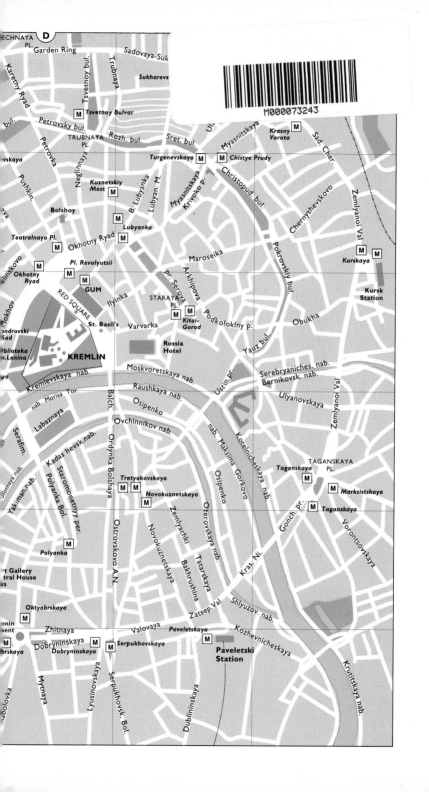

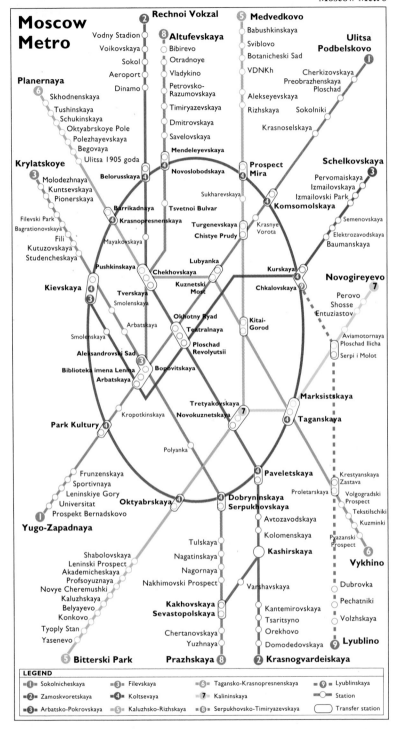

Moscow Metro

Moscow Metro

Rechnoi Vokzal

Medvedkovo

Ulitsa Podbelskovo

Altufevskaya

Vodny Stadion
Voikovskaya
Sokol
Aeroport
Dinamo

Bibirevo
Otradnoye
Vladykino
Petrovsko-Razumovskaya
Timiryazevskaya
Dmitrovskaya
Savelovskaya

Babushkinskaya
Sviblovo
Botanicheski Sad
VDNKh
Alekseyevskaya
Rizhskaya
Krasnoselskaya

Cherkizovskaya
Preobrazhenskaya Ploschad
Sokolniki

Planernaya

Skhodnenskaya
Tushinskaya
Schukinskaya
Oktyabrskoye Pole
Polezhayevskaya
Begovaya
Ulitsa 1905 goda

Mendeleyevskaya
Novoslobodskaya

Prospect Mira

Schelkovskaya

Pervomaiskaya
Izmailovskaya
Izmailovski Park

Krylatskoye

Molodezhnaya
Kuntsevskaya
Pionerskaya

Belorusskaya

Sukharevskaya

Komsomolskaya

Semenovskaya

Filevski Park
Bagrationovskaya
Fili
Kutuzovskaya
Studencheskaya

Barrikadnaya
Krasnopresnenskaya

Tsvetnoi Bulvar

Turgenevskaya
Chistye Prudy

Krasnye Vorota

Elektrozavodskaya
Baumanskaya

Mayakovskaya

Kievskaya

Pushkinskaya
Tverskaya
Smolenskaya

Chekhovskaya
Kuznetski Most

Lubyanka

Kurskaya
Chkalovskaya

Novogireyevo

Perovo
Shosse Entuziastov

Arbatskaya

Okhotny Ryad
Teatralnaya
Ploschad Revolyutsii

Kitai-Gorod

Aviamotornaya
Ploschad Ilicha
Serpi i Molot

Smolenskaya

Aleksandrovski Sad
Biblioteka imena Lenina
Arbatskaya

Borovitskaya

Marksistskaya

Tretyakovskaya
Novokuznetskaya

Taganskaya

Park Kultury

Kropotkinskaya

Frunzenskaya
Sportivnaya
Leninskiye Gory
Universitat
Prospekt Bernadskovo

Polyanka

Paveletskaya

Krestyanskaya Zastava
Volgogradski Prospect
Tekstilschiki
Kuzminki

Oktyabrskaya

Dobryninskaya
Serpukhovskaya

Proletarskaya

Yugo-Zapadnaya

Avtozavodskaya
Kolomenskaya

Pyazanski Prospect

Shabolovskaya
Leninski Prospect
Akademicheskaya
Profsoyuznaya
Novye Cheremushki
Kaluzhskaya
Belyayevo
Konkovo
Tyoply Stan
Yasenevo

Tulskaya
Nagatinskaya
Nagornaya
Nakhimovski Prospect

Kashirskaya

Vykhino

Varshavskaya

Dubrovka
Pechatniki
Volzhskaya

Kakhovskaya
Sevastopolskaya

Kantemirovskaya
Tsaritsyno
Orekhovo
Domodedovskaya

Lyublino

Chertanovskaya
Yuzhnaya

Bitterski Park

Prazhskaya

Krasnogvardeiskaya

LEGEND

1 Sokolnicheskaya	3 Filevskaya	6 Tagansko-Krasnopresnenskaya	9 Lyublinskaya
2 Zamoskvoretskaya	4 Koltsevaya	7 Kalininskaya	Station
3 Arbatsko-Pokrovskaya	5 Kaluzhsko-Rizhskaya	8 Serpukhovskovo-Timiryazevskaya	Transfer station

Москвоский Метро

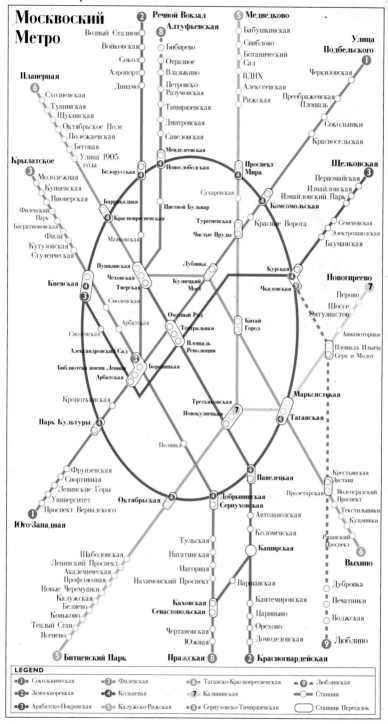

Moscow

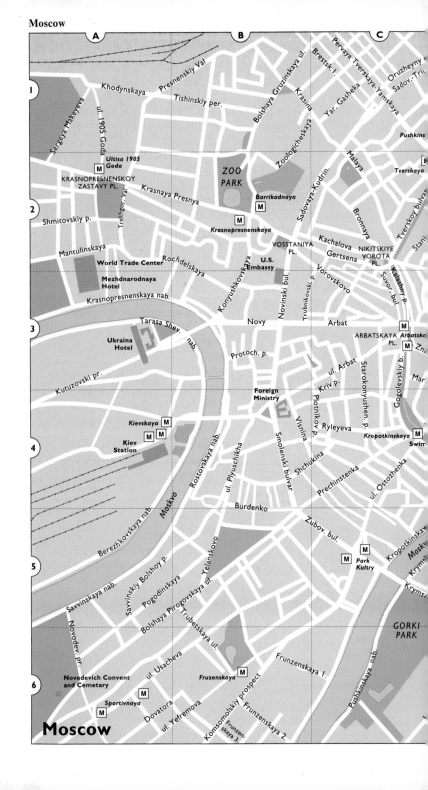

Moscow

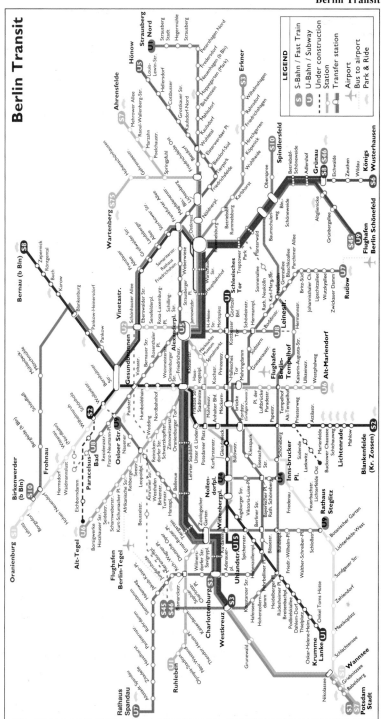

Munich Transit

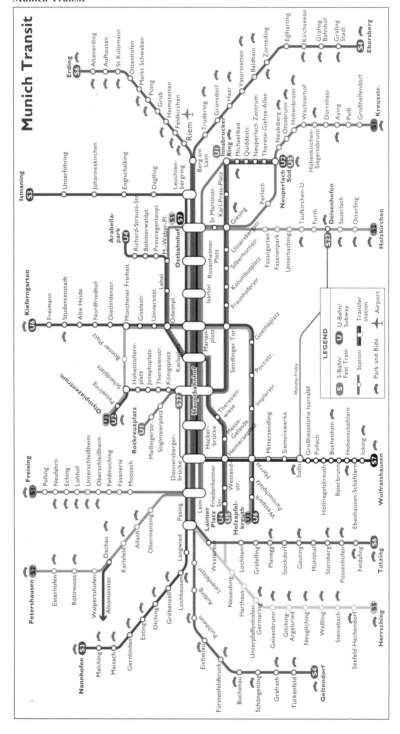

Hamburg Transit

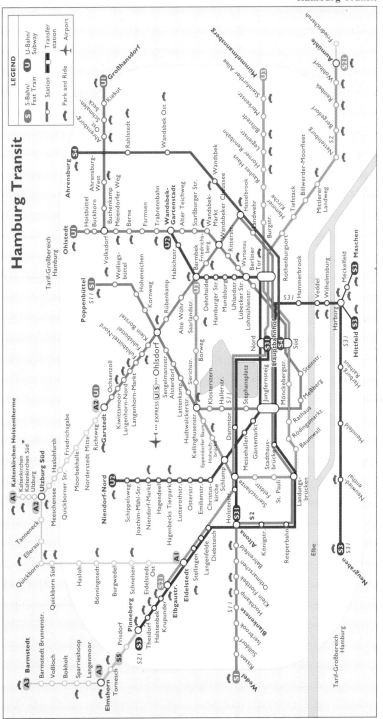

Frankfurt Transit

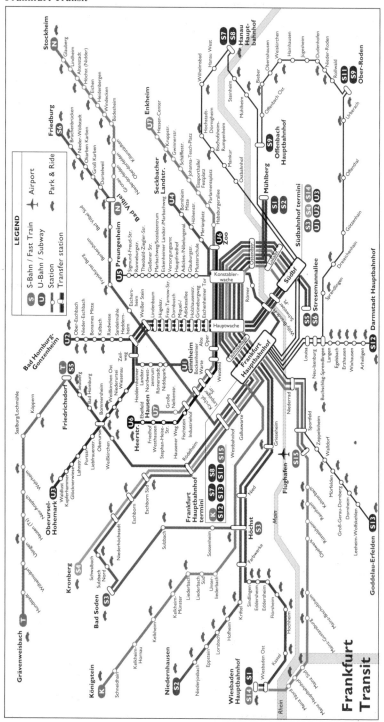

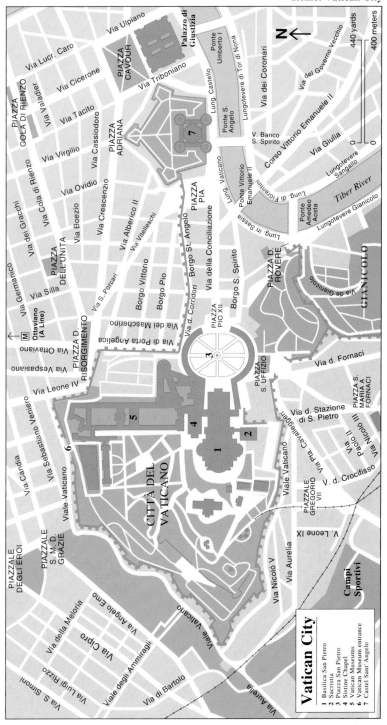

Rome: Vatican City

Vatican City

1 Basilica San Pietro
2 Sacristia
3 Piazza San Pietro
4 Sistine Chapel
5 Vatican Museums
6 Vatican Museum entrance
7 Castel Sant'Angelo

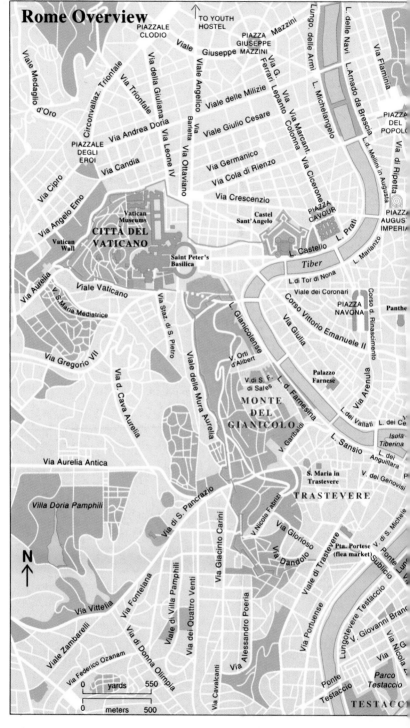

Rome Overview

Rome: Transportation

Rome Transport

VILLA BORGHESE

SALARIO
CASA PRETORIO
B-LINE
TERMINI
A-LINE
B-LINE
REPUBBLICA
BARBERINI
SPAGNA
FLAMINIO
A-LINE
LEPANTO
OTTAVIANO
A-LINE
S. PIETRO

Urban Train Service (F.S.)

TO YOUTH HOSTEL
PIAZZA GIUSEPPE MAZZINI
PIAZZA DEL POPOLO
PIAZZA CAVOUR
PIAZZA COLONNA
PIAZZA VENEZIA
PIAZZA NAVONA
Castel Sant'Angelo
St. Peter's Basilica
Vatican
Pantheon
Trevi Fountain
Palazzo del Quirinale
Palazzo Farnese
C. d. Rinascimento
Tiber

Viale Regina Margherita
V. Dalmazia
Via Nomentana
Via Nizza
Via Salaria
Via Piave
Via XX Settembre
Via Po
Corso d'Italia
Via Castro Pretorio
Via Marsala
Via Merulana
Via Giov. Lanza
Via Cavour
Stazione Termini
Via V. Veneto
Via Barberini
V. d. Quattro Fontane
Via Sistina
Via Nazionale
V. del due Macelli
Via del Tritone
Via del Babuino
Via del Corso
Via di Ripetta
Via Flaminia
Viale del Muro Torta
Via Marcant. Colonna
Via Cicerone
Viale dei Coronari
Corso Vittorio Emanuele II
Via Giulia
Via G. Ferrari
Via Lepanto
Via Giulio Cesare
Viale delle Milizie
Viale Giulio Cesare
Via Cola di Rienzo
Via Crescenzio
V. Ottaviano
Via Leone IV
Viale Angelico
Viale Giuseppe Mazzini
P. D. CINQUECENTO
P. D. INDIPENDENZA
P. D. REPUBBLICA

•61•65•
•490•495•
•60•61•62•
•65•
•95•
•95•490•495•
•119•
•90•90b•
•26•81•
•492•913•
•87•
•280•
•34•49•492•990•
•81•
•23•34•
•23•49•492•
•23•
•990•
•19•70•490•913•
•32•
•41•
•64•
•49•
•34•46•46b•
•62•65•98•
•56•60•62•81•85•90•90b•
•52•53•56•
•58•61•62•80•
•95•116•492•
•71•81•
•70•71•
•93b•93•
•93•93b•
•16•93•
•70•
•70•
•71•
•71•
•57•64•65•
•70•75•170•
•170•
•6•61•62•492•
•95•119•492•
•119•
•26•44•46•56•60•64•62•64•70•81•492•
•23•

Rome: Transportation

1/2 mile

500 meters

MANZONI

V. Appia

Via Concordia

Via Etruria

Via Magnagrecia

Via Statilia

V. Emanuele

Fiberto

NE

Palazzo Lateranense

S.Giovanni Laterano

S. GIOVANNI

Via d. Laterani

•85•87•

Via di S.Giovanni in Laterano

•85•87•

•85•118•

Via Labicana

P. D. COLOSSEO

V. Claudia

Via della Navicella

Via dell'Amba Aradam

Via di S. Stefano Rotondo

Via Gallia

Via Satrico

Via Vetulonia

Viale Metronio

Via di Porta Latina

Via di Porta Sebastiano

•118•

•118•

•90b•118•

Via Druso

Viale di Terme di Caracalla

•93•93b•613•671•

CELIO

Celio

Parco del

Colosseum

B-LINE

CIRCO MASSIMO

V. delle Terme

•90•90b•118•

Terme di Caracalla

Viale Guido Baccelli

OSTIENSE

Urban Train Service (F.S.)

TO AIRPORT

Via di S. Gregorio

MONTE PALATINO

Via dei Cerchi

Via del Circo Massimo

•15•90•90b•

•90b•94•

•90•

•15•

Via Aventina

Terme di Caracalla

•94•

Via di S. Prisca

AVENTINO

Viale Aventino

Via Gracio

PIRAMIDE

•57•95•318•

Via Aventino

Viale di Piramide Cestia

•11•15•27•118•673•

TO LAURENTINA

B-LINE

Isola Tiberina

•57•90•

•23•57•92•95•716•

Via Marmorata

•13•23•57•

Via Nicola Zabaglia

Parco Testaccio

TESTACCIO

V. Giovanni Branca

Via Galvani

•92•

Via Ostiense

•11•92•115•

•673•

TRASTEVERE

•28•44•75•97•170•280•

Viale di Trastevere

Via Glorioso

Via Dandolo

•710•

•44•75•

V. Nicola Fabrizi

Via Alessandro Poerio

TRASTEVERE

Urban Train Service (F.S.)

•1•3•23•27•31•228•280•710•719•

Via di S. Pancrazio

•41•

Via Giacinto Carini

•75•

V. Cavalcanti

Viale di Villa Pamphili

Via dei Quattro Venti

Via di Donna Olimpia

N←

Rome: "Walks"

Walks

1 Piazza del Popolo
2 Ara Pacis
3 Mausoleum of Augustus
4 Palazzo Borghese
5 Spanish Steps
6 Trevi Fountain
7 Vittorio Emanuele Monument
8 Campidoglio
9 Teatro Marcello
10 Isola Tiberina
11 Palazzo Doria Pamphili
12 Church of Santi Apostoli
13 Church of San Marcello
14 Church of S. Ignazio
15 Piazza di Pietra
16 Piazza Colonna/ Column of Marcus Aurelius
17 Palazzo Chigi
18 Pantheon
19 Giolitti
20 Piazza Minerva
21 Church of Santa Maria Sopra Minerva
22 Church of San Luigi dei Francesi
23 Piazza Navona
24 Church of Sant'Antonio dei Portoghesi
25 Museo Napoleonico
26 Il Gesù
27 Largo Argentina
28 Church of Sant'Andrea delle Valle
29 Palazzo del Cancelleria
30 Chiesa Nuova
31 Piazza Sforza Cesarini
32 Campo dei Fiori
33 Piazza Farnese
34 Piazza della Quercia
35 Monte di Pieta
36 Church of Santissima Trinità dei Pellegrini

VILLA BORGHESE
VILLA MEDICI

V. del Muro Torto
Via Belvedere
Via Trinità del Monti

Spagna M
PIAZZA TRINITÀ D. MONTE
Via d. Due Macelli
PIAZZA DI SPAGNA
Via Propaganda
Via Mario de' Fiori
Via del Tritone
Via della Mercede
PIAZZA S. SILVESTRO
LARGO

Via del Babuino
Via della Croce
Via della Carozze
Via d. Condotti
Via Borgogna
Via Frattina
Via delle Vite

Via Vittorio
Via del Corso
Via Borghese
Via Campo Marzo

PIAZZA DEL POPOLO ①
Via di Ripetta
Via Brunati
Via del Vantaggio
Via Canova
LARGO D. SCHIAVONI
PIAZZA AUGUSTO IMPERATORE ③
PIAZZA D. PORTO DI RIPETTA
②
Via Tomacelli
④
PIAZZA DEL PARLIAMENTO
Via Prefetti

Via F. di Savoia

Lung. in Augusta
Tiber River
Ponte Margherita
PIAZZA D. LIBERTA
Via Orsini
Via Feder. Cesi

Lung. dei Mellini
Ponte Cavour
Lung. Prati
Via Clementino
Via della Scrofa
②④
Via dell'Orso

Via Cola di Rienzo
Via G. Belli
Via P. Cossa
Via V. Colonna
Via Ulpiano
Lungotevere Marzio
Ponte Umberto I
②⑤
Tor di Nona

Via Orsini
Via E. Q. Visconti
Via Lucr. Caro
Via Cicerone
PIAZZA CAVOUR
PIAZZA DEI TRIBUNALI

Via Tacito
Via Triboniano
Lungotevere Castello

Via Cassiodoro
Via Ovidio
Via Crescenzio
PIAZZA ADRIANA
Castel Sant' Angelo
Ponte S. Angelo

Via Boezio
Via Alberico II
Via Vitelleschi
PIAZZA PIA
Via della Conciliazione
Via Vaticano
Lung.

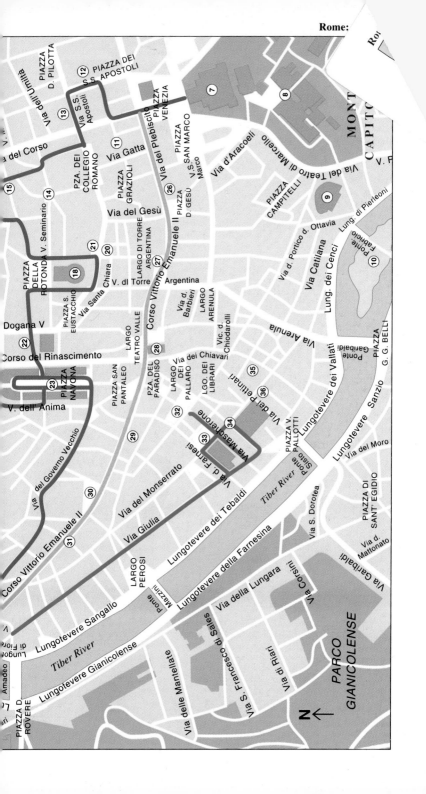

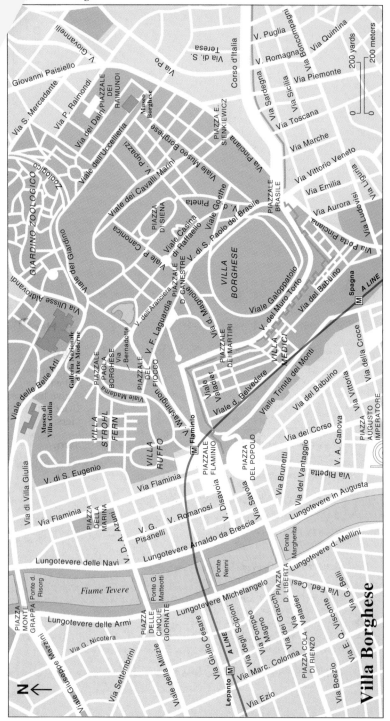

Villa Borghese

Let's Go

EUROPE

is the best book for anyone traveling on a budget. Here's why:

▨ No other guidebook has as many budget listings.

In Europe we list over 10,000 budget travel bargains. We tell you how to get there the cheapest way, whether by bus, plane, or bike, and where to get an inexpensive and satisfying meal once you've arrived. We give hundreds of money-saving tips that anyone can use, plus invaluable advice on discounts and deals for students, children, families, and senior travelers.

▨ Let's Go researchers have to make it on their own.

Our Harvard-Radcliffe researcher-writers travel on budgets as tight as your own—no expense accounts, no free hotel rooms.

▨ Let's Go is completely revised each year.

We don't just update the prices, we go back to the place. If a charming café has become an overpriced tourist trap, we'll replace the listing with a new and better one.

▨ No other guidebook includes all this:

Honest, engaging coverage of both the cities and the countryside; up-to-the-minute prices, directions, addresses, phone numbers, and opening hours; in-depth essays on local culture, history, and politics; comprehensive listings on transportation between and within regions and cities; straight advice on work and study, budget accommodations, sights, nightlife, and food; detailed city and regional maps; and much more.

▨ Let's Go is for anyone who wants to see Europe on a budget.

Books by Let's Go, Inc.

EUROPE

Let's Go: Europe

Let's Go: Austria & Switzerland

Let's Go: Britain & Ireland

Let's Go: Eastern Europe

Let's Go: France

Let's Go: Germany

Let's Go: Greece & Turkey

Let's Go: Ireland

Let's Go: Italy

Let's Go: London

Let's Go: Paris

Let's Go: Rome

Let's Go: Spain & Portugal

NORTH & CENTRAL AMERICA

Let's Go: USA & Canada

Let's Go: Alaska & The Pacific Northwest

Let's Go: California

Let's Go: New York City

Let's Go: Washington, D.C.

Let's Go: Mexico

MIDDLE EAST & ASIA

Let's Go: Israel & Egypt

Let's Go: Thailand

Let's Go

The Budget Guide to

EUROPE

1995

Declan Fox
Editor

Anna Dahlstein
Associate Editor

Tina Tseng
Associate Editor

Written by
Let's Go, Inc.
A subsidiary of
Harvard Student Agencies, Inc.

St. Martin's Press ■ **New York**

HELPING LET'S GO

If you have suggestions or corrections, or just want to share your discoveries, drop us a line. We read every piece of correspondence, whether a 10-page e-mail letter, a velveteen Elvis postcard, or, as in one case, a collage. All suggestions are passed along to our researcher-writers. Please note that mail received after May 5, 1995 will probably be too late for the 1996 book, but will be retained for the following edition.
Address mail to:

Let's Go: Europe
Let's Go, Inc.
1 Story Street
Cambridge, MA 02138
USA

Or send e-mail to:

letsgo@delphi.com

In addition to the invaluable travel advice our readers share with us, many are kind enough to offer their services as researchers or editors. Unfortunately, the charter of Let's Go, Inc. and Harvard Student Agencies, Inc. enables us to employ only currently enrolled Harvard-Radcliffe students.

Maps by David Lindroth, copyright © 1995, 1994, 1993, 1992, 1991, 1990, 1989, 1986 by St. Martin's Press, Inc.

Distributed outside the U.S. and Canada by Macmillan Reference Books.

Let's Go: Europe. Copyright © 1995 by Let's Go, Inc., a wholly owned subsidiary of Harvard Student Agencies, Inc. All rights reserved. Printed in the United States of America. No part of this book may be used or reproduced in any manner whatsoever without written permission except in the case of brief quotations embodied in critical articles or reviews. For information, address St. Martin's Press, 175 Fifth Avenue, New York, NY 10010.

ISBN: 0-312-11403-6

First edition
10 9 8 7 6 5 4 3 2 1

Let's Go: Europe is written by the Publishing Division of Let's Go, Inc., 1 Story Street, Cambridge, MA 02138.

Go ® is a registered trademark of Let's Go, Inc.
the U.S.A. on recycled paper with biodegradable soy ink.

About Let's Go

Back in 1960, a few students at Harvard University got together to produce a 20-page pamphlet offering a collection of tips on budget travel in Europe. For three years, Harvard Student Agencies, a student-run nonprofit corporation, had been doing a brisk business booking charter flights to Europe; this modest, mimeographed packet was offered to passengers as an extra. The following year, students traveling to Europe researched the first full-fledged edition of *Let's Go: Europe*, a pocket-sized book featuring advice on shoestring travel, irreverent write-ups of sights, and a decidedly youthful slant.

Throughout the 60s, the guides reflected the times: one section of the 1968 *Let's Go: Europe* talked about "Street Singing in Europe on No Dollars a Day." During the 70s, *Let's Go* gradually became a large-scale operation, adding regional European guides and expanding coverage into North Africa and Asia. The 80s saw the arrival of *Let's Go: USA & Canada* and *Let's Go: Mexico*, as well as regional North American guides; in the 90s we introduced five in-depth city guides to Paris, London, Rome, New York City, and Washington, DC. And as the budget travel world expands, so do we; the first edition of *Let's Go: Thailand* hit the shelves last year, and this year's edition adds coverage of Malaysia, Singapore, Tokyo, and Hong Kong.

This year we're proud to announce the birth of *Let's Go: Eastern Europe*—the most comprehensive guide to this renascent region, with more practical information and insider tips than any other. *Let's Go: Eastern Europe* brings our total number of titles, with their spirit of adventure and reputation for honesty, accuracy, and editorial integrity, to 21.

We've seen a lot in 35 years. *Let's Go: Europe* is now the world's #1 best selling international guide, translated into seven languages. And our guides are still researched, written, and produced entirely by students who know first-hand how to see the world on the cheap.

Every spring, we recruit over 100 researchers and 50 editors to write our books anew. Come summertime, after several months of training, researchers hit the road for seven weeks of exploration, from Bangkok to Budapest, Anchorage to Ankara. With pen and notebook in hand, a few changes of underwear stuffed in our backpacks, and a budget as tight as yours, we visit every *pensione*, *palapa*, pizzeria, café, club, campground, or castle we can find to make sure you'll get the most out of *your* trip.

We've put the best of our discoveries into the book you're now holding. A brand-new edition of each guide hits the shelves every year, only months after it is researched, so you know you're getting the most reliable, up-to-date, and comprehensive information available. The budget travel world is constantly changing, and where other guides quickly become obsolete, our annual research keeps you abreast of the very latest travel insights. And even as you read this, work on next year's editions is well underway.

At *Let's Go*, we think of budget travel not only as a means of cutting down on costs, but as a way of breaking down a few walls as well. Living cheap and simple on the road brings you closer to the real people and places you've been saving up to visit. This book will ease your anxieties and answer your questions about the basics—to help *you* get off the beaten track and explore. We encourage you to put *Let's Go* away now and then and strike out on your own. As any seasoned traveler will tell you, the best discoveries are often those you make yourself. If you find something worth sharing, drop us a line. We're at Let's Go, Inc., 1 Story Street, Cambridge, MA, 02138, USA (e-mail: letsgo@delphi.com).

Happy travels!

LONDON ACCOMMODATION

WESTPOINT HOTEL

170 SUSSEX GARDENS, HYDE PARK, LONDON W2 1PT.
TEL: 071-402 0281 (RESERVATIONS) FAX: 071-224 9114
Open all year. Central heating.Most rooms with private shower & toilet,
radio/intercom & colour. T.V. Children welcome. TV lounge

*This hotel has long been a popular choice amongst tourists because of it central location,
being near to Hyde Park and only 2 minutes from Paddington and Lancaster Gate tube
stations. The West End's tourist attractions, including theatres, museums and Oxford Street
stores are within easy reach. Individuals, families and groups are all welcome.*

• PRIVATE CAR PARK • PARKING •

Rates: *Low Season*
Singles from £18.00 per person
Doubles from £15.00 per person
Family from £12.00 per person

High Season
Singles from £22.00
Doubles from £18.00 per person
Family rooms from £15.00 per person

ABBEY COURT HOTEL

**174 SUSSEX GARDENS, HYDE PARK,
LONDON W2 1PT.**
TEL: 071-402 0704 FAX: 071-262 2055

Open all year. Radio/Intercom in every
room. Children welcome. Most rooms with
private shower, toilet and colour TV.

• CAR PARKING •

*This hotel has long been popular with tourists because
of it central location, near to Hyde Park and two
minutes from Paddington and Lancaster Gate tube
stations. The tourist attractions, of the West End
including theatres, museums and Oxford Street stores
are within easy reach. Individuals, families, school
parties and groups are all welcome and group tours
can be arranged.*

Rates per person:

High Season
Singles from £28.00
Doubles from £18.00 p.p.
Family from £15.00 p.p.

Low Season
Singles from £24.00
Doubles from £16.00 p.p.
Family from £15.00 p.p.

SASS HOUSE HOTEL

**11 CRAVEN TERRACE, HYDE PARK,
LONDON, W2 3QD.**
TEL: 071-262 2325 FAX: 071-262 0889

Centrally located - within easy reach of
London's most famous tourist attractions
Nearest underground Paddington and
Lancaster Gate Served by a network of bus
routes Colour television lounge Centrally
heated Radio and intercom in all rooms.
Special group and party booking rates Parking
facilities available.

Rates per person:

Singles from £18.00 Double room from £14.00
p.p. and Family room or party hooking rate
from £13.00 p.p. inc bed & breakfast

BATH ACCOMMODATION

Old Mill Hotel & Revolving Waterwheel Restaurant

Tollbridge Road, Bath, Avon. BA1 7DE (0225) 858476 Fax: (0225) 852600

Riverside Experience On the banks of the River Avon, beside the historic
tollbridge and overlooking the weir with breathtaking views - **yet only 1.5
miles from the centre of Bath**. Luxurious en-suite rooms, with
river views. Fourposter beds for 'honeymooners'.
Turn with the Wheel, **Unique
Revolving Restaurant** - floor turned
gently by huge waterwheel showing
diners the varied river views.

...rk **Fishing Special short**
... Single from £35.00
... 8.00

Contents

This guidebook teaches you how to budget your money.

This page is for slow learners.

We all make mistakes. So if you happen to find yourself making a costly one, call Western Union. With them you can receive money from the States within minutes at any of our European locations. Plus, it's already been converted into the appropriate currency.

Just call our numbers in Austria 0222 892 0380, Belgium 02 753 2150, Denmark 800 107 11, Finland 9 800 20440, France 161 43 54 46 12, Germany 069 2648201, 0681 933 3328, Greece 01 687 3850, Ireland 1 800 395 395*, Italy 02 95 457 305, Netherlands 06 0566*, Poland 2 231 7008, Spain 93 301 1212, Sweden 020 741 742, United Kingdom 0 800 833 833*, or if you are in the United States 1 800 325 6000*.

And since nobody's perfect, you might want to keep these numbers in your wallet, for those times when nothing else is in there.

WESTERN UNION | MONEY TRANSFER
The fastest way to send money worldwide.℠

©1994 Western Union Financial Services, Inc.   * Toll free within country.

Maps

Researcher-Writers

Mayanthi Fernando   *Finland, Sweden, and Bornholm (Denmark)*
Sophisticated and cosmopolitan, Mai braved postmodern architecture, drunken revelers, and screaming blond schoolkids in the course of an adventure in Finland and Sweden. From the self-conscious glamour of Stockholm and the kitsch of Santa's Arctic village to reindeer and mosquitoes, she braved the elements and the cities, sending us rewarding and frank appraisals of the regions she covered. Mai now has a USSR passport and a job offer to work in a museum in Finland.

Lars Kroijer   *Denmark (except Bornholm) and Norway*
The Great Dane tapped into his Viking heritage and embarked on a voyage through his native Denmark and Norway. His instincts drew him to the hotspots of Scandinavia from Copenhagen to the Arctic Circle and beyond. Somehow, he always found the beautiful people and a place for the night; the drawback was the astronomical price of beer in Norway. Lars now works on Wall Street.

Daniel Williams   *Belgium, Iceland, Luxembourg, and the Netherlands*
Consummate explorer, Dan dashed through Belgium, the Netherlands, and Luxembourg before hopping on a plane to Iceland. With a keen sense of what was fun, he braved Dutch rail strikes, found an infernal bar in Brussels, witnessed a lesbian wedding in Amsterdam, and cooked a Reuben sandwich in the ashes of a volcano somewhere close to the testing grounds of the Apollo space program in Iceland. His imagination and wit dazzled us; how we looked forward to his copy and how we wished he could have researched even more countries.

Regional Researcher-Writers

Fifty-seven researchers documented the other 23 countries in this book for 12 regional guides, picking out highlights for the 928 pages here. Adventurers, wits, hikers, sophisticates (though not necessarily all at the same time), they made us alternately giggle, commiserate, and cuss some awful handwriting.

Lisa Anne Abend	*Tuscany, Umbria, Sardinia*
Kelly Adams	*Bulgaria*
Ingrid V. Basset	*Rome*
Sonia Batra	*Portugal*
Paul Berger	*Hungary*
Ross Blank	*Athens, Cyclades, Sporades*
Daniela Bleichmar	*Andalucía*
Rebecca Boggs	*Burgundy, Champagne, North and Central France*
Marios Veletzas Broustas	*Northern Greece, Northeast Aegean & Ionian Islands*
Amy Brown	*Languedoc-Roussillon, Basque Country, Aquitaine*
Anne Colby Carman	*Provence, French Riviera, Corsica*
Jonathan Caverly	*French Switzerland & Vienna*
Heather Clark	*Western Ireland*
Elisabetta Coletti	*Lombardy, Italian Riviera, Emilia-Romagna*
Laura Cooley	*Salzburg, Salzkammergut*
Michael S. Costanzo	*Sicily*
Sarah Dryden	*Northern & Central Germany*
Justyna Fife	*Poland*
Jonathan Wade Goldman	*Southern Italy*

Susan Gray	*Crete, Dodecanese*
Harris Tzvi Hartman	*İstanbul, Turkish Aegean & Mediterranean Coasts*
David Jeorg	*Balearic Islands, Catalonia*
Plamen Jordanoff	*Baden Württemberg*
Charlotte Kaiser	*Russia*
Adam Kirsch	*Dublin and Southeast Ireland*
Deborah L. Kory	*Rome*
Natasha Leland	*Russia*
Vivian Lin	*London*
Andrew Liu	*Oxford, Southwest England, Wales*
Daryna McKeand	*Andalucía*
Bruce McKinnon	*Paris*
Jeffrey C. Milder	*Southwest and Southeast Ireland*
Mark Moody	*Estonia, Latvia, Lithuania*
Şerban Nacu	*Romania, Slovenia*
Maria Ordoñez	*Italian and German Switzerland, Liechtenstein*
Michael Patrick O'Shea	*Berlin, Eastern Germany*
Krzysztof Owerkowicz	*Normandy, Brittany*
Rosalie Parker	*Peleponnese, Ionian Islands*
Kelli Rae Patton	*Southwest, Southeast, & Heart of England*
Tripler Pell	*Loire Valley, Aquitaine*
Gabriel Piedrahita	*Andorra, Basque Country, Catalan Pyrenees*
Grigore Pop-Eleches	*Central & Eastern Germany*
Joel M. Rainey	*Alsace-Lorraine, Burgundy, Lyon, the Alps*
Nat Riley	*Anatolia*
Geneviève Roach	*Ukraine*
Stephanie Rosborough	*The Marches, Veneto, Friuli-Venezia Giulia, Emilia Romagna*
Colleen Ryan	*Northwest Ireland, Northern Ireland, Isle of Man*
Mimi Schultz	*London*
Kurt Schumacher	*Galicia, Central Spain*
Shira Springer	*Innsbruck, Kitzbühel*
Karen Todd	*Paris*
Tracey Tomlinson	*Scotland*
Raimond Tulius	*Czech Republic*
Julianna Tymoczko	*Paris, Rouen*
Tristanne L. Walliser	*Eastern Germany, Bavaria*
Erica Werner	*Central Spain*
Elizabeth Yellen	*Central & Northern England, Southern Scotland*

█ Staff

Editor	Declan *"Wunderhund"* Fox
Associate Editor	Anna "Roxette" Dahlstein
Associate Editor	Tina "Perky" Tseng
Managing Editor	Joseph E. Mullin III
Publishing Director	Pete Keith
Production Manager	Alexis G. Averbuck
Financial Manager	Matt Heid
Assistant General Manager	Anne E. Chisholm

Regional Guide Staffs

Austria & Switzerland	Sucharita Mulpuru
	Melissa Liazos
Britain & Ireland	Daniel C. G. Glover
	Emily Hobson
Eastern Europe	Luiza Chwiałkowska
	Katarzyna Drozd
	Samuel P. Trumbull
	Jol Andrew Silversmith
France	Natalie Tatiana Boutin
	Olivia Gentile
	Elizabeth "Fifi" Squires
Germany	Tanya Vivienne Bezreh
	Kardyhm Anne Kelly
Greece & Turkey	Eleni Gage
	Alp Aker
	Michael Cisneros
Ireland	Sean Fitzpatrick
	Jed Willard
Italy	Howie Axelrod
	Elizabeth Theran
	Samantha Kent
London	Julie E. Cooper
Paris	Miranda Frances Spieler
Rome	Garen Eileen Thomas
Spain & Portugal	María Colbert
	Yael Schenker
	Manuel Cachán

Sales Group Manager	Sherice R. Guillory
Sales Department Coordinator	Andrea N. Taylor
Sales Group Representatives	Eli K. Aheto
	Timur Okay Harry Hiçyılmaz
	Arzhang Kamerei
	Hollister Jane Leopold
	David L. Yuan
President	Lucienne D. Lester
General Manager	Richard M. Olken

Acknowledgments

Club Europa thanks

Euro-Pop. The extremely helpful staffs of the the tourist boards of Belgium, Denmark, Finland, Iceland, Luxembourg, Netherlands, Norway, and Sweden. Alexis for cheerful commiseration and support through the vagaries of fonts and format; also fellow compufreak, Liz. The Spanish File Salvage Crew, María and Yael. Natalie for beret-bereft France. Tanya and K2 *für Gemütlichkeit*. Such for Alps. Laconic Alp. Miranda, glam, glib, and glorious. Liz Squires for the quagmire of maps. Sam, Luiza, & Kasia for the Eastern Europe condom patrol. Dan, Eleni, Garen, Howie, Julie, Sean, Emily, Jed, Livy, LizT, Jol, Manny. Joe, who dealt with a lot and managed to survive. Pete for bagels and weathering the occasional storm. Anne Chisholm for keeping the office on an even keel.

Declan thanks

Cosmo-Swede Anna, who brought me Roxette and Abba. Tina—how do I keep roping you into things? The Europe room had no view and our salaries were compared to the linen manager's, but we creative types will survive all the "cool" people who sell ads. No footie sagas or bawdy puns for us, but enthusiasm for the project if not for summer camp. Dave for four years of friendship and dain bramage but, alas, little time at the Bow this summer. Roommates Vonnie, Geoff, and baby Frank. Radhika for beach, beer, and a bun in my oven. Miranda for many cigarettes and post-graduation support. Thanks to the academy, but what next? Joan for years of encouragement and support. Dad, Mam, Enda, Sinéad, Eimear, Gráinne, and Donnacha, thanks for everything; this one's for you. Yeah, yeah, yeah.

Anna thanks

European Studies major, well-traveled Irishman, occasional frequenter of what Americans inexplicably call "Euro" clubs, connoisseur of literally everything from Florentine tripe recipes to Berlin squatter movements, Declan was even sighted smoking Gauloises this summer. *Let's Go* won't find a better editor. Tina (Eurosnob by default) approached Icelandic fonts, unhighlighted copy, and food fests with an enthusiasm that was contagious. María: ídola. Natalie, fellow rave nerd at 5am. Pepe Mullin, por tu modo de apreciar lo kitsch, el pastiche, y la onda "glitter." Tack ma' och Jenny för era insatser på Sverigefronten, och för hallonsnörena. Ecstatic Wendy. Deborah Yashar, for great company (though you were in our rival town). Torsten "il y a des chanwis dans le mini-bar" Fetzer and Frida "Topolino" Kollberg for the trip. Pero chabones, la próxima vez tenemos que pasar por Hotel Gronchi (Pisa) y la Riviera di Levante. For Doug, kilted travel companion, since you'll never use it.

Tina thanks

Chartmaster Declan, my partner in crime and lament—alternately savior and entertainer through the years. Anna, my partner in late-night incoherence, bad singing, and hysterical laughter. Who would've thought that Icelandic water, soft rock, and transportation hubs could ever be so funny? Ada for being just a little overcommitted, indecisive, and nutty right there beside me. Kat for crazy schemes, impossible plans, and dreams of the future that come true. Lauri for four fabulous years of friendship, angst, and food. Liza for day trips, caffeinated frenzies, and moral support. Roommates at one time or another, Jodi, Tom T., and Jeremy. Tom G. for lending me his house and his cat. Steph, for being my fellow romantic entering the world. And, finally, Mump and Smoot, the classy, crazy clowns from hell, who added the all-healing god Ummo to my life. Oh yeah.

How To Use This Book

Thirty-five years ago, a pamphlet on European travel appeared; the following year, 1961, *Let's Go: Europe* made a recognizable appearance, told readers to travel in West Germany soon "since you face the possibility of fighting there for Berlin" and reliably informed that in Poland, it was "legal to play bridge with dollars: you can lose dollars and win back lots of złoty." Times have obviously changed; 1995 ushers in *Let's Go: Eastern Europe*, a comprehensive guide to the region and you no longer need to get permission from the Selective Service Commission to travel abroad. What hasn't changed is a belief in economical travel and the value of honesty in appraisal and integrity of editing.

   Let's Go: Europe opens with a chapter of **Essentials** to guide you through the quagmire of preparations, with tips on passport and visa acquisition, packing, getting to Europe, and the budget travel opportunities once you're there. It also addresses specific concerns, such as those of women, bisexuals, gays, lesbians, travelers with disabilities, senior citizens, and travelers with kids.

   The rest of the book lists individual countries in alphabetical order. For geographical efficiency, Estonia, Latvia, and Lithuania are listed as the Baltic States, and England, Wales, and Scotland are grouped under Great Britain, while Northern Ireland and the Isle of Man are in the Ireland chapter. Each chapter begins with an overview of that country's history and culture as well as country-specific Essentials, where you'll find such tidbits as visa requirements and the lowdown on transportation, accommodations, and regional cuisine.

   For each major city, the **Orientation and Practical Information** section gives you a clue about the city's layout, as well as how to get there, how to communicate with folks back home, and where to seek transportation and help in medical emergencies and crisis situations. Then we shower you with information on **Accommodations, Camping, Food, Sights,** and **Entertainment.** Smaller towns are usually divided in half: first we describe the sights and entertainment hotspots, then we dig into the nitty-gritty: practical information, accommodations, and food.

   Although our intrepid researcher-writers beat a trail across the continent annually, there are countless undiscovered travel gems in Europe. Please keep an eye out for any amazing places we've missed, follow your own spirit and imagination, and feel free to write us about what you find.

A NOTE TO OUR READERS

The information for this book is gathered by *Let's Go*'s researchers during the late spring and summer months of 1994. Each listing is derived from the assigned researcher's opinion based upon his or her visit at a particular time. The opinions are expressed in a candid and forthright manner. Other travelers might disagree. Those traveling at a different time may have different experiences since prices, dates, hours, and conditions are always subject to change. You are urged to check beforehand to avoid inconvenience and surprises. Be prepared for fluctuations in currency exchange rates and inflation. Travel always involves a certain degree of risk, especially in low-cost areas. When traveling, especially on a budget, you should always take particular care to ensure your safety.

Fortunately, when you travel on Rail Europe, there are some sights you'll miss.

No goofy hats. No big sunglasses. No plaid shirts with striped shorts. Instead, on Rail Europe, you'll experience Europe the way Europeans do. You'll enjoy scenic countryside no one else can show you. And meet unique and interesting people. In short, you'll explore Europe the way it was meant to be explored. When it comes to visiting 33 European countries, get real. Go Rail Europe. Because traveling any other way could end up showing you some pretty dreadful sights. To learn more, call your travel agent or 1-800-4-EURAIL. (1-800-438-7245)

Rail Europe

Europe. To the trained eye.

■ Essentials

■■■ PLANNING YOUR TRIP

Touring through the entirety of Europe, or even just a large chunk of it can be a daunting, albeit exciting, prospect. Where to begin? Fortunately, there are countless resources devoted to helping travelers tackle the project of planning a journey through Europe. The organizations, publications, and national tourist offices listed below can provide you with more than enough literature on your destination countries. All you need to do is dive in and plan a trip tailored to your specific interests and needs without losing sight of the fact that this is your vacation and you're doing it for fun. Don't overplan your itinerary so that the trip becomes one big blur; just relax and wander through Europe at your own particular pace.

Give careful consideration to those with whom you travel and the time of year in which you travel. Friends can insulate you from local culture, but they also provide an invaluable source of energy and comfort, offer extra safety, and share in food and lodging costs. If you choose to travel with others, discuss your trip in detail before you leave to make sure your interests are compatible. Going solo can be the best way to travel as well as the worst. Freedom of movement is counterbalanced by the danger of loneliness and need for extra safety precautions, particularly for women (see Women Travelers). A budget travel subculture fills Europe's hostels and ensures that you will only be as lonely as you want to be, with or without travel companions. Also, when planning your trip, remember that summer is the high season for traveling in Europe, with the masses coming in around July and August; June or September may be a better time to go.

■■■ USEFUL ADDRESSES

The following organizations, offices and agencies contain a wealth of information. They can help familiarize you with your destination countries before you get there and help you organize your travel plans.

USEFUL TRAVEL ORGANIZATIONS

Campus Travel, 52 Grosvenor Gardens, London SW1W 0AG (tel. (0171) 730 88 32, fax 730 57 39). Offices across the U.K. Student and youth fares on travel by train, boat, and bus, as well as flexible airline tickets. Offers telephone booking service from **London/Europe** (tel. (0171) 730 34 02), from **North America** (tel. (0171) 730 21 01), and **worldwide** (tel. (0171) 730 81 11). Supplies maps, guides, ID cards for youths, and special travel insurance for students and those under 35.

Council on International Educational Exchange (CIEE), 205 East 42nd St., New York NY 10017 (tel. (212) 661-1414). A private, non-profit organization, CIEE administers work, volunteer, academic and professional programs worldwide. Offers identity cards (including the ISIC and the GO 25) and a range of publications, among them *Student Travels* (free, postage $1) and *Going Places: The High School Student's Guide to Study, Travel and Adventure Abroad* ($13.95, postage $1.50).

Council Travel. CIEE subsidiary. Specializes in student and budget travel. Offers charter flight tickets, guidebooks, ISIC, ITIC, and GO 25 cards, hostelling cards, and travel gear. Forty-one U.S. offices, including: 729 Boylston St. #201, **Boston,** MA 02116 (tel. (617) 266-1926), 1153 N. Dearborn St., 2nd Fl., **Chicago,** IL 60610 (tel. (312) 951-0585), 6715 Hillcrest, **Dallas,** TX 75205 (tel. (214) 363-9941), 1093 Broxton Ave., Suite 220, **Los Angeles,** CA 90024 (tel. (310) 208-3551), 205 East 42nd St., **New York,** NY 10017 (tel. (212) 661-1450), 715 SW Morrison #600, **Portland,** OR 97205 (tel. (503) 228-1900), 530 Bush St., Ground Fl., **San Francisco,** CA 94108 (tel. (415) 421-3473), 1314 Northeast

TOP 5 Ways to Save Money While Traveling

5. Ship yourself in a crate marked "Livestock." Remember to poke holes in the crate.

4. Board a train dressed as Elvis and sneer and say "The King rides for free."

3. Ask if you can walk through the Channel Tunnel.

2. Board the plane dressed as an airline pilot, nod to the flight attendants, and hide in the rest room until the plane lands.

1. Bring a balloon to the airline ticket counter, kneel, breathe in the helium, and ask for the kiddie fare.

But if you're serious about saving money while you're traveling abroad, just get an ISIC—the International Student Identity Card. Discounts for students on international airfares, hotels and motels, car rentals, international phone calls, financial services, and more.

For more information:

In the United States:

 Council on International Educational Exchange
205 East 42nd St.
New York, NY 10017
1-800-GET-AN-ID
Available at Council Travel offices (see inside front cover)

In Canada:

 Travel CUTS
243 College Street,
Toronto, Ontario M5T 2Y1
(416) 977-3703
Available at Travel CUTS offices nationwide

43rd St. #210, **Seattle,** WA 98105 (tel. (206) 632-2448). Also in San Diego, CA, Tempe, AZ, Washington, DC, Miami, FL, Ann Arbor, MI, Providence, RI, and Cambridge, MA. In **Europe,** 28A Poland St. (Oxford Circus), **London** W1V 3DB (tel. (0171) 437 77 67), 22, rue des Pyramides, 75001 **Paris** (tel. (1) 44 55 55 44), and 18, Graf-Adolf-Str., **Düsseldorf** (tel. (0211) 32 90 88).

Council Charter, 205 East 42nd St., New York, NY 10017 (tel. (212) 661-0311 or (800) 800-8222). CIEE subsidiary. Offers a combination of inexpensive charter and scheduled airfares from a variety of U.S. gateways to most major European destinations. One-way fares and open jaws (fly into one city and out of another) are available. Council Charter also offers a US$30 cancellation waiver which allows passengers to cancel for any reason up to three hours prior to departure from the U.S. and receive a full refund.

Federation of International Youth Travel Organizations (FITYO), Bredgade 25H, DK-1260, Copenhagen K, Denmark (tel. 33 33 96 00, fax 33 93 96 76). International organization promoting educational, cultural and social travel for young people. Member organizations include language schools, educational travel companies, national tourist boards, accommodation centers and other suppliers of travel services to youth and students. Sponsors the GO 25 Card, which offers various discounts and benefits worldwide. Like the ISIC, this card can be obtained from local student travel services, and from some hostel associations.

International Student Travel Confederation, Store Kongensgade 40H, 1264 Copenhagen K, Denmark (tel. 33 93 93 03, fax 33 93 73 77). Sells ISIC. Affiliated organizations include International Student Rail Association (ISRA), Student Air Travel Association (SATA), ISIS Travel Insurance, and the International Association for Educational and Work Exchange Programs (IAEWEP).

Let's Go Travel, Harvard Student Agencies, Inc., 53-A Church St., Cambridge, MA 02138 (tel. (800) 5-LETS GO (553-8746) or (617) 495-9649). Offers railpasses, HI/AYH memberships, ISICs, International Teacher ID cards, GO 25 cards, guidebooks, maps, bargain flights, and a complete line of budget travel gear. All items available by mail; call or write for a catalog. Also, see insert in this book.

STA Travel, 5900 Wilshire Blvd. #2110, Los Angeles, CA 90036 (tel. (800) 777-0112 nationwide). Discount airfares for travelers under 26 and full-time students under 32, railpasses, accommodations, tours, insurance & ISICs. 11 offices in US, including: 297 Newbury St., **Boston,** MA 02116 (tel. (617) 266-6014), 48 E. 11th St., **New York,** NY 10003 (tel. (212) 477-7166), 51 Grant Ave., **San Francisco,** CA 94108 (tel. (415) 391-8407), and 2401 Pennsylvania Ave., **Washington,** DC 20037 (tel. (202) 887-0912). In the **U.K.,** 117 Euston Rd., **London** NW1 2SX (tel. (0171) 937 99 21l). In **Australia,** 222 Faraday St., **Melbourne,** VIC 3053 (tel. (03) 349 24 11). In **New Zealand,** 10 High St., **Auckland** (tel. (09) 398 99 95).

Travel CUTS (Canadian University Travel Services, Ltd.), 187 College St., Toronto, Ont. M5T 1P7 (tel. (416) 798-CUTS (798-2887), fax 979-8167). Offices across Canada. Also, in the **U.K.,** 295-A Regent St., London W1R 7YA (tel. (0171) 637 31 61). Discounted transatlantic and domestic flights; ISIC, GO 25, and HI hostel cards; and discount travel passes. Special student fares with valid ISIC. Offers free *Student Traveller* magazine, and info on Student Work Abroad Program (SWAP).

University and Student Travel (USTN). A national association of university travel agencies (in most cases located on campus in student unions) who specialize in student travel. Offers ISICs, GO 25 Cards, youth hostel cards, STA and CIEE student tickets, USTN student discount airline tickets, Eurail and BritRail passes, student tours, etc. Member agencies across the U.S, including Berkeley Northside Travel, 1824 Euclid Ave., **Berkeley,** CA 94709 (tel. (510) 843-1000, fax 843-7537), James Travel Points, UMC/Rm. 162, Campus Box 207, **Boulder,** CO 80309 (tel. (303) 492-5154, fax 492-2183), Mid America Travel, 515 East Green St., **Champaign,** IL 61820 (tel. (217) 344-1600, fax 344-6171), and ASUCLA Travel Service, Ackerman Union, 308 Westwood Plaza, **Los Angeles,** CA 90024 (tel. (310) 825-9131, fax 206-3212),

USIT Ltd., 19-21 Aston Quay, O'Connell Bridge, Dublin 2 (tel. (01) 679 88 33, fax 677 88 43). Sells ISIC, HI hostel cards and *Let's Go*. In addition to selling dicounted student fares on scheduled flights, USIT books its own charter flights in the summer for some of the best flight deals going.

ESSENTIALS

SPECIALIZING IN STUDENT TRAVEL

SCHEDULED FLIGHTS TO EUROPE AND BEYOND
Asia, Africa, Latin America, South Pacific and around the world.
Experienced staff. Best prices!

EURAIL/EURAIL YOUTH PASSES ISSUED IMMEDIATELY
TICKETS VALID UP TO ONE YEAR
I.D. INFORMATION

PRISM·TRAVEL
342 Madison Ave., Suite 1930, New York, NY 10173
1-800-272-9676
1-212-986-8420 in NYC

EUROPE
NO FRONTIERS

Usit student and youth travel specialists have been helping young Europeans find their way around the globe for over 30 years. Low cost, fully flexible travel options combined with a service second to none.

When in Europe call into the nearest Usit travel shop where our English speaking staff will be delighted to help.

Major credit cards accepted.

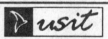

TRAVEL OFFICES
ATHENS:
Usit, 3 Filellinon Street (off Syntagma Square) 105 57 Athens Tel: 324 1884
BRUSSELS:
Connections-Eurotrain N, Head Office, 19/21 Rue du Midi, Brussels 1000 Tel: 02/512 50 60
DUBLIN:
Usit, Aston Quay, O'Connell Bridge, Dublin 2 Tel: 01-679 8833
LONDON:
Campus Travel, 52 Grosvenor Gardens, London SW1W 0AG Tel: Europe: 071-730 3402 Worldwide : 071-730 8111
PARIS:
Usit Voyages, 12 Rue Vivienne, 75002 Paris Tel: 1-42 96 0603

Low Cost Flexible Fares for the Independent Traveller

NATIONAL TOURIST OFFICES

Austrian National Tourist Office: U.S.: P.O. Box 1142, New York, NY 10108-1142. Tel. (212) 944-6880. Fax 730-4568. **Canada:** 2 Bloor St. East #3330, Toronto, Ont. M4W 1A8. Tel. (416) 967-3381. Fax 967-4101. **U.K.:** 30 St. George St., London W1R 0AL. Tel. (0171) 629 04 61. Fax 499 60 38. **Ireland:** Honorary Representation for Ireland, Merrion Hall, Strand Rd., Sandymount, P.O. Box 2506, Dublin 4. Tel. (01) 283 04 88. Fax 283 05 31. **Australia and New Zealand:** 36 Carrington St. 1st Fl., Sydney NSW 2000. Tel. (02) 299 36 21. Fax 299 38 08. **South Africa:** Private Bag X18, Parklands, 2121 Johannesburg. Tel. (11) 442 72 35. Fax 442 83 04.

Belgian Tourist Office: U.S.: 780 Third Ave. #1501, New York, NY 10017-7076. Tel. (212) 758-8130. Fax 355-7675

British Tourist Authority: U.S.: 551 Fifth Ave., 7th Fl., New York, NY 10176-0799. Tel. (800) 462-2748. **Canada:** 111 Avenue Rd., Ste. 450, Toronto, Ont. M5R 3J8. Tel. (416) 925-6326. **Australia:** The University Centre, 210 Clarence St., Sydney NSW 2000. Tel. (02) 267 45 55.

Balkan Holidays (Bulgaria): U.S.: 41 E. 42nd St. #508, New York, NY 10017. Tel. (212) 573-5530. Fax 573-5538. **Canada (Consulate):** 65 Overlea Blvd. # 406, Toronto, Ont. M4H 1P1. Tel. (416) 696-2420 or 696-2778. Fax 696-8019. **U.K.:** Sofia House, 19 Conduit St., London W1R 9TD. Tel. (0171) 491 44 99. Fax 491 70 68. **Ireland (Trade Representation):** 22 Burlington Rd., Dublin. Tel. (01) 68 40 10. **Australia (Consulate):** 1/4 Carlotta Rd., Double Bay, NSW 2028. Tel. (612) 327 75 92 or 327 44 40. Fax 327 80 67.

Čedok (Private Czech Tourist Agency): U.S.: 10 E. 40th St., New York, NY 10016. Tel. (212) 689-9720. Fax 481-0597. **U.K.:** 17-18 Old Bond St., London W1X 4RB. Tel. (0171) 629 60 58. For other countries contact the local embassy or consulate of the Czech Republic. **Canada (Consulate):** 1305 Av. des Peins ouest, Montréal, Qué. H3G 1B2. Tel. (514) 849-4495. Fax 849-4117. **Ireland (Consulate):** Trade Mission of the Czech Republic, Confederation House of Irish Industry, Kildare St., Dublin 2. Tel. (3) 71 49 81. Fax 679 86 38. **Australia (Embassy):** 38 Culgoa Circuit, O'Malley, Canberra, ACT 2606. Tel. (06) 290 13 86. Fax 290 00 06. **South Africa (Embassy):** 936 Pretorius St., Arcadia, Pretoria 0083, or P.O. Box 3326, 0001 Pretoria. Tel. (12) 342 34 77. Fax 43 20 33.

Danish Tourist Board: U.S.: 655 Third Ave., 18th Fl., New York, NY 10017. Tel. (212) 949-2333. **Canada:** PO/CP 636, Mississauga, Ont. L5M 2C2. Tel. (905) 820 8984.

Estonian Consulate-General: U.S.: 630 Fifth Ave. #2415, New York, NY 10111. Tel. (212) 247-7634. **Canada:** 958 Broadview Ave., Toronto, Ont. M4K 2R6. Tel. (416) 461-0764. **U.K.:** 16 Hyde Park Gate, London SW7 5D6. Tel. (0171) 589 34 28.

Finnish Tourist Board: U.S.: 655 Third Ave., New York, NY 10017. Tel. (212) 949-2333. Fax 983-5260. **U.K.:** 66/68 Haymarket, London SW1Y 4RF. Tel. (0171) 930 58 71.

French Government Tourist Office: U.S.: 610 Fifth Ave., New York, NY 10020. Tel. (900) 990-0040; costs US50¢/min. **Canada:** 1981 av. McGill College #490, Montréal, Qué. H3A 2W9. Tel. (514) 288-4264. **U.K.:** 178 Piccadilly, London W1V 0AL. Tel. (71) 493 66 96. **Ireland:** 35 Lower Abbey St., Dublin 1. Tel. (353) 17 03 40 46. **Australia:** BNP building, 12th Fl., 12 Castlereagh St., Sydney NSW 2000. Tel. (02) 231 52 44.

German National Tourist Office: U.S.: 122 E. 42nd St., 52nd Fl., New York, NY 10168-0072. Tel. (212) 661-7200. Fax 661-7174. **Canada:** 175 Bloor St. E., North Tower #604, Toronto, Ont. M4W 3R8. Tel. (416) 968-1570. Fax 968-1986. **U.K.:** Nightingale House, 65 Curzon St., London W1Y 7PE. Tel. (0171) 495 39 90. Fax 495 61 29. **Australia:** Lufthansa House, 9th Fl., 143 Macquarie St., Sydney NSW 2000. Tel. (012) 367 38 90. Fax 367 38 95. **South Africa:** c/o Lufthansa German Airlines, 22 Girton Rd., Parktown, Johannesburg 2000. Tel. (011) 643 16 15. Fax 484 27 50.

Greek National Tourist Office: U.S.: Olympic Tower, 645 Fifth Ave., 5th Fl., New York, NY 10022. Tel. (212) 421-5777. Fax 826-6940. **Canada:** 1300 Bay St., Toronto, Ont. M5R 3K8. Tel. (416) 968-2220. Fax 968-6533. **U.K.:** 4 Conduit St.,

ESSENTIALS

PRESENTING AN INDEPENDENT APPROACH TO TRAVEL.

If you have independent ideas about travel, we specialize in putting you exactly where you want to be. And with over 100 offices worldwide, we'll take care of you when you're there. So when it's time to plan your trip, call us at 1.800.777.0112.

New York: 212-477-7166
Washington DC: 202-887-0912
Philadelphia: 215-382-2928
Boston: 617-266-6014
Los Angeles: 213-934-8722
San Francisco: 415-391-8407

STA
STA TRAVEL
We've been there.

London W1R DOJ. Tel. (0171) 734 59 97. **Australia: 5**1-57 Pitt St., Sydney, NSW 2000. Tel. (02) 241 16 63.

IBUSZ (Hungarian Tourist Organization): U.S.: 1 Parker Plaza #1104, Fort Lee, NJ 07024. Tel. (201) 592-8585. Fax 592-8736. **U.K.:** Danube Travel, 6 Conduit St., London W1R 9TG. Tel. (0171) 493 02 63. Fax 493 69 63. **Canada (Consulate):** 102 Bloor St. W. #1001, Toronto, Ont. M5S 1M8. Tel. (416) 923-8981. Fax 923-2732. **Ireland (Consulate):** 2 Fitzwilliam Pl., Dublin 2. Tel. (01) 61 29 03. Fax 61 28 80. **Australia (Consulate):** Edgecliff Centre #405, 203-233 New South Head Rd., Edgecliff NSW 2027. Tel. (02) 328 78 59 or 328 78 60. Fax 327 18 29.

Icelandic Tourist Board: U.S.: 655 Third Ave., New York, NY 10017. Tel. (212) 949-2333 ext. 130. Fax 983-5260.

Irish Tourist Board: U.S.: 345 Park Ave., New York, NY 10154. Tel. (800) 223-6470 or (212) 418-0800. Fax 371-9052. **Canada:** 160 Bloor St. E. #1150, Toronto, Ont. M4W 1B9. Tel. (416) 929-2777. Fax 929-6783. **U.K.:** 150 New Bond St., London W1Y 0AQ. Tel. (0171) 493 32 01. Fax 493 90 65. **Australia:** Level 5, 36 Carrington Street, Sydney NSW 2000. Tel. (02) 299 61 77. Fax 299 63 23.

Italian Government Travel Office: U.S.: 630 Fifth Ave. #1565, New York, NY 10111. Tel. (212) 245-4822. Fax 586-9249. 12400 Wilshire Blvd. #550, Los Angeles, CA 90025. Tel. (310) 820-0098. Fax 820-6357. **Canada:** 1 Pl. Ville Marie #1914, Montréal, Qué. H3B 3M9. Tel. (514) 866-7667. Fax 392-1429. **U.K.:** 1 Princes St., London W1R 8AY. Tel. (0171) 408 12 54. Fax 493 66 95. **Ireland:** 47, Merrion Square, Dublin 2. Tel. (01) 76 63 97. Fax 76 45 14. **South Africa:** Enit Casella Postale 6507, Johannesburg 2000.

Latvian Embassy and Honorary Consul: U.S. (Embassy): 4325 17th St., NW, Washington, DC 20011. Tel. (202) 726-8213. Fax 726-6785. **Canada (Consulate):** 230 Clemow Ave., Ottawa, Ont. K1S 2B6. Tel. (613) 238-6868. **U.K. (Embassy):** 72 Queensborough Terr., London W23 SP. Tel. (0171) 727 16 98. **Australia (Consulate):** P.O. Box 23, Kew, Victoria, 3101, Melbourne. Tel. (03) 499 69 20.

Lithuanian Embassy, Consulate, and Honorary Consul: U.S. (Embassy): 2622 16th St. NW, Washington, DC 20009. Tel. (202) 234-5860. Fax 328-0466. **U.S. (Consulate):** 420 5th Ave., NY 10018. Tel. (212) 354-7849. Fax 354-7911. **Canada (Honorary Consul):** 235 Yorkland Blvd., Willowdale, Ont. M2J. Tel. (416) 494-4099. Fax 494-4382. **U.K. (Embassy):** 17 Essex Villas, London W8 7BP. Tel. (0171) 937 15 88 or 938 24 81. Fax 938 33 29. **Australia (Honorary Consul):** 26 Jalanga Crescent, Aranda ACT 2614. Tel. and fax (616) 253 20 63.

Luxembourg National Tourist Office: U.S.: 17 Beekman Pl., New York, NY 10022. Tel. (212) 935-8888. Fax 935-5896. **U.K.:** 122 Regent St., London W1R 5FE. Tel. (0171) 734 12 05.

Netherlands Board of Tourism: U.S.: 225 N. Michigan Ave. #326, Chicago, IL 60601. Tel. (312) 819-0300. **U.K.:** 25-28 Buckingham Gate, London SW 1E 6LD. Tel. (0171) 828 79 00.

Northern Ireland Tourist Board: U.S.: 551 Fifth Ave., New York, NY 10176-0799. Tel. (212) 992-0101. Fax 922-0099. **Canada:** 111 Avenue Rd. #450, Toronto, Ont. M5R 3J8. Tel. (416) 925-6368. Fax 961-2175. **U.K.:** 11 Berkeley St., London W1X 5AD. Tel. (0171) 493 06 01. Fax 499 37 31. **Australia:** 36 Carrington St., Sydney NSW 2000. Tel. (02) 299 61 77. Fax 299 63 23.

Norwegian Tourist Board: U.S.: 655 Third Ave., New York, NY 10017. Tel. (212) 949-2333. **U.K.:** Charles House, 5-11 Lower Regent St., London SW1Y 4LR. Tel. (0171) 839 26 50.

Polish National Tourist Office: U.S.: 275 Madison Ave. #1711, New York, NY 10016. Tel. (212) 338-9412. Fax 338-9283. Or, 333 N. Michigan Ave. #224, Chicago, IL, 60601. Tel. (312) 236-9013. Fax 236 1125. **Canada (Embassy):** 1500 Pine Ave., Montréal, Qué. H3G 1B4. Tel. (514) 937-9481.

Portuguese National Tourist Office: U.S.: 590 Fifth Ave., 4th Fl., New York, NY 10036-4704. Tel. (212) 354-4403. Fax 764-6137. **Canada:** 60 Bloor St. W. #1005, Toronto, Ont. M4W 3B8. Tel. (416) 921-7376. Fax 921 1353. **U.K.:** 22/25A Sackville St., London W1X 1DE. Tel. (0171) 494 14 41. Fax 494 18 68. **Ireland:** Portuguese Embassy, Knocksinna, Foxrock, Dublin 18. Tel. and Fax (01) 289 68 52. **Australia (Embassy):** 6 Campion St., 1st Fl., Deakin ACT, 2600, Canberra. Tel.

ESSENTIALS

(062) 85 20 84. **New Zealand (Embassy):** 117 Arney Rd., Remuera, Auckland 5. Tel. (649) 524 82 66. **South Africa:** Diamand Corner, 8th fl., 68 Eloff St., P.O. Box 70, 2000 Johannesburg. Tel. (11) 337 47 75 or 337 47 82. Fax 337 16 13.

Romanian National Tourist Office: U.S.: 342 Madison Ave. #210, New York, NY 10173. Tel. (212) 697-6971. Fax 697-6972. **U.K.:** 17 Nottingham St., London W1M 3RD. Tel. (0171) 224 36 92. **Canada (Embassy):** 655 Rideau St., Ottawa, Ont. K1N 6A3. Tel. (613) 789-3709 or 789-5345. Fax 789-4365.

Intourist Travel Information Office (Russia): U.S.: 610 Fifth Ave. #603, New York, NY 10020. Tel. (212) 757-3884/5; for reservations (800) 982-8416. Fax (212) 459-0031. **Canada:** 1801 McGill College Ave. #630, Montréal, Qué. H3A 2N4. Tel. (514) 849-6394. **U.K.:** 219 Marsh Wall, London E14 9FJ. Tel. (0171) 538 86 00.

Slovakia Travel Service: U.S.: 10 E. 40th St. #3601, New York, NY 10016. Tel. (212) 213-3865/2. Fax 213-4461 or 684-7648.

Slovenian Tourist Office: U.S.: 122 E. 42nd St. #3006, New York, NY 10168. Tel. (212) 682-5896. Fax 661-2469. **U.K.:** 57 Grosvenor St., London, W1X 9DA. Tel. (0171) 499 74 88. Fax 355 48 28.

Tourist Office of Spain: U.S.: 665 Fifth Ave., New York, NY 10022. Tel. (212) 759-8822. Fax 980-1053. **Canada:** 102 Bloor St. W. #1400, Toronto, Ont. M5S 1M8. Tel. (416) 961-3131. Fax 961-1992. **U.K.:** 57-58 St. James St., London SW1A 1LD. Tel. (0171) 499 09 01. Fax 629 42 57. **Australia:** 203 Castlereagh St. #21A, Sydney, NSW 2000. Tel. (02) 264 79 66. Fax 267 51 11.

Swiss National Tourist Office (including Liechtenstein): U.S.: 608 Fifth Ave., New York, NY 10020. Tel. (212) 757-5944. Fax 262-6116. **Canada:** 154 University St. #610, Toronto, Ont. M5H 3Y9. Tel. (416) 971-9734. Fax 971-6425. **U.K.:** Swiss Centre, Swiss Court, London W1V 8EE. Tel. (0171) 734 19 21. Fax 437 45 77.

Turkish Cultural and Information Office: U.S.: 821 United Nations Plaza, New York, NY 10017. Tel. (212) 687-2194. **U.K.:** 170-173 Piccadilly, London W1V 9DD. Tel. (0171) 734 86 81/2.

IT'S THE

Incredibly low rates on travel to:

NEW

EUROPE • TAHITI • INDIA

ATTITUDE

• SKIING IN THE FRENCH ALPS

CALL NOW! OPEN 7 DAYS A WEEK
EAST: 800-366-6387
WEST: 800-677-0720

NEW FRONTIERS

Ukrainian Embassies: U.S.: 3350 M St., NW, Washington, DC 20007. Tel. (202) 333-0606. Fax 333-7510. **Canada:** 331 Metcalfe St., Ottawa, Ont. K2P153. Tel. (613) 230-2961. Fax 230-2400. **U.K.:** 78 Kensington Park Rd., London W112PL. Tel. (0171) 727 63 12. Fax 792 17 08. **Australia:** 4 Bloom St., Moonee Pons, 3039, Melbourne. Tel. (613) 326 01 35. Fax 326 01 39.

■■■ DOCUMENTS AND FORMALITIES

Be sure to file all applications several weeks or months in advance of your planned departure date. Remember, you are relying on government agencies to complete these transactions. A backlog in processing can spoil your plans.

When you travel, always carry on your person two or more forms of identification, including at least one photo ID. A passport combined with a driver's license or birth certificate usually serves as adequate proof of your identity and citizenship. Many establishments, especially banks, require several IDs before cashing traveler's checks. Never carry all your forms of ID together, however; you risk being left entirely without ID or funds in case of theft or loss. Also, carry half a dozen extra passport-size photos that you can attach to the sundry IDs or railpasses you will eventually acquire. If you plan an extended stay, register your passport with the nearest embassy or consulate.

U.S. citizens seeking information about documents, formalities and travel abroad should request the booklet *Your Trip Abroad* from the U.S. Dept. of State, Bureau of Consular Affairs, Public Affairs, Room 5807, Washington, DC 20520-4818.

ENTRANCE REQUIREMENTS

Citizens of the U.S., Canada, the U.K., Ireland, Australia, New Zealand, and South Africa all need valid passports to enter any European country and to re-enter their own country. Some countries will not allow entrance if the holder's passport will expire in less than six months, and returning to the U.S. with an expired passport may result in a fine. Some countries in Europe will also require a visa.

When you enter a country, dress neatly and carry **proof of your financial independence,** such as a visa to the next country on your itinerary, an airplane ticket to depart, enough money to cover the cost of your living expenses, etc. Admission as a visitor does not include the right to work, which is authorized only by a work permit (see Alternatives to Tourism, below). Entering certain countries to study requires a special visa, and immigration officers may also want to see proof of acceptance from a school, proof that the course of study will take up most of your time in the country, and as always, proof that you can support yourself.

Passports

Before you leave, photocopy the page of your passport that contains your photograph and identifying information, especially your passport number. Carry this photocopy in a safe place apart from your passport, and leave another copy at home. These measures will help prove your citizenship and facilitate the issuing of a new passport if you lose the original document. Consulates also recommend you carry an expired passport or an official copy of your birth certificate in a part of your baggage separate from other documents. You can request a duplicate birth certificate from the Bureau of Vital Records and Statistics in your state or province of birth.

If you do lose your passport, it may take weeks to process a replacement, and your new one may be valid only for a limited time. In addition, any visas stamped in your old passport will be irretrievably lost. If this happens, immediately notify the local police and the nearest embassy or consulate of your home government. To expedite its replacement, you will need to know all information previously recorded and show identification and proof of citizenship. Some consulates can issue new passports within two days if you give them proof of citizenship. In an

ESSENTIALS

emergency, ask for immediate temporary traveling papers that will permit you to reenter your home country.

Your passport is a public document belonging to your nation's government. You may have to surrender it to a foreign government official; but, if you don't get it back in a reasonable amount of time, inform the nearest mission of your home country.

Applying for a Passport

U.S. and Canada U.S. citizens may apply for a passport, valid for 10 years (five years if under 18) at any federal or state **courthouse** or **post office** authorized to accept passport applications, or at a **U.S. Passport Agency,** located in Boston, Chicago, Honolulu, Houston, Los Angeles, Miami, New Orleans, New York, Philadelphia, San Francisco, Seattle, Stamford, or Washington, DC. Refer to the "U.S. Government, State Department" section of the telephone directory or call your local post office for addresses. Parents must apply in person for children under age 13. You must apply in person if this is your first passport, you're under age 18, or if your current passport is more than 12 years old or was issued before your 18th birthday. It will cost US$65 (under 18, US$40). You can **renew** your passport by mail or in person for US$55. Processing usually takes three to four weeks. Passport agencies offer **rush service** if you have proof that you're departing within five working days (e.g. an airplane ticket). For more info, contact the U.S. Passport Information's **24-hour recorded message** (tel. (202) 647-0518). If your passport is lost or stolen in the U.S., report it in writing to Passport Services, U.S. Department of State, 1111 19th St., NW, Washington, DC 20522-1705, or to the nearest passport agency.

Canadian application forms in English and French are available at all passport offices, post offices, and most travel agencies. Citizens may apply in person at any one of 28 regional Passport Offices across Canada. Travel agents can direct the applicant to the nearest location. Canadian citizens residing abroad should contact the nearest Canadian embassy or consulate. You can apply by mail by sending a completed application form with appropriate documentation and the CDN$35 fee to Passport Office, Foreign Affairs, Ottawa, Ont., K1A OG3. Processing takes approxi-

More Europe... for less money.

Call us for low rates on trips from 23 days to 6 months. Our minimum age is only 18 years.

RENAULT *EURODRIVE*
l'Europe en Liberté
The Alternative to Car Rental

Call 1-800-221-1052
From Western states, call 1-800-477-7116
650 First Avenue, New York, NY 10016

To see the insider's Europe, take to the roads.

To save money with the insider's car plan, call Eurodrive.

Our *low, tax-free rates* on comfortable, brand-new cars are truly all-inclusive and can save you hundreds of dollars off rental car costs.

Travel Agent inquiries welcome

LG 8/94

mately five business days for in-person applications and three weeks for mailed ones. A passport is valid for five years and is not renewable. Keep in mind that some countries require a child to carry his or her own passport whether traveling with a parent or not. If a passport is lost abroad, Canadians must be able to prove citizenship with another document. For additional info, call (800) 567-6868 (24 hrs; from Canada only). In Metro Toronto call 973-3251. Montrealers should dial 283-2152. Refer to the booklet *Bon Voyage, But...* for further help and a list of Canadian embassies and consulates abroad. It is available free of charge from any passport office or from Info-Export (BPTE), External Affairs, Ottawa, Ont., K1A OG2.

U.K., Ireland, Australia, New Zealand, and South Africa British citizens, British Dependent Territories citizens, and British Overseas citizens may apply for a **full passport.** Residents of the U.K., the Channel Islands and the Isle of Man also have the option of applying for a more restricted **British Visitor's Passport.** For a full passport, valid for 10 years (five years if under 16), apply in person or by mail to a passport office, located in London, Liverpool, Newport, Peterborough, Glasgow, or Belfast. The fee is UK£18. Children under 16 may be included on a parent's passport. Processing by mail usually takes four to six weeks. The London office offers same-day walk-in rush service; arrive early. A Visitor's Passport, valid for one year in some western European countries and Bermuda only, is available from main post offices in England, Scotland and Wales, and from passport offices in Northern Ireland, the Channel Islands and the Isle of Man. The fee is UK£12.

   Irish citizens can apply for a passport by mail to either the Department of Foreign Affairs, Passport Office, Setanta Centre, Molesworth St., Dublin 2 (tel. (01) 671 16 33), or the Passport Office, 1A South Mall, Cork (tel. (021) 27 25 25). You can obtain an application form at a local Garda station or request one from a passport office. Passports cost IR£45 and are valid for 10 years. Citizens under 18 or over 65 can request a three-year passport that costs IR£10.

   Australian citizens must apply for a passport in person at a post office, a passport office, or an Australian diplomatic mission overseas. An appointment may be necessary. Passport offices are in Adelaide, Brisbane, Canberra, Darwin, Hobart, Melbourne, Newcastle, Perth, and Sydney. A parent may file an application for a child who is under 18 and unmarried. Application fees are adjusted every three months.

   Applicants for **New Zealand** passports must contact their local Link Centre, travel agent, or New Zealand Representative for an application form, which they must complete and mail to the New Zealand Passport Office, Documents of National Identity Division, Department of Internal Affairs, Box 10-526, Wellington (tel. (04) 474 81 00). The application fee is NZ$80 for an application submitted in New Zealand and NZ$130 for one submitted overseas (if under age 16, NZ$40 and NZ$65, respectively). Standard processing time is 10 working days from receipt of completed application. Overseas citizens should send the application to the nearest embassy, high commission, or consulate that is authorized to issue passports.

   South African citizens can apply for a passport at any Home Affairs Office. Two photos, either a birth certificate or an identity book, and the SAR38 fee must accompany a completed application. For further information, contact the nearest Department of Home Affairs Office.

Visas

A visa is an endorsement that a foreign government stamps into a passport; it allows the bearer to stay in that country for a specified purpose and period of time. Most visas cost US$10-30 and allow you to spend about a month in a country, within six months to a year from the date of issue.

   Most Western European nations do not require visas of American, Canadian, British, Irish, Australian, or New Zealand citizens staying for less than three months; France requires a visa from Australians. Eastern European countries' visa requirements have been eroding steadily since 1989 but vary greatly for citizens of different countries. We list specific visa requirements and consulate addresses in the Getting

IF YOU CAN'T AFFORD TO TRAVEL, JOIN THE CLUB.

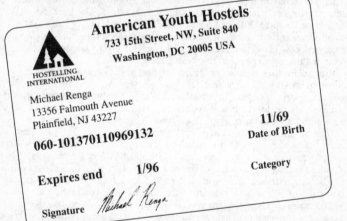

American Youth Hostels
733 15th Street, NW, Suite 840
Washington, DC 20005 USA

HOSTELLING INTERNATIONAL

Michael Renga
13356 Falmouth Avenue
Plainfield, NJ 43227

11/69
Date of Birth

060-101370110969132

Expires end   1/96   Category

Signature   *Michael Renga*

Traveling doesn't have to mean snobby hotels that cost $200 a night. With a Hostelling International card you can stay in Paris for just $20, New York for $20 or Tokyo for $32. Hostels even offer special discounts on everything from museum fees and ski lifts to air, rail and ferry tickets. Plus they have fully equipped do-it-yourself kitchens, which not only save you money but also are great for meeting fellow world travelers. So if you're looking for a less expensive way to travel, join the club. Call 1-800-444-6111 in the U.S., or 1-800-663-5777 in Canada.

HOSTELLING INTERNATIONAL
The new seal of approval of the International Youth Hostel Federation.

HOSTELLING INTERNATIONAL®

There section of each Eastern European country introduction. Check the country's visa requirements and restrictions as close to your departure date as possible.

Some visas are incompatible: Greece won't let you in if you have a passport stamp from Northern Cyprus; Morocco and most Arab countries turn away those with Israeli stamps; and South Africans have been denied entry to Scandinavia. You may ask that these visa or entry stamps be placed on a removable page in your passport. Border officials run the gamut from not nice to downright nasty, so stay informed about visa requirements and restrictions.

If you want to stay for longer, apply for a visa at the country's embassy or consulate in your home country well before your departure. Unless you are a student, extending your stay once you are abroad is more difficult. You must contact the country's immigration officials or local police well before your time is up, and show sound proof of financial resources (see Entrance Requirements).

For more information, send for *Foreign Visa Requirements* (US$0.50) from **Consumer Information Center,** Dept. 454V, Pueblo, CO 81009 (tel. (719) 948-3334), or contact **Center for International Business and Travel (CIBT),** 25 West 43rd St. #1420, New York, NY 10036 (tel. (800) 925-2428 or (212) 575-2811 from NYC). This organization secures visas for travel to and from all countries. The service charge varies; the average cost for a U.S. citizen is US$15-20 per visa.

HOSTEL MEMBERSHIP

Hostelling International (HI), 9 Guessens Rd., Welwyn Garden City, Hertfordshire AL8 6QW, England (tel. (01707) 33 24 87). A worldwide federation of youth hostels (more than 5000 total) and of individual national hostelling associations. All of the organizations listed below are HI national affiliates, and thus comply with any standards and regulations set by HI. Official youth hostels worldwide will normally display the HI logo (a blue triangle) alongside the symbol of one of the 70 national hostel associations.

A one-year HI membership permits you to stay at youth hostels all over Europe at unbeatable prices. And, despite the name, you need not be a youth; travelers over 25 pay only a slight surcharge for a bed. Save yourself potential trouble by procuring a membership card at home; some hostels don't sell them on the spot. For the most part, membership must be acquired through the HI affiliate in one's own country, not abroad. For more details on youth hostels, see Accommodations in each country's Essentials section.

One-year hostel membership cards are available from some travel agencies, including Council Travel, Let's Go Travel, and STA Travel (see Useful Travel Organizations, above), and from the following organizations:

American Youth Hostels (HI-AYH), 733 15th St., NW, #840, Washington, DC, 20005 (tel. (202) 783-6161; fax 783-6171). Comprised of 39 local councils which, in addition to licensing hostels (150 in 36 states and the District of Columbia), provide local members and visitors with special programs, events, trips, and activities. HI-AYH membership cards cost US$25, renewals US$20. (under 18, US$10; over 54, US$15; family cards, US$35). Membership valid for one year from date of issue. Contact AYH for ISIC, student and charter flights, travel equipment, literature on budget travel, and information on summer positions as a group leader for domestic outings.

Hostelling International—Canada (HI-C), 400-205 Catherine St., Ottawa, Ont. K2P 1C3 (tel. (613) 237-7884, fax 237-7868). One-year membership fee CDN$26.75, under 18 CDN$12.84, two-year CDN$37.45.

Youth Hostels Association of England and Wales (YHA), Trevelyan House, 8 St. Stephen's Hill, St. Albans, Herts. AL1 2DY (tel. (01727) 85 52 15) or 14 Southampton St., Covent Garden, London WC2E 7HY (tel. (0171) 836 10 36). Enrollment fees are UK£9, under 18 UK£3, two-day introductory membership (over 18) UK£3, children 5-18 enrolled free when a parent joins.

An Óige (Irish Youth Hostel Association), 61 Mountjoy St., Dublin 7 (tel. (01) 830 45 55, fax 830 58 08). One-year membership is IR£7.50, under 18 IR£4, and family IR£15.

Youth Hostels Association of Northern Ireland (YHANI), 22-32 Donegall Rd., Belfast BT12 5JN, Northern Ireland (tel. (01232) 32 47 33, fax 43 96 99).

Scottish Youth Hostels Association (SYHA), 7 Glebe Crescent, Sterling FK8 2JA (tel. (01786) 45 11 81, fax 45 01 98). Membership UK£6, under 18 UK£2.50.

Australian Youth Hostels Association (AYHA), Level 3, 10 Mallett St., Camperdown, NSW, 2050 (tel. (02) 565 16 99, fax 565 13 25). Fee AUS$40, renewal AUS$24; under 18 fee and renewal both AUS$12.

Youth Hostels Association of New Zealand (YHANZ), P.O. Box 436, 173 Gloucester St., Christchurch 1 (tel. (03) 379 99 70, fax 365 44 76). Annual memberships: Senior (adult) NZ$34, Youth (15-17) NZ$12, under 15 free. Rates are lower for 2- and 3-year memberships. Life membership NZ$240. New Zealand memberships not renewable overseas.

Hostel Association of South Africa, 606 Boston House, Strand St., Cape Town 8001 (tel. (21) 419 18 53).

Budget Accommodation Vol. 1: Europe and the Mediterranean (US$11, CDN$13, UK£7, AUS$15), lists up-to-date information on HI hostels; it's available from any hostel association.

HI has recently instituted an **International Booking Network** which allows you to make confirmed reservations at any of almost 200 hostels in the U.S. and abroad. To reserve space in high season, obtain an International Booking Voucher from any national youth hostel association (in your home country or the one you will visit) and send it to a participating hostel four to eight weeks in advance of your stay, along with US$2 in local currency. You can contact some hostels, indicated in the guide, by fax. If your plans are firm enough to allow it, pre-booking is wise. Reservations can be made for up to three consecutive nights and for groups of up to nine

Are you Ready for Europe?

Let Bitter Root outfit you for your journey

Extra bags, too much gear, and heavy luggage can slow you down.
You want to have the time of your life, not a load of bad memories!
We carry a full line of travel gear that is designed to make your trip a success! We will even include a free packing guide so you will be sure to take along only the things you need. Our prices and shipping are among the lowest you will find. We want to make your trip a great one!

Call anytime, day or night, or write for a FREE Catalog
(800) 688-9577

All products are unconditionally GUARANTEED. If for any reason, you are unhappy with your purchase, return item for a full refund!

Bitter Root
Travel Gear
P.O. Box 3538
Dana Point, CA 92629-8538

Travel Backpacks
Shoulder Bags
Sleeping Gear
Fanny Packs
Laundry Kits
Money Belts
Luggage Tags
Film Protectors
Coffee/Tea Kits
Eating Utensils
Leatherman Tool
Electrical Adapters
Bath & Shower Bag
Lightweight Ponchos
Currency Calculators
Language Translators
Alarm Clocks
Curling Irons
Steam Irons
Hair Dryers
1st Aid Kits
Flashlights
Booklights
Umbrellas
Trip Diary
Toiletries

people, and changes can be made up to three or more days before the date of the reservation. Credit card (MC or Visa) guarantee required.

YOUTH, STUDENT, & TEACHER IDENTIFICATION

The **International Student Identity Card (ISIC)** is the most widely accepted form of student identification. Flashing this card can garner you discounts for sights, theaters, museums, accommodations, train, ferry, and airplane travel, and other services throughout Europe. Present the card wherever you go, and ask about discounts even when none are advertised. It also provides accident insurance of up to US$3000 as well as US$100 per day of in-hospital care for up to 60 days. In addition, cardholders have access to a toll-free Traveler's Assistance hotline whose multilingual staff can provide help in medical, legal, and financial emergencies overseas.

Many student travel offices issue ISICs, including Council Travel, Let's Go Travel, and STA Travel in the U.S.; Travel CUTS in Canada; and any of the organizations under the auspices of the International Student Travel Confederation (ISTC) around the world (see Useful Travel Organizations, above). When you apply for the card, request a copy of the International Student Identity Card Handbook, which lists by country some of the available discounts. You can also write to CIEE for a copy (see Useful Travel Organizations). The card is valid from September to December of the following year. The fee is US$16. Applicants must be at least 12 years old and must be a degree-seeking student of a secondary or post-secondary school. Because of the proliferation of phony ISICs, many airlines and some other services now require other proof of student identity: have a signed letter from the registrar attesting to your student status and stamped with the school seal, and carry your school ID card. The new, US$16 **International Teacher Identity Card (ITIC)** offers similar but limited discounts, as well as medical insurance coverage.

Federation of International Youth Travel Organisations (FIYTO) issues a discount card to travelers who are not students but are under 26. Also known as the **International Youth Discount Travel Card,** or the **GO 25 Card,** this one-year card offers many of the same benefits as the ISIC, and most organizations that sell the ISIC also sell the Go 25 Card. A brochure that lists discounts is free when you purchase the card. To apply, bring: (1) proof of birthdate (copy of birth certificate, passport, or valid driver's license); and (2) a passport-sized photo (with your name printed on the back). The fee is US$16, CDN$12, or UK£4. For information, contact CIEE in the U.S. or FIYTO in Denmark (addresses in Useful Travel Organizations, above)

DRIVING PERMITS AND INSURANCE

Unless you have a valid driver's license from an EU country, you must have an **International Driving Permit** (IDP) to drive in Europe, though certain countries allow travelers to drive with a valid American or Canadian license for a limited number of months. Most car rental agencies don't require the permit. A valid driver's license from your home country must always accompany the IDP. Call an automobile association to find out if your destination country requires the IDP. Even if it doesn't it may be a good idea to get one anyway, in case you're in a position (such as an accident or stranded in a smaller town) where the police may not read or speak English.

Your IDP must be issued in your own country before you depart. U.S. license holders can obtain an International Driving Permit (US$10), valid for one year, at any **American Automobile Association (AAA)** office or by writing to its main office, AAA Florida, Travel Agency Services Department, 1000 AAA Drive (mail stop 28), Heathrow, FL 32746-5080 (tel. (407) 444-4245; fax 444-7823). For further information, contact a local AAA office.

Canadian license holders can obtain an IDP (CDN$10) through any **Canadian Automobile Association (CAA)** branch office in Canada, or by writing to CAA Toronto, 60 Commerce Valley Dr. East, Markham, Ont., L3T 7P9 (tel. (416) 771-3170).

If you are renting a car in Europe chances are that your rental company will supply insurance. Be sure, however, that if you are traveling through more than one country, your insurance is valid in all countries on your itinerary. For those using

ESSENTIALS

Don't forget to write.

Now that you've said, "Let's go," it's time to say
"Let's get American Express® Travelers Cheques." If they are lost or
stolen, you can get a fast and full refund virtually anywhere you
travel. So before you leave be sure and write.

© 1994 American Express Travel Related Services Company, Inc.

their own cars while traveling, the **green card,** or **International Insurance Certificate,** to prove that you have liability insurance, is necessary. Contact any AAA or CAA office to find out which countries have special restrictions on green card auto insurance. European drivers should contact their car insurance companies to check the limitations of their policies for international driving. If you have a collision while in Europe, the accident will show up on your domestic records. Theft insurance is not paid by the rental agency in some countries (especially in Spain and Italy, where cars are stolen more often); in any case, you will be required to pay for insurance when the agency does not.

■■■ MONEY

If you stay in hostels and prepare your own food, expect to spend anywhere from US$12-50 per day plus transportation, depending on the local cost of living and your needs. Don't sacrifice your health or safety for a cheaper tab. Also remember to check the financial pages of a large newspaper for up-to-the-minute exchange rates before embarking on your journey.

CURRENCY AND EXCHANGE

Banks in Europe often use a three-letter code based on the name of the country and the name of the currency (for example, New Zealand dollars are NZD and Norwegian kroner are NOK). We list this code at the beginning of each country section, with the abbreviation we use for that country's currency and the September, 1994 exchange rate for U.S. dollars (US$), Canadian dollars (CDN$), British pounds (UK£), Irish pounds (IR£), Australian dollars (AUS$), New Zealand dollars (NZ$) and South African Rand (SAR).

It is more expensive to buy foreign currency than to buy domestic; i.e., pounds will be less costly in the U.K. than in the U.S. Converting some money before you go, however, will allow you to breeze through the airport while others languish in exchange lines, and is a good practice in case you find yourself stuck with no money after banking hours or on a holiday. It's generally wise to bring at least enough foreign currency to last for the first 24-72 hours of a trip, depending on the day of week you will be arriving. Also, observe commission rates closely, and check newspapers to get the standard rate of exchange. Bank rates are generally the best. Of course, services vary; in Germany, post offices usually offer the best exchange rates, while in Britain and Ireland, they're the worst.

Since you lose money with every transaction, convert in large sums (provided the exchange rate is either staying constant or deteriorating), but not more of any one currency than you will need. Save transaction receipts; some countries require them to reconvert local currency. Exchanging some of your old currency before moving on to a new country, is, although a little more costly, good insurance against arriving after hours in a bankless town.

American Express offices usually charge no commission, but often have slightly poorer rates. Carry some bills or checks in small denominations, especially for those moments when you are forced to exchange money at train stations or, worse yet, at luxury hotels or restaurants. In general, you should carry a range of denominations since, in some countries, charges are levied per check cashed.

Australian and New Zealand dollars and Irish pounds are impossible to exchange in some countries. Keep a few U.S. dollars or German marks handy when heading into Eastern Europe; they can prevent some sticky situations. Western currency will often be the preferred payment in Eastern European hotels; find out which hotels and restaurants require hard currency before going there, and don't use Western money when you don't need to. Don't throw dollars around visibly to gain preferential treatment, however; besides being offensive, it'll make you an instant target for theft. Some restaurant owners, proprietors, or even taxi drivers may pick up on the fact that you're a foreigner and try to force you to pay in hard currency when it's not necessary. Stick to your guns or go somewhere else.

ESSENTIALS

What to do when your *money* is done traveling before you are.

Don't worry. With MoneyGram,℠ your parents can send you money in usually 10 minutes or less to more than 15,500 locations in 75 countries. So if the money you need to see history becomes history, call us and we'll direct you to a MoneyGram agent closest to you.

MoneyGram℠
INTERNATIONAL MONEY TRANSFERS.

USA: 1-800-MONEYGRAM • Canada: 1-800-933-3278 • France: (331) 47-77-70-00
England: (44) Ø*-71-839-7541 • Germany: (0049) Ø*-69-21050 • Spain (91) 322 54 55
When in Europe, contact the nearest American Express Travel Service Office.

"DIAL "0" WHEN CALLING WITHIN COUNTRY. ©1994 IPS INC. MONEYGRAM℠ IS A SERVICE MARK OF INTEGRATED PAYMENT SYSTEMS INC. AMERICAN EXPRESS®
IS A REGISTERED SERVICE MARK OF AMERICAN EXPRESS COMPANY.

TRAVELER'S CHECKS

Traveler's Checks are the safest way to hold money; if they get lost or stolen, travelers get reimbursed by the checks' issuers. They should be ordered well in advance, especially if large sums are being requested. Keep check receipts and a record of which checks you've cashed in a separate place from the checks themselves. Leave a photocopy of check serial numbers with someone at home as back-up in case you lose your copy. Never countersign checks until you're prepared to cash them. Be sure to keep cash on hand in less touristy regions, because smaller establishments may not accept traveler's checks. Finally, be sure to bring your passport with you any time you plan to use the checks.

American Express: Call (800) 221-7282 in U.S. and Canada, (0800) 52 13 13 in the U.K., (008) 25 19 02 in Australia, and (0800) 44 10 68 in New Zealand. Elsewhere, call U.S. collect (801) 964-6665. AmEx traveler's checks are now available in 9 currencies: British, Canadian, Dutch, French, German, Japanese, Saudi Arabian, Swiss, and U.S. They are the most widely recognized worldwide and easiest to replace if lost or stolen. Checks can be purchased for a small fee at American Express Travel Service Offices, banks and American Automobile Association offices. Cardmembers can also purchase checks at American Express Dispensers at Travel Service Offices, at airports, and by ordering them via phone (tel. (800) ORDER-TC (673-3782)). AmEx offices cash their checks commission-free (except where prohibited by national governments) and sell checks which can be signed by either of 2 people traveling together. AAA members can obtain AmEx traveler's checks commission-free at AAA offices. Request AmEx's booklet "Traveler's Companion," listing travel office addresses and stolen check hotlines for each European country.

Barclays Bank: Call (800) 221-2426 in the U.S. and Canada. Sells Visa traveler's checks in U.S. and Canadian dollars, British pounds, and German marks; a 1-3% commission is charged depending on the bank at which the checks are purchased. When the checks are issued, you will receive the number to call from outside the U.S. for lost or stolen checks. Branches throughout Britain. Barclays branches cash any Visa brand checks for free.

Citicorp: Call (800) 645-6556 in the U.S. and Canada, (0171) 982 40 40 in the U.K. Elsewhere, call the U.S. collect at (813) 623-1709. Sells both Citicorp and Citicorp Visa traveler's checks in U.S. and Australian dollars, Japanese yen, German marks, and British pounds. Commission 1-2% on check purchases. Citicorp's World Courier Service guarantees hand-delivery of traveler's checks anywhere in the world.

MasterCard International: Call (800) 223-9920 in U.S. and Canada; elsewhere call U.S. collect (609) 987-7300; from abroad, call collect (44) 733 50 29 95. Offers checks in British, German, Canadian, Australian, Hong Kong, Japanese, French, Swiss, Dutch, Spanish, and U.S. currencies. Commission 1-2% for purchases. Try buying the checks at a Thomas Cook office (see below) for potentially lower commissions.

Thomas Cook: Call (800) 223-7373 for refunds and (800) 223-4030 for orders in the U.S. Elsewhere call U.S. collect (212) 974-5696. Distributes traveler's checks with both the MasterCard and Thomas Cook names printed on them. Checks available in U.S. dollars as well as 10 other currencies. 0-2% commission on purchase. Rates often better than those for Mastercard International.

Visa: Call (800) 227-6811 in the U.S. and Canada, (0171) 937 80 91 in the U.K., and elsewhere, call New York collect (212) 858-8500. Any kind of Visa traveler's checks (Barclays or Citicorp) can be reported lost at the general Visa number.

CREDIT CARDS AND CASH CARDS

Credit cards are not always useful to the budget traveler, but they can prove invaluable in a financial emergency. Many small, cheap establishments don't take them, but many foreign banks will allow you to withdraw money from ATM machines with a credit card. Visa and MasterCard are the most common, followed by American Express and Diner's Club. The British "Barclaycard" is equivalent to Visa and Mastercard is better-known in Europe as "EuroCard" or "Access." You can often

ESSENTIALS

reduce conversion fees by charging a purchase instead of changing traveler's checks. With credit cards such as American Express, Visa, and MasterCard, associated banks will give you an instant cash advance in the local currency as large as your remaining credit line, but in most cases, you will pay devastating rates of interest for such an advance.

American Express (tel. (800) CASH-NOW (528-4800)) has a hefty annual fee (US$55) but offers a number of services. AmEx cardholders can cash personal checks at AmEx offices abroad. Global Assist, a 24-hour hotline offering information and legal assistance in emergencies, is also available (tel. (800) 554-2639 in U.S. and Canada; from abroad call U.S. collect (202) 783-7474). Cardholders can also take advantage of the American Express Travel Service; benefits include assistance in changing airline, hotel, and car rental reservations, sending mailgrams and international cables, and holding your mail at one of the more than 1500 AmEx offices around the world. **MasterCard** (tel. (800) 999-0454) and **Visa** (tel. (800) 336-8472) credit cards are sold by individual banks, and each bank offers different services in conjunction with the card.

Automatic Teller Machines (ATMs; operated by bank cards) in Europe are not quite as prevalent as in North America, but most banks in larger cities are connected to an international money network, usually **CIRRUS** (U.S. tel. (800) 4-CIRRUS (424-7787)) or **PLUS** (U.S. tel. (800) 843-7587). Cirrus now has international cash machines in 43 countries and territories. It charges US$5 to withdraw non-domestically. However, depending on the amount of the withdrawal, the fee might be worth it because ATMs offer low exchange rates. PLUS is not as extensive as Cirrus, but can also be accessed in some foreign countries. Soon, traveler's checks will be available from ATM machines through a new **American Express** service (tel. (800) 528-4800). Call to find out if this service is available near you.

Depending on your home bank's system, you will probably be able to access your own personal bank account whenever you're in need of funds. Do this whenever possible, because ATM machines get the wholesale exchange rate which is generally 5% better than the retail rate most banks use. An important note: European ATMs may not have letters on their keypads, so be sure you memorize your PIN by its numbers before you take off.

SENDING MONEY ABROAD

The easiest way to get money from home is to bring an **American Express card;** AmEx allows green-card holders to draw cash from their checking accounts at any of its major offices and many of its representatives' offices, up to US$1000 every 21 days (no service charge, no interest). AmEx also offers the **American Express Moneygram Service** through which money can be sent from the U.S. to Europe. Fees are commensurate with the amount of money being sent and the particular service requested: ten-minute delivery, overnight, or three to five days. For details about your particular country, call (800) 543-4080 in the U.S. or (800) 933-3278 in Canada.

Western Union (tel. (800) 325-6000 in the U.S., Mexico, and Canada and (448) 17 41 36 39 or (0800) 83 38 33 in Europe) cables money. Service takes longer in certain parts of Portugal (two business days instead of two to three minutes). Again, fees for sending money depend not on where the money's going, but on how much is being sent. Rates are US$29 to send US$250, US$40 to send US$500, and US$50 to send US$1000.

Another option is to **cable money** from bank to bank. Find a local bank big enough to have an international department; bring the address of the receiving bank and the destination account number. Both sender and receiver must usually have accounts at the respective institutions. Transfer can take up to a few days; the fee is usually a flat US$20-30. Outside an AmEx office, avoid trying to cash checks in foreign currencies; they take weeks and a US$30 fee to clear.

If you're an American and suddenly find yourself in big trouble, you can have money sent to you via the State Department's **Citizens Emergency Center** (tel. (202) 647-5225 or 647-7000 after business hours). The State Department, 2201 C St.,

NW, Washington, DC 20520, will cable a modest amount of money to foreign consular offices, which will then disburse it accordingly. Those wishing to send money abroad through the State Department can drop it off at the department itself or cable money to the department through Western Union. Similar contingencies are available to citizens of other countries. In an emergency, contact the nearest consulate and they will contact your home country for a transfer of funds.

■■■ PACKING

PACK LIGHT! Before you leave, pack your bag, strap it on, and imagine yourself walking uphill on hot asphalt for the next three hours. At the slightest sign of heaviness, unpack something. A good rule is to set out what you think you'll need, then take half of it and more money. *The Packing Book* (US$7.95), by Judith Gilford, teaches you how to overcome the "overpacking syndrome", provides various checklists and suggested wardrobes, addresses safety concerns, imparts packing techniques, and more. Order from Ten Speed Press (tel. (800) 841-2665).

If you plan to cover a lot of ground by foot, a sturdy **backpack** is hard to beat. Internal frames stand up to airline baggage handlers and can often be converted to shoulder bags; external frames distribute weight more evenly. Whichever style you choose, avoid extremely low economy prices and go for quality (good packs usually cost at least US$100). If checking a backpack on your flight, tape down loose straps, which can catch in the conveyer belt. Take a light **suitcase** or a large **shoulder bag** if you will not be doing much walking. A plastic bag packed inside your luggage will be useful for dirty laundry, while a small **daypack** is indispensable on plane flights, and for carrying your camera, lunch, and *Let's Go*. Keep your valuables in a **money-belt** or **neck pouch** that sits inside your clothing. (See Safety and Security, below.)

Comfortable **shoes** are crucial. In sunny climates, sandals or other light shoes serve well. For heavy-duty hiking, sturdy lace-up walking boots are necessary. Make sure they have good ventilation. A double pair of socks—light absorbent cotton inside and thick wool outside—will cushion feet, keep them dry, and help prevent blisters. Bring a pair of light flip-flops for protection against the fungal floors of some station and hostel showers.

In wet regions, **raingear** is essential. A waterproof jacket plus a backpack rain cover will take care of you and your pack at a moment's notice; a rain poncho is more cumbersome but lightweight.

Also consider taking a pocketknife (with all the gizmos), needle and thread, safety pins, a sturdy plastic water bottle, a flashlight, detergent soap, an alarm clock, a bath towel, bags that seal shut (for damp clothing, soaps or messy foods), and a padlock. Carry extra toiletries—especially aspirin, razor blades, and tampons—in Eastern Europe. The toilet paper in some areas of Europe can be rough on tender Western bottoms—if you're concerned, bring your own.

Bringing along a camera, while it allows you to immortalize those raucous Vikings you met on the train, can invite a lot of extra worry. If you do, pack some rolls of **film** as well, since it can be quite expensive in well-touristed areas. A less stressful option is the **disposable camera,** available at most supermarkets and drug stores — it will be less tragic if it is stolen, since it is not much more than a paper box. More expensive models include a flash or wide-angle lens.

In most European countries, **electricity** is 220 volts AC, enough to fry any 110V North American appliance. Visit a hardware store for an adapter (which changes the shape of the plug) and a converter (which changes the voltage). Do not make the mistake of using only an adapter, or you'll melt your radio. Contact **Franzus,** Murtha Industrial Park, P.O. Box 142, Railroad Ave., Beacon Falls, CT 06403 (tel. (203) 723-6664) for their free pamphlet *Foreign Electricity is No Deep Dark Secret.*

ESSENTIALS

*From the corporate offices of Tokyo
to the beaches of Bali...*

TEACH ENGLISH IN FOREIGN COUNTRIES

No Second Language Necessary

- TEFL Teaching Certificate Course
- One-month Intensive or Three-month Part-Time
- Practical Training with Foreign Students
- European Direct Method
- Job and Travel Guidance
- Student Housing Available
  Transworld Guest House

SUE E. MACKARNESS
Director / Trainer
22 Years in EFL/ESL
14 Years Training Teachers
Taught in 14 Countries
Internationally Certified

TRANSWORLD TEACHERS
TRAINING CENTER
683 Sutter Street, San Francisco, CA 94102
Near Union Square

America's Leading
TEFL Training School

1-800-241-8071
TWT HOTLINE
A Recorded Newsletter
(415) 995-2554

Teachers

Get A Piece of the Peace...

ISRAEL

...Come See For Yourself

Exciting opportunities for students and young adults:

- **PROGRAMS FOR COLLEGE CREDIT:**
  STUDY IN ENGLISH OR HEBREW
  UNDERGRADUATE OR GRADUATE
  SEMESTER, YEAR & DEGREE PROGRAMS
- **INTENSIVE HEBREW STUDY**

- **SUMMER TOURS**
- **KIBBUTZ**
- **INTERNSHIPS**
- **JUDAIC STUDIES**
- **ARCHAEOLOGY**

USD/AZYF
University Student Department
110 E. 59th Street, Suite 301
New York, NY 10022
(212) 339-6940/1

1 (800) 27-ISRAEL

■■■ ALTERNATIVES TO TOURISM

STUDY

Foreign study programs vary tremendously in expense, academic quality, living conditions, degree of contact with local students, and exposure to the local culture and language. Most American undergraduates enroll in programs sponsored by U.S. universities, and many colleges staff offices to give advice and information on study abroad. Take advantage of these counselors and put in some hours in their libraries. Ask for the names of recent participants in the programs, and get in touch.

American Field Service (AFS), 220 East 42nd Street, 3rd Fl., New York, NY 10017 (tel. (800) 237-4636). Summer, semester, and year-long homestay exchange programs for high school students. Short-term adult programs also offered. Financial aid available. Austria, Belgium, Czech Republic, Denmark, Finland, France, Germany, Great Britain, Hungary, Iceland, Italy, Latvia, Netherlands, Norway, Portugal, Russia, Slovak Republic, Spain, Switzerland, Turkey.

American Institute for Foreign Study/American Council for International Studies, 102 Greenwich Ave., Greenwich, CT 06830 (tel. (800) 727-2437; for high school students, (800) 888-2247). Organizes high school and college study in European universities. Minority and merit scholarships available. Programs in Paris, Grenoble, Cannes, London, Berlin, Salzburg, Florence, Salamanca, Granada and St. Petersburg.

Association of Commonwealth Universities, John Foster House, 36 Gordon Square, London WC1H 0PF, England (tel. (0171) 387 85 72). Administers scholarship programs such as the British Marshalls and publishes information about Commonwealth universities.

Central Bureau for Educational Visits and Exchanges, Seymour Mews House, Seymour Mews, London W1H 9PE, England (tel. (0171) 486 51 01, fax 935 57 41). Publishes *Study Holidays* (£ 8.99) with basic information on over 600 language study programs in 25 European countries. Distributed in North America by IIE Books (see below).

Eurocentres, 101 N. Union St. #300, Alexandria, VA 22314 (tel. (800) 648-4809, fax 684-1495) or Eurocentres, Head Office, Seestrasse 247, CH-8038 Zurich, Switzerland. Coordinate language programs and homestays for college students and adults in French (Paris, La Rochelle, Amboise, Lausanne, Neuchâtel), Italian (Florence), Spanish (Madrid, Salamanca, Barcelona), German (Cologne, Weimar, Lucerne), Russian (Moscow), and English (London, Bournemouth, Brighton, Cambridge, Oxford, Bath, Edinburgh, Dublin). Program fees range from about US$400-5000 and last from 2 weeks to 3 months. Some financial aid is available.

Institute of International Education Books (IIE Books), 809 United Nations Plaza, New York NY 10017-3580 (tel. (212) 984-5412; fax 984-5358) puts out several annual reference books on study abroad, including *Academic Year Abroad* (US$43 plus US$4 postage) and *Vacation Study Abroad* (US$37 plus US$4 postage) which detail over 3,600 programs offered by U.S. colleges and universities overseas. Distributes several books published by the **Central Bureau for Educational Visits and Exchanges** in the U.K., including *Study Holidays*, *Working Holidays*, and *Home from Home* (US$23 plus US$4 postage each.) They also operate the International Education Information Center at the UN Plaza address, open Tues.-Fri. 11am-4pm.

Unipub Co., 4611-F Assembly Dr., Lanham, MD 20706-4391 (tel. (800) 274-4888, fax (301) 459-0056). Distributes UNESCO's *Study Abroad*, an unwieldy but excellent guide to international scholarships and courses for students of all ages (US$24, plus postage and handling).

World Learning, Inc., Summer Abroad, P.O. Box 676, Brattleboro, VT 05302 (tel. (802) 257-7751 ext. 3452, or (800) 345-2929). Founded in 1932 as The Experiment in International Living, it offers high school programs in France, Germany, Greece, Italy, Spain and Switzerland, as well as language-training programs with elective homestays. Positions as group leaders are available world-wide if you are over 24, have previous in-country experience, and are fluent in the language.

Q. WHY CHOOSE EDUCATIONAL TRAVEL CENTRE FOR YOUR BUDGET TRAVEL NEEDS?

A. BECAUSE WE HAVE NO SHIPPING OR HANDLING FEES FOR RAILPASSES, HOSTEL CARDS AND AIRLINE TICKETS.

EURAIL YOUTHPASS (under age 26)
15 day–$398, 1 month–$578, 2 month–$768;
EURAIL YOUTH FLEXIPASS 5 days in 2 months–$255,
10 days in 2 months–$398, 15 days in 2 months–$540;
FIRST CLASS EURAILPASS 15 day–$498, 21 day–$648, 1 month–$798;
FIRST CLASS FLEXIPASS 5 days in 2 months–$348,
10 days in 2 months–$560, 15 days in 2 months–$740;
HOSTEL 1-YEAR MEMBERSHIP $25 ($10 if under age 17).
(Hostel card orders only by mail with check or money order.

■ Additional Eurailpasses, Britrail
and individual country passes available, also!

■ Student and teacher airfares to many
European destinations.

Call toll free 1-800-747-5551
(9–5 Monday–Friday) to place your
rail or flight order on Visa or
MasterCard. Identify yourself as a
Let's Go reader and your order
will be shipped free of charge.

For mail orders send certified check
or money order to **Educational Travel
Centre,** 438 N. Frances Street, Madison,
WI 53703. Orders will be processed
within 72 hours. Indicate items needed,
birthdate, address, telephone number and
date of departure from the U.S.

Most U.S. colleges will transfer credit for semester work done abroad. Some financial aid is available.

WORK

There's no better way to submerge yourself in a foreign culture than to become part of its economy. The good news is that it's very easy to find a temporary job abroad; the bad news is that unless you have connections, it will rarely be glamorous and may not even pay for your plane ticket over.

Officially, you can hold a job in European countries only with a **work permit,** applied for by your prospective employer (or by you, with supporting papers from the employer). Many countries are tight-fisted with work permits due to large numbers of working-age immigrants; often, an employer must demonstrate that a potential employee has skills that locals lack. The real catch-22 is that normally you must physically enter the country in order to have immigration officials validate your work permit papers and note your status in your passport. This means that if you can't set up a job from afar (which requires contacts and time) and have the work permit sent to you, you must enter the country to look for a job, find an employer, and have them start the permit process, then leave the country until the permit is sent to you (up to six weeks), and finally reenter the country and start work.

In practice, it's rarely so complicated. Friends in Europe can help expedite work permits or arrange work-for-accommodations swaps. Many permit-less agricultural workers go untroubled by local authorities, who recognize the need for seasonal help. European Union citizens can work in any other EU country, and if your parents or grandparents were born in an EU country, you may be able to claim dual citizenship or at least the right to a work permit. (Beware, however, of countries where claiming citizenship obligates you to do military service.) Students can check with their universities' foreign language departments, which may have official or unofficial connections to job openings abroad.

If you are a full-time student at a U.S. university, the simplest way to get a job abroad is through work permit programs run by **CIEE** and its member organizations (see Useful Travel Organizations, above). For a US$160 application fee, CIEE can procure 3- to 6-month work permits (and a handbook to help you find work and housing) for Britain, France, Germany, and Ireland. French and German positions require evidence of language skills; the British program is the best for neophytes, since a special CIEE office helps with finding openings and making friends. **Travel CUTS's** Canadian program is similar, but does not include Germany.

The number of books listing work-abroad opportunities has ballooned recently. Start with CIEE's free booklet "Work Abroad," then graduate to the excellent publications put out by **Vacation Work,** 9 Park End St., Oxford OX1 1HJ, England (tel. (01865) 24 19 78, fax 79 08 85), available in U.S. bookstores. **World Trade Academy Press,** 50 East 42nd St.., New York, NY 10017 (tel. (212) 697-4999), publishes *Looking for Employment in Foreign Countries* (US$16.50) which gives info on federal, commercial, and volunteer jobs abroad and advice on resumes and interviews. Other publications to check out are *Working Holidays*, an annual guide to short-term paid and voluntary work in Britain and worldwide, and *Home From Home*, a guide to international homestays, termstays, and exchanges, both available from the Central Bureau for Educational Visits and Exchanges or IIE Books (see Study, above).

InterExchange, 161 Sixth Avenue, New York, NY 10013 (tel. (212) 924-0446), provides information in pamphlet form on international work programs and *au pair* positions in Austria, the Czech Republic, Finland, France, Germany, Hungary, Italy, Norway, Poland, and Spain. **Childcare International, Ltd.,** Trafalgar House, Grenville Place, London NW7 3SA (tel. (0181) 959 36 11 or 906 31 16, fax 906 34 61) arranges 6-12 month *au pair* and nanny placements throughout Europe in selected host families and provides full back-up. Application fee £60.

The best tips on jobs for foreigners come from other travelers, so be alert and inquisitive. Many travelers follow the grape harvest in the fall—mostly in France, but

ESSENTIALS

IN LONDON: 2 for 1 THEATRE MUSEUM (COVENT GARDEN) • 25% OFF SMOLLENSKY'S BALLOON • 2 for 1 L'AMIRAL RESTAURANT • 25% OFF XENON NIGHTCLUB • 2 for 1 VAL TARO RISTORANTE • 25% OFF WIDOW APPLEBAUMS • 25% OFF SMITH'S RESTAURANT • FREE MEMBERSHIP 100 CLUB • 25% OFF SMOLLENSKY'S ON THE STRAND • 25% OFF SOL Y SOMBRA • 25% OFF FERRI'S RESTAURANT • 2 for 1 DINO'S • 25% OFF ROCK GARDEN • 2 for 1 ADMISSION LE PALAIS • 2 for 1 ADMISSION THE HIPPODROME • 2 for 1 CAFE ST PIERRE • 2 for 1 LEONI'S QUO[...]DLANDS • 2 for 1 ROYAL [...]GETARIAN RESTAURANT [...] • 2 for 1 ADMISSION S[...]HTINGALE MUSEUM • HA[...]HOUSE • 2 for 1 • 2 for 1 [...]ICKET • 2 for 1 OLD ROY[...]SE • 2 for 1 THE DESIGN[...]THE CLINK • 2 for 1 WINS[...]UM SHOP • 50% OFF THE [...]TMINSTER • **IN EDINBU**[...]TLE • 50% OFF ROYAL SC[...]USTEAUS SEAFOOD • 2 [...]UDES: THE ROYAL OBSER[...]DSTONE'S LAND • 2 for [...] • 2 for 1 CHARLOTTE S[...] **GLASGOW**: 2 for 1 NATIONAL TRUST FOR SCOTLAND INCLUDES: GREENBANK GARDEN HUTCHESON'S HALL, AND THE VICEROY • 2 for 1 GANDHI • 2 for 1 THE TENEMENT HOUSE • **IN DUBLIN**: 2 for 1 THE FLAME ON THE HILL • 2 for 1 THE IRISH WHISKEY CORNER • 2 for 1 FRY MODEL RAILWAY • 2 for 1 THE PINK BICYCLE • 2 for 1 CHIMES RESTAURANT • 50% OFF ADMISSION ROCK GARDEN • **IN PARIS:** 30% OFF FARE BATEAUX PARISIENS • **IN AMSTERDAM:** 2 for 1 ADMISSION VAN GOGH MUSEUM • 2 for 1 ALLARD PIERSON MUSEUM • 2 for 1 ADMISSION AMSTELKRING OUR LORD IN THE ATTIC • 2 for 1 ADMISSION JEWISH HISTORICAL MUSEUM • 30% OFF ADMISSION THE OLD CHURCH • 2 for 1 THE ROYAL PALACE • 30% OFF DE BRAKKE GROND • 30% OFF FRASCATI THEATER • 25% OFF ADMISSION JOSEPH LAM • **IN FL**[...]d DE[...]E CE[...]1 MA[...]F SO[...]F CR[...]d DE[...]E TH[...]E EN[...]**E:** 2 [...]1 ALCAZABA • **IN LISBON:** FREE ENTRY ALCANTARA MAR • FREE ENTRY DISCO PALM BEACH • 50% OFF SOLCLUB • 50% OFF TRANS

Just order your rail pass from 800-444-8400 and we'll send you 2,000 discount certificates for **FREE!**

Its simple: Your rail pass, shipped within one business day, via overnight mail with the best FREE Certificates!

Only through The Rail Connection: 800-444-8400

*1994 Prices.... YOUTHPASS: 15 day $398 • 30 day $578 • 60 day $768
YOUTH FLEXIPASS: 5 days in 2 months $255 • 10 days in 2 months $398 • 15 days in 2 months $540
EURAILPASS: 15 day $498 • 21 day $648 • 30 day $798 • 60 day $1,098 • 90 day $1,398
FLEXIPASS: 5 days in 2 months $348 • 10 days in 2 months $560 • 15 days in 2 months $740

*Subject to 1995 price increases

also in Switzerland and in Germany's Mosel Valley. More or less menial jobs can be found anywhere in Europe; for instance, Swiss ski resorts leave much of the grunt-work to foreigners. (Be aware of your rights as an employee; should a crafty national try to refuse payment at the end of the season, it'll help to have a written confirmation of your agreement.) Youth hostels frequently provide room and board to travelers willing to stay a while and help run the place. *Au pair* baby-sitting and household jobs abound in Great Britain, France, and, to some extent, in Germany and Scandinavia. Look for newspaper ads and bulletin board notices.

In non-English-speaking countries, consider **teaching English.** Post a sign in markets or learning centers stating that you are a native speaker, and scan the classifieds of local newspapers, where residents often advertise for language instruction. Teaching English may be your only option in Eastern Europe. Various organizations in the U.S. will place you in a (low-paying) teaching job, but securing a position will require patience and legwork, because teaching English abroad has become enormously popular in the past few years. Professional English-teaching positions are harder to get; most European schools require at least a bachelor's degree and most often training in teaching English as a foreign language. Call or write **WorldTeach,** HIID, 1 Eliot St., Cambridge, MA 02138 (tel. (617) 495-5527) for information on volunteer teaching in Poland or Russia. The **Office of Overseas Schools**, A-OS, Room 245, SA-29, Department of State, Washington DC 20522 (tel. (703) 875-7800), maintains a list of elementary and secondary schools abroad and agencies which arrange placement for Americans to teach abroad.

VOLUNTEERING

Volunteer jobs are readily available almost everywhere. You may receive room and board in exchange for your labor, and the work can be fascinating. Opportunities include archeological digs and community and workcamp projects. Keep in mind: the organizations that arrange placement sometimes charge high application fees in addition to the workcamps' charges for room and board. You can sometimes avoid this extra fee by contacting the individual workcamps directly; check with the organization. Listings in Vacation Work's *International Directory of Voluntary Work* (£8.95; see ordering information under Work, above) can be helpful.

Council on International Educational Exchange (CIEE) publishes *Volunteer! The Comprehensive Guide to Voluntary Service in the U.S. and Abroad* (US$9, US$1.50 postage). Available from Council Travel offices and CIEE (for further information see Useful Travel Organizations, above).

Service Civil International (SCI-VS), Rte. 2, Box 560B, Crozet, VA 22932 (tel. (804) 823-1826). Arranges placement in workcamps in Europe (ages 18 and over). Registration fees US$40-200, depending on the camp location.

Volunteers for Peace, 43 Tiffany Rd., Belmont, VT 05730 (tel. (802) 259-2759, fax 259-2922). Arranges speedy placement in over 800 10-15 people workcamps in 40 countries, primarily in Europe. Gives perhaps the most complete and up-to-date listings in the annual International Workcamp Directory (US$10 postpaid). Registration fee US$150. Some workcamps are open to 16-18 year-olds for a slightly higher fee (US$175). Free newsletter.

■■■ BOOKS, GUIDES, MAPS, ETC.

You might supplement your *Let's Go* library with publications that serve more specific purposes. **Handy Dictionaries** (US$7-9) in over 90 languages and language tapes can be obtained through Hippocrene Books, Inc. 171 Madison Ave., New York, NY 10016 (orders: tel. (718) 454-2366, fax 454-1391). Request their free catalog, which lists maps and travel reference books too. Hard-to-find **maps** are stocked by Wide World Books and Maps, 1911 N. 45th St., Seattle, WA 98103 (tel. (206) 634-3453). Copernicus Press, 1089 Dunbarton, P.O. Box 190084, Atlanta, GA 30319, puts out *Destination Europe*, a comprehensive **travel planner and journal** for the intensely organized, including maps, travel tips, common phrases in 10 languages, a section for recording new friends' addresses, and more. The booklet **Festivals** from the European Festivals Association, 120B, rue de Lausanne, 1202 Geneva, Switzerland (tel. (022) 732 28 03, fax 738 40 12) lists dates and programs of major music, theatre and dance festivals for which student rates are often available.

Michelin's *Green Guides for Western Europe* are in-depth sightseeing guides with star ratings, maps, suggested tours, historical and cultural background, and more. Visit your bookstore or contact Michelin Travel Publications, Davy House, Lyon Rd., Harrow, Middlesex HA1 2DQ, England (tel. (0181) 861 21 21); in the U.S., P.O. Box 19008, Greenville, SC 29602-9008 (tel. (800) 423-0485). Peruse *Mona Winks: Self-Guided Tours of Europe's Top Museums* (U.S.$17) or take *Europe 101: Art and History for the Traveler* (US$16) with "Professor" Rick Steves, a veteran traveler who offers great advice on the dos and don'ts of budget travel in *Europe Through the Back Door* (US$18). All three can be obtained from John Muir Publications, P.O. Box 613, Santa Fe, NM 87504 (tel. (505) 982-4078 or (800) 888-7504).

For the inside story on *Charming Small Hotels* in Austria, Germany or Spain or *Hiking in Poland & the Ukraine* or *Spain & Portugal by Rail* (US$17), write to Hunter Publishing, 300 Raritan Center Parkway, Edison, NJ 08818 (tel. (908) 225-1900, fax 417-0482) for their catalog. Travel gear as well as maps, guidebooks, railpasses, timetables, and youth hostel memberships can also be purchased from the Forsyth Travel Library, P.O. Box 2975, Shawnee Mission, KS 662011 (tel. (800) 367-7984; fax (913) 384-3553). MC, Visa, Discover, no COD.

■■■ HEALTH

PREPARING FOR A HEALTHY TRIP

Common sense is the simplest prescription for good health while you travel: eat well, drink enough, get enough sleep, and don't overexert yourself. If you're going to do a lot of walking, take some quick-energy foods to keep your strength up. You'll need plenty of protein (for sustained energy) and fluids (to prevent dehydration and constipation, two of the most common health problems for travelers). Carry a canteen or water bottle and drink frequently. If you are prone to sunburn, use a potent sunscreen, cover up with long sleeves and a hat, and drink plenty of fluids. Finally, remember to treat your most valuable resource well: lavish your feet with attention. Make sure your shoes are appropriate for extended walking, change your socks often, and pad hotspots before they become excruciating blisters.

For minor health problems, a compact **first-aid kit** should suffice. Some hardware stores carry ready-made ones, but it's just as easy to assemble your own: include bandages, aspirin, antiseptic soap or antibiotic cream, a thermometer in a sturdy case, tweezers, medicine for stomach problems, sunscreen, and insect repellent.

Always go prepared with any **medication** you may need, as well as a copy of the prescription and/or a statement from your doctor, especially if you will be bringing insulin, syringes, or any prescribed narcotics into European countries. Travelers with chronic medical conditions should consult with their physicians before leaving. It's often useful to carry separate batches, stored in different parts of your luggage, in case of loss or theft.

If you wear **glasses** or **contact lenses,** take an extra prescription with you and arrange for someone at home to send you a replacement pair in an emergency. If you wear contacts, take along a pair of glasses to rest tired eyes. Bring extra solutions, enzyme tablets, and eyedrops; the price for lens solution can be exorbitant.

Any traveler with a medical condition that cannot be easily recognized (i.e. diabetes, epilepsy, heart conditions, allergies to antibiotics) may want to obtain the internationally recognized **Medic Alert Identification Tag,** which indicates the bearer's condition and the number of Medic Alert's 24-hour hotline. Contact Medic Alert Foundation (tel. (800) 432-5378). The **American Diabetes Association,** (tel. (800) 232-3472) provides diabetic ID cards with messages in 18 languages.

All travelers should be concerned about **Acquired Immune Deficiency Syndrome (AIDS),** transmitted through the exchange of body fluids with an infected (HIV-positive) individual. Remember that there is no assurance that someone is not infected: HIV tests only show antibodies after a six-month lapse. Do not have sex without using a condom or share intravenous needles. The U.S. Center for Disease Control's **AIDS Hotline** can refer you to organizations with information on European countries (tel. (800) 342-2437). Travelers who are HIV-positive or have AIDS should inquire about country-specific immigration restrictions from the **U.S. State Department** (tel. (202) 647-1488, fax 647-3000).

Reliable **contraception** may be difficult to come by while traveling. Women on the pill should bring enough to allow for possible loss or extended stays. Although **condoms** are increasingly available, you might want to stock up on your favorite national brand before you go; availability and quality vary in European countries, and it's best to be prepared in case you need some during the flight over. Attitudes towards and availability of **abortions** vary from country to country in Europe. Contact your country's embassy or consulate to receive a list of ob/gyn doctors who perform abortions.

For additional information before you go, you may wish to contact the **International Association for Medical Assistance to Travelers (IAMAT).** IAMAT provides several brochures on health for travelers, an ID card, a chart detailing advisable immunizations for 200 countries and territories, and a worldwide directory of English-speaking physicians. Membership to the organization is free (although donations are welcome) and doctors are on call 24 hours a day for IAMAT members. Contact chapters in the **U.S.,** 417 Center St., Lewiston, NY, 14092 (tel. (716) 754-4883), in **Canada,** 1287 St. Clair Ave. West, Toronto, M6E 1B8 (tel. (416) 652-0137), or **New Zealand,** P.O. Box 5049, 438 Pananui Rd., Christchurch 5 (tel. (03) 352 90 53, fax 352 46 30).

STAYING HEALTHY

While you travel, pay attention to the signals of pain and discomfort that your body may send you. This may be due to a new climate, diet, water quality, or pace when you first arrive, or even after a couple of weeks. Once you get going, some of the milder symptoms that you may safely ignore at home may be signs of something more serious on the road; your increased exertion may wear you out and make you more susceptible to illness. Check with the publications and organizations listed above for more information.

When traveling in summer, protect yourself against **heatstroke;** in the early stages, sweating stops, body temperature rises, and an intense headache develops, followed by confusion. To treat heatstroke, cool the victim off immediately with fruit juice or salted water, wet towels, and shade. Rush the victim to the hospital. Extreme cold is no less dangerous. The signs of **hypothermia** are uncontrollable shivering, poor coordination, and exhaustion, followed by slurred speech, hallucinations, and amnesia. Do not let victims fall asleep—unconsciousness can lead to death. To avoid hypothermia, keep dry, wear wool, dress in layers, and wear a hat. **Frostbite** turns skin white, waxy, and cold. *Never* rub frostbite—the skin is easily damaged. See a doctor as soon as possible. Travelers in **high altitudes** should allow a couple of days to adjust to lower oxygen levels before engaging in strenuous activity, particularly long hikes. Those new to high altitudes may feel drowsy; alcoholic beverages will have stronger effects.

Food poisoning can spoil any trip. Some of the cheapest and most convenient eating options are also most prone: street vendors, tap water, and carrying perishable food for hours in a hot backpack. **Diarrhea** has unmistakable symptoms but also, thankfully, some means of relief, such as the over-the-counter remedy Immodium. Since dehydration is the most common side effect of diarrhea, those suffering should drink plenty of fruit juice and water. The simplest anti-dehydration formula is still the most effective: 8 oz. of water with a ½ tsp. of sugar or honey and a pinch of salt. Down several of these a day, rest, and let the disease run its course. If it does not subside within a few days, see a doctor immediately. Traveler's diarrhea may be the symptom of dysentery, giardia, or other parasitic conditions which can haunt your gastro-intestinal tract for years after your trip is over.

Women traveling in unsanitary conditions are vulnerable to **urinary tract and bladder infections**, common and severely uncomfortable bacterial diseases which cause a burning sensation and pain during urination. Drink tons of juice rich in vitamin C, plenty of water, and urinate frequently. If symptoms persist, see a doctor.

■■■ INSURANCE

Beware of unnecessary coverage—your current policies might well extend to many travel-related accidents. **Medical insurance** (especially university policies) often cover costs incurred abroad. Canadians are protected by their home province's health insurance plan: check with the provincial Ministry of Health or Health Plan Headquarters. Australians are covered by Medicare in countries with which the government has signed reciprocal agreements: Finland, Italy, the Netherlands, Sweden, and the U.K. Consult Medicare's brochure "Health Care for Australians Travelling Overseas" to find out the extent of coverage and how to obtain benefits. Contact the Commonwealth Department of Health, Housing and Community Services, GPO Box 9848 in your capital city. Take out travel insurance to cover those eventualities not covered by reciprocal agreements such as ambulance coverage and medical evacuation. EU citizens are covered for emergency medical treatment throughout the EU by holding an E111 form, available from your local national health authority. Your **homeowners' insurance** (or your family's coverage) often covers theft during travel. Homeowners are generally covered against loss of travel documents (passport, plane ticket, railpass, etc.) up to US$500.

ISIC provides US$3000 worth of accident and illness insurance and US$100 per day up to 60 days of hospitalization. **CIEE** offers the Trip-Safe plan, with options covering medical treatment and hospitalization, accidents, baggage loss, and even

NEW!

LET'S GO AMSTERDAM!!

THE FLYING PIG

Travellers HOSTEL Amsterdam

from fl. 23,50 a night

In the City Centre!!

No curfew

Clean/Laid back

Free use of kitchen facilities

No dorms but shared rooms

Cheapest beer in town in...

● *THE TRAVELLERS CAFÉ* ●

Vossiusstraat 46-47, 1071 AJ Amsterdam, HOLLAND
Phone: 0031 20 · 400 41 87, Fax: 0031 20 · 400 41 05

THE PIG'S A PALACE!

(Tram 1, 2 or 5 to the 'Leidseplein' - cross 'Stadhouderskade' - turn left - take the 3rd street to the right.)

charter flights missed due to illness; **STA** offers a more expensive, more comprehensive plan. **American Express** cardholders receive car-rental and flight insurance on purchases made with the card. (For addresses, see Useful Travel Organizations and Money, above.)

Insurance companies usually require a copy of police reports for thefts, or evidence of having paid medical expenses (doctor's statements, receipts) before they will honor a claim, and may have time limits on filing. Always carry policy numbers and proof of insurance. Check with each insurance carrier for specific restrictions.

Globalcare Travel Insurance, 220 Broadway, Lynnfield, MA, 01940 (tel. (800) 821-2488, fax (617) 592-7720). Complete medical, legal, emergency, and travel-related services. On-the-spot payments and special student programs.

Travel Assistance International, Worldwide Assistance Services, Inc., 1133 15th St., NW, Washington DC 20005-2710 (tel. (800) 821-2828, fax (202) 331-1530). Provides on-the-spot medical coverage (US$15,000-US$90,000) and unlimited medical evacuation insurance, 24-hr. emergency multilingual assistance hotline and worldwide local presence. Trip cancellation/interruption, baggage and accidental death and dismemberment insurance are also offered.

Travel Insured International, Inc., 52-S Oakland Avenue, P.O. Box 280568, East Hartford, CT 06128-0568 (tel. (800) 243-3174, fax (203) 528-8005). Insurance against accident, baggage loss, sickness, trip cancellation/interruption, travel delay, and default. Covers emergency medical evacuation and automatic flight insurance.

■■■ SAFETY AND SECURITY

Tourists are particularly vulnerable to crime for two reasons: they often carry large amounts of cash, and they are not as savvy as locals. To avoid such unwanted attention, the best tactic is, therefore, to blend in as much as possible: the gawking camera-toter is much easier prey than the casual local look-alike. This is often harder than it sounds—chances are you will not be able to fully hide the fact that you're a tourist. Muggings are more often impromptu than planned; walking with nervous, over-the-shoulder glances can be a tip that you have something valuable to protect. Carry all your valuables (including your passport, railpass, traveler's checks, and airline ticket) either in a money belt or neckpouch stashed securely inside your clothing. This will protect you from skilled thieves who use razors to slash open backpacks and fanny packs (particular favorites of skilled bag-snatchers), and they should be kept on your person at all times, including trips to the shower if you are staying in the dorm-style rooms of most hostels. Making photocopies of important documents will allow you to recover them in case they are lost or filched. Carry one copy separate from the documents and leave another copy at home. A simple, but effective, theft deterrent is a small padlock readily available in luggage stores that is small enough to ensure your backpack or daypack remains shut as you walk about.

When exploring new **cities,** extra vigilance may be wise, but don't let fear inhibit your ability to experience another culture. When walking at night, turn day-time precautions into mandates. Stay near crowded, well-lit places and do not attempt to cross through parks, parking lots, or any other large, deserted areas. Among the more colorful aspects of many large cities are the **con artists.** Be aware of certain classics: sob stories that require money, rolls of bills "found" on the street, ice-cream or mustard spilled (or saliva spit) onto your shoulder distracting you for enough time to snatch your bag. Always carry a shoulder bag so that the strap passes over your head and runs diagonally across your torso. Hustlers often work in groups, and children are among the most effective. A firm "no" should communicate that you are no dupe. Contact the police if a hustler acts particularly insistent or aggressive.

Trains are other notoriously easy spots for thieving. Professionals wait for tourists to fall asleep and then carry off everything they can. When traveling in pairs, sleep in alternating shifts; when alone use good judgment in selecting a train compart-

We See Europe In Your Future

...and it won't cost you a fortune !

Student
Discount
Airfares!

We Will
Save You
Money!

AESU & Contiki Student Tours

All Student Tours

• Eurail & Britrail Passes • Intn'l I.D. & Hostel Cards

USTN agencies are located on or near University campuses, and specialize in student travel to Europe. Our agents will help you plan your trip to Europe and help you decide the best way to go!

University and Student Travel
A National Organization

• Arizona State University–ASU	(800) 815–6455
• California State Polytechnic, San Luis Obispo–CPSLO	(800) 321–8728
• California State University, Fullerton–CSUF	(800) 222–7411
• California State University, Long Beach–CSULB	(310) 985–4000
• California State University, Los Angeles–CSULA	(800) 448–8111
• California State University, Northridge–CSUN	(800) 452–3666
• Long Beach City College–LBCC	(800) 462–8004
• Oregon State University, Corvallis–OSU	(800) 858–3399
• San Diego State University–SDSU	(800) 862–6220
• University of California, Berkeley–UCB	(510) 843–1000
• University of California, Irvine–UCI	(800) 278–1132
• University of California, Los Angeles–UCLA	(800) 235–6876
• University of California, Santa Barbara–UCSB	(805) 968–5151
• University of Colorado, Boulder–CU	(303) 492–5154
• University of Colorado, Boulder–Hill	(800) 284–0292
• University of Illinois, Urbana–UIU	(800) 747–8990
• University of Northern Colorado–UNC	(303) 352–2700
• University of Oregon, Eugene–UO	(800) 835–4745
• University of Southern California–USC	(800) 634–7394
• University of Washington, Seattle–UW	(800) 788–0829

For Student Travel Count on USTN

ment: never stay in an empty one, and try to get a top bunk. When sleeping, wrap the straps of your luggage securely about you.

Sleeping in your **automobile** is one of the most dangerous ways to get your rest. Park in a well-lit area as close to a police station or 24-hour service station as possible. **Sleeping outside** is often illegal and exposes you to ever more hazards—camping is recommendable only in official, supervised, campsites.

There is no sure-fire set of precautions that will protect you from all situations you might encounter when you travel. A good self-defense course will give you more concrete ways to react to different types of aggression, but it might cost you more money than your trip. **Model Mugging** (East Coast tel. (617) 232-7900, Midwest tel. (312) 338-4545, West Coast tel. (415) 592-7300), a U.S. national organization with offices in several major cities, teaches a comprehensive course on self-defense (US$400-500; women's and men's courses offered). The **U.S. Department of State's** (tel. (202) 783-3238) pamphlet *A Safe Trip Abroad* (US$1) summarizes safety information for travelers. For official Dept. of State **travel advisories** on European countries, call their 24-hour hotline at (202) 647-5225. **Travel Assistance International** provides its members with a 24-hr. hotline for emergencies and referrals (see Insurance below.)

■■■ GETTING THERE

The first challenge in European budget travel is getting there. The **airline industry** attempts to squeeze every dollar from customers; finding a cheap airfare in their computerized jungle will be easier if you understand the airlines' systems better than they think you do. Call every toll-free number and don't be afraid to ask about discounts. Have a knowledgeable travel agent guide you; better yet, have several knowledgeable travel agents guide you. Remember that travel agents may not want to do the legwork to find the cheapest fares (for which they receive the lowest commissions). Students and people under 26 should never need to pay full price for a ticket. Seniors can also get great deals; many airlines offer senior traveler clubs or airline passes and discounts for their companions as well. Sunday newspapers have travel sections that list bargain fares from the local airport. Australians should consult the Saturday travel section of the *Sydney Morning Herald*, as well as the ethnic press, where special deals may be advertised. Outsmart airline reps with the phonebook-sized *Official Airline Guide* (at large libraries), a monthly guide listing every scheduled flight in the world (with prices). *The Airline Passenger's Guerrilla Handbook* (US$15; last published in 1990) is a more renegade resource.

Most airfares peak between mid-June and early September. Midweek (Mon.-Thurs.) flights run about US$30 cheaper each way than on weekends. Traveling from hubs such as New York, Atlanta, Dallas, Chicago, Los Angeles, San Francisco, Vancouver, Toronto, Sydney, Melbourne, Brisbane, Auckland, or Wellington to London, Frankfurt, Paris, Brussels, Luxembourg, Rome, or Amsterdam will win a more competitive fare than from smaller cities. Flying to London is usually the cheapest way across the Atlantic, though special fares to other cities such as Amsterdam, Luxembourg, or Brussels can be even lower. Return-date flexibility is usually not an option for the budget traveler; except on youth fares purchased through the airlines, traveling with an "open return" ticket can be pricier than fixing a return date and paying to change it. Be wary of one-way tickets, too: the flight to Europe may be economical, but the return fares are outrageous. Whenever flying internationally, pick up your ticket well in advance of the departure date and arrive at the airport at least two hours before your flight.

To get to the Continent from Ireland or Britain, cross the English Channel by **ferry** (Stena Sealink Line, Head Office, Adelaide House, 7 Haddington Terrace, Dun Laoghaire, Co., Dublin, Ireland) or take an **express bus** from London to over 270 destinations in Europe with Euroline (UK) Ltd., 52 Grosvenor Gardens, Victoria, London SW1 (tel. (0171) 730 0202). (London to Paris UK£38, return UK£55, youth UK£3 less.) The Air Travel Advisory Bureau, Strauss House 41-45, Goswell Rd., Lon-

ESSENTIALS

East Coast<>Europe $169
West Coast<>Europe $249
Other Places in
the USA<>Europe $199

If You Can Beat These Prices Start Your Own Damn Airline.

Air-Tech, Ltd.
(800)575-TECH
info@aerotech.com

don EC1V7DN, England (tel. (0171) 636 29 08) will put you in touch with the cheapest carriers out of London for free. In May 1994, the **Channel Tunnel** was completed, physically connecting England and France, to the horror of some. By spring 1995, the limited *Discovery* train service between London and Paris/Brussels through the Chunnel will give way to a full *Eurostar* service with approximately fifteen daily departures to either destination. Consult Thomas Cook's European Timetable or, in the U.K., call (01233) 61 75 75 for more information. Ask whether railpasses and BIJ tickets (see Getting Around) will be valid.

COMMERCIAL AIRLINES

Even if you pay an airline's lowest published fare, you may waste hundreds of dollars. The commercial airlines' lowest regular offer is the **APEX** (Advance Purchase Excursion Fare); specials advertised in newspapers may be cheaper, but have more restrictions and fewer available seats. APEX fares provide you with confirmed reservations and allow "open-jaw" tickets (landing in and returning from different cities). Reservations usually must be made at least 21 days in advance, with 7- to 14-day minimum and 60- to 90-day maximum stay limits, and hefty cancellation and change penalties. Payment must be made within 72 hours of departure. For summer travel, book APEX fares early; by May you will have a hard time getting the departure date you want.

Most airlines no longer offer standby fares, once a staple of the budget traveler. Standby in the United States has given way to the **3-day-advance-purchase youth fare,** a cousin of the one-day variety prevalent in Europe. It's available only to those under 25 (sometimes 24) and only within three days of departure, a gamble that can backfire. Return dates are open, but you must come back within a year, and again, can book your return seat no more than three days ahead. Youth fares in summer aren't really cheaper than APEX, but off-season prices drop deliciously.

Look into flights to less-popular destinations or on smaller carriers. **Icelandair** (tel. (800) 223-5500) has last-minute offers and a stand-by fare from New York to Luxembourg (April-June 15 and Sept.-Oct. $398; June 15-Aug. $598) for travelers under 25 years of age. Reservations must be made within three days of departure.

STUDENT TRAVEL AGENCIES

Students and people under 26 with proper ID qualify for enticing reduced airfares. These are rarely available from airlines or travel agents, but instead from student travel agencies like **Let's Go Travel, STA, Travel CUTS, USTN** and CIEE's **Council Travel** (see Useful Travel Organizations, above). These agencies negotiate special reduced-rate bulk purchases with the airlines, then resell them to the youth market; in 1994, peak season round-trip rates from the East Coast of North America to even the offbeat corners of Europe rarely topped US$700 (though flights to Russia were higher), and off-season fares were considerably lower. Round-trip fares from Australia or New Zealand through STA or Flight Centres International cost between AUS$1600 (low season) and AUS$2500 (high season). Return-date change fees also tend to be low (around US$50 through Council or Let's Go Travel). Most of their flights are on major airlines, though in peak season some seats may be on less reliable chartered aircraft. Student travel agencies can also help non-students and people over 26, but probably won't be able to get the same low fares.

CONSOLIDATORS AND CHARTER FLIGHTS

Ticket consolidators resell unsold tickets on commercial and charter airlines. Look for their tiny ads in weekend papers (in the U.S., the *Sunday New York Times* is best), and start calling them all. There is rarely a maximum age; tickets are also heavily discounted, and may offer extra flexibility or bypass advance purchase requirements, since you aren't tangled in airline bureaucracy. But unlike tickets bought through an airline, you won't be able to use your tickets on another flight if you miss yours, and you will have to go back to the consolidator to get a refund, rather than the airline. Phone around and pay with a credit card so you can stop pay-

ESSENTIALS

ment if you never receive your tickets. Don't be tempted solely by the low prices; find out everything you can about the agency you're considering, and get a copy of their refund policy in writing. Ask also about accommodations and car rental discounts; some consolidators have fingers in many pies. Insist on a **receipt** that gives full details about the tickets, refunds, and restrictions, and if they don't want to give you one or just generally seem clueless or shady, use a different company. A 10% fee will usually be deducted from any refunds.

The theory behind a **charter** is that a tour operator contracts with an airline (usually one specializing in charters) to fly extra loads of passengers to peak-season destinations. Charter flights fly less frequently than major airlines and have more restrictions, particularly on refunds. They are also almost always fully booked, and schedules and itineraries may change or be cancelled at the last moment (as late as 48 hours before the trip, and without a full refund); you'll be much better off purchasing a ticket on a regularly scheduled airline. As always, pay with a credit card if you can; consider travelers insurance against trip interruption.

It's best to buy from a major organization that has experience in placing individuals on charter flights. One of the most reputable is the CIEE-affiliated **Council Charter,** 205 E. 42nd St., New York, NY 10017 (tel. (800) 800-8222); their flights can also be booked through Council Travel offices. Also try **Interworld** (tel. (800) 331-4456; in Florida, (305) 443-4929); **Rebel** (tel. (800) 227-3235); and **Travac** (tel. (800) 872-8800). Don't be afraid to call every number and hunt for the best deal.

If budget travel inspires your utmost bravery and patience, **Airhitch,** 2641 Broadway, New York, NY 10025 (tel. (212) 864-2000) and 1415 Third St., Santa Monica, CA 90410 (tel. (310) 394-0550), will add a certain thrill to the prospects of how you will get to Europe and where exactly you will end up. Complete flexibility on both sides of the Atlantic is necessary; flights cost US$169 each way when departing from the East Coast, US$269 from the West Coast, and US$229 from most places between. The snag is that you must choose a five-day period in which to travel and draw up a list of preferred destinations. There are several offices in Europe so you can wait to register for your return; the main one is in Paris (tel. (1) 44 75 39 90). A

Time-Tested * Student Originated * No Restrictions

ABSOLUTELY POSITIVELY CHEAPEST WAY TO JET TO

EUROPE

If all you want to do is get to Europe and you don't care precisely where or when!

* Especially good when you have a Eurail™ pass *

For no more than:

$169	From the East Coast	Coast to Coast - **$129**
$269	From the West Coast, Northwest	Chicago or Dallas - **$79**
$229	From the Southeast, Midwest	Hawaii - **$129**

Caribbean/Mexico - **$189 R/T**

For information and a FREE program description, call:

East Coast: 1-800-326-2009

West Coast: 1-800-397-1098

As reported in Consumer Reports TL, NY Times, LA Times, Wash Post, etc.

very similar service is offered by **Air-Tech, Ltd.,** 584 Broadway #1007, New York, N.Y. 10012 (tel. (212) 219-7000, fax 219-0066) and 2, rue Dussoubs, 75002 Paris (tel. (1) 42 21 14 77). This company has agreements with certain carriers to accept their Air-Tech FlightPass for boarding designated flights on a space-available basis. Again, flexibility is required; you choose 3 destination preferences and a Travel Window of 2 to 5 days, and are only guaranteed to end up within the region of your choice, within that time, departing from JFK (N.Y.). Travel Windows and rates to and from Europe (continually updated; call and verify) are: Northeast 2-4 days, $169; West Coast 5 days, $249; Midwest/Southeast 5 days, $229. Upon registration and payment, Air-Tech sends you a FlightPass with a contact date falling soon before your Travel Window, when you are to call them for flight instructions. Note that the service is one-way—you must go through the same procedure to return—and that *no refunds* are granted unless the company fails to get you a seat before your Travel Window expires. Air-Tech also arranges courier flights and regular confirmed-reserved flights at discount rates. Be sure to read all the fine print in your agreements with either company. The Better Business Bureau of New York City has received complaints about Airhitch; be warned that it is difficult to receive refunds, and that clients' vouchers will not be honored when an airline fails to receive payment in time. The Bureau has not yet received any complaints about Air-Tech, Ltd.; it was established in 1993.

Eleventh-hour **discount clubs** and **fare brokers** offer members savings on European travel, including charter flights and tour packages. Research your options carefully. **Last Minute Travel Club,** 1249 Boylston St., Boston, MA 02215 (tel. (800) 527-8646 or (617) 267-9800), and **Discount Travel International** (tel. (212) 362-3636) are among the few travel clubs that don't charge a membership fee. Others include **Moment's Notice** (tel. (212) 486-0503; US$25 annual fee), **Traveler's Advantage** (tel. (800) 835-8747; US$49 annual fee), and **Worldwide Discount Travel Club** (tel. (305) 534-2082; US$50 annual fee). For a ticketing fee of 5-12%, depending on the number of travelers and the itinerary, **Travel Avenue** (tel. (800) 333-3335) will search for the lowest international airfare available and then take 7% off the base price. Study these organizations' contracts closely; you don't want to end up with an unwanted overnight layover.

COURIER FLIGHTS AND FREIGHTERS

Those who travel light should consider flying to Europe as a **courier.** The company hiring you will use your checked luggage space for freight; you're only allowed to bring carry-ons. Restrictions to watch for: you must be at least 18, most flights are round-trip only with fixed-length stays (usually short); you may not be able to travel with a companion (single tickets only); and most flights are from New York (including a scenic visit to the courier office in the 'burbs). Round-trip fares to Western Europe from the U.S. range from US$200-350 (during the off-season) to US$400-550 (during the summer). **NOW Voyager,** 74 Varick St., New York, NY 10013 (tel. (212) 431-1616), acts as an agent for many courier flights worldwide from New York, with some flights available from Houston. They offer special last-minute deals to such cities as London, Paris, Rome, and Frankfurt for as little as US$300 round-trip plus a US$50 registration fee. Other agents to try are **Able Travel,** (tel. (212) 779-8530), **Halbart Express,** 147-05 176th St., Jamaica, NY 11434 (tel. (718) 656-8279), **Courier Travel Service,** 530 Central Avenue, Cedarhurst, NY 11516 (tel. (516) 763-6898), and **Discount Travel International**, (NY tel. (212) 362-3636, Miami tel. (305) 538-1616).

You can also go directly through courier companies in New York, or check your bookstore or library for handbooks such as *The Insider's Guide to Air Courier Bargains* (US$15). *The Courier Air Travel Handbook* (US$13.50) explains how to travel as an air courier and contains names, phone numbers, and contact points of courier companies. It can be ordered directly from Bookmasters, PO Box 2039, Mansfield, OH 44905 (tel. (800) 507 2665). **Travel Unlimited**, P.O. Box 1058, Allston, MA 02134-1058, publishes a comprehensive, monthly newsletter detailing all possible options for courier travel (often 50% off discount commercial fares). A one-year subscription is US$25 (outside of the U.S. US$35).

If you really have travel time to spare, **Ford's Travel Guides,** 19448 Londelius St., Northridge, CA 91324 (tel. (818) 701-7414) lists **freighter companies** that will take trans-Atlantic passengers. Ask for their *Freighter Travel Guide and Waterways of the World* (US$15, plus US$2.50 postage if mailed outside the U.S.).

■■■ GETTING AROUND

BY TRAIN

European trains retain the charm and romance their North American counterparts lost long ago. Bring some food and a plastic water bottle you can fill at your hostel and take with you on all train trips; the train café can be expensive, and train water undrinkable. Trains are not theft-proof; lock the door of your compartment if you can, and keep your valuables on your person at all times.

Many train stations have different counters for domestic and international tickets, seat reservations, and information; check before lining up. On major lines, reservations are always advisable, and often required, even with a railpass; make them at least a few hours in advance at the train station (usually less than US$3). Faster trains, such as France's famed TGV and Germany's ICE, require a special supplement (US$3-18), which you can sometimes pay for on board, but it'll cost a bit more. Eurailpasses include unlimited use of EuroCity, InterCity and TGV trains as well, but without the reservation fee.

A sleeping berth in a couchette car is an affordable luxury (about US$10; reserve at the station at least several days in advance). Very few countries give students or young people discounts on regular domestic rail tickets, but many will sell a student or youth card valid for one-half or one-third off all fares for an entire year. Check the introductory sections of each country chapter for details.

On a budget? Don't rough it! Explore London, Enjoy London and make lots of friends too!

London's a big place and when you arrive you'll want to get your bearings, make some friends and find a comfortable place to stay. You'll have no worries if you travel with the London Explorers Club because we offer...

● Airport transfer in the club minibus
● Lively, exclusive club bar in our own Porchester Hotel
● Comfortable central London hotel accommodation
● Introductory half day Tour of London
● Information desk and travel seminars
● Plus discounts on trips, special events and loads more!

Make your trip to London safe, memorable and of course lots of fun.

Bookable in the USA through Council/CIEE Travel and in other countries through leading travel agents. To book Vienna Budget Hotels only call 0171 286 5294

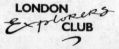
LONDON *Explorers* **CLUB**

WITH VIENNA BUDGET HOTELS
16 Leinster Square, London W2 4PR
TEL 0171 286 5294. Fax 0171 229 3917

Railpasses Buying a railpass is both a popular and sensible option under many circumstances. Ideally conceived, a railpass allows you to jump on any train in Europe, go wherever you want whenever you want, and change your plans at will. The handbook that comes with your railpass tells you everything you need to know and includes a timetable for major routes, a map, and details on ferry discounts. In practice, of course, it's not so simple. You still must stand in line to pay for seat reservations, supplements, and couchette reservations, as well as to have your pass validated when you first use it. More importantly, railpasses don't always pay off. Find a travel agent with a copy of the **Eurailtariff manual** to weigh the wisdom of purchasing them. Add up the second-class fares for your planned routes and deduct 5% (listed prices automatically include commission) for comparison. If under age 26, the BIJ tickets described below are probably a viable option.

You may find it tough to make your railpass pay for itself in Belgium, Greece, Ireland, Italy, Luxembourg, Netherlands, Portugal, Spain, and all of Eastern Europe, where train fares are reasonable or distances short. If, however, the total cost of your trips nears the price of the pass, the convenience of avoiding ticket lines may well be worth the difference. Avoid an obsession with making the pass pay for itself; you may come home with only blurred memories of train stations.

Eurailpass, P.O. Box 10383, Stamford, CT 06904, remains the best option in European rail passes for North American travelers. Eurailpasses are valid in most of Western Europe (not in Britain, however). The first class **Eurailpass** rarely pays off; it is offered for durations of 15 days (US$498), 21 days (US$648), 1 month (US$798), 2 months (US$1098), or 3 months (US$1398). If you are traveling in a group, you might prefer the **Eurail Saverpass,** which allows unlimited first-class travel for 15 days (US$430), 21 days (US$550), or one month (US$678) per person in groups of two or more (three or more April-Sept.). Travelers under age 26 on their first day of travel can buy a **Eurail Youthpass,** good for 15 days (US$398), one month (US$578), or two months (US$768) of second-class travel. It's tough to get your money's worth from a one-month pass; the two-month pass is more economical. **Eurail Flexipasses** allow limited first-class travel within a two-month period: five days (US$348), 10 days (US$560), or 15 days (US$740). **Youth Flexipasses** are available for US$255, US$398, or US$540, respectively. They offer discounts similar to Eurail Flexipasses, but with a second-class youth option.

The new **Europass** allows travelers to combine the most popular of European countries in one travel plan: France, Germany, Italy, Spain, and Switzerland. This option offers rail travel through a limited number of countries determined by the number of travel days selected. For instance, a five-day trip allows you unlimited travel in three of the participating countries, an eight- to ten- day trip allows you four and an 11- to 15-day trip allows unlimited travel in all five countries. However, if you take one of the first two options, the three or four countries you visit must be adjacent to each other. First class prices begin at US$280 and the second class youth version at US$198. All passes are valid for two months.

You'll almost certainly find it easiest to buy a Eurailpass before you arrive in Europe; contact Council Travel, Travel CUTS, or Let's Go Travel (see Useful Travel Organizations, above), or any of many other travel agents. If you're stuck in Europe and unable to find someone to sell you a Eurailpass, make a transatlantic call to an American railpass agent, who should be able to send a pass to you by express mail. Eurailpasses are not refundable once validated; you will be able to get a replacement if you lose one only if you have purchased insurance on the pass from Eurail, something that cannot be done through a travel agent. You can, however, obtain specifics through a travel agent since this insurance program is relatively new. All Eurailpasses can be purchased from a travel agent. Also, **Rail Europe,** 226 Westchester Ave., White Plains, NY 10604 (tel. (800) 4-EURAIL (438-7245) in the U.S., and (800) 361-RAIL (361-7245), fax (416) 602-4198 in Canada) provides extensive information on pass options and publishes the *Europe on Track* booklet.

If you plan to focus your travels in one country, consider a national railpass. Also look into regional passes such as the ScanRail passes, which give you unlimited rail travel in Scandinavia, the BritFrance passes, the Benelux Tourrail Pass for Belgium, the Netherlands, and Luxembourg, and the European East Pass, which covers Poland, the Czech Republic, Slovakia, Hungary, and Austria. Some of these passes can be bought only in Europe, some only outside of Europe, and for some it doesn't matter; check with a railpass agent or with national tourist offices.

Rail tickets For travelers under 26, **BIJ** tickets (Billets Internationals de Jeunesse, sold under the names **Wasteels, Eurotrain,** and **Route 26**) are a great alternative to railpasses. Available for international trips within Europe and for travel within France as well as most ferry services, they knock 30-45% off regular second-class fares. Tickets are all good for 60 days after purchase and allow an unlimited number of free stopovers along the normal direct route of the train journey. Issued for a specific international route between two designated points in different countries, they must be used in the direction and order of the designated route without side- or back-tracking. You can buy BIJ tickets at Wasteels or Eurotrain offices (usually in or near train stations). For international journeys departing from the U.K., France, and Germany, tickets can be issued in the U.S. by **Wasteels Travel,** 7041 Grand National Dr. #207, Orlando, FL 32819 (tel. (407) 351-2537, fax 363-1041); for departure from other countries, tickets can be purchased through many European agents or directly at the ticket counter in some nations.

Useful Resources The ultimate reference is the *Thomas Cook European Time-table* (US$25; US$34 includes a map of Europe highlighting all train and ferry routes; plus $US4 for postage). The timetable, updated monthly, covers all major and many minor train routes in Europe. In the U.S., order it from **Forsyth Travel Library,** P.O. Box 2975, Shawnee Mission, KS 66201 (tel. (800) 367-7984 or (913) 384-3440), which provides other useful travel books as well. Also look for Lenore Blaken's *Camp Europe by Train* (US$15), which covers all aspects of train travel and includes sections on railpasses, packing, and the specifics of rail travel in each country. The *Eurail Guide* (US$15, postage US$3), available in bookstores, lists train schedules

LET'S GO
TRAVEL

1995 Eurail Passes
Starting at
$198

Mention this ad and receive free shipping!

800-5-LETSGO

and brief cultural information for almost every country on earth. Requests can also be directed to **Eurail Guide Annual,** 27540 Pacific Coast Highway, Malibu, CA 90265 (tel. (310) 457-7286). Rick Steves's free *Europe Through the Back Door* travel newsletter and catalog, 109 Fourth Ave. N., P.O. Box 2009, Edmonds, WA 98020 (tel. (206) 771-8303, fax 771-0833) provides comprehensive information on rail-passes (both Eurail and national/regional passes). **Hunter Publishing,** 300 Raritan Center Parkway, Edison, NJ 08818 (tel. (908) 225-1900, fax 417-0482) provides a comprehensive catalog of handy rail atlases, travel maps, and guidebooks that might pertain directly to your guide. Titles on hand include *Britain on the Backroads, Eastern Europe by Rail,* and other country-specific materials.

BY BUS

Though European trains and railpasses are extremely popular, the long-distance bus networks of Britain, Ireland, Portugal, Morocco, Greece, Turkey, and Yugoslavia are more extensive, efficient, and often more comfortable than train services; in Spain, Hungary, Albania, and northern Scandinavia, the bus and train systems are on a par; and in Iceland, bus service is the only ground transportation available. In the rest of Europe bus travel is more of a crapshoot, where scattered offerings from private companies are often cheap, but unreliable. All over Europe, short-haul buses reach rural areas inaccessible by train.

The biggest problem with European bus travel is deregulation; since there is little pan-European organization, it can be difficult to negotiate the route you need. Amsterdam, Athens, İstanbul, London, Munich, and Oslo are centers for lines that offer long-distance rides across Europe and, from time to time, all the way to India; see the Buses listings under the Practical Information sections for those cities.

The new **Eurobus** program offers two months of unlimited travel on continental style coaches with an English-speaking driver and guide. Destinations include major cities throughout continental Europe, such as Paris, Amsterdam, Cologne, Prague, Munich, Venice, Rome, and Milan. Travelers can hop on and off, and move on as often as they wish. The buses also stop door to door at a selection of campsites, hostels, and hotels, as well as offer on-board video presentation of various regions. Eurobus offers a "supersaver" discount book offering deals throughout Europe. For more info, contact Eurobus at 33 Princes Square, London W2 4NG (tel. (0171) 792 37 70, fax 792 37 66).

BY CAR AND VAN

Yes, there really is no speed limit on the Autobahn. Cars offer great speed, great freedom, access to the countryside, and an escape from the town-to-town mentality of trains. Unfortunately, they also insulate you from the *esprit de corps* European rail travelers enjoy. Although a single traveler won't save by renting a car, four usually will. If you can't decide between train and car travel, you may benefit from a combination of the two; Avis and Hertz offer rail and car packages, and Rail Europe and other railpass vendors (see above) offer economical "Euraildrive" passes.

You can **rent** a car from either a U.S.-based firm (Avis, Budget, or Hertz) with its own European offices, from a European-based company with local representatives (National and American International represent Europcar and Ansa, respectively), or from a tour operator (Europe by Car, Auto Europe, Foremost, Kemwel, and Wheels International), which will arrange a rental for you from a European company at its own rates. Not surprisingly, the multinationals offer greater flexibility, but the tour operators often strike good deals and may have lower rates. Rentals vary considerably by company, season, and pick-up point; expect to pay at least US$140 a week, plus tax, for a teensy car. (Picking up your car in Brussels or Luxembourg is usually cheaper than renting from Paris.) Reserve well before leaving for Europe and pay in advance if you can; rates within Europe are harsh. Always check if prices quoted include tax and collision insurance; some credit card companies will cover this automatically. Ask about student and other discounts and be flexible in your itinerary. Ask your airline about special packages; sometimes you can get up to a week of free

ESSENTIALS

WHERE IN THE WORLD ARE YOU GOING?

✈ **SPECIAL AIRFARES FOR STUDENTS, YOUTH, TEACHERS & GROUPS**

🏠 HOSTEL PASSES   ☼ VACATION PACKAGES

🐚 TRAVEL INSURANCE   🚆 EURAILPASSES

🚢 CRUISES   📷 TOURS

🚗 CAR RENTALS   📖 GUIDEBOOKS

AND MORE...

travelcraft

591 BROADWAY
NEW YORK, NY 10012

(800)777-CRAFT or (212) 431-7280

LONDON HOTEL

BEST RATES

SINGLES FROM £28
DOUBLES FROM £19 PP
FAMILIES 3/4/5 FROM £15 PP

WINDSOR HOUSE HOTEL,
12 PENYWERN RD, LONDON SW5 9ST
Tel 44-171-373-9087 Fax 44-171-385-2417

5 mins to Piccadilly

Call, fax or write now!
WELCOME TO LONDON!

rental. Minimum age restrictions vary by country; rarely, if ever, is it below 21. Try **Auto Europe,** 10 Sharp's Wharf, P.O. Box 1097, Camden ME 04843 (tel. (800) 223-5555); **Avis Rent a Car** (tel. (800) 331-1084); **Budget Rent a Car** (tel. (800) 472-3325); **Europe by Car,** Rockefeller Plaza, New York, NY 10021 (tel. (800) 223-1516 or (212) 581-3040); **Europcar,** 145 Avenue Malekoff, 75016 Paris (tel. (1) 45 00 08 06); **Foremost Euro-Car** (tel. (800) 272-3299; in Canada (800) 253-3876); **France Auto Vacances** (tel. (800) 234-1426); **Hertz Rent a Car** (tel. (800) 654-3001), **The Kemwel Group** (tel. (800) 678-0678); **Maiellano Tours,** 441 Lexington Ave., New York, NY 10051 (tel. (212) 687-7725); or **Payless Car Rental** (tel. (800) PAY-LESS (729-5377)). **The French National Railroad (SNCF),** 610 5th Ave., New York, NY 10020 (tel. (800) 848-7245 or (212) 582-2110) has a train-plus-car-rental package in about 200 cities in Europe. U.S. office answer s questions about overseas locations.

For longer than three weeks, **leasing** can be cheaper than renting; it is sometimes the only option for those aged 18-20. The cheapest leases are actually agreements where you buy the car and then sell it back to the manufacturer at a pre-agreed price. As far as you're concerned, though, it's a lease and doesn't entail enormous financial transactions. Leases include insurance coverage and are not taxed. The most affordable ones usually originate in Belgium or France and start at around US$500 for 23 days and US$1000 for 60 days. Contact **Foremost**, **Europe by Car,** and **Auto Europe**. You will need to make arrangements in advance.

If you're brave or know what you're doing, **buying** a used car or van in Europe and selling it just before you leave can provide the cheapest wheels on the Continent. Check with consulates for different countries' import-export laws concerning used vehicles, registration, and safety and emission standards. David Shore and Patty Campbell's annually updated *Europe By Van And Motorhome* (US$14, US$1 postage, US$8 overseas airmail) guides you through the entire process, from buy-back agreements to insurance and dealer listings. To order, write to 1842 Santa Margarita Dr., Fallbrook, CA 92028 (tel. (800) 659-5222 or (619) 723-6184). *How to Buy and Sell a Used Car in Europe* (US $6.00 plus US$0.75 postage, from Gil Friedman, P.O. Box 1063, Arcata, CA 95521, tel. (707) 822-5001), also contains practical information on the process of avoiding rental and lease hassles with a bit of wrangling.

Driving a camper-van or motorhome gives the advantages of car rental without the hassle of finding lodgings or cramming six friends into a Renault. You'll need those friends to split the gasoline bills, however, although many European vehicles use diesel or propane, which are cheaper. The car rental firms listed above have more information. *Moto-Europa,* by Eric Bredesen (US$20 plus US$3 shipping to North America, US$7 overseas), available from Seren Publishing, P.O. Box 1212 Dubuque, IA 52004 (tel. (800) EUROPA-8 (387-6728)) is a new comprehensive guide to all of these moto-options. From itinerary suggestions to a motorists' phrasebook, the guide provides all sorts of useful tips on the whole undertaking, whatever the chosen mode of transport. More general information is available from the **American Automobile Association (AAA),** Travel Agency Services Dept., 1000 AAA dr., Heathrow, FL 32746-5080 (tel. (800) 222-4357 or (417) 444-7380); the **American Automobile Touring Alliance,** Bayside Plaza, 188 The Embarcadero, San Francisco, CA 94105 (tel. (415) 771-3170); and, the **Canadian Automobile Association (CAA),** 60 Commerce Valley Dr. East, Markham, Ont. L3T 7P9.

Before setting off, be sure you know the laws of the country in which you're driving (for instance, both seat belts and headlights must be on at all times in Scandinavia, and remember to keep left in Ireland and the U.K.). Scandinavians and Western Europeans use unleaded gas almost exclusively, but it's almost nonexistent in Eastern Europe and North Africa. At most agencies in Europe, all that's needed to rent a car is a U.S. license and proof that you've had it for a year. See the International Driving Permits section, above, for details on who needs the IDP and how to get one.

FLYING AROUND

Unless you're under 25, flying across Europe on regularly scheduled flights will eat your budget. If you are 24 or under, special fares on most European airlines requir-

ESSENTIALS

THE WORLD'S BIGGEST TRAVEL COMPANY FOR 18-35 YEAR OLDS

Contiki offers you two hassle-free ways to see EUROPE from US$60 per day:

SUPERIOR TOURS
✓ Superior tourist class hotels with private facilities.
✓ Daily breakfast and dinners as per itinerary
✓ Luxury air-conditioned motor coach.
✓ Experienced professional tour manager and driver.

BUDGET TOURS
✓ Stay in unique Contiki special stopovers and Contiki villages.
✓ Daily breakfast and dinners as per itinerary
✓ Free sleeping bag – yours to keep.
✓ Luxury air-conditioned motor coach.
✓ Experienced professional tour manager and driver.

ADDITIONAL CONTIKI BONUS:
Contiki is on sale in over 30 countries, ensuring you will travel with 18-35 year olds from around the world.

For your free 1995 Europe brochure call
1 800 CONTIKI

ing ticket purchase either the day before or the day of departure are a lovely exception to this rule. These are often cheaper than the corresponding regular train fare, though not always as cheap as student rail tickets or railpasses. Student travel agencies also sell cheap tickets, and budget fares are also frequently available in the spring and summer on high-volume routes between northern Europe and resort areas in Spain, Italy, and Greece. Consult budget travel agents and local newspapers and magazines. The **Air Travel Advisory Bureau,** 41-45 Goswell Road, London EC1V 7DN England (tel. (0171) 636 5000), can put you in touch with discount flights to worldwide destinations, for free. **Virgin Atlantic Airways,** 96 Morton St., New York, NY 10041 (tel. (800) 862-8621) offers a package deal for European touring that allows U.S. purchasers of tickets to Europe to buy voucher coupons for travel within Europe. These tickets bought "in bulk" generally end up cheaper than buying them leg by leg once in Europe.

BY BOAT

Travel by boat is a bewitching alternative much favored by Europeans but overlooked by most foreigners. Most European ferries are comfortable and well-equipped; the cheapest fare class sometimes includes use of a reclining chair or couchette where you can sleep the trip away. You should check in at least two hours early for a prime spot and allow plenty of time for late trains and getting to the port. It's a good idea to bring your own food and avoid the astronomically priced cafeteria cuisine. Fares jump sharply in July and August. Always ask for discounts; ISIC holders can often get student fares and Eurail passholders get many reductions and free trips (check the brochure that comes with your railpass). You'll occasionally have to pay a small port tax (under US$10). Advance planning and reserved ticket purchases through a travel agency can spare you several tedious days of waiting in dreary ports for the next sailing.

Ferries in Europe divide into four major groups. **Mediterranean** ferries may be the most glamorous, but are also the most treacherous. Reservations are recommended, especially in July and August, when ships are insufferably crowded and expensive (bring some toilet paper). Ferries run on erratic schedules, with similar routes and varying prices; shop around and watch out for dinky, unreliable companies which will often not accept reservations. Ferries across the **English Channel** are frequent and dependable; see the Great Britain and Ireland Getting There sections for more details. Ferries in the **North Sea** and **Baltic Sea** are prized by Scandinavians for their duty-free candy and alcohol shops; they also offer student and youth discounts, are universally reliable, and go everywhere (in summer, you can go from St. Petersburg to Iceland or Scotland without once using land transport). Those content with deck passage rarely need to book ahead. The best American source for information on Scandinavian ferries and visa-free cruises to Russia is **EuroCruises,** 303 W. 13th St., New York, NY 10014 (tel. (212) 691-2099 or (800) 688-3876). **Riverboats** acquaint you with many towns that trains can only wink at. The Moselle, Rhine, and Danube steamers have been overrun by gaudy tourists; less commercial-looking lines can be more seductive.

BIKING

Today, biking is one of the key elements of the classic budget Eurovoyage. Everyone else in the youth hostel is doing it, and with the proliferation of mountain bikes, you can do some serious natural sight-seeing. Be aware that touring involves pedaling both yourself and whatever you store in the panniers (bags which strap to your bike). Take some reasonably challenging day-long rides at home to prepare yourself before you leave. Have your bike tuned up by a reputable shop. Wear visible clothing, drink plenty of water (even if you're not thirsty), and ride on the same side as the traffic. Learn the international signals for turns and use them. Learn how to fix a modern derailleur-equipped mount and change a tire, and practice on your own bike before you have to do it overseas. A few simple tools and a good bike manual will be invaluable. For information about touring routes, consult national tourist offices or any of the numerous books available. **The Mountaineers Books,** 1011 Klickitat Way #107, Seattle, WA 98134 (tel. (800 553-4453) offers several nation-specific tour books (especially Germany, Ireland, France and England), as well as *Europe By Bike,* by Karen and Terry Whitehill (US$15), a great source of specific area tours in 11 countries. Send for a catalog. *Cycling Europe: Budget Bike Touring in the Old World,* by N. Slavinski (US$13) may also be a helpful addition to your library. **Michelin road maps** are also clear and detailed guides.

If you are nervous about striking out on your own, **CBT Bicycle Tours** (tel. (312) 404-1710 or (800) 736-BIKE (736-2453) in the U.S. and Canada, fax (312) 404-1833) offers bicycle tours through Belgium, England, France, Germany, Holland, Luxembourg and Switzerland that are exclusively for the college-aged and arrange discounted airfares for their participants.

Most airlines will count your bike as your second free piece of luggage (you're usually allowed 2 pieces of checked baggage and a carry-on). As an extra piece, it will cost about US$85 each way. Policies on charters and budget flights vary; check with the airline. The safest way to send your bike is in a box, with the handlebars, pedals, and front wheel detached. Within Europe, most ferries let you take your bike for free. You can always ship your bike on trains, though the cost varies from a small fixed fee to a substantial fraction of the ticket price.

Riding a bike with a frame pack strapped on it or on your back is about as safe as pedaling blindfolded over a sheet of ice; panniers are essential. The first thing to buy, however, is a suitable **bike helmet.** At about US$50-100, they're a much better buy than head injury or death. To lessen the odds of theft, buy a U-shaped **Citadel** or **Kryptonite** lock. These are expensive (about US$20-55), but the companies insure their locks against theft of your bike for one to two years. **Bike Nashbar,** 4112 Simon Rd., Youngstown, OH 44512 (tel. (800) 627-4227), has excellent prices on equipment and cheerfully beats all competitors' offers by US5¢.

Renting a bike beats bringing your own if your touring will be confined to one or two regions. **The French National Railroad (SNCF),** 610 5th Ave., New York, NY 10020 (tel. (800) 848-7245 or (212) 582-2110) rents bicycles for inter/intra-national

travel. They have representatives in 11 different countries. With a train ticket or rail-pass and ID, anyone can rent a bike for about US$3/day (plus a US$20 deposit). Let's Go lists bike rental shops in most cities and towns. Some youth hostels (especially in France) rent bicycles for low prices. In many countries (including France and Belgium), train stations rent bikes and often allow you to drop them off elsewhere without charge.

BY MOPED AND MOTORCYCLE

Motorized bikes have long spiced southern European roads with their flashy colors and perpetual buzz. They offer an enjoyable, relatively inexpensive way to tour coastal areas and countryside, particularly where there are few cars. They don't use much gas, can be put on trains and ferries, and are a good compromise between the high cost of car travel and the limited range of bicycles. However, they're uncomfortable for long distances, dangerous in the rain, and unpredictable on rough roads or gravel. Always wear a helmet and never ride with a backpack. If you've never been on a moped before, a twisting Alpine road is not the place to start. Expect to pay about US$15-35 per day; try auto repair shops and remember to bargain. Motorcycles normally require a license. Before renting, ask if the quoted price includes tax and insurance or you may be hit with an unexpected additional fee. Avoid handing your passport over as a deposit; if you have an accident or mechanical failure you may not get it back until you cover all repairs. Pay ahead of time instead.

HITCHING

> *Let's Go* strongly urges you to seriously consider the risks before you choose to hitch. We do not recommend hitching as a safe means of transportation and none of the information presented here is intended to do so.

No one should hitch without careful consideration of the risks involved. Not everyone can be an airplane pilot, but almost any bozo can drive a car. Hitching means entrusting your life to a random person who happens to stop beside you on the road and risking theft, assault, sexual harassment, and unsafe driving. In spite of this, there are gains to hitching. Favorable hitching experiences allow you to meet local people and get where you're going, especially in northern Europe and Ireland, where public transportation is sketchy. In many areas of Eastern Europe, the line between hitching and taking a taxi is quite thin. The choice, however, remains yours.

Depending on the circumstances and the norms of the country, men and women traveling in groups and men traveling alone might consider hitching (called "autostop" in much of Europe) to locations beyond the scope of bus or train routes. If you're a woman traveling alone, don't hitch. It's just too dangerous. A man and a woman are a safer combination, two men will have a harder time finding a ride, and three will go nowhere.

If you do decide to hitch, consider where you are. Britain and Ireland are probably the easiest places in Western Europe to get a lift. Hitching in Scandinavia is slow but steady. Long-distance hitching in the developed countries of northwestern Europe demands close attention to expressway junctions, rest stop locations, and often a destination sign. Hitching in southern Europe is generally mediocre; France is the worst. Hitching remains common in Eastern Europe, though Westerners are a definite target for theft. In Russia, the Baltics, and some other Eastern European countries, there is no clear difference between hitchhiking and hailing a taxi.

Where you stand is also vital. Experienced hitchers pick a spot outside of built-up areas, where drivers can stop, return to the road without causing an accident, and have time to look over potential passengers as they approach. Hitching (or even standing) on super-highways is generally illegal: you may only thumb at rest stops, or at the entrance ramps to highways. In the Practical Information section of many cities, we list the tram or bus lines that will take travelers to strategic points for hitching out.

ESSENTIALS

ASTOR
H O S T E L S
London
2 1   y e a r s   e x p e r i e n c e

FORGET THE REST STAY AT **LONDON'S** BEST

SUPERB BUDGET ACCOMMODATION

Four great Student Hostels in the heart of London offer superb budget accommodation in sharing rooms. Meet fellow Travellers for lots of fun, parties and inexpensive trips in and around London. Also help for job hunters.

Sharing Room from **£11.00**

Weekly Rate* from **£55.00**

Prices include Tax and Continental Breakfast
*Not available in Summer

Quest — Next to Hyde Park/Queensway

45 Queensborough Terrace W2
Tel: (071) 229 7782   Fax: (071) 727 8106
Bayswater (Circle Line), Queensway (Central Line)

Museum — Opp. British Museum/West End Theatres

27 Montague Street WC1
Tel: (071) 580 5360   Fax: (071) 6367948
Tottenham Court Road (Central and Nothern Line)

Victoria — Near Buckingham Palace/Parliament

71 Belgrave Road SW1
Tel: (071) 834 3077   Fax: (071) 932 0693
Victoria (Central District and Victoria Lines)

Maree — British Museum/West End Clubs/Soho

25 Gower Street WC1
Tel: (071) 636 4868
Tottenham Ct. Rd. (Central Line)
Goodge Street (Nothern Line)
Russell Square (Piccadilly Line)

RESERVATIONS

You can Just arrive Or, to pre-book, Call/Write/Fax
to Hostel of choice: Your name, address, arrival date,
Credit Card Number and Expiry Date

DISEÑO.MEX (22) 450-658

ENQUIRES: Tel (071) 229 7866   Fax (071) 727 8106

Finally, success will depend on what you look like. Successful hitchers travel light and stack their belongings in a compact but visible cluster. Most Europeans signal with an open hand, rather than a thumb; many write their destination on a sign in large, bold letters and draw a smiley-face under it. Drivers prefer hitchers who are neat and wholesome. No one stops for anyone wearing sunglasses.

Safety issues are always imperative, even when you're traveling with another person. Avoid getting in the back of a two-door car, and never let go of your backpack. Hitchhiking at night can be particularly dangerous; stand in a well-lit place and expect drivers to be leery of nocturnal thumbers. Don't get into a car that you can't get out of again in a hurry. If you ever feel threatened, insist on being let off, regardless of where you are. If the driver refuses to stop, try acting as though you're going to open the car door or vomit on the upholstery.

Europe: A Manual for Hitchhikers gives directions for hitching out of hundreds of cities, rates rest areas and entrance ramps, and deciphers national highway and license plate systems. It's available from Vacation Work Publications (see Work section, above, for complete address).

Most Western European countries offer a ride service, a cross between hitchhiking and the ride boards common at many university campuses, which pairs drivers with riders, with a fee to both agency (about US$25) and driver (per km). **Eurostop International** (called **Verband der Deutschen Mitfahrzentralen** in Germany and **Allostop** in France) is one of the largest in Europe. Not all of these organizations screen drivers and riders; ask in advance.

WALKING AND HIKING

Europe's grandest scenery can often be seen only by foot. *Let's Go* describes many daytrips for those who want to hoof it, but native inhabitants (Europeans are fervent, almost obsessive hikers), hostel proprietors, and fellow travelers are the best source of tips. Many European countries have hiking and mountaineering organizations; alpine clubs in Germany, Austria, Switzerland, and Italy, as well as tourist organizations in Scandinavia, provide inexpensive, simple accommodations in splendid settings. One good book is J. Sydney Jones' *Tramping in Europe: A Walking Guide* (US$8); check your local bookstore for others.

■■■ ACCOMMODATIONS

If you arrive in a town without a reservation, your first stop should be the local tourist office. These offices distribute extensive accommodations listings free of charge and will also reserve a room for a small fee (though some favor their friends' establishments). As a rule, expect all prices to rise each January.

Often, hostel proprietors or locals with rooms to rent will approach you in ports or train stations. This may seem dangerous, but it is an accepted custom in many areas. However, there is no guarantee of these hawkers' trustworthiness or of the quality of their establishments. Carry your own baggage, ask for their identification, and have them write down the offered price.

HOSTELS

Especially in summer, Europe is overrun by young, budget-conscious travelers. Hostels are the hub of this gigantic subculture, providing innumerable opportunities to meet students from all over the world, find new traveling partners, trade stories, and learn about places to visit. At US$7-20 per night, prices are extraordinarily low; only camping is cheaper. Guests tend to be in their teens and twenties, but most hostels welcome travelers of all ages. In northern Europe, where hotel prices are astronomical, hostels have special family rooms, a higher standard of cleanliness, and correspondingly less of a student atmosphere. In the average hostel, though, you and anywhere from 1 to 50 roommates will sleep in a gender-segregated room full of bunk beds, with common bathrooms and a lounge down the hall. The hostel war-

P A R I S

YOUNG & HAPPY
——HOSTEL——

107 F
Bed & Breakfast

Run by young people
for young people!!
80, rue Mouffetard
75005 Paris

✆ **(1) 45 35 09 53**

Fax: (1) 47 07 22 24
Metro: "Place Monge" Line n°7

IDEALLY LOCATED • ENGLISH SPEAKING STAFF • STUDENT DISTRICT • SAFE DISTRICT • STUDENT RESTAURANTS • COMFORTABLE ROOMS • HOT SHOWERS • SAFE DEPOSIT BOX • SUPERMARKETS, LAUNDROMATS, POST OFFICE, CAFÉ NEARBY • ONE OF THE OLDEST OPEN MARKETS OF PARIS OPENED DAILY • CLEANED DAILY •

ALOHA HOSTEL

Prices:
Summer: 97F
Winter: 87F

☑ 10 MIN. WALK FROM EIFFEL TOWER
☑ ENGLISH SPEAKING STAFF
☑ NEWLY RENOVATED
☑ CLEANED DAILY
☑ SAFE DISTRICT
☑ FREE MAPS
☑ LARGE INFOSTAND
☑ COOKING FACILITIES
☑ SAFE DEPOSIT BOX
☑ SUPERMARKETS, BAKERIES NEARBY
☑ LAUNDROMATS
☑ FAX SERVICE
☑ BIKE RENTAL & BIKE TOUR IN ENGLISH

✆ **(1) 42 73 03 03**
Fax: (1) 42 73 14 14

1, rue Borromée - 75015 Paris
(Corner 243 rue de Vaugirard)
Metro: "Volontaires" Line n°12

*Summer: April - Oct. Winter: Nov. - March

den may be a laid-back student, a hippie dropout, or a crotchety disciplinarian. Most hostels have well-equipped kitchens; some serve hot meals.

The basic disadvantage of hostels is their regimentation. Most have an early curfew—fine if you're climbing a mountain the next morning, but a distinct cramp in your style if you plan to rage in town. There is also usually a lockout from morning to mid-afternoon. Conditions are generally spartan and cramped, with little privacy, and you may run into more screaming pre-teen tour groups than you care to remember. Hostel quality also varies dramatically. Some are set in strikingly beautiful castles, others in run-down barracks far from the town center. Rural hostels are generally more appealing than those in large cities. Hostels usually prohibit sleeping bags for sanitary reasons and provide blankets and sheets instead. Some require **sleepsacks;** make your own by folding a sheet and sewing it shut on two sides. If you're lazy or less domestic, you can order one (about US$14) from Let's Go Travel or a youth hostel federation.

Large hostels are reluctant to take advance telephone reservations because of the high no-show rate; citing an exact train arrival time or promising to call again and confirm can sometimes help. In large city hostels in Western Europe, take advantage of hostel-to-hostel fax booking services where the hostel you're staying at faxes another to see if there's space, then charges you the overnight fee plus a booking fee (less than US$1) and finally issues you a confirmation slip which you present to the other hostel.

Prospective hostel-goers should become members of the official youth hostel association in their country; all national hostel associations are part of **Hostelling International (HI).** (For HI headquarters or national member association addresses, see Documents and Formalities, above.) If you haven't become a member in advance, show up at an HI hostel and ask for a blank membership card with space for six validation stamps. Each night you'll pay a nonmember supplement (equal to one-sixth the membership fee) and earn one Guest Stamp; get six stamps and you're a member. This system works well in most of Western Europe, though in some countries you may need to remind the hostel reception to issue you a guest card. In Eastern Europe, most hostels are not HI members. Most student travel agencies sell HI cards on the spot; otherwise, contact one of the national hostel organizations listed below. Ask about the *Budget Accommodation: Volume I: Europe and the Mediterranean* (US$11).

Privately owned hostels are found in major tourist centers and throughout some countries (particularly Ireland). No membership is required, and you won't always have to contend with early curfews or daytime lockouts, but their quality varies widely. The YMCA runs 29 **Interpoint** hostels in major northern European cities (July-Aug.); membership cards are available at each location.

HOTELS, GUESTHOUSES, AND PRIVATE HOMES

Hotels are quite expensive in Britain, Switzerland, Austria, and northern Europe: rock bottom for singles is US$14-17, for doubles US$18-22. In the rest of Europe, couples can usually get by fairly well (rooms with a double bed are generally cheaper than those with two twin beds), as can groups of three or four. Inexpensive European hotels may come as a rude shock to pampered North American travelers. You'll share a bathroom down the hall; one of your own is a rarity and costs extra when provided. Hot showers may also cost more. Don't confuse the toilet with the *bidet*. In Britain and Ireland a large breakfast is generally included; elsewhere a continental breakfast of a roll, jam, coffee or tea, and maybe an egg is served. Some hotels offer "full pension" (all meals) and "half pension" (breakfast and dinner). Unmarried couples will generally have no trouble getting a room together, although couples under age 21 may occasionally encounter resistance.

Smaller, family-run **guesthouses** and **pensions** are usually a little cheaper than the cheapest hotels. Even less expensive are rooms in **private homes,** of which the local tourist office usually has a good list. If you're traveling alone, this is an economical way to get your own room and meet real Europeans. The British and Irish **bed**

ESSENTIALS

REST EASY

Call this number... **1-800-444-6111**

BOOK AHEAD

IBN INTERNATIONAL BOOKING NETWORK

HOSTELLING INTERNATIONAL

IBN is a computerized advance reservation system operated by Hostelling International to simplify your ongoing travel with advance reservations.

- Immediate reservation and confirmation, worldwide
- Pay in local currency where you make the reservation – no exchange fees or bank charges!

For reservations call 1-800-444-6111 or simply contact any participating hostel or travel center.

Budget accommodations you can trust!

VISITING LONDON?

MIDDLESEX UNIVERSITY

Need somewhere to stay?

Middlesex University offers single-room, self-catering accommodation at the University's Wood Green Hall of Residence, only 20 minutes by underground from the heart of London. **£9.50 a night** (bed only, per person), July to September. Group bookings welcome – one free place for every 10.

**Accommodation Manager
Wood Green Hall
Middlesex University
London N22 6UZ, UK
+44 181 888 4866**

CENTRAL LONDON SIX MILES

and breakfast is a breed of private room that's extra heavy on the bacon and eggs. Private rooms are an excellent option in Eastern Europe, where youth hostels are primitive and hotels in flux; in the absence of good tourist offices, travel agencies book most private rooms in the east, and proprietors flag down tourists at the train station (try not to get stuck in a distant, vapid suburb).

If you reserve in writing, indicate your night of arrival and the number of nights you plan to stay. The hotel will send you a confirmation and may request payment for the first night. Not all hotels take reservations, and few accept checks in foreign currency. Enclosing two International Reply Coupons (available at any post office) will ensure a prompt reply, but will cost as much as a short transatlantic phone call.

CAMPING

Camping in Europe can rock or suck. **Organized campgrounds** exist in almost every European city, most accessible by foot, car, or public transportation. Showers, bathrooms, and a small restaurant or store are common; some sites have more elaborate facilities. Prices range from US$1-10 per person with an additional charge for a tent. Money and time expended in getting to the campsite may eat away at your budget and your patience; if you're doing the Eurail thing, hostels are probably more pleasant.

Europa Camping and Caravanning, an annually updated catalog of campsites in Europe, is available through Recreational Equipment, Inc., REI, P.O. Box 1700, Sumner, WA 98352-0001 (tel. (800) 426-4840) for US$20. Finally, the Automobile Association, Norfolk House, Basingstoke, Hampshire RG24 9NY, England (tel. (01256) 201 23), publishes *Camping and Caravanning in Europe* (UK£7.99). An **International Camping Carnet** (membership card) is required by some European campgrounds but can usually be bought on the spot. The card entitles you to a discount at some campgrounds, and often may be substituted for your passport as a security deposit. In the U.S., it's available for US$30 through Family Campers and RVers, 4804 Transit Rd., Bldg. #2, Depew, NY 14043 (tel. (716) 668-6242; carnet price includes a FCRV membership fee).

Prospective campers will need to invest a lot of money in good camping equipment and a lot of energy carrying it on their shoulders. Use the reputable mail-order firms to gauge prices; order from them if you can't do as well locally. In the fall, the previous year's merchandise may be reduced by as much as 50%. **Campmor**, 28 Park Way, Upper Saddle River, NJ 07458-0770 (tel. (800) 526-4784), has name-brand equipment at low prices. **Cabela's**, 812 13th Ave., Sidney, NE 69160 (tel. (800) 237-4444), also offers great prices. **REI** (listed above) stocks a wide range of the latest gear and holds great seasonal sales. And 24 hours a day, 365 days a year, **L.L. Bean,** Freeport, ME 04033 (tel. (800) 341-4341), supplies its own equipment and national-brand merchandise.

Most of the better **sleeping bags**—down (lightweight and warm) or synthetic (cheaper, heavier, more durable, and warmer when wet)—have ratings for specific minimum temperatures. The lower the mercury, the higher the price. Estimate the most severe conditions you may encounter, subtract a few degrees, and then buy a bag. Expect to pay at least US$65 for a synthetic bag and up to US$270-550 for a down bag suitable for use in sub-freezing temperatures. **Sleeping bag pads** range from US$15-30, while **air mattresses** go for about US$30-60. The best **tents** are free-standing, with their own frames and suspension systems. They set up quickly and require no staking. Remember to use the tent's protective rain fly and seal the seams to protect against water seepage. Backpackers and cyclists will require especially small, lightweight models, costing US$145 and up. **Sierra Design**, 2039 4th St., Berkeley, CA 94710, sells a two-person tent that weighs less than 1.76kg (4lbs.).

Other camping basics include a battery-operated **lantern** (*never* gas) and a simple plastic **groundcloth** to protect the tent floor. When camping in autumn, winter, or spring, bring along a "space blanket," a lightweight silvery sheet that helps you retain your body heat. Large, collapsible **water sacks** will significantly improve your lot in primitive campgrounds and weigh practically nothing when empty. **Camp-**

ESSENTIALS

- JET SKIS - VOLLEYBALL - BILLIARDS - INNER TUBING - WEIGHT ROOM - BASKETBALL - MOTORCYCLES - MOPEDS -

BOAT EXCURSIONS - SCUBA DIVING - WATERSKIING - BASKETBALL - JET SKIS - VOLLEYBALL - MOTORCYCLES - MOPEDS - FOOZBALL - BILLIARDS - INNER TUBING - CLIFF DIVING - WATERSKIING - BASKETBALL

BASKETBALL - BOAT EXCURSIONS - WATERSKIING - SCUBA DIVING - BILLIARDS - WEIGHT ROOM - FOOZBALL - MOPEDS - MOTORCYCLES - VOLLEYBALL - JET SKIS - BASKETBALL - WATERSKIING

Take a Vacation from Your Vacation ...

Experience

THE **Pink Palace**

CORFU, GREECE

Recommended
by
LET'S GO
and
FROMMERS

The World's Largest Youth Resort

Tel: (661) 53103/53104

ONLY $18 per night*

Breakfast, Dinner & Night Club Included

Private Rooms
Hot Showers - Laundry Service
Giant Jaccuzi - Dancing til Dawn
Breakfast til Noon - Long Distance Calling
Commission-Free Money Exchange

Get a voucher for ONE NIGHT FREE**
when you book your railpass or flight at:

in the United States

Council Travel

in Canada

TRAVEL CUTS
VOYAGES CAMPUS

*Price in $US at time of printing.
** Based on a minimum stay of 3 nights. Voucher must be stamped by issuing office. One per person per stay.

The Pink Palace accepts:

- CLIFF DIVING - FOOZBALL - SCUBA DIVING - INNER TUBING - WEIGHT ROOM - JET SKIS - VOLLEYBALL - BILLIARDS -

stoves come in all sizes, weights, and fuel types, but none are truly cheap (US$30-120) or light. Consider GAZ, a form of bottled propane gas that is easy to use and widely available in Europe and remember waterproof matches. A canteen, Swiss army knife, and insect repellent are small, essential items. For further information about camping equipment and other camping concerns, contact **Wilderness Press**, 2440 Bancroft Way, Berkeley, CA 94704-1676 (tel. (800) 443-7227 or (510) 843-8080), which publishes useful books such as *Backpacking Basics* (US$11, including postage) and *Backpacking with Babies and Small Children* (US$11).

THE GREAT OUTDOORS

The first thing to preserve in the wilderness is yourself—health, safety, and food should be your primary concerns. See the Health section for information about basic medical concerns and first-aid. One comprehensive guide to outdoor survival is *How to Stay Alive in the Woods*, by Bradford Angier (Macmillan, $8). Many rivers, streams, and lakes are contaminated with bacteria such as giardia, which causes gas, cramps, loss of appetite, and violent diarrhea. To protect yourself from the effects of this microscopic trip-wrecker, always boil your water vigorously for at least five minutes before drinking it, or use a purifying iodine solution. Filters do not remove all bacteria. *Never go camping or hiking by yourself for any significant time or distance.* If you're going into an area that is not well-traveled or well-marked, let someone know where you're hiking and how long you intend to be out. If you fail to return on schedule, searchers will at least know where to look for you.

The second thing to protect while you are outdoors is the wilderness. Because firewood is scarce in popular areas, campers are asked to make small fires using only dead branches or brush; using a campstove is the more cautious way to cook. Some parks/sites prohibit campfires altogether. Pitch your tent on high, dry ground, don't cut vegetation, and don't clear campsites. If there are no toilet facilities, bury human waste at least four inches deep and 100 feet or more from any water supplies and campsites. Use only biosafe soap or detergents in streams or lakes. Always pack up your trash in a plastic bag and carry it with you until you reach the next trash can; burning and burying pollute the environment.

ALTERNATIVE ACCOMMODATIONS

In university and college towns, **student dormitories** may be open to travelers when school is not in session. Prices are usually comparable to those of youth hostels, and you usually won't have to share a room with strangers or endure stringent curfew and eviction regulations. Also, many **monasteries** and **convents** will open their doors to those seeking corporeal or spiritual relief, particularly in Italy. A letter of introduction from a clergy member could facilitate matters.

A number of host networks will help you find lodging with families in Europe. **Servas** is an organization devoted to promoting world peace and understanding among people of different cultures. Traveling members may stay free for two nights in other members' homes in over 100 countries. You contact hosts in advance, and you must be willing to fit into the household routine (membership US$55, for a US$25 deposit get up to 5 host lists, which provide self-description of hosts). Write: U.S. Servas, Inc., 11 John St., #407, New York, NY 10038-4009 (tel. (212) 267-0252, fax 267-0292). **Willing Workers on Organic Farms**, Speerstrasse 7, 8305 Dietlikon, Switzerland (tel. (01) 834 02 34) compiles a list of organic farms in Denmark, England, Ireland and Germany which provide beds and meals in exchange for labor.

Sleeping in European train stations is a time-honored tradition. While it's free and often tolerated by authorities, it's neither comfortable nor safe. Don't spend the night in an urban park unless you place a similarly low value on your life.

■■■ WOMEN TRAVELERS

Women exploring any area on their own inevitably face additional safety concerns. In all situations it is best to trust your instincts: if you'd feel better somewhere else,

ESSENTIALS

LET'S GO TO BALMER'S
The first private hostel in Switzerland

Balmer's Hostel   Balmer's Guesthouse

A home away from home — open all year round

Special Discount Excursions, Balmer's Bus
Shuttle service available
Swiss Army Knives «VICTORINOX»
(best prices / best selection) free engraving!
Typical Swiss dishes for reasonable prices
Ski rent discount, Laundry facilities
All major credit cards welcome
Balmer's club
No age limit, no curfew

BALMER'S HERBERGE
Fam. E. + K. Balmer, Hauptstr. 23—25
3800 Interlaken / Switzerland
☏ 036 - 22 19 61, Fax 036 - 23 32 61

NEW: BALMER'S TENT

The Balmer family and their Super Crew are looking forward
to your visit!

Balmer's Ticket office

Tandem Paragliding   Mountain Biking   Bungy Jumping   Riverrafting   Canyoning   Rockclimbing   Hiking   Dry Canyoning   Waterskiing

Sport + Adventure local professional guides only! Booking office here don't hesitate to move on. Always carry extra money for a phone call or taxi. Consider staying in hostels, YWCAs, or religious organizations which offer single rooms that lock from the inside or in religious organizations that offer rooms for women only. Stick to centrally-located accommodations and avoid late-night treks or metro rides. Hitching is never safe for lone women, or even for two women. Choose train compartments occupied by other women or couples. In some parts of the world, women (foreign or local) are frequently beset by unwelcome and tenacious followers. Exercise reasonable caution without feeling that you must avoid all local men.

To escape unwanted attention, follow the example of local women. In general, dress conservatively, especially in more rural areas. If you spend time in cities, you may be harassed no matter how you're dressed. Look as if you know where you're going (even when you don't) and ask women or couples for directions if you're lost. Your best answer to verbal harassment is no answer at all (a reaction is what the harasser wants). In crowds, you may be pinched or squeezed by oversexed slimeballs; wearing a wedding band may help prevent such incidents.

Don't hesitate to seek out a police officer or a passerby if you are being harassed. Memorize the emergency numbers in the countries you visit, and always carry change for the phone and enough extra money for a bus or taxi. Carry a whistle or an airhorn on your keychain, and don't hesitate to use it in an emergency. A **model mugging** course will not only prepare you for a potential mugging, but will also raise your level of awareness of your surroundings as well as your confidence. (See Safety and Security, above.) Women also face additional health concerns when traveling (see Health, above). All of these warnings and suggestions should not discourage women from traveling alone. Don't take unnecessary risks, but don't lose your spirit of adventure either.

For general information, contact the **National Organization for Women (NOW)**, which boasts branches across the country that can refer women travelers to rape crisis centers, and counselling services, and provide lists of feminist events in the area. Main offices include: 22 W. 21st St., 7th Fl., **New York**, NY 10010 (tel. (212) 807-0721), 425 13th St., NW, **Washington**, DC 20004 (tel. (202) 234-4558, and 3543 18th St., **San Francisco**, CA 94110 (tel. (415) 861-8880). The following publications also offer tips for women travelers:

Handbook for Women Travelers by Maggie and Gemma Moss (UK£9). Encyclopedic and well-written. From Piaktus Books, 5 Windmill St., London W1P 1HF (tel. (0171) 631 07 10).

Index/Directory of Women's Media. Lists women's publishers, bookstores, theaters, and news organizations. Published by the Women's Institute for the Freedom of the Press, 3306 Ross Place, NW, Washington, DC 20008 (tel. (202) 966-7793).

A Journey of One's Own by Thalia Zepatos (Eight Mountain Press, US$15). The latest on the market, interesting and full of good advice, plus a specific and manageable bibliography of books and resources.

Women Going Places (US$14). From Inland Book Company, P.O. Box 12061, East Haven, CT 06512 (tel. (203) 467-4257). A women's travel and resource guide emphasizing women-owned enterprises. Geared toward lesbians, but offers advice appropriate for all women.

Women Travel: Adventures, Advice & Experience by Davies & Jansz (Penguin, US$13). Info on specific foreign countries, decent bibliography & resource index.

Wander Women, 136 N. Grand Ave. #237, West Covina, CA 91791 (tel. (818) 966-8857), travel/adventure networking organization for women over 40. Quarterly newsletter *Journal 'n' Footnotes*. US$29 annual membership fee.

■■■ OLDER TRAVELERS

Seniors are eligible for a wide array of discounts on transportation, museums, etc. Many car rental agencies have discounts that vary depending on city, car size, and travel time. Proof of senior citizen status is required for many of the services below.

AARP (American Association of Retired Persons), 601 E St., NW, Washington, DC 20049 (tel. (202) 434-2277 or (800) 927-0111). U.S. residents over 50 and their spouses receive benefits which include the AARP Travel Experience from American Express (tel. (800) 927-0111), the AARP Motoring Plan from Amoco (tel. (800) 334-3300), and discounts on lodging, car rental, and sight-seeing. US$8 annual fee per couple.

Elderhostel, 75 Federal St., 3rd Fl., Boston, MA 02110-1941 (tel. (617) 426-8056). You must be 60 or over, and may bring a spouse. Programs at colleges and universities in over 47 countries focus on varied subjects and generally last one week.

National Council of Senior Citizens, 1331 F St., NW, Washington, DC 20004 (tel. (202) 347-8800). For US$12 a year, US$30 for three years, or US$150 for a lifetime, an individual or couple can receive hotel and auto rental discounts, a senior citizen newspaper, use of a discount travel agency, supplemental Medicare insurance (if you're over 65), and a mail-order prescription drug service.

Gateway Books, 2023 Clemens Road, Oakland, CA 94602 (tel. (510) 530-0299, fax 530-0497). Publishes *Get Up and Go: A Guide for the Mature Traveler* (US$11) and *Adventures Abroad* (US$13) which offer general hints for the budget-conscious senior considering a long stay or retiring abroad. For credit card orders call (800) 669-0773.

Pilot Books, 103 Cooper St., Babylon, NY 11702 (tel. (516) 422-2225). Publishes *The International Health Guide for Senior Citizens* (US$5, postage US$1) and *The Senior Citizens' Guide to Budget Travel in Europe* (US$6 postage US$1).

Unbelievably Good Deals and Great Adventures That You Absolutely Can't Get Unless You're Over 50 by Joan Heilman (Contemporary Books, US$8). After you finish reading the title page, check inside for some great tips on senior discounts and the like.

■■■ TRAVELERS WITH CHILDREN

Restaurants often have kids menus and discounts. Virtually all museums and tourist attractions also have a children's rate. Be sure to make sure your child carries some sort of ID in case of an emergency or if he or she gets lost.

By airplane, children under two generally fly free on domestic flights and for 10% of the adult fare on international flights (this does not, however, necessarily include a seat). Children 2 to 12 usually fly half price.

Some of the following publications offer tips for adults traveling with children or distractions for the kids themselves. You can also contact the publishers to see if they have other related publications which you might find useful.

Backpacking with Babies and Small Children (US$11). Published by Wilderness Press, 2440 Bancroft Way, Berkeley, CA 94704 (tel. (800) 443-7227 or (510) 843-8080).

The Kidding Around series (US$10 to US$13, postage under US$4.25). A series of illustrated books for children includes some about major U.S. cities, Spain, Paris and London that could be educational and distracting on long trips. Published by John Muir Publications, P.O. Box 613, Santa Fe, NM 87504 (tel. (800) 285-4078).

Take Your Kids to Europe by Cynthia W. Harriman (US$14). A budget travel guide geared towards families. Even includes cartoon illustrations. Published by Mason-Grant Publications, P.O. Box 6547, Portsmouth, NH 03802 (tel. (603) 436-1608, fax 427-0015).

Travel with Children by Maureen Wheeler (US$11, postage US$1.50 in the U.S.). Published by Lonely Planet Publications, Embarcadero West, 155 Philbert St., Suite 251, Oakland, CA 94607 (tel. (510) 893-8555 or (800) 275-8555, fax (510) 893-8563). Also P.O. Box 617, Hawthorn, Victoria 3122, Australia.

■■■ DISABLED TRAVELERS

Countries vary in their general accessibility to travelers with disabilities. Some national and regional tourist boards provide directories on the accessibility of various accommodations and transportation services. If these services are not available, contact institutions of interest directly. Those with disabilities should also inform airlines and hotels of their disabilities when making arrangements for travel; some time may be needed to prepare special accommodations.

Rail is probably the most convenient form of travel. Large stations in Britain are equipped with wheelchair facilities, and the French national railroad offers wheelchair compartments on all TGV (high speed) and Conrail trains. Contact your destination's station in advance for specific information, or call **Rail Europe** in the U.S. at (800) 345-1990 (fax (914) 682-2821). Most countries require a six-month quarantine for all animals, including guide dogs. To obtain an import license, owners must supply current certification of the animal's rabies, distemper and contagious hepatitis inoculations, and a veterinarian's letter attesting to its health. They should inquire as to the specific quarantine policies of each destination country. The following organizations provide information or publications that might be of assistance:

American Foundation for the Blind, 15 W. 16th St., New York, NY 10011 (tel. (212) 620-2147). Provides ID cards (US$10); write for an application, or call the Product Center at (800) 829-0500. Also call this number to order AFB catalogs in braille, print, or on cassette or disk.

Directions Unlimited, 720 North Bedford Rd., Bedford Hills, NY 10507 (tel. (800) 533-5343 or (914) 241-1700, fax 241-0243). Specializes in arranging individual and group vacations, tours, and cruises for those with disabilities.

Facts on File, 460 Park Ave. S., New York, NY 10016 (tel. (800) 829-0500 or (212) 683-2244 in Alaska and Hawaii). Publishers of *Access to the World* (US$16.95), a guide to accessible accommodations and sights. In bookstores or by mail order.

Flying Wheels Travel Service, P.O. Box 382, 143 W. Bridge St., Owatonne, MN 55060 (tel. (800) 535-6790, fax (507) 451-1685). Arranges international trips for groups or individuals in wheelchairs or with other sorts of limited mobility.

Graphic Language Press, P.O. Box 270, Cardiff by the Sea, CA 92007 (tel. (619)944-9594). Publishes *Wheelchair Through Europe* (US$12.95, postage paid), which provides comprehensive advice for wheelchair-bound travelers. Specifics on wheelchair-related resources in various cities throughout Europe.

The Guided Tour, Inc. Elkins Park House #114B, 7900 Old York Road, Elkins Park, PA 19117-2339 (tel. (215) 635-2637 or (800) 738-5841). Year-round travel programs (domestic and international) for persons with developmental and physical challenges as well as those geared to the needs of persons requiring renal dialysis. Call or write for a free brochure.

Mobility International, USA (MIUSA), P.O. Box 10767, Eugene, OR 97440 (tel. (503) 343-1284 voice and TDD, fax 343-6812). International headquarters in Britain, 228 Borough High St., London SE1 1JX (tel. (0171) 403 56 88). Contacts in 30 countries. Information on travel programs, international work camps, accommodations, access guides, and organized tours. Membership costs US$20 per year, newsletter US$10. Sells updated and expanded *A World of Options: A Guide to International Educational Exchange, Community Service, and Travel for Persons with Disabilities* (US$14, nonmembers US$16, postpaid).

Moss Rehabilitation Hospital Travel Information Service, 1200 W. Tabor Rd., Philadelphia, PA 19141 (tel. (215) 456-9603). Telephone info resource center. Nominal fee charged for packet of information on tourist sights, accommodations, and transportation. Makes referals if they cannot provide information.

Society for the Advancement of Travel for the Handicapped, 347 Fifth Ave. #610, New York, NY 10016 (tel. (212) 447-7284), fax 725-8253). Publishes quarterly travel newsletter SATH News and information booklets (free for members, US$3 each for nonmembers). Advice on trip-planning for people with disabilities. Annual membership is US$45, students and seniors US$25.

Twin Peaks Press, P.O. Box 129, Vancouver, WA 98666-0129 (tel. (206) 694-2462, fax 696-3210). Publishes *Travel for the Disabled,* (US$20) which lists tips and resources for disabled travelers. Also available: *Directory for Travel Agencies of the Disabled* (US$20), *Directory of Accessible Van Rentals* (US$10), and *Wheelchair Vagabond* (US$15). Postage US$2 for first book, US$1 for each additional.

60 ■ DISABLED TRAVELERS

Rick Steves' Europe Through the Back Door

FREE VIDEO, GUIDEBOOK AND ▲ ADVICE WITH EVERY EURAILPASS.

Rick Steves' 1995 Back Door Guide to
EUROPEAN RAILPASSES

I t's easy to see why we've become America's leading Eurailpass retailer. Buy your pass from us and we'll throw in a copy of Rick Steves' hour-long *"How to get the most out of your railpass" video,* plus one of his ten regional *"Best of..." guidebooks and phrasebooks,* plus our *sage advice* on your 1-page trip itinerary, plus a *colorful* Europe Through the Back Door patch. Even with all these extras our Eurailpasses still cost the same as everyone else's — sometimes less! Before you order your pass from anyone else, *call us for a free copy of our 64-page 1995 Back Door Guide to European Railpasses.*

RICK STEVES' FREE TRAVEL NEWSLETTER-CATALOG.

Wait, there's more... Call us and we'll send you Rick Steves' *free newsletter-catalog* packed full of information on European destinations, budget travel skills, railpasses, guidebooks, videos, travel accessories (including our svelte moneybelts and radical convertible backpacks) and free-spirited tours.

EUROPE THROUGH THE BACK DOOR

▼ ▼ ▼ ▼ ▼

120 Fourth Ave. N, Box 2009, Edmonds, WA 98020 USA
▶ Phone: (206) 771-8303   Fax: (206) 771-0833

ESSENTIALS

■■■ BISEXUAL, GAY, AND LESBIAN TRAVELERS

Attitudes toward bisexual, gay, and lesbian travelers are, naturally, particular to each country and to the cities within it. Listed below are contact organizations and publications which offer materials addressing those concerns.

Are You Two Together? A Gay and Lesbian Travel Guide to Europe (Random House, US$18). Travel guide with anecdotes and tips for gay and lesbians traveling in Europe. Overviews of regional laws relating to gays and lesbians, lists of gay/lesbian organizations and establishments. Available in bookstores.

Ferrari Publications, P.O. Box 37887, Phoenix, AZ 85069 (tel. (602) 863-2408). Publishes **Ferrari's Places of Interest** (US$16), **Ferrari's Places for Men** (US$15), **Ferrari's Places for Women** (US$13), and **Inn Places: USA and Worldwide Gay Accommodations** (US$15). Available in bookstores or by mail order (postage US$3.50 for the first item, US50¢ for each additional).

Gay's the Word, 66 Marchmont St., London WC1N 1AB, England (tel. (0171) 278 76 54). Open Mon.-Fri. 11am-7pm, Sat. 10am-6pm, Sun. and holidays 2-6pm. Gay/lesbian bookshop. Mail order service. No catalogue of listings, but will provide a list of titles germane to a given subject.

Giovanni's Room, 345 S. 12th St., Philadelphia, PA 19107 (tel. (215) 923-2960, fax 923-0813). International feminist, lesbian, and gay bookstore with mail-order service carrying many of the publications listed here. Call or write for free catalogue.

Inland Book Company, P.O. Box 120261, East Haven, CT 06512 (tel. (203) 467-4257). Publishes **Women Going Places** (US$14), an international travel and resource guide emphasizing women-owned enterprises, geared toward lesbians, but offering advice appropriate for all women. Available in bookstores.

International Gay Travel Association, Box 4974, Key West, FL 33041 (tel. (800) 448-8550).

International Lesbian and Gay Association, 81 rue Marcheau Charbon, 7000 Bruxelles 7, Belgium (tel. (02) 502 24 71).

Renaissance House, P.O. Box 533, Village Station, New York, NY 10014 (tel. (212) 674-0120, fax 420-1126). Gay bookstore which carries many of the titles listed in this section. Send self-addressed stamped envelope for a free catalogue.

■■■ MINORITY TRAVELERS

In certain regions, tourists of color or members of certain religious groups may feel unwelcomed by local residents. Furthermore, either historical or newly-developed discrimination against established minority residents may surface against travelers who are members of those minority groups. In your travels, you may find signs stating things such as "Interdit aux Africains" ("No Africans"). Let's Go asks that our researchers do not include such establishments in our guides. If, in your travels, you encounter discriminatory treatment, do not push the matter. Move on; the last thing you want is conflict in a country that isn't yours. Native residents have the upper hand because they are comfortable on their own turf.

In terms of general safety, we don't have any easy answers. We have been hard-pressed to find any resources that advise members of visible minorities on specific travel concerns since social climates differ for different minorities in different places; essentially, use your own common sense. No publications have thus far specifically addressed the matter; the best bet is to check out the travel columns of magazines such as Black Enterprise and American Visions, which often carry advice and tips for overseas as well as domestic travel. Keep abreast of current events before you set off on your trip so that you have an idea of the general cultural attitudes of your destination country. When you're there, if you find yourself in need of assistance, contact the nearest embassy or consulate of your home country. Traveling in groups and taking a taxi whenever you are uncomfortable are always good ideas; your personal safety should always be your top priority. For the traveler, the best answer to xenophobic comments and other verbal harassment is no answer at all. But above all, keep in mind that your ethnicity or religion will not necessarily be problematic; you may find your vacation trouble-free and your hosts open-minded.

■ ■ ■ KOSHER AND VEGETARIAN TRAVELERS

Before you head off, contact national tourist offices. They often publish lists of kosher and vegetarian restaurants in their respective countries.

The European Vegetarian Guide: Restaurants and Hotels is available from the Vegetarian Times (tel. (800) 435-9610, orders only).

The International Vegetarian Travel Guide (UK£3) was last published in 1991, but copies are still available from the **Vegetarian Society of the UK,** Parkdale, Dunham Rd., Altringham, Cheshire WA14 4QG (tel. (61) 928 07 93). VSUK also publishes other titles; call or send a self-addressed, stamped envelope for a listing.

The Jewish Travel Guide (US$12, postage US$1.75) lists synagogues, kosher restaurants, and Jewish institutions in over 80 countries. Available in the U.K. from **Jewish Chronicle Publications,** 25 Furnival St., London EC4A 1JT (tel. (0171) 405 92 52, fax 831 51 88), and in the U.S. from **Sepher-Hermon Press,** 1265 46th St., Brooklyn, NY 11219 (tel. (718) 972-9010).

North American Vegetarian Society, P.O. Box 72, Dolgeville, NY 13329 (tel. (518) 568-7970) publishes several titles related to travel in the U.S. and Canada. Call or write for a free catalogue of titles available by mail order.

■ ■ ■ STAYING IN TOUCH

MAIL

Mail can be sent internationally through **Poste Restante** (the international phrase for General Delivery) to any city or town; it's well worth using and much more reliable than you might think. Mark the envelope "HOLD" and address it, for example, "Tonya <u>HARDING</u>, Poste Restante, City, Country." The last name should be capitalized and underlined. The mail will go to a special desk in the central post office, unless you specify a post office by street address or postal code. In Central and Eastern Europe, you should put a "1" after the city name to ensure mail goes to the central post office. As a rule, it is best to use the largest post office in the area; when possible, it is safer, quicker, and more reliable to send mail express or registered.

It helps to use the appropriate translation of Poste Restante (*Lista de Correos* in Spanish, *Fermo Posta* in Italian and *Postlagernde Briefe* in German). When picking up your mail, bring your passport or other ID. If the clerk insists that there is nothing for you, try checking under your first name as well. In a few countries you will have to pay a minimal fee (perhaps 0.50) per item received. *Let's Go* lists post offices in the Practical Information section for each city and town's towns.

The cheapest letters you can send are aerograms, which provide a limited amount of writing space and fold over into envelopes (no enclosures allowed). It helps to mark air mail in the appropriate language if possible (*par avion* in French, *por avion* in Spanish, *mit luftpost* in German, *per via aerea* in Italian, *lotnicza* in Polish), though *par avion* is universally understood.

Sending mail c/o **American Express** offices is quite reliable; they will hold your mail for free if you have AmEx Traveler's Cheques or a card. Even if you use another brand of traveler's checks, you can use this service by buying some AmEx Cheques. Mail will automatically be held 30 days; to have it held longer, write "Hold for x days" on the envelope. Again the sender should capitalize and underline your last name, marking the envelope "Client Letter Service." Check the Practical Information section of the countries you plan to visit; we list AmEx office locations for most large cities. A complete list is available for free from AmEx (tel. (800) 528-4800) in the booklet *Traveler's Companion*.

Airmail from Europe to the U.S. averages a week to 10 days. Allow at least 2 weeks for Australia, New Zealand, Eastern Europe, North Africa, and South Africa. Mail to and from parts of Eastern Europe can require up to 4 or 6 weeks.

Surface mail is by far the cheapest and slowest way to send mail. It takes one to three months to cross the Atlantic, appropriate for sending large quantities of items you won't need to see for a while. It is vital, therefore to distinguish your airmail from surface mail by explicitly labeling air mail in the appropriate language. When ordering books and materials from another country, include one or two **International Reply Coupons (IRC)**, available at the post office, with your request. IRCs provide the recipient of your order with postage to cover delivery.

TELEPHONES

In Essentials and country listings, the **country code** is not included with phone numbers; please consult the beginning of each country's chapter, where the country code is listed with exchange rates. In the Practical Information section for large cities, **city codes** are listed under Telephones; and, in smaller cities and regions, the codes are listed in parentheses with the phone numbers.

Some countries in Eastern Europe do not have an international dialing code; you must go through the operator. In some other countries you must wait for a tone after the international dialing code. Denmark, Luxembourg, and most of Europe's microstates have neither city codes nor domestic long-distance prefixes; just skip that step. For more information, see each country's Practical Information section.

You can usually make direct international calls from a pay phone, but you may need to feed money in as you speak. In some countries, pay phones are card-operated; some even accept major credit cards. The best places to call from are phone booths and post offices since phones in cafés, hotels, and restaurants tend to carry surcharges of 30% or more.

English-speaking operators are often available for both local and international assistance. Operators in most European countries will place **collect calls** for you. It's cheaper to find a pay phone and deposit just enough money to be able to say "Call me" and give your number (though some pay phones in Europe can't receive calls).

A **calling card** is another alternative; your local long-distance phone company will have a number for you to dial while in Europe (either toll-free or charged as a local call) to connect instantly to an operator in your home country. The calls (plus a small surcharge) are then billed either collect or to a calling card. For more information, call **AT&T** about its **USADirect** and **World Connect** services (tel. (800) 331-1140, from abroad (412) 553-7458), **Sprint Express** (tel. (800) 877-4646), or **MCI's WorldPhone** program (tel. (800) 996-7535). Similar services are available for Canada, the U.K., Australia, New Zealand, and South Africa. Contact your local phone company for details.

Phone rates tend to be highest in the morning, low in the evening, and lowest on Sunday and at night. (AT&T's and MCI's phone rates remain constant.) Also, remember **time differences** when you call. Britain, Ireland, Portugal, and Iceland are on Greenwich Mean Time (GMT)—5 hours ahead of Eastern Standard Time. Finland, Estonia, Latvia, Lithuania, western Russia, Romania, Bulgaria, Greece, Turkey, Israel, and Egypt are 2 hours ahead of GMT. Moscow is 3 hours ahead. Everywhere else in this book is 1 hour ahead of GMT. Some countries (like Iceland) ignore daylight savings time, and fall and spring switchover times vary between those countries that do use it.

OTHER COMMUNICATION

In Eastern Europe, domestic and international telegrams can be faster and cheaper than using the phone. Fill out a form at any post or telephone office; cables to North

America arrive in two days. In Western Europe, telegrams are slower, more expensive, and much less fun. Major cities across Europe also have bureaus where you can pay to send and receive **faxes.**

If you're spending a year abroad and want to keep in touch with friends or colleagues in a college or research institution, **electronic mail** ("e-mail") is an attractive option. It takes a minimum of computer knowledge a little prearranged planning, and it beams messages anywhere for free.

Between May 2 and Octoberfest, EurAide (P.O. Box 2375, Naperville, IL 60567; tel. (708) 420-2343) offers **Overseas Access**, a service most useful to travelers without a set itinerary. The cost is US$15 per week or US$40 per month for an electronic message box, plus a US$15 registration fee. To reach you, people call the "home base" in Munich and leave a message; you receive it by calling Munich whenever you wish, which is cheaper than calling overseas. For an additional US$20 per month, EurAide will forward mail sent to Munich to any addresses you specify.

Published media dailies including the London *Times*, *Financial Times*, *Observer*, *International Herald-Tribune*, *Wall Street Journal* (European Edition), and, less frequently, *USA Today* are available at train stations and kiosks in major European cities. Furthermore, the *Economist* and international versions of *Time* and *Newsweek* are easy to come by.

■■■ WEIGHTS AND MEASURES

1 centimeter (cm) = 0.39 inches	1 inch = 2.54cm
1 meter (m) = 3.28 feet	1 foot = 0.31m
1 kilometer (km) = 0.62 miles	1 mile = 1.61km
1 gram (g) = 0.04 ounces	1 ounce = 28g
1 kilogram (kg) = 2.2 pounds	1 pound = 0.45kg
1 liter (l) = 0.26 gallons	1 gallon = 3.76l
1 Imperial Gallon (U.K.) = 1.2 gallons	1 gallon = .83 Imperial Gallons
°F = (°C x 1.8) + 32	°C = (°F-32) x .56

■■■ CUSTOMS

Upon entering a country as well as returning home, you must declare all articles you acquired abroad and must pay a duty on the value of those articles that exceed the allowance established by your country's customs service. Holding onto receipts for purchases made abroad will help establish values when you return. It is wise to make a list, including serial numbers, of any valuables that you carry with you from home; if you register this list with customs before your departure and have an official stamp it, you will avoid import duty charges and ensure an easy passage upon your return. Be especially careful to document items manufactured abroad.

Goods and gifts purchased at duty-free shops abroad are not exempt from duty or sales tax at your point of return; you must declare these items, as well. "Duty-free" merely means that you need not pay a tax in the country of purchase.

United States citizens returning home may bring US$400 worth of accompanying goods duty-free and must pay a 10% tax on the next US$1000. You must declare all purchases, so have sales slips ready. Goods are considered duty-free if they are for personal or household use (this includes gifts) and cannot include more than 100 cigars, 200 cigarettes (Cuban tobacco products may only be included if purchased in Cuba), and 1l of wine or liquor. You must be over 21 to bring liquor into the U.S. To be eligible for the duty-free allowance, you must have remained abroad for at least 48 hours and cannot have used this exemption or any part of it within the preceding 30 days.

You can mail unsolicited gifts duty-free if they are worth less than US$100, though you may not mail alcohol, tobacco, or perfume. Officials occasionally spot check parcels, so mark the price and nature of the gift and the words "Unsolicited Gift" on the package. If your package exceeds the duty-free limit, the U.S. Postal Service will collect customs duties and handling charges in the form of "postage due" stamps. Duty on gifts or other packages mailed from abroad cannot be prepaid. If you mail home personal goods of U.S. origin, you can avoid duty charges by marking the package "American goods returned." For more information, consult the brochure *Know Before You Go,* available from the U.S. Customs Service, P.O. Box 7407, Washington, DC 20044 (tel. (202) 927-6724). Foreign nationals living in the U.S. are subject to different regulations; refer to the leaflet *Customs Hints for Visitors (Non-residents).*

Canadian citizens who remain abroad for at least one week may bring back up to CDN$300 worth of goods duty-free once every calendar year; goods that exceed the allowance will be taxed at 12%. You are permitted to ship goods home under this exemption as long as you declare them when you arrive. Citizens over the legal age (which varies by province) may import in-person (not through the mail) up to 200 cigarettes, 50 cigars, 400g loose tobacco, 1.14l wine or alcohol, and 355ml beer; the value of these products is included in the CDN$300 allowance. For more information, contact Canadian Customs, 2265 St. Laurent Blvd., Ottawa, Ont. K1G 4K3 (tel. (613) 993-0534). Or, from within Canada, call (800) 461-9999.

British citizens or visitors arriving in the U.K. from outside the European Union must declare any goods in excess of the following allowances: 1) 200 cigarettes, 100 cigarillos, 50 cigars or 250g tobacco; 2) 2l still table wine; 3) 1l liquor, 2l fortified or sparkling wine, or an additional 2l still wine; 4) 60ml perfume; 5) 250ml toilet water; 6) UK£136 worth of all other goods including gifts and souvenirs. You must be over 17 to import liquor or tobacco. These allowances also apply to duty-free purchases within the EU, except for the last category, other goods, which then has an allowance of UK£71. Goods obtained duty- and tax-paid for personal use (regulated according to set guide levels) within the EU do not require any further customs duty. For more information about U.K. customs, contact Her Majesty's Customs and Excise, Custom House, Heathrow Airport North, Hounslow, Middlesex TW6 2LA (tel. (0181) 910 37 44, fax 910 37 65). HM Customs & Excise Notice 1 explains the allowances for people travelling to the U.K. both from within and without the European Union.

Irish citizens must declare everything in excess of the following allowances for goods obtained outside the EU or duty and tax free in the EU: 1) 200 cigarettes, 100 cigarillos, 50 cigars, or 250g tobacco; 2) 1l liquor or 2l wine; 3) 2l still wine; 4) 50g perfume; 5) 250ml toilet water; 6) IR£34 of other goods per adult traveler (IR£17 per traveler under age 15). A maximum of 25l beer may be imported as a part of, but not in addition to, the adult allowance. Goods obtained duty and tax paid in another EU country, within certain limits set out for personal use, will not be subject to additional customs duty. Travelers under 17 are not entitled to any allowance for tobacco or alcoholic products. For more information, contact The Revenue Commissioners, Dublin Castle (tel. (01) 679 27 77; fax 671 20 21) or The Collector of Customs and Excise, The Custom House, Dublin 1.

Australian citizens may import AUS$400 (under 18 AUS$200) of goods duty-free, in addition to the allowance of 250 cigarettes, 250g tobacco, and 1l alcohol. You must be over 18 to import either. There is no limit to the amount of Australian and/or foreign cash that may be brought into or taken out of the country. However, amounts of AUS$5000 or more, or the equivalent in foreign currency, must be reported. For information, contact the Australian Customs Service, 5 Constitution Ave., Canberra, ACT 2601 (tel. (06) 275 62 55, fax 275 69 89).

New Zealand citizens may bring home up to NZ$700 worth of goods duty-free if they are intended for personal use or are unsolicited gifts. The concession is 200 cigarettes (1 carton) or 250g tobacco or 50 cigars or a combination of all three not to exceed 250g. You may also bring in 4.5l of beer or wine and 1.125l of liquor. Only travelers over 17 may bring tobacco or alcoholic beverages into the country. For more information, consult the *New Zealand Customs Guide for Travelers,* available from customs offices, or contact New Zealand Customs, 50 Anzac Avenue, Box 29, Auckland (tel. (09) 377 35 20, fax 309 29 78).

South African citizens may import duty-free: 400 cigarettes, 50 cigars, 250g tobacco, 2l wine, 1l of spirits, 250ml toilet water, and 50ml perfume, and other items up to a value of SAR500. Golf clubs and firearms do not fall within the duty-free allowances for travelers who have been absent from the Republic for less than six months, and goods acquired abroad and sent to the Republic as unaccompanied baggage do not qualify for any allowances. You may not export or import South African bank notes in excess of SAR500. Persons who require specific information or advice concerning customs and excise duties can address their inquiries to: The Commissioner for Customs and Excise, Private Bag X47, Pretoria, 0001. This agency distributes the pamphlet *South African Customs Information,* for visitors and residents who travel abroad. South Africans residing in the U.S. should contact: South African Mission, 3201 New Mexico Ave. #380, NW, Washington, DC 20016 (tel. (202) 364-8320/1, fax 364-6008).

■■■ PARTING WORDS

The best way to sample a new culture is to dissolve discreetly in it; there's no faster way to learn about new people than to let them think you're one of them. As a foreigner, you'll probably be conspicuous—but you will be welcomed if you make a sincere effort to fit in. An afternoon of quiet relaxation at a park in Prague or a café in Colmar will often teach you more about a country and its people than a museum. Make the effort to actually meet people. A photo of Wolf and Gisela Kügelbrecher who put you up for the night in Munich will contain many more memories than a postcard of the Eiffel Tower. Europeans are earnestly interested in other lands and cultures but have a very strong sense of their own cultural history; if you insult or belittle it, you'll only seem ignorant. Don't expect things to work the way they do in your own country; half the fun is untangling a new system. Culture shock can really happen, but go for the *pâté* and goulash anyway and leave McDonald's for when you get home. Running into compatriots on the road can be fun, but if you associate with them exclusively, you might as well have stayed at home—an even cheaper option to budget travel. Unfortunately, particularly Americans have gained notoriety abroad; this may explain the little red maple leaves Canadians are careful to sew on to their backpacks. By now, even U.S. citizens have taken to disguising themselves as Canucks. That shouldn't be necessary—simply avoid behaving like an Ugly American, and you will be received warmly.

A word of warning. Many travelers find themselves succumbing to budget obsession on the road: to stay in the cheapest lodgings, no matter how miserable, to eat grim, tasteless food, and to make each day's goal to spend less than yesterday. Perhaps the worst sin of the entire *Let's Go* series is that it perpetuates this mindset among our readers. When you hit the doldrums, use some of your money to cushion the shock. A hearty meal or a quiet evening in a soothing pension might add 10 dollars to your bill, but it will make you feel rich and pampered rather than destitute and ignored. You're on a vacation, not a crusade.

Falling into the mentality that "they all speak English" can offend; every time you address Europeans in English, you're asking a favor that you probably couldn't return were they to visit your home town. Humbly ask "Do you speak English?" before launching into a question. Better yet, try to learn a little about the foreign languages you'll be encountering. Except for Finnish, Estonian, and Hungarian (related to each other), Turkish (related to Central Asian tongues), and Basque (related to nothing in particular), all the languages in Europe are part of the Indo-European language family. Indo-European languages are remarkably similar: for instance, the words for "three" in French, Lithuanian, Norwegian, and Russian are *trois, trys, tre,* and *tri,* respectively. You can learn any pronunciation system, plus the words for yes, no, where is, how much, and the numbers up to 10, in about 15 minutes. Really. Or at least you can make some new friends in the attempt.

Andorra

Embracing fewer than 250 sq. km between France and Spain in the hermetic confines of the Pyrenees, pint-sized Andorra is Europe's greatest anomaly: French President François Mitterand and Bishop of Urgell Dr. Joan Martí Alanis share the title "Co-Princes" of Andorra, while a popularly elected, 28-member "General Council of the Valleys" conducts day-to-day government. Andorra offers soaring peaks and near-pristine wilderness, but it is the humility of its sales taxes rather than the grandeur of its sights that draws most visitors. European tourists overrun the capital in search of bargains in the duty-free perfume and electronics shops lining the main avenue of **Andorra la Vella,** the capital city and the Hong Kong of the Pyrenees. Andorran establishments are legally bound to accept French and Spanish currencies, but there is a conspicuous preference for pesetas (exchange rate is about 130ptas to the U.S. dollar, 24 pesetas to the franc). Spanish is widely spoken and French will get you by, but Catalan is the country's official language. **Phones** require an STA *teletarja* (telecard), which costs a minimum of 500ptas, available at any post office or kiosk. From Spain, Andorra's **area code** is 9738. Collect calls are not available, and AT&T does not access Andorra.

All highway traffic from France must enter Andorra at the town of **Pas de la Casa;** on the Spanish side, **Sant Julià de Lòria** is the gateway. To approach Andorra by train from **France,** stop at l'Hospitalet or Ax-les-Thermes (both stops on the Toulouse-Ax-les-Thermes-Barcelona line). **Société Franco-Andorrane de Transports (SFAT)** (tel. 213 72), runs a bus from Ax-les-Thermes through l'Hospitalet to Andorra la Vella (2hr., 40F). From **Spain,** reach Andorra by bus from Barcelona (3-4 per day, 4-4½hr., 2245-2555ptas); call **Alsina Graells** in Andorra la Vella (tel. 273 79) or Barcelona (tel. 265 68 66).

To best appreciate Andorra, visit the picturesque Lilliputian villages cradled within a Brobdignagian mountain range. Most towns are connected by an efficient bus system. Additionally, an extensive network of hiking trails and cabins make the country's beauty accessible to those on foot. Pick up the tourist office's booklet *Andorra: the Pyrénéan Country* for a complete list of cabin and *refugio* locations within the principality. **Canillo** and **La Massana** provide a base for skiing from December to April on a wide range of downhill and cross-country terrain.

Andorra la Vella and La Massana Built in the 16th century and graced with mini-Barbican towers, the **Casa de la Vall** (House of the Valleys) is the tiniest little parliament you ever saw (obligatory guided tour every hr. Mon.-Fri. 10am-1pm and 3-6pm, Sat. 10am-1pm; free). The main **tourist office** (tel. 202 14), on Av. Doctor Villanova at the foot of the **Barri Antic** (Old Quarter), dispenses information on lodgings and hiking in English (open Mon.-Sat. 9am-1pm and 3-7pm; Oct.-June Mon.-Sat. 10am-1pm and 3-7pm, Sun. 10am-1pm). **Pensió La Rosa,** Antic Carrer Major, 18 (tel. 218 10), just south of av. Príncep Benlloch, provides immaculate rooms, all with cheery wallpaper (singles 1700ptas, doubles 3000ptas, breakfast 350ptas).

An excellent base for exploring Andorra's spectacular mountains, the parish of **La Massana** lies but a 10min. bus ride from Andorra la Vella (every ½hr. until 8:30pm, 95ptas). Find the **tourist office** (tel. 35 693) by the bridge just ahead of the bus stop (open Mon.-Sat. 9am-1pm and 3-7pm, Sun. 9am-1pm and 3-6pm). A 20-30min. climb takes you to the **Alberg Borda Jovell,** av. del Jovell (tel. 365 20) in **Sispony,** a mountain-clinging hamlet of gray stone houses. To get there from La Massana's bus-stop, go back towards Andorra la Vella 75m and turn right at the main intersection. Follow the signs south for 1.3km until the *alberg*, a 700-year-old stone house, appears on the left. The friendly owner holds court in the restaurant downstairs and is a great source of information on the area. (1050ptas, *pensío completa* 2450ptas. Sheets 550ptas. Curfew midnight.)

Austria (Österreich)

US$1 = 10.42AS (schilling, or ATS)
CDN$1= 7.76AS
UK£1 = 16.55AS
IR£ = 16.40AS
AUS$1 = 7.98AS
NZ$1 = 6.32AS
SAR1 = 2.92AS
Country Code: 43

10AS = US$0.96
10AS = CDN$1.29
10AS = UK£0.60
10AS = IR£0.61
10AS = AUS$1.25
10AS = NZ$1.58
10AS = SAR3.42
International Dialing Prefix: 00
from Vienna: 900

The Federal Republic of Austria binds Eastern and Western Europe. For centuries, the Austrian lands have sheltered Magyars, Germans, Italians, and myriad other ethnic groups under a common political order. The Danube's majestic flow reflects the commercial conduit between the industrial democracies of Western Europe and the fledgling market economies of the east. This Alpine nation, swathed in edelweiss, nurtured the ineffable genius of Mozart, Schönberg, Beethoven, Brahms, Strauss, Freud, Klimt, and Kokoschka, as well as the xenophobic mania of Adolf Hitler.

The once-sprawling Austro-Hungarian empire is now a tiny fragment of its imperial self, but the Court's cultural footprints remain. Despite the lack of a prior democratic tradition, postwar Austria has seen a successful, stable blend of social welfare and democratic pragmatism. The country has created a marriage of socialism-with-a-brain and conservatism-with-a-heart that will serve it well in the European Union.

For extensive and entertaining information on the country, pick up a copy of the truly inimitable *Let's Go: Austria and Switzerland*.

GETTING THERE AND GETTING AROUND

Rail travel in Austria is extraordinarily reliable and efficient, but can be expensive. Eurail is valid. The **Rabbit Card** gives four days of unlimited travel over a 10-day period (2nd-class 1130AS; juniors (under 27) 700AS). Seniors (men over 65, women over 60) are entitled to **half-price tickets** (*Umweltticket für Senioren*) on trains, long-distance buses, Danube steamers, and many cable cars; you must show an official **Reduction Card** *(Ermässigungsausweis)*, valid for one year (240AS). All cards are available at major post offices and train stations.

The Austrian **bus** system consists of orange **Bundesbussen** and yellow **Post buses.** Both are efficient and cover mountain areas inaccessible by train. They usually cost a bit more than trains, and railpasses are not valid. Tickets may be purchased onboard, or at the multitude of *tabak* stands dotting every town.

Austria is a **hitchhiker's** nightmare—Austrians rarely pick them up, and many mountain roads are all but deserted. Generally, hitchhikers stand on highway *Knoten* (on-ramps) and wait. The thumb signal is recognized, but signs with a destination and the word *bitte* (please) are just as common. More formal arrangements for longer, inter-city routes can be arranged through a **Mitfahrzentrale** office, which charges roughly half the going rail fare to match travelers with somebody traveling by car in the same direction.

About 160 Austrian rail stations rent **bikes.** They can be returned to any participating station and cost 90AS per day—half-price if you have a train ticket *to* the station from which you are renting and have arrived on the day of rental. Look for signs with a bicycle and the word *Verleih.* Pick up the list *(Fahrrad am Bahnhof)* of participating stations at any station. Tourist offices provide regional bike route maps. 30AS will get your bike aboard a train; look for the *Gepäckbeforderung* symbol on departure schedules to see if bikes are permitted. All Austrian train stations offer luggage storage (up to several months) for 20AS per piece; many offer lockers as well (10-20AS, depending on size).

AUSTRIA ESSENTIALS

The Austrian government operates a network of chipper and knowledgeable **tourist offices** *(Verkehrsamt* or *Verkehrsverein);* even the smallest towns have them. Most tourist offices will reserve private rooms, usually for free.

Banks throughout Austria are usually open weekdays 8am to 12:30pm and 2 to 5:30pm. In Vienna, most banks are open Monday to Wednesday and Friday 8am to 3pm, Thursday 8am to 5:30pm. Many banks offer cash advances to Visa holders (the **Zentralsparkasse und Kommerzialbank** does this at most branches). A town's main post office *(Hauptpostamt)* is usually the best place to exchange money. Remember, however, that all institutions which exchange money (AmEx, post offices, banks, etc.) are legally required to charge at least a 14AS commission for cashing foreign traveler's checks. Also, beware that commissions vary wildly: expect to pay at least 100AS per check in large cities. Commissions in small towns, however, are significantly less.

Stores in Austria close Saturday afternoons and Sundays; many museums take Mondays off. Stores in many small towns take most of the afternoon off for lunch (usually noon-3pm). Everything closes on New Year's Day (Jan. 1), Epiphany (Jan. 6), Easter Monday (April 17, 1995), Whit Monday (May 29, 1995), Corpus Christi (June), Assumption (Aug. 15), Austrian National Day (Oct. 26), All Saints' (Nov. 1), Immaculate Conception (Dec. 8), and Christmas and St. Stephen's Day (Dec. 25-26). The first Saturday of each month is a long shopping day: stores close at 5pm, not noon.

Communication should not be a tremendous problem; English is the most common second language. Any effort, however incompetent, to use the mother tongue will win loads of fans; *Grüss Gott* (God bless) is the typical Austrian greeting.

You can make international **phone** calls at telephone centers (usually only in the larger cities), in most post offices, and from pay phones. **Telephone cards** *(Wertkarten),* available in post offices, train stations, and some stores, come in 50AS, 100AS, and 200AS denominations. For AT&T's **USADirect,** dial 022 90 30 11; for MCI's **WorldPhone,** dial 022 90 30 12; for **SprintExpress,** dial 022 90 30 14; for **Canada Direct,** dial 022 90 30 13; for **BT Direct,** dial 022 90 30 44; and for **New Zealand Direct,** dial 022 90 30 64. Note that the use of any of these services is considered a local call, so you have to keep dropping shillings into the phone or have an Austrian phone card. For assistance calling abroad, dial 08. For directory assistance, call 16 11. For the **police** anywhere in Austria, dial 133; for an **ambulance,** dial 144; in case of **fire,** dial 122; and, for **train info,** dial 17 17. With older pay phones, you must push the red button when your party answers.

Accommodations and Camping Rooms in Austria are usually spotless; even the most odious of Austria's 120-odd **youth hostels** *(Jugendherbergen)* are, by international standards, quite tolerable. Most charge about 130AS per night (160AS in larger cities), continental breakfast included. Nonmembers are normally charged an extra 40AS and sometimes turned away completely.

Hotels are expensive; look for *Zimmer Frei* or *Privat Zimmer* signs; they advertise typically inexpensive rooms in private houses (150-300AS per person). Otherwise, smaller pensions and *Gasthäuser* are often within the budget traveler's range. Local tourist offices will help set you up and also give advice on camping. **Campgrounds** are the cheapest option, charging about 30-80AS per person, tent, or car. Lists are available at tourist offices.

Skiing and Hiking Western Austria is one of the world's best **skiing and hiking** regions. The areas around Innsbruck and Kitzbühel in the Tyrol are saturated with lifts and runs. High season runs from mid-December to mid-January, from February to March, and from July to August. Local tourist offices provide information on regional skiing and can point you to budget travel agencies that offer ski packages; the tourist offices will generally pre-arrange packages for you if you write in advance. Lift tickets generally run 250-500AS per day.

Unless you're on top of a mountain, Austria doesn't usually get brutally cold, even in the dead of winter. Nevertheless, warm sweaters are the rule from September to May, with a parka, hat, and gloves added in the winter months. Summertime brings frequent rains and high humidity (especially east of Salzburg)—almost every other day in Salzburg—so suitable gear is a must.

The various Alpine associations in Austria currently maintain more than 1100 **huts** *(Schutzhütten)* which provide accommodations, cooking facilities, and, occasionally, hot meals. Prices for an overnight stay are 50-150AS and no reservations are necessary; if they're crowded, you may end up sleeping on a cot, but you won't be turned away. Topographic maps *(Alpenvereinskarten),* available in most bookstores, show hut locations. If you plan carefully, you can undertake week-long hikes that bring you to a hut every night, thus freeing yourself from the burden of carrying a tent and cooking gear. Several guides such as *Walking Austria's Alps Hut to Hut* by Jonathan Hurdle (US$11) plot out such hikes. Those planning extensive walking tours of the Austrian Alps may want to purchase membership in the largest of the Alpine associations, the **Österreichischer Alpenverein** (430AS, under 26 300AS, under 18 120AS). This will entitle you to a 50% discount at their refuges, all of which have beds, as well as discounts on some cable car rides and organized hikes. Their main office is at Wilhelm-Greil-Str. 15, Innsbruck 6010 (tel. (0512) 595 47).

Many cities, like Innsbruck, offer free guided hikes if you stay in the town for three days. Even if you're going for only a day hike, check terrain and weather conditions; weather in the Alps changes instantaneously. *Always* carry waterproof clothing and some high-energy food, wear durable footwear, and tell someone where you're going. If you get into serious trouble, use the *Alpinenotsignal* (Alpine Distress Signal)—six audible (such as blows on a whistle) or visual signals spaced evenly over one minute and followed by a break of one minute before repetition. Paths marked "Für Geübte" are for experienced climbers only. Finally, remember that those gorgeous Alpine meadows are extremely fragile habitats. Leave trails and campsites exactly as you found them.

Food and Drink One of life's great enigmas is how a country with such unremarkable cuisine can produce such heavenly desserts. In mid-afternoon, Austrians flock to *Café-Konditoreien* to nurse the national sweet tooth with *Kaffee und Kuchen* (coffee and cake). Try *Sacher Torte*, a rich chocolate pastry layered with marmalade, or *Linzertorte*, a nutty pastry with raspberry filling, or a multitude of other delights such as *Apfel Strudel.* Staple foods include *Schweinfleisch* (pork), *Kalbsfleisch* (veal), *Wurst* (sausage), *Eier* (eggs), *Käse* (cheese), *Brot* (bread), and *Kartoffeln* (potatoes). Austria's best-known dish is *Schnitzel*, a meat cutlet (usually veal or pork) fried in butter with bread crumbs. The best discount supermarkets in Austria are **Billa, Spar, Hofer,** and **Konsum.** Most restaurants expect you to seat yourself; a small tip (usually rounding up the bill) is customary. The server won't bring your check without first being asked. Say *zahlen, bitte* (TSAH-len BIT-uh) to settle up.

Imbibing in Austria is trouble-free—beer is sold more commonly than soda, and anyone old enough to see over the counter can buy it (although those under 18 will have trouble purchasing liquor and getting into nightclubs). Eastern Austria is famous for its white wine. Grüner Veltliner's *Klosterneuburger* is both reasonably priced and dry. Austrian beers are outstanding; try *Stiegl Bier*, a Salzburg brew, *Zipfer Bier* from upper Austria, and *Gösser Bier* from Graz. Austria imports lots of Budweiser beer, a.k.a. *Budwar*—the Czech original, not the watery American imitation. For a more potent potable, try the whopping 180 proof *Ströh Rum.*

■■■ VIENNA (WIEN)

An imposing and dominating metropolis ever since it ruled over a vast and heterogeneous empire, Vienna dwarfs the rest of Austria—culturally, historically, and demographically—to a degree unmatched even by Paris or London. Vienna, the *prima donna* of Austria, governs a nation but inhabits a world all its own. The empire's standing trailed the rising stars of Viennese society; as history was created and rewritten within the Ringstraße, the Viennese acquired a sense of self-importance at once grossly inflated and wholly justified.

Before the First World War, Vienna balanced a troubled allegiance between the imperial tradition of Kaiser Franz Josef and the optimistic liberalism of a burgeoning bourgeoisie. The 20th century saw the shedding of the empire and a brief liberal tradition, as intellectuals struggled to define a national identity within the new bureaucratic ethic of modernization. In 1938, Austria joined ranks with Germany under the command of Adolf Hitler. Today, the Viennese struggle with the same *Vergangenheitsbewältigung* (confronting the past) that haunts many Germans.

Despite its checkered political history, Vienna can look with unabashed pride on the art and culture pulsing through every cobblestone. Almost all composers in the classic Germanic tradition lived here at some point and subsequently lent their names to every third street in the *Altstadt*. The birthplace of the Viennese waltz is still abuzz with balls from December to March. Monuments to playwrights, musicians, and poets are scattered throughout the city on desultory corners.

ORIENTATION AND PRACTICAL INFORMATION

Vienna is in eastern Austria, 40km from the Hungarian, Czech, and Slovak borders. The city is divided into 23 **districts** (*Bezirke*); the oldest area, *die Innere Stadt*, is the first. The **Ringstraße** separates the 1st district from the 2nd through 9th districts. The districts spiral around the center in a clockwise formation; the 10th through 23rd districts begin once one crosses the **Gürtel** (literally "belt," a larger ring and 2-way thoroughfare). Street signs indicate the district number in either Roman or Arabic numerals (e.g. "XIII, Auhofstr. 26" is in the 13th district) and postal codes depend on the district number (1010 represents the 1st district, 1020 the 2nd, etc.). *Let's Go* lists the district number where possible in this format. The epicenter of Viennese life, the intersection of the **Opernring, Kärntner Ring,** and **Kärntner Straße,** is home to the Opera House, tourist office, and the **Karlsplatz** U-Bahn stop. Vienna is a metropolis with crime like any other; use common sense, especially if you venture out after dark. Be extra careful in the beautiful Karlsplatz, home to many pushers and junkies—avoid the area after dark. Beware of pickpockets in the parks and on **Kärntner Straße,** where the hordes of tourists make tempting targets; this avenue leads directly to **Stephansplatz** and the **Stephansdom,** the center of the city and its *Fußgängerzone*.

Tourist Offices: I, Kärntner Str. 38, behind the Opera House. A rather small bureau dispensing an assortment of brochures. The free city map is comprehensive, but lacks a much needed index. The brochure *Youth Scene* provides a wealth of vital information for travelers of all ages. The restaurant and club sections are particularly useful. Books rooms (350-400AS) for a 35AS fee and the first night's deposit. Open 9am-7pm. Other offices at Westbahnhof (open 6:15am-11pm), Sudbahnhof (open 6:30am-10pm, Nov.-April until 9pm), the airport (open 8:30am-11pm; Oct.-May until 10pm), and at the Richtung Zentrum exit off the A1 Westautobahn. **Jugend-Info Wien (Youth Information Service),** Bellariapassage (tel. 526 46 37), in the underground passage at the Bellaria intersection. Entrance at the Dr.-Karl-Renner-Ring/Bellaria tram stop (lines 1, 2, 46, 49, D, and J). Additional entrance from the Volkstheater U-Bahn station. Info on cultural events. Hip and knowledgeable. Pick up the hostels and pensions list, as well as cheap tickets to rock and pop music events. Open Mon.-Fri. noon-7pm, Sat. 10am-7pm. **Tourist Information Number:** 211 14 54 or 211 14 27. Patience is rewarded.

Budget Travel: ÖKISTA, IX, Türkenstr. 6 (tel. 40 14 80). Books sharply-discounted flight and train tickets. Young staff understands budget travel and English. Open Mon.-Fri. 9:30am-5:30pm. Branch office, IV, Karlsgasse 3 (tel. 505 01 28), same hours.

Consulates and Embassies: U.S. Embassy, IX, Boltzmangasse 16, off Währingerstr. **U.S. Consulate,** I, Gartenbaupromenade 2, off Parkring (tel. 313 39). Open Mon.-Fri. 8:30am-noon and 1-5pm. **Canada,** Laurenzerburg 2 (tel. 533 36 91). Open Mon.-Fri. 8:30am-12:30pm and 1:30-3:30pm. **U.K.,** III, Jauresgasse 10, near Schloß Belvedere (tel. 714 61 17). Open Mon.-Fri. 9:15am-noon, for British citizens 9:15am-noon and 2-4pm. **Ireland,** III, Hilton Center, 16th floor, Landstraßer Hauptstr. 2 (tel. 715 42 46 0). **Australia,** IV, Mattiellistr. 2-4 behind the Karlskirche (tel. 51 28 58 01 64). Open Mon.-Fri. 8:45am-1pm and 2-5pm. **New Zealand,** I, Lugeck 1 (tel. 52 66 36). Open Mon.-Fri. 8:30am-5pm. **South Africa,** XIX, Sandgasse 33 (tel. 326 49 30). **Czech Republic,** XIV, Penzingerstr. 11-13, in Hütteldorf (tel. 894 37 41 or 894 62 36). Open Mon.-Fri. 9-11am. **Hungary,** I, Bankgasse 4-6 (tel. 533 26 31). Open Mon.-Fri. 8:30am-12:30pm.

Currency Exchange: Banks open Mon.-Wed. and Fri. 8am-3pm, Thurs. 8am-5:30pm. Bank and airport exchanges use same official rates (min. commission 65AS for traveler's checks, 10AS for cash). Longer hours (Mon.-Fri.) and lighter commission at train stations: Opernpassage 9am-7pm, Westbahnhof 4am-10pm, Südbahnhof 6:30am-10pm, the City Air Terminal 8am-12:30pm and 2-6pm, and Schwechat airport 6am-11pm. Cash advance with Visa at numerous banks. Most ATMs in the inner city accept Cirrus and MC.

American Express: I, Kärntnerstr. 21-23 (tel. 515 40), down from Stephansplatz. Holds mail. 40AS min. for traveler's checks, 15AS min. for cash. Open Mon.-Fri. 9am-5:30pm, Sat. 9am-noon.

Post Office: I, Fleischmarkt 19. Also has currency exchange (60AS per traveler's check, no charge for cash). Open 24hrs., as are branches at Westbahnhof, Süd-bahnhof, and Franz-Josefs Bahnhof. All change currency. **Postal Codes:** A-1010.

Telephones: I, Börseplatz 1, near the Schottenring. Open 6am-midnight. Also at 4 main post offices. Buy telephone cards at post offices and train stations (48AS and 95AS). Push red button on older pay phones to connect. 1AS and up for local calls, 9AS for long-distance. **City Code:** in Austria, 0222; from abroad, 1.

Flights: Wien Schwechat airport (tel. 711 10 22 33), 18km from the city center, linked by bus (60AS) to Westbahnhof, Südbahnhof, and the City Air Terminal (next to the Hilton in district III; take U-3 or U-4 to Landstr. or train to Wien-Mitte). S-Bahn railway also runs hourly from Wien Mitte or Wien Nord stations (30AS, Eurail and Vienna public transport passes valid).

Trains: tel. 17 17, 24hrs. English spoken. **Wien-Mitte,** in the center, handles commuter trains. **Franz-Josefs-Bahnhof** handles local trains and trains to Berlin via

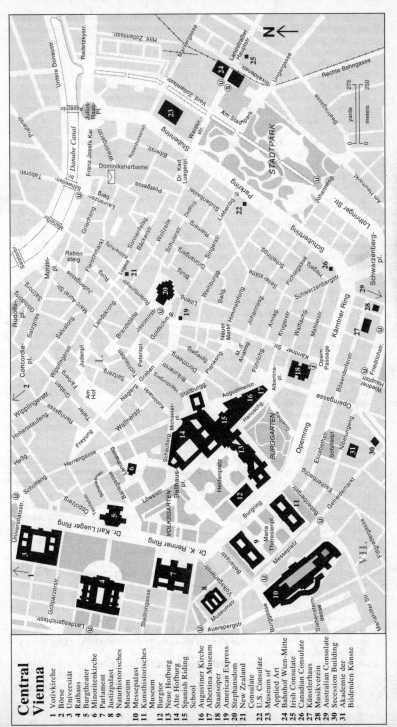

Central Vienna

1 Votivkirche
2 Börse
3 Universität
4 Rathaus
5 Burgtheater
6 Minoritenkirche
7 Parlament
8 Justizpalast
9 Naturhistorisches Museum
10 Messepalast
11 Kunsthistorisches Museum
12 Burgtor
13 Neue Hofburg
14 Alte Hofburg
15 Spanish Riding School
16 Augustiner Kirche
17 Albertina Museum
18 Staatsoper
19 American Express
20 Stephansdom
21 New Zealand Consulate
22 U.S. Consulate
23 Museum of Applied Art
24 Bahnhof Wien-Mitte
25 Irish Consulate
26 Canadian Consulate
27 Künstlerhaus
28 Musikverein
29 Australian Consulate
30 Secession Building
31 Akademie der Bildenden Künste

AUSTRIA

Prague; tram D "Südbahnhof" runs to the Ring. **Westbahnhof** serves France, western Germany, Switzerland, the Netherlands, Belgium, the U.K., Bulgaria, Romania, Hungary, and western Austria; take U-6 then U-4 to Karlsplatz or take tram 52 or 58 to the Ring. **Südbahnhof** has trains to Italy, Greece, Czech Republic, Slovakia, Poland, and (June-Sept.) Bulgaria and Hungary; take tram D "Nußdorf" to the Ring. To Prague (5-6hr., 410AS), Berlin (1hr., via Prague 790AS, via Munich 1314AS), Budapest (4-5hr., 372AS plus 80AS InterCity supplement). Showers and baths in the Westbahnhof at **Friseursalon Navratil,** on the ground floor. 48AS per 30min. shower; 60AS per 30min. bath. 10AS extra on Sun. Open Mon.-Sat. 10am-8pm, Sun. 8am-1pm.

Buses: City bus terminal at **Wien-Mitte** rail station. Post and Bundesbahn buses across Austria; private international buses. Currency exchange and lockers available. Domestic ticket desk open 6:15am-6pm; international private lines maintain travel agencies in the station. Call 711 01 for info (6am-9pm).

Public Transportation: Excellent **U-Bahn** (subway), bus, and tram systems. Single fare is 20AS, 17AS if purchased in advance at ticket office or tobacco shop; a 24-hr. pass is 50AS, and a 72-hr. pass is 130AS. The 7-day pass (142AS) requires a passport-sized photo, and is valid from Mon. at 9am to 9am the next Mon (i.e. if you buy it Sat. you only have 2 days left). An 8-day ticket costs 265AS; it must be stamped for each ride. With this card, 4 people can ride for 2 days, 8 for 1, etc. All passes allow unlimited travel on the system, except on special night buses. To validate a ticket, **punch the ticket immediately** upon entering the bus, tram, etc. in the orange machine; if you possess a ticket that is not stamped, it is invalid, and plain-clothes inspectors may fine you up to 500AS. Tickets can be purchased from *Tabak* kiosks or *automaten* in major U-Bahn stations. Most of the system closes shortly before midnight. Special **night buses** run Fri.-Sat. 12:30-4am between the city center, at Schwedenplatz, and various outlying districts (25AS, day-transport passes not valid). Night bus stops are designated by "N" signs. Streetcar lines and U-Bahn stops are listed on a free city map, available at the tourist office. There is a public transportation **information** number (tel. 587 31 86, English-speaking operator available upon request) that will give you directions to any point in the city by public transportation. Open Mon.-Fri. 7am-6pm, Sat.-Sun. 8:30am-4pm.

Ferries: Cruise with **DDSG Donaureisen** to Budapest for 750AS, round-trip 1100AS (daily April 24-Sept. 18). Buy tickets at tourist offices. Boats dock at the Reichsbrücke on the New Danube. Take U-1 to Reichsbrücke.

Taxis: tel. 313 00, 401 00, 601 60, or 910 11. Base charge 22AS. 12AS surcharge for taxis called by radiophone, 10AS for trips 11pm-6am, on Sun. and holidays, 12AS for luggage over 20kg, 24AS surcharge for luggage over 50kg.

Bike Rental: Best bargain at **Wien Nord** and **Westbahnhof** train stations. 90AS per day, with train ticket 45AS from day of arrival. Elsewhere in the city rental averages 30AS per hr. Pick up the Vienna By Bike brochure at tourist office.

Hitchhiking: Those who hitch to Salzburg take the tram to the end of the line at Hütteldorf station and walk over to the beginning of the Autobahn. Those hitching south try the traffic circle near Laaerberg (tram 67 to the last stop). **Mitfahrzentrale Wien,** III, Invalidenstr. 15 (tel. 715 00 66), pairs drivers and riders (Salzburg 230AS, Innsbruck 280AS). Open Mon.-Fri. 9am-6pm, Sat. 10am-2pm.

Luggage Storage: Lockers at all train stations (30AS per 24hr.). Adequate for sizable backpacks. Checked luggage 20AS. Open 4am-1:15am.

Lost Property: Central lost property office, IX, Wasagasse 22 (tel. 313 44 91 11). Open Mon.-Fri. 8am-noon. For objects lost on public transport system, call 50 13 00 within 3 days.

Bookstore: Shakespeare & Company, I, Sterngassse 2 (tel. 353 50 53). Open Mon.-Fri. 9am-6pm, Sat. 9am-noon. **British Bookshop,** I, Weihburggasse 8. Stocks *Let's Go.* Open Mon.-Fri. 9am-6pm, Sat. 9am-noon.

Gay and Lesbian Information: Rosa Lila Villa, VI, Linke Wienzeile 102 (tel. 586 81 50). A favored resource for Viennese homosexuals and tourists. Lending library available. Open Mon.-Fri. 5-8pm.

Laundromat: Münzwäscherei Kalksburger & Co., III, Schlachthausgasse 19 (tel. 78 81 91). Wash 90AS per 6kg, dry 10AS. Soap 10AS. Open Mon.-Fri. 7:30am-6:30pm, Sat. 7:30am-1pm. **Münzwäscherei Margaretenstraße,** IV, Margaretenstr. 52 (tel. 587 04 73). Wash 85AS per 6kg, dry 10AS. Soap included. Open Mon.-Fri. 7am-6pm, Sat. 8am-noon.

Crisis Lines: House for Threatened and Battered Women, emergency hotline 545 48 00 or 408 38 80. 24hrs. **Rape Crisis Hotline,** tel. 93 22 22. Mon. 10am-1pm, Tues. and Thurs. 6-9pm. **English-language Suicide Hotline,** tel. 713 33 74.

Medical Assistance: Allgemeines Krankenhaus, IX, Währinger Gürtel 18-20 (tel. 404 00). Your consulate can provide a list of physicians.

Emergencies: Police, tel. 133. **Ambulance,** tel. 144. **Fire,** tel. 122.

ACCOMMODATIONS AND CAMPING

The only unpleasant aspect of Vienna is the hunt for cheap rooms. The June crunch abates slightly from July to September, when university dorms metamorphose into hostels. Write ahead or call the day before for reservations, and pick up the lists of hostels and hotels from the tourist office. Beware of offers made at the station and shady talk of *Studentenzimmer* (student rooms), which are often closet-sized. **Tourist offices** handle private homes (3-day min. stay) in the 180-250AS range, but many of these are in the 'burbs. **ÖKISTA** (see Budget Travel, above) finds cheaper rooms and charges no commission. The office is at IX, Türkenstr. 46 #314 (tel. 40 14 80), adjacent to the travel office (open Mon.-Wed. and Fri. 9:30am-4pm, Thurs. 9:30am-5:30pm). In summer, the **Mitwohnzentrale** at Laudongasse 7 (tel. 402 60 61) will find you a room or apartment from 200AS per day (commission included); for stays of a month or longer, rooms start at 2500AS (book 4 weeks in advance). Bring your passport. (Open Mon.-Fri. 10am-2pm and 3-6pm.)

Hostels

Myrthengasse (HI), VII, Myrthengasse 7 (tel. 523 94 29 or 523 63 16, fax 523 58 49). From Westbahnhof, take U-6 to Burggasse, then bus 48A to Neubaugasse; walk back on Burggasse about a block, and take the 1st right. About 15min. by bus to city center or Westbahnhof. Sparkling modern rooms with 2-6 beds, washroom, and big lockers. Enthusiastic management, game room. Reception open 7:30am-1am. Lockout 9am-2pm. Curfew 1am. 140AS. Breakfast (7-8:30am) and sheets included. Reservations recommended. Wheelchair access.

Believe-It-Or-Not, VII, Myrthengasse 10, #14 (tel. 526 46 58). Across from Myrthengasse hostel (above). Cramped but sociable quarters. Fully equipped kitchen, sheets, down quilts, hot water, and very thoughtful owner. Believe it. Lockout 10:30am-12:30pm. 160AS; Nov.-Easter 110AS. Call ahead.

Gästehaus Ruthensteiner (HI), XV, Robert-Hamerlinggasse 24 (tel. 893 42 02 or 893 27 96). From Westbahnhof, walk down Mariahilferstr., take 1st left at Palmgasse, then 1st right (3min.). Small, sunny rooms. Courtyard and kitchen. Reception open 24hrs. Dorm bed (bring sheets or sleeping bag) 129AS. Singles and doubles 209AS per person. Breakfast 25AS. Lockers and kitchen facilities. Reservations recommended.

Neustiftgasse (HI), VII, Neustiftgasse 85 (tel. 523 74 62, fax 523 58 49). Around the corner from Myrthengasse hostel (above) and managed by the same folks. Reception open 7:30am-1am. Lockout 9am-noon. Curfew 1am. Members only. 140AS. Breakfast and sheets included. Laundry 50AS per load.

Jugendgästehaus Wien Brigittenau (HI), XX, Friedrich-Engels-Platz 24 (tel. 33 28 29 40, fax 330 83 74). U-1 or U-4: Schwedenplatz and then tram N to Floridsdorfer Brücke/Friedrich-Engels-Platz. Efficient and helpful management oversees brigades of high-school kids. 334 beds. Reception open 24hrs. Lockout 9am-3pm. Curfew 1am. Members only. 140AS. Breakfast included. 3-night max. stay.

Kolpingfamilie Wien-Meidling (HI), XIII, Bendlgasse 10-12 (tel. 83 54 87, fax 812 21 30). U-4 or U-6: Niederhofstr. Head right on Niederhofstr. and take the third right onto Bendlgasse. Well-lit and modern rooms with 4, 6, and 8 beds are 140AS, 125AS, and 95AS per person respectively. Doubles 405AS. Sheet rental 65AS. Breakfast 42AS. Reception open 6am-midnight. Curfew midnight. Doors locked midnight-4am. No daytime lockout. Check-out by 9am.

Hostel Zöhrer, VIII, Skodagasse 26 (tel. 43 07 30, fax 408 04 09). From the Westbahnhof, take U-6: Alserstr., then take tram 43 "Dr. Karl Lueger Ring" 2 stops to Skodagasse. From the Südbahnhof, take bus 13A to Alserstr./Skodagasse. About 10min. from the city center. Crowded but comfortable, in a good location. Dorm beds, singles, 4-, 6-, or 7-bed rooms, each with showers, all 160AS per person. Laundry 70AS. Reception open 7:30am-10pm. Checkout 9am. Front door/locker key deposit 50AS. Breakfast (7:30-9:30am), sheets, and kitchen facilities included.

Jugendgästehaus Hütteldorf-Hacking (HI), XIII, Schloßberggasse 8 (tel. 877 02 63, fax 877 026 32). U-4 or S-50: Hütteldorf, walk over the footbridge and follow the signs (10min.). Often packed with student groups, but there are two separate buildings for individual travelers to escape from the little monsters. There is no curfew in these buildings. 139AS. Laundry 70AS per load. Large closets without locks—it's *much* wiser to use the safes available at reception (10AS per day). Reception open 7am-11:45pm. Curfew 11:45pm, but it can be loud for an hour or two. Lockout 9am-4pm. Breakfast and showers included.

Schloßherberge am Wilhelminenberg (HI), XVI, Savoyenstr. 2 (tel. 458 50 37 00). From U-6 "Friedensbrücke" to tram 46: Maroltingerstraße, then bus 46B or 146B: Schloß Wilhelminenberg. On a hill, abutting a beautiful palace. 164 beds in comfortable quads, all with shower and toilet. Reception open 7am-11:45pm. 205AS. Breakfast included. Open March-Oct. Wheelchair access.

University Dormitories

The following dorms usually become summer hostels from July to September. Expect mass-produced university cubicles.

Porzellaneum der Wiener Universität, IX, Porzellangasse 30 (tel. 34 72 82). From the Südbahnhof, take streetcar D "Nußdorf" and get off at Fürstengasse. From the Westbahnhof, take streetcar 5 to the Franz-Josefs Bahnhof, then streetcar D "Südbahnhof" to Fürstengasse (20min.). The Crazy Eddie of hotels, these prices are an insanely good deal. Reception open 24hrs. Singles and doubles 160AS per person, with some triples and quads. Sheets and showers included. Reservations recommended.

Rudolfinum, IV, Mayerhofgasse 3 (tel. 505 53 84). Just a few yards down Mayerhofg. from U-1: Taubstummengasse. Reception open 24hrs. Rock on dude! Buy a beer at the reception and veg in front of MTV. Great location. Singles 250AS. Doubles 420AS. Triples 540AS. Sheets, showers, and breakfast included.

Katholisches Studentenhaus, XIX, Peter-Jordanstr. 29 (tel. 34 92 64). From Westbahnhof, U-6: Nußdorferstr., then streetcar 38: Hardtgasse, and turn left onto Peter-Jordanstr. From Südbahnhof, streetcar D: Schottentor, then streetcar 38: Hardtgasse. Unexciting rooms, but the price is right. Reception on 2nd floor. Singles 220AS. Doubles 166AS per person. Showers and sheets included. Call ahead.

Gästehaus Pfeilgasse, IV, Pfeilgasse 6 (tel. 408 34 45). U-2: Lerchenfelderstr. Head right on Lerchenfelderstr., first right on Lange Gasse, and then first left on Pfeilgasse. The home-sick will not be reminded of home, but of their freshman dorms. Singles 250AS, doubles 420AS, triples 540AS. Showers and breakfast included. Reception open 24hrs.

Hotels and Pensions

Irmgard Lauria, VII, Kaiserstr. 77, #8 (tel. 522 25 55). U-6: Burggasse-Stadthalle, then take a right onto Burggasse, and then the second left onto Kaiserstr. About 15min. from center. A great place for a private room or a dorm bed. Eclectically decorated but attractive rooms with murals ranging from the African plains to a crazily-pastelled forest. Dorms 160AS. Doubles 530AS. No curfew. Coed rooming possible. Reservations strongly recommended but require a 2-day min. stay.

Pension Falstaff, IX, Müllnergsse 5 (tel. 317 91 27, fax 349 18 64). U-6: Roßauer Lände. Cross Roßauer Lände and head down Grünentorgasse, taking the third left onto Müllnergasse. Quieter than its boisterous namesake. Singles 345-465AS. Doubles 565-680AS. Triples 680AS. Extra bed 200AS. Breakfast included.

Pension Kraml, VI, Brauergasse 5 (tel. 587 85 88, fax 586 75 73), off Gumpendorferstr. From the Westbahnhof, walk across the Gürtel and up Mariahilferstr., and take the third right onto Otto-Bauerstr.; make the first left on Königseggasse, then the first right (15min.). About 10min. from the city center. Tidy, comfortable, new, and run by a cordial family. Singles 260AS. Doubles 530-660AS. Triples 720-930AS. Quads 1120AS. Continental breakfast included. Call ahead.

Pension Hamminger, XVIII, Türkenschanzstr. 34 (tel. 470 19 39). Quiet, feels safe, 8min. from the city center. Doubles 500AS, shower included. English spoken.

Hedwig Gally, XXV, Arnsteingasse 25 (tel. 892 90 73, fax 833 10 28). By the West-bahnhof, but the U-3 to the city center is a short walk away. Singles 250-300AS. Doubles 400-460AS. Triples 540-600AS. Quads 720-760AS. Breakfast 50AS.

Hospiz-Hotel CVJM, VII, Kenyongasse 15 (tel. 93 13 04). From the Westbahnhof, cross the Gürtel, walk 1 block down Stallgasse and turn left on Kenyongasse (3 min.). This large old building, part of the Austrian YMCA, provides a quiet location close to the station. Singles 350-380AS. Doubles 620-680AS. Triples 870-990AS. Quads 1120-1280AS. 40AS surcharge for one-night stay. Ample parking. Key to entrance and room provided.

Camping

Wien-West I (tel. 94 14 49) and **II** (tel. 94 23 14), at Hüttelbergstr. 40 and 80, respectively, are the most convenient campgrounds; both lie in the 14th *Bezirk* about 8km from the city center. For either, U-4: Hütteldorf, then bus 52B "Campingpl. Wien West." 58AS per person, children 33AS; 53AS per tent; 53AS per car. Both offer laundry machines, grocery stores, and cooking facilities. I is open July 15-Aug. 28; II year-round.

FOOD

Food and drink are inseparably linked in Vienna; both are consumed in large quantities. Viennese culinary offerings reflect the patchwork empire of the Habsburgs. *Serbische Bohnensuppe* (Serbian bean soup) and *Ungärische Gulaschsuppe* (Hungarian spicy beef stew) are two examples of eastern European influence. *Knödel,* bread dumplings found in most side dishes, originated in the former Czechoslovakia. Even the famed *Wiener Schnitzel* (fried and breaded veal cutlets) was first cooked in Milan. The *Gästehaus* and the *Beisel* serve inexpensive rib-sticking meals that are best washed down with much beer. *Würstelstands,* found on almost every corner, provide a quick, cheap lunch. Vienna is perhaps most renowned for its sublime desserts and chocolates; they're unbelievably rich, but priced for patrons who are likewise blessed. *Sacher Torte, Imperial Torte,* and even *Apfelstrudel* cost up to 40AS, though most residents adamantly maintain that they are worth every *Groschen*.

Restaurants in the touristy **Kärntnerstraße** area are generally overpriced. A better bet is the neighborhood just north of the university where **Universitätsstraße** and **Währingerstraße** meet; reasonably priced *Gaststätten, Kneipen* (bars), and restaurants are easy to find. Otherwise, nibble the aromatic delicacies at the open-air **Naschmarkt,** an especially filling option for vegetarians who travel to this carnivorous city (U-4: Kettenbrückengasse; open Mon.-Fri. 7am-6pm, Sat. 7am-1pm). For discount supermarket fare, try the ubiquitous **Billa, Konsum,** or **Hoffer.** Except at train stations, all grocery stores close from Saturday afternoon to Monday morning. To conquer the summer heat, try **Gelateria Hoher Markt,** I, Hoher Markt just off Rotenturmstr (open March-Oct. 9am-11pm).

Restaurants

Trzesniewski, I, Dorotheergasse 1, 3 blocks down the Graben from the Stephansdom. A famous stand-up restaurant, this unpronounceable establishment has been serving petite open-faced sandwiches for more than 80 years. 7AS per *Brötchen.* Open Mon.-Fri. 9am-7:30pm, Sat. 9am-1pm.

Maschu, I, Rabenstr. U-1 or U-4: Schwedenpl. Facing away from the canal, head right on Franz-Josefs-Kai, then left. Surrounded by 5 bars, smack in the middle of the Triangle, this stand-up restaurant is ideal for a bite before, during, or after the night's revels. Succulent *Schwarma* (38AS) and delicious falafel (55AS). Open 10am-2am.

Bizi Pizza, I, Rotenturmstr. 4 (tel. 513 37 05), on the corner of Stephanspl. Self-service restaurant boasts a deliciously fresh salad bar (small plate 30AS, large plate

50AS) and huge individual pizzas (60-75AS, slices 27AS). Open 11am-11pm. Branch with the same hours at Franz-Josefs-Kai (tel. 535 79 13).

Fischerbräu, XIX, Billrothstr. 17 (tel. 319 62 64). From U-2: Universität or U-2 or 4: Schottentor, take tram 38 to Hardtgasse, and walk back 50m. Popular spot for youngish locals. The leafy courtyard, accompanied by jazz music, makes this an ideal spot to consume the home-brewed beer (large glass 38AS) and delicious food. The veal sausage (56AS) is excellent, and the chicken salad (78AS) has made more than one New Yorker squeal with glee. Open Mon.-Sat. 4pm-1am, Sun. 11am-1am.

Tunnel, VIII, Florianigasse 39 (tel. 42 34 65). U-2: Rathaus, and with your back to City Hall, head right on Landesgerichstr., then left on Florianigasse. Dark and smoky, with funky paintings and the occasional divan instead of chairs. Cheap eats featuring Italian, Austrian, and Middle-Eastern dishes. Vegetarian options. The best affordable breakfast in Vienna—29AS buys anything from a Spanish omelette to an "Arabian" selection. Entrees 35-120AS. Open 9am-2am.

Schnitzelwirt Schmidt, VII, Neubaugasse 52 (tel. 93 37 71). From the Burgring, take bus 49 to the end station at Neubaugasse (5min.). Every kind of *Schnitzel* imaginable (56AS). Huge portions and low, low prices will sate your most carnivorous desires and spare your budget. Open Mon.-Fri. 11am-11pm, Sat. 11am-2:30pm and 5-11pm.

Cafés and Konditoreien

The café is a centerpiece of Vienna's unhurried charm. Choose a piece of cake at the counter before sitting down; often you'll pay for it immediately and give your receipt to the server when you order beverages. The server then returns with your pastry. Coffee can be ordered *schwarzer* (black), *brauner* (a little milk), *melange* (light), and *mazagron* (iced with rum).

Demel, I, Kohlmarkt 14. Walk 5min. from the Stephansdom down Graben. *The* Viennese coffeeshop. The atmosphere is near-worshipful in this legendary *fin-de-siècle* cathedral of sweets. Waitresses in convent-black serve divine confections (35-48AS). Don't miss the *creme-du-jour*. Open 10am-6pm.

Hotel Sacher, I, Philharmonikerstr. 4 (tel. 512 14 87), around the corner from the main tourist information office. This historic sight has been serving the world-famous *Sacher Torte* (45AS) in red velvet opulence for years. Exceedingly elegant; most everyone is refined and bejeweled. Open 6:30am-midnight.

Café Central, I, at the corner of Herrengasse and Strauchgasse, inside Palais Ferstel. Former patrons include Leon Trotsky, Theodor Herzl, Sigmund Freud—the list goes on. And they serve coffee. Open Mon.-Sat. 9am-8pm.

Café Hawelka, I, Dorotheergasse 6, 3 blocks west from the Stephansdom. Come here for the incredible *buchteln* (sweet dumplings filed with preserves, 25AS, served only after 10pm). Coffee 30-40AS. Open Mon., Wed.-Sat. 8am-2am, Sun. 4pm-2am.

Café Drechsler, VI, Linke Wienzeille 22 (tel. 587 85 80). By Karlspl., where Operngasse meets Linke Wienzeille. *The* place to be the morning after the night before. Early birds and night owls roost here over pungent cups of *mokka*. Open Mon.-Sat. 4am-8pm.

Café Willendorf, VI, Linke Wienzeile 102, in the Rosa Lila Villa (tel. 587 17 89). A café, bar, and restaurant with an outdoor terrace that attracts a mainly gay and lesbian clientele. Open 7pm-2am.

SIGHTS

Vienna from A to Z (30AS from the tourist office, more in bookstores) gives all you need for a self-created tour. The free *Museums* brochure from the tourist office lists all opening hours and admission prices. Individual museum tickets usually cost 15AS; 150AS will buy you a book of 14.

Ecclesiastic and Imperial Vienna Start your odyssey at the Gothic **Stephansdom** (U-1 or U-3: Stephansplatz). The smoothly tapering stone lace spire of this magnificent cathedral has become Vienna's emblem, appearing on every second postcard. (Tours in English Mon.-Sat. 10:30am and 3pm, Sun. and holidays 3pm; 30AS. June-Aug. spectacular evening tour Sat. 7pm; 100AS.) View Vienna from the **Nordturm** (North Tower; open 9am-5:30pm; elevator ride 30AS).

The enormous **Hofburg** (Imperial Palace) rising from the southeast of the **Michaelerplatz** was home to the Habsburg emperors until 1918, and is currently the Austrian president's office. Wander through the *Burggarten* (Gardens of the Imperial Palace), *Schweizerhof* (Swiss Courtyard), the *Schatzkammer* (treasuries), the *Burgkapelle* (chapel, where the Vienna Boys' Choir sings Mass on Sun. and religious holidays), the Neue Burg (New Palace, now the *Kunsthistorisches Museum*—see Museums, below), built 1881-1913, and the the *Schauräume* (state rooms; open Mon.-Sat. 8:30am-noon and 12:30-4pm, tours 40AS, students 20AS.) Between Josefsplatz and Michaelerplatz, the Palace Stables *(Stallburg)* are home to the Royal Lipizzaner stallions of the **Spanische Reitschule** (Spanish Riding School). Performances (April-June and Sept. Sun. at 10:45am and Wed. at 7pm; March and Nov. to mid-Dec. Sun. at 10:45am) are always sold out; you must reserve tickets six months in advance. Write to Spanische Reitschule, Hofburg, A-1010 Wien. Write only for reservations; don't send money. (Tickets 200-600AS, standing-room 150AS.) Watching the horses train is much cheaper. (March-June and Nov. to mid-Dec. Tues.-Sat. 10am-noon; Feb. Mon.-Sat. 10am-noon, except when the horses tour. Tickets sold at door at Josefsplatz, Gate 2, from about 8:30am. 50AS, children 15AS. No reservations.)

Fin-de-Siècle and Cosmopolitan Vienna The Hofburg's Heldenplatz gate presides over the northeastern side of the Burgring segment of the **Ringstraße.** In 1857, Emperor Franz Josef commissioned this 187-foot-wide and 2½-mile-long boulevard to replace the city walls that separated Vienna's center from the suburban districts. Follow Burgring west through the **Volksgarten's** hundreds of varieties of roses to reach the Neoclassical, sculpture-adorned **Parliament** building. Just up Dr.-Karl-Renner-Ring is the **Rathaus,** an intriguing remnant of late 19th-century neo-Gothic with Victorian mansard roofs and red geraniums in the windows. The **Burgtheater** opposite contains frescoes by Klimt. Immediately to the north on Dr.-Karl-Lueger-Ring is the **Universität.** The surrounding sidestreets gush cafés, bookstores, and bars.

Kärntner Straße connects Stephansdom to the **Staatsoper** (State Opera House). During the summer, street music fills the air with everything from Peruvian folk to Bob Dylan to Schubert. If you miss the shows (standing-room tickets 15-20AS) at the Opera House, tour the glittering gold, crystal, and red velvet interior (featured in the movie *Amadeus* and once home to Mahler's skilled conducting). (Tours 11am-3pm on the hour; Sept.-June on request 40AS, students 25AS.) Alfred Hrdlicka's poignant 1988 sculpture **Mahnmal Gegen Krieg und Faschismus** (Memorial Against War and Fascism), behind the opera in the Albertinapl., memorializes the suffering of Austria's people—especially its Jews—during World War II.

Outside the Ring Music lovers might trek out to the **Zentralfriedhof** (Central Cemetery), XI, Simmeringer Hauptstr. 234, where Beethoven, Wolf, the Strausses, and Schönberg are buried. Take tram 71. (Open May-July 7am-7pm; Sept.-Oct. and March-April 7am-6pm; Nov.-Feb. 8am-5pm.) One of the more unforgettable buildings in Vienna is the **Hundertwasser Haus,** at the corner of Löwenstr. and Kegelgasse in the third district, a municipal housing project named for the artist who designed it in 1983. The structure is a wild fantasia of pastel colors, ceramic mosaics, and tilted tile columns.

Another must-see is the **Schloß Schönbrunn** and its surrounding gardens, which encompass 1.6 sq. km of glorious space. This former summer residence of the Habsburgs holds the **Wagenburg** (coach collection), where the coronation carriage and the imperial hearse are on display. A tour through the palace interior brings you to the **Bergl** rooms, where frescoes of peacocks perched on rose bushes create the

AUSTRIA

impression of a refined royal jungle. (Palace apartments open 8:30am-5:30pm; Nov.-
March 8:30am-5pm; 80AS, tours available in English. Wagenburg open 9am-6pm,
April and Oct. 9am-5pm, Nov.-March 10am-4pm; 30AS.)

The **Prater,** extending southeast from the Wien-Nord Bahnhof, is a notoriously
touristed amusement park that functioned as a private game reserve for the Imperial
Family until 1766 and as the site of the World Expo in 1873. The park boasts ponds
and meadows and is dotted with various rides, arcades, restaurants, and casinos
(entry to the complex is free, but each attraction charges admission). Rides range
from garish thrill machines to merry-go-rounds to the stately-moving 65m **Riesenrad**
(Giant Ferris Wheel). The wheel, which has one of the prettiest views of Vienna, is
best known for its cameo role in Carol Reed's postwar thriller, *The Third Man.*
(Ride lasts 20min. Open Feb.-Nov. 10am-10pm, sometimes 11pm.) Beloved by children during the day, the Prater becomes less wholesome after sundown: peepshows and prostitution abound.

Museums On the Burgring in what used to be the *Neue Hofburg* is the world-
famous **Kunsthistorisches Museum,** home to one of the world's best art collections,
including entire rooms of prime Brueghels, Vermeer's *Allegory of Painting,* and
numerous works by Rembrandt, Rubens, Titian, Dürer, and Velázquez. Cellini's
famous golden salt cellar is here, along with a superb collection of ancient art and a
transplanted Egyptian burial chamber. Gustav Klimt decorated the lobby. (Picture
gallery open Tues.-Wed., Fri.-Sun. 10am-6pm, Thurs. 10am-9pm. Egyptian and Near-
Eastern, Greek and Roman, and sculpture collections open Tues.-Sun. 10am-6pm.
95AS, students 45AS.) Fans of Klimt and his fellow radicals, Egon Schiele and the
always colorful Oskar Kokoschka, should visit the **Austrian Gallery,** in the **Belvedere Palace,** entrance at Prinz-Eugen-Str. 27. Also check out the *Biedermeier* paintings and the breathtaking view of the city from the upper floors. (Open Tues.-Sun.
10am-5pm. 60AS, students 30AS.)

Kunst Haus Wien, III, Untere Weißgerberstr. 13, built for the works of Hundertwasser, is one of his greatest works in and of itself. Crazily pastiched building also
hosts international contemporary exhibits. (Open 10am-7pm. Hundertwasser exhibition 60AS, students 44AS.) **Historisches Museum der Stadt Vienna** (Historical
Museum of the City of Vienna), IV, Karlspl. 5, to the left of the Karlskirche houses
collection of historical artifacts and paintings that document the city's evolution
from the Roman Vindobona encampment through 640 years of Habsburg rule to the
present (open Tues.-Sun. 9am-4:30pm; 30AS).

The greatest monument of *fin-de-siècle* Vienna is the **Secession Building,** I,
Friedrichstr. 12, built by Wagner's pupil Josef Maria Olbrich to accommodate the
artists, led by Gustav Klimt, who scorned historical style and broke with the uptight
Viennese art establishment. Olbrich designed this extraordinary ivory-and-gold edifice as a reaction against the overblown neoclassicism of the Ring museums. Exhibits by contemporary artists adorn the walls, as does Klimt's 30m *Beethoven Frieze.*
Note the inscription above the door: *Der Zeit, ihre Kunst, der Kunst, ihre Freiheit*
(to the age, its art; to art, its freedom). (Open Tues.-Fri. 10am-6pm, Sat.-Sun. 10am-
4pm. 30AS, students 15AS.) The **Künstlerhaus,** from which the Secession seceded,
is to the east at Karlsplatz 5. This is the conservative museum in Vienna, and you can
tell by the statues of Old Masters on either side of the entrance.

For more of the art nouveau movement, visit the **Österreichisches Museum für
Angewandte Kunst** (Museum of Applied Art), I, Stubenring 5, the oldest museum of
applied arts in Europe. Otto Wagner furniture and Klimt sketches pose amid crystal,
china, furniture, and rugs from the Middle Ages to the present. (Open Tues.-Wed.
and Fri.-Sun. 10am-6pm, Thurs. 10am-9pm. 90AS, students 45AS.) Unmissable creations are Otto Wagner's **Pavilion** at Karlsplatz, the major U-Bahn station, his **Kirche
am Steinhof,** XIV, Baumgartner Höhe 1 (take bus 48a to the end of the line), and his
Postsparkassenamt (post office savings bank), on the Postgasse.

ENTERTAINMENT

Music and Theater

You can enjoy Viennese opera in the imperial splendor of the **Staatsoper** (State Opera House) for a mere 15-35AS. Get in line on the west side about 3:30-4pm for standing room (*Stehplätze*, sold only on day of performance, 15AS balcony, 20AS orchestra). Get tickets for the center; you see nothing standing at the side. Bring a scarf to tie on the rail to save your place during the show. Costlier advance tickets (100-850AS) are on sale at the **Bundestheaterkassen**, I, Goethegasse (tel. 514 44 22 18; open Mon.-Fri. 8am-6pm, Sat. 9am-2pm, Sun. 9am-noon). Students with ID (not ISIC) can buy unsold seats ½hr. before curtain. They also sell tickets for Vienna's other public theaters: the **Volksoper, Burgtheater,** and **Akademietheater.** Discount tickets for these go at the door an hour before performances (50-400AS). The **Wiener Philharmoniker** (Vienna Philharmonic Orchestra) is world-renowned, performing in the **Musikverein**, I, Dumbastr. 3, on the northeast side of Karlsplatz.

Vienna, the most musical of cities, wanes somewhat in summer; the **Staatsoper** and the **Wiener Sängerknaben** (Vienna Boys' Choir) vacation during July and August. During the rest of the year, the pre-pubescent prodigies sing 9:15am mass each Sunday at the **Burgkapelle** (Royal Chapel) of the Hofburg. Reserve tickets (50-250AS) at least two months in advance from Verwaltung der Hofmusikkapelle, Hofburg, Schweizerhof, A-1010 Wien. Do not enclose money. Unreserved seats are sold starting at 5pm on the preceding Friday. Standing room is free. Sunday High Masses in the major churches (Augustinerkirche, Michaelerkirche, Stephansdom) are accompanied by choral or organ music that approaches the celestial.

The **Theater an der Wien**, VI, Linke Wienzeile 6 (tel. 58 03 02 65), opens with musicals in July (performances 7:30pm; 100-990AS), and the **Wiener Kammeroper** (Chamber Opera) performs during the summer in Schönbrunner Schloßpark (tickets 50-350AS). To get a full listing of what's offered, consult the monthly *Programm* available at the tourist office.

English-language drama is offered at **Vienna's English Theater,** VIII, Josefsgasse 12 (tel. 402 12 60 or 42 82 84; box office open Mon.-Sat. 10am-6pm, evening box office opens at 7pm; tickets 150-420AS, students 100AS on night of performance). Something of a tradition in Vienna, this theater still has enough artistic vision to host world premieres; Edward Albee debuted his most recent play, *Three Tall Women*, here. If you yearn to hear still more English, head to the **International Theater,** IX Porzellangasse 8 (tel. 31 62 72; tickets 220AS, students under 26 120AS).

Heurigen and Nightlife

Vienna is almost as famous for its *Heurigen* (outside seating at picnic tables, with mugs of wine hung over the door) as for its art and music. Unique to Vienna, *Heurigen* began when Emperor Joseph II, in a fit of largesse, allowed the local wine-growers to sell and serve their wine in their homes at certain times of the year. The worn picnic benches and old shade trees provide an ideal spot to contemplate, converse, or listen to *schrammelmusik* (sentimental, wine-lubricated folk songs played by aged musicians inhabiting the *Heurige).* Once upon a time, patrons would bring picnics with them, but sadly those days seem to be gone. However, a *Heurige* generally serves simple buffets (grilled chicken, salads, pretzels, etc.) that make for an enjoyable and inexpensive meal. In the middle of the summer, *Stürm* (cloudy, unpasteurized wine) is available; the drink is very sweet, but quite potent. Learn the word for "dry," *trocken*. After the Feast of the Martins on November 11, the wine remaining from last year's crop becomes "old wine," no longer proper to serve in the *heurigen*; the Viennese do their best to spare it this fate by consuming the beverage in Herculean quantities before time's up.

Heurigen freckle the northern, western, and southern suburbs, where grapes are grown. **Grinzing** is the largest *Heurigen* area, but atmosphere and prices are better in **Nußdorf** (tram D from the Ring), in **Sievering, Neustift am Wald** and in **Stammersdorf.** Hidden from tourists and therefore beloved by locals, **Buschenschank**

AUSTRIA

Heinrich Niersche, XIX, Strehlgasse 21, overlooks the field of Grinzing. (Take bus 41A from the U-6: Währingerstraße/Volksoper to Pötzleindorfer Höhe; walk one block and make a left on Strehlgasse. Open Thurs.-Mon. 3pm-midnight.) Ask the tourist office for its list of *Heurigen*. Most are open from 4pm to midnight; wine costs about 30AS per mug.

Areas of Vienna contain notoriously high concentrations of cafés, bars, and *Biesel*. The city parties until dawn, though the public transportation closes at midnight. An extensive club scene every night; the door game is minimal, the cover charges reasonable, and the theme nights varied enough to please most tastes. Rock me, Amadeus! No matter what the diversion for the evening, most roads lead to an all-night *Beisel* or café for a strudel or toast. Pick up a copy of *Falter* for the best entertainment listings, be it an opera schedule, or club theme nights. Revelers tend to lose themselves in the infamous **Bermuda Dreieck (Triangle),** a collection of about thirty bars crammed into an area northwest of Stephanspl. bordered by Rotenturmstr. and Wipplingerstr. The action moves indoors at 10pm, until 2am or even 4am. The area around the U-3: Stubentor station is also a solid stomping ground of the hip. Other locals congregate in the region surrounding **Bäckerstraße** behind the Stephansdom. The **8th District** behind the university, is also a target area for thirsty night-owls. In the outer districts, Spittleberg's sleepy cafés pick up enormously when the sun goes down.

Zwölf Apostellenkeller, I, Sonnenfelsgasse 3, behind the *Stephansdom* (tel. 52 62 77). To reach this underground tavern, walk into the archway, take a right, go down the long staircase, and discover grottoes that date back to 1561. One of the best *Weinkeller* in Vienna, and a definite must for catacomb fans. The complex has many levels—the lowest is the liveliest. Beer 34AS. *Viertel* of wine starts at 25AS. Open Aug.-June 4:30pm-midnight.

Santo Spirito, I, Kampfgasse 7 (tel. 512 99 98). From Stephanspl., walk down Singerstr. and make a left onto Kumpfgasse (5min.). The stereo here pumps out Rachmaninoff's second piano concerto while excited patrons co-conduct. Open 6pm until people leave.

Jazzland, I, Franz-Josefs-Kai 29 (tel. 533 25 75). U-1, U-4: Schwedenplatz. Jazz music—Austrian style. Excellent live music filters into soothingly cool grottoes. Hefty cover 120-200AS. Open Tues.-Sat. 7pm-2am. Music 9pm-1am.

Fischerbräu, XIX, Billrothstr. 17 (tel. 31 962 64). A rare Viennese beer garden.Stained and lacquered hardwood interior and the leafy garden outside. Open Mon.-Sat. 4pm-1am, Sun. 11am-1am.

Tunnel, VIII, Florianigasse 39 (tel. 42 34 65). Frequented by students for the bohemian, Euro-chic atmosphere, and live music in the cellar (from 8:30pm, cover 30-100AS, Mon. free). The upper level holds a regular bar/restaurant with a plethora of drinks and food. Open 9am-2am.

P1, I, Rotgasse 9, (tel. 535 99 95). From the Stephansdom, head down Rotenturm, left on Fleischmarkt, and left on Rotgasse. A younger crowd dances the night away to assortments of house, hip-hop, and acid jazz. Cover 50-100AS. Open Sun.-Thurs. 9pm-4am, Fri.-Sat. 9pm-6am.

Volksgarten, I, Burgring/Heldenpl. (tel. 63 05 18). Nestled on the edge of the Volksgarten Park, near the Hofburg. Comfy red couches where wallflowers can watch the Viennese shake their *hintern*. Open-air bar after midnight, and students enter free and nosh the free buffet on Tues. Cover 70AS, students 60AS. Open 10pm-5am.

Café Berg, IX, Berggasse 8 (tel. 319 57 20). A mixed gay café/bar at night. Casual hang-out by day. Open 10am-1am.

■■■ SALZBURG

Protected by forested mountains, Salzburg is a city of castles, horse-drawn carriages and church towers, whose voice is the sublime music of favorite son Wolfgang Amadeus Mozart. Salzburg's adulation of the composer crescendoes during its annual summer music festival, the **Salzburger Festspiele.** For those wishing to pay homage to moviedom's sweetly trilling Von Trapp family of singers, Salzburg is the place to be; *The Sound of Music* was largely filmed here, as tour guides won't let you forget.

ORIENTATION AND PRACTICAL INFORMATION

Salzburg straddles the **Salzach River** a few km from the German border. The expansive *Altstadt* (old town) clusters around **Mozartplatz** and **Residenzplatz** on the west bank of the river. The train station is on the northern edge of the (relatively) new town, which centers around **Mirabellplatz** and **Marktplatz**, east of the river. Both towns are a 15- to 20-min. walk down **Rainerstraße** from the train station. You can also get to either by taking bus 1, 5, 6, 51, or 55 from the bus stop across the street from the station.

Tourist Office: Mozartplatz 5 (tel. 84 75 68 or 88 98 73 30; fax 88 98 73 42), in the *Altstadt.* Open 8am-10pm; Sept.-Oct. and April-June 9am-7pm; Nov.-March Mon.-Sat. 9am-6pm. Hours may vary in spring and autumn. Free hotel map is the same as the 10AS city map. Branch at the train station, platform 2a (open Mon.-Sat. 8:45am-8pm).

Budget Travel: Ökista, Wolf-Dietrich-Str. 31 (tel. 88 32 52; fax 88 18 19), near the International Youth Hotel. Open Mon.-Fri. 9:30am-5:30pm. **Young Austria,** Alpenstr. 108a (tel. 62 57 58 00; fax 62 57 58 21). Open Mon.-Fri. 9am-5pm, Sat. 9am-noon. Many discounts, especially for travelers under 26.

Consulates: U.S., Giselakai 51 (tel. 286 01). Closed in 1994. For emergency help, contact the U.S. Consulate, Herbert von Karajan Platz 1 (tel. 84 8776) in the Altstadt. Open Mon., Wed., and Fri. 9am-noon. **U.K.,** Alter Markt 4 (tel. 84 81 33). Open Mon.-Fri. 9am-noon.

Currency Exchange: Banking hours are Mon.-Fri. 8am-12:30pm and 2-4:30pm. Currency exchange at train station open 7am-9pm. Banks offer better rates for cash; AmEx has better rates on traveler's checks.

American Express: Mozartplatz 5-7 (tel. 84 25 01, fax 842 50 19). All banking services. Mail held. Open Mon.-Fri. 9am-5:30pm, Sat. 9am-noon.

Post Office: Train station (tel. 88 97 00). Open 24hrs. **Postal code:** A-5010. Large branch office downtown at Residenzplatz 9 (tel. 844 12 10). Open Mon.-Fri. 7am-7pm, Sat. 8-10am.

Telephones: At the train station post office. Open 24hrs. **City Code:** 0662.

Airport: Flughafen Salzburg (tel. 85 20 91). Bus 77 "Bahnhof" (20AS) runs to the train station every 15-30min. (5:54am-11:11pm).

Trains: Hauptbahnhof, on Südtiroler Platz in the new city. For train info call 17 17. Trains run to Vienna (396AS), Munich (272AS), Budapest (670AS), Innsbruck (336AS), and Graz (396AS).

Buses: Main depot across from the train station on Südtiroler Platz (tel. 87 21 45). For schedule info, call 167 or 87 21 50.

Local Public Transportation: Information at Griesgasse 21 (tel. 62 05 51, ext. 553). Extensive 18-bus network. 21AS per ride if you pay the driver, 14AS if you purchase at a *Tabak/Trafik* stand, 17AS if you buy from an automatic vending machine, 7AS for children 6-15. A 24hr. pass costs 30AS.

Bike Rental: At the train station, platform 3 (tel. 88 87 54 27). Five-day rental packages 200AS.

Hitchhiking: Hitchers headed to Innsbruck, Munich, or Italy (except Venice) first take bus 77 to the German border. Thumbers bound for Vienna or Venice take bus 29 "Forellenwegsiedlung" to the *Autobahn* entrance at Schmiedlingerstr. They also take bus 15 "Bergheim" to the *Autobahn* entrance at Grüner Wald.

Luggage Storage: At the train station. Large lockers 30AS for two calendar days (not 48hrs). Small lockers 20AS. Luggage check 20AS per piece per calendar day for max. 30 days. Open 24hrs.

Bookstore: Bücher Schneid, Rainerstr. 24 (tel. 87 17 85). Sells *Let's Go* and other English-language books. Open Mon.-Fri. 8:30am-6pm, Sat. 8am-noon.

Laundromat: Wäscherei Constructa, Kaiserschutzenstr. 10 (tel. 87 62 53), opposite the station. 92AS per load for wash and dry. Open Mon.-Fri. 7:30am-6:30pm, Sat. 8am-noon.

Pharmacies: Elisabeth-Apotheke, Elisabethstr. 1 (tel. 87 14 84), a few blocks left of the train station. Pharmacies open Mon.-Fri. 8am-12:30pm and 2:30-6pm, Sat. 8am-noon. List of pharmacies on call posted on pharmacy doors.

Gay, Lesbian and Bisexual Organizations: Homosexuelle Initiative (HOSI), Müllner Hauptstr. 11, (tel. 43 59 27). Discussion groups. Open Wed. 10pm-midnight, Fri. 9pm-midnight, and Sat. 10pm-midnight. **HUK-Salzburg** (Gay Christian Organization), Philaharmonikerg. 2 (tel. 84 13 27). **Frauenkulturzentrum** (Women's Center), Markus-Sittikusstr. 17 (tel. and fax 87 16 39). Open Mon. 12-4pm, Tues.-Thurs. 10am-4pm. Women's café Wed.-Sat. 8pm-midnight.

Crisis Lines: Rape: tel. 88 11 00. **AIDS:** tel. 88 14 88.

Medical Assistance: Hospital, Müllner-Hauptstr. 48 (tel. 448 20).

Emergencies: Ambulance: tel. 144. **Fire:** tel. 122. **Police:** tel. 133. Headquarters at Alpenstr. 90 (tel. 638 30).

ACCOMMODATIONS AND CAMPING

Ask for the tourist office's list of private rooms (*not* the hotel map). During the summer festival (late July-Aug.), hostels fill by mid-afternoon; call ahead. The tourist office charges 30AS to reserve accommodations, plus a 50AS deposit. Beware people who approach you n the train station; often they'll drag you far out of town and saddle you with a nasty room.

Gasthaus Naturfreundehaus, Mönchsberg 19c (tel. 84 17 29). Take bus 1 or 2 "Maxglan" to Mönchsbergaufzug, then take the elevator built into the cliff (round-trip 25AS). At its summit, turn right, go down paved path through stone arch of the old fortress, and take the small dirt path to the left. Look for the red umbrellas. Reception open 7:30am-10pm. 110AS. Showers 10AS per 4min. Breakfast 30AS. Sheets 5AS. Open May to mid-Oct.

International Youth Hotel, Paracelsusstr. 9 (tel. 87 96 49), off Franz-Josef-Str. From town, take bus 15 "Bergheim" to Paracelsusstr. Full of drinking Americans. Reception open 8am-10pm. No curfew; theoretical quiet time 10pm. Dorms 120AS. Doubles 160AS per person. Quads 140AS per person. Showers 10AS per 6min. Breakfast 15-40AS. Lockers 10AS. Stylish sheetsacks 20AS.

Jugendgästehaus Salzburg (HI), Josef-Preis-Allee 18 (tel. 842 67 00 or 84 68 57, fax 84 11 01). Take bus 5, 51, or 55: Justizgebäude. Sunny, spacious rooms. Often overrun with school groups. Reception open sporadically between 7am and midnight. No lockout. Curfew midnight. 130AS. Doubles with shower 225AS per person. Quads 177AS per person. Shower, breakfast, and sheets included. *Sound of Music* tour 230AS. Reservations by mail, fax, or HI network booking. Wheelchair access.

Haunspergstraße (HI), Haunspergstr. 27 (tel. 87 50 30). From Kaiserschützenstr., which becomes Jahnstr., turn left to Haunspergstr. Reception open 7am-2pm and 5pm-midnight, but fills by late afternoon. Curfew midnight. 135AS per person in doubles, triples, and quads. Sheets and breakfast included. Wash 25AS, dry 25AS. Members only. Open July-Aug.

Glockengasse (HI), Glockengasse 8 (tel. 87 62 41, fax 876 24 13). From station walk down Gabelsbergerstr., turn right on Bayerhamerstr. to the foot of the Kapuzinerberg (mountain). A labyrinth of dorms with few showers. Reception open 7-9am and 3:30pm-midnight. Lockout 9am-3:30pm. Curfew midnight. First night 115AS, 105AS after. Showers, breakfast, and sheets included. Lockers 100AS deposit. Open April-Sept.

Eduard-Heinrich-Haus (HI), Eduard-Heinrich-Str. 2 (tel. 62 59 76, fax 62 79 80). Clean, modern facilities, but a bit out of the way. Take bus 51 "Alpensiedlung Süd" to Polizeidirektion. Walk down Billrothstr., turn left on Robert Stolz Promenade. Reception open 7-9am and 5-11pm. Lockout 9am-5pm. Curfew 11pm. Dorms 135AS. Showers and lockers included. Breakfast 7-8am.

Aigen (HI), Aignerstr. 34 (tel. 6 232 48, fax 232 48 13). Take bus 5 from the station to Mozartsteg, then bus 49 to Finanzamt and walk 10min. Enormous 6-bed rooms with jungle-like potted plants. Reception open 7-9am and 5-11pm. Curfew 11pm. 145 AS, nonmembers 175 AS. Breakfast, showers and sheets included.

Haus Lindner, Kasern Berg 64 (tel. 45 66 81 or 45 67 73). 30 private beds in three separate houses, all sharing a breakfast room in Haus Lindner. Delicious all-you-can-eat breakfasts. No singles. 150-180AS per person in doubles, triples, and quads. Showers included.

Haus Rosemarie Seigmann, Kasern Berg 48 (tel. 500 01). Welcoming, English-speaking hostess. Stone terrace overlooks the Alps. 170-180AS per person for doubles and triples. Breakfast and showers included.

Germana Kapeller, Kasern Berg 44 (tel. 45 66 71). *Dirndl*-clad hostess oversees enchanting traditional rooms and screens *The Sound of Music* daily. 160-180AS per person, or quads 600AS. Showers and complete breakfast included.

Haus Moser, Kasern Berg 59 (tel. 45 66 76), above Haus Rosemarie Seigmann. Dark-timbered home with spacious rooms. 160-180AS per person for singles, doubles, triples, and quads. Fortifying breakfast and shower included.

Haus Ballwein, Moostr. 69 (tel. 82 40 29). Take bus 60 which stops directly in front of the pension. Relaxing rural reprieve from the bustle of city tourism. 200AS per person for rooms with hall showers, 240AS with private shower.

Haus Kernstock, Karolingerstr. 29 (tel. 82 74 69). Bus 77 to Karolingerstr. Friendly hostess, commodious rooms, and an ample breakfast. 220-250AS per person for doubles, triples, and quads, including.

Hotel Merian, Merianstr. 40 (tel. 87 006-11; fax 22 12 915). Exit the station from the staircase on Platform 13 (not out the front door). Turn right on the footbridge, then right again onto Lastenstr. Marianstr. is the first left. Noisy (directly behind the train station), but ideal locale. A dorm during the year, and open to travelers July-Sept. Mostly narrow single bedrooms off a corridor with common shower and toilet. Singles 240AS. Doubles 370AS. Breakfast included.

Haus Elisabeth, Rauchenbichlerstr. 18 (tel. 507 03). Take bus 51 to Itzling-Pflanzmann, walk up Rauchenbichlerstr. over the footbridge, and continue right along the gravel path. Amazing rooms with great views of the city. Singles with shower 300AS. Doubles 260AS per person. Breakfast included.

Camping Stadtblick, Rauchenbichlerstr. 21 (tel. 506 52), next to Haus Elisabeth. Sweeping view of the city. Reception open 7:30am-10pm. 60AS per person, 15AS per tent, 15AS per car, 80AS for a bed in a tent.

Camping Nord-Sam, Samstr. 22-A (tel. 66 04 94). Take bus 33 "Obergnigl" to Langmoosweg. Shady, flower-bedecked campsites, and a small swimming pool. Laundry 75AS. 50AS per person, 95AS per site; April to mid-June and Sept.-Oct. 40AS per person, 76AS per site.

FOOD

Blessed with fantastic **beer gardens** and innumerable **Konditoreien** (pastry shops), Salzburg begs its guests to eat outdoors. The Salzburger *Nockerl* is the local specialty—a large soufflé of eggs, sugar and raspberry filling, baked into three mounds representing the three hills of Salzburg. *Knoblauchsuppe*—creamy soup loaded with croutons and pungent garlic—shouldn't daunt the confident. **Hofer,** at Schallmooser Hauptstr. and Franz-Josef-Str., is a discount supermarket (open Mon.-Fri. 8am-6pm, Sat. 8am-noon). **Konsum** and **SPAR** are widespread and can be found in the Getreidegasse and Mirabellplatz. Look for **open-air markets** held Mon.-Fri. 6am-7pm, Sat. 6am-1pm in Universitätsplatz in the *Altstadt*. Fresh *semmel* (rolls), stuffed with tomatoes, cheese, *wurst,* and leafy greens are particularly filling.

Humboldt-Stuben, Gstättengasse 6 (tel 84 31 71). Giant hamburgers and cheeseburgers for 39AS. Other hot entrees under 60AS. Over 20 vegetarian salad offerings. Located right under the Mönchberg elevator. Open 10am-2am.

Shakespeare, Hubert Sattlergasse 3, off Mirabellplatz (tel. 87 91 06). Sit around with university students and partake in intellectual discourse. Sip white-wine or cocktail. Try a *galette,* a pancake-like wrapper filled with cheese, ham, fried egg, or just about anything else for 23-36AS. Doubles as a bar. Open 10am-1am.

Restaurant Zur Bürgerwehr-Einkehr, Mönchberg 19c (tel. 84 17 29). From the Mönchberg elevator at Anton Newmayer Platz, go up to Café Winkler and follow the signs. The best view in town of Salzburg and the Festung. Entrees 65-110AS. Try the Fitnessmeal, a light salad topped with chicken breast filet. Open May to Oct., Tues.-Thurs. 11am-9:30pm; Oct. to May Thurs.-Tues. 10:30am-8pm.

Der Wilder Mann, Getreidegasse 20 in the passage (tel. 84 17 87). Huge portions of *wiener schnitzel*, potatoes, and *Stiegl Bier*. Entrees 70-120AS and worth every groschen. Pleasantly less-touristed than nearby bistros. Open 11am-9pm.

University Mensa, Sigmund Haffnergasse 6 (tel. 24 1 39), in the *Altstadt*, inside the courtyard of the law school. Three hot dishes available. Menu I (28AS) is forgettable. Go for Menu II (39AS) or III (55AS). Vegetarian meal 39AS. Read menus carefully so you don't choose extras. Desserts and drinks not included. Open Mon.-Fri. 11:30am-2pm. Student ID required. ISIC accepted.

Fischmarkt, at Hanuschplatz on the *Altstadt* side of the river. Two mammoth trees reach through the roof. Partake in the pleasures of imported Danish seafood. Very casual and very crowded. *Fischbrötchen* 16-25AS, beer 20AS. Open Mon.-Fri. 9am-6pm, Sat. 9am-12:30pm.

Vegy, Schwarzstr. 33 (tel. 87 57 46). A Harley in a garage of cars. Pricey, but a rarity in this sausage-filled city. A vegetarian Shangri-La. Grab some asparagus soup and spinach pancakes. Health shakes at the bar. Open Mon.-Fri. 10:30am-6pm.

SIGHTS

Salzburg sprang up under the protective watch of the hilltop fortress **Hohensalzburg,** built atop the imposing *Mönchberg* between the 11th and 17th centuries by the ruling archbishops. The first-rate tours (15AS) wind through medieval torture chambers and the castle's impressive staterooms and pregnate its impregnable watchtower. (Fortress open 8am-7pm; Oct.-May 8am-6pm. 50-min. tours daily 9am-5:30pm; April-June and Sept.-Oct. 9:30am-5pm; Nov.-March 10am-4:30pm. 30AS, ages 16-19 20AS; seniors 30AS.) **The Rainer Museum,** inside the fortress, displays more medieval weapons and instruments of torture. (Open May-Oct. Free with tour. Otherwise 30AS, students and children 15AS.) The cable car from Festungsgasse to the fortress runs every 10min. (22AS, round-trip 32AS).

At the bottom of the Festungsbahn is **Kapitelplatz,** housing a giant chess grid and horse-bath fountain. Standing at the chess grid, the entrance to **St. Peter's Monastery,** through the cemetery, is at the back right corner. The cemetery, **Petersfriedhof,** is one of the most peaceful places in Salzburg and is best known as the spot where Liesl's Nazi boyfriend Rolf blew the whistle on the von Trapp family in *The Sound of Music* (open 9am-8pm, Sept.-May 10am-7pm). On the left side of the cemetery is the entrance to the **Katakomben** (catacombs), where Christians allegedly worshipped as early as 250AD. The guided tours drones for half an hour. (Tours in English and German May-Sept. 10am-5pm; Oct.-April 11am-noon and 1:30-3:30pm every hour. 12AS, students 8AS.) Exit the cemetery down the little path in the opposite corner from the entrance off Kapitelplatz, to the courtyard in front of the church. **St. Peter's Church** itself, once a stoic collegiate church, received a Rococo face-lift in the 18th century. (Open 9am-12:15pm and 2:30-6:30pm.)

Wolfgang Amadeus Mozart was unleashed upon the world from what is now called **Mozarts Geburtshaus** (birthplace) at Getreidegasse 9. The street itself is worth a look; the guild signs and painted walls remain as they were when the composer was just a tyke. The house exhibits pictures, letters, stage sets for Mozart's operas, and the Hammerklavier on which he composed *The Magic Flute*. (Open 9am-7pm; Sept.-March 9am-6pm. 60AS, students and seniors 45AS.) Mozart's **Wohnhaus** (residence), Marktplatz 8, suffered major damage in WWII air raids, but has periodically undergone renovations; unfortunately, it is not scheduled to reopen until January 1996.

Turn right at the Alter Markt and venture down to Residenzplatz where you'll find Archbishop Wolf Dietrich's palace, the **Residenz,** Residenzpl. 1, which features baroque staterooms and a gallery filled with works by Rembrandt, Rubens, Brueghel, and Titian (gallery open 10am-5pm. 40AS, students and seniors 30AS, under 15 free). Mozart was christened in the adjacent baroque **Dom** in 1756 and later worked here as *Konzertmeister* and court organist. The connecting **Dom Museum** holds the **Kunst- und Wunderkammer** (art and miracles chamber), which includes conch shells, mineral formations, and a 2-ft. whale's tooth. (Open May to mid-Oct. Mon.-Sat. 10am-5pm, Sun. 11am-5pm. 30AS, ages 16-18 10AS, ages 6-15 5AS.)

Cross the river on the *Staatsbrücke* into the *Neustadt* (new city). It is the only bridge from the *Altstadt* over the Salzach open to motorized traffic; in the new city, the bridge opens into **Linzer Gasse,** an enchanting, less-touristed medieval street. Ascend the stairs from under the stone arch on the right side of Linzer Gasse 14 to the **Kapuzinerkloster** (Capuchin Monastery), built in the late 16th century. The etymology of the word *cappuccino* lies in the resemblance of coffee topped with steamed milk to the trademark brown robes and white hoods of the resident monks.

Continue up this street to Mirabellplatz to discover the marvelous **Schloß Mirabell.** Archbishop Wolf Dietrich built this rosy-hued wonder in 1606 for his mistress Salome Alt and their ten children, christening it "Altenau" in her honor. Unfortunately, the only way to catch a glimpse of the gorgeous interior is by attending one of the concerts held there. Next to the palace, the delicately manicured **Mirabellgarten** includes extravagant rose beds, labyrinths of groomed shrubs, and 15 grotesque marble likenesses of Wolf Dietrich's court jesters. Often students from the nearby Mozarteum will perform here. Maria also made this one of her stops in *The Sound of Music* as the children danced around and sang "do-re-mi."

In 1964, Julie Andrews, Christopher Plummer, and a gaggle of 20th-Century Fox crew members arrived in Salzburg to film **The Sound of Music,** based on the true story of the von Trapp family. Salzburg hasn't hesitated to cash in on the celluloid notoriety. **Salzburg Sightseeing Tours** (tel. 88 16 16, fax 88 21 20) traces the movie through the city. They reduce the 300AS price to 250AS for students. Non-students using *Let's Go* get a 10%. Just bring the guide with you when you "book" the tour (the discount is only for the Sound of Music Tour).

ENTERTAINMENT

The renowned **Salzburger Festspiele** (Summer Music Festivals) run from late July to the beginning of September. In the month of festivities, almost every public space is overrun with operas, dramas, films, concerts, and tourists. The complete program of events is printed a year in advance (10AS) and available from any tourist office. Inside are all crucial concert locations and dates. For the best seats, requests must be made in person or by mail months in advance. Remaining tickets are distributed to ticketing agencies, who sell them at 30-40% mark-ups. To place orders, write to Kartenbüro der Salzburger Festspiele, A-5010 Salzburg, Postfach 140, fax 84 66 82. Operas run upwards of 1000AS and theater tickets can be 400AS. At **Salzburger Marionettentheater,** Schwarzstr. 24, a lighthearted show is accompanied by tapes of past festival opera performances (tickets 250-400AS).

For a particularly enchanting atmosphere, attend one of the **Festungskonzerte** (Fortress Concerts) up in the ornate Fürstenzimmer (Prince's chamber) and Goldener Saal (Golden Hall) in the Fortress. There is a concert nightly (270AS). For more info contact: Festungkonzerte Anton-Adlgasserweg 22, A-5020 Salzburg (tel. 82 58 58, fax 82 58 59; open 9am-9pm). For those without the foresight to plan ahead of time, the day before the first day of performances is an **Eröffnungsfest** (opening celebration), usually around July 24-26. On this day, cheap, cheap, cheap tickets are sold for many of the final dress rehearsals of various operas, concerts, and plays. These can be bought the same day from the cashier at the Festspielhaus. Some events exclude people over 26 from buying tickets. These tickets vary, but usually hover around 50AS. Stop by the Festspielhaus to see exactly what is available for the opening celebration. In addition, there is a lot going on for free in the Residenzplatz. Traditional folksingers begin performing at 8pm and at 10pm.

Salzburg prides itself on the charm of its **beer gardens,** many of which often serves generous portions of food. They do, however, tend to close early. For those who want to tipple later, simply head to one of the more conventional bars.

Stieglkeller, Festungsgasse 10, off Kapitelplatz near the Festungsbahn (tel. 84 26 81). Host of the local Stiegl beer. Good beer on tap, reasonably-priced food. Perched half-way up the mountain on the way to the Festung, this garden has a fantastic view of the roofs and spires of the *Altstadt*. Open 11:30am-9:30pm.

Sternbräu, Getreidegasse 23 (tel. 84 21 40). Formally a place where beer was brewed, it's now just a place to drink and eat in mass quantities. Located in the *Altstadt*, has two beer gardens, a restaurant and a snack bar with sausages and smaller meals. Get there by ducking into any number of passages at the end of Getreidegasse. All these bars are located in corridors of the "mall". Open 8-11pm.

Augustiner Bräu, Augustinergasse 4 (tel. 43 12 46). Take buses 27, 49, 60, 80, and 95 to Bärenwirt. Salzburg's most legendary garden. Great beer brewed by the Müllner Kloster, poured into massive steins from even more massive wooden kegs. Reasonably priced snacks available to placate grumbling stomachs. The brewery is inside the kloster building with the big tower. Open 3-11pm.

Pub Passage, Rudolfskai 22, right under the Radisson Hotel by Mozartssteg. A shopping promenade of sorts for clubbing. Come here to bar hop. **Speedy Bar** has a Mexican theme, **Tom's Bierklinik** brags beers from all over the country, **The Black Lemon** has Latino night every Wed. and carries 15 varieties of whisky, **Bräu zu frommen Hell** is a bastion of 80s music, with lots of beer and young people, and **Vis A Vis** is for the more Euro-artistic types.

Pepe Gonzales, Steingasse 5. Cool western interior. Order beer, cocktails, or margaritas to go with your order of chips and salsa or tacos. Open 5:30pm-3am.

■ HALLEIN

The tremendous wealth provided by the **Salzbergwerke** (salt mines) around the Salzkammergut long buttressed the ruling bishops' political hegemony. The closest mines, at **Bad Dürrnberg** near Hallein, are quite an experience. On the 90min. tour, don traditional miner's clothes, slide down passages in the dark, take a miniature train ride, and ride a raft on the salt lakes. The Salzbergbahn cable car ride to the entrance provides an outstanding view. (Open April-Oct. 9am-5pm. 230AS, students 200AS, under 15 115AS. Includes round-trip cable car, tour, and museum. For more info, call (06245) 852 85 15.) You can reach the mines at Bad Dürrnberg by bus (from Salzburg's train station, take bus 3083 or 3081; 45min., 34AS) or rail (20min., 34AS, round-trip 53AS). The cable car will then take you from Salzbergbahn Parkplatz on Dr.-Viktor-Zatloukal-Str. From the train station, walk straight down Bahnhofstr., turn right at the intersection, and cross the Salzach via the Staatsbrücke. Then walk straight down to Bayrhamer Platz, bear left on Raitenaustr., and turn left on Gampertorplatz.

■ LUSTSCHLOß HELLBRUNN

Just south of Salzburg lies the unforgettable **Lustschloß Hellbrunn,** a one-time pleasure palace for Wolf Dietrich's nephew, the Archbishop Markus Sittikus. The neighboring **Wasserspielen** (Water Gardens) are perennial favorites; Markus amused himself with elaborate water-powered figurines and a booby-trapped table, which could spout water on his drunken guests. Prepare yourself for an afternoon of wet surprises. (Open July-Aug. 9am-10pm; May-June and Sept. 9am-5pm; April and Oct. 9am-4:30pm. 48 AS, students 24 AS.) The **Steintheater,** on the palace grounds, is the oldest natural theater north of the Alps. To reach the palatial grounds, take bus 55 "Anif" from the train station or Mozartsteg to Hellbrunn, or bike 40min. down Hellbrunner Allee, a beautiful tree-lined path.

■ ■ ■ SALZKAMMERGUT

East of Salzburg, the landscape swells into towering mountains pockmarked by frigid, unfathomably deep lakes. The Salzkammergut is named for the abandoned salt mines which, in their glory days, underwrote Salzburg's architectural treasures.

AUSTRIA

Transportation and Accommodations The Vienna-Salzburg rail line skirts the northern edge of the Salzkammergut. At Attnang-Puchheim, 50km east of Salzburg, a spur line begins its way south through Gmünden, Ebensee, Bad Ischl, Obertraun, and Bad Aussee to Steinbach. If you're traveling by bus or have your own wheels, you can enter directly from Salzburg along Highway 158. Within the region there is a dense network of **buses;** most run 4-12 times per day. Ask at the Salzburg kiosk for a comprehensive schedule, or call for info: Salzburg tel. (0662) 167, St. Gilgen tel. (06227) 425, and Bad Aussee tel. (06152) 20 50. The pamphlet *Wandern mit dem Postbus,* available at the main bus stations in these towns, details hikes that coincide with the bus network. The **Salzkammergut Ticket** is valid for unlimited travel on all trains and buses in the Salzkammergut region (3 days travel in 10-day period 220AS). **Hitchers** from Salzburg reportedly take bus 29 to Gnigl and come into the Salzkammergut at Bad Ischl. The lake district itself is known as one of the rare Austrian regions in which hitchhikers make good time. Most train stations in the region rent **bikes.** Reasonably priced **ferries** serve each of the larger lakes. The **Wolfgangsee** line is operated by the Austrian railroad, so railpasses get you free passage; on the **Attersee** and **Traunsee** lines, Eurailers receive a discount.

Hostels abound, though you can often find far superior rooms in private homes and *pensionen* at just-above-hostel prices. **Campgrounds** dot the region, but many are trailer-oriented; away from large towns, some travelers camp discreetly almost anywhere without trouble. Hikers can capitalize on dozens of **cable cars** in the area to gain altitude before setting out on their own, and almost every community has a local trail map publicly posted or available at the tourist office. At higher elevations there are **alpine huts** leased through the **Österreichischer Alpenverein,** which supplies mountain information of all sorts; the number in Linz is (tel. (0732) 77 32 95).

St. Gilgen Erstwhile hometown of Mozart's mother and sister, **St. Gilgen** in the western Salzkammergut lies at the foot of **Mt. Zwölferhorn** (1520m); in summer, it avails itself for hiking, and at the top has a spell-binding panorama of the entire region. (Cable car round-trip 180AS, 160AS with guest card. One way 120AS, 110AS with guest card.) The **tourist office** tel. (06227) 348 or 72 67, fax 726 79), in the *Rathaus,* details alternative budget accommodations. (Open Mon.-Fri. 9am-noon and 2-6pm, Sat. 9am-noon, Sun. 10am-noon; Sept.-June Mon.-Fri. 9am-noon and 2-5pm.) The **Haus Schafbergblick (HI),** Mondseestr. 7 (tel. (06227) 365), is positively luxurious, with dreamy, lakeside rooms and balconies. (Reception open 8-9am and 5-7pm. No lockout. Curfew 11pm. Dorms 100AS. Singles 180-240AS. Doubles 300-380AS per person. Triples 420-510AS. Quads 480-600AS.) **Camping Wolfgangblick,** Staudachwaldstr. 24 (tel. (06138) 24 75), and **Camping Lindenstrand,** Gschwand 36 (tel. (05342) 72 05), both offer peaceful shore locations, warm showers, and food. (Wolfgangblick 45AS per person, under 14 25AS, 25AS per tent or car. Lindenstrand 45AS per person, under 15 25AS, 50-65AS per site. Showers 10AS for 6min.) For good, cheap local cuisine in a surprisingly modern interior, try **Gasthof Rosam,** Fronfestgasse 2-4 (tel. 591). Sample omelettes for 56AS, light entrees for 54AS, and large *wiener schnitzel* for 90AS.

Hallstatt In a valley surrounded on all sides by the sheer rocky cliffs of the Dachstein mountains, **Hallstatt** is, in the words of Alex V. Humboldt, "the most beautiful lakeside village in the world." In the 19th century, Hallstatt was the site of one of the largest Iron Age archeological finds in history. Depending on one's point of view, a visit to St. Michael's Chapel at the **Pfarrkirche** is macabre, poignant or intrusive; next to the chapel is the parish "charnel house"—a bizarre repository for sundry skeletons. (Open May-Sept. 10am-6pm. To visit in winter, call the church at (06134) 82 79 for an appointment. 10AS.) The 2500-year-old **Salzbergwerke** is the oldest saltworks in the world still in operation. (Open June to mid-Sept. 9:30am-4:30pm; May and mid-Sept. to mid-Oct. 9:30am-3pm. 130AS, with guest card 115AS, students 60AS.) To reach the mines, take the **Salzberg Tram**—just follow the yellow eyes to the bottom of the train station (9am-6pm; Oct.-April 9am-4:30pm; 55AS,

AUSTRIA

with guest card 45AS, students 35AS; round-trip 95AS, 80AS, and 50AS, respectively). For outdoor activities, take a long walk to the **Glacier Gardens.** Located in Echnertal, it takes about an hour from the salt mines on foot (no other transportation is available).

The Hallstatt **tourist office** (tel. (06134) 82 08, fax 83 52), in the **Kultur und Kongresshaus,** off Seestr., finds cheap rooms for no fee (open Mon.-Fri. 9am-5pm, Sat.-Sun10am-2pm; Sept.-May Mon.-Fri. 9am-noon and 1-5pm). If you arrive by **train,** alight at the Hallstatt Bahnhof, across the lake from the village itself. To escape the town by rail, ferries depart roughly ½hr. before the train. The **hostel (Jugendherberge, HI)** at Salzbergstr. 50 (tel. (06134) 82 12), 10min. from the town center, offers basic, inexpensive lodgings in a tidy, flower-bedecked house. (Reception open 6-9pm. Lockout 10am-6pm. Curfew 9pm. 90AS. Open May-Sept.) **TVN Naturfreundeherberge,** Kirchenweg 36 (tel. (06134) 83 18), also called *Gasthaus Zur Mühle,* is a quasi-hostel with cheap 3- to 8-bed rooms. (Reception open 8am-2am and 4-10pm. 100AS.) *Privatzimmer* at just-above-hostel-prices speckle the town. **Frühstuckspension Sarstein** (tel. (06134) 82 17) offers the prettiest accommodations in town, luring visitors with homey rooms, wonderful vistas of the lake and village, a beachside lawn for sunning and swimming, and a TV (180-200AS; hall showers 10AS; breakfast included).

Dachstein Ice Caves At the other end of the lake in Obertraun, the prodigious Dachstein Ice Caves, though marred by cheesy names like "Cave Venus" and "Hall of Oblivion," give eloquent testimony to the geological hyperactivity that forged the region's natural beauty. (Open May to mid-Oct. 9am-5pm. To Giant Ice Cave 76AS, to Mammoth Cave 70AS, combined 106AS.) From Hallstatt, take the boat to Obertraun (35AS) and ride the Dachstein cable car up 1350m to Schönbergalm (round-trip 150AS, with guest card 135AS). For info on the caves, call (06131) 362.

■■■ KITZBÜHEL

Kitzbühel (or "Kitz" as witty tourist officials have tried to popularize as a nickname) is a cross between glitzy St. Moritz and gaudy Atlantic City—wealthy visitors pump enough cash into the local casinos to keep the cobblestone streets in good repair and the sidewalk cafés flourishing. At night, affluent international playchildren gather in Kitzbühel's tiny pubs to squander inherited money on drink and debauchery in this land of Visa and EuroCard.

An extensive network of hiking trails snakes up the surrounding mountains. To reach some of the lower trails and meadow walks, ride the **Hahnenkammbahn** to reach some of the loftier paths (150AS, with guest card 130AS; children 75AS). Or climb up yourself; the descent is free on all area cable cars. The **Kitzbüheler Hornbahn** cable cars will take you up to the **Alpenblumengarten,** where over 120 different types of Alpine flowers blossom each season. (Open late May to mid-Oct.; each of 2 sections of the cable car 65AS.) Guest-card holders can take advantage of the tourist office's *wunderbar* free mountain hiking program. Guided hikes begin June to mid-Oct. at 9am at the office (2½-6hr.; free). The Kitzbühel **ski area** is simply one of the world's best; 64 lifts and shuttle buses are yours with a 1-day ski pass (320-340A, under 15 ½-price). Downhill ski rental runs 95-140AS per day, and lessons cost 340AS per day. For a **snow report** (in German), call (05356) 181 or 182.

Practical Information, Accommodations, and Food Tiny Kitzbühel has 2 **train stations,** one at either side of the "U" formed by the rail tracks. From Salzburg, you arrive first at **Hauptbahnhof;** from Innsbruck or Wörgl, at **Hahnenkamm.** From there, go left, turn right at the end of the street, and walk toward the shops. When you reach the *Fußgängerzone,* turn right to see the **tourist office,** Hinterstadt 18 (tel. (05356) 22 72 or 21 55, fax 23 07). The office doesn't make reservations; use the free phone at the electronic accommodations board outside. (Open June 20-Oct. 2 Mon.-Fri. 8:30am-7pm, Sat. 8am-noon and 4-8pm, Sun. 10am-

8pm; Christmas-Easter Mon.-Sat. 8am-8pm, Sun. 10:30am-4pm; April 5-19 and Oct. 3-Christmas Mon.-Fri. 8:30am-noon and 3-6pm, Sat. 8:30am-noon. Accommodations board open 6am-10pm.) Opposite the tourist office, **Reisebüro Eurotours** exchanges money. (Open Mon.-Fri. 8:30am-noon and 3-6:30pm, Sat. 8:30am-noon and 4:30-6:30pm, Sun. and holidays 10am-noon and 4:30-6:30pm.)

Kitzbühel has more guest beds (10,000) than inhabitants (8070), but you'll pay for the convenience; the only youth hostel is far from town and restricted to groups. Call the **Gasthof Alpenhof,** Aurach 176 (tel. (05356) 45 07), 3km outside Kitzbühel, and they'll pick you up at the rail station. The Australian, New Zealander, and Brit staff creates an English-speaker's paradise in the Austrian heartland. (150-200AS. Open mid-Nov. to Dec. 20.) To get to **Camping Schwarzsee,** take the train to Schwarzsee (just before Hahnenkamm), and flit toward the lake. (July 1-Aug. 15 75AS per person; off-season 68AS). Grocery shoppers can hit the **SPAR Markt** on Bichlstr. (Open Mon.-Fri. 8am-6:30pm, Sat. 8:30am-1pm.)

■■■ INNSBRUCK

Thrust into the international limelight by the Winter Olympics of 1964 and 1976, the ancient capital of the Tyrol is lined with Baroque façades, over-laden with rose bushes, and ringed by snow-capped mountains. More than 150 cable cars and chair-lifts and an extensive network of mountain paths radiate from Innsbruck, making the Alps surrounding the city accessible to winter skiers and summer hikers alike.

ORIENTATION AND PRACTICAL INFORMATION

Because of Innsbruck's compact size, nearly any two points lie within easy walking distance of each other, and public transportation, though available, is largely unnecessary. To reach the *Altstadt* from the main train station, turn right and walk until you reach Museumstr., then turn left and walk about 10min. Or take trams 1 or 3, or city bus K or O from the train station to Maria-Theresien-Str. You can join **Club Innsbruck** (summer 310AS; winter 280AS) at no charge if you register at any central-Innsbruck accommodation for at least 3 nights, and membership has privileges: you get cable car and museum discounts, free bike tours, and the option of participating in the club's fine hiking program (June-Sept.; ask at the tourist office or where you're staying).

Tourist Office: Innsbruck-Information, Burggraben 3 (tel. 53 56; fax 53 56 43), on the edge of the *Altstadt,* just off the end of Museumstr. Arrange tours and concert tickets, but don't count on budget accommodations. Staff helps bewildered tourists with quick questions. Open 8am-7pm. **Tirol Information Office,** Wilhelm-Greil-Str. 17 (tel. 532 01 70, fax 532 01 50). Specializes in providing accommodations listings and information on attractions and schedules. Open Mon.-Fri. 8:30am-6pm, Sat. 9am-noon.

Currency Exchange: Best rates at main post office and its main train station branch. Open 7:30am-noon, 12:45-6pm, and 6:30-8pm. Innsbruck's banks are open Mon.-Fri. 7:45am-12:30pm and 2:15-4pm.

American Express: Brixnerstr. 3 (tel. 58 24 91), in front of the main train station. Mail held. All banking services. Open Mon.-Fri. 9am-5:30pm, Sat. 9am-noon.

Post Office: Maximilianstr. 2, down from the Triumph Arch. Open 24hrs. Poste Restante. Branch next to the train station. Open Mon.-Sat. 8am-9pm, Sun. 9am-noon. **Postal Code:** A-6020.

Telephones: Atthe post office. **City Code:** 0512.

Trains: Hauptbahnhof, Südtiroler Pl. (tel. 17 17), a 10min. walk down Museumstr. from the *Altstadt.* Buses J, K, O, 4, and S take you there. Lockers, luggage storage, bike rental, and showers.

Buses: Post buses leave for all areas of Tyrol from the station on Sterzinger Str., adjacent to the *Hauptbahnhof.* Open Mon.-Fri. 7am-5:30pm, Sat. 7am-1pm. For information, contact the *Postautodienst,* Maximilianstr. 23 (tel. 57 66 00).

Bike Rental: At the main train station. 90AS per day, 50AS per day with Eurailpass. Open April to early Nov. 9am-11pm.

Ski Rental: Skischule Innsbruck, Leopoldstr. 4 (tel. (05222) 58 23 10). 250AS including insurance.

Hitchhiking: Hitchers go to the Shell gas station by the DEZ store off Geyrstr. near Amras; bus K delivers to Geyrstr. Most cars leaving Innsbruck take this exit.

Laundromat: Waltraud Hell, Amraserstr. 15, behind the station. Wash and dry 95-106AS. Open Mon.-Fri. 8am-6pm.

Medical Assistance: University Hospital, Anichstr. 35 (tel. 50 40).

Emergencies: Ambulance: tel. 144 or 26 77 55. **Fire:** tel. 122. **Police:** tel. 133. Headquarters at Kaiserjägerstr. 8 (tel. 590 00).

ACCOMMODATIONS AND CAMPING

Beds are scarce during June, when only three hostels are open. In July, university housing opens up to travelers, making lodgings somewhat easier to find.

Jugendherberge Innsbruck (HI), Reichenauer Str. 147 (tel. 461 79 or 461 80). Bus O: Rossbachstr. Often crowded with Americans, but they'll honor phone reservations as long as you show up by 5pm. 4- to 6-bed dorms. Reception open 5-8pm. English spoken. Lockout 10am-5pm. Curfew 11pm. Kitchen and laundry (45AS including soap), but notify the desk by 5pm if you intend to do laundry. Members 130AS, non-members 170AS. Breakfast (7-8am) and sheets included.

Jugendheim St. Paulus (HI), Reichenauerstr. 72 (tel. 442 91). Bus R: Pauluskirche. 50 beds and trough-like bathroom sinks. But, comfortable lounge, kitchen facilities, helpful staff, and the cheapest beds in town. 3-night max. stay. Open mid-June to mid-Aug. Reception 7-10am and 5-10pm. Lockout 10am-5pm. Curfew 10pm, but leave passport for a key. Doors locked until 7am. 95AS per person. Breakfast 25AS. Sheets 20AS. Showers included.

Jugendherberge St. Nikolaus (HI), Innstr. 95 (tel. 28 65 15, fax 28 65 15 14). Walk across the river from the *Altstadt* along Rennweg to Innstr., or take bus K: St. Nickolaus. Clean rooms and a party-hearty, English-speaking crowd. Reception open 9-11am and 5-8pm. No curfew or lockout; Eurail ticket, passport or 200AS deposit required for key. Silence after 10pm. Checkout 9am. Members 115AS first night, 100AS subsequent nights. Nonmembers 145AS first night, then 130AS. Sheets included. Shower 10AS. Breakfast 15-75AS.

Hostel Torsten Arneus-Schwedenhaus (HI), Rennweg 17b (tel. 58 58 14, fax 585 81 44), along the river. Bus C: Handelsakademie. Convenient location and a front-yard view of the Inn River. Open July and August. Reception open 5-10 pm. Lockout 9am-5pm. Curfew 10 pm. Breakfast 45AS. Sheets 20AS. 100AS per person per night. Written reservations recommended.

Jugendherberge MK (HI), Sillgasse 8a (tel. 57 13 11). From the station, walk up Museumstr., and take your first right onto Sillgasse. A funky place with friendly management, a café next door, and a basketball court on the 3rd floor. Open July-Sept. 15. Reception open 7-9am and 4-11pm. Lockout 9am-4pm. Curfew 11pm. 130AS, non-members 140AS. Sheets 10AS. Breakfast and showers included.

Internationales Studentenhaus, Rechengasse 7 (tel. 501). Bus B: Innsbruck Universität Bibliotek and turn right on Rechengasse. Modern 560-bed dorm with English-speaking staff. Parking nearby. Open July-Sept. Reception open 24hrs. Singles 290-360AS. Doubles 480-320AS. Students with ID 120AS. All-you-can-eat buffet breakfast 40AS. Laundry 20AS per wash, dry free.

Haus Wolf, Dorfstr. 48 (tel. 58 40 88), in the suburb of Mutters. Take the Stubaitalbahn (STB) to "Birchfeld," and walk down Dorfstr. There's no place like home, but this comes close. And eat, eat, eat at breakfast. Singles, doubles, and triples 180AS per person. Breakfast and shower included.

Haus Rimml, Harterhofweg 82 (tel. 28 47 26), a 20min. bus ride from the train station. Follow directions to Camping Innsbruck Kranebitten below. Consummately comfortable—private showers, TV room, and large singles. Jolly owners have breakfast waiting for you. 300AS per person. Breakfast included. Call ahead.

Pension Paula, Weiherburggasse 15 (tel. 29 22 62). Satisfied guests frequently return to this inn-like home down the hill from the Alpenzoo. Take bus K from the Hauptbahnhof to "St. Nikolaus," and then walk uphill. Singles 200-400AS. Doubles 480-620AS. Breakfast included. Reservations strongly recommended.

Camping Innsbruck Kranebitten, Kranebitten Allee 214 (tel. 28 41 80). Bus LK from Boznerpl. to Klammstr. Follow the signs to the camping area. Or, switch to LK from bus O at Lohbachsiedlung West. Reception open 7am-8pm. 61AS per person, children under 15 55AS. Tent 35AS. Car 35AS.

FOOD

Most tourists first glimpse cosmopolitan Innsbruck from the glamour of **Maria-Theresienstr.;** rather than gawk at overpriced delis, however, escape the over-touristed *Altstadt* and cross the river to the university district. An indoor **market** is in the *Markthalle,* behind the *Altstadt* (open Mon.-Fri. 7am-6 ;30pm, Sat. 7am-1pm).

Philippine Vegetarische Küche, Müllerstr. 9, (tel. 58 91 57), a block from the post office. A vegetarian rest stop on a highway of meat. Entrees 60-100AS. Mid-day specials include soup, entree, dessert 120AS. Open Mon.-Sat. 10am-midnight.

Al Dente, Meranestr. 7 (tel. 58 49 47). Although quarters are cramped, the food and its aroma more than make up for it. After finishing your entree (78-106AS), polish your meal off with yummy *tiramisú* (46AS). Plenty of vegetarian options. English menus. Open Mon.-Sat. 7am-11pm, Sun. and holidays 11am-11pm.

Crocodiles, Maria-Theresienstr. 49 (tel.58 88 56). 33 different pizza, all baked in an old-fashioned brick oven. English menus available. Small pizzas 55-65AS, large 75-85AS. Open Mon.-Fri. 11am-10pm, Sat. 11am-2pm.

Gasthof Weißes Lamm, Mariahilfstr. 12 (tel. 28 31 56). Home-style, Tirolian restaurant, popular with local crowd. 100AS can go a long way with their heaping portions and special menus which serve soups, entree and salad for 80-135AS. Open Mon.-Wed., Fri.-Sun. noon- 2pm and 6-10pm.

China-Restaurant Asia, Angerzellgasse 10 (tel. 58 08 01). Traditional Chinese dishes like house Crispy Duck (115AS) in the heart of Austria. Other entrees 105-130AS. Open 11:30am-3pm and 6pm-midnight.

Ebi's Uni Café-Bistro, Innrain 55 (tel. 57 39 49), near Innsbruck Universität Bibliothek. Hip students sporting shades and *schwarz* contemplate existence, all over coffee and sandwiches. Entrees and salads 68-90AS. Breakfast menu; extensive beverage list. Open Mon.-Fri. 9am-1am, Sat.-Sun. noon-1am.

Wienerwald, Museumstr. 24 (tel. 58 89 94), and another branch at Maria-Theresienstr. 12 (tel. 58 41 65). *Schnitzelhaus!* Wienerwald *schnitzel* (112AS), salads (36-78AS), chicken wings (83AS). English menus. Open 10am-midnight.

University Mensa, Herzog-Siegmund-Ufer 15, 2nd fl. of new university between *Markthalle* and Blasius-Hueberstr. Student cafeteria open to public; no ID necessary. Meals 30-60AS. Open in summer 11am-1:30pm; in winter, 11am-2pm.

SIGHTS

Beneath 2657 gold shingles, the **Goldenes Dachl** (Golden Roof), on Herzog Friedrichstr., is the center of the *Altstadt* and commemorates the marriage of Habsburg couple Maximilian I and Bianca. Inside, on the mezzanine level, the **Olympia-museum** commemorates the 1964 and 1976 Winter Games with mannequins modeling Austrian ski kits, an Austrian bobsled from 1964, stamps from scores of participating countries, and a video filmed from the boots of a ski jumper. (Open 9:30am-5:30pm. Nov.-Feb. Tues.-Sun. 9:30-5:30pm. 22AS, students with ID 11AS, children 15AS). Climb the narrow stairs of the 14th-century **Stadtturm** (city tower) to soak in the panorama. Look up before you climb—on a sunny day the tower can be as crowded as a New York dance club and even harder to move around in. (Open 10am-5pm. Tower 18AS, children 9AS. Tower and Olympiamuseum 32AS, students 16AS.) The 16th-century **Goldener Adler Inn** (Golden Eagle Inn) is just to the left of the Goldenes Dachl; Goethe, Heine, and Sartre ate, drunk, and made merry here. Behind the Goldenes Dachl stands the Baroque **Dom St. Jakob** (currently under construction), with its superb *trompe l'oeil* ceiling depicting the life of St. James and an altar decorated with Lukas Cranach's *Intercession of the Virgin.*

AUSTRIA

At Rennweg and Hofgasse stand the grand **Hofburg** (Imperial Palace) and **Hofkirche** (Imperial Church). Built between the 16th and 18th centuries, the Hofburg brims with Habsburgs. (Open 9am-5pm; mid-Oct. to mid-May Mon.-Sat. 9am-4pm. 30AS, students 10AS. English guidebook 5AS.) Emperor Maximilian I wished to have the coterie stand guard over his tomb, the **Kaisergrab,** which lies in the middle of the church. A funeral cortege of sorts granted his wish: 28 mammoth bronze statues stare blankly at the sarcophagus. Dürer is responsible for the likenesses of King Arthur, Theodoric the Ostrogoth, and Count Albrecht of Habsburg. (Open 9am-5pm; Oct.-April 9am-noon and 2-5pm. 25 AS, students 14 AS.) A combi-ticket (40AS, students 25 AS) will also admit you to the collection of the **Tiroler Volkskunstmuseum** (Tirolean Handicrafts Museum) next door. Dusty implements, peasant costumes, and furnished period rooms provide a brief introduction to Tirolean culture, though the ornate wood carvings in the "Peasants' Room" are suspiciously posh. (Open Mon.-Sat. 9am-5pm; Oct.-April Mon.-Sat. 9am-noon and 2-5pm. Museum also open Sun. 9am-noon. Museum 20AS, students 15AS.) Walk through the **Triumphpforte** (Triumphal Arch) near the Altstadt, built in 1765 to commemorate the betrothal of Emperor Leopold II. The nearby **Hofgarten** is a pleasant, shaded picnic and chess spot by day.

Backtrack a bit, cross the covered bridge over the Inn, and follow the signs up to the **Alpenzoo,** the loftiest zoo in Europe, with every vertebrate species indigenous to the Alps. Descend on the network of scenic trails that weave across the hillside. If you'd rather ride to the zoo, catch tram 1 or 6, or the train to Hungerburg Funicular Railway and take the cable car up the mountain. (Zoo open 9am-6pm; mid-Nov. to March 9am-5pm. 56AS, students 28AS.)

Outside the city proper, Archduke Ferdinand of Tirol left behind mounds of 16th-century armor and artwork (including pieces by such masters as Velazquez and Titian) at **Schloß Ambras.** The medieval castle dates back to between the 11th and 15th centuries but was rebuilt by Ferdinand into one of the most beautiful Renaissance castles in Austria. A portrait gallery depicts European dynasties from the 14th to the 19th centuries. To go it alone, take tram 6 "Pradl": Schloß Ambras, and follow the signs (open April-Oct. Mon. and Wed.-Sun. 10am-5pm). Feel queasy thinking of all the daredevils who have propelled themselves over the **Olympische Schischanze** (Olympic Ski Jump) in Bergisel. Take tram 1, 6, or the STB to Bergisel. Further down the Brennerautobahn spanning the Sil River is the tallest bridge on the continent, the 2330ft high **Europabrücke.**

ENTERTAINMENT

Many private groups and *Pensionen* in Innsbruck offer package deals for a day's **skiing,** usually including transportation to and from the mountain; decide whether the convenience they offer is worth the extra cost (usually about 100AS). Innsbruck-Information offices at the train station or in the *Altstadt* offer ski packages that include round-trip bus fare to the glacier, an all-day lift ticket, and equipment (about 660AS per day). To go it alone, take the Omnibus Stubaital bus (leaves the bus station at 7:25 and 9:45am) to Mutterbergalm-Talstation (150AS); then buy a daypass (230-295AS) and ride the gondola to the top station, where you can rent equipment.

During August, Innsbruck hosts the **Festival of Early Music,** featuring concerts by some of the world's leading soloists on period instruments at the Schloß Ambras, and organ recitals on the Hofkirche's 16th-century Ebert organ. (For tickets, call 535 60, fax 53 56 43.) Several of the festival's performances are held at the **Tiroler Landestheater,** across from the Hofburg on Rennweg (tel. 52 07 44; tickets Mon.-Sat. 8:30am-8:30pm, or 1hr. before the performance at the door; 40-250AS.)

Innsbruck's late-night opportunities are limited; most visitors collapse into bed after a full day of stomping around the mountains. The most lively nightlife revolves around the students; wander around the university quarter for sundown activity. The 20-year-old **Hof Garten,** hidden inside the Hof Garten park, is quickly becoming the focal point of nightlife for both students and professionals. The crowd starts gathering around 7pm, and by 9pm close to 1000 people fill the outdoor tents, which shelter different bars and dance floors. (Snack food 50-100AS, beer 28AS, wine spritzers 31AS. Open 10am-1am.) **Treibhaus,** Angerzellgasse 8, in an alley to the right of China Restaurant, is Innsbruck's favorite student hangout. Left-wing protest music serenades the crowd in the evening; jazz reigns on Sunday mornings. Sommergarten series includes concerts every Saturday evening; jazz and blues festivals in June. (Food 50-95AS. Mon.-Sat. 11am-1am, Sun. 10am-1am.

Baltic States

Baltic States: Estonia

US$1 = 12.67kr (kroons)	10kr =	US$0.79
CDN$1= 9.43kr	10kr =	CDN$1.06
UK£1 = 20.11kr	10kr =	UK£0.50
IR£1 = 19.93kr	10kr =	IR£0.50
AUS$1 = 9.70kr	10kr =	AUS$1.03
NZ$1 = 7.67kr	10kr =	NZ$1.30
SAR1 = 3.55kr	10kr =	SAR2.81
Country Code: 372	International Dialing Prefix: 810	

Estonia took a historic step in the summer of 1992 when it became the first Baltic state to acquire its own post-Soviet constitution and currency. As the kroon gains some stability and a collection of Western ventures fills Tallinn with Volvos, cellular phones, and Jehovah's Witnesses, stoic Estonians deliberate over the best ways of reversing a 50-year social process that Russified their culture and Sovietized their supermarkets. After overcoming successive centuries of domination by the Danes, Swedes, and Russians, the Estonians' serene, patient pragmatism has matured into a dynamic and (some would say) Scandinavian attitude. Language is a stray link among ethnic Estonians (60% of the population) but divides them from the Russian immigrant community, who have to pass strict Estonian language tests in order to obtain citizenship in this new state. With a maximum span of less than 300km, Estonia is the smallest of the Baltic nations. Tallinn, its cosmopolitan, fast-paced capital, is home to half a million; Tartu, the Estonian Oxbridge, is a daytrip away; and Pärnu and the islands of Saaremaa and Hiiumaa shine as Baltic Coast resort areas.

For a more encompassing tour through the Baltic States, pick up a copy of *Let's Go: Eastern Europe*.

GETTING THERE AND GETTING AROUND

Citizens of the U.S., Canada, Great Britain, and Australia can visit Estonia visa-free for up to 90 days. You're likely to meet a lot of Australians in Tallinn, since Estonia is one of the few East European nations that don't require visas of them. Keep in mind that since early 1993, the three Baltic states have been united in a common visa zone; a visa from any one of the three countries should be sufficient for travel to the other two. Latvian visas tend to be cheapest. Most Estonian consulates can issue a 30-day, single-entry tourist visa (US$10) or a 1-year, multiple-entry visa (US$50) to citizens of Ireland, New Zealand, and South Africa. It is possible to obtain a visa upon arriving in Estonia, but it is wiser to obtain one beforehand.

Several **cruise lines** reach Tallinn from Helsinki. Tallink Finland Oy, Eteläranta 14, 00130 Helsinki (tel. 358 (0) 63 58 22, fax. 63 53 11) sends ferries and catamarans to Tallinn (US$22-27). The **Estonian New Line,** Kalevankatu 1 C 51, 00100 Helsinki (tel. 358 (0) 680 24 99, fax 680 24 75) speeds catamarans across (1½-2hr., US$24-36). From Stockholm, **Estline,** Estlineterminalen i Frihammnen, 11556 Stockholm (tel. 46 (8) 667 00 01), sails the *Nord Estonia* to Tallinn and back 3-4 times a week at 5:30pm. (14½hr., from US$48). **Buses** and **trains** radiate from Tallinn across Estonia, with connections to Russia, Latvia, and Lithuania. **Taxis** will take you anywhere for hard currency, although it is cheaper to pay in kroons.

ESTONIA ESSENTIALS

Try to get all the brochures and travel literature you can in Tallinn; most small towns offer only city maps. *The Baltic States: A Reference Book* offers data ranging from maps and hotels in every major town to a small *Who's Who* section for each country. Buy it for 200kr at Hotel Viru or in bookstores, where it'll be cheaper. All over the Baltics, St. John's (Jaanipäev), the eve of the summer solstice, inspires bonfires, festivals of song, and open-air revelry. In Estonia, Saaremaa throws the best bash. The main frolicking usually takes place on June 24th. Other important holidays include Independence Day (Feb. 24), Victory Day (June 23—how convenient) and the Day of Rebirth (Nov. 16).

Postcards and letters to the U.S. require 4kr stamps. In summer 1994, public **telephones** were (usually) free outside of Tallinn, as they still have not been converted to take Estonian senti pieces. Within Tallinn, a few phones in the most obvious locations (the bus station, train station, airport, etc.) require a 20-senti coin for local calls. Theoretically, all phones nationwide will soon be converted to a **phonecard** system. Make calls to from the central post office to the U.S. for a steep 24kr per minute. Estonia's currency is the **kroon**, divided into 100 senti. Consider carrying a small backup supply of hard currency, as traveler's checks can be difficult to cash.

Estonians speak the best English in the Baltic states; most young people know at least a few phrases. Try familiarizing yourself with these words and phrases: *Kas*

Teie raagite inglis keelt? (Kahs Teh-yeah REH-git-teh EEN-glis kehlt; "Do you speak English?"); *bussijaam* (BUSS-ee-yahm; "bus station"); *raudteejaam* (ROWD-tee-yahm; "train station"); *postkontor* (pohst-KON-tohr; "post office"; *avatud* (AH-vah-tuht; "open"); *suletud* (SUH-leh-tuht; "closed").

■■■ TALLINN

An active port just 80km from Helsinki, Tallinn already feels Scandinavian, achieving a slowly growing western feel that is more solid than the ephemeral cellular phones and BMWs of Rīga or Vilnius. Still, there is a discernable Soviet legacy here. In the past 30 years, immigrants from Russia more than doubled the city's population to half a million; ethnic Russians now number 40% of the city. But in Tallinn, the signs of Estonian-Russian friction you might expect are absent, and clerks switch fluently from Estonian to Russian or even English without skipping a beat.

ORIENTATION AND PRACTICAL INFORMATION

Tallinn's **Vanalinn** (Old Town) is an egg-shaped maze of streets from which four main roads branch forth. **Põhja puiestee,** which joins with Sadama, leads to the sea terminal, **Mere puiestee** follows the eastern side, running south from Põhja to join **Pärnu maantee,** which heads south. **Toom puiestee** leads west, and **Narva maantee** will take you to east from the junction of Mere and Pärnu towards the looming Hotel Viru, the central landmark in Tallinn. The Old Town peaks in the fortress-rock of **Toompea,** whose 13th-century streets are level with the church steeples in the **All-linn** (low town).

Tourist Office: Tallinna Turismiamet, Raekoja Plats 8 (tel. 44 88 86 or 66 69 59, fax 44 12 21), across from the Town Hall in Old Town. City maps (in English 18kr), hotel lists, and other useful brochures. The friendly English- and German-speaking staff will quote schedules and prices and make reservations for transportation. They also have info on package tours. Open 10am-5pm.

Embassies: U.S., Kentmanni 20 (tel. 45 53 28 or 825 24 40 91). Open Mon.-Fri. 8:30am-5:30pm. **U.K.,** Kentmanni 20 (tel. 31 20 21 or 825 24 02 04). Open Mon.-Fri. 9:30am-12:30pm and 2-4:30pm. **Russia,** Pikk 19 (tel. 44 30 14). Open Mon.-Fri. 9am-12pm. **Latvia,** Tõnismägi 10 (tel. 68 16 68). Open Mon.-Fri. 8am-1:30pm and 2:30-5pm. **Finland,** Liivalaia 12 (tel. 44 95 22). Open Mon.-Fri. 9am-2pm.

Currency Exchange: Five *valuutavahetus* inside the central post office, offer rates that are among the best in Tallinn.

Post Office: Main office at Narva maantee 1, across from the Hotel Viru. Poste Restante. Open Mon.-Fri. 8am-8pm, Sat. 9am-5pm. **Postal Code:** EE-0001.

Telephones: Central office on 1st floor of post building at Narva maantee 1. Open 7am-10pm. Fax service. Local phones are sometimes free of charge, or sometimes need a 20-senti coin, but usually just don't work. A phonecard system should be in place soon. **City Code:** 249, and sometimes 6 on digital lines.

Trains: The **Balti jaam** (Baltic station) on Toom puiestee can be reached by trams 1 and 2. To St. Petersburg (10hr., 66-108kr), Minsk (23hr., 178-282kr), Narva (4hrs. 25kr), Tartu (3-4hr., 22kr), and, Warsaw (21hr., 551-851kr). Rent lockers in the **luggage storage** area for 3kr.

Buses: The **Autobussijaam** (station) is on Masina, 1.5km southeast of the Old Town. Tram 2 or 4 and bus 22 connect to the city center. Call 31 32 22 for info. To Rīga (7hr., 71kr), Tartu (2½hr., 38kr). Open 4:30pm-midnight.

Ferries: Tallinna Reisisadam (Tallinn Harbor) is a 15min. walk from the city center. Bus 65 from Hotel Viru or train station. **Tallink** (tel. 60 19 60) services **Helsinki** (4hr., 120FIM); and, **Estline** (tel. 31 36 36) runs to Stockholm (14½hr.; 385SEK, 295SEK one way student deck fare).

Public Transportation: Buses, trams, and trolleybuses cover the entire Tallinn suburban area and each category has separate stops marked with ideograms. They run 6am-midnight and require tickets which can be purchased only at newsstands (0.85kr). Punch them on board. You can get a *Tallinna Transpordi Teatmik* (transportation schedule) from some kiosks, but without a route map, it's not very helpful; a route map exists, but only on a Russian-language map of Tallinn.

Taxis: Around **Hotel Viru,** they'll rip you off. Find a *Takso* stand, or call 60 30 44 (state-run). Rides around Tallinn, as far out as the bus station or ferry terminal should run no more than US$6.

Emergencies: Ambulance, tel. 03. **Police,** tel. 02. **Fire,** tel. 01.

ACCOMMODATIONS

While other prices skyrocket in rapidly westernizing Tallinn, affordable rooms are still plentiful. Anticipated renovations at the Agnes and the Vitamin may change the picture somewhat by summer 1995, but the new hostel opening up should even things out. The **Agnes youth hostel (HI),** Narva mnt. 7 (tel. 43 88 70), offers 34 rooms with communal showers and bathrooms, complemented by a friendly Russian-speaking staff who also know some English and German. From the bus or train station, take tram 2. The hostel is in the courtyard. Knock on the door to get in after midnight. (100kr, 90kr with ISIC or student ID. Open June 1-Aug. 24.) The **ETK Hotel Vitamin,** Narva mnt. 7 (tel. 43 85 85), 2 doors down from Agnes, offers roughly the same facilities as the hostel, but the bathrooms are shared by fewer people. There's no English spoken here. (Singles 200kr. Doubles 400kr.) **Family Hotel Service (Hua Ai Trade Ltd.),** Mere puiestee 6 (tel. and fax 44 11 87), arranges rooms with families and access to bathrooms and kitchen. (Singles 100-190kr. Doubles 180-290kr. Office open 10am-5pm.) **CDS Reisid (Baltic Bed and Breakfast),** Raekoja Plats 17 (tel. 44 52 62, fax 31 36 66), sets up private rooms with English-speaking hosts (breakfast included). They'll pick you up on arrival in Tallinn. (Singles 265kr. Doubles 400kr. Reserve ahead. Office open Mon.-Fri. 10am-6pm, Sat.-Sun. 10am-3pm.) Contact the Karol travel firm (tel. 45 49 00) about the new **HI Youth Hostel** on the corner of Pärnu and Liivalaia, which was slated to open in late summer 1994. Also not to be overlooked are the rooms at the **bus station.** Inquire at the info desk in the main hall, and you can snag a perfectly clean bed for 40kr.

FOOD

The Old Town is beginning to fill with small restaurants where low prices and large portions guarantee budget travelers' satisfaction. On Uus 7, the Roosakas Panter (Pink Panther) **24hr. store** beckons the night owl. Tallinn also has quite a few Western-style supermarkets. The largest is Kaubahall, Aia tn. 7, a stone's throw from the Viru Gates into the Old Town (open Mon.-Sat. 9am-8:30pm, Sun. 9am-3pm).

Paks Margareeta (Fat Margaret's), Pikk 70, in the gate-tower housing the Maritime museum. A genuine American sub shop run by two gents from California. Small subs 12-15kr, large 28-34kr. After the meal, climb up to the observation deck on top of the tower for a great view. Open 10am-6pm.

Sanjay's, Rataskaevu 5, on the 2nd floor of a four-restaurant complex. A palate-pleasing mix of Indian and Chinese food. Spicy Singapore fried rice 34kr, most other main dishes 50-70kr. Open noon-11pm.

Foster's (The Tex-Mex Place), Tartu mnt. 50, one tram stop west of the bus station. Hidden inside the Flexer Sports Club, the only Mexican food in the Baltics, so get it while you can. Burrito 35kr. Chili cheeseburgers 25kr. Fresh baked pies 13kr a slice. Open Mon.-Fri. 9am-9pm, Sat.-Sun. 10am-9pm.

Baar Vegan, Uus 22, serves (can you believe it?) several vegetable and grain dishes from which you compile your meal; each heaping ladleful costs 0.60-3kr. Fruit and veggie juices are also available. Open 10am-6pm.

Eeslitall, Dunkri 4. Meat and vegetarian dishes 20-50kr, tasty omelets 9-20kr, in a crazy pomo interior. Open Sun.-Thurs. noon-midnight, Fri-Sat. noon-1am.

SIGHTS AND ENTERTAINMENT

You can get acquainted with the **Old City** by starting at Hotel Viru, walking down Narva maantee then continuing on along Viru past the 15th-century Viru City Gate to **Raekoja plats,** where handicrafts are sold on summer evenings and folk songs and dances are performed on a small outdoor stage. The **Raekoda** (Town Hall) was

BALTIC STATES

built 1371-1404 and is guarded by **Vana Toomas** (Old Thomas), a cast-iron figurine of the legendary defender of Tallinn, which dates from 1530. Behind the Raekoda, at Raekoja 4/6, you'll find the **Raemuseum,** which served as the town jail in the middle ages. Nowadays it houses an interesting exhibit on early Estonian photography and some contemporary Estonian sculptures. (Open Thurs.-Tues. 10:30am-5:30pm. 3kr.) For a view of the northern towers and bastion of the medieval city, go up Vene, take a right on Olevimägi and up Uus. In front of the smaller tower, *Paks Margareeta* (Fat Margaret), you'll find the **Meremuuseum** (maritime museum), Pikk 70, changing exhibits on Tallinn's history as a busy port. (Open Wed.-Sun. 10am-6pm. 5kr.) If you go down Pikk, you'll run into the **Oleviste kirik** (St. Olav's Church) on your right, the tallest church in town. (Open Sun 10am-5pm, services on Mon. and Thurs. at 6:30pm.) Go to the end of Pikk and take a left onto Rataskaevu to see the mighty spire of **Niguliste kirik** (St. Nicholas Church), Oleviste's only rival among city churches. Inside is a fragment of Bernt Nothe's medieval masterpiece, *Danse Macabre.* (Open Wed. 2-9pm, Thurs.-Sun. 11am-6pm. 3kr.) If you walk down Rüütli, on your left you'll see **Kiek in de Kök** (Peek in the Kitchen) tower, an allusion to the fact that from this height, you could see into everyone's home in 16th-century Tallinn. (Open Tues.-Fri. 10:30am-5:30pm, Sat.-Sun. 11am-4:30pm. 3kr.) Straight ahead is the **Neitsitorni** (Virgin Tower), where you can drink *höögviin* and hobnob with bohemians. The doorman extracts a 3kr entrance fee, and you'll get nailed with another 3kr if you wander out onto the balcony. Up the street and to the left, the **Alexander Nevsky Cathedral** was begun under Tsar Alexander III and finished a few years before the Bolshevik Revolution. (Open 8am-7pm.) At the **Tallinn City Museum,** 17 Vene, you can bore yourself silly with rooms full of 19th-century knickknacks (open Wed.-Fri. 10:30am-5:30pm, Sat.-Sun. 10:30am-4:30pm; 2kr). In **Rocca-Al-Mare,** a peninsula 12km west of Tallinn, you'll find the quaint **Estonian Open-Air Museum,** Vabaõhumuuseumi 12 (tel. 55 91 76), a collection of wooden mills and farmsteads from the 18th-20th centuries. Take bus 21 from Balti jaam (30min.) or a taxi (70kr). (Open May-Oct. Wed.-Sun. 10am-6pm. 10kr, students 6kr.) In July, **Rock Summer** draws students and bands from around the world to Tallinn for a weeklong music fest. In 1994, over 30 bands played and the Pogues, Phil Collins, and Phish showed up. For more info, call Makarov Music management at 23 85 03.

When it comes to a night on the town, Tallinn is light-years ahead of the rest of the former Soviet Union. **Hell Hunt (The Gentle Wolf),** 39 Pikk, is a rocking Irish pub with Guinness and Killian's on tap and live music nightly. (No cover. Open Sun.-Mon. 10am-1am, Tues.-Thurs. 10am-2am, Fri.-Sat. 10am-3am.) In the cavernous cellar of the restaurant, sailors, tourists, and intellectuals wander through a labyrinth of colored lights, archways, nooks and crannies to imbibe and dance the night away at **Eesli Tall Baar,** Dunkri 4 (open 4pm-4am). The avant-garde **Von Krahli Teater/ Baar,** Rataskaevu 10, on the western edge of the lower Old Town, showcases Baltic talent ranging through Lithuanian jazz, experimental dance, and cutting-edge music (bar open 6pm-4am; theater shows most nights 8pm or 10pm; tickets 15-20kr).

■ ■ ■ KURESSAARE

Sleepy but charming Kuressaare became the seat of the Saare-Laane bishopric in the 16th century. The town is small; you can walk from the west side's medieval episcopal castle (complete with moat), to the modern bus station on the eastern border in less than 15min. From the station, downtown is a short 3 blocks along Tallinna. On the way toward the castle, at **Raekoja plats,** stands a monument to the 1918-1920 struggle for independence. Walk through the park on Lossihoovi towards the **Kuressaare Linnus-Kindlus** (Episcopal Castle), the town's main attraction. The castle houses the **Saaremaa Regional Museum** (18kr, students 6kr). Pick up a map (2kr) at the castle entrance. (Castle and museum open Wed.-Sun. 11am-7pm. Last entry 5:30pm.) The quiet and clean beaches of **Mändjala** and **Järve** cover an 8-12km stretch from Kuressaare.

Baltic Tours, Tallinna 3 (tel. (245) 554 80), isn't exactly a tourist office, but they can help with ferry info, English-language tours, hotels, and the like (open Mon.-Fri. 9am-1pm and 2-5pm). If you want to bike across town or around Saaremaa, rent one (50kr per day) from **Steady Ltd.,** Vallimaa 5A (tel. (245) 558 78). Catch a **bus** at the *Autobussijaam,* Pihtla tee 2 (tel. (245) 573 80 for info, 562 20 for reserves), to Haapsalu (3hr., 34kr), Pärnu (3hr., 36kr), and Tallinn (3-4hr., 52kr).

The **Panga Pansionaat** (tel. (245) 579 89) at Tallinna 27, has sparkling, airy rooms in a clean and modern place that feels like home. It's best to reserve ahead. From the bus station, go around the back and cross Tallinna. (Singles 190kr. Doubles 380kr. Large room-service breakfast included.) The **Mardi Öömaja,** Vallimaa 5A (tel. (245) 574 36), has spacious, clean, institutional-style rooms that share a toilet and shower (no hot water) with one other room. A café downstairs serves breakfast for 30kr. (Singles 100kr. Doubles 200kr. Triples 300kr, Quints 500kr.) **Kohvik Kursaal,** Pargi 2, is undoubtedly the best restaurant in town. Located in an 1889 dance hall with high windows, ceiling fans, it conjures the air of a bygone era. (Entrees 7-19kr. Open noon-midnight.) Fan your appetite at **Kohvik (Café) Veski,** in the old windmill at Pärna 19, with its ludicrously Soviet "service," but food well worth the wait. (Entrees 7-13kr. Open noon-midnight.)

■■■ PÄRNU

Located 130km south of Tallinn on Estonia's western coast, the medieval center of Pärnu has rapidly become commercialized. Discover the charm of this coastal city by walking on the *Rand* (beach) or through the parks; the beach pavilions and beautiful houses on the *Esplanaadi* (boulevard) were built in the 19th century when Pärnu was famed for its waters and mud baths.

Facing Hotell Pärnu on Rüütli, you'll find the **Museum of the City of Pärnu,** a quintessential municipal museum full of old clothes and arrowheads (open Wed.-Sun. 11am-6pm; 6kr). This and the **Lydia Koidula Museum,** Jannseni 37, located at the childhood home of the 19th-century poet who led a revival in Estonian-language verse and drama, are the only museums in town (open Wed.-Sun. 10am-5pm; 6kr). If you turn left on Nikolai, you'll find the stern **Eliisabeti Kirik,** built in 1747. On Midsummer Night *(Jäänipaev),* Pärnu hosts the week-long **Fiesta International Jazz Festival,** along with the **Baltiscandal,** a modernist Baltic and Scandinavian theater extravaganza.

Pärnu is best reached by **bus** since the station is in the very center, down Ringi from the bus parking lot on your right. Buses regularly serve Rīga (41kr), Tallinn (30kr), Tartu (40kr), Kuressaare (36kr), and Haapsalu (24kr). Grab maps and info about Pärnu at **Reiser Travel Agency,** Rüütli 35 (tel. (244) 445 00; fax 448 85). From the bus station, walk down Kirji and take a right on Rüütli; the **post and telephone office** on Akadeemia 7 is at the street's end (open 7am-10pm).

The most central rooms are at the **Hotell Pärnu,** Rüütli 44 (tel. (244) 509 00, fax 509 05), right by the bus station. All rooms include TV and private bath. (Singles 210kr. Doubles 290kr. Renovated singles and doubles aren't worth 510kr for Danish furniture.) Change money 8am-midnight, but the rates aren't great. The **Hotell** at Seedri 4 (tel. (244) 430 98), near the beach is a small and plain place with hall showers and toilets (singles/doubles 120kr). Just off the beach, the high-ceilinged **Rannasalong** was a 1930s dance hall and restaurant (open noon-midnight). **Trahter Postipoiss,** Vee 12, has a courtyard café and restaurant in a 19th-century post office (open 11am-midnight). Dance it up in the outdoor **Disoklubs "Hamilton"** at Rüütli 1, which boasts different DJs from across Estonia every night (open 9am-5pm in summer; cover 25kr).

■■■ TARTU

Since the town has been burned to the ground 55 times, very little remains of medieval Tartu. The **Town Hall** dominates the center square of Tartu, which dates from after 1775 when the medieval market which previously stood on the site burned down in a gigantic fire. **Tartu University** to the north, founded in 1632, is the oldest in northern Europe. The **Museum of Classical Art,** a small but charming gathering of Roman and Greek art, is inside. (Open Mon.-Fri. 11am-4:30pm. 5kr.) The ruins of the 14th-century **Jaani Kirik** (St. John's Church) can be found on Ülikooli (which turns into Jaani). On top of the **Toomemägi** (Cathedral Hill) are the majestic remainders of the 13th-century **Toomkirik** of St. Peter and Paul. The **Estonian National Museum** is at Veski 32 (open Wed.-Sun. 11am-6pm; 7.50kr), and features ethnographic exhibits from all over Estonia.

Tartu is starting to reassign all of its phone numbers, going from a 5-digit to a 6-digit code. Currently the **city code** is 234 plus the 5-digit number, but soon it will be 7 plus the 6-digit number. The **tourist office** is just off the main square (Raekoja plats) at Küütri 3 (tel. 321 41. Open Mon.-Fri. 10am-6pm). There are virtually no **buses** going to destinations outside Estonia. Mondays, a private bus line runs to Berlin. (28hr., 900kr, students 765kr. Call 47 22 46 for info.)

There aren't many budget options left in Tartu in the aftermath of the 1994 Song Festival, which prompted many hotels to revamp their rooms (and their prices). The tourist office can help ferret out cheaper accommodations. Behind the bus station, try **Tartu Võõrastemaja,** Soola 3 (tel. 320 91), both a hotel and a youth hostel; the showers are communal, but there's also a sauna (54kr per hr., singles 170kr, doubles 230kr; with hosteling card, prices drop by 50kr). **Hotle Salimo,** Kopli 1 (tel. 47 08 88), has plain rooms with bare-bones furnishings and no-nonsense white paint (singles and doubles 75kr with private toilet and shower); be forewarned that no buses run even close. A cavernous 18th-centrury gunpowder cellar, **Püssirohukelder,** is now a two-level *baar* and the jolliest restaurant in town. A full meal costs 100kr. Make reservations on Wednesday, Friday, and Saturday nights, because the variety show (9-11pm) usually draws a full house.

■ Baltic States: Latvia (Latvija)

US$1 = 0.54LS		1LS =	US$1.85
CDN$1= 0.40LS		1LS =	CDN$2.48
UK£1 = 0.86LS		1LS =	UK£1.17
IR£1 = 0.85LS		1LS =	IR£1.18
AUS$1 = 0.41LS		1LS =	AUS$2.42
NZ$1 = 0.33LS		1LS =	NZ$3.05
SAR1 = 0.15LS		1LS =	SAR6.60
Country Code: 371		International Dialing Prefix: 810	

Latvia, a vibrant nation of 2.6 million situated on the Baltic coast between Lithuania and Estonia, is no exception to the region's history of foreign domination; since the 13th century, the country has suffered under Germans, Swedes, Poles, and Russians. Fifty years of Soviet occupation has left deep marks, as massive influxes of Russian workers reduced Latvians to a near-minority in their own country. But Latvia has managed to retain its national identity, as reflected in its music, art, and folk culture; again independent, Latvia is quickly becoming a player in world business markets.

With a population of nearly a million, Rīga is the largest (not to mention most exciting) city in the Baltics, a resplendent mixture of medieval Hanseatic influences and 19th-century Art Nouveau.

GETTING THERE AND GETTING AROUND

Citizens of the U.K. can visit Latvia visa-free for up to 90 days. Citizens of the U.S., Canada, Ireland, Australia, New Zealand, and South Africa require a visa (free to Americans and Canadians), which can be obtained at the airport or on the border. Keep in mind that the three Baltic states have formed a common visa zone, meaning that a visa from any one of the three countries should be sufficient for travel to the other two. Latvian visas are the cheapest of the three. If you want to visit the Baltics for a long time, you should also plan to get a Latvian visa; negotiations currently underway should make it possible for U.S. citizens to obtain 12-month, multiple-entry visas for Latvia by summer 1995. Latvian embassies or consulates are located at 4325 17th St. NW, Washington, DC 20011 (tel. (202) 726-8213, fax 726-6785), 230 Clemow Ave., Ottawa, Ont. K1S 2B6. (tel. (613) 238-6868), 72 Queensborough Terrace, London W2 3SP (tel. (0171 727 16 98), and P.O. Box 23, Kew, Victoria 3101, Melbourne (tel. (03) 499 69 20).

Latvia is well-connected by **train** to Moscow, St. Petersburg, Vilnius, Tallinn, and even Berlin. **Buses** also have an efficient long-distance network running to Estonia and Lithuania, though with fewer routes to other countries. **Ferries** run to Rīga from Stockholm and Kiel, though it is cheaper from Stockholm to go to Tallinn and take a train; from Kiel, it's often better to go to Klaipėda and catch a bus. **Flights** to Latvia use the overworked Rīga Airport, whose only runway was short enough to cause safety concern when President Clinton visited in 1994.

Buses and **trains** run everywhere in Latvia; getting from town to town is rarely a problem. You can buy complete schedules *(Saraksts)* of the diesel-train, bus, ferry, and electric-train systems radiating from Rīga at bookstores for 40 santims. The electric suburban train system centered in Rīga actually covers nearly half the country, stretching between the Lithuanian and Estonian borders. To cross Latvia by train, from Liepaja to Daugavpils, via Rīga, takes about nine hours. Buses are faster on the whole, though more expensive. In the vast eastern region of Latgale, there are virtually no trains, leaving buses the only option.

LATVIA ESSENTIALS

Tourist offices are uncommon in Latvia. Rīga has *Rīga this Week,* an unhelpful English/German compendium of casino ads that is published every 5-8 months. Matthias Lûfkes, creator of the *Vilnius in Your Pocket* series, has been talking about doing a Rīga guide; keep your eyes open for it. When you're there, take full advantage of the **Tourist Club of Latvia,** Skārņu iela 22 (tel. (2) 22 17 31, fax 22 76 80), right behind St. Peter's Church; immense amounts of information on travel to Russia, Ukraine, Belarus, Lithuania, Latvia, Germany, and other destinations flow from the manager. He only speaks German, Latvian, and Russian, but other office staff know some English (open 9am-5pm). The **Latvijas Universitäte Türists Klubs,** in the main University building at Raiņa bulv. 19, room 107 (tel. (2) 22 52 98, fax (8) 82 01 13), is another great source of info on Latvia, especially on hiking and bicycling options (open 9-am-6pm). Stores sometimes close for an hour or two between noon and 3pm, and restaurants may take a break between 5 and 7pm. Major holidays in Latvia include the National Day (Nov. 18), celebrating the anniversary of Latvia's independence (1918), but the most important date is June 23, the Midsummer's Eve Festival called *Ligo* or *Jāni* (St. John's Day).

The Latvian **LS** (100 santims=1LS) has an almost unreal value; at press time, one LS was worth significantly more than a unit of any other currency in the world, attesting to the amount of business being transacted in Latvia. Fortunately, this economic precociousness means that traveler's checks can be cashed in Rīga.

The **phone** system in Latvia is currently a mess, but extensive renovations mean that public phones throughout Latvia are expect to be replaced by cardphones in late 1994 or 1995, but the conversion may not proceed on schedule. In summer 1994, local phones in Latvia required special *Žetoni*, purchasable at kiosks and post offices for 1 santims each (good for a 3min. local call). Long-distance calls within Latvia can be made from some of the old gray public phones with the double-grooved *Žetoni* sold at post offices (6 santims each, good for ½-2min.). For international calls to the West, the only options at present are at the post office or from your hotel room. To do it yourself, dial 81 94, and talk to the operator in Latvian or Russian; you'll be asked where you want to call, the number, your number, your name, and when you want to talk (or you may just be told to wait). International calls within the former Soviet Union can be placed directly by dialing 8, followed by the old Soviet city code (usually the same as the current code). In general, try and avoid making international calls from Latvia; it's really expensive. Most young Latvians study English or German but probably aren't fluent. Start off in your own language, and break into Russian only after your native tongue has failed. Key words and phrases include *lūdzu* (LOOD-zoo; "please"), *paldies* (PAHL-dee-yes; "thank you") and *Vai jūs runājiet angliski?* (VIE yoos roo-nah-yet ahn-GLEES-kee; "Do you speak English?").

Homemade Latvian bread and pastries are delicious and worth asking for; try *speka rauói,* a warm pastry, or *biezpienmaize,* bread with sweet curds. Latvian beer is strong and bitter, but very cheap.

■■■ RĪGA

Cosmopolitan Rīga has a history of conquest that left Swedes, Germans, Poles, and Russians successively in control of Latvia's capital since the early 1200s. Only in the 20th century have Latvians come to rule their own city, but just as the famed Jugendstil architecture of the city reflects vanished German influences, the metropolitan population, nearly two-thirds of which is Russian, is the inescapable legacy of Soviet-era immigration. **Vecrīga** (Old Rīga), full of 18th- and 19th-century architectural landmarks, occupies a small part of the city: the area between Kr. Valdemāra iela and Marijas iela can be covered in a 15min. walk.

ORIENTATION AND PRACTICAL INFORMATION

To reach **Vecrīga** (the Old Town) from the bus station, go under the bridge at your left and across the street. From the train station, walk down Marijas iela toward the river 3-4min., then turn right on Vaļņu iela, followed by a left on Audēju iela and you'll come to **Pēter baznīcas** (St. Peter's Church) on your right after a few blocks.

Tourist Office: Elizabetes iela 6 (tel. 32 60 09, fax 32 33 21). Brochures and prices on accommodations and transportation. Open Mon.-Sat. 9am-8pm. **Tourist Club of Latvia,** Skārņu iela 22 (tel. 22 17 31, fax 22 76 80), behind St. Peter's Church, is the best for all-encompassing knowledge of the Baltics. Only Aira Andriksone speaks English, but the rest of the staff knows Latvian, Russian, German, and French. Open 9am-5pm.

American Express: Latvia Tours, Grēcinieku iela 22/24 (tel. 22 18 96), is the Latvian AmEx rep, but can't cash cheques. Open Mon.-Fri. 9am-5pm. **Deutsch-Lettische Bank,** Jēkaba iela 3/5 (tel. 22 24 05) cashes cheques. Open Mon.-Fri. 9am-5pm.

Embassies: U.S., Raiņa bulv. 7 (tel. 21 00 05 or 22 03 67). Open Mon.-Fri. 9am-noon and 2-5pm. **U.K.,** Elizabetes iela 2 (tel. 32 07 37). Open Mon.-Fri. 9am-1pm and 2-5pm. **Canada,** Doma Laukums 4 (tel. 33 33 55). Open Mon.-Fri. 10am-1pm. **Russia,** Antonijas iela 2 (tel. 22 06 93). Open Mon.-Fri. 10am-1pm. **Lithuania,** Elizabetes iela 2 (tel. 32 15 19). Open Mon.-Fri. 10am-1pm. **Estonia,** Skolas iela 13 (tel. 22 68 45). Open Mon.-Fri. 10am-1pm.

Currency Exchange: At any of the innumerable *Valutos Maiņa* kiosks or shops in the city. Also, a 24hr. exchange with good rates on Aspazijas bulv.

Post Office: Stacijas Laukums 1, near the railway station. Open Mon.-Fri. 8am-8pm, Sat. 8am-6pm, Sun. 10am-4pm. **Postal Code:** LV-1000.

Telephones: Office at Brīvības bulv. 21. Open 24hrs. **City code:** 2 (sometimes 8 for digital lines).

Flights: Lidosta Rīga (Rīga Airport), 8km southwest of the Old Town. Take bus 22 from Arhitektu iela and punch 3 tickets. Flight info tel. 20 70 09.

Ferries: Sea terminal (tel. 32 98 82) located 1km north of the Rīga castle along Eksporta iela. **Mercuri** arrives from Kiel, Germany (360DM one-way).

Trains: Rigas Centrālā Stacija, Stacijas laukums, just east of the Old Town and north of the canal. To Moscow (17½hr., 8.14LS), St. Petersburg (15hr., 6.59LS), Kaliningrad (12hr., 5.12LS), Vilnius (8hr., 5.77LS), and, Berlin (35hr., 48LS). Get train info at the window or by calling 007.

Buses: Autoosta, 200m south of the train station along Marijas iela. To Tallinn (6hr., 2.80LS), Vilnius (5½hr., 2.70LS), Pärnu (3½hr., 1.90LS), and, Klaipēda (2-4hr., 1.02LS). For info, call 21 36 11.

Public Transportation: Buses, trams, and trolleybuses all require 6-santims tickets, available at kiosks. The city has 3 travel zones, each requiring a ticket.

Taxis: A crosstown ride should cost no more than 3LS. Call 33 40 41.

Emergencies: Ambulance, tel. 03. **Fire,** tel. 01. **Police,** tel. 02.

ACCOMMODATIONS

The old Intourist haunts have dusted their counters, and now, easily fooled Western businessmen shell out US$100 a night to stay in them. But if you don't absolutely need CNN or MTV, you can still bunk down for as little as US$5. **Patricia,** Elizabetes iela 22-4a (tel. 28 48 68), places travelers into private homes for US$15 per person per night (open 8am-8pm).

Rīga Hostel, Kalnciema iela 10/12 (tel. 22 64 63, fax 22 47 85). Take train 4 or 5. On the 3rd floor of a music and ballet school. Spartan accommodations, hot water, and a friendly, English-speaking staff. Singles 5LS. Doubles 10LS. The hostel is perennially uncertain about its future, and may not exist in 1995; if it does, it will be open June -Aug.

Victorija, A Čaka iela 55 (tel. 27 62 09 or 27 23 05), 8 blocks from the railway station on Marijas iela, or 2 stops on trolleybus 11 or 18. Singles 8-13LS. Doubles 10-18LS.

Latvijas Universitāte Turists Klubs, Raiņa bulv. 19, rm. 107 (tel. 22 52 98), Student dorms for 4-8LS per person per night, in 3 locations throughout the city. Rooms share hall showers/bath; the more expensive are more central.

Avrora, Marijas iela 5 (tel. 22 44 79), across from the railway station. An unreformed Soviet hotel, but it's the cheapest in town that will accept Westerners. Hall showers and toilets. Singles 2.72LS. Doubles 5.44LS.

FOOD

For the most part, food in Rīga is a blur of the same *karbonades, kotletes,* and *bifšteks* you'll find elsewhere in the Baltics, but you may come across menus featuring roast suckling pig for 120LS. Between extremes, there are plenty of options for a good meal in Vecrīga, and most of the time you can get away for under US$5. One of the most jealously guarded secrets in the Baltics is that the **U.S. embassy** canteen is open to US citizens and their guests; it's also the only place in Rīga with clam chowder (open Mon.-Fri. noon-2pm).

Fredis Café, Audēju iela 5, near the Pēterbaznīcas. Subs (0.80-1.30LS), spaghetti with mushrooms (2LS), and french onion soup (0.70 LS) make this the premier choice for fast and tasty café dining in Rīga. Open 9am-midnight.

Pie Kristapa, Jauniela 25/27 (tel. 22 75 30), on the main street south from Doma Laukums. Incredible beer hall downstairs serves hearty portions of simple and delicious Latvian cuisine. Open noon-6pm and 7pm-midnight.

Pie Kaleja, Kalēju 50, was one of the better state-run cafeterias during the Soviet era, and has been successfully making a transition to a good money-grubbing café, popular among the university students. Most entrees 1.25-1.60LS. Open Mon.-Fri. 8am-8pm, Sat.-sun. noon -7pm.

Zilais putns, Tirgoṇ iela 4. The "bluebird" has good thin-crust pizza downstairs or outside, and upstairs is the best pasta in Rīga. With a great view of the Doma laukums. *Pasta con mare* (a shrimp, oyster, and squid-stuffed masterpiece), 3LS. Open noon-11pm.

SIGHTS AND ENTERTAINMENT

For an amazing view of Rīga's rooftops and the Baltic Sea, climb the 72m **tower** of **St. Peter's Church** in **Vecrīga.** (Open Tues.-Sun. 10am-7pm in summer, in winter Tues.-Sun. 10am-4:30pm. 0.75LS.) Just behind the church at Jāṇa 7 stands the Sv. **Jāṇa baznīca** (St. John's Church), a small 13th-century chapel (open 10am-1pm). The vast, irregular, and cobblestone expanse of **Doma laukums** (Cathedral Square) appeared on Rīga's map in 1936. Looming over one end of the square is **Rīgas Doms** (Rīga cathedral), the largest church in the Baltics. First consecrated in 1226, it has since been modified by architects of various persuasions. Notice the German pipe organ that dates from 1844; boasting 6786 pipes, it's among the biggest (and best) in the world. (Church open to visitors Mon. and Fri. 10am-2pm, Tue.-Thurs. and Sat. 1-4pm. 0.30LS.) On leaving the church, go back to the square and walk north along Jēkaba iela. Take your first left, Mazā Pils iela. **Rīga Pils** (Rīga Castle) awaits you at the end of the street; nowadays, it houses three museums. The **Museum of Latvian History** and the **Museum of Foreign Art** house Latvian paintings, works of German and Dutch masters, and exhibits on the decorative arts (both open Tues.-Thurs. 11am-5pm; 0.40LS each). Torņa iela, lined with galleries and shops, leads to the **Pulvertornis** (Powder Tower), one of Rīga's oldest landmarks and the only city wall tower left. Nine cannonballs are still lodged in its 14th-century walls. Inside, visit the **Latvian Museum of War,** with exhibits on Latvian armed forces. (Open Tues.-Sun. 11am-6pm. 0.30LS.) Down Basteja bulv. and then left on Brīvības, you'll come across **Brīvības Piemineklis,** the beloved Latvian Freedom Memorial that was dedicated in 1935 when Latvia was an independent republic. A few blocks up Brīvības, in the Esplanāde, the **Orthodox Metropolitan Cathedral** rises over the greenery. Across the Esplanāde, near the corner of kr. Valdemāra and Elizabetes, you'll find the **State Museum of Latvian Art,** Rīga's foremost art museum boasting 19th- and 20th-century works by such artists as Kazaks, Tone, and colorful Rēriks. (Open Wed.-Mon. 11am-6pm in summer; in winter Wed.-Mon. 11am-5pm. 0.50LS.)

Nightlife in Rīga is better than in any of the other Baltic cities. The undisputed king of beer gardens is the **Carlsberg garden** that fills Doma Laukums year-round. **Jāṇa Sēta,** in the small courtyard behind St. John's church, is a local jewel, great for afternoon coffee or evening suds. Birthplace of Mikhail Baryshnikov, Rīga is home to the **Latvian National Opera** and the excellent **Rīga Ballet,** but with the Opera house under reconstruction at least until the next millennium, both companies are currently performing in the *Kongress zāle*, in the Kronvalda parks. Posters throughout the city announce upcoming events, or call 61 57 73. Tickets are all under 2LS, some as low as 0.35LS.

■ NEAR RĪGA

Only 20km west of Rīga, the sandy beaches of **Jūrmala** beckon on hot summer days. To get there, take a bus or one of the frequent trains (every 15-20min., 4am-11pm) from the rail station in Rīga. A handful of towns dot the Jūrmala coast; **Majori** (the 4th stop after crossing the river, 40min., 0.28LS), with its beaches and lively shopping area, is the largest and one of the most enjoyable. From the train stop, walk down the closest street you see, take the first right, to reach Jomas iela, Majori's main street, which is lined with shops, cafés, restaurants, and bars.

Located less than 60km northeast of Rīga and serviced by frequent trains (1hr., 0.45LS), **Sigulda** stands at the entrance to the **Gauja National Park,** 920 sq. km of woods, caves, brooks, lakes, and ancient oaks. From the stations, walk up Raiṇa iela through the center of town. Pils iela leads off to the ruins of the **Siguldas pilsdrupas** (Sigulda Castle), built by the German Knights of the Sword in the early 13th century.

A great view from the ruins peers across the river. Ride on the cable car for a memorable crossing of the **Gauja gorge** (10min., 0.25LS); the castles and cave await you on the other bank. Inside the park, the walls of **Gūtmaņa ala** (Gūtmaņis's Cave), the largest cave in Latvia, are covered with inscriptions, some dating to the 17th century. Go 500m up Turaidas road to reach the **Turaidas Castle Complex;** tickets are sold at the gate (open 9:30am-6pm in summer; Tues.-Sun. 10am-5pm in winter; 0.40LS). The main tower holds a historical exhibit of various castle occupants' belongings, dating back to 1214; climb to the top for a magnificent view of the Gauja and the surrounding hills.

Baltic States: Lithuania (Lietuva)

US$1 = 4.00LT (litas)	10LT = US$0.25
CDN$1 = 2.98LT	10LT = CDN$0.34
UK£1 = 6.36LT	10LT = UK£0.16
IR£1 = 6.30LT	10LT = IR£0.16
AUS$1 = 3.07LT	10LT = AUS$0.33
NZ$1 = 2.43LT	10LT = NZ$0.41
SAR1 = 1.12LT	10LT = SAR0.89
Country Code: 370	International Dialing Prefix: 810

BALTIC STATES

You're not likely to associate Lithuania with the word "empire," but Lithuania, now long forgotten by most of the world, was once the superpower of Eastern Europe. The grand duchy of Lithuania, which included Belarus, western Ukraine, and modern-day Lithuania, was one of the most influential powers in the entire region during the 14th through 16th centuries. Today, Lithuania (pop. 3.5 million) is struggling to chart a new political and economic course in the vacuum of Soviet collapse.

Visitors to Lithuania will be pleasantly surprised by its scenery and historical attractions. Vilnius is one of the most habitable capital cities in the Baltic Republics, graced by green parks, relaxed cafés, and a low, unassuming skyline. Ruined medieval castles and fortifications stand as mute reminders of Lithuania's glorious past; not far away are the sophisticated, modern, cosmopolitan cities of Kaunas and Klaipėda. The best beaches in the Baltics await at Palanga, which is also home to lovely botanical gardens and relaxing mineral springs. The Curonian Spit offers more sun and fun, featuring dunes of fine white sand framed by dense forests.

Get all the dirt on Lithuania in the premier edition of *Let's Go: Eastern Europe.*

GETTING THERE AND GETTING AROUND

Citizens of the U.S. and the U.K. can visit Lithuania visa-free for up to 90 days; others will need a valid passport to receive a visa. Ten-day visas may be obtained at the border for a fee of US$40—it is always wise, however, to obtain a visa from your local embassy prior to your departure. Citizens of the U.S. and the U.K. can visit Lithuania visa-free for up to 90 days. The Baltics now constitute a "common visa zone:" Lithuanian visas are valid in Estonia and Latvia, and vice versa. Latvian visas are the cheapest of the three. Lithuanian embassies and honorary consuls are located at 2622 16th. St. NW, Washington, DC 20009 (tel. (202) 234-5860, fax 328-0466), 235 Yorkland Blvd., Willowdale, Ont. M2J (tel. (416) 494-4099, fax 494-4382), 17 Essex Villas, London W8 7BP (tel. (0171) 937 15 88 or 938 24 81, fax 938 33 29), and 26 Jalanga Crescent, Aranda ACT 2614 (tel. and fax (616) 253 20 63).

Klaipėda, Kaunas, and Vilnius are easily reached by train or bus from Latvia, Poland, and Russia. If travelling from Poland, note that all trains to Vilnius go through Belarus, requiring a transit visa (US$30). Only a few rail options circumvent a Belarussian interlude by a complicated pre-World War II rail route across the Polish-Lithuanian border, requiring a change of trains because of the different rail gauges in Poland and the former Soviet Union. The *Baltic Express* plys the rails from Warsaw to Tallinn and back, departing Warsaw at 2:30pm, passing through Kaunas, Lithuania at midnight, and arriving in Tallinn the next day at 1:10pm. One overnight train runs between Warsaw and Šeštokai, Lithuania arriving at 6:30am, 2¼hr. before a Šeštokai-Kaunas-Vilnius train departs (arrival in Vilnius 12:30pm). Buses from Poland to Lithuania do not go through Belarus.

Currently, **trains** to Poland go through Belarus, requiring a transit visa of US$25. Several airlines service the decaying Vilnius airport: SAS flies from Copenhagen, Lufthansa from Frankfurt, and the Polish carrier LOT from Warsaw. You can also reach Klaipėda, on the Baltic Sea coast, by **ferry** from Saßnitz, Germany (20hr. alternate days) with Deutsche Touristik (tel. 49 (381) 458 42 72).

Buses, though slightly more expensive, are better for travel within Lithuania; the trains are slow, noisy, and often horridly crowded. Two major train lines cross Lithuania: one runs north-south from Latvia through Ťiauliai and Kaunas to Poland; the other runs east-west from Belarus' through Vilnius and Kaunas to Kaliningrad, or on a branch line from Vilnius through Ťiauliai to Klaipėda. Buses, however, radiate from all the cities of Lithuania, and unlike in Latvia, Belarus, and other post-Soviet countries, bus services in Lithuania have yet to be seriously pruned, leaving seeming zillions of buses zipping around the byroads of the nation.

LITHUANIA ESSENTIALS

There may eventually be tourist offices in Lithuania; in the meantime, read the excellent English-language *Vilnius in Your Pocket,* an exhaustive compendium about the capital city produced by enterprising German journalist Matthias Lûfkens. It's thoroughly updated every two months and is available at newsstands in Vilnius (3LT). Also check out its sister guides *Kaunas in Your Pocket* and *Klaipėda in Your Pocket,* currently published only annually, but just as comprehensive. Be sure to take advantage of Lithuanian Youth Hostels (LJNN), an organization of eight hostels across Lithuania. HI membership is nominally required, but a LJNN guest card (US$3 at any of the hostels) will suffice. The head office is in Vilnius, Kauno 1A-407 (tel. (22) 26 26 60, fax 26 06 31; open 8am-6pm). Grab a copy of their *Hostel Guide,* a handy little booklet with info. on bike and car rentals, advance booking, and city maps showing how to reach various hostels.

St. John's Eve (Rasos), celebrated as elsewhere in the Baltics on the eve of the summer solstice (the night of June 23), is a beer-drinking, folk-dancing, song-singing, countryside party. The highlight of the evening is wandering into the woods to search for *fern flowers,* a Lithuanian herb best shown to you by someone of the opposite sex, if you know what we mean. Other big **holidays** that you'll see streets named after are: Vasario 16 (Feb. 16; Independence Day, 1918); Kovo 11 (Mar. 11; Independence Restoration Day, 1990); Day of Mourning and Hope (June 14); and Mindaugas's Day (July 6, 1253 the day the first King of Lithuania was crowned).

The unit of currency is the **Lit** (1 Lit = 100 centų.) Since March 1994, the Lit has been tied to the U.S. dollar (US$1=4LT).Traveler's checks can be cashed at most banks (for a 2-3% fee); Thomas Cook seems to be the company of choice.

Local **phones** in Lithuania are mostly free (and mostly broken), though in some locations in Kaunas and Vilnius the phones have been mysteriously maintained to require old Soviet 15-kopeck coins, which nearby kiosk vendors conveniently keep on hand for 0.15LT. Long-distance calls can be made from certain of the old grey public phones with the wide-grooved gold Šetoni sold at post offices (0.24LT). For **international calls,** it is often best to use the Norwegian card phones which have been installed at some locations, such as the main phone offices and railway terminals of the larger cities; cards are sold at the phone offices in denominations of 15,

17.70, 32, 96, and 196LT. Rates for international calls: U.S. 10.50LT per minute; Latvia and Estonia 0.95LT per minute; Europe 5.80LT per minute. You can also book international calls through the operator at the central phone office (pay when finished), but you'll have to wait 20-45min. for the call to go through.

Direct dialing has arrived in Lithuania, though only to some countries. Dial 8, wait for the second tone, and dial 10 followed by the country code and number. Calls to cities within the former Soviet Union can be placed directly by dialing 8, followed by the old Soviet city code. For countries to which direct dialing is not available, dial 8, wait for the second tone, and dial 195 (English-speaking operators available). To reach the AT&T **USADirect operator,** dial 196; **SprintExpress** 197.

Lithuanians pride themselves on the fact that their national language is the most archaic among the Indo-European tongues, more closely related to Latin and Sanskrit than to modern languages. One of only two surviving languages in the Baltic branch (Latvian is the other), it has a rolling, hearty sound full of wonderful letters like ų, ė, ę, š, and ą. A few Lithuanian words will secure instant goodwill. "Do you speak English?" is *Ar kalbate Angliškai?* (AHR KAHL-bah-teh AHN-gleesh-kye), *prašau (*prah-SHAU) means "please" while *Ačiū* (AH-choo) is "thank you." "Hotel" is *viešbuti,* and "market" is *turgus.* If you can, try and tune in everyone's favorite radio program in Lithuania, *Sister Barbara's English Lesson;* Sister Barbara, a Lithuanian-American from New Orleans, comes on daily to teach Lithuanians important phrases in English like "Is this cheese hot?"

■■■ VILNIUS

Multilingual, sprawling and defiant, the capital city of Lithuania has stood at the crossroads of foreign influences for centuries without losing its preeminence as Lithuania's major cultural and social center. Called Wilno by Poles, Vilnius also played had a major role in Polish cultural development, reflected by its inclusion as part of Poland until 1939. The multinational flavor of the city today embraces ethnic Russians, Poles, and Belarussians though religiously, it is firmly Catholic.

ORIENTATION AND PRACTICAL INFORMATION

The River **Neris** winds through the city center; most of the **Senamiestis** (Old Town) is on the left bank. The railway and bus stations are only a few steps from the heart of the old city. A long street called **Aušros Vartų,** then **Didžioji,** then **Pilies,** runs 200m north from the station to the cathedral square and east of the Cathedral.

Tourist Offices: Not yet; try the Lithuanian Youth Hostels office, Kauno 1A-407 (tel. 26 26 60; open 8am-6pm) or the service desks of the **Hotel Astorija,** Didžioji 35/2, or **Hotel Lietuva,** Ukmergės 20. You don't need a tourist office if you're toting *Vilnius In Your Pocket* (3LT).
Embassies: U.S., Akmenų 6 (tel. 22 30 31, fax 22 27 79). Open Mon.-Fri. 9am-5:30pm. **U.K.,** Antakalnio 2 (tel. 22 20 70, fax 35 75 79). Open Mon.-Fri. 9am-5pm. **Poland,** Aušros Vartų 7 (tel. 22 44 44). Open Mon.-Fri. 9am-1pm.
Currency Exchange: Central Currency Exchange Office, inside central Post Office, Gedimino pr. 7 (tel. 22 28 15), offering the best rates in town on non-US$, non-DM currencies, including the Polish *złoty.* Open Mon.-Fri. 8am-8pm, Sat.-Sun.11am-7pm.
Post Office: Central Post Office at Gedimino pr. 7 (tel. 61 66 14). Open Mon.-Fri. 8am-8pm, Sat.-Sun. 11am-7pm. Postcards abroad 0.80LT. **Postal Code:** LT-2001.
Telephones: Place calls abroad at the **Central Telegraph Office,** Vilniaus 33/2 (tel. 61 99 50). **City Code:** 22, from the West 2.
Trains: Station at Geležinkelio 16, (tel. 63 00 88 or 63 00 86). Reservation bureau, Šopeno 3, near the station (tel. 62 30 44). To Moscow (18hr., 120LT), Kaliningrad (7½hr., 38LT), Warsaw (12hr., 85LT), Rīga (8hr., 56LT), Klaipėda (9hr., 10.50LT).
Buses: At **Autobusų Stotis,** Sodų 22, 50m from the railway station. To: Klaipėda (5hr., 14LT), Rīga (6hr., 19LT), Minsk (5hr., 9.40LT), Tallinn (12hr., 38LT), War-

saw (11hr., 55LT), Kaunas (1½hr., 5LT). Advance booking (tel. 26 29 77); international booking (tel. 63 52 77).

Public Transportation: Good system; doesn't run (but isn't necessary) in the Old Town. Rides on buses and trolleybuses 0.30LT, monthly passes 12LT. Buy tickets at kiosks. Runs roughly 6am-midnight.

Taxis: State taxi service tel. 22 88 88. Set rate of 1LT plus 1LT per km (double after 11pm). Private taxis have a green light in windshield; debate fare before you go.

Emergency Numbers: Ambulance, tel. 03. **Fire,** tel. 01. **Police,** tel. 02.

ACCOMMODATIONS

There's a room crunch in Vilnius, but the new International Youth Hostel should open soon in Old Town (hopefully by summer 1995). In the meantime there are plenty of budget options, but they fill quickly.

Lithuanian Youth Hostels (HI), Filaretų 17 (tel. 69 66 27). Reached by bus 34 from the train station (7 stops); in a peaceful neighborhood in the outskirts of the Old Town. Hot breakfast served 9-10am in the sunny dining room. Clean communal showers, often lacking hot water. Midnight lockout. 20LT with HI card or LJNN guest card (US$3).

Hotel Vilnius, Gedimino pr. 20/1 (tel. 62 36 65). This centrally located, unremodeled, state-run hotel is in fact, up for sale. Rooms include sink, TV, phone; floor showers. Singles 70LT. Doubles 140LT. Double room with private bath goes for 240LT.

Litinterp, Bernardinų 72 (tel. 22 32 91, fax 22 35 59), a little south of the Old Town. Arranges private accommodations with English-speakers and apartments. Reservations preferred. Singles 75LT. Doubles 125LT.

FOOD

Vilnius has a handful of marvelous restaurants with excellent food and contrasting atmospheres. Order appetizers, ice cream, and an extra entree with your meal; it still won't cost more than US$3-4.

Café Stikliai, Stiklių 18. Bright and shining example of how to get decent spaghetti (5LT), small pizzas (4-7LT), and a damned good cappuccino (2.50LT) for not much money. Open Mon.-Fri. 9am-11pm, Sat. noon-10pm, Sun. 10am-10pm.

Viola, Kalvarijų 3, across from St. Raphael's Church. A lively Armenian restaurant, serving possibly the best food in Vilnius. Try the *shashliki,* the *kebab,* Armenian cheese, and Armenian meat salad. Menu in Russian and Lithuanian. Live Russian jazz band at night. Entrees 2-6LT. Open 1pm-midnight.

Blyninė, Pilies 8. Look for 2 bronze arms holding a plate of pancakes above the door. Great *blynai* (pancakes) with meat or cheese fillings smothered in cream or jelly. (0.60-1.30LT) Open Mon.-Fri. 11am-8pm, Sat.-Sun 9am-6pm.

SIGHTS

One block north of the railway station, the **Aušros Vartai** (Gates of Dawn) leads into Vilnius's **Old Town,** the largest in the Baltics. Built in the 16th century, the gates are the only surviving entrance from the old city wall and feature griffins and the crest of Lithuania on their outer façade. Through the gates and the first door to the right, the **Chapel of Our Lady of Vilnius** is a 17th-century shrine built around an icon variously said to have been captured in Ukraine by Grand Duke Vytautas, or to actually be a portrait of a 16th-century Lithuanian princess. The **Šv. Kazimiero** church, named after the country's patron saint, can be found further along Aušros Vartų. The oldest Baroque church in town, the Soviets turned it into a museum of atheism in 1966; it was restored as a church in 1989. After this landmark, Aušros becomes Didžioji and broadens to form **Town Hall Square.** On its center stands the **Town Hall,** home to the **Lietuvos Dailės Muziejus** (Lithuanian Art Museum) and a collection of late 19th- and 20th-century Lithuanian paintings. (Open Tues.-Sun. noon-6pm. 0.40LT, Wed. free.)

At the corner of Pilies and Šv. Jono, you'll find the **University of Vilnius.** Go through the arches opposite from St. John's church and you'll see the remarkable **Astronomical Observatory,** a 17th-century building with zodiac signs on the frieze atop the façade. If you turn right on Šv. Mykolo and walk for a block from Pilies, you'll face **St. Michael's,** a Renaissance church dating to 1625, which now houses a bland Soviet-style **Museum of Architecture.** (Open Wed.-Mon. 11am-5pm. 1LT.) Across the street shines Vilnius's Gothic treasure, **St. Anne's Church and Bernardine Monastery,** the church Napoleon wanted to carry back to France. Today, it partly houses the Art Academy and Design School of the University of Vilnius. At the end of Pilies, on Šventaragio, you'll find the white-walled, majestic **Katedros Aikštė** (Cathedral Square). Inside, notice the early Baroque **Chapel of St. Casimir,** which houses a royal mausoleum. (Open Wed.-Fri. 10am-6pm in summer, 11am-5pm in winter. 1LT.) Up the Castle Hill, **Gediminas Tower** offers an unparalleled view of Vilnius's spires and a modest historical museum. (Open Wed.-Mon. 10am-6pm in summer, 11am-5pm in winter. 1LT.) Across the Neris River, you'll find the **Lithuanian State Museum,** with exhibits on the January 1991 crackdown in Vilnius. (Open Wed.-Sun. 11am-6pm. 1LT.) One final must-see is the Baroque **St. Peter and St. Paul Church,** built around 1688. Located on Antakalnio, before the British embassy, it's a 10min. walk from Cathedral Square. Look up at the ceiling, where over two thousand figures dance, sing, and levitate.

■ TRAKAI

Don't miss a visit to the peaceful lakeside village of Trakai, 20km west by bus and train service from Vilnius. The capital of the Grand Duchy of Lithuania in the 14th century, **Trakai Castle** sits on an island in Lake Galvė, accessible by footbridge. From the bus station take a right, walk down Vytantos St. for 1½km and then take the bridge on your right. The watch tower is 30m high. (Open Tues.-Sun. 10am-6pm. 4LT, students 2LT; photo permission 1LT.) Rent a **rowboat** on the lake shores for 2LT per hour. Four trains (40min., 0.80LT) and 15 buses (50min., 1.10LT) link Trakai and Vilnius.

■■■ KAUNAS

Over 90% Lithuanian, many claim that Kaunas is the true heart of Lithuania. The "provisional capital" during Lithuania's first period of independence (1918-1940), Kaunas matured from a German-oriented trade center into a clean, modern city of pedestrian design and graceful architecture that still charms with provincial spirit. Getting around central Kaunas is simple, since it lies on either side of one long thoroughfare: the pedestrian street **Laisvės aleja,** 2km long, lined with shops, restaurants, cafés, and bars. When the street bears left, it joins also-pedestrianized **Vilniaus gatvė** at the entrance to the Old Town, leading to Town Hall Square.

The massive, majestic **St. Michael the Archangel Church** commands the eastern end of Laisvės aleja; its sumptuous Neo-Byzantine interior is a feast for the eyes while the exterior undergoes much-needed renovation. Walk down Laisvės for 2 blocks, turn right on Daukanto, and then take your first left to reach the **Freedom Monument,** deported by the Soviets in the 1940s and returned to its pedestal in 1989. Through the arcade with the cannons on the right as you leave the museum, the **M. K. Čiurlionis Museum** commemorates the work of the prolific avant-garde artist who sought to combine painting and music into a single artistic medium. (Open Tues.-Sun. noon-6pm. 2.50LT, Wed. free.) Across the street, at Putvinskio 64, the **A. Žmuidzinavičiaus Museum,** better known as the **Kaunas Devil's Museum,** houses a collection of nearly 2000 devil figures, most of them folk carvings. Don't miss the sculpture that shows Devil Hitler and Mephisto Stalin chasing each other through a playground littered with human bones. (Open Tues.-Sun. 11am-5pm. 1.50LT.) Where Laisvės ends, Kaunas's Old Town begins; venture through the underpass to get to the **Kaunas Basilica,** the largest Gothic building in Lithuania with a interior that is pristine, dynamic late Baroque.

Practical Information, Accommodations, and Food At Laisvės 102, you'll find the **Central Post Office.** (Open Mon.-Sat. 9am-7pm.) To change money, look for *Valintos Keitykla* signs. Kaunas's **bus station** is at Vytanto pr. 24/26, near the train station. Catch buses here for Minsk (7hr., 13.50LT) and Vilnius (1½-2hr., 4-5LT). One and a half blocks down Vytanto, at the corner with Čiurlionio stands the **train station,** with connections to Kaliningrad (6hr., 20LT) and Vilnius (2hr., 3.20LT). Kaunas doesn't have a lot for the overnight visitor; thankfully there's a youth hostel, Prancūzų gatvė (tel. (27) 74 89 72), 1km uphill behind the train station. Inside the Viešbutis Republika, you can get a suite of your own with bedroom, bathroom, kitchen, and balcony for 40LT. At the grayish but comfortable **Baltija Hotel** at Vytanto pr. 71 (tel. (27) 29 32 02); spartan singles go for 60LT, doubles for 120LT; convince them you're Latvian and get in for 25LT. Dining in Kaunas offers no frills, but at Laisvės 68, the well-known **Metropolis** beckons with red decor, meat-and-potatoes entrees (4-7.50LT), and live Lithuanian music after 9pm. Arrive early and be prepared to wait. (Open noon-5pm and 6pm-midnight.)

■PAŽAISLIS MONASTERY

The **Pažaislis Monastery and Church,** a vibrant Baroque ensemble with rich frescoes, lounges on the right bank of the Nemunas, 10km east of central Kaunas. The church was commissioned by the Chancellor of Lithuania, Kristunas Pacas, and was dedicated in 1674 after 60 years of labor and an expenditure of 2 million ducats. (Open Mon.-Sat. 10am-5pm, Sun. 10am-6pm.) Take trolleybus 5 from the Historical Museum or the railway station to the end of the line; then walk down the main road for 1km. The church is just past a small beach.

■■■ KLAIPĖDA

The third-largest city in Lithuania is rather cosmopolitan—it's one of the few places in Lithuania where you can dance 'til 3am. Klaipėda is the capital of "Lithuania Minor," the western coast of the country which was, until quite recently, German territory. Razed during the war, the city was heavily rebuilt, and the population today is almost 90% Lithuanian, but the zillions of German tourists may confuse you.

Klaipėda faces a narrow peninsula that separates the Kuršių Marios, Lithuania's largest lake, from the Baltic Sea. The **Smiltynė beach** is on the peninsula and faces the Baltic; ferries drift off from the mainland frequently in summer (0.40LT). The **ferry terminal** is near the city canal in the Old Town, not far from Tiltų. From the ferry landing, a road leads 1½km north towards Kopgalis (literally, the head"), where the Curonian Lagoon meets the Baltic See.

Klaipėda's nightlife makes Lithuania's other cities pale, and is one of the city's prime attractions. **Pas Alberta,** at the corner of Sukilėlių and Daržų in the Old Town, is the most popular place in town, despite the hefty cover charge. Dance every night to the DJ's favorite Pet Shop Boys album. (Open noon-6pm and 8pm-2:30am. Cover 12LT.) Originally cleared for a new town market in the 18th century, the classical **Klaipėda Theater** now dominates from the north end. Built in 1857, the theater is famous as one of Wagner's favorite haunts, and infamous for the *Anschluß* (annexation) speech Hitler gave from its balcony in 1939.

Practical Information, Accommodations, and Food Walk right from the railway station along Priestočio to reach **Manto gatvė,** the main thoroughfare. Manto continues north across the city channel and into the Old Town, where it becomes Tiltų. You can **exchange currency** in kiosks surrounding the train station and the bus station, or in one of the multitudinous banks in the city. From the **bus station,** Butkų Juzės 9 (tel. (261) 114 34, info 148 63), within sight of the train station, buses head for Liepāja (3½hr., 5.40LT), Kaliningrad (5hr., 12LT), Vilnius (7½hr., 14LT), and Palanga (½hr., 1.80LT). **Trains** chug from the station at Priestočio 7 (tel. (261) 963 56, info 146 14) to Vilnius (5-9hr., 12.40LT).

Klaipėda has a few cozy hotels; the best deal is **Hotel Vėtrungė,** Taikos 28 (tel. (261) 548 08), 1½km away from the Old Town, serviced by buses 8 and 10. Rooms come with bathroom, shower, and phone (singles/doubles 48LT). **Hotel Baltija,** Janonio 4 (tel. (261) 149 67), is located closer to the bus and train stations but has communal showers (singles 26LT, doubles 35LT). The café **Juoda-Balta,** H. Manto 15, has a black and white interior with mirrors and red, green, and cool blue lighting, as well as delicious food. The flaming ice cream (6LT) is liquor-coated volcano perfect for an afternoon's indulgence. (Open 11am-midnight.) **Prūsija,** Šimhaus 6, has a softer, less modern decor, with MTV blaring for jarring contrast (main courses 7-9LT, open 10am-4pm, 5pm-midnight).

■■■ CURONIAN SPIT (NERINGA)

The Spit's 60m-high dunes of white sand, deep forests of pine and birch, and wide beaches facing the Baltic are the perfect getaway. Getting there is easy; frequent **ferries** from Klaipėda sail to Smiltynė, at its northern terminus. Another option is to go by **hydrofoil** from Kaunas to Nida. A paved road runs south from Smiltynė, passing through the four towns of Juodkrantė, **Pervalka, Preila,** and Nida; a toll point at the entrance to the Park restricts traffic in Neringa with a fee of 4.50LT per car and 0.80LT for pedestrians or bicyclists. **Public transportation** on the Spit consists of the various buses and route-taxis *maršrutinis taxis)* that ply the road from Smiltynå. Be warned also that catching these buses or taxis at points *en route* is difficult as they often fill up; you may have to wait through 6-7 buses before one has room.

Twenty km south of Smiltynå, **Juodkrantė** is a quiet grouping of summer cottages among the pine-covered dunes, and home to the spit's youth hostel, 12 beds in an unused kindergarten classroom. Walk south from the bus stop and turn right onto Ievos Kalno gatvė. Reception is at no. 18, apt. 6 (tel. 533 14). 16LT per person. For an extra 8LT, the school cook will make you a *massive* breakfast that will leave you full for the rest of the day.) Food is hard to come by in Juodkrantė, so stock up before you arrive. One excellent way to explore the forests here is by hiking up the **Raganú kalnas** (Witches' Hill), where carved wooden sculptures of wood spirits, monsters, and local personalities line the trails to the top. Entrance to the trail is on a marked side road south of the main section of town. Dozens of other good trails lead across the Spit towards fabulous beaches on the Baltic side.

Buried three times by shifting dunes, **Nida** is the most famous town on the whole of the Curonian Spit. Outside the center, just past the junction of Skruzdynės gatvė with Pamario, the **Thomas Mann House** marks where the famous German lived from 1930-33. It is now a museum devoted to the author, with his books, photos, and writing desk (open Tues.-Sun. 10am-5pm; 2LT). A walk down Naglių leads through the old artists' colony of Nida, a collection of well-kept wooden cottages now interspersed with cafés and souvenir shops. The Russian border is just 500 meters or so beyond this dune, but there are no controls on this side of the Spit. German tour groups now routinely book entire hotels in Nida for the entire summer, leaving few choices for travelers without reservations. **Auksinės Kopos,** Kuverto gatvė 17 (tel. 522 12), is a remodeled Soviet-era resthome primarily frequented by Lithuanians, with private baths and a fridge. (Singles 35LT. Doubles 58LT. Luxury suites featuring a TV 75LT. Breakfast included.) One thing you shouldn't miss is smoked fish, a Nida specialty. At **Rūkyta Žuvis,** to the right of the disco, one giant fish costs 5LT (open "days"). The **Disco Baras,** in the large grey Agila building on central square, is the only point for nightlife in town, regularly filled to bursting with "Spiting" teenagers (open noon-3am).

BALTIC STATES

Belgium
(Belgique, België)

US$1	= 31.95BF (francs, or BEF)	10BF =	US$0.31
CDN$1	= 23.80BF	10BF =	CDN$0.42
UK£1	= 50.77BF	10BF =	UK£0.20
IR£1	= 50.29BF	10BF =	IR£0.20
AUS$1	= 24.50BF	10BF =	AUS$0.41
NZ$1	= 19.37BF	10BF =	NZ$0.52
SAR1	= 8.96BF	10BF =	SAR 1.12
Country Code: 32		**International Dialing Prefix: 00**	

From a train speeding through the Belgian countryside, you may wonder whether any urban development interrupts the miles after miles of rolling countryside spread over the hills, lined with rows of trees, and interrupted only by the occasional farmhouse in the distance. Suddenly, however, the swift blur of gold and green is replaced by grey, red and brown brick, and you'll have arrived. Large metropolitan areas appear quickly and vanish almost as suddenly into the wide expanse. Major centers such as Antwerp and Brussels bustle and thrive as any comparable major city. Brussels—today's "capital of Europe"— home to NATO and the European Union hums with a bureaucratic buzz as diplomats and leaders stream to and from work quietly making the decisions you'll read about in tomorrow's paper.

The first stop on the military tours of so many would-be European conquerors, Belgium bears the scars of a troubled European history. Today, the small nation continues to argue with itself as nationalist Flemish-speaking residents of the northern province of Flanders demand independence from the southern Walloons.

Belgium's real allure, however, comes from the beautiful scenery and medieval villages, not the major cities. Such treasures as Bruges and Ghent are reminders of Belgium's long cultural history. So, forget the tensions and bask in Belgium's beauty, watching the sunlight reflected in the meandering canals.

GETTING THERE AND GETTING AROUND

Belgium's **train network** is one of the most reliable in Europe. Prices are low, if only because the country is small (at most four rail-hours across). **Eurail** is valid on inter-city buses as well as trains. The **Benelux Tourrail Pass** is a decent option, covering five days of travel in Belgium, the Netherlands, and Luxembourg during a one-month period (4040BF, under 26 3030BF). The best deal could be the **Go Pass** (1290BF for 10 trips within Belgium). A **Half-Fare Card** (550BF for one month) is also available, and tourist offices sell a **24-hr. pass** covering all municipal transport in the country (200BF).

Biking is very popular, and many roads are equipped with bike lanes (which you must use even if they're studded with potholes). When you see two paths next to the street, the one by the street is for bicycles and mopeds, the one by the storefront is for pedestrians. Of Belgium's 150 train stations, 65 rent bikes (150BF per day, 280BF per day without rail ticket); you can return them to any of 115 designated stations (100BF to return a bike to a station that doesn't lend them). Pick up the brochure *Train et Vélo/Trein en Fiets* at any station. **Hitching** in Belgium is generally auspicious. Bilingual signs ("please" is *s.v.p.* in French, *a.u.b.* in Flemish) are reportedly more successful. **Taxi Stop** (tel. (02) 646 86 10) has offices in major cities and matches travelers with Belgian drivers to destinations all over Europe (1.3BF per km, 150-500BF per trip). **Ferries** from Zeebrugge and Oostende, near Bruges, cross to Dover and other British ports.

BELGIUM ESSENTIALS

Belgium's network of efficient tourist offices is supplemented by **Infor-Jeunes/Info-Jeugd,** a nationwide information service which helps young people with short- or long-term accommodations in Belgium. The English-language weekly *Bulletin* (75BF at newsstands) lists everything from movies in English to job opportunities.

National holidays in Belgium are Jan. 1, April 17, May 1, Ascension Day (May 25, 1995), Whit Monday (June 5, 1995), July 21, Aug. 15, Nov. 1, Nov. 11, and Dec 25. Most public **phones** require a phone card (200BF or 1000BF) which can be purchased at **PTT** (post, telephone, and telegraph) offices or at magazine stands; the few remaining coin-operated phones take an initial deposit of 10BF. Belgium's MCI **WorldPhone** number is 0800 100 12, AT&T **USADirect** 0800 100 10, **Sprint Express** 0800 100 14, **Canada Direct** 0800 100 19, **BT Direct** 0800 100 44, **Ireland Direct** 0800 103 53, **SA Direct** 0800 100 27. In an **emergency** anywhere in Belgium, dial 100 for medical service or the fire brigade, and 101 for the police. To reach the domestic operator, dial 13 07; the European operator, 13 04; the international operator, 13 22. Note that the digit "3" in the preceding numbers becomes a "2" in Flemish areas.

Accommodations, Camping, Food, and Drink Most visitors to Belgium make the mistake of staying in Brussels and day-tripping to neighboring cities. Try using Bruges or Ghent as a base instead. Private hostels in Bruges are fun and lively, and the city is a welcoming refuge at night. Not as many opportunities for nightlife exist in these cities, however, so if your aim is to party, park yourself in

Brussels. **Hotels** in Belgium are exorbitantly expensive, with "trench-bottom" prices for singles starting at 800BF and doubles at 1000-1100BF. Avoid bankruptcy by staying in one of the 31 **HI hostels,** which charge about 335BF per night and are generally quite modern, clean, and loads more fun, usually boasting extremely cheap bars. Pick up *Budget Holidays* at any tourist office for complete hostel listings. **Campgrounds** charge about 100BF per night. The pamphlet *Camping,* with complete listings and prices, is available free at tourist offices. Belgian cuisine can be wonderful, but a native dish may cost as much as a night in a decent hotel. Steamed mussels are usually tasty and reasonably affordable (a whole pot for around 395BF). Belgian beer provides both national pride and a national pastime; more varieties (over 500) are produced here than in any other country and they range from the ordinary to the religiously brewed Chimay. Regular or quirky blonde goes for as little as 30BF, and dark beers cost about 60BF. Leave room in the wallet and the belly for Belgian *gaufres* (waffles) and those famous Godiva chocolates.

■■■ BRUSSELS (BRUXELLES, BRUSSEL)

Instantly associated with the home of the European Union and NATO, and for the less enlightened, with the sprout, Brussels breathes beyond the confines of offices and vegetables. Where Antwerp lays claim to Rubens, Brussels's cultural icon is no less than Hergé and his world-famous, studly-yet-androgynous creation Tintin. Throughout the city, he and his little dog Snowy peer and smile at you—often comforting but at the same time somewhat eerie. Even if you don't understand exactly what Art Nouveau architecture entails when you leave, you'll still be able to recognize a Victor Horta building as well as many experts. The great architect was the innovator of and the inspiration for many of Brussels's most fascinating interiors and exteriors. Unfortunately, many of Brussels's more recent architects went to the 1970s school of design and, consequently, garish concrete and glass boxes pop up without warning from behind less functional, but more artistic, gothic arches and spires.

ORIENTATION AND PRACTICAL INFORMATION

Brussels's trinity of train stations consists of **Brussels Midi** (serving the southern part of the city), **Brussels Central** (your gateway to the Grand-Place, and the rest of the action in tourist Brussels), and **Brussels Nord** (in the heavy construction area around the Botanical Gardens). Most of Brussels's major attractions are clustered around this backbone, the **Bourse** (Stock Market) to the west, and the **Parc de Bruxelles** to the east. Travel within the center of the city is easy, but trekking from the northern end to the southern is quite a hike. If you will only be in Brussels for a short time, a **tourist passport** may be a good option. For 200BF you get one day's free public transportation, a free map, and an army of reductions for the city's museums, etc. (available at the TIB or at almost any bookshop). Multiday travelers may want to attack the city an area at a time. Be aware that public transportation stops at midnight and there are no night buses; having to walk from a disco in the south back up to Gare du Nord will not be fun, especially if your senses are a bit blurred from the night's "festivities." Also, be aware that Brussels is a bilingual city, and some maps may only have the Flemish street names (*Let's Go* uses French since it is usually more familiar to travelers).

Tourist Offices: National, 61, rue du Marché aux Herbes (tel. 504 03 90). From the Grand-Place, walk 1 block away from Town Hall. Books rooms throughout Belgium. Comprehensive *What's On* brochure (free). Open Mon.-Fri. 9am-7pm; Oct.-June 9am-1pm and 2-7pm. **TIB (Tourist Information Brussels),** in the Town Hall on the Grand-Place (tel. 513 89 40). Helpful, but crowded. Free room reservations, *Brussels Guide and Map* (70BF). Theater, opera, and ballet tickets sold Mon.-Sat. 11am-5pm. Open 9am-6pm; Oct.-March Mon.-Sat. 9am-6pm.

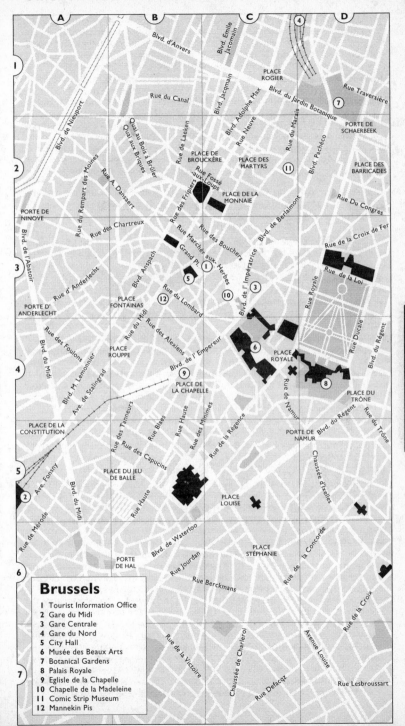

BELGIUM

Brussels

1 Tourist Information Office
2 Gare du Midi
3 Gare Centrale
4 Gare du Nord
5 City Hall
6 Musée des Beaux Arts
7 Botanical Gardens
8 Palais Royale
9 Eglisle de la Chapelle
10 Chapelle de la Madeleine
11 Comic Strip Museum
12 Mannekin Pis

Tours: Le Bus Bavard/De Babbelbus (tel. 673 18 35, fax 675 19 67). Walking tour of the old city, then a bus to attractions on the outskirts. Tours (3hrs.) leave daily May 20-Sept. 26 at 10am (in July also at 2pm) from the entrance to the St-Hubert Galleries at 90, rue Marché aux Herbes. 300BF; discount if staying in a youth hostel.

Budget Travel: Acotra World, 51, rue de la Madeleine (tel. 512 70 78). Free room-finding; budget flights for those under 26. Open Mon.-Sat. 10am-5:30pm. **Infor-Jeunes,** 27, rue du Marché-aux-Herbes (tel. 512 32 19). Budget bonanza. Open Mon.-Fri. noon-5:45pm. Also at Gare du Midi (tel. 522 58 56) March-Oct.

Embassies: U.S., 27, bd. du Régent (tel. 513 38 30). Open Mon.-Fri. 9am-6pm. **Canada,** 2, av. Tervueren (tel. 741 06 11). Open Mon.-Fri. 9am-noon and 2-5pm. **U.K.,** 85, rue Arlon (tel. 287 62 11). Open Mon.-Fri. 9:30am-noon. **Australia,** 6, rue Guimard (tel. 231 05 16). Open Mon.-Fri. 9am-noon. **New Zealand,** 47, bd. du Régent (tel. 512 10 40). Open Mon.-Fri. 9am-1pm and 2-5pm. **South Africa,** 26 rue de la Loi (tel. 230 68 45). Open Mon.-Fri. 9-11:30am.

Currency Exchange: At **Gare du Nord** (open 7am-9:45pm, 20BF commission), **Gare Centrale** (open 8am-8pm; no commission, mediocre rates) and **Gare du Midi** (open 7am-11pm, 20BF commission). Almost every bank and change booth charges 100-150BF to cash checks, but banks have better rates.

American Express: 2, pl. Louise (tel. 512 17 40). M: Louise. Decent exchange rates. Open Mon.-Fri. 9am-5pm, Sat. 9:30am-noon. Holds mail for 30 days. Charges 50BF to retrieve mail if you don't have an AmEx card or Cheques.

Post Office: M: de Brouckère. **Main office** on the 2nd floor of the Centre Monnaie, the tall building on pl. de la Monnaie. Open Mon.-Fri. 9am-6pm, Sat. 9am-noon. **Postal Code:** 1000 Bruxelles 1.

Telephones: 17, bd. de l'Impératrice, near Gare Centrale. Open 8am-10pm. Far superior rates to privately owned competitors. **Public Phone** (a private company) at 30a, rue de Lombard, open 10am-8pm. High rates in a more pleasant atmosphere. For operator assistance in Brussels, dial 1280. **City Code:** 02.

Flights: (tel. 722 31 11; flight info tel. 723 60 10). Trains to **Brussels International Airport** (80BF) depart Gare Centrale 5:39am-11:14pm; all stop at Gare du Nord.

Trains: (tel. 219 28 80). Most trains stop at **Gare Centrale,** and many stop at either **Gare du Nord** or **Gare du Midi** as well. Traffic to **Gare du Quartier Leopold** generally passes through one of the main stations. Trains regularly leave for Amsterdam (900BF), Bruges (355BF), and Antwerp (180BF).

Buses: STIB (Société des Transports Intercommunaux Bruxellois). Offices in Gare du Midi (open Mon.-Fri. 7:30am-6pm, Sat. 8:30-4:30pm), and at 20, Galeries de la Toison d'Or, 6th Fl. (tel. 515 30 64). **L'Épervier,** 50, pl. de Brouckère (tel. 217 00 25). M: Brouckère. Belgian representative of Europabus; low fares to major cities. Open Mon.-Fri. 9am-6pm, Sat. 9am-12:30pm and 1:30-4:30pm.

Car Rental: Hertz, 8 Blvd. Lemonnier. Open 9am-5pm.

Luggage Storage: Lockers and offices at the 3 major train stations. Bag check 60BF, lockers 80BF.

Public Transportation: 50BF buys 1hr. of travel on buses, the **Métro** (M), and trams. Tickets at any Métro or train station, or on the bus. Public transportation runs 6am-midnight.

Hitchhiking: Hitchhiking is on the decline in Belgium; it is illegal to hitch on motorways and sliproads. Those hitching to Antwerp and Amsterdam take tram 52 from Gare du Midi or Gare du Nord to Heysel, the terminus. About 300m from the terminus, they fork right for Antwerp. Those going to Liège and Cologne take tram 90 from the Gare du Nord to M: Diamant to reach the E40. Those headed to Ghent, Bruges and Oostende take bus 85 from the Bourse to one stop before the terminus and follow the E40 signs. Those going to Paris take tram 52 "Gare du Midi" to rue de Stalle and walk toward the E19.

Bookstore: W.H. Smith, 71-75, bd. Adolphe Max (tel. 219 27 08). M: de Brouckère. Vast and pricey. Open Wed.-Mon. 9am-6:30pm, Tues. 10am-6:30pm.

Laundromat: Salon Lavoir, 5, rue Haute, around the corner from Bruegel's youth hostel. M: Gare Centrale. Wash and dry 210BF. Open Mon.-Fri. 8am-6pm.

Crisis Hotline: SOS-Jeunes, 27, rue Mercellis (tel. 512 90 20). 24hrs. **Helpline** (tel. 648 40 14). English crisis line. 24hrs.

Gay Services: Gay Switchboard (tel. 233 25 02). 9am-9pm.
Pharmacies: Pharma-Congrès, 56, rue du Congrès, at rue du Nord, near the
Jacques Brel hostel. M: Gare Centrale. Open Mon.-Fri. 8:30am-1pm and 1:30-
5:30pm. **Neos-Bourse Pharmacie,** bd. Anspach at rue du Marché-aux-Polets. M:
Bourse. Open Mon.-Fri. 8:30am-6:30pm, Sat. 9am-6:30pm.
Medical Assistance: Free Clinic, 154a, chaussée de Wavre (tel. 512 13 14). Don't
be misled by the name; you do have to pay for medical attention. Open Mon.-Fri.
9am-6pm. **24-hr. medical services** (tel. 479 18 18 or 648 80 00).
Emergencies: Ambulance or **First Aid:** tel. 112. **Police:** tel. 101.

ACCOMMODATIONS AND CAMPING

Accommodations in Brussels are fairly easy to come by, since there is a slew of inexpensive hostels. However, with the exception of just a few hotels and bed and
breakfasts, accommodations are geared toward the more expensive. Most places to
stay are relatively close to the center of town with the exception of those in and
around pl. Louise. The tourist office will point you in the right direction.

Sleep Well, 23, rue du Daumier (tel. 218 50 50, fax 218 13 13). 1995 will be the
first full year in its new home for Sleep Well. The light and airy modern building
is a radical departure from its claustrophobic predecessor. Tintin and Snowy are
still the official mascots. Singles 620BF. Doubles 490BF. Triples or quads 410BF. 6-
bed dorm 360BF. Laundry facilities available and discounts abound. 10% off with
your ISIC card, 25% if you have the number "23" on your passport, 50% if you
have the letters S-L-E-E-P-W-E-L-L in your name, and still free if it's your birthday.
Whew. Breakfast included. Wheelchair accessible.
CHAB, 8, rue Traversière (tel. 217 01 58). M: Botanique. From Gare du Nord, take
bus 61 or walk 10min. From Gare Centrale, take bus 65 or 66 to rue du Méridien.
Vincent Van Gogh wrote that "my modest room costs 50 francs a month. Bread is
included, and a cup of coffee every morning..." Prices may have changed, but
breakfast is still free. Colorful, artsy rooms and a small garden. Kitchen. Lockout
10am-4pm. Curfew 2am. Large dorms 300BF. Smaller dorms 370BF. Singles
620BF. Doubles 510BF per person. Triples and quads 430BF per person. Large
lockers free with your own lock. Sheets 100BF. Laundry 150BF.
Bruegel (HI), 2, rue du St-Esprit (tel. 511 04 36), behind Notre-Dame-de-la-
Chapelle. M: Gare Centrale. Excellent location. One of the most modern youth
hostels around with showers that are to die for. High-tech lockers but you pay
accordingly (90BF for a large locker). Lockout 10am-2pm. Curfew midnight.
Dorms 395BF. Singles 660BF. Doubles 540BF. Quads 440BF. Showers and breakfast included. Dinner 260BF. Packed lunch 140BF. Sheets 120BF. Wheelchair
accessible. Make reservations in summer.
Gîtes d'Etape: Auberge de Jeunesse "Jacques Brel" (HI), 30, rue de la
Sablonnière (tel. 218 01 87), on the pl. des Barricades; 10min. from Gare du Nord,
15min. from Gare Centrale. M: Madou. Institutional rooms, each with shower. Bar
and terrace. Other amenities include a game room, a TV and video room, and a
good-sized cafeteria. Reception open 7am-1am. Curfew 1am. Dorms 395BF. Singles 660BF. Doubles 540BF. Triples and quads 440BF. Breakfast included. Sheets
120BF. Wheelchair accessible. Call ahead since hostel fills up quickly.
Hôtel Pacific, 57, rue Antoine Dansaert (tel. 511 84 59). M: Bourse. Fine location
and friendly, English-speaking management. Flexible midnight curfew. Tasty Belgian breakfasts included. Jackson Pollock copies on the walls. Singles 950BF. Doubles 1300-1500BF. Showers 100BF.
Pension Bosquet, 70, rue Bosquet (tel. 538 52 30). M: Hôtel des Monnaies. Plaster
falling off the walls, but fairly inexpensive rooms, some with small terraces.
Reception open 8am-11pm. Singles 900BF, with shower 1200-1300BF. Doubles
1200BF, with shower 1650BF. Quads with shower 2600BF. Hall showers 100BF.
Breakfast included. Reserve in summer.
Camping: All sites are outside Brussels. First choice is **Paul Rosmant,** 52 Warande-
berg (tel. 782 10 09), in Wezembeck-Oppem. Reception open 9am-12:30pm and
2-10pm. 120BF per person. Open April-Sept. Just north of Brussels in Grimbergen

BELGIUM

is **Veldkant,** 64 Veldkantstr. (tel. 269 25 97). Take bus G or H from Gare du Nord; alight at Grimbergen. 100BF per person, 100BF per tent. Open April-Oct.

FOOD

Restaurants in Brussels run the gamut from the charmingly cheap to the egregiously expensive. Many, many restaurants are found in the blocks around the Grand-Place. Worth a visit is the **rue des Bouchers,** about a block north of the Place, if only to admire the exotic dead fish peering out of their blankets of ice. Farther down, the restaurants on the rue Grétry serve up plentiful Italian grub. You'll find everything from pizza to pita and hoagies to gyros if you spend some time wandering about. If you're about a quart low on grease, check out the city's many *fritte* stands; you name it, it's fried. Open air markets can be found at **pl. Ste.-Catherine** (7am-5pm), **pl. Emile Bockstael** (Sat. 7am-2pm), and **chaussée d'Anvers** (Wed. 7am-1pm). **GB supermarkets** are at 248, rue Vierge Noire (M: Bourse; open Sat.-Thurs. 9am-7:50pm, Fri. 9am-8:50pm) and in the "City 2" shopping center, 50m from Sleep Well. (M: Rogier. Open Sat.-Thurs. 10am-7pm, Fri. 10am-8pm.)

Sole d'Italia, 67, rue Grétry, serves up a whopping plate of spaghetti, with all the bread and water you like for 165BF. Other Italian specialties are not much more expensive. Open noon-late.

Chez Léon, 18-20, rue des Bouchers, just off the Grand-Place. M: Gare Centrale. Deep in the tourist maelstrom, but fun. Hamburgers and Brussels's famed mussels (large portions 315-595BF). *Plat du jour* 315BF. Open noon-1am.

Le Grand Café, 78, bd. Anspach, on the other side of the Stock Exchange. M: Bourse. Generous *menus* include appetizer, main course and dessert (465-695BF). Open Sun.-Mon. 7am-midnight, Fri.-Sat. 7am-1am.

L'Ecole Buissonnière, 13, rue de Traversière (tel. 217 01 65), opposite CHAB youth hostel. M: Botanique. Great lunch menus (300BF). You could get a bit more for your money, however, from the dinner menu. Ask to dine on the patio. Open Mon.-Fri. noon-2:30pm and 6:30-10:00pm.

't Kelderde, 6, Grand-Place (tel. 513 73 44). This little *sous-terre* restaurant doles out temptingly large entrees from as little as 195BF. Good ambience and the place usually has a crowd. Open noon-2am.

Le Forestier, 2 rue Haute (tel. 512 75 22), just around the corner from Bruegel youth hostel. Home to large Italian entrees and various salads and quiches. Open noon-11pm.

SIGHTS

One look at Brussels's **Grand-Place** and it isn't surprising to learn that it was dubbed "the most beautiful square in the world" by Victor Hugo. Framed by ornate gold-trimmed architecture, the Place is a masterpiece in itself; enclosing a daily flower market and feverish tourist activity. The jewel in the crown is the 15th century **Town Hall,** with its Gothic spires piercing the sky. Not to be missed is the Place's light show held at around 10pm and 11pm. Pulsing to the beat of 15th century chants and awe-inspiring instrumentals, the Hall is lit with over 800 multi-colored floodlights, bathing the building in an eerie, psychedelic glow. (Hall open Tues.-Fri. 9:20am-12:15pm and 1:45-5pm, Sun. 10am-noon and 2-4pm; Oct.-March 9:30am-12:15pm and 1:45-4pm.)

Three blocks behind the Town Hall on rue de l'Etuve at rue du Chêne is Brussels's most giggled-at sight, the impudent figure of the **Mannekin-Pis,** a statue of a small boy (with an apparently gargantuan bladder) steadily urinating. One story goes that a 17th century mayor of Brussels promised to build a statue in the position that his young son was found; another says it commemorates a young boy who (à la Gulliver) ingeniously defused a bomb that had been lit to blow up the Town Hall. Either way, you've got to admire the lad's courage. More comically, the locals have hundreds of outfits made up for him, from Napoleon to a Eurocrat, each with a little hole for you-know-what.

BELGIUM

For more intellectual stimulation, the **Musée d'Art Ancien,** 3, rue de la Régence (M: Gare Centrale or Parc) houses a huge collection of the great Flemish masters including Brueghel the Elder's *Fall of Icarus* and *Census in Bethlehem* and Rubens's *Martyrdom of St. Levinius* and *Calvary* (open Tues.-Sun. 10am-noon and 1-5pm; free). Next door is the sister-museum, the **Musée d'Art Moderne.** Here, you'll find everything from the brilliant to the boring to the banal. This museum-houses an extensive Magritte collection in addition to works by Miró, Picasso, and Dalí. A veritable must for those who find meaning in women painted green, plain black canvases, or jumbled masses of stone and wire. (Open Tues.-Sun. 10am-noon and 1-5pm. free.) The **Musées Royaux d'Art et d'Histoire,** 10, parc du Cinquan-tenaire (M: Mérode), cover a wide variety of periods and genres—Roman torsos lacking heads, Syrian heads without torsos, and Egyptian caskets with protruding wooden feet (open Tues.-Fri. 9:30am-5pm, Sat.-Sun. and holidays 10am-5pm; free).

For those who lived for chemistry class and the chance to invent a compound with plastic straws and balls, the **Atomium** (M: Heysel, in the Bruparck entertain-ment complex) is for you. The symbol of the 1958 World's Fair, the shining alumi-num-and-steel Atomium is meant to represent a cubic iron crystal structure magnified 165 billion times and serves as Brussels's answer to the Eiffel tower. Now it's a science museum (open 9:30am-8pm, Sept.-March 9:30am-6pm; 160BF).

The **Musée Horta,** 25, rue Américaine, is Art Nouveau master Baron Horta's home (open Tues.-Sun. 2-5:30pm; 100BF during the week, 200BF on the weekend). For more examples of Art Nouveau architecture, plus all the French and Belgian comic strips you can read, check out the surreal **Belgian Comic Strip Centre,** 20, rue des Sables, in a renovated warehouse just a couple blocks from Sleep Well. Brussels, the "Comic Strip Capital of the World," does its moniker proud by providing gobs of comic strip (*bande desinée*) art, including, of course, plenty of Tintin comics. There is also a comic strip library for your "studious activities." They even have Tintin's rocket ship! (Open Tues.-Sun. 10am-6pm. 150BF.) Escape from the glass and con-crete of the city to the lush greenery of the **Botanical Gardens,** rue Royale (M: Bot-anique; open 10am-10pm; free).

ENTERTAINMENT

Theatre and Cinema

The flagship of Brussels's theatre network is the beautiful **Théâtre Royal de la Mon-naie,** pl. de la Monnaie (tel. 218 12 11), M: de Brouckère. Renowned throughout the world for it's opera and ballet, the theatre actually has affordable performances (open Tues.-Sat. 11am-6pm; 250BF-3000BF). The **Cinema Museum,** 9, rue Baron Horta (tel. 513 41 55), M: Gare Centrale, shows two silent movies per night with piano accompaniment and three talkies, sometimes in English with French subtitles (open 5:30-10:30pm; 80BF per 2hrs.). In the shadow of the Atomium, **Kinepolis** (M: Heysel) shows movies on its 26 screens making it the largest movie theatre in Europe. The main attraction here is the 600sqm Imax screen which routinely blows people away with its incredible panoramas. (Open daily, evenings and matinées. Expect to pay upwards of 300BF for a seat.) From June through September, con-certs frequently pop up on the **Grand-Place,** and in the **Parc de Bruxelles.** The **Théâtre Royal des Galleries** offers popular theatre but presents it only in French (tel. 513 23 28; tickets 150-800BF). For more events information, snag a calendar at the tourist office or call **BBB Agenda** (tel. 512 82 77).

Bars and Nightclubs

The Brussels bar and club scene is relatively fresh, with many opportunities for the bored backpacker. Most night spots are clustered around the Grand-Place, within about four blocks. Another good place for nocturnal frenzy is the area around av. Louise, but remember, it's a long walk back to the hostels.

BELGIUM

La Mort Subite, 7, rue Montagne-aux-Herbes-Potagères, is one of Brussels's oldest and best-known cafés, across the street from the entrance to Galeries St. Hubert, opposite the Grand-Place. Open 10:30am-midnight. Beer 50BF, coffee 55BF.

Le Cercueil, 10, rue des Harengs, just off the Grand-Place, literally means "the coffin" and the mood and ambience here is unparalleled. Lit only by blacklights, the place may ruin your eyes, but it will make your shoes and clothes glow with an unearthly light. Temptation in the form of cocktails such as Demon's Sperm and Cadaver's Urine. The brooding, dark mood music doesn't help either. But the Satan imagery doesn't stop there; the drinks are expensive as Hell. Open 11am-3am, weekends until 5am. Beer from 100BF, cocktails from 250BF.

Ultième Hallucinatie, 316, rue Royale (tel. 217 06 14). Tram 92 or 94. Art Nouveau temple. Showing its age a little, but still just as nice inside. Open Mon.-Fri. from 11am, Sat-Sun. from 4pm.

Au Bon Vieux Temps, 12, rue Marché-aux-Herbes, just off the Grand-Place. Live jazz in a mellow 17th century tavern. Open Sun.-Thurs. 11am-11pm, Fri.-Sat. 11am-2am. Beers from 70BF.

La Fleur en Papier Diré, 53-55 rue des Alexens. Quiet, mellow, and adorned with pictures of all sorts on the walls. Just relax. A somewhat older clientele. Open 11am-11pm.

The Garage, 16, rue Dequesnoy, is a panic of sweaty bodies, and that's just to go through the cover charge line. Live bands often. Open Wed.-Sun. 11pm-late. 200BF cover includes a free drink. Sun. is gay only.

L'Ecume des Nuits, 122a galerie Louise, at pl. Stéphanie, is home to funky tunes and throbbing house music. Open Fri.-Sat. 10pm-dawn.

■ LOUVAIN (LEUVEN)

About half an hour out of Brussels, just over the language border stands the ancient university town of Louvain (Leuven). Impressive Flemish Renaissance buildings and ostentatious Gothic façades conceal the clubs and hangouts of the teeming student population. Louvain's most ostentatious display of masonry is the sculpture-burdened **Stadhuis** (Town Hall). (Guided tour only. Mon.-Fri. 11am and 3pm. Sun. 3pm; March-Oct. 3pm.) Across from the Town Hall is **St. Pieterskerk,** a 15th century church with a collection of paintings by Dick Boutz, including his *Last Supper* (open Mon.-Sat. 10am-noon and 2-5pm, Sun 2-5pm; Oct.15-March 15 Tues.-Sat. 10am-noon and 2-5pm). The 50BF admission also includes entrance to the **Museum Vander Kalen-Mertens** at Savoyestr. 6. The **Groot Begijnhof,** is a lovely "city within a city" down Naamestr. Built during the 17th and 18th centuries, the buildings once housed *Beguines*, women scorned because they insisted on keeping their own property and supporting themselves (*mon dieu,* what brazenness!); university students now frolic in the area. Louvain has Belgium's largest (Interbrew) and smallest (Domus) **breweries.** The latter, at Tiensestr. 8, has taps running directly from its brewery to its tavern (beer 45BF). Thursday means party, since most students return home for the weekend. Each Friday in July is a different festival; the first is a **classical music festival,** with violinists playing on rooftops and balconies. August 13-15 Louvain busts loose for the **Markt Rock festival** (most concerts free; finale 100BF).

Trains leave hourly from Brussels (130 BF, round-trip 180BF). From the station, walk down Bondgenotenlaan to pick up a map (10BF for a good one, 5BF for a not-so-good one) at the **tourist office,** Naamsestr. 1a (tel. (016) 21 15 39; open Mon.-Fri. 9am-5pm, Sat. 10am-5pm; March-Oct. also Sun. 10am-5pm). Students in Louvain live in *Kots,* houses overseen by often stern women known as *Kotmadams;* during the summer, some of them open their doors to travelers. Try the *Kot* at De Beriotstraat 13 (tel. (016) 40 02 88; singles 800BF, doubles 1400BF, triples 200BF).

■ WATERLOO

Napoleon was caught with both hands in his shirt at Waterloo, just south of Brussels. If you aren't interested in Napoleon, you won't have much fun here because the whole town is devoted to him. The town is a tourist magnet, sucking you in and sucking the spare change out of your pocket. Start at the **Musée Wellington,** right in the center of town, for an explanation of European politics before and after the short, "dead French dude," plus an hour-by-hour account of the battle (open 9:30am-6:30pm; mid-Nov. to March 10:30am-5pm; 70BF, students 50BF, children 40BF). Next, take bus W, across the street from the Musée Wellington, a few km and 38BF down the road to the **Lion Mound,** an imposing edifice of earth that gives you (and about 50 other tourists) a spectacular view of the battlefields (open 9:30am-6:30pm; Nov.-March 10:30am-4pm, last entry ½hr. before closing; 40BF). While at the Lion Mound, check out the **battlefield panorama** (275BF, students 220BF, includes admission to the other museums) to immerse yourself in the fighting—complete with surround sound.

To get to Waterloo, take bus W (every 1½-2hrs.; 40BF each way) from pl. Rouppe in Brussels (accessible via tram 90), or take the train from Brussels (130BF round-trip) and walk 1km to the center of town. For a discount pass to all the museums and sights, go to the **Tourist Office,** 149, chausée de Bruxelles (tel. (02) 354 99 10, fax (02) 354 22 23) and buy a pass for 300BF (250BF for students) that gets you admission to all six museums, the panorama, and the Lion Mound.

■■■ BRUGES (BRUGGE)

Bruges, the capital of Flanders, fulfills the postcard critera for the idyllic European town, with vaulting Gothic steeples, cobblestone roads (complete with horse-drawn carriages), and brisk bike-riding locals. You may think you've walked straight into the pages of a travel brochure. Behind the picturesque façade, however, thrives a healthy, exciting nightlife and a city more cosmopolitan than initial impressions might suggest. But, arrive prepared for the weather: there is a saying that if you can see the belfry, it's going to rain and if you can't, it's already raining.

ORIENTATION AND PRACTICAL INFORMATION

Although it might seem logical to make Bruges a daytrip from Brussels, there is good reason to stay in Bruges and make Brussels an excursion from there. Highways encircle the town, as canals cut and wind their way through and around it. The dizzying **belfort** (belfry) towers high at the center of town, presiding over the **Markt,** a handsome square. Outside the ring of canals, south of the center of the city, stands the train station.

Tourist Office: Burg 11 (tel. 44 86 86), just east of the Markt, in the town's other main square, the Burg. Turn left out of the station and enter 't Zand Sq., then turn right on Zuid-Zuidzandstr. Books rooms (400BF deposit) and sells a good map for 20BF. Open Mon.-Fri. 9:30am-6:30pm, Sat.-Sun. and holidays 10am-noon and 2-6:30pm; Oct.-March Mon.-Fri. 9:30am-5pm, Sat. 9:30am-12:45pm and 2-5pm. Smaller office at the **train station** also sells maps and books hotels. Open Mon.-Sat. 2:45-9pm; Nov.-Feb. Mon.-Sat. 1:45-8pm. **Youth Information Center: JAC,** Kleine Hertsbergestr. 1 (tel. 33 83 06), near the Burg, the 2nd right off Hoogstraat. Lists cheap rooms and restaurants. Also a youth crisis center. Open Mon. and Wed. 9am-noon and 1:30-8pm, Tues. 1:30-8pm, Fri. 9am-noon and 1:30-6pm, Sat. 10am-12:30pm.

Post Office: Markt 5. Poste Restante. Open Mon.-Fri. 9am-6pm, Sat. 9am-noon. **Postal Code:** 8000.

Telephones: There aren't many public phones in Bruges. Find one at the Tourist Office, outside the post office, or at your hostel. **City Code:** 050.

Trains: Train station on Stationsplein (tel. 38 23 82), a 15min. walk south of the city center. Open 6:30am-10:30pm. Frequent connections to Antwerp (360BF), Brussels (345BF), and Ghent (155BF).

Bike Rental: At the train station, 150BF per day with train ticket, 280BF without. **Koffieboontje,** Hallestr. 4 (tel. 33 80 27), off the Markt, next to the belfry, charges 250BF per day, students 110BF; 850BF per week.

Hitchhiking: Despite the (relatively) low cost of the train system, hitching is said to be quite effective once you get on the main highways. Those hitching to Brussels take bus 7 to St. Michiels or pick up the highway behind the station.
Luggage Storage: At the train station, 60BF. Lockers (15BF) at the tourist office.
Laundromat: Belfort, Ezelstr. 51, next to Snuffel's Traveller's Inn. Wash 'n' dry 120-240BF. Open 7am-10pm.
Emergencies: Ambulance tel. 100, **Police,** tel. 101.

ACCOMMODATIONS AND CAMPING

Hostels fill up quickly in June, July, and August; it's advisable to call ahead or at least to show up in the morning. You won't be disappointed by the quality; the private hostels are clean, fun, and social.

The Passage, Dweersstr. 26 (tel. 34 02 32, fax 34 01 40), 1 block north of 't Zand, first right off of Noordzanstr. Clean and airy rooms with exceptionally nice blankets. The large, hardwood bar is quite pleasant, and the restaurant serves typical Belgian cuisine and vegetarian meals. Dining available 6pm-midnight (entrees 195BF-370BF); for guests, free Belgian beer with meal. Reception open 8:30am-midnight; bar open 5pm to whenever the party dies down. No lockout or curfew. Rooms range from 310BF for a dorm to 375BF per person for a four-person room. Free t-shirt if you stay 4 days, and a free city map to everyone. 5% discount off more expensive rooms with a *Let's Go* or a youth hostel card. Free if it's your birthday. Lockers available for 20BF and a security deposit; same for room keys.
Bauhaus International Youth Hotel, Langestr. 135-137 (tel. 34 10 93, 33 41 80), 10min. from the Markt. Bus 6 from the station (40BF). The Bauhaus is a piece of America transplanted into a few square feet. Huge current music selection from the Stones to the Stone Temple Pilots. A frenzy of activity at night. Restaurant open 6pm-midnight (entrees 185BF-400BF). Co-ed dorms 295BF. Singles 550BF. Doubles 950BF. Triples and quads 320BF per person. Showers and breakfast included. Lockers available (30BF). Reception open 8am-2am.
Snuffel's Traveller's Inn, Ezelstr. 49 (tel. 33 31 33), 10min. from the Markt; follow Sint-Jakobstr., which turns into Ezelstr. Bus 3, 8, 9, or 13 from the station. The downstairs bar stays active until the wee hours of the morning. Expect road noise if you have a room by the street. Reception open 10am-midnight. No lockout or curfew. Co-ed dorms 325BF. Doubles 450BF. Showers and breakfast included, but the showers are in a separate building. Ask about doing chores in exchange for a free night's stay, but this space fills up quickly.
Europa Jeugdherberg (HI), Baron Ruzettelaan 143 (tel. 35 26 79), 25min. south from the Markt; take bus 2 to Wantestr. (2nd stop). Walk up the road 75m, left at the HI sign. Clean and slick, but comparatively dull and far away. Attracts grammar-school groups. Reception open 7:30-10am and 1-11pm. Lockout 10am-1pm. No curfew. Dorms 335BF. 4-bed rooms with shower 1700BF. Nonmembers add 100BF. Showers and breakfast included. Dinner 230BF. Wheelchair access. Free lockers. Sheets 120BF. Bar open 6pm-midnight. Cheapest beer in the city (30BF). Reserve ahead.
Hotel Lybeer, Korte Vulderstr. 31 (tel. 33 43 55), just off 't Zand Sq., first right off Zuidzandstr., then a quick left. Fresh, pretty rooms and an elegant reception area. Reception open 8am-midnight. Singles 900BF (1990BF with private bathroom). Doubles 1500BF (2300BF with private bath). Triples 2100BF (3500BF with private bath). Breakfast and showers included. Those who take the more expensive rooms get a slightly larger breakfast and a generally nicer room.
Camping: Memling, Veltemweg 109 (tel. 35 58 45), 2km from town center. Bus 11 or 58A from the station. Cramped, crowded campground catering to tired tourists in tacky trailers. 95BF per person, 115BF per tent. Restaurant open 6-10:30pm (130BF-450BF).

FOOD

In general, Bruges is not the cheapest place in the world to eat, but there are inexpensive restaurants out there if you take the time to search a bit. Don't be shocked if you spend more for dinner than you did on your room. To avoid high prices, stay

away from the many cafés lining the Markt and 't Zand. Instead, look for deals starting about one block from these two town centers. Try the **Vismarkt** (from the Burg,
cross the river and turn left) to find fresh seafood. An even cheaper option is one of
Bruges's renowned supermarkets; try the **Nopri Supermarket,** Noordstr. 4, just off
't Zand (open Mon.-Thurs. and Sat. 9am-6:30pm, Fri. 9am-7pm), or **EDI Supermarket,** 55 Langestr., close to Bauhaus (open Mon.-Fri. 9am-12:30pm, 1:30pm-6:30pm,
Sat. 9am-6pm). You'll find great deals when **markets** open on **'t Zand** every Saturday morning and the **Burg** every Wednesday morning.

> **Ganzespel,** Ganzestr. 37, from the Burg, up Hoogstr., cross the river and it's your
> 3rd right. Very cheap and very tasty. 230BF will buy you soup, an entree, salad
> and a side of rice or potatoes. Open Wed.-Sun. noon-2pm and 6-10pm.
> **Chicken-In,** 31 Sint-Amandsstr., directly off the Markt. Rotisserie chicken and
> other poultry from 255BF in a casual atmosphere. Open noon-2pm and 5-
> 10:30pm.
> **Ristorante Riva Del Sole,** 22 Wollestraat. A nice, little Italian restaurant serving
> pizza for 230BF. Other meals start from 320 BF. Open noon-3pm and 6-11pm.
> **The Lotus,** Wappenmakerstr. 5, 3rd left off Philipstockstr. from the Markt. Serves
> vegetarian lunches in an attractive building. Open mid-Aug. to July 10am-2pm.
> Meals from 210BF-230BF.

SIGHTS AND ENTERTAINMENT

Bruges is best seen on foot; the tourist office suggests excellent walking tours. Rising precipitously out of the Markt, the **belfort** towers magnificently as the literal hub
of Bruges. Climb its dizzying 366 steps during the day for a view of surrounding
areas and come back at night when it serves as the city's torch (open 9:30am-5pm;
Nov.-March 9:30am-12:30pm and 1:30-5pm; tickets sold only until 4:15pm; 100BF,
students 80BF, family 200BF). Up the street, at the Burg, the 14th-century **Stadhuis**
(Town Hall) has some typically beautiful paintings and furniture behind its flamboyant Gothic front (open 9:30am-5pm; Oct.-March 9:30am-noon and 2-5pm; 60BF).
For those fascinated by death and torture, check out the **Groeninge Museum** on
Dijverstr. Decapitation, flaying, boiling in oil, drawing and quartering, and others, by
the Flemish Primitives (Jan van Eyck, Hans Memling) and the master of medieval
macabre, Hieronymous Bosch (open 9:30am-5pm; Oct.-March Wed.-Mon. 9:30am-
noon and 2-5pm; 130BF, students 100BF). Next door is the **Gruuthuse Museum,** in
the 15th-century residence of wealthy beer magnates. Today, the museum hosts a
collection of historic weapons, musical instruments, pottery, lace, and coins (open
9:30am-5pm; Oct.-March Wed.-Mon. 9:30am-noon and 2-5pm; 130BF, students
100BF, family 230BF; tickets sold only until 4:40pm). Hidden away in the **Church of
Our Lady** is the oft-photographed Michelangelo sculpture *Madonna and Child,* his
only work to leave Italy during his lifetime (open Mon.-Sat. 10-11:30am and 2:30-
5pm, Sun. 2:30-5pm; Oct.-March closes ½hr. earlier in the evenings; 30BF, students
15BF). A relic supposedly containing the blood of Christ is held in the **Basilica of the
Holy Blood,** on the corner of the Burg. Free entrance to the chapel, but there is a
small museum inside that charges 40BF, students 20BF (open 9:30-noon and 2-6pm;
Oct.-March 10am-noon and 2-4pm, closed Wednesday afternoon). **Minnewater** (the
Lake of Love) lies on the southern end of the city. Be prudent; this romantic spot is
more for the contemplation, not the consummation, of love. The area around the
bridge was once the home of a not-so-romantic ammunition dump.

If you're geared up for cycling and aren't too tired, try **Bruges with Bart** bike
tours, which leave from the Markt at 10am (350BF includes bike, raingear, and insurance; buy tickets at Boekhandel De Reyghere, Markt 12). **The Back Road Bike Co.**
explores remote windmills and castles by mountain bike. Tours leave the tourist
office on op de Burg. (10am, 400BF; 2pm, 450BF; March-June and Sept.-Oct. at 1pm,
400BF. Groups limited to 15 and fill quickly. Call 34 30 45 for more information.)
Boat tours along Bruges's picturesque and winding canals leave every ½-hour
(10am-6pm) from five points on the main canal (150BF); call the tourist office for
more information.

BELGIUM

The best nightlife in Bruges is free—wandering through romantic streets and over cobblestone bridges after sunset. Ogle over a mind-blowing 300 varieties of beer at **Brugs Beertje,** Kemelstr. 5; just the menu will blow you away (open Mon.-Tues. and Thurs. 4pm-1am, Sat.-Sun. 4pm-2am; prices from 50BF). Next door, try the many tantalizingly fruity flavors of *jenever* (cleverly masking the very high alcohol content) at **Dreiple Huis. L'ObCéDé,** right on 't Zand, is a good place for pulsating music, low purple lights, and dancing (8pm-3am, no cover). Near the Hotel Lybeer, on Korte Vuldersstr., is a cool jazz and blues bar, **bistrorant Lokkedize,** a pleasant locale to simply mellow for a few hours (open Tues.-Thurs. 7pm-1am, Fri. 7pm-3am, Sat. 6pm-3am, Sun. 6pm-1am).

During the **Festival van Vlaanderen** (July 29-Sept. 24), the entire town pulses with the **International Fortnight of Music.** On Ascension Day, while the rest of Belgium snoozes, Bruges oozes with medieval fare during the **Festival of the Holy Blood** (May 25 in 1995). Snatch the monthly program *Agenda Brugge* (free) at the tourist office for a schedule of local events.

■ NEAR BRUGES

Informative **Quasimodo** tours (tel. (050) 37 04 70) are an excellent way to explore Flanders while keeping Bruges as a base. "Flanders Fields" somberly patrols the battlefields of World War I where thousands of Allied soldiers died in the trenches (Tues., Thurs., and Sat. 1300BF), while "Triple Treat" offers a little of everything, stopping for waffle, chocolate, and beer along the way (Mon., Wed., and Fri. 1300BF—samples included). Conducted in English, these tours leave various hostels and hotels around 9am, return around 5pm, include a picnic lunch, and are highly recommended by their older customers. Show *Let's Go* and get 300BF discount.

The towns of the North Sea coast of Belgium win fans largely for their beaches. Ferries, ships, and jetfoils chug daily to the U.K. from **Zeebrugge** and **Oostende,** easily accessible by train from Bruges. Get tickets from travel agents, at ports, or in the Oostende train station. **P&O European Ferries** (Brussels tel. (02) 231 19 37; Oostende tel. (059) 70 76 01; Zeebrugge tel. (050) 54 22 22) sails between Oostende and Dover, Zeebrugge and Dover, and Zeebrugge and Felixstowe. Another option is the classy **Oostende Lines,** with its mighty freighter, the Prins Filip (tel. (059) 55 99 55, fax (059) 80 94 17). They sail between Oostende and Ramsgate, England (about 2hrs. from London: Victoria Station) six times a day, plus jetfoil service. (1200BF, 2300BF round trip.) In Oostende, the **De Ploate youth hostel (HI),** Langestr. 82 (tel. (059) 80 52 97), is 5min. from the station (reception open 8am-6pm; dorms 400BF). Campgrounds freckle the coast; two options are **De Vuurtoren,** Heistlaan 168, in Knokke (tel. (050) 51 17 82; 90BF per person, 190BF per tent; open mid-March to mid-Oct.) and **Jamboree,** Polderlaan 55, in Blankenberge (tel. (050) 41 45 45; 120BF per person, 150BF per tent).

■■■ GHENT (GENT)

Back in the 14th century, when the feudal system was all the rage, and kings and queens were more than just ceremonial figureheads, Ghent was the center of Europe's garment industry. Back in those glory days, the city erected its three magnificent towers, testaments to its wealth and power. At the time, Ghent was second only to Paris in size and prestige. Today, Ghent is no longer a European powerhouse, but it can still challenge Paris as *la ville lumière*. By night, the city is a vibrant spectacle not to be missed; most buildings are bathed in multicolored splendor.

PRACTICAL INFORMATION

Tourist Office: Municipal Tourist Office, in the crypt of the town hall on Botermarkt (tel. 224 15 55). Take tram 1 or 12 from the train station to the main post office (looks more like a castle than a post office), then head down Klein Turkije towards the belfry. Maps and informative walking-tour booklets. Open 9:30am-12:30pm and 1:15-4:30pm.

Budget Travel: JOKER/Acotra, Overpoorstr. 58 (tel. 221 97 94). BIJ tickets and helpful advice. Open Mon.-Fri. 10am-1:15pm and 2-6pm, Sat. 10am-1pm; Sept.-April Mon.-Fri. 10am-1:15pm and 2-6pm. **Taxi-Stop,** Onderbergen 51 (tel. 223 23 10). Matches drivers with riders (1.3BF per km), books cheap last-minute flights (tel. 224 00 23) and sells **Eurolines** bus tickets. Open Mon.-Fri. 9am-6pm.

Post Office: Korenmarkt 16 (tel. 225 20 34). Poste Restante. One of the lovelier buildings in town. Open Mon.-Fri. 8am-6pm, Sat. 9am-noon. **Postal Code:** 9000.

Telephones: Keizer Karelstr. 1. Buy telephone cards here or at any newsstand. Open Mon.-Thurs. 8am-4pm, Fri. 8am-6pm. **City Code:** 09.

Trains: Trams 1, 10, 11 and 12 run between **Sint-Pieters Station** (tel. 222 44 44) on the southern edge of the city, and Korenmarkt, the center of the old city. Frequent trains to Bruges (160BF), Brussels (215BF), and Antwerp (235BF).

Hitchhiking: Ghent lies at the intersection of the E40, connecting Brussels and Germany with Oostende, and the E17, linking Paris and Amsterdam. Hitchers turn right out of the station onto Clementinalaan, which becomes Burggravenlaan, and continue until they reach the E17.

Laundromat: St. Jacobsnieuwstr. 85. Open 8am-10pm. Wash and dry 140BF; bring plenty of 20BF coins.

Emergencies: Ambulance: tel. 100, **Police:** tel. 101; headquarters: tel. 266 61 11.

ACCOMMODATIONS AND CAMPING

Ghent's new youth hostel, **De Draeke** (The Dragon), St-Widostraat 11 (tel. 09 233 70 50, fax 233 80 01), is elegant and modern. Lying in the shadow of Gravensteen, its location is perfect. 355BF gets you into a 2-, 3-, 4- or 6-person room with personal bathroom and shower. The dining hall serves delicious all-you-can-eat meals if there are groups staying (230BF). Lockout 10am-3pm, front door locks at 11pm, but know the code and you'll get in. Take tram 12 to the castle and take your next left. You can also get a room at Ghent's **university** from mid-June to mid-September, while the students are away. Single with sink 500BF, breakfast and shower included. Call the office at Stalhof 6 (tel. 222 09 11) for information and reservations. If all the rooms are full, and you are forced to sleep in the manger, then **De Ijzer,** Vlaanderenstr. 177 (tel. 225 98 73) may be your best choice. The cloisters are small, but not too shabby. Take tram 12 from the station to Kouter. Singles and doubles 1150BF. Showers and breakfast included. **Camping Blaarmeersen,** Zuiderlaan 12 (tel. 221 53 99), is 15 blocks or a bus ride (38) northwest of Sint-Pietersstation. Open March to mid-Oct.; 100BF per person, 110BF per tent.

FOOD

Ghent is an inexpensive place to eat. With luck, you'll be able to find a good meal for about 200BF. The best areas are around **Korenmarkt,** just in front of the post office and **St.-Pietersnieuwstraat,** down by the University. When bread and cheese just won't satisfy, treat yourself to a meal at **De Appelier,** Citadellaan 47 (tel. 221 67 33), near the Museum of Fine Arts. Their vegetarian plates (240-290BF) are scrumptious; ask to sit in the rose garden in back. (Open Sun.-Fri. 11:30am-2pm and 5:30-8pm, Sat. 11:30am-2pm.) At the student cafeteria **Overpoort,** in the Restaurant Rijksuniversiteit Gent building on Overpoortstr., near Citadellaan, you'll find typical student subsistence: macaroni, spaghetti and hamburgers (100-200BF; open 10:30am-2:30pm). **Backstage,** on the corner of St.-Pietersnieuwstr. and J. Plateaustr. serves mouth-watering salads from 200BF and omelettes from 130BF. This place also doubles as a theater (open 11:30am-1am). Next door at **La Rustica,** they dole out tasty, cheap pizza from about 200BF-250BF (open 12:30-2:30pm and 6-11pm; closed Sat. and Sun. afternoons). Sample freshly-made **Australian ice cream,** on Hoogstr., just off Groentenmarkt—it's delicious and only 25BF a scoop. While you're down there, check out the fresh fruits and vegetables at **Groentenmarkt** (open Mon.-Fri. 7am-1pm, Sat. 7am-7pm).

BELGIUM

SIGHTS AND ENTERTAINMENT

Ghent has more protected monuments than any other city in Belgium, so connoisseurs of fine architecture will not be disappointed. **Gravensteen, the Castle of the Counts,** is a winding, sprawling medieval fortress complete with ramparts to climb, dozens of rooms to explore, and a torture room with rack, thumbscrews, and other barbarities (open April-Sept. 9am-6pm, Oct.-March 9am-5pm; 80BF). Wind your way up the towering **belfort** (belfry) and experience some classic Hitchcock vertigo as you gaze over the surrounding landscape. The dragon weathervane that sits atop the belfry is the *de facto* symbol of Ghent. In medieval times, a man hiding inside the great bronze dragon shot fire from its mouth with a torch and fireworks. (Open 10am-12:30pm and 2-5:30pm. 100BF with guide, 80BF without, students 60BF.) The **Stadhuis** (Town Hall) is an arresting juxtaposition of Gothic and Renaissance architecture. A block away on Limburgstr. stands **Sint-Baafskathedraal,** built between the 14th and 16th centuries; its real pearl is Jan van Eyck's *Adoration of the Mystic Lamb,* an imposing polyptych on wood panels (open Mon.-Sat. 9:30am-noon and 2-6pm, Sun. 1-6pm; Oct.-March Mon.-Sat. 10:30am-noon and 2:30-4pm, Sun. 2-5pm; Cathedral free; *Adoration* 50BF, students 40BF). Also worth a visit is the **Museum voor Schone Kunsten** (Museum of Fine Arts), in the Citadel Park, which lodges a strong Flemish collection and an outstanding exhibit of contemporary art (open Tues.-Sun. 9:30am-5pm; 80BF, students 40BF).

Ghent houses a large university, the **Rijksuniversiteit Ghent,** and the city's nightlife lives and dies by its student population. From October to July 15, students cavort in the cafés and discos near the university restaurant on Overpoortstr. **Vooruit,** on St-Pietersnieuwstr., is a huge art-deco bar popular with collegiates. Its concert hall (tel. (09) 223 82 01 for reservations) features everything from rock to jazz to avant-garde. The café is always crowded (open Aug. 13-July 16 10pm-3am). By the youth hostel, **De Tap en de Tepal,** on Gewand, serves up wine and cheese from around 100-200BF.

■■■ ANTWERP (ANTWERPEN)

Antwerp gained much fame from being an early European commercial center and later a major hub for the diamond and garment trade. Artistically, it lays claim to Peter Paul Rubens, with whom you will be inundated throughout your visit. According to legend, the river ports of the city were once guarded by a merciless giant called Druoon Antigroon, who punished toll evaders by cutting off their hands. His reign of terror was ended by a brave Roman soldier who cut the giant's hand off and threw it in the river. The name "Antwerp", some claim, comes from a combination of the Dutch "hand" and "werpen" (to throw). Less colorful linguists dismiss this derivation, claiming the actual derivation from the term for a sandbank or silt deposit.

ORIENTATION AND PRACTICAL INFORMATION

Antwerp rests 40km north of Brussels on the Amsterdam-Brussels-Paris rail line. **Centraal Station** stands smack in the middle of town. The **Meir,** an avenue lined with shops and eateries, connects the station to the **Grote Markt** and **Groenplaats,** Antwerp's two major squares.

Tourist Office: Municipal Tourist Office, Grote Markt 15 (tel. 232 01 03). From the train station, turn left onto DeKeyserlei, which becomes Meir, and follow it to Groenplaats; turn right past the cathedral. Free hotel reservations. City map 10BF; whopping package of info plus map 20BF. Not-so-detailed free map also available. Open Mon.-Sat. 9am-7:45pm, Sun. 9am-4:45pm.
Budget Travel: VTB, St. Jacobsmarkt 45-47 (tel. 234 34 34). Travel info and youth tickets. Open Mon.-Fri. 9am-5:30pm, Sat. 9am-12:30pm. **Jeugd-Info-Antwerpen,** Apostelstr. 20-22 (tel. 232 27 28). Open Mon.-Fri. 10am-7:30pm, Sat. 2-5pm.

Currency Exchange: Bureaus at Centraal Station have poor rates (10-50BF commission for cash, 50BF for traveler's checks). One, however has extended hours (open 8am-11pm). If the banks aren't open, you'll find the best rates at **American Express** and the **Thomas Cook** bureau on Koningen Astridplein, in front of the train station.

American Express: Frankrijklei 21 (tel. 232 59 20). Exchange and mail desks close at 5pm Mon.-Fri. 50BF to retrieve mail without AmEx card or Traveler's Cheque.

Post Office: Main office and Poste Restante on Groenplaats. Open Mon.-Fri. 7am-7pm, Sat. 7am-noon. Open Mon.-Fri. 9am-6pm. **Postal Code:** 2000.

Telephones: RTT, Jezusstr. 1. Open 8am-8pm. Also at Centraal Station. Open Mon.-Fri. 9am-noon and 12:30-5:15pm. **City Code:** 03.

Trains: Centraal Station, 15min. from the Grote Markt and most of the sights. 20 trains per day to Rotterdam (540BF) and Amsterdam (890BF), 4 trains per hr. to Brussels (180BF). Lockers are quite pricey at 100BF for a large, 80BF for medium, and 60BF for small. By comparison, the baggage check is only 60BF per day.

Public Transportation: Most public transportation in Flanders is run by the same company, de Lijn; a pass from one city will work in another. Trams and buses 40BF; buy a 10-ride ticket for 250BF at Centraal Station, tram and subway stops, or at the tourist office. Subway runs 6am-midnight.

Hitchhiking: Those heading to Germany, the Netherlands, and Ghent, take bus 20 from the train station to the big interchange (Plantin en Moretuslei) outside town. Those going to Brussels and points south, take tram 2 to the intersection of Jan Devoslei and Jan van Rijswijklaan.

Laundromat: Was-A-Tom, 34 Lange Koepoort, near the Grote Markt. Wash 80-110BF, dry 10-20BF. Open 7am-11pm.

Pharmacy: Apoteek devollesmacht, Nationalestr. 119. Open Mon.-Fri. 9am-12:30pm and 2-6:30pm. Pharmacies post the current *pharmacie de garde.* Pharmacies are everywhere; look for big, green, neon crosses.

Medical Assistance: Saint Elisabeth Hospital, Lange Gasthuisstr. 45 (tel. 223 56 11 or 223 56 20).

Emergencies: Ambulance: tel. 100. **Police:** tel. 101; headquarters, Oudlaan 5 (tel. 202 55 11).

ACCOMMODATIONS AND CAMPING

Budget accommodation possibilities are less than spectacular. Some cafés around the train station advertising "rooms for tourists" rent lodgings by the hour.

Boomerang Youth Hostel, Volkstr. 49 (tel. 238 47 82). From Centraal Station, take bus 23 to Museum, or walk 25min. Eclectic, trippy atmosphere. A movie every night chosen from over 300 by the first lucky traveler. The rooms are clean and the showers are hot. Reception open 9am-10pm. Free lockers need padlocks. Backyard terrace with barbecue. Dorms 360BF. Doubles 1100BF. Breakfast included. Dinner 200BF. Sheets 100BF.

Jeugdherberg Op-Sinjoorke (HI), Eric Sasselaan 2 (tel. 238 02 73). Take tram 2 "Hoboken" to Bouwcentrum or bus 27 to Camille Huysmanslaan. Turn around, face the statue, take first left and follow the HI signs over the river and through the woods. Clean, modern, and somewhat strict. Kitchen, laundry and ping-pong table. Work 3 hours and stay free. Work 2 hours more and get 3 meals. Lockout 10am-5pm. Midnight curfew. 335BF, nonmembers 435BF. Breakfast included. Reserve a bag lunch (120BF) and call ahead to see if dinner (230BF) will be served. Bar open 5-11:30pm.

New International Youth Home, Provinciestr. 256 (tel. 230 05 22). Take tram 11 from Centraal Station or walk left down Pelikaanstr., 4th underpass under the railroad tracks, turn right at Pizza Hut. Clean and comfortable, but painfully dull. Reception open 8am-11pm. No lockout. Curfew 11pm, but night key available for a 200BF deposit. Dorms 410BF. Singles 870BF. Doubles 1250-1350BF. Triples 1950BF. Quads 2200BF. Dinner (330BF) at 7:30pm, but only served to groups. Sheets 120BF. Phone reservations encouraged.

Scoutel, Stoomstr. 3 (tel. 226 46 06, fax 232 63 92), only 5min. from Centraal Station. Follow Pelikaanstr., go under 2nd underpass, it's the first right. New and sporting some creatively decorated meeting rooms. Bedrooms are neat and comfortable. All rooms come with a personal bathroom and shower. Kitchen and TV room. Reception open from 9am-6pm. Check in before 8pm (Fri.-Sat. before 10pm). Doubles 1300 BF. Triples only 1650BF. Over 25 1500BF and 1900BF, respectively. Breakfast included. Reservations without deposit held until 6pm.

Camping: Jan van Rijswijklaan, on Vogelzanglaan (tel. 238 57 17). Reception open 7am-9pm. 65BF per person, 35BF per tent. Shower included. **De Molen,** on St. Annastrand (tel. 219 60 90). Reception open 7am-10pm. 35BF per person, 35BF per tent. Shower 20BF. Both open April-Sept.

FOOD

Finding inexpensive food in Antwerp can be quite a crusade. Avoid the cafés surrounding Groenplaats—most are pricey. Your best bet is to avoid the more touristed areas and head to less known spots north and south of Groenplaats. Wander south along the river until you reach the area around the **Waalse Kaai** and the **Museum of Fine Arts,** or head north to **Suiker Rui.** A meal for about 200BF is a good deal. **GB,** Groenplaats's subterranean supermarket is the place to go if you're on a tight budget. (Go down into the Groenplaats tram station and follow the signs for Winkelcentrum. Open Mon.-Thurs. and Sat. 9am-8pm, Fri. 9am-9pm.) Following Pelikaanstr. south, next to Centraal Station, will bring you to the kosher world of the **Jewish District.**

Pizzeria Toni, across from the Stadhuis in Grote Markt. Serves all varieties of (extremely) thin crust pizza for 230BF and up. Students can get a special Mon.-Fri. noon-3pm: their choice of pizza for 200BF.

Atlantis, Korte Nieuwstr. 6, serves vegetarian meals such as omelettes and cheese toast at the bargain prices (about 125-220BF). Open Mon. and Wed.-Fri. noon-2pm and 5-9:30pm, Sat.-Sun. 5-9:30pm.

De Ware Jacob, Vlasmarkt 19, is called a "brown pub" because of its oak interior. Check it out more for the wood; its prices start at about 350BF. Open Mon.-Thurs. 5pm-late, Fri.-Sat. noon-late, Sun. 4pm-late.

Gringo's Mexican Restaurant, Ernest van Dijckaai, is a great deal for Mexican food. The restaurant itself has a great look. Meals from around 180BF. Open Wed.-Sun. 5-11pm.

't Oerwoud, hip little place on the corner of Suiker Rui and Ernest van Dijckaai. Serves pub fare as well as spaghetti and others from about 200BF. Open 5pm-late.

SIGHTS AND ENTERTAINMENT

Many of the best sights in Antwerp are free. A walk down the **Cogels Osylei** will bring you past some outrageous Art Nouveau mansions that practically scream "Blatant display of wealth!" **Centraal Station** itself is one of the most beautiful examples of Antwerp's architecture. The shops and buildings lining the **Meir** are excellent examples of Antwerp old and new.

Antwerp does have its requisite beautiful buildings and museums, as well. The **Stadhuis** (Town Hall), in Grote Markt in the **oude stad** (old city), is a dignified example of Renaissance architecture (open for tours Mon.-Fri. 11am, 2pm and 3pm, Sat. 2pm and 3pm; closed during frequent official functions). The nearby **Kathedraal van Onze-Lieve-Vrouw,** Groenplaats 21, has a showy Gothic tower. Its interior is decorated with stained glass and Flemish masterpieces, notably Rubens's *Descent from the Cross* and *Exaltation of the Cross* (open Mon.-Fri. 10am-6pm, Sat. 10am-3pm). The little-known **Mayer van den Bergh Museum** at Lange Gasthuisstr. 19 harbors Brueghel's *Mad Meg* and other works (open Tues.-Sun. 10am-5pm; 75BF, students 30BF). Antwerp's famed son built **Rubens Huis,** Wapper 9 (off Meir), and filled it with a trove of art (open Tues.-Sat. 10am-5pm; 75BF, students 30BF). The **Royal Art Gallery,** Leopold De Waelplaats 1-9, showcases one of the best collections of Old Flemish Masters in the world (from the 14th-17th centuries), as well as some monumental Rubens canvases. Natural lighting and the originality of its

BELGIUM

exhibit designs have made this gallery a model for many others (open Tues.-Sun. 10am-5pm; main galleries free; special exhibits can be pricey).

The reason most people come to Antwerp is for its 300 bars and nightclubs. One of the most famous is **Café d'Anvers,** Ververrui 16, where international DJs come and spin house music in near-rave conditions. Unfortunately, a 200BF cover (open Sat.-Sun. midnight-very late). Another good spot is the **Swing Café,** on Suikerrui, where live jazz bands play on Mon., Tues., and Sat. nights (open noon-late; no cover). **Bierland,** Korte Nieuwstr. 28, offers over 400 varieties of Belgian beer (from 40BF; open Sun.-Thurs. 8am-late, Fri.-Sat. noon-late).

From June to mid-July the **Whitsun Fair,** across from the Museum of Fine Arts, is a tangle of carnival food, bright neon, and gut-wrenching rides. Celebrating its 150th birthday, the **Antwerp Zoo** provides a serene and exotic natural environment for its potpourri of wildlife (open 9am-6pm; 340BF; students 270BF). For movie listings or a guide to events, pick up the monthly *Antwerpen* at the tourist office.

■■■ NAMUR AND THE ARDENNES

The small city of **Namur,** in the heart of Wallony is the last remaining outpost before the vast wilderness of the Ardennes. The Ardennes, with their bountiful opportunities for hiking, biking, caving, climbing should be visited by any lover of the outdoors, but Namur itself deserves some exploration as well.

Only about an hour's train ride from Brussels, Namur can easily be made either a day trip or a home base. The first sight you'll probably notice is the foreboding **citadel,** firmly rooted on the top of a rocky hill to the south. You can do the adventurous thing and climb your way to the top, or you can wimp out and ride the *téléférique* (cable car). (Open 10am-7pm, Oct.-May Sat.-Sun. 10am-7pm. 160BF, round-trip 190BF.) For another 195BF, you can go on a whirlwind tour of the fortress, including a historical film, a museum, a guided tour through the damp underground passages, and a train ride around the fort. For a little adrenaline (and to save your legs), rent a mountain bike from the high station of the *télésiège* (150BF per hr., 450BF per ½-day, 600BF per day). All sorts of museums populate Namur. For some holy spirits, check out the hallowed halls of the **Abbage de Floreffe,** where tours are given of the 18th century monastery, and also of the brewery. Take bus 10 "Chatelineau" to Floreffe. (Open March-Oct. Mon.-Fri. 11am-6pm, Sat.-Sun. 11am-8pm. 80BF, students 60BF. Beer 60BF.)

Practical Information, Accommodations, and Food A list of all the 13 museums can be found at the **city tourist office,** 1 Square de l'Europe Unie (tel. (081) 22 28 59; open 9am-6pm). Here, or at the train station, you can buy a map for 10BF. The **provincial tourist office,** 3 rue de Notre Dame (tel. (081) 22 29 98; open Mon.-Fri. 8am-5pm) should be your first stop if you are planning on venturing into the deep green Ardennes forest. Youth travel information can be found at **Infor-Jeunes,** Beffroi 4 (tel. (081) 22 38 12; open 11:30am-6pm), tucked away in the recesses of Namur's belfry.

Namur's youth hostel, the **Auberge Félicien Rops (HI),** 8, av. Félicien Rops (tel. (081) 22 36 88), is named for one of Namur's best known artists. It is loaded down with services and facilities, such as laundry (240BF), kitchen facilities, and tasty meals (see if you can get some homemade apple sauce). It also rents bikes 8-9am for 100BF, and books kayak trips at a 10% discount. Ask about working for free room and board if you are planning an extended stay. (Take bus 3 directly to the door, or take bus 4 or 5 to Les Marroniers, better directions can be found at the Infobus parked in front of the station. 335BF, nonmembers 435BF. Packed lunch 120BF. Dinner 230BF. Sheets 120BF. Midnight curfew.) **Les Trieux,** 99, rue des Tris (tel. (081) 44 55 83), in Malonne, is your best "wilderness" option. Take bus 6 for 6km to Malonne. (75BF per person, 50BF per tent. 30BF per hot shower. Cold showers free. Brrrr. Open April-Oct.) **Le Parisien,** 16, rue Emile Cuvelier, has a lunchtime menu for 290BF (open noon-2pm).

Bulgaria (България)

US$1	= 55Lv (leva, or BGL)	10Lv =	US$0.18
CDN$1	= 39Lv	10Lv =	CDN$0.25
UK£1	= 82Lv	10Lv =	UK£0.12
IR£1	= 80.5Lv	10Lv =	IR£0.12
AUS$1	= 40.4Lv	10Lv =	AUS$0.25
NZ$1	= 32.45Lv	10Lv =	NZ$0.31
SAR1	= 15.2Lv	10Lv =	SAR0.66
Country Code: 359		**International Dialing Prefix: 00 (EU)**	

Come to Bulgaria and you'll find a nation where southern European charm and tranquility belie the sometimes inefficient nature of many institutions, where hospitality can win you lifelong friends, and where education is valued above all else.

In 681, Bulgar tribes imposed their state traditions over the more agricultural Slavic tribes settled in the Balkans, thus forming the first of the Slavic nations. Brothers Cyril and Methodius created the first Bulgarian alphabet, called *glagolitsa;* their disciple Kliment Ohridski was the author of the modern-day Cyrillic alphabet. With the recognition of Bulgarian church autonomy in 870, the country joined Christian Europe. After over 100 years of Byzantine rule, the powerful Second Bulgarian Kingdom emerged in 1187, stretching from the Black Sea to the Aegean and the Adriatic Seas. In the 14th century, the country was crushed by Ottoman invaders who valued the region's agricultural output and ruthlessly kept Bulgaria a nation of peasants for almost 5 centuries.

During the National Revival of the 19th century, Bulgarians reestablished an independent church and founded a school system. While Britain and France insisted on preserving the integrity of the Ottoman Empire, Russia began to be seen as Bulgaria's defender—a factor in Bulgaria's eventual alliance with the Soviet Union. The Soviets, however, dealt a crushing blow to the Bulgarian economy by making it dependent on Russian imports.

On November 10, 1989, the Bulgarian Communist Party retired Todor Zhivkov, the unpopular, conservative, and much-ridiculed leader, changed its name to the Socialist Party (BSP), and held elections. After the parliamentary elections of November 1991, Bulgaria established a non-Communist government. The country's first presidential elections in January 1992 re-elected philosopher Zhelyn Zheler and poet Blaga Dimitrova as president and vice-president. Personal freedoms in Bulgaria have bounded ahead, yet many Bulgarians are starting to feel the stranglehold of financial limitations and skyrocketing inflation. For tourists, some of the onerous regulations, such as visa requirements, have been relaxed, while others—like the statistical card issued at the border—remain.

For more detailed coverage of Bulgaria, peruse *Let's Go: Eastern Europe*.

GETTING THERE

As of July 1994, American citizens could visit Bulgaria **visa**-free for up to 30 days; but Canadian, British, Irish, South African, Australian, and New Zealand citizens need either a 1-month tourist visa (US$34) or a 30hr. transit visa (US$24). Even in European capitals, visas usually take a week or more to process, so try to get one from the Bulgarian Embassy in your home country. For more info, contact an **embassy or consulate** are at 1621 22nd St., NW, Washington, DC 20008 (tel.(202) 387-7969, fax (202) 234-7973), 65 Overlea Blvd. #406, Toronto, ON M4H 1P1 (tel. (416) 696-2420 or 696-2778, fax 696-8019), Sofia House, 19 Conduit St., London W1R 9TD (tel. (0171) 491 44 99, fax 491 70 68), and 1/4 Carlotta Rd., Double Bay, Sydney, NSW 2028 (tel. (02) 327 75 92 or 327 44 40, fax 327 80 67).

GETTING AROUND

Public transportation in Bulgaria costs about 15Lv per 100km. The **train** system is quite comprehensive, but very slow, crowded, and shows its age. Direct trains run between Sofia and all major towns. Trains come in three varieties: express (експрес), fast (бързи), and slow (пътнически). Couchettes are an option (usually 15Lv); purchase spots in advance. To buy an international ticket, you must go to the appropriate office, usually in the town center; look for **Rila Travel** (РИЛА). In Sofia, Rila is at ul. General Gurko 5 (tel. 87 07 77) and at NDK, the Palace of Culture (tel. 59 31 06). Rila no longer gives any ISIC discounts. You can only buy domestic tickets at train stations, except for the Sofia Central Railway Station (Централна Гара-София) where there is an international ticket counter. Stations are poorly marked, and signs are often only in Cyrillic. Try to find out the exact time you are due at your destination or take along a current map that shows your route. Be prepared for smoke-filled corridors, nasty bathrooms, breathtaking views of the Bulgarian countryside, and friendly fellow travellers. Some useful words are влак *(vlak,* "train"), автобус *(avtobus,* "bus"), гара *(gara,* "station"), перон *(peron,* "platform"), коловоз *(kolovoz,* "track"), билет *(bilet,* "ticket"), заминаващи *(zaminavashti,* "departure"), пристигащи *(pristigashti,* "arrival"), пушачи *(pushachi,* "smoking"), непушачи *(nepushachi,* "non-smoking"), and спален вагон *(spalen vagon,* "sleeping car").

Rising train ticket prices have made travel by **bus** an attractive option. Prices are often lower and travel times up to three hours less from the capital to the Black Sea coast. Tourist offices such as **Balkantourist** have comfortable express buses—ideal for long distances. Even better are private bus companies such as **Group Travel Ltd.** Buy tickets ahead of time from the agency office (the recommended procedure) or pay as you board. Some buses have set departure times, while others, especially on busy routes, leave whenever they are full. Agents usually speak some English.

The once-cheap **Balkan Air** fares have increased a lot over the past year. (Sofia to Varna or Burgas: US$65 one-way). There are no youth discounts on Balkan Air within Bulgaria. Unless you are in a hurry to get to the coast, take the bus or train.

Renting a car is a great way to see many of the off-the-beaten-track places in Bulgaria. Like air travel, however, this option is prohibitively expensive. **Taxis** are usually a pretty good deal in cities and larger towns. Avoid private taxis (private cars which have been turned into taxis for the day or week) in favor of the cab companies. Taxi drivers, in theory, meter their fares. In practice the fare structure depends on the company, the honesty of the driver, and the age of the meter. Always refuse to pay in dollars and insist that you want the ride metered (*"sus apparata"*). The one exception is at Sofia airport. Taxi drivers will wait for you at the door, asking for US$20 to take you to the center. Do not pay more than US$10.

Hitchhiking, once popular and reliable in Bulgaria, is now a growing risk with worsening economic conditions, particularly for Westerners who are targets for theft. *Let's Go* cannot recommend hitchhiking as a safe means of transportation. There have also been reports about attacks on drivers from hitchhikers recently. Consequently, male hitchhikers will have little luck finding a ride. Transportation is so cheap that having to wait and possibly getting stuck under the scorching Balkan sun makes hitchhiking simply not worth it.

BULGARIA ESSENTIALS

Balkantourist, the former national tourist bureau, maintains offices throughout the country, although many have new names as a result of privatization. The staff changes money, and books hotel rooms and private accommodations. Hotels throughout the country often maintain tourist offices which can be of great help. They usually speak English.

One lev (Lv; plural: leva), the standard monetary unit, is divided into 100 stotinki (st), but we list most prices in U.S. dollars (US$). Inflation has made stotinki obsolete, except for the old 20st. coin (*not* the new) which is worth its weight in gold since it is the only coin that can be used in public telephones. Hoard them. New leva bills are now being introduced. The official rate of US$1 to approximately 55Lv closely coincides with the rates offered by private banks and numerous private exchange bureaus. The private exchange bureaus often take most major credit cards and **American Express** traveler's checks. Hotels have worse rates and people who approach you on the street to change money usually do not have the best intentions. You can cash American Express checks in dollars or leva at major banks such as the **First Private Bank** which has branches throughout the country, or at the **Bulgarian Foreign Trade Bank** on **Ploshtad Sveta Nedelya (St. Nedelya's Square,** площад Света Неделя) opposite the Sheraton in Sofia (Commission: US$10 for every US$1000 regardless of the number of checks). Businesses open around 8-9am. Banking hours are usually 8:30am-4pm, but some banks close around 2pm. Tourist bureaus, post offices, and shops remain open to about 6 or 8pm; in more touristy areas and bigger cities shops may close as late as 10pm, but they're often shut on Sundays. In government offices and state agencies, expect an hour lunch break around 1pm. Private shops, restaurants, cafés, and bars have more extended hours and are usually open on weekends. "Non-stop" signs in English indicate that the place is open 24hrs. National **holidays** are: January 1-2 (New Year's Day), March 3 (Liberation from the Ottoman Yoke), a few days around Orthodox Easter, May 24 (Saints Cyril and Methodius's Day), and 3-4 days around Christmas.

Don't find out about the state of public **bathrooms,** some of which consist of nothing more than a hole in the ground, the hard way; pack a small bar of soap and some toilet paper. Public bathrooms often require a 1 or 2Lv note as a toilet paper charge. Have small bills ready. **Safety concerns** are of special importance in a country where hard currency is desirable. Avoid currency speculators. If you take a taxi, choose your driver carefully. On the same note, avoid walking alone after dark, even if you're sure of where you're going. There is a general lack of tolerance towards homosexuals in the country though the chances of being attacked are minimal. Discretion will make life easier. Bulgaria's Black Sea coast is a thriving pick-up scene; beware, however, that safe sex isn't universal.

Communication See the Cyrillic transliteration table in the Russia chapter; Bulgarian is much the same as the Russian except that х is *h*, ш is *sht*, and ъ is sometimes transliterated as *â* (pronounced as in English b*u*g). Key phrases include добър ден (DO-bur den, "hello"), кога (ko-GA, "when"), къде (kuh-DEH, "where"), колко (KOL-ko, "how much"), благодаря (blahg-oh-dahr-YAH, "thank you"), моля (MOE-lya, "please"), довиждане (doh-VEEZH-dan-eh, "good bye"), колко струва (KOHL-ko STROO-va, "how much does it cost?"), извинете (izvenete, "excuse me"), говорите ли английски? (Go-VO-ri-te-li ang-LIY-ski?, "Do you speak English?"), Аз не разбирам (az ne raz-BI-iram, "I don't understand"), and the all-purpose phrase Добре (dobreh; "good" or "OK," used in almost every sentence). Russian is widely understood, but it is best to ask permission before using it. Many Bulgarians are learning English and it is widely spoken in travel agencies and tourist areas. Bulgarian-English phrasebooks are sold at bookstands and bookstores for about 30Lv. Since Bulgarian head movements for "yes" and "no" are the reverse of the West's, try to confirm everything with *da* (yes) or *ne* (no). Also be aware that many street names will be changed as the country moves further from its communist past, but many old signs have not yet been replaced. Use both the old and new street names, and, once there, try to find the most recent map that you can. In smaller towns, new maps may not yet be available and residents may have no idea what the new name of a street or square is; confusion often abounds.

Making international **telephone** calls from Bulgaria requires tremendous patience. To reach the new **AT&T USADirect operator,** dial 00 18 00 00 10. To call collect, dial 0123 for an international operator or have the telephone office or hotel receptionist order the call for you. You can usually make international calls at any post office. All lines go through Sofia, though, so getting a call through often takes a while. Calls to the U.S. average about US$1 per minute, but you can expect to pay as much as US$4 per minute from hotel phones. **Betkom** direct dial telephones with digital display screens are found at most major hotels and resort areas. They serve only Europe and the Middle East and require a special calling card sold from a kiosk near the phone. In an emergency (such as visa complications or urgent phone calls) go to the consular section of your embassy.

Accommodations and Camping When you cross the border you will be given a yellow **statistical card** to document where you stay each night. If you lose it, you may have difficulty getting a hotel room. The establishment in which you stay will add its stamp to the card, which is collected when you leave the country. Years ago, tourists were fined if they didn't have a stamp for each night they had spent in Bulgaria; now, Bulgarian border officials tend to be much less strict, so many find that a card with at least a couple of stamps on it may suffice.

Private rooms are arranged through Balkantourist or other tourist offices for US$8-13 a night. Be sure to ask for a central location and try to find out if any family members speak English. Bulgarian **hotels** are classed by stars; rooms in one-star hotels are almost identical to those in 2- and 3-star hotels but have no private bathrooms; they average about US$8 for singles and US$17 for doubles. Foreigners are always charged higher prices than Bulgarians and you can usually pay in hard currency or leva. The majority of Bulgarian **Youth Hostels** are located in the countryside and are popular with student groups; try to make reservations through **ORBITA,** 48 Xristo Botev (Христо Ботев; tel. 80 01 02, fax 88 58 14), or **Pirin Tours,** bul. Stamboliiski 30 (tel. 87 06 87) in Sofia. Outside major towns, **campgrounds** give

BULGARIA

you a chance to meet backpackers (US$3-5 per person). Spartan wooden bunga-lows await at nearly every site but are often full, and many have closed. Free-lance camping is popular, but you risk a fine. Camping in reserve areas is strictly prohib-ited; watch for the signs (Национален Парк, national park; or Резербат, reserve).

Food And Drink Food from kiosks is cheap (35-50Lv for a sandwich or burger and a Coke), and restaurants average 100Lv per meal. Kiosks sell *kebabcheta* (small hamburgers, 10Lv), salami sandwiches (7Lv), pizzas (12Lv), and *banitsa* (cheese-filled breads, 5Lv). Fruits and vegetables are usually sold in vegetable shops (зелен-чуков магазин, *zelenchukov magazin*), in markets (пазар, *pazar*) or directly on the streets from stalls. 24hr. mini-markets sell cheese, bread, milk, and snack foods. In the summer Bulgaria is blessed with delicious fruits and vegetables. Try *shopska sal-ata*, an addictive salad of tomatoes, peppers, and cucumbers covered with feta cheese. *Kiopolou* and *imam bayaldu* are eggplant dishes. There is a heavy empha-sis on meat in the Bulgarian menu. The Bulgarians are known for their cheese and yogurt. Try *Sirene*, a feta cheese, and *kashkaval*, a hard yellow cheese. You can get desserts like baklava and *sladoled* (ice cream) in sweetshops called Sladkarnitsi (сладкарнии). Bulgarian coffee is served Turkish style. Well-stirred *airan*, Bulgarian yogurt with a little water and a few ice cubes, can bring you back to life on a hot summer day. The water is probably purer than the stuff you're used to drinking back home. Bring a water bottle and a hearty spirit. Delicious red and white wines are produced in various regions of the country. Even the most expensive bottles are less than US$1.

■■■ SOFIA (СОФИЯ)

Affordable and undiscovered, feeding on cool jazz and cheap, delicious wine, Sofia offers an unequaled night on the town for pennies. With the overthrow of the com-munists, youth has come to dominate business and control the tempo of life in the city. Western visitors are few, but it's only a matter of time. The center of town, with its grid of enormously wide *bulevards* paved with yellow bricks lends an air of Oz. At the crossroads of Europe and Asia, the city has changed hands many times and has been known also as Serdika, Sredetz, and Triaditza. Today, Western influ-ences abound and often seem out of place. Sofia is for the most part a new city—a carnival of Socialist architecture where only a few medieval churches and 2 mosques survive—but its architecture, often a cross between German Baroque and Russian Imperial styles, reflects Bulgaria's role as a bridge between East and West.

ORIENTATION AND PRACTICAL INFORMATION

Sofia's 1.2 million inhabitants occupy the center of the Balkan peninsula, 500km southeast of Belgrade. International trains run to Belgrade, Thessaloniki, Athens, İstanbul, and Bucharest. **Ploshad Sveta Nedelya** (St. Nedelya Square, площад Света Неделя), once named for Lenin, is the center of Sofia. Most sights are within walking distance of the city center and easily found with the aid of a map. The central district is ringed by a road that changes names as it circles the city. Incoming roads intersect this ring; the most important starts life as **bul. Vitosha** (Витоша) and runs north through Pl. Sveta Nedelya, where it changes its name to **bul. Knyaginya Maria Luiza** (Княгиня Мария Луиза) and bends around to reach the train station at the northern end of the city. Perpendicular to bul. Knyaginya Maria Luiza, bul. Stamboliiski (Стам-болийски) and bul. Dondukov (Дондуков) are two other major thoroughfares. Resi-dents orient themselves by the **radio tower** on Mt. Vitosha. Maps are sold at tourist offices and at stalls on the street (30Lv). Useful English-language **Sofia city guides** (published every month) are available at major hotels for about US$1.

Tourist Offices: Balkantourist, bul. Stamboliiski 27 (tel. (02) 88 55 43, fax 83 30 58). From Pl. Sveta Nedelya, walk up Stamboliiski three blocks and it's on your left. English-speaking staff books accommodations in hotels and private houses,

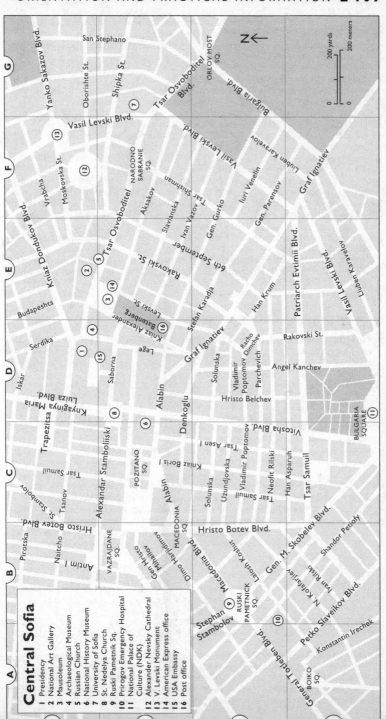

Central Sofia

1 Presidency
2 National Art Gallery
3 Mausoleum
4 Archaeological Museum
5 Russian Church
6 National History Museum
7 University of Sofia
8 St. Nedelya Church
9 Ruski Pametnik Sq.
10 Prirogov Emergency Hospital
11 National Palace of Culture (NDK)
12 Alexander Nevsky Cathedral
13 V. Levski Monument
14 American Express office
15 USA Embassy
16 Post office

BULGARIA

exchanges money, and sells out-of-date maps. Open Mon.-Fri. 8:30am-5pm, Sat.-Sun. 9am-8pm. The office at bul. Vitosha 1 (tel. 97 51 92, fax 80 01 34) will give you cash advances from all credit cards *except* American Express. It is the former American Express office and is still collecting cardmember mail. Excellent English spoken. Open Mon.-Fri. 8am-8pm, Sat. 8:30am-1:30pm. **Pirin Tours (HI),** bul. Stamboliiski 30 (tel. 87 06 87, fax 65 00 52), across from Balkantourist, helps arrange transportation and accommodations and provides youth hostel information, homestays, and university housing. Open Mon.-Fri. 9am-5:30pm.

Budget Travel: ORBITA Travel, Hristo Botev 48 (tel. 80 01 02 or 87 91 28, fax 88 58 14). From Pl. Sveta Nedelya, walk up Stamboliiski, and make a left on Hristo Botev. Can make hotel reservations and will help you find university, hotel, and hostel accommodations. English spoken. Open Mon.-Fri. 9am-5:30pm.

Embassies: U.S., ul. Suborna 1a (tel. 88 48 01 through 05), 3 blocks from Pl. Sveta Nedelya behind the Sheraton Hotel. Consular section at ul. Kapitan Andreev 1 (tel. 65 94 59), behind the Economic Tehnikum, near Hotel Hemus. Americans are recommended to register with the consular section when they arrive in Bulgaria (open Mon.-Fri. 9am-4:30pm for American citizens). **U.K.,** bul. Vasil Levksi 65 (*not* Vasil Levski Street; tel. 88 53 61), 3 blocks northwest of the Palace of Culture (open Mon.-Thurs. 8:30am-12:30pm and 1:30-5pm, Fri. 8:30am-1pm). Citizens of **Canada, Australia,** and **New Zealand** should contact the British embassy. **Romania,** ul. Sitniakovo 4 (tel. 70 70 46).

Currency Exchange: At **Balkantourist** offices and all large hotels. Generally open 8am-10pm. Better rates than private exchange places like **Lindor,** bul. Vitosha 31 (tel. 88 14 92), **Inter,** bul. Vasil Levski 72 (tel. 81 57 40), or **7M** (branches throughout Sofia). Traveler's checks cashed at the **First Private Bank** at ul. Suborna 2a (tel. 46 51 28; open Mon.-Fri. 9am-12:30pm), and at the **Bulgarian Foreign Trade Bank,** Pl. Sveta Nedelya 7 (tel. 84 91, fax 88 46 36 or 88 53 70), across from the Sheraton. Open Mon.-Fri. 8:30am-12:30pm and 2-4pm.

American Express is located at Megatours, 1 Levski St. (tel. 88 04 19, fax 87 25 67) across from Dimitrov's Mausoleum on Pl. Aleksander Batenberg (Александр Батенберг). Cashes traveler's checks, collects mail, and issues airplane tickets. Flawless English. Open Mon.-Fri. 9am-6:30pm, Sat. 9am-noon.

Post Office: ul. General Gurko 2, at the park east of Pl. Sveta Nedelya. Poste Restante generally open 7am-8:30pm. Many hotels also provide postal services.

Telephones: Across from the post office. Expect long lines. Open 7:30am-1am. To avoid them, call from the Sheraton Hotel's lobby phones, but expect to pay nearly four times as much. For local calls, use 20st coins. Local phone numbers have between 4 and 7 digits. **City Code:** 02.

Flights: Airport Sofia (tel. 793 21). Call 72 06 72 or 79 80 35 for international departure information; 79 32 11 for international arrivals; 72 24 14 for domestic flight information. Buses 84 and 284 run regularly. **Bulgarian Balkan Airlines** has an office at Pl. Narodno Subranie 12 (tel. 88 06 63). Always ask for **youth fares** if you're under 26; the savings can be more than 50% on international flights.

Trains: Sofia's central train station is north of the center on bul. Knyaginya Maria Luiza. Trams 1, 7, and 15 travel to pl. Sveta Nedelya. Windows at station sell domestic tickets only. For info, international tickets, and couchette reservations, visit **Rila Travel** at ul. General Gurko 5 (tel. 87 07 77; open Mon.-Fri.7am-7pm, Sat. 8am-1pm). One way fares to Athens US$63, Thessaloniki US$31, Bucharest US$15, Budapest US$40, and İstanbul US$32. No ISIC discounts.

Buses: Terminal at bul. Gen. H. Mihailov 23 (tel. 52 50 04) handles tickets for international routes. **Group Travel,** a private bus company, will take you practically anywhere you want to go in Bulgaria and Eastern Europe, from ul. Rakovski 85 (tel. 83 14 54, fax 83 24 26). Round-trip fares to the Black Sea Coast, US$5; Budapest, US$23; Warsaw, US$36; and Prague, US$29. All Group Travel buses and other private buses leave from the **Novotel Europa,** directly across from the central train station.

Public Transportation: The system of trams, trolley buses, and buses is gleefully cheap (3Lv per ticket, 10Lv for an all-day ticket). Buy tickets at kiosks or from the driver and punch 'em in the small machines between the bus windows. Open 4am-1am (although many routes stop before midnight).

Hitchhiking: Hitching in the Sofia area is getting increasingly dangerous. *Let's Go* does not recommend hitchhiking as a safe means of transportation. Those hitching to Rila Monastery take tram 5 to highway E79. Those headed to Koprivshtitsa take tram 3 from Sofia. They leave early to return the same day.

Laundromats: There aren't any *per se* in Bulgaria. The larger hotels are often unwilling to wash non-guests' clothing, even for hard currency. A good **dry cleaner** is Svezhest (Свежест) at Vasil Kolarov 19. From pl. Sveta Nedelya, walk up Vitosha and make a left on Vasil Kolarov. Open Mon.-Fri. 7am-7pm.

Pharmacy: Pl. Sveta Nedelya 5, (tel. 81 50 89). Open 24hrs. Night pharmacies throughout the city generally open 10pm-7am. Try **1st Private Pharmacy** at the intersection of Neofit Rilski and Tsar Asen. Pharmacists can usually recommend doctors.

Medical Assistance: In a medical emergency, contact a hotel receptionist. Emergency aid for foreigners, offered by state-owned hospitals, is free of charge. If you have an emergency go to **Pirogov emergency hospital,** bul. Totleben 21, across from the Rodina Hotel (tel. 53 31; open 24hrs). For more information about medical care in Bulgaria, ask for a handout when you register at your embassy.

Emergencies: Police, tel. 166. **Ambulance,** tel. 150. **Fire,** tel. 160.

ACCOMMODATIONS

Balkantourist and ORBITA (see above) arrange private rooms for US$8-15 per night. So do our friends at the train station (but remember that these "cheap private room" pushers may not stamp your yellow card). If you arrive in Sofia after Balkantourist closes, you're on your own. **Private accommodations** are the smartest option in Sofia. Hotels are not always worth their prices and the cheapest ones can be unsafe. Apart from the Balkantourist office at bul. Stamboliiski 27, you may also find private lodgings at **Markela**, bul. Knyaginya Maria Luiza 17, across from the Central Department Store (tel. 81 52 99). Average cost: US$6-7.50 per person; full apartments for US$13-14.50 per night. They will stamp your statistical card and give you the keys to your apartment along with directions. (Open Mon.-Sat. 10am-7pm.) After hours you may call English-speaking Hristo or Daniella (tel. 54 69 69 or 62 35 02).

Hotel Baldjieva (Балджиева), 23 Tsar Asen St., (tel. 97 29 14). A private hotel in the city center right off bul. Vitosha. Clean, small rooms with shared bath. Pay in dollars or leva. Singles US$18. Doubles US$32.

Hotel Nicky, ul. Neofit Rilski 16, off bul. Vitosha (tel. 51 19 15). Private showers and beautiful restored Bulgarian architecture. Pay in dollars or leva. Singles US$20. Doubles US$40. Ask for the 10% student discount.

Orbita Hotel, bul. James Bourchier 76 (tel. 65 74 47 or 88 10 19). Take tram 9 south past the Palace of Culture to the intersection with bul. Anton Ivanov and look behind the Hotel Vitosha. A 2-star Communist behemoth which offers clean, plain rooms with private bath. A rocking disco awaits you downstairs. Singles US$26. Doubles US$34. Discounts can be had through Balkantourist.

Hotel Hemus (Хемус), bul. Cherni Vruh 31 (Черни Връх; tel. 66 13 19 or 639 51). A 3-star hotel past the Palace of Culture at the southern extreme of downtown. Take tram 1, 7, or 15 to Palace of Culture, then head for the high-rise up bul. Cherni Vruh. Lots o' groups. Friendly English-speaking receptionists. Singles US$40; doubles US$60 (US$25 and US$40 through Balkantourist). MC and Visa.

Slavianska Beseda (Славянска Беседа), Slavianska St. 3 (tel. 87 21 23, fax 87 56 38). In the center near the post office. Unattractive halls lead to clean rooms with showers and tubs. Pay in dollars or leva. Singles US$30. Doubles US$40. Ask for a student discount.

FOOD

From fast food to Bulgarian specialties, inexpensive meals are easy to find. Tipping is not expected. If there are no empty tables, it is customary to sit with others.

BULGARIA

Pizza Palace (Пица), bul. Vitosha 34 (tel. 81 08 69). Delicious, medium-sized pizzas for US$2-4. Menu in English. Also sells *USA Today* and the *International Herald Tribune*. Open 11am-2am.

Café Luciano (Лучано), ul. Rakovski, two blocks from hotel Sevastopol and various other locations in Sofia. A chain of pastry cafés worth visiting each time you pass a new one. Amazing *tortes,* whole cakes US$3.75. Open Mon.-Fri. 7:30am-11pm, Sat. and Sun. 9am-11pm.

Eddy's Tex-Mex Diner, bul. Vitosha 4 (tel. 87 67 83). Interpreted Mexican dishes, including burritos, and margaritas. Nightly jazz or country music. The hippest place in town. When famous bands play there is a 50Lv cover. Entrees US$3-4. Open 10am until the last customer leaves. Dinner served until 11pm.

Wiener Café, Sheraton Hotel, first floor, on pl. Sveta Nedelya. Sandwiches served from 10am-2pm. Otherwise, a full selection of *tortes,* ice cream, and alcohol. Menu in English. Open 10am-11pm.

Venezia Pizzeria (Венеция), 12 Benkovski St. (tel. 87 63 64). Head up Dondukov from pl. Sveta Nedelya, and turn right on Benkovski at the "Pizzeria" sign. Brick oven pizzas, ravioli, and lasagne. Famous throughout Sofia. English menu. Open noon-midnight.

SIGHTS AND ENTERTAINMENT

Sofia's two most venerable churches, the late Roman **St. George's Rotunda** and the early Byzantine **St. Sofia,** sprang up in the 4th and 6th centuries, respectively. St. George's hides in the courtyard of the Sheraton Hotel, while St. Sofia, the city's namesake, stands several blocks behind the Party house. Both are closed for restoration but worth seeing from the outside. Across the square from St. Sofia looms the massive, gold-domed **St. Alexander Nevsky Cathedral** (open Sun.-Fri. 8am-6pm, Sat. 8-10am and 4-8pm), erected in the early 20th century in memory of the 200,000 Russians who died in the 1877-78 Russo-Turkish War. The main attraction is in the **crypt,** a monstrous collection of painted icons and religious artifacts from the past 1000 years. (Open Wed.-Mon. 10am-6pm.) In an underpass at pl. Sveta Nedelya is the tiny 14th-century **Church of Saint Petka Samardzhiiska,** which contains some eye-grabbing frescoes; despite its size, this is one of Sofia's finest churches. (Open 8am-6pm. Donations encouraged.)

Along the way to the central train station from the Central Department Store towers the **Banya Bashi Mosque.** Built in the 16th century and named after the mineral baths nearby, the mosque has one minaret and is once again used as a place of worship. The former **Georgi Dimitrov Mausoleum,** on pl. Aleksander Batenberg (Александър Батенберг) is a memorial to Stalin's former henchman, long-hated and now officially vilified. While debate still rages over the fate of the building, Bulgarians have put it to practical use as a public bathroom. The labels in the **National Museum of History,** off pl. Sveta Nedelya on Vitosha 2, are in Bulgarian only, but the magnificent Thracian treasures need no commentary (open Mon.-Fri. 9:30am-5:15pm; 5Lv, 3Lv with ISIC). For a look at traditional Bulgaria, be sure to check out the **National Ethnographic Museum** (open Wed.-Sun. 10am-noon and 1:30-6pm; 20Lv) and the **National Museum of Fine Arts** (open Tues.-Sun. 10am-6pm, 20Lv), also located on the square. (10Lv each with ISIC.)

The **nightlife** in Sofia gets wilder every year. Outdoor cafés and bars share **Bul. Vitosha** with musicians, gypsies and dancing bears. At **Frankie's Jazz Club/Piano Bar,** right off bul. Vitosha across from the American Center, there is a 40Lv cover for the best jazz east of New Orleans (open 10am-2am). Smartly-dressed Sofians go to the cafés around the park outside **NDK** to see and be seen. Euro-techno pop brings down the house at the **Orbilux** disco at the Orbita hotel, bul. James Boucher 76 (tel. 66 89 97). Music starts around 10pm. The **disco** underneath the Palace of Culture rocks until 4am (small cover). More bars and dance floors await at the **Angel Club** at 9 Narodni Sabranie, near Balkan Airlines and the Hotel Sofia.

The opera and theater seasons run September-June. Good seats at the **Opera House** are under US$1 (tel. 87 70 11; box office open 9:30am-7pm). There are no performances on Mondays. You can get tickets for the **Ivan Vazov National The-**

ater at 5 Levski St. (tel. 88 28 84) for 15-30Lv. Movie theaters are plentiful and films are usually in English. Two good theaters are at bul. Vitosha 62 (tel. 88 58 78) and the **Serdica** at 1 Vasil Levski Sq. (tel. 43 17 97).

■ RILA MONASTERY (РИЛСКИ МАНАСТИР)

The Rila Monastery, 120km south of Sofia, is the largest and most famous monastery in Bulgaria. Founded by the hermit Ivan of Rila in the 10th century, it maintained the arts of icon painting and manuscript copying during the Turkish occupation. The 1200 frescoes on the central chapel and surrounding walls form an outdoor art gallery. Try to make one of the services at 7am or 4:30pm. (Open 6am-dusk.) The monastery also houses 3 museums with ornate religious objects and items from Bulgaria's past (20Lv). In the hills surrounding the monastery there are excellent opportunities for both short and long **hikes.** Inquire at Pirin Tours in Sofia or any of the monastery's souvenir shops for more info.

To reach the monastery from Sofia, take the lone **direct bus** at 6:30am from the Ovcha Kupel (Овча Купел) station in Sofia (accessible by tram 5); or take the train to Blagoevgrad, then a bus to Rila town (hourly) and another to the monastery (7 per day). To stay in the **monastery** itself, inquire in room 169, next to the museum. (US$6.50 per person, heated room, no showers or hot water.) Right outside the back gate there is a small **hostel** (US$4.50 per person, open 24hrs.). If you're hungry, buy a piping hot loaf of bread from the **monastery bakery** for only 10Lv. **Restaurant Rila,** just outside the western gate of the monastery, serves up a beautiful view of the mountains and monastery and delicious local trout (US$2-4).

■ KOPRIVSHTITSA (КОПРИВЩИЦА)

Wood-and-stone cottages and a proud history of revolution make Koprivshtitsa one of Bulgaria's most enchanting villages, one of the few remaining where horses cart more than a histrionic duty. In 1876, Todor Kableshkov drafted his momentous "letter of blood" here, announcing the April uprising against Ottoman rule—the most passionately glorified event in Bulgarian history. The Turks savagely crushed the insurgency, but their brutality sparked the Russo-Turkish War of 1877-78, leading to Bulgarian independence.

Koprivshtitsa flaunts brilliant examples of **National Revival** architecture; several houses now serve as **museums.** Buy a map and a guidebook in one of the little **souvenir shops** just off the main square. Check out the two types of cottages: the first are sturdy, half-timbered, early 19th-century houses with open porches, high stone walls, and sparse ornamentation; the more common type features enclosed verandas and delicate woodwork. (Most open 8am-noon and 1:30-5:30pm, closed Mon. or Tues. 20Lv ticket from museum ticket office in the central square provides entrance to all houses.)

Trains from Sofia to Varna stop at Koprivshtitsa station, 8km away from the town, which is the station after Anton (2hr., 30Lv). A bus awaits to take you into town (10min.). All your accommodation needs can be met at the reception desk of the **Hotel Koprivshtitsa** (Хотел Копривщица; tel. (99768316) 21 82). Cross the second stone bridge from the center and ascend the steps. They can arrange **private rooms** for US$5 per person or book rooms in the hotel itself for US$6 per person, breakfast included. Some devious maps show a nonexistent campground. The **Restaurant Diado Liben** (ресторант Дядо Либен) in the blue house across the river from the center serves grilled specialties including *sirene po trakiski* (сирене по тракийски; cheese with sausage) and *diado liben* (Дядо Либен: a pork and vegetable dish, 70Lv). The restaurant complex in the town center houses an excellent **cafeteria.** Above the cafeteria is the **disco** that rocks little Koprivshtitsa every night.

BULGARIA

■■■ PLOVDIV (ПЛОВДИВ)

At first glance, Bulgaria's second city sprawls with gray housing complexes and exhaust-ridden boulevards. Hold your disappointment until you stroll into the rambling stairway-streets of the **Old Town** via the **Trimontsium** (Тримълмието), where the upper stories of National Revival houses hang over cobblestones, windows stare down into alleyways at impossible angles, and churches and mosques hide in secluded corners. From the train station, take trolley 102 to the town center (5 stops). Start at the **Dzhumaya Mosque** (Джумая джамия) on ul. Knyaz Aleksandr I (Княз Александър I), and wander up ul. Suborna (Съборна). Turn to find the 2nd-century **Amphitheater of Philippopolis,** at the entrance to the tunnel that runs under the old town. If at all possible, try to see a performance in the amphitheater, such as June's Theater Festivities or the summer run of the National Opera (about 25Lv at the box office, ul. Gurko 19 (ул. Гурко; tel. (32) 22 55 53). Back on Suborna, continue a bit farther to the **National Ethnographic Museum** (Етнографски Музей), which contains a well-presented collection of artifacts from this period (open Tues.-Thurs. and Sat.-Sun. 9am-noon and 2-5pm, Fri. 2-5pm). Ask at the Puldin Tours office about tickets to the **Plovdiv Chamber Music Festival** (June-July).

Practical Information, Accommodations, and Food The English-speaking staff at the **Puldin Tours** office, bul. Bulgaria 106 (България; tel. (32) 55 38 48), proffers a city map and guides to Plovdiv's history (45Lv), arranges private accommodations (singles US$10, doubles US$15), and changes traveler's checks (US$5 commission). To reach the office from the train station, take trolley 102 to bul. Bulgaria (the 9th stop) near Plovdiv's fairgrounds. Walk back one block—it's on your right. (Open Mon.-Fri. 9am-8pm, in winter Mon.-Fri. 8am-6pm.) Public transportation in Plovdiv consists of buses and trolleys (3Lv). **Private buses** to Sofia, the Black Sea Coast, Athens, İstanbul, and capitals in Eastern Europe depart from the **Yug** bus station (Avtogara ½g). International buses also leave from Park-Hotel Saint-Petersburg (Парк-хотел Санкт-Петербург) or the Rodopi bus station (автогара Родопи). **Trains** from Sofia to İstanbul stop in Plovdiv, as do most Sofia-Burgas trains. Sofia-Plovdiv service runs about every 2 hours (2½hr., US$1).

Hotel Leipzig (Хотел Лайпциг), bul. Ruski 70 (Руски; tel. (32) 23 22 50, fax 45 31 60), is just three blocks from the rail station and 10min. from the town center. Though located in a noisy area, the hotel has excellent prices and clean rooms. (Singles US$18. Doubles US$34.) For US$15-20 rooms with satellite TV, bath, and access to kitchen and laundry facilities, walk from pl. Centralen across bul. Vzrazhdane and track down **Hotel Feniks** (Феникс) Kapitan Raicho 79 (Капитан Райчо; tel. (32) 22 47 29 and 23 69 60). Take bus 23 from the train station to **Trakia Camping** (tel. (32) 55 13 60), open year-round. The bar doubles as a reception desk. (2-3 people bungalows US$7 a night.) Unless you have a fetish for East European tractor demonstrations, avoid Plovdiv during the biannual trade fairs (beginning on the first Mon. of May, and the last Mon. of Sept.) when accommodation prices swell by up to 500%.

In the heart of the Old Town, **Taverna Puldin** (Пълдин), ul. Knjaz Tseritelev 3 (Княз Церетелев), is built right into the Roman walls. Take ul. Maksim Gorky (Максим Горки) to its 4th right through the Turkish gate; it's your second right. (Full meal US$6-9. Open 10am-midnight.) Also in the Old Town, try the **Restaurant Alafrang-ite** (Алафрангите), ul. Kiril Nektariev 17 (Кирил Нектариев), in an eye-catching National Revival house. Their specialty is *vreteno,* a pork or veal steak with a cheese and mushroom filling. From behind the Dzhumaya Mosque follow ul. Maxim Gorki; make the 3rd right. (Full meal around US$3. Open 11:30am-midnight.) On a cool evening, head to the fountainside **café** in the Public Garden (formerly the Garden of King Boris), within walking distance from the Old Town. Multicolored strobes illuminate the fountain—the most popular hangout in town—and you can rent rowboats to splash your way around the small lake.

BULGARIA

■ BACHKOVO MONASTERY

About 28km south of Plovdiv is the Bachkovo Monastery, second largest in the country after Rila, where visitors can spend the night for under US$1. (Call (3327) 277 and ask for Brother Gurman.) Take a bus from the main station in Plovdiv to **Asenovgrad**, where you can catch a bus to the monastery.

■■■ VALLEY OF ROSES (РОЗОВА ДОЛИНА)

Two and a half hours east from Sofia along the Sofia-Varna rail line is the small town of **Karlovo** (Карлово), huddled at the foot of the Stara Planina. The first weekend of June sees the annual **Rose Festival** (Празник на розата) featuring performances by traditional Bulgarian song-and-dance troupes and comedians, as well as soccer matches, bazaars, and the like. Ask travel agents for details. For a grand view of the festivities, book a room in the **Rozova Dolina Hotel.** (tel. (335) 33 80, fax 68 90; singles US$17, doubles US$25). Karlovo's **Roza Tours** office occupies the hotel lobby.

Trains connect Karlovo with **Kazanlak** (Казанлък), the largest town in the valley, several times a day (1½hr., US$0.50). During the summer months the air of Kazanlak is filled with the fragrance of roses. Check out the ethnographic **Rose Museum** (Музей на Розата) by jumping on bus 2 from the central square; ask the driver to stop at the museum (open 8:30am-5pm, students 20Lv). The **Kazanlak Tomb,** in Tyulberto Park, is actually a copy of the tomb that dates back to the late 4th century BC (open 8am-noon and 1:30-6pm, students 25Lv). A local tale has it that young men drinking water from the fountain off the city's central square are destined to marry a local maiden.

The **tourist office** (tel. (431) 251 52 or 210 87) is located on the 1st floor of Hotel Kazanlak, on the central square (open Mon.-Fri. 8:30-11:30am and 2-5pm). Many private **bus** lines to nearby towns and cities (such as Karlovo, Gabrovo, and Stara Zagora) start from the bus and railway station just south of the center of town; buses to further points depart from the parking lot in front of the Hotel Kazanlak. Snag the best hotel deal in town at the **Hotel Roza,** ul. Rozova Dolina 2 (tel. (431) 246 05, fax 400 29), facing the central square (singles US$28, doubles US$40). Make reservations for the festival. Or try the **Campground Kazanlushka Roza** (Къмпинг "Казанлышка роза"), 4km north of Kazanlak (open May-Sept.). Escape the gray socialist blocks in the **women's monastery** (Женския Манастир), Tsar Osvoboditel 9 (tel. (431) 222 16), which rents rooms to both men and women for donations only (reception open until 6:30pm). For budget dining, search out the restaurant **Strata Kushta** (Старата Къща) on ul. Dr. Baev 19. Heading into the central square, take your second left onto ul. Gen. M. Skobelev and then the first right on ul. Gen Gurke. (Open 10am until last customer leaves; meals under US$1.)

Ten km south of Kazanlak (US$6 by taxi) is **Lake Koprinka** (Копринка), formerly Georgi Dimitrov, a scenic, brownish lake on whose bottom lie the remains of the Thracian city Sevtopolis. At the northern extreme of the Valley of Roses looms the legendary **Shipka Pass** (Шипченски Проход), site of the bloody and pivotal battle where Russian and Bulgarian forces prevented the Turks from advancing beyond the Balkan Mountains. Take bus 6 from Kazanlak to get to Shipka town.

■■■ VELIKO TURNOVO (ВЕЛИКО ТЪРНОВО)

Perched on the steep hills above the twisting Yantra River, Veliko Turnovo was once the capital of the powerful Second Bulgarian Kingdom. Amid the ruins of the palaces of Bulgarian tsars and patriarchs are fragments of mural paintings and mosaics that testify to the vibrancy of this center of medieval culture. The ruins of the fortress **Tsarevets** (Царевец), which once housed the royal palace, litter the top of a

BULGARIA

large hill (open 8am-7pm, 50Lv). You can explore the battle towers and the newly-restored **Ascension Church,** which has some amazing murals, or stand on the rock from which traitors were hurled to their death. A ticket kiosk at the bottom of the hill sells brochures. As you wander to or from the fortress, stop at the **Archeological Museum,** off ul. Ivan Vazov (Иван Вазов), which contains wonderful Thracian pottery, a fine collection of medieval crafts from the Turnovo ruins, and copies of the most famous Bulgarian religious frescoes (open Tues.-Sun. 9am-noon and 1-6pm, 50Lv). Next door in the light-blue building is the **Museum of the National Revival** (Музей на Възраждането). Come learn about Bulgaria's great cultural and religious resurgence of the 19th century. (Open 7am-noon and 1-5pm.) You can see 20th-century depictions of Veliko Turnovo over the ages at the municipal **art museum,** situated on the peninsula within the river's bend (open 10am-6pm; 10Lv, students 5Lv, free on Thursdays).

Practical Information, Accommodations, and Food Veliko Turnovo is about 5 miles off the main international train route. Trains stop in **Gorna Oryahovitza** (Горна Оряховица), from which there is a continual bus service into town (bus 10 or 14, 4Lv). There are six direct trains from Sofia to Veliko Turnovo's smaller train station as well. From the Veliko Turnovo train station, take bus 4 to the town center (2Lv) or brace yourself for the uphill climb to the city (1km). From the bus station, take bus 7 or 10 five stops to the center. The privatized version of Balkantourist, **Yantra Tourist,** is located next to the Hotel Etur (tel. (62) 202 36 or 281 65). They have useful brochures and 50Lv maps of the city, and can arrange private accommodations. (Open Mon.-Fri. 8am-noon and 1-5:30pm.) Just off the main square, **Orbita Hotel,** 15 Hristo Botev (Христо Ботев), 4th fl., (tel. (62) 220 41), offers clean rooms with shared baths at amazingly cheap rates (US$2.60 per person). **Hotel Trapezitsa** (Хотел Трапезица) houses an excellent **youth hostel** at 79, ul. Stefan Stambolov (Стефан Стамболов) (tel. (62) 220 61). All rooms have private bathrooms. (Singles US$10, with ISIC US$7. Doubles US$19, with ISIC US$16.)

For a superb meal complete with quick, friendly service and a fantastic view, get a window seat at the **Panorama Complex** (Комплекс Панорама), next door to Hotel Trapezitsa (full meal under US$3, open 6am-midnight). In the small square across from there, the **Mehana Hadji Mincho** (Механа Хаджи Минчо) is a fine place to sample *shishlik* (lamb kebab) and live Bulgarian music (full meal US$2.50, open 6am-11:30pm). There's a *pazar* (market) at ul. Vasil Levski and ul. Dimitur Ivanov.

■ ETURA

About 50km southwest of Veliko Turnovo lies this **ethnographic museum park,** established in the 1960s to preserve the awareness of arts and crafts from the National Revival period; here you can watch the manual production of flour, sheets, gold jewelry, and wool carpets. It's a bit out of the way, but well worth a half-day's visit; take the train west from Gorna Oryahovitsa and get off in **Gabrovo.** Etura is just on the outskirts of town. (Tickets 50Lv. You can hire a guide for another 50Lv.)

■ ■ ■ RUSE (РУСЕ)

For centuries, foreigners have drifted down the Danube into Ruse, bringing with them their strange and varied tastes in music, art, and architecture. The city eagerly adopted the Baroque, Renaissance, and Art Deco styles of its guests and used the money spent by the wealthy Austro-Hungarians to support local rebels struggling against the Turks. Ruse is still known for its outstanding musical traditions, which have made it the setting of Bulgaria's biggest symphonic music festival—the **March Musical Days** (Мартенски Музикални Дни).

At Pl. Svoboda you will find a beautiful Italian-style monument and a magnificent theater building reminiscent of Vienna. Unique to Ruse, however, is former **Communist Party headquarters,** aptly named *Koraba* ("the ship") behind the statue on

BULGARIA

pl. Svoboda. To the left is the **Opera House** and next to it the **Holy Trinity Church** (Света Троица; main building open Sat.-Sun. 6am-8:30pm). Erected in 1632 during the Ottoman occupation, the church couldn't be built higher than any Turkish mosque in the city. One of the few Catholic churches in Bulgaria, **St. Paul's Church** (Света Павел), is currently under reconstruction. At night, take a stroll in **Mladezhki Park** (Младежки Парк) or disco in the Riga and Dunav hotels.

Practical Information, Accommodations, and Food Ruse can be reached by **train** from Bucharest (618Lv) and by train or **bus** from Sofia (4 per day, 143Lv), Varna (2 per day, 84Lv), or Veliko Turnovo. The bus and train stations are adjacent to each other about 2km south of the city center. Take bus 1 or 101, or trolley 23 or 25, from in front of the rail station for 3 stops. Walk 2 blocks up that street, ul. Borisovska (Борисовска), to reach the central square, most recently called Svoboda (Свобода). The tourist office **Dunav Tours** (Дунав Турс), 13 Rakovska (Раковска; tel. (82) 22 42 68, fax 27 71 77), right off pl. Svoboda (Свобода) should be your first stop. Friendly and fluent in English, they can arrange **private accommodations** for a US$5 fee, provide maps, and sell tickets to the opera and theater (US$0.50) and the March Musical Days (US$1). If they're closed, try **Hotel Helios** (Хелиос), Nikolaevska 1 (tel. (82) 22 56 61); to get there from Pl. Svoboda, walk past the post office on Alexandrovska to the end, walk diagonally through the park, and make a left on Nikolaevska. (Singles US$20. Doubles US$30.) **Campground Ribarska Koliba** (Рибарска Колиба; tel. (82) 22 40 68) is located about 8km west of the city center. To get there, hop on bus 6 or 16 from the city center. (Open April-Oct., US$3 per bed in bungalows.)

For a solid, inexpensive meal, stop at any of the restaurants along the main street. **Restaurant Potsdam** (Ресторант Потсдам) is located to the east of the main square at ul. Aleksandrovska 79 (full meal US$3, open 8am-midnight). **Panorama Café,** at the top of the Riga Hotel on the Danube, serves up sublime mixed drinks and great views of the city (open 6pm-3am). By the campground, **Restaurant Ribarska Koliba** (Рибена Колиба), is a Ruse institution. A seafood place known for its fish soup (рибска чорба, 18Lv), it features bamboo ceilings and a wine cellar (open 11am until the last customer leaves).

BLACK SEA COAST

Many Eastern and a growing contingent of Western Europeans come to the Black Sea Coast to bronze themselves in July and August; Varna and Burgas are the principal transportation centers. Go north if you like rocky cliffs and small villages; go south for seaside campgrounds and untouched beaches. To meet Bulgarians, avoid the pricey Balkantourist resorts and instead rent a private room (US$4-6) or bungalow (US$3-10) in one of the small fishing hamlets or campgrounds that dot the coast and then commute by bus or hike along the beach to jet ski, sunbathe, and party your brains out. **Love** is free and rampant on Bulgaria's biggest pick-up scene; unfortunately, birth-control is not. Pack your own along with sunscreen and bug spray— the mosquitoes can be merciless. Street names are often—thankfully—written in the Latin script, and many signs are even in English and German.

Train travel from Sofia is excruciatingly crowded and slow, yet still a bargain at under US$4; express buses are quicker (5-6hr.), more comfortable, and affordable (US$4.35 with Globe Travel). The resorts have **minivans** running from the major villages and cities (US$0.50).

■■■ VARNA (ВАРНА)

Varna, known as Bulgaria's sea capital, is understandably crowded in summer. It harbors an alluring old town, seaside gardens, and a beach ideal for rollerblading. By

BULGARIA

the time the Romans arrived in the 2nd century AD, Varna was already a trade and cultural center. In 1402, it was the last city to surrender to the Ottoman invaders, and remained the least influenced by them under their oppression. As you stroll along Varna's **seaside gardens,** have a look inside the **Marine Museum** (Военно-Морски Музей; open 10am-5:30pm; 50Lv) and check out the **Aquarium** (Аквариум; open Mon. noon-5pm, Tues.-Sat. 9am-7pm; 20Lv). In the old part of the city, known as the Greek neighborhood (Грыцка Махала), you can see the impressive **Roman baths** (Римски Терми; open Mon.-Sat. 10am-5pm, winter Tues.-Sat. 10am-5pm; 30Lv). The second-largest cathedral in the country, **Sv. Bogoroditsa,** is in the center of the city, where you can also have a look at the exquisite **art gallery** at 1, ul. L. Karavelov (Л. Каравелов) . Chamber concerts are often held here; inquire at the tourist bureau for a schedule. (Open Tues.-Sun. 10am-7pm; the sign "free day Monday" means it's closed then.)

Varna's **beach** charges a nominal 10Lv entrance fee; pay up or get pounded by bouncers. For more serious sunbathing and lots of water sports, head to one of the nearby resorts. You'll either hate or love **Golden Sands** (tel. (52) 85 56 81, fax 85 55 87), 17km north of Varna, where you can play sports, hear folk music at the **Gypsy Hideaway** (Цигански Табор), sample *souvlaki* at **Dionysos,** a Greek tavern, don some *Lederhosen* at DAB, a **German Beer Hall,** or quaff some warm beer at the **Golden Lion,** an English pub. Later, spin the roulette wheel at the **Shipka Casino**, or dance to the fierce rhythms at the **Astoria Disco.** All this, and no danger from predatory animals (or so the brochures reassure). To get there, hop on bus 9 (15Lv) or any of the private minivans leaving from the Cathedral.

Practical Information, Accommodations, and Food Balkantourist has been transformed into several small travel agencies; one of the best is **Varnenski Bryag Co.** (Варненски Бряг), ul. Musala 3 (tel. (52) 22 55 24, fax 25 30 83). The English-speaking clerks can arrange **private accommodations** (US$5-6). From the train station, go through the underpass and walk straight up ul. Tsar Simeon I until you come to the large Independence Sq. (пл. Независимост). The bureau is on the 2nd side street to your right. (Open 8am-9pm, winter Mon.-Sat. 8am-6pm). There is a helpful **Rila** international trains bureau at ul. Shipka 3 (Шипка; tel. (52) 22 62 73), a side street off ul. Knyaz Boris I (open Mon.-Fri. 8am-4:30pm). The **post office** and **telephones** can be found behind the Cathedral. (Telephones open 7am-10pm. Post office open Mon.-Fri. 7am-7pm, Sat. 7:30am-7pm, Sun. 8am-noon.)

There are several **private room** bureaus on Knyaz Boris 1. Look for the sign "*Chastni Kvartiri*" (Частни Квартири). Prices range from US$4-6 per night, and most of them double as **change bureaus. Hotel Idilia,** 3 Bratya Skorpil (Братя Шкорпил; tel. (52) 23 20 92), a short walk from the center, has clean rooms with private baths for US$6.50 per person.

Restaurants and **nightlife** center around Pl. Nezavisimost and along ul. Knyaz Boris I. A very popular hangout for younger crowds is the festival complex (Фестивалния Комплекс). International relations are also conducted at the Orbita Hotel discotheque. In the summer a good number of discos and bars open up by the beach.

■■■ BURGAS (БУРГАС)

The Black Sea coast's other transportation hub, Burgas offers easy access to nearby villages and beaches. The town's seaside gardens are quieter than those in Varna, and kids of all ages enjoy the giant **water slide** (open 9am-10pm, 5Lv). Next door is the hottest open-air disco on the coast, the **Black Sea Nightclub** (open 24hrs., performances at 1am, 3am, and 4:30am). Burgas is accessible from Varna by **bus** (6 per day, 2½hr., 120Lv) and from Sofia by bus (2-3 per day, 235Lv) or **train** (8 per day, 175Lv). The **Garderobs** at the stations will store your stuff for 5-6Lv per bag per day. The English-speaking staff at the **tourist office,** 2, ul. Aleksandrovska (Александровска) (tel. (56) 472 75), gives out old maps in English, and sells bus tickets to Sofia and İstanbul (US$18). There is a **bank** right inside the train station (open Mon.-Fri.

BULGARIA

8:30am-noon and 12:45-7:15pm); no banks are open weekends, but all change bureaus take AmEx traveler's checks. International **phone** calls can be placed only from the new **post** office at Bul. Osvobozhdenie (Бул. Освобождение). The tourist office books **private rooms** (US$4); otherwise, the best idea is to head for the clean beach of **Kraimone Campground** and stay in a motel room (doubles US$10) or bungalow (US$8). Take the hourly bus 17 from the bus station. Chow seafood at **Starata Gemiya** (Старата Гемия) restaurant called "Fregata" in town. It's behind the Hotel Primorets in the Maritime Park. (Full meal US$3. Open 9am-midnight.) Feast on curry dishes (US$2.50) and chop suey (US$1), identifiable on the English menu at the Chinese restaurant **"The Garden,"** 16 Aleksandrovska (open 11am-midnight). Avoid tap water in Burgas; its metal content burns tender tourist stomachs.

■ SOZOPOL AND NESEBUR

The area south of Burgas is becoming increasingly popular; the stretch between Burgas and **Ahtopol** (Ахтопол) is lined with enchanting bays and beaches. There are about 15 campgrounds, and many small and inexpensive private hotels are now appearing. **Sozopol** (Созопол), 34km south of Burgas, is Bulgaria's oldest Black Sea town, settled in 610BC and later called Appollonia. The yet untouristed **Old Town** sits on a rocky peninsula with a Mediterranean mystique; old women still sell beautiful handmade lace on the street. The bus from Burgas (30Lv) lets you off near the **Sozopol Tourist Office** (tel. (5514) 17 84), but you may have trouble finding someone who speaks English. On the other hand, English-speaking staff in the large white building of **Helio Tours,** Ropotamo ul. (tel. (5514) 251), can arrange **private rooms** (US$6) and reserve beachside bungalows with bath (US$5-6) at nearby **campgrounds** Kavacite, Gradina, or Cherno Moretz (open 8am-10pm). **Hotel Radik** (Хотел "Радик"), at 4, ul. Republikanska (Републиканска) (tel. (5514) 17 06, has a gorgeous panoramic view of the harbor (US$5 per bed). For a delicious meal and a romantic view of the sea, walk to the northern end of the Old Town until you reach the ivy-covered **Restaurant Vyaturna Melnitsa** (Вятърна Мелница), on ul. Morski Skali (Морски Скали). (Menu in English. Meals US$3. Open 8am-1am.)

The area north of Burgas caters to family and package-vacation crowds, making it grueling to find cheap lodgings. The big tourist ghetto here is the crowded **Sunny Beach** (Слънчев Бряг), reached by minivans from Varna or Burgas. The **accommodation complex** across the street from the huge Hotel Cuban (Кубан) will navigate you to rooms, food, and fun. **Nesebur** (Несебър) is a charming museum town perched atop the peninsula at the southern end of Sunny Beach, a sweet alternative for a few nights' stay. **Buses** from Burgas run every hour, and from Sunny Beach every 15min. Just across the street from the bus station, the **tourist bureau** sells tickets for a daily bus to Sofia (US$5), and books private **rooms** in the old and new town (US$8). Or do as the Bulgarians, and knock on doors in the new town yourself. Many families have rooms to rent (US$3-5).

BULGARIA

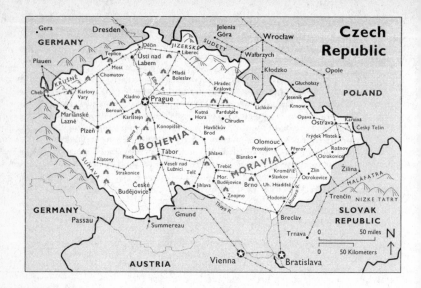

Czech Republic
(Česká Republika)

US$1 = 28.33kčs (koruny, or CSK)		10kčs =	US$0.35
CDN$1= 21.10kčs		10kčs =	CDN$0.47
UK£1 = 45.01kčs		10kčs =	UK£0.22
IR£1 = 44.59kčs		10kťs =	IR£0.22
AUS$1 = 21.71kčs		10kčs =	AUS$0.46
NZ$1 = 17.18kčs		10kčs =	NZ$0.58
SAR = 7.95kčs		10kťs =	SAR1.26
Country Code: 42		International Dialing Prefix: 00	

On New Year's Day, 1993, after more than three quarters of a century of relatively unabrasive coexistence, the Czech and Slovak Republics, formerly known as Czechoslovakia, split, bloodlessly. The notion of self-determination is a fairly new thing to the Czech people; from the Holy Roman Empire to the Nazis and the Soviets, foreign powers have driven their internal affairs: even Alexander Dubček's 1960s "Prague Spring" refroze in 1968 with the iron rumble of Soviet tanks. After the demise of communist governments in Hungary and Poland, and after the fall of the Berlin Wall in 1989, the Velvet Revolution came to Czechoslovakia. Despite Communist crackdowns, Czechs increasingly demonstrated in Prague and other cities in November, and within a month, the Communist government had resigned and Václav Havel emerged as the main political leader. The transformation to constitutional democracy, a market economy and the departure of Soviet troops were overseen by Havel and his Civic Forum Party, which united with the Slovak Public Against Violence Party in the free elections of June 1990. Havel attempted to preserve the Czech-Slovak union but three years of debate and a popular vote resulted in the separation of the two nations on January 1, 1993.

Although he temporarily stepped down during the divorce with Slovakia, Czechs today have much respect for their playwright-president and for the most part are embracing the westernization process that continues at a dizzying pace. The Czech

Republic boasts Eastern Europe's most stable currency and the regions second-largest GDP per capita, after Slovenia.

Check out the Czech Republic in further detail in *Let's Go: Eastern Europe.*

GETTING THERE AND GETTING AROUND

Visas American citizens may visit the Czech Republic visa-free for up to 30 days; citizens of the U.K. and Ireland for up to 90 days. Australians, Canadians, New Zealanders and South Africans require visas available from their **Czech Embassy** or from one of three border crossings: **Rozvadov, Dolni Dvoriste** or **Hate.** Single-entry or transit visas cost US$21 (US$44 for Canadians), multiple-entry visas US$49, and require two photos and two days to process. Upon arrival in the Czech Republic, Canadian citizens are required to register with the police and have their visa stamped. In Australia contact the Czech Embassy, 38 Culgoa Circuit, O'Malley, Canberra, ACT 2606 (tel. (06) 290 13 86, fax 290 00 06). The embassy in South Africa is located at 936 Pretorius St., Arcadia, Pretoria 0083, or P.O. Box 3326, 0001 Pretoria (tel. (12) 342 34 77 or 43 36 01, fax 43 20 33).

Transportation Eurail became valid in the Czech Republic in 1994, and **Eastrail** has been accepted since 1991. Because rail travel remains such a bargain (about 30kč per 100km on a 2nd-class *rychlik* train), however, railpasses are less of a necessity here than in Western Europe. The fastest trains are the *expresný.* The *rychlík* trains cost as much as the express, while the few *spešný* (semi-fast) trains cost less; avoid *osobný* (slow) trains. **ČSD,** the national transportation company, publishes the monster *Jízdní řád* (train schedule, 74kč), helpful if only for the two-page English explanation in front. *Odjezd* (departures) are printed in train stations on yellow posters, *prijezd* (arrivals) on white. **ČEDOK** gives ISIC holders up to 50% off international tickets bought at their offices. If you're heading to **Austria** or **Hungary,** it's generally less expensive to buy a Czech ticket to the border, and then buy a separate ticket from the crossing to your destination once inside the foreign country. **Seat reservations** *(místenka,* 6kč) are required on almost all express and international trains, and for all 1st-class seating; snag them at the counter labeled by a boxed "R." A slip of paper with the destination, time, date, and a capital letter "R" expedites the transaction.

Buses can be significantly faster and only slightly more expensive than trains, especially near Prague and for shorter distances, but be sure to check how many stops they make. **ČSAD,** the national bus company, also runs international routes. From Prague, buses run a few times per week to Munich, Milan, etc., and from Brno to Linz, Austria. Consult the timetables posted at stations or buy your own (25kč) from bookstores and newsstands. **Hitchhiking** is popular in the Czech Republic, especially during the morning commuting hours (6-8am).

CZECH REPUBLIC ESSENTIALS

The importance of **ČEDOK,** the state tourist company and relic of centralized communist bureaucracy, has seriously diminished since the 1989 revolution. **CKM,** its junior affiliate, remains helpful for the student and budget traveler by serving as a clearinghouse for youth hostel beds and issuing ISICs and HI cards. The quality and trustworthiness of private tourist agencies varies. **Information offices** in major cities provide tons of print on sights, cultural events, hostels, and hotels. City maps *(plán mésta)* are available for almost all tourist destinations (28-60kč).

There is no longer any mandatory foreign **currency exchange** requirement, but keep a couple of exchange receipts in order to change money back upon leaving. Though still operating, the black market is graying around the temples; since the official exchange rate has almost reached street levels, it's hardly worth the risk. Bring some western currency in small denominations, as it is often preferred as payment in larger hotels and private accommodations in bigger cities. Banks are generally open from 8am to 4pm. Czech money is not valid in Slovakia.

CZECH REPUBLIC

Crime has climbed dramatically since the 1989 revolution; be especially aware of snatch-and-run and pickpocketing. In **emergencies,** make use of your embassy; local police may flounder in English. Lost wallets and purses sometimes appear at embassies with only the cash missing. The **emergency phone number** throughout the country is **158.** To reach the AT&T **USADirect operator,** dial 00 42 00 01 01; **MCI WorldPhone** 00 42 00 01 12; **Canada Direct** 00 42 00 01 51; **BT Direct** 00 42 00 44 01. The **mail** works fine; letters reach the U.S. within 10 days. International **phone** calls are possible, though finding a grey and blue pay phone that works can be challenging. Look for a phone with a globe above it; most in post offices work. Buy phone cards (100kč) at most newsstands or at the post office. Local calls cost 2kč regardless of length. For inter-city calling, insert additional coins when the warning tone sounds.

National holidays include New Year's Day, Easter Sunday and Monday, May Day (May 1), the Anniversary of Soviet-American Liberation (May 8), July 5-6, October 28 (Independence Day), and Christmas (Dec. 25-26). Many establishments now close on other religious holidays such as Ascension Day (late May or early June).

Communication Russian *was* every student's mandatory second language, but English will win you more friends. A few German phrases go even further, especially in Prague. Pronunciation of Czech words can be difficult. The č is "ch," as in ČEDOK (CHE-dok), the š is "sh," as in *gulaš* (GOU-lash), ž sounds like "zh" as in "azure" or *nádraží* (NAH-dra-zhee), ň sounds like the Spanish ñ, though more subtle, ě is "yeh" as in "náměstí" (NAH-myes-tee). Before you leave home, pick up a "Say it in Czech" phrasebook. A few handy phrases in Czech will make you sound like less of an oaf: *Dobrý den!* (doh-BREE den, "hello"); *Na shledanou* (nah-SLEH-dah-noh-oo, "goodbye"); *Děkuji* (DYEH-koo-yih, "thank you"); *Prosím* (PROH-seem, "please" and "you're welcome"); *Kolik?* (KOH-lik, "how much?"); and *Zaplatíme* (ZAH-plah-tyee-meh, "We're ready to pay"). Just this once, *no* (NOH) or *ano* (ah-NOH) means "yes," and *ne* (NEH) means "no."

Accommodations and Camping Converted **university dorms** run through CKM are the cheapest option in July and August. Comfy 2-to 4-bed rooms go for 200-400kč per person. CKM also runs **Junior Hotels,** year-round hostels loosely affiliated with HI, which give discounts to both HI and ISIC holders and which are comfortable but often full. Private hostel operations have usurped CKM's monopoly on youth lodgings, but not necessarily surpassed its reliability. Showers and bedding are usually included, and breakfast is too, especially outside of Prague.

Across the country, **private homes** have become a legal and feasible lodging option. In Prague, hawkers offer expensive rooms (US$16-30, but don't agree to more than US$25), sometimes including breakfast. Scan train stations for "hostel," "*zimmer*," or "accommodations" ads. Quality varies widely; *don't* pay in advance. Make sure anything you accept is easily accessible by public transport; be prepared for a healthy commute to the center of town. Outside of Prague, **ČEDOK** handles private room booking, although private agencies are burgeoning around train and bus stations. If you're sticking to **hotels,** consider reserving ahead of time from June to September in Prague and Brno, even if it requires pre-payment. Outside major cities, it's easier to find a bed. Hotels come in 5 flavors: A-star, A, B-star, B, and C. As cities scramble to attract tourists, many of the grungy C hotels have begun to disappear. In 1994, singles in a B hotel averaged 650kč, doubles 900kč (within Prague 950kč and 1400kč, respectively). Inexpensive **camping** is available everywhere (most sites open only mid-May to Sept.), ranging from 60-100kč per person. The book *Ubytování ČSR,* in decodable Czech, comprehensively lists the hotels, inns, hostels, huts, and campgrounds in Bohemia and Moravia. Bookstores also sell a fine hiking map of the country, *Soubor Turistických Map,* with an English key.

Food and Drink The health food craze has yet to hit the Czech Republic: the 4 basic food groups here are sausages (*párek, klobosa*), cheese (*sýr*), ice cream (*zmr-*

zlina), and beer (*pivo*). The *Hotová Jídla* (ready dishes) section on menus consistently includes variations on *gulaš*, pork, or beef doused in a creamy sauce. Some key words are: *vepřová* (pork), *hovězi* (beef), *klobása* (sausage), *kuře* (chicken), *ryby* (fish), *kapr* (carp), *pstruh* (trout), and *zelenia* (vegetables). Meat can be *pečeně* (roasted), *vařené* (boiled) or *mleté* (ground). Signs which should command your salivary attention are *bufet*, *samoobsluha* (self-service), and *občerstveni*, all variations on the stand-up snack bar. A *hostinec* caters to a steady clientele of beer drinkers; a *kavárna* or *cukrárna* serves coffee and exquisite pastry, but note that *káva* (coffee) is often a Turkish-style thick layer of grounds topped with boiling water. A *pivnice* is a beer hall and a *vinárna* a wine bar; both are good places to eat. Czech beers are among the world's best. The most famous are *Plzeňský Prazdroj* (Pilsner Urquell) and *Budvar* (the original Budweiser), but the *Velképopovický Kozel* is a local favorite. It is customary to round the bill up by a few crowns—often it will be done for you. At finer eateries, you should add a 10% tip as you pay; do not leave the tip on the table. Vegetarians can munch on *smaženy sýr* (fried cheese), a scrumptious Czech specialty sold at food stands, and produce from *ovoce zelenina* stores (greengrocers) or *potraviny* (general grocery stores). Vegetarian restaurants have begun to pop up in larger cities. From Saturday noon to Sunday morning, all grocery stores and some restaurants close.

■■■ PRAGUE (PRAHA)

The Princess Libuše stood atop a hill overlooking the River Vltava and declared, "I see a city whose glory will touch the stars; it shall be called *Praha* (threshold)." Prague is the "city of a hundred spires," of soaring cathedrals and lavish 14th-century palaces. Its lively squares and avenues give the city a festival atmosphere which few can rival, and its museums, concert halls, and ballet and opera performances are world-class. Since the Velvet Revolution of 1989, the city has exploded from relative obscurity and isolation behind the Iron Curtain into a tourist destination rivalling the great capitals of Western Europe. Over 20,000 Yappies ("Young Americans in Prague") call the city home, and more than 750,000 visitors left envying them last year. While many locals can't keep up with the rising prices, Prague is still a fabulous bargain by Western standards. Just don't flaunt your affluence; instead, immerse yourself as seamlessly as possible into the humbling magnificence of this 1000-year-old metropolis.

ORIENTATION AND PRACTICAL INFORMATION

Prague straddles the **River Vltava** (Moldau in German), with direct rail and bus links to Vienna, Berlin, Munich, and Warsaw. High on the western bank of the river lies **Hradčany,** Prague's castle district. Below it huddle the palaces and gardens of **Malá Strana** (Lesser Town). From Malá Strana, the pedestrian-only **Karlův Most** (Charles Bridge) crosses the river and leads into **Staré Město** (Old Town), at the center of which is the resplendent plaza, **Staroměstské náměstí.** North of Staroměstské náměstí lies **Josefov,** the old Jewish quarter. South of Staré Město are the rich 19th-century façades of the more commercial **Nové Město** (New Town).

The center of Prague is dominated by 3 streets which form a leaning *T*. The long stem of the *T*, separating the Old and New Towns, is **Václavské náměstí** (Wenceslas Square; actually a grand boulevard); at the bottom of the *T* towers the **National Museum.** The busy pedestrian street **Na příkopě** forms the right arm and leads to **náměstí Republiky.** On the left, 28 Října becomes **Národní** after a block, leading to the **National Theater** on the river. A maze of small streets leads to Staroměstské nám. 2 blocks above the *T*.

Tabak stands and bookstores sell an indexed *plán mésta* (city map).

Prague will undergo a much-needed telephone system overhaul until 1996; many of the numbers listed may change.

CZECH REPUBLIC

Tourist Offices: CKM, Žitná 12 (tel. 29 12 40), next to the Junior Hotel Praha. Has information, accommodations, and transportation tickets. Beware of old maps that show CKM branch offices that no longer exist. Open 9am-1pm, 2-7pm. **ČEDOK,** Na příkopě 18 (tel. 212 71 11, fax 290 798 or 242 277 18). Information on private accommodations and sightseeing in Prague. Also sells train, bus, and plane tickets. Open Mon.-Fri. 9am-7pm, Sat. 8:30am-2pm. **Prague Information Service** (Pražská Informační Služba), Staroměstske nám. 22 (tel. 22 44 523). Sells a massive variety of maps and booklets on Prague and the Czech Republic. English and German spoken. Open 9am-5pm. **American Hospitality Center**, Na Mustkú 7 (tel. 26 15 74 or 26 20 45), just north of the end of Vácklavske nám. Message board posted with requests for English tutors, cycling companions, notes to friends, and whatnot. Nurse a coffee and chat with folks who think they're in 1920s Paris. CNN, MTV, popcorn, and pizza. No apple pie. Open 10am-10pm.

Embassies: U.S., Tržiště 15, Praha 12548 (tel. 24 51 04 47, after-hours 52 12 00). M: Malostranská. From Malostranské nám. turn into Karmelitská and then right on Tržiště. Open Mon.-Fri. 8am-1pm and 2-4:30pm. **Canada,** Mickiewiczova 6 (tel. 312 02 51). Open Mon.-Fri. 8:30am-noon, 2-4pm. Citizens must register with the police at Olšanska 2 within 3 working days of arriving in the Czech Republic. Your compulsory visa must be stamped. **U.K.,** Thunovská 14 (tel. 24 51 04 39). Open Mon.-Fri. 8:30am-12:30pm and 1:30-5pm. Travelers from **Australia** and **New Zealand** should contact the British embassy in an emergency. **Hungary,** Badeního 1 (tel. 36 50 41). Same-day visa for citizens of Australia and New Zealand, US$20 plus 2 photos. Open Mon.-Wed. and Fri. 9am-noon. **Poland,** Valdštejnská 8 (tel. 53 69 51). Consular section, Václavské nám. 49 (tel. 26 44 64). Same-day visa service for citizens of Australia and New Zealand; US$28 plus 2 photos, students US$21 with ISIC. Open Mon.-Fri. 9am-1pm. **Russia,** Pod kaštany 1 (tel. 38 19 45). Consular section around corner at Korunovační 34 (tel. 37 37 23). Visas US$25 (invitation required); citizens of Australia pay US$50. Open Mon., Wed., and Fri. 9:30am-1pm.

Currency Exchange: State bank, Na příkopě 14 (tel. 23 31 11 11), cashes U.S. dollar or DM traveler's checks. Open Mon.-Fri. 7:30am-noon and 1-3:30pm. **Živnostenská bank,** Na příkopě 2 (tel. 24 12 11 11). Also MC and Visa cash advances. Commission 1% on notes, 2% on traveler's checks. Open Mon.-Fri. 8am-5pm. **Chequepoint,** in all of Prague's touristed areas. About 10% commission on top of a service charge. Branches at intersections of Václavské nám. and Vodičková and of Václavské nám. and 28 Října open 24hrs. **Thomas Cook,** Václavské nám 47 (tel. 26 31 06 and 24 22 86 58). Cash your Thomas Cook Eurocheques here. Flexible hours. Open Mon.-Fri. 9am-9pm, Sat. 9am-4pm, Sun. 10am-2pm. Beware the **black market;** you may end up with a wad of counterfeit bills that no one will take.

American Express: Václavské nám. 56 (tel. 26 17 47). M: Muzeum. Mail held at U.S. visitors counter. Cardholders' personal checks cashed for kč only. MasterCard advances. Express cash machine. Open Mon.-Fri. 9am-6pm, Sat. 9am-noon.

Post Office: Jindřišská 14. M: Můstek. Poste Restante at window 28, stamps at windows 20-23, letters and parcels under 2kg at windows 10-12. Open 24hrs. **Postal Code:** 110 00. **Parcels** over 2kg can be mailed only at **Pošta-Celnice,** Plzeňská 139. Take tram 9 west, and ask for the stop. Open Mon.-Tues. and Thurs.-Fri. 7am-3pm, Wed. 7am-6pm, Sat. 8am-noon.

Telephones: At the post office and most train and metro stations. Phone cards (100kč) available at post offices and many newsstands, giving about 2min. calling time to the U.S. **City Code:** 02.

Flights: Ruzyně Airport (tel. 334 33 14), 20km northwest of city center. Take bus 119 from the M: Dejvická. Various private companies offer expensive (expect 100kč) buses from the airport to downtown Prague. **ČSA** (tel. 36 78 14), the Czech airline, is located on Revoluční north of nám. Republiky.

Trains: Train information in Czech (tel. 24 44 41 or 26 49 30). Four train stations; always ask what your point of departure will be. **Praha-Holešovice** is the main international terminal—you'll probably arrive here or at Hlavní Nádraží. M: Nádraží Holešovice. **Praha Hlavní Nádraží** (Wilsonovo Nádraží). M: Hlavní nádraží. Some international and many domestic routes. To Berlin (6hr.), Budapest

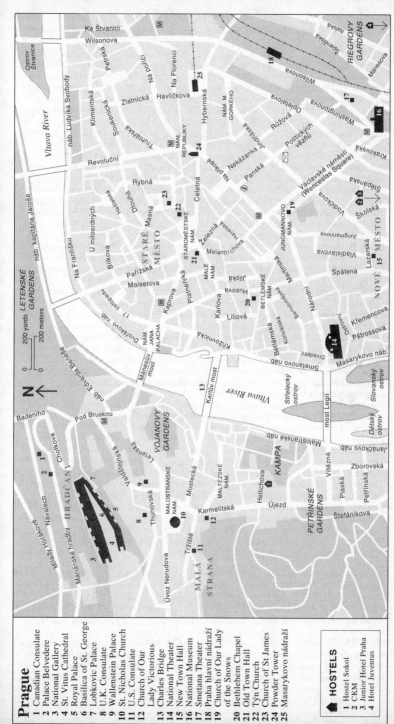

Prague
1 Canadian Consulate
2 Palace Belvedere
3 National Gallery
4 St. Vitus Cathedral
5 Royal Palace
6 Basilica of St. George
7 Lobkovic Palace
8 U.K. Consulate
9 Wallenstein Palace
10 St. Nicholas Church
11 U.S. Consulate
12 Church of Our
   Lady Victorious
13 Charles Bridge
14 National Theater
15 New Town Hall
16 National Museum
17 Smetana Theater
18 Praha hlavní nádraží
19 Church of Our Lady
   of the Snows
20 Bethlehem Chapel
21 Old Town Hall
22 Tyn Church
23 Church of St James
24 Powder Tower
25 Masarykovo nádraží

HOSTELS
1 Hostel Sokol
2 CKM
3 Junior Hotel Praha
4 Hotel Juventus

CZECH REPUBLIC

(9hr.), Vienna (5hr.), Warsaw (10hr.). **Masarykovo Nádraží,** at Hybernská and Havličkova. M: nám. Republiky. **Praha-Smíchov,** M: Smíchovské Nádraží. Domestic routes.

Buses: ČSAD has 3 terminals *(autobusové nádraží)*. The central one is **Praha-Florenc,** on Křižíkova (tel. 22 86 42 or 22 26 29), behind the Masarykovo nádraží railway station. M: Florenc. Staff speaks little English, but posted schedules are legible and extensive. Buy tickets at least a day in advance, as they often sell out. To Milan and Munich (2 per week), Venice (4 per week), Vienna (daily). Extensive service throughout the Czech Republic and Slovakia. Open Mon.-Fri. 6am-6:30pm, Sat. 6am-1pm, Sun. 8:30am-noon and 12:30-3:30pm.

Public Transportation: The metro, tram, and bus systems serve the city well. **Tickets,** good for all forms of transportation, cost 6kč; stock up at newspaper stands and *tabak* shops as the orange *automat* machines in metro stations require exact change. **Punch your ticket** when boarding, and punch a new ticket when switching vehicles—except in the Metro, where your ticket is valid for 1hr. after punching on all lines as long as you don't go above ground. Fine for riding without a punched ticket: 200kč. Three **Metro (M)** lines run 5am-midnight: on city maps, line A is green, line B is yellow, and line C is red. Můstek (lines A and B), Muzeum (lines A and C), and Florenc (lines B and C) are the primary junctions. **Night** trams 51-58 and buses 500-510 run midnight-5am (every 40min.); look for their dark blue signs at transport stops. The municipal transit authority (DP, at Jungmannovo nám., M: Můstek, and at Palackého nám., M: Karlovo náměstí; both open 7am-9pm), sells **tourist passes** valid for the entire network. 1-day 50kč, 2-day 85kč, 3-day 110kč, 4-day 135kč, 5-day 170kč.

Taxis: tel. 35 03 20, 35 04 91, 202 95 19, or 203 94 19. Check to see that the meter starts at "0." On shorter trips, make sure the meter is running by saying "Zapněte taxametr, prosím," and for longer trips set a price beforehand.

Hitchhiking: Hitchhiking in and around Prague has become increasingly dangerous. Hitchers going east take tram 1, 9, or 16 to the last stop. To points south, they take Metro C to Pražskeho povstání, then go left 100m, crossing náměstí Hrdinů to 5 Květná, (a.k.a. highway D1). To Munich, they take tram 4 or 9 to the intersection of Plzeňská and Kukulova/Bucharova, then hitch south. Those going north take a tram or bus to Kobyliské nám., then bus 175 up Horňátecká.

Luggage Storage: Lockers (10kč) in every train and bus station. Those in the main train station are usually full—try 24hr. baggage storage in basement (25kč per day for 1st 15kg). Beware of nimble thieves, who might relieve you of heavy baggage while you concentrate on setting your 4-digit locker code.

Laundromat: If you stay in a private flat, ask if your laundry can be included with the family's. Often it will come back darned and ironed, even your underwear. Otherwise, go to **Laundry Kings** at Dejvická 16, 1 block from M: Hradčanská. Self-service wash 50kč per load, dry 15kč per 8min. Soap 10-20kč. Full-service is an additional 30kč and takes 24hr. Filled with similarly soiled and thirsty travelers. Throw back a few cold ones while waiting (beer 11 kč). Open 8am-10pm.

Bookstore: The Globe Bookstore, Janovského 14. M: Vltavská, then walk under the overpass on your right and turn right onto Janovského. Large selection of used paperbacks (avg. 80kč); will trade and buy yours. Open 9am-5pm.

Pharmacy: *(Lékárna),* Na příkopě 7 (tel. 22 00 81). Open 24hrs. Don't hesitate to ask for contraceptives *(kontrcepční prostředky),* bandaids *(náplast),* or tampons *(dámské vložky).*

Emergencies: Ambulance, tel. 155. **Fire,** tel. 150. **Police,** tel. 158. **Medical Emergency Aid** in English and German (tel. 29 93 81). **Police** headquarters at Olšanská 2 (tel. 21 21 11 11). M: Flora, then walk down Jičinská and right onto Olšanská; the station is about 200m ahead on your right. Or take tram 9. Come here to get a **visa extension.** Open Mon.-Fri. 7:30am-2pm.

ACCOMMODATIONS AND CAMPING

Prices in Prague are rising rapidly; the prices listed below are certain to increase (perhaps 50-100kč). Besides private flats (see agencies below), budget travelers have three main options: youth hostels, class B (2-star) or C (1-star) hotels, and campgrounds. In late June, universities empty for the summer, freeing up hundreds of cheap—albeit sterile and boxy—dorm rooms.

Private Agencies

Many of the hawkers who besiege visitors at the train station are actually agents for other people. Their going rate hovers at about US$15-30 (500-1000kč), depending primarily on proximity to downtown. Try haggling. These are generally safe arrangements, but if you're wary of bargaining on the street, use private agencies. Make sure you understand just what sort of room you are paying for—have the staff write it down—and that it is reachable by public transportation. Payment is usually accepted in Czech, U.S., or German currency.

CKM, Žitná 12 (tel. 29 12 40). M: I.P. Pavlova, and then backtrack down Žitná. The definitive place to find youth-hostel-esque lodging. Expect to pay 220-400kč per person per night. Open 9am-1pm and 2-7pm.

Hello Ltd., Senovážné nám 3 (formerly Gorkého nám. 3) between Na Příkopě and Hlavní Nádraží (tel. and fax 242 727 61). DM fetishists. Private apartments (from 30DM per person) and rooms at youth hostels (from 15DM per person). Private rooms start at 370kč per person, although most cost 620kč, 740kč and 860kč. Open 9am-10pm.

CK OK, Wilsonova (tel. 24 61 71 19, fax 54 90 21), on the top floor of the Hlavní Nádraží train station. Offers lodging in private flats and pricey hotels. Most rooms are "in the city" but without private bathrooms. Singles start at 680kč per person and doubles start at 425kč. Open 6am-10pm.

Pragotur, U Obecního domu 2 (tel. 232 22 05 or 232 51 28, fax 24 81 16 51), a side street off nám. Republiky, across from the Hotel Paříž. M: nám. Republiky. Rooms with shared bathrooms start at 460kč per person (double) and 605 kč (single) in downtown, 385kč and 460kč on the periphery. Makes hotel and motel reservations. Open Mon.-Sat. 9am-6pm, Sun. 9am-3pm.

Vesta, Wilsonova (tel. 236 81 90 or 236 81 92, fax 236 81 28 or 24 22 57 69), on the top floor of the Hlavní Nádraží train station. 58 hostel beds. Private doubles start at 700kč per person; hotel rooms start at 900kč (single), 1200kč (double), or 1500kč (triple). Open Mon.-Sat. 8:30am-7:30pm, Sun. 8:30am-4:30pm.

Prague Suites, Melantrichova 8 (tel. and fax 24 22 99 61), 2 blocks north of the Václavské nám. and Na Příkopě intersection. Singles, doubles, and triples (with shared bath) all start at US$20 per person in central Prague and at US$12 on the periphery. Open Mon.-Fri. 9am-6pm and Sat. 9am-2pm.

Wolff Travel, Na Příkopě 24 (tel. 26 15 05 or 24 22 79 89, fax 24 22 88 49). Singles in central Prague with shared bathroom 700kč (with private bath 800kč); central doubles with shared bath 1000kč (with private bath 1200kč). Also makes hotel reservations. Open Mon.-Fri. 9:30am-6:30pm, Sat. 10am-6pm, Sun. 10am-4pm.

Slunečko CK Travel Service, Ostrov Štvanice Hlávkův Most (tel. 37 16 92 or 26 42 08, fax 35 13 66) where Wilsonova crosses the Vltava River. Lots to choose from. Hostels start at US$8 per person per night. Private rooms start at US$12.50 per night and become more expensive as you approach central Prague. B&B from US$16.50 per person per night and hotel rooms with private bathrooms at US$27 per night. Open 10am-10pm.

Hostels (Studentska Kolej)

An enormous cluster is west of the river in the Strahov neighborhood, next to the Olympic stadium. These may be the best bet for travelers who arrive in the middle of the night without a clue. Call ahead and inquire about vacancies.

ESTEC Hostel, Vaníčkova 5 (formerly Spartakiádní 5), blok 5 (tel. 52 73 44). Take bus 217 or 143 from M: Dejvická, or bus 176 from M: Karlovo nám. to Koleje Strahov. Recently renovated; you can smell the fresh paint. Lively bars and discos in the adjacent village of communist-era blocks. English spoken. Reception open 24hrs. Check-out 10am. No curfew. Singles 360kč. Doubles 240kč. 500 beds from July to mid-Sept., 70 beds from mid-Sept. to June.

Interjunior Travel: Juniorhostel Strahov, Vaníčkova 5 (formerly Spartakiádní 5), blok 7 (tel. and fax 252 08 51). Next to the ESTEC Hostel. Reception open 9:30am-1pm and 2-6pm. Check-out 10am. Doubles and triples 220kč per person. Open year-round. In the summer, they will reserve doubles in ugly but functional buildings throughout Prague.

Oasa, Posepného nám. (tel. 792 63 15). M: Roztyly, or ride bus 505 from M: Muzeum. Reception open 24hrs. No curfew. 170kč per person per night. Showers, lockers, kitchen, sauna, and weight room.

Pension Unitas, Bartolomějská 9 (tel. 232 77 00, fax 232 77 09), a short walk through the Old Town from M: Národni. From Jesuit monastery where Beethoven performed, to state prison where Václav Havel was repeatedly jailed. Thoroughly renovated but you can still visit the "torture room." Reception open 6am-1am. Check-out 10am. Singles 920kč. Doubles 1100kč. Breakfast included.

TJ Slavoj, Vnáklích (tel. 46 00 70). Take tram 3 or 17 from M: Braník. Lonely 10min. walk from the tram stop; go there in daytime especially if traveling alone. About 50 beds in a boathouse by the river. 3- to 5-bed rooms. No lockout or curfew. A mere 170kč per body. Hearty meals 40kč.

Domov Mládeže, Dykova 20 (tel. 25 06 88, fax 25 14 29). Take tram 16 from Ječná to the fourth stop, or ride tram 16 from M: nám. Míruto to the second stop. From the streetcar stop, head right on Nitranská, and turn left on Dykova. 60 beds in the peaceful Vinohrady district. Hall showers. Open 24hrs. No lockout or curfew. 260kč. Breakfast 30kč.

Hostel Braník, Urbova 1233 (tel. 46 26 41 or 46 26 42, fax 46 26 43). M: Smíchovské nádraží, then take bus 196 or 198 to Ve Studeném and walk 100m up the hill. 180 beds in singles, doubles, triples, and quads. Open 24hrs. No lockout or curfew. 280kč per person. Breakfast included.

Pension Novodvorská, Novodvorská 151 (tel. 47 18 414). M: Smíchovské nádraží, then bus 196 or 198 to Sídl. Novodvorská. Many floors of student housing, often full. Reception open 24hrs. 420 kč.

Hotels

With so many Western tourists infiltrating Prague, hotels are upgrading both service and appearance. Budget hotels are fading faster than you can say *demokracia.* The difference in price between B- and C- hotels is often dramatic, though quality levels are comparable. Beware that hotels may try to bill you for a room more expensive than the one in which you stayed. Come armed with pen, paper, and receipts.

Hotel Madape, Malešická 74 (tel. 89 31 04, fax 77 13 55). Take bus 234 from M: Želivského to Vackov (5 stops). Beside the cemetery where Kafka is buried. B-category. Private baths. Doubles off hospital-like corridors 610kč. Breakfast 100kč. Often full. Some German spoken.

Hotel Kafka, Cimburkova 24 (tel. 273 101, fax 272 984) in the Žižkov district, near the television tower. Brand new hotel in a pleasant 19th-century neighborhood with nearby restaurants and *pivnice.* Reception open 24hrs. Singles 900kč. Doubles 1300kč. Breakfast 55kč.

Hotel Bílý Pev, Cimburkova 20 (tel. 271 126, fax 273 271), also in the Žižkov district. Another freshly renovated hotel. Reception open 24hrs. Singles 1240kč. Doubles 2360 kč. Breakfast included.

Betlem Club, Betlémské náměsti 9 (tel. 242 16 872, fax 242 18 054). Recently renovated Romanesque and Gothic parlors from the 13th century in central Prague. Reception open 24hrs. Singles 1530kč. Doubles 2720kč. German spoken.

Camping

For a roundup of camping options, visit **Slunečko CK Travel** (tel. 37 16 92), on the left-hand side of Hlávkův Most, where Wilsonova crosses the Vltava River (open 10am-10pm). For a tranquil setting along the banks of the Vltava River, try the **Císařska Louka** campground, located on an island between Smíchov and Vyšehrad (tel. 54 50 64 or 54 09 25, fax 20 40 21 or 54 33 05). Currency exchange and tennis courts. US$6 per person.

FOOD

Restaurants in Prague eat careless travelers alive. After numerous hidden charges are added in, the bill can be nearly twice what you expected. *Anything* offered with your meal (even french fries) will cost extra, as will everything placed on your table, including bread and ketchup. Check the bill scrupulously. The further you are from the mobs of tourists in the Old Town, the less you'll spend. *Hotová Jídla* (prepared meals) are least expensive. For a quick bite, the window stands selling tasty *párek v rohlíku* (sausage in a roll) for 7-15kč are a bargain. Outlying metro stops become impromptu marketplaces during the summer; look for the daily **vegetable market** at the intersection of Havelská and Melantrichova in the Old Town. For picnic supplies, the **supermarket** in the basement of **Kotva department store,** at the corner of Revoluční and Náměstí Republiky (M: nám. Republiky) is consistently well-stocked (open Mon.-Wed. and Fri.-Sun. 8am-7pm, Thurs. 8am-9pm). Run by a friendly fellow named Merxbauer, the corner store **Potraviny,** Zlatnická at Na Pořtěr, near Musarykovo train station, has a great selection of food and drink at decent prices (open Mon.-Fri. 8am-9pm, Sat. 9am-9pm).

Restaurace U Dvou Koćek, Uhelný trh 10, in the Old Town. Menu rotates among *paprikáš, guláš,* and schnitzel, starting at 39kč. Beware the 25kč service charge. ½l Pilsner Urquell costs 15kč. Open 11am-11pm.

U Radnických Restaurace, Havelská 9, in the historic *radnice* (old town hall). Dishes for under 50kč. ½l of Prague's very own *Staropramen* lager a mere 15kč.

Bitburger Pils Snack Bar, Husova 5, in the Old Town. Spaghetti 69kč. Duck hovers around 120kč. Imported *Bitburger Pils* is on draft. Open Mon.-Fri. until 8pm.

Restaurace U Parvdů, Žitná 15, in the New Town. Best schnitzel (*řízek*) in Prague. Wood and plaster decor, chandelier and high ceiling take you back in time. Friendly, young staff is eager to practice English and German. Open 11am-10pm.

Krab Haus, Jungmannovo námĕsti. Cheap and close to Wenceslas Square. Sandwiches and pastries from 10kč. Open Mon.-Fri. 9am-8pm, Sat.-Sun. 10am-6pm.

U Benedikta, Benediktská 11. From M: nám. Republiky, walk down U Obecního domů and turn right on Rybná. Enjoy Czech and other European entrees (70-150 kč) on the pleasant terrace. Open 11:30am-11pm.

Malostranská Hospoda, Karmelitská 25, two blocks south of Malostranské nám. Quality Bohemian pub fare, including sirloin, roast pork, and *guláš,* for less than 50kč. Open Mon.-Sat. 10am-midnight, Sun. 11am-midnight.

Café Espresso Paulus, Malostranské náměstí, right behind Dienzenhofer's famous Baroque St. Nicholas Church. Wonderful location; hip and happening café. Coffee 15kč. Vodka 30kč. Open 10am-8pm.

SIGHTS

Staré Město Surrounded by a labyrinth of Old World alleyways, the luminous Baroque elegance of **Staroméstské námĕstí** is truly startling. This sweeping space is dominated by the **Old Town Hall,** which expanded from the original 14th-century tower to include several neighboring buildings. The town hall used to extend to within a few meters of the baroque **St. Nicholas Church,** but that section was demolished by the Nazi tanks on the very last day of WWII. Townspeople and tourists gather on the hour to see its fabulous **Astronomical Clock,** with 12 peering apostles and a bell-ringing skeleton representing death. The clockmaker's eyes were put out by his patron so he could not craft another. A statue of martyred Czech theologian and leader **Jan Hus** occupies the place of honor in the center of the square. Across from the Town Hall is **Týn Church.** The tower on the right represents Adam, who shields Eve, the tower on the left, from the midday sun. To the left of the church, the creamy 14th-century **House at Stone Bell** shows the Gothic core which may lurk under many of Prague's Baroque façades, and exhibits works from the Municipal Gallery of Prague (open Tues.-Sun. 10am-6pm). Between Maiselova and Týn church is **Franz Kafka**'s former home, marked with a plaque. (Hard-core Kafka devotees can visit the writer's final resting place at the Jewish Graveyard right outside M: Želivského.) A short detour down Jilská will bring you to the **Bethlehem**

Chapel, where Jan Hus preached to his loyal congregation from 1402 until he was burnt at the stake.

Prague's historic Jewish neighborhood, Josefov, is located north of Staroměstí náměstí along Maiselova and several side streets. It's cultural wealth lies in five well-preserved synagogues. To gain access to all five and to the historic Jewish cemetery, purchase a comprehensive ticket at the **State Jewish Museum** (Státní Židovské Muzeum), Jáchymova 3; the desolate remains of this formerly vibrant community are reproduced in the scattered buildings (80kč, students 30kč). At U starého hřbitova and Maiselova is the **Old-New Synagogue** (Staronová synagogá), one of the few remaining early Gothic synagogues in Europe. The eclectic **Ceremonial Hall,** dating from 1906, currently holds exhibits from the Jewish museum. Next to the Old-New Synagogue is the **High Synagogue** (Vysoká synagoga) from the 16th century. Today it holds several exhibits of ceremonial items and religious tapestries. The neighboring **Jewish Town Hall** (Židovnická radnice) has a clock that runs counterclockwise in its pink Rococo exterior of the Town Hall. Walk down Maiselova and turn right on Široka until you reach the **Pinkas Synagogue** (Pinkasova synagogá) which displays a **memorial** to the Jews of Bohemia who perished in the Holocaust.

Karlův most (Charles Bridge) may be Europe's most festive. Artisans, classical guitarists, and other street musicians fill the bridge day and night above a bevy of swans. Depicted at the base of hero Jan Nepomuk's statue in the center of the bridge is hapless Jan being tossed over the side for guarding his queen's confidences. Climb the Gothic **defense tower** on the Malá Strana side for a super view of Prague (open 10am-5:30pm; 20kč, students 10kč). Head down the stairs on the left side of the bridge (as you face the castle district) to **Hroznová,** where a mural honors John Lennon and the peace movement of the 1960s. **Slovanskù ostrov** (island) and the larger **Střelecky ostrov** (accessible from **most Legíí**) offer soothing shade.

Malá Strana The Lesser Town is rich in palaces, ornate gardens, and grand Baroque churches. The grandest is the 18th-century **St. Nicholas' Church,** the highest achievement of Czech Baroque art. Mozart played the organ here. (Open 9am-5pm. 20kč, students 10kč.) Nearby on Karmelitská rises the more modest **Church of Our Lady Victorious,** repository of the porcelain statue of the Infant Jesus of Prague, reputed to have miraculous powers. A simple wooden gate at Letenská 10 (off Malostranské nám.) opens onto the **Valdštejnská zahrada** (Wallenstein Garden), one of Prague's best-kept secrets. This tranquil 17th-century garden, adorned with statues and frescoes depicting scenes from the Trojan War, is enclosed by old buildings that glow golden on sunny afternoons (open 9am-7pm).

Hradčany You can spend days wandering about the edifices that comprise the **Pražský hrad** (Prague Castle), on Nerudova. All the styles of architecture that have made Prague so astonishingly beautiful are well-represented. The castle is crowned by the soaring **Katedrála sv. Vita** (St. Vitus's Cathedral), completed in 1930 after 600 years of construction. To the right of the high altar stands the **tomb of St. John Nepomuk**, three meters of solid, glistening silver, weighing in at two tons. Stroll across the third interior courtyard to enter the **Starý královský palác** (Old Royal Palace). Inside is the vast **Vladislav Hall,** with ample room for the jousting competitions that once took place here. Climb the 287 steps of the **Cathedral Tower** for a breathtaking view of the castle and the city (open 10am-4pm; 15kč, students 8kč). In the nearby **Chancellery of Bohemia,** two Catholic Habsburg officials were supposedly lobbed out the window by fed-up Protestant nobles in 1618 in the notorious **Defenestration of Prague.** Though a dungheap broke their fall, the die was cast, and war ravaged Europe for the next 30 years. The Romanesque **Basilica of St. George** (Bazilika sv Jiří) was erected in 921 just behind the Starý královský palác. Immediately on the right as you enter, note the wood and glass tomb enclosing St. Ludmila's skeleton. (Basilica open 9am-4:45pm).

The **Lobkovic Palace,** at the bottom (northeast) of Jiřská, contains a replica of the coronation jewels of Bohemia and an exhibit recounting the history of the lands that

CZECH REPUBLIC

today comprise the Czech Republic (30kč, students 15kč; not included in the combined admission ticket). Halfway up is a tiny street carved into the fortified wall—Kafka held an office on this **Zlatá ulička** (Golden Lane), where the court alchemists supposedly toiled (all palace-related buildings open Tues.-Sun. 9am-5pm, Oct.-March Tues.-Sun. 9am-4pm).

A model of the Eiffel Tower tops the **Petřínské sady,** gardens on the hills to the south (open May 9am-10pm, July-Aug. 9am-11pm; 20kč, students 5kč). A funicular to the top (4kč—look for *lanové dráhy* signs) leaves from just above the intersection of Vítézná and Žjezd. Not far from the station at the top is a wacky little castle offering juvenile bliss—a hall of mirrors (open April-Oct. 9am-6pm; 10kč, students 5kč). Just east of the park lies **Strahov Stadium,** the world's largest, enclosing the area of 10 soccer fields.

Nové Město Václavské náměstí (Wenceslas Square), the modern nexus of Prague, was actually designed as a quiet promenade in the late 19th century. The statue of the king and saint **Wenceslas,** has presided over a century of turmoil and triumph,watching no less than five full revolutions from his south-east standpoint, in front of the National Museum. The present version of this equestrian statue of Saint Václav was completed in 1912, though a Wenceslas monument of some sort has graced the square since 1680. The statue was the site for student Jan Palach's 1969 self-immolation protesting Soviet intervention in the Prague Spring; his sacrifice sparked a series of similar demonstrations around the country.

Stretching north from the Wenceslas monument, Art Nouveau houses are scattered among the modernist offices at the sides of the Václavské náměstí. The premier example of Bohemian Jugendstil is the 1903 **Hotel Evropa,** just before the intersection with Jindřišská on the right-hand side. Most of the other art nouveau structures along the square were designed by Jan Kotěra, the noted disciple of Viennese architectural giant Otto Wagner.

A half-hour walk south of Nové Město is the quiet fortress **Vyšehrad,** the Czech Republic's most revered landmark, which is delightfully tourist-free. On the mount above the river, the fortress encompasses a neo-Gothic church, a Romanesque rotunda, and the Vyšehrad Cemetery. (Complex open 24hrs.) Take Metro C to Vyšehrad. Even the subway stop has a movie-sweep vista of Prague.

Museums

National Museum, Václavské nám. 68. M: Muzeum. Vast collection including meteorites, enormous minerals, fossils, and a skeleton horse and rider. Open Mon. and Wed.-Fri. 9am-5pm, Sat.-Sun. 10am-6pm. 20kč, students 10kč.

National Gallery collections are housed in 9 different historical buildings. The **National Gallery of European Art** is in the **Šternberk Palace,** Hradčanské nám. 15, just outside the front gate of the Prague Castle. Includes works by Rubens, Breughel, Dürer, Picasso, and your favorite Impressionists. The **National Gallery of Bohemian Art,** Gothic to Baroque, is housed in **St. George's Monastery,** Jírské nám. 33, inside the Castle. Showcases works by Czech artists including Master Theodorik, court painter for Charles IV. More Bohemian creations are exhibited at the **Anežský areal,** at the corner of Anežka and Řásnovka; the structure was the Cloister of St. Agnes for centuries. All collections open Tues.-Sun. 10am-6pm; each gallery 40kč, students 10kč.

Betramka Mozart Museum, Mozartova 169. M: Anděl, then make a left on Pleňská, and turn left on Mozartova. In the Villa Bertramka, where Mozart lived in 1787 and reputedly wrote *Don Giovanni.* Open 9:30am-6pm. Garden concerts July-Aug. on Fri. at 7:30pm. Call ahead for tickets. 50kč, students 30kč.

The Prague Municipal Museum (Muzeum Hlavního Města Prahy), Na poříčí 52. M: Florenc. Holds the original calendar board from the Town Hall's Astronomical Clock and a 1:480 scale model of old Prague, meticulously precise to the last window pane. Other exhibits from the same collection reside in the **House at Stone Bell,** in Staroměstské nám. just to the left of Týn Church. Both buildings open Tues.-Sun. 10am-6pm. 10kč, students 5kč.

CZECH REPUBLIC

ENTERTAINMENT

For a listing of current concerts and performances, consult the *Prague Post,* the *Prague News, Prognosis, Prager Zeitung,* or *Český Böhmen Expres.* The grandest of Prague's theaters are the **National Theater** (Národní Divadlo), Národní třída 2-4 (tel. 24 91 34 37; box office open Mon.-Fri. 10am-8pm, Sat.-Sun. 3-8pm), and the newly renovated **Estates Theater** (Stavorské divadlo), Ovocný trh 6, between Celetná and Železná in the Old Town (M: Můstek), which premiered *Don Giovanni* in 1787, with Mozart himself conducting (box office open Tues.-Sat. 10am-6pm, Sun.-Mon. noon-6pm; provides earphones from simultaneous English translation). Most opera, drama, and ballet productions begin at 7pm; unsold tickets are sometimes available 30min. before showtime.

From mid-May to early June, the **Prague Spring Festival** draws musicians from around the world and outdoor concerts animate the city. Tickets (270-540kč) can be bought at **Bohemia Ticket International,** Na příkopě 16 (tel. 22 87 38), next to ČEDOK (open Mon.-Fri. 9am-6pm, Sat. 9am-3pm, Sun. 9am-2pm).

Nightlife in Prague is fluid—sometimes a dark, quiet brew, sometimes a charged molten metal—but always slipping through your fingers like beads of quicksilver. Hotspots appear and evaporate overnight. **Václavské náměstí** quakes with numerous dancefloors, but often the best way to enjoy Prague at night is to find a *pivnice* (beer hall) or a *vinárna* (wine hall).

V Masné, Mansá 17. Go up Rybná from nám Republiky and then turn left onto Masná. Authentic Czech *pivince* with Budweiser *Budvar* (the real thing) on tap, happily removed from tourists and high prices. Open 10am-10pm.

U Švejka, Újezd 22 in Malá Strama (tel. 52 56 20). An impressive beer garden with die-hard pivo-loving patrons. Half a liter of draft *Urquell* costs 19kč. Open 11am-midnight.

In Vino Veritas, Havelská 12 in the fruit and vegetable market area. Find your truth in this pleasant *vinárna's* wide selection of wine. Great location in the Old Town. Open until 10pm.

Highlander-Blue Note, Národní tř. 28 (tel. 24 21 35 55) down Národní from M: Můstek. Possibly the most popular jazz club in Prague. Live music starts at 9pm. Open Mon.-Sat. 11am-2am and Sun. 11am-midnight.

Rock Club Bunkr, Lodecká 2 (tel. 231 31 23). M: nám. Republiky, then walk down Na Poříčí, and left on Zlatnická. Hot Czech and American rock-n-roll bands in an erstwhile Communist-regime nuclear bunker. Cover usually 50kč. Open 7pm-5am. Café upstairs open 11am-3am.

Radost FX, Bělehradská 120, below Café FX. Comes with a "virtual reality light show" and driving techno beat. Cover 50kč. Open 9pm-6am.

Reduta, Národní 20 (tel. 24 91 22 46). Live jazz nightly and a clientele of artists drowning in tourists. Cover 80kč. Open Mon.-Sat. 9pm-2am.

Rock Café, right next to Reduta (tel. 24 91 44 16). MTV pumped in on satellite, and the occasional rockumentary. Open Mon.-Fri. 10am-3am, Sat. noon-3am.

■ NEAR PRAGUE

The Central Bohemian hills surrounding Prague contain 14 castles, some built as early as the 13th century. A 45min. train ride from Prague (8kč) brings you to **Karlštejn,** a walled and turreted fortress built by Charles IV to house his crown jewels and holy relics. The **Chapel of the Holy Cross** is decorated with more than 2000 inlaid precious stones and 128 apocalyptic paintings by medieval artist Master Theodorik. Take the metro to Smíchovské nádraži (Praha-Smíchov station), where trains cart gawkers hourly to Karlštejn. (Open Tues.-Sun. 9am-4pm. With foreign language guide 90kč, students 40kč; in Czech 10kč, students 5kč.) A **campground** (tel. (0311) 942 63) is located on the left bank of the River Berounka (open 24hrs.).

An hour and a half southeast of Prague by bus is the former mining town of **Kutná Hora.** Soon after a silver vein was struck here in the 13th century, a royal mint—**Vlašský dvůr**—was established to produce the Prague *groschen* (silver coin). The uninteresting coin museum has commentary written entirely in Czech, but up the stairs from the courtyard is a magnificent **Gothic Hall** with frescoes and lovely carved wooden triptychs. The most convincing evidence of the wealth that once flowed through the town is the fantastic, begargoyled **Cathedral of St. Barbara,** built to rival St. Vitus in Prague. Buses leave nearly hourly from platform #2 of Prague's M: Želivského, and from Praha-Florenc station.

At the end of the 18th century, Austrian Emperess Maria Theresa had a fortress built at the confluence of the Labe (Elbe) and Ohře (Eger) known as **Terezín** or Theresienstadt. Little did she know the miseries to which this fortress would bear witness. The Nazis established a concentration camp here in 1940 in which 32,000 prisoners were held. Among the inmates were Jews, Poles, dissident Germans, British POWs, and Communists. Nearby, the Nazis constructed Terezín ghetto, a sham "model village" to satisfy the International Red Cross (all Terezín residents were murdered after the Red Cross visit). After the Red Army captured the camp in May, 1945, the Czech regime used Terezín as an internment camp for Sudeten and Bohemian Germans. The fortress is now a monument and museum. Buses leave the Jewish Town Hall, Maiselova 18, twice per week (every Sun. and Thurs. at 10am, returning at 3pm) and daily from the Florenc bus station (Buses 17 and 20). The ride takes about an hour. (Terezín fortress open 8am-4:30pm. Museum open 9am-6pm.)

BOHEMIA

Bohemia, the western half of the Czech Republic, is the traditional homeland of the Czech people. Common heritage did little to prevent squabbles, as the hundreds of prickly castles guarding former feudal principalities attest.

■■■ LIBEREC

In the 19th century, Liberec was known as Reichenberg and was one of the most rapidly industrializing regions of Austria-Hungary. In 1888, the Liberec city council commissioned Viennese architect F. V. Neumann to build a new **City Hall** *(radnice)* on náměstí Benešovo. While the 65m tower is not open to the public, the foyer of the building welcomes visitors who admire the intricate stained-glass windows. Železná leads to **Sokolovské náměstí,** another square surrounded by 19th-century buildings, but far more run-down than those on nám. Benešovo. The timbered houses on Větrná visible from Sokolovské náměstí are the oldest buildings in Liberec. Known as the **Wallenstein Houses** *(Valdštejnské domky),* the plaster and timber buildings, which date to 1670. To the east of nám Benešovo, down Felberova, rises the attractive but not memorable **Castle** *(Zámek).* Originally built in 1582, the castle building has been renovated so many times that virtually nothing of the original remains. Pedestrian-laden **5. května** is a pleasant capitalist promenade which opens into **Nerudovo náměstí,** a square with a beer garden on each side. Guzzle some *Bud Budvar* at **Pivnice Parlament,** a neo-Gothic beer hall in the town hall *(Radnice)* on Benešovo nám. (open 1-10pm).

The helpful **tourist office,** nám. Benešovo 14 (tel. and fax (048) 298 54) speaks English and sells several maps, guidebooks, and pamphlets on Liberec and Northern Bohemia (open Mon.-Fri. 9am-5pm). They also book well priced rooms (250-300kč per person). **ČEDOK,** Soukenné nám. 8 (tel. (048) 210 47), offers a full range of travel agency services and finds rooms for 300-400kč per person (open Mon.-Fri. 9am-4pm, Sat. 9am-noon). At **Hotel Česká Beseda,** Na rybničku 143 (tel. (048) 231 61) near the bus station, rooms start at 390kč per person. **Radničkní Sklep,** in the town hall *(radnice)* on nám. Benešovo, serves authentic Czech cuisine (open 11am-10pm). For Chinese food Czech-style, try **Restaurant Hotel Eden,** Chrastavská 13 (entrees 80-90kč). **Cukrárna,** 5. května 15, between nám. Benešovo and nám.

CZECH REPUBLIC

Šaldovo, is a popular shop selling all sorts of pastries, sweets, and baked goods (open Mon.-Fri. 8am-6pm, Sat. 9am-6pm, Sun. 1-6pm).

■■■ KARLOVY VARY (KARLSBAD)

The springs of Karlovy Vary (Karlsbad) beckoned the icons of the 19th century: Goethe, Schiller, Tolstoy, Gogol, Beethoven, Metternich, and Marx sampled the waters here. People still throng to the town to attempt to cure their ailments and to enjoy the air of Victorian luxury and grandeur. The product of the town's "13th spring" is a potent liqueur with a pastoral aftertaste called *Becherovka*, distilled from herbs, sugar and Karlovy Vary water. A fitting accompaniment to all Karlovy Vary rituals are the circular *oplatký* wafers which look like beer coasters; they taste divine plain or chocolate-covered.

Mararyka and Nabřeží Osvobozeni fuse into **Zahradní** (literally "Garden Street"), bubbling *fin-de-siècle* apartments on one side, while the gray Hotel Thermal stagnates on the other. In the heart of the pedestrian spa area, the pavilion of **Freedom Spring** (*Pramen Svobody*) emerges. Bring your own cup or buy one from a souvenir shop (40-200kč). Next door, the impressive **Mill Colonnade** (*Mlýnská kolonáda*) gushes forth six different springs. Across the river, the Baroque **Church of Mary Magdalene,** unlike so many in the republic, is open to visitors. The most potent of the town's springs, the **Sprudel Fountain** (*Vřídlo;* formerly the Yuri Gagarin Colonnade) can spew over thirty liters of 72°C water per second several meters into the air. Follow Stará Louka (Old Meadow) until you reach Mariánská; at the dead end, a funicular rises to the **Diana Watchtower** (every 15min. 10am-6pm; 25kč one way). You can also hike to Diana on the forested hill's pathways. Nová Louka (New Meadow) features the **Karlsbad Museum,** which documents the local Becherovka liquor industry and manufacture of porcelain (open Wed.-Sat. 9am-noon and 1-5pm; 16kč, students 8kč).

Practical Information, Accommodations, and Food The **bus** takes 2½hr. from Prague's Praha-Florenc station; buy tickets 2 or 3 days in advance. Leave your bags at **dolní nádraží** train station, a block down Varšovká (which becomes Západní) from the bus station. **ČEDOK,** Moskerská 2 (tel. (017) 222 92), distributes small but free town **maps** and books **rooms** for 369kć per person (open Mon.-Fri. 8am-noon and 1-5pm, Sat. 8am-noon). The young staff at **Cestovní Kancelář Therma,** Varšavska 2 (tel. (017) 280 89) also offers maps, advice and **rooms** for DM (yep, only DM) 15-20 per person (open Mon.-Fri. 9-11am and noon-4pm). Friendly faces welcome you round-the-clock in **Hotel Adria,** Západní 1 (tel. (017) 237 65; singles 554kč, doubles 820kč, triples 1230kč) and **Hotel Turist,** Dr. David Bechera 18 (tel. (017) 268 37; 400kč per person) two great deals near the bus station. **Penzion Kosmos,** Zahradní 39 (tel. (017) 231 68), by the prim and proper Dvořák Gardens (*Dvořákovy Sady),* also scores big on location. (Reception closes midnight. Singles 400kč. Doubles 700kč.) Popular with the locals, **Česka Restaurace,** Jaltská 19, offers refreshing *Velkopopovicky Kozel* (13kč per glass) to go with your 60-100kč beef, *schnitzel,* and steak entrees (open 10am-11pm). Centrally located and affordable, **Café Radio Restaurant,** Stará Louka 38, supplements the schnitzel with Italian options for 60-80kč (open 11am-11pm). In the evening, switch from water to booze and hear the happy Czech DJ at **Tom Bar,** Jaltská 7 (open 4pm-6am).

■■■ CHEB (EGER)

As capital of the erstwhile autonomous region of Egerland, the culture and style of Bohemia, Bavaria, and Saxony congregated in Cheb. Historical coexistence ended with Nazi occupation of the area and the expulsion of the Sudeten Germans from Bohemia after WWII. Not a large city, the narrow winding streets of Cheb's **Staré Město** (Old Town), reflect its cosmopolitan history and its strategic importance.

CZECH REPUBLIC

The commercial thoroughfare **Svobody** leads from the main train station to the heart of historic Cheb, **náměstí Jiřího z Poděbrad.** The 11 small half-timbered **Špalíček-Stöckl** in the square functioned as shops and storage houses in the late Middle Ages. Behind Špalíček-Stöckl, the **city museum** tells the story of General Albrecht of Wallenstein, whose murder in the building 350 years ago was decisive in the course of the Thirty Years War (open Tues.-Sun. 9am-noon and 1-5pm, 5kč). The alley by the city museum and Gabler House leads to the **Church of St. Nicholas** (*Kostel sv. Mikuláše*), one of the finest Romanesque structures in Bohemia. The **Imperial Castle of Barbarossa** offers fine views of Cheb and the Ohře River valley; climb the 20m high **Black Tower** (open Tues.-Sun. 9am-noon and 1-4pm; 10kč, students 2kč). The stony cold interior of the 800-year-old castle **chapel** (*Hradní Kaple*) builds a stark contrast with the often overbearingly ornate churches of later epochs.

The **Square of the Franciscans** is named for the cloister that borders on the square. The tall, gray, Gothic building is striking, but sadly closed to public inspection. Across the square sits the Baroque Church of **St. Clara** (*Kostel sv. Kláry*), a masterpiece by Bohemian architect Kristof Dienzenhofer (also closed to visitors).

Rail lines from Karlovy Vary, Mariánské Lázně, and Františkovy Lázně converge in Cheb. The city also rests on the Paris-Frankfurt-Nuremberg-Prague route. On the way to the Old Town from the train station, **ČEDOK,** Májova 31 (tel. (0166) 339 51), off Svobody, does not book private rooms, but can direct you to pensions (open Mon.-Fri. 8:30am-5pm, Sat. 8am-11pm). **Hotel Hradní Dvůr,** Dlouhá 12 (tel. (0166) 224 44 or 220 06), shelters singles, doubles, triples and quads one block from nám. Jiřího z Poděbrad in the heart of the Old Town. (Reception open 24hrs. From 400kč per person. Showers 60kč.) At **Hotel Slávie,** Svobody 32 (tel. (0166) 332 16), on the main pedestrian street, each room is priced differently; expect to pay 515-715kč per person (open 24hrs.). A similar pricing system is in effect at **Hotel Hvězda,** right on nám. Jiřího z Podwbrad (tel. (0166) 225 49, fax 225 46; about 500kč per person, open 24hrs.). Also on the square, appealing **Restaurace Roland** serves roast pork and schnitzel for under 70kč (open 10am-10pm).

■■■ PLZEŇ

Eighty km southwest of Prague, Plzeň (Pilsen) is a mecca for beer-aficionados. The town that blessed the world with **Pilsner Urquell** will savor its **700th anniversary** throughout 1995. In February, there will be a ball and a *Fasching*-type carnival. In June, the best of Czech pop and rock bands will congregate in the city for a three-day **music festival.** The merriment will conclude with **"Beer Days"** from October 2-7. Drown the city's industrial aspect with several rounds of the town's finest (13kč per ½l) at the **U Kanónu,** Rooseveltova 18, an atmospheric beer-hall which fills with increasingly attractive young people. *Helena miluji vás* (cheers). (Open Mon.-Fri. 10am-11pm, Sat.-Sun. 10am-10pm.) And there's ne'er a quiet moment in **Pivnice U Žumbery,** Bezručova 14, were you can sip your Gambrinus draft (13kč) in an outdoor beer garden (open Mon.-Sat. 9am-10pm, Sun. 9am-7pm). While you were sober, you should have taken a tour of the **Brewery Museum,** housed in a 15th-century malthouse at Veleslavínova 6. The collection of 19th-century pub signs and memorabilia is most impressive. (Open Tues.-Sun. 10am-6pm; 30kč, students 15kč.) From the northeast part of nám. Republiky, the short street Pražská takes you to the former **Slaughter House** (*Masné Krámy*), an impressive late-Gothic building that is nowadays a division of the West Bohemian Gallery. Across the street is the **Water Tower** (*vodárenská věž*), built in 1532 as part of the city's medieval water works. Today the tower and the **Historic Underground Cellars** (*Plzeňské podzemí*) can be visited on a guided tour that starts inside Perlova 4, a building near the tower. The cellars were used primarily for the storage and the covert mass consumption of beer. (Open Tues.-Sun. 9am-4pm. 30kč.)

Practical Information, Accommodations, and Brewski Plzeň lies conveniently on the Prague-Munich **train** line, 2hr. from Mariánské Lázné. Tourist

CZECH REPUBLIC

information can be garnered either from **MIS,** náměstí Republiky 41 (tel. (019) 22 44 73), on the main square (open 9am-5pm), or from **ČEDOK,** Prešovská 10 (tel. (019) 366 48; open Mon.-Fri. 9am-noon and 1-5pm, Sat. 9am-noon). The latter also finds **private rooms** for about 300kč per person. Less than a block from the cathedral, though, **Penzion J. Bárová,** Solnjí 8 (tel. (019) 366 52) is *wunderschön.* (Reception open 9am-6pm. Singles 510kč. Doubles 850kč. Breakfast 85kč.) South of the Old Town in Bory, **Penzion Müllerová,** U svépomoci 23 (tel. (019) 27 52 06), is cheaper at 350kč (DM20) per person, breakfast included. If that's full, you needn't leave the Bory district; try **Penzion Slavia,** U borského parku 21 (tel. (019) 27 17 70; 370kč or DM22 per person). You needn't leave the Pilsner Urquell brewery complex for food: **Na spilce,** U Prazdroje, is one of the largest restaurants in Europe. (Traditional Bohemian specialties 50-100kč. Open Mon.-Fri. 10am-11pm, Sat. 11am-10pm, and Sun. 11am-9pm.) The usual carnivorous fare costs 40-55kč in **U Kanónu,** Rooseveltova 18 (open Mon.-Fri. 10am-11pm and Sat.-Sun. 10am-10pm).

■■■ ČESKÉ BUDĚJOVICE

No quantity of beer will help you correctly pronounce České Budějovice (CHESS-kay BOOD-yay-yov-ee-tzeh); luckily for the paunchy world-wide, the town was known as Budweis in the 19th century when it inspired the name of the popular but pale North American *Budweiser.* The most famous beer brewed today in the city is the sweet and malty **Budweiser Budvar.** You can weave through medieval alleys and challengingly straight 18th-century streets in the **Old Town,** a fascinating *guláš* of architecture surrounded by the Vltava and Malše Rivers. The center is **nám. Přemysla Otakara II,** lined with arcaded Baroque burghers' homes crawling with small businesses. Note the pained expressions on the faces which spew water from the Baroque **Samson Fountain** *(Samsonova Kašna).* You don't want to look that way tonight. The narrow medieval alley Hradební or the route along the **Mill Stream** *(Mlýnská stoka)* provides an interesting walk through one of the oldest parts of town. From either street, turn right onto U Černé věže, which leads to the **Black Tower.** You can climb the 72m-high tower (Tues.-Sun. 9am-5pm) for a mere 6kč. Next to the tower is the Baroque 17th-century **Church of St. Nicholas** *(Kostel sv. Mikuláše)* and farther along Kněžska the Renaissance former **Church of St. Anne.** The **Bishop's Residence** *(Sídlo biskupa),* down Karla IV, across the square and south on Biskupská, is in a plain and utilitarian former pianist college.

Practical Information, Accommodations, and Food The jolly yellow **train** station east of the Old Town welcomes thirsty travelers coming from Prague (3hr.), Plzeň (2hr.) Brno (5hr.) and Linz, Austria. **CTS Travel Service,** Lannova třída 6 (tel. (038) 276 39), on the main pedestrian street between the train station and the Old Town books **private rooms** from 130kc, but those in the center cost 500kč per capita (open Mon.-Fri. 9am-6pm, Sat. 9am-noon). **AT Pension,** Dukelská 15 (tel. (038) 731 25 29), has fabulous 2- and 3-bed rooms, some with private bath. From the train station, walk down Žižkova, then left on U třílvů, and left on Dukelská. (Reception open 24hrs. 400kč per person includes breakfast.) The rooms in **Hotel Grand,** Ndražní 27 (tel. 365 91, fax 525 68), across the street from the train station, have private showers. (Reception open 24hrs. Singles 580kč. Doubles 835kč. Breakfast included.) No meal in České Budwjovice goes unaccompanied by Budweiser Budvar or Samson. The řízek (schnitzel, 40kč) is freshly cooked and the draft Samson a modest 9kč per ½l at **Pivnice U Zlatého Soudku,** Široká 29 (open Mon.-Sat. for lunch and dinner). The famous **Masné Krámy** beer hall crams tables into former Renaissance meat shops. Daily specials (50kč) are a good deal, albeit posted in Czech. (Entrees 90-130kčs. Budvar 15kč per ½l. Open Sun.-Thurs. 10am-11pm, Fri.-Sat. 10am-midnight.) Self-service Bohemian dishes cost under 30kc at **U Kneisslů,** on the corner of Česká and Panská (open Mon.-Thurs. 9am-6pm and Fri. 9am-4pm).

CZECH REPUBLIC

MORAVIA

Moravia is the wine-making eastern half of the Czech Republic. The word "Český," grates on the ears in these parts; it describes both Bohemia as a historic territory and the Czechs as an ethnic community. Though some wanted the new Czech Republic to be called "Czechomoravia" *(Českomorávska)*, there is no threat of Moravian separatism. The sub-regions of Moravia are equally finicky. The university town of **Olomouc** proudly describes itself as the capital of the Hanák region; the Hanáks eagerly distinguish themselves from the Horňáks and the "Moravian Slovaks" to the east. Each group speaks a different dialect and has a unique style of dress.

■■■ BRNO

On the rail line between Prague (3¼hr.) and Bratislava (1½hr.), Brno is the political and cultural capital of Moravia, the wine-making eastern half of the Czech Republic. To find the principal sights, simply look up: the **Cathedral of Sts. Peter and Paul** rears above the city in a kaleidoscope of stained-glass. Atop the hill behind the cathedral, the **Spielberg Castle** fell to both Napoleon and later Hitler; over 80,000 prisoners were executed in the castle's dungeons. (Open Tues.-Sun. 9am-6pm. Last entry at 5:15pm. 20kč, students 10kč.) **Masarykova,** the main pedestrian street that begins in front of the train station leads to Kapucínské námestí, site of the **Capuchin Church,** where local personalities are remembered in glass-enclosed coffins. The rows of smiling Capuchin monk mummies were not embalmed, but rather dried naturally by an innovative ventilation system designed by the monks themselves. (Open Tues.-Sat. 9am-noon and 2-4:30pm, Sun. 11-11:45am and 2-4:30pm. 10kč.) **Nám. Zelnýtrh** hosts the daily **produce market** and the **Dietrichstein Palace,** which holds the **Moravian Museum** of regional history (open Tues.-Sun. 9am-6pm; 20kč, students 10kč). From Šilingrovo náměstí, a walk along **Pekařská** (literally Baker Street) leads to the heart of the "Old Brno" neighborhood, **Mendel Square** *(Mendlovo námwstí).* The High Gothic **Augustinian Monastery** was home to **Johann Gregor Mendel,** who fudged his way to fame in genetics. Next door is the **Starobrno Brewery** and **beer-hall,** built in 1872 to replace the monastery brewery.

    ČEDOK, Nádražní 10/12 (tel. (05) 42 21 15 61), in front on the main train station, books rooms for 369kč per person (open Mon.-Fri. 8am-6pm and Sat. 9am-5pm). Stay in the heart of historic Brno over a hip local pub at **Hotel Pegas,** Jakubská 4 (tel. and fax (05) 42 21 12 32), near St. James's Church (open 24hrs.; singles 880kč, doubles 1400kč) or develop an appreciation for 60s decor and communal toilets in the **Hotel Astoria,** Novobranská 3 (tel. (05) 225 41), where singles are 510kč, doubles with shower 680kč (also open 24hrs.). Sample traditional Moravian dishes in **Restaurace U Mioritů,** Orlíat Minoritská (open Mon.-Fri. 10am-10pm and Sat. 10am-11pm) or **Pivnice Pegas,** Jakubská 4 (open 9am-midnight).

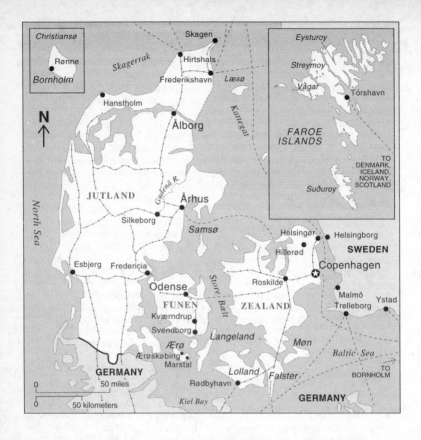

Denmark (Danmark)

US$1 = 6.62kr (kroner, or DKK)	10kr = US$1.51
CDN$1 = 5.03kr	10kr = CDN$1.99
UK£1 = 10.30kr	10kr = UK£0.97
IR£1 = 9.60kr	10kr = IR£1.04
AUS$1 = 4.31kr	10kr = AUS$2.32
NZ$1 = 3.66kr	10kr = NZ$2.73
SAR1 = 1.38kr	10kr = SAR7.26
Country Code: 45	International Dialing Prefix: 009

Within the borders of Denmark the landscape changes from green farmland to beech forests to chalk cliffs and sand dunes—the sea is always nearby. Danes joke that if you stand on a case of beer, you can see from one end of the country to the other. Denmark is neither that flat nor that small. The word "Dane" once struck fear into hearts all over Europe, but today the Vikings are but ghosts in the long history of a nation. The Danes of today are much more civilized and genial. On a short visit, Denmark seems such an overwhelmingly *good* country: the Danes (who rarely jay-walk) saved their Jews from the Nazis, invented Legos, spend tons of money on education, and make wonderful ice cream. The only threat Denmark poses is its cuteness. To immunize yourself against the onslaught of Hans Christian Andersen knickknacks, peruse *The Present Age*, by the wry Danish philosopher Søren Kierkegaard.

Well into the 16th century, the Danish crown ruled an empire that united Norway, Sweden, Iceland, and parts of Germany. Strategically positioned at the northern tip of continental Europe, Denmark was the bridge across which first Christianity, then the Protestant Reformation, and then the socialist movements of the late 19th century crossed into Scandinavia. During the 19th century, a series of failed military escapades eroded Denmark's borders and in 1864 the province of Schleswig-Holstein was snatched from the Danes by Bismarck's ascendant Prussia. During WWI, Denmark managed to remain neutral, but in 1940, with Hitler on the doorstep, the Danes capitulated and retained some autonomy rather than risk a full invasion. In 1943, Germany took direct control of Denmark and it was then that the Danish resistance smuggled 7000 Danish Jews into neutral Sweden. Since 1972, Queen Margarethe II has been on the throne and has often been spotted biking around the country. In 1973, Denmark joined the EEC, but in 1992 the nation refused to ratify the Maastricht Treaty, launching a Europe-wide debate on the nature of European union.

GETTING THERE AND GETTING AROUND

Eurailpasses are valid on all state-run **DSB** routes. The *buy-in-Scandinavia* **Scanrail pass,** which replaced the Nordturist Railpass, allows 5 days within 15 (1264kr, under 26: 948kr) or 21 consecutive days (1930kr, under 26: 1450 kr) of unlimited rail travel through Denmark, Norway, Sweden, and Finland, as well as many free or discounted ferry rides. This differs from the *buy-outside-of-Scandinavia* **Scanrail pass** which offers 5 out of 15 days (US$159, under 26: US$119), 10 out of 21 days (US$275, under 26: US$206), or 30 consecutive days (US$399, under 26: US$299) of unlimited travel. In Denmark, seniors over 65 and groups of 3 or more traveling together get discounts.

If you're under 26 and make your journey during the first 2 weeks of the Danish university's summer vacation (usually late June-early July), you can take advantage of the **UNG pass** (435kr), good for train travel throughout Denmark (Bornholm and Faroe Islands excluded). Check ahead of time with a tourist office, or call **Dan Rail** at 33 14 17 01. Seat reservations are compulsory on some trains, including the plush InterCity (IC) and some international trains (prices vary with destination). They sometimes require long waits, so you may want to stick to the seat-yourself IR and RE trains. Towns not on rail lines are often served by regional buses that stop at the nearest train station.

To reach Copenhagen by train from the rest of Denmark or from any other country you'll need to use at least one **ferry;** however, you may hardly notice, since these ships are specially equipped with rails, and the trains just roll on and off. Trains from Odense cross from Nyborg to Korsør, trains from Hamburg cross from Puttgarden to Rødby Færge, trains from Berlin from Warnemünde to Gedser, and trains from Stockholm and from Helsingborg to Helsingør. Eurail and Scanrail passes are valid on many Scandinavian international boat crossings for discounts (sometimes free rides); ask when you're booking a berth. The *Denmark Ferry Guide*, available at tourist offices, can help you sort out the dozens of smaller ferries that serve Denmark's outlying islands. Also, remember that while Denmark proper is small, it can take up to 11 hours to travel from the northernmost point of Jutland to Copenhagen.

Flat terrain, bike paths in the countryside, and bike lanes in the towns and cities make Denmark a cyclist's dream. **Bicycles** can be rented for 35-50kr per day from some tourist offices (not Copenhagen's), ubiquitous bicycle rental shops, and a few railway stations in North Zealand (Copenhagen, Helsingør, Hillerød, Klampenborg, and Lyngby). A 200kr deposit is ordinarily required. For quality maps (20-80kr, country map 49kr) and tour information, contact the **Dansk Cyklist Førbund** (Danish Cycle Federation), Rømersgade 7, 1362 Copenhagen K (tel. 33 32 31 21; open in summer Mon.-Wed. and Fri. 10am-5pm, Thurs. 10am-7pm, Sat. 10am-2pm; in winter

DENMARK

Mon.-Wed. and Fri. 10am-3pm, Thurs. 10am-5pm). It's often possible to tote bicycles on the train; check the pamphlet "Bikes and Trains in Denmark" for rules and prices.

DENMARK ESSENTIALS

Stacks of free tourist information in English, published by tourist boards, are an extra bonus when visiting Denmark. Good street maps and comprehensive city guides are waiting at almost every tourist office. Denmark celebrates national holidays on Jan. 1, Easter (April 13-17, 1995), Common Prayer's Day (May 12, 1995), Ascension (May 25, 1995), Whit Monday (June 5, 1995), Dec. 24-26 and 31. **Cirrus** cash cards work in the red "*Dankort automater*" cash machines in Denmark. Danish **phone** numbers are all 8 digits long, and you must dial the whole thing regardless of where you're calling from (no city codes). From pay phones, local calls require a minimum of 1kr, often 2kr. For directory information, dial 118 (free from pay phones). For international information, dial 113. For AT&T's **USA Direct** dial 80 01 00 10; MCI's **World Phone** 80 01 00 22; **SprintExpress** 80 01 08 77; **Canada Direct** 80 01 00 11; **BT Direct** 80 01 14 44; and **SA Direct** 80 01 00 27. Denmark's **emergency** number is **112**; no coins are required.

Almost every Dane speaks English, and a simple "Pardon?" will generally prompt a switch. The Danish alphabet adds *æ* (like the "e" in "egg,"), *ø* (like the "i" in "first,"), and *å* (still sometimes written as *aa;* like the "o" in "lord") at the end; thus Århus would follow Viborg in an alphabetical listing of cities. One particularly useful word to know is *ikke* ("not"), which will help you to figure out such signs as "No smoking" and "Don't walk on the grass." If you're feeling more confident, try *tak* ("thank you"), *undskyld* (UND-scoold, "I'm sorry" or "Excuse me"), and *vær venlig* (VER VEN-li, "please").

Accommodations and Camping The 100 **HI youth hostels** *(vandrerhjem)* throughout Denmark are well-equipped and well-run, have no age limit, and generally include rooms for families. All charge 60-90kr per bed; nonmembers pay 35kr extra for a guest stamp. You can generally feast on an unlimited breakfast for 38kr. Reception desks normally close between noon and 4pm and close for the day at 9 or 11pm. Reservations are required from September to mid-May, recommended in summer, and essential in hostels near beaches. They can be made by phone without a deposit, but you will be asked to show up by 5pm on the first night of the reservation or call that day to confirm. Cards (90kr, family 140kr) and an official hostel guide (free and in English) are available at **Danmarks Vandrerhjem,** Vesterbrogade 39, 1620 København V (tel. 31 31 36 12, fax 31 31 36 26). (Open Mon. - Thurs. 9am-4pm, Fri. 9am-3pm.) Other options are **hotels,** the cheapest of which run about 250kr for a single without shower, and rooms in **private homes,** which can often be arranged through tourist offices (100-150kr, 25kr fee).

Before you pitch a tent in Denmark, you must get the landowner's OK. You can also stay at one of the many official **campgrounds** (about 40kr per person per night). Campgrounds rank from one star (basic facilities) to three (the works). You'll need a camping pass; the Danish version is available at all campgrounds (24kr, family pass 48kr) and expires in January; one-time guest passes are 6kr (families 12kr), and international passes are accepted, too. The **Dansk Camping Union,** Gammel Kongevej 74d, Copenhagen (tel. 31 21 06 04), will sell you passes and a campground handbook (60kr; also available in bookstores; open Mon.-Fri. 10am-5pm; May 15-July 15 Mon. and Wed.-Fri. 10am-5pm, Tues. 10am-6:30pm). Sleeping in train stations, parks, and streets is illegal.

For a fee of US$25, **Friends Overseas** will connect you with families along your itinerary in Denmark, Sweden, Norway, and Finland who are eager to introduce you to their communities; send a self-addressed, stamped envelope to 68-04 Dartmouth Street, Forest Hills, NY 11375, USA, for more information.

Food and Drink Beyond the "Danish," called *wienerbrød*, there are oodles of other baked goodies: flaky *kringle*, syrupy *brunsvigerkage*, and more. Danish ice cream, especially nut flavors like pistachio, is generally quite good, but better still are the cones it comes in, fresh-baked and filled with whipped cream, plus more cream and jam on top. Remember: ice cream doesn't have any calories if you eat it in a foreign country. For more substantial fare, Danes favor *smørrebrød* (pronounced "smorebro" as one syllable)—small, open-faced sandwiches with such toppings as cheese, smoked salmon, pickled herring, or raw beef. Wash these down with the national brews, Carlsberg and Tuborg. The many varieties of *akvavit*, a distilled liquor, are so expensive that they are served one shot (0.02 liter) at a time. The legal drinking age in Denmark is 18.

Menus and restaurant checks include both tax and service; what you see is what you pay. All-you-can-eat buffets are very popular in Denmark. Youth hostels offer unlimited breakfasts of cereal, rolls, cheese, and meat for around 36kr; restaurants may have buffets of pizza, herring, or other seafood.

■■■ COPENHAGEN (KØBENHAVN)

A plethora of parks, waterways, and teeming pedestrian streets, the Danish capital is sensuous and exuberant—especially in summer. Copenhagen's countless street performers, outdoor cafés, ice cream vendors, and all-night discos epitomize Nordic *joie de vivre.* In winter, the outdoor seating is packed away and the harsh realities of life above the 55th parallel set in.

ORIENTATION AND PRACTICAL INFORMATION

Copenhagen lies on the east coast of the Danish island of **Zealand** (Sjælland). Malmö, in Sweden, is just across the sound (Øresund). Copenhagen's **Hovedbanegården** (Central Station) lies close to the city's heart. One block north of the station, **Vesterbrogade** passes **Tivoli** and **Rådhuspladsen** (the city's central square, where most bus lines originate) and then leads into **Strøget** (STROY-yet), the longest pedestrian thoroughfare in the world. The districts of Vesterbro, Nørrebro, Østerbro, and Christianshavn fan out from this central area.

Tourist Office: Danmarks Turistråd, Bernstorffsgade 1, 1577 København V (tel. 33 11 13 25), in the corner of Tivoli nearest the train station on the left. Everything you need to know about Copenhagen and the rest of Denmark (much of it hidden behind the counter), plus a free map and the indispensable *Copenhagen This Week,* which lists sights, prices, and hours. For a small fee, they will book private accommodations and hotel rooms. Open 9am-8pm; mid-April to mid-May 9am-6pm; mid-Sept. to mid-April Mon.-Fri. 9am-5pm, Sat. 9am-2pm. **Use It,** Rådhusstræde 13 (tel. 33 15 65 18), on the 2nd floor of the Huset complex 2 blocks east of Rådhuspladsen. A youth-oriented info office with heaps of free assistance, from bed-finding to passport retrieval. Mail held, ride and message boards, flash reports on rooming availability (list posted after-hours), and free baggage storage (1 day; 10kr each day thereafter; 50kr deposit). Publishes 3 helpful guides: *Copenhagen By Bike, Copenhagen By Foot,* and *Copenhagen By Bus.* Get their map (superior to the Turistråd's) and a copy of their guide *Playtime.* Open 9am-7pm; mid-Sept. to mid-June Mon.-Fri. 10am-4pm.

Budget Travel: Waastel, at Skoubogade 6 (tel. 33 14 46 33), sells student and youth discount tickets for trains and flights. Open Mon.-Fri. 10am-5pm. Similarly reduced ferry and plane fares also at **Kilroy Travel,** Skindergade 28 (tel. 33 11 00 44). Open Mon. 10am-7pm, Tues.-Fri. 10am-5pm, Sat. 10am-1pm. **Spies,** Nyropsgade 41 (tel. 33 32 15 00), arranges cheap charters to southern Europe. Open 6am-midnight.

Embassies: U.S., Dag Hammarskjölds Allé 24 (tel. 31 42 31 44; bus 1 or 6). Open Mon.-Fri. 8:30am-5pm. **Canada,** Kristen Bernikowsgade 1 (tel. 33 12 22 99; bus 27, 28, or 29). **U.K.,** Kastelsvej 36-40 (tel. 35 26 46 00; bus 1, 14, or 40). **Australia,** Kristianiagade 21 (tel. 35 26 22 44; bus 1, 6, or 9). Travelers from **New**

Zealand should contact the British embassy. **Ireland,** Østerbanegade 21 (tel. 31 42 32 33). **South Africa,** Gammel Vartovvej 8 (tel. 31 18 01 55). **Estonia** (tel. 33 93 34 62), **Latvia** (tel. 33 93 18 67), and **Lithuania** (tel. 33 93 48 17) all at H.C. Andersens Blvd. 38. **Poland,** Richelieusallé 10 (tel. 31 62 77 02).

Currency Exchange: At Central Station (open 6:45am-10pm; Oct. to mid-April 7am-9pm; 22-28kr commission on cash, 20kr per check with a 40kr minimum), the Tivoli office (open in summer noon-11pm), or the airport (open 6:30am-10pm; traveler's checks and cash only). Avoid the countless change counters on the Strøget, which charge up to 9.5% commission. Most banks are clustered on Vesterbrogade, between the train station and Rådhuspladsen, and in the pedestrian district. Regular bank hours Mon.-Wed. and Fri. 9:30am-4:00pm, Thurs. 9:30am-6pm. Commissions on traveler's checks are high (30-35kr min.), except at American Express.

American Express: Neither a borrower nor a lender be at their office on Amagertorv 18, on the Strøget (tel. 33 12 23 01). No commission on Traveler's Cheques (15kr commission on cash). Holds mail for AmEx card and Chequeholders only. Open Mon.-Fri. 9am-5pm, Sat. 9am-2pm, Sun. 10am-2pm; Sept.-May Mon.-Fri. 9am-5pm, Sat. 9am-noon.

Post Office: Tietgensgade 37-39, behind Central Station. Poste Restante. Open Mon.-Fri. 10am-6pm, Sat. 9am-1pm. **Postal Code:** 1500 København V. Branch office at Central Station. Open Mon.-Fri. 8am-10pm, Sat. 9am-4pm, Sun. and holidays 10am-5pm.

Telephones: Telecom Denmark, at Central Station. Call first and pay later (even by credit card). (Open Mon.-Fri. 8am-10pm, Sat.-Sun. 9am-9pm.) **Faxes** and **telegrams** can also be sent from here.

Flights: tel. 31 54 17 01. Bus 32 (32min.; 14kr or 1 stamp on yellow stripcard) from Rådhuspladsen and the SAS bus (20min.; 28kr) from Central Station both run to and from **Kastrup Airport.** SAS buses run to the airport 5:40am-9:45pm every 10-15min. and from the airport 6:30am-11:10pm every 10-15min.

Trains: All trains stop at **Hovedbanegården.** For information, call 33 14 17 01. To: Stockholm (437kr, under 26 319kr); Oslo (528kr, under 26 346kr); Berlin (323kr, under 26 208kr). The **InterRail Center** in the station, for all holders of BIJ, Scanrail, or Eurailpasses, is one of Copenhagen's most useful and friendly assets. Relax in a special lounge, wait for late-night connections, make phone calls, get information, and take showers (15kr per 10min.). Free stove use (no oven) but no utensils. Message board great for finding lost travelers and making new friends. Open mid-June to mid-Sept. 5:40am-2am.

Public Transportation: Bus information: tel. 36 45 45 45. **Train** information: tel. 33 14 17 01. Buses and S-trains (a cross between subways and suburban trains) operate on a shared zone system. Three zones cover central Copenhagen; 11 zones get you all the way to Helsingør. Buy tickets (2 zones 9.50kr, each additional zone 4.75kr) or, better, a yellow *rabatkort* (rebate card), which gets you 10 "clips" for 85kr (each clip good for 1 ride within 3 zones; more zones require more clips). Purchase the cards at kiosks or from bus drivers; they must be clipped in the machines provided each time you begin a journey. Ticket or clipped clip gives 1hr. of unlimited transfers on buses and trains. The 24hr. bus and train pass permits free use of public transportation in nearly half of Zealand; buy it at the Tivoli tourist office or any railway station (65kr). All railpasses allow free travel on S-trains but not on buses. The **Copenhagen Card** allows unlimited free travel throughout North Zealand, discounts on ferries to Sweden, and free admission to most sights, including Tivoli (1 day 140kr, 2 days 230kr, or 3 days 295kr; available at hotels, travel agencies, tourist offices, and large train stations). Free maps issued by tourist office and Use It both show bus routes and include S-train network maps. Buses and trains run approx. Mon.-Sat. 5am-12:30am, Sun. 6am-12:30am; **night buses** cost an extra 9.50kr and run through the night, but less frequently and on fewer routes.

Ferries: The variety and number of ferry services from Copenhagen boggle the mind; consult the tourist office for more complete details. There are 4 basic groups. To **Norway: DFDS/Scandinavian Seaways** (tel. 33 11 63 00) sails daily departing at 5pm from Copenhagen to Oslo (16hr.; 630kr with berth, 405kr with-

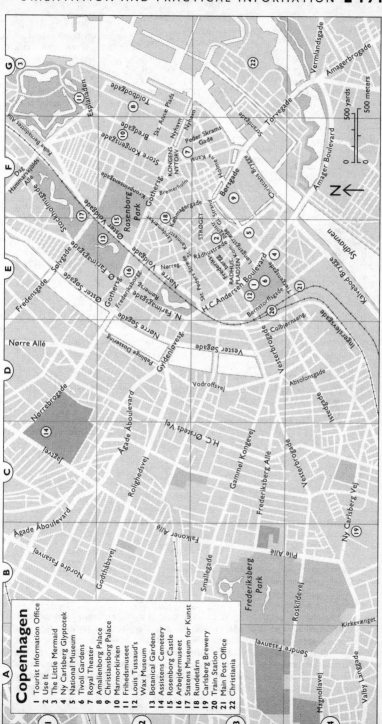

Copenhagen

1 Tourist Information Office
2 Use It
3 The Little Mermaid
4 Ny Carlsberg Glyptotek
5 National Museum
6 Tivoli Gardens
7 Royal Theater
8 Amalienborg Palace
9 Christiansborg Palace
10 Marmorkirken
11 Frihedsmuseet
12 Louis Tussaud's Wax Museum
13 Botanical Gardens
14 Assistens Cemetery
15 Rosenborg Castle
16 Arbejdermuseet
17 Statens Museum for Kunst
18 Rundetårn
19 Carlsberg Brewery
20 Train Station
21 Main Post Office
22 Christiania

out, 20% Eurail discount, bigger student discounts through Kilroy Travel; see Budget Travel, above). To **Sweden:** trains from Copenhagen to the rest of Scandinavia cross over the Helsingør-Helsingborg **Scandlines** ferry at no extra charge. **Hydrofoils** (tel. 33 12 80 88) cross hourly between Havnegade (at the end of Nyhavn in Copenhagen) and Malmö, Sweden (45min.; 85kr, 64kr with railpasses). To **Poland: Polferries** (tel. 33 11 46 45) sails Mon., Wed., and Thurs. at 10pm, Sun. at 11:30am from Nordre Toldbod off Esplanaden in Copenhagen to Świnoujście in the northwest corner of Poland, where there are rail connections to the rest of the country (9½-10½hr.; 280kr, 230kr with ISIC). To **Bornholm:** See the Bornholm section.

Taxis: tel. 31 35 35 35. Expensive. Central Station to Kastrup Airport, 130kr.

Bike Rental: Dan Wheel, Colbjørnsensgade 3 (tel. 31 21 22 27). From 35kr per day, 165kr per week; 200kr deposit. Open Mon.-Fri. 9am-5:30pm, Sat.-Sun. 9am-2pm. **DSB Cykelcenter,** Reventlowsgade 11 (tel. 33 14 07 17), in the train station building. From 40kr per day, 185kr per week; 200kr deposit. Repairs too. Open Mon.-Fri. 7am-6pm.

Hitchhiking: You have a better chance of ice skating across Egypt in July. Try **Use It's** ride boards (see Tourist Offices above) instead. **Interstop,** 54A Vesterbrogade (tel. 31 23 24 40), hooks hitchers up with drivers for a fee of 0.30kr per km.

Luggage Storage: Use It is good but has limited hours (see Budget Travel above). In **Central Station,** luggage lockers accessible Mon.-Sat. 5:30am-1am and Sun. 6am-1am (20kr per 24hrs.), and the **DSB Garderobe** is open 6:30am-12:15am (suitcases 10kr, backpacks 15kr per 24hrs.).

Bookstores: The Book Trader, Skindergade 23 (tel. 33 12 06 69), sells secondhand English books (20-30kr) and offers a 50% discount on exchanges. Open Mon.-Fri. 11am-6pm, Sat. 10am-2pm. Pick up the latest English tabloids at **The British Bookshop,** 8 Badstrustræde (tel. 33 93 11 15). Open Mon.-Thurs. 10am-5:30pm, Fri. 10am-6pm, Sat. 10am-2pm.

Laundromats: Just about everywhere; look for the sign *"møntvask."* At Borgergade 2, Nansensgade 39, and Istedgade 45. Most open 8am-10pm (25-30kr). Facilities at the 2 main HI hostels (25kr).

Women's Centers: Kvindehuset, Gothersgade 37 (tel. 33 14 28 04), runs a bookstore-café. Open Mon.-Fri. noon-7:30pm. **Kvindecentret Dannerhuset,** Nansensgade 1 (tel. 33 14 16 76). Overnight shelter for women who have been attacked.

Gay and Lesbian Services: National Organization for Gay Women and Men, Knabrostræde 3 (tel. 33 13 19 48), provides information and advice. Distributes *Copenhagen Gay and Lesbian Guide,* a listing of gay/lesbian nightspots and services in Copenhagen (free). Also operates a small bookstore and library (open Mon.-Tues. and Thurs.-Fri. 5pm-7pm, Wed. 5-8pm).

Crisis hotline: tel. 33 66 33 33. **Den Sociale Døgnvagt** offers counseling for travelers experiencing difficult times.

Pharmacy: Steno Apotek, Vesterbrogade 6c (tel. 33 14 82 66). Open 24hrs. From 8pm-8am Mon.-Fri., 2pm-8am Sat., and all day Sun., ring for entrance; 10.25kr fee on purchases except for prescriptions written that day.

Medical Assistance: Doctors on Call (tel. 33 93 63 00) provides appointments with medical practitioners. (Mon.-Fri. 9am-4pm; at other times, call 31 12 00 41.) Doctor's visits cost 120-350kr.

Emergencies: Police, Ambulance, and **Fire:** tel. 112. No coins needed from public phones. **Police station** is at Nyropsgade 20 (tel. 33 91 14 48).

ACCOMMODATIONS

Like all of Scandinavia, Copenhagen is rich in hostels and campgrounds but poor in budget hotels. In summer the 3 HI hostels fill early, despite their remote locations. (Allow for at least 19kr to cover bus fare there and back.) Reservations are especially advisable during Karneval (mid-May), the Roskilde Festival (late June), and the Copenhagen Jazz Festival (early July). Failing that, consult **Use It** or **Værelseanvisning,** a hotel reservation service located in the Copenhagen Tourist Information office near Tivoli. (Open 9am-midnight; mid-Sept. to mid-April Mon.-Fri. 9am-5pm,

Sat. 9am-2pm. 13kr fee per person.) Both give a listing of hostels and budget hotels. Slumbering in a park or the station is not a good idea, nor is it legal.

Hostels

YMCA Inter Point, KFUK, Store Kannikestræde 19 (tel. 33 11 30 31). Super-central location. 60 beds in a ballroom divided into 5-bed cubicles. You'll need an Inter Point pass, which costs 25kr and is good for one calendar year. Reception open 8am-noon, 2:30p-6pm, and 7pm-1:30am. Lockout 10am-2pm. Curfew 12:30am. 50kr. Breakfast 20kr. Sheets 20kr. Bike rental 50kr. Open July to mid-Aug. Also at **Vesterbros KFUM,** Valdemarsgade 15 (tel. 31 31 15 74). Approx. 40 beds. Open July 15-Aug. 15.

Københavns Vandrerhjem (HI), Herbergvejen 8 (tel. 31 28 97 15, fax 35 89 02 10), in Bellahøj. In a park with a small lake, 15min. bus or bike ride from Rådhuspladsen. Take bus 2 ("Bronshøj" or "Bellahøj") to Fuglsang Allé, or night bus 902. The Godthåbsvej S-train stop is about a 15min. walk south down Godthåbsvej, but you'll have to transfer at Ryparken to get downtown. 290 beds (in 4- to 6-bed dorms) fill quickly. Reception and lobby open 24hrs. Lockout 10am-1pm. No curfew. 65kr, nonmembers 87kr. Breakfast 35kr. Backpack-size lockers, optional lock rental 5kr, deposit 20kr. No kitchen. Laundry 20kr per load. Open mid-Feb.-Dec. Wheelchair-accessible.

Sleep-In, Per Henrik Lings Allé 6 (tel. 31 26 50 59, fax 35 43 50 58). From central station, S-train to Østerport and walk up Hammarskjölds to Rådhuspladsen and take bus 1 to Parken, or 6 or night bus 906 to Sankt Jakobs Plads. 385 beds in a converted ice rink (it's not cold) partitioned into 2- to 4-bed cubicles. Clean, fun and not too far out of town (about 15min.). The best last-minute place; they'll virtually always find you a spot to crash. Lockout noon-4pm. Dorms 85kr. Singles 120kr. Doubles 240kr. Breakfast included. Thursday night BBQs (25kr) and a great juice bar. Free lockers, deposit 20kr. Open July-Aug. At the highest point of the high season (July 25-Aug.15), another 320 beds open up down the street.

Copenhagen Youth Hostel (HI), Vejlandsallé 200 (tel. 32 52 29 08, fax 32 52 27 08). Take bus 46 (Mon.-Fri. 6am-5pm) from Central Station or 37 "Valby Station" from Holmens Bro (across the street from the front of Christiansborg Castle) to Sjællandsbroen, or take the S-train to Valby station and bus 37 from there. Good place to meet screaming Scandinavian children and their overly permissive parents. 528 beds—the largest hostel in Europe. Slow reception and long lines mean 20-40min. wait to check in. Hotel-like, lockable 2- and 5-bed rooms. Reception open 1pm-10am, bathrooms closed 9am-1pm. No curfew. 65kr, nonmembers 87kr. Breakfast 35kr. Dinner 55kr. Sheets 25kr. Laundry 25kr per load. Kitchen. Free use of safe. Wheelchair access. Open Jan. 2-Dec. 20.

City Public Hostel, Absalonsgade 8 (tel. 31 31 20 70, fax 31 23 51 75), in the Vesterbro Ungdomsgård. From the station, walk away from the Rådhuspladsen on Vesterbrogade (10 min.). Central location makes it worth the price. Not the best part of town (near the red light district), but within walking distance of Copenhagen's nightlife. 206 beds. Room size varies; the largest has 68 beds. Reception open 24hrs. Lockout 10am-noon. 95kr, with all-you-can-eat breakfast 110kr. Kitchen, BBQ facilities. Small unlocked lockers free, locks sold for 30kr. Sleeping bags allowed. Open early May-Aug.

Private Homes and Hotels

Værelseanvisning will find you a room in a hotel or private home (often a haul from the center of town) for a booking fee of 13kr per bed. Private home prices start at 150kr per person. Use It can often beat these prices and does not charge a fee.

Mike's Guest House, Kirkevænget 13 (tel. 36 45 65 40), near Frederiksberg Castle and the Zoological Gardens. Take bus 6 from Rådhuspladsen. Lush gardens and some private balconies are paradise for the weary traveler. Reception open 24hrs. Singles 200kr. Doubles 260kr. Triples 350kr. Guest kitchen (30kr), laundry facilities (25kr), and free showers. Several cheap supermarkets in the vicinity.

Søfolkenes Mindehotel, Peder Skramsgade 19 (tel. 33 13 48 82), near Nyhavn. A seafarer's hotel with clean, simply furnished rooms and an earnest, affable staff.

DENMARK

Expensive for the budget traveler but in a central location. Reception open 24hrs.
Singles 300kr, with shower 395kr. Doubles 430kr, with shower 520kr. Triples
600kr. Breakfast included.

Hotel Jørgensen, Rømersgade 11 (tel. 33 13 81 86), in a quiet area about 20min.
from Central Station. Cramped but clean. Reception open 8am-midnight. Coed
basement dorm 89kr. Singles 360kr. Doubles 460-575kr. Lockers free (20kr
deposit). Huge breakfast included. Bike rental 50kr, with 300kr deposit.

Camping

Bellahøj Camping, Hvidkildevej (tel. 31 10 11 50), 5km from the center. Take bus
2 ("Bellahøj") or night bus 902 from Rådhuspladsen. Reception open 24hrs. 40kr.
Kitchen facilities and free showers. Danish breakfast 25kr. Café and market open
7am-midnight. Bike rental 35kr. Open June-Aug.

Absalon Camping, Korsdalsvej 132 (tel. 31 41 06 00), 9km from the city. Take S-
train line B or L to Brøndbyøster, then walk 10min. north through the housing
projects (ask for directions at the station). Reception open 7am-10pm. 48kr. Also
has cabins (195kr plus 42kr per person), store, and laundry.

Nærum Camping, Ravnebakken (tel. 42 80 19 57), 20min. north of Copenhagen
by bus or train. Kitchen, TV room, laundry, bike rental, and mini-golf. Good location to explore the northern parts of Zealand. 44kr.

FOOD

In Copenhagen, food is a party. Stroll down the **Strøget** with peach juice dripping
down your chin, munch pickled herring by the waterfront, and sample the goodies
staring out of every bakery window. Around **Kongens Nytorv,** elegant cafés serve
satisfying sandwiches at lunchtime for around 35kr. North of Nytorv, the university
district shelters many cheaper places to eat. Eating out is expensive; avoid the touristy sit-down restaurants, especially in the pedestrian district and Tivoli. Picnic in a
park or by the harbor on take-out *smørrebrød* (from 20kr each, but you'll need
more than one), or shop for your own in the discount supermarket, **Fakta,** Lan-
demærket 3, near the round tower (open Mon.-Fri. 8am-7pm, Sat. 8am-2pm). Supermarkets—except the one in Central Station (open 8am-midnight)—are closed
Sundays. An open **market** occurs daily except Sunday in Israels Plads near Nørreport Station for much of the year (Mon.-Fri. 7am-6pm, Sat. 7am-2pm), and scads of
fruit stalls line Strøget. For cheap hot meals, your best bet will be pizza or pasta at
one of the many Italian joints that line the city's open spaces, some with outdoor
seating.

Centrum Smørrebrød, Vesterbrogade 6c, near Scala and Tivoli. Scrumptious
take-out sandwiches for 20-30kr. Open 24hrs. The affiliated **City Smørrebrød** at
Gothersgade 10 is open Mon.-Fri. 8am-7pm.

Nyhavns Færgekro, Nyhavn 5 (tel. 33 15 15 88). Sit indoors or along the canal.
Lunch on all-you-can-eat herring (65kr), over a dozen varieties. You can't get
much more Danish than that. Dinners around 130kr. Open 11:30am-4pm and 5-
11:30pm.

Riz Raz, Kompagnistræde 20. Savory all-you-can-eat vegetarian Mediterranean buffet often includes pizza and falafel. 39kr before 5pm, 59kr thereafter. Dinner
kebabs 69-145kr (includes buffet). Open 11:30am-midnight.

ReeF N' BeeF, Landemarket 27, near Kultorvet. A little piece of Australia in the
middle of Denmark. Serves up the best alligator (188kr) and kangaroo (155kr) in
Copenhagen. Dinner entrees 85kr-166kr. Open 5-10pm.

Det Lille Apotek, St. Kannike Stræde 15 (tel. 33 12 56 06). Traditional Danish
atmosphere and fare. Dinner entrees run 85-120kr, but a lunchtime *platte* costs
only 59kr.

Gråbrødre Restaurent, Gråbrødretorv 1 (tel. 33 32 83 83), allows you to select
three courses from their à la carte menu for 98kr.

Den Grønne Kælder, 10 Klarehoderne. Fights the good vegetarian fight. Specializes in hummus (small plate 18kr, large 35kr) and veggie burgers (28kr, served
with 2 salads). Daily vegetarian dishes 28-45kr. Open Mon.-Sat. 11am-9pm.

DENMARK

SIGHTS

A fairly compact city, Copenhagen is best seen on foot or by bike. Pick up *Copenhagen This Week* and begin with the celebrated **Tivoli** amusement park. Founded in 1843, it doesn't have the most thrilling rides in the world, but parts are awfully pretty. The wild swans—each painted differently—give a terrific, spinning panorama of the city's skyline. In the evening, the park becomes a spectacle of colorful, illuminated ponds, and outdoor concerts ending with fireworks at midnight as the park closes (Wed. and Fri.-Sun.). (Open late April to mid-Sept. 10am-midnight. Children's rides begin at 11:30am, more serious rides from 1:30pm. 35kr, 10kr discount before 1pm. Single-ride tickets 8kr, 10 for 70kr; most rides cost 2 tickets. Ride-pass 125kr.)

Next to Tivoli, the **Ny Carlsberg Glyptotek,** funded by the Carlsberg beer empire, displays ancient, classical, and impressionist art, including a fine collection of Roman busts. The museum centers on a glass-domed tropical plant conservatory. (Open Tues.-Sun. 10am-4pm; Sept.-April Tues.-Sat. noon-3pm, Sun. 10am-4pm. 15kr, free with ISIC, Sun. and Wed. free.) Nearby, the **National Museum,** at Ny Vestergade 10, contains Danish and European archaeological discoveries, including ones from the Viking Age. (Open Tues.-Sun. 10am-5pm. 30kr. Closed on national holidays.) Across the canals on Slotsholmen Island is **Christiansborg Palace,** the meeting place of the *Folketing* (Parliament). (Hourly tours Sun.-Fri. 10am-4pm; Oct.-May Sun. 10am-4pm. Free.)

Continuing north, you'll reach **Kongens Nytorv,** the departure point for harbor and canal boat tours (July-Aug. every ½hr. 10am-7:30pm; May-June and Sept. hourly 10am-6pm; 50min.; 15-36kr). Boats also leave from **Gammel Strand** (tel. 33 13 31 05 for info) across the canal from Thorvaldsens Museum. Kongens Nytorv marks the ritzy endpoint of **Strøget,** the pedestrian street; the **Royal Theater** here is home to the world-famous Royal Danish Ballet. Half-price tickets for this treater and most others in the city are available the day of the performance at **Nørreport Kiosk** on the corner of Fiolstræde and Nørrevold opposite the Nørreport Rail Station. (Open Mon.-Fri. noon-7pm, Sat. noon-3pm; 40-100kr. Call 36 66 22 22 for info.) East of the square is **Nyhavn,** a picturesque canal crammed with yachts and lined with restaurants, where Hans Christian Andersen wrote his first fairy tale. Farther north is **Amalienborg Palace,** a group of four 18th century Rococo mansions that serves as the official royal residence. Some of the splendid official and private rooms of the palace are open to the public. (Open 11am-4pm, Nov.-March closed Mon. 35kr.) The changing of the palace guard takes place at noon on the brick plaza. The western approach to the plaza frames a view of the impressive dome of the 19th-century Romanesque Baroque **Marmorkirken** (marble church). The inside of the dome is almost as elaborate. (Open Mon.-Sat. 11am-2pm. Sunday mass 10:30am. Free.) A few blocks north of Amalienborg is the intriguing **Frihedsmuseet** (Resistance Museum), Churchillparken, which chronicles the Nazi occupation of 1940-1945. While proudly documenting Denmark's heroic rescue of almost all its Jews, the museum also examines the initial period of resigned acceptance of German "protection," when the Danish government arrested anti-Nazi saboteurs. (Open Tues.-Sat. 10am-4pm, Sun. 10am-5pm; mid-Sept. to April Tues.-Sat. 11am-3pm, Sun. 11am-4pm. Free.) On the other side of **Kastellet,** a 17th-century fortress-turned-park (open 6am-dusk), is Edvard Eriksen's statue of **Den Lille Havfrue** (The Little Mermaid), the model for all those souvenir paperweights you've been seeing. Watch the sun set over posing tour groups.

The area around Østervoldgade and Sølvgade houses Copenhagen's finest parks and gardens. The **Botanisk Have** (Botanical Gardens), at the corner of Østervolgade and Gothersgade, flower daily from 8:30am-6pm (Sept.-late March 8:30am-4pm; free). Across the street is **Rosenborg Palace and Gardens** (Rosenborg Slot); the palace (entrance on Østervoldgade) houses the rest of the collection of royal treasures, including the crown jewels and 3 life-size silver lions. (Open 10am-4pm; Sept.-late Oct. and May 11am-3pm; late Oct.-April Tues., Fri., and Sun. 11am-2pm. 35kr.) Nearby, at Rømersgade 22, the gripping **Arbejdermuseet** (Workers' Museum)

DENMARK

graphically portrays the lives of those who could not afford royal treasures. (Open Tues.-Fri. 10am-3pm, Sat.-Sun. 11am-4pm. 25kr.) Three blocks north, at Østervoldgade and Sølvgade—in yet another garden—is the **Statens Museum for Kunst** (State Museum of Fine Arts), worth a visit for its Matisses and Dutch Masters (open Tues.-Sun. 10am-4:30pm; 20kr, students and seniors 10kr).

Back in the pedestrian district, climb the unique spiral ramp of the **Rundetårn** (round tower) for a good view of the city's spires. (Open 10am-8pm; Sept.-March Mon.-Sat. 10am-5pm. 12kr.) Southeast of downtown, in the Christianshavn district, lies **Christiania** (entrances on Prinsessegade). This utopian "free city" was founded in 1971 by youthful squatters in abandoned military barracks. With lots of hash and pot and mess, it's not everyone's cup of tea. Always ask before taking pictures and exercise caution at night. Beer enthusiasts can tour the city's breweries: **Carlsberg,** Ny Carlsbergvej 140 (take bus 6 west from Rådhuspladsen; tours Mon.-Fri. at 11am and 2pm; meet at the Elephant Gate), and **Tuborg,** Strandvejen 54 (take bus 6 north from Rådhuspladsen; ½hr. tours Mon.-Fri. at 10am, 12:30pm, and 2:30pm). Both tours are free and offer free beer (about 2 bottles per person) and soda at the end of the tour. Interact with science for hours at the **Eksperimentarium,** Tuborg Havnevej 7 (tel. 39 27 33 33; bus 6 north from Rådhuspladsen), to the north of the city. Visit the automatic diet exhibit and lose 20kg in just one second or dance in the reverse disco where the music follows your movement. (Open Mon., Wed., and Fri. 9am-6pm, Tues. and Thurs. 9am-9pm, Sat.-Sun. 11am-6pm. 55kr, students and seniors 49kr, under 15 39kr.)

ENTERTAINMENT

Copenhagen's weekends often begin on Wednesday, and nights rock until 5am. The central pedestrian district reverberates with populous bars and discos, while Kongens Nytorv contains fancier joints, and Nyhavn exudes the salty charisma of moored ships. For current events listings, consult *Copenhagen This Week* or contact Use It, which also distributes a lesbian and gay guide to the city. The Scala complex across the street from Tivoli features a multitude of bars and restaurants. Avid drinkers might consider the "death route," including Vestergade and Skt. Petersstræde just off the Strøget. University students liven up the cheaper bars in the Nørrebro area.

Huset, Rådhusstræde 13. A relaxed, unpretentious cultural center. Use It is on the 2nd floor. The cinema often features film series for around 45kr. On the ground floor, **Kafé pår Zalü** overflows into a student-filled courtyard. Coffee 10kr, beer 17kr. Open noon-2am. **Bar Blue,** a techno disco/club jolts to a start later in the evening. Open mid-Aug. to mid-June Mon.-Fri. 10pm-2am, Sat.-Sun. 6pm-2am. Cover 80kr. Upstairs, **Græshoppen** screens American and Danish films (with English subtitles) for 30kr. Open 5:30pm-midnight.

Mojo, Løngangstræde 21. A jamming spot for blues. Open Sun.-Thurs. 8pm-4am, Fri.-Sat. 8pm-5am. Cover Fri.-Sat. 40kr.

Pan Café, Knabrostræde 3. A popular lesbian and gay center in an area with several gay bars and clubs. Open Sun.-Tues. 2pm-3am, Wed.-Thurs. 2pm-4am, Fri.-Sat. 2pm-6am. Cover on weekends 55kr. Dancing nightly after 10pm. Café and disco only for women on Thurs.

Montmartre, Nørregade 41. Regular live music and exhausting all-night dancing. Café open Mon.-Sat. 3pm-midnight. Club night (Thurs.-Sat. midnight-5am) followed by breakfast for the sore and sleepy (served Sat.-Sun. 5-8am). Cover Fri.-Sat. 20kr. Live music on irregular weekdays (9am-1am; cover 50-250kr; call the ticket office (3-7pm) at 33 12 78 36 for more info).

Krasnapolski, Vestergade 10 (tel. 33 32 88 08). Student hangout in the university area. Always crowded with the enlightened elite of Copenhagen.

Park Café, Østerbrogade 79 (tel. 31 42 62 48). Large, classic bar-nightclub combo. Popular with everyone, it seems.

Cafe Victor, Ny Østergade/Hovedvagtsgade 8 (tel. 33 13 36 13). The place to be seen at your best. The mutual-admiration society of Copenhagen's young and beautiful.

Café Sommersko, Kronprinsensgade 6 (tel. 33 14 81 89), is one of the most popular student hangouts in the city. Open Mon.-Wed. 9am-1am, Thurs.-Sat. 9am-2am, Sun. 10am-1am; beer 18kr. **Bananrepublikken,** Nørrebrogade 13 (tel. 31 39 79 21), is another good place to explore student nightlife.

X-Ray, Baron Boltens Gård, off Kongens Nytorv. Alive and happening nightclub. Very hip, New York style. Open Thurs.-Sat. 11pm-5am. Cover 40kr.

The **Copenhagen Jazz Festival** draws top musicians from around the globe (early July); make accommodations reservations early. **Karneval,** a Brazilian dance extravaganza, is slated for Whitsund. The **Mermaid Theater,** 27, Skt. Pederstræde (tel. 33 11 43 03), presents everything from Twain to Kierkegaard (in English), after which the audience is invited to discuss their reactions to the play with the performers over coffee. (Performances Mon.-Sat. 8:30pm; tickets 65-125kr.)

■ NEAR COPENHAGEN

Royal castles, scenic beaches, and a stunning museum are all within easy reach of Copenhagen by train. Two rail lines go north from Copenhagen: a more or less coastal line up to Helsingør (paralleled by the very coastal and more scenic bus 388), and an S-train line to Hillerød. **Klampenborg** and **Bellevae,** close in on the coastal line (alternatively, at the end of S-train line C), both offer topless beaches, while **Bakken,** the world's oldest amusement park, though far less ornate than Tivoli, delivers more thrills (magnified by untranslated warning signs and unknown safety codes) and offers a wide selection of bars and restaurants to boot. (Open March-Aug. 2pm-midnight. Just north from the train station, turn left, cross the bridge over the road, and head through the park. Free entry.)

Rungsted and Humlebæk Rungsted, a picturesque harbor town up the coast from Klampenborg, is home to the **Karen Blixen Museum,** Rungsted Strandvej 111, which occupies the home of the late author, who wrote as Isak Dinesen; Meryl Streep portrayed her in the film *Out of Africa.* Many of Blixen's Gothic tales paint a sweeping picture of 19th-century Denmark. (Open 10am-5pm; Oct.-April Wed.-Sun. 1-4pm. 30kr.) **Humlebæk,** yet a stretch further up the coast, would be completely undistinguished were it not home to the spectacular **Louisiana Museum of Modern Art.** Named after the 3 wives of the estate's original owner, all called Louisa, the museum contains works by Picasso, Warhol, Giacometti, Lichtenstein, and other 20th-century deities. Overlooking the sea and the Swedish coast, the remarkable building and its sculpture-studded grounds are themselves well worth the trip. Follow the signs 1.5km north from the Humlebæk station or snag bus 388. Evening classical concerts on summer Wednesdays cost 85kr, including museum admission. Call 42 19 07 19 for information. (Open Mon.-Tues. and Thurs.-Fri. 10am-5pm, Wed. 10am-10pm, Sat.-Sun. 10am-6pm; mid-Sept. to late Jan. Mon.-Tues. and Thurs. 10am-5pm, Wed. and Fri. 10am-10pm, Sat.-Sun. 10am-6pm. 45kr, students with ISIC and seniors 35kr.)

Helsingør, Hornbæk, and Hillerød Farther north, castles give evidence of the Danish monarchy's fondness for lavish architecture. Take arms against your sea of troubles at **Helsingør** (Elsinore in Shakespeare's *Hamlet),* the major ferry departure point for Sweden; its many liquor stores cater to Swedes seeking to avoid their country's outrageous fortune of an alcohol tax (from Central Station 3 per hr., 50min., 11 zones). **Kronborg Slot** was built in the 15th century to collect tolls from passing merchant ships. Viking chief and Danish national hero Holger Danske sleeps in the castle's dungeon; legend has it that he arises to face menaces to Denmark. The royal apartments boast some impressive furnishings, including a pair of fascinating Renaissance globes. The castle also houses the Danish maritime museum. (Open

DENMARK

10:30am-5pm; April and Oct. Tues.-Sun. 11am-4pm; Nov.-March Tues.-Sun. 11am-3pm. To castle 20kr, to casemates and dungeons 10kr, to maritime museum 34kr.) The **tourist office** (tel. 49 21 13 33) in Helsingør is to the left of the train station as you exit. They book rooms (25kr fee) and provide ferry info. (Open Mon.-Fri. 9:30am-7pm, Sat. 10am-6pm; mid-Aug. to mid-June Mon.-Fri. 9:30am-5pm, Sat. 10am-1pm.) An **HI youth hostel** (tel. 49 21 16 40, fax 49 21 13 99) stands by the beach at Ndr. Strandvej 24. Take bus 340 from the station. (Reception open 8am-noon and 4-9pm. 64kr, non-members 86kr. Sheets 40kr. Free showers and kitchen. Open Feb.-Nov.) **Borgerkron,** Strandvejen 75, is a typical Danish inn where you can eat and drink well for a reasonable price.

A very short distance from Helsingør, **Hornbæk** is a charmingly relaxed beach town about an hour north of Copenhagen. The town comes alive during the summer when city-weary urbanites flock to the beach for a day or weekend. Danish people at their most beautiful are on display when the sun shines. Wild antics surround the **harbor party** on the fourth weekend in July.

Moated **Frederiksborg Slot** in **Hillerød** is the most impressive of the castles north of Copenhagen, featuring exquisite gardens, brick ramparts, and the **National Historical Museum,** exhibiting portraits of several centuries' worth of prominent Danes. Concerts are given on the famous **Esaias Compenius organ** in the chapel Sundays at 5pm. Call 42 26 04 39 for information. (Castle open 10am-5pm; Oct. 10am-4pm; Nov.-March 11am-3pm; April 10am-4pm. 30kr, students with ID 10kr.) Along the train line halfway between Hillerød and Helsingør is **Fredensborg Castle,** built in 1722 and still in use as the spring and autumn royal residence. When Queen Margarethe is in, there is a colorful changing of the guard. The park is free and open year-round. (Castle open July 1-5pm. 10kr.) You can peek into the palace gardens from the **Fredensborg Youth Hostel (HI),** Østrupvej 3 (tel. 42 28 03 15), 1km from the train station. (Reception open 8am-11pm. 84kr, non-members 106kr.) Hillerød is at the end of S-train lines A and E from Copenhagen (40min. via Lyngby, 32.25kr or 3 clips on the yellow *rabatkort)* and also accessible direct from Helsingør by train (30min.).

Roskilde   Roskilde, 25-30 minutes west of Copenhagen (33.25kr or 3 clips on the yellow *rabatkort),* is home to much Danish history; King Harald Bluetooth built the first Christian church in Denmark here in 980, and 38 Danish monarchs repose in the **Roskilde Domkirke** cathedral. The **Viking Ship Museum,** down on the shore of Roskilde Fjord, houses the dinosaur-like remains of 5 vessels. The ships were sunk about 1060 AD and are somewhat the worse for wear, but the reconstructions moored in the harbor outside aid the imagination. (Open 9am-5pm; Nov.-March 10am-4pm. 28kr includes 15min. film.) A vegetable, fruit, flea, and flower **market** transforms Roskilde on Wed. and Sat. (8am-2pm). Over the last weekend in June, Roskilde hosts one of northern Europe's largest **music festivals** (tel. 42 36 14 00), with rock, jazz, and folk bands from all over the planet. U2 and Talking Heads played here before they were big. The **tourist office** (tel. 42 35 27 00) near the cathedral sells tickets to the 4-day festival, makes bookings in local hotels (25kr fee), and can suggest walking tours around the enchanting old quarter (open Mon.-Fri. 9am-8pm, Sat. 9am-5pm, Sun. 10am-1pm). Roskilde's **HI youth hostel,** amid rolling fields on Hørhusene 61 (tel. 42 35 21 84, fax 42 35 66 90; bus 601 or 604, then a 1.5km walk), is geared toward young families (75kr, non-members 97kr; breakfast 38kr). You can **camp** by the beach at **Vigen Strandpark,** Baunehøjvej 7-9 (tel. 46 75 79 96), 4km north of town on bus 602. If you don't have the required 24kr camping card, they'll accept an HI hostel card. (40kr per person. Open early April to mid-Sept. Reception open 7am-10pm.)

Møns   To see what H.C. Andersen called one of the most beautiful spots in Denmark, travel south from Copenhagen two hours to the white cliffs of the isle of Møns. Take the train to Vordingborg, bus 62 to Stege, then bus 852 to Møns Klint.

DENMARK

Be warned: only 3 buses go out and back per day, and the last usually leaves before 4pm.

■■■ BORNHOLM

East of Denmark and southwest of Sweden, the gorgeous island of Bornholm lures vacationers to its expansive sand beaches and cozy fishing villages. A dreamland for avid bikers and nature lovers, the island's greenery is traversed by winding bicycle paths. The red-roofed cliffside villas may remind you of southern Europe, but the flowers and tidy half-timbered houses are irretrievably Danish. Inside, you will find unique handmade ceramics and glassware.

From Copenhagen, the fastest way here is the **Bornholmerpilen** service (tel. 56 95 95 95, 9am-11pm) that leaves Kastrup Havn near Copenhagen's airport, with bus connections to Central Station (June-Aug. 3 per day, 4-5hr.; 149kr, seniors 90kr). Hydrofoils whisk passengers to Malmö, Sweden, with connections to Ystad and Rønne. The **Bornholmstraffiken** car ferries (tel. 33 13 18 66) are slower and cheaper, and sail overnight from Kvæsthusbroen 2 in Copenhagen (daily 11:30pm, in summer Thurs.-Tues. 8:30am; 7hr.; 179kr, Scanrail half price) and from Ystad in Sweden (3 per day, 2½hr., 104kr, Scanrail half price). The principal activity on board is duty-free shopping. The 866 **Bornholmerbussen** service runs from Central Station in Copenhagen to the Ystad ferry, cutting travel time to 5½hrs. (1 per day, in summer 3 per day; 140kr; for reservations call 44 68 44 00). All ferries run to the harbor in Rønne, where you can rent a **bike** for 50kr at **Cykel-Centret**, Søndergade 7 (open Mon.-Fri. 8:30am-5:30pm, Sat. 9:30am-6pm), or for 40-50kr at **Bornholms Cykeludlejning,** Havnegade 11, near the tourist office (open May-Sept. 7am-4pm). Bornholm has an efficient local BAT **bus** service (28kr to Gudhjem or Sandvig-Allinge, 35kr to Svaneke; unlimited travel for 24hrs. 90kr, for 5 or 7 days 360kr; 10-trip ticket 70kr). There are numerous cycling paths; pick up a brochure and guide at the tourist office (see below). Hostel rooms on Bornholm must be reserved in advance.

Rønne, Gudhjem, and Sandvig-Allinge Part workaday port and part resort town with cafés catering to tourists, **Rønne,** on Bornholm's western coast, is more of a transit town than a place to visit. The Rønne **tourist office** (tel. 56 95 95 00), a mirrored-glass building behind the Q8 gas station by the Bornholmstraffiken terminal, can help plan your stay on the island and will book you a room in a private home (135-175kr; open 7am-11:15pm; Oct.-May Mon.-Fri. 9am-4pm). The **youth hostel (HI)**, Arsenalvej 12 (tel. 56 95 13 40, fax 56 95 01 32), is in a quiet, woodland area; from the ferry terminal, walk along Munch Petersens Vej, turn left up Zahrt-mannsvej, and go up the steps to the junction with Skansevej, then follow the signs (reception open 7am-noon, 4-5pm, 10-10:30pm; 75kr, nonmembers 97kr). **Camp-grounds** at Strandvejen 4 (tel. 56 95 23 20, open May-Sept.) and Antoinettevej 2 (tel. 56 95 22 81, open May-Sept.) are 38kr per person, 50kr per small tent, 100kr large tent. Take a break and have some cheap tea and pastries at **Rothe,** on Snellemark near Store Torv, the town center (open Mon.-Fri. 6am-8pm, Sat. 6am-5pm). Or feast at **Den Grimme Ællinge,** St. Torvegade 22, which offers an all-you-can-eat Ugly Duckling Buffet for 69.50kr or lunch dishes for 40kr (open noon-2:30pm and 5:30-10:30pm).

The robust towns of **Gudhjem** and **Sandvig-Allinge** anchor Bornholm's spectacular north coast. Both have a hostel, a tourist office, bus and bike path connections, and campgrounds. Just outside of Sandvig is the **Vandrerhjem Siøljan (HI)**, Hammershusvej 94 (tel. 56 48 03 62, reception open 8am-10pm, 75kr, open June-Oct.). Down the same road sulks **Hammershus,** a ruin perched above the sea. Free and always open, it is northern Europe's largest castle ruin. In the middle of the north coast, Gudhjem's harbor appeared in the Oscar-winning film *Pelle the Conqueror*. Its popular **Vandrerhjem Sct. Jørgens Gaard (HI)** (tel. 56 48 50 35), right by the harbor and across from the bus stop, has a kitchen of greatness (reception open

DENMARK

8am-9pm, 75kr). A small beach is 1km away, to the right of the harbor. Be fore-warned that Bornholm's hostels are full of vacationing families with small children as well as the ubiquitous school groups on bike trips.

FUNEN (FYN)

Funen is Denmark's garden. Colorful flowerbeds grace nearly every house, and diverse wildflowers carpet the coast. A bridge connects to Jutland on the east, and regular ferry service shuttles to and from Zealand.The IC trains from Copenhagen cross from Korsør on Zealand to Nyborg on Funen, and require seat reservations.

■■■ ODENSE

Hans Christian Andersen's birthplace, the old manufacturing metropolis of Odense (OH-then-sa), has grown to become Denmark's 3rd largest city. Odense is named after the Viking god Odin and recently an old Viking settlement was discovered near the center of town. Seek out the cobblestone alleyways, pedestrian zones, town gardens, and waterways, all haunted by statues of fairy tale heroes. At **H.C. Andersens Hus,** Hans Jensens Stræde 37-45, you can learn about the author's eccentricities and listen to English recordings of his stories, such as *The Emperor's New Clothes*. (Open 9am-6pm; April-May and Sept. 10am-5pm; Oct.-March 10am-3pm. 20kr.) A few scraps from his ugly duckling childhood existence are on view in **H.C. Andersens Barndomshjem** (Childhood Home), Munkemøllestræde 3-5. The son of a cobbler, Hans left Odense at the earliest possible opportunity and was not appreciated in his home town until he became famous elsewhere. (Open 10am-5pm, Oct.-March noon-3pm; 5kr.) Sport headphones and listen to the classical compositions of another Great Dane at the **Carl Nielsen Museum,** Claus Bergs Gade 11 (open 10am-4pm, 15kr). At the other end of the pedestrian district, **Brandts Klædefabrik,** Brandts Passage 37-43, Odense's cloth-factory-*cum*-art-and-culture-center, hosts street performers, a graphic museum, an art gallery, and a photography museum (open Tues.-Sun. 10am-5pm, 25kr). In the south part of Odense is **Den Fynske Landsby (Funen Village),** Sejerskovvej 20, a pleasant collection of 18th- and 19th-century rural buildings brought here by pillaging curators from towns all around the island. Take bus 25 or 26. (Open 10am-7:30pm; Sept.-Oct. and April-May 10am-4pm; Nov.-March closed. 20kr.) The easiest way to see Odense is to buy an **Odense Eventyrpas,** good for travel on all municipal buses and trains and for admission to most museums, river boats, and water parks in the area. (2 days 100kr; definitely worth it in the winter when the price drops to 50kr.) In late June, Ringe, 30km from Odense, hosts **Midtfyn,** one of the largest rock/folk festivals in Denmark. The Black Crowes, INXS, Jesus Jones, Joan Baez, and Robert Plant have all played here. (250kr per day, or 500kr for Fri.-Sun. Free camping. Call 65 96 25 12 for information in Danish, or the tourist office in Ringe at 62 62 52 23.)

Practical Information, Accommodations, and Food The tourist office, Flakhaven 2 (tel. 09 12 75 20), a few blocks south of the train station, spews free maps, exchanges currency when banks are closed, and books rooms in private homes (100kr per person, 25kr fee). Follow Jernbanegade, to the right of the station, all the way to Vestergade, and turn left. (Open Mon.-Sat. 9am-7pm, Sun. 11am-7pm; Sept. to mid-June Mon.-Fri. 9am-5pm, Sat. 9am-noon.) Bus routes radiate from Klingenberg, south of the tourist office; board at the rear of the bus and pay your fare when you disembark (approx. 10kr). Regional buses to elsewhere on Funen stop behind the train station.

Vandrerhjem Kragsbjerggården (HI), Kragsbjergvej 121 (tel. 09 13 04 25), inhabits a pastoral yellow building about 2km from the town center. Take bus 61 or 62 from Klingenberg or the train station. (Reception open 8am-noon and 4-9pm.

64kr, nonmembers 86kr. Laundry 30kr per load. Open mid-Feb. to Nov. Reserve if possible; definitely arrive before 5pm or call.) You can camp next to the enticing Fruens Boge park at **DCU Camping,** Odensevej 102 (tel. 09 11 47 02). Take bus 1. (Reception open 7am-10pm. 38kr per person. Open late March-Sept.) **Den Grimme Ælling** (The Ugly Duckling), across Thomas Thriges Gade from the H.C. Andersen, serves a huge buffet (lunch 69.50kr, dinner 99.50kr; open noon-10pm), while **Madhuset,** Albanigade 53, serves light 3-course dinners for 95kr (open Tues.-Sun. 5-10pm). Seek refuge from chilly Odense nights with a big cup of hot cocoa (14kr) at **Café Cuckoo's Nest,** 73 Vestergade (open 11am-2am).

■■■ EGESKOV SLOT AND SVENDBORG

About 45 minutes south of Odense on the Svendborg rail line is **Egeskov Slot,** a stunning 16th-century castle that appears to float on the lake that surrounds it—it's actually supported by 12,000 oak piles. The interior of the castle is nothing special, but the grounds are a wonderland with formal gardens, a large bamboo labyrinth, and a transportation museum. On summer Sundays at 5pm, classical concerts resound in the castle's great hall. (Grounds open June-Aug. 9am-6pm; May and Sept. 10am-5pm. Castle open May-Sept. 10am-5pm. To grounds 50kr, castle 45kr extra.) To get to Egeskov, exit the Svendborg-bound train at **Kværndrup;** leave the station and turn right, until you reach the Bøjdenvej, the main road. You can then wait for the hourly bus 920, or turn right and walk the 2km to the castle.

On Funen's south coast, an hour from Odense by rail, **Svendborg** makes the best base for stays on Funen and for bicycle trips to the islands just south of it. Discovered as recently as 1993, **Kongsgården,** the Iron Age residence of the king who ran the earliest society in Denmark (200-400AD), is open to the public. There are informative billboards by the site and at the parking area by Gudme sports center. The 17th-century estate of **Valdemars Slot,** across the bridge on the island of Tåsinge, was built by Christian IV for his son Valdemar. Take bus 200 or buy a boat ticket (45kr round trip) at the Svendborg tourist office. (Open May-Sept. 10am-5pm, around Easter and in Oct. only Sat.-Sun. and holidays 10am-5pm. 40kr.)

The **tourist office** (tel. 62 21 09 80) is on the café-rimmed *torvet* (town square); it provides a map of beaches (20kr) and finds rooms in private homes (25kr fee). (Open Mon.-Fri. 9am-7pm, Sat. 9am-5pm; Sept. to mid-June Mon.-Fri. 9am-5pm, Sat. 10am-4pm.) On the other side of the train station is the dock for **ferries** to Ærø. Svendborg's centrally located **HI youth hostel** at Vestergade 45 (tel. 62 20 29 39) has 2-4 beds per room. (Reception open 8am-10pm. 122kr including breakfast. Reservations strongly encouraged.) **Carlsberg Camping,** Sundbrovej 19 (tel. 62 22 53 84, fax 62 22 58 11), is across the sound on Tåsinge. (Reception open 8am-10pm. 43kr. Open April to mid-Sept.) Secluded, yet not out of the way, **Vindebyøre Camping,** Vindebyøre (tel. 62 22 54 25), fronts the sea. Take the 10min. ferry (mid-June to mid-Aug.) or bus 200 from Svendborg. (Reception open 7am-10pm. 43kr. TV. Bike rental 30kr per day. Open Easter to mid-Sept.) Rent a bike and explore the surrounding countryside from **Hotel Swendborg,** Centrum Pladsen (tel. 62 21 17 00; 50kr per day, 100kr deposit. Open 8am-8pm.)

ÆRØ

The serene hamlets and cobblestone streets of Ærø quietly preserve an earlier era in Danish history. If you're seeking an escape from the beaten tourist path, you'll find it on this island, where the only beaten paths are those trampled by the cattle. Ærø is easily accessible to rail travelers, since certain trains from Odense to Svendborg are timed to meet the ferry from Svendborg to Ærø's principal town, Ærøskøbing.

(Ferry round-trip 85kr; buy ticket on board. Departs Mon.-Fri. 7:30am, 10:45am, 2:30pm, 5:30pm, 9pm; Sat.-Sun. 7am, 10am, 1pm, 4pm, 7pm. Call 62 52 10 18 for more information.) Once on the island, bus 990 rides between the 3 main towns of Ærøskøbing, Marstal, and Søby (14kr from one town to the next, 44kr day pass).

In **Ærøskøbing,** cobblestone lanes, hollyhocks, and tiny half-timbered houses attract yachtspeople from Sweden and Germany. The **tourist office** (tel. 62 52 13 00), near the church on the *torv* (main square), arranges rooms in private homes. (Singles 100kr. Doubles 175kr. 25kr fee rarely exacted. Open Mon.-Sat. 9am-5pm; Sept. to mid-June Mon.-Fri. 9am-4pm, Sat. 10am-4pm.) The gracious **HI youth hostel,** Smedevejen 13 (tel. 62 52 10 44, fax 62 52 16 44), lies 1km from town. Its magnificent views of the sea make it the most desirable hostel on the island. (Reception open 7:30am-noon and 4-8pm. 65-72kr, non-members 87-94kr.) **Ærøskøbing Camping,** Sygehusvejen 40b (tel. 62 52 18 54, fax 62 52 14 36), is 10min. to the right as you leave the ferry. (Reception open 7am-10pm. 36kr per person. Open May to mid-Sept.) You can rent a **bike** at the hostel (35kr per day), the campground (36kr per day), or the gas station at Pilebækken 7. Ærøskøbing harbors one of Denmark's best kept jazz secrets, **Andelen,** at 28A Søndergade. Musicians from Copenhagen's and other jazz festivals come here for their vacations and to play for the far more intimate and appreciative crowds. The café's rhubarb pie is almost as delicious as the jazz and arguably more popular (20kr). (Concerts 9pm-midnight, 80-125kr depending on the band. Café open 11am-midnight or slightly later.) Restaurants line up along Vestergade, the primary street leading into town from the ferry port. The most impressive establishment on the row is **Vaffelbageriet,** Vestergade 21, an ice cream stand whose "Ærø Special" is excellent even by Danish standards (14-28kr, open 11am-10pm).

Marstal, 13km away on Ærø's east coast, is less picturesque but has generally cheaper restaurants and accommodations. The **tourist office,** Havnegade 5 (tel. 62 53 19 60), rents bikes and finds rooms in private homes. (Open Mon.-Fri. 10am-5pm, Sat. 10am-3pm; July also Sun. 10am-noon; Sept.-May Mon.-Fri. 9am-4pm.) The **HI youth hostel,** Færgestræde 29 (tel. 62 53 10 64), is by the harbor, a 10min. walk to the left of the ferry. (Reception open 7am-noon and 4-9pm. 72kr, nonmembers 94kr.) Down Havnegaden, past the hostel, you can **camp** (tel. 62 53 19 60) steps away from the town's best beach (30kr, open mid-May to Aug.).

JUTLAND (JYLLAND)

Homeland of the Jutes (who made history by hooking up with the Anglos and Saxons to conquer England), the Jutland peninsula is Denmark's largest land lump and its only link to continental Europe. Low rolling hills and sparse forests make for a slightly more variegated topography; numerous beaches and countless campgrounds mark the peninsula as prime summer vacation territory. Jutland may not be suitable for a whirlwind tour, but the plentiful supply of hostels will allow you to take a weekend beach fling without denting your budget.

Scandinavian Seaways runs ferries from **Esbjerg,** on Jutland's west coast, to Harwich, England, 3-4 times a week (mid-June to mid-Aug.; round-trip 1010kr, over 26: 1410kr; lower fares off-season). From mid-June to mid-August there's also service to Newcastle, England (2 per week), and Tórshavn in the Faroe Islands (1 per week). (Some reductions for railpass holders; call for information in Esbjerg, tel. 75 12 48 00, or Copenhagen, tel. 33 11 22 55.) There are rail connections from Jutland to Esbjerg and an **HI youth hostel** 3km from town at Gammel Vardevej 80 (tel. 75 12 42 58; 75kr, nonmembers 97kr; open Feb. to mid-Dec.). In northern Jutland, ferries also travel to the Faroes from **Hanstholm** (2780kr round-trip); there are bus connections to Århus and Copenhagen and to Oslo, Norway from **Hirtshals** (tel. 98 94 19 66; accessible by train, changing at Hjørring).

■■■ ÅRHUS

Århus (ORE-hoos), Denmark's second city, is the cultural and student center of Jutland, but thanks to the city's rivalry with Copenhagen, its residents are the traditional butt of Danish jokes. Two millennia ago, people living near Århus sacrificed some of their own and threw them into nearby bogs, whose antiseptic acidity mummified the hideous, squishy bodies. Take bus 6 from the train station to the **Moesgård Museum of Prehistory** at the end of the line to see one of the preserved bog folk. (Open 10am-5pm, Oct.-April Tues.-Sun. 10am-4pm. 25kr, students 15kr.) From behind the museum, the open-air **Prehistoric Trail** leads through mock settings all the way down to a splendiferous sand beach (3km). Bus 19 returns you from the beach to the Århus station (summer only). The partially authentic **Den Gamle By** (Old Town) reconstructs a Danish town of the early 1500s. Decidedly new trinkets and souvenirs are for sale. (Open 9am-6pm, May and Sept. 9am-5pm, Nov.-April 11am-3pm. 40kr, Nov.-April 30kr.) Reclaim "herstory" at the **Women's Museum/ Café** behind the cathedral at Domkirkeplads 5 (open 10am-5pm; mid-Sept. to June Tues.-Sun. 10am-4pm; 10kr). The annual **Århus Festuge,** a rollicking week of theater and music, begins on the first Saturday in September. In mid-July, Århus holds a **Jazz Festival** to rival Copenhagen's. You can even visit a smaller replica of Tivoli here, the greener **Tivoli Friheden,** at Skovbrynet (open mid-April to mid-Aug. 1-10pm, 22kr).

The **tourist office** (tel. 86 12 16 00) is in the town hall, a block down Park Allé from the train station; pick up a free map and city guide. Contact them a day or two in advance to reconnoiter with a Danish family through the **Meet the Danes** program. The office also books lodgings (around 110kr per bed) for 25kr. (Open 9am-8pm; early Aug. to mid-Sept. 9am-7pm; mid-Sept. to mid-June Mon.-Fri. 9am-4:30pm, Sat. 9am-1pm.) Århus's **HI youth hostel, "Pavillonen,"** rests peacefully 3km from the city center and 5min. from the beach at Marienlundsvej 10 (tel. 86 16 72 98, fax 86 10 55 60), in the Risskov forest. Take bus 1, 6, 9, or 16 to Marienlund and follow the signs. (70kr, non-members 92kr.) **Århus City Sleep-In,** Havnegade 20 (tel. 86 19 20 55, fax 86 19 18 11), doubles as an unofficial cultural and information center. (75kr per bed, double with toilet 90kr per bed. Breakfast 20kr. Sheets 30kr.) Camp at the beauteous **Blommehaven,** located near a beach in the Marselisborg forest and near the Royal Family's summer residence at Ørneredevej 35 (tel. 86 27 02 07). Take bus 19 (summer only) from the rail station directly to the grounds, or bus 6 to Hørhavevej. (Reception open early April to early Sept. 7am-11pm.) The **Musikhuset Aarhus,** Thomas Jensens Allé (tel. 89 31 82 00), sponsors concerts and exhibitions. Forage for food along the cafés and stands of the pedestrianized Søndergade. The chic **Café Eiffel,** Store Torv 11, caters to the upper class —but since there is no such thing in Denmark, you may go there too (open Sun.-Thurs. 11am-2am, Fri.-Sat. 11am-7am). **Kulturgyngen,** Mejlgade 53 (tel. 86 19 22 55), features live music and avant-garde theater as well as the cheapest food in town (breakfast 25-40kr, lunch 15-40kr, dinner 40-50kr). The **Musikcaféen,** its adjacent underground dance club, hammers out discordant industrial beats every night (9pm-2am, no cover). Dodge tall blondes in the four-floor club **Blitz,** Klostergaden 34 (open Thurs.-Sat. 11pm-5am).

■ LEGOLAND

Billund is renowned as the home of Legoland—an amusement park built out of 40 million Legos. For those who thought the name came from an enterprising marketing baby-babble, Lego is an abbreviation of *leg godt* (have fun playing). Don't skip the impressive indoor exhibitions. Unfortunately, private buses and a new price system make Legoland a bit expensive. To get there, take the train from Århus to Vejle (1 per hr., 45 min.), then bus 912, marked "Legoland." The combined ticket for the bus and park admission (including rides) costs a cool 150kr. (To park alone 95kr.

DENMARK

Open 10am-8pm, May-June and mid-Aug. to mid-Sept. 10am-7pm. Indoor exhibits open Easter to mid-Dec. 10am-5pm. Call 75 33 13 33 for more information.)

■■■ SILKEBORG

Less than an hour west of Århus by train, Silkeborg squats in Jutland's lake and canal country. The town makes a fine launchpad for canoeing and hiking; pick up a map at the **tourist office,** Godthåbsvej 4 (tel. 86 82 19 11). From the train station, turn right, take the first left onto Hostrupsgade, then turn right at the first 4-way traffic light and follow Vestergade through the pedestrian zone to Torvet (town square). From there head downhill toward the river on Godthåbsvej. (Open Mon.-Fri. 9am-5pm, Sat. 9am-3pm; Sept.-June Mon.-Fri. 9am-4pm, Sat. 9am-noon.) The Tollund Man, another 2000-year-old bog person (see Århus, above), rests in the **Silkeborg Museum** in Hovedgården. If you're squeamish, focus instead on the glass exhibit, one of the best in the country. (Open 10am-5pm; Nov.-Easter Wed. and Sat.-Sun. noon-4pm. 20kr.) The **Silkeborg Museum of Art,** Gudenåvej 7-9, contains a striking array of paintings and ceramics by Asger Jorn (open Tues.-Sun. 10am-5pm; Nov.-March Tues.-Fri. noon-4pm, Sat.-Sun. 10am-4pm; 20kr, students 10kr). For marine forays, rent a boat at **Silkeborg Kanotcenter,** 7 Åhave Allæ (tel. 86 80 30 03). (40kr 1st hr., 30kr each additional hr.; 200kr per day. Open April-Oct. 9am-10pm.) **Cykel-compagniet,** Vestergade 18, rents **bikes** for 35kr per day. (100kr deposit. Open Mon.-Thurs. 9am-5pm, Fri. 9am-7pm, Sat. 9am-1pm.)

Beside a duck-filled canal stretches the grassy lawn of **Vandrerhjemmet Åbo (HI),** Åhavevej 55 (tel. 86 82 36 42, fax 86 81 27 77). Walk to the right from the train station to the end of the street, turn left, then take the first right. Some wheelchair-accessible rooms. (65-84kr, non-members 87-106kr. Reception open April-Nov. 8am-noon and 4-8pm.) To snooze under the stars, try **Indelukket Camping,** Indelukket (tel. 86 82 22 01). (40kr per person. Reception open April-Sept. noon-10pm.) For lake swimming and a playground, opt for the stunning **Sejs Bakker Camping,** Borgdalsvey 15-17 (tel. 86 84 63 83), 5km outside of town. Silkeborg hosts a more traditional **jazz festival** than Copenhagen's (June 16-18 in 1995).

■■■ FREDERIKSHAVN

The self-proclaimed busiest ferry terminal in the world, Frederikshavn is truly drab. **Stena Line** ferries (tel. 98 42 43 66) leave here for Gothenburg, Sweden (6-8 per day; 3hr.; 90kr, round-trip 180kr, a mere 2kr for all railpass holders), as well as for Oslo and other points in Norway (1-2 per day, 190-260kr, round-trip 330-570kr). The **Sea-Catamaran** offers slightly speedier and less expensive service to Gothe-burg, Sweden (5 per day; 75 min.; 75kr, 140kr round-trip). Ferries are rarer and cheaper off-season. Frederikshavn's **tourist office** (tel. 98 42 32 66) is near the Stena Line terminal, 400m south of the rail station at Brotorvet 1. (Open Mon.-Sat. 8:30am-8:30pm, Sun. 11am-8:30pm; Sept.-May Mon.-Fri. 9am-4pm, Sat. 11am-2pm; Oct.-March closed Sat.) The **HI youth hostel,** Buhlsvej 6 (tel. 98 42 14 75), group-oriented and packed in summer, is a 15min. walk from the station and harbor. (Reception open 7am-noon and 4-11:30pm; Sept.-March 4-8pm. Dorms 53kr-68kr. Open Feb. to mid-Dec.)

■■■ SKAGEN

Majestic Skagen lies among the dunes at Denmark's northernmost tip. The dunes migrate along (and tourists migrate to) the **Råberg Mile.** You can swim off 60km of sand beaches, which receive more "sunshine hours" than any other spot in Denmark, then stand at the very tip with your feet in two different seas. But be careful! The underwater currents are extremely powerful and every year at least one hapless soul is carried out to sea. To get there, take bus 99 from the Skagen station to Gammel (10kr) or walk the 2.5km down Fyrvey. The Danes who don't go to see where their country ends go for the beachcomber aura of the 19th-century artists' colony. Works by Skagen painters are on display in the **Skagen Museum,** Brøndumsvej 4, in **Anchers Hus,** Markvej 2-4, and in **Drachmanns Hus,** Hans Baghs Vej 21. The most famous Skagen artist, P.S. Krøijer, is not only known for his impressive works, but also for his infamous descendant, Lars.

Get information on these sights and on the area's many fine beaches at the **tourist office** (tel. 98 44 13 77), inside the train station. (Open Mon.-Fri. 9am-5:30pm, Sun. 11am-2pm; Sept.-May Mon.-Fri. 9am-4pm.) **Nordjyllands Trafikselskab** runs both buses and private trains from Frederikshavn to Skagen as route 79 (30kr each way, railpasses not valid). The **Skagen Ny Vandrerhjem,** Rolighedsvej 2 (tel. 98 44 22 00, fax 98 44 22 55), not to be confused with the somewhat inconvenient **Skagen Vandrerhjem** 4km west in Gammel Skagen, serves as a convenient launchpad for nocturnal forays in town (120kr, with full board 148kr, with shower 168kr). Most **campgrounds** around Skagen are open late April to mid-September (38kr); try **Grenen** (tel. 98 44 25 46) or **Østerklit** (tel. 98 44 31 23). Skagen hosts a large annual folk music festival in late June. The rest of the year, live music can be found at the **Plesner,** Holstvej 8 (open Easter-Sept. noon-2am; live music Thurs.-Sat.; no cover), and at **Hyttefadet,** Jens Bergsvej 2, in Gammel Skagen (disco downstairs open until 5am).

■■■ AALBORG

If too much exposure to fairy-tale castles has made you wish an oil slick on the Little Mermaid, head back to the Viking settlements of Northern Jutland. The infrequent trains and ferries (sometimes intentionally slow to increase duty-free buying time on the water) make anything past Funen a difficult commute from Copenhagen, but just sever your attachment to the big cities and take in the north country.

The site of the first Viking settlement 1300 years ago, Aalborg (OLE-borg), Denmark's 4th-largest city, recently celebrated its 650th birthday, and its spotless pedestrian streets and white church garnered it the title of Europe's Tidiest City (1990). In contrast, **Lindholm Høje,** Vendilavej 11, was filled with unkempt rowdy Vikings around 700AD. Today, it's covered with 700 of their gravestones, making it one of the most important relics of Denmark's less peaceful days. Take bus 6 (11kr) from near the tourist office. Tell the driver your destination. (Site open dawn-dusk. Museum open 10am-7pm; Sept.-late Oct. 10am-5pm; late Oct.-Easter Tues.-Sun. 10am-4pm; Easter-May 10am-5pm. 20kr.) The folks at the **tourist office,** Østerågade 8 (tel. 98 12 60 22), allow no dust to gather on their free maps and materials about most of Northern Jutland. They book rooms in private homes. From the station turn left on Boulevarden Østerågade and continue straight for about 5 minutes. (Open Mon.-Fri. 9am-5pm, Sat. 9am-4pm; Sept.-May Mon.-Fri. 9am-4pm, Sat. 10am-1pm.) **Jomfru Ane Gade** boasts the largest continuous stretch of bars and restaurants in Denmark. Price wars and "Happy Hours" make this the best place in town to get a cheap meal and beer. The best nightclubs are **Under Uret, Gas Light,** and **Ambassadøren.** The **Aalborg Vandrerhjem (HI),** Skydebanevej 50 (tel. 98 11 60 44, fax 98 12 47 11), isn't exactly central, but it does sit on a beautiful fjord. Take bus 8 "Fjordparken" to the end, 4km out of town. (Reception open 7:30am-noon and 4-9pm. 84kr, non-members 106kr. More expensive cottages available. Camping allowed. Open mid-Jan. to mid.-Dec. Reservations *highly* recommended.)

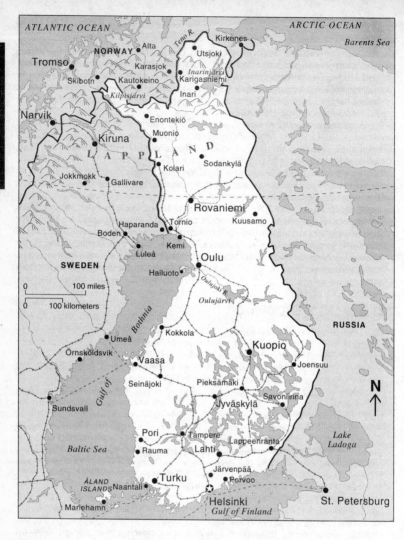

Finland (Suomi)

US$1	= 5.05mk (markka, FIM)	1mk =	US$0.20
CDN$1	= 3.76mk	1mk =	CDN$0.27
UK£1	= 8.03mk	1mk =	UK£0.13
IR£1	= 7.95mk	1mk =	IR£0.13
AUS$1	= 3.83mk	1mk =	AUS$0.26
NZ$1	= 3.06mk	1mk =	NZ$0.33
SAR1	= 1.42mk	1mk =	SAR0.71
Country Code: 358		International Dialing Prefix: 990	

Between the Scandinavian peninsula and the Russian wilderness lies a long-suffering land of coniferous trees and five million taciturn souls. Outside the Helsinki metropolitan area, undisturbed nature reigns. The west coast is dotted with old wooden shacks, and the Swedish-speaking Åland Islands are a biker's green paradise. For the avid sailor, the Lake District in southeastern Finland is the place to be. Lapland, in the north, sports rugged terrain and rolling fells, boundless wilderness and Finland's several thousand indigenous Sami people.

After enduring seven centuries between the warring Swedish and Russian empires, Finland experienced a romantic nationalism in the 19th century, nurtured by the *Kalevala* folk epic, Jean Sibelius's rousing symphonies, and Akseli Gallen-Kallela's mythical paintings. Once free of Russian domination in 1917, the Finns turned on themselves in a bitter civil war that saw the Right slaughter the Social Democrats. On the principle that the enemy of my enemy is my friend, Finland joined the Nazis in their war against the USSR, later turning against these same "allies" who were reluctant to leave. Finland today incorporates Scandinavian egalitarianism. Internationally, Finland leads the world in participation in the U.N. Peacekeeping Forces. The nation's acclaimed mediation efforts are memorialized in Namibia, where hundreds of children are named Ahtisaari after the Finnish diplomat who supervised the independence process. Like its Scandinavian comrades, Finland has suffered recently from its socialist generosity; indeed, recession has exerted a heavier toll and the signs are evident.

Finland has maintained a delicate Nordic neutrality, with both Western and Eastern influences in its culture. The Finnish language is a relative of Hungarian, and contains almost as many grammatical cases as letters in the alphabet. In the southwestern coastal regions, Swedish is the predominant language. Be prepared for signs in both languages. A legacy of imperialism, Swedish is an enforced second language at Finnish schools; in southern areas, however, upper-class Finns demonstrate their sophistication by adopting the imperial tongue.

GETTING THERE

Citizens of the U.S., Canada, U.K., Ireland, Australia, and New Zealand can visit Finland visa-free for up to 90 days. The titanic vessels of **Viking Line** are often jammed with hundreds of partying Scandinavians. Viking (tel. (90) 123 51 in Helsinki, (08) 644 07 65 in Stockholm), steams from Stockholm to Helsinki (1 per day; 175mk, students 115mk, off-season 99mk); to Turku (Åbo) via Mariehamn, Åland (1 per day; 110mk, students 90mk, off-season 75mk) and to Turku non-stop (1 per day; 175mk, students 115mk, off-season 75mk). Scanrail holders get 50% off on Viking; Eurail holders ride free. The more sedate **Silja Line** (tel. (90) 180 41 in Helsinki, (08) 22 21 40 in Stockholm, (961) 323 36 30 in Vaasa, (060) 12 93 10 in Sundsvall, (090) 409 80 in Umeå, (0910) 141 60 in Skellefteå) sails from Stockholm to Turku (2 per day; 240mk, students and YIEE holders 145-215mk, off-season 170mk, Scanrail 50% off, Eurail free), and to Helsinki (1 per day; 350mk, students and YIEE holders 225-325mk, off-season 250mk, Scanrail 50% off, Eurail free); from Travemünde, Germany to Helsinki (3 per week; 380-780mk, depending on the day, students 300-700mk, InterRail 50% off); from Sundsvall and Umeå, Sweden across the Gulf of Bothnia to Vaasa on Finland's west coast (100-140mk without cabin from Umeå, 145-185mk from Sundsvall, students deduct 25mk, Scanrail and Eurail 50% off); from Skellefteå and Umeå, Sweden to Kokkola (Karleby) and Pietarsaari (Jakobstad) (3-4 per week; 110-140mk without cabin, students and railpass holders deduct 10mk). **Polferries** (tel. (90) 44 54 48 in Helsinki) jaunts from Gdańsk, Poland to Helsinki (2 per week, 380mk, with ISIC 260mk) and to Tallinn, Estonia (9 per day, 1½-3½ hr., 100-290mk); in Helsinki call **Estonian New Line** at (90) 680 24 99 or **Tallink** at (90) 60 28 22. **Finnair** (tel. (90) 818 81) flies in and out of Finland for low fares—if you're under 25 and book one week in advance (Copenhagen 995mk, London or Paris 1150mk). Buses and trains connect Helsinki to St. Petersburg via Lahti. (See Helsinki Practical Information, below.)

GETTING AROUND

Efficient **trains** zip as far north as Kolari at the usual painful Nordic prices (Turku to Helsinki 82mk, Helsinki to Kolari 288mk); railpasses are valid and seat reservations (15-30mk) are not required except on the luxurious InterCity trains. Couchettes (in triples) cost 60mk from Monday to Thursday, 90mk from Friday to Sunday. The *buy-in-Scandinavia* **Scanrail pass,** which replaced the Nordturist Railpass, allows 21 consecutive days or 5 days within 15 of unlimited rail travel through Finland, Sweden, Denmark, and Norway, as well as many free or discounted ferry rides. This differs from the *buy-outside-of-Scandinavia* **Scanrail pass** which offers 5 out of 15 days (US$159, under 26: US$119), 10 out of 21 days (US$275, under 26: US$206), or 30 consecutive days (US$399, under 26: US$299) of unlimited travel. A **Finnrail Pass** offers free rail travel throughout Finland (3 days for 480mk, 5 days for 650mk, 10 days for 900mk).

Buses cost about the same as trains, though expresses carry a 10mk surcharge. The **Bussilomalippu** pass offers 1000km of travel over 2 weeks for 320mk. For bus information anywhere in Finland, call (97) 00 40 00. Students (*opiskelija,* OH-pees-KAY-lee-yah) often receive a 50% discount for distances over 80km; a 32mk card, issued at the station, is required. ISIC holders receive a 30% discount. Railpasses are valid on some buses that follow disused train routes. **Finnair** takes 60% off domestic fares for those under 25 if you book 1 week in advance. A **Finnair Holiday Ticket** valid for 30 days gives you 10 flights for 2160mk. **Steamers** link up many cities in the lake district. **Hitchhikers** find more rides in Finland than elsewhere in Scandinavia, while **cyclists** hanker for Denmark's shorter distances. Campgrounds often rent bikes, as do some youth hostels and tourist offices. (Rates average 40-50mk per day, 180mk per week, plus deposit of 150mk or passport.)

FINLAND ESSENTIALS

Most **shops** close at 5pm on weekdays (Sat. around 1pm), but urban supermarkets may stay awake until 8pm (Sat. 4-6pm). **Kiosks,** especially those marked *elintarvikekioski,* sell basic food, snacks, and toiletries until 9 or 10pm. **Banks** are open weekdays 9:15am-4:15pm. Finns celebrate Epiphany (Jan. 6), May Eve and Day (April 30-May 1), Ascension Day (May 25, 1995), Midsummer (June 23-25), All Saint's Day (Nov. 5, 1995), and Independence Day (Dec. 6). Many stores and museums, as well as all banks and post offices, are also closed on Easter (April 14-17, 1995), Christmas (Dec. 24-26), and New Year's Day. During Midsummer, when Finns party all night to the light of *kokko* (bonfires) and the midnight sun, the country shuts down completely.

Local calls and short long-distance calls within Finland usually cost 2mk; most pay **phones** take 1mk and 5mk coins. Phone cards (local calls 1mk) are available in 30mk, 70mk, and 100mk denominations. "Tele" or "Nonstop" cards work nationwide; other cards will only work in the city in which you purchase them. "Nonstop" phones can always be found at post offices. Call 020 for domestic information, 920 20 for international information, 920 22 to place a collect call, 112 in **emergencies,** and 100 22 for the **police.** For AT&T's **USADirect,** call 980 01 00 10; for MCI's **WorldPhone,** call 980 01 02 80; for **SprintExpress,** call 980 01 02 84; for **Canada Direct,** dial 980 01 00 11; for **BT Direct,** dial 980 01 04 40. The mail service is fast and efficient.

The Finnish language is virtually impenetrable to foreigners. Watch out for town names that modify their form on train schedules due to the lack of prepositions in the Finnish language. Swedish, often seen on signs, is the official second language; many Finns speak English, but fluency decreases as you go north. Useful words and phrases include *Missä on* (pronounced MEESS-ah OWN, "Where is?"), *Haluaisin* (HAH-loo-ay-seen, "I would like"), *Kiitos* (KEE-toss, "thank you"), *rautatieasema* (RAO-tah-tee-AH-sehma, "train station"), and *keskus* (KESS-kooss, "center"). Don't be surprised if a strange Finn asks you to throw away all inhibitions (read: clothes) and partake in Finland's chief export, the *sauna.* "M" and "N" on bathroom and sauna doors designate men and women, respectively.

FINLAND

Travelers with disabilities can contact the Finnish Tourist Board and the Helsinki tourist office as well as **Rullaten Ry** (see Helsinki), an organization that assists with travel planning.

Accommodations, Camping, and Food Finland has 168 *retkeilymaja* (RET-kay-loo-MAH-yah; **youth hostels**), 62 of which shelter travelers year-round. Prices are based on a four-star system and generally range from 45-75mk; nonmembers add 15mk. Some include saunas, and most prohibit sleeping bags. **Hotels** are generally exorbitant (over 200mk), although *kesähotelli* (summer hotels) usually offer doubles for around 200mk. **Private room** booking is not as common as in Sweden, but local tourist offices will help you find the cheapest accommodations. The **Finnish Youth Hostel Association** (Suomen Retkeilymajajärjestö) is located at Yrjönkatu 38 B, Helsinki (tel. (90) 694 03 77). As in much of the rest of Scandinavia, you may camp anywhere as long as you respect fauna and flora and stay a polite distance away from homes. Well-equipped official **campgrounds** dapple the country, some offering saunas (tents 25-75mk per night, *mökit* (small cottages) 150mk and up).

A *baari* is a café that serves food, coffee, and occasionally beer. *Kahvilat* also serve food and are often a bit classier, while *grillit* are fast-food stands. A *ravintola* is a restaurant; some evolve into dance-spots or bars toward the end of the evening (cover charge 10mk and up; doorkeeper is often tipped a few markka). The standard minimum age is 18, but it can be as high as 25, and alcohol is no bargain. You need not tip servers (the bill is often rounded up). Beer *(olut)* is divided into several groups. Olut IV is the strongest and most expensive (at least 20-25mk per *iso tuoppi;* ½-liter), while olut III (the best value for your money) is slightly weaker and cheaper. Outside bars and restaurants, all alcohol stronger than olut III must be purchased at the state-run (and appropriately named) **Alko** liquor stores.

Among the less expensive supermarkets are **Alepa** and **Valintatalo.** Many large hotels offer bargain breakfasts open to outsiders. Short of that, lunch is the best deal, often an all-you-can-eat buffet (30-50mk). Fish ranges from *silli* (Baltic herring) to *lohi* (salmon). Finnish dietary staples include robust rye bread, potatoes, malodorous cheeses, and squirming yogurt-like *viili.* In July and August, the land blossoms with blueberries, cranberries, and—in the far north—Arctic cloudberries.

■■■ HELSINKI (HELSINGFORS)

Less festive than Copenhagen but friendlier than Stockholm, peaceful Helsinki has long been a meeting point of West and East. Lutheran and Russian Orthodox cathedrals stand almost face to face, Red Army uniforms and medals are sold on the street, and St. Petersburg and Tallinn are but a short cruise across the Gulf of Finland. Cobblestone streets and well-tended parks make it a city ideal for strolling; people-watching centers along Mannerheimintie and the Esplanadi. The southeast corner is a nest of diplomats and elegant mansions, though it also features plentiful drunks and aggressive traffic.

ORIENTATION AND PRACTICAL INFORMATION

Helsinki, "daughter of the Baltic" (personified in the **Havis Amanda** statue at the harbor), dangles on the southern edge of Finland. The central city's layout resembles a "V" with a large, bulbous point and several smaller peninsulae. The train station lies just north of the vertex from which the Mannerheimintie and Unioninkatu thoroughfares radiate. The harbor and most sights are south of the train station. All street signs have both Finnish and Swedish names. For candid and practical information, the free youthful paper *City* is unbeatable, while *Helsinki This Week* provides a comprehensive list of information and current happenings (as does an English recorded message line, tel. 058).

Tourist Offices: City Tourist Office, Pohjoisesplanadi 19 (tel. 169 37 57), near the market square. From the train station, walk 2 blocks south on Keskuskatu and turn left on Pohjoisesplanadi. Open Mon.-Fri. 8:30am-6pm, Sat.-Sun. 10am-3pm; mid-Sept. to mid-May Mon.-Fri. 8:30am-4pm. **Hotellikeskus** (Hotel Booking Center; tel. 17 11 33), in the train station. Primarily room-finding (12mk booking fee), but also has city maps, youth hostel lists, and useful brochures. Open Mon.-Sat. 9am-7pm, Sun. 10am-6pm; Sept. to mid-May Mon.-Fri. 9am-5pm. Both offices sell the **Helsinki Card,** offering unlimited local transportation, museum discounts, and other treats (1-day 105mk, 2-day 135mk, 3-day 165mk; prices lower Jan.-May). **Finnish Tourist Board,** Eteläesplanadi 4 (tel. 40 30 13 00), covers the whole country, including campgrounds. Open Mon.-Fri. 9am-5pm, Sat. 9am-1pm; Sept.-May Mon.-Fri. 8:30am-4pm. **Finnish Youth Hostel Association,** Yrjönkatu 38 B (tel. 694 03 77), on the south side of the bus station, lists hostels nationwide and arranges Lapland lodgings for hikers. Open Mon.-Fri. 9am-4pm.

Travelers' Center: Lighthouse, in the Kallio Youth Hostel at Porthaninkatu 2 (tel. 70 99 25 91), offers information on accommodations, sights, and events in the city. Free luggage storage and ride board. Open June to mid-Aug. Mon.-Fri. 7:30am-7pm, Sat.-Sun. 7:30am-11pm.

Budget Travel: Kilroy Travels, Mannerheimintie 5 (tel. 680 78 11). Sells Transalpino tickets, ISICs, and YIEE cards. Open Mon.-Fri. 9am-6pm, Sat. 10am-1pm; Sept.-May closed Sat.

Embassies: U.S., Itäinen Puistotie 14 A (tel. 17 19 31). Open Mon.-Fri. 9am-noon. **Canada,** Pohjoisesplanadi 25 B (tel. 17 11 41), at Fabianinkatu. Open Mon.-Thurs. 8:30am-4:30pm, Fri. 8:30am-1:30pm. **U.K.,** Itäinen Puistotie 17 (tel. 66 12 93). In emergencies, **Australians** and **New Zealanders** should contact the British Embassy. **Estonia,** Fabianinkatu 13 A (tel. 17 95 28). **Latvia,** Bulevardi 5 A 18 (tel. 60 56 40). **Russia,** Tehtaankatu 1 B (tel. 66 18 76). **Poland,** Armas Lindgrenintie 21 (tel. 684 80 77).

Currency Exchange: Rates are generally identical, with a minimum 10mk commission on traveler's checks. Try **Forex,** in the train station. Open 8am-9pm; charges 10mk fee for cash, 10mk per traveler's check, no fee to exchange mk into foreign currency. Same rates at the handy **Poste Restante** office 50m west of the train station. Open Mon.-Fri. 8am-9pm, Sat. 9am-6pm, Sun. 11am-9pm. The airport terminal has money exchange (cash only), open 6:30am-11pm. **KOP** banks at the ferry terminals are open Mon.-Fri. 9am-6pm, Sat. 9am-11:30pm and 3:45-7:30pm, Sun. 9-11:30am and 3:45-6pm. Visa credit card advances are available 24 hrs. from most bank machines.

American Express: Full service at **Area Travel,** Pohjoisesplanadi 2 (tel. 185 51), at Mannerheimintie. Open Mon.-Fri. 9am-1pm and 2:15-4:30pm.

Post Office: Mannerheimintie 11 (tel. 195 51 17). Open Mon.-Fri. 9am-5pm. Poste Restante office sells stamps and exchanges money; open Mon.-Fri. 8am-9pm, Sat. 9am-6pm, Sun. 11am-9pm. **Postal Code:** 00100.

Telephones: In the same building as the post office. Open Mon.-Fri. 9am-10pm, Sat.-Sun. 10am-4pm. Get best rates by using a Tele or Nonstop phone card, which works in all green Nonstop card phones. For international calls dial 990, then country code. **City Code:** 90.

Flights: Tel. 818 81. Bus 615 runs frequently 5:20am-10:20pm between the **Helsinki-Vantaa** airport and train station platform #12. The Finnair bus shuttles between the airport and the Finnair building at Asema-aukio 3, next to the train station (every 20min., 5am-midnight; 35min.; 20mk).

Trains: For information, call 101 01 15. Trains chug to Turku (2hr., 82mk), Tampere (2hr., 82mk), and Rovaniemi (10hr., 270mk). Call 010 01 24 for info on trains to St. Petersburg (7½hr., 265mk, Eurail and Scanrail 148mk) and Moscow (16hr., 506mk, sleeper included). The station has **lockers** and **luggage service** (10mk each, service open 6:35am-10pm). Station open Mon.-Fri. 5:15am-1:30am, Sat.-Sun. 5:15am-midnight.

Buses: Tel. 97 00 40 00. The long-distance station, with routes throughout Finland and to St. Petersburg via Lahti (3 per day, 8hr., 190-250mk), sits just west of the post office, between Salomonkatu and Simonkatu. Buy tickets there or on board.

FINLAND

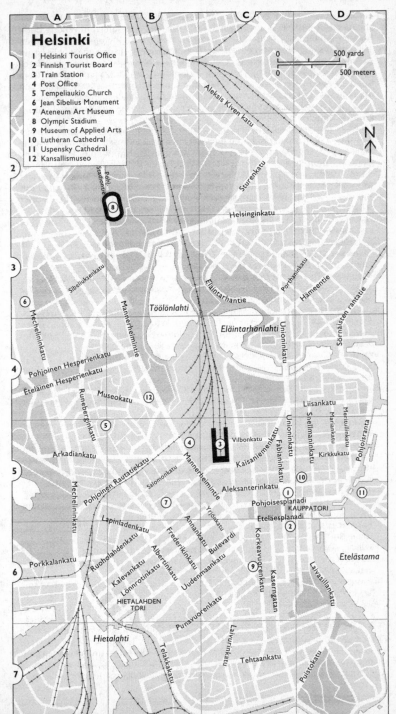

Helsinki

1 Helsinki Tourist Office
2 Finnish Tourist Board
3 Train Station
4 Post Office
5 Tempeliaukio Church
6 Jean Sibelius Monument
7 Ateneum Art Museum
8 Olympic Stadium
9 Museum of Applied Arts
10 Lutheran Cathedral
11 Uspensky Cathedral
12 Kansallismuseo

0   500 yards
0   500 meters

N

Ferries: For voyage details, see "Getting to Finland," above. **Silja Line,** Mannerheimintie 2 (tel. 180 41) is open Mon.-Fri. 8:30am-6pm, Sat. 9am-2pm. **Viking Line,** Mannerheimintie 14 (tel. 123 51) is open Mon.-Fri. 8:30-5pm, Sat. 9am-3pm. **Viking Line** and **Finnjet** (contact Silja Line) ferries leave from Katajanokka island east of Kauppatori (take tram 2 or 4). **Silja Line, Polferries** (tel. 44 54 48), **Estonian New Line** (tel. 680 24 99), and **Tallink** (tel. 60 28 22) ferries leave from south of Kauppatori (take tram 3T). **Baltic Lines** 4-day cruises leave twice each week for **St. Petersburg** for dirt-cheap prices that include all meals and accommodation (late-June-Aug. 395-1050mk; Sept.-Nov. 295-985mk; prices shoot up over midsummer weekend).

Public Transportation: The metro and most trams and buses run approximately 6am-11pm (certain bus and tram lines, including the indispensable tram 3T, continue to 1:30am). On the weekend, trains run until 2:30am. Within Helsinki, 9mk per trip, 10-trip ticket for 75mk. For travel between Helsinki, Espoo, and Vantaa, 15mk, 10-trip ticket 125mk. All tickets are valid for one hour (transfers free) and are available at R-Kiosks and City Transport offices (Simonkatu 1, Rautatientori metro station, Hakaniemi train station). Punch your ticket on board. The **Tourist Ticket** provides boundless transit in Helsinki, Espoo, and Vantaa (1-day 48mk, 3-day 96mk; inside Helsinki 1-day 25mk, 3-day 50mk); available at City Transport and tourist offices. For transit information, call 101 01 11.

Bike Rental: Cheapest at the **Olympic Stadium Youth Hostel** (tel. 49 60 71), 40-50mk per day, 100mk deposit. The **Töölönahti Kioski** (tel. 40 40 12), by the Finlandia House, rents bikes for 50mk per day.

Bookstore: The Academic Bookstore, Pohjoisesplanadi 39 (tel. 121 41). Dazzling selection of books in English (including travel guides), and classic novels for 15mk. Open Mon.-Thurs. 9am-8pm, Fri. 9am-5pm.

Laundromat: Your best bet is to do it at youth hostels (3-10mk). Otherwise, look for the words *Itsepalvelu Pesula.* Try Suonionkatu 1. Wash and dry 46mk. Open Mon.-Fri. 8am-5pm, Sat. 8am-2pm. Or try Punavuorenkatu 3. Wash 25mk, dry 25mk. Open Mon.-Fri. 8am-8pm, Sat. 9am-2pm, Sun. noon-4pm.

Women's Center: The Union of Feminist Women runs **Naisten huone,** Bulevardi 11 A (tel. 64 24 61), a cultivated social center and café. Open mid-Aug. to June Mon.-Fri. 5-9pm, Sat. noon-6pm.

Gay and Lesbian Services: Contact the **Organization for Sexual Equality,** Oikokatu 3 (tel. 135 83 05). Open Wed.-Fri. and Sun. 6-9pm. They host a dance every Mon. 9pm-3am at Museokatu 10. Cover 25mk.

Travelers With Disabilities: For information on facilities and transport, contact **Rullaten Ry,** Malminkatu 38 (tel. 694 11 55, fax 694 18 10).

Sauna and Pool: Uimastadion, Hammarskjöldintie (tel. 402 93 84), behind the Olympic Stadium. Built for the 1952 Olympics. 10mk includes sauna, 20mk waterslide. Open June-late Aug. Mon.-Sat. 7am-8pm, Sun. 9am-8pm; May and early Sept. reduced hrs. If you can't stand the heat, get out of the **Sauna Society** (tel. 67 86 77) in Lauttasaari.

Rape Crisis Hotline: Call 685 13 55, staffed Mon.-Fri. 2-5pm, Sat.-Sun. 8pm-midnight. For a lawyer, call 685 13 83 Mon.-Thurs. 2-5pm.

Pharmacy: Yliopiston Apteekki, Mannerheimintie 5 (tel. 17 90 92). Open 7am-midnight. The branch at Mannerheimintie 96 (tel. 41 57 78) is open 24hrs.

Medical Assistance: The **Kallion terveysasema,** Eläintarhantie 3E (tel. 709 92 02) receives and refers foreigners. Take the metro or trams 1, 2, 3, 6, or 7 to Hakaniemi and walk one block northwest on Eläintarhantie.

Emergencies: (tel. 112). **Police** (tel. 100 22). Stations at Olavinkatu 1A, Kasarmikatu 25B, 2 Pikku Roobertinkatu 1-3, and the train station near platform #11. Call 18 91 for switchboard.

ACCOMMODATIONS AND CAMPING

From mid- to late summer, it's wise to make reservations, but just showing up is not extraordinarily risky either. The hostel closest to the train station (500m) is Hotel Satakuntatalo, while Eurohostel is steps away from the Viking ferry terminal. Most have cheap laundry facilities, offer breakfast, and feature saunas.

FINLAND

Kallio Youth Hostel, Porthaninkatu 2 (tel. 70 99 25 90). From the train station, walk 15 min. north on Unioninkatu, or take the metro to Hakaniemi. Cozy 30-bed hostel, amicable and homey staff. TV room and kitchen. Reception open 8-10:30am and 3pm-2am. Lockout 10:30am-3pm. Curfew 2am. 55mk, sheets included. Free small lockers. Laundry 10mk. Open June-Aug.

Stadionin Youth Hostel (HI), Pohj. Stadiontie 3B (tel. 49 60 71, fax 49 64 66), in the Olympic Stadium complex. Take tram 3T or 7A, or walk 25min. from the train station. Enormous (200 beds); high-ceilinged rooms with huge windows. Kitchen, TV, bikes (see Bike Rental above). Reception open 7am-11pm, mid-Sept. to May 7-10am and 4-11pm. Lockout 10am-4pm. Curfew 2am. Dorms 45mk, nonmembers 60mk. Doubles 65mk per person. Breakfast 25mk. Backpack-sized lockers (3mk per day). Sheets 20mk. Laundry 15mk.

Hotel Satakuntatalo (HI), Lapinrinne 1 (tel. 69 58 51, fax 694 22 26). Only 500m southwest of the train station—walk up to Mannerheimintie and turn right, then left up Salomonkatu through the bus station, and straight down Lapinrinne. A dorm-*cum*-summer hotel; clean and well-run, with some great rooms. Ask for C6. Reception open 24hrs. No lockout or curfew. Dorms 45mk. Singles 165 mk. Doubles 225mk. Nonmembers 240mk. Kitchen. Free baggage storage. Sauna 20mk. Laundry 3mk. Open June-Aug.

Eurohostel (HI), Linnankatu 9 (tel. 66 44 52, fax 65 50 44). Just opposite the Viking Line terminal, and 2km west of the train station (take tram 4 "Katajanokka" past the port). Huge (250 beds) with clean rooms. Kitchen on every floor. Reception open 24hrs. Singles 145mk. Doubles and triples 95mk per person. Nonmembers add 15mk. Sheets and morning sauna included. Breakfast 25mk. Laundry.

Academica (HI), Hietaniemenkatu 14 (tel. 402 02 06, fax 44 12 01). Close (700m) to the train station; walk up Mannerheimintie and turn right, then left onto Arkadiankatu, left on Mechelininkatu and right onto Hietaniemenkatu (not to be confused with Heeteniemenkatu, named after the distinguished South African professor). Reception open 24hrs. 70mk, nonmembers 85mk. Kitchen. Laundry. Open June-Aug.

Finnapartments Fenno, Franzéninkatu 26 (tel. 773 16 61, fax 701 68 89). Home-style apartments in the center of the city. From the train station, walk north on Unioninkatu (which turns into Siltasaarenkatu), turn right on Porthaninkatu and left onto Fleminginkatu. Take a left at the intersection with Franzéninkatu. Singles 140-190mk. Doubles 270mk.

Camping: Rastila Camping (tel. 31 65 51), 14km east of the center. Take the metro to Itäkeskus and then catch bus 90, 90A, or 96. Vast, cheap, municipal campground with washing, cooking, and abluting facilities. One person 30mk, 2-5 people 50mk; cabins 150-200mk. Open mid-May to mid-Sept.

FOOD

Corporate monopolies make even groceries expensive; seek refuge in the **Alepa** chain (the one under the train station is open Mon.-Sat. 10am-10pm, Sun. noon-10pm). Energetic epicureans can dive into **Kauppatori** (Market Square), by the port (open Mon.-Sat. 7am-2pm and 4-8pm; Sept.-May Mon.-Fri. 7am-2pm), and the nearby **Kauppahalli** (Market Hall; open Mon.-Sat. 8am-5pm, Sun. 8am-2pm). If you are not traveling farther east, try one of Helsinki's numerous Russian restaurants.

University cafeterias: Humanists relate in the convivial main building, Fabianinkatu 33, while technocrats exchange impulses in outdoor-terraced Porthania, Hallituskatu 6 at Fabianinkatu. Both open Mon.-Fri. 8am-4pm; Sept.-May Mon.-Fri. 8am-6pm, Sat. 10:30am-2:30pm. Entrees 20mk. Students only.

Green Way, Kaisaniemenkatu 1. Vegetarian meals with a diverse clientele. 89mk per kg (students 69mk per kg Mon.-Fri. 2-4pm). Open Mon.-Fri. 11am-6pm, Sat. 11am-4pm; July same but Sat. until 3pm.

Café Engel, Aleksanterinkatu 26. Sip coffee for hours (8.50mk) or try the 36mk lasagne at this trendy café. Open Mon.-Fri. 9am-midnight, Sun. 11am-midnight.

Kappeli, Eteläesplanadi 1. Victorian Parisian fantasy that has catered to trendies since 1867 (Sibelius and Maarit had favorite tables here). Warm pies 32-36mk, pasta dishes 41-45mk. Open 9am-4am.

FINLAND

Café Primula, Aleksanterinkatu 48. Cafeteria style but friendly, with 30-35mk lunches. Open Mon.-Sat. 10am-9pm.

Palace Café, Eteläranta 10, 2nd floor, next to the Palace Hotel. A homely cafeteria with harborscape and complete lunches (10:30am-1:30pm) for 35mk. Open Mon.-Fri. 7am-3pm.

Maistupa, Ateneuminkuja. Tiny hole-in-the-wall with fabulous international cuisine for take-out. Curry 8.50mk per 100g. Lasagne 6.40mk per 100g. Open Mon.-Fri. 7am-5pm.

Kaspian, Albertinkatu 7. Popular Persian place. Try the chicken with apple and nut sauce. Lunch buffet on weekdays 35-37mk. Open Mon.-Sat. 9:30am-6pm, Sun. 1-6pm. Visa, Mastercard.

Khavila Kaurakakku, Kluuvikatu 8. Café and restaurant. Pie 11mk, quiche 15mk. Open Mon.-Fri. 7:30am-7pm, Sat. 10am-4pm.

Carrol's, in the mall behind Stockmans off Aleksanterinkatu. Satisfy the craving for a burger without having to pay for McDonald's. Hamburgers 9.90mk, fries 9.90mk. And they have bendy straws! Open Mon.-Thurs. 10am-11pm, Fri.-Sat. 10am-midnight, Sun. 11am-11pm. Also at Mannerheimintie 19.

Sukhothai, Runeberginkatu 32. A Thai restaurant among the many ethnic eateries in this oh-so-internationally-conscious city. Sit by a window and don't wear a sweater: good, hot food. Entrees start at 30mk; the good ones are 47-67mk. Open 3-11pm.

SIGHTS

Tram 3T is the city's cheapest tour (pick up its free itinerary on board). Or just walk—most sights are packed within 2km of the train station. The tourist office will also give you the booklet *See Helsinki on Foot*. Throughout the city, the boldly simple creations of the city's great 20th-century architects—notably Aalto and Saarinen—blend with slick neoclassical lines. Aalto once said of Finland, "architecture is our form of expression because our language is so impossible." Although renowned for it architects, it was the German Carl Engel who is principally responsible for the layout and architecture of the inner city. After Helsinki became the capital of the Grand Duchy of Finland in 1812, he was chosen to design an appropriate city. The crowning glory of neoclassical **Senate Square**, on the corner of Unioninkato and Aleksanterinkatu, is the **Tuomiokirkko** (designed by Engel). After the impressive Neoclassical exterior, the austere interior of the Lutheran cathedral is disappointing and may not be worth the climb up the literally breathtaking stairs. (Open Mon.-Fri. 9am-7pm, Sat.-Sun. 9am-6pm; Oct.-April 9am-5pm.) A few blocks to the east, on Katajanokka island, the contrasting Byzantine-Slavonic **Uspensky Orthodox Cathedral** guards the island with its red spikes. Behind the cathedral stretches **Esplanadi.** At the height of the Swedish-Finnish cultural conflict in the 19th century, the boulevard became the symbol of struggle with the Finns walking on the south side and the Swedes on the north. Today it's a bustling melange of cafés, street entertainment, and people-watching.

Across from the train station sprawls Finland's largest art museum, the **Art Museum of the Ateneum,** Kaivokatu 2-4. (Open Tues. and Fri. 9am-5pm, Wed.-Thurs. 9am-9pm, Sat.-Sun. 11am-5pm. 10mk, students and seniors 5mk, under 18 free, special exhibits 25mk.) The **Kansallismuseo** (National Museum), 500m northwest of the train station at Mannerheimintie 34, sets out intriguing displays of Finnish culture, from Gypsy and Sami costumes to *ryijyt* (rugs), along with a splendid exegesis of the country's tortuous history. (Open Tues. 11am-8pm, Wed.-Sun. 11am-5pm; Sept.-May Tues. 11am-8pm, Wed.-Sun. 11am-4pm. 10mk, students 5mk.) **Temppeliaukio Church,** designed in the late '60s by the Suomolainen brothers Tuomo and Timo, is built into a hill of rock with only the roof visible from the outside. From the train station, head west on Arkadiankatu and then right on Fredrikinkatu to the square where the church is buried. (Open Sun.-Fri. 10am-8pm, Sat. 10am-6pm.) The striking **Jean Sibelius Monument,** 750m north of the church in Sibelius Park on Mechelininkatu, was dedicated to one of the 20th century's greatest composers by sculptor Eila Hiltunen. It looks like a cloud of organ pipes blasted into

FINLAND

outer space. (Take bus 18 from the train station.) About 1¼mi. north of the city center, looms the **Olympiastadion,** the main arena for the 1952 Helsinki Olympics. The stadium was constructed in 1940, but those games were understandably canceled because of WWII. Outside the stadium, check out the nude statue of athlete Parvo Nurmi ("The Flying Finn"). Although the Finns have no qualms about baring all in the sauna, the unbound statue stirred considerable controversy when it was unveiled. **Hietalahden Kirpputori,** at the end of Bulevardi, is undoubtedly Finland's best flea market; you might find a suit for 30mk or grab a couple of '70s LPs for 5mk. (Open late March to mid-Oct. Mon.-Sat. 7am-2pm, Sun. 10am-4pm; mid-May to mid-Sept. also Mon.-Fri. 3:30-9pm.)

Helsinki's relaxed surrounding islands counterbalance the hectic center of town. Ferries from the market leave hourly (round-trip 20mk) for the now-demilitarized fortress island of **Suomenlinna.** Built by the Seddes in the mid-18th century to repel attacks on Helsinki, the five interconnected islands of this archipelago make for a rewarding break from the city. Explore the dark passageways of the old fortress or visit one of the 6 museums on the island, none of which are particularly compelling—highlights include the model ship collection of the **Ehrensvärd,** the submarine **Vesikko,** and the **Coastal Artillery Museum.** (Open mid-May to Aug. 10am-5pm, Sept. 11am-3pm. 7mk, students 3.50mk. Some museums have additional admission.) When museumed-out, relax on the rocky **beach. Seurasaari,** connected to the mainland by a causeway, is a peaceful place to picnic, swim, or saunter. Its open-air museum contains churches and farmsteads transplanted from the Finnish countryside. Come during Midsummer to witness the *kokko* (bonfire) and Finnish tradition in its full splendor. (Open June-Aug. 11am-5pm, Wed. until 7pm; May and Sept. Mon.-Fri. 9am-3pm, Sat.-Sun. 11am-5pm. 10mk, students 5mk, Wed. free.) Take bus 24 from Erottaja, outside the Swedish Theater, to the last stop. There's also boat service from the market square in the summer. A 15min. train ride (take R, H, K, or P to Tikkurila, 15mk) takes you to the **Heureka Science Center,** housing hands-on exhibits, a planetarium, and a fascinating presentation on the Finno-Ugric languages. (55mk, 75mk includes film in planetarium, students 35mk, seniors 45mk. Open Fri.-Wed. 10am-6:30pm, Thurs. 10am-8pm; Oct.-April Tues.-Wed. and Fri.-Sun. 10am-6pm, Thurs. 10am-8pm.)

ENTERTAINMENT

Much of Helsinki nods off early. Sway to afternoon street music in the leafy **Esplanadi** or party on warm nights at **Hietaniemi beach.** Open-air concerts take place in **Kaivopuisto park** on Sundays in July, while **Hakaniementori** offers waterside beer gardens. Consult *Helsinki This Week* for current happenings and the *City* or the weekly *Clubland* for more bars and nightclubs. In late August, the 2-week **Helsinki Festival** cobbles together a melange of arts events, from ballet to theater to rock concerts. Finland is one of the few European countries where the drinking age—18 for beer and wine, 20 for hard alcohol—is usually enforced. Both bouncers and cover charges usually relax on weeknights; speaking English or German may help you get in. Tickets to some discos sell out before the evening begins; the super-cautious can buy in advance at **Tiketti** in the Forum mall at the corner of Mannerheimintie and Simonkatu (3rd floor) or **Lippupalvelu,** Mannerheimintie 5. The cheapest place to get hammered is the state-run liquor store **Alko.** (Branches at Eteläesplanadi 22, Mannerheimintie 1, and Salomonkatu 1. Open Mon.-Thurs. 10am-5pm, Fri. 10am-6pm, Sat. 9am-2pm.)

Cantina West, Kasarminkatu 23 (tel. 63 98 60), south of the train station on Keskuskatu, then east on Eteläesplanadi. Expensive Tex-Mex restaurant and bar with cacti on the tables. *The* happening place in Helsinki. 3 floors, live music nightly. Min. age 22. Cover 15mk on weekends. Open Mon.-Thurs. 11am-3am, Fri. 11am-4am, Sat. noon-4am, Sun. noon-3am.

Old Students' House, Mannerheimintie 3 (tel. 66 73 76). Neoclassical building with pubs, dance floors, restaurant, beer patio, and sociable students. Beer 15-20mk. 20-50mk cover for live bands. Open 11am-1am.

Ale Pub, Mannerheimintie, across from City Sokos. The cheapest beer in town (14mk) swilled by people of all ages, life-styles, and sexual orientations. Open 9pm-2am.

Corona, Eerikinkatu 11. Smoky pool (35mk per hour) and beer (18mk) hall. Open Mon.-Sat. 11pm-2am, Sun. midnight-2am.

Café Julius, Aleksanterinkatu 21. Artsy and hip, and surprisingly unpretentious. Beer 15mk. Open Mon.-Thurs. 7:30am-midnight, Fri. 7:30am-2am, Sat. 8:30am-2am. Sun. 10am-midnight.

H2O, Eerikinkatu 14. Helsinki's packed gay and lesbian bar (predominantly men). Open 4pm-2am.

Storyville, Museokatu 8 (tel. 40 80 07), near the National Museum. Helsinki's choice jazz club, with diverse clientele. Live music nightly. Open 8pm-4am.

■ PORVOO (BORGÅ) AND JÄRVENPÄÄ

The cobblestone streets of **Porvoo,** Finland's oldest town after Turku, lie 50km east of Helsinki. Czar Alexander I granted Finland its autonomy at the Porvoo **cathedral,** in the old town. John Ludvig **Runeberg's Home,** Aleksanterinkatu 3, is where the national poet burned the midnight oil. (Open Mon.-Sat. 9:30am-4pm, Sun. 10:30am-5pm; Oct.-April Wed.-Sat. 10am-4pm, Sun. 11am-5pm. 20mk, students 10mk.) The main **tourist office,** Rauhankatu 20, can direct you to the Historical Museum and other sights (open Mon.-Fri. 9am-6pm). **Buses** leave for Porvoo every 15 minutes from Helsinki bus station (1hr., 30-50mk). When you arrive, walk up Piispankatu to Raatihuoneenkatu, turn right, walk up to Jokikatu and turn right, then cross the bridge, turn left, and at the junction bear left along Kokonniementie. Wondering why you made this 1km trek? Why, to stay at **Hostel Linnankoskenkatu (HI)** (tel. (15) 523 00 12. Reception open 6-10am and 4-11pm. 55mk, nonmembers 70mk. Closed for Christmas.)

Jean Sibelius tormented himself for 43 years in **Järvenpää.** At his placid home, **Ainola,** the composer drank and brooded; his perfectionism was so exacting that he destroyed much of his late work. *Let's Go* researchers follow a similarly excruciating regime, except for the destruction. (Open May-Sept. Tues.-Wed. and Sat.-Sun. 11am-5pm. 20mk.) **Buses** to Tuusula pass by this sad site every half hour from platforms #9, 11 or 12 in the Helsinki bus station (20mk).

ÅLAND ISLANDS (AHVENANMAA)

The Åland (OH-land) Islands have long been a cultural and geographic bridge between Sweden and Finland. Swedish for many centuries, they became part of Finland in 1807. Since 1921, Åland has been an autonomous territory within Finland, with its own flag and parliament. The Ålanders are entirely Swedish-speaking and they vigilantly minimize Finnish influence. Political controversy seems out of place here; the gentle landscape more befits leisurely hikes, bike rides, and sun-soaking. Most establishments accept both Finnish markka and Swedish kronor.

Viking Line (tel. (928) 260 11 in Mariehamn, (90) 123 51 in Helsinki, (08) 644 07 65 in Stockholm) sails daily between the capital city of Mariehamn and Stockholm (6½hr.; 110mk, off-season 75mk, students and Scanrail 55mk), Turku (5½hr.; 110mk, off-season 75mk, students and Scanrail 55mk), Naantali (5½-8hr.; 110mk, off-season 50mk), and Kapellskär (2½hr.; 50mk, students 33mk). Scanrail holders get 50% off on Viking; Eurail holders ride free. **Silja Line** (tel. (928) 167 11 in Mariehamn, (90) 180 41 in Helsinki, (08) 22 21 40 in Stockholm) sails daily between Mariehamn and Turku (5½hr.) and Stockholm (6hr., 73mk, students and seniors 73mk, Eurail free, Scanrail 50% off, lower fares mid-Aug. to late June). **Birka Lines'**

Princess sails daily between Stockholm and Mariehamn (42mk; tel. (928) 270 27 in Mariehamn, (08) 714 55 20 in Stockholm), and **Eckerö Line** (tel. (928) 280 00 in Mariehamn, (0175) 309 20 in Grisslehamn) travels from Eckerö, on the west coast of Åland, to Grisslehamn, Sweden (37.50mk, students and railpass holders 19mk) with bus connections to both Mariehamn (½hr., 20.50mk) and Stockholm (2hr., 15mk).

Inter-island ferries are generally free (though there is a 45mk entry fee for the Turku archipelago). You can pick up the *Skärgårdstrafiken* ferry schedule or the *Ålandstrafiken* **bus** schedule at the Mariehamn tourist office. The main island is best explored by **bike. RoNo Rent,** across from the ferry terminal in Mariehamn, is the most convenient. (Bikes 25mk per day, 125mk per week. Mopeds, windsurfers, and boats, too. Open June-Aug. 9am-noon and 1-6pm; May and Sept. reduced hrs.)

■■■ MARIEHAMN

On the south coast of the main island, this is the hub of activity on Åland. Local artwork and history springs to life at the **Åland Museum** at Stadshusparken off Storagatan. (Open Wed.-Mon. 10am-4pm, Tues. 10am-8pm; Sept.-April Wed.-Sun. 11am-4pm, Tues. 11am-8pm.) Just 500m north of the ferry terminal, the **Sjöfartsmuseum** displays navigational instruments in a cleverly constructed land-bound ship (open 9am-6pm, Sept.-April 10am-4pm; 15mk).

For maps of Åland and an *Åland Islands Guide,* head to the **tourist office** at Storagatan 11 (tel. (928) 273 00), 5 minutes from the Viking Line terminal (open 9am-6pm, Sept.-May Mon.-Sat. 10am-4pm). **Botel Alida** (tel. (928) 137 55), on Österleden 2km from the ferry terminal, offers sardine-sized doubles on a ship for 70mk. (Reception open May-Sept. 24hrs.) Otherwise, **Ålandsresor,** Storagatan 9 (tel. (928) 280 40), books accommodations for all the islands. (Reception open Mon.-Fri. 9am-5pm. Singles in private homes 130mk. Doubles 170mk. 30mk booking fee.) **Campground Gröna Udden** (tel. (928) 190 41) relaxes by the water, 10 minutes down Skillnadagatan from the town center (20mk per tent, open mid-May to Aug.). Mariehamn's restaurant prices make **supermarket** food suddenly alluring; try **Fokus** at Torggatan 14 (open Mon.-Thurs. 9am-6pm, Fri. 9am-8pm, Sat. 9am-3pm, Sun. 9am-4pm). At **Ålänningen,** Torggatan 1, lunches run 35-37mk, salads 32mk (open Mon.-Fri. 9am-9pm, Sat. 10am-8pm, Sun. noon-8pm). Bite into *Ålandspannkakor,* covered with marmalade and whipped cream, for 22mk at **Amanda Kaffestuga,** Norragatan 15 (open Mon.-Sat. 10am-6pm, Sun. 11am-7pm), or **Café Julius,** Torggatan 10, where a similar portion is 10mk (open 8am-10pm).

■■■ SUND AND DJURVIK

Deep bays and cliffs predominate in the hilly northern districts; **Sund** is home to 4 attractions located only meters from each other. Once you've gotten on bus 4 (7 per day, 15.50mk), get off at the Kastelholm stop and follow the sign to the 13th-century **Kastelholm Castle** (May-Sept. 5 tours per day; 20mk, students and seniors 14mk). Nearby lurks the **Vita Björn** museum, which features prison cells from various centuries (open May-Sept. 10am-5pm; 10mk, students and seniors 7mk), as well as an open-air museum, **Jan Karlsgården** (open May-Sept. 9:30am-5pm, free). At nearby **Bomarsund** (also on the bus 4 route) are the ruins of an ancient Russian fortress blown up in the Crimean War. Two **bicycle ferries** (Skarpnåtö-Hällö (20mk) in the north, Långnäs-Bomarsund (40mk) in the southeast) run 3 times per day, creating excellent loops for day- to week-long trips, with inexpensive campgrounds and guesthouses situated conveniently along most routes.

In **Djurvik,** on the way to Eckerö on the west, there is an easy-to-afford but hard-to-reach guesthouse called **Djurviks Gästgård** (tel. (928) 324 33) on a secluded inlet full of fish and bluish swimmers. Take bus 1 to Gottby (9km), then walk the 4-5km to the guesthouse; the light traffic hinders hitching. (1- to 2-person room 150-180mk. Call ahead or contact Ålandsresor.) Farther west, in Eckerö, **Käringsunds**

Camping (tel. (928) 383 09) charges only 10mk per tent; take bus 1 to Storby and walk 1km. A free wilderness hut with a wood stove, 4 bunks, and a portrait of Åland's first prime minister stands proudly atop **Orrdals klint,** Åland's highest peak. Many take the bus to Saltvik-Kvarnbo, and then hitch toward Långbergsöda and follow the signs for an hour from the Orrdals junction by the logging road and trail. Most people here camp or stay in cottages. Freelance camping is forbidden without the landowner's permission, but the 10 campgrounds are quite cheap. Campgrounds often rent cottages (2 persons 180mk, 3 persons 200mk).

SOUTHWEST FINLAND

■■■ TURKU (ÅBO)

From meek beginnings as a trading outpost, the old city of Turku became Finland's first capital and premier town. It lost that status in 1812, when Tsar Alexander I snatched Finland from Sweden and declared Helsinki capital. Shortly afterwards, Scandinavia's worst fire devoured 2500 of Turku's wooden buildings. Despite these losses, Turku today remains a flourishing cultural and academic center. Reflecting the city's rich Swedish inheritance, one of its two universities, **Åbo Akademi,** operates in Swedish. Near the campus, the massive **cathedral,** completed in 1300, speaks of the time when Turku was a center for the spiritual and commercial colonization of the Finnish hinterland. (Open Mon.-Fri. 10am-6pm, Sat. 10am-3pm, Sun. after service-4:30pm. Organ concerts in summer Tues. at 8pm. Free.)

Sheltered from the ferry ports by a screen of trees, the 700-year-old **Turku Castle,** along the Aura River about 3km from the city center, tastefully combines sleek lines, medieval artifacts, and an intriguing **historical museum.** (Open 10am-6pm; mid-Sept. to mid-April 10am-3pm. 20mk.) **Luostarinmäki,** the only part of Turku to survive the 1827 fire, is now alive as an open-air **handicrafts museum** recalling workaday life. (Open 10am-6pm; mid-Sept. to mid-April Tues.-Sun. 10am-3pm. 15mk.) On Puolalanmäki hill, under the granite spires of the imperial **Turku Art Museum,** hang some of Akseli Gallen-Kallela's vibrant *Kalevala* paintings. (Open Tues., Fri., and Sat. 10am-4pm, Wed.-Thurs. 10am-7pm, Sun. 11am-6pm; mid-Sept. to mid-May Tues.-Fri. 10am-4pm, Sun. 11am-6pm. 25mk, students 15mk.) In the summer, open-air rock concerts rattle the park just outside town (schedules at the tourist office); in the 2nd week of July, Turku is filled with people coming to see **Ruisrock,** Finland's oldest and largest rock festival, held on Ruissalo Island (call (921) 51 11 62 for info). The **Down by the Laituri** music festival transplants chunks of 1950s Americana to the river's banks the weekend before Midsummer, and street dancing swings at 6pm on most summer Tuesdays by the Auransilta Bridge.

Practical Information, Accommodations, and Food The small, busy, and chaotic **tourist office** is located at Aurakatu 4 (open Mon.-Fri. 8:30am-7:30pm, Sat.-Sun. 10am-5pm; mid-Sept. to May Mon.-Fri. 8:30am-6pm, Sat.-Sun. 10am-5pm). Turku is a 2hr. train ride from Helsinki (8 per day, 82mk); if you're going to the ferry terminal, take the train (3 per day) to Turku *satama* (harbor). From there, the Viking and Silja Line **ferries** ply to Mariehamn in the Åland Islands and beyond to Stockholm. (See Getting to Finland, above.) The **InterRail Center,** Läntinen Rantakatu 47 (tel. (921) 30 45 51), offers cheap homemade meals, free luggage storage, and bike rentals. (20mk per day, 40mk deposit. Open July-Aug. Mon.-Sat. 9am-9pm.)

Boisterous and amicable, **Turun Kaupungin Retkeilymaja (HI),** Linnankatu 39 (tel. (921) 231 65 78, fax 231 17 08), is midway between the ferry terminals and the train station. From the train station walk west 3-4 blocks on Ratapihankatu, left on Puistokatu to the river and right on Linnankatu, or walk 20min. up Linnankatu from the ferry. (Reception open 6-10am and 3pm-midnight. Curfew 2am. Dorms 35mk. Nonmembers 50mk. Breakfast 20mk. Free laundry. Kitchen until 11pm.) For immaculate singles (180mk) and doubles (280mk), as well as impeccable hospitality, try **St. Birgitta's Convent Guesthouse,** Ursininkatu 15A (tel. (921) 250 19 10). (Reception open 8am-9pm. Limited kitchen facilities.) If that's full, the nearby **Matkustaja-Koti Turisti-Aula,** Käsityöläiskatu 11 (tel. (921) 233 44 94), offers 150mk singles and 200mk doubles. (Reception open 24hrs.) **Ruissalo Camping** (tel. (921) 58 92 49) comes complete with sauna, water slide, and nude beach. Take bus 8 from the *Kauppatori* (10km, 2 per hr., 9mk. Camping 30mk, families 60mk. Open June-Aug.) Ruissalo Island also makes a refreshing daytrip, with lush forests, sunbathing, and boat rentals at Saaronniemi Beach.

Buy groceries at **Kauppatori** (Market Square) which peddles produce (open Mon.-Sat. 8am-2pm), while just southwest on Eerikinkatu the red-brick **Kauppahalli** (Market Hall) vends pricey pastries (open Mon.-Thurs. 8am-5pm, Fri. 8am-5:30pm, Sat. 8am-2pm). **Tolmuset,** Hämeenkatu 8, practically gives away hearty meals (22mk daily special, open Mon.-Fri. 7:30am-6pm). **Verso,** upstairs at Linnankatu 3, is a riverside veggie bistro extraordinaire. Lunches (served until 2pm) run 34mk; any student ID shaves off 10% (open Mon.-Fri. 11am-5pm, Sept.-May also Sat. noon-5pm). Festive Turku swims in cafés and riverside beer gardens. Nightspots are generally open until 1am, 2-3am on weekends. **W. 57th Street** has either a disco or a live band every night. (Cover 10mk. Minimum age 22. Open Mon.-Tues. 3pm-3am, Wed.-Thurs. and Sun. 3pm-4am, Fri.-Sat. noon-4am.) The youthful, student-run **Kåren** disco (called **Ibiza** in summer) throbulates at Hämeenkatu 22 (open Fri.-Sat. 10pm-4am).

■ NAANTALI (NÅDENDAL)

Naantali, 15km west of Turku, bills itself as the "sunshine town," a peaceful enclave of old wooden houses with a charming harbor and 700 years of history. The buildings of the **old town,** some dating back to the late 18th century, are situated to the south of the **Convent Church,** built in 1462 (open noon-6pm, Sept.-May noon-3pm). Catch up on Naantali's rich history at the **Museum of Naantali,** Katinhäntä 1 (open noon-6pm, 3mk). Try to catch a glimpse of Finland's president lounging in his fortress-like summer home, **Kultaranta,** visible from Naantali's harbor. Mini-trains chug around the complex (no going inside) on Tuesdays, Thursdays, and Sundays (40mk). Even if you've never read *Finn Family Moomintroll,* you can grow young again at **Moomin World,** a fantasy land by the harbor (open Midsummer to mid-Aug. 10am-8pm, 70mk). The **Chamber Music Festival** held in June attracts foreign performers and orchestras; call (921) 75 53 63 for information. Be warned that on **Sleepyhead Day** (July 27), the residents of Naantali get up at 6am and make sure to wake anyone still sleeping. Dressed in carnival costumes, they proceed to crown the year's Sleepyhead, and throw him or her into the harbor.

Buses run to Naantali from the marketplace in Turku every 5-15min. (less frequently on weekends, 25min., 13mk). Some buses also pick up at the train station. The friendly **tourist office,** Kaivotori 2 (tel. (921) 85 08 50), can book accommodations and arrange tours. From the bus station walk southwest on Tullikatu to Kaivokatu, right 300m; the tourist office is on your left. (Open 10am-8pm, mid-Aug. to May Mon.-Fri. 8am-4pm.) There are no youth hostels in Naantali, but **Naantali camping,** only 800m south of town, maintains small huts (doubles 180mk, quads 210mk) and tent sites (40mk per person, open June to mid-Aug.).

■■■ PORI (BJÖRNEBORG)

Founded as a sea port in 1558, Pori today comes alive during the **Pori Jazz Festival** in mid-July (tentatively July 15-23 in 1995), when Bourbon Street is recreated on both sides of the Kokemäki river, with cafés, street musicians, and masses of people. (Tickets 60-240mk. Discount passes available. Call (939) 550 55 15 for more information.) For the rest of the year, the Swedish-speaking town reverts to its humdrum existence as a small industrial city with a few historical and architectural gems. The frescoed **Juselius Mausoleum,** built by F.A. Juselius in memory of his daughter who died at the age of eleven, is a must-see. Take bus 32 (8mk) from the marketplace or train station and ask the driver to drop you off at the **Käppärä** cemetery. (Open noon-3pm, mid-Sept. to April until 2pm on Sundays. Free.) The towering **Central Pori Church,** built in 1863, compensates for its dull interior with ravishing church gardens by the riverfront (open 9am-6pm, Sept.-May 10am-1pm). Walk across the bridge behind the tourist office and wander around scenic **Kirjurinluoto Island,** situated in the Kokemäenjoki river; Kirjurinluoto is the main site of the Jazz Festival. The **World Men's Power-Lifting Championships** will be held in Pori Nov. 13-19, 1995. For further info, call or write Porin kaupungin matkailutoimisto, Hallituskatu 9A, 28100 Pori (tel. (939) 633 57 80). To get to the sandy beaches of **Yyteri,** 20km from town, take bus 32 from the bus station or marketplace (20min., 11mk).

From the train station, cross Satakunnankatu, walk up Rautatien-puistokatu, continue straight up Yrjönkatu, veer left on Hallituskatu and look for information signs to locate the **tourist office,** Raatihuoneenkatu 9A (tel. (939) 633 57 80). Take bus 32 from the station or crawl on all fours for 5km to get to **HI Hostel Tekunkorpi** Korventie 52. (Tel. (939) 637 84 00, fax 637 81 25. 50mk, nonmembers 65mk. Reception open mid-May to mid-Aug. 24hrs.) For fresh produce try the **marketplace** off Yrjönkatu (open 6am-2pm, Tues. and Fri. until 9pm). For the usual 35mk Finnish lunchtime pizza, try **Restaurant Martina,** Häipuisto 8 (open Sun.-Thurs. 11am-midnight, Fri.-Sat. 11am-1am) or **Havi Retki,** on the corner of Yrjönkatu and Itsenäisyydenkatu (open Mon. 11am-11pm, Tues.-Sat. 11am-midnight, Sun. 11am-10pm). Get odd-sounding beef and potato pastries (5-15mk) or salad (20mk) at **Sarpi Konditoria,** Pohjoiskauppatori 3 (open Mon.-Fri. 7am-6pm, Sat. 7am-2pm).

LAKE DISTRICT

In the Southeast stretches the vast Lake District from which Finland has earned its fame as the "land of a thousand lakes." Canoe, hike, camp, cross-country ski, and swat mosquitoes amid the boundless stretches of water and forest. To truly experience the beauty of the region, avoid the cities; the region is dotted with isolated youth hostels. Tourist offices can also arrange rooms in farmhouses and point out wilderness huts.

■■■ TAMPERE

Though officially founded in 1779, Tampere is best described as a child of the industrial revolution. When in 1820 Scotsman James Finlayson harnessed the power of the nearby Tammerkoski rapids for a textile mill, he transformed a provincial town into the country's most industrialized city. Today industry is no longer the centerpiece of "the Manchester of Finland." Some of the red-brick factory buildings on the banks of Tammerkoski now house restaurants, and the old working-class neighborhood of Pispala, perched on a ridge between two lakes, has gentrified into the trendy abode of wealthy artists. Preserved workers' housing can be found in the museum of **Amuri,** Makasiininkatu 12, a fascinating showcase of 25 representative living quarters spanning the century before 1973. (Open early May to mid-Sept. Tues.-Sat. 9am-5pm, Sun. 11am-5pm. 10mk, students 3mk.) The proletarian spirit burns most brightly at the unforgettable **Lenin Museum,** established and still managed by the Finnish-Soviet Friendship Society at Hämeenpuisto 28, site of the first conference of Lenin's revolutionary party. It was here that Lenin met Stalin, although that's not the most-publicized nugget of info. (Open Mon.-Fri. 9am-5pm, Sat.-Sun. 11am-4pm. 10mk, students 3mk. Lenin pins 5mk.) Round off your Socialist tour with exhibitions on the history of workers' movements at the **Central Museum**

of Labour in Finland, Kuninkaankatu 3 (open Tues.-Sun. 11am-6pm, 15mk). Climb up the world's highest *esker* (a glacier-formed ridge) at **Pyynikki** park, and catch a view of both Näsijärvi lake and Pyhäjärvi lake from the observation tower (2mk), which also serves a delicious *munkki,* a Finnish doughnut-like pastry. Tampere's **Short Film Festival** (March 8-12 in 1995), featuring contestants from 30 different countries (5-day pass 300mk, seat tickets extra; for info call (931) 219 61 49), is rivaled in cosmopolitan content only by the **International Theater Festival.** (Aug. 15-20 in 1995. Tickets 40-80mk. For info call (931) 219 69 58.) See the results of years of erging at the **World Rowing Championships,** Aug. 18-26, 1995 (for info call (90) 15 81).

Practical Information, Accommodations, and Food The mega-helpful **tourist office** is located on Verkatehtaankatu 2 (tel. (931) 212 66 52); from the train station, walk up Hämeenkatu, turn left just before the bridge, and look for the information sign. They offer 2hr. guided tours of Tampere for 25mk, departing at 2pm. (Open Mon.-Fri. 8:30am-8pm, Sat.-Sun. 11:30am-6pm; Sept.-May Mon.-Fri. 8:30am-5pm.) Tampere connects south by **train** to Helsinki (9 per day, 2hr., 82mk) and to Turku (7 per day, 2hr., 74mk), and north by train to Oulu (6 per day, 5hr., 188mk), or by the **steamers** that sail thrice a week to Ruovesi (4½hr., 164mk) and beyond to Virrat (7½hr., 222mk). If you're planning a return trip, your best bet is a package tour that includes traveling one way by bus (Ruovesi 170mk, Virrat 310mk). For more information, call (931) 212 48 04.

When your Marxist yearnings have faded, treat yourself to the 4-star **Domus hostel (HI),** Pellervonkatu 9 (tel. (931) 55 00 00), 2km east of the train station, where every room comes equipped with kitchenette and bathroom, and where the sauna, indoor pool (both open 7-10am), laundry room, and bike rental are free. From the train station, follow Itsenäisyydenkatu and Sammonkatu and turn left onto Joukahaisenkatu, or take bus 25. (Reception open 24hrs. Dorms 55mk, nonmembers 70mk. Breakfast 24mk. Open June-Aug.) The alternative is the stark edifice of **Tampeeren NNKY (YWCA),** Tuomiokirkonkatu 12 (tel. (931) 22 54 46), 400m north on Tuomiokirkonkatu perpendicular to Hämeenkatu a block from the train station. (Max. stay 5 nights. Reception open 8-10am and 4pm-midnight. Dorms 45mk. Triples and quads 50mk per person. Nonmembers add 15mk. Breakfast 25mk. Kitchen. Open June to late Aug.) Five km southwest on bus 1, **Camping Härmälä** (tel. (931) 65 12 50) overlooks Lake Pyhäjärvi. (Tents 60-62mk, cottages 100-275mk. Open early May to late Aug.)

Sample *mustamakkara,* a Tampere sausage containing flour and cow's blood at **Kauppahalli** (market hall), Hämeenkatu 19 (open Mon.-Thurs. 8am-5pm, Fri. 8am-6pm, Sat. 8am-2pm). Stock up on inexpensive groceries at **Vesa Vikkula,** opposite the train station (open Mon.-Fri. 8am-8pm, Sat. 8am-4pm). At **Kaks Mattia,** Ilmarinkatu 16, you can heap a plate to your heart's content for 39mk (open Mon.-Fri. 7am-5pm), and at **Myllärit,** Åkerlundinkatu 4, four salads and an all-you-can-eat buffet lunch costs 40mk (open Mon. 11am-3:15pm, Tues.-Sat. 11am-midnight). At **Tullikamari,** live music resonates 3-4 nights a week (cover 15-100mk, beer 15mk, min. age 18) in a warehouse where you can lunch during the academic year for 35mk. (Open Mon. and Fri. 11am-4pm, Tues.-Thurs. 11am-2am, Sat. 9pm-4am.)

■■■ JYVÄSKYLÄ

The capital of Finland's lake district, Jyväskylä (YOO-ves-kill-eh) is famous as the home of architect Alvar Aalto. If you like his stuff, this town's the place for you; the compact and modern city is sprinkled liberally with buildings designed by Aalto, which, if you can't pick them out yourself, are presented in a guide (5mk) offered by the **tourist office,** Asemakatu 6 (tel. (941) 62 49 03), one block up from the train station (open Mon.-Fri. 8am-5pm, Sat.-Sun. 9am-4pm; Sept.-May Mon.-Fri. 8am-5pm). The **Alvar Aalto Museum,** at Alvar Aallon Katu 7, left on Vapaudenkatu to the end, will help you follow the development of his style through furniture, photographs, plans, and models (open Tues.-Sun. 11am-6pm; 10mk, Fri. free). The building itself was also designed by the architect. Nearby, the **University of Jyväskylä,** largely designed by Aalto, occupies an isolated campus in piney woods near the museum. The unique **Finnish National Costume Center,** Gummeruksenkatu 3E, displays a changing selection of national costumes not designed by Aalto (open Tues.-Sun. 11am-6pm; 10mk, Fri. free). Jyväskylä is a student-oriented town; show your student ID, and admission to any of its 9 museums is free. For 20mk, you can get a joint ticket for the Alvar Aalto Museum, the Finnish National Costume Center, the Museum of Central Finland, and the Crafts Museum of Finland.

During the 2nd week of June, Jyväskylä hosts an **Arts Festival,** with concerts, film screenings, and exhibitions. (Call (941) 61 56 24 1 for info. Ticket prices 30-110mk, students win 25-50% discounts.) Throughout the summer, three parks (Yrttisuo, Mäki-Matti and the Church Park) host **free concerts** ranging from gospel to marching band music (ask tourist office), while the Hippos Sports Park hosts Finnish **baseball** games on Sunday and Wednesday afternoons. During the last week of July, a **summer carnival** is held on Kauppakatu, interestingly titled "Jyväskylä Cultural Brats." **Cruises** on Lake Päijänne are 50mk (departing Tues.-Sun. 11:30am-3pm). Boats also leave once daily Tues.-Sat. except Thurs. (190mk, round-trip 280mk). For more information, call (914) 26 34 47.

Trains from Tampere (8 per day, 2hr., 75mk) and Helsinki (8 per day, 3½hr., 140mk) plus **bus** connections to towns throughout the Lake District make Jyväskylä a regional transport hub. Sporty **Laajari (HI),** Laajavuorentie 15 (tel. (941) 25 33 55), has a ski slope and skateboard ramp in its backyard and a free sauna in the basement. Take bus 25 from the park across from the tourist office. (Dorms 40mk, nonmembers 55mk. Kitchen; ask for cooking pot at reception.) Lakeside **Tuomiojärvi Camping** (tel (941) 62 48 96) lies 2km north of town by bus 8 (40mk per person, cabins 185mk for 4 persons; open June-Aug.). Treat yourself to a lunch special at **Rosso Ristorante,** Kauppakatu 19 (pizza 39mk, lunch 35-45mk; open Mon.-Thurs. 11am-11pm, Fri.-Sat. 11am-midnight, Sun. noon-11pm). For more macho beer, pizza, and TV, try **Magic Sandy Pita Bar,** Kauppakatu 41 (pizza 33mk; open Sun.-Thurs. 10:30am-3am, Fri.-Sat. 10:30am-4am).

■■■ LAHTI

Although Lahti truly comes alive during the winter, it is no less active in the summertime; Aleksanterinkatu is crowded with people during the day, and at night, the junction of Aleksanterinkatu and Vesijärvinkatu crawls with bars. Lahti is a winter wonderland for the athletically inclined. The **Lahti Sports Center** has hosted the Nordic World Ski Championships five times since 1928 and is a candidate for 2001; it may also host the 2006 Winter Olympics. You can visit the sports complex and go to the top of the highest ski jump for 20mk. The **Ski Museum** at the Sports Center has a rather nifty ski-jump simulator (open Mon.-Fri. 10am-5pm, Sat.-Sun. 11am-5pm; 20mk). The **Radio and TV Museum,** Radiomäki, predictably exhibits old radios and televisions (open Mon.-Fri. 10am-5pm, Sat.-Sun. 11am-5pm; 20mk). For a quick fix of Aalto, check out the towering, macabre **Church of the Cross,** Kirkkokatu 4 (open 10am-3pm). In mid-July, Lahti hosts a **Jazz Festival** in the marketplace; for more information call (918) 782 86 90. Otherwise, the **market** only features fruit and vegetable stands (Mon.-Sat. 7am-2pm).

Lahti, a transportation center, is easily accessible by both bus and train. **Buses** depart for Jyväskylä (3hr., 100mk) and Savonlinna (4hr., 135mk). **Trains** chug to Helsinki (1½-2 hr., 56mk), Tampere (2hr., 78mk), Jyväskylä (134mk), Savonlinna (130mk), and St. Petersburg, Russia (6hr., 214mk). The city **tourist office** is located at Torikatu 3B (tel. (918) 818 25 80; open Mon.-Fri. 8am-7pm, Sat.-Sun. 10am-2pm; Sept.-May open Mon.-Fri. 8am-4pm). The laid-back **Hostel Onnela (HI),** Onnelantie 10 (tel. (918) 883 33 00) is 500m from the train station and even closer to town. (Reception open 6am-11pm. 50mk, nonmembers 65mk. Sheets 10mk. Laundry 7mk. Kitchen.) If that's full, try the **Lahti City Youth Hostel (HI),** Kivikatu 1 (tel.

(918) 782 63 24; 50mk, nonmembers 65mk). Take bus 31 to Mäntsäläntie and follow the signs. There's a **campground** at the **Mukkula Tourist Center** (tel. (918) 30 67 30), accessible by bus 30 (8mk; 40mk per tent, open June-Aug.). If you're staying at Hostel Onnela, breakfast at the **Esso gas station** for 6mk (coffee and croissant/doughnut), at the intersection of Karjalankatu, Ahtialantie, and Viipurintie. Esso also houses a 24hr. **mini-mart** with cheap, cheap food (sandwich and coffee 13.50mk). **Bellamani,** Kauppakatu 9, has 25mk lunch specials and an outdoor café (open 10am-1am). **Café Farra,** Aleksanterinkatu 16, offers pizza and other lunch specials for 35mk (open Mon.-Sat. 11am-midnight).

■■■ SAVONLINNA

The tsarist aristocracy turned Savonlinna into a fashionable resort 150 years ago and it has remained true to form; its Mediterranean flair will make you forget you are in Scandinavia and only the local cuisine will bring your senses back to Finland. While the other Lake District towns merely border lakes, Savonlinna, a chain of small islands, is surrounded by crystal waters. During the magnificent **Opera Festival** (July 8-Aug. 5 in 1995), divas come from all over the world to perform in the courtyard of Olavinlinna Castle. Tickets to performances cost 200-500mk and should be ordered as early as the preceding October. Write to Savonlinna Opera Festival, Olavinkatu 35, SF-57130 Savonlinna (tel. (957) 51 47 00, fax (957) 218 66) or contact the tourist office (see below). Unclaimed tickets are sold at the ticket booth on Tallisaari (before castle) at 5pm the day of the show, but individual scalpers often charge less, and prices plunge nearer to showtime. The **Retretti Arts Center** takes culture to new depths; a summer concert series resounds in the wonderful acoustics of a deep cave. (Tickets 30-90mk, students 20-70mk. Inquire at the Opera Festival Ticket Office.) The 1.5km of caverns feature paintings and sculpture amid shimmering reflecting pools. (Open late May to June and Aug. 10am-6pm, late June-July 10am-7pm. 60mk, students and seniors 55mk.) Most trains to Savonlinna stop at Retretti. During July, special *lättähattu* trains shuttle between Savonlinna and Retretti (½hr., 20 mk, railpasses valid). Head east from the bus and train stations on Olavinkatu and cross the bridge, then hug Linnankatu along the south shore until you reach **Olavinlinna Castle,** a weatherworn but intact medieval fortress. A guided tour sallies through steep defense passages, winding stairways, and three 16th-century towers. (Open 10am-5pm, mid-Aug. to May 10am-3pm. 14mk.) For some peace and sun, hop north via the two footbridges to the pine-covered isle of **Sulosaari.**

Practical Information, Accommodations, and Food Savonlinna is yours by **train** from Helsinki (5 per day, 160mk) or **bus** (railpasses not valid) from Pieksämäki (2 per day, 57mk) or Kuopio (3 per day, 75mk). The train stops first at Savonlinna-Kauppatori in the center of town and near the tourist office, then continues to the Savonlinna stop by the main train station. **Water travel** costs a pretty *penni* but provides the best access to the pristine regions of the lakes; vessels cruise between Savonlinna and Kuopio (Tues.-Sun. 10am, 11½hr, 250mk). The friendly but busy **tourist office** (tel. (957) 27 34 92) occupies the yellow building across the bridge from the market at Puistokatu 1 off Olavinkatu. They will help you find accommodations (and reserve them, no fee) and change money when banks are closed. (Open 8am-8pm, Sept.-May Mon.-Fri. 9am-4pm.) Despite its location behind the casino, **Vuorilinna Hostel (HI),** Kylpylaitoksentie (tel. (957) 575 00), snoozes peacefully on the island 200m across the footbridge from the market. (Reception open June-Aug. 6:30am-11pm. 75mk, nonmembers 90mk. Breakfast 25mk.) **Retkeilymaja Malakias (HI),** Pihlajavedenkuja 6 (tel. (957) 232 83), is 1.5km from town. Going up Tulliportinkatu, veer right on Savonkatu, or take bus 1, 2, 3, or 4. (Reception open July to mid-Aug. 7am-11pm. 75mk, nonmembers 90mk. Breakfast 22mk.) **Vuohimäki Camping** (tel. (957) 53 73 53) is 7km out, but bus 3 (2 per hr.) runs there. (Camping 35mk per person, June and Aug. 33mk. Open early June to late Aug.)

Eating and imbibing centers around Olavinkatu. For a great breakfast deal, visit **Pietari Kylliäinen** at Olavinkatu 15, on the castle side of town. (All-you-can-eat, 20mk. Open Mon. and Sat. 7-9:30am, Tues.-Fri. 6:30-9:30am, Sun. 7-11am.) For lunch, try **Steakhouse San Martin,** Olavinkatu 46. (Salads 28mk, lunch special 34-40mk. Open Mon.-Fri. 10:30am-8pm, Sat. 11am-8pm, Sun. noon-6pm.) Across Olavinkatu from the market, throw back a few beers at **Happy Time Pub,** Kauppatori 1. (Open Sun.-Mon. noon-midnight, Tues.-Thurs. noon-1am, Fri.-Sat. noon-2am. No cover. Live bands Wednesday.)

■ VALAMO, KERIMÄKI, AND RAUHALINNA

The stretch of land and water between Savonlinna and Kuopio includes many worthwhile stops. At the handsome **Valamo Monastery** (tel. (972) 619 59), 35km from Heinävesi along the Savonlinna-Kuopio boat route, guests often outnumber monks 20 to 1. Stay in the guest house for 100mk per night (breakfast included), and chow at the restaurant for 40-65mk. (No shorts or photographs.) The largest wood church in the world in **Kerimäki,** 24km east of Savonlinna, seats over 3000 people. (Bus 20mk. Free entry.) A more worldly retreat is **Rauhalinna,** a wooden palace built in the 19th century by a Russian commander for his wife. Cruises to this elegant island leave the market square in Savonlinna several times daily (1¼hr., 30mk round-trip).

OSTROBOTHNIA

■■■ VAASA (VASA)

An active harbor town on the Gulf of Bothnia, Vaasa is no cultural metropolis, featuring two main attractions: **Wasalandia,** an amusement park for children, and **Tropiclandia,** a fun-fest of fake tropical paradises for their lame parents. An antidote to the touristy kitsch is the **Tikanoja Art Gallery,** Hovioikeudenpuistikko 4, which exhibits Finnish art (open Tues.-Sat. 11am-4pm, Sun. noon-5pm; 10mk, students free). Learn about the region at the **Museum of Ostrobothnia,** Museokatu 3 (open Mon. noon-4pm, Tues.-Fri. noon-8pm, Sat.-Sun. noon-5pm; 10mk, seniors and students 5mk).

From Vaasa, Silja **ferries** sail to Umeå (1-2 per day, 123mk) and Sundsvall (1 per day, 120mk), Sweden (railpasses 50% off). For more information contact **Silja Line,** Alatori (tel. (961) 323 36 30; open Mon.-Fri. 8:30am-6pm, Sat. 9am-2pm). Cruises around the idyllic **Vaasa Archipelago** depart from Kalaranta (mid-June to mid-Aug. at 1 and 4pm, 50mk). Find out more at the **tourist office,** Hovioikeudenpuistikko 11 (tel. (961) 325 11 45; open Mon.-Fri. 8am-7pm, Sat.-Sun. 10am-7pm; Sept.-May Mon.-Fri. 8am-4pm). To get to the tourist office from the train station, walk up Hovrätt-sesplanaden to the yellow building on the right. The nearest **HI hostel, Tekla** (tel. (961) 317 78 50, fax 13 21 39 89), is a bit far out; from the station or town center take bus 1 or 3 to Tekla. (Reception open 24hrs., Sept.-May 8am-10pm. 80mk, non-members 95mk. Kitchen. Laundry. Free sauna.) Get an authentic Finnish lunch at **Bertels Panorama** (don't be fooled; there's no panorama, it's just on the second floor), Vasaesplanaden 16 (open Mon.-Fri. 9am-5pm, daily special 35mk).

■■■ OULU

A lively university city by Finnish standards, Oulu's flower-bordered streets and well-tended bike paths lend it a Mediterranean grace that belies the city's history as one of Finland's busiest ports and the world's leading tar exporter during the 19th century. See and sniff exotic flora from around the world at the University of Oulu's

Botanical Gardens, 7km north of the center along bus route 4, or 6. Twin glass pyramids, named Romeo and Julia, house citrus, olive, and cocoa trees. (Pyramids open Tues.-Fri. 8am-5pm, Sat.-Sun. 10am-5pm; Sept.-May Tues.-Fri. 8am-3pm, Sat.-Sun. noon-3pm. Open-air gardens open 8am-9pm. Free.) **Nallikari,** Finland's Côte d'Azur, rims an island 5km northwest of town. The largely untouristed and splendiferous beach is the best place in Northern Finland to enjoy the Bothnian waters, despite its tacky amusement park. You can stay at nearby **Nallikari Camping** (tents 40mk per person, 4-person cabins 290mk, May and Sept.-Oct. cabins 240mk). Take bus 5 (hourly) from Kajaanintie outside the hostel heading toward the center of the city.

All **trains** between north and south Finland pass through Oulu's clutches; 4-5 per day leave south to Helsinki (230mk) and north to Rovaniemi (97mk). The **municipal tourist office,** Torikatu 10 (tel. (981) 314 12 94), greets with good-natured help. Take Hallituskatu, the broad avenue perpendicular to the train station, for 6 blocks, then go left on Torikatu (open Mon.-Fri. 9am-4pm). **Retkeilymaja Välkkylä (HI),** Kajaanintie 36 (tel. (981) 37 77 07, in winter 311 52 47, fax 311 65 72), offers the only inexpensive lodgings in town; terrific quads (not bunk beds) ensure a comfy stay. From the train station, turn right and walk down Rautatienkatu parallel to the railway, take a right (under the overpass) onto Kajaanintie, and continue until the cemetery ends and a hostel sign appears. (Reception open 7:15am-11pm. 50mk, nonmembers 65mk. Breakfast 25mk. Kitchen. Free laundry. Sauna 15mk.) A bizarre cultural phenomenon awaits at the shopping center between the rail station and the youth hostel: hundreds of Finnish teens drive cars back and forth for hours on end, with friends jumping in and out of back seats, in an unusual form of "cruising." **Kahvila Konditoria,** Kirrkokatu 17, serves fast food, but also good salads and sandwiches and fantastic desserts (open Mon.-Fri. 8:30am-5pm, Sat. 9am-2:30pm). Dungeonesque rock club **45 Special,** Saaristonkatu 12, complete with iron bars and shackles, serves "Jailhouse Rock" hamburgers (38mk) and hosts Finnish bands. (open 8pm-4am, cover Fri.-Sat. 20mk, students 15mk). Hang with the locals at **Leskinen,** Saaristonkatu (opposite 45 Special), and down some damn good 18mk beer (open Sun.-Thurs. 4pm-1am, Fri.-Sat. 3pm-2am).

LAPLAND (LAPPI)

The sun never sets on Lapland during the pleasant 2- to 3-month summer. In winter the sun rises for only a few hours a day, but the dry air abates the effects of the low temperatures. Clear sky, moonlight, and white snow produce an eerie blue glow, and the green, red, and yellow streaks of the Northern Lights illuminate a surreal snowscape. In the south you'll find crashing river rapids and whitefish. To the north lies 80km-long *Inarijärvi* (Lake Inari) and its countless islands; even farther north, the steep tundra slopes of the Teno River Valley. Skiing is ideal from February to mid-May, with facilities and rental outlets at almost every tourist center (Pallas, Pyhä, Ruka, Saariselkä, Ylläs, and Ounasvaara, near Rovaniemi). In summer, guides lead hiking expeditions from the same places. Only experienced groups should undertake independent excursions. Hikers should plan their routes around the mountain huts run by the Finnish Youth Hostel Association. The best source for maps, hiking routes, locations of huts and cabins, and information regarding fishing licenses is **Etiäinen** (tel. (960) 36 25 26), located 8km north of Rovaniemi in Santa Claus's Village (see Rovaniemi, below).

Most of the Sami (Finnish Lapps) and Kolttas (originally Russian Lapps) live in the 4 northernmost parishes of Sodankylä, Enontekiö, Inari, and Utsjoki; at least 800 families still make a living from reindeer herding. Local delicacies include *poroliha* (Rudolph meat), *lohi* (salmon), and liqueurs made from Arctic *lakka* (cloudberries).

■■■ KUUSAMO AND THE KARHUNKIERROS

For foaming rapids and bottomless gorges, lace up your hiking boots and head for the **Karhunkierros** (The Bear's Ring), a 75km hiking trail through untainted landscape near the Russian-Finnish border. To get started, head by bus to Kuusamo from either Oulu (6 per day, 3½hr., about 120mk), Kajaani (4 per day, 4½hr., 116mk) or Rovaniemi (2 per day, 2½hr., 90mk). In **Kuusamo**, stay at **Kuusamon Kansanopisto (HI)** (tel. (989) 221 32), a yellow house across from the bus station. (Reception open June-Aug. 5-9pm. 45-60mk, nonmembers 60-75mk. Kitchen. Laundry.) Stock up on food at **Kitkan Viisas** in the same building as the bus station (open Mon.-Fri. 9am-8pm, Sat. 9am-6pm). The Kuusamo **tourist office,** Torangintaival 2 (tel. (989) 850 29 10), 2km from town at the corner of highways 20 (Ouluntie) and 5, peddles maps (50mk) and proffers information about the trail, which takes 4-6 days, depending on your condition. If you want to hike just part of the trail, they'll show you which buses to catch. (Open 9am-8pm; Sept.-May Mon.-Fri. 9am-5pm.) There are free 10- to 20-person cabins every 10km or so along the way, but bring a tent during the summer in case they're full. You may want rubber boots for the boggy stretches. Bring food and mosquito repellent—there are only 2 supply stations on the trail and billions of pesky pests ready to eat you alive. To fish, you need both a local (50mk per day, 200mk per week) and a national license (30mk per year; get both at the tourist office in Kuusamo.

■■■ ROVANIEMI

Tucked 8km south of the Arctic Circle, Rovaniemi is the capital of Finnish Lapland. Don't expect to see quaint old buildings, though; as a farewell gesture, retreating Germans razed Rovaniemi to the ground in 1944. The city was rebuilt using blueprints conceived in the mind of Aalto, who shaped the city's layout to resemble reindeer antlers. Take bus 8 or 10 from the train station (11mk) to **Santa Claus's Village,** from which destinations around the world are served by reindeer shuttle (departures yearly in late Dec., youths free if you've been good). You can meet the elves and pet the reindeer too, if you manage to fight your way through the hordes of eager tourists. Santa also sells certificates (5mk) that prove that you've been to the Arctic Circle, and Santa's Main Post Office sends letters and gifts on your preferred date, stamping them with a unique postmark. (Open 8am-8pm, Sept.-May 9am-5pm, free.) A visit to the brand-new **Arktikum** center, Pohgoisranta 4, is a must; it houses the **Arctic Science Center,** with exhibits on life and culture in the north, as well as the **Provincial Museum of Lapland.** The research room holds fascinating books on the Arctic and computer programs that can entertain you for hours. (Open 10am-7pm, Sept. to mid-June Tues.-Sun. 10am-6pm; 40mk, students 20mk, films 15mk.)

The **tourist office** at Koskikatu 1 (tel. (960) 322 22 79) finds rooms in private homes (about 130mk) and dishes up a weekly events listing amusingly titled *Let's Go,* as well as information on boat (95-250mk) and snowmobile (220-530mk) safaris (open Mon.-Fri. 8am-6pm, Sat.-Sun. 11:30am-4pm; Sept.-May Mon.-Fri. 8am-4pm). From the train station, head right on Ratakatu and turn right on Hallituskatu; follow Hallituskatu to the end and turn right onto Koskikatu. Rovaniemi's **HI youth hostel,** Hallituskatu 16 (tel. (960) 34 46 44), is friendly but lacks facilities: no kitchen, no TV, no showers after 10pm. Turn right from the station, go up the hill, and turn right on Hallituskatu just after the bus station. (Reception open 6:30-10am and 5-10pm. 55mk, nonmembers 70mk. Breakfast 24mk.) Across the river from the town center, **Ounaskoski Camping** (tel. (960) 34 53 04) has a prime location and river swimming (40mk, open June-Aug.). In the Sampokeskus shopping center, **Ristorante Il Bel Giovanni** serves up pasta dishes and Finnish lunch specials (43mk, open 11am-10pm). **Rinnemarket** is the closest market to the station, with a huge selection including several types of *lapinleipä* (Lappish bread). (Open Mon.-Fri. 8am-8pm, Sat. 8am-6pm.)

Buses head east to Kuusamo (2½hr., 90mk), and north to Inari (5½hr., 165mk), Karigasniemi (7hr., 200mk), Kilpisjärvi (6½hr., 185mk), and Muonio (3½hr., 110mk) with connections to Norway. Travel to Sweden by train to Kemi, then by bus (railpasses valid) 25km west to the border town of Tornio. Some buses continue across the border into Haparanda. Stay at the Tornio **HI hostel** (tel. (9698) 416 82), at Kirkkokatu, 1.6km north of the Finnish customs post. Rovaniemi is easily accessible by **trains** coming northward through Oulu (Helsinki-Rovaniemi, 4 per day, 270 mk) and by southbound buses from Inari, Muonio, Enontekiö, and Karasjok, Norway. **Finnair** also flies here from Helsinki (youth fare booked 1 week in advance 500mk, round-trip 660mk).

■■■ NORTHERN LAPLAND

When you set out for northern Lapland, plan ahead; connections will be difficult. From Rovaniemi, there are 2 routes to the north, traversed by buses and hitchers: Highway 79 leads towards Muonio and Enontekiö in the northwest, Highway 4 to Inari and Utsjokidue north. At the info office in the Rovaniemi train station, borrow timetables for Lapland's 2 bus companies: the **Postilinjat** (postal buses), and **J.M. Eskelisen Lapin Linjat Oy.** Prices are fairly similar; the postal line is slower.

Next to Lake Inari, the minute town of **Inari** is both a tourist spot and an old Lapp center. Seaplanes roar off the lake, and befuddled reindeer wander the streets. A well-kept and friendly (but small) **retkeilymaja (HI)** (tel. (9697) 512 44) welcomes travelers. It's a few hundred meters north from the center of town; turn left at the gas station. (Reception open 8am-noon and 4-11pm. Dorms 45mk. Nonmembers 60mk. Open March-Sept.) Six official **campgrounds** punctuate the wilderness. The tiny **tourist office** (tel. (9697) 511 93; open mid-June to mid-Sept. Mon.-Sat. 9am-8pm) sits next to a gallery of regional art in the town center. Ask them about **Lemmenjoki River** hiking, about 40km from Inari (daily bus connection), and about boat trips (70mk). The **Ravadasköngäs Falls** resound for kilometers; make day-hikes and return to Inari, or crash out in the wilderness huts along the trails. A few professional gold-panners still work claims along the river.

North of Inari, the River Teno winds along the Norwegian border below dwarf birches and tundra-covered fells. **Karigasniemi,** an isolated outpost, has an **HI retkeilymaja** (tel. (9697) 611 88) right in the center of "town." (45mk, nonmembers 60mk.) Use your railpass to its max at **Kolari,** the northernmost rail point in Finland. (In summer and ski season 2 trains per week.) The train station is 4km north of town, although all buses stop at the TB gas station 400m west of the train station. Stay at **Vaattovaaran retkeilymaja (HI)** (tel. (9695) 610 86) in town. Buses run from Kolari and Rovaniemi to **Muonio,** then continue either north to Kautokeino in Norwegian Lapland (7½hr. from Rovaniemi), or northwest through **Kilpisjärvi** in Finland's most mountainous region (7hr.) before emerging an hour later at Skibotn on the Norwegian coast and connecting with the bus to Tromsø. Hiking in this pure, untainted part of the world is stunning, but the freedom to explore uninhabited wilderness carries with it the responsibility not to fall off the edge of it all: carry a map and compass. Hike from Kilpisjärvi across the gently rounded peaks of the **Malla Nature Reserve** and to the **Three Countries Frontier,** where Finland, Norway, and Sweden meet on the shores of a lonely lake.

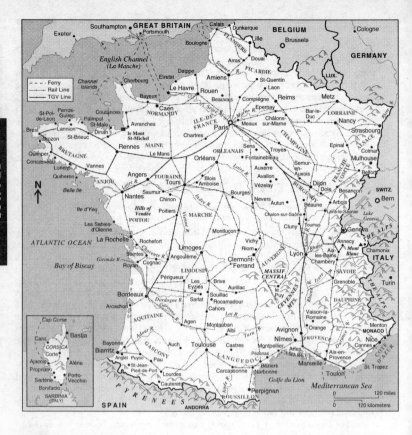

France

US$1	= 5.33F (francs)	1F =	US$0.19
CDN$1	= 3.97F	1F =	CDN$0.25
UK£1	= 8.48F	1F =	UK£0.12
IR£1	= 8.39F	1F =	IR£0.12
AUS$1	= 4.09F	1F =	AUS$0.25
NZ$1	= 3.23F	1F =	NZ$0.31
SAR1	= 1.50F	1F =	SAR 0.67
Country Code: 33		**International Dialing Prefix: 19**	

Temple of culture, cuisine, fashion, snobbery, and cheese, France is an extraordinary mosaic of tiny villages, walled medieval cities, sleazy ports, and, of course, Paris. Charles de Gaulle, WWII Resistance hero and French President for much of the postwar era, summed up the French spirit with the words, "France cannot be France without greatness." In the center of all this, the crowded brilliance of Paris presents only one of France's many facets. The cliffs and fertile countryside of Normandy posed for the Impressionists and embraced an Anglo-American liberation, while Brittany and Corsica clung to distinct cultural identities. The Loire Valley blossoms with the architecture of the French Renaissance, while the Alps illustrate the architecture of raw geological force. The Dordogne River Valley, dubbed "The Capital of Prehistory," shelters 20,000-year-old cave paintings, while the Côte d'Azur is just too glorious for its own good.

France was originally inhabited by the Gauls, a Celtic people who fell prey first to Caesar's legions and then to decentralized turmoil after the collapse of the Roman Empire. Charlemagne brought renewed unity to France in the 8th century, and over the next several centuries, the feudal lords of Paris consolidated power over the rest of the region, forging for the first time a true French "nation." During the Renaissance, the nation grew grand, as François I planted the Loire Valley with luxurious châteaux. The opulence crescendoed during the reign of Louis XIV, the Sun King, whose ostentatious palace at Versailles was imitated across the continent. By 1789, the French citizens could no longer support such extravagance; the ensuing years of furious barricade-building, rabble-rousing, and violence served as the inspiration for later revolutions in France and across Europe.

In the afterglow of the Revolution, Napoleon's armies mastered Europe, and the marching song of Marseille's tattered regiment became the country's national anthem—*La Marseillaise.* The unstable 19th century saw France swap republic for monarchy, for republic, for empire, and for republic once again.

French and German armies ripped through the countryside in the Franco-Prussian War (1870-71) and both World Wars. Impressionists such as Monet and Renoir redefined painting, and after WWI, Paris became the shrine of Hemingway, Gertrude Stein, and the rest of the Lost Generation.

President Charles de Gaulle pursued his claims to French Greatness as the foremost public figure of the post-WWII era, and his words still ring in French ears. Today, although France's political scene is as rocky as ever, the country holds its position as a world leader in the avant-garde of aesthetic, cultural, and intellectual movements, and its tourist industry, as always, is poised and waiting to receive.

For more detailed, fact- and flavor-filled coverage, pick up a copy of *Let's Go: France* or *Let's Go: Paris.*

GETTING THERE AND GETTING AROUND

France does not require visas of U.S., Canadian, New Zealand, or EU citizens, but it does of Australians. Contact the French consulate in Australia at 31 Market St., 20th floor, Sydney NSW 2000 (tel. (02) 261 5779).

With over 15,000 departures daily, the **Société Nationale de Chemins de Fer (SNCF)** manages one of Europe's most extensive rail networks. Timetables are complicated but well-organized, consisting of 3 color-designated periods. "Blue periods" have minimum train traffic, usually Monday afternoon through Friday morning and Saturday afternoon to Sunday afternoon; "white periods" coincide with heavier train use (most other times). Point-to-point ticket prices vary according to the period. Train tickets are not valid for use until inserted in the orange machine at the entrance to the platforms. Seat **reservations,** recommended for international trips, are mandatory on France's legendary TGV *(train à grande vitesse).* Reservation fees run about US$8. The SNCF's premier pass offering, the **France Railpass,** allows 3 days of 2nd-class travel within a 15-day period (US$125), with up to 6 additional days available (US$29 each), and must be purchased outside France; contact a travel agent for details. Other special tickets apply during specified periods. Bring a photo when you make your purchase.

French **buses,** usually slow and affordable, are useful for filling the gaps in the rail network. The bus station, usually located near the train station, is called the *gare routière.* France is one of the worst countries in Europe for **hitching.** The larger the city, the more difficult it will be to get a ride. **Allostop-Provoya** is a nationwide service that pairs drivers and riders. It charges 230F for 8 trips within a 2-year period, or 30-70F for individual trips depending on the distance traveled. Gas and tolls are 20 centimes per km extra. Their main office at 84, passage Brady, 75010 Paris (tel. (1) 42 46 00 66), can give you the addresses of offices throughout the country.

With a wealth of well-paved minor routes, French roads are terrific for **cycling.** Prime regions include the Loire Valley, Normandy, Provence, the Dordogne River

Valley, Alsace-Lorraine, and Burgundy. SNCF's pamphlet *Guide du train et du vélo* offers details on combining cycling and railroading in France. Bikes cost 42F to transport on trains, and they often take 3 days to arrive. Some train stations rent bikes (around 50F per day); you may sometimes return it to another station.

FRANCE ESSENTIALS

The extensive French tourism support network revolves around **syndicats d'initiative** and **offices de tourisme,** both of which *Let's Go* labels as "tourist office." Either will help you find accommodations (for about 15F), distribute maps, and suggest excursions to the countryside. The basic unit of currency in France is the franc, subdivided into 100 centimes and issued in both coins and paper notes.

Just about everything snoozes in France from noon to 2pm and closes on Sundays, and many provincial areas also shut down on Mondays. Most museums close for at least one day per week, usually Tuesday. The major national holidays in France, on which banks, museums, and other public buildings close, are: January 1, Easter Monday (April 17, 1995), May 1 (Labor Day), May 8 (Victory in Europe Day), Ascension Day (May 25, 1995), Whit Monday (June 5, 1995), July 14 (Bastille Day), August 15 (Assumption Day), November 1 (All Saints' Day), November 11 (Armistice Day), and December 25 (Christmas).

Summer brings daytime highs of around 23°C to most of France, although it is cooler in the North and in the Alps, and southern France basks in 32°C scorchers every summer. Winters are generally mild, with temperatures rarely dipping below freezing, although frequent rains will dampen more than just spirits.

Communication Be polite: before addressing a French person in English, first ask *Parlez-vous anglais, Madame/Monsieur?* (PAR-lay VOO an-GLAY, mah-DAHM/muh-SYUR; "Do you speak English, ma'am/sir?"). Contrary to popular opinion, even flailing efforts to speak French will be appreciated, especially in urban areas. Be lavish with your *Monsieurs, Madames,* and *Mademoiselles;* greet people with a friendly *bonjour (bonsoir* after 6pm). Other helpful phrases include *combien* (kohm-BYEHN, "how much"), *je voudrais* (ZHUH voo-DRAY, "I would like"), *Où est/sont* (OO AY/SOHN, "where is/are"), and *je ne comprends pas* (ZHUH NUH kohm-PRAHN pah, "I don't understand").

France's **telephone** system splits into 2 halves: Paris (city code 1) and everything else (no city code). To dial the provinces from Paris, preface the 8-digit number with 16; in reverse, dial 1 and then the 8-digit Paris number. To operate payphones, buy a *télécarte* (telephone credit card). Available at train stations, post offices and *tabacs,* they cost 40F *(petite)* or 96F *(grande).* To call collect, tell the operator *"en PCV"* (on-PAY-say-VAY). For AT&T's **USADirect,** dial 19, wait for the tone, then dial 00 11. For MCI's **WorldPhone,** dial 19 00 19; **SprintExpress,** 19 00 87; **Canada Direct,** 19 00 16; **BT Direct,** 19 00 44; **SA Direct,** 19 00 27. Anywhere in France, dial 10 for an **operator,** 12 for **directory assistance,** 15 for **medical emergencies,** 17 for **police assistance** and 18 for the **fire department.** Dial 19 33 11 for the **international operator,** and be prepared to wait for up to an hour.

Accommodations and Camping Youth hostels *(auberges de jeunesse)* cover France, ranging from well-kept, centrally located castles to run-down barracks. Most are affiliated with HI and charge nonmembers slightly more. Hostels run 40-80F per person, with breakfast about 20F (usually not obligatory). The quality of **hotels** in France generally matches their standardized rating on the government scale of zero to 4 stars. Rock-bottom hotels start at about 80-100F for singles, 90-110F for doubles, both without private bath or breakfast. Rates are often the same for single- and double-occupancy. Showers are usually not included in the price, and can run 10-25F. Inquire whether the breakfast or meals at the hotel are *obligatoire.* Breakfast (15-25F) usually means bread, jam, and coffee or hot chocolate. Make reservations (confirm with 1 night's deposit) for the larger cities in summer.

Campgrounds, plentiful in France, are also rated on a 4-star system. *Michelin's Camping and Caravanning in France* details the best sites. The **Club Alpin Français** maintains a network of mountain huts in upland regions. For further information, contact the office at 24, av. de Laumière, 75019 Paris (tel. (1) 42 02 68 64, fax 42 03 55 60).

Tourist offices list local *gîtes d'étape* (shelters inacessible to motorists) and *chambres d'hôte* (rustic farmhouse accommodations). Most tourist offices in rural areas have a list of *campings à la ferme*—campsites located on private farms.

Food and Drink French chefs cook for one of the most finicky clienteles in the world: the French. Traditionally, the complete French dinner includes an *apéritif* (pre-dinner drink), an *entrée* (appetizer), a *plat* (main course), salad, cheese, dessert, fruits, coffee, and a *digestif* (after-dinner drink); it takes several hours. A meal to tell your grandchildren about will run about 160F. The French generally take wine with their meals.

In restaurants, fixed-price 3-course meals (called *menus*) begin at a reasonable 55F. Service is always included; tips are only necessary for (rare) sensational treatment. Be careful when ordering *à la carte; l'addition* (the check) may exceed your weekly budget. You can buy sandwiches at most French bakeries and cafés; for 12-25F you get a foot-long *baguette* with cheese or meat inside. Cafés are a forum for continuous conversation, but you pay for the right to sit and watch the world go by: drinks and food are often 10-30% more if served in the dining room *(salle)* or outside *(sur la terrasse)* rather than at the bar *(comptoir)*.

Boulangeries, pâtisseries, and *confiseries* tempt with bread, pastries, and candy, respectively. *Fromageries* and *crèmeries* present an astonishing array of cheeses. *Charcuteries* sell meats. For supermarket shopping, look for **Uniprix, Prisunic, Casino Rallye,** or **Monoprix.** The many local markets *(marchés)* are picturesque, animated, and often offer better quality than supermarkets.

■■■ PARIS

Paris is a place that exists in most peoples' imaginations before they ever see the city—Paris as the City of Lights, the romantic Paris of the movies, the mysterious city described in books and letters. The actual city, though different from the imaginary one, is not a disappointment. Constantly evolving, Paris is the center of the changing French political landscape and ground for artistic innovation as well as tradition. Baudelaire called Paris a "teeming city, city full of dreams, where the specter in full daylight, accosts the passerby." Such phantasms are part of the city's mystery. And while Paris may not be the mythical city full of dreams (it is quite possible to go to Paris and not fall in love; you may not even finish your novel), its complexities are part of its charm, and the web of myth is part of its everyday realities. It is, in Hemingway's words, "a moveable feast," a city with a flavor so irresistible that once you taste it, you will carry memories of the experience around with you forever after.

For dazzling, detailed, definitive coverage of the wonders of Paris and its environs, pick up a copy of *Let's Go: Paris*.

ORIENTATION AND PRACTICAL INFORMATION

Coursing languidly from east to west, the Seine River forms the heart of modern Paris. The **Ile de la Cité** and neighboring **Ile St-Louis** remain the geographical center of the city, while the Seine splits Paris into two large expanses—the renowned *rive gauche* (Left Bank) to its south and the *rive droite* (Right Bank) to its north. By the time of Louis XIV, the city had grown to 20 *quartiers*; Haussmann's 19th-century reconstructions shifted their boundaries but kept the number, dividing Paris into 20 *arrondissements* (districts) which spiral clockwise (like a snail's shell) around the **Louvre.** In the majority of *Let's Go* listings, the *arrondissement* is included; thus 8ᵉ signifies the *huitième,* or eighth, *arrondissement*.

FRANCE

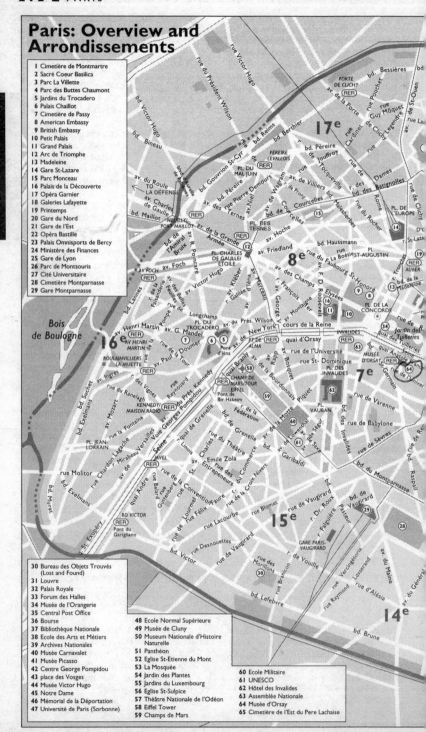

Paris: Overview and Arrondissements

1 Cimetière de Montmartre
2 Sacré Coeur Basilica
3 Parc La Villette
4 Parc des Buttes Chaumont
5 Jardins du Trocadero
6 Palais Chaillot
7 Cimetière de Passy
8 American Embassy
9 British Embassy
10 Petit Palais
11 Grand Palais
12 Arc de Triomphe
13 Madeleine
14 Gare St-Lazare
15 Parc Monceau
16 Palais de la Découverte
17 Opéra Garnier
18 Galeries Lafayette
19 Printemps
20 Gare du Nord
21 Gare de l'Est
22 Opéra Bastille
23 Palais Omnisports de Bercy
24 Ministère des Finances
25 Gare de Lyon
26 Parc de Montsouris
27 Cité Universitaire
28 Cimetière Montparnasse
29 Gare Montparnasse

30 Bureau des Objets Trouvés (Lost and Found)
31 Louvre
32 Palais Royale
33 Forum des Halles
34 Musée de l'Orangerie
35 Central Post Office
36 Bourse
37 Bibliothèque Nationale
38 Ecole des Arts et Métiers
39 Archives Nationales
40 Musée Carnavalet
41 Musée Picasso
42 Centre George Pompidou
43 place des Vosges
44 Musée Victor Hugo
45 Notre Dame
46 Mémorial de la Déportation
47 Université de Paris (Sorbonne)

48 Ecole Normal Supérieure
49 Musée de Cluny
50 Museum Nationale d'Histoire Naturelle
51 Panthéon
52 Eglise St-Etienne du Mont
53 La Mosquée
54 Jardin des Plantes
55 Jardins du Luxembourg
56 Eglise St-Sulpice
57 Théâtre Nationale de l'Odéon
58 Eiffel Tower
59 Champs de Mars

60 Ecole Militaire
61 UNESCO
62 Hôtel des Invalides
63 Assemblée Nationale
64 Musée d'Orsay
65 Cimetière de l'Est de Pere Lachaise

FRANCE

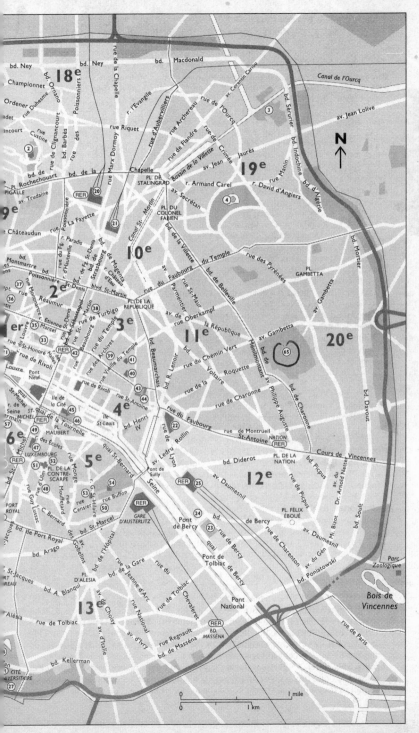

Tourist Offices: Bureau d'Accueil Central, 127, av. des Champs-Elysées, 8ᵉ (tel. 49 52 53 54). M: Charles de Gaulle-Etoile. Helpful, English-speaking, and packed. Open 9am-8pm. Branches at Gare de Lyon, Gare de l'Est, Gare d'Austerlitz, Gare Montparnasse, and the Eiffel Tower. **Tourist Information:** tel. 49 52 53 56 (English), 49 52 53 55 (French). A taped message gives the week's major events.

Budget Travel: Accueil des Jeunes en France (AJF), 119, rue St-Martin, 4ᵉ (tel. 42 77 87 80), in front of the Pompidou Center. M: Rambuteau. Reduced-price student train and bus tickets. Open Mon.-Sat. 9:30am-5:30pm; Oct.-May Mon.-Sat. 9am-6pm. Also 139, bd. St-Michel, 5ᵉ (tel. 43 54 95 86), in the *quartier latin.* M: Port-Royal. Open Tues.-Sat. 10am-1pm and 1:30-6pm. **Council Travel,** 16, rue de Vaugirard, 6ᵉ (tel. 46 34 02 90). M: Odéon. 22, rue des Pyramides, 1ᵉʳ (tel. 44 55 55 44). M: Pyramides. English-speaking travel service for young people. International flights, student train tickets, guidebooks, and ISIC. Offices open Mon.-Fri. 9:30am-6:30pm; Vaugirard branch open Sat. 10am-5pm. Pyramides branch open Sat. 9:30am-5:30pm. MC, Visa.

Embassies and Consulates: U.S., 2, av. Gabriel, 8ᵉ (tel. 42 96 12 02 or 42 61 80 75), off pl. de la Concorde. M: Concorde. **Consulate,** 2, rue St-Florentin (tel. 42 96 12 02), 3 blocks away. Open Mon.-Fri. 9am-3pm. **Canada,** 35, av. Montaigne, 8ᵉ (tel. 44 43 29 00). M: Franklin-Roosevelt or Alma-Marceau. Open Mon.-Fri. 9-10:30am and 2-3pm. **U.K.,** 35, rue du Faubourg-St-Honoré, 8ᵉ (tel. 42 66 91 42). M: Concorde or Madeleine. **Consulate,** 9, av. Hoche (tel. 42 66 91 42), near Parc Marceau. M: Charles de Gaulle-Etoile. Open Mon.-Fri. 9am-noon and 2-5pm. **Ireland,** 12, av. Foch, 16ᵉ (tel. 45 00 20 87). M: Charles de Gaulle-Etoile. Open Mon.-Fri. 9:30am-5:45pm. **Australia,** 4, rue Jean-Rey, 15ᵉ (tel. 40 59 33 00). M: Bir-Hakeim. Open Mon.-Fri. 9am-noon and 2-5pm. **New Zealand,** 7*ter,* rue Léonard-de-Vinci, 16ᵉ (tel. 45 00 24 11). M: Victor-Hugo. Open Mon.-Fri. 9am-1pm and 2-5:30pm. **South Africa,** 59, quai d'Orsay, 7ᵉ (tel. 45 55 92 37).

Currency Exchange: Best rates at the Banque de France (1ᵉʳ) and around the Opéra, on rue Scribe, rue Auber, and rue de la Paix (8ᵉ). Many post offices will change cash and AmEx traveler's checks at competitive rates and without commission; bureaus at train stations (except Montparnasse) and airports offer less favorable rates, but do have longer hours; the Gare de Lyon and both airports are open 6:30am-11:30pm. American Express cards work in ATMs at **Credit Lyonnais** banks. Most cash machines will give you francs off MasterCard or Visa.

American Express: 11, rue Scribe, 9ᵉ (tel. 47 77 77 07). M: Opéra or Auber. Across from the back of the Opéra. Receives moneygrams and will hold mail for cardholders or for those with AmEx traveler's checks; otherwise 5F per inquiry. English spoken. Open Mon.-Fri. 9am-5:30pm, Sat. 9am-5pm.

Post Office: 52, rue du Louvre, 1ᵉʳ (tel. 42 80 67 89), by the Bourse du Commerce. M: Châtelet-Les-Halles. Poste Restante. Only urgent telegrams, and no mailings over 2kg outside normal business hours. Open 24hrs. The **postal code** can be formed by adding the *arrondissement* to the number 750 (e.g., 1ᵉʳ becomes 75001, 16ᵉ becomes 75016, etc.).

Telephones: At the main post office. Open 24hrs. No collect calls to the U.S. on Sun. Buy a *télécarte* (40 or 96F) at any rail station ticket window, post office, or *tabac;* coin-operated phones are scarce. For calls outside Paris, dial 16. To Paris from the provinces, dial 161. From abroad, use the **city code:** 1.

Flights: Most international flights land at **Aéroport Roissy-Charles de Gaulle** (tel. 48 62 22 80), 23km northeast of Paris. Terminal 2 serves Air France (tel. 43 20 14 55; real-live telephone operator tel. 44 08 24 24, 9am-9pm). The cheapest, fastest way to get into town is by Roissy Rail, a bus-train combination to central Paris. Take the free shuttle bus from Aérogare 1, gate 28; Aérogare 2A, gate 5; Aérogare 2B, gate 6 or Aérogare 2D, gate 6 to the Roissy train station, and ride the RER B3 to the city (45min., 37F, includes transfer to metro). **Aéroport Orly** (tel. 49 75 15 15), 12km south of Paris, handles charters and many European flights. From Orly Sud, Gate H or Orly Ouest, Gate F, take the free shuttle bus to Orly train station and the RER C2 to central Paris (35min., 27F).

Trains: SNCF (tel. 45 82 50 50 for info; 45 65 60 60 for reservations). Guard your valuables; don't buy train or metro tickets from anyone except the uniformed personnel in the booths. **Gare du Nord** for northern France, Belgium, Netherlands,

Scandinavia, and northern Germany. To: Brussels (3hr., 220F); Amsterdam (5-6hr., 356F); Cologne (5-6hr., 332F); Copenhagen (16hr., 1030F). **Gare de l'Est** for eastern France, Luxembourg, northern Switzerland, southern Germany, and Austria. To: Zürich (6hr., 375F). **Gare de Lyon** for southeastern France, southern Switzerland, Italy, and Greece. To: Geneva (4hr. by TGV, 402F plus 16-80F reservation); Rome (14-16hr., 678F). **Gare d'Austerlitz** for southwestern France, Spain, and Portugal. To: Barcelona (11-14hr., 575F); Madrid (12-16hr., 561F). **Gare St-Lazare** for Normandy. **Gare de Montparnasse** for Brittany and the TGV to southwestern France. All train stations are also metro stops for at least 2 lines.

Buses: Many international buses arrive at **Gare Routière Internationale,** av. du Général de Gaulle, Bagnolet (tel. 49 72 51 51; M: Gallieni; formerly at Porte de la Villette). Check with your company for the precise location. For international bus info, call **International Express Eurolines Coach Station** (tel. 40 38 93 93).

Public Transportation: The Paris subway, **Métropolitain** or **Métro (M),** is quick and efficient. Lines are referred to by final destination and connections are called *correspondances.* Tickets anywhere within the city cost 6.50F; a *carnet* of 10 is 39F. Several passes allow unlimited travel on the metro and buses. At 90F for 3 days and 145F for 5, the *Paris Visite* tourist ticket probably isn't worth it (valid for unlimited travel on bus, metro, and RER, and discounts on sight-seeing trips, bicycle rentals, and more). *Formule 1* is valid for one day (27F). The weekly *(hebdomadaire)* **Coupon Vert** allows unlimited travel (starting on the first day of the week) but must be accompanied by the ID-style **Carte Orange.** To get your *carte orange,* bring an ID photo to the ticket counter and then purchase your handsome *coupon vert* (59F). *Hold onto your ticket* until you exit the metro. If caught without one, you must pay a hefty fine. Any changes to the **RER** (Réseau Express Régional—commuter train to the suburbs, express subway within central Paris) require inserting your validated (and uncrumpled) ticket into a turnstile. Metro service runs approximately 5:30am-12:15am (check the *Princi-pes de Tarification* poster on every platform for specifics on each line). **Buses** require their own 6F tickets (purchased from driver, *tabacs,* or metro stations); on trips crossing 2 zones (refer to route map on buses) you'll need 2 tickets, both of which must be validated in the machine by the driver's seat. Buses run until 8:30pm, *autobus du soir* until 12:30am and a few *noctambus* (3-4 tickets) run all night to the *portes* of the city from the Châtelet stop. For info on the services of RATP, contact the **Bureau de Tourisme RATP,** pl. de la Madeleine, 8ᵉ (tel. 40 06 71 45; M: Madeleine; open Mon.-Sat. 7:30am-7pm). An English-speaking representative is usually available.

Taxis: Cab stands near train stations and major bus stops. 3-person max. Taxis are expensive, especially if you don't speak French. When you call (tel. 47 39 47 39, 42 41 50 50, or 42 70 41 41), the meter starts running immediately (i.e., before you are picked up). A 12-15% tip is customary.

Hitchhiking: Thumbing out of Paris is difficult and unsafe. Hitchhikers ask around at youth hostels for tips on where to hitch. They don't wait at *portes* (city exits); traffic is too heavy for cars to stop safely. Because of decreased traffic, hitchers find summer a better time to hitchhike. A sign clearly stating the destination, with the letters "S.V.P." *(s'il vous plaît)* helps ingratiate drivers. Hitchhikers sometimes ask customers at gas stations if they are going their way. For a more formal "hitch," **Allostop-Provoya,** 84, passage Brady, 10ᵉ (tel. 42 46 00 66; M: Strasbourg-St-Denis), will try to match you with a driver going your way. An economical way to go; price varies according to destination.

Luggage Lockers: At all train stations. 15F.

Lost Property: Bureau des Objets Trouvés, 36, rue des Morillons, 15ᵉ (tel. 45 31 98 11). M: Convention. When you visit or write, describe the object and when and where it was lost. No information given by phone. Open Mon. and Wed. 8:30am-5pm, Tues. and Thurs. 8:30am-8pm.

Bookstores: Shakespeare and Co., 37, rue de la Bûcherie, 5ᵉ, across the Seine from Notre-Dame. M: St-Michel. A quirky and wide-ranging selection of new and used books. Bins outside offer a mixed bag of bargains, including many French classics in English (30F). Open noon-midnight.

FRANCE

Gay and Lesbian Services: Maison des Homosexualités, 25, rue Michel-le-Compte, 3e (tel. 42 77 72 77). M: Rambuteau. Provides info on gay and lesbian activities. Open Mon.-Sat. 3-8pm.

Public Baths: Beat the high cost of hotel showers at 8, rue des Deux Ponts, 4e (tel. 43 54 47 40). M: Pont-Marie. Showers 6F, with soap and towel 18F. Open Thurs. noon-7pm, Fri. 8am-7pm, Sat. 7am-7pm, Sun. 8am-noon.

Crises: SOS Friendship (tel. 47 23 80 80). Assistance in English for the depressed and lonely. Open 3-11pm. **Rape: SOS Viol** (tel. 05 05 95 95). Call free from anywhere in France. Open Mon.-Fri. 10am-6pm.

Pharmacy: Les Champs Elysées, 84, av. des Champs-Elysées, 8e (tel. 45 62 02 41). M: George V. **Grande Pharmacie Daumesnil,** 6, pl. Félix-Eboué, 12e (tel. 43 43 19 03). M. Daumesnil. Visible as you exit the metro. Both open 24 hrs.

Medical Assistance: Hôpital Franco-Britannique de Paris, 3, rue Barbès, in the suburb of Levallois-Perret (tel. 46 39 22 22). M: Anatole France. Consultations with English-speaking doctors. **Hôpital Americain,** 63, bd. Victor Hugo, Neuilly (tel. 46 41 25 25), also in the 'burbs. M: Porte Maillot, then bus 82 until the end of the line. More expensive. Blue Cross-Blue Shield accepted if you fill out the forms first. Dental service.

Emergency: Ambulance: tel. 15. **Fire:** tel. 18. **Police:** tel. 17. Police station in every *arrondissement;* call the operator (tel. 12) for the nearest.

ACCOMMODATIONS

If at all possible, make a reservation *before* coming to Paris; it will make your first day in the luminous city far more pleasant, and you just might be able to stay in the city center without paying a fortune for it. The **Office du Tourisme** listed in the Practical Information section can also book rooms, although the lines may be long and the selections not the cheapest in Paris. Otherwise, don't panic. Instead of calling around or showing up at hotels, try the booking services listed below:

La Centrale de Réservations (FUAJ-HI), 4, bd. Jules Ferry, 11e (tel. 43 57 02 60, fax 40 21 79 92). M: République. The best way to secure a bed in a hostel or to book any other budget accommodation in Paris. Rooms for 90-130F per night per person. Same-day reservations in one of their affiliated youth hostels or budget hotels—a total of 10,000 beds in and around the city. The earlier you show up, the better, but they can usually help anyone, any time. Books beds throughout France and Europe and arranges excursions. Open Mon.-Sat. 9am-6pm.

Accueil des Jeunes en France (AJF), 119, rue St-Martin, 4^e (tel. 42 77 87 80). M: Rambuteau. Walk away from rue Rambuteau along side of Centre Pompidou; turn left down street opposite plaza in front of the museum; AJF is halfway down this street, facing the Pompidou. Guarantees "decent and low-cost lodging with immediate reservation" for the same day only. You must pay the full price of the *foyer* room when making your reservation, even before seeing the room. AJF can also help find a hotel room, though not always for the full duration of your stay. English spoken. 10F fee. Open Mon.-Sat. 9am-5:30pm; Oct.-May Mon.-Sat. 9:30am-6pm. Other offices: 139, bd. St-Michel, 5^e (tel. 43 54 95 86; M: Port-Royal; open Mon.-Fri. 10am-12:30pm and 1:30-6:15pm) and Gare du Nord, 10^e (tel. 42 85 86 19; open June-Sept. 8:30am-5:15pm).

Hostels and Foyers

Paris's big-city hostels don't bother with many of the restrictions—sleep sheets, curfews and the like—that characterize most hostels in the world, but they do have maximum stays (though even these are flexible). There are only two HI hostels in the city proper. The rest of the dorm-like accommodations in Paris are either non-HI hostels or *foyers,* many of which are full-time dorms during the academic year, and have different characters, rules, and prices.

Centre International de Paris (BVJ). Relatively luxurious chain of youth hostels. **Paris Louvre,** 20, rue J.-J. Rousseau, 1er (tel. 42 36 88 18, fax 42 33 40 53). M: Louvre. Lunch or dinner 50F. **Paris Opéra,** 11, rue Thérèse, 1er (tel. 42 60 77 23, fax

42 33 40 53). M: Pyramides. 68 beds. Bigger rooms with fewer beds; more subdued than Paris Louvre. Open March-Sept. **Paris Les Halles,** 5, rue du Pélican, 1er (tel. 40 26 92 45; fax 42 33 40 53). M: Palais Royal. Low-ceilings, somewhat cramped rooms. Open March-Sept. **Paris Quartier Latin,** 44, rue des Bernardins, 5e (tel. 43 29 34 80, fax 42 33 40 53). M: Maubert-Mutualité. Filled with a friendly, boisterous crowd. All hostels open 6am-2am. No families. Rooms available at 2:30pm. Singles, doubles, triples, and quads 120F per person, breakfast and showers included. No singles in Paris Louvre. Weekend reservations accepted up to one week in advance; reserve one day ahead for weekday bookings.

Maisons des Jeunes Rufz de l'Avison, 18, rue J.-J. Rousseau, 1er (tel. 45 08 02 10). M: Louvre (not "Musée du Louvre") or Palais-Royal. Summer coed foyer. Stunning open-air courtyard looks like a king's picnic area. Doubles, triples, and quads 95F per person. 3-day min. stay. Reception open 7am-7pm. No curfew. Shower and breakfast included. Reserve by mail with 1 night's payment or arrive early.

Hôtel des Jeunes (MIJE) (tel. 42 74 23 45, fax 42 74 08 93) Three first-rate *foyers* located in former aristocratic residences of the Marais. **Le Fourcy,** 6, rue de Fourcy, 4^e. M: St-Paul. **Le Fauconnier,** 11, rue du Fauconnier. M: St-Paul or Pont Marie. A luxury in modern hostelry. **Maubuisson,** 12, rue des Barres. M: Hôtel-de-Ville. Ages 18-30. 7-day max. stay. English spoken. Reception open 7am. Check-out noon. Lockout noon-4pm. Silence after 10pm. Curfew 1am. 115F. Individuals may reserve rooms only in person and by paying in full in advance. Rebooking must be requested before 10pm the day before.

Young and Happy (Y&H) Hostel, 80, rue Mouffetard, 5^e (tel. 45 35 09 53, fax 47 07 22 24). M: Monge. Lively hostel with clean, cramped rooms in the heart of the raucous student quarter. Lockout 11am-5pm. Curfew 1am. 95F per night, 600F per week. Sheets 12F. Reservations with 1 night's deposit or show up at 8am.

Foyer International des Etudiantes, 93, bd. St-Michel, 6^e (tel. 43 54 49 63). M: Luxembourg. Across from Jardin du Luxembourg. Marbled reception area and elegant wood panelling everywhere. Oct.-June women only; open Sun.-Fri. 6am-1:30am, Sat. 24hrs.; singles 133F, doubles 82F per person, breakfast and shower included. July-Sept. men and women; open 24 hrs.; singles 155F, doubles 105F per person, breakfast and shower included. Reserve in writing 2 months in advance, 200F deposit if confirmed. Call ahead or arrive around 9:30am.

Auberge de Jeunesse "Jules Ferry" (HI), 8, bd. Jules Ferry 11e (tel. 43 57 55 60). M: République. Walk east on rue du Faubourg du Temple and turn right on the far side of bd. Jules Ferry. Wonderfully located. Clean, large rooms. Most spaces full by 10am. If they are full, they'll help you find other city lodgings; they work with the **Centrale de Réservations,** located at 4, bd. Jules Ferry. 3-night max. stay (sometimes extended during the winter). Reception open 24hrs. Lockout noon-2pm. No curfew. 4-6 bed dorms 105F. Doubles 115F per person. Showers and breakfast included. Lockers 5F. Sheets 14F (paper in summer '94; by winter '94-'95, they may have 25F cotton sheets).

Résidence Bastille (AJF), 151, av. Ledru-Rollin, 11e (tel. 43 79 53 86). M: Voltaire. Attractive rooms and a friendly multilingual staff. Ages 18-35 only, though not strictly enforced. Reception open 7am-1am. Lockout noon-4pm. Curfew 1am. 113F. Showers, breakfast, and sheets included. No reservations, so arrive early in the morning. A welcoming station at the Gare du Nord, inside the suburban station (tel. 42 85 86 19) can make same-day reservations.

Maison Internationale des Jeunes, 4, rue Titon, 11^e (tel. 43 71 99 21, fax 43 71 78 58). M: Faidherbe-Chaligny. Well-located, exceptionally clean, airy, and tranquil, with a garden in back whose bushes hide a pair of pet bunnies. Big, bright, clean rooms with 2-8 beds for ages 18-30 (flexible). Coed bathrooms. Family housing. Handicapped access. 3- or 4-day max. stay. Reception open 8am-2am. Lockout 10am-5pm. Curfew 2am. Silence 10pm-8am. 110F. Showers and breakfast included. Sheets 15F.

Association des Foyers de Jeunes: Foyer des Jeunes Filles, 234, rue de Tolbiac, 13e (tel. 44 16 22 22, fax 45 65 46 20). M: Glacière. Large, modern *foyer* for young women (ages 18-30) with great facilities. Reception open 24hrs. July-Aug. 110F. Showers and breakfast included. Sept.-June 100F. Breakfast and dinner included. 30F registration fee (good for a year) required of all first-time visitors.

FIAP Jean-Monet, 30, rue Cabanis 14ᵉ (tel. 45 89 89 15, fax 45 81 63 91). M: Glacière. Comfortable, well-furnished rooms with toilet and shower. Some rooms wheelchair accessible. 3-day max. stay. Singles 250F. Doubles 165F per person. Quads 145F per person. 8-bed rooms 120F per person. Open April-Sept. MC, Visa.

Aloha Hostel, 1, rue Borromée, 15ᵉ (tel. 42 73 03 03), on a tiny side street across from 243, rue de Vaugirard. M: Volontaires. Despite the cheesy name, one of the best in the city. Bright rooms with new beds, new mattresses, and freshly painted interiors. Lockout 11am-5pm. 85F per person. 537F per person per week. Arrive at 9am or send 1 night's deposit for reservations.

Three Ducks Hostel, 6, pl. Etienne Pernet, 15ᵉ (tel. 48 42 04 05). M: Commerce. Without a doubt one of the most rowdy and fun hangouts in the city for young vacationing backpackers during the summer months. Central courtyard becomes a loud, fun café hangout on summer nights when a young, mostly Anglo crowd drinks cheap beer from the hostel's watering hole, **Richie's Bar.** Flexible 1-week max. stay. Lockout 11am-5pm. Curfew 1am. 93F. 630F per week. Reservations accepted with 1 night's deposit. Witty, worthwhile 6hr. guided **mountain bike tours** (tel. 48 42 57 87) of Paris begin here (118F per person includes insurance).

Auberge de Jeunesse "Le d'Artagnan" (HI), 80, rue Vitruve, 20ᵉ (tel. 43 61 08 75, fax 43 61 75 40). M: Porte de Bagnolet or Porte de Montreuil. A cross between a hostel and a mall. Mostly triples; a few doubles; some 8-bed rooms. English spoken. Wheelchair access. Flexible 3-day max. stay. Open 24hrs. Lockout 10am-2pm. Triples and dorms 100F per person. Doubles 115-125F per person. Breakfast and sheets included. Lockers 15F. Reservations a must; hostel is packed Feb.-Oct.

Hotels

Of the three classes of Parisian budget accommodations, hotels may be the most practical for the majority of travelers. There are no curfews, no school groups, total privacy, and often concerned managers—features hostels and *foyers* usually can't offer. Groups of 3 and 4 may actually find it more economical to stay in a hotel. Note that Parisian law forbids hanging laundry from windows or over balconies to dry; proprietors will remind you that food in the rooms attracts mice. Expect to pay at least 150F for a single, but only 40-60F more for a single-bedded double; 2-bed doubles are rare and cost considerably more. In less expensive hotels, few rooms come with private bath. If you book a room without a shower, you will usually have to pay 15-25F for the key to the hall shower.

Rooms disappear quickly after morning checkout (generally 10am-noon), so try to arrive early or reserve ahead; all hotels accept reservations unless otherwise noted and generally require one night's deposit payable by credit card of check in francs. Instead of parading yourself and your bags around town all morning, call first.

Marais-Bastille-République

The Marais has emerged as a pivot for sometimes upscale, alternative nightlife. Around **Opéra Bastille,** inexpensive hotels cluster close to alterno-chic clubs, bars, and other signs of misspent youth.

Grand Hôtel des Arts et Métiers, 4, rue Borda, 3ᵉ (tel. 48 87 73 89, fax 48 87 66 58). M: Arts-et-Métiers. Decent location, clean linen, clean bathrooms, and mostly clean rooms. Minimal English. Singles 130-2700F. Doubles 200-270F. 10-20% *Let's Go* discount. Showers 20F. Breakfast 20F. MC, Visa.

Hôtel Picard, 26, rue de Picardie, 3ᵉ (tel. 48 87 53 82, fax 48 87 02 56). M: République. Cheerful, smallish rooms. Twin doubles are bunk-bed style. 10% *Let's Go* discount for stays of more than 1 night. Singles 200-320F. Doubles 240-390F. Triples 510F. Extra bed 120F. Showers 20F. Breakfast 30F. MC, Visa.

Hôtel Bretagne, 87, rue des Archives, 3ᵉ (tel. 48 87 83 14). M: Temple. Cheaper rooms are simple; pricier ones have TVs and snazzy bathroom fixtures. Singles 155-300F. Doubles 195-350F. Triples 330-500F. Quad 440-600F. Breakfast 30F.

Castex Hôtel, 5, rue Castex, 4ᵉ (tel. 42 72 31 52, fax 42 72 57 91). M: Bastille. Affable family management tends to these tidy, streamlined rooms. English spoken.

Check-in 1pm. Singles 215-265F. Doubles 280-340F. Triple 440F. Reserve 7-8 weeks in advance. MC, Visa.

Hôtel de la Herse d'Or, 20, rue St-Antoine, 4^e (tel. 48 87 84 09). M: Bastille. Expect pared-down decor and only rudimentary English from the desk clerk. Singles and doubles 150-270F. Triples 375-405F. 10% less Nov.-May. Breakfast 25F. Reserve 1-3 days in advance.

Hôtel Practic, 9, rue d'Ormesson, 4^e (tel. 48 87 80 47, fax 48 87 40 04). M: St-Paul. Clean, practical little rooms make good on the hotel's name. Basic English spoken. Singles 150F. Doubles 230-340F. Free showers for guests in rooms without them. Breakfast 25F, served 7-11am.

Palace Hôtel, 3, rue Bouchardon, 10^e (tel. 42 06 59 32). M: Strasbourg/St-Denis. Lots of sunny doubles and triples. Safe back-street location. English spoken. Singles 100F. Doubles 140-250F. Triples 180-280F. Quad 230-350F. Breakfast 20F. Reserve two weeks in advance in summer. Visa.

Cambrai Hôtel, 129*bis*, bd. de Magenta, 10e (tel. 48 78 32 13, fax 48 78 43 55). M: Gare du Nord. Clean, airy rooms with high ceilings. Singles 133-204F. Doubles 181-251F. Triples 344-367F. Showers 20F. Breakfast included.

Hôtel de Belfort, 37, rue Servan, 11e (tel. 47 00 67 33, fax 43 57 97 98). M: Père Lachaise. Especially attractive for its *Let's Go* special: only 100F per person per night in doubles, triples, and quads. English spoken. Lizard King's tomb is a stone's throw away. Breakfast 15F with *Let's Go* special. MC, Visa.

Louvre-Palais Royal

Henri IV, 25, place Dauphine, 1er (tel. 43 54 44 53). M: Cité. Last outpost of cheap accommodations on Ile de la Cité; one of the best-located hotels in the city. Somewhat dilapidated, average-sized rooms with squishy beds. Singles 105-135F. Doubles 140-195F. Triples 190-220F. Quads 250F. Reserve 2 months in advance.

Hôtel de Lille, 8, rue du Pélican, 1er (tel. 42 33 33 42). M: Palais-Royal. Functional rooms with slightly worn mattresses and decor. Outside door locked at 9pm; arrive before 7pm to pick up your personal and main door keys. Singles 170F. Doubles 200-250F. Showers 30F. Reserve 1 month in advance.

Hôtel du Palais, 2, quai de la Mégisserie, 1er (tel. 42 36 98 25, fax 42 21 41 67). M: Châtelet. Location by the Seine gives all rooms (except those on top floor) splendid views. Double-glazing reduces street noise from animal market outside (no joke). Singles 280-350F. Doubles 320-380F. Triple 420F. Large quad (480F) and quint (550F). Garret-like top floor: singles 180F, doubles 230F. Shower included for top-floor rooms. In summer, reserve 3 weeks in advance. MC, Visa.

Rue Montmartre-Faubourg Montmartre

Hôtel La Marmotte, 6, rue Léopold Bellan, 2e (tel. 40 26 26 51). M: Sentier. Well-kept rooms with firm beds and high ceilings. Singles 180-260F. Doubles 200-290F. 2-bed double with shower and toilet 300F. Extra bed 80F. Breakfast 20F. Shower 15F. Reserve 2-3 weeks in advance. AmEx, MC, Visa.

Hôtel des Trois Poussins, 15, rue Clauzel, 9^e (tel. 48 74 38 20). M: St-Georges. Quiet family-owned hotel with a lovely courtyard and clean rooms. Singles 140-150F. Doubles 220–260F. Basic English spoken. Showers 15F. Breakfast 25F. Reserve 2-4 weeks in advance.

Latin Quarter

Revolving around the **Sorbonne** and the **Ecole des Beaux-Arts,** the *quartier latin* shelters café-filled squares, markets, and an explosive nightlife.

Hôtel d'Esmeralda, 4, rue St-Julien-le-Pauvre, 5e (tel. 43 54 19 20, fax 40 51 00 68). M: St-Michel. Homey, traditionally furnished rooms and friendly, multilingual staff. Singles 160-320F. Doubles 420-490F. Triples 550F. Quads 600F. Shower 10F.

Hôtel des Médicis, 214, rue St-Jacques, 5e (tel. 43 54 14 66). M: Luxembourg. Rooms are in better repair than the lobby. Conveniently located near cafés and groceries. Singles and doubles 75-160F. Showers 10F. Reception open 9am-10pm.

Hôtel des Grandes Ecoles, 75, rue Cardinal Lemoine, 5e (tel. 43 26 79 23, fax 43 25 28 15). M: Cardinal Lemoine. Impeccably clean, tasteful rooms to the great pleasure of its faithful guests. Singles 450-480F. Doubles 530-550F. Breakfast 40F. Reserve well in advance. MC, Visa.

Hôtel des Alliés, 20, rue Berthollet, 5e (tel. 43 31 47 52; fax 45 35 13 92), off bd. Port Royal. M: Censier-Daubenton. Clean, comfortable rooms for next to nothing. Singles 135-145F. Doubles 180–295F. Showers 15F. Breakfast 28F. Reserve with 1 night's deposit. MC, Visa.

Hôtel Gay Lussac, 29, rue Gay-Lussac, 5e (tel. 43 54 23 96). M: Luxembourg. Carefully cleaned, sunlit rooms with sculpted plaster ceilings. Doubles and singles 150-350F. Triples or quads 500F. Breakfast 25F. Reserve by phone; no deposit required.

Hôtel Nesle, 7, rue du Nesle, 6e (tel. 43 54 62 41). M: Odéon. Through-the-looking-glass excursion away from the monotony of Paris' like-seeming budget hotels. Singles 200F. Doubles 160-350F. Toilets in the hall if not in your room. Shower 25F. Breakfast 25F. No reservations accepted.

Hôtel Stella, 41, rue Monsieur-le-Prince, 6e (tel 43 26 43 49, fax 43 54 97 28). M: Odéon. Wood-trimmed bedrooms are pleasant and breezy. Singles 198F. Doubles 274F.

Hôtel St-André des Arts, 66, rue St-André-des-Arts, 6e (tel. 43 26 96 16, fax 43 29 73 34). M: Odéon. Beautiful, unusual fabric is used for walls, curtains, and bedding. Central location. Singles 220-320F. Doubles 410- 430F. Triples 500-520F. All rooms have toilets. Breakfast included. MC, V.

Champs de Mars-Eiffel Tower

You'll be close, but don't expect a view.

Hôtel de la Paix, 19, rue du Gros Caillou, 7e (tel. 45 51 86 17). M: Ecole Militaire. Some worn carpets, soft mattresses, and peeling paint, but fairly clean and quiet. Reception open 9am-10pm. Check-out at noon. Singles 145-210F. Doubles 270-340F. Triples 440F. Shower 15F. Breakfast 32F. Reservations recommended.

Grand Hôtel Lévêque, 29, rue Cler, 7e (tel. 47 05 49 15, fax 45 50 49 36). M: Ecole Militaire. Small rooms have beautifully tiled bathrooms and wake-up-call service. Reception open 24hrs. Singles and doubles 195-355F. Triples 420F. Extra bed 80F. Breakfast 25F. Reserve by phone, confirm in writing. MC, Visa.

Montparnasse

Renowned for its nightlife, Montparnassse lured Picasso and his cronies from Montmartre. Today, areas closest to flashy **bd. du Montparnasse** maintain their vitality while adjoining neighborhoods are residential and sedate.

Hôtel de Blois, 5, rue des Plantes, 14e (tel. 45 40 99 48, fax 45 40 45 62). M: Mouton-Duvernet. Full bathrooms, TVs, telephones, and pseudo-Laura Ashley décor. Doubles 220-270F. Triples 350F. Shower 15F. Breakfast 25F. AmEx, MC, Visa.

Hôtel du Midi, 4, av. René-Coty, 14e (tel. 43 27 23 25, fax 43 21 24 58), off pl. Denfert-Rochereau. M: Denfert-Rochereau. A large, professionally run hotel that recalls a Holiday Inn. Doubles 228-328F. Breakfast 30F. MC, Visa.

Hôtel Plaisance, 53, rue de Gergovie, 14e (tel. 45 42 11 39 or 45 42 20 33, fax 41 13 74 42). M: Pernety. Good value if not inspirational. Singles 135-210F. Doubles 170-250F. Showers 20F. Breakfast 25F. AmEx, MC, Visa.

FOOD

Neither budget travelers nor most Parisians have the time, appetite, or cash for the Rabelaisian (or Spielerian) stupor that six-course meals require. Both affordable and eminently French are the breads, cheeses, and pastries that appear as standard fare. With a bakery on every corner and dozens of open-air markets, food is a high-profile, high-quality affair. The restaurants of Paris are a diverse lot; don't hesitate to try one of the many wonderful and inexpensive Vietnamese, North African, or Middle Eastern restaurants that dot the city. Otherwise, crunch a *croque monsieur* or a plate of quiche at a sidewalk café. Or absorb the best of both at a *bistro,* an amusingly pretentious café-restaurant hybrid. For a light meal accompanied by excellent wine, hit one of Paris's many wine bars, cozy places that seem to sidestep the tourist onslaught. Every *arrondissement* has at least one outdoor market (most last Mon.-Sat. 7am-noon). Ask at your hotel or hostel for the nearest one. When assembling a picnic, visit some of the many speciality shops throughout the city. For concentration of shops selling everything from warm baguettes to eggs in aspic, head for **rue Montorgeuil**, 2ᵉ, or **rue Mouffetard**, 5ᵉ. Exotic mushrooms and other produce overflow at the **Marché Bastille** on bd. Richard-Lenoir (M: Bastille; Thurs. and Sun. 7am-1:30pm). Beer and soda, including your fave *eau minérale,* are really cheap in supermarkets. Above all, be bold, be adventurous, and treat yourself at least once: you may never get another chance to slurp snails by the Seine.

Restaurants

Marais-Bastille-République

Even with prices on the rise, budget restaurants are holding their ground in the Marais. Filling, inexpensive meals are easily culled from the delis and falafel stands on **rue des Rosiers,** pulse of the Marais's Jewish quarter. Catering to locals rather than tourists, restaurants in the 10ᵉ permit visitors to soak up a Paris that doesn't revolve around the Eiffel Tower or the Louvre. **Passage Brady,** filled with Indian eateries, offers a festival of the palate for rock-bottom prices. The eleventh's restaurants fill to capacity with young and chic regulars who stay through the night.

La Dame Tartine, 2, rue Brisemiche, 4ᵉ (tel. 42 77 32 22). M: Rambuteau. Next to the Stravinsky fountain. Also at 69, rue de Lyon, 12ᵉ (tel. 44 68 96 95). Just a stone's throw from the Pompidou's album-cover street life, the terrace fills with a mostly young, dressed-down crowd. Main courses 25-40F. Open noon-11:30pm.

Chez Marianne, 2, rue des Hôspitalières-St-Gervais, 4ᵉ (tel. 42 72 18 86). M: St-Paul. Folksy canteen and specialty store offering Israeli and Eastern European specialties. *Falafel* (30F), blini (10F). Sample 4, 5, or 6 specialties (55F, 65F, or 75F). Take-out available. Open Sat.-Thurs. 11am-midnight.

Auberge de Jarente, 7, rue de Jarente, 4ᵉ (tel. 42 77 49 35). M: St-Paul. Basque specialties like *cailles* (quail) and *cuisses de grenouilles* (frogs' legs). 115F *menu* includes appetizer, main course, salad or cheese, and dessert. 75F lunch *menu.* Open Tues.-Sat. noon-2:30pm and 7:30-10:30pm. AmEx, MC, Visa.

L'as du Falafel, 34, rue des Rosiers, 4ᵉ (tel. 48 87 63 60). M: St-Paul. In *Rolling Stone,* Lenny Kravitz credited this little take-out sandwich shop with "the best falafel in the world, particularly the special eggplant falafel with hot sauce." Gonna go his way with the falafel (20F)? Hummus (18F), schwarma (32F).

Le Piano Show, 20, rue de la Verrerie, 4ᵉ (tel. 42 72 23 81). M: Hôtel-de-Ville. Welcome to the lipstick-smacking world of drag. It'll knock your pantyhose off! It may be a bit expensive, but divas cost and here's where you start paying. Dinner consists of *rôti de veau brisé, filet de dinde,* and *banane brésilienne* (*brésilien* is a French insider's slang for gay, and *banane* denotes, well, you know). Dinner and show Sun.-Thurs. 8:45pm-11:30pm. 199F. Reservations required. MC, V.

Paris-Dakar, 95, rue du Faubourg St-Martin, 10ᵉ (tel. 42 08 16 64). M: Gare de l'Est. African masks and batiks decorate this popular, family-run restaurant. Try *Yassa* (chicken with lime and onions, 70F) or *Tiep Bou Dieone,* the "national dish of Senegal" (fish with rice and veggies, 92F). Weekday lunch *menu* 59F, dinner *menu* 99F. Open Tues.-Sun. noon-3pm and 7pm-midnight. MC, V.

Kamathenu, 69, passage Brady, 10ᵉ (tel. 42 46 47 90). M: Château d'Eau or Strasbourg St-Denis Affordable South Asian restaurant. Tandoori plate 35F. Curries 43-63F. Take-out available. Open noon-midnight.

Au Trou Normand, 9, rue Jean-Pierre Timbaud, 11ᵉ (tel. 48 05 80 23). M: Oberkampf. Unbelievably low-priced, no-fuss French food. The *onglet rocquefort* and *frites* (30F) is a favorite. Appetizers 10-13F, *plats du jour* 29-39F, tasty desserts 9-13F. Open Sept.-July Mon.-Fri. noon-2:30pm and 7:30-11pm, Sat. 7:30-11pm.

Louvre-Palais Royal-Ile St-Louis

L'Incroyable, 26, rue de Richelieu or 23, rue de Montpensier, 1ᵉʳ (tel. 42 96 24 64). M: Palais-Royal. An intimate restaurant with an incredibly cheap 3-course *menu* (60F, 70F in the evening). Terrace and quaintly decorated interior. Open Tues.-

Fri. noon-2:15pm and 6:30-9pm, Sat. and Mon. noon-2:15pm. Closed late Dec. and for the first 2 weeks of Jan.

Berthillon, 31, rue St-Louis-en-l'Ile, 4ᵉ (tel. 43 54 31 61), on Ile-St-Louis. M: Cité or Pont Marie. The best ice cream and sorbet in Paris. Choose from dozens of *parfums* (flavors), ranging from chocolate to *tiramisu* to *cassis* (black currant). Since lines at the main store are quite long in summer, look for nearby Berthillon take-out windows. Open Sept.-July Wed.-Sun. 10am-8pm.

Montmartre

Touristy cafés and restaurants of the place du Tertre are pricey for dinner but perfect for coffee breaks. Otherwise, descend the *butte* toward cheaper eateries that circuit the lower hillside.

Refuge des Fondues, 17, rue des Trois Frères, 18ᵉ (tel. 42 55 22 65). M: Abbesses. A small, finger-food restaurant with only two main dishes: *fondue bourguignonne* (meat fondue) and *fondue savoyarde* (cheese fondue). Wine served in baby bottles; Freudian revulsion/American puritanism drive many to remove the nipples. The 85F *menu* includes a kir *apéritif,* half a jug of wine, appetizer, fondue, and dessert. Open 5pm-2am, dinner after 7pm.

Au Grain de Folie, 24, rue la Vieuville, 18ᵉ. M: Abbesses. A vegetarian restaurant for one and all, with a vast array of dishes from couscous to salads to every kind of cheese. On a quiet street. Dinner ala carte about 100F; also 65F and 100F *menus.* Open Tues.-Sun. noon-3pm and 7:30pm-1:30am, Mon 7:30-11:30pm.

La Villa du Poulbot, 10, rue Dancourt, 18ᵉ (tel. 42 55 28 44). M: Abbesses. Sumptuously elegant, scrumptiously cheap. Plush velvet chairs. 42F, 68F, 95F, and 120F *menus,* with specialties like *magret* (breast) of duck, seafood lasagna, and chicken in banana sauce. Open Tues.-Sun. noon-3pm and 6-9pm. MC, Visa.

Latin Quarter

Foraging for food in the 5ᵉ requires no special skills. Traditional French, Greek, and Lebanese restaurants dovetail along **rue Mouffetard** extending down **rue Descartes** all the way to **bd. St-Germain.** Budget restaurants line **rue du Pot-de-Fer.** In the 6ᵉ, tiny restaurants with rock-bottom *menus* jostle each other for space and customers in the area bounded by bd. St-Germain, **bd. St-Michel,** and the Seine.

L'Apostrophe, 34, rue de la Montagne Ste-Geneviève, 5ᵉ (tel. 43 54 10 93). M: Maubert-Mutualité. 3 well-priced *menus:* at 49F, served until 8pm; at 65F, served until 9pm; at 85F, served all night. The first two *menus* include an appetizer and main course (10F supplement for dessert or cheese course). The third offers 3 courses, with an all-you-can-eat buffet as an appetizer choice. Open 6pm-2am.

Restaurant Perraudin, 157, rue St-Jacques, 5ᵉ (tel. 46 33 15 75). M: Luxembourg. Gamble on *le plat du jour selon l'humeur du chef* (daily special according to the chef's mood), or try old favorites like *sautée d'agneau aux flageolets* (sautéed lamb with white beans) 58F. 3-course lunch *menu* 60F. Main dishes 58F. Open Tues.-Fri. noon-2:15pm and 7:30-10:15pm, Mon. and Sat. 7:30-10:15pm.

Café Le Volcan, 10, rue Thouin, 5ᵉ (tel. 46 33 38 33). M: Cardinal Lemoine. Boisterous restaurant heats up at night with a youthful crowd of regulars. Specializes in Greek dishes. 55F *menu* (served until 9pm) includes appetizer, main course, and dessert; at lunch it includes a glass of wine as well. Dinner *menus* 80-100F. Open noon-2pm and 7-11:30pm. MC, Visa.

Le Petit Vatel, 5, rue Lobineau, 6ᵉ (tel. 43 54 28 49). M: Odéon or Mabillon. Tiny restaurant but delicious, inexpensive meals. At lunch and on weekdays, choose a main dish plus an appetizer or dessert from the 59F *menu* on the chalkboard. Vegetarian plate is always offered. Take-out available. Open Mon.-Sat. noon-3pm and 7pm-midnight, Sun. 7pm-midnight. Closed 1 week in Aug. AmEx, MC, Visa.

Orestias, 4, rue Grégoire-de-Tours, 6ᵉ (tel. 43 54 62 01). M: Odéon or Mabillon. French food with heavy Greek influence: *dolmata,* Greek wine, and *baklava* are offered alongside more traditional French foods. 44F *menu.* Open Mon.-Sat. noon-2:30pm and 6-11:30pm. MC, Visa.

Kiotori, 61, rue Monsieur-le-Prince (tel. 43 54 48 44). M: Odéon or Luxembourg. A youthful international crowd packs this Japanese restaurant for succulent skewers of grilled beef, chicken, and shrimp, and picture-perfect plates of *sushi* and *maki*. *Menus* 40-90F. Open Mon.-Sat. noon-2:30pm and 7-11pm. MC, Visa.

Crémerie Restaurant Polidor, 41, rue Monsieur-le-Prince, 6ᵉ (tel. 43 26 95 34). M: Cluny-Sorbonne or Luxembourg. Traditional French cuisine cooked perfectly. *Menu* 100F. 3-course à la carte 120-130F. Open Mon.-Sat. noon-2:30pm and 7pm-12:30am, Sun. noon-2:30pm and 7-10pm.

Montparnasse

At the turn of the century, Bretons flocked into Montparnasse bringing their speciality *crêpes* and *galettes* (a larger, buckwheat version). Eateries in the 15ᵉ remain treasured local establishments, where owners personally welcome their regulars.

Aquarius Café, 40, rue de Gergovie, 14ᵉ (tel. 45 41 36 88). M: Pernety. Serene, slightly hip vegetarian restaurant. "Mixed grill" includes tofu sausages, cereal sausages, wheat pancakes, wheat germ, brown rice, and vegetables in a mushroom sauce for 65F. Aquarius salad (55F) with *chèvre*, avocado, egg, vegetable pâté, potato salad, *crudités,* and vinaigrette. Open Mon.-Sat. noon-2:30pm and 7-10:30pm. AmEx, MC, V.

Le Château Poivre, 145, rue du Château, 14ᵉ (tel. 43 22 03 68). M: Pernety. Generous portions, enhanced by 80 varieties of wine 89F *menu* (lunch and dinner, but not served after 10pm). Open Mon.-Sat. noon-2:30pm and 7-10:30pm.

Crêperie St-Malo, 53, rue de Montparnasse, 14ᵉ (tel. 43 20 87 19). M: Edgar Quinet. Perhaps a higher concentration of *crêpes* and *galettes* than in all of Brittany. *Menu—galette*, dessert *crêpe*, hard cider and coffee 49F. Open Mon.-Fri. noon-3pm and 6pm-1am, Sat.-Sun. noon-midnight.

Café Aux Artistes, 63, rue Falguière, 15ᵉ (tel. 43 22 05 39). M: Falguière. Cheap restaurant with an extensive menu. 2-course lunch *menu* 55F, 3-course dinner 75F. Open Mon.-Fri. noon-2:30pm and 7pm-1am, Sat. 7pm-1am. MC, Visa.

Sampieru Corsu, 12, rue de l'Amiral Roussin, 15ᵉ. M: Cambronne. Run by a Marxist Corsican separatist. Simple tables which you might share with other visitors. Pay according to your means, though the suggested price for the simple, but copious, 3-course *menu* is 40F (beer or wine included). Open Mon.-Fri. 11:45am-1:45pm and 6:45-9:45pm.

Cafés

Even visitors to Paris who don't drink coffee should still think of cafés as a worthwhile haunts. Remember that café prices are two-tiered; it's cheaper at the counter *(comptoir* or *zinc)* than in the seating area, whether inside *(salle)* or on the *terrasse* (terrace). Both these prices should be posted. Aside from coffee and wine, other popular drinks include *citron pressé,* freshly squeezed lemon juice (with sugar and water on the side). Cafés also offer Coke, but charge lots. You can also order a wide range of spring, mineral, and soda waters. If not too famous and tourist-ridden, cafés serve light lunches and snacks that are definitely affordable. A *croque monsieur* (grilled ham-and-cheese sandwich), a *croque madame* (the same with a fried egg), and assorted omelets cost about 15-20F. A more popular choice is a salad. Listed here are some of the most historically important and currently fashionable cafés. By no means is this a list of budget establishments. Think of these cafés as museums, since the price of coffee or soda here is comparable to the average admission fee.

Café Beaubourg, 100, rue St-Martin, 4ᵉ (tel. 48 87 63 96). M: Rambuteau. An indoor-outdoor showcase for alternative chic, designed by Phillip Starck. Order whatever you can afford and linger. By all means check out the bat-cave-like bathrooms; boys, don't confuse the sinks and urinals. Coffee 17F, *café crème* or tea 25F, desserts 30F. Open Sun.-Thurs. 8am-1am, Fri.-Sat. 8am-2am.

La Closerie des Lilas, 171, bd. du Montparnasse, 6ᵉ (tel. 43 26 70 50). M: Port-Royal. One-time favorite of Hemingway and of the Dadaists and Surrealists before him. Picasso came here weekly to hear Paul Fort recite poetry. Coffee 15F, house wine 26F, *marquise au chocolat* 65F. Open noon-1am.

La Coupole, 102, bd. du Montparnasse, 14ᵉ (tel. 43 20 14 20). M: Vavin. Enormous Art Deco café. Former patrons include Lenin, Stravinsky, Hemingway, and Einstein. The *menus* are outrageously expensive, but you can still afford a coffee (10F). *Café crème* 20F, beer 20-27F, sandwiches 15-25F. Open noon-2am.

Les Deux Magots, 6, pl. St-Germain-des-Prés, 6ᵉ (tel. 45 48 55 25). M. St-Germain-des-Prés. Home to Parisian literati since it opened in 1875, Les Deux Magots is now a favorite among Left Bank Parisian youth. *Café des Deux Magots* 21F, *café-crème* 24F, *chocolat des Deux Magots* (a house specialty) 28F, beer 26-38F, ham sandwich 34F. Open 7am-1:30am.

SIGHTS

You're not the first person to be fascinated by Paris. Over the centuries people have sung her praises, painted her portrait, and immortalized her in film and photographs. What is it about this city that creates such mystique and evokes such attraction? With map in hand, comfortable shoes on feet, and adventurous spirit, you are ready to discover what makes Paris tick. Sights in Paris, however impressive by day, achieve new glamor once dark falls. At night, spotlights go up over everything from the Panthéon to the Eiffel Tower, Notre Dame, and Obélisque; Paris' monuments transform into glittering chandeliers.

Ile de la Cité and Ile St-Louis If any one location could be called the sentimental and physical heart of Paris, it is the **Ile de la Cité.** Since the third century BC, when it was inhabited by a primitive Gallic tribe of hunters, sailors, and fisherfolk called the Parisii, it has been the administrative center of Paris and the home of kings. When Baron von Haussmann rolled through, he destroyed the island's traditional appearance, reducing its medieval monuments to misplaced relics. Now the island sinks under the weight of countless tour buses whose passengers spill into souvenir shops to buy the only berets you're likely to see in Paris. The **Cathédrale de Notre-Dame de Paris** (M: Cité) was begun in 1163 but not completed until 1361. After the Revolution, the building fell into disrepair and was even used to shelter livestock, but Victor Hugo's 1831 novel, *Notre-Dame-de-Paris (The Hunchback of Notre Dame)* inspired thousands of citizens to push for restoration. The modifications by the architect Eugène Viollet-le-Duc (including the addition of the spire, the gargoyles, and a statue of himself admiring his own work) remain highly controversial. Thousands of visitors float in sweeping torrents past the doors of the cathedral, overlooking one the most glorious aspects of the entire structure: the **façade.** Inside, the soaring light and apparent weightlessness of the walls—effects produced by brilliant engineering and optical illusions—inspire awe in even the most church-weary. The cathedral's biggest draw is the enormous stained-glass **rose windows** that dominate the north and south ends of the transept. A rousing **tour** in English is led by Irving Levine, "the only non-Roman Catholic to give tours at Notre-Dame." A 60-year-old psychiatric social worker from Atlantic City and Washington, D.C., he has been living in Paris for the last 28 years (tours in English Wed. and Thurs. noon, in French daily noon; free). A perilous and claustrophobic staircase inside the **towers** emerges onto a spectacular perch, where weather-worn gargoyles survey a stunning view of the city's heart. (Towers open 9:30am-6pm. 31F, seniors and students 20F, under 17: 7F. Cathedral open Mon.–Sat.8am-7pm, Sun. 8am-8pm. Confession in English.)

The **Palais de Justice** has harbored Paris district courts since the 13th century. Obscured somewhat by the Palais, **Ste-Chapelle** remains one of the foremost examples of 13th-century French architecture, built to house the most precious of King Louis IX s possessions, the crown of thorns from Christ's Passion. (Open 9:30am-6:30pm. 25F, students and seniors 17F, under 17: 6F.) **The Conciergerie,** one of Paris's most infamous prisons, lurks ominously around the corner of the Palais from the entrance to the Chapelle, brooding over the souls and memories of the prisoners who died here during the Revolution, including Marie Antoinette and Robespierre. (Open 9:30am-6:30pm; Oct.-March 10am-5pm. 26F, students and seniors 17F, under 17: 7F. Combo ticket to Conciergerie and Ste-Chapelle 40F.)

A short walk across the Pont St-Louis will take you to **Ile St-Louis,** among the city's most charming and elegant neighborhoods. Some of the most privileged of Paris's exceedingly privileged elite, including the Rothschilds and Pompidou's widow, now call this scrap of land home. At night, Ile St-Louis comes alive with the glow of cast-iron lamps, outlined against the shadows of the Seine.

The Latin Quarter and St-Germain-des-Prés Home since the 13th century to the famed **Sorbonne,** the *quartier latin* evokes bookish bohemians scribbling works-in-progress in attic apartments or corner cafés. After the student uprisings of May 1968, the University of Paris was decentralized, and in one blow, the *quartier* lost many of its inhabitants. Then a tidal wave of tourist gold swept over the area and crushed many of its small bookstores and cafés. Much of the area now resembles any other Parisian commercial center.

The Panthéon, its proud dome visible from any point in the Latin Quarter, towers over the highest point of the Left Bank (M: Cardinal Lemoine). In the **crypt** you'll find the remains of Voltaire, Rousseau, Victor Hugo, Emile Zola, Jean Jaurès, and Louis Braille decaying peacefully in their stone tombs, which can be viewed from behind locked iron gates at each of their niches. The **dome** lavishes you with an up-close view of a horrifyingly garish set of Neoclassical frescoes and a disappointing view of the surrounding neighborhood. One ticket provides entry to both. (Crypt and dome open 9:30am-6:30pm. 26F, students 17F.)

If an average walk in the park bores you, stroll through the **Jardin des Plantes,** 57, rue Cuvier (M: Jussieu). Opened in 1640 for the sole purpose of growing medicinal plants to promote His Majesty's health, it now supports a conglomeration of museums and a dejected-seeming **zoo.** A walk through the park is, of course, free, but the many museums charge admission. (Zoo open in summer 9am-6pm, in winter 9am-5pm. 25F, students and under 17: 15F.) The **boulevard St-Michel,** with its fashionable cafés, restaurants, bookstores and movie theaters, courses with student life. **Place St-Michel,** at the northern tip of this *grand avenue,* stands as a medley of the surrounding neighborhood, attracting tourists, students, and drunken indigents

West of the Panthéon, the **Jardin du Luxembourg** is one of the most beautiful parks in Europe. A block north of the garden's northern edge is the awesome **Eglise St-Sulpice** (M: St-Sulpice), containing Delacroix frescoes and one of the world's largest organs (open 7:30am-7:30pm). The **Eglise St-Germain-des-Prés,** pl. St-Germain-des-Prés (M: St-Germain-des-Prés), showing the wear of its many centuries, is officially the oldest standing church in modern-day Paris, dating from 1163 (open 9am-7:30pm).

The Faubourg St-Germain The green, tree-lined **Esplanade des Invalides** runs from Pont Alexandre III, lined with gilded lampposts, to the gold-leaf dome of the **Hôtel des Invalides,** 2, av. de Tourville (M: Invalides), which includes the **Musée de l'Armée** (see Museums, below); the same ticket admits you to **Napoleon's Tomb,** lovingly placed under Jules Hardouin-Mansart's royal dome. (Open 10am-7pm; Oct.-March 10am-5pm; April-Dec. 10am-6pm.)

Of the **Tour Eiffel** (Eiffel Tower), Gustav Eiffel wrote in 1889, "France is the only country in the world with a 300m flagpole" (M: Bir-Hakeim). Built in 1889 to celebrate the centennial of the storming of the Bastille, the world's largest Gallic symbol is breathtaking. Don't miss out on one of the most satisfying experiences in Paris, even if it seems tacky or "touristy." Try it at night—even the most blasé will be impressed. (Tower open July-Aug. 9am-midnight; Sept.-June 9:30am-11pm. Elevator to: 1st floor 20F, 2nd floor 36F, 3rd floor 52F. Over 60: 1st floor 10F, 2nd floor 18F, 3rd floor 25F. Wheelchair access.)

The Louvre, the Opéra, the Marais, and the Bastille Hugging the Seine, the **Louvre**—world-famous art museum and former residence of kings—occupies about one seventh of the 1er *arrondissement* (see Museums). **Le Jardin des Tuileries** (M: Palais-Royal/Musée du Louvre), at the western foot of the Louvre, was built in 1649 and has since become one of the most popular open spaces in Paris. The **place Vendôme,** 3 blocks north along the rue de Castiglione, hides 20th-century office buildings behind 17th-century façades. In the center of the *place* is a column cast from 1,250 Austrian and Russian bronze cannon captured in battle by Napoleon. The **Palais-Royal,** across rue de Rivoli from the Louvre was constructed in 1639 for Cardinal Richelieu. In 1784, the addition of the elegant buildings that enclose the palace's formal garden made the palace a shopping arcade. Today, the galleries of the venerable buildings contain small shops and a few cafés with a splendid view of the palace fountain and flower beds.

North of the Louvre, feast your eyes on Charles Garnier's grandiose **Opéra** (M: Opéra), built under Napoleon III in the showy eclecticism of the Second Empire. The magnificent and eclectic interior is adorned by Gobelin tapestries, gilded mosaics, a 1964 Chagall ceiling, and the six-ton chandelier, which fell on the audience in 1896. (Open for visits Mon.-Sat. 10am-4:30pm. 33F, under 17: 20F.) East of the Opéra lie the 3e and 4e *arrondissements,* known together as **Le Marais.** With Henry IV's construction of the **place des Vosges** (M: St-Paul) at the beginning of the 17th century, the area became the center of fashionable living. Several of the many mansions left in the area now house museums. In the northwest corner of the fourth, the **Centre Pompidou** (also referred to as the **Palais Beaubourg**) looms like an oversized engine abandoned next to the Seine (see Museums, below). In afternoon and early evening, the vast cobblestone plaza in front of the complex gathers a mixture of caricature artists, street musicians, monologuists, and more. Consult the big numerical display that counts the seconds until the year 2000; if you want a precise record of your visit, buy a postcard which will tell you the date and time to the millisecond (30F).

Further east, Charles V built the **Bastille** prison to confine his enemies and to guard the eastern entrance to his capital. On July 14, 1789, Revolutionary militants stormed the Bastille for the prison's supply of gunpowder. Demolition of the prison was completed in 1792. On July 14, 1989, François Mitterand inaugurated the glittering **Opéra Bastille,** 120, rue de Lyon (M: Bastille) to celebrate the destruction of Charles's hated fortress 200 years earlier.

Champs-Elysées, Bois de Boulogne, and La Défense The **place de la Concorde** (M: Concorde), Paris's largest and most infamous public square, forms the western boundary of the Tuileries. Constructed between 1757 and 1777 to provide a home for a monument to Louis XV, the vast area soon became the place de la Revolution, the site of the guillotine that severed 1,343 necks. The gargantuan, rose-granite **Obélisque de Louqsor** dates back to the 13th century BC and recalls the deeds of Ramses II.

Stretching west, the **avenue des Champs-Elysées** is lined with salons and boutiques of *haute couture* and sprinkled with embassies. This is the Paris you've seen in *Vogue* and in *Cosmo,* where the scarf is always Hermès, the watch is pure Cartier, and everyone has had a busy day at the boutique. At its western terminus, the **Arc de Triomphe,** pl. Charles de Gaulle, moves every heart not made of stone (M: Charles de Gaulle-Etoile). The world's largest triumphal arch was commissioned in 1806 by Napoleon in honor of his Grande Armée. The terrace at the top provides a terrific view of av. Foch and the sprawling city. (Observation deck open 9am-6pm. 31F, students 18-25 and over 59: 20F, under 18: 6F. Expect lines even on weekdays and buy your ticket before going up to the ground level.)

Avenue Foch, one of Haussmann's finest creations, runs from l'Arc de Triomphe to the **Bois de Boulogne,** 16^e (M: Porte Maillot, Sablons, Pont de Neuilly, Porte Dauphine, or Porte d'Auteuil), a popular place for jogs, picnics, and sex crimes after dark. For joggers and walkers, maps can be found at regular intervals on the periphery of the park. A long path, marked in red and yellow, follows the periphery of the park. A shorter one, marked in blue and white, circles about half of it. Although the police have recently cleaned out many of the drug dealers and prostitutes who once did business here, it's still a poor choice for a romantic moonlight stroll.

Outside the city limits, La Défense (M: La Défense, zone 2; RER, zone 3) is the comic-book city of the future. The headquarters of 14 of France's top 20 corporations vie to outdo each other with sleek, modern design. The boldest is that of the **Grande Arche,** a 35-storey office block in the shape of a hollowed cube. Go through the roof for a great view. (Open Sun.-Thurs. 9am-8pm, Fri.-Sat. 9am-9pm; roof closes 1hr. after ticket office. 32F, under 18: 25F. Wheelchair access.) Shops, galleries, trees, and bizarre sculpture make the large pedestrian esplanade a pleasant place for a stroll. Major roads run underneath the esplanade, but you'll feel less oppressed by pollution and cars here than you ever will in central Paris.

Montmartre and Père-Lachaise The **Basilique du Sacré-Coeur** (Basilica of the Sacred Heart), 35, rue du Cheval de la Barre (M: Anvers, Abbesses, or Château-Rouge), crowns the **butte Montmartre** like an enormous white meringue. Its onion dome is visible from almost any corner of Montmartre and from much of the city down below. Climb the 112m bell tower for the highest point in Paris and a view that can stretch as far as 50km. (Open 7am-11pm. Free. Dome and crypt open 9am-7pm; in winter 9am-6pm. To dome 15F, students and seniors 8F. To crypt 10F, students and seniors 5F.)

The **Cimetière Père-Lachaise,** on bd. de Ménilmontant (M: Père-Lachaise), encloses the remains of Balzac, Colette, Corot, Danton, David, Delacroix, La Fontaine, Haussmann, Molière, Sarah Bernhardt, and Proust within its peaceful, winding paths and elaborate sarcophagi. Foreigners inhumed here include Chopin, Gertrude Stein, Modigliani, and Oscar Wilde. The most visited grave is that of **Jim Morrison** (lead singer of The Doors). His fans' graffiti fills the cemetery. In summer, dozens of young people bring flowers, joints, beer, or poetry to leave on his tomb. *Poseurs* in brand-new, well-ironed Lizard King t-shirts linger for hours, looking really, really sad. Some take hits, others photographs, but there's a rule against filming Morrison's grave. French Leftists make ceremonious pilgrimage to the **Mur des Fédérés** (Wall of the Federals), where 147 Communards were executed and buried. (Cemetery open Mon.-Fri. 7:30am-6pm, Sat. 8:30am-6pm, Sun. and holidays 9am-6pm; in winter Mon.-Fri. 8am-5:30pm, Sat.-Sun. and holidays 9am-5:30pm.)

Museums

Every Parisian institution, artistic movement, ethnic group, and custom seems to have a museum devoted to its history, art, and memorabilia. For listings of temporary exhibits, consult the bimonthly *Bulletin des musées et monuments historiques,* available at the tourist office. *Paris Museums and Monuments* published by the tourist office, describes the museums and indexes them by theme and *arrondissement. Pariscope, 7 à Paris* and *L'Officiel des spectacles* also list museums with hours and temporary exhibits. Frequent museum-goers, especially those ineligible for discounts, may want to invest in a **Carte Musées et Monuments,** which grants entry to 65 Parisian museums *without waiting in line.* The card is available at major museums and metro stations (1-day 60F, 3-day 120F, 5-day 170F).

Musée de l'Armée, 2, av. de Tourville, 7ᵉ (M: Invalides, Latour-Maubourg, or St-François Xavier), in the Hôtel des Invalides, celebrates centuries of French military history, examining heroes ranging from Napoleon to de Gaulle. Open 10am-6pm; Oct.-March 10am-5pm. Entrance free with admission to Napoleon's tomb. 34F; students, seniors, and under 18: 24F. The ticket is valid for two days

Musée Carnavalet, 23, rue de Sévigné, 3ᵉ (M: Rivoli or Carnavalet), in a 16th-century *hôtel*, is Paris's main display of its own history. Open Tues.-Sun. 10am-5:30pm. 25F, 19-25 and over 60: 10F, all on Sun. free. Temporary exhibits extra. Wheelchair access.

Les Catacombs, 1, pl. Denfert-Rochereau, 15e (M: Denfert-Rochereau), contain the bones of 5-6 million Parisians in former limestone mines. Bring a sweater, a flashlight, and a friend for support. Open Tues.-Fri. 2-4pm, Sat.-Sun. 9-11am and 2-4pm. 27F, students 15F.

Centre National d'Art et de Culture Georges-Pompidou (Palais Beaubourg), 4e (M: Rambuteau, Hôtel de Ville, or Châtelet-Les Halles). Shameless building-turned-inside-out bares its circulatory system to all passers-by, and has inspired architectural controversy ever since its inauguration in 1977. Zip up and down on the escalators. The **Musée National d'Art Moderne,** the center's main attraction, houses a rich selection of 20th-century art, from Fauves and Cubists to Pop and Conceptual art. Open Mon. and Wed.-Fri. noon-10pm, Sat.-Sun. 10am-10pm. Wheelchair access through back entrance on rue Beaubourg. 30F, under 26 20F, under 18 free, Sun. 10am-2pm free. Admission to temporary exhibits varies. Buy your tickets downstairs; they are not available at the museum entrance.

Hôtel de Cluny, 6, pl. Paul-Painlevé, 5e, not only houses one of the world's finest collections of medieval art, jewelry and tapestries, but is itself a perfectly preserved medieval manor, built on top of restored Roman ruins. Open Wed.-Mon. 9:15am-5:45pm. 27F; under 25, over 60, and Sun. 18F; under 18 free.

Cristalleries Baccarat, 30-32, rue de Paradis, 10^e (M: Gare de l'Est). The impressive building, built under the Directory between 1798 and 1799, houses both the Baccarat crystal company headquarters and the Baccarat museum. The museum houses an array of every imaginable crystal object, including a life-size chandelier-woman at the entrance. With exquisite vases, goblets, and sculptures reflected in mirrored tables, the display looks like an ice palace. Open Mon.-Fri. 9am-6pm and Sat. 10am-noon and 2pm-5pm. Free.

Musée Salvador Dalí (Espace Montmartre), 11, rue Poulbot, 18e (M: Anvers, Blanche, or Pigalle). Right off pl. du Tertre, this space dedicated to the "Phantasmic World of Salvador Dalí" is full of lithographs and sculptures by the Spanish surrealist, with scads of incarnations of the famous droopy clocks. The museum is laid out in "Surrealist surroundings," which amounts to wonderful spacing, interesting lighting and slightly ridiculous "space-music" in the background. Open daily 10am-6pm. 35F, students 25F.

Musée des Egouts de Paris (Sewers Museum), actually inside the sewers at the corner of the quai d'Orsay and the place de la Résistance, 7e (M: Pont de l'Alma). Take a self-guided tour with a French, English, German, and Spanish pamphlet, or one of the impromptu tours led by a real live *égoutier* (sewer worker). Open Sat.-Wed. 11am-6pm; winter 11am-5pm. Last ticket sold 1hr. before closing. 25F, students 20F. Closed for 3 weeks in Jan.

Musée du Louvre, 1er (M: Palais-Royal/Musée du Louvre). Spending a full day in the museum is more likely to dull your powers of perception than to sharpen your appreciation of the art; the most satisfaction you're likely to derive is seeing the *Mona Lisa* through a forest of golf hats. Enter through I.M. Pei's controversial pyramid in the Cour Napoléon. Try to take in a few galleries over the course of several days. The extra admission charges are a small price to pay for the satisfaction. Better yet, come on Mon. or Wed. evening, when there are more paintings than people. Open Thurs.-Sun. 9:30am-5:30pm, Mon. and Wed. 9am-9:30pm. Last entry 45min. before closing. 40F before 3pm, 20F after 3pm and Sun., under 18 free. Tours in English Mon. and Wed.-Sat. at 10am, 11:30am, 2pm and 3:30pm, 33F, ages 13-18: 22F. Meet at the "Acceuil des Groupes" area. Recorded tours museum highlights—available in English—30F, driver's license, passport, or 500F deposit.

Musée de l'Orangerie, 1er (M: Concorde). A small collection of Impressionist paintings nestled in the southwest corner of the Tuileries. Though less spectacular than Orsay, this museum is also less crowded, so you can admire the Cézannes, Renoirs, Matisses, Picassos, and other greats in comfort. Open Wed.-Mon. 9:45am-5:15pm. 26F; ages 18-25, over 60, and all on Sun. 14F.

Musée d'Orsay, 1, rue de Bellechasse, 7e (M: Solférino; RER: Musée d'Orsay). Often reckoned as Paris's Impressionist museum, though its most engaging displays highlight the lesser-known artists who anticipated Impressionism's revolutionary approach. Contrasting architecture, sculpture, painting, and furniture all show-

*Very good.
Restaurant for neighborhood at 49 Rue de Turenne.
Cafe Des Muses
Excellent food, friendly*

cased beneath the breathtaking iron-and-glass ceiling of a former train station. Manet's *Olympia* awaits on the ground floor. Open June 20-Sept. 20 Tues.-Wed. and Fri.-Sun. 9am-6pm, Thurs. 9am-9:45pm; Sept. 21-June19 Tues.-Wed. and Fri.-Sat. 10am-6pm, Thurs. 10am-9:45pm, Sun. 9am-6pm. Last tickets 45min. before closing. 35F; ages 18-25, over 60, and all on Sun. 24F; under 18 free. Permanent collection and temporary exhibits 55F, reduced 38F. Wheelchair access.

Musée Picasso, 5, rue de Thorigny, 3e (M: Chemin Vert). Many works of minor significance, but the collection as a whole is fascinating, thanks to the tasteful and informative layout. Open Wed.-Mon. 9:30am-6pm; Oct.-March 9:30am-5:20pm. 33F; 18-25, over 60 and all on Sun. 24F. Wheelchair access.

Musée Rodin, 77, rue de Varenne, 7e (M: Varenne), in elegant 18th-century Hôtel Biron. Containing all the major works of France's most famous sculptor, Auguste Rodin, it ranks among the top attractions in Paris. Open Tues.-Sun. 10am-5:45pm; Oct.-March Tues.-Sun. 10am-5pm. Last entry 30min. before closing. To museum and park 26F; under 18, students, and seniors 17F. To park alone 4F.

ENTERTAINMENT

Paris teems with cabarets, discos, and smoky jazz clubs; with U.S. and European cinema; with avant-garde and traditional theater; with rock and classical concerts. Consult the two bibles of Paris entertainment: the magazine **Pariscope** (3F) and the **Officiel des Spectacles** (2F), both on sale weekly at any newsstand. Even if you don't understand French, you should be able to decipher the listings of times and locations. Or, contact **Info-Loisirs,** a recording that keeps tabs on what's on in Paris (English tel. 49 52 53 56; French tel. 49 52 53 55).

While it's not London or Berlin, Paris has a lively and venerable bi, gay, and lesbian scene. The indisputable center of the action is still the **Marais,** but also consider the quieter restaurants and cafés that line the **rue Vieille-du-Temple.** For the most comprehensive listing of bi, gay, and lesbian restaurants, clubs, hotels, organizations, and services, consult Gai Pied's *Guide Gai 1995* (50F at any kiosk). *Lesbia's* ads are a good gauge of what's hot, or at least what's open (24F at kiosks).

Fortunately, the most traditional Parisian entertainment—people-watching—is free. The area around the **Pompidou Center** fills with an aging, rotund fire-eater, sword-swallowers, Chilean guitar bands, and other performers. Around **pl. St-Germain,** you'll find throngs of people parading by in the latest fashions and a few bars where unlimited jazz comes with the price of one drink. At **Ile St-Louis** you'll find more refined tourists strolling the banks of the Seine. To see a movie or to linger in the more fashionable cafés, wander around **Montparnasse,** the touristy **Champs-Elysées,** and the streets radiating from **bd. St-Michel, bd. St-Germain,** and **bd. Sébastopol.** Keep in mind that several sections of Paris have developed entertainment businesses of a different sort. The areas around Pigalle, Gare St-Lazare, and Beaubourg fill nightly with prostitutes and drug dealers. Everyone should avoid the Bois de Boulogne after dark.

Theater tickets can run as high as 200F, but students can often pay lower prices, and some theaters sell standby tickets a half-hour before the performance. Most theaters close for August. *Pariscope* and *l'Officiel des Spectacles* print complete listings of current shows. Far and away the best place for reduced-rate theater tickets is the **Kiosque-Théâtre,** 15, pl. de la Madeleine, 8e (M: Madeleine), which sells tickets at half-price the day of the show (open Tues.-Sat. 12:30-8pm, Sun 12:30-4pm). Another useful service for theater, concert, and festival tickets is **Alpha FNAC: Spectacles** at 136, rue de Rennes, 6e (tel. 49 45 30 00; M: Montparnasse-Bienvenue); Forum des Halles, 1-7, rue Pierre Lescot, 1er (M: Châtelet-Les Halles); 26-30, av. des Ternes (tel. 44 09 18 00; M: Ternes); and 71, bd. St-Germain, 5ème (tel. 44 41 31 50). They sell tickets for theater, concerts, and festivals. Their *Carte FNAC* (150F for 3 years, students 100F) entitles you to discounts of up to 40% on classical music and theater tickets. (Open Mon.-Sat. 10am-7pm.) Finally, contact the theater itself—many offer last minute rush tickets.

FRANCE

Cinema

Paris is famous the world over for a movie scene that rivals—some say surpasses—that of New York. Don't expect to find many megaplexes and greasy popcorn; film-going in Paris is an evening on the town. Cafés, bars, and restaurants cohabit with projector rooms in some of the city's smaller theaters, whose intimate rooms can have as few as twenty or thirty seats (almost always plush, roomy, and comfortable). Proof of Paris' movie enthusiasm are the mile-long lines for anything from Robert Mitchum to Bambi. Catering to the city's enormous student population, Paris' cinemas offer a range of ticket discounts. On Mondays and Wednesdays prices drop about 10F. Check *Pariscope* for details—days and reductions vary with the theater. The entertainment weeklies list show times and theaters. Film festivals are listed separately. The notation *v.o. (version originale)* after a non-French movie listing means that the film is being shown in its original language with French subtitles; watching an English-language film with French subtitles is a great way to pick up new (and sometimes very interesting) vocabulary. *v.f. (version française)* means that it has been dubbed—an increasingly rare and entirely avoidable phenomenon. Make sure you tip the person who points you to your seat (about 2F). An old law assuring service workers 12-15% inadvertently bypassed ushers and taxi drivers. Most foreigners are not aware they are expected to tip ushers and often encounter hostility when they fail to do so.

Action Christine, 4, rue Christine, 6ᵉ, off rue Dauphine. M: Odéon. Plays a variety of artsy films, American and otherwise. 40F; students, large families, on Mon. and Wed. 30F. For 110F (plus a 30F fee at the first purchase), buy a pass good for 1 year that admits you to 6 movies. One of the 2 rooms is wheelchair-accessible; descend down a steep, twisting staircase to get to the other.

Dôme IMAX, La Défense, to the right of L'Espace Marques. Programs in-the-round which compensate for lack of plot, substance, or taste with their immediacy; past features include *The Fires of Kuwait* and *In Space.* Admission (for 2 films) 55F during the day, 75F at night. Students 45F, 65F at night. Upstairs, the Spider cafeteria (open 10am-4pm) offers a good lunch deal at 50F.

Musée du Louvre, 1ᵉʳ. M: Palais Royal/Musée du Louvre. A perhaps unlikely venue for cutting-edge film series. Also hosts silent movies with live musical accompaniment. Movies 25F. Open Sept.-June.

Jazz

Some critics mourn that Paris is no longer the jazz center it once was. Although big names find it more profitable to play huge summer festivals in southern France and in Switzerland, Paris still nourishes dozens of interesting clubs. Not only do many excellent, lesser-known American musicians play here, the variety of music—including African, Antillean, and Brazilian—is astounding. For complete listings, check out the monthly *Jazz Magazine* or *Jazz Hot* or one of the entertainment weeklies.

New Morning, 7-9, rue des Petites-Ecuries, 10ᵉ (tel. 45 23 51 41). M: Château d'Eau. All the greats have played here; expect long lines. Open Sept.-July from 9:30pm; times vary. 110-130F.

Le Petit Opportun, 15, rue des Lavandières-St-Opportune, 1ᵉʳ (tel. 42 36 01 36). M: Châtelet. Relaxed and unpolished, featuring the best modern jazz around. Come early to get a place in the tiny 60-seat club. Open Sept.-July Tues.-Sat. from 11pm; bar open until 3am. 1st drink 100F, 50F thereafter.

Au Duc des Lombards, 42, rue des Lombards, 1ᵉʳ (tel. 42 33 22 88). M: Châtelet. French jazz groups, occasional American singers or soloists. Dark, smoky, and overflowing with enthusiastic crowds. Call for prices—1st drink about 60F. Open 7:30pm-4am.

Bars and Dance Clubs

Paris is not Barcelona, Montréal, or Buenos Aires; you won't find streets filled with young people waiting to get into discos. Instead, the clubs are small, private, and nearly impossible to sniff out unless you're a native. In general, word of mouth is the best guide to the current scene. Many Parisian clubs are officially private, which means they have the right to pick and choose their clientele. Parisians tend to dress up more than Americans for a night on the town; haggard backpackers might be wise to try a bar instead. Almost as common as cafés, the bars feature heavier drinking and heavier socializing. Law dictates a price increase after 10pm, but no one really goes out to drink before then.

Les Bains, 7, rue de Bourg l'Abbée, 3e (tel. 48 87 01 80). M: Réaumur-Sébastopol. Ultra-selective and ultra-expensive, but worth it—if you can get in past the fearless bouncers. Models and super-attractive people. Patrons have included Madonna, Mike Tyson, Roman Polanski, and he-who-was-Prince. 140F (includes 1st drink), second drink 100F. Open Tues.-Sun.11:30pm-6am.

Le Café Majéstic, 34, rue Vieille-du-Temple, 4e (tel. 42 74 61 61). M: Hôtel-de-Ville. A vibrant, eclectic young crowd of bi, gay, lesbian, and straight people converge to show off and look around. Rock/pop mix provides soundtrack for sometimes clothed, often buff Beautiful People. Drinks 16-46F. Open 9am-2am.

Le Bar Central, 33, rue Vieille-du-Temple, 4e (tel. 48 87 99 33). M: Hôtel-de- Ville. A comfortable gay bar. Drink draft beer (15F), check out the boys, and eye the black marble torso. Open Sun.-Thurs. 2pm-1am, Fri.-Sat. 2pm-2am.

James Joyce Pub, 71, bd. Gouvion-St-Cyr. 17e, near the Palais des Congrès. M. Porte Maillot. The James Joyce is one of Paris' three most lively Irish pubs (next to Kitty O'Shea's and Finnegan's Wake). The mahogany bar and tall green barstools create a warm backdrop to the daily and nightly crowd of Irish, British, and American expatriates downing a pint. Run by a friendly Irish staff, the pub is full of James Joyce paraphernalia, including a number of letters and pages penned in his own hand. Live Irish music every Mon. beginning at 8:30pm. Lunch served noon-2:30pm; dinner from 7:30pm on. Open noon-1:30am.

La Perla, 26, rue François-Miron, 4^e (tel. 42 77 59 40). M: Hôtel-de-Ville. The best of the Parisian Tex-Mex rage, La Perla mixes a superb margarita (50F) and attracts laid-back, turned-out twentysomethings with money and time on their hands. Draft beer 20F, bottled 32F. Quesadillas 32-40F. Fajitas 48F. Open noon-2am.

Le Bar sans Nom, 49, rue de Lappe, 11e (tel. 48 05 59 36). M: Bastille. There's nothing cooler than this bar—cavernous, deep crimson, and packed with the hippest of the hip. Beer 20F. Cocktails 44F. Open 10:30pm-2am.

Pub St-Germain-des-Prés, 17, rue de l'Ancienne Comédie, 6e (tel. 43 29 38 70). M: Odéon. Maybe the largest pub in Europe, a fave with American students looking for a good time. Over 450 types of bottled beer and 25 varieties on tap. At night beers and cocktails start at an outrageous 75F per bottle. Open 24hrs.

Subway, 35, rue Ste-Croix-de-la-Bretonnerie, 4e (tel. 42 77 41 10). M: Hôtel-de- Ville. New and in vogue, A dark, cramped, loud, gay bar in the Marais. Beer 14-18F, mixed drinks 39-48F. Getting in can be a hassle, especially for women, even accompanied. Open 2:30pm-2am.

Le Palace, 8, rue du Faubourg Montmartre, 9^e (tel. 42 46 10 87). M: Rue Montmartre. A funky disco, though past its prime. Very top-40. Huge (up to 2000 people per night), with multi-level dance floors, each with separate bars and different music. Sun. features the **Gay Tea Dance,** a 15-year institution of the Parisian gay scene. Cover and 1 drink Tues.-Thurs. 100F, Fri.-Sat. 130F, Sun. 130F for men, women free. Subsequent drinks 60F. Open Tues.-Sun. 11:30pm-6am.

Scala de Paris, 188bis, rue de Rivoli, 1er (tel. 42 61 64 00 and 42 60 45 64). M: Palais-Royal. Halfway between a disco and a rollercade; strings of lights and 2 disco balls hang above the central, two-story dance floor. Mixes house and techno for an 18-24 crowd. Lots of foreigners. Cover Sun.-Thurs. 80F, women free, Fri. 80F, Sat. 90F. Additional drinks 45F. Open 10:30pm-dawn.

Le Balajo, 9, rue de Lappe, 11e (tel. 47 00 07 87). M: Bastille. Formerly the favorite stage of Edith Piaf. Founded in 1936. Jammed with a youthful crowd. Cover and first drink 100F. Open Mon. and Wed.-Sat. 11pm-5am.

Le Queen, 102, av. des Champs-Elysées, 8ᵉ (tel. 42 89 31 32). The closest Paris comes to the New York scene. Flashing purple on the Champs Elysées, it's easy to see but hard to get into. Transvestites dance on tables to excellent house music. Dress your most (insert adjective) and try to look nonchalant. Open daily.

Le Club, 14, rue St-Denis, 1ᵉʳ. M: Châtelet-Les Halles. Found in a less chic, but *très* gay area of Beaubourg. A dark, subterranean, intimate place to dance. Bouncers only admit women and straight men if accompanied by a gay man, preferably one they recognize. Wed. garage-techno. Thurs. theme parties. Cover 48F (including 1st drink) Fri.-Sat. only. Drinks 32-50F. Open 11:30pm-dawn. MC, Visa.

Le Privilège, 3, cité Bergère, 9ᵉ (tel. 42 46 50 98). M: Rue Montmartre. The place for a glam all-female crowd; dance all night and into the morning, when the club becomes an after-hours joint for the boys from the KitKat upstairs. Selective door policy. Drinks 100F. Open Tues.-Wed. and Sun. 11pm-dawn, Fri.-Sat. 11pm-noon.

■ VERSAILLES AND CHARTRES

The magnificent palace of Louis XIV, **Versailles** perfectly embodies the Sun King's absolute power and his famous statement, *"L'État, c'est moi"* (I am the State). Louis gathered the aristocracy of France to this glorified hunting lodge, forcing them to vie for his attention while paying crippling taxes. The incredibly lavish building embodies the Old Regime's extravagance that led to the Revolution. Le Nôtre's geometric gardens are studded with unforgettable fountains, which spurt every Sunday May through September. (Château open Tues.-Sun. 9am-6:30pm; Oct.-April 9am-5:30pm. Last admission 30 min. before closing. Gardens open 7am-sunset. General admission to the palace 40F; ages 18-25, over 60, and Sun. 26F.) Trains run from M: Invalides on RER Line C5 to the Versailles Rive Gauche station (every 15min., 35-40 min., 19F round-trip). From the Invalides metro stop, take trains with labels beginning with "V." Buy your RER ticket *before* going through the turnstile to the platform, even though your metro ticket will get you through these turnstiles; it will not get you through the RER turnstiles at Versailles.

The stunning **Cathédrale de Chartres,** spared by bureaucratic inefficiency after being condemned during the Revolution, survives today as one of the most sublime creations of the Middle Ages. Arguably the finest example of Gothic architecture in the world, the cathedral gained fame for its stained-glass windows and the magnificent sculptures adorning each of the main doors. (Cathedral open 7:30am-7:30pm, in winter 7:30am-7pm.) The town of Chartres provides a refreshing change from the grand boulevards and cosmopolitan atmosphere of Paris. Chartres is accessible by frequent trains from Gare Montparnasse (1hr., round-trip 132F). Many trains run only on certain days or occasions—make sure you aren't caught waiting in vain.

■ EURODISNEY®

It's a small, small world® and Disney® seems hell-bent on making it even smaller. When EuroDisney® opened on April 12, 1992, Peter Pan, Mickey Mouse, Cinderella, and Snow White were met with the jeers of French intellectuals and the popular press. Regardless, the park is an exciting place to spend a day, even for the budget traveler; every show, attraction, and ride is included in the admission price. Cash-strapped tourists should consider visiting the park at night; EuroDisney® Resort has started offering a discounted admission after 5pm (150F). Although Disney® may eventually develop its 600 hectares, it takes only ten minutes to walk to the farthest point inside the park. On the other hand, this Disney® park is the most technologically advanced yet, and the special effects on some rides are enough to knock your Reeboks® off. Ticket windows close repeatedly for hours at a time to keep lines down during the summer. Try to get there on a weekday—Tuesdays and Thursdays are the least crowded. Line-cutting families duck under barriers and worm their way up front. Crowds thin out toward 5pm, when parents start crying to go home, reducing the wait in line—save the bigger rides for the evening; you'll still have plenty of time to do all your favorite rides several times over. For the wildest rides,

THE CHANNEL PORTS ■ 233

look for those accorded the greatest warnings. While "may frighten certain young children" might sound promising, it only means that the ride is dark and things pop out at you. Warnings directed at pregnant women and people with chronic heart problems, are the hallmarks of the more exciting rides.

Instead of selling tickets, EuroDisney® issues *Passeports,* available at the 50 windows located on the ground floor of the Disneyland Hotel. You can also buy *Passeports* at the Paris tourist office on the Champs-Elysées. Pursue this option if you plan on coming out on a weekend day, so you won't risk wasting a couple of hours while the windows remain closed due to the crowds. (250F, under 12: 175F. 150F after 5pm.) The easiest way to get to the EuroDisney® Resort is by taking the RER A4 from M: Gare de Lyon or Châtelet-Les Halles (direction: Marne-la-Vallée) to the last stop, Marne-la-Vallée/Chessy (50min., 70F round-trip). The last train to Paris leaves Disney® at 12:22am, but you may have trouble getting the metro at the other end.

THE NORTH

■■■ THE CHANNEL PORTS

Calais and Boulogne Ever since Richard the Lion-Heart and his crusaders passed through en route to Jerusalem, **Calais** has been the Continent's primary portal to Britain. The tourist mobs will only get denser now that the long-awaited **Channel Tunnel** linking Calais with Dover, England has been completed. Calais is the most frequently used transfer point for **ferries** to Dover, England (1½hr.): **Sealink** (tel. 21 34 55 00; 290F, students 140F) and **P&O** (tel. 21 46 04 40; 230F). **Hoverspeed,** in the Hoverport (tel. 21 46 14 14), fires its space-age craft to Dover every hour (35min., 240F, with Interrail 172F). Free shuttle buses connect the hoverport and ferry terminal with the train station. By spring 1995, the limited *Discovery* train service between London and Paris/Brussels through the Chunnel will give way to a full *Eurostar* service with approximately fifteen daily departures to either destination. Consult Thomas Cook's European Timetable or, in the U.K., call (0233) 61 75 75 for more information. Ask whether railpasses and BIJ tickets will be valid. There are 24hr. **currency exchanges** at both the ferry terminals and the Hoverport, but rates are obscene. The town's **tourist office,** 12, bd. Clemenceau (tel. 21 96 62 40), changes money (no commission for less than 200F, 10F commission for 200-500F; open Mon.-Sat. 9am-7pm). Should you have to stay the night, try the brand-new **Centre Européen de Séjour/Auberge de Jeunesse (HI),** av. Maréchal de Lattre de Tassigny (tel. 21 34 70 20; open 24hr.; 65F), or drop your bags at **Hôtel le Littoral,** 71, rue Aristide Briand (tel. 21 34 47 28), with its huge, comfy rooms. (Singles 100-120F. Doubles 120-160F.) The budget traveler should make a beeline for the **market** at pl. Crèvecœur (Thurs. and Sat. mornings) or pl. d'Armes (Wed. and Sat. mornings). Otherwise, resort to the hostel cafeteria or the **Match supermarket,** pl. d'Armes (open Mon-Fri. 9am-12:30pm and 2:30-7:30pm, Sat.9am-7:30pm).

Local legend claims that in 636, a glow-in-the-dark, unpiloted boat carrying a statue of the Virgin Mary washed up on the beach at **Boulogne.** Towering over the *vieille ville* is the 19th-century **Basilique de Notre-Dame.** Beneath it are labyrinthine crypts containing the remains of a Roman temple. (Church open Mon.-Sat. 8am-noon and 2-7pm, Sun 8:30am-12:30pm and 2:30-7pm. Crypts open Tues.-Sat. 2-5pm, Sun. 2:30-5pm. 10F.) **Hoverspeed** crafts (tel. 21 30 27 26) shuttle to Folkestone (every 3hr., round-trip 240F). The **tourist office,** pl. Frédéric Sauvage (tel. 21 31 68 38), has good maps (2F), a free accommodations service, and ferry brochures (open Mon.-Sat. 9am-8pm, Sun. 10am-7pm; Oct.-May Mon.-Sat. 9am-7pm, Sun. 10am-12:30pm and 1:30-5pm). Boulogne's **auberge de jeunesse (HI),** 36, rue de la Port Gayole (tel. 21 31 48 22, fax 21 80 94 23), just outside the *vieille ville,* offers cramped but clean dorms. (Reception open 8-10am and 5-11pm. Curfew 11pm, but manager will give you code to open door. 60F, nonmembers 80F. Camping 24F.) Restaurants and bistros line rue de Lille in the *vieille ville*. At **Le Cyne**, 30, rue des Pipots (tel. 21 30 01 63), the friendly and hard-working management serves tasty seafood in huge portions (open noon-3pm and 7-9pm).

Dunkerque A fishing town since the 10th century and now the 3rd-largest port in France, Dunkerque endured Flemish, Spanish, and English rule before becoming French in 1662. The **Musée d'Art Contemporain,** rue des Bains, across the bridge from the hostel, has eccentrically manicured paths with fake sheep enclosing a modern sculpture garden (open Wed.-Mon.9am-6pm, Oct.-March Wed.-Mon. 10:30am-5:30pm; 12F, students 6F). The **tourist office,** rue Amiral Ronarch (tel. 28 66 79 21), books rooms for free (open Mon.-Fri. 9am-12:30pm and 1:30-7:30pm, Sat. 9am-6pm, Sept.-April also open Sun. 3-5:30pm).

The **auberge de jeunesse (HI),** pl. Paul Asseman (tel. 28 63 36 34, fax 28 63 24 54), by the beach (15min. walk or take bus 3 to Piscine), has single-sex rooms but co-ed bathrooms. (Lockout 9am-5:30pm. Curfew 11pm. Members only, 43F.) Take bus 3 (every 20min., 6am-9pm) to the campsite **Dunkerque Camping Municipal** for grounds with shower, TV, and swimming pool. (Office open Mon.-Sat. 9am-noon and 2-7pm. 11F per person, 7F per tent or car. Open March-Nov.) Fresh fish and seafood are served on the waterfront at **Pavois,** 175, digue de Mer (tel. 28 29 06 07; open March-Oct. 9am-10:30pm).

■■■ FROM LILLE TO PARIS

Lille The largest city in the north, Lille (1hr. from Paris by train) puts aesthetics before practicality, but possesses the best features of a city: an ultra-modern metro, a huge shopping district, sidewalk cafés, street festivals, and enough students to foster a fun nightlife. Acknowledged as one of France's finest museums, Lille's **Musée des Beaux-Arts** shelters works by Rubens, Goya, El Greco, David, Delacroix, and Renoir in a majestic 19th-century building on pl. de la République. (Renovations should be completed by now.) **Charles de Gaulle's birthplace** at 9, rue Princesse, now marred by graffiti, has a vast collection of photographs and newspaper clippings on the leader of the Resistance and two-time French president (open Wed.-Sun. 10am-noon and 2-5pm, 7F). The **tourist office,** pl. Rihour (tel. 20 30 81 00), haunts a 15th-century castle (open Mon.-Sat. 9am-7pm, Sun. 10am-noon and 2-5pm). If you are staying in town, ask **CROUS** (tel. 20 88 66 00) about summer university housing (min. stay 3 nights, 35F). **Hôtel Faidherbe,** 42, pl. de la Gare (tel. 20 06 27 93), offers clean 110F singles and 130F doubles near the station. Sample Flemish favorites, mussels (45-55F) and beer, at **Aux Moules,** 34, rue de Béthune (open 11:30am-12:30am). Join in the rambunctious singing at **L'Irlandais,** 160-162, rue Sulferino, a big-hearted beer joint.

Arras Built over the **Les Boves** tunnels that have sheltered both medieval chalk miners and British WWII soldiers, Arras lies 35min. by train from Lille (35min. by train). The friendly folks of the **tourist office** (tel. 21 51 26 95) in the 15th-century **Hôtel de Ville** provide free accommodations service (open Mon.-Sat. 9am-6pm, Sun. 10am-6:30pm; winter Mon.-Sat. 9am-noon and 2-6pm, Sun. 10am-noon and 3-6:30pm). Ask the concierge of the building to show you the marriage chamber (a church wedding is not legally sufficient, and most French have both ceremonies). The town has a central **auberge de jeunesse (HI),** 59, Grande Place (tel. 21 22 70 02, fax 21 07 46 15), with pleasant dorm-style rooms in a Flemish townhouse. (Reception open 8-10am and 5-11pm, Oct. and March-April 7:30-10am and 5-10pm. Curfew 11pm. Members only, 43F.) Inexpensive cafés skirt pl. des Héros; more elegant restaurants are found on the Grande Place. Ten km northeast of Arras lies the monument of **Vimy,** a memorial to the 60,000 Canadians killed in WWI. The somber 11,285 trees planted in the park represent the number of Canadian soldiers whose final resting place is unknown. (Open 10am-5pm. Tours April-Nov. 15. Free.) Frequent buses and trains serve Vimy (15min., 15F), but you have to hike about 2km from the station to the memorial.

Laon Perched dramatically on an upstart *butte* in the middle of a flat prairie, Laon huddles under the tremendous **Cathédrale de Notre Dame,** the first of the great Gothic cathedrals. Its five towers display the heads of oxen, in memory of the ox who mysteriously appeared to help cart building materials to the top of the hill. (Open 8am-7pm.) Ask at the **tourist office** (tel. 23 20 28 62), beside the cathedral in what was France's first hospital, about guided tours in French, and request a free map of town (open 9am-7pm and 2-6:30pm, Sun. 10am-12:30pm and 2:30-6:30pm). The pumpkin-colored hallways inside the nearby **Maison des Jeunes,** 20, rue du Cloître (tel. 23 20 27 64), lead to simple singles and doubles (65F; call ahead).

NORMANDY (NORMANDIE)

Inspiration to Impressionists and generals, fertile Normandy is a land of gently undulating farmland, tiny fishing villages, and soaring cathedrals. Vikings seized the region in the 9th century, and invasions have twice secured Normandy's place in military history: in 1066, when William of Normandy conquered England, and on D-Day, June 6, 1944, when Allied armies began the liberation of France here.

Normandy supplies a fat percentage of the country's butter. Try the creamy, pungent *camembert* cheese, but be sure it's ripe (soft in the middle). Eating *tripes à la normandaise* (made from cow guts) requires intestinal fortitude (yours, that is). The province's traditional drink *(cidre)* is fermented apple juice that comes both dry *(brut)* and sweet *(doux)*. A harder cousin is *Calvados,* aged apple brandy, whose fumes alone are lethal.

■■■ ROUEN

Best known as the city where Joan of Arc was burned and Emma Bovary was bored, Rouen is no provincial town. Rouen witnessed a flowering of Gothic architecture in its heady days as capital of the Norman empire. Victor Hugo dubbed Rouen "the city of 100 spires," the most famous of which are the needles, gargoyles and gables of the **Cathédrale de Notre-Dame,** with the tallest tower (151m) in France. The now-grimy Gothic façade so fascinated Monet that he painted it over and over again in varying lights and seasons. Behind the cathedral lies **Eglise St-Maclou,** a fine example of the later, flamboyant Gothic style. Its charnel house, **Aitre St-Maclou** (turn left into 186, rue de Martainville), decorated with *danse macabre* wood carvings, has also been preserved. The Rouennais buried a live cat within the building's walls to exorcise dead spirits; visitors may now gape at the perfectly preserved cat cadaver through a glass panel to the right of the cloister's entrance. (Open 8am-9pm. Free.) Joan of Arc sizzled on **place du Vieux Marché,** east of the center of town; a cross near the ugly **Eglise Jeanne d'Arc,** designed to resemble an overturned boat, marks the spot. Pedestrian precincts full of cafés and restaurants radiate from the charmingly inaccurate **Gros Horloge,** a 14th-century clock tower and Renaissance gatehouse (open Thurs.-Mon. 10am-noon and 2-6pm, Wed. 2-6pm; 11F includes Musée des Beaux-Arts, students free). The **Musée Flaubert et d'Histoire de la Médecine,** 51, rue de Lecat, houses a gruesome array of pre-anesthesia medical instruments, including gallstone crushers and a battlefield amputation kit (open Tues.-Sat. 10am-noon and 2-6pm, free).

Practical Information, Accommodations, and Food From Rouen's train station (lockers 15-30F), walk straight down rue Jeanne d'Arc and turn left onto rue du Gros Horloge for pl. de la Cathédrale and the **tourist office** (tel. 35 71 41 77). Their free map, and watching out for pick-pockets, are essential. Rouen is easily accessible by frequent **train** from Paris's Gare St-Lazare (1¼hr., 97F), Lille (3hr., 160F), Le Havre (1hr., 67F), and Caen (2hr., 116F).

For information on university **CROUS** lodgings, which are cheap but usually available only on summer weekends, ask the tourist office or call 35 74 18 68. Rouen's clean, modern **auberge de jeunesse (HI)** is at 118, bd. de l'Europe (tel. 35 72 06 45), deep in the heart of industrial Rouen. Take bus 12 from the station to Diderot or walk (½hr.) straight across the river on rue Jeanne d'Arc and its extensions, av. Jacques Cartier and av. de Bretagne, to bd. de l'Europe. (Reception open 5-10pm. Lockout 10am-5pm. Curfew midnight. Members only, 55F. 100F deposit for linen and a locker key.) **Hôtel Normandya,** 32, rue du Cordier (tel. 35 71 46 15), offers, well, perfect rooms and genial hospitality only 10min. from the train station. (Singles and doubles 90-100F, with shower 130-140F.) Attractive campsites with squeaky-clean bathrooms await at **Camping Municipal de Déville,** rue Jules Ferry in Déville-les-Rouen (tel. 35 74 07 59), 4km from Rouen. Take bus 2 from the station. (22F per person, 7F per tent or car. Open March-Oct. for tents.)

A **market** enlivens pl. du Vieux Marché (Tues.-Wed. and Fri.-Sun. 7am-12:30pm). Buy fish, cheese, and fresh produce there or at **Monoprix supermarket,** 67, rue du Gros Horloge (open Mon.-Sat. 8:30am-8pm). Buy ferocious *Calvados* liqueur directly from the farmers in the Norman countryside. Even the most bloodthirsty carnivores will wish they were vegetarian after trying the full, well-balanced meals at **Pixie,** 48, rue aux Ours (dishes 38-48F, desserts 12-25F; open Mon.-Sat. noon-2:30pm and 7:30-11:30pm). Crêpes are made right before your eyes at **La P'tite Flambée,** 24, rue Cauchoise, off pl. du Vieux-Marché (open Tues.-Sat. noon-2:30pm and 7-11:30pm, Sun. 7-11:30pm).

■■■ NORMANDY COAST

One of the largest passenger ports in Europe, **Dieppe** has attracted hordes of sun-starved Britons to its long pebbly **beach,** bordered by protective cliffs to the west and the port to the east. The city's **tourist office,** pont Jehan Ango (tel. 35 84 11 77) is to the left of the Sealink/Stena ferry passenger terminal. The **auberge de jeunesse (HI),** 48, rue Louis Fromager (tel. 35 84 85 73), has recently been renovated. From the station, take bus 1 "Les Bruyères" and ask the driver to drop you at the *auberge;* or call ahead for directions fo the 30min. walk. (Reception open 8-11am and 5-11pm. Members only, 43F.) Sealink/Stena **ferries** chug across the English Channel to Newhaven from quai Henri IV (tel. 35 84 80 54; 4 per day, Jan.-Feb. 3 per day; 180F, students 160F, ages 4-14 90F; bicycles free).

Fécamp is famous for the massive **Abbatiale de la Trinité,** whose 127m nave is as long as that of Paris's Notre-Dame (open 9am-7pm, free). The relic of the **Précieux Sang,** a fig trunk that allegedly carried a few drops of Christ's blood and washed ashore in the 6th century, rests within the nave. Another precious liquid (originally distilled from 27 plants and spices by the town's monks) is produced in the **Palais Benedictine,** 110, rue Alexandre Le Grand (including sample 25F, students 20F). The **tourist office,** 113, rue Alexandre Le Grand (tel. 35 28 51 01), books rooms (10F) and dispenses free maps (open Mon.-Fri. 9am-12:15pm and 1:45-6pm, Sept.-June Mon.-Sat. 9am-12:15pm and 1:45-6pm). Fécamp's most affordable rooms are found in the vicinity of Eglise St-Etienne. Try **Hôtel Moderne,** 3, av. Gambetta for pleasant, antique-filled surroundings (tel. 35 28 04 04; 110-140F, with bath 170F).

Le Havre connects France with Rosslare and Cork in Ireland and Portsmouth in England. **P&O European Ferries,** av. Lucien Corbeaux (tel. 35 19 78 50), serves Portsmouth year-round. (Ticket and info office open 6:30am-11:30pm.) **Irish Ferries,** quai de Southampton (tel. 35 53 28 83), alternates service to Rosslare and Cork (Eurail valid, but 30F tax required). Take bus 3 from Hôtel de Ville or train station to Marceau. Avoid walking alone at night in Le Havre, especially near the station and the port. The **tourist office** (tel. 35 21 22 88) is across the bridge from the train station in the Hôtel de Ville (open Mon.-Sat. 8:45am-12:15pm and 1:30-7pm, Oct.-March 8:45am-12:15pm and 1:30-6:30pm). Rest at **Hôtel le Relax,** 97, rue de la

République (tel. 35 26 53 07), close to the station (80-85F, with shower 120F) or the pleasant **Hôtel Séjour Fleuri,** 71, rue Emile Zola (tel. 35 41 33 81), where singles and doubles are 100-130F, with shower 145-160F. **Trains** (at cours de la République) connect Le Havre to Rouen, Paris, and Fécamp.

■■■ CAEN

Despite a punishing Allied bombardment during WWII, the Romanesque churches of **Caen** recall the prosperous 11th century, when the town was William the Conqueror's ducal seat. In the town center, the imposing ruins of William's **château** (open 6am-9:30pm, Oct.-April 6am-7:30pm) enclose two notable museums: the **Musée des Beaux-Arts,** with 19th-century impressionist tableaux of Normandy by Monet, Courbet and Boudin; and the **Musée de Normandie,** which traces Norman peasant life. (Beaux-Arts open Wed.-Mon. 10am-6pm. 20F, students 10F, under 18 free. Normandie open Wed.-Fri. 10am-12:30pm and 2-6pm, April-Sept. Sat.-Mon. 9:30am-12:30pm and 2-6pm. 10F, students 5F. Wed. free.) In the shadow of the château stands the **Eglise St-Pierre,** whose bell tower and detailed exterior illustrate the evolution of the Gothic style from the 13th through the 16th centuries (open 9am-noon and 2-6pm). Perched above the city center, the **Abbaye-aux-Dames** and its twin, the **Abbaye-aux-Hommes,** were built by William and his cousin Mathilda to expiate the sin of their incestuous marriage. North of the center, the excellent **Mémorial: Un Musée Pour la Paix** makes a cogent plea for world peace with high-tech audio-visual aids and actual WWII footage. Take bus 17 "Mémorial" from *centre ville.* (Open 9am-9pm, Sept.-May 9am-7pm. 58F, students 48F.)

Practical Information, Accommodations, and Food From pl. de la Gare (tel. 31 83 50 50) **trains** depart to Paris (5-7 per day, 2hr.) and Rouen (4 per day, 1½hr), and **Bus Verts** (tel. 31 44 77 44) leave for Bayeux (3 per day, 1hr., 35F) and Le Havre (4 per day, 2½hr., 115F). The super-organized, English-speaking **tourist office,** pl. St-Pierre (tel. 31 27 14 14), finds rooms. (15F in town. Open Mon.-Sat. 9am-7pm, Sun. and holidays 10am-12:30pm and 3-6pm; mid-Sept. to May Mon. 10am-noon and 2-7pm, Tues.-Sat. 9am-noon and 2-7pm.) To reach Caen's **auberge de jeunesse (HI),** Foyer Robert Reme, 68*bis,* rue Eustache-Restout (tel. 31 52 19 96) from the station, walk right, take a left up the hill at the end of the street, and catch bus 5 or 17 "Fleury" or "Grâce de Dieu" to Lycée Fresnel. (Reception open 5-10pm. Members only, 57F. Reserve ahead. Open June-Aug.) The more conveniently located **Hôtel du Havre,** 11, rue du Havre (tel. 31 86 19 80), is close to Eglise St-Jean. (Singles 80-105F, with shower 125F. Doubles 85-113F, with shower 150F. Hall showers 13F.) The quiet, clean rooms of the **Hôtel St-Jean,** 20, rue des Martyrs (tel. 31 86 23 35), are right next to Eglise St-Jean. (Singles and doubles with shower 150-170F. Triples 200F.)

Inexpensive *crêperies* and *brasseries,* as well as a smattering of ethnic restaurants, line the cobblestone streets of **quartier Vaugeux,** near the château. **La Petite Auberge,** 17, rue des Equipes-d'Urgence, next to Eglise St-Jean, offers excellent *menus* (open Tues.-Sat. noon-2pm and 7-9pm, Sun. noon-2pm). Caen's staid old streets pulsate by moonlight, especially by the university. The brochure *Le Mois à Caen* lists plays, concerts, and exhibitions for the month. Free copies are available at the youth hostel and at the student center, **CROUS,** 23, av. de Bruxelles (tel. 31 94 54 50).

■■■ BAYEUX, D-DAY BEACHES, AND CHERBOURG

Bayeux Beautiful, ancient Bayeux is an ideal launching pad for the D-Day beaches, and is itself renowned for the **Bayeux Tapestry,** which recounts the Norman conquest of Britain at the 1066 Battle of Hastings. The linen embroidery, probably commissioned for Bayeux's cathedral, now hangs in the **Centre Guillaume le**

Conquérant on rue de Nesmond. (Exhibitions and audio cassette in French and English. Open 9am-7pm; Sept. 16-Oct. 15 and March 16-April 30 9am-12:30pm and 2-6:30pm; Oct. 16-March 15 9:30am-12:30pm and 2-6pm. 30F, students 13F.) The **Musée de la Bataille de Normandie,** bd. Fabian Ware (tel. 31 92 93 41), recounts the events of June-August 1944 through old American, English, French, and German newspapers, photographs, uniforms, and weapons. A 30min. film, "Images of the Battle of Normandy," in English and French, shows footage of the battle front and includes shots from land, air, and sea. (Open 9am-7pm; Jan.-March 15 and Oct. 16-Dec. 10am-12:30pm and 2-6pm; March 16-May and Sept.-Oct. 15 9:30am-12:30pm and 2-6:30pm. 24F, students 11F.)

The helpful, English-speaking staff of the **tourist office,** on the corner of rue St-Jean and rue Larcher (tel. 31 92 16 26), books rooms and changes money when banks are closed. (Open Mon.-Sat. 9am-noon and 2-6pm, Sun. 10am-12:30pm and 3-6:30pm; Sept. 15-July 1 closed Sun.) The coziest place to stay is the converted 17th-century residence, **Family Home (HI),** 39, rue Général de Dais (tel. 31 92 15 22), off rue de la Juridiction. (Follow signs from the train station. Reception open 7:30am-11pm. 85F, nonmembers 95F. Make reservations.) The **Centre d'Accueil Municipal,** 21, rue des Marettes (tel. 31 92 08 19), has sterile singles for 80F (reception open 7am-10pm). For traditional Norman cuisine, try **Le Petit Normand,** 35, rue Larcher (tel. 31 22 88 66), overlooking the cathedral; *menus* start at 49F. (Open noon-2:30pm and 7-10pm; Oct.-March closed Sun. nights.)

D-Day Beaches and Cherbourg Ten km north of Bayeux on the D514 is **Arromanches,** easternmost of the **D-Day beaches.** Arromanches's fascinating **Musée du Débarquement,** on the beach, displays relics and photographs of the British and Canadian landings. (Open April-May 7 9-11:30am and 2-6pm; May 8-Sept. 4 9am-6:30pm; Feb., March, Sept.12-Dec. 9-11:30am and 2-5:30pm; closed Jan. 30F, seniors 25F.) The high cliffs of **Omaha Beach,** scaled by invading American troops, lie to the west. The American Cemetery is in **Colleville-sur-Mer;** the Canadian Cemetery is at **Bény-sur-Mer-Reviers,** near Courseulles; there are British cemeteries at **Hermanville-sur-Mer** and **Ranville.** English-speaking tours based in Bayeux are more convenient than buses. **Normandy Tours** (tel. 31 92 10 70) runs flexible tours for 1-8 people (100F for a 3-4hr. tour) and **Bus Fly** (tel. 31 22 00 08) tours leave daily from the Family Home, 39, rue Général de Dais (9am and 2pm; 150F, students 120F, fee includes admission to the Musée du Débarquement).

Northwest of Bayeux at the northern tip of the Cotentin peninsula lies **Cherbourg,** WWII's "Port de la Libération," which shuttles passengers to and from Portsmouth, Poole, and Southampton, England. Contact **P&O European Ferries** (tel. 33 88 65 70) for Portsmouth, **Brittany Ferries** (tel. 33 22 38 98) for Poole, and **Sealink** (tel. 33 20 43 38) for Southampton. **Irish Ferries** (tel. 33 44 28 96) run to Cork and Rosslare, Ireland. The **train station** is a 15min. walk from the ferry terminal; trains run to Paris (7 per day, 3½hr.), Rouen (3 per day, 3hr.), Caen (6 per day, 1½hr.), Bayeux (9 per day, 1hr.), and points south in Normandy and Brittany. The helpful **tourist office** (tel. 33 93 52 02), is at the northern end of the Bassin du Commerce near the bridge Pont Tournant (open Mon.-Sat. 9am-noon and 1:30-6:30pm, off-season Mon.-Fri. 9am-noon and 2-6pm). If you stay overnight in this city of concrete blockhouses, try the **Hôtel Divette,** 15, rue Louis XVI (tel. 33 43 21 04), 5min. from the station. From pl. Jaurès, follow quai Alexandre III, turn left onto av. Delaville and then right before the square (95-110F, with shower or bath 150F). For cheap provisions, stock up at the **Continent supermarket,** next to the station (open Mon.-Sat. 8:30am-9:30pm).

■ ■ ■ MONT SAINT-MICHEL

Rising abruptly out of a huge expanse of sea, the fortified island of Mont St-Michel is visible for kilometers in all directions. A venerable abbey and exquisite cloister balance precariously on the jutting rock, surrounded by military fortifications and a *ville basse* built to serve medieval pilgrims. Pack a lunch and make the Mont a day-trip; ignore its tourist swarms. You can pay to visit just limited parts of the abbey on your own or take a 1hr. guided tour to see more. (Open 9:30am-6pm; Sept. 16-Nov. 10 and Feb. 16-May 14 9:30-11:45am and 1:45-5pm; Nov. 12-Feb. 15 9:30-11:45am and 1:45-4:15pm. Tours in English at 10am, 11am, noon, 1:30pm, 2:30pm, 3:30pm, 4:30pm, and 5:30pm. Tours in French every ½hr. 36F, ages 18-25 and over 60 23F, under 18 7F, Sun. ½-price.) The 2hr. *visites conférences* (French only) are a special treat; they allow you to walk atop a flying buttress and creep inside the pre-Roman crypts. (Tours at 10am, 11am, 2:30pm, and 3:30pm. 56F, ages 18-25 and over 60 43F, under 18 27F.) The tide rushes in to envelop the Mont at 2m per second; an extraordinary sight. Try to time your visit with the highest tides: 36-48hrs. after the new and full moons respectively. You must be on the Mont two hours ahead of time, as the causeway becomes impassable. Mont St-Michel is stunningly illuminated at night (dusk-11pm); the spectacle is at its best at the entrance to the causeway or from Avranches on the other side of the bay.

To get to Mont St-Michel, take a train to **Pontorson;** from Paris, change at Rennes (4hr., 235F), or Caen (4½hr., 219F). The last train from Pontorson to Rennes leaves around 7pm. Conquer the remaining 9km to the Mont by boarding the **STN bus** outside the Pontorson station (the last leaves the Mont at 6:30pm) or by renting a **bike** at the station (44-55F per day with a 100F deposit or major credit card). Lock your baggage at the station (3F).

Prices rise higher than the bay's famous tides, but the **Centre Duguesclin (HI)** (tel. 33 60 18 65), rue Gén. Patton, a 10min. walk from the Pontorson station, has good facilities. (Members only, 41F. Reception open 9-11am and 6-10pm. Lockout 9am-6pm. Open June to mid-Sept.) In **Pontorson**, stay in the comfortable rooms of the **Hôtel de l'Arrivée**, 14, rue du Docteur Tizon (tel. 33 60 01 57), across from the station. (Singles and doubles 80-150F. 3-4 people 150-170F.)

BRITTANY (BRETAGNE)

This rugged peninsula tugs away from mainland France, intent on its own direction. Locals insist that they are Bretons first and French second, and lilting *Breizh* (Breton) is spoken energetically at the pubs and ports in the western part of the province. The region's 1800-odd *crêperies* set their tables with the regional specialty, accompanied by *cidre brut* (the local cider) or by the sweeter *cidre doux*.

While getting to Brittany is hardly a problem, getting around Brittany is a different matter. Cycling is the best way to travel. Hikers can choose from a number of routes, including the long-distance footpaths *(Grandes Randonnées)* GR341, GR37, GR38, GR380, and the spectacular GR34 along the northern coast. Tourist offices can help you coordinate your hiking or biking tour.

■■■ RENNES

In 1720, a drunken carpenter knocked over his lamp and set most of Rennes ablaze. Since then, the closest Rennes gets to burning is the revelry of students who return to the city when the summer tourists have left. The **Musée de Bretagne** and the **Musée des Beaux-Arts** are housed in the same building at 20, quai Emile Zola, by the canal. The Musée de Bretagne provides an informative introduction to the region's history and traditions; the Musée des Beaux-Arts displays local landscapes as well as an interesting (if obscure) collection of art from the 14th century to the present. (Both open Wed.-Mon. 10am-noon and 2-6pm. To each 15F, students 7F50; to both 20F, students 10F.) The pamphlet *Spectacles, Informations* at the tourist office lists everything going on around town. In early July, Rennes hosts **Les Tombées de la Nuit**, 9 days of non-stop music, dance, theater, song, and mime by international performers who prowl the streets from noon to midnight. For information, write to the Office de Tourisme, Festival de TN, 8, pl. du Maréchal Juin, 35000 Rennes (tel. 99 79 01 98 or 99 30 38 01). The **Association Bretonne des Relais et Itinéraires (ABRI)**, also known as Maison de la Randonnée, 9, rue de Porte-Morde-laise (tel. 99 31 59 44), is devoted to helping you discover Brittany on foot, by horse-back, or by canoe, offering information on GR *(Grande Randonnée)* trails and *gîtes d'étape* (open Mon.-Fri. 9:30am-12:30pm and 2-7pm).

Practical Information, Accommodations, and Food Rennes is 2hr. from Paris's Gare Montparnasse by TGV (3½hr. by regular train) and accessible from Normandy via Caen. The **train station** on pl. de la Gare (tel. 99 65 50 50; reserva-tions 99 65 18 65), schedules departures to St-Malo (1hr., 65F), Nantes (2hr., 110F); Caen (3hr., 170F), Brest (160F plus 36-98F TGV reservation), and Paris (210F plus 36-90F TGV reservation). **Buses**, bd. Magenta (tel. 99 30 87 80), off pl. de la Gare, serve St-Malo (5 per day, Sat.-Sun. 1-2 per day, 1½hr., 55F) and Vannes (Mon.-Fri., 2 per day, 2½hr., 88F). **Les Courriers Bretons** (tel. 99 56 79 09) run to Mont-St-Michel (4 per day, 1 on Sun., 2½hr., 60F) via Pontorson.

To reach the inviting **auberge de jeunesse (HI)**, 10-12, Canal St-Martin (tel. 99 33 22 33), walk (30min. from station) or take bus 20 (on weekends, 1 or 18) "Centre Commercial Nord" to Pont de Legraverend. (Reception open Mon.-Fri. 7:45am-11pm, Sat.-Sun. 8-10am and 6-11pm. Curfew midnight or 30F key deposit. Members only, 70F. Singles 120F. Doubles 75F per person. Sheets 18F.) The well-kept **Hôtel de Léon**, 15, rue de Léon (tel. 99 30 55 28), near the Vilaine River off quai de Riche-mont, has 120F singles and 130F doubles (hall showers 17F, breakfast 24F; closed July 24-Aug. 20). Formerly a prison, the **Crêperie au Boulingrain**, 25, rue St-Melaine, serves *galettes* worth doing time for (*crêpes* 35F; open Mon.-Fri. 11:30am-2pm and 6:30-11pm, Sat.-Sun. 6:30-11pm). Otherwise, take some bread and cheese to a bench in the beautiful **Jardin du Thabor.** The **Stoc supermarket** is close to the sta-tion at 2, rue d'Isly (open Mon.-Sat. 9am-7:30pm).

■■■ ST-MALO

Once the refuge of pirates, the port town of St-Malo continues to attract its share of tourists. Today, visitors come not to drink rum and visit brothels but to walk on the high walls, explore the tiny streets, duck into the many small restaurants and shops, and luxuriate on its miles of beach. Porte St-Thomas looks out onto the **Fort National,** accessible only at low tide. Climb down to the beach and continue along the stone walkway to **Le Grand Bé,** the small island that holds Romantic scribbler Châteaubriand's lonely grave. Within the walls of the *vieille ville,* the **Musée de la Ville,** at the Hôtel de Ville near Porte St-Vincent, leads you through hoards of maps, models, maritime documents, and other pirate paraphernalia. The turret has a phe-nomenal panorama of St-Malo. (Open 10am-noon and 2-6pm; Nov.-March Wed.-Mon. 10am-noon and 2-6pm. 19F, students 9.50F.)

The **tourist office,** Esplanade St-Vincent (tel. 99 56 64 48), near the entrance to the old city, distributes a city map and a list of campsites. (Open Mon.-Sat. 9am-8pm, Sun. 10am-6pm; Sept.-June Mon.-Sat. 9am-noon and 2-7pm, Sun. 10am-noon and 2-5pm.) **Trains** chug daily to Paris-Montparnasse (5hr., 236F) and the TGV zips to Paris via Rennes (3½hr., 236F plus 36-90F reservation fee). **Ferries** chug to Ports-mouth, Weymouth, and Poole in England and to Cork, Ireland. The pavilion oppo-site the tourist office doles out information on buses and ferries.

During July and August, sleeping space is scarce and in great demand. To get to the **auberge de jeunesse (HI),** 37, av. du Père Umbricht (tel. 99 40 29 80), walk (25min. from station) or catch bus 5 "Paramet" (last bus at 7:30pm) and get off after the hostel flags on the left. (Open 24hrs. No lockout. Members only. 66F. Doubles 74F per person.) Basic, comfortable rooms in the old town await you at **Les Chiens du Guet,** 4, pl. du Guet (tel. 99 40 46 77; singles and doubles 150-170F, with shower 180-240F; during low season 140-150F, 150F). **Camping Municipal de la Cité d'Aleth,** near promenade de la Corniche in **St-Servan** (tel. 99 81 60 91), is the closest and most scenic site, equipped with running water and hot showers. (Take bus 1 or 6 to Aleth. 18F per adult, 9F per child, 9F per tent.) *Crêperies* litter the city. Try **Le Petit Malouin,** 6, rue de la Vieille Boucherie (three-crêpe *menu* for 48F or 59F; open 11am-11pm, Oct.-May closed Thurs.).

■■■ DINAN

Tranquil Dinan boasts proudly of its reputation as the best preserved medieval town in Brittany. The **Promenade des Petits-Fossés** begins near the post office and follows the looming ramparts to the 13th-century **Porte du Guichet,** the entrance to the formidable **Château de la Duchesse Anne.** Inside its oval tower, the **Musée de Dinan** displays 18th-century multicolored statuettes and bas-reliefs and a selection of medieval and Roman weapons and artifacts. (Château and museums open June-Oct. 15 10am-6pm; Oct. 16-Nov. 15 and March 16-May Wed.-Mon. 10am-noon and 2-6pm; Nov. 16-Dec. 31 and Feb. 7-March 15 Wed.-Mon. 1:30-5:30pm. 20F, students 10F.) In the *vieille ville,* rue Général de Gaulle leads to the **Promenade de la Duchesse Anne,** at the end of which stands the beautiful **Jardin Anglais.** From the port, re-enter the walled city by **rue de Petit Fort,** which becomes **rue du Jerzval,** one of Dinan's prettiest roads.

Dinan is accessible by train (change at Dol) from Rennes (2hr., 67F) and St-Malo (1¼hr., 44F). From July to September, 3 daily buses run to St-Malo (1hr., 32F). The **tourist office,** 6, rue de l'Horloge (tel. 96 39 75 40), in the *vieille ville,* offers walking tours of the town (July-Aug. 10am and 3pm; 25F) and excellent guides (10F) and maps. (Open Mon.-Sat. 9am-6:45pm, Sun. 10am-1pm and 3-5:45pm; Oct.-May. Mon.-Sat. 8:30am-12:30pm and 2-5:45pm.) A bus runs from the train station in the morning and the evening to the **auberge de jeunesse (HI),** Moulin du Méen in Vallée de la Fontaine-des-Eaux (tel. 96 39 10 83). If you're walking (½hr.), turn left from the train station's main exit, then turn left across the tracks and follow the signs. (Reception open 9-11am and 3-11pm. Curfew 11pm; tell the receptionist the day before if you will be back later. Members only, 46F. Sheets 16F.) **Hôtel-Restaurant de l'Océan,** pl. du 11 Novembre 1918 (tel. 96 39 21 51), across from the station, offers spacious, bright, clean rooms. (Singles and doubles 110-170F. Triples170F. Quads with shower and toilet 200F. Extra bed 30F. Showers free. Breakfast 25F.) **Camp** at the youth hostel amidst beautiful, rustic scenery (24F per night). Featured in the *New York Times,* **the Crêperie des Artisans,** 6, rue du Petit Fort, serves a feast of *galettes* and *crêpes.* (*Menus* 47-64F. Open noon-10:30pm; Sept.-June closed Mon.)

■■■ NORTHERN COAST (CÔTES D'ARMOR)

Brittany's northern coast features some of the most spectacular scenery in France. Transportation poses problems, but don't let it deter you; many tourist offices give out the *Guide Régional des Transports,* which lists regional bus, train, and boat connections, and is issued twice a year.

CÔTE D'EMERAUDE AND CÔTE DE GRANITE ROSE

St-Brieuc is a great place to launch a tour of the Côte d'Emeraude and even the eastern part of the Côte de Granite Rose, but not for much else. It has a train station (rare in the area) and is serviced by several buses. Frequent **trains** arrive from Paris as well as Rennes (1hr., 80F), Morlaix (1hr., 70F), and Dinan (2-3 per day, 55F). If you're in search of a bed for the night, try **Manoir de la Ville Guyomard (HI)** (tel. 96 78 70 70). Take bus 3 "Les Villages" (last one around 7:45pm, 6F) to Van Meno or Jean Moulin. (No lockout or curfew. 53F, over 26 60F. Breakfast 22F. Sheets 21F. Bike rental 45F per day.).

Northeast of St-Brieuc, **Cap Fréhel** marks the northern point of the Côte d'Emeraude, a windswept peninsula whose tip drops 70m into the ocean below. **CAT**

buses go to Le Vieux Bourg, not far from the Cap (1 per day from St-Brieuc, 39F).
Hitchhikers report easy rides to the cape. If your spirit is as rugged as the cape's
cliffs, you'll love the **Auberge de Jeunesse Cap Fréhel (HI)**, la Ville Hadrieux,
Kerivet, in Plévenon (tel. 96 41 48 98 or 96 78 70 70), where most guests and even
the employees choose to sleep outside. Take a bus to the Cap and walk 20min.
toward Plévenon on D16. (Lockout 11am-4pm. 40F. Camping 22F. Sheets 20F.
Breakfast 18F. Open May-Sept.) The hostel also rent **bikes** (45F per day); if you ask at
St-Brieuc's hostel, you can leave a rented bike at Cap Fréhel and vice-versa.

The sweet town of **Paimpol** anchors the eastern end of the Côte de Granite Rose.
Trains connect to St-Brieuc (1hr., 60F) via Guincamp (45min., 35F). Five **CAT
buses** run daily direct from St-Brieuc to Paimpol (1¼hr., 38F). Paimpol's **auberge de
jeunesse/gîte d'étape (HI),** an old manor house at Château de Keraoul (tel. 96 20 83
60), is 20min. from the station. (Members only, 43F. Camping 24F. Sheets 16F.)

NORD FINISTÈRE

Morlaix and Brest **Morlaix,** whose motto is *"S'ils te mordent, mords-les!"* ("If
they bite you, bite them back"), clings picturesquely to the high green hills that
flank the edge of 2 merging rivers. **Trains** arrive from St-Brieuc (45min., 70F), Brest
(45min., 50F), and Quimper (via Landerneau, 2hr., 91F). The helpful **tourist office,**
pl. des Otages (tel. 98 62 14 94), offers a free city map and self-guided walking tour
info (open Mon.-Sat. 9am-12:30pm and 1:30-7:30pm, Sun. 10am-12:30pm; Sept.-
June Mon.-Sat. 9am-noon and 2-6pm). **Espace Nature,** 88, rue Gambetta (tel. 98 88
14 11), down the street from the train station, rents bikes (60F per day, 315F per
week; deposit 3000-5000F; open Mon.-Sat. 9am-7:30pm). The **auberge de jeunesse
(HI),** 3, rte. de Paris (tel. 98 88 13 63), is a 20min. walk from the station. (Reception
open 8-11am and 6-9pm. Lockout 10am-6pm. Curfew midnight, off-season 11pm.
Members only, 43F. Sheets 15F.) Next to the hamlet of Garlan, 5km from town, lies
Camping Croas-Men (tel. 98 79 11 50). Buses do not run there. From the *centre
ville,* follow signs first to Plouigneau and then to Garlan. (14F per person. Tent 15F.
Open 24hrs. year-round.) People without camping equipment can stay in one of the
four area **gîtes d'étape** (30-45F per night). Ask at the tourist office for more info.

Situated on the southern side of Finistère's northern peninsula, **Brest** has a natural
harbor so ideal that in 1631 Cardinal de Richelieu designated it as France's major
naval base. The **auberge de jeunesse (HI)** (tel. 98 41 90 41) is about 4km from the
train station and right near Océanopolis. From the Port de Plaisance bus 7 stop, take
the first left and turn left again at the first street. (Reception open Mon.-Fri. 7-9am
and 5-8pm, Sat.-Sun. 7-10am and 5-8pm. Lockout 10am-6pm. Curfew 11pm. Members only, 70F.)

Camaret, Morgat, and Crozon At the western end of the Crozon peninsula, little **Camaret** is a jewel; once you see the beach below the hostel, you'll want
to stay forever. Just beyond the edge of town on the D8 is a modest circle of stone
menhirs. The **Pointe de Penhir,** 3½km away on the D8, is one of the finest capes in
Brittany. Climb out onto the rocks for a blood-boiling view of the isolated rock
masses of the **Tas de Pois.** Farther north, the road passes another stone circle, the
Alignements de Lagatjar, some 100 *menhirs* arranged in intersecting lines and ending in a Stonehenge-like circle. Camaret's **tourist office,** quai Toudouze (tel. 98 27
93 60), is in the *Gendarmerie* barracks next to pl. Charles de Gaulle (open Mon. 2-
5pm, Tues.-Fri. 9am-noon and 2-5pm, Sat. 9am-noon). Hotels here are good but few
and expensive. Make Camaret a daytrip from Brest or come with a tent and pitch it
at **Camping Municipal de Lannic** (tel. 98 27 91 31), off rue du Gronnach, close to
the town center (9.25F per person, 8.25F per site; showers 7F; open May-Sept.).

Morgat and **Crozon** are practically indistinguishable, although for the record,
Crozon leads a busy commercial life whilst Morgat sunbathes on its enormous
beach in the summer The 9F bus ride from Camaret will drop you by the **tourist
office** (tel. 98 27 07 92), which has a slew of info on both towns and the surrounding area (open Mon.-Sat. 9:15am-7:30pm, Sun. 10am-noon; Sept.-June Mon.-Sat.
9:15am-noon and 2-6:30pm). Morgat's **tourist office,** across from the beach on bd.

de la France Libre (tel. 98 27 07 92), waylays visitors as they enter from Crozon (open June and Sept. Mon.-Sat. 9:30am-noon and 2-6pm; July-Aug. Mon.-Sat. 9:30am-7:30pm, Sun. 4-6:30pm).

Crozon has only one hotel, **Hôtel Moderne**, rue Alsace-Lorraine (tel. 98 27 00 10). (Singles 146-170F, with bath 234-278F. Doubles 210-219F, with bath 300-318F. Simple triples or quads 210F. Triples with bath 384F. Showers 20F. Breakfast 31F.) **ULAMIR**, rte. de Camaret (tel. 98 27 01 68), in the SIVOM building, can inform you about the location and accessibility of the four *gîtes d'étapes* (40F per night). The whole Crozon peninsula is strewn with **campgrounds.** Ask at the Crozon tourist office for a complete listing. **Pen-Ar-Ménez** (tel. 98 27 12 36), on bd. de Pralogan toward Camaret, is closest to this town-and-beach (16F per person, 20F per tent).

■■■ SOUTHERN BRITTANY

Quimper Although staunch, half-timbered houses with crooked façades share cobblestone streets in the *vieille ville* (old town) with legions of tourists and hordes of fashion-conscious teens, Quimper (kem-PEAR), capital of La Cornouaille, has managed to retain its Breton flavor. During the week preceding the fourth Sunday of July each year, Quimper recalls its heritage with the *Festival de Cornouaille,* a cavalcade of mirth and music in Breton costume. The **tourist office,** 7, rue de la Déesse (tel. 98 53 04 05), has free maps and a concise *guide pratique,* and sells bus excursion tickets to nearby sights such as Pointe du Raz (open Mon.-Sat. 8:30am-8pm, Sun. 9:30am-12:30pm; Sept.-June Mon.-Sat. 9am-noon and 1:30-6pm). **Trains** leave the station on av. de la Gare for Paris (7½hr.; TGV 5hr.; 305F, plus 36-90F reservation for TGV), Nantes (3hr., 165F), and Brest (1½hr., 80F). All **buses** leave from the *gare* next to the train station or across the street in front of the Café Nantais.

To reach the **auberge de jeunesse (HI)**, 6, av. des Oiseaux (tel. 98 55 41 67), about 2km out of town, take bus 1 "Penhars" to Chaptal from the station or the rue du Parc stop across from the tourist office. (Reception open 8-10am and 6-8pm. Lockout 10am-6pm. 42F. Open April-Oct.) Near the train station, the **Hôtel de l'Ouest,** 63, rue le Déan (tel. 98 90 28 35), offers clean rooms in a quiet neighborhood. (Singles 100-180F. Doubles 150-190F. Triples 220F.) Next to the hostel, **Camping Municipal,** av. des Oiseaux in the Bois du Séminaire, is clean but crowded. (Reception open Mon. 4:30-8:30pm, Tues.-Sat. 9-11am and 3:30-8:30pm, Sun. 9am-noon. 15F per person. Tent 3F.)

Quiberon All roads in Quiberon lead to the sandy and wonderfully clean **Grande Plage** at the heart of town. To escape the congested port area, head for smaller, rockier **Plage du Goviro** near the campgrounds. From the port, follow bd. Chanard east along the water as it becomes bd. de la Mer and then bd. du Goviro. **Train** service to Quiberon from Auray operates only in July and August; in the off-season, buses are frequent and dependable. **TIM buses** (tel. 97 47 29 64) run to Auray (10 per day, 1 hr., 34F) via Carnac (½hr., 21F). To find the **tourist office,** 14, rue de Verdun (tel. 97 50 07 84) from the train station, turn left and walk down rue de la Gare. Veer to the right of the church, down rue de Verdun; the tourist office is on the left. The professional staff can help you find a B&B for 100-200F per night.

To reach the small, centrally located **auberge de jeunesse (HI),** 45, rue du Roch-Priol (tel. 97 50 15 54), turn left at the station, then take rue de la Gare through pl. du Repos, take rue de Lille, turn left on rue Roch-Priol, and continue bearing left about two blocks. (Lockout 10am-6pm. 41F. 2-person tents 70F. Kitchen. Open May-Sept.) **Au Bon Accueil,** 6, quai de L'Houat (tel. 97 50 07 92), lets inexpensive rooms above a busy restaurant. (Singles and doubles 100-145F. Doubles and triples 140-250F.) Recently renovated **Camping Bois d'Amour** (tel. 97 50 13 52, off-season 97 30 24 00) boasts a heated swimming pool. Reservations are advisable in summer. (15-28F per person. 2-person tents 15-25F. Open April-Sept.)

FRANCE

Belle-Ile At least 5 boats depart daily from Quiberon's Port-Maria for Belle-Ile, an island that merges high cliffs, narrow creeks, and crashing seas. The crossing takes 25-45 min. (83F per person, 36F per bike round-trip.) Biking is the best way to tour the island. **Peugeot Location,** 14, rue de l'Eglise (tel. 97 31 84 19), rents them next to the church (40F per day; open 9am-12:15pm and 2-7pm, Sept.-June closed Sun.-Mon.). An impressive 15th-century walled citadel protects **Le Palais,** once a strategic port and currently the island's largest town. The **tourist office** (tel. 97 31 81 93) at the end of the quay distributes free guide in English (open Mon.-Sat. 8:30am-7:30pm, Sun. 8:30am-1:30pm; Sept.-June Mon.-Sat. 9am-12:30pm and 2-6:30pm, Sun. 9am-12:30pm). Bike 6km to **Sauzon,** a tiny fishing port with picture-book façades. From Sauzon, continue another 4km to the **Pointe des Poulains,** at the northernmost tip of the island. Four km southwest on the Côte Sauvage lies the impressive **Grotte de L'Apothicairerie.** From the grotto, follow D25 south to the rough **Aiguilles de Port-Coton,** which Monet captured in an 1886 painting, and the nearby **Plage de Port-Donnant.**

Inexpensive accommodations on the island include numerous campgrounds, 2 *gîtes d'étapes,* and an **HI youth hostel.** The hostel and one campsite are located near the citadel, a 20min. hike from Le Palais port. Turn right from the port and follow the quay to the footbridge leading to the citadel; cross the bridge, walk diagonally left through the parking lot, and enter **Camping Les Glacis** (tel. 97 31 41 76; 13F per person, 23F per tent, 2F per bike.) To reach the **hostel** (tel. 97 31 81 33), continue on and turn right at the road by the showers, climb another hill, follow the road through a small residential neighborhood and look for the sign to the *auberge* on the right. (Reception open 8:30-10am and 6-8pm. Members only, 47F. Tent 35F. Breakfast 18F. Sheets 16F.) Besides selling fresh vegetables, the *gîte d'étape* in **Port Guen** (tel. 97 31 55 88), about 3km south of Le Palais, rents beds (47F) in dorm-style rooms in a colorful barn. Reservations are recommended.

■■■ NANTES

Politically, Nantes is part of the Pays de la Loire. Culturally, most *nantais* feel an allegiance to Brittany. Architecturally, the city resembles Paris, with public parks and gardens, and wide boulevards marking the boundaries between administrative *arrondissements.* Thanks to their lightweight Vendée stone, the Gothic vaults of **Cathédrale St-Pierre** soar 37.5m into the heavens, higher than the arches of Notre-Dame in Paris (open 8:45am-7pm). Built by François II, Nantes's heavily fortified 15th-century **château** once held Gilles de Rais (Bluebeard), who was convicted of sorcery in 1440. Henri IV signed the Edict of Nantes here in 1598, granting religious freedom to Protestants. The better of two museums inside the château, the **Musée des Arts Populaires Régionaux** displays traditional Breton costumes and furniture. The **Musée des Salorges** presents Nantes's commercial history since the 18th century. Take tram 1 or bus 24, 26, 28, or 29 to Duchesse Anne. (Open 10am-noon and 2-6pm, Sept.-June Wed.-Mon. 10am-noon and 2-6pm. Courtyard and ramparts open 10am-7pm; Sept.-June 10am-noon and 2-6pm. 30F, students 15F, free on Sun.) West of the château is a *quartier* of elegant 18th-century buildings. Prosperous sea merchants relied on the slave trade profits to build lavish houses on the **Ile Feydeau,** between allée Turenne and allée Tuouin.

Two blocks from the cathedral at 10, rue Georges Clemenceau, is Nantes's **Musée des Beaux-Arts,** with a large collection of fine canvases by Courbet, Delacroix, Ingres, and Kandinsky. Take bus 11, 12, 21, or 23 to Trébuchet. (Open Mon., Wed.-Thurs., and Sat. 10am-6pm, Fri.10am-9pm, Sun. 11am-6pm. 20F, students 10F, free on Sun.) Let your imagination run wild at the innovative **Musée Jules Verne,** 3, rue de l'Hermitage, near the river in pl. M. Schwob, which re-creates the fictional worlds of hometown boy, Jules Verne. Take bus 21 to Garennes. (Open Mon. and Wed.-Sat. 10am-noon and 2-5pm, Sun. 2-5pm. 8F, students 4F, Sun. free.) Nearby is the **planetarium,** 8, rue des Acadiens. (Showings Tues.-Sat. 10:30am, 2:15pm, and 3:45pm; Sun. 2:15pm and 3:45pm. 24F, students and seniors 12F.) Ask the tourist office about the **global pass** to the château museums, the Musée des Beaux-Arts, the Musée d'Histoire Naturelle, and the Musée Jules Verne.

At night, rows of white and yellow lanterns lead you to lively pubs, bars, and cafés in the area between the château and pl. Graslin. The area north of rue Crébillon and around rue Scribe is most popular in the evening. Nightly at 11pm, a live band tunes up at **The Tie Break Club,** 1, rue des Petites Ecuries (open Mon.-Sat. 6pm-4am). The popular mixed gay club, **Le Temps d'Aimer,** 14, rue Alexandre Fourny, off pl. de le République, rocks till dawn in a mirrored interior (open Tues.-Sun. 11pm-5am; 40F, weekends 70F).

Practical Information, Accommodations, and Food To get to the center of town and the tourist office, turn left out of the north exit of the station onto bd. de Stalingrad, which becomes cours John Kennedy. Place du Commerce and the tourist office are 1km ahead. The **tourist office** (tel. 40 47 04 51), in the 19th-century commerce building, doles out good town maps (open Mon.-Fri. 9am-7pm, Sat. 10am-6pm). **Trains** leave from the station at 27, bd. Stalingrad (tel. 40 08 50 50), running to Paris (3-4hr., TGV 2hr.; 220F plus 36-90F TGV reservation); Bordeaux (5-8 per day, 4hr., 220F), and Rennes (7 per day, 2 on Sun., 2hr., 110F).

The spacious **auberge de jeunesse (HI),** 2, pl. de la Manufacture (tel. 40 29 29 20), is open July-Sept. From the station, turn right onto bd. de Stalingrad, left onto rue Manille and then left onto pl. de la Manufacture (10min.). Or take the tram from the train station (7F) to Manufacture. (Reception open 7am-noon and 2-11pm. Curfew 1am. Members 70F. Sheets 16F.) Small, sterile rooms await you at the **Centre Jean Macé,** 90, rue du Préfet Bonnefoy (tel. 40 74 55 74). To get there, turn left onto cours John Kennedy, then right at pl. de la Duchesse Anne onto rue Henri IV, which becomes rue Sully. The Centre is on rue Sully at rue du Préfet Bonnefoy. Otherwise, take bus 12 from the SNCF station to pl. Maréchal Foch and continue up rue Sully. (Reception open 9-11:30am and 2:30-6pm. 55F, with bath 60F.) To reach the superb **Camping du Val de Cens,** 21, bd. du Petit Port (tel. 40 74 47 94), take a 10min. ride north on tram 2 from pl. du Commerce to Marhonnière. (Reception open 7-11pm. 15F per person. 20F per tent. No phone reservations; in summer, arrive early.)

Try Nantes's delicious seafood, prepared *au beurre blanc* (with butter sauce), and *canard nantais* (duck) made with grapes, as well as the white wines *Muscadet* and *Gros Plant.* **Markets** erupt daily except Monday from 9am to 1pm in pl. du Bouffay and at the **Marché de Talensac,** along rue de Bel Air near pl. St-Similien. A **Decré supermarket** is in the basement of Nouvelles Galeries, rue du Moulin, in the *centre ville* (open Mon.-Sat. 9am-7pm). **Crêperie Jaune,** 1, rue des Echevins, off pl. du Bouffay, is packed with students scarfing down the 42F *plat du jour* or the house specialty, an immense, meaty, 42-55F double-decker *galette* called *pavé nantais* (vegetarian version available; open Mon.-Sat. noon-3pm and 7pm-2am).

LOIRE VALLEY (PAYS DE LA LOIRE)

For years, people have come to the region between Paris and Brittany to see the Loire River and the châteaux. The surprisingly sordid history of many of these dignified mansions presents a mixed bag of mischief, genius, promiscuity, and dirty-dealing. While the dukes and the counts chased stags with armies of hounds, their wives hosted bacchanalian orgies and decorated the castles with the finest Italian masters, fostering an opulence never before imagined.

The hostels in Blois, Saumur, and Orléans are comfortable bases, but pose daunting logistical challenges to those without their own wheels; public transportation routes fan out of the larger cities, but infrequent service can leave you stranded. SNCF's *Châteaux pour Train et Vélo,* with train schedules, distances, and information on bike and car rental, is invaluable. Hitching to the isolated châteaux, such as

246 ■ LOIRE VALLEY

Chambord and Chenonceau, is difficult; fortunately, many châteaux lie near well-traveled roads.

■■■ ORLÉANS

In 1429, Joan of Arc wrested Orléans, then the most important city in France after Paris, from the English. Today, the city proudly sports her name on restaurants, cafés, and hotels. Stop in Orléans en route to châteaux country, if only to witness Orléans's modern battle between cobblestone and plastic. The stained-glass windows telling Joan's story in the **Cathédrale Ste-Croix** will knock your smelly socks off (open 9am-noon and 2-6pm). The **Maison de Jeanne d'Arc,** 3, pl. de Gaulle, features period costumes and an audio-visual recreation of the siege of Orléans. (Open Tues.-Sun. 10am-noon and 2-6pm; Nov.-April Tues.-Sun. 2-6pm. 10F, students 5F, under 16 free.) When you tire of Joan, view the extraordinary collection of Gallo-Roman bronze animals at the **Musée Archéologique et Historique de l'Orléannais,** in the Hôtel Cabu, at pl. Abbé Desnoyers, near the intersection of rue de Bourgogne and rue de l'Empereur (open Wed.-Sun. 10am-noon and 2-6pm, Oct.-March Wed.-Mon. 10am-noon and 2-5pm; 11F, students 5.50F).

The **tourist office,** pl. Albert 1er (tel. 38 53 05 95), next to the train station, sponsors walking tours in French (35F, students 18F) and has info on local summer music and theater productions (open Mon.-Sat. 9am-7pm, Sun. 9:30am-12:30pm and 3-6:30pm; Sept.-June Mon.-Sat. 9am-7pm). One of the brightest spots in Orléans is the homey, well-appointed **auberge de jeunesse (HI)** at 14, rue Faubourg Madeleine (tel. 38 62 45 75), on the west side of town; take bus B "Paul Bert" from in front of the train station (7.50F). (Reception open 7-9:30am and 5:30-10pm. Lockout 9:30am-5:30pm. Members only, 38F. Feb.-March open Sun.-Fri. only.) The owner of the **Hôtel de Paris,** 29, bd. du Faubourg Bannier (tel. 38 53 39 58), speaks English and can be a useful source of information for visitors. (Singles and doubles 100-180F. Showers 15F. Breakfast 20F.) Pizzeria **L'Arlequin,** at the corner of rue des Minimes and rue du Columbier, off of bd. du Bannier (tel. 38 62 38 62), becomes a popular bar later at night (open Mon.-Sat. 11am-3pm, 5pm-midnight).

■■■ BLOIS

The **Château de Blois** glistens as a result of a massive restoration project. The octagonal spiral staircase crawls with King François I's stone salamanders. (Open 9am-6:30pm, last admission at 5:30pm; Nov.-March 9am-noon and 2-5pm. 27F, students 15F.) A mid-sized city bursting at its seams, Blois corrals a herd of attractive churches and gardens. One of the most well-preserved examples of medieval architecture, the abbey of **Ste-Laumer** (today called St-Nicholas) impresses inside and out. Don't miss the old quarter around the **Cathédrale St-Louis.**

The **tourist office,** 3, av. Jean Laigret (tel. 54 74 06 49 or 54 78 23 21), will change money for an 18F commission. (Open Mon.-Sat. 9am-7pm, Sun. 10am-1pm and 4-7pm; Oct.-March Mon.-Sat. 9am-noon and 2-6pm.) Ask here about bus passes to create your own itinerary of châteaux. Accommodations in Blois fill up fast. The homey and rustic **auberge de jeunesse (HI),** 18, rue de l'Hôtel Pasquier (tel. 54 78 27 21), is 7½km outside Blois in Les Grouets. Take bus 4 "Les Grouets" (last bus at 7:30pm; 6F) from pl. Valin by the river. (Lockout 10am-6pm. 40F, nonmembers 60F. Open March-Nov. 15.) Get bright, tidy rooms at the **Hôtel St-Jacques,** 7, rue Ducoux (tel. 54 78 04 15; singles and doubles 100-120F). To find the quiet, newly renovated **Hôtel du Bellay,** 12, rue des Minimes (tel. 54 78 23 62), turn left onto Minimes at the top of porte Chartraine. (Singles and doubles 112-200F. Breakfast 24F. Call in advance.)

Eating is most blissful on lively, restaurant- and bar-lined rue Foulerie, in the shadow of the cathedral. **Côté Sel Côté Cour,** 5, rue du Grenier à Sel (tel. 54 56 17 08), is left off rue de la Foulerie walking away from the rond pont de la Résistance.

Every wackily carved glass-holder in the eatery is for sale (80F full *menu*, open Tues.-Sat. 1-4pm and 6:30pm-midnight). For 58F, enjoy the all-you-can-eat buffet with dessert at **La Forge**, 18, rue Bourg Neuf. Their specialty is meat cooked over a wooden fire. (Open Mon. noon-2pm, Tues.-Sat. noon-2pm and 7:30-11pm.)

■ CHAMBORD, CHEVERNY, AND AMBOISE

Built by François I for his hunting trips and orgiastic fêtes, **Chambord** is the largest and most extravagant of the Loire châteaux. Access to the grounds and surrounding wildlife preserve is free and unlimited. Seven hundred of François I's trademark stone salamanders, symbols of bravery, lurk on Chambord's walls, ceilings, and ingenious staircase, while the 365 fireplaces scattered through the 400 rooms create a miniature rooftop city of decorated chimneys (open 9:30am-6:15pm, Sept.-June 9:30am-12:15pm and 2-5:15pm; 33F, students 22F). Chambord is accessible by bus or bike from Blois; take the D956 south for 2-3km and turn left onto the D33 for 11km (about 1hr.).

Cheverny, also served by bus from Blois, soothes with stately classical lines and the most elegant interior of all the châteaux. A compound on the ground houses 70 bloodhounds; watch them ravenously devour their dinner. (Feedings Mon-Sat. at 5pm; Sept.-March Mon. and Wed.-Fri. at 3pm. Château open 9:15am-6:45pm; mid-Sept.-May 9:30am-noon and 2:15-5pm. 35F, students 20F.) Those hitching to Cheverny from Blois follow the D956 south.

The château at **Amboise** marks the beginning of the decorative Renaissance style that later inspired Blois and Chambord. It also saw two Kings expire: The 4-ft. Charles VIII fatally bumped his head on a *really* low door here, and Charles V tripped onto a torchbearer and burned himself alive. Leonardo da Vinci spent the last 3 years of his life in the nearby Clos Lucé, and his bones are said to rest in the flamboyant **Chapelle St-Hubert,** the gem of the château's remaining structures. (Open 9am-6:30pm; Sept.-March 9am-noon and 2-5pm; April-June 9am-noon and 2-6:30pm. 28F, students 18F.) Amboise's comfortable **auberge de jeunesse (HI)** (tel. 47 57 06 36) lies on the delightful Ile d'Or. (Reception open Tues.-Sun. 3-8pm. 48F. Nov.-Feb. 34F. In summer, arrive early or call ahead.) About half the trains on the Blois-Tours route stop midway at Amboise.

■■■ TOURS

Tours is too large to be cute, and too impersonal to be endearing. But with a large, cosmopolitan student population, it's the hot spot of the Loire, and an excellent base from which to explore the Valley. East of pl. Plumereau, **Cathédrale St-Gatien,** rue Jules Simon, may be the most dazzling compilation of stained glass in the Loire. (Open 7:15am-7pm; Oct.-Easter 7:15am-noon and 2-6:45pm.) The amazing **Musée du Gemmail,** 7, rue du Murier, flaunts several *gemmaux* (a step beyond stained glass) signed by Picasso. (Open April-Oct. 15 Tues.-Sun. 10am-noon and 2-6:30pm. 25F, students 15F.)

Tours's **tourist office,** rue Bernard Palissy (tel. 47 70 37 37), arranges bus tours to the châteaux. (Open Mon.-Sat. 8:30am-7pm, Sun. 10am-12:30pm and 3-6pm; Sept.-May Mon.-Sat. 8:30am-6:30pm.) The **auberge de jeunesse (HI)** (tel. 47 25 14 45), 4km from the station in a park by the highway, is accessible via buses 1 and 6 (last one at 8:15pm) from the stop on the right side of av. de Grammont, 30m down from pl. Jean Jaurès. (Reception open 5-11pm, off-season 5-10pm. Lockout 10am-4pm. Curfew 11pm. 62F includes breakfast.) The quiet **Mon Hôtel,** 40, rue de la Préfecture (tel. 47 05 67 53), left off rue Bernard Palissy, has bright, newly decorated rooms. (Singles 100-170F. Doubles 115-170F. Showers 15F. All-you-can-eat breakfast 25F.) Inexpensive hotels cluster near the train station. Tasty treats abound on rue Colbert and around pl. Plumereau. **Les Trois Canards,** 16, rue de la Rôtisserie, serves an elegant 47F 3-course *menu* and a more delicate 69F *menu* (open Mon.-Fri. noon-2pm and 7:30-10pm, Sat. 7:30-10pm).

FRANCE

■ CHÂTEAUX NEAR TOURS

The graceful château of **Chenonceaux** (tel. 47 23 90 07) arches effortlessly over the languid River Cher. Three women overlooked and influenced the construction of this romantic palace: Catherine Briçonnet, Diane de Poitiers (Henri II's mistress), and Cathérine de Médicis (Henri's wife). The long gallery served as a military hospital during WWI, and a passageway from annexed France to Vichy France during WWII. Chenonceaux's stunning exterior will move even the most jaded castle-goer. (Open March 16-Sept. 15 9am-7pm; call for closing times in off-season. 40F, students 25F.) Your best bet is to make Chenonceaux a daytrip from Tours (3 trains per day, 1 on Sun., 45min., 32F).

Azay-le-Rideau château gazes vainly at its reflection from an island in the Indre river. Colorful 16th-century French tapestries ornament the interior, while outside, the old moat has been replaced by a decorative expanse of water. (Open July-Aug. 9am-6:30pm, April-June and Sept. 9:30am-6pm, Oct.-March 9:30am-12:30pm and 2-5:30pm; 31F, students 20F.)

Engulfed by the thick woods of the Forêt de Chinon, **Ussé's** pointed towers, white turrets, and chimneys inspired *Sleeping Beauty.* The château is decorated with wax figures which give a sense of theme to the place, but if 54F for the whole ball of wax seems a little steep, just relish the view from outside. (Open March-Oct. 9am-noon and 2-7pm, Oct.-Nov. 10am-noon, 2-6pm. 54F, students 22F.)

Villandry maintains fantastic formal gardens with vine-covered walkways and 3 terraces of sculpted shrubs and flowers, but the château pales before its regal cousins. (Gardens open 9am-8pm; Sept.-May 9am-nightfall. Château open March15-Nov. 11 9am-7pm. To gardens 26F, students 20F. To château and garden 40F.)

■■■ SAUMUR

Saumur's picture-book 14th-century **château** stands above the city's otherwise modest skyline. Inside, the **Musée des Arts Décoratifs** displays a collection of medieval and Renaissance painting and sculpture, 15th- and 16th-century tapestries, and brightly decorated porcelain. The **Musée du Cheval** upstairs, with bridles, bits, horseshoes, saddles, and horse skeletons from all over the world, will appeal to even those who aren't fanatic horse lovers. (Château and museums open June 15-Sept. 15 9am-7pm, Wed. and Sat. in July-Aug. until 10pm ; Sept. 16-Sept. 30 and April-June 14 9am-noon and 2-6pm; Oct.-March Wed.-Mon. 10am-noon and 2-5pm. 32F, students 23F.) Saumur's proud name adorns a fine white, a subtle rosé, and an earthy red wine. One of the most impressive *caves,* **Gratien et Meyer**, route de Chinon (tel. 41 51 01 54), founded in 1864, stretches for several km in the limestone caves cut into the hills. Take bus D from pl. Bilange to La Grue. Check out the millions of bottles of wine in the cave, then try some for free. You can sign up for a 45min. wine-tasting course for 40F. (Open Sept.-July 9-11:30am and 2-5pm, Aug. 9am-6pm, Nov.-Feb. Mon.-Fri. 9-11am and 2-5:15pm, Sat.-Sun. 10-11:45am and 3-5:15pm.) Once you have had enough to drink, continue 4km down the road to the **Musée du Champignon** (tel. 41 50 25 01) where exotic fungi await. Tours in French, English, and German trace the history of the mushroom. (Open Feb.-Nov. 10am-7pm. 20F.)

Ask at the **tourist office,** pl. Bilange (tel. 41 51 03 06), for information about horse exhibitions, wine *dégustations,* and fungus tours. (Open Mon.-Sat. 9:15am-7pm, Sun. 10:30am-12:30pm and 3:30-6:30pm; Sept. 16-June 14 Mon.-Sat. 9:15am-12:30pm and 2-6pm.) The modern **auberge de jeunesse (HI)** (tel. 41 67 45 00), on Ile d'Offard between the station and tourist office, has a free swimming pool and a superb view of the château. (Reception open 8-10am and 5-10pm. Lockout 10am-5pm. Curfew 10pm. 8-berth rooms 82F, 2-berth rooms 105F. Sheets and breakfast included.)

■■■ ANGERS

The massive stone walls of Anger's **château** once daunted Norman hordes, then narrowly escaped destruction during the Wars of Religion; today they remain imposing despite a stifling urban onslaught. The 17 formidable towers of the château and the deep moat's waters have been replaced with formal gardens and a deer park. Inside, the **Tapestries of the Apocalypse** depict the Book of Revelations. Spun in gold thread, this triumph of medieval art is large enough to carpet a small street. (Château open 9am-7pm, Sept. 16-April 9:30am-12:30pm and 2-6pm. 31F, students 17F.)

Angers's **tourist office,** pl. Kennedy (tel. 41 23 51 11), across from the château, organizes castle trips and changes money for a 20F fee when banks are closed. (Open Mon.-Sat. 9am-7pm, Sun. 10am-1pm and 3-6pm; Oct.-May Mon.-Sat. 9am-12:30pm and 2-6:30pm.) The largest hostel in France, the **Foyer des Jeunes Travailleurs (HI),** is on rue Darwin (tel. 41 72 00 20), 4km from the station. Take bus 8 "Beaucouzé" to the CFA stop (48F, nonmembers 65F). At **Hotel des Lices,** 25, rue des Lices (tel. 41 87 44 10), near the cathedral and château, welcoming owners present immaculate, small singles and doubles for 125F, with shower and toilet 170F (reserve ahead in summer). Appetizing eateries garnish the pedestrian district around pl. Romaine. Remarkably inexpensive fare awaits at Les Halles, a covered **market** at rue Plantagenet behind the cathedral (open Tues.-Sat. 9am-7:30pm, Sun. 7am-1:30pm, Mon. 2-7:30pm).

AQUITAINE

Forested hills, soporific river valleys, and dramatic cliffs first drew people here some 150,000 years ago. Today, the Dordogne, Vézère, Isle, and Lot Rivers snake past 12th-century Byzantine-Romanesque churches, chapels clinging to the rocks in the pilgrimage town of Rocamadour, *bastides* (fortified mountaintop towns) built during the Hundred Years War, and pastoral villages near Sarlat and Périgueux.

■■■ PERIGORD

Périgueux and Les Eyzies-de-Tayac The capital of the Périgord region, **Périgueux** makes a good base for the local prehistoric caves. In town, modern façades mask the labyrinthine *vieille ville* and the multi-domed **Cathédrale St-Front** (10F, tours in French at no extra charge 8am-noon and 2:30-7:30pm). The town receives several **trains** a day from Bordeaux (2½hr., 95F); Paris via Limoges (7hr., 260F), and Toulouse (180F). Ask the **tourist office,** 26, pl. Francheville (tel. 53 53 10 63), for their invaluable free brochures, *La Fête en Périgord* and *Guide des Commerces* (open Mon.-Fri. 9am-7pm, Sat. 9am-noon and 2-7pm, Sun. 10am-5pm; Sept.-May Mon.-Sat. 9am-noon and 2-6pm). The **Foyer des Jeunes Travailleurs Résidence Lakanal,** off bd. Lakanal (tel. 53 53 52 05) offers a comfortable bed for the night. From the tourist office, turn left down cours Fénélon and take a right onto bd. Lakanal; 15m before the dead-end at the train tracks, turn right and walk around the club Périgueux and through the gate out back. (Reception open Mon.-Fri. 5-7pm, Sat.-Sun. noon-1pm and 7-8pm. 60-85F per person. Sheets, showers, and breakfast included.) Get value for your coins at **Au Bon Coin,** 78, rue Chanzy (tel. 53 53 43 22), off rue Denis Papin en route to the *centre ville.* (Reception closed Sun. Singles and doubles 100F per person. Free hall showers. Breakfast 20F.) Camp 1½km away in Boulazac at **Barnabé-Plage,** 80, rue des Bains (tel. 53 53 41 45). Hop the city bus D "Cité Belaire" (6F, last one 7:30pm) from cours Montaigne. (Open 9am-midnight. 14F per person, 15F per tent.)

Five trains per day from Périgueux (40min., 39F) make **Les Eyzies-de-Tayac** a perfect daytrip. **Prehistoric caves**—nearly bursting with tourists from July to mid-September—house fascinating paintings and carvings, as well as spectacular stalagmites and stalactites. Call at least 2 weeks in advance to get tickets during summer. The best paintings near town are at the **Grotte de Font-de-Gaume** (tel. 53 06 90 80), 1km out of town, where 15,000-year-old horses, bison, reindeer and woolly mammoth cavort along the cave walls. (Open Wed.-Mon. 9am-noon and 2-6pm, Oct.-March Wed.-Mon. 9:30am-noon and 2-5:30pm. 31F, ages 18-25 and over 60 20F, under 18 6F, children under 7, artists, and art students free.) About 9km north-west of Les Eyzies on route D66, the **Roque St-Christophe** (tel. 53 50 70 45) is the most extensive cave dwelling discovered yet. A 30-45min. visit (brochures in English) allows you to examine the cave's tools, ovens, monastic remains, and weapons. (Open 10am-6:30pm, Oct.-March 11am-5pm. No waiting period or reservation. 35F.) In town, the **Musée National de La Préhistoire** has an excellent collection of weapons, skeletons, and Cro Magnon artwork. (Open Wed.-Mon. 9:30am-6pm; April-June and Sept.-Nov. 9:30am-noon and 2-6pm; Dec.-March 9:30am-noon and 2-5pm. 20F; ages 18-25, over 60, and Sun. 12F; under 18 free.) The **tourist office,** pl. de la Mairie (tel. 53 06 97 05), rents bikes, exchanges currency, and sells hiking guides. (Open Mon.-Sat. 9am-7pm, Sun. 10am-noon and 2-6pm; March-June and Sept.-Oct. Mon.-Sat. 9am-noon and 2-6pm; Nov.-Feb. Mon.-Fri. 10am-noon and 2-6pm.)

Sarlat and Rocamadour Despite the dense mobs swarming **Sarlat** each summer, its remarkable *vieille ville,* a medieval sculpture of golden sandstone, merits a mosey. Sarlat's movie-set perfection attracts the gaze of more than a few cameras—*Cyrano de Bergerac* and *Manon of the Spring* were both shot here. The Saturday **market** is renowned throughout France (7:30am-12:30pm, 2-6pm). Stop by the **tourist office,** pl. de la Liberté (tel. 53 59 27 67), for a free copy of the *Guide Pratique,* which includes transportation schedules and useful practical info (open Mon.-Sat. 9am-7pm, Sun. 10am-noon and 2-6pm; Oct.-May Mon.-Sat. 9am-noon and 2-7pm). **Trains** run to Bordeaux (2½hr., 115F) and Périgueux (1½hr., 70F) via Les Eyzies (1hr., 39F). **SCETA buses** truck to Souillac (50min., 25F), and from there trains chug to Toulouse and Paris. Sarlat's run-down **auberge de jeunesse (HI),** 77, av. de Selves (tel. 53 59 47 59), 30min. from the train station but only 10min. from the *vieille ville,* has outdoor showers and toilets, but is the only budget option in town. Go straight along rue de la République until it becomes av. Gambetta; follow it for another 100m, then bear left at the fork onto av. de Selves. The hostel will be on your right, behind a green gate. (Reception open 6-8pm, but you can drop off your bags anytime. 40F. Camping 23F. Sheets 16F. Kitchen. Open March 15-Nov.) Camp at **Le Montant** (tel. 53 59 18 50), 2.5km from town on the D57 (18F per person, 20F per tent; open Easter-Sept.).

Built into the face of a sheer cliff, the sanctity and staggering beauty of historic **Rocamadour** bring 1½ million pilgrims and tourists a year to this town of 5000. **Le Grand Escalier** climbs from the town's lone street; some devotees still journey here to kneel at each of its 216 steps. At the top hovers the 12th-century **Cité Religieuse,** a complex of chapels including the **Chapelle de Notre-Dame,** home to the venerated Black Virgin. (Cité open 9am-6pm and 6:30-10pm; June-Sept. 9am-6pm.) Perched precariously at the top of the cliff—and more zig-zagging steps—is the 14th-century **château.** Its ramparts (the only part open to the public) command exceptional views of the valley, but the free view of the town from the road will do. (Ramparts open July-Aug. 9am-7pm; April-June and Sept.-Oct. 9am-noon and 1:30-8pm. 10F, students 8F.) Less pious pilgrims can ascend to both Cité and château on convenient **elevators** for 25F. Rocamadour is most easily reached by **train** (45min., 40F), via Brive, to the north. Coming from Sarlat or Souillac, catch a bus to St-Denis-Près-Martel (25F), then a train from St-Denis (17F). The main **tourist office** (tel. 65 33 62 59) is in the old Hôtel de Ville, on the pedestrian street of the medieval *cité* (open July-Aug. 10am-8pm; Sept.-Oct. and March-June Thurs.-Tues. 10am-noon and 2-7pm; service by phone Nov.-Feb.). Expect to pay at least 200F for a single or double. If trying to reserve less than 2 weeks in advance in July or August, you'll be laughed at. The **Hôtel Panorama** (tel. 65 33 62 13), up in L'Hospitalet, has 5 nice rooms with showers and TV for 170F (open April-Nov. 15). Luckily, there are seven campsites nearby; the closest is the **Relais du Campeur** (tel. 65 33 63 28) in l'Hospitalet, which also has a small, expensive grocery store. (Reception on rte. de Lacave open 8am-10pm. 17F per person, 19F per site. Free showers. Open Easter-Sept.)

■■■ BORDEAUX

Like many of the fine vintage reds for which it is renowned, Bordeaux has grown noticeably darker with age, an apparent victim of its own success. Nearly 900 years after its consecration by Pope Urban II, **Cathédrale St-André** remains the *grande dame* of Bordeaux's high Gothic masterpieces. (Free organ concerts every other Tues. evening, mid-May to mid-Sept. Cathedral open 9am-noon and 2-6pm.) Two blocks from cours de Maréchal Foch, the far-out **Musée d'Art Contemporain** and the **Arc en Rêve Centre d'Architecture** provide a sensitive and surprisingly versatile setting for exhibits of funky modern painting, sculpture, design and photography, complemented by exhibits focusing on specific architects or architectural movements (open Tues.-Sun. noon-7pm, Wed. until 10pm; free, but this might have changed in Dec. 1994). The **Maison du Vin/CIVB**, 1, cours du 30 Juillet, pours free samples of regional labels, answers any wine questions, and distributes a list of the smaller wine-producing châteaux in the area. You, too, can swish whites and reds around in your mouth while sitting in a wine-conference room complete with foot-pedal operated spitting sinks. Just take the 2hr. "Initiation to Wine Tasting" course given in French. (Twice weekly in summer, 60F. Maison open Mon.-Fri. 8:30am-6pm, Sat. 9am-12:30pm and 1:30-5pm.) Bordeaux's nightlife during the school-year revolves around the student cafés near pl. de la Victoire. The sidestreets around pl. Gambetta also have their share of bars. A new hangout is the **Virgin Megastore** at 15-19, pl. Gambetta. In addition to a monolithic collection of music-related stuff, it houses a Tex-Mex café at the top called "The Mexican Road Cafe" with saddle-shaped cowhide bar stools, a pool table, and a rooftop patio. (Store and café open 10am-midnight.)

Practical Information, Accommodations, and Food   Trains arrive in Bordeaux's Gare St-Jean, rue Charles Domercq, from Paris (5-8hr., 290F; TGV 3¼hr., 375F), Nantes (4hr., 220F), Toulouse (2½hr., 165F), and Nice (9½hr., 405F). Storage lockers cost 15-30F. From the train station, take bus 7 or 8, get off at the Grand Théâtre, and walk toward the Monument des Girondins to reach the **tourist office,** 12, cours du 30 Juillet (tel. 56 44 28 41). (Open Mon.-Sat. 9am-8pm, Sun. 9am-7pm, Oct.-May Mon.-Fri. 9am-7pm.) **CGFTE** urban and suburban buses criss-cross the city (tickets 7.50F). An **American Express** office can be found at 14, cours de l'Intendance (tel. 56 81 70 02; open Mon.-Fri. 8:45am-noon and 1:30-6pm). Exchange currency at the **post office**, 52, rue Georges Bonnac (tel. 56 48 87 48). (Open Mon.-Fri. 8am-7pm, Sat. 8am-noon. Postal code: 33065.)

Relatively inexpensive hotels (look around **place Gambetta** and **cours d'Albret** and an elegant student *maison* are tempting alternatives to the hostel. Reserve at least a day or two in advance during the hectic summer months. To get to the clean, classy, and central **Maison des Etudiants,** 50, rue Ligier (tel. 56 96 48 30), take bus 7 or 8 from the train station to Bourse du Travail and continue in the same direction on cours de la Libération to rue Ligier. Or, walking, follow cours de la Marne through pl. de la Victoire to cours Aristide Briand and turn right onto rue Ligier (30min.). (24hr. reception. No lockout or curfew. 70F, with ISIC 50F. Showers and sheets included. Oct.-June primarily monthly residents.) The **auberge de jeunesse (HI)**, 22, cours Barbey (tel. 56 91 59 51), is reasonably clean but rules will hinder nighttime raging. Take Cours de la Marne from the right end of the station about 5 blocks and turn left onto cours Barbey. (Reception open 8-9:30am and 6-11pm. Lockout 9:30am-6pm. Curfew 11pm. 40F. Sheets 16F.) For spacious, comfortable rooms with all the mod-cons, consider **Hôtel la Boétie,** 4, rue de la Boétie (tel. 56 81 76 68, fax 56 81 24 72), between pl. Gambetta and the Musée des Beaux-Arts.

FRANCE

(Reception open 7am-10pm. Singles 120-135F. Doubles 135-160F. Triples 180F.) In the center of town, **Hôtel d'Amboise,** 22, rue de la Vieille Tour (tel. 56 81 62 67), offers attractive singles (85-110F), doubles (90-110F). If you're armed with a tent, haul butt to **Camping les Gravières,** Pont-de-la-Maye (tel. 56 87 00 36), in Ville-neuve D'Ornon. Take bus B "Courrégean" from pl. de la Victoire for 30min. (Reception open 8am-11pm, off-season 8am-10pm. 19F per person and per tent.)

Bordeaux, known as *La Région de Bien Manger et de Bien Vivre* (The Region of Fine Eating and Living), has affordable restaurants in which to do so, especially along and just off the pedestrian **rue Ste-Catherine.** Won't you feel suave when you hear jazz and sample the 100F *menu* with oysters, *tourtière landaise* (a quiche-like dish), and dessert at **La Boîte à Huîtres,** 8, rue de la Vieille Tour, right off cours de l'Intendance from pl. Gambetta (open 10am-2pm and 6pm-midnight). Or take a plate and knife, descend into the cool cellar of **Baud et Millet,** 19, rue Huguerie, off pl. Tournu., and take as much as you want from the immense selection of fromages (cheese plus dessert 95F, open Mon.-Sat. 9am-2am). When hunger is choosing, **Le Bistrot Romain,** 65, cours de l'Intendance, at pl. Gambetta, offers a 55F 3-course menu with a glass of wine and all-you-can-eat fries or pasta. (Open Mon.-Sun. 11:30am-3pm and 6:30pm-midnight.)

■ DUNE DU PILAT

Trains leave Bordeaux daily for **Arcachon** (1hr., 48F), the first leg of a daytrip to the **Dune du Pilat.** A mountain of sand that brings out the acrobat in everyone, the Dune may be the most sublime beach in the world. Its 60 million sandy tons, 104-114m high, pose an encroaching threat to the homes lying at its base. Buses leave from the Arcachon station for **Pyla-sur-Mer** (last return around 8pm; 30min.; 16F round-trip), which is a 10-15min. walk from the Dune.

BASQUE COUNTRY (PAYS BASQUE)

■■■ BAYONNE

A grand port with small-town appeal, Bayonne enjoys a prominent position on the Gulf of Gascony, close to the Spanish border. Its spiny twin steeples biting into Bay-onne's skies, the northern-Gothic **Cathédrale Sainte-Marie** intimidates from afar and impresses from within (open Mon.-Sat. 8am-7:15pm, Sun. 8:30am-7pm). High-lights of the unbeatable **Musée Bonnat,** 5, rue Jacques Laffitte, in Petit-Bayonne, include the lecherous mythical men in the superbly lit Rubens room, a ghoulish El Greco portrait, and Goya's grim *La Dernière Communion de San José de Calasanz* (open Wed.-Mon. 10am-noon and 3-7pm, Fri. open until 9pm; Sept. 11-June 14 reduced hours; 15F, students 5F).

Bayonne is linked by **train** to Bordeaux (2hr., 130F). The **tourist office,** (tel. 59 46 01 46), pl. des Basques, provides a shoddy map and can help find rooms (open Mon.-Sat. 9am-7pm, Sun. 10am-1pm; Oct.-May Mon.-Fri. 9am–6:30pm, Sat. 9am-5pm). Inexpensive hotels abound in Bayonne. The **Hôtel Paris-Madrid,** pl. de la Gare (tel. 59 55 13 98), features personalized rooms. (Reception open 6am-12:30am. Singles and doubles 85-145F. Triples and quads 195-215F.) Huge portions of the most authentic and delicious regional cuisine you will ever find at these prices are served in a classy atmosphere at **Le Bistrot Ste-Cluque,** 9, rue Hugues, across from the station. (Eat-like-royalty *menu* at 55F. *Paella* 50F. *Gazpacho* 15F. Big salads 35F. Open 11am-11:30pm.)

■■■ BIARRITZ

Originally a whaling village at the base of the Pyrenees and now home to the "queen of French beaches," Biarritz embodies all that is regal. While not a budgeteer's dream, a little ingenuity makes it affordable. At the **Grande Plage**, you'll find a wealth of surfers and bathers. Just north are **plage Miramar**, cozied against the base of the cliffs, and **Pointe St-Martin**, where bathers peacefully repose *au naturel*. Jutting out from the plateau, the craggy peninsula of the **Rocher de la Vierge** gazes over magical views at sunset. At low tide, the **plage des Basques** boasts the cleanest water and the most open sand in Biarritz.

Trains cruise through **Biarritz-la-Négresse**, 3km out of town. To get to the *centre ville*, take blue bus 2 "Bayonne via Biarritz" (6:30am-7:38pm every 20-40min.) or bus 9 "Biarritz HDV"). Both buses leave directly across from the station. Since many Paris-Hendaye trains don't stop in Biarritz, another option is to get off the train in Bayonne and hop a bus to downtown Biarritz (30min.). All buses cost 7F. The **tourist office,** Javalquinto, 1, square d'Ixelles (tel. 59 24 20 24), dispenses the *Biarritzcope* with monthly events listings and will track down a room or a campsite for you (open 8am-8pm, Oct. 4-May 9am-6:45pm). Biarritz hotels have more stars than the Milky Way. Affordable accommodations go fast, so commuting from Anglet or Bayonne may be your best bet. The 12-bed dorm room (75F) with no meal obligations in **Hôtel Barnetche**, 5bis, rue Floquet (tel. 59 24 22 25, fax 59 24 98 71), is the best deal in town. (Doubles 210-220F. Triples and quads 110F per person. Obligatory breakfast 27F. In Aug., 85F obligatory *demi-pension*. Open May-Sept.) Centrally located **Hôtel Berhouet,** 29, rue Gambetta (tel. 59 24 63 36), offers singles and doubles for 100-180F.

■■■ ANGLET

Anglet's *raison d'être* is its 4km of fine-grained white sand, parcelled out into nine beaches—each with its own name and personality, from the perfect waves of the *plage* **Les Cavaliers** to the rocky jetty of the **Chambre d'Amour,** where two legendary lovers perished when the tide came in. The **Rainbow Surfshop,** just above the beach on the border of *plages* **Chambre d'Amour** and **Sables d'Or** (tel. 59 03 35 62) rents a colorful spectrum of tools of the trade: bodyboards (70F per day), surfboards (100F per day), and wetsuits (50F per day). Lessons for one or two people cost 170F for the first hour and 150F for each subsequent hour. (Open Mon.-Sun. 9:30am-11:30pm.) For walking or jogging, the **Fôret du Pignada's** pine needle-covered trails are easy on the knees. The only hostel within 100km is in **Anglet**; the well-equipped, carefree **auberge de jeunesse (HI),** 19, rte. de Vignes (tel. 59 63 86 49, fax 59 63 38 92), lies directly uphill from the beach. From the Hôtel de Ville in Biarritz, take line 4 "Bayonne Sainsontain" (every 50min.). From pl. de la République or pl. de Réduit in Bayonne, take line 4 to La Barre, then change to bus 4N "Mairie Biarritz." (Reception open 8:30-10am and 6-10pm. No lockout. 70F per person. Cot 65F. Camping 50F. Surfboard rental 75F.) Try to arrive at least an hour before opening.

LANGUEDOC-ROUSSILLON

Languedoc and Roussillon have never been comfortable with Parisian authority, and it's easy to see why. This is a rugged southern land and its people are as much Spanish as French in origin, accent, and architecture. Once, an immense region called Occitania (today Languedoc) stretched from the Rhône all the way to the foothills of the Pyrénées, and from the Catalan coastal region of Roussillon in the southeast to Toulouse in the west. Its gentle people spoke the *langue d'oc* (named for its word for "yes," *"oc"*) as opposed to the *langue d'oïl* spoken in northern France, which evolved into modern French. Independent of France or Spain, the area was lorded over by the Count of Toulouse, whose court enjoyed tales of adventure and courtly love recounted by wandering troubadours. In the mid-12th century, when the Cathar religion was introduced by immigrants from Asia, Occitania's nobles and peasants alike were intrigued. Accustomed to war and frustrated by unsuccessful crusades, the Catholic nobility of northern France needed little prodding to turn on their rivals in the south. Cathars sought refuge in the châteaux of the many nobles sympathetic to their cause, but castles full of non-violent dissenters were no problem for de Montfort and his troops. With the region's integration into the French kingdom, the *langue d'oc* faded , and in 1539, the Edict of Villiers-Cotterets made the northern *langue d'oïl* official.

■■■ TOULOUSE

Toulouse's eclectic architecture, streets, alleys, squares, and people greet you like a breath of fresh air. The city came of age in the 16th and 17th centuries when many merchants who had amassed large fortunes through the pastel (a plant used to dye fabrics blue) trade gained appointments as consuls or *capitouls* and built extravagant townhouses to symbolize their new power and status. Today one of the fastest growing cities in France, Toulouse is known not only for its beauty but also for its technology—Aérospatiale, creator of *Ariane* rocket systems and *Airbus,* calls the town home.

A defiant Catholic stronghold in a region torn by wars of religion, Toulouse boasts some of France's most architecturally distinctive and historically important religious monuments. St. Dominique, most vigilant of Cathar-hunters, led his inquisition from the magnificent **Basilique St-Sernin,** the longest Romanesque structure in the world. (Open Mon.-Sat. 8-11:45am and 2-5:45pm, Sun. 2-5:45pm. Tours July-Aug. at 2pm and 3:15pm. 35F.) Named for the religious order rather than revolutionaries, **Les Jacobins,** rue Lakanal, is an excellent example of the southern Gothic style. A modest crypt inside contains the ashes of philosopher and theologian St. Thomas Aquinas. (Church open Mon.-Sat. 10am-6:30pm, Sun. 2:30-6:30pm; Sept-June Mon.-Sat. 10am-noon and 2:30-6pm, Sun. 2:30-6pm. Admission to cloister 10F.)

The **Musée des Augustins,** 21, rue de Metz, off rue Alsace-Lorraine, exhibits exquisite Romanesque and Gothic sculpture. Especially noteworthy are the 15 sniggering gargoyles from Les Cordeliers, an abbey that was pillaged mercilessly after it burned to the ground in the 19th century. (Open Thurs.-Mon. 10am-6pm, Wed. 10am-10pm; Oct.-May Thurs.-Mon. 10am-5pm, Wed. 10am-9pm. 10F, students free.) **Place St-Georges** is the heart of *toulousain* student life. The weekly journal of entertainment, *Flash,* gives complete club listings (10F at newsstands) while the free *Regard* magazine, available in newsstands and *tabacs,* lists concerts and theater events in the area.

Practical Information, Accommodations, and Food Trains arrive in Toulouse's **Gare Matabiau,** bd. Pierre Sémard from Paris (7hr., 340F); Bordeaux (2¼hr., 165F); Lyon (6hr., 295F); Marseille (4½hr., 230F); and Perpignan (2½hr., 140F). The flustered **tourist office,** rue Lafayette (tel. 61 11 02 22), in the park behind the Capitôle, changes money when banks are closed and books rooms. (Open Mon.-Sat. 9am-7pm, Sun. 9am-1pm and 2-5:30pm; Oct.-April Mon.-Fri. 9am-6pm, Sat. 9am-12:30pm and 2-6pm, Sun. and holidays 10am-12:30pm and 2-5pm. Currency Exchange open May-Sept. Sat.-Sun. and holidays 11am-1pm and 2-4:30pm.) **Hôtel des Arts,** 1bis, rue Cantegrol (tel. 61 23 36 21), at rue des Arts, near pl. St-Georges, offers lively, central rooms with artsy posters. Take the metro to pl. Esquirol, walk down rue du Metz; Rue des Arts is the 3rd street on the left. (Singles and doubles 80-125F, with shower 125-145F, with shower and toilet 135-170F. Triples and quads 150F, with shower 180F. Hall shower 10F.) Tall, bright, and cheap rooms halfway between the train station and pl. Wilson await inside the **Hôtel Beauséjour,** 4, rue Caffarelli (tel. 61 62 77 59), just off allée Jean Jaurès. (Singles 60F, with shower 135F. Doubles 95F, with shower 150F.) St-Exupéry (best known for his book *Le Petit Prince*) stayed in room 32 of the **Hôtel du Grand Balcon,** 8, rue Romiguières (tel. 61 21 48 08), at a corner of the pl. du Capitôle. (Singles 120F, with shower 150F. Doubles 125F, with shower 150-195F. Triples and quads 150F, with shower 200F. Shower 11F. Closed much of Aug.; call first.) Pitch your tent at **Pont de Rupé,** 21, chemin du Pont de Rupé (tel. 61 70 07 35), at av. des Etats-Unis (N20 north). Take bus 59 "Lespinasse" to Rupé. (16F per person, 25F per tent.)

Markets line bd. Victor Hugo, pl. des Carmes, and bd. de Strasbourg (Tues.-Sun. 9am-1pm), and food stands spill over at Les Halles, on the ground floor of the Parking Victor Hugo. Restaurants thrive on the tiny streets on either side of rue St-Rome, but the most economical eateries lie along the **rue du Taur** on the way to the university. Let the regional specialties of **Salade Gasconne,** 75, rue du Taur, tantalize your taste buds. Students love it. (Salads 30-50F. 50F *menu.* Open Mon.-Fri. 11:30am-3pm and 7-10:30pm, Sat. 11:30am-3pm.) **Auberge Louis XIII,** 1bis, rue Tripière, with its shaded terrace and country cuisine, draws a student crowd. (65F and 75F *menus.* 50F lunch *menu.* Open Sept.-July Mon.-Fri. noon-2pm and 7-10pm.) Creatively prepared healthy salads (30-42F) and 1001 versions of pasta (39-58F) are served in the youthful **Mille et Une Pâtes,** 3, pl. du Peyrou, two blocks from St-Sernin. (Open Mon. 11:30am-2pm, Tues.-Fri. 11:30am-2pm and 7:30-10pm, Sat. 11:30am-2pm and 7:30-10pm.)

■■■ ALBI

Albi, which derived its name from the bloody 13th-century inquisition against Catharism initiated by the Pope against its population, today presides over culture instead of carnage. The extraordinary **Musée Toulouse-Lautrec,** in the Palais de la Berbie, presents a stunning collection of the controversial artist's work, including the lithographs that earned him his international reputation. The extraordinary museum contains not only all 31 of the famous posters of Montmartre nightclubs, but also dozens of oils, pastels, sketches, and drawings. (Open 9am-noon and 2-6pm, Oct.-March Wed.-Mon. 10am-noon and 2-5pm, April-May 10am-noon and 2-6pm. 20F, students 10F.) Across from the museum, the enormous **Basilique Ste-Cécile** was designed to be a fortress as well as a church. Just below the organ, an immense fresco depicts *Le Jugement Dernier* (The Last Judgment), demonstrating in horrific detail—complete with boiling oil—what will happen to visitors who don't obey the "Silence" signs liberally sprinkled throughout the church. (Open 8:30am-7pm; Sept.-May 9-11:30am and 2-5:30pm.)

Fifteen **trains** from Toulouse screech to a halt in Albi every day (1hr., 60F). The **tourist office,** pl. Ste-Cécile (tel. 63 54 22 30), has rooming info and a generic brochure that includes a good map. (Open Mon.-Sat. 9am-7:30pm, Sun. 10:30am-1pm and 3:30-5:30pm; Sept.-June Mon.-Sat. 9am-noon and 2-6pm, Sun. 10:30am-12:30pm and 3:30-5:30pm.) The **Maison des Jeunes et de la Culture,** 13, rue de la République (tel. 63 54 53 65), offers well-supported bunks for 26F. Take bus 1 "Cantepapu" to République. (Reception open 6-7pm. No lockout or curfew, but 20F key deposit.) **Hôtel La Régence,** 27, av. Maréchal-Joffre (tel. 63 54 01 42), a block from the station, offers singles and doubles with antique furniture and Laura Ashley wallpaper from 110-190F. Camp at **Parc de Caussels** (tel. 63 60 37 06), 2km east of Albi on rte. de Millau (50F per 2 people). At **Le Petit Bouchon,** 77, rue Croix Verte, owner Claude serves 40-60F quality menus and shakes up a secret mixed drink that'll leave beer fanatics hollering for fuzzy navels (open Mon.-Fri. 11:30am-2:30pm and 7-9:30pm, Sat. 11:30am-2:30pm).

■■■ CARCASSONNE

The **Cité de Carcassonne** is a life-sized toy castle, a double-walled, fortified city with towers and turrets rising from a precipitous plateau in the Garonne valley. First attacked by Roman invaders (and subsequently by Visigoths, Invisigoths, and Arabs), Europe's largest fortress fell into an egregious state of disrepair following the 13th-century Wars of Religion. A revived interest in medieval France spurred the rebuilding of the Cité in 1844, directed by architect Viollet-le-Duc.

On the black line, bus 4 serves the medieval **cité** from both the train station and pl. Gambetta (every ½hr. until 7pm, 5F); you can also hike 30min. up the hill. Originally constructed as a palace, the **Château Comtal** fortress overlooks the south side of the Cité. Admission is by guided tour. (Open July-Aug. 9am-7pm; Sept. and June 9am-6:30pm; Oct.-March 10am-12:30pm and 2-5pm; April-May 9:30am-12:30pm and 2-6pm. 26F, ages 18-25: 17F.) The **Basilique St-Nazaire,** with its radiant stained-glass windows and delicate Gothic ribbed vaulting, is considered the finest in southern France. Sadists and masochists alike will be aroused by a visit to the torture chamber at the **Exposition Internationale,** 9, rue Saint-Jean. Marvel at the objects of gentle persuasion used by Catholics to show the Cathars the errors of their ways. (Historical explanations in English. 20F, students 15F.) On **Bastille Day** (July 14), Carcassonne outdoes any normal display of fireworks—a complex lighting effect makes the Cité look as if it's going up in flames when viewed from the *basse ville,* commemorating the villages burned under Carcassonne's stern mandate when the city's Tour de l'Inquisition was the seat of the papal jury. The entire city medievalizes during the **Médiévales** festival in August (tickets 30F).

Practical Information, Accommodations, and Food To reach the **tourist office,** 15, bd. Camille Pelletan (tel. 68 25 07 04), from the train station, walk over the canal on rue G. Clemenceau; turn left onto rue de la Liberté and then right onto bd. Jean Jaurès; the office is on the right. (Open Mon.-Sat. 9am-7pm; Sept., April–June Mon.-Sat. 9am-12:15pm and 1:45-7pm; Oct.-March Mon.-Sat. 9am-noon and 2-6:30pm.) The immaculate **auberge de jeunesse (HI)** (tel. 68 25 23 16, fax 68 71 14 84) is on rue Vicomte Trencavel in the Cité. (Reception open 7am-noon and 5pm-1am. Members only, 67F. Call a few days in advance; July-Aug. a few *weeks* in advance.) At the intersection of rue Montpellier and rue Tourtel, the **Hôtel Astoria** (tel. 68 25 31 38, fax 68 25 31 38) doles out pristine singles for 85F (min. stay 2 nights) and doubles for 105F (with shower 130F; reception open 6am-midnight).

Cassoulet, the local specialty, is a hearty/greasy stew with white beans, herbs, and meat (usually lamb or pork). A running courtyard fountain refreshes diners at **Les Fontaines du Soleil,** 32, rue du Plo, in the Cité. (55-155F menus specialize in fish and cassoulet. Open 11am-2am.) **L'Ostal des Troubadours,** 5, rue Viollet-le-Duc, posts one of the cheapest *menus* around (49F, plus service) and stays animated with live performers nightly at 8pm (open noon to midnight; *menus* served noon-2pm and 7-11pm). **L'Hippocampe,** 38, rue du 4 Septembre, is a relaxed counter-top restaurant with miraculously low prices (pizza 26F, 4-course menus with wine 50F; open Mon.-Sat. 11:30am-2pm and 6:45-10pm). For provisions, truck to the **market** on pl. Carnot (Tues., Thurs., and Sat. 7am-1pm).

PROVENCE

■■■ AVIGNON

The walled city of Avignon sparkles with artistic brilliance among the lush vineyards of the Rhône Valley. Film festivals, street musicians, and the famed **Festival d'Avignon** keep this university town shining. The **Palais des Papes,** built in the 14th century when the popes moved from Rome, stands in white-granite majesty at the highest point in Avignon. (Open Aug. 20-Sept. 9am-8pm, Oct.-March 9am-noon and 2-5pm, April-Aug. 19 9am-7pm. 38F, students and seniors 29F. English tours daily 10am and 3pm; 46F, students 37F.)

From early July to early August, the **Festival d'Avignon** (tel. 90 82 67 08) puts on everything from avant-garde plays to Gregorian chants to all-night readings of the *Odyssey*. (Tickets 90-165F per event; some are free. Events start 9:30-11pm.) The cheaper and more experimental **Festival Off** presents over 400 plays, some in English, from July 9-August 3. Contact the OFF-ice, pl. du Palais (tel. 90 82 28 62), for more info (open 11am-8pm).

Practical Information, Accommodations, and Food The **tourist office,** 41, cours Jean Jaurès (tel. 90 82 65 11), three blocks from the train station, lists accommodations, restaurants, and museums (open Mon.-Fri. 9am-1pm and 2-6pm, Sat. 9am-1pm and 2-6pm; during festival, Mon.-Fri. 10am-7pm, Sat. 9am-1pm and 2-5pm). Avignon lacks an HI youth hostel, but **Foyer Bagatelle** (tel. 90 86 30 39, fax 90 27 16 23), Ile de Barthelasse, just over Pont Daladier, has spacious dorm rooms (53F, sheets 16F). The managers at the **Squash Club,** 32, bd. Limbert (tel. 90 85 27 78), will give you a 10% discount on lodgings if you can beat them at squash. (Reception open 8-11am and 5:30-11pm. Lockout 11am-5pm. Curfew 11pm. 46F. Mandatory breakfast on squash courts 15F. Sheets 14F. Call ahead during festival and off-season.) Pet the narcoleptic dog at **Hôtel Innova,** 100, rue Joseph Vernet (tel. 90 82 54 10, fax 90 82 52 39). From the station, go left from rue de la République. (Singles and doubles 140F, with shower 160F. Breakfast 25F.) Next door to the public pool (18F), **Camping Bagatelle** (tel. 90 86 30 39, fax 90 27 16 13), features a cafeteria, laundromat, and supermarket (26F per person, 20F per tent).

Buy provisions in **Les Halles,** the large indoor **market** on pl. Pie (open Tues.-Sun. 8am-1pm), at the less expensive open-air market outside the city walls near porte St-Michel (Sat.-Sun. 7am-10pm), or at **Codec supermarket,** rue de la République (open Mon.-Sat. 8:30am-7:25pm). **Restaurant Oanh,** 31bis, rue Bonneterie, is a family-run Vietnamese restaurant with great food at great prices, such as curry chicken for 31F (open 11am-2pm and 6-11pm). For the musically inclined, try **Tache d'Encre,** 22, rue des Teinturiers, a pleasant *café-théâtre* with live jazz and blues on most weeknights. The excellent French cuisine can be enjoyed as 49F (lunchtime), 74F, and 89F menus. (Open Mon.-Fri. noon-2pm and 7:30pm-midnight, Sat.-Sun. 7:30pm-midnight.)

■■■ ARLES

Roman grandeur haunts the sun-baked remnants of Arles's **Roman baths,** lingers in the amphitheater **arenas** (now used for bullfights), and endures in the city's **Théâtre Antique** (now used for frequent summer concerts). Arles proudly inscribes plaques in the regional tongue and celebrates the **Fête de la Tradition** (the last weekend in June and the first in July) in local costume, with bonfires blazing in the streets. Arles's beautiful monuments and vistas lured both Picasso and Van Gogh, who spent his final years—and his ear—here. The **Musée Réattu,** rue du Grand Prieuré, exhibits contemporary art including 57 Picasso drawings donated by the master himself. (Open 8:30am-7pm; Oct. and March 9am-12:30pm and 2-6pm; Nov.-Feb. 9am-noon and 2-4:30pm; April 9am-12:30pm and 2-7pm; May 9am-12:30pm and 2-7pm. 15F, students 9F.) The mid-July **Rencontres Internationales de la Photographie** (tel. 90 96 76 06) courts photographers and agents alike (10-20F per exhibit, global ticket 140F, students 110F).

The **tourist office** (tel. 90 18 41 20), in esplanade Charles de Gaulle at bd. des Lices finds rooms for a 4F fee (open Mon.-Sat. 9am-7pm, Sun. 9am-1pm; Sept.-June Mon.-Sat. 9am-1pm and 3-7pm). There is also a **branch office** at the train station (open Mon.-Sat. 9am-noon and 2-6pm). Frequent **buses** run from the *gare routière* (next to the train station) to the **Camargue,** an enormous natural reserve where flamingoes and wild horses run free (1hr., 32F) and the beaches at nearby **Les Stes-Maries-de-la-Mer** (same bus). Trains roll from the **train station,** av. P. Talabot, to Avignon (20min., 34F), Marseille (1hr., 70F), Nîmes (25min., 39F), and Aix-en-Provence (1¾hr., 90F). Inexpensive **hotels** cluster around rue de l'Hôtel de Ville and pl. Voltaire, and fill in a flash during the photography festival. The sleek **auberge de jeunesse (HI)** is on av. Maréchal Foch (tel. 90 96 18 25, fax 90 96 31 26), 20min. from the station by foot, or by the Fournier stop of bus 8 from pl. Lamartine. (Reception open 7-10am and 5pm-midnight. Curfew 1am. 75F 1st night, 65F thereafter. Arrive early.) **La Gallia Hôtel,** 22, rue de l'Hôtel de Ville (tel. 90 96 00 63), is a real gem in an excellent location (singles or doubles with shower 120F, doubles with shower and toilet 140F). Regional produce fills the **open markets** on bd. Emile Courbes (Wed. 7am-1pm) and on bd. des Lices (Sat. 7am-1pm). A **Monoprix supermarket** faces pl. Lamartine, near the train station. You can kill an entire evening in the cinema-bookstore-gallery-eatery **Le Restaurant du Méjan,** quai Marx Dormoy. (Films in original language 33F, students 25F. *Formule rapide:* salad, dessert, wine, and coffee 55F. Open noon-2pm and 7-11pm.) For people-watching, head to the cafés on **pl. du Forum;** avoid the overpriced ones on bd. des Lices.

■■■ AIX-EN-PROVENCE

Blessed with plentiful restaurants, elegant cafés, spellbinding museums, and exuberant festivals, Aix (pronounced "Ex") truly marks the spot as the gastronomic and cultural core of Provence. Pass the afternoon sitting in a café on the **cours Mirabeau,** or walk the **Chemin de Cézanne,** a walking tour that transforms the city into an open-air museum of the artist and his work. Pick up the pamphlet *In the Footsteps of Cézanne* and follow the bronze markers in the sidewalk. The **Musée Granet,** pl. St-Jean-Marie-de-Malte, displays bushels of Dutch and French works and 10 paintings by Cézanne (open Wed.-Mon. 10am-noon and 2-6pm; 25F, students 15F). Beginning in the second week of June, all of Aix celebrates with **Aix en Musique,** a casual two-week jamboree of big-band jazz, classical quartets, and wind ensembles. Many concerts are free, others have discounts for students. The tourist office lists concerts and locations; call 42 16 11 61 or 42 23 34 04 for more information. When the sun sets, **Le Scat,** 11, rue Verrerie, is a terrific club with live jazz and blues 10:30pm (open Mon.-Sat. 10pm-whenever). **Bistro Aixois,** Cours Sextius, off la Rotonde, attracts students with live bands (10pm-3am). A little outside town, **La Chimère,** montée d'Avignon, quartier des Plâtrières, attracts a sizeable gay crowd to its bar and disco (open Tues.-Sun. 10pm-6am).

Practical Information, Accommodations, and Food The **tourist office,** 2, pl. du Général de Gaulle (tel. 42 16 11 61), makes hotel reservations (5F) and has the comprehensive guide *Aix la Vivante*, which suggest walking tours, museums, and local recipes. From the train station, bear left up av. Victor Hugo for the tourist office and the central city bus terminus. (Open Mon.-Sat. 8am-10pm, Sun. 9am-1pm and 2-10pm; Sept. 16-June Mon.-Sat. 8am-7pm.) To get anywhere by **train** from Aix, one must first go to Marseille by train (hourly, last one 9:30pm, 40min, 34F) or on the cheaper **bus** (every 15min., 30min., 22F). Four buses per day run to Avignon (1½hr., 83F).

The crowded **auberge de jeunesse (HI),** 3, av. Marcel Pagnol (tel. 42 20 15 99, fax 42 59 36 12), is next to the Fondation Vasarely. Follow av. des Belges from la Rotonde and turn right on av. de l'Europe. At the first rotary after the highway overpass, bear left and climb the hill. The hostel is on your left. To avoid the 35min. walk, take bus 12 (every 15min. until 8pm, 7F) from La Rotonde to Vasarely. (Reception open 7:30am-noon and 5:30pm-midnight. Lockout 10am-5:30pm. Curfew midnight. 80F 1st night, 70F thereafter. 66F if you have your own sheets.) Friendly **Hôtel du Casino,** 38, rue Victor Leydet (tel. 42 26 06 88, fax 42 27 76 58), is way cool, and clean (singles 180F, doubles 240F). The singles and doubles (175F) of **Hôtel Paul,** 10, av. Pasteur (tel. 42 23 23 89, fax 42 63 17 80), past the Cathédrale St-Sauveur, are simple but spacious.

The streets north of cours Mirabeau are packed with restaurants for all palates and wallets. **Hacienda,** 7, rue Mérindol, in the pl. des Fontêtes, is a good value; the delicious 60F *menu* includes wine and dessert. (Open Sept.-Aug. Mon.-Sat. noon-2pm

FRANCE

and 7:30-10pm.) **La Table Provençale,** 13, rue Maréchal Joffre, offers another viable version of a 60F menu (open Mon.-Sat. noon-2pm). Buy a picnic lunch at the **market** at pl. de Verdun (Tues., Thurs., and Sat. 7am-1pm), or stock up at **Monoprix,** 25, cours Mirabeau (open Mon.-Sat. 9am-8:30pm). Be sure to sample Aix's famed almonds, used in cakes and cookies, at one of the numerous *pâtisseries* along rue d'Italie or rue Espariat.

FRENCH RIVIERA (CÔTE D'AZUR)

Paradises are made to be lost. Sparkling between Marseille and the Italian border, the sun-drenched beaches and waters of the Mediterranean form the backdrop for this fabled playground of the rich and famous. But its seductive loveliness has almost been its undoing, as shrewd developers have turned the coast's beauty to profit and its pleasures into big business. Today, the area is as crammed with low-budget tourists as with high-handed millionaires, and many French condemn it as a shameless Fort Lauderdale, a mere shadow of its former self.

The coast is well-served by frequent, inexpensive trains and buses. Trains for the Côte leave Paris's Gare de Lyon every hour in summer; the trip takes 5 hours on the TGV to Marseille and 7-8 hours to Nice. Trains and roads are packed in summer; you might want to base yourself in the less expensive coastal towns and take daytrips to the purse-emptying cities. Like western Provence, the Riviera is best visited during early June and in September when crowds are low and hotel vacancies high.

■■■ MARSEILLE

France's third city, Marseille is sort of like the *bouillabaisse* for which it is famous: steaming hot and full of spice. Unlike *bouillabaisse,* the town is hardly delectable. The city enjoys a universal reputation for roguishness and danger. Although racial tensions pervade Marseille, it remains charged throughout with color and commotion. Its daily fish market, nearby beaches, wild nightclubs, and big-city adventure merit a (brief) stop-over on the way to Nice or Avignon.

The city's heart is the humming **Vieux Port** (old port) and the adjacent streets of the *vieille ville.* Extending straight out of the port is Marseille's main artery, **La Canebière,** affectionately known to English sailors as "Can o' beer." The **North African quarter** twists through the narrow, dusty streets between the train station and La Canebière. At night these areas can be dangerous for travelers of either sex.

Practical Information, Accommodations, and Food The **tourist office,** 4, La Canebière (tel. 91 54 91 11), near the *vieux port*, has a free accommodations service and sells a 20F bus/metro day pass (open 8:30am-8pm; Oct.-June Mon.-Sat. 9am-7:30pm, Sun. 10am-5:30pm). The **annex** at the train station (tel. 91 50 59 18) performs the same services (open Mon.-Sat. 10am-2:30pm and 3:30-7pm, Sept.-June Mon.-Fri. 10am-1pm and 1:30-6pm). Marseille maintains **train** connections with Paris (TGV 4¾hr., 400F plus 18F reservation) and Lyon (3½hr., 200F). A cheaper but slower option are the **buses** that leave from pl. Victor Hugo, behind the train station. For information on **ferries** to Corsica, Sardinia, and North Africa, try the **SNCM** office at 61, bd. des Dames (tel. 91 56 30 10, for reservations 91 56 80 20). To reach the local **hospital,** Hôpital Timone, bd. Jean Moulin (tel. 91 38 60 00), take metro line 1 to Castéllane, then bus 91. The **police** are at 2, rue du Commissaire Becker (tel. 91 39 80 00).

Inexpensive hotels abound in Marseille, especially on rue Breteuil and rue Aubagne. A herd of 1- and 2-star hotels grazes on allée Gambetta. A former château now houses the well-kept but isolated **Auberge de Jeunesse de Bois-Luzy (HI),** allée des Primevères (tel. and fax 91 49 06 18); take bus 6 from cours J. Thierry at the top of La Canebière (away from the port) to Marius Richard, or take bus 8 from

La Canebière by day (or bus K at 10pm, 11:20pm, or 12:45am) to Bois-Luzy and head to the end of av. Bois-Luzy and walk left along the gravel path. (Reception open 7:30am-noon and 5-10:30pm. Curfew 10:30pm. 42F. Cooking facilities.) Turn right off rue Paradis to arrive at the great location of **Hôtel Montgrand**, 50, rue Montgrand (tel. 91 33 33 81, fax 91 33 75 89). Immaculate rooms are white and blue. (Singles 110-155F. Doubles 200-240F. Triples 250-280F.) Chow down on a *bouillabaisse* or a 5-course seafood *menu* (each 75F) at **Racasse-Dauphin**, 6, quai de Rive-neuve, in the *vieux port* (open Fri.-Wed. noon-2pm and 7-11pm).

FRANCE

■■■ ST-TROPEZ

To be sure, mansions abound in a town that even the French have nicknamed *Saint Trop d'Aise* (St. Too Much Luxury). This coastal village shimmers and glitters while clinging to centuries-old architecture and traditions establishing a tasteful and understated ambience where grubby kilted buskers like Doug Cameron can exist comfortably alongside the exquisite and wealthy "natives." To reach the beaches, take a **Sodetrav bus** from the *gare routière* on av. du Général de Gaulle ("St-Tropez-Ramatuelle," Mon.-Sat. 3 per day). Or, rent a pair of wheels from **Louis Mas**, 3-5, rue Quarenta. (Bicycles 45F per day, deposit 1500F. Mopeds 90-165F, deposit 2500-5000F. Open Easter-Oct. 15 Mon.-Sat. 9am-7:30pm, Sun. 9am-1pm and 5-7:30pm).

To reach St-Tropez take the **bus** (tel. 94 95 24 82) from St-Raphaël (1½-2¼hr., 44F50) or Toulon (3hr., 90F). The faster, more scenic boat ride from St-Raphaël is much more suave, and not much more expensive (50min., 100F round-trip, only 80F if you stay at the Fréjus hostel). Call **Gare Maritime de St-Raphaël** at 94 95 17 46 for details. Hitching is poor; they'd soil the upholstery, darling.

The **tourist office** (tel. 94 97 41 21), between av. Général de Gaulle and av. Général Leclerc, has an invaluable free room-finding service (open 10am-12:30pm and 2:30-7pm). Budget hotels do not exist in St-Tropez; the closest youth hostel is in Fréjus. **Camping** is by far the cheapest option, but again, make reservations. The tourist office can tell you which sites have space, but few will in July and Aug. Try 4-star **La Croix du Sud,** route de Pampelonne (tel. 94 79 80 84; 90F for 1-2 people, 120F for 3; open Easter-Sept.), or **Kon Tiki** (tel. 94 79 80 17; 80F per tent). Both lie just behind the Pampelonne beach.

The **Vieux Port** and the narrow cobblestone streets of the hillside *vieille ville* behind the waterfront form the hub of St-Tropez's culinary activity. **Au Regalé**, 12, rue du Colonel Guichard, next to the Eglise Paroissiale, serves pasta, roast chicken and *ratatouille* on its 50F *menu* (open noon-2:30pm and 7-11pm). To create your own ambience, head to the **Prisunic supermarket**, 7, av. du Général Leclerc (tel. 94 97 07 94; open Mon.-Sat. 8am-9pm, Sun. 9am-1pm and 5-9pm). Great slacking spots lounge along the water 10min. from the *Vieux Port.*

■■■ ST-RAPHAËL AND FRÉJUS

Sandwiched between St-Tropez and Cannes, the twin cities of St-Raphaël and Fréjus boast all the wide, sandy beaches, seafood restaurants, and coastal charm of their swanky Côte d'Azur cousins at half the cost. Bake in the sun along the long and sandy **Plage Fréjus,** just 10min. along the waterfront from the St-Raphaël train station. You can visit the huge **Parc Zoologique Safari de Fréjus** by car or—if you're brave—by foot. Take the "Fayence-St-Raphaël" bus line from St-Raphaël to Le Camps le Coq. Go right at the fork and continue for about 10min. (Open 10am-5:30pm. 50F.) The first weekend in July is the **Competition International de Jazz New Orleans** in St-Raphaël. Over 400 musicians face off in the streets and by the port in front of a panel of judges—and the shows are free. (Tickets only needed for the final round of competition; call 94 82 15 68 or ask at the tourist office for more info.)

The **tourist office** in St-Raphaël (tel. 94 19 52 52), across the street from the train station, has the scoop on transportation and room availability (open Mon.-Sat. 8am-

8pm, Sun. 8am-noon, Sept.-June Mon.-Sat. 8am-6:30pm). St-Raphaël sends frequent **trains** to Toulon (50min., 75F), Cannes (25min., 32F), and Nice (1hr., 55F). **Sodetrav buses** connect St-Raphaël to St-Tropez (15 per day, 2hr., 45F), and **Forum Cars** (tel. 94 95 16 71) makes the scenic trip from Cannes to St-Raphaël (8 per day, 70min., 31F). **Les Bateaux de Saint Raphaël,** at the *vieux port* (tel. 94 95 17 46), cruise to St-Tropez 4-5 times per day in summer (50min., 100F round-trip). If you are staying at the youth hostel in Fréjus, ask about ticket reductions. Buses leave from quai #7 for the St-Raphaël to Fréjus voyage every ½hr. (Mon.-Sat. 7:30am-7pm, Sun. 7am-6pm; 6F).

Kind managers and a great crowd of backpackers hang out at the **Auberge de Jeunesse de St-Raphaël-Fréjus (HI),** chemin du Counillier (tel. 94 52 18 75, fax 94 51 50 91), 4km from the St-Raphaël train station. A direct shuttle bus runs from quai #6 of the *gare routière* to the hostel at 6pm (5F); a return shuttle leaves at 9:15am. (Lockout 10am-6pm. Curfew 11pm. 65F. Camping 27F per person.) Or, head to the simple but well-located **La Bonne Auberge,** 54, rue de la Garonne (tel. 94 95 69 72) in St-Raphaël. (Singles 130F. Doubles 150F, with shower 200F. Open March-Oct.) In the center of town, **Le Mistral,** 80, rue de la Garonne (tel. 94 95 38 82), lowers the price the longer you stay. (Singles 130F-170F. Doubles 170-250F. Triples 240-350F.) Affordable restaurants center around the *vieux port* and bd. de la Libération. **Restaurant La Grillade,** 32, rue Boëtman, serves delicious *brochettes d'agneau* (lamb skewers, 65F) and a 78F seafood *menu.* Pizzas run 36-55F. (Open Mon.-Fri. and Sun. noon-2:30pm and 7-10:30pm, Sat. 7-10:30pm.)

■■■ CANNES

All preconceived notions of the French Riviera materialize in Cannes. Sister city to Beverly Hills, Cannes is a favorite stop of the international jet-set. Less reclusive, however, than St-Tropez, Cannes allows even the unshaven budget traveler to tan on the beach with Gérard Depardieu or browse in boutiques with Madonna. In May, Cannes's **Festival International du Film** skims the cream of Hollywood across the ocean. None of the festival's 350 screenings is open to the public (that means you). Most of Cannes's daytime activity (and spending) pulses between rue Félix-Faure and the waterfront. **Rue d'Antibes,** running parallel to the sea, and **bd. de la Croisette,** passing right along the shore, contain high-priced shops sporting familiar names—Christian Dior, Hermès and Gianni Versace. Farther west, the **Castre Cathédrale** and its courtyard stand on the hill on which *vieux* Cannes was built.

Of Cannes's 3 casinos, the most accessible is **Le Casino Croisette,** 1, jetée Albert Eduoard (tel. 93 38 12 11), next to the Palais des Festivals, with slots, blackjack, and roulette. (Gambling 5pm-3am; open for slots at 11am. No shorts. Min. age 18. Admission free.) If your luck sours, take to the clubs, but prepare to feel underdressed. From 11pm to dawn, dance at **Jane's,** 38, rue des Serbes, in the Hôtel Gray d'Albion. (Cover and 1st drink 120F.) Ask around for the newest places, and look for posters advertising clubs and events.

Practical Information, Accommodations and Food The info-effusive **tourist office** at 1, bd. de la Croisette (tel. 93 39 01 01 or 93 39 24 53, fax 93 99 37 06), next to the *vieux port*, has a free accommodations service (open 9am-7:30pm, Sept.-June Mon.-Sat. 9am-6:30pm). Find a **branch office** at the train station (open July 4 to Sept. 4 Mon.-Sat. 8:30am-12:30pm and 2:30-6:30pm.) On the major coastal **train** line, Cannes has frequent connections to Nice (35min., 29F), Monaco (50min., 40F), and Marseille (2hr., 125F). The station, 1, rue Jean-Jaurès (tel. 93 99 50 50), has **baggage service** (30F) for those who want to make Cannes a daytrip. Buses leave from the **gare routière** (Buz Azur; tel. 93 90 67 50) every 20min. to Antibes (30min., 13F), Nice (1½hr., 28F), and St-Raphaël (70min., 23F).

Cannes's beds sleep enough stars to produce the next brat pack, but a few bargains lurk just off rue d'Antibes and close to the beach. Try to book ahead—an absolute must in July and August. At **Hôtel du Nord,** 6, rue Jean Jaurès (tel. 93 38 48 79, fax 92 99 28 20), across from the station, eat breakfast among pictures of the Grand Canyon and get sight-seeing advice from the English-speaking owner. (Singles 140-180F. Doubles 200-240F, with shower 280F. Triple 360F. Quads with shower 370F. Breakfast 25F. Open Dec.-Oct.) **Hôtel Chanteclair,** 12, rue Forville (tel. 93 39 68 88), off the Forville market to the right of the station, has modern rooms overlooking an enclosed courtyard. (Reception closes at 8pm. Singles 180F, with shower 200F. Doubles 180-210F, with shower 240F. Prices 50-100F lower off-season. Breakfast 20F.) The best **camping** is the 3-star site at **Le Grand Saule,** 24, bd. Jean Moulin (tel. 93 90 55 10), in nearby Ranguin. Take bus 9 (7F) from pl. de l'Hôtel de Ville toward Grasse. (70F per person, 125F for two, tent included. Open April-Oct.)

The elegant sidewalk cafés on bd. de la Croisette, Cannes's runway of conspicuous consumption, cost an arm and a leg and will probably demand your soul as cover charge. Smaller cafés and restaurants on **rue Meynardier** are just as lovely and much less expensive. The delightful **Chez Mamichette,** 11, rue St-Antoine, has *fondue savoyarde* (65F), a 70F *menu,* and a 40F *plat du jour* (open Mon.-Sat. noon-3pm and 7-11pm). **Rue Rouguière** is lined with other bargain restaurants; try **des Artistes** or **La Voute.** For a picnic, buy supplies at **Monoprix supermarket,** 9, rue Maréchal Foch, across from the train station (open Mon.-Sat. 9am-8:30pm), and head to the breezy, palm-tree-filled **Jardin de la Croisette. Outdoor markets** find happy homes on pl. Gambetta and marché Forville (Tues.-Sun. 7am-1pm).

■■■ NICE

Blessed with a beautiful beach and a vibrant arts and entertainment scene, Nice is the unofficial capital of the French Riviera. Don't let the city's popularity and crowds scare you away; it's big and there's room for everyone, with decently priced hotels, excellent local and regional transport, and a population amenable to visitors. Nice erupts into song and dance during the annual *Carnaval* (Feb. 16-March 5, 1995), the grandparent of New Orleans's *Mardi Gras.* Even if you can't make it then, you'll find plenty of revelry in the labyrinth of tiny streets in the old city.

ORIENTATION AND PRACTICAL INFORMATION

With excellent rail connections, Nice is a fab place from which to make daytrips to surrounding coastal towns. The SNCF train station (Gare "Nice-Ville") is in the center of town, next to the tourist office on **avenue Thiers.** To the left, **avenue Jean-Médecin** runs toward the water to **place Masséna.** Vieux Nice lies just south of pl. Masséna. Heading right from the train station, you'll run into **boulevard Gambetta,** the other main street running directly to the water. Sweeping along the coast, the majestic and festive **promenade des Anglais** is rock-covered, crowded, and noisy. Unfortunately, Nice's big-city appeal is coupled increasingly with big-city crime. Women should avoid walking alone after sundown, and everyone should exercise caution at night near the train station and Vieux Nice. Never leave your belongings unattended. If you are leaving a club late at night, be particularly careful as teams of pickpockets have been known to hone in on the night-life districts.

Tourist office: av. Thiers (tel. 93 87 07 07), beside the station. Books a limited number of rooms after 8am (12-24F). Stake out a place in line early. Ask for the English-language pamphlet *Nice: A Practical Guide* and the detailed city map (very helpful in Vieux Nice). Open 8am-8pm; Sept. 16-June 30 Mon.-Sat. 8am-7pm, Sun. 8am-noon and 2-6pm. **Branch offices** at 2, rue Massenet (tel. 93 87 60 60) near the **beach** and pedestrian zones. Open 8am-8pm, Sept.16-June 30 Mon.-Sat. 8:45am-12:30pm and 2-6pm; **Aéroport I** (tel. 93 21 44 11). Open 8am-10pm; and at the **promenade des Anglais** (tel. 93 83 32 64), near Ferber parking area. Open 8am-8pm, Sept. 16-June 30 Mon.-Sat. 8am-7pm.
Currency Exchange: Cambio, 17, av. Thiers (tel. 93 88 56 80), across from the train station. No commission, good rates. Open 7am-11pm, Sept.-June 8am-8pm.

American Express: 11, promenade des Anglais (tel. 93 16 53 53), at the corner of rue des Congrès. Open Mon.-Fri. 9am-noon and 2-6pm, Sat. 9am-1pm and 2-6pm.

Post Office: 23, av. Thiers (tel. 93 88 52 52), near the train station. Open Mon.-Fri. 8am-7pm, Sat. 8am-noon. Poste Restante and **telephones. Postal code:** 06000.

Flights: Aéroport Nice-Côte d'Azur (tel. 93 21 30 30). Take Sunbus 23 (6am-9pm, every 15min., 8F) from train station. The airport bus (tel. 93 56 35 40) runs between bus station by pl. Leclerc and airport every 20min. (21F).

Trains: Gare SNCF Nice-Ville, av. Thiers (tel. 93 87 50 50). Trains about every 20min. (5:40am-midnight) to Cannes (35min., 29F) and Antibes (18min., 20F); about every 15min. (6:30am-11:30pm) to Monaco (25min., 17F) and Menton (35min., 23F). Also to other coastal towns, northern France, Italy, and Spain. In summer, about 11 per day connect with the TGV from Marseille to Paris (7hr., 465F plus 18F required reservation). **Showers** 12F. Open 7am-7pm. **Lockers** 20F for 72 hr. **Luggage storage** 15F per day per piece. Open 5:30pm-midnight.

Buses: Gare Routière, promenade du Paillon (tel. 93 85 61 81), between av. Félix-Faure and bd. Jean Jaurès. Buses every 20min. (6:30am-7:30pm) to Monaco (45min., 18F), Antibes (1hr., 28F), and Cannes (1¼hr., 35F).

Public Transportation: Sunbus, 10, av. Félix Faure (tel. 93 16 52 10), near pl. Leclerc and pl. Masséna. Long treks to museums and youth hostels make the 21F day pass, 31F *carnet* of 5 tickets, 87F five-day pass, or 117F week pass well worth it. Buy passes at the agency (open Mon.-Fri. 7am-7pm, Sat. 7am-6pm) or the information kiosk at pl. Leclerc (open Mon.-Fri. 6:30am-9:30pm). Otherwise, tickets cost 8F. Bus 12 goes from train station to pl. Masséna and the beach every 12min. Ask tourist office for the *Guide Infobus* which lists schedules and routes.

Ferries: SNCM, quai du Commerce (tel. 93 13 66 66), at the port. Take bus 1 or 2 from pl. Masséna. Passage to and from Corsican cities: Bastia (4-5hr., one-way 255F, students 190F) and Ajaccio (6-7hr., same prices). Open Mon.-Fri. 8am-noon and 1:30-6:30pm, Sat. 8am-noon.

Bike Rental: Nicea Location Rent, 9, av. Thiers (tel. 93 82 42 71), near the train station. Bikes 120F per day, 2000F deposit. Open Mon.-Sat. 9am-7:30pm. **Cycles Arnaud,** 4, pl. Grimaldi (tel. 93 87 88 55), near the pedestrian zone and the beach. Bikes 90F, credit card deposit. Open Mon.-Fri. 8am-noon and 2-7pm.

Laundromats: Suisse Laundrette, rue de Suisse (tel. 93 88 78 52), between rue Paganini and rue d'Angleterre. Close to hotels around the station. Wash 18F. Dry 2F per 5min. Open 7am-9pm.

Pharmacy: 7, rue Masséna (tel. 93 87 78 94). Open 7:30pm-8:30am.

Hospital: St-Roch, 5, rue Pierre Devoluy (tel. 92 03 33 33). From av. Jean Médecin, turn left on rue Pastorelli, which turns into rue P. Devoluy.

Medical Services: SOS Medical Service (tel. 93 53 03 03). Available 24 hrs.

Emergency: tel. 17. **Police,** tel. 93 92 62 22, at the opposite end of bd. Maréchal Foch from bd. Jean Médecin. English interpreter on call.

ACCOMMODATIONS

Rooms in summer are like Marlboros in Moscow: gone as soon as they're on sale. Arrive at the av. Thiers tourist office early for help in finding a room, or call individual hotels in advance. Although police sporadically enforce a law that prohibits sleeping on the beach, groups of young people often check their baggage at the *consigne* and head for the rocky waterfront. The largest concentrations of decent, affordable hotels cluster around Notre-Dame, on rue d'Angleterre, rue de la Suisse, and rue de Russie. Nice's two youth hostels and two *résidences* (temporary youth hostels set up in university dorms) are great, but often full.

Auberge de Jeunesse (HI), rte. Forestière du Mont-Alban (tel. 93 89 23 64, fax 92 04 03 10), 4km away from it all, but bubbling with the bronzed and the beautiful. Take bus 14 from the *gare routière* on bd. Jean Jaurès (Mon.-Fri. every 15min., Sat.-Sun every 30min., last bus 7:30pm), or a 50min. walk. Reception opens at 5pm. Lockout 10am-5pm. Curfew midnight. 61F. Showers and breakfast included. Kitchen. Laundry 35F.

Relais International de la Jeunesse "Clairvallon," 26, av. Scudéri (tel. 93 81 27 63), in Cimiez, 4km out of town. Take bus 15 from train station or pl. Masséna (every 10min.; 20min.). A large, luxurious hostel in an old villa with a free swimming pool. Check-in 5pm. Curfew 11pm. Lockout 9:30am-5pm. 75F the first night, 65F thereafter. Breakfast included. Three-course dinner 50F.

Pado Tourisme, 26, bd. Rimbaldi (tel. 93 80 98 00), a 5min. walk from train station. For 55F per night, you get a friendly, happy atmosphere, free use of the kitchen, a bed, hot shower, and info on happening pubs, clubs, and restaurants. Two mountain bikes available for 50F per day. Reception open 8-11am and 5-8:30pm. No curfew. Lockout 11am-5pm. All-you-can-eat pancake breakfast 15F.

Résidence Les Collinettes (HI), 3, av. Robert Schumann (tel. 93 89 23 64, fax 93 37 19 86; if these numbers don't work, call the HI Auberge de Jeunesse). Take bus 17 from the train station and get off at Châteauneuf. Summer hostel in a great location. Open for reservations all day. No lockout. 95F. Open July 7-Aug. 31.

Espace Magnan, 31, rue de Coppet (tel. 93 86 28 75), near the promenade des Anglais and the beach. From the train station, take bus 12, 22, 23 or 24 to Rosa Bonheur (8F). Clean and efficient, if somewhat impersonal. Reception open 8:30am-12:30pm and 2pm-midnight. Lockout 10am-6pm. 50F. Baggage rooms 10F per day. Open June 12-Sept. 15.

Hôtel Belle Meunière, 21, av. Durante (tel. 93 88 66 15), near the station. This quasi-villa was a gift from one of Napoleon's generals to his mistress. 75F per person in 3- to 5-bed rooms. Singles 90F. Doubles 140-250F. Showers 10F. Breakfast included. Baggage room 10F. Open Feb.-Dec.

Hôtel Notre Dame, 22, rue de Russie (tel. 93 88 70 44, fax 93 82 20 38), at the corner of rue d'Italie. Renovations galore make for an extremely professional look. All 18 rooms are clean and quiet and have telephones. Singles 130F, with private bathroom 150F. Doubles 160F, with shower 220F.

Hôtel Lyonnais, 20, rue de Russie (tel. 93 88 70 74, fax 93 16 25 56). Spacious, and clean rooms. Some face a courtyard. Elevator for the weary. Singles 150F, with shower 180F. Doubles 200F. Breakfast 20F.

Hôtel Idéal Bristol, 22, rue Paganini (tel. 93 88 60 72), off rue Alsace-Lorraine. Dorm-style rooms (4-5 people per room) with kitchenettes, refrigerators and showers. 87F. Fifth-floor dorm leads to a terrace overlooking Nice's tile rooftops. Singles 120F. Doubles 150F, with shower 185F.

FOOD

Nice offers a smorgasbord of seafood, North African and Italian gastronomic delights. Niçois specialties include *bouillabaisse, pissaladière* (onion, olive, and anchovy pizza), and, of course, the *salade niçoise.* Avoid the cheap, touristy places near the train station in favor of the fine restaurants that cluster around the Vieux Port. Most restaurants' cheapest *menus* are reasonable enough to justify treating yourself to a feast (55-80F); shop around. Filling meals at Nice's university cafeterias cost about 36F. The convenient **Restaurant Université,** 3, av. Robert Schumann, is open from September through June. The cafeteria at **Montebello,** 96, av. Valrose, near the Musée Matisse, is open until mid-August. All student cafeterias are open daily 11:30am-1:30pm and 6-8pm. Stock up at the **Prisunic supermarket,** 42, av. Jean Médecin (open Mon.-Sat. 8:30am-8pm). **Restaurant de Paris,** 28, rue d'Angleterre, near the train station offers generous menus for 38F, 48F, and 58F (open 11:30am-2:30pm and 7pm-midnight). Budget travelers find the right prices in **Cafétéria Flunch,** av. Thiers, next to train station (crêpes 10-22F; open 11am-10pm). For generous portions of typical niçois food in a friendly atmosphere, eat at **Passez à Table,** 30, rue Pertinax (*menu* 52F; open 11:30am-2:30pm and 6:30-11pm).

SIGHTS

Even museum-haters will have a hard time resisting Nice's varied collections. Since most are hidden among attractive houses in quiet suburbs, visiting them gives you a respite from the beach and a glimpse of the luxurious residential areas. Moreover almost all are free. The newly renovated **Musée Matisse,** 164, av. des Arènes de Cimiez, showcases books illustrated by the artist, preliminary sketches for the *Chapelle du Rosaire in Vence,* and several of his famous happy, wall-sized cut-outs (open Wed.-Mon. 11am-7pm, Oct.-March Wed.-Mon. 10am-5pm; 25F, students 10F). The

FRANCE

elegant **Musée National Marc Chagall,** av. du Docteur Ménard, is a 15min. walk north of the station. Or take bus 15 (every 20min., 8F) to the Docteur Moriez stop. The 17 oil paintings devoted to Old Testament themes, including the vivid *Song of Songs,* exemplify Chagall's colorful whimsy. (Open Wed.-Mon. 10am-7pm, Oct.-June 10am-12:30pm and 2-5:30pm. 17F; students, seniors, and Sun. 8F.) The **Musée des Beaux-Arts,** 33, av. Baumettes, is a must-see for fans of the surreal and of Degas, Monet, Sisley, and Renoir. Take bus 38 from the train station to Chéret, or 12 to Grosseo. (Open Tues.-Sun. 10am-noon and 3-6pm, Oct.-April Tues.-Sun. 10am-noon and 2-5pm. Free.) The **Musée d'Art Moderne et d'Art Contemporain,** promenade des Arts, at the intersection of av. St-Jean Baptiste and Traverse Garibaldi (take bus 5 from the station) features over 400 French and American avant-garde pieces from 1960 to the present. Modernism has never been so friendly; the rooftop entrance, while covered in minimalist white marble and shining metal, is also decorated with purple-flowered trees and anthropomorphic steel sculptures with cute little polka-dot cutouts. (Open Sat.-Mon. and Wed.-Thurs. 11am-6pm, Fri. 11am-10pm. Free.)

Fiddle with your rosaries at the **Cathédrale Orthodoxe Russe St-Nicolas,** 17, bd. du Tsarévitch, off bd. Gambetta, a 5min. walk east of the train station. This gorgeous church was built in 1912 under the patronage of Tsar Nicholas II. (Open Wed.-Thurs. and Sat.-Mon. 11am-6pm, Fri. 11am-10pm. 25F, students 10F. Free Oct.-June.) The **Monastère Cimiez,** pl. du Monastère, housed Nice's Franciscan brethren from the 13th to the 18th centuries. The monastery's cloister, the Eglise Gothique, and 350 works of religious art are open to the public. Take bus 15 or 17 from the station. (Open Mon.-Sat. 10am-noon and 3-6pm. Free.)

Nice maintains many beautiful parks and public gardens, the most central of which is the sprawling **Jardin Albert Ier.** Located at promenade des Anglais and quai des Etats-Unis, this quiet refuge has benches, fountains, plenty of shade, and the ornate 18th-century Triton fountain. The fragrant, equally sprawling **Esplanade du Paillon,** near pl. Masséna, surrounds a spectacular central fountain and is an ideal setting for a picnic. Like many centers on the Côte, Nice has a colorful, convoluted old section, known to residents as **Vieux Nice.** Just east of Vieux Nice lies **Le Château,** a hillside public park where you can enjoy a spectacular view of the city, its beaches, the port, and the Baie des Anges (Bay of Angels).

ENTERTAINMENT

Nice's party crowd swings long after the folks in St-Tropez and Antibes have called it a night. The bars and nightclubs around rue Masséna and Vieux Nice are constantly rollicking with jazz, snazz, and rock 'n' roll. The area around the clubs in Vieux Nice can be dangerous at night and should not be visited alone. Nice's nightclubs are relentlessly expensive. The **Hot Spot,** 10, Cité du Parc, deserves its name. The party lasts from 9pm 'til dawn but only for those in proper attire—no shorts or sandals. (60F, free most Sundays.) If you left your Sunday best at home, **Subway,** 19, rue Droite in Vieux Nice will let you dance and save money too (cover 30-50F, free to students with ID on Wed.). Gay nightlife in Nice is fun, flamboyant, and *cher.* Try **Quartz Underground,** 18, rue de Congrès (tel. 93 88 88 87), a mixed disco in the center of town, or **The Blue Boy,** a gay disco on rue Spinetta in West Nice. For pubs, crawl into the lively **Hole in the Wall,** 3, rue de l'Abbaye, near rue de la Préfecture in Vieux Nice (open Tues.-Sun. 8pm-midnight). **Scarlet O'Hara's,** 22, rue Droite, off rue Rossetti in Vieux Nice, is a friendly Irish pub with live music which serves Guiness Pie and beef cooked in Guiness (open Mon.-Sat. 6pm-2am).

Nice's **La Grande Parade du Jazz** in mid-July at the Parc et Arènes de Cimiez (tel. 93 37 17 17), near the Musée Matisse, attracts world-famous European and American jazz musicians to its 3 stages. Past performers have included Miles Davis, The Manhattan Transfer, and Wynton Marsalis. The **Festival de Folklore International** and the **Batailles des Fleurs,** pageants of music and flowers along promenade des Anglais, bloom every year on the last weekend of July (reserved seats 80F). *Semaine des Spectacles,* published every Wednesday, carries entertainment listings for the entire Côte and is available at newsstands (8F). The **Comité des Fêtes,** 5, promenade des Anglais (tel. 93 87 16 28), has festival information (open Mon.-Fri. 10am-noon and 2-5pm). The **FNAC** in the Nice Etoile shopping center on 24, av. Jean Médecin, sells tickets for virtually every performance in town. Call the tourist office for more information.

■ VILLEFRANCHE-SUR-MER

The narrow streets and pastel houses of Villefranche-sur-Mer, only two stops from Nice on the local train, enchanted Aldous Huxley, Katherine Mansfield, and a bevy of other writers. Trains run from Nice every half-hour (10F). On quai Courbet stands the 14th century **Chapelle St-Pierre,** decorated by film director Jean Cocteau with boldly executed scenes from the life of St-Peter and the Camargue gypsies of Stes-Maries-de-la-Mer. (Open 9:30am-noon and 3-7pm; Oct.-June 9:30am-noon and 3-5pm. 14F.) Both of the town's excellent museums are located in the 16th-century **Citadelle,** near the waterfront. The **Musée Volti** displays the contemporary art and sculpture of Villefranche resident Antoniucci Volti, while the **Musée Goetz-Boumeester** traces the work of Villefranche painter and sometime Surrealist Henri Goetz and his wife, Christine Boumeester. (Both open Wed-Mon. 10am-noon and 3-5pm; June and Sept. 9am-noon and 3-6pm; Oct.-May 10am-noon and 2-5pm; closed Nov. and all Sun. mornings.)

■ ANTIBES AND JUAN-LES-PINS

Antibes boasts beautiful beaches, new theater and music festivals, and a seaside youth hostel. Once home to celebrated English writer Graham Greene, the town has become one of the Riviera's newest budget backpacker hotspots. If you've gotten your share of the sun, retreat to the charming *vieille ville.* Old Antibes, which stretches between bd. Maréchal Foch and the port d'Antibes, is a haven for pricey boutiques but inexpensive and well-curated museums. The **Musée Picasso,** in the Château Grimaldi on pl. Mariejol, displays works by the master and his contemporaries. (Open 10am-6pm; Sept 16-June 14 10am-noon and 2-6pm. Closed Mon. and Nov. 20F, students 10F.) **Trains** connect Antibes with Cannes (15min., 10F), Marseille (2½hr., 125F), Nice (20min., 20F) and Juan-les-Pins. The color-coordinated staff at the **tourist office,** 11, pl. de Gaulle (tel. 92 90 53 00), has information on accommodations, camping, and the frequent festivals. Exit the train station, turn right onto av. Robert Soleau, and follow signs for the *Maison du Tourisme.* (Open Mon.-Sat. 8:30am-8pm, Sun. 10am-1pm; Oct.-June Mon.-Sat. 9am-noon and 2-6pm.) Cheap rooms and a view of the ocean make the **Relais International de la Jeunesse,** at the intersection of bd. de la Garoupe and av. l'Antiquité (tel. 93 61 34 40), a good option. Take bus 2A (5F40) from the *gare routière* to the L'Antiquité stop on bd. de la Garoupe. (Lockout 10am-6pm. Curfew midnight. 65F. 4-course dinner 50F. Sheets 20F. Open June-Sept.) Place Nationale, in the heart of the *vieille ville,* holds a great selection of cheap restaurants. Try the *crêpes* (50-70F) at **Adieu Berthe,** 26, rue Vauban (open Wed.-Mon. 6-11pm.) Or resign yourself to the **Codec supermarket,** 8, av. Niquet, near pl. de Gaulle. (Open Mon.-Sat. 8am-7:30pm, Sun. 8am-noon.)

Though communally joined as one—a city known as Antibes-Juan les Pins (pop. 70,000)—Antibes and **Juan-les-Pins** are 2-3km apart and sport separate train stations, post offices, and tourist offices. They also beat to a different rhythm, Juan-les-Pins being the younger, hipper, and more hedonistic of the two. No place burns the midnight oil like Juan-les-Pins. Boutiques remain open until midnight, cafés until 2am, and nightclubs until past sunrise. The streets are packed with seekers of sea, sun, and sex (order varies), and nightclubs pulse with promises of decadence. The cafés are much cheaper and almost as lively as the clubs, so even the most miserly budget traveler can be included in Juan-les-Pins's nightly bash. In winter, Juan-les-Pins virtually becomes a ghost town. Five of Juan-les-Pins's six *discothèques* are in the center of town. They all open around 11pm, and their cover charges are all around 100F (first drink included). Look for posters around town advertising special events at the clubs. **Voom Voom,** 1, bd. de la Pinède and **Whiskey à Gogo,** la

Pinède use balloons and throbbing bass to out-do nearby competitor **Le Bureau,** av. de la Gallice. **Joy's Club,** av. Dautheville, has dance revues as well as a disco. (Cover 100F, second drink 70F.) The **Soft Club,** av. Guy Maupassant, often has all-male nights. **Les Pêcheurs,** bd. Edouard Baudoin, is about a 10min. walk along the coast from the center of town. Dress code at all the clubs is simple: be chic.

The **train station** is on av. l'Esterel where av. du Maréchal Joffre joins it. Trains leave about every 20min. for Nice (25F) and Cannes (10F). To get from Antibes' pl. du Général de Gaulle to Juan-les-Pins by foot, follow bd. Wilson (about 1.5km) and turn left on av. Dautheville. You'll be in nightlife heaven, but you won't be able to afford to spend the night there. Instead party all night and take the train to Cannes or Nice in the morning (trains start running at 5:30am).

■ ■ ■ MONACO/MONTE-CARLO

All the wealth, mystery, and intrigue of Monte-Carlo revolves around the famed **Casino,** where Mata Hari once shot a Russian spy. The slot machines open at noon, and the *salle américaine* (where blackjack, craps, and roulette require a 30F min. bet) at 4pm; hard core veterans don't arrive until after 10pm. Admission to the main room—or "kitchen"—is free (you must be over 21 and cannot wear shorts, sneakers, sandals, or jeans), but it costs 50F to enter the chic *salons privés.* After losing your shirt, admire the royal robes at the **Palais Princier,** the some-time home of Prince Rainier and the one-time home of his bride, Princess Grace. Guards change outside the palace daily at 11:55am. When the flag is down, the prince is away and the doors open to tourists. Take a tour of the small but lavishly decorated palace. (Open 9:30am-6:30pm, Oct. 10am-5pm, closed Nov.-May. 30F, students 15F.) Next door is the stately **Cathédrale de Monaco,** 4, rue Colonel Bellando de Castro. Each of the former Princes of Monaco is buried within this Romanesque-Byzantine church; Grace Kelly's simple grave is behind the altar. (Open Mon.-Sat. 10am-6pm, Sun. 2-6pm.) Once directed by Jacques Cousteau, the tremendous **Musée Océanographique,** av. St-Martin, houses thousands of species of fish and marine animals from every sea on earth (open 9am-8pm; April-May and Sept. 9am-7pm; Oct. and March 9:30am-7pm; Nov.-Feb. 10am-6pm. 60F, under 18 and students 30F.)

Practical Information, Accommodations, and Food The **tourist office,** 2a, bd. des Moulins (tel. 92 16 61 66), near the Casino, provides a helpful map of the city and makes room reservations. **Annexes** are set up in the train station and in the port in summer. (Open Mon.-Sat. 9am-7pm, Sun. 10am-noon.) The **train station** at av. Prince Pierre (tel. 93 25 54 54), connects Monaco to Nice (25min., 15F), Antibes (45min., 30F), and Cannes (70min., 45F) from 5:30am to 11pm. (Information desk open 9am-7pm.) In emergencies, call the **police,** 3, rue Louis Notari (tel. 93 30 42 46 or if urgent tel. 17).

To stay in Monaco, you'll need to seduce royalty or win big to afford the price of a bed for the night. Try the **Centre de Jeunesse Princesse Stéphanie,** 24, av. Prince Pierre (tel. 93 50 83 20, fax 93 25 29 82), 100m up the hill from the train station. In summer, arrive before 9am if you want a bed; reservations are accepted off-season only. The age limit is 26 for non-students and 31 for students with ID. (Reception open 7am-12:45am, off-season 7am-11:45pm. Curfew 12:45am. 70F. Breakfast and sheets included.) Sitting by the ocean in the shade with a breeze blowing, you'll look like you stepped straight out of an Orangina commercial at **Le Calypso,** off bd. Louis II. Savor especially the *escalope de veau* (veal cutlet, 65F) or the lasagna (50F). The **Carrefour supermarket** is in Fontvieille's *centre commercial* (shopping plaza). From the train station, turn right onto rue de la Colle until you reach pl. du Canton. Cross the street and go down one level. (Open Mon.-Sat. 8:30am-9pm.)

FRANCE

CORSICA (CORSE)

Appropriately called Kallysté, "the most beautiful," by the Greeks, the island combines the mountainous splendor of the Alps with the beaches and crystal-blue Mediterranean water of the Riviera. Try to visit in the off-season; although ferries and other tourist services multiply between June 15 and the end of September, prices soar by 50%. Half the island's one million annual tourists (mostly French, Italian, and German) visit then, and the beaches and hotels in the coastal resorts are packed.

Getting There and Getting Around The **Société National Maritime Corse Méditerranée (SNCM)** sends car ferries from Marseille, Toulon, and Nice on the continent to Bastia, Calvi, Ajaccio, and Propriano on Corsica. About 2 boats per day travel between Corsica and the mainland in the off-season, a few more per day during summer. The trip from Marseille or Toulon costs 266-296F; from Nice, 240-266F. Discounts are available if you are under 25, a student under 27, or over 60. SNCM has offices in Ajaccio, quai l'Herminier (tel. 95 29 66 99, -88); Bastia, Nouveau Port (tel. 95 54 66 99); Calvi, quai Landry (tel. 95 65 01 38). On the mainland, SNCM offices are in Nice, quai du Commerce (tel. 93 13 66 99); Marseille, 61, bd. des Dames (tel. 91 56 30 10); Toulon, 21, av. de l'Infanterie de Marine (tel. 94 16 66 66); and Paris, 12, rue Godot-de-Mauroy, 9ème (tel. 49 24 24 24). **Corsica Ferries** crosses from the Italian ports of Livorno, Genoa, and La Spezia to Bastia (145-175F).

Air France and **Air Inter** fly to Bastia, Ajaccio, and Calvi from Paris (1230F, with discounts 525-800F), Nice (with discounts 273-397F), and Marseille (with discounts 315-447F). Discounted fares apply to everyone under 25 or over 60, and to students under 27, for off-peak "blue flights" (several/week, boxed in blue on the schedule). Air France maintains offices at 3, bd. du Roi-Jérôme in Ajaccio (tel. 95 29 45 45) and at 6, av. Emile Sari, in Bastia (tel. 95 54 54 95). Air Inter's offices are at the airports in Ajaccio (tel. 95 29 45 45), Bastia (tel. 95 54 54 95), and Calvi (tel. 95 65 20 09). Reservations are advisable; call between 8am and 6pm.

Train service in Corsica is slow and limited. It doesn't serve all the major towns (no rail to Bonifacio or Porto-Vecchio) and accepts no passes. **Buses** mire in a seemingly endless maze of carriers, connections, and times (many before 8am). Bus services connect major towns but are neither cheaper nor more frequent than trains. **Hitchhiking** is reportedly near impossible. Renting a **car** is convenient but costs 360-450F per day for the least expensive models, plus 2-4F per km. Weekly rentals (from 2200F) usually include unlimited free mileage. **Hiking** is the best way to explore the island's mountainous interior. The longest marked route, the **Grande Randonnée 20,** is a difficult, 160km, 15- to 21-day trail which takes hikers across the island from Calenzana (southeast of Calvi) to Conca (northeast of Porto-Vecchio). There are about 25 hostels on Corsica; most are inland and far from the major towns. Hostel cards are rarely necessary, and most set no age restrictions. Campgrounds lie close to most major cities, and many rent tents. The government ban on unofficial camping is strictly enforced.

Ajaccio, Calvi, and Bastia Ajaccio is both a picturesque beachside resort and a humming industrial center, whose claim to fame is its notorious son, Napoleon Bonaparte. The **tourist office** (tel. 95 21 40 87, 95 21 53 39), Hôtel de Ville, pl. Maréchal Foch, hands out free maps, schedules, and accommodation lists (open 8am-8pm, Sept. 16-June 14 Mon.-Sat. 9am-6pm). The **Hôtel Bonaparte,** 1-2, rue Etienne-Conti (tel. 95 21 44 19), has neat, tiny rooms with a view of the port (singles 250F, doubles 290F, triples 360F, quads 390F). **Hôtel Kallysté,** 51, cours Napoléon (tel. 95 51 34 45) offers firm beds and lots of light (singles from 200F, doubles 260F, triples 300F). *Boulangeries, pâtisseries, charcuteries,* and Corsican specialty shops congregate along rue Cardinal Fesch, flanked by pizzerias. The morning **market** on bd. Roi Jérome and in pl. César Campinchi behind the tourist office will fill your picnic basket (8am-noon).

With its well-preserved Genoan citadel and stretches of white-sand beaches, **Calvi** is an ideal place to bask in the island's sun and beauty—ideal, that is, until July and August, when tourists flood in. During the second week of June, Calvi hosts a **jazz festival** and performers often give impromptu concerts near the port. For more information, call the **tourist office**, at Port de Plaisance (tel. 95 65 16 67), which also describes excursions and hotel availability and distributes the indispensible *Guide Calvi*, which includes a map and a list of hotels (open 10am-6pm; Sept.-June Mon.-Fri. 9am-noon and 2-6pm, Sat. 9am-noon). The bustling **BVJ Corsotel,** av. de la République (tel. 95 65 14 15), has clean, airy rooms with 2-8 beds (no curfew or lockout, 120F, open late March-Oct.). Pickings are slim, as far as cheap food goes, in Calvi. Gather the elements for a picnic feast at **Super U,** av. C. Colomb, 5min. from the train station, which sells a wide array of Corsican cuisine (open Mon.-Sat. 8:30am-12:15pm and 3-7:15pm).

The sections of **Bastia** that aren't under construction look like they should be. Don't let the **tourist office** (tel. 95 31 00 89), at pl. St-Nicolas (open 8am-6pm; Oct.-April 9am-noon and 2-5pm) convince you to stay in town; if you must, try **Hôtel l'Univers,** 3, av. Maréchal Sebastiani (tel. 95 31 03 38), down the street from the train station (singles 150F, doubles 170F). Instead, ask the tourist office for the useful *Guide Pratique* to Cap Corse, containing bus schedules, accommodations, and a description of *La Route des Vins*. **Cap Corse** is a 48km peninsula north of Bastia, strung with fishing villages and quiet inlets. **Macinaggio,** 40km from Bastia, is one of the few port towns where you can find services and supplies. **Cars Micheli** (tel. 95 35 61 08) offers a tour of Cap Corse beginning in late June and running until late September for 80F. (Tours leave from 1, rue du Nouveau Port at 9am on Mon., Thurs., and Sat.) In Calvi **Autocars Mariani** (tel. 95 65 05 32) runs excursions to the Cap.

THE ALPS

After museum corridors, the Alps come as a refreshing relief. Snow-capped crests, tumbling waterfalls, and rich pastures exhilarate the weary soul, and crystal-clear air makes Paris smog seem a distant memory. **Skiing** in the Alps has always been expensive. Make arrangements 6-8 weeks in advance or, better yet, in late summer. The least crowded and cheapest months to go are January, March, and April. Most resorts close in October and November, between the hiking and skiing seasons. **FUAJ,** the French Youth Hostel Federation, offers affordable week-long winter skiing and summer sports packages. For more info, contact local FUAJ offices, youth hostels, or the central office at 27, rue Pajol, 75018 Paris (tel. (1) 46 07 00 01).

The beauty of the Alps does little good to the traveler who wants to go anywhere quickly or directly. While TGV **train** service will whisk you from Paris to Aix-les-Bains or Annecy at the gateway to the serious mountains, from there it's either slow trains, special mountain trains, or more often, torturously slow **buses. Hiking** ranges from simple strolls through mountain meadows to some of the most difficult climbing in the world, including Europe's highest mountain, Mont-Blanc. Many towns maintain chalet dorms, as well as hostels and campgrounds; in less accessible spots, the **Club Alpin Français** runs refuges. Get a list from one of their offices: 136, av. Michel-Croz, Chamonix (tel. 50 53 16 03); 38, av. du Parmelan, Annecy (tel. 50 45 52 76); 32, av. Félix Vialet, Grenoble (tel. 76 87 03 73). *Always* check with local hiking bureaus (listed in each town) before setting out on *any* hike; even in summer, you can encounter snowstorms and avalanches.

■ ■ ■ ANNECY

With winding cobblestone streets, overstuffed flower boxes, and the purest mountain lake in France, Annecy approaches a photogenic cataclysm. Hordes of vacation-

FRANCE

ers enjoy the lakeside beaches and stroll along the flower-dotted canals around the **Palais d'Isle,** a 12th-century prison rising out of a tiny island. Climb up to the **Château d'Annecy,** which doubles as a museum, for a splendid view of the old town's aquatic labyrinth. (Open 10am-noon and 2-6pm, Oct.-May Wed.-Mon. 10am-noon and 2-6pm. To museum and observatory 30F, students 10F. Museum or observatory alone 20F, students 10F. Free Wed. Sept.-May.) Penniless sun-seekers can use the free beach, the **plage des Marquisats,** while restless sailors might want rent a boat or windboard on the transparent **Lac d'Annecy.** The **Fête du Lac** enlivens the first Saturday in August with fireworks and water shows (35-250F). Take a train to Lovagny (3 per day, 10min., 10F) and then walk 800m to the **Gorges du Fier,** a canyon carved by prehistoric glaciers. (Open June-Oct. 9am-7pm, March-May 9am-noon and 2-6pm. 22F for the 40min. walk. Call 50 46 23 07 for info.)

Practical Information, Accommodations, and Food The **tourist office,** 1, rue Jaurès (tel. 50 45 00 33), at pl. de la Libération on the ground floor of the Bonlieu, dispenses a bevy of brochures on both Annecy and nearby towns (open 9am-6:30pm; Sept.-June Mon.-Sat. 9am-noon and 1:45-6:30pm, Sun. 3-6pm). Room reservations are vital, particularly during July and August. The **Auberge de Jeunesse "La Grande Jeanne" (HI),** route de Semnoz (tel. 50 45 33 19, fax 50 52 77 52), is a super-chalet in the woods but requires a 45min. uphill haul. From the tourist office, walk down quai Chappuis to the Hôtel de Ville, across from where bus 91 "Semnoz" (7F, summer only, last bus at 7pm) stops. (Reception open 5-10pm. 65F, non-members 84F. No lockout. Curfew 11pm. Sheets 16F.) **Hôtel Plaisance,** 17, rue de Narvik (tel. 50 57 30 42), caters to young internationals who favor bright, pleasant rooms in excellent condition. (Singles 120F. Doubles 135F, with shower 180F. Quad 285F. Showers 10F. Breakfast 25F.) **Hôtel Savoyard,** 41, av. de Cran (tel. 50 57 08 08), in a residential area behind the train station, is hospitable and rustic. (Singles 100F, with luxurious bathroom 180F. Doubles 100F, with shower 180F. Showers 10F. Breakfast 20F.) On the road to the HI youth hostel is the oft-mobbed **camping area,** rte. de Semnoz (tel. 50 45 48 30, fax 50 45 55 56; 20F per person, 31F per tent or car; open Dec. 15-Oct. 15). Dozens of small campgrounds border the lake in the town of **Albigny,** reachable by Voyages Crolard buses or by following av. d'Albigny from the tourist office (1.5km).

Lakeside picnics are the only real budget options; a **Prisunic supermarket** fills the better part of the pl. de Notre-Dame (open Mon.-Sat. 8:30am-12:30pm and 3-7:30pm), and **open-air markets** are held on pl. Ste-Claire (Tues., Fri. and Sun. mornings) and on bd. de Taine (Sat. mornings). Try *fondue savoyarde* (52-95F) and *raclette* (57F) at **Taverne le Freti,** 12, rue Ste-Claire (open Tues.-Sun. 7-11:30pm).

■■■ CHAMONIX

As Nice epitomizes the Riviera, Chamonix, propped between the bookend peaks of Le Brévent to the west and L'Aiguille du Midi to the east, captures the Alps. Both shrink before the majesty of nearby Mont Blanc, which at 4807m is Europe's highest peak. Even if hiking and skiing aren't your thing, don't forsake this town; numerous *téléphériques* (cable cars) will take you on breathtaking tours over the cloud-covered peaks of France and even Italy.

For *télépherique* travel, get going as early as possible—crowds and clouds gather by late morning. The simplest trip takes you to **Plan de l'Aiguille** (50F, round-trip 65F), but the **Aiguille du Midi** is much more spectacular (160F). From the Midi, you can continue to a 3rd stage, **Gare Helbronner** in Italy (170F, round-trip 240F; take your passport). Ask the tourist office for information on smaller, cheaper *téléphériques* like **Le Brévent** (68F round-trip; tel. 50 53 13 18) and **Col De Balme** (60F round-trip; tel. 50 54 00 58). Bring warm clothes and lunch, don't forget your camera, and remember that mountain weather can change rapidly. Special trains run from a small station next to the main train station to the huge **Mer de Glace** glacier (May-Sept. 8am-6pm; 42F, round-trip 56F), but you might prefer the 2hr. hike. A more rewarding hike is to **Lac Blanc,** a turquoise pool encircled by jagged peaks and Alpine flowers. To get there, walk 25min. along rue Vallot/route de Praz to the town of Les Praz, then board the *téléphérique* for La Flégère (round-trip 46F). From there it's 1½hrs. to the lake.

Practical Information, Accommodations, and Food The **tourist office,** pl. du Triangle de l'Amitié (tel. 50 53 00 24), lists hotels and dormitories and a map of campgrounds; they sell good 25F hiking maps. (Open July-Aug. and winter vacation weeks 8:30am-7:30pm; otherwise 8:30am-12:30pm and 2-7pm.) Across the street, the **Maison de la Montagne** houses the **Compagnie des Guides** (tel. 50 53 00 88) and a ski school. Upstairs in the **Office de Haute Montagne** (tel. 50 53 22 08), there's vital information on trails and mountain refuges.

Mountain chalets with dormitory accommodations combine affordability with splendid settings, but many of them close off-season (Oct.-Nov. and May). All hotels and many dormitories require reservations (preferably 6 weeks in advance) for the hectic school vacations (Dec. and Feb.). For breathtaking views and hordes of schoolchildren, try the **auberge de jeunesse (HI)** in Les Pélerins (tel. 50 53 14 52, fax 50 55 92 34). Take the bus from pl. de l'Eglise in Chamonix toward Les Houches; get off at Pélerins Ecole, and follow signs uphill. If coming by train, get off at Les Pélerins and follow the signs. (Reception open 8am-noon and 2-10pm. 70F, nonmembers 89F. Doubles 200-220F per person. Wheelchair access. Sheets 17F. Breakfast included.) From the train station, go under bridge, take a right across the tracks, a left on chemin des Cristalliers, and a right on route de la Frasse (15min.) to no. 152 to reach the sparkling new **Gîte d'Etape La Tapia** (tel. 50 53 18 19, fax 50 53 67 01), which serves regional dinners of fondue or *raclette* for 65F. (Reception open 9am-noon and 5:30-9pm. Bunk dorms 65F. Breakfast 25F.) The global village gathers at **Chalet le Chamoniard Volant,** 45, rte. de la Frasse (tel. 50 53 14 09; reception open 10am-10pm; dorms 65F, sheets 20F). The **Chalet Ski Station,** 6, rte. des Moussoux (tel. 50 53 20 25), is near the Télécabine de Planpraz, up the hill from the tourist office. (Reception open Dec. 20-May 10 and June 25-Sept. 26 9am-11pm. 50F. Showers 5F. Sheets 30F.)

Poco Loco, 45, rue du Dr. Paccard, serves 12-38F sandwiches and 32-45F pizza (open 10am-4am, Oct.-May 10am-2am). **Le Sabot,** 254, rue Paccard, serves tasty cuisine in a wooden chalet-type place. (Pasta 40, *galettes* 15-45F, salads 16-40F, *menu* 70F. Open noon-2pm and 7-10pm.) Frugal folks retreat to **Supermarché Payot Pertin,** 117, rue Joseph Vallot (open Mon.-Sat. 8:15am-7:30pm, Sun. 8:30am-12:15pm).

■■■ GRENOBLE

The historic capital of Dauphiné, Grenoble combines an active nightlife with plenty of opportunities to enjoy the mountains. Take the bubble-shaped cable car (the *téléphérique de la Bastille*) up to the **Bastille** for a jarring view of Grenoble and the landscape that inspired Shelley to ethereal free verse. Several mountain **hikes** begin here. (Open Mon. 10am-midnight, Tues.-Sun. 9am-midnight; Sept. 13-Oct. and April-June 13 Mon. 10am-7:30pm., Tues.-Sat. 9am-midnight, Sun. 9am-7:30pm; Nov.-Dec. and Feb.-March Mon. 11am-6pm, Tues.-Sun. 10am-6pm. 20F, round-trip 31F; students 11F, round-trip 16F50. Wheelchair access.) In town are several interesting museums, including the **Musée de Grenoble,** 5, pl. de Lavalette (open Wed.-Mon. 11am-10pm, Thurs.-Mon. 11am-7pm.; 25F, students 15F, Wed. free), and the disturbing **Musée de la Résistance et de la Déportation,** 14, rue Hébert (open Wed.-Mon. 9am-noon and 2-6pm, Sept.-June Wed.-Sat. 2-6pm; free).

The **tourist office,** 14, rue de la République (tel. 76 42 41 41), has excellent maps, accommodations information, and *Grenoble Magazine,* a guide to events in town (open 9am-12:30pm and 1:30-7pm, Oct.-May closes 6pm). The *Guide DAHU,* a guide to restaurants, shopping, sports, and nightlife written in a hip and witty style by Grenoble students, is available at some *tabacs* and the tourist office (20F). To reach the **auberge de jeunesse (HI),** 18, av. du Grésivaudan (tel. 76 09 33 52, fax 76

09 38 99), 4km out of town, take bus 8 "Pont Rouge" to La Quinzaine. (Reception open Mon.-Sat. 7:30am-11pm, Sun. 7:30-10:30am and 5:30-11pm. 65F, nonmembers 84F. Sheets 16F.) Peach accents prevail in the well-kept rooms of **Hôtel Beau Soleil,** 9, rue des Bons Enfants (tel. 76 46 29 40), off bd. Gambetta near pl. Victor Hugo. (Singles 100F, with shower 155F. Doubles 140F, with shower 170F. Shower 15F. Breakfast 20F.) In the center of town, **Hôtel de la Poste,** 25, rue de la Poste (tel. 76 46 67 25), has friendly management, purple petunias, and spacious rooms. (Singles 90F. Doubles 140F. Triples 180F. Quads 200F. Hearty breakfast 30F.) Wander around **rue Chenoise** for cheap North African eats, or try the regional delights at **Bleu Nuit,** 9, pl. de Metz (open Mon. 11:30am-2pm, Tues.-Sat. 11:30am-2pm and 7:30-10:30pm; closed 1st half of Aug.). The **Prisunic supermarket** sits across from the tourist office (open Mon.-Sat. 8:30am-7:15pm).

CENTRAL FRANCE

■■■ LYON

One would expect France's second-largest city to quiver in the gargantuan shadow of Paris, but Lyon has established itself as a cultural and economic alternative to, rather than subordinate of, the capital. Moreover, the city lays claim to a renowned culinary tradition; some of the greatest chefs in the world—Paul Bocuse, Georges Blanc, Jean-Paul Lacombe—call Lyon home, and even the cheapest restaurants seem always to delight the palate. Off-beat neighborhoods, a slew of museums, energetic nightlife, and reasonably priced accommodations all make for a fine destination.

ORIENTATION AND PRACTICAL INFORMATION

The Saône and the Rhône cleave Lyon into 3 parts. **Vieux Lyon** (the old city) unfolds on the west bank of the Saône. East of the Rhône spreads a quieter residential neighborhood, an extensive shopping district, and the mammoth Part-Dieu commercial center and train station. Between the rivers, the pedestrian zone runs from the Perrache train station north to pl. Carnot, up rue Victor Hugo to pl. Bellecour, and along rue de la République to pl. des Terreaux. Lyon is divided into nine *arrondissements;* the first and second sit between the Saône and the Rhône, the fifth is the *vieille ville,* and the third, sixth, and seventh lie east of the Rhône. Exercise caution at night, especially inside Perrache and at pl. des Terreaux.

Tourist Office: pl. Bellecour, 2^e (tel. 78 42 25 75). Distributes the handy *Lyon Vous Aimerez,* and the *Guide de Lyon.* Superb map. Open Mon.-Fri. 9am-7pm, Sat. 9am-6pm; mid-Sept to mid-June Mon.-Fri. 9am-6pm, Sat. 9am-5pm. **Central office** at Saint Jean, av. Adolphe Max, 5^e. Open 10am-6pm; mid-Sept. to mid-June Mon.-Fri. 9am-6pm, Sat. 10am-6pm, Sun. 10am-5pm.

Budget Travel: La Bigerie Wasteels (tel. 78 37 80 17), in the Perrache's **Galerie Marchande.** BIJ and Transalpino tickets. Open Mon.-Fri. 9am-7pm, Sat. 9am-6pm.

Currency Exchange: AOC, in the tourist offices on pl. Bellecour and Perrache. **Thomas Cook** (tel. 78 33 48 55), in the Part-Dieu train station. Open Mon.-Sat. 8am-8pm, Sun. 10am-7pm.

American Express: 6, rue Childebert (tel. 78 37 40 69), up rue de la République from pl. Bellecour. Open Mon.-Fri. 9am-noon and 2-6:15pm, Sat. 9am-noon; Oct.-April Mon.-Fri. 9am-noon and 2-6:15pm. Currency exchange closes at 5:30pm.

Post Office: pl. Antonin Poncet (tel. 72 40 65 22), next to pl. Bellecour. Open Mon.-Fri. 8am-7pm, Sat. 8am-noon. **Telephone** and telegraph services open Mon.-Sat. 8am-midnight, Sun. 8am-2pm. **Postal Code:** 69002.

Flights: Aéroport Lyon-Satolas (tel. 72 22 72 21), 25km east of Lyon. **Buses** leave from Perrache via Part-Dieu (every 20min. 6am-11pm, 45min., 50F).

Trains: Lyon has 2 train stations. TGV trains to Paris pass through both. Check the schedule posters at either station to find out about other destinations. **Perrache**

FRANCE

FRANCE

(tel. 78 92 50 50), between the Saône and Rhône rivers, is more central of the two. Mall with currency exchange. SNCF information and reservation desk open Mon.-Sat. 8am-7:30pm. **Part-Dieu** (tel. 78 92 50 50), in the business district on the east bank of the Rhône. SNCF information desk open Mon.-Sat. 8am-7:30pm, Sun. 9am-6:30pm. To Paris (most are TGV, 4½hr., 265F plus 36-90F TGV reservation), Dijon (2¼hr., 135F), Grenoble (1½hr., 95F), Strasbourg (5hr., 250F), Geneva (2hr., 115F), Marseille (3hr., 200F), and Nice (6hr., 290F).

Buses: (tel. 72 41 09 09), on the bottom floor of the Perrache train station. Open Mon.-Sat. 7:30am-6:30pm, Sept.-June Mon.-Sat. 6:30am-5pm. Service to Annecy and Grenoble.

Public Transportation: TCL (tel. 78 62 67 69). Information offices at both train stations and major metro stops. Generally open Mon.-Fri. 7:30am-6:30pm, Sat. 9am-5pm. **Metro** (M) operates 5am-midnight. Tickets (7.50F) good for 1hr. in 1 direction, bus and trolley connections included. *Ticket Liberté* (20F) for 1 day's unlimited travel (available at tourist and TAG offices, not in stations). **Trolleys** *(funiculaires)* operate until 8pm and run from pl. St-Jean to the Théâtre Romain.

Taxis: Allô Radio de Lyon (tel. 78 30 86 86). 24hrs. Around 150F to the airport.

Hitchhiking: *Let's Go* cannot recommend hitchhiking as a safe means of transportation. *Autoroute* ramps are difficult places to catch rides; taking bus 2, 5, 19, 21, 22, or 31, and standing past pont Monton at the intersection with the N6 is easier. Those heading to Grenoble usually take bus 39 as far as the rotary at bd. Pinel.

English Bookstore: Eton, 1, rue du Plat (tel. 78 92 92 36), 1 bl. toward the Saône from pl. Bellecour. Open Mon. 2-7pm, Tues.-Sat. 10am-12:30pm and 1:30-7pm.

Laundry: Salon Lavadou, on rue Ste-Hélène, near the museums. Wash 16F per 6kg. Dry 2F per 8min. Change machines. Open 7:30am-8:30pm. **Lav 123,** 123, rue Jean Jaurès. Wash 16F. Dry 2F per 5min. Soap 2F. Open 7am-8pm.

Gay and Lesbian Services: Maison de L'Homosexualité, 16, rue St. Polycarpe, 1er (tel. 78 47 10 10). Open Mon.-Fri. 6:30-8:30pm. **ACT-UP,** tel. 78 42 05 15.

Crisis Lines: CISL (tel. 78 01 23 45), an international center for visitors to Lyon. **SOS Racisme** (tel. 78 39 24 44).

Pharmacy: Pharmacie Blanchet, 5, pl. des Cordeliers (tel. 78 42 12 42), in the *centre ville* between pont Lafayette and rue de la République. M: Cordeliers. If you need something from midnight-7am, call ahead.

Medical Assistance: For non-emergencies, go to **Hôpital Hôtel-Dieu,** 1, pl. de l'Hôpital, 2e (tel. 72 41 30 00), near quai du Rhône. In a dire emergency, **SAMU,** 9, pl. Arsenal (tel. 15 or 78 33 15 15) is on the scene in 10min.

Emergencies: tel. 17. **Police,** 47, rue de la Charité (tel. 78 42 26 56).

ACCOMMODATIONS AND CAMPING

France's second financial center, Lyon fills with business folk during the week. The centrally located hotels are often packed Monday to Thursday nights but then empty over the weekend. Even if the hotels near Perrache are full, cheap rooms should be available near pl. des Terreaux. Plan ahead.

Auberge de Jeunesse (HI), 51, rue Roger Salengro, Vénissieux (tel. 78 76 39 23, fax 78 77 51 11), just outside the city limits. Take bus 35 from pl. Bellecour to George Lévy (½hr.); after 9pm, take bus 53 "St-Priest" from Perrache to Etats-Unis-Viviani and walk 500m along the abandoned train tracks (but not alone at night). From Part-Dieu, take bus 36 "Hinguettes" to Viviani Joliot-Curie (last bus at 11:15pm, but call ahead if you'll be late). Friendly modern hostel with comfort dorms, kitchen, bar, TV, laundry facilities, and international crowd. Reception open 9-11:30am and 5-11:30pm. Lockout 11:30am-5pm. 50F, non-members 69F. Sheets 16F. Laundry 30F. Breakfast 17F. Phone reservations accepted.

Résidence Benjamin Delessert, 145, av. Jean Jaurès, 7e (tel. 78 61 41 41, fax 78 61 40 24). From Perrache, take any bus that goes to J. Macé, walk under the train tracks, and look to your left after 2½bl. From Part-Dieu, take the metro to Macé. Large, plain dorm rooms, all with telephones and comfortable beds. TV room. 60F, mid-Sept. to June 95F. Showers and sheets included. Reserve a week ahead in the summer; 6 months ahead for the school year.

Centre International de Séjour, 46, rue du Commandant Pegoud, 8ᵉ (tel. 78 01 23 45, fax 78 77 96 95), near the youth hostel. From Perrache, take bus 53 "St-Priest" to Etats-Unis-Beauvisage (last bus at 11:30pm). From Part-Dieu, take bus 36 "Minquettes" (last bus 11:15pm). A hopping polyglot spot with 24hr. reception. Modern rooms with showers. Singles 120F. Doubles 180F. Triples 240F. Quads 300F. Self-service meals from 25F. Reserve well ahead; priority given to groups.

Hôtel Vaubecour, 28, rue Vaubecour, 2e (tel. 78 37 44 91, fax 78 42 90 17). M: Ampère/Victor Hugo. Cozy and cheap. Singles 90F, with shower 120F. Doubles 120F, with shower 180F. Breakfast 22F. Showers 15F.

Camping: Dardilly (tel. 78 35 64 55). From the Hôtel de Ville, take bus 19 "Ecully-Dardilly" to Parc d'Affaires. One of the most beautiful campgrounds in the Rhône Valley. Hot showers, swimming pool, grocery store, bar, and restaurant. 50F per tent and car. Open year-round.

FOOD

Lyon's galaxy of *Michelin* stars acclaims the gastronomic capital of western civilization. There are plenty of options for budget travelers. Head for a *bouchon,* descendant of the inns; today, the 20 or so remaining serve *cochonailles* (hot pork dishes), *tripes à la lyonnaise* (heavy on the onions and vinegar), and *andouillettes* (sausages made of chitterlings). Original *bouchons* congregate around pl. des Terreaux (the oldest is **Le Soleil,** 2, rue St-Georges). The most pleasant (and tourist-laden, and expensive) places in Vieux Lyon will seat you outdoors on narrow, cobblestone streets. The diverse restaurants on rue St-Jean provide affordable alternatives.

The market at **Les Halles,** 102, cours Lafayette, 3ᵉ, sells celery, *escargots,* and truffles to the great chefs, as well as to mere mortals (open Tues.-Sat. 7am-noon and 3-7pm., Sun. 7am-noon). Open **markets** are held at quai St-Antoine and on bd. de la Croix Rousse (both held Tues.-Sun. 7:30am-12:30pm). The **Carrefour Supermarché,** one of the largest in France, looms across the highway from the hostel.

Chez Mounier, 3, rue des Marroniers, 2ᵉ (tel. 78 42 88 92), on the street across from the post office. A *bouchon.* The *gnafron* (sausage in fresh cream sauce) alone justifies the visit. 60F, 80F, and 90F *menus* change daily. Open Tues. and Thurs.-Sun. noon-2pm and 7-10:30pm; Sept.-June noon-2pm and 7-10pm.

Chez Carlo, 22, rue du Palais Grillet, 2ᵉ (tel. 78 42 05 79), near Garioud. Recommended by locals for the greatest pasta and pizza (42-44F) in Lyon. Awesome *osso bucco* (60F) and a big dessert list (25-30F). Open Tues.-Sat. noon-1:30pm and 7-11pm, Sun. noon-1:30pm.

Le Pâtisson, 17, rue Port du Temple, 2ᵉ (tel. 72 81 41 71). M: Bellecour. A rarity in France: a vegetarian and non-smoking restaurant. Salads 25-34F. Medallions de tofu exotique 60F. 85F menu. Open Mon.-Fri. 11:30am-2pm and 7-9:30pm

L'Etoile de l'Orient, 31, rue des Remparts d'Ainay, 2ᵉ. M: Ampère/Victor Hugo. Cozy restaurant full of regulars; the best North African cuisine in town. Fresh *couscous* 50-100F. 120F *menu.* Open Thurs.-Tues. noon-2pm and 7-11pm.

Garioud, 14, rue du Palais-Grillet, 2ᵉ (tel. 78 37 04 71). M: Cordeliers. Great *cuisine lyonnaise* by Paul Griard, a Bocuse acolyte. 140F *menu* includes wine. Dress appropriately (no shorts). Open Mon.-Fri. noon-2pm and 7:15-10:30pm, Sat. 7:15-10:30pm. Reservations recommended.

SIGHTS

To enjoy Lyon, cultivate a taste for strolling. Start at **place Bellecour,** a barren Sahara of red gravel fringed by shops and flower stalls that encircles Louis XIV on horseback. At pl. des Terreaux, the ornate Renaissance **Hôtel de Ville** stands guard opposite the **Musée des Beaux-Arts,** in the Palais St-Pierre, whose strengths include a small but distinguished collection of French painting, works by Spanish and Dutch masters, and a wing devoted to the Italian Renaissance. (Open Wed.-Sun. 10:30am-6pm. 20F, students 15F, under 18 free. Day pass for most museums in town 30F, students 15F.) The **Musée d'Art Contemporain,** located in the same building but with an entrance at 16, rue Edouard-Herriot, displays excellent temporary exhibits of work since 1960 (open Wed.-Mon. noon-6pm; 20F, students 15F, under 18 free). A

FRANCE

few blocks north of the museums on rue Burdeau, 1er, lie the ruins of the Roman **Amphithéâtre des Trois Gaulles,** built in 19 AD and site of the martyrdom of lots of Christians in 177 AD (open dawn-dusk, free).

Lyon revels in its long-standing dominance of the European **silk** industry. At the turn of the 18th century, 28,000 looms operated in Lyon, and although silk manufacturing is based elsewhere today, an extraordinary collection of silk and embroidery ranging from the Coptic to the Oriental remains at the **Musée Historique des Tissus,** 34, rue de la Charité, 1er (open Tues.-Sun. 10am-5:30pm; 25F, students 12F, Wed. free). Weave through the **Musée Lyonnais des Arts Décoratifs,** down the street at 30, rue de la Charité, which displays furniture, porcelain, silver, and tapestries from the 17th and 18th centuries (open Tues.-Sun. 10am-noon and 2-5:30pm, free with ticket from Musée des Tissus). **La Maison des Canuts,** 10-12, rue d'Ivry, 4e demonstrates the actual weaving techniques of the *canuts lyonnais* (open Mon.-Fri. 8:30am-noon and 2-6:30pm, Sat. 9am-noon and 2-6pm; 6F).

Vieux Lyon A brief walk across the Saône leads to the most intriguing part of town, Vieux Lyon. The *bourguignon* **Cathédrale St-Jean's** northern transept holds a 14th-century astronomical clock that shows the feast days from 600 years ago all the way through 2000. (Open Mon.-Fri. 7:30am-noon and 2-7:30pm, Sat.-Sun. 2-5pm. Free 15min. tours June 20-Aug. 15 at 10-11:30am and 2-5:30pm.) Gaze over Lyon's urban sprawl from the **Fourvière Esplanade,** high above the old city. The most scenic route follows rue de la Bombarde to rue du Boeuf. Take the montée des Chazeaux staircase and turn left on montée St-Barthélémy. On the right lie the **Jardins du Rosaire,** from which a beautiful uphill path climbs to the extravagant 19th-century **Basilique Notre-Dame de Fourvière** (open 8am-noon and 2-6pm). This hillside was the site where Julius Caesar founded Lugdunum—the commercial and military center of Gaul—in 43 BC. Lyon's funkiest museum, the **Musée Gallo-Romain,** 17, rue Cléberg, 5e, on the Fourvière hill, displays an impressive array of mosaics, swords, rings, statues, and money from Lyon's Roman past in serpentine concrete halls. A hip, young staff guides you through it all. (Open Wed.-Sun. 9:30am-noon and 2-6pm. 20F, students 10F, under 18 free.)

The **Centre d'Histoire de la Résistance et de la Déportation,** 14, av. Bertholet, 7e, has assembled documents and photos of the resistance to the Nazis, which was centered in Lyon (open Wed.-Sun. 9am-5:30pm; 20F, students 10F). Film and photography buffs will want to see the **Institut Lumière,** 25, rue du Premier-Film, 8e, a museum which examines the lives of the brothers who invented the first film projector (open Tues.-Sun. 2-7pm, 25F).

ENTERTAINMENT

To find out what's up in Lyon, pick up a copy of the weekly *Lyon Poche* (9F) at a newsstand. July 1 kicks off the **Festival du Jazz à Vienne,** a two-week celebration that welcomes international jazz celebrities to **Vienne,** just outside Lyon, accessible by bus or train. For info, call 74 85 00 05 or the Vienne **tourist office** (tel. 74 85 12 62) on 11, quai Reonded. Lyon is a terrific place to see silver screen classics. The **Cinéma Opéra,** 6, rue J. Serlin (tel. 78 28 80 08), and **Le Cinéma,** 18, impasse St-Polycarpe (tel. 78 39 09 72), specialize in black-and-whites, all in the original language (30-40F). Avant-garde flicks and more classics roll at the **CNP Terreaux Cinéma,** 40, rue Président Edouard Herriot (37F).

Lyon may well have more pubs per capita than any other French city. Students kill the night at the so-called *"pub anglais,"* **Albion,** 12, rue Ste-Cathérine, 1er (open Mon.-Sat. 5pm-2am, Sun. 5pm-1am). For a wide variety of music (rock, blues, Brazilian, African) in a refined atmosphere, try **Mozart,** 53, rue Mercière, 2e. (Open Mon.-Sat. 10:30pm-dawn; concerts in summer. Cover 25-75F. No jeans or sneakers.)

BURGUNDY (BOURGOGNE)

Burgundy's best ambassadors to the world are its annual 40 million bottles of wine, which graciously represent a grand, sparse landscape splashed with vineyards and peppered by monasteries, cathedrals, and châteaux. Burgundy was an ecclesiastical center in medieval times, and the religious orders that constructed the monumental abbeys at Tournus, Cluny, and Vézelay also planted the green vineyards that now carpet the hills.

■■■ DIJON

Synonymous with the spicy, wine-based mustards it produces, Dijon survives not on Grey Poupon alone. An important industrial center and home to a respected university, Burgundy's animated capital stands at the tip of one of the Côte d'Or wine region. A colorful and tastefully restored *vieille ville,* myriad churches, museums, festivals, and lively sidewalk cafés keep this ancient city fresh.

Dijon's greatest attraction is the **Musée des Beaux-Arts,** occupying a wing of the splendid **Palais des Ducs de Bourgogne.** Its most famous gallery is the **Salle des Gardes,** dominated by the huge sarcophagi of Philippe le Hardi and Jean sans Peur. (Open Mon. and Wed.-Sat. 10am-6pm, Sun. 10am-12:30pm and 2-6pm. 15F. Students, under 18, and Sun. free. A 17F card, available at the Musée des Beaux-Arts, admits you to all of Dijon's museums.) Its façade a morass of gargoyles, the 13th-century **Eglise de Notre-Dame** exemplifies Burgundian Gothic, while the **Eglise St-Michel** is crosses from Gothic to the Renaissance. The elegant 93m apse and spire of the **Cathédrale St-Bénigne,** on pl. St-Bénigne, recall the 2nd-century missionary priest whose martyred remains were exhumed near Dijon in the 6th century. Next door, the **Musée Archéologique,** 5, rue Docteur Maret, unearths the history of the Côte d'Or (open Wed.-Mon. 9:30am-6pm, Oct.-May Wed.-Sun. 9am-noon and 2-6pm. 11F, students 5F50.) And no trip to Dijon is complete without a stop at the **Grey Poupon** store, 32, rue de la Liberté, where they've been making *moutarde au vin* since 1777 (jars cost half as much in any supermarket).

In June, Dijon's **Eté Musical** stages many of the world's best symphony orchestras and chamber groups. From mid-June to mid-August, **Estivade** (call 80 30 31 00 for info) brings dance, music, and theater to the streets. Dijon devotes a week in the first half of September to the **Fête de la Vigne** (call 80 30 37 95 for info), a well-attended celebration of the grape with various folklore ensembles. For information on all things artistic and cultural in Dijon, pick up the thorough, bi-monthly *Spectacles à Dijon* and *Dijon Nuit et Jour,* free at the tourist office. Students flock to the **Club International d'Etudiants,** 7, rue Audra, a combination bar, pool hall, nightclub, and *discothèque* (open 3pm-3am).

Practical Information, Accommodations, and Food The **tourist office,** pl. Darcy (tel. 80 43 42 12), a 5min. walk down av. Maréchal Foch from the train station, has a 15F accommodations service (open 9am-9pm; mid-Oct. to April 9am-1pm and 2-7pm). The **Foyer International d'Etudiants,** 6, rue Maréchal Leclerc (tel. 80 71 51 01, fax 80 71 60 48), has TV rooms, laundry, a kitchen, and a cafeteria. Take bus 4 "St-Apollinaire" to Parc des Sports. (Good singles 65F.) Join screaming school groups at the **auberge de jeunesse (HI),** 1, bd. Champollion (tel. 80 72 95 20, fax 80 70 00 61), a concrete mega-hostel with laundry, bar, and self-service dinner. Take bus 5 "Epirey" from pl. Grangier. (Dorms 65F. Singles 150F. Doubles 185F.) Hotels in the center fill quickly in summer. Find spotless rooms with air-conditioning at **Hôtel Montchapet,** 26-28, rue Jacques Cellerier (tel. 80 55 33 31), north of av. Première Armée Française off pl. Darcy. (Singles 130-175F. Doubles 160-210F. Triples 260F. Quads 340F.) **Hôtel du Théâtre,** 3, rue des Bons Enfants (tel. 80 67 15 41), is no luxury resort, but what a location (off pl. de la Libération), what a price (singles and doubles 90F, with shower 100F)! Take bus 12 to Chartreux to arrive at

FRANCE

Camping Municipal du Lac (tel. 80 43 54 72), at bd. Kir and av. Albert 1er, on a pretty lake (9F per person, 4F per tent. Open April-Nov. 15).

The most elegant way to sample Burgundy's fabulous wines is with a gourmet meal. **Au Bec Fin,** 47, rue Jeannin, has an outstanding 55F *menu* at lunch and 76F and 85F *menus* at dinner (open Mon.-Fri. noon-1:30pm and 7:15-10:30pm, Sat. 7:30-10:30pm). Otherwise, pick up vital victuals in the well-stocked **Prisunic supermarket** at 11, rue Piron, off pl. J. Mace (open Mon.-Sat. 9am-7:15pm).

■ BEAUNE AND CÔTE D'OR

The well-touristed town of **Beaune,** half an hour south of Dijon on the Lyon rail line (35F), has disgorged wine for centuries. Surrounded by the famous **Côte de Beaune** vineyards, the town itself is packed with wineries offering free *dégustations.* Visit the **Marché aux Vins,** near the Hôtel-Dieu. For 40F (imitation-silver tasting spoons 10F), you can sample 37 of Burgundy's finest wines, the best of which come last, so don't get too rocked on the early labels. (Open 9:30-11:30am and 2:30-6:30pm; Nov.-March 9:30am-noon and 2:30-4:30pm.) The **Hôtel-Dieu,** built in the 15th century as a hospital for the poor, is a landmark of Burgundian architecture with colorful roof tiles (open 9am-6:30pm, Nov. 22-March 23 9-11:30am and 2-5:30pm; 27F, students 21F). The **tourist office,** rue de l'Hôtel-Dieu (tel. 80 22 24 51), lists *caves* in the region offering tours (open Sun.-Thurs. 9am-8pm, Fri.-Sat. 9am-9pm; March-May and Oct.-Nov. 9am-10pm; Dec.-Feb. 9am-7:15pm). The 60km **Côte d'Or,** dubbed the "golden hillside," has produced some of the world's greatest wines. The fascinating **Château du Clos de Vougeot,** 16km south of Dijon, is home to the Confrérie des Chevaliers du Tastevin, a fraternity founded in 1934 to defend the honor of Burgundian wines. At the ritualized initiation rites (based on those described in the works of Molière and Rabelais), over 500 guests in black tie sing, toast, and poke fun at each other. (Open Sun.-Fri. 9am-6:30pm, Sat. 9am-5pm; Oct.-March Sun.-Fri. 9-11:30am and 2-5:30pm, Sat. 9-11:30am and 2-5pm. 15F.)

ALSACE-LORRAINE

■■■ STRASBOURG

Sophisticated and elegant, Strasbourg impressed both Goethe and Rousseau. Seat of several European Union agencies including the European Parliament, the city today symbolizes international cooperation, yet retains a distinctive local flavor with its half-timbered houses, covered bridges, and flower-lined canals. Start a tour at the **cathedral,** whose airy spire soars 142m above the historic center. While you wait for the tuneful tinkle of the **Horloge Astronomique** (astrological clock) at 12:30pm, take a gander at the **Pilier des Anges** (Angels' Pillar), a masterpiece of Gothic sculpture; both are in the south transept. (10F, students 7F to see the tiny apostles parade around and the rooster crow. Tower open 9am-6:30pm.) **Maison de l'Oeuvre Notre-Dame,** opposite the cathedral, is more interesting for its architecture than for its collection of sculpture, stained glass, and other period artifacts. The **Musée d'Art Moderne,** also across from the cathedral, has an excellent collection of Modernist and Impressionist sculpture and painting. Artists include Gaugin, Picasso, Tzara, Klimt, Chagall, Klee, Rodin, and Arp (a *strasbourgeois*). The palatial **Château des Rohan,** 2, pl. du Château, houses a trio of small, noteworthy museums: the **Musée des Beaux-Arts,** the **Musée des Arts Décoratifs,** and the **Musée Archéologique.** (All museums open Mon.-Sat. 10am-noon and 1:30-6pm, Sun. 10am-5pm. 15F, students 8F. In the Château, 2 museums 22F, students 10F.)

Practical Information, Accommodations, and Food Strasbourg is a major European rail junction; **trains** go to Paris (4hr., 254F), Luxembourg (2hr.,

143F), Frankfurt (3hr., 195F), and Zürich (2½hr., 213F). **Tourist offices** across from the station and next to the cathedral dispense the monthly booklet *Strasbourg actualités* (open Mon.-Sat. 8:30am-7pm, Sun. 9am-6pm; Oct.-May 9am-6pm.) **CROUS youth center,** 1, quai du Maire-Dietrich (tel. 88 21 28 00), can set you up in a **dorm** for 55F per night if you have student ID (July-Aug. only; call a week in advance) and sells **meal** vouchers (19F) Mon. 9am-noon and Tues.-Fri. 11:30am-1pm (open Mon.-Fri. 9-11:30am and 1:30-6pm).

Everyone stays the night here, so make reservations, call ahead, or arrive early. The **Auberge de Jeunesse René Cassin (HI),** 9, rue de l'Auberge de Jeunesse (tel. 88 30 26 46, fax 88 30 35 16), 2km from the station, has a friendly and fun young staff, and a bar open until 1am. Take bus 3 or 23 (7F, every ½hr.) from rue du Vieux-Marché-aux-Vins. (Reception open 7-11:30am and 2pm-midnight. Curfew 1am. No lockout. Members only. 6-bed dorms 65F. Doubles, triples, and quads 95F per person. Singles 145F. Sheets 17F. Camping 40F per person. Breakfast included.) The sparkling **CIARUS (Centre International d'Accueil de Strasbourg),** 7, rue Finkmatt (tel. 88 32 12 12, fax 88 23 17 37), flags terrific rooms just 15min. from the train station. Take rue du Maire-Kuss to the canal, turn left, then make a left onto rue Finkmatt. (Curfew 1am. No lockout. 4- to 12-bunk dorms 75-100F. Singles 175F. Breakfast included. Free luggage storage. Wheelchair-accessible.) In a 16th-century house, **Hôtel Patricia,** 1a, rue du Puits (tel. 88 32 14 60, fax 88 32 19 08), in the *vieille ville* behind Eglise St-Thomas, gloats over a perfect location. (Reception closes 8pm. Singles from 120F. Doubles from 180F. Room with shower 70F more.)

Strasbourgeois restaurants are known for delicious *choucroute garnie,* spiced sauerkraut served with meat. You can't miss the triple-decker **Au Pont St-Martin,** at 13-15, rue des Moulins. Sit overlooking the canal locks and savor huge servings of seafood, salads, and *choucroute.* (Mon.-Fri. 3-course 54F lunch *menu.* Open noon-2pm and 7-11pm, no Sat. lunch.) **Pizzeria Aldo,** 8, rue du Faisan, is a wildly popular joint where you design your own 42F pizza or salad (open noon-2pm and 6:30pm-1:30am).

■■■ COLMAR AND METZ

Ringed by vineyards and overshadowed by the craggy Vosges Mountains, **Colmar** slices Alsatian life authentically, but the word is out, and the streets are flooded with tourists. The restored tanners' lodgings and **La Petite Venise** area preserve the feeling of a medieval town. Carved wooden doors and a rainbow of muted colors accentuate the houses that line the canals, and geraniums hang from the window boxes above cobblestone streets. Don't miss the extraordinary **Musée Unterlinden,** on pl. Unterlinden, a former Dominican convent housing medieval religious art, including Mathias Grünewald's gruesome polyptch, *Isenheim Altarpiece* (open 9am-6pm, Nov.-March Wed.-Mon. 9am-noon and 2-5pm; 28F, students 18F). The annual **Alsatian Wine Festival,** held in early August, spouts wine, beer, and agricultural equipment for all. Colmar is 30min. south of Strasbourg by frequent **train** (55F). A 10min. walk from the station, the **Maison des Jeunes (Centre Internationale de Séjour),** 17, rue Camille Schlumberger (tel. 89 41 26 87), is the best deal in town. (Registration Mon.-Sat. 7am-noon and 2-11pm, Sun. 8am-noon and 5-11pm. Curfew 11pm. 40F. Call ahead.)

In the neighboring region of Lorraine, the public buildings of **Metz** are constructed of a regional stone, *pierre de jaumont,* which lends the city its warm mustard overtone. The 6500 square meters of sensational stained-glass windows, including several by Chagall, have earned the **Cathédrale St-Etienne** the moniker "Lantern to God." (Info office open Mon.-Sat. 9am-7pm, Sun. noon-7pm; Oct.-April Mon.-Sat. 9am-noon and 2-5:30pm, Sun. 2-5:30pm.) Nearby, the fascinating **Musée d'Art et d'Histoire,** 2, rue du Haut-Poirier, built over ruins of Roman baths, reconstructs medieval and Renaissance home interiors. (Open 10am-noon and 2-6pm. 20F, students 15F. Wed. and Sun. mornings free.) **Trains** run to Paris (3hr., 200F), Strasbourg (1½hr., 105F), and Lyon (5hr., 270F). The **tourist office,** pl. d'Armes (tel.

87 75 65 21) issues a confusing map; try the free map of the local bus system. (Open Mon.-Sat. 9am-9pm, Sun. 10am-1pm and 2-5pm; Sept.-Oct. and April-June Mon.-Sat. 9am-7pm, Sun. 10am-1pm and 3-7pm; Nov.-March Mon.-Sat. 9am-7pm, Sun. 10am-1pm.) The fantastic **auberge de jeunesse (HI)**, 1, allée de Metz Plage (tel. 87 30 44 02, fax 87 33 19 80), is on the river across town from the station. Hop bus 3 "Metz-Nord" or 11 "St-Eloy" (last bus 8:50pm) from the station to Pontiffroy. (Reception open 7-10am and 5-10pm. Lockout 10am-5pm. No curfew. 60F per person in dorms, 70F in single or double. Sheets (required) 17F. Laundry service 35F.) Surprisingly reasonable restaurants gather on prime people-watching turf on rue des Clercs, including the *crêperie* **St-Malo**, 14, rue des Clercs (tel. 87 74 56 85), which serves *galettes* crammed with ham and *gruyère*, salads, and crêpes smothered with ice cream. (Open Mon.-Sat. 11:45am-11pm).

CHAMPAGNE

Champagne, the region between Lorraine and Paris, is under French law the only source of real champagne, which must be aged according to the rigorous *méthode champenoise*. The best way to see and taste the results is to visit the underground *caves* of Reims and Epernay, both a little over an hour from Paris's Gare de l'Est, where prestigious champagne houses carefully guard their precious troves.

■■■ REIMS

Pounded to rubble during WWI, Reims has been tenaciously reconstructed; the modern city gracefully combines contemporary structures (such as funky egg-shaped fountains) with a restored fleet of Gothic and Roman buildings. The **Cathédrale de Notre-Dame,** ornamented with dreamlike Chagall windows, was built with blocks of golden limestone quarried beginning in 1211. From Clovis to Charles X, 25 kings of France were crowned beneath its vaulted roof. (Open Mon.-Sat. 7:30am-7:30pm, Sun. 8:30am-7:30pm.) The **Palais du Tau** next door, once the archbishop's palace, houses medieval sculptures and cathedral treasures including Charlemagne's 9th-century talisman and the 12th-century chalice from which 20 kings received communion. (Open 9:30am-6:30pm; March 16-June and Sept.-Nov. 14 9:30am-12:30pm and 2-6pm; Nov. 15-March 15 Mon.-Fri. 10am-noon and 2-5pm, Sat.-Sun. 10am-noon and 2-6pm. 26F, students and seniors 17F.) To the east lies the **Basilique St-Remi,** reputed resting place of France's earliest kings. The graceful **Musée des Beaux-Arts,** 8, rue Chazny, built in the 18th century as an abbey, has a fine Corot collection and some Impressionist works (open Wed.-Mon. 10am-noon and 2-6pm; 10F, students free). For a look at the simple schoolroom where the Germans surrendered to the Allies on May 8, 1945, head over to the **Salle de Reddition.** It shows maps, period newspapers, photos, and an excellent film. (Open Wed.-Mon. 10am-noon and 2-6pm. 10F, students free.) Snag a brochure with maps and hours of Reims's underground city of **champagne caves** from the tourist office. Most offer free tours in French and English. The most engaging *caves* (and perhaps the best wines) belong to **Pommery,** 5, pl. du Général Gouraud (tel. 26 61 62 55). Set in a magnificent group of 19th-century English-style buildings, its free tours live up to the elegant expectations generated by the exterior (by appointment 10am-5:30pm). Beware when touring *caves* that tasting usually obliges you to buy. For more reasonably priced champagne, look for the occasional sales on local brands at shops around the cathedral—check first at a supermarket. A good bottle can usually be had for about 70F.

Throughout July and August, Reims hosts the fantastic **Flâneries Musicales d'Eté,** with almost-daily classical concerts, all of which are free. For more free fun, head to the cathedral every Saturday night in July and August for **Cathédrale de Lumière,** an impressive 1hr. spectacle illuminating the cathedral and nearby buildings and culminating in a light show on the cathedral façade. (For information call 26 47 30 40.) The trendy set sips *espresso* at **Café Gaulois,** on the corner of rue Condoret and pl. d'Erlon, examining the laminated hairdos of punkers and poodles alike as they saunter past (open 8am-1am).

Practical Information, Accommodations and Food The **tourist office,** 2, rue Guillaume de Machault (tel. 26 47 25 69), is in the ruins of the old char-terhouse (open Mon.-Sat. 9am-8pm, Sun. 9:30am-7pm; Easter-June and Sept. closes ½hr earlier; Oct.-Easter closes 1½hr earlier.) They have info on Reims's numerous *foyers,* which start at about 60F and may accept travelers for 1 or 2 nights. **Au Bon Accueil,** 31, rue Thillois (tel. 26 88 55 74), right off pl. d'Erlon, has large, bright rooms with comfy beds—if you make it up the amusingly perilous staircase. (Singles from 70F. Doubles from 80F.) The **Centre International de Séjour (HI),** 1, chaussée Bocquaine (tel. 26 40 52 60), next to La Comédie-Espace André Malraux, is a 15min. walk from the station. Continue straight through the park (1 block) then turn right onto bd. Général Leclerc. Follow it to the canal and cross the first bridge (pont de Vesle). Chaussée Bocquaine is your first left. The place is as close to heaven as a hos-tel gets, and just as hard to get into. (Reception open 7am-11pm. Curfew 11pm. Singles 78F. Doubles 63F.) Only a 10min. walk from the centre ville, **Hôtel Linguet,** 14, rue Linguet (tel. 26 47 31 89), has singles from 85F, doubles from 110F, and 240F quints.) Fast-food joints, cafés, and bars abound on pl. Drouet-Erlon. **Monoprix supermarket** is a sure crowd-pleaser, housed in a graceful 19th-century building on the corner of rue de Vesle and rue de Talleyrand, one block from the cathedral (open Mon.-Sat. 8:30am-8pm). **Les Brisants,** 13, rue de Chativesle, is right off pl. d'Erlon; sit in the pastel dining room or bask in the courtyard. (75F and 125F *menus.* Open Mon.-Sat. noon-2pm and 7pm-midnight, Sun. 7-11pm. Reservations recommended on weekends.)

■ EPERNAY

There are no cathedrals in Epernay, but the golden *caves* under av. de Champagne inspire worship of a different sort. The best known is **Moët et Chandon,** 20, av. de Champagne, home of James Bond's preferred vintage, *Dom Perignon.* For informa-tion on Epernay's bubbly makers and about lodging (25F), consult the **tourist office,** 7, av. de Champagne (tel. 26 55 33 00; open Mon.-Sat. 9:30am-12:30pm and 1:30-7pm, Sun. and holidays 11am-4pm; mid-Oct. to mid-April Mon.-Sat. 9:30am-12:30pm and 1:30-5:30pm). Epernay is not the place for the budget traveler to stay; instead, rest your bones in Reims, only 20min. and 30F away.

Germany (Deutschland)

US$1 = DM1.56 (Deutschmarks)	DM1 = US$0.64
CDN$1 = DM1.16	DM1 = CDN$0.86
UK£1 = DM2.48	DM1 = UK£0.40
IR£1 = DM2.45	DM1 = IR£ 0.41
AUS$1 = DM1.20	DM1 = AUS$0.84
NZ$1 = DM0.95	DM1 = NZ$1.06
SAR1 = DM0.48	DM1 = SAR2.29
<u>Country Code: 49</u>	<u>International Dialing Prefix: 00</u>

It seems somehow appropriate that as the world reinvents itself, Germany once again stands at the center of it all. Despite its history of reactionary governments, Germany has always been a wellspring of revolutionaries—for better and for worse. One of the greatest heroes of German history, Karl der Große (Charlemagne), was the first to unify post-Roman Europe under enlightened rule. An obscure German monk, Martin Luther, stands as one of the most influential figures in Western history for the revolutionary forces unleashed when he triggered the Protestant reformation. Lessing, Bach, and Beethoven turned the worlds of drama and music upside-down. Socialist pioneers Karl Marx and Friedrich Engels equipped the revolutionary ground swell of 19th-century Europe with an ideology and a goal whose power has only been blunted and redirected, never defused. Adolf Hitler, the most loathsome figure in Western history, organized in this country the capacity to perform deeds—the seizure of power, the conquest of Europe, the Holocaust—that simply defy explanation. This last image, of course, indelibly colors all subsequent German history. Germans must grapple with the wrenching fact that the cradle of Goethe and Beethoven also nurtured Dachau and Buchenwald. As the only country to collectively acknowledge the moral bankruptcy of its nationalism, Germany brings a unique perspective—and a unique motivation—to the revolutionary transformation of Europe into a democratic super-state. Although eternally burdened with the crimes of the Third Reich, Germany is also blessed with a cultural tradition without compare. No major European artistic movement of the last 500 years is entirely without debt to Germans, and quite a few would be unthinkable without German influence.

While the historical truths underlying popular stereotypes do provide some insight into what it means to be German, the nation that has finally emerged from the horrors of World War II and the surreal bipolarism of the Cold War is decidedly non-stereotypical. There are, to be sure, certain "German" characteristics—industriousness, efficiency, and a mystifying refusal to cross the street against the light, even in the absence of traffic—but the broad social and political range that comprises the nation defies easy categorization.

Although now a unified country, the differences between east and west have not been eliminated by the shoddy and opportunistic annexing of the former GDR by the capitalist Federal Republic. The world is continually stunned by reports of racist attacks on immigrants and foreigners in the country and the inability (or unwillingness) of the right-wing government to establish a basis for multicultural society. Across the political spectrum, some wish the wall had never come down.

It's worth remembering all of this as you pass through the country—that the legacy represented by the wealth of artistic, historical, and cultural treasures that Germany has managed to accumulate throughout centuries of war and division defines a healthy chunk of Western civilzation's collective past, but may conceal more than just of a glimpse into the future.

For more comprehensive and stimulating coverage of the region, treat yourself to *Let's Go: Germany.*

GETTING THERE AND GETTING AROUND
German Train Systems and Rail Passes While integrating the western **Deutsche Bundesbahn (DB)** and old eastern **Reichsbahn (DR)**, Germany is also on planning to privatize its federal rail system as the new unified **Deutsche Bahn.** Signs of this process may already be visible, but "*Ein Land, zwei Bahnen,*" (one country, two railroads) remains the motto to travel by. Moving from west to east, there is significant variance in quality and service. The DB network is one of Europe's finest (and most expensive) systems, averaging over 120km per hour with stops. The **Reichsbahn** is improving, but still lags behind. Commuter trains, marked "City-Bahn" (CB), "S-Bahn", or, "Nahverkehrszug" (N), are very slow; "D" and "E" (Eilzug) trains are slightly faster and "FD" trains faster still. "Interregio" (IR) trains, speed comfortably between neighboring cities while "IC" (inter-city) trains approach the luxury and speed of airplanes. However, unless you have a full-fare railpass, you

must purchase a supplementary "IC Zuschlag" to ride an IC or EC train (DM6 when bought in the station, DM8 on the train). For a price, the super-sleek InterCity Express (ICE) zips from Hamburg to Munich in six hours flat, surpassing even these quickies.

If you decide to purchase a **railpass,** there are a few that can be purchased only in Germany. For anyone under age 23 and for students under age 27, the best deal going is the **tramper-Monats** ticket, good for one month of unlimited 2nd-class travel on all DB trains (except the ICE), railroad-run buses (*Bahnbusse*), and the local S-Bahn (DM300; combined DB/DR ticket DM350; with ICE DM465). Bring proof of age and a student ID. The **Bahncard,** available to travelers ages 18-22 and students under 27 (DM110), is valid for one year and gets you a 50% discount on all rail tickets, DB and DR alike. It offers the same deal for everyone between 12 and 17 (DM50), and anyone over age 60 (DM110). Passes are only available at major train stations, and all require a small photo.

Eurail, Buses, Flights, Bikes, and Cars   Eurail holders are entitled to free passage on the **S-Bahn** (commuter rail) and **DB bus lines** (marked *Bahn*). Regional bus systems of the west tend to be quite helpful, while private long-distance bus travel is less reliable. Domestic air travel is quite expensive, and the few student discounts levy severe restrictions that exclude most non-native Germans.

Bikes are sight-seeing power tools; Germany makes it easy with its wealth of trails and bike tours. Cities and towns usually have designated bike lanes. German rail's **Fahrrad am Bahnhof** ("bikes at the station") program offers cycle rentals throughout the country (DM6-10 per day). Inter-station rental and return makes bike travel easy and efficient. For information about bike routes, regulations and maps, contact **Allgemeiner Deutscher Fahrrad-Club,** Postfach 10 77 47, 28077 Bremen. A bike tour guidebook, including extensive maps, is available from **Deutsches Jugendher-bergswerk (DJH)** (see address in Accommodations).

It is permitted and quite common to **hitch** on the German *Autobahnen* (expressways), but hitchers may stand only at **Raststätten** (rest stops), **Tankstellen** (gas stations), and in front of the *Autobahn* signs at on-ramps.

Mitfahrzentralen offices in many cities pair drivers and riders. For a fee of DM10-25, the MFZ will give you the telephone number of the driver, whom you can then call to make arrangements and set a price (usually determined by splitting gas costs). Check in the white and yellow pages (*Gelbe Seiten*) under "Mitfahrzentrale."

Urban **public transit** is excellent in the west and middling in the east. You'll see four types: the **Straßenbahn** (streetcar), **S-Bahn** (commuter rail), **U-Bahn** (subway), and regular **buses.** Consider purchasing a day card (*Tagesnetzkarte*) or multiple-ride ticket (*Mehrfahrkarte*); they usually pay for themselves by the 3rd ride.

GERMANY ESSENTIALS

In certain regions, tourists of color or members of certain religious groups may feel threatened by local residents. Neo-Nazi skinheads in the large cities of former East Germany, as well as in Western Germany, have been known to attack foreigners, especially travelers of color. Furthermore, either historical or newly-developed discrimination against established minority residents may be directed towards travelers who are members of those minority groups. In any situation, however, common sense will serve better than paranoia.

Every city in western Germany has a **tourist office,** usually located near the main train station (*Hauptbahnhof*) or central market square (*Marktplatz*) and marked with signs reading "*Verkehrsamt*" or "*Verkehrsverein*"; they provide city maps and book rooms (usually for a small fee).

Currency exchange (*Wechsel*) can be found in all large train stations and virtually all banks. (Open Mon.-Fri. 9am-noon and 2-4pm.) The best rates are often at post offices (in major cities usually open Sat.-Sun.), which will cash American Express checks for DM3 per check. **Credit card** acceptance is markedly less common in Germany than in the U.S. or U.K.; locals tend to carry large wads of hard cash in their wallets.

Shops are generally open weekdays from 8:30am to 6pm, and Saturday from 8:30am to 1pm. In some smaller towns, stores close from noon to 3pm for *Mittagspause*. In larger cities, stores stay open until 6pm on the first Saturday of each month *(langer Samstag)*. Germany celebrates the following public holidays: Jan. 1, Good Friday (April 14, 1995), Easter Monday (April 17, 1995), May 1, Ascension Day (May 25, 1995), Whit Monday (Jun 5, 1995), Oct. 3 and Dec. 25-26.

Communication English **language** ability is common in the west, but far less so in the east. In all cases, introduce yourself with a polite, universally applicable *bitte* ("please," "excuse me," "thanks," "help"), the even politer *bitte schön* or the definitive *Entschuldigung* ("excuse me," "sorry I bumped into you," or "help me *now*"). The letter *ß* is equivalent to a double *s*.

In the west, most **post offices** are open Monday through Friday from 8am to 6pm, Saturday from 8am to noon; all accept **Poste Restante,** known as *Postlagernde Briefe*. In **phone** booths, a local call costs 30 pfennigs. Deposit coins first, even for toll-free calls. Change will not be returned, but if you hang up then quickly pick up the receiver again, you can make another call. The *Kartentelefon* accepts cards sold at the post office in DM12 and DM50 denominations; it saves loose change and time in line, and is displacing coin-ops in many cities. Only phones marked "international" can be used for international calls. The old national information number, 11 88, has been replaced by 011 88. For information within the EU, call 00 11 88. For international collect calls, go to the post office; for AT&T's **USA Direct,** dial 01 30 00 10. AT&T recently issued new cards for European service. Old cards may no longer work; call AT&T before you go to make sure. The MCI **WorldPhone** number is 01 30 00 12; for **SprintExpress** call 01 30 00 13; for **Canada Direct** 01 30 00 14; for **BT Direct** 01 30 80 00 44; for **SA Direct** 01 30 80 00 27. Keep these phone numbers in mind: **police** (tel. 110) and **fire or medical emergency** (tel. 112).

Accommodations and Camping A German schoolteacher founded the world's first youth hostel in 1909, and there are now more than 750 *(Jugendherberge)* throughout eastern and western Germany. Beds normally cost DM13-19 for "juniors" (under 27) and 2 or 3 Marks more for "seniors" (27 and up). Bavarian hostels accept *only* juniors; elsewhere, they are given priority (until 7pm). Curfews are normally between 9:45pm and 11pm, and a small breakfast is almost always included. Sheetless guests must rent bed linen (DM3.50-5); foam- or down-filled sleeping bags are usually unacceptable. All hostels are required to hold extra beds for unannounced individual travelers, although these can fill quickly. In some western cities, the new-generation **Jugendgästehaus** is displacing the hostel; with higher prices (from DM21.50, sheets included) and later curfews, these cater more to young adults than schoolchildren. **DJH** publishes a guidebook (DM6) that details all federated German hostels; it is available at all German bookstores and many newsstands, or write DJH-Hauptverband, Bismarkstr. 8, Postfach 1455, 32704 Detmold, Germany.

Campgrounds are common and usually cost only DM4-7 per person, DM3-4 per tent; ask at the local tourist office for the most convenient sites. Freelance camping is now illegal for environmental reasons.

Food and Drink Though German cuisine is generally fatty and ponderous, it is far from taste bud torture. *Deutsche* delights often include *Schnitzel* (a lightly fried veal cutlet), *Spätzle* (a southern noodle), or almost any seafaring creature. However, pork and potatoes are the more steady staples of the family table. Most notable is Germany's broad palette of breads and cheeses that puts the baguette to shame. The fresh rolls (*Brötchen* or *Semmeln*) sold in any bakery will satisfy even the most discriminating of dough *dilettantes*.

German breakfasts *(Frühstück)* are simple, consisting of coffee and buttered rolls with cheese or salami and an occasional hard-boiled egg. The main meal, *Mittagsessen,* is served at noon. Around 4pm, you will probably notice Germans with sweet tooths and coffee addictions heading to the *Konditorei* for *Kaffee und Kuchen* (coffee and cake). The evening meal, *Abendbrot* or *Abendessen,* is traditionally a reprise of breakfast—bread, cheese, and cold cuts.

In restaurants, you order from the *Tageskarte* (daily menu). All restaurant prices include tax and service *(Mehrwertsteuer und Bedienung)*; if you wish to tip, round the bill up to the nearest Mark or two. For inexpensive food, look into a department-store cafeteria or *Mensa* (dining halls located at most universities). Most *Mensas* are supposed to admit only their own students, but you'd never guess it. Stop at an *Imbiß* (they pepper the pedestrian zones) for anything fast.

In good weather, Stein-hoisters flock to the ubiquitous open-air *Biergarten. Ein Helles* is a standard light-colored beer; *Dunkles* is darker and sweeter. *Weißbier* or *Weizenbier* is a delicious, smooth, rich wheat beer. *Pilsner* or *Pils* gets its clear complexion and bitter taste from the addition of extra hops. *Radler* is a tasty, thirst-quenching mix of beer and lemon soda. Also try the largely overlooked particularly German wines, particularly the sweet *(lieblich* or *süß)* whites of the Rhine and Mosel Valleys and the comparatively unknown dry *(trocken)* whites of southwestern Baden.

EASTERN GERMANY

Those visiting Eastern Germany for the first time will be surprised to find that the lion's share of Germany's cultural and historic monuments lie in the east. That's the good news. The bad news is that the corpse of Communism still rots across most of the former GDR. The disparity in living standards between Eastern and Western Germany is still astounding: the majority of Eastern homes lack telephones and central heating. However, those who have been here before will marvel at how quickly things are changing—how much cleaner the air is and how much difference a little paint can make. Everywhere businesses are opening, remodeling, or closing.

■■■ BERLIN

Berlin is one of the most fascinating cities on Earth. Raised in the shadow of the Cold War, Berliners responded with a glorious storm of cultural activity and the sort of nightlife you might expect from a population that has its back against the wall. When Communist governments fell across Eastern Europe, Berlin suddenly found itself it in a unique position: straddling the border of two distinct but no longer separate worlds. The result has been a period of dizzying change, and Berlin is both better and worse off as a result. Eastern Berlin currently suffers from massive unemployment as the transition from communism to capitalism proves more painful than the Kohl government predicted in the heady days before Germany's first united elections. Hopelessness and social alienation have encouraged many young Berliners in their fascination with xenophobic neo-Nazi movements. There's something about the city that doesn't make sense; it sneaks up on you and hides things. But Berlin's dark side pales in comparison to the exhilaration of riding on the cutting edge. As Weimar decadent Karl Zuckmayer wrote, "Berlin tasted of future, and for that, one happily accepted the dirt and coldness as part of the bargain."

ORIENTATION AND PRACTICAL INFORMATION

Berlin surveys the Prussian plain in the northeastern corner of reunited Germany about four rail hours southeast of Hamburg and double that time north of Munich, sporting excellent rail and air connections to Eastern and Western European capitals. Berlin is *immense*, and its eastern and western halves are two worn puzzle pieces that no longer fit together smoothly, connected by the grand tree-lined boulevard, **Straße des 17 Juni,** which runs through the massive **Tiergarten** park. For stays of more than a few days, the blue and yellow **Falk Plan** (DM8.80; at most kiosks) is indispensable.

The commercial district of Western Berlin centers around **Bahnhof Zoo** (Zoo Station) and **Breitscheidplatz,** site of the bombed-out Kaiser-Wilhelm-Gedächtniskirche, the boxy tower of Europa Center, and the main tourist office. A star of streets radiates from Breitscheidpl. Toward the west run **Hardenbergstraße, Kantstraße** and the **Kurfürstendamm,** or **Ku'damm.** Down Hardenbergstr. 800m is Steinpl. and the enormous Berlin Technical University. Down Kantstr. 800m is **Savignyplatz,** home to cafés, restaurants, and pensions. The newly asphalted **Ebert Straße** runs uncomfortably along the path of the deconstructed Berlin Wall from the Reichstag to **Potsdamer Platz**. The landmark **Brandenburg Gate** and surrounding Pariser Platz, reconstructed with the aid of EU funds, open onto **Unter den Linden,** which leads to the historic heart of Berlin around **Lustgarten,** and the neighboring commercial district of **Alexanderplatz.** The region near the Brandenburg Gate still shows the scars of what Berliners called "wall sickness." The alternative **Kreuzberg** and **Mitte,** for 40 years fringe back-against-the-wall neighborhoods of the West and East respectively, are once again at the crossroads.

Tourist Offices: Berlin-Touristen-Information, Europa Center, in the Europa Center at Budapesterstr. 45 (tel. 262 60 31). From Bahnhof Zoo, walk along Budapesterstr. past the Kaiser-Wilhelm-Gedächtniskirche about 5min. Open Mon.-Sat. 8am-10:30pm, Sun. 9am-9pm. **Bahnhof Zoo** (tel. 313 90 63) and **Tegel Airport** (tel. 41 01 31 45) open 8am-11pm. **Hauptbahnhof** in the east (tel. 279 52 09) open 8am-8pm. All offices provide a simple city map, *Berlin Tut Gut* (a pamphlet about the city), and the useful *Unterkünfte für Junge Besucher,* a list of Berlin's budget accommodations with directions and prices (a little outdated; add DM3-5 to their listings). All offices will also book rooms for a DM5 fee.

Budget Travel: ARTU Reisebüro, Hardenbergstr. 9 (tel. 31 04 66), down the street from Bahnhof Zoo. Transalpino and other passes. Books flights; last minute specials. Open Mon.-Tues. and Thurs.-Fri. 10am-6pm, Wed. 11am-6pm, Sat. 10am-1pm. **SRS,** Marienstr. 25 (tel. 281 67 61; fax 281 51 33); U-Bahn 6: Friedrichstr. Books student flights; binder of last minute specials. Open Mon.-Fri. 9am-6pm, Sat. 9am-2pm.

Embassies and Consulates: U.S. Consulate, Clayallee 170 (tel. 832 40 87). Consulate Section (tel. 819 74 54). Open Mon.-Fri. 2:30-4pm. **Canadian Consulate,** Friedrichstr. 95 (tel. 261 11 61). Open 8:30am-noon and 2-4pm. **U.K. Embassy Berlin Office,** Unter den Linden 32-34 (tel. 201 840). Open Mon.-Fri. 8:30am-5pm. **Irish Consulate,** Ernst-Reuter-Platz 10 (tel. 348 00 822). Open Mon.-Fri. 10am-1pm. **Australian Consulate,** Uhlandstr. 181-3 (tel. 880 08 80). Open Mon.-Thurs. 8:30am-12:30pm and 1:30-5pm, Fri. 8:30am-12:30pm and 1:30-4:15pm. **South African Consulate,** Douglasstr. 9 (tel. 82 50 11). Open Mon.-Fri. 8am-4:15pm. **Bulgaria,** Leipzigerstr. 20 (tel. 200 09 22). Open Mon.-Fri. 10am-12:30pm and 2-5pm. **Czech Republic,** Wilhelmstr. 44 (tel. 220 04 81). Open Mon.-Fri. 8:30-11am. **Hungary,** Unter den Linden 76 (tel. 220 25 61). Open Mon.-Fri. 9am-noon. **Poland,** Under den Linden 72-74 (tel. 220 25 51). Visa section open Mon., Wed.-Fri. 9am-1pm. Main section Mon.-Fri. 8am-4pm. **Russia,** Under den Linden 63-65 (tel. 229 11 10). Open Mon.-Fri. 8am-noon and 2-5pm. Visa section is at Reichensteiner Weg 34-36 (tel. 832 70 04). Open Mon., Wed., and Fri. 9am-1pm; Tues. and Thurs. 2-5pm.

American Express: Uhlandstr. 173 (tel. 882 75 75). The usual. On Fridays and Saturdays, expect out-the-door lines of American students carrying *Let's Go* guides. Open Mon.-Fri. 9am-5:30pm, Sat. 9am-noon.

Currency Exchange: Deutsche Verkehrs-Kredit Bank (tel. 881 71 17), at Bahnhof Zoo on Hardenbergstr. Decent rates for exchange; 1% commission on traveler's checks (DM7.50 minimum). Open Mon.-Sat.7:30am-10pm, Sun. 8am-7pm. Branch also at **Hauptbahnhof** (tel. 426 70 29), open Mon.-Fri. 7am-7:30pm, Sat.-Sun. 8am-4pm. **Berliner Bank** in Tegel Airport is open 8am-10pm.

GERMANY

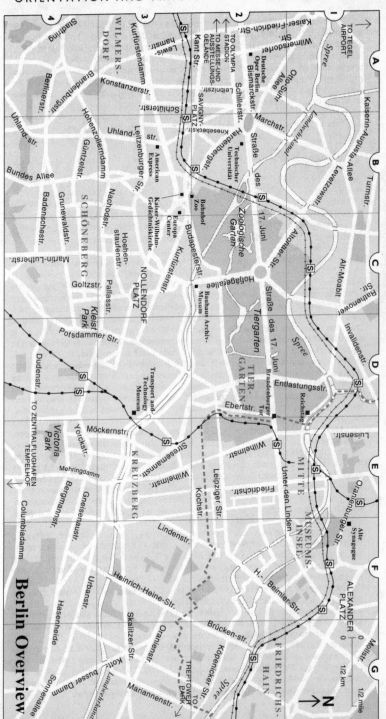

GERMANY

Berlin Overview

Post Offices: In the **Bahnhof Zoo.** Open Mon.-Fri. 6am-midnight, Sat.-Sun. 8am-midnight. Poste Restante at window 9. **Postal Code:** 10612. Branch office at **Tegel Airport** (tel. 430 85 23) open 6:30am-9pm. **Hauptbahnhof,** Postamt Berlin 17. Open Mon.-Fri. 7am-9pm, Sat. 8am-8pm. **Postal Code:** 10243.

Telephones: At Bahnhof Zoo. Near the post office, with same hours. Note that public phones are rarer in the eastern part of the city. **City code:** 030. With the shortage of new phone lines, many homes and businesses in East Berlin use mobile phones. It's very expensive to call these numbers.

Flights: Flughafen Tegel (tel. 410 11), Bus 109 (from Bahnhof Zoo or Jakob-Kaiser-Platz U-Bahn station): Tegel. Western Berlin's main airport. **Flughafen Tempelhof** (tel. 690 91). Bus 119: Kurfürstendamm. **Flughafen Schönefeld** (tel. 678 70), in Eastern Berlin, is connected by S-Bahn 3 to the city center.

Trains: Bahnhof Zoo is Berlin's principal station for trains to the west, while **Hauptbahnhof** is the focus of eastern and southern-bound trains. Stations are connected by S-Bahn. Trains from the east also arrive at **Bahnhof Lichtenberg. Bundesbahn and Reichsbahn Information** (tel. 194 19). Be prepared for a long wait. Similarly long lines at offices in **Bahnhof Zoo** (open 5:30am-10:30pm) and **Hauptbahnhof.**

Buses: ZOB, the central bus station (tel. 301 80 28), is by the Funkturm near Kaiserdamm. U-Bahn 1: Kaiserdamm. Check *Zitty* and *Tip* for deals on long-distance buses; often buses are only slightly cheaper than train or plane travel.

Public Transportation: Indispensable, efficient, and relatively inexpensive. Information and tickets are available at the **BVG Pavillon,** Bahnhof Zoo (tel. 256 24 62). Open 8am-8pm. A single ticket *(Einzelfahrschein Normaltarif)* costs DM3.50 and is good for 2hr. after validation. An *Einzelfahrschein Kurzstreckentarif* (short-trip fare, DM2.30) allows travel through up to 6 bus stations (with no transfers; not valid on airport bus lines) or 3 U- or S-Bahn stops (with unlimited transfers). A 4-trip *Sammelkarte* (Multiple Ticket) costs DM12; each "click" is good for 2hr. A short-trip 4-ride *Kurzstreckensammelkarte* is also available for DM6.40, though logistics make it a poor value. Buy tickets from machines, bus drivers, or ticket windows in the U- and S-Bahn stations. The **Berlin Tagesticket** (DM13, ages 6-14 DM6.50) is a 24hr. pass for the bus, U- and S-Bahn. A **6-Day Ticket** (DM33) is good for a Mon.-Sat. period. A monthly **Umweltkarte** costs DM82, a good value for longer stays. The cost of cheating is steep (DM60 and tremendous humiliation). *All tickets must be canceled in the red validation box before boarding to be valid.* U- and S-Bahn do not run 1-4am, except for the **U-1** and **U-9,** which run all night Fri.-Sat. An extensive system of **night buses,** centered on Bahnhof Zoo stop every ½hr.; look for the signs with a moon and stars or pick up the free *Nachtliniennetz* map. All night bus numbers are preceded by **N.**

Bike Rental: Near Ernst-Reuter-Platz, **Herr Beck** at Goethestr. 7 (tel. 312 19 25). DM12 per day, mountain bikes DM20 per day. Call for selection and deposit information. Bring passport. No English spoken. In Lichtenberg, **Pedal-Power,** Psarrstr. 122, has a wide selection for rent. Bikes DM15 per day, DM100 deposit; mountain bikes DM24 per day, DM200 deposit. At S-Bahn 5 and 7: Nöldnerplatz. Fri. 10am-6pm, Sat. 10am-1pm.

Hitchhiking: Those who hitch west and south (Hanover, Munich, Weimar, Leipzig) take S-Bahn 1 or 3: Wannsee, then bus 211: *Autobahn* entrance ramp. Those headed north (Hamburg, Rostock) take U-Bahn 6: Tegel, then bus 224 and ask the driver to be let out at the *Trampenplatz.* Both have huge crowds, but someone gets picked up every few minutes.

Mitfahrzentrale: City Netz, Kurfürstendamm 227, in the Ku' Eck mall, has a computerized ride-share database (tel. 194 44 or 882 76 04). Open 8am-9pm. **Mitfahrzentrale Alex** (tel. 242 36 42), in the Alexanderplatz U-Bahn station, specializes in the East. Open Mon.-Fri. 8am-8pm, Sat. 8am-6pm, Sun. 10am-6pm.

Luggage Storage: In the Bahnhof Zoo train station; lockers DM2, larger DM4, 72hr. max. At **Hauptbahnhof;** lockers DM2, larger DM4, 72hr. max. At Bahnhof **Lichtenberg** and S-Bahnhof **Alexanderplatz:** Lockers DM2. 24hr. max.

Lost Property: BVG Fündbüro, Lorenzweg 5 (tel. 751 80 21). For items lost on the bus or U-Bahn. Open Mon.-Tues. and Thurs. 9am-3pm, Wed. 9am-6pm, Fri. 9am-2pm. **Fundbüro Deutsche Reichsbahn,** in the Hackescher Markt S-Bahn station (tel. 29 72 16 71). For items lost on trains or S-Bahn. Open Mon., Wed.-Thurs. 10am-4pm, Tues. 10am-6pm, Fri. 8am-noon. **Zentrales Fundbüro,** Platz der Luftbrücke 6 (tel. 69 90).

Bookstores: The **British Bookshop,** Mauerstr. 83-84 (tel. 238 46 80), is a new, artfully stocked addition to Berlin's English book club. Magazines too. Open Mon.-Fri. 9am-6:30pm, Sat. 9am-2pm.

Laundromat: Wasch Centers (tel. 852 37 96) are at Leibnizstr. 72 in Charlottenburg; Wexstr. 34 in Schöneberg, Bergmannstr. 61 in Kreuzberg; Markstr. 4 in Wedding; Behmstr. 12 in Mitte; and Jablonskistr. 21 in Prenzlauer Berg. All open 6am-10pm. Wash DM6 per 6kg, dry DM2 for 30min. Soap included.

Pharmacies: Europa-Apotheke, Tauentzienstr. 9-12 (tel. 261 41 42), by Europa Center (close to Bahnhof Zoo). Open 9am-9pm. Closed *Apotheken* post signs directing you to the nearest one open.

Crisis Lines: Sexual Assault Hotline: tel. 251 28 28. Open Tues. and Thurs. noon-9pm, Sun. noon-2pm. **Schwüles Überfall** (gay bashing) hotline and legal help: tel. 216 33 36. Open Sun.-Fri. 6-9pm, Sat. 6pm-4am. English speakers at both. **Drug Crisis,** tel. 192 37.

Medical Assistance: The tourist office has a list of English-speaking doctors. **Emergency Doctor:** tel. 31 00 31 (Western), tel. 12 59 (Eastern). **Emergency Dentist:** tel. 11 41.

Emergencies: Police: tel. 110. Headquarters at Platz der Luftbrücke 6 (tel. 69 90). **Ambulance and Fire:** tel. 112.

ACCOMMODATIONS AND CAMPING

The immediate euphoria and tourist influx after the fall of the Wall have leveled out and the prices and quality of Berlin accommodations have stabilized. For a DM5 fee, **tourist offices** will find you a hotel room. Count on spending at least DM60 for a single, DM100 for a double; the really cheap pensions will already be booked. There are also over 4000 private rooms *(Privatzimmer)* available in the city; the overwhelming majority are controlled by the tourist offices. A recent price-fixing has set all such rooms at DM40 for singles, DM65 for doubles, plus a single-night surcharge of DM5. They often prefer to fill up the *Pensionen* first, so you may have to ask specifically for private rooms. Reserve a room by writing directly to a *Pension* or to the **Verkehrsamt Berlin,** Martin-Luther-Str. 105, 10825 Berlin (tel. 212 34, fax 21 23 25 20; note that this is a *different* address from the main tourist office). The *Verkehrsamt* requires that you state precisely how much you want to spend (minimum DM60 for a single, DM100 for a double). Write at least four weeks in advance.

For longer visits (more than four days) the various **Mitwohnzentralen** can arrange for you to housesit or sublet someone's apartment. Prices start at DM35 per night plus a percentage fee, and go down the longer you stay. The **Mitwohnzentrale,** Kurfürstendamm 227/228, in the Ku'damm Eck mall, 2nd (tel. 88 30 51, fax 882 66 94) is the biggest (open Mon.-Fri. 10am-6:30pm, Sat.-Sun. 11am-2pm).

Hostels

Hostels fill quickly with German school groups (especially in summer and on weekends); call ahead. All HI-affiliated hostels are for members only, tend to attract school groups, and are liable to be overbooked. For an extra DM4, some hostels will give nonmembers a stamp and let you spend the night. HI hostels also have curfews which hinder night-ragers and tend to be strict in their regulations. Read the nightlife section before you decide where to stay—consider location and curfew before booking. Many hostels accept written reservations.

Jugendgästehaus (HI), Kluckstr. 3 (tel. 261 10 97, fax 262 95 29). Bus 129 "Hermannpl." from Kurfürstendamm: Jugendgästehaus, or U-Bahn 1: Kurfürstenstr., then walk up Potsdamerstr., left on Pohlstr., right on Kluckstr. Clean and central, many school groups. Reception open 1-1:45pm, 2:35-9:45pm, and 10:15pm-midnight. Lockout 9am-noon. Curfew midnight; stragglers admitted at 12:30am and 1am. DM28, over 26 DM35. Sheets and breakfast included. Key deposit DM10.

Lockers, laundry facilities. Reservations strongly recommended; call 262 30 24 more than 2 weeks in advance.

Jugendgästehaus Central, Nikolsburgerstr. 2-4 (tel. 87 01 88, fax 861 34 85). U-Bahn 9: Güntzelstr. or U-Bahn 2: Hohenzollernplatz. Determinedly clean with drab green walls. Curfew 1am. 2-6 bed rooms. DM32. Breakfast included. Sheets DM7, free for stays of more than 2 nights.

Jugendherberge Ernst Reuter (HI), Hermsdorfer Damm 48 (tel. 404 16 10). U-Bahn 6: Tegel, then bus 125 "Frohnau/Invalidensiedlung": Jugendherberge. Distant from the center in a placid suburb, on the edge of the forest. Curfew midnight. Stragglers admitted until 1am. 6-bed rooms. DM23, over 26 DM28. Sheets and breakfast included. Key deposit DM10.

Jugendgästehaus Tegel, Ziekowstr. 161 (tel. 433 30 46, fax 434 50 63). U-Bahn 6: Tegel, then bus 222 or night bus N22: Titusweg. Old brick outside, new and bright inside, with wide, high schoolish linoleum halls. Under 27 only. No curfew. DM35. Breakfast and sheets included. Written reservations only.

Jugendgästehaus Nordufer, Nordufer 28, 13351 Berlin (tel. 451 70 30, fax 452 41 00). U-Bahn 9: Westhafen, left over the bridge and left onto Nordufer. Away from the center, but on the pretty, blue, swimmable Plötzensee Lake. Some singles, but more 4-bed rooms. Free use of next-door *Freibad.* Reception open 7am-midnight. No curfew. DM35. Buffet breakfast and sheets included.

Jugendgästehaus am Wannsee (HI), Badeweg 1 (tel. 803 20 34, fax 803 59 08). S-Bahn 1, 3: Nikolassee, walk 10min. toward the Strand Bad Wannsee beach. Far from the center, but likely to have space, and Wannsee has its own charm. Large groups of jolly German kids. Lockout 9am-noon. Curfew 1am. DM28, over 26 DM35. Sheets and breakfast included. Key deposit DM20.

Jugendgästehaus am Zoo, Hardenbergstr. 9a (tel. 312 94 10, fax 401 52 83), directly opposite the Technical University *Mensa.* Bus 145, or a short walk from Bahnhof Zoo out the back exit and straight down Hardenbergstr. Within spitting distance of Zoo Station, the rooms and beds are extremely sparse. Graffiti by U.S. frat boys. Reception open 24hrs. No curfew. Singles DM53, over 26 DM58. Doubles DM91, over 26 DM96. Dorms (4-12 beds) DM41, over 26 DM54. Breakfast included. No reservations, but tends to have room if you call in the morning.

Hotels and Pensionen

Prices have finally stabilized as small pension and hotel owners once more cater to small budgets. Most *Pensionen* and small hotels listed in *Let's Go* are amenable to *Mehrbettzimmer,* where extra beds are moved into a large double or triple. The best place to find cheap hotel rooms is around Savignyplatz or down along Wilmersdorfstr. and its side-streets.

Hotel Transit, Hagelbergerstr. 53-54 (tel. 785 50 51; fax 785 96 19). U-Bahn 6,7: Mehringdamm, bus 119, or night bus N19 (every 10-15min.). Bright and high-ceilinged rooms in a converted factory with showers and safes. Reception and big-screen (M)TV lounge open 24hrs., bar open until 2-3am. Curfew? Don't make them laugh. Revel all night, sleep all day—there's no lockout and breakfast is available until noon or later. Singles DM80. Doubles DM99. Triples DM130. Quads DM170. "Sleep-In" deal offers dorm accommodation DM33. Breakfast included.

Hotelpension Cortina, Kantstr. 140 (tel. 313 90 59, fax 31 73 96). S-Bahn 3, 5, 6, 9 or bus 149: Savignyplatz. Bright, convenient and hospitable. Reception open 24hrs. Singles DM65-70. Doubles DM90-120. *Mehrbettzimmer* DM40-45 per person. Breakfast included.

Pension Knesebeck, Knesebeckstr. 86 (tel. 312 72 55, fax 313 95 07). S-Bahn 3, 5, 6, 9: Savignyplatz. Just north of the park. Friendly, large *Alt-Berliner* rooms, all with sinks. Hearty buffet-style breakfast. Reception open 24hrs. Singles DM85, off-season DM75. Doubles DM120. *Mehrbettzimmer* DM40-45 per person. Phone reservations must be confirmed in writing. Book ahead.

Hotel-Pension München, Güntzelstr. 62 (tel. 857 91 20, fax 853 27 44). U-Bahn 9: Güntzelstr. Small pension decorated cleverly with drawings and paintings. White-walled rooms with colorful comforters and telephones. Singles DM64. Doubles

DM84-124. DM5-10 surcharge for one-night stays. Breakfast included. Written reservations recommended.

Charlottenburger Hof, Stuttgarterpl. 14 (tel. 32 90 70; fax 323 37 23). S-Bahn 3, 5, 6, 9: Charlottenburg or U-Bahn 7: Wilmersdorferstr. Spotless modern rooms with phones, safes, and TVs. Singles DM70–110. Doubles DM100-160. Breakfast (in the jointly-owned Café Voltaire; see Food, below) DM5. Winter discounts.

Hotel-Pension Hansablick, Flotowstr. 6 (tel. 391 40 48, fax 392 69 37). Near Tiergarten. A bit pricey, but it's a century-old Berliner Jugendstil pearl, from the decorative ceilings to the marble entrance and antique-looking lamps gracing the cobblestone streets in front. Few places like this survived WWII bombing, so call, write, or fax ahead for reservations. Reception open 24hrs. Singles DM150. Doubles DM170-190. Mehrbettzimmer DM55 per person. 5% *Let's Go* discount.

Hamburger Hof, Kinkelstr. 6 (tel. 333 46 02), in the old quarter of Spandau. U-Bahn 7: Altstadt Spandau (2nd-to-last stop). Easily accessible. A tiny, comfortable hotel with only 15 beds. Small-town charm, but no English spoken. Singles DM50. Doubles DM100. Showers and breakfast included.

Camping

Kladow, Krampnitzer Weg 111-117 (tel. 365 27 97), is in Spandau; take U-Bahn to Rathaus Spandau, then bus 135 to the end and follow Krampnitzer Weg another 500m. Closer to the center of Spandau is **Haselhorst,** Pulvermühlenweg (tel. 334 59 55); take U-Bahn to Haselhorst, then head north on Daumster to Pulvermühlenweg. Perhaps the most unusual is **Dreilinden** (tel. 805 12 01), which is surrounded on 3 sides by the vestiges of the Berlin Wall. Take the U-Bahn to Oskar-Helene Heim, then bus 118; follow Kremnitzufer to Albrechts-Teergfen (about 20min.). All charge DM6.90 per person, DM5.50 per tent. All are open year-round. Make reservations with **Deutscher Camping Club,** Mandlstr. 28, 80802 München, or call in advance. For hippie, international *esprit de tente,* try the **Internationales Jugendcamp,** Ziekowstr. 161 (tel. 433 86 40), U-Bahn 6: Tegel, then bus 222 or night bus N22: Titusweg. Next to Jugendgästehaus Tegel (see Hostels, above), it's far away, but gets you a mat under a giant tent with shower facilities. (Under 27 only. Lockout 9am-5pm. DM9. No written reservations accepted. Open July 1-Sept 4.)

FOOD

Berlin's restaurant scene is as international as its population; German food should be a second priority here. Much typical Berlin food is Turkish: almost every street has its own Turkish *Imbiß* or restaurant. The *Imbiß* stands are a vital lifeline for the late-night partier; most are open ridiculously late, some 24hrs. The *Döner Kepab,* a sandwich of lamb and salad, has cornered the fast food market, with *Falafel* running a close second. For DM4-5, either makes a small meal, but other Turkish dishes are also worth a shot. A second wave of immigration has brought quality Indian restaurants to Berlin, and Italian is always a safe choice.

A gloriously civilized tradition in Berlin cafés is *Frühstück,* breakfast served well into the afternoon, sometimes 24hrs. Budget eateries have traditionally been scarce in Eastern Berlin, but this is rapidly changing. New cafés in Mitte and Prenzlauer Berg are rapidly providing stiff competition for their western counterparts; prices tend to be lower and portions larger. In addition, street vendors with all shapes, sizes, and flavors of cheap eats fill **Alexanderplatz** every day.

Aldi, Bolle, and **Penny Markt** are the cheapest supermarket chains, along with **Plus** stores which are omnipresent in Wilmersdorf, Schönberg, and Kreuzberg. Supermarkets are usually open Mon.-Fri. 9am-6pm, Sat. 9am-1pm. The best **open-air market** fires up Saturday mornings in Winterfeldplatz, though almost every neighborhood has one; there's a kaleidescopic **Turkish market** in Kreuzberg on the banks of the Landwehrkanal (near U-Bahn 1: Kottbusser Tor) every Friday. In Eastern Berlin, markets often set up under S-Bahn platforms.

Café Hardenberg, Hardenbergstr. 10. Big Belle Epoque spot, opposite the TU *Mensa.* Cheap food, lots of German and American students. Breakfast (served

9am-5pm) a good value at DM4-8; entrees mostly well under DM13. Also good for a few drinks. Open 9am-1am.

Restaurant Marché, Ku'damm 14-15, just a couple of blocks down from the Zoo and the *Gedächtniskirche.* The colorful, upscale cafeteria area is full of fresh produce salads, grilled meats, pour-it-yourself wines, and hot pastries. Expect to pay DM12-25. Free ice water! Open 8am-midnight.

KaDeWe, Tauentzienstr. 21 (tel. 212 10). U-Bahn 1, 3, or 4: Wittenbergpl. A tremendous department store. Satiate any desire in the 6th floor food emporium. Bright, beautiful stands happily heaped with cabbages and caviar. Open Mon.-Wed. and Fri. 9:30am-6:30pm, Thurs. 9:30am-8:30pm, Sat. 9am-2pm.

Schwarzes Café, Kantstr. 148 (tel. 313 80 38), near Savignypl. Art-speckled interior full of hip, young folks. It's not so cool to pay DM4.20 for 0.2l of apple juice. Breakfast at all hours (DM7-13). Open 24hrs., except Tues. early morning-6pm.

Baharat Falafel, Winterfeldtstr. 37. U-Bahn 1 or 4: Nollendorfplatz. Quite possibly the best falafel in Berlin. Plump, freshly-made chickpea balls in a fluffy pita, covered with veggies and heavenly sesame, mango, or chili sauce DM5. Open Mon.-Sat. noon-2am, Sun. 1pm-2am. Closed the first 2 weeks in August.

Indus, Martin-Luther-Str. 47 (tel. 213 38 33). U-Bahn 7: Bayerischer Platz. Excellent, sit-down Indian restaurant. Immense selection of vegetarian meals (DM11-16). Cool the spice with creamy mint-yogurt sauce. Open noon-midnight.

Mediencafé Strada, Potsdamerstr. 131 (tel. 215 93 81). U-Bahn 1: Kurfürstenstr. Italian-accented café with soothing golden walls and great coffee (DM3). Lavish brunch menu Fri.-Sun. Breakfast served 10am-2pm. Open Sun.-Thurs. 10am-2am, Fri.-Sat. 10am-3am.

Graeffitti, Graefestr. 92 (tel. 692 74 02). U-Bahn 8: Schönleinstr. Airy, lazy café with original watercolors dotting the walls. Splendid *Frühstücksbuffet* served 9am-4pm (just DM12). Artsy crowd has been known to wear light colors and upbeat dresses from time to time. Open 9am-midnight.

Restaurant V, Lausitzer Platz 12 (tel. 612 45 05). U-Bahn 1: Görlitzer Bahnhof. Reasonably priced vegetarian restaurant. Serves great breakfasts until 3pm. *Tofu-Würstchen* with scrambled eggs and tomato sauce (DM10.50). Open 10am-2am.

Café Ici, Augustr. 61. U-Bahn 6: Oranienburger Tor. Blessedly peaceful little café brims with character: beat-up chandeliers, framed chalk drawings and photos, old floral rugs, and mismatched wooden chairs and sofas to sit on. Haiku-simple menu of soups and salads. Open 3pm-3am.

Valentino, Auguststr. 84. U-Bahn 6: Oranienburger Tor or S-Bahn 1, 2: Oranienburgerstr. Crumbling pre-war buildings are the backdrop for this active art deco café, with food until late and changing exhibits by young Berliner artists. Large gay presence. Brunch Sundays 10am-3pm at the *Frühstücksbuffet* (DM10). Open Mon.-Sat. 6pm-3am, Sun. 10am-3am.

Zur Letzten Instanz, Waisenstr. 14 (tel. 242 55 28). U-Bahn, S-Bahn: Alexanderplatz. Wonderfully preserved old Berlin restaurant, established in 1621. Topnotch *Deutsche Küche* served in small, wood-panelled rooms. Entrees DM17-30. Open Mon.-Sat. noon-1am, Sun. noon-11pm.

Café Restauration 1900, Husemannstr. 1 (tel. 44 940 52), at Kollwitzplatz. U-Bahn 2: Eberswalderstr. Alternative interior on a Potemkin-village-esque street. Decent food at reasonable prices. German, French, and Italian wines. In the afternoon families mix with *Szene*-folk. Open noon-2am. Kitchen open until midnight.

Die Krähe, Kollwitzstr. 84 (tel. 442 82 91), off Kollwitzplatz. Bright crowd orders from the daily menu on the blackboard. Excellent breakfasts: the *Gemischtes Frühstück* (DM8.50) comes with fruit, ham, sausages, cheese, excellent rolls, and *Vollkornbrot,* plus a stuffed tomato. Open Tues.-Sun. 10am-2am, Mon. 5pm-2am.

SIGHTS

Between Eastern and Western Berlin

For decades a gateway to nowhere, the **Brandenburger Tor** (Brandenburg Gate) is the structure that most commonly symbolizes the future of Berlin and a united Germany. It is now the center point of the city, opening east onto Unter den Linden (S-Bahn: Unter den Linden). Built during the reign of Friedrich Wilhelm II as a symbol of peace, the gate became a symbol of East-West division as a locked door embedded in the Berlin Wall. The gate was not actually opened until December 22, 1989, more than a month after the wall came down. The **Berlin Wall** itself is a dead dinosaur, with only fossil remains still visible. Fenced in overnight on August 13, 1961, the 160-km-long wall separated families and friends, sometimes running through people's homes. Portions of it are preserved near the *Hauptbahnhof* and the Reichstag. The longest remaining bit is the brightly painted **East Side Gallery** (S-Bahn: Hauptbahnhof), the world's largest open-air gallery.

The demolished Wall has left an incompletely healed scar across the city center. From the western side, trees have been planted extending the Tiergarten a few meters more. But the eastern side, a grassy no-man's-land strewn with cinder blocks awaits construction workers. **Potsdamer Platz,** cut off by the Wall, was once a major transportation hub of Berlin designed under Frederick Wilhelm I. The land surrounding the *Platz* was recently purchased by Sony and Daimler-Benz.

The **Haus am Checkpoint Charlie,** Friedrichstr. 44 (U-bahn: Kochstr. or bus 129), narrates the history of the Wall through film and photo. Upstairs there are exhibits on human rights, as well as artistic renderings of the Wall. (Open 9am-10pm. DM7.50, students DM4.50.)

Western Berlin

The Reichstag and Tiergarten Just to the north of the Brandenburger Tor sits the **Reichstag** building, the once and future seat of unified Germany's parliament. In August 1914, Karl Liebknecht's famous "Nein!" was one of a few votes in its halls against the impending First World War. In 1918, after Kaiser Wilhelm II had abdicated, the Social Democrat Philip Scheidemann proclaimed the German Republic from one of its windows. His move turned out to be wise, since two hours later Karl Liebknecht announced a German Socialist Republic down the street in **Palast der Republik.** Civil war conditions in Berlin and much of the rest of Germany resulted. In February 1933, just one month after Hitler became chancellor, the Reichstag mysteriously burnt down. Hitler used the Reichstag fire to woo support for the infamous Enabling Act, managing to convince the "moderate" parties in parliament to help him become legal dictator of Germany. At the moment, the Reichstag is not a government building, although the major political parties have opened offices here. The lush **Tiergarten,** a vast landscaped park formerly used by the Prussian monarchs for hunting, spreads itself over the northeast corner of western Berlin. In the heart of the Tiergarten, the **Siegessäule** (victory column) celebrates Prussia's campaign against France in 1870. In 1938, the Nazis moved the monument from its spot in front of the Reichstag to increase its height and make it more impressive. Climb the 285 steps to the top for a panorama of the city. (Open April-Nov. Mon. 1-5:30pm, Tues.-Sun. 9am-5:30pm. DM1.50, students DM1.) The **Soviet Army Memorial** (yes, you're still in Western Berlin) stands at the end of Str. des 17 Juni, flanked by a pair of giant toy tanks.

Ku'damm, Schöneberg and Charlottenburg A sobering reminder of the devastation caused by World War II, the shattered **Kaiser-Wilhelm-Gedächtniskirche** now houses an exhibit dedicated to peace which has lost some of its didactic force amidst the giddy neon of the Ku'damm and the Europa Center. (Exhibit open Tues.-Sat. 10am-4pm.) The renowned **Zoo,** entrance at Budapesterstr. 34 (the Elephant Gate), across from the tourist office in the Europa Center, houses an exotic collection of fauna as well as the spectacular **Aquarium,** Budapesterstr. 32. (Zoo open 9am-6pm; Oct.-Feb. 9am-4:45pm; March-April 9am-5:15pm. Aquarium open 9am-6pm. To zoo DM10, students DM8. To aquarium DM9, students DM7.50. Combined admission DM15, students DM12.)

South of Nollendorfpl. is the **Rathaus Schöneberg,** where West Berlin's city government convened. On June 26, 1963, 1½ million Berliners swarmed the streets to hear John F. Kennedy reassure them of the Allies' continued commitment to the city 15 years after the 11-month Berlin Airlift. Kennedy's speech ended with the now-famous words, "All free men, wherever they may live, are citizens of Berlin. And therefore, as a free man, I take pride in the words *'Ich bin ein Berliner.'"*

Schloß Charlottenburg, the vast Baroque palace built by Friedrich I for his second wife, presides over a carefully landscaped Baroque park. The ornate **Knobelsdorff Wing** is the most lavish of the palace suites. Take U-Bahn 2 to Sophie-Charlotte-Pl. or bus 145 from Bahnhof Zoo. Seek out the **Palace Gardens,** with their carefully planted rows of trees, small lake, footbridge, and fountains which surround the **Royal Mausoleum; Belvedere,** an 18th-century residence housing a porcelain exhibit; and the **Schinkel Pavilion,** with furniture designed by Schinkel. (All open Tues.-Sun. 9am-5pm. To palace complex DM8, students DM3.)

Kreuzberg Indispensable for a sense of Berlin's counterculture is a visit to Kreuzberg, an area loaded with cafés and bars. For its more respectable face, get off at U-Bahn 6 or 7: Mehringdamm and wander around; Bergmannstr. features an especially large number of old buildings and second-hand shops. At night many bohemian and punk clubs overflow onto Yorckstr., which heads west from its intersection with Mehringdamm. The cafés and bars on Oranienstr. (U-Bahn: Kottbusser Tor) boast a more radical element; the May Day parades always start on Oranienplatz. The **Landwehrkanal,** a channel which runs from Tiergarten into Kreuzberg, is where Rosa Luxemburg's body was thrown after her murder in 1919; it was recovered only recently. The tree-dotted strip of the canal near Hallesches Tor, **Paul-Linke Ufer,** may be the most beautiful street in Berlin with its shady terraces and old apartment facades. The east end of Kreuzberg, near the old Wall, is home to Turkish (half of Western Berlin's foreign population) and Balkan neighborhoods, and boasts a correspondingly large number of ethnic cafés and restaurants, popular with the radicals and students. From the Schlesisches Tor U-Bahn station, a 3min. walk takes you to the recently reopened **Oberbaumbrücke,** through a fragment of the wall, and into the Friedrichshain district of the former East.

Eastern Berlin

Unter den Linden and Gendarmenmarkt
The Brandenburg Gate opens eastward onto **Unter den Linden,** once one of Europe's best-known boulevards and the spine of old Berlin. All but the most famous buildings have been destroyed, but farther down many 18th-century structures have been restored to their original Prussian splendor. Past Friedrichstr., the first massive building on your left is the **Deutsche Staatsbibliothek** (library), with a pleasant café inside. Beyond the library is **Humboldt Universität,** once one of the finest in the world. Next door, the old **Neue Wache** (New Guard House), designed by the renowned Prussian architect Friedrich Schinkel, is today the somber **Monument to the Victims of Fascism and Militarism.** Buried inside are urns filled with earth from the Nazi concentration camps of Buchenwald and Mauthausen and from the battlefields of Stalingrad, El Alamein, and Normandy. The honor guard in front changes on the hour, with the full ceremony Wednesdays at 2:30pm. The building with the curved façade is the **Alte Bibliothek.** The most striking of the monumental buildings is the **Zeughaus,** now the **Museum of German History.** From the museum you can enter the courtyard and see the tormented faces of Andreas Schlüter's *Dying Warriors.*

Berlin's most impressive ensemble of 18th-century buildings is a few blocks south of Unter den Linden at **Gendarmenmarkt,** graced by the twin cathedrals of the **Deutscher Dom** and the **Französischer Dom.** Enclosing the far end of the square, the classical **Schauspielhaus,** designed by Schinkel, is Berlin's most elegant concert space and hosts many international orchestras and classical performers. Destroyed by an air attack in 1945, it was painstakingly reconstructed and reopened in 1984.

Lustgarten, the Museumsinsel, and Alexanderplatz
As it crosses the bridge, Unter den Linden opens out onto the **Museumsinsel** (Museum Island). To the left is the **Altes Museum,** with a big polished granite bowl in front, and the poly-domed **Berliner Dom** (Berlin Cathedral). Severely damaged by an air raid in

GERMANY

1944, the cathedral emerged from 20 years of restoration in 1993; the interior is gaudy. (Open 9am-7:30pm. Free.) Behind the Altes Museum lie three other enormous museums and the ruins (now being restored, to be reopened in 1995) of a fourth. At the center of this jungle of pediments, porticoes, and colonnades is the **Lustgarten** park, formerly Marx-Engels Platz.

Across the Liebknecht Brücke, in the middle of a park stands a park and "conceptual memorial" consisting of steel tablets engraved with images of worker struggle and protest surrounding a twin statue of Marx and Engels. The park and the street behind it used to be collectively known as the **Marx-Engels Forum;** the park has yet to be renamed, while the street is now called **Rathausstr.**

On the other side of the Museumsinsel, Unter den Linden leads into the teeming, concrete **Alexanderplatz.** This atrociously ugly square was meant to be a showpiece for socialism; construction has begun to remove the edge from the buildings, but it's unclear whether the revamped version will be any more satisfying. Friends from both Germanies often meet at the plaza's **Weltzeituhr,** the international clock, but the undisputed landmark of the district is the Death-Star-on-a-Swizzle-Stick **Fernsehturm** (television tower), the tallest structure in Berlin. (Open 9am-midnight; open the 2nd and 4th Tues. of each month 1pm-midnight only. Last entry 11:30pm. Expect a 20-60min. wait. DM6.)

Nikolaiviertel and Scheuenviertel-Oranienburger Str. The graceful 15th-century church, **Marienkirche,** stands on the wide open plaza behind the *Fernsehturm.* Nearby is the gabled **Rotes Rathaus,** Old Berlin's famous red-brick town hall. Behind the *Rathaus,* the twin spires of the **Nikolaikirche** mark Berlin's oldest building. Inside the 13th-century structure, a small museum documents the early history of the city. (Open Tues.-Fri. 9am-5pm, Sat. 9am-6pm, Sun. 10am-5pm.) The church gives the surrounding **Nikolaiviertel,** a carefully reconstructed *Altstadt,* its name; among the two dozen historic buildings are the **Knoblauchhaus** and the rococo **Ephraim-Palais.**

Northwest of Alexanderpl. is the **Scheuenviertel,** the former ghetto of Berlin. It was later home to the Jews who fled the Eastern European pogroms only to end up in Hitler's concentration camps, and it contains many reminders of Berlin's former Jewish community, once the most emancipated and cultured in the world. It later became a showpiece for the East German government; many buildings have been restored, and some new constructions have a flair unusual for Berlin. The area has also become a center of the squatter scene, with a corresponding amount of cultural and café life. Down Oranienburgerstr. at no. 30 is the burnt-out shell of Berlin's major **synagogue,** once the center of West European Judaism. Torched by Nazis during *Kristallnacht* (November 9, 1938) and flattened by the Allies during the Battle of Berlin, the building is being restored, to reopen in 1995. The façade and dome remain nonetheless gorgeous. A sign on the side reads "Never forget this."

Prenzlauer Berg and Treptow East of Oranienburgerstr. is **Prenzlauer Berg,** a former working-class district largely neglected by East Germany's reconstruction efforts. Many of its old buildings are falling apart; others still have shell holes and embedded bullets from WWII. The result is the charm of age and graceful decay, slightly less charming for phoneless local residents with bad plumbing. Home to cafés, restaurants, and a few museums, restored **Husemannstraße** is especially worthy of a stroll. The area's population belies the aging architecture; there are heaps of students, artists, cafés, clubs, and communes, but the city government's anti-commune policy is in danger of destroying this counter-cultural renaissance.

The powerful **Sowjetische Ehrenmal** (Soviet War Memorial) is a mammoth promenade built with marble taken from Hitler's Chancellery (S-Bahn: Treptower Park). The Soviets dedicated the site in 1948, honoring the soldiers of the Red Army who fell in the "Great Patriotic War." The memorial sits in the middle of **Treptower Park,** a spacious wood ideal for morbid picnics. The neighborhood adjoining the park is known for its pleasant waterside cafés and handsome suburban mansions.

GERMANY

Museums

With 85 museums, Berlin is one of the world's great museum cities. Four major complexes—Charlottenburg, Dahlem, Museumsinsel, and Tiergarten—form the hub of the city's museum culture; smaller museums deal with every subject imaginable. The Charlottenburg complex is closed Friday, the Museumsinsel, Dahlem, and Tiergarten Monday. Regrettably, the traditionally-free *Preußischer Kulturbesitz* have recently begun to charge admission to their regular collections. Special exhibits can be particularly expensive (DM6-10); when museum-hopping, be sure to bring student ID.

Pergamonmuseum, Kupfergraben, Museumsinsel. One of the world's great ancient history museums. The scale of the exhibits is mind-boggling: the Babylonian Ishtar Gate (575 BC), the Roman Market Gate of Miletus, and the majestic Pergamon Altar of Zeus (180 BC). Also has extensive collection of Greek, Islamic, and Far Eastern art. Open Tues.-Sun. 9am-5pm; Islamic art section open Tues.-Sun. 10am-6pm. Last entry 30min. before closing. DM4, students and seniors DM2. Tours of Pergamon Altar 11am and 3pm.

Alte Nationalgalerie, Bodestr. Recently exchanged its mixed 20th-century collection for a purely 19th-century (and mostly German) one, with the former exhibits moving into the Tiergarten's *Neue Nationalgalerie.* Comprehensive and scholarly; lots of busts and mythological landscapes. Open Tues.-Sun. 9am-5pm. DM4, students and seniors DM2.

Bodemuseum, Monbijoubrücke. A world-class exhibit of Egyptian art as well as late Gothic wood sculptures, early Christian art, 15th- to 18th-century paintings, and an exhibit on ancient history. Open Tues.-Sun. 9am-5pm. Egyptian and papyrus collections open Tues.-Sun. 10am-6pm.

Dahlem Museum, Arnimallee 23-27 and Lansstr. 8. U-Bahn: Dahlem-Dorf. Huge complex of 7 museums, each worth a ½day. Particularly superb are the **Gemäldegalerie** (painting Gallery), a collection of Italian, German, Dutch, and Flemish Old Masters (including 26 Rembrandts), and the **Museum für Indische und Islamische Kunst,** extensive collections of South Asian and Islamic art. Open Tues.-Fri. 9am-5pm, Sat.-Sun. 10am-5pm. DM4, students and seniors DM2.

Schloß Charlottenburg, Spandauer Damm (U-Bahn 2: Sophie-Charlotte-Pl. or bus 145) contains several museums. The **Ägyptisches Museum,** across Spandauer Damm from the castle's main entrance, houses a fascinating collection of ancient Egyptian art, including the 3300-year-old bust of Queen Nefertiti. Also check out the **Antikensammlung** and the **Galerie der Romantik.** All open Mon.-Thurs. 9am-5pm, Sat.-Sun. 10am-5pm. DM4, students and seniors DM2.

Neue Nationalgalerie, Potsdamerstr. 50 (tel. 266 26 51). Bus 129 from the Ku'damm or S-Bahn 1 or 2 or U-Bahn 2: Potsdamer Platz. Part of the Tiergarten complex. All the 20th-century paintings of the *Preußischer Kulturbesitz,* a world-class collection. Brilliant works by Kokoschka, Kirchner, Beckmann, de Chirico, and more, plus a roomful of American abstractions. Open Tues.-Fri. 9am-5pm, Sat.-Sun. 10am-5pm. DM4, students DM2.

Martin-Gropius Bau, Stresemannstr. 110 (tel. 25 48 60). S-Bahn or U-Bahn: Anhalter Bahnhof. The **Berlinische Galerie** is it's heart on the second floor, a collection of paintings by 20th-century Berlin artists. On the top floor, the **Jüdisches Museum,** hosts extremely varied exhibits of painting, sculpture, and design related to Jews in Germany. (Most exhibits in both open Tues.-Sun. 10am-8pm. DM6, students DM3.) Adjacent to the museums, a Gestapo annex built by inmates of Sachsenhausen houses the exhibit **Topographie des Terrors,** detailing the use of various local buildings by the Nazis and describing the development of fascism in Germany. Open Tues.-Sun. 10am-6pm. Free. **Prinz-Albrecht-Gelände** is a deserted wasteland near the site of the wall, adjacent to the Topographie des Terrors which used to be a concentrated clump of Nazi ministries including the Gestapo, SS, and Reich Security. Rubble and signs mark the sites of the headquarters. Open Tues.-Sun. 10am-6pm. Free.

Bauhaus Archiv-Museum für Gestaltung, Klingenhöferstr. 13-14. Take bus 129 to Lützowpl. Designed by Walter Gropius, this shimmering modern building a plays exemplary works by Bauhaus members. Open Wed.-Mon. 10am-5pm. DM3, students DM1.

Brücke Museum, Bussardsteig 9. From the Zoo, take bus 249 a few stops to Güntzelstr., then take bus 115 to Pücklerstr. at Clayallee. *The* Expressionist museum in Berlin, with works by the Brücke school that flourished in Dresden and Berlin from 1909 to 1913. Open Wed.-Mon. 11am-5pm. DM4, students DM2.

Deutsches Historisches Museum, Unter den Linden 2, Zeughaus. Across from the Museumsinsel. Once a paean to the advent of socialism, now the site of provocative multi-media exhibitions on recent German history. Open Thurs.-Tues. 10am-6pm. DM4, students DM2.

Lesben-Archiv Spinnboden, Burgsdorfstr. 1. U-Bahn: Wedding; or bus 120. Lesbian history archive and information center. Open Wed. and Fri. 1-8pm. DM5.

ENTERTAINMENT

Berlin is *wild,* all night, every night. The best guides to theater, cinema, nightlife, and the extremely active musical scene are the biweekly magazines *Tip* and *Zitty.* The monthly *Berlin Program* lists more "cultural" events and includes good theater information. The free magazine *Siegessaüle* details gay events for the month and is available in gay bars and bookstores.

Nightlife

In Western Berlin, the best places to look are the **Savignypl., Schöneberg, Wilmersdorf,** and **Kreuzberg.** Mainstream activity centers around two areas to the north and south of the Ku'damm. The north is a bit more inviting; the middle point is **Savignyplatz** and includes Grolmanstr., Knesebeckstr., Bleibtreustr., and Schlütterstr., as well as Steinpl. South of the Ku'damm, the area between Uhlandstr. and Olivaer Platz is littered with crowded late-night cafés. Traditionally, the social nexus of bisexual, gay, and lesbian life has centered around the **Nollendorfplatz**—Christopher Isherwood lived at Nollendorfstr. 17 while writing his collection of stories *Goodbye to Berlin,* later adapted as the Broadway musical *Cabaret.* The *Szene* in **Kreuzberg** clusters around Viktoria Park, along Yorckstr. and Gneisenaustr., and along Oranienstr. between U-Bahn 1: Kottbusser Tor and U-Bahn 1: Görlitzer Bahnhof.

Despite Kreuzberg's funky appeal, the center of gravity of the *Szene* is shifting inexorably eastward. The east, in a word, is hot: low rents and a fascinating new "alternative" population give it an edge in nurturing new spots that the expensive west can't match. Its cafés and bars have a grittier, more vital feel and attract an exciting mixture of people. Some of the more interesting bars abound in the **Scheuenviertel,** especially along Oranienburger Str. (not to be confused with Kreuzberg's Oranienstr.) near the old Synagogue. The **Prenzlauer Berg** area also boasts some fun, interesting places along Prenzlauer Allee, Schönhauser Allee, Kastanienallee, and especially the area around Kollwitzplatz. Streetlights are sparse on many of the residential streets of the east, making a midnight club crawl a little creepy. Eastern Berlin is still safer than most American cities, but it's wise to avoid empty alleys and parks and travel in groups when possible. Most of the listings in *Let's Go* lean toward the alternative; if you want a beer hall, go to Munich.

Quasimodo, Kantstr. 12a (tel. 312 80 86). S-Bahn 3, 5, 6, 9: Savignyplatz. One of Berlin's most crucial Jazz venues, drawing in big names and lively crowds. Totally dead until 10pm when the shows begin; then surges to life. Cover depends on performance, ranging from free to DM30. Concert tickets available from 5pm or at Kant Kasse ticket service (tel. 313 45 54). Open from 8pm.

Metropol, Nollendorfplatz 5. U-Bahn 1 or 4: Nollendorfplatz or night buses N19, N29, or N85. Berlin's most famous disco; still *the* place to go, with all the pluses and minuses that entails. Three sections, each with a bar: dazzlingly-lit disco/DJ floor; a concert hall (the *Loft);* and an absurdly popular rumba/Glenn Miller-themed dance floor. Cover DM12; tickets to shows DM15-25 (tel. 216 27 87).

Disco open Fri. 9pm-6am, Sat. 9pm-8am. *Konzertkasse* open Mon.-Fri. 11am-3pm and 3:30-6pm. *Loft* days and times vary.

M, Goltzstr. 33. U-Bahn 7: Eisenacherstr. One of the more interesting Schöneberg bars, stark and neon-lit, slightly wild late at night. Black is eternally "in." Open Sun.-Thurs. 8:30am-midnight, Fri.-Sat. 8:30am-3am.

Yorck-Schlößchen, Yorckstr. 15). U-Bahn 7 or S-Bahn 1or 2: Yorckstr. Fun, Jazz-happy pub in a wedge-shaped Kreuzberg tenement. Endearing local jazz acts play every Sunday at 2pm. Open Sun.-Thurs. 9am-3am, Fri.-Sat. 9am-4am.

Flammende Herzen, Oranienstr. 170. U-Bahn 1 or 8: Kottbusser Tor. Black-and-torn denim-clad crowds spill out of this innovative *Kneipe* and block traffic on O-Str. Compare nose, ear, and body rings. Open from 10am. Food served until 5pm, in summer until 11pm.

Alibi, Oranienstr. 166. U-Bahn 1 or 8: Kottbusser Tor. Crowded bar with orange walls and offbeat regulars, up to something at all hours. A step down in intensity from *Flammende Herzen* 3 doors down, but still fun. Open Sun.-Thurs. 10pm-2am, later Fri.-Sat.

Ex, Mehringhof, Gneisenaustr. 2a (tel. 693 58 00). U-Bahn 6 or 7: Mehringdamm or night bus N19. Nascent bands rattle the little stage on weekends; punk/hip-hop disco on Saturdays. Open 7pm-2am.

SO 36, Oranienstr. 190 (tel. 615 26 01). U-Bahn 1: Görlitzer Bahnhof. Hard, Death, Metal, and Grind core, plus a healthy dose of Reggae/world music. Open from 10pm.

Silberstein, Oranienburgerstr. 27. U-Bahn 6: Oranienburger Tor or S-Bahn 1 or 2: Oranienburger Str. Next door to the synagogue. The theme is wrought-iron and rust, with vaguely human bronze statues that seem to creep around. So do the art-loving patrons. Drink beer and don't look surprised. Open noon-4am.

Tacheles, Oranienburgerstr. 53-56 (tel. 282 61 85). U-Bahn 6: Oranienburger Tor. Sprawling, majestically-decrepit 5-storey building may be the single-most concen-trated source of alternative energy in Berlin. It houses a legendary **art commune** which has decorated every square inch of the multi-level interior with graffiti, col-lage, or *papier-mâché*. Three separate **bars.** Also a *Kinobar* and cinema wing that hosts mightily entertaining film series with such themes as "Distraught Out-siders." Bands, innovative raves, and bizarre performances all find their place here. Dress as weirdly as possible. Complex opens at 4pm.

Franz-Klub, Schönhauser Allee 36-39 (tel. 442 82 03). U-Bahn 2: Eberswalder Str. One of the east's most reliable rock venues—a favorite among Prenzlauer Bergers and *Wessies* in the know. Cover varies. Live music every night starting around 10pm, followed by dance and DJ until late.

Lipstick, Richard-Wagner-Platz 5 (tel. 342 81 26). U-Bahn 7: Richard-Wagner-Platz. A teeming lesbian dance hall, the hottest in the city. Men (many gay) can sneak in Thurs., Fri., or Sun. nights only. Open from 10pm.

Pool, Motzstr. 19 (tel. 213 45 70). U-Bahn 1 or 4: Nollendorfplatz. Hottest, main-stream gay dance club in the city. The place to find Berlin's young beauties. Open 10pm-6am. Two doors down is **Tom's,** a techno-playing leather bar.

Hafen, Motzstr. 19. A mellower, more chat-oriented gay spot than Tom's, with bet-ter drink prices. Happy hour 9-10:30pm. Open 9pm-4am.

Anderes Ufer, Hauptstr. 157 (tel. 784 15 78). U-Bahn 7: Kleistpark. German for "the other shore." Stylish gay/lesbian/mixed café splashed with rotating art exhib-its. Also serves an excellent breakfast. Open 11am-2am.

Concerts, Opera, and Dance

Berlin reaches its musical zenith during the fabulous **Berliner Festwochen,** lasting almost the entire month of September and drawing the world's best orchestras and soloists, and the **Berliner Jazztage** in November. For more information on all these events (and tickets, which sell out far in advance), write to Berliner Festspiele, Budapesterstr. 48-50, 10787 Berlin 30 (tel. 25 48 92 50; open noon-6pm). In mid-July, **Bachtage** (Bach Days) offer an intense week of classical music; every Saturday night in August, **Sommer Festspiele** turns the Ku'damm into a multifaceted concert hall with punk, steel drum, and folk groups competing for attention.

In the monthly pamphlet *Kultur in Berlin* and *Berliner Programm,* as well as the biweekly magazines *Tip* and *Zitty,* you'll find notice of concerts in the courtyard of the old Arsenal, on the **Schloßinsel Köpenick** (Castle Island), or in the parks. Tickets for the *Philharmonie* and the *Oper* are often impossible to acquire through conventional channels. Instead, try standing out in front before performances with a small sign saying, *"Suche Karte"* (I seek a ticket).

Philharmonie, Matthäikirchstr. 1 (tel. 882 76 22). Bus 129 from Ku'damm: Potsdamerstr. or S-Bahn 2:Potsdamerplatz. The big yellow building is as acoustically perfect within as it is unconventional without. It's nigh impossible to get a seat; check an hour before concerts or write far in advance. Closed during the summer months. Ticket office open Mon.-Fri. 3:30-6pm, Sat.-Sun. and holidays 11am-2pm.

Deutsche Staatsoper, Unter den Linden 7 (tel. 200 47 62). U-Bahn 6: Friedrichstr. East Berlin's leading opera company. Ballet and classical music, too. Box office open Mon.-Sat. noon-6pm and Sun. 2-6pm. Tickets DM18-35.

Deutsche Oper Berlin, Bismarckstr. 35 (tel. 341 02 49). U-Bahn 1: Deutsche Oper. Berlin's best opera. Main box office open Mon.-Sat. 11am-1hr. before performance. 10min. before performances, you can get student discounts of up to 50%. Tickets DM10-125.

Theater and Film

Berlin has a lively English-language theater scene; look for listings in *Tip* or *Zitty* that say *"in englischer Sprache"* next to them. On any night in Berlin, you can choose from 100 different films, many in the original language. ("O. F." next to a movie listing means "original version"; "O.m.U." means original with German subtitles. Everything else is dubbed.) Check *Tip, Zitty,* or the subway posters. There is an international **Film Festival** (late Feb.-March) and a **Theater Festival** (May).

Deutsches Theater, Schumannstr. 13a (tel. 28 44 12 25). U- or S-Bahn: Friedrichstr. The best theater in the country. Innovative productions of both classics and newer works. The **Kammerspiel des Deutschen Theaters** (tel. 28 44 12 26) has smaller productions. Tickets DM15-40; 50% student discount often available.

Maxim Gorki Theater, Am Festungsgraben 2 (tel. 208 27 83), just off Unter den Linden. Excellent contemporary theater. Box office open Mon.-Sat. 1-6:30pm, Sun. 3-6:30pm. Tickets DM5-25.

Die Distel, Friedrichstr. 101 (tel. 200 47 04). A cabaret of political satire. Box office open Mon.-Fri. noon-6pm, Sat.-Sun. 2hr. before performance.

Filmtheater Babylon, Rosa-Luxemburg-Str. 30. U-Bahn 2: Rosa-Luxemburg-Platz. Classics and art films often in original language. DM8, students DM7.

Kino-Arsenal, Welserstr. 25. U-Bahn 1: Wittenbergpl. Berlin's best repertory film house. DM9.

■ POTSDAM

Potsdam, city of Frederick the Great and getaway spot for the Kaisers, is an essential foray from Berlin. S-Bahn 3 and 7 run from Berlin to both Potsdam-Stadt, near the town center. Berlin rapid transit tickets are valid on the S-Bahn and for public transportation within Potsdam, but are not valid for the bus lines to the tourist areas; a surcharge of around DM3 is levied.

The 600-acre **Sanssouci Park** houses four baroque palaces and countless exotic pavilions. The largest of the quartet, the **Neues Palais,** was built by Frederick the Great while pouting over several unsuccessful wars. Inside is the 19th-century Grottensaal, a reception room whose ribbed walls glitter with seashells and semi-precious stones. At the opposite end of the park stands **Schloß Sanssouci,** where Fred used to escape his wife and other troubles. Romantic **Schloß Charlottenhof** melts into its landscaped gardens and grape arbors. Overlooking the park from the north, the pseudo-Italian **Orangerie-Schloß** is famous for its 67 dubious Raphael imitations and for the **Neue Kammern** (royal guest chambers). The most bizarre of the park's pavilions are its "oriental" houses; the **Chinesisches Teehaus** is a gold-plated opium dream, complete with rooftop Buddha. (Park open 6am-sundown; free. Palaces open 9am-5pm; Oct. and Feb.-March 9am-4pm; Nov.-Jan. 9am-3pm. Neue Kammern closed Fri. All palaces closed 1st and 3rd Mon. of each month. To each palace DM8, students DM4. Compulsory German tours of Sanssouci, Neue Kammern, Schloß Charlottenhof; in others you can wander on your own.)

The **Brandenburger Tor,** a less famous cousin of Berlin's Brandenburg Gate, sits awkwardly in the middle of Luisenplatz. From here, **Brandenburger Str.** leads down to the 19th-century **Peter-Pauls-Kirche.** One block before the church, Friedrich-Ebertstr. heads left to the red-brick **Dutch Quarter.** Potsdam's second park, the Neuer Garten, contains several former royal residences. Take tram 95 from Platz der Einheit. **Schloß Cecilienhof** exhibits the **Potsdam Treaty,** signed at the Palace in 1945. (Open 9am-5:15pm; Nov.-April 9am-4:15pm; closed 4th Mon. of each month. DM3, students and seniors DM2, under 6 free.)

The **tourist office,** Friedrich-Ebertstr. 5 (tel. (0331) 29 11 00), is near the Pl. der Einheit or the Alter Markt tram stops. The office provides info on local events, a modest map, and private rooms. (Accommodations tel. (0331) 29 33 85. Rooms DM20-40 per person. Booking fee DM5. Open Mon.-Fri. 9am-8pm, Sat.-Sun. 9am-6pm; Nov.-March Mon.-Fri. 9am-6pm, Sat.-Sun. 11am-3pm.)

■■■ DRESDEN

No matter where you go in Dresden, you will not be able to forget the fact that the "Florence on the Elbe," a city of minimal military importance but formidable cultural value, was incinerated by Allied bombers during World War II, claiming over 50,000 lives. For 40 years, Dresden lived in the shadow of its former glory and great destruction; unlike Munich or Hamburg, where reconstruction obscured the wounds of war, the city remained scarred. The Dresden of the 1990s is still a haunted city—by the war, the DDR, and the pollution that accompanied years of socialism. But the metaphor of the phoenix-from-the-ashes is uncannily appropriate. With a skyline dominated by construction cranes and long-term renovation plans stretching well past the year 2000, Dresden is poised to regain its prewar elegance. If you've come to see the ruins, you'd better hurry.

ORIENTATION AND PRACTICAL INFORMATION

The capital of Saxony, Dresden stands magnificently on the Elbe River about 80km northwest of the Czech border and 180km south of Berlin. The *Altstadt* is on the same side as the *Hauptbahnhof;* the *Neustadt,* to the north, escaped most of the bombing and is now paradoxically the oldest part of the city. South of the *Altstadt* are the contrasting suburbs of Plauen and Strehlen. Dresden has just about completed the process of removing socialist-era names from streets and squares. Pick up a map at the tourist office, or any postcard stand—if you pay less than DM5, ask how old it is.

Tourist Offices: Dresden Information, Pragerstr. 10 (tel. 495 50 25, fax 495 12 76). Turn left out of the Hauptbahnhof, cross Wiener Platz and walk down Pragestr. 5min.; the office is on the right. Helpful city map DM1.50. Open Mon.-Sat. 9am-8pm, Sun. 9am-noon; Nov.-Feb. Mon.-Sat. 9am-6pm, Sun. 9am-noon.

Currency Exchange: Deutsche Verkehrs Bank AG Hauptbahnhof, in the train station. Open Mon.-Fri. 7:30am-7:30pm, Sat. 8am-4pm. More banks on Pragerstr. After hours, the self-service exchange machine in the station, but rates are poor.

American Express: Köpckestr. 15 (tel. 566 28 65), in the Bellevue Hotel across the Elbe from the Opera. Open Mon.-Fri. 10am-noon and 1-5:30pm, Sat. 9am-noon.

Post Office: Hauptpostamt fills several trailers on Hertha-Lindner-Str.; during renovation, the office is in Dresden-Neustadt, Königbrückerstr. 21/29, 01099 Dresden (tel. 594 40). Open Mon.-Fri. 8am-6pm, Sat. 8am-noon. **Postal Code:** 01099
Telephones: At the post offices. **City Code:** 0351.

Trains: (tel. 471 06 00 for info) or use the computerized schedule center in the *Hauptbahnhof.* From the **Dresden Hauptbahnhof** travelers shoot off to Warsaw, Paris, Kraków, Berlin, Budapest, Copenhagen, Munich, and Frankfurt. Trams 3, 11, and 26 connect it to **Bahnhof Dresden Neustadt,** which sits on the other side of the Elbe and bears a striking physical resemblance to its mate; trains leave from here to Leipzig and other Eastern German cities. Don't be fooled.

Public Transportation: Extensive but noisy. As you board, punch your ticket (one ride DM1, day pass DM5, week pass DM12).

Hitchhiking: Those headed to Berlin take streetcar 3 or 6: Liststr., then bus 81: Olter and walk back to the Autobahn interchange. Those headed to Prague take bus 76: Südhöhe, then hitch southbound on Innsbruckerstr. Those headed to Eisenach and Frankfurt am Main take streetcar 1: Zschonergrundstr. (four stops past "Dresden Cotta"—tell the driver you want to get off at the Autobahn to make sure the bus stops), then walk left (away from the river) to the interchange. **Mitfahrzentrale SMZ**, Nürnbergerstr. 57 (tel. 463 60 60). Call one day in advance. DM0.03 per km (Berlin DM18; Frankfurt an der Main DM44; Munich DM46; Hamburg DM46). Open Mon.-Fri. 10am-7pm, Sat. noon-2pm.

Crisis Lines: Frauen in Not (tel. 33 22 33) for women in emergency situations. Open Mon. 1-3pm, Thurs. 4-7pm for counseling. **Ausländer in Bedrängis** (tel. 484 55 08) for victims of racial violence.

Emergencies: Ambulance: tel. 115. **Fire:** tel. 112. **Police:** tel. 110.

ACCOMMODATIONS, CAMPING, AND FOOD

Arrive early and expect a struggle. Contact the tourist office for private rooms. (Singles DM20-50. Doubles DM40-100. DM5 fee.) To reach the **Jugendherberge Dresden Rudi Arndt (HI),** Hübnerstr. 11 (tel. 471 06 67, fax 472 89 59), take tram 5 "Südvorstadt" or 11 "Plauen": Nürnberger Platz, continue down Nürnbergerstr. and turn right onto Hübnerstr. From the train station, walk down 2 blocks on Fritz-Löffler-Str., turn right on Reichenbach, which becomes Rugestr., bear right to Altenzellerstr., and turn left onto Hübnerstr. The 73-bed hostel was built by the sewing machine magnate Isaac Singer. (Reception open Mon.-Sun. 10am-3pm, 1am-6am. Checkout 9am. DM19, over 26 DM23.50. Mandatory sheet rental DM5.) **Jugendherberge Oberloschwitz (HI),** Sierksstr. 33 (tel. and fax 366 72), has a beautiful location well worth the trip. From the train station, take S-Bahn 3 or 5: Pirnaischer Platz, change to S-Bahn 1: Schillerplatz, then ride the *Schwebebahn* (hill train; 1hr.; DM2.50) from Körnerplatz across the Elbe to Sierkstr. (Reception open 7-10am and 4-8pm. DM18.50, over 26 DM22.50.) **Campingplatz Mockritz,** Boderitzerstr. 8 (tel. 471 82 26), is an hour away from the *Hauptbahnhof:* take the bus "Moritzburg" or "Moritzburg/Radeburg": Sonnenland. (Reception open until 10pm. DM10 per person, DM6 per tent. Bungalows with kitchens DM20 per person.)

Restaurants open and close daily in Dresden, as the new market mentality shuffles the status quo. The cheapest eats are at supermarkets or *Imbiß* stands on Pragerstr. In a run-down, pre-war brownstone, **Raskolnikov** is hard to find in all its underground glory, hidden beneath a sign for Galerie Erhard; it offers Russian and Afghani fare for DM5-12 in an outdoor garden with homemade candles (open 10pm-1am). A refined vision of punk, **Planwirtschaft,** Louisenstr. 20, serves marvelous eastern teas, steak, *soljanka,* and mozzarella sandwiches (open Mon.-Thurs. 4pm-1am, Fri.-Sat. 4pm-3am).

SIGHTS AND ENTERTAINMENT

From the banks of the Elbe, the **Electors of Saxony** once ruled nearly the whole of central Europe. The extravagant collection of Emperor Augustus the Strong and the magnificent palace he built to house it, the **Zwinger,** once rivalled the Louvre in Paris. The northern wing of the palace, a later addition, was designed by revolutionary activist and master architect Gottfried Semper, whose famed opera house, the **Semper-Oper,** echoes the robust style of the palace wing and has premiered many of Strauss and Wagner's greatest works. Its painstaking restoration, both inside and out, has made it Dresden's major attraction. Near the Zwinger lie the ruins of the

Palace of Saxony's Electors and Kings, leveled by the firebombing on February 13, 1945; since the fall of 1990, restoration has been proceeding at near-light speed. Part of the **Residenzschloß** is now open to the public, featuring a display on the Renaissance and Baroque eras of the palace. (Open Fri.-Wed. 10am-6pm. DM3, students and seniors DM1.50. *Tageskarte* valid.) A private walkway connects the palace to the **Katholische Hofkirche** (Catholic Cathedral), originally the royal family's private chapel built to hide the family's Catholic pageantry from their Protestant subjects. (Tours Mon.-Thurs. 11am and 2pm, Fri.-Sat. 1pm and 2pm, Sun. 1pm, but times flexible.) Adorning the alley leading to the main entrance of the Catholic cathedral, the **Fürstenzug** (Procession of Kings) is a 150m pictorial in Meißner porcelain tiles tracing the history of Saxony since the Middle Ages.

From the cathedral, the 16th-century **Brühlsche Terrasse** offers a prime photo opportunity of the Elbe River (best at sunset). Turn right at the end of the terrace to reach the **Albertinum,** another fabulous museum complex, created out of a former arsenal with a courtyard collection of Greek and Roman sculpture. From the there, a walk to the *Neumarkt* leads to the shell of the **Frauenkirche,** once Germany's most splendid Protestant church. Plans are underway to reconstruct it, with a completion date estimated around 2006. In the **Neustadt,** look for the **Dreikönigskirche** (Church of the Three Kings) on Hauptstr., one of the oldest original structures in the city (open 9am-6pm; free organ concerts Mon.-Fri. 5:30-6pm.) In the direction of Blasewitz, Loschwitz, and Striesen you'll find the haunting grounds of the author Friedrich Schiller; his fans can check out the **Schillerhaus,** Schillerstr. 19 (open May-Sept. Sat.-Sun. 10am-5pm or by appointment; DM1, students and seniors DM0.50).

The **Gemäldegalerie Alte Meister,** Zwinger Palace, houses one of the world's premiere collections of painting from 1500 to 1800 (open Tues.-Sun. 10am-6pm; free tours Sun. 4pm; DM7, students and seniors DM3.50). Out the back gate of the Zwinger courtyard, visit the **Porzellansammlung** (porcelain collection), which traces the history of Saxony's famous porcelain industry through a never-ending procession of outlandishly delicate but lifeless tureens, vases, and knick-knacks (open Mon.-Wed., Fri.-Sun. 10am-6pm; DM3, students and seniors DM1.50).

The *Altstadt* (especially the area near Brühlscher Terrasse) and Hauptstraße are home to Dresden's more mainstream burgeoning café culture. But the city's most exciting offering is its rock scene. For everything from techno-pop disco to live guitar rock and heavy metal, go to **Klub Neue Mensa,** Bergstr. 47, beneath the Neue Mensa (open Mon. 10am-6pm, Tues.-Thurs. until midnight, Fri. until 4pm, Sun. 5pm-midnight; July-Sept. closed Mon.; no cover). The heart of the *Neustadt* scene is **Scheune,** Alaunstr. 36-40, a piano-stocked Pee Wee's Playhouse that serves Indian food cooked by the German Shiva Team; its culturally eclectic mix permits you to disco to West African roots and Baltic and Yiddish piano songs (club entrance from 8pm; call for schedule of events). For a night of theater, visit **Dresdner BREttL,** Maternistr. 17, famous for its satirical cabaret (DM10-15, students DM5-7.50).

■ MEIßEN

The town of Meißen became the center of the porcelain craft in the 18th-century; many have been obsessed with the eerie beauty of Meißen dolls. The **Albrechtsburg** is a castle overlooking the city (open Feb.-Dec. 10am-6pm; DM5, students and seniors DM3). Augustus the Strong built Europe's first top-secret porcelain factory here; today anyone can tour the **Staatliche Porzellan Manufaktur** at Talstr. 9. (open Tues.-Sun. 8:30am-4:30pm; DM5, students and seniors DM4). In the village, the porcelain bells of the **Frauenkirche** will lead you to the **tourist office,** An der Frauenkirche 3 (tel. (03521) 45 44 70), which arranges rooms and guides wayward tourists to the **Jugendherberge (HI)** at Wilsdrufferstr. 28 (tel. (03521) 45 30 65; reception open 7-10am and 5-8pm, Sat.-Sun. 7-9am and 6-8pm; DM13.50, over 26 DM16).

■■■ WITTENBERG

The Protestant Reformation, which catapulted Europe into centuries of convulsive upheaval, began quietly in Wittenberg on October 13, 1517, when local professor Martin Luther nailed his 95 theses to the wooden door of the **Schloßkirche** (castle church). This small town on the Leipzig-Berlin train route makes for a relaxing day-trip from either city. Plan your sightseeing around **Collegienstraße.** On your right, note the sickly elm tree; under it, Luther proudly burned a papal order of excommunication. At no. 54 stands Luther's former home, the **Lutherhalle,** where he lived from 1508. Inside is a truly formidable museum that follows the course of the Reformation, from Luther's first misgivings about papal indulgences through his fiery refusal to recant before the Pope. The family living room has been preserved intact, as has obnoxious tourist Peter the Great's signature, scribbled on the door when he stopped by in 1702. (Open Tues.-Sun. 9am-6pm. Last entry 5:30pm. DM6, students and seniors DM3.) Farther down the street is **St. Marienkirche** (St. Mary's Church); its distinctive altar, painted by pharmacist-*cum*-artistic genius Lucas Cranach the Elder, incorporates Luther in the biblical scene (open Mon.-Sat. 9am-noon and 2-5pm, Sun. 11am-noon and 2-5pm). Nearby rises the town's **Rathaus,** with an imposing Renaissance façade and statues to Luther and the philosopher-humanist Melancthon. Also in the square is the **Jungfernröhrwasser** (fountain of youth), a 16th-century well whose refreshing (and potable) waters still flow through the original wooden pipes. Farther down the street, a sumptuous baroque cupola crowns the tower of the **Schloßkirche.** It was here that Luther nailed his theses to the door; his original draft is inside.

 Wittenberg Information, Collegienstr. 29 (tel. (03491) 22 39 or 41 48 48), between the Lutherhalle and the market, finds rooms for a DM3 fee (open Mon.-Fri. 9am-6pm, Sat. 10am-2pm, Sun. 11am-3pm). The **Jugendherberge (HI)** in the castle has a unique atmosphere and reasonable prices (tel. (03491) 32 55; reception open 7-10am and 5-10pm; lockout 10am-3pm; DM15, over 26 DM10; breakfast included). Even the most stubborn papist will enjoy the *Luthersuppe* (creamy tomato and potato soup, DM4) at **Zur Schloßfreiheit,** Coswigerstr. 24 (open Sun.-Fri. noon-2pm and 6pm-midnight). Wittenberg is a mere 1½hr. by train from Berlin (DM15), Halle, or Leipzig (both around DM10), making it an excellent daytrip.

■■■ LEIPZIG

Badly bruised in WWII, Eastern Germany's second-largest city compensates for its lack of beauty with one of Europe's more brilliant cultural pedigrees. Originally, Leipzig gained its fame through music and letters: the university, founded in 1409, upholds an illustrious tradition that embraces the names of Leibniz, Lessing, and Nietzsche. More recently, Leipzig has become Germany's *Heldenstadt* (city of heroes) for its role as the crucible of *die Wende,* the sudden toppling of the GDR in 1989. Dozens of bookstores recall Leipzig's pre-war position as capital of European publishing, and several major international book fairs take place here annually.

 Leipzig's historic *Innenstadt* suffered less from the bombing of World War II than from the frenzied and poorly planned building of the socialist era. But in **Sachsenplatz,** the sooty façades of early 18th-century **Bürgerhäuser** can be seen clearly if you look past the tired cement of the Platz itself. Behind the *Altes Rathaus,* on Nikolaistr., the 800-yr.-old **Nikolaikirche** witnessed the birth of Bach's *Johannes Passion* and the GDR's peaceful revolution (open Mon.-Sat. 10am-6pm, Sun. after services; free). The **Museum der Bildenden Künste,** Georg-Dimitroff-Platz 1, hosts a ponderously impressive 2500 paintings and sculptures, including works by van Eyck, Dürer, Rubens, Kolbe, Rembrandt, and Rodin (open Tues.-Sun. 9am-5pm, Wed. 1-9:30pm; DM5, students DM2.50, free on Sun.). The striking but unattractive **Neues Rathaus** covers an entire city block at the end of Schillerstr. Just north is the **Thomaskirche,** where Bach's remains were interred in front of the altar after his original burial site was destroyed in WWII, and where a stained-glass win-

GERMANY

dow commemorates Martin Luther's trip here in the early stages of the Reformation. Mozart and Mendelssohn performed in this church, and Wagner was baptized here in 1813. (Open 8am-6pm; in winter 9am-5pm.)

The **Museum der "Runden Ecke,"** Dittrichring 24, former headquarters of the **Stasi,** the East German Ministry for State Security, houses a permanent exhibition "Stasi: Macht und Banalität" (Power and Banality). The 10,000 names of Stasi-suspects on one wall sums up the experience with eloquent force (open Wed.-Sun. 2-6pm; free). Outside the city, a towering stone monument commemorates Leipzig's first self-liberation; the **Völkerschlachtdenkmal** on the *Süd-Friedhof* remembers the 400,000 soldiers engaged in the 1813 Battle of Nations. From the top, on clear days, you can see the Harz Mountains. Take streetcar 15 or 20 "Meusdorf" or "Probstheida" to Völkerschlachtdenkmal (open 10am-5pm; DM3.50, students DM2).

Leipzig's classical music offerings are among the best in Europe. Above all, try to hear the **Gewandhaus Orchestra,** a major international orchestra since 1843. Some concerts are free, but usually only when a guest orchestra is playing; otherwise buy tickets (DM7 and up; 30% student discount) at the Gewandhaus box office, Augustusplatz 8 (tel. (0341) 127 02 80; open Mon. 1-6pm, Tues.-Fri. 10am-6pm, Sat. 10am-2pm; no concerts in August).

Locals complain that the nightlife isn't what it used to be in the days before the Wall fell, since those most willing to walk on the wild side went west after the borders opened. All the same, the remaining students keep things hopping. The **Moritzbastei,** Universitätsstr. 9, is a complex of various-sized café, bar, and concert areas, most of which are underground, with hip, curved brick walls and ceilings. Everybody meets everybody here. (Ticket counter open Mon. noon-6pm, Tues.-Fri. noon-2pm and before shows; DM4-10.) **Killywilly,** Karl-Liebknecht-Str. 44, is a ballsy Irish pub in the southern part of town (open 6pm-2am). At **Kabarett "Academixer,"** Kupfergasse 6, the Leipzig student body recreates a 1920s Cabaret atmosphere—very Joel Grey, very late Weimar. The **Academixer-Club** opens up for drinks each night after the show (open around 10:30pm-late).

Practical Information, Accommodations, and Food Leipzig's **tourist office,** Sachsenpl. 1 (tel. (0341) 795 90), books private rooms (DM45 fee). Ask for the useful free map of the *Innenstadt* and suburbs. From the train station, walk through Pl. der Republik and bear right past the Park Hotel. (Open Mon.-Fri. 9am-7pm, Sat. 9:30am-2pm.) Leipzig lies on the Berlin-Munich **rail** line with regular Inter-City service to Frankfurt am Main. The information counter is near track 15. **Trams** cover the city, running from 5:30am until around 12:30-1am. Tickets come in three brands: 10min. for DM1, 30min. for DM1.50, and 60min. for DM1.50

Budget travelers are still a novelty here, though they are not, unfortunately, as rare as budget rooms. The large and well-run **Jugendherberge Leipzig Centrum (HI)** is at Käthe-Kollwitz-Str. 64 (tel. (0341) 47 05 30, fax 47 58 88). Take tram 1 or 2 west 4 stops to Marchenstr. and continue down the street. (Reception open 7-9am and 2:30-10pm. Curfew 1am. DM19, over 26, DM23.50.) Unfortunately, this hotel is slated to be closed in the summer of 1995; call ahead. The **Hotel Grünau,** Gärtnerstr. 177 (tel. (0341) 412 61 50, fax 412 61 58), has newly renovated rooms, and a restaurant downstairs; but Grünau isn't Leipzig's loveliest suburb—don't wander too far (reception open until 11pm, but call ahead; singles DM52, doubles DM82; breakfast included). **Campingplatz am Kulkwitzer See** (tel. (0341) 941 13 15) is on Seestr. in Markrandstadt; take tram 8 "Lausen" to the last stop and bear right (open April 15-Oct. 15). The **Innenstadt** is well-supplied with **Imbiß** (snack joints), bistros, and restaurants, but an ever-increasing number are of the DM4-for-a-glass-of-juice variety. A lifesaver is the **Tengelmann Supermarkt** on the Brühl, 5min. from the station. Local farmers and Greek and Turkish merchants offer a **market** of fresh produce Tuesdays and Fridays in *Sachsenplatz,* in front of the tourist office. Two blocks left of the Centrum hostel, **Antiquitäten Café Galerie "Kleinod,"** Käthe-Kollwitz-Str. 71, offers small but well-prepared dishes among elegant mismatched chairs and eleven different clocks showing eleven different times (open 2-10pm).

■ NAUMBURG

Despite its beauties, Naumburg is best as a day-trip; well-situated along the rail network, it's an excellent sidelight to a visit to Leipzig, Halle, Weimar, or Erfurt. Between Leipzig and Weimar, the phenomenal **Naumburger Dom**, cathedral extraordinaire, merits a visit. Begun in the 11th century, it was glamorized two centuries later with 12 striking stone figures by one of Germany's greatest sculptors. The still, echoing space inside the *Dom* is interrupted only by the constant construction on the exterior. (Open Mon.-Sat. 9am-6pm, Sun. noon-6pm. DM3.50, students and seniors DM2. DM10 for the right to take photos or use video cameras inside.) Naumburg has recovered well from its 45 years as a backwater Red Army post. A jaunt on Steinweg leads to Naumburg's bright, lively **market** and then to the **Wenzelkirche**, the *Dom's* earnest runner-up. It features a couple of Cranach paintings and an impressive 18th-century organ (open Mon.-Sat. 10am-4pm, Sun. and holidays noon-4pm; free).

The **tourist office**, right on the market square under the big "*Fremdenverkehrsamt*" sign can also help find a room for the night. The best bets here are definitely rooms with private families (open Mon.-Fri. 9am-6pm, Sat. 10am-4pm, Sun. 10am-2pm). Cheap meals can be found on Steinweg past the *Dom*. Naumburg's most interesting culinary surprise is indubitably **China-Garten**, 4 Rosbacher Str., an extremely authentic American-Chinese restaurant that flaunts the obligatory muted lacquer trim, mirrors, and pseudo-Asian instrumental pop. (Open 11:30am-2:45pm and 5:30-11:30pm).

■■■ HALLE

Halle an der Saale, the fortunate town saved by Katrin's drumming in the climactic scene of Brecht's *Mother Courage and Her Children,* was also lucky enough to emerge from WWII more or less unscathed. The city's luck ran out 3 months later, however, when the occupying Americans traded the city to the Soviets for a piece of Berlin. Halle has two favorite sons: composer Georg Friedrich Händel and political *Wunder* Hans-Dietrich Genscher, Germany's well-respected ex-foreign minister. The city revolves around the **Marktplatz,** which buzzes with traffic, vegetable stands, con artists, and international vendors around the haunting **Roter Turm,** a 400-year-old bell tower. Across from the tower stands the **Marktkirche unsere lieben Frauen,** with the organ where little Händel began his studies. (Open Mon.-Wed. and Fri. 10am-noon and 3-6pm, Thurs. 4-5pm, Sat. 9am-noon and 3-5pm, Sun. service at 10am. Free 30min. organ concerts Tues. at 4:30pm and Fri. at 5:30pm.) The **Händelhaus,** the composer's family home at Große Nikolaistr. 5-6, offers high-quality stereo soundtracks in 19 languages to guide pilgrims through Händel's career in Germany, Italy, and England. (Open Mon.-Wed. and Fri.-Sun. 9:30am-5:30pm, Thurs. 9:30am-7pm. DM2, students DM0.50, seniors DM1; Thurs. free.) From Händel's home to the **Dom** (cathedral) is a 5min. walk down Nikolaistr. Just a few steps from the *Dom* lies the 15th-century **Moritzburg fortress,** most of which is dedicated to the **Staatliche Galerie Moritzburg Halle,** the largest art museum in Sachsen-Anhalt; although much of the collection was burnt or sold off by the Nazis, the salvaged works remain an impressive monument to artistic freedom. (Open Tues. 11am-8:30pm, Wed.-Fri. 10am-5:30pm, Sat.-Sun. 10am-6pm; last admission ½hr. before closing; DM5, students DM3, Tues. free).

The **tourist office** (tel. (0345) 233 40), in the *Roter Turm* on the Marktplatz, sells maps and books rooms (open Mon.-Tues. and Thurs.-Fri. 9am-6pm, Wed. 10am-6pm, Sat. 9am-1pm; April-Sept. also Sun. 10am-2pm). From the main train station, cross beneath the underpass to the left as you exit the building, follow the pedestrian tunnel, and follow Leipzigerstr. past the *Leipziger Turm* to the Marktplatz (15min). Or take tram 4 "Heide/Hubertuspl." or 7 "Kröllwitz" to Markt (4 stops). The **Jugendherberge (HI),** August-Bebel-Str. 48a (tel. (0345) 247 16), is in a newly restored mansion north of the market. Take tram 7 "Kröllwitz" 6 stops from the train station or 2 from the market. Follow Geistsstr. 1 block, turn right onto Pusch-kinstr., and turn right onto August-Bebel-Str. (Reception open 7-10am and 5-11pm. Lockout 10am-5pm. Curfew 10pm. DM13, over 26 DM18.50. Breakfast included.)

■■■ WEIMAR

The name **Weimar** still evokes many contradictory pictures: the 1919 well-inten-tioned Constitution that proved disastrous, ultimately leading to the rise of the Nazis; the birthplace of the Bauhaus art school; site of the Buchenwald concentra-tion camp; the city where Germany's first republic was founded; and the city where Goethe, Schiller, Herder, Liszt, and Nietzsche all unleashed their genius.

Goethe, Germany's very own Renaissance man, still reigns over these streets 150 years after his death. Especially impressive are his flawless manuscripts and private chambers in the **Goethehaus,** Frauenplan 1 (open Tues.-Sun. 9am-5pm; Nov.-Feb. 9am-4pm; DM8, students DM5). A handy English guide, *Goethe's House on the Frauenplan at Weimar* (DM3) will guide you through the rooms where Goethe entertained, wrote, studied, and eventually died. Between the Frauenplan and the **Marktplatz** is the beginning of Weimar's central artery, **Schillerstraße,** a pedestrian zone crammed with antique shops and bookstores. At the end of the street, **Schiller-haus,** Schillerstr. 12, the former residence of the playwright, displays original drafts, early editions of plays, and a biographical chronicle of the life of Goethe's friend and rival (open Wed.-Mon. 9am-5pm; Nov.-Feb. Wed.-Mon. 9am-4pm; DM5, students DM3). Around the corner, the pair are reconciled in stone before the **Deutsches Nationaltheater,** which first breathed life into their stage works (tel. (03643) 75 53 34; box office open Mon. 2-6pm, Tues.-Fri. 10am-1pm and 4-6pm, Sat. 10am-noon and 3-6pm; tours of the interior Sat. 3-5pm; tickets DM20-60, student rush tickets as low as DM7).

The **Bauhaus School,** now at the **Hochschule für Architektur und Bauwesen** (College for Architecture and Construction), offers no exhibits related to the icono-clastic design movement. Bauhaus work is better represented by the **Denkmal der Märzgefallenen,** designed by Gropius to honor those killed in the 1919 revolution. Of particular note are Goethe's fake ruins and the statue of William Shakespeare at the **Park an der Ilm,** still bearing the scars of a coat of black paint applied by the Nazis in 1939. On the park's slopes rests Goethe's **Gartenhaus,** Corona-Schröter-Str., the poet's first home in Weimar and later his retreat from the city (open Tues.-Sun. 9am-noon and 1-5pm; DM3, students DM1). At the edge of the park is the **Franz Liszt Haus,** Marienstr. 17, where the composer spent his last years. The instruments and furnishings are supposedly original, but given Liszt's torrid love life, the small single bed seems unlikely (open Tues.-Sun. 9am-1pm and 2-5pm; Nov.-Feb. 9am-1pm and 2-4pm. DM2, students and seniors DM1).

Practical Information, Accommodations, and Food Weimar's intelligently-designed bus system runs virtually all lines through two nerve centers: the train station and the Goetheplatz in the center of town. **Weimar Information,** Marktstr. 10 (tel. (03643) 21 73, fax 612 40), within view of the city's *Rathaus,* pro-vides maps, brochures, theater tickets and the like (open Mon.-Fri. 9am-7pm, Sat. 9am-4pm, Sun. 10am-4pm; Nov.-Feb. Mon.-Fri. 9am-6pm, Sat. 9am-1pm). Weimar's three youth hostels make finding a place to stay here easier than in other Eastern cit-ies. Try the friendly, convenient **Jugendherberge Germania (HI),** Carl-August-Allee 13 (tel. (03643) 20 76), 2min. from the station (reception open 3-11pm; lockout 10am-1pm; curfew 11pm; DM16.50, over 26 DM20.50; includes breakfast). The **Jugendgästehaus Maxim Gorki (HI),** Zum Wilden Graben 12 (tel. and fax (03643) 34 71) is pleasantly located amid old villas (reception open 4-8pm; DM19.50, over 26 DM23.50; 4-bed "family" rooms with showers DM50; includes breakfast). Weimar serves up very rich cooking for tourists; console yourself at the daily **pro-duce market** in the Marktplatz, or at the **Ladenmarkt** grocery store at the corner of Markstr. and Windischenstr.; facing the tourist office, turn left and walk a block (open Mon.-Fri. 8am-6pm, Sat. 8am-noon). For pizzas and salads in a jazzy venue, try **Scenario,** Carl-August-Allee 15 (tel. (03643) 41 96 40), at the corner of Meyerstr. (open 11am-1am; kitchen closes at 11pm; DM7-12).

■ BUCHENWALD

From 1937 to 1945, the **Buchenwald** concentration camp held over 250,000 Jews, political prisoners, gypsies, and gays; most did not survive the Holocaust. What remains is the **Nationale Mahn- und Gedenkstätte Buchenwald** (National Buchenwald Memorial). Signs point to the **KZ Lager** and the **Gedenkstätte:** the former refers to the remains of the camp; the latter is a solemn monument overlooking the valley. Since reunification, the focus of the camp exhibits has shifted from the internment of German communists under the Third Reich to the Soviet use of the camp from 1945-50, when 32,000 Germans were interned here by the Soviet Army—almost no mention is made of the other victims of the camp. **Memorial stones,** on the site of a former Jewish children's barracks, read in English, German, and Hebrew: "So that the generation to come might know; that the children, yet to be born, may rise and declare to their children." (Museum and film buildings open 9:45am-5:15pm; Oct.-April 8:45am-4:15pm.)

■■■ ERFURT

Erfurt offers a stunning cathedral, a handful of museums, and a cultural life fueled by its three colleges. Because of its political importance and its recent 1250th birthday celebration, most of the inner city has been beautifully restored, giving Erfurt a look of style all too rare in the cities of the East. Towering above the city skyline on the Domhügel hill is one of Eastern Germany's most impressive cathedrals, the mammoth Erfurt **Dom.** Luther was invested as a priest here and interrupted his first mass by throwing a Bible across the altar. He claimed that his target was the devil himself. The simple sandstone interior of the **Church of St. Severi** is dominated by the Saint's sarcophagus. (Cathedral and church open Mon.-Fri. 9-11:30am and 12:30-5pm, Sat. 9-11:30am and 12:30-4:30pm, Sun. 2-4pm; Mass Sun. 11am and 6pm.) From the sprawling Domplatz, a broad **Marktstr.** leads down to the Fischmarkt, bordered by former guild houses with rather wild façades, and the 1869 **Rathaus.** Marktstr. runs to the Gera River, spanned by the **Krämerbrücke,** a covered medieval bridge teeming with small shops dating from the 12th century. From the far side of the bridge, follow Gotthardstr., and cut left through Kirchengasse to reach the **Augustinerkloster,** where Martin Luther spent 10 years. He got his way; the cloister now functions as a Protestant college.

The **tourist office (Erfurt Fremdenverkehrsamt),** Bahnhofstr. 37 (tel. (0361) 262 67; fax 233 55), is 5min. straight from the train station. They sell maps and book rooms in private homes (open Mon.-Fri. 10am-6pm, Sat. 10am-1pm; singles DM30-40; doubles DM40-60; DM5 fee). Housing options are limited. Try the **Jugendherberge (HI),** Hochheimerstr. 12 (tel. (0361) 265 67 05), whose newly renovated interior is much more accommodating than the dilapidated exterior. Take tram 5 from the train station to "Steigerstr.", backtrack a bit, turn left onto Hochheimerstr., and the hostel is on the left corner at the first intersection (reception open 6-9am and 3-10pm; lockout 10am-3pm, curfew 10pm; DM18, over 26 DM21.50; breakfast included). In a pinch, Weimar's hostels are only a 15min. train ride away. Sample the succulent regional speciality *Thüringer Bratwurst* from the countless stands at street corners (DM2-3).

■■■ THURINGIAN FOREST

Stretching south of Eisenach, Weimar, and Erfurt to the border with Bavaria, the time-worn mountains and the peaceful pine woods of the Thuringian Forest fostered and inspired many of Germany's composers, philosophers, and poets. The

Rennsteig, a 168km-long scenic hiking trail, snakes from Hörschel near Eisenach right into Bavaria; history books date the trail at 1330, but locals claim that it was first worn down by prehistoric hunter-gatherers.

Arnstadt Just beyond Erfurt lies Arnstadt, Thuringia's oldest town. J.S. Bach began his career as an organist in what is now the **Bachkirche** (open March-Sept. 10:30am-12:30pm and 2-4pm). The **Neues Schloß** (new palace), Schloßplatz 1, houses the **doll museum "Mon Plaisier."** More than 400 dolls are displayed in 24 dollhouses, in a total of 82 furnished rooms. (Open Tues.-Sun. 8:30am-noon and 1-4:30pm; Nov.-April Tues.-Sun. 9:30am-4pm. DM2.50, students DM1.50.) The **tourist office, Arnstadt Information,** Markt 3 (tel. (03628) 20 49), finds rooms from DM30 (DM3 fee); turn left from the station and then right on Bahnhofstr., and walk up Ledermarkt (open Mon.-Fri. 9:30-noon and 12:30-6pm, Sat. 9am-noon). They also organize bus tours (DM5-10) to the **Drei Gleichen** (3 matching castles), and have info on hiking trails. Near Arnstadt, the ruined monastery of **Paulinzella,** on the train line to Saalfeld and Rudolstadt, remains one of Thuringia's most striking monuments of the Romanesque period.

Ilmenau and the Goethe Trail

By far Thuringia's favorite posterboy genius is Johann Wolfgang Goethe, who first worked in **Ilmenau** reorganizing the area mining industry, only to return to the area later in life as a self-searching poet. South of the city center, parallel to Waldstr., stretches the 18½km **Goethe Trail (Goethewanderung),** marked by Goethe's over-flourished **"G"** monogram, leading through the forest to Stützerbach. About 4km uphill is his hut on the **Kickelhahn,** where you can read the poetry he scratched on the walls as a young man. A year before his death at age 83, Goethe himself returned to the hut on a tour of his past. The hike ends in **Stützerbach,** where the local glass-works magnate hosted the poet. His house is now a **Goethe Memorial,** with demonstrations of traditional **glass-blowing** on the 1st floor (open Tues.-Sun. 9am-noon and 1-5pm; DM3, students DM2). Ilmenau also makes a good starting point for a hike along the **Rennsteig.** (Take the train to Schmiedefeld.)

Ilmenau's **tourist office** is at Lindenstr. 12 (tel. (03677) 23 58, fax 25 02); walk down Bahnhofstr. across Wetzlarer Platz and follow the pedestrian zone (15min.). It provides maps and hiking brochures (DM5) and books private rooms (from DM15) for DM2 per person (open Mon.-Fri 9am-6pm, Sat. 9am-noon). The **youth hostel,** Waldstr. 22 (tel. (03677) 24 13), lies at the beginning of the trail straight ahead from Bahnhof Ilmenau-Bad (reception open 7am-8pm; curfew 10pm; DM14.50, over 26 DM18.50). Behind the Raiffeisenbank on the right side of Bahnhofstr., the **market** offers fresh fruits and vegetables (open Mon.-Fri. 8am-5pm, Sat. 8am-11am).

Rudolstadt and Bad Blankenburg

Below Weimar, the Saale River Valley winds to **Rudolstadt,** where Richard Wagner got his first break as the local choir director. **Schillerstraße 25** marks the spot where Goethe and Schiller first met, thus beginning one of literature's greatest symbiotic relationships. During the 18th century, social life centered on the Baroque-towered **Heidecksburg palace,** accessible by Vorwerkgasse, a path behind the *Rathaus* (open Tues.-Sun. 10am-6pm; Oct.-April 9am-4pm; DM6, children DM3). Rudolstadt is also a route to **Schloß Kochberg,** once the summer home of **Charlotte von Stein,** the inspiration for many of Goethe's powerful love poems; take bus 21. (Open Tues.-Sun. 9am-noon and 1-5pm; Sept.-April Wed.-Sun. 9am-noon and 1-5pm. DM6, students DM4. Last bus from Groß Kochberg to Rudolstadt around 5:08pm.)

To reach the **tourist office,** Marktstr. 57 (tel. and fax (03672) 245 43), walk down Bahnhofstr. to Marktstr. and turn left (open Mon.-Fri 9am-6pm, Sat. 9am-1pm). Trains and buses from Weimar (bus 14) and Erfurt (bus 13) take about an hour. The nearest **hostel** is in **Bad Blankenburg,** Am Kesselberg 1 (tel. (03674) 25 28), a 20min. bus ride away. From Anton-Sommer-Str. (across from the Rudolstadt station) take bus A, B, or C "Bad Blankenburg" to the *Bahnhof.* Walk straight on Bahnhofstr., then right on Zeigerheimer Weg onto Burgweg. Turn right on Unterehausbergstr. and left onto Am Jesuborn. (Reception open 2-7pm. Curfew 10pm. 5-day max. stay. DM15.50, over 26 DM19.)

Saalfeld Just 25min. by train from Rudolstadt lies Saalfeld, famous for its underground **Feengrotten** (fairy grottoes), Feengrottenweg 2. The phosphorescent caverns are intensely colorful; the main orange and amber **Märchendom** (fairy cathedral) chamber branches off into the **Blaugrüne Grotte** (blue-green grotto) that glows with teal light. From the marketplace go straight on Brudergasse and then on to Pfortenstr.; take a left on Melanchthonstr. and follow the signs. (Open Feb. to mid-Nov. 9am-5pm. Tours every 45min. DM6, students DM4.50.)

Saalfeld's **tourist office,** Blankenburger Str. 4 (tel. and fax (03671) 339 50), scouts out rooms (from DM25) for a DM3 fee. From the station, walk left on Bahnhofstr. and across the bridge; at the Saaltor gate, take Saalstr. and turn right at *Markt* (open Mon.-Fri 9am-6pm, Sat 9am-noon). Saalfeld's **youth hostel,** Schieferhof 4 (tel. (03671) 28 02 or 51 03 94), is a 25min. hike from the station. At the Saaltor gate, go right on Am Bleichanger and follow it until Schieferhof. (Reception open 7am-8pm. Curfew 10pm. DM14, over 26 DM17.) **Roter Hirsch,** Markt 6 (tel. 22 85), offers Thuringian wild game (open 9am-10pm; lunch DM10-14, dinner DM11-18).

■■■ EISENACH

Birthplace of Johann Sebastian Bach and home-in-exile of Martin Luther, Eisenach boasts impressive humanist credentials. Its medieval half-timbered houses ornament the northwestern slope of the Thuringian forest. The Romanesque **Wartburg Schloß** sheltered Martin Luther after his excommunication while the reformer translated the Bible into German. The castle's **Festsaal** commemorates the 1817 meeting of university fraternities. The view from the top of the Wartburg's courtyard tower is amazing; the 1st floor is a former dungeon. Wartburg sits on the south side of Eisenach, down Wartburger Allee from the train station. A plethora of city-sponsored tourist buses run back and forth between the city center, the castle, and the hill every 15min. (rountrip DM2.50, one-way DM1.50). For the more adventurous, there are a number of well-cleared footpaths up the hill.

The **Bachhaus,** Frauenplan 21 (tel. (03691) 20 37 14), where Johann Sebastian stormed into the world in 1685, recreates the family quarters with period instruments. Turn off Wartburger Allee at Grimmelgasse (open Mon. noon-5:45pm, Tues.-Sun. 9am-5:45pm; DM5, students and seniors DM4). Town life centers on the **Markt,** bounded by the **Lutherhaus,** Lutherplatz 8, home to young man Martin from 1498 to 1501 (open 9am-1pm and 2-5pm; DM3, students DM1.50).

Practical Information, Accommodations, and Food The **tourist office,** Bahnhofstr. 3-5 (tel. and fax (03691) 69 04 15), books private rooms for no fee (open Mon. 10am-6pm, Tues.-Fri. 9am-6pm, Sat. 10am-2pm). **Jugendherberge Artur Becker (HI),** Mariental 24 (tel. (03691) 20 36 13), fills an old villa beyond the castle. From the station, take Bahnhofstr. to Wartburgallee, to Mariental; the hostel is 15min. down and to the right. Or, take the infrequent bus 3 from the station, get off at Lillenstr., and the path to the hostel will be a few meters in front of you. (Reception open 9am-8pm; curfew 10pm; DM16, over 26 DM19.50; breakfast included.) **Camp** at **Am Altenberger See** (tel. (03691) 741 37), in the hamlet of Eckardshausen. From the Eisenach station, take the Bad Liebenstein bus (4 per day 7:35am-5:35pm); tell the driver your destination. (Reception open until 8pm. DM10 per person.) Take in well-priced local food specialties at the **Gastätte Zum Schwan,** Bahnhofstr. 12, with lunch deals starting around DM8 (open Mon.-Fri. 8am-6pm).

BAVARIA (BAYERN)

From hidden villages in the Bavarian Forest and glittering Baroque cities along the Danube to medieval churches punctuating the Romantic Road and turreted castles of the Alps, Bavaria is the Germany of fairy tale, Teutonic myth, and Wagnerian opera. In fact, when many foreigners conjure up images of Germany, they imagine the Bavaria-land of beer halls, oom-pah bands, and *Lederhosen.* Nevertheless, the fiercely independent locals have always been Bavarians first and Germans second. *Remember that HI-affiliated hostels in Bavaria do not admit guests over age 26.*

■■■ MUNICH (MÜNCHEN)

The capital and cultural center of Bavaria, Munich is a sprawling, liberal metropolis in the midst of solidly conservative southern Germany. World-class museums, handsome parks and architecture, a rambunctious arts scene, and an urbane population combine to create a city of astonishing vitality. The ebullient, arrogant mixture of sophistication and earthy Bavarian *Gemütlichkeit* keeps the city awake at all hours. *Münchners* party particularly zealously during *Fasching* (Jan.1-Feb. 28 in 1995), Germany's equivalent of Mardi Gras, and during the legendary *Oktoberfest.*

ORIENTATION AND PRACTICAL INFORMATION

Touring by foot is easy in Munich's compact center. **Schützenstraße,** straight ahead from the main train station, leads towards **Neuhauser Straße,** the main pedestrian shopping street. Neuhauser Str. connects **Karlsplatz** (called **Stachus** by the *Münchener)* and the famed **Marienplatz. Im Tal** leads further to Zweibrückenstr., and to the Isar River. North of Marienplatz, the pedestrian zone ranges to **Odeonsplatz,** next to the *Residenz* palace. **Ludwigstraße,** an avenue of lordly homes, leads to the Siegestor, where Munich's strip of iniquity and chic nightlife, **Leopoldstraße,** continues north through **Schwabing,** once the center of student life but now rivaled by other urban centers like the culturally fertile **Haidhausen** southeast of the Isar. Further southwest sits posh **Nymphenburg,** built around **Nymphenburg Palace.** Southwest of Marienplatz, **Sendlingerstraße** leads past shops and the Baroque **Asamkirche** to the Sendlingertor. Lindwurmstr. proceeds onward to Goetheplatz, from which Mozartstr. leads to **Theresienwiese,** site of the *Oktoberfest.*

Tourist Office: Fremdenverkehrsamt (tel. 239 12 56 or 239 12 57), opposite track 11 in the main train station. A must, but you'll wait 5-15min. or more in summer. Books rooms (DM5 per room plus DM3-9 deposit) and sells accommodations lists (DM0.50). Excellent free map. Open Mon.-Sat. 8am-10pm, Sun. 11am-7pm. Branch office at the **Flughafen München** airport (tel. 97 59 28 15) in the *Zentralgebäude.* Open Mon.-Sat. 8:30am-10pm, Sun. 1-9pm. **Fremdenverkehrsband München-Oberbayern,** Sonnenstr. 10 (tel. 59 73 47), has brochures, maps, and info for the upper Bavaria region (open Mon.-Thurs. 9am-noon, 1-5pm, Fri. 8am-noon). **EurAide in English** (tel. 59 38 89), in the station at track 11. Provides free train info and reserves rooms (DM6). Their free *Inside Track* is available at their office and at the *Reisezentrum.* Eurailpasses validated. Open May 7:30-11:30am and 1-6pm and 1-4:30pm; June-Oct. 7:30-11:30am and 1-6pm.
Budget Travel: Studiosus Reisen an der Uni, Amalienstr. 73 (tel. 50 06 05 40 or 50 06 05 43, ext. 544), near the university. Open Mon.-Fri. 9am-6pm. Sells ISIC Mon.-Fri. 9:30-11:30am. **Travel Overland,** Leopoldstr. 13 (tel. 34 67 21 or 27 27 60), behind the pink library in the university cafeteria. Open Mon.-Fri. 10am-2pm.
Consulates: U.S., Königinstr. 5 (tel. 288 80). Open Mon.-Fri. 8-11:30am. **Canada,** Tal 29 (tel. 22 26 61). Open Mon.-Fri. 9am-noon, 2-5pm, Fri. 9am-1:30pm. **U.K.,** Bürkleinstr. 10 (tel. 21 10 90). Open Mon.-Fri. 8:45-11:30am and 1-3:15pm. **Ireland,** Mauerkircherstr. 1a (tel. 98 57 23 25). Open Mon.-Fri. 9am-noon and 2-4pm.
Currency Exchange: Go to the **post office** across from the station to exchange large denomination traveler's checks (DM6 per check). **Deutsche Verkehrs-**

Munich (München)

Bank (DVB), at the main station, also changes currency and checks and advances cash with Visa and MasterCard. Open 6am-11pm. Pick up the *Inside Track* at the EurAide office for a 50% commission reduction for U.S. traveler's checks totaling over US$50 at the Deutsche Verkehrs-Bank.

American Express: Promenadepl. 6 (tel. 29 09 00). From the train station, walk straight through Karlsplatz to Neuhauserstr. and turn left on Ettstr. Cashes AmEx checks for no fee. Open Mon.-Fri. 9am-5:30pm, Sat. 9:30am-12:30pm.

Post Office: Post/Telegrafamt, Bahnhofplatz 1, 80335 München (tel. 54 54 27 32), opposite the train station. **Poste Restante** open Mon.-Fri. 6am-10pm, Sat.-Sun. 7am-10pm.

Telephones: Make credit card and collect calls from the **post office** on the 2nd level of the train station or across the street. **City code:** 089.

Flights: The spiffy new **Flughafen München** is accessible from the train station by S-Bahn 8 every 20min. 3:22am-12:42pm. DM12.50 or 8 stripes on a 12-stripe ticket *(Streifenkarte);* railpasses valid. For flight info call 97 52 13 13.

Trains: Munich connects to all major cities in Germany and throughout Europe several times per day. For schedules and fare info, call 194 19; reservations (in German only), 12 23 23 33. Station open 5am-12:30am. To: Frankfurt (3½hr.); Berlin (9½hr.); Prague (7hr.); Vienna (5½hr.); and Zürich (4½hr.).

Public Transportation: Runs from about 5am-12:30am on weekdays, until 1:30am on weekends. Eurail is valid on S-Bahn (commuter rail), but *not* on the U-Bahn (subway), *Straßenbahn* (trams), or buses. Single rides within the *Innenraum* (inner city) cost DM3.20. The *Tageskarte Innenraum* (inner-city day pass) is valid for up to 5 people (max. 2 adults) and a dog—no joke—from 9am until the last U-Bahn (DM10). Cancel your ticket in the boxes marked with an "E" *before* you go to the platform. Transit maps can be found at the tourist office, EurAide, and the MVV counters near the subway entrance in the train station.

Bike Rental: Rent bikes from the **Deutsche Bahn** at 15 S-Bahn locations and return them to stations throughout Upper Bavaria. DM12 per day, DM8 for rail-ticket holders. Most convenient to town is English-speaking **Radius Touristik** (tel. 59 61 13), near platform 35 at the station. Bikes DM10 for up to 2hr., DM20 per day (10am-6pm), DM80 per week. DM50 deposit. Students and Eurailpass holders get a 10% discount. Open 9am-6pm.

Hitchhiking: Hitchers try *Autobahn* on-ramps; *standing behind the blue sign with the white auto may incur heavy fines.* Hitchers who've gotta get to *Autobahn* E11 "Salzburg-Vienna-Italy" start with U-Bahn 1 or 2: Karl-Preis-Platz. For E11 "Stuttgart/France", they take U-Bahn 1: Rotkreuzplatz, then tram 12: Amalienburgstr.; *or* S-Bahn 2: Obermenzing. Thumbers who want to get to the *Autobahn* E6 interchange for all points north take U-Bahn 6: Studentenstadt and walk 500m to the Frankfurter Ring. For the *Autobahn* to Lake Constance and Switzerland, these intrepid souls take U-Bahn 4 or 5: Heimeranplatz, then bus 33: Siegenburgerstr. For Garmisch-Partenkirchen, hitchers head for the *Autobahn* E6 south; U-Bahn 3 or 6: Westpark, and from bus 33: Luise-Kesselbach-Platz. To ride-share, you can try **McShare Treffpunkt Zentrale,** Lämmerstr. 4 (tel. 59 45 61), near train station. Open Mon.-Sat. 8am-8pm. **Känguruh,** Amalienstr. 87 (tel. 194 44), in the Amalienpassage. Open Mon.-Fri. 8:30am-7pm, Sat. 9am-3pm, Sun. 10am-7pm. Also scan bulletin boards in the *Mensa* at Leopoldstr. 13.

Laundromat: Münz Wäschsalon, Amalienstr. 61, near the university. Wash DM6, dry DM1. Soap DM1. Open Mon.-Fri. 8am-6:30pm, Sat. 8am-1pm.

Pharmacy: Bahnhof Apotheke (tel. 59 41 19 or 59 81 19), on the corner outside the station. Open Mon.-Fri. 8am-6:30pm, Sat. 8am-2pm. 24-hr. service rotates; call 59 44 75 for info or get a free schedule from the tourist office or EurAide.

Medical Assistance: University clinic, across the river on Ismaningerstr. U.S. and British consulates have lists of English-speaking doctors.

Emergencies: Ambulance: tel. 192 22. **Emergency medical service:** tel. 55 86 61. **Police:** tel. 110.

ACCOMMODATIONS AND CAMPING

Munich accommodations fall into one of three categories: seedy, expensive, or booked. Reserve in advance in summer and during *Oktoberfest,* when all three often apply. Sleeping in the *Englischer Garten* is unsafe and illegal. With a railpass, Augsburg's hostel (30-45min. by train) is a viable option, but mind the 11pm curfew.

Hostels and Camping

Jugendlager Kapuzinerhölzl ("The Tent"), Franz-Schrank-Str. (tel. 141 43 00). U-Bahn 1: Rotkreuzplatz, then tram 12 "Amalienburgstr.": Botanischer Garten (ticket inspections are especially rigorous along this route). Sleep with 400 other people in a big circus tent. DM13 for foam pad, blankets, dry spot on the floor, bathrooms, shower, and hot tea. Spontaneous merrymaking around bonfire at nightfall. Tent's future is in doubt; call ahead. 3-day max. stay. Reception open 5pm-9am. Under 24 only (flexible). No reservations. Open late June-early Sept.

Jugendherberge (HI), Wendl-Dietrich-Str. 20. (tel. 13 11 56). U-Bahn 1: Rotkreuzplatz. Central location attracts crowds. Check-in 10:30am, but lines form before 9am. Reception open 10am-1am. Lockout 9am-12:30pm. Curfew 1am. Under 27 only. Men only dorm DM21.50. All else DM22.50 (4-6 beds per room). DM20 key deposit. DM50 safe deposit. Breakfast and sheets included.

Jugendherberge Pullach Burg Schwaneck (HI), Burgweg 4-6 (tel. 793 06 43, fax 793 79 22). S-Bahn 7 "Wolfratshausen": Pullach. Romantic surroundings swarms with schoolkids. Reception open 5-11pm. Curfew 11:30pm. Under 27 only. DM15.50 plus DM4 for sheets if 1-night stay. More nights, sheets free. Buy shower tokens (DM1) early to beat crowds. Breakfast included.

Jugendgästehaus München (HI), Miesingstr. 4 (tel. 723 65 50, fax 724 2567). U-Bahn 1 or 2: Sendlinger Tor, then U-Bahn 3 "Forstenrieder Allee": Thalkirchen (Tierpark). Crowded and distant, but rooms spacious and immaculate. Reception 7am-1am. Curfew 1am. Under 27 only. 8- to 15-bed rooms DM24.50-26.50. Singles DM32.50. Doubles DM28.50 per person. Triples DM26.50 per person. Quads DM26.50 per person. Sheets and breakfast included. July no phone reservations.

Haus International Youth Hotel, Elisabethstr. 87, 80797 München (tel. 12 00 60, fax 12 00 62 51). U-Bahn 2 "Dülferstr.": Hohenzollernpl., then tram 12 or bus 33: Barbarastr. Everything's clean. Disco with flashing lights and palm trees. Reception open 24hrs. Singles DM52-81. Doubles DM98-136. Triples DM133.50. Quads DM160. Quints DM195. Reserve by mail or fax.

CVJM (YMCA) Jugendgästehaus, Landwehrstr. 13, 80336 München (tel. 552 14 10, fax 550 42 84). Take Schillerstr. 2 blocks; it's on the left. Convenient, clean, no-frills rooms. Slightly seedy neighborhood. Reception 8am-12:30am. Curfew 12:30am. Singles DM45-49. Doubles DM78. Triples DM108. Over 27 15% surcharge. After 3-6 nights cheaper. Breakfast included. Reserve by phone and mail.

Jugendhotel Marienberge, Goethestr. 9 (tel. 55 58 91), south of the train station. Rough neighborhood but generally secure building staffed by nuns. *Only women 18-25.* Reception open 8am-midnight. Curfew midnight. Singles DM35. Doubles DM60. Triples DM90. 7-bed rooms DM25 per person. Showers and breakfast.

Camping: Campingplatz Thalkirchen, Zentrallandstr. 49 (tel. 723 17 07, fax 724 31 77). U-Bahn 1 or 2: Sendlinger Tor, then U-Bahn 3: Thalkirchen, then change to bus 57. Large grounds well-run but crowded. Laundry facilities, snack shop, TV lounge, billiards, and cheap restaurant (meals DM3-8). Curfew 11pm. DM7 per person. Under 4 DM2.50. Small tent DM5.50. Tent for 2 or more DM7. Motorcycle DM4. Car DM8. Trailer DM17.50. Showers DM1. Open mid-March to end of Oct.

Hotels and Pensions

When the city is full, finding singles under DM50-60 or doubles under DM80-100 is nearly impossible. The tourist office finds rooms (DM5 fee). At the train station, EurAide also finds rooms (DM6 fee).

Pension am Kaiserplatz, Kaiserplatz 12 (tel. 34 91 90). U-Bahn 2 or 5: Odeonsplatz, then U-Bahn 3 or 6: Münchner Freiheit. Elegantly decorated, high-ceilinged rooms. Reception open 7am-8pm. Singles DM45-59. Doubles DM69-79. Triples DM98-105. Quads DM120. Quints DM150. 6-person room DM160-170. Breakfast (room service) and showers included. Phone reservations only.

GERMANY

Pension Geiger, Steinheilstr. 1 (tel. 52 15 56), across from the Technische Universität. Homey, with big fluffy pillows. Reception open 8am-10pm. Singles DM45-65. Doubles DM84-96.

Pension Theresia, Luisenstr. 51 (tel. 52 12 50), 40 paces up Luisenstr. from Pension Geiger. Rooms plain but clean. Reception open 6:30am-10pm. Singles DM44-68. Doubles DM77-118. Breakfast included. Showers off hall DM3; no showers between 9pm-7am. DM3 surcharge on one-night stands.

Hotel-Pension am Markt, Heiliggeiststr. 6 (tel. 22 50 14, fax 22 40 17), in the town center next to *Heiliggeist Kirche.* Sparsely furnished but thoroughly clean rooms. Reception open 10am-7pm. Singles DM62-95. Doubles DM110-150. Breakfast included. Reserve rooms 3-4 weeks early by phone.

Hotel Haberstock, Schillerstr. 4(tel. 55 78 55, fax 550 36 34), right below the train station. Snazzy rooms with soft, expansive pillows. Reception open 24hrs. Singles DM60–98. Doubles DM104-165. Breakfast included. Prices 10% higher during *Oktoberfest.*

Hotel Helvetia, Schillerstr. 6 (tel. 55 47 45, fax 55 02 381), next door to Hotel Haberstock. Sparse but neat rooms. Central location. Singles DM65. Doubles DM95. Triples DM120. Quads DM160. Quints DM200. Showers and breakfast included. Phone reservations only. In summer call ahead for singles and doubles.

FOOD

Munich's gastronomic center is the vibrant **Viktualienmarkt,** 2min. south of Marienplatz, with a rainbow of bread, fruit, meat, pastry, cheese, wine, vegetable, and sandwich shops. (Open Mon.-Fri. 6am-6:30pm, Sat. 6am-noon.) Try Munich's *Leberkäs* (a mixture of beef and bacon) and *Weißwurst* (veal sausage).

Münch'ner Suppenküche, at the Viktualienmarkt; also at Schellingstr. 24 near the university. A Munich institution; warm hearty soup meals (DM4.90-7.80). *Krustis* (sandwiches) DM3.50-4.80. Open Mon.-Fri. 8am-6:30pm, Sat. 10am-5pm.

Türkenhof, Türkenstr. 78, to the left of the university. A favorite hangout for the university crowd. Smoky and packed in the evenings. Varying menu. Creative entrees *(Schnitzels,* omelettes, soups) DM7-15. Open 11am-1am.

La Boheme, Türkenstr. 79, just across from Türkenhof. Waiter, there's an antique knick-knack in my Italian food. Pastas DM10.50. Pizzas DM7-11. Salads DM5-9.50. At dinner add DM1 to all dishes. Beer DM3.50 (0.5L).

Gaustätte Engelsburg, Türkenstr. at Schellingstr. Low key mix of students and locals. Bavarian specialties including *Weißwürste, Nürnberger Rostbratwürstl,* and *Spätzle.* Daily special 3-course lunches DM9.90-15.90. Take-out window with its own menu, including pizza (DM8.50-12.50). Open 9:30am-1am.

Schelling Salon, Schellingstr. 54. Bavarian *Knödel* and billiard balls. Founded in 1872, this pool joint has racked the balls of Lenin, Rilke, and Hitler; Franz Josef Strauss came occasionally for a snack. Open Thurs.-Mon. 6:30am-midnight.

Me.t., Leopoldstr. 44. Right on the main drag near the Gisela Str. U-bahn. Cheap and good; a student magnet. Delicious pizza DM5-7.20. Pasta dishes DM5-6.50. Beer starts at DM2.80. Open Mon.-Sat. 5pm-1am, Sun. 11am-1am.

Gollier, Gollierstr. 83. Gollier and its sister establishment **Der Ignatz,** Georgenstr. 67, serve delicious homemade vegetarian fare. Gollier open Mon.-Fri., Sun. 11:30am-midnight and Sat. from 5pm. Der Ignatz open 10am-10pm. Sunday brunch 'til 1pm.

SIGHTS

The 15th-century **Frauenkirche** has long been one of Munich's most notable landmarks (towers open April-Oct. Mon.-Sat. 10am-5pm; DM4, students DM2, under 6 free). At the neo-Gothic **Neues Rathaus** (open Mon.-Fri. 9:30am-7pm, Sat., Sun. 10am-7pm; DM2, under 14 DM1), the **Glockenspiel** makes its booty boom with jousting knights and dancing coopers. At 9pm, a mechanical watchman marches out and the Guardian Angel escorts the *Münchner Kindl,* Munich's symbol, to bed. (Performances 11am, noon, 5, and 9pm; Nov.-April 11am and 9pm. Tower open Mon.-Fri. 9:30am-7pm, Sat.-Sun. 10am-7pm. DM2, under 14 DM1.)

Munich's ritual past is represented by the 11th-century **Peterskirche,** at Rinder-markt and Petersplatz; 294 steps scale the saintly tower, christened *Alter Peter* (Old Peter) by locals. Those clever Bavarians. (Tower open Mon.-Sat. 9am-6pm, Sun. 10am-6pm; DM2.50, students DM1.50, children DM0.50). Ludwig II of Bavaria (of dumbwaiter fame) rests in peace in a crypt of the 16th-century Jesuit **Michaels-kirche,** on Neuhauserstr. (crypt DM0.50). A Bavarian Rococo masterpiece, the **Asamkirche,** Sendlinger Str. 32, is named after the brothers who created it; Cosmas Damian Asam painted the frescoes while Egid Quirin Asam carved the sculptures. The dozens of richly decorated rooms built from the 14th to the 19th centuries in the magnificent **Residenz,** Max-Joseph-Platz 3 (U-Bahn 3, 4, 5 or 6: Odeonsplatz), form the material vestiges of the Wittelsbach dynasty. The **Schatzkammer** (trea-sury) contains jeweled baubles, crowns, swords, china, ivorywork, and other trin-kets from the 10th century on (open Tues.-Sun. 10am-4:30pm; DM4, students and group members DM2, children under 15 with adult free).

The royal summer residence of **Schloß Nymphenburg** is worth the trip north-west of town (U-Bahn 1: Rotkreuzplatz, then streetcar 12 "Amalienburgstr."). A Baroque wonder set in a winsome park, the palace hides a number of treasures, including a two-story granite marble hall seasoned with stucco, frescoes, and a Chi-nese lacquer cabinet. Check out King Ludwig's "Gallery of Beauties"—whenever a woman caught his fancy, he would have her portrait painted. (*Schloß* open Tues.-Sun. 9am-12:30pm and 1:30-5pm; Oct.-March 10am-12:30pm and 1:30-4pm. Main palace DM3, students DM5; entire complex DM6; children under 15 with adult free. Wander the grounds for free.) Next door is the immense **Botanischer Garten,** whose greenhouses shelter rare and wonderful flora from around the world. (Open 9am-7pm. Greenhouses open 9am-11:45am and 1-6:30pm. DM3, students DM1.50, under 15 DM0.50.) Abutting the city center is the vast **Englischer Garten,** one of Europe's oldest landscaped public parks.

Museums Munich is a supreme museum city. The **Deutsches Museum,** on the *Museumsinsel* (Museum Island) in the Isar River, is one of the world's most exten-sive museums of science and technology; the planetarium (DM2) and daily electrical show will warm the cockles of any physicist's heart (open Tues.-Sun. 9am-5pm; DM8, students DM3). The **Alte Pinakothek,** Barer Str.27, 13th-17th century Wittels-bacher family storage which covets works by Giotto, Titian, da Vinci, Dürer, Rem-brandt, and Rubens, is closed until 1997 for renovations, but main works are shown next door in the **Neue Pinakothek,** a sleek space for the 18th-19th centuries (open Tues. 10am-8pm, Wed., Fri.-Sun. 10am-5pm; DM6, students DM3.50. Sun. free). **Lenbachhaus,** Luisenstr. 33, houses Munich cityscapes, along with the works of Kandinsky, Klee, and the *Blaue Reiter* school, which disdained Impressionism and forged the modernist aesthetic of abstraction (open Tues.-Sun. 10am-6pm; DM6, stu-dents DM3; Sun. free). **Staatsgalerie moderner Kunst,** Prinz-Regenten-Str. 1, in the Haus der Kunst, showcases Beckmann, Kandinsky, Klee, Picasso, and Dalí, among others. Originally constructed by the Nazis as the Museum of German Art, it housed the famous exhibit of *Entartete Kunst* (degenerate art) that included works of Cub-ists, Expressionists, and Dadaists. (Open Tues.-Wed. and Fri.-Sun. 9:15am-4:30pm, Thurs. 9:15am-4:30pm and 7-9pm. DM5, students DM3, Sun. free. Visiting exhibits extra.) The **ZAM: Zentrum für Außergewöhnliche Museen (Center for Unusual Museums),** Westenriederstr. 26, hogties under one roof such treasures as the Cork-screw Museum, the Museum of Easter Rabbits, and a chamberpot museum. (Open 10am-6pm. DM8, students, seniors, and children DM5.)

ENTERTAINMENT

Munich's streets erupt with bawdy beer halls, rowdy discos, and cliquey cafés every night of the week. Gads of culture and nightlife guides are available to help you sort out the Munich scene. Pick up *Munich Found* (DM4.20), *in München* (free), or *Prinz* (monthly for DM5, the hippest) at any newsstand to find out what's up.

GERMANY

Beer To most visitors, Munich means beer. The six great city labels are *Augustiner, Hacker-Pschorr, Hofbräu, Löwenbräu, Paulaner-Thomasbräu,* and *Spaten-Franzinskaner.* Each brand supplies its own beer halls. Beer is served by the *Maß* (about a liter, DM8-11). The biggest keg party in the world, Munich's **Oktoberfest** runs late-September to early-October (Sept. 16-Oct. 1, 1995). The world-famous **Hofbräuhaus,** Am Platzl 9, 2 blocks from Marienpl., has been tapping barrels for the commoners since 1859, and is now hopelessly touristy; 15,000 to 30,000 liters of beer are sold per day. (*Maß* DM9.20. Most meals DM9-15. Open 10am-midnight.) Most *Müncheners* are quick to claim **Augustiner,** Arnulfstr. 52, as the finest beer garden in town, with its lush grounds and 100-year-old chestnut trees overhead. (*Maß* DM8.50-9. Open 10am-1am; food until 10pm; beer garden open 10:30am-midnight.) **Am Seehaus,** Kleinhesselohe 3, is loved by students and locals for the dearth of tourists (open 10am-1am; beer garden open until 11pm; *Maß* DM9). The largest beer garden in Europe, **Hirschgarten,** Hirschgartenallee 1, is boisterous and verdant, but somewhat far out; lots of families head here for the grassy park with a carousel (*Maß* DM9; open 9am-midnight; restaurant open Nov.-Feb. only Tues.-Sun.). The small size of the **Taxisgarten,** Taxisstr. 12, has hidden it from tourists and kept it a favorite of locals and students (*Maß* DM8.40; open 10am-10pm).

Nightlife and Performances Munich's nightlife is a curious collusion of Bavarian *Gemütlichkeit* and trendy cliquishness. The trendy bars, cafés, cabarets, discos, and galleries plugged into Leopoldstr. in the **Schwabing** district attract tourists from all over Europe. The area in Schwabing around **Münchener Freiheit** is the most touristy, but you'll also find the most serious partying and loudest discos. The blocks between **Viktualienmarkt** and **Gärtnerplatz** are the center of the gay and lesbian scene.

At **Master's Home,** Frauenstr. 11, navigate the homey geography of a *faux*-private house *cum* subterranean bar (open 6pm-1am). Singles flock to **Wunderbar,** Hochbrückenstr. 3, especially for telephone night on Wed; there's a phone on every table, just like in *Cabaret.* (Open Tues.-Thurs., Sun. 8pm-3am; Mon., Fri.-Sat. 8pm-4am. Wed. only cover DM8. Disco Fri. and Sat.) **Nachtcafé,** Maximiliansplatz 5, plays live jazz, funk, soul, and blues until the wee hours. (Breakfast after 2am. No cover. Karaoke every Sunday. Beer DM4-6. Open 7pm-5am.) **Park Café,** Sophienstr. 7, is a pleasant beer garden by day (open 10am-1am, *Maß* DM9.50), and a bumping disco come nightfall (open Tues., Thurs., Sun. 10pm-4am, Fri.-Sat. 10pm-7am. DM10 on weekends, weekdays DM5-8.) Raucous revelers of all genders and sexual orientations fill **Villanis Café-Bistro,** Kreuzstr. 3b, every night, though Sunday is unofficially "gay night." (Beer DM5. Open Mon.-Sat. 10am-1am, Sun. and holidays 11am-1am.)

The tourist office's *Monatsprogramm* lists schedules for all of Munich's stages. Stages sprinkled throughout the city span styles and tastes from dramatic classics at the **Residenztheater** and **Volkstheater** to comic opera at the **Staatstheater am Gärtnerplatz** on to experimental works at the **Theater im Marstall** in Nymphenburg. Leftovers tickets run around DM10. Munich's **Opera Festival** (July 1-31, 1995) is held in the **Bayerische Staatsoper** (tel. 55 59 33), accompanied by a concert series in the Nymphenburg and Schleissheim palaces (regular season standing-room and student tickets DM15-20; box office open Mon.-Fri. 10am-1pm and 3:30-6pm, Sat. 10am-1pm). **Gasteig,** Rosenheimer Str. 5, hosts musical performances ranging from classical to non-Western avant-garde on the former site of the *Bürgerbräukeller* where Adolf Hitler launched his abortive "Beer Hall *Putsch.*" (Box office in the Glashalle (tel. 48 09 86 14) open Mon.-Fri. 10:30am-2pm and 3-6pm, Sat. 10:30am-2pm, and 1hr. before the beginning of a program.)

■ DACHAU AND ANDECHS

"Once they burn books, they'll end up burning people," wrote the 19th-century German poet Heinrich Heine. This eerily prophetic statement is posted at **Konzentrationslager-Gedenkstätte,** the concentration camp (Germany's first) at **Dachau,**

GERMANY

next to a photograph of one of Hitler's book burnings. Though most of the buildings were destroyed in 1962, the walls, gates, guard towers, and crematoria remain. The terrifying legacy of Dachau lives on in photographs and film in the museum, the two reconstructed barracks, and the several memorials and chapels on the grounds. Take S-2 "Petershausen" to Dachau and catch bus 722 (DM2) in front of the station to the *KZ Gedenkstätte,* a 20min. ride. (Grounds open Tues.-Sun. 9am-5pm.) EurAide offers a guided tour in English that leaves at 9:30am from the Munich *Hauptbahnhof.* (June-Aug. 21 Tues. and Thurs. DM27, with railpass DM20.)

The monastery at **Andechs** combines Bavaria's two most acclaimed attributes—Catholicism and beer gardens—on a gorgeous mountaintop. The monks brew a tasty light beer and a strong *Bockbier* that isn't served on Sundays or Saturdays Easter-Oct. *(Maß* DM10.40). The adjacent **Klosterkirche Heiliger Berg** (Abbey Church of the Holy Mountain) houses over 250 centuries-old votive candles—giant, ornate candles commemorating departed brothers. Take S- to Herrsching; switch to the private bus line **Omnibus-Verkehr Rauner** (10min., DM2). Or take public transportation. You can also take a 3km hiking trail up the mountain. Follow the signs marked "*Fußweg nach Andechs*" and stick to the trail.

■■■ CHIEMSEE ✓

For almost 2000 years, artists, architects, and musicians have focused on the Chiemsee (Lake Chiem), Bavaria's largest lake, with its picturesque islands, meadows, and dramatic crescent of mountains. Ferries ply the waters of the Chiemsee from the port in Prien to the **Herreninsel** (Gentlemen's Island), the **Fraueninsel** (Ladies' Island), and towns on the other side of the lake. The architecture of **Königsschloß Herrenchiemsee** on Herreninsel, King Ludwig II's third and last "fairy-tale castle" is fabulously overwrought. Concerts are given in the **Hall of Mirrors** throughout the summer. (Open April-Sept. 9am-5pm, Oct.-March 10am-4pm. Obligatory guided tour DM6, seniors, students, and disabled persons DM3.50, under 15 free with adult.) Fraueninsel offers subtler pleasures. Its miniature world has no room for cars; only footpaths wander this village of fishermen and nuns. The **abbey** dates back to at least 866. Various artifacts, including the impressive 8th-century Merovingian **Cross of Bischofhofen,** are on display in the room above the Torhalle, the oldest surviving part of the cloister. (Open 11am-6pm, Oct.-May 11am-6pm. DM3, students and seniors DM1.50.)

Use **Prien** as a base to orient yourself for trips to the sights on the lake.The large, modern **tourist office,** Alte Rathaus 11 (tel. (08051) 690 50 or 69 05 35), is full of free maps, bumper stickers, and brochures; it also finds rooms in private houses for no fee (open Mon.-Fri. 8:30am-6pm, Sat. 9am-noon). The cheapest bed in town is at the **Jugendherberge (HI),** Carl-Braun-Str. 46 (tel. (08051) 29 72, fax 634 85), a 10min. walk from the lake. (Reception open 5-7pm. Lockout 9am-1pm. Curfew 10pm. DM17.50. Sheets DM5.50. Open Jan.-Oct.) There is a campsite, **Campingplatz Hofbauer** at Bernauer Str. 110 (tel. and fax (08051) 41 36). Walk up Bahnhofstr. from the train station and turn left, then walk 800m. Most of the restaurants in Prien cater to vacationing bourgeoisie. Eat cheap at **La Spaghettata,** Seestr. 7, where they make a decent pizza (DM7), and better tortellini (open Tues.-Sun. noon-2pm and 6pm-midnight). Gather groceries from **Norma's,** on Hallwanger Str. coming from the station take Seestr., and then the first left after the railroad tracks (open Mon.-Fri. 8am-noon and 2-6pm, Sat. 8am-noon).

■■■ NUREMBERG (NÜRNBERG)

Though the city officially cites *Bratwurst,* Albrecht Dürer, and the local soccer team as its most memorable attractions, in the eyes of many, Nuremberg is a city inextricably bound to a darker past. The very mention of Nuremberg—which hosted massive annual Nazi party rallies from 1927-1935, lent its name to the 1935 racial purity

GERMANY

laws that paved the way for the Holocaust, and also hosted the 1949 war criminal trials—still conjures up totalitarian imagery of the sort immortalized in Leni Riefenstahl's film *Triumph des Willens* (Triumph of the Will). It was Nuremberg's long association with the imperial traditions of the Holy Roman Empire that first attracted Hitler to the city. Its checkered past aside, contemporary Nuremberg is now a model of postwar prosperity; the second-largest city in Bavaria (after Munich), the city's wide variety of attractions beckon visitors of every stripe.

Allied bombing didn't leave much of old Nuremberg for posterity. The churches, castle, and buildings were reconstructed from the original stone between 1945 and 1966. During WWII, the **Lorenzkirche,** on St. Lorenzplatz, was completely destroyed except for the towers, but the beautiful Gothic church has since been completely restored (open Mon.-Sat. 9am-5pm, Sun. 1-4pm). Across the river on Hauptmarktplatz is the **Frauenkirche** (Church of Our Lady), a Gothic church with beautiful stained glass windows (open Mon.-Sat. 8am-6pm, Sun. and holidays 12:30-6pm). Every day at noon you can watch the antics of Emperor Karl IV and his seven elector-princes on the church clock. Beneath the *Rathaus* are the **Lochgegängnis-sen** (dungeons), containing an exhibit of medieval torture instruments (obligatory 25min. tour every 30min; open April 1-Sept. 30 Mon.-Fri. 10am-4pm, Sat.-Sun. 10am-1pm; DM3, students DM1.50). Across from the *Rathaus* is the **Sebalduskirche,** where once a year the Catholic congregation is allowed to fetch St. Sebaldus's relics (his corpse) for his feast-day, whereupon they parade through the streets with him (open Jan.-Feb, Nov. 9:30am-4pm, June-Aug. 9:30am-8pm; all other months 9:30am-6pm). Up the hill is the **Kaiserburg** (Emperor's castle), which housed all the Holy Roman Emperors after Konrad III. (45min. tour (in German) covers all parts of the Kaiserburg. DM3.50, children DM2.50. Open 9am-noon and 12:45-5pm; Oct.-March 9:30am-noon and 12:45-4pm. Last entrance 1hr. before closing.) The **Albrecht Dürer Haus,** Albrecht-Dürer Str. 9, is the last residence of Nuremberg's favorite son; the *Fachwerk* house contains period furniture along with Dürer etchings and copies of his paintings, as well as an exhibit of Dürer-derived works by modern artists alongside the originals. (Open Tues.-Sun. 10am-5pm. DM4, students DM2.)

The ruins of **Dutzendteich Park,** site of the Parteitage (Nazi Party Convention) rallies in the 1930s, remind visitors of a darker time in German history. (R-Bahn 5 "Neumarkt": Dutzendteich Bahnhof; or take streetcar 9 "Luitpoldhain": last stop, and continue to your left until you reach the artificial lake Dutzenteich.) Many areas are fenced off with electrified wire, so be careful. **Zeppelin Field** sits on the far side of the lake near the massive marble platform from which Hitler addressed throngs. The overwhelming emotional power of these events can be seen in the exhibit *Faszination und Gewalt* ("Fascination and Violence") located inside the Zeppelin **Tribune** in the Golden Hall (open July-Oct. Tues.-Sun. 10am-6pm; free).

Practical Information, Accommodations, and Food Nuremberg's **tourist office** (tel. (0911) 233 61 32), in the main train station, finds rooms for a DM3 fee (open Mon.-Sat. 9am-7pm). The comfortable and well-run **Jugendgästehaus (HI),** Burg 2 (tel. (0911) 22 10 24), was once a grain storage house of the imperial castle. From the train station, continue north through the *Altstadt* to Burgstr.; the hostel is on top of the hill. (Reception open 7am-1am. Curfew 1am. Checkout 9am. Under 27 only. DM25.50.) The recently opened **Jugend-Economy Hotel,** Gostenhofer Hauptstr. 47-49 (tel. (0911) 926 20, fax 926 21 30), caters to both student crowds and business folk, with comfortable modern rooms for privacy and luxury at only slightly steeper prices than the hostel (under 27 singles DM32, doubles DM64; over 27 singles DM38-43, doubles DM76-86). **Campingplatz am Stadion,** Hans-Kalb-Str. 56 (tel. (0911) 81 11 22), waits behind the soccer stadium; take the U-Bahn south to Messenzentrum (DM7 per person, DM6 per tent, DM5.50 per car; call ahead). *Rostbratwurst,* a mild sausage, is the thing to eat in Nuremberg, and the place to do so is beneath the smoking chimney of the tiny **Bratwurst-Häusle,** Rathausplatz 1, next to St. Sebald's Church (6 *Rostbratwürst* DM8-15 with sauerkraut or spiced potato salad; open Mon.-Sat. 9:30am-10pm). Eat crêpes, drink cappuccino, and enjoy stimulating conversation in the orange and green art deco **Café Mohr,** Färberstr 3 (open Mon.-Thurs. 9am-midnight, Fri.-Sat. 9am-1am, Sun. 2pm-midnight). Join the *Szene* and wiggle it in **Das Boot,** Hafenstr. 500, a club in a former DDR steam ship (cover and music vary; Mon-Sat. open 10pm-4am).

■ ■ ■ ROMANTIC ROAD (ROMANTISCHE STRAßE)

Between Würzburg and Füssen, at the foothills of the Alps, lies a beautiful country-side of walled cities, castles, and elaborate churches. Sensing opportunity, the German tourist industry christened these bucolic backwaters the Romantic Road in 1950. The world has responded—this is the most visited region in Germany, so be prepared for a group experience. DB's **Europabus** runs daily from Frankfurt to Munich (11hr.) and from Würzburg to Füssen (11hr.) April-October. The trip can also be done in segments, or you can stop anywhere along the line and catch the bus the next day. Eurail and all DB passes cover the charge. Regular *Linienbusse* go to all the towns on the Europabus route and then some (3-10 per day) and are far less crowded. Schedules are posted in train stations and tourist offices. For general information, contact the **Romantische Straße Arbeitgemeinschaft,** Marktplatz, 91550 Dinkelsbühl (tel. (09851) 902 71).

Würzburg Straddling the Main River and surrounded by vineyards, Würzburg sports an expansive baroque palace, a muscular fortress, and numerous alcohol-oriented festivals. **Marienburg Fortress,** the striking symbol of the city, keeps its vigil high on a hillside over the Main. German paintings, furniture, and *objects d'art* cluster in the **Fürstenbau Museum** (open Tues.-Sun. 9am-12:30pm and 1-5pm, Oct.-March Tues.-Sun. 10am-12:30pm and 1-4pm; DM3, students DM2). The fortress also houses the **Mainfränkisches Museum,** with statues by Würzburg's native son, Tilman Riemenschneider, the Master of Würzburg (open Tues.-Sun. 10am-5pm, Nov.-March Tues.-Sun. 10am-4pm; DM3, students DM1). Masochists can make the climb to the fortress in under an hour. Alternatively, take bus 9 from the Spitäle stop at the western end of the bridge (every ½hr.; May to mid-Oct. 9:43am-5:43pm; DM1.80). The **Residenz** palace, containing the largest ceiling fresco in the world, stands over the sweeping Residenzplatz (open Tues.-Sun. 9am-5pm; Oct.-March Tues.-Sun. 10am-4pm; last admission ½hr. before closing; DM4.50, students and seniors DM3). The **Residenzhofkirche** is astounding: the gilded moldings, pink marble, and frescoes make this little church the apex of Baroque fantasy (open Tues.-Sun. 9am-noon and 1-5pm, Oct.-March Tues.-Sun. 10am-noon and 1-4pm; free).

In front of the train station, a **tourist office** (tel. (0931) 374 36) helps find rooms for a DM3 fee (open Mon.-Sat. 8am-8pm). Würzburg's **Jugendgästehaus (HI),** Burkarderstr. 44 (tel. (0931) 425 90), is in the lee of St. Burkard's Basilica, across the river from downtown. Take tram 3 "Heidingsfeld" or 5 "Heuchelhof" from the station to Löwenbrücke. (Reception open 8am-10pm. Curfew 1am. Under 27 only. Top floor beds DM21.50, others DM24. Breakfast and sheets included.) **Uni Café,** Neubaustr. 2, has a relaxed student atmosphere and outdoor sidewalk seating (cakes, baguettes, frozen yogurt all DM3-8; open Mon.-Sat. 8am-1am, Sun. 9am-1pm). Alternatives guzzle their healthy ethnic foods at **Kult,** Landwehrstr. 10 (open Mon.-Fri. 9am-1am, Sat. 6pm-1am, Sun. 11am-1am).

Rothenburg to Augsburg Though **Rothenburg ob der Tauber** is undoubtedly the most touristed spot in Germany, it may be your only chance to ever see a completely intact walled medieval city without a single modern building.The **tourist office,** Marktplatz 1 (tel. (09861) 404 92), next to the Rathaus supplies handy maps and books rooms (open Mon. Fri. 9am-noon and 2-6pm, Sat. 9am-noon and 2-4pm.) Stay at the **Jugendherberge Rossmühle (HI),** Mühlacker 1 (tel. (09861) 45 10). From the *Marktplatz,* make a left onto Obere Schmiedgasse and go straight until you see the sign to the right. (Reception open 7-9am, 5-7pm and 8-10pm. Curfew 11:30pm. DM 18.50. Under 27 only.) Not as pre-packaged as Rothenburg, **Dinkelsbühl,** 40km south, maintains a full complement of half-timbered houses. The walled city of **Nördlingen im Ries,** 35km south of Dinkelsbühl, sits near the center of a circular meteor crater, the **Ries,** nearly 12km in diameter, which you can eye from **Der Daniel,** the tower of the 15th-century **St. Georgskirche** (DM2.50, children and groups DM1.50).

Founded by Caesar Augustus in 15 BC, **Augsburg** became the financial center of the Holy Roman Empire through the industry of the Fugger banking dynasty, later the personal financiers to the Habsburgs. The **Fuggerei** quarter was founded by Jakob Fugger the Rich as the first welfare housing project in the world, a haven for the elderly destitute, who earn their keep by praying for the departed souls of the Fuggers and pay DM1.72 annual rent. The **Fuggerei Museum** documents this classic piece of urban planning, as well as the financial adventures of its patrons (open March-Dec. 9am-6pm; DM1, students and seniors DM0.70). The **Bertolt Brecht Haus** on Auf dem Raim, birthplace of the influential 20th-century playwright, now chronicles his life through photos, letters, and his own poetry (open Tues.-Fri. 10am-1pm and 2-5pm, Sat.-Sun. from 11am; Oct.-April Tues.-Fri. 10am-3pm, Sat.-Sun. 10am-1pm and 2-4pm; DM2.50, students and children DM1.50).

Augsburg's resourceful **tourist office,** Bahnhofstr. 7 (tel. (0821) 50 20 70, fax 502 07 45), is about 300m in front of the station, and will book rooms for a DM3 fee (open Mon.-Fri. 9am-6pm). There's also an office at Rathauspl. (tel. (0821) 502 07 24; open same hours, also Sat. 10am-4pm, Sun. 10am-1pm). To find the clean, cramped, and central **Jugendherberge (HI),** Beim Pfaffenkeller 3 (tel. (0821) 339 03), take tram 2 "Kriegshaber" from the station to Stadtwerke, and continue on foot in the same direction; turn right onto Inneres Pfaffengäßchen. (Reception open 7:30am-11pm. Curfew 11pm. Under 27 only. DM16.50. Call ahead. Open Jan 20-Dec. 12.)

■■■ BAVARIAN ALPS (BAYERISCHE ALPEN)

South of Munich, the land buckles into dramatic peaks and valleys which stretch through Austria into Italy. Rail lines are scarce in this terrain; buses fill the gaps. For regional info, contact the **Fremdenverkehrsverband Oberbayern,** Sonnenstr. 10, in Munich (tel. (089) 59 73 47; open Mon.-Fri. 9am-4:30pm, Sat. 9am-noon).

Füssen The town's proximity to Mad King Ludwig's famed **Königsschlösser** (royal castles) is part of what lures legions here each year. Lingering reminders of the prince-bishops' medieval reign include such architectural astonishments as the inner walls of the **Hohes Schloß** (High Castle) courtyard, decorated with arresting *trompe l'oeil* windows and towers. Inside is the **Gemäldegalerie,** a collection of regional late-Gothic and Renaissance art, residing in what were once the work and love dens of late-medieval bishops and knights (open Tues.-Sun. 11am-4pm, Nov-March Tues.-Sun. 2-4pm; DM4, students and seniors DM2).

The **tourist office,** Kaiser-Maximilian-Platz 1 (tel. (08362) 70 77 or 78), dispenses hiking advice and finds rooms for free (open Mon.-Fri. 8am-noon and 2-6pm, Sat. 9-12:30pm, Sun. 10am-noon, Oct.-May Mon.-Fri. 8am-noon and 2-6pm, Sat. 10am-noon). Budget singles in *Gasthäuser* run DM30-35; in *Pensionen* DM40 and up. Füssen's **Jugendherberge (HI),** Mariahilferstr. 5 (tel. (08362) 77 54, fax 27 70), is blessed by a lovely location. Turn right from the station and follow the railroad tracks. (Reception open 7-9am and 11am-10pm. Curfew 11pm. DM17.50, plus DM1.40 resort tax. Sheets DM5.50. Closed Nov.)

Across the river, in the village of **Hohenschwangau,** visit the *Königsschlösser.* From Füssen, take the bus ("Königsschlösser"), which departs from the train station more or less hourly (DM2.20). **Schloß Neuschwanstein,** inspiration for the Disney

World "Fantasyland" castle and pinnacle of Ludwig's desperate building spree across Upper Bavaria, is impressive in its excesses. Lines tend to be endless for the obligatory tours. Consider taking the tour early in the morning and spending the afternoon hiking around the spectacular castle environs, particularly the **Pöllat Gorge** behind the castle. (Castles open 8:30am-5:30pm; Oct.-March 10am-4pm. DM9, students, seniors, and disabled persons DM6.) Other **buses** to the castles depart from the Garmisch-Partenkirchen train station and stop in Hohenschwangau (8am, 12:10pm, and 4:50pm; 2hr.; DM12.10, round-trip DM18.70). From Munich, take a **train** to Buchloe and transfer to the regional train to Füssen (2hr., DM30).

Garmisch-Partenkirchen The small resort villages of **Garmisch** and **Partenkirchen** united in 1935 for the following year's Winter Olympics; today Garmisch-Partenkirchen, in the shadow of the **Zugspitze,** Germany's highest mountain, is a thriving ski paradise. There are three ways up the peak. Take the cog railway from the *Zugspitzbahnhof* to Hotel Schneefernerhaus, then the *Gipfelseilbahn* (cable car), to the Zugspitzplatt (80min., 65min. to ski area; round-trip DM60), and continue with the *Gletscherbahn* cable car. Or, get off the cog railway at Eibsee and take the *Eibseeseilbahn,* one of the steepest in the world, to the top (round-trip tickets DM67 and are interchangeable among the three *Bahnen*; combo ticket including the train from Munich/Augsburg and *Zugspitze* tour DM84). The cheapest way is to hike for about 10hr. Get a free map of local hiking trails at the **tourist office** *(Verkehrsamt der Kurverwaltung),* Richard-Strauss-Pl. (tel. (08821) 18 06); walk left from the train station, then turn left on Von-Brug-Str. (open Mon.-Sat. 8am-6pm, Sun. 10am-noon). When the office is closed, check out the *automat* in front of the building or call (08821) 194 12. Awaken to church bells at the **Jugendherberge (HI),** Jochstr. 10 (tel. (08821) 29 80, fax 585 36); take bus 6 or 7 "Farchant" to Burgain. (Reception open 7-10am and 5-10pm. Curfew 11:30pm. Under 27 only. DM16.50. Open mid-Dec. to Oct.) **Camping Zugspitze** (tel. (08821) 31 80) is on highway B24 at the base of the Zugspitze; take the blue-and-white bus from the station to Schmölzabzweigung (DM7.20 per person, DM10 per site, DM5 per tent). The cheapest **ski equipment rental** is at **Ski-Schule,** am Hausberg 8, next to the Hausbergbahn. **Ski passes** in the Zugspitz area cost DM56 per day, DM42 with railpass. More advanced leg-breakers ski in the **Verbundgebiet,** home of the World Cup Kandehar run, for DM45 per day. A week pass costs DM272, two weeks DM430.

Berchtesgaden At the easternmost point of the Bavarian Alps, Berchtesgaden profits from a somewhat sinister attraction—Hitler's **Kehlsteinhaus,** a mountaintop retreat christened "Eagle's Nest" by occupying American troops, with an Alpine panorama from the 1834m summit (open mid-May-mid-Oct., weather permitting). The Berchetesgaden **Schloß,** a monastic priory until Bavarian rulers usurped the area and appropriated the property, now houses a collection of art and weaponry (open Sun-Fri. 10am-1pm and 2-5pm, last admission 4pm, Oct.-Easter Mon.-Fri. 10am-1pm and 2-5pm; DM7, students DM3.50, under 16 DM3). Hitler used the **Berghof** in Obersalzberg to entertain foreign dignitaries. It was here in 1938 that the Nazi dictator browbeat Austrian Chancellor Kurt von Schuschnigg into giving the Nazis control of the Austrian police, paving the way for the *Anschluß*.

The **tourist office,** *Kurdirektion* (tel. (08652) 96 70), is opposite the train station at Königsseerstr. 2. The hiking pass (DM2) includes tips on walking trails and climbs (open June-Oct. Mon.-Fri. 8am-6pm, Sat. 8am-5pm, Sun. 9am-3pm; Nov.-May Mon.-Fri. 8am-5pm, Sat. 9am-noon). Berchtesgaden is 3hrs. from Munich by train. (Day excursion Tues.-Thurs. and Sat.-Sun. DM50. Round-trip DM86, under 26 DM68.) The **Jugendherberge (HI),** Gebirgsjägerstr. 52, (tel. (08652) 21 90, fax 663 28), is to the right as you emerge from the train station, 20min. down the road in nearby Strub. (Reception open 5-7pm. Flexible curfew 10pm. DM16.50. Breakfast included. Sheets DM5.50. Open Dec. 27-Oct.) Pick up a *Wurst* sandwich from a vendor, or groceries at the **Edeka Markt,** Dr.-Imhof-Str. near Griesstätterstr. (open Mon.-Fri. 8am-6pm, Sat. 8am-noon).

■■■ THE DANUBE

Northeast of Munich, the Danube Valley, with baroque Passau and Gothic Regensburg, is every bit as inviting as the Romantic Road. Rolling hills and lovely riverscapes attract visitors year-round—Germans themselves summer in cottages here.

Regensburg and the Bavarian Forest Regensburg was once the capital of Bavaria; it later became the administrative seat of the Holy Roman Empire. The halls where the Imperial Parliament met live on in the **Reichstags Museum,** housed in the Gothic **Altes Rathaus** (tours every ½hr. Mon.-Sat. 9:30am-4pm, English tour 3:15pm; Nov.-March Mon.-Sat. 9:30, 10:30am, 2, 3, and 4pm, Sun. 10, 11am, and noon; DM5, students DM2.50). The splendid high-Gothic **Cathedral of St. Peter** towers over the city (open 6:30am-6pm; Nov.-March 6:30am-4pm). The **tourist office** *(Fremdenverkehrsamt),* Altes Rathaus (tel. (0941) 507 44 10) finds rooms (DM1.50), provides a free map and sells tickets to city events. From the station, walk down Maximilianstr. and take a left on Grasgasse. Take a right onto Obere Bachgasse and follow it to Rathauspl. **Trains** depart to Munich via Landshut (2-3hr., DM31), to Nurmberg (1½hr., DM24), and to Passau (1hr., DM29). The **Jugendherberge (HI),** Wöhrdstr. 60 (tel. (0941) 574 02), has been renovated into pleasant but sterile modernity. (Reception usually open 7am-11:30pm. Lockout 9am. Curfew 11:30pm. DM18.50. Reservations encouraged. Partial wheelchair access.) Campers should head for the **Campingplatz** (tel. (0941) 27 00 25) on Weinweg 40 outside of town. Take the Hochweg or bus 6 out of town and turn right on Hans-Sachs-Str., go about 2½km and the campsite will be on your right. (DM5 per person, DM3.50 per tent, DM3 per car. Open March-Oct.) Eat at **Goldene Ente,** Badstr. 32, a beer garden with steaks, spare-ribs, *Würstchen,* and *Schnitzel* grill for student-friendly prices (DM7-11) (open 11am-2pm and 5pm-1am, Sun. breakfast buffet 10am-2pm; beer from DM3.50). Leftists argue over vegetarian fare and salads (DM6-14) at the **Antagon Kneipe,** Rote-Hahnen-Gasse 2.

Northeast of Regensburg and Passau along the Austrian and Czech borders, the **Bavarian Forest** (Bayerischer Wald) is Central Europe's largest range of wooded mountains. The **Bavarian Forest National Park** is strictly protected from any activities that may alter the forest ecosystem. You can hoof it alone or sign up for guided walking tours, botanical tours, natural history tours, and tours of virgin woodlands. For information and schedules, contact the **Nationalparkverwaltung Bayerischer Wald,** Freyunger Str. 2, 8352 Grafenau (tel. (08552) 427 43). For news of the rest of the forest, contact the **Fremdenverkehrsverband Ostbayern,** Landshuterstr. 13 (tel. (0941) 571 86), a 10min. walk from the station in Regensburg (open Mon.-Sat. 9am-noon and 2-6pm, Sun. 10am-noon). The park's thick, cool woods conceal glass factories and 17 **HI youth hostels;** Regensburg's tourist office has an omniscient brochure. **Jugendherberge Mauth (HI),** Jugendherbergstr. 11 (tel. (08557) 289), is accessible from Passau (under 27 only; DM16.50; breakfast included).

Passau Elegant, baroque Passau spans two peninsulas formed by the confluence of the Danube, Inn, and Ilz Rivers. A center of trade and of both sacred and profane power for centuries, Passau teems with beautiful churches, palaces and cloisters. Its Baroque architecture reaches its apex in the sublime **Stephansdom** (St. Stephen's Cathedral). Hundreds of cherubs are sprawled across the ceiling, and the world's **largest church organ,** gilded and filigreed, looms above the choir. (Cathedral open Mon.-Sat. 8-11am and 12:30-6pm. Free. Organ concerts May-Oct. Mon.-Fri. noon, DM3, students and seniors DM1; Thurs. 8pm, DM6, students and seniors DM3; no concerts on holidays.) The **Domschatz** (cathedral treasury) within the *Residenz* has an extravagant collection of gold and tapestries purchased by the bishops with the wealth they tithed from their flocks. (Open May-Oct., Christmas to early Jan., and the week after Easter Mon.-Sat. 10am-4pm. DM2, children DM1.) Nearby stands the Baroque church of **St. Michael,** built by the Jesuits and covered with gold (open Tues.-Sun. 9am-5pm; Nov.-Jan. and March 10am-4pm; admission DM3, students DM1.50). The 14th-century Gothic **Rathaus** is decorated with less opulent colors, but is still stunning. (Great Hall of *Rathaus* open Easter-May 15 10am-4pm, May 16-Sept. 30 10am-5pm, Oct. Mon.-Fri. 10am–4pm. DM1.)

The **tourist office,** Rathauspl. 3 (tel. (0851) 334 21), has free maps, schedules, and hiking and camping info, and can find you a room for a DM2.50 fee (open Mon.-Fri. 8:30am-6pm, Sat.-Sun. and holidays 10am-2pm). **Trains** run to Munich (DM46) and Vienna (DM53). **Steamers** cruise to Linz, Austria, (5½hr., round-trip DM47). The **Jugendherberge (HI),** Veste Oberhaus 125 (tel. (0851) 413 51, fax 437 09), is an aging hostel redeemed by the fantastic view of Austria through the windows. Take the shuttle ("Pendelvekehr") from Rathauspl. to the front door. (Reception open 6:30am-11:30pm. Curfew 11:30pm. DM16.50. Breakfast included. Reservations recommended.) The **Rotel Inn** (tel. 951 60, fax 951 61 00), a bizarrely bright modern hotel was built in 1993 in the shape of a sleeping man. Wide beds fill the tiny rooms for surprisingly little. (Reception open 24 hrs. Singles DM25. Doubles DM50. Breakfast DM8.) **Café Kowalski,** Gottfried Schäffer Str. across from the Innpromenade leading up to the Innbrücke, is filled with dark wood, students and stacks of newspapers; a vine-covered balcony provides breezy seating (open 10am-1am; sandwiches and baguettes DM5-8, salads DM7-11, and steaks DM11-14). Also, try **Café Museum,** Bräugasse 17, for its baguettes, soups, and salads (DM5-9) (open Tues.-Sat. 10am-midnight, Sun. 10am-8pm, Mon. in summer 10am-8pm; breakfast until 4pm).

■■■ BAYREUTH AND BAMBERG

Bayreuth When composer Richard Wagner first moved to Bayreuth (buy-ROIT) in 1872, he saw in the small provincial town the perfect setting for his music and the perfect wealthy patroness (the Margravine Wilhelmine) to support him. Every year in late summer (July 25-late Aug. 28), thousands of visitors pour in for the **Bayreuth Festspiele,** a vast and bombastic celebration of Wagner's works in the **Festspielhaus,** the theater Wagner built for his "music of the future." Tickets (DM77-290, obstructed view DM39-44) go on sale a year in advance and sell out almost immediately. To order, write to Bayreuth Festspiele, 95402 Bayreuth, preferably well before November of the preceding year. Reserve a room as soon as you get tickets. Ticketless visitors can console themselves with a tour of Wagner's house, *Haus Wahnfried,* now the **Richard Wagner Museum,** Richard-Wagner-Str. 48. Snippets from Wagner's compositions are performed in the drawing room at 10am, noon, and 2pm. (Open 9am-5pm. DM4, students DM1.50; Sept.-June DM3, students DM1.50.)

The **tourist office,** Luitpoldpl. 9 (tel. (0921) 885 88), to the left and about 4 blocks from the train station, provides city maps, hotel listings, and area info. (Open Mon.-Fri. 9am-6pm, Sat. 9am-noon.) The town is an easy day trip by frequent **trains** connecting it to Nuremberg. Except during the Festspiele, accommodations in Bayreuth are abundant and reasonable. To reach the roomy and modern **Jugendherberge (HI),** Universitätsstr. 28 (tel. (0921) 252 62), take bus 4 (DM1.60) from the Marktpl. to Mensa, walk past the buildings straight ahead, take the first left after the *Mensa,* then take a right after the bridge underpass. (Reception open 7am-1pm and 5-10pm. Curfew 10pm. Under 27 only. DM12.50, with breakfast DM19. Open March to mid-Dec.) **Gastätte Porsch,** Maximilian Str. 56 (tel. 649 19), piles delicious portions at the best prices in town. (*Bratwürtschen,* cabbage, and fresh bread, DM7.50. Open Mon.-Sat. 7am-8pm.)

Bamberg Few travelers think to explore the treasures of the Franconian cathedral city of Bamberg. The **Altes Rathaus** guards the middle of the Regnitz River like an anchored ship. Stand on one of the two bridges to gaze at this half *Fachwerk* (timbered), half Baroque facade with a Rococo tower in between. Across the river and up the hill is the **Dom** (cathedral), on which construction began in 1004. The most famous object within the *Dom* is the equestrian statue the **Bamberger Reiter** (the Bamberg Knight), dating from the 13th century, depicting the chivalric ideal of the medieval warrior-king. (Open 9am-6pm except during services. Closed June 29-30. ½hr. organ concerts Sat. noon. Free. Call 50 23 30 for info on group tours.) Across the square, the **Neue Residenz,** Domplatz 8, the former Episcopal palace, poses amongst roses; from its prim rose garden, the town stretches out like a sea of roofs and the air smells rosy from 40 paces (open 9am-noon and 1:30-5pm, Oct.-March 9am-noon and 1:30-4pm; DM3, students DM2). The **Franconian Brewery Museum,** Michaelsberg 10f, explains everything you ever wanted to know about beer and its brewing (open Thurs.-Sun. 1-4pm; DM3, students DM1.50).

The **tourist office** at Geyerwörthstr. 3 (tel. (0951) 87 11 61, fax 87 19 60) dispenses city maps (free inside, DM0.50 at machine outside; open Mon.-Fri. 9am-7pm, Sat. 9am-5pm.) Frequent **trains** connect Bamberg to Würzburg (DM24) and Nuremberg (DM15). Though far from the center of town, **Jugendherberge Wolfsschlucht (HI),** Oberer Leintritt 70 (tel. (0951) 560 02 or 563 44, fax 552 11), is fairly tidy and pleasant; take bus 18 from the *Zentralomnibusbahnhof* (ZOB) to Am Regnitzufer. (Reception open 3-5pm and 6-10pm. Curfew 10pm. Under 26 only. DM19. Sheets DM5.50. Breakfast included. Open Feb. to mid-Dec. Call up to 6 months early for summer reservations.) The **Maisel-Bräu-Stübl,** Obere Königstr. 38 (tel. and fax (0951) 255 03), has large rooms overlooking a serene courtyard. (Reception 9am-midnight. Singles DM35. Doubles DM65, with shower DM75. Breakfast included; delectable dinners from DM11.) At the **Hofcafé,** Ausstr. 14, sit upstairs on the balcony or inside the light rooms of this student aerie and relax (open Mon.-Fri. 8am-7pm, Sat. 9am-6pm, Sun. 10am-6pm; soup DM5.50, salads DM6.50-11.50). For a funky mix of gothic, alternative, punk, grunge, and mystic music on Thursdays and the local jazz scene on weekends, go to the **Jazzclub,** Obere Sandstr. 18 (DM10, students DM6; Thurs. DM4).

BADEN-WÜRTTEMBERG

Two of the most prominent German stereotypes—the brooding romantic of the Brothers Grimm and the economic empowerment exemplified by Mercedes Benz—shake hands in Baden-Württemberg. Pretzels, cuckoo clocks, and cars were all invented here, and the region is as diverse as its products. Rural custom and tradition are still widely evident in the scenic, foreboding hinterlands of the Black Forest and the Swabian Jura, while the modern capital city of Stuttgart is rooted in the latter-day ascendancy of the German industrial machine. The province also hosts the snooty millionaires' resort of Baden-Baden, the vacation getaways of Lake Constance, and the ancient university towns of Freiburg, Tübingen, and Heidelberg.

■■■ STUTTGART

Covered with luscious parks and an extensive vineyard that stretches to the train station, you can bike along tree-lined paths from one end of Stuttgart to the other, without ever crossing a busy street. Founded as a stud farm 1000 years ago, the city enshrouds itself in both industry and bureaucracy, while at the same time entertaining throngs on busy streets and in peaceful parks. Now Porsche, Mercedes, and a host of high-tech coffee makers all live out their corporate lives here.

The **Schloßgarten,** Stuttgart's main municipal park, runs from the train station northeast to the Neckar, and south to the elegant baroque **Neues Schloß,** now infested with bureaucrats. This and the 16th-century **Altes Schloß,** across the street on Schillerplatz, comprise the whole of Stuttgart's architecturally notable sights, but Stuttgart's dearth of venerable buildings is more than compensated for by numerous excellent museums, most of them free. Across from the *Schloßgarten* at Adenauer-

Str. 30 is the superb **Staatsgalerie Stuttgart;** the modern wing contains works by Picasso, Kandinsky, Beckmann, and Dalí (open Wed. and Fri.-Sun. 10am-5pm, Tues. and Thurs. 10am-8pm; free; special exhibits DM8, students DM5). The **Mercedes-Benz Museum** (tel. (0711) 172 25 78; bus 56: Stadion or S-Bahn 1: Daimler-stadion) is housed in the workshop where Herr Daimler, the inventor of the automobile, built the first generation of Mercedes-Benz (open Tues.-Sun. 9am-5pm; free). Not to be outdone, Dr. Porsche's **Porsche-Museum** tells the same story about different cars (S-Bahn 6: Neuwirkshaus; open Mon.-Fri. 9am-4pm, Sat.-Sun. 9am-5pm; free). The **Staatstheater** (box office tel. (0711) 22 17 95), across the plaza from the *Neues Schloß,* is Stuttgart's most famous (tickets available Mon.-Fri. 10am-6pm, Sat. 9am-1pm; DM10-90). The 25 other local theaters are usually much cheaper (DM10-25, students DM5-15). The tourist office provides schedules and sells tickets.

Practical Information, Accommodations, and Food The **tourist office, I-Punkt,** Königstr. 1 (tel. (0711) 222 82 40), directly in front of the escalator down into the Klett-Passage, books rooms for free and sells the *Monatsspiegel* (in German, DM1), which lists museum hours, cultural events, and musical performances, and includes a guide to restaurants and nightlife (open Mon.-Fri. 9:30-8:30pm, Sat. 9:30am-6pm, Sun. and public holidays 11am-6pm; Nov.-Apr. Sun. and holidays 1-6pm.) The main **post office** (tel. (0711) 206 74 72) is at the Hauptbahnhof, 2 Arnulf-Klett (open Mon.-1 ri. 8am-6pm, Sat. 9am-noon, Sun. 11am-noon). The **American Express** office, Lautenschlagerstr. 3 (tel. (0711) 187 50), is 1 block south of the station (open Mon.-Fri. 9am-5:30pm, Sat. 9am-noon). Stuttgart's **public transportation** system offers single-ride tickets for buses, streetcars, U-Bahns and S-Bahns ranging from DM2.50-8.20; the 24hr. *Tageskarte,* valid for trains and buses (except night buses), is DM16.

Most of Stuttgart's budget beds are on the two ridges surrounding the downtown area and are easily accessible by tram. The busy **Jugendherberge Stuttgart (HI),** Haußmannstr. 27 (tel. (0711) 24 15 83, fax 60 83 51), is left from the station on Schillerstr. and up the hill; or, take U-Bahn 15 or 16 to Eugensplatz and walk right down Kernerstr. (Reception open 7-9am and noon-11pm. Strict lockout 9am-noon. Curfew 11:30pm. DM19.50, over 26 DM24.50. Sheets DM5.50. Sleepsack DM3.50. Reserve by mail or fax.) If the hostel's full, try **Jugendgästehaus Stuttgart,** Richard-Wagner-Str. 2 (tel. (0711) 24 11 32). Take U-Bahn 15 or 16 to Bubenbad; continue in the direction of the U-Bahn on the right side of the street, then veer right; it's on the right. (Reception open Mon.-Fri. 9am-8pm, Sat.-Sun. 11am-8pm. No curfew. Singles DM35, with bath DM45; doubles DM60, with bath DM70; triples DM90, with bath DM100. Breakfast, showers, and lockers included. Key deposit DM20.)

At the **University Mensa,** Holzgartenstr. 9-11, quantity compensates for quality (meals DM3-4). Get a *Mensa* credit card at the entrance and leave a DM20 deposit. (Open 11:15am-2:30pm; Aug.-Sept. until 1:30pm. Any form of student ID will do.) **Litfass,** Eberhardstr. 37 (tel. (0711) 24 30 31), serves delicious and relatively inexpensive Turkish and Swabian food in this cross between a sophisticated *Biergarten* and a sultan's harem; live bands play Fri. and Sat. after midnight (open 11:30am-5am; cheese baked in foil DM11.50). The walls sweat and the music blasts at **OZ,** on Büchsenstr. 10 (entrance on Kronprinzstr.; open Wed. 8pm-5am, Fri.-Sat. 8pm 'til they feel like closing). Two discos, **Kings Club,** Calverstr. 21 (tel. (0711) 22 45 58), and **Lauras Club,** Lautenschlagerstr. 20 (tel. (0711) 29 01 60), cater to gay men and lesbians, respectively (open 10pm-5am).

■■■ HEIDELBERG

In 1386, the sages of Heidelberg turned from illuminating manuscripts to illuminating young German minds. This, the oldest of Germany's university towns, is perhaps also the most quintessentially German. Set against a backdrop of wooded hills along an ancient river, the crumbling edifices of the once-majestic *Schloß* and the cobblestone streets of the *Altstadt* exert a magnetism that draws thousands of shutter-click-ing, beer-swilling tourists every year.

ORIENTATION AND PRACTICAL INFORMATION

To get to the *Altstadt* from the station, take almost any bus or streetcar going into the city. (From Bismarckplatz, bus 33 "Köpfel" to Bergbahn, or bus 11 to Universitätsplatz.)

Tourist Office: Directly in front of the station (tel. 277 35, fax 16 7318). Rooms reserved (DM4 fee plus a 5% down payment). Call hotels yourself; the office steers guests toward more expensive places. Open Mon.-Sat. 9am-7pm, Sun. 10am-6pm; Nov.-Dec. same but Sun. until 3pm; Jan.-Feb. same but closed Sun.

Budget Travel: HS Reisebüros, am Bismarckplatz (tel. 271 51), next to Woolworth's. Student deals and specials; any student ID will do. Open Mon.-Fri. 9am-12:30pm and 2-6pm, Sat. 9am-noon.

American Express: Friedrich-Ebert Anlage 16 (tel. 912 70). Member mail held, but not packages. All banking services. Open Mon.-Fri. 9:30am-5:30pm, Sat. 9am-noon. Banking services closed noon-2pm.

Post Office: Main office on Belfortstr., diagonally to the right across from the front of the station. Held mail can be picked up at counter 17. Open Mon.-Fri. 7am-6pm, Sat. 7am-noon. Limited services Mon.-Fri. 6-9pm. **Postal Code:** 69115

Telephones: At the post office and at the main train station. **City Code:** 06221.

Trains: Frequent trains run from Stuttgart (45min.) and Frankfurt (1hr.); Mannheim is less than 10min. away. Trains run regularly to towns in the Neckar Valley.

Public Transportation: To get in, out, and around Heidelberg, buy a 24hr. pass good on all streetcars and buses (DM8), available at the HSB Kiosk, halfway across the street (Gneisenaustr.) that runs by the side entrance to the train station or simply from any bus or streetcar. Single-ride tickets are DM2.80.

Bike Rental: At the *Expreßgut* counter at the back of the train station. DM12, with railpass DM8. Open April-Sept. Mon.-Fri. 7am-7pm, Sat. 7-11:30am.

Hitchhiking: People have been known to walk to the western end of Bergheimer-str. for all directions. The **Mitfahrzentrale,** Kurfürstenanlage 57 (tel. 246 46 or 194 44), 200m in front of the station, matches drivers and riders in a more orderly fashion. Open Mon.-Fri. 9am-6:30pm, Sat. 10am-2pm, Sun. 11am-2pm.

Laundromat: Wasch Salon SB, Post-Str. 49, next to Kurfürst Hotel. Wash DM7, dry DM1 per 20min. Open Mon.-Sat. 7am-11pm.

Emergencies: tel. 110 for all emergencies, including medical. **Police:** Rohrbacher-str. 11 (tel. 52 00).

ACCOMMODATIONS AND CAMPING

Finding accommodations (even expensive ones) can be a nightmare in Heidelberg. In the summer, save yourself a major headache by arriving early in the day. If Heidelberg fills up, the tourist office's listings in nearby Kirchheim (bus 40, 20min.) may be worth investigating. Those with a rail pass should try the countless little towns and villages scattered around at short distances from Heidelberg. Many Neckar Valley towns which have youth hostels lie along the Heidelberg-Heilbronn railroad, and train service is reliable between them. Heidelberg's tourist office does not always have correct information about whether or not a place is full; check again by phone.

Jugendherberge (HI), Tiergartenstr. 5 (tel. 41 20 66). From the station or Bismarckplatz, bus 33 "Zoo-Sportzentrum: Jugendherberge. Small, poorly lit rooms and hordes of school children; small disco can be fun. Lockout from 9am-1pm. Curfew 11:30pm, but flexible; arrange with the receptionist. Members only. DM19, over 26 DM23. Sheets DM5.50. Partial wheelchair access. Reserve ahead.

Jeske Hotel, Mittelbadgasse 2 (tel. 237 33). From train station, bus 33 "Köpfel" or 11 "Karlstor": Bergbahn. Perfect location. The amazingly low price and Erika Jeske's charming style of management draw a whole subculture of students to this quiet, respectable overnighter. 2- to 5-bed rooms DM22 per person. Floor with sleeping bag and cushion DM11. Showers DM2. Open Feb. to mid-Nov.; other times call ahead, the owner may be in Barbados.

Hotel-Pension Elite, Bunsenstr. 15 (tel. 257 33). Truly sweet rooms. One narrow single DM75; doubles DM95; DM15 per extra person. Shower and breakfast in the little garden included. Reserve by mail and phone.

Camping: Haide (tel. (06223) 21 11), between Ziegelhausen and Kleingemünd. Bus 35: Orthopedisches Klinik; cross the river. DM7 per person, DM6 per tent, DM2 per car. Cabins DM14-16. Or, camp on the other side of the river at **Camping Heidelberg-Schlierbach** (tel. (06221) 80 25 06) near the Orthopedic Clinic. Bus 35 "Neckargmünd": Im Grund. DM7 per person, DM6 per tent, DM3 per car.

FOOD

Eating out is costly in Heidelberg. Avoid the pedestrian zone; just outside its confines are historic student pubs and restaurants that offer better value. Buy groceries at **Handelshof,** Kurfürsten-Anlage 60, 200m in front of the train station on the right (open Mon.-Wed. and Fri. 8am-6:30pm, Thurs. 8am-8:30pm, Sat. 8am-2pm).

Mensa, on Marstallstr. perpendicular to the river. State-subsidized cafeteria turned café in the afternoon. Cheap food, beer and cheesecake. Those who forgot their student IDs often ask a student hanging out on the green in front to buy them Mensa Marks (each one DM3; sold in fives).

Gastätte Essighaus, Plöck 97 (tel. 224 96). Service relatively quick by German standards; tasty food. Specials includes soup, salad, and an entree for DM11-16. Open 11:30am-midnight, Wed. 11:30am-5:30pm.

Wirsthaus Zum Spreisel, Neckarstaaden 66. Individual meals are not cheap (DM15-40) but the portions are so huge and the food so good that it may be good to split a dish. The place may be teeming with tourists, but it hasn't lost its typically German flavor. Open Sun.-Thus. 5pm-midnight, Fri.-Sat. 2pm-midnight.

Vetters, Steingasse 9 (tel. 16 58 50). Snuggle up with working brewing machinery. Meals DM9-20, beer DM4-6.

SIGHTS AND ENTERTAINMENT

The jewel in the crown of an already beautiful city, the **Heidelberger Schloß,** has survived the ravages of both war (1622 and 1693) and nature (lightning struck the tower arsenal in 1764). Best viewed from the *Philosophenweg* high above the northern bank of the Neckar, it is easily accessible by foot or by *Bergbahn* (cable car), which runs from "Bergbahn/Rathaus" (bus 11 or 33) to the castle (round-trip DM4.50) and farther up to Königstuhl (DM7). (Every 10min. from Kornmarkt 9am-6:20pm.) The obligatory tour of the *Schloß* includes a visit to the **Faß,** reputedly the world's largest wine barrel. (Tours in English and German 9am-4pm. Castle and *Faß* open 9am-5pm; Nov.-March 9am-4pm. DM2, students and children DM1.) The **Apothekenmuseum** in the castle features a 17th-century pharmacy and alchemist's lab (open 10am-5pm; Nov.-March Sat.-Sun. 11am-5pm; DM3, students DM1.50).

In town, several sights cluster near the **Marktplatz,** a cobbled square that holds an open air market every Wednesday and Saturday. In the center stands the **Hercules Fountain,** where accused witches and heretics were burned in the 15th century. The two oldest structures in the city border the Marktplatz: the 15th-century **Heiliggeistkirche** and the 16th-century **Hotel zum Ritter.** The stately **Rathaus** presides over the far end of the square. From the square, take Hauptstr. west for more Heidelbergian beauty; five blocks down, the **Universitätsplatz,** centered around a stone-lion fountain, is the former headquarters of the **Alte Universität.** Between 1778 and 1914, naughty students were jailed in the **Studentkarzer** (enter via Augustinergasse behind the old university building; open Tues.-Sat. 10am-noon and 2-5pm; Nov.-March Sat. 10am-1pm; DM1.50, students and children DM1). At Hauptstr. 97, the **Kurpfälzisches Museum** features the jawbone of *homo Heidelbergensis* ("Heidelberg Man," one of the oldest humans unearthed), works of art by Van der Weyden and Dürer, and a spectacular 15th-century Gothic altarpiece (open Tues.-Sun. 10am-5pm, Wed. 10am-9pm. DM4; students DM2; children and Sun. free).

A stroll across the elegant **Karl-Theodor-Brücke** reveals a statue of the Prince-Elector himself, which he commissioned as a symbol of his modesty. From the far end of the bridge, clamber up the **Schlangenweg,** a winding stone stairway, to the **Philosophenweg,** a famous pedestrian walkway where Hegel indulged in afternoon promenades. Atop the **Heiligenberg,** the mountain traversed by the *Philosophenweg,* lie the ruins of the 9th-century **St. Michael Basilika,** the 13th-century **St. Stephen Kloster,** and an **amphitheater** built under Hitler in 1934 on the site of an ancient Celtic gathering place.

Heidelberg's **Faschings Parade** struts through the city on Shrove Tuesday, the day before Ash Wednesday. The two-week **Spring Festival** begins at the end of May. A **wine festival** is held in mid-September, and the **Christmas market** runs from late November to December 22.

At night, venture to one of the many area pubs. Conversations in the **Roter Ochsen,** Haupstr. 217, inspired Twain's caustic essay, "The Awful German Language" (open Mon.-Sat. 5pm-midnight; DM4.50-25). You'll hear no English at the **Max Bar,** Marktplatz 5, with its big, happy, mostly young German crowd (open 8pm-1am). **Bierbrunnen,** 21 Kettergasse, is a popular destination for the German *X-Generation* (open 6pm-1am, weekends until 2am). Opened in 1954, **Cave 54,** Krämergasse 2, is the current club for 70's paraphernalia (open 10pm-3am; beer DM4.50; cover DM5). **Schwimmbad Musik Club,** Tiergartenstr. 13, is the city's main catwalk; Nirvana played here a few moons ago—alas no more (open Wed. and Thurs. 8pm-2am, Fri. and Sat. 8pm-3am). **Whiskey á go go,** Fahrtgasse 18, is a gay and lesbian club; mucho techno, black lights, and smoke (open Wed.-Mon. 9pm-3am; strictly gay scene on Tues. 9pm-1am).

■ SPEYER AND NECKAR VALLEY

The cathedral town of **Speyer** to the west and the ancient castles of the **Neckar Valley** to the east are both simple day trips from Heidelberg. The Rhein-Neckar-Fahrgastschiffahrt (tel. (06221) 201 81) runs boat tours early June through early September between Heidelberg (departing from in front of the *Stadthalle*) and Neckarsteinach (daily, round-trip DM15.50). You can also view the valley from the Heidelberg-Heilbronn rail line, which follows the river with frequent stops in the medieval towns of **Neckarsteinach** and **Hirschhorn.**

Bus 7007 travels from Heidelberg to **Speyer** (1½hr.), which can also be reached by train via Mannheim (30-50min.). The 12th-century **Kaiserdom** (Imperial Cathedral) is the largest structure of the Romanesque period. The crypt under its east end retains the remains of eight Holy Roman Emperors. (Open Mon.-Sat. 9am-5pm, Sun. 9am-1:30pm; Nov.-March 9am-5pm.) Just south of the *Dom* is the **Historisches Museum der Pfalz,** whose adjacent wine museum harbors what is touted as the oldest bottle of wine in the world, from a wild Roman bash around 300 AD (open Tues. and Thurs.-Sun. 10am-6pm, Wed. 10am-8pm; free except for some visiting exhibitions). Speyer's **tourist office** (tel. (06232) 143 92) is on Maximilianstr. 11, near the main entrance to the cathedral; take the city shuttle from the train station (open Mon.-Fri. 9am-5pm, Sat. 10am-noon).

■ ■ ■ TÜBINGEN

Leftist graffiti smeared across 15th-century public buildings leaves no doubt that Tübingen is one of Germany's venerable academic towns. The students are gone in August and September, but at other times the buzz of young people and a relative lack of tourists enhance the city's charm. The focal point of the *Altstadt,* the 15th-century **Stiftskirche,** is surrounded by winding alleys and gabled houses. The church's chancel contains the tombs of 14 members of the former House of Württemberg; climb the rickety stairs of the church tower for an amazing view. (Church open 9am-5pm. Chancel and tower open April-July and Oct. Fri.-Sun. 10:30am-5pm; Aug.-Sept. 10:30am-5pm. To chancel and tower DM2, students DM1.) The ornate,

So, you're getting away from it all.

Just make sure you can get back.

AT&T Access Numbers
Dial the number of the country you're in to reach AT&T.

*AUSTRIA[†††]	022-903-011	*GREECE	00-800-1311	NORWAY	800-190-11
*BELGIUM	0-800-100-10	*HUNGARY	00◇-800-01111	POLAND[†]◆[2]	0◇010-480-0111
BULGARIA	00-1800-0010	*ICELAND	999-001	PORTUGAL[†]	05017-1-288
CANADA	1-800-575-2222	IRELAND	1-800-550-000	ROMANIA	01-800-4288
CROATIA[†]◆	99-38-0011	ISRAEL	177-100-2727	*RUSSIA[†] (MOSCOW)	155-5042
*CYPRUS	080-90010	*ITALY	172-1011	SLOVAKIA	00-420-00101
CZECH REPUBLIC	00-420-00101	KENYA[†]	0800-10	S. AFRICA	0-800-99-0123
*DENMARK	8001-0010	*LIECHTENSTEIN	155-00-11	SPAIN•	900-99-00-11
*EGYPT[†] (CAIRO)	510-0200	LITHUANIA◆	8◇196	*SWEDEN	020-795-611
*FINLAND	9800-100-10	LUXEMBOURG	0-800-0111	*SWITZERLAND	155-00-11
FRANCE	19◇-0011	F.Y.R. MACEDONIA	99-800-4288	*TURKEY	00-800-12277
*GAMBIA	00111	*MALTA	0800-890-110	UKRAINE[†]	8◇100-11
GERMANY	0130-0010	*NETHERLANDS	06-022-9111	UK	0500-89-0011

Countries in bold face permit country-to-country calling in addition to calls to the U.S. **World Connect**℠ prices consist of **USADirect**® rates plus an additional charge based on the country you are calling. Collect calling available to the U.S. only. *Public phones require deposit of coin or phone card. ◇Await second dial tone. †May not be available from every phone. †††Public phones require local coin payment through the call duration. •Not available from public phones. • Calling available to most European countries. [1]Dial "02" first, outside Cairo. [2]Dial 010-480-0111 from major Warsaw hotels. ©1994 AT&T

Here's a travel tip that will make it easy to call back to the States. Dial the access number for the country you're visiting and connect right to AT&T. It's the quick way to get English-speaking AT&T operators and can minimize hotel telephone surcharges.

If all the countries you're visiting aren't listed above, call **1 800 241-5555** for a free wallet card with all AT&T access numbers. Easy international calling from AT&T. **TrueWorld Connections.**

AT&T

These people are only a third of the 150 students who bring you the *Let's Go* guides. With pen and notebook in hand, a few changes of underwear stuffed in our backpacks, and a budget as tight as yours, we visited every *penstone*, *palapa*, pizzeria, café, club, campground, or castle we could find to make sure you'll get the most out of *your* trip.

We've put the best of our discoveries into the book you're now holding. A brand-new edition of each guide hits the shelves every year, only months after it is researched, so you know you're getting the most reliable, up-to-date, and comprehensive information available.

But, as any seasoned traveler will tell you, the best discoveries are often those you make yourself. If you find something worth sharing, drop us a line. We're at Let's Go, Inc., 1 Story Street, Cambridge, MA 02138, USA (e-mail: letsgo@delphi.com).

H A P P Y   T R A V E L S !

painted façade of the **Rathaus** faces the old market square in the middle of the *Altstadt.* On top of the hill that rudely separates the university from most of the city stands the **Schloß Hohentübingen,** a castle with a rough stone balcony overlooking the old town. From the *Rathaus,* follow the signs marked "*Schloß*" leading up to the right in order to reach the castle. On the northern riverbank is the **Hölderlinturm,** a tower where 18th-century poet Friedrich Hölderlin lived out the final 36 years of his life in a state of clinical insanity. The tower now houses a memorial museum. (Open Tues.-Fri. 10am-noon and 3-5pm, Sat.-Sun. 2-5pm. Tours Sat.-Sun. 5pm. DM3, students DM2.)

Practical Information, Accommodations, and Food Tübingen's **tourist office**, Neckarbrücke (tel. (07071) 350 11 or 913 60), sits on the south side of the Eberhardt Bridge. From the front of the train station, turn right and walk to Karlstr., turn left, and walk to the river. The office books hotel rooms and private rooms (DM25-40), both for a DM5 fee. (Open Mon.-Fri. 9am-6:30pm, Sat. 9am-5pm, Sun. 2-5pm.) The large, worn **Jugendherberge (HI),** Gartenstr. 22-2 (tel. (07071) 230 02, fax 250 61), overlooks the Neckar just downstream from the bridge at the tourist office. Take bus 11 from the station (DM2.50) to Jugendherberge. (Reception open 7:30-9am, noon-1pm, 5-8pm, and 10-10:15pm. Curfew midnight. Members only. DM18.50, over 26 DM24. Breakfast included. Wheelchair access.) Camp at **Rappernberghalde** (tel. (07071) 431 45) on the river. Go upstream from the old town or left from the station, cross the river on the Alleenbrücke, and turn left again. Follow the blue camping signs (20-25min.). (Reception open April to mid-Oct. 8am-12:30pm and 2:30-10pm. DM8 per person, DM6-7 per tent.)

Tübingen's students keep a number of superb yet inexpensive restaurants busy. The student-run **Marquardtei,** Herrenbergstr. 34, serves whole-wheat pizza and a vast selection of vegetarian and meat dishes to a mostly Red and Green clientele (open Sun.-Fri. 11:30am-1am, Sat. 6pm-1am; entrees DM7-17). **Kelter,** on the corner of Kelterustr. and Schmiedtorstr, is a covered market carrying the full picnic assortment, even calamari salad (100g DM6) (open Mon.-Fri. 9am-6:30pm, Sat. 9am-1pm).

Nearly every block in Tübingen claims one or two student pubs. Neckarmüller, Garlenstr. 4, serves its own brew in a beer garden under big shady trees on the river (open 1pm-1am). The **Zentrum-Zoo** disco, Schliefmühleweg 86, a 10min. walk from the old city, is popular with college students but occasionally gets overrun by a younger crowd (open Tues.-Sat. 9pm-2am, Sun. 8:30pm-1am, Sun. 8:30pm-1am; beer DM3.50-4; cover varies, usually DM5).

■■■ FREIBURG IM BREISGAU

A political football that has spent most of its 800-odd years under Austrian or French control, the undisputed metropolis of the Black Forest maintains a relaxed and cosmopolitan air. The pride of Freiburg is the **Münster,** a tremendous stone cathedral with a 116m spire built at intervals between the 13th and 16th centuries. (Cathedral open 9am-7pm. Tower open Mon.-Sat. 9:30am-5pm, Sun. 1-5pm; Nov.-April Tues.-Sat. 9:30am-5pm; DM1.) A stroll through the surrounding *Altstadt* will uncover several **Bächle,** narrow streams of swiftly flowing water that run through the city. In medieval times, these open gutters were used to water cattle and protect against fires; today, they exist only to soak the shoes of unwary tourists. Two medieval gates—the **Schwabentor** and the **Martinstor**—still stand within a few blocks of one another in the southeast corner of the *Altstadt.* The latter is indelibly profaned by a McDonald's sign. From the Schwabentor, take the pedestrian overpass across the heavily trafficked Schloßbergring and climb the **Schloßberg** for an excellent view of the city. Freiburg's museums cater to a variety of interests. The **Augustiner Museum,** housed in a former monastery on Augustinerplatz has a large collection of mostly medieval artifacts (open Tues.-Fri. 9:30am-5pm, Sat.-Sun. 10am-5pm; DM4, students DM2). Farther south at Marienstr. 10a is the **Museum für Neue Kunst**

(Museum of Modern Art), with a modest collection of 20th-century German works (open Tues.-Fri. 9:30am-5pm, Sat.-Sun. 10:30am-5pm; free).

Practical Information, Accommodations, and Food The **tourist office** at Rotteckring 14 (tel. (0761) 368 90 90, fax 37 00 37), 2 blocks down Eisenbahnstr. from the train station, finds rooms and distributes the comprehensive *Freiburg Official Guide* (DM5, German or English; open Mon.-Fri. 9:30am-8pm, Sat. 9:30am-5pm, Sun. 10am-noon; Oct.-May Mon.-Fri. 9:30am-6pm, Sat. 9:30am-2pm, Sun. 10am-noon.) Accommodations in Freiburg tend toward the pricey; the tourist office books cheaper rooms (single DM25-45, doubles DM45-80) in private homes, but a stay of at least 3 nights is usually required. The **Jugendherberge (HI)**, Kartäuserstr. 151 (tel. (0761) 676 56, fax 603 67), provides modern institutional accommodations in an arboreal setting. Take S-Bahn 1 "Littenweiler" to Römerhof, walk down Fritz-Geiges-Str., cross the stream, and turn right. (Reception open 7am-11:30pm. Curfew 11:30pm. Members only. DM17, over 26 DM22.50.) **Hotel Schemmer,** Eschholzstr. 63 (tel. (0761) 27 24 24), is friendly and centrally located. From the train station, take the overpass that crosses over the tracks, then go past the church and turn left. (Singles DM45. Doubles DM75.) For a little suburb living, take S-Bahn 1 "Littenweiler": Lassbergstr., then hop on bus 17 to Kleintalstr. and follow Peterhof up to the large wooden farmhouse and **Haus Lydia Kalchtaler,** Peterhof 11 (tel. (0761) 671 19; DM18 per person). The conveniently located brewery **Bromerei Gauter,** Schwarzwaldstr. 43, conducts tours tracking the production process of the malt beverage; the grand finale of the ½hr. tour consists of food and lots of beer atop one of the factory buildings.

■■■ BLACK FOREST (SCHWARZWALD)

Stretching west of the Rhine from Karlsruhe to Basel, the Black Forest looms large in the German cultural consciousness. Fairy tales, storybooks, and romantic lyrical poetry all owe their inspiration to the tangled expanse of evergreens where Hänsel and Gretel were left to their own devices. Hiking is a favorite pastime here; trails are frequent and well-marked, and many are used in winter for cross-country skiing.

The main entry points to the Black Forest are Freiburg, at its center, Baden-Baden to the northwest, Stuttgart to the east, and Basel, Switzerland to the southwest. Public transportation is sparse in this mountain region; rail lines run along the perimeter from Baden-Baden to Freiburg and east from Freiburg to Donaueschingen and Stuttgart, but many of the innermost regions are accessible only by infrequent bus service. Check return connections in advance before setting off on daytrips. Many bus lines are privately owned, rendering railpasses invalid.

Titisee and Schluchsee Thirty km east of Freiburg lies the resort town of **Titisee** along the lake of the same name, attractively set against a backdrop of dark pine-forested ridges, but somewhat marred by the kitsch trappings of consumer tourism. Hourly trains connect Freiburg to Titisee; the train ride, running through the **Höllental** (Hell's Valley), is one of the most scenic in Germany. The **tourist office** is in the *Kurhaus,* Strandbadstr. 4 (tel. (07651) 980 40, fax 98 04 40); to reach the building, turn right in front of the train station, walk to the first intersection and turn right at the entrances to the pedestrian zone. Look for the flags dotting the lawn. The office books rooms for DM4; detailed maps (DM7.80-DM9.80) of the 130km of hiking trails surrounding the lake are also available. (Open Mon.-Fri. 8am-6pm, Sat. 10am-noon and 3-5pm, Sun. 10am-noon; Oct. -March Mon.-Fri. 8am-noon, 12:30-5:30pm, Sat.-Sun. 10am-noon.) **Paddleboats** can be rented from several vendors along Seestr. for DM11-15 per hour, and **guided boat tours** of the lake (DM5, 25min.) depart from the same area. **Jugendherberge Veltishof (HI),** Bruderhalde 27 (tel. (07652) 238, fax 756), is comfortable but inconveniently located at the far end of the lake. From the train station, take the Südbaden bus "Todtnau" (every 2hr., DM2) to Feuerwehrheim. By foot, it's a 30min. walk along the main road from the *Kurhaus.* At DM8, the hostel serves the cheapest meal in the area. (Reception open 5-6pm and 7:30-8pm. Curfew 10pm. Members only. DM18, over 26 DM23.) Several campgrounds lie along the same road; **Campingplatz Weiherhof** (tel. (07652) 14 68) is on the water near the hostel and has laundry facilities. (April-Oct. DM7 per person, DM9 per tent.)

South of Titisee is the comparably picturesque, less-touristed **Schluchsee,** whose **Jugendherberge Schluchsee-Wolfsgrund (HI)** (tel. (07656) 329, fax 92 37) is ideally situated on the shore; from the station, facing away from the water, turn left and follow the tracks across the bridge to Wolfsgrund 28. (Reception closed 2-5pm. Curfew 11pm. DM18.50, over 26 DM23.50. Dinner DM8.50. Laundry DM6.)

St. Peter, St. Märgen, and Triberg North of Titisee and about 15km east of Freiburg, the twin villages of **St. Peter** and **St. Märgen** lie within the High Black Forest. Buses run regularly from Freiburg (line 7216, DM7.60, DM 3.80 with rail pass). **St. Peter's,** designed by architect Peter Thumb, perches up where a halo of green farmland breaks through the dark crust of pine forests. Its **Klosterkirche** may not be much on the outside, but inside it's rocking with Baroque angels. (Tours Mon., Wed. 11am, Tues., Thurs. 2:30pm. DM2.) The bus puts you near the **tourist office** (tel. (07660) 91 02 29, fax 91 02 44; open Mon.-Thurs. 8am-noon and 2-5pm; June-Oct. also Sat. 11am-1pm). Well-marked **trails** cover the surrounding area; one of the trails from the abbey leads directly to St. Märgen, 8km away.

At the center of the High Black Forest is **Triberg,** a hiker's paradise accessible by a half-hour train ride from Donaueschingen to the southeast. From the train station, the city center is 15min. uphill walk; turn right in front of the station, head down the stairs at the overpass and follow the road past the large post office building. At the top of the street is Triberg's prime attraction, the largest **waterfall** in Germany. Mobs of visitors shell out DM2.50 (students DM1) to see the water plunge 162m in 7 separate drops (open 9am-7pm). One-and-a-half-blocks to the left of the waterfall's entrance is the **tourist office,** Luisenstr. 10 (tel. (07722) 95 32 30, fax 95 32 30), in the *Kurhaus.* It books rooms and sells city maps (in English, DM1) and detailed hiking maps (DM5; open Mon.-Fri. 8am-noon and 2-5pm; May-Sept. also Sat. 10am-noon.) Triberg's **Jugendherberge (HI),** Rohrbacherstr. 37 (tel. (07722) 41 10), is scenically located, but the journey there—a grueling 20min. walk uphill from the waterfall—may dismay. (Reception open 5-7pm and at 9:45pm. Curfew 10pm. Members only. DM18, over 26 DM23.)

■■■ BADEN-BADEN

If you're fabulously wealthy, Baden-Baden can be a lot of fun. Even if you're not, it can still be a great place to visit, as long as you get at least some pleasure out of watching rich people on vacation; minor royalty and the like convene here to bathe in the curative mineral spas and drop fat sums of money in the casino.

Baden-Baden's history as a resort goes back nearly two millennia, when the Romans built the first **thermal baths** here. The **Friedrichsbad,** Römerplatz 1, is a palatial 19th-century bathing palace where you can enjoy a 2hr. "Roman" or "Irish Bath." Not a stitch of clothing is permitted. (Open Mon.-Sat. 9am-10pm. Last entry 7:30pm. Baths are coed Tues. and Fri. 4-10pm and all day Wed. and Sat. DM28, with soap and brush massage DM38.) More modest and budget-minded cure-seekers should try next door at the also astoundingly beautiful **Caracalla-Thermen,** Römerplatz 11, which offers placid soaking in the same water (and in bathing suits) at half the price. (DM18, with youth hostel coupon DM14.40. Open 8am-10pm.)

When not getting all pruny at the baths, Baden-Baden's affluent guests head to the **Casino,** whose opulent decor—modeled on the palace at Versailles—can be viewed during guided tours (open 10am-noon; Oct.-March 9:30am-noon; last tour at 11:30am; DM4). Attendance during gaming hours (Sun.-Thurs. 2pm-2am, Fri.-Sat.

2pm-3am) costs DM5; and, you must be 21 (or married to someone who is), present ID proving you're not a Baden-Baden resident, and wear appropriate dress (coat and tie for men). Technically, students are not allowed.

For a sumptuous view of the Black Forest, mount the 668m **Merkur** peak east of town. Take bus 5 to the Merkurwald stop, then take the railway to the top. (Combined round-trip DM6.) On the hill, the **Neues Schloß** houses a museum of the town's history (tours Mon.-Fri. 3pm; open Tues.-Sun. 10am-12:30pm, 2-5pm; DM2, students DM1). From the neighboring garden, you can get an excellent view of the entire town; there's an even better one, extending all the way to France, from the 12th-century ruins of the **Altes Schloß** in the upper hills a few km from the Neues Schloß (bus 15 from Augustaplatz).

Practical Information, Accommodations, and Food The opulent **tourist office** is at Augustapl. 8 (tel. (07221) 27 52 00, fax 27 52 02), inside the massive Haus des Kurgastes (open Mon.-Sat. 9am-10pm, Sun. 10am-10pm). Baden-Baden's **train station** is several km northwest of town. To avoid the blistering 90min. walk, take bus 1 "Lichtental/Oberbeuren": Augustaplatz (DM2.50, 24-hr. pass DM6.50). The **post office** on Leopoldpl. has phones (open Mon.-Fri. 8am-6pm, Sat. 8am-noon, Sun. 10:30am-11:30am) and changes money, as does the casino.

The cheapest bed in town is at the modern **Jugendherberge (HI)**, Hardbergstr. 34 (tel. (07221) 522 23, fax 600 12), halfway between the station and the town center; take bus 1 to Große-Dollen-Straße and follow the signs uphill. (Reception open 5-6pm and briefly at 8 and 10pm. Curfew 11:30pm. Members only. DM19, over 26 DM24. Wheelchair-accessible.) Rooms in the center of town are ritzy and overpriced, with the exception of the **Hotel Löhr**, Adlerstr. 2 (tel. (07221) 313 70). Reception is 1½ blocks away at **Café Löhr**, Lichtentalerstr. 19, across the street from the Augustaplatz bus stop. (One single at DM35, other singles DM60, with shower DM65. Doubles DM90, with shower DM100.) Most restaurant prices in Baden-Baden aren't compatible with budget travel, but daily specials often run for under DM12. Another option is to fill up a picnic basket at **Pennymarkt** at the Grosse-Dollenstr. bus stop.

■■■ LAKE CONSTANCE (BODENSEE)

The third-largest lake in Europe, the Bodensee forms a graceful three-cornered border at the conjunction of Austria, Switzerland, and Germany. Ancient castles, manicured islands, and endless opportunities to tan to a crisp draw residents of all three countries to the lake all summer long.

Spanning the Rhine's exit from the lake, the elegant university city of **Konstanz** is among the few German cities never struck by a bomb, and the local architecture shows it. Particularly inspiring is the **Münster** (cathedral); don't miss the view from the top of its Gothic spire (open mid-April to mid-Oct. Mon.-Fri. 9am-5pm, Sat. 10am-5pm, Sun. 1-5pm; free, tower DM2, students DM1). Konstanz's free public beaches are packed in good weather. **Strandbad Horn** is the largest and most popular. (Take bus 5.) The twentysomething set frolics on the beach at the university. (Take bus 4 to Egg and walk past the playing fields.)

The **tourist office** (tel. (07531) 90 03 76, fax 90 03 64), in the arcade to the right of the train station, provides an excellent walking map (open Mon.-Fri. 9am-6pm, Sat. 9am-1pm; Nov.-March 9am-noon, 2-6pm.) Konstanz has two **HI youth hostels. Jugendherberge Kreuzlingen,** (tel. (072) 75 26 63), rests in an old manor south of the border in Kreuzlingen, Switzerland. The best way there is by foot; the bus is no faster. (Reception open 5-9pm. DM19-70.) The hostel in Konstanz proper, **Jugendherberge "Otto-Moericke-Turm"** at Allmannshöhe 18 (tel. (07531) 322 60), is housed in a former water tower. Take bus 4 from Marktstätte stop (around the corner from the post office in front of the station) to Jugendherberge. (Reception open 4:30-5:30pm, 7-7:10pm and 9:45-9:55pm. Curfew 10pm. DM17.50, over 26 DM20.50. Open March-Oct. Call ahead.) For good *Biergarten* atmosphere and cheap snacks, try **Seekuh,** Kouzilstr. (across from the old *Rathaus;* open Mon.-Fri. 10am-1am, Sat. 11am-1am). Health food stores, leftist graffiti, and student cafés pepper the area around **Rheingasse.**

CENTRAL GERMANY

■■■ FRANKFURT AM MAIN

A city of skyscrapers and investment bankers, Frankfurt belongs properly to the Germany of the future; it has the reputation of being the most Americanized city in Europe, a dubious distinction given Frankfurt's designation as the crime and hard-drugs capital of Germany. Not much of the historic city escaped WWII bombings and Frankfurters didn't much care to restore the buildings of the past. One of the best zoos in Europe and a variety of museums may, however, be enough to draw the visitor away from the comfy reclining chairs in the local airport.

What's left of old Frankfurt is in the **Römerberg** area, a cluster of surviving historical buildings in the city center overshadowed by the **Dom,** a huge red Gothic cathedral that was the site of coronation ceremonies for German emperors between 1562 and 1792. The view from the cathedral's tower is worth the climb to the top (open 9am-noon and 2:30-5pm, in summer until 6pm; tower DM3, students and children DM1, closed in winter). The **Römer,** a distinctively gabled red sandstone structure at the west end of Römerberg, has been Frankfurt's city hall since 1405. The upper floors contain the **Kaisersaal,** a banquet hall whose walls are adorned with portraits of 52 German emperors (open Tues.-Sun. 11am-3pm; obligatory tour on the hour DM3). Near the Römer at Saalgasse 19, the **Historisches Museum** (tel. (069) 21 23 46 11) presents a first-rate series of exhibitions on the history of the city and the German nation (open Tues. and Thurs.-Sun. 10am-5pm, Wed. 10am-8pm. DM5, students DM2.50). A few blocks from the Römer at Großer Hirschgraben 23-25 stands the **Goethe Haus,** birthplace of the poet and now a carefully preserved museum. (Due to renovations of unspecified duration, the museum is closed, but the house is still open to the public, entrance through the Volkstheater, Mon.-Sat. 9am-6pm and Sun. 10am-1pm; Oct.-Mar. Mon.-Sat. 9am-4pm, Sun. 10am-1pm; DM4, students DM3.)

From Römerberg, a 10min. walk across the Eiserner Steg footbridge leads to the **Museumsufer,** home to a string of seven museums along Schaumainkai on the southern bank of the Main and Frankfurt's weekly flea market (Sat. 10am-5pm). (Museums open Tues. and Thurs.-Sun. 10am-5pm, Wed. 10am-8pm.) For less cerebral entertainment, head to Frankfurt's **Zoo** on the eastern side of town (U-6 or U-7; open 8am-7pm, Oct. to mid-March 8am-5pm; DM9.50, students DM4.50).

The **Alt Sachsenhausen** district between Dreieichstr. and Brückenstr. is crawling with pubs and outdoor restaurants. Frankfurt's renowned jazz scene centers around Kleine Bockenheimer Str.—also known as Jazzgasse—in the city center. The most famous of the venues is **Der Jazzkeller,** Kleine Bockenheimer Str. 18a (tel. (069) 28 85 37; open Tues.-Sun. 9pm-3am; cover varies). Gay nightlife flourishes in the area between Zeil and Bleichstr.

Practical Information, Accommodations, and Food Frankfurt's airport and train station are among the busiest in Europe. From the **airport,** S-Bahn lines 14 and 15 travel every 10min. to the main train station (DM4.40 from a blue automat, Eurail valid). Frequent **trains** leave the station for all the other major cities in Germany and the rest of central Europe. The **tourist office,** in the main train station across from track 23 (tel. (069) 21 23 88 49 or 21 23 88 51), will book rooms for

DM5, plus a DM10 deposit (open Mon.-Sat. 8am-9pm). **American Express** is at Kaiserstr. 8 (tel. (069) 210 50; open Mon.-Fri. 9:30am-5:30pm, Sat. 9am-noon). There's a 24hr. **post office** on the 2nd floor of the train station; fetch **Poste Restante** at counter 6 or 7 of the main branch at Zeil 110, 60313 Frankfurt (U-Bahn: Hauptwache; open Mon.-Fri. 8am-6pm, Sat. 8am-noon).

The very institutional **HI youth hostel,** Deutschherrnufer 12 (tel. (069) 61 90 58, fax 61 82 57), is conveniently located near the Sachsenhausen pubs. From the station, take bus 46 (DM2.10, during rush hours DM2.80) to Frankensteinerplatz. The hostel is 50m west in the large yellow building. After 7:30pm, take S-bahn 5, 6, or 14 to the Lokalbahnhof, walk north on Dreieichstr. and take a right on Deutschherrnufer. (Reception open 11am-10pm. Lockout 9am-1pm. Curfew midnight. DM20.50, over 20 DM24.50. Sheets DM10. Key deposit for smaller rooms DM10.) **Pension Bruns,** Mendelssohnstr. 42 (tel. (069) 74 88 96), has tastefully decorated, comfortable rooms. Facing the train station, turn right down Düsseldorfer Str., which will become Friedrich-Ebert-Anlage, turn right on Mendelssohnstr., and it's on the right. (Singles DM56, doubles DM76, triples DM96; showers DM2; breakfast included; call ahead if you arrive after 6pm.) **Pension Backer,** Mendelssohnstr. 92 (tel. (069) 74 79 92), offers clean rooms and a pleasant locale near the university (U-Bahn: Westend; singles DM40, doubles DM60; showers 7am-10pm DM3 per 8min.; breakfast included.)

Frankfurter sausages (the locals know them as *Wieners*) are not a Frankfurt specialty and should probably be avoided; try instead *gegrillte Rippchen* (grilled ribs) or *Handkäse mit Musik* ("handcheese with music"; really curd cheese with raw onions). Many of the taverns and pubs in the Alt Sachsenhausen district also serve food, and you can always find fairly cheap cuisine around Lipzigerstr. in the Bockenheim district (U-Bahn 6 or 7). **Restaurant Marché,** Zeil 112-114, offers staple and fresh (though not terribly exciting) food at reasonable prices (open Mon.-Sat. 9am-11pm).

■■■ MARBURG

The Brothers Grimm spun their fairy tales in these rolling hills; from a distance Marburg an der Lahn seems more of their world than ours. The world's first Protestant university was founded here in 1527 and is still the heart of the town. Its alumni include Martin Heidegger, Boris Pasternak, T.S. Eliot, and Richard Bunsen (of burner fame). Climb more than 250 steps or take bus 16 to the exalted **Landgrafenschloß,** former haunt of the Teutonic knights. **Elisabethkirche,** the oldest Gothic church in Germany (c.1285), commemorates the town patron, a countess-and-widowed-child-bride-turned-altruist-and-saint (open 9am-6pm, Oct. 9am-5pm; Nov.-March 10am-4pm, Sun. after 11am; church free; reliquary DM2, students DM1).

The **tourist office** (tel. (06421) 20 12 49 or 20 12 62), to the right of the train station, finds rooms from DM35 free of charge. (Open Mon.-Fri. 8am-12:30pm and 2-5pm, Sat. 9:30am-noon; Nov.-March closed Sat.) Marburg is served by frequent **trains** from Frankfurt (1hr.) and Kassel (1hr.). The riverside **Jugendherberge (HI),** Jahnstr. 1 (tel. (06421) 234 61, fax 121 91), catches the nighttime music of the *Altstadt* from across the Lahn. From the train station, take bus 1-6, 16, or S to Rudolfpl., cross the river and turn immediately right onto Trojedamm, then follow the riverside road until you turn left onto Jahnstr. (10min.). To find Rudolfspl. on foot, head up Bahnhofstr., turn left on Elisabethstr., which becomes Pilgrimstein, and walk 10min. (Reception officially open 7am-11:30pm. DM22, over 26 DM26.) **Camping Lahnaue** (tel. (06421) 213 31) is on the Lahn River; take bus 1 "Sommerbad": Mensa. (DM5 per person, DM4 per tent.) **Café Local,** Steinweg 1, is a pleasant, relaxed café with an outdoor terrace in the pedestrian zone; pizza, pasta, salads, and *Aufläufe* are mostly under DM10 (open 11am-1am).

■■■ THE RHINE: MAINZ TO KOBLENZ

The Rhine River may run all the way from Switzerland to the North Sea, but in the popular imagination it exists only in the 80km of the **Rhine Gorge** that stretches from Mainz to Bonn. This is the Rhine of legend, a sailor's nightmares, a poet's dreams, and often the rhetorical storms of nationalism. From the Lorelei Cliffs, legendary sirens lured passing sailors to their deaths on the sharp rocks below, and the Rhine wines from the hillside vineyards have inspired many a lesser illusion.

The Mainz-Koblenz train affords excellent views, but the best way to see the Rhine is by boat. The **Köln-Düsseldorfer (KD) Line** makes the complete Mainz-Koblenz run thrice daily in summer and along shorter stretches more frequently. (Fewer trips off-season. Mainz-Koblenz one-way DM72.60, round-trips discounted, free with Eurailpass.) English copies of the schedule are available at local tourist offices or at the docks; for more information call (0221) 208 83 18 or 208 83 19.

Mainz and Bacharach The capital of the Rhineland-Palatinate region, **Mainz** makes a convenient starting point for Rhine tours; **Köln-Düsseldorfer ferries** depart from the docks across from the ultramodern *Rathaus*. Mainz's most famous son and the father of movable type, Johannes Gutenberg, is immortalized along with his most important creations in the **Gutenberg Museum** on Liebfrauenpl. (open Tues.-Sat. 10am-6pm, Sun. 10am-1pm; movie shown at 11:15am; free). Across the square stands the colossal 11th-century red sandstone **Martinsdom,** one of the most impressive cathedrals in Germany and the final resting place of several Archbishops of Mainz, whose extravagant tombs line the walls. (Open Mon.-Fri. 9am-6:30pm, Sat. 9am-4pm, Sun. 1-2:45pm and 4-6:30pm; Oct.-March Mon.-Fri. 9am-5pm, Sat. 9am-4pm, Sun. 1-5pm.) The adjacent **Dom Museum** houses sculptural artifacts dating from the early years of the Holy Roman Empire (open Mon.-Wed. and Fri. 10am-4pm, Thurs. 10am-8pm, Sat. 10am-2pm; free). On a hill several blocks to the south, in the opposite direction from the river, the **Stephanskirche** is noted for its stunning set of stained-glass windows created by Marc Chagall in the eight years prior to his death in 1984 (open 10am-noon and 2-5pm).

To make the maze of Mainz more maneuverable, streets running parallel to the Rhine have blue nameplates and streets running toward the river have red ones. The **tourist office,** Bahnhofstr. 15 (tel. (06131) 28 82 10 or 286 21 55), down the street opposite the train station, reserves rooms for DM5; unfortunately, the town offers few inexpensive ones. (Open Mon.-Fri. 9am-6pm, Sat. 9am-1pm.) Mainz's well-run **Jugendgästehaus (HI),** Otto-Brunsfels-Schneise 4 (tel. (06131) 853 32, fax 824 22), is in the *Volkspark* in Weisenau (bus 1: Jugendgästehaus or 22: Viktorstift). (Reception open 5-10pm. Curfew 11:30pm. DM19.50, over 26 DM23.50.) **Campingplatz Maaraue** (tel. (06131) 629 71), lies close to the Theodor-Heuss bridge; cross it and turn right. (Reception open 7am-1pm and 3-10pm. DM6 per person, DM4-6 per tent. Open April-Sept.)

On the west bank of the Rhine between Mainz and Koblenz is the cozy village of **Bacharach,** whose many **Weinkeller** (wine cellars) and **Weinstuben** (wine pubs) do their best to live up to the town's name ("altar to Bacchus"). From the Gothic **Peterskirche** in the center of town, stairs lead up to the **Wernerkapelle,** the red sandstone frame of a chapel that took 140 years to build (1294-1434) but only a few hours to destroy during the War of Palatine Succession in 1689. The **tourist office,** Overstr. 1 (tel. (06743) 12 97), has maps of area hiking trails and a detailed list of wine cellar and pub offerings (open Mon.-Fri. 8:30am-12:30pm and 2-5pm). A 15min. walk uphill from the *Wernerkapelle* ends at **Jugendherberge Stahleck (HI)** (tel. (06743) 12 66), a gorgeous 12th-century castle with a fabulous view of the Rhine Gorge. The manager will bowl you over with friendliness. (Curfew 10pm. DM19.50, over 26 DM23.50.)

Koblenz The city's strategic location at the confluence of the Rhine and the Mosel has kept it in the limelight since Roman days; Koblenz turns 2003 in 1995. The annual **Rhein in Flammen** (Rhine in Flames) festival on the second weekend in August features a burst of pyrotechnics.

Koblenz is a popular jumping-off point for Rhine and Mosel **cruises.** Bus 1 connects the train station to the main docks at the Rheinfähre stop (one-way DM1.60); on foot, it's a 25min. walk from the station down Markenbildchen Weg and then left along the river. Cruises lasting anywhere from one hour to all day depart frequently from the docks. The **tourist office** (tel. (0261) 313 04), across the street from the station, gladly gives away boat schedules and city maps complete with hotel, restaurant, and pub listings (open Mon.-Sat. 8:30am-8:15pm, Sun. 2-7pm; Nov.-April Mon.-Fri. 8:30am-1pm and 2:15-5pm).

The focal point of the city is the **Deutsches Eck** (German Corner), the peninsula that supposedly saw the birth of the German nation when the Teutonic Order of Knights settled there in 1216. The monumental **Mahnmal der Deutschen Einheit** (Monument to German Unity) now dominates this little corner of history; first erected in 1897 in honor of Kaiser Wilhelm I, the 14m equestrian statue that once crowned it was destroyed in 1945. Most of the nearby *Altstadt* was flattened during WWII, but several important buildings have been carefully restored. The **Rhein Museum,** Florinsmarkt 15-17, contains a reputable collection of German art and antiquities (open Tues. and Thurs.-Sun. 10am-5pm, Wed. 10am-8pm; free). From the docks on the Rhine, a frequent ferry (DM1.20) runs across the river to **Festung Ehrenbreitstein,** a fortress that in Prussian days was the largest in Europe. The 25min. climb to the battlements is worth it for the view; a chairlift *(Sesselbahn)* also makes the trip. (May-Oct. 9am to about 5pm. DM5, round-trip DM8.)

Inside the fortress is the recently renovated **Jugendherberge Koblenz (HI),** which may have the most scenic location of any hostel in Germany (tel. (0261) 737 37). From the train station, take bus 7, 8, 9, or 10 to Charlottenstr., then continue up the river and turn right onto the "main road" towards the castle (follow the signs). (Curfew 11:30pm. DM19.50, over 26 DM23.20.) **Campingplatz Rhein-Mosel** (tel. (0261) 80 24 89) is across the Mosel from the *Deutsches Eck;* a ferry journeys across the river during the day. (DM5 per person, DM4 per tent. Open April to mid-Oct.)

■■■ THE MOSEL VALLEY (MOSELTAL)

An arresting landscape, a smattering of ancient castles, and many fewer tourists make the Mosel Valley as intriguing as the Rhine. The river meanders northeast across more than 200km of German territory from Trier on the Luxembourg border to Koblenz, where it flows into the Rhine. See the valley's splendid scenery by boat, bus, or bicycle, since the train line between Koblenz and Trier strays frequently from the river into remarkably dull countryside. Some train stations will rent you a sturdy, heavy one-speed for DM12 per day, DM6 per day with a train ticket, Bundesbahn bus ticket, or railpass. You can drop off the bike at another train station at no extra charge and have your baggage sent ahead. Although passenger boats no longer make the complete Koblenz-Trier run, several companies run daily summer trips along shorter stretches; local tourist offices will provide details.

Cochem and Beilstein The town of **Cochem** seems to survive solely to produce wine and coddle tourists. High on a vineyard-blanketed hill above the town, the majestic turrets of the **Reichsburg** castle reign over the setting. Originally built in the 11th century, the castle—like much of the Palatinate—was destroyed in 1689 by French troops led by Louis XIV. In 1868, it was rebuilt in neo-Gothic style by a wealthy Berlin merchant. The interior can be seen today only on a guided tour. (Frequent tours last 40min; written English translations available. Open mid-March to Oct. 9am-5pm. DM4, students DM3.50.) Even if you bag the tour, the view from the castle grounds alone is worth the 15min. uphill climb along Schloßstr. from the Marktpl. Cochem itself is a maze of twisting streets and tourist establishments. The flower-lined **Promenade** along the river offers some respite from the endless succession of beer Steins and postcard trees.

The **tourist office** (tel. (02671) 39 71) is on Enderpl. right next to the bridge; from the train station, head to the river and turn right. The office will book rooms for DM2. (Open Mon.-Fri. 9am-1pm and 2-5pm, Sat. 10am-3pm; Nov.-May closed Sat.) Cochem's friendly but minimalist **Jugendherberge (HI)** is 10-15min. from the station on the opposite shore at Klottener Str. 9 (tel. (02671) 86 33 or 85 68: reception open 8-9am and 6-6:30pm. Latecomers should ring the bell. Curfew 10pm. DM18.10, over 26 DM25.30.) **Campingplatz am Freizeitzentrum** (tel. (02671) 44 09) is on Stadionstr. just below the youth hostel. (Reception open 8am-10pm. DM4.50 per person, DM3.50-7.50 per site. Open April-Oct.)

Ten km upstream from Cochem lies **Beilstein,** an attractive hamlet with little-touristed half-timbered houses and crooked cobblestone streets. A private bus line (railpasses not valid) makes several trips a day between Cochem (stopping at the train station and on Endertpl.) and Beilstein (15min., one-way DM3.60); the passenger boats of **Personenschiffahrt Kolb** (tel. (02673) 15 15) make 4 round-trips per day. (1hr., round-trip DM15. Railpasses not valid.) **Wine cellars** abound in Beilstein; make it a point to try one of the full-bodied local whites. Not to be missed here are the ruins of **Burg Metternich,** another casualty of the pyromaniacal French troops of 1689; the view from its broken-down edifices sweeps the valley (open April-Oct. 8:30am-7pm; DM2, students DM1).

Trier At the western end of the Mosel Valley lies **Trier,** the oldest city in Germany. Now just over 2000 years old, Trier had its heyday in the 4th century as the capital of the Western Empire and residence of Emperor Constantine. It's been a long but graceful 1600-year decline; today, some of the most extensive Roman ruins outside Italy and an *Altstadt* that's as attractive and well-preserved as they come make Trier more than worth the time. The natural point of departure for any tour of the city is the 2nd-century **Porta Nigra** (Black Gate), named for the centuries of grime that have turned its sandstone face varying shades of gloomy (open April-Sept. 9am-5:30pm; Oct.-Nov. and Jan.-March 9am-4:30pm. DM4, students DM1.50). From there, stroll down Simeonstr. to the **Hauptmarkt,** which is the northern leg of Trier's remarkably large pedestrian shopping district. A left onto Sternstr. brings you to the impressive interiors of the 11th-century **Dom** (open 6am-6pm; Nov.-March 6am-noon and 2-5:30pm; free). From the *Dom,* Liebfrauenstr. leads to the **Konstantin Basilika,** Constantine's 4th-century throne room, now about as exciting as an airplane hangar (open Mon.-Sat. 9am-1pm and 2-6pm, Sun. 11am-1pm and 2-6pm; free). From here, it's a 5-minute walk uphill along Olewiger Str. to the remains of the 2nd-century **amphitheater,** a 20,000-seat venue which would have been a required stop on any Roman world tour. The masses may want to make a pilgrimage to the **Karl-Marx Haus,** Brückenstr. 10, the birthplace of the bearded philosopher; it now houses a slightly dry account of his life (open Mon. 1-6pm, Tues.-Sat. 10am-6pm. DM3, students DM2).

In the shadow of the *Porta Nigra* is Trier's **tourist office** (tel. (0651) 97 80 80; open Mon.-Sat. 9am-6pm, Sun. 9am-3:30pm; Nov.-March Mon.-Sat. 9am-6pm, Sun. 9am-1pm). Several **trains** a day make the 1½-hour trip from Trier to Koblenz in the east and the 35min. jaunt from nearby Luxembourg to the west (day excursion DM10.90). **Personen-Schiffahrt** sails daily for Bernkastel-Kues in the Mosel Valley (9:15am, DM41). Trier's **Jugendgästehaus (HI),** An der Jugendherberge 4 (tel. (0651) 292 92, fax 240 80), has all the comforts of home. From the station, it's a 30min. walk; take Theodor-Heuss-Allee to the *Porta Nigra,* turn right on Paulinstr., take the first left onto the narrow, poorly marked Maarstr. and follow it until it ends. Or take bus 2 or 8 "Trierweilerweg" or "Pfalzel/Quint" to Moselbrück and walk 10min. downstream on the path along the top of the river embankment. (Reception open 3-11:30pm. Lockout 9:30am-1pm. Curfew midnight. Quads with toilet and shower in room DM25.30, over 26 29.30. Breakfast included.) The **Jugendhotel Kolpinghaus,** with dorm rooms, and the adjacent **Hotel Kolpinghaus** with singles and doubles, are clean, friendly, and one block off the *Hauptmarkt* at Dietrichstr. 42 (tel. (0651) 751 31, fax 746 96; reception open 8am-11pm; dorm bed DM22; singles DM30, doubles DM60; call ahead). Camp at **Schloß Monaise,** at Monaiser Str. (tel. (0651) 862 10) on the grounds of an 18th-century castle (DM5 per person, DM6 per car). **Astarix,** Karl-Marx-Str. 11, serves ridiculously inexpensive meals in a casual student-dominated environment (open Mon.-Sat. 11am-1am, Sun. 6pm-1am).

■■■ COLOGNE (KÖLN)

Cologne, whose eight bridges straddle the Rhine just north of Bonn, began as a Roman colony, gaining fame and fortune as a medieval crossroads rich in academic life. The city pulled itself up by its bootstraps after WWII, which left 90% of Cologne in ruins; the defiant survival of the city's magnificent *Dom* became a symbol of German reconstruction.

PRACTICAL INFORMATION

Tourist Office: Verkehrsamt, Unter Fettenhennen 19 (tel. 221 33 40, fax 221 33 20), across from the main entrance to the cathedral. Free city maps. Books rooms (DM3-5 fee). Pick up the *Monatsvorschau* (DM2), with essential info and complete monthly schedule of events. Open Mon.-Sat. 8am-10:30pm, Sun. 9am-10:30pm; mid-Oct. to April Mon.-Sat. 8am-9pm, Sun. 9:30am-7pm.

Currency Exchange: At the train station (open 7am-9pm), but the service charges are lower at the post office.

American Express: Burgmauerstr. 14 (tel. 257 74 84), near the *Dom.* ATM. Client letter service. DM5 per letter for non-cardmembers. Open Mon.-Fri. 9am-5:30pm, Sat. 9am-noon; cashier closed noon-2pm.

Post Office: Main office, An den Dominikanern, straight out of the station and to the right of the cathedral. Open Mon.-Fri. 7am-9pm, Sat.-Sun. 11am-8pm. **Postal Code:** 50668.

Telephones: In the train station. **City Code:** 0221.

Flights: tel. (02203) 40 40 01 or 40 40 02 for flight info. Bus 170 runs from the *Hauptbahnhof* to the Köln-Bonn Airport (15min.; DM7.20, children DM3.70).

Trains: Hauptbahnhof, next to the cathedral. To: Düsseldorf (25min.), Hamburg (4hr.), Frankfurt (2½hr.), Brussels (2½-3hr.), and Amsterdam (2hr.).

Public Transportation: VRS (Verkehrsverbund Rhein-Seig) offices have a plan of the S- and U-Bahn lines, as well as a map of city bus and streetcar lines. Tickets are priced by distance; the short-ride single cards (DM1.80), 4-ride cards (DM6.80), and day-cards (DM9.50) are available at automats and designated stations.

Hitchhiking: Hitchers who seek to reach Aachen, and then Holland or Belgium, take the U-Bahn 1 from Neumarkt to Junkersdorf. Look for the signs to Autobahn 4 (A4), direction Weiden. All those headed south, take bus 132 to the last stop **Citynetz Mitfahrzentrale,** Saarstr. 22 (tel. 194 44). Open Mon.-Sat. 9am-7pm.

Laundry: Öko-Express, Neue Weyerstr. 1. Wash DM6, dry DM1 per 15min. Soap included. Open Mon.-Sat. 6am-11pm.

Pharmacy: Dom Apotheke, Komodienstr. 5, near the station. Their *Pharmacie-Internationale* advises in English. List of after-hours pharmacies posted outside. **Police:** tel. 110.

ACCOMMODATIONS AND FOOD

Cologne's two hostels are both filled to the beams from June to September.

Jugendherberge Köln-Deutz (HI), Siegesstr. 5a (tel. 81 47 11, fax 88 44 25), just over the Hohenzollern Bridge. S-Bahn 6, 11, or 12 from the station: Köln-Deutz, cross Ottoplatz and you're there. Cramped rooms in a prime location, free laundry, and a great jukebox. Fills quickly. Check in 6-9am. Riskier reception noon-9:30pm. Curfew 12:30am. DM25, over 26 DM29. Sheets and breakfast included.

Jugendgästehaus Köln-Riehl (HI), An der Schanz 14 (tel. 76 70 81, fax 76 15 55), on the Rhine north of the zoo. From the station, take S-Bahn 5 or U-Bahn 16 or 18 "Ebertplatz/Mülheim": Boltensternstr.; or walk 40min. along the Rhine on Konrad-Adenauer-Uferstr., which becomes Niederländer-Ufer and finally An der Schanz. More luxurious but less convenient than Köln-Deutz, and fairly crowded. 24hr. reception. No curfew. DM 30.50. Sheets and breakfast included. The **Köln-Treff Café** sells beer, baguettes, and fries. Open 8pm-12:30am.

Hotel Rossner, Jakordenstr. 19 (tel. 12 27 03). From the back of the station (2min.), 4th left off of Johannisstr. Good value and convenient. Classic noble German rooms. Singles DM55, with shower DM75. Doubles DM80, with shower DM110. Triples DM95-130. Breakfast included.

Camping: Campingplatz Poll (tel. 83 19 66), southeast of the *Altstadt* on the Rhine. U-Bahn 16: Marienburg, and cross the Roddenkirchener Bridge. Reception open 8-11am and 4-8pm (later in the summer). DM3 per tent, DM5.50 per person.

Don't pass through Cologne without sampling the city's eponymous and extraordinarily smooth beer, *Kölsch*. Inexpensive food is available along **Schildergasse** and **Hohe Straße,** the main pedestrian shopping thoroughfares by the cathedral. The most interesting area for cheap food is on **Weidengasse,** in the Turkish district. Although in the middle of the chi-chi shopping district, **Spitz,** Ehrenstr. 43, is proudly alternative, serving dinners for under DM8 (open Sun.-Thurs. 9am-1am, Fri.-Sat. 9am-2am). **Café Waschsalon,** Friesenstr. 80, is filled with washers that might actually be made operational, but for now, no spin cycle will spill your drink (open Sun.-Thurs. 10am-1am, Fri.-Sat. 10am-3am; breakfast (DM 5.50 and up) until 4pm).

SIGHTS AND ENTERTAINMENT

Overwhelming in intricacy and scale, the colossal **Dom** (cathedral) took six centuries to build. Inside is the **Shrine of the Magi,** a reliquary of the Three Kings in blinding gold brought to Cologne in 1164. While in the *Dom,* look for the 976 **Gero Crucifix,** the oldest intact sculpture of the Crucifixion in the world. (Cathedral open 6am-7pm. Tours Mon.-Sat. 10, 11am, 2:30, and 3:30pm. For info call 52 19 77. Free organ concerts mid-June to Sept. Tues. 8pm.) It only takes 509 steps to reach the top of the **Südturm** (south tower) and peer down at the river below. Catch your breath at the *Glockenstübe,* chamber for the tower's nine bells. Four of the *Glocken* date to the Middle Ages, but the upstart 19th-century bell known affectionately as **Der große Peter** (at 24 tons, the world's heaviest swinging bell) rings the loudest. (Tower open 9am-5:30pm, March-April and Oct. 9am-4:30pm, Nov.-Feb. 9am-3:30pm; DM3, students DM1.50). The 12th-century **Groß St. Martin,** once on an island surrounded by the then-Rhine-flooded pedestrian zone, rises like a medieval castle beside the *Dom* despite extensive wartime damage (DM1, students and children DM.50). The squares and crooked streets of the old **Fischmarkt** district open onto paths along the Rhine; crowded café patios give way to a wide stretch of grass bordering the river, perfect for a picnic. The **Rathaus** (Town Hall) was partially bombed, but has been reconstructed in the original style (or styles).

The quirky museums of Cologne display an intriguing fanaticism of specialization. **Heinrich-Böll-Platz**, Bischofsgartenstr. 1, a building designed to provide a maximum of natural light, houses three separate museums, including **Museum Ludwig,** which travels from Impressionism to Picasso, Dalí, Klee, and Lichtenstein to art where the glue and paint is not quite dry. (Free tours Wed. 4:30pm, Sat. and Sun. 11am. Museums open Tues.-Fri. 10am-6pm, Sat.-Sun. 11am-6pm. Comprehensive admission DM10, students DM5. Special exhibits extra.) **EL-DE-Haus,** Am Appellhofplatz 23/25, memorializes the victims of the secret police in the basement of aformerly Gestapo-owned house (open Tues.-Sun. 10am-4pm; tours first Sat. of each month 2pm; free).**Das Mmmuseum (Imhoff-Stollwerk Museum),** Rheinauhafen, near the Severins bridge, is better than Willie Wonka's; salivate at every step of chocolate production, and enjoy the free samples (open 10am-6pm, last entry 5pm; DM10, students, seniors, children DM5; tours Sun. 11am, 2, and 4pm, DM3).

Cologne becomes a living spectacle during **Karneval,** a week-long pre-Lenten festival. The weekend builds up to the bacchanalian, dancing-in-the-streets parade on **Rosenmontag,** the last Monday before Lent (Feb. 27 in 1995). Everyone's in costume and everyone gets a couple dozen *Bützchen*—that's Kölsch for a kiss on a stranger's cheek. For info on the festival and tickets to events, inquire at the **Festkomitee des Kölner Karnevals,** Antwerpenerstr. 55. Also pick up the *Köln, Karneval* booklet at the tourist office, crammed with helpful hints.

Cologne does everything, including nightlife, on a large scale, but the closer you venture to the Rhine and the *Dom,* the more that scale directly applies to your wallet. Students congregate in the **Quartier Lateng,** a.k.a. the *Bermuda Dreieck* (triangle), the area bounded by Zülpicherstr., Zülpicher Platz, Roonstr. and Luxemburgstr. The center of gay nightlife runs up Matthiasstr. to Möhlenbach, Hohe Pforte, Marienplatz, and up to Heumarkt in the area by the Deutzer Brücke. Visit **Museum,** Zülpicherplatz 9; no temple of science is complete without a 2-story dinosaur looking out over blood alcohol level experiments (open Sun.-Tues. 4pm-1am, Wed.-Thurs. 4pm-2am, Fri.-Sat. 4pm-3am). **Filmdose,** Zülpicherstr. 39, is a café-bar with a creative performance space (performances Tues.-Thurs. and Sun. 8pm, Fri.-Sat. 7:30pm; *Kneipe* open Sun.-Thurs. 6pm-1am, Fri.-Sat. 6pm-3am). Sink into a couch, beer in hand (DM1.80), and show your skill at Monopoly, Mastermind, or German games at **Café Störchen,** Ursula Kloster 46 (open Mon.-Fri. 11am-1am, Sun. 10am-1am). **Moulin Rouge,** Maastrichterstr. 6-8, is a red velvet ex-brothel that draws in the sexy and the freaky for roaring good times; gets going around 1am. Belly dancing or poetry performances (3 per week) can cost DM15-20, but Fri.and Sat. cost DM5 whether it's just the café or a transvestite diva singing TV's greatest theme songs. (No cover most weeknights. Open 11pm-4:30am.)

■■■ BONN

A historical nonentity for most of its 2000 years, Bonn, the so-called *Hauptdorf* (capital village) made it big by chance: since Konrad Adenauer, the revered postwar chancellor, had a house in its suburbs, the ever-considerate occupying powers promoted humble Bonn to capital status. Easy come, easy go; newly resurgent Berlin is poised to become what it always really was, Germany's capital. Before the *Bundestag,* Bonn had Beethoven. Ludwig wailed his first notes in what's now called **Beethovens Geburtshaus** (Birthplace), Bonngasse 20, now a museum dedicated to his life and work (open Mon.-Sat. 10am-5pm, Sun. 10am-1pm; Oct.-March Mon.-Sat. 10am-4pm, Sun. 10am-1pm; last entry ½hr. before closing; DM5, students DM1.50; call ahead for English tours). The 18th-century pastel **Rathaus** presides over the Marktplatz; in the similarly colorful 1960s, de Gaulle, Kennedy, and Elizabeth II all made the building their photo-op backdrop. Nearby stands the **Kurfürstliches Schloß,** an 18th-century palace later converted into the central building of Bonn's university. The **Kunstmuseum Bonn,** Friedrich-Ebert Allee, showcases a superb assembly of Expressionist and contemporary German art (open Tues.-Sun. 10am-6pm; DM5, students DM3). From the bank of the Rhine, you can see the **Bundeshaus,** Germany's Parliament, on Görrestr., the "Least Prepossessing Parliament Building" in the whole world (open Mon.-Fri. 9am-4pm, Sat.-Sun. 10am-4pm; Jan. to mid-March Mon.-Fri. 9am-4pm; obligatory tours on the hour at Hermann-Ehlers-Str. 29, opposite the Hochhaus; bring your passport).

Bonn's **tourist office,** Münsterstr. 20 (tel. (0228) 77 34 66) books hotels for a DM3-5 fee. Take the Stadtmitte exit from the station, walk 60m up Poststr., turn left at Münsterstr. and it's to your right (open Mon.-Sat. 8am-9pm, Sun. 9:30am-12:30pm; Oct.-Feb. Mon.-Sat. 8am-7pm, Sun. 9:30am-12:30pm). The newly renovated **Jugendgästehaus Bonn-Venusberg (HI)** is at Haager Weg 42 (tel. (0228) 28 99 70, fax 289 96 14). Take bus 621 "Ippendorf Altenheim". (Curfew 1am. DM30.50. Sheets and breakfast included. Wheelchair access.) The more central **Jugendgästehaus Bonn-Bad Godesberg (HI),** Horionstr. 60 (tel. (0228) 31 75 16, fax 31 45 37), is just as spiffy. Take U-Bahn 63 or 16 from the main station to Rhein-allee or bus 615 "Stadtwald/Evangelische Krankenhaus" from the Bad Godesberg station to Venner Str. and look for the sign. (Curfew 1am. Same prices and perks.)

Young Bonners stomach inexpensive but barely palatable meals (DM1.80-3.50, DM1 extra without student ID) at the **University Mensa,** Nassestr. 11, a 15min. walk from the train station along Kaiserstr., with a ridiculously cheap (DM5 per kg) salad bar upstairs (open for lunch Mon.-Thurs. 11:30am-2:15pm, Fri. 11:30am-2pm, Sat. noon-1:45pm; open for dinner Mon.-Fri. 5:30-8pm). The **Pizzeria la Piccola,** Bonngasse 4 (tel. (0228) 63 78 16) has a neverending list of pizzas, salads, and pasta dishes, mostly under DM10 (open 11am-1am). **Cassius Garten,** Maximilianstr. 28d, at the edge of the *Altstadt* facing the station, will fulfill your wildest vegetarian fantasies (DM2.32 per 100g; open Mon.-Wed. and Fri. 11am-7pm, Thurs. 11am-8pm, Sat. 11am-3pm).

■■■ AACHEN

Tramping across 8th-century Europe, Charlemagne fell in love with Aachen and made it the capital of the nascent Frankish empire. Its octagonal neo-Byzantine **Dom,** in the center of the city circle, is one of the world's immortal cathedrals. Stained-glass panels ring the 15th-century Gothic choir; beneath the chancel lie the bones of the big guy himself. (Open 7am-7pm.) On the northern façade of the 14th-century **Rathaus,** over the Marktpl. beside the cathedral, stand 50 statues of former German sovereigns (open Mon.-Fri. 8am-1pm and 2-5pm, Sat.-Sun. 10am-1pm and 2-5pm; 2DM, students and children DM1). The **Ludwig Forum für Internationales Kunst,** Jülicherstr. 97-109, in a converted Bauhaus umbrella factory, opened just in time to invest in a stunning Eastern European collection. Warhol looks stodgy by comparison. (Open Tues.-Wed. and Fri.-Sun. 11am-7pm, Thurs. 11am-10pm. DM6, students DM3. Free tours Thurs. 8pm and Sun. 11:30am.)

Practical Information, Accommodations, and Food At the crossroads between Germany, Belgium, and the Netherlands, Aachen is also a departure point for **trains** to France, and Cologne is less than an hour away. The **tourist office** (tel. (0241) 180 29 60), in the Atrium Eliserbrunnen on Friedrich-Wilhelm-Pl., books rooms for a DM3 fee (open Mon.-Fri. 9am-6:30pm, Sat. 9am-1pm). Aachen's whitewashed brick **Jugendherberge (HI),** Maria-Theresia-Allee 260 (tel. (0241) 711 01, fax 70 82 19), sits on the edge of a forest south of the city. From the station, walk left on Lagerhausstr. to the Finanzamt at the corner of Mozartstr.; from there, take bus 2 "Preusswald" to Ronheide or bus 12 "Diepenbendem" to Colynshof and walk uphill. (Reception open until 10pm. Curfew 11:30pm. DM18.50, over 26 DM22.) **Pontstraße** is lined with restaurants and student pubs. **Café Seminar,** Templergraben 46, across from the university, is crowded with students on a quest for cheap, palatable eats; here, a "small" (read: good-sized) pizza runs DM6.50 (open Mon.-Sat. 9am-1am, Sun. 9am-6pm; kitchen open Mon.-Sat. noon-3pm and 6-11:30pm, Sun. noon-3pm). **Café Kittel,** 39 Pontstr. offers bowls of *Milchkaffee* and light snack on its outdoor patio or indoors against a backdrop of graffiti and concert posters. Pocket some *Aachner Printen,* trademark nut-studded ginger cookies, at local bakeries.

■■■ DÜSSELDORF

Germany's fashionable advertising center and multinational corporate base, Düsseldorf teems with German patricians and poseur aristocrats. Residents jibe that Düsseldorf isn't on the Rhine, but on the **Königsallee** ("the Kö"), a km-long fashion runway that leads down either side of the old town moat. At the upper end of this see-and-be-seen promenade, the **Hofgarten** park adds an oasis of green and culture to all the urbanity. West of the Hofgarten is the mirror-glass **Kunstsammlung Nordrhein-Westfalen,** Grabbepl. 5, an exceptional modern art museum with *the* definitive Paul Klee collection. Take U-Bahn 70, 75, 76, 78, or 79 to Heinrich-Heine-Allee and walk north 2 blocks. (Open Tues.-Sun. 10am-6pm. DM5, students DM3.) **Burg-platz** was the site of a glorious castle, but tired citizens only saved a single tower; given the structure's history, you can't blame them. The castle was built in 1324, burnt in 1490, rebuilt in 1559, razed in 1794, rebuilt in 1851, and flattened in 1872, at which point the townsfolk gave up—only the tower was reconstructed in 1900, and bombed into rubble during the WWII. Pessimistic citizens waited until 1984 to rebuild. North on the Rhine are the well-preserved ruins of Emperor Friedrich's palace in the tiny town of **Kaiserwerth.** Built in 1184, the palace was destroyed in 1702 during the War of Spanish Secession, but the romantic Kaiserpfalz frame remains. Take U-Bahn 79 to Klemensplatz, follow Kaiserwerther Markt to the Rhine and walk left another 150m. (Open Mon.-Fri. 3-7pm, Sat.-Sun. 10am-7pm. Free.)

Coolibri and *Biograph* are free cultural guides, less complete but still more than you'll ever need to keep it (your thang, that is) shakin' all night long. **Das Kommöd-chen** (tel. (0211) 32 94 43) is a tiny, extraordinarily popular theater behind the Kunsthalle at Grabbeplatz. (Box office open Mon.-Fri. 11am-2pm and 4-8pm, Sat. 2pm until performance time.) Ballet and opera tickets are best bought (without service charge) at the **Opernhaus** (tel. (0211) 890 82 11), on Heinrich Heine Allee. (Box office open Mon.-Fri. 11am-6:30pm, Sat. 11am-1pm, and 1hr. before performances. Tickets can be purchased by phone (Mon.-Fri. 9am-5pm). **Black Box,** Schulstr. 4 (tel. (0211) 899 24 90), off Rathaus-Ufer along the Rhine, services the art film aficionado with languages unadulterated. (DM7, students DM5. Seminars DM2.)

Practical Information The main **tourist office** is on Konrad-Adenauer-Pl. (tel. (0211) 17 20 20), to the right of the train station in the towering Immermanhof building. Its free monthly *Düsseldorf Monatsprogramm* is packed with information. (Open for ticket sales (fee 12%) and general services Mon.-Fri. 8:30am-6pm, Sat. 9am-12:30pm; for hotel reservations (DM6) Mon.-Sat. 8am-10pm, Sun. 4-10pm.) The **American Express** office is at Heinrich-Heine-Allee 14 (tel. (0211) 802 22; open Mon.-Fri. 9am-5:30pm, Sat. 9am-noon). The central **post office** is on Konrad-Adenauer-Pl. (open Mon.-Fri. 8am-6pm, Sat. 9am-2pm, Sun. noon-1pm). Forward Brenda's hate mail to the Poste Restante at **Düsseldorf 40210.**

Frequent S-Bahns and a Lufthansa shuttle travel to the **airport** (tel. (0211) 421 22 23 for flight info; 5am-12:30am). **Change money** at the airport (6am-10pm) or at **Deutsche Verkehrs Credit Bank** in the Hauptbahnhof (7am-9pm). Better rates with no extra charge are available at AmEx. Regional transportation, the *Rheinbahn,* includes subways, trams, buses, and the S-Bahn. Single rides cost DM1.60-10, depending on distance. The *Tagesticket* (DM8, higher prices for longer distances) is the best value around: groups of up to 5 people can travel all day on any line.

Accommodations Düsseldorf is a convention city; if you're considering a budget hotel stay, call the tourist office for trade fair dates and avoid them. Most rooms go for at least DM40 per person even in the off-season. Check the area around the train station or consider taking a room in nearby Mönchengladbach or Neuss. The conjoined **Jugendherberge und Jugendgästehaus Düsseldorf (HI),** Düsseldorfer Str. 1 (tel. (0211) 55 73 10, fax 57 25 13), is conveniently located, just over the Rheinkniebrücke from the *Altstadt.* Take U-Bahn 70, 75, 76, or 77 to Lugeplatz and walk 500m down Kaiser-Wilhelm-Ring. Choose between the cheaper but above-average **Jugendherberge** (DM25, over 26 DM29; breakfast included) or the possibility of a single in the adjacent **Jugendgästehaus.** (Singles DM37.50. Double DM63. Quads DM122. At both, reception open 7:15-9:45am, 10-11:30am, noon-2:30pm, 3-5:30pm, and 6-11pm. Curfew 1am, but open briefly at 2, 3, 4 and 6am. Open mid-Jan. to mid-Dec.) Bible literature is the only frill at the standard **CVJM-Hotel,** Graf-Adolf-Str. 102 (tel. (0211) 36 07 64, fax 361 31 60), down the street to the left of the train station (24hr. reception; singles DM55; doubles DM90). **Hotel Manhattan,** Graf-Adolf-Str. 39 (tel. (0211) 37 02 44, fax 37 02 47), is straight up from the station. The mirror-plated lobby glows with 1970s dance fever, but the clean, desk-equipped rooms are surprisingly charming (singles DM60-95; doubles DM100-140;

call in advance). Stake out **Camping Unterbacher See,** Kleiner Torfbruch 31 (tel. (0211) 899 20 38). Take the S-Bahn to Düsseldorf Geresheim and change to bus 737 "Stamesberg" to Seestr. (DM27.50 per site for up to 3 people, DM7 per extra person. Call ahead.)

Food The busy streets of the *Altstadt* are lined with restaurants and fast-food joints. The **Markt** on Karlsplatz offers all sorts of produce and foods, including *Sauerbraten* (pickled beef) with greens on the side (open Mon.-Sat. 8am-5pm). **Breweries** sell cheap meals in addition to their house concoctions; **Hausbrauerei "zum Schlüssel"** and **Schumacher Bräu "Im Goldenen Kessel",** at Bolkerstr. 45 and 44 respectively, are huge and happening. Dine with the glitzy clientele at **Galerie Burghof,** Burgallee 1-3 (open Mon.-Sat. 5pm-1am, Sun. noon-midnight; pancakes DM 13). **Asia Grill,** Hunsrückenstr. 20, has plastic dragon-lamps and a good selection of filling meals; duck is the most expensive at DM10.50 (open Wed.-Sat. 10am-5am). Line up with the locals to try the house specialties of *Blutwurst* (black pudding) DM2.80 or *Mainzer* (Mainz cheese) DM3.25 at **Uerige,** Bergerstr. 1 (open Mon.-Fri. 5pm-midnight, Sat. 11am-midnight).

Folklore holds that Düsseldorf's 500 pubs make up *die längste Theke der Welt* (the longest bar in the world). *Prinz* magazine (DM4) is Düsseldorf's fashion cop and scene detective; it's often available free at the youth hostel. **Zum Goldenen Einhorn** and **Brauerei zum Uel,** Rattingerstr. 16-18, in the *Altstadt,* are papered with listings for musical happenings. (Requisite *Schlösser Alt*—0.2 liter for DM2.20. Open Sun.-Tues., Thurs. 10am-1am, Wed., Fri.-Sat. 10am-3am.) Or head over to **Rheingold,** to the right of the main train station; it shakes the atmosphere with an ensemble of bars, cafés, balconies, and a dance floor (Thurs.-Sun. from 10pm). Meet Germans practising their brogues at **McLaughlin's,** Kurzestr. 11 (open Mon.-Sat. 11am-3am, Sun. 11am-1am).

■ ESSEN

Düsseldorf owes a good deal of its modern prosperity to the wealth of the **Ruhr Valley** *(das Ruhrgebiet),* a sprawling conglomeration of cities joined by the densest concentration of rail lines in the world. Between the 1850s and the 1970s, riverside coal deposits were mined to feed Germany's breakneck industrialization. Infamous 19th-century railroad and armaments mogul Alfred Krupp perfected steel-casting in industrial **Essen.** The **Villa Hügel,** for decades the Krupp family home, was given to the city in the '50s in an attempt to brighten a company image sooted by unsavory wartime activities. (S-Bahn 6: Essen-Hügel. Grounds open 8am-8pm. Villa open Tues.-Sun. 10am-6pm. DM1.50, special exhibits DM10.) Essen's massive **Alte Synagoge,** Steelerstr. 29, was gutted by Nazis in 1938, but remained standing as the largest synagogue north of the Alps (U-Bahn: Porchepl.; open Tues.-Sun. 10am-6pm; free; tours Wed. 3pm).

NORTHERN GERMANY

Northern Germany has a history of prosperity and fierce independence that dates back to the medieval Hanseatic League. Hamburg is an immense port and frenzied metropolis; Bremen and Lübeck preserve the heritage that infected all of Scandinavia with German culture and medieval mercantilism.

■■■ HAMBURG

Birthplace of Brahms and the largest German city after Berlin, Hamburg has the oldest democratic structure in the country and a liberal atmosphere—from the licentious sex industry in St. Pauli to a vociferous ecological movement. Though partially

GERMANY

devastated in World War II, the copper-roofed architecture so characteristic of northern Germany survives, due in large part to the old money that makes Hamburg Germany's richest city. Germany's largest port has been welcoming and bidding farewell to goods and passengers from all over the world for centuries; the result is a vibrant and cosmopolitan metropolis.

ORIENTATION AND PRACTICAL INFORMATION

The center of Hamburg lies on the north bank of the **Elbe River.** Most major sights lie between the **St. Pauli Landungsbrücken** ferry terminal in the west, and the tourist office and main train station in the east.

Tourist Offices: The **Hauptbahnhof office**, Kirchenallee exit (tel. 30 05 12 30), open 7am-11pm, and the Fühlsbüttel **airport office,** Terminal 4 arrivals (tel. 30 05 12 40), open 8am-11pm, will book rooms for a DM6 fee. Info also available at the **St. Pauli Landungsbrücken,** between piers 4 and 5 (tel. 30 05 12 00), open 9am-6pm, Nov.-Feb. 10am-5pm; and in the **Hansa-Viertel mall,** Poststr. entrance (tel. 30 05 12 20), open Mon.-Fri. 10am-6:30pm, Sat. 10am-3pm, Sun. 11am-3pm.

Budget Travel: SSR Reiseladen, Rothenbaumchaussee 61 (tel. 410 20 81), near the university. Student discounts up to 50%. Open Mon.-Fri. 9am-6pm, Sat. 9am-noon.

Currency Exchange: Long hours but high prices at the train station. Open 7:30am-10pm. Better rates at downtown banks (open 9am-4pm).

American Express: Rathausmarkt 5 (tel. 33 11 41). The usual. Open Mon.-Fri. 9am-5:30pm, Sat. 9am-noon.

Post Office: At the Kirchenallee exit of the train station. **Poste Restante** at window #1. Open Mon.-Sat. 7am-9pm, Sun. 8am-8pm. **Postal Code:** 20099

Telephones: At the *Hauptbahnhof* post office. **City Code:** 040.

Flights: tel. 50 75 25 57. Buses zoom off to **Fuhlsbüttel Airport** from outside the Kirchenallee exit of the train station (5:40am-9:20pm every 20min., 30min., DM8), or take the U-Bahn to Ohlsdorf, then a bus (every 10min., DM3.40).

Trains: The **Hauptbahnhof** handles most traffic. **Dammtor** station is across the Kennedy/Lombardsbrücke. Most trains to and from Kiel, Schleswig, Flensburg, and Westerland stop only at **Altona** station, in the west of Hamburg. Frequent trains and S-Bahn connect all three. **Information:** 194 19.

Buses: Near Hauptbahnhof on Adenauerallee. Long-distance buses to Berlin (3½hr., DM50) and points farther afield.

Public Transportation: Efficient buses, the U-Bahn and the S-Bahn cost DM1.40-7.70. U-Bahn and S-Bahn day tickets DM7.20 from orange automat machines or at tourist office. A 3-day ticket is DM20.70. Only a few night buses run past midnight although the U-Bahn begins to roll again at 5am. The **Hamburg Card** can be good value—it includes unlimited public transportation, including night buses, free admission to 11 museums, and other perks (1-day card DM10.80 for 1 adult and 3 kids, 3-day DM21)

Ferries: Landungsbrücken, pier 9 (tel. 38 90 71), 2km west along the shore from St. Pauli Landungsbrücken. Overnight connections with **Scandinavian Seaways,** Van der Smissenstr. 4 (tel. 389 03 71), to Harwich, England (every other day; tickets DM130-500; students under 26 and seniors 20% off).

Hitchhiking: Hitchers to Berlin, Copenhagen, and Lübeck take S-1 to Wandsbeker Chaussee and walk along Hammerstr. until the Hamburg Horn, a large, treacherous traffic rotary at the base of the *Autobahn.* For points south, hitchers take S-3 "Harburg" to Veddel and walk 5min. to the *Autobahn.*

Mitfahrzentrale, Lobuschstr. 22 (tel. 39 17 21), at the Altona train station. Open Mon.-Wed. 9am-7pm, Thurs.-Fri. 9am-8pm, Sat. 9am-7pm, Sun. 10am-6pm.

Bookstore: Thalia, Hermannstr. 18-20 (tel. 302 07 01). Good-sized English section. Open Mon.-Wed., Fri. 9:30am-6:30pm, Thurs. 9:30am-9:30pm.

Laundry: Wasch-Center, Nobistor 34, near the Reeperbahn. Wash DM6, dry DM2 per 15min. Open 6am-10pm.

Lesbian and Gay Center: Magnus Hirschfeld Centrum, Borgweg 8 (tel. 279 00 60). U-Bahn 3 or bus 108 to "Borgweg." Daily films and counseling sessions. Evening café open Mon.-Sat. 3pm-midnight, Sun. and holidays 4pm-midnight. Lesbians and gays alike are clued in on special events by the *Dorn Rosa* journal and *Gay Life* (both available at newsstands).

Emergency: Police: tel. 110. Headquarters at Kirchenallee 46, opposite the train station. **Ambulance:** tel. 112.

ACCOMMODATIONS AND CAMPING

Hamburg is not a cheap place to stay; single rooms start at about DM50, with doubles from DM75. A stew of small, inexpensive pensions line **Steindamm, Bremer Weg** and **Bremer Reihe** north of the train station. Check out your hotel before you accept a room—half the establishments along this strip are of dubious quality. For help, pick up a *Hotelführer* (DM1) from the tourist office.

Jugendherberge auf dem Stintfang (HI), Alfred-Wegener-Weg 5 (tel. 31 34 88; fax 31 54 07). S-Bahn 1, 2, or 3 or U-Bahn 3 (from the main station): Landungsbrücke. Hike up steps to hill above. Large, busy hostel attracts travelers from all over the globe. Take security advice to heart. Reception open 7-9am and 1pm-1am. 3-day max. stay. Curfew 1am. DM18.50, over 26 DM22.50, nonmembers DM5 extra. Breakfast included.

Jugendgästehaus Horner-Rennbahn (HI), Rennbahnstr. 100 (tel. 651 16 71; fax 65 56 516). U-Bahn 3: Horner-Rennbahn, then walk 10min. or take the bus toward Wandsbek (DM2.80). Clean and peaceful, but a bit far. Reception open 7:30-9am, 1-6pm and 12:30pm-1am. Curfew 1am. DM26, over 26 DM32. Open March-Dec.

Annerhof, Lange Reihe 23 (tel. 24 34 26). From the station's Kirchenallee exit, the second street on your right. High corniced ceilings in spacious, comfortable rooms. Call ahead. Singles DM46, doubles DM76. Breakfast DM8.

Pension Sarah Peterson, Lange Reihe 50 (tel.24 30 24). Small, artsy pension in an old building with bohemian flair. Singles DM79, doubles DM96, triples DM140.

Campingplatz Buchholz, Kielerstr. 374 (tel. 540 45 32). S-Bahn 3 "Pinneberg" or S-Bahn 21 "Elbgaustr.": Stellingren. Reception open 7am-11pm; Oct.-May 8-10am and 4-8pm. DM6 per person, DM12.50 per tent. Showers DM2.50. Call ahead.

FOOD

Walk along **St. Pauli's Quai, Landungsbrücke,** for small fish restaurants. In the middle of the square of the same name, the **Rathausmarkt** offers all things edible at honest prices. Find good deals in the numerous inexpensive cafés and restaurants in the university area around **Renteelstr., Grindlehof,** and **Grindallee**. In **Altona** a plethora of inexpensive cafés and restaurants can be found on **Schanzenstr**.

Geo, Beim Schlump 27 (tel. 45 79 29), serves possibly the best pizza in the world (open 11am 'til you've had enough; DM7.70-14).

Da Rocco & Pietro Ristorante, Talstr. 10 (tel. 317 10 19). From the bright lights of the street, step into the candle-lit, cozy den where pasta dishes (DM8-10) include garlic bread (open 6pm-4am).

Fischerhaus, St. Pauli Fischmarkt 14 (tel. 31 40 53). Fresh fish and superb service explain this restaurant's appeal. Meals DM11-30. Open 11am-11pm.

Sunset, Fischmarkt 14 (tel. 31 45 67). Right by the Fischmarkt pavilion. Bask in the contempo teal and funky jazzed-up versions of Queen's Greatest Hits. Meals DM6-19.50. Open 9am-1am.

Gorki Park, Grindelallee 1, near the university at Bundesstr. (tel. 45 70 17). The new face of socialism serves up a *proletarier* fest (DM8-15) amidst red velvet drapes, antique furniture, communist kitsch, and Russian folk music. Open 5pm-3am.

SIGHTS

The sight of Hamburg's seven copper towers tells visitors they've arrived. At night the **Hamburg Hafen,** the largest port in Germany, is lit up by ships from all over the world. After sailing the East Indies, the 19th century **Windjammer Rickmer Rickmers** was docked at pier 1 and restored as a museum ship. Come for the old naviga-

GERMANY

tion equipment, all brass and polished, alongside the newer technology. (Open 10am-6pm. DM6.50, children DM3.50.)

The richly ornamented **Rathaus,** a 19th-century monstrosity, dominates the city center. Tours pass through gorgeous rooms, still used for receptions and meetings (hourly in English Mon.-Thurs. 10:15am-3:15pm, Fri.-Sun. 10:15am-1:15pm; *Rathaus* open Mon.-Thurs. 10am-3pm, Fri.-Sun. 10am-1pm; DM2). Just south of the *Rathaus* on Ost-West-Str. stand the somber ruins of the **St. Nikolaikirche.** One of the earliest examples of neo-Gothic architecture, it was flattened by Allied bombing raids in 1943. A tad farther west is the imposing 18th-century **Große Michaeliskirche,** whose baroque tower is Hamburg's city emblem (tower open May-Oct. 9am-6pm; Nov.-April 10am-4pm; church free). A block south of the *Hauptbahnhof*, the **Museum für Kunst und Gewerbe** boasts a fantastic, rich collection of handicrafts, china, and furnishings, ranging from ancient Egyptian and Roman to Asian and *Jugendstil* (open Tues.-Sun. 10am-6pm; DM6, students and seniors DM1). One block north of the train station, the **Hamburger Kunsthalle,** Glockengiesserwall 1, holds a huge selection of paintings and drawings ranging from medieval to modern (open Tues.-Wed. and Fri.- Sun. 10am-6pm, Thurs. 10am-9pm. DM8-15, students DM6-10). At the end of the restored baroque **Peterstraße,** the **Museum of Hamburgische History,** Holstenwall 24, is the parent of the **Historic Emigration Office,** Bei den St. Pauli Landungsbrücken 3, an archive that recorded the names and home towns of the 5 million Germans and East Europeans who emigrated through Hamburg between 1850 and 1914. Take the U-Bahn to the St. Pauli stop. (Open Tues.-Sat. 10am-6pm. DM6, students DM1.)

ENTERTAINMENT AND NIGHTLIFE

The cultural capital of the North, Hamburg invests a great deal in the arts. The **Staatsoper,** Dammtorstr. 28, houses one of the best opera companies in Germany, and the attached **ballet** company is the nation's acknowledged dance powerhouse. **Orchestras** abound: the **Philharmonie,** the **Symphony,** and the **Nord-Deutscher-Rundfunk** are the big 3. Lighter music, popular musicals, and transvestite cabarets play the **Operettenhaus Hamburg,** the **Neue Flora Theater,** and smaller venues. Call the tourist office for info on dates and tickets.

Hamburg has an extensive live music scene which spans all tastes. Traditional jazz is at its best at the **Cotton Club,** Alter Steinweg 10 (tel. 319 19 99; open Mon.-Sat. 8pm-midnight; cover DM5-10), and on Sunday mornings at the Fish Auction Hall at the **Fischmarkt.** International rock groups frequently play at **Große Freiheit** 36, (tel. 319 36 49), and at **Docks,** Spielbudenplatz 19 (tel. 319 43 78). The renowned **Fabrik,** Barnerstr. 36 (tel. 39 10 70) in Altona, features everything from funk to punk. The best sources of information about what's happening are *Szene, Oxmox,* or *Prinz* (available at newsstands for DM5, and free in hostels).

The nexus of Hamburg's nightlife is at the heart of St. Pauli on the **Reeperbahn.** Known as the home of the St. Pauli girls, the area features the best clubs and bars in Hamburg, as well as seamy sex-clubs and peepshows. **Große Freiheit,** a street lined with explicit revues and cabarets, might be one of the most concentrated sinks of sleaze in the world. **Herbertstraße,** just south of the Reeperbahn of Davidstr., is a legalized prostitution strip. Only men over 18 are permitted down the street.

Clusters of popular student bars can be found along Grindelallee and Schanzenstr. Swarms of street-side cafés line the three squares **Gänsemarkt** (U-Bahn 2), **Rodningsmarkt** (U-Bahn 3), and **Großneumarkt** (S-Bahn 1 or 2: Stadthausbrücke). In general, clubs open late and close late, with some techno and trance clubs staying open until noon the following day. For some jazz, try the **Mojo Club,** Reeperbahn 1 (tel. 319 19 99), deemed the best club in Germany by MTV; the attached **Jazz Café** attracts the trendy and has stylish bar-tenders (club open Fri.-Sat. from 11pm; cover usually DM10; café open Wed.-Sat. from 10pm; no cover). Drink beer by candlelight with the local students while listening to funky new-age German music at the **Frank und Frei,** Schanzenstr. 93 (tel. 43 48 03; open Mon.-Sat. 11am-3am, Sun. 10am-3am). Meanwhile, **Logo,** Grindelallee 5 (tel. 410 56 58) is a dance hall which features a host of alternative live music (open from 9:30pm; cover varies). **Front,** Heiden-kampsweg 1 (tel. 23 25 23) is a hip, largely gay house club (open Fri.-Sat. from 11pm; cover DM10). **Frauenkneipe,** Stresemanstr. 60, is a bar and meeting place for women of all orientations (open Mon.-Fri. 8pm-1am, Sat. 9pm-3am, Sun. 2pm-1am). Check *Szene, Oxmox,* and *Prinz* for more info.

■■■ SCHLESWIG-HOLSTEIN

Lübeck Once the robust capital of the Hanseatic League, Schleswig-Holstein's most exciting city, Lübeck, flourished in the Middle Ages, linking the prosperous Baltic trade. Thomas and Heinrich Mann drew the inspiration for their literary critiques of the German bourgeoisie while living among the wealth and hypocrisy of this city. On Mengestr., the **Buddenbrooks House** is now a hi-tech museum dedicated to the life and work of the brothers (open Tues.-Sun. 10am-5pm; DM4, students DM2).

Since its destruction by Allied bombers in WWII, Lübeck has been renovating and rebuilding its *Altstadt,* whose **Rathaus,** a 13th-century structure of glazed black bricks sets off the technicolor fruit and flower market in the square. (Tours Mon.-Fri. at 11am, noon, and 3pm. DM4, students DM2.) Across the *Marktplatz,* the North-German Gothic **Marienkirche** displays a partially restored section of its famous **Totentanzbild,** or death-dance mural (open 10am-6pm, off-season 10am-4pm; free).

Between the inner city and the train station is the **Holstentor,** one of the four gates built in the 15th century to guard the entrance to Lübeck. Inside, the **Museum Holstentor** exhibits ship construction, trade, and quaint local implements of torture (open Tues.-Sun. 10am-5pm; Oct.-March 10am-4pm; DM3, students DM1.50, under 18 free). The steeple of the 750-year-old **Petrikirche** on Schmiederstr. gives a sweeping view of the *Altstadt.* (Church open Tues.-Sun. 11am-4pm. Elevator open April-Oct. 9am-6pm. DM3, students DM1.50.) The well-preserved houses of sea captains adorn **Engelsgrubestraße,** opposite Jacobkirche. For entertainment listings, pick up *Piste, Journal,* or *Zentrum* from the tourist office.

At the **tourist office** (tel. (0451) 86 46 75, fax 86 30 24) in the train station (open Mon.-Sat. 9am-6pm), grab a free map and make for the larger **main office** at Am Markt 1 (tel. (0451) 122 81 06), across from the *Rathaus.* (Open Mon.-Fri. 9:30am-6pm, Sat.-Sun. 10am-2pm.) Frequent **trains** connect Lübeck and Hamburg's Hauptbahnhof (40min.).

Sleep-In (CVJM), Große Petersgrube 11 (tel. (0451) 789 82), near the Petrikirche, is a shiny, earnest YMCA in the old area of town, 10min. from the station. (Reception open Mon.-Fri. 9am-noon and 5pm-midnight, Sat.-Sun. 9-10am and 5pm-midnight; Sept.-June until 10pm. 10-bed dorms for DM15 per person. Sheets DM5. Breakfast DM5.) Peter and Kalli welcome you to their clean and friendly **Rucksack Hotel,** Kanalstr. 70 (tel. (0451) 70 68 92), in the *Altstadt* by the canal. From the train station walk past the Holstentor, turn left on An der Untertrave, and right on Beckergrube. (Reception open 9am-10pm. Doubles DM75. Quads DM120. Dorms DM19-22.) **Café Affenbrot,** Kanalstr. 70, is a tropical collective-vegetarian restaurant (open 9am-midnight). Don't miss Lübeck's famous marzipan from **I. G. Niederegger,** Breitestr. 89, opposite the Rathaus (open Mon.-Fri. 9am-6:30pm, Sat. 9am-6pm, Sun. 10am-6pm).

Kiel Capital of Schleswig-Holstein, industrial Kiel boasts the Kiel locks, the largest in the world. The end of June sees the annual **Kieler Woche,** an internationally renowned regatta that enlivens the harbor and fills the town with people, music, food and beer, particularly around the Olympia Zentrum (bus 4 or 44 north). Near the **St. Nicolaskirche** (open Mon.-Fri. 10am-1pm and 2-6pm, Sat. 10am-1pm; free) stands Barlach's haunting statue, the **Geistkämpfer** (ghost-fighter). If shipping and other maritime activities (including sunbathing) aren't for you, every 2hr. a bus leaves from the station for the Hamburg airport (1½hr., DM20). Leaving from the wharf on the west bank of the city, **Stena Line** (tel. (0431) 90 90) sails to Gothenburg, Sweden daily at 7pm (14hr., DM98-194), and **Color Line** (tel. (0431) 97 40 90) journeys to Oslo, Norway (daily, every other day in Jan.; 18hr.; DM304-1448, students 50% off selected sailings). Reach the **Jugendherberge,** Johannesstr. 1 (tel. (0431) 73 57 23) on bus 4 or 34. Get off at Karlstr., walk a block, and go left on Johannesstr. (Reception open 7am-11:30pm. DM18, over 26 DM22.)

■■■ BREMEN

Bremen lies along the Weser River, and owes its living to the North Sea, preserving its medieval heritage while capitalizing on such modern assets as Beck's Beer brewery. The early 15th-century **Rathaus** survived World War II because the English pilot ordered to bomb the downtown deliberately dodged his target (tours, the only access to the building interior, Mon.-Fri. at 10am, 11am, and noon, Sat.-Sun. at 11am and noon; DM4; children DM2). Also a war survivor, the impressive **St. Petri Dom,** Sandstr. 10-12, dates from 798 when Charlemagne had the first foundation stone laid. The cathedral hosts a mosaic interior of orange, gold, and gray stone arches. (open Mon.-Fri. 10am-5pm, Sat. 10am-noon, Sun. 2-5pm). Cross the Domsheide to the **Schnoorviertel,** a gingerbread quarter of craft shops and red-roofed houses. Bremen's **Kunsthalle,** Am Wall 207, contains a bouquet of art from the Renaissance to the present, including a strong collection of moody early 20th-century German expressionists (open Tues. 10am-9pm, Wed.-Sun. 10am-5pm; DM6, students DM3).

Practical Information, Accommodations, and Food The **tourist office** (tel. (0421) 30 80 00; fax 308 00 30), across from the train station carries guides to museum exhibits and the like (open Mon.-Wed. and Fri. 9:30am-6:30pm, Thurs. 9:30am-8:30pm, Sat. 9:30am-2pm., Sun. 9:20am-3:30pm). The **post office** and **telephones** are at Domsheide 15, near the Markt. **American Express** (tel. (0421) 141 71) has a travel agency and full cardmember service at Am Wall 138. (Open Mon.-Fri. 10am-5:30pm, Sat. 10am-noon.) Up the Weser and to the north, **Bremerhaven** and **Cuxhaven** work deep-sea ports with ferry connections to the vacation isle of **Helgoland.** About an hour to the east, **Oldenburg** opens up the "Southern-North-Sea-Land," an embarkment point for trips to the low-lying **East Frisian Islands.**

The sleek **Jugendgästehaus Bremen (HI),** Kalkstr. 6 (tel. (0421) 17 13 69, fax 17 11 02), can be reached by bus 26 or tram 6: Am Brille stop; then take Bürgermeister-Smidt-Str. to the river, turn right, and walk 2 blocks (reception open 24hrs.; DM24.50, over 26 DM29). **Hotel Enzensperger,** Brautstr. 9 (tel. (0421) 50 32 24), has tidy rooms with some street-side terraces. From the Markt, cross the Wilhelm-Kaiser Bridge, turn right on Osterstr. and right again on Brautstr. (Singles DM47, with shower DM48, doubles DM69, with shower DM80; breakfast included.) Otherwise, rooms in Bremen are ruinously expensive. **Camping** is distant, at Am Stadtwaldsee 1 (tel. (0421) 21 20 02); take bus 22 or 23 to the last stop (15min.), then walk along Kuhgangweg to Anwieseck and turn left (DM6.50 per person, DM4-8 per tent; open Easter-Oct.).

In the *Rathaus* visit Bremen's renowned **Ratskeller** (tel. (0421) 32 16 76), dating to 1408, one of the oldest wineries in Germany; sip one of each of the 600 German labels (DM4.20 per 0.2l glass). Meals here cost at least DM20, but merit every mark. (Open 11am-midnight.) Café Torno, Am Dobben 71, satifies hunger for a little less with rich *panini*, pasta, and *gyros* (DM5-12; open Mon.-Fri. noon -2am, Sat. noon-4am, Sun. noon-1am). Student pubs await farther east on and around **Ostertorsteinweg,** just beyond Goethepl. Litfass, Ostersteinweg 22, is an all-day, all-night bastion of alternative chic. The place to be seen on your European tour. (Open Sun.-Thurs. 10am-2am, Fri.-Sat. 10am-4am.)

■■■ HANOVER (HANNOVER)

Hanover, a hyper-modern industrial and commercial center, rose phoenix-like from the ashes of World War II. Among the few architectural gems remaining is the spectacular **Neues Rathaus,** which spent 1943 to 1945 as a parking lot. This perfectly recreated palace has an amazing tower view. (Tower open April-Oct. 10am-12:30pm and 1:30-4:30pm. DM3, students DM2.) The **Sprengel Museum,** Am Maschseeplatz, between the lake and the Rathaus is a modern art lover's dream: Turrell, Moore, Dalí, Picasso, Magritte, and Antes (open Tues. 10am-10pm, Wed.-Sun. 10am-6pm; free except for special exhibits). The city's crown jewel is the **Herrenhausengarten,** a baroque garden with manicured rose gardens, geyser-inspired fountains, and the **Herrenhausen Palace**. The frequent concerts, ballets, and plays held in the palace often spill outside in the summer. (Open 8am-8pm; in winter 8am-4:30pm entrance to gardens DM3.) Inquire at the **tourist office,** Ernst-August-Pl. 28 (tel. (0511) 30 14 22; fax 30 14 14), across from the train station, about tickets to performances at the Herrenhausen and the Opera. The amiable staff also finds rooms (DM5 fee) and gives regional transport information.

The **Jugendherberge Hannover (HI)** at Ferdinand-Wilhelm-Fricke-Weg 1 (tel. (0511) 131 76 74; fax 185 55) is the cheapest and most central place to crash. Take bus 24 to Stadionbrücke to the front door or U-Bahn 3 or 7 "Mühlenberg" to Fischerhof/Fachhochschule, cross the tracks and follow the signs along the bike path. (Curfew 11:30pm. DM19, over 26 DM23.50. Camping DM12.25.) Most of Hanover's cheap eats lie in or near the pedestrian zone between the *Altstadt* and Kröpcke. **Café Klatsch,** Limmerstr. 58 (tel. (0511) 45 52 31) offers fresh sandwiches and salads, pastries, great coffee, and board games with alternative, ecologically friendly flair (open Mon.-Fri. 9am-6:30pm, Sat. 10am-6:30pm, Sun. 11am-6:30pm). To rock the night away, head to **Rottkäpchen,** Limmerstr. 44 (tel. (0511) 45 12 30); watch out for the Satan head watching you from the doorway (open Mon.-Fri. 3pm-2am, Fri.-Sat. 3pm-3am, Sun. 11am-6pm (brunch); warm food Mon.-Thurs. 5pm-1am). For more info on nightlife, pick up a free copy of *MagaScene* at the tourist office. For 10 days in late June and early July, Hanover crawls with locals for the **Schützenfest** (shooting festival), which dates back to the summer of 1539. Shooting quickly gives way to drinking as celebrants get *Schützen*-faced on the traditional festival drink: the *Lutje Lager*. Without spilling, you drink from two glasses at the same time—held side by side. One glass contains dark beer, the other Schnapps. Hold onto your hat!

■■■ HARZ MOUNTAINS

Heinrich Heine wrote that even Mephistopheles trembled when he approached the mist-draped Harz, the devil's dearest mountains. Unification lifted a less tangible but more palpable veil from the range, which stretches from the western **Oberharz** to the eastern **Ostharz** and to sun-sheltered health resorts in the south. Spring thaws turn ski slopes into webs of hidden hiking trails. The **Harzerquerbahn,** a stylishly antique narrow-gauge railway, steams through gorgeous Harz scenery from Nordhausen to Wernigerode.

Goslar In 922 AD, Holy Roman Emperor Heinrich stumbled upon Goslar, and the dusty town, 40min. by train from Hanover, still fancies itself the unofficial capital of the Harz. Guarded by a pair of stone Braunschweig lions, the **Kaiserpfalz,** at Kaiserbleek 6, is a massive Romanesque palace that served as the ruling seat for 11th- and 12th-century emperors (open 10am-5pm; Nov.-March 10am-4pm; DM3.50, students DM2). Each day, the small mechanical figures of court nobles and the miners whose work made the region prosperous dance to the chime of the **Glocken- und Gigurenspiel** at 9am, noon, 3pm, and 6pm, opposite the Rathaus. The **Mönchehaus,** Mönchestr. 3, is an outstanding modern art museum inside a small house with a sculpture garden (open Tues.-Sat. 10am-1pm and 3-5pm, Sun. 10am-1pm. DM 3.50, students and children DM2.)

The **Harzer Verkehrsverband regional tourist office,** Marktstr. 45 (tel. (05321) 340 40), is inside the Industrie und Handels Kammer building (open Mon.-Thurs. 8am-4pm, Fri. 8am-1pm). Their indispensable *Grüner Faden für den Harz-Gast* pamphlet (DM3) lists attractions, and *Jugend und Freizeitheime im Harz und im Harzvorland* is a compilation of area youth hostels and student centers. The **local tourist office,** Markt 7 (tel. (05321) 28 47, fax 230 05), across from the *Rathaus,* finds rooms (from DM30) for no fee. From the station, walk to the end of Rosentor-str. (open Mon.-Fri. 9am-6pm, Sat. 9am-2pm; Nov.-April Mon.-Fri. 9am-5pm, Sat. 9am-1pm). The **Jugendherberge (HI),** Rammelsbergerstr. 25 (tel. (05321) 222 40), wins the prize for most confusing location. From the bus C stop at Theresienhof, walk up Rammelbergerstr. past numbers 27-49. After no. 49, make a sharp left at the *"Jugendherberge"* sign and walk uphill to no. 25. (Reception open 8:30-11am, 4-7pm and 9:30-10pm. Curfew 10pm. Members only. DM17.80, over 26 DM21.80.) **Campingplatz Sennhütte,** Clausthalerstr. 28 (tel. (05321) 224 98), 3km from town along the B241 highway, has a restaurant and sauna. (DM5 per person, DM4 per tent, showers DM1.)

Bad Harzburg, Torfhaus, and Braunlage

The train from Hanover to the mountains ends at **Bad Harzburg,** about 10min. past Goslar. Next to the station, the **tourist office** is always happy to find you a room (DM5 fee). **Torfhaus,** a humble crossroads 3km from the former inter-German border, offers naught but an airy mountain hostel, near-perfect hiking trails, and the Harz's highest mountain (the 1142m **Brocken**). The Bad Harzburg-Braunlage **bus** pauses here every 1½hrs. (Mon.-Fri. 7:45am-9pm, DM3.90). Turn right at the "Altenau-8km" sign for the exceptional **Jugendherberge (HI),** Torfhaus 3 (tel. (05320) 242; reception open 12:15-1pm and 6:15-7pm; curfew 10-11pm; DM19, over 26 DM23.20). A left turn from the "Altenau 8km" sign leads to **Goethe Weg** and the 16km trail to Brocken's peak. Along the way it skirts the stream that used to divide the two Germanies; look for the abandoned **Soviet Radar Station.**

Twelve km south of Torfhaus, the larger town of **Braunlage** also makes an ideal launchpad for hikes and winter sports. The **tourist office** *(Kurverwaltung),* Elbingeroderstr. 17 (tel. (05520) 10 54), attends to accommodations (open Mon.-Fri. 7:30am-12:30pm and 2-5pm, Sat. 9:30am-noon). After hours, check the board outside the office. The **Jugendherberge (HI),** von-Langenstr. 63 (tel. (05520) 22 38), is an uphill climb from town. Take the bus to Marienhof and walk up Am Marienhof to the dirt path; or walk von-Langenstr. past the soccer fields and turn left on the first paved path. (Reception open 9am-1pm and 5-7pm. DM17.30, over 26 DM21.30.)

Wernigerode

One of Goethe's secret spots in the hills and the best east-west connection within them, a worthy stop on the **Harzquerbahn** route. The Kaiser came to the *Schloß* above town for the hunting; his room is a wildly brocaded suite of red, green, and gold. Rule the mountains with the view from the terrace. (Open 10am-6pm; Oct.-April Tues.-Sun. 9am-4pm. DM5, students DM4; tour DM1 extra.) Wernigerode's busy **tourist office,** on Breitstr. (tel. (03943) 330 35) around the corner from the *Rathaus,* books rooms for DM3 (open Mon.-Fri. 9am-6pm, Sat.-Sun. 10am-3pm). To reach the **Jugendgästehaus,** Friedrichstr. 53 (tel. (03943) 320 61), take bus line A or D to Kirchstr., or walk from the Westerntor station right on Unter den Zindeln, then turn right on Friedrichstr. (25min.). Guests sleep in motel-style rooms. (Reception 5-7pm. DM20.50, reduced rates for children.)

GERMANY

US$1 = £0.63 (British pounds)	**£1** = **US$1.59**
CDN$1= £0.47	**£1** = **CDN$2.13**
IR£1 = £0.99	**£1** = **IR£1.01**
AUS$1 = £0.48	**£1** = **AUS$2.08**
NZ$1 = £0.38	**£1** = **NZ$2.62**
SAR1 = £0.18	**£1** = **SAR5.67**
Country code: 44	**International Dialing Prefix: 00**

A language of many, sometimes fragmented, dialects created by invaded and colonized peoples, English today is also the word of international power. It has always been a mongrel voice. First considered too common for real scholarship or rule, the tongue later became a tool in England's subjection of Wales, Scotland, and Ireland, and was integral to the creation of the modern British state—from mercantilism to Empire and beyond. "England" originally referred to a group of Anglo-Saxon principalities united in the 9th century, though it came to refer to the areas of most centralized power. In 1603, barren Elizabeth I died and James VI of Scotland added the title of James I of England and Wales, although the kingdoms were not to be merged for another century. In 1801, after the French Revolution and revolt in Ireland, Ireland was denied its provincial government and the "United Kingdom of Great Britain and Ireland" was proclaimed. But in the 20th century, this union began to disintegrate, foreshadowing the collapse of the overseas Empire. Most of Ireland won its independence in 1921; only six counties in the northeast of the island remain in the U.K. As the ongoing Troubles in Northern Ireland reflect, questions of union and nationalism will likely be contested for years to come—just as they are in Britain's old holdings on more foreign turf. It's been a while since the Union Jack flew over two-fifths of the earth's surface, and the Empire's heirs retain a proud, even arrogant detachment toward the rest of the world.

Names, like language, hold a certain political force. Deciding just what to call this part of the world can incite local tempers and fuel debates. "Great Britain" refers to England, Scotland, and Wales (and don't call a Scot or Welshman "English"—it's neither accurate nor polite); the political terms "United Kingdom" and "Britain" refer to these regions, Northern Ireland, and the Isle of Man. Because of distinctions in laws and currency, *Let's Go* uses the term "Great Britain" to refer to England, Scotland, and Wales. Coverage of Northern Ireland is in the Ireland chapter for geographical convenience; no political statement is imputed or intended. Britain may be small but is clearly not homogeneous. For the traveler, such topographical, cultural, and economic difference so close together makes for an extremely rich journey. Allow yourself time to take in both the cities and the isolated, wild hills and sea.

For more detailed, exhilarating coverage of Great Britain, pore over *Let's Go: Britain & Ireland* or *Let's Go: London*.

GETTING THERE

In May 1994, the bi-national Franco-British company Eurotunnel completed the **Channel Tunnel (Chunnel),** connecting England and France. Eurotunnel's **Le Shuttle** service carries passengers with cars, buses, or campers. By spring 1995, the limited *Discovery* train service between London and Paris/Brussels through the Chunnel will give way to a full *Eurostar* service with approximately 15 daily departures to either destination. It has yet to be determined what rail passes (BritRail or Eurail) will be accepted for the journey. Consult Thomas Cook's European timetable or, in the UK, call (01233) 61 75 75 for info.

Sealink Stena Line (tel. (01233) 64 70 47 or 24 02 80) and **P&O European Ferries** (tel. (01233) 20 33 88) offer extensive ferry service across the channel between France (Calais, Cherbourg, and Le Havre) and England (Dover or Portsmouth). Always ask about reduced fares—flashing an HI card or ISIC with Travelsave stamps might win a 25-50% discount on your fare. Other routes between the Continent and England include Bergen, Norway, to Newcastle; Esbjerg, Denmark, to Harwich or Newcastle; Gothenburg, Sweden, to Harwich or Newcastle; Hamburg to Harwich or Newcastle; Le Havre to Southampton; Oostende, Belgium, to Dover; and Zeebrugge, Belgium to Felixstowe.

Ferries are also the best way to get to Britain from **Ireland.** Boats run from Fishguard and Pembroke in South Wales to Rosslare in southeastern Ireland; from Holyhead in North Wales to Dún Laoghaire (dun LEAR-y) near Dublin (one way IR£16-26); and from Stranraer, Scotland, to Larne, Northern Ireland (one way £18-20). Almost all sailings in June, July and August must be booked a day in advance. Contact **B&I Line** in London (tel. (0171) 734 46 81) or in Dublin at 16 Westmoreland St.

(tel. (01) 679 79 77). Their after-hours information line in England is (0161) 236 39 36, in Ireland (01) 660 66 66. Reach **Stena Sealink** at 15 Westmoreland St., Dublin 2 (tel. (01) 280 88 44).

GETTING AROUND

In general, fares on all modes of public transportation in Britain are either "single" (one way) or "return" (round-trip). "Period returns" require you to return within a specified number of days; "day return" is equivalent to same-day round-trip. An "APEX" (return) is a cheaper rate and must be purchased at least a week early.

Long-distance **coach** travel in Britain is more extensive than in most European countries and the cheapest option. **National Express** is the principal operator of long-distance coach services. For info contact Eurolines (UK) Limited, 23 Crawley Road, Luton LU1 1HX, England, or in London, (tel. (0171) 730 02 02). Those 60 or over or 16-25 are eligible for Seniors' and Young Persons' **Discount Coach Cards** (£7), valid on National Express, which reduce standard coach fares by about 30%.

Britain's nationalized **British Rail** service is extensive but expensive. If you plan to travel a great deal within Britain, the **BritRail Pass** is a good buy. *You must buy BritRail Passes before arriving in Britain.* They allow unlimited travel in England, Wales, and Scotland; British Rail does not operate in Northern Ireland or the Republic of Ireland. In 1994, BritRail passes cost US$219 for 8 days (ages 16-25 US$179), US$339 for 15 days (ages 16-25 US$269). BritRail Travel also offers **Flexipasses,** allowing travel on a limited number of days within a specific time period. The **Young Person's Railcard** (£16, valid for one year) offers 33% off most fares and discounts on Sealink Stena Line to Continental and Irish ports. You can buy this pass at major British Rail Travel Centres in the U.K. You must prove you're either between 16 and 23 (with a birth certificate or passport) or a full-time student over 23 at a British school, and submit 2 passport-sized photos. Families, seniors, and travelers in wheelchairs have their own Railcards. The **Eurailpass** is *not* accepted in Britain.

Freewheelers is a "lift agency" which can match you up to a driver going your way. Membership is required, and costs £5. Each match-up costs you £1, and the price for the trip itself is agreed between the passenger and driver, though the agency recommends a passenger contribution of 3.5p per mile (£6.90 London to Manchester). Members must abide by a safety procedure to confirm each other's identity, and keeps records of all members and matches made. Single-sex matching can be arranged. Freewheelers does not take responsibility for members' safety— you are still getting in a car with a stranger. For more details, call (0191) 222 00 90, or write to Freewheelers, 25 Low Friar St., Newcastle upon Tyne, NE1 5UE.

To really see Britain, you must get off the rail or coach routes and **bike** or **hike.** Most cities and villages have bike rental shops and maps of local cycle routes; ask at the tourist office. Britain is the most-mapped, most-written-about island in the world; take along a large-scale Ordnance Survey map of the area you plan to cover, and ask tourist offices and National Park Information Centres about routes. For those who've chosen to sample British **hitching,** Vacation Works Publications publishes the *Hitch-Hikers' Manual: Britain,* which contains practical information on hitching laws, techniques, and the best places to hitch in 200 British towns (£4).

GREAT BRITAIN ESSENTIALS

There are local **tourist offices** everywhere in Great Britain; many will book you a place to stay for around £1.50. Most offices also offer a "book-a-bed-ahead" service; for about £2.50 (less in Wales), they'll reserve a room in the next town you visit. Many offices post an accommodations list after closing.

The pound sterling (£) is the main unit of **currency** in the United Kingdom. One pound equals 100 pence (p). Northern Ireland, Scotland, the Isle of Man, and the Channel Islands have their own bank notes, which are identical in value to other British notes and can be used interchangeably with standard currency. However, you may have difficulty using Scottish £1 notes outside Scotland, and Northern Ireland currency is not accepted in the rest of Britain. Most banks are closed on Saturday, Sunday, and all public holidays. Usual weekday bank hours are Monday through Friday 9:30am to 3:30pm, although more and more banks are opening Saturdays as well. Great Britain closes for **"Bank Holidays"** on Jan. 1, Easter (April 14-17, 1995), May 29, 1995, Aug. 28, 1995, and Christmas (December 25-16). The U.K. charges **value-added tax (VAT),** a national sales tax on most goods and some services; the rate is 17.5% on many services (such as hairdressers, hotels, restaurants, and car rental agencies) and on all goods (except books, medicine, and food). Should you, as a visitor to the U.K., wish to receive a VAT refund, you must ask the shopkeeper from whom you buy your goods for the appropriate form, which British officials will sign and stamp when you take your purchases through customs. Once home, send the form and a self-addressed, British-stamped envelope to the shopkeeper, who will then mail your refund. (Whew!)

Communication The newly remodeled **British pay phone** charges 10p for local calls. A series of harsh beeps will warn you to insert more money when your time is up. For the rest of the call, the digital display ticks off your credit in 1p increments so you can watch your pence in suspense. Unused coins (not change) are returned. You may use remaining credit on a second call by pressing the "follow on call" button (often marked "FC"). Phones don't accept 1p, 2p, or 5p coins. If you'll be making more than a few calls during your stay in Britain, pick up a **Phonecard,** available in denominations of £2, £5, £10, and £20. Get them at post offices, newsagents, or John Menzies stationery shops. Phone booths that take cards are labeled in green and are common except in rural areas; coin booths are labeled in red.

To make **international direct calls** from Great Britain, dial the **international access code (00),** the country code for where you're calling, the area/city code and then the local number. Another option is to access an operator in the country you're dialing—rates are often cheaper than those for direct calls, and service a bit speedier. Long-distance companies in your home country may have economical arrangements for their clients calling home from overseas. The following services allow you to place **collect calls** (expensive) or charge them to a **calling card** (less so): AT&T **USA Direct** (tel. 0800-89-0011), MCI **WorldPhone** (tel. 0800 89 02 22), **Canada Direct** (tel. 0800 89 00 16), **New Zealand Direct** (tel. 0800 89 06 40) and **Australia Direct** (tel. 0800 89 00 61). In case of sudden illness or an accident, dial **999,** the general **emergency** number for Britain and Ireland; it's free from any pay phone.

Accommodations and Camping Great Britain has hundreds of **youth hostels,** both HI and independent. The hostel associations of England and Wales (YHA), and Scotland (SYHA) publish inexpensive, essential guides with full maps and descriptions for all their hostels. Hostels are generally closed from 10am-5pm and impose an evening curfew (usually about 11pm). All require sleep sacks, which they sell or rent for a nominal fee. If these regulations cramp your style, stick to looser independent establishments. Always book ahead in high season.

Native to Britain, the term "bed and breakfast" generally means a small place that offers basic accommodations and breakfast at a reasonable price, often in private homes, or in guest houses. B&Bs (£10-12, in London £16-60) are so widespread that it is absurd to single out the establishments we list; when they're full, ask for a referral. Some proprietors grant considerable rate reductions to guests who pay in advance or by the week and offer discounts between September and May. Practically all tourist offices book rooms for a fee (usually £1 or 10% deposit); *Let's Go* notes those that don't charge. **Aunties (Great Britain) Limited,** 56 Coleshill Terrace, Llanelli, Dyfed, Wales SA15 3DA (tel. (01554) 77 00 77) will scout out B&Bs in London suburbs and other areas of England, Scotland, and Wales, and caters to vegetarians. **Bed and Breakfast (GB),** P.O. Box 66, Henley-on-Thames, Oxon, England RG9 1XS (tel. (01491) 57 88 03, fax 41 08 06) covers London, England, Scotland, Wales, and Ireland.

Food and Drink Although enormous traditional breakfasts get all the fame and glory, the rest of English cuisine is not simply a cauldron of boiled blandness. After recovering from your morning tea or coffee, orange juice, cereal, eggs, bacon, sausage, toast, butter, marmalade, grilled tomatoes, mushrooms, kippers (smoked herring), and, in winter, porridge, you will discover that England is a nation of meat-eaters; the best native dishes are roasts—beef, lamb, and Wiltshire hams. Vegetables are the weakest and mushiest part of the meal; go with salads.

Pub grub (meals served in bars) is the classic, fast, and filling lunch. The *ploughman's lunch* (the product of a 1960s advertising campaign) is inexpensive: cheese, bread, pickled onions, chutney, and a tomato or two. Fish and chips are traditionally drowned in vinegar and salt. To escape English food, try Asian, Greek, Middle Eastern, or Indian cuisines. Ubiquitous "wholefoods" shops cater to vegetarians. You don't have to tip in those restaurants that include service charge (10-12½%).

Britain may be surrounded by water, but tea keeps it afloat. Tea is the preferred remedy for exhaustion, ennui, a rainy morning, or a hot afternoon. It is served strong and milky; if you want it any other way, say so in advance. "Tea" is also a meal. Afternoon high tea as it is still served in rural Britain includes cooked meats, salad, sandwiches, and dessert.

If tea remains the focus of family life, the pub is where individual and community come together, a place to catch the latest news or gossip, air an opinion, or relax with your mates. Although exact times vary from pub to pub, the most common hours are from 11am to 11pm, noon to 10:30pm on Sundays. Beer is the standard pub drink. Bear in mind that British beer may have a higher alcohol content than that to which you are accustomed. It is also usually served warm. Lager is served at a colder temperature. Traditional cider, a fizzy fermented apple juice, served either sweet or dry, is a potent and tasty alternative to beer.

■■■ LONDON

At first glance, London is kind to the expectations of visitors stuffing their mental baggage with bobbies and Beefeaters, nursery rhymes and "Masterpiece Theatre," Sherlock Holmes and history books. The relatively small area embraced by the Underground's Circle Line seems filled to bursting with the "big sights" and all the city's double-decker red buses do seem to spin around the mad whirl of Piccadilly Circus. But central London is just a speck on the Greater London map. Beyond Tower Bridge looms the glossy, pyramid-tipped Canary Wharf skyscraper, centerpiece of the world's largest and most controversial redevelopment. Those clunky cabs are actually state-of-the-art traffic-dodging equipment, able to turn 360° in a smaller space than any other car on the road. The Victorian doorway inscribed with an Anglican piety may belong to a Sikh or a Muslim in a city internalizing its imperial past. What makes London not just "quite interesting," but rather, enthralling, can be found partly in this, a tension between the close quarters of central London and the expansive boroughs, between the cluttered, "familiar," and sometimes fictional past of the heritage industry and a riotously modern present. For an absolutely dapper little book packed with first-rate info on this city, grab a copy of *Let's Go: London*.

ORIENTATION AND PRACTICAL INFORMATION

London is divided into boroughs and postal code areas, and into informal districts. Both the borough name and postal code prefix appear at the bottom of most street signs. The city has grown by absorbing nearby towns, which is reflected in borough names such as "City of Westminster" and "City of London" (or simply "The City").

Central London, on the north side of the Thames and bounded roughly by the Underground's Circle Line, contains most of the major sights. Within central London the vaguely defined **West End** incorporates the understated elegance of Mayfair, the shopping streets around Oxford Circus, the theaters and tourist traps of Piccadilly Circus and Leicester Square, the exotic labyrinth of Soho, chic Covent

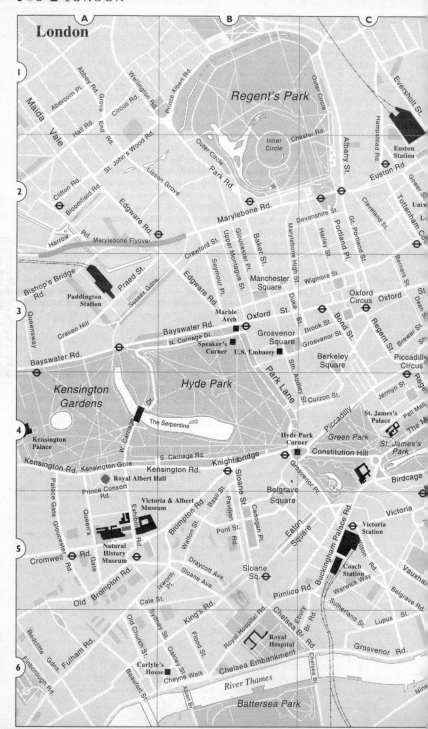

London

A

1
Maida Vale
Abbey Rd.
Abercorn Pl.
Hall Rd.
Grove End Rd.
Circus Rd.
Wellington Rd.
Prince Albert Rd.

Regent's Park

Outer Circle
Hampstead Rd.
Eversholt St.

Inner Circle
Chester Rd.
Albany St.
Euston Station

2
Clifton Rd.
Bloomfield Rd.
St. John's Wood Rd.
Lisson Grove
Edgware Rd.
Park Rd.
Outer Circle
Marylebone Rd.
Devonshire St.
Harley St.
Gt. Portland St.
Portland Pl.
Cleveland St.
Euston Rd.
Gower St.
Tottenham Co
Univ
L
Berners St.

Harrow Rd.
Marylebone Flyover
Crawford St.
Seymour Pl.
Upper Montague St.
Gloucester Pl.
Baker St.
Marylebone High St.
Wigmore St.
Oxford Circus
Oxford
St
Dean St
Regent St.
Brewer St

Bishop's Bridge Rd.
Praed St.
Sussex Gdns.
Edgware Rd.
Manchester Square
Duke St.
Bond St.
Brook St.
3
Paddington Station
Craven Hill
Bayswater Rd.
Marble Arch
Oxford St.
Grosvenor Square
Grosvenor St.
Berkeley Square
Piccadilly Circus

Queensway
Bayswater Rd.
N. Carriage Dr.
Speaker's Corner
U.S. Embassy
5th Audley St.
Park Lane
Curzon St.
Piccadilly
Jermyn St.
Rege

Kensington Gardens

Hyde Park
W. Carriage Dr.
The Serpentine

St. James's Palace
Pall Mall
The M

4
Kensington Palace
Hyde Park Corner
Green Park
Constitution Hill
St. James's Park

Palace Gate
Kensington Rd.
Kensington Gore
Kensington Rd.
S. Carriage Rd.
Knightsbridge
Birdcage

Queen's Gate
Gloucester Rd.
Royal Albert Hall
Prince Consort Rd.
Victoria & Albert Museum
Exhibition Rd.
Brompton Rd.
Sloane St.
Belgrave Square
Grosvenor Pl.
Buckingham Palace Rd.
Victoria
Victoria Station

5
Cromwell Rd.
Natural History Museum
Walton St.
Basil St.
Pont St.
Pavilion Rd.
Cadogan Pl.
Eaton Square
Coach Station
Vauxha

Old Brompton Rd.
Draycott Ave.
Sloane Ave.
Sloane Sq.
Pimlico Rd.
Warwick Way
Belgrave Rd.

Redcliffe Gdns.
Fulham Rd.
Ixworth Pl.
Cale St.
Sydney St.
King's Rd.
Royal Hospital Rd.
Ebury Br. Rd.
Chelsea Br. Rd.
Sutherland St.
Lupus St.

6
Emborough Rd.
Beaufort St.
Old Church St.
Oakley St.
Flood St.
Carlyle's House
Cheyne Walk
Royal Hospital
Chelsea Embankment
Grosvenor Rd.
Chelsea Br.

Albert Br.
River Thames
Nine

Battersea Park

B

C

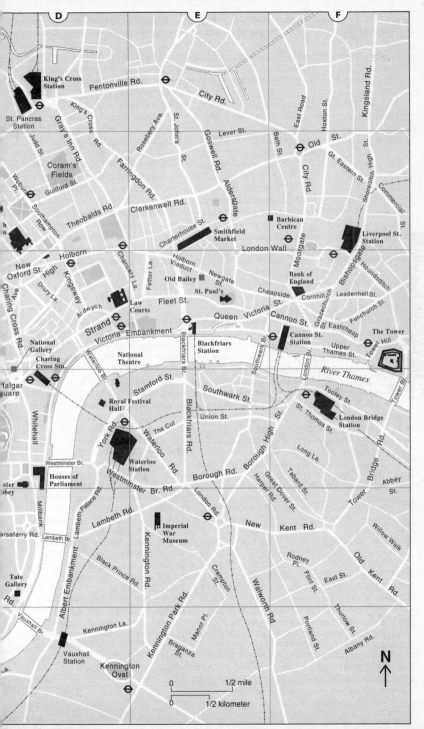

D E F

King's Cross Station

St. Pancras Station

Pentonville Rd.

City Rd.

King's Cross Rd.

Rosebery Ave.

St. John's St.

Goswell Rd.

Lever St.

Bath St.

Old St.

Hoxton St.

East Road

City Rd.

Kingsland Rd.

Gt. Eastern St.

Shoreditch High St.

Commercial St.

Coram's Fields

Gray's Inn Rd.

Farringdon Rd

Clerkenwell Rd.

Aldersgate

Judd St.

Woburn Pl.

Southampton Row

Guilford St.

Theobalds Rd.

Charterhouse St.

Smithfield Market

Barbican Centre

Moorgate

London Wall

Liverpool St. Station

Bishopsgate

Houndsditch

New Oxford St.

Holborn

High

Kingsway

Chancery La.

Fetter La.

Holborn Viaduct

Old Bailey

Newgate St.

St. Paul's

Cheapside

Bank of England

Cornhill

Gracechurch St.

Leadenhall St.

Fenchurch St.

Drury La.

Charing Cross Rd.

Aldwych

Law Courts

Fleet St.

Queen Victoria

Cannon St.

St. Eastcheap

The Tower

Strand

Victoria Embankment

Blackfriars Br.

Blackfriars Station

Cannon St. Station

Upper Thames St.

London Br.

Tower Hill

National Gallery

Charing Cross Stn.

National Theatre

Southwark Br.

River Thames

Tower Br.

Trafalgar Square

Whitehall

Royal Festival Hall

Waterloo Br.

Stamford St.

Blackfriars Rd.

Southwark St.

Union St.

Tooley St.

St. Thomas St.

London Bridge Station

York Rd.

The Cut

Waterloo Rd.

Borough High St.

Long La.

Bridge Rd.

Abbey St.

Westminster Br.

Houses of Parliament

Waterloo Station

Westminster Br. Rd.

Borough Rd.

London Rd.

Great Dover St.

Harper Rd.

Tabard St.

Tower

Millbank

Lambeth Palace Rd.

Lambeth Rd.

Kennington Rd.

New Kent Rd.

Walworth Rd.

Willow Walk

Old Kent Rd.

Horseferry Rd.

Lambeth Br.

Imperial War Museum

Rodney Pl.

Flint St.

East St.

Tate Gallery

Albert Embankment

Black Prince Rd.

Kennington Park Rd.

Crampton St.

Manor Pl.

Thurlow St.

Portland St.

Albany Rd.

Vauxhall Br.

Kennington La.

Vauxhall Station

Kennington Oval

Braganza St.

N

0   1/2 mile

0   1/2 kilometer

Garden, and London's unofficial center, Trafalgar Square. East of the West End lies **Holborn,** center of legal activity, and **Fleet Street,** the traditional journalists' haunt.

Around the southeastern corner of the Circle Line is **The City,** London's financial district, with the Tower of London at its eastern edge and St. Paul's Cathedral nearby. Farther east is the **East End,** ethnically diverse and working-class, and the epic construction site of the **Docklands.** Moving back west, along the river and the southern part of the Circle Line is the district of **Westminster,** the royal, political, and ecclesiastical center of England, where you'll find Buckingham Palace, the Houses of Parliament, and Westminster Abbey. In the southwest corner of the Circle Line, below the expanse of **Hyde Park,** are gracious **Chelsea,** embassy-laden **Belgravia,** and **Kensington,** adorned with London's posher shops and restaurants.

Around the northwest corner of the Circle Line, tidy terraces border **Regent's Park;** nearby are the faded squares of **Paddington** and **Notting Hill Gate,** home to large Indian and West Indian communities. Moving east towards the Circle Line's northeast corner leads to **Bloomsbury,** which harbors the British Museum, London University colleges, art galleries, and specialty bookshops. Trendy residential districts stretch to the north, including **Hampstead** and **Highgate,** with the enormous Hampstead Heath and fabulous views of the city.

Trying to reach a specific destination in London can be frustrating. Numbers often go up one side of a street and then down the other. One road may change names four times in fewer miles, and a single name may designate a street, lane, square, and row. A good map is key. For a day's walk, London Transport's free map will do, but those staying a week or longer ought to buy a London street index. *London A to Z* (that's "*ay* to *zed,*" by the way), *Nicholson's Streetfinder,* and the *ABC London Street Atlas* (all £2 and up) are excellent.

For the most part, London is a tourist-friendly city. It's hard to wander unwittingly into unnerving neighborhoods; these areas, in parts of Hackney, Tottenham, and South London, lie well away from central London. The areas around King's Cross/St. Pancras and Notting Hill Gate tube stations are a bit seedy at night. Late trains on the tube out of central London are usually crowded and noisy, but waiting late at night at less central stations can be unsettling. In general, unattended packages will be taken either by thieves or by the police, who are paranoid—and rightly so—about terrorist bombs. Obey the constant warnings regarding suspicious packages; leave nothing unattended.

Tourist Offices: London Tourist Board Information Centre: Victoria Station Forecourt, SW1 (tel. (01839) 12 34 32, recorded message only, 48p per min.). Tube: Victoria. Info on London and England and an accommodations service (hefty £5 booking fee, plus 15% refundable deposit). Open 8am-7pm; Dec.-March Mon.-Sat. 8am-7pm, Sun. 8am-5pm. Branches at **Heathrow Airport** (open 9am-6pm; Dec.-March 9am-5pm), **Harrods,** and **Selfridges** department stores. **British Travel Centre:** 12 Regent St., SW1. Tube: Piccadilly Circus. Down Regent St. from the Lower Regent St. tube exit. Ideal for travelers bound for destinations outside of London. Pleasantly relaxed compared to LTB, but similarly long queues. Open Mon.-Fri. 9am-6:30pm, Sat. 9am-5pm, Sun. 10am-4pm; Nov.-April Mon.-Fri. 9am-6:30pm, Sat.-Sun. 10am-4pm. **City of London Information Centre:** St. Paul's Churchyard, EC4 (tel. 606 30 30). Tube: St. Paul's. Specializes in the City of London. Helpful, knowledgeable staff. Open 9:30am-5pm; Nov.-March Mon.-Fri. 9:30am-5pm, Sat. 9:30am-12:30pm.

Budget Travel: London is *the* place to shop for cheap bus, plane, and train tickets to North America, Africa, Asia, Australia, and the moon. Browse the ads in *Time Out* or the *Evening Standard.* See also Essentials—Useful Travel Organizations for many London agencies, including **Council Travel, Travel CUTS,** and **Campus Travel. Trailfinders,** 42-50 Earl's Ct. Rd., W8 (tel. 937 54 00). Tube: High St. Kensington. Busier branch at 194 Kensington High St., W8 (tel. 938 32 32; tube: High St. Kensington). Travel services. Both branches open Mon.-Wed. and Fri.-Sat. 9am-6pm, Thurs. 9am-7pm; Sun. 10am-2pm (telephone only at Earl's Ct.). **Lon-**

GREAT BRITAIN

don Student Travel, 52 Grosvenor Gdns., WC1 (tel. 730 34 02). Tube: Victoria. Competitive rail, coach, and air fares on the Continent and beyond.

Embassies and High Commissions: U.S., 24 Grosvenor Sq., W1 (tel. 499 90 00). Tube: Bond St. **Canada,** MacDonald House, 1 Grosvenor Sq., W1 (tel. 629 94 92). Tube: Bond St. or Oxford Circus. Visas Mon.-Fri. 8:45am-2pm. **Australia,** Australia House, The Strand, WC2 (tel. 379 43 34; in emergency, tel. 438 81 81). Tube: Aldwych or Temple. Visa and passport inquiries tel. 438 88 18. Open Mon.-Fri. 10am-4pm. **Ireland,** 17 Grosvenor Pl., SW1 (tel. 235 21 71). Tube: Hyde Park Corner. Open Mon.-Fri. 9:30am-5pm. **New Zealand,** New Zealand House, 80 Haymarket, SW1 (tel. 930 84 22). Tube: Charing Cross. Open Mon.-Fri. 10am-noon and 2-4pm. **South Africa,** South Africa House, Trafalgar Sq. WC2 (tel. 930 44 88). Tube: Charing Cross.

Currency Exchange: Go to banks, *never* to *bureaux de change* (such as Chequepoint), which have high fees and/or ridiculously bad rates. If you're stuck outside banking hours, stick to American Express, **Thomas Cook,** 15 Shaftesbury Ave., Piccadilly Circus (24hrs.), or **Exchange International,** Victoria Station (24hrs.).

American Express, 6 Haymarket, SW1 (tel. 930 44 11). Tube: Piccadilly Circus. Message and mail services open Mon.-Fri. 9am-5pm, Sat. 9am-noon. Currency exchange open Mon.-Fri. 9am-5:30pm, Sat. 9am-6pm, Sun. 10am-5:45pm. Bring ID to pick up mail (60p; free for AmEx Cheque or cardholders). Other offices at Victoria Station (147 Victoria St., SW1; tel. 828 74 11); Cannon St. (54 Cannon St., EC4; tel. 248 26 71); Knightsbridge (78 Brompton Rd., SW3; tel. 584 61 82); and at the British Tourist Centre.

Post Office: Save hassle and have mail sent to Trafalgar Sq., 24-28 William IV St., London WC2N 4DL (tel. 930 95 80). Tube: Charing Cross. Open Mon.-Sat. 8am-8pm. If you don't specify a post office, mail will be sent to either Trafalgar Square or London Chief Office, King Edward Bldg., EC1 (tel. 239 50 47). Tube: St. Paul's. Open Mon.-Tues. and Thurs.-Fri. 8:30am-6:30pm, Wed. 9am-6:30pm.

Telephones: You can make international calls from any pay phone; use a Phonecard for convenience. The blue Mercurycard phones are cheaper than BT phones, but harder to find. For London directory information call 142; operator 100; international operator 155. London has 2 **city codes:** 0171 (central London) and 0181 (outer London). Use the code only if you are calling from one area to the other. All London numbers listed in *Let's Go* are (0171) unless otherwise indicated.

Flights: Heathrow Airport (tel. (0181) 759 43 21), is the world's busiest airport. From Heathrow, take the **Underground** to central London (45min.). London Transport's **Airbus** (tel. 222 12 34) zips from Heathrow to central points, including hotels (1hr., £5). Most charter flights land at **Gatwick Airport** (tel. (01293) 53 53 53). From there, take the BR Gatwick Express train to Victoria Station (every 15min., £8.50, £7.50 from Council Travel). **National Express** buses run 5:30am-11pm from Victoria Station to Gatwick (1hr., £7.50). Taxis take twice as long and cost 5 times as much. British Rail's Stansted Express runs to **Stansted Airport** (tel. (01279) 68 05 00) from Liverpool St. station (£10).

Trains: 8 major stations: **Charing Cross, Euston, King's Cross, Liverpool St., Paddington, St. Pancras, Victoria,** and **Waterloo.** All stations linked by the Underground. **Travel Centres** at the Tube's mainline stations and at 12-16 Regent St. (tube: Piccadilly Circus); The Strand (tube: Charing Cross); Victoria St.; and King William St. (All open Mon.-Fri. 9am-5pm.) Talking timetables. To East Anglia, Essex, Southern England, Northeast, East, and South London: tel. 928 51 00. To the South Midlands, West of England, South Wales, West London, and Republic of Ireland via Fishguard: tel. 262 67 67. To the East and West Midlands, North Wales, Northwest England, Scotland via West Coast, Northwest London, Northern Ireland, and Republic of Ireland via Holyhead: tel. 387 70 70. To East and Northeast England, Scotland via East Coast, and North London: tel. 278 24 77. To Europe: tel. (01891) 88 87 31.

Buses: Victoria Coach Station (tube: Victoria), on Buckingham Palace Rd., is the hub of Britain's denationalized coach network. **National Express coaches** (tel. 730 02 02) service an expansive network which links cities big and small. Outer London area served by **Green Line** (tel. (0181) 668 72 61) coaches, which leave frequently from Eccleston Bridge behind Victoria Station. Purchase tickets from the driver. Discounts include the one-day **Rover** ticket (£6, valid on almost every Green Line coach and London Country bus Mon.-Fri. after 9am, Sat.-Sun. all day); and the **Three-Day Rover** (£16.50).

Luggage Storage: Very restricted, due to recent bomb threats. **Students-Tourists Storage** (tel. (0800) 62 22 44) has branches near all major tube, train, and coach stations. Storage companies in the London area charge £3-5 per item per week (check the Yellow Pages under "Storage Service").

Public Transportation: The **Underground** (or **tube**) is fast, efficient and crowded. It opens about 6am; the last train runs around midnight. Buy your ticket before you board and pass it through automatic gates at both ends of your journey; on-the-spot £10 fine if you're caught without a valid ticket. The **Travelcard** is a must for budget travelers. One-day Travelcards cannot be used before 9:30am Mon.-Fri., and are not valid on night buses (adult one-day Travelcard, zones 1 and 2, £2.70). The one-week and one-month Travelcards can be used at any time, and are valid for Night Bus travel. (Adult 1 week Travelcard, zones 1&2, £13; adult 1 mo. Travelcard, zones 1&2, £50. Bring a passport-sized photo). **Night buses** (the "N" routes) run frequently throughout London 11pm-6am. All pass through Trafalgar Square, and many stop at Victoria as well. Free brochure about night buses, which includes times of the last British Rail and Underground trains. The **bus** network is divided into 4 zones. In and around central London, one way fares range from 60p to £1.20, depending on the number of zones you cross. Travelcards purchased for the Underground are valid on buses; armed with a Travelcard, you can hop on or off as often as you like. Pick up free maps and guides at **London Transport's Information Centres** (look for the lowercase "i" logo at info windows and on signs) at the following major tube stops: King's Cross, Piccadilly Circus, Oxford Circus, St. James's Park, Liverpool St., Hammersmith, and Heathrow Terminals 1, 2, 3 station (most open weekdays 8am-6pm; central London stations also have weekend hours).

Taxis: Hail your own or call a radio-dispatched taxi (tel. 272 02 72 or 253 50 00). London fares are steep, and 10% tip is standard. In addition to licensed black cabs, there are tons of unregulated "minicabs" in the Yellow Pages. **Ladycabs** (tel. 272 30 19) has only women drivers.

Bike Rental: Mountain Bike and Ski, 18 Gillingham St., SW1 (tel. 834 89 33). Tube: Victoria. From the station, go down Wilton Rd. and right on Gillingham St. £7 per day, £13 per weekend, plus £1 per day for insurance. £50 deposit required. Open Mon.-Thurs. 8:30am-5pm, Fri. 8:30am-7:30pm, Sat. 8:30am-4pm.

Hitchhiking: Anyone who values safety will take a train or bus out of London. Hitchers check the University of London Union's **ride board,** on the ground floor of 1 Malet St., WC1 (tube: Russell Sq.), or ask at youth hostels for possibilities. **Freewheelers** is a ride-share agency. Membership is required, and costs £10 per year. You must pay for 5 match-ups (each £1) in advance. Single-sex matching can be arranged. For more details, call (0191) 222 00 90, or write to Freewheelers, Ltd., 25 Low Friar St., Newcastle upon Tyre, NE1 54E.

Disabled Travelers: Disability Information and Advice Service, tel. 275 84 85. **RADAR,** tel. 637 54 00. **Disability Information Service,** tel. 630 59 94 (Mon.-Fri. 10am-4pm).

Bisexual, Gay, and Lesbian Services: London Lesbian and Gay Switchboard (tel. 837 73 24). 24-hr. advice and support service. **Bisexual Helpline:** tel. (0181) 569 75 00.

Crises: Samaritans, 46 Marshall St., W1 (tel. 734 28 00). Tube: Oxford Circus. 24hr. crisis hotline. **London Rape Crisis Centre,** (tel. 837 16 00). Open 24hrs.

Pharmacy: Every police station keeps a list of emergency doctors and pharmacies in its area. Listings under "Chemists" in the Yellow Pages. **Bliss Chemists,** 5 Marble Arch, W1 (tel. 723 61 16) open 9am-midnight.

Medical Assistance: You can receive free treatment in the casualty ward (emergency room) of any hospital. Try **Westminster Hospital,** Dean Ryle St., Horseferry Rd., SW1 (tel. 746 80 00; tube: Pimlico) or **Royal London Hospital,** Whitechapel Rd., E1 (tel. 377 70 00; tube: Whitechapel).

Emergencies: Police, fire, or ambulance: **999.** No coins required.

ACCOMMODATIONS

Write well in advance to reserve rooms for summer. Among London's spectrum of accommodations, private hostels and university halls of residence are the best buys; check for reduced weekly rates in hotels. Sleeping outdoors is unsafe and illegal.

YHA/HI Hostels

Cheap, cheery, and chock full o' youths, London's YHA hostels can be a welcome relief from dreary B&Bs; despite daytime lockouts and curfews, they're buzzing meeting places. Groups gobble space early, but some beds are kept free for individuals. Reserve ahead for July and August; if not, it's still worth calling (central tel. 248 65 47). All hostels have personal lockers requiring a padlock. An **International Guest Pass** (£1.50) permits residents of places other than England and Wales to stay at hostel rates without joining the hostel association. After you purchase six Guest Passes, you attain full membership. A membership card for residents of England and Wales costs £9 for age 18 and over, £3 otherwise.

Oxford Street, 14-18 Noel St., W1 (tel. 734 16 18). Tube: Oxford Circus. Heart of London and Soho. Small, plush rooms for 2-4. 24hr. security. Currency exchange. Baggage room. Reception open 7am-11pm. No curfew. £16.70, under 18 £13.70.

City of London, 36 Carter La., EC4 (tel. 236 49 65, fax 236 76 81). Tube: St. Paul's. From the City Information Centre on the opposite side of St. Paul's Cathedral, go left down Godliman St. Take the first right onto Carter Lane. Centrally located and newly refurbished. Reception open 7am-11pm. Single or double £22, under 18 £18.50. Triple or quad £19, under 18 £16.50. Standard dorm (5-8 beds) £18.90, under 18 £15.90. Economy dorm (10-15 beds) £14, under 18 £11.

Hampstead Heath, 4 Wellgarth Rd., Hampstead, NW11 (tel. (0181) 458 90 54). Tube: Golder's Green. Despite peaceful surroundings, the hostel can fall victim to school parties. Currency exchange. Reception open 7am-midnight. No curfew. £13.90, under 18 £11.80. Wheelchair access.

Holland House (King George VI Memorial Youth Hostel), Holland Walk, Kensington, W8 (tel. 937 07 48, fax 376 06 67). Tube: High St. Kensington. Half is a restored Jacobean mansion; the other half, a late 60s cement block. Reception open 24hrs. No curfew. £16.90, under 18 £14.90, breakfast included. Book ahead through central HI reservations.

Earl's Court, 38 Bolton Gns., SW5 (tel. 373 70 83). Tube: Earl's Court. Townhouse in leafy neighborhood. Kitchen. 24hr. security. Currency exchange. Reception open 7:30am-10:30pm. 4-16 per room. No curfew. £16.90, under 18 £14.90.

Highgate, 84 Highgate West Hill, N6 (tel. (0181) 340 18 31). Tube: Archway. Out-of-the-way Georgian house in beautiful neighborhood—worth the trek. 9- to 16-bed rooms. Reception open 8:45-10am, 1-7pm, and 8-11:30pm. Strict midnight curfew. £11.75, under 18 £7.85.

Rotherhithe, Island Yard., Salter Rd., SE16 (tel. 232 21 14). Tube: Rotherhithe. 15min. walk down Brunel Rd. to Salter. Welcome to *2001: A Space Odyssey*. Light, immaculate rooms. Bar and video games. Reception open 7am-11:30pm. No curfew. 24-hr. security. £16.50, under 18 £13.50. Wheelchair access.

Private Hostels

These places aren't as crammed with schoolkids, do not require membership cards, and tend to have fewer rules. Open all year, their facilities compare to HI hostels'.

Palace Court Hotel, 64-65 Prince's Sq., W2 (tel. 229 47 47 or 44 12, fax 727 92 28). Tube: Bayswater or Notting Hill Gate. Free keg parties every Wed. night, outdoor patio area, and airy, comfortable rooms. One bed in a 6-bed room £9, in a 4-bed room £10, in a double £12; corresponding weekly rates are £50, £55, and £60. Sheets and cozy duvets included. English breakfast included. Call ahead.

Centre d'Echanges Internationaux, 61-69 Chepstow Pl., W2 (tel. 221 81 34, fax 221 06 42). Tube: Notting Hill Gate or Bayswater. Immaculate hostel in a chic residential area. Bilingual staff and spacious, well-kept rooms. Lockout 10am-5pm.

No curfew. Dorm (8-12 beds) £14, singles £25, doubles £20 per person, and triples £17.50 per person. Prices lower in off-season. Breakfast included. Call ahead.

Palace Hotel, 31 Palace Ct., W2 (tel. 221 56 28, fax 243 81 57). Tube: Notting Hill Gate or Queensway. Shiny, happy young'uns in bright 8-bed rooms. No curfew. £10 per night, £55 per week. English breakfast included.

Quest Hotel, 45 Queensborough Terrace, W2 (tel. 229 77 82). Tube: Queensway. Communal, clean, and sociable; staff throws one theme party a month. No curfew. 4-8 bed rooms £11.50-13.50, continental breakfast included. English breakfast £2. Pool room and kitchen open 24hrs. Key deposit £3. Call ahead.

Curzon House Hotel, 58 Courtfield Gdns., SW5 (tel. 581 21 16). Tube: Gloucester Rd. Exceptionally friendly staff attracts diverse clientele. Kitchen, TV lounge. Single-sex dorms £13. Singles £26. Doubles £38. Triples £45. Quads £64. Continental breakfast included.

Albert Hotel, 191 Queens Gate, SW7 5EU (tel. 584 30 19). Tube: South Kensington or Gloucester Rd. Near Royal Albert Hall. Victorian rooms with private facilities. Reception open 24hrs. No lockout. Checkout 10am. Dorms £9.50-12. Twins £32. Continental breakfast included. Reserve ahead with 1 night's deposit.

Central University of Iowa Hostel, 7 Bedford Pl., WC1 (tel. 580 11 21, fax 580 56 38). Tube: Holborn or Russell Sq. Bright, spartan, clean rooms. 2-week max. stay. Reception open 8am-1pm and 3-8pm. Dorms £15.50. Laundry. Open mid-May to mid-Aug.

Victoria Hotel, 71 Belgrave Rd. SW1 (tel. 834 30 77; fax 932 06 93). Tube: Victoria or Pimlico. Closer to Pimlico; from the station, take the Bessborough St. (south side) exit and go left along Lupus St. Take a right at St. George's Sq.; Belgrave Rd. starts on the other side. Whimsical splashes of color brighten the standard rooms with bunk beds. Dorms £13-14.

International Student House, 229 Great Portland St., W1 (tel. 631 32 23, fax 636 55 65). Tube: Great Portland St. Ugly '60s exterior conceals thriving international network of events and facilities. Well-maintained rooms. No curfew. 4-bed dorm £12. Singles £22.70. Doubles £38.30. Triples £48.30. English breakfast. Reserve well ahead.

Elizabeth House (YWCA Hostel), 118 Warwick Way, SW1 (tel. 630 07 41). Tube: Victoria. Anyone over 5 welcome. Friendly. Dorms £15. Singles £21. Doubles £40-45. Continental breakfast included. Reserve early with £10 deposit.

Tonbridge School Clubs, Ltd., corner of Judd and Cromer St., WC1 (tel. 837 44 06). Tube: King's Cross. Right price for desperadoes. Seedy neighborhood. Blanket and foam pads on gymnasium floor. Non-British students with passports only. Reception open 10-11:30pm. Check-out 10am. Hot showers, storage. £3.

University Halls of Residence

London's university residences often accommodate visitors for limited periods during the summer break and during Easter vacations. Many of these halls are characterized by boxlike rooms and institutional furniture. Most charge around £20 and contain all singles, offering more privacy than a hostel. Call well in advance (by April for July reservations), as conference groups tend to snatch up rooms early. The **King's Campus Vacation Bureau,** 552 King's Rd., London SW10 0UA (tel. 351 60 11, fax 352 73 76), controls bookings for a number of residence halls where students of **King's College** of the University of London live during the academic year. Rooms are available from early June to mid-September.

Carr Saunders Hall, 18-24 Fitzroy St., W1 (tel. 580 63 38). Tube: Warren St. Turn right off Tottenham Ct. Rd. onto Grafton Way, then left onto Fitzroy St. A newer London School of Economics building. Singles £20.50. Doubles £41. English breakfast. Min. 4 nights. Self-catering apartments. Doubles £33. Triples £48. Quads £62. Quints £75.

Connaught Hall, 36-45 Tavistock Sq., WC1 (tel. 387 61 81, fax 383 41 09). Tube: Russell Sq. Head left from the station and turn right onto Woburn Pl.; the first left is Tavistock Sq. Graceful London University Hall often filled by academic groups. Reception open Mon.-Sat. 8am-11pm, Sun. 9am-11pm. Singles £19.50. English breakfast. Reservations recommended. Open July-Aug.

John Adams Hall, 15-23 Endsleigh St., WC1 (tel. 387 40 86, fax 383 01 64). Tube: Euston. Heading right on Euston Rd., turn right onto Gordon St., and first left onto Endsleigh Gdns.; Endsleigh St. is the second right. Elegant London University building. Reception open 7:30am-10pm. Singles £21.40. Doubles £37. Open July-Aug., Easter.

Ingram Court, 552 King's Rd., SW10 (tel. 351 65 13). Tube: Sloane Sq. or Fulham Broadway. From Sloane Sq., take bus 11 or 22 to Lot's Rd.; or walk 10min. from Fulham Broadway. Singles £19.50, twin £15.25 per person.

Lightfoot Hall, Manresa Rd. at King's Rd., SW3 (tel. 333 48 98 or 351 60 11 for booking, fax 333 49 01). Tube: Sloane Sq. or South Kensington. From South Kensington, take bus 49; from Sloane Sq., bus 11 or 22. With student ID, singles and doubles are £13 per person. Singles £20. Twins £16 per person. Rooms may be available during school year.

Queen Alexandra's House, Kensington Gore, SW7 (tel. 589 36 35 or 589 40 53). Tube: South Kensington, or bus 52 to Royal Albert Hall; the hostel is just behind the Royal Albert Hall. Women only. Cozy rooms, mostly singles. £22. Write weeks in advance for a booking form.

University of North London, Arcade Hall, Holloway Rd. Tube: Holloway Rd. The University of North London offers self-contained flats with kitchens for groups of 4-6 people on a weekly basis. All reservations must be made at the **Accommodations Advisory Office,** Stapleton House, 277-281 Holloway Rd., N7 (tel. 753 50 41), and all payments must be made in advance. £40 per person per week, with a deposit of £40 for each week's stay. (Deposit of £120 for stays of over 2 weeks.) Open July-Sept.

Bed and Breakfasts

Most B&Bs in London cluster around the railway stations. Although abundant and convenient, rooms in these areas tend to be well-worn. Less obvious but equally convenient areas offer more humane surroundings. Don't be put off by B&Bs located in areas which seem removed, residential, or peripheral; rooms in these outlying areas are often well-decorated and in good repair, neighboring special pubs and restaurants that don't cater to an exclusively tourist crowd.

Bloomsbury

Despite its proximity to the West End, Bloomsbury maintains a fairly residential demeanor. Gracious, tree-filled squares and a prime location (within Zone 1 on the tube) cause hotel prices to be a pound or two higher here. All Bloomsbury B&Bs accept reservations with one night's deposit.

Regency House Hotel, 71 Gower St., WC1 (tel. 637 18 04, fax 323 50 77). Tube: Goodge St. Color-coordinated rooms and spotless bathrooms. Singles £27-37. Doubles £37-52. Triples £52-65. Quads £60. Quint £68. Breakfast included. Winter discounts. Book in advance. MC, Visa.

Ridgemount Hotel, 65-67 Gower St., WC1 (tel. 636 11 41 or 580 70 60). Tube: Goodge St. Radiantly clean throughout. Rooms with TV. Laundry facilities, a garden in back, and tea and coffee in the TV lounge. Singles £26-35. Doubles £38-47. Triples £51-60. Quads £60-70. Quints £68. English breakfast. Call in advance.

Cosmo House Hotel, 27 Bloomsbury Sq., WC1 (tel. 636 46 61 or 636 05 77). Tube: Holborn. Clean, comfortable rooms with color TVs and fringed pink lampshades that look like Rococo Batman logos. Furnishings are a bit worn. Singles £27. Doubles £40. Triples £50. English breakfast. AmEx.

Thanet, 8 Bedford Pl., WC1 (tel. 636 28 69 or 580 33 77, fax 323 66 76). Tube: Holborn. Simple and spacious, and all come with TV, radio, phone, and hot pot. Singles £37-47. Doubles £50-62. Triples £75. Quads £85. MC, Visa.

Celtic Hotel, 62 Guilford St., WC1 (tel. 837 92 58). Tube: Holborn or Russell Sq. Pastel color scheme gives the place a fresh feel, balancing out the darkly lit walkways. Front rooms can be a bit noisy. TV lounge. Singles £30.50. Doubles £42.50. English breakfast.

Hotel Apollo, 43 Argyle St., WC1 (tel. 837 54 89, fax 916 18 62). Tube: King's Cross. Bright white with blue trim, this hotel stands out from the others on the street. Singles £24. Doubles £32. English breakfast.

Earl's Court

The area feeds on the tourist trade; beware the hustlers. Travel agencies, take-away eateries, Australians, and souvenir shops dominate. Earl's Court is also home to a significant gay population.

White House Hotel, 12 Earl's Ct. Sq., SW5 (tel. 373 59 03). Glassed-in porch. Bedrooms are pleasant and much cheaper than most of their equals. Laundry. Singles £15. Doubles £25-30. Triples £30. Continental breakfast.

York House Hotel, 27-29 Philbeach Gdns., SW5 (tel. 373 75 19). Helpful, experienced manager. French, Spanish, and Arabic spoken. Reception open 7am-11pm. Singles £24.70. Doubles £38.80-55. Triples £49-65. Quads £56. English breakfast. Reserve in advance with 1 night's deposit.

Kensington and Chelsea

The snazzy Royal Borough of Kensington and Chelsea is hardly a gold mine of budget B&Bs. The few exceptions to this rule are particularly impressive.

Vicarage Hotel, 10 Vicarage Gate, W8 (tel. 229 40 30). Tube: Notting Hill Gate. Posh! Red velvet and gold frame a sweeping staircase. Small, comfy, immaculate bedrooms. Luxurious TV lounge. Singles £30. Doubles £52. Triples £65. Quads £70. Full English breakfast included. Reserve in advance.

Hotel Europe, 131-137 Cromwell Rd., SW7 (tel. 370 23 36/7/8). Tube: Gloucester Rd. Classy dining room and lounge. Fax service. Singles £30-35. Doubles £40-45. Triples £45-55. Continental breakfast. Reserve ahead.

Paddington and Bayswater

These neighborhoods are located near many of London's finest attractions. Whiteley's, London's first large, indoor shopping mall, is within walking distance. Slightly decrepit B&Bs cluster around Norfolk Sq. and Sussex Gdns. As you travel west, the hotels increase in character. (Tube: Paddington, unless otherwise noted.)

Compton House Hotel and Millard's Hotel, 148-152 Sussex Gardens, W2 (tel. 723 62 25 or 723 29 39). One of the most respectable and clean budget hotels in this area. Singles £25, with shower £30. Doubles £35, with shower £40. Triples £45-48, with shower £50-55. Prices negotiable for longer stays. Reserve ahead.

Ravna Gora, 29 Holland Park Ave., W11 (tel. 727 77 25). Tube: Holland Park. Sedate and family-run, with room for 50 guests. Convenient to, yet removed from Holland Park and the crowds of Portobello. 24-hr. reception. Singles £27. Doubles £44-54. Triples £51-63. Quads £64-76.

Hyde Park House, 48 St. Petersburgh Pl., W2 (tel. 229 16 87). Tube: Queensway or Bayswater. Quiet residential surroundings. Cozy, sun-filled rooms with TV and washbasin. Singles £20. Doubles £30.

Hyde Park Rooms Hotel, 137 Sussex Gdns., W2 (tel. 723 02 25 or 723 09 65). Recently renovated rooms are bright and airy. Singles £20. Doubles £30. Family £15 per person. Discount for small children.

Garden Court Hotel, 30-31 Kensington Gdns. Sq., W2 (tel. 229 25 53, fax 727 27 49). Tube: Bayswater. Refreshingly tasteful decor. Budget travelers can only afford the rooms without private toilets and showers; these rooms are still a bit pricey, but worth it. Reception 7:30am-11pm. Singles £26-38. Doubles £38-51. Triples £49-57. Quads £57-62.

Near Victoria Station

In exchange for fairly expensive accommodations, travelers checking in to the B&Bs around Victoria Station receive a convenient location, within close proximity to several of London's major attractions. In the summer, prudent visitors make reservations at least two weeks in advance.

Luna and Simone Hotel, 47-49 Belgrave Rd., SW1 (tel. 834 58 97, 828 24 74), past Warwick Sq. Tube: Victoria. Immaculate, cheap rooms with color TV. English breakfast. Singles £20-22. Doubles £30-44. Triples £39-51. Winter discounts.

Melbourne House, 79 Belgrave Rd., SW1 (tel. 828 3516; fax 828 7120). Past Warwick Sq. Closer to Pimlico than Victoria; from Pimlico station take the Bessborough St. (south side) exit and go left along Lupus St. Turn right at St. George's Sq.; Belgrave Rd. starts on the other side of the square. Sparkling bedrooms, all of which come with TV, phone, and hot pot. Singles £22-25. Doubles £45-55. Triples £65-70. 2-room quads £75-80. Winter discount. MC, Visa.

Georgian House Hotel, 35 St. George's Dr., SW1 (tel. 834 14 38). Tube: Pimlico. Well decorated. Friendly. Wacky student discounts. TV, phone, tea/coffee maker too. Reception open 8am-11pm. Singles £25-29. Doubles £35-44. Triples £48-53. Quads £59-67. Students: singles £15, doubles £28, triples £39. English breakfast.

Oxford House, 92-94 Cambridge St., SW1 (tel. 834 64 67), near the church. Tube: Victoria Sta. Quiet residential area; it's home-like, with pets. TV lounge. Good cooking, commodious rooms, and firm beds. Singles £28-30. Doubles £38-40. Triples £48-51. Quad £64-68. English breakfast. Reserve 3-4 weeks ahead.

FOOD

London presents a tantalizing range of foreign and English specialties. With Indian, Lebanese, Greek, Chinese, Thai, Italian, West Indian, and African food inexpensive and readily available, the city has few rivals when it comes to diversity. If you eat but one meal in London, let it be Indian—British Indian food is rivaled only by India's and Sarala's. Meals are cheaper on Westbourne Grove (tube: Bayswater), or near Euston Station (tube: Euston) than in the West End.

Supermarkets are cheaper than corner shops and stock inexpensive pre-fab dishes. **Safeway** stores punctuate King's Rd., Edgware Rd. (not far from Paddington), and the Brunswick Shopping Centre opposite the Russell Sq. tube stop. **Sainsbury** has a branch on Victoria Rd. not far from Victoria Station, and another on Cromwell Rd. (tube: Gloucester Rd.). Ubiquitous **Europa Food** stores are expensive but stay awake until 11pm.

The West End

Food for Thought, 31 Neal St., WC2. Tube: Covent Garden. Generous vegetarian servings straight from the pot in an intimate plant-filled restaurant. Daily specials from £3.25. Open Mon.-Sat. 9am-7pm.

Neal's Yard Dining Room, 14-15 Neal's Yard, WC2. Wide international selection in an airy room, overlooking a vegetarian paradise: nearby are Neal's Yard's takeaway **Soup and Salad Bar** and **Bakery.** Tortilla heaped with cheese £3.10. Open Tues.-Fri. noon-8pm, Mon. and Sat. noon-5pm.

Scott's, corner of Bedfordbury St. and New Row, WC2. Tube: Covent Garden. Crowds line up at lunchtime to get into this sophisticated *pâtisserie*. Sandwiches £1.50-3.50. Open 8am-11:30pm.

Alpha One Fish Bar, 43 Old Compton St., W1. Tube: Leicester Sq. or Piccadilly Circus. Good, greasy fun. Fresh fish and chips, "not a deep freeze on the premises." Large cod £2.40. Open Sun.-Thurs. 11:30am-1am, Fri.-Sat. 11:30am-2am.

Old Compton Café, 34 Old Compton St., W1. Tube: Leicester Sq. Open 24hrs. in the geographic epicenter of Soho, this is *the* gay café.

Pollo, 20 Old Compton St., W1. Tube: Leicester Sq. or Piccadilly Circus. Packed Italian restaurant/madhouse. Pizzas £3.30. Open Mon.-Sat. 11:30am-11:30pm.

Chuen Cheng Ku, 17 Wardour St., W1. Tube: Leicester Sq. Considered by some to be one of the planet's best. *Dim sum* dishes £1.65. Open 11am-midnight.

Pizza Express, 10 Dean St., W1. Tube: Tottenham Ct. Rd. Great pizza £3.15-5.30. Live jazz Mon.-Thurs. from 9pm and Fri.-Sat. from 8pm. Open noon-midnight.

City of London and East End

The Place Below, in St. Mary-le-Bow Church crypt, Cheapside, EC2 (tel. 329 07 89). Tube: St. Paul's. Hip executives enjoy attractive and generous vegetarian dishes. Quiche and salad £5.25. Savory tomato, almond, and saffron soup £2.70.

GREAT BRITAIN

Dinner is more expensive (£15 for a two-course meal and coffee). Open Mon.-Fri. 7:30am-3pm, dinner Thurs.-Fri. 6:30-10:30pm. £3.50 min. noon-2pm.

Croissant Express, Unit 20-22, Leadenhall Market, EC3 (tel. 623 88 04). Tube: Bank. (Another branch at the Moorgate tube station.) A good place for a quick bite or cheap take-away. Open Mon.-Fri. 7am-5pm.

The East-West Restaurant, 188 Old St., EC1 (tel. 608 03 00). Tube: Old St. Sublime macrobiotic cooking. Main meals, such as deep-fried tofu with sweet carrots or stuffed peppers with tahini sauce, come in small (£4.50) or large (£6) portions. Open Mon.-Thurs. 11am-9pm, Fri.-Sat. 11am-10 pm, Sun. 11am-4pm.

The Cherry Orchard Café, 247 Globe Rd., E2 (tel. (0181) 980 66 78). Tube: Bethnal Green. Un-Chekhovian restaurant run by Buddhists. Entrees (like broccoli and almond filo pie) average £3.50. Hot meals served Mon. and Thurs.-Fri. noon-3pm, Tues.-Wed. noon-7pm.

Bloom's, 90 Whitechapel High St., E1 (tel. 247 60 01). Tube: Aldgate East. A London institution, this traditional kosher restaurant sells good salt (corned) beef sandwiches for £3.20. *Haimishe* family atmosphere. The take-away counter also sells canned food. Popular on Sun. Open Sun.-Thurs. 11am-9pm, Fri. 11am-2pm.

Kensington, Knightsbridge, Chelsea, and Victoria

Mima's Sandwiches and Salads, 9 Knightsbridge Green, SW1. Tube: Knightsbridge. Understandably packed during lunch hours. Practically every sandwich under the sun, each £2 or less. Open Mon.-Sat. 7am-5:30pm.

Knightsbridge Express, 17 Knightsbridge Green, SW1. Tube: Knightsbridge. Upbeat eatery. Most sandwiches £1-2. Sandwich platters with coleslaw and potato salad under £4. Open Mon.-Sat. 6:30am-5:30pm.

Ambrosiana Crêperie, 194 Fulham Rd., SW10. Tube: South Kensington. Airy storefront with cane chairs and small tables. Savory crêpes £4.60-6 (try the combination of salami, asparagus, onions, and cheese). Sweet crêpes slightly cheaper. Open Mon.-Fri. noon-3pm and 6pm-midnight, Sat.-Sun. noon-midnight.

Bar Escoba, 102 Old Brompton Rd., SW7. Tube: South Kensington. Lively Spanish restaurant and bar; just a 10min. walk from the South Kensington tube. *Tapas* £1.50-4. Grilled chicken breast with lemon and chili sauce, chips, and salad £8. Gazpacho £1.95. Full bar. Open noon-11pm.

Aquarius, 163 Old Brompton Rd., SW7. Tube: South Kensington. Spare vegetarian and whole-food restaurant in a quiet locale. Most entrees, like vegetable paella or Mexican bean stew (£5.50 each) combine lentils, beans, rice, pasta, and/or soya. Veggie burger with salad £3.55. Open Mon.-Sat. 8:30am-11pm, Sun. noon-10pm.

Chelsea Kitchen, 98 King's Rd., SW3. Tube: Sloane Sq., then bus 11 or 22. 5-10min. walk from the tube. Locals rave about the eclectic menu of cheap, filling, tasty food: *spaghetti bolognese* or Spanish omelet £2.30. Breakfast served 8-11:25am. Open Mon.-Sat. 8am-11:30pm, Sun. noon-11:30pm.

The Stock Pot, 273 King's Rd., SW3. Tube: Sloane Sq., then bus 11or 22. The minimum per person is £2.20, but most meals won't cost you more than that anyway. All entrees, from lamb chops to fillet of trout, under £3.50. Open Mon.-Sat. 8am-midnight, Sun. 10am-midnight.

Planet Poppadum, 366 King's Rd., SW2. Tube: Sloane Sq., then bus 11or 22. Hipsters crowd in late at night. Most vegetarian and chicken dishes under £5. All entrees include complimentary salad, yogurt, mango chutney, mixed pickle sauce, and, from a galaxy far, far away, poppadum. Renowned *nan* bread £1.50. Open Mon.-Wed. 4pm-midnight, Thurs.-Sun. noon-midnight.

Bloomsbury and Euston

Wagamama, 4 Streatham St., WC1. Tube: Tottenham Ct. Rd. Go down New Oxford St., taking a left onto Bloomsbury St. "Positive Eating & Positive Living." Strangers sit elbow-to-elbow at long tables slurping happily from their massive bowls of ramen. Pan-fried noodles, rice dishes, and vegetarian soups also available. Noodles in various combinations and permutations £3.80-5.70. No smoking. Open Mon.-Fri. noon-2:30pm and 6-11pm, Sat. 1-3pm and 6-11pm.

Greenhouse, 16 Chenies St. basement, WC1. Tube: Goodge St. Fresh vegetarian dishes. Thick pizza £2.10. Open Mon. 10am-7pm, Tues.-Fri. 10am-9pm, Sat. 10am-8pm, Sun. noon-3pm.

GREAT BRITAIN

Mille Pini Restaurant, 33 Boswell St., WC1. Tube: Holborn. Take Southampton Row and turn right onto Theobald's Row. Boswell St. is the second left. Terrific brick-oven pizza (£3.80-4.50), pasta (£4.50-4.80), and homemade ice cream. Take-away available. Open Mon.-Fri. noon-3pm and 6-11pm, Sat. 6-11pm.

Chutney's, 124 Drummond St., NW1. Tube: Warren St. A cheerful café serving vegetarian dishes from Western and Southern India. Lunch buffet Mon.-Sat. noon-2:45pm and Sun. noon-10:30pm, £3.95. *Dosas* (filled pancakes) £2.45-3.50. Take-away 6pm-11:30pm. Open noon-2:45pm and 6-11:30pm.

The Fryers Delight, 19 Theobald's Rd., WC1. Tube: Holborn. One of the best chippies around. Funky diner decor—ensconce yourself in red and green vinyl booths while you munch. Large portions of fish and chips just £2.85. Open Mon.-Sat. noon-10pm, until 11pm for take-away.

North London

Parkway Pizzeria, 64 Parkway, NW1. Tube: Camden Town. Exit the station to the right, then head left along Camden High St.; Parkway is the immediate right. Juicy pizzas. With capers, pine nuts, tomato, and mozzarella, £3.65. Take away available. £3 min. when the restaurant is full. Open noon-midnight.

The New Culture Revolution, 42 Duncan St., N1. Tube: Angel. Exit right from the station and take the first right onto Duncan St. Dumpling and noodle bar with slick black tables, plush chairs, and Matisse prints on the walls. Fried dishes are zestier. Dumplings £3.50-4. Noodles £3.50-5.50. Open Mon.-Fri. noon-2:30pm and 6-11pm, Sat. 1-11pm. 20% off if you pay before 7pm.

The Angel, 65 Graham St., N1. Tube: Angel. One of few gay places with a consistently balanced male-female ratio. Eclectic menu of light meals. Free live music Sun. Open Mon.-Sat. noon-midnight, Sun. noon-11:30pm.

Bar Gansa, 2 Inverness St., NW1. Tube: Camden Town. Exit the station to the right and head right; Inverness is the first left. Small *tapas* bar with cream-colored walls, bright prints, and Spanish ceramics. *Tapas* £1.95-3.50. Grilled goat cheese sandwich £4. Open Mon.-Thurs. 10:30am-11:45pm, Fri.-Sat. 10:30am-midnight, Sun. 10:30am-11pm.

Paddington and Bayswater

The Garden, 1 Hillgate St., W8. Tube: Notting Hill Gate. A small, tasteful establishment with the cheapest lunches around. Homemade pasta with chicken and mushrooms £2.25. Sandwiches £1-1.95. Open Mon.-Sat. 8am-4pm.

Geale's, 2 Farmer St., W8. Tube: Notting Hill Gate. Spirited locals crowd this reputable wood-paneled restaurant with award-winning fish and chips (around £3.50). Often a wait; sit it out in the bar upstairs. Open Tues.-Sat. noon-3pm and 6-11pm.

Cafe Grove, 253 Portobello Rd., W11. Tube: Ladbroke Grove. House music pulses through this art gallery/coffeehouse. Sandwiches £1.75-2.75. Omelets £3-5. BYOB. Open Mon.-Fri. 9:30am-11pm, Sat. 10am-11pm, Sun. 10:30-11pm.

Khan's, 13-15 Westbourne Grove, W2. Tube: Bayswater. Cavernous, noisy, and crowded and the best bargain around for delicious Indian cuisine. Chicken *saag* (chicken cooked with spinach) £2.95. *Nan* bread 95p, rice £1.40. Chicken *tikka masala* £3.50. Open noon-3pm and 6pm-midnight.

The Café, 106 Westbourne Grove, W2. Tube: Bayswater or Notting Hill Gate. No-nonsense British-style breakfasts (served all day) and lunches. Soothing in its unaffectedness, with a friendly, maternal waitstaff. Standard breakfast (bacon, beans, a fried egg, a grilled tomato, buttered bread, and coffee or tea) £3. Open 8am-8pm.

SIGHTS

London is best explored on foot. When your soles begin to ache, the **London Transport Sightseeing Tour** (tel. 222 12 34), provides a cursory, but convenient, overview of London's sights. (9:30am-5:30pm every ½hr. from Baker St., Haymarket, Marble Arch, and Victoria St., near the station. £9, children £5. Pay conductor.)

Mayfair to Parliament An auspicious beginning to a day's wander is **Piccadilly Circus** and its towering neon bluffs (tube: Piccadilly Circus). At the center of the Nash's swirling hub stands a fountain topped by a statue everyone calls Eros but

GREAT BRITAIN

is actually supposed to be the Angel of Christian Charity. North are the tiny shops of Regent St. and the renovated seediness of **Soho,** a region which sports a vibrant sidewalk café culture where pornography once reigned. Outdoor cafés, upscale shops and slick crowds huddle in **Covent Garden,** to the northeast. **Piccadilly,** running off the Circus, is lined with exclusive stores, including **Fortnum and Mason,** with its Earl Greys. Paths across **Green Park** lead to **Buckingham Palace** (Tube: Victoria or Green Park), now open to tourists. (Tours Aug.-Sept.; £8, seniors £5.50, children £4.) The Changing of the Guard occurs daily (April-July) or every other day (Aug.-March) at 11:30am unless it's raining; arrive early or you won't see a thing. The extravagant "Trooping the Colour" is on a Saturday in June, the Queen's official birthday.

    The Mall, a wide processional, leads from the palace to **Admiralty Arch** and Trafalgar Square. **St. James's Park,** south of the Mall, shelters a duck preserve and a flock of lawn chairs. The center of a vicious traffic roundabout, **Trafalgar Square** (tube: Charing Cross), centers on Nelson's Column, a 40-ft. statue astride a 132-ft. column. Political Britain branches off **Whitehall,** just south of Trafalgar. Draped in black Velvet, Charles I was led out of the **Banqueting House** (corner of Horse Guards Ave. and Whitehall) and beheaded; the building now hosts less lethal state dinners. (Open Mon.-Sat. 10am-5pm. £2.90, students and seniors £2.25.) The Prime Minister resides off Whitehall at **10 Downing Street,** now closed to tourists and other terrorists. In the middle of Whitehall is the **Cenotaph,** a monument to Britain's war dead. Whitehall ends by the sprawling **Houses of Parliament** (tube: Westminster). Access to the House of Commons and the House of Lords is restricted since a member was killed in a bomb blast in 1979; your best bet is to send a written request to the Public Information Office, 1 Derby Gate, Westminster, SW1. Pedantically speaking, **Big Ben** is neither the tower nor the clock, but the 14-ton bell, cast when a similarly proportioned Sir Benjamin Hall served as Commissioner of Works. Church and state tie the knot in **Westminster Abbey,** coronation chamber to English monarchs for the past 684 years, as well as the site of **Poet's Corner,** the **Grave of the Unknown Warrior,** and the elegantly perpendicular **Chapel of Henry VII.** Britain bestows no greater honor than burial within these walls. The abbey plumber is buried here among such greats as Elizabeth I, Darwin, Dickens, and Ben Jonson (whose last name is misspelled with an *h* on his tomb). Ask about the story surrounding the Stone of Scone. (Abbey nave open Mon.-Sat. 7:30am-6pm, Wed. 6-7:45pm, Sun. in between services; free. Chapels and transepts open Mon.-Fri. 9am-4:45pm, also Wed. 6-7:45pm, Sat. 9am-2:45pm and 3:45-5:45pm. £4, concessions £2, children £1, all parts of the abbey free Wed. 6-7:45pm. Photography permitted Wed. evenings only.)

Hyde Park and Kensington to Chelsea   Hyde Park shows its best face on Sundays from 11am to dusk, when soapbox orators take freedom of speech to the limit at **Speaker's Corner** (tube: Marble Arch, *not* Hyde Park Corner). To the west, **Kensington Gardens,** an elegant relic of Edwardian England, celebrates the glories of model yacht racing in the squarish Round Pond. From the gardens you can catch a glimpse of Kensington Palace, home of those models of royal family values, Charles and Diana. The **Royal Albert Hall,** on the south edge of Hyde Park, hosts the Proms, a gloriously British festival of music (see Entertainment, below). Up Brompton Rd. near Knightsbridge, **Harrods** (tube: Knightsbridge) vends under their humble motto, *Omnia Omnibus Ubique* ("All things for all people, everywhere"). (Open Mon.-Tues., and Sat. 10am-6pm, Wed.-Fri. 10am-7pm.) Still-fashionable **King's Road** (tube: Sloane Sq.), to the south in **Chelsea,** attempts to do justice to its bohemian past. If you're pressed for time, be aware that the tube is practically nonexistent around here, so you'll have to rely on **buses** (11 or 22).

Regent's Park to Fleet Street   Take a picnic from Harrods to the expanse of **Regent's Park,** northeast from Hyde Park across Marylebone (tube: Regent's Park). The **London Zoo,** in the north end, has mambos, Asian lions, and piranhas.

(Open 10am-5:30pm; Oct.-March 10am-4pm. £6.50, students and seniors £5.) **Camden Town** (tube: Camden Town), bordering the park to the northeast, sports some of the hemisphere's rollickingest street markets.

Bloomsbury—eccentric, erudite and disorganized—is known for its literary and scholarly connections, including the **British Museum** (see Museums, below). **Fleet Street** is the traditional den of the British press, though nearly all the papers have moved to cheaper real estate. Close by are the **Inns of Court,** which have controlled access to the English Bar since the 13th century.

City of London Once upon a time, "London" meant the square-mile enclave of the **City of London;** the rest of today's metropolis were far-flung towns and villages. The **Tower of London** was the grandest fortress in medieval Europe and the palace and prison of English monarchs for over 500 years. Its best-known edifice, the **White Tower,** is also the oldest, begun by William the Conqueror. In 1483, the "Princes in the Tower" (Edward V and his brother) were murdered in the **Bloody Tower** in one of the great unsolved mysteries of history; two of the wives of jolly King Henry VIII were beheaded in the courtyard, and in 1941 Rudolf Hess was sent to the Tower after his parachute dumped him in Scotland. The **Crown Jewels** include the Stars of Africa, cut from the enormous Cullinan Diamond, which was mailed 3rd-class from the Transvaal in an unmarked brown paper package. (Tube: Tower Hill. Open Mon.-Sat. 9:30am-5pm, Sun. 2-5pm; Nov.-Feb. Mon.-Sat. 9:30am-4pm. £6.70, students and seniors £5.10.) Next to the Tower is **Tower Bridge,** one of London's best-known landmarks. The walkways provide one of London's best views and a new exhibition inside the bridge explains its history. (Tube: Tower Hill. Open 10am-6:30pm; Nov.-March 10am-5:15pm. £5.) Other shrapnel of history are scattered throughout the City, among them 24 Christopher Wren churches interspersed with the soaring steel of modern skyscrapers. Peruse smaller churches, such as The Strand's **St. Clement Danes** of "Oranges and Lemons" fame, or the superb **St. Stephen Walbrook** near the Bank of England (tube: Bank). True-blue cockney Londoners are born within earshot of the famous bells of **St. Mary-le-Bow,** Cheapside. In the German Blitz in 1940, **St. Paul's Cathedral** stood firm in a sea of fire. Climb above the graves of Wren, Nelson, and Wellington in the crypt to the dizzying top of the dome; the view is unparalleled. (Tube: St. Paul's. Open Mon.-Sat. 8:30am-4pm; ambulatory and crypt open Mon.-Sat. 8:45am-4:15pm; galleries open Mon.-Sat. 10am-4:15pm. Cathedral, ambulatory, and crypt £3, students £2.50. Cathedral, ambulatory, crypt, and galleries £5, £4.)

The South and the Outskirts Lesser-known but equally rewarding treasures lie south of the river. **Southwark Cathedral,** a smallish, quiet church, boasts London's second-best Gothic structure and a chapel dedicated to John Harvard (tube: London Bridge). West along the riverbank, a reconstruction of Shakespeare's Globe Theatre is underway; it should open in August 1995. South London's entertainment history lives on in the externally drab but internally festive **South Bank Arts Centre** (tube: Waterloo).

The transport system that encouraged London's urban sprawl blurs the distinction between the city and its surroundings. If Hyde Park seemed but a small bit of green, **Highgate** and **Hampstead Heath** will prove that there is an English countryside. Nestled in the midst of Hampstead, **Keats House,** Keats Grove, is one of London's finest literary shrines. The house is furnished as it was during Keats's life, complete with his manuscripts and letters. (Tube or BR: Hampstead. Open Mon.-Fri. 2-6pm, Sat. 10am-1pm and 2-5pm, Sun. 2-5pm; Nov.-March Mon.-Fri. 1-5pm, Sat. 10am-1pm and 2-5pm, Sun. 2-5pm. Free.) To the east, Karl Marx and George Eliot repose in the gothic tangle of **Highgate Cemetery,** Swains La., a remarkable monument to the Victorian fascination with death. (Tube: Archway. Eastern Cemetery open Mon.-Fri. 10am-4:45pm, Sat.-Sun. 11am-4:45pm. £1.50. Western Cemetery access by guided tour only Mon.-Fri. at noon, 2pm, and 4pm, Sat.-Sun. hourly from 11am to 4pm. £2. Camera permit £1, valid in both sections.)

GREAT BRITAIN

Head by train or boat to red-brick **Hampton Court** for a quirky change of pace; its grounds contain the famous hedgerow maze (BR: Hampton Court). **Windsor Castle** is the Queen's country retreat. **Greenwich,** home of the Prime Meridian, is on the Thames, east of central London. You can visit Wren's **Old Royal Observatory,** Inigo Jones' grand **Queen's House,** as well as the suprisingly elaborate **National Maritime Museum** (BR: Greenwich). Just west of central London on the Thames lie the serene and exotic **Kew Gardens.** Lose yourself in the controlled wilderness of the grounds, or explore the Victorian and modern glasshouses containing thousands of plant species. (Tube or BR: Kew Gardens. Open Mon.-Fri. 9:30am-6:30pm, Sat.-Sun. 9:30am-7:30pm).

Museums

British Museum, Great Russell St. Tube: Tottenham Ct. Rd. or Holborn. The closest thing this planet has to a complete record of the rise and ruin of world cultures. Among the plunder on display are the Rosetta Stone (whose inscriptions allowed French scholar Champollion to decipher hieroglyphics) and the Elgin Marbles. Also hoards an early manuscript of *Beowulf* and 2 of 4 surviving copies of the *Magna Carta.* Open Mon.-Sat. 10am-5pm, Sun. 2:30-6pm. Free. Special exhibits £3, students and seniors £2.

National Gallery, Trafalgar Sq. Tube: Charing Cross. One of the world's finest collections of European painting; heavyweight works by da Vinci, Turner, and Velázquez. The new Micro Gallery, a computerized, illustrated catalogue, will print out a free personal tour. Open Mon.-Sat. 10am-6pm, Sun. 2-6pm. Free.

National Portrait Gallery, St. Martin's Pl., opposite St. Martin's in the Fields. Tube: Charing Cross. Doubles as *Who's Who in Britain.* Open Mon.-Fri. 10am-5pm, Sat. 10am-6pm, Sun. 2-6pm. Free.

Tate Gallery, Millbank, up the Thames from Parliament Sq. Tube: Pimlico. The best of British artists such as Gainsborough, Reynolds, and Constable, along with works by Monet, Dalí, and Matisse. The vast J.M.W. Turner collection rests in the Clore Gallery, an extension of the main building. Both open Mon.-Sat. 10am-5:50pm, Sun. 2-5:50pm. Free.

Victoria and Albert Museum, Cromwell Rd. Tube: South Kensington. A mind-boggling array of fine and applied arts from all periods and places. Open Mon.-Sat. 10am-5:50pm, Sun. 2:30-5:50pm. "Donation" £4.50, students and seniors £1.

Imperial War Museum, Lambeth Rd. Tube: Lambeth North. Despite its jingoistic name, a moving reminder of the human cost of conflict. Open 10am-6pm. £3.90, students £2.90 and children £1.95, free after 4:30pm.

London Transport Museum. Tube: Covent Garden. Transforms the tube from frustrating to fascinating. Open 10am-6pm, last entry 5:15pm. £3.95, students and seniors £2.50.

Madame Tussaud's, Marylebone Rd., NW1. Tube: Baker St. The classic waxwork museum. Open Mon.-Fri. 10am-5:30pm, Sat.-Sun. 9:30am-5:30pm. £7.40, children £4.75, seniors £5.50.

Museum of London, 150 London Wall, EC2. Tube: St. Paul's or Barbican. From Londinium to the Docklands. Free lectures Wed.-Fri. 1:10pm. Open Tues.-Sat. 10am-6pm, Sun. noon-6pm, bank holidays 10am-6pm, last entry 5:30pm. £3, students £1.50. Free after 4:30pm.

Museum of Mankind, 6 Burlington Gdns. Tube: Piccadilly Circus. Engrossing assemblage of artifacts from non-Western societies. Open Mon.-Sat. 10am-5pm, Sun. 2:30-6pm. Free.

Science Museum, Exhibition Rd. Tube: South Kensington. A hands-on extravaganza irresistible to kids of all ages. Open Mon.-Sat. 10am-6pm, Sun. 11am-6pm. £4.50, students and seniors £2.40, free after 4:30pm.

ENTERTAINMENT

On any given day or night, Londoners and visitors can choose from the widest range of entertainment a city can offer. For guidance, consult the weekly *Time Out* (£1.50), or *What's On* (£1).

Theater, Music, and Film

London **theater** is unrivalled. Seats cost £8-22 and up, and student/senior standby (with an "S" or "concessions" in listings) puts even the best seats within reach—around £7-10 shortly before curtain (come 2hr. early to get a seat). **Day seats** are sold cheaply (9-10am, the day of) to all; queue up earlier to snag one. The **Leicester Square Ticket Booth** sells ½-price tickets on the day of major plays. (Open Mon.-Sat. noon-2pm and 2:30-6:30pm; long wait. £1.50 fee. Cash only.) Standby tickets for the **National Theatre,** on the South Bank (tel. 928 22 52; tube: Waterloo) sell 2hrs. beforehand (£8-10; students and seniors £6, 45min. before). The **Barbican Theatre** (tel. 628 22 95; tube: Barbican or Moorgate), the London home of the Royal Shakespeare Co. sells student and senior standbys for £6.50-8 from 9am on the day of performance. Often, more exciting performances for significantly less cash are to be found in the **Fringe,** an assemblage of smaller less commercial theaters.

Most major **classical music** is staged at the acoustically superb **Royal Festival Hall** (tel. 928 88 00; tube: Waterloo) and the **Barbican Hall** (tel. 638 41 41; box office 638 88 91). Hampstead Heath's **Kenwood House** (tel. (0181) 348 12 86; booking 973 34 27) and the **Marble Hill House** have low-priced outdoor concerts on summer weekends (tel. 973 34 27; booking 413 14 43). Opera and ballet embellish the **Royal Opera House** (tel. 240 19 11 or 240 10 66; tube: Covent Garden) and the **London Coliseum** (tel. 836 3161; tube: Charing Cross or Leicester Sq.). Londoners have been lining up for standing room in the **Royal Albert Hall's "Proms"** (BBC Henry Wood Promenade Concerts), the most popular and endearing feature of the London music scene, for nearly a century. So, how many holes *does* it take to fill the Albert Hall? (Tube: South Kensington. July-Sept. Gallery £2, arena £3; join line at 6pm; regular tickets £4-16. Box office 9am-9pm.)

Every **pop music** phenom that didn't take off in London gets there at some point. Ticket offices and record shops list concerts. **The Marquee,** 105 Charing Cross Rd., WC2 (tel. 437 66 01; Tube: Leicester Sq. or Tottenham Ct. Rd.), is a loud, band-churning machine (cover £5-7). **Brixton Academy,** 211 Stockwell Rd., SW9 (tel. 326 10 22; tube: Brixton) is a larger, rowdy venue for a variety of music including rock and reggae (advance tickets £9-15). **Ronnie Scott's,** 47 Frith St., W1 (tel. 439 07 47; Tube: leicester Sq. or Piccadilly Circus), has London's greatest jazz (cover from £14). Bob Dylan played in the **Troubadour Coffee House,** 265 Old Brompton Rd., SW5 (tel. 370 14 34); you'll still find great acoustic entertainment. (Tube: Earl's Ct. Folk and jazz Fri.-Sat. £4.50, concession £3.50. Open 8pm-11pm.)

Electric Cinema, 191 Portobello Rd. (tube: Ladbroke Grove or Notting Hill Gate) is the first Black cinema in Britain. (£5. Discounted tickets (£4) available Mon.-Thurs. for students, seniors, and children; bring your ID.) **Gate Cinema,** Notting Hill Gate (tube: Notting Hill Gate) screens recent foreign language and art films. (Tickets £5.50, Mon.-Fri. before 6pm students £3. Rotating Sunday matinees, £4.)

Sports

In late June and early July, London aces **Wimbledon** (tel. (0181) 946 22 44; tube: Southfields; to grounds £5-7, less after 5pm; important matches up to £30). Final matches sell out centuries in advance. **Football** (soccer) matches are electric, and the "terraces" are simply fierce: beware! International matches are played at **Wembley** (tel. (0181) 900 12 34); half-a-dozen other fields are scattered around the city: check out **Arsenal** (tel. 359 01 31; tube: Arsenal) or **Tottenham Hotspur** (tel. (0181) 808 30 30; BR: White Hart Lane). **Lord's** (tel. 289 16 15; tube: St. John's Wood) hosts stuffy cricket matches; in contrast, watch **rugby,** a revelrous melee of mud, blood, and drink, at Wembley (above).

Pubs

London's 7000 pubs are as colorful as their country counterparts, but in London the clientele varies widely from one neighborhood to the next. Avoid pubs near train stations; they prey on naïve tourists. For the best prices, head to the East End or south of the Thames. Posh prevails in Chelsea and Hampstead. For people-watching, hit the West End. Besides as many as a dozen potent ales and two ciders, many pubs offer cheap, standard British "pub grub," juices, and soft drinks.

Freud's, 198 Shaftesbury Ave., WC2. Tube: Tottenham Ct. Rd. or Covent Garden. A downstairs bar with leftover late-80s decor: concrete walls, slate tables, and art for sale. In early evenings, a comfortable place, even for the single traveler. Beer £1.95-2.75. Cocktails £3.10-4.55. Live jazz Sun. eve. Open Mon.-Sat. 11am-11pm, Sun. noon -10:30pm.

The Water Rats, 328 Grays Inn Rd., WC1. Tube: King's Cross/St. Pancras. Ordinary appearance belies radical historical connections—this used to be one of Marx and Engels' favorite haunts. Average pint £2.10. Moonlights as the **Splash Club** Wed.-Sat. nights, a venue for indie rock, punk, and occasional acoustic gigs. 3 bands a night. £5, concessions £3.

The Dog & Duck, 8 Bateman St., W1. Tube: Tottenham Ct. Rd. The smallest pub in Soho, it fills up with a "punter" (British jargon for "alternative") crowd. Fireplace in back.

Lamb and Flag, 33 Rose St., WC2, off Garrick St. Tube: Covent Garden or Leicester. Bygone fights earned it the name "Bucket of Blood"; poet John Dryden was thrashed here by a mob of angry readers.

Riki Tik, 23-24 Bateman St., W1. Tube: Leicester Square, Tottenham Ct. Rd., or Piccadilly Circus. A hyped, hip, and tremendously swinging bar specializing in flavored vodkas (£2 per shot). Closed Sun.

Admiral Codrington, 17 Mossop St., SW3. Tube: South Kensington. This old, handsomely appointed pub with a peaceful patio off the back is brimming with girls in platform shoes and boys in baggy suits.

Freedom, 60-66 Wardour St., W1. Tube: Piccadilly or Leicester Sq. A hyper-trendy Soho haunt frequented by a predominantly gay crowd. Open Mon.-Sat. 9am-11pm, Sun. 9am-10:30pm.

First Out Café/Bar, 52 St. Giles High St., WC2. Tube: Tottenham Ct. Rd. Off of New Oxford St. Casual, mainly gay crowd. Open Mon.-Sat. 10am-11pm, Sun. noon-10:30pm. Fri. night women only in the bar 8-11pm.

The Lamb, 94 Lamb's Conduit St., WC1. Tube: Russell Sq. Discreet cut-glass "snob screens" render this pub ideal for dangerous liaisons and illicit assignations. Limited outdoor seating. Hot food served noon-2:30pm.

Black Friar, 174 Queen Victoria St., EC4. Tube: Blackfriars. Directly across from the station. Art Nouveau monument to the medieval monks whose vestments are celebrated in the pub's name. Average pint £1.90.

Slug and Lettuce, 1 Islington Green, N1. Tube: Angel. Upper St. changes its name to Islington Green as it passes by the Green. Good observation post for spotting Islington trendies (inside or outside). Try upstairs for a comfy, cozy setting.

Babushka, 173 Blackfriars Road, SE1. Tube: Waterloo. Art. High ceilings. Bottled beers £2, wine £1.60 per glass. Spirits served. Live music (mostly jazz) Mon.-Sat. 6-9:30pm. Open Mon.-Sat. noon-11pm, Sun. noon-6pm.

Bar Central, 131 Waterloo Rd., SE1. Tube: Waterloo. Near the Old Vic. Cosmopolitan full bar and brasserie. Barkeep will mix you any drink that you know the name of. Open Mon.-Sat. noon-midnight, Sun. noon-11:30pm.

Dance Clubs

London pounds to 100% Groovy Liverpool tunes, ecstatic Manchester rave, hometown soul and house, imported U.S. hip-hop, and Jamaican ragga. Many clubs host a variety of provocative one-night stands (like "Get Up and Use Me") throughout the week. If you're looking for a truly underground dance experience, keep your ear to the ground. While news of serious raves travels exclusively by word of mouth, they can attract thousands of revelers in the know, who congregate in abandoned warehouses or in open fields outside the city. As always, check listings in *Time Out* and *What's On*.

The Fridge, Town Hall Parade, Brixton Hill, SW2. Tube: Brixton. Night bus N2. A serious dance dive with a multi-ethnic crowd. Popular weekly "Love Muscle"

GREAT BRITAIN

every Sat. night crowds with busy mixed-gay clientele. The Fridge cools down during the summer months. Open 10pm-4 or 6 am.

Gossips, 69 Dean St., W1. Tube: Piccadilly Circus or Tottenham Ct. Rd. A dark basement club renowned for a wide range of great one-nighters. Anything goes, from heavy metal to ska to psychedelia to reggae. Open Mon.-Sat. 10pm-3:30am.

Heaven, Villiers St., WC2, underneath The Arches. Tube: Embankment or Charing Cross (Villiers is off of the Strand). Still the oldest and biggest gay disco in Europe. Three dance floors, high-tech lighting, bars, and a capacity of 4000 means you'll never get bored. Open 10pm-4am. £8, £7 before 11:30pm.

Subterania, 12 Acklam Rd., W10 (tel. (0181) 960 4590). Tube: Ladbroke Grove. This is where it's at—directly beneath the Westway flyover. Relaxed, multi-ethnic crowd comes to dance to wicked house and garage music. Club classics and "90s disco." Sat. is **Bump** and mainly gay. £5-8. Open 10pm-3am.

Turnmills, 63B Clerkenwell Rd., EC1. Tube: Farringdon. Walk up Turnmill St. and turn right onto Clerkenwell Rd. Three hugely popular clubs. Sat. is **Pumpin' Curls,** a women's night of hard house. Gay men allowed as guests. (Open 10pm-3am. £5 or £10 joint ticket with "Trade.") At 3am, **Trade,** a high-NRG house party takes over. (Open 3am-noon. £10. Tickets available at Rox on Old Compton St., Trax on Greek St., and the Dispensary on Newburgh St.) Sun. night at **ff,** music tends to be more techno, the crowd younger, male, and cruisy. (Open 9:30pm-5am. £7, £5 students before midnight.)

The Vox, 9 Brighton Terrace, SW9. Tube: Brixton. Behind Red Records on Brixton Rd. "Institute of Dubology" rages every Thursday 10pm-3am. Most nights headline dub, techno, and psycho-trance. £3-6. Open until 3am, Fri.-Sat. until 6am.

The Garage, 22 Highbury Corner, N5. Tube: Highbury and Islington. Night bus N19, N73, N96. Local club specializing in indie rock. Saturday nights women only. £3-6. Open 7:30pm-2am.

SOUTH AND SOUTHEAST ENGLAND

■■■ KENT

Canterbury In the Middle Ages, the route from London to Canterbury was England's busiest road, lined with pilgrims striding to Thomas à Becket's shrine in **Canterbury Cathedral.** (Open Mon.-Sat. 8:45am-7pm; Nov.-Easter 8:45am-5pm. Donation £2. Check nave pulpit for times of guided tours: tickets £2.40, students £1.20. 25-min. headphone tour £1.70. Services Sun. 11am and 6:30pm.) The rest of the city brims with more religious monuments: the gardens of **Greyfriars,** on Stour St.; **St. Augustine's Abbey,** near the medieval wall; and, round the corner, **St. Martin's,** the oldest parish church in England. Canterbury's **tourist office,** 34 St. Margaret's St. (tel. (01227) 76 65 67), books accommodations (£3 or 10% deposit) and carries maps and guides for the rest of Kent (open 9:30am-5:30pm; Nov.-March 9:30am-5pm). B&Bs bunch near both train stations and on London and Whitstable Rd. Try the **HI youth hostel** at 54 New Dover Rd. (tel. (01227) 46 29 11). (Reception open 7-10am and 1-11pm. £8.70, under 18 £5.80. Open Feb.-Dec. Book a week in advance July-Aug. Call for off-season openings.) **The Tudor House,** 6 Best Ln. (tel. (01227) 76 56 50), sports bright rooms with TV (£16). The **London Guest House,** 14 London Rd. (tel. (01227) 76 58 60), is a spacious Victorian house in immaculate condition (£16). **St. Martin's Touring Caravan and Camping Site,** Bekesbourne Lane (tel. (01227) 46 32 16), off A257 (Sandwich Rd.), lies 1½mi. east of the city center. (£3 per tent, £3.30 per person. Open April-Oct.) The streets around the cathedral seethe with bakeries and sweet shops. The tasty selections are fresh at **Fungus Mungus,** 34 St. Peter's St., despite the name. (Main dishes £4.95, starters £2.10. Open 10am-11pm.) **The White Hart,** Worthgate Pl., near East Station, is a congenial pub with homemade luncheon specials (£3-6). Live a little and ask to eat in the rose garden. (Open Mon.-Sat. noon-2:30pm.)

Trains run from London's Victoria Station to Canterbury East Station and from Charing Cross and Waterloo to Canterbury West Station (1½hr.; £11.70). Reach both Canterbury stations at (01227) 77 01 11. **Buses** to Canterbury (station tel. (01227) 47 20 82) leave London's Victoria Coach Station (1¾hr., £6.75).

Dover The "melancholy roar" of the English Channel at Dover has been drowned out by the puttering of ferries and the squabbling of French families *en vacances*. The view from Castle Hill Rd. reveals why **Dover Castle** is famed both for its setting and for its impregnability. Dover's **tourist office,** Townwall St. (tel. (01304) 20 51 08), spews info on available accommodations, ferry tickets, hoverport tickets, and rental cars (open 9am-6pm). The **Charlton House Youth Hostel (HI),** 306 London Rd. (tel. (01304) 20 13 14), is a ½mi. walk from the train station. (10am-1pm. Curfew 11pm. £8.80, under 18 £5.95.) At Elmo Guest House, 120 Folkestone Rd. (tel. (01304) 20 62 36), a proprietor with a calming presence offers airy rooms near the train station for £12-16. Rough it with a pallet on the floor at the YMCA, 4 Leyburne Rd. (tel. (01304) 20 61 38); it's perfect if you have a sleeping bag (men and women; no curfew; reception open 9am-noon and 5-10pm; £5 with bed and breakfast). Cheap **food** fries from dawn to dusk in the fish-and-chip shops on London Rd. and Biggin St., and a decent pub lunch can be had almost anywhere in the city center.

Trains for Dover's Priory Station (tel. (01732) 77 01 11) leave from London's Victoria, Waterloo, Cannon St., London Bridge, and Charing Cross stations approximately every 45min. (2hr., £15, return £15.60). From Victoria, express lines continue to the Western Docks Station. **Buses** run regularly from London's Victoria Coach Station; they continue to the Eastern Docks after stopping at the bus station on Pencester Rd. (tel. (01227) 24 00 24, info (01813) 58 13 33; 2¾hr., £10). Buses also make trips to Canterbury (£3). Most **ferries** sail from Eastern Docks; Stena Sealink (tel. (01233) 64 70 47 for reservations, or 24 02 80) and P&O (tel. (01233) 20 33 88) both serve Calais (return £50). **Hovercrafts** hover from the Hoverport (tel. (01304) 20 80 13; reservations 24 02 41), for Calais or Boulogne (35min.). Book a few days in advance. (Single £26, 3-day return £26, 5-day return £38.) In May 1994, the **Channel Tunnel (Chunnel)** was completed, connecting England and France. By spring 1995, the full *Eurostar* service will be operational with approximately 15 daily departures to either destination. It has yet to be determined what rail passes (BritRail or Eurail) will be accepted for the journey. Call (01233) 61 75 75 for info.

■■■ SUSSEX

Brighton The undisputed home of the "dirty weekend," Brighton sparkles with a risqué, tawdry luster all its own. According to legend, the soon-to-be King George sidled into Brighton for some hanky-panky around 1784. Having staged a fake wedding with a certain "Mrs. Jones" (Fitzherbert), he headed off to the farmhouse known today as the Royal Pavilion and the Royal rumpus began. Recently restored, the **Royal Pavilion** shimmers on Pavilion Parade, next to Old Steine (open 10am-6pm; Oct.-May 10am-5pm; £3.75, children £2.10). Around the corner stands the **Brighton Museum and Art Gallery** on Church St., featuring paintings, English pottery, and a wild deco and Art Nouveau collection. Leer at Salvador Dalí's incredibly sexy, red, pursing sofa, *Mae West's Lips.* (Open Mon.-Tues. and Thurs.-Sat. 10am-5:45pm, Sun. 2-5pm. Free. Partial wheelchair access.) At the **tourist office,** 10 Bartholomew Sq. (tel. (01273) 32 64 50), book a bed. (£2.50 plus deposit. Open Mon.-Fri. 9am-6pm, Sat. 10am-5pm, Sun. 10am-4pm; mid-July to late Aug. Mon.-Fri. same, Sat.-Sun. until 5:30; Sept.-May Mon.-Fri. 9am-5pm, Sat. 10am-5pm, Sun. 10am-4pm.) Brighton's best bets for budget lodging are its three hostels. Cheaper and shabbier B&Bs snuggle in the **Kemp Town** area, on the streets opposite Palace Pier. The **Brighton Backpackers Hostel,** 75-76 Middle St. (tel. (01273) 77 77 17), is an independent hostel run by two young English chaps at a great location. (No curfew. £9; weekly rates negotiable, usually £40 per week. 4-8 per room.) **Moonrider's Rest,** 33 Oriental Place (tel. (01273) 73 37 40) gives discounts on windsurfing and bike hire nearby (£8 per person, £45 per week; doubles £20; ask about the "pay for 3 nights, get 1 free" promotion). The **HI Youth Hostel,** Patcham Pl. (tel. (01273) 55 61 96) is a big country house with rooms that look new though they're 400 years old (£7.50, ages 16-20 £6.30; call ahead July-Aug.). Prowl "The Lanes" between North and Prince Albert St. in search of sustenance. **Food for Friends,** 17a Prince Albert St., has cheap, well-seasoned vegetarian meals (£2.50-4. Open Mon.-Sat. 9am-10pm, Sun. 9:30am-10pm). Trendy types dance at **The Escape Club,** near the pier at 10 Marine Parade. **The Queen's Arms,** 8 George St., packs an enthusiastic gay and lesbian crowd into its Sunday night cabaret. On Wednesday and Saturday nights the disco ball spins.

Trains escape regularly from London to Brighton (1¼hr., £11, day return £17.10). They depart for Brighton station (tel. (01273) 20 67 55) to other southern locales including Arundel via Ford (½hr., £4.90, day return £4.80) and Portsmouth (1½hr., £9.30). National Express **buses** go from London to Brighton (2hr., £6.75).

Arundel and Chichester A Merchant-Ivory movieset town, **Arundel** fills with wealthy Brits on holiday and white-vested, pale-thighed cricketers. **Arundel Castle** is the third oldest in Britain and seat of the Duke of Norfolk, Earl Marshal of England (open April-Oct. Sun.-Fri 11am-5pm; last entry 4pm. £4.50, students and seniors £4, children £3.50). In late August, the castle hosts the Arundel Festival—10 days of concerts, jousting, and outdoor theater. A fringe schedule offers less expensive events. For more info, call (01903) 88 36 90). Pick up a free *Town Guide* at the **tourist office,** 61 High St. (tel. (01903) 88 22 68; open Mon.-Fri 9am-5pm, Sat.-Sun. 10am-5pm; off-season Mon.-Fri. 9am-3pm, Sat.-Sun. 10am-3:30pm). If you're up for a walk, the **Warningcamp Youth Hostel (HI)** (tel. (01903) 88 22 04), 1½mi. from town, cheerfully offers a place to prop up your feet. (Lockout 10am-5pm. Curfew 11pm. £7.15, under 18 £5. Kitchen. Open April-Aug; Sept.-Oct. and March Tues.-Sat.) Otherwise, prepare to pay at least £14 for B&B along the River Arun. Locals frequent **Belinda's,** 13 Tarrant St., off High St.; a barn on the 1560 town map, its herds today consume steak and kidney pie (£4.50; open Tues.-Sat. 9am-5:30pm, Sun. 11am-5:30pm). **Trains** leave London's Victoria Station for Arundel (1¼hr., day return £12.30-14.10). Most other train and bus routes require connections at Littlehampton to the south or Barnham to the east.

After centuries of confinement within the remains of Roman walls, the citizens of **Chichester** seem peculiarly content with their lot, basking in the shade of the immense Norman cathedral and meandering around Market Cross in the town's center. The **Cathedral,** begun in 1091, has a Chagall stained-glass window. (Open 7:40am-7pm, in winter until 5pm. £1 donation encouraged. Wheelchair accessible.) The **Roman Palace** in nearby Fishbourne is the largest Roman residence yet excavated in Britain. Fishbourne is an easy walk from Chichester; go west along Westgate, which becomes Fishbourne Rd. (the A259) for 1½mi., or take bus 700 or 701 from Chichester center. (Palace open May-Sept. 10am-6pm; March-April and Oct. 10am-5pm; Feb. and Nov.-Dec. 10am-4pm; Jan. Sun. only 10am-4pm. £3.40, students and seniors £2.70.) The **tourist office,** South St. (tel. (01243) 77 58 88, fax 53 94 49; open Mon.-Sat. 9:15am-5:15pm; April-Sept. also Sun. 10am-4pm), has a 24hr. computer information guide listing vacancies. Rooms for under £15 are virtually nonexistent here. **Hedgehogs,** 45 Whyke Lane (tel. (01243) 78 00 22), is run by affable owners with an enthusiastic hound named Sooty (£16-17). Camping is available at **Southern Leisure Centre,** Vinnetrow Rd. (tel. (01243) 78 77 15), a 5min. walk southeast of town. (£5 per tent, £1.25 per person. Open April-Oct.) **Noble Pot,** 3 Little London off East St., crouches in 200-year-old wine cellars, serving great food at low prices. (Open Mon.-Sat. noon-2:30pm, Mon.-Thurs. 5:30-11pm, Fri.-Sat. 5:30-midnight.)

Trains run to and from London's Victoria Station (1½hr., day return £13.40); Brighton (1hr., day return £6.10), and Portsmouth (40min., day return £3.80). National Express **buses** run less frequently to London (return £12.25); Coastline buses serve Brighton (bus 700, 2hr., £2.90) and Portsmouth (bus 700, 1hr., £2.50).

The bus station (tel. (01243) 78 32 51) lies diagonally across from the train station (tel. (01243) 20 67 55) on Southgate.

■■■ HAMPSHIRE

Portsmouth 1994 marked both the 50th anniversary of D-Day's launching from Portsmouth and the 900th birthday of this bawdy king of the British maritime. Henry VIII's **Mary Rose** set sail from Portsmouth in 1545 only to keel over before the monarch's eyes, not to be raised from its watery grave until 1982 (open 10am-5:30pm, Nov.-Feb. 10am-5pm; wheelchair access). Admiral Nelson's flagship **HMS Victory** won the Battle of Trafalgar against the French and Spanish in 1805 (open 10am-4:50pm; Nov.-Feb. 10:30am-4:20pm). Entrance to the **Historic Dockyard** is free (open 10am-7pm; March-June and Sept.-Oct. 10am-6pm; Nov.-Feb. 10am-5:30pm). But the ships are worth the admission expense (to one ship £4.75, seniors £4.25, students and children £3.50; two ships £9, £8, £6.50).

Portsmouth's **tourist office** is on The Hard (tel. (01705) 82 67 22), right next to the entrance to historic ships (open 9:30am-5:45pm). **Trains** from London's Waterloo station stop at both Portsmouth and Southsea station ("town station") and at Portsmouth harbor station (tel. (01703) 22 93 93, 1½hr., day return £15.70). National Express **buses** run from London (2½hr., £12.25). Moderate **B&Bs** clutter Southsea, a contiguous town 1½mi. east along the coast. Cheaper lodgings lie 2 or 3 blocks inland. Cosham, a bus or train ride away, harbors the **HI youth hostel**, Wymering Manor, Old Wymering Lane, Medina Rd. (tel. (01705) 37 56 61). (Lockout 10am-5pm. £7.75, under 18 £5.20. Open July-Aug. and Jan.1-4 daily; March-June Mon.-Sat.; Sept.-Nov. Tues.-Sat.; mid-Jan.-Feb. Fri.-Sat.) Mrs. Parkes presides at **Testudo House,** 19 Whitwell Rd., Southsea (tel. (01705) 82 43 24; £16). Decent **restaurants** bunch along Osborne, Palmerston, and Clarendon Rd. in the Southsea shopping district. A **Waitrose** supermarket supplies goods on Marmion Rd.

Winchester Once the axis of ecclesiastical, political, and economic power during the Dark and Middle Ages, Winchester yearns for its former days of glory. Strategically located in the center of southern England, it makes an excellent daytrip from less-expensive Salisbury or Portsmouth. **Winchester Cathedral,** at 556ft., is the longest medieval building in Europe, and **Winchester College** was founded in 1382 as England's first "public" school. (College open 10am-1pm, 2-5pm. £2, seniors, students, and children £1.50.) The **tourist office,** The Guildhall, Broadway (tel. (01962) 84 05 00 or 84 81 80), gives guided tours. (£2, children 50p. Open Mon.-Sat. 9:30am-6pm, Sun. 11am-2pm; Oct.-May Mon.-Sat. 10am-5pm.) **Trains** run to Winchester from London (1hr., £13.30-15.90), and depart for Chichester (1hr., £7.60), Portsmouth (45min., £5.50), and Bath (2hr, day return £12.50-£17.50). National Express **buses** run to London via Heathrow (2hr., £7.50-11.50) as well as to Oxford and Gatwick. Hampshire buses head to Salisbury (1½hr., £3.50), Southampton (50min., return £2.55), and Portsmouth (1½hr., return £3.50). Call the train station in Southampton (tel. (01703) 22 93 93) or the bus station (tel. (01962) 85 23 52) for all the sordid details. **B&Bs** cluster southwest of the office on Christchurch and St. Cross Rd. near Ranelagh Rd. The **HI youth hostel** is well-located at 1 Water Ln. (tel. (01962) 85 37 23). (Lockout 10am-5pm, with stringent curfew 11pm. Expect a chore or two. £6.90, under 18 £4.60. Kitchen. Open July-Aug. daily; March-June and Sept. Tues.-Sat. Call ahead.) **Mrs. P. Patton,** 12 Christchurch Rd. (tel. (01962) 85 42 72), has graceful, classy doubles. (£12.50, £10 for multiple nights.) Camp at **River Park Leisure Centre,** Gordon Rd. (tel. (01962) 86 95 25; 3-night max. stay; £6.10 per 1-2 person tent; open June-Sept.) **Restaurants** line Jewry St., and most of Winchester's many pubs serve good fare. The **Royal Oak** is another of countless English bars that claim fame as the oldest. Descend into the 900-year-old subterranean foundations.

■■■ SALISBURY AND STONEHENGE

Salisbury Cathedral rises monolithically from its grassy close to the neck-breaking height of 404ft. The free 45min. tours feature the oldest working clock in Britain. One of 4 surviving copies of *Magna Carta* rests in the **Chapter House,** to King John's eternal chagrin (open Mon.-Sat. 9:30am-4:45pm, Sun. 1-4:45pm; Nov.-Feb. Mon.-Sat. 11am-3pm, Sun. 1-3:15pm; 30p, students and seniors 20p). The folks at the **tourist office,** Fish Row (tel. (01722) 33 49 56), in the Guildhall in Market Sq., are especially helpful. (Open Mon.-Sat. 9:30am-7pm, Sun 11am-5pm; June and Sept. 9:30am-6pm, Sun. 11am-4pm; Oct.-April Mon.-Sat. 9:30am-5pm; May Mon.-Sat. 9:30am-5pm, Sun. 11am-4pm.) The **HI youth hostel** at Milford Hill House, Milford Hill (tel. (01722) 32 75 72) is surrounded by 2 acres of garden (lockout 10am-1pm; curfew 11:30pm; £11.30, under 18 £8.40; camping £4.35 per person). **Ron and Jenny Coats**, 51 Salt Lane (tel. (01722) 32 74 43), just up from the bus station, keep welcoming and clean 400-yr.-old house. (2-, 3- and 6-bed rooms. No curfew. £7.50, with breakfast £9-9.50. Sheets 80p.) **Reeve the Baker** (next to tourist office) stocks all the strolling sightseer could crave, from Cornish pasties to caterpillar meringues.

Trains depart Salisbury station (tel. (01703) 22 93 93) to Winchester (change at Southampton, 1½hr., £8); Southampton (40min., £5.50); Portsmouth (1½hr., £10) and London (£16.90-18.40). National Express **buses** run from Victoria (2½hr., £12.25; call the Salisbury bus station at (01722) 33 68 55). **Wilts and Dorset** service X4 runs from Bath, 40mi. northwest of Salisbury (2hr., £3.90); buses also drive to Stonehenge (½hr., return £3.75).

The much-touted **Stonehenge,** only 22ft. high, may initially be disappointing. Consider, however, that these geometrically-arranged gray slabs were lifted by an infinitely tedious process over many lifetimes (2800-1500 BC), representing an enduring religious and aesthetic dedication that defies modern explanation. Capture the finest view of the site from Amesbury Hill, 1½mi. up the A303. On clear Tuesdays and Fridays in winter the ropes around the stones are taken down to allow a closer view. (Open 10am-6pm; Nov.-late March 10am-4pm. £2.85, students and seniors £2.15.) **Wilts & Dorset** (tel. (01722) 33 68 55) runs buses from Salisbury center and Salisbury train station (return £3.75). The last leaves Stonehenge at 4:20pm (Sun. 3:50pm, ½hr.).

SOUTHWEST ENGLAND

Mists of legend shroud the counties of Dorset, Somerset, Devon, and Cornwall in England's **West Country.** While it is easy to lose the spirit of legend among "King Arthur" parking lots and "Mayflour" bake shops, the terrain itself is unfailingly beautiful. The sunny coast of Cornwall is particularly popular with older travelers.

British Rail **trains** from London pass through Exeter (3hr., £34) and Plymouth (3½hr.,£39), and end at Penzance (5½hr.,£46). From Edinburgh, trains roll through Bristol, Taunton, and Exeter before continuing through Plymouth to Penzance. National Express **buses** run to major points along the north coast via Bristol and to points along the south coast (including Penzance) via Exeter and Plymouth. Within the region, local bus service is less expensive and more extensive than local trains.

The longest coastal path in England, the **South West Peninsula Coast Path,** originates in Dorset and passes through South Devon, Cornwall, and North Devon, ending in Somerset; the final section, **Somerset and North Devon Coastal Path,** offers views from the highest seaside cliffs in Southwest England.

■■■ EXMOOR NATIONAL PARK

Dramatic sea-plunging cliffs, tranquil woodlands, and purple-heathered moorland cover **Exmoor,** the 265 sq. mile national park on the north coast of England's south-western peninsula. Access is made easy by frequent buses and trains from Plymouth, Bristol, and London to Barnstaple and Minehead, Exmoor's western and eastern gateways. Once you reach the outskirts of the park, exploring its innards by public transport is a nightmare; the meager offerings of the area's sundry bus companies have been collected in a booklet available at the tourist and park offices. The park is best toured on foot (on the **Somerset and North Devon Coast Path**) and by bike (on the **coastal path** that follows the ghost of the Barnstaple railroad).

Stop at one of the many **National Park Information Centres** to pick up detailed Ordnance Survey maps (about £4) and the free *Exmoor Visitor,* an annual park publication that includes a map and a detailed list of accommodations. The headquarters is at the **Dulverton Heritage Centre,** Guild Hall, Dulverton (tel. (01398) 238 41), and handles all postal inquiries. Other centers are at **Combe Martin** (tel. (01271) 88 33 19), **County Gate** (tel. (015987) 321), **Dunster** (tel. (01643) 82 18 35), and **Lynmouth** (tel. (01598) 525 09). Additionally, there are **tourist offices** in **Barnstaple** (tel. (01271) 38 85 83), **Ilfracombe** (tel. (01271) 86 30 01), **Lynmouth and Lynton** (tel. (01598) 522 25), and **Minehead** (tel. (01643) 70 26 24).

Little villages (some hundreds of years old) interrupt the coastal path about every 15 miles; B&Bs line the streets. **HI youth hostels,** practically all with a lockout (10am-5pm), a curfew (11pm-midnight), and kitchen and laundry facilities, string out along the path in **Crowcombe Heathfield** (tel. (019847) 249; £6.50, under 18 £4.35; open mid-July to Aug.; March to mid July Fri.-Sun.), **Exford** (tel. (0164383) 288; £7.75, under 18 £5.20; open July-Aug. daily; April-June and Sept. Mon.-Sat.; Jan.-March and Oct.-Nov. Tues.-Sat.), **Ilfracombe** (tel. (01271) 653 37; £6.30, ages 16-20 £5.10; open July-Aug. daily; April-June and Sept. Mon.-Sat.) and **Minehead** (tel. (01643) 70 25 95; £7.15, under 18 £4.75; open July-Aug. daily; April-June Mon.-Sat.; Sept.-Oct. Tues.-Sat). Campsites are easy to find along the coastal road, but be sure to ask the owner's permission.

■■■ DARTMOOR NATIONAL PARK

The lush, green forests and windy moors of the Dartmoor National Park (south of Exmoor, 10 miles west of Exeter and 7 miles east of Plymouth) will make you forget how hard it was to get there. Call the **Exeter bus station** at (01392) 562 31, the **Plymouth bus station** at (01752) 22 26 66, or the Devon County Council's **Public Transportation Helpline** (tel. (01392) 38 28 00; open Mon.-Fri. 8:30am-5pm) for advice. Also be sure to grab a copy of the free Dartmoor Visitor at one of the following National Park Information Centres: **Dartmoor (Tavistock)** (tel. (01822) 61 29 38), **Ivybridge,** (tel. (01752) 89 70 35), **Okehampton** (tel. (01837) 530 20), **Newbridge** (tel. (013643) 303), **Parke Barn** (tel. (01626) 83 20 93), **Postbridge** (tel. (01822) 882 72), **Princetown** (tel. (01822) 89 04 14), and **Steps Bridge** (tel. (01647) 520 18).

Prehistoric remains are scattered about the moor around **Princetown,** the setting for the famous Sherlock Holmes tale *The Hound of the Baskervilles*. The eastern part of the park is a rugged area centered around **Hay Tor.** Dartmoor's celebrated medieval ruins at **Hound Tor,** where excavations unearthed the remains of 13th-century huts and longhouses, lie 2 miles north of Hay Tor village. **Dartmoor Letterboxes,** each complete with an inkpad, rubber stamp, and visitors book, are scattered about the moors, though finding them is hardly elementary, my dear Watson. (Collect as many different stamps as possible; cluebooks available.)

B&B signs frequently hang in pubs and farmhouses along the roads; the less adventurous can check the *Dartmoor Visitor*. Both Dunsford village and Yelverton have HI hostels, **Steps Bridge** (tel. (01647) 524 35; £6.50; April-June and Sept. £5.90; open July-Aug.; April-June and Sept. Thurs.-Tues.) and **Bellever** (tel. (01822)

882 27; £7.75; open July-Aug.; April-June and Sept.-Oct. Mon.-Sat.), respectively. If you want to camp on the open moor, ask permission before crossing or camping on private land.

■■■ PLYMOUTH

The blackened shell of **Charles Church,** destroyed by an incendiary bomb in March of 1941, stands in the middle of the Charles Cross traffic circle half a block east of the Plymouth bus station. The roofless walls are Plymouth's memorial to her citizens killed in the Blitz; grass grows where the altar used to stand. However, the harbor from which both Sir Francis Drake and the *Mayflower* began their famous voyages from Plymouth's harbor remains untouched, now lined with restored Elizabethan buildings, a *Mayflower* passenger list, and the "journey through time" of the **Plymouth Dome,** which deploys the latest technology to revive the stench of Elizabethan England (open 9am-6pm; £3.40, seniors £2.70).

The **tourist office,** Island House, 9 The Barbican (tel. (01752) 26 48 49) hocks piles of overpriced pamphlets; city map £1 (open Mon.-Sat. 9am-5pm, Sun. 10am-4pm). Low-priced B&Bs line Citadel Rd. and Athenaeum St., between the north end of Royal Parade and the Hoe; prices run from £10 to £16. The **HI youth hostel,** Devonport Rd., Stoke (tel. (01752) 56 21 89), 2mi. from the city center offer spacious rooms in a former banker's mansion. Take bus 14, 14A, 15 or 15A from Royal Parade to Molesworth Rd., then go left onto Devon port, pass through Stoke Village and the hostel is on your left. (Lockout 10am-4pm; Sept.-June 10am-1pm. Curfew 11pm. £7.75. Breakfast £2.60. Evening meals £3.90.) **Cap'n Jaspers,** a stand by the Barbican side of the Harbor, sells local catch to sea-salts and schools of tourists (open Mon.-Sat. 6:30am-11:45pm, Sun. 10am-11:45pm). **Trains** run hourly to London's Paddington station, Exeter, Bristol, and Penzance. National Express **buses** serve London, Exeter, and Bristol. **Brittany Ferries** run from **Millbay Docks** (tel. (01752) 22 13 21) to **Roscoff, France** and **Santander, Spain**.

■■■ THE CORNISH COAST

Penzance and St. Ives The largest town on Cornwall's Penwith peninsula, **Penzance** manages to combine Cornish Market Town and Mediterranean Resort. A stone sailor greets visitors to the **Maritime Museum** halfway down chapel St. (open June-Oct. Mon.-Sat. 10am-5pm; £1.50, children £0.75). A few hundred yards off the coast at Marazion is the **St. Michael's Mount** monastery (tel. (01736) 71 05 07), accessible by ferry (open April-Oct. Mon.-Fri. 10:30am-5:45pm, most weekends during summer and clement days during winter; to island £3.) Penzance's **rail station** (tel. (01872) 762 44), **bus station** (tel. (01736) 660 55), and **tourist office** (tel. (01736) 622 07) stand conveniently together in the same square, adjacent to both the harbor and the town. The **HI youth hostel,** Castle Horneck (tel. (01736) 626 66), provides barracks-style accommodation on iron-framed beds in what was formerly a gracious 18th-century mansion (reception open 5-11pm; lockout 10am-5pm; £8.70). **The Turk's Head,** 46 Chapel St., provides delicious food in a 13th-century pub. In the 17th century, a smuggler's tunnel allegedly wound from the harbor to the inn. (Open Mon.-Sat. 11am-2:30pm and 6-10pm, Sun. noon-2:30pm and 7-10pm. Lunch £4-5, seafood dinners from £5, pricey drinks.)

Ten miles north of Penzance, the peaked roofs and breathtaking views of **St. Ives** grant a partial reprieve from the commercialization of neighboring towns. Peaked roofs line the hillside and brazen seagulls divebomb toward the harbor. The **tourist office** is in the Guildhall at Street-an-Pol (tel. (01736) 79 62 97; open Mon.-Sat. 9am-5:30pm, closed in winter). **Trains** run daily to St. Erth, connecting to Penzance (£2.60). Three **buses** per hour run from Penzance (daily; off-season Mon.-Sat.). Although the closest youth hostel and YMCA to St. Ives are in Penzance, **B&Bs** line every alley for £13 and up. Prices are usually lower for rooms farther from the water

GREAT BRITAIN

and higher up the gusty hillside. Try **Clodgy View** and **West Place** for fine sea views. B&Bs also cluster on **Park Avenue** and **Tregenna Terrace.** Camping is abundant in Hayle. Try **Trevalgan Camping Park** (tel. (01736) 79 64 33), with laundry and cooking facilities, and access to the coastal path. Miniscule **Ferrell's Bakery,** at 15 Fore St. (tel. (01736) 79 77 03), bakes a delicious version of the Cornish pasty (PASS-tee). (Open Mon.-Sat. 9am-5pm).

Falmouth Two spectacular castles guard the bland town of Falmouth which reclines along the Penryn River next to the world's third-largest natural harbor. **Pendennis Castle,** built by Henry VIII to keep French frigates out of Falmouth, now features a walk-through the diorama (open 10am-6pm, Nov.-March 10am-4pm; £2.10). The **tourist office** in Falmouth is located at 28 Killigrew St. (tel. (01326) 31 23 00; open Mon.-Thurs. 8:45am-5:15pm, Fri. 8:45am-4:45pm, Sat. 9am-5pm; Oct.-March closed Sat). The **HI youth hostel,** Pendennis Castle (tel. (01326) 31 14 35) is a 30min. walk from town ending with an uphill hike by the sea, but after 6pm, guests have the star-shaped castle to themselves (reception open 8:30-10am, 5-6:45pm, 8-10:30pm; curfew 11pm; £8.70, Sept.-Jun. £7.75; breakfast £2.60, dinner £3.90; open daily July-Aug.; Sept.-June Mon.-Sat.). **St. Mawes Castle,** a 20min. ferry ride from Falmouth to the village of St. Mawes, was built by Henry VIII to blow holes through any Frenchman the gunners of Pendennis spared (open daily 10am-6pm, Nov.-March Wed.-Sun. 10am-4pm; £1.35). Ferries leave from the Prince of Wales Pier and Customs House Quay (every ½ hr., Sun. every hr., in winter every hr., return £3).

Newquay "Surf City" is an outpost of surfer subculture, an enclave of neon youth in a region of blue-haired bus tours. The town overlooks six beaches, each with its own particular crowd and character. The town's **tourist office** sits atop Marcus Hill (tel. (01637) 87 13 45; open Mon.-Sat. 9am-6pm, Sun. 10am-5pm, shortened hours in winter). All **trains** to Newquay run through Par off the main London-Penzance line. National Express **buses** run from Plymouth via Bodmin, St. Austell, and St. Ives. Sack out at the **HI youth hostel,** Alexandra Court, Narrowcliff (tel. (01637) 87 63 81; £8.70, children £5.80; open daily April-Aug.), or at the more cramped and centrally located **Towan Beach Backpackers,** 15 Beachfield Ave. (tel. (01637) 87 46 68; £5). The restaurants in Newquay pour tea and pasties into tourist who want a quick, bland, and costly fill-up. Keep your eye out for signs advertising three-course "early bird" specials. **Food for Thought** on Beachfield Ave. offers take-away California-style salads, sandwiches, and meat subs, all for under £1.50 (open 8:30am-10pm). Newquay is notorious for its after-hours activities; even stores extend their hours well into the night. Almost every hotel offers some type of dancing, and innocuous doorways by day open up onto flashy clubs by night.

HEART OF ENGLAND

■■■ OXFORD

Shrouded in 800 years of tradition, Oxford shook off those dusty cloths and found itself a city. Unfortunately, a measure of mayhem, squealing bus brakes, and rattling bicycle chains have forced directors of BBC dramas to shoot Oxford's "dreaming spires" from very select camera angles.

ORIENTATION AND PRACTICAL INFORMATION

Queen, High, St. Aldates, and Cornmarket Streets intersect at right angles in **Carfax,** the town center, surrounded by the colleges; bus and train stations lie to the west.

Tourist Office: St. Aldates Chambers, St. Aldates St. (tel. 72 68 71, after hours 25 26 64). A pamphleteer's paradise. *Welcome to Oxford* (£1) is the official guide; *Vade Mecum* (£1), put out by Oxford undergrads, includes a helpful list of restaurants. Accommodations list 40p, comprehensive map 70p. Books rooms for £2.50 and a 10% deposit. Oxbridge Blackcurrant Conserve £2.40 per jar. *Bureau de Change.* Open Mon.-Sat. 9am-5pm, Sun. 10am-3:30pm.

Currency Exchange: Banks crowd in on Carfax. **Barclays,** 54 Cornmarket St. (tel. 791 33). Open Mon.-Fri. 9:30am-4:30pm, Wed. 10am-5:30pm, Sat. 10am-5pm.

American Express: Keith Bailey Travel Agency, 99 St. Aldates St. (tel. 79 00 99). Client mail held. Open Mon., Wed.-Fri. 9am-5:30pm, Tues. 9:30am-5:30pm, Sat. 9am-5pm.

Post Office: 102/104 St. Aldates St. (tel. 81 47 83). Open Mon.-Fri. 9am-5:30pm, Sat. 9am-12:30pm. **Postal Code:** OX1 1ZZ.

Telephones: City Code: 01865.

Trains: Botley Rd., west of Carfax. Travel Centre open Mon.-Fri. 8am-7:30pm, Sat. 8am-6pm, Sun. 11am-6pm. Station open Mon.-Fri. 5:50am-8pm, Sat. 6:50am-8pm, Sun. 8am-8pm. Intercity trains run from Paddington (1hr., day return £12.40, period return £16.40).

Buses: Gloucester Green. **Oxford Tube** (tel. 77 22 50), **Oxford CityLink** (tel. 71 13 12, 77 22 50 for timetable), and **National Express** (tel. 79 15 79). **Carfax Travel,** 138 High St. (tel. 72 6 172), books for National Express, British Rail, and ferries. Open Mon.-Fri. 9am-5pm, Sat. 9am-1pm. Oxford Tube sends buses to Grosvenor Gardens in London (1½ hr., day return £6, students, children, and seniors £5.50). Oxford CityLink shuttles between Oxford and Heathrow (1hr., day return £10) and between Oxford and Gatwick (2 hr., day return £10).

Crises: Samaritans, 123 Iffley Rd. (tel. 72 21 22). Phone 24hrs.; drop in 8am-10pm. **Drug and Alcohol Hotline** (tel. 74 98 00). 24hrs. **Rape Crisis** (tel. 72 62 95). Open Mon.-Tues., Thurs. 7-9pm, Wed. 4-6pm, Sun. 6-8pm.

Gay Switchboard: tel. 79 39 99. Mon.-Tues., Fri., and Sun. 7-9pm. **Oxford Lesbian Line,** tel. 24 23 33. Wed. 7-10pm.

Pharmacy: For late-night pharmacies, check the weekly Rota Service listings on pharmacy doors around town.

Hospital: John Radcliffe Hospital, Woodstock Rd. (tel. 74 11 66). Take bus 10.

Emergencies: Dial 999. **Police:** St. Aldates and Speedwell St. (tel. 26 60 00).

ACCOMMODATIONS, CAMPING, AND FOOD

B&Bs line the main roads out of town, all of them a 15-20min. walk from Carfax. You'll find cheaper B&Bs on Iffley Rd. and Cowley Rd., both served by buses from Carfax. Expect to pay at least £15-18 per person, and book ahead.

HI youth hostel, Jack Straw's Lane, Headington (tel. 629 97). Catch any minibus departing from the post office south of Carfax (every 15min., last bus 11:10pm, 55p). Remote but well-equipped, with showers, kitchen, and food shop. Camping in backyard. Lockout 10am-1pm. Curfew 11:30pm (but night guard on duty to let in stragglers). £8.70, under 18 £5.80.

Bravalla, 242 Iffley Rd. (tel. 24 13 26). Sunny rooms hung with soothing, nonintrusive floral patterns and pastels. Dining room has glass walls. Singles £18-20, doubles with bath £36-42. If full, the proprietress will help find a room elsewhere.

Whitehouse View, 9 Whitehouse Rd. (tel. 72 16 26), off Abingdon Rd. Only 10min. from Carfax. Size and decor of the rooms vary greatly; ask to see rooms if you can. Solicitous proprietors and excellent breakfasts. Doubles with TV £17-18.

Old Mitre Rooms, 48 Turl St. (tel. 27 98 21). Lincoln College dorm rooms with authentic ripped-down poster decor. 1 bathroom for every 6 people. Continental breakfast. Singles £18. Doubles £35.20, with bath £38. Open July-early Sept. Inquire at the Mitre Pub and Restaurant at the corner of Turf and High St.

Camping: Oxford Camping International, 426 Abingdon Rd. (tel. 24 65 51), behind the Texaco Station. 129 nondescript sites on a manicured lawn. Laundry and warm showers. 1 person £3.75, 2 people £5.15, car £1.60 extra.

Oxford virtually explodes with restaurants and cheap cafés to distract students from disagreeable college food. For fresh produce, deli, and baked goods, visit the **Covered Market** between Market St. and Carfax (open Mon.-Sat. 8am-5:30pm). **The Nosebag,** 6-8 Michael's St., serves heaping plates of salad and meat served cafeteria-style for under £5, £6.50 at dinner (open Mon. 9:30am-5:30pm, Tues.-Thurs. 9:30am-10pm, Fri.-Sat. 9:30am-10:30pm, Sun. 9:30am-9pm). For spicy Thai food and an extensive vegetarian menu, head for **Chiang Mai,** in an alley at 130A High St. (entrees £4.30-6.50; open Mon.-Sat. noon-2:30pm, 6-11pm). **Parmenters,** 58 High St., near Magdalen College, serves mighty sandwiches to take away (open Mon.-Fri. 8:30am-5:30pm, Sat.-Sun. 9am-5:30pm). Hordes of England's finest stuff themselves with sandwiches with a wide variety of fillings at **Heroes,** Ship St. (open Mon.-Fri 8am-7pm, Sat. 8:30am-5pm, Sun. 10am-5pm; breakfast 8am-11am).

SIGHTS AND ENTERTAINMENT

A tour of Oxford University, founded in 1167, begins at the college with the grandest quad and the most distinguished and obnoxious students, **Christ Church** (open Mon.-Sat. 9:30am-5:30pm, Sun. noon-5:30pm; £2.50, students and seniors £1), whose **Picture Gallery** collects Italian primitives and Dutch paintings (open Mon.-Sat. 10:30am-1pm and 2-5:30pm, Sun. 2-5:30pm; Oct.-March, closes at 4:30pm. £1, students 50p). **Merton College,** off Merton St., features a fine garden, and the college's 14th-century library holds the first printed Welsh *Bible.* **Magdalen College** is traditionally considered Oxford's handsomest. Its spiritual patron is probably alumnus Oscar Wilde; the place has always walked on the flamboyant side. (Open July-Sept. 11am-6pm; other months Mon.-Fri. 2-6pm, Sat.-Sun. noon-6pm. £1.50, children and seniors £1.) **New College** has become one of Oxford's most prestigious.

Turn up Catte St. to the **Bodleian Library,** Oxford University's principal reading and research library, which does not lend out its over 6 million books. Across Broad St. you can browse more freely at **Blackwell's,** the famous bookstore. The **Sheldonian Theatre,** set beside the Bodleian, is the Roman-style home of the graduation ceremonies (open Mon.-Sat. 10am-12:45pm and 2-4:45pm; Nov.-Feb. until 3:45pm. 50p, children 25p). The **Ashmolean Museum,** Beaumont St., was Britain's first public museum, and brandishes an outstanding collection of European art (open Tues.-Sat. 10am-4pm, Sun. 2-4pm; free). By far the most self-indulgent of Oxford's neighborhoods is the five blocks of **Cowley Road** near the Magdalen Bridge roundabout, a fascinating clutter of alternative lifestyles, Marxist bookstores, junk shops, and scruffy ethnic restaurants.

Music at Oxford is a particularly cherished art; try to attend a concert or a service at one of the colleges, or a performance at the **Holywell Music Rooms.** The **Jericho Tavern,** at the corner of Walton and Jericho St., features local rock and jazz bands (open Mon.-Sat. 11am-3pm and 6-11pm; cover charge £3.50-5). A favorite pastime in Oxford is **punting** on the River Thames (known in Oxford as the Isis) or on the River Cherwell. The university celebrates **May Day** at the beginning of May, and **Eights Week** at the end of May.

Pubs far outnumber colleges in Oxford, and many consider them the city's prime attraction. *Good Pubs of Oxford* (£1.99 at bookstores and the tourist office) is an indispensable guide to the town's beer dungeons. Try the **Turf Tavern,** 4 Bath Pl., with extensive outdoor seating by the ruins of the old city wall, and many beers, punches, ciders, and country wines. At **The Bear,** Alfred St., 5000 ties from England's brightest and most boastful cover every flat surface but the floor. Sit on the terrace at the **Head of the River,** Folly Bridge, and watch the Sweet Thames run softly by.

■ NEAR OXFORD

The largest private home in England (also one of the loveliest), **Blenheim Palace,** features rambling grounds designed by Capability Brown, a lake, and a fantastic garden center. Whilst attending a party here, Churchill's mother gave birth to the future cigar smoker and Prime Minister in a closet. (Palace open mid-March to Oct. 10:30am-4:45pm. Grounds open 9am-5pm. £6.90, children £3.30, includes a boat trip on the lake.) Blenheim sprawls in **Woodstock**, 8mi. north of Oxford on the A34; **Thames Transit** (tel. (01865) 72 70 00) runs buses from bay 2 at the Oxford bus station (2hr.; 25min.). **Spires and Shires** (tel. (01865) 25 17 85) offers daily bus tours to Blenheim from Broad St. and the Oxford train station (2 per day, both in the morning; £7.50, children £5). Geoffrey Chaucer once lived here, and Winston Churchill is buried in the nearby village churchyard of **Bladon.**

■■■ COTSWOLDS

Stretching across the west of England from the River Humber to the Dorset coast, the rolling hills of the Cotswolds, origin of the famed Cotswold stone, are flecked with tiny villages dating from the Saxon times. The hills lie mostly in Gloucester-shire, bounded by **Banbury** in the northeast, **Bradford-upon-Avon** in the south-west, **Cheltenham** in the north, and **Malmesbury** in the south. Local roads are perfect for biking; the frequent villages make ideal watering holes. Cotswold Way, spanning just over a 100 miles, should appeal to those interested in hiking the hills and staying in unspoiled villages. The *Cotswold Way Handbook* (£1) lists B&Bs along the Way. Campsites congregate close to Cheltenham; the villages Bourton-on-the-Water, Stow-on-the-Wold, and Moreton-on-the-Marsh also provide convenient places to bivouac. Get the annually updated *Cotswolds and Gloucestershire Cara-van and Camping Guide* free from local tourist offices.

While they ought not to be omitted from any itinerary, the Cotswolds are not eas-ily accessible by public transportation. Major cities within the area (Cheltenham, Bath, Gloucester, and Cirencester) can be reached by train or bus; the smaller vil-lages are linked by a bus service that is infrequent and slow. Snag the inclusive and far-reaching *Connection* timetable free from all area bus stations and tourist offices.

Stow-on-the-Wold, Winchcombe, and Cirencester Stow-on-the-Wold flourished with the sheep trade and erected buildings of honey-colored stone. A **HI youth hostel** (tel. (01451) 304 97) occupies the center of town (£6.50, under 18 £4.35; open March-Oct. daily; Nov.-Dec. and Feb. Fri.-Sun.). West of Stow-on-the-Wold and 6mi. north of Cheltenham on the A46, **Sudeley Castle** dominates **Winchcombe.** Regular falconry shows are held here. (Open April-Oct. noon-5pm. £4.75.) Archaeologists have found prehistoric tracks and some 70 habitation sites across the Cotswolds. **Belas Knap,** a 4000-yr. burial mound, stands about 1½mi. southwest of Sudeley Castle.

The Cotswolds contain some of the best examples of Roman settlements in Brit-ain—most notably in **Cirencester,** the site of "Corinium," founded in 49 AD. The **Corinium Museum,** Park St., houses a formidable collection of Roman artifacts (open Mon.-Sat. 10am-5pm, Sun. 2-5pm; Oct.-March Tues.-Sat. 10am-5pm, Sun. 2-5pm; £1.25, students and seniors £1). On Fridays, the town turns into a rollicking market. **Duntisbourne Abbots hostel (HI)** (tel. (01285) 82 16 82) is 5mi. outside town (£7.15, under 18 £4.75; open March-early Nov. Mon.-Sat.; Dec. 24-28 daily). The **tourist office** is in Corn Hall, Market Pl. (tel. (01285) 65 41 80).

Cheltenham The Cotswold's largest town epitomizes elegance and proudly possesses the only naturally alkaline water in Great Britain. Enjoy the diuretic and laxative effects of the waters at the **Town Hall** (open Mon.-Fri. 9am-1pm and 2:15pm-5pm; free). The **Gustav MacCallum Holst Birthplace Museum,** 4 Clar-ence Rd., presents an interesting picture of middle-class family life in the Regency and Victorian periods (open Tues.-Sat. 10am-4:20pm; £1.50, children 50p). The **tourist office,** 77 Promenade (tel. (01242) 52 28 78), lies one block east of the bus station (open June-Sept. Mon.-Fri. 9:30am-6pm, Sat. 9:30am-5pm; July-Aug. also Sun. 10am-4pm; Oct.-May Mon.-Sat. 9:30am-5pm). **Trains** (tel. (01452) 52 95 01) run reg-ularly to London (2½hr., £22.50), Bristol (1¾hr., £5.70), Bath (1½hr., £9.50), and

GREAT BRITAIN

Exeter (2hr., £21). Frequent **buses** (tel. (01242) 58 41 11) run to London (3hr., £16), Bath (2½hr., £7.50), and Exeter (3½hr., £17). Four miles north of town, the **Cleeve Hill hostel (HI)** (tel. (01242) 67 20 65), provides bunks (£6.50; under 18 £4.35; open April-Sept. Tues.-Sun.). Both men and women can stay at the **YMCA,** Victoria Walk (tel. (01242) 52 40 24), for £12.25. Supermarkets and the aptly named **Fruity Fruit Store** are strung along High St. and Clarence St.

■■■ STRATFORD-UPON-AVON

Die-hard fans should purchase the joint ticket to the five **Shakespeare properties** (£7.50, students £7). The least-crowded way to pay homage is to visit his grave in **Holy Trinity Church,** Trinity St. (50p, students 30p). Start your walking tour at **Shakespeare's Birthplace** on Henley St., half period recreation and half Shakespeare life-and-work exhibition (open Mon.-Sat. 9am-5:30pm, Sun. 10am-5:30pm; Nov.-Feb. Mon.-Sat. 9:30am-4pm, Sun. 10:30am-4pm; £2.60). **New Place,** Chapel St., was Stratford's hippest home when Shakespeare bought it in 1597 (open Mon.-Sat. 9:30am-5:30pm, Sun. 10:30am-5:30pm; Nov.-Feb. Mon.-Sat. 10am-4pm, Sun. 1:30-4pm; £1.80). Shakespeare's eldest daughter once lived in the impressively furnished **Hall's Croft,** Old Town Rd. (same hours and admission).

All the world's a stage (and you a player) at the **Royal Shakespeare Company Collection** museum (open Mon.-Sat. 9:15am-8pm, Sun. noon-5pm. £2, students and seniors £1.50). Backstage tours allow you to fiddle with the props and costumes. (Tours 1:30 and 5:30pm. £4, students £3.) The well-respected **Shakespeare Centre,** Henley St., has a library, a bookshop (across the street), and archives open to students and scholars. The center also holds madrigal concerts and hosts a fine poetry festival in July and August. (For festival info, call (01789) 20 40 16. Concerts £1-£1.50. Poetry readings Sun. at 8pm; tickets £3.50-5.50.) **Anne Hathaway's Cottage,** the birthplace of Shakespeare's wife, lies about a mile from Stratford in Shottery (open Mon.-Sat. 9am-5:30pm, Sun. 10am-5:30pm; Nov.-Feb. Mon.-Sat. 9:30am-4pm, Sun. 6:30am-4pm; £2.20, children £1). **Mary Arden's House,** the farmhouse restored in a style that a 19th-century entrepreneur determined to be that of Shakespeare's mother, stands 4mi. from Stratford in Wilmcote (open Mon.-Sat. 9:30am-5pm, Sun. 10:30am-5pm; Nov.-Feb. Mon.-Sat. 10am-4pm, Sun. 1:30-4pm; £3). After enduring the cultural-commodity fetishism, seek solace in a performance by the sublime **Royal Shakespeare Company** (tel. (01789) 29 56 23; seats £4.50-41). The **Swan Theatre** RSC productions of plays by Shakespeare's contemporaries (tickets £8-25, standing room £4.50). **The Other Place** is the RSC's newest branch, producing modern dramas (£8-14).

Practical Information, Accommodations, and Food The **tourist office** is located at Bridgefoot (tel. (01789) 29 31 27; open Mon.-Sat. 9am-6pm, Sun. 11am-5pm; Oct.-March Mon.-Sat. 9am-5pm). Stratford lies 2¼hrs. from London Euston by rail or by the bus/rail **Shakespeare Connection** (2hr., £22.50, round-trip £21). Only the **Shakespeare Connection** (tel. (01789) 29 44 66) operates at night after plays. **National Express buses** run to and from London's Victoria Station (3hr., day return £13.75). Buy National Express tickets at the tourist office.

Guest houses (£14-18) line Grove Rd., Evesham Pl., Evesham Rd., and Shipston and Banbury Rd. across the river. The tourist office will put you in touch with local farms that take paying guests (£12.50-16); they also book B&B accommodations. The **HI youth hostel,** Hemmingford House, Wellesbourne Rd., Alveston (tel. (01789) 297 093), is 2mi. from Stratford (reception open 7am-midnight; curfew midnight; £12, under 18 £8.80; breakfast included). Enjoy **Nando's,** 18 Evesham Pl. (tel. and fax (01789) 20 49 07) delightful owners and homey rooms with TVs (£16.50-20.50 per person; singles £19). Find refreshing lodgings at **Field View Guest House,** 35 Banbury Rd. (tel. (01789) 29 26 94), an immaculate country home (singles £14, doubles £28). Camp at **Avon Caravan Park,** Warwick Rd. (tel. (01789) 29 34 38), 1mi. east of town on the A439. (£4.50, £1.50 per additional person. Showers. Open March-Oct.) **Café Natural,** 10 Greenhill St., prepares elaborate vegetarian foods. (Tues. 10% discount for students and seniors. Entrees £2.50-3.15. Open Tues.-Sat. 9am-4:30pm.) **Vintner Bistro and Café Bar,** 5 Sheep St., serves satisfying salads and delightful desserts. (£4.75-4.95. Open Mon.-Sat. 10:30am-11pm, Sun. 10:30am-10:30pm.)

■■■ BATH

Immortalized by Fielding, Smollet, Austen, and Dickens, Bath once stood only second to London as a social capital of England. Queen Anne's visit to the natural hot springs here in 1701 established Bath as one of the great meeting places for British artists, politicians, and intellectuals of the 18th century. Sewer-diggers uncovered the **Roman Baths** in 1880, and recent excavation has yielded a splendid model of Roman engineering. (Open March-July and Sept. 9am-6pm; Aug. also 8-10pm; Nov.-Feb. Mon.-Sat. 9am-5pm, Sun. 10am-5pm. Last admission ½hr. before closing. £5. Partial wheelchair access.) Next door, the 15th-century **Bath Abbey** seems an anomaly among Bath's first-century Roman and 18th-century Georgian sights (open 9am-6pm; £1). Walk up Gay St. to **The Circus,** which has attracted illustrious residents for two centuries; blue plaques mark the houses of Thomas Gainsborough, William Pitt, and David Livingstone. Proceed up Brock St. to **Royal Crescent** and its upended saucer of a lawn. The interior of **No. I Royal Crescent** has been painstakingly restored to a near-perfect replica of a 1770 townhouse (open Tues.-Sun. 10:30am-5pm; Nov.-Dec. until 4pm; £3, children, students, and seniors £2.50).

Pubs sit along Walcot St.; locals favor **The Bell,** where the best local bands (from rock to jazz) perform live nightly, and the trendy **Hat and Feather,** with two levels of indie and rave as well as mind-expanding light decorations. Before a pub-and-club crawl, gather at the Huntsman Inn at North Parade Passage nightly at 8pm for the **Bizarre Bath Walking Tour;** punsters lead locals and tourists alike around Bath pulling pranks for about 1¼hrs. (£3, students £2.50).

Practical Information, Accommodations, and Food The **train and bus stations** are near the south end of Manvers St. Trains make the journey London-Paddington (1½hr., single £26) and Bristol (15min., £3). National Express buses depart for London-Victoria (3hr., return £12.25), Oxford (2hr., £12.25), and Salisbury (1½hr., £4.30). From either terminal, walk up Manvers St. to the Orange Grove rotary and turn left to the efficient **tourist office** in the Abbey Churchyard (tel. (01225) 46 28 31; open Mon.-Sat. 9:30am-6pm, Sun. 10am-4pm; mid-Sept. to mid-June Mon.-Sat. 9:30am-5pm).

B&Bs (£14-17) cluster on **Pulteney Rd.** and **Pulteney Gdns**. For a more relaxed setting, continue past Pulteney Gdns. to **Widcombe Hill**. The graciously clean Italianate **youth hostel (HI),** Bathwick Hill (tel. (01225) 46 56 74) over looks the city. From N. Parade Rd., turn left onto Pulteney Rd., then right onto Bathwick Hill. A footpath takes you up the steep hill to the hostel (20min. walk). (No lockout. £8.70; Sept.-May £7.50.) **YMCA International House,** Broad St. Place (tel. (01225) 46 04 71) is heavily booked in summer. Walk under the arch and up the steps from Walcot St. across from Beaufort Hotel. (Men and women allowed. Singles £12. Doubles £22. Triples available as well. Dorm rooms with continental breakfast £9.50 per person; key deposit £5.) Savor **Mrs. Guy's** Georgian house, 14 Raby Pl. (tel. 46 51 20), with its light, cool interiors, and a modern art collection (singles £16, doubles £32).

For fruits and vegetables, visit the **Guildhall Market,** between High St. and Grand Parade (open Mon.-Sat. 9:30am-5:30pm). Splash out for cream tea (£4.25) in the palatial Victorian **Pump Room,** Abbey Churchyard (open Mon.-Sat. 10am-5pm). Scoff not at **Scoff's** lunches, served in a woody dining room on Monmouth and Westgate St. (open Mon.-Sat. 9am-5pm). **Café Retro,** at Orange Grove, offers a sophisticated atmosphere and a chic smoked chicken and orange salad (£3.90; open Mon.-Sat. 10am-10:30pm, Sun. 10am-6pm).

GREAT BRITAIN

EAST ANGLIA

The plush green farmlands and dismal watery fens of East Anglia stretch northeast from London, cloaking the counties of Cambridgeshire, Norfolk, and Suffolk. While high-tech industry modernizes the economies of Cambridge and Peterborough, the college town and cathedral city are still linked by flat fields, hedges, and stone walls. East Anglia's flat terrain and relatively low annual rainfall are a boon to bikers and hikers. The area's longest, most popular walking trails are **Peddar's Way** and **Weaver's Way**. If you plan to see a lot of the region by public transport, buy an **Anglia Rover** ticket (about £35, discount with railcard), available only at rail stations within East Anglia, good for a week's rail travel. The **Explorer** ticket (£4.50) is good for a day's travel on all Eastern Counties bus routes in East Anglia, which serve many areas not covered by British Rail; however, buses run infrequently.

■■■ CAMBRIDGE

Cambridge the university has lorded over Cambridge the town for 785 years. Competing in most everything with Oxford, Cambridge loses in age and boat races but wins on charm and spectacle; the countrified Backs on the west bank of the River Cam lend a pastoral air to the city.

ORIENTATION AND PRACTICAL INFORMATION

Cambridge, about 60 miles north of London, has two main avenues. The main shopping street starts at **Magdalene Bridge** (MAWD-lin) and becomes Bridge St., Sidney St., St. Andrew's St., Regent St., and finally Hills Rd. The other—alternately St. John's St., Trinity St., King's Parade, Trumpington St., and Trumpington Rd.—is the academic thoroughfare, with several colleges lying between it and the River Cam.

Tourist Office: Wheeler St. (tel. 32 26 40), 1 block south of the marketplace. Open Mon.-Tues. and Thurs.-Fri. 9am-6pm, Wed. 9:30am-6pm, Sat. 9am-5pm; Nov.-March closes at 5:30pm. Also open Easter-Sept. Sun. 10:30am-3:30pm. Information on Cambridge events also available at **Corn Exchange** box office (tel. 35 78 51), Corn Exchange St., opposite the tourist office.

American Express: Abbot Travel, 25 Sidney St. (tel. 35 16 36). Client mail held. Open Mon.-Tues., Thurs.-Fri. 9am-5:30pm, Wed. 9:30-5:30pm, Sat. 9am-5pm.

Post Office: 9-11 St. Andrew's St. (tel. 32 33 25). Open Mon.-Tues. and Thurs.-Fri. 9am-5:30pm, Wed. 9:30am-5:30pm, Sat. 9am-12:30pm. Poste Restante and currency. **Postal Code:** CB2 3AA.

Telephones: City Code: 01223.

Train Station: Station Rd. (tel. 31 19 99). Purchase tickets 5am-11pm. Travel Centre open Mon.-Sat. 4:30am-11pm, Sun. 6am-11pm. To get to Market Sq. from the train station, take a Cityrail Link bus (60p) or walk down Hills Road (25min.).

Bus and Coach Station: Drummer St. Station. **National Express** (tel. 46 07 11). **Cambus** (tel. 42 35 54) handles city and area service (40p-£1). Some local routes serviced by **Miller's** or **Premier** coaches. **Whippet Coaches** run daytrips from Cambridge. Travel Centre open Mon.-Sat. 8:15am-5:30pm.

Bike Rental: University Cycle, 9 Victoria Ave. (tel. 35 55 17). £7 per day, £15 per week. Cash deposit £25. Open Mon.-Sat. 9am-5:45pm.

Crisis Lines: AIDS, tel. 697 65. Open Tues.-Wed. 7:30-10pm. **Crime Victims,** tel. 630 24. **Rape Crisis,** tel. 35 83 14, 24hr. **Samaritans,** tel. 644 55.

Emergency: tel. 999; no coins required. **Police:** Parkside, (tel. 35 89 66). **Addenbrookes Hospital,** Hills Rd. (tel. 24 51 51).

ACCOMMODATIONS, CAMPING, AND FOOD

Cambridge has no shortage of rooms (albeit expensive ones) for visitors, but it's advisable to book ahead during the high season. Many of the cheap B&Bs hover around **Portugal St.** and **Tenison Rd.** Check the comprehensive list in the tourist office window, or pick up their guide to accommodations (50p).

HI youth hostel, 97 Tenison Rd. (tel. 35 46 01, fax 31 27 80), entrance on Devonshire Rd. Relaxed, welcoming atmosphere; well-equipped kitchen, laundry room, and TV lounge. Mostly 3-4-bed rooms. Small lockers in some rooms. £12, under 18 £8.80, breakfast and sleep sack included. Call in advance and arrive by 6pm.

Home from Home B&B, Mrs. Flora Miles, 39 Milton Rd. (tel. 32 35 55). Mrs. Miles graciously welcomes guests into her sunny, immaculate, well-decorated home, 15min. from bus station and city center. Singles £20. Doubles £32. Full English breakfast included. Call a few days ahead.

Warkworth Guest House, Warkworth Terrace (tel. 636 82). A charming and gracious hostess has 16 sunny rooms near the bus station. Singles £17. Doubles £30. Family £45. Breakfast included. Kitchen, laundry, telephone.

Tenison Towers, Mr. and Mrs. Madeira, 148 Tenison Rd. (tel. 56 65 11). Clean and comfy rooms located near the train station. Singles £14-18, doubles £24-28, triples £35-39, quads £44-52. Prices vary with season. Reductions for long-term stays.

Highfield Farm Camping Park, Long Rd., Comberton (tel. 26 23 08). Head west on A603 for 3mi., then left on B1046. Or take Cambus 118 from the Drummer St. station (every 45min.). Flush toilets, showers, and a washing machine. £7-8 per tent. Call ahead. Open April-Oct.

Market Square has bright pyramids of fruit and vegetables for the hungry budgetarian (open Mon.-Sat. approximately 8am-5:30pm). Students buy their gin and cornflakes at **Sainsbury's,** 44 Sidney St., the only grocery store in the middle of town. (open Mon.-Wed. 8:30am-7pm, Thurs.-Fri. 8:30am-8pm). **Rajbelash,** 36-38 Hills Rd., serves up a spectacular array of curries, *tandooris,* and *biryanis* (open noon-2:30pm and 6pm-midnight, £2.60-6.40; Sunday buffet noon-2:30pm, £6.50, children £4.50). The **Corner House Restaurant,** 9 King St., serves up generous portions for low prices (open Mon.-Fri. 11:30am-2:30pm and 5-9:30pm, Sat.-Sun. 11:30am-9:30pm). Practice your Esperanto over cappuccino at **Clown's,** 54 King St., a meeting place for foreigners, bozos, and beautiful people (open 9am-11pm).

SIGHTS AND ENTERTAINMENT

Cambridge is an architect's dream, packing some of the most breathtaking examples of English architecture into less than 1 sq. mile. If you are pressed for time, visit at least one chapel (preferably King's), one garden (try Christ's), one library (Trinity's is the most interesting), and one dining hall. Cambridge is most busy (read: most interesting) during the university's three terms: Michaelmas (Oct.-Dec.), Lent (Jan. -March), and Easter (April-June). Most of the colleges are open from 9am to 5:30pm, though virtually all are closed during exam period (mid-May to mid-June).

Cambridge's colleges stretch along the River Cam. **King's College,** on King's Parade, possesses a spectacular Gothic chapel; Rubens's magnificent *Adoration of the Magi* hangs behind the altar (college open June-Oct. Mon.-Fri. 9:30am-4:30pm, Sun. 9am-5pm; £2, students and children £1; chapel open term-time Mon.-Sat. 9:30am-3:30pm, Sun. 1:15-2:15pm and 4:45-5:15pm; free). **Trinity College,** on Trinity St., the wealthiest college in Cambridge, houses the stunning **Wren Library,** which keeps such notable treasures as A.A. Milne's handwritten manuscript of *Winnie-the-Pooh* and less momentous works such as John Milton's *Lycidas* and Wittgenstein's journals (library open Mon.-Fri. noon-2pm, free; college and library closed during exams). **Queens' College** was founded not once, but twice, and possesses the only unaltered Tudor courtyard in Cambridge (college open 1:45-4:30pm; summer vacation also 10:30am-12:45pm; closed during exams; £1). **Christ's College,** founded as "God's house" in 1448, has won fame for its gardens (open Mon.-Fri. 10:30am-12:30pm and 2-4pm; in summer Mon.-Fri. 9:30am-noon).

The splendor of the colleges is indeed distracting, but Cambridge's museums also merit attention. The **Fitzwilliam Museum,** Trumpington Rd., houses paintings by da Vinci, Michelangelo, Dürer, Monet, and Seurat (open Tues.-Fri. ground floor

GREAT BRITAIN

10am-2pm, upper floor 2-5pm, Sat. both floors 10am-5pm, Sun. both floors 2:15-5pm; free). The **Scott Polar Research Institute,** Lensfield Rd., commemorates icy expeditions with photographic and artistic accounts and equipment (open Mon.-Sat. 2:30-4pm; free).

Students drink local bitters IPA (India Pale Ale) and Abbott at the **Anchor,** Silver St., on rainy days, and **The Mill,** Mill Lane, off Silver St. Bridge, on sunny ones. The Anchor boasts live jazz bands on Tuesdays and Thursdays, and at the neighboring Mill, you can partake of a pint along the banks of the Cam while punt-and-people watching. The **Burleigh Arms,** 9-11 Newmarket Rd., serves up beer and lager to a primarily gay, lesbian, and bisexual clientele. The best source of information on student activities is the *Varsity.* Try the **Arts Cinema,** Market Passage, which screens comedy classics and undubbed foreign films (tickets £2.90-3.80; tickets £7.50-16, 50% off for student standby day of performance for certain concerts; box office open Mon.-Sat. 10am-9:15pm, Sun. 1-9:15pm). You can get an earful of concerts at the **Cambridge Corn Exchange,** at the corner of Wheeler St. and Corn Exchange, a venue for jazz, and classical concerts (box office tel. 35 78 51; open Mon.-Sat. 10am-6pm;). On a sunny afternoon, the river is almost always stocked with narrow, flat-bottomed **punts,** England's retort to the gondola. Rent one from **Scudamore's Boatyards,** at Magdalene Bridge or Silver St.; hourly rates are £6-8 for punts, rowboats, and canoes, plus a £40 cash deposit (open 9am-6pm).

■ ELY AND BURY ST. EDMUNDS

Fifteen miles north of Cambridge, **Ely** earned national tourist notoriety as the first town in England to charge admission to its **cathedral,** but the massive building and its separate stained glass museum are well worth the pence. (Cathedral open Mon.-Fri. 7:30am-6pm, Sun. 7:30am-5pm; in summer 7am-7pm. Tours Easter-Oct. Mon.-Sat. 11:15am and 2:15pm; July-Aug. also 3:15pm. Museum open March-Oct. Mon.-Sat. 10:30am-4pm, Sun. noon-3pm. £1.50, students 70p.) Trains run between Cambridge and Ely (20min., day return £3.10). Twenty-five miles southeast of Cambridge, the less-touristed streets of **Bury St. Edmunds** arrange themselves according to the original 12th-century street plan and house an exquisite **abbey flower garden.** (Abbey and gardens open 7:30am-sunset. Free.)

CENTRAL ENGLAND

The 19th century swept into central England, revolutionizing quiet village life with its industrial sandstorms; the "dark satanic mills" that William Blake foresaw indeed overran the Midlands. Manchester and Liverpool are now home to innovative music and arts scenes as well as some of the U.K.'s most vibrant nightlife while cities like Lincoln and Chester tell some of their tales in Latin.

■ ■ ■ LINCOLN

All roads in Lincoln lead to the spectacular Gothic cathedral (or so it seems). Built in the 12th century on the ruins of a Norman structure, **Lincoln Minster** was, for many centuries, the tallest building in Europe. (Open Mon.-Sat. 7:15am-8pm, Sun. 7:15am-6pm; in winter Mon.-Sat. 7:15am-6pm, Sun. 7:15am-5pm. Near-obligatory donation £2.50, students and seniors £1. Tours Mon.-Fri. 11am, 1 and 3pm; March-April and Oct.-Dec. Mon.-Fri. 11am and 2pm; Jan.-Feb. Sat. 11am and 2pm.) Roof tours (£2.50) must be booked in advance. **Lincoln Castle** still retains its Norman walls and houses the best preserved of the four copies of the *Magna Carta.* (Open Mon.-Sat. 9:30am-5:30pm, Sun. 11am-5:30pm; Nov.-March Mon.-Sat. 9:30am-4pm. Last entry ½hr. before closing. £2, students, seniors, and children £1.20.)

GREAT BRITAIN

The **main tourist office,** 9 Castle Hill (tel. (01522) 52 98 28), perches at the top of the hill near the cathedral (open Mon.-Thurs. 9am-5:30pm, Fri. 9am-5pm, Sat.-Sun. 10am-5pm; Oct.-March same weekday hrs., Sat.-Sun. 11-3pm). **Trains** (tel. (01522) 53 95 02) run to London via Newark (£30, return £31-38) and to York (1½-3½hr., £14.50, return £16.50-21.50). National Express sends **buses** (tel. (01522) 53 44 44) to London (5hr., £22, return £23-27.50).

Carline Rd. and Yarborough Rd., west of the castle and cathedral, are lined with B&Bs (£12-18). The **HI youth hostel,** 77 S. Park (tel. (01522) 52 20 76), opposite South Common at the end of Canwick Rd., is a top-notch hostel across the street from a park. (Reception closed 10am-5pm. Curfew 11pm. £7.75, under 18 £5.20. Open July-Aug. daily; April-June Mon.-Sat.; Sept.-Oct. and mid- Feb. to March Tues.-Sat.; Nov. to mid-Dec. Fri.-Sat.) Sit by the window in a house built on a medieval bridge at **Stokes High Bridge Café,** 207 High St. (£3-4 lunchtime specials 11:30am-2pm. Open Mon.-Wed. 9am-5pm, Thurs.-Sat. 9am-5:30pm.) Or down a pint and some grub at the **Lion and Snake,** 79 Bailgate, up by the cathedral. (Food served Mon.-Fri. noon-2pm and 6-8pm.) **Kiss,** Newland Ave., and **Ritzy,** Silver St., supply music and a flat surface.

■■■ PEAK NATIONAL PARK

Covering 555 sq. mi., Peak National Park lies at the southern end of the Pennines, with Manchester, Sheffield, Nottingham, and Stoke-on-Trent at its corners. Devoid of towering peaks, the area in fact derives its name from the Old English *peac,* meaning hill. Wedged between large urban centers, nature is the cardinal attraction for visitors to the Peak.

Practical Information To accommodate the pumped-up volume of human traffic, public transport and commercial bus tours move the mobs on sunny summer weekends; for a more tranquil visit, try to catch the infrequent buses to the bleaker northern moors, out of the reach of the commuter-rail lines. Although protected from development by national park status, the land is still privately owned, so be respectful and stay to designated rights-of-way. Ramblers' guidebooks and other useful publications are available at National Park Information Centres, and can be ordered by mail. Write to Peak Park Joint Planning Board, National Park Office, Aldern House, Bakewell DE4 1AE for a list of publications. For an information pack on the park, write to the Tourism Officer, Town Hall, Matlock, Derbyshire, DE4 3NN. **Information centers** in the park distribute free park-wide and regional accommodations guides; a camping guide costs 35p. The **National Park Information Centres** at **Castleton** (tel. (01433) 62 06 79), **Edale** (tel. (01433) 67 02 07), and **Fairholmes** should be helpful. You can also ask questions at area **tourist offices: Ashbourne** (tel. (01335) 343 66), **Bakewell** (tel. (01629) 81 32 27), **Buxton** (tel. (01298) 251 06), and **Matlock Bath** (tel. (01629) 550 82). There are over 20 **HI youth hostels** in the park, including **Bakewell** (tel. (01629) 81 23 13) and **Buxton** (tel. (01298) 222 87). The park authority operates seven **Cycle Hire Centres,** where you can rent a bike (£3.80 per 3hr., £6 per day; under 16 £3.80 per 3hr., £4.30 per day, £10 deposit; 10% discount for HI members and Wayfarer ticket holders; open in summer 9:30am-6pm, off-season hours vary). Call **Ashbourne** (tel. (01335) 34 31 56) for information.

Southern and Northern Peaks The **Southern Peak** is better served than the Northern Peak by buses and trains and is consequently more trampled than the its counterpart. The former spa town of **Buxton** is reliable for cheap accommodations, though it enjoys neither the pastoral scenery nor the small-town atmosphere of its more touristy neighbors. The **tourist office** (see information centers above) on the Crescent offers guided walks of the town (85p), free accommodations booking, and public transportation schedules. An **HI Hostel** (tel. (01298) 222 87) on Harpur Hill Rd. is a short walk from the city center. Like the Romans, you, too, can bathe in the mineral water now famous throughout England. Bathe as the Romans did in the **Buxton "Spa Water" Swimming Pool** (tel. (01298) 265 48; hours and prices vary). To the east lies **Bakewell,** the best base from which to explore the southern portion of the park and to eat Bakewell pudding (created when a flustered cook, trying to make a tart, poured an egg mixture over strawberry jam instead of mixing it into the dough). Try gracious Mrs. Holden's **Erica Cottage,** Butts Rd. (tel. (01629) 81 32 41), for rooms starting at £13. On Rutland Sq., **The Old Original Bakewell Pudding Shop** sells lunches and delicious desserts in a paneled restaurant above the shop (open 8:30am-9pm; Sept.-June Mon.-Thurs. 9am-6pm, Fri-Sat. 8:30am-9pm, Sun. 8:30am-6pm).

The **northern district** area contains some of the wildest and most rugged hill country in England. Cradled in the deep dale of the River Noe, with gentle, gray-green hills sweeping up on two sides, **Edale** has little in the way of civilization other than a church, café, pub, school, and nearby youth hostel. Its natural environs, however, are arguably the most spectacular in Northern England. Your tent could be your best friend in this town, where the only accommodations are at the 140-bed **HI youth hostel** (tel. (01433) 67 03 02). (Lockout 10am-5pm. Curfew 11pm. £5.70-£8.40.) Picturesque **Castleton,** in the shadow of the ruined Peveril Castle, has four caverns that are the source of the town's characteristic Blue John stone. The **Blue John Cavern** (tel. (01433) 206 38) and **Treak Cliff Cavern** (tel. (01433) 620 571) are about 1½ mi. west of town on the A625. (Blue John open 9:45am-6pm; in winter 9:45am-about 4pm; closed Jan-Feb; £4, seniors £2.50, children £2. Treak Cliff open 9:30am-5pm; Nov.-Easter 9:30am-4pm; £3.80, seniors £3, children £1.90.) Gigantic **Peak Cavern** (tel. (01433) 62 12 85) right in town, was known in the 18th century as the "Devil's Arse" and features the second-largest aperture in the world (open Easter-Oct 10am-5pm; closed Mon. in winter; £3, children and seniors £2).

■■■ MANCHESTER

Manchester recently declared itself a "nuclear-free city," and countless placards and posters reveal that the labor movement and environmentalism are the norm here. An intense cultural core and vibrant arts community pulses beneath the buffed façade, sending its rhythms across the nation and the world in the form of bands with funny names. Behind the Town Hall Extension is Manchester's jewel, the **Central Library,** one of the largest municipal libraries in Europe (open Mon.-Wed. and Fri. 10am-8pm, Sat. 10am-noon and 1-5pm). In the **Museum of Science and Industry,** on Liverpool Rd., working steam engines and looms provide a dramatic sense of the awesome speed, power, danger, and noise of Britain's industrialization (open 10am-5pm; £3.50, students, seniors, and disabled £1.50; includes entrance to all galleries for 1 day). The **City Art Galleries** consist of two adjacent buildings: the Mosely St. gallery gives a whirlwind tour of western art from 14th century Italian religious painting to modern art; the Princess St. building houses touring shows and other temporary exhibits (both open Mon.-Sat. 10am-5:45pm, Sun. 2-5:45pm; free; disabled access). The Spanish and Portuguese Synagogue turned **Jewish Museum,** 190 Cheetham Hill Rd., north of Victoria Station, traces the history of the city's sizeable Jewish community (open Mon.-Thurs. 10:30am-4pm, Sun. 10:30am-5pm; £1.75, seniors, students, and children £1, disabled access ground floor only).

Pick up a free copy of the biweekly *Uptown* at the Central Library's information center or *City Life* (£1.20) at the tourist office for a comprehensive schedule of arts events (from Mozart to dance clubs) before entering the whirlpool of Manchester nightlife. Its club scene remains a national trend-setter, and it centers on the notorious **Hacienda,** 11-13 W. Whitworth St., close to G-Mex (for concert info call (0161) 236 50 51; open 9pm-2am). Buses run to outlying areas regularly until 11pm; less frequent night service runs until 2:30am.

Practical Information, Accommodations, and Food The **tourist office,** Town Hall Extension on Lloyd St. (tel. (0161) 234 31 57 or 234 31 58), pro-

GREAT BRITAIN

vides brochure guides on accommodations, food, and sights (open Mon.-Sat. 10am-5:30pm, Sun. 11am-4pm). The office also offers dozens of guided walks (£2, students and seniors £1) on such topics as "Murders and Mysteries of Manchester" and "Feminine Influence." **Trains** (tel. (0161) 832 83 53) run to London (2½hr., return £24-42), Liverpool (45min., £5.70, day return £6.50), Chester (1hr., £6.20, day return £6.50) and York (1hr., £11.50, day return £12). **Buses** (tel. (0161) 228 78 11) roll to Sheffield (1½hr., £5.50, day return £5.75), Glasgow (4½-5hr., £18, Fri. £22, return £21-25), and London (4hr., £24-42, return £22.50).

Manchester sends its budget travelers packing to the outskirts of town. YHA plans to complete a 150-bed **hostel** on Potato Wharf, Castlefield, Manchester by March 1, 1995; book via their Central Reservations Office (tel. (0171) 248 65 47). The disabled-access hostel will be open 24hrs., charging £6.50-£12 per person. The highest concentration of budget accommodations is found 2 or 3 miles south of the city center in the suburbs of **Fallowfield, Withington,** and **Didsbury. University of Manchester, St. Gabriels Hall,** 1-3 Oxford Pl., Victoria Park (tel. (0161) 224 70 61) is a self-catering dorm available during school vacations (singles £10, students £6; twins £20, £12; reserve ahead). Or try the **Holly House Hotel,** 140 Palatine Rd., West Didsbury (tel. (0161) 434 64 42; singles £12-15, including breakfast; twins/doubles £28-30; £2 off for students). In the Rusholme area, before the university on bus 40, numerous Middle Eastern and Indian restaurants and take-away counters line Wilmslow Rd. At the **Cornerhouse Café,** 70 Oxford St., get quiche and salad for £2.40, and scrumptious desserts from 70p (open 11am-8:30pm; hot meals served noon-2:30pm and 5-7pm). Join the lively crowd at the **Lass-O-Gowrie,** Charles St., where you can watch your bitter brew.

■■■ CHESTER

With fashionable shops tucked away in medieval houses, guides in full Roman armor leading tours around the city's walls, and a Barclays Bank occupying a wing of the cathedral, Chester sometimes resembles an American theme-park pastiche of Ye Olde English Village. Chester's famous **city walls** completely encircle the town. The original **Northgate,** with a fine-grained view of the Welsh hills, was rebuilt in 1808 to house the city's jail, 30 ft. below ground level. Just outside Newgate lie the half-unearthed foundations of the largest **Roman amphitheater** in Britain (open 10am-6pm; Oct.-March Tues.-Sun. 10am-1pm and 2-4pm; free). Chester's brooding and massive Gothic **cathedral** began its life in the 11th century as the burial place for St. Werburgh, a Mercian abbess, and one of the early founders of the northern monasteries (open 7am-6:30pm). The last week in June and the first week of July, Chester is home to the **Sports and Leisure Fortnight.** Celebrations center around a river carnival and raft race down the winding Dee. Write the tourist office or contact Joan Houghton, Holly Cottage, Nomansheath, Malpas (tel. (0194) 88 53 25). Begun in the 18th century as a forum for Chester's minstrels to audition, the **Chester Summer Music Festival** now draws orchestras and musical groups from across Britain during the third week of July. Contact the Chester Summer Music Festival Office, Gateway Theatre, Hamilton Pl., Chester CH1 2BH (tel. (01244) 34 03 92).

Practical Information, Accommodations, and Food The **tourist office,** Town Hall, Northgate St. (tel. (01244) 31 83 56 or 31 31 26), offers brochures and info (open Mon.-Sat. 9am-7:30pm., Sun. 10am-4pm; Oct.-April Mon.-Sat. 9am-5:30pm, Sun. 10am-4pm). British Rail **trains** (tel. (01244) 34 01 70) run to London's Euston (3hr., £38.50, return £32-42); Holyhead (£12.60, return £13-19.50), and Manchester (1hr., £6.20, day return £6.50). National Express **buses** (tel. (01244) 38 15 15) run to London (4½hr., £22.50, return £23.50), Manchester (2hr., £4.35, return £4.60), and Bristol (3hr., £17.50, return £18.50).

The highest concentration of decent B&Bs (average price £12) is along **Hoole Road,** 5min. from the train station. Buses 21, C30, and C53 run to this area of town. The **HI youth hostel,** Hough Green House, 40 Hough Green (tel. (01244) 68 00

56), is in a beautiful, recently renovated Victorian house on a quiet street (lockout 10am-3pm; £11.90, under 18 £7.80; open Jan.-Nov.). **Dutton's Health Foods,** 8 Godstall Lane, near the cathedral entrance, has packed lunches—a roll with cheese or paté, apple, and Brazil nuts—for a pittance (open Mon.-Sat. 8:30am-5pm). **Hattie's Tea Shop,** 5 Rufus Ct., off Northgate, has scrumptious cakes and inexpensive lunchtime snacks. Ravish the "giant topless" ham salad sandwich. (£3.25. Open Mon.-Sat. 9am-5pm. Wheelchair access.) **Rendezvous,** 12-16 Northgate St. (open Thurs.-Sat. 9:30pm-2am), and **Blimper's,** City Rd. (open Wed.-Sat. 9:30pm-2am), both blast a good variety of music.

■■■ LIVERPOOL

The city that clings tightly to its status as the birthplace of the Beatles maintains a thriving cultural life that has diminished little since the 1960s, when Allen Ginsberg described it as "the center of human consciousness." The Anglican **Liverpool Cathedral,** begun in 1904 and completed in 1978, is vast. A Trumpian wonder, it has the highest Gothic arches ever built, the largest vault and organ, and the highest and heaviest bells in the world. View north Wales from the top of the tower. (Cathedral open 7:45am-6pm; tower open 10am-3:30pm, weather permitting. Tower £1.50, children £1. Free organ recitals in summer Fri. 12:30pm.) Liverpool's efforts to bring its waterfront out of the rusty age of freight have yielded **Albert Dock,** an 1846 series of warehouses transformed into a complex of shops, restaurants, and museums. A cornerstone of this development is the **Tate Gallery,** a branch of the London institution (open Tues.-Sun. 10am-6pm; free; some special exhibits £1, seniors, students, and children 50p). Also at Albert Dock, **The Beatles Story** presents a chronological look at the four guys that shook the world (open 10am-6pm; Oct.-March until 5pm; £4.25, students, seniors, and children £2.95). Pick up the **Beatles Map** (£1.50) at the tourist office, which gives directions to Strawberry Fields and Penny Lane. Nearby, the **Beatles Shop,** 31 Mathew St., is stuffed to the gills with souvenirs and memorabilia (open Mon.-Sat. 9:30am-5:30pm).

The **tourist office** (tel. (0151) 709 36 31) resides in the Clayton Sq. Shopping Centre (open Mon.-Sat. 9:30am-5:30pm; bank holidays 10am-5pm). A smaller branch is located at **Atlantic Pavilion,** Albert Dock (tel. (0151) 708 88 54; open 10am-5:30pm). **Trains** (tel. (0151) 709 96 96) run to Manchester (1½hr., £5.70, return £8.20), Birmingham (£16, return £20.50), and London (3hr., £47, return £42). **Buses** (tel. (0151) 709 64 81) head to London (4hr., £21.50, return £22.50), Manchester (1hr., £3.35, return £3.60), and Birmingham (2½hr., £8.75, return £9.25).

Enjoy a relaxed atmosphere in a beautiful old house at the **Embassy Youth Hostel,** 1 Faulkner Sq. (tel. (0151) 707 10 89; no curfew £8.50). Passable lodgings are on offer at the **YMCA,** 56-60 Mt. Pleasant (tel. (0151) 709 95 16; singles £12.50; doubles £21.50; full breakfast included). Women will find sparkling clean rooms at the **YWCA,** 1 Rodney St. (tel. (0151) 709 77 91; singles £9.50, doubles £16). Try **St. John's Market** (above the shopping mall) for fresh produce and local color. Liverpool has many a budget restaurant, especially along Hardman St. **Everyman Bistro,** 9-11 Hope St. off Mt. Pleasant by the university is a bouncy allegorical hangout below the theater, even if they nuke their food. Hot meals run about £3-6. (Open Mon.-Sat. noon-midnight.) Grab a pint at the **Black Horse & Rainbow,** 21-23 Berry St., near Chinatown, which is named after its two home-brewed bitters (open Mon.-Sat. 11:30am-2am; disabled access).

Liverpool's oft-grim demeanor is brightened by a thriving arts scene and an energetic nightlife. The *Liverpool Echo,* a local evening newspaper sold on streetcorners, has the most up-to-date arts information as well as local news and banal royal family gossip (25p). Fight your way inside **Flanagan's Apple,** Matthew St., which offers the best Irish music in town nightly.

NORTH ENGLAND

Between Central England's industrial belt and Scotland's rugged wilderness is a quiet area of natural beauty. Vertically sliced by the Pennine Mountains, North England's main attractions lie enshrined in four national parks and several calm coastal areas. Walkers and ramblers flock here, and no trail tests their stamina more than the Pennine Way, the country's first official long-distance path and still its longest. Isolated villages along the trails continue a pastoral tradition that contrasts with the polluted enormity and din of many English cities to the south.

■■■ PENNINE WAY

The Pennine (PEN-eyen) Peaks form the spine of England. They arch, like any quality backbone would, south to north up the center of Britain from the Peak National Park to the Scottish border. The **Pennine Way,** the Countryside Commission's 250mi. path, crowns the central ridge of the watershed. Hikers (with a capital "H") have completed the hike in 10 days, but most walkers spend 3 weeks on the long, green trail. The classic Wainwright's *Pennine Way Companion* (£6.50), a pocket-sized volume available from bookstores, supplements Ordnance Survey maps, which run about £5, available at Peak Information Centers. Sudden mist and rain on the Peaks can reduce visibility to under 20 ft. After a storm, the low-level paths can become boggy, and some paths will leave you knee-deep (or worse) in hungry peat.

HI youth hostels are spaced within a day's hike (7-29 mi.) of one another. Any National Park Information Centre can supply details on trails and alternative accommodations. The *Pennine Way Accommodations and Catering Guide* (90p) could prove as valuable as moleskin. Camping in the open is also permitted.

South Pennines In the midst of the barren **South Pennines,** the tiny villages of **Haworth** and **Hebden Bridge** provide hospitable civilization breaks for an overnight or daytrip from Manchester. From Hebden Bridge, you can make day-hikes to the nearby villages of Blackshaw Head, Cragg Vale, or **Hepstonstall,** where you'll find the ruins of a 13th-century church and a 1764 octagonal church, the oldest Methodist house of worship in the world. The **Birchcliffe Centre,** in a former Baptist chapel on Birchcliffe Rd. (tel. (01422) 84 36 26), allows travelers who call ahead to fill beds not needed by groups (£11-15). Hebden Bridge's **tourist office,** 1 Bridge Gate (tel. (01422) 84 38 31), is equipped with maps (25p) and many free walking guides and leaflets on local attractions. (Open Mon.-Sat. 9am-5pm, Sun. 10am-5pm; Oct. to mid-March daily 10am-4pm.) Brontë fans must stop in Haworth to see the **parsonage** near the tourist office, where Emily, Charlotte, and Anne lived with their father and their brother Branwell. (Open 10am-5pm; Oct.-March 11am-4:30pm. £3.60, students and seniors £2.60.) Haworth's **tourist office,** 2 West Lane (tel. (01535) 64 22 39; open 9:30am-5:30pm; Nov.-March until 5pm), at the summit of Main St., stocks plenty of maps and guides. The town's **HI youth hostel,** Longlands Dr. (tel. (01535) 64 22 34), tops a hill a mile from the tourist office. (11pm curfew; 11:30pm lights out; lockout 10am-5pm or £1.50 for day access; £7.75, under 18 £5.20; open March-Oct. daily; Nov. and mid- to late Feb. Sun.-Thurs.) B&Bs for about £16-17 are at 4, 6, and 8 Main St., and up the hill to the tourist office.

High Pennines This area stretches from below Barnard Castle in the south to Hadrian's Wall in the north, about 20mi. west of Durham City. It's best suited to hiking and cars can successfully navigate the roads, but buses tackle the region with distressing hesitancy. Twenty miles southwest of Durham along the River Tees, the busy market town of **Barnard Castle** makes an excellent base for exploring the castles of Teesdale and the North Pennine peaks and waterfalls (open 10am-6pm; Oct.-March Tues.-Sun. 10am-1pm and 2-4pm; £1.80, under 16 90p). Just northeast of Barnard Castle looms **Raby Castle,** an imposing 14th-century fortress with a superb medieval kitchen and gardens (open July-Sept. daily, May-June Wed. and Sun.; castle 1-5pm, park and gardens 10am-5pm; no admission to either after 4:30pm; castle £3.30, seniors £3, children £1.50; park £1, seniors and children 75p). In town, stay with **Mrs. Fry,** 66 Newgate (tel. (01833) 372 40; £13). The **tourist office,** 43 Galgate (tel. (01833) 69 09 09), will tell you about nearby scenic walks.

■■■ DURHAM CITY

Windy, medieval streets, inconspicuous alleyways, walking bridges, and restricted vehicle-access make Durham a foot-friendly and lively town, even when students give way to tourists in the summer months. Built in 1093, **Durham Cathedral** is the greatest Norman cathedral in England (open Mon.-Sat. 7:15am-8pm, Sun. 8am-8pm, closes at 6pm from Oct.-April; free). At one end of the church lies the **tomb of the Venerable Bede,** author of *Ecclesiastical History of the English People.* The spectacular view from the top of the **Tower** merits the 325 steps it takes to get there (same hours as cathedral in summer; £1, child 50p). **Durham Castle,** once a key defensive fortress against Scotland, has become a residence for students at the University of Durham. (Hourly tours 10am-noon and 2-4pm; Oct.-June Mon., Wed., and Sat. 2-4pm; £1.50, children £1). For a cheap evening under the stars, £2 buys an hour in a **rowboat** from **Brown's Boathouse Centers,** Elvet Bridge (£1 children). Wind around the horseshoe curve of the River Wear, dodging scullers and ducks.

The **tourist office** (tel. (0191) 384 37 20) is at Market Place (open Mon.-Sat. 9:30am-6:30pm, Sun. 2-5pm; June and Sept. Mon.-Fri. 10am-5:30pm, Sat. 9:30am-5:30pm; Oct.-May Mon.-Fri. 10am-5pm, Sat. 9:30am-1pm). **Trains** (tel. (0191) 232 62 62) run to London, York, and Newcastle. **Buses** (tel. (0191) 384 33 23) also regularly serve London and Newcastle. A boon for travelers is the large supply of inexpensive dormitory rooms that ring the cathedral, available from July to September and during school vacations. The **HI youth hostel,** Durham Sixth Form Centre, The Sands, Providence Row (tel. (0191) 384 22 17), performs Durham's version of musical beds; check the tourist office for the hostel's current location (£6.30, under 18 £4.20; open late July-Aug). Bakeries with £1 sandwiches and pizzerias peddling £3 pies occupy prime Durham real estate near places of interest. Fruits and vegetables fill the stands of the weekend **market** near the tourist office (Thurs.-Sat.).

■■■ YORK

Well-preserved city walls that once foiled many a marauding invader are, today, impressive fortifications which greet York's equally stubborn hordes of tourists. Their quarry is a city strewn with medieval cottages and Georgian townhouses, presided over by Britain's largest Gothic cathedral. The **York Visitor Card** (£1), available at the tourist office, offers discounts on many of the museums and buildings in York; it will pay for itself if two adults use it at just one or two sites. Of the bewildering array of organized tours, a few merit attention: the free 2hr. **walking tour** emphasizes York's architectural legacy (meet in Exhibition Sq., April-Oct. at 10:15am and 2:15pm; June-Aug. also at 7pm); and a fascinating **haunted walk** covers some of York's ghostlier spots (meet at King's Arms Pub, King's Staith at 8pm; £2.50, children £2; call (01904) 64 64 63 for more info). For information on the narrated open-top **Guide Friday bus tour,** call (01904) 64 08 96.

Everyone and everything in York converges on **York Minster,** the largest Gothic cathedral in Britain. An estimated half of all the medieval stained glass in England glitters and holds the walls together. It's a mere 275 steps to the top of the **Central Tower,** from which you can stare down at the red roofs of York (open 9:30am-6:30pm; tower £2, children £1). Housed in a former debtor's prison, the huge York **Castle Museum,** by the river and Skeldergate Bridge, contains everything from excavations to, quite literally, the kitchen sink. Visit **Kirkgate,** an intricately reconstructed Victorian shopping street, and the **Half Moon Court,** its Edwardian counterpart. (Museum open Mon.-Sat. 9:30am-5:30pm, Sun. 10am-5:30pm; Nov.-March Mon.-Sat. 9:30am-4pm, Sun. 10am-4pm. £3.95, students and seniors £2.85.) Across from the Castle Museum is the strange, squat silhouette of **Clifford's Tower,** one of the last remaining pieces of York Castle (open 10am-6pm; Oct.-March 10am-4pm; £1.20, seniors and students 90p, children 60p).

For the most current information, pick up the weekly *What's On* guide and the seasonal *Evening Entertainment* brochure from the tourist office. The free bi-monthly *Artscene* is a good resource for arts information throughout Yorkshire.

Practical Information, Accommodations, and Food Trains arrive from London, King's Cross Station (2hr., £47, return £54-95), Manchester's Picca-dilly (1½hr., £11.50, return £15), and Edinburgh (3-4hr., £39.50, return £53). **Buses** London (4hr., £30, return £25), Manchester (3hr., £8, return £8.50), and Edinburgh (5hr., £26, return £27.50) stop at the Rougier St. York. The main **tourist office** in De Grey Rooms, Exhibition Sq. (tel. (01904) 62 17 56) finds rooms for a £2 fee. (Open June-July Mon.-Sat. 9am-5pm, Sun. 10am-1pm; Aug. Mon.-Sat. 9am-7pm, Sun. 10am-1pm; Oct.-May Mon.-Sat. 9am-5pm.)

Competition for inexpensive B&Bs (from £12) can be fierce from June through August. Try **The Mount** area (out past the train station and down Blossom St.); **Haxby Road** (take bus 2a, or walk from the tourist office out to the end of Gillygate and take the right fork); or any of the sidestreets along **Bootham/Clifton.** For charming chambers with wrought-iron frames, walk ½mi. up Bootham from Exhibi-tion Sq. or take the bus to Clifton Green to reach **the Old Dairy,** 10 Compton St. (tel. (01904) 62 38 16; £12, breakfast included). The superior-grade **HI Youth Hos-tel,** Water End, Clifton (tel. (01904) 65 31 47), is 1mi. from the center of town. From Exhibition Sq. tourist office, walk about ½mi. out Bootham/Clifton; or take the bus to Clifton Green and walk ¼mi. (Reception open 7am-11:30pm. Bedroom lock-out 10am-1pm. No curfew. £12.90, under 18 £9.40, includes breakfast. Open mid-Jan. to Dec.) Room 12 of the **York Youth Hotel,** 11-13 Bishophill Senior (tel. (01904) 62 59 04 or 63 06 13) is an excellent place to meet fellow travelers; the rest of the building is often booked by youth groups. (24hr. reception. Dorm beds £8-11 (sheets £1). Singles £13-16.50. Twins £24-30. Continental breakfast £1.30, full break-fast £2.50.)

Expensive tea rooms, medium-priced bistros, and cheap eateries bump elbows in even the remote alleyways of York. The **Gillygate Vegetarian Restaurant,** at Mill-ers Yard off Gillygate, serves tasty hot dishes (open Mon.-Sat. 10am-4:30pm; £2.50-3). Grab a massive plate to load with salads, meats, and desserts (£5-7) at **Oscar's Wine Bar and Bistro,** Little Stonegate, (open 11am-11pm). The **Roman Bath,** St. Sampson's Sq., serves pints among the ruins. The **Old Starre** is the city's oldest pub, with a license that goes back to 1644. It also dishes up the best pub grub.

■■■ LAKE DISTRICT NATIONAL PARK

In the Lake District, mortarless cottages, livestock, literary legacy, and even tourists fade in the reflections of jagged peaks, windswept fells and primeval forests. Wind-ermere, Ambleside, Grasmere, and Keswick all make convenient bases for explor-ing the region. Ascend into the hills and wander through smaller towns, especially those in the more remote northern and western areas; the farther west you go from the busy bus route serving the towns along the A591, the more countryside you'll have to yourself. These days, hikers, bikers, and boaters are almost as numerous as sheep and cattle, at least during the summer. The ratio is particularly disastrous in July and August, when an exhaustive cloud of tour buses spew their contents onto the lakeshores.

Getting There and Getting Around The most sensible option for reaching the Lake District is either to head straight to Windermere and Keswick or to cross the perimeter of the park at Oxenholme and Penrith and connect from there. **National Express** and **British Rail** run to and through the park. Two rail lines flank the park: the **Preston-Lancaster-Carlisle** line runs south to north along the eastern edge, while the **Barrow-Carlisle** line serves the western coast. The free *Explore Lakeland by Bus,* available at tourist offices, presents a list of timetables. The **Lakeside and Haverthwaite Railway** (tel. (015395) 315 94) can take you through the scenic River Leven Valley by steam locomotive (March-Sept. 6-7 per day; £1.80, return £3, children £1.15-1.80). The **Ravenglass and Eskdale Railway** (tel. (01229) 71 71 71) is England's oldest and narrowest (15in.) narrow-gauge railway (40min., return £5.60, children £2.80). It connects with British Rail's Barrow-Carlisle line.

Hilly terrain comes with the territory in the Lake District; expect aching muscles if you decide to **bike.** Two-wheelers can be rented in almost all the area towns. **Hikers** will find an abundance of trails and often an overabundance of fellow walkers. If you plan to take a long or difficult hike, check with the Park Service, call for weather information (tel. (015394) 451 51; 24hrs.), and leave a plan of your route with your B&B proprietor or hostel warden before you set out.

Practical Information and Accommodations For an introduction to the area, including exhibits, talks, films, and special events, visit the beautiful landscaped grounds and house of the **National Park Visitor Centre** (tel. (015394) 466 01) in **Brockhole,** halfway between Windermere and Ambleside (open July-Aug. 10am-8pm; Sept.-Oct. and Easter-June 10am-5pm; free). The free newspaper *Lake District Guardian* includes a comprehensive calendar of guided walks and events. The following **National Park Information Centres** provide expert information on the Lakes, sell a camping guide (95p), and book accommodations: **Pooley Bridge** (tel. (017684) 865 30), **Ullswater** (tel. (017684) 824 14), **Seatoller Barn** (tel. (017687) 772 94), **Grasmere** (tel. (015394) 352 45), **Ambleside (Waterhead)** (tel. (015394) 327 29), **Hawkshead** (tel. (015394) 365 25), **Coniston** (tel. (015394) 415 33), and **Bowness Bay** (tel. (015394) 428 95).

Although plentiful, accommodations in the Lake District fill in July and August. **B&Bs** line every street in every town (£13-15) and the Lakes have the highest concentration of **HI youth hostels** in the world (27 at last count). You should call to reserve—most places will hold a bed until 6pm. Some hostels have short lockout hours, reopening at 1pm. Campers should pick up the National Park Authority's comprehensive guide (95p), which includes listings of **camping barns** (£3-5).

Windermere and Bowness A first stop for most travelers, Windermere and Bowness together are vacation towns-*cum*-tourist centers. **Bowness Bay Boating** (tel. (015394) 433 60) and the **Windermere Iron Steamboat** (tel. (015395) 311 88) run cruises from the pier; from Easter to October, boats sail north to Waterhead pier in Ambleside (½hr., 10am-6pm; return £4.95, children 5-15 ½-price) and south to Lakeside (40min., 10:25am-6:30pm; same prices as to Ambleside). The **Windermere tourist office** near the rail station is game for questions (tel. (0153945) 464 99; open 9am-6pm; Nov.-Easter 9am-5pm; wheelchair access). The nearest **HI youth hostel** is in **Troutbeck** (tel. (015394) 435 43), 2mi. north of Windermere. (£7.10, under 18 £4.75. Open mid-March to mid-Sept daily, mid-Sept. to early Nov. and Jan. to mid-March Wed.-Mon.) Both Windermere and Bowness are chock-full of **B&Bs,** all convenient to train and town. The nearest campground, **Limefitt Park** (tel. (015394) 323 00), lies 4½mi. south of Bowness on the A592 and has all the necessary amenities except access by public transportation (2-person tent £5-6). In Windermere, eat at the cheery **The Coffee Pot,** 15 Main Rd. (open Mon.-Sat. 9:30am-6:30pm). In Bowness, try the **Hedgerow Teashop,** on Lake Rd. (open 10:30am-5pm; Nov.-Easter Wed.-Mon. 10:30am-5pm.)

GREAT BRITAIN

Ambleside and Grasmere The lake-bound villages of Ambleside and Grasmere both do their thing at a slower, less frenetic pace. The easy hike between the
two is not to be missed. Serious hikers can tackle the path from **Rydal** (halfway
between Ambleside and Grasmere) to **Legburthwaite** in one full athletic day. This
route passes by several of the highest peaks in the area, including **Great Rigg** and
the spectacular **Helvellyn**. The **tourist office** awaits on Church St. (tel. (015394)
325 82; open 9am-5pm; Oct.-Easter Fri.-Sat. only). Lodging seems to be Ambleside's
principal industry; there are almost as many B&Bs and guesthouses here as private
residences. Nonetheless, call ahead in summer. The nearest **HI hostel** (tel. (015394)
323 04), 1mi. south on Windermere Rd. (the A591), has a distinctive country-club
feel; you can even swim off the pier. (£8.40, under 18 £5.60. Open April-Aug. daily;
Sept. to mid-Dec. and mid-Feb. to March Thurs.-Tues.) **The Old Smithy,** The Slack,
off Market Pl. at the Queen's Hotel, serves cheap and excellent fish and chips and
has the lengthy queues to prove it (open 11:30am-2pm and 5-8:30pm).

Every establishment in **Grasmere** tries to cash in on William Wordsworth's legacy, occasionally falling back on the more easily digested Beatrix Potter. Visit **Dove
Cottage,** where Wordsworth lived with his wife, sister, Coleridge, De Quincey, and
up to a dozen kids, opium-eaters, and literati (open 9:30am-5pm; closed mid-Jan. to
mid-Feb., £3.90, children £1.95; tickets cover admission to museum next door).
There are two **HI youth hostels** within a mile of Grasmere. **Butterlip How** (tel.
(015394) 353 16) is a Victorian house with flowering gardens north of Grasmere village. (£7.75, under 18 £5.20. Open mid-March to mid-Sept. daily; mid-Sept. to early
Nov. and Jan. to mid-March Tues.-Sun.) **Thorney How** (tel. (015394) 355 91) is a
converted farmhouse; follow the road to Easedale, turn right at the fork, then turn
left. (£7.75, under 18 £5.20. Open mid-March to mid-Sept. daily; mid-Sept. to Oct.
Wed.-Sun.; Nov. to mid-Dec. Wed.-Sat.; mid-Feb. to mid-March Fri.-Sat.) Sarah Nelson's famous Grasmere Gingerbread is a bargain at 20p per slice in **Church Cottage,** just by St. Oswald's.

Keswick Sandwiched between towering Skiddaw peak and the northern edge of
Lake Derwentwater, once-quiet Keswick (KEZ-ick) rivals Windermere as the Lake
District's tourist capital. The **tourist office,** Moot Hall, Market Sq. (tel. (017687) 726
45), provides a 90p accommodations booklet and a 20p map (open 9:30am-7pm;
April-June and Sept.-Oct. 9:30am-5:30pm; Nov.-March 10am-4pm). The Keswick
and Derwentwater hostels grace this town. To get to **Barrow House,** Borrowdale,
Keswick (tel. (017687) 772 46), take the Borrowdale bus to Seatoller (£8.70, under
18 £5.80; open mid-Feb. to mid-Sept. daily; mid-Sept. to early Nov. Mon.-Sat.; Jan. to
mid-Feb. Thurs.-Tues.). The **Keswick hostel (HI),** Station Rd. (tel. (017687) 724
84), is a former hotel with balconies over the river, new rooms, a lenient staff, and a
decent kitchen (curfew 11:30pm; £8.70, under 18 £5.80; open mid-March to Oct.
and late Dec. daily; Nov. to mid-Dec. and mid-Feb. to mid-March Wed.-Sun.). B&Bs
are sandwiched between the A591, Station St., St. John St., and Ambleside Rd. **May-
son's,** Lake Rd., serves heaping plates of veggie lasagna and stir fry (£4-6) under a
thicket of hanging plants (open 10:30am-9pm, Nov.-June 10:30am-4pm).

A 9mi. hike south of Keswick and Derwent Water lies the harrowing **Honister
Pass,** gateway to the wildest parts of the Lake District: Wasdale, Eskdale, and
Langdale. **Honister Hause youth hostel** (tel. (017687) 772 67) sits at the Pass' sum-
mit (£6.50, under 18 £4.35; open July-Aug. Fri.-Wed.; late March-June and Sept.-early
Nov. Fri.-Tues.). Of course, no serious mountain climber's Lakeland experience
would be complete without a hike up nearby **Scafell Pike** in the magnificent
Langdale Fells, at 3221ft., the highest peak in England.

GREAT BRITAIN

WALES

Wales clings steadfastly to its Celtic heritage, continuing a struggle for independence that has been surging for over a millennium. Especially in the North, which is even more fiercely nationalistic and linguistically independent of England than South Wales, the Welsh language endures in conversation, in commerce, and through a fiercely-revived literature. As churning coal and steel mines fall victim to the vicissitudes of Britain's economy, Wales has turned its economic base from heavy industry to tourism. Avoid calling the Welsh "English" at all costs.

Getting Around Two rail lines in the south and two in the north connect the coast with many towns in England, and buses fill the gaps. **Cardiff Bus** (tel. (01222) 39 65 21) serves the area around Cardiff; **Red and White** (tel. (01291) 62 29 47) buses run the routes from Gloucester and Hereford in England west through the Wye Valley, past Abergavenny and Brecon in the north. **South Wales Transport** (tel. (01492) 47 55 11) operates between Swansea and Haverfordwest in South Pembrokeshire in the West. **TransCambria** (tel. (01222) 39 87 00) is a north-south bus line. Many travelers **hitchhike** in summer. Cars often stop for hitchers who stand in lay-by areas along narrow roads.

Wales has hundreds of well-marked **footpaths.** Check the booklets *Walking in Wales,* available in Welsh tourist offices, and *Wales: Walking* (£1.10), available from the British Tourist Authority. The **Offa's Dyke Path** and the **Pembrokeshire Coast Path** are popular long-distance walks through glorious and often remote countryside. For more info, write the Countryside Commission Dispatch Dept., Prinworks Lane, Levenshulme, Manchester, England M19 3JP. Bikers will value the *Cyclists Guide to North Wales* at tourist offices; bicycles can be rented from the occasional dealer. Betws-y-Coed, Llanberis, and Shrewsbury all make good biking bases.

■■■ CARDIFF (CAERDYDD)

The only urban center in a land of small villages, Cardiff expresses its intense Welsh pride through a lively arts scene and beautifully restored architecture. The preposterously opulent interior of **Cardiff Castle** is no less flamboyant than the peacocks that mewl inside the gates and pester tourists for food. (Open May-Sept. 10am-6pm, tours every 20min.; Oct.-Nov. and Feb.-April less frequently. £3.30, seniors and children £1.70.) The domed grandeur of the **National Museum of Wales** overwhelms its collection, which includes a hoard of pastoral paintings and Impressionists (open Tues.-Sat. 10am-5pm, Sun. 2:30-5pm; £2.50, students and seniors £1.85).

The **tourist office** (tel. (01222) 22 72 81) doles out information at Cardiff Central Railway Station and 8-14 Bridge St. (both open Mon.-Sat. 9am-6:30pm, Sun. 10am-4pm.) **Buses** roll into the station at Wood St. National Express Rapide buses (tel. 34 47 51) run between Cardiff and London (3hr., £21), Bristol (1¼hr., £7), and Glasgow (8½hr., £45). Store your luggage or jump on a train at **Central Station,** Wood St. (tel. (01222) 22 80 00), behind the bus station. British Rail **trains** leave from London's Paddington Station (2hr., £34.50).

Budget accommodations are scarce at the center of Cardiff, but the tourist office lists reasonably priced B&Bs (£13-15) on the outskirts. The smaller neighborhoods around Cathedral Rd. are the best bet for less expensive B&Bs (bus 32, 62, or a 15min. walk from the castle). Room at the comfortable **Cardiff youth hostel (HI),** 2 Wedal Rd., Roath Park (tel. (01222) 46 23 03), 2mi. from the city center; take bus 78, 80, or 82 from Central Station. (Check-in after 3pm. Curfew 11pm. £8.70, under 18 £5.80. Open March-Oct. daily; Jan.-Feb. and Nov. Mon.-Sat.) **The Homade,** 26 Dumfries Pl., at the end of Queen St., and **Bistro One,** Quay St., off St. Mary St. near the castle, both serve large rolls enlivened by a variety of fillings (open Mon.-Sat. 7:30am-6pm). Head to the **Four Bars Inn** on Castel St. for a Brains booze-fest—the upstairs houses one of Britain's only all-jazz clubs outside of London (cover £3-4, student discounts 50p).

■■■ WYE VALLEY

The River Wye (Afon Gwy) joins the broad River Severn at Beachley near **Chepstow,** running through both England and Wales. The **Wye Valley Walk** runs between the picturesque towns of Chepstow and Monmouth along cliffs, wooded hills, and farmland, while across the river **Offa's Dyke Path** runs the entire length of the English-Welsh border, offering over 177mi. of hiking trails.

Chepstow Castle guards the ancient entrance to the valley by stretching its massive bulk right along the river (open 9:30am-6:30pm; mid-Oct. to March Mon.-Sat. 9:30am-4pm, Sun. 11am-4pm; £2.90, seniors and students £1.80). The **tourist office** (tel. (01291) 62 37 72), confronts the castle from its car park (open in season 9am-5pm). In Chepstow, stay at the **Lower Hardwick House,** Mt. Pleasant (tel. (01291) 62 21 62), a wonderful old mansion run by the delightful Eileen Grassby (singles £17, doubles £26), or camp in her exquisite garden (£5 per tent). Alternatively, stay at the **HI youth hostel** at **St. Briavel's Castle,** (tel. (01594) 53 02 72) 4mi. from Tintern, complete with dog-turning spit. Take bus 69 from Chepstow and get off at Bigsweir Bridge; walk 2mi. from there. (£7.75, under 18 £5.20. Open March-Oct.)

Five miles north of Chepstow along the A466, find the delicate walls of **Tintern Abbey,** the majestic 12th-century monastery that inspired Wordsworth (open 9:30am-6:30pm; mid-Oct. to mid.-March Mon.-Sat. 9:30am-4:pm, Sun. 11am-4pm; £2, seniors and children £1.50). Often crowded with tourists, the abbey retains its mystical appearance if viewed from the surrounding hills—hike to the **Devil's Pulpit** (1hr.), an enormous stone from which Satan is said to have tempted the monks.

The market town of **Monmouth** lies 8mi. north of Tintern Abbey, birthplace of Henry V and Geoffrey of Monmouth (who gave what little historical credibility there is to King Arthur and Merlin in his *History of the Kings of Britain*). Fascinated by its own history, the Monmouth is always excavating some piece of turf. Monmouth's **HI youth hostel,** Priory St. School (tel. (01600) 71 51 16), occupies a 15th-century building in the center of town (lockout 10am-5pm, curfew 11pm, last booking 10:30pm; open March-Oct. £6.50, under 18 £4.35).

Presided over by a stubby town clock that rings hollow chimes, **Hay-on-Wye** seeds its confusing streets with the world's largest clutter of secondhand book stores. Stay 8 mi. outside of town at **Capel-y-Ffin** (tel. (01873) 89 06 50), along Offa's Dyke Path (£6.50; open March-Oct. Thurs.-Tues., Nov. and Feb. weekends only). The delightful low-ceilinged **Jasmine Cottage,** on Brook St. behind the Wheatsheaf pub (tel. (01873) 82 11 68), displays a 500-yr.-old dresser in a breakfast-room crammed with antiques (single £15, double/twin £27). Hay's oldest pub, the **Three Tuns** on Broad St., has one bench and one table.

■■■ BRECON BEACONS NATIONAL PARK (BANNAU BRYCHEINIOG)

The Brecon Beacons National Park encompasses roughly 519 sq. mi. of varied terrain and is crisscrossed by four mountain ranges. Storms rise within minutes, so guard against hypothermia. At the center of the park, the **Brecon Beacons** mountain range beckons hikers with its beauty. The most convenient route to the top of the 2907ft. **Pen-y-Fan,** the highest mountain in South Wales, starts at **Storey Arms;** or take the trail that skirts **Llyn** (Lake) **Cwm Llwch** (koom-hlooch), a small pool at an altitude of 2000 ft. The **Black Mountains** make great ridge-walking. At **Porth-yr-Ogof** (Welsh for "mouth of the cave"), less than a mile from the HI hostel, the River Afon Mellte flows into a cave at the base of a cliff and emerges in an icy pool. Near **Abercrave,** midway between Swansea and Brecon off the A4067, the **Dan-yr-Ogof**

Showcaves are huge and stunning, with enormous stalagmites. Although not actually in the mountains, **Brecon** is the best base for hiking through the surrounding craggy peaks. The **National Park Information Centre** (tel. (01874) 62 31 56) is in Cattle Market Car Park (open April-Oct. 9:30am-5:30pm).

Five **HI youth hostels** dot the park: **Llwyn-y-Celyn youth hostel (HI),** Brecon Beacons (tel. (01874) 62 42 61), 8mi. south of Brecon (£6.50; open July-Aug. daily, March-June and Sept.-Oct. Mon.-Sat.); **Ystradfellte youth hostel (HI)** (tel. (01639) 72 03 04), south in the waterfall district (£5.90; open April-Oct. Fri.-Wed.; Nov.-March for groups of 10 or more only); **Llanddeusant hostel (HI)** (tel. (015504) 634 or 619), in the Black Mountains by Llangadog village, accessible from the Trecastle-Llangadog mountain road (£5.90; open daily Easter-Sept., year-round advance booking; reserve ahead); **Capel-y-Ffin youth hostel (HI)** (tel. (01873) 89 06 50), near the River Honddu, at the eastern edge of the Black Mountains (£6.50; open April-Sept. Thurs.-Tues.); and **Ty'n-y-Caeau youth hostel (HI)** (tel. (01874) 862 70), 3mi. from Brecon, on a lane leading from the A470 through Groesffordd to the A38 (£6.50; open March to mid-July and Oct. Mon.-Sat., mid-July to mid-Sept. daily).

■■■ PEMBROKESHIRE COAST NATIONAL PARK AND ABERYSTWYTH

The **Pembrokeshire Coast National Park** offers 225 sq. mi. of lovely coastal scenery broken only by little harbors, stone villages, and Milford Haven's towering oil refineries. Pre-Cambrian cliffs, sheltered beaches, natural sea arches, and islands spotted with birds and seals line the 186mi. coastal path from Amroth to Cardigan. Inland, swaths of farmland separate small towns like Tenby and St. David's, where the best Welsh bakers and craftsmen labor among the country's ancient shrines. Enter the region at centrally located **Haverfordwest,** on the main rail line from London (£48) and Cardiff (£12.10). There are National Park Information Centres in Haverfordwest, Pembroke, and Tenby. For short hikes, stick to the more accessible **St. David's Peninsula,** in the northwest. Otherwise, set out on the coastal path, which is marked with acorn symbols and covers mostly manageable terrain. It passes **St. David's Head,** the site of pre-Cambrian formations.

Near the western extremity of the coast path, **St. David's** stands as the largest and richest diocese in medieval Wales and now Britain's smallest city. A chest in the **cathedral** holds the bones of St. David, the patron saint of Wales (£1 donation appreciated). The **Bishop's Palace,** a few yards away, resembles more a castle (open 9:30am-6:30pm; Nov.-March Mon.-Sat. 9:30am-4pm, Sun. 11am-4pm; £1.50, seniors, students, and children £1).

Another point of entry into the park is the tiny town of **Pembroke,** which clings to the huge 13th-century **Pembroke Castle.** It is among the most impressive fortresses in South Wales and the birthplace of Henry VII. (Castle open 9:30am-6pm; March and Oct. 10am-5pm; Nov.-Feb. Mon.-Sat. 10am-4pm. £2.) **B&I ferries** (tel. (01646) 68 41 61) sail twice a day from Pembroke Dock to Rosslare, Ireland.

Along the sweeping Cardigan Bay coastline, **Aberystwyth's** elaborate pier and promenade hark back to its heyday as a Victorian seaside resort; now, the city serves as a hub for travel by bus or train to all of Wales. The **National Library of Wales,** off Penglais Rd., houses nearly all books and manuscripts written in or pertaining to Wales (open Mon.-Fri. 9:30am-6pm, Sat. 9:30am-5pm; free). The **Electric Cliff Railway** will whisk you to the top of **Constitution Hill** to see the *camera obscura* gazebo, an enormous wide-lens telescope that offers dizzying views of the town. (Open 10am-6pm; July-Aug. 10am-9pm; train every 10min. Rail fare return £1.85, students and seniors £1.60. Last entry to *camera obscura* 5:30pm. Free.)

The **tourist office,** Terrace Rd. (tel. (01970) 61 21 25), has photos of area B&Bs (open 10am-5pm; July-Aug. 10am-6pm; June 10am-5:30pm). The nearest **HI hostel** (tel. (01970) 87 14 98) lies 9mi. north in Borth (£7.75; open April-Aug. daily; Sept.

Mon.-Sat.; Oct. Tues.-Sat.). Or, stay with **Mrs. E. V. Williams,** 28 Bridge St. (tel. (01970) 61 25 50) for £11. For food, head to **Y Graig Wholefood Café,** 34 Pier St. (open Mon.-Sat. 9am-midnight, Sun. from 2pm, but hours unreliable). Forty-two **pubs** make Aberystwyth more than just a dayspot.

■■■ SNOWDONIA FOREST AND NATIONAL PARK

Stretching from Machynlleth in the south to Bangor and Conwy in the north, Snowdonia is the reason you came to Wales. A total of 840 square sheep-dotted miles, the park encompasses coastal areas as well as the rugged hills of the interior. The mountain of **Snowdon** itself, at 3560 ft., is the highest, barest peak in England and Wales. Half a million climbers reach the summit of Mt. Snowdon every year; the result has been the erosion of the mountain and disruption of its ecosystem. Stick to well-marked trails to avoid damaging the area further. Since other climbs will be less crowded and probably more scenic, it might be wise to skip Snowdon altogether and try a hike up **Tryfan** or nearby **Devil's Kitchen.** Contact the **Snowdonia National Park Information Centre** (tel. (01766) 77 02 74), Penrhyndeudraeth (pen-rin-DOY-dryth), Gwynedd LL48 6LS, Wales for details. Other National Park Information Centres are at Betws-y-Coed, Harlech, Blaenau Ffestiniog, Dolgellau, Aberdyfi and Bala. Call **Mountaincall Snowdonia** (tel. (01839) 50 04 49) for local forecast, ground conditions, and a national 3- to 5-day forecast (36-48p per min.).

The 8 **HI youth hostels** in the mountain area are some of the best in Wales. **Pen-y-Pass** (tel. (01286) 87 04 28) sits at the head of Llanberis Pass between the Snowdon and Glyders peaks. (£8.70, Open April-Oct. daily; Feb.-March and Nov. Tues.-Sat.) The **Llanberis hostel** (tel. (01286) 87 02 80; £7.75; open April-Sept. daily; Oct. and Feb.-March Fri.-Tues.; Nov.-Dec. Fri.-Mon.) and **Snowdon Ranger** (tel. (01286) 65 03 91; £7.75; open April-Sept. daily; Oct. and Feb.-March Thurs.-Mon.) are near main walking trails up Snowdon. Save yourself the hike by taking the **Snowdon Mountain Railway** (tel. (01286) 87 02 23), which runs from Llanberis. (Round-trip 2hr., single £9.50, return £13.20. Weary hikers can try for a £5 standby back down.) The **Snowdon Sherpa,** a service of Crosville bus lines on which all Crosville passes are valid, offers relatively easy access to the various Snowdon trailheads, where parking is almost impossible to find. Inform the driver if you intend to switch buses; connections often fail due to late or impatient buses.

Distinguished mainly by the Mountain Railway, **Llanberis** is the largest town in the park and the best place to stock up on food and gear. To reach **Ceunant Mawr,** one of Wales's most impressive waterfalls, take the public footpath on Victoria Terrace by Victoria Hotel, then the first right and then the first left (about 1mi.). The **tourist office,** Museum of the North building (tel. (01286) 87 07 65), in the bypass at the end of High St., doles out tips on hikes and sights. (Open Easter-Sept. 10am-5:45pm.) Stoke your engine with a dose of gut-nuking chili (£3.90) at **Pete's Eats.** (Open 9am-8pm; off-season Mon.-Fri. 9am-6:30pm.Sat.-Sun. 8am-8pm.)

■■■ LLEYN PENINSULA AND NORTHERN COAST

Lleyn has thrived on tourism since the Middle Ages, when crowds of religious pilgrims tramped through on their way to Bardsey Island off the peninsula's western tip, but much of the hilly region is still remote and unsullied. **Porthmadog,** a resort town at the southeastern end of the peninsula, is linked by the steam **Ffestiniog Railway** to Blaenau Ffestiniog (March-Oct. 2-8 per day; 1hr., return £4.50-11.40). Porthmadog's **tourist office** is at the end of High St. (tel. (01766) 51 29 81; open 10am-6pm; Nov.-Easter Fri.-Wed. 10am-5pm). An eccentric landmark of British Italy-fixation, the private Italianate village of **Portmeirion** stands 2 mi. east of Porthmadog, a stage-set project of the late potter Sir Clough Williams-Ellis (1925-1972).

Caernarfon and Bangor Perched on the edge of the bay of the same name, **Caernarfon** (can-AR-von) lures visitors with Wales's grandest medieval **castle,** dating from 1283. Built by Edward I of England, the castle features the Middle Eastern double gatehouses he discovered while crusading. Prince Charles was appointed Prince of Wales at the castle in 1969. (Open 9:30am-6:30pm; Nov.-March Mon.-Sat. 9:30am-4pm, Sun. 11am-4pm. £3.50, students and seniors £2.50.) The **tourist office,** Castle Pitch, Oriel Pendeitsh (tel. (01286) 67 22 32), stands opposite the castle entrance (open 10am-6pm, Nov.-March Thurs.-Tues. 10am-5pm). **Buses** 5, 5A, and 9 shuttle between Caernarfon and Bangor every 20min. (£1.05). The **Snowdon Sherpa bus** runs southwest to Beddgelert and Llanberis, while buses 1 and 2 head south to Porthmadog (£1.65). Stay with **Mrs. Hughes,** Pros Kairon, Victoria Rd. (tel. (01286) 67 62 29), and you'll be treated like one of the family (£11). **Camping** is available about ½mi. from town at **Cadnant Valley,** Llanberis Rd. (tel. (01286) 67 31 96; tents £3.30-4.40 per person). **Stones Bistro,** 4 Hole-in-the-Wall, near Eastgate, is candlelit and crowded on weekends; the Welsh lamb is worth wounding your wallet (£8.95; open 6-11pm, Jan.-Feb. Tues.-Sat. only).

Huddled in a valley by the Menai Strait, the pleasant university town of **Bangor** makes the best bus base for forays into all corners of North Wales. Just outside Bangor, where the A55 splits off the A5 (walk about 2mi. or catch any bus heading north), **Penrhyn Castle** is the best buy for your castle-going pound. (Open July-Aug. Wed.-Mon. 11am-5pm; Sept.-Oct. and April-June noon-5pm. Grounds open 11am-6pm. £4.40, children £2.20.) The **tourist office** at Theatr Gwynedd, off Deiniol Rd. (tel. (01248) 35 27 86), provides loads of bus schedules, maps, and other good things. (Open Easter-Sept. 9:30am-5pm.) Call (01492) 58 51 51 for **train** info and (01248) 37 02 95 for **bus** info in Bangor. Buses fan out everywhere; trains run along the North Wales Coast rail line that connects Holyhead with Chester. Stay at the **Tany y Bryn youth hostel (HI)** (tel. (01248) 35 35 16), ½mi. from the town center, with its aristocratic view of Penrhyn Castle (£7.75; open March-Jan. daily; Feb. Tues.-Sat.), or try the B&Bs along Garth Rd.

Holyhead, Conwy, and Llangollen Holyhead, on the Isle of Anglesey (Ynys Môn), is a one-horse town with **ferries** to Ireland. **B&I** (tel. (0171) 734 46 81) runs to Dublin (4hr., £16-26). **Sealink** (tel. (01407) 76 67 65) sails to **Dún Laoghaire** (3½hr., £16-26), with bus and commuter rail connections to Dublin. If you miss the boat, check the list of B&Bs (from £12) posted at Holyhead's **tourist office,** Marine Sq., Salt Island Approach (tel. (01407) 76 26 22), in a caravan down the main road from the terminal (open 10am-6pm, winter 9:30am-5pm). Holyhead can be reached by Crosville Bus 4 or 44 from Bangor via Llangefni (1¼hr., £2.45). The town is also the end of the North Wales Coast rail line with hourly **trains** to Bangor (½hr., £4.60), Chester (1½hr., £12.60), and London (6hr., £49). British Rail runs from Holyhead to Cardiff (£45.90).

Conwy has an agelessness that even the visitor buses that scrape through its13th-century arches cannot touch. Fourteenth-century **Aberconwy House** on Castle St. is the oldest dwelling in town, where tilted floors and windows frame displays of armor and period furnishings (open April-Oct. Wed.-Mon. 11am-5:30pm, last entry 5pm; £1.80, children 90p). Mind your head as you step into **Ty Bach,** Britain's smallest house, with a mere 72 in. of frontage on the quay. (Open July-Aug. 10am-9pm, Easter-June and Sept.-Oct. 10am-6pm. 50p, students and children 30p.) Conwy's **tourist office** (tel. (01492) 59 22 48) is at the entrance to the castle (open Easter-Oct. 9:30am-6pm; Nov.-Easter 10am-4pm). **B&Bs** cluster in the Cadnant Park area, a 10min. walk from the castle. Try **Colwyn Bay youth hostel,** Foxhill, Nant-y-Glyn (tel. (01492) 53 06 27), 8mi. east of town. (£6.50. Open July-Aug. daily; mid-Feb. to March Fri.-Sat.; Sept-late Oct. Tues.-Sat.; April-June Mon.-Sat.) Crosville **buses** 5 and 5A serve a northern coastal route from Caernarfon to Llandudno, stopping in Bangor and Conwy along the way (Bangor-Conwy £1.80).

Halfway to Shrewsbury, England, is the emphatically Welsh town of **Llangollen** (hlan-GOTH-len), which overflows with tourists during the **Llangollen Interna-**

tional Eisteddfod (July 4-9 in 1995), when competitors from over 50 countries sing, shout, and dance until the fields and hills can take no more. Book tickets and accommodations far in advance through the International Musical Eisteddfod Office, Llangollen, Clwyd, Wales LL20 8NG (tel. (01978) 86 02 36, fax 86 13 00; office open Mon.-Fri. 9:30am-12:30pm and 1:30-4:30pm). The friendly wardens at the **HI hostel,** Tyndwr Hall (tel. (01978) 86 03 30), 1½mi. out of town, frequently plan days of climbing, archery, or water sports. (£7.75. Open mid-Feb. to Oct.)

SCOTLAND

Scotland at its best is a world apart, a defiantly distinct nation within the United Kingdom with a culture and worldview all its own. Exuberant Glasgow is the most Scottish in character, Aberdeen is a postcard, set-piece of grand architecture and delightful gardens, and Edinburgh is the epicenter of Scottish culture during its famed International Festival in August. A little over half the size of England but with one tenth its population, Scotland revels in stark and open space that varies with the geography of the land. The heather-covered mountains and glassy lochs of the west coast and luminescent mists of the Hebrides demand worship, while the farmlands to the south and the rolling river valleys of the east coast display a gentler beauty.

Getting There and Getting Around The cheapest way to Scotland from outside Britain is usually through London. Although the **bus** trip from London's Victoria Station takes more than seven hours, fares are half that of trains. Recently combined, **Scottish Citylink** and **National Express** (tel. (0171) 730 02 02)—look for either logo—serve Scotland via Glasgow and Edinburgh (£29.50, return £36-38; one-week APEX return £25). The cheapest options are Citylink's **Londonliner** or the independent **Night Rider** (tel. (0171) 833 44 72). Both depart King's Cross at 11pm (£15, return £22). Reserve in advance. From London, **trains** to Scotland take only 5-6 hours, but fares are steep: trains to Edinburgh (most from King's Cross Station) and to Glasgow Central (most from Euston Station) both cost £57 (return £57-67).

  Bus travel in Scotland is a steal. **National Express** and **Scottish Citylink** have merged; their prices are the same and tickets may be bought at either counter, but routes still run under separate names, and neither company has printed a comprehensive timetable. Bus stations are often closed or nonexistent, but tickets can always be bought on board. In rural areas, wave to signal the driver to stop. **Scottish Rail** trains are clean and punctual, if not especially cheap. Their comprehensive timetable costs 40p (available at all stations); alternatively, pick up free timetables to services in particular regions. The excellent **Go Blue Banana** minibus service (tel. (0131) 220 68 68) drives a circular route from Edinburgh through Skye and back, stopping at hostels on its way. A complete circuit, completed in under a month, costs an unbeatable £39. Many **hitchhike** in Scotland, except in places like the Northwest and Inverness, where cars crammed full of tourists make up a large percentage of the traffic.

  Scotland offers scenic, challenging terrain for **biking.** The area of Fife and regions south of Edinburgh and Glasgow offer gentle pastoral pedaling, while the Highlands are tremendously challenging. You can usually rent bikes even in very small towns and transport them by ferry for little or no charge. Beginning in April, the **Bike Bus** (tel. (0131) 229 62 74) will take you and your bike from Edinburgh to different points north and south on weekends (£18, plus £2 if you need to rent a bike).

  For info on Scotland's two long-distance footpaths, the **West Highland Way** and the **Southern Upland Way,** write to the **Scottish Tourist Board,** 23 Ravelston Terr., Edinburgh EH4 3EU. Or you can join in the hiking sport of "Munro bagging" by collecting any of the 280 Scottish peaks logged in 1891 by Hugh T. Munro.

GREAT BRITAIN

Essentials SYHA hostels, part of the Hostelling International stable, are the most economical lodgings in Scotland; hostel standards are perhaps the best in the world. The price range is low (£3.15-9.80, including breakfast), and there are hostels in or near almost every city and region described in this section. Hostels are carefully graded: grade 1 hostels have laundry facilities, free hot showers, shorter lockouts, and a microwave in the kitchen. Most grade 2 hostels charge for hot showers, may have more primitive clothes-washing facilities, and have lockouts until 5pm. Grade 3 hostels, usually more remote, lack hot showers and clothes washers, but compensate with coziness and lenience. A sleep sack (rentable for 60p) and an HI membership card (purchasable as you go) are required at all grades. From June to August, advance booking is *essential*. Hostels generally accept telephone reservations between 7 and 10pm (never on the same day as arrival) and hold them until 6pm (sometimes later if you can specify a train or bus arrival time). The SYHA has introduced a **fax booking system** between its most popular hostels (mostly grade 1); 70p plus the prepaid unrefundable overnight fee assures you a bed up to 10pm on your date of arrival. Some travelers prefer the growing Scottish network of **independent hostels.** Though their atmosphere and rules are usually more relaxed than those at SYHA hostels, facilities vary considerably.

B&Bs are a comfortable but more expensive alternative. It's best to book B&Bs using tourist office literature. Most tourist offices charge £1 for local booking (with a 10% deposit), except in Edinburgh where the same service costs £2.50. You can **camp** free on all public land, but make sure you know which areas are restricted (i.e., preserves or other protected land). Always ask the landowner's permission if you suspect you're on privately owned land.

Weekend clan gatherings, bagpipe competitions, and Highland games occur frequently during the summer here. Check at the tourist office and in the local newspaper for dates of local events. Above all events towers the **Edinburgh International Festival** (Aug.13-Sept. 2, 1995), the largest international festival in the world and its much less costly sibling, the **Festival Fringe**. (See Edinburgh Entertainment below.)

■■■ EDINBURGH

Scotland's magnificent capital since the 15th century, Edinburgh is still the administrative center of Scotland. The stunningly beautiful city—a concert of stone, wild landscapes and tidy gardens—marks the point where nature and human art intersect. The city's beauty is augmented by a cultural wealth: Edinburgh boasts a year-round mixture of superb museums, bookstores, and pubs, and transforms into a gallery of thrills during August's festival season.

ORIENTATION AND PRACTICAL INFORMATION

Short distances and quiet streets make Edinburgh an ideal walking city. Princes St. is the main thoroughfare in the New Town, the northern section of Edinburgh; "**The Royal Mile**" (Lawnmarket, High St., and Canongate) links **Edinburgh Castle** and **Holyrood Palace** and is the main road of the Old Town, the city's southern half.

Tourist Office: Edinburgh and Scotland Information Center, Waverley Market, 3 Princes St. (tel. 557 17 00), next to the train station. Busy but efficient accommodations service (£2.75-3); a 24-hr. computer outside gives updates on availability. Pick up *The Essential Guide to Edinburgh* (25p), *Day by Day* (free), and a free accommodations booklet. Open July-Aug. Mon.-Sat. 9am-8pm, Sun. 10am-8pm; May-June and Sept. Mon.-Sat. 9am-7pm, Sun. 11am-7pm; April and Oct. Mon.-Sat. 9am-6pm, Sun. 11am-6pm; Nov.-March Mon.-Sat. 9am-6pm.

Budget Travel Services: Edinburgh Travel Centre, Potterow Union, Bristol Sq. (tel. 668 22 21). Branches at 196 Rose St. and 92 S. Clark St. Open Mon.-Fri. 9am-5:30pm; Rose St. and S. Clark St. also open Sat. 10am-1pm.

Currency Exchange: When banks are closed, go to the tourist office.

Edinburgh

1 Edinburgh Castle
2 Outlook Tower
3 Gladstone's Tower
4 Parliament House and Law Courts
5 High Kirk of St. Giles
6 Royal Scottish Museum
7 Festival Fringe Office
8 Tourist Information Center
9 John Knox's House
10 Canongate Tolbooth
11 General Post Office
12 Nelson Monument
13 National Monument
14 Portrait Gallery
15 Scott Monument
16 National Gallery
17 Royal Scottish Academy
18 Georgian House
19 Royal Lyceum
20 St. Mary's Cathedral
21 Palace of Holyroodhouse
22 Scotch Whisky Heritage Center
23 Lady Stair's House
24 Greyfriars Kirk
25 Huntly House
26 Museum of Childhood
27 Register House
28 Royal Botanic Garden
29 Assembly Rooms
30 Edinburgh University
31 City Observatory
32 National Library of Scotland
33 Outlook Tower and Camera Obscura

GREAT BRITAIN

Map locations and street labels:

Easter Rd., Royal Terrace, Regent Terrace, Monatgomery St., Hillside Cr., London Rd., Windsor St., Royal Terrace, Regent Gardens, CALTON HILL, Regent Rd., Calton Rd., Tolbooth Wynd, New St., Canongate, Holyrood Rd., Pleasance St., Richmond Pl., Nicolson St., Dumbiedykes Rd., Queen's Dri., Holyrood Park, Queen's Dri.

E. London St., Broughton Pl., Forth St., Broughton St., Union St., Leith Walk, Greenside Row, Waterloo Pl., Leith St., St. Andrew's Hospital, Waverley Station, North Bridge, E. Market St., St. Mary's St., South Bridge, S. Coll., S. Coll. St., Lothian, TO POLLOCK, HALLS OF RESIDENCE, TO RESIDENCE

E. London St., Barony St., Albany St., Duke St., York Pl., St. James Centre, St. Clyde St., Bus Station, Cockburn St., High St., Cowgate, Chambers St., Greyfriars Pl., Heriot Pl.

London St., S. Drummond Pl., S. St. Andrew St., ST. ANDREW SQUARE, David St., Waverley Br., Market St., George IV, Lawnmarket, Victoria St., Candlemaker Row, Grassmarket, Heriot Pl.

Nelson St., Hanover St., The Mound, Royal Mile, Johnston Terr., Lawson St.

Abercromby Pl., Frederick St., Rose St., Princes St., West Princes Street Gardens, King's Stable Rd., Castle Terr., Lady, West Port Ter., Bread St.

Fettes St., Dundas St., Great King St., Northumberland St., Queen Street Gardens, Queen St., Thistle St., Castle St., George St., Charles St., American Express, Grindlay St., Lothian Rd., Cumberland, Howe St., ROYAL CIRCUS, India St., N. W. Circus Pl., Gloucester La., MORAY PLACE, AINSLIE PLACE, RANDOLPH CRES., CHARLOTTE SQUARE, Queensferry St., Rutland, Alva St., Melville St., Shandwick Pl., William St., Manor Pl., Chester St., Palmerston Pl., West Maitland St., Morrison St., Cumming St., TO SYHA, EGLINTON

Raeburn Pl., India Pl., Doune Terr., Stuart, St., Queensferry Rd., Water of Leith, St. Stephen's St.

220 yards / 200 meters

N

American Express: 139 Princes St. (tel. 225 78 81). Holds mail. Open Mon.-Fri. 9am-5:30pm, Sat. 9am-4pm.

Post Office: 2-4 Waterloo Place (tel. 550 82 53), at North Bridge and Princes St. Open Mon.-Fri. 9am-5:30pm, Sat. 9am-12:30pm. **Postal Code:** EH1 1AA.

Telephone Code: 0131.

Flights: LRT's Airlink 100 (tel. 220 41 11; £3) and the Edinburgh Airbus Express (tel. 556 2244; £3.20) both depart from Waverley Bridge for Edinburgh Airport. Journey time is about 25min.

Trains: Waverley Station, in the center of town. 24hr. info tel. 556 24 51. Ticket and info office open Mon.-Sat. 8am-11pm, Sun. 9am-11pm. To Glasgow (£5.50), Stirling (£3.70), Aberdeen (£26, return £30), Inverness (£23, return £31), Thurso (£30.50, return £40), Oban (£20, return £34.10), and London (£58, reserve 2 weeks in advance for £29; return £69, reserve 1 week in advance for £44). For schedule information, call Scotrail at 556 24 51.

Buses: St. Andrew Square Bus Station, St. Andrew Square. For Scottish Citylink info call 557 57 17, SMT tel. 654 07 07, National Express tel. 452 87 77. After hours, or to avoid lines, buy tickets on the bus. SMT and National Express office open Mon.-Tues. and Thurs.-Sat. 8:40am-5pm, Wed. 9am-5pm. Scottish Citylink open Mon.-Sat. 9am-5pm, Sun.9am-4pm. **Scottish Citylink** to Glasgow (£4), Aberdeen (£11.70), Inverness (£11.20). **National Express** to London (£29.50; reserve 7 days in advance for £25 return). **Londonliner** to London (£15).

Taxi: Taxi stands at both stations and on almost every corner on Princes St. Or call **City Cabs** (tel. 228 12 11) or **Central Radio Taxis** (tel. 229 24 68).

Bike Rental: Central Cycle Hire, 13 Lochrin Place (tel. 228 63 33), off Home St. in Tollcross near Cameo Cinema. 12-speed town bikes £8 per day, 21-speed touring bikes £10 per day, mountain bikes £15 per day. £60 per week. Open Mon.-Sat. 10am-5:30pm; Sept.-May Mon. and Wed.-Sat. 10am-5:30pm.

Laundromat: Bruntsfield Laundrette, 108 Bruntsfield Pl. (tel. 229 26 69), near Bruntsfield hostel. Wash £2, dry 20p. Open Mon.-Fri. 9am-5pm, Sat. 9am-4pm, Sun. 10am-4pm.

Bisexual, Gay, and Lesbian Services: Gay Switchboard, tel. (556 40 49), 7:30-10pm. **Lesbian Line,** tel. 557 17 51, open Mon.-Thurs. 7:30-10pm. Pick up a copy of *Gay Scotland,* ask the tourist office for their information sheet, or drop by the **Bisexual Resource Center** (tel. 556 1471), on Broughton St.

Services for Disabled: Lothian Coalition of Disabled People, 13 Johnston Ter. (tel. 220 68 55). Info available on disabled access to restaurants and sights.

Crisis Lines: Nightline, tel. 557 44 44, 6pm-8am. **Rape Crisis Center,** tel. 556 94 37, Mon. 7-9pm, Tues. 1-4pm, Thurs. 6-8pm.

Pharmacy: Boots, 48 Shandwick Pl. (tel. 225 67 57), past west end of Princes St. Emergency medication Mon.-Fri. 8:30am-9pm, Sat. 8:45am-9pm, Sun. 9am-5pm.

Emergency: Dial 999. **Police:** Headquarters on Fettes Ave. (tel. 311 31 31).

ACCOMMODATIONS

Edinburgh's **B&Bs** cluster in three well-stocked colonies. The **Bruntsfield** district lies south of the west end of Princes St.; take bus 11, 15, 16, or 17 and try around Gilmore Pl., Viewforth Ter., or Huntington Gdns. **Newington** is south of the east end of Princes St. Hunt along Dalkeith Rd. and Minto St.; take bus 3, 8, 18, 31, 36, 62, 69, 80, 81, or 89. **Leith** lies northeast of the east end of Princes St. Try Pilrig St.; take Leith Walk from the east end of Princes St. or bus 11 or 14. Most B&Bs in the city open between May and September and cost £11-16. Edinburgh's **hostels** are cheap and convenient but fill up fast.

High Street Hostel, 8 Blackfriars St. (tel. 557 39 84), just off the Royal Mile. Hostel paradise. Australian cheer and priceless advice. 24hr. reception Check-out 10:30am. No curfew. 4-16 beds per room. £8.50, 7th night free. Continental breakfast £1.20. Laundry (£2.50) and kitchen facilities. Opening the spring of 1995, the **Backpackers' Royal Mile Hostel** at 117 High St. (tel. 557 61 20), run by the High Street Hostel management, will offer the same services (£8.90).

14 Argyle Pl. (Iolaire) (tel. 667 99 91), south of the Meadows and the Royal Mile. Heather and Jed Dignan have lovingly renovated 2 old houses and furnished them with good, solid wooden furniture and oriental rugs. No curfew. £9-10. TVs and unlimited kitchen access.

Belford Youth Hostel, 6-8 Douglas Gardens (tel. 225 62 09). Elegant, 100-yr.-old church which has been converted into a clean, welcoming, modern hostel. Reception open 8am-11pm. Check-out 10am. No curfew. 4- to 6-person rooms £8.50. Doubles with private bathrooms £25 per room. Kitchen, laundry machines. Bus picks up groups from train or bus stations with prior notice.

Hostel Bruntsfield (HI), 7 Bruntsfield Crescent (tel. 447 29 94). A trek from town, but the sparkling facilities, amiable staff, and wonder-dog Jedda make it all worthwhile. Reception open 7am-11:30pm. Curfew 2am. 8- to 24-bed rooms. £7.25, under 18 £5.95. Kitchen, laundry facilities. Open Feb.-Dec.

Camping: Silverknowes Caravan Park, Marine Drive, by the Forth (tel. 312 68 74). Take bus 1 from North Bridge (70p). Tents from £4.70. Toilets, showers and a shop in the campground. Open April-Oct.

FOOD

Most traditional Scottish fare in Edinburgh is served in restaurants that will have you in the alms house for a week, but you can get haggis—if you want to, that is—at many inexpensive cafés. **Littlewoods Department Store,** 92 Princes St., has a basement supermarket where you can pack a container full of salad for a fixed price (open Mon.-Wed. 9:30am-5:30pm, Thurs. 9am-7pm, Fri.-Sat. 9am-6pm; £1.19-2.59).

Corner Stone Coffee House, Lothian Rd. (tel. 229 02 12), at Princes St., beneath St. John's Church. Savory vegetarian meals served in a converted crypt for £3.05. Open Mon.-Sat. 10am-4:30pm, during Festival Mon.-Sat.10am-6:30pm.

Teviot Restaurant, Teviot Row Union, in Bristo Sq. The best of the university unions. Filling main dishes around £2. Open Oct.-June Mon.-Fri. 8:30am-6:45pm, Sun. 12:30-6:30pm. During the Festival, it becomes the **Fringe Club.**

Kalpna, 2 St. Patrick's Sq. (tel. 667 98 90). Superb Indian vegetarian fare, in a subdued, smoke-free setting. Buffet lunch £3.50. Wildly exotic vegetable dishes, £3.25-7. Dinner reservations are wise. Open Mon.-Fri. noon-2pm and 5:30-11pm.

Larry's Diner, 26 Nicolson St. (tel. 667 57 12). Good french fries. Steak pie and chips (£2.50), fish and chips (£2.75). Set lunch noon-2pm with soup, main dish, chips, and tea (£2.50). Open Mon.-Sat. 8am-5pm, Sun. 9am-2pm.

Seeds Café, 53 W. Nicolson St. (tel. 667 86 73). Hardcore vegetarian fare. Daily specials under £3. Open Mon.-Sat. 10am-9pm, Fri. 10am-10pm; during the Festival 10am-midnight.

Parrots, 3-5 Viewforth (tel. 229 32 52). Tasty, inexpensive dishes (and a good vegetarian selection). *Moussaka* (£3.25), seafood gratia (£4.25). Open Sun.-Thurs. 6-10:30pm, Fri.-Sat. 5-10:30pm. Non-smoking. Reserve ahead.

SIGHTS

Princes St. Gardens split Edinburgh into gray-stone **Old Town,** where centuries of piecemeal construction overlap haphazardly, and the classically Georgian **New Town,** a marvel of rational city planning. Great locations for people-watching. The **Royal Mile** spills downhill through the middle of the Old Town, from Edinburgh Castle to the Palace of Holyrood.

At one end of the Royal Mile, **Edinburgh Castle** scowls atop an extinct volcano at the city it once protected. Inside, **St. Margaret's Chapel,** dates back to the 12th century and is believed to be the oldest structure in Edinburgh. (Open Mon.-Sun. 9:30am-6pm; Oct.-March Mon.-Sun. 9:30am-5pm; last admission 45min. before closing; £4.) Everything in the 1620 tenement **Gladstone's Land,** behind the pig at 483 Lawnmarket, remains as it was almost 400 years ago (open April-Oct. Mon.-Sat. 10am-5pm, Sun. 2-5pm; last admission 4:30pm; £2.40, students £1.20). Through the passage at 477 Lawnmarket, the 17th-century **Lady Stair's House** harbors relics of Robert Burns, Sir Walter Scott, and Robert Louis Stevenson (open Mon.-Sat. 10am-6pm, during Festival also Sun. 2-5pm; Oct.-May Mon.-Sat. 10am-5pm; free).

Where Lawnmarket becomes High St., the Mile is dominated by the principal church of Scotland, **St. Giles Cathedral,** where John Knox delivered the fiery Presbyterian sermons that drove Mary Queen of Scots into exile. (Open 9am-7pm; Sept.-Easter 9am-5pm. Free. Donation requested in Thistle Chapel.) The **Museum of Childhood,** 42 High St., displays dolls, games, toys, rods and canes (open Mon.-Sat. 10am-6pm, during Festival also Sun. 2-5pm; Oct.-May Mon.-Sat. 10am-5pm; free).

For a self-guided tour of Edinburgh's **New Town,** start at **St. Andrew Square,** walk west up George St. to the **Georgian House,** 7 Charlotte Sq., a well-restored townhouse (open April-Oct. Mon.-Sat. 10am-5pm, Sun. 2-5pm; £3, students and children £1.50). Between the Mound and Waverley Bridge is the **Walter Scott monument,** a somewhat grotesque Gothic spire once pithily described as "a steeple without a church." Climb its winding 287-step staircase for £1 and get an eagle's-eye view of Princes St. Gardens, the castle, and Old Town's Market St. (open Mon.-Sat. 9am-6pm; Oct.-March Mon. and Sat. 9am-3pm).

The *Edinburgh Gallery Guide* at the tourist office will guide you through the marble halls of Edinburgh's vast and varied collections. On **The Mound** between the two halves of Princes St. Gardens, the **National Gallery of Scotland** stashes a small but superb collection of works by Renaissance, Romantic, and Impressionist masters (open Mon.-Sat. 10am-5pm, Sun. 2-5pm; during Festival Mon.-Sat. 10am-6pm, Sun. 11am-6pm; free). The **Scottish National Portrait Gallery,** 1 Queen St., just north of St. Andrew Sq., displays likenesses of famous Scots, including Robert Burns, Sean Connery, and Mary Queen of Scots (open Mon.-Sat. 10am-5pm,; free).

Just off the eastern end of the Royal Mile, get a whiff of the Highlands with a stroll through **Holyrood Park** or a manageable 45min. climb up **Arthur's Seat** (823 ft.); the exposed volcanic summit offers a stunning view. Edinburgh's requisite romantic oasis is the **Royal Botanic Gardens** on Inverleith Row. Take bus 23 or 27 from Hanover St. and stroll around the splendid rock garden and plant houses. (Open 10am-8pm; Sept.-Oct. and March-April 10am-6pm; Nov.-Feb. 10am-4pm.)

ENTERTAINMENT

The summer season overflows with music in the gardens, theater and film events, and *ceilidhs* (KAY-lees, bouts of dancing, singing, and drinking)—and that's all before the Edinburgh International Festival comes to town. In winter, light thickens; shorter days and the crush of students promote a flourishing nightlife. For details, pick up a copy of *The List* (£1.30), a bi-weekly comprehensive guide to events in Glasgow and Edinburgh, at any local bookstore, newsstand or record shop. *Day by Day,* free from the tourist office, is also useful.

The **Royal Lyceum Theatre,** Grindlay St. (tel. 226 96 97), presents well-known comedies. The **Traverse Theatre,** Cambridge St. (tel. 228 14 04), performs innovative, sometimes controversial, drama, and the **Playhouse Theatre,** Greenside Place (tel. 557 25 90), often hosts musical shows. Tickets for these theaters run £5-25.

Thanks to an overabundance of hip university students who never let books get in the way of a good night out, Edinburgh's music scene is alive and well. For jazz and blues, head to **Preservation Hall,** 9A Victoria St. (open 1pm-1am). You'll find Scottish bands and country dancing most evenings at the **Ross Open-Air Theatre** (info. tel. 529 79 05), under the tent in Princes St. Gardens (usually begins about 7pm), and at a number of smaller local pubs.

It's difficult to find yourself without a pub in view anywhere in Edinburgh, but *The List* directs you to the most authentic ones. The **Grassmarket,** at the base of Candlemaker Row has frequent live music and an array of ales. Royal Mile pubs tend to attract an older crowd, but **Scruffy Murphy's,** 49 George IV Bridge, and **The Ceilidh Bar,** off High St., are notable exceptions, both with spontaneous Irish and Scottish folk music. **Deacon Brodie's Tavern,** nearby at 435 Lawnmarket, pays homage to the respectable yet multiple-personalitied Scot who inspired Stevenson to write *Dr. Jekyll and Mr. Hyde.* The **Blue Moon Café** (60 Broughton St.) and **Madisons** (Greenside Place) are good bi, gay, and lesbian meeting places while **The Laughing Duck** at 24 Howe St. offers a hectic gay and lesbian scene on Thursday nights.

GREAT BRITAIN

Festivals The extraordinary **Edinburgh International Festival** (Aug. 13-Sept. 2, 1995) ignites a massive bonfire of music, art, drama, and dance. For tickets and a full schedule of events, contact the **Festival Box Office,** 21 Market St. EH1 1BW (inquiries tel. 226 40 01, bookings tel. 225 57 56, fax 226 76 69). Tickets (£2-44) are sold by phone and over the counter starting the 3rd week in April, and by post or fax the 2nd week in April. You can also get them at the door for most events. Look for ½-price tickets in the Princes St. Gardens (1-5pm on day of performance).

Around the established festival has grown a more spontaneous **Festival Fringe,** which is generally more weird and whimsical; you may find it more interesting than the official offerings. The *Fringe Programme* (available from the end of June) and the *Daily Diary* list necessary information on performances; get brochures and tickets by mail from the **Fringe Festival Office,** 180 High St., Edinburgh, Scotland EH1 1QS. (From outside Britain, include £1 (from EU countries) or £2 postage; cash, stamps, and foreign currency accepted; from within Great Britain, 60p.) Bookings can be made by mail starting June 26, by phone (with a credit card) beginning July 3, and in person from Aug. 1 (inquiries tel. 226 52 57, bookings tel. 226 51 38; box office open Mon.-Fri. 10am-6pm; in Aug. and during the Festival daily 10am-7pm). You can sometimes get free tickets from desperate actors who give them away outside the Fringe Festival Office. Full price tickets seldom run over £6.

The **Edinburgh International Jazz Festival** (Aug. 5-12 in 1995) opens with a day of free outdoor jazz at the Princes St. Gardens. Tickets (£8-15) are available at the Ticket Centre on Waverley Bridge from five days before the festival, by phone (tel. 557 16 42; credit card required) and by mail from the Festival Office, 116 Canongate EH8 8DD. The office stocks complete listings of events and venues.

■ ST. ANDREWS

Scotland's oldest university, the cathedral and castle ruins, restored medieval streets, and active nightlife make St. Andrews equally compelling to golf fanatics and the sports averse. The most imposing sights are concentrated by the North Sea at the east end of town. **St. Andrews Cathedral,** once Scotland's religious nexus, now lies in ruin (open Mon.-Sat. 9:30am-6pm, Sun. 2-6pm; Oct.-March Mon.-Sat. 9:30am-4pm, Sun. 2-4pm; £1.50, students and seniors 80p). The high stone walls of **St. Andrews Castle** now crumble down to the North Sea; once the local bishop's residence, the castle still maintains a network of explorable secret tunnels, bottle-shaped dungeons, and high stone walls (same hours as cathedral; £2, students and seniors £1.25). **St. Andrews University,** founded in the 15th century, stretches just west of the castle between North St. and The Scores. For a 1-hr. official **tour,** show up to meet the guide at St. Salvator's Chapel Tower on North St. (June 20-Aug. 1 Mon.-Sat. 10:30am and 2:30pm. £2.50). The tour is your key to the interiors of most university buildings.

Golf pilgrims' holy shrine is the St. Andrews **Old Course,** the oldest golf course in the world. According to disputed historical evidence, Mary Queen of Scots played here only days after her husband was murdered. Nonmembers must present a handicap certificate or a letter of introduction from a golf club to play the Old Course (call (01334) 47 57 57 to enter the lottery or reserve a time; £50 per round on the Old Course, £12-18 on less prestigious courses). Learn about the ancient origins of golf next door at the **British Golf Museum** (tel. (01334) 47 88 80; open 10am-5:30pm; Nov.-Feb. Thurs.-Mon. 11am-3pm; March-April Thurs.-Tues. 10am-5pm; £3.50, students and seniors £2.50, under 15 £1.50; disabled access).

Fife Scottish buses (tel. (0131) 556 84 64) take the cheapest and most scenic route from Edinburgh to St. Andrews (2hr., £4, students £2.60). **Scotrail** stops 5mi. away at **Leuchars** on its London-Edinburgh-Dundee-Aberdeen line. The marvelous **tourist office** is at 70 Market St. (tel. (01334) 47 20 21, 24-hr. answering service, fax 47 84 22; open July-Aug. Mon.-Sat. 9:30am-7pm, Sun. 11am-5pm; June and Sept. Mon.-Sat. 9:30am-6pm, Sun. 11am-5pm; Oct.-April Mon.-Fri. 9:30am-1pm, Sat. 2-5pm; May Mon.-Sat. 9:30am-1pm and 2-5pm, Sun. 2-5pm). The trek to **Mr. Penning-**

GREAT BRITAIN

ton's **Bunkhouse** (tel. (01333) 31 07 68), 8mi. south of town, is well worth the effort. The owner, a diving expert-*cum*-historian, and his family warm the coldest hearts (£5.50; bicycles available). **Brambles,** 5 College St., is anything but prickly; vegetarians may never want to climb back out (lasagne with salad £4.35, omelets from £2.70; open Mon.-Sat. 9am-5pm, Sun. noon-5pm).

■■■ GLASGOW

Scotland's largest city matches Edinburgh's capital class with boundless energy and Continental elegance. Glasgow University, half a millennium old, overlooks Kelvingrove Park; its student population of 13,000 overlaps with an innovative arts community to breed a lively atmosphere.

ORIENTATION AND PRACTICAL INFORMATION

The **city center,** with the remains of medieval Glasgow and a newer, gridded street system, is not at the center of the city, but rather on the north bank of the River Clyde. **George Square** is the physical center of town; the train and bus stations, tourist office, and cathedral are within a few blocks.

Tourist Office: 35 St. Vincent Place, off George Sq. (tel. 204 44 00) and south of Buchanan and Queen St. Stations, northeast of Central Station. U: Buchanan St. Pick up *What's On,* a free schedule of local events; the *Official Quick Guide to Glasgow* (£1) and *Where To Stay,* a guide to accommodations (90p). Open July-Aug. Mon.-Sat. 9am-8pm, Sun. 10am-6pm; June and Sept. Mon.-Sat. 9am-7pm, Sun. 10am-6pm; Oct.-May Mon.-Sat. 9am-6pm, Sun. (in May) 10am-6pm.

American Express: 115 Hope St. (tel. 221 43 66, fax 204 26 85). Mail held. Open Mon. and Wed.-Fri. 9am-5pm, Tues. 9:30am-5pm, Sat. 9am-noon.

Post Office: 1-5 George Sq. (tel. 242 42 60). Open Mon.-Fri. 9am-5:30pm, Sat. 9am-12:30pm. **Postal Code:** G2 1AA.

Telephones: City Code: 0141.

Flights: Glasgow Airport (tel. 887 11 11), 10mi. west in Abbotsinch. Frequent buses (service 500/501) run to Glasgow's Buchanan (20min., £2) and Anderston stations, as well as to Edinburgh (1¾hr., £6).

Trains: Central Station, Gordon St. (U: St. Enoch). To Stranraer (2½hr., £17.30) and Dumfries (1¾hr., £14.50). **Queen St. Station,** beside Coppthorne Hotel, George Sq. (U: Buchanan St.). To Edinburgh (50min., £6.20), Aberdeen (2½hr., £31.50), Inverness (3¼hr., £25), and Thurso (7½hr., £32.50). For connections between the two stations, take bus 398 (every 15min., 50p); take a taxi (£1.50) or walk (8-10min.). For 24hr. passenger info, call 204 28 44. **Luggage storage** £1-2.

Buses: Buchanan Station (tel. 332 91 91), 2 blocks north of Queen St. Station on N. Hanover St. To Edinburgh (50min., £4), Oban (3hr., £9), and Inverness (3-4hr., £10.30).

Public Transportation: Glasgow's transportation system includes suburban rail, a confusing variety of private local bus services and the **Underground (U),** a circular subway line. (U open Mon.-Sat. 6:30am-10:30pm, Sun. 11am-5:50pm. 50p.) Wave your hand to stop buses and carry exact change (45-55p).

Taxi: TOA Taxis tel. 332 70 70.

Laundry: Park Laundrette, 14 Park Rd. Wash £1.40, dry 20p per 10min. Express service £3. Open Mon.-Fri. 8:30am-8pm, Sat.-Sun. 9am-6:30pm.

Gay and Lesbian Switchboard: tel. 221 83 72, 7-10pm.

Pharmacy: Boots, 200 Sauchiehall St. (tel. 332 19 25). Open Mon.-Wed. 9am-5:30pm, Thurs. 8:45am-7pm, Fri.-Sat. 8:45am-6pm.

Medical Assistance: Glasgow Royal Infirmary, 82 Castle St. (tel. 552 35 35).

Emergencies: Dial 999; no coins required. **Police:** Stewart St. (tel. 332 11 13).

ACCOMMODATIONS

On the debit side of Glasgow's growing popularity is a perennial bed shortage, most acute in August. Reserve in advance; if you'd rather go a-wandering, most B&Bs lie scattered on the streets to either side of the Great Western in the University area.

HI youth hostel, 7-8 Park Terrace, (tel. 332 30 04), in a beautiful residential district overlooking Kelvingrove Park. U: St. George's Cross. Bus 44 or 59 to first stop on Woodlands Rd. (Lynedoch St.). From Queen St. Station or Buchanan station, take bus 11. Newly renovated hostel with an air of luxury—plush halls, carved banisters, and a mirror-walled dining room. TV and game rooms, bike shed, and inhouse disco; no lockout; curfew 2am. £9.80, includes breakfast. Sheets 60p.

Glasgow Backpackers Hostel, Kelvin Lodge, 8 Park Circus, (tel. 332 54 12). U: St. George's Cross. Sunny and spacious, mostly 3-bed rooms. Laid-back atmosphere. Roomy kitchen; no lockout; free night key if out after 2:30am. Dorms £7.90, doubles £8.90 per person. Open July to mid-Sept.

University of Glasgow, administrative offices at 52 Hillhead St. (tel. 330 53 85; open Mon.-Fri. 9am-5pm). Summer housing at 6 college dorms. **Queen Margaret Hall,** 55 Bellshaugh Rd. (tel. 334 21 92), near Byres Rd. Free laundry. B&B: £20.50, students £14.45. Without breakfast £11, students £9.40. **Maclay Hall,** 18 Park Terrace (tel. 332 50 56), overlooking Kelvingrove Park, in an attractive, old building with big rooms, is nearer to the city center. £11, students £9.40. No breakfast. Open Easter and late June-late Sept.

YMCA Aparthotel, David Naismith Court, 33 Petershill Dr. (tel. 558 61 66). Take bus 12A, 16, or the M11 from Queen St. Station. Clean, institutional rooms. TV lounge; game room; no curfew. B&B: singles £16, doubles £13.50 per person.

Iona Guest House, 39 Hillhead St. (tel. 334 23 46), near "The Hub," on a street lined with B&Bs. U: Hillhead. Subterranean breakfast nook and Laura Ashley rooms. Convenient city center. Singles £20, doubles £16 per person.

FOOD

As with many university towns, Glasgow has plenty of cheap hole-in-the-wall restaurants with great food. Professors hold *tête-à-têtes* in the cafés behind Byres Rd. on **Ashton Lane,** a cobblestone alley lined with 19th-century brick façades.

The Bay Tree Vegetarian Café, 403 Great Western Rd. Vegans and vegetarians rejoice! Superb hot meals (£3.50) and a selection of salads (large plate £3), hummus, and sinful desserts. Open Tues.-Sun. 10am-9pm.

Grosvenor Café, 31-35 Ashton Lane. Behind U: Hillhead. Students flock to this café's unbelievable subterranean bargains. Stuff yourself silly: most dishes dive under £1. Open Mon.-Sat. 9am-10:30pm, Sun. 11am-6pm.

The Basement Restaurant, 14 Otago St. beneath a contemporary art gallery. U: Kelvinbridge. Cluttered with paintings and gallery posters. Delicious, homemade vegetarian dishes. Quiche 95p, salads 70-90p. Open Mon.-Sat. 9:30am-5:30pm.

Magnus Dining Room, in the Glasgow University Refectory ("The Hub"), on Hillhead St. just above University Ave. U: Hillhead. The central student cafeteria with salad, snacks, and meals. Open Mon.-Thurs. 8:30am-6:10pm, Fri. 8:30am-3:30pm.

Strathclyde University Students' Union, on John St., 2 blocks from George Sq. Any student ID will allow you access. **Petit 4** is the cafeteria and **Red's** is the bar. Petit 4 Open Mon.-Fri. 8am-3pm (until 6pm during the term). Red's open Mon.-Wed. 11am-1am and Thurs.-Sat. 11am-2am.

SIGHTS

The Gothic **Glasgow Cathedral,** near the center of town on Castle St., was the only full-scale cathedral spared by the fury of the mid-16th century Scottish Reformation (open Mon.-Sat. 9:30am-6pm, Sun. 2-5pm; Oct.-March Mon.-Sat. 9:30am-4pm, Sun. 2-4pm; free). Nearby, the newly-opened **St. Mungo Museum of Religious Life and Art** surveys world religions from Mormon to Hindu to Native American and Yoruba (open 10am-5pm, Sun. 11am-5pm; free). The **People's Palace,** a museum with attached greenhouse on Glasgow Green by the river, recreates much of the medieval past the city eagerly cast aside during the Industrial Revolution (open Mon.-Sat. 10am-5pm, Sun. 11am-5pm; free).

Rounded crescents and elegant parks in the West End's residential **Park Circus** area present intact examples of early Victorian terracing. The **Tenement House,** a late 18th-century apartment on 145 Buccleuch St., has been carefully restored to its pristine state by the National Trust for Scotland (open 1:30-5pm, last entry 4:30pm; Nov.-Easter Sat.-Sun. 2-4pm; £2, children and seniors £1). A block west is **Kelvingrove Park,** a large wooded expanse on the banks of the River Kelvin, where locals tan on the grassy slopes and university students make out behind trees. Just off the intersection of Argyle and Sauchiehall St., the spired **Art Gallery and Museum** displays an art collection that ranges from Rembrandt to Dalí while the ground floor is devoted to natural history and wildlife (open Mon.-Sat. 10am-5pm, Sun. 11am-5pm; free). **Kelvin Hall** combines a complete public sports complex and a dazzling museum on Dumbarton Rd. The **Museum of Transport,** in the Hall's rear half, houses a collection of full-scale original trains, trams, and automobiles inside an immense warehouse (open Mon.-Sat. 10am-5pm, Sun. 11am-5pm; free).

ENTERTAINMENT

Glaswegians party hard. Nab *What's On* at the tourist office. The **Ticket Centre,** City Hall, Candleriggs, will tell you what's playing at the city's dozen-odd theaters (tel. 227 55 11; phone 9am-9pm; office open Mon.-Sat. 10am-6:30pm, Sun. noon-5pm). *The List,* available from most city newsagents, is a detailed fortnightly guide to the arts and other events in Glasgow and Edinburgh (80p).

At the sweating **Sub Club,** 22 Jamaica St., students and the under-30 crowd bump and grind. Saturday is house and garage night; other nights are gay or mixed scenes (open Fri.-Sat. 11pm-3am, Thurs. during the term; cover £5-8). Nightly gyrations to the latest club music shake **Tunnel,** 84 Mitchell St., which offers student discounts (Thurs.), and **Club Industria,** 15 Union St. **Bennet's,** 90 Glassford St., and **Club Xchange,** 23 Royal Exchange Square, attract mixed crowds. Club hours are generally 11pm to 3:30am; cover charges run £3-7 with occasional student discounts.

Mayfest, an arts festival (April 28-May 20, 1995), offers a program of Scottish and international theater and music. Contact Mayfest, 18 Albion St., Glasgow, G1 1LH. The annual **Glasgow International Jazz Festival,** in late June or early July, brings such greats as B.B. King and Herbie Hancock to town (same address as Mayfest). Folk and traditional music thrive throughout Glasgow, especially during the **Glasgow International Folk Festival** at the beginning of July; contact the Festival Office, 4 Blackfriars St., Glasgow. During the annual **World Pipe Band Championships,** in mid-August, the skirling of bagpipes may be heard for miles.

The Byres Road pub crawl ("The path is long an' the ale is strong") usually starts with a trip to **Tennant's Bar** and then proceeds in the direction of the River Clyde. Alternatively, try the jazzy **Halt Bar,** 106 Woodlands Rd., or the groovy **O'Brien's Pub,** steps from the HI hostel. **The Variety Bar,** 401 Sauchiehall St., is an older men's pub by day, art students' hangout by night (open 11am-midnight). **The Horseshoe Bar,** 17-21 Drury St., in the city center, is a magnificent Victorian bar with etched mirrors and carved wooden walls; it's the longest continuous bar in the U.K. (open Mon.-Sat. 11am-midnight, Sun. 12:30pm-midnight).

■■■ STRANRAER

Located on the westernmost peninsula of Dumfries and Gallaway, Stranraer (stren-RAHR) is *the* place to get a **ferry to Northern Ireland,** but don't count on much beyond that. **Sealink ferries** (tel. (01776) 70 22 62 or (01233) 64 70 47) leave for Larne, Northern Ireland (2hr. 20min., £18-20, students and seniors £10; bikes free). Show up 45min. before scheduled departures; ferries will occasionally leave early depending on weather conditions. Trains connect Glasgow to Stranraer (2½hr., £17.30). The **Seacat Hoverspeed** (tel. (01776) 70 22 55) travels year-round to Belfast, Northern Ireland. (1½hr., £20-22, students and seniors £13-14, children £11-12. Bikes free.)

Stranraer is well-stocked with **B&Bs;** check the supplies on the A75 toward Newton Stewart (London Rd.). The **tourist office** (tel. (01776) 70 25 95), at 1 Bridge St., books accommodations and posts a list of B&Bs. (Open June-Sept. 9:30am-6pm; April-May and Oct. 9:30am-5pm.) From Stranraer, **buses** run to Dumfries (3hr.,

£6.30), Ayr (2hr., £4.90) and Glasgow (4hr., £6.60). They also lumber once or twice a day to London (9½hr.), Manchester (6hr.), and Birmingham (7½hr.).

■■■ ABERDEEN

The center of Britain's North Sea oil industry, Aberdeen is a practical commercial city that somewhat offsets its dirt and smog with attractive parks and a vibrant university. The tourist office offers **guided tours of Old Aberdeen** (early June-early Sept. Wed. 7pm and Sun. 2:30pm. £2, children 50p). Pick up a copy of the tourist office's monthly *What's On in Aberdeen*, or call the 24hr. info line (tel. (01224) 63 63 63). **The Aberdeen Art Gallery,** Schoolhill, houses a wide range of English, French, and Scottish paintings; its 20th-century British collection is particularly impressive (open Mon.-Sat. 10am-5pm, Thurs. 10am-8pm, Sun. 2-5pm; free). **Provost Skene's House,** on Guestrow near the tourist office, is a beautifully restored 17th-century townhouse "among buildings of lesser vintage" (open Mon.-Sat. 10am-5pm; free). Aberdeen has a fine **sandy beach** that stretches about 2mi. north from the old fishing community of Footdee (fi-TEE) to the Don estuary.

The **tourist office,** St. Nicholas House, Broad St. (tel. (01224) 63 27 27), has a mountain of leaflets; ask for *It's Free in Aberdeen* (open Mon.-Fri. 9am-8pm, Sat. 9am-6pm, Sun. 10am-6pm; Sept. and June Mon.-Sat. 9am-6pm, Sun. 10am-4pm; Oct.-May Mon.-Fri. 9am-5pm, Sat. 10am-2pm). **National Express** travels to Edinburgh (£11.70, return £15.50) and Glasgow (£12.10, return £16). **Bluebird Northern** serves Inverness (£8.40, return £10). **ScotRail** (tel. (01224) 59 42 22) provides service to Edinburgh (£27.50, return £31); Glasgow (£31.50, return £35); Inverness (£16, round-trip £23) and London (£67, return £68).

King George VI Memorial Hostel (HI), 8 Queen's Rd. (tel. (01224) 64 69 88; grade 1) is spacious and comes equipped with ping-pong and pool tables. (Strictly enforced 11:30pm lights-out and 8:30am wake-up call. Lockout 10:30am-1:30pm. Curfew 2am. £7.25. Open mid-Feb. to early Jan.) **Great Western Road,** 20min. from the train and bus stations on foot and also accessible by bus 17, 18, or 19, is loaded with B&Bs (£15-23). **The Grill,** 213 Union St., is authentically Aberdonian (open Mon.-Thurs. 10am-11pm, Fri.-Sat. 11am-midnight, Sun. 7:30-11pm). **Gannet's,** on the 2nd floor of the Students' Union on Broad St., offers tasty pizza (open mid-June to early July and mid-Aug. to Sept. Mon.-Sat. 10:30am-5pm; Oct. to mid-June Mon.-Fri. 9am-6pm, Sat. 11am-6pm).

The Aberdeen Ferry Terminal, Jamieson's Quay (tel. (01224) 57 26 15), is the only place on mainland Britain to catch a ferry to the Shetland Islands. Ferries to Lerwick (Mon. and Wed.-Fri. 6pm, Tues. and Sat. at noon via Orkney; 14hr.; June-Sept. £49, with berth £58-99; Oct.-May £43, with berth £52-89.50) and Stromness (Sat. at noon or 6pm; June-Aug. also Tues. at noon; 8hr., £34.50, with berth £38-71; off-season £31.50, with berth £34-65). Go down Market St., turn left at the traffic light past the P&O Scottish Ferries warehouse (open Mon.-Fri. 8:45am-6pm, Sat. 9am-6pm).

■■■ INVERNESS

The charms of Inverness, like Nessie herself, are somewhat elusive—Banquo's ghost has no ruin to haunt, and Nessie lives five miles to the south. Unfathomably deep and unbelievably famous, **Loch Ness** guards its secrets 5mi. south of town. For a full dose of Nessie-hunting lore and a hearty welcome to the Highlands, take a tour on **Gordon's Minibus.** The entertaining narrative of marine biologist and historian Dr. Gordon Williamson is a refreshing break from the usual area tourist traps. His minibus leaves from the Inverness tourist office at 10:30am and returns at 4:30pm. (£9.90; students, seniors and hostelers £6.90.) **Cawdor Castle** has been the residence of the Thane's descendents since the 15th century; don't miss the "wild" garden and the stunning nature walks (open May-early Oct. 10am-5:30pm. £3.50, grounds only £1.80.)

The helpful **tourist office** in Castle Wynd (tel. (01463) 23 43 53, fax 71 06 09) has probably heard far too much about Nessie already. (Open late April-late May and Oct. Mon.-Sat. 9am-5pm, Sun. 10am-4pm; late May-late June and mid-Sept.-end of Sept. Mon.-Sat. 9am-6pm, Sun. 10am-5pm; late June to mid-Sept. Mon.-Sat. 9am-8:30pm, Sun. 9:30am-6pm; Nov.-Dec. and Jan.-late April Mon.-Fri. 9am-5pm, Sat. 10am-4pm). **Scottish Citylink** provides service to Edinburgh (4hr., £11.20, return £18.50), Glasgow (4¼hr., £11.30, return £20.50); Thurso and Wick (3½hr., £8.10, return £13.50). **Gaelicbus** runs to Fort William and **Morrison's Coaches** serves Thurso and Wick. For more travel information call **Highland Bus and Coach** (tel. (01463) 71 10 00) or the **train** station (tel. (01463) 23 89 24).

While in town, stay at the friendly **Inverness Student Hotel**, 8 Culduthel Rd. (tel. (01463) 23 65 56; open 6:30am-2:30am; £7.50-7.90). The quiet **HI youth hostel** (tel. (01463) 23 17 71) is across from the Student Hotel at 1 Edinburgh Rd. (check-out 10:30am; curfew 2am; £7.25) Near the youth hostel, **The Castle Restaurant** serves filling British meals (shepherd's pie £3.25; open Mon.-Sat. 8am-8:25pm.)

■■■ HIGHLANDS AND ISLANDS

The Highlands Boundary Fault stretches northeast from Arran Island to Aberdeen, marking the southern boundary of the Highlands and Islands. Scotland's frayed northwestern coast, cut by sea lochs and girded by innumerable islands, remains the most beautiful region in Scotland and one of the last stretches of true wilderness in Europe. Even in tourist season, you can easily hike for a full day without seeing another human being. The Mainland towns of Oban, Fort William, Glencoe, Ullapool, and Thurso act as points of access to the islands. Although bus routes criss-cross the region and boat services connect more than 40 islands to the mainland, you can't count on making more than one or two journeys per day on any form of transportation, even in high season.

Most ferries on the west coast are run by **Caledonian MacBrayne** (head office tel. (01475) 65 01 00, fax 63 76 07), which publishes an excellent, widely available free timetable and fare sheet; their open-dated **Island Hopscotch** service provides discounts on a succession of ferry trips. Bikes can cross without reservation for a fee of £1-2, but advance booking for cars is strongly recommended.

OBAN, MULL, AND IONA

Oban (OH–ben; 3hr. by bus or train from Glasgow), the busiest ferry port on the west coast, endears itself with sporadic outbursts of small-town warmth. If you tire of the busy pier, gaze at the bay from **McCaig's Tower** (built in the 19th century to employ local masons), or walk 15min. north of town to the crumbling tower of **Dunollie Castle**. The **tourist office**, Argyll Sq. (tel. (01631) 631 22), is unflaggingly friendly despite the milling throngs. (Open Mon.-Sat. 9am-8:45pm, Sun. 9am-5pm; May and Sept. Mon.-Sat. 9am-5:30pm, Sun. 10am-5pm; Oct. and April Mon.-Fri. 9am-5:30pm; Nov.-March Mon.-Fri. 9am-1pm and 2-5:30pm.) Sleep like royalty in the giant bunks at **Oban Backpackers Lodge**, Breadalbande St. (tel. (01631) 621 07 or 633 23), a clean, comfortable, new hostel with the most amiable of managers (open 24hrs., check out and check in 10:30am; £7.50; continental breakfast £1.50). The **HI youth hostel**, on Corran Esplanade (tel. (01631) 620 25), presides over the bay. (Curfew 2am. £7.25. Open March-Oct.; frantically busy July-Aug.)

Most visitors leave from the Oban pier for **Mull**, the largest of the southern isles. Several ferries sail each day in summer for **Craignure** (40min., £2.70). There's not much to do in Craignure, but climb aboard Mull's 10¼-in.-gauge steam train to **Torosay Castle**, a graceful Victorian mansion nearby (open Easter-Oct. 10:30am-5:30pm; £3.50, students and seniors £2.75), or else bus it to **Tobermory** (Mull's main town) or **Fionnphort** (where ferries to Iona leave). The Tobermory **HI youth hostel** (tel. (01688) 24 81) on Main St., has a magnificent panorama of the bay. (£3.85. Open mid-March to Sept.) The isle of **Iona** was the first Christian settlement in Scotland (St. Columba founded its abbey in 563). For B&B, try the **Bishop's**

GREAT BRITAIN

House (tel. (016817) 306; £24.50, students 15% off) or **Finlay, Ross Ltd.** (tel. (016817) 357; £16-18).

FORT WILLIAM AND MALLAIG

Fort William no longer has a fort, but it could use one to fend off summer tourists. Mountaineers come for the challenge of **Ben Nevis** (4418 ft.), the highest peak in Britain. The main tourist path starts just up Glen Nevis past the town park. The **tourist office** (tel. (01397) 70 37 81) functions as the central depot for information of the West Highlands. (Open Mon.-Sat. 9am-8pm, Sun. 9am-6pm; Oct. Mon.-Thurs. 9am-5:30pm, Fri.-Sat 9am-5pm; Nov.-Dec. Mon.-Thurs. 9am-5:30pm, Fri. 9am-5pm; Jan.-March Mon.-Sat. 9am-5:30pm; April to mid-May 9am-5:30pm.) Just 5min. from train, bus, and town, the snug and fun-loving **Ft. William Backpackers Guesthouse** (tel. (01937) 70 07 11) welcomes visitors back from Ben Nevis with a hot cup of tea and a cozy bed (£7.90, breakfast £1.20). The **Glen Nevis HI youth hostel** (tel. (01397) 70 23 36) stands 3mi. east of town on the Glen Nevis Rd.; book 2 days ahead in July and August (£6.50; Dec.-Oct.). On the opposite side of the River Nevis, the **Ben Nevis Bunkhouse** (tel. (01397) 70 22 40) lies 1½mi. from town along Achintee Rd. (£6). The **Glen Nevis Caravan & Camping Park** (tel. (01397) 70 21 91) stretches canvas on the same road, ½mi. before the HI hostel. (Tents £4.50, £1.20 per person. Open mid-March to mid-Oct.)

Trains wind coastwards from Fort William to **Mallaig** along the famous "Road to the Isles," through mountains and past lochs and the Silver Sands of Morar (white beaches more at home in the Caribbean). Disembark from the train either at Arisaig or the next stop, Morar, to reach the comfortable **Garramore youth hostel (HI)** (tel. (016875) 268; grade 1; £6.50; open March-Oct.), a 3mi. walk along the A830 from either station; it's next to a campsite and close to secluded sandy beaches with misty views of the Inner Hebrides. From Mallaig, ferries shuttle to Skye and the **Small Isles** of Muck, Eigg, and Canna.

SKYE

Often described as the shining jewel in the Hebridean crown, Skye radiates unparalleled natural splendor. The **Cuillin Hills,** volcanic peaks surging boldly into a halo of clouds, are perhaps the most dramatic mountain vistas in Britain. Lush peninsulas and bays mark the extremes of the island near Staffin and Armadale. Until a bridge is completed in mid-1995, sole access to the island is provided by **ferry.** They sail from Kyle of Lochalsh on the mainland to Kyleakin on Skye (free, cars £5), and from Mallaig to Armadale (£2.30, cars £11.60). Transportation on the island is not easy; bus service is infrequent and expensive. Biking or hiking may be better options; many hitch. A thoroughly enjoyable way to get around Skye's scattered sights is with **Badger Tours** (tel. (014716) 228). Australian Ted Badger, a former divorce lawyer and urban refugee, knowledgeably and wittily guides you around the island on full-day tours by foot and minibus for £10 per person. The **tourist office** in Kyle of Lochalsh (tel. (01599) 42 76) books B&Bs for £1 on either side of the channel. (Open July-Sept. Mon.-Sat. 9am-7pm; Aug. Mon.-Sat. 9am-9:30pm, Sun. 12:30-4:30pm; Easter-June and Oct. Mon.-Sat. 9am-5:30pm.)

Once you've seen the harbor in Kyleakin, you've seen all you can there. Move on to the ruins of the **Castle Moil;** legend relates that the original castle on this site was built by "Saucy Mary," a Norwegian princess who stretched a stout chain across the Kyle and charged ships a fee to come through the narrows. On an islet in Loch Duich, **Eilean Donan Castle** perches, the restored 13th-century seat of the Mac-Kenzies. Or visit the ruins of **Duntulm Castle,** which guard the tip of the peninsula. The castle was the MacDonald's formidable stronghold until a nurse dropped the chief's baby boy from the window to the rocks below.

Skye's five **HI hostels** are sweetly situated but distressingly oversubscribed in the summer. Try to call at least one night in advance. **Glenbrittle** (tel. (01478) 64 02 78) is in the heart of the Cuillins, accessible only to hikers and those with their own transportation. (£5.05. Open mid-March to Sept.) **Uig** (tel. (0147042) 211), overlooking the bay on the northern peninsula, is a tough 30min. walk from the ferry on the A586. (£5.05. Open mid-March to Oct.) **Broadford** (tel. (014712) 82 44 42) is the most central, close to both mountains and beaches. (£4.80. Open early March-Oct.) **Armadale** (tel. (014714) 260), on the southern tip of Skye, is near the Mallaig ferry and serves well as a base for touring the verdant **Sleat Peninsula.** (£5.05. Open mid-March to Sept.) **Kyleakin** (tel. (01599) 45 85), Skye's only grade 1 hostel fills very quickly in the summer, so book weeks ahead. (£6.50. Breakfast £2.65, dinner £3.55.) Several independent hostels have recently sprung up in Skye to help cope with excess demand. The **Backpacker's Guesthouse** (tel. (01599) 45 10) in Kyleakin offers low-key comfort for £7.50. Near Broadford, the tiny **Fossil Bothy** (tel. (01471) 82 26 44 or 82 22 97) sleeps 8 cozily (£6).

OUTER HEBRIDES

The landscape of the Outer Hebrides is astoundingly ancient. The culture and customs of the Hebridean people have also resisted change; most old and some young islanders still speak Gaelic among themselves. The vehemently Calvinist islands of Lewis, Harris, and North Uist observe the Sabbath strictly: all shops, pubs, and restaurants close, and public transportation stops on Sundays. According to legend, Bafinn, a Norwegian princess, rests in a 3000-year slumber under a knoll on North Uist. When she wakes, the weather on the Outer Isles will improve. Until then, expect a regular riot of high winds and rain.

 Caledonian MacBrayne ferries travelers out, while spasmodically scheduled buses and ferries connect the islands lengthwise; hitching and cycling are excellent but often rain-soaked. Since ferries arrive at odd hours, try to arrange a bed ahead. The Outer Hebrides are home to the very special **Gatliff Hebridean Trust Hostels** (Urras Osdailean Nan Innse Gall Gatliff), five 19th-century thatched croft houses converted into simple hostels, open year-round, whose authenticity and atmosphere more than compensate for crude facilities. Camping is allowed on any public land, but freezing winds and sodden ground often make it miserable. For more light on the islands, snag a copy of *The Outer Hebrides Handbook and Guide* (£4.25 at all tourist offices).

Lewis, Harris, and Barra Lewis island is famous for its atmosphere: pure light and drifting mists off the Atlantic Ocean shroud the untouched miles of moorland and small lochs in quiet luminescence. The unearthly setting is great for exploring the **Callanish Stones,** an extraordinary Bronze Age circle as isolated as Stonehenge is overrun. **Caledonian MacBrayne** ferries from Ullapool on the mainland serve **Stornoway,** the biggest town in the Outer Hebrides (Mon.-Sat. 2-3 per day, £10.05). The **tourist office** (tel. (01851) 70 30 88) is at 26 Cromwell St.—turn right from the ferry terminal, then left on Cromwell St. (Open Mon.-Sat. 9am-6pm and 9-10pm; Nov.-March Mon.-Fri. 9am-5pm; April Mon.-Thurs. 9am-5:30pm and 9-10pm, Fri.-Sat. 9am-5pm and 9-10pm.)

 Although **Harris** is part of the same island as Lewis, it preserves its separate identity behind the curiously treeless **Forest of Harris** (actually a mountain range). Open hills, softened by a carpet of *machair* and wildflowers, make for wonderful off-trail rambling. **Ferries** (tel. (01859) 50 24 44) serve the town of **Tarbert** from Uig on Skye (£6.65) and Lochmaddy on North Uist (direct service Tues. and Fri. only, £6.65). A **tourist office** sits on Pier Rd. (tel. (01859) 20 11; open April to mid-Oct. roughly 9am-5pm and for late ferry arrivals). The nearest **HI youth hostel** is 7mi. away in **Stockinish** (tel. (01859) 53 03 73; £3.85; open April-Sept.).

 Little **Barra,** the southern outpost of the outer isles, is unspeakably beautiful; on a sunny day, the island's colors are unforgettable—grassy sand dunes and flawless beaches edge waters flecked unnameable shades of light-dazzled blue, wreathed below by dimly-visible red, brown, and green kelp. **Kisimul Castle,** bastion of the old Clan MacNeil, inhabits an islet in Castlebay Harbor (boat trips out Mon., Wed., and Sat. 2-5pm; £2). West of Castlebay, near Borve (Borgh), are **standing stones.** Locals say that these stones were erected in memory of a Viking galley captain who lost a bet with a Barra man; Scandinavian archaeologists who excavated the site did indeed find a skeleton and Nordic armor. A chambered cairn, **Dún Bharpa,** and the better-preserved **Dún Cuier,** north of Allasdale (Allathasdal), are also near Borve. A **Caledonian MacBrayne ferry** stops at Castlebay (Bagh A Chaisteil) on Barra on its way between Oban on the mainland and Lochboisdale on South Uist (Mon.-Thurs., and Sat.; return Tues., Thurs.-Fri., and Sun.; to Oban 5¼hr., £14.30; to Lochboisdale 1¾hr., £4.45). The Castlebay **tourist office** (tel. (01871) 81 03 36) is around the bend and to the right from the pier (open roughly April to mid-Oct. Mon.-Fri. 9am-5pm, Sat. 9am-4pm, Sun. 11:30am-12:30pm, and for late ferry arrivals).

ORKNEY ISLANDS

Less well known than the more northerly Shetland, Orkney rarely fails to enchant its visitors with its impressive mix of nature, history, and hospitality. Two **ferries** connect mainland Scotland to Orkney. P&O's St. Ola car ferry (tel. (0224) 572 615 in Aberdeen, (0856) 850 655 in Stromness; 1¾hr., £12, Oct.-May £11) runs past the great cliffs of Hoy on its runs from Scrabster to Stromness. A bus leaves from Thurso railway station for Scrabster before each crossing (65p). Thomas & Beros (tel (095581) 353) runs from John O'Groats to Burwick on South Ronaldsay (45min., £10, return £16). Buses connect Kirkwall with all ferry arrivals and departures at Burwick (£2). There are more bus companies populating the roads of Mainland than there are islands in the surrounding sea. Ferries to the smaller islands run from Kirkwall and Tingwall for the north, Houton and Stromness for the south. The Orkney Islands Shipping Company (OISC; tel. (0856) 87 29 21) operates most ferries. (Return fares range from £2-14.) An Island Explorer Ticket gives the intrepid traveler 10 days of unlimited ferry travel for £20 (seniors and travelers with disabilities £15, children £10). Ask about student discounts on all ferry journeys.

Home to one-third of Orkney's 21,000 souls, **Kirkwall** in East Mainland is Orkney's largest and busiest town. The **tourist office,** 6 Broad St. (tel. (01856) 87 28 56), books B&Bs down the main road from the cathedral. Behind an abandoned British Telecom building on old Skapa Rd. is the **Kirkwall Youth Hostel (HI)** (tel. (01856) 87 22 43; open mid-March-Oct.; £6.50). Camping is available near Kirkwall off A965 at the **Pickaquoy Caravan & Camping Site** from £4 (tel. (01856) 87 35 35). You can pitch your tent almost anywhere on the islands, but ask the landowner first. Stock up on supplies during the week at the **Presto Supermarket** on Broad St. (open Mon.-Sat. 9am-6pm). The **Atholl Coffee Shop,** Albert St., is the cheapest sit-down in town (sandwiches £1.50, open Mon.-Fri. 9:30am-7pm, Sat. 9am-6pm).

Stromness, Orkney's second metropolis is a small port that reeks of fish. The **Stromness Museum** on Alfred St. tackles the history of the sea with artifacts and memorabilia from the whaling and fishing industries (open Mon.-Sat. 10:30am-5pm; Oct.-April Mon.-Sat. 10:30am-1pm, 2-4pm; 80p). The helpful **Stromness tourist office** (tel. (01856) 85 07 16) resides in an 18th-century rice warehouse on the pier (open for ferry arrivals and departures; call for hours). Fewer than five minutes from the tourist office, **Brown's Hostel (HI),** 45-7 Victoria St. (tel. (01856) 85 06 61) is as warm and toasty as the night is cold and damp (£6.50). The **Ness Point Caravan and Camping Site** (tel. (01856) 87 35 35) juts just south of Stromness (£4). Arguably the most happening place in Stromness, **The Café** at 22 Victoria St. serves cheap meals (£3-4) and warm soup (£1.05; open Mon.-Sat. 9am-9pm).

SHETLAND ISLANDS

Getting There and Getting Around British Airways flies from Aberdeen; **Loganair** flies from Edinburgh, and Glasgow. All flights are met by buses which run to Lerwick (1hr., £2.90). Inter-Shetland flights use **Tingwall Airstrip** just outside Lerwick (tel. (0159548) 246 for reservations).

P&O Scottish Ferries leave weekdays at 6pm (June-Aug. Tues. at noon) from Aberdeen for Lerwick (14hr., £49; Oct.-May £43.50, berth from £47). A P&O ferry also runs from Stromness on Orkney to Lerwick (Tues. 10pm and Sun. noon, Sept.-May Sun. noon; 8hr., £31.50). P&O leaves Scotland behind with runs to Bergen,

Norway (June-Aug. Sat. 11am; £55, berth from £5). From June through August, the **Smyril Line** ferry sails from Lerwick to the Faroe Islands (Tues. 2pm, £56) and Hanstholm, Denmark (Sun. 1pm, £73). Connect to Iceland from Faroe. Ferries run from Lerwick to Berger, Norway early June to late August Saturdays 10am (£55). Students get 25% off these fares, which are lower in early June and late August. Bookings and information for P&O and Smyril Line are available from P&O Scottish Ferries. P.O. Box 5. Jamieson's Quay, Aberdeen AB9 8DL (tel. (01224) 57 26 15).

Shetland's main bus companies are **John Leask & Son** (tel. (01595) 31 62) and **Shalder Coaches** (tel. (0159588) 217). The tourist office has the indispensable *Inter-Shetland Transport Timetable* (80p) listing bus, ferry, and plane schedules.

Practical Information, Accommodations, and Food Shetland **Islands Tourism** (tel. (01595) 34 34), at Market Cross in Lerwick, will book you a bed anywhere in the islands for a £1 fee, or free for 3 or more nights (open Mon.-Fri. 8am-6pm, Sat. 8am-5pm; Oct.-March Mon.-Fri. 9am-5pm). The relaxed Lerwick **HI youth hostel,** Islesborough House at King Harald and Union St., is closed for renovations until mid-1995. Other hostel-style accommodations are available outside of town. While the hostel is closed, treat yourself to B&B, yellow Shetland tomatoes, and a backyard view of Clickimin Broch at **Mrs. Wiseman's** (tel. (01595) 39 30) at 27 Russell Crescent (£12.50). There are three **campgrounds** on Mainland, but you can camp almost anywhere with the landowner's permission. **Clickimin Caravan and Camp Site** (tel. (01595) 45 55) is closest to the Lerwick ferry terminal—turn left on the A970, then right on the A969 (tents £5.25-7; open late April to Sept.).

Inexpensive eats cluster in the heart of Lerwick. **Central Bakery** offers fresh filled rolls in a non-smoking environment (open Mon.-Tues. and Thurs.-Fri. 9am-4:15pm, Wed. 9am-1:30pm, Sat. 9am-4pm). The **Fort Café,** 2 Commercial Rd., fries up the local catch (open Mon.-Fri. 11am-8pm, Sat. 11am-6pm, Sun. 5-8pm).

Lerwick, Bressay, and Tingwall Nowhere on Shetland's desolate, tireless terrain can you be farther than three miles from the sea. **Lerwick** lies on the eastern coast of the main island ("Mainland") and is served by the A970 which runs the length of the island. The best views of Lerwick and its harbor are from the giant pentagonal **Fort Charlotte** in the center of town, a relic of the Cromwellian era. Only a mile west of the city center on Clickimin Rd., the ruins of **Clickimin Broch,** a stronghold from the 4th century BC, rest on a strand cutting into a loch. Hourly **ferries** (65p) sail from Lerwick to the isle of **Bressay,** a gentle spot ideal for a slow amble. Hike up conical **Ward of Bressay** (743ft.) for a sweeping view of the sea. **Tingwall,** 5mi. north of Lerwick, houses the cluttered **Tingwall Agricultural Museum** (open July-Sept. 2-5pm; £1, seniors 50p). The view from the top of nearby Wamadale Hill will shatter your camera lens—in clear weather, you can see 40mi. into the distance.

Greece (Ελλας)

US$1	= 237dr (drachmas, or GRD)	**100dr =**	**US$0.42**
CDN$1	= 176dr	**100dr =**	**CDN$0.57**
UK£1	= 377dr	**100dr =**	**UK£0.27**
IR£1	= 373dr	**100dr =**	**IR£0.27**
AUS$1	= 182dr	**100dr =**	**AUS$0.55**
NZ$1	= 144dr	**100dr =**	**NZ$0.70**
SAR1	= 66dr	**100dr =**	**SAR1.50**
Country Code: 30		**International Dialing Prefix: 00**	

Even before Odysseus made his epic voyage across the Mediterranean, Greece was a place for wanderers. Wanderers today should know they will not be alone, although finding a heavenly piece of solitary Greece remains a possibility. Some areas of Greece are plowed over by the heaviest tourist industry in Europe, while others nearby retain authenticity. The West's oldest, most sacred monuments cringe over conspicuously tacky tourist strips, while untrodden mountainsides arch above beaches resembling human rugs.

In some ways, Greece is an aggressively western country whose capital rivals London, Paris, and Rome. As proud guardians of the classical inheritance, Greeks consider western civilization a homespun export. But to step into Greece is to walk east—into a stir of Byzantine icons, Orthodox priests trailing long dark robes, and air spiced with the strains of *bouzouki*. Greece's Eastern flavor is the result of four centuries of Ottoman rule. Thanks mostly to the integrity of the Orthodox Church, the Greek national identity survived Turkish captivity. Memories of the 1821 War of Independence still excite Greek nationalism; 400 years are not easily forgotten.

Only in the last 20 years has Greece rebounded from a battering century that brought Nazi occupation, mass starvation, civil war, and military rule. Villages began seeing automobiles and electric lights only in the 1960s. Greece still faces severe problems, however; despite its recent entry into the Common Market, per capita income and productivity are half the EU average, and inflation continues to rage. Consequently, volatility and ferocity characterize Greek politics.

Macedonia is the latest issue to inflame Greek public opinion. After the former Yugoslav province declared itself the independent Republic of Macedonia, Greeks felt an important part of their history and culture usurped. Ancient Macedonia, home to Alexander the Great, was very probably a Hellenic civilization and certainly not a Slavic one. Albanian refugees have also recently encountered resistance in Greece. Although initially greeted with open arms, outbreaks of crime and anger at the persecution of ethnic Greeks in Albania have turned sympathy into hostility.

For more extensive coverage of Greece than we can offer here, plunge in the 1995 edition of *Let's Go: Greece and Turkey*.

GETTING THERE

One of the least expensive ways to reach Greece is by **train,** even without a railpass. From Venice or Vienna, expect a 36hr. trip and huge crowds in summer; insist on a seat reservation. Buses are even cheaper, but a real marathon. **London Student Travel,** 52 Grosvenor Gardens, London SW1W OAG (tel. (071) 730 34 02), runs a bus from London to Athens for about UK£75. **Magic Bus,** 20 Filellinon St., Athens (tel. (01) 323 74 71 or 322 68 10), sells discounted bus tickets from Athens to London.

Certainly the most popular way of getting to Greece is by **ferry** from Italy. Boats travel primarily from Ancona and Bríndisi to Corfu (9hr., deck class in high-season 11,500-15,500dr, low-season 8500-8970dr), Igoumenitsa (11hr., same prices), and Patras (18hr., high-season 15,500-16,300dr, low season 8970-10,600dr). Ferries also stop at Piraeus; Iraklion; Rhodes; Limassol; Cyprus; Haifa, Israel (from Piraeus high season 21,000dr); and İzmir, Turkey. From Patras, buses leave for Athens frequently and also for points throughout the Peloponnese. If you plan to travel from Bríndisi in the summer, make reservations and arrive at the port well before your departure time. Those 26 and under, and ISIC-holders 30 and under, can usually obtain student deck fares for 1000dr less than the regular price. Senior citizens may get a 10% discount, and children under 12 pay ½-price (under 4 ride free). **Eurail** passholders may receive 30% off regular fares. Regardless of the ticket, everyone pays the port tax (TL11,000-18,000 in Bríndisi, about 1000dr at Greek ports).

Flying from northern European cities is also a popular way of getting to Greece. Watch for special package fares offered by travel agents or advertised in newspapers, especially from London, Amsterdam, and major cities in Germany and Scandinavia. These are often the cheapest deals available, even if you must take a hotel package. In addition, you may be able to fly aboard charters to island destinations otherwise inaccessible by direct flight.

GETTING AROUND

Train service in Greece is slow and infrequent compared with the rest of Europe, and no lines go to the western coast. Though Eurail is valid, even Eurail holders should take buses. **OSE** (tel. (01) 524 06 01), the national train network, offers discounts of up to 20% to those under 26 and 50% for kids.

Faster, more extensive, and only slightly more expensive, **buses** are a good alternative to train travel; most are run through **KTEL.** While large towns all have their own bus stations, smaller ones usually use cafés as bus stops. Along the road, little blue signs marked with white buses or the word "ΣΤΑΣΙ" indicate bus stops, but drivers usually stop anywhere if you signal. Let the driver know ahead of time if you want to get off; if your stop is passed, yell "Stasi!"

Greeks are not eager to pick up foreigners. Sparsely-populated areas simply have little or no traffic. Those who do choose to **hitchhike** write their destination on a sign in both Greek and English, and hitch from turn-offs rather than along long stretches of straight road. *Women should never hitch alone.* The mountainous terrain and unpaved roads make **cycling** in Greece difficult. A better means of transport is the humble **moped,** which is perfect for exploring.

There is frequent **ferry** service to the Greek islands, but schedules can be exasperating, misinformation is common, and direct connections exist only between major islands. Don't plan to follow a strict schedule. Wild competition exists between ferry lines and travel agencies. No Greek ferry agent has ever breathed a word about the competition's schedule (or even their existence), so you'll have to visit several—or all—agencies in town to plan your trip. To avoid hassles, go to **limenarxeio** (port police)—every port has one, and they all carry complete ferry information. **Hydrofoils** are speedier, but costlier. In Piraeus, the situation is considerably better, since the GNTO publishes a schedule; however, the schedule loses meaning as the summer progresses. And finally, keep an ear to the ground for boat strikes.

The national airline, **Olympic Airways** (tel. (01) 929 21 11), operates efficient and reasonably priced flights between many islands. Note that these flights are often booked weeks in advance in summer, however. Coverage to remote areas is spotty.

GREECE ESSENTIALS

The **Greek National Tourist Organization (GNTO),** which the Greeks call **EOT,** is far from standardized. Some cities have full-fledged offices that distribute brochures, maps and bus schedules, and help with accommodations. Other towns have no office at all. In the islands, "Tourist Information Centers, Inc." often masquerade as official offices. Although they aggressively market their local package tours, they can supply useful information and are often the best places to locate a place to stay. Many towns have branches of the **tourist police,** who can give information and assist travelers in trouble. Regular police will step in if there isn't a tourist police officer around; most, however, speak no English. **Tourist information** is available in English by calling 171 (24hrs.). The **emergency** number for **police** is 100 throughout most of Greece; for **medical assistance,** it's 166.

Though many Greek men are notorious *kamaki* (playboys), women traveling in Greece are relatively safe. If you find yourself in an emergency, call out "vo-EE-thee-a" ("help"). Modest dress (no shorts, short skirts, or revealing tops) is required of both sexes at monasteries and churches. Normal **business hours** in Greece include a break from about 2pm until 5 or 6pm, with **evening hours** usually on Tuesday, Thursday, and Friday. Banks are normally open Monday through Thursday from 8am to 1:30pm, Friday from 7:45am to 2pm. The major **national holidays** in Greece—during which all banks and shops are closed—are New Year's Day, Epiphany (Jan. 6), National Holidays (March 25 and Oct. 28), Labor Day (May 1), The Assumption of the Virgin Mary (Aug. 15) and Christmas (Dec. 25).

Communication Greece's **telephone** company is **OTE.** Their offices are usually open from 7:30am to 3pm in small towns and from 7:30am to 10pm in larger towns. In cities, OTE offices are open 24hrs., but you must bang on the door after midnight. For AT&T's **USA Direct,** dial 00 800 1311, MCI **WorldPhone** 00 800 12 11, **SprintExpress** 00 800 14 11, **Canada Direct** 00 800 16 11, **BT Direct** 00 800 44 11, **Ireland Direct** 00 800 353 11, and **Australia Direct** 00 800 6111. Post offices are generally open Monday through Friday from 7:30am to 2pm; some larger offices keep longer hours. A letter or postcard to the U.S. costs 120dr and takes about 9 to 11 days, sometimes longer from small villages. **Poste Restante** may be filed under your last name, first name, or randomly.

GREECE

Although many Greeks in Athens and other resort towns speak English—particularly young people—those living off the beaten path are unlikely to. Be forewarned that "né" means "yes" in Greek. The following transliteration table should help you decipher things, although prepare for some exceptions to it (for instance, Φ and φ are often spelled *ph*).

Greek	Roman	Greek	Roman	Greek	Roman
A, α	A, a	I, ι	I, i	P, ρ	R, r
B, β	V, v	K, κ	K, k	Σ, σ, ς	S, s
Γ, γ	G, g	Λ, λ	L, l	T, τ	T, t
Δ, δ	D, d	M, μ	M, m	Y, υ	Y, y
E, ε	E, e	N, ν	N, n	Φ, φ	F, f
Z, ζ	Z, z	Ξ, ξ	X, x	X, χ	Ch, ch
H, η	I, i	O, o	O, o	Ψ, ψ	Ps, ps
Θ, θ	Th, th	Π, π	P, p	Ω, ω	O, o

Learn a few helpful phrases, given here phonetically: "I don't speak Greek" (dhen mee-LAHO el-leen-ee-KAH), "Do you speak English?" (mee-LAHS ahn-glee-KAH?), "how much?" (PO-so KAH-nee), "I would like" (thah EE-the-lah), "can I see a room?" (bo-RO nah DHO E-nah dho-MAH-tee-o), "what time is it?" (tee O-rah EE-ne) and "do you have?" (E-che-te).

Even more important to know is Greek body language, which can lead to endless misunderstandings. To say no, Greeks silently close their eyes or click their tongues while lifting their heads and/or eyebrows. To indicate a yes, they tilt and bow the head in one motion. A hand waving up and down that seems to say "stay there" actually means "come." Be careful when waving good-bye; if you do so with your palm forward, the gesture may be interpreted as an insult.

Accommodations and Camping Lodging in Greece is a bargain; the country's two dozen or so **youth hostels** cost about 1000dr per night. Curfew is usually midnight or 1am, and HI membership requirements are not enforced. Since bartering is common, **hotels** are also reasonable; expect to pay 5000dr for a double without bath in a D or E class hotel. GNTO offices invariably have a list of inexpensive accommodations with prices. In many areas, *dhomatia* (rooms to let) are an attractive and perfectly dependable option. Although you may lack locks or towels, the possibility of sharing coffee or some intriguing conversation with your proprietor is worth it. Often you'll be approached by locals as you enter town or disembark from your boat; see their rooms before you decide. Greece hosts plenty of official **campgrounds,** and discreet freelance camping—though illegal in Greece—is sometimes tolerated. Under these warm, dry skies, camping may become your favorite way to spend the night, but only if you remember to bring mosquito spray. **Tourist Guide of Greece,** 137 Patission St., Athens 11251 (tel. (01) 864 16 88), in conjunction with the Greek Camping Association, publishes a list of official campsites in Greece.

Food and Drink Greek food is simple and healthy. Most restaurants in Greece work from the same culinary palette, but create original masterpieces with subtle shadings of taste. A Greek restaurant is known as either a *taverna* or *estiatorio,* while a grill is a *psistaria.* Breakfast can be bread, *tiropita* (cheese pie), or a pastry with *marmelada* (jam) or *meli* (honey), along with a cup of coffee. Lunch, the largest meal of the day, is eaten in the mid to late afternoon. The evening meal is a leisurely affair; served late relative to American standards, usually after 8 or 9pm, and as late as 11pm-1am during the summer in the larger cities. Greek restaurants divide food into two categories, *magiremeno,* meaning cooked, or *tis oras,* (of the hour) to indicate grilled meat. The former is generally cheaper. *Tis oras* includes grilled *moskari* (veal), *arni* (lamb), or *kotopoulo* (chicken), served with *patates* (french fries), *rizi* (rice), or *fasolia* (beans). Popular *magiremeno* dishes include *mousaka* (chopped meat and eggplant mixed with a cheese and tomato paste), *pastitsio* (a lasagna-like dish of thick noodles covered with a rich cream sauce), *yemista* (stuffed tomatoes and peppers), *dolmadhes* (stuffed grape leaves with rice and minced meat, and *youvrelakia* (meatballs covered with egg and lemon sauce). You can hardly avoid *souvlaki,* a large skewer of steak, generally pork or lamb. A *souvlaki pita,* appropriately known as "the budget food of the masses," consists of a pita crammed full of skewered meat and fillings (only about 120dr). Gyros also abound in street vendor fast-food stands (approximately 120dr). A favorite Greek snack combination is *ouzo* with *mezes,* tidbits of cheese, sausage, cakes, and octopus. *Ouzo* is a distilled spirit to which anise is added, giving it a licorice taste. Some people drink it as an aperitif, all afternoon long; others have it after dinner as a liqueur. Mixed with water, it's sweet but not overwhelming.

One of the great arts in Greece is wine-making, and every region has its own specialty. Long ago, the Greeks discovered that when wine was stored in pitch pine-sealed goatskins, it developed a fresh, sappy flavor. After much deduction, they discovered that adding pine resin in varying amounts during fermentation achieved the same result. The resulting wine became known as *retsina.* Resinated wines now come in three varieties: white, rosé, and red *(kokkineli).*

■■■ ATHENS (ΑΘΗΝΑ)

Athens boggles the mind less because of its dimension in space than its dimension in time. Under the watchful eye of the ancient Acropolis, this city of five-million-plus slowly drags itself towards the high-tech Age of Efficiency. Visitors harboring mental images of togas and philosophers may be disappointed; Athens is a city in the 20th-century sense of the word—crowded, modern, and polluted. Yet one glimpse of the Parthenon from the grimy streets is enough to remind you of Athens's more ethereal incarnation. The structures of the Acropolis are majestic. They evoke images of gods, reminding you that there's more out there than hordes of Vespas.

ORIENTATION AND PRACTICAL INFORMATION

Athens is impossible to negotiate without a map. **Syntagma (Constitution) Square** is the focal point for tourists, with the transportation terminals and construction for a subway station. **Filellinon Street** and **Nikis Street,** parallel streets which head out from Syntagma toward the Plaka, contain the city's budget travel offices, cheap hotels, and dance clubs. The Parliament, facing Syntagma Square, is bordered on the south side by the tranquil **National Garden.** The **Plaka,** between Syntagma and the **Acropolis,** is the oldest section of the city, now brimming with shops, restaurants, and hotels. Ermou St. leads from Syntagma to **Monastiraki,** home of the Athens **flea market.** Adjacent to the flea market is the **Agora** (marketplace). Women shouldn't stroll alone at night; actually, no one should. South of the Acropolis, separated by **Andrea Singrou,** are the **Koukaki** and **Kinossargous** regions. **Piraeus,** a seedy port, is a 15min. subway ride to the southwest.

Make use of the two quality maps available at the GNTO; their free map of the city is clear and includes bus and trolley routes, and their magazine *Greece-Athens-Attica* has a more detailed street plan. The Acropolis provides a useful reference point. *This Week in Athens,* also available at the GNTO, is a trove of addresses and phone numbers. The daily *Athens News* (150dr) and the monthly *Athenian* magazine both provide helpful information on sights and events.

Tourist Offices: Greek National Tourist Office (GNTO), 2 Karageorgi Servias St. (tel. 322 25 45), inside the National Bank on Syntagma Sq. All-encompassing info sheets on transportation, embassies, and museums. Open Mon.-Fri. 8am-2pm and 3:30-8pm, Sat. 9am-2pm. The **Hellenic Chamber of Hotels,** at the same location, will give advice on rooming. Open Mon.-Thurs. 8:30am-2pm, Fri. 8:30am-1:30pm. A less harried GNTO office is 1 block away at 1 Ermou St. (tel. 325 22 67/68), inside the **General Bank of Greece.** Open Mon.-Fri. 8am-8pm, Sat. 8am-2pm. The GNTO office in the **East Terminal** of the airport (tel. 961 27

GREECE

22) is open in summer Mon.-Fri. 8am-10pm, Sat. 10am-5pm; off-season Mon.-Fri. 9am-6pm, Sat. 10am-5pm.

Budget Travel: Travel agencies along Nikis and Filellinon St. off Syntagma Sq. offer student discounts on international plane and train travel. There are *no* discounts for foreign students on domestic travel in Greece. **Magic Bus,** 20 Filellinon St. (tel. 323 74 71), has an extremely competent, English-speaking staff. Open Mon.-Fri. 9am-5pm, Sat. 9am-1pm.

Embassies: U.S., 91 Vassilissis Sofias (tel. 721 29 51 or 721 84 00). Open Mon.-Fri. 8:30am-5pm. **Canada,** 4 Ioannou Genadiou St. (tel. 725 40 11). Open Mon.-Fri. 7:30am-3:15pm, consular section Mon.-Fri. 9am-noon. **U.K.,** 1 Ploutarchou St. (tel. 723 62 11), at Ypsilantou St. **Ireland,** 7 Vas. Konstantinov Ave. (tel. 723 27 71). **Australia,** 37 D. Soutson St. (tel. 644 73 03). 8:30am-12:30pm. **Turkey,** 8 Vassileos Gheorgiou B. St. (tel. 724 59 15).

Currency Exchange: National Bank of Greece, 2 Karageorgi Servias St., Syntagma Sq. (tel. 323 64 81, 322 27 38) Open Mon.-Thurs. 8am-2pm and 2:30-6:30pm, Fri. 8am-1:30pm and 3-6:30pm, Sat. 9am-3pm, Sun. 9am-1pm. Branch at the Airport East Terminal open 24hrs.

American Express: 2 Ermou St., above McDonald's in Syntagma Sq. (tel. 324 49 75 or 79). The usual services. Open Mon.-Fri. 8:30am-4pm, Sat. 8:30am-1:30pm (only travel and mail service on Sat.).

Central Post Office: 100 Aiolou St., Omonia Sq. (tel. 321 60 23). Poste Restante on right as you enter. **Postal code:** 10200. Branch office on Syntagma Sq. Open Mon.-Fri. 7:30am-8pm, Sat. 7:30am-2pm, Sun. 9am-1:30pm.

Telephones: OTE, 15 Stadiou St., 24hrs. Offices at Omonia Sq., at the end of Stadiou St., and at 85 Patission/28 October St. are open 7am-11pm (Omonia closed Sun.). International collect calls (to countries other than the U.S.) take up to 1hr. to go through (2-3hrs. on weekend); you must wait there during that time. Most phone booths in the city operate by telephone cards that can be purchased for 1000, 4500, or 8000dr at OTE offices and some kiosks. **City Code:** 01.

Flights: East Terminal, all foreign airlines and charters; **West Terminal,** Olympic Airways domestic and international service. From Athens, the double-decker Express buses 091 from either Syntagma Sq., in front of the Bank of Macedonia, or Stadiou St. near Omonia Sq serve both terminals (200dr). From airport to Athens, look to your left after exiting customs for the blue and yellow express buses.

Trains: Larissis Station serves northern Greece (Thessaloniki 3500dr). Take yellow trolleybus 1 from Panepistimiou St. (also called Eleftheriou Venizelou) in Syntagma (every 10min., 5am-midnight, 75dr). **Peloponnese Station** (tel. 513 16 01), is in a Victorian-style building with a silver roof. From Larissis, exit to your right and go over the bridge, or you can catch blue bus 057 from Panepistimiou St. (every 15min., 5:30am-11:30pm, 75dr). Serves Patras and elsewhere in the Peloponnese. For more info, call **OSE, Hellenic Railways** (tel. 524 06 01).

Buses: Kifissou Station, (terminal A), 100 Kifissou St. (tel. 514 88 56), serves most of Greece, including the Peloponnese and northern Greece. Take blue bus 051 from the corner of Zinonos and Menandrou near Omonia Sq. **Liossion St. Station** (terminal B), 260 Liossion St. (tel. 831 70 59), serves Delphi, Evia, Lamia and Larissa. Take bus 024 from Panepistimiou St. (Eleftheriou Venizelou).

Ferries: Most dock at **Piraeus.** To reach Syntagma (in Athens) from Piraeus, walk left (facing inland) along the waterfront to Roosevelt St., take the subway to Monastiraki (75dr), turn right up Ermou St., and walk 5min. Boats also leave from **Rafina,** a port suburb east of Athens, to Andros, Tinos, and Mykonos. Always check ferry schedules available at GNTO or in the *Athens News* just prior to departure. **Hydrofoils** speed above water between islands and from some ports, serving the Argosaronic, Sporades, and Cyclades groups. **Ceres's Flying Dolphins** (tel. 428 00 01 through 10) and **Ilios Lines' Ilios Dolphins** (tel. 322 51 39) are the two main companies. Hydrofoils leave from **Zea Port** near Piraeus, Agios Konstantinos, and Volos.

Public Transportation: Blue buses, designated by 3-digit numbers, and yellow trolley rides cost 75dr. Note that money is not accepted on trolleys; buy tickets ahead of time at a kiosk. From Syntagma trolleys 1, 2, 4, 5 and 11 run to Omonia

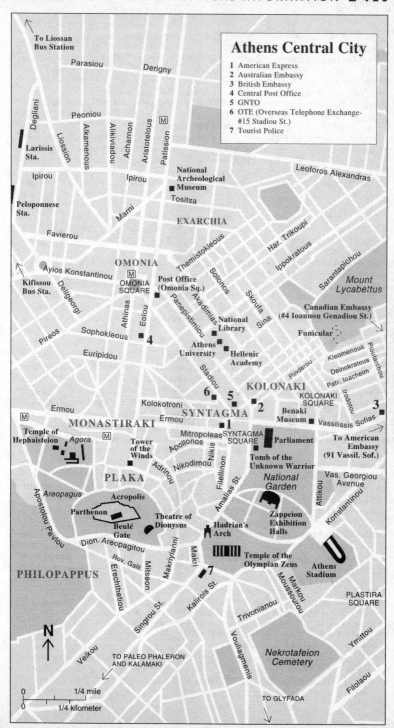

Athens Central City

1 American Express
2 Australian Embassy
3 British Embassy
4 Central Post Office
5 GNTO
6 OTE (Overseas Telephone Exchange-#15 Stadiou St.)
7 Tourist Police

To Liossan Bus Station

Parasiou

Derigny

Peoniou

Degliani

Liossion

Alkamenous

Alikiadou

Acharnon

Aristotelous

Patission

Larissis Sta.

Ipirou

Ipirou

National Archeological Museum

Tositsa

Marni

EXARCHIA

Peloponnese Sta.

Favierou

Leoforos Alexandras

Har. Trikoupi

Ippokratous

Ayios Konstantinou

OMONIA

Themistokleous

Kifissou Bus Sta.

Deligeorgi

OMONIA SQUARE

Post Office (Omonia Sq.)

Solonos

Skoufa

Sina

Sarantapichou

Mount Lycabettus

Pireos

Athinas

Eolou

Panepistimiou

Akadimias

National Library

Canadian Embassy (#4 Ioannou Genadiou St.)

Sophokleous

Funicular

Euripidou

4

Athens University

Hellenic Academy

Pindarou

Kleomenous

Ploutarchou

Deinokratous

Patr. Ioacheim

Stadiou

KOLONAKI

Irodotou

Kolokotroni

6

5

KOLONAKI SQUARE

3

Ermou

MONASTIRAKI

Ermou

SYNTAGMA

2

Benaki Museum

Vassilisis Sofias

Temple of Hephaisteion

Agora

1

Mitropoleas

SYNTAGMA SQUARE

To American Embassy (91 Vassil. Sof.)

Tower of the Winds

Apollonos

Nikodimou

Adrinou

Nikis

Parliament

Tomb of the Unknown Warrior

Vas. Georgiou Avenue

PLAKA

Filellinon

Amalias St.

National Garden

Attikou

Areopagus

Acropolis

Apostolou Pavlou

Parthenon

Beulé Gate

Theatre of Dionysus

Hadrian's Arch

Zappeion Exhibition Halls

Konstantinou

Dion. Areopagitou

Erechthaliou

Rov. Galli

Mitseon

Makriyianni

Makri

Temple of the Olympian Zeus

Athens Stadium

PLASTIRA SQUARE

PHILOPAPPUS

7

N

Singrou St.

Kalirois St.

Markou Moussourou

Trivonianou

Nekrotafeion Cemetery

Ymittou

Veikou

TO PALEO PHALERON AND KALAMAKI

Vouliagmenis

Filolaou

0   1/4 mile

0   1/4 kilometer

TO GLYFADA

GREECE

Sq. A subway system runs from Piraeus harbor to Kifissia in northern Athens with stops at Monastiraki, Omonia, and Victoria, among others. Fare 75-100dr.

Hitchhiking: Hitchhiking out of Athens is nigh impossible and extremely dangerous for women traveling alone. Hitchers have the most luck at the truck parks at the cargo wharves in Piraeus. Those going to northern Greece take the subway to the last stop (Kifissia), walk up to the town's central square, take the bus to Nea Kifissia, walk to the National Road (Ethniki Odos) and start praying. Those heading to the Peloponnese take bus 873 from Eleftheras Sq. to the National Road.

Luggage Storage: At the airport for 130dr per piece per day. Several offices on Nikis and Fillellinon St. Usually 200dr per piece per day.

English Bookstores: Eleftheroudakis Book Store, 4 Nikis St. (tel. 322 93 88). Air-conditioned and shiny, this book store is a true pleasure. Open Mon.-Fri. 9am-8pm, Sat. 9am-3pm. **Pantelides Books,** 11 Amerikis St. (tel. 362 36 73). Open Mon. and Wed. 8am-4pm, Tues. and Thurs.-Fri. 8:30am-8:30pm, Sat. 9am-3pm.

Laundromats: The Greek word for laundry is *plinitirio,* but most places have signs saying "Laundry." Self-serve laundromats include one at 10 Angelou Geronta St. in Plaka, and 41 Kolokinthous and Leonidou St. (tel. 522 62 33), near the train stations. Expect to pay about 2000dr per load for wash, dry, and detergent.

Pharmacies: Indicated by a Byzantine-style red or green cross hanging into the street. The daily *Athens News* (150dr) lists each day's emergency pharmacies and their hours in its "useful information" section.

Medical Assistance: Free emergency medical care for tourists at **Evangelismos Hospital,** 45-47 Ipsilandou St. (tel. 722 00 01), opposite the Hilton.

Emergencies: Tourist Police, tel. 171. English spoken. Greek-speakers can phone the **Athens Police,** tel. 100 or **Medical Emergency,** tel. 166. **Red Cross First Aid Center,** #21, 3 Septemvriou St. (tel.150 or 522 55 55) is three blocks north of Omonia Sq., on the left. Open 24hrs. English spoken.

ACCOMMODATIONS

In July and August prices may be at least 1000dr higher than those quoted here. If you arrive late in the tourist season, venture beyond the Syntagma Sq. area, where there are many hotels on out-of-the-way streets. In the past, hotel owners would allow guests to sleep on the roof when the rooms filled up, for a small fee. *Although the practice is still in effect at some hotels, it is illegal.* Many hotel hawkers meet trains at the station. Most distribute pamphlets with maps for decent places near the station, some of which are listed here. Others, however, have been known to lure tourists into fleabags miles from anywhere and then charge exorbitant rates. Have the hawker point out the place on a large map of the city and set a firm price, in writing if possible, *before* leaving the station. Most of the city's cheap hotels cluster in Plaka-Syntagma area of town. Stay here if sights and nightlife are a priority. If you are planning to stay fewer than three nights, a hotel owner can legally add a 10% surcharge to your bill. Athens proper has no **camping** facilities. Do not sleep in the parks, even as a last resort; it's illegal and extremely unsafe.

Athens International Hostel (HI), 16 Victor Hugo St. (tel. 523 10 95 or 523 20 49). From Omonia Sq., walk down Third September St., take a left on Veranzerou; it will become Victor Hugo after crossing Marni St. The only HI-affiliated youth hostel in Athens, now in a new location. In 1995, expect laundry service and restaurant. HI membership required (2600dr at hostel; get photo from nearby booth). 2000dr. Lockout 10am-2pm. Reservations recommended.

Hotel Tempi, 29 Eolu St. (tel. 321 31 75). From Syntagma Sq., follow Ermou St. and take a right on Eolu (also spelled Aiolou and Eolou). Airy rooms, many with Parthenon views. A gracious couple oversees the hotel. Singles 3600-5000dr. Doubles 5800-6800dr. Triples 7500dr. 24hr. hot water. Laundry service 800dr.

Hotel Festos, 18 Filellinon St. (tel. 323 24 55). Festive and extremely popular with students, Festos' neon letters seize attention on one of the busier streets off Syntagma Sq. As a result, it may be hard to find vacancy in summer without a reservation. Bar with happy hour. Payment by 10am to secure bed. Check-out 9am.

Curfew 2am. No singles. Dorm beds 2000dr. Doubles 6000dr. Triples 9000dr. Quads 10,000dr. Hot showers morning and evening. Free luggage storage.

Thisseos Inn, 10 Thisseos St. (tel. 324 59 60). From Syntagma Sq., take Karageorgi Servias (which becomes Perikleous), and Thisseos St. is on the right. Popular with students who want to stay near Syntagma's attractions but insulated from its noise. TV in reception area, communal kitchen, common showers (hot 24hrs.). Check-out noon. Curfew 2am. Dorm beds 1800-2000dr. Doubles 4000dr.

Student-Travelers Inn, 16 Kidathineon (tel. 324 48 08). In the middle of one of the Plaka's busiest streets, this hotel targets backpackers. The exuberant owner touts his clean, blue rooms and courtyard café. Singles 3000dr. Doubles 5000dr. Triples 6000dr. Quads 8000dr. Breakfast 200-600dr.

George's Guest House, 46 Nikis St. (tel. 322 64 74). Several blocks down Nikis off Syntagma Sq. Spacious pink-and-green rooms make up for the dizzying spiral stairs. Dorm beds (4 to a room) 2000dr. Doubles 5000dr. Triples 6000dr.

Hotel Phaedra, 16 Herefondos St. (tel. 322 77 95). From Hadrian's Arch on Vas. Sofias, walk 1 block up Lysikrateus St. to the intersection with Cherefoutos. Many rooms have balconies with Acropolis views. Check-out noon. Singles 5200dr. Doubles 7000dr. Triples 8500dr. Quads 9900dr. Breakfast 900dr.

Acropolis House, 6 Kodrou St. (tel. 322 23 44 or 322 62 41). Turn left off Mitropoleos onto Voulis and follow it to the end, at the base of a small hill. A truly elegant (and crowded) hotel. Centrally located, thus noisy both morning and night. Check-out noon. Singles 4912-5133dr. Doubles 6650-6950dr. Breakfast 695dr. Luggage storage 50dr per day. Reservations are a must.

Hotel Rio, 13 Odisseos St., (tel. 522 70 75 or 522 67 95). From train stations, follow Deligiani St. to Odisseos; from Omonia Sq., follow Agiou Konstandiou to Karaiskaki Sq. Convenient for travelers who need to stay between one of the two train stations and Omonia Sq., home of the subway to Piraeus and most ferries. All rooms have showers, telephones, and central heating. 15% discount with youth hostel membership. No curfew. Singles 3600dr. Doubles 4800dr. Triples 6000dr. Quads 8000dr. Breakfast 700dr. Free luggage storage. (Expected 1995 prices.)

FOOD

Athens offers a mélange of stands, open-air cafés, outdoor sidestreet tavernas and intriguing dim restaurants frequented by grizzled Greek men. Athens's culinary claim to fame is cheap and plentiful street food. *Souvlaki* (200dr), either on a *kalamaki* (skewer) or wrapped in *pita*, is the Greek alternative to fast-food. A *tost*, a grilled sandwich of variable ingredients (normally ham and cheese) for 200-500dr, is considered "strollable" as well. Locally brewed beer runs about 150dr per half-liter. *Tiropita* (hot cheese pie) and *spanakopita* (hot spinach pie) go for around 250dr. Ice cream is sold at almost every kiosk. A *koulouri,* a donut-shaped, sesame-coated roll, makes a quick breakfast for 50dr.

The best place to eat—and the place where solicitors are in full force—is the Plaka. Although crowded in peak season, outdoor *tavernas* and roof gardens make for terrific people-watching. You'll find a plethora of interesting places up and down Adrianou and Kidatheneon St. Women should know that the Plaka is a popular spot for *kamakia* (literally, "harpoons") who enjoy making catcalls at women as they walk by. Keep walking.

To Gerani, 14 Tripodon St. (tel. 324 76 05). From Kidatheneon, one of the Plaka's busiest strips, Tripodon is a side street. The perfect place to sample Greek delicacies; actually, they're your only choice. A waiter will bring out a large tray of the day's offerings and ask you to pick. Decisions, decisions. Don't miss the flaming sausages (500dr). Full meals range from 1500-2000dr.

Byzantino, 18 Kidathineon St. (tel. 322 73 68). A few blocks below Fillelinon in a small square, strategically located in the midst of one of the Plaka's main pedestrian thoroughfares. Excellent traditional Greek dishes. Greek salad 900dr. *Mousaka* 900dr. *Souvlaki* 1400-1700dr.

Embassy, 105-7 Vasilissis Sofias (tel. 643 67 22). Near (surprise!) the American and Australian embassies. Look for the orange and green motif and outdoor seating. Omelets 500-800dr. *Mousaka* 980dr.

Eden Vegetarian Restaurant, 12 Lissiou (tel. 324 88 58). On the corner of Minissikleous in the western side of Plaka. Airy and secluded. Popular with both herbivores and omnivores. Tofu-meat in dishes like *mousaka* and lasagna (both 800dr). Crusty, tasty bread included. Outside terrace.

Restaurant Gardenia (ΓΑΡΔΕΝΙΑ), 31 Zini St., Koukaki (tel. 922 95 83). Around the corner from the Marble House Pension. No frills. Cheap, good food. Spaghetti with meat sauce 500dr. *Mousaka* 550dr. Beer 250dr.

SIGHTS

The **Acropolis,** or "high city," with its strategic position overlooking the Aegean Sea and Attic Plains, has served throughout history as both a military fortress and a religious center. Today, the hilltop's remarkable ruins grace otherwise rubble-strewn grounds. The ramp that led to the Acropolis in classical times no longer exists. Today's visitors make the 10-min. climb to the ticket-window, enter through the crumbling **Beulé Gate** (added by the Romans and named after the French archaeologist who unearthed it), and continue through the **Propylaea,** the ancient entrance. Unfortunately, the site is not wheelchair-accessible. The marble can be slippery, so be careful if you are wearing shoes that have seen better days. At the cliff's edge, the tiny **Temple of Athena Nike** was built during a respite from the Peloponnesian War, the so-called Peace of Nikias (421-415 BC). Looming over the hillside, the **Parthenon,** or "Virgin's Apartment," keeps vigil over Athens. The temple intentionally features many almost imperceptible irregularities; the Doric columns bulge in the middle and the stylobate (pedestal) of the building bows slightly upward in order to compensate for the optical illusion in which straight lines, viewed from a distance, appear to bend. The **Erechtheum,** to the left of the Parthenon as you face it, was completed in 406 BC, just prior to Athens's defeat by Sparta. Lighter than the Parthenon, the Erechtheum is a unique two-leveled structure that housed a number of cults. On the south side of the Erechtheum, facing the Parthenon, are the **Caryatids,** six columns sculpted in the shape of women. The **Acropolis Museum** (tel. 323 66 65), footsteps away from the Parthenon, contains a superb collection of sculpture, including five of the original Caryatids of the Erechtheum (the sixth was stolen, and now resides in the British Museum). Only a few pieces from the Parthenon are here—Lord Elgin helped himself to the rest, and they are now in the British Museum. The collection is nonetheless impressive. (Acropolis open Mon.-Fri. 8am-6:30pm, Sat.-Sun. 8:30am-2:45pm; winter 8:30am-4:30pm. 1500dr, students 800dr with ISIC. Free on Sun. and holidays. Museum open Mon. 11am-6:30pm, Tues.-Fri. 8am-6:30pm, Sat.-Sun. 8:30am-2:30pm. Cameras with flash allowed, but no posing next to the objects; it's considered disrespectful.)

The **Athenian Agora,** at the foot of the Acropolis, was the administrative center and marketplace of Athens from the sixth century BC through the late Roman Period (5th and 6th centuries AD). The **Temple of Hephaestus,** on a hill in the northwest corner, is the best-preserved Classical temple in Greece. Built around 440 BC, it is especially notable for its friezes which depict the labors of Hercules and the adventures of Theseus. To the south, the elongated **Stoa of Attalos,** a multipurpose building for shops, shelter, and informal gatherings, was rebuilt with new materials between 1953 and 1956 and now houses the **Agora Museum.** The museum contains a number of relics from the site and offers a cool sanctuary from the sweltering summer sun. (Agora and museum open Tues.-Sun. 8:30am-3pm. To both 800dr, students 400dr.) There are several entrances to the Agora, including one at the edge of Monastiraki, one on Thissio Sq. and one on Adrianou St. One of the world's finest selections of classical sculpture, ceramics and bronzework is found in the **National Archeological Museum,** 44 Patission St. Pieces that would shine elsewhere impact only dimly amid the general magnificence. The "Mask of Agamemnon," from Heinrich Schliemann's Mycenae digs, is a must-see. (Museum open Mon. 12:30-7pm,

Tues.-Fri. 8am-7pm, Sat.-Sun. and holidays 8:30am-3pm. 1500dr, students 800dr, free on Sun. and holidays. No flash photography.) A precious collection of simple marble figurines can be viewed at the air-conditioned **Goulandris Museum of Cycladic and Ancient Greek Art,** 4 Neophytou Douka St., near Kolonaki (open Mon.-Fri. 10am-4pm, Sat. 10am-3pm. 250dr, students 125dr). The cool, pleasant **National Garden** (open sunrise to sunset), adjacent to Syntagma Square, is a great escape from the noise, heat, and frantic pace of Athens. Walk along its tranquil paths and visit the duck pond and zoo. Women should avoid strolling alone. When you're passing through Syntagma Sq., don't miss the changing of the guard in front of the **Parliament** building. Every hour on the hour two sets of enormously tall *evzones* (guards) slowly wind up like toy soldiers, kick their heels about, and fall backwards into symmetrical little guard houses on either side of the **Tomb of the Unknown Warrior.** Unlike their British equivalents, *evzones* occasionally wink and even smile at tourists. Their jovial manner is as delightful as their curious attire—pom-pom-laden clogs, short pleated skirts *(foustanela),* and pony-tail-tasselled hats. Every Sunday at 10:45am, the ceremony occurs with the full troop of guards, a band, and even greater pomp than usual.

ENTERTAINMENT

Every evening the cafés near the **Zappeion** (Exhibition Hall) present musicians, comedians, and acrobats on an outdoor stage. Standing is free; you can also get a table. Athens's two principal markets attract everyone from bargain-hunters to inveterate browsers. The **Athens Flea Market,** adjacent to Monastiraki Sq., has a festive bazaar-like atmosphere and offers a potpourri of secondhand junk, costly antiques, and everything in between. Although parts of it have become overtouristed, there is still the occasional treasure to be found, and lots of neo-hippies to watch besides. The market is open daily (8am-2pm), and Sunday is the grand bazaar: the flea market overflows the square and Fillis Athinas St. A huge indoor-outdoor **food market** lines the sides of Athinas St. between Evripidou and Sofokleous St. A sight, to be sure, the meat market is huge, but not for vegetarians or the faint of heart. The **Athens Festival** runs annually from June until September, featuring classical theater groups performing in the **Odeon of Herodes Atticus.** Performances are also staged in **Lycabettos Theater** at the top of Lycabettos Hill, and in Epidavros (see Peloponnese section). The Greek Orchestra plays during this festival, as do visiting groups, which have ranged from the Bolshoi to B.B. King; from the Alvin Ailey Dance Company to the Talking Heads. The **Festival Office** (tel. 322 14 59 or 322 31 11, ext. 240) is in the arcade at 4 Stadiou St.; a line forms by 9am so arrive early. Student tickets are generally cheap (500-1500dr with student ID; open Mon.-Fri. 8:30am-2pm and 5-7pm, Sun. 10am-1pm).

■ NEAR ATHENS

The sublime view of the Aegean from the **Temple of Poseidon** makes a visit here a spiritual experience, even for lapsed Poseidon worshippers. The 16 remaining Doric columns of this sanctuary, built by Pericles in 440 BC, sit on a promontory high above the coast at **Cape Sounion,** 70km from Athens. (Open Mon.-Sat. 9am-sunset, Sun. 10am-sunset. 600dr, students 300dr, EU students free. Last Athens bus departs according to hr. of sunset; check schedules at bus station upon arrival.) Two buses travel to Cape Sounion. One travels the Apollo Coast, leaving every hour on the half-hour from Manromateon St. (6:30am-6:30pm, 2¼hr., 800dr). The other bus, following a much less scenic inland route, leaves from Areos Park (every hr. on the hr., 6am-6pm, 2¼hr., 850dr). Don't forget water and a lunch.

The masterful mosaics in the monastery at **Daphni** deserve a visit. The **monastery** has served as both an army camp and a lunatic asylum (open 8:30am-3pm. 500dr, students 300dr; video 1000dr, flash camera 600dr). **Camping Daphni** (tel. 581 15 63) is on the road to the monastery. (Reception open 7am-10pm. Check-out 2pm. 800dr per person, 550dr for a small tent, 800dr for a large tent, shower 500dr.) To

GREECE

reach Daphni from Athens, take bus 855, 862 or 880 from Thermopylou on P. Tsalderi (Pireos) St. (every 20min., 6am-10pm, ½hr., 75dr) to Psychatreio.

Troubled denizens of the ancient world journeyed to the Oracle of Apollo at **Delphi,** where the *Pythia* gave them profound, if cryptic, advice. If modern Delphi is the center of anything, it's of the tour-bus circuit. Billions of tourists seek the sanctuary, so visit early in the morning. **Buses** leave Athens for Delphi from the 260 Liossion St. station (5 per day, 3hr., 2250dr). If you have a railpass, take the **train** to Levadia and catch the Delphi bus there (550dr).

NORTHERN GREECE

The northern provinces of **Macedonia, Thessaly, Thrace,** and **Epirus** adamantly cling to the charm that the Greek Islands long ago relinquished. Here, unlike on the islands, no one caters to visitors or puts on a show: nobody whitewashes the buildings, translates the menus, or accepts American Express cards with a smile.

Thessaloniki A clean, green, and delightfully moped-free city of shops and cafés, Thessaloniki is simultaneously low-key and energetic. The capital of Macedonia and second-largest city in Greece, Thessaloniki is riddled with Byzantine churches and Roman ruins, and contains one of the best **archeological museums** in Greece, full of opulent artifacts from the significant Macedonian finds at Vergina (open Mon. 12:30-7pm, Tues.-Fri. 8am-7pm, Sat.-Sun. 8:30am-3pm; in winter Mon. 10:30am-5pm, Tues.-Fri. 8am-5pm, Sun. 8:30am-3pm; 1000dr).

The **GNTO** (tel. (031) 27 18 88 or 22 29 35), off Aristoelous Sq. at #8, 1 block from the water, has city maps, hotel listings and transport information (open Mon.-Fri. 8am-8pm, Sat. 8:30am-2pm). The **tourist police,** 10 Egnatia St. (tel. (031) 45 32 23), are less helpful than the GNTO, but are available 24hrs. **Trains** leave from Monastirou St., in the western part of the city (tel. (031) 51 75 17). Destinations include Athens (8hr., 3440dr); Sofia, Bulgaria (9hr., 10,000dr); and İstanbul (23hr., 11,800dr). The **KTEL bus** company operates out of stations across the city. One, across from the train station, sees buses off to Athens (7½hr., 6300dr). Several bargain hotels cluster on Egnatia St., near the railway station. The **HI youth hostel** (tel. (031) 22 59 46) is at 44 Alex. Svolou St., also known as Nikolaou St. (Reception open 9-11am and 6-11pm. Lockout 11-6pm. Curfew 11pm. 1500dr per person. Showers 6-10pm only.) Stock up at the lively **agora** (marketplace), bordered by Aristotelous, Irakliou, Egnatia, and Venizelou St.

Mt. Olympus, Meteora, and Kalambaka Greece's loftiest peak, **Mt. Olympus** (Ολυμπος), rises from the coastal plain 90km southwest of Thessaloniki. The mountain's eerily beautiful summits require two days of challenging hiking but no special equipment. Get there from Thessaloniki via Katerini (2hr., 1250dr). In **Litohoro,** the gateway village to Olympus, information on hiking may be obtained from the **SEO Mountaineering Club of Greece,** located past the taxi stand and the Ereto Restaurant (tel. (0352) 823 00). Most youthful climbers stay at the small **Youth Hostel (HI)** (tel. (0352) 813 11), by following the signs 200m up the hill from the square (reception open 9am-2pm and 6-11pm; 1350dr; hiking equipment for rent).

Southwest of Olympus is **Meteora** (Μετεωρα), where several Orthodox monasteries grip the tops of 500m rock formations. The **Monastery of Agia Triada** (Holy Trinity), the setting for the 1981 James Bond flick *For Your Eyes Only,* is one of the top tourist attractions in northern Greece, and it's easy to see why. The most popular base for exploring Meteora is the town of **Kalambaka** (Καλαμπακα), where the **Hotel Astoria,** 93 G. Kondilli St. (tel. (0432) 222 13), across from the train station, has comfortable singles for 3000dr and doubles for 4000dr. Buses travel regularly from Kalambaka to the **Grand Meteoron Monastery,** the oldest and largest of the monasteries (5 per day, 1 per day in winter, 160dr). Three others loom nearby,

GREECE

remaining active, while two others now serve as convents. (All monasteries open 9am-1pm and 3:20-6pm but most stay open until midnight or until all visitors have safely gone, 300dr. Closing days are staggered; all are open Sunday, Wednesday and Thursday.) The regulations against picture-taking and revealing dress are enforced with severity. Closer to Meteora, the village of **Kastraki** has the **Hotel Kastraki** (tel. 222 86; singles 4000dr, doubles 6000dr) and two swell campgrounds. The swimming pool at **Camping Vrachos** (tel. 222 93) provides welcome relief from the parching sun (750dr per person, 400dr per tent).

THE PELOPONNESE (ΠΕΛΟΠΟΝΝΗΣΟΣ)

The Peloponnese, a divine union of *vouna* (mountains) and *thalassa* (sea), is the Greece of legend. History slumbers in the ruins at Mycenae, Epidavros and Corinth, the Byzantine remains at Mystra and Monemvassia and the Turko-Venetian castle-fortresses at Methoni, Koroni and Pylos. Stay in the serene mountain villages in Arcadia, the lively port towns of Gythion and Nauplion, or the bland but central modern cities of Sparta, Tripolis, Patras and Kalamata. The rugged should explore barren but fascinating Mani, with its dramatic tower houses. Most enter the Peloponnese by sea from Italy to Patras, or by land from Athens to Corinth. The easiest way to explore is by car, but tour buses make trips to the monuments daily. You'll know when you're in the Peloponnese because the air pollution will have dissipated and the oil refineries outside your window will be replaced by fragrant olive leaves.

■■■ ARGOLIS AND CORINTHIA (ΑΡΓΟΛΙΔΑ ΚΑΙ ΚΟΡΙΝΘΙΑ)

Chronicled in the pages of ancient writers, Argos—a grotesque beast covered with 100 unblinking eyes—once stalked vast stretches of the northern Peloponnese, subduing unruly satyrs and rampaging bulls. Today's Argolis and Corinthia hold many of the most impressive monuments of the Peloponnese's 3500 years of history.

Corinth The first stop for most visitors to the Peloponnese from Athens is Corinth (Κορινθος), a town thrice crumpled by earthquakes and rebuilt as a squat, secure, but uninspiring city. The **ruins** of Ancient Corinth are 7km from town; follow either the road to Patras or the one to Argos and look for signs. Alternately, **buses** travel from Modern Corinth to Ancient Corinth, at the mountain's base, every hour, returning on every half-hour (160dr). Begin your visit at the **Ministry of Culture Archaeological Museum,** which houses mosaics from the site and, in the Asclepion Room, a collection of cured body parts, votive offerings to the god of medicine. As you exit the museum, to your left the 6th-century BC **Temple of Apollo** keeps a quiet vigil over the city's Roman ruins. (Site and museum open 8am-7pm high season; July-Aug. 8:45-3pm. To both 1000dr, students 500dr; free on Sun. and holidays.) The Turko-Venetian fortress of **Acrocorinth** towers 575m over the classical site; you can take a taxi directly from Corinth or tough the one-hour hike up. The upper summit originally held a **Temple to Aphrodite,** which was served by 1000 "sacred courtesans." From here you could, until about 20 years ago, see all the way to the Acropolis in Athens, but pollution took care of that.

If you stay in New Corinth, try the **Hotel Belle-vue,** 41 Dimaskinou St. (tel. (0741) 220 88) on the waterfront (singles 2500dr, doubles and triples 4000dr, all without bath). An authentic choice for food is the restaurant **Kanita,** a lively *taverna* filled with travellers from the hotels (Greek salads 700dr, entrees 800-1300dr).

GREECE

Buses leave Athens for Corinth from 100 Kifissou St. (5:30am-9:30pm every 30min., 1½hr., 1150dr). Returns are from Ermou St. at Koliatsou St.

Nauplion Plentiful bus connections and beautiful architecture make this the ideal base for exploring the ruins of the Argolid Peninsula. From the bus terminal, walk right (facing the bus station) down Singrou to the harbor. The area behind Bouboulinas and Singrou is the old part of town, where reasonably priced hotels dapple the streets. The **HI youth hostel,** Neon Vyzantion St. (tel. (0752) 277 54), is a hike (15-20min.) from the bus stop (curfew 11pm; 1000dr per person). **Hotel Epidavros** (tel. (0752) 275 41) offers clean rooms on Ipsilandou St., 1 block below Amalias St. (doubles 5000dr, with private bath 6500dr). Or, if you are in the new part of town, try the clean and airy rooms of the **Hotel IRA** (HPA in Greek), 9 Vas. Georgiou B St. (doubles 6000dr, triples 7000dr, off-season doubles 2300dr).

Restaurants, *tavernas,* and fast-food joints are interspersed throughout the town with particular concentrations in certain areas, like the waterfront and Syntagma Square. These tend to be overpriced and overcrowded; better dining options are a street above the square on Plapouta-Staikopoulou. Noteworthy is **Taverna Basiles** behind the National Bank of Greece. The house specialty, rabbit in onions (1100dr), will delight even the most avid Beatrix Potter fan. Soften your arteries on the nearly 999 steps to the **Palamidi Fortress,** with intricate walls and a stunning view (open Mon.-Fri. 8am-6:30pm, Sat.-Sun. 8:30am-2:30pm; low season Mon-Fri. 8:45am-2:30pm, Sun. 8:45am-2pm; 400dr, students 200dr).

Mycenae and Epidavros Mycenae (Μυκηνες), Greece's supreme city from 1600 to 1100 BC, was once ruled by Agamemnon, commander of the Greek forces during the Trojan War. His wife Clytemnestra and her fatal attraction Aegisthus axed him in a bathtub. Most of the treasures from the excavation are in the Athens Museum, but the **Lion's Gate** and the **Treasury of Atreus** number among the most celebrated archeological finds in modern history. (Site open Mon.-Fri. 8am-7pm; Oct.-March 8am-5pm. 1000dr, students 500dr, free on Sun.) Arrive ahead of the midday heat and tourist swarms, and hold on to your ticket so you won't have to pay twice. The **Belle Helene Hotel** (tel (0751) 662 25) is on the main road, is a bus stop, and offers clean and spacious rooms (doubles 4500dr, triples 5500dr). The **bus** rambles daily to Mycenae from Nauplion (400dr) and Argos (300dr).

In **Epidavros** (Επιδαυρος), visit the ruins of the **Sanctuary of Asclepius** as well as the best preserved of all Greek theaters. Built in the 4th century BC and still acoustically impeccable, the theater has total capacity of 14,000. Henry Miller wrote that he heard "the great heart of the world" beat here; while you may not have the same experience, you can stand on the top row of seats and hear a *drachma* dropped on stage. In the museum, between the theater and the ruins, you'll find sculpture fragments from the temples of Asclepius and Artemis, a reconstruction of the *tholos* floor, and a spectacular Corinthian column collection. (Theater, site and museum open Tues.-Sat. 7:30am-7pm; Nov.-Apr. 8am-5pm. 1000dr, students 500dr.) Classical drama (in Greek) is still performed at the theater by the **National Theater of Greece** and visiting companies on Friday and Saturday evenings from July to mid-August (usually at 9pm). Tickets start at 3000-4500dr (2000dr for students) and may be purchased at the theater from 5pm, or in advance at the Athens Festival Box Office, 4 Stadiou St.

■■■ PATRAS (ΠΑΤΡΑ)

Mountains encircle the eastern and western edges of the noisy harbor of Patras. The older, more sedate streets encompassing the *kastro* look down on a homogeneity of high-rises languishing under a shroud of smog. If you must stay, you'll find a decent amount of diversion, especially if you visit during Carnival (mid-January to Ash Wednesday), when the city becomes one huge party. A scenic traipse leads to **Achaïa Clauss winery,** 9km southeast of town. Its German founder, Baron von

Clauss, was dazed with lust for a drowned woman named Daphne. He took his blackest grapes, and made a sweet wine in her honor, called *Mavrodaphne*, "Black Daphne." (Tours 9am-7:30pm; off-season 9am-5pm. Free.) Take bus 7 (20min., 95dr) from the intersection of Kolokotroni and Kalakari St.

The helpful staff at the **GNTO** (tel. (061) 65 33 58), outside customs, on the waterfront just before Iron Polytechniou, gives free maps, brochures, and help with accommodations. Check here for complete bus and boat timetables. (Open Mon.-Sat. 7am-9pm, Sun. 2-9pm.) **Trains** roll into town from Athens (2600dr) via Corinth (1600dr); Kalamata (6hr., 1500dr); and Pirgos (2hr., 820dr). **KTEL buses,** 3½ blocks to the right, down the waterfront from customs, on Agiou Andreou sets out for Athens (4hr., 2750dr), Kalamata (4hr., 3100dr); Pirgos (1350dr), and Thessaloniki (6350dr). From Patras, **boats** go to Cephalonia, Ithaki, and Corfu, in addition to Italy's Bríndisi, Bari, and Ancona. Ticket prices fluctuate tremendously. The waterfront is coated with travel agencies selling tickets for roughly the same prices. There is a stopover on Corfu for Italy-bound ferries.

Cheap accommodations are threaded through the tangle of buildings on Agiou Andreou St., a block up and parallel to the waterfront. The cramped but convenient **HI Youth Hostel,** 68 Iron Polytechniou St. (tel. (061) 42 72 78) was used as German officers' headquarters in World War II. From the ferry, turn left and walk 1½km. (No curfew. Check-out 10:30am. Bed 1400dr. Sheets 100dr.) For huge old rooms, try **Hotel Parthenon,** 25 Ermou St. (tel. (061) 27 34 21), off Agiou Andreou. (Singles 3340dr. Doubles 5100dr. Triples 6600dr.) Pitch your tent at **Kavouri Camping** (tel. (061) 42 21 45), 2km east of town, next to the Patras swimming pool. It's crowded, but cheap. (500dr per person, 200dr per tent.) Stop by the new **Europa center,** at the corner of Othonos Amalias and Karolou, east past the KTEL bus station. This bright pink establishment caters to all the needs of a traveler: tickets to Italy, tourist information, a café and restaurant, stores, a disco, and clean toilets. (Open 6:30am-3am.) There are decent fast food places near **Platia Trion Simahon**. The best *souvlaki* grills are past Platia Georgiou along Korinthou St.

■■■ OLYMPIA (ΟΛΥΜΠΙΑ)

From the unexciting but inevitable **Pirgos,** take a bus (40min., 350dr) to Olympia, the religious sanctuary that hosted the original Olympics. From 776 BC young men from cities all over Greece gathered here for the quadrennial festival of Olympian Zeus and the athletic competition that accompanied it. Today the site is scattered and poorly labeled but still lovely; the gleaming **New Museum** is excellent. Inside is Praxiteles' statue of Baby Dionysus, in addition to the famous Little Man with the Big Erection. (Site open Mon.-Fri. 8am-7pm, Sat.-Sun. 8:30am-3pm. 1000dr. Museum hours same as site, except Mon. 12:30-7pm. 1000dr, students 500dr.) In the center of town is a 50-bed **youth hostel (HI)** (tel. (0624) 225 80; 800dr). **Camping Diana** (tel. (0624) 223 14), just 200m above town, charges 1100dr per person, 700dr per tent. In the center of town near the taxi stand, **Ambrosia** offers tasty, reasonably priced meals and a 10% *Let's Go* discount.

■■■ LACONIA (ΛΑΚΩΝΙΑ)

Sparta and Mystra Outside of war, **Sparta** (Σπαρτη) contributed little to Greek history; little philosophy, poetry, or art ever flourished here. Great ruins are lacking; the Spartans considered monumental architecture a luxury that made strong citizens weak. They would have been scandalized by the Byzantine opulence 6km west in **Mystra** (Μυστρα), where 3 tiers of tiled churches and ghostly palaces grope up a steep hillside (site open Mon.-Fri. 8am-7pm, Sat.-Sun. 8:30am-3pm; spring and fall 8am-5pm; winter 9am-3:30pm; 1000dr, students 500dr; Sun. free). Camp at **Camping Mystra** (tel. (0731) 227 24) between Sparta and Mystra (500dr per person, 400dr per tent). The modern **Camping Castle View** (tel. (0731) 933

03) is also nearby, with a pool, wonderful modern showers, a minimarket, and amiable owners (650dr per person, 350dr per tent). In Sparta, on Paleologou, just past Lykourgou, **Hotel Panellinion** (tel. (0731) 280 31) has clean rooms with balconies (singles 3500dr, doubles 5000dr). **Dhiethnes** is in a corner of the main square across from the **GNTO** office in the town hall; it has good spaghetti (800dr) and standard *taverna* fare. **Buses** run to Athens (5hr., 2850dr), stopping in Corinth (4hr., 1850dr); Monemvassia (2½hr., 1350dr; change in Molai); and Gythion (1hr., 600dr). The new **Tourist Police** speak English and are polite and earnestly helpful.

Mani and Monemvassia The bold can plunge south into the sparsely settled territory of **Mani** (Μανη), the middle peninsula of the southern Peloponnese, known for a bloody past of family feuds and savage piracy. The entire region is stark; bald mountains drop to a jagged coast, and forbidding, hooded towers guard the abandoned towns. From **Areopolis,** you can make daytrips to the spectacular **Glyfatha Lake Cave** (also known as *Pirgos Dirou* or *Spilia Dirou).* The ticket includes a 30min. boat ride and walk through the dense forest of stalactites and stalagmites. The caves are 4km away from the town, accessible by bus, and make for an easy trip from Gythion by moped. Many hitchhike, especially in summer when hordes of tourists converge. You may not get in after 4pm. (Open June-Sept. 8am-6pm; off-season 8am-3pm. 1800dr.) For a bed in **Areopolis,** take Kapetan Matapa St. off the main square and look for a sign dangling off a balcony that advertises rooms to rent. Beneath the sign, **George Versakos** has an impressive antique gun collection and a wonderful sense of humor. (Doubles 5000dr. Quints 10,000dr.) If you don't mind a much bleaker room, George will rent you lodgings across the street. (3000dr for 2-3 people).

The capital of the Mani is the picturesque port of **Gythion** (Γυθειο). Swim off the wooded islet nearby or in many of the desolate rocky coves to the southeast. In town, try the comfortable, super-clean rooms of **Xenia Karlaftis** (tel. (0733) 227 19) near the port police (doubles 5000dr, off season 4000dr; bed on the veranda 1500dr). The most luxurious campgrounds are **Meltemi** (tel. (0733) 228 33; 750dr per person, 700dr per tent) and **Gytheio Beach Campgrounds** (tel. (0733) 225 22; 800dr per person, 600dr per tent). Also try **Mani Beach** (tel. (0733) 234 50; 750dr per person, 550dr per tent) or **Kronos** (tel. (0733) 930 93; 785dr per person, 550dr per tent; off-season 685dr per person, 640dr per tent). The campgrounds are south of town and, except for Kronos, accessible by bus. There is a **laiki agora** (fruit and produce market) every Tuesday and Friday starting at 4:30am between Herakles and Archaia Theatrou St. **Ferries** depart from the quay to the right of Mavromichaeli Sq. and run to Kythera (daily, 800dr) and Crete (Wed. and Sat., 3600dr). Contact **Olympia Travel** on the waterfront (open 9am-11pm; tel. (0733) 245 01).

Off the easternmost peninsula of the Peloponnese, the ancient Byzantine city **Monemvassia** (Μονεμβασια) juts out from a rocky island. Still inhabited, this charming medieval village revolves around the church that clings to its rocky summit. Stay in the new town on the mainland at **Hotel Akrogiali** (tel. (0732) 613 60) which wears a sign bearing the owner's name, S. Sofos (singles 3500dr; doubles 5350dr). **Buses** connect Monemvassia with Sparta (2½hr., 1350dr), and Athens (6½-7½hr., 4200dr) via Molai (½hr., 360dr).

IONIAN ISLANDS
(ΝΗΣΙΑ ΤΟΥ ΙΟΝΙΟΥ)

Collectively, the Ionian Islands are distinct from the rest of Greece; individually, they differ from each other. All escaped the Turkish occupation the rest of Greece underwent, only to become the subjects of other varied foreign powers, including the Venetians, the British, the French and the Russians. Historical ties make them a favorite among British holiday-makers and Italian villa-renters, as well as the usual run of ferry-hopping backpackers.

■■■ CORFU (KERKYRA, KEPKYPA)

A verdant island bordered by sparkling beaches, lush **Corfu** is traditionally a favorite haunt of European royalty and aristocrats, and is the most eclectically international of the Ionians. Only here do British palaces sit on an esplanade modeled after the Rue de Rivoli in Paris and next to the shuttered alleyways of an *ersatz* Venice.

Corfu Town Ferries from Patras and Italy dock in Corfu Town's new port. Follow the water to your left to get to the old town, where you'll find an informative **GNTO** in the agricultural Bank Building (tel. (0661) 375 20; open Mon.-Sat. 7am-2:30pm). Decent, reasonably priced rooms are available in Corfu, but hotel managers sometimes fill their rooms with camp beds, which they then offer as dorms but charge the price for singles. Prices drop about 100dr per person in off-season. A little remote, but still the cheapest place to stay (1000dr) is **Youth Hostel Kontokali (HI)** (tel. (0661) 912 02), 4½km north on the main road from the port on the edge of Kontokali Village. Take the 7 Dassia bus from Platia Sanrocco or across from the Hotel Constantinoupolis near the Old Port (every ½hr. until 10:45pm, 20min., 155dr). For centrally located small rooms, try **Hotel Cyprus,** 13 Agion Pateron (tel. (0661) 406 75). Walking from the Esplanade to Platia Sanrocco, turn right at the National Bank on Voulgareos and follow the signs. (Singles 3000dr. Doubles 5000dr. Triples 6000dr. Quads 7000dr.) Corfu has several official campsites, and prices are strictly regulated. All campsites here should charge 830dr per person, 700dr per tent, and 700dr per car. Rates should be about 100dr less in the off-season. **Camping Kontokali** (tel. (0661) 912 02), by the HI hostel, is the nearest to Corfu Town. The premier restaurant areas are at the two ends of **N. Theotoki Street,** near the Spianada and by the Old Port. **To Nautikon,** 150 N. Theotoki, near the Old Port serves a delicious *mousaka* (1100dr) that will impress even palates tired of this ancient Greek standby. (Most entrees 1300-1500dr. Open April-Oct. noon-midnight.) Try the "Pete special" pizza (1400dr) at **Pizza Pete,** 19 Arseniou St., on the waterfront halfway between the Spianada and the Old Port. (Open April-Oct. 10am-3am.)

Elsewhere on Corfu KTEL buses leave frequently from New Fortress Sq. in Corfu Town for most of the island's major spots (some are reached by city buses from Platia San Rocco); it's easier but more dangerous to travel by moped. A trip west takes you to **Paleokastritsa** and its whitewashed mountaintop monastery, **Panayia Theotokos** and **Bella Vista,** a natural balcony with a great view. (Monastery open April-Oct. 7am-1pm and 3-7pm.) Nearby are the knee-weakening beaches of **Glyfada** and **Pelekas** and the nearby nude beach **Myrtiotissa.** (Topless sunbathing is the rule on just about all of Corfu.) Pelekas swings at night and has several inexpensive pensions. **Agatha's Travel Service** (tel. (0661) 942 83 or 946 02) on the main street in town, to the left of the church, rents mopeds (2500dr per day) and can help you find a room. (Open April-Oct. 8:30am-2am; off-season 9am-midnight.) Doubles generally run 2500-5000dr. The western exposure and elevation of Pelekas offer an ideal vantage for rejoicing with the sunsets. **Agios Gordios,** accessible by bus (45min., 225dr), with its steep cliffs and impressive rock formations, is the setting for the **Pink Palace** (tel. (0661) 530 24, fax 530 25). Run by Greek "Dr." George, his sister Magda, and an energetic crew of Aussies, Brits, Canucks, and Swedes, this resort has legendary status among English-speaking, beer-guzzling travelers with weekly toga parties in a disco which grooves all night as pink *ouzo* flows. Some enjoy the pink party and the nightly dirty-joke and spin-the-bottle games, others feel isolated and disgusted. Rooms vary in quality. (4000dr per person. Terrace cots 3200dr. Breakfast, dinner, and nightclub included.)

■■■ CEPHALONIA (ΚΕΑΛΦΛΩΝΙΑ)

If Corfu whets your appetite for islands, visit rugged Cephalonia, larger and far less touristed. All boats leave you on the east coast of the island in **Sami,** a tranquil port town surrounded by lush green hills. Though smaller than the capital, Sami has a beach and is closer to the beauty of the island's northern region. The main town of **Argostoli** is the island's transportation center. A **GNTO** at the port gives candid advice on accommodations. (Open Mon.-Fri. 8am-10pm.) The surprisingly interesting and eclectic **Historical and Folk Museum** shows pictures of the town before it was wiped out by a 1953 earthquake. (Open Mon.-Sat. 8:30am-2:30pm.400dr.) Hotels here are expensive. The **Hotel Parthenon** (tel. (0671) 222 46) offers sunny balconies and is by far the cheapest option (singles 2500dr, doubles 4500dr). Both Sami and Argostoli have superb **campgrounds.** Sami's (700dr per person, 550dr per tent) is right by the town's uncomfortable pebble beach; Argostoli's (1100dr per person, 750dr per tent) is a 1½km trek. In summer, **ferries** link Cephalonia with Patras and Zakinthos. Boats from Corfu and Bríndisi stop here in July and August on their way to Patras.

■■■ ITHAKA (ITHAKI, ΙΘΑΚΗ)

The placid beauty of the island's northern villages explain Odysseus's compulsive homesickness for this small, steep, rocky place. The main town of **Vathi** is an amiable cluster of shops and houses in the center of a horseshoe harbor. There's no GNTO office here, but the tourist agencies can be of help. Helpful, friendly **Lazarus Tours** (tel. (0674) 306 74 or 325 87), open 9am-10pm, rents the cheapest rooms (doubles with bath 5000dr). Some travelers **camp** on the nearby beach.

Those of poetic imagination and adequate footwear will want to climb 45min. up to the **Cave of the Nymphs,** where Odysseus hid the treasure the Phaeacians bestowed upon him; bring a flashlight or you'll see only the entrance. (200dr.) The site of Odysseus's palace is farther north in **Stavros.** Swim in the tingling waters of the gentle pebble coves of the east coast between charming **Frikes** and **Kioni.** An exhilarating **bus** route serves these villages from Vathi.

Boats run back and forth from Frikes on Ithaka to Nidri on Lefkada (2½hr., 870dr). From Vathi there are ferries to Agios Efimia on Cephalonia (1hr., 900dr), Sami on Cephalonia (1hr., 870dr), and Astakos on the mainland (2hr., 1220dr). There are also boats from Piso Ateos to Sami (2 and 8:30pm, 465dr) and to Bríndisi in Italy (12-14hr., 10,500dr for deck fare, 14,500dr in August, no student discounts). Be sure to check boat schedules at your port of departure.

CYCLADES (ΚΥΚΛΑΔΕΣ)

Chances are, when people wax rhapsodic about the Greek islands, they're talking about the Cyclades. Whatever your idea of Greece—winding cobblestone streets and whitewashed houses, *ouzo* sipped outside during warm sunsets, inebriated revelry—you can find it here. The islands are practically international colonies during the summer, when every American student on the continent seems to convene here for the post-Eurailpass party, along with shipping tycoons, hippies, and perennial backpackers.

■■■ MYKONOS AND DELOS (ΜΥΚΟΝΟΣ ΚΑΙ ΔΗΛΟΣ)

Chic and sleek, **Mykonos's** sole purpose is partying and sunning, but its sophistication and sense of history (pirates, churches) make it bearable—even pleasant. Social life, both gay and straight, may be easy but it's not cheap on this favorite among the Cyclades islands—you'd need a wallet thicker than your *Let's Go* to enjoy all the flash. But you needn't pay to savor the beaches and the labyrinthine streets of Mykonos Town, dotted with the odd confused mule and pompous pink pelican.

For most visitors, "beach" is synonymous with the renowned, largely gay naked-ness of **Paradise Beach** and **Super Paradise Beach.** Take a bus to **Plati Yialos,** not a bad beach in its own right, and a boat from there (250dr to Paradise, 320dr to Super Paradise). The beaches at **Megali Ammos, St. Stefanos,** and **Psarou** are closer to town and have less of a meat-market atmosphere. At night, the sprawling **Skandinavian Bar** is always packed (open 7:30pm-3am; beers 400-600dr, cocktails 1000dr). At **Pierro's** on Matogianni St., the mainly gay crowd spills out into the square (beer 900dr, cocktails 2000dr). Step into a Toulouse-Lautrec at **Montpar-nasse,** on Agion Anargyron St. in the Little Venice district (wine 800dr, cocktails 1600-1800dr).

Practical Information, Accommodations, and Food The **National Bank of Greece** is in the center of the waterfront (open Mon.-Thurs. 8am-2pm, Fri. 8am-1:30pm; exchange window open Mon.-Thurs. 8am-2pm and 6:30-9pm, Fri. 8am-1:30pm and 6:30-9pm, Sat.-Sun. 10am-1pm and 5:30-8:30pm). The **tourist police** (tel. (0289) 224 82 for tourist info, 222 35 for general info; open 24hrs.) have an office at the ferry landing. **Buses** are the best way to cover the island. The **North Station** next to the beach serves the northern and eastern beaches; **South Station,** oddly enough, serves the south. Schedules are posted.

Pushing past the hawkers and their shuttle vans as you step of the ferry, bear right 10m along the water; you can't miss the offices for hotels (tel. (0289) 245 40), rooms-to-let (tel. (0289) 248 60), camping, and the port police. Hotels are expen-sive. The official **campground** on **Paradise Beach** (tel. (0289) 221 29 or 228 52) is a spacious and clean self-sufficient community (800dr per person, 500dr per tent; prices higher in high season). **Chez Maria Pension,** 30 N. Kalogera St. (tel. (0289) 224 80) is cheap but often full (doubles 9000-10,000dr, triples 13,000dr). Next door, **Hotel Phillippi** (tel. (0289) 222 94) boasts friendly owners, more magnificent gardens, and spacious rooms (doubles 9800-11,500dr, triples 13,500-16,000dr).

On Mykonos, self-consciously trendy food is the rule, but several cheap and/or good places persist nonetheless. **Niko's Taverna** hops with traditional Greek cui-sine (tel. (0289) 243 20; open noon-1am; baked calamari with cheese 1000dr); **La Scala** serves big plates of Italian food (tel. (0289) 245 60; open noon-2am; 3990dr for huge mixed grill); and, **Ta Kiouria** has some interesting specials (tel. (0289) 228 66; veal *souvlaki* 1350dr).

Delos The nearby island of **Delos,** legendary birthplace of Apollo and his twin sis-ter Artemis, was one of the great spiritual centers of the ancient world. Extensive ruins cover the island, but they can only be visited on a daytrip from Mykonos or Naxos, as overnight stays are forbidden. Boats leave from Mykonos Tues.-Sun. morn-ings starting at 8:30am (1500dr round-trip).

■■■ PAROS AND NAXOS
(ΠΑΡΟΣ ΚΑΙ ΝΑΞΟΣ)

Paros The geographical center of the islands, Paros is the place for those who want a taste of everything. To enjoy such variety, however you'll have to skimp on quality—its interior and villages are less picturesque than on Naxos and its nightlife less raucous than on Ios. **Paroikia,** the main port of the island, has two redeeming features: a healthy nightlife and the wonderful Byzantine **Panagia Ekatontapiliani** (Church of Our Lady of 100 Gates), which houses three adjacent churches, clois-ters, and a large peaceful courtyard (open 8am-1pm and 4-9pm). Ten km south of town is the cool, spring-fed **Valley of the Butterflies,** home to an enormous spawning swarm of the brown-and-white critters. Take the bus from Paroikia to Aliki (10min., 160dr), ask to be let off at the butterflies *(petaloudes)*, and follow the signs. (Open Mon.-Sat. 9am-8pm, Sun. 9am-1pm and 4-8pm, 200dr.) You can also take a tour from one of the various travel agents (2500dr). Beautiful **Chrissi Akti** (Golden Beach) is a short bus or windsurf jaunt from town. The next beach south, lovely **Drios,** is quieter and more isolated. Also worth a visit is the adjacent island of **Antiparos** and its ancient stalactite caves, with graffiti from as far back as 1776.

The **Hotelier's Association of Paros** (tel. (0284) 245 55 or 244 56) is just to the right of the windmill, facing inland, and lists hotel prices, helps with rooms-to-let, and provides general info. Paros is 5-6 **ferry** hours from Piraeus (3060dr) and in summer is linked to all the neighboring islands by frequent service. Olympic Airways has **flights** between Paros and Athens (15,800dr). **Hotel Dina** (tel. (0284) 213 25) is quiet, immaculate, and right off Market St. (singles 5000-8000dr, doubles 6000-9500dr, triples 7000-10,500dr, reserve ahead). The **Festos Hotel** (tel. (0284) 216 35) boasts a marble terrace and private showers in the rooms (2000-4000dr per person). A slew of fairly cheap pensions and rooms-to-let boarding houses have opened up behind the town beach. There are also official **campgrounds: Koula** (tel. (0284) 220 81) is near town on the beach (1000dr per person, 500dr per tent), and **Parasporas** (tel. (0284) 219 44) lies south of the port with frequent shuttle bus service (700dr per person, 400dr per tent). Restaurants are everywhere, so you won't go hungry in Paroikia. Try **To Tamarisko,** near the National Bank and Market St., with its romantic garden setting (meatballs 1100dr, pork "Tamarisko" 1400dr).

Naxos After Ariadne, daughter of King Minos of Crete, saved Theseus from her father's labyrinth, he expressed his gratitude by abandoning her on **Naxos**. Don't worry about self-centered demi-gods on this largest and least spoiled of the major Cyclades. The twining streets of **Naxos Town** dazzle with flashes of blue ocean behind ice-white walls. Be sure to stroll around the old **Venetian Kastro,** a series of mansions still inhabited by the descendants of the original Frankish and Venetian nobility. The **Portara,** an impressive 6th-century marble archway on the hilltop peninsula near the port, is a perfect photo and picnic spot.

On the waterfront across from the boat dock is a **Tourist Information Center** (tel. (0285) 252 00 or 243 58 or 229 93 after hours; open 8:30am-10pm) where you can store luggage (300dr), change money, make phone calls, and trade used books. Walk down the waterfront with the water on your right for the **National Bank of Greece** (open Mon.-Thurs. 8am-2pm, Fri. 8am-1:30pm). To reach the **post office,** walk down the waterfront (water on your right), turn left after Hotel Hermes, then take your first right (open Mon.-Fri. 7:30am-2pm). The **bus depot** is directly in front of the ferry dock; schedules are posted. You can rent **mopeds** from **Theoharis** (tel. (0285) 234 98), in the same office as CIAO Travel (open 8am-midnight); bikes run from 2500-3500dr per day). Dock hawks charge about 3000dr for singles and 5000dr for doubles. Look for painted red hands pointing the way is the **Hotel Dionysos** (tel. (0285) 223 31) in the old market section, near the Venetian *kastro*—it's cheap, friendly, and boho, but a little run-down (dorm beds 1500-2500dr, singles 3500-4800dr, doubles 3500-6000dr, triples 5000-7200dr). **Anna Legaki's Rooms** (tel. (0285) 228 37) are small, the owner's hospitality more than compensates (singles 2000dr, doubles 3500-5000dr, triples 4500-6000dr). Take the first left before the post office and look for the sign on the right. **Naxos Camping** (tel. (0285) 235 00), off Agios Giorgios Beach, is closest to town (2km) (1000dr per person).

Picnicking is a good idea in Naxos, especially since the town's markets are brimming with outstanding cheese, wine, fruits, and vegetables. **Manolis Garden Taverna,** in the maze of Old Naxos—find it with patience or a local's assistance—serves delicious chicken *souvlaki* wrapped in bacon (1300dr). **Elli,** up the street from CIAO Travel on the left, heaps huge portions of unique offerings. Naxos's nightlife isn't as frenetic as some of the other islands; try **Mike's Bar,** behind the OTE, and the **Ocean Club** disco behind the National Bank.

Naxos's bewitching **interior** is easily traversed by bus or, with some difficulty, by moped. **Buses** (in front of the Naxos Town ferry dock) are cheap and frequent. The main road across the island passes through the resplendent **Tragea,** a vast arcadian olive grove. Stop in **Chalki's** parish church, **Panayia Protothonis,** where restoration has uncovered wall paintings from the 11th through the 13th centuries. If the church is closed, find a local priest to admit you. In **Apiranthos,** visit the **Folk Art Museum** and **Michael Bardani Museum** of Cycladic art (both open 8am-2pm, but hours vary), which lie in the shadows of the two castles commanding the town. The road ends at the enticing beach town of **Apollonas** on the west coast. Don't miss the 10.5m-high *kouros* (sculpture of an idealized male figure) outside of town.

Amorgos Solitude-seekers should head east of Naxos to rugged **Amorgos,** home of the stunning **Chozoviotissa Monastery,** 20min. by foot or 5min. by bus from **Chora,** and built so flawlessly into the sheer face of a cliff that it appears to have grown there. Be sure to observe the dress code: long pants for men, dresses or skirts for women, no bare shoulders. If you complete the hike between sunrise and 2pm (also 5-7pm in summer), the monks will greet you with water, Naxion liqueur and sweets. **Ferries** sail to the port villages of **Katapola** and **Aegiali** from Piraeus (8-13hr., 3665dr), Naxos (4-7hr., 1886dr), and Paros (1-2 per day, 2200dr). Buses connect Katapola and Chora (15min., 160dr). Contact one of the several tourist offices in Katapola or Aegiali for more info.

■ ■ ■ IOS (ΙΟΣ)

You'll be hearing about Ios long before you arrive—some love it, some loathe it, some fear it. If your idea of paradise is to beach-wallow all day and cavort drunkenly all night, Ios is your island: this place, in the words of Spinal Tap's Nigel Tufnell, goes to eleven. Most of Ios's bars are packed into the old village area. Some bars offer happy hours early in the evening, but the real drinking doesn't begin until at least 11pm. **The Slammer Bar,** just uphill from the main square in the village specializes in tequila slammers (500dr). **Disco 69,** on the main village street has cheap drinks and a crowded dance floor (cocktails 500dr, 300dr during 8-11pm happy hour). Or try the **Sweet Irish Dream,** with two stories of Irish partying with billiards, darts, and video games downstairs and tables made for dancing on them upstairs (beer 500-600dr, cocktails 700-800dr). After that, try the **Scorpion Disco,** *the* outdoor dance emporium (700dr cover includes 1st drink).

You can take care of business in Ios within a 3-block radius of the bus stop. The **Tourist Information Center** (tel. and fax (0286) 911 18) at the stop sells ferry and hydrofoil tickets, provides currency exchange, helps with accommodations, and offers free luggage storage and safety deposit boxes (open 7am-1am). Behind the tourist office are the English-speaking **police** (tel. (0286) 912 22; open 24hrs.) and the **Medical Center** (tel. (0286) 912 27; open Mon.-Fri. 10:30am-1pm and 7-9pm, Sat.-Sun. 11am-1pm and 8-9pm). **Buses** shuttle continuously between the port, the village, and the beach (8am-midnight, 160dr).

Ios has outlawed the dock hawks who seem to meet every other ferry in Greece. Coming off the boat on your left is the **Community Tourist Information Office** (tel. (0286) 910 28), a booth generally staffed by helpful English speakers who will call the proprietors of rooms anywhere in Ios and arrange to have them come pick you up for free. **Francesco's** (tel. (0286) 912 23), uphill from the bank, has been recently renovated (doubles 3000-4000dr, with bath 4000-8000dr, triples 4500-6000dr, with bath 6000-9000dr). **Pension Markos** (tel. (0286) 910 59), behind the bus stop on the small hill, is lively and clean (doubles 4000-7000dr, triples 5000-9000dr, quads 7000-10,000dr). If you arrive late, go to **Camping Ios** at the port (800dr per person including tent). Aptly named **Far Out Camping** (tel. (0286) 914 68, fax 915 60) at the far end of Mylopotas beach is the hippest, most luxurious choice (700dr per person, 1000dr with tent). For great Greek fare, try **Pithari,** near

GREECE

the bank or **Saïni's,** near the bars. *Souvlaki* and gyros joints are cheap, greasy, and always satisfying alternatives (*souvlaki* 300dr).

■■■ SANTORINI (THIRA, ΘΗΡΑ)

Santorini's landscape is as wildly beautiful and dramatic as the cataclysm that carved it: a massive volcanic eruption that gave rise to the Atlantis legend and is believed by many to have destroyed the Minoan civilization on Crete. Modern Santorini is really only the eastern crescent of what was a circular island. You can climb New Kameni, which remains an active volcano. In **Thira,** the **Archeological Museum** holds an impressive collection of vases, most from the site of ancient Thira (open Tues.-Sun. 8:30am-3pm. 400dr, students 200dr, free Sun. if accompanied by guide). More fascinating are the excavations at **Akrotiri,** a late Minoan city preserved virtually intact under layers of volcanic rock (open Tues.-Sun. 8:30am-3pm. 1000dr, students 500dr, free on Sundays). Bus tours (3000-3500dr) are often coupled with a visit to the **Profitias Ilias Monastery** and a local wine-tasting. From Profitias Ilias, it's about an hour's hike to the **Ancient Thira.** The ancient theater, church, and forum of the island's old capital are still visible, though less spectacular than the Akrotiri excavations. (Open Tues.-Sun. 9am-3pm. Free.)

Ferries arrive on Santorini from Piraeus (10hr., 4334dr), Ios (1½hr., 1137dr), Paros (5hr., 2469dr), Mykonos (7hr., 2756dr), and Crete (8hr., 2373dr). Most ferries land at **Athinios** harbor, where you can strike a deal for a room with the homeowners who meet each boat. Try for one of the small towns near **Thira,** the island's dramatically situated capital. **Kontohori Youth Hostel** (tel. (0286) 227 22/23 or (0286) 225 77), down a slope about 400m north of the square offers friendlier and slightly nicer than the official (HI) youth hostel, but still not the most soothing place to spend time (single-sex dorm beds with thin mattresses; reception open 8am-1pm and 5-11pm; dorm beds 1000-1400dr, doubles 4000dr; hot showers 6-10pm). **Kamares Youth Hostel (HI),** also north of the square has a roof snack bar (reception open 8am-1pm and 5-9pm; dorm beds 1000dr; hot showers 5-9pm). **Pension Andreas** (tel. (0286) 225 88) is one of a line of new, clean, affordable, and nearly identical pensions lining the road to Santorini Camping. (Doubles 5000-8000dr. Triples 7500-10,000dr.) Follow the blue "camping" signs further to **Santorini Camping** (tel. (0286) 229 44; 900-1200dr per person; 550-700dr per tent). The **tourist police** station (tel. (0286) 226 49; open 24hrs.) is on the main road south of the bus depot.

SPORADES (ΣΠΟΡΑΔΕΣ)

Lush islands of fragrant pines, luxurious beaches, and abundant fruit orchards, the Sporades ("the scattered ones") offer travelers a smorgasbord of earthly delights. Although word has gotten out about the Sporades, this small archipelago remains relatively quiet and inexpensive.

For Skiathos, Skopelos and Alonissos it's easiest to travel by bus from Athens to Agios Konstantinos (2½hr., 2300dr) and from there by ferry (to Skiathos 3½hr., 2775dr; to Skopelos 4½hr., 2924dr; to Alonissos 5½hr., 3232dr). Skyros is linked to the charming town of **Kimi,** on Evia (3½hr., 2250dr). Most buses to Kimi should continue on to the port area, Paralia Kimi. From there a ferry makes sporadic trips, but at least 2 boats per week serve the group; Skiathos (4½hr., 3398dr); Skopelos (4hr., 3050dr); and Alonissos (3hr., 2870dr). Skyros can be reached by daily ferry from Kimi (2hr., 1630dr), or by hydrofoil from any of the other Sporades (5 times per week, 3700-5500dr).

Skiathos and Skopelos Cosmopolitan and expensive, **Skiathos** (Σκιαθοσ) is the place to ogle and be ogled in the Sporades. A bus runs every 15-20min. along Skiathos's main paved road to the many **beaches** on the southern coast. Between stops

19 and 20 on the bus route, **Camping Koukounaries** (tel. (0427) 492 50) offers a restaurant, beach access, and a playground for the kiddies (500dr per person, 700dr per tent). At the end of this line, **Koukounaries** beach and nearby nudist **Banana** beach feature pine trees, golden sand, and big crowds. For relative peace 'n' quiet, take one of the treacherous paths continuing away from the Koukounaries to the less populated **Eleni beach.** Rooms are scarce in late July and August; homes advertising "rooms to let" *(dhomatia)* have the cheapest rates. You'll find restful rooms at **Hadula Tsourou,** 17 Mitrop. Ananiou St., at the end of Pandra St. (doubles 5000dr). Friendly **Australia House** (tel. (0427) 224 88), on the first left off Evangelistrias St., offers rooms with private baths (singles 3000dr, doubles 4000dr). For inexpensive food, try **Tsaprounis** (tel. (0427) 226 85), to the uphill end of Papadiamadi St. (local *mousaka* baked and served in a clay pot 900dr). Skiathos bursts with drink and dance. **La Piscine,** 600m down Evangelistrias St., favors a Love Boat-style atmosphere, complete with swimming pool, piano, slick dancers, cleavage-exposing barmaids, (Senator) Gopher, and restaurant (open for breakfast, swim, and booze 10am-6pm and 9pm-2am; cover 1000dr, beer 500dr, drinks 1000dr). Across from the Taverna Stavros, the **Adagio Bar** features classical music until midnight, when it gears up to jazz and light pop (open 8:30pm-2:30am, beer 400dr, drinks 1000-1303dr).

The looming cliffs rising from the coastline of **Skopelos** (Σκοπελος) gave the island its name: "steep rock from the sea." Tourism here has been kept within sane limits: only the harbor area of Skopelos Town has been transformed to suit foreign expectations. For a superb hike, take the bus to Glossa and walk the dirt track across the island to the **Monastery of Agios Ioannis** clinging to a massive boulder above the ocean. Beaches line the coast south of Skopelos up to Loutraki; the best is the far less crowded **Velanio Beach,** advertised as the only legal nude beach on Skopelos (the inhibited bather need not fear—many beach-goers opt for clothing).

Tourist offices on the island are primarily interested in selling their own excursions and rooms; shop around. For the lowest prices, bargain with the *dhomatia* owners. On a waterfront corner, the **Sotos Pension** (tel. (0424) 225 09) offers rooms with private baths, plus an orange-tree-shaded courtyard (doubles 7000dr). The restaurants in town are fairly expensive, but **Ta Kymata,** at the end of the jetty, has a busy family atmosphere and serves tasty fresh fish and *tzatziki* (squid 100dr). For hefty pasta portions and tangy pizza, try **Aktaion** in the center of the waterfront (spaghetti dishes 500-1000dr).

Alonissos and Skyros

Though it lacks polished beauty, **Alonissos** is one of the friendliest and least touristed islands in Greece. The beaches are magnificent, and the mountains and cliffs maintain a pristine, almost icy, emptiness. Set high on the hill to ward off pirate attacks, the rebuilt old town of **Old Alonissos** is a jewel among the craggy rock. While there, stop at the **Paraport Taverna** at the end of the central street for a drink and equally intoxicating views. Among the myriad beaches kissing the Aegean, **Chrissi Milia** is the best.

In Patitiri, **Ikos Travel** (tel. (0424) 653 20 or 656 48/9) is run by an amiable English-speaking couple who will help find rooms, give info, book excursions, and exchange money. Ask at **Boutique Mary,** on Pelagson Ave., about rooms at **Dimakis Pension** (tel. (0424) 652 94; doubles 4000dr, with bath 5000dr). Or try **Hotel Alykon** (tel. (0424) 656 02 or 653 66, fax 651 95), with inviting beds and gorgeous rooms (singles 5000-7000dr, doubles 6500-8500dr). At the waterfront *tavernas,* you have the choice of dining under canvas or a canopy of leaves. Your sweet tooth will appreciate the decadent desserts at **Pub Dennis,** also on the waterfront. The **Balcony Bar,** set on a ledge overlooking the harbor (follow the inescapable signs throughout town), serves fresh peach juice (500dr) as refreshing as the view. (Both open May-Sept. 9am-2am.)

Skyros (Σκυρος) is the most beautiful of the Sporades, and its hardy island culture outlasts burgeoning tourism. **Skyros Travel** (tel. (0222) 911 23 or 916 00) on Agoras St. organizes expensive (6500dr) boat trips to the south of the island, can

GREECE

help to locate accommodations, and sells maps of the island (350dr) better than those sold on the street (open 9am-2pm and 6:30-11pm). In **Skyros Town,** visit the **Monastery of St. George** and the ruins of the Byzantine fortress the **Castle of Licomidus.** Both sites afford spectacular views of the island's eastern coast. The **Archeological Museum** (tel. (0222) 913 27) shows a cult ceramic ring with two snakes devouring a series of ducks (open Tues.-Sun. 8:30am-3pm; 400dr; free on holidays). Not to be outdone, the **Faltatis Museum** exhibits a superior folk art collection (open 10am-1pm and 5:30-8pm; guided tour in English, free).

Both Skyros town and **Molos** beach, 1km away, offer affordable rooms. Buses run to both places (get off at the Xenia Hotel). Town residents with *dhomatia* may greet the bus; if you prefer to look around on your own, wander the streets of Skyros Town or comb through the dirt roads behind the beach. Sack out near the beach on a **campground** (tel. 924 58) in a pleasant field (1000dr per person). Rent a **motorbike** (3000dr per day) at any of the dealers in town. **On The Rocks,** near the beach, plays Top 40 until 2 or 3am, when Greek music attracts the local youths.

CRETE (KRITI, KPHTH)

Greece's largest island embraces an infinite store of mosques and monasteries, mountain villages, gorges, grottoes, and beaches. Crete has produced a culture distinct from the rest of Greece; Cretans have their own folk dances, crafts, and costumes. Most travelers arrive in Crete by **ferry.** The island is well-served during the summer. Boats arrive regularly in **Iraklion** from Piraeus, Santorini, Ios, Paros and Naxos. Leaving Crete, you can make connections in Santorini to almost any other island in the Cyclades. Boats also run from Piraeus to Chania; from Gythion on the Peloponnese to Kastelli; from Rhodes to Agios Nikolaos; and from Piraeus to Agios Nikolaos, via Milos, Folegandros, Santorini, and Anafi. The **hydrofoil** *Nearchos* connects Iraklion with Santorini, Ios, Paros, and Mykonos.

■■■ CENTRAL CRETE

Iraklion Many visitors' first impression of Crete is the overdeveloped mess of Iraklion (Ηρακλειο). All that is impressive in this town is its past: the superb museum and spectacular ruins will explain why Crete is considered the cradle of Western civilization. The **Archaeological Museum** (tel. (081) 22 60 92) off Eleftherias Sq. houses colorful Minoan frescoes (open Mon. 12:30-7pm, Tues.-Sun. 8am-7pm; 1000dr, students 500dr, Sun. free).

Across from the Archaeological Museum, the **GNTO** office, 1 Xanthoudidou St. (tel. (081) 22 82 03) has maps of the city, hotel lists and schedules (open Mon.-Fri. 8:30am-2:30pm). The **tourist police,** 10 Dikeosinis St. (tel. (081) 28 31 90), will provide general tourist information as well (open 7am-11pm). The main **post office** is off Gianani St. Most of Iraklion's cheap accommodations cluster around **Handakos St.,** at the center of town. Others are on Evans and 1866 St., near the market. **Hotel Rea,** Kalimeraki St. (tel. (081) 22 36 38 or 24 21 89), off Handakos St., has spotless pastel-colored doubles for 4500dr, with bath 5500dr. The **hostel,** 5 Vironos St. (tel. (081) 28 62 81 or 22 29 47), is just off 25th Augustou Ave. It's family-run, cleanish, cool, and quiet (curfew 11:30pm, 700dr per person). The best food show in town is the open-air **market** on 1866 St., just off Venizelou Sq. There you can either amass a picnic or sample one of 10 colorful *tavernas* on **Theodosaki Street,** the first left as you enter the market. **Ta Psaria,** at the base of 25th Augustou Ave. provides decent seafood at moderate prices (open 10am-midnight; kalamari 900dr, shrimp 1300dr). At **Minos Restaurant,** Dedalou St., the manager will personally guide you to have a look in the kitchen and *then* he will let you sit down (lemon swordfish 1800dr).

VOSLWEIDERSTR.93
5020 SALZBURG/ AUSTRIA

4828 5700 1711 202

04/97 CV

THOMAS G BURSON

OGLWEIDERHOF

VOGLWEIDERSTR.93
5020 SALZBURG/ AUSTRIA
940 012 668 6

VISA-SERVICE

KREDITKARTEN-AKTIENGESELLSCHAFT
POSTFACH 147, A-1011 WIEN

B
A

Dur
die
sich
gur

*The
and
the*

Unterschrift/*Signature*

VISA

VERKAUFSBELEG
SALES DRAFT

Datum
Date 26.5.95

Autorisierungs-Nummer/*Code*

3 64500

...ag in öS
...nt in AS 980.—

...nterschrift anerkennt der Karteninhaber
...tigkeit dieses Beleges und verpflichtet
...n angeführten Betrag gemäß den Bedin-
...zur Verwendung der Karte zu bezahlen.

...lholder agrees to accept this transaction
...es to pay the Total amount shown as per
...nt agreement with the cardissuing bank.

Kopie für den Karteninhaber / Cardholder's copy

Knossos, Phaestos, and Matala Bus 2 travels from 25th Augustou Ave. to **Knossos,** 6km south. Here the mytho-historical palace of King Minos and the ancient capital of the Minoan civilization have been imaginatively reconstructed (open 8am-7pm; 1000dr, students 500dr, Sun. free). Buses travel from Terminal B in Iraklion to the Minoan ruins at **Phaestos,** which may be a disappointment to those not well-versed in Minoan archaeology because it's hard to visualize what the palace must have looked like in its prime (open Mon.-Fri. 8am-7pm, Sat.-Sun. 8am-6pm; 800dr, students 400dr, Sun. free). The sandy beach and spacious caves of **Matala** are also accessible by bus from Iraklion (Terminal B, 2hr., 1150dr). The grottoes surrounding the town were cut by the Romans, used by the Nazis as hideouts, and became summer homes for 1960s flower children. At the moment, most of the caves are sealed with thin netting. Most travelers stay legally at **Matala Camping** on your right as you enter the town center (550dr per person, 500dr per tent), or at one of Matala's few pensions. Flash your *Let's Go* at **Rent Rooms Dimitris** and he'll give you a discount on his posh, clean rooms (singles 2500dr, doubles 3300dr; inquire at Matala Travel in the center of town).

■■■ WESTERN CRETE

Rethymnon and Chania 81km west of Iraklion, **Rethymnon** (Ρεθυμνο) is an enchanting slice of Crete's past spiced with vestiges of Turkish and Venetian influence. Be sure to visit the colossal **Venetian Fortezza,** dating from around 1580, and if you are traveling in July and August, don't miss the **Renaissance Festival,** held in the fortress. The **GNTO** (tel. (0831) 291 48), on the waterfront, supplies maps and bus and ferry schedules (open Mon.-Fri. 9am-3:30pm). The **HI youth hostel,** 41 Tombasi St. (tel. (0831) 228 48), is cheerful, relaxed, and crammed in summer (reception open 8am-noon and 5-8pm; no curfew; 1000dr per person). **Olga's Pension,** 57 Souliou St. (tel. (0831) 298 51), is an eternal party, with homemade wine (150dr) at the terrarium café (singles 4000dr, doubles 4500dr, triples 5500dr, quads 6000dr; private bath included). Pitch tents on the grass at **Elizabeth Camping** (tel. (0831) 286 94), 3km east of town, (1200dr, 600dr per tent, 500dr per car; frequent buses from the bus station).

In the lively harbor town of **Chania** (Χανια), Ottoman and Venetian architecture converge. Check out the **Venetian Inner Harbor** for a thriving social scene, as well as a **Venetian lighthouse** restored by the Egyptians during their occupation of Crete in the 1830's. The **GNTO** (tel. (0821) 264 26) is on the 4th floor of the Megaro Pantheon, Platia 1866, above the Greek Agricultural Bank (open Mon.-Fri. 8am-2:30pm). For pleasant housing, try the **Hotel Piraeus,** 10 Zambelou St. (tel. (0821) 946 65), with friendly management and a view of the harbor (singles 3000dr, doubles 4300dr, triples 6000dr). Or, check out the **Kydonia Pension,** 15 Isodion St. (tel. (0821) 571 79; singles 3500dr, doubles 4500dr). When you first get off the bus, head to **Yordanni's,** 18 N. Plastira, the insider's place for *bougatsa*, a pie filled with the creamy, slightly salty white cheese unique to Crete (300dr). **Discos** and live music enliven at the eastern end of the harbor beyond the tourist office.

Samaria Gorge, Agia Roumeli, and Environs One of the "musts" in Crete is a 5hr. hike through the 16km **Samaria Gorge,** a spectacular ravine that cuts through heavy forests and sheer granite cliffs (open May-Oct. Winter flash floods have claimed many lives; 1000dr). **Buses** run from Chania via Omalos to **Xyloskalo** at the mouth of the gorge four times a day. A hot, dusty hike beyond the official exit from the gorge will bring you to **Agia Roumeli,** a seedy oasis for tired and thirsty hikers. Energetic hikers should explore Crete's unspoiled southwest coast. Peaceful **Loutro** is accessible only by ferry from Agia Roumeli (620dr) or Chora Sfakion (390dr). **Sougia** and **Paleochora,** to the west of Agia Roumeli, are likewise beautiful, though more crowded. In Paleochora, stay at the cozy **Lissos Hotel** (tel. (0821) 412 66) on Venizelou St. (singles 5000dr, doubles 6700dr).

GREECE

■■■ EASTERN CRETE

Visit the largely unremarkable resort town of **Malia** (Μαλια) for the ruins of the **Minoan Palace,** one of the three great cities of Minoan Crete, or for the **Hypostyle Crypt,** believed to have been a social center for Malia's intelligentsia (open Tues.-Sun. 8:30am-3pm; 400dr, Sun. free). Find lodgings on 25 Martiou St. at **Pension Aspasia** (tel. (0897) 312 90; doubles 6000dr, triples 8000dr; common baths) or at **Pension Menios** (tel. (0897) 313 61; doubles 6000dr, triples 7500dr; small balconies and private baths; no reception—ask at adjacent market or call). **Camping Sissi** (tel. (0897) 712 47 or 712 62/3) is 12km to the east on an uncrowded stone beach with grassy tent-pitches (700dr per person, 550dr per tent, 400dr per car). Eating in Malia is cheap compared to the rest of Crete; many places on the Paraliakos (Beach Rd.) serve an English breakfast for 600dr and offer dinners for under 1500dr.

Agios Nikolaos (Αγιος Νικολαος) exudes an appealing mix of humility and pretension. The **tourist office** (tel. (0841) 223 57), at the bridge between the lake and the port, changes money and makes room reservations (open 8:30am-9:30pm.) **The Green House,** 15 Modatsou St. (tel. (0841) 220 25), has a tangled garden, and the multilingual proprietors often proffer homemade Italian ice (doubles without bath 3500dr). For nightlife, stroll around the harbor; check out **Charlie Chan's** nightclub (beer 400dr, mixed drinks 700dr).

Sitia (Σητεια), at the island's east end, is an etherized port town with a good **HI Youth Hostel,** 4 Therissou St. (tel. (0843) 226 93; 1000dr per person; reception open 9am-1:30pm and 4:30-9pm; if no one is around, find a bed and register later). For **ferry** tickets to the Dodecanese, Amorgos, Paros, and Piraeus (Wed.); and Kassos, Karpathos, Chalki, and Rhodes (Sat.); try **Porto Belis Travel,** 3 Karamanli St. (tel. (0843) 223 70), near the bus station (open 8:30am-9pm). From Sitia, it's an easy trip to the fortified monastery of **Toplou.** Notice the holes above the gate where gentle monks poured boiling oil on the heads of invaders. Also nearby are the ravishing and touristy beaches of **Kato Zakros** and **Vai.**

NORTHEAST AEGEAN AND DODECANESE ISLANDS

The intricate, rocky coastlines of the Northeast Aegean Islands enclose thickly wooded mountains and isolated valleys. Proximity to Turkey explains the presence of guns, camouflage, and large numbers of young soldiers.

Lesvos, Samos, and Nearby Islands Once home of the sensual poet Sappho, **Lesvos** (ΛΕΣΒΟΣ) is Greece's third-largest island. Legend holds that the island was once populated solely by women. The towns of **Plomari,** in the south, and **Molyvos,** in the north (dominated by a Genoese fortress) are two good destinations. Coming from the main port of Mitilini, the bus stops at Molyvos's **tourist office** (tel. (0253) 710 79), which finds private rooms starting at about 4000dr. **Plomari,** the island's second- largest city, is at once a no-holds-barred resort town (with discos, cheery *tavernas,* and all the other accoutrements of package tour groups) and an all-out fishing village. Manolis Stefanis at **Plomari Travel** on Lesviou St. (tel. (0252) 329 46) has lots of information about everything from accommodations to excursions. **Boats** run daily to Lesvos via Chios from Piraeus (12-14hr., 4700dr), as do several **flights** from Athens (14,600dr) and Thessaloniki (18,600dr).

Samos is perhaps the most beautiful and certainly the most touristed island in the area, although it's quiet compared to most of the Dodecanese and the Cyclades. On the northeastern end of the island, **Samos Town** is among the northeast Aegean's more attractive ports. Ferries run from Samos Town to Piraeus (12hr., 4500dr), Chios (2-4 per week, 1920dr), and Paros; less frequently to Lesvos, Mykonos, and

GREECE

Syros. Ferries leave from quieter **Pythagorion,** the former capital of Samos, for Patmos and points south. **Samos Tours** (tel. (0273) 277 15), right at the end of the ferry dock, has all the information you'll need. (Open 6am-midnight and usually whenever a boat arrives.) The **tourist office** (tel. (0273) 285 30) is signposted from the waterfront (open July-Aug. Mon.-Sat. 9am-1pm and 6-8:30pm). There are barely enough rooms to go around on Samos. The best place to stay is the clean, cheap **Pension Ionia,** 5 Manoli Kalomiri St. (tel. (0273) 287 82; singles 2500dr; doubles 3000dr). **Hotel Artemis,** Pythagoras Sq. (tel. (0273) 277 92), run by the affable, English-speaking Mr. Kostas, affords travelers clean rooms and helpful service. (Doubles 4000dr, with bath 5000dr.) **Buses** run every hour from Samos Town to Pythagorion, where you can see the magnificent remains of Polykrates's 6th-century BC engineering projects: the **Tunnel of Eupalinos,** a rock pier built in 40m of water, and the **Temple of Hera,** one of the 7 wonders of the ancient world. The beautiful beaches that rim the northern coast are, excepting picturesque **Kokkari,** uncrowded. **Psili Ammos** on the southern coast becomes nicer after 4pm, when the excursion buses return to Samos Town.

Samos is the main transit point to **Ephesus** on the Turkish coast, the site of perhaps the most extensive classical ruins in the Mediterranean (see Turkey). Ferries leave twice daily in summer (8am and 4:30pm) to Kuşadası (about 6000dr). The Turkish port tax (not included) is about US$10 but can fluctuate wildly; if you stay overnight you have to pay the tax again. Just a 2hr. ferry hop west from Samos, **Ikaria** is famous for its therapeutic waters and wax-winged namesake. The verdant, untouristed **Chios** lies midway between Samos and Lesvos. Green **Thassos** and small, mysterious **Samothraki** are easily accessible from northern Greece.

Rhodes Bunched off the coast of Asia Minor, the **Dodecanese** have historical significance, gorgeous beaches and throngs of tourists. **Rhodes** (Ροδοσ) today is the undisputed tourist capital of the Dodecanese. The island is famous for its unparalleled medieval architecture, impressive ancient ruins and splendid coves. The best beaches (**Faliraki, Tsambika,** and **Haraki**) stretch along the east coast toward Lindos. Five km north of Faliraki is **Kalithea,** once an exclusive spa for European aristocrats; during the day, you can use the shower on the park's beach. On the northern coast are the ruins of an ancient town at **Kamiros,** and farther west, the majestic hilltop castle at **Monolithos.** You can walk around inside the castle and small chapel of St. Panteleimon, but mind the steep drop when the views knock you off your feet (24hrs., free). The interior and southern half of the island are quieter, subsisting on agriculture rather than tourism.

One look at the **Old City** and it's clear that the Knights of St. John were building for keeps. Replacing Hellenistic structures with their own incredible array of medieval castles and fortresses, the knights left the most enduring mark on the city. The best place to begin exploring this quarter is at **Symi Square,** inside Liberty and Arsenal Gates, the main passages between the Old and New Towns and the waterfront. The beautiful halls and courtyards of the former **Hospital of the Knights** now house the **Archeological Museum** in **Museum Square** (open Tues.-Sun. 8:30am-3pm. 600dr, students 300dr; free on Sun.). At the top of the street is a second pride of the city, the **Palace of the Knights of St. John.** Also called the Palace of the Grand Masters, the complex has 300 rooms, moats, drawbridges, huge watch towers, and colossal battlements. (Palace open Tues-Sun. 8:30am-3pm; 800dr, students 400dr.) The modern **new town** has only hotels and expensive shops, but the old town welcomes budget travelers with small pensions and inexpensive restaurants. The **tourist office** (tel. (0241) 359 45) is on Rimini Sq. The **GNTO** (tel. (0241) 232 55 or 236 55) is several blocks up the street. In the Old Town, stay at **Pension Sofia,** 27 Aristofanous St., which is family-run, clean, and bright, and the rooms have private baths (doubles 4500-6000dr, triples 5000-6600dr). Also, **Hotel Andreas,** 28 D. Omirou, with its nifty loftbeds affords an excellent view of the city (doubles 5000-7000dr, triples 6500-9000dr). In the New Town, try **Tina's Studios,** on the corner of Katho-

GREECE

pouli and Constantopedos, with beautiful studios with private kitchenettes and bath (doubles 3000-4000dr, triples 6000-7000dr).

Rhodes is the most accessible island in the Dodecanese. Regular **ferries and hydrofoils** connect it with Piraeus, Crete, some Cyclades, the Northeast Aegean islands, Kavala, and the other Dodecanese islands. Schedules here vary from day to day and should be checked at travel agencies. Rhodes is also the air hub of the islands, with connections to Athens, Kos, Karpathos, Kassos, Crete, Santorini, and Mykonos. There are **ferries** from Rhodes to all of the Dodecanese islands and Athens (Piraeus) and to Marmaris in Turkey (6000dr). For tickets and schedules, go to **Triton Tours,** 9 Plastira St. (tel. (0241) 306 57; open 8am-8pm). Regular **flights** in summer leave from Rhodes to Athens, Crete, Kos, Santorini, Mykonos, Karpathos, and Kassos. The airport (tel. (0241) 929 81) is on the west coast, 17km from town near the city of Paradisi; public buses run hourly (280dr).

Kos, Patmos, and Karpathos Keeping the island of **Kos** (Κως) a secret from travel agents is like hiding truffles from a pig. In summer visitors throng to the classical and Hellenic ruins, carpet the wide, sandy beaches, and frisk about bars. The most popular beach is shady **Tingaki,** 10km west of **Kos Town,** which is notable only for a boisterous nightlife. If you're here to party, try **Pension Alexis,** 9 Irodotou St. (tel. (0242) 287 98, 255 94, or 293 51); if his rooms are full (doubles 4000-5000dr; triples 6000-7500dr), he'll put you up with a mattress and sheets on the patio (1200dr) or give you a deal at his elegant **Hotel Afendoulis** (tel. (0242) 253 21) in the ritzier part of town (doubles with bath 6000-6500dr). The continuous sands of the south of the island are broken into many beaches, depending on where you enter. **Paradise beach** has a small bus stop and, therefore, the greatest crowds. For more open space, try **Magic** beach or **Camel** beach north of Paradise. The main archaeological sites are in town and at **Asclepion,** Hippocrates's school of medicine, 4km away. (Open summer Tues.-Sun. 8:30am-3pm. 600dr, students 300dr; free on Sun.) The mountain villages of **Asfendiou** and the surrounding hills are great for hiking. For a quieter beach town than Kos, try **Mastihari** on the northern coast or petite **Kamari,** near the southern tip. **Ferries** from Kos go to Piraeus (11-15hr., 5900dr), Rhodes (4hr., 2770dr), Thessaloniki (17hr., 9720dr), Paros (3190dr), and Naxos (3230dr). Boats also leave for Bodrum, Turkey (12,000dr round-trip).

Patmos, the northernmost of the Dodecanese islands, is where St. John is said to have written the Book of Revelation. The sprawling monastery dedicated to him, just above the charming and labyrinthine hilltop village of **Chora,** presides over the austere beauty of the island. Stay in the pleasant port of **Skala.** Even boats arriving at 1am are greeted by a battalion of locals offering rooms (average prices: singles 3000dr, doubles 4000-5000dr). **Ferries** from Patmos travel to Piraeus (10hr., 4763dr), Kos (4hr., 2225dr), Rhodes (10hr., 4315dr) while **hydrofoils** service Leros (2615dr), Kos (4801dr), Samos (4396dr), and Chios (6946dr).

Karpathos (Κάρπαθος), south of Rhodes, is more isolated and features **Olymbos,** a town with two working windmills, women in traditional garb, and the pretty, stony beach at **Vananda.** Both are accessible from the small port of **Diafani** in the northern part of the island; the main administrative port is **Karpathos** in the south. In **Ta Pigadia,** stay at the family-run, English-speaking **Harry's Rooms to Rent** (tel. (0245) 221 88), just up the hill and to the left of the Arva Hotel. (Singles 2400dr. Doubles 3500dr.) The beautiful, nearly deserted beaches of **Ahata** and **Amopi** are perfect for camping and bathing. **Boats** from Karpathos go to Rhodes (4½hr., 3100dr). Boats also chug to Kassos (1½hr., 1110dr) and Iraklion, on Crete (Wed. and Sat., 6hr., 3109dr). Departures are infrequent in winter and always at the mercy of the weather in this, the roughest stretch of the Aegean.

Hungary (Magyarország)

US$1 = 108Ft (forints, or HUF) 100Ft = US$0.93
CDN$1 = 80Ft 100Ft = CDN$1.25
UK£1 = 171Ft 100Ft = UK£0.59
IR£1 = 169Ft 100Ft = IR£0.59
AUS$1 = 82Ft 100Ft = AUS$1.21
NZ$1 = 65Ft 100Ft = NZ$1.53
SAR1 = 30Ft 100Ft = SAR3.32
Country Code: 36 International Dialing Prefix: 00

The people of Hungary combine an exacting attention to detail with a warm Mediterranean affability that has miraculously survived the troubles of its rocky past. Academic minds will marvel at the centuries-old tension between Magyar ethnicity and foreign control. Mongols invaded the country in the 13th century, and in the 16th and 17th centuries, Turks and Habsburgs overtook it. World War I redistributed two thirds of its territory, and during World War II, the Nazis occupied it, until the two-month Soviet siege of 1945. The short-lived Hungarian republic of 1946-49 gave way to the Communist People's Republic, under which the country became strongly tied to the USSR. In 1956, Hungarian patriots led by Imre Nagy rose up against the new government, paving the way for yet another communist government, this time led by János Kádár. In the fall of 1989 the Hungarian people fulfilled the aspirations of the previous generation and broke away from the Soviet orbit in a bloodless revolution. Eager to further privatize Hungary's hybrid economy and sensing the changes sweeping Eastern Europe, the reforming Communists relinquished their party's monopoly on power and took the ironic "People's" out of the People's Republic of Hungary. The 1990 elections transferred power to the center-right Hungarian Democratic Forum, led by Prime Minister József Antall and President Arpád Göncz, a former Soviet political prisoner. The renamed-and-revamped Socialists were again trusted with power in 1994. Change continues at a dizzying pace, but Hungarians have adapted and thrived admirably since the last Soviet troops departed in June 1991.

Hungarian culture has flourished throughout the country's tumultuous history: musical contributions include 19th-century composer Ferenc (Franz) Liszt, as well as 20th-century geniuses Zoltán Kodály and Béla Bartók. Many current musical groups enjoy worldwide respect, and theater and film also thrive under the direction of such luminaries as István Szabó and Miklós Jancsó. Folk music collectors should look for tapes by Márta Sebestyén.

GETTING THERE AND GETTING AROUND

Citizens of the United States, Canada, U.K., Ireland, and South Africa can travel to Hungary visa-free with a valid passport. Australians and New Zealanders must obtain 30-day tourist visas from their Hungarian Embassy valid for 6 months after the date of issue, for US$15 (single entry), US$30 (double entry), US$60 (multiple entry) and US$15 (transit). Add US$5 for rush (on-the-spot) service. Obtaining a visa takes one day, requires a valid passport, 2 photographs (4 for multiple entry) and payment by cash or money order. You can apply for a visa extension at police stations in Hungary, but tourist visa holders cannot stay more than 90 days.

Budapest's **Ferihegy airport** handles all international traffic, including **MALÉV**, the national airline. Hungary's domestic transportation network radiates out from Budapest; most rail lines swerve through the capital. Use buses to travel among the outer provincial centers, or plan on returning to Budapest to make connections.

Hungarian **trains** *(vonat)* are reliable and inexpensive; Eurail is valid. *Személyvonat* are excruciatingly slow; *gyorsvonat* trains (listed on schedules in red) cost the same and move at least twice as fast. All of the larger provincial towns are accessible by the blue express rail lines *(expressz)*. The express fare from Budapest to any of the provincial cities costs 400-900Ft each way, including a seat reservation (required on trains marked with an "R" on schedules). Hungarian train terms include *érkezés* (arrival), *indulás* (departure), *vágány* (track), and *állomás* or *pályaudvar* (station, abbreviated *pu.*). Travelers under 26 are eligible for a 33% discount on domestic train fares. The ISIC earns discounts on international tickets from IBUSZ, Express, and station ticket counters. Show your card and repeat "student," or the Hungarian, *diák* (DEE-ahk). The student discount on international trains is roughly 30%, but sometimes you need to be persistent to get it.

The extensive **bus** system is cheap but crowded; it links many towns whose only rail connection is to Budapest. The **Erzsébet tér** bus station in Budapest posts schedules and fares. Buy intercity bus tickets on the bus (get there early if you want a seat), while tickets for local city buses must be bought in advance from a newsstand (30-35Ft) and punched on board. Either IBUSZ or Tourinform can provide a brochure about **cycling** in Hungary that includes maps, suggested tours, sights, accommodations, bike rental locations, repair shops, and recommended border-crossing points. Write to the **Hungarian Nature-Lovers' Federation (MTSZ)**, 1065 Budapest, Bajcsy-Zsilinszky út 31, or the **Hungarian Cycling Federation**, 1146 Budapest, Szabó J. u. 3, for more info. Some rail stations rent bicycles to passengers.

HUNGARY ESSENTIALS

Perhaps the best word for foreigners in Hungary to know is **IBUSZ**, the Hungarian national travel bureau. Their offices throughout the country make room arrangements, change money, sell train tickets, and charter tours. Snare the pamphlet *Tourist Information: Hungary* and the monthly entertainment guides *Programme in Hungary* and *Budapest Panorama* (all free and in English). **Express,** the former national student travel bureau, handles youth hostels and changes money. Regional travel agencies are more helpful than IBUSZ and Express in outlying areas. **Tourinform** is a fantastically helpful nonprofit info service with locations in 15 of Hungary's 19 counties. They have free, helpful brochures, and answer all your questions about Budapest and the rest of Hungary, often serving as interpreters.

Change money only as you need it. Keep some Western cash to purchase visas, international train tickets, and (less often) private accommodations (hard currency sometimes results in lower prices and better service). **American Express** offices in Budapest, and IBUSZ offices around the country, cash traveler's checks for a 6% commission. All major credit cards are accepted at more expensive hotels and at many shops and restaurants; smaller ones accept only American Express. The best rates in summer 1994 were found at branches of the OTP, IBUSZ, Mezőbank, and MKB in Budapest. New Zealand dollars cannot be exchanged here, so pack another currency. At the few offices with extended hours, the rates are generally poor. Black market exchanges are illegal yet common, but the rates are rarely favorable enough (an extra 10%) to risk the large chance of being swindled.

Over 600 street names in Budapest alone have changed since the 1989 revolution, so it's advisable to get the most recent maps available. Hungarian addresses usually involve one of the following: *utca,* abbreviated *u.* (street); *út,* or *útja,* (avenue); *tér,* or *tere,* (square, but may be a park, plaza, or boulevard); *híd* (bridge); and, *körút,* abbreviated *krt.* (ring-boulevard). Numbers on either side of the street are not always in sync; some streets are numbered odd and even while others are numbered up one side and down the other.

Business hours in Hungary are Monday to Friday 9am-5pm (7am-7pm for food stores). Banks close around 3pm on Friday, but hours continue to expand. Larger shopping centers and food stores may also sell food on Sundays. Tourist bureaus usually open Monday to Saturday 8am-5pm (some open until noon on Sun.) in summer; in winter these hours shrink to Monday to Friday 10am-4pm. Museums are usually open Tuesday to Sunday 10am-6pm, with occasional free days on Tuesday. With an ISIC you can often get in free or pay 50%. Nothing is open on national **holidays:** Christian holidays, May 1, and August 20, March 15, and Oct. 23.

Communication Hungarian belongs to the Finno-Ugric family of languages. English is the country's very distant third language after Hungarian and German—much of western Hungary is set up for German-speaking tourists. In eastern Hungary, however, even German may fail. A few starters for pronunciation: *c* is pronounced "ts" as in ca*t*s; *cs* is "ch" as in *Ch*alupa; *gy* is "dy" as in the French a*di*eu; *ly* is "y" as in *y*am, *s* is "sh" as in *sh*ovel; *sz* is "s" as in "*S*eattle"; *zs* is "jh" as in plea*s*ure, and *a* is "a" as in *a*lways. The first syllable usually gets the emphasis. Some useful tidbits: *jó napot* (YOH naw-pot, "hello"); *köszönöm* (KUR-sur-nurm, "thank you"); *mikor?* (MI-kor? "when?"); *hol?* (where?); *kérem* (KAY-rem, "please"); *kérek* (KEH-rek, "I'd like..."); *viszontlátásra* (VI-sohn-tlah-tah-shraw, "goodbye"); *fizetni szeretnék* (VI-zet-ney SEH-ret-nayk, "I'd like to pay"); *nem értem* (NEM AYR-tem, "I don't understand"); *beszél angolul/németül* (BES-el AWN-gohlul/NAY-met-yuhl, "Do you speak English/German?"); *víz* ("water"); *sör* (SHUR, "beer").

Almost all telephone numbers in the countryside now have six digits and begin with a "3." Hungary's pay **phones** require 10Ft per minute for local calls, 25 Ft per minute for long-distance calls within Hungary. Wait for the tone and dial slowly. For long distance, dial 06 before the area code (2 digits long, except in Budapest). International calls require red phones or new, digital-display blue ones, found at large post offices, on the street, and in metro stations. The blue phones tend to cut you off after 3-9min. At 160Ft per minute to the U.S., telephones suck money so fast you need a companion to feed them. Direct calls can also be made from the telephone office in Budapest, with a 3min. minimum to the U.S. To reach AT&T's **USADirect** operator, put in a 5, 10, or 20Ft coin (which you'll get back), dial 00, wait for the second dial tone, then dial 80 00 11 11. To reach the MCI **WorldPhone** operator, dial 80 00 14 11; **SprintExpress** 80 00 18 77; **Canada Direct** 80 00 12 11; **BT Direct** (UK) 80 04 40 11; **Ireland Direct** 80 00 35 31; **Australia Direct** 80 00 61 11; **New Zealand Direct** 80 00 64 11.

The **mail** is perfectly reliable (airmail—*légiposta*—to the U.S. takes 5-10 days). Because Hungary's per capita telephone rate is the second-lowest in Europe (Albania wins), it is very common to send **telegrams,** even across town. Ask for a telegram form *(távirati ürlapot)* and fill it out before returning to the counter. Post offices are indicated by the sign **POSTA** (usually open Mon.-Fri. 8am-7pm, Sat. 8am-1pm). When using hand signals for numbers, remember to start with the thumb for "1"—holding up your index finger means "wait."

Accommodations and Camping Most travelers stay in **private homes** booked through a tourist agency. (Singles 500-2000Ft. Doubles 800-3000Ft.) Singles are scarce; it's worth finding a roommate, because solo travelers often must pay for a double room. Know that agencies may initially try to foist off their more costly quarters on you. Outside Budapest, the best and cheapest office is usually the regional one. After a few nights, you can often make arrangements with the owner directly, and avoid the tourist agencies' 20-30% commission. You can also find your own room where there is a sign for *Szoba Kiadó* or *Zimmer frei*. Make sure any private room you rent is near the center or easily accessible by public transport.

Some towns have cheap **hotels** (doubles 1200-1600Ft), but most are disappearing. As the hotel system develops and room prices rise, **hostels** become more attractive. Many can be booked at **Express** or sometimes the regional tourist office after you arrive (250-700Ft). Late June through August, **university dorms** metamorphose into hostels. Locations change annually; book with an Express office in the off-season, at the dorm itself during the summer. The staff at Express generally speak German, sometimes English. Over 100 **campgrounds** are sprinkled throughout Hungary (about 500Ft per day for 2 people). They also often rent bungalows: 2-person for 800-1200Ft and 4-person for about 2000Ft. Most sites are open May-Sept. Tourist offices offer the comprehensive booklet *Camping Hungary,* which is revised annually. For more information and maps, contact the **Hungarian Camping and Caravanning Club** in Budapest, or **Tourinform.**

Food and Drink With its fantastic concoctions of meat, spices, and fresh vegetables, many find Magyar cuisine among the finest in Europe. Paprika, Hungary's chief agricultural export, colors most dishes red. In Hungarian restaurants, called *vendéglő* or *étterem,* you may begin with *gulyásleves,* a delicious and hearty beef soup seasoned with paprika—often a meal in itself for only 100-200Ft. *Borjú-paprikás* is a veal dish with paprika, often accompanied by small potato-dumpling pastas called *gnocchi*. Vegetarians can find the tasty *rántott sajt* (fried cheese) and *gombapörkölt* (mushroom stew) on most menus. *Túrós táska* is a chewy pastry pocket filled with sweetened cottage cheese.

Finding a genuine, "local" eatery is hard. Gypsy music often spells tourist trap. A 10% gratuity has become standard, even if the bill includes a service charge (which goes to the management); tip as you pay. A gypsy musician expects about 150Ft from your table, depending on the number of listeners. A *csárda* is a traditional inn, a *bisztró* an inexpensive restaurant, and an *önkiszolgáló étterem* a cheap cafeteria. Since few menus outside Budapest are written in English, a dictionary can spare you from a point-and-pray meal. For pastry and coffee, look for a *cukrászda,* where a sweet-tooth can fulfill relentless desire for dangerously few forints. *Kávé* means espresso. **Salátabárs** vend deli concoctions. Vegetarians may have trouble filling up in Hungarian restaurants, but fresh fruit and vegetables abound on stands and in produce markets. Supermarkets (look for the **"ABC"** sign) sell dry goods and dairy products; **Julius Meinl** is the largest national chain. Except "non-stops," which are open 24hrs., most shops close from 1pm Saturday to Monday morning.

Hungarians are justly proud of their wines. Most famous are the red *Egri Bikavér* ("Bull's Blood of Eger") and the white *Tokaji* wines (150Ft per bottle at a store, 300Ft at a restaurant). Fruit schnapps *(pálinka)* are a national specialty; you can try them in most cafés and bars. Local beers are good; the most common is *Dreher.*

BUDAPEST ■ 451

■■■ BUDAPEST

At once a cosmopolitan European capital and the stronghold of Magyar nationalism, Budapest has awakened from its 40-year Communist coma with the same vigor that helped rebuild the city from the rubble of WWII. Endowed with an architectural majesty befitting its former high status in the Habsburg empire, it also retains an intellectual and cultural scene often compared to that of Paris. Today, the city refuses to buckle under the relentless siege of Western glitzification—while pursuing the total abnegation of all things Russian.

ORIENTATION AND PRACTICAL INFORMATION

Budapest straddles the **Danube River** (Duna) in north-central Hungary, 250km downstream from Vienna. **Óbuda** (Old Buda), in the northwest, was the center of the original Roman settlement. Hilly **Buda** on the west bank embraces the **Castle District;** on the east side buzzes **Pest,** the heart of the modern city. Three central bridges, **Széchenyi lánchíd** (Chain Bridge), slender, white **Erzsébet híd** (Elizabeth Bridge), and green **Szabadság híd,** bind the halves together.

Moszkva tér (Moscow Square), is where virtually all trams and buses start or end their routes. One metro stop away, **Batthyány tér** lies opposite the Parliament building on the west bank; this is the starting node of the HÉV commuter railway. Budapest's three metro lines converge at **Deák tér,** at the core of Pest's loosely concentric ring boulevards, beside the main international bus terminal at **Erzsébet tér.** Streets arbitrarily change names from one block to the next. The city is divided into 22 districts, and addresses are preceded by the city area code; central Buda is I while downtown Pest is V. Many street names occur more than once in town; always check the district as well. Streets are in the process of shedding their Communist names; an up-to-date map is essential. The American Express and Tourinform offices have excellent free tourist maps, or pick up the *Belváros Idegenforgalmi Térképe* at any metro stop (80Ft).

Tourist Offices: Tourinform, V, Sütő u. 2 (tel. 117 98 00). Off Deák tér around the corner from Porsche Hungaria. M: Deák tér. Remarkably helpful, multilingual tourist office providing info ranging from sight-seeing tours to opera performances to the location of Aikido dojos. Open 8am-8pm. Sight-seeing, accommodation, and travel services available at **IBUSZ, Coptourist,** and **Budapest Tourist** (offices in train stations and tourist centers). Ask for their free, very helpful quarterly *For Youth*.

Budget Travel: Express, V, Zoltán u. 10 (tel. 111 64 18), 2 blocks south of the Parliament. M: Kossuth Lajos. Reduced international plane fares for those under 26, youth and ISIC fares on trains to Eastern Europe (same reductions available at station ticket offices). Open Mon.-Thurs. 8:30am-4:30pm, Fri. 8:30am-3pm. **Main office,** V, Szabadság tér 16 (tel. 131 77 77), sells ISIC (250Ft). Open 7am-7pm.

Embassies: Unless otherwise noted, embassy and consulate services are in the same building. **U.S.,** V, Szabadság tér 12 (tel. 112 64 50, after hrs. 153 05 66). M: Kossuth Lajos, then walk 2 blocks down Akadémia and take a left on Zoltán. Open Mon.-Tues. and Thurs.-Fri. 8:30am-noon. **Canada,** XII, Budakeszi út 32 (tel. 176 77 11). Take bus 22 5 stops from Moszkva tér. Open Mon.-Fri. 9-11am. **U.K.,** V, Harmincad u. 6 (tel. 118 28 88), near Café Gerbeaud. M: Vörösmarty tér. Open Mon.-Fri. 9am-noon and 2-4:30pm. **New Zealanders** should contact the British embassy. **Australia,** VI, Délibáb u. 30 (tel. 153 42 33), parallel to Andrássy ut. M: Hősök tere. Open Mon.-Fri. 9am-noon. **Czech Republic,** VI, Rózsa u. 61.4 (tel. 132 55 89). Open Mon.-Fri. 8:30am-1pm. **Slovakia,** Embassy XIV, Stefánia út 22-24 (tel. 251 18 60). Consulate XIV, Gervay u. 44 (tel. 251 79 73). **Poland,** VI, Városligeti fasor 16 (tel. 268 17 21). **Russia,** VI, Bajza út. 35 (tel. 252 12 28). Open Mon., Wed., and Fri. 10am-3pm.

Currency Exchange: Larger exchange offices will turn traveler's checks into hard currency for 6% commission. Generally open Mon.-Fri. 8am-6pm. **OTP Bank** or **Penta Tours,** on Váci u. 19-21. Probably the best rates in town. Open Mon.-Fri. 9am-12:30pm and 1:30-5pm. **IBUSZ,** at V, Petőfi tér 3, just north of Elizabeth

HUNGARY

(Erzsébet) Bridge. Cash advances on Diners Club and Visa (forints only). Most AmEx services. Open 24hrs.

American Express: V, Deák Ferenc u. 10 (tel. 266 86 80). M: Vörösmarty tér. ATM for AmEx cards; cashes traveler's checks in US$ for 6% commission. Cash advances only in forints. Free maps; on Thurs. and Fri. pick up the free *Budapest Week* here. Holds mail. Open Mon.-Fri. 9am-6pm, Sat. 9am-2pm; Oct.-June Mon.-Fri. 9am-5pm, Sat. 9am-1pm.

Post Office: Poste Restante at V, Városház u. 18 (tel. 118 48 11). Open Mon.-Fri. 8am-8pm, Sat. 8am-3pm. **Branches** at Nyugati station, VI, Teréz krt. 105-107 and Keleti station, VIII, Baross tér 11c. 24hrs. After-hours staff does not speak English.

Telephones: V, Petőfi Sándor u. 17. English-speaking staff. Fax service. Open Mon.-Fri. 8am-8pm, Sat.-Sun. 8am-3pm. Budapest numbers begin with 1 or 2. Many of the public phones now use **phone cards**, available at newsstands and post offices. (50-message cards 250Ft, 120-message cards 600Ft.) Use card phones for international calls. **City code:** 1.

Flights: Ferihegy Airport, tel. 157 89 08 reservations, 157 71 55 flight info, 157 75 91 check-in. *Volánbusz* takes 30min. to terminal 1 and 40min. to terminal 2 (200Ft) from Erzsébet tér. The **airport shuttle-bus** service (tel. 157 89 93), picks you up anywhere in the city (any time, day or night), or takes you anywhere in the city from the airport, (600Ft). Call for pick-up a few hours in advance.

Trains: (tel. 122 78 60 domestic, 142 91 50 international). Those under 26 get a 33% discount on international tickets. Show your ISIC. The 3 main *pályaudvar* (stations), **Keleti pu., Nyugati pu.,** and **Déli pu.,** are also metro stops. Trains to and from a given location do not necessarily stop at the same station. 2nd class to **Vienna** (3½hr.; US$27), **Prague** (8hr.; US$47), Warsaw (US$53), Berlin (US$62), Belgrade (US$26) and Bucharest (US$88). Catch the **Orient Express** in Budapest—1 train per day arrives from Berlin and continues on to Bucharest.

Buses: Volánbusz Main station, V, Erzsébet tér (tel. 118 21 22). M: Deák tér. One bus daily to İstanbul (14½hr., US$60) and one per day Tues.-Sat. to Venice (13½hr., US$55). Buses to the Czech Republic, Slovakia, Poland, Romania, Turkey and Ukraine depart from the **Népstadion** terminal on Hungária körút 48-52. M: Népstadion. Domestic buses are usually cheaper than trains, but may take slightly longer. Buses to the Danube Bend leave from the **Árpád Híd** station.

Public Transportation: The **Metro (M)** is rapid and punctual. There are three numbered lines—M1 is yellow, M2 is red, and M3 is blue. "M" indicates a stop, but you won't always find the sign on the street; look for stairs leading down. The metro officially closes at 11:30pm. Metro, buses and trams all use the same yellow tickets, sold in metro stations, at all *Trafik* shops and by some sidewalk vendors. A single-trip ticket *(jegy)* is 25Ft; punch it at the gate of the metro or on board buses and trams. (10-trip *tíz jegy* 225Ft, 1-day *napi jegy* 200Ft, 3-day *három napos jegy* 400Ft.) The **HÉV commuter rail** runs between Batthyány tér in Buda and Szentendre, 40min. north on the Danube Bend about every 15min.

Hydrofoils: MAHART International Boat Station, V, Belgrád rakpart (tel. 118 17 04 or 118 15 86, fax 118 77 40), near the Erzsébet bridge, has information and ticketing. Open Mon.-Fri. 8am-4pm. Or try the **IBUSZ** office at Károly Krt. 3 (tel. 122 24 73). M: Astoria. Open Mon.-Fri. 9am-5pm. Arrive at the docks 1hr. before departure for customs and passport control. Eurailpasses get a 50% discount.

Taxis: Főtaxi, tel. 222 22 22. 50Ft plus distance. **Volántaxi,** tel. 166 66 66. 36Ft per km. Avoid the Mercedes-Benz taxis, which charge double the jalopy fee. A new night tariff has recently been added to all evening fares.

Hitchhiking: Hitching in the Budapest area has become especially dangerous of late. Those who are hitching south to Szeged and Belgrade (along M5 and E75) take tram 2 from Soroksári út to the end of the line, then switch to bus 23, then bus 4. Hitchers heading west to Győr and Vienna or southwest to Lake Balaton and Zagreb take bus 12 from Moszkva tér out to Budaörsi út, then switch to bus 72. **Kenguru,** VIII, Kőfaragó u. 15 (tel. 138 20 19; M: Astoria) is a carpool service charging 4Ft per km. Open Mon.-Fri. 8am-6pm, Sat. 8am-2pm.

Bookstore: Kossuth Könyvesbolt, V, Vörösmarty tér 4, to the right of Café Gerbeaud. English-language tourist books and paperbacks. Open 10am-6pm.

Budapest

1 Déli pu Train Station
2 Military Museum
  (Hadtörténeti
  Múzeum)
3 Musical Instruments
  Museum
4 St. Anne's Church
5 Fisherman's Bastion
  (Halász Bástya)
6 Matthias Church
7 National Gallery
  (Magyar Nemzeti
  Galéria)
8 Ludwig Museum
9 Budapest History
  Museum
10 Citadella
11 Chain Bridge
  (Széchenyi Bridge)
12 House of Parliament
13 Nyugati Train Station
14 Szépmüvészeti
  Museum
15 Kelet (Eastern Train
  Station)
16 Ferenc Liszt
  Memorial Museum
17 Ferenc Liszt Academy
  of Music
18 Hungarian State
  Opera House
19 St. Stephen's Basilica
20 Erzsébet tér Bus
  Station
21 City Hall
22 Great Synagogue and
  Museum of Hungarian
  Jewry
23 Hungarian National
  Museum
24 Franciscan Church
25 University Church
26 Inner City Parish
  Church
27 Vigadó tér Boat
  Station

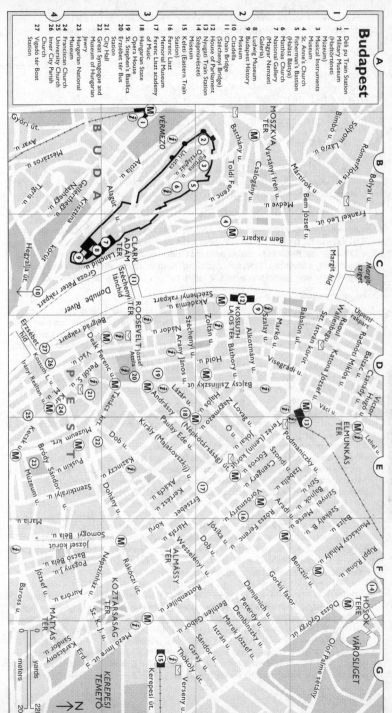

HUNGARY

Laundromats: Mosószalon, V, József Nádor tér 9. Wash: 5kg 210Ft. Dry: 15min 90Ft. Look for the gumball-hue tile column in the window. Open Mon., Wed., and Fri. 7am-3pm, Tues. and Thurs. 11am-7pm.

Pharmacies: The following are open 24hrs.: I, Széna tér 1 (tel. 202 18 16); VI, Teréz krt. 41 (tel. 111 44 39); IX, Boráros tér 3 (tel. 117 07 43); and IX, Üllői út 121 (tel. 133 89 47). At night, call the number on the door or ring the bell to summon the sleepy manager; you will be charged a slight fee for the service.

Medical Assistance: (English spoken) tel. 118 82 88 or 118 80 12. Open 24hrs.

Emergencies: Police, tel. 07. **Fire,** tel. 05. **Ambulance,** tel. 04. Emergency care free for foreigners. List of English-speaking doctors available at U.S. embassy.

ACCOMMODATIONS AND CAMPING

Travelers arriving July and August will be swarmed at the train station by representatives of various hostels. If you'd rather rent a private room or flat, seek out a less voracious onlooker; just make sure the room is near public transportation, preferably tram or metro which run more frequently than buses, and see it before you pay.

Hostels

Most hostel-type accommodations, including university dorm rooms, are under the aegis of **Express.** Try their office at V, Semmelweis u. 4 (tel. 117 66 34 or 117 86 00); leave Deák tér on Tanács krt., head right on Gerlóczy u., and the first left is Semmelweis u. Before accepting lodging at the rail station, make sure you're not being brought to a private hostel trying to wedge many people into a tiny 2-room closet.

Open year-round

Back Pack Guesthouse, XI, Takács Menyhért u. 33 (tel. 185 50 89). From Keleti pu. or city center take bus 1, 7, or 7A heading toward Buda to Tétenyi u., after the rail bridge. Go back under the bridge, turn left, and follow the train tracks for 3 blocks. Look for the small green signs. No curfew. 450-520Ft per person. Hot showers, breakfast, private locker, kitchen. Sheets 50Ft. Call ahead.

ASMARA youth hostel, XVIII, Bajcsy-Zsilinszky u. 51, near the airport. M: Kőbánya-Kispest, then bus 9: Majus 1. tér; Bajcsy-Zsilinszky u. is 2 blocks to the right. 560Ft per person. Common bathroom and kitchen. Supermarket, restaurant, and swimming pool in the area

Donáti, I, Donáti u. 46 (tel. 201 19 71). M: Batthyány tér. Walk up Batthyány u. 3 blocks, and cross the park. Good location. Uncrowded rooms. 12-bed dorms. Reception open 24hrs. 460Ft per person.

Diaksportszálló, XIII, Dózsa György út. 152 (tel. 140 85 85 or 129 86 44). M: Dózsa György. Enter on Angyaföldi, 50m from the stop. Huge and social, but neither the cleanest nor the quietest. Bar and reception open 24hrs. Singles 780Ft. 550Ft for a spot in a room with 8-12 bunk beds. Belongs to the More Than Ways chain; if you don't like this one, you won't like the others.

Summer hostels

Almost all dorms of the **Technical University** (*Műegyetem*) become hostels in July and August; they're conveniently located in district XI, around Móricz Zsigmond Körtér (M: Kálvin Tér, then tram 47 or 49 to Móricz Zsigmond). For more info, call the **International Student Center** at 166 77 58 or 166 50 11, ext. 1469. During the summer the center also has an office in Schönherz.

Schönherz, XI, Irinyi József u. 42 (tel. 166 54 60), one metro stop after Universitas. The largest and most ambitious dorm around. High-rise with well-kept quads with bathrooms and refrigerators. 500Ft per person. 70Ft surcharge without HI membership. Quads can also be booked as doubles (750Ft per person) or triples (650Ft per person). Breakfast 150Ft. Office open 8am-midnight. Sauna 100Ft.

Strawberry Youth Hostels, IX, Ráday u. 43-45 (tel. 138 47 66) and Kinizsi u. 2-6 (tel. 117 30 33). M: Kálvin tér. Converted university dorms a block apart in Pest, on a smaller street running south from Kálvin tér. 24hr. reception. Check-out

10am. Doubles 690Ft per person. Triples and quads 640Ft per person. 10% off with HI card.

Baross, XI, Bartók Béla út 17 (tel. 185 14 44), a block from Géllert tér. Lived-in college dorms. Ranges from simple singles to quads with sink and refrigerator. Hall bathroom. Reception open 24hrs. Check-out 9am. 590Ft per person.

Vásárhelyi, XI, Krusper u. 2-4 (tel. 185 37 94), on the southwestern corner of the Technical University. Bliss in dorm-land—all rooms have a refrigerator and private shower. Doubles 790Ft per person, quads 690Ft per person.

Bakfark hostel, I, Bakfark u. 1-3 (tel. 201 54 19). M: Moszkva tér. Centrally located. Stroll along Margit krt. (formerly Mártírok út); take the first side street after Széna tér. Reception open 24hrs. Checkout 9am. No curfew. Dorm beds 520Ft. Sheets, locker, storage space and washing machine. Van will pick backpackers up at the Keleti rail station; call ahead. A More than Ways affiliate.

Private Accommodations Services

Accommodation services and new branches of established organizations that find travelers lodging in private rooms are overrunning Budapest. The rates (700-2000Ft per person) depend on the quality and location. Be stubborn about getting the lowest possible price. Arrive early (around 8am) and you may get a single for 900Ft or a double for 1500Ft. It's hard to find a cheap, centrally located room for only one or two nights. Travelers who stay for more than four nights can haggle for a better rate.

IBUSZ: 24hr. accommodation office, V, Petőfi tér 3 (tel. 118 39 25 or 118 57 76, fax 117 90 99). The streets outside IBUSZ offices swarm with Hungarians pushing "bargain" rooms; quality varies widely, but they're perfectly legal. Branches at all train stations.

Budapest Tourist, V, Roosevelt tér 5 (tel. 117 35 55, fax 118 66 02), near the Forum Hotel, on the Pest end of the Chain Bridge. No min. stay. Singles 2000-3000Ft. Doubles 4000Ft. Open Mon.-Thurs. 9am-7pm, Fri. 9am-4pm, Sat. 9am-1pm; Oct.-June closed Sat. Same hours at branches throughout the city.

Coleopterist, VI, Bajcsy-Zsilinszky út 17 (tel. 156 95 67 or 111 70 34 or 111 32 44, fax 111 66 83), supplies doubles (2000Ft). Claims that all of the rooms are in districts VI and VII. 30% surcharge for stays fewer than 3 nights. Hotel rooms 300-500DM. English spoken. Open Mon.-Fri. 9am-4pm.

Duna Tours, next to Coleopterist (tel. 131 45 33 or 111 56 30), allows travelers to see rooms before accepting them (doubles from 1500Ft). The English-speaking staff claims their rooms are located only in district V and VI. Open Mon.-Fri. 9:30am-noon and 12:30pm-5pm. Limited hours in winter.

To-Ma Tour, V, Oktober 6. u. 22 (tel. 153 08 19), promises to find you a central room, even if only for 1 night (doubles 1800-3000Ft, with private bathroom 2500Ft; triples 2200Ft). Winter prices 10% less. Reservations recommended in summer. Open Mon.-Fri. 9am-noon and 1-8pm, Sat.-Sun. 9am-5pm.

Hotels

Budapest still has a few inexpensive hotels, often clogged with groups. Call ahead. Proprietors generally speak English. All should be registered with Tourinform.

Hotel Citadella, 1118 Gellérthegy, atop Gellért Hill (tel. 166 57 94, fax 186 05 05). Tram 47 or 49: Móricz Zsigmond Körtér, then bus 27 to Citadella. Perfect location. Dorm beds 500Ft; doubles, triples and quads 2700Ft-3300Ft. Usually packed, so call ahead.

Lido Hotel, III, Nánási út 67 (tel. 250 45 49, fax 250 45 76). M: Arpád híd, then bus 106 to Nánási. Near the river bank and the Aquincum ruins. Singles 800Ft, doubles 1600Ft. Hall showers on all floors. Breakfast included.

Aquincum Panzió, III, Szentendrei u. 105 (tel. 168 64 26, fax 250 23 94). HÉV from Batthyány tér: Köles út. Presentable rooms with hall bathrooms. Singles 2600Ft, doubles 2860Ft. Breakfast included.

Unikum Panzió, XI, Bod Péter u. 13 (tel. 186 12 80). M: Deli pu., then bus 139 south to Zólyom Köz; walk 2 blocks on Zólyom Köz and turn left. 15min. south of the castle. Showers, toilets and TVs in rooms. Singles US$20, doubles US$30.

Camping

Camping Hungary, available at tourist offices, describes Budapest's campgrounds.

Római Camping, III, Szentendrei út 189 (tel. 168 62 60, fax 250 04 26). HÉV from Batthyány tér: Római fürdő. Disco, swimming pool, and huge green park on the site; Roman ruins nearby. Reception open 24hrs. Bungalows mid-April to mid-Oct. Doubles 1100Ft. 2-person tent, 1150Ft. Open all year.

Hárs-hegy, II, Hárs-hegy út 7 (tel. 115 14 82, fax 176 19 21). Bus 22 from Moszkva tér: Dénes u. 2-person tent 1050Ft; bungalows 1200-3800Ft; cars 350Ft. Good, cheap restaurant. Currency exchange, traveler's checks.

Diák Camping, III, Királyok út 191. HÉV from Batthyány tér: Római fürdő, then bus 34 for 10min. You'll see it. 160Ft per person, 80Ft per tent. Doubles, triples, quads, and 10-bed dorm rooms 240Ft per person. Rents bikes (30Ft per hr., 180Ft per day) and canoes (40Ft per hr., 240Ft per day).

FOOD

Even the most expensive restaurants in Budapest may be within your budget, though less costly family eateries may offer superior cuisine. An average meal runs 400-600Ft. Cafeterias lurk under **Önkiszolgáló Étterem** signs (entrees 50Ft, meat entrees 120-160Ft). Seek out the *kifőzde* or *kisvendéglő* in your neighborhood for a taste of Hungarian life. Though hardly Hungarian, fast food joints can prove lifesavers with their late hours and quick service. Travelers may also rely on markets and raisin-sized 24hr. "Non-Stop" stores. Good places to head for include the **produce market,** IX, Vámház krt. 1-3 at Fővám tér (open Mon. 6am-3pm), the **ABC Food Hall,** I, Batthyány tér 5-7 (open Sun. 7am-1pm), or the **Non-Stops** at V, Október 6, u. 5, and at V, Régi Posta u., off Váci u. past McDonald's.

Vegetárium, V, Cukor u. 3. M: Ferenciek tere. Walk up Ferenciek tere to Irányi u. on the right; a quick left onto Cukor u. Vegetarian and macrobiotic dishes *(tempura* dinner 300Ft). Classical guitar in the evening. Vehemently non-smoking. Menu in English. Open noon-10pm.

Alföldi Kisvendéglő, V, Kecskeméti u. 4. M: Kálvin tér. Traditional Hungarian folk cuisine; even the booths are paprika-red. Sumptuous homemade rolls (24Ft each) are reason enough to come. Entrees 180-300Ft. Open 11am-midnight.

Claudia, V, Bástya u., off of Kecskeméti u. M: Kálvin tér. Subterranean family restaurant with hearty, inexpensive food (entrees 220-510Ft). Generous helpings of exotic specials are a highlight. Open 11am-11pm.

Bohémtanya, V, Paulay Ede u. 6. M: Deák tér or Bajcsy-Zsilinszky. Packed at lunchtime for its large portions of delicious Hungarian food. Traditional brooding Hungarian atmosphere. Entrees from 230Ft. English menu and English-speaking staff. Open noon-11pm.

Picasso Point Kávéház, VI, Hajós u. 31. M: Arany János utca, then walk 2 blocks north and turn right onto Hajós u. A bohemian hang-out for students, intellectuals and foreigners. Eclectic mix of traditional Hungarian and everything else. Live music. Open noon to some vaguely defined point after 3am.

New York Bagels, IX, Ferenc körút 20. M: Ferenc körút, then a 200m walk toward the river. Eastern Europe's first and only bagel shop. Assorted bagels baked hourly, freshly made spreads, sandwiches, salads and the only chocolate chip cookies in Budapest. Bagel with lox, cream cheese and onions 379Ft. Counter service. Open 9am-midnight.

Fészek Művész Klub Étterem, VII, Kertész u. 36. M: Oktogon or tram 4, 6: Király u.; it's at the corner of Dob u. Excellent Hungarian food and very low prices; the menu ranges from beef and fowl to venison and wild boar. Entrees 270-600Ft. English menu. Open noon-1am.

Söröző a Szent Jupáthoz, II, Dékán u. 3. M: Moszkva tér; the entrance is on Retek 50m away. Venture down the modest stairway, then right back up into a lively garden. Portions are gargantuan—be ready to roll yourself home. "Soup for Just Married Man" 139Ft. Entrees 300-900Ft. Open 24hrs.

LET'S GO® TRAVEL

CATALOG

1995

WE GIVE YOU THE WORLD... AT A DISCOUNT

Discounted Flights, Eurail Passes,
Travel Gear, Let's Go™ Series Guides,
Hostel Memberships... and more

Let's Go Travel

a division of
Harvard Student
Agencies, Inc.

**Bargains
to every
corner of
the world!**

Travel Gear

A ## Let's Go T-Shirt...$10
100% combed cotton. Let's Go logo on front left chest. Four color printing on back. L and XL. Way cool.

B ## Let's Go Supreme...........$175
Innovative hideaway suspension with parallel stay internal frame turns backpack into carry-on suitcase. Includes lumbar support pad, torso, and waist adjustment, leather trim, and detachable daypack. Waterproof Cordura nylon, lifetime gurantee, 4400 cu. in. Navy, Green, or Black.

C ## Let's Go Backpack/Suitcase.....................$130
Hideaway suspension turns backpack into carry-on suitcase. Internal frame. Detachable daypack makes 3 bags in 1. Waterproof Cordura nylon, lifetime guarantee, 3750 cu. in. Navy, Green, or Black.

D ## Let's Go Backcountry I..$210
Full size, slim profile expedition pack designed for the serious trekker. New Airflex suspension. X-frame pack with advanced composite tube suspension. Velcro height adjustment, side compression straps. Detachable hood converts into a fanny pack. Waterproof Cordura nylon, lifetime guarantee, main compartment 3375 cu. in., extends to 4875 cu. in.

E ## Let's Go Backcountry II............................$240
Backcountry I's Big Brother. Magnum Helix Airflex Suspension. Deluxe bi-lam contoured shoulder harness. Adjustable sterm strap. Adjustable bi-lam Cordura waist belt. 5350 cubic inches. 7130 cubic inches extended. Not pictured.

800-5-LETSGO

Discounted Flights

Call Let's Go now for inexpensive airfare to points across the country and around the world.
EUROPE • SOUTH AMERICA • ASIA • THE CARRIBEAN • AUSTRALIA • AFRICA

Eurail Passes

Eurailpass (First Class)

5 days	$498
1 month (30 days)	$798
2 months (60 days)	$1098

Unlimited rail travel anywhere on Europe's 100,000 mile rail network. Accepted in 17 countries.

Eurail Flexipass (First Class)

A number of individual travel days to be used at your convenience within a two-month period.

Any 5 days in 2 months	$348
Any 10 days in 2 months	$560
Any 15 days in 2 months	$740

Eurail Youthpass (Second Class)

15 days	$398
1 month (30 days)	$578
2 months (60 days)	$768

All the benefits of the Eurail Pass at a lower price. For those passengers under 26 on their first day of travel.

Eurail Youth Flexipass (Second Class)

Eurail Flexipass at a reduced rate for passengers under 26 on their first day of travel.

Any 5 days in 2 months	$255
Any 10 days in 2 months	$398
Any 15 days in 2 months	$540

Europass (First & Second Class)

First Class starting at	$280
Second Class starting at	$198
For more details	CALL

Discounted fares for those passengers travelling in France, Germany, Italy, Spain and Switzerland.

Hostelling Essentials

F **Undercover Neckpouch............$9.95**
Ripstop nylon with soft Cambrelle back. Three pockets. 6 x 7". Lifetime guarantee. Black or Tan.

G **Undercover Waistpouch.........$9.95**
Ripstop nylon with soft Cambrelle back. Two pockets. 5 x 12" with adjustable waistband. Lifetime guarantee. Black or Tan.

H **Sleepsack.................................$13.95**
Required at all hostels. 18" pillow pocket. Washable poly/cotton. Durable. Compact.

I **Hostelling International Card**
Required by most international hostels. For U.S. residents only. Adults, $25. Under 18, $10.

J **Int'l Youth Hostel Guide.......$10.95**
Indispensable guide to prices, locations, and reservations for over 4000 hostels in Europe and the Mediterranean.

K **ISIC, ITIC, IYTC..........$16, $16, $17**
ID cards for students, teachers and those people under 26. Each offers many travel discounts.

800-5-LETSGO

Order Form

Please print or type — Incomplete applications will not be processed

Last Name	First Name	Date of Birth

Street   *(We cannot ship to P.O. boxes)*

City	State	Zip

Country	Citizenship	Date of Travel

(   )   -

Phone   School (if applicable)

Item Code	Description, Size & Color	Quantity	Unit Price	Total Price
		SUBTOTAL:		

Domestic Shipping & Handling	Shipping and Handling (see box at left):	
Order Total: Add:	Add $10 for RUSH, $20 for overnite:	
Up to $30.00 $4.00	MA Residents add 5% tax on books and gear:	
$30.01 to $100.00 $6.00		
Over $100.00 $7.00	GRAND TOTAL:	
Call for int'l or off-shore delivery		

MasterCard / VISA Order

CARDHOLDER NAME _____

CARD NUMBER _____

EXPIRATION DATE _____

Enclose check or money order payable to:
Harvard Student Agencies, Inc.
53A Church Street
Cambridge, MA 02138

Allow 2-3 weeks for delivery. Rush orders guaranteed within
one week of our receipt. Overnight orders sent via FedEx the same afternoon.

Missing a Let's Go Book from your collection?
Add one to any $50 order at 50% off the cover price!

Let's Go Travel
1-800-5-LETSGO

(617) 495-9649   Fax: (617) 496-8015
53A Church Street
Cambridge MA 02138

Cafés

The café in Budapest is more a living museum of a bygone era than just a place to be spoiled by scrumptious desserts and coffee; these amazing institutions were the training grounds for Budapest's literary, intellectual, and cultural elite. A visit to a café is part of the Budapest experience; moreover, the ornate pastries are absurdly inexpensive, even in the most pretentious establishments.

Café New York, VII, Erzsébet krt. 9-11. M: Blaha Lujza tér. Turn of the century "starving" *artistes* fed under its exquisite gilded ceilings. Cappuccino 100Ft. Ice cream and coffee delights 100-350Ft. Open 9am-midnight. Full, Hungarian-style meals are served downstairs noon-midnight. Entrees from 700Ft.

Művész Kávéház, VI, Andrássy út 29. M: Opera. Diagonally across the street from the National Opera House. Lauded café draws the pre- and post-Opera crowds. Pastries start at 60Ft. Open 9am-midnight.

Lukács Cukrászda, VI, Andrássy út 70. M: Vörösmarty u. Near Hősök tere. One of the most stunning cafés in Budapest. Heavenly cakes and tortes 30-50Ft. Seated service costs more. Open Mon.-Fri. 9am-8pm.

Gerbeaud Cukrászda, V, Vörösmarty tér 7. M: Vörösmarty tér. Formerly the meeting place of Budapest's literary elite, this café retains a stunning 19th-century elegance. You can write your own obscure novel by the time you're served. No menus in some sections. Pastries for about 90Ft. Open 7am-9pm.

SIGHTS

Buda Várhegy (Castle Hill), 100m above the Danube is the site of Budapest's **Castle District.** From Pest, cross the **Széchenyi lánchíd** (chain bridge) and ride the 19th-century *sikló* (cable car) to the top of the hill (7:30am-10pm, 80Ft; closed 2nd and 4th Monday of the month). Built in the 13th century, the castle was razed and rebuilt after during successive invasions of the city; the Germans were the last to level it in 1945. Today the **Budavári palota** (Royal Palace) houses several notable museums. During recent reconstruction of the palace, excavations revealed artifacts from the earliest castle on this site; they are now housed in Wing E of the **Budapest History Museum** (open Mon., Wed.-Sun. 10am-5pm; 60Ft, students 30Ft). Wing A houses the **Museum of Contemporary History** and the **Ludwig Museum,** a collection of international modern art, while Wings B-D shelter the **Hungarian National Gallery,** a vast hoard of the best Hungarian painting and sculpture. (Museums open Tues.-Sun. 10am-6pm. Wing A 100Ft, students 50Ft. Wings B-D 60Ft, students 30Ft.)

From the palace, stroll down Színház u. and Tárnok u. to **Trinity Square,** site of the Disney-esque **Fisherman's Bastion.** This arcaded stone wall supports a squat, fairy-tale tower with a magnificent view across the Danube. Behind the tower stands the neo-Gothic **Mátyás templom** (Matthias Church); it spent 145 years as a mosque after the Turks seized Buda. These days, High Mass, with orchestra and choir is celebrated Sundays at 10am. (Open 7am-7pm.) Intricate door-knockers and balconies adorn the Castle District's other historic buildings; ramble through **Úri u.** (Gentlemen's Street) with its Baroque townhouses, or **Táncsics Mihály u.** in the old Jewish sector. Enjoy a tremendous view of Buda from the Castle District's western walls.

The **Liberation Monument** crowns neighboring **Gellért Hill,** just south of the Castle. This 30m bronze statue honors Soviet soldiers who died "saving" Hungary from the Nazis. The hill itself is named for St. Gellért, an 11th century bishop sent by the Pope to help King Stephen convert the Magyars. A statue of him overlooks the **Erzsébet híd** (Elizabeth Bridge), near the base of the hill, complete with colonnaded backdrop and glistening waterfall. The **Citadella** was built by the Habsburgs after the 1848 Revolution to remind their subjects exactly who wore the pants; to get there, climb the hill from beside the Gellért Hotel or take bus 27 from Móricz Zsigmond Körter to two bus stops beyond the hotel.

East of the Vadaskert, the fabulous **Pál-völgyi caves** boast 15m-high caverns and remarkable stalactite formations. Take the HÉV rail line from Batthyány tér to Szépvölgyi, and walk away from the river to Kolosy tér, then take bus 65 or 65a, across from the yellow church, to Pál-völgyi barlang. (Guided 45min. tours leave

HUNGARY

May.-Sept. Tues.-Sun. every hr. 9am-4pm; Oct.-Dec. and Feb.-April Sat.-Sun. only. 50Ft, students 30Ft.) Between the caves and the Castle, the **Margit híd** spans the Duna to the lovely **Margitsziget.** Off-limits to private cars, the island offers thermal baths, luxurious garden pathways, and numerous shaded terraces. Take bus 26 from Szt. István krt. to reach the island.

Pest Across the river, Pest throbs as the commercial and administrative center of the capital. The river bank sports a string of luxury hotels leading up to the magnificent neo-Gothic **Országház** (Parliament) in Kossuth tér. (Tours by IBUSZ and Budapest Tourist; 1200-1500Ft). Nearby, at Kossuth tér 12 in what used to be the Hungarian Supreme Court, the **Néprajzi Múzeum** (Museum of Ethnography) hosts an outstanding exhibit of Hungarian folk culture, from the late 18th century to WWI, and an exceptional collection of cultural artifacts from Asian, African, and Aboriginal peoples. (Open Tues.-Sun. 10am-5:30pm. 50Ft, students free; Tues. free.)

St. **Stephen's Basilica,** two blocks north of Deák tér, is by far the city's largest church, with room for 8500 worshippers. St. Stephen's mummified right hand, one of the Hungary's most revered relics, is on display. Climb 323 spiraling steps to the Panorama tower for a 360° view of the city. (Basilica open 8am-7pm. Hand on view Mon.-Sat. 9am-5pm, Sun. 1-4pm; Oct.-March Mon.-Sat. 10am-4pm, Sun. 1-4pm. Free. Tower open 9am-6pm; 100Ft.) To the east of the basilica, **Andrássy út,** Hungary's grandest boulevard, extends from the edge of the **Belváros** in downtown Pest to **Hősök tere** (Heroes' Square), some 2km away. The **Magyar Állami Operaház** (Hungarian National Opera House), VI, Andrássy út 22, was ornately decorated with sculptures and paintings in the 1880s; the Opera House is still one of the leading centers for the performing arts. (Tours in English 3 and 4pm. 300Ft, students 150Ft.)

The **Millennary monument,** commemorating the nation's most prominent leaders and national heroes from 896 to 1896, dominates Hősök tere. The **Szépművészeti Múzeum** (Museum of Fine Arts) on the square maintains a fine collection; highlights include an entire room devoted to El Greco and an exhaustive display of Renaissance works. (Open Tues.-Sun. 10am-6pm.) Behind the square, the **Városliget** (City Park) is home to a circus, amusement park, zoo, castle, as well as the impressive **Széchenyi Baths.** The **Vajdahunyad Castle** was also built for the Millennium Exhibition of 1896 and now houses the **Museum of Agriculture,** which displays artificial fruit and stuffed animals (open Tues.-Sun. 10am-6pm; 50Ft, free with ISIC and on Tues.).

Back toward the center of Pest at the corner of Dohány and Wesselényi u., the **Great Synagogue** is the largest temple in use in Europe and the second largest in the world (open Mon.-Fri. 10am-6pm, in winter until 3:30pm). Next door, the **Jewish Museum** juxtaposes magnificent exhibits dating back to the Middle Ages with harrowing documentation of the Holocaust (open April-Oct. Mon. and Thurs. 1-4pm, Tues.-Wed. and Fri. 10am-1pm).

The ruins of the northern Budapest garrison town, **Aquincum,** continue to crumble in the outer regions of the third district. These are the most impressive vestiges of the Roman occupation, which spanned the first four centuries AD. The **museum** on the grounds contains a model of the ancient city as well as musical instruments and other household items. (Open April-Sept. 9am-6pm, Oct. 9am-5pm. 20Ft.) The remains of the **Roman military baths** are displayed to the south of the Roman encampment, beside the overpass at Flórián tér near the Árpád híd HÉV station. From the stop, just follow the main road away from the river.

ENTERTAINMENT AND NIGHTLIFE

Budapest offers a vast cultural program year-round. Pick up a copy of the English-language monthly *Programme in Hungary* or *Budapest Panorama,* both available free at tourist offices; they contain listings of all concerts, operas, and theater performances in the city. The "Style" section of the weekly English-language *Budapest Sun* is another excellent source for schedules of entertainment happenings.

The **Central Theater Booking Office,** at VI, Andrássy u. 18, next to the Opera House (tel. 112 00 00), and the branch at Moszkva tér (tel. 135 91 36) both sell tickets without commission to almost every performance in the city. (Open Mon.-Thurs. 10am-1pm and 2-6pm, Fri. 10am-3pm.) An extravaganza in the gilded, neo-Renaissance **State Opera House,** VI, Andrássy út 22 (tel. 153 01 70; M: Opera) can cost as little as 50Ft; the box-office sells any unclaimed tickets for amazing discounts (up to half-price) ½hr. before showtime. (Ticket office open Tues.-Sun. 10am-7pm.) The city's **Philharmonic Orchestra** is also world renowned; their concerts thunder through town almost every evening from September to June. The **National Philharmonic Ticket Office,** is located at Vörösmarty tér 1 (open Mon.-Fri. 10am-6pm, Sat. 10am-2pm; tickets 600Ft).

When the weather turns warm, the Philharmonic takes a summer sabbatical, but the tide of culture never ebbs; **summer theaters** are located throughout the city. Classical music and opera are performed in the **Hilton Hotel Courtyard,** I, Hess András tér 1-3, next to the Matthias Church in the Castle District. The **Margitsziget Theater,** XIII, on Margaret Island, features opera and Hungarian music concerts. Take tram 4 or 6 to Margitsziget. Try **Zichy Mansion Courtyard,** III, Fő tér 1, for orchestral concerts. Folk-dancers stomp across the stage at the **Buda Park Theater,** XI, Kosztolányi Dezső tér. Brochures and concert tickets flood from the ticket office at Vörösmarty tér 1. (Open Mon.-Fri. 11am-6pm; tickets 70-250Ft.) For a psychedelic evening, try the laser shows at the **Planetárium,** M: Népliget. Performances—they even play Floyd on occasion—are Tues.-Sat. 6:30 and 9pm (350Ft).

After a few drinks, you'll forget you ever left home. A virtually unenforced drinking age and cheap drinks may be the only cause for culture shock.

Tilos az Á, VIII, Mikszáth Kálmán tér 2. M: Kálvin tér, then walk down Baross u. 2 blocks and turn left. Live music ranges from jazz to funk to alternative and dancing. Cover charge 150-300Ft depending on the band. Open 8pm-4am.

Morrison's Music Pub, VI, Révay u. 25, just to the left of the State Opera House. M: Opera. Half pub, half hip dance club with cheap beer (80Ft). A young, international crowd. Cover 100-200Ft. Open noon-4am.

Fregatt Pub, V, Molnár u. 26, off Váci u. near the Ferenciek tere Metro station. Popular pub, usually filled with English-speaking twenty-somethings. Beer 110Ft. Shuts down at midnight.

Jazz Café, V, Balassi Bálint u. 25. M: Kossuth tér, then walk across the square past the Parliament. Live jazz under blue lights nightly at 8pm. Club closes at midnight.

Véndiák (Former Student), V, Egyetem tér. M: Kálvin tér, then walk up Kecskeméti u. This late-night bar also has a lively dance floor. Popular with local students. Really picks up around 2am. Open 9pm-4am.

Tánchaz, an itinerant folk-dancing club, where you can stomp with Transylvanians. They invariably have a beginners' circle and an instructor. Locate them in *Pesti Műsor* (Budapest's weekly entertainment guide, in Hungarian) or ask at Tourinform.

■■■ DANUBE BEND (DUNAKANYAR)

North of Budapest, the Danube sweeps south in a dramatic arc known as the Danube Bend *(Dunakanyar)* as it flows down from Vienna along the Slovak border. Roman ruins from settlements of the first century dapple the countryside, and medieval palaces gaze upon the river in **Esztergom** and **Visegrád.** An artist colony thrives today amid the museums and churches of **Szentendre.** Less than 45km from Budapest, the region offers numerous possibilities for excursion.

Hourly **buses** from Budapest's Árpád Híd metro station link these towns with the capital. If you're going directly to Esztergom, take the bus through Dorog; the 1¼hr. ride is almost an hour shorter than the route winding along the river through Visegrád (139Ft, stretches between the 3 cities cost 74Ft each). The suburban railway

(HÉV) to Szentendre (¾hr., 64Ft) starts from Batthyány tér in Budapest. **River boats** from Budapest are a pleasurable, if painstaking, way to visit the region; they cast off from Budapest's Vigadó tér dock 4 times per day and steam to Visegrád (3hr., 180Ft) and Esztergom (5hr., 200Ft), making short stops along the way. Not all boats stop at Szentendre (1hr., 160Ft). **Dunatours,** V, Bajcsy-Zsilinszky út. 17 (tel. 131 45 33), in Budapest, books private rooms in Szentendre (open Mon.-Thurs. 9:30am-noon and 12:30-5pm, Fri. 9:30am-noon and 12:30-4pm).

Szentendre Despite an active artistic community, superior galleries and art museums, and a near-overload of folk crafts, Szentendre lacks much of the easy charm and sense of history that towns outside Budapest's shadow boast. The town's first stone church, built in the 13th century, sits on **Templomdomb** (Church Hill) above Fő tér. Facing the church, **Czóbel Museum** exhibits the works of Hungary's foremost impressionist, Béla Czóbel (open Tues.-Sun 10am-4pm; 30Ft). Across Alkotmány u. is the Baroque **Serbian Orthodox Church;** the church is open only for Sunday services, but the grounds house a museum of 18th-century Serbian religious art (open Wed.-Sun. 10am-6pm; 30Ft). The **Kovács Margit Múzeum,** Vastagh György u. 1 exhibits brilliant ceramic sculptures and tiles by the 20th-century Hungarian artist Margit Kovács, including the renowned *Pound Cake Madonna* (open 10am-6pm;100Ft, students 25Ft).

HÉV commuter trains link the town with Budapest (¾hr., 45Ft); **buses** run to Budapest's Árpád Bridge station (½hr., 70Ft) and continue to Visegrád (¾hr.) and Esztergom (1½hr.). From the bus and train station, use the underpass and continue 10min. up Kossuth Lajos u. to the triangular center of the old town, Fő tér. The **Tourinform** office, Dumtsa Jenő 22, south of the square provides maps, brochures, and advice (open 10am-4pm). **Dunatours,** Bogdányi u. 1 (tel. (26) 31 13 11), speaks rough-hewn English but can usually secure doubles starting at 1300Ft (open 9am-6pm). **Pap-szigeti Camping** (tel. (26) 31 06 97), 1km north of Fő tér offers camping facilities (2 people with tent 830Ft), but also rents doubles in motel rooms for 990-1190Ft and triples in bungalows for 1990Ft.

Visegrád Thirteen km upriver between the Pilis and Börsöny mountains, Visegrád was once the high-water mark of the Roman Empire. **Salamon-Torony** (Solomon's Tower) is the hexagonal monolith standing at the foot of the hill. Formerly part of a fortress that regulated river traffic, it now houses the **King Matthias Museum,** which contains fountains and wall reliefs and other relics taken from the grounds of the palace. (Open May-Sept. 9am-5pm. 50Ft.) Now partially reconstructed, the **Royal Palace,** above the western end of Fő u., was abandoned for centuries and used as a source of building stones. (open April-Oct. Tues.- Sun. 9am-5pm; 50Ft, free with ISIC). High above the Danube, the **Citadel** houses exhibits on folkcraft, hunting, and local history, but the real attraction is the castle itself and the view it commands of the river and surrounding hills (open April-Nov. 8:30am-6pm; 50Ft, 30Ft with ISIC). You can reach the Citadel on foot or by bus—look for signs that say "Fellegvár." Several hiking paths take about ½hr; the easiest starts at the end of Kálvária u. Some of the southbound buses on Rt. 11 turn left and head up Nagy Lajos u. Catch one at the stop in front of the ferry pier (¼hr., 28Ft).

Buses to Esztergom (¾hr.) and to Budapest (1½hr.) pass through Visegrád at least once per hour. **MAHART boats** run to Esztergom (2hr.), Szentendre (1¼hr.), and Budapest via Szentendre (2½hr.) **Visegrád Tours,** Rév u. 13 (tel. (26) 39 81 60), between the ferry and Nagy Lajos u., books private rooms for 1200-2000Ft. and supplies tourist information (open 10am-8pm, Sept.-May 10am-6pm). The village is usually visited as a day trip, but accommodations are easy to find; Fő u. is lined with *panzió* and private homes displaying *Zimmer Frei* signs. **Camping Visegrád,** Fő u. 70 (tel. (26) 39 81 02), has entrances both on Fő u. and on Route 11 (55Ft per tent and 165Ft per person; open May 1-Oct. 11).

Esztergom If you can't find the Esztergom **cathedral,** you're either too close or in the wrong town; take a step back and look up. The biggest church in Hungary and one of the largest in Europe was consecrated in 1856. (Franz Liszt composed and conducted the consecration mass.) Climb to the 71.5m-high **cupola** for a view of Slovakia (10Ft) or descend into the Egyptian-style **crypt** to walk among the ranks of Hungary's archbishops. The **cathedral treasury** through the passage on the north side of the main altar, holds the most extensive ecclesiastical collection in Hungary (open 9am-4:30pm; 60Ft, 30Ft with ISIC.) Next door, the restored 12th-century **Esztergom Palace,** now the **Vármúzeum** (Castle Museum), tells its own story and the town's from Roman times (open Tues.-Sun. 9am-4:30pm, winter 10am-3:30pm; 50Ft, 25Ft with ISIC). Simor János u., north of the bus terminal, is an open-air food and clothing **market** with a country-town atmosphere (6am-5pm).

The **train station** is at the southern edge of town. Get to Rákóczi tér by walking up Baross Gábor út, making a right onto Kiss János altábornagy út, and keeping straight as it becomes Kossuth Lajos u. Trains leave Esztergom for Budapest (1½hr., 300Ft), but buses are generally more convenient. The **bus** terminal is a few blocks south of the square—walk straight up Simor János u. Buses leave for Budapest via Dorog (1½hr., 200Ft), Visegrád (½hr., 90Ft), and Szentendre (1¼hr., 200Ft). **Gran Tours,** Széchenyi tér 25 (tel. (33) 31 37 56), at the edge of Rákóczi tér, provides maps, English information, and books doubles for around 1500Ft (open Mon.-Fri. 8am-3:30pm; in summer also Sat. 8am-noon). **IBUSZ,** Lőrinc u. 1 (tel. (33) 31 25 52) will change currency or find you a doubles for about 1000Ft (open Mon.-Thurs. 8am-4pm, Fri. 8am-3pm). **Platán Panzió,** Kis-Duna Sétány 11 (tel. (33) 31 13 55), between Rákóczi tér and Primate Island, is one of several pensions in the center of town (doubles from 2500Ft). For the hostel-thing, **Martos Flóra Kollégium,** Szent Istvan tér 16 (tel. (33) 31 28 13), just northeast of the cathedral, lets you sleep in a room with three complete strangers (400Ft; open weekends during the school year and late-June to early Sept.). **Gran Camping,** Nagy-Duna Sétány (tel. (33) 31 13 27), is in the middle of Primate Island (doubles 4000Ft; hostel 320Ft per person; campsite 270Ft per tent, 300Ft per person). **Alabárdos Restaurant,** Bajcsy-Zsilinszky út 49, serves excellent Hungarian specialties (entrees 350-580Ft; English menu; open noon-11pm). For dessert, coffee, and people-watching, head for **Belvárosi Kávéház,** Rákóczi tér (open Mon.-Sat. 8am-midnight, Sun. 8am-11pm). The bus terminal is surrounded by various seedy **non-stop büfé,** as well as a **non-stop ABC** convenience store.

■ ■ ■ EGER

In 1552, Captain Dobó István and his tiny army held off the invading Ottomans for an entire month in Eger. Credit for their fortitude is given to the potent *Egri Bikavér* ("Bull's Blood of Eger" wine) they downed before battle. With good company or sheer determination, you can spend an entire afternoon and evening in the wine cellars of **Szépasszonyvölgy,** the Valley of the Beautiful Women. The valley is lined with the doors of hundreds of tiny cellars dug into the hills. Most cellars open at 1pm and begin to close around 8pm, or whenever their owners have had enough. One-deciliter glasses cost 30Ft, and little glasses for tasting are free. Get there by walking west from Deák u. down Király u., which eventually becomes Szépasszonyvölgy u. and leads into the valley.

The yellow **cathedral** on Eszterházy tér is a good place to start a walking tour of Eger. The second-biggest church in Hungary, it was built in 1836 by Joseph Hild, who also built Hungary's largest—the Esztergom cathedral. Organ concerts are held here Mon.-Sat. at 11:30am and Sun. 12:30pm (60Ft). Opposite the cathedral is the Rococo **Lyceum.** The fresco in the magnificent library on the first floor depicts an ant's eye view of the Council of Trent, which spawned the edicts of the Counter-Reformation. (Open Mon.-Fri. 9:30am-1:30pm, Sat.-Sun. 9:30am-12:30pm. 60Ft, 15Ft with ISIC.) On the southern side of Dobó tér stands the luxuriously Baroque

HUNGARY

Minorite Church, which overlooks a statue of Captain Dobó and two co-defenders, one of them a woman poised to hurl a rock upon an unfortunate Turk.

Hungarians revere medieval **Eger Castle;** it was here that Dobó István and his 2000 men repelled the unified Ottoman army, halting their advance for another 44 years. An 80Ft ticket (40Ft with ISIC) buys admission to the **picture gallery,** the **Dobó Istvan Castle museum,** which displays excavated artifacts, armor, and an impressive array of sharp, spiky, and pointy weapons; in summer, a **prison museum** is thrown in—inspiration to sadists and masochists alike. Ascend the 40m **Turkish minaret,** the Ottoman Empire's northernmost phallic symbol, for a great view; beware that the steep spiral staircase is not much wider than the average 20th-century person (open 1am-6pm; 20Ft). The 18th-century **Serbian Orthodox church** on Vitkovics u. (at the northern end of the town center, parallel to Széchenyi u.) houses a magnificent altar and beautiful murals (open 10am-4pm; free).

Eger revels in its Baroque heritage during the **Baroque Festival** held throughout July. Nightly performances of operas and operettas and medieval and Renaissance court music are held in the courtyard of the Franciscan church, the cathedral, and in Dobó tér. An international folk-dance festival called **Eger Vintage Days** is held daily throughout September. See the Tourinform office for schedules and tickets.

Practical Information, Accommodations, and Food The upbeat **Tourinform** office, at Dobó tér 2 (tel. (36) 32 18 07) has stacks of brochures, pamphlet and maps (the good one costs 50Ft) and information about all the accommodations in town (open Mon.-Fri 9am-6pm, Sat 9am-2pm, in summer also Sun 10am-1pm). The **bus station** is 5min. west of Dobó tér. Fifteen **buses** a day take the highway to Budapest (2½hr., 462Ft) and several others take local routes. To get there from the **train station,** take a bus to the bus terminal (bus 10, 11 or 14) or walk: make a right onto Deák Ferenc u., make a right and then a quick left onto Széchenyi u. at the Cathedral, and then a right onto Érsek u., which leads into the square (20min.). Trains depart for Budapest-Keleti station. Trains split in Hatvan so make sure you're in the right car. **Eger Tourist,** Bajcsy-Zsilinszky u. 9 (tel. (36) 31 17 24) can arrange doubles in private homes in the center of town for 1040Ft, or 1560Ft with private bath. (2-3 person apartments 2470Ft. Open Mon.-Fri. 8:30am-7:30pm, Sat. 9am-1pm; Sept.-May: Mon-Fri. 9am-5pm, Sat. 9am-1pm.) **IBUSZ** (tel. (36) 31 26 52), in the courtyard next door called Bajcsy-Zsilinszky tömb-belső, has doubles from 1000Ft. **Express,** Széchenyi u. 28 (tel. (36) 31 07 57), relays information about summer rooms in university dorms (open Mon.-Fri. 8am-4pm). Eger Tourist operates the very basic **Tourist Motel,** Mekchey u. 2 (tel. (36) 31 00 14; doubles with bath and breakfast 2300Ft; doubles with shared bath and no breakfast 1200Ft). **Hotel Romantik,** Csik S. u. 26 (tel. (36) 31 04 56), is a small pension with doubles equipped with TV and refrigerator for 2400-4000Ft. The **Eszterházi Károly Kollégiuma,** Léanyka u. 2 (tel. (36) 41 20 66), east of the castle, charges 300-400Ft per night in a room with 3-4 beds (open July1-Sept. 5). Eger Tourist also operates **Autós Caravan Camping,** Rákóczi u. 79 (tel. (36) 31 0558), north of the center. Walk there in 20min., or take bus 5, 10, 11, or 12. (Motel doubles 1250Ft. Campsite 280Ft per tent and 220Ft per person.)

For quick and inexpensive gourmet food, go to the **MBM Bajor Söház,** Bajcsy-Zsilinszky u. 19, off Dobó tér, a Bavarian beer house that serves Hungarian specialties (entrees 229-459Ft; English menu; open 10am-10pm, Nov.-March Mon.-Sat. 10am-10pm). **The Belvárosi Étterem,** Bajcsy-Zsilinszky u. 8, is a *csárda* that attracts a mix of tourists and locals (entrees 200-750Ft; open 11am-11pm). **Gyros Étterem,** Széchenyi u. 10, serves recognizable gyros, *souvlaki* and Greek salads (gyros pita 120Ft, entrees 235-480FtFt; open 9am-10pm).

■ AGGTELEK

The **Baradla** caves are a 24km-long system of limestone tunnels that wind between Hungary and Slovakia. Each chamber is a forest of dripping stalactites and stalagmites and fantastically shaped stone formations. **Cave tours** begin from Aggtelek. A large chamber with perfect acoustics has been converted into an auditorium, and the tours pause here for a light-and-sound show. Wow. (Hour-long tours leave at 10am, 1pm, 3pm, and 5pm, but others are added on busy days. 180Ft, 90Ft with ISIC.) The one **bus** from Eger leaves at 8:40am, and arrives in Aggtelek around 11am (390Ft) in the front of the Cseppkő Hotel, a 200m uphill from the cave entrance. The bus back to Eger leaves around 3pm.

■■■ SZEGED

Szeged straddles the Tisza River about 10km north of the Yugoslav border. Its easy-going charm belies its status as Hungary's only planned city; after an 1879 flood practically wiped out the town, streets were laid out and lined with row after row of colorful neo-Renaissance and Art Nouveau buildings. Walk east to the river to find the **Móra Ferenc Múzeum,** Roosevelt tér 1-3, which boasts an exhibit of folk art from the 18th century to the present—keep an eye out for the waffle irons that look like giant salad tongs (open Tues.-Sun. 10am-5pm; 40Ft, students 20Ft). On Dóm tér, the red brick **Votive Church** pierces the city's skyline with its twin 91m towers (open 9am-6pm, except during services, Sun. 10-11am). Beside the church is the 12th-century **Demetrius Tower.** Smaller and brighter than the Votive Church is the 1778 **Serbian Orthodox Church** across the street, home to 60 gilt-framed paintings (open whenever there's someone around to collect the 40Ft admission fee). At the corner of Hajnóczi u. and Jósika u. stands the eclectic **Great Synagogue,** built in 1903. English-speaking guides explain every detail of the building, which is now used mainly for concerts and memorials (open May-Sept. 9am-noon and 2-5pm; 50Ft, students 25Ft). The Szeged **Open-Air Theater Festival,** running from mid-July to mid-August, is the country's largest outdoor theatrical festival. Traveling troupes perform folk dances, operas, and musicals in the amphitheater in Dóm tér. Tickets are available at the Ticket Office, Deák Ferenc u. 28-30 (tel. (62) 47 14 66).

Practical Information, Accommodations, and Food Tourinform, Victor Hugo u. 1 (tel. (62) 31 17 11), has free maps and hires English-speaking staff in summer (open Mon.-Fri. 8am-6pm, Sat. 10am-2pm). **Trains** chug to Budapest (2¼-3hr., 600-710Ft). **Buses** leave the terminal on Mars tér just west of Londoni körút, a 10min. walk west of the center for Budapest (3½hr. 650Ft) and Pécs (4½hr., 720Ft). **Szeged Tourist,** at Klauzál tér 7 (tel. (62) 32 18 00), has English speakers year-round and the cheapest private accommodations, starting at 500Ft for singles and 1000Ft for doubles (open Mon.-Fri. 8:30am-1pm and 1:30-5pm, Sat. 9am-1pm). For doubles with private bath for 2300Ft, and triples with shared bath for 1650Ft, try **Hotel Petro,** Kállay u. 6-10 (tel. (62) 43 14 28), in Újszeged near the river. **Fortuna Panzió,** Pécskai u. 8 (tel. (62) 43 15 85), one block west, has doubles with private baths for 2200Ft. **Pölös Panzió,** Pacsirta u. 17/a (tel. (62) 31 38 61), one block west of Páriszi körút, charges 1500Ft for one person, 2800Ft for two. **Apáthy István Kollégium,** Apáthy István u. 1 (tel. (62) 32 31 55), is conveniently located next to Dóm tér (singles and doubles 1400Ft, triples 1800Ft; open July-Aug.) **Eötvös Loránd Kollégium,** Tisza Krt. 103 (tel. (62) 31 06 41), just down the road from Hősök Kapuja has singles for 477Ft and doubles for 901Ft.

For late-night munchies and supplies on weekends, there is a **non-stop ABC market** at 17 Mars tér, near the corner of Londoni krt. and Mikszáth Kálmán u. **Roosevelt téri Halászcsárda,** Roosevelt tér 14, is *the* place to sample Szeged's famous spicy fish soup (entrees 230-490Ft; English menu; open 11am-10pm). **Boszorkány Konhya** (The Witch's Kitchen), Híd u. 8, just off Széchenyi tér, is a cafeteria that serves entrees for 120-160Ft (open 6:30am-9pm). Get excellent pastries (50Ft) and a dollop of ice cream (15Ft per scoop) at **Kisvirág Cukrászda,** in Klauzál tér (open 8am-10pm).

HUNGARY

■■■ PÉCS

Home to five universities and colleges, several galleries with well-known collections, and acclaimed ballet and opera companies, Pécs (PAYTCH) is renowned as a refuge of students and artists. During the Middle Ages, Pécs was a bishopric whose city walls encircled an area larger than modern-day Vienna. Pécs was taken by the Turks in 1543 and made into a cultural center for the next 143 years. Remnants of the Ottoman occupation are quite visible in Pécs. The main square, **Széchenyi tér,** is dominated by the nation's largest **mosque,** dating from the 16th century. An impressive **synagogue** on Kossuth tér recalls a once-thriving Jewish community (open May-Oct. Sun.-Fri. 9:30am-1pm and 1:30-5pm; 35Ft, students 25Ft). West of Széchenyi lies the distinctive four-towered **Cathedral,** whose earliest parts date back to the 4th century; it was restored in Romanesque style in the 1880s (open Mon.-Sat. 9am-1pm and 2-5pm, Sun. 1-5pm; 40Ft, students 20Ft.) Eight museums and galleries, some quite exceptional, are all clustered along Káptalan u. The **Zsolnay Porcelain Museum** houses some exquisite creations, while the **Viktor Vasarely Museum** showcases arresting works by the famous Hungarian op-artist. Not to be missed is the **Csontváry Museum,** which houses the works of Tivadar Csontváry Kosztka, Hungary's two-eared answer to Van Gogh. (Museums open Tuesday to Sunday 10am to 6pm. Free with ISIC.) Pécs's **ballet** and **opera** companies perform locally between October and May. The best way to find out what's going on is to pick up a schedule of regional events at Tourinform. **Clubs** and **discos** come and go in a matter of months here, so ask at Tourinform for hotspots.

Practical Information, Accommodations, and Food Pécs sits on the knees of the Mecsek mountain range; conveniently, north and south correspond to up and down the hillside. The middle of the city is **Széchenyi tér** where most of the tourist offices are located. What little tourist information is available is geared towards German-speakers; your best bet is to drop by **Tourinform,** Széchenyi tér 9 (tel. (72) 31 21 76). They sell two tourist **maps** of Pécs for 100Ft and 180Ft, as well as a slightly dated but informative guide to the city that discusses its history building by building (100Ft). (Open Mon.-Fri. 9am-7pm, Sat. 9am-4pm; Sept.-May Mon.-Fri. 9am-5pm, Sat. 9am-4pm.) The Pécs **train station** is located just beyond the bottom of the city's historic district, a 10min. bus ride (30 or 34) from the center of town. Trains zip to Budapest four times per day (2½hr., 693Ft plus 130Ft reservation fee, 30% discount for ISIC holders.)

Private accommodations are usually arranged through the tourist offices in Széchenyi tér. For stays of less than three nights, a 30% fee is added to the first night's price. As well as Tourinform, try **MÁV travel office** (tel. (72) 32 45 23) in the railway station, 10min. from the city center by bus, which rents beds in its tourist hostel for 500Ft per night (open Mon.-Thurs. 9am-4:30pm, Fri. 9am-4pm; Sept.-May Mon.-Thurs. 8am-4:30pm, Fri. 8am-3:30pm). The **student dormitory,** Rákóczi út 52, across from the Konzum department store (tel. (72) 31 59 57) is bare but liveable (doubles, triples and quads all 400Ft per person; open July-Aug.). Early in the day or outside of peak season, take bus 34 directly to the **campground** (tel. (72) 31 59 81), in the hills above the city, where tent sites (500Ft for 2 people), 3-bed bungalows (1600Ft) and doubles (2000Ft) in a one-star hotel are located at the entrance to hiking trails into the Mecsek Hills (open mid-April to mid-Oct.). Although it looks cruddy from the outside, the interior of **DÓM Vendéglő Restaurant,** Király u. 3, is an impressive two-level wooden reproduction of a church, complete with stained-glass windows (entrees 350-500Ft; menu in German; open 11am-11pm). **Salibár,** Bartók Béla u. 34, offers mostly herbivore fare: salads and rice. Ask for the English menu—it's kicking around somewhere. (Entrees 120-260Ft. Open 11:30am-10pm.)

HUNGARY

■ NAGYHARSÁNY

From Pécs, consider a daytrip to the incredible sculpture park in **Nagyharsány**, 37km south, hard by the Croatian border. Located in and around a former quarry, the park contains work by artists from around the world. Facing the quarry, follow the path on the right for a climb to even better views of the town and the fruited plains below. First take a train to Villány (1hr., round-trip 220Ft); from the station, turn left and follow the main road (towards Siklós) about 4km. There is a map across from the ABC supermarket 1km along, or just ask for the *szoborpark*.

■ ■ ■ GYŐR

Usually associated with heavy industry, Győr (JYUR) nonetheless manages to retain an aura of charm; some of the finest 17th- and 18th-century buildings in all of Hungary crowd the inner city, and the occasional horse-drawn cart still plods through rush-hour traffic. Bécsi Kapu tér is the site of the very yellow **Carmelite church** and the remains of a medieval **castle** built to defend against the Turks. At the top of Káptalandomb is the **Episcopal Cathedral,** originally built in 1030. Generations of embellishments have resulted in a not particularly coherent hybrid of architectural styles. The miraculous **Weeping Madonna of Győr,** in the altar in the north nave, was brought from Ireland in the 1650s by a priest fleeing the regime of Oliver Cromwell. The **Imre Patkó Collection,** in the **Iron Log House** at Széchenyi tér 4, proudly displays two floors of the works of modern Hungarian artists, and a small room of foreign masters including Picasso and Chagall. (open Tues.-Sun. 10am-6pm; 20Ft, students 10Ft). The **Margit Kovács Museum,** Rózsa Ferenc u. 1, a block north of the square, is one of Győr's hidden treasures, displaying the artist's distinctive ceramic sculptures and tiles (open Tues.-Sun.10am-6pm, Nov.-March 10am-5pm; 20Ft, students 10Ft). The marketplace on the river erupts into a **bazaar** on Wed., Fri., and Sat. mornings. Győr frolics away the June and July with **Győri Nyár,** a festival of daily concerts, theater, and ballet. Buy tickets at the box office on Baross Gábor út, or at the performance venue. Schedules are available at Ciklámen Tourist and IBUSZ.

Practical Information, Accommodations, and Food By train, Győr is 2½hr. from Budapest (418Ft). Other trains steam to Vienna and Sopron (1½hr., 264Ft). **Buses** depart from the terminal beside the train station for Budapest (2½hr., 393Ft) and Sopron (1½hr., 342Ft). One block up from the train station, **Ciklámen Tourist,** Aradi Vértanúk u. 22 (tel. (96) 31 76 01 or 31 15 57) offers English-speakers who market free brochures and new maps for 180Ft. They also find private accommodations (singles from 600Ft, doubles from 1000Ft). (Open Mon.-Thurs. 8am-4:30pm, Fri. 8am-3:30pm, Sat. 8am-12:30pm.) A few blocks east, **IBUSZ,** Szent István út 29 (tel. (96) 31 17 00 or 31 12 24), is bigger and has singles for 880Ft, and doubles for 990Ft (open Mon., Tues. and Thurs. 8am-3:30pm, Wed. and Fri. 8am-3pm. **Express,** Bajcsy-Zsilinszky út 41 (tel. (96) 32 88 33), can help make hostel reservations (open Mon.-Fri. 8am-3:45pm). **Hotel Szárnyaskerék,** Révai Miklós u. 5 (tel. (96) 31 46 29), is right outside the train station; it's gloomy but clean and the staff speaks English (doubles with shared bath 1320Ft, with private bath 2200Ft). For hostel-type accommodation, try **2sz. Fiú Kollégium** (Boy's Dormitory No. 2), Damjanich u. 58 (tel. (96) 31 10 08), just north of the Mosoni-Duna River (400Ft; open weekends and June 13-Aug. 31). **Kiskút-ligeti Camping,** Kiskútliget (tel. (96) 31 89 86), has a motel with triples for 1800Ft. Camping and bungalows are open April 15-Oct. 15 (4-person bungalows 1200Ft; 250Ft per tent, 200Ft per person).

For emergency supplies, there is a tiny **non-stop market** in the train station, near the stairs to the underpass. **Piero,** Munkácsy Mihály u. 6, just south of the Petőfi Bridge, is a decent French restaurant, slightly upscale (entrees 365-595Ft; English menu available; open noon-midnight). **Komédiás,** Czuczor Gergely u. 30, is a cozy, family-run restaurant with wonderful food (entrees 180-500Ft; English menu; open

Mon.-Sat. 11am-midnight, Sun. 7pm-midnight). **Vaskakas Tavern** (Iron Rooster), Bécsi Kapu tér 7, is in a huge, dark dungeon built into the castle wall. Deserted during the day, it's jammed with Austrian tourists at night. (Entrees 150-500Ft. Open Mon.-Sat. 11am-4am, Sun. 11am-midnight.)

■■■ SOPRON

Neither the invading Mongols nor the Turks were able to reach the center of Sopron, so buildings dating to the 14th century are common, and many structures have foundations that were laid by the Romans. Most of Sopron's historic sights lie within the horseshoe shaped old town—with its four churches, two medieval synagogues and 10 museums—and are concentrated in Fő tér. The **Fire Tower,** on the north side of the square, is a 17th-century spire atop a 16th-century tower, sitting on a 12th-century base that straddles a Roman gate (open Tues.-Sat. 10am-6pm; 40Ft, 20Ft with ISIC). Across the square is the **Bencés Templom** (Goat Church) which was originally built in the 13th century with funds from a happy herder whose goats found gold. The small **Franciscan Monastery** next door dates from the late 13th century. Visitors can enter its **Chapter's Hall,** a room of textbook Gothic architecture enriched by 10 sculptures of human sins, and the latest Gregorian chant release. (Church and the Chapter's Hall open 10am-noon, 2pm-5pm. Free, but donations encouraged.)

At Fő tér 8, the **Storno House** is the best museum in town. The Stornos were 19th century Swiss-Italian restorers of monuments and cathedrals; their taste in churches is often less than impressive, but their home and personal collection of furniture and artwork spanning the Renaissance to the 19th century is exquisite. (Compulsory prerecorded tour; English-speakers get a fact sheet. 60Ft, 40Ft with ISIC. Open Tues.-Sun. 10am-6pm.) Down Új u., once known as Zsidó utca (Jew street), the **Old Synagogue,** at #22, was built around 1300. It has been reconstructed and includes the stone Torah niche and the wooden pulpit, and in a small building in the courtyard, the deep well used as the ritual bath. (Open Wed.-Mon. 9am-5pm. 40Ft, 20Ft with ISIC.) Learn the history of baking in the **Bakery Museum,** Bécsi út. 5, north of the old town (open Wed., Fri., Sun. 10am-2pm and Tues., Thurs., Sat. 2pm-6pm; 40Ft, 20Ft with ISIC).

Practical Information, Accommodations, and Food Sopron rises from fertile farmland only a few **rail** hours from Budapest's Déli station (3hr., 682Ft) and Vienna's Südbahnhof (1hr., 131AS). From the train station, walk north on Mátyás Király út for 10min. to reach Várkerület. The **bus station** is north of Ciklámen Tourist on Lackner Kristóf. **IBUSZ,** Várkerület 41 (tel. (99) 31 24 55), has doubles in private homes starting at 1300Ft (open Mon.-Fri. 8am-1pm, 1:30pm-4pm, Sat 8am-12:30pm). **Ciklámen Tourist,** Ógabona tér 8 (tel. (99) 31 20 40) has one single for 1050Ft, and doubles for 1400Ft. **Express** tourist office at Mátyás Király u. 7 (tel. (99) 31 20 24, open Mon.-Fri. 8am-3:30pm, Sat 8am-noon) can help with hostel accommodations. **Hotel Locomotiv,** Lővér Krt. 1 (tel. (99) 31 41 80), not surprisingly near the train station rents doubles for 2400Ft per night. **Talizmán Panzió,** Táncsics u. 15 (tel. (99) 31 16 20) offers doubles for 1200-1500Ft. Show 'em your *Let's Go* and get a 200Ft discount on rooms. **Lővér Campground** at the south end of town on Kőszegi u. (tel. (99) 31 17 15) has 4-person bungalows for 3000Ft, 3-person bungalows for 1200Ft, and 2-person bungalows for 700-800Ft. For campsite use, it charges 200Ft per tent, and 180Ft per person. (Open April 15-Oct. 15.) **Rondella Étterem,** Szent György u. 14, serves excellent steaks for 320-560Ft, pizza and spaghetti for 130-280Ft to lots of young Austrians (open 11am-11pm). **Cézár Pince,** Hátsókapu 2, is a wine cellar that serves great light meals and snacks, including sausage platters and cheese platters for 90-190Ft. A little non-stop **grocery store** lingers on the corner of Móricz Zsigmond u. and Magyar u.

■ FERTŐD

Twenty-seven km east of Sopron, in tiny **Fertőd,** stands the magnificent Rococo **Eszterházy Palace,** Bartók Béla u. 2. Miklós Eszterházy, known as Miklós the Sumptuous before he squandered his family's vast fortune, ordered the palace built in 1766 to hold his multi-day orgiastic feasts. Josef Haydn wrote and conducted here, and stellar concerts still resound within (open Tues.-Sun. 8am-noon, 1pm-5pm). Buses leave hourly for Fertőd from stage five in the station on Lackner Kristóf in Sopron (45min., 105Ft). Fertőd has dorm beds and a few doubles, but groups often fill them. Book with Ciklámen Tourist in Sopron.

■■■ LAKE BALATON

Shallow Balaton is the largest lake and one of the most coveted vacation spots in Central Europe. Villas first sprouted along its shores during the Roman Empire. When a railroad linked lake to cities in the 1860s, it was transformed into a favored summer playground. Today, the region's rich scenery and comparatively low prices draw mobs of German, Austrian, and Hungarian vacationers; as soon as schools let out, the lakeside becomes raucous and crowded with the young and the restless.

Siófok The largest town by Lake Balaton, Siófok's lakeside is the playground of surf-starved Germans and Austrians. Several high-rise, high-priced hotels line the crowded beachfront, making it the most modern, if least scenic, of Balaton's resorts. Public and private **beaches** (up to 100Ft) alternate along Siófok's expensive coastline; both are equally packed in the summers. Numerous nightclubs line the lakefront, while amphibious boppers revel on the **Disco Boat** from July 9-August 21, leaving the docks at 9:30pm (300Ft).

The bus and train stations are next to each other off the town's main drag, Fő u. **Trains** arrive from Budapest-Déli station roughly every hour (2hr., 304Ft). From the stations, go right down Fő u. toward the large octagonal water tower. **Tourinform** (tel. (84) 31 01 17) is inside the tower's base. (Open Mon.-Sat. 8am-8pm, Sun. 8am-1pm; Sept.-June Mon.-Fri. 9am-4pm, Sat. 9am-noon.) Nearby **IBUSZ,** Fő u. 174 (tel. (84) 31 10 66), has doubles near the center for 1500Ft (open Mon.-Sat. 8am-6pm, Sun. 8:30am-1pm). Camp 5km east of the center at **Aranypart Camping** (tel. (84) 31 18 01), where two people can pitch a tent near the water for 630Ft (open April-Sept.). You can also pitch a tent in the backyard of the **Tuja Panzió,** Szent László u. 74 (tel. (84) 31 49 96), for 400Ft per person or rent a doubles inside (1200Ft per person). **Szent László u.,** just one block from the beach, is lined with *panziós* and *Zimmer Frei* signs; doubles here fetch 1500-2700Ft. The **Csárdás Restaurant,** Fő u. 105, offers traditional Hungarian dishes in a friendly atmosphere (entrees 275-500Ft; open mid-May to mid-Oct. 11:30am-midnight). The outdoor cafeteria counter near the ferry station serves a respectable *spaghetti bolognese* (120Ft).

Keszthely Certainly the most civilized town on the whole lake and its largest port, the pride of Keszthely (KESS-tay) is the **Festetics Palace.** Built by one of the most powerful Austro-Hungarian families, it exemplifies the beauty, grandeur, and gaudiness of the Baroque. Concerts are often held in the mirrored ballroom hall during summer. (Open Tues.-Sun. 9am-6pm. 250Ft, 70Ft with ISIC.) The surrounding park is a vast and well-kept strolling ground. The **Georgikon Major Múzeum** at Bercsényi u. 67 is an amusing apotheosis of György Festetics, who founded Europe's oldest agricultural university here in 1797. (Open April-Oct. Tues.-Sat. 10am-5pm, Sun. 10am-6pm. 30Ft, free with ISIC.)

Five **trains** per day head to and from the Budapest-Déli station in Budapest (3hr., 600Ft). The bus station is beside the train station; **buses** leave for nearby towns as well as places as far away as Győr and Budapest. Walk straight ahead along Mártírok u. until you reach the city's main street, Kossuth Lajos u. Turn right and head for its pedestrian section. Try **IBUSZ,** Széchenyi u. 1-3, for doubles from 1320Ft (open

HUNGARY

Mon.-Sat. 8am-6pm, Sun. 9am-1pm; Sept.-May Mon.-Thurs. 8am-4pm, Fri. 8am-3pm.)
Tourinform, Kossuth Lajos u. 28, will find apartments for four people for 3000Ft
(open Mon.-Fri. 9am-6pm, Sat.-Sun. 9am-1pm; Sept.-Jun. Mon.-Sat. 9am-5pm). The
Forrás Panzió (tel. (83) 31 14 18), Római út 1, is social and popular with students
(singles 1300Ft, doubles 2340Ft). **Mr. Attila Lukic's** cozy *panzió*, Jókai Mór u.16
(tel. (83) 31 12 32) has doubles for 3000Ft—*Let's Go* readers get 20% off. **Vajda J.
Középiskola Kollégiuma,** Gagarin u. 4 (tel. (83) 31 13 61), charges 350Ft for a bed
in a dormitory room (open June-Aug.). **Sport Camping,** Csárda u. (tel. (83) 31 28
42), is a 5min. walk south from the train station and across the tracks; 2-person bungalows cost 700Ft, 1500Ft with bathroom (140Ft per person,150Ft per tent; open
May-Sept). The **Park Vendéglő,** Vörösmarty u.1/a, has an English menu (entrees
280-550Ft; 10% *Let's Go* discount or free glass of wine; open 11am-11pm). **Béke
Vendéglő,** Kossuth Lajos u. 50, has a large, shady courtyard and live gypsy music in
the evenings (entrees 140-460Ft; open 8am-10pm.)

Tihany High on its peninsular hilltop, Tihany (TEE-hawn) is the most luscious
spot on Lake Balaton. The price of paradise is predictably high and Tihany's isolation means fewer hedonistic diversions. The two **ferry** landings, Tihany and, to the
southwest, Tihanyi-rév, are easy to confuse; don't. Take the **bus** (departing frequently from both ferry wharves, or stay on the bus from Balatonfüred) to the village proper, or **hike** up the winding paths toward the church. Lording over the
peninsula, the 1754 **Abbey Church** has Baroque altars, pulpit, and organ (open
10am-5pm; 20Ft, students 10Ft). Next door, an 18th-century monastery now exists
as the **Tihany Museum,** with psychedelic dreamscapes, colorized etchings, and
Roman inscriptions displayed in a cool, subterranean lapidarium. (open March-Oct.
Tues.-Sun. 10am-6pm; 30Ft). Far from the madding crowd is the bizarre **garage-gal-
lery** of "painter artist, writer, professor" Gergely Koós-Hutás, at Fürdőtelep 43, a
5min. climb from Tihany wharf. Works include massive canvases of a didactic Lenin
and several of the artist himself in front of famous edifices around the world, such as
Grauman's Chinese Restaurant in Hollywood. Signed photos are a steal at 20Ft.

The promenade behind the church also leads to the **beach** (follow the "strand"
signs).The beach is open 7am to 7pm (50Ft), though the side gate remains unlocked
after hours. If you have been enchanted, **Balatontourist,** Kossuth u. 20 (tel. (86) 34
85 19) arranges private rooms in the village. (Doubles 1570Ft; private apartments
with kitchen, bath, and two double rooms 3500-4000Ft. Open summer Mon.-Sat.
8am-6:30pm, Sun. 8am-1pm.)

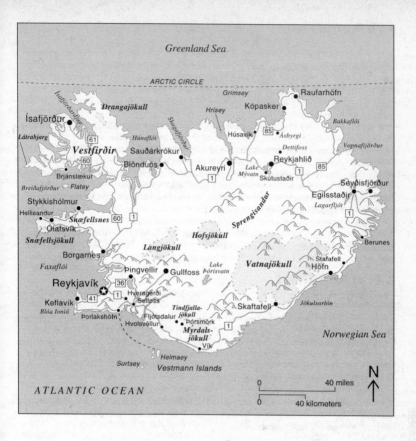

Iceland (Ísland)

US$1 = 69.28kr (krónur, or ISK)
CDN$1 = 52.66kr
UK£1 = 107.38kr
IR£1 = 100.48kr
AUS$1 = 45.08kr
NZ$1 = 38.31kr
SAR1 = 14.41kr
Country Code: 354

10kr =   US$0.15
10kr = CDN$0.19
10kr =   UK£0.09
10kr =   IR£0.10
10kr = AUS$0.22
10kr =   NZ$0.26
10kr =   SAR0.66
International Dialing Prefix: 90

Iceland is rugged. Continually reshaped by the fiery force of volcanoes and the slow digging of glaciers, the land is contorted into fantastic natural contrasts. From the alien moonscapes of the Keflavík and Mývatn areas to the soaring black mountains, colorful Rhyolite hills, and spectacular waterfalls of the coastal regions, nature itself is the best attraction. Trees, however, are almost nonexistent, and those that *are* living are weather-hardened and wiry, focusing all their resources on the fine art of survival.

The same can be said of the people of Iceland themselves. Cast in the fierce Viking mold of ancient times, they continue to struggle, and triumph, over the raw power of nature; taming it, and bending its will to theirs. Today, most of the country is heated by geothermal power and Icelanders have an almost limitless supply of electricity. Roads have been built through the interior and airplanes zip from city to city. With a population of 265,000, Iceland is the most sparsely populated nation in Europe. The Icelanders work hard, however, for their way of life; indeed, their 54-hour work week is the longest in Europe, but their standard of living is among the highest in the world.

Icelanders may not disembowel enemies over a bit of slander anymore, but much of the strong Viking heritage that inspired the world's first democracy still exists today. A language committee systematically banishes foreign words, and, instead of surnames, people follow the patronymic custom of identifying themselves as the sons or daughters of their fathers (phone books are ordered by first name). Much of their economy depends on the sea, and a high fish diet means Icelanders lead some of the longest lives in the world. Almost everyone in Iceland is literate and loves the president, Vigdís Finnbogadóttir, who in 1980, was the first woman elected president of any nation and has been reelected three times since. Paradoxically, modern Icelanders maintain a strong belief in the supernatural; over 900 years after the introduction of Christianity, the belief continues that elves and fairies live in the rocks and fields, and road projects have been canceled so as "not to disturb the fairy-folk."

GETTING THERE

From North America, flying is the only option. **Icelandair** (tel. (800) 223-5500) flies from New York all year (Thurs.-Tues. in summer), from Orlando (in summer 1 per week, early Sept.-late May 1-2 per week), from Baltimore (April-late Oct. 3-4 per week), and from Fort Lauderdale (1-2 per week). These planes connect each morning with flights to Icelandair's European destinations; Luxembourg is the most popular. Often, the airline will give you a free 3-day layover in the country. The only scheduled non-Icelandair flights to Iceland are on **SAS** from Copenhagen (3 per week) and on **Lufthansa** from Frankfurt (1 per week, summer only).

The only opportunity to feel the sea wind off Iceland's rugged shores is on the ferry *Norröna*, which circles the North Atlantic via Seyðisfjörður (East Iceland), Tórshavn (Faroe Islands), Bergen (Norway), and Hanstholm (Denmark); see the East Iceland section for more information.

GETTING AROUND

Icelanders make it as easy as possible to travel in their country. One tour company, **BSÍ**, coordinates all bus schedules and prices into a single system. There are no trains. Free schedules are available in hostels and tourist offices. The *Iceland 1994* brochure lists selected bus schedules as well as tours and ferry routes.

Buses Though flying is more comfortable, **bus travel** can be cheaper and allows you to appreciate the rugged terrain up close. Land travel focuses on the 1411km **Highway I,** completed in 1974, which circles the island. (Only partially paved, it often has just one lane.) Plan on at least a week in Iceland if you want to circle the country on the Ring Road; buses do it in four 5- to 9-hour stages (Reykjavík to Akureyri to Egilsstaðir to Höfn and back to Reykjavík, and vice versa), with daily service on each leg from mid-June through August. You can buy tickets in the stations *(umferðarmiðstöð)* in Reykjavík and Akureyri, or from the driver. **BSÍ**, based in the Reykjavík bus station, sells two passes that simplify bus travel greatly. The **Full Circle Passport** (14,000kr) allows you to circle the island at your own pace (available mid-May to Sept.). The **Omnibus Passport** (available all year) entitles you to a period of unlimited travel on all scheduled bus routes (1 week 14,300kr, 2 weeks 21,500kr, 3 weeks 27,500kr, 4 weeks 30,800kr). Both passes entitle you to 10% discounts on many ferries, campgrounds, farms, and *hótel edda* sleeping bag accommodations. Plus, you can purchase vouchers at BSÍ for a greater discount on accommodations. If you're on the whirlwind tour and plan to go off the Ring Road (to the West Fjords), the Omnibus pass is the best deal, but if you're taking your time, you'll find that the Full Circle will end up a better bargain. In the off-season, one-week Omnibus Passports are cheaper, since fewer routes are available.

Flights The only quick way to travel in Iceland is by air; flights are on propeller planes with occasionally stellar views over glaciers, mountains, and lava fields, though more often of puffy cumulonimbus clouds. **Flugleiðir** (Icelandair's domestic service) flies primarily between Reykjavík and major towns, **Flugfélag Norðurlands** out of Akureyri, and **Flugfélag Austurlands** between towns in the east. The two available air packages may be cheaper than the bus. The first, the **Air Rover,** is only sold abroad at Icelandair offices, and offers 4 stops from Reykjavík for US$320. The second option, the **Four Sector Icelandair Pass,** allows 3 destinations from Reykjavík and is available in Iceland (US$190). Both are valid on the regional airlines as well as Icelandair. Another option is the **Air/Bus Rover** (fly one-way, bus the other), offered by Icelandair and BSÍ Travel. Valid from June 1 to Sept. 30, a ticket from Reykjavík to Akureyri costs 8000kr. Icelandair offers 20% student discounts on all flights, and a 50% companion discount. Flugfélag Norðurlands offers 25% student discounts on all flights. Iceland's dicey weather can ground flights on short notice, so *do not* plan to fly back to Reykjavík the day before your plane leaves Iceland.

Cars Seeing the country by **car** (preferably 4-wheel-drive) allows you the most freedom. Car rental *(bílaleiga)* starts at about 4000kr per day and 30kr per km (ask about special package deals). Patient **hitchers** try the busiest roads in summer, but rides can be hard to come by, especially in the East. The traffic is sparse and the weather unpredictable. A tent, a map and awareness of recent road closings help. **Cycling** is becoming increasingly popular, but ferocious winds, nonexistent road shoulders, and thousands of aimless sheep conspire to make the going difficult. The cheapest and most rewarding way to see Iceland is on foot. Well-marked trails are rare, but many areas of the country are suitable for hiking. (See The Interior, below, for more information.)

ICELAND ESSENTIALS

The tourist season in Iceland lasts June through August. Many accommodations, transport and tourist information offices hibernate until June 1. The summer is *the* best time to travel here since many roads aren't even open before July or after early September. Plus, it's always night in the winter and you won't be able to see anything unless you bring a flashlight. In the summer, though the sun technically dips beneath the horizon for a few hours each night, it never gets really dark, there's no snow, and it's warm enough to camp and hike. The Gulf Stream keeps temperatures moderate: the mercury rarely rises above 60°F (16°C) in summer, or dips below 20°F (-6°C) in winter. Bring watertight, lightweight clothing that can be layered. A rain jacket, woolen sweaters, and sturdy shoes are a must any time of the year since the weather is very capricious, and the most common evil is rain. It *will* rain. Iceland's hot water wells spawn an extensive outdoor bathing culture, so pack a swimsuit. Every town has comfortable pools with special hot pools on the side.

Seek out the tourist information offices in large and important towns for mounds of schedules and brochures, and request information at hotel reception desks in smaller towns for local information. Must-haves are the free brochures *Around Iceland,* with accommodations, restaurant, and museum listings for every town, and *Iceland A-Z,* which presents relevant practical information concisely. The Icelandic language has changed little from Old Norse, but fortunately most Icelanders speak English. Icelandic's two extra letters need not confuse: Þ (lowercase þ) is pronounced as in *th*orn, Ð (lowercase ð) as in *the*.

On June 17, Independence Day festivals are held all over Iceland, the best of them in Reykjavík. Other legal holidays in 1995, when most everything closes, include Jan. 1, Easter (April 14-17), Ascension Day (May 25), Whit Sunday (June 4), Whit Monday (June 5), Bank Holiday Monday (Aug. 7), and Christmas (Dec. 24-26). Regular business hours are weekdays from 9am to 5pm, 6pm in summer. **Banks** open

ICELAND

weekdays from 9:15am to 4pm. Currency exchange commissions vary only slightly between banks (except at the airport), and the rates are set by the government. **Post offices** *(póstur)* are generally open on weekdays from 8:30am to 4:30pm, as are **telephone** *(sími)* offices (often in the same building). Post offices and hostels normally hold mail. Pay phones take 5, 10 and 50kr pieces; local calls cost 10kr. For assisted international calls, dial 09. For AT&T **USADirect** dial 99 90 01, MCI **World-Phone** 99 90 02, **Canada Direct** 99 90 10, and **BT Direct** 99 90 44 (calls cost 5kr). **Emergency numbers** vary across the country; they are listed on the inside front cover of the *símaskrá* (phone book), or you can call the operator 24hrs. by dialing 03. The phone book lists people by first name. Iceland does not observe daylight savings time—it is even with London in winter but stays an hour behind in summer.

In May, 1995, all telephone numbers in Iceland will change. All numbers will have 7 digits and there will be no regional codes. In **Reykjavík:** 6-digit numbers, add a 5 to the beginning (e.g. 64 27 19 becomes 564 27 19); 5-digit numbers, add 55. **Outside Reykjavík:** 5-digit numbers, add 4, followed by the regional code (the first "9" does not *officially* count as part of that code). **West Fjords:** 4-digit numbers, add 456. **Toll-free numbers:** replace 99 with 800. **International calls:** dialing prefix 90 becomes 00 (country code remains the same).

Accommodations and Camping Iceland has 25 **HI youth hostels** (get the free *Hostelling in Iceland* brochure at the tourist office for a complete listing) which charge 1000kr (nonmembers 1100 or 1250kr) and are invariably clean, with kitchens and common rooms. **Sleeping bag accommodations** *(svefnpokapláss)*, widely available on farms, at summer hotels, and in guesthouses *(gistiheimili)*, are a viable and competitively priced alternative (most often you get at least a mattress); consult the free *Around Iceland* and *Icelandic Farm Holidays* brochures (the latter lists about 100 farms nationwide). Starting in early June, many schoolhouses become *Hótel Eddas,* which offer sleeping bag accommodations from 1100kr (no kitchens, 10% discount for bus-pass holders). Most of these places also offer breakfast and made-up beds (both of which are *quite* expensive). Be warned: while staying in a tiny farm or hostel may be the highlight of your Icelandic trip, the nearest bus may be 20km away and run once a week. Check the bus schedules *very* carefully and try not to hurry through your trip. Many remote lodgings offer to pick up car-less tourists at the nearest town, sometimes charging a small fee.

In cities and nature reserves, **camping** is permitted only at designated campsites. Outside of official sites, camping is free but discouraged; watch out for *Tjaldstæði bönnuð* (No Camping) signs and *always* ask in the nearest farm before you camp anywhere else. Use gas burners; Iceland has no firewood and it is illegal to burn the sparse vegetation. Always bring your waste with you to the nearest disposal. **Official campsites** (summer only) range from rocky fields with cold water taps to the sumptuous facilities in Reykjavík. Upper-crust sites run 400kr per person, more basic ones about 250kr. Rent camping gear suited to Iceland's climate from **ALP Rentals,** located beside BSÍ bus station in Reykjavík (tel. (91) 175 70; open 8am-6pm; sleeping bag 2000kr per week, 2-person tent 4000kr per week). For all camping items, go to **Skátabúðin** in Reykjavík at Snorrabraut 60 (tel. (91) 61 20 45), between Egilsgata and Bergþórugata (open Mon.-Fri. 9am-6pm, Sat. 10am-2pm).

Food and Drink Icelandic cuisine celebrates animals you might normally have considered wonderful and exotic pets. Check supermarkets or ask around for traditional foods such as *lundar* (puffin), *rjúpa* (ptarmigan) and *selshreifar* (seal flippers). Conservative eaters can stick to fish and lamb, or bust out and try *svið* (singed and boiled sheep's head), *hrútspungur* (ram's testicles), or *hákarl* (rotten, years-old shark). Icelanders drink mostly on weekends and pay through the nose for the privilege; a beer at almost any pub costs more than 450kr. Alcoholic beverages are sold only in state-run monopoly outlets (located in few places and open very few hours) and in pubs and restaurants. The drinking age is 20 (though rarely enforced), and driving under the influence is severely punished.

Grocery stores are the basic hunting grounds for travelers in Iceland; most every town has a **Kaupfélag** (cooperative store) and usually a fast-food kiosk. Gas stations (usually open from 9am until 10 or 11pm) sell snacks too. Groceries in many small towns close for an hour at lunch (noon-1pm). Larger towns commonly have supermarkets: the best deal is the comprehensive **Hagkaup**. Most larger towns also have restaurants which serve fish and meat courses. Remember that food is extremely expensive in Iceland; a *cheap* restaurant meal will cost you no less than 800kr. There's no tipping in Iceland.

■■■ REYKJAVÍK

"To ill purpose we crossed good land to settle this spit." Those were the words of Reykjavík's founder, the Norwegian adventurer, Ingólfur Amarson, upon arriving at the land the gods had chosen for him. Three years earlier, before landing on Iceland, he threw his high seat pillars overboard, imploring the gods for their help in city planning, and promising to settle wherever the pillars washed up on shore. After years of beachcombing, he and his slave finally settled in the Bay of Smoke, the desolate area of Reykjavík. Today, that "smoke" (or, rather, geothermal steam) heats all the houses in the Reykjavík area, and Reykjavík has transformed from a lovely "spit" to the governmental, economic, and cultural capital of the country, with two-thirds of the entire Icelandic population. Amarson chose wisely, since this geothermal energy keeps Reykjavík the cleanest capital in Europe. Where else can you find an excellent salmon river flowing right through the city limits? However, the superb air quality is often overshadowed by the thick rainclouds that stay for 360 days a year. On a good day, the view from Reykjavík can capture much of Iceland's natural splendor, and fill you with the warm, fuzzy feeling of cohabitation with the environment, but on a bad day, you'll just get wet.

ORIENTATION AND PRACTICAL INFORMATION

Lækjartorg, the main square of old Reykjavík, sits on the northern side of a stubby peninsula on Iceland's southwest coast. To the north and across the harbor looms Mount Esja. Roughly south of Lækjartorg are the lake, the long-distance bus station, and the Reykjavík Airport on the peninsula's south shore. Radiating east and west from Lækjartorg is the pedestrian thoroughfare which forms the axis of the city; the street name varies, called **Austerstræti** to the west and **Bankastræti** to the immediate east, then transforming into **Laugavegur**.

All international flights arrive at **Keflavík Airport,** 55km from Reykjavík. Forty-five minutes after each arrival, a "Flybus" (tel. (91) 62 10 11; US$9.50 or 500kr) shuttles passengers to the domestic **Reykjavík Airport** and the adjacent Hótel Loftleiðir, from which bus 17 (100kr) leaves every 20min. for Lækjartorg, and bus 5 goes to the Sundlaugarvegur Youth Hostel. Outgoing Flybuses leave the Holiday Inn 2½hrs. and Hótel Loftleiðir 2hrs. before each departure from Keflavík as well as from the youth hostel at 4:45am June 1 to September 10. Many flights depart before city buses run, so allow time for walking to the Flybus stops or book a cab in advance. From Hótel Loftleiðir's Reykjavík Excursions desk (open 24hrs.), which runs the Flybus and many tours, you can pick up a free city map and a free copy of *What's On in Reykjavík*. After-hours currency exchange is cheapest at the hotel's **Landsbanki Íslands** branch (open Mon.-Fri. 8:15am-4pm and 5-7:15pm, Sat. 8:15am-7:15pm, Sun. 2-6pm; commissions double on weekends and holidays).

Tourist Office: Upplýsingamiðstöð Ferðamála á Íslandi, Bankastræti 2 (tel. 62 30 45), at the end of the small courtyard immediately to your right as you walk uphill from Lækjartorg. Free maps, tons of brochures, and extensive information on tours, accommodations, cultural events, and weather conditions. Open Mon.-

Fri. 8:30am-6pm, Sat. 8:30am-2pm, Sun. and holidays 10am-2pm; Sept.-May Mon.-Fri. 10am-4pm.

Budget Travel: Ferðaskrifstofa Stúdenta, Hringbraut (tel. 61 56 56), next to the National Museum. Same building as the university bookshop. Discounts on international travel only; sells ISIC and InterRail. Open Mon.-Fri. 9am-5pm.

Embassies: U.S., Laufásvegur 21 (tel. 291 00). Open Mon.-Fri. 8am-12:30pm and 1:30-5pm. **Canadian consulate,** Suðurlandsbraut 10, 3rd floor (tel. 68 08 20). Open Mon.-Fri. 8am-4pm. **U.K.,** Laufásvegur 49 (tel. 158 83). Open Mon.-Fri. 9am-noon; phones answered until 5pm. **Ireland,** Þverholt 19-21 (tel. 62 63 00 or 423 55). Open Mon.-Fri. 9am-noon. **South Africa,** Hafnarstræti 7 (tel. 62 95 22 or 67 87 97). Open Mon.-Fri. 8:30am-11:30am.

Currency Exchange: Banks open Mon.-Fri. 9:15am-4pm; there are many on Austurstræti and Laugavegur. After-hours exchange at the Hótel Loftleiðir bank (see Orientation, above). Also at the tourist office (June-Sept. Mon.-Fri. 4:30-6pm, Sat. 9am-1pm) and at the Salvation Army (May-Oct.).

American Express: Úrval-Útsýn Travel, Lágmúli 4, P.O. Box 8650, 128 Reykjavík (tel. 69 93 00). Brand-new state o' the art offices. Mail held, traveler's checks not cashed; no wired money accepted.

Post Office: Póstur, Pósthússtræti 5 (tel. 63 60 00), in the town center. Open Mon.-Fri. 8:30am-4:30pm, Sat. 10am-2pm; Sept.-May Mon.-Fri. 8:30am-4:30pm for poste restante. Branch at BSÍ bus station open Mon.-Fri. noon-6pm, Sat. 9am-1pm. **Postal code:** Reykjavík 101.

Telephones: Póstur og Sími Afgreiðsla, across from Kirkjustræti 8, in the center. Open Mon.-Fri. 8:15am-7pm, Sat. 10am-6pm, Sun. noon-6pm. **City Code:** 91.

Flights: Keflavík Airport, for international flights (see above). The Icelandair ticket office is at Lækjargata 2 (info tel. Reykjavík (92) 502 00; open Mon.-Fri. 9am-5pm). Domestic **Reykjavík Airport,** just south of town, has 2 distinct halves. On the *western* side of the runways, **Flugleiðir (Icelandair)** (tel. 69 02 00) has regular flights to Iceland, Greenland, and the Faroe Islands. Take bus 5 from Lækjartorg or Sundlaugarvegur, or walk (15min. along the dirt road near the bus station, at the junction of Hringbraut and Vatnsmýrarvegur). From the *eastern* side of the airport, next to Hótel Loftleiðir, **Íslandsflug** (tel. 61 60 60) flies to several small towns in Iceland, including Vestmannaeyjar. Take bus 1 or walk (15min. from the bus station).

Buses: Umferðarmiðstöð, Vatnsmýrarvegur 10 (tel. 223 00), off Hringbraut near Reykjavík Airport. Terminal open 7am-midnight, tickets sold from 7:30am. Upstairs, **BSÍ Travel** has bus passes and schedules, as well as bike rentals. Open June-Aug. Mon-Fri. 7:30am-7pm, Sat. 7am-2pm, Sun. 7am-1pm and 5-7pm.

Public Transportation: Strætisvagnar Reykjavíkur (SVR) runs yellow city buses (tel. 127 00). Fare 100kr. Ask the driver for a free transfer ticket *(skiptimiði),* good for 45min. Kiosks at 4 terminals sell sheaves of schedules and bunches of tickets; the 2 main ones are at Lækjartorg (in the building on the north side of the square) and at Hlemmur (in the building between Hverfisgata and Laugavegur at Rauðarárstígur). Buses run at 20-30min. intervals Mon.-Sat. 7am-midnight, Sun. and holidays 10am-midnight.

Taxis: BSR, Skolatröð 18 (tel. 117 20). 24hr. service. About 500kr from Lækjartorg to Hótel Loftleiðir.

Bike Rental: Reiðhjólaverkstæðið Borgarhjól, Hverfisgata 50 (tel. 156 53). 3-speeds 390kr per ½-day, 800kr per 24hrs.; mountain bikes 580 per ½-day, 1180kr per day, and 6800kr per week. All bikes come with free repair kit. Open Mon-Fri. 8am-6pm, Sat. 10am-2pm, or try BSÍ Travel (see Buses).

Hitchhiking: Those hitching take buses 15a, 15b, 10 or 100 to the east edge of town, then stand on Vesturlandsvegur for the north, Suðurlandsvegur to go southeast. Exposure is risked if not picked up quickly.

Luggage Storage: At the Sundlaugarvegur hostel. 50kr per day, even for non-guests. Also at the BSÍ terminal. Open Mon.-Fri. 7:30am-11:30pm, Sat. 7:30am-2:30pm; 100kr per day, 310kr per week.

Laundromat: Ask your hostel about special arrangements with nearby cleaners. Otherwise, visit Þvoið Sjálf, Barónsstígur 3, below Hverfisgata (tel. 314 41).

Wash 350kr, dry 250kr. Open Mon.-Fri. 8am-7pm, Sat. 10am-6pm; Sept.-May Mon.-Fri. 8am-7pm, Sat. 10am-6pm.

English Bookstore: Most every bookstore has a strong English-language section. A good one is Eymundsson, Austurstræti 18. Open 10am-10pm.

Weather: Daily radio broadcasts in English on FM 92.4 and FM 93.5, June-Aug. 8:55am. Also try the tourist office or call an English recording (tel. 69 36 90).

Women's crisis hotline: tel. 99 62 05.

Gay/Lesbian Center: SAMTÖKIN 78, Lindargata 49 (tel. 285 39). Small coffeeshop and library (largest of its kind in Scandinavia) which are open Mon. and Thurs. 8-11pm and Fri.-Sat. 10pm-late. Call for info Mon.-Fri. 11am-noon, Mon. and Thurs.-Sat. also 8-11pm.

Disabled Visitors: Icelandic Association of the Disabled, Hátún 10, IS-105, Reykjavík (tel. 267 00).

Pharmacies: Vesturbaëgur Apótek, Laugávegur 16. Open Mon.-Fri. 9am-5pm. Or just look for *apótek* signs. For the location of a 24-hr. pharmacy, call 188 88.

Medical Assistance: The Medical Center (Laeknavaktin) at Heilsuverndarstöðin, Barónsstigur 47 (tel. 212 30). Open Mon.-Fri. 8am-5pm, Sat.-Sun. and holidays 24hrs. Also, **Borgarspítalinn** (City Hospital), on Sléttuvegur. Take bus 6, 7, 8 or 9. Or call 69 66 00. Telephone number and emergency ward open 24hrs.

Emergencies: Ambulance and **Fire** tel. 111 00. **Police** tel. 111 66.

ACCOMMODATIONS AND CAMPING

The city is littered with dozens of guesthouses that offer sleeping bag accommodation. In most cases, this means you get a nice room with a nice bed, *sans* sheets and blanket. This can range from a double to a room with six people, from a bunkbed to a double bed. The tourist office has gobs of info on all accommodation. A cheap hotel will cost no less than 4000kr and breakfast is often not included in the price.

Reykjavík Youth Hostel (HI), Sundlaugarvegur 34 (tel. 381 10). Stay on the Flybus to the Holiday Inn, or take bus 5 from Lækjargata to Sundlaugarvegur. The top floor sports some nice hardwood floors that are saved by the strict no-shoe policy. Large kitchen. Reception open Mon.-Fri. 8am-11am; Sat.-Sun. 8-11am and 4pm-midnight. Curfew midnight. Sells bus and air tickets and stores baggage (50kr per day). 1100kr, nonmembers 1350kr. No sleeping bags; sheets 250kr. Reservations recommended; held until 7pm or later with advance notice. Breakfast 600kr.

Hjálpræðisherinn Gesta- og Sjómannaheimili (Salvation Army Guest and Seamen's Home), Kirkjustræti 2 (tel. 61 32 03). A pale yellow house on the same street as the Parliament. Cheap, friendly place. Everything is immaculately laid out; you get free soap and a towel waiting on your bed when you check in. Reception is always helpful and friendly even though they work as long as 10-11hr. shifts. *Big* breakfast. 2- to 5-bed rooms. Reception open 7am-1am, but try the doorbell if you arrive later. Sleeping bag accommodations 1100kr. Sheets 200kr. Reservations needed July-Aug.

Baldursbrá, Laufásvegur 41 (tel. 266 46). Only 5-7min. from the BSÍ terminal. Clean sleeping bag rooms with a German translation of Martin Luther King, Jr.'s "I have a dream" speech on the wall. Good, well-stocked kitchen and amicable owner. 6-bed room 1500kr per person. No curfew. Reserve ahead.

Guesthouse Smárar, Snorrabraut 52 (tel. 62 33 30). A bit far from the old city center, but closer to the new business district. Large rooms with double beds and a refrigerator. Sleeping bag accommodations 1700kr. Breakfast 600kr. No curfew. Reserve ahead.

Hótel Garður, Hringbraut (next to the National Museum; tel. 156 56 or 159 18, reservations 347 00). About as cheap as you'll get for a made-up bed, and right in the middle of town. Beds with linen 4200kr. sleeping bag accommodation 2000kr (breakfast included). No curfew. Open June-Aug.

Camping: (tel. 68 69 44). Right behind the Sundlaugarvegur hostel; take bus 5. The only site in town, but quite nice and not very expensive. Showers, laundry, and cooking facilities. 200kr per tent, 200kr per person. Reservations recommended. Open June-Aug. Free buses run from the campsite to the BSÍ terminal at 7am.

ICELAND

FOOD

Iceland's culinary landscape is as diverse as its geological one, although most of the traditional foods center on seafood and lamb products. Reykjavík's seafood restaurants serve fish that may have been caught that very day, but you pay the price: fresh fish is often no less than 1000kr. Many inexpensive restaurants cluster around Tryggvagata by the harbor. The supermarket giant is **Hagkaup** (branch at Laugavegur 59; open Mon.-Thurs. 9am-6pm, Fri. 9am-7pm, Sat. 10am-4pm).

Café Sólon Íslandus, Bankastræti 7 (tel. 126 66). Trendy café with avant-garde art on the walls and artists in the seats. Mostly fish and surprisingly inexpensive. From 480kr. Open Mon.-Fri. 10am-1am, Sat.-Sun. 11am-3am.

Múlakaffi Cafeteria, on Hallarmúli near Ármuli (tel. 377 37). Ask a waiter to translate the traditional Icelandic menu; the low prices make it worthwhile. From 680kr. Open 7am-11pm.

Thailandi, just by Laugavegur 11 on Smiðustígur. Step off the monochromatic streets of Reykjavík into a crowded, bright orange, green, and blue Bangkok alley complete with parking meter. Eight Thai dishes; large servings 490-880kr. Open 11:30am-10pm.

Á Næstu Grösum, Laugavegur 20b (tel. 284 10), entrance on Klapparstígur (1st door on your right coming from Laugavegur). Simple 2nd-floor macrobiotic restaurant—the aroma of boiled lentils and wild rice meets your nostrils as you enter. Iceland's only vegetarian restaurant. Limited selection. Large portions 800kr; small portion without refills 400kr. Open Mon.-Fri. noon-2pm and 6-8pm.

Sveinn Bakari. Many locations of this bakery chain, including one on Laugavegur and one on Lækjargata. Generally open 9am-7pm. *Kleina* (doughnuts) 47kr, orange juice 70kr.

SIGHTS AND ENTERTAINMENT

Your best deal for sights is the **Reykjavík Card,** which allows free and unlimited admission to the swimming pool, the Farm Animal Zoo, the Sculpture Museum, the National Museum, and others. Plus, it gives unlimited free public transportation (which is almost enough reason to buy the card). The card is on sale at the tourist offices for 400kr for 1 day, 500kr for 2, and 600kr for 3. For a better idea of the layout of the city, hike up Skólavörðustígur to the **Hallgrímskirkja** (Hallgrímur's Church), modeled after the ubiquitous basalt columns, and visible from almost anywhere in town. The observation deck in the steeple shows how minuscule Reykjavík is compared to Mount Esja. (Open Tues.-Sun. 10am-6pm; 200kr to ascend). For over 2hrs. of seismographic delight, see the **Volcano Show** at Hellusund 6a (almost a continuation of Skothúsvegur as you walk from the lake; tel. 299 75 for info, 132 30 for bookings). A collection of well-filmed documentaries show Ósvaldur Knudsen and his son Vilhjálmur searching out all volcanic activity on the island; they've filmed the Mývatn eruptions for 17 years. (Shows in English at 10am, 3pm, and 8pm; Sept.-May Tues., Thurs. and Sat. at 8pm. 750kr.)

The **Þjóðminjasafn Íslands** (National Museum of Iceland), at Hringbraut and Suðurgata beside the university, packs a millennium of history into a few well-arranged rooms, written and described only in Icelandic—from disintegrating iron swords of the 10th-century Norse settlers to models of 19th-century fishing boats (open Tues.-Sun. 11am-5pm; mid-Sept. to mid-May Tues., Thurs., and Sat.-Sun. noon-5pm; 200kr). The bright **Listasafn Íslands** (National Gallery of Iceland) by the lake at Fríkirkjuvegur 7 (entrance on Skálholtsstígur) shows Icelandic paintings and frequent international shows (open Jan. to mid-Dec. Tues.-Sun. noon-6pm; free, special exhibits 300kr). **Árbæjarsafn,** a collection of old buildings from all over the country, traces the history of daily life in Iceland. Take bus 10 or 100 to Rofabær and walk back to the end of the street and through the underpass. (Open June-Aug. Tues.-Sun. 10am-6pm. 250kr, seniors and under 16 free.) The **Ásmundur Sveinsson Sculpture Museum,** Sigtún, is a collection of huge concrete paeans to the working man carved by the great Icelandic sculptor (open June-Sept. 10am-4pm, Oct.-May 1-4pm. 200kr). **Light Nights,** Tjarnargata 10e, by the lake and across from the concrete town hall monstrosity, is a multimedia show based on Icelandic history and sagas (performances mid-June to Aug. Thurs.-Sun. at 9pm; 1500kr, students 900kr).

You haven't experienced Iceland without a plunge into one of Reykjavík's geo-thermally heated pools. The outdoor **Laugardalslaug**, on Sundlaugarvegur next to the campground, is the largest (open Mon.-Fri. 7am-9pm, Sat. 7:30am-5:30pm, Sun. 8am-5:30pm; closed holidays; 150kr, children 75kr). Get in touch with your warm, cuddly side next door at the **Icelandic Farm Animal Zoo** in the Laugardalur Park, near the Botanical Garden. See all those cute little sheep that your bus almost ran over, plus horses, cows, and other typical and atypical farm animals. (Open in sum-mer 10am-7pm. 300kr.)

Reykjavík nightlife busts out over the weekend, but have a keg o' krónur handy if you want to join in; alcohol is frighteningly expensive and cover charges are down-right hostile. Expect to pay anywhere from 800-1000kr cover and then 500-600kr for a beer. But if you have strong financial backing, you'll find that the Icelanders really love their weekends. Clubs typically open about 10 or 11pm and go until 3 or 4am. Things are usually hopping by midnight. Try **Casablanca**, Skúlagata 30, a bit out of town but a university hangout and a general meeting point for hipsters (open 11pm-late). **Rosenberg**, Amsturstræti 22b, is right in the middle of town, stuffed in next to Berlin. Twentysomethings rage in a relatively glamorous location. (Open 10pm-3am.) **22**, Laugavegur 22, is an artsy mirrors hangout that's predominantly gay over the weekend (open Thurs. until 1am, Fri. until 3am). **Gaukur Á Stöng**, Tryg-gvagata 22, was Iceland's first pub, and has thrived ever since. Live music often. Weekends are better for meeting young people. (Open 11:30am-2:30pm and 6pm-1am, Fri.-Sat. until 3am.) **Tveir Vinir**, Laugavegur 45, is hidden away in a nonde-script building next to a housing development. However, it's good for live music and the cutting edge of the Reykjavík scene that spawned the Sugarcubes (Thurs.-Sun. 10pm-2am).

■ NEAR REYKJAVÍK

Some of Iceland's stellar attractions are within an hour or two from downtown Reykjavík, and just about every hostel, guesthouse, tourist office, and travel agent sells some kind of tour to get you out there. There is no need, however, to empty your wallet for a guided tour when the scheduled buses are just as good. BSÍ coordi-nates all the scheduled buses, and there are schedules galore at the bus terminal. **Þingvellir National Park**, 50km east of Reykjavík, is home to Iceland's ancient par-liament, the Alþing. Here, at the junction of the European and American tectonic plates, Icelandic warriors, priests, and farmers gathered once a year for almost nine centuries in the shadow of Lögberg (Law Rock) to discuss matters of blood, money, and justice. The river Öxará slices through the lumpy lava fields and deep, jagged fis-sures of the area to the Drekkingarhylur (Drowning Pool), where convicted women were drowned, finally dumping into Lake Þingvallavatn, the largest lake in Iceland. The river, according to legend, changes mysteriously into wine for one hour every year, and portends doom by changing into blood. (Buses from Reykjavík to Þingvel-lir May-Sept. at 1:30pm, returning at 5pm; July-Aug. also at 9am, returning at 6:15pm, 500kr one way.) Call the Ranger's Office at (98) 226 77 for more informa-tion and touring suggestions.

The powerful neighbors **Gullfoss** and **Geysir** lie on the same road, past the lush green valleys and bright red clay paths, and are one of the most popular day trips from Reykjavík. The Geysir area is a rocky, rugged tundra, with steaming, gurgling pools of hot water every few yards. Most are small and are content to bubble away, but two of them are more fickle and ferocious. Geysir, "The Gusher", grandaddy of them all, is the biggest geyser in the world, and their etymological parent. It used to spray water almost 250 ft. into the air, but now sits and simmers quietly, unless large quantities of soap are added to break the surface tension to make it erupt. These eruptions are announced in the papers and at tourist offices. Just a few steps away, the smaller **Strokkur** makes up for its size with the energetic frequency of its eruptions (every 5-10min.). Look for the water beginning to swell and then take cover. Across the road, **Hotel Geysir** (tel. (98) 689 35) provides a free pool offering a sweeping panorama of the valley, and sleeping bag accommodations (with breakfast 1000kr). The hotel also runs the nearby campsite. Get serenaded to sleep by the falling water as you pitch your tent on a soft, grassy field close to all the action. (200kr per person, 100kr per tent; camping open mid-May to mid-Sept.; call ahead.) A tourist shop/grocery store/gas station/bus stop sells all the supplies you'll need to make it through the night. Nine km uproad lies the torrential **Gullfoss** (Golden Falls), so named for the golden hue it acquires from the mud it carries downstream, which is surrounded by a steady mist. You can get as close as you dare, but bring raingear if you're going to get right in the thick of things. (Buses leave for Geysir and Gullfoss May-Sept. at 9 and 11:30am, returning from Gullfoss 12:45 and 4:15pm and from Geysir 2:30pm (except Sun.) and 5pm; Geysir 1040kr, Gullfoss 1100kr.)

On the road to Gullfoss and Geysir, and sheltered in a little green valley, lies **Hveragerði,** the "Flower Town," home to geothermally heated greenhouses which raise such "Icelandic" specialties as bananas and tropical flowers, and a popular vegetarian rheumatism rehabilitation center that utilizes mud baths, hot springs, new-age herbal remedies, and probably mantra-chanting. Hiking in this sheltered area is pleasant since the whipping winds are blocked and the streams are always warm. (Scheduled buses run at 9am, 1, 3, 6, 8, and 11pm; June-Aug. also at 11:30pm, returning 7:50 and 10:50am, and 2:20, 5:20, 7:50 and 10:50pm, 380kr one way.) **Tourist Information** is at Breiðamörk 10 (tel. (98) 345 88). Sleeping bag accommodations are at **Ból Youth Hostel,** Hveramörk 14 (tel. (98) 341 98; open May-Sept.).

Tourists and locals alike flock to **Bláa Lónið,** the Blue Lagoon, in the lunar landscape near Keflavík. But, don't expect to find Brooke Shields lounging on the deck, *this* Blue Lagoon is the runoff from a geothermal power plant, and seems to have curative effects on victims of skin conditions such as eczema and psoriasis. Sitting in the steamy white-blue water and letting your feet sink into the squishy silica muck on the bottom is an experience not to be missed. Be sure to bring lots of shampoo for after your swim or your hair will dry into one large sticky mass. (Open 10am-10pm, 300kr. Buses leave 10:30am and 1:30pm; July-Aug. 1:30pm. Returns 1:20 and 9:20pm; July-Aug. also 4:50pm. 500kr.).

VESTMANN ISLANDS (VESTMANNAEYJAR)

Vaulting boldly and majestically from the icy blue depths of the North Atlantic, the precipitous black cliffs off the Vestmann Islands (named after the Irish slaves of the first Viking settler) are the newest product of the volcanic fury that created Iceland. Forged in fire and baptized in the salty sea water, these 15 jagged monoliths are barely inhabited by humans. However, the steep, angular ledges are a teeming sanctuary of bird life. Rare seabirds from all over the north come here to nest and feed from the rich Icelandic waters churning below. Humans are also fully aware of the plentiful seafood; the town of **Vestmannaeyjar,** on the largest island, **Heimaey,** is one of the most important fishing ports in the country. However, the islanders have had far from an easy life—in the early 17th century, pirates from North Africa rampaged through the town, leaving a bloody trail, killing most of the men and stealing the rest of the population for slaves in Algiers. The town was repopulated and continued to thrive until 1973, when a fiery volcanic fault tore through the northern sector of the island, spewing forth glowing lava and hot ash in an eruption that lasted nearly five months. Through perseverance, ingenuity, and a bit of good fortune, the entire population was evacuated and saved before the volcano **Eldfell** had covered 20% of the town in a lava flow and the rest under 15 ft. of ash. Today, the town stands once again, rebuilt and modernized, framed by still-cooling lava and the black and green mountains that enclose the town and shelter its harbor. However,

ICELAND

buildings, half-crushed by the lava, still stand as a chilling reminder of how quickly a city's borders can be redrawn.

Hiking is possible, and encouraged, on the lumpy grey-brown lava fields. Though much of the lava has already cooled, there are still hot spots near the top. Face the chilling gale that constantly whips across the peak, and hike up the loose sand to the summit for a great feeling of accomplishment and an awe-inspiring view. Bring an egg or a sandwich with you and have yourself a natural boiled egg or hot reuben. (Wrap in a thick layer of aluminum foil and bury in a hot patch. Eggs take nearly 2hrs. to boil, but sandwiches can be ready in a ½hr.) A shot of pure adrenaline and one of the greatest thrills is leaping down the steep sandy crater of the volcano. Dump the stones out of your boots and head over to the country's only **aquarium,** near the gas station, on Heiðarvegur, where you can ogle at the strange and wonderful sealife without having to get your feet wet (open in summer 11am-5pm; 200kr). Wrap up the night with the **Volcanic Film Show,** at the corner of Faxastígur and Heiðarvegur. Two documentaries are shown in English: one on the exploits of an Icelandic sailor and the other on the eruption. Both include plenty of blood and violence (especially against puffins), but no gratuitous sex. (Films 45min. total. June 2pm and 4pm, July-Aug. also 9:15pm. 400kr.)

Getting to Vestmannaeyjar is relatively easy. Five Flugleiðir flights per day arrive from Reykjavík (20min., 8050kr round-trip), but prepare for cancellations in bad weather. The airport sits below Eldfell's twin peak **Helgafell,** a short uphill walk from town. A slower, but much cheaper, option is the **ferry,** a stomach-churning 2½hr. carnival ride, that leaves from **Þorlákshöfn.** (Noon, Fri. and Sun. also 7pm, June-July also Thurs. at 7pm; 1300kr. Buses from Reykjavík connect and leave 1½hr. before the ferry sails; 500kr.) Vestmannaeyjar's **tourist office** is in the Samvinnuferðir-Landsýn travel agency, Vestmannabraut 38 (tel. (98) 112 71; open June-Sept. Mon.-Fri. 9am-6pm, Sat.-Sun. 1-6pm). The **HI hostel,** Faxastígur 38 (tel. (98) 129 15), is a typical Icelandic hostel: meticulously clean, and warm and friendly. (1000kr, nonmembers 1250kr; sheets 280kr. Open June to mid-Sept. Flexible midnight curfew. Kitchen for guests' use, but no breakfast served. Sleeping bags allowed.) Pick up some cheap eats at **Eyja Kjör** supermarket, Hólgata 28, 3min. north of the hostel (open Mon.-Fri. 9am-10pm, Sat. 10am-10pm, Sun. 11am-10pm).

SNÆFELLSNES AND THE WEST FJORDS

Nowhere is the awesome power of the Ice Age glaciers more vividly exposed than in the deeply striated northwest. Raking through the Greenland Sea like the curved talons of a hawk, the Snæfellsnes Peninsula and the Western Fjords (Vestfirðir) are Iceland's most isolated coastal landscapes. With the land quickly rising high above the sea in mossy, snow-covered cliffs, the area affords few places for permanent settlements and the so-called "towns" are few and far between. In the midst of this desolation, beats the heart of Iceland's vital fishing industry; fishermen prowl the waters night and day, trawling for the cod or herring that will make the difference between profit and loss. At the western tip of the Snæfellsnes, the extinct glacier-capped volcano **Snæfellsjökull** provides the dramatic entrance to the mysterious, subterranean inner-world (or so claimed Jules Verne in *Journey to the Center of the Earth*). To the north, **Breiðafjörður,** the bay of a thousand islands (whose exact number is said to be incalculable) provides the border between Snæfellsnes and the magnificent **West Fjords,** where the ever-changing terrain provides a stunning backdrop to its myriad glacial pools and waterfalls.

The best way to reach the fjords (only 150km north of Reykjavík) is by the scheduled buses and ferries, where the views are often gorgeous but the roads are rarely paved. Daily bus departures from Reykjavík (Mon.-Fri. 9am, Sat. 1pm, Fri-Sun. 7pm) serve the entire peninsula. To see Snæfellsjökull, connect to Ólafsvík (3hr. 15min.; 2000kr, 3600kr round-trip) or Hellissandur (3hr. 45min.; 2100kr, 3700kr round-

ICELAND

trip). Ask at the Reykjavík tourist office about sleeping bag accommodation and snow-cat glacier tours. Otherwise, stay on the bus to Stykkishólmur (3hr.; 1850kr, 3300kr round-trip). Daily buses return to Reykjavík from Ólafsvík (Sun.-Fri. 5:30pm, Mon.-Sat. 8am; Hellissandur ½hr. earlier) and from Stykkishólmur (Sun., Tues., Thurs. 6pm, Mon., Wed., Fri. 4pm and 6pm, Sat. 8:30am).

■■■ STYKKISHÓLMUR

The fact that Stykkishólmur is the largest town on the peninsula, and its principal port, only illustrates just how sparsely populated and desolate the Snæfellsnes actually are. The town, however, is rich in folk-history and is home to the mysterious hill, **Helgafell,** the Holy Mountain. According to legend, anyone who climbs this hill for the first time will be granted one wish (provided it is not of evil intent or one of those "world peace" or "10 million more wishes" wishes). In order for the wish to be granted, the wisher must *not* look back on the way up the hill, has to face east while making the wish (bring a compass), and must never reveal the wish to another living soul. The only other real sight in this town is the **church,** which resembles a Viking ship, or perhaps a plastic toy that got caught in a lawnmower.

To get to the **HI Hostel,** Höfðagata 1 (tel. (93) 810 95), follow Aðalgata around to the left and then take another left up the hill. The hostel is pleasant and spotless, offering 50 beds in 1-, 2-, 3-, or 4-bed rooms. **Hótel Egilshús** (tel. (93) 814 50), the high price alternative in the red and white building at the end of Aðalgata (the main street and continuation of the intercity road), offers sleeping bag accommodations (11 rooms; 1900-3000kr). Ask the Reykjavík tourist office or the boat office (tel. (93) 811 20) beside Egilshús about **tours** of Breiðafjörður on the speedboat *Eyjafirðir*.

Your link to the West Fjords is the ferry *Baldur* (tel. (93) 811 20), which chugs across the bay twice a day to the tiny settlement of **Brjánslækur,** to the south of the fjords. The ride is cheap, scenic, and generally calm. (Mid-May to Aug. leaves Stykkishólmur 10am and 4:30pm, returns from Brjánslækur 1 and 7:30pm. 1300kr one-way, 10% off for bus passes and student cards.) On Mondays, Wednesdays and Fridays (mid-June to Aug.), buses run from Ísafjörður to Bránslækur and back (3hr. each way), connecting to the *Baldur's* 1pm arrival and departure. Tuesdays, Thursdays and Saturdays, a similar service travels to the "bird cliffs" of **Látrabjarg** (upon request, 3½hr.), Europe's westernmost point, where daring, swinging cragsmen gather thousands of bird eggs each June. The *Baldur* stops briefly (too short to disembark unless you want to wait for the later ferry) at the small, rocky island of **Flatey,** once home to an ancient monastery where many of Iceland's great works of literature were composed. Today, the island is remarkably well-preserved, with old fisherman's houses dotting the rocky shore. The **Café Vogur** stocks some food and has space for sleeping baggers.

■■■ ÍSAFJÖRÐUR

The best part of Ísafjörður may be the bus ride there. The ride from Brjánslækur carries you through striking natural contrasts. In the highlands, above the fjords, dry rocky plains, sepia-toned trails, and crystal-clear mountain ponds stretch off into the horizon. The scene could be lifted straight from an Arizona desert if it weren't for the small snowbanks that sit like little islands in the dusty, barren expanse. Plunging once again into the emerald-hued glacial rifts, sparkling waterfalls and sapphire fjords wrap around the tiny road. Waterfalls rip through the natural tapestry, slashing thin fissures into the cliffs. The bus stops at the mighty **Dynjandi** waterfall, actually one large waterfall and five smaller ones, before continuing on to Ísafjörður.

The town itself is walled in by the twin cliffs of **Eyrafjall** and **Ernir,** and is the center of all things in the West Fjords. From mid-June through August, buses connect it to Reykjavík via ferry *Baldur* (12hr.; schedules at the BSÍ office and are also mentioned above). Flugleiðir flies daily from Reykjavík to Ísafjörður, while Ernir (tel. (94)

49 00), and Norðurlands (tel. (94) 30 00) provide regular service between Ísafjörður and other Icelandic cities. New bus lines make it possible to get to Akureyri by bus if you time things right (leaves June-Aug. Tues. and Thurs. 11:45am via Homavík and Brú; 12hr.; 5300kr). Otherwise, you'll have to backtrack to Borgarnes.

The main part of Ísafjörður rests on a narrow sliver of land that curves out into **Skutulsfjörður,** forming a natural harbor. There are no HI hostels, but there is an excellent **summer hotel,** in a converted schoolhouse, the *Menntaskólin á Ísafirði,* a two-story white building with red trim and a funky yellow statue out front. The sleeping bag accommodations range from a well-equipped double (2 desks, a mirror, and a sink) to a dorm-like schoolroom. Everything is tidy and friendly, and the management is helpful (tel. (94) 38 76; doubles 1650kr per person, dorms 800kr; open mid-June to Aug.). Beside the hotel is a small, quiet **campsite** (350kr per 1-person tent, 150kr per additional person). There are two **guest houses** in town, **Austurstræti 7** (tel. (98) 38 68; sleeping bag accommodation 800kr, singles 1500kr) and **Föndurloftið,** above a little tourist shop at Mjallargötu 5 (tel. (94) 36 59; sleeping bag accommodation 1000kr, bed 1500kr). The **tourist office** is at Hafnarstræti 8 (tel. (94) 51 21; open Mon.-Fri. 8am-6pm, Sat.-Sun. 10am-2pm). The café-restaurant **Frabær,** on Hafnarstræti at the main intersection, serves all types of cheap, greasy food (meals from 700kr) and the **Hotel Ísafjörður** has a relatively cheap tourist menu (lunches from 600kr, dinner from 900-1500kr; 10% off if staying at the summer hotel). Two supermarkets, **Kaupfélag** (at the corner of Austurvegur and Hafnarstræti) and **Björnsbuð** (on Silfurgata, just off of Hafnarstræti; open Mon.-Thurs. 9am-12:30pm and 1-6pm, Fri. 9am-12:30pm and 1-7pm, Sat. 10am-4pm, Sun. 1-4pm) stock all the bread, cheese, pasta, and soda that the strapped-for-cash desire. After you realize that there's really nothing to do in Ísafjörður besides watch the cliffs and the ships, there are two ways to tour the **Ísafjarðarjúp** (the West Fjord's main inlet) and the fjords branching off of it: the regular ferry *Fagranes* (tel. (94) 31 55; full-day tour 2000kr, reservations necessary) and the speedboat *Eyjalín* (a 3½hr. tour for 2800kr, refreshments included; reserve ahead). Inquire at the tourist office.

NORTH ICELAND (NORÐURLAND)

Gently caressing the harsh boundary of the north, the arctic circle, and basking in the glow of the midnight sun, North Iceland has a paradoxically mild climate. Thanks to a well-placed mountain range and warm southern currents, the weather is often nicer than on the sometimes bleary and cloudy south shore. Roads connecting the north to the west are lined with hillside fields where the sturdy Iceland horse still runs unhindered. Rugged, long-haired sheep, and the occasional cow, are often seen tramping across grass-covered boulders, past the cobweb of short, black, stone fences that radiate from little barns and the turf-covered farmhouses that are still built in the way of the ancient Norse settlers. Volcanic activity has turned much of the north into a wild melee of steam and stone, but wispy birch forests claim many patches of the still fertile land.

■■■ AKUREYRI

Akureyri, with slightly less than 15,000 inhabitants, is the second largest city in Iceland and the hub of the north. The snow-capped mountains that define the city limits rise high above the city skyline, at once asserting nature's dominance over the isolated city, and sheltering it from nature's chilling effects. The city's **Lystigarður** (botanical garden), on Eyrarlandsvegur, provides a welcome respite from the area's stark and often treeless surroundings. The sweet aroma of lush flora and the calming fountains and streams can easily transform a brief visit into a full afternoon. Originally designed as simply a grove of trees, the garden has developed into a sanctuary for many colorful varieties of arctic plants. (Open June-Sept. Mon.-Fri. 9am-9pm,

Sat.-Sun. 10am-9pm. Free.) A short jaunt down the hill takes you to the **Minjasafn Akureyrar** (folk museum), Aðalstræti 58, a placid little building that chronicles the town's history from early settlements to the rise of Danish trade, the growth of the cooperative movement, and the literary age that fostered some of Iceland's most famous poets (open June-Aug. 11am-5pm; 200kr).

Akureyri is easily accessible by land and by air. **Buses** connect it to Reykjavík all year, leaving Reykjavík at 8am and Akureyri at 9:30am (6½hr., 3500kr one-way, 6700kr round-trip); June to August, extra evening buses shuttle in both directions (5pm). **Flugleiðir** flies to and from Reykjavík five times a day (50min., 6530kr one-way) while **Flugfélag Norðurlands** flies direct from Keflavík to Akureyri (5 per week) and from Akureyri to smaller towns. Akureyri also makes a good base for exploring northern Iceland's other attractions; ask about getting to the islands of **Hrísey**, in the fjord north of Akureyri, and **Grímsey**, Iceland's only territory north of the arctic circle, or to Europe's most powerful waterfall at **Dettifoss** and the cliffs of **Ásbyrgi** and **Hljóðaklettar.** Find your way through this prodigious list of place names at the **tourist office,** Hafnarstræti 82 (tel. (96) 277 33; open Mon.-Fri. 7:30am-9pm, Sat.-Sun. 7:30-11:30am and 3-6:30pm; Sept.-May Mon.-Fri. 8:30am-5pm). This is the same building as the **bus station** at the south end of town. Pick up an **SVA** bus schedule when you're there (75kr per ride) or hoof it around while you're still young. The **post office/telephone building** is farther north at Hafnarstræti 108 (open Mon.-Fri. 9am-4:30pm; phones open Mon.-Fri. 9am-6pm, Sat. 10am-3pm). Some **American Express** services can be found at **Úrval-Útsýn Travel,** Ráðhústorgi 3 (right in the town center, across from the bank). They will hold mail, and clear card-member's personal checks (for cashing at the nearby bank), but won't sell or cash traveler's checks nor accept wire money (go to the bank instead).

Akureyri has two **HI hostels;** the closest is a 20min. walk from the bus station at Stórholt 1 (tel. (96) 236 57). Go left (facing the water) on Drottningarbraut, the busy street along the shore; it will change into Glerágata after the town center and again into Horgárbraut before you get to a small traffic circle, and Stórholt is on the right. The hostel is on the second floor, has comfortable doubles and a well-equipped kitchen. (Reception 8am-11:30pm, 11:30pm curfew is flexible. 1000kr, nonmembers 1100kr.) A second hostel is 3km north of town in Lónsá. If you call (tel. (96) 250 37), the owners will pick you up (same prices). Clean guesthouses, right in the center of town, have **sleeping bag accommodations** for 1200kr, if the rooms are unoccupied at the higher bed and breakfast rate; the tourist office has an exhaustive list. Try friendly **Skala,** Skipgata 1, 3rd floor (tel. (96) 226 97) or **Ás,** Hafnarstræti 77, just as you step off the bus (tel. (96) 122 49). The huge, sprawling **campsite** downtown is new and takes up most of Þórunnarstræti, beside the outdoor swimming pool (400kr per person). Try **Bautinn,** Hafnarstræti 92, which serves meals with soup and salad (open 9am-11pm, from 1050kr) or head across the street to **Súlnaberg Cafeteria,** which does serve-it-up meat, fish, and sandwiches (fish from 850kr, meat from 1050kr, sandwiches from 350kr). The mighty **Hagkaup** superstore, at Norðurgata and Grenivellir has the cheapest prices on everything from baked beans to boxer shorts, but is a bit remote (open Mon.-Fri. 9am-9pm, Sat. 10am-6pm, Sun. noon-7pm). Red, orange, and purple line buses bring you right to the door.

■ ■ ■ MÝVATN

The beauty and fury of Iceland's fiery past explodes into view in the area surrounding Mývatn, a shallow volcanic lake 100km east of Akureyri. Buses there pass the turbulent turquoise waters of **Goðafoss,** the waterfall of the pagan gods. It was here, in the year 1000, that the Icelanders sent the symbols of the ancient Viking gods to their doom, down into the churning deep, in order to better welcome Christianity. Mývatn, the lake, sits placidly among the rocky tumult surrounding it. Its clear, cool waters reflect the stark black islands that pierce through its mirrored skin, as its serpentine coastline wriggles and writhes its way through the countryside. Directly to the west of the lake, the gnarled dark towers of the **Dimmuborgir** disappear over the hills. Scientists still can only theorize as to how these mysterious lava formations came into existence. To the north, dark red lava fields still steam from the most recent eruption and a bright white lagoon, not unlike Bláa Lonið (see Near Reykjavík, above), surrounds the Krafla geothermal power plant. Farther on, over the small mountain range, is one of Iceland's most hellish wonders, **Devil's Kitchen.** Here, amidst a backdrop of red, orange, and yellow mountains, the air is thick with the stink of sulfur, putrification, and decay. The horrid stench combines with the thick jets of steam to create an atmosphere of death and disease like Puritan minister Jonathan Edwards's frightening vision of damnation. Instead of fire and brimstone, massive holes in the earth belch and bubble scalding, fetid blue sludge. Best heed the posted warnings and stay to the marked paths, lest you fall into the boiling sulfur pits below. Escape, ye sinners, from the hands of this angry god to the surrounding woods and streams, or descend further to the giant craters of the **Krafla** volcano, where you can bathe in the warm lake **Víti** (hell).

On foot, you'll need several days to appreciate all the area's sights, but renting a bicycle will speed your progress considerably. **Mountain bike rental** can be found at the gas station in front of the Hótel Reynihlíð (900kr per ½day (6hrs.), 1500kr per full day. 2000kr deposit and passport required). For those short on time but long on cash, regular one-day bus tours are available that leave daily from Akureyri (mid-May to Sept. 8:15am; 4000kr, 10% off with bus pass). Regular buses depart for Mývatn daily from Akureyri (May-July 8:15am, July-August 8pm; returns May-July 4:15pm, July-Aug. 8am and 6pm; 2hrs.; 1100kr).

Buses stop at the small communities of **Skútustaðir** on the southern side, and the preferable **Reykjahlíð,** on the northern side, in the thick of it all. Camp in among the lichen-stained lava rocks, but be wary of their past. It is said that long ago, an old man and his wife went to bring porridge to the Virgin Mary by means of an infinitely long ladder that reached all the way up to Heaven. Midway up, vertigo overtook them. They lost their balance and fell, plummeting the long way to the hard earth below them. The impact of landing splattered their brains and the porridge far over the land. Today, the brains have turned into white lichen and the porridge into yellow lichen. So, look out for falling objects if you camp by the rocks. (Tel. (96) 441 03; both sites 400kr per person.) Sleeping bag accommodation is readily available at both towns. Stay at **Guesthouse Skútustaðir** (tel. (96) 442 12; 900kr) or at the **campsite** in Reykjahlíð which offers cozy little log cabins that each sleep four people and also a larger complex that looks shabby from the outside, but is ultra-spiffy on the inside and has doubles. Cooking facilities available. (Beds from 1200kr.) Information on accommodations and tours is available from the Hótel Reynihlíð, the camping site, and at Eldá travel agency (tel. (96) 442 20), 300m to the left of the hotel, by the lake (open summer 10am-3pm, winter Mon., Wed., Fri. 10:30am-3pm).

EAST ICELAND (AUSTURLAND)

Crossing the inland road to East Iceland from Akureyri, you may think you'll never see vegetation again. Dull, flat planes of lifeless earth stretch into the horizon, the only terrain being the scattered stones and the rolling hills of unbroken beige. Suddenly, however, glacial rivers appear, bringing water and life to the barren wastelands. Grasses and bushes spring from the earth, blossoming into leafy fields and open pastures. These areas are little used by the East Icelanders, who cling to the bristling fjördside villages, still dependent on the fishing industry. Major ports and minor cities dot the coastline, but for the most part, all's quiet on the eastern front.

■■■ EGILSSTAÐIR

The main town in the east is landlocked Egilsstaðir, at the northern tip of the narrow lake **Lögurinn,** actually just a widening of the river Lagarfljót. According to the locals, this lake is home to a monster, rarely sighted in recent times, but that once wreaked much havoc. The **Kaupfélag Héraðsbúa supermarket** and its parking lot make a good reference point; just uphill are the post office and bank, while the **tourist office** (tel. (97) 123 20; open June-Sept. Mon.-Sun. 9am-5pm and 7-11pm) and **campsite** (400kr per person) are at the far end of the parking lot. Looking lakewards from the Kaupfélag, you can easily spot red-roofed **Egilsstaðir Farm,** a 5- to 10-min. walk away, which has **sleeping bag accommodations** for 1200kr (tel. (97) 111 14). Other sleeping bag accommodations can be found at the **campsite,** which runs a small guesthouse with warm, tidy rooms, a TV, toilet, and small kitchen (1200kr). Egilsstaðir is the opposite node of the bus ring from Reykjavík, with service to Akureyri (3000kr) and Höfn. (3000kr, 5-6hr. Leaves Höfn 9am, Egilsstaðir 4pm. Mid-May to mid-June and Sept. 3-4 per week; mid-June to Aug. daily.) Planes arrive from Reykjavík (3-4 per day) and Akureyri (1 per day).

■■■ SEYÐISFJÖRÐUR

Twenty-six km from Egilsstaðir, Seyðisfjörður's curving, sheltered fjord harbors Iceland's only international car and passenger ferry, the *Norröna* (tel. (97) 211 11; in Reykjavík (91) 62 63 62; in U.S. through Eurocruises, tel. (800) 688-3876). The ship sails to Tórshavn in the Faroe Islands (16hr., about US$190, with 25% student discounts), and continues to Bergen (Norway, 20,450kr one way), and Hanstholm (Denmark, 23,950kr one way). (Arrives Seyðisfjörður June-Aug. Thurs. at 8am, departing at noon.) Seyðisfjörður's excellent **HI hostel** (tel. (97) 214 10) is in the pink house on the north shore of the fjord and has all the *Twin Peaks* episodes on video (1000kr, nonmembers 1250kr; sheets 350kr; make reservations on nights before and after the ferry). Buses connect Egilsstaðir and Seyðisfjörður over a fog-bound pass that sometimes stays snowy all summer. (740kr one way, Mon.-Fri. leaving Seyðisfjörður between 8:30 and 9:30am, check hostel or ferry office for exact times. Egilsstaðir between 9:30 and 10:30am, check tourist office for times, late June- late Aug. also Sat.-Sun. at 2:45pm and 4:15pm; extra service Wed.-Thurs.)

■■■ THE EASTERN COAST

The coast between Egilsstaðir and Höfn will make you glad you came east. Lush fields, the sparkling green of a serpent's eye, envelop the area surrounding Egilsstaðir. Small ravines dart under the twisting road, carrying crystalline water down from the high mountains. The little valleys are quickly swallowed up by the dark coastal crags, looming ominously over the grey-blue ocean, like a row of judges before a courtroom. Buses that stop at **Reyðarfjörður** take Highway 96, which meanders through small fjord villages before joining Highway 1 at **Breiðalsvík.** There are two isolated **HI hostels** along the way, at Berunes (off Highway 1; tel. (97) 889 88; 20 beds) and at Stafafell (tel. (97) 817 17; 45 beds).

SOUTHERN ICELAND (SUÐURLAND)

The southern coast of Iceland washes down like a green wave from the mountains and glaciers of the interior. Long, flat pastures made from the accumulated silt of great ancient glacial rivers provide ample space for sheep, horses, cows, and the occasional farmer to mosey around. Dozens of spidery waterfalls cascade over the rocky caves and columns where the elves and trolls make their homes. Commerce and tourism dominate the local economies, diminishing the importance of fishing and increasing the importance of black sand beaches and (mostly) good weather.

■■■ HÖFN

This treacherous fishing town (whose harbor frequently capsizes errant ships) links the southern coast to the eastern fjords; it's the terminus for buses from both Egilsstaðir (see above) and Reykjavík (leaves Reykjavík 8:30am, Höfn 9am; mid-Sept. to May Sun., Tues., and Fri. leaves Reykjavík 8:30am, Höfn 10am; 9-10hr., 3900kr), as well as the launching point for tours to **Vatnajökull** (Europe's largest glacier), which dwarfs the town and shimmers a robust gold at sunset. The **campsite** (on your left as you come into town) doubles as a **tourist information center** (tel. (97) 817 01; open June-Sept.) and intercity bus stop. Look on your right for cheap **sleeping bag accommodations** in the local theater on the main road at Hafnarbraut 17 (tel. (97) 811 61; open June to mid-Sept. Sun.-Thurs.). Further along the street is the **HI youth hostel,** Hafnarbraut 8, which is cramped and a bit claustrophobic; prepare to rub elbows as you use the kitchen, the TV, the bedroom, etc. (tel. (97) 817 36; reception open 7:30-11:30am and 5-11:30pm; 1000kr, nonmembers 1250kr; open mid-May to mid-Sept.; 30 beds).

■■■ SKAFTAFELL PARK

Amid the icy tongues of the Vatnajökull glacier are the numerous hiking paths and thick birch forests of Skaftafell National Park. As an Icelandic national park, it is little more than just a small part of the all-encompassing landscape that has had some trails built on it. However, following these trails will lead you through dense greenery and Iceland's stunted trees, and past spectacular waterfalls and rock formations. The most impressive of these is **Svartifon,** "Black Falls", where glacial water pours out over vaulting basalt columns which resemble the pipes of an immense Brobdingnagian organ. In the background, snow-covered peaks block the sun and keep much of the park in the deep-freeze. The park is just off Highway 1 (3hrs. west of Höfn; buses from Reykjavík 1860kr, from Höfn 500kr). The extremely popular and often quite crowded **campsite** serves as home base for exploration of the park (tel. (97) 816 27; 400kr per person, 100kr for showers) and also houses a well-stocked information center and a comprehensive grocery store. The facilities are wheelchair accessible, but the terrain often isn't. Nearby, the farmhouse **Bolti** (tel. (97) 816 26) offers all the comforts of home and year-round sleeping bag accommodation from 1300kr. Between Skaftafell and Höfn, buses stop at the glacial lake **Jökulsárlón,** where floating blue icebergs give you an idea what Henry Moore would have sculpted if he were an Eskimo. Boat tours are available, but steer clear of any boats named *Titanic.*

■■■ THE SOUTHERN COAST

The coastline to Reykjavík is mostly owned by farmers whose sheep graze freely on the slopes. The Reykjavík-Höfn bus stops at every little town. There are **HI youth hostels** in **Reynisbrekka** (tel. (98) 711 06), **Fljótsdalvr** (tel. (98) 784 98), **Leirubakki** (tel. (98) 765 91), and **Selfoss** (tel. (98) 688 31). Ask about sleeping bag accommodations in **Vík** or in the farm country near **Selfoss,** center of Iceland's dairy industry.

THE INTERIOR

The home of elves, trolls, bandits, and backpackers, Iceland's interior is the most forbidding and desolate wilderness in Europe. Today, as 1000 years ago, people rarely venture into the deepest of the interior and you could easily walk for days without seeing a settlement. There are no paved roads, bridges, markets, or gas stations. Limitless stretches of sand rise into mountains, peaked with glaciers, that dissolve into waterfalls, that melt into rivers. Most travel here is done by special 4-

ICELAND

wheel-drive buses that plow through rivers. Jeeps and vans with huge tires and 30ft. tall antennas kick up clouds of reddish dust. Alien landscapes of craters and lava are so out of this world that Apollo astronauts trained here for lunar landings. Valleys fill with sand as black as the night that, in the summer, never comes, and in the winter, never leaves.

An oasis in the long dry plains of the interior, the lush green birches of **Þórsmörk** (Thor's Forest) are the most popular vacation spot for tourists and locals alike. An idyllic camping spot (450kr per person) and **sleeping bag accommodations** (1200kr) are run by the Iceland touring club, but can often be filled up. Call ahead of time to reserve a spot (tel. (91) 67 85 45). Save up your cash for the 200kr hot showers. A four-day hike from Þórsmörk or a 3hr. bus ride from Reykjavík, the technicolor rhyolite mountains of **Landmannalaugar** rise into the distance. Bright crimson, orange, and gold streaks cut great swaths of color across the stone and highlight the many snowfields of the area. Hot springs and streams provide a great place to relax after a long day. The **campsite** is, again, run by the Iceland Touring Club (400kr per person) and large bunkrooms with **sleeping bag accommodation** are available (1100kr). Call the touring club for more info. Further on, past Landmannalaugar is the **Eldgjá** volcanic fissure, a 40km gash that once produced almost 300 sq. miles of lava. On the western side, a spectacular double-waterfall had cut a land bridge out of the stone, until a flood in 1993 washed it away. Other attractions in the interior are the volcano **Hekla** (in medieval times thought to be the entrance to Hell) and the summer-skiing at **Kerlingarfjöll,** west of Mýrdalsjökull. Interior routes to Akureyri are available, but only in guided-tour form. Consult BSÍ Travel in Reykjavík for more information (tel. (91) 223 00) and reservations. (Buses to Þórsmörk in summer 8:30am and Mon.-Thurs. also 5pm; return to Reykjavík 3:30pm and Mon.-Thurs. also 8am; 3½hrs; 4600kr round-trip. To Landmannalaugar 8:30am, return from Reykjavík 2:30pm; 4½hrs.; 5400kr round-trip. To Eldgjá passing through Landmannalaugar and continuing to Skaftafell; from Reykjavík 8:20am, return from Skaftafell 8am; 7½hrs.; 5400kr one way.)

Any traveler in the interior should know some basic safety precautions. You *must* pack in all food and gas needed for your trip since there are *no* places to buy anything. Anyone driving in the interior should get a copy of *Mountain Roads* (available at most tourist offices), which details all the "cans" and "cannots" of interior driving. Never venture out without a detailed map, an all-season sleeping bag, a sturdy windproof tent, and a compass. Several companies can help you out by organizing interior tours. **Útivist,** Hallveigarstig 1, P.O. Box 236, 121 Reykjavík (tel. (91) 614 330), or **Austurland Travel,** Draghals 6, 110 Reykjavík (tel. (91) 67 85 45). Without professional guidance, prepare well. The **Ferðafélag Íslands** (Icelandic Touring Club), at Mörkinni 6, 108 Reykjavík (tel. (91) 68 25 33), can help. **Landmælingar Íslands** (the Iceland Geodetic Survey) runs a complete and up-to-date map shop at Laugavegur 178 in Reykjavík (tel. (91) 68 09 99; open Mon.-Fri. 9am-6pm). Leave an itinerary with the **Landssamband Hjálparsveita Skáta** (Association of Icelandic Rescue Teams) at Snorrabraut 60, above the Skátabúðin camping store, in Reykjavík (tel. (91) 250 22; 24-hr. hotline (91) 68 60 68; open Mon.-Fri. 9am-5pm). There are many huts in the interior (marked on good maps) and popular places like Þórsmörk and Landmannalaugar have campsites.

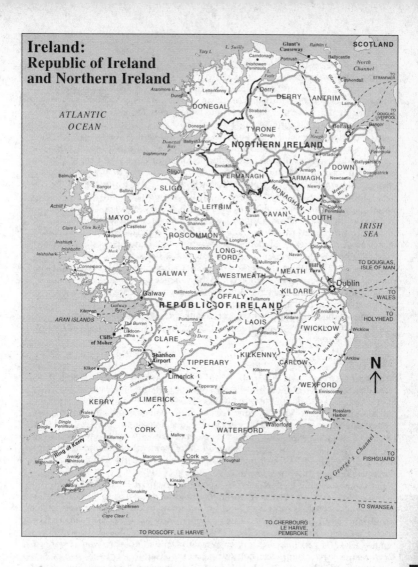

Ireland:
Republic of Ireland
and Northern Ireland

Ireland (Éire and Northern Ireland)

US$1 = IR£0.64 (pounds, or IEP)
CDN$1 = IR£0.47
UK£1 = IR£1.01
AUS$1 = IR£.49
NZ$1 = IR£0.39
SAR1 = IR£0.17
Country Code: 353

IR£1 = US$1.57
IR£1 = CDN$2.11
IR£1 = UK£0.99
IR£1 = AUS$2.06
IR£1 = NZ$2.60
IR£1 = SAR5.61
International Dialing Prefix:00

IRELAND

Shrouded in the mists of stereotype, Ireland has struggled to come to terms with its identity, both within the island and on the world stage. Many of those stereotypes have some basis in truth: the rain, most of the green fields, and friendly people. Nonetheless Ireland, north and south, are modern states with an ever-increasing urban culture that ties cities like Dublin and Belfast more to major European centers than to the rolling hills and unspoiled countryside.

In 1171, Henry II claimed the Emerald Isle for the English throne in a less-than-decisive victory, and both English feudal and Gaelic Irish influences split Ireland during the Middle Ages. Following the Reformation in England, the defiant Catholic population was ruthlessly suppressed by the English. The trail to independence and emancipation was blazed by Daniel O'Connell in the 1830s; by the turn of the century, nationalist Fenians agitated passionately for home rule. Following the abortive proclamation of the Irish Republic in Easter 1916, a five-year Anglo-Irish War ended in the partition of the island into the Irish Free State and Northern Ireland, part of the United Kingdom. In 1949, the Free State officially proclaimed itself the Republic of Ireland (*Éire* in Gaelic), an independent country that nonetheless still stakes a territorial claim over the six counties that remain under British rule.

By the end of the 1960s, the tension between Catholic Nationalists and Protestant Unionists in Northern Ireland erupted into the violence that tragically define the Ireland of today. In recent years, the British and Irish governments' attempts to defuse the situation have only led to indiscriminate sectarian attacks by paramilitaries on both sides of the debate in Northern Ireland and on both sides of the border.

For more detailed coverage of Ireland, snag a copy of *Let's Go: Ireland* or *Let's Go: Britain & Ireland.*

GETTING THERE

Brittany Ferries, Tourist House, 42 Grand Parade, Cork (tel. (021) 27 78 01), sail from Roscoff, France (14hr.). **Irish Ferries** sail from quai Joseph Hamel, Cherbourg, France (tel. 33 44 28 96) to Rosslare (16hr. overnight; 390-685F, students 310-605F) and to Cork (18½hr. overnight, same prices). From quai de Southampton, Le Havre, France, the same company sails to Rosslare (20hr. overnight, Jan.-April and Oct.-Dec. 390F, students 475F; May-June and Sept. 500F, students 420F; July 1-8 and Aug. 15-31 555F, students 475F; July 10-Aug. 14 685F, students 605F) and Cork (June-Aug. 1 per week, 20½hr. overnight, same prices as Rosslare). From either port, Eurailpass holders may board free after paying a tax (30F).

For those traveling to Ireland from Great Britain, **Irish Ferries/B&I Line** (tel. (01646) 68 41 61) sail twice daily from Pembroke Dock, Wales to Rosslare. (Walk-on passengers UK£20 each way; UK£198 return with car.) **Sealink ferries** (tel. (01348) 87 28 81 or 87 36 72) sail twice daily to Rosslare from Fishguard Harbor, also in Wales. (3½hr. Foot passengers single UK£20, return UK£40; car with 5 passengers UK£104.) Sealink also runs four **catamarans** to Rosslare daily. **Swansea-Cork ferries** leave from Keys Dock, Swansea in Wales to Cork (10hr.; foot passengers UK£20-26, bikes UK£7; call (01792) 45 61 16 for info). Two ferry lines operate out of Holyhead, Wales. **B&I** leaves Holyhead for Dublin (4hr.; UK£21-26; June to mid-July and Sept. to mid-Oct. UK£17-20; low season UK£16-18). Call B&I in Liverpool at (0151) 227 31 31 to book tickets, or in Holyhead at (01407) 76 02 22 or 76 02 23 for inquiries only. Tickets are available from the B&I office in the Holyhead train station (open when the ship is in, usually 12:30-3:30am and 12:30-3:30pm), and from most travel agents on the North Wales coast, or any tourist office in North Wales. **Sealink** (tel. (01407) 76 67 65) has a 24hr. booking office at the train station on Turkeyshore Rd. Ferries sail to **Dún Laoghaire** in Ireland (3½hr.) with bus connections to nearby Dublin. (UK£21-26; June to mid-July and Sept. to mid-Oct. UK£17-20; low season UK£16-18). Sealink runs a high-tech **catamaran** between Holyhead and Dun Laoghaire (1¼hr., UK£4 more than standard slow ferry).

Stena-Sealink ferries (Stranraer tel. (01776) 22 62) shuttle from Stranraer, Scotland, to Larne, Northern Ireland (2½hr.; UK£18, students UK£13, seniors and children UK£8). **P&O Ferries** (Carnryan tel. (015812) 276) run between Carnryan,

Scotland and Larne. (UK£18, seniors and children UK£9.) The **Hoverspeed Seacat** leaves Stranraer (tel. (01776) 22 55) and arrives in Belfast (tel. (01232) 31 20 02; 1½hr.; UK£18-19, seniors and students UK£14-15, ages 4-15 UK£9-10, bikes and tykes under 4 free).

Many **flights** of British Airways, Aer Lingus, British Midlands, Manx Air, and Ryan Air hop between Gatwick, Stansted, Heathrow, Luton, Manchester, Birmingham, Liverpool, and Glasgow airports (in Britain) and Dublin, Shannon, Cork, Kerry, Galway, Knock, Sligo, Waterford, and Belfast.

GETTING AROUND

Trains run by **Iarnród Éireann (Irish Rail)** branch out from Dublin to larger cities, but there is limited service. For schedule information, pick up an *InterCity Rail Traveler's Guide* (50p), available at most train stations. By far the most useful student travel pass in Ireland is the **Travelsave stamp,** available from USIT (see Dublin, below) with an ISIC and IR£7. Affixed to your ISIC, this stamp decreases single fares by about 50% on national rail and 15% on bus services in Ireland (except fares less than IR£1). **Eurailpass** is valid on trains in Ireland.

Buses in the Republic of Ireland, operated by **Bus Éireann** (tel. (01) 284 47 68), reach more destinations than trains. The company operates both long-distance **Expressway** buses, which link larger cities, and **provincial** buses, which serve the countryside and smaller towns. The bus timetable book (50p) is available at Busáras in Dublin. Ireland has its share of **Rambler** tickets, but you have to move fast to make them pay off.

Northern Ireland Railways (tel. (01232) 89 94 11) service isn't extensive, but covers the northeastern coastal region well. The **Travelsave** stamp (UK£5.50) is valid on this rail line and is available at the Student Travel Office, 136 Fountain St., Belfast. It offers 50% off all trains and 15% off bus fares over UK£1. **Ulsterbus**, Oxford St., Belfast (tel. (01232) 32 00 11), runs service throughout the province; coverage expands in summer, when open-top buses cover a northeastern coastal route. Full- and half-day tours leave for key tourist spots from Belfast.

You can rent bikes from **Raleigh Rent-a-Bike** shops almost anywhere in the country (IR£7 per day, IR£30 per week; IR£40 deposit). Their one-way rental plan allows you to rent a bike at one shop and drop it off at any of eight others for IR£42 per week. A list of Raleigh dealers is available at most tourist offices and bike shops. Ireland offers rugged hills and small mountains to its **hikers.** The best hiking maps are the Ordnance Survey ½in.-to-1mi. series (IR£3.70), available at tourist offices.

IRELAND ESSENTIALS

Bord Fáilte (the Irish Tourist Board) operates a nationwide network of offices, selling maps and detailed local guidebooks. They also distribute the free *Calendar of Events* in Ireland. Their accommodations booking service (locally IR£1, nationwide IR£2; deposit 10%) can be helpful, but do your homework: many fine hostels and B&Bs are not "approved," so the tourist office can't tell you about them.

Weather in Ireland is both temperate (summer temperatures 10-27°C or 50-80°F) and temperamental. Keep a rain poncho or umbrella handy, and carry a warm sweater, as warm sunshine often suddenly yields to chilly dampness.

Ireland has nine bank holidays: New Year's Day, St. Patrick's Day (March 17), Good Friday (April 14, 1995), Easter Monday (April 17, 1995), first Monday in June (June 5), First Monday in August (Aug. 7), last Monday in October (Oct. 30), Christmas Day (Dec. 25), and St. Stephen's Day (Dec. 26). Also check for local half-day holidays, when banks and stores close. **Banks** are generally open from Monday to Friday 10am to 12:30pm and 1:30 to 3pm; in Dublin, banks stay open until 5pm on Thursday. To make **international direct calls** from the Republic of Ireland, dial the **international access code:** 00; then the country code, area code, and local number. You can access an international operator at 114. AT&T's **USA Direct** can be reached at 1 800 550 000; MCI's **WorldPhone** at 1 800 55 10 01; **SprintExpress** at 1 800 55 20 01; **Canada Direct** 1 800 55 50 01; **BT Direct** 1 800 55 00 44; **Austra-**

lia **Direct** 1 800 55 00 61; and **SA Direct** 1 800 55 00 27. Dial 190 for the operator and 1190 for directory inquiries. Dial 999 in an **emergency.**

Accommodations, Camping, and Food Hostelling is the way to go in Ireland. **An Óige,** the Irish Hostelling International affiliate, runs 44 hostels nation-wide. The annually-updated *An Óige Handbook* (IR£1.50) lists, locates, and describes all the An Óige hostels; its standard pricing system isn't always followed by all the hostels listed, however. Recently, two non-HI hostel organizations in Ireland merged to form **IHH.** IHH hostels have no lockout or curfew, accept all ages, require no membership card, and have a mellow atmosphere; all are Bord Fáilte-approved. **B&Bs** are a wonderful, luxurious break from hostelling. Expect to pay IR£10-18 for singles and IR£20-30 for doubles. "Full Irish breakfasts"—eggs, bacon, sausage, bread, cereal, orange juice, and coffee or tea—are often filling enough to get you through until dinner.

Camping in Irish State Forests and National Parks is not allowed; camping on public land is allowed only if there is no official campsite in the area. Most caravan and camping parks are open from April through October, though some stay open year-round. The Ireland Accommodation Guide, published by Bord Fáilte and available at all tourist offices (IR£4), lists all approved campgrounds in the Republic.

Pubs in Ireland are the forum for banter, singing, and *craic* (KRAK), meaning simply "a good time." In the evening, many pubs play impromptu or organized traditional music; there's quite a bit of variety to these watering holes. Aside from the Holy Trinity, **Guinness,** a rich, dark stout, is the most revered thing in Ireland. **Irish coffee** is sweetened with brown sugar and whipped cream and laced with Irish whiskey, which is sweeter and more stinging than its Scotch counterpart. Pubs are generally open Monday to Saturday 10:30am to 11:30pm (11pm in winter), Sunday 12:30 to 2pm and 4 to 11pm.

Food in Ireland is expensive, especially in restaurants. The basics—and that is what you'll get—are simple and filling. Soda bread is delicious and will keep for about a week, and Irish dairy products are addictive. Vegetarianism has yet to make a major impact in Ireland (although this is changing fast); expect meat, especially lamb, pork, bacon, and some form of beef an the average menu.

■■■ DUBLIN

Dublin is where the Irish nation meets international urban trends, traditions, and economies, and where (counting the suburbs) over a third of the Republic's population resides. Its buildings belong to 18th-century England, but its culture belongs to the Dubliners: the life of packed pubs, long walks, and walk-ups recorded in James Joyce's *Dubliners* and *Ulysses*. Subcultures flourish here in a way they couldn't in the rest of the country, making Dublin's social life both more hidden and more varied than the rest of Ireland's, while the economics of trade, transport, and education draw the young here from other counties, just as they did 100 years ago.

ORIENTATION AND PRACTICAL INFORMATION

The **River Liffey** cuts central Dublin in half. Most of the best food and famous sights stick to the **South Side,** though plenty of hostels (and the bus station) sprout up in the **North Side.** When streets split into "Upper" and "Lower" Such-and-Such Street, "Lower" is always closer to the mouth of the Liffey. Be safety-conscious on the far North Side, in parks at night, and on the far west of the South Side around the Guinness Brewery; compared to most of Ireland, Dublin has plenty of crime. Most of the city's attractions are located on or close to the north-south axis comprised of O'Connell St. on the North Side, which turns into Westmoreland St. after it crosses the Liffey, leading to Grafton St., and ending on St. Stephen's Green.

Tourist Office: Main Office: 14 Upper O'Connell St. (tel. 284 47 68). From Connolly Station, follow Talbot St. Accommodations service (IR£1 fee and 10% book-

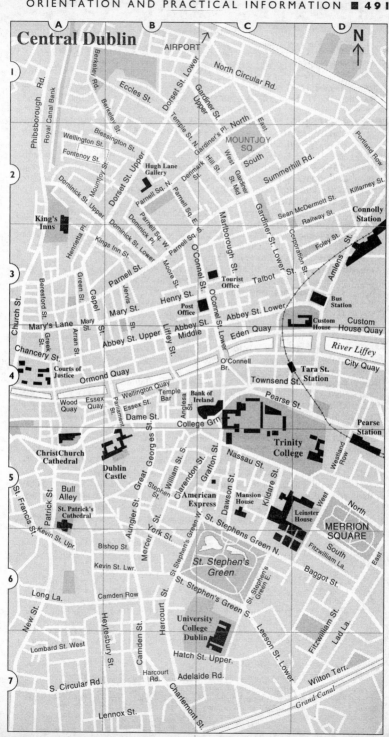

Central Dublin

AIRPORT

N

IRELAND

ing deposit). *Map of Greater Dublin* (IR£4). Open June Mon.-Sat. 8:30am-6pm; July-Aug. Mon.-Sat. 8:30am-8pm, Sun. 10:30-2pm; Sept.-Feb. Mon.-Fri. 9am-5pm., Sat. 9am-3:30pm; March-May Mon.-Sat. 9am-5pm. **Bord Fáilte Éireann (Irish Tourist Board),** Baggot St. Bridge (tel. 676 58 71 or 661 65 00). Maps and stuff on the rest of the Republic. Open Mon.-Sat. 9am-5pm.

Budget Travel: USIT (Irish Student Travel Agency), 19-21 Aston Quay (tel. 679 88 33), near the O'Connell Bridge. ISICs, HI cards. Travelsave stamps IR£7. Plethora of discounts, especially for under 26. Open Mon.-Fri. 9am-6pm, Sat. 11am-4pm.

Embassies: U.S., 43 Elgin Rd., Ballsbridge (tel. 668 87 77). Open Mon.-Fri. 8:30am-5pm. **Canada,** 65 St. Stephen's Green South, (tel. 478 19 88; emergencies, call 285 12 46). Open Mon.-Fri. 10am-noon and 2-4pm. **U.K.,** 31 Merrion Rd., Dublin 4 (tel. 269 52 11). Open Mon.-Fri. 10am-noon and 2-4pm. **Australia,** Fitzwilton House, Wilton Terrace (tel. 676 15 17). Open Mon.-Fri. 10am-noon and 2-4pm. **New Zealanders** and **South Africans** should contact their embassies in London.

Currency Exchange: Best rates at banks, otherwise try the *bureau de change* in the **General Post Office.**

American Express: 116 Grafton St. (tel. 677 28 74). Client mail held. Open Mon.-Sat. 9am-5pm, June-Sept. also Sun. 11am-4pm.

Post Office: General Post Office, O'Connell St. (tel. 705 70 00), near the tourist office. Dublin is the only city in Ireland with postal codes. Open Mon.-Sat. 8am-8pm. **Postal Code** for **Poste Restante:** Dublin 1.

Telephones: In the General Post Office. International pay phones open Mon.-Sat. 8am-8pm, Sun. and holidays 10:30am-6:30pm. **City Code:** 01.

Flights: Dublin Airport, 7 mi. north of the city center (tel. 844 99 00). Catch Dublin bus 41, 41A, or 41C (every 20min., IR£1.10) to Eden Quay in the city center.

Trains: Most trains arrive at **Heuston Station** (tel. 703 21 32), just south of Victoria Quay. The other main terminus is **Connolly Station** (tel. 703 23 58), centrally located on Amiens St. **Pearse Station,** on Pearse St. and Westland Row, is served by fewer trains. **Irish Rail Information,** 35 Lower Abbey St. (tel. 836 62 22). Open Mon.-Fri. 9am-5pm, Sat. 9am-1pm; phones open Mon.-Sat. 9am-6pm, Sun. 10am-6pm.

Buses: Busáras, Store St. (tel. 836 61 11), directly behind the Customs House. Central station for intercity buses. Day **luggage lock-up** IR£1.50, rucksack IR£2.

Public Transportation: Dublin Bus (Bus Átha Cliath). Fares IR£0.55-1.10; some buses require exact change. **Dublin Area Rapid Transportation (DART),** an electric light-rail train system serves coastal suburbs from Howth to Bray; fares IR£0.75-1.50. Buses and DART run 6am to 11:30pm. **NiteLink** services shuttle nightowls back to the suburbs (Fri.-Sat. hourly, midnight-3am; IR£2, no passes valid). Among passes, choose between the **One Day Travel Wide** (IR£2.80; Dublin buses only), the **One Day Bus/Rail** (IR£4, valid on buses, DART, and rail service between Kilcoole, Balbriggan, and Maynooth), and the **Four Day Explorer** (IR£10, 4 days; otherwise same as One Day Bus/Rail). Insert your pass into the scanner on the right side of the bus entrance as you get on.

Ferries: Stena-Sealink ferries arrive in Dún Laoghaire, where the DART shuttles weary passengers to Connolly Stn., Pearse Stn., and Tara St. in the city center for about IR£1.20. **B&I** ferries dock at the mouth of the River Liffey; from there, buses 53 and 53A run by Alexandra Rd. and arrive near the Custom House (80p). **B&I,** 16 Westmoreland St. **Sealink,** 15 Westmoreland St.

Car Rental: Practical Car and Van Rental, 19 Nassau St. (tel. 671 55 40). Convenient location. IR£35 per day, IR£154 per week. Ages 25-70 can rent. 100 miles free. Open Mon.-Fri. 9:30am-6pm, Sat. 9:30am-12:30pm.

Bike Rental: Rent-A-Bike, 58 Lower Gardiner St. (tel. 872 59 31 or 872 53 99). Cross-country and mountain bikes IR£6 first day, IR£5 per subsequent day, IR£30 per week, deposit IR£30. Panniers, helmets, and childseats IR£5 per week. For IR£5 extra, return the bike to depots in Rosslare, Cork, Limerick, Killarney, Sligo, Galway, or Westport. Open Mon.-Sat. 9am-6pm.

Laundromat: The Laundry Shop, 191 Parnell St. (tel. 872 35 41). Wash IR£1.90, dry IR£1, soap 50p. Open Mon.-Sat. 8:30am-6pm, Thurs. 8:30am-8pm.

Crisis Lines: Samaritans, 112 Marlborough St. (tel. (1850) 60 90 90 or 872 77 00). **Rape Crisis Centre,** 70 Lower Leeson St. (tel. 661 49 11; after 5:30pm and weekends, call 661 45 64). **Women's Aid** (tel. 872 37 56). Open Mon.-Fri. 10am-10pm, Sat. 10am-6pm.

Bisexual, Gay and Lesbian Information: Gay Switchboard Dublin, Carmichael House, North Brunswick St., Dublin 7 (tel. 872 10 55). Open Sun.-Fri. 8-10pm, Sat. 3:30-6pm.

Late-Night Pharmacy: O'Connell's, 55 Lower O'Connell St. (tel. 873 04 27). Open Mon.-Sat. 8:30am-10pm, Sun. 10am-10pm.

Hospital: Meath Hospital, Heytesbury St. (tel. 453 65 55 or 453 60 00 or 453 55 94). 24 hrs.

Emergency: Dial 999 for police, fire, or ambulance; no coins required.

ACCOMMODATIONS

Dublin accommodations fill to bursting during Easter weekend, British school holidays, and periodically during the summer—it never hurts to reserve in advance. Summertime singles in B&Bs are especially hard to come by. Most hostels are north of the River Liffey and east of O'Connell St., in a working-class neighborhood. Most are independent—not affilliated with HI. In busy summer months, call ahead. A pride of august B&Bs covers Dublin and the surrounding suburbs, charging from IR£12 up to IR£25 and clustered along Upper and Lower Gardiner St. Bord Fáilte's Ireland Accommodation Guide (IR£4) lists all approved B&Bs and their rates.

Avalon House (IHH), 55 Aungier St. (tel. 475 00 01). From Dame St. take South Great George St. to Aungier St. One of the best hostels in Dublin, with groovy comforters and terracotta decor. Unbeatable location between Trinity and Temple Bar. Coed showers, toilets, and dorms. 4-bed dorm IR£11, July-Aug. IR£11.50. Twin IR£13, July-Aug. IR£13.50. 4-bed and twin rooms with bath, add 50p. Wheelchair-accessible double (2 beds) IR£13.50. 24-bed, co-ed room IR£7.50, July-Aug. IR£10.50. 10% off with European Youth Card. Kitchen with microwave.

Kinlay House (IHH), 2-12 Lord Edward St. (tel. 679 66 44), continue down Dame St. past Dublin Castle. Located in hip 'n' happening Temple Bar. No lockout, no curfew. Single IR£16.50. Double IR£11.50 per person, with bath IR£12.50. 4-bed unit in large dorm IR£7.50 per person. 4-6 bed room IR£9.50. July-Sept. extra IR£1 for dorm rooms, 50p for single and twins. Lockers, laundry (IR£4), kitchen. Bike hire available. Luggage storage with 24hr. access. Breakfast, towel, linen, and soap included.

Isaac's (IHH), 2-4 Frenchman's Lane (tel. 874 93 21), first right on Lower Gardiner St. walking up from the Custom House. Floor upon floor of attractively decorated rooms, and everyone mingles in the bustling, inexpensive café on the ground floor. Reception open 24hrs. Lockout 11am-5pm. No curfew; lockers in rooms 50p deposit, free sheets. Single IR£15.25. Double IR£23. Triple IR£33.75. Dorms with 12-14 people per room IR£5.75. 6-8 people per room IR£6.50. 4-6 people per room IR£7.50. Reservations recommended for Fri. and Sat. night stays.

Dublin International Youth Hostel (HI), 61 Mountjoy St. (tel. 830 17 66 or 830 13 96), walk north on O'Connell St. continuing on Frederick St. past Dorset St., take next left onto Mountjoy St. A convent converted to a comfortable, institutional hostel. Large rooms with squeaky wooden bunks. Currency exchange, kitchen, secure parking. No lockout, no curfew. Max. 3-night stay. Dorm IR£9, non-members IR£9.50; 3- to 6-bed room IR£10; twin IR£12. Oct.-May, subtract IR£2. Continental breakfast.Sheets 50p; luggage storage 50p.

Marlborough Hostel (IHH), 81-81 Marlborough St. (tel. 874 76 29 or 874 78 12), next to the pro-Cathedral, and directly behind the O'Connell St. tourist office. Large, light, airy rooms with super-comfy beds. Check-out 10:30am. Singles IR£14. Doubles IR£22. 4-10 person dorm IR£7.50 per person. Includes continental breakfast. Sheet rental 50p, laundry 50p. Bike shed, kitchen with microwave. Free luggage storage.

Mrs. Bermingham, 8 Dromard Terr. (tel. 668 38 61). Take bus 3 from O'Connell St. or DART to Sandymount stop. Old-fashioned rooms, one with a bay window overlooking the garden, and a TV in the sitting room. Owner is a ball of fire. Soft beds with great comforters. Singles IR£14. Doubles IR£23.

IRELAND

Leitrim House, 34 Blessington St. (tel. 830 87 28), Walk up O'Connell St., which becomes Parnell Sq. East and then Frederick St. Cross Dorset St. and continue straight on Blessington St.; Leitrim House is 1 block past the false teeth repair shop, or take bus 10 to the top of Mountjoy St. Lilac walls in the bedrooms, flowers on the windowsill, and reliquaries in the parlor, but the real charm lies in the grandmotherly touch. IR£12.

Mrs. Carmel Drain, Bayview, 265 Clontarf Rd. (tel. 833 98 70). Take bus 30 to Clontarf Rd. Palm tree in front yard. Hello, knick-knacks! Pretty view of Dublin Bay and Wicklow Mountains from the front windows. Orthopedic beds and instant hot water in showers. IR£14, with bath IR£15.

FOOD

Dublin's open air **Moore St. Market** provides fresh and cheap fixings for those on a tight budget (open Mon.-Sat. 9am-5pm). On-the-go food is quick, greasy, and very popular; you can't escape the "Take Away: Fish and Chips" signs. Pub grub is always a good choice for a quick and inexpensive meal, especially at lunchtime. The cheapest **supermarkets** around Dublin are **Dunnes Stores** at St. Stephen's Green Shopping Center; ILAC Center, off Henry St.; and on North Earl St., off O'Connell St. (tel. 848 33 48; all open Mon.-Wed. and Fri.-Sat. 9am-6pm, Thurs. 9am-8pm).

The Well Fed Café, 6 Crow St., off Dame St. (tel. 677 22 34). Inventive vegetarian dishes served by a worker's cooperative in a stripped-down boho atmosphere. Brown bread and soup IR£1, main courses IR£2, small salad 55p, large salad 80p, apple pie with cream IR£1.10. Wheelchair accessible. Open Mon.-Sat. noon-8pm.

Leo Burdock's, 2 Werburgh St. (tel. 454 03 06), uphill from Christ Church Cathedral. Lucky the steps of the Cathedral are nearby—Burdock's is take-out only, and eating Burdock's fish and chips is a religious experience. Every Dubliner's pick for fish and chips. Haddock and cod IR£2, whiting IR£1.50, plaice and ray IR£2.50, large chips IR£0.85. Open Mon.-Fri. 12:30-11pm, Sat. 2-11pm.

Bewley's Cafés, (tel. 677 67 61), 3 locations at Grafton, Westmoreland, and South Great George's St. A Dublin institution: a delightful crowd of Dublin characters, dark wood paneling, marble table tops, and mirrored walls. Wild pastries (IR£1); outstanding coffee. 4 branches: 78 Grafton St. is the largest (open Sun.-Thurs. 7:30am-1am, Fri.-Sat. 7:30am-2am). James Joyce frequented the branch at 12 Westmoreland St. (open Mon.-Sat. 7:30am-9pm, Sun. 9:30am-8pm). Also at 13 South Great Georges St. (open Mon.-Sat. 7:45am-6pm) and at Mary St. (past Henry St.; open Mon.-Wed. 7am-9pm, Thurs.-Sat. 7am-2am, Sun. 10am-10pm).

Marks Bros., 7 South Great Georges St. (tel. 667 10 85), off Dame St. Thick sandwiches (IR£1.30-1.70) and salads for starving artists and punks among artsy posters. Contemplate Joyce and social stratification. Legendary cinnamon buns 40p; sandwiches IR£1.30-1.70. Open Mon.-Sat. 10am-5pm.

Bad Ass Café, Crown Alley, off Temple Bar (tel. 671 25 96). Huge warehouse converted into a Viewmaster of American culture. Trendy young crowd basks in the glow of fire-engine red trim. Lunch IR£3-5. Medium pizza IR£5, large IR£7. Student menu (with ISIC): coleslaw, scone and butter, "magic mushrooms," medium pizza, drink (IR£5.50). Open daily 9am-"late" (past midnight).

The Winding Stair Bookshop and Café, 40 Lower Ormond Quay (tel. 873 32 92), near Bachelor's Walk. Unhurried café amidst 2 floors of bookshelves, overlooking the Liffey. Big portion of Greek salad IR£2.60, sandwiches IR£1.50, soup and bread IR£1.60. Open Mon.-Sat. 10:30am-5:30pm.

SIGHTS

Dublin is a walkable city; most of the sights lie within a one-mile radius of O'Connell Bridge. The tourist office sells *Visitor Attractions in Dublin* (IR£1) as well as information-stuffed brochures (IR£1) for self-guided walking tours. The **Historical Walking Tour** (tel. 845 02 41; IR£4, students IR£3) is a 2hr. crash course in Dublin's history from the Celts to the present. The witty and irreverent **Trinity College Walking Tour** also covers Dublin's history, but concentrates on university lore (30min.; IR£5, students IR£4). **Trinity College,** alma mater of Swift, Beckett, and

Wilde, houses the *Book of Kells,* in the **Old Library,** built in 1712 (open Mon.-Sat. 9:30am-5:30pm, Sun. noon-4:30pm. IR£2.50, students IR£2). South of the city, on the block between Kildare St. and Upper Merrion St., Irish history and culture reign. Ireland treasures including the Ardagh Chalice and the Tara brooch reside at the **National Museum** (open Tues.-Sat. 10am-5pm, Sun. 2-5pm; free). Down the street on Merrion Sq., the **National Gallery's** 4-floor winding staircase is lined with portraits of Lady Gregory, Eliza O'Neill, Joyce, Shaw, and Yeats (open Mon.-Sat. 10am-6pm, Thurs. 10am-9pm, Sun. 2-5pm; free).

Kildare St., Dawson St., and Grafton St. all lead from Trinity south to **St. Stephen's Green.** The big, well-landscaped park was a private estate until the Guinness clan bequeathed it to the city; here are acres of arched bridges, an artificial lake, couples, flowerbeds, fountains, gazebos, pensioners, punks, strollers, swans, more swans, trees, even more trees, and waterfalls. On sunny days, half of Dublin fills the lawns, in various stages of undress. During the summer, the ducks enjoy outdoor theatrical productions near the old bandstand. (Open Mon.-Sat. 8am-dusk, Sun. 10am-dusk.)

At the west end of Dame St., at its confluence with Parliament and Castle St., is **Dublin Castle,** built in 1204 by King John, and seat of English rule for more than 700 years (State Apartments open Mon.-Fri. 10am-12:15pm and 2-5pm. Sat.-Sun. and holidays 2-5pm; hours vary during official functions; IR£1.75, students and children IR£1, rest of castle free). Ironically, Dublin's only official cathedrals, **Christ Church Cathedral** (on Dame St.; open daily 10am-5pm except during services; choral evensong Thurs. at 6pm, except July-Aug, IR£1 donation) and **St. Patrick's Cathedral** (open Mon.-Fri. 9am-6pm, Sat. 9am-5pm, Sun. 10am-4:30pm; IR£1, students 40p), are both Protestant.

If you crave alcoholic nectar, the huge **Guinness Brewery,** St. James Gate, pumps 2½ million pints a day to sate your thirst (open Mon.-Fri. 10am-4pm, last tour 3:30pm; IR£2, students IR£1.50). To get there, take bus 21A, 78, or 78A west along the quays, where murky river water seems to resemble the beverage.

ENTERTAINMENT

The *Dublin Event Guide* (free from the tourist office) and *In Dublin* (IR£1.50) offer a smorgasbord of choices: music listings, theater reviews, exhibitions, and comedy shows. The national theater of Ireland, the **Abbey Theatre,** 26 Lower Abbey St. (tel. 878 72 22), was founded in 1904 by Yeats and Lady Gregory to promote Irish culture and modernist theater (box office open Mon.-Sat. 10:30am-7pm; tickets IR£8-13; student standby discounts IR£5, available 1hr. before Mon. and Thurs. shows.) The **Gate Theatre,** 1 Cavendish Row (tel. 874 40 45), produces everything from Restoration comedies to Irish classics (box office open Mon.-Sat. 10am-7pm; tickets IR£10-12; student standby IR£6 Mon.-Thurs. at curtain).

In Dublin should be your bible to Dublin's music world. Scheduled concerts usually start at 9pm, impromptu ones even later. Traditional music is not always a tourist gimmick. **The Rock Garden,** 3a Crown Alley (tel. 679 91 14), the current core of Dublin's aspiring rock world. Bigger bands entertain at the **Baggot Inn,** 143 Baggot St. (tel. 676 14 30), where U2 played in the early 80s. For classical, the **National Concert Hall,** Earl's Fort Terrace (tel. 671 15 33), hosts touring orchestras. (July-Aug. 8pm; tickets IR£7-10, students ½-price).

Dublin returns to 1904 each year on **Bloomsday,** June 16, the day on which the action of Joyce's Ulysses takes place. Festivities take place in the week leading up to Bloomsday. The **Joyce Center** (tel. 873 19 84) sponsors a mock funeral and wake, a lunch at Davy Byrne's, and a breakfast with Guinness as part of its Bloomstime program. On the day itself, a Messenger Bike Rally culminates in St. Stephen's Green with drink and food. "Good puzzle would be cross Dublin without passing a pub," wrote James Joyce. As a rule, dance spots open at 10:30 or 11pm, but the action gets moving only after 11:30pm, when partiers swarm from closing pubs to the dance floors; most clubs close down at 3 or 4am. Cover runs from IR£4-8, pints IR£2.

McDaid's, 3 Harry St., off Grafton St., across from Anne St. Writer Brendan Behan frequented this cheery place; besides literary pilgrims, the pub draws ribald buskers who contribute to the happy din with impromptu ballads. Occasional rock gigs.

The Bailey, 2 Duke St., off Grafton St. In the lobby, see the preserved front door of #7 Eccles St., fictional home of Leopold Bloom. A popular gay and lesbian meeting place at teatime, especially Sat. afternoons.

Davy Byrne's, 21 Duke St., off Grafton St. "Nice quiet bar. Nice piece of wood in that counter. Nicely planned. Like the way it curves there." Come see what Joyce meant in *Ulysses*.

The Buttery, Trinity College. Dark, smoky, and crammed with students, even at 3pm. Open Mon.-Fri. noon-11pm.

The Brazen Head, 20 Lower Bridge St., off Merchant's Quay. Dublin's oldest pub, established in 1198 as the first stop after the bridge on the way into the city. The courtyard is quite the pickup scene on summer nights.

The Long Hall, 51 South Great Georges St. A beautiful and very lengthy old bar with a carved polished wood bar, ornate mirrors, and neighborly local socializing and *craic*.

The Norseman, 29 East Essex St., corner of Sycamore St. behind Wellington Quay. Trendies: musicians, actors, entourage. Ballads Sun. 9-11am.

The Stag's Head, Main St., Ashbourne (tel. 835 01 12). Often confused with its name sake on Dame Ct., near Temple Bar, this Stag's Head is located 10mi. outside Dublin on the N2. Take a bus from Busáras or stop by en route to northern Ireland. Happenin' place with something for all. Pub grub galore and a convivial atmosphere. The hip'n'trendy throng the back lounge weekend nights.

■ HOWTH

Nine miles north of Dublin, easily accessible by DART, Howth is a quick fix of the best of Ireland—scenery, pubs, history, literature, a castle, an abbey, and fresh fish. Orient yourself with the *Guide to Howth Peninsula,* posted at the harbor entrance, across from the St. Lawrence Hotel. **Glenn na Smol** (tel. 832 29 36), on the left at the end of Nashville Rd. is a full-service B&B (IR£15, with bath IR£16). After a day on your feet, stop for a pint in town at the classy **Cock Tavern,** 18 Church St. (tel. 832 3237), opposite St. Mary's Abbey. Rock bands play Wed. and Sun. nights at 9pm, and ballads Sun. afternoons.

A **cliff walk** rings the peninsula, following heather-crossed cliffs. The views, and especially the springtime blooms of the slopes, are amazing. For the less hardy, bus 31B cruises from Lower Abbey St. to the cliffs' summit (1 per hr.). Aside from its spectacular views, Howth's primary attraction is **Howth Castle,** on the outskirts of town, a patchwork of different styles, giving it an awkward charm. Farther up the hill, follow the path to the right around the Deer Park Hotel to reach the fab **Rhododendron Gardens.** When the flowers are in bloom (June-July), a climb to the top is a must; visitors emerge from the dark trail into a dazzling panorama of sea, sky, Howth harbor, and Dublin, framed by spectacular flowers.

SOUTHEAST IRELAND

THE WICKLOW MOUNTAINS

Just inland from the east coast jut the gorse- and heather-covered summits of the **Wicklow Mountains,** pleated by rivers rushing through wooded glens. The 70mi. **Wicklow Way** hiking trail starts near Dublin and jogs south all the way to Clonegal in County Carlow, located at the bottom of the Blackstairs mountains. Though the path is well-posted with yellow arrows, pick up the Wicklow tourist board's free *Info Sheet 26B* and the Ordnance Survey's *Wicklow Way* (IR£3.75) at tourist offices, bookstores, and mountaineering stores. **Glendalough** (GLEN-da-lock), a spectacularly uninhabited valley in the midst of the mountains, cradles two lakes, a pine forest, and the best preserved of Ireland's ruined monastic settlements. Stay at the **Glendalough Hostel (HI)** (tel. (0404) 453 42; IR£5.50, Oct.-May IR£4.50) or the **Old Mill Hostel (IHO)**, Rathdrum Rd., Glendalough (tel. (0404) 451 56; IR£5.90-7.50, camping IR£3). **St. Kevin's Bus Service** (tel. (01) 281 81 19) runs there from Dublin (return IR£8) or from Bray town hall (return IR£6).

ROSSLARE HARBOUR

The population of the **Rosslare Harbour** area is transient by nature—at any given time, most people are either coming or going. The Rosslare area has two **tourist offices:** the manic-panic one in the ferry terminal (tel. (053) 336 23), and the over-staffed one 1mi. from the harbor on the Wexford Rd. in Kilrane (tel. (053) 332 32). Avoid the ferry office one at all costs during rush times. (Ferry office open 6:30am-9:30am and 11am-8:30pm or 1-8:30pm, depending on ferry arrival times. Kilrane office open May-mid-Sept. 11am-8pm.) **Irish Ferries** (tel. (053) 331 58) chug to Cherbourg and Le Havre, France (to Le Havre 21hr, to Cherbourg 17hr.; IR£55-80). Stena Sealink and B&I ferries connnect Rosslare with PEmbroke and Fishguard in Wales. **Buses** run to Cork (IR£12),Limerick (IR£12, return IR£16), Waterford (IR£5, return IR£7), Dublin (3hr.; IR£9), and Wexford (20min.; IR£2.40). **Trains** connect the ferry port to Dublin (2hr., IR£10), Limerick (3½hr., IR£18), Waterford (20min., IR£8.50), and Wexford (20min.; IR£3). The **Rosslare Harbour youth hostel (HI),** Goulding St. (tel. (053) 333 99), offers modern facilities and a concentration of continental youth. (Check-in 5:30pm. Lockout 9:30am-5:30pm. Curfew 11:30pm, lights out midnight. IR£6, Sept.-May IR£5.)

KILKENNY

Touted as the best preserved medieval town in Ireland, **Kilkenny's** ancient architecture and rocking nightlife draw hordes of tourists —it's a not-to-be-missed stop on everyone's southeastern circuit. Beware the ghost of 13th-century **Kilkenny Castle.** (Open 10am-7pm; April-May 10:30am-5pm; Oct.-March Tues.-Sat. 10:30am-5pm, Sun. 11am-5pm. IR£2, seniors IR£1.50, students and children IR£1.) The stone steps of **St. Canice's Cathedral** are lined with fragments of sculpture from the cathedral itself. (Open 10am-6pm, except during services. cathedral free, donations requested.) Get the free *Kilkenny City and County Guide* at the **tourist office,** Rose Inn St. (tel. (056) 515 00; open Mon.-Sat. 9am-6pm, Sun. 11am-5pm; Oct. Mon.-Sat. 9am-1pm and 2-5:30pm; Nov.-March Tues.-Sat. 9am-1pm and 2-5:15pm; March-April Mon.-Sat. 9am-1pm and 2-5:15pm). Kilkenny is on the Dublin-Waterford rail line. Stay at the **Kilkenny Town Hostel (IHO),** 35 Parliament St. (tel. (056) 635 41; IR£5.50-6; 50p discount to *Let's Go* users except July-Aug.).

CASHEL

South of Kilkenny, the **Rock of Cashel** rises like a fairy castle out of Cashel town. A huge limestone outcrop with a jumble of secular and ecclesiastical buildings on top, the Rock is truly magical when lit at night. On the Rock, **Cormac's Chapel,** a majestic, dual-towered structure, was built between 1127 and 1134. The interior displays gorgeous Romanesque carvings and a richly decorated sarcophagus. The 13th-century **Cashel Cathedral** overshadows all the other ruins in grandeur. The museum at the entrance to the castle complex preserves the 13th-century **St. Patrick's Cross;** Kings of Munster were crowned on the site marked by the *croix faux.* (Rock open mid-June to mid-Sept. 9am-7:30pm; mid-March to mid-June 9:30am-5:30pm; mid-Sept. to mid-March 9:30am-4:30pm. Last admission 40min. before closing. IR£2, students IR£1.) Hostels are your best bet in Cashel and B&Bs tend to be pricey. **O'Brien's Farmhouse Hostel,** off Dundrum Rd. (tel. (062) 610 03) is set in the shadow of the Rock near Hore Abbey (6-bed dorms IR£6, private rooms IR£9; camping IR£3.50 per person). The **Cashel Holiday Hostel,** 6 John St. (tel. (062) 623 30), off Main St., is more central (4- to 8-bed dorm IR£5, 4-bed with bath IR£6; private rooms IR£8 per person).

IRELAND

SOUTHWEST IRELAND

■■■ CORK CITY

Originally no more than an island surrounded by marsh, Cork remains compact in geography. In the early 17th century, the citizens of Cork refused to recognize the English monarchy, and through the first decades of the 20th century, Cork remained a center for Republican activities. Modern Cork is vibrant: coffeehouses spill patrons onto the streets, the young gather here in gaudy 70s flares and platforms, and everyone tells you how much finer a place it is than dreary Dublin.

The River Lee is a physical and economic divide between the north side (Shandon) and the more affluent commercial south side. Good pubs are generally to be found in the latter area, while the shopping district is in and around Patrick St.

St. Finbarr's Cathedral, the South Gate entrance to medieval Cork, incorporates a zoo's worth of animals, griffins, and angels into its limestone gingerbread-house façade (open Mon.-Sat. 10am-1pm and 2-5:30pm; Oct.-April Mon.-Fri. 10am-1pm and 2-5pm). North of the River Lee, the red sandstone and white limestone **Shandon Tower** of **St. Anne's Church** rises high above the hodgepodge of factories and warehouses, sporting an 11-ft. salmon weathervane. Climb it for a view of the city and harbor (open Mon.-Fri. 9:30am-5pm, Sun. open just for services; IR£1.50). Just opposite the church, artisans practice weaving, porcelain-making, crystal-cutting, and pottery in the **Shandon Craft Centre.** In the city center, the **Crawford Municipal Art Gallery** (tel. (021) 270 433) is one of Ireland's finest public art museums (open Mon.-Sat. 10am-5pm; free).

Practical Information, Accommodations, and Food Cork's **tourist office** (tel. (021) 27 32 51) is on Grand Parade at South Mall St. (open June-Sept. daily 9am-7pm; winter Sun.-Fri. 9:15am-5:30pm, Sat. 9am-1pm). **Trains** chug into **Kent Station,** Lower Glanmire Rd. (tel. (021) 50 47 77; across the river in the northeast part of town; open 7am-8pm), from Dublin (5-7 per day, 3hr.), Limerick City (3-5 per day, 1½hr.); Killarney (3-4 per day, 2½hr.); and Tralee (3-4 per day, 2½hr.). **Ferries** to France and England dock at **Ringaskiddy Terminal,** 9 mi. south of the city. The 40min. city bus from the terminal to the bus station costs IR£3. **Bus Éireann** also runs the "Supabus" (tel. (021) 50 60 66) which connects Cork to London and Birmingham by bus and ferry. Buses leave Cork at 5:15pm, London and Birmingham at 7:30pm, and arrive at their respective destinations 15hr. later (IR£35-40 single, IR£44-59 return).

Cork is blessed with wonderful hostels; B&Bs run IR£11-13. Both are concentrated on **Western Rd.,** west of the Grand Parade (take bus 8) near the bus and train stations, and the less attractive **Lower Glanmire Rd. Campus House (IHO),** 3 Woodland View, Western Rd. (tel. (021) 34 35 31), is the tops for friendly owners (IR£5.50). **Isaac's,** 48 MacCurtain St. (tel. (021) 50 00 11) rents 220 rooms in the splendor of hardwood floors, brick arches and contemporary paintings (reception open 24hrs; dorms IR£5.50, 4- to 6-person dorms with bath IR£4.50, singles IR£18.50, doubles IR£13.50; wheelchair access). Campers head for **Cork City Caravan and Camping Park** (tel. (021) 96 18 66), southwest of the city center on Togher Rd., ½mi. beyond Lough Rd. Bus 14 runs every 20min. (IR£5.50 per tent, IR£1 per person, IR£7.50 per caravan, children under 7 25p; open Easter-Oct.).

Try the **arcade** (entrances off Grand Parade, Patrick St., and Princes St.) for fresh meat, cheese, and fruit, and the armada of bakeries along Oliver Plunkett St. and Washington St. for pastries and sandwich breads. **Quay Co-op,** 24 Sullivan's Quay, serves up vegetarian and vegan entrees (open daily 9:30am-10:30pm). **Kelly's,** 64 Oliver Plunkett St., fills you with huge portions of *real* Irish food (open noon-9pm). Pop a cork at any of the many pubs in town serving local brews **Murphy's Stout** and **Beamish.** For nightclub action, pick up a copy of *Razz* at **The Harlequin,** 21 Paul St.; popular clubs include **Gorby's** and **Norma Jean's,** both on Oliver Plunkett St.

■ BLARNEY

Five mi. northwest of Cork is **Blarney,** home of **Blarney Castle** and the terrifically overrated **Blarney Stone** (open Mon.-Sat. May 9am-6:30pm, June-Aug. 9am-7pm, Sept. 9am-6:30pm, Oct.-April: 9am-sundown; Sundays in summer 9:30am-5:30pm, in winter 9:30am-sundown; IR£3, seniors and students IR£1.50, children IR£1).

■ ■ ■ SOUTHWEST COAST

KINSALE

A ½hr. drive southwest of Cork lies Kinsale, a ritzy seaside resort town where you don't need money to have fun because the highlights—spectacular vistas and peaceful walking trails—are free. The prickly, overgrown ruin of **James Fort** holds secret passageways; its thrilling 30ft. limestone walls give panoramic views of Kinsale. Or try **Charles Fort,** 2 mi. east of town (open mid-June to Sept. daily 9am-6pm; mid-April to mid-June Tues.-Sat. 9am-4:30pm, Sun. 11-5:30pm; IR£1, students 50p). Take the **Scilly walk** on your way back; the view of the harbor and ocean is one of the best in Europe. Stay at **Dempsey's Hostel (IHO),** just outside town on Cork Rd. (tel. (021) 77 21 24), beside Dempsey's Garage (8 beds per room, IR£4).

BEARA PENINSULA

Southwest of Kinsale, off the coast of the tiny fishing village of **Baltimore,** lie Sherkin Island and Cape Clear Island (where Irish is still spoken). North of the islands, the Beara Peninsula juts into the sea with similar majesty to the more northerly Iveragh Peninsula, and fewer tourists. Don't even bother trying to hitchhike; rent a bike.

   Bantry makes a fine base for exploring Beara's scenic surroundings. Buses connect with Cork City (return IR£8.80, students IR£5). The **Bantry Independent Hostel (IHH),** Bishop Lucey Pl. (tel. (027) 510 50), is a small, friendly establishment with a darn good view of the hills (dorms IR£5.50, private rooms IR£7.50; open mid-March to Oct.).

   A fishing village and the largest town on the peninsula, **Castletownbere** reverberates with the sounds of ferry engines, cars, loud children, and wind. Two mi. west of town on Allihies Rd., the **Beara Hostel (IHH)** (tel. (027) 701 84) offers comfortable beds for IR£5 (private rooms IR£7) and less comfy ground to camp on for IR£3.50. Four mi. further, and a good deal more isolated, is the **Garranes Farmhouse Hostel** (tel. (027) 731 47), a luxurious, welcoming cottage perched above the sea (dorms IR£5, singles and doubles IR£7 per person). Phone ahead to make sure the Buddhist retreat center next door hasn't gobbled up all the space.

   Kenmare, a colorful town at the elbow of the Beara and Iveragh peninsulas, offers access to both. Sink into the cushy **Fáilte Hostel (IHH),** Henry St. (tel. (064) 410 83; dorms IR£5.50, private rooms IR£7.50).

RING OF KERRY

The Ring of Kerry once embodied the tough, romantic spirit of Ireland, but has now more or less sold out to attract the masses. **Killarney** is lively but touristy, a good base for exploring the spectacular National Park nearby. Try the cozy rooms at **The Súgán (IHH),** Lewis Rd. (tel. (064) 331 04; dorms IR£6), or the **Bunrower House Hostel (IHH)** (tel. (064) 339 14), right next to the park (6-bed dorms IR£6, coubles IR£8, camping IR£3.50). The **Aghadoe Hostel (HI)** (tel. (064) 312 40), three mi. west on the Killorglin Rd. near the stunning Killarney National Park, hides in a magnificent mansion with a view and offers a frees bus from the train and bus station (IR£6, Oct.-May. IR£4; breakfast IR£2). Down a meal at **An Taelann,** Bridewell Lane, off New St., which serves incredible vegetarian food amid philosophy books (open Tues.-Sat. 12:30-3pm and 6:30-10pm). **Bus Éireann** runs a counterclockwise summer circuit through all the major towns on the Ring (2 per day). Cyclists, drivers, and hitchers should try to travel the ring clockwise to avoid bus traffic.

IRELAND

The easiest way to reach the deservedly hallowed **Gap of Dunloe** is to follow the Killorglin Rd. for 5mi., and then turn left on the road to Beaufort. You will pass the entirely ruined Dunloe Castle, an Anglo-Norman stronghold on which Cromwell's armies did a very effective demolition job. Before the Gap, you'll pass **Kate Kearney's Cottage**, once home to the mountain-dwelling independent woman famous for brewing *poteen* (moonshine); now, her former home is usually full of souvenir-mad tourists (open 9am-midnight). Past the cottage, your options are walking or cycling; cars are banned along the 7mi. stretch of road near the Gap. The Gap itself divides the epic **Macgillycuddy's Reeks** (the tallest mountain range in Ireland) from the lake-studded **Purple Mountains.** Locals say the best time to "do" the Gap is during late afternoon, after the masses have cleared the road and the mountains are left to themselves for the night.

What tiny **Caherdaniel** lacks in greeting-card charm it makes up for with the inspiring **Derrynane Strand,** and Daniel O'Connell's **Derrynane House.** The **Village Hostel** (tel. (066) 752 77), sits near the town's crossroads (midnight curfew; IR£5; showers 50p; open Feb.-Nov.). The best reasons to halt around **Ballinskelligs Bay** are the groovy **Peter's Place** hostel on Main St. in Waterville (no phone, he hates 'em), a self-described madhouse (IR£5; camping IR£3), and **Skellig Michael,** a 6th-century monastic settlement jutting out of the Atlantic, 8mi. offshore (boats IR£15-20 and worth it; info tel. (066) 742 68 or 761 55). **Cahersiveen** is worth a stop for the friendly **Sive Hostel (IHH),** 15 East End, Main St. (tel. (066) 727 17), and the very Irish **Anchor Bar** and **Mike Murt's** pubs. In **Killorglin,** cleanliness abounds at the **Laune Valley Farm Hostel** (tel. (066) 614 88), a farm 1mi. from Killorglin on the Tralee road (IR£5).

DINGLE PENINSULA

Dingle Peninsula, County Kerry's northernmost, has one of Ireland's few surviving Irish-speaking communities. Base yourself in **Dingle Town,** abundant in traditional music, craft shops, and small restaurants, before the growing tourist flood drowns all the charm. While the town is well-connected to Killarney and Tralee, public transport within the peninsula is scarce. **Buses** to towns run daily in July and August, but only two or three times per week the rest of the year. For info, call the Tralee station (tel. (066) 235 66). The **Rainbow Hostel** (tel. (066) 510 44), ½mi. west of town on Strand Rd., is a small, friendly setup (IR£6, Sept.-June IR£5; doubles IR£7.50; camping IR£2.50). For exotic wholefoods and great live traditional music, go to **Café Ceol,** Green St., opposite the church, behind Dick Mack's pub (open 1-3pm and 6-9pm, later when there's music). Though fewer than 1500 people live in Dingle, the town has 52 pubs—drink up.

No matter how tight you think your schedule is, you will inevitably be waylaid by glorious **Slea Head** and its inviting, though clandestine, strand. *The Quiet Man* and parts of *Far and Away* were filmed in the area. The scattered settlement of **Dunquin** has stone houses, a pub, and plenty of spoken Irish. Just down the road to Ballyferriter, the **hostel (HI)** (tel. (066) 561 21) provides adequate bunks and a spacious, window-walled sitting and dining room overlooking the Atlantic. (Lockout 10:15am-5pm; curfew 11:30pm. IR£6, Oct.-May IR£5. Sheets 60p. Breakfast IR£1.60) Across the way, the **Blasket Center** hosts exhibits about life on the islands. (Open July-Aug. 10am-7pm, Easter-June and Sept. to mid-Oct. 10am-6pm; IR£2, students IR£1). From Dingle Town to the northern side of the peninsula, the 1500-ft.-high **Conor Pass,** a winding cliffside road too narrow for buses to traverse, crosses the mountains and affords ripping views of the bays and valleys.

TRALEE

In contrast to the painfully visitor-oriented feel of Tralee's sights, the rest of the town is quite authentic: locals handily dilute the smattering of tourists in pubs, restaurants, and shops. Ireland's second-largest museum is **Kerry the Kingdom,** Ashe Memorial Hall, Denny St., where all the resources of modern display technology are marshalled to tell the story of Co. Kerry from 8000 BC to the present. (Open March-

July and Sept.-Oct. Mon.-Sat. 10am-6pm, Sun. 2-6pm; Aug. Mon.-Sat. 10am-7pm, Sun. 2-6pm, Nov.-Dec. Mon.-Sat. 2-5pm. IR£3.90, students IR£3.50.) Budding sociologists should save the last week of August for the **Rose of Tralee International Festival.** A maelstrom of entertainment surrounds the central event, a competition between young women of Irish ancestry for the title "Rose of Tralee." The Rose office, 5 Lower Castle St. (tel. (066) 213 22), can wolf-whistle about it.

It's not difficult to get to Tralee; **trains** link the town with Cork (2½hr.; IR£16, students IR£7), Killarney (40min.; IR£5, students IR£3.50), and Dublin (3-4hr.; IR£33.50, students IR£12). Buses run to Cork (2½hr.; IR£9 students IR£6), Dingle (1¼hr.; IR£5.90, students IR£3.50), Killarney (40min.; IR£5.90, students IR£3.50), and Limerick (2hr.; IR£9 students IR£5.30). **Finnegan's Hostel (IHH),** 17 Denny St. (tel. (066) 276 10), in a majestic 19th-century townhouse, offers bunks for IR£6, and doubles for IR£7.50 a head.

WESTERN IRELAND

The undesirability of Western land limited foreign influence, preserving spoken Irish in the Connemara, although it's the rugged scenery there that most travelers are understandably seeking. The West was hardest hit by the potato famine: entire villages emigrated or died, and the population is still less than half of what it was in 1841. Hikers, cyclists, and hitchhikers observe rural depopulation in boggy, rocky, or brilliantly mountainous landscapes.

■■■ LIMERICK AND ENNIS

Limerick City is in the middle of a facelift—it has been for years—but a number of factors keep it sagging: high unemployment, grimy industry, and an unimaginative grid of streets strewn with neon and plastic, as well as a slew of abandoned buildings. At **King John's Castle,** Nicholas St., pre-Norman excavations and scale models of battle machinery are, however, worth exploring (open 9:30am-5:30pm, last admission 4:30pm; IR£3.30, students IR£1.70). Go to the **tourist office,** Arthurs Quay (tel. (061) 31 75 22) for excellent free city maps (open Mon.-Fri. 9am-7pm, Sat.-Sun. until 6pm; March-June and Sept.-Oct. Mon.-Sat. 9:20am-5:30pm; Nov.-Feb. Mon.-Fri. 9:30am-5:30pm, Sat. until 1pm). The **train and bus stations** are both in Colbert Station (train info tel. (061) 41 86 66; bus info tel. (061) 31 33 33; open Mon.-Sat. 8:45am-6pm, Sun. 9:45am-6pm; Oct.-May Mon.-Sat. 8am-6pm, Sun. 3-7pm), just off Parnell St. **Trains** leave Limerick for Dublin (2½hr.; IR£24, students IR£9.50), Cork (2½hr.; IR£12.50, students IR£6), Killarney (3½hr. IR£14, students IR£6.50), Tralee (2¼hr.; IR£14, students IR£6.50) and Waterford (2hr.; IR£16, students IR£7). Antiseptic doubles and private rooms are available across town on George's Quay at the **Limerick Holiday Hostel,** Barrington House (tel. (061) 41 52 22), near St. Mary's Cathedral (singles IR£6.50, doubles IR£5). Better yet, **St. Anthony's,** 8 Coolraine Terrace, Ennis Rd. (tel. (061) 45 26 07) offers pleasant rooms overlooking a flourishing garden (*Let's Go* special: IR£11.50, with bath IR£13). Ask at the tourist office about new hostels slated to open on Arthurs Quay, Cruises St., and next to Colbert station in 1995.

Eight miles northwest of Limerick along the Ennis Rd. (N18), **Bunratty Castle** claims to be Ireland's most completely medieval castle, with superbly restored furniture, tapestry, and stained-glass windows. Further west of Limerick off the Ennis Rd. (15mi.), **Shannon Airport** (tel. (061) 47 14 44; Aer Lingus info tel. (061) 47 16 66), ends jets to North America and Europe. The airport provides direct ground transport to Ennis, Galway, Westport, Tralee, and Killarney.

The narrow, high-walled streets and buzzing crowds of **Ennis** reside 20mi. northwest of Limerick; the town is also the gateway to the Clare coastal region. Ask questions at the tourist office in the **Upstairs Downstairs shop,** O'Connell Sq. (open

IRELAND

9am-9pm; Oct.-May 9am-6pm, Sun. 10am-6pm). **Buses** run frequently from Station Rd. to Limerick (IR£5, students IR£3) and Galway (IR£7.30, students IR£4.30). Ask for a map at the rambling **Abbey Tourist Hostel (IHH),** Harmony Row (tel. (065) 226 20; reception open 9:30am-10:30pm. Laundry. IR£5. Sheets IR£1.) **O'Connell Street** is the place for cheap eats.

■■■ CLARE COAST

Meadows freckled with hollyhocks, dandelions, and B&Bs roll down to the sea along the coast from Kilkee in the south to Miltown Malbay; the 15mi. stretch north of Milltown to Doolin is far more dramatic. To get to the coast, take the Ennis post bus or the bi-daily buses from Limerick and Ennis to the many coastal towns.

Halfway up the coast, past Lahinch, cold blue waves crash against the majestic **Cliffs of Moher,** limestone masses that tower 700ft. over the Atlantic. Vaguely-marked paths meander the cliffs; tourists drop away after the first curve. A mile from the cliffs, the **Old Hostel** (tel. (065) 813 82), a gabled schoolhouse, keeps a collection of musical instruments around the peat stove. (Kitchen. Dorm beds IR£5.50. Doubles IR£10.)

Lisdoonvarna hosts one of Ireland's last remaining **Matchmaking Festivals.** At these traditional fêtes, farmboys and farmgirls, their crops already harvested (but with wild oats left to sow), throw their rakes and buckets aside to collide in uninhibited climax. Irish women tend to stay home and mock the randy bachelors who attend. The **Burren Holiday Tourist Hostel,** Doolin Rd. (tel. (065) 743 00), ranks among the finest in Ireland, with oak handrails, high ceilings, and antique decor. (IR£6. Delicious meals IR£3-6. Laundry IR£3. Bikes IR£5.)

Doolin (called **Fisherstreet** on some maps) is why you came to Ireland. World-class folk music fills the pubs, and the single mile-long street is one hand-painted storefront after another. **O'Connor's,** in the lower village, and **McGann's,** in the upper, have both won awards for the best traditional music in Ireland. Always book ahead for accommodations. The **Aille River Hostel (IHH),** ¼mi. downhill from the Upper Village (tel. (065) 742 60) is a small hostel with groovy ambience (IR£5.50 per person, private room IR£6.50, camping IR£3.50, free laundry; open mid-March to Oct.). **Westwind B&B,** Upper Village (tel. (065) 742 27), advises spelunkers or other would-be Burren explorers (IR£11, Sept.-May IR£10).

Around Lisdoonvarna, the **Burren** begins when bare limestone starts to appear amid the grasses and sheep. Inland and in-between, the limestone plains, spines and outcroppings dominate; this 100-square-mile region is the Burren, whose elaborate *karst* moonscape includes rare wildflowers, flat stone pedestals, and jagged hills resembling grey skyscrapers bombed to rubble. Respect the Burren landscape; do not interfere with the flora and fauna since some species are unique to the region. A small town 8km southeast of Lisdoonvarna along the R478, **Kilfenora** calls itself "the heart of the Burren;" it's certainly a useful base. Tourists, most of them on bicycles, stop here for a pint, some grub, and a walk through the **Burren Display Center,** which explains the formation of the Burren, displays artifacts, and shows an excellent film on the biology of the Burren, which may help you recognize the species you'll walk by. (Open July-Aug. 9:30am-7pm; mid-March-May and Sept.-Oct. 10am-5pm; June 9:30am-6pm. Center and film IR£2, students IR£1.) A tourist office sits next to the Center (tel. (065) 881 98) and sells the helpful *Burren Rambler* map series (IR£2). (Open June-Oct. 9:30am-6pm.)

Prehistoric bears once inhabited the two-million-year-old **Aillwee Cave,** 2mi. south of **Ballyvaughan,** a small village on the N67 abutting Galway Bay; you'll hear all about bears on the tour, but the spectacular rocks and waterfalls are what you'll be gaping at. (Open July-Aug. 10am-6:30pm; mid-March to June and Sept. to early Nov. Mon.-Fri. 10am-5:30pm. IR£3.85, students IR£3.)

■■■ GALWAY CITY

Galway meanders between rivers and sea, full of old merchant houses, traditional music pubs, active independent theaters, and gaggles of hip young people. In summer you must parry and thrust with your furled umbrella to clear space on the tourist-filled streets. Galway's **cathedral** dominates the city's skyline and postcards, looming above the Salmon Weir Bridge. Two blocks south, the restored **Nora Barnacle House,** Bowling Green, exposes the correspondence and photos of James Joyce and his wife (open May-Sept. Mon-Sat. 10am-5pm; IR£1). Sixteenth-century **Lynch's Castle,** an elegant stone mansion with incongruous gargoyles, now houses the Allied Irish Bank (bank and exhibits open Mon.-Wed. and Fri. 10am-3pm, Thurs. 10am-5pm; free). By the river, the **Spanish Arch** is the only surviving gateway to the old trading town. The Arch is more famous than it is impressive—just a worn, one-story stone curve, yet half the town's stores seem named for it. Around Dominick St. is the neighborhood called the **Claddagh;** until the 1930s, this area was an independent, Irish-speaking, thatched-cottage fishing village. The cottages have since been replaced by stone bungalows, but the area still retains a certain charm, not to mention great views of Galway Bay. Claddagh rings, the traditional wedding rings of the old neighborhood, are mass-marketed but still-remarkable examples of Celtic metalworking.

Theaters, musicians, and literary events crowd Galway itself; music both rowdy and sedate barrages Salthill's clubs. The big nights are Wednesday, Friday, and Saturday; come here on any other night and the clubs will be more or less empty. For twelve days in mid-July the **Galway Arts Festival** attracts famous trad musicians, rock groups, theater troupes, filmmakers and comedians; ask the Festival Box Office, Eyre Sq. (tel. (091) 672 11) for information. **The Quays,** Quay St., is a bar popular with everyone under 25, including large numbers of scamming yuppie types and Americans. Home to the alternative nation, **Monroe's,** Dominick St., features a bat-cave interior replete with bandanas, long hair, body piercings, and dreadlocks. Wear black.

The main **tourist office,** Victoria Pl. (tel. (091) 630 81), lies a block west of the bus and train station (tel. (091) 621 41; open 9am-7pm; Easter-July and Sept.-Oct. Mon.-Sat. 9am-5:45pm, Sun. 9am-12:45pm; Nov.-March Mon.-Fri. 9am-5:45pm, Sat. 9am-12:45pm). Another office hides in **Salthill** (same phone; open June to mid-Sept.; 9am-5:45pm; July-Aug. 9am-8:30pm). Rent bikes at **Europa Cycles,** Hunter's Building, Earls' Island (tel. (091) 633 55; open Mon.-Sat. 9am-6pm, Sun. 10am-2pm and 4-6pm; IR£3 per day, IR£25 per week, IR£30 deposit). **Trains** run from Eyre Square Station (tel. (091) 614 44; open Mon.-Sat. 7:40am-6pm) to Athlone (1hr. IR£8, students IR£6) and continue to Dublin (3hr., IR£12, students IR£8); transfer at Athlone for other lines. **Buses** depart to Dublin (IR£8, students IR£6.50), Ennis (IR£7.30, students IR£4.30), and Shannon Airport (IR£9, students IR£5.30).

Hostels are conveniently located downtown. **Salmon Weir Hostel,** Woodquay (tel. (091) 611 33), is the best hostel in Galway; one-night visitors have been known to stay for months (curfew 3am; laundry IR£4; IR£5.90). **The Westend** (formerly Owen's Hostel), Upper Dominick St. (tel. (091) 636 36), offers clean, comfortable rooms, extremely laid back atmosphere, with storytelling and live music in summer (laundry IR£3.50. IR£6.50, Sept.-May IR£5.50; private rooms IR£10, Sept.-May IR£8). B&Bs hide in the Galway suburb **Renmare.** Be sure to book lodgings ahead, especially in July and August. For affordable eats, stick east of the river near the short blocks in and around Quay St., High St., Shop St., and Abbeygate St.

■■■ ARAN ISLANDS (OILEÁIN ÁRANN)

Fifteen miles off the coast of Galway, Irish-speaking Inishmore, Inishmaan, and Inisheer rise defiantly out of the Atlantic. Unless you're a jolly good swimmer, boats and planes are your only transport options. Frequent **ferries** run from Galway, Ros-

IRELAND

saveal, and Doolin (in County Clare). Direct your ferry queries to the Galway **tourist office** (tel. (091) 689 03, after business hours (091) 924 47; ferry desk open 9am-7pm, Oct.-May 9am-6pm). For flight information, call Aer Árann (tel. (091) 930 34 or 930 54), or make reservations in person at the Galway Tourist Office (IR£33 return, students IR£25). Dozens of ruins, forts, and churches, as well as "minor sites" like holy wells, lighthouses, and kelp kilns, rise from the stony terrain of **Inishmore.** The 18-ft. thick walls of **Dún Aengus Fort** (Dún Aonghasa), 5mi. west of the pier at Kilronan, guard Inishmore's northwest quarter and the strangely brilliant turquoise waves that hollow the base of the surrounding cliffs. Stay at the wonderful **Mainistir House (IHH)** (tel. (099) 611 69), which perches ½mi. from Kilronan; go up the hill and take a right after the supermarket (IR£7; doubles IR£20). **An Sean Chéibh,** with outdoor seating and fresh Aran fish, is a short walk left from the harbor. Ferries land at the pier in **Kilronan** (Cill Rónáin), the island's main harbor; the **tourist office** (tel. (099) 612 63) is at the pier. (Open June to mid-Sept. 10am-7pm.)

Tourists are a rarer breed on the smaller islands, **Inishmaan** and **Inisheer,** than on Inishmore. Here one finds stunning scenery and locals who construct *curraghs* (small boats made from curved wicker rods tied with string and covered with cowskin and black tar). On Inishmaan, stay with **Mrs. Faherty,** Creigmore (tel. (099) 730 12), who runs a jolly good B&B. (IR£10. Open April-Oct.)

■■■ CONNEMARA

A lacy net of inlets and islands along the coast and a rough gang of inland mountains make up the famously rugged Connemara, the thinly populated western arm of Co. Galway, flexing west from Galway City to the Atlantic. Like much of the western coast, the most rewarding way to absorb Connemara is on bike. Otherwise, take the 3hr. public bus from Galway to Clifden via Cong, which passes through the most miraculous areas of the region. On the southern coast of Connemara, Ireland's largest Gaelic-speaking population inhabits an area stretching westward from Galway City to Carna perfect for camping. Throngs arrive in summer for the *curragh* races, the largest of which is held in **Spiddal** (An Spidéal), 12mi. west of Galway City on the main Connemara coast road. The landscape becomes progressively starker west of Spiddal. Stay at the **Connemara Tourist Hostel,** Aille, Inverin (tel. (091) 931 04), 2 mi. west of Spiddal (IR£5.50). The coastal bus from Galway stops outside.

CLIFDEN

Connemara's western outpost is the only spot in the region that could be properly classified as a town. Clifden has become a miniature Killarney, boasting six hostels, tour buses, and countless *bureaux de change*. In summer you're almost certain to see more tourists than natives. **Connemara Heritage Tours,** Market St. (tel. (095) 213 79), foray into the history, folklore, and archeology of the region (leave Easter-Oct. 9:30am and 2pm; IR£10, students IR£8; 4hr.). The amiable **tourist office** (tel. (095) 211 63) is at the bottom of Market St. (open May and Sept. Mon.-Sat. 10am-5:30pm; June Mon.-Sat. 9am-6pm; July-Aug. Mon.-Sat. 9am-6pm, Sun. 12-4pm). Rent bikes at **Mannion's,** Bridge St. (tel. (095) 211 60; IR£7 per day, IR£30 per week, IR£40 deposit; open Mon.-Sat. 9am-6:30pm, Sun. 10am-1pm and 5-7pm). **Buses** run to Clifden from Galway through Oughterard.

What the **Clifden Town Hostel,** Market St. (tel. (095) 210 76) lacks in character, it makes up with clean, uncrowded rooms and a helpful, friendly staff (4-5-bed bunkroom IR£6; private rooms low season IR£6.50, high season IR£7.50). The reputation of the "loo with a view" at sunny, whitewashed **Leo's Hostel** (tel. (095) 214 29) has spread far and wide (IR£5, private room IR£5.50; cabin for 2 IR£6). Sit on honey-colored wooden picnic benches at **My Teashop,** Main St. (open 9am-6pm). For a little drink and wink, try **The Central,** Main St.

CLEGGAN AND THE TWELVE BENS

Ten miles northwest, **Cleggan,** the center of Connemara's fishing industry, offers the charms of Clifden without the tourists. Explore the pleasant sandhills and small ruins of **Omey Island,** just offshore to the southwest and accessible by foot at low tide. People remain for days at the airy **Master House Hostel** (tel. (095) 447 46), full of plants, bright wood, and exposed stone. (IR£6. Private room IR£7. Fishing rods IR£2.50.)

The **Twelve Bens** (*Na Benna Beola*, also known as the Twelve Pins) are a range of rugged hills 1700-2400 ft. high in the heart of the Connemara. Hikers can base themselves at the **Ben Lettery youth hostel (HI)** (tel. (095) 346 36) in Ballinafad, 8mi. east of Clifden, off the N59 west of the Roundstone turn-off (April-June and Sept. IR£4.50, July-Aug. IR£5.50). Farther east along the N59, **Killary Harbour,** Ireland's only fjord, breaks through the mountains to the town of **Leenane,** wrapping itself in the skirts of the **Devilsmother Mountain.** The remote **Killary Harbour youth hostel (HI)** (tel. (095) 434 17) is at the very mouth of the harbor, 7mi. west of Leenane (March-May and Sept IR£4.50, June-Aug. IR£5.50).

WESTPORT

Westport is a quintessentially pleasant town with a satisfactory pub life and plenty of good cafés; its location at the elbow-crook of Clew Bay, with Connemara to its south and Co. Mayo's islands a short jaunt northwest, makes it a likely stop. **Croagh Patrick's** perfect cone of a mountain rises 2510 ft. over Clew Bay; the summit has been considered holy for thousands of years. Most climbers start from the village of Murrisk, west of Westport on the R335 to Louisburgh; buses traverse the route all year. The **tourist office** (tel. (098) 257 11) occupies the North Mall, down by the river (open Easter-Sept. Mon.-Fri. 9am-6pm, Sat. 10am-6pm; winter Mon.-Fri. 9am-12:45pm, 2-5:15pm). **Bike World,** the Octagon (tel. (098) 59 61 79), rents 2-wheelers (IR£6 per day, IR£30 per week; open Mon.-Sat. 10am-6:30pm, Sun. noon-6pm). **Trains** (tel. (098) 252 53 or 253 29; inquiry line open. Mon.-Sat. 9:30am-6pm) arrive from Dublin via Athlone and Castlebar (IR£12, students IR£9) at the Altamont St. Station. **Buses** leave from the Octagon for Galway (IR£9.70); and Sligo, continuing on to Belfast (May-Sept. only).

The **Old Mill Holiday Hostel (IHH),** James St. (tel. (098) 270 45), offers firm pine-framed beds and shockingly hot showers in a renovated mill and brewery (bedroom lockout 11am-1pm; IR£6, Sept.-June IR£5). **Club Atlantic (HI),** Altamont St. (tel. (098) 266 44 or 267 17) , is a massive 140-bed complex across from the train station that "has it all" (6- to 8-bed rooms June-Aug. IR£5.50-5.90; March-May and Sept.-Oct. IR£4.50; singles IR£9, doubles IR£14).

NORTHWEST IRELAND

The upper Shannon's strips of farmland interrupted by monasteries and islands are a gradual windup to the punch of Sligo, a fun bay town close to the heart of the poet William Butler Yeats. Donegal's windy mountains and winding coasts may be your wildest dream come true, and don't leave the country without having seen the Inishowen Peninsula. From there, it's easy to cross into Derry, a history-soaked Northern city filled with nervous energy.

Sligo Town, Donegal Town, and Killybegs South of County Donegal, **Sligo town,** childhood haunt of W.B. Yeats, is a convenient stopover for northern wanderers and a happening pub town to boot. Yeats fanatics hike up rocky **Knocknarea** but, simply admire more severe **Benbulben,** which broods over Yeats's grave in **Drumcliff churchyard,** 4mi. north of town. Back in Sligo, the **bus/train station** (bus tel. (071) 600 66; train tel. 698 88) is centrally located on Lord Edward St. and the **tourist office** (tel. (071) 612 01) is past the cathedral on Temple

St. (open Mon.-Fri. 9am-6pm, Sat. 10am-2pm; July-Aug. Mon.-Sat. 9am-8pm, Sun. 10am-6pm; Sept.-April Mon.-Fri. 9am-5pm). The hippest hostel in town, the **White House Hostel (IHH),** Markievicz Rd. (tel. (071) 451 60), has 3 young, fast-talking wardens, and bunks named after the likes of Jimi Hendrix, James Connolly, and Socrates (IR£6; key deposit IR£2). Wonderful lunches vary daily at ever-authentic **Hardogan's** on O'Connell St.

Gateway to the stunning cliffs and inlets to the west, **Donegal town** is a good springboard for northwest Ireland. The **tourist office** (tel. (073) 211 48) sits south of the Diamond (the central town square and home of the **bus depot**) on Quay St. (Open Mon.-Sat. 9am-8pm, Sun. 10am-1pm and 2-8pm; Sept.-Oct. and Easter-June Mon.-Fri. 9am-5pm, Sat.-Sun. 10am-1pm.) With its wide patio, the **Donegal Town Hostel (IHH)** (tel. (073) 28 05), 1mi. down Killybegs Rd., seems as if it should overlook the sea, not the main road (checkout 11am; IR£5.50). The best dinner deal is at **Errigal Restaurant,** Main St. (open Mon.-Sat. 9am-10:20pm, Sun. 3-10:20pm; fish and chips IR£2-4, chicken dinner IR£3.50). For basics, head to **Foodland Supermarket,** in the Diamond (open Mon.-Thurs. 9am-8pm, Fri. 9am-9pm, Sat. 9am-7:30pm). **Schooner's** on Main St. has live music and good conversation.

The road heading west along Donegal's southern coast (the N56), from Donegal town to Rossan Point at the peninsula's tip, is scenic and varied. Buses run from Donegal town to **Killybegs** (5 per day, Sept.-early July Mon.-Sat. 3 per day). Several miles farther on the coast road between Kilcar and Carrick, **Dun Ulun House** provides a luxurious alternative to hostel life. Large flowery beds accompany a continental (IR£11) or full (IR£13) breakfast. Down the road, the **Derrylahan Hostel (IHH)** (tel. (073) 380 79), welcomes guests like long-lost cousins. With a well-stocked shop and hot showers, this hostel makes a great stopover. (IR£5. Private room IR£7. Camping IR£3.) The road south from Carrick leads to **Slieve League,** a 2000ft. mountain that drops precipitously into Donegal Bay. On one side of One Man's Pass, the cliffs drop 1800ft. straight to the sea; on the other side they fall 1000ft. to a rocky floor. The N15 provides a considerably safer, if less dramatic, route to **Glencolumbcille** at the westernmost point of the peninsula.

Derryveagh Mountains and Letterkenny The bulky **Derryveagh Mountains** isolate the northwest corner of Donegal, the country's largest Irish-speaking area. On the road to Gweedore via Church Hill, 14mi. northwest of Letterkenny, stretches the **Glenveagh National Park** (tel. (074) 370 88)—10,000 hectares of glens, mountains, and nature walks, plus a castle. (Park and castle open April-May 10am-6:30pm; June-Aug. Mon.-Sat. 10am-6:30pm, Sun. 10am-7:30pm; Oct. Sat.-Thurs. 10am-6:30pm. IR£1.50, students 60p.)

Letterkenny is Donegal's commercial center and the fastest growing town in Europe. You'll want to stop here between peninsular jaunts, on you way to Glenveagh National Park, or coming to or from Donegal. The **Chamber of Commerce Visitors Information Centre,** 40 Port Rd. (tel. (074) 228 66), looks like a china shop, but bull on in for the pamphlets and friendly advice (open Mon.-Fri. and some Sat. 9am-7pm; Sept.-June Mon.-Fri. 9am-5pm.) The **Rosemount Hostel (IHH),** 3 Rousemount Terrace (tel. (074) 262 84), is predictably friendly (6- to 8-bunk dorms; IR£5; open June-Oct.).

Donegal Peninsulas Between Lough Swilly and Mulroy Bay the **Fanad Peninsula** juts into the Atlantic, somewhat in the shadow of its larger neighbor, the Inishowen. North of Rathmullan, the land rises over the Knockala Hills and Glenvar, beyond which the coast is at its most arresting as it arcs between mountain and shore. Follow the signs to **Bunnaton Hostel,** Glenvar (tel. (074) 501 22; IR£5, private rooms IR£6.50 per person). It would be a crime to leave Ireland without experiencing the **Inishowen Peninsula.** A mosaic of rugged mountains, lush forests, sumptuous beaches, and sheep, the peninsula is a microcosm of Ireland. Any tour of the area must begin with a visit to the hilltop fort of **Grianán of Aileach,** the "stone palace of the sun," built in 1700 BC. **Buncrana,** on the west side of the peninsula along the shores of Lough Swilly, is an energetic resort where sweeping beaches repose in the long shadow of **Slieve Snacht,** a 2019-ft. peak. About 6mi. north of Buncrana, the **Gap of Mamore** sits 800ft. above sea level, offering torrid views of the entire peninsula. Vivid **Malin,** winner of Ireland's cut-throat Tidy Town Competition, is Inishowen's northernmost outpost before the peninsula reaches out to tag **Malin Head,** from which you can see all the way across to the Paps of Jura on a clear day. Make a pitstop at **Farren's Pub,** Malin Head, Ireland's northernmost pub. A mile from the head is **Hell's Hole,** a 250-ft. chasm that roars with the incoming tide.

Situated on a lovely estuary, the village of **Culdaff** exudes a friendly warmth from its beaches and the great **McGrory's Pub.** The McGrory family also runs a splendid **Guest House** above the pub (tel. (077) 791 04; IR£14). Nearby **Kinnagoe Bay,** site of the 1588 wreckage of the Spanish Armada, will take your breath away. On the southeast coast of the Inishowen Peninsula, 5mi. over the border from Derry in Northern Ireland, lies **Muff Hostel (IHH)** (tel. (077) 841 88), run by the gentle Martin Cooke; it's a hosteler's best base for most of Inishowen and for seeing Derry (IR£5; hot showers; open March-Oct.).

NORTHERN IRELAND

The strife that makes the North famous hides the land's beauty and appeal from international travelers. What they're missing includes the string of seaside villages on the Ards Peninsula; the pockets of womblike green collectively called the Glens of Antrim; one of the world's strangest geological sights, the Giant's Causeway; the beautiful Fermanagh Lake District; and an amazing folk park in Omagh. Pub culture and urban neighborhoods show everyday life in a divided (and, for most people most of the time, peaceful) society. You haven't seen the North until you've seen all these: not just the coastal resorts, but certainly not just the Troubles either.

> As part of the United Kingdom, Northern Ireland uses British pounds ("pounds sterling"); its banks print their own sterling notes, which are *not* accepted in the rest of the U.K., though English, Scottish, and Manx notes *are* accepted in Northern Ireland. Irish pounds are not ordinarily accepted; make a trip to the bank and change your *punts.*

SECURITY

If you're planning to cross the border on a bike or in a car, be sure to do so at one of the approved **border-crossing checkpoints,** of which there are many; crossing at an unapproved point can get you followed by the army. Always bring ID and check that the road you mean to use hasn't been blown up near the border. Hitching is unsafe around Dundalk in the Republic and the little towns of South Armagh, especially Crossmaglen. Do not ever take **photographs** of soldiers or of military installations or vehicles; if you do, your film will be confiscated, and you may be detained for questioning. Some urban areas have **"control zones,"** where there's no parking due to fear of car bombs. Since **unattended luggage** can also conceal a bomb, it's viewed with suspicion and may be blown up by the security forces.

■■■ BELFAST

The second largest city on the island, Belfast is in some ways more cosmopolitan than Dublin. Over one-fifth of the North's population lives in Belfast, making the city the center for Northern Ireland's active and separate commercial, artstic, and paramilitary worlds.

IRELAND

ORIENTATION AND PRACTICAL INFORMATION

Belfast is loosely centered on **City Hall** in **Donegall Square,** six blocks from the River Lagan and the harbor. To the north of the center lies the city's snazzy shopping district and two blocks west on Great Victoria St. is the **Golden Mile.** The working class neighborhoods of West Belfast are sharply divided by the **"peace line"**—a physical wall that runs halfway between the Catholic Falls Rd. and the Protestant Shankill Rd. If you must visit, do so during the day and under no circumstances cross the peace line. If you want to visit both areas of West Belfast, you must return to the city center and take a black cab to the other area. Those planning to visit the docks for the nightlife should go to and from their chosen clubs in a taxi.

Tourist Office: St. Anne's Court, 59 North St. (tel. 24 66 09). Info, brochures, and a terrific free map of the city with bus schedules. A computer set into the office's exterior gives 24hr. tourist info. Open Mon.-Sat. 9am-5:15pm, July-Aug. Mon.-Fri. 9am-7:30pm, Sat. 9am-5:15pm, Sun. noon-4pm.

Budget Travel Office: USIT, 136 Fountain Centre, College St. (tel. 32 40 73), near Royal Ave. Open Mon.-Fri. 9:30am-5:30pm, Sat. 10am-1pm.

U.S. Consulate General: Queens House, Queen St. (tel. 22 82 39). Open Mon.-Fri. 1-5pm.

Currency Exchange: Thomas Cook, British Airways, College St. (tel. 89 91 31). Open Mon.-Fri. 9am-5pm, Sat. 9am-4:15pm.

American Express: Hamilton Travel, 10 College St. (tel. 32 24 55). Client mail held. Open Mon.-Fri. 9am-5pm, Sat. 10am-1pm.

Post Office: 25 Castle Pl. (tel. 32 37 40). Open Mon.-Fri. 9am-5:30pm, Sat. 9am-1pm. **Postal Code:** BT1BB.

Telephones: City Code: 01232.

Flights: Belfast International Airport (Aldergrove). A shuttle bus runs to Central Station (every ½hr., Sun. every hr.; UK£3.50).

Trains: Belfast Station (tel. 230 310). From Dublin's O'Connolly Station (UK£13, return UK£19.50). From Derry (UK£7, return UK£9.70).

Buses: Central Station (tel. 32 00 11). To Dublin (Mon.-Sat. 4/day, Sun. 3/day; UK£9.50, return UK£12). From Derry (Mon.-Sat. 6/day, Sun 4/day; UK£5.30, return UK£9.30). All others arrive at **Europa/Glengall St. Station.**

Ferries: The Seacat and ferries cross from Scotland to Belfast and Larne, north of the city. (See Ireland—Getting There, above.)

Taxi: Huge **black cabs** run set routes to West Belfast, collecting and discharging passengers along the way (standard 50p charge). Easily identifiable by either a Falls Rd. or Irish-language sign (Catholic), or a red poppy (Protestant), the cabs are heavily partisan. If you're not going their way, call an ordinary metered cab (all 24hr.): **City Cab** (tel. 24 20 00)

Crisis Lines: Samaritans: tel. 66 44 22, 24hrs. **Rape Crisis Center:** 41 Waring St. (tel. 32 18 30). Open Mon.-Fri. 10am-6pm, Sat. 11am-5pm.

Emergencies: Dial 999; no coins required. **Police:** 65 Knock Rd. (tel. 65 02 22; often faster than 999 in an emergency).

ACCOMMODATIONS AND FOOD

Look for safe and convenient lodgings near the university, south of the center.

YHANI Belfast Hostel (HI), 22 Donegal Rd. (tel. 32 47 33). Clean, spacious, ultra-modern rooms with 2-6 beds, some with private bathrooms. No lockout or curfew. Wheelchair access. UK£8.50, with private bath UK£10. Book 2 weeks in advance for weekends.

Mrs. Davidson's East-Sheen Guest House, 81 Eglantine Ave. (tel. 66 71 49). The best deal in Belfast, if you can get a room. Mrs. D. will nurse you with scones; every room has a teapot, sugar cubes, and biscuits. UK£14.

Queen's University Accommodations, 78 Malone Rd. (tel. 38 16 08). Take bus 70 or 71 from Donegall Sq. East, or walk down Great Victoria Rd., which runs into Malone Rd. Spartan rooms on long corridors. No curfew. Single rooms: UK students UK£7, international students UK£8.23, non-students UK£11-16. Twins UK£17.63. Open mid-June to mid-Sept., also Christmas and Easter vacations.

Dublin Rd. and the **Golden Mile,** stretching from the Grand Opera House down Great Victoria St. to University Rd., have the highest concentration of places to eat; **Bookfinders,** 47 University Rd., a smoky, atmoshperic bookstore/café, offers *moussaka* and salad (UK£3.20) or soup and bread (UK£1.40) amidst stacks of old books, as well as the occasional poetry reading (open Mon.-Sat. 10am-5:30pm). **Café Equinox,** 32 Howard St., behind the arts gift store, is a sleek black café with double espressos and the best sandwiches in Belfast (open Mon.-Wed. and Fri.-Sat. 9:30am-5pm, Thurs. 9:30am-9pm). For wholesome veggie fare, try **Spice of Life,** 62 Lower Donegall St., across from St. Anne's Cathedral, which serves soups and sandwiches (UK£1.50) and vegan ice cream (55p per scoop); nothing is over UK£3 (open Mon.-Sat. 10am-5pm).

SIGHTS AND ENTERTAINMENT

Belfast's main attraction, the **Ulster Folk and Transport Museum,** lies five miles east of the city center, in Cultra. This fascinating open-air museum contains traditional buildings from all over Northern Ireland that were dismantled at their original locations and carefully reconstructed on the museum's 180 acres of parkland. (Open Mon.-Sat. 10:30am-6pm, Sun. noon-6pm; April-June and Sept. Mon.-Fri. 9:30am-5pm, Sat. 10:30am-6pm, Sun. noon-6pm; Oct.-March Mon.-Fri. 9:30am-4pm, Sat.-Sun. 12:30-4pm. Closed Christmas week. UK£2.60, HI discount 50%.)

Belfast's ornate **City Hall** stands set apart by a grassy square, with a 173-ft. green copper dome that can be seen from anywhere in the city. (Free tours Wed. 10:30am; July-Aug. Mon.-Fri. also 2:30pm; by advance booking only. Call 32 02 02.) The northwest corner of Donegall Square holds the **Linen Hall Library,** 17 Donegall Sq., famous for its comprehensive collection of political materials relating to the Troubles (open Mon.-Wed. and Fri. 9:30am-5:30pm, Thurs. 9:30am-8:30pm, Sat 9:30am-4pm). Just across College Square, **Old Museum Arts Center** mounts rotating art exhibits, and holds frequent concerts and performances (open Mon.-Fri. 9am-5:30pm, Sat. 10am-5pm; free). Follow Great Victoria St. south from City Hall to **Queen's University,** whose attractive Tudor buildings overlook the **Botanic Gardens** (open 7:30am-dusk; free). The **Ulster Museum** has an astounding collection of silver and gold looted from the *Girona,* a Spanish Armada ship wrecked off the Giant's Causeway in 1588 (open Mon.-Fri. 10am-5pm, Sat. 1-5pm, Sun. 2-5pm; free).

Belfast's nightlife changes with the wind; the best sources of information are the *Arts Council Artslink,* Thursday's *Irish News* and the daily *Belfast Telegraph.* You'll find pubs all over the city, but they'll practically bump into you around Great Victoria St. and the city center, or in the vicinity of the university. Try the **Crown Liquor Saloon,** 46 Great Victoria St., or **Kelly's Cellars,** 30 Bank St. Students hop back and forth between **The Botanic Inn** ("The Bot"), 23 Malone Rd., and **Eglantine Inn** ("The Egg"), 32 Malone Rd. They dance at **Lavery's,** 12 Bradbury Pl.

The truly **Grand Opera House,** Great Victoria St. (tel. 24 19 19; 24hr. info 24 91 25), boasts an impressive mix of opera, ballet, musicals, and drama. During opera season in September tickets may be booked at tel. 38 12 41 (UK£8-30, student standbys 45min. before performance UK£5). Tickets for other events are available at the box office, 17 Wellington Pl. (open Mon.-Sat. 9:45am-5:30pm). In November, Queen's University hosts the **Belfast Festival at Queen's,** a three-week extravaganza of drama, music, and art. (Contact the Festival House, 25 College Gardens, Belfast BT9 6BS by Aug.; tel. 667 687. Ticket sales by mail begin Sept. 15; from Oct. 15 on, tickets available by phone at tel. 66 76 87.)

■■■ FERMANAGH LAKE DISTRICT

Located in the southwestern corner of Northern Ireland, the Fermanagh Lake District is the perfect place for an amphibious jaunt. Hiking, biking, canoeing, windsurf-

IRELAND

ing, and orienteering all make this an invigorating region; everything cool is within 20mi. of **Enniskillen,** the region's main town. **Erne Tours Ltd.** (tel. (01365) 32 28 82) sets out from Round O Jetty, Beleek Rd., and stops on **Devenish Island,** with its 12th-century castle. (May-June Sun. 2:30pm; July-Aug. daily 10:30am, 2:15pm, and 4:15pm; plus Tues., Thurs., and Sun. 7:15pm. Sept. Tues., Sat., and Sun. 2:30pm. UK£3.50.) Visit Enniskillen's well-equipped **Lakeland Visitors Center** (tel. (01365) 32 31 10) on Shore Rd. (Open Mon.-Fri. 9am-5:30pm, Sat. 10am-6pm, Sun. 11am-5pm; Oct.-May Mon.-Fri. 9am-5pm.) **Ulsterbus** (tel. (01365) 32 26 33) leaves from its swanky new station across from the tourist office to Belfast (3 per day; 2¼hr.; UK£5.50, students UK£4.70) and Dublin (Mon.-Sat. 2-5 per day, Sun. 3 per day; 3hr.; UK£9, students UK£6). Stay at the modern **Castle Archdale Youth Hostel (HI)** (tel. (013656) 281 18) in a restored 19th-century house 1mi. off the road from Enniskillen to Kesh (UK£6, wash and dry UK£2).

■■■ DERRY

Nicknamed "Stroke City" because it's sometimes written "L'derry" so as not to offend rival factions of Unionists and Nationalists, Derry (also known as Londonderry) is a city divided—the River Foyle keeps the predominantly Protestant east side and the predominantly Catholic west side from running into each other. At the highest point in the city, **St. Columb's Cathedral** of 1633 was the first in Britain and Ireland after the Reformation (open Mon.-Sat. 9am-5pm; free; call ahead to arrange a free tour). The political murals painted around the streets are sights themselves. Look for "The Auld's Days," which is painted at the junction of William and Rossville St. The **tourist office,** 8 Bishop St. (tel. (01504) 26 72 84), distributes *Derry Visitors Guide* (open Mon.-Sat. 9am-8pm, Sun. 10am-6pm; Oct.-June Mon.-Fri. 9am-5:15pm). Trains from The Waterside station on the east bank of the river only travel east, to Belfast (2½hr.; UK£7) and Antrim Town; a sideline from Coleraine zips north to Portrush. **Ulsterbus** (tel. (01504) 26 22 61) also services all points in Northern Ireland. The very institutional, but central, **Oakgrove Manor (HI),** Magazine St. (tel. (01504) 37 22 73), is modern, spacious, and centrally located (curfew 2am, checkout 10am strictly enforced; large dorm UK£6, with shower UK£7; singles with shower and breakfast UK£15; doubles with shower and breakfast UK£8). Just 5mi. outside of Derry is the relaxed, homey **Muff Hostel** (UK£5 per person). **The Sandwich Co.,** the Diamond, at the corner of Ferryquay St. and Bishop St., offers *real* sandwiches with loads of fresh fillings (95p-£2.45; open Mon.-Thurs. and Sat. 9am-5pm, Fri. 9am-6pm).

■■■ CAUSEWAY COAST

As the Northern Irish coast rounds Torr Head, between Ballycastle in the east and Portstewart in the west, 600-ft. cliffs plummet into the restless surf. **Ulsterbus** runs tours through the area, and during July and August the open-topped **Bushmills Bus** (tel. (01265) 433 32) follows the coast between Coleraine (5mi. south of Portrush) and the Giant's Causeway (4 per day, Sun. 2 per day). Ulsterbus 172 runs along the coast from Ballycastle to Portrush (1hr.).

The glens end and the Causeway Coast begins in **Ballycastle,** a tired but friendly resort stopover point. The **tourist office** is in Sheskburn House at 7 Mary St. (tel. (012657) 620 24; open Mon.-Fri. 9:30am-7pm, Sat. 10am-6pm, Sun. 2-6pm; Sept.-May Mon.-Fri. 9:30am-5pm, Sat. 10am-4pm). Ballycastle's best asset is actually the **ferry** that runs to **Rathlin Island,** the ultimate in escapism for 20,000 puffins, one golden eagle, and about 100 human beings. The **Castle Hostel,** 62 Quay Rd. (tel. (012657) 623 37), has a central location and overcrowded bunk room. (UK£5; free laundry; camping out back UK£3).

Five miles west of Ballycastle is the village of **Ballintoy,** with a picturesque church and a tiny harbor. Just off the shore is **Carrick-a-rede Island** ("rock in the road").

Crossing the flimsy bridge that connects the mainland to the islands (over a dizzying 80ft. drop to rocks and sea) is now a popular activity for tourists. To find the bridge, take the sign-posted turnoff from the coast road about a mile east of Ballintoy.

Advertised as the eighth natural wonder of the world, the **Giant's Causeway** is deservedly Northern Ireland's most famous sight. Forty thousand hexagonal columns of basalt form a honeycomb path from the foot of the cliffs into the sea. Many paths loop to the causeway from the nearby **YHANI Youth Hostel (HI)** (tel. (012567) 317 45; no lockout or curfew; UK£6, nonmembers UK£7.50). Visit the **Causeway Visitors Centre** (tel. (012657) 315 82) to pick up the excellent trail leaflet (40p) that will guide you the 8mi. back. (Center open July-Aug. 10am-7pm; Sept.-Oct. 10:30am-6pm; mid-March to May 11am-5pm. Causeway always open.)

Two miles west of the National Trust Visitor's Centre is **Bushmills,** home of the oldest functioning whiskey distillery in the world, open since 1609. (Tours, with free sample, every 15min. Mon.-Thurs. 9am-noon and 1:30-4:15pm, Fri. 9am-3:45pm, Sat. 10am-3:45pm; Sept.-May Mon.-Thurs. 9am-noon and 1:30-3:30pm, Fri. 9-11:45am. UK£2.)

■■■ GLENS OF ANTRIM

Between the Causeway Coast and Belfast, the rolling green hills and high moors of County Antrim drop through nine deep valleys lush with greenery—the Glens of Antrim—down to the rocky coast. Two **bus** lines serve the area: the 162 service from Belfast (Mon.-Fri. 10 per day, Sat. 8 per day, Sun. 2 per day) and the Antrim Coaster from Belfast to Coleraine (June-Sept. Mon.-Sat. 2 per day). Most rides within the Glens average UK£2-4. Many hitch a ride along these lovely roads; cycling is, as always, fabulous.

Ballygally and Waterfoot Ballygally is an excellent gateway to the Glens. Both the Larne-Cushendall and Antrim Coaster buses stop right outside the friendly **Ballygally Youth Hostel (HI)** (tel. (01574) 58 33 77; UK£6, under 18 UK£5; open March-Dec.). Outside Ballygally, nearer to Larne, is the **Carnfunnock Country Park** (tel. (01574) 27 62 55), which provides campsites (UK£5). Pathways lead from the sundials of the time garden to a carefully constructed hedge maze.

Five miles down the coast, the village of **Waterfoot** (Glenariff) guards Antrim's broadest glen and the town's namesake, Glenariff. Another 4mi. down the road in **Glenariff Forest Park,** waterfalls feed the River Glenariff (taxonomic originality was not an Irish strength). If you don't want to camp at **Glenariff Forest Park Camping,** 98 Glenariff Rd. (tel. (0126673) 232; tents UK£4.50), find one of the many farmers in the area who welcome campers (ask in town), or stay in Waterfoot. The Bally-mena-Cushendun **bus** (Mon.-Fri. 4 per day, Sun. 1 per day) passes the park entrance.

Cushendall, Cushendun, and Fair Head Cushendall, 2 mi. north of Waterfoot, offers plenty of rooms and practical convenience for the glen explorer. The **Cushendall HI youth hostel** (tel. (012667) 713 44) is a mile from town on Layde Rd. (Lockout 10:30am-5pm. Curfew 11:30pm. Members UK£6, under 18 UK£5. Open March-Dec.) It would be hard to imagine a warmer welcome than the one you will receive from Mrs. O'Neill at **Glendale,** 46 Coast Rd. (tel. (012667) 714 95). Bikes and the like can be rented from **Ardclinis Activity Center,** 11 High St. (tel. (012667) 713 40; mountain bikes UK£10 per day, no deposit).

Farther north via an inland road that climbs up through the moors, the National Trust preserves the tiny village of **Cushendun.** The vast sandy beach and a set of pudding stone sea caves makes the village a terrific afternoon stopover. The **National Trust** (tel. (0126674) 506) maintains an office, with displays on the history of the village and the sea caves, at 1 Main St. (open 1-5pm; Sept.-June Sat.-Sun. 1-5pm.) **The Villa,** 185 Torr Rd. (tel. (0126674) 252), has a great B&B a mile from town on a particularly scenic portion of the Ulster Way (UK£15 per person). Seven miles north of Cushendun, just south of Ballycastle, **Fair Head** draws international hikers to its majestic basalt cliffs. On a clear day, you can see Rathlin Island, Donegal, and Scotland.

ISLE OF MAN

Floating in the Irish Sea, the Isle of Man is British without being part of the U.K. The island proudly touts its own legislature, flag, currency, and language. **Douglas,** the capital, is really just a grape-sized metropolis. Popularity as a resort among the Victorians endures in the form of the railway and horse tram network, promenades, and the **Gaiety Theater,** where three ghosts purportedly wander—one of them a little old lady in seat D-14 (tours every Sat. 10:30am, July-Aug. also Thurs. 2:30pm; free, but donation encouraged). Just south of the theater, visit the **Manx Museum,** which chronicles the natural and human history of the island, from the Ice Age to the present (open Mon.-Sat. 10am-5pm; free).

Three miles down the Castletown Rd. from Douglas, fields full of happy old horses draw visitors to the **Isle of Man Home of Rest for Old Horses,** Bulhrenny. The horses, most of whom used to pull the trams back and forth across Douglas, are happy because the Home has saved them from the slaughterhouse. (Open June-Sept. Mon.-Wed. 10am-4:50pm.)

The Isle of Man is connected to the British telephone system and uses British currency; note that Manx notes are not accepted in the rest of the U.K. The Isle of Man Steam Packet Company monopolizes **ferry** service on the island, sailing to Douglas and Heysham, Liverpool, and Fleetwood, England; Ardrossan, Scotland; and, Belfast and Dublin. For reservations, call the Douglas office (tel. (01624) 66 16 61; open Mon.-Sat. 7am-9pm, Sun. 9am-9pm), or the Belfast office (tel. (01232) 35 10 01; open Mon.-Fri. 9am-5:15pm). **Combination Sea/Rail tickets** from any British Rail station to Douglas are available through travel agents (London UK£88-99 return; Edinburgh UK£69-84; higher fares weekends in summer). The island also has an excellent public transport system. The 7-day **Freedom Ticket** allows you to ride any public transport (buses, railways, and horse trams) for UK£22.90.

In Douglas, the **tourist office,** Harris Promenade (tel. (01624) 68 67 66), provides a dizzying array of leaflets and lists, as well as bus and rail timetables and passes (open 9am-7:30pm; Sept. to mid-May Mon.-Fri. 9am-5pm, Sat. 9am-1:30pm). Inexpensive guesthouses cluster along the promenades. Try **Merridale Guest House,** 30 Castlemona Ave., with its large, clean bedrooms with sinks and coffee/teapots (UK£12 per person; open March-Dec.; sometimes fills weeks in advance for June-Aug.). Or try the small and cozy **Pat's B&B,** 27 Derby Rd., with its well-maintained garden and the cheapest rates in town (open March-Oct. UK£10 per person). **L'Experience,** Summer Hill, near the Electric Railway station, serves surprisingly good French cooking at reasonable lunchtime prices (French ploughman's lunch with Brie UK£2.75; lunch Mon.-Sat. noon-2pm).

IRELAND

Italy (Italia)

US$1 = L1587 (lire)	**L1000 = US$0.63**
CDN$1 = L1182	**L1000 = CDN$0.85**
UK£1 = L2522	**L1000 = UK£0.40**
IR£1 = L2498	**L1000 = IR£0.40**
AUS$1 = L1217	**L1000 = AUS$0.82**
NZ$1 = L962	**L1000 = NZ$1.04**
SAR1 = L445	**L1000 = SAR2.25**
Country Code: 39	**International Dialing Prefix: 00**

Stolid, rough-hewn medieval walls still encircle many of Italy's cities. In past centuries they insulated communities from the mayhem of the world beyond, facilitating the development of local dialects and customs and original artistic and architectural styles. Though the 20th century has left an indelible mark on Italian culture, the outward appearance of many cities has remained virtually unchanged, and a proud individualism still exists within each region. If it's not politics, it's soccer, and if not soccer, then it's wine that provokes heated discussion. Since the fall of Mussolini and the fascists, Italy has seen no fewer than 48 governments, the result of an electoral system that gives power to even the smallest of parties and necessitates unwieldy, tenuous coalitions. Added to this state of near-anarchy is the persistence of politically motivated acts of violence intended to disrupt the slow process of reforming the government. Despite this, Italy perseveres, with all of its pleasures and laid-back elegance intact.

A trip through the history of Italy begins beneath the grassy hills of Tarquínia, in the brightly painted tombs of the Etruscans; this highly developed civilization ruled central Italy centuries before the birth of Christ. Meanwhile, in Sicily, the Greeks honored their gods with soaring temples in white marble. Traces of the vast Roman Empire define the landscape, from the monumental amphitheaters of Rome and Verona to the volcanically embalmed towns of Pompeii and Herculaneum. Sparkling with Byzantine frescoes, simple early Christian churches distinguish Ravenna as a treasure house of early medieval culture, while San Gimignano bristles with the forbidding towers of the later Middle Ages. In Florence the remnants of the Italian Renaissance can be experienced at its most intoxicating.

For more detailed coverage than can be offered here, peruse *Let's Go: Italy* and *Let's Go: Rome*.

GETTING THERE AND GETTING AROUND

The **Ferrovie dello Stato (FS),** the Italian State Railway, runs more or less on time and its network is comprehensive. A *locale* train stops at nearly every station; the *diretto* is more direct, while the *espresso* stops only at major stations. The *rapido* zips along but costs a bit more (Eurailpass and BTLC holders exempt). The *Biglietto Chilometrico* (Kilometric Ticket) is good for 20 trips or 3000km, whichever comes first, and can be used for 2 months by as many as 5 people. (1st-class US$264, 2nd-class US$156, plus US$10 per pass.) If you have no railpass and are under 26, the **cartaverde** (L40,000, good for 3 years) should be your first purchase. Showing this card entitles you to a 20% discount on rail tickets. Trains, however, are not the safest means of travel. When traveling in groups, sleep in shifts, and always keep documents and valuables concealed on your person.

Intercity **buses** are often more convenient for shorter hauls off the main rail lines, and they serve countryside points inaccessible by train. The most beautiful rides are, unfortunately, the most nauseating—no fun for motion-sick types. For **city buses,** buy tickets in *tabacchi* stores or most newsstands, and validate them on board. The relatively uncrowded *autostrade* (super-highways) are gorgeous celebrations of engineering, but gas and tolls are prohibitive, and Italian drivers are often crazed speed demons. **Mopeds** (rates L25,000-50,000 per day) can be a great way to see the islands and the more rural areas of Italy, but are potentially disastrous in major cities, where you should stick to public transportation. **Bicycling** is a popular national sport, but bike trails are rare, drivers often reckless, and, except in the Po Valley, the terrain challenges even the fittest. **Women traveling alone should never hitchhike.** Hitchers should *never* fall asleep—it's tantamount to giving some drivers a blatant sexual invitation.

ITALY ESSENTIALS

Italian tourist offices come in two varieties: the bureaucratic **Ente Provinciale per il Turismo (EPT)** in the largest cities, and the fuzzier **Azienda Autonoma di Sogiorno e Turismo (AST)** nearly everywhere else. Most offices can usually help you find a room, often free of charge. Recently, a new brand of tourist office, the

Azienda di Promozione Turismo (APT), has popped up. Watch out for these—they're allowed to present you with a list of only those hotels that have paid to be listed, and some of the hotels we recommend may not be on the list.

Take **holidays** both legal and religious into account when planning your stay in Italy. The country officially closes on the following dates: Jan. 1, Jan. 6, Easter (April 17, 1995), April 25, May 1, Aug. 15, Nov. 1, Dec. 8, and Dec 25-26. August, especially the weeks around the 15th, is vacation month for most Italians; the cities shut down and empty out. Summers are humid and hot in the north, drier and hotter with every step south. In general, early afternoon is good for nothing but a *siesta* (snooze). Winters are ferocious in the Alps and cold and damp in Venice, Florence, and Rome, but Sicilian waters are swimmable year-round.

Nearly everything closes from 1 to 3 or 4pm. Most museums open from 9am-1pm and some again from 4-7pm; Monday is their *giorno di chiusura* (day of closure). Banks are usually open from 8:30am-12:30pm and 2:30-4pm.

Italy's cathedrals and churches are religious institutions and not museums. Don't visit during mass, and cover your legs and shoulders; the more conservative your appearance, the more likely you are to see what you came for.

Italian men, generally speaking, have earned their tarnished reputation. For tips on how to handle unwanted attention and sexual harassment, see Essentials—Women and Travel.

Communication Any knowledge of Spanish, French, Portuguese, or Latin will help you understand Italian. Most tourist office staff speak at least some English. If your conversation partner speaks Italian too quickly, ask her or him to *rallenta* (rah-LEN-ta; "slow down"). Useful phrases include: *Quanto costa* (KWAN-toe CO-stah; "How much does it cost?"); *Dov'è* (doh-VAY; "Where is...?"); *Che ore sono* (Kay oreh SO-no; "What time is it?"); *Non capisco* (noan cah-PEE-sko; "I don't understand"); *Grazie* (GRAHT-zee-yeh; "Thank you") and *Il conto, per favore* (ill KON-to pehr fah-VO-reh; "The bill, please").

Everyone is at the mercy of the Italian **phone** system, which this year is undergoing yet another series of major overhauls. In Rome, phone numbers change as quickly as traffic lights. There are 3 types of phones in Italy. Dark ages phones take only tokens (*gettoni*), available for L200 from machines in bus and train stations. (One *gettone* per 5min.) *Scatti* calls are made from a phone run by an operator. A meter records the cost of the call, and you pay when you finish. Check first for a service fee. The most common type of phone accepts either coins or **phone cards** (L5000 or L10,000 from machines). For AT&T's **USADirect,** use your phone card or deposit L200 (which will be returned), then dial 172 10 11; MCI **WorldPhone** 172 10 12; **SprintExpress** 172 18 77; **Canada Direct** 172 10 01; **BT Direct** 172 00 44; **Ireland Direct** 172 03 53; **Australia Direct** 172 10 61; **SA Direct** 172 10 27. **Fermo Posta** is Italian for Poste Restante.

Accommodations and Camping Associazione Italiana Alberghi per la Gioventù (AIG), the Italian **hostel** federation, operates dozens of youth hostels (*ostelli Italiani*) across the country, especially in the north. A complete list is available from most EPT and CTS offices and from many hostels. Prices average about L15,000 per night, including breakfast. Hostels that require HI cards charge L5000 extra for nonmembers or sell the cards for L30,000. Hostels are the best option for solo travelers (single rooms are relatively scarce in hotels), but curfews, lockouts, and out-of-the-way locations detract from their appeal. Two or more people can often stay almost as cheaply in a hotel.

The **hotel** industry is rigorously controlled in Italy; prices are set not by private owners but by the state. Under Italian law all guests must be registered by passport on a special form; check the room *first,* and then don't be afraid to hand the passport over for a while (usually overnight), but ask for it as soon as you think you will need it. One-star *pensioni* are the best budget option. Prices fluctuate by region, but singles usually start around L23,000, doubles L36,000. By law, the price must be posted on the door of each room; if it isn't, get it in writing from the management. Always check to see if tax (IVA), breakfast, and shower privileges are included and/or mandatory. For doubles, specify *doppia* (2 beds) or a *letto matrimoniale* (double bed). A triple should cost no more than 135% the price of a double. A private bath *(con bagno)* usually costs at least L5000 extra. **Affitta camere** (rooms to let in private residences) can be significantly less.

An even better value in most large cities are the **Protezione della Giovane,** dorms run by religious orders for women travelers only. Quality is high, and beds average only L14,000, but the curfew is generally early. Try to reach your destination and begin looking for accommodations before noon, especially in summer. If you must arrive late, call and reserve a day ahead. **Convents** are an alternative to hostels (and sometimes admit men as well as women). Singles are quiet and clean and cost about L17,000, doubles L22,000. Their curfews are even earlier than the hostels, usually around 10pm. No naked Twister, either.

Camping sites tend to be loud and modern and average L7000 per person plus L7000 per car, much higher in big cities. An annual guide to the country's campsites, *Campeggi in Italia,* is available in bookstores across Italy.

Food and Drink *"Mangia, mangia!"* The production, preparation, and loving consumption of food are all close to the core of Italian culture. For simple, hearty, and inexpensive eating, try *alimentari* stores; they often prepare *panini* (sandwiches) with fresh local salami and slices of excellent Italian cheese: *Bel Paese, provolone,* or the divinely rich *parmigiano* (parmesan). *Rosticcerie* sell hot food to take-out and are often the cheapest option for a filling dinner. Local markets *(mercati)* also offer these delicacies, along with the freshest produce, but supermarkets are often cheaper. A *tavola calda* is a cheap, sit-down option, as is the student *mensa* in every university town. *Osterie, trattorie,* and *ristoranti* are, in ascending order, fancier and more expensive. They are usually open 12:30-2pm and 7-11pm (later in the south). Menus in smaller restaurants are often incomplete or nonexistent; ask for the *piatti del giorno* (daily specials). A *menù turistico,* when offered, might run only L14,000-18,000 for a full meal, but variety is limited. Sit-down establishments charge *pane e coperto* (a bread and cover charge), usually not much more than L1500-2500. Check whether service is included *(servizio compreso).*

A full meal consists of an *antipasto* (appetizer), a *primo piatto* (pasta or soup), a *secondo piatto* (meat or fish) with a vegetable *(contorno),* and usually salad, fruit, and/or cheese. In the north, butter and cream sauces dominate. As one travels south, tomatoes and spices play an increasingly significant role. By the time you reach Naples, the standard pasta dish beads the brow with sweat. Pastries also get progressively sweeter, reaching an all-time glucose high in the sinfully sugary *marzipan* of Sicily.

Coffee is another focus of Italian life. *Espresso* is meant to be quaffed quickly. *Cappuccino,* a mixture of *espresso* and hot, frothy milk, is the normal breakfast beverage. *Caffè macchiato* ("spotted") is *espresso* with a touch of milk, while *latte macchiato* is milk with a splash of coffee. Perhaps the best finish to a meal is a *caffè corretto* ("corrected"), *espresso* spiked with your favorite liqueur.

Starting with the delicate white *Asti Spumante* from Piedmont and *Soave* from Verona, Italian local wines get rougher and earthier as you proceed south, although there are several exceptions. Italian beer leaves something to be desired; drink *Peroni* or *Würbrer* only if there are no imports in sight.

Bars are good places to sample wines, eat breakfast, or stop for snacks. They also serve a wide collection of Italian liqueurs. Try *grappa,* the gut-wrenching liqueur of the Veneto flavored with various fruits, and Roman *sambuca,* a sweet anise concoction served flaming, with coffee beans floating on top. Sitting down at a table doubles the price of anything you order.

In almost every Italian town you can find numerous shops selling Italy's greatest contribution to civilization: *gelato* (ice cream). Look for the *produzione propria* (homemade) sign. Also delicious on hot summer days are *granite* ("Italian ices") and *frullati* (cool fruit shakes), both guaranteed to please.

■■■ ROME (ROMA)

Wandering through Rome can really make you feel like Alice in Wonderland. Networks of tiny alleys open suddenly and startlingly into grandiose Baroque *piazze*, and a turn of your head can change the view from a cosmopolitan modern city to an ancient forum or a medieval street. A surprise awaits around almost every corner, and there are a *lot* of corners. From the earliest times onward, the concept of large-scale city planning was completely alien to Rome; the most substantial attempt at marshalling the twisted web of streets was Mussolini's, which resulted in depressingly rectilinear EUR, by far the least seductive part of the city. As a result, navigating Rome may leave you feeling more like an explorer than a tourist, as each new sight or "wrong" turn takes on the thrill of new discovery. It may also leave you weary and irritated; don't worry, you're not alone. Choose a piazza, park, or archaeological site and take a break, relax, and bask in the atmosphere—the one aspect of Rome that *is* consistently easy to find.

ORIENTATION AND PRACTICAL INFORMATION

No longer defined by the Seven Hills, modern Rome sprawls over a large area between the hills of the **Castelli Romani** and the beach at **Ostia.** From Termini, the central locus and arrival point for most visitors to Rome, **Città Universitaria** and the student area of **San Lorenzo** are to the east, while most of the major tourist sights slope down between the hills to the west toward the Tiber. **Via Nazionale** is the central artery connecting Termini with the city center. At its base, Via Nazionale joins the immense **Piazza Venezia.** From here, Via dei Fori Imperiali leads southeast to the **Forum** and **Colosseum;** Corso Vittorio Emanuele heads west into the historic districts that fill the bend in the Tiber; **Via del Corso,** the backbone of the city, stretches straight north to **Piazza del Popolo** and the **Spanish Steps.**

The fourteen *rioni* (districts) of Rome, distinct in appearance and character, emerge from the snarl of traffic that fills these boulevards. To the north, the enormous **Villa Borghese** and **Pincio** parks border the Piazza del Popolo, the high-class shopping streets centering round the Spanish Steps, and the faded glamour of the **Via Veneto.** South of here, between Via Tritone and Via Nazionale, **Piazza Barberini** points the way to the stunningly restored **Trevi Fountain.** The **Forum** and **Colosseum** lead out of the city toward the ruins of the **Circus Maximus,** the **Appian Way** and the **Catacombs.** From Piazza Venezia to the west, **Largo Argentina** marks the start of Corso Vittorio Emanuele, which leads into the medieval and Renaissance tangle of alleys around the **Pantheon** and **Piazza Navona** (north of the street) and **Campo dei Fiori** and **Piazza Farnese** (between Via Giulia and the river), before crossing the Tiber to the overwhelming prospect of **Castel Sant'Angelo** and the **Vatican City.** South of the Vatican is the medieval **Trastevere** quarter, home to countless *trattorie* and the best streets for wandering in the city. Back across the river, the historic **Tiber Island** and **Jewish Ghetto** lie in ruinous calm behind the Victor Emanuele Monument. Bounding the historic city at the south are the peaceful **Aventine Hill** and the delicious **Testaccio** district.

Rome's circuitous streets make maps indispensable for the traveler. The tourist office, American Express, Enjoy Rome, and **McDonald's** at Piazza di Spagna, 46/47 offer good maps at no charge. (McDonald's maps are actually very good for sights and general areas, but not so good for streets.) The **Lozzi Roma Metro-Bus Office** publishes a good map of the city plus a booklet containing all metro, bus, and tram routes; it is also available at newsstands and bookstores (L5000).

For a major city, Rome is relatively safe. Exercise common sense and be especially aware around the Forum and the Colosseum, where people are blindly admiring the architecture, and on the crowded buses 64 and 492. At night women and men will generally feel safe walking through the center of town during all but the darkest

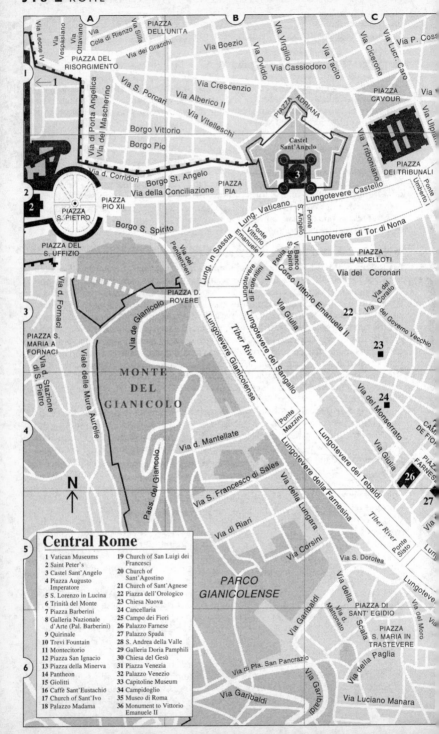

Central Rome

1 Vatican Museums
2 Saint Peter's
3 Castel Sant'Angelo
4 Piazza Augusto Imperatore
5 S. Lorenzo in Lucina
6 Trinità del Monte
7 Piazza Barberini
8 Galleria Nazionale d'Arte (Pal. Barberini)
9 Quirinale
10 Trevi Fountain
11 Montecitorio
12 Piazza San Ignacio
13 Piazza della Minerva
14 Pantheon
15 Giolitti
16 Caffè Sant'Eustachio
17 Church of Sant'Ivo
18 Palazzo Madama
19 Church of San Luigi dei Francesci
20 Church of Sant'Agostino
21 Church of Sant'Agnese
22 Piazza dell'Orologico
23 Chiesa Nuova
24 Cancellaria
25 Campo dei Fiori
26 Palazzo Farnese
27 Palazzo Spada
28 S. Andrea della Valle
29 Galleria Doria Pamphili
30 Chiesa del Gesù
31 Piazza Venezia
32 Palazzo Venezio
33 Capitoline Museum
34 Campidoglio
35 Museo di Roma
36 Monument to Vittorio Emanuele II

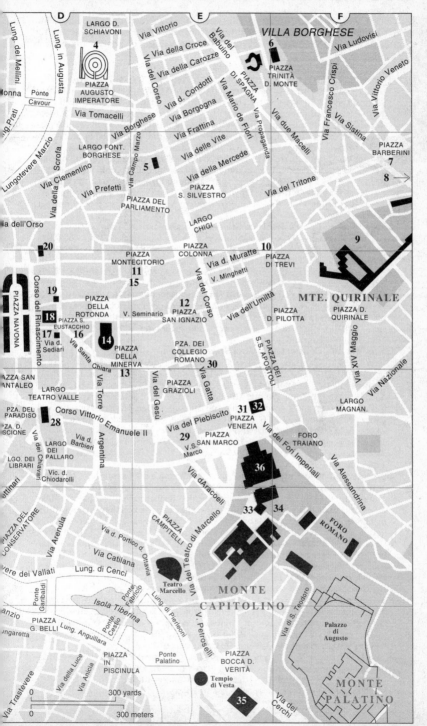

VILLA BORGHESE

D

LARGO D. SCHIAVONI

4

PIAZZA AUGUSTO IMPERATORE

Via Tomacelli

Lung. dei Mellini

Lung. in Augusta

Ponte Cavour

Lung Prati

Lungotevere Marzio

Via della Scrofa

Via della Clementino

Via dell'Orso

LARGO FONT. BORGHESE

Via Borghese

Via Campo Marzo

Via Prefetti

PIAZZA DEL PARLAMENTO

5

20

Corso del Rinascimento

19

18

17 16

PIAZZA NAVONA

PIAZZA S. EUSTACCHIO

PIAZZA DELLA ROTONDA

V. Seminario

14

PIAZZA DELLA MINERVA

13

Via d. Sediari

Via Santa Chiara

Via Torre Argentina

E

Via Vittorio

Via della Croce

Via della Carozze

Via del Corso

Via d. Condotti

Via Borgogna

Via Frattina

Via delle Vite

Via della Mercede

PIAZZA S. SILVESTRO

LARGO CHIGI

Via del Babuino

Via Mario de' Fiori

Via Propaganda

PIAZZA DI SPAGNA

6

PIAZZA TRINITÀ D. MONTE

Via due Macelli

PIAZZA COLONNA

PIAZZA MONTECITORIO

11

15

12

PIAZZA SAN IGNAZIO

PZA. DEI COLLEGIO ROMANO

30

Via del Corso

V. Minghetti

Via d. Muratte

10

PIAZZA DI TREVI

Via del Tritone

Via Francesco Crispi

Via Sistina

F

Via Ludovisi

Via Vittorio Veneto

PIAZZA BARBERINI

7

8 →

9

MTE. QUIRINALE

Via dell'Umiltà

PIAZZA D. PILOTTA

PIAZZA DEI S.S. APOSTOLI

PIAZZA GRAZIOLI

Via del Gesù

PIAZZA D. QUIRINALE

Via XIV Maggio

Via Nazionale

LARGO MAGNAN.

PIAZZA SAN ANTALEO

LARGO TEATRO VALLE

PZA. DEL PARADISO

PZA. D. SCIONE

28

Corso Vittorio Emanuele II

Via d. Barbieri

LARGO DEI PALLARO

LGO. DEI LIBRARI

Vic. d. Chiodarolli

Via del Plebiscito

29

PIAZZA SAN MARCO

V.S. Marco

31 32

PIAZZA VENEZIA

36

Via dei Fori Imperiali

FORO TRAIANO

Via Alessandrina

PIAZZA DEL CONSERVATORE

Via Arenula

Via d. Portico d. Ottavia

Via Catilana

Lung. di Cenci

Ponte Garibaldi

PIAZZA G. BELLI

Lung. Anguillara

Isola Tiberina

Ponte Fabricio

Ponte Cestio

Lung. di Pierleoni

PIAZZA CAMPITELLI

Via d'Aracoeli

Teatro Marcello

33

34

FORO ROMANO

Via di S. Teodoro

Palazzo di Augusto

MONTE CAPITOLINO

V. Petroselli

PIAZZA IN PISCINULA

Via della Luce

Via Anicia

Via Trastevere

Ponte Palatino

PIAZZA BOCCA D. VERITÀ

Tempio di Vesta

35

Via dei Cerchi

MONTE PALATINO

0 ____ 300 yards

0 ____ 300 meters

hours. Outside the *Centro Storico* (historical center), however, use caution. The area around Termini and to its south (especially near P. Vittorio Emanuele and the colle Oppio, notorious drug areas) and Testaccio deserve special care; walk in groups at night.

Tourist Office EPT, in the Termini Station (tel. 487 12 70 or 482 40 78), between tracks #2 and 3. Lines can be horrendous. **Central Office,** Via Parigi, 5 (tel. 48 89 91 or 48 89 92 28, fax 481 93 16). Walk from the station diagonally to the left across P. dei Cinquecento (filled with buses) and go straight across P. della Repubblica. Via Parigi starts on the other side of the basilica, at the Grand Hotel. English spoken. Offices open Mon.-Sat. 8:15am-7:15pm. Pick up a map and copies of *Romamor.* All these offices will help you find a room; arrive early. **Enjoy Rome,** Via Varese, 39, (tel. 445 18 43, fax 445 07 34). From Termini station, cross Via Marsala (adjacent to the station to the right as you exit the train terminal), and head three blocks up to Via Varese. Hotel accommodations, walking, cycling, and bus tours throughout the city. Open Mon.-Fri. 7:30am-1:30pm and 3:30-7pm, Sat. 7:30am-1:30pm. Oct.-May Mon.-Fri. 8:30am-1:30pm and 3:30-6:30pm, Sat. 8:30am-1:30pm.

Budget Travel: Centro Turistico Studentesco Giovanile (CTS), Via Genova, 16 (tel. 467 91, fax 467 92 05). Branch offices at Termini (at track #22, tel. 467 92 54; open 8:30am-8:30pm), Via Appia Nuova, 434 (tel. 780 84 49; open 9:30am-1pm, 3-7pm), and Corso Vittorio Emanuele II, 297 (tel. 687 26 72). Travel, accommodation, and sight-seeing discounts. Sells the *Carte Verde* for discount train fares, ISIC, GO25, and EYC. Open Mon.-Fri. 9am-1pm and 3:30-7pm, Sat. 9am-1pm. **Compagnia Italiana di Turismo (CIT)** books discount train tickets and tours. In Termini (tel. 488 16 78, combined with *Sestante* travel agency); P. della Repubblica, 64 (tel. 473 43 93, fax 479 44 10); Via Veneto, 14c (481 43 82); Cinecittà (tel. 72 28 91), a stop on Metro A; general information tel. 479 41. All offices open Mon.-Fri. 9am-1pm and 2-5:30pm.

Embassies and Consulates: United States, Via Veneto, 121 (tel. 467 41). Open Mon.-Fri. 8-11:30am, and 1:30-3pm. **Canada,** Consulate, Via Zara, 30 (tel. 44 59 81 or 44 59 84 21, fax 44 59 89 05). Open 10am-noon and 2-4pm. Embassy, Via G.B. De Rossi, 27 (tel. 44 59 81). **U.K.,** Via XX Settembre 80A (tel. 482 55 51, fax 487 33 24), near the Porta Pio and the corner with Via Palestro. Open Mon.-Fri. 9:30am-12:30pm and 2-4pm; mid-July and Aug. open Mon.-Fri. 8am-1pm. **Ireland,** Largo del Narzareno, 3 (tel. 678 25 41). **Australia,** Via Alessandria, 215 (tel. 85 27 21, fax 85 27 23 00). Consular and passport services around the corner at Corso Trieste 25. Open Mon.-Thurs. 9am-noon and 1:30-4pm, Fri. 9am-noon. **New Zealand,** Via Zara, 28 (tel. 440 29 28, fax 440 29 84). Open Mon.-Fri. 8:30am-12:45pm and 1:45-5pm.

Currency Exchange: Large banks like **Banco Nazionale del Lavoro** have offices all around the city. **Termini** has *cambi* with poor rates and/or high commissions. The one by the train information booth is open daily 8am-8pm. If at all possible, avoid the usurious rates at **automatic tellers** that exchange foreign bills: machines in Termini; at Via Marsala, 4; Via del Corso, 230 and 283; Via degli Uffici del Vicario, 78; P. San Silvestro; Via di Conciliazione; Via Veneto 7, 74, and 115. Some **ATMs** accept Visa and MasterCard around Via Veneto, the Vatican, P. Barberini, and Via Giovanni Giolitti near Termini.

American Express, P. di Spagna, 38 (tel. 676 41). Chaotic at times, but perfect English spoken. Mail held. Same rates as any of the small *cambi* all over Rome. Good free maps. Open Mon.-Fri. 9am-5:30pm, Sat. 9am-12:30pm.

Post office: P. San Silvestro, 19 (tel. 67 71), between P. di Spagna and the Corso. Stamps at booths #31-33, *Fermo Posta* booth #65. Currency exchange (no checks) booths #25-28. Stamp machines and computer information in English in lobby. Open Mon.-Fri. 8:25am-7:10pm, Sat. 8:20-11:50am. *Cambio* open Mon.-Fri. 8:20am-5:30pm, Sat. 8:20-11:50am. **Postal code:** 00186.

Phones: SIP, in the Villa Borghese parking lot. Open 8am-9:30pm. Phone booths throughout the city. Booth in Termini across from aisle 6. Open Mon.-Sat. 8am-11pm, Sun. 9am-noon and 5-10pm. Sells magnetic phone cards in L5000 or L10,000 units (also available at *tabacchi* and newsstands around the city).

Flights: International flights at **Leonardo da Vinci Airport (Fiumicino)** (tel. 659 51). Currency exchange, baggage check (24hrs.; L4650 per day). Follow the signs marked "Treno" after exiting customs to reach the **train** to Rome's Termini train station (7am-10pm, every hr.; L12,000). If you arrive at the airport during the time in which the trains to Termini don't run (10pm-7am), take a **COTRAL bus** from the airport (11:30pm-6am, every hr.) to **Tiburtina station** where you then take the **42N bus** to **Termini,** the heart of Rome. Most charter and domestic flights arrive at **Ciampino** (tel. 79 49 41). From here take the blue COTRAL bus to the Anagnina stop on Metro A (6am-11:30pm, every 30min.; L2000).

Trains: Termini is the focal point of most train and both subway lines. Crowded railway information and Eurail offices at the front. Make reservations in person. Various stations on the fringe of town **(Tiburtina, Trastevere, Ostiense, San Lorenzo, Roma Nord, Prenestina, Stazione S. Pietro)** connected by bus and/or subway to Termini. Watch out for pickpockets in and around the station. **Luggage storage** along tracks 1 and 22. L1500 per piece per day. Open 5am-1am. *Diretto* trains to **Florence** (2hr., L41,200), **Naples** (2hr., L16,100), **Milan** (5hr., L44,000), **Bologna** (3hr., L31,200), **Verona** (5hr., L37,900), **Brindisi** (10hr., L44,600), **Palermo** (night train, L64,400).

Buses: COTRAL bus service between Rome and the province of **Lazio** (tel. 591 55 51) has moved its departure points outside of the city proper; you need to take the subway to an outlying area and catch the bus from there. Take Metro A to **Anagnina** for buses to Frascati and the Colli Albani; Metro B to **Rebibbia** for Tivoli and Subiaco; and Metro A to **Lepanto** for Cervéteri, Tarquinia, Bracciano, Lago Vico, and Civitavècchia.

Public Transportation: ATAC *(Aziende Tramvie Autobus Communali),* intracity **bus** company (tel. 469 51), P. del Cinquecento. English spoken. Detailed map of bus routes L1000. Buses run until midnight, followed by *servizio notturno.* Signal night buses by waving an arm at one of their stops (black rather than daytime red). Tickets L1200. Stamp ticket in orange machine at back of bus as you board (only from front or back doors); ticket good for transfers over the next 90min. If you exceed 90min. during your last ride, stamp other end of ticket to prove it was still valid when you boarded. Buy tickets at newsstands, *tabacchi,* or kiosks. **B.I.G.** daily ticket valid for 24hrs. on metro and buses (L5000). **Weekly bus pass** *(biglietto settimanale),* valid for 8 nights and days (L12,000), sold at P. del Cinquecento. **Trams** use same tickets as buses; metro does not. L50,000 fine for riding without ticket. After midnight, ticket salesmen will sell you a ticket onboard buses. **Metro** (M) entrances marked on the street by white "M" on red square. Open 5:30am-11:30pm. Tickets L1000; buy them at newsstands, *tabacchi,* or at coin-operated machines in stations.

Taxis: Expensive. Ride only in yellow or white taxis, and make sure there's a meter. L7500 for first 3km or 9min. waiting period, then L1500 per km. Night surcharge L3000; Sunday surcharge L1000; each suitcase L500. **Radio taxis** (tel. 35 70, 66 45, 49 94, or 881 77). Taxis to and from the airport cost around L70,000.

Bike Rental: I Bike Rome, Via Veneto, 156 (tel. 322 52 40), in the Villa Borghese's underground parking garage; entrance near the intersection of Via di S. Paolo del Brasile and Via della Magnolie. Bikes L5000 per hour, L13,000 per day, L38,000 per week. Mopeds L30,000 per 4hr., L45,000 per day. Open 9am-8pm.

Lost Property: Oggetti Rinvenuti, Via Nicolo Bettoni, 1 (tel. 581 60 40), north of P. di Ponte Testaccio. Open Mon.-Sat. 8:30-11:30am, Tues. also 2:30-6pm. **Termini** (tel. 47 30 66 82), at track #22. Open 7am-11pm.

Bookstores: Economy Book and Video Center, Via Torino, 136 (tel. 474 68 77), off Via Nazionale. Open Mon.-Fri. 9:30am-7:30pm, Sat. 9:30am-1:30pm; Oct.-May Mon. 3-7:30pm, Tues.-Sat. 9:30am-7:30pm.

Laundromat: OndaBlu, Via Principe Amedeo, 70/b, off Via Cavour 2 blocks south of Termini. Wash L6,000 per 6.5kg. Dry L6,000 per 20min.

Crisis Line: Samaritans, Via San Giovanni in Laterano, 250 (tel. 70 45 44 44). Native English speakers. Open for calls and visits 4-10pm.

Pharmacies: The closed pharmacies usually post a list. **Farmacia Grieco,** Piazza della Repubblica, 67 (tel. 488 04 10 or 48 38 61), steps from Termini. **Farmacia Risorgimento,** P. Risorgimento, 44 (tel. 372 46 22).

Medical Assistance: Rome-American Hospital, Via Emilio Longoni, 69 (tel. 22 55 71). Private emergency and lab services. English-speaking physician on call 24hrs. **International Medical Center,** Via Amendola, 7 (tel 488 23 71, nights and Sun. 488 40 51) English doctor referral (L105,000 per visit). Open Mon.-Sat. 8am-8:30pm; telephones open 24hrs.

Emergency: First Aid *(Pronto Soccorso)* and **Police:** tel. 113. **Fire** *(fuoco)* tel. 115. **Foreigner's Office** *(Ufficio Stranieri),* Via Genova, 2 (tel. 46 86 28 76). English spoken. Report thefts in person. Open 24hrs. **Police Headquarters,** Via San Vitale, 15 (tel. 468 61). **Green Line** tel. 167 86 32 77 to report gay-bashing; toll-free.

ACCOMMODATIONS AND CAMPING

A huge quantity of rooms meets the tourist demand, but quality varies significantly and hotel prices are often astronomical. Although reservations help, they don't always guarantee that a room awaits you for the full length of your intended stay, or at the decided price, since large groups frequently take precedence over a reserved double in the minds of some proprietors. Make sure the hotel charges you no more than the price posted on the back of your room's door; it's the law.

The **tourist offices** in Rome will scrounge (reluctantly in peak season) to find you a room, as will the **Centro Turistico Studentesco e Giovanile (CTS)** and the **Enjoy Rome** agency (see Practical Information, above). **Protezione delle Giovane,** Via Urbana, 158 (tel. 488 14 19), will help women under 25 find convent accommodations and moderately priced rooms. Termini is full of "officials" swarming around to find you a place. Many are the real thing and have photo IDs issued by the tourist office. Stay on the safe side: ask for maps and directions (real officials will always have maps), and *always insist on seeing a room first.*

It is illegal and stupid to "rough it" in public areas of Rome. It is also a good idea to be careful even at designated campgrounds.

Hostels

If you are looking for a raucous time in Rome, institutions are not the place to go. While providing affordable accommodations, most of them are inconveniently located and difficult to arrange, and curfews at the HI hostel and various religious organizations keep you locked away from *la dolce vita*.

Ostello del Foro Italico (HI), Viale delle Olimpiadi, 6 (tel. 32 36 267, fax 32 42 613). M: Ottaviano, then exit onto Via Barletta and take bus 32 (in the middle of the street) to Cadorna. Inconvenient location but 350 beds with huge red lockers big enough for two packs. Bar downstairs open 7:30am-11pm. 3-day max. stay when full. Reception noon-11pm. Lockout 9am-2pm. Curfew midnight. L19,000 per person, nonmembers L26,000. Breakfast included. Handicapped access.

YWCA, Via Cesare Balbo, 4 (tel. 488 04 60 or 488 39 17, fax 487 10 28), off Via Torino, south of Termini. A fantastic place for women travelers who appreciate safety in numbers. Curfew midnight. No men allowed unless they are married to their roommates. Singles L38,000. Doubles L64,000. Triples L78,000. Quads L104,000. Showers and breakfast included. No breakfast offered Sunday.

Hotels and Pensions

North of Termini

There are clusters of clean, reasonably priced *pensioni* and hotels waiting within 15 minutes of Termini in a somewhat run-down but not particularly dangerous area.

Pensione Papa Germano, Via Calatafimi, 14A (tel. 48 69 19), off Via Volturno between Via Gaeta and Via Montebello. Deservedly popular with backpackers and students, reservations are a must during the summer months. Singles L35,000. Doubles L55,000-L70,000. Triples L80,000. Quads L22,000 per person. 10% less Nov.-March.

Hotel Castelfidardo and **Hotel Lazzari** (tel. 446 46 38, fax 494 13 78), Via Castelfidardo, 31. Completely new rooms, clean showers, and helpful management. Singles L40,000-50,000. Doubles L55,000-70,000. MC, Visa, and AmEx.

Pensione Tizi, Via Collina, 48 (tel./fax 474 32 66 or 482 01 28). A 15min. walk from the station. Take Via Goito from P. dell'Indipendenza, cross Via XX Settembre onto Via Piave, and turn left onto Via Flavia, which leads to Via Collina. Sinfully comfortable singles (L40,000) and doubles (L55,000-70,000). Triples L80,000-90,000.

Pensione Alessandro, Via Vicenza, 42 (tel. 446 19 58). Near the corner with Via Palestro. Buzz #6 to get in. The rooms aren't much to look at, but it's close to the station and the price is right. Check in 8am-midnight. No curfew, but ask for a key. L20,000 per person.

Pensione Lachea, Via San Martino della Battaglia, 11 (tel. 495 72 56), off P. dell'Indipendenza. *Let's Go's* biggest fan, the warm-hearted owner will ensure every comfort, claiming that he considers his guests to be his own children. Doubles L50,000-72,000. Triples L65,000-90,000.

Pensione Piave, Via Piave, 14 (tel. 474 34 47, fax 487 33 60). Off Via XX Settembre. Worth the extra *lire*. All rooms have private bath, telephone, and carpeted floors. Check-out at 10:30am but luggage can be left all day. Singles L40,000-52,000. Doubles L75,000. Triples L95,000-120,000. Quads L85,000-115,000.

Pensione Fawlty Towers (formerly Il Nido), Via Magenta, 39 (tel. 445 03 74), off Via Marghera, parallel to Via Marsala, just North of Termini. An enthusiastic English-speaking staff (that doesn't include Basil and Sybil, nor the steward from Baaarcelona) runs this hostel-like backpacker's haven with genuine affection. L22,000-25,000 per person. Winter: L18,000-21,000 per person.

Pensione Restivo, Via Palestro, 55 (tel. 446 21 72). *La donna simpatica* who runs the place takes great pride in the blinding whiteness of her sheets. Singles L30,000-40,000. Doubles L50,000-60,000. Triples L75,000. Credit cards accepted.

South of Termini

The closer you get to P. Vittorio Emanuele, the seedier the area becomes at night. Use extra caution if you're a woman traveling alone. In general, the farther one gets from the station, the better the neighborhood becomes.

Hotel Chèrie, Via Cavour, 238 (tel. 474 17 89). Located across from Largo Visconti Venosta, not far from the Colosseum. Endearing airy rooms with painted ceilings and plant-laden balconies. Minimal English spoken. Singles L50,000-60,000. Doubles L65,000-80,000. Triples L95,000.

Hotel Ferraro, Via Cavour, 266 (tel. 474 37 55), just past Via degli Annabaldi. Charming hotel, a stone's throw from the Colosseum. Singles L40,000-65,000. Doubles L50,000-L90,000.

Hotel San Paolo, Via Panisperna, 95 (tel. 474 52 17, fax 474 52 18), at Via Caprareccia. Modestly sized rooms in recently renovated building. Singles L35,000. Doubles L50,000-60,000. Reservations accepted.

Hotel Kennedy, Via Filippo Turati, 62 (tel. 446 53 73). Hip, English-speaking staff. Private bath, TV, phone, and A/C are bonuses. Singles L60,000, with bath L75,000. Doubles L85,000. Triples L110,000. Breakfast L5,000.

Pensione Pezzotti, Hotel Contilia, and **Hotel Tony,** Via Principe Amedeo, 79D (tel. 446 69 42 or 446 68 75, fax 446 69 04). Choose between three establishments run by the same courteous management. Pastel and pleasing. **Pezzotti:** Singles L50,000. Doubles L65,000. Triples L90,000. **Contilia:** Singles L55,000-65,000. Doubles L90,000. **Tony:** Singles L50,000. Doubles L60,000-70,000. MC, Visa, AmEx.

Hotel Giugiu, Via del Viminale, 8 (tel./fax 482 77 34). Large airy rooms with frescoed ceilings. Singles L40,000-50,000. Doubles L65,000-80,000.

Pensione Sandy, Via Cavour, 136 (tel. 488 45 85), near Santa Maria Maggiore. No sign; look for the Hotel Valle next door. Bursting with youthful energy. Rooms are for 3, 4, or 5 people. L20,000 during the summer, L18,000 in winter (no heat but lots of blankets). Showers included.

Around Piazza Navona and Campo dei Fiori

Il Centro Storico (The Historic Center) is the ideal, if increasingly expensive, base for living as the Romans do. Expect to pay about 10-15% more to finance the charm and the deeper sense of Roman history absent from Termini accommodations.

Albergo della Lunetta, P. del Paradiso, 68 (tel. 686 10 80, fax 689 20 28), near the Church of Sant'Andrea della Valle. Take Via Chiavari off Corso Vittorio and then the first right off Via Chiavari. Homey, tidy rooms with armoires, phones, and desks. Singles L45,000-65,000. Doubles L80,000-110,000. Triples L110,000-145,000. Reservations recommended but not accepted for a single night's stay.

Pensione Mimosa, Via Santa Chiara, 61 (tel. 68 80 17 53, fax. 683 35 57), off P. di Minerva behind the Pantheon. Haphazard decoration but a fantastic location. Curfew 1am. Singles L50,000. Doubles L80,000. Triples L122,000. Quads L150,000. Breakfast (8-9am) L5000 per person.

Albergo Pomezia, Via dei Chiavari, 12 (tel./fax 686 13 71). The recently renovated section on the first floor is far nicer than the old one. Singles L60,000-100,000. Doubles L90,000-140,000. Triples L110,000-180,000. Prices drop in winter (Nov.-Feb., except for Christmas). Breakfast included.

Hotel Piccolo, Via dei Chiavari, 32 (tel. 689 23 30 or 68 80 25 60), off Corso Vittorio Emanuele II, behind Sant'Andrea della Valle. Clean, quiet and comfortable. Curfew 1:30am. Singles L58,000-70,000. Doubles L85,000-120,000. Triples L95,000-120,000. Breakfast L5,000. Reservations recommended. Visa, MC.

Pensione Navona, Via dei Sediari, 8 (tel. 686 42 03, fax 680 38 02; call before faxing). Take Via dei Canestrari off P. Navona, cross over Corso del Rinascimento, and continue straight. Helpful Italian-Australian family runs a tight ship in this 16th-century Borromini building. All of the rooms are quiet and clean and most have bathrooms (ask for a room facing the courtyard). Checkout 11am. Singles L65,000. Doubles L90,000-95,000. Each extra person thereafter L43,000.

Albergo del Sole, Via del Biscione, 76 (tel. 654 08 73, fax 689 37 87). Off P. Campo dei Fiori. Top-notch furniture, plush lounging chairs, and matching bedsteads and dark wood armoires. Checkout at noon. Singles L70,000-85,000. Doubles L95,000-130,000. Triples L160,000.

Near the Spanish Steps

Silk suits, leather loafers, mini-skirts, and face-lifts abound; inexpensive accommodations do not.

Residenza Brotsky, Via del Corso, 509 (tel. 361 23 39 and 323 66 41). Antique furniture for weary travelers. Climb up to the roof terrace for a spectacular view of St. Peter's. Singles L60,000. Doubles L80,000-95,000. Triples L140,000. Breakfast L8000. Reservations recommended.

Pensione Parlamento, Via delle Convertite, 5 (tel. 679 20 82, for reservations 69 94 16 97), off Via del Corso, one block before the post-office. High ceilings and balconies, plush velvet lounge with magazines galore. Singles L61,000-85,000. Doubles L80,000-105,000. Each additional person L25,000. Reserve in advance.

Pensione Panda, Via della Croce, 35 (tel. 678 01 79 or 69 94 21 51), between P. di Spagna and Via del Corso. Bright and airy—a refuge from the fashion chaos below. Single L50,000. Doubles L85,000. Triples L110,000. Reservations recommended.

Ottaviano and Trastevere

The *pensioni* on the other side of the Tiber aren't the cheapest in Rome, but they tend to be comfortable, clean and friendly. Many have plans for or are in the process of renovation, which may raise prices. Those in **Ottaviano,** near the Vatican, are attractive for their proximity to popular sights and a safer, residential area. Hedonists and bohemians might prefer to stay in **Trastevere,** scene of much nighttime revelry and home to many young expatriates.

Hotel Alimandi, Via Tunisi, 8 (tel. 39 72 39 48 or 39 72 39 41 or 39 72 63 00, fax 397 239 43). Take the steps off Viale Vaticano and go straight—literally meters away from the Vatican Museum. A gorgeous place with a beautiful garden terrace on the roof. Singles L60,000-75,000. Doubles L85,000-105,000. Triples L133,000. L10,000 per extra bed. Reserve ahead.

Hotel Pensione Joli, Via Cola di Rienzo, 243, 6th floor (tel. 324 18 54 or 324 18 93, fax 324 18 93). At Via Tibullo. Slick and snazzy. Singles L55,000-70,000. Doubles L95,000. Triples L128,000.

Pensione Ottaviano, Via Ottaviano, 6 (tel. 39 73 72 53 or 39 73 81 38), off P. del Risorgimento north of P. San Pietro. The only hostel-style *pensione* in the area—3-6 beds per room and that's it. A fine home for the budget traveler. L18,000-L23,000 per person (depending on the time of year).

Hotel Florida, Via Cola di Rienzo, 243 (tel. 324 18 72, fax 324 18 57). On the 2nd and 3rd floor, below Hotel Joli. Charming, modern rooms. Expect maximum prices in July and August. Singles L63,000-L90,000. Doubles L85,000-120,000.

Pensione Manara, Via Luciano Manara, 25 (tel. 581 47 13). Take a right off Viale di Trastevere onto Via delle Fratte di Trastevere to Via Luciano Manaro. Homey pension overlooking P. San Cosimato in the heart of Trastevere. Singles L50,000-60,000. Doubles L68,000-85,000. Triples and quads 35% per extra person.

Pensione Esty, Viale Trastevere, 108 (tel. 588 12 01), about 1km down Viale di Trastevere from the Ponte Garibaldi (you're almost there when you pass the towering stone municipal building on your right). Clean, airy hotel sits somewhat removed from the rowdy heart of Trastevere. Singles L55,000. Doubles L71,000.

Camping

You probably won't catch the malaria that killed Daisy Miller, but there are still plenty of mosquitoes in campgrounds near the city. In August, arrive early—well before 11am—or you may find yourself without a spot.

Seven Hills, Via Cassia, 1216 (tel. 303 627 51 and 303 31 08 26, fax 303 31 00 39), 8km north of Rome. Take bus 910 from Termini to Piazza Mancini and transfer to bus 201; get off on Via Cassia and walk 1.5km down Via Italo Piccagli from Via Cassia. A camping commune in the hills that harkens back to the '60s. Bar, restaurant, convenience store, and pizzeria. Ask about direct bus service from Termini. L9500 per person, L8000 per tent. Open March 15-Oct. 30.

Flaminio, Via Flaminia Nuova, 821 (tel. 333 14 31) is about 7km outside of Rome. Take bus 910 from Termini to Piazza Mancini, then transfer to bus 200. Get off on Via Flaminia Nuova when you see the "Philips" or EUCLID building on your right. Shady grass strewn with closely knit enclaves of tents, campers, and bungalows. Pool, market, restaurant, bar, and a disco that rages long into the night. L10,500 per person. L5200 per tent. Open March-Oct.

FOOD

Meals in Rome are prolonged affairs (breakfast—a quick gulp of caffeine—is the exception). Stay away from the area near the train station; most ostensibly "bargain" restaurants (offering dirt-cheap fixed-price menus) are actually second-rate tourist snares serving nothing resembling Italian cuisine. Explore the winding streets around **Piazza Navona,** particularly around **Via del Governo Vecchio,** and **Campo dei Fiori.** Some of the best *pizzerie* known to man call **Trastevere** home. The university district of **San Lorenzo** and the traditional neighborhood of **Testaccio,** on the eastern banks of the Tiber, are the last untouristed restaurant districts in Rome. Romans generally eat dinner around 9pm. For daytime snacks, try any of the numerous places that sell *pizza rustica* (the cruder square pizza, sold by weight) or *panini* (bulging sandwiches). Try P. Vittorio, near the station, or Campo dei Fiori. **Giolitti,** Via degli Uffici del Vicario, 40, is revered as the home of Rome's best *gelato.* From the Pantheon, follow Via del Pantheon to its end and then take Via della Maddelena to the end; Via degli Uffici del Viccario is on the right. (Open Tues.-Sun. 7am-2am.) **Palazzo del Freddo Giovanni Fassi,** Via Principe Eugenio, 65/67, off P. Emanuele west of Termini, is a worthy challenger. (Open Tues.-Sun. noon-midnight. Open Mondays only in the summer, 6pm-midnight.) Campo dei Fiori hosts the liveliest food **market;** there's an indoor market off Via Cola di Rienzo, near the Vatican, and outdoor ones on Via Montebello, near Termini, and at P. di S. Cosimato, in Trastevere. (Markets open Mon.-Sat. 6am-2pm.) Supermarket **STANDA** offers a huge selection of foodstuffs; there's one on Viale Trastevere, and one on Via Cola di Rienzo, several blocks down from the Ottaviano metro stop and several blocks up from P. del Popolo.

Palladini, Via del Governo Vecchio, 29. Really a *salumiere* (deli) rather than a bona fide restaurant. No sign or place to sit, but bustling with a Roman lunch crowd eating seconds-old *panini*. Hearty sandwich L2500-5000. Open Sept.-July Mon.-Sat. 8am-2pm and 5-8pm.

Il Giardinetto, Via del Governo Vecchio, 125 (tel. 686 86 93). Take your time over the well-seasoned pastas—try the *gnochetti* (L7000) or the *pennette alla gorgonzola* (L8500). Portions generous enough to skip the *secondi* (L11,500-16,000). Open Tues.-Sun. 12:30-3pm and 7:30pm-midnight. MC, Visa, DC.

Pizzeria Baffetto, Via del Governo Vecchio, 114 (tel. 686 16 17), on the corner of Via Sora. Once a meeting place for '60s radicals; now all political persuasions queue for *pizza gigante*. Pizzas L5000-9000. Cover L1000. Open Mon.-Sat. 6:30pm-1am.

L'Insalata Ricca, Largo di Chiavari, 85 (tel. 688 036 56), off Corso Vittorio Emanuele near P. Sant'Andrea della Valle. Funky modern art, innovative dishes, and an off-beat ambience. Try the *gnocchi al sardi* (L7000) or request their title dish *insalata ricca,* a robust salad with everything on it (L6500, smaller portion L5500). Cover L2000. Open Thurs.-Tues. noon-3pm and 7-11:15pm.

Filetti di Baccalà, Largo dei Librari, 88 (tel. 686 40 18). Take Via dei Giubbonari off P. Campo dei Fiori; Largo dei Librari will be on your left. The ideal spot for informal *antipasti* and wine, this self-service favorite makes an unforgettable *filetto di baccalà* (deep fried cod filet, L4000). Cover L1500. Open Sept.-July Mon.-Sat. 5:30-10:30pm.

Pizzeria Vergillo, Campo dei Fiori, 10 (tel. 68 80 27 46). One of the cheaper spots in a row of bustling cafes and *trattorie.* Delicious pizzas (L7000-12,000) and rich pasta dishes *(fettucine al salmone* and *gnocchi alla gorgonzola* L12,000 each). Cover L2500. Open Thurs.-Tues. noon-3pm and 7pm-midnight.

La Cappricciosa, Largo dei Lombardi, 8 (tel. 687 86 36), right off Via del Corso and across from Via della Croce. The dark wood decor and paintings of old Rome will give you a taste of pre-chaos days. *Primi* L6000-9000. Pizza from L7000. Cover L2000. Open Wed.-Mon. 12:30-3pm and 7pm-1am. Closed Aug. 24-31.

Er Buco, Via del Lavatore, 91 (tel. 678 11 54), steps from P. di Trevi. Possibly the oldest pizza oven in the city. Pizza "Er Buco" (tomatoes, cheese, parmigiano and basil) L8000. *Bruschetta alla crema di carciofi* (toast with creamed artichoke) L3000. Salmon calzone L10,000. Open Mon.-Sat. noon-2:30pm and 7:30-11:30pm.

Al Piccolo Arancio, Vicolo Scanderberg, 112 (tel. 678 61 39), near the Trevi Fountain in an alley off Via del Lavatore (off P. di Trevi). Unusual and delicious pastas and appetizers. Thurs. *gnocchi al salmone* (L7000) or *linguini all'aragosta* (lobster linguini). Cover L2500. Open Sept.-July Tues.-Sun. 12:30-3pm and 7-11:30pm.

Taverno del Moro, Via del Moro, 43 (tel. 580 91 65), off Via Lungaretta in Trastevere. Large, airy restaurant with in- and outdoor dining. *Pizza con verdura* L12,000. Cheesecake L4000. Cover L2000. Open Tues.-Sun. 5:30pm-12:30am.

Mario's, Via del Moro, 53 (tel. 580 38 09). Take Via della Lungaretta off Viale Trastevere, and turn right after the church. Excellent pasta L4500-6500. *Fettucini ai funghi porcini* (with porcini mushrooms) L6500. Tourist menu, which includes pasta, meat, salad and fruit, L11,000. Wine L4400. Cover L1000. Open Sept. to mid-Aug. Mon.-Sat. noon-3pm and 7-11pm.

Pizzeria Ivo, Via di San Francesca a Ripa, 158 (tel. 581 70 82). Take Via delle Fratte di Trastevere off Viale Trastevere. The mouth-watering pizza's still well worth the long wait (L9500-13,000). Outdoor dining in summer. Cover L1500. Open Sept.-July Wed.-Mon. 1:30-3:30pm, 6pm-2am.

Il Tulipano Nero, Via Roma Libera, 15 (tel. 581 83 09), in P. San Cosimato. A friendly, rowdy pizzeria—dine outdoors in the summer. Try the innovative pizza combos. *Pizza tonno, mais, e rughetta* (with tuna, corn, and arugula, L10,000). Small or gigantic *(gigante)* portions. Open Thurs.-Tues. 5pm-1:30am.

Armando, Via degli Ombrellari, 41 (tel. 686 16 02). North of Via di Conciliazione. Delicious lasagne is the house specialty at L8500. Cover L2500. Open Thurs.-Tues. 12:30-3pm and 7-11pm.

Trattoria da Bucantino, Via Luca della Robbia, 84/86 (tel. 574 68 86). Take Via Vanvitelli off Via Marmorata, then take the first left. A Testaccio tavern with fabulous antipasta. Wrestle with the *coda alla vaccinara* (L10,000). Wine L5000 per liter. Open Aug. 27-July 21 Tues.-Sun. noon-3pm and 7:30-11pm.

Trattoria Turiddo, Via Galvani, 64 (tel. 575 04 47), in the Mattatoio district of Testaccio (take bus 27 from Termini or the Colosseum). Locals come here for food they grew up on, like *rigatoni con pagliata* (with tomato and lamb intestine, L8000), *coda alla vaccinara* (stewed oxtail, L14,000), and *animelle alla griglia* (grilled calf's veins, L11,000). Cover L2000. Open mid-Sept. to mid-Aug. Mon.-Tues. and Thurs.-Sat. 1-2:30pm and 7-10:30pm, Sun. 1-2:30pm.

Via Claudia, 24 (tel. 700 05 50). Start at Piazza del Colosseo on the side of the Colosseum opposite the entrance. Head 2 blocks toward the ancient walls of Claudio (and the grassy hill behind it). In the shade of the mighty amphitheater. *Melanzane alla piastra* (grilled eggplant) L5000. *Linguini al pesto* L7500. ½l wine L3500. Open noon-3pm and 8pm-midnight.

Il Pulcino Ballerino, Via degli Equi, 66/68 (tel. 49 03 01), off Via Tiburtina. Artsy, with cuisine to match. Specialities include *tagliolini del pulcino* (pasta in lemon cream sauce, L9000) or *risotto alla fragola* (strawberry rice, L10,000). Cover L2000. Open Mon.-Sat. 8pm-midnight. Closed first two weeks of August.

Pizzeria L'Economica, Via Tiburtina, 46 (tel. 445 66 69), on the main road of the bus route. Tourists throng to this United Nations pizza convention. *Antipasto salad* L6,000. *Pizza con funghi* L6,000. Crowded, with lots of outdoor tables. Go early or late to avoid waiting. Open Sept.-July Mon.-Sat. 6:30-11pm.

Il Ristorante Tudini, Via Filippo Turati, 5 (tel. 446 72 97), one block from Termini on corner of Via Gioberti. Appetizing reprieve from Termini fare with marble tables and greenery. *Veal scalloppine* L10,000. *Lasagne al carciofi* (artichoke lasagna) L5500. Cover L2000. Service 15%. Open 6pm-2am.

SIGHTS

Rome wasn't built in a day, and it's not likely that you'll see much of it in 24 hours either. No city can lay claim to so many masterpieces of architecture from so many different eras of history—not to mention the treasures of painting and sculpture inside. A hot and dusty place in summer (and crowded and chaotic year-round), Rome is likely to sap the energy of even the most hardened sightseer. Pace yourself, make time for a stop in a bar or *caffè*, and carry a bottle of water (refillable at any of Rome's corner water-spouts; you'll see Romans bending to drink from the streams). With the exception of the Vatican, museums are closed Mondays. When visiting churches, dress modestly—those in shorts, short skirts, sleeveless dresses, or sleeveless shirts will not be welcome and in some cases will not be admitted.

Vatican City Occupying 108½ acres entirely within Italy's capital, the **Vatican City** is the last remaining territory under direct control of the Roman Catholic Church. Under the Lateran Treaty of 1929, the pope remains supreme monarch of this tiny theocracy, exercising all legislative, judicial, and executive powers over the 300 souls who hold Vatican citizenship; by the same agreement, the church stays out of national and municipal politics. The state maintains an army of Swiss Guards—all descended from 16th-century mercenaries hired by Pope Julius II. Michelangelo designed their resplendent costumes. (Take Metro A to Ottaviano—walk south on Via Ottaviano toward the colonnade—or buses 64 and 492 from Termini, 62 from P. Barberini, or 19 from San Lorenzo.)

Approach the **Basilica di San Pietro** (St. Peter's Basilica), the largest Roman Catholic cathedral in the world, through Bernini's peerless Baroque colonnades. Begun by Bramante on the site of St. Peter's tomb, the basilica's design changed hands from da Sangallo to Michelangelo, Raphael, and finally Maderno, who added the present façade. Michelangelo's sorrowful *Pietà* now sits in grace on the ground level behind bullet-proof glass (a maniac attacked the sculpture with an ax in 1978).

Downstairs, the **Vatican Grottoes** harbor the tombs of innumerable popes and saints. The cavernous **dome** of St. Peter's, for centuries the world's largest, was Michelangelo's final opus. To enjoy a matchless view of Rome, make the climb to the top. You *must* wear long pants and clothing that covers your shoulders when visiting St. Peter's. (Open daily 8am-7pm. Dome closes 1hr. earlier. To the dome on foot L5000, by elevator L6000.) **Mass** is celebrated several times per day, with a particularly beautiful vespers service Sunday at 5pm.

When in town, the Pope grants **public audiences** in P. San Pietro on Wednesdays (10am; Sept.-May 11am). Get free tickets (Mon.-Tues. 9am-1pm) at St. Peter's Gate (bronze doors to right of Basilica), or apply in writing to the **Prefetture della Casa Pontificia,** 00120 Città del Vaticano.

A short walk down Via d. Conciliazione from St. Peter's stands the massive **Castel Sant'Angelo.** Built by the Emperor Hadrian (117-138 AD) as a mausoleum for himself and his family, the edifice has served the popes of Rome as a convenient and forbidding fortress, prison, and palace. It now contains a museum of arms and artillery, but the papal apartments and the incomparable views of Rome seen from them are the real reasons to visit. (Open 9am-7pm, last entry 1hr. before closing. L8000.) The marble **Ponte Sant'Angelo,** lined with Bernini's angels, leads back across the river, and is the starting point for the traditional pilgrimage route from St. Peter's to the Basilica of San Giovanni in Laterano on the other side of Rome.

A 10min. walk around the Vatican City walls, or the bus from the Piazza, brings you to the **Vatican Museums.** Of the four color-coded paths through the museums, Tour A hits only the barest essentials, while tour D hits absolutely everything. The most famous works of classical sculpture cluster in the **Pio-Clementine Museum.** In the **Belvedere Court** stand the *Apollo Belvedere* and the evocative *Laocoön,* which was carved from a single piece of marble; these two statuaries provided the chief inspiration for much of the Renaissance sculpture throughout Rome and Italy. The remarkable **Etruscan Museum,** a floor above, displays the contents of the splendid **Regolini-Galassi Tomb,** found intact and full of such treasures as an extraordinary bronze chariot and bed.

All routes in the museum lead through the breathtakingly frescoed **Raphael Stanze** (Raphael rooms). The **Stanza della Segnatura** contains the *School of Athens,* in which Raphael painted the features of his contemporaries onto those of great philosophers. The climax of any tour is the **Sistine Chapel.** In the *Creation of Adam,* eight Old Testament scenes climax in the electric touch of God's and Adam's fingers. Refrain from taking flash photos, even if you see others doing it; it's detrimental to the fresco and you can buy much better shots (cheaper than using your own film) on professional postcards. Get there early to avoid the mobs. The altar wall is covered by Michelangelo's newly restored *The Last Judgement.* This somber vision shows humanity, blessed and damned, huddled before a wrathful God.

Once out of the Sistine Chapel, linger at the **Pinacoteca;** Raphael's *Transfiguration* alone is worth the stop. (Museums and Sistine Chapel open Mon.-Sat. 8:45am-1:45pm; Easter and July-Sept. Mon.-Fri. 8:45am-4pm, Sat. 8:45am-1:45pm. Last entry 45min. before closing.L13,000, with ISIC L8000. Closed on major religious holidays. Last Sun. of every month open 8:45am-1pm, free.)

Piazza del Popolo to Piazza Quirinale The northern entrance to the city, **piazza del Popolo** (the people's square) is a favorite arena for communal antics. Tucked away on the north side of the *piazza* near the Porta del Popolo, the small **Church of Santa Maria del Popolo** contains two canvases by Caravaggio: the *Conversion of St. Paul* and the *Crucifixion of St. Peter.* (Open Mon.-Sat. 7am-noon and 4-7pm, Sun. 8am-1:30pm and 4:30-7:30pm.)

Designed by an Italian, paid for by the French, occupied by the British, and now haunted by Americans, the **Spanish Steps** (M: Spagna) have a truly international atmosphere. Ideal for people-watching, the Spanish Steps and **Piazza di Spagna** take their names from the Spanish Embassy, located since 1647 in the hourglass-shaped *piazza.* Today you're more likely to see con artists, but in its day the area attracted Stendhal, Balzac, Wagner, and Liszt; Henry James and the Brownings lived on Via Bocca di Leone, a small sidestreet in the area. Above Via Frattina, 50, a plaque announces James Joyce's former residence. Another small plaque on the side of P. di Spagna, 26, marks the place where Keats died in 1821. The second floor of the house now houses the charming **Keats-Shelley Memorial Museum,** full of curious relics from the poets' lives (open Mon.-Fri. 9am-1pm and 3-6pm; L5000). Despite its simple design (by Carlo Maderno), the rosy façade of the **Church of Santa Trinità dei Monti** provides a worthy climax to the stairs' grand curves, not to mention a sweeping view of the city.

Rome's largest park, the **Villa Borghese** (M: Spagna), contains three major museums. The **Museo Borghese,** undergoing restoration, houses Bernini's greatest early sculpture (including *Apollo and Daphne* and *David*). (Take bus 910 from Stazione Termini and get off on Via Pinciana. Open Tues.-Sat. 9am-7pm, Sun. and holidays 9am-1pm. L4000.) The **Galleria Nazionale d'Arte Moderna** is filled with the best Italian art of the 19th and 20th centuries (open Tues.-Sat. 9am-2pm, Sun. and holidays 9am-1pm; L8000, EU nationals under 18 free). The **Museo di Villa Giulia** (within walking distance of the main gate, or take tram 19 from Via Flaminia to Viale delle Belle Arti), hides a vast trove of Etruscan art discovered in burial grounds north of Rome (open Tues.-Sun. 9am-7pm, Sept.-May 9am-2pm; L8000).

East along Via Sabina from the Spanish Steps rises the newly restored **Fontana di Trevi** (Trevi Fountain), at its aesthetic best at night. In the most famous scene of Fellini's *La Dolce Vita,* the bodacious Anita Ekberg takes a midnight dip in the fountain with Marcello Mastroanni and a kitten. Northwest of the fountain, **Piazza Barberini** showcases the Bernini **Fontane delle Api** (Bee Fountain, for the "use of the public and their animals"). The Palazzo Barberini's **Galleria Nazionale d'Arte Antica** in Via Quattro Fontane, near the Barberini Fountain, houses a superb collection of paintings from the 13th to 18th centuries. (Open Tues.-Sun. 9am-2pm; Thurs. and Sat. open until 7pm, but after 2pm, visitors are allowed only in the 1st floor galleries, and are admitted in small groups on the ½hr. L6000.)

Piazza del Quirinale, at the end of Via del Quirinale, running from Via XX Settembre, occupies the summit of the tallest of Rome's seven hills. In the middle of the piazza, the heroic statues of **Castor and Pollux** (mythical warrior twins embraced by ancient Romans as their protectors) flank yet another of Rome's many obelisks. The **Palazzo del Quirinale** is the official residence of president of the Italian Republic. Via del Quirinale leaves the *piazza* to the north, passing the modest façade of Bernini's **Sant'Andrea al Quirinale,** whose oval interior departs from traditional church plans (the nave is wider than it is long). (Open Wed.-Mon. 8am-noon and 4-7pm.) Further down the street is the undulating façade of Borromini's **Church of San Carlo alle Quattro Fontane** ("San Carlino"). (Open Mon.-Fri. 9am-12:30pm and 4-6pm, Sat. 9am-12:30pm. If interior is closed, ring at the convent next door.)

Closer to Termini at P. della Repubblica, the **Church of Santa Maria degli Angeli** presides over the ruins of the ancient Baths of Diocletian. (Church open 7:30am-12:30pm and 4-6:30pm.)

Via del Corso to Piazza Navona and Beyond

The majestic **Pantheon,** between Via del Corso and Piazza Navona, has presided over its busy *piazza* for nearly 2000 years, its marble columns and pediment, bronze doors, and soaring domed interior (save superficial decorative changes) all unchanged from the day it was erected by Hadrian. (Open Mon.-Sat. 9am-6:30pm, Sun. 9am-1pm; Oct.-May Mon.-Sat. 9am-4pm, Sun. 9am-1pm. Free.) Around the left side of the Pantheon another obelisk marks the center of tiny **Piazza Minerva,** supported by Bernini's winsome elephant statue. Behind, the unassuming façade of the **Church of Santa Maria Sopra Minerva** hides some of Renaissance Rome's artistic masterpieces, including the **Carafa Chapel,** with a brilliant fresco cycle by Filippino Lippi. Michelangelo's great *Christ Bearing the Cross* stands guard near the altar. (Open 7am-noon and 3:45-7pm. Under restoration.)

A few blocks west, across Corso Rinascimento, **Piazza Navona** is the finest Baroque space in Rome. Modern times have maintained the true-to-Rome uproar of the ancient chariot track and 15th-century festival and marketplace, home to 3 Bernini fountains, most notably the **Fountain of the Four Rivers.** This centerpiece represents the Nile, Ganges, Danube, and Río de la Plata (all identifiable by representative flora and fauna). One story holds that Bernini designed the Nile and Plata statues to shield their eyes from the sight of the **Church of Sant'Agnese** opposite, which was designed by Bernini's great rival Borromini. Off the northeastern corner of the *piazza* sits the 15th-century **Church of Sant'Agostino,** which shelters Raphael's *Prophet Isaiah* and Caravaggio's *Madonna of Loreto* (open 4:30-8pm).

Corso Vittorio Emanuele II, Campo dei Fiori, and Via Giulia The baroque **Gesù,** on Corso Vittorio Emanuele, is the parent church of the Jesuit order (open 6am-12:30pm and 4-7:15pm). Continuing up the Corso, find the recently restored **Church of Sant'Andrea della Valle,** which was begun in 1591 by Grimaldi and completed in 1665 by Baroque bigwig Carlo Maderno (open Mon.-Sat. 7:30am-noon and 4:30-9:30pm, Sun. 7:30am-12:45pm and 4:30-7:45pm).

Across corso Vittorio Emanuele II from Piazza Navona (down Via della Cancelleria), **Campo dei Fiori** is a flower-filled clearing in the middle of a dense medieval quarter. During papal rule, the area was the site of countless executions; now the only carcasses that litter the *piazza* are those of the fish in the colorful **market** that springs up every day but Sunday from 7am to 2pm. Behind the elaborate Baroque façade of the **Palazzo Spada,** in Piazza della Quercia, you'll find the opulent assortment of sculpture and painting of the **Galleria Spada** (open Tues.-Sat. 9am-2pm, Sun. 9am-1pm; L4000). Head toward the river to find the harmonious **Piazza Farnese** and wander down the elegant Renaissance **Via Giulia,** the first direct route to the Vatican commissioned by Julius II in 1508.

The Ancient City Across the River Tiber from the Vatican lie the few tangible remnants of ancient Rome. The physical center and the most sacred part of the ancient city, the **Campidoglio** (Capitoline Hill) still serves as the seat of the city's government and is crowned by a spectacular *piazza* of Michelangelo's design. From the back of P. del Campidoglio, behind Rome's **City Hall** (the central building), there's a great daytime view of the Forum. The **Musei Capitolini,** in the twin *palazzi* on either side of the *piazza,* display one of the largest collections of ancient sculpture in the world, including the famous *Capitoline Wolf,* an Etruscan statue which has symbolized Rome since antiquity. You may find the *pinacoteca*'s lackluster assortment of 16th-century Italian paintings a bit disappointing. (Museums open Tues.-Sun. 9am-1:30pm; in summer, also Tues. 5-8pm and Sat. 8-11pm; in winter, also Tues. and Sat. 5-8pm. Last entry ½hr. before closing. L10,000, with student ID L5000; free last Sun. of the month.)

Enter the Roman **Forum** (M: Colosseo or bus 27), once the center of the Empire, from Via dei Fori Imperiali, behind the white neoclassical horror of the **Victor Emanuel Monument** (popularly known as "the wedding cake" or "the typewriter"). Once a marshy valley prone to flooding, the area which is now the Forum evolved first into an Etruscan market and later into Rome's chief square, and was at its busiest in the 2nd century, after the conquest of ancient Greece. The Forum endured its first excavations in 1803, and they continue today; unfortunately, archaeologists have rendered the site extremely confusing. To really understand the chaotic collage of stone and brick, invest in a map (L4000). Brace yourself for the traditional headaches of visiting the Forum: slow tour groups, confusing sites, heat, and dust. Go early and take a bottle of water. (Forum, Palatine, and Antiquarium open Mon.-Sat. 9am-7pm, Sun. 9am-1pm; in winter Mon.-Sat. 9am-3pm, Sun. 9am-1pm. Last entry ½hr. before closing. L10,000.)

The Forum houses dozens of significant monuments. The Senate met at the **Curia;** male citizens voted at the **Comitum Well,** or assembly place, in front of the Curia, until Julius Caesar moved the gathering point to the *campus martius,* today's

Campo dei Fiori. At the end of the oldest street in Rome, the **Via Sacra,** the hefty **Arch of Septimius Severus** (203 AD) commemorates the emperor's victories in the Middle East. Visit the **Imperial Rostra,** from which politicians orated, and the **Arch of Titus,** which features the famous frieze of Roman legionnaires making off with the great Menorah from the Temple of Jerusalem. Bordering the south side of the Forum is Julius Caesar's **Basilica Julia** (54 BC), from whose halls justice was administered. Look for inscribed grids and circles in the steps where Romans, anxiously awaiting verdicts, distracted themselves with an ancient form of tic-tac-toe. The **Column of Phocas,** in front of the basilica, honors the man who seized the throne of Byzantium and awarded the Pantheon to Pope Boniface IV. At the east end of the Basilica Julia, the **Temple of Castor and Pollux** celebrates the Roman rebellion against their Etruscan king in 510. According to legend, the twin gods descended and routed the Etruscan army at the Battle of Lake Regilles in 499 BC. At the far end of the Forum, the **Palatine Hill** houses a complex of imperial palaces surrounded by parks and gardens. The most impressive structure here is the **Palace of Domitian,** divided into the Domus Flavia (official palace), the Domus Augustana (private residence), and the Stadium. At the southern base of the Palatine is the **Circus Maximus;** you can still see the start and finish lines for the chariot races once held here.

Fori Imperiali and the Colosseum The **Fori Imperiali** sprawl across the street from the old Forum Romanum, a vast conglomeration of temples, basilicas, and public squares constructed by the emperors of the first and 2nd centuries AD. In the 1930s, Mussolini, with imperial aspirations of his own, cleared the area of medieval constructions and built the Via dei Fori Imperiali to pass over the newly excavated remains; the broad, barren thoroughfare cuts across the old foundations at an awkward angle. The largest and most impressive of the lot is the **Forum of Trajan** (107-113 AD), including the **Trajan Column;** it is the greatest specimen of Roman relief-sculpture ever carved, narrating the Emperor's victorious campaigns against the Dacians, denizens of present-day Romania. **Trajan's Market,** a semi-circular ancient shopping mall that housed 150 *tabernae* (single-room stores), holds frequent art exhibits. (Open Mon.-Wed, Fri., and Sun. 9am-1:30pm, Thurs. and Sat. 9am-6pm; winter Tues.-Sat. 9am-1:30pm. L3750. EU citizens under 18 and over 60 free. Entrance at Via IV Novembre, 94.) The **Forums of Caesar** and **Nerva** are best appreciated from street level, as is the **Forum of Augustus,** dedicated by the Emperor in 2 BC in honor of Mars Ultor (Mars the Avenger). (All *fora* except Trajan's Markets closed for renovation in 1994.)

Dominating the heart of ancient Rome, the **Colosseum** (M: Colosseo), erected in 80 AD by Emperor Flavius, is the city's grandest symbol. In its heyday, the Colosseum accommodated more than 50,000 spectators, and could be filled with water for mock naval battles. The floor (now gone) lay over a labyrinth of brick cells, corridors, ramps, and elevators used for transporting wild animals from their cages up to the level of the arena. The interior is a bit of a disappointment, since Renaissance popes used most of the marble stands for their own grandiose constructions. (Ground level open Mon.-Tues. and Thurs.-Sat. 9am-7pm, Wed. 9am-1pm, Sun. 9am-6pm, Sept.-May Sun. 9am-1pm. Free. Upper floors open Sun.-Tues. and Thurs. 9am-6pm, Wed. 9am-1pm, Fri.-Sat. 9am-7pm; winter Sun.-Tues. and Thurs. 9am-3pm. L6000, EU nationals under 18 free.)

From P. di Porta Capena, Via delle Terme di Caracalla passes the hulking remains of the **Baths of Caracalla,** the largest and best-preserved imperial baths in the city. (Open Tues.-Sat. 9am-7pm; in winter Tues.-Sat. 9am-3pm and Sun.-Mon. 9am-1pm. L6000, EU citizens under 18 or over 60 free.)

Outside the city proper lie the **catacombs,** mysterious multi-story condos for the dead. The most notable are those of **San Sebastiano, San Callisto,** and **Santa Domitilla,** next door to one another on Via Appia Antica south of the city. Take bus 118 from Via Claudia near the Colosseum, or more frequent bus 218, also on Via Appia Antica; get off before it takes a sharp right turn up Via Ardeatina. (Open

8:30am–noon and 2:30-5pm. San Sebastiano closed Tues., Santa Domitilla closed Thurs., San Callisto closed Wed. Obligatory tour L8000.)

The grandiose **Church of San Giovanni in Laterano,** the cathedral of the diocese of Rome, lies east of the Colosseum at the end of Via San Giovanni in Laterano, in the *piazza* of the same name. The traditional pilgrimage route from St. Peter's ends here at the city's oldest Christian basilica. The church, accorded the same rights of extraterritoriality as the Vatican, is used by the pope for mass on certain feast days; the cathedral reopened in 1994, but restoration to repair severe damage inflicted by a bomb attack is ongoing. (Open 7am-5pm; in winter 7am-6pm.)

Trastevere Across the river, with its meandering streets, hidden churches, lively cafés, and crumbling medieval homes, Trastevere (bus 170 from Termini or bus 56 from Via Claudio in front of P. San Silvestro) proclaims its independence and unrivaled vitality. Today, Trastevere attracts hordes of expatriates, bohemians, and artists, but thanks to rent control and centuries of fiery patriotism, the area retains its local gusto. Right off the Ponte Garibaldi, on busy Viale di Trastevere, stands the **Torre degli Anguillara,** the only medieval town tower left of those that once forested the area. Via di Giulio Cesare Santini leads east into Via dei Genovesi (left of the McDonald's). The **Church of Santa Cecilia in Trastevere** lies two blocks ahead, on Via di S. Cecilia. Rococo restorers wreaked untold damage on the medieval frescoes by Pietro Cavallini which once covered the church, but his magnificent *Last Judgement* (1293) has no contemporary parallel in Europe. (Open 10am–noon and 4-6pm.) At the end of Via della Lungaretta, the **Church of Santa Maria in Trastevere** dominates the *piazza* of the same name. It claims to be the first of Rome's churches dedicated to the Virgin, and is the site of the oldest Christian structure in Rome, tracing back to 222 AD. The 13th-century mosaics on the 12th-century façade are only a prelude to those within. (Open 7am-1pm and 3:30-7pm.)

The easiest way to ascend **Gianicolo Hill** is by the medieval Via Garibaldi on its tortuous route up from the Via della Scala in Trastevere (10min.). Atop the hill sits the **Church of San Pietro in Montorio,** on the spot once believed to be the site of St. Peter's upside-down crucifixion. It's home of one of Italy's smallest and most exquisite buildings, the **Tempietto** (1499-1502), a brilliant marriage of Renaissance theory and ancient architecture. At Via della Lungara, 10 (on the left as you descend Via Garibaldi), is the **Palazzo Corsini,** home to one half of the **Museo Nazionale d'Arte Antica** (the rest of the collection is in the Palazzo Barberini). Spanning the 13th through 18th centuries, the museum contains no fewer than 41 portrayals of the Virgin Mary, by Fra Angelico, Breughel, van Dyck, Titian, and Poussin. (Open Tues.-Sat. 9am-2pm, Sun. 9am-1pm. L6000.) Across the street, the magnificent **Villa Farnesina** houses several rooms frescoed by Raphael, Peruzzi, il Sodoma, and Giulio Romano (open 9am-1pm; free).

ENTERTAINMENT
Music, Dance, and Theater The **Accademia Nazionale di Santa Cecilia** (tel. 679 03 89) performs symphonies and chamber music in its auditorium at Via di Conciliazione, 4 (the street leading up to the Vatican). In summer, the company moves outdoors to the *nymphaeum* in the Villa Giulia, a spectacular setting. Special concerts are sometimes also held in P. di Campidoglio. Tickets cost L15,000 or L30,000. Call (tel. 322 65 71) 9am-1pm and 4-7pm in order to buy tickets for the Villa Guilia concerts. An annual international classical concert festival sails through Rome Aug. 27-Sept. 18. Though the concerts are costly (L30,000-95,000), there are student discounts available. Call the **Palazzo dei Congressi** (tel. (0323) 310 95), where the concerts are held, for more details. From mid-June through the first week in August, the **Cortile della Basilica di San Clemente,** features the **Rome Festival,** a highly acclaimed orchestra and opera series in the Piazza San Clemente at 8:30pm. Call (tel. 561 15 19) between 10am-noon and 4-6pm.

The **Alexander Platz Jazz Club** (tel. 70 45 07 91) features *free* open-air jazz concerts at the lush **Villa Celimontana,** between the Colosseum and the Terme di Caracalla. The concerts, which attract large crowds of music-loving Romans, are held at 9pm at P. della Navicella. Jazz greats jam away from June 25 to Aug. 15; when the most famous names play, there is sometimes a small fee. For info on pop, rock and jazz clubs and gigs around Rome, check under "music box" in *TrovaRoma*, published weekly by *La Reppublica*.

The **Rome Opera Ballet** shares the stage and ticket office with **Teatro dell'Opera** (tel. 48 16 01 or 481 70 03). Call there for information. Tickets cost L20,000-250,000. For **theater** listings check with the tourist office or call the information number at **Teatro delle Arti,** Via Sicilia, 59 (tel. 474 35 64), **Teatro delle Muse,** Via Forli, 43 (tel. 44 23 13 00), or **Teatro Ghione,** Via delle Fornaci, 37 (tel. 637 22 94).

Nightlife Clubs are not necessarily an integral part of nightlife—the real social scene spills out-of-doors. Check the various local listings for films, shows, concerts, and special events or check out Thursday's *TrovaRoma*, a comprehensive list of concerts, plays, clubs, movies, and special events. Romans adore summer and hold myriad celebrations. At night, subdued Dionysian revelry claims the streets. Festivals erupt spontaneously in different *piazze*. In **Piazza della Repubblica,** there's often a Vegas-style crooner, while in **Piazza S. Maria in Trastevere,** you may run across the last vestiges of the flower children. **Via Giulia** makes a quiet and romantic evening *passeggiata*, or you can head over to the **Campo dei Fiori** for some low-key schmoozing. The **Gianicolo** serves as Lover's Lane, lined wall to wall with quivering Fiats. Somewhat removed from the historical center, **Testaccio** is renowned for its hip club scene, yet you'll find the best mix of foreigners and Romans outdoors strolling, and in funky bars in **Trastevere.**

During weekdays, most Romans rush into a *caffè*, down an *espresso*, and leave, but at night, the *caffès* come alive. The streets around Campo dei Fiori and Trastevere hide some of the best places. Rome's music clubs attract a much hipper Italian crowd than the pubs; some even have dancing and are usually much cheaper than discos. Relatively speaking, Roman discos are cheesy; the cooler ones open and close as often as their clientele changes outfits. Rome has only a handful of gay and lesbian bars, and most keep late hours. Pick up a *Pianta Gay di Roma* at any gay bar or disco for complete entertainment listings.

Bar S. Calisto, P. S. Calisto, 4, in Trastevere (tel. 583 58 69). *Il favorito* across the river, where Trasteverean youth, expatriates, and Roman elders socialize over incredible yet inexpensive *cappuccino* (L1200) and *granita di limone* (L2000). Open Mon.-Sat. 6am-1:30am, Sun. 4pm-1:30am; winter closed Sun.

Jonathan's Angels, Via della Fossa, 16 (tel. 689 34 26). West of P. Navona. Live music and a hip, young crowd, enjoying the campy, candlelit ambience. Medium beer on tap L10,000. Open Tues.-Sun. 11pm-2am.

Druid's Den, Via San Martino ai Monti, 28. Traveling south on Via Merulana from Via Santa Maria Maggiore, take your second right. An Irish hangout where Romans get to be tourists. Pints of Guinness L5000. Open 8pm-1am.

The Drunken Ship, Via dei Leutari, 34 (tel. 68 30 05 35), off Corso Vittorio Emanuele II before P. Pasquino. Two American women run this facsimile of a fraternity bar. Sit outside and sip a Bud on tap (L5000) or Jamaican beers (L5000). American musical favorites drown out conversation. Open 8pm-2am.

Yes Brasil, Via San Francesco a Ripa, 103 (tel. 581 62 67), in Trastevere. Foot-stomping live Brazilian music. A fave with young Romans. Drinks L8000-10,000. No drink, no dance. Open Mon.-Sat. 3pm-2am. Music 10pm-midnight.

American Bar Bilbò, Via Salita del Crescenzi, 3 (tel. 687 74 04) off P. della Rotonda. White piano in the bar downstairs. Multiple, chic, lounging nooks. Outdoor restaurant seating where you can even find a cheeseburger (L10,000). Beautiful people. Cocktails L15,000. Open 11am-2am.

Uonna Club, Via Cassia, 871, off Via del Foro Italico, north of the Stadio Olimpico. Rock-n-roll of various kinds, from reggae to garage-bands, underground music, and New Wave. Prices and hours vary.

Gilda, Via Mario de Fiori, 97 (tel. 678 48 38 or 679 73 96), near the Spanish Steps. Dubbed by foot-stompin' Romans as "the best" in 1994. Gilda becomes **Gilda on the Beach,** Lungomare di Ponte, 21, in the summer, an exhilarating, hip disco in Fregene, a beach with its share of hedonistic Roman commuters.

RadioLondra, Via di Monte Testaccio, 67 (tel. 57 50 04). Funky, lively and friendly club for straight, gay, striped and wild types. The best part is that it's free, as are the best things in life. No drink purchase required. Mixed drinks L10,000. Beer from the tap, L6000. It's crowded, so get there early. Caffè open daily 9:30pm-4am. Club open 11:30pm-6am.

L'Alibi, Via Monte di Testaccio, 44 (tel. 574 34 48), in the Testaccio district (M: Piramide). *The* gay club in Rome. Mostly men, but popular with women too. Mainstream-looking types not welcome. Wednesday is '70s night. The 20N and 30N night buses pass nearby Piramide all night long. On Wed., Fri., Sat., Sun. nights there is a steep L20,000 cover. Tues., Thurs. the first drink (L10,000) is mandatory. Open 11pm-5am.

Hangar, Via in Selci, 69 (tel. 488 13 97, fax 68 30 90 81). M: Cavour, or any bus down Via Cavour from Termini, or up from the Colosseum. Gay bar run by Philadelphia emigré. Blaring music and a cheery crowd. No cover, and the drinks are the cheapest in Rome. Open Wed.-Mon. 10:30pm-2am. Closed 3 weeks in Aug.

■ NEAR ROME

Do as the (ancient) Romans did to escape urban commotion; retreat to **Tivoli,** summer resort for such archaic big-wigs as Horace and Hadrian. The 16th-century **Villa d'Este** is a dazzling, splashy park overflowing with fountains and waterfalls (open 9am to 1hr. before sunset; L5000). Just outside of Tivoli is the **Villa Adriana,** where the Emperor Hadrian reconstructed the architectural wonders of his far-flung empire (open 9am-dusk; L8000). **COTRAL buses** depart from M: Rebibbia for Tivoli (5am-midnight, ½hr., L4600). To get to Villa Adriana, get off the COTRAL bus before it reaches Tivoli at Bivio Adriana or take bus 4 from Largo Garibaldi in Tivoli.

The romantic remains of **Ostia Antica** offer a cooler, closer, and cheaper alternative to the more famous ruins at Pompeii and Herculaneum. The ruins are so sparsely visited you'll have no trouble finding a spot for a picnic. Take Metro B to the Magliana stop (L1200), change to the Lido train, and get off at Ostia Antica (20min., same ticket). Cross the overpass and continue to the "T" intersection. Make a left and follow the signs. (Open 9am-6pm; in winter 9am-4pm. L8000.)

Overlooking Rome from the volcanic Alban hills, the **Castelli Romani** are famous for their white wines, Renaissance villas, and annual festivals. **Frascati,** famed for its fruity white wines, is the closest to Rome (20min. by bus). Beneath the Villa Aldobrandini, the road leading left out of town climbs 5km over winding country roads to the ruins of **Tusculum,** an ancient resort town that hosted such Roman luminaries as Cato and Cicero. Down the other side rests the hamlet of **Grottaferrata,** 3km from Frascati, whose handsome Romanesque **abbey** is inhabited by Greek Orthodox monks who run an ancient winery and a museum of Byzantine mosaics. Catch the bus here back to Rome (last one at 10:10pm). Buses leave Rome for Frascati, Grottaferrata, or Marino (5am-10:30pm, about every ½hr., L1500).

A few km across the hills from Frascati and Grottaferrata, the rest of the Castelli Romani cling to the sides of an extinct volcanic crater, now filled with the shimmering blue (and swimmable) waters of **Lago Albano.** Buses leave for **Marino** (for a clockwise tour of the lake) or **Castel Gandolfo** (to go counterclockwise) and other *castelli* locations every half hour from the Anagnina stop at the end of Metro Line A (L1500 each way).

VENETO

The Veneto stretches from the Austrian Alps down across the foothills of the Dolomites and the Venetian Alps to the fertile plain of the Po and its delta. It encompasses a wide variety of terrains, as well as a multitude of culturally independent towns and cities which were lumped together by Venetian rule in the 14th century. A good indicator of the ultimate unity of the region can always be found in local cuisine. Rice and *polenta* provide the starch base, the latter a cornmeal concoction used with most local seafood dishes. Wine is strictly regional, featuring the dry white *soave,* the sparkling *prosecco,* the light red *bardolino,* and the full-bodied *valpolicella.*

■■■ VENICE (VENEZIA)

It is with good reason that Venetians call their city *La Serenissima*—the most serene. Venice awakes each morning with a refreshing absence of the speeding cars and roaring mopeds that infest other Italian cities. Her citizens make their way on foot or by boat through an ancient maze of narrow streets and winding canals. Only recently has the serenity been broken by the swarms of tourists that collect in the *campi* (squares) and thoroughfares of the city, searching out its wealth of museums and landmarks. These visitors often overlook the real Venice, which lies hidden in the romantic backstreets and residential quarters of the city. Venice cannot help but beckon visitors to her grand Renaissance architecture and stately legacy as queen of the Adriatic.

ORIENTATION AND PRACTICAL INFORMATION

Situated at the northern tip of the Adriatic, Venice is linked by ferry to Greece and the Middle East, and by rail to major European cities. The **Santa Lucia train station** lies on the northwestern edge of the city, while the garages, car rentals, and bus terminals are across the Grand Canal in nearby **Piazzale Roma.** To get to **Piazza San Marco** (and the central tourist office) directly, take *vaporetto* (canal boat) 82 from the station or Piazzale Roma. For a splendid introduction to the *palazzi* along the stately **Canale Grande,** take boat 1 or follow the signs for 40min. on foot to San Marco. The city is a confusing maze; the *edizioni Storto* map-guide of Venice (L5000) shows all the major streets, is color-coded, and has an invaluable street index. The main part of Venice is divided into *sestieri* (districts): **San Marco, Castello, San Polo, Santa Croce, Santa Elena, Cannaregio,** and **Dorsoduro.** Within each section, there are no individual street numbers, but one long sequence of numbers (roughly 6000 per *sestiere*) that winds its way haphazardly through the district. Every building is located on a "street"—*fondamenta, salizzada, calle, campi, canale, rio, ponte,* and *rio terrà—Let's Go* also lists these wherever possible. Always be sure you're looking in the proper *sestiere;* some street names are duplicated and no *sestiere* boundaries are marked. Yellow signs posted all over town will direct you to and from **Piazza San Marco** (at the border of San Marco and Castello), the **Rialto Bridge** (linking San Marco to San Polo), the **train station** (in Cannaregio), **Piazzale Roma** (in Santa Croce), and the **Accademia** (in Dorsoduro).

The **Grand Canal,** the central artery of Venice, can be crossed on foot only at the **ponti** (bridges) **Scalzi, Rialto,** and **Accademia.** *Traghetti* (gondola-like ferry boats) are used fairly frequently for canal crossings where there is no bridge. High tides (usually Nov.-April) cause *acque alte,* the periodic floods that swamp parts of the city, notably San Marco, under as much as 3 feet of water.

> **Tourist Offices: APT, Palazzetto Selva** (tel. 522 63 56). Exit P. S. Marco and turn right along the waterfront. The office is just past the park. Ask for *A Guest in Venice,* an indispensable booklet listing current exhibitions and shows. Open Mon.-Sat. 9:30am-12:30pm and 2-5pm. Also at the **train station** (tel. and fax 71 90 78).

Usually mobbed. Get in line at the left side of the booth. Open Mon.-Fri. 9am-noon and 3-6pm, Sat. 8am-2pm. On **Lido** at Gran Viale 6/A (tel. 526 57 21). Open Mon.-Sat. 9am-2pm. **Youth Discount Card: Rolling Venice,** Comune di Venezia, Assessorato alla Gioventú, San Marco, 1529 (tel. 270 76 50, fax 270 76 42), on Corte Contarina. Discount card for ages 14-29 (L5000), valid at many hotels, restaurants, shops, and museums in Venice; also gives a 20% discount on the 3-day *vaporetto* pass (normally L20,000). Guidebook and map included. Worth it if you're in Venice more than a couple of days.

Budget Travel: CTS, Dorsoduro, 3252 (tel. 520 56 60, fax 523 69 46) on Fondamenta Tagliapietra. Off the Dorsoduro-to-San Marco route, near Campo S. Margherita. Open Mon.-Fri. 9am-12:30pm and 3:30-7pm. **Transalpino** (tel. and fax 71 66 00), for international train tickets, is to the right as you exit the station. Open Tues.-Fri. 8:30am-12:30pm and 3-7pm, Sat. 8:30am-12:30pm, and Mon. 3-7pm.

Currency Exchange: Better rates are found in Padua. In Venice try **Banca d'America e d'Italia** on Calle Larga XXII Marzo, San Marco, between San Marco and the Accademia. L2000 commission on cash, L5000 on traveler's checks. Open Mon.-Fri. 8:30am-1:30pm and 2:45-4pm. If you insist on changing money at the station, get slightly better rates by walking 400m to **Banco San Marco,** on the corner near the bridge spanning the canal. L5000 commission. (Open Mon.-Fri. 8:10am-1:10pm and 2:45-4:15pm).

American Express: San Marco, Sal. S. Moise, 1471 (tel. 520 08 44), between S. Marco and the Accademia (look for the AmEx directional mosaic underfoot). L2000 inquiry charge on mail for those without card or traveler's checks. Mediocre exchange rates, but no commission. Office open Mon.-Fri. 9am-5:30pm, Sat. 9am-12:30pm. Exchange service open in summer Mon.-Sat. 8am-8pm.

Post Office: San Marco, 5554 (tel. 528 62 12), on Salizzada Fontego dei Tedeschi near the eastern end of the Rialto bridge off Campo San Bartolomeo. *Fermo Posta* at desk 4; stamps at 12. Open Mon.-Sat. 8:15am-6:45pm. **Branch office** through the arcades at the end of P. San Marco. Open Mon.-Fri. 8:15am-1:30pm, Sat. 8:15am-12:10pm. Stamps are sold in *tabacchi* all over town. **Postal Code:** 30124.

Telephones: SIP, train station. Booths open 24hrs. Also at San Marco, Fontego dei Tedeschi, 5550, next to the main post office (open Mon.-Sat. 8am-7:45pm), and in P. Roma and along Viale Santa Maria Elisabetta on the Lido. Open 8am-9:30pm. **Telephone Code:** 041.

Flights: Aeroporto Marco Polo (tel. 541 54 91). ACTV (tel. 528 78 86) local bus 5 runs to the airport every 1½hr. (30min., L1500), or take the ATVO coach (tel. 520 55 30) with luggage space for L5000.

Trains: Stazione di Santa Lucia (tel. 71 55 55, lost and found 71 61 22). Information office in station across from tourist office. Open 7:10am-9:30pm. To: Padua (every 15min., 30min., L3200); Bologna (14 per day, 1½hr., L12,700); Milan (18 per day, 3hr., L19,500); Florence (6 per day, 3hr., L19,500); Rome (4 per day, 5¼hr., L41,200). **Luggage Storage:** L1500 per day. Open 24 hrs.

Buses: ACTV, the local line for buses and boats (tel. 528 78 86) in P. Roma. Open Mon.-Sat. 8am-2:30pm. Closed the last 2 weeks in Aug. **ATP** is the long distance carrier. Buses roughly every 30min. to the villas on the Riviera del Brenta (Malcontenta L1000, Mira L2500, Strà L4000), Padua (L4000), Mestre (L1000), Treviso (L2800). Ticket office open 6:40am-10pm. Information office open Mon.-Sat. 8am-6:30pm. Fine for riding without a ticket: L30,000.

Public Transportation: The alternative to walking is taking the *vaporetti* (motorboat buses), which cruise the Venetian waterways. Most principal boats run 24hrs. but frequencies are reduced after 11pm. A 24hr. *biglietto turistico,* available at any ticket office, allows you unlimited travel on all boats (L14,000). You can also purchase a three-day ticket for L20,000. Neither is really worthwhile unless you're on a kamikaze tour. The ACTV office offers a special three-day ticket for holders of the **Rolling Venice Card** (see tourist offices under Practical Information) for L16,000. Not all stations sell tickets all the time—buy extras, but make sure to get the type that can be machine-validated at any station. Tickets may be bought at the booths in front of the *vaporetti* stops and at various self-serve dispensers (located at the ACTV office at P. Roma and at the Rialto stop). Tickets may also be bought from the conductor after boarding (L500 surcharge).

ITALY

N ←

TO MURANO ←

TO LIDO →

Isola di
S. Giorgio
Maggiore

Canale di S. Marco

TO MAINLAND ←

CASTELLO

SAN MARCO

SAN POLO

SANTA CROCE

DORSODURO

Canal Grande

Canale della Giudecca

R. d. Pietà
R. d. S. Lorenzo
C. Lion
R. d. Greci
Riva degli Schiavoni
Fond. Osmarin
R. d. S. Severo
Barbaria delle Tole
Ruga Giuffa
Rio di San Marina
R. del Mendicanti
R. d. Palazzo della Paglina
Molo
Piazza San Marco
Frezzaria
Calle dei Fabbri
Rio di San Moisé
Rio della Ostreghe
Rio d. Fornace
Sal. di S. Lio
Rio della Guerra
Rio di S. Salvador
Merceria
C.lle Mandola
S.Luca
CAMPO MANIN
CAMPO S. BORTOLOMIO
CAMPO S. ANGELO
CAMPO SAN STEFANO
Riva del Vin
Rio di S. Barnaba
Rio Foscari
F.Minotto
C. d. Lacca
Rio Marin
Rio della Sacchere
Corte Anatomia
R. di San Polo
CAMPO DI SAN POLO
CAMPO S. ROCCO
CAMPO DEI MORTI
CAMPO DI SAN MARGHERITA
Calle Avogaria
Fondamenta delle Zattere
Rio di Ognissanti
Rio d. S. Vio
Rio d. San Sebastiano
C. d. Carrozze
Ramo dei Torri
R. di San Cassiano
CAMPO DEI S.S. APOSTOLI
Rio S. Caterina
R. di Noal
Strada Nuova
Lista d. Bari
Riva di Biasio
Canal Grande
Lista di Spagna
Fond. di Santa Lucia
Fond. di S. Simeon Piccolo
Ponte Scalzi
Canale di Santa Chiara
Rio Nuovo
Rio di Santa Marta

Venice
1 Train Station
2 Post Office
3 Amex
4 IYHF
5 Piazza San Marco
6 Palazzo Ducale (Doge's Palace)
7 Campo San Salvaatore
8 Gallerie dell' Accademia
9 Church of s. Maria Della Salute
10 Church dei Frari
11 Church of San Zaccaria
12 Campo S. Giorgio
13 Campo SS. Giovanni e Paolo
14 Church of S. Maria Formosa
15 Teatro Goldoni
16 Tourist office (APT),
17 Tourist office
   (APT), Stazione S. Lucia
18 Piazzale Roma
19 Questura di Venezia
20 Hospital (Ospedale Civili)
21 Ponte Rialto

0   200 yards
0   200 meters

The fine for riding the *vaporetti* without a ticket is L30,000. Enforcement can be lax, but tourists are much more prone to being checked (and fined) than locals.

English Bookstores: Libreria Editrice Cafoscarina, Dorsoduro, 3243 (tel. 523 89 69, fax 522 81 86) on Ca' Foscari along the Rialto-to-Accademia route. The largest selection in Venice, including *Let's Go*. 10% discount with Rolling Venice. Open Mon.-Fri. 9am-7pm, Sat. 9am-12:30pm.

Laundromat: Lavaget, Cannaregio, 1269 (tel. 71 59 76), on Fondamenta Pescaria. Take a left from the station, cross 1 bridge, and turn left along the canal. L15,000 per 3 kilos, soap included. Open Mon.-Fri. 8:30am-12:30pm and 3-7pm.

Late-Night Pharmacy: check *A Guest in Venice* or call 192.

Emergencies: tel. 113. **Police: Carabinieri,** P. Roma (tel. 523 53 33 or 112 in an emergency). **Medical Assistance:** tel. 520 32 22. **Hospital: Ospedale Civili,** Campo SS. Giovanni e Paolo (tel. 529 45 17). **Boat ambulances:** tel. 523 00 00.

ACCOMMODATIONS AND CAMPING

Plan on spending slightly more on rooms here than elsewhere in Italy. Reservations, preferably made as much as a month in advance, will preserve your sanity in summer. To avoid the crowds and expense of summertime stays in Venice, visit the city while based in one of the towns nearby (Padua and Treviso, each 30min. away, are good places to secure a room). Dormitory-type accommodations are always available in Venice without reservations, even during August and September. Such accommodations often have irregular operating seasons, so check with the tourist offices to see which are open. In *pensioni,* look out for L12,000 breakfasts and other forms of bill-padding, and always agree on what you'll pay (and whether you want breakfast etc.) before you hit the sack or surrender your passport. Remember that prices are likely to have risen since this book's publication; for better or for worse, the price quoted at the hotel is what you'll have to pay.

Hostels and Dormitories

Ostello Venezia (HI), Fondamenta di Zitelle, 86 (tel. 523 82 11, fax 523 56 89), on Giudecca. Take *vaporetto* 82 from the station (25min., L3500), or 5 (*destra),* 82 or 52 from San Zaccaria near San Marco (5min., L2500). Get off at Zitelle and walk right. A recently renovated warehouse on the canal. English spoken. Check-in 2-11pm—the tourist office at the train station will let you know if they're already full. Lockout 9am-4pm. Curfew 11pm. Members only, L20,000 per person. HI cards available. Breakfast included. Full meals L12,000. No phone reservations.

Foresteria Valdese, Castello, 5170 (tel. 528 67 97). Take the *vaporetto* to San Zaccharia, then walk to Campo Santa Maria Formosa (5min.). From the *campo,* take Calle Lunga S. M. Formosa, just over the 1st bridge. The 18th-century guesthouse of Venice's biggest Protestant church. Check-in 9am-1pm and 6-8pm. Lockout 10am-1pm. Dorms with bunk beds L25,000 per person, L22,000 each additional night. Breakfast included. Reserve 1 mo. ahead for their 2 beautiful doubles (L60,000). Phone reservations suggested. Closed 15 days in November.

Domus Civica, ACISJF, San Polo, 3082 (tel. 72 11 03/52 40 46), across the street from a bar in both directions, on the corner of Calle Chiovere, Calle Campazzo, and S. Rocco, between the Frari Church and Piazzale Roma. Along the road, follow the yellow arrows between Piazzale Roma and the Rialto. Both men and women welcome. Run by a church-affiliated organization. Curfew 11:30pm. Singles L30,000. Doubles L50,000. Rolling Venice: 20% discount. Open mid-June to mid-Oct.

Suore Cannosiano, Fondamenta del Ponte Piccolo, 428 (tel. 522 21 57), also on Giudecca. Take boat 82 to Palanca/G and walk left just over the bridge. Women only. Nun-run. Arrive any time of day to leave your bags. Check-out 7:30-8:30am. Lockout 9am-3pm. Curfew 10pm. Large dorm-style rooms L16,000 per person.

Hotels

Locanda Antica Casa Carettoni, Cannaregio, 130 (tel. 71 62 31), along Rio Terrà Lista di Spagna, to the left of the station. Rooms steeped in antiquity described by the proud proprietor as "truly Venetian." Curfew midnight. Singles L30,000. Doubles L52,000. Triples L75,000. Closed either August or October.

Hotel Minerva and Nettuno, Cannaregio, 230 (tel. 71 59 68, fax 524 21 39), on your left on Lista di Spagna from the station. Spacious, remodeled rooms and convenient locale make this a prime choice. Singles L45,000, with bath L62,000. Doubles L60,000, with bath L96,000. Triples L75,000, with bath L120,000. Quads L90,000, with bath L144,000. Breakfast (L9000) is added to the price unless you arrange otherwise at check-in. AmEx, MC, Visa.

Albergo Adua, Cannaregio, 233/A (tel. 71 61 84), on Lista di Spagna. Small, family-run, and quiet for the neighborhood. Singles L44,000. Doubles L60,000, with bath L95,000. Triples L81,000, with bath L120,000. Extra beds: 35% more per bed. Breakfast L8000. MC, Visa.

Cà Foscari, Dorsoduro, 3887/B (tel. and fax 522 58 17), on Calle della Frescada. Take *vaporetto* 1 or 82 to San Tomà. Go straight off the boat, turn left over the bridge, and follow the road right, then left. Family-run, with pride. Tastefully decorated rooms. Singles L42,000. Doubles with toilet or shower L75,000. Triples L105,000. Quads L125,000. Breakfast included. Closes at 1am. Call in advance—rooms held until noon. Open Feb.-Nov.

Locanda Casa Petrarca, San Marco, 4386 (tel. 520 04 30). Take vaporetto 1 or 82 to the Rialto, walk inland and to the right until you reach Campo San Luca, then go south on Calle dei Fuseri, take the 2nd left and then turn right onto Calle Schiavone. English spoken. Singles L45,000. Doubles L75,000, with bath L100,000. Extra beds: 35% more per bed. Breakfast L5000. 5% discount with *Let's Go*. Phone ahead; rooms held until 3pm.

Locanda San Salvador, San Marco, 5264 (tel. 528 91 47), on Calle del Galliazzo, off Campo San Bartolomeo. Take vaporetto 1 or 82 to Rialto. Good views and a spacious terrace. Right in the middle of the action. Singles L45,000. Doubles L75,000-99,000. Triples L105,000-120,000. Extra bed: 35% more. Phone ahead. Proprietor may be able to find another room for you if they're booked.

Pensione Casa Verardo, Castello, 4765 (tel. 528 61 27). Take Rimpetto la Sacrestia out of Campo SS. Filippo e Giacomo (just east of San Marco) across the bridge. Without a doubt *the* find in this part of town—run by a hospitable, outgoing family. Singles L45,000. Doubles L75,000-85,000. Triples L110,000-120,000. Quads L130,000-140,000. Breakfast L7000. Reserve with 1 night's deposit. MC, Visa.

Locanda Sant'Anna, Castello, 269 (tel. 528 64 66). Take Via Garibaldi, which becomes Fondamenta Santa Anna, turn left on Ponte Santa Anna, then right at Corte del Bianco (*vaporetto:* 1 or 4 to Giardini). Worth the hike. Friendly family proprietors and a refreshing absence of tourists. Starched sheets and sparkling rooms. TV downstairs. Curfew midnight. Singles L55,000. Doubles L76,000-103,000. Triples L110,000-135,000. Quads L135,000-160,000. Breakfast included. Reserve ahead with 1 night's deposit. MC, Visa.

Camping

Cà Pasquali, Via Poerio, 33 (tel. 96 61 10), charges a mere L4700 per person and L12,400 per tent space. Open May-Sept.

Campeggio Fusina, Via Moranzani, in the locality of Malcontenta (tel. 547 00 55). From P. Roma, take bus 4 (L1100) to Mestre and change to bus 13 (across the street from Supermarket Pam); ride to the last stop (1hr., last bus at 9pm). The boat trip is more picturesque and convenient but also more expensive. Take *vaporetto* 82 or 52 (L2800) left to Zattere and then take #16 (L3500) for 20min. to Fusina. L8200. L6200 per tent. L19,000 per tent and car. Call ahead.

FOOD

It is becoming difficult to sit down to a good meal in Venice without emptying your wallet. To avoid paying a fortune, visit any *bar* or *osteria* in town and make a meal from the vast display of meat-and cheese-filled pastries, tidbits of seafood, rice, and meat, and *tramezzini*, triangular slices of soft white bread with every imaginable filling. (Venetians have long cultivated the tradition of just such a between-meal repast, known as the *cicchetto,* always washed down by *un'ombra,* a glass of local wine). Good deals on tourist *menùs* abound along the broad **Via Garibaldi,** a lovely 15min.

walk along the waterfront from P. San Marco. Seafood is the local speciality. *Seppie in nero* is a tasty, soft squid coated with its own ink and usually served with *polenta*, a bland cornmeal mush. *Fegato alla veneziana* is a simple but celebrated dish of liver and onions.

There are a few **street markets** in town. Located in the area surrounding the **Rialto** (San Polo side), the most famous market is the former center of trade and merchandise for the old Venetian Republic. Fruit stands line the Ruga degli Orefici. Locals shop on the side streets near **Campo Beccarie** in San Polo near the Rialto. Less entertaining but more convenient are the *alimentari*. In Cannaregio, **STANDA**, on Strada Nova, 3660, near Campo S. Felice, has groceries in the back (open 8:30am-7:20pm). In Castello near San Marco, there's **Su. Ve.**, 5816, on Calle del Mondo Novo, off Campo Santa Maria Formosa. (Open Mon.-Tues. and Thurs.-Fri. 8:30am-1:30pm and 4-7:30pm, Wed. 8:30am-1:30pm, and Sat. 8:30am-7:30pm.)

Mensa Universitaria di Cà Foscari, S. Polo, 2480 (tel. 71 80 69), on Calle del Magazen. From the main entrance of the Chiesa dei Frari, go over the bridge, turn left, over the next bridge, and left again. Without a doubt the best meal deal in Venice. Full meals including drink L5000 with student ID (ISIC) or L7100 with Rolling Venice card. Open Mon.-Sat. 11:45am-2:30pm and 6:30-8:30pm, Sun. noon-2pm.

Ai Pugni, Dorsoduro, 2839 (tel. 523 98 31), along the Rio di S. Barnaba, off the *piazza* of the same name. Take *vaporetto* 1 to Cà Rezzonico. A fun, newly-remodeled place with huge pizzas. *Primi* L6000-8000, *secondi* L11,000-13,000, pizza L5500-8000. No cover charge. Open for drinks Tues.-Sun. 10am-1am, for eats Tues.-Sun. noon-3pm and 7pm-1am.

Caffè Poggi, Campo della Maddalena, 2103 (tel. 71 59 71). On the main route, left from the station, across two bridges. A popular student hangout with loud music. *Panini* L3000-5000, wine L800-2500 per glass. Open Mon.-Sat. 9am-midnight.

L'Arca di Noe, Cannaregio, 5401 (tel. 523 81 53). On Calle Gallina, 2 bridges from Campo SS. Giovanni e Paolo. Vegetarian restaurant. Indian food every Wed. *Primi* L8000-12,000. Combination dishes L13,000-18,000. *Menù* L28,000. No cover. Open Mon.-Sat. 9am-3pm and 5-11pm. AmEx, MC, Visa.

Rosticceria San Bartolomeo, San Marco, 5424/A (tel. 522 35 69), in Calle della Bissa off Campo San Bartolomeo near the Rialto Bridge, under a sign for Rosticceria. Top-notch self-service. Venetian specialties such as *seppie con polenta* (L13,000). *Primi* L6000-7000, *secondi* L8000-13,000. Cover L2000. 15% discount with Rolling Venice. Open Feb.-Dec. Tues.-Sun. 9:30am-2:30pm and 4:50-8:50pm.

Antiche Botteselle, Via Garibaldi, 1621 (tel. 523 72 92), a broad street that penetrates Castello near the Arsenale stop. A 15min. waterfront walk from S. Marco. *Menù* L14,000 plus cover (L1500) and service (12%). 36 types of pizza (L5000-8000). *Primi* L6000-12,000. *Secondi* and fish L8000-19,000. Open Thurs.-Tues. 8:30am-3pm and 6-10pm (bar til midnight).

Gelateria Mille Voglie, San Polo, 3033 (tel. 524 46 67), on Salizada S. Rocco. In the shadow of the Chiesa dei Frari on the way to the Chiesa di S. Rocco. The best and cheapest in Venice. Cones L1000-3000. Plate-sized pizzas L2500. Open 9am-7pm.

Gelati Nico, Fondamenta Zattere, 922 (tel. 522 52 93), in Dorsoduro near the *vaporetto* stop of the same name, is the pride of Venice. *Gianduiotto*, a slice of dense chocolate hazelnut ice cream dunked in whipped cream, is their specialty (L3400). Cones L2000-4000. Open in summer Fri.-Wed. 7am-11pm; mid-Jan. to mid-Dec. 7am-9pm.

SIGHTS

In Venetian churches a strict dress code applies. No shorts, sleeveless shirts or miniskirts allowed.

San Marco and Environs **Piazza San Marco** is the city's nucleus. Construction of the **Basilica of San Marco** began in the 9th century, when two Venetian merchants stole St. Mark's remains from Alexandria. The basilica's main treasure is the **Pala d'Oro,** a Veneto-Byzantine gold bas-relief encrusted with precious gems. The ticket to this area will also get you into the small **treasury,** a hoard of gold and relics

ITALY

from the Fourth Crusade. (Basilica open 9:45am-7:30pm; free. Treasury open Mon.-Sat. 9:45am-5pm, Sun. 2-5pm; L3000.) The **Galleria della Basilica** displays the recently restored Horses of St. Mark (open 10am-6:30pm, L3000). The **Torre dell' Orologio** (clock tower), left of San Marco, is an florid arrangement of sculpture and sundials. Two oxidizing bronze Moors still strike the hour. You can ascend the brick **Campanile** in front of San Marco for a Kodak moment of the whole city. (Open 9:30am-7pm. L5000.) Better views, cheaper admission, and shorter lines are available from the **Campanile di San Giorgio** (see below).

The **Palazzo Ducale** (Doge's Palace), next to San Marco, faces Sansovino's exquisite **Libreria.** Admire the exhaustive display of Titians, Veroneses, and Tintorettos (especially his *Paradiso*), as well as the armor museum and the ominous **Ponte dei Sospiri** (Bridge of Sighs), leading out to the prison. (Open 9am-7pm. L10,000, students L6000.)

Art Galleries, Churches, and the Lagoon The **Accademia** in Dorsoduro displays the best of Venetian painting. The world-class collection includes the superb Bellini *Pala di San Giobbe*, Giorgione's enigmatic *Tempest,* and Titian's last work, a brooding *Pietà.* Go early to get your money's worth. (Open Mon.-Sat. 9am-7pm; off-season Mon.-Sat. 9am-1pm. L13,000, students L10,000.) For very different art, visit the **Collezione Peggy Guggenheim,** Dorsoduro, 701, housed in the late Ms. Guggenheim's Palazzo Venier dei Leoni, near the tip of Dorsoduro. All the major names in modern art are here, shown in glorious surroundings. (Open Wed.-Mon. 11am-6pm. L10,000; seniors, students with ISIC, or Rolling Venice card L5000.) Another art-filled area surrounds the Gothic **Basilica dei Frari** in San Polo (*vaporetto* to San Tomà). The basilica houses a moving wooden sculpture of St. John by Donatello, Bellini's *Madonna and Saints,* and Titian's dramatic *Assumption.* (Open Mon.-Sat. 8:30-11:45am and 2:30-6pm, Sun. 3-6pm. L1000, Sun. and holidays free.) The *scuole* of Venice, a cross between guilds and fraternities, erected ornate "clubhouses" throughout the city. The richest *scuola* was the **Scuola Grande di San Rocco** (across the campo at the end of the Frari), which boasts 56 Tintorettos. To see the paintings in chronological order, start on the 2nd floor in the Sala dell'Albergo and follow the cycle downstairs. (Open 9am-5:30pm; off-season Mon.-Fri. 10am-1pm, Sat.-Sun. 10am-4pm. L8000, Rolling Venice L5000.)

Across the Giudecca canal on the island of Giudecca stand 2 churches designed by the great late-Renaissance architect Palladio: **San Giorgio Maggiore,** on the Isola di San Giorgio, and the **Chiesa del Redentore,** on Giudecca itself and built after one of the many Venetian plagues. The **campanile** at San Giorgio offers a superb view of the islands (open 9:30am-12:30pm and 2-6pm, L2000). Take *vaporetto* 52 or 82 from P. San Marco.

North of Venice stretches the **lagoon.** With a *vaporetto* ticket you can visit the island of **Murano** (52), famous for its glass since 1292, the fishing village of **Burano** (12), and **Torcello,** an island with an enchanting Byzantine cathedral and some of the finest mosaics in Italy. The **Lido** separates the Venice lagoon from the Adriatic. Its long sandy beach was the setting for Thomas Mann's *Death in Venice.*

■ ■ ■ PADUA (PÁDOVA)

By the middle of the 12th century, Padua had overcome its penchant for tyrannical rule and had become one of the intellectual hubs of Europe. The university, host to Dante, Petrarch, and Galileo, still enlivens this small city whose friendly youth hostel, within close reach of Venice, makes Padua an ideal base camp.

The train station is at the northern edge of town, a 10min. walk down the Corso del Popolo, which becomes Corso Garibaldi; the latter leads to the modern, commercially minded heart of town. On the way you'll pass the **Cappella degli Scrovegni,** the masterpiece of medieval innovator Giotto. The 36 panels illustrating the lives of Mary and Jesus constitute the painter's only fresco cycle to have escaped even partial deterioration. (Open 9am-7pm, Oct.-March Tues.-Sun. 9am-6pm.

L10,000, students L7000. To chapel on Mon. L4000. Tickets are sold and also valid at the **Museo Civico.)** Next door, the **Church of the Eremitani** boasts an imposing exterior and a beautiful carved wooden ceiling that was successfully reconstructed after a devastating bombing in 1944 (open Mon.-Sat. 8:15am-noon, Sun 9am-noon and 3:30-6:30pm; Oct.-March Mon.-Sat. 8:15am-noon and Sun. 9am-noon and 3:30-5:30pm; free). Take Via Antenore, then turn down Via del Santo to get to the **Basil-ica di Sant'Antonio,** Piazza del Santo, a quirky melange of medieval architectural styles and a popular pilgrimage destination. The tongue and voice box of St. Anthony are fittingly preserved in a head-shaped reliquary in the apse of the church (open 6:30am-7:45pm). Next door, the **Oratorio di San Giorgio** houses some fine examples of Giotto-school frescoes, and the **Scuola del Santo** on the corner con-tains three by a very young Titian. (Both open 9am-12:30pm and 2:30-7pm, Oct.-Jan. 9am-12:30pm, Feb.-March 9am-12:30pm and 2:30-4:30pm. L3000.)

Practical Information, Accommodations, and Food The **tourist office** (tel. (049) 875 20 77) in the train station provides free maps and accommoda-tions and entertainment listings (open Mon.-Sat. 8am-6pm, Sun. 8am-noon; main branch is in Museo Civico). The **bus station** at Via Trieste, 42, is 5 minutes from the train station; buses run to Venice every half hour (45min., L4300). **Trains** chug reg-ularly to Venice (every 15min., ½hr.) and to Milan (every hr., 2hr.).

In summer, start looking for rooms early and call ahead. If you arrive late, try call-ing (049) 65 42 99 to check on availability of summer housing at the university. The friendly, crowded **Ostello Città di Padova,** Via Aleardi, 30 (tel. (049) 875 22 19, fax 65 42 99), has tidy, capacious rooms. From the station, take bus 3 and get off when you cross the bridge. (Open 8-9:30am and 6-11pm. Curfew 11pm. L17,000. Show-ers and breakfast included.) **Albergo Verdi,** Via Dondi dall'Orologio, 7 (tel. (049) 875 57 44), offers simple rooms in the center of town (singles L35,000, doubles L45,000; reserve 2-3 days ahead in summer). **Pensione Bellevue,** Via L. Belludi, 11 (tel. (049) 875 55 47), off Prato della Valle, has gorgeous rooms on an ivy-covered courtyard (singles L35,000-49,000, doubles with bath L45,000).

Tame your hunger at **Mensa Universitaria,** Via San Francesco, 122. (Full meal L11,000. Open Mon.-Sat. 11:45am-2:30pm and 6:45-9pm, Sun. 11:45am-2:30pm.) Check here for info on the other *mensas'* schedules. The self-service **Brek,** in the *piazza* off Via VII Febbraoi, rivals the university *mensa's* prices. (Full meal including wine L11,000. Open Sat.-Thurs. 11:30am-3pm and 6:30-10:30pm.) **Al Pero,** Via Santa Lucia, 72, is a neighborhood eatery with fantastic food. (*Salamini arrosti con polenta* (small roasted sausages), L5000. Cover L1500. Open Mon.-Sat. noon-2:30pm and 7:30-9:30pm.)

■■■ VERONA

The city of rose-colored marble is no less romantic today than it was in Shakes-peare's *Romeo and Juliet*. In fact, the city's artistic strength is in part inherited from its two-thousand-year stint as a major metropolis. Even during its formative years as a Roman colony, Verona was an important crossroads, and the remarkably well-pre-served remains from this period are tangible evidence of the colony's preeminence. In the 13th and 14th centuries, Verona experienced another cultural heyday under the rule of the della Scala clan.

The majestic pink **Arena** (tel. 800 32 04) in Piazza Brà dates back to 100 AD, and among Roman amphitheaters it is surpassed in size only by the one at Capua and the Colosseum in Rome. In July and August, it hosts an annual opera and ballet extrava-ganza. (Open Tues.-Sun. 8am-6:30pm, in opera season 8am-1:30pm. Admission L6000, students L1500. Admission to opera and ballet L30,000. Tickets available from Arch #8 or 9 or call (045) 59 01 09 or 59 07 26.) From **Piazza Brà,** which defines the center of Verona, Via Mazzini takes you into **Piazza delle Erbe,** where vendors hawk fruit and hokey trinkets amid the Renaissance *palazzi* constructed by several gentlemen of Verona. The **Arco della Costa,** called the "Arch of the Rib" for the whale rib hung from it, separates P. delle Erbe from **Piazza dei Signori** and the **Tombs of the Scaligeri,** the peculiar Gothic remnants of the Scala family, top dogs in medieval Verona. The equestrian statue of the Cangrande della Scala, a glorification of raw power, preens in the museum of the **Castelvecchio,** the family fortress (open Tues.-Sun. 8am-6:30pm; L5000, students L1500). Upstream from the Castelvecchio looms **Chiesa di San Zeno Maggiore,** a Romanesque church noted for its Mantegna altarpiece (open 8am-noon and 3-7pm). Don't shell out a small fortune for a moment of disillusionment at **Casa di Giulietta (Juliet's House),** Via Cappello, 23; you'll stand on a diminutive balcony and thrill to a view of camera-happy tourists only to find out that the feuding dal Capellos (Capulets) never lived here. (Open Tues.-Sun. 8am-6:30pm. L5000, students L1000.) **Casa Romeo (Romeo's House),** Via Arche Scaligori, 2, is now a coffee bar.

Practical Information, Accommodations, and Food The train station is a 20min. walk on Corso Porta Nuova or a L1200 ride on AMT bus 2 from Verona's center, P. Brà. The **tourist office,** Via Leoncino, 61 (tel. (045) 59 28 28), in Piazza Brà, on the left side of the large yellow building with columns, has an English-speaking staff (open Mon.-Sat. 8am-8pm). To reach the unbeatable **Ostello Verona (HI),** Salita Fontana del Ferro, 15 (tel. (045) 59 03 60), hop on bus 72 or night bus 90 (from the "f" platform of the train station). Get off in P. Isolo, turn right at Via Ponte Pignolo, walk 3 blocks, turn left, then right, then left again. The best hostel in Italy has both 15th-century frescoes and spotless bathrooms. (Curfew 11pm, later if you're at the opera. L15,000. Amazing dinners L12,000. Camping in the garden L7000. 5-night max. stay.) Women might try **Casa della Giovane,** Via Pigna, 7 (tel. (045) 59 68 80; curfew 10:30pm, extended for opera-goers; L15,000-L20,000). **Locanda Catullo,** Vicolo Catullo, 1 (tel. (045) 800 27 86), has gorgeous singles for L35,000; doubles go for L50,000-70,000. Camp at **Campeggio Romeo e Giulietta,** Via Bresciana, 54 (tel. (045) 851 02 43), on the road to Peschiera de Garda (check in 8am-11pm; L11,300 for one person and one tent, L5000 per additional person).

Across the river beckons the fine *menù* at **Trattoria Al Cacciatore,** Via Seminario, 4. (Cover L2000. Open Mon.-Fri. 8:30am-2:30pm and 6:30-10pm, Sat. noon-2:30pm.) **Trattoria Fontanina,** Piazzetta Chiavica, 5 (tel. 803 11 33), down the street from the tombs of the Scaligeri boasts a streetside terrace and pleasant atmosphere (cover L1500; open Wed.-Sun. 12:15-2pm and 7-9:30pm, Mon. noon-2pm). **Il Grillo Parlante,** Vicolo Seghe San Tomaso, 10, is a vegetarian hotspot. (Cover L2500. Open Fri.-Sun. and Tues.-Wed. noon-2pm and 7:30-10pm, Thurs. noon-2pm.) **Supermarket PAM** is at Via dei Mutilati, 3, off Corso Porta Nuova (open Mon.-Tues. and Thurs.-Sat. 8:30am-7:30pm, Wed. 8:30am-noon).

FRIULI-VENEZIA GIULIA

■■■ TRIESTE

Evidence of Trieste's multinational history lingers in the numerous buildings and monuments of Habsburg origin and the Slavic nuances in the local cuisine. The 15th-century Venetian **Castle of San Giusto** presides over **Capitoline Hill,** the city's historic center. You can take bus 24 (L1100) from the station to the last stop at the fortress, and ascend the hill via the daunting **Scala dei Giganti** (Steps of the Giants— all 265 of them) rising from P. Goldoni. Directly below are the remains of the old Roman city center, and across the street is the restored **Cathedral of San Giusto.** Walk around the ramparts of the castle (open 8am-7pm), or peek into the museum, which has temporary exhibits in addition to a permanent collection of weaponry (open Tues.-Sun. 9am-1pm; admission L2000). The city's Italian identity is aggressively asserted by the persistence of fascist and anti-Slav parties, and more passively in **Piazza dell'Unità d'Italia,** the largest square in Italy.

The product of these conflicting forces is a cosmopolitan transportation hub—a logical departure point for travelers to Eastern Europe. Trieste is a direct train ride from Venice or Udine, and several trains and buses cross over daily to neighboring Slovenia and Croatia. Less frequent ferry service runs the length of the Istrian Peninsula. The **train station,** in P. della Libertà (tel. (040) 41 82 07), serves Venice (2hr., L12,700), Milan (7½hr., L31,200), and Ljubljana (3½hr., L15,000). **Agemar Viaggi,** P. Duca degli Abruzzi, 1/A (tel. (040) 36 37 37), will arrange ferry bookings with **Adriatica Navigazione** to Durres in Yugoslavia. The **Ostello Tegeste (HI),** Viale Miramare, 331 (tel. (040) 22 41 02), stacks only members in its bunks. From the station, take bus 36 (L1000). (Registration open noon-11:30pm. Curfew 11:30pm. Checkout 9:30am. L17,000, shower and breakfast included.) **Centrale,** Via Ponchielli, 1 (tel. (040) 63 94 82), offers clean, no-frills rooms. (Singles L30,000-45,000. Doubles L50,000-65,000. Triples L73,000. Showers L3000. Many dishes in Trieste's restaurants have Eastern European overtones (usually Hungarian) and are often loaded with paprika. **Paninoteca Da Livio,** Via della Ginnastica, 3/B, inland off Via Carducci, boasts monster *panini* (L2500-7000) and dozens of brands of beer. (Open Mon.-Sat. 9am-3pm and 5-10pm.)

THE LAKES AND THE DOLOMITES

When Italy's monuments and museums all start to blur together, take a breather and explore the natural beauty of the country's lakes and mountains. The Dolomites dominate the landscape in the province of Trentino-Alto Adige, rising from Austrian-influenced valley communities to lofty peaks equipped for skiing, hiking, and awestruck admiration. The Lake Country, by contrast, has long attracted a less athletic breed of tourist (windsurfers being a prominent exception). Contemplate the meaning of life in the shade of a lake or the isolation of a mountain hut before descending upon Italy's human wonders with renewed enthusiasm.

The Lakes An oddly forked amalgam of 3 lesser lakes, **Lake Como** (Lago di Como) is ½hr. north of Milan by train (L4600) en route to the nearby Swiss border. The city of **Como** is the lake's largest urban outpost; its stately **duomo** harmoniously combines Gothic and Renaissance elements, and is accompanied by a multitude of luxurious *ville* which overlook the dreamy waters amid the secular splendor of shoreside parks and gardens. Contact the tourist office for information and visiting hours. For excellent hiking and eye-exploding views, take a *funicolare* up to **Brunate.** The cars leave from the piers of Lungo Lario Trieste, in front of P. Cavour (L6100 round-trip, L4000 at the hostel). Como's **tourist office** distributes information near the waterfront at P. Cavour, 16 (tel. (031) 27 40 64; open Mon.-Sat. 9am-12:30pm and 2:30-6pm). In Como, stay in the **Ostello Villa Olmo (HI)** behind imposing Villa Olmo, Via Bellinzona, 6 (tel. and fax (031) 57 38 00; L14,000). In Menaggio, **Ostello La Prinula (HI),** Via IV Novembre, 86 (tel. (0344) 323 56), is one of the jollier and better-kept hostels around. (Lockout 10am-5pm. Curfew 11:30pm. L13,000. Open mid-March to mid-Nov.) The **hostel (HI)** in Domaso is at Via Case Sparse, 12 (tel. (0344) 960 94). It lies 16km from Como by bus, but the boat is more convenient. (L13,000 per person. Open March-Oct.)

Lake Garda (Lago di Garda) is the grandest and most popular of the lakes. In the north, **Riva del Garda** has thus far escaped complete commercialization, but **Sirmione,** the southern peninsula, has become a zoo of summer tourists. Buses run to Sirmione every half-hour from Brescia and Verona (1hr., L3900 and L4400 respectively), and from Desenzano, the closest train station (L2000). Get accommodations information at the **tourist office** in Riva (tel. (0464) 55 44 44) or Sirmione (tel. (030) 91 61 14), or choose the indoor economy option at Riva's **Ostello Bena-**

ITALY

cus (HI), P. Cavour, 9 (tel. (0464) 55 49 11; L14,000). The lake's impressive castles include the **Rocca** at Riva and an equivalent at Sirmione. **Desenzano** lies 2 hours from Venice, 25 minutes from Verona, and 1 hour from Milan. Once there, it's easy to get to the lake towns by bus, hydrofoil, and ferry.

The Dolomites Trent (Trento, Trient) is an hour north of Verona on the Bologna-Brenner train line. Italian prevails culturally and linguistically, but you'll see Austrian influence in the local cuisine and interest in all things mountainous. The Azienda Autonoma **tourist office** is across the park from the train station at Via Alfieri, 4 (tel. (0461) 98 38 80). Stay at the hotel-turned-hostel **Ostello Giovane Europa (HI),** Via Manzoni (tel. (0461) 23 45 67), for L15,000 (closed for renovation 1994; expected to reopen 1995). **Monte Bondone** rises majestically over Trent and begs for pleasant daytrips and overnight excursions. Check with the tourist office (tel. and fax (0461) 94 71 88) in **Vanzene,** halfway up the mountain, about accommodations, ski lifts, and maps.

Only an hour and a half north of Trent, also en route to the Brenner Pass, **Bolzano** (Bozen) attempts to ease linguistic feuds with mandatory instruction in both Italian and German for its youth, but the disproportionately large number of fair, rosy-cheeked bilinguals reveals the city's true Austrian bent. The historic center is a combination of spacious *Plätze/piazze* and arcaded alleys, and is an ideal place to acclimate to South Tyrol valley culture and stock up on essentials for a mountain escape. The **tourist office** at P. Walther, 8 (tel. (0471) 97 56 56), has local information, including some easy hiking recommendations in the neighboring hillsides. To prep for serious mountaineering, go to the **Provincial Tourist Office for South Tyrol,** P. Parrocchia, 11 (tel. (0471) 99 38 08), just down from P. Walther, across from the *duomo.* Also pick up their volume of regional accommodations services. For housing in Bolzano itself, head for the hills (you'll find great views and lower prices). **Pensione Reiseggerhof,** Sta. Maddalena di Sotto, 24 (tel. (0471) 97 86 94), offers doubles and breakfast for L28,000 per person. The **Swiss Alps** offer a return to nature just 1½ hours away by bus.

LOMBARDY (LOMBARDIA)

Although cosmopolitan Milan may loom largest in foreigners' perceptions of Lombardy, it does not epitomize the region. Mantua, with its hints of Venetian influence, is culturally foreign to its western neighbor. The beginnings of the Alps are not far away, combining an Italian climate with strains of Swiss and Austrian culture.

■■■ MILAN (MILANO)

It's said that for every church in Rome, there's a bank in Milan. But there's more to Milan than money; there's the preoccupation with *haute couture* and rampant industrial expansion. The steel and glass face of the city's center reflects its fixation with modernity; the city's adolescents exude an epidemic vanity.

ORIENTATION AND PRACTICAL INFORMATION

Milan is linked by train to all major cities in Western Europe. The layout of the city resembles a giant target, encircled by concentric ancient city walls. The **duomo** and **Galleria Vittorio Emanuele II** comprise the bull's-eye, roughly at the center of the downtown circle. The huge Stazione Centrale sprawls on a radial street to the northeast, and the **Metropolitana Milanese (MM)** makes it easy to get around. From the station, a scenic ride on bus 60 takes you to the downtown hub, as does the more efficient commute on metro line 3.

Tourist Office: APT, Via Marconi, 1 (tel. 80 96 62), in the Palazzo di Turismo in P. del Duomo, to the right as you face the *duomo*. Comprehensive local and regional information, useful map and museum guide. Open Mon.-Sat. 8am-8pm, Sun. 9am-12:30pm and 1:30-5pm. Branch offices at **Stazione Centrale** (tel. 669 05 32; open Mon.-Sat. 8am-6pm) and **Linate Airport** (tel. 74 40 65; open Mon.-Fri. 9am-4:30pm). For hotel information and reservations, call **Hotel Reservation Milano** (tel. 76 00 60 95), which may request a deposit during busy periods.

Currency Exchange: Banca Nazionale delle Comunicazioni at Stazione Centrale has standard rates. Open Mon.-Sat. 8am-6:30pm, Sun. 9am-1pm. L3000 fee.

American Express: Via Brera, 3 (tel. 855 71), on the corner of Via dell'Orso. Mail held free for AmEx members, otherwise L800 per inquiry. Accepts wired money for a fee of US$30 per US$1000. Open Mon.-Fri. 9am-5pm.

Post Office: Via Cordusio, 4 (tel. 869 20 69), near P. del Duomo toward the castle. Stamps at #1 and 2. *Fermo Posta* c/o CAI-POST office to the left upon entering. Open Mon.-Fri. 8:30am-7:30pm, Sat. 8:30am-5:30pm. **Postal Code:** 20100.

Telephones: SIP, in Galleria Vittorio Emanuele. **IRITEL,** in Stazione Centrale. Both open 7am-midnight (IRITEL international calls 8am-9:30pm). **City Code:** 02.

Flights: Malpensa Airport, 45km from town. Intercontinental flights. Buses leave every ½hr. in the morning, hourly in the afternoon from P. Luigi di Savoia, on the east side of Stazione Centrale (L12,000). **Linate Airport,** 7km from town. Domestic and European flights. Much easier logistically: the bus to Linate leaves Stazione Centrale every 20min. from 5:40am-7pm (L4000). It's cheaper (L1200) to take bus 73 from M: P. San Babila. **Flight info** for both airports, tel. 74 85 22 00.

Trains: Stazione Centrale, P. Duca d'Aosta (tel. 675 00). The primary station. To: Genoa and Turin (1½-2hr., L12,000); Venice (20 per day, 3hr., L18,700); Florence (3hr., L33,500 with supplement); Rome (5hr., L59,300 with supplement.) **Information office** open 7am-11pm. **Luggage storage** L1500. Open 4am-2am.

Buses: Intercity buses are less convenient and more expensive than trains; **Autostradale** and others depart from P. Castello and environs (M: Ciroli).

Public Transportation: The 3 **Metropolitana Milanese** (M) lines serve much of the city. Buses and trains fill the gaps. Purchase tickets in advance at newsstands or from ticket machines—bring small change. Tickets (L1100) are good for one subway ride or 75min. of surface transportation. All-day passes (L3500) are available from the **ATM** office at the Duomo and Centrale stops. L56,000 fine for riding without a ticket.

Laundromat: Lavanderia Automatica, Corso Porta Vittoria, 51 (tel. 55 19 23 15), beyond Largo Augusto behind the *duomo,* is the most central.

Late-Night Pharmacy: Though nocturnal duty rotates, the one in Stazione Centrale (tel. 669 07 35 or 669 09 35) stays open 24hrs.

Hospital: Ospedale Maggiore Policlinico, Via Francesco Sforza, 35 (tel. 550 31), 5min. from the *duomo* on the inner ring road.

Emergencies: tel. 113. **Police:** tel. 772 71. **"SOS for Tourists":** tel. 545 65 51 for legal complaints. **Medical Emergency:** tel. 38 83. **Ambulance:** tel. 77 33.

ACCOMMODATIONS

Every season is high season in Milan (except Aug.), and a single in an upright establishment for under L35,000 is a real find. For the best deals, head for the city center or the southern periphery. In all cases, make reservations well ahead of time. The **Ostello Pietro Rotta (HI),** Viale Salmoiraghi, 2 (tel. 39 26 70 95; M "Molino Dorino": QT8), is modern but very regimented. (Reception open 7-9am and 5pm-midnight; no morning check-in. Inflexible daytime lockout. Curfew 12:30am. Members only, L20,000. Breakfast, sheets, and lockers included. Laundry L12,000. Open Jan. 13-Dec. 20.) From the station, head left to P. Caiazzo and turn onto Via Pergolesi (which becomes Piccinni) to find the **Hotel San Marco,** Via Piccinni, 25 (tel. 29 51 64 14, fax 29 51 32 43; M: Loreto), where comfortable singles (L50,000) and doubles (L68,000-90,000). **Albergo "Villa Mira,"** Via Sacchini, 19 (tel. 29 52 56 18; M: Loreto), off Via Porpora 2 blocks from P. Loreto, boasts rooms out of a Mr. Clean commercial, plus a bar downstairs. (Singles L40,000. Doubles L55,000.) At Viale Tunisia, 6, equidistant from the station and the city center, you'll find both **Hotel S.**

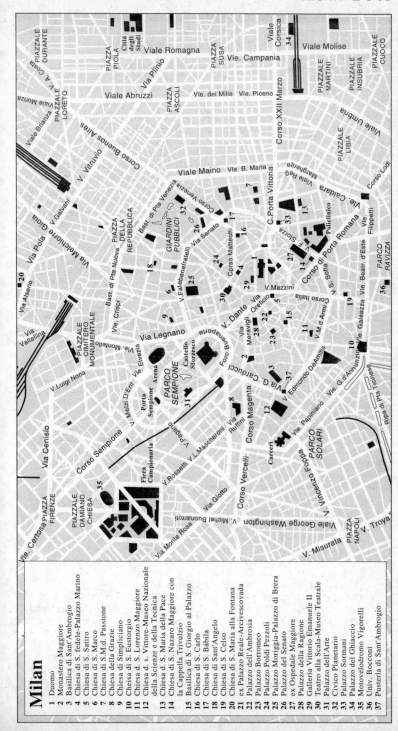

ITALY

Milan

1 Duomo
2 Monastero Maggiore
3 Basilica di Sant'Ambrogio
4 Chiesa di S. fedele-Palazzo Marino
5 Chiesa di S. Satiro
6 Chiesa di S. Marco
7 Chiesa di S.M.d. Passione
8 Chiesa della Grazie
9 Chiesa di Simpliciano
10 Chiesa di S. Eustorgio
11 Chiesa d. S. Lorenzo Maggiore
12 Chiesa d. s. Vittore-Museo Nazionale
    della Scienze e della Tecnica
13 Chiesa d. S. Maria della Pace
14 Chiesa di S. Nazaro Maggiore con
    la Cappella Trivulzio
15 Basilica di S. Giorgio al Palazzo
16 Chiesa di S. Carlo
17 Chiesa di S. Babila
18 Chiesa di Sant'Angelo
19 Chiesa di S. Celso
20 Chiesa di S. Maria alla Fontana
21 ex Palazzo Reale-Arcivescovada
22 Palazzo dell'Ambrosia
23 Palazzo Borromeo
24 Palazzo Poldi Pezzoli
25 Palazzo Moriggia-Palazzo di Brera
26 Palazzo del Senato
27 ex Ospedale Maggiore
28 Palazzo della Ragione
29 Galleria Vittorio Emanuele II
30 Teatro alla Scala-Museo Teatrale
31 Palazzo dell'Arte
32 Civico Planetario
33 Palazzo Sormani
34 Palazzo del Ghiaccio
35 Motovelodromo Vigorelli
36 Univ. Bocconi
37 Pusterla di Sant'Ambrogio

Tomaso (tel. 29 51 47 47), on the 3rd floor (singles L30-40,000, with bath L45,000; doubles L48-70,000) and, on the 6th floor, **Hotel Kennedy** (tel. 29 40 09 34) with '60s dreamscape decor (singles L50,000-65,000; doubles L70,000-140,000). Simple camping facilities await at **Autodromo** (tel. (039) 38 77 71), in the park of the Villa Reale in Monza. From Monza, take a city bus to the campground. (L4000 per person and per tent. Open April-Sept.)

FOOD

Like its fine *couture,* Milanese cuisine is sophisticated and overpriced. Specialties include *risotto giallo* (rice with saffron) and *cotoletta alla milanese* (breaded veal cutlet with lemon). For **supermarkets,** try **Pam,** off Corso Buenos Aires at Via Piccinni, 2, or the air-conditioned store at Via Piane, 38B (both open Mon. 2-7:30pm, Tues.-Sat. 8:30am-7:30pm). For the freshest and fanciest, take your taste buds to the jolly **Viel Frutti Esotici Gelati** on the left as you face the *castello* from Largo Cairoli (M: Cairoli). Sit down with Milanese office workers at one of the countless self-service restaurants that cater to them; the convenient **Ciao** in P. del Duomo serves cheap, balanced meals (*primi* average L4500, *secondi* L7500), and **Brek,** Via Lepetit, 20, by Stazione Centrale, is becoming increasingly popular with a varied crowd (tourist menu L13,000; open Mon.-Sat. 11:30am-3pm and 6:30-10:30pm).

Immense specialty salads (L10,000) add more foliage to leafy **Tarantella,** Viale Abruzzi, 35, just north of Via Plinio (open Sun.-Fri. noon-2:30pm and 7-11:30pm; closed in Aug.). Choose among 47 different kinds of super-fresh *panini* for just L3500-5000 at **Isola del Panino,** Via Felice Casati, 2, at the corner of Corso Buenos Aires (open Tues.-Sat. 7:30am-midnight). Enormous pizzas (L7000-10,000) keep rowdy patrons' mouths full in the **Pizzeria del Nonno,** Via Andrea Costa, 1 (M: Loreto), off P. Loreto (open Tues.-Sat. noon-2:30pm and 7pm-midnight, Sun. 7pm-midnight). Night owls get similarly-priced pizza at **La Piccola Napoli,** Viale Monza, 13 (M: Loreto) until 3am (open mid-Aug. to mid-July Tues.-Sun. at 6pm).

SIGHTS AND ENTERTAINMENT

The **duomo,** with its 135 spires and 96 gargoyles, is a terrifying, radically vertical Gothic creation whose grand stained-glass windows are said to be the largest in the world. Climb to the top of the cathedral to find yourself surrounded by florid outbursts of turrets and spires. (Open 7am-7pm; Oct.-May 9am-4:30pm. L4000, with elevator L6000. Proper dress.) Beside the *duomo* is the monumental entrance to the **Galleria Vittorio Emanuele II,** a colossal iron-and-glass arcade housing cafés and shops. Meander through the gallery from the *duomo* to the **Teatro alla Scala (La Scala),** the world's premier opera house. Innumerable opera titans, from Maria Callas to Pavarotti, made their international debuts here. Enter the lavish hall through the **Museo Teatrale alla Scala,** which includes plaster casts of the hands of famous conductors (open Mon.-Sat. 9am-noon and 2-6pm, Sun. 9:30am-12:30pm and 2:30-6pm; Oct.-April closed Sun.; L5000).

Via Verdi leads to Via Brera and the **Pinacoteca di Brera,** one of Italy's finest museums, a 17th-century *palazzo* with works by Caravaggio, Bellini, and Raphael. (open Tues.-Sat. 9am-2pm, Sun. 9am-1pm; L8000). The **Museo Poldi-Pezzoli,** at Via Manzoni, 12, houses a superb private collection whose masterpieces reside in the Golden Room (open Tues. and Fri. 9am-12:30pm and 2:30-6pm, Sat. 9:30am-12:30pm and 2:30-5:30pm, Sun. 9:30am-12:30pm; L5000).

The **Castello Sforzesco** (M: Cairoli) is the huge 15th-century castle of Milan's Renaissance dukes. Its excellent sculpture collection includes Michelangelo's unfinished *Pietà Rondanini.* (Open Tues.-Sun. 9:30am-5:30pm. Free.) Leonardo da Vinci created his *Last Supper* for the refectory wall of the **Church of Santa Maria delle Grazie** (M: Cairoli). You can glimpse Leonardo's characters and use of perspective through the scaffolding. (Closed for renovations through mid-1995.) Da Vinci is also the attraction at the **Museo Nazionale della Scienza e della Tecnica "Leonardo da Vinci,"** Via San Vittore, 21 (M: San Ambrogio, or bus 50 or 54), off Via Carducci. A large section is devoted to applied physics, and a huge room is filled with models of

Leonardo's most ingenious and visionary inventions. (Open Tues.-Sun. 9am-5pm. L6000.)

Populism and posh converge for the **Musica in Metro** series of summer concerts performed by local music students dressed in their black-tie best in metro stations. These kids probably hope to perform someday at **La Scala,** where gallery seats (notorious for inducing altitude sickness) go for as little as L30,000. (Box office tel. 72 00 37 44, open Tues.-Sun. 10am-1pm and 3:30-5:30pm. Cheap tix go on sale 1hr. before curtain. Season Dec. 7-June; fewer shows July-Sept.)

The **Navigli** and **Porta Ticinese** areas, once home to prostitutes and black-marketeers, are now alive with clubs, *birrerie* (beer halls), and *paninoteche* (sandwich bars). Another safe, attractive, and chic district lies by **Via Brera;** here you'll find art galleries, small clubs, and restaurants. The majority of young Milanese head to discos in nearby Brescia and Bergamo. One of Milan's top discos, **Gimmi's,** Via B. Cellini, 2, near Corso Porta Vittoria, brimming with beautiful people, is suitably expensive (cover and first drink L30,000; open Wed.-Sun. 10:30pm-3:30am). **Contatto,** Corso Sempione, 76 (M: Cairoli, then bus 57), behind the Castello Sforzesco, is a gay club.

After Bologna, Milan supports the best rock scene in Italy. Attend **Plastic** (officially *Il Killer Plastico*), close to Viale Umbria, 120, which swings between a punk/ New Wave and a fashionable New York crowd (cover L15,000, Sat. L18,000; open Tues.-Sun. until 3am), or the nearby **New Magazine,** Strada Via Piceno, 3, where the crunchy atmosphere is accentuated by peanut shells on the floor (cover Fri. L12,000, Sat. L15,000.; closed Mon.). New bands looking for a break start out at **Magia Music Meeting,** Via Salutati, 2 (M: San Agostino). Dine while you listen. (About L8000. Open until 3am.)

■■■ MANTUA (MANTOVA)

Mantua had its heyday as the court of the extravagant Gonzaga dynasty. During their 400-year reign, the Gonzaga loaded the center of town with palaces, churches and towers, and lured some of the most important Renaissance artists to their court. The **Church of Sant'Andrea** is acclaimed as the most brilliant creation of Florentine architect Leon Battista Alberti. The plan—a vaulted church with a single aisle, flanking side chapels, and a domed crossing—served as the model for ecclesiastical architecture for the next 200 years. Cobblestone **Piazza Sordello** forms the center of a vast complex built by the Gonzaga.The **Palazzo Ducale** is one of the largest and most sumptuously decorated palaces in Europe. Its more than 500 rooms include a series of miniature chambers designed for court dwarves. Near the entrance in the Hall of Dukes hang Antonio Pisanelli's frescoes (1439-44), discovered in 1969 under thick layers of plaster. (Open Mon.-Sat. 9am-1pm and 2:30-6pm, Sun. 9am-1pm. L10,000 lets you into everything in the Palazzo.) A trek through P. Veneto and down Largo Patri leads to the opulent **Palazzo del Tè,** built in the early 16th century as the Gonzaga family's suburban villa. One wing of the palace features regular exhibits by modern Italian artists alongside a collection of Egyptian art. (Open Tues.-Sun. 10am-6pm. L10,000, under 18 L4000.)

Mantua is two hours southeast of Milan by train. The **tourist office** is at P. Mantegna, 6 (tel. (0376) 32 82 54), adjacent to the church of Sant'Andrea. From the train station, take a left on Via Solferino through P. S. Francesco to Via Fratelli Bandiera, and turn right on Via Verdi. Request the invaluable *Mantova: Directions for Use,* which comes with a fabulous map, and ask about **agriturismo** lodgings, around L20,000 a night. (Open Mon.-Sat. 9am-noon and 3-6pm.) Mantua's youth hostel and its campsite were closed during the summer of 1994, but may re-open in 1995. For as long as it remains closed, **Hotel ABC Moderno,** P. Don Leoni, 25 (tel. and fax (0376) 32 23 29), right across from the station, is offering a special bargain to everybody with a certain ticket (*biglietto*) from the tourist office (L20,000 per person, including breakfast). Nearby, some chic singles (from L45,000) and doubles (from L85,000) in **Albergo Bianchi Stazione,** P. Don Leoni, 24 (tel. (0376) 32 64 65, fax 32 15 04) overlook a private garden. For cheap sit-down meals go to the **Self-Service**

Virgiliana, P. Virgiliana, 57 (meals under L11,000; open Mon.-Fri. noon-2:30pm).
Pizzeria Capri, Via Bettinelli, 8 (tel. 36 32 38), immediately on your right as you exit
the train station, specializes in Neapolitan cuisine—that means *real* pizza—and seafood. (*Margherita* (plain cheese) pizza L6000; with *porcini* mushrooms L10,500.
Open Fri.-Wed.)

ITALIAN RIVIERA (LIGURIA)

Genoa divides Liguria, the Italian Riviera, neatly in half—**Riviera di Ponente** (setting
sun) to the west and the more splendid **Riviera di Levante** (rising sun) to the east,
with its colorful fishing villages and clear turquoise water. This crescent-shaped
coastal stretch differs greatly from its French counterpart; here you'll find elegance,
not arrogance, and much less hype. Especially lovely are the **Portofino peninsula**
(about ½hr. by train from Genoa) and the **Cinque Terre** area (immediately west of
La Spézia). In July and August, only reservations or amazingly good fortune will get
you a place for the night. Don't miss the *pasta alla genovese,* commonly known as
"al pesto," and *focaccia,* a delicious oily bread topped with onions or tomato sauce.

■■■ GENOA (GENOVA)

The descendant of a proud and piratical maritime republic, Genoa's commercial
center does not necessarily merit a visit. Stick to the entanglement of narrow footpaths that wind their way among houses and overhanging gardens; these trails offer
a peaceful respite from the chaos of the modern city. The **centro storico** (historical
center) preserves many of Genoa's most important monuments; unfortunately, it is
also the city's most dangerous quarter. The sights are worth seeing, but do it with a
map, during the day. North of P. de Ferrari is P. Fontane Marose, off which runs **Via
Garibaldi,** along which the splendid *palazzi* **Bianco, Rosso, Municipale,** and **Parodi**
house many of the Flemish and Dutch masterpieces amassed by the Genovese merchants. (Bianco and Rosso share staff, so open alternately in am or pm; L4000, EU
nationals free. Municipale open Mon.-Fri. 8:30am-noon and 1-4:30pm; free.) The
Palazzo Ducale on P. Matteotti was once the home of the city's rulers. **Villetta di
Negro,** spreads over the hill next to P. Corvetto with grottoes, waterfalls, and terraced gardens. On its summit, the **Museo d'Arte Orientale** houses impressive sculptures (open Tues.-Sat. 9am-7pm, Sun. 9am-12:30pm; L4000, under 18 and EU
nationals free).

Practical Information, Accommodations, and Food   Genoa is easily
accessible by rail from Rome (5-6hr., L33,600) and Turin (2hr., L12,100). The
French border lies 2 hours westward. There are 2 train stations: **Stazione Principe,**
P. Acquaverde, to the west near the port, and **Stazione Brignole,** P. Verdi, farther
east. Call (010) 28 40 81 for train information. Bus 40 from Brignole and 41 from
Principe run to P. de Ferrari. Via Balbi extends from Stazione Principe to **Piazza de
Ferrari,** the center of town, while **Via XX Settembre** runs east towards Stazione
Brignole. Street numbers are marked in red (commercial establishments) or black
(residences or offices), in double sequence. To get to the **tourist office,** Via Roma,
11 (red) (tel. (010) 54 15 41) from Brignole, go right on Via de Amicis to P. Brignole,
then continue up Via Serra to P. Corvetto (open Mon.-Fri. 8am-1:30pm and 2-5pm,
Sat. 8am-1:30pm). There is a **branch** (tel. 26 26 33) at the Principe train station
(open 8am-8pm). Make sure to head to the **travel office for youth** in the Palazzo
Ducale to pick up a better map and the invaluable "Genovagiovane" guide (open
Mon.-Fri. 9am-noon and 1-5pm).

Genoa's youth hostel, **Ostello per la Gioventù (HI),** Via Costanzi, 120 (tel. and
fax 242 24 57), offers panoramic views and incredible facilities. Take bus 35 five
stops from Principle, then transfer to bus 40 (which goes directly from Brignole)

and ride to the end. (Lockout 9am-4pm. Curfew 11:30pm. Members only. L19,000. Wheelchair access.) **Pensione Mirella,** Via Gropallo, 4/4 (tel. 839 37 22), is in a beautifully maintained and secure building. From Stazione Brignole, go right on Via de Amicis to P. Brignole and go right again (singles L35,000, doubles L50,000). Avoid the hotels in the *centro storico,* many of which rent rooms by the hour.

Genoa's culinary claim to fame is *pesto,* made from basil, cheese, pine nuts, garlic, and olive oil. Try *pansotti,* ravioli filled with cheese and herbs served with a walnut sauce. **Trattoria da Maria,** Vico Testadoro, 14r, off Via XXV Aprile serves the best of quintessential Genovese cuisine (*Menù* L12,000; open Sun.-Thurs. noon-2pm and 4:30-10pm). In summer the action moves to nearby **Nervi,** where the Genovese bar-hop or stroll along the *lungomare* lapping *gelato.*

■■■ RIVIERA DI PONENTE AND RIVIERA DI LEVANTE

Finale Ligure Eschewing the glamor and arrogance of other Rivería towns, Finale Ligure welcomes weary backpackers with soft sand and luxurious flora. **Finalborgo,** enclosed within ancient solid walls, is a 1km walk up Via Brunenghi from the train station. Frequent **trains** head to Genoa (L5300), Ventimiglia (L6700), and Santa Margherita Ligure (L7400). To the left of the train station, **SAR buses** run to neighboring beachside towns. The **IAT tourist office,** Via S. Pietro, 14 (tel. (019) 69 25 81), on the street parallel to the waterfront, provides a free map and loving advice. (Open Mon.-Sat. 8am-1pm and 3:30-6:30pm; off-season Mon.-Sat. 8am-1pm and 3-6pm.) Rent **bikes** at **Oddone,** Via Colombo, 20 (tel. (019) 69 42 15), behind the tourist office.

The **Castello Wuillerman (HI)** (tel. and fax 69 05 15), on Via Generale Caviglia is in a red brick castle overlooking the sea. From the station, take a left onto Via Mazzini, which turns into Via Torino. Turn left onto tiny Via degli Ulivi when you hit the Esso gas station, and climb up the Gradinata delle Rose. (Reception open 7-9:30am and 5-11pm. Curfew 11:30pm. Check-in 5pm, but you can leave bags 7-9:30am. L16,000, nonmembers L21,000. Open March 15-Oct. 15.) The cheaper culinary options are on Via Rossi and Via Roma, inland from the waterfront. **Spaghetteria Il Posto,** Via Porro, 21, is an elegant locale with an unusual menu and vegetarian options. (Cover L1500. Open Tues.-Sun. 7-10:30pm.) Locals enjoy filling pizza at **La Grotta,** Vico Massaferro, 17, off Via San Pietro (along the waterfront), right across the alley from the tourist office (open Wed.-Mon. 7pm-2am).

Camogli With a fabulous pebble beach and festive atmosphere, Camogli takes its name from the wives who ran the town while their husbands sailed its once-huge fishing fleet. (Camogli is a contraction of *casa mogli*—wives' house.) Reach Camogli by train (L1500) or bus (L1700) from Santa Margherita. The **tourist office,** Via XX Settembre, 33 (tel. 77 10 66), looms to your right as you exit the station. (Open Mon.-Sat. 9am-12:30pm and 4-6:30pm, Sun. 3:50-6:20pm; Sept.-June Mon.-Sat. 9am-12:30pm.)

Stay at **Albergo La Camogliese,** Via Garibaldi, 55 (tel. (0185) 77 14 02, fax 77 40 24), down the loooong stairway near the train station. The owner offers *Let's Go* 10% discounts on luxurious rooms. (Singles with bath L45,000; doubles with bath L75,000-90,000.) For great pizza and a maritime motif, try **Moro Mare,** Via Garibaldi, 133 (tel. 77 50 09). (L2000 cover. A/C. Pals with the gang over at La Camogliese, they offer *Let's Go* 10% discount off as well! Open Tues.-Sun. 7-11pm.)

Portofino and San Fruttuoso Gorgeous yacht- and boutique-filled **Portofino** merits a daytrip from Santa Margherita. Though you won't be able to afford to stay or eat, the harbor view is enthralling. The town is accessible by **bus** from Santa Margherita (every 20min., L1700)—get off at Portofino Mare, not Portofino Vetta. Trek up to the **Chiesa di San Giorgio** or the **castle** for enchanting vistas of the bay, or follow the "Al faro" signs to reach the **lighthouse** for a breathtaking view of the coastline. Isolated **San Fruttuoso** is a verdant village at the peninsula's western corner. Boats run here (about every hr.) from Camogli (round-trip L10,000), or you can venture on foot (1½hr.) from Portofino.

Santa Margherita Ligure Come here for an affordable taste of what a real Italian Riviera holiday is supposed to be. Evocative of the elegance of an era now past, you can still experience the fantasy of glamour which has not been ruined by tourist development. Frequent trains from Genoa (L2500) make this an excellent base for exploration of the Portofino peninsula. The English-speaking, efficient **tourist office**, Via XXV Aprile, 2b (tel. (0185) 28 74 85), provides accommodations service and a town map. Turn right from the train station onto Via Roma, then right again on Via XXV Aprile. (Open 8:45am-12:30pm and 3:30-7pm.) A beautiful old villa, **Hotel Nuova Riviera,** Via Belvedere, 10 (tel. (0185) 28 74 03) has spacious, elegant rooms (singles L45,000-55,000, doubles L65,000-85,000; breakfast included; ½-pension sometimes required in summer at L65,000 per person.) Also an 18th-century villa, **Hotel Conte Verde,** Via Zara, 1 (tel. (0185) 28 71 39, fax 28 42 11), right from Via Roma, lends bikes to guests (singles L40,000-65,000, doubles L70,000-90,000). Buy bread, cheese, meat, and produce along Corso Matteotti; on Fridays from 8am to 1pm, the shops spill out onto the *corso.* For a hearty meal, try **Trattoria Baicin,** Via Algeria, 9, off P. Martiri della Libertà. Mamma Carmela's *Trofie alla Genovese,* gnocchi mixed with potato, string beans, and pesto (L6500) is stupendous. (Open Tues.-Sun. noon-3pm and 6:45pm-midnight.) **Rosticceria Revelant,** Via Gramsci, 15, east of P. Martiri della Libertà, offers scrumptious take-out meals (open 8am-noon and 4:30-8pm, closed Sun.-Mon. in the winter).

Cinque Terre and La Spézia Tripping down the coast, don't miss the **Cinque Terre**, a group of five connected villages clinging to the cliffs above the sea. The towns, in order of increasing distance from Genoa, are **Monterosso, Vernazza, Corniglia, Manarola,** and **Riomaggiore,** of which Monterosso is the biggest, easiest to reach, and least charming. The **tourist office** (tel. (0187) 81 75 06) in Monterosso below the train station, provides accommodations service and currency exchange (open April-Oct. Mon.-Sat. 10am-noon and 5-7:30pm, Sun. 10am-noon). In Riomaggiore, sack out at sign-less **Hostel Mamma Rosa,** P. Unità, 2, (tel. (0187) 92 00 50), across from the bar at the train station (L20,000), or check out the *affitta camere* (private rooms) in Corniglia and Vernazza. **Albergo Barbara,** P. Marconi, 21 (tel. 81 22 01), at the port in **Vernazza** offers bright, airy rooms with fantastic views of the port. (Singles L40,000-50,000. Doubles L60,000-70,000.) Munch happily on any of the seafood dishes that abound in the Cinque Terre, and wash them down with *sciacchetrà,* the sweet local white wine. Wood-burning ovens deliver every kind of *focaccia* imaginable at **Foccacceria Il Frontoio,** Via Goberti, 1, in **Monterosso.** (Slices L1500-2500. Open Fri.-Wed. 9am-1:30pm and 4-8pm.)

 La Spézia is more commercial and less pleasant than the smaller towns of the surrounding coast, but it serves as a departure point to Corsica. **Corsica Ferries** (tel. (0187) 212 82) and **Navarma Lines** (tel. (0187) 218 44), both at the Molo Italia dock, offer comparable services to Bastia, Corsica (L34,000-38,000). If you must stay here, **Albergo Terminus,** Via Paleocapa, 21 (tel. (0187) 71 49 35), has lofty singles (L35,000) and doubles (L47,000). The **tourist office** in the station lists official *affita camere* for all five villages of Cinque Terre (open Sun. and Tues.-Thurs. 9:30am-1:30pm and 3-6pm., Fri.-Sat. 9:30am-6pm). A good place to sample *mescuia,* a thick soup of beans, cornmeal, olive oil, and pepper is **Trattoria da Sandro,** V. del Prione, 268. (*Trittico della casa,* combo plate of seafood pastas, L9500; open Sat.-Thurs. noon-2pm and 7:30-10pm.).

EMILIA-ROMAGNA

Italy's wealthiest wheat- and dairy-producing region covers the fertile plains of the Po river valley and fosters the finest in culinary traditions. Plan to go over budget, as you gorge on Parmesan cheese and *prosciutto* and Bolognese fresh pasta and *mortadella*, washing it all down with red wines like the sparkling *lambrusco*.

■■■ BOLOGNA

With one forkful of Bologna's *tortellini*, it becomes clear that this city appreciates the better things in life. The city founded the first university in Europe 900 years ago; the **Università di Bologna** has since graduated the likes of Dante, Petrarch, Copernicus, and Tasso. A general opulence belies wealthy Bologna's contradictory position as the outpost of the Italian Communist Party.

Bologna's most remarkable sight is the endless series of porticoes that line buildings throughout the city, a 14th-century solution to an urban housing crisis. The tranquil expanse of **Piazza Maggiore** is the city's heart and center. It adjoins the **Piazza del Nettuno,** whose **Palazzo del Podestà** was remodeled by Fioravanti's son Aristotle, who later designed Moscow's Kremlin. The bronze *Neptune and Attendants* by Giambologna splash happily in the fountain outside. Follow the afternoon shade to the steps of the **Basilica of San Petronio,** a huge Gothic structure that some claim would have been bigger than St. Peter's had the Pope not been peeved (open 7:30am-7pm). You can climb the less tipsy of the two towers on **Piazza Porta Ravegnana** (open 9am-6pm, winter 9am-5pm; L3000).

Down Via Santo Stefano, the triangular **Piazza Santo Stefano** opens into a complex of Romanesque churches of austere beauty. The grandest is the round **Chiesa del San Sepolcro;** San Petronio, patron of Bologna, rests under a carved pulpit. In the courtyard behind is the **Basin of Pilate,** in which Pontius supposedly cleansed his hands. The **Pinacoteca Nazionale,** Via delle Belle Arti, 56, one of Italy's major galleries, contains a beguiling bevy of Bolognese paintings and a spread of Renaissance masterpieces (open Tues.-Sat. 9am-2pm, Sun. 9am-1pm; L3000).

The university ensures classical concerts and a hopping nightlife during the academic year. Get *Bologna Spettacolo News* from the tourist office for listings and times, and bar-hop the university quarter around P. Verdi or Via delle Belle Arte.

Practical Information, Accommodations, and Food Bologna's **tourist office,** in the train station (tel. (051) 24 65 41), books rooms for free. Pick up a copy of *Bologna Dove* for the latest information and a respectable free map. (Open Mon.-Sat. 9am-7pm.) The **main office** in Palazzo Comunale at P. Maggiore, 6 (tel. (051) 23 96 60), is more exhaustive. One of Italy's biggest rail hubs, the **train station** (tel. (051) 24 64 90) is in P. delle Medaglio d'Oro at the northern end of town, a 20min. walk from the center (or hop on bus 25 or 30; L1300).

Prices are high and rooms scarce due to the glut of students and business travelers. Bologna's clean, congenial **Ostello San Sisto (HI),** Via Viadagota, 5 and 14 (tel. and fax (051) 50 18 10), overlooks fertile farmland 6km away. Ask at the tourist office for the map with specific directions or call the English-speaking hostel. (Reception open 7-9am and 5-11:30pm. Lockout 9am-5pm. L17,000, nonmembers L22,000. Breakfast included.) In the heart of town, try the clean and friendly **Albergo Panorama,** Via Livraghi 1 (tel. (051) 22 18 02; singles L45,000, doubles L70,000, triples L95,000). On the second right off Via Orefici from P. Maggiore, **Albergo Apollo** couldn't be closer to the center of town (clean white singles L43,000, doubles L70,000-91,000; closed first 2 weeks in Aug.).

Don't miss Bologna's namesake dish, *spaghetti alla Bolognese,* pasta with a hefty meat and tomato sauce; or, perhaps, "bologna," known locally as *mortadella.* The areas around Via Augusto Righi and Via Piella, as well as the neighborhood of Via Saragozza, are especially good for cheap, traditional *trattorie.* The touristy but affordable snack bar **Lazzarini,** Via Clavature, 1, off P. Maggiore, has an exquisite self-service restaurant upstairs. (Pasta dishes L4000-8000. *Secondi* L4000-7500. Restaurant open Mon.-Fri. 11:30am-3pm. Snack bar open Mon.-Sat. 7am-8pm.) **Ristorante Clorofilla,** Strada Maggiore, 64, serves up innovative vegetarian specialties and imaginative salads (L6500-12,000). (Open Mon.-Sat. 12:15-3pm and 6pm-midnight.) **Antica Trattoria Roberto Spiga,** Via Broccaindosso 21/A, a modest, miraculous Bolognese relic, serves complete meals with wine or water (L18,500), *primi* (L4500-6000), and *secondi* (L7000-12,5000). (Cover L1500. Open Sept.-July Mon.-Sat. noon-2pm and 7-10pm.) Or mingle with the student crowd at the **Mensa Universitaria Irnerio,** Via Zamboni, 47, where you can load up on a full meal for only L2000-8000. (Show any student ID to buy a ticket. Open Sept.-July Mon.-Fri. 11:45am-3pm and 7-10pm, Sat.-Sun. 11:45am-3pm.) For picnic fare, the vast indoor market, **Mercato Ugo Bassi,** Via Ugo Bassi, 27, sells produce, cheese and meats (open Mon.-Wed. 7am-1:15pm and 5-7pm, Fri. 7am-1:15pm and 4:30-7:30pm, Thurs. and Sat. 7am-1:15pm).

■■■ PARMA

Conveniently located on the Bologna-Milan rail line, Parma rivals Bologna as Italy's food capital and is home to the most refined *prosciutto* ham and fragrant *parmigiano* cheese, as well as *lambrusco,* a deliciously intoxicating red wine. Try to arrive famished. Parma's **duomo** contains two medieval masterpieces: the moving *Descent from the Cross,* precursor of several Renaissance versions, and the *Episcopal Throne* by Benedetto Antelami, Parma's medieval master sculptor (open 9am-noon and 3-7pm). Correggio painted the interior of the dome of the **Church of San Giovanni Evangelista** (open 6:30am-noon and 3:30-8pm), while Antelami festooned the exterior of the **baptistry** with bas-reliefs of fantastic animals and biblical allegories (open 9am-12:30pm and 3-8pm). Nearby, the **Palazzo della Pilotta** houses the **Galleria Nazionale,** with works by da Vinci and Correggio (open 9am-1:45pm. L10,000). Make sure to see the premier **opera house** of Parma, the **Teatro di Reggio,** next to P. della Pace. Check with the tourist office for prices of cheaper standing-room-only tickets during their Oct.-May season.

Via Garibaldi, Parma's main street, runs from the station to the center of town. The **Azienda Promozione Turistica,** P. Duomo, 5 (tel. (0521) 23 47 35), has lists of Parmesan accommodations (open Mon.-Fri. 9am-12:30pm and 3:30-6:30pm, Sat. 9am-12:30pm, Oct.-April Mon.-Fri. 9am-12:30pm and 3-6pm, Sat. 9am-12:30pm). The **Ostello Cittadella (HI),** Via Passo Buole (tel. (0521) 58 15 46), occupies a 15th-century fortress; get on bus 9 in front of the station or snag bus 2 or 6 from P. Garibaldi. (3-day max. stay. Strict curfew 11pm. Members only, but sometimes accepts student ID. L13,000. **Camping** (April-Oct.) L6800 per person, L6500 per tent.) Women under 25 only are allowed stay in the first-class rooms (L17,000) at **Casa Della Giovane,** Via del Conservatorio, 11 (tel. (0521) 28 32 29). There's a lovely restaurant downstairs from **Albergo Croce di Malta,** Borgo Palmia, 8 (tel. (0521) 23 56 43), off Strada Farini, next to an old church. (Singles L40,000. Doubles L60,000. Triples L75,000. *Menù* L20,000. Open 12:30-3pm and 7:30-10:30pm.)

Eat lustily. The delightful **Sorelle Pachini,** Strada Farini, 27, near P. Garibaldi, hides the best lunchtime *trattoria* in town under the cover of a salami shop (*primi* L8000, *secondi* L10,000-12,000; open Mon.-Sat. noon-2:30pm). For dinner, hit **Trattoria Corrieri,** Via Conservatorio, 1. Wash down the exceptional *tortelli di zucca* (ravioli made with sweet squash in cheese sauce, L6000) with L6000 carafes of *lambrusco.* (Open Mon.-Sat. noon-2:30pm and 7:30-10:30pm.) An **open-air market** can be found at P. Ghiaia, off Viale Mariotti, past Palazzo Pilotta (8am-1pm and 3-8pm).

TUSCANY (TOSCANA)

Tuscany is the stuff Italian dreams (and more than one romantic Brits-in-Italy movie) are made of. With rolling hills covered with olives and grapevines, bright yellow fields of sunflowers, and inviting cobblestone streets, it's hard not to wax poetic. Tuscany's Renaissance culture, an unprecedented explosion of art, architecture, and humanist scholarship, became the culture of Italy, while Tuscan, the language of Dante, Petrarch, and Machiavelli, is today's textbook Italian. The region has only one drawback: it's too popular. Though Tuscans are generally very gracious, your English may induce sighs from natives, especially in Florence. Efforts to speak Italian, however mangled, will be much appreciated.

■■■ FLORENCE (FIRENZE)

Since the High Renaissance kicked in, nearly every visitor to walk Florence's cobblestone streets has fallen in love with the city. Henry James, Stendhal, Albert Camus, and even cranky Mark Twain were all won over by its beauty. Fueled by an innovative banking system, the city evolved from a booming, 13th-century wool- and silk-trading town into the archetype of political experimentation and artistic rebirth. Periodic civil wars disrupted Florentine civic life until the ascendancy of the Medici clan and their establishment of peace in the 15th century under Lorenzo the Magnificent. At its apex in the mid-15th century, Florence was the unchallenged European capital of painting, sculpture, architecture, medicine, astronomy, physics, commerce, and political thought.

ORIENTATION AND PRACTICAL INFORMATION

Major arteries radiate from the Duomo and its two *piazze:* **Piazza San Giovanni** encircling the baptistry and **Piazza del Duomo** around the cathedral. The pedestrian walkway, **Via dei Calzaiuoli,** runs from the *duomo* to **Piazza Signoria** towards the river Arno. Parallel to Via dei Calzaiuoli on the west, **Via Roma** leads from P. S. Giovanni through **Piazza della Repubblica** to the **Ponte Vecchio,** which spans the Arno to the district called the **Oltrarno.** For guidance through Florence's tangled center, pick up a free map (ask for the one with the street index) from inside the train station or from one of the tourist offices.

Florence has two entirely independent sequences of street numbers: red indicates a commercial building (noted here with an "r"), and blue or black a residential one (including most *pensioni* and most sights); always note which color you're after.

Tourist Offices: Azienda Consorzio I.T.A. (tel. 28 28 93 and 21 95 37), in the train station by track #16, next to the pharmacy. Come in person and they'll find you a room. L3000-5000 fee. Open 8:30am-9pm. **Informazione Turistica,** inside the squat round glass-and-concrete building outside the train station (exit by track #16). No booking service, but plenty of up-to-date info on entertainment and cultural events. Open April-Oct. 9am-7pm, Nov.-Mar. 9am-2pm.

Budget Travel: STS (Student Travel Service), Via Zanetti, 18r (tel. 28 41 83). Student discounts on rail, bus, and plane tickets. Open Mon.-Fri. 9:30am-12:30pm and 3:30-6:30pm, Sat. 9:30am-12:30pm.

Consulates: U.S., Lungarno Vespucci, 38 (tel. 239 82 76), near the station. Open Mon.-Fri. 8:30am-noon and 2-4pm. **U.K.,** Lungarno Corsini, 2 (tel. 28 41 33). Open Mon.-Fri. 9:30am-12:30pm and 2:30-4:30pm.

Currency Exchange: Banks have the best rates. Open Mon.-Fri. 8:20am-1:20pm and 2:45-3:45pm. Banks open on Sat. mornings close by 11:20am. **Cassa di Risparmio di Firenze** now has ATMs to change money at Via de' Bardi, 73r; Via de' Tornabuoni, 23r; Via degli Speziali, 16r; and Via dei Servi, 40r. Open 24hrs.

American Express: Via Dante Alighieri, 20-22r (tel. 509 81). From the Duomo, walk down Via dei Calzaiuoli; turn left onto Via dei Tavolini. AmEx is on the little *piazza* at its end. Open Mon.-Fri. 9am-5:30pm, Sat. 9am-12:30pm.

Post Office: Via Pellicceria, off P. della Repubblica. *Fermo Posta* at windows #23 and 24. Open Mon.-Fri. 8:15am-6pm, Sat. 8:15am-12:30pm. **Postal Code:** 50100.

Telephones: ASST, at the post office. Make international collect calls here. Open 8am-9:45pm. Phones also at Via Cavour, 21r. Open 9am-9pm, winter 9am-8pm. **City Code:** 055.

Trains: Santa Maria Novella Station, near the center of town. Information office (tel. 27 87 85) open 7am-9pm. Try the (English-speaking) computers outside the office to plan your trip. Every hr. to: Bologna (1hr., L7700, *rapido* L11,000); Venice (3½hr., L19,500, *rapido* L25,900); Milan (3½hr., L22,800, *rapido* L32,100); and Rome (2½hr., L22,800). All trains arrive here except a few to and from Rome, which use the **Campo di Marte** station on the east side of town. Bus 19 connects the 2 stations about every 20min. around the clock (25min.).

Buses: SITA, Via Santa Caterina da Siena, 15r (tel. 48 36 51, Sat.-Sun. tel. 21 14 87). Frequent buses to Siena (2hr., L8300); San Gimignano (L8800). **LAZZI,** P. Via Stazione, 4-6r (tel. 21 51 54), to Pisa (L9200), Prato (L2500), and Lucca (L7400). **LAZZI Eurolines** travels to Rome and Naples.

Public Transportation: ATAF buses run 6am-1am. Tickets (L1300 for 1hr.; L5000 for 24hr.), available at most kiosks, must be bought *before* boarding and validated by the punch-machine on board, or pay a L50,000 fine. Get a bus map at the ATAF office outside the train station.

Bike and Moped Rental: MotoRent, Via S. Zanobi, 9r (tel. 49 01 13). Bikes start at L8000 per 3hr., L15,000 per day. Mopeds begin at L7000 per hr., L35,000 per day, L200,000 per week. No license necessary, but min. age 16 (bring ID).

Hitchhiking: Those going on the A-1 to Bologna and Milan or the A-11 to the Riviera and Genoa take bus 29, 30, or 35 from the train station to the feeder near Peretola. For the A-1 to Rome and the Siena extension take bus 31 or 32 from the station to exit #23. The **International Lift Center,** Corso Tintori, 39 (tel. 28 06 21), matches passengers with drivers for a fee. Open Mon.-Sat. 9am-7:30pm, Sun. noon-3pm.

Luggage Storage: at the station, by track #16. Open 4:30am-1:30am. L1500.

Bookstores: BM Bookstore, Borgo Ognissanti, 4r (tel. 29 45 75). Great selection of English language books. Open Mon.-Sat. 9am-1pm and 3:30-7:30pm, Sun. 9am-1pm; Nov.-Feb. closed Sun.

Laundromat: Wash and Dry Lavarapido, Via dei Servi, 105, two blocks from the Duomo. Self-service L11,000 for wash, dry, and detergent. Open 8am-9pm.

Public Baths: Bagno S. Agostino, Via S. Agostino, 8, off P. Santo Spirito. Bath L3000. Soap and towel L1500. Open Tues. and Thurs. 3:30-6:45pm, Sat. 8:30am-noon and 3:30-6:45pm.

Pharmacy: Farmacia Comunale, by track #16 in the station (tel. 28 94 35). **Molteni,** Via Calzaiuoli, 7r (tel. 28 94 90). Both open 24hrs.

Medical Assistance: Misericordia, P. del Duomo, 20 (tel. 21 22 22). **Tourist Medical Service,** Via Lorenzo il Magnifico, 59 (tel. 47 54 11). House calls 24hrs.

Emergency: tel. 113. **Police: Questura** (headquarters), Via Zara, 2 (tel. 497 71). On weekends or after hours go around the corner to Via Duca D'Aosta. English-speaking personnel usually available. **Fire:** tel. 115.

ACCOMMODATIONS AND CAMPING

Florence abounds with one-star *pensioni* and private homes with *affitta camere.* Sleeping in Florence's train stations, streets, or parks is a poor idea, and police discourage it. The city's best budget lodgings can be found at the **Ostello Archi Rossi** near the train station and at **Pensionato Pio X** and **Istituto Gould** in the Oltrarno, but clean and inexpensive lodgings are dispersed throughout the city. If you arrive late in the afternoon, check with the accommodations service at the train station; they'll know who still has room and at what prices. The best places go early, so reservations are wise, especially if you plan to visit at Easter or in summer. The vast majority of *pensioni* prefer to take reservations in the form of a letter with at least 1 night's deposit by postal money order. Prices are uniformly raised by 5% or so every year, with the increase taking effect in March or April. If you have any complaints

ITALY

N

Florence

1 Piazza M. D'Azeglio
2 Giardino Della Gherardesca
3 Giardino dei Semplici
4 S. Maria Novella Station
5 San Lorenzo
6 Duomo
7 S. Spirito
8 S. M. Del Carmine
9 Uffizi Gallery
10 Palazzo Vecchio
11 Palazzo Riccardi
12 S. Marco Università
13 Fortezza Da Basso
14 Pal. Pandolfini
15 S. Croce
16 S. S. Annunziata
17 S. Maria Novella
18 Palazzo Strozzi
19 Palazzo Corsini
20 Badia
21 Bargello
22 Museo Bardini
23 Camping
24 Azienda Autonoma di Turismo
25 Post Office
26 American Express
27 Bus Station
28 Palazzo Pitti
29 Forte Belvedere

Fiume Arno

Giardino Torrigiani

talk first to the proprietor, and then to the **Ufficio Controllo Alberghi,** Via Cavour, 37 (tel. 276 01).

Hostels

Ostello Archi Rossi, Via Faenza, 94r (tel. 29 08 04, fax 230 26 01), 2 blocks from the train station. Exit left from the station onto Via Nazionale and turn left at Via Faenza. Look for the blue neon "ostello" sign. A brand-new hostel with a TV room and a courtyard patio. Lockout 11am-2:30pm. Curfew 12:30am. L20,000 per person in dorm room. L23,000 in room with bath. Management doesn't accept phone reservations; arrive by noon to get a bed in summer. Wheelchair access.

Istituto Gould, Via dei Serragli, 49 (tel. 21 25 76), across the river in the Oltrarno. Leave the station by track #16, turn right and walk to P. della Stazione. Go straight down Via degli Avelli, with the church Santa Maria Novella on your immediate right. Cross P. Sta. Maria Novella and continue straight down Via dei Fossi, over the Ponte alla Carraia, and down Via dei Serragli (15min.). Or take bus 36 or 37 from the station to the 1st stop across the river. One of the best lodgings in Florence: staff is happy to answer questions and the sunny rooms are spotless. Office open Mon.-Fri. 9am-1pm and 3-7pm, Sat. 9am-1pm; closed Sunday. No curfew, no lock-out. Prices per person: Singles L42,000. Doubles L28,000-30,000. Triples L27,000. Quads L24,000. Quints L22,000.

Pensionato Pio X, Via dei Serragli, 106 (tel. 22 50 44). Follow the directions to the Istituto Gould (above) then walk a few more blocks down the street. Quiet, with clean rooms and bathrooms. Max. stay 5 days, min. stay 2 days. Check-out 10am. No lockout. Curfew midnight. L18,000 per person includes showers. L21,000 with bath. No reservations. Usually full in summertime, but turnover is high. On weekends arrive before 9am.

Ostello della Gioventù Europa Villa Camerata (HI), Viale Augusto Righi, 2-4 (tel. 60 14 51), northeast of town. Leave the station by track #5, then take bus 17B (20-30min.). You can also catch this bus from P. del Duomo. In a gorgeous villa with *loggia* and gardens. Reception open Mon.-Fri. 9am-1pm and 3-7pm. Check-out 9am. Curfew midnight. L18,000 per person. L14,000 to stay in beds in tents outside without breakfast. Nonmembers L5000 extra. Sheets and breakfast included. Reserve by letter only.

Ostello Santa Monaca, Via S. Monaca, 6 (tel. 26 83 38), off Via dei Serragli near Istituto Gould in the Oltrarno. This hostel tends to crowd many beds into high-ceilinged rooms, but it's the best price for such a central location. Max. stay 1 week. Open 6-9:30am and 4pm-12:30am. Curfew 1am. L18,000 per person. Shower included. Laundry L12,000. Sign-up sheet posted 9:30am-1pm, with as many spaces as there are beds open. No reservations.

Hotels

Piazza Santa Maria Novella, Via Nazionale, and Environs

Beyond the Basilica of Santa Maria Novella and in the immediate vicinity you'll find excellent budget accommodations galore, close to the Duomo and *centro,* a short walk from the station. Here, along **Via Nazionale, Via Faenza, Via Fiume, Via Guelfa,** and nearby, cheap establishments abound—often several to a building.

Pensione La Mia Casa, P. Santa Maria Novella, 23 (tel. 21 30 61). A 17th-century *palazzo* with clean rooms and fabric-covered walls. 300 years and innumerable backpackers have worn it down a bit. Curfew midnight. Singles L30,000. Doubles L45,000-55,000. Triples L60,000-74,000. Quads L76,000-92,000.

Locanda La Romagnola and **Soggiorno Gigliola,** Via della Scala, 40 (tel. 21 15 97 and 28 79 81). Leave the station by track #5, walk across the street to V.S. Caterina de Siena and turn right onto Via della Scala after a block. Simple rooms with ample space. Curfew midnight. Singles L37,000-45,000. Doubles L58,000-68,000. Triples L81,000-91,000. Showers L3000. May be closed in Jan. or Feb.—call first.

Albergo Montreal, Via della Scala, 43 (tel. 238 23 31). Clean and friendly, with TV lounge. Curfew 1:30am. Singles L40,000. Doubles L63,000-70,000. Triples L90,000. Quads L110,000.

Hotel Visconti, P. Ottaviani, 1 (tel. 21 38 77). You'll know you're in the right place when you see the towering marble nudes. Singles L37,000. Doubles L54,000-67,000. Triples L84,000.

Hotel Elite, Via della Scala, 12 (tel. 21 53 95). Proprietor is deservedly proud of his well-maintained 8-room hotel. Singles with shower L60,000. Doubles with bath L95,000. Triples L102,000. Breakfast included. To reserve, send 1 night's deposit or call ahead.

Via Faenza, 56 houses no fewer than 6 separate pensioni, all of which are among the best budget lodgings in the city. From the station follow the directions to Via Nazionale, on which Via Faenza is the 2nd intersection. **Pensione Azzi** (tel. 21 38 06) styles itself as the *locanda degli artisti*—the artists' inn. Large, immaculate rooms, and elegant dining room and terrace. Curfew 1am. Singles L55,000. Doubles L85,000. Triples L95,000. Breakfast L5000. Prices lower in off-season. **Locanda Paola** (tel. 21 36 82). Newly renovated rooms, many of which offer lovely views. All rooms with shower. Doubles L90,000. Triples L120,000. Quads L150,000. AmEx. **Albergo Merlini** (tel. 21 28 48). Light and airy, hip and breezy. Tremendous views of the Duomo—E. M. Forster must've seen this one. Breakfast (L7000) served amidst grand windows and funky artwork. Singles L40,000. Doubles L60,000-70,000. Triples L75,000. **Albergo Marini** (tel. 28 48 24). Polished wood hallway leads to simple white rooms with brass beds. Curfew 1am. Doubles L65,000-80,000. Triples L87,000, with bath L108,000. Quads with bath L136,000. **Albergo Anna** (tel. 239 83 22). Lovely rooms—some ceilings with frescoes, others with fans. Singles L60,000. Doubles L95,000. Breakfast included. Prices lower in winter. **Albergo Armonia** (tel. 21 11 46). Clean, with decoratively tiled walls. Pay in advance. Singles L70,000. Doubles L100,000. Triples L125,000. Prices significantly lower in winter.

Hotel Nazionale, Via Nazionale, 22 (tel. 238 22 03), near P. Indipendenza. Sunny rooms and quilted bedspreads. Breakfast included. No curfew. Singles L50,000, with bath L60,000. Doubles L78,000-88,000. Triples L105,000-118,000.

Pensione Daniel, Via Nazionale, 22 (tel. 21 12 93), above the Hotel Nazionale. Basic, white-washed rooms; recently renovated bathrooms. No curfew. Breakfast included. Doubles L50,000.

Via Faenza, 69: Locanda Nella e Pina (tel. 21 22 31 and 28 42 56). Passable rooms occupy two floors—there's usually one available. Curfew midnight. Singles L38,000. Doubles L70,000. **Locanda Giovanna** (tel. 238 13 53). 7 basic, well-kept rooms, some with garden view. Kitchen facilities. Singles L35,000. Doubles L55,000. Triples L70,000.

Ausonia e Rimini, Via Nazionale, 24 (tel. 49 65 47). Welcoming owners. The spotless rooms are nicely decorated and well-lit. Curfew 1am. Singles L45,000-65,000. Doubles L69,000-89,000. Triples L92,000-115,000. Breakfast included. Nov. 10-Jan. prices should be about 10% lower. AmEx, Visa.

Kursaal, Via Nazionale, 24 (tel. 49 63 24). A one-star on its way to becoming a two; take advantage of its lovingly decorated rooms while they're still affordable. Singles L45,000-65,000. Doubles L69,000-89,000. Triples L92,000-115,000. Breakfast included. Handicapped accessible. AmEx, DC, Visa.

The University Quarter

This area is considerably calmer and less tourist-ridden than its proximity to the center would suggest.

Hotel Tina, Via San Gallo, 31 (tel. 48 35 19 or 48 35 93). Small *pensione* with high ceilings and artsy posters. Singles L45,000. Doubles L65,000-75,000. Triples with bath L95,000. Gargantuan breakfast included.

La Colomba, Via Cavour, 21 (tel. 28 91 39). Sunny, white modernity. Windows peer out across a picturesque Florentine roofscape. Negotiable curfew 1:30am. Singles L60,000. Doubles L90,000-110,000. MC, Visa.

Hotel Enza, Via S. Zanobi, 45 (tel. 49 09 90). From Via Nazionale, turn right on Via Guelfa—Via Zanobi is the 1st cross-street. Tidy, ascetic rooms with pristine sea-blue bathrooms. Singles L45,000. Doubles L65,000-80,000.

Albergo Sampaoli, Via San Gallo, 14 (tel. 28 48 34). Proprietor proud of her enduring relationship with American tourism since the 50s. A little faded, but antique furniture and spic-n-span bathrooms make the *pensione* an enduring gem. Singles L40,000. Doubles L50,000-65,000. Triples with bath L90,000. No written reservations; call the night before you arrive.

Near the Duomo

The tourist deluge misses many of these establishments; the atmosphere benefits.

Locanda Orchidea, Borgo degli Albizi, 11 (tel. 248 03 46). Take a left off Via Proconsolo, which begins behind the Duomo. Dante's wife was born in this 12th-century *palazzo*. 7 cozy rooms, 4 of which open onto garden views. Singles L38,000. Doubles L60,000. Triples L82,000. Closed 2 weeks in Aug.; reservations *strongly* recommended for the rest of the summer.

Hotel Il Perseo, Via Cerretani, 1 (tel. 21 25 04), one block from the Duomo as you head toward P. Santa Maria Novella. Enthusiastic Australian owners joyfully welcome travelers to their light, immaculate rooms-with-a-view. Singles L45,000-55,000. Doubles L80,000-95,000. Triples L100,000. Quads L120,000-160,000. Ample breakfast included. AmEx, MC, Visa.

Soggiorno Panerai, Via dei Servi, 36 (tel. 26 41 03). Facing the Duomo's entrance, Via dei Servi radiates out from the cathedral's left-hand corner. Serene, white-washed rooms, each with a few antiques. Doubles L55,000. Triples L70,000.

Soggiorno Brunori, Via del Proconsolo, 5 (tel. 28 96 48), off P. del Duomo. Beautiful and conveniently located building. Curfew 12:30am. Doubles L59,000-74,000. Triples L89,000-105,000. Quads L105,000-132,000. Breakfast (L8000) served in your room.

Camping

Italiani e Stranieri, Via le Michelangelo, 80 (tel. 681 19 77), near P. Michelangelo. Take red or black bus 13 from the station (15min., last bus 11:55pm). Extremely crowded, but offers a spectacular panorama of Florence. Well-stocked food store and bar. They may post a *completo* sign or tell you the same by phone, but if you show up on foot they will often let you in. L6000 per person, L7500 per tent, L5000 per car, L3000 per motorcycle. Open mid-March to Nov. 6am-midnight.

FOOD

White beans and olive oil form the two main staples, and most regional dishes will come loaded with one or the other, if not both. Specialties include such *antipasti* as *bruschetta* (grilled Tuscan bread doused with olive oil and garlic, and sometimes topped with tomatoes and basil). Florentines have perfected the Tuscan classics *minestra di fagioli* (a delicious white bean and garlic soup), *trippa alla fiorentina* (tripe cooked in a tomato and cheese sauce), *pecorino* (a cheese made from sheep's milk), and the premium wine, *chianti classico*. For lunch, visit one of the many *rosticcerie gastronomie*, stop by the **students' mensa** at Via dei Servi, 52, or browse over pushcarts throughout the city. Buy your own fresh produce at the **Mercato Centrale**, between Via Nazionale and the back of San Lorenzo. (Open Mon.-Sat. 8am-1pm; Oct.-May Mon.-Sat. 6:30am-1pm and 4-8:30pm.) For staples, head to **Supermercato STANDA,** Via Pietrapiana, 1r (open Tues.-Sat. 8:30am-8pm, Mon. 3-8pm), or to any of the small markets throughout the city.

No dinner in this gelato capital of Italy would be complete without a luscious lick from one of the many *gelaterie*. You know you've found a true Florentine *gelateria* when the banana gelato is slightly off-grey, indicating only real live bananas are inside. Test **Vivoli,** Via della Stinche, 7, behind the Bargello (open Sept.-July Tues.-Sun. 8am-midnight); **Gelateria dei Neri,** Via dei Neri, 20-22r (open 10:30am-midnight).

Trattoria Contadino, Via Palazzuolo, 69r. Filling, home-style meals, including *primo, secondo,* salad, and wine, L14,000. Open Mon.-Sat. 11am-3pm and 7pm-midnight.

Trattoria da Garibaldi, P. del Mercato Centrale, 38r. Fresh, tasty, and way cheap. Huge, crisp salads. *Menù* includes *primo, secondo, contorno*, and wine or water (L13,000). Open Mon.-Sat. noon-2:30pm and 7:30-9:30pm.

Trattoria Mario, Via Rosina, 2r, right around the corner from P. Mercato Centrale. Share huge wooden tables with the crowds of locals that flock here for lunch. *Primi* L5000-7000, *secondi* L6000-10,000. Open Mon.-Sat. noon-3:30pm.

Ristorante Il Vegetariano, V. Ruote, 30, off V. San Gallo. Pretty landscape scenes surround you in this meat-free zone as you dine on fresh, healthy cuisine. Open Tues.-Sun. 11am-3pm and 8pm-midnight.

Acqua al Due, Via Vegna Vecchia, 40r, behind the Bargello. Florentine specialties in a cozy, air-conditioned place popular with young Italians. The *assaggio*, a dish of 5 types of pasta, demands a taste (L9800); getting a table, however, usually demands a reservation. Open Tues.-Sun. 7pm-1am. MC, Visa.

La Maremmana, Via dei Macci, 77r (tel. 24 12 26), near the Mercato Sant'Ambrogio. A rare combination: well-prepared, generous, and affordable. *Menù* starting at L20,000. Tablecloths, cut flowers, pasta, *secondo,* side dishes, a fruit dessert, and wine included. Open Sept.-July Mon.-Sat. 12:30-3pm and 7:30-10:30pm.

Trattoria l'che c'è c'è, Via de Mangalotti, 11r (tel. 21 65 89). The owner/chef cares about his food, as you'll taste. *Topini (gnocchi) alla gorgonzola,* L8000. Try a Tuscan *secondo* like *salsicce e faglioli* (sausage and beans, L10,000). Cover L2000. Open Tues.-Sun. 12:30am-2:30pm and 7:30-10:30pm.

I Latini, Via Palchetti, 6r. From the Ponte alla Carraia, walk up Via del Moro; V. Palchetti is on the right. Patrons dine on delicious Tuscan classics beneath an abundance of dangling hams. *Primi* L8000-10,000; *secondi* L9000-15,000. Open Tues.-Sun. noon-2:30pm and 7pm-midnight. (Be prepared to wait for a table.)

Oltrarno Trattoria Casalinga, Via Michelozzi, 9r, near P. Santo Spirito. Delicious Tuscan specialties in relaxed, if crowded, atmosphere. Ravioli made with spinach and ricotta, L6000. *Secondi* L7000-12,000. Menu changes daily. Cover L1500. Open Mon.-Sat. 11am-3pm and 7pm-midnight.

SIGHTS

Piazza del Duomo Florentines often refer to their cathedral as "Santa Maria del Fiore"; asking a local about *"il duomo"* may leave both of you confused. Filippo Brunelleschi directed the construction of the largest dome in Europe since the Roman Pantheon. His revolutionary idea involved building a double-shelled dome with interlocking bricks that would support itself during construction. The church has the world's third longest nave, behind St. Peter's in Rome and St. Paul's in London. The fresco in the left aisle, by a student of Fra Angelico, illustrates the *Divine Comedy* in tribute to Dante. The **orologio,** on the cathedral's back wall, a 24hr. clock designed by Paolo Uccello, runs backwards. Climb up the 463 steps around the inside of the dome to the **lantern,** and on the way survey the city from the external gallery. (Duomo open 10am-5:30pm. Mass held 7-10am and 5-7pm. L5000.) The much older **Battistero** (Baptistry), just in front of the Duomo, is famous for its bronze doors (the southern set by Andrea Pisano, the others by Ghiberti). Entering the cool, cavernous interior, note the mosaics in the cupola—the devils beneath Christ's feet and the intricate tortures of Hell are worthy of Dante, who was baptized here. (Open Mon.-Sat. 1-6pm, Sun. 9am-1pm.) Next to the Duomo rises the 82m **campanile,** the "lily of Florence blossoming in stone." Giotto, then the official city architect, drew up the design and laid the foundation, but died soon after construction began. The 414-step endurance test is worth the effort—the views are magnificent. (Open 8:30am-6:50pm; Nov.-March 9am-5:30pm. L5000.)

Bargello to Ponte Vecchio The heart of medieval Florence lies between the Duomo and P. Signoria around the 13th-century **Bargello,** in P. San Firenze, once the chief magistrate's residence. It now houses the **Museo Nazionale,** with Donatello's delicate *David* and Ghiberti and Brunelleschi's *Sacrifice of Isaac.* (Open Tues.-Sun. 9am-2pm. L6000.)

The fortess-like **Palazzo Vecchio** in P. della Signoria forms the civic center of Florence. (Open Mon.-Fri. 9am-7pm, Sun. 8am-1pm. L8000.) Sculptures adorn the area, including an awkward Neptune statue to whose sculptor Michelangelo quipped: "Oh Ammannato, Ammannato, what lovely marble you have ruined!" Michelangelo's **David** used to stand here in self-assured perfection, but it now graces the **Accademia,** Via Ricasoli, 60 (open Tues.-Sat. 9am-7pm, Sun. 9am-2pm; L10,000).

In May 1993, a bomb exploded in the **Uffizi,** killing 5 people in nearby buildings and destroying priceless works of art. Half the rooms in the Uffizi remain closed to the public and will not open for several years while reconstruction of the bombed out rooms carefully progresses. But don't skip the Uffizi because of the closed rooms: it continues to display an unparalleled collection of art. The city can thank the Medici for the most stunning collection of Renaissance art in the world. The collection is arranged chronologically, and provides a complete education on Florentine painting in the Renaissance, with detours into a select collection from the German and Venetian Renaissances. Highlights of the museum include Rooms 10-14, a vast Botticelli shrine: *Primavera, Birth of Venus, Madonna della Melagrana,* and *Pallas and the Centaur* glow with luminous color after their recent restoration. Discover Leonardo da Vinci's remarkable *Annunciation* and perhaps more remarkable (though unfinished) *Adoration of the Magi.* (Open Tues.-Sat. 9am-7pm, Sun. 9am-2pm. L10,000.)

From the Uffizi, turn left onto Via Georgofili, then right when you reach the water. The nearby **Ponte Vecchio** has spanned the Arno at its narrowest point since Roman times. The commander leading the German army's retreat across the river in 1944 could not bear to blow up the bridge, and instead destroyed the medieval towers and nearby buildings on either side to make the bridge impassable.

Palazzo Davanzati to Santa Maria Novella As Florence's 15th-century economy expanded, its bankers and merchants showed off their new wealth by erecting palaces grander than any seen before. The great Quattrocento boom commenced with the construction of the **Palazzo Davanzati,** Via Porta Rossa, 13. Today the *palazzo* has been reincarnated as the **Museo della Casa Fiorentina Antica** and illustrates the lives of affluent 15th-century merchants. The building houses furniture, tapestries, utensils, and paintings typical of a wealthy family during the Renaissance. (Open Tues.-Sun. 9am-2pm. L4000.)

The Medici staked out an entire portion of the city north of the Duomo in which to build their own church, the spacious **Basilica of San Lorenzo** and the Palazzo Medici. San Lorenzo was begun in 1419 following Brunelleschi's plans. Michelangelo designed the church's exterior, but the profligate Medici ran out of money to build it, so it stands bare. Inside the basilica, two massive bronze pulpits by Donatello command the nave. (Open 7am-noon and 3:30-5:30pm.) To reach the **Cappelle Medicee,** go out the front entrance and walk around the church through the market to the back entrance on P. Madonna degli Aldobrandini. Michelangelo's **New Sacristy** (1524) is a starkly simple architectural design reflecting the master's study of Brunelleschi (open Tues.-Sun. 9am-2pm; L9000).

The wealthiest merchants built their chapels in the **Church of Santa Maria Novella,** near the train station. Built from 1246 to 1360, the church boasts a green and white Romanesque-Gothic lower façade. Frescoes covered the interior until the Medici commissioned Vasari to paint others in their honor; they ordered most of the other walls whitewashed so their rivals would not be remembered. The **Cappella di Filippo Strozzi,** just to the right of the high altar, contains frescoes by Filippo Lippi, including portrayals of a rather green Adam, a woolly Abraham, and an excruciatingly accurate *Torture of St. John the Evangelist.* (Open 7-11:30am and 3:30-6pm.)

Oltrarno Historically disdained by downtown Florentines, the far side of the Arno remains a lively, unpretentious quarter. A few blocks west of P. Santa Spirito stands the **Church of Santa Maria del Carmine.** Inside, the **Brancacci Chapel** houses a group of revolutionary 15th-century frescoes that were declared masterpieces in their time. Note especially the *Expulsion from Paradise* and *The Tribute Money*. (Open Mon. and Wed.-Sat. 10am-4:30pm, Sun. 1-4:30pm. L5000.)

Brunelleschi originally envisioned an exciting four-aisled nave encircled by hollow chapels for the **Church of Santo Spirito.** However, he died before the project was completed, and the plans were altered to make the building more conventional. Nonetheless, it remains a masterpiece of Renaissance harmony, similar to but far less busy than San Lorenzo. (Open 8am-noon and 3:30-6:30pm, in winter 4-6pm.)

Luca Pitti, a *nouveau-riche* banker of the 15th century, built his *palazzo* east of Santo Spirito, against the Bóboli hill. The Medici acquired the *palazzo* and the hill in 1550, and enlarged everything possible. Today, the **Pitti Palace** now houses no less than five museums. The **Museo degli Argenti** on the ground floor exhibits the Medici loot (open Tues.-Sun. 9am-2pm; L6000 gets you into the costume as well). The **Museum of Costumes** displays more Medici debris (open Tues.-Sat. 9am-2pm, Sun. 9am-1pm; L6000 combined ticket with Museo degli Argenti). The **Royal Apartments** on the main floor preserve the furnishings from the residence of the Royal House of Savoy, together with a few treasures from the Medici period (open Tues.-Sun. 9am-2pm, L8000). The **Galleria Palatina** was one of only a handful of public galleries when it opened in 1833. Today its collection includes a number of Raphaels (most, unfortunately, behind glass), and works by Titian, Andrea del Sarto, Rosso, Caravaggio, and Rubens. (Open Tues.-Sun. 9am-2pm. L8000.) The fifth and final museum, the **Galleria d'Arte Moderna,** houses one of the big surprises of Italian art: the early 19th-century proto-impressionist works of the Macchiaioli school (open Tues.-Sat. 9am-2pm and Sun. 9am-1pm, L4000).

The elaborately landscaped **Bóboli Gardens** behind the palace stretch to the hilltop **Forte Belvedere,** once the Medici fortress and treasury. Ascend Via di Costa San Giorgio (off P. Santa Felicità, to the left after crossing Ponte Vecchio) to reach the villa, an unusual construction with a central *loggia* designed by Ammannati. (Gardens open Tues.-Sun. 9am-7:30pm; April-May and Sept. 9am-6:30pm; March and Oct. 9am-5:30pm; Nov.-Feb. 9am-4:30pm. L5000. Fort open 9am-10pm; in winter 9am-5pm. Free.)

ENTERTAINMENT

For reliable information on what's hot and what's not, consult *Firenze Spettacolo* (L2500). The **passeggiata** promenades along Via dei Calzaiuoli; afterwards Florentines frequent the ritzy *caffè* in P. della Repubblica. Street performers draw crowds to the steps of the Duomo, the arcades of the Mercato Nuovo, and P. Michelangelo. P. Santo Spirito hops with a good selection of bars and restaurants. A chattering crowd of beautiful people frequents **Lo Sfizzio,** on Lungarno Cellini, 1, where they carouse over enormous drinks on the outdoor terrace (open until 1am). If you prefer a little guitar-strumming with your chianti, check out **Chiodo Fisso,** Via Dante Alighieri, 16; music begins at 10:30. **The Red Garter,** Via dei Benci, 33r, is a raucous mix of American students, Italians, flying peanut shells, and classic American rock. **Angie's Pub,** Via dei Neri, 35r, is an Italian place (despite the name) catering mostly to students, and therefore usually uncrowded in the summer months (open Tues.-Sat. 12:30-3pm and 7pm-1am). When it behooves to groove, *the* spot for Italian students is **Rockafè,** Borgo degli Albizi, 66, American infiltration not yet complete. (Cover L15,000. Open Sept.-June Tues.-Sun. 10pm-4am.) In a tiny alleyway across P. della Signoria from the Palazzo Vecchio is **Tabasco Gay Club,** P. S. Cecilia, 3r, Florence's most popular gay disco. (Min. age 18. No cover, but min. 1 drink. Open Tues.-Sun. 10pm-3am.) For live jazz and a slick scene, try the **Jazz Club,** Via Nuova dei Caccini, 3; disregard the "members only" sign. (Open Sept. 21-July 14.)

The festival of **St. John the Baptist** (June 24) centers around a tremendous fireworks display which rips over the city from P. Michelangelo. The last week of June also brings the traditional games of **Calcio Storico in Costume,** an archaic, hilarious form of soccer played in historical dress. Contact the tourist office for ticket info. The summer swings with music festivals, starting in May with the **Maggio Musicale,** which draws many of the world's eminent classical musicians. The **Estate Fiesolana** fills the old Roman theater in **Fiesole** with concerts, opera, theater, ballet, and movies (June-Aug.). For information on tickets, contact the Biglietteria Centrale in the Teatro Communale, Corso Italia, 16 (tel. 21 62 53, 277 92 36), or Universalturismo, Via degli Speziali, 7r (tel. 21 72 41), off P. della Repubblica.

■■■ SIENA

Today, Siena cowers in Florence's shadow, but during the 13th century its flourishing wool trade, crafty bankers, and sophisticated civil administration made it easily its rival's equal. The city remains a living masterpiece; even in Italy, few places are as aesthetically harmonious. The salmon-colored, shell-shaped **Piazza del Campo** is the focus of Sienese life. At the bottom of the shell is the **Palazzo Pubblico,** a graceful Gothic palace over which soars the **Torre del Mangia,** named for the gluttonous bellringer, "Mangiaguadagni" (literally, "eat the profits"). Inside, the **Museo Civico** contains some of Siena's finest Gothic painting; don't miss the *Allegories of Good and Bad Government* by Pietro and Ambrogio Lorenzetti. (*Palazzo* and museum open Mon.-Sat. 9:30am-7:45pm, Sun. 9:30am-1:45pm; Nov.-March 9am-1:45pm. L6000, students L3000. Torre del Mangia open 10am-6pm; mid-March to mid-April and mid-Oct. to mid-Nov. 10am-5pm; mid-Nov. to mid-March 10am-1:30pm. L4000.)

The construction of Siena's **duomo** took so long that it spanned two architectural eras, incorporating Romanesque arches and Gothic pinnacles. The **pulpit** is one of Andrea Pisano's best, with allegorical and biblical reliefs wrapping around the barrel. The lavish **Libreria Piccolomini,** off the left aisle, holds frescoes by Pinturicchio and some 15th-century illuminated musical scores. (*Duomo* open mid-March-Sept. 7:30am-7:30pm, Nov. to mid-March 7:30am-5pm. No tank-tops or shorts above the knee. Library open mid-March to Sept. 9am-7:30pm, Nov. to mid-March 10am-1pm and 2:30-5pm. L2000.) The **Museo dell'Opera della Metropolitana,** next to the cathedral, displays the foremost Gothic statuary of Italy, all by Giovanni Pisano, as well as Duccio di Buoninsegna's splendid *Maestà* (open mid-March to Oct. 9am-7:30pm, Oct. to early Nov. 9am-6pm, Nov. to mid-March 9am-1pm; L5000).

All day on **il Palio,** July 2 and August 16, Sienans parade around in 15th-century costume; the central event is a traditional bare-back horse race around the packed P. del Campo. Get there three days early to watch the rambunctious horse selection in the *campo* (10am) and to pick a *contrada* ('hood) to root for. The night before the race everyone revels until 3am or so, strutting and chanting their way around the city, pausing only to eat and drink. You can stand in the "infield" of the *piazza* for free, but access closes early, so stake out a spot early in the day. For tickets and a list of rooms-to-let write to the tourist office by March; arrive without a reservation and you'll be sleeping on the streets.

Practical Information, Accommodations, and Food Siena lies off the main Florence-Rome **rail** line. From Florence, change at Empoli (L7800); from Rome, at Chiusi (L19,900). Take any bus passing across the street from the station to the center of town (L1100), or prepare for a 45min. uphill trek. Express **TRA-IN/SITA** buses, often faster than the train, link Siena with Florence (L9000) and other Tuscan destinations. The **tourist office,** P. Il Campo, 56 (tel. (0577) 28 05 51), has a list of *affitta camere* (about L30,000 per person). (Theoretically open Mon.-Sat. 8:30am-7:30pm.) Its travel agency **changes money** for outrageous rates and sells bus, train, and boat tickets (open Mon.-Fri. 9am-1pm and 3:30-7pm, Sat. 9am-1pm). Finding a room in Siena is usually simple, but call a few days ahead during July and August and book months ahead for either *Palio*. The rather inconveniently located **Ostello della Gioventù "Guidoriccio" (HI),** Via Fiorentina, 89 (tel. (0577) 522 12, fax 561 72), in Località Lo Stellino, is a 20min. ride on bus 15 from the station or P. Matteotti; if coming from Florence by bus, get off at the stop just after the large black and white sign announcing that you've entered Siena. (Curfew 11pm. L19,000. Breakfast included.) The **Casa del Pellegrino,** Via Camporegio, 3 (tel. (0577) 441 77), behind P. San Domenico, is a spotless establishment run by nuns;

ITALY

the rooms have fantastic views of the *duomo.* (Opens at 7:30am. Curfew 11pm. Singles L35,000-43,000. Doubles L64,000. Triples L85,000. Quads L102,000. Reservations preferred.) **Albergo Tre Donzelle,** Via Donzelle, 5 (tel. (0577) 28 03 58) offers airy singles (L32,000), doubles (L53,000-67,000) and triples (L71,000-115,000).

Siena specializes in rich pastries, most notably *Panforte,* a concoction of honey, almonds, and citron. Sample it at **Bar/Pasticceria Nannini,** Via Banchi di Sopra, 22-24. Shoestringers can pick up supplies at the **Consortio Agrario** supermarket, Via Pianigiani, 5, off P. Salimberi (open Mon.-Fri. 7:45am-1pm and 5-8pm, Sat. 7:45am-1pm). **Osteria Le Logge,** Via Porrione, 33, is highly reputed and affordable. *(Secondi* around L15,000. Cover L2000. Service 10%. Open Mon.-Sat. noon-3pm and 7-10:30pm.) Savor *tagliatelle* with asparagus cream sauce (L7000) under the vaulted ceilings of **Ristorante Guidoriccio,** Via Duprè, 2, off P. Il Campo. (Tourist menu L21,000, cover L3000. Open Mon.-Sat. noon-2:30pm and 7:30-10:30pm.)

■ SAN GIMIGNANO AND ELBA

The medieval towers of **San Gimignano** bristle skyward only an hour from Siena by bus (L6700). The towers and the walled *centro* testify to a 13th-century building competition between San Gimignano's two wealthiest families. Of the original 72 edifices, 14 remain. Scale the **Torre Grossa,** the tallest of the remaining towers, attached to **Palazzo del Popolo,** for a 360° panorama of Tuscany (open 9:30am-7:30pm, Oct.-March Tues.-Sun. 9:30am-1:30pm and 2:30-4:30pm; L6000, students L4000). *Affitta camere* **private rooms** (singles around L40,000, doubles L70,000) are an alternative to overpriced hotels in this hostel-devoid town. Get a list from either the tourist office or **La Rocca,** an accommodations service at Via dei Fossi, 3/A (tel. (0577) 94 03 87), outside the walls near Parco della Rocca (open 9am-1pm and 3-9pm). **Albergo/Ristorante Il Pino,** Via S. Matteo, 102 (tel. (0577) 94 04 15), in the quiet quarter near the convent, is a study in contrasts: red plastic bedframes against a rustic beamed ceiling (doubles L60,000). Pitch a tent at **Il Boschetto,** at Santa Lucia (tel. 94 03 52), 2½km downhill from Porta San Giovanni. Buses run from town to the site (L1000), but it's not a bad hike. (Office open 8am-1pm, 3-8pm, and 9-11pm. L6000 per person, L6500 per small tent. Hot showers included. Open April 1-Oct. 15.) Wolf down *panini* with fennel and locally-made salami (L4000) at **Gustavo Enoteca,** Via San Matteo, 29, downhill from P. Duomo (open 8am-8pm).

If you've had it with city-hopping, soak in a few days of sun and swimming on the island of **Elba,** just off the coast of Tuscany, where Napoleon spent his exile. Take the train to Piombino Marittima, where you can hop on one of the frequent Toremar or Navarma ferries (about 18 per day, 1hr., L9000-13,000). Talk directly to Toremar (tel. (0565) 91 80 80) or Navarma (tel. 22 12 12) at Piazzale Premuda, 13, in Piombino. Avoid Elba in July and August, when half of Italy and more of Germany cram onto its limited shores.

■ ■ ■ PISA

Every year millions of tourists descend on Pisa's Campo dei Miracoli into a seething, T-shirt-buying, ice-cream-licking, photo-taking mob. Not that the Leaning Tower isn't worth seeing; it's a prime example of the innovative architecture of the Pisan Romanesque period. Throughout the Middle Ages, Pisa was a major port city, whose Mediterranean empire extended to Corsica, Sardinia, and the Balearics. Unfortunately for Pisa, the Arno began to silt up, and the city's power and wealth declined accordingly. Pisa's most revered monuments lie in the **Campo dei Miracoli** (Field of Miracles), a grassy expanse on the northern side of the Arno. A L14,000 ticket lets you into all of the Campo's sights, while L8000 will get you into any two. The dazzling **duomo** is a treasury of fine art, including Giovanni Pisano's elaborate pulpit and its burlesque Gothic reliefs. (Open 7:45am-12:45pm and 3-6:45pm; in winter until 4:45pm. Closed for mass 10-10:45am.) Next door is the **baptistry;** astoundingly, the dome's acoustics are such that an unamplified choir can be heard

20km away. (Open 8am-7:40pm, in winter 9am-4:40pm.) The adjoining **Camposanto,** a long white-walled cemetery, has many Classical sarcophagi and a series of haunting frescoes by an unidentified 14th-century artist known only as "Master of the Triumph of Death" (open 8am-7:40pm, off-season 9am-4:40pm). Though the famous **Leaning Tower** continues to slip 1-2mm every year, it's losing little ground as a tourist hotspot. To delay the tilt of the tower, visitors are no longer allowed to enter. The **Museo delle Sinopie,** across the square from the Camposanto, displays *sinopie* (sketches preliminary to the fresco process) discovered during restoration after World War II (open 8am-7:40pm; off-season 9am-12:40pm and 3-4:40pm). The **Museo dell'Opera del Duomo,** behind the Tower, displays works by Giovanni Pisano and Guardi, alongside archeological finds (open 8am-7:30pm, off-season 9am-12:30pm and 3-4:30pm). One hidden treasure in town is the Gothic church of **Santa Maria della Spina,** which faces Lungarno Gambacorti against the river. Its bell tower inclines slightly, not unlike its more famous cousin, and claims to house a thorn from Christ's crown (open 8am-noon and 4-6:30pm).

Practical Information, Accommodations, and Food The **tourist office,** P. della Stazione, 11 (tel. (050) 422 91) doles out maps with directions to the tower (open Mon.-Sat. 8am-8pm, Sun. 9am-noon). There's a **branch office** in P. del Duomo (tel. (050) 56 04 64), behind the Tower (open Mon. and Fri. 8:30am-3pm and 3:30-6:30pm, Tues.-Thurs. 9:30am-3pm, Sat. 9:30am-noon and 3-6pm).

The **Centro Turistico Madonna dell'Acqua** hostel, Via Pietrasantina, 15 (tel. (050) 89 06 22), awaits beneath an old sanctuary. Take bus 3 from the station and ask to be let off at the *ostello.* (Reception open 6-11pm. L18,000, in double or triple L20,000 per person. Singles L30,000.) The **Albergo Gronchi,** P. Archivescovado, 1 (tel. (050) 56 18 23), just off P. del Duomo, has frescoed ceilings and a pretty garden. (Curfew midnight. Singles L28,000. Doubles L46,000. Triples L62,000.) The **Casa della Giovane,** Via F. Corridoni, 29 (tel. (050) 430 61), a 10min. walk from the station (turn right immediately), offers beds to women only. (Reception open 7am-10pm. Curfew 10pm. L20,000 in clean doubles or triples.) **Campeggio Torre Pendente,** Viale delle Cascine, 86 (tel. (050) 56 06 65) is 1 km away. Follow the signs from P. Manin. (L8000 per person, L5000 per tent. Open mid-March to Sept.) Pisa's cheaper and more authentic restaurants certainly aren't located near the *duomo.* Pisans prefer the **open-air market** in P. Vettovaglie (take Via Vigina off Lugarno Pacinotti). To eat well, head for the river or the university area. Delicious, innovative, veggie-based food is served inside the garden-like **Ristoro al Vecchio Teatro,** V. Collegio Ricci, 2, off P. Dante. (*Primi* L7000, *secondi* L8000. Open Mon.-Fri. 12:30-2:30pm and 8-10:30pm.) At **Trattoria da Matteo,** Via l'Aroncio, 46, off Via S. Maria, the prix fixe lunch for L15,000 includes *primo, secondo,* and *contorno* (open Sun.-Fri. noon-3pm and 7-10:30pm).

UMBRIA

Christened the "Green Heart of Italy," Umbria has enjoyed renown since ancient times for its wooded hills, valleys, and rivers. Often shrouded in an ethereal silvery haze, the landscape also nurtured a mystic tradition that stretches from prehistory through to St. Benedict, who preached the doctrine of the marriage of work and worship, and to Umbria's most famous visionary, the nature-adoring ascetic St. Francis. Generations of visual artists also clambered about these hills, among them Giotto, Signorelli, Perugino and Pinturicchio.

■■■ PERUGIA

The exceedingly polite population of Perugia may be trying to make up for several millennia of excessive nastiness, during which they regularly stoned each other for fun and even threw tree-hugging St. Francis of Assisi into a dungeon. Perugia gets dubious religious points as the birthplace of the Flagellants, who wandered Europe whipping themselves in public, and as the deathbed of three popes (two were poisoned). Perugia has since mellowed into a university town, host of a popular 10-day world-class jazz festival in July, and core of the Italian chocolate-making industry.

The city's most noteworthy sights frame **Piazza IV Novembre.** The grand fountain in the center is adorned with sculptures and bas-reliefs by Nicolà and Giovanni Pisano. The 13th-century **Palazzo dei Priori** presides over the *piazza*, sheltering the **Galleria Nazionale dell'Umbria,** where Pinturicchio's gleeful use of color and disdain for Renaissance seriousness in his *Miracles of San Bernardino* is the visual equivalent of eating a *bacio* (open Mon.-Sat. 9am-1:45pm and 3-7pm, Sun. 9am-1pm; L8000). Perugia's austere Gothic **duomo** looms at the end of the *piazza;* its façade was never completed because the *Perugini* were forced to return the marble they had stolen to build it. At the end of Corso Cavour, the street leading out of the P. IV Novembre, lie the well tended **Giardini Carducci,** the place to clutch your *amore.* A walk down Via Ulisse Rocchi leads to the perfectly preserved Roman **Arch of Augustus,** now sporting a 16th-century portico to boot.

Practical Information, Accommodations, and Food Perugia awaits three hours by train from both Rome (changing at Teróntola, L23,000) and Florence (L15,800), and only 25min. from Assisi (L2500). City buses 26, 27 and 36 (L1000) regularly connect the station, in the valley, with P. Matteotti, in the center of town. Note that phone numbers in Perugia have recently been changed; if you have no luck with the one listed, try adding 57 to the front of those that begin with a "2" and see if that works. The **tourist office** on P. IV Novembre (tel. (075) 572 53 41) provides travel and accommodations information, an artsy but misleading city map, and a detailed walking guide (open Mon.-Sat. 8:30am-1:30pm and 4-7pm, Sun. 9am-1pm; in winter Mon.-Sat. 3:30-6:30pm). The **currency exchange** in the train station charges no commission for amounts under L80,000, but has worse rates than banks. The spacious kitchen in the independent youth hostel, **Centro Internazionale di Accoglienza per la Gioventù,** Via Bontempi, 13 (tel. (075) 572 28 80) is a prime meeting spot. (Lockout 9:30am-4pm. Curfew midnight. L14,000. Showers included. Sheets L1000. Open mid-Jan. to late Dec.) The clean, cool rooms in **Albergo Anna,** Via dei Priori, 48, 4th floor (tel. (075) 573 63 04), are 300 years old, but have been renovated since. (Singles L33,000. Doubles L46,000. Triples L85,000.) **Paradis d'Ete** (tel. (075) 517 21 17), 5km away in Colle della Trinità, is indeed a summer **camping** paradise, with hot showers and a pool at no extra charge. Take bus 36 from the station. (L7000 per person, L6000 per tent.)

Though renowned for chocolate, Perugia also serves up a variety of delectable breads and pastries; try **Ceccarani,** P. Matteotti, 16, or the **Co.Fa.Pa.** bakery, at no. 12 (both open Fri.-Wed. 7:30am-1pm and 5-7:45pm). Tsk, tsk, no dessert before dinner. Quite possibly the best pizza by the slice in all Italy (with potatoes and rosemary L1500) can be found at **Pizzeria Cuccio,** Via Mazzini (open Mon.-Sat. 9am-1:30pm and 4-8:30pm). **Trattoria Dal Micocco,** Corso Garibaldi, 12, gives the weirdest names to its food, but is understandably popular. (L20,000 tourist menu. Open Tues.-Sun. 12:30-2:30pm and 7:30pm-midnight.)

■■■ ASSISI

Assisi's serenity originates with the legacy of St. Francis, the eco-friendly monk who preached poverty, obedience, and love 8 centuries ago. After his death in 1226, eminent Florentine and Sienese painters decorated the **Basilica di San Francesco** with a spectacular ensemble of frescoes illustrating his life. The basilica is actually a double decker; the Upper Church is elaborate and sumptuously decorated, while the Lower Church, built around the crypt housing the saint's tomb, is more subdued and pious, like the good saint himself. (Open sunrise to sunset, no tourists on Holy Days. English-language Mass Sun. 8:30am. English tours Mon.-Sat. 10am and 3pm.

Modest dress; no photography.) The modern **Museo Tesoro della Basilica** is worth a visit (open April-Oct. 9:30am-noon and 2-6pm; Nov.-March closed Sun.; L3000). Towering above town, the recently restored fortress **Rocca Maggiore** overwhelms with huge proportions and tremendous views (open 10am-dusk, in winter 10am-4pm; closed in very windy or rainy weather; L5000). The pink-and-white **Basilica of Santa Chiara** stands at the other end of Assisi, on the site of the ancient basilica where St. Francis attended school. Downstairs, St. Clare lies preserved in a glass tomb. (Open Mon.-Sat. 6:30am-noon and 2-7pm; in winter until 6pm.)

Assisi is on the Foligno-Teróntola **rail** line, 30min. from Perugia (L2500). From Florence (L15,600), change at Teróntola; from Rome (L14,500), change at Foligno. Buses run to Perugia (L4200) and other Umbrian towns. Check with the **tourist office,** P. del Comune, 12 (tel. (075) 81 25 34), for rooming help, musical events info, and bus and train schedules (open Mon.-Fri. 8am-2pm and 3:30-6:30pm, Sat. 9am-1pm and 3:30-6:30pm, Sun. 9am-1pm). The tremendous **Ostello della Pace (HI),** Via San Pietro Campagna (tel. (075) 81 67 67), charges L17,000 for bed and breakfast (open 7-9:15am and 5-11pm). Superb **Ostello Fontemaggio** (tel. (075) 81 36 36) lies a few km from Assisi in the hamlet of the same name. (Hostel L19,000. **Camping** L6000 per person, L4500 per tent.) Several houses off P. Matteotti offer *camere* (rooms) for about L25,000 per person. **Albergo Anfiteatro Romano,** Via Antifeatro Romano, 4 (tel. (075) 81 30 25), off P. Matteotti, is built into the old Roman amphitheater. (Singles L29,000. Doubles L40,000, with bath L60,000.) Tasty pizzas (L5000-9500) are served bubbling straight from the wood-burning oven in **Pizzeria Il Duomo,** Via Porta Perlici, 11, up a block from P. Rufino (open Thurs.-Tues. noon-3pm and 7-11pm; AmEx, MC, Visa).

THE MARCHES (LE MARCHE)

■■■ URBINO

If you visit only one town in Italy, make this the one. A perfectly harmonious ensemble created under the aegis of philosopher/warrior Federico da Montefeltro (1444-1482), Urbino exemplifies the finest in Renaissance style and tradition. Urbino's most remarkable monument is the Renaissance **Palazzo Ducale** (Ducal Palace). The façade, which overlooks the edge of town, boasts a unique design attributed to Ambrogio Barocchi: two tall, slender towers enclosing three stacked balconies. Enter the palace from P. Duca Federico; the interior **courtyard** is the quintessence of Renaissance harmony and proportion. To the left, a monumental staircase takes you to the private apartments of the Duke, which now house the **National Gallery of the Marches,** whose exhibits are incorporated through the meandering hallways of his palace and include Raphael's *Portrait of a Lady,* Paolo Uccello's tiny, strange *Profanation of the Host* and Piero della Francesca's unsettling *Flagellation.* The **Archeological Museum,** on the far side of the palace's courtyard, is free with admission to the National Gallery, but you can only enter during the sporadic hours when the guide is on duty. (*Palazzo* open July-Sept. Tues.-Sun. 9am-7pm, Mon. 9am-2pm. L8000.) At the end of Via Barocci stands the 14th-century **Oratorio di San Giovanni Battista,** decorated with brightly colored Gothic fresco-work representing events from the life of St. John the Baptist (open 10am-noon and 3-5pm; L3000, but you will be obliged to see S. Giuseppe next door for another L2000). **Raphael's house,** Via Raffaello, 57, is now a vast and delightful museum with period furnishings. His earliest work, a fresco entitled *Madonna e Bambino,* can be found in the *sala.* (Open Mon.-Sat. 9am-1pm and 3-7pm, Sun. 9am-1pm. L4000.)

Urbino's **P. della Repubblica** serves as a modeling runway for local youth in their oh-so-fine threads. Throughout July the Church of S. Domenico hosts an **Antique Music Festival.** August brings the ceremony of the **Revocation of the Duke's Court,** complete with Renaissance costumes. Check at the tourist office for the exact dates for 1995.

Practical Information, Accommodations, and Food The **SAPUM bus** from Pésaro's P. Matteotti or train station (on the main Bologna-Leece line along the Adriatic coast) is cheap, frequent, and direct (1hr., L3500). After winding up steep hills, the bus will deposit you at Borgo Mercatale, above which lies the beautiful city center. A short uphill walk or a ride in the elevator (open summer 9am-9pm; L300) takes you to **Piazza della Repubblica**, the heart of the city. The **tourist office**, P. Duca Federico, 35 (tel. (0722) 24 41), distributes a list of hotels and a small map (open Mon.-Sat. 9am-1pm and 3-6pm, Sun. 9am-1pm; off-season Mon.-Sat. 8:30am-2pm). Cheap lodging is rare in Urbino and reservations are essential. **Albergo Italia,** Corso Garibaldi, 52 (tel. (0722) 27 01), off P. della Repubblica, near the Palazzo Ducale, is home to 48 elegant singles (L35,000-48,000) and doubles (L48,000-68,000). Small, charming rooms without bath are available at **Pensione Fosca,** Via Raffaello, 67, on the top floor (tel. (0722) 32 96 22; singles L30,000-35,000, doubles L42,000-45,000). Pitch your tent 2km from the city walls at **Camping Pineta,** Via San Donato (tel. (0722) 47 10), in Cesane, (L7000, L14,000 per tent; open April to mid-Sept.). Many *paninoteche, gelaterie* and burger joints lurk around P. della Repubblica. Do all your shopping at **Supermarket Margherita,** Via Raffaello, 37 (open Mon.-Wed. and Fri.-Sat. 7:45am-12:45pm and 5-7:45pm; closed Thurs. afternoon). **Ristorante Rustica,** Via Nuova, 3, serves up delicious pizza from L4500 (open Thurs.-Tues. noon-3pm and 7pm-1am; closed July 5-25).

ADRIATIC PORTS

Ancona, Bari, and Bríndisi—all on the Bologna-Lecce train line—are Italy's principal departure points for Greece, Cyprus, and Israel. Bríndisi is redeemed only by its cheap fares to Greece for Eurailpass holders. Bari is the South's most vibrant city, and has the cheapest passage to Greece for those without railpasses.

Ancona Named by the Greeks for the elbow (*ankon*) shape of its harbor, Ancona is the archetype of a port city. Its value as a center of trade was first recognized by the Roman emperor Trajan, who developed the city in the first century AD. Today, the cargo is ferry-borne tourists, not spices and silks; yet Ancona still retains a certain appeal. Get complete and accurate ferry schedules at the **Stazione Marittima** on the waterfront just off P. Kennedy; bus 1 runs to and from the train station (L1000). All the ferry lines operate ticket and information booths.

Most travel agents have up-to-date schedules, but ferry service can be fickle, so call and check on dates and prices. An arrivals/departures board for the upcoming week hangs inside the main entrance of the station. Most lines give discounts (up to 50%) for round-trip tickets, and student and senior reductions are usually available. Make reservations if you're traveling during July or August. Be at the station at least 2hr. before departure. The main lines are: **Karageorgis** (tel. 27 45 54 or 27 72 04), **Marlines** (tel. 20 25 66, fax 411 77 80), **Minoan Lines** (tel. 567 89, fax 20 19 33), **Strintzis** (tel. 286 43 31, fax 20 66 75), **G.A. Ferries** (tel. 20 10 80 or 20 36 37, fax 20 63 31), **Hellenic Mediterranean Lines** (tel. 552 18, fax 29 26 18 or 20 40 41).

In summer, people waiting for ferries often spend the night at the Stazione Marittima, but you'll find lots of reasonably priced hotels in the lively town center. Avoid the overpriced lodgings in the area by the train station. Make reservations or arrive early—rooms fill quickly in the summer. **Pensione Centrale,** Via Marsala, 10 (tel. 543 88), 1 block from P. Roma, on the 4th floor, is but a 10min. stroll from the Stazione Marittima. (Singles L35,000. Doubles L45,000, with bath L65,000.) The port harbors a good number of inexpensive restaurants. Regional specialties include *brodetto* (fish stew), *pizza al formaggio* (cheese bread), and *vinisgrassi* (lasagna

ITALY

with chicken livers and white sauce). Pack a meal for your ferry ride at the old-fashioned **Mercato Pubblico** (across from Corso Mazzini, 130), where you'll find the four food groups well-represented (open Mon.-Wed. and Fri. 7:30am-12:45pm and 5:15-7:30pm, Thurs. and Sat. 7:30am-12:45pm).

Bríndisi Bríndisi (2hr. by train from Bari, 8hr. from Rome via Fóggia) has a lone redeeming feature: great Eurailpass discounts on ferries to Greece. **Adriatica,** Via Regina Margherita, 13 (tel. (0831) 52 38 25), near the ferry terminal, and **Hellenic Mediterranean Lines,** Corso Garibaldi, 8 (tel. (0831) 52 85 31), have high regular prices but offer **Eurailpass** holders free deck passage (space-available basis—you could get bumped by a paying passenger). You still must pay the L10,000 port tax, and June 10-Sept. 30 there's a L22,000 supplement in addition to the tax. Don't spend money on anything posher than deck class; in summer you'll actually be more comfortable there than in an upright seat in a large, smoke-filled cabin. Bicycles travel free. Railpass holders should go directly to the main offices listed above for tickets; travel agents will try to charge commission. Those without railpasses should consider departing from more palatable Bari, where departures can be cheaper. If you're intent on leaving from Bríndisi, Hellenic Mediterranean Lines (see above), **Fraglines,** Corso Garibaldi, 88 (tel. (0831) 56 82 32), and **Ventouris,** Via F. Consiglio, 55 (tel. (0831) 52 48 69), offer various types of discounts. Check in at the embarkation office at least 2hr. before departure or risk losing your reservation. Allow plenty of time for late trains and the 1km station-to-port walk.

Bríndisi is generally unsafe and crime-ridden; lone backpackers and women should beware in the evenings. The **EPT tourist office,** Lungomare Regina Margherita, 5 (tel. (0831) 52 19 44), is at the dock. Avoid staying in Bríndisi; if you're stuck, don't risk sleeping outdoors. Duck into **Hotel Altair,** Via Tunisi, 4 (tel. (0831) 52 49 11), off Corso Garibaldi (singles L25,000, doubles L40,000). **Spaghetti House Osteria Cucina Casalinga,** Via Mazzini, 57, serves a full meal of pasta, beverage, and bread for about L7000 (cover L500; open 9am-9pm, mid-Sept. to June closed Sun.). At **Trattoria da Emilia Spaghetti House,** Vico dei Raimondo, 11, L7000 meals include fresh pasta, salad, bread, and a beverage if you flash your *Let's Go* (open 9am-10pm). The **Supermarket Sidis,** Corso Garibaldi, 106, is convenient for boat-ride provisions (open Fri.-Wed. 8am-1pm and 4:30-8:30pm, Thurs. 8am-1pm).

Bari Yes, dear, there is a Santa Claus, but he's dead. The burial place of St. Nicholas, Bari offers a terrific program designed to serve under-30 backpackers. From mid-June to mid-September, the **"Stop-Over in Bari Program"** (24hr. English-speaking summer hotline (080) 577 23 49) will cater to your every need. Booths by the train and ferry stations have info on ferries, free events and discounts (open Mon.-Sat. 8:30am-8:30pm, Sun. 9am-6pm); pick up their daily English newsletter. They also offer free **camping** and showers (tent provided) and free but insufficient bus service throughout the city; take bus 5 (last one 10:45pm). If you hate tents, Stop-Over's English-speaking staff will put you up in an apartment **room** (L30,000 for 2 nights; call (080) 521 45 38 to reserve). There are no ferry discounts for Eurailpasses, but **Marlines** (tel. (080) 521 7699), **Ventouris Ferries** (tel. (080) 521 0556), and **Poseidon Lines** (080) 521 00 22) offer student discounts. You must check in at the ferry terminal 2hr. before departure. In the **old town,** stop in at the **Church of San Nicola** to view the remains of dear old Santa, but do not wander into the area unaccompanied or at night. Santa's remains themselves are stolen goods—plundered from Asia Minor by Baresi sailors in 1087. St. Nicholas is renowned not only for Christmas loot but also for resurrecting three children who were sliced to bits and plunged into a barrel of brine by a nasty butcher. (Open 8am-noon and 4-7pm.)

SOUTHERN ITALY

South of Rome, the sun gets brighter, the meals longer and the passions more intense. Though long subject to the negative stereotypes and prejudices of the more industrialized North, the so-called "Mezzogiorno" (midday) region remains justly proud of its open-hearted and generous populace, strong traditions, classical ruins, and enchanting beaches.

■■■ NAPLES (NAPOLI)

Naples has gotten a bad rap. True, you'll probably see more crazy, strung-out panhandlers here than in the rest of Italy combined. True, traffic jams follow one after the other like recurring nightmares, stoplights are taken as mere suggestions, and mopeds race down the sidewalk almost as often as down the street. But somehow the Neapolitans thrive on this chaos. The city has an almost-palpable vitality that can be seen at the street markets off Piazza Dante and tasted in the world's best pizza. Superb art and archaeological museums and wonderful Renaissance and Baroque churches reward your patience with Naples' rough edges.

ORIENTATION AND PRACTICAL INFORMATION

Naples is on the west coast of Italy, 2 hours south of Rome. It sends regular ferries to Sicily and Sardinia, and trains to and from Rome, Calabria, Sicily, and the Adriatic. Immense **Piazza Garibaldi,** on the eastern side of Naples, contains the central train station and the major city bus terminal. Broad, tree-lined **Corso Umberto I** leads southwest from P. Garibaldi, ending at **P. Bovio.** From here Via Depretis branches to the left, leading to P. Municipio and nearby **P. del Plebiscito,** an area of stately buildings and statues. On the water at the foot of P. Municipio lie **Molo Beverello** and the **Stazione Marittima,** the point of departure for ferries. Turn right from P. del Plebiscito and go up Via Toledo (also called Via Roma) through the old quarter and to **Piazza Dante,** the **university district,** and **Spaccanapoli** (literally "splitting Naples"), a straight, narrow street that changes names every few blocks. Lined with palaces and churches, Spaccanapoli follows the course of the ancient Roman road through the middle of historic Naples. Along the coast past P. Plebiscito, you'll find the **Santa Lucia** and **Mergellina** districts and the public gardens, **Villa Comunale.** Farther west are the most scenic areas of Naples: hillside Via Posillipo (in fact, older than the old quarter), Via Petrarca winding up above Mergellina, and Via Manzoni running along the crest of the ridge.

Neapolitans' vivacity and unruliness at times seem to transform the city into an anarchical landscape of haggling market crowds, hell-bent motor vehicles, and volatile youngsters known as *scugnizzi*. Like its *scugnizzi*, Naples possesses an unkempt and dangerous charm that is often difficult to appreciate, especially for the many visitors who fall prey to *lo scippo*, the local term for petty thievery.

Tourist Office: EPT (tel. 26 87 79), at the central train station. Helps with hotels and ferries. English spoken. Pick up the invaluable *Qui Napoli* (Here's Naples) and a city map. Open Mon.-Sat. 8am-8pm. **AAST information office,** P. Gesù Nuovo (tel. 552 33 28). Take bus 185 up Via Roma toward P. Dante, get off at Via Capitelli, and follow it to the *piazza*. The most helpful and professional office in the city. Open Mon.-Sat. 9am-7pm, Sun. 9am-2pm.

Budget Travel: CTS, Via Mezzocannone, 25 (tel. 552 79 75), near P. Bovio. Student travel information, ISIC and FIYTO cards, and booking service. Open Mon.-Fri. 9:30am-1pm and 3-6pm, Sat. 9:30am-noon.

Consulates: U.S., P. della Repubblica (P. Principe di Napoli on some maps) (tel. 761 43 03; 24hr. emergency tel. (0337) 79 32 84). Open Mon.-Fri. 8am-noon.

Currency Exchange: Neapolitan banks charge high commissions. Closest to the train station is **Banca Nazionale del Lavoro,** P. Garibaldi (tel. 799 71 13). Open for exchange Mon.-Fri. 8am-1:30pm and 2:30-8pm.

ITALY

Post Office: P. Matteotti (tel. 552 00 67), on Via Diaz. *Fermo Posta* (L250 per letter). Open Mon.-Fri. 8:15am-7:15pm, Sat. 8:15am-noon. **Postal Code:** 80100.

Telephones: SIP, at Via Petronio, 16, off Via N. Sauro along the water in Santa Lucia. Open Mon.-Fri. 9am-noon and 4-7:30pm. **ASST,** Via Depretis, 40, off P. Bovio at the end of Corso Umberto. Open 24hrs. Shorter lines. **City Code:** 081.

Trains: Consult the info booths (open 7am-9pm), use the Digiplan machines, or call 553 41 88. To: Rome (1-2 per hr., 2½hr., L16,100); Syracuse (9hr., L47,900); and Bríndisi for ferries to Greece (6½hr., L31,200).

Ferries: Caremar, Molo Beverello. To: Cápri (4 per day, 70min., L8500). **Tirrenia,** Molo Angioino (tel. 761 36 88). To: Palermo (11hr; daily at 8pm; L68,400, Oct.-May L53,100; L2000 Naples port tax) and Cagliari (16hr.; Thurs. and Sat. at 5:30pm, L54,900; Sept. 16 to June 23 Thurs. 7:15pm, L43,300).

Hitchhiking: Hitching in or out of Naples is extremely risky.

Emergency: tel. 113. **Ambulance:** tel. 752 06 96. **Police:** tel. 794 11 11. English-speaking **Ufficio Stranieri** (foreigners' office) at the *Questura* (police station), Via Medina, 75, off Via Diaz.

ACCOMMODATIONS AND FOOD

In Naples, consider paying a little more for added comfort, security, and respectability. Always agree on the price before you unpack, never give up your passport before seeing your room, and watch out for shower charges, obligatory breakfasts, and the like. Call the EPT (tel. 40 62 89) if you have complaints. Naples's lone youth hostel is the **Ostello Mergellina (HI),** Salita della Grotta, 23 (tel. and fax 761 23 46), 2 quick rights onto Via Piedigrotta from M: Mergellina. (Lockout 9:30am-4pm. Curfew 12:30am. Check-out 9am. L18,000. Doubles L40,000.) For reasonably priced beds, snoop around the **university area,** between **P. Dante** and the **duomo.** Take bus 185, CS, or CD from p. Garibaldi. **Albergo Imperia,** P. Miraglia, 386, 4th floor (tel. 45 93 47), has clean, recently renovated rooms. (Singles L21,000. Doubles L34,000.) Near noisy but safe Piazza Bovio is the **Albergo Orchidea,** C. Umberto, 7 (tel. 551 07 21), scala B, on the 5th floor, whose dazzling, high-ceilinged rooms (all with private showers) have small balconies. (Doubles L80,000. Triples L100,000. Quads L120,000.) The area around the train station should be your last choice—some hotels are of the by-the-hour variety. Ironically, the **Casanova Hotel,** Via Venezia, 2 (tel. 26 82 87) is a good option (doubles L42,000). **Hotel Ginevra,** Via Genova, 116 (tel. 28 32 10), has bright, pleasant rooms. Walk two blocks up Corso Novara, and take the second right onto Via Genova. (Singles L30,000. Doubles L50,000. 10% *Let's Go* discount.)

Pizza-making is an art born in Naples. At **Antica Pizzeria da Michele,** Via Cesare Sersale, 1/3, off Corso Umberto not far from the train station, they've perfected the craft. Try their L3000 *Marinara.* (Open Sept. to mid-Aug. Mon.-Sat. 8am-10pm.) Spaghetti, too, was first cooked up by Neapolitan chefs. Have it *alle vongole* (with clams) or *alle cozze* (with mussels). Some of the best *trattorie* and *pizzerie* are near P. Dante. **Pizzeria Port'Alba,** Via Port'Alba, 18, is the oldest *pizzeria* in Italy. Their *vecchia pizza Port'Alba* (L10,000) is split into quarters, one with shrimp and calamari, one with tomato and mozzarella, one with capers and olives, and one with mushrooms, and a little surprise in the center. (Open Thurs.-Tues. 9am-2am.) **Ristorante-Pizzeria Bellini,** Via Costantinopoli, 79, by Port'Alba, is the archetypal Italian restaurant (open Mon.-Sat. noon-4pm and 7:30pm-2am). At **Avellinese da Peppino,** Via Silvio Spavneta, 31/35 (from the train station, take the 3rd left on P. Garibaldi), locals and tourists dine in harmony at the outdoor tables. Unparalleled *spaghetti alle vongole* is L6500. (Cover L1000. Service 10%. Open 11am-midnight.) For a *trattoria* true to the Neapolitan style despite its proximity to the train station, try **Trattoria Da Maria,** Via Genova, 115, the 2nd right off Corso Novara (pasta L5000-6000; open Mon.-Sat. noon-3:30pm and 6:30-10pm, closed Aug. 15-30).

SIGHTS

The renowned **Museo Nazionale Archeologico,** near the Cavour metro stop, houses a stunning collection of mosaics, frescoes, and jewelry excavated from

Pompeii and Herculaneum. Look for the famous painting of the *Brawl in the Amphitheater,* depicting a riot which took place at the amphitheater in Pompeii in 59 AD between Pompeian and Nucerian (soccer?) fans. (Open 9am-7pm; Sept.-May Mon.-Sat. 9am-2pm, Sun. 9am-1pm. L8000.) Occupying a restored 18th-century royal palace in the hills to the north is the **Museo e Gallerie di Capodimonte;** take bus 110 or 127 from station, bus 160 or 161 from P. Dante. Masterpieces and kitsch compete for attention along the walls; the former are usually on the second floor, the latter on the first. (Open Tues.-Sat. 9am-2pm, Sun. 9am-1pm. L8000. May be temporarily closed; call 744 13 07 first.) The **Museo Nazionale di San Martino,** in a Carthusian monastery on the hill of Sant'Elmo, documents the art and history of Naples since the 16th century (open Tues.-Sun. 9am-2pm; L6000, under 18 and over 65 free). For a nature break, head to the **Villa Floridiana,** on a hill overlooking the bay, where you'll find a lovely park and the pottery-filled **Museo Duca di Martina** (open Tues.-Sat. 9am-2pm, in June 9am-7pm; L4000, EU citizens under 18 and over 65 free).

Walk along the bay in the late afternoon or early evening to see the Villa Comunale fill with locals taking their *passeggiata*. Via Sauro in the Santa Lucia section is the traditional place to watch the sunset. The 12th-century **Castel dell'Ovo** (Egg Castle; open for exhibits only), a massive Norman structure of yellow brick and incongruously converging angles, stands on the promontory of the port of Santa Lucia, dividing the bay into two parts. To the west lies the **Villa Comunale,** a waterfront park dotted with sycamores and palms and graced by sculptures, fountains, and an **aquarium.** The oldest in Europe, it features a collection of 200 species of fish and marine fauna native to the Bay of Naples. (Open in summer Tues.-Sat. 9am-5pm, Sun. 9am-6pm. L3000.)

Naples slumbers at night, except for the Sunday evening *passeggiata,* when the Villa Comunale along the bay fills with folks taking in the cool air. The young elite strut their new threads around **Piazza Amedeo.** Join legions of amorous couples at the scenic park at Capo di Posillipo (take bus 140 to the end). While strolling Via Posillipo, sample an ice cream from **Bilancione,** Via Posillipo, 398/B (tel. 769 19 23), near P. San Luigi. It's a Naples tradition. (Open Sept.-July Thurs.-Tues. 10am-11pm.)

■ POMPEII

Immense **Mount Vesuvius** looms indomitably over the area east of Naples. The eruption of the great volcano in 79 AD buried the nearby Roman city of Herculaneum (Ercolano) in mud, and its neighbor Pompeii (Pompei), in ashes. Excavation continues to uncover the lives of the ancients with astonishing precision. The findings have provided us with our most vivid picture of daily life in the Roman era.

The west entrance leads past the Antiquarium (permanently closed since the 1980 earthquake) to the **Forum,** surrounded by a colonnade which retains a portion of what was once a second tier. Once dotted with numerous statues of emperors and gods, this was the commercial, civic, and religious center of the city. Showcases along the western side display some of the gruesome body casts of the volcano's victims. Exit the Forum to the north by the cafeteria, and enter the **Forum Baths** to the left on Via di Terme. The body casts displayed here are so complete that you can even see teeth through their grimaces. Continue to the left on Via della Fortuna and turn left on Vico di Vetti to see the **House of the Vettii,** home to some of the most vivid frescoes in Pompeii. In the vestibule is a depiction of Priapus (the god of fertility) displaying his colossal member; phalli were believed to scare off evil spirits in ancient times, but now they seem only to invite hordes of tittering tourists. Walk back on Vico di Vetti and continue on Vico del Lupanare, where there is a small **brothel** with several bed-stalls. Above each of the stalls a pornographic painting depicts with unabashed precision the specialty of the woman who inhabited it (or so archaeologists think). Continue down the street to the main avenue, Via dell'Abbondanza. Turn right down Via dell'Abbondanza and note the red writing scribbled on the walls. You'll see everything from political campaign slogans to declarations of love—apparently graffiti hasn't changed much in 1900 years. At the end of the street the **House of Tiburtinus** and the **House of Venus** are sprawling complexes with wonderful frescoes and gardens replanted according to our knowledge of ancient horticulture. The nearby **amphitheater,** the oldest one still standing (80 BC), held 12,000 spectators, and the **Great Palestra** was a gymnasium complete with a pool.

Most travelers take the *circumvesuviana's* Naples-Sorrento **rail** line, which lets you off at the Pompeii-Villa dei Misteri stop just outside the west entry (L2500, Eurail valid). A comprehensive walk-through will probably take four or five hours; pack a lunch and a water bottle, as the cafeteria is hideously expensive. Consider buying the informative *New Practical Guide of Pompeii* (ed. Bonechi) for L7000, available outside all site entrances. To reach the site, head downhill from the Villa dei Misteri station and take your first left. (Entrances open 9am 'til 1hr. before sunset, off-season until 3:45pm. L10,000.) There is no reason to stay in dull, modern Pompei; make the site a daytrip from Naples or Sorrento. Stock up at the **GS Supermarket,** Via Statale, km. 24, on the main road between the east and west entrances to the archaeological site. They've got good prices and great air-conditioning. (Open Mon.-Sat. 8am-8:30pm; closes Thurs. 2pm.)

■■■ AMALFI COAST

South of Naples on the far side of the Amalfi Peninsula, clinging cliffside roads and tiled towns make the **Amalfi Coast** the most beautiful stretch of shoreline in Italy. **Sorrento,** at the western end of the peninsula (1½hr. by *circumvesuviana* train, L3900), and **Salerno** at its eastern base (1hr. by regular rail, L4600) are easy jaunts from Naples; buses between them (every 2hr.) pass through all the coastal towns. The westerly orientation of the beaches near Sorrento makes sunset swims truly memorable. For a free swim, take the bus all the way to **Punta del Capo** and walk 10 minutes down the footpath to the right. On the coast you will also see the remains of the ancient Roman **Villa di Pollio.** The Villa's not much, but they knew how to pick a swimming hole! **Trains** arrive from Naples, passing Pompeii and Torre Annunziata, every 30min. 4am-11pm (L3900). Savvy young management, wild decorations, and a waterfront location redeem **Ostello Surriento (HI),** Via Capasso, 5 (tel. (081) 878 17 83). From the train station, take a right on Corso Italia. After 200m, look for the old church on your left; Via Capasso runs along its side. (Lockout 9:30am-5pm. Curfew midnight. L13,000 per person. Breakfast L2000. Open March-Nov.) Take the 2nd left off Via Giuliani, which runs off Corso Italia at the cathedral to get to **Ristorante e Pizzeria Giardiniello,** Via Accademia, 7. Mamma Luisa does all the cooking. (*Gnocchi* L6000. 10 tiny oven-baked pizzas with prosciutto and mushrooms L7000. Cover L1500. Open 10:30am-3pm and 7pm-2am, Oct.-May Wed.-Mon. 10:30am-3pm and 7pm-2am.)

The towns to see are Positano, Amalfi and Ravello. Beware though—affordable beds are available only in Praiano and Atrani. **SITA buses** depart for towns on the Amalfi coast from the *circumvesuviana* station every 2 hours from 6:30am-9:45pm to Positano (L1800), Praiano (L2500), Amalfi (L3200), and Salerno (L5000). Buy tickets at bars and *tabacchi,* and validate them in the yellow box when you board the bus. Rent a moped from **Sorrento Rent-A-Car,** Corso Italia, 210/A to explore the coast. (Mopeds about L45,000 per day, L260,000 per week. Vespa 125s (for 2 people), L67,000 per day, L382,000 per week. Helmet and insurance for damage to other cars included. Passport, credit card, and driver's license required.) In **Praiano,** between Sorrento and Amalfi, marvel at the coastal views from **La Tranquilità,** Via Roma, 10 (tel. (089) 87 40 84), a campground-hotel. (Camping L14,000 per person. Clean, new bungalows with bath L30,000-50,000 per person including breakfast. Open Easter-Nov.) Above La Tranquilità is the open-air **Ristorante Continental,** whose package deal of mountain air, endless views, and exquisite meals will leave you in Amalfi Coast bliss. (Cover L2000. 15% *Let's Go* discount. Open Easter-Nov. noon-3pm and 8pm-midnight.) In **Atrani,** a 10min. walk from the town of **Amalfi,**

stay in **A Scalinatella,** P. Umberto 12 (tel. (089) 87 19 30), in the town's only
piazza. (Curfew midnight. L15,000 for bed and shower. Sheets L5000. Laundry
L7000.) Students and those with *Let's Go* can partake of a fixed-price menu
(L16,000 including beverage and service) at **Ristorante La Piazzeta,** P. Umberto I.

■■■ BAY OF NAPLES ISLANDS

Cápri Since imperial times, the divine landscapes and azure waters of the island of
Cápri have beckoned wayfarers from the Italian mainland. The **Grotta Azzura** (Blue
Grotto) is the island's symbol, but avoid the rip-off motorboat tours (L8000 round-
trip); instead take a bus (L1500 from Ánacapri). You can swim in the fluorescent
cave when the boats aren't running (before 9am or after 6pm). When the surf is
high, the boats don't run and you shouldn't swim. To appreciate Cápri's Mediterranean beauty from on high, take Via Longano from P. Umberto in Cápri center and
then make the trek up to the left on Via Tiberio to **Villa Jovis** (1hr.). This is the
Roman emperor Tiberius's ruined but still magnificent pleasure dome. Legend has it
that Tiberius tossed those who displeased him over the precipice. (Open 9am-1hr.
before sunset. L4000.)

   Caremar ferries run from Naples' Beverello port to Cápri (hourly from 7:55am-
7:25pm, last return 6:35pm, L8500) and from Sorrento (5 per day, 7:55am-7:40pm,
last return 6:45pm, L5100). **Linee Lauro's** hydrofoil runs to and from Íschia once
daily (L16,000). **Ánacapri,** literally "over Cápri," sits high on a plateau of **Monte
Solaro** (589m). It is less frequented by daytrippers, and qualifies as a budget version
of paradise; take the bus (L1500) there from Marina Grande where most boats dock.
Get tourist information in Cápri, at the end of the dock at Marina Grande (tel. (081)
837 06 34; open Mon.-Sat. 8am-8pm, Sun. 8:30am-2:30pm). In Ánacapri, the tourist
office is at Via Orlandi, 19/A (tel. (081) 837 15 24), off the main *piazza*, to the right
as you get off the bus (open Mon.-Sat. 8am-8pm; Nov.-May 9am-3pm). **Villa Eva,** Via
della Fabbrica, 8 (tel. (081) 837 15 49, fax 837 20 40), is 5min. from P. Vittoria and a
scenic 30min. walk from the Grotta Azzurra. Call from the port and the warm-
hearted Mamma Eva or her husband Vicenzo will pick you up. (Pool, small kitchen
and barbecue for your use. L25,000 per person. *Let's Go* prices: L18,000-L25,000
per person. Private doubles L50,000.) The management of **Hotel il Girasole,** Via Lin-
ciano, 47 (tel. (081) 837 36 20, fax 837 23 51) loves *Let's Go* and its readers. Call
from Marina Grande and they'll pick you up. (Doubles L50,000. Triples L69,000.
Quads L80,000.) Dine in style in Ánacapri at **Trattoria il Solitario,** Via Orlandi, 96,
an outdoor ivy-covered hideaway serving homemade pasta for L8000. (Cover
L2000. Open 12:15-3pm and 7pm-midnight; Sept. 21-June 19 closed Mon.)

Íschia Across the bay from overrun Cápri, larger, less glamorous Íschia offers a
variety of landscapes, including beautiful beaches, natural hot springs, ruins, forests,
vineyards, lemon groves, and a once-active volcano. **Caremar ferries** arrive from
Naples almost every hour (8am-7pm, L8500) and **Linee Lauro** runs from Sorrento to
Íschia (L12,000) and connects the island to Cápri with a hydrofoil once daily
(L16,000). The bus (route 1) follows the coast in a counterclockwise direction from
Íschia Porto to **Fório,** the hippest area on Íschia thanks to its tree-lined streets and
popular bars. Buy tickets in P. Trieste (just off Íschia Porto), also the main departure
point. (Buses leave every ½hr. 5am-midnight; one-way L1200. Morning passes
L2500, afternoon L2800, and full day L4000.)

   Hotels in Íschia can be expensive. By late July and August rooms are hard to come
by without reservations made at least one month in advance. In Fório, try **Pensione
Di Lustro,** Via Filippo di Lustro, 9 (tel. (081) 99 71 63), a short walk from the beach
(doubles with bath L70,000, including breakfast; half-pension required in July,
L60,000 and Aug. L65,000). Also consider camping at **Eurocamping dei Pini,** Via
delle Ginestre, 28 (tel. (081) 98 20 69), a 10min. walk from the port. Take Via del
Porto onto Via Alfredo de Luca, walk uphill and take a right on Via delle Terme,

where you will see the arrow indicating camping. (Sept.-June L8000 per person, L4000 per small tent. Small price increase July-Aug. Open year-round.)

SICILY (SICILIA)

Every great Mediterranean civilization of the past 2500 years has left its mark on Sicily: the ancient Greeks scattered temples and theaters; the Romans, bridges and aqueducts; the Saracens, mosques and towers; the Normans, churches and castles. Unlike citizens of other parts of Italy, Sicilians don't revel in their island's traditions: today they speed unabated toward the future, installing condom-vending machines in front of medieval cathedrals and demonstrating against their most well-known institution, the Mafia. A series of seismic and volcanic catastrophes have periodically wiped clean the gains of Sicily's inhabitants, but the island has remained intact through centuries of occupation, creation, and destruction.

The cheapest way to reach Sicily is a train-ferry combination to Messina (from Rome via Règgio di Calabria, L47,900). **Tirrenia** sails from Naples to Palermo (8pm; 11hr.; L53,100-68,400) and from Messina to Règgio di Calabria (20 per day, 20 min., L4000) and Villa San Giovanni (20 per day, 35 min., L1800). Two bus companies, the private, air-conditioned **SAIS** and the public, often steamy **AST** serve many of the destinations inaccessible by train. Expect delays and confusion. **Hitchhiking** is difficult on long hauls; hitchers are reputed to have better luck near turn-offs, on short trips. Moreover, it's very risky—*Let's Go* strongly cautions against it.

■■■ PALERMO

The people and palaces of Palermo proclaim it as a crossroads of Mediterranean cultures. In modern times, Palermo has earned notoriety as the cradle of *Cosa Nostra* (the Mafia). Sicily's capital and cultural center features brightly-lit avenues masking a labyrinth of dark, older streets; despite the dilapidation, the *palazzi* strewn about the town contain some of the most wondrous courtyards in Italy. To reach the exuberant **cattedrale** from the station, head straight on Via Roma, bearing left on Corso Vittorio Emanuele (open 7am-noon and 5-7pm). Nearby, the **Palazzo dei Normanni** exhibits an impressive fusion of artistic styles and a mucho-mosaicked *cappella palatina*. Go for baroque at the **Church of San Giuseppe dei Teatini,** with its fantastic interior decoration (open 7:30am-noon and 6:30-8:15pm).

For maps and information, visit the **APT** office in the train station, or the main branch 2km north (tel. (091) 58 38 47). Take bus 101 or 107 "Teatro Politeamo"; it's the building with the huge *Sicilcassa* sign (open Mon.-Fri. 8am-8pm, Sat. 8am-2pm; train station Mon.-Fri. 8am-8pm). **Hotel Cortese**, Via Scarpelli, 16, (tel. (091) 33 17 22), a 10min. walk from the train station down Via Maqueda to Via dell'Università, has impeccable rooms. (Singles L25,000-30,000. Doubles L45,000-L55,000.) **Albergo Orientale,** Via Maqueda, 26 (tel. (091) 616 57 27), just a few blocks from the station, is a gloriously run-down 17th-century *palazzo*. (Singles L25,000. Doubles L40,000, with bath L50,000. Triple with bath L60,000.) **Albergo Letizia,** Via Bottai, 30, (tel. (091) 58 91 10), is a little out-of-the-way, but the rooms are as fresh as the bottles of rainwater the owner collects in his spare time. From Via Roma head along Corso Vittorio Emanuele toward the water; take the eighth street on the right. (Singles L33,000-40,000. Doubles L50,000-60,000.)

Despite its name, **Trattoria Shanghai,** Vicolo de Mezzani, 34, overlooking P. Caracciolo, is pure Palermo, with great *gamberi* (shrimp; L8000). (Cover L1000, service 10%; open Mon.-Sat. 11am-4pm and 6:30-midnight.) **Hostaria al Duar 2,** Via E. Amari, 92, off Via Roma as you angle towards the port, serves up Tunisia's finest, the *Completo Tunisio* (L13,000, food, drink, and cover included), as well as the more Italian *penne all'arrabiata*, pasta so hot it's "rabid." (Cover L1000. Open Thurs.-Tues. 10am-3pm and 7pm-midnight.) After dinner, hike up town to Frankie's **Bar**

Fiore, Via Principe di Belmonte, 84, where Palermo's greatest extrovert will give you a *frullato* (frothy Italian milkshake) for only L4000 (open 6am-midnight). Sip it while lounging on the tree-lined avenue watching time go by. Most of Palermo's nightlife is outside the city proper in nearby **Mondello;** take bus 6, 14, or 15 from Via della Libertà or the station, and get off at Mondello Paese.

■ MONREALE AND CEFALÙ

If you like mosaics, don't pass up **Monreale,** 10km southwest of Palermo, where the cathedral mixes Norman architecture with Sicilian and Arabian motifs. From Palermo take bus 9 (L1000) from Via Lincoln, across from the train station and to the left. (Open 8am-12:30pm and 3:30-6:30pm.) The **Benedictine Cloister** next door frames a garden with fanciful medieval columns. (Open 9am-7pm; Nov.-March Mon.-Sat. 9am-1:30pm, Sun. 9am-12:30pm. L2000.) Bus 389 leaves from Palermo's P. Indipendenza and drops you off right by the cathedral.

About an hour from Palermo by train (L5300), **Cefalù** boasts a cache of Arab, Norman, and medieval architecture. In P. Duomo off Corso Ruggero you'll find Cefalù's austere 11th-century Norman **cathedral.** Inside, 16 Byzantine and Roman columns support superb capitals, as well as elegant horseshoe arches that exemplify the Saracen influence on Norman architecture in Sicily. (Open 9am-noon and 3:30-7pm. Proper dress required.) Opposite the cathedral, the private **Museo Mandralisca,** Via Mandralisca, 13, houses a fine collection of paintings, Greek ceramics, Arab pottery, antique money, and Antonello da Messina's *Ritratto di Ignoto.* (Open 9am-12:30pm and 3:30-7pm. L4000.) For a bird's-eye view of the city, make the half-hour haul up the **Rocca** by way of the Salita Saraceni, which begins near P. Garibaldi off Corso Ruggero. Follow the brown signs for "*pedonale Rocca.*" On the mountain, walkways lined with ancient stone walls lead to the **Tempio di Diana** (Temple of Diana). Dating back to the 4th century BC, it was first used for sea-cult worship and later as a defensive outpost.

■ ■ ■ AGRIGENTO

Among Sicily's classical remains, the **Valley of Temples** at Agrigento shares top honors with those at Syracuse. **Temple of Concord,** one of the world's best-preserved Greek temples, owes its survival to consecration by St. Gregory of the Turnips. On the road to the archaeological park from the city center, the **Museo Archeologico Nazionale,** contains a notable collection of artifacts, especially vases from all over central Sicily (open Mon., Wed.-Thurs., and Sat 9am-1pm, Tues. and Fri. 9am-5pm; free). Take bus 8, 9, 10, or 11 from the train station (last bus back at 9:45pm; L600) and ask to be dropped off at the *Quartiere Ellenistico-Romano.*

The **tourist office** (tel. (0922) 204 54) is on the main street at Via Atenea, 123 (open Mon.-Sat. 9am-1:45pm and 5:30-8pm). **Trains** arrive from Palermo (1½hr., L10,900). **Hotel Bella Napoli,** P. Lena, 6 (tel. (0922) 20 435), off Via Bac Bacat the north end of Via Atenea, has clean, refurbished rooms and a terrace overlooking the valley. (Singles L25,000-30,000. Doubles L40,000-60,000.) Closer to the train station is spotless **Concordia,** Via San Francesco, 11 (tel. (0922) 59 62 66; singles L25,000-30,000, doubles L40,000-60,000). If you're lucky, you'll overhear the chef sing Verdi at **Trattoria Black Horse,** Via Celauro, 8, off Via Atenea. *Tronchetto dello chef* (L6500) is the specialty: a thick lasagna packed with peas, ham, and meat sauce. (Cover L2000. Open Mon.-Sat. noon-3pm and 7-11pm. AmEx, MC, Visa.) **Trattoria Atenea,** Via Ficani, 32, the 4th right off Via Atenea from P. Moro, has a quiet courtyard and extensive seafood offerings. *Calamari* (squid) and *gamberi* (shrimp) are L9000. (Open Mon.-Sat. noon-3pm and 7pm-midnight.)

■■■ SYRACUSE (SIRACUSA)

Founded in 734 BC by Corinthians who fancied its splendid harbor, the Hellenic city of Syracuse produced Pindar, Archimedes, and the world's first cookbook. Cross the bridge on Corso Umberto to the island of **Ortigia** to pay homage to the Temples of **Apollo** and **Athena**. The latter, now part of the city's cathedral, has a richly embellished façade, added in the 18th century. From P. del Duomo, a trip down Via Picherale leads to the ancient **Fonte Aretusa**, a "miraculous" freshwater spring by the sea. Syracuse's larger monuments are in or near the **Archaeological Park** on the north side of town; follow Corso Gelone until it is intersected by Viale Teocrito; the entrance to the park is down Via Augusto to the left. The park contains the world's largest ancient **Greek Theater**. (Park open 9am-6pm; winter 9am-3pm. L2000.) Check out the **Orecchio di Dionigi** (Ear of Dionysius), a giant artificial grotto with an earlobe-shaped entrance. The cave's acoustics reputedly allowed one to overhear prisoners talking in the lower room. Nearby, the **Altar of Hieron II** (241-215 BC) was used for public sacrifices. At 198m by 23m, it is the largest altar known. The **Roman amphitheater,** constructed in the 2nd century AD, is occasionally used for dance and dramatic performances. Bus the 20km to **Fontane Bianche** (bus 21 or 22, L600), an endless, silken beach (camping L7000 per person, L7000 per small tent at Viale dei Lidi, 476). More popular with the locals but less spectacular is **Arenella,** 8km from the city (bus 23, every 45min., L600).

Near the **Catacombs of San Giovanni** (open 9am-1pm and 3-6pm, mid-Nov. to mid-March 9am-1pm; L2000), the **tourist office,** Via San Sebastiano, 45 (tel. (0931) 677 10), distributes maps and brochures (open Mon.-Sat. 8am-2pm and 4-7pm). **Trains** arrive from Taormina (2hr., L10,900), while **buses** pull into town from Palermo (4hr., L20,000) **Pensione Bel Sit,** Via Oglio, 5 (tel. (0931) 602 45), on the 5th floor, has modern, basic singles (L30,000, with bath L35,000) and doubles (L40,000, with bath L50,000). Room size varies at **Hotel Milano,** Corso Umberto, 10 (tel. (0931) 669 81), but it has low prices and a convenient location near the bridge to Ortigia. (Singles L28,000, with bath L38,000. Doubles L45,000, with bath L60,000.) For staples, invade the **Supermercato Linguanti,** Corso Umberto, 174, a block from the train station (open Mon.-Sat. 7:30am-1pm and 3:30-8pm). An ancient Syracusan institution, **Spaghetteria do Scugghiu,** Via D. Sciná, 11, off P. Archimede, serves up 22 delicious kinds (all L6000; open Tues.-Sun. noon-3pm and 7pm-midnight).

■■■ TAORMINA

Perched precariously on a cliff high above the Mediterranean, with the massive profile of Mt. Etna looming nearby, Taormina has drawn visitors since the 8th century BC when it was founded by a shipwrecked Greek sailor on the rocky shore below; it later became a destination for European aristocrats who transformed the town into a resort community. These days it's a precious combination of mansions, pine trees and purple flowers, with a hazy-blue coastline stretching out beyond. The 3rd-century **Greek Theater,** at the very edge of the cliff, is arguably the most dramatically situated theater on earth (open 9am-7pm; L2000, under 18 or over 60 free). Nearby is the **Roman Odeon,** a small theater now partly covered by the Church of Santa Caterina next door. A small set of steep steps snake up the mountainside to the **castello,** with Taormina's finest view.

Reach Taormina by **bus** from Messina or Catania (L5100). **Trains** are twice as frequent, and only L3900—but the train station is far below town with access controlled by buses (L2500) that make the climb every 15-75min. until 10:20pm. A helpful and well-organized **tourist office** waits on P. Santa Caterina (tel. (0942) 232 43), in Palazzo Corvaia off Corso Umberto (open Mon.-Sat. 8am-2pm and 4-7pm). Accommodations can be hard to come by in summer, so arrive early and have the tourist office book a room for you. The **Pensione Svizzera,** Via Pirandello, 26 (tel. (0942) 237 90, fax 62 59 06), is kept so neat, even the Swiss would be impressed. (Singles L35,000. Doubles L56,000. Triples L75,000. Breakfast L5000. Open March-

Nov.) Another option is the **Villa Pompei,** Via Bagnoli Croci, 88 (tel. (0942) 238 12), across from the public gardens. (Singles L30,000. Doubles L48,000, with bath L54,000. Extra bed L15,000. Showers L2000. Reservations for June-Sept. required a month in advance with deposit.) Dining can be expensive; consider stocking up at the **Standa** supermarket on Via Apollo Arcageta, at the end of Corso Umberto, a block from the post office (open Mon.-Sat., 8:30am-1pm and 5-9pm). The sign in front of **Trattoria da Nino,** Via Pirandello, 37, reads "Stop, you have found the best home-made cooking and pasta in Taormina." It may well be correct. (*Primi* from L5500. Open noon-3:30pm; closed Fri. in winter.)

■■■ AEOLIAN ISLANDS (ISOLE EOLIE)

Home of the smithy god Hephaistos, the wind god Aeolus, and the Sirens, the Aeolian (or Lipari) Islands are an enchanting volcanic archipelago off northern Sicily. On **Lípari,** the largest and most beautiful of the islands, the picturesque town of the same name is crowned by the walls of a medieval *castello*, the site of an ancient Greek acropolis. Lípari is renowned for its beaches and panoramas—to explore, rent a bike or moped from **Foti Roberto,** Via F. Crispi, 31 (tel. (090) 981 23 52 or 981 25 87), on the beach to the right of the ferry port. (Bicycles L5000 per hr., L20,000 per day. Mopeds and scooters L12,000 per hr., L30,000-40,000 per day. L100,000 deposit. Open Easter-Oct. 15 daily 9am-6pm.) The **tourist office,** Corso Vittorio Emanuele, 202 (tel. (090) 988 00 95), up the street from the ferry dock, doles out useful free handouts (open Mon.-Fri. 8am-2pm and 4:30-7:30pm, Sat. 8am-2pm, July-Aug. Mon.-Fri. until 10pm). Inside the walls of the fortress, the **Ostello Lípari (HI)** (tel. (090) 981 15 40, winter 98 12 527) strictly enforces the curfew, but is probably the best deal on the island. (Reception open 7:30-9am and 6pm-midnight. Midnight curfew. L10,000 includes sheets and cold showers. Open March-Oct.) **Il Galeone,** Corso Vittorio Emanuele, 220, tempts with 32 types of pizza (L5000-12,000; open 8am-midnight, Oct.-May Thurs.-Tues. 8pm-midnight). Reach Lípari by ferry (2hr., L10,600) from the city of **Milazzo,** on the Messina-Palermo train line (from Messina L3500, from Palermo L13,800). **Siremar** (tel. (090) 928 32 42 in Milazzo) and **Navigazione Generale Insulare** (tel. (090) 928 34 15) run reliable ferries out of Milazzo. Take the quicker, more expensive hydrofoils (*aliscafi*) to the nearby islands (Vulcano, Salina and Panarea), but use the slow ferries for visits to Strómboli, Filicudi and Alicudi.

The island of **Vulcano,** easily accessed from Lípari (by hydrofoil L3900, by ferry L2200), is the perfect daytrip, with thermal springs and bubbling mud baths. From the dock at Porto di Levante, head to the left up the snaking path to the crater and past the sulfur fumaroles for a breathtaking view of the other isles. Just up Via Provinciale from the port sits the **Laghetto di Fanghi** (mud pool) to your right, a bubbling pit where hundreds of zealots come to spread the allegedly therapeutic goop all over their bodies. **Strómboli** (take the less expensive *nave*—L12,700—rather than the ferry from Lípari) is the most dramatic and enticing of the islands, with an active volcano, streams o' lava, voluptuous vegetation, and alluring beaches. There's nothing to see but smoke during the day—see the crater at dusk. Although hiking the volcano is officially illegal, lots of people do and escape unscathed. A night spent at the summit watching red-hot lava against pitch-black sky is unforgettable. Nights are crisp and windy at the crater; the wise bring a plastic groundsheet and sleeping bag, a heavy sweater, water, and a flashlight with an extra set of batteries, as the path isn't lit. The hike takes 3 hours up, 2 hours down. **Guide Alpine Autorizzate** leads official tours from their office in P. Vincenzo at 5pm (L25,000; April-Oct.). Travelers are likely to have trouble stashing bags in town; some try leaving them in the Lípari hostel or, in a pinch, ask very nicely at the Villa Petrusa further down the road. The aforementioned conditions make winter travel on Strómboli particularly impractical. Get away from it all on **Filicudi** or **Alicudi;** neither supports more than

400 people, and electricity only came recently. The beautiful, expensive beaches and crystal-clear waters of **Panarea** and **Salina** are also good daytrips from Lípari.

SARDINIA (SARDEGNA)

Phoenicians, Byzantines, Pisans, Genoans, the Aragonese, and NATO have all tried to mainstream the island, but to no avail; Sardinia unabashedly retains its honor and proclaims its autonomy. Sardinia's beaches rival Europe's finest, and the island is still a refuge for marine seals and pink flamingos. Tourism has vanquished the northeastern **Costa Smeralda;** stick to the stunning beaches and ancient ruins farther south.

Tirrenia runs the most extensive ferry network, with service from Civitavécchia to Olbia 7hr., L33,400) and Cagliari (13hr., L52,200); Genoa to Olbia (13hr., L57,400); Genoa to Cagliari (20hr., L80,200); and Naples to Cagliari (16hr., L53,500). Prices listed above are for reserved seats; *posto ponte* (deck class) is cheaper. **Flights** arrive in Olbia and Cagliari (Rome-Olbia about L131,500 one way, night flights L106,000). On the island, **ARST** buses link villages while **PANI** buses connect only major cities. **Trains** are picturesque and much cheaper, but can be slow and unreliable. Most ignore railpasses. **Car rental** is most convenient, and gives you access to magnificent campgrounds. The best car rental deals are found in larger cities. (Prices start at around L90,000 per day; look for weekend deals.) Ask any tourist office for the semi-reliable and comprehensive *Annuario Alberghi,* which lists prices for all hotels, *pensioni,* and official campsites on the island.

Cagliari, at the southern tip of the island, lies near exquisite beaches, ancient ruins, and flamingoed lagoons. Stay at **Albergo Firenze,** Corso Vittorio Emanuele, 50 (tel. (070) 65 36 78; singles L30,000, doubles L36,000), or **Locanda Las Palmas,** Via Sardegna, 14 (tel. 65 16 79; singles L30,000; doubles L42,000/45,000). Try legendary **Antica Hostaria,** Via Cavour, 60, for traditional Sardinian dishes (open Mon.-Sat. noon-2:30pm and 8-10:30pm).

Alghero, "the Barcelonetta of Sardinia," induces nostalgia and is a great base for daytrips. On the corner of Via Cagliari and Via Mazzini, a **market** offers the freshest of produce (open Tues.-Sun. 7am-1pm). Try **Hotel San Francesco,** Via Machin, 2 (tel. (079) 98 03 30; singles L40,000, doubles L65,000). **Núoro** is an authentic Sardinian town in the heart of the island, largely unblemished by tourism. From Núoro, a 1hr. bus trip will connect you with **Cala Gonone,** a take-off point to sandier, less-populated beaches down the coast and **Grotta del Bue Marino,** a stunning cave where seals still romp at night.

Liechtenstein

Famous chiefly for its postage stamps, wines, and royal family, Liechtenstein's minute size renders the principality its own chief tourist attraction. In the capital city of **Vaduz,** exhibits rotate about four times a year at **Staatliche Kunstsammlung,** Städtle 37, next to the tourist office (open 10am-noon and 1:30-5pm; April-Oct. until 5:30pm. 3SFr, students 1.50SFr). The **Walser Heimatmuseum** in nearby **Triesenberg** chronicles the simple lifestyle of the Walsers, a group of 13th-century Swiss immigrants (open Tues.-Fri. 1:30-5:30pm, Sat. 1:30-5pm, Sun. 2-5pm; Sept.-May closed Sun; 2SFr, students 1SFr). The Triesenberg **tourist office** (tel. 219 26) is in the same building and has the same hours. **Malbun,** a mountain resort dubbed "the undiscovered St. Moritz," offers secluded and affordable ski slopes, and has served as a training ground for many an Olympian. Highlights are two chairlifts, four T-bars, two ski schools, and a dearth of other skiers. (Daypass 30SFr. Weekly pass 124SFr.) Contact the Malbun **tourist office** (tel. 263 65 77) for specifics (open June-Oct. and mid-Dec. to mid-April Mon.-Wed. and Fri. 9am-noon and 1:30-5pm., Sat. until 4pm). See *Let's Go: Austria & Switzerland* for in-depth coverage of this little country.

Practical Information Though its people have enjoyed the status of a sovereign nation since 1806, a customs agreement with Switzerland makes border passage hassle-free. Liechtenstein uses Swiss currency and the Swiss phone system; its **city code** is 075. **Postal buses** speed visitors to Vaduz from Buchs or Sargans in Switzerland, or from Feldkirch in Austria (all 4SFr). Liechtenstein's **national tourist office,** Städtle 28 (tel. 392 11 11 or 232 14 43; fax 392 16 18), just steps from the Vaduz-Post bus stop, stamps passports (2SFr), locates rooms for free, distributes free maps and advice on hiking, cycling, and skiing in the area, and makes hotel reservations for 2SFr (open Mon.-Fri. 8am-noon and 1:30-5:30pm, Sat.-Sun. 9am-noon and 1-4pm; Sept.-June Mon.-Fri. 8am-noon and 1:30-5:30pm). **Cycling** enthusiasts can rent trusty steeds at the train station in Buchs or Sargans for 19SFr per day, leaving an ID as a deposit. Although biking is a dream in this flat, green principality, one can also opt for the efficient and cheap **postal bus system** that links all 11 villages (most trips 2SFr; Swisspass valid).

Accommodations and Food The lone **Jugendherberge (HI),** Untere Rütigasse 6 (tel. 250 22), is in **Schaan.** Take the "Schaan" bus from Vaduz to Hotel Mühle; from there, turn on Marianumstr. and follow the signs. (Reception open Mon.-Sat. 7-9:30am and 5-10pm, Sun. 6-10pm. Curfew 10pm. Members only. 20.30SFr. Lockers, laundry (6SFr). Showers and breakfast included; dinner 10SFr. Open Jan.-Nov. 15.) If the hostel is full, walk about 10min. back up the main road toward Vaduz or take the "Schaan" bus to Falknis for **Hotel Falknis** (tel. 263 77) right near the stop (singles and doubles 40SFr per person; breakfast and showers included). Liechtenstein's two **campgrounds,** peaceful to a fault, are easily accessible by postal bus. **Bendern** (tel. 312 11) is on the Schellenberg line (3SFr per person, 2-4SFr per tent). **Camping Mittagspitze** (tel. 392 36 77 or 392 26 86) lies between Triesen and Balzers on the road to Sargans (reception open 7am-noon and 2-10pm; 5SFr per person, 3-5SFr per tent). Eating in Liechtenstein is an absolute nightmare; shop at **Denner Superdiscount,** Aulestr. 20, in Vaduz, and find a shady tree (open Mon.-Fri. 8:30am-1pm and 1:30-6:30pm, Sat. 8am-4pm).

Luxembourg

US$1 = 34.50LF (francs, or LUF)		10LF =	US$0.29
CDN$1= 26.20LF		10LF =	CDN$0.38
UK£1 = 53.40LF		10LF =	UK£0.19
IR£1 = 50.00LF		10LF =	IR£0.20
AUS$1 = 22.40LF		10LF =	AUS$0.45
NZ$1 = 19.10LF		10LF =	NZ$0.52
SAR1 = 7.17F		10LF =	SAR1.39
Country Code: 352		International Dialing Code: 00	

Founded in 963, the Grand Duchy of Luxembourg was first named Luclinburhuc, or "little castle." By the time successive waves of Burgundians, Spaniards, French, Austrians, and Germans had receded, the little castle had become a bristling armored mountain, and the countryside was saturated with fortresses. Only after the last French soldier returned home in 1867 and the Treaty of London restored its neutrality did Luxembourg begin to cultivate its current image of peacefulness and independence. Today Luxembourg is an independent constitutional monarchy, a member of the European Community, and a tax-haven for investors from around the globe, with the Grand Duke and his Cabinet of 12 ministers still wielding supreme executive power over the country's 400,000 residents. From the wooded and hilly

Ardennes in the north to the fertile vineyards of the Moselle Valley in the south, the country's unspoiled rural landscapes markedly contrast with the high-powered banking industry of its capital city.

LUXEMBOURG ESSENTIALS

Luxembourg is only 2600km square, but the tiny territory is split into even smaller travel zones; the price of a trip is calculated according to the number of zones crossed. A *billet courte distance* (short distance ticket) costs 35LF and allows you to traverse up to six zones. Most intercity trips will require at least two or three tickets. Train and bus stations sell network tickets, **Billets Reseaux** (140LF), which allow a day's unlimited 2nd class travel on any train or national bus. A **Benelux Pass,** good for unlimited travel any 5 days in a 17 day period in Belgium, the Netherlands, and Luxembourg, costs only 3030LF, 4040LF if over 26. **Bicycles** are permitted on any train for 35LF. **Hitching** is fair; distances are short, but traffic is light.

The **tourist office** network is exhaustive and highly skilled at ferreting out bargain rooms. Youth hostels frequently offer discounts on tours. The hostel association maintains trails marked with white triangles between each of their houses.

Luxembourg's official **languages** are French and German, but the most common language is Letzebuergesch, a German dialect with a slew of French loanwords. French is often preferred over German. Most banks are open Mon.-Fri. from 8:30am to 4:30pm; most shops Tues.-Sat. from 9:30am to 6pm and Mon. from 2 to 6pm. Many shops close at noon for 2 hours, especially in the countryside, where only taverns may be open after 6pm. Luxembourg francs are worth the same as Belgian francs; you can use Belgian money in Luxembourg, and Luxembourg bills are valid in Belgium. For AT&T **USA Direct,** call 08 00 01 11; for MCI **WorldPhone** 08 00 60 63; for **SprintExpress** 08 00 01 15; **Canada Direct** 09 00 01 19; and **BT Direct** 08 00 00 44. **Business holidays** are Jan. 1, Carnival (in Feb.), Easter Monday (April 17, 1995), May 1, Ascension Day (May 25, 1995), Whit Sunday and Monday (June 4 and 5, 1995), June 23, Aug. 15, Nov. 1-2, and Dec. 25-26.

Accommodations, Camping, and Food The 13 **HI youth hostels** in Luxembourg charge between 300 and 380LF, ages over 26 350-440LF, nonmembers 90LF extra. Breakfasts are included, packed lunches cost 110LF, and dinners are 230LF; eating a meal in the hostel wins a 15LF discount. Sheets are 100LF. Lockers require 500LF or your passport deposit. All hostels (except the one in Grevenmacher) have kitchens. Many hostels are clogged with traveling tots in early summer, and many of them also close during December and January; phone ahead. Luxembourg hotels run 600-1500LF per night. **Campgrounds** abound; almost all have hot showers. Two people with a tent will pay 250-300LF. Restaurant prices will devour your budget. Luxembourg cuisine is closely linked to that of the neighboring Lorraine region of France, with sliced Ardennes ham a national specialty.

■■■ LUXEMBOURG CITY (VILLE DE LUXEMBOURG)

Rising triumphantly from the lush valleys of the Pétrusse and Grund Rivers, the city of Luxembourg is profoundly shaped by the awesome power of nature, thus creating one of the most attractive and dramatic capitals in Europe. The omnipresent force of the topography cradles a mix of ancient castles and fortifications, modern buildings and sculpture making the city a feast for the eyes. Sitting in one of the outdoor terraces in the evening, listening to the music and watching the people bustle about, it's sometimes hard to remember that you're in one of the smallest and most rural nations on the continent, and that the European Court of Justice, international banking firms, and a few well-placed rivers are all that separate you from the forest beyond.

PRACTICAL INFORMATION

Tourist Offices: Grand Duchy National Tourist Office, pl. de la Gare (tel. 48 11 99), in the Luxair office. Turn right as you leave the train station. Indispensable map, hotel listings, and reservations service—all free. Open Mon.-Fri. 9am-7:15pm, Sat.-Sun. and holidays 9am-noon and 2-6pm; Sept.-May Mon.-Sat. 9am-6pm. The **Municipal Tourist Office,** pl. d'Armes (tel. 22 28 09), in the center of town, offers info on and services for the city only. Open Mon.-Sat. 9am-7pm, Sun. 10am-noon and 2-6pm; mid-Sept. to Mid-June Mon.-Sat. 9am-1pm and 2-6pm. The Municipal tourist office has more staff and more specific info, and the crowds are not so bad.

Budget Travel: SOTOUR, 15, pl. du Théâtre (tel. 46 15 14). BIJ and other discount tickets. Open Mon.-Fri. 9am-6pm, Sat. 9am-noon.

Embassies: U.S., 22, bd. E. Servais (tel. 46 01 23). **U.K.,** 14, bd. Roosevelt (tel. 22 98 64). Open Mon.-Fri. 9am-12:30pm and 2-5pm. Answering machine gives a 24hr. emergency number. Travelers from **Canada, Ireland, Australia, New Zealand,** and **South Africa** should contact their embassies in France or Belgium.

Currency Exchange: Mediocre rates at the train station *bureau de change*. Open Mon.-Sat. 8:30am-9pm, Sun. 9am-9pm. Banks have similar rates. Many have offices in front of the train station. Standard charge of around 50LF per check. An **automatic currency exchange machine** is across from the station at Banque UCL.

American Express: 34, av. de la Porte-Neuve (tel. 22 85 55). Mail held. Traveler's checks cashed, sold, and replaced; wired money accepted. Exchange rates similar to banks. Open Mon.-Fri. 9am-1pm and 2-5pm, Sat. 9:30am-noon.

Post Office: Main office, 38, pl. de la Gare, across the street and to the left of the train station. Poste Restante open Mon.-Sat. 6am-8pm. **Branch office,** 25, rue Aldringern, 2 blocks from pl. d'Armes. Poste Restante open Mon.-Sat. 8am-7pm. **Poste Restante Code:** L-1009 Luxembourg for the main office.

Telephones: At both post offices. Main office open Mon.-Fri. 6am-7:15pm, Sat. noon-8pm. The branch on rue Aldringern has the same hours as the post office.

Flights: Bus 9 to the airport (35LF plus a rarely enforced 35LF charge for baggage) is cheaper than the Luxair bus (120LF) and runs the same airport-hostel-train station route more frequently (every 20min.).

Trains: Gare CFL, av. de la Gare (tel. 49 24 24), near the foot of av. de la Liberté. In the southern part of the city, 10min. from the city center. Bus 9 runs between the railway station, the hostel, and the airport. Pick it up on your right as you leave the station, in front of the Luxair office. Luxembourg lies on major train routes from Brussels to Basel, and from Amsterdam to Milan.

Buses: Buy tickets from the driver (35LF; valid 1hr.), or get a package of 10 (270LF) at banks or at the bakery around the corner from the national tourist office.

Luggage Storage: At the station. Check your bags (60LF; open 6am-10pm) or use the lockers (80LF, oversized lockers 100LF, both good for 2 days).

Laundromat: Quick Wash, 31, rue de Strasbourg, near the station. Wash 230LF, dry 20LF for 7min. Open Mon.-Sat. 8am-7pm (closed holidays).

Pharmacy: Pharmacie du Globe, 12, rue Jean Origier (tel. 48 70 09), off av. de la Gare. Open Mon.-Fri. 7:40am-noon and 1:30-6pm. Dial 112 on weekends to find an open pharmacy or look in any pharmacy window for the name and address of the current *pharmacie de garde*.

Crisis Lines: (tel. 54 16 16) for emotional and psychological problems. Open Mon.-Fri. 9am-5pm. **Rape Crisis:** (tel. 54 57 57) 24hrs. English spoken. **Drug problems: Infor-Drogue** (tel. 47 57 47) and **Youth Drug Help** (tel. 49 10 40).

Medical Assistance: Tel. 112. Open 24hrs. (English spoken).

Emergencies: Ambulance: Tel. 112. **Police:** 58-60, rue Glesner (tel. 40 94 01). Call 113 for police emergencies.

ACCOMMODATIONS, CAMPING, AND FOOD

Inexpensive hotels jam the streets near the train station. Hotels become increasingly pricey and posh as you move north of the ravine. Both the main and branch tourist offices find rooms for free, but the main (Luxair) office is less crowded.

LUXEMBOURG

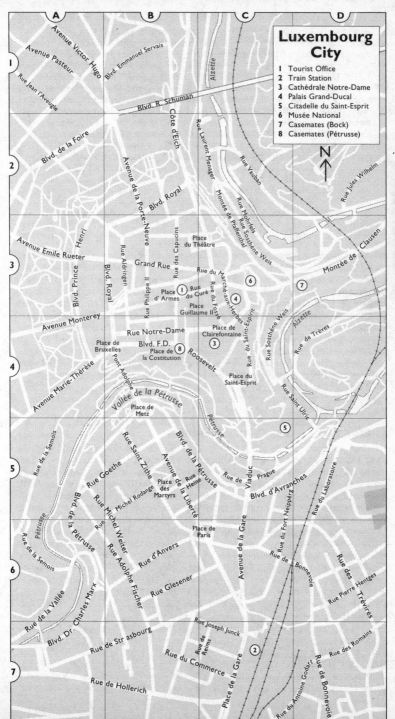

Luxembourg City

1 Tourist Office
2 Train Station
3 Cathédrale Notre-Dame
4 Palais Grand-Ducal
5 Citadelle du Saint-Esprit
6 Musée National
7 Casemates (Bock)
8 Casemates (Pétrusse)

N

LUXEMBOURG

Avenue Victor Hugo
Avenue Pasteur
Rue Jean l'Aveugle
Blvd. Emmanuel Servais
Alzette
Blvd. R. Schuman
Côte d'Eich
Blvd. de la Foire
Avenue de la Porte-Neuve
Blvd. Royal
Rue Laurent Menager
Rue Vauban
Rue Jules Wilhelm
Avenue Emile Rueter
Henri
Rue des Capucins
Blvd. Royal
Grand Rue
Blvd. Prince
Blvd. Aldringen
Rue Philippe II
Place du Théâtre
Rue du Marché-aux-Herbes
Rue du Fossé
Rue Mohrfels
Rue Sosthène Weis
Montée de Pfaffenthal
Montée de Clausen
Avenue Monterey
Place d'Armes
Rue du Curé
Place Guillaume II
Rue Notre-Dame
Blvd. F.D. Roosevelt
Place de Clairefontaine
Rue du Saint-Esprit
Rue Sosthène Weis
Alzette
Rue de Trèves
Place de Bruxelles
Place de la Constitution
Avenue Marie-Thérèse
Pont Adolphe
Vallée de la Pétrusse
Place de Metz
Place du Saint-Esprit
Pétrusse
Rue Saint Ulric
Rue de la Semois
Rue Goethe
Rue Saint Zithe
Avenue de la Liberté
Blvd. de la Pétrusse
Rue Heine
Rue de Prague
Viaduc
Blvd. d'Avranches
Rue du Laboratoire
Blvd. de la Pétrusse
Rue Michel Rodange
Place des Martyrs
Rue de la Semois
Rue Michel Welter
Rue Adolphe Fischer
Rue d'Anvers
Place de Paris
Avenue de la Gare
Rue du Fort Neipperg
Rue de Bonnevoie
Rue des Trèvires
Rue de la Vallée
Rue Glesener
Rue Pierre Hentges
Blvd. Dr. Charles Marx
Rue de Strasbourg
Rue Joseph Junck
Rue de Reims
Rue du Commerce
Place de la Gare
Rue des Romains
Rue du Antoine Godart
Rue de Bonnevoie
Rue de Hollerich

Auberge de Jeunesse (HI), 2, rue du Fort Olisy (tel. 22 68 89). Take bus 9 from airport or train station to Vallée d'Alzette below rue Sigefroi. Can be noisy, but has exceptionally friendly staff. Clean dorms and rooms for families and groups. 3 day max. stay if it's full. Reception open 7:30-9:30am and 3pm-midnight. Lockout 9:30am-2pm. No curfew. 350LF, over 26 420LF. Breakfast included. Packed lunch 110LF. Dinner 230LF. Lockers 500LF or passport deposit. Bike rental 400LF.

Hotel Carlton, 9, rue de Strasbourg (tel. 48 48 02). From the station, up av. de la Liberté and left on rue de Strasbourg. Cheapest rooms in the city and beautiful ones, at that. A hearty breakfast is included in an elegant dining room. Lobby with stained-glass windows; clean rooms. 24hr. reception. Singles 650-850LF, with shower 1100-1250LF. Doubles 1500LF. Make reservations.

Hotel Papillon, 9, rue Jean Origier (tel. 49 44 90). From the station, north on av. de la Gare and left on rue Jean Origier. Decently large rooms, each with shower and plastic furniture resembling a Barbie doll play set. Singles 1050LF. Doubles 1600LF. Breakfast included.

Auberge Le Parisien, 46, rue Ste. Zithe (tel. 49 23 97), 5min. from the station, off pl. de Paris. Small rooms, all with TV. Singles 1000LF, with shower 1150LF. Doubles 1600LF, with shower 1750LF. Breakfast included. Open Jan. 9-Dec. 22.

Camping: Kockelscheuer (tel. 47 18 15). Bus 2 from the station. 90LF, children 50LF, 100LF per tent. Hot showers included. Wheelchair access. Open Easter-Oct.

Most restaurants in the area are crowded with Luxembourgeois with money to spend. But, with a little searching, you can get back down to earth. **EMS,** 30, pl. de la Gare, packs in the locals with local specialties such as smoked Ardennes ham. **Bella Napol,** 4, rue de Strasbourg, is home to cheap pizza and pasta. 180LF will get you a basic pizza. **Le Gaugin,** 8, pl. Guillaume, may turn out to be your "fauve-erate" restaurant, with all sorts of Italian delights. From pizza to tortellini and lasagna, you'll get cheap dishes from 200LF. (Open 11am-midnight.) For a touch of high class without those prices, try **Restaurant Bacchus,** 32, Marché-aux-Herbes, situated directly across from the Grand-Ducal palace, where you can get meals from 200LF. In general, the area around the **Place d'Armes** is nice for dining since the area is filled with terraces and frequent live music. For a more tranquil meal, try packing a picnic lunch from the giant subterranean supermarket **Nobilis,** 47, av. de la Gare, and finding a nice spot in the parks by the ravine (open Mon.-Fri. 9am-7:30pm, Sat. 9am-7pm).

SIGHTS AND ENTERTAINMENT

Luxembourg is gearing up for its year as 1995's Cultural Capital of Europe. Visitors should expect newly renovated buildings, and a myriad of art and music shows. The tourist office offers two different well-organized walking tours: one that begins and ends at the station, and another that traipses around the outskirts of the city. Both tours include Luxembourg's precious **Bock-Casemates,** which are actually a good sight despite the fact that every Luxembourg brochure is saturated with "visit the casemates!" pleas. Looming imposingly over the Alzette River valley, this fortress (part of Luxembourg's original castle, dating back to the 10th century) sheltered 35,000 people while the rest of the city was pounded during WWII. (Entrance on rue Sigefroi near the bridge that leads to the hostel. Open March-Oct. 10am-5pm. 50LF.) If that isn't enough, follow up by descending into the **Pétrusse Casemates,** on the place de la Constitution. Dating back to the 1600s, these fortifications were built by the Spanish and later improved by the Austrians. (Open July-Sept.) Get back above ground and check out the **Citadel of the Holy Ghost,** visible from the Viaduc bridge or from the valley, an imposing medieval barracks planted midway up the side of a cliff, or the **Notre Dame Cathedral,** off bd. F.D.R. You won't find Quasimodo lumbering around the eaves of this church's three towers, only the centerpiece of a 17th-century Jesuit college. Both sights are closed to visitors. The **Musée National d'Histoire et d'Art,** houses a curious mix of local art (mostly modern), ancient ruins, and all sorts of rocks, minerals, and scientific equipment. Most importantly, it's free. (Open Tues.-Fri. 10am-4:45pm, Sat. 2-4:45pm, and Sun. 10-11:45am and 2-4:45pm.) The most beautiful and impressive sights in the city may well be in the many parks lining the valleys. Walk along windy, shady paths to multiple splendid viewpoints. *La Semaine à Luxembourg,* available in the city tourist office, provides a guide to the week's events. You'll have to bust out of the old city if you want to bust out at all at night. Some sleepy bars line the intensely beige **Bisserweg** and **rue St. Ulric** down in the valley, but **Scott's Pub and Restaurant,** 4, Bisserweg (tel. 22 64 74) defies stodgy Luxembourg traditions and really rocks. It's just like a bit of England planted in the heart of Luxembourg, where pints of Guinness flow freely and the locals shoot the bull at the bar and shoot darts at the board. (Open noon-1am; English pub grub 300-350LF.)

Across the valley lie the city's clubs. Mosh in Morocco or dance to Techo in Tunisia at the **Casablanca,** 36, bd. d' Avranches (open Wed., Fri., Sat. 10pm-3am). **Melusina,** 145, rue Tour Jacob, is more of a student's dance club, substituting more rock for techno (open 7pm-late). Expect about a 200LF cover charge at both clubs.

■■■ THE COUNTRYSIDE

In 1944, the bloody Battle of the Bulge raged through the country, mashing the Ardennes forest into slime and mud. Now, 50 years later, the new-growth forest is as verdant as ever, its thick greenery only broken by Luxembourg's many small, shallow rivers. Sun, water, and ancient castles draw hordes of German tourists, and visitors from all over the rest of the world. However, bus and train travel is relatively intermittent and infrequent. Buy a one-day pass for 140LF and try to cover all the one-sight towns in one sweep. Trains do grind regularly between Luxembourg and Ettelbrück (1 per hr., 1hr., 105LF), but you'll need to take the hot, brown CFL buses to the smaller towns. (Luxembourg-Echternach 1hr., 105LF; Ettelbrück-Echternach 30min., 105LF; Echternach-Vianden 50min., 105LF; Ettelbrück-Vianden 30min., 70LF; Echternach-Grevenmacher 40min., 105LF, railpasses valid.)

■ ETTELBRÜCK

Ettelbrück offers little more than sleepy cafés and uninteresting shops, but its train and bus stations serve as a hub for the rest of the country. The **tourist office** is right by the station at 1, pl. de la Gare (tel. 820 68; open Mon.-Fri. 9am-noon and 1:30-5pm). The **HI Youth Hostel,** (tel. 822 69) off rue Grande Duchesse Joséphine-Charlotte (a street name that's much more impressive than the hostel) about halfway up the hill at #48. After tromping 1½km from the station, the climb up the steep staircase may give you that coronary you've been looking for. The rooms are clean and comfortable, but the staff could be more friendly. (Reception open 5-6pm and 8:16-9:15pm. Curfew 11pm. 320LF; 380LF if over 26. Open mid-March to mid-Oct. and early Dec. to mid-Feb.) **Camp** in Ettelbrück at **Kalkesdelt** (tel. 821 85; 100LF per person, 100LF per site; free showers; open April-Sept.). **Hostels** lurk in the woods at **Beaufort,** 6, rue de l'Auberge (tel. 860 75); **Bourglinster,** 2, rue de Gonderange (tel. 781 46); **La Rochete,** 45, Osterbour (tel. 870 81); **Hollenfels,** 2, rue du Château (tel. 30 70 37); **Lultzhausen,** (tel. 894 24); and **Wilz,** 6, rue de la Montagne (tel. 95 80 39). Most tourist offices have a brochure with all hostels, their addresses, and a brief description of their facilities.

■ THE MOSELLE AND SURE VALLEYS

The **Moselle Valley,** with its sunny weather and abundance of water, was discovered by French winemakers as a suitable substitute for the Champagne region of France. Now, the region is itself renowned for its still wines like *Riesling* and *Pinot Gris,* and for its sparkling wines (only wines made in the Champagne region of France can use the term *champagne;* often you'll find sparkling wines marked *méthode champenoise*). The village of **Grevenmacher,** once home to a training ground for the *greven* (a second-class form of nobility), is right in the center of this

LUXEMBOURG

wine culture and makes an excellent base to explore the famous vineyards. The best place to begin your exploration is on a tour of the **Bernard-Massard winery,** rue du Vin, right next to the bridge. Here, you'll get a long visual presentation (in English) about the history of the area, and then head into the dark fermentation cellar where thousands of bottles wait up to three years to become just right. You'll learn all about the champagne method, but more importantly, you'll indulge in a glass at the end of the tour. (Open April-Oct. 9am-noon and 2-6pm; 80LF.)

The **HI Hostel** at Grevenmacher, 15 Gruewereck (tel. 752 22) is an excellent hostel co-owned by a friendly man who sounds uncannily like Arnold Schwarzenegger. The rooms are clean and intimate, and the family makes you feel at home. Turn left from the bus stop and walk through the pedestrian district to the fountain, then turn right and follow that road to the end. At the "T" turn right and 5m away are rickety steps leading up to the hostel. (Rooms 320LF; no curfew; reception open after 5pm. Say "hi" to Ricky, who'll be 3 in Sept.) Few buses or trains run through this secluded valley, but **riverboats** glide along regularly on the placid Moselle (Grevenmacher-Remich 240LF, round-trip 370LF). Pick up a schedule at the fully stocked hostel. Buses run to Grevenmacher from Echternach throughout the day (105LF).

If you tire of the Moselle, tackle the **Sûre River,** where kayaking is readily available. Be forewarned, there will be no barrel-rolling in these plastic rental behemoths, just a lot of paddling. **The Outdoor Center,** by the station in **Diekirch** (a short ride from Ettelbrück) at 34, ave de Gare. It's a 6hr. paddle to the destination, so get there early. (1-seaters 650LF; 2-seaters 1000LF; lifejacket 50LF; 50LF *Let's Go* discount.) The shop will pick up kayaks but not people at the final destination, so stay in Echternach to avoid the bus trip back to Diekirch.

■ VIANDEN

Victor Hugo found Vianden "consoling and magnificent." There's no arguing with the man that the city has more than its share of beauty. The village spills down a steep hill beneath a renovated 9th-century **château** containing an exhibit on its own history. Dutch tourists crowd the riverside and Dutch dishes are served in the restaurants, all because Vianden is the ancestral home of the Orange-Nassau dynasty, rulers of Holland and (in the person of William III) England as well. (Château open 10am-6pm. Oct. 10am-5pm, Nov.-Dec. 10am-4pm, Jan.-Feb. open only on weekends and holidays, March daily 11am-5pm. 110LF, students 80LF.) The **tourist office** (tel. 842 57) is in the **Victor Hugo House,** on rue de la Gare, beside the bridge over the River Our (open July-Aug. and April-Oct. Fri.-Wed. 9:30am-noon and 2-6pm, Nov.-March Wed. and Fri. 2-6pm, Sat. 9:30am-noon). Ride Vianden's **télésiège** (chairlift) from rue de Sanatorium, 500m upstream from the tourist office (round-trip 150LF, one-way with easy hike down 90LF, students 90LF and 60LF; open Easter to mid-Oct. 10am-6pm, July-Aug. 10am-7pm). The ascent affords a phenomenal photo opportunity of the château and, with a small hike, Europe's largest hydroelectric plant, the **Barrage.** The **HI youth hostel,** 3, Montée du Château (tel. 841 77), sits atop a large hill beneath the castle; cross the bridge from the tourist office and follow the Grande Rue until it curves to the left and ends. In early summer the hostel accepts many groups and often has no space left for individual trekkers; call ahead. (Reception open 5-9pm or later if you call ahead. 320LF, over 26 380LF. Sheets 100LF. Open Feb.-Nov.) Numerous cheap hotels litter the Grande Rue; the tourist office lists rooms in private homes (singles from 800LF, doubles 1000LF), but you can find cheaper rooms yourself. **Camp op dem Deich** (tel. 843 75), a 5min. hike downstream from the tourist office, offers campsites in the shadows of the château on both banks of the river. (120LF per person and per tent. Open Easter-Sept.)

The Netherlands (Nederland)

US$1	= fl.74 (guilders, or NLG)	fl =	US$0.57
CDN$1	= fl.29	fl =	CDN$0.77
UK£1	= f2.76	fl =	UK£0.36
IR£1	= f2.73	fl =	IR£0.37
AUS$1	= fl.13	fl =	AUS$0.75
NZ$1	= fl.05	fl =	NZ$0.95
SAR1	= f0.49	fl =	SAR2.05
Country Code: 31		**International Dialing Prefix: 09**	

The Dutch say that God created the rest of the world but that they created the Netherlands. The country is, indeed, a feat of engineering, and since most of it is below sea level, vigorous pumping and a series of dikes have created thousands of square kilometers of land (including Amsterdam) that were once under water. What was once inhabited by seaweed and cod is now littered with cows, cheese, windmills, and the occasional city. During the Age of Exploration, Dutch conquerors fanned out over the globe, as the Dutch East and West India companies traded as far afield as Java, the Caribbean, and Africa. This exploration resulted in the prosperity and wealth of the Dutch Golden Age. During this time, Holland became home to Europe's religious and political dissidents. This intellectual freedom spawned the masterpieces of Rembrandt and Vermeer and the philosophies of Descartes and Spinoza. Since then, the Dutch have continued to race ahead and push social frontiers. Recovering from the devastating effects of two world wars, the Dutch raised their cities with the stark, modernistic influence of Mondriaan's De Stijl school and the architecture of Mies van der Rohe. Now, where craters and rubble once lay, modern buildings gleam and tower. But, outside of the cities, the countryside is still dotted and crossed with the same ancient towns and winding canals that have existed for centuries.

GETTING THERE AND GETTING AROUND

Trains, Buses, and Trams NS, the efficient rail authority, runs up to four trains per hour between major cities. Intercity trains generally cruise nonstop, *sneltreins* trace the fastest route between two points, and *stoptreins* pause in most or all of the villages along the way. **Eurail** is valid. A round-trip ticket is valid only on the day of issue. **Day Trip** (or **Rail Idee**) programs, available at train stations in spring and summer, allow you to pay an all-inclusive, reduced price for a round-trip train ticket, entrance fees for attractions, and often, connecting transport and a snack.

Euro Domino Holland is a card for 3 (f83), 5 (f138.50), or 10 (f277) days unlimited rail travel in the period of 1 month. During June, July, and August, the **Zomertoer** pass kicks in with 3 travel days in a 10-day period for 1 (f104) or 2 (f149) people. Travel like hell, or it may not pay off. More feasible may be the **Multi Rover** card that 2-6 people can use for one day of unlimited travel (f96-162). So, grab some friends and get to it. If you have no friends, get a 1 or 7 day **Rail Rover** which allows unlimited travel for 1 or 7 consecutive days (1 day f63, with public transportation f69.50; 7 days f152, with public transportation f177). Other passes offer a "plus" package, where for 20% extra, you get use of trams and other public transportation.

A nationalized fare system covers city buses, trams, and long-distance buses. The country is divided into zones; you need a certain number of *strippenkaart* (strip tickets) depending on the number of zones through which you travel. The base charge is 2 strips, and travel to smaller towns can exceed 20 strips. Bus and tram drivers sell 2-strip (f3), 3-strip (f4.25), and 8-strip tickets (f11). Tickets are *much* cheaper (15-strip ticket f11, 45-strip ticket f31) from public transportation counters, post offices, and some tobacco shops and newsstands (look for a *strippenkaart* sign). You can have the bus driver validate two 10-strip tickets as a day-ticket, good for unlimited travel anywhere in the country, or, during the summer, buy a *Zommer Zwerfkaart* from the driver with the same effect (f15). Riding without a ticket can result in a f60 fine plus the original cost of the ticket.

Cycling and Hitchhiking Cycling is the way to go in the Netherlands. Distances between cities are short, the countryside is flat, and most streets have separate bike lanes. One-speed bikes abound (f8 per day or f40 per week, deposit f50-200); utter flatness (except near the coast) renders 3-speeds unnecessary. Eighty train stations rent bicycles (same prices) upon presentation of your train ticket or railpass. Call the station a day ahead to reserve; phone numbers are in the free booklet *Fiets en Trein*. Purchasing a used bike (about f140) and then reselling it may prove more thrifty than renting one. **Hitchhiking,** where allowed, appears to be generally swift, except out of Amsterdam, where competition is cutthroat.

NETHERLANDS ESSENTIALS

The **VVV** tourist information offices inhabit buildings marked by blue triangular signs. The VVV, as well as museums themselves, sell the one-year **Museumkaart,** good for admission to over 400 Dutch museums (except special exhibitions) and discounts on various cultural events (f40, under 18 f15, over 64 f25). The **Cultureel Jongeren Paspoort (CJP)** entitles those under 26 to reduced rates at museums and cultural events (f20, valid 1 yr.) and is available at the VVV or the **Amsterdam Uit Buro (AUB),** Leidseplein 26. Bring a passport-size photo for either card.

A profusion of women's centers, coffeehouses, and crisis lines exist, particularly in Amsterdam and the university towns. Check *Man to Man* (f15), available in book-stores or directly from the publisher at Spuistr. 21, Amsterdam, for listings of ser-vices for gay men. Travelers with disabilities should obtain the VVV's free and thorough pamphlet, *Holiday in Holland for the Handicapped.*

Drugs are illegal in this country, despite what you may see, hear, and smell. Although police largely ignore the soft drug scene, possession of up to 30g of hash-ish will make you subject to fines, and possession of more than this amount is a seri-ous offense. Dutch police consider hard drugs a different category altogether and punish offenders accordingly.

Although most Dutch speak English extremely well, do try out their native tongue, which resembles German. "Yes" = *ja;* "no" = *nee;* "please" = *alstublieft;* "thanks a lot" = *dank u wel;* "hello" = *hallo;* "bathroom" = *toiletten;* "bread" = *broodje;* and "cheese" = *kaas.* Most Dutch (especially those in service jobs) will use *alstublieft* as "thank you"; a simple "hi" is *hoy;* and, avoid looking like an idiot at doors by knowing *duwen* = "push" and *trekken* = "pull." Dutch coins have names, just like in the U.S. and Canada: the *stuiver* (5¢), *dubbeltje* (10¢), *kwartje* (25¢), and *rijksdaalder* (f2.50). You can make international calls from pay **phones,** which take 25¢ and f1 coins. For directory assistance, dial 06 80 08 (within the Nether-lands) or 06 04 18 (international); for collect calls, dial 06 04 10. To reach AT&T's **USADirect,** dial 06, wait for a tone then dial 022 91 11. For MCI's **WorldPhone,** dial 06 022 91 22; for **SprintExpress** 06 022 91 91; for **Canada Direct** 06 022 91 16; for **BT Direct** 06 022 99 44; and for **SA Direct** 06 022 02 27.

Banks are open weekdays from 10am to 4pm and usually on Thursday from 6 to 8pm or 7 to 9pm. Post offices, generally open weekdays from 9am to 5pm, exchange money at reasonable rates for a commission. Most shops and supermar-kets are open Monday afternoons, Tuesday to Friday from 9am to 6pm, and Saturday 9am to 5pm. Most museums are open Tuesday to Sunday from 9am to 5pm. Shops close for standard European holidays, as well as the Queen's Birthday (April 30), Ascension Day (May 25, 1995), and Whit Sunday and Monday (June 4-5, 1995). All of Holland flocks to Amsterdam to celebrate the Queen's birthday, New Year's Day, and Liberation Day (May 5).

Accommodations and Camping The VVV supply accommodations lists, can nearly always find you a room, and will make reservations in other cities (f4 fee). A room in a private home costs about two thirds as much as a hotel, but may not be available everywhere; check with the VVV. During July and August many cities levy a f2.50 "tourist tax," added to the price of all rooms. The country's best values are the 42 **youth hostels** run by the **NJHC (Dutch Youth Hostel Federation),** set into three price categories based on quality and charm (f20-23 for bed and breakfast, plus high-season and prime-location supplements). The VVV has a hostel list and the useful *Jeugdherbergen* brochure describes each one (both free). Contact the NJHC at Prof. Tulpplein 4, Amsterdam (tel. (020) 551 31 55; open Mon.-Fri. 9am-5pm). Youth hostel cards are available at hostels (f27.50; bring a passport photo). **Camp-ing** is possible all over the country (the VVV lists campgrounds), but many sites are crowded and trailer-ridden in summer.

Food and Drink Dutch food is hearty and simple: plenty of meat, potatoes, vegetables, bread, cheese, and milk. Pancakes, salted herring, and pea soup are national specialties. Dutch cheeses transcend *gouda* and *edam;* nibble *leiden,* the mild *belegen,* and the creamy *kernhem,* too. Slices of cold meat and fresh cheese on bread with a soft-boiled egg make for a typical breakfast. For a hearty brunch, order an *uitsmijter,* a dish which piles salad, ham, cheese, and eggs on one plate. At din-ner, reap the benefits of Dutch imperialism: *rijsttafel* is an Indonesian specialty comprising up to 25 different dishes, such as curried chicken or lamb with pineap-

NETHERLANDS

ple, served on a mountain of rice. Or try *pannekoeken,* the traditional Dutch supper of buttery, sugary, golden brown pancakes. Wash it all down with a foamy mug of hometown beers Heineken and Amstel or *jenever,* a strong gin made from juniper berries and traditionally accompanied by eel. In any of the many university towns in Holland, you can eat cheaply and plentifully at student *mensas* when school is in session.

■■■ AMSTERDAM

Amsterdam. Just the name conjures up more images of sugarplums in young travellers' heads than any night before Christmas could. The reputation is so great that you don't really know what to expect as you step off the train in Centraal Station. You half expect to be marauded by an army of pushers and dealers, while simultaneously being solicited by those who live behind the red-light glass. And, in a way, you're pretty disappointed when all you're greeted by are huge lines at the VVV, sadistic bell-ringing cyclists, a maze of twisting streets, identical canals, and, God forbid, old buildings, beautiful museums, and *culture.*

Some people say that the best vacation to Amsterdam is the one you can't remember, but a stay in the city can yield much more than bacchanalian pleasure. You'll remember the orange-clad Dutch soccer fans and quiet walks through the artsy Jordaan, admiring the quirky cafés and galleries. Ah, and who will ever forget the museums—the stirring Anne Frank house, and the inspired Van Goghs? More than these sights however, you'll remember the atmosphere: the heavy aroma of cannabis wafting from the coffeeshops, the red-light district, crazy people from every corner of the planet, and fast-food vending machines. Explore the city—let curiosity, not intimidation, be your guide to one of the most exciting cities in the world.

ORIENTATION AND PRACTICAL INFORMATION

Amsterdam is a major international transportation center, with budget flights all over the world (especially southeast Asia) and trains all over Europe. Emerging from the train station, you will land on **Damrak,** a key thoroughfare that leads to the **Dam,** Amsterdam's main square. Concentric canals ripple out around the Dam and **Centraal Station,** so that the city resembles a horseshoe with the train station at the open northern end. Radiating out from the station, the canals lined by streets of the same name are **Singel, Herengracht, Keizergracht,** and **Prinsengracht.**

The areas around the train station and up Damrak are the easiest places to lose money, cameras, and credit cards. Don't head immediately left of the train station (into the red light district) until you've locked up your bags either at the train station or where you'll be staying. Pickpockets run rampant between the VVV and the station, and unattended baggage may disappear. Take an extra minute to organize yourself—the hash isn't going anywhere. Women traveling alone should avoid the train station at night. Seek out larger coed dorms; there's often safety in numbers. Amsterdam has some of the best nightlife in Europe, but use your brains as well as your beer-drinking skills. The police are extremely helpful, so report all thefts.

Amsterdam is best conquered by foot or bike. The names of streets change capriciously; buy a *Falk Plan* (f7.50) at the VVV or more cheaply at magazine stands (f4.95). *Use It* (f2.50) includes a map, info on inexpensive accommodations, an index of youth agencies, and news about the city. While illegal, marijuana and hashish are tolerated and readily available at cafés and coffeeshops (listed in the *Mellow Pages,* available at bookstores). Ignore street dealers who will undoubtedly approach you; street hash is usually of poor quality or laced with something else. For information on the legal ins and outs of the Amsterdam drug scene, call the Jellinek clinic at 570 23 55. Anyone with drug-related health problems should call 555 55 55.

Tourist Office: VVV, Stationsplein 10 (tel. 06 340 340 66; open 9am-5pm), in front of Centraal Station, to the left. Try to book your own rooms; they can be ret-

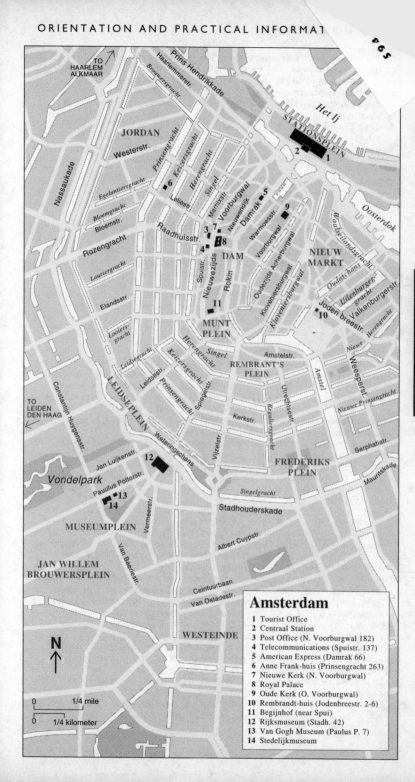

Amsterdam

1 Tourist Office
2 Centraal Station
3 Post Office (N. Voorburgwal 182)
4 Telecommunications (Spuistr. 137)
5 American Express (Damrak 66)
6 Anne Frank-huis (Prinsengracht 263)
7 Nieuwe Kerk (N. Voorburgwal)
8 Royal Palace
9 Oude Kerk (O. Voorburgwal)
10 Rembrandt-huis (Jodenbreestr. 2-6)
11 Begijnhof (near Spui)
12 Rijksmuseum (Stadh. 42)
13 Van Gogh Museum (Paulus P. 7)
14 Stedelijkmuseum

N
↑

0 _____ 1/4 mile
0 _____ 1/4 kilometer

icent about budget alternatives (hefty f5 fee plus a f5 deposit). Sells maps (f3.50) and tickets, changes money (poor rates), and plans excursions. Get *What's On,* a fabulous listing of all events in Amsterdam (f3.50). Go early to skirt long lines. Open 9am-11pm; Easter-June and Sept. Mon.-Sat. 8am-8:30pm; Oct.-May 9am-5pm. **Branch offices,** Leidestr. 106, at Korte Leidsedwarsstr, open 9am-9pm and in Centraal station, open 8am-9pm.

Budget Travel: NBBS, Rokin 38 (tel. 624 09 89 or 620 50 71). Budget student flights. Open Mon.-Fri. 9:30am-5:30pm, Sat. 10am-4pm; mid-Aug. to mid-May closes Sat. at 3pm. Credit cards not accepted. **Budget Bus/Eurolines,** Rokin 10 (tel. 627 51 51). Good deals on Euroline buses. Open Mon.-Fri. 9:30am-5:30pm, Sat. 10am-4pm.

Consulates: U.S., Museumplein 19 (tel. 664 56 61). Open Mon.-Fri. 8:30am-noon and 1:30-3:30pm. **U.K.,** Koningslaan 44 (tel. 676 43 43). Open Mon.-Fri. 9am-noon and 2-4pm. **Australian, Canadian, New Zealand,** and **South African** embassies are in The Hague.

Currency Exchange: Your best bet is the American Express office (see below). For after-hours banking try **Change Express,** Damrak 86 (tel. 624 66 82), for fine rates with a 3% commission. Open 8am-midnight. **Branch offices** at Kalverstr. 150 (open 8am-8pm), and Leidestr. 106 (open 8am-midnight). The **GWK** office at Centraal Station has worse rates but is open 24hrs. Avoid the **Chequepoint** booths' outrageous commissions (up to 10%).

American Express: Damrak 66 (tel. 520 77 77). Excellent rates, no commission on any brand of traveler's checks. Open Mon.-Fri. 9am-5pm, Sat. 9am-noon. Cash machine for cardholders. **Branch Office,** Van Baerlestr. 28, is near the museums and much less crowded. Both cash checks, but only Damrak holds mail. Open Mon.-Fri. 9am-5pm, Sat. 10am-4pm.

Post Office: Singel 250-256 (tel. 556 33 11), at Raadhuisstr. behind the Dam, holds Poste Restante. Open Mon.-Fri. 9am-9pm, Sat. 9am-noon. **Postal Code:** 1016 AB.

Telephones: Public phones can be found outside Centraal Station or at the post office. Call first and pay afterward at **Telehouse,** Raadhuisstr. 48-50, near the Dam (open 24hrs.), or **TeleTalk Center,** Leidsestr. 101, near the Leidseplein (open 10am-midnight). Both handle faxes. **City Code:** 020.

Flights: Schiphol Airport (tel. 06 350 33 08 for charters; 350 34 05 for other flights). Trains connect to Centraal Station (every 15min., 16min., f2.50).

Trains: Centraal Station, Stationsplein 1, at the end of the Damrak opposite the tourist office. Lockers f4, large f6. For international information and reservations, get a number at the booth, then wait in the office until you're called. In summer, expect waits as long as 1hr. Open for domestic and international information Mon.-Fri. 8am-10pm, Sat.-Sun. 9am-8pm; reservations Mon.-Fri. 8am-8pm, Sat.-Sun. 9am-5pm. For info, call (02) 92 96 (international) or (06) 92 92 (domestic).

Buses: Trains are usually quicker and more convenient. The **GVB** (see Public Transportation) will tell you if your destination lies on a rail line. If it doesn't, they'll direct you to a bus departure point. **Muiderpoort** (2 blocks east of Ooster-park) serves destinations to the east; **Marnixstation** (at the corner of Marnixstr. and Kinkerstr.), the west; and **Stationsplein depot,** the north and south.

Public Transportation: Trams, buses, *nachtbussen* (night buses), and 2 subway lines. Most tram and bus lines radiate from Centraal Station and retire at midnight; get a separate schedule for the *nachtbussen.* Don't buy your *strippenkaart* and *dagkaart* (Amsterdam day-passes, f12) on the bus because they charge up to 4 times as much. The **GVB,** Amsterdam's public transportation company, has an office on Stationsplein (tel. (06) 92 92 for transport info) which sells tickets and distributes the handy flyer *Public Transport.* Best deal for light travel over several days is the 15-strip card (f11). Open 8am-10:30pm, Sat.-Sun. 8am-10:30pm.

Taxis: tel. 677 77 77. Fares start at f5.80 plus f2.75 per km or min.; more at night.

Bike Rental: All **train stations** rent plain ol' bikes (f8 per day, f30-40 per week). **Damstraat Rent-a-Bike,** Pieter Jacobstr. 11, just off Damstr. (tel. 625 50 29), near the Dam; f12.50 per day, f50 per week, deposit f50 and passport; sells used bikes for f140-200. **Yellow Bike Tours,** N.Z. Voorburgwal 66 (tel. 620 69 40), offers 3hr. city tours at 9:30am and 1pm (f29) and 6½hr. countryside tours at 9am

and noon (f42.50) April-Oct. (reservations nece~~~
from Amstel station (tel. 692 35 84) for 7hr. trips~~~

Hitchhiking: Those hitching to Utrecht, central and~~~
gium take tram 25 to the end and start at the bridge.~~~
and northern Germany take bus 56 to Prins Bernhardp~~~
and start along Gooiseweg. Those going to the airport,~~~
take tram 16 or 24 to Stadionplein and start on the oth~~~
Amstelveenseweg. Those going to Haarlem, Alkmaar, and N~~~
22 to Haarlemmerweg and start from Westerpark. The **Inte**
ter, Nieuwezijds Voorburgwal 256, 1st floor (tel. 622 43 42),~~~
drivers for destinations all over Europe. Riders pay a f10 memb~~~ for a
year) plus money for gas. Open Mon.-Fri. 10am-6pm, Sat. 10am-2~~~

Bookstores: Mountains of paperbacks at the **American Discount Book Center,**
185 Kalverstr. Open Mon.-Wed. and Fri.-Sat. 10am-8pm, Thurs. 10am-10pm, Sun.
11am-6pm. Students get a 10% discount.

Laundry: Look for a *Wasserette* sign, or Oude Doelenstr. 12. Open Mon.-Fri.
8:30am-7pm, Sat. 10am-4pm; last load 1hr. before closing.

Gay and Lesbian Services: COC, Rozenstr. 14 (tel. 623 40 79 or 626 30 87). The
main source of info. Open Wed.-Thurs. 1-5pm, Fri. 9pm-4am, Sat.1-5pm. Coffee-
house on Wed. 8pm-midnight. The *Man to Man* guide (f15) has a "gay map" listing bars, shops, saunas, and more. Help for victims of violence or discrimination
available Wed. and Sun. 8pm-midnight (tel. 624 27 49). **Intermale,** Spuistr. 251
(tel. 625 00 09), is a gay bookstore. Open Mon. noon-6pm, Tues.-Sat. 10am-6pm.
Gay and Lesbian Switchboard (tel. 623 65 65) is answered 10am-10pm.

Crises: The **Opvang Sexueel Geweld** counsels women threatened by violence
and is a **rape crisis** hotline (tel. 612 75 76; 10:30am-11:30pm). **Drug counseling,**
Binnenkant 46 (tel. 624 47 75), 10min. from Centraal Station, near the Oosterdok.
Open Mon.-Fri. 10am-5pm.

Medical Assistance: Tourist Medical Service (tel. 695 56 38), 24hr. For hospital
care, call **Academisch Medisch Centrum,** Meibergdreef 9 (tel. 566 91 11), near
the Holendrecht metro stop. For free emergency medical care, visit the **Kruis-**
post, Oudezijds Voorburgwal 129 (tel. 624 90 31). Open 10am-12:30pm and
6:45pm-11pm. **Sexually Transmitted Disease Clinic** at Groenburgwal 44 (tel.
555 58 22; open Mon.-Fri. 8-10:30am). Free and confidential. **AIDS Hotline,** (tel.
060 22 22 20; open Mon.-Fri. 2pm-10pm).

Pharmacies: Everywhere. Open Mon.-Fri. 8:30am-5pm. When closed, each
apotheek (pharmacy) posts a sign directing you to the nearest open one.

Emergencies: tel. 06 11. **Police headquarters:** Elandsgracht 117 (tel. 559 91 11).

ACCOMMODATIONS AND CAMPING

Amsterdam is packed from late June to mid-September, but you can almost always
find a bed at the Sleep-In if the bazillions of hostels and student hotels are full. For
most, the best shot is to show up early in the morning or to book a room from
another HI hostel and pay for it in advance. Both the HI and Christian hostels have
huge, clean rooms, and curfews; the Christian hostels' single-sex dorms are safer,
less wild, and easily the best bargain in town. Private hostels generally charge more
for later (or nonexistent) curfews, and more laid-back atmospheres. Almost all
places lower their rates about f2.50 in the off-season; *Let's Go* lists summer prices. If
you arrive at night, just stay in a neighboring city.

In both institutional and private hostels, keep tabs on your valuables at all times.
Use the lockers wherever provided; some will require your own padlock, available
at **HEMA** (a department store behind the Damrak American Express) for f7-25. At
the station and tourist office you'll be accosted by people offering all kinds of lodgings; many are from reputable hostels, but be cautious. The legitimate ones usually
carry printed cards bearing their hostel's address and prices: always ask to see the
card before you follow, carry your own luggage, and never pay before you look.

NETHERLANDS

...nal Hostels

...an Youth Hostel Eben Haëzer, Bloemstr. 179 (tel. 624 47 17), 1 street ...om Rozengracht. Take tram 13 or 17 to Marnixstr. A pristine bargain with a clean-cut, cheery staff. Happiness will be pummeled into your head with a mallet of love, but you can always vent your Generation-X anger elsewhere. Hot, filling breakfasts with French toast. Rooms close 10am-2pm, but the lobby and snack bar stay open. Curfew midnight, Fri.-Sat. 1am. Ages 16-35 f15. Showers and breakfast included. Dinner f8.50. Lockers f10 deposit.

Jeugdherberg Vondelpark (HI), Zandpad 5 (tel. 683 17 44), on a sleepy street bordering Vondelpark. Take tram 1, 2, or 5 to Leidseplein, then cross the Stadhouderskade and walk 2 streets to the left. Facilities include kitchen and small library. Recently renovated and lookin' pretty slick. They have a new hi-tech locker system. Avoid the park at night. Bar open 7pm-12:30am, happy hour 8-9pm. Reception open 7am-12:30am. Lockout 10:45am-3:30pm. Curfew 2am. f24, nonmembers f29. Breakfast included. Sheets f6. Lockers f1 per day; deposit f10.

Christian Youth Hostel "The Shelter," Barndesteeg 21-25 (tel. 625 32 30), off the Nieuwmarkt, amid the red lights. Larger and looser than Eben Haëzer, with snack bar (open 8am-2pm and 2:30-11:30pm) and cozy courtyard. Huge clean dorms with happy religious slogans. Strictly enforced midnight curfew, 1am on Fri. and Sat. Ages 16-35 f15. Showers, sheets, and breakfast included. Lockers f1; deposit f10.

Jeugdherberg Stadsdoelen (HI), Kloveniersburgwal 97 (tel. 624 68 32, fax 639 01 35), between Nieuwmarkt and Rembrandtsplein. Take tram 4, 9, 16, 24, or 25 to Muntplein. Spacious, clean, and central but becoming a bit shabby and worn. Rebuffs tour groups. Bar with pool table and daily happy hour (8-9pm; beers f1.50). Reception open 7am-12:30am. Curfew 2am. f22.50, nonmembers f27.50 (July-Aug. f2.50 surcharge). Breakfast included. Sheets f6. Free lockers with passport or f25 deposit. Open mid-March to Jan. Reservations accepted but you must arrive by 4pm.

Private Hostels

The Flying Pig, Vossiusstr. 46-47 (tel. 400 41 87, fax 400 41 05) Take tram 1, 2, or 5 to the Leidseplein, cross the "Stadhouderskade," turn left, and it's your 3rd left. Next to the park, the newest of Amsterdam's hostels is clean and comfortable. Such modern touches as carpets set the pig apart from others. Dorm rooms start at f23.50 and go up to f26.50 for 6-person rooms. Sheets and lockers for a f10 deposit. Laundry and kitchen facilities available. Unfortunately, breakfast is an extra f6.50. Reserve ahead.

International Budget Hotel, Leidsegracht 76 (tel. 624 27 84). Take tram 1, 2, or 5 to Prinsengracht and walk 1 block to the right facing Leidseplein. Beautiful canal location. Reception open 9am-11pm. No curfew. f32.50 per person in 4-person dorm. Doubles f115. Showers and TV included.

Euphemia Budget Hotel, Fokke Simonszstr. 1-9 (tel. 622 90 45), 10min. from Leidseplein. Take tram 16, 24, or 25 to Prinsengracht (Weteringcircuit), cross back over Lijnbaansgracht, and turn right. Safe and comfortable, near the museums. Dorms f35. Doubles f95. Triples f135. Sheets included. Breakfast 9am-noon (f6.50). Reception open 8am-11pm. Bikes stored safely in the garden.

't Ancker, De Ruijterkade 100 (tel. 622 95 60). From the back exit of Centraal Station, walk to your right 80m. Super-fun Irish woman and her Dutch husband keep these rooms in shipshape condition, though somewhat noisy. Reception and bar open 24hrs. Dorms f35. Doubles f80. Sheets, lockers (deposit f10), and all-you-can-eat breakfast included. Free maps. Restaurant open 1-10pm (meals f4-20); bar food available all night.

Sleep-In, 's-Gravesandestr. 51-53 (tel. 694 74 44). Take trams 3, 6, 9, 10, or 14 to Mauritskade and walk back down Sarphatistr., or hop night bus 77. Major renovations have turned this place into a palace, complete with marble columns and art deco staircases, a recording studio, concert hall, and art gallery. However, plan to spend your experience with 60 of your closest friends. Can we say bedlam? Hip bands play Wed.-Sun. (f2.50 off cover if you're staying here); dances on Fri. Reception closed noon-1:30pm. f20 per person (60-bed dorms), f22.50 per per-

NETHERLANDS

son (8-20 bed dorms), f45 per person for a double. Breakfast f7. Lunch f8.50. Dinner f15. Sheets f5, f20 deposit. Information office open 9am-1pm and 4-9pm. Bike rental (f10 per day) open 10am-noon and 7-8pm. Free lockers.

Hotel Kabul, Warmoesstr. 38-42 (tel. 623 71 58), 5min. from Centraal Station, in the Red Light District. Huge, clean, and right in the thick of things. Bring a roll of string and use it, or you may never make it out of the dark maze of hallways again. Two swinging bars (meals f12.50); live bands Fri. and Sat. 24-hr. reception. No curfew. Dorms f23-32. Singles f67. Doubles f79-94. Triples f116. Breakfast f6.50 or f12.50. Key deposit f15. Safe for valuables (f1) and free lockers in the rooms.

Bob's Youth Hostel, Nieuwezijds Voorburgwal 92 (tel. 623 00 63), near the Dam and Centraal Station. Take tram 1, 2, 5, 13, or 17. Reception open 7:30am-3am. No smoking in rooms; you'll inhale enough going up the stairs. This is the place that keeps all the Amsterdam stories going. f10 deposit for door key. Curfew 3am. Dorms f21. Mattress on floor f18. Breakfast included. Dinner f5 (July-Aug. only). Free lockers (f25 deposit). No reservations.

Frisco Inn, Beursstr. 5 (tel. 620 16 10), brushing the Red Light District, close to the station. Cramped rooms and noisy bar but central location. Dorms f30-35. Doubles f70-75. Triples f90. Quads f120. Some rooms have private showers. Breakfast f12.50. Reception and bar open Mon.-Fri. 9am-1am, Sat.-Sun. 9am-2am.

Hotels

Hotel van Onna, Bloemgracht 102 (tel. 626 58 01), in the Jordaan. Take tram 13 or 17 from Centraal Station. Sparkling and new, the building was razed and built again from scratch. Ask for room 24 in the old section to see where the movie *Twice a Woman* with Anthony Perkins was filmed. Singles, doubles, triples, and quads f60 per person. Big breakfast in a canal-view dining room included. Reception open 8am-midnight. Phone reservations recommended.

Hotel Museumzicht, Jan Luykenstr. 22 (tel. 671 29 54). In a quiet neighborhood near the museums and chock-full of similar budget hotels. Doubles f100, with shower f115. Triples f120-145. Breakfast included. Reserve in advance.

Hotel Bema, Concertgebouwplein 19 (tel. 679 13 96, fax (020) 662 36 88), across from the Concertgebouw. Take tram 16 to Museumplein. Spacious, spotless rooms in an expensive part of town, near the museums. Friendly American owner. Singles f55-65. Doubles f85-110. Triples f125-135. Quads f170. Breakfast in bed included. Reserve in advance.

Hotel Groenendael, Nieuwendijk 15 (tel. 624 48 22), near the station. Friendly, clean, comfortable, and surrounded by the best Amsterdam vices. Singles f60. Doubles f85. Triples f120. Breakfast included. Reserve at least a week or two ahead—year-round.

Hotel Hortus, Plantage Parklaan 8 (tel. 625 99 96). Take tram 9 seven stops to the zoo. Dennis will fix you up in a pleasant, comfy room and see to it that you aren't bored by giving you free rein of the VCR, laserdisc player, and CD player. You may even get a room overlooking the botanical gardens. 24hr. reception. No curfew. Singles f55, doubles, triples, quads, and quints f40 per person. Most rooms have showers. Breakfast from 8:30-10am.

City Hotel, Utrechtsestr. 2 (tel. 627 23 23). Great location near Rembrandtsplein will move you away from tourist invasion. Reception open 8am-10pm. Singles f65. Doubles f95. Triples, quads, and quints f45 per person. No breakfast, but free coffee. Coin-operated TVs in every room.

Hotel Tamara, Nieuwezijda Voorburgwal 144 (tel. 624 24 84). Nice central location in the thick of it all. Run by a helpful Irish couple. The place shows its age a little, though. 24hr. reception. No curfew. Dorms f25. Singles f50. Doubles f70. Triples f90. Quads f120. Breakfast, shower, and sheets included. Bar happy hour from 7-8pm.

Hotel Ronnie, Raadhuisstr. 41b (tel. 624 28 21). Clean, but a bit rickety. Perhaps the staff could be a *bit* more informed. Singles f40-45. Doubles f80-90. Triples f120-135. Breakfast f7. 24hr. reception. Book in advance.

Pensions and Private Accommodations

Roommate's snoring keeping you up all night? Hate being part of the masses at the local Sleep-In? Sick of absorbing more noxious fumes than a catalytic convertor? Pack out to the cheap and wonderful pensions surrounding the city; it's well worth the time.

Ursula Schoniau, 134 Jan Evertstr. (tel. 612 25 27). Take tram 13 to Mercatorplein and you're right there. Staying with Ursula is a bit out of the ordinary; expect the unexpected. Breakfast will be a travel experience not to forget, and husband Henry cooks up a fantastic fried egg (provided you say "Good Morning" to him). Clean rooms, shower (8min.) and a great breakfast. f25. Only for stays of more than one night.

Pension Kil, Volendammerpad 19 (tel. (02993) 718 27). Take the NZH bus to Edam (7 strips). Violently verdant and eclectically eccentric, the living room has been transformed into a replica of the deepest jungle, complete with an aviary of songbirds. Helpful owner. Reception open 9am-11pm. f40 per person, Oct.-June f35-40 per person. Reserve ahead, especially in July-Sept. Breakfast and showers included.

Gerda Rikker-Kouwenhoren, Iepenlaan 16 (tel. (02993) 639 33). About 35min. by bus in beautiful downtown Volendam. Tastefully decorated living room and nice bedrooms with those dizzying 3-D pictures. Knowledgeable, helpful, and friendly owner. Central to Edam, Hoorn, and Zaanse Schaus for all you windmill lovers. f27.50 per person.

Camping

Camping Zeeburg, Zuider-Ijdijk 44 (tel. 694 44 30), next to the Amsterdam Rijn-canal. Direct ferry to Centraal Station, or take buses 22 or 37, or night bus 170. Youth-oriented, with periodic live music. Reception open 8am-11pm, April-June and Sept.-Aug. 9am-1pm and 5-9pm. f5 per person, f2.25 per tent. Showers f1.50.

Gaasper Camping, Loosdrechtdreef 7 (tel. 696 73 26), in the idyllic Gaasper Park, 20min. from Centraal Station by metro ("Gaasperplas") to the end, or night bus 75. Vast and fully rigged. f5 per person, f4.25 per tent. Showers f1.25. Washers and dryers f11. Reception open 9am-12:30pm and 1:30-9pm. Open mid-March to Dec.

FOOD

Dutch food ranges from the hopelessly bland to the oddly tasty. The closest you'll come to Dutch cuisine is the local **FEBO**. These self-service fast food stands are reasonably priced and vend little brown fried things that all look the same. Some are good, some are gross—steer clear of the burgers. *Frikandel* (fried sausage) usually costs as little as f1.50. Amsterdam is filled with restaurants of all different styles and nationalities. Taste Surinamian, Indonesian, Chinese, and Indian food in the red light district around the Nieuwmarkt and off the Dam, on streets such as Hartenstr. Indonesian *rijsttafel* here is ambrosia. *Eetcafés* strewn through Amsterdam purvey good meat-and-potatoes fare for f12-20, especially in the Jordaan. Bakeries vending inexpensive cheese croissants and magnificent breads cluster along Utrechtsestr. south of Prinsengracht.

Fruit, cheese, flowers, and sometimes even live chickens take over the **markets** on Albert Cuypstr., near the Heineken brewery (open Mon.-Sat. 9:30am-5pm); the VVV publish a list of markets in its Amsterdam brochure (f6.50). Shop for grocery essentials at the **Mignon Supermarket** at Leidsestr. 74-6 near Prinsengracht (open Mon. 11am-5pm, Tues.-Wed. and Sat. 9am-6pm, Thurs. 9am-9pm, and Fri. 9am-6:30pm); the **Big Banana Nightshop** across the street is more expensive, but open until 1am. Health food nuts will shop 'til they drop at **Met de Natuuraan Tafel,** Weteringschans 135 (open Mon. 11am-5pm, Tues.-Wed. and Fri. 9am-6pm, Thurs. 9am-9pm, and Sat. 9am-5pm). Some restaurants close during school vacations.

Atrium, Oude Zijds Achterburgwal 237, at Binnengasthuisstr. A huge, spotless university trough on the fringe of the red light district. Dinner f7.75. Meals served noon-2pm and 5-7pm; snack bar open 9am-7pm. Open Aug.-June.

Bojo, Lange Leidsedwarstr. 51, near the Leidseplein. Crowded at dinner-time with those seeking the terrific *rijstafel* (f13.50-15.50) and other Indonesian fare (f10-16.50). Open Sun.-Thurs. 5pm-2am, Fri.-Sat. 5pm-4am.

Vegetarish Eethuis "Sisters," Nes 102, 300m from Dam Sq. Two women and one cat run this cavernous, bohemian eatery. Daily vegetarian special (f12.50) usually disappears by 7pm. Open Mon.-Fri. noon-4pm and 5-9:30pm, Sat.-Sun. 2-9:30pm. Dinner f16-17. Dinner salads f8.50-11.

Egg Cream, Sint Jacobstr. 19, an alley off N.Z. Voorburgwal. Custom-built sandwiches f3-6.50; complete vegetarian dinner with salad f17. The apple crumble (f3.50) is the sweetest of Amsterdam's many sins. Open 11am-8pm.

The Pancake Bakery, Prinsengracht 191 (tel. 625 13 33), a canal-side block down from the Anne Frank Huis. Crowded with locals and out-of-towners. More than 50 filling varieties of the classic Dutch supper f6.50-18.50; omelettes f10-14. *Kersen* (cherry) or *mokkakaramel* pancakes make a killer dessert. Open noon-9:30pm.

Vishandel de Kreeft, Vijzelstr. 3, near Muntplein. A stand-up seafood counter that'll satisfy your salty, wet desires cheaply. Open Tues.-Sat. 10am-5:30pm.

Bolhoed, 60-62 Prinsengracht, across the canal from the Anne Frank house, specializes in organic vegetarian food (f10-20). Open noon-10pm.

Say Saté, Amstelstr. 26, a convenient hop from the *iT* disco. Specializing in the Indonesian *Rijstafel* (rice table, a collection of rice, noodles, and spices), and it's trademark *Saté,* a dish of skewered meat. Delicious and cheap at only f18-25 for a full meal. Open noon-11pm.

Pacifico, Warmoesstr. 31 (tel. 624 29 11). Remember the Alamo in this stucco Mexican eatery, the first in Europe. You *can* drink the water. Open 5:30-10pm. Dishes f15-35. Reserve ahead.

Leto, Haarlemmerijk 114. Out of the way and a bit hard to find. Their motto: "Don't keep the customer satisfied!" So, using reverse psychology, you should give it a try. Or don't. Open 5-11pm, Sat. 6-11pm, closed Mon.

SIGHTS

Amsterdam's former town hall, **Koninklijk Palace,** in the Dam, may be a symbol of the city's 17th century commercialism, but its majesty is topped by the **Magna Plaza** behind it, today's homage to commercialism (open Jun.-Aug. 12:30-4pm; f5). A visit to Amsterdam would be incomplete without a visit to the **Rijksmuseum,** and that's precisely why you'll have to use guerrilla fighting skills to make your way past the crowds to Rembrandt's famed militia portrait *The Night Watch (The Company of Captain Frans Banning Cocq).* Slide Shows every 25min. make it possible to handle such a bevy of art. (Open Tues.-Sat. 10am-5pm, Sun. 1-5pm; f10, under 18, over 65, and CJP holders f5.) **Rembrandthuis,** Jodenbreestr. 4-6 (at the corner of the Oude Schans Canal), is where the master lived, worked, and taught until the house was confiscated by the city for taxes. It holds 250 of Rembrandt's etchings and drypoints, as well as many of his tools and plates. (Open Mon.-Sat. 10am-5pm, Sun. 1-5pm; f5, under 17 f3.50.) Trace how a painter can fall deeper and deeper into insanity while his art gets better at the renowned **Van Gogh Museum** where you can ogle over 200 of his paintings (open Mon.-Sat. 10am-5pm, Sun. 1-5pm; f10, under 18, over 65, and CJP holders f5). Pull yourself up by your bootstraps and visit the **Tropenmuseum** (Museum of the Tropics), Linnaeusstr. 2, a seemingly incongruous center devoted to the emergence and problems of developing countries. Great for a guilt trip. (Open Mon.-Fri. 10am-5pm, Sat.-Sun. noon-5pm; f7.50, under 18, over 65, and CJP holders f3.50.)

Queue it up for the **Anne Frank Huis,** Prinsengracht 263, where thousands of visitors file through the rooms where the famous girl hid from the Nazis with her family until their capture in 1944. The 30-45min. line may quell some of your enthusiasm, why not read her diary while you wait? (Open Mon.-Sat. 9am-6:45pm, Sun. 10am-6:45pm; f8, under 17 and CJP holders f4.) Of related interest is the **Verzetsmuseum Amsterdam,** Lekstr. 63, which relates the poignant story of the Nazi resistance in the Netherlands. Take trams 4 and 25. (Open Tues.-Fri. 10am-5pm, Sat.-Sun. and holidays 1-5pm. f3.50, free with Museumkaart.) More obscure is the **Joods-Portuguese Synagogue** at Jonas Daniël Meijerplein, near Waterlooplein. A handsome 17th-century building, the synagogue was founded by Portuguese Jews expelled from their country. (Open Sun.-Fri. 10am-4pm. f2.) Next door at Jonas Daniël Meijerplein 2-4 is the **Joods Historisch Museum,** with exhibits on Jewish history and culture (open 11am-12:30pm and 1pm-4pm; f7, with ISIC f3.50). The **Museum Amstelkring "Ons' Lieve Heer op Solder"** ("Our Lord in the Attic"), O.Z. Voorburgwal 40, in the red-light district, dates from the days of the Reformation, when it was forbidden for Catholics to practice their faith in public. The former Catholic priest's *grachtenhuis* (house on a canal) houses a hidden church in its attic. (Open Mon.-Sat. 10am-5pm, Sun. 1-5pm. f4.50, students and over 65 f3.)

Probably the best f2 you can spend in Amsterdam is on a visit to the retired **Heineken Brewery,** Stadhouderskade 78. You'll probably leave still a little clueless as to exactly how beer is made but the presentation is slick and you get 45min. at the end of the tour to suck down as much free beer as you can. If it's your birthday, you get to enter a beer-guzzling contest to get a free mug. If it makes you feel better, the f2 admission fee goes to charity. (Tours at 9, 9:45, and 10:30am, 1, 1:45, and 2pm; get your tickets early.) See sex in any way you dreamed possible (and many you didn't) to the tune of tasteful porno music played in the background at the **Amsterdam Sex Museum.** Upstairs you can watch movies in the shadow of a 7ft. plastic penis. Yee ha! Directly on the Damrak. (Open 10am-11:30pm; f3.95.)

To continue your "Only in Amsterdam" tour, visit the **Hash Marihuana Hemp Museum,** Oudezijds Achterburgwal 148. To quote their newspaper ad: "If you come on the right day, you will see fat ripe buds glistening with the rich resin and smell air heavy with the fragrance of the crop. What an experience!" If you come on the wrong day, you may be subject to the frequent police raids. (Open Sun.-Wed. 11am-6pm, Thurs.-Sat. 11am-10pm; during summer daily 11am-10pm. f7.)

Lose the tourist crunch in the artsy narrow streets of the **Jordaan.** Bounded roughly by Prinsengracht, Brouwersgracht, Marnixstr., and Lauriersgracht, the Jordaan holds small cafés, unique shops, and vine-laden buildings. Built as an artisan district in the Golden Age, the streets still reflect times past. Take refuge from Amsterdam's mobbed sights and seamy streets in **Begijnhof,** a beautifully maintained, grassy courtyard surrounded by 18th-century buildings; walk down Kalverstr. and turn onto Begijnensteeg, a small side street between Kalverstr. 130 and 132. Spend a day people-watching in the grassy **Vondelpark.** Amid all the trees, cafés, and cows there are plenty of spots to relax, have a quick nap, and hopefully not get your pocket picked. On sunny days, expect crowds around the waterfront and plenty of skin.

Amsterdam's art scene is not confined to cramped old galleries, populated by crusty old tourists, and filled with the same "old masters" you've seen a hundred times already. Some of the most exciting stuff in Amsterdam is free and open to the public, painted on the doors, walls, and trams of the city. Graffiti and psychedelic murals dot the façades of several of the area's buildings. Check out the **Vrankrijk** building, Spuistr. 216, for some angry anarchistic menages surrounded by rampaging dragons, idiotic tourists, and angst-ridden youths. At the neck of Vondelpark, where it widens, a bridge displays more of the trippy kaleidoscope of wacked-out bodies and swirling colors that could only have come from a mind under the influence of some harsh chemicals. The area around **Mr. Visserplein,** near Waterlooplein and the Hortus Botannicus, yields further evidence that graffiti is much more than writing your name and a vulgar phrase. Continue your psychedelic survey of the city at the **3D Hologram Store,** Grimburgwal 2. This place has some excellent images that'll make your eyes bug out. (Open Tues.-Fri. noon-6pm, Sat. noon-5:30pm, Sun. 1-5:30pm.)

The **red light district,** bounded by Warmoestr., Gelderskade, and Oude Doelenstr., is the vice sink of Europe; it'll either repulse you or fulfill your wettest dreams. Pushers, porn shops, and live sex theaters do a brisk business. Red neon marks houses of legal, if ill, repute. Unlike the illegal streetwalkers, these prostitutes have regular gynecological exams—but forget not that HIV/AIDS takes 6 months to detect. During the day, the red-light district is comparatively flaccid, with tourists milling about, consulting their maps, bringing their children. As the sun goes down, the lights get brighter, the people get braver, and the area is much more stimulating. Cops patrol the district until midnight, and there's a police station on Warmoestr. Women may feel uncomfortable walking through this area. Walk quickly and avoid eye contact with the numerous sleazy characters.

To round off your tour of Amsterdam, pet a stray cat at the **Poezenboot** (the Cat Boat), moored off Singel 40, a home to cuddly pussies, and the movement to keep them from multiplying. It's amazing how much stress a cat can relieve, unless, of course, you are allergic. (Open 1-3pm. Free, but donations accepted.)

ENTERTAINMENT

Cafés and Bars

Amsterdam's finest cafés are the old, dark, wood-paneled *bruine kroegen* (brown cafés) of the Jordaan, where denizens gather under the nicotine-stained ceilings and dim brass lamps to trade stories and crack jokes. Bars at Leidseplein are predominantly tourist traps, but the jazz is good. **Rembrandtsplein** has become *the* place to watch soccer and sing with drunk revelers; just pretend you know the words. Gay bars line Reguliersdwarsstr.; look for the pink velour. Most cafés open at 10 or 11am and close at 1am on Fridays and 2am Saturdays.

Café Twee Prinsen, Prisenstr. 27, on the edge of the Jordaan. Crowded at night with upscale Dutch partygoers. Beer from f2.75. Open Sun.-Thurs. 11am-1am, Fri.-Sat. 11am-2am.

Café de Tuin, Tweede Tuindwarsstr. 13 (open Sun.-Thurs. 10am-1am, Fri.-Sat. 10am-2am), and **de Reiger,** Nieuwe Leliestr. 34 (Sun.-Mon. 6pm-1am, Fri.-Sat. 11am-2am; beer from f2.75), both in the Jordaan, attract a young, artsy set.

Saarien, Elandstr. 119, is a hip bar in the Jordaan. Bi, lesbian, and straight women only. Open Mon. 8pm-1am, Tues.-Thurs. and Sun. 3pm-1am, Fri.-Sat. 3pm-2am.

Grand Café Dulac, Haarlemserstr. 118, near the station. A decorative fantasy from "1001 Nights." Erotic statues jump out of every metallic corner. Open 4pm-1am or 2am.

The Sound Garden, Maruixstr. 164. Grunge café near the Christian Youth Hostel where you can recharge on anger before you enter happyland. But, can you eat where there's a larger-than-life poster of a half-naked Iggy Pop? Open 1pm-1am, Sat.-Sun. 1pm-2am.

Koekeloere, Leisedwarsstr. 41, next to McDonald's, is officially a coffeeshop, but the atmosphere is much different at night. Laid-back, with dancing and a giant screen for soccer games. Now about all those clocks... Open Sun.-Thurs. 2pm-1am, Fri.-Sat. 2pm-2am.

April, Reguliersdwarsstr. 37; **Havana,** Reguliersdwarsstr. 17-19; and, **Downtown,** Reguliersdwarsstr. 31 are gay bars in a neigborhood notorious for its watchers and its watched. All open from 3 or 4pm until 1am on weekdays and 2am on weekends.

Coffeeshops

Yes, the rumors are true: marijuana and hashish, though technically illegal, are so decriminalized that coffeeshops don't just sell coffee (unless one counts the green leafy coffee with names like "mother's milk" and "super skunk" or the little coffee-cakes baked the way grandma used to do it, with just a pinch of hashish). Most places will also supply rolling papers and filter tips. A bag typically costs about f25 and the better you buy, the less you get. In general, hash is more common than marijuana and comes in two varieties: blond and black. Black hash hits a little harder. Only tourists smoke from pipes; locals roll burnt, powdered hash into cigarettes with tobacco. The farther you travel from the popular and over-touristed spots, the better, the mellower, and less expensive it becomes. Watch out for those space-cakes unless you have a day or so to spare.

The **Coffeeshop 36,** Warmoesstr. 36, next to the Hotel Kabul in the red-light district, is as much an Amsterdam institution as the Anne Frank Huis. All types hang out here amid the blaring music. (Open Sun.-Thurs. 10am-1am, Fri.-Sat. 10am-2am.) **The Grasshopper,** Nieuwezijds Voorburgwal 57, gently simmers across the street from Bob's Youth Hostel and is much frequented by its guests (open Sun.-Thurs. 9am-midnight, Fri.-Sat. 9am-1am). Bumblebees, schoolbuses, and just about everything else vanish against the yellow-and-black decor of the **Mellow Yellow,** Vijzelstr. 33. A short walk up Vijzelstr. (away from the center) takes you to a calm canalside park to chill. (Open Sun.-Thurs. 8:30am-1am, Fri.-Sat. 8:30am-2am.) Fly over to **Lucky Mother's,** Keizergracht 695, for a super-mellow atmosphere and "the best food and coffee" in a coffeeshop as judged in the 1994 *High Times* Cannabis Cup. Great location, away from the melee of tourism. (Open 10am-8pm.) If only to gaze at the bitchin' façade, check out the original **Bulldog,** Oudezijds Voorburgwal 90. Madonna and Willie Nelson have both been here. Loud, touristy, and not so mellow. (Open Sun.-Thurs. 9am-1am, Fri.-Sat. 9am-2am.)

Live Music

Though Amsterdam may lack a thriving, world-class music scene, it does offer you a great deal of variety and occasionally headlines some mainstream pop and jazz groups. The **Jazzlijn** gives information (tel. 626 77 64) about concerts in the Amsterdam area. Many clubs avoid a cover charge by inflating beer prices.

Melkweg, Lijnbaasgracht 234a (tel. 624 17 77), in an old factory off Leidseplein, across from the police station. Amsterdam's legendary nightspot retains a cutting-edge aura despite the crowds. Live bands, theater, films, an art gallery, and a snack bar fashion the joint's multimedia attack on the senses. Open Wed.-Thurs. and Sun. 7pm-2am, Fri.-Sat. 7pm-4am. Cover charge f7-15 plus membership fee (f4, good for 1 month), f13-21 plus membership on the weekends. Box office open Mon.-Fri. noon-5pm, Sat.-Sun. 4-7pm and while the club is open.

Paradiso, Weteringschans 6-8 (tel. 626 45 21). Some of the foremost international punk, new-wave, and reggae bands play here. f10-27, depending on the band. Shows start at 10pm; check outside or call to learn the evening's guests.

De Kroeg, Lijnbaansgracht 163 (tel. 420 02327). Vibrant crowds writhe to live reggae, salsa, rock, and blues. Open Sun.-Thurs. 8pm-2am, Fri.-Sat. 8pm-3am. DJ on Fri. Periodic jam sessions (usually Mon. and Wed.). Music starts at 10pm. f5 cover on nights with live music, f2.50 on DJ night, jam sessions free.

The Bimhuis, Oude Schans 73-77 (tel. 623 13 61). The hub of Dutch jazz. More than 200 concerts held yearly. Sun.-Tues. jazz workshops. Wed.-Sat. concerts after 9pm. f10, students f7.50.

Odeon Jazz Kelder, Singel 456, near Leidsestr. Men in sharp suits and women in heels come here to bebop. Open Sun.-Thurs. 10pm-4am, Fri.-Sat. 10pm-3am. Cover f7.50, weekends f12.50.

Dancing

Many nightclubs in Amsterdam charge a membership fee in addition to the normal cover, so the tab can be hefty. Be prepared for arrogant, cocky doormen who like nothing better than turning away tourists. Be a beautiful woman or show up early. There are expensive discos aplenty on Prinsengracht, near Leidsestr., and on Lange Leidsedwarsstr. Gay discos line Amstelstr.

RoXY, Singel 465. The hippest crowd in town busts a move to acid house. Obvious tourist attire rebuffed. Open Wed.-Thurs. around 9am-4am, Fri.-Sun. 9am-5am. Cover Wed. and Sun. f7.50, Thurs. f10, Fri.-Sat. f12.50.

MAZZO, Rozengracht 114 (tel. 26 75 00), in the Jordaan. Artsy disco that is constantly revolving its DJs and the style of music. Display and slideshow change every 3 weeks. Open Sun.-Thurs. 11pm-4am, Fri.-Sat. 11pm-5am. Live music Tues. Cover f7.50, weekends f10.

Dansen bij Jansen, Handboogstr. 11, near Spui. Location near the university makes it popular among students (officially, a student ID is required). Happy hour Sun.-Wed. 11pm-midnight. Open Sun.-Thurs. 11pm-4am, Fri.-Sat. 11pm-5am. Cover f4, weekends f5.

iT, Amstelstr. 24, near Waterlooplein. Clients tout this as one of the best and most decadent gay discos in Europe. Open Thurs. and Sun. 11pm-4am, Fri.-Sat. 11pm-5am. Free to members, otherwise f15. Gay only on Sat.

Theater, Dance, and Music

VVV puts out *What's On* (f3.50), with comprehensive cultural listings. In summer, there are free performances Wednesday through Sunday at the **Vondelpark Openluchttheater** (tel. 673 14 99); jazz and folk concerts dominate, but children's theater, political music, and mime also grab the limelight. Check posters at park entrances. The June **Holland Festival** of dance, drama, and music is closely followed by the **Summer Festival** of small theater companies in July. (Contact the Balie Theatre on Leidseplein, tel. 623 36 73. Tickets f10-15.) The sparkling new **Muziektheater,** perched over the junction of the Amstel and the Oude Schans (tel. 625 54 55), hosts the **Netherlands Opera** and the **National Ballet.** The **Royal Concertgebouw Orchestra,** one of the world's finest, is conducted by Ricardo Chailly at the Concertgebouw on Van Baerlestr. (Concerts start at 8:15pm. Tickets f25.) There is English-speaking theater year-round in **De Stalhouderij,** eerste Bloemdwarsstr. 4 (tel. 626 22 82). Frequent English-language performances and cabarets are given at the theater/café **Suikerhof,** Prinsengracht 381 (tel. 22 75 71; open from 5pm, Sun. from 2pm). Make reservations for any cultural event, in person only, at the **Amsterdams Uit Buro** (AUB) Ticketshop (tel. 621 12 11). The VVV Tourist Office theater desk, Stationsplein 10 (open Mon.-Sat. 10am-4pm) and the larger tourist bureaus in Holland (VVV I) also operate ticket-reservation services.

Organ concerts resound Wednesday evenings at 8:15pm during the summer at **Westerkerk,** where Rembrandt is buried, at Prinsengracht 281 (tel. 624 77 66), and **Nieuwe Kerk,** where Dutch monarchs are sworn in (they're not crowned), on the Dam (tel. 626 81 68). Prices are f5-12.50. The free monthly publication *UITKRANT* list all concerts, films, theater, and club events.

There's no escaping **Boom Chicago,** their *Boom Paper* turns up in more places than all the ABN/Amro banks and FEBO outlets put together. With two different shows and a gut-busting Saturday night "Boom Chicago Unplugged" (totally improvised hour and a half sketch), you ought to find something there that you like. "Boom Chicago is a great time with cool people—and it's funny too," raves Dan Williams from *Let's Go.* Also chock full of tourist info and cool books and videos the VVV only wishes they had. Find it all at the **Boom Café,** Lijnbaansgracht 238. (Café open Tues.-Sun. 11:30am-8:30pm. Shows Tues.-Sun. 8:30pm; tickets f15 if you buy before 6pm and f20 at the door; snag a couch seat for f20, f25 at the door if you come early enough.)

■ ALKMAAR AND EDAM

When you tire of free and easy Amsterdam, explore the surrounding countryside. Trains are expensive, so buy a cheap day return or get a one-day bus pass (f18.10). **Alkmaar,** 45min. away by train (4 per hr.), holds a large open-air **cheese market** every Friday from 10am to noon (mid-April to mid-Sept.). When the market is over, there is still plenty to buy along the narrow canal-lined streets. Die-hard windmill fans should flock to **Zaanse Schaanz,** a traditional (and touristy) town sitting alongside a river. Five windmills stand accompanied by a cheese-making facility and traditional crafts (from Amsterdam 15min., round-trip f6).

Discover picturesque cottages and soaring stone towers in **Edam,** Holland's sleeping beauty just outside Amsterdam, accessible by NZH bus from Centraal Station (7 strips). The 15th century **Grote Kerk,** or St. Nicholaaskerk, is the largest three-ridged church in Europe and has 30 superb stained-glass windows. Farmers still bring their famed edam cheese to market by horse and by boat on Wednesdays in July and August (10am-12:30pm). Rent a bike at **Ronald Schot,** Kleine Kerkstraat 9-11 (f10 per day), and head to the source yourself. **Alida Hoeve,** Zeddewed 1, is a **traditional cheese factory** across the street from the bike path as you head toward Volendam (pass by the first touristy cheese factory you see), where Edam cheese is still made by hand and the generous samples are free. (Open 9am-6pm. Free.) Further down the same bike path stands a towering **windmill.** For f1, you can climb the steep ladder to the top (while it's turning) and catch a great view of the surrounding pastures. (Open April-Aug. 9am-4pm.)

■■■ HAARLEM

This ain't the home of the Globetrotters or African-American culture. Haarlem, 20km from Amsterdam, is home to a completely different kind of culture—the beautiful Renaissance façades and placid canals that inspired Dutch artists during the Golden Age. Seek out the 17th and 18th century *hofjes* (almshouses for elderly women), with their elegant brickwork and comfortable, grassy courtyards. Try secluded **Hofje van Bakenes,** Wijde Appelaarsteeg 11, near the Teylers Museum, or the **Hofje van Oirschot,** at the end of Kuisstr., where it becomes Barteljorisstr. These are private property and still inhabited—be tactful. From the station, Kruisweg leads to the **Grote Markt** and the glorious medieval **Stadhuis** (Town Hall), originally the 13th-century hunting lodge of the Count of Holland. When the Hall of Counts is not in use, you can sneak a free peek at the lavishly furnished interior; ask at the reception desk. The **Grote Kerk** graces the opposite end of the Grote Markt and still houses the Müller organ, which Mozart played at age 11 (the organ was 28). (Church open Mon.-Sat. 10am-4pm. f2, children and students f1. Free organ recitals May-Oct. Tues. 8:15pm; July-Aug. also Thurs. 3pm.)

From the church, walk down Damstr. to the Netherlands' oldest museum, the **Teylers Museum** at Spaarne 16. Looking like something out of an H.G. Wells novel, the museum lets you see what people in 1788 thought a museum should be: a blend of scientific instruments of the era, fossils, coins, paintings, and superb drawings, including works by Raphael and Michelangelo. (Open Tues.-Sat. 10am-5pm, Sun. 1-5pm. f6.50, seniors and CJP holders f4.50.) The legacy of Haarlem's brash portraitist Frans Hals lives on in the **Frans Hals Museum,** Groot Heiligland 62. Housed in a charming 17th-century almshouse, the collection includes Hals's lively group portraits and a permanent collection of modern art. (Open Mon.-Sat. 10am-5pm, Sun. 1-5pm. f6, seniors and CJP holders f2.) The **Corrie Ten Boomhuis,** better known as The Hiding Place, Barteljorisstr. 19, is where Corrie Ten Boom and her family hid Jewish refugees during WWII. The refugees were never discovered, but the entire Ten Boom family was removed to concentration camps; Corrie was the only survivor. (Tours every hour on the ½ hour Tues.-Sat. 10am-4:30pm; Nov.-April Tues.-Sat. 11am-3:30pm. Free, but donations appreciated.) On Saturdays, a technicolor **flower and fruit market** fills the Grote Markt (9am-4pm).

Practical Information, Accommodations, and Food The **VVV,** Stationsplein 1 (tel. (023) 31 90 59), sells an excellent map of Haarlem for f2.50 (open Mon.-Sat. 9am-5:30pm; Oct.-March Mon.-Fri. 9am-5:30pm, Sat. 10am-4pm). Haarlem is easily accessible from Amsterdam by **train** (4 per hr., f5.25) or by **bus** 80 from Marnixstr., near Leidseplein (2 per hr., 6 strips). Five night buses (86) cruise from Amsterdam's Leidseplein to Haarlem (12:42am-3:20am), but none go from Haarlem to Amsterdam.

A super-cheery staff keeps the clean and comfortable **Jeugdherberg Jan Gijzen (HI),** Jan Gijzenpad 3 (tel. (023) 37 37 93). Bus 2 "Haarlem-Nord" will drive you the 3km from the station to the hostel; tell the driver your destination. In July and August, no groups are accepted. (Reception open 7:30am-midnight. f21.50, nonmembers f26.50. Flexible midnight curfew. Open March-Oct.) Haarlem apparently has not heard of budget hotels, but the VVV can find you a private room from about f28 plus a f9 fee for all their hard work. But if no place has room for you, and you're tired of the hostile hostels, try the ideally located **Hotel Carillon,** Grote Markt 27 (tel. (023) 31 05 91). (Singles f50-85, doubles f85-110. Breakfast included. Reception and bar open 7:30am-1am.) The **Stads Café,** Zijlstr. 56-58 (tel. (023) 32 52 02), offers Dutch cuisine (daily *dagschotel* f9.75) and commodious sleeping quarters. (Singles f50, doubles f75-100. Breakfast f8.50. Café open Mon.-Thurs. 11am-10:30pm, Fri.-Sat. 11am-11:30pm, Sun. 2-11pm.) When these hotels fill, seek out the cheap pensions in nearby Zandvoort (see Near Haarlem). A **campground** is located at **De Liede,** Liewegje 17 (tel. (023) 33 23 60). Take bus 2 "Zuiderpolder" and walk 10min. (f4 per person, f4 per tent).

Pannekoekhuis De Smikkel, Kruisweg 57, serves plump buttery pancakes (f6.75-16.75) dripping with anything from bananas to seafood (open Mon.-Sat. 11am-8pm, Sun. 2-8pm). For healthier fare, try out **Eko Eetcafé,** Zijlstr. 39 (open 5:30-9:30pm). They serve a verdant vegetarian plate for f16 and pizzas for f12-16.50.

■ NEAR HAARLEM

Haarlem is only 10min. by train from **Zandvoort** beach (2-6 per hr., round-trip f3.50). South of here, between *paal* (wooden posts) 68 and 71, is a popular nude beach. Zandvoort hosts scads of cheap pensions and hotels. The **VVV,** at Schoolplein 1, in the village center, a downhill walk from the beach and the station, sells a indispensable guide to lodgings (f3.50). (Open Mon.-Fri. 9am-7pm, Sat. 9am-5pm; April-June and Sept. Mon.-Sat. 9am-5pm; Oct.-March Mon.-Fri. 10am-12:30pm and 1:30-5pm, Sat. 10am-12:30pm and 1:30-3:30pm.) **Hotel-Pension Noordzee,** Hogeweg 15 (tel. (02507) 131 27), is located only 100m from the beach and the casino (singles f40, doubles f60-70). **Hotel van der Aar,** Brederodestr. 44, (tel. (02507) 148 02) is a good second choice (singles f32.50, doubles f65; reception open 8am-midnight). **Bloemendaal** is a more repressed beach, accessible by bus 81 (1 per hr.) from the Haarlem train station. An international flower auction is held year-round in the nearby town of **Aalsmeer.** From Haarlem, take bus 140. (Open Mon.-Fri. 7:30-11am; the most germinal budding flowers from 8-9am.) The **Frans Roozen Gardens** bloom with 500 different types of flowers and plants; summer flower shows are free. Bus 90 "Den Haag" stops in front of the gardens. (Open July-Oct. Mon.-Fri. 9am-5pm. Tulip show April-May daily 8am-6pm.) Bus 50 or 51 runs past some of Holland's famous flower fields. Daffodils blossom in early to late April, hyacinths in mid- to late April, and tulips from late April to mid-May.

■■■ LEIDEN

As William of Orange's 1574 reward to the people of Leiden for withstanding a Spanish siege, the University of Leiden is Holland's oldest institute of higher learning. The resourceful residents threw open local dikes, flooding the surrounding plain and thwarting the Spanish armies. Leiden is an archetypal college town, brimming with bookstores, cafés, bicycles, and 11 diverse museums. The **Rijksmuseum voor Volkenkunde** (National Museum of Ethnology), Steenstr. 1, one of the oldest anthropological museums in the world, boasts a collection of fantastic artifacts from the Dutch East Indies (open Tues.-Fri. 10am-5pm, Sat.-Sun. noon-5pm; f5, students f3.50). The **Rijksmuseum van Oudheden** (National Antiquities Museum), Rapenburg 28, harbors the complete, lovingly restored Egyptian Temple of Taffeh, which the Dutch removed from the reservoir basin of the Aswan Dam and opened to the public in 1979 (open Tues.-Sat. 10am-5pm, Sun. noon-5pm; f5, over 65, under 18, and CJP holders f4). The university's garden, the **Hortus Botanicus** at Rapenburg 73, is one of Europe's oldest. It includes greenhouses and a Japanese garden. (Garden open Mon.-Sat. 9am-5pm, Sun. 10am-5pm; Oct.-March Mon.-Sat. 9am-5pm. Some greenhouses close at 4:30pm. f3.50; seniors f1.50, CJP holders free.) Propel yourself to the top of a functioning Dutch windmill and inspect its mechanical

NETHERLANDS

innards at the **Molenmuseum "De Valk,"** 2de Binnenvestgracht 1, built in 1743 (open Tues.-Sat. 10am-5pm, Sun. 1-5pm. f3.50; over 65, under 16, and CJP holders f2; free with Museumkaart).

Practical Information, Accommodations, and Food The **VVV,** Stationsplein 210 (tel. (071) 14 68 46), across the street and to the right of the train station, doles out maps (f1) and can locate rooms in private homes (f3.50 fee). Their *Rembrandt Tour* (f3.50) and *Pilgrim Tour* (f1) brochures offer creative ways to see the town on foot. (Open Mon.-Fri. 9am-5:30pm, Sat. 9am-4pm.) A student housing crunch has made finding inexpensive rooms difficult in Leiden, but not impossible. Idyllic **Jeugdherberg De Duinark (HI),** Langevelderlaan 45 (tel. (02523) 729 20), is 18km from Leiden in Noordwijk. Take bus 60 to Kappellebosiaan or bus 61 to Sancta Maria and walk 15min. Reserve ahead. (Reception open 8am-1am. Curfew 1am. f24, nonmembers f29. f2.50 tourist tax July-Aug. Sheets f6.) The surest bargain is the **Lits Jumeaux Jeugdhotel,** Lange Scheistr. 9 (tel. (071) 12 84 57), off Oude Singel and just outside the pedestrian district. (Reception open 8:30am-12:30am. 4- to 10-bed dorms f25, f5 extra for a hearty breakfast. Singles f50 and doubles f75 come with breakfast, shower and TV. Doors lock at 12:30am but keys to outside door available upon request.) If you need a break from hostels, set yourself up in either **Hotel Pension Witte Singel,** Witte Singel 80 (tel. (071) 12 45 92; singles f45, doubles f80, plus a f2.50 tourist tax), or the nearby **Pension Bik,** Witte Singel 92 (tel. (071) 12 26 02; singles f47, doubles f80; breakfast included; reception open 7:30am-10pm; no one-night stays). Both offer immaculate rooms overlooking gardens and canals. If it hasn't already filled, try **Pension In de Goede Hoek,** Diefsteeg 19a (tel. (071) 12 10 31), with tidy rooms and a great location near the Stadhuis. You'll have to make your own breakfast, but plenty of good food is available in the kitchen. Reserve ahead of time; guests with longer stays are given priority. (Reception open 7am-10pm. Singles f40, doubles f70.)

For Leiden's cheapest bite, try the university *mensas:* **Augustinus,** Rapenburg 24 (open Sept.-June Mon.-Fri. 5:30-7:15pm), and **De Bak,** Kaiserstr. 23-25 (open mid-Aug. to late July Mon.-Fri. noon-2pm and 5:30-6:30pm), offer dishes starting at f5. **Café de Illegale,** Hooigracht 72, draws an intellectual crowd with scrumptious vegetarian and Dutch cuisine (f15-22). Someone will usually be crooning and playing guitar on Tuesday and Wednesday nights. (Open 5pm-midnight; kitchen closes at 10pm.) Or eat a bag lunch culled from the **Dagmarkt** supermarket, on the corner of Stationsweg and Stationsplein, just across from the station (open Mon. 1-6pm, Tues.-Fri. 9am-6pm, Sat. 9am-5pm). The renovated area near Pieterskerk harbors sedate coffee shops. The **Duke,** Oude Singel 2 (tel. (071) 12 19 72), on the canal down the street from the Jeugdhotel, rounds up live jazz nightly at 9:30pm and open jam sessions on Sundays (open Sun.-Thurs. 7pm-1am, Fri.-Sat. 7pm-3am; beer from f2.25).

Leiden makes an appealing **rail** daytrip from Amsterdam (4 per hr. from Centraal Station, 30min., f11.50) or the Hague (2 per hr., 20min., f4.50).

■ LISSE

Arriving in Lisse, you'll feel as Dorothy did when she left her black-and-white Kansas and landed in technicolor Oz. However no flying monkeys will hinder your progress through nature's awesome display of beauty. In late March, April, and May, the splendiferous **Keukenhof** garden (f15) blossoms into a spectacular kaleidoscope of color as over 5 million bulbs explode into life. Take bus 50 or 51 toward Lisse from the Haarlem train station; a combination bus and admission ticket bought at Centraal Station (f21) saves money. The rest of the year you can examine what goes on under the soil at the **Museum Voor de Bloembollenstreek,** which is devoted entirely to the history and science of tulip raising (open Tues.-Sun. 1-5pm. f2.50). On April 22, 1995, Lisse will stick its petals to the metal in the annual flower parade.

■■■ THE HAGUE (DEN HAAG)

Although Amsterdam is the economic center of the Netherlands, the seat of government is The Hague. Here the streets are broader, the buildings grander, and the roses redder. Where else do the horses have their own special day where they walk freely through the city and eat from silver plates? Centuries of wealth have bestowed many beautiful buildings and parks to The Hague's streets and canals, and left the city with fine museums. This cool city of diplomats also harbors the royal residence and the International Court of Justice, which meets at the Peace Palace. Many of the locals ship out to nearby beachfront night spot, **Scheveningen** (a city so difficult to pronounce correctly, it was used as a code word by the Dutch in WWII). Here, you'll find beaches, casinos, and a newly restored boardwalk.

PRACTICAL INFORMATION

Tourist Offices: VVV, Kon. Julianaplein 30 (info hotline tel. (06) 34 03 50 51), in front of Centraal Station, on the right side under the Hotel Sofitel. Distributes tourist brochures (f1.50), peddles maps (f2.75), books rooms (f3.50 fee) and publishes events listings. Open Mon.-Sat. 9am-9pm, Sun. 10am-5pm; mid-Sept. to March Mon.-Sat. 9am-6pm, Sun. 10am-5pm.

Budget Travel: NBBS, Schoolstr. 24 (tel. 346 58 19). Long lines pay off in cheap tix. Open Mon.-Fri. 9:30am-5:30pm, Sat. 10am-4pm; Sept.-Dec. Mon.-Fri. 9:30am-5:30pm, Sat. 10am-3pm.

Embassies: U.S., Lange Voorhout 102 (tel. 310 92 09). Open Mon.-Fri. 8:30am-5:15pm. **Canada,** Sophialaan 7 (tel. 361 41 11). Open Mon.-Fri. 9am-1pm, 2-5:30pm. **U.K.,** Lange Voorhout 10 (tel. 364 58 00). Open Mon.-Fri. 9am-1pm and 2:15-5:30pm. **Australia,** Carnegielaan 12 (tel. 310 82 00). Open Mon.-Fri. 9am-12:30pm and 2-5:30pm. **New Zealand,** Carnegielaan 10 (tel. 346 93 24). Open Mon.-Fri. 9am-12:30pm and 1:30-5:30pm. **South Africa,** Wassenarseweg 40 (tel. 392 45 01). Open 8am-4:30pm.

American Express: Venestr. 20 (tel. 370 11 00), near the Binnenhof. Open Mon.-Fri. 9am-5pm, Sat. 9:30am-12:30pm. Published rates and no charge on traveler's checks. Mail held (f2.50 charge without AmEx card or checks).

Post Office: Nobelstr. and Prinsenstr. (tel. 384 58 45), near the Grote Kerk. **Postal Code:** 2513 AZ. Open Mon.-Wed. and Fri. 8:30am-6:30pm, Thurs. 8:30am-8:30pm, Sat. 9am-noon. Branch office at Koningin Julianaplein 6, to the left of the station. Open Mon.-Fri. 8am-6pm.

Telephones: Public phones (and fax!) at the Post Office or across the street from the Kurhaus in Scheveningen. **City Code:** 070.

Trains: Call 06 92 92 for information. Trains serving Amsterdam and Rotterdam use **Holland Spoor;** most others use **Centraal Station.** Reach Centraal Station and the VVV from Holland Spoor by *stoptrein* or tram 9 or 12. Both have **lockers** (small f4, large size f6).

Bike Rental: At both Holland Spoor (tel. 389 08 30) and Centraal Station (tel. 385 32 35). f8 per day, deposit f100 or passport. Grab cycling maps (f8) at VVV.

Pharmacies: Hofstad Apotheek, 7a Korte Poten (tel. 346 47 48), just off the Plein. Open Mon.-Fri. 8:30am-10pm, Sat. 10am-6pm, Sun. noon-5pm.

Emergencies: tel. 0611. English spoken.

ACCOMMODATIONS AND FOOD

Staying in The Hague is not an easy thing to do. Budget accommodations are sparse and distant, and their quality is not as good as those in neighboring cities, such as Rotterdam. Thus, The Hague makes a good daytrip; in fact, it'll be a daytrip even if you're staying at the local hostel. There is always the option of finding a **private home** through the VVV, but they will be f40 at the cheapest and far from the center of town. **Jeugdherberg Ockenburgh (HI),** Monstersweg 9 (tel. 397 00 11), 8km from town in Kijkduin, 40min. by bus 122, 123 or 124: Ockenburgh and another 10min. walk down the road. Huge, institutionalized to the max, and overflowing with groups. Similar to booking a room in a hospital, but not as clean, and a hospital gives you more food. (Reception open 7am-11pm. Curfew midnight, but door

NETHERLANDS

opens briefly at 1, 2, and 3am. Dorms f26, singles f36, doubles f67, triples f95. Non-members add f5.) The Hague's cheap hotel rooms cluster in the seedy and some-what dangerous neighborhood around the Holland Spoor train station; ship out to more pleasant quarters in nearby Scheveningen. Five minutes from a beautiful beach and huge casino, **Hotel Pension Lobèl,** Haagsestr. 53 (tel. 354 58 03), will set you up in a tidy single (f45) or double (f90). Take tram 1, 7, or 9 from the station ("Scheveningen," 3 strips) and tell the driver your destination. Also available is the **Hotel Scheveningen,** Gevers Deynootweg 2 (tel. 354 70 03), which can get you a single for f40 or double for the low, low price of f60. Just don't look down the street at the extravagant five-star hotel. Pitch a tent near the beach at **Ockenburgh,** Wijndaelerweg 25 (tel. 325 23 64). Take tram 3 from Centraal Station. (f5 per adult, f12 per site. Under 18 *(Jeugdplaats)* f12.75. Open April to mid-Oct.)

In The Hague, the horses may dine off silver plates, but you'll have to really search for a plate of your own. Ordinary folk flock for Flemish favorites, fresh fruit and fish, at the nearby covered market **Markthof,** Spuistr., a few blocks from Binnenhof, along Groete Marktstr. (open Mon. 11am-6pm, Tues.-Wed. and Fri. 9am-6pm, Thurs. 9am-9pm, Sat. 9am-5pm). Enjoy a stroll along **Denneweg,** a street lined with tiny exotic restaurants. For more traditional fare, **Le Perroquet,** Plein 12a (tel. 363 97 86), has entrees from f22.50. On the beach at Scheveningen, expect to pay f12-16 for a *halve kip* (half chicken) or, if you are the brave sort, swallow a herring for f3-4.

SIGHTS

A visit to the **Binnenhof,** the courtyard whose buildings house the Netherlands's Parliament, is enough to make you want a career in Dutch politics. Guided tours (leaving from Binnenhof 8a) begin with an audiovisual presentation and move on to the **Ridderzaal** (Hall of Knights), and usually one or both of the chambers of the States General. (Open Mon.-Sat. 10am-4pm, last tour at 4:45pm; f5.) Just outside the north entrance of the Binnenhof, the 17th-century **Mauritshuis** features a heavy-weight collection of Dutch paintings, including Rembrandt's *The Anatomy Lesson* and Vermeer's *Lady with a Turban* (open Tues.-Sat. 10am-5pm, Sun. 11am-5pm. f7.50; seniors, under 18, and CJP holders f4.50). The **Haags Gemeentemuseum,** Stadhouderslaan 41 boasts the largest collection of Mondriaans in the world (open Tues.-Sun. 11am-5pm. f7, seniors and children f6, CJP holders f5).

The extravagant **Peace Palace,** donated by Andrew Carnegie when he was expe-riencing a bout of industrialist guilt, and home to the International Court of Justice, glistens at Carnegieplein, 10min. from the Binnenhof. The palace is usually closed when the Court is in session; call ahead to check if it's open to the public (tel. 302 42 42). Guided tours (required) leave Mon.-Fri. at 10, 11am, 2, 3, and 4pm. (Oct.-May last tour leaves at 3pm; f5, under 13 f3.)

The **Haags Filmhuis,** Spui 191, features oldies and the best of current movies; all films are shown in their original language with Dutch subtitles (f11-15, students and seniors f8.50-12.50; screenings nightly at 7:30pm and 9:45pm). The best deal in The Hague may just be the **MGM Odeon Theatres,** Herengracht 13, where one movie is always f2.50. **Muziekcafé La Valletta,** Nwe. Schoolstr. 13a, is a jazz café that fea-tures live shows Thursday nights at 10pm (open 5pm-1am; no cover). **Fireworks** explode from the pier (f1 entrance fee) in Scheveningen every Friday night in July and August, and in mid-June the beach hosts the **Nationale Nederlanden Kite Fes-tival** and the **International Sandcastle Festival. Parkpop** in late June is the largest free mainstream rock concert in Europe. In July, the annual **North Sea Jazz Festival** brings four straight days of jazz, gospel concerts, and dance contests to The Hague. For a smurfy good time, check out the incredibly tacky and cheesy **Smurf Festival** in Scheveningen in early July, or the weekly brochure *Over Uit.* For a complete list of cultural events, pick up the brochure *Info* from the VVV.

■■■ DELFT

With the exception of a few stray soda bottles and assorted trash, Delft's canals are still as they were back when hometown boy Jan Vermeer froze them on canvas over 300 years ago. Biologists have Delft to thank for Antoni van Leeuwenhoek, the inventor of the microscope. More commonly, however, Delft is renowned for Delftware, the jaw-dropping, blue-on-white china developed in the 16th century to compete with the newly-imported Chinese porcelain. You can gawk at the pricey plates in the main boutique at **Koniklijke Porceleyne Fles,** Rotterdamseweg 196 in South Delft, where there are also hourly painting demonstrations. Take bus 60 from the station. (Open Mon.-Sat. 9am-5pm, Sun. 10am-4pm. Free.) For more in-depth study, tour the factory at **De Delftse Pauw,** Delftweg 133, in the northern reaches of the city, where artisans still painstakingly hand-paint the porcelain. Take tram 1 from the station. (Open 9am-4pm; mid-Oct. to March Mon.-Fri. 9am-4pm, Sat.-Sun. 11am-1pm. Free.) Both places unload seconds at 25% off.

Built in 1381, the **Nieuwe Kerk** looms over Delft's central **Markt.** It contains the mausoleum of the Dutch liberator, William of Orange, flanked by a statue of his loyal dog, who starved to death out of despair after his master died. (Church open Mon.-Sat. 9am-5pm; Nov.-March. Mon.-Sat. 11am-4pm. f2.50, seniors f2.) Ascend the church tower to see the 48-bell carillon and a ripping view of old Delft. (Tower open Mon.-Sat. 10am-4:30pm; April 30-June 12 Tues.-Thurs. 10am-4:30pm. f3.25.) Built in the 15th century as a nun's cloister, **Het Prinsenhof,** at Sint Agathaplein, was William's abode until a crazed Spanish sympathizer assassinated him in 1584. Today it exhibits paintings, tapestries, Delft pottery, and a touch of adventurous contemporary art. In mid-October, the museum sponsors an **antique fair** famous throughout Holland. (Open Tues.-Sat. 10am-5pm, Sun. 1-5pm. f3.50; seniors, under 14, and CJP holders f1.75.)

Practical Information, Accommodations, and Food Delft is one hour southwest of Amsterdam by train, with connections at The Hague (f3.50) and Leiden (f6.25). For train or bus info in Delft, call 06 92 92. Snag a complete pamphlet on Delft (f3), as well as hiking and cycling maps of the area, from the **VVV,** Markt 85 (tel. (015) 12 61 00; open Mon.-Fri. 9am-6pm, Sat. 9am-5pm, Sun. 11am-3pm; Oct.-March closed Sun.).

Delft may be renowned for its china, but it sure isn't known for its budget accommodations. The sage choice is cozy **Van Leeuwen,** Achterom 143 (tel. (015) 12 37 16), overlooking a canal near the train station and the Markt. Don't worry if you don't see a hotel sign, just ring the bell. (Singles f35, doubles f65-70. Breakfast included.) Surprisingly, several hotels dotting the Markt offer spiffy rooms at decent prices. **La Dalmacija,** Markt 39 (tel. (015) 12 37 14), posts singles at f40-60 and doubles at f70-100 (reception open 9am-11pm). Try the housing wheel of fortune at **Let Krakeelhof,** Jacoba von Bierernlaan. The guys in room 39 will try to find you a place to stay, even though technically their services are exclusively for students at Delft's university. You may have a bed, you may have a couch—who knows? Expect to pay about f20, more or less, depending on how well you get to know your host. Delft also has a private **campground** on Korftlaan (tel. (015) 13 00 40), in the Delftse Hout recreation area (reception open 9am-10pm, mid-Sept.-May 9am-6pm; f3.50 per person, f17.50 per tent; laundry facilities available). The camp restaurant serves *Dagschotel* for f13.50 (open noon-10pm). Take bus 60 or 64 from the station to the Korftlaan stop.

A large **market** erupts every Thursday (9am-5pm) in the town center; on Saturdays, a **fruit and vegetable market** fills the Brabantse Turfmarkt. The student *mensa* **Eettafel Tyche,** Oude Delft 123 (tel. (015) 12 21 23), practically gives away meat-and-potatoes fare (open Sept.-May Mon.-Sat. 5:15-7:15pm; f5.25). For f5.95, you can savor any one of the small yet tasty sandwiches voted the best *broodje* in the Netherlands at **Kleyweg's Stads-Koffyhuis,** down the street at no. 133-135 (open Mon.-Fri. 9am-7pm, Sat. 9am-6pm). After dark, the dim, yet inviting, **Bebop**

Jazzcafé, Kromstr. 33, near the Markt, draws local hepcats. (Open Mon.-Thurs. 7pm-1am, Fri.-Sun. 3pm-2am. Live jazz Sept.-June Sun. and the 1st and 3rd Wed. of the month.) Delft also has a central square full of activity, especially in the summer. The **Straattheater festival** in June summons street performers from every corner of the city. The third week in August brings the **Oude Stijl Jazz Festival** and the cultural **Delftdag.**

■■■ ROTTERDAM

A barrage of German bombs obliterated Rotterdam's center on May 14, 1940, cowing the Netherlands into a hasty surrender. Rising like a phoenix from the dust and ashes, this gleaming city of metal and glass is testament to the resilience and perseverance of its inhabitants. In the gleam of the skyscrapers, however, are solemn reminders of the city's tortured past. Grim and contorted faces peer sternly from the stark and austere statues that dot its streets and squares. However inspired you are by the sparkling columns of glass, or amused by the avant-garde architecture of the bridges and buildings, the faces on the statues will always make you look again, and think of the past.

PRACTICAL INFORMATION

The city of Rotterdam sprawls out over a vast area, but a good 70% of the beautiful f4 map will be totally useless, since the main tourist area is very small by comparison. The borders can roughly be defined as **Centraal Station** to the north, **Blaak Station** to the east, the road **'s Gravendijkwal** to the west and the river **Maas** to the south. Most sights inside this perimeter are within walking distance, so don't waste your *strippenkaarten*. Get the exercise; it's good for you.

Tourist Offices: VVV, at the train station (tel. 436 57 63), sells a guide and street map (f2.50) and books rooms (f2.50). Open Mon.-Sat. 9am-10pm, Sun. 10am-10pm. The **main office** at Coolingsel 67 (tel. (063) 403 40 65), near Stadhuisplein, publishes the free cultural calendar *This Month* and does theater bookings (f2.50). Open Mon.-Thurs. 9am-5:30pm, Fri. 9am-9pm, Sat. 9am-5pm, Sun. 10am-10pm.

Budget Travel: NBBS, Meent 126 (tel. 414 94 85), near the Town Hall, gives out budget travel info. Open Mon.-Fri. 9:30am-5:30pm, Sat. 10am-4pm.

American Express: The office on Meent 92 does all the average AmEx things like check cashing, mail-holding (f2.50 charge if you don't have The Card or traveler's checks), etc. Good exchange rates. Open Mon.-Fri. 9am-5pm, Sat. 10am-1pm.

Post Office: Located across the street from the VVV at Delftsplein 31. Equipped with phones, faxes and all the conveniences of home. Open Mon. 11am-6pm, Tues.-Thurs. 9am-6pm, Fri. 9am-8:30pm.

Telephones: The PTT office is in the post office; phones take cards and coins. Fax also available. **City Code:** 010 for the city center.

Trains and Buses: All trains pass through **Centraal Station** and some stop at **Blaak Station** also. Buses also use Centraal Station for a hub. Call 06 92 92 for train information, 411 71 00 for buses. Daily connections to The Hague (f13.50), Amsterdam (f20.75), and Utrecht (f13.50).

Luggage Storage: Lockers at the train stations; small f4, large f6. The baggage check will hold a bag for f4 per day.

Public Transportation: Rotterdam's metro is nothing extravagant, but fast and efficient. Most rides will cost you 2 strips. The metro and the trams spread over the entire city and run from 6am-midnight. Night buses also run Friday and Saturday nights. *Strippenkaarten* will cost you f11 (15 strips).

Emergencies: 06 11 will get you in touch with a general emergency switchboard.

ACCOMMODATIONS AND FOOD

For such a large city, the possibilities for sleeping cheaply are limited. However, the two budget accommodations, which do exist, are quite centrally located. Your best bet is the **NJHC City-Hostel Rotterdam (HI),** Rochussenstr. 107-109 (tel. 436 57 63), M: Dijkzigt, or tram 6. The place may be showing its age a bit, but the staff is very courteous and friendly. To make your stay more comfortable, the hostel offers a lounge, game room, TV, bar, and more of those high-tech lockers (f3.50). No groups are accepted in July and August. (Reception open 7am-2am. Lockout 10am-3pm. Curfew 2am. f24, nonmember f29. Shower and breakfast included. Sheets f6.) For even cheaper accommodation, there's always the **Sleep-In,** hidden away at Mauritsweg 29 (tel. 412 14 20 or 414 32 56). A bit grimy, but the cheapest beds in town (f15). Open mid-June to mid-August. Reception open 4pm-1am. Curfew 1am. Lockout 10am-4pm. Breakfast and showers included. No reservations.

There are many eating options in Rotterdam, and most of them cluster around **Nieuwe Binnenweg** (close to both accommodations), or in the **Oude Haven. Lux,** 's Gravendijkwal 122, gives you a really classy atmosphere in which to wolf down your hearty Italian meal (open 7:30-11pm; entrees f7-20). **Congo Bongo,** 's Gravendijkwal 136a, is home to a Caribbean menu, with a mood that is decidedly wicker and home of beautiful people (open Tues.-Sun. 6-11pm; menu f5-25). **Aqui,** on the Oude Haven, offers a Spanish menu, tile mosaics, and a great view of the harbor (open Wed.-Sun. 5pm-late; meals f7-22). Olé! **De Eend,** Mauritsweg 28, right next to the Sleep-In, serves up affordable Dutch meals. The menu changes daily (open Mon.-Fri. 4:30-7:30pm; prices f10-17).

When the wallet is thin, **Jac Hermans Supermarket,** 30a Nwe. Binnenweg, vends all your basic sustenance (open Mon. 11am-6pm, Tues.-Thurs. 9am-6pm, Fri. 9am-6:30pm, Sat. 9am-5pm). Markets also pop up in squares all over the city. Your options after about 6pm are quite limited; late-night convenience stores haven't quite caught on yet.

SIGHTS AND ENTERTAINMENT

Much of Rotterdam's attraction lies in its architecture. Heavily influenced by the de Stijl school, Rotterdam was built as a futuristic abstraction. Although there are no rocket cars, man-eating monsters, or jet packs to be seen, Rotterdam nonetheless ruthlessly pushes ahead to become more advanced and modern.

The city is in a state of constant construction; it seems that around every corner, you're met with forklifts and excavation. What has been completed, however, should not be missed. For a dramatic example of the eccentric approach of some recent architecture, check out the freaky **cube houses,** designed by Piet Blom and built in 1984. Looking like something out of *Alice in Wonderland,* these odd living quarters are strangely reminiscent of the inside of a *Yahtzee* dice cup: jumbled cubes perched precariously around one another. You can even tour one if you like. Take the metro to Blaak, and follow the signs to **Kijks-Kubus** (open Mon.-Fri. 10am-5pm, Sat.-Sun. 11am-5pm; Oct.-Dec. and April-May Tues.-Sun. 10am-5pm; Jan.-March Sat.-Sun. 11am-5pm; f2.50). Such modern architecture strikes a strange contrast with nearby **Oude Haven** (old harbor), home to nice restaurants populated with swanky youths reclining and watching the ships go by.

Perhaps the most powerful monument in the city is Ossip Zadkine's incredible **Monument for the Destroyed City,** a statue of a man screaming, his arms raised in self-defense, his entrails spilling out onto the ground. This vision vividly embodies the pain and terror of the 1940 bombing raid. Take the metro to Churchillplein, walk toward the Blaak, and the statue is directly behind the Mariteim Museum. While you're here, check out the **Mariteim Museum** as well, a collection of memorabilia related to sailing from paintings to models to masts (open Tues.-Sat. 10am-5pm, Sun. 11am-5pm; f6).

To the north, across the street from the Mariteim Museum, stands the stately manor of the **Schielandshuis** (Historical Museum), 31 Korte Hoogstr. Inside, you'll find the history of Rotterdam through painting, sculpture, and other artifacts of the times (open Tues.-Sat. 10am-5pm, Sun. 11am-5pm; f6). For an astoundingly comprehensive collection of art, try out the **Museum Bogmans-van Bogningen,** Museumpark 18-20, M: Eendractsplein or tram 5. Home to everything from before Bosch, past Picasso, with a row of Rubens, a vault of Van Gogh, and a mix of Magritte (open Tues.-Sat. 10am-5pm, Sun. 11am-5pm; admission f6).

Chill for a couple of hours in **Dizzy Jazz Café,** 's Gravendijkwal 127. Hang out with a cup of cappuccino and sweet live jazz on Tuesday nights. (Open 8am-2am, dinner served until 10pm; f5-15.) To mingle with all the other cool people in Rotterdam, head to the **Westerpaviljoen,** at the corner of Nwe. Binnenweg and Mathenesserlaan. If the weather's nice, there's usually a big crowd outside. Inside, the service is fast and friendly. (Open Mon.-Fri. 7am-1am, Sat.-Sun. 7am-2am; cappuccino f2.50, meals f7-15.) Another popular Rotterdam institution is **de Pijp,** on Gaffelstr. 90, just off Nwe. Binnenweg. The inside is decked out in neckties and coasters, creating a rather strange ambience. Rumor has it that the Rolling Stones ate here. (Open Mon.-Sat. noon-1am.)

For a little less talk and a lot more sweat, check out one of Rotterdam's dance clubs. (Word to the wise, dancing with your wallet in your back pocket is like painting "sucker" on your back.) For Rotterdam's most active club life, try **Night Town,** West Kruiskade, 28. Alternative and Indie bands play here and the mood is frenetic. Expect a f5 "membership fee" and then another f10-35 cover depending on the band. (Open Fri.-Sat. 11pm-late.) For a good time without the entrance fee, try **Beat Corner,** at the corner of Nwe. Binnenweg and 's Gravendijkwal (open 10pm-late).

■ GOUDA

Gouda's late Gothic splendor revolves around the monstrous **St. John's Church.** Ravaged by everything from lightning to Reformation iconoclasts, it has managed to maintain a stunning collection of 70 16th-century stained-glass windows. (Open Mon.-Sat. 9am-5pm; Nov.-March Mon.-Sat. 10am-4pm; f2.50, students f1.50.) The **Goudse Pottenbakkerij,** 76 Peperstr., has been producing traditional Dutch clay pipes since the 17th century. Behind the factory that makes these long, almost lascivious pipes, the **Het Trefpunt Hostel,** at Westhaven 46 (tel. (01820) 128 79), sits primly along a canal (reception open Mon.-Sat. 8am-11:30pm, Sun. 8am-7pm; f19, sheets f5.50; no wheelchair access). Great Dutch pancakes are served to hungry souls at **Het Goudse Winkeltje,** across from the church at 9a Achter de Kerk (open Tues.-Wed. 9am-6pm, Thurs. 9am-9pm, Fri.-Sat. 9am-6pm; f3-11). Gouda is also one of the few places in Holland where you can climb inside a working windmill, **De Roode Leeuw,** while it's turning (open Tues.-Sat. 9am-2pm; f2.50, children f1).

■■■ UTRECHT

At the geographical center of the Netherlands, Utrecht presents comely canals, a grandiose cathedral, and a university that is a leftist bastion in a liberal country. Its students support a dynamic cultural scene and nightlife. If you arrive by train, hang out in the **Hoog Catharijne,** the huge modern shopping complex around Centraal Station. For something a little different from the mall, bail out to Utrecht's older quarters. At the center of Utrecht rises the **Domkerk,** begun in 1254 and finished 250 years later (open 10am-5pm; Oct.-April Mon.-Sat. 11am-4pm; free). The **Domtoren,** originally attached to the cathedral but freestanding since a nasty medieval storm blew away the church nave, is the highest tower in the Netherlands. Climb all 465 steps to see Amsterdam on a clear day. (Tower open Mon.-Fri. 10am-5pm, Sat.-Sun. noon-4pm; Nov.-March open Sat.-Sun noon-4pm. Obligatory guided tours on the hour. f4, children under 12 f2.) The **Pandhof,** the church's 15th-century cloister garden, has been converted into a rustic herb garden (open Mon.-Fri. 10am-5pm, Sat. 11am-5pm, Sun. noon-5pm; Nov.-March Sat.-Sun. noon-5pm; free). At the **Centraal Museum,** Agnietenstr. 1, you can marvel at a 9th-century Viking and paintings of the Utrecht school (open Tues.-Sat. 10am-5pm, Sun. noon-5pm. f5; seniors, children, and CJP holders f2.50). **Het Catharijneconvent,** Nieuwe Gracht 63, documents the progress of Christianity in the Netherlands with a comprehensive collection of Dutch religious artwork (open Tues.-Fri. 10am-5pm, Sat.-Sun. 11am-5pm. f5, students, seniors, and those under 18 f3.50).

Practical Information, Accommodations, and Food Utrecht has a lamentable dearth of cheap hotels; the **VVV** charges f3.50 (plus f1 for the phone calls) to locate lodgings, but they can secure special discount rates. Visit the main office, Vredenburg 90 (tel. (06) 34 03 40 85), at the end of the shopping mall—if you arrive by train, ask at the information booth in the station for a free walking map (subsequent maps f1.50) to help you find it (open Mon.-Fri. 9am-6pm, Sat. 9am-4pm; a machine outside spews a map and information for f2 at other times). The delightful **Jeugdherberg Rhijnauwen (HI),** Rhijnauwenselaan 14 (tel. (03405) 612 77), is set in a majestic medieval manor house surrounded by countless country canals. Take bus 40, 41 or 43 from Utrecht's Centraal Station (several per hr., 3 strips; tell driver your destination) and walk 5min. (Reception open 8am-12:30am. Curfew officially 12:30am, but it's flexible. f22, nonmembers f27. Sheets f6. Lockers f1, with f5 deposit. Showers and breakfast included. Pizza and cheeseburgers f2-7 at the bar.) **Camping De Berekuil,** Ariënslaan 5-7 (tel. (030) 71 38 70), is not far from the center of town; take bus 57 from the station to the Veemarkt stop (f4 per person and f4 per tent; reception open 9am-10pm; open April-Oct.).

Café De Baas, Lijnmarkt 8, just across the canal from the Domtoren, features yummy vegetarian dishes from f9.50 with occasional live music (open Wed. 5pm-10pm, Thurs. 5pm-1am, Fri. 5pm-10pm, Sat. noon-10pm). The two main student *mensas,* open to all, are **Veritas,** Kromme Nieuwe Gracht 54, and **Unitas,** Lucasbolwerk 8 (meals f5-9; both open mid-Aug. to late June Mon.-Fri. 5-7:30pm). **De Goey-Koot,** Nobelstr. 22, vends exotic fruits at basement prices (open Mon. noon-6pm, Tues.-Sat. 9am-6pm). The restaurants lining the Oude Gracht are more atmospheric, but their ambience will cost you. Try the hip and happening **Toque Toque,** Oude Gracht 138, at Vinkenburgstr. A mongo plate of pasta, with salad and bread, runs f12.50. (Open Mon.-Fri. 10am-midnight, Sat. 9am-midnight, Sun. noon-midnight.)

Utrecht presents ample opportunity to get wild and let loose. Things get hopping around 11pm at two popular bars: intellectual **De Kneus,** Nobelstr. 303 (open 4pm-4am), and the earthier **'t Pandje,** Nobelst. 193 (open 10pm-4am; beers from f2.50; bar food f2.50-4.50). If you're yearning for Americana, escape to the jungle at **Mad Mick and Big Mamou,** Oudekerkhof 29, a rocking Cajun bar and restaurant with drinks like the "Slippery Nipple" and live music every Monday at 9:30pm (dishes f7.50-15; open Sun.-Thurs. 2pm-2am, Fri.-Sat. 11am-3am).

■■■ ARNHEM AND THE HOGE VELUWE NATIONAL PARK

Rebuilt after punishing WWII bombings, **Arnhem,** 100km southeast of Amsterdam (2 trains per hr., 70min.) is now one huge outdoor shopping center with little to offer. Let the wild rumpus begin as you check out where the wild things are at the contiguous **Hoge Veluwe National Park,** a 13,000 acre preserve of woods, heath, dunes, red deer, and wild boars. This may well prove one of the highlights of your trip to Europe. Tucked deep within the park and a 35min. walk from the nearest entrance lies the **Rijksmuseum Kröller-Müller,** one of the finest modern art museums in Europe, with 276 Van Goghs and superb paintings by Seurat, Mondriaan, and many others, as well as a sculpture garden including pieces by Maillol, Moore, and Lipchitz. Visitors can pedal the park's white bikes for free—pick one up at the visitor center and drop it off at any bike stand. The newly-opened **Museonder,** at the visitor center, is the world's first underground museum, dedicated to the study of the subterranean ecosystem (exhibits open 9am-5pm, Nov.-April 10am-5pm). From June through August, and at selected times throughout the rest of the year, bus 12 "Hoge Veluwe" leaves from the Arnhem train station; board and alight as often as you wish (1 per hr., 9:40am-4:10pm, 7 strips). The bus will zoom you directly to the

NETHERLANDS

museum's doorstep, or you can ride another 1200m to **Koperen Kop,** the visitor center and bike rental station. At other times, take bus 107 to Otterlo and walk 45min. from there. (Park open 8am-sunset. Museum and sculpture park open Tues.-Sat. 10am-5pm, Sun. 11am-5pm; Nov.-March Tues.-Sat. 10am-5pm, Sun. 1-5pm. Park f7.50, children f3.75; museum and sculpture park free.)

The **VVV,** to the left of the station on Stationsplein (tel. (085) 42 03 30), finds accommodations and distributes information about the park (open Mon.-Fri. 9am-5:30pm, Sat. 9am-4pm). The placid **Jeugdherberg Alteveer (HI),** Diepenbroeklaan 27 (tel. (085) 42 01 14), is in a crunchy rural setting but gives special attention to groups and families. The rooms are clean and every room has a shower. Take bus 3 toward Alteveer and ask the driver to let you off at the hostel, then follow the signs. (Reception open 8am-12:30am. Curfew 12:30am. f24, nonmembers f29, July-Aug. add f2.50, f0.65 tourist tax. Sheets f6. Breakfast included.) **Hotel-Pension Parkzicht,** Apeldoornsestr. 16 (tel. (085) 42 06 98), is about 15min. from the station (singles f45, doubles f80-90; breakfast included). Camp at **Kampeercentrum Arnhem,** Kemperbergerweg 771 (tel. (085) 43 16 00), accessible by bus 2 "Schaarsbergen." (f10 per person, no site charge. Open March-Sept.) The **Old Inn,** Stationsplein 39a (tel. (085) 42 06 49), is a café and restaurant with a f11.70 *dagmenu* (open 11am-1am; kitchen closes at 11pm).

■■■ MAASTRICHT

Derived from the Latin *Mosae Trajectum* meaning "the crossing of the Meuse (or Maas) River," the city of Maastricht continues to thrive after over 2000 years of history. Situated on the narrow finger of land copping a feel on Belgium and Germany in the southern part of Holland, the city has seen its share of interstate rivalries. In 1991, Maastricht was the scene of the signing of the Maastricht Treaty, the latest in a series of attempts to unite Europe further. The path of Maastricht's own culture and history is well preserved in many of the city's ancient buildings. The **Onze Lieve Vrouwe Basiliek,** O.L. Vrouweplein, is an impressive medieval basilica, home to a potpourri of religious paraphernalia (open Easter-Oct. Mon.-Sat. 11am-5pm, Sun. 1-5pm; admission to the vaults f3.50). In the spring of 1995, the **Bonnefanten Museum** will move across the river to the Céramique Center. Artifacts of the Limburg area such as bits of architecture, paintings, and sculpture will be proudly honored. Finally, amateur spelunkers should really dig the **Casemates,** dug between the 16th and 19th centuries for mining and escaping sieges. Tramp through the labyrinth of tunnels for an hour on a guided tour (2pm, July16-Aug. 21 also at noon; f5.25). Another way to see the caves is by **boat,** on the Maas (April-Sept. every hr. on the hr. 10am-3pm, Sun. 1-3pm; f13).

Arriving in Maastricht, you'll end up on the eastern side, across the river from all the action, at Centraal Station. Buses run frequently from the station, across the river to the Markt. The **VVV** is about one block south of the Markt at Het Dinghuis, Kleine Staat 1 (tel. (043) 25 21 21). Pick up a super-informative info brochure for f1.75 and use the free map to navigate around. They'll also book hotel rooms free of charge. (Open Mon.-Fri. 9am-6pm, Sat. 9am-5pm.) The **HI Hostel Sportel de Dousberg,** Dousbergweg 4 (tel. (043) 43 44 04) is 20min. out of town by bus 8 to De Dousberg at a popular recreation park with an indoor/outdoor pool that guests can use for free. Slick and entertaining. (Curfew 1am. f26 plus f10 key deposit. Reserve ahead.) Sleep on the Maas at **de Hotelboot,** moored at Maasboulevard 95 (tel. (043) 21 90 23). Get rocked to sleep as you're serenaded by the thoroughfare. (Singles f55, doubles f70-80; breakfast included.)

Wallow in cheap pasta at **Stap in,** Kesselskade 61, where a full three-course meal is only f17 (open 10am-9pm). The city's cafés and nightlife are centered around the pedestrian district and especially around the **Vrijthof Square. De Bobbel,** Wolfstr. 32, is a fun café not far from the Vrijthof (open Mon.-Sat. 10am-midnight; meals from f10). **Momus,** Vrijthof 8, holds a cellar restaurant, a decidedly upper-crust first-floor dining room, and a beautiful café that is transformed into a dance hall Thurs.-Sun. nights (open Tues.-Sun. 5-10pm; meals from f15-30).

■■■ GRONINGEN

At the spritely young age of 955, Groningen (approx. 2hrs. northeast of Amsterdam) on the northern coast of Holland, shows a brash flamboyancy that has attracted bold and beautiful young people from all over Holland. Principally a college, with a city built around it, Groningen is home to all the bars, bistros, and bookstores that one would expect from a college town. Because of the German bombing of the city, most of the old buildings are now just part of the ground you're walking on, but one that survives is the **Martinitoren,** a 97m high tower that weathered everything from German bombs to a victory celebration that got out of hand (open Easter-Oct. noon-4:30pm; f2.50). Groningen's newest building, however, is certainly its most decadent. A pastel assemblage of squares cylinders, and slag metal is the quirky palace that is the new **Groninger Museum,** scheduled to open in November 1994. The art that it holds (from ancient Chinese to cutting-edge modern) will have quite a challenge competing with the building itself. (No times available yet; call (050) 18 33 43 for more info.) Groningen is also within easy biking distance from many **lakes** and **forests.** Rent a bike at the station (f8 per day), buy a map at the VVV (f7), and have at it. Also, the island of **Shiermonnikoog** (where cars are forbidden) can be reached by bus 65 (leaving at 6:20, 9:20, and 11:20am; 1:20, 5:20 and 7:20pm). A pass purchased at the VVV for f32.25 will pay for bus and ferry fares.

The **VVV** (tel. (063) 202 30 50) is at Ged. Kattendiep 6; just turn right out of the station and follow the signs (open 9am-5:30pm). The city's vitality is reflected in the perky **Simplon Youth Hotel,** Boteidiep 73 (tel. 050 15 52 21). Bestowed with funky ceiling art, this youth hotel has many other things to offer, such as laundry facilities and a weight room. Sadly, the coin-op showers could leave you all lathered up with no place to go. (24hr. reception; no curfew; dorms f17.50, breakfast f5, dinner f7.) This student's city is well-endowed with a selection of nightlife that would do for a city twice its size. The best areas for action are Poelstr. and Peperstr. (off the Groete Markt) and Zwanestr. (by the University). There, you'll find crowds of students and even impromptu volleyball games. Grab a bite to eat at the mellow café **Ugly Duck,** on Zwanestr., where a meal (with soup and quackers) will only set you back f12-15 (open 11am-2am). Or try the more stylish double-decker grand café **De Opera.** Chow your delicious meal with other beautiful people till the fat lady sings for only f14.75 for daily *dagschotel,* and from f19 for vegetarian meals. Aria having a good time? Enjoy a can of Campbell's soup and dance till the sun comes up at **Warhol,** Peperstr. 7 (open Sun.-Wed. midnight-5am, Thurs.-Sat. 11:30pm-6am). Enjoy some live jazz with other local funksters at **Jazzcafé De Spieghel,** just down the street on Peperstr., with live jazz Thurs.-Sat. at about 10:30-11pm. Most have no cover. (Open 9am-late.)

■■■ WADDEN ISLANDS (WADDENEILANDEN)

Wadden means "mudflat" in Dutch, and the land is indeed as flat as a *pannekoeken* (until you reach the lumpy sand dunes of the coast). In summer, however, sand rather than mud defines the islands. The long sandy beaches of the Wadden Islands attract hordes of German and Dutch tourists, hoping to escape the rain-drenched mainland, usually finding a rain-drenched island.

Texel You can visit Texel, the southernmost and largest island, on a daytrip from Amsterdam if you get your act together. Take the train to Den Helder (70min., f20), then bus 3 from the station to the ferry. Boats leave at 35min. past the hour, every hour from 6am to 9pm (last boat back 9:05pm, round-trip f11.55). After the ferry drops you at **'t Horntje,** on the southern tip of the island, rent a bike (f7) to pedal between Texel's three major villages: **Den Berg,** the largest town, squats in the center of island; **De Koog** lolls on the beaches on the western edge; and **De Cocksdorp** isolates itself at the northern end of the isle. Texel is a voyeur's paradise: there are two popular nude beaches (one south of Den Hoorn and one off De Cocksdorp at paal 28) plus fine bird watching. You can visit the **nature reserves** only on a two-hour guided tour organized by the State Forest Department (f7.50). Book in advance from **Ecomare,** Ruyslaan 92 (tel. (02220) 177 41), in De Koog, and specify English-speaking tours not requiring rubber boots.

Both of Texel's **HI youth hostels** are immaculate and within walking distance of Den Burg; snag bus 27 or 28 from the ferry landing to reach either one (tell the driver your destination). **Panorama,** Schansweg 7 (tel. (02220) 154 41), snuggles in a nature reserve complete with Texel's own breed of sheep. (Curfew midnight, but night key available with f50 deposit. f25.20, f30.20 nonmembers, f2 tourist tax in July. Dinner f16.) **De Eyercoogh,** Pontweg 106 (tel. (02220) 154 41), is conveniently near the town center. (Curfew midnight, but night key available. f22.50, nonmembers f27.50, f2 tax in July. Reception open 9am-midnight. Open March-Oct.) If both the hostels are full, your best bet is **Hotel de Merel,** Warmoestr. 22 (tel. (02220) 131 32), around the corner from the main square in Den Burg (f40 per person; f10 surcharge per person for 1 night stay; f2 tourist tax in summer). The **VVV** in Den Burg, 66 Emmalaan (tel. (02220) 147 41), sells excellent maps (f5.95) of biking and walking routes and updates you on the island's 20 **campgrounds** and several farms that allow camping. (Open Mon.-Fri. 9am-6pm, Sat.-Sun. 9am-5pm.) Sample the local seafood at **Theodorahoeve,** Kogerstr. 26 in Den Burg (fish soup f7.50), which also dishes out great Dutch pancakes (f8.50-15.50). (Open 11am-9pm.) **De 12 Balcken Tavern,** at 20 Weverstr. in Den Burg, is a snug and dimly lit pub that specializes in *'t Jutterje,* the island's wildly popular alcohol, blended from herbs and wheat (open Mon.-Sat. 10am-2am, Sun. noon-2am; beer f2.75). On June 17, 1995, Texel will host **Ronde Van Texel,** the largest catamaran race in Europe and the culmination of a week-long **jazz festival.** Another jazzfest is held during the first week in October.

The Friese Islands The four other islands (the Friese Islands) all have extensive dunes and wildlife sanctuaries. **Schiermonnikoog** and **Vlieland** are the most deserted, while **Terschelling** and **Ameland** offer more nightlife. On boat excursions to Vlieland from Texel, you must return the same day. Schiermonnikoog's **VVV,** Reeweg (tel. (05195) 312 33), finds rooms in private homes for about f30 per person. Reserve ahead, even in off-season. (Open Mon.-Fri. 9am-1pm and 2:30-6:30pm.) There are **HI youth hostels** on three of the islands: the **Terschelling Hostel (HI),** van Heusdenweg 39 (tel. (05620) 23 38; open year-round), the Ameland **De Kleine Grie (HI),** Oranjeweg 59 (tel. (05191) 41 33; open mid-June to late Aug. plus a week at Easter), and Schiermonnikoog's **Rijsbergen,** Knuppeldam 2 (tel. (05195) 312 57; closed in Jan.). For Terschelling or Vlieland, take the main train line from Amsterdam to **Leeuwarden** (2½hr.), then continue to Harlingen (f7), where you can catch the ferry to either island (2hr., round-trip f30.60, bikes f11). To reach Ameland, take bus 66 from Leeuwarden (6 strips, 50min.) to Holwerd and then the ferry (8-11 per day; Sept.-May 4-6 per day; 45min., f14.30 round-trip). Reach Schiermonnikoog from Lauwersoog (40min., f14.80 round-trip), itself reached by bus 51 from Leeuwarden (75min., 11 strips). In July and Aug., ferries also run between the islands, making it possible to see several in two or three days.

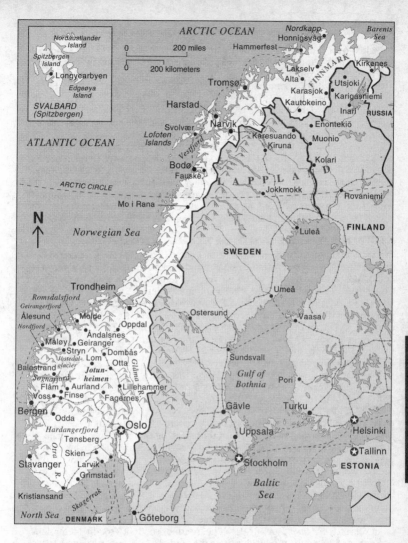

Norway (Norge)

US$1	= 6.81kr (kroner, or NOK)		1kr =	US$0.15
CDN$1	= 5.07kr		1kr =	CDN$0.20
UK£1	= 10.82kr		1kr =	UK£0.09
IR£1	= 10.72kr		1kr =	IR£0.09
AUS$1	= 5.22kr		1kr =	AUS$0.19
NZ$1	= 4.13kr		1kr =	NZ$0.24
SAR1	= 1.91kr		1kr =	SAR0.52
Country Code: 47			International Dialing Prefix: 095	

Stretched over the northwest rim of Europe, Norway is the continent's ineffable encounter with nature. Piney valleys and farming homesteads soften severe fjords and mountains. From Norway's rugged coast, fierce Norsemen spread across the Atlantic and "settled" communities in England, Ireland, and France. The pagan pillaging party subsided in the 10th century, when King Harald Hårfagre (Harold the Fair-haired) unified the realm and Olav Haraldsson imported Christianity (duty free). Runestones, stave churches, and preserved Viking ships still survive from this age, while sagas chronicle it and its myths in rich poetry and epics.

The closing years of the 19th century spawned great luminaries of art, drama, and music, from Munch to Ibsen, Hamsun to Grieg. After oppressive German occupation in WWII, Norway developed into a modern welfare state. Today its four million people pay outrageous taxes but officially enjoy the highest standard of living in the world. Northern Norway's simple, striplike geography contrasts with the country's wider southern parts, where long valleys run between Oslo and Trondheim, connected by passes over Scandinavia's highest mountains to the fjords in the west.

GETTING THERE AND GETTING AROUND

Every coastal town of any significance from Oslo to Bergen has **ferry** service to Denmark, England, or Germany (more frequent and expensive in summer and on weekends). Most foreigners, cowed by the ferry system, take the **train** to Oslo from Copenhagen (3-4 per day, 10hr., 580kr) or Stockholm (1-3 per day, 6hr., 484kr). Eurail is valid on all trains in Norway. The new **Norway Rail Pass** grants you unlimited travel within the country for 3 days (US$129, Oct.-April US$115), 7 days (US$180, Oct.-April US$144), or 14 days (US$243, Oct.-April US$195). The *buy-in-Scandinavia* **Scanrail pass,** which replaced the Nordturist Railpass, allows 5 days within 15 (1335kr, under 26: 1000kr) or 21 consecutive days (2040kr, under 26: 1530 kr) of unlimited rail travel through Norway, Sweden, Denmark, and Finland, as well as many free or discounted ferry rides. This differs from the *buy-outside-of-Scandinavia* **Scanrail pass** which offers 5 out of 15 days (US$159, under 26: US$119), 10 out of 21 days (US$275, under 26 US$206), or 30 consecutive days (US$399, under 26 US$299) of unlimited travel. No free brochure gives you a complete, comprehensive picture of the complex domestic transportation scene; you'll have to collect sheaves of free regional schedules, or ask travel agents or train stations for a look at their all-fathoming *Rutebok for Norge.* Norwegian trains run only up to Bodø; the only trains farther north move along the Swedish rail line through Kiruna, which dead-ends at Narvik on the Norwegian coast, and along a line from Murmansk in Russia. You need a seat to ride trains, so book ahead (20kr, sleeping berths 100-200kr).

For those under 25, special youth fares make **flying** a viable option, often cheaper than the train. **SAS** and **Braathens SAFE** are the main airlines, and both offer standby tickets (*chance billet*) for any trip either north or south of Trondheim for 400kr one way, or 800kr if the trip involves both the northern and southern zones. A "Visit Norway Pass" purchased in the U.S. (from Scanam World Tours, call 800-545-2204), which is not really a flight pass but rather a type of discount, costs US$70 per flight segment (north or south of Trondheim) and is valid from May through September. **Buses** are usually quite expensive (about 1kr per km), but are the only firm surface option north of Bodø and in the fjords. Always ask for student discounts and try flashing your railpass.

Car ferries *(ferjer)* are usually much cheaper (and slower) than the many **hydrofoils** *(hurtigbåte)* that cruise the coasts; both occasionally allow student discounts. Throughout the chapter you'll see references to the **Hurtigruten** (the famed Coastal Steamer), which takes 6 days for its fantastic voyage from Bergen to Kirkenes; each of the 25 stops en route have one northbound and one southbound departure per day. The *Hurtigruten* often have a free sleeping-bag room; empty cabins run from 70 to 110kr per night (50% off in off-season). Many Norwegians **hitch** beyond the rail lines in northern Norway and the fjord areas of the west. Those hitching use a sign or flag and try to find a ride before or during a ferry trip to avoid getting stuck at the landing. In all of Nordland province (including Bodø, Fauske, the Lofotens, and Narvik), Scanrail takes 50% off bus fares. In the Lofotens, students only get the 50% discount, Eurail gets nothing, and car ferries give a 50% student discount, while hydrofoils give no discounts to non-Norwegians.

NORWAY ESSENTIALS

Most towns in Norway have *Turistinformasjon* offices; look for the blue signs with black lower-case "i"s. Try to go the night before planning an excursion, as buses often leave early in the morning. **Banks** are open Monday through Friday from 8:15am to 3pm in summer and 3:30pm in winter, Thursday 9am to 5pm. Large **post offices** exchange money and usually charge less commission. (Generally open Mon.-Fri. 8am-5pm, Sat. 8am-1pm.) Legal **holidays,** when everything closes, include New Year's Day, Easter (April 13-17, 1995), Labor Day (May 1), Constitution Day (May 17), Whit Monday (June 5, 1995), Midsummer (June 23-25, 1995) and Christmas.

For a few weeks around the summer solstice (June 21), Norway north of Bodø basks in the midnight sun. Skiing is best just before Easter, when the winter has slackened somewhat, and the sun returns after months of darkness. Oslo averages 63°F (17°C) in July, 24°F (-4°C) in January; up north, summer temperatures dip to about 50°F (10°C) while winter temperatures are much the same as in the south. Hikers should bring heavy clothing and four-season sleeping bags.

Domestic and international **telephone** calls can butcher the budget in Norway. Pay phones take 1, 5, and 10kr coins and local calls require at least 2kr; buying a *telekort* card is more economical in the long-run. For operator assistance dial 093 (English- and German-speaking) or 091 (Nordic). To make collect calls internationally, dial 01 15, within Norway 01 17. AT&T **USADirect's** number is 800 19 011, MCI **WorldPhone** 800 19 912, **Canada Direct** 800 19 111, **BT Direct** 800 19 044, **Ireland Direct** 800 19 353, **Australia Direct** 800 19 961, and **South Africa Direct** 800 19 927. Norway is officially a bilingual country. Reacting to the Danish-influenced *bokmål* Norwegian used in Oslo, 19th-century linguists constructed an alternative standard language *(nynorsk)* based on the more archaic dialects of rural western Norway; the two are taught on an equal footing in schools. Fortunately, the great majority of Norwegians speak fluent English.

Accommodations and Camping When in Norway, camp. Norwegian law allows you to camp for free anywhere you want for two nights, provided you keep 150m from all buildings and fences and leave no traces of your frolicking. Take advantage of **Den Norske Turistforening** (DNT, the Norwegian Mountain Touring Association); their Oslo and Bergen offices are particularly helpful. They sell excellent maps and maintain a series of mountain huts *(hytter)* throughout the country. (40-65kr per night. Open to nonmembers for a 45kr surcharge. Membership 270kr, under 25: 150kr.) Staffed huts serve full meals and are akin to hostels but have a consistently more attractive ambience and more Norwegian guests than international tourists. Get the entrance key for unattended huts (deposit required) from a DNT or tourist office before heading out. DNT huts are open during Easter and from the end of June to the beginning of September. The indispensable *Vandrerhjem i Norge* brochure lists prices, phone numbers, and so much more for Norway's 94 **HI youth hostels** *(vandrerhjem)*. Beds run 70-165kr; breakfast (often mandatory) costs 40-50kr. Usually only rural hostels have curfews, but only a few are open year-round. Most tourist offices in Norway can book you a room in a private home; they're roughly 160kr for singles, 240kr for doubles. **Campgrounds** usually have cabins at 200-400kr for groups of 2 or 4.

Food and Drink Norwegian food is murder on the wallet; markets and bakeries may become your dearest friends. Seek out the nationwide discount **REMA 1000** supermarkets. (Usually open Mon.-Fri. 9am-8pm, Sat. 9am-6pm.) Though hostel breakfasts are usually dull, they almost always provide the cheapest grub around. Restaurants often have inexpensive *dagens ret* (dish of the day) specials (60-70kr for a full meal); otherwise you're lucky to get out for less than 100kr. Tips are included. Self-service *kafeterias* are a less expensive option. Fish in Norway—cod, salmon, and herring—is unusually fresh, good, and cheap. National specialties include cheese *(ost;* try *Jarlsberg* and the brown *geitost),* pork and veal meatballs *(kjøtkaker)* with boiled potatoes, and (for lusty carnivores) controversial *kval* (whale meat). In most Norwegian restaurants, alcohol is served only after 3pm and never on Sundays. Beer is heavily taxed and *very* expensive (50kr in a bar is quite reasonable). *Gløgg,* a Scandinavian mulled wine, is popular in winter.

■■■ OSLO

Founded in 1050, Oslo has burned down several times since. Although the city has a dull reputation, a mine of attractions await excavation. Moreover, the city abounds with nightlife and diversions, which although expensive become scarce when you leave for the wilds. Oslo is one of the largest cities in the world, in terms of area and boasts verdant vistas and broad boulevards, making it a cosmopolitan center of culture, cuisine, and style.

ORIENTATION AND PRACTICAL INFORMATION

Karl Johans gate, running from Sentralstasjon to the *Slottet* (Royal Palace), is Oslo's principal boulevard and a useful reference point. Several pedestrian streets originate from it. The city is small enough to manage by foot; only excursions to places like Holmenkollen (the ski jumps you can see in the distance) require use of the well-developed public transportation system.

Tourist Office: The **Main Tourist Office,** Vestbaneplassen 1 (tel. 22 83 81 50), in a yellow former train station toward the piers, sports gigantic "NORWAY" signs and books rooms (20kr fee). Free maps and guides. Sells the Oslo Card, which covers public transit and admission to many sights for 1 day (110kr), 2 days (190kr), or 3 days (240kr). Open Mon.-Fri. 9am-8pm, Sat.-Sun. 9am-4pm; March-May and Sept.-Nov. Mon.-Fri. 9am-4:30pm; Jan.-Feb. and Dec. Mon.-Fri. 9am-4pm. The branch at **Sentralstasjon** (tel. 22 17 11 24) also books rooms. Open 8am-11pm. For hikers, **Den Norske Turistforening,** Stortingsgata 28, with entrance around the corner on Olav V gate (tel. 22 83 25 50), rents mountain huts and sells trail maps. Open Mon.-Wed. and Fri. 8:30am-4pm, Thurs. 8:30am-6pm. Youth-oriented **USE IT,** Møllergata 3, (4 blocks up Karl Johans gate from the station, then right; tel. 22 41 51 32), offers listings of cheap lodgings and restaurants, travel tips, and the useful *Streetwise* youth guide. Open Mon.-Fri. 7:30am-6pm, Sat. 9am-2pm; Sept.-May Mon.-Fri. 11am-5pm.

Budget Travel: Kilroy Travels, Universitetssentret (tel. 22 85 32 00). The cheapest deals in town. **Reisebyrået Terra Nova,** Dronningens gate 26 (tel. 22 42 14 10). Discounted rail and plane tickets on international routes. Open Mon.-Fri. 9:30am-4pm, Sat. 10am-2pm.

Embassies: U.S., Drammensveien 18 (tel. 22 44 85 50). Take tram 1, 2, or 9, or bus 27, 29, or 30. Open Mon.-Fri. 9am-3pm. **Canada,** Oscarsgate 20 (tel. 22 46 69 55), near Bislett Stadium. Take tram 2 or 11. Open Mon.-Fri. 8am-3:30pm. **U.K.,** Thomas Heftyesgate 8 (tel. 22 55 24 00). Open Mon.-Fri. 9am-4pm. Travelers from **Australia** or **New Zealand** should contact the British Embassy. **Ireland,** contact embassy in Copenhagen. **South Africa,** Drammenveien 8c (tel. 22 44 79 10).

Currency Exchange: Lowest commissions on traveler's checks other than AmEx (see below) at post offices (10kr per check, 15kr for cash). Rail station office open Mon.-Fri. 7am-5:30pm, Sat. 9am-2pm, and central post office open late (see below). After-hours exchange in **Bankveksling** next to the post office in the station—but 15-20kr per traveler's check. Open 7am-11pm.

American Express: Winge Reisebyrå, Karl Johans gate 33 (tel. 22 41 95 00; emergency number: 05 01 10 00). All services. Address mail to American Express, P.O. Box 54, Majorstuen, 0304 Oslo. Open Mon.-Fri. 9am-6pm, Sat. 10am-3pm.

Post Office: Dronningens gate 15 (tel. 22 40 78 23); enter at Prinsens gate. Open Mon.-Fri. 8am-8pm, Sat. 9am-3pm. **Postal Code:** 0101 Oslo 1.

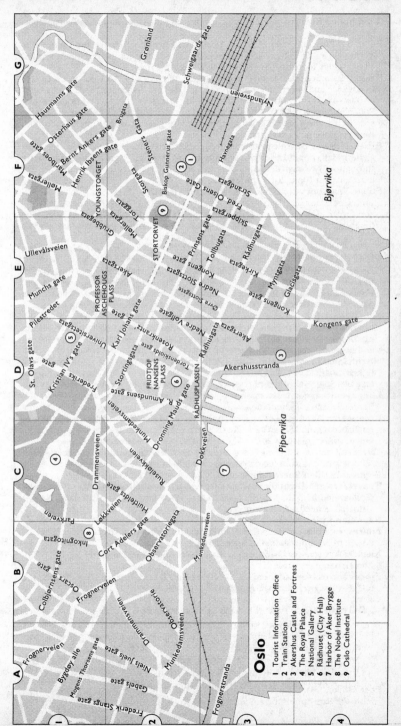

NORWAY

Oslo

1 Tourist Information Office
2 Train Station
3 Akershus Castle and Fortress
4 The Royal Palace
5 National Gallery
6 Rådhuset (City Hall)
7 Harbor of Aker Brygge
8 The Nobel Institute
9 Oslo Cathedral

Telephones: Kongens gate 21, enter at Prinsens gate. Open Mon.-Fri. 8:30am-8pm, Sat. 10am-5pm.

Flights: White SAS buses (35kr) run between **Fornebu Airport** and the Air Bus Terminal (tel. 59 62 20) at Galleri Oslo opposite the station. Frequent service 6am-9:30pm. Municipal bus 31 runs to Fornebu (15kr).

Trains: Oslo Sentralstasjon (Central Station, tel. 22 17 14 00). Book at least 1 day in advance and get reduced *minipriser* any day but Fri. or Sun. Trains to Bergen (7-8hr., 480kr), Trondheim (7-8hr., 550kr, *minipris* 380kr), and Bodø (17hr., 860kr, *minipris* 490kr). Open 6:30am-11pm. The **InterRail Center** at Sentral-stasjon has **showers** (20kr), a kitchen, and **luggage storage** (free). Open mid-June to late Sept. 7am-11pm.

Buses: Norway Bussekspress, Schweigårdsgate 10 (tel. 22 17 52 90) in the Oslo Galleri Mall, behind the train station and to the right, sends buses scurrying throughout Norway (Bergen 500kr) and across Europe. Terminal open Mon.-Fri. and Sun. 8am-10pm, Sat. 8am-5:30pm.

Public Transportation: Info at **Trafikanten** (tel. 22 17 70 30), in front of the station. Open Mon.-Fri. 7am-8pm, Sat.-Sun. 8am-6pm. All forms (bus, tram, subway, and ferry) 15kr per trip. A 24hr. **Dagskort** allows unlimited travel (35kr). For longer stays, the **7-day card** (130kr) makes sense. The **Oslo Card** (see Tourist Offices, above) is economical only for a *lot* of sight-seeing.

Ferries: Passenger ferries arrive at the port, a 15min. walk from the center. **Color Line** (tel. 22 83 60 10) has daily ferries to Kiel, Germany (400kr) and Hirtshals, Denmark (330kr, weekends 460kr). No student discount July to mid-Aug. **DFDS Scandinavian Seaways** (tel. 22 41 90 90) sails to Helsingborg, Sweden and Copenhagen daily (from 425kr in summer; higher on weekends). **Stena Lines** (tel. 22 33 50 00) has 1 daily run to Frederikshavn, Denmark (370kr in summer).

Bike Rental: Den Rustne Eike, Vestbaneplassen 2 (tel. 22 83 72 31), behind the tourist office. 95kr per day, 465kr per week. Mountain bikes 120kr per day, 600kr per week. Deposit 500kr (mountain bike 1000kr) or passport. Open 10am-6:30pm, Oct.-May Mon.-Fri. 10am-3:30pm. 15% discount with Oslo card.

Hitchhiking: Leaving Oslo by thumb is often a losing proposition; some try the USE IT ride board. Those heading south try outside West Station. Those going north take bus 30 or 31 to Sinsenkrysset, main intersection of north-bound highways.

Luggage Storage: Train station lockers 20-30kr. Open 7am-11pm. Free at the InterRail Center in the station.

Bookstore: Tanum Libris, Karl Johans gate 43 (in Paléet). Wide selection of English paperbacks and *Let's Go*s. Open Mon.-Fri. 10am-8pm, Sat. 10am-5pm. **Norli,** Universitetsgata 20-24. Cheap books for starving students.

Laundromat: Look for the word *Myntvaskeri*. **Selvbetjent Vask,** Ullevålsveien 15, a few blocks from the city center. Wash 30kr, dry 10kr. Soap included.

Gay and Lesbian Services: tel. 22 11 33 60, after 8pm, weekdays.

Travelers with Disabilities: The **Norwegian Association of the Physically Challenged** (tel. 22 17 02 55, fax 22 17 61 77), P.O. Box 9217 Vaterland, N-0134 Oslo, has general information.

Rape Crisis Line: Legevakt, tel. 22 20 10 90. Also, see Emergencies.

Pharmacy: Look for the word *Apotek*. **Jernbanetorvets Apotek** (tel. 22 41 24 82), in front of the station, is open 24hrs.

Medical Assistance: Oslo Kommunale Legevakt, Storgata 40 (tel. 22 11 70 70). 24hr. emergency care.

Emergencies: Ambulance: tel. 003. **Fire** and **Accidents:** tel. 001. **Police:** tel. 002. Headquarters at Grønlandsleiret 44 (tel. 66 90 50).

ACCOMMODATIONS AND CAMPING

Ask at the **Innkvartering** accommodations office in the station, and at the **USE IT** office, which has a list of cheap sleeps. Innkvartering books rooms in private homes for multi-night stays. (Singles 315kr. Doubles 415kr. 20kr fee.) *Pensjonater* (pensions) are usually less expensive than hotels; call for reservations. Many hotels slash prices from late June to mid-August. Wilderness huts outside Oslo are a deal (from 60kr), but 45 minutes from public transport. Inquire at USE IT.

YMCA Sleep Inn, Møllergata 1 (tel. 22 42 10 66, fax 22 42 39 56); enter on parallel Grubbegata. The cheapest spot in town. Sleeping bag accommodations. 60 mats in 2 dorms. Reception open 8-11am and 5pm-midnight. Lock-out 11am-5pm. Lax curfew 2am. 100kr. Kitchen facilities and baggage storage. Open July to mid-Aug.

Haraldsheim (HI), Haraldsheimveien 4 (tel. 22 15 50 43, fax 22 22 10 25). Take tram 10 or 11. Friendly, cozy, and crowded. No sleeping bags. Reception closed 11am-2pm. Lock-out 11am-4pm. 145kr, nonmembers 170kr. Breakfast included. Sheets 35kr. Laundry 40kr (soap included). Reservations essential in summer.

Ellingsens Pensjonat, Holtegata 25 (tel. 22 60 03 59, fax 22 60 99 21). Take tram 1 direction "Majorstuen" or walk 3km from the city center. Clean, tight ship. Singles 200kr. Doubles 3000kr. Call ahead.

Cochs Pensjonat, Parkveien 25 (tel. 22 60 48 36, fax 22 46 54 02), corner of Hegdehaugsveien by the royal park. Triples 450kr. Quads 520kr. Triple 570kr and quad 640kr (with kitchenette and bathroom). Reservations recommended.

OSI-Chalet, Kjellerberget (tel. 22 49 90 36). Sleeping-bagged students snooze in sylvine sanctuary. Bus 41 to Sørhedalen School, then a 45min. walk. Call for directions and reception hours. 70kr, with student ID 50kr.

Camping: Ekeberg Camping, Ekebergveien 65 (tel. 22 19 85 68), about 3km from town, with marvelous view. Take tram 1 or 9 from Central Station. Tent sites 90kr, including showers. Open June-Aug. **Free camping** in the forest north of town as long as you avoid public areas. Try the end of the Sognsvann subway line.

FOOD

A full meal in a restaurant may impoverish you. The cheapest shopping area is the **Tøyen/Grønland** immigrant district northeast of Central Station; try along Tøyengata and Urtegata. Another option is the lunch specials (from 44kr) in the **Paléet Shopping Center** (Karl Johans gate 37-41, next to the American Express office). Three discount supermarket chains bring an inexpensive selection: **Rimi,** Rosenkrantzgate 20 (open Mon.-Fri. 9am-5pm); **Rema 1000,** Holmesgata 7 (open Mon.-Wed. and Fri. 9am-6pm, Thurs. 9am-8pm); **Tempus,** Youngsgata 11 (open Mon.-Fri. 8am-7pm, Sat. 10am-6pm). The **7-Eleven** stores and **Narvesen** kiosks are open late.

Vegeta Vertshus Frisksportrestaurant, Munkedamsveien 3b, off Stortings gate. *Jeg er vegetaner.* Unpretentious vegetarian delight with an awesome array of salads, soups, pizzas, and hot dishes. All-you-can-jam-on-a-plate 75kr, all-you-can-jam-in-your-face buffet 110kr. Open 10am-11pm.

Kafé Celsius, Rådhusgata 19. Pale-yellow buildings shelter a cozy courtyard. Omelet 68kr, pasta from 80kr. Open Tues.-Wed. 11:30am-12:30am, Thurs.-Sat. 11:30am-2am, Sun. 1pm-12:30am.

Darbar Mat & Vinhus, Smedgata 45. Take subway to Tøyen station, walk down path to Sørligata, and continue to Smedgata. Authentic Indian restaurant full of aroma. Vegetarian dishes 60-90kr, meat dishes 100-150kr. Open Mon.-Sat. 4-11pm, Sun. 2-11pm.

Gamle Rådhus Restaurant, Nedre Slottsgate 1 (tel. 22 42 01 07). The oldest restaurant in Oslo. Smells fishy, in a positive sense—Norwegian cuisine. Tourist menu 120kr. Open Mon.-Fri. 11am-11pm, Sat. 5-11pm.

SIGHTS

Akershus Castle and Fortress was built in 1300 and transformed into a Renaissance palace by Christian IV. You can explore the castle's underground passages, banquet halls, dungeons, and courtyards. There are concerts on summer Sundays. (Open May to mid-Sept. Mon.-Sat. 10am-4pm, Sun. 12:30-4pm; mid-Sept. to Oct. and April 15-30 Sun. 12:30-4pm. 10kr, students 5kr. Tours in summer at 11am, 1pm, 3pm; spring and fall at 1 and 3pm.) The poignant **Hjemmefrontmuseet** (Resistance Museum) in the fortress documents Norway's efforts to subvert Nazi occupation. (Open Mon.-Sat. 10am-5pm, Sun. 11am-5pm; Oct. to mid-April Mon.-Sat. 10am-3pm, Sun. 11am-4pm. 15kr, students and seniors 5kr.)

From the castle, head toward the island of **Bygdøy;** take ferry 91 from pier #3, or bus 30 from Nationaltheatret. The island's **Folkemuseum** collection of traditional houses amounts to seeing all of Norway in two hours—how's that for a budget tip? (Open 10am-6pm, mid-Sept. to mid-May 10am-4pm, mid-May to mid-June 11am-5pm. 35kr, students 25kr. English tours at 11am, noon, and 2pm.) Embark on the nearby **Polar Ship "Fram,"** which Arctic explorer Roald Amundsen chilled on in 1892 (open 9am-5:45pm, 20kr). The ethnologist **Thor Heyerdahl's** crafts *Kon-Tiki, Ra I,* and *Ra II* have their own museum, featuring the original *Kon-Tiki* and a fake full-scale whale. Heyerdahl recreated ancient, often mythical voyages; in 1947, the Kon-Tiki expedition set out to prove that the first Polynesian settlers had sailed from pre-Inca Peru. (Open 10am-6pm; Sept. to mid-May closes 1-3hr. earlier. 20kr, students 10kr.) The three vessels of the **Viking Ship Museum** include the 9th-century ring-prowed, dragon-keeled *Oseberg* barge used to bury a queen. (Open 10am-6pm, Sept. 11am-5pm, April and Oct. 11am-4pm, Nov.-March 11am-3pm. 20kr, students 10kr.) Weather permitting, plunge in the bracing water off **Huk Beach,** Oslo's most popular, located about 1km from the Viking Ship Museum. Or bare it all at nude **Strandskogen,** across the inlet from Huk.

The blunt, powerful sculptures at **Vigeland Park (Frognerpark)** depict each stage of the human life cycle; the park is a playground of grassy knolls, duck ponds, and tennis courts. Gustav Vigeland's obelisk resides here: an eerie, erotic tower of contorted human shapes. (Open 24hrs. Free.) Take tram 2 or bus 20 from National-altheatret, or walk up **Hegdehaugsveien,** with its markets, cafés, and shops. The **Munch Museum,** Tøyengata 53 (open Mon.-Sat. 10am-6pm, Sun. noon-6pm; Oct.-May Tues.-Sat. 10am-4pm, Sun. noon-6pm; 40kr, students 10kr; take the subway to Tøyen) may be a scream, with an outstanding collection of Edvard Munch's unsettling paintings, woodcuts, and lithographs, but his "Scream" is actually at the **National Gallery,** Universitetsgaten 13. (Open Mon., Wed., and Fri.-Sat. 10am-4pm, Thurs. 10am-8pm, Sun. 11am-3pm. Free.)

For a panorama of Oslofjord and the city, take subway 15 from Stortinget to the stop on the Frognerseteren line and walk to the ski jump **Holmenkollen.** Grease your body and slide on down. As you sail through the air, note that forest and lakes cover over half of the "city" of Oslo. (Open May and Sept. 10am-5pm; June 9am-8pm; July 9am-10pm; Aug. 9am-8pm; Oct-April Mon-Fri. 10am-3pm, Sat.-Sun. 11am-5pm. 15kr, students 10kr.) To bask in Norway's natural grandeur, take the Sogns-vann subway from Nationaltheatret to the end of the line. USE IT provides free trail maps; in winter, ask the tourist office about cross-country ski rental.

Enjoy a delightful and inexpensive daytrip on one of the islands in the inner Oslofjord. In summer, you can visit the ruins of an old monastery on **Hovedøya; Langøyene** offers Oslo's best beach. Boats leave from the piers in front of City Hall and from **Vippetangen,** reached by bus 18. (Round-trip 32kr, free with city transport pass.) The evening cruise is especially enchanting.

ENTERTAINMENT

For information on daily events in Oslo, consult *What's on in Oslo,* free at the tourist offices. Summer sends the opera, philharmonic, and numerous theatre companies scurrying for shade, and the Oslo hordes head for the pubs, bars, and cafés which line **Aker Brygge** quay and the area along Karl Johans gate. Revelry comes with its price; beer is expensive, and cover charges are often outrageous. **The Beach Club,** Bryggetorget 14, is a quiet outdoor bar at the end of the courtyard in Aker Brygge (open Mon.-Sat. noon-1am, Sun. 1pm-1am). **Sebastian's Rock Cafe,** on Karl Johans gate next to the American Express office, features dancing, live music, and outdoor tables for people-watching (open Mon.-Tues. 11am-1am, Wed.-Thurs. 11am-2am, Fri.-Sat. 11am-4am, Sun. 3pm-1am). A young, trendy set drinks to the red rum of Jack Nicholson in **Café Nichol and Son,** Olav V's gate 1, while emulation of another brand is carried on at **Woodstock** and neighboring **Underhuset,** on the pedestrian section of Karl Johans gate. Hunt or be hunted in **Barock,** Universitetsgata 2b, a hip restaurant, bar, and club. University students booze it up at **Café Amsterdam,** Universitetsgata 11, while radical freethinkers ruminate on an outdoor terrace during long summer nights at **Café Nordraak,** St. Olavs gate 2. The gay scene shifts constantly; **Recepten,** Prinsens gate 22, is a popular haunt.

SOUTHERN NORWAY

Norway's southern coast substitutes serenity for drama. *Skjærgård,* archipelagos of water-worn rock hugging the shore, stretch from Oslo south to Kristiansand. From Kristiansand to Stavanger, the shoreline smooths to an endless white beach. This coast is Norway's premier summer holiday resort, but foreign tourists are less common here. Inland, dense woods swathe the high cliffs; fishing, hiking, rafting, and canoeing are summer options, as is cross-country skiing in the winter, especially in Telemark, where the sport was born. Two train lines run south from Oslo. The main one extends through Kristiansand around to Stavanger; the other loops through Tønsberg to Skien before reconnecting with the main line at Nordgatu. Most towns along the south coast without rail service are connected by buses (check the NSB schedules). Larger towns have ferry service to Denmark and sometimes Britain.

Tønsberg and Larvik Reputedly the oldest town in Scandinavia, **Tønsberg** brings the beach to within a daytrip from Oslo. Buses run from the station to **Nøtterøy** (15kr) and **Tjøme** islands (30kr), where *skjærgård* and bathing unite. The Slottsfjellet tower offers a voluptuous vista (12kr). The **Vestfold Fylkemuseum,** Farmannsveien 30, a museum of regional history, has skeletons in the closet. Of big whales. (Open May-Sept. Mon.-Sat. 10am-5pm, Sun. noon-5pm.) The terminally helpful **tourist office** (tel. 33 31 02 20) is on Nedre Langgate 36B; follow Tolbod from the station, and turn left on Nedre Langgate a block before the harbor. Ask them about renting a hut on one of the 672 islands. (Open June and Aug. Mon.-Sat. 10am-5pm; July 10am-8pm; Sept.-May Mon.-Fri. 10am-4pm.) The welcoming **HI youth hostel,** Dronning Blancas gate 22 (tel. and fax 33 31 28 48), is near the station. Take a right on Farmannsveien, then left on Peder Lagmannsgate. (Reception open 6am-11pm. 140kr, nonmembers 165kr. Closed Christmas week.)

Larvik, the small and industrial birthplace of explorer and author Thor Heyerdahl, lies 2½ hours south of Oslo. The **tourist office,** Storgata 48 (tel. 33 13 01 00), 50m east of the station, helps you find accommodations in *hytte* (pensions). (Open Mon.-Sat. 8am-6pm, Sun. 3-6pm; early Aug.-late June Mon.-Fri. 8:30am-4pm.) **Jahrengård og Færiehytter** (tel. 33 19 90 30) offers doubles for 250kr, a 10km bus ride (20kr) from town. Closer to Larvik, **Seierstad Gjestegaard** (tel. 33 11 10 92, fax 33 11 12 60) offers rustic singles for 180kr, doubles for 260kr. The closest **camping** is at **Gon** (tel. 33 12 65 11), 4km out of town. Consult the gratis *Larvik Distrikt* booklet for happenings. There are many excellent beaches along the district's 123km coastline, mostly consisting of *svaberg,* smooth rounded rocks sloping into the sea.

Skien and Kristiansand **Skien,** the gateway to the Telemark province, lies before **Nordgatu** at the junction of the two train lines. Birthplace of iconoclast playwright Henrik Ibsen, its **tourist office** is at Henrik Ibsen gata 2 (tel. 35 52 82 27). From the train station, walk down Rektor Ørns gate and follow the signs. Venstøp Farm, 3mi. north of the town center was Ibsen's childhood home and is furnished with objects used by the Ibsen family as well as period pieces. Ibsen didn't like Skien so much, leaving Skien when he was 15 and only returning to scrounge some money for school in Oslo. (Open June-Aug. Mon.-Sat. noon-5pm, Sun. noon-6pm. 15kr.) **Dag Bondeheim,** a hotel at Prinsessegate 7 near the tourist office, offers the cheapest accommodations at 240kr a room; to get to the two **camping sites,** take the Ulefoss bus (**Gåsodden camping**) or the Klyve bus (**Skien camping**).

Kristiansand, "Norway's #1 Vacation Town," lies at the southern tip of Norway. Here the sun shines more often—on tourists and touristy shops. Day hikes wind along the cliffs above the town, and the beach is jumping on a warm day. The helpful **tourist office** on Dronningensgate 2 (tel. 38 02 60 65), is a 5-block walk from the train station along Vestre Strandgate. (Open Mon.-Sat. 7am-7:30pm, Sun. noon-7:30pm; Sept.-May Mon.-Fri. 8am-4pm.) The **Kristiansand Youth Hostel (HI),** Kongsgårds Allé 33c (tel. 38 09 53 69), is a long trek across the Otra River from the city center. Take bus 15 or 16 from Henrik Wergelandsgate (direction "Lund"). (Reception open 4-10pm. 125kr, nonmembers 150kr. Open May-Sept.) **Ferries** run to Hirsthals, Denmark. (Bookings tel. 38 07 88 88. 3-4 per day. 4hr. From 84kr in the winter and 294kr in July and Aug., 50% Eurail discount, students ½-price except July to mid-Aug.).

Stavanger At the end of the southern rail line, Stavanger radiates oil-boom wealth. North Sea cash provided the tax revenue to restore the be-cobbled **old quarter,** Northern Europe's best preserved wooden-house settlement. Built by King Sigurd the Crusader in 1125, the Gothic **cathedral** retains medieval solemnity amidst Stavanger's light-hearted center. (Open Mon.-Sat. 9am-6pm, Sun. 1-6pm; late Sept.-May Mon.-Fri. 9am-2pm.) At the spectacular **Pulpit Rock,** a cliff plunges over 600m into the Lysefjord. From Stavanger, take the frequent ferry to Tau (tel. 51 56 71 71; 23kr, 40min.), a bus (30kr, departs every 40min.) to the base of the mountain, and hike the 2 hours to the top. The **tourist office** (tel. 51 53 51 00), 2 blocks from the train station (turn left as you leave the station), can provide maps, a city guide, and essential ferry information. (Open Mon.-Fri. 9am-5pm; Sept.-May also Sat. 9am-2pm; booth by the fisher's market open June-Aug. 10am-8pm.) The **Mosvangen Youth Hostel (HI),** Ibsengate 22 (tel. 51 87 09 77), is one of Norway's poshest (110kr, nonmembers 135kr). The most central campsite is **Mosvangen camping** (tel. 51 53 29 71) by the youth hostel. Take bus 130 to both. (Tents 60kr. Open June-Sept.) Nothing is cheap in the center of town, but for budget food, try **Rema 1000, Mauritz,** and **Obs** markets, or **Breitorget Bistro** on Breitorget. Stavanger's streets teem with young people; clown-car-like hordes emerge on weekends, frequenting the **pubs** along Nedre Strandgate and the **waterfront.** Dance club **Berlin,** Lars Hertervigsgate 5, tries really hard, and pulls it off.

Catamarans run from Stavanger to **Bergen** (4hr.; 450kr, 50% off for students, 25% off with Scanrail). Slower **ferries** connect the 2 cities, shipping out from Randaberg in Stavanger (6hr.; 175kr, students 25% discount); **buses** meet Rondaberg-Bergen ferry sailings; inquire in the tourist office for information. **Color Line** (tel. 51 52 45 45) runs ships from Stavanger to **Newcastle,** England (18hr., from US$57 in winter and US$114 July-Aug.).

EASTERN NORWAY

■■■ GUDBRANDSDALEN, RONDANE, AND DOVREFJELL

Two train lines shoot north from Oslo to Trondheim; the slower goes eastward through the Østerdalen valley and Røros, the faster one through the **Gudbrandsdalen** valley that runs from Lillehammer northwestward through Otta and Dombås. Traditionally one of Norway's great thoroughfares, Gudbrandsdalen is also famous as the origin of the brown *Gudbrandsdalsost* cheese, for its skiing, hiking, and canoeing, and old churches and wooden houses. Lillehammer is the largest town and marks the southern edge; farther up the valley, the old, soft slopes of the mountain ranges of **Dovrefjell** and **Rondane** provide easy access to untrampled scenery. Both areas have national parks; the one in Dovrefjell is famous for its musk oxen.

Lillehammer In February 1994, Norway's second winter Olympic Games were hosted in Lillehammer and across the valley in the neighboring towns of Kvitfjell,

Faberg, Hunder, Hamar, and Gjøvik. Despite the construction of several billion kroner's worth of infrastructure, Lillehammer maintains a natural atmosphere; all the sports facilities were designed to be environmentally friendly, and the Olympic housing has been recycled for use by the army. Any aspiring Eddie the Eagle can reach the top of the **ski jump** (15kr; Sat.-Sun. only). A **bobsled simulator** in the Olympic park takes you on a terrifying run (open 10am-7pm, 35kr). The adventurous, or perhaps just stupid, can ride the **real bobsled run** in summer on wheels and in winter on ice. (Take the bus from the station to Hunder, 20kr. Open 1-6pm, 100kr.) "Olympic Sight-seeing" tours departing from the tourist office (2½hr., 90kr) include these thrills, and provide an overview of the town (call 61 25 25 49). If you hate sports altogether, slack in the **Banken Cultural Center,** Kirkegate 41, where you can enjoy art works and the only vegetarian buffet in town.

The **tourist office** lies at the North end of Storgata (tel. 61 25 92 99; open Mon.-Fri. 9am-9pm, Sat. 9am-7pm, Sun. 11am-7pm; Sept.-May Mon.-Fri. 9am-5pm, Sat. 10am-2pm). **Trains** run up to a dozen times daily for Oslo (2½hr.), and service also runs to Trondheim and Åndalsnes. **Gjeste Bu,** Gamleveien 110 (tel. 61 25 43 21), is central, snug, and cozy (sleeping bag accommodations 65kr); open all year, it's your best rooming bet, but call ahead. **Speidersenter,** Zystgårdsveien 23 (tel. 61 25 97 24), provides a view of the Olympic facilities, but closes August 15 to July 2 (sleeping bag accommodations 55kr). The **Lillehammer Youth Hostel (HI),** in the **Smestad Sommerhotell,** Smestadreien 4 (tel. 61 25 09 87), is both distant and institutional (105kr, nonmembers 125kr). **Restaurants** line the pedestrian thoroughfare. Decent fast food near the tourist information office at **M-Burger,** Lysgadsveien 89, including hot dogs from 13kr and hamburgers from 33kr.

Otta and Dombås Rondane is most accessible from **Otta,** 1½hrs. north of Lillehammer. The **tourist office** (tel. 61 23 03 65), in the station, has maps and tips on accommodations, white water rafting on the Sjoa River, and hints on the Rondane hiking trails at **Mysuseter** and **Høvringen** (open Mon.-Fri. 8:30am-7:30pm, Sat. 10am-6pm, Sun. noon-6pm; mid-Aug. to mid-June Mon.-Fri. 8:30am-4pm). The **Guesthouse Sagatun** (tel. 61 23 08 14) offers singles (160kr), doubles (220kr), and triples (325kr). Spectacular **bus** routes snake from Otta across the Jotunheimen mountains to Sogndal in Sognefjord and Stryn in Nordfjord.

The slightly more challenging **Dovrefjell** is best reached from the rail town of **Dombås.** The **Dombås tourist office** (tel. 61 24 14 44), in the shopping mall at the end of the hill, can help you plan tours along the trails (open 10am-8pm, late Aug.-early June Mon.-Fri. 9am-4pm). The **Dombås Youth Hostel (HI)** (tel. 61 24 10 45) is uphill from the train station; turn right, away from the city, on the main street. (Reception open 8-10am and 4-11pm. Lockout 10am-4pm. 85kr, nonmembers 110kr. Reservations necessary in summer. Open late June to mid-Aug.)

■■■ VALDRES AND JOTUNHEIMEN

The **Valdres** valley, running parallel and to the west of Gudbrandsdalen, has six of Norway's 25 medieval wooden stave churches. It terminates in the highest mountain range in Europe north of the Alps, the jagged, reindeer-inhabited **Jotunheimen** massif. Covered by endless boulder fields, the region looks like the home of the troll giants for whom it is named. While only two of the several hundred peaks require technical gear to climb, only experienced hikers should attempt anything longer than a daytrip. It snows even in July, so always bring warm, wool clothes and raingear, even on short jaunts. Also visit the DNT offices in either Oslo or Bergen for maps and info on trails, huts, and safety precautions. On the east side of Jotunheimen, Route 51 winds north from Fagernes to meet Route 15 at Vågåmo; **Gjendesheim,** an hour north of Fagernes by bus, is the best hiking base. The DNT hut here provides a sleeping bag and lodging (125kr). Buses also run to Gjendesheim from the Oslo-Trondheim train line at Otta, 30km downvalley from

NORWAY

Vågåmo. From the **hut** at Gjendesheim, you can hike across the **Besseggen,** a spectacular ridge with a deep blue lake at 1200m and an emerald green one at 984m.

Fagernes is the center of things in the valley. Reach Fagernes by **bus** from Gol on the Oslo-Bergen rail line (70min., 45kr, students 33% off), from Lillehammer (2hr., 93kr, students 33% off), or by *Valdresekspressen* bus from Oslo (3hr., 174kr). The **tourist office** (tel. 61 36 04 00), by the bus station, will gladly hand over the comprehensive *Valdres Summer* (or *Winter*) *Guide* (open Mon.-Fri. 8am-9pm, Sat. 10am-6pm, Sun. 11am-6pm; late Aug.-late June Mon.-Fri. 8am-4pm). Ask at the tourist office about the **stave churches** (30kr each). The more mobile should request a map and further info about the *Vardevandring* (watchtower hike), through most of the valley. The **Fagernes Youth Hostel (HI),** Valdres Folkhøjskole (tel. 61 36 20 25), is 4km south of town in Leira (80kr, nonmembers 105kr; open June-Sept.).

Lom, Bøverdalen, and Turtagrø The northwest approach means a spectacular bus ride along Routes 15 and 55 over the main massif of Jotunheimen between Otta on the rail line and Sogndal on Sognefjord (2 per day). Sixty-two km out of Otta, the bus stops in **Lom** (52kr), just to the north of Jotunheimen, the branching point for buses to Stryn in Nordfjord. Lom's **tourist office** (tel. 61 21 12 86), 300m from the bus stop, does the info thing (open Mon.-Sat. 9am-9pm, Sun. 10am-6pm; Sept.-May Mon.-Fri. 7:30am-3:30pm). In **Bøverdalen,** 15km from Lom, stay at the **youth hostel (HI)** (tel. 61 21 20 64; 90kr, nonmembers 140kr; open June-Sept.) and make daytrips to **Galdhøpiggen** (2469m) and its sibling summit **Glittertinden** (2464m), the highest points in Norway. Eighteen km off Route 55, the **tourist chalet** (tel. 61 21 14 80) at Spiterstulen is closer to Glittertinden, with cheap beds and story-filled hikers (60kr, camping 40kr per person). **Buses** run daily (mid-July to mid-Aug., 55kr) from Lom at 4:05pm, and from Galdesand (across from youth hostel) at 5pm (35kr). They return to Lom from Spiterstulen at 11am (74kr). Southwest of Bøverdalen, the plateau between **Krossbu** and **Sognefjellhytta** is strewn with rock cairns tracing the way between snow-covered lakes; cross-country skiing is often possible even in July. Near **Turtagrø,** just above the tip of the Sognefjord system, is one of Norway's premier rock-climbing areas. From the road there's a steep but well-maintained 4hr. path to **Fannaråkhytta** (2069m), the highest hut in the DNT system, on Smørstabreen Glacier.

THE FJORDS AND WEST COUNTRY

All along the western coast, sapphire sea and severe mountain ranges will tax your supply of camera film. Bergen is an ideal starting point; the tourist office there will help you plan a trip. Ferries wind through labyrinths of islands and peninsulas, catamarans go to Sognefjord and Nordfjord to the north, and buses connect to Hardangerfjord and the uninhabited Hardangervidda plateau to the southeast. To avoid excruciating train zig-zags, a good way to explore the fjords is to take a coastal voyage *(Hurtigruten)* which steam from Bergen, through the fjords, all the way to the Northern Cape (see Norway Essentials, above).

■■■ BERGEN

Bergen's scenery exalts it above most cities in the world, and its Germanic heritage sets it apart from most of Norway. Until the railway to Oslo was completed, it was easier to travel from Bergen to London, and the city acquired an international flair. Originally the capital of Norway, Bergen became a center of commerce in the 14th century and more recently a focal point of resistance to the Nazis. Trees soften the commercial frenzy; from the hills, Bergen looks more like a wooded settlement than a thriving trade and university city.

ORIENTATION AND PRACTICAL INFORMATION

Bergen's train station lies several blocks above the gleaming harbor, at the top of the city center. Looking towards the water, **Bryggen** (the extension of Kong Oscars gate) and the town's most imposing mountain are to your right; most of the main buildings are to the left. **Torget**—an outdoor market—is at the harbor's tip.

Tourist Office: Bryggen 7, on the harbor's right side, just past the Torget (tel. 55 32 14 80). Books rooms, exchanges currency, and sells the Bergen Card (100kr for 1 day). Pick up the all-knowing *Bergen Guide 1995.* Open Mon.-Sat. 8:30am-9pm, Sun. 10am-7pm; Oct.-April Mon.-Fri. 9am-4pm. **DNT** (see Oslo section, tel. 55 32 22 30), Tverrgaten 4-6, off Marken, a pedestrian thoroughfare beginning at the railroad station and leading to the harbor, is a must for travelers headed for the highlands. Open Mon.-Wed. and Fri. 10am-4pm, Thurs. 10am-6pm.

Budget Travel: Kilroy Travels, in the Studentsentret, Parkveien 1 (tel. 55 32 64 00). Discounts on international travel, sells ISIC and Interrail. Open Mon.-Fri. 8:30am-4pm.

Currency Exchange: At the tourist office when banks and post offices are closed; 4% commission.

American Express: Winge Travel Bureau, Christian Michelsensgate 1-3 (tel. 55 90 12 90). Mail held (address to: P.O. Box 1226, 5001 Bergen), but no currency exchange (see Tourist Office). Open Mon.-Fri. 8:30am-4pm, Sat. 9:30am-2pm.

Post Office: In the green building with the clock on Småstrand gate, 1 block from the Torget. Open Mon.-Wed. and Fri. 8am-5pm, Thurs. 8am-6pm, Sat. 9am-2pm. **Postal Code:** N-5000.

Telephones: Tele Building, Starvhusegate 4, across Rådhusgate from the post office. Open Mon.-Fri. 8am-8pm, Sat. 9am-2pm.

Trains: tel. 55 96 60 60 or 55 96 60 50. To Voss (4-6 per day, 1hr., 110kr), Myrdal (1¾-2½hr., 155kr), and Oslo (7-8hr., 470kr, seat reservations compulsory). **Luggage storage** 10kr. Open 6:45am-10:45pm.

Buses: Bystasjonen, Strømgaten 8 (tel. 55 32 67 80). Service to neighboring areas and the Hardangerfjord district, as well as to Oslo, 470kr.

Public Transportation: Yellow buses chauffeur you around the city (13kr per ride, free between Post Office, Bus Station, and Railway Station).

Ferries: To Stavanger and fjords: from the train station, boats leave from the left side of the harbor. **To other countries:** ships leave from Skoltegrunnskaien, a 20min. walk past Bryggen along the right side of the harbor. **Smyril Line,** with offices in Engelgården at Bryggen (tel. 55 32 09 70), departs June-Aug. Tues. at 3pm for the Faroe Islands (21hr., 800-2000kr) and Iceland (42hr., 1610kr). Student discount 25%, another 25% off early to mid-June and Aug. **Color Line,** Skuteviksboder 1-2 (tel. 55 54 86 60), sails to Newcastle via Stavanger May-Sept. US$57-114, 50% off with student ID in winter. **P & O Scottish Ferries,** reservations made through Color Line, sails June 4-Aug. 28 to the Shetland Islands (12hr., 660kr, 25% student discount). The **Hurtigruten** leaves daily at 10pm from a separate harbor at Frieleneskaien, behind the Natural History Museum.

Gay and Lesbian Services: Gay Movement, 2a Nygårdsgaten, (tel. 55 31 21 39). Open Mon.-Thurs. 7-10pm.

Pharmacy: In the bus station. Open 8:30am-midnight.

Medical Assistance: Accident Clinic, Lars Hilles gate 30 (tel. 55 32 11 20). Open 24hrs.

Emergencies: Ambulance, tel. 003. **Police,** tel. 002.

ACCOMMODATIONS, CAMPING, AND FOOD

The tourist office books rooms for a 15kr fee (20kr for 2 people) in private homes. (Singles 145-180kr. Doubles 235-260kr.)

Intermission, Kalfarveien 8 (tel. 55 31 32 75). A 15min. walk from the center up Kong Oscars gate, which turns into Kalfarveien past the train station at the Old Gate House; or take bus 2,4, 7, or 11. Co-ed dorm, friendly staff, kitchen, showers, and ghost. Lockout 11am-5pm. Flexible curfew. 95kr. Breakfast 20kr. Free laundry. Open mid-June to mid-Aug.; leave name on sign-up sheet or call ahead.

YMCA Interrail Center, Nedre Korskirkealmenningen 4 (tel. 55 31 73 32). Spacious and central; 2- to 50-person rooms. Reception open 7:30am-midnight. Lockout 11am-4:30pm. 80kr for mattress on floor. Open June 15-Sept. 1. Reserve.

Vågenes, J.L. Mowinckelsvei 95 (tel. 55 16 11 01), 10min. on bus 60 (13kr). In a private home; call for reservations and directions. Doubles with kitchens and made-up beds 100kr per person.

Montana Youth Hostel (HI), Johan Blyttsveien 30 (tel. 55 29 29 00, fax 55 29 29 00), halfway up Mt. Ulriken, 4km from center. Take bus 4 to Lægdene (13kr). Motel-esque. 145kr, nonmembers 165kr. May-Sept. 95kr. Breakfast included. Open early May-early Oct. Reservations recommended.

Camping: Bergenshallen Camping, Vilhelm Bjerknesveien 29 (tel. 55 27 01 80), in the city. Take bus 3 from Strandgate. 65kr per tent. Open late June to mid-Aug. If that's full, call **Bergen Camping Park,** Haukås om Åsane (tel. 55 24 88 08).

Mekka, a discount supermarket, at Marken 3, 5min. from the station on the street parallel to Kaigaten, saves the hungry traveler. (Open Mon.-Fri. 9am-8pm, Sat. 9am-6pm.) Hunt around for *dagens ret* restaurant specials (70-100kr), or try one of the seafood restaurants. **Kaffistova,** on the 2nd floor across from the Torget, offers large hot entrees. As can be expected, there is a heavy emphasis on fish. (*Dagens ret* 75kr. Open Mon.-Fri. 10am-6pm, Sat. 11:30am-3:30pm, Sun. noon-6pm.) **Spisestedet Kornelia,** Fosswinckelsgate 8, serves vegetarian food in a whole-wheat atmosphere. (Salads from 45kr, pasta from 60kr, student specials Tues. and Fri. Open Mon.-Fri. 11:30am-7:30pm, Sat. 12:30-5:00pm, Sun. 2-6pm; in summer closed weekends.) **Ola's Inn,** Vaskerelvsmuget 1, at the end of Torgalmenningen, in the alley behind "Dickens," is a quiet, inexpensive cafeteria. (Fish and chips 60kr. Open Mon.-Fri. 10am-10pm, Sat. 10:30am-5pm.)

SIGHTS AND ENTERTAINMENT

Looking toward the right side of the harbor from the Torget, you'll see the pointed gables of **Bryggen,** a row of medieval buildings that's survived half a dozen disastrous fires and the explosion of a Nazi munitions ship on Hitler's birthday in 1944. Listed by UNESCO as one of the world's most significant showcases of the Middle Ages, it now features restaurants, offices, and artsy-craftsy workshops. The former city fortress **Bergenhus** teeters at the end of the quay, and the **Rosenkrantz Tower** stands in late medieval splendor. **Håkonshallen,** built by Håkon Håkonsson in the 13th century, is what is left of the original castle. (Open 10am-4pm; mid-Sept. to mid-May Sun. noon-3pm; closed during the festival. 15kr.) The **Theta Room,** Enhjørningsgården Bryggen, chronicles the Resistance operations during the Nazi occupation (open mid-May to mid-Sept. Tues. and Sat.-Sun. 2-4pm. 15kr).

Lose your head over the **Leprosy Museum,** Kong Oscars gate 59. Since 1970, the university has tastefully documented the history of the disease in a 19th-century hospital. (Open mid-May to Aug. 11am-3pm. 15kr, students 6kr.) On the western shore of **Lille Lungegårdsvatnet,** a shimmering pond in the middle of town, the **Rasmus Meyer's Collection** provides a quality overview of Norwegian Naturalists, Impressionists and Expressionists. (Open Mon.-Sat. 11am-4pm, Sun. noon-3pm; mid-Sept. to mid-May Tues.-Sun. noon-3pm. 15kr.) A quick bus trip from downtown is **Gamle Bergen** (Old Bergen), a collection of wooden buildings from the last century. Of the 40 old houses, 17 are open to the public via guided tours. Take city bus 1 or 9 "Løn-____rg" from outside Den Norske Bank to the first stop past the second tunnel. ____s open mid-May to Aug. 11am-6pm. 25kr, students 15kr.)

____ntains on three sides and vast archipelagos to the west, you can take ____ of nearby nature. The ever-popular **Fløibanen** takes you from the ____aze of mountaintop paths and views (open 7:30am-11:30pm,

14kr one way). Consult **Bergen Touring Association,** Bergen Turlag, at the DNT office, for detailed maps and inspiration. Take a bus from the Bergen bus station 8km to Hop, turn right, walk about 200m, then turn left and walk for about 20min. to reach **Troldhaugen** (Troll Hill), Edvard Grieg's summer villa. The house still contains many of the composer's belongings, including his Steinway piano, which is used at summer concerts in Troldsalen Hall next door (tel. 55 91 17 91; open May-Oct. 9:30am-5:30pm; 30kr).

Nightclubs and discos pack the town center. Work your way down Norway's longest bar counter (36m) in **Banco Rotto,** 16 Vågalmenningen. Then frolic at **Galeien,** 3 Bradbenken, Brygger Orion (open 8:30pm-3am). Consult your *Bergen Guide* for other distractions. All the stops are pulled out for the annual **Bergen International Festival,** a 12-day program of music, ballet, folklore, and drama from May 25-June 5 in 1995. Try calling the ticket office (tel. 55 31 09 54 or 55 31 31 04); uncollected tickets are sold at half-price on the day of performance.

■■■ SOGNEFJORD

The longest of the fjords (200km), Sognefjord's deep, slender fingers penetrate all the way to the foot of the Jotunheimen mountains. A short ride north of the stunning Oslo-Bergen rail line, Sognefjord is ideal for those seeing Norway by train. A natural starting point tucked deep within Sognefjord, **Flåm** is the only fjord town accessible by rail (connecting to the Oslo-Bergen line through **Myrdal;** 50min., 60kr). This train route, Flåmbanen, spirals down the steep descent of the mountain, and stops at scenic spots. Catamarans also run between Flåm and Bergen (5hr., 440kr, 50% off with railpass or ISIC), traveling through **Balestrand** and on to Aurland. A jumble of ferries also tie Flåm to its fjord-bound friends: Godvangen, Aurland, and Balestrand. Flåm has a small, friendly **tourist office** (tel. 57 63 21 06), in the hut beside the train station (open June to mid-Aug. 8:15am-8:30pm). You can buy a fishing license at **Flåm Camping and Hostel (HI)** (tel. 57 63 21 21, fax 57 63 23 80), 5min. into the valley along the tracks (75kr, nonmembers 100kr; open May to mid-Oct.).

The boots 'n' shorts set hop off the Oslo-Bergen train at **Finse,** just east of Myrdal, and hike for 3 or 4 stunning days down the Aurlandsdalen Valley to **Aurland,** 7km from Flåm, sleeping warmly all the way in evenly spaced DNT *hytter.* For maps and prices, inquire at DNT in Oslo or Bergen; they range from 45kr for a mattress on the floor (nonmembers 95kr) to 355kr for a bed with breakfast and a pack lunch with thermos and dinner. Buses also connect Aurland and Flåm (17kr). There is a fantastic view of the Aurland fjord from **Otternes Bygdetun** (tel. 57 63 33 00), a unique cluster of 27 17th-century houses between the two towns (open mid-June to mid-Aug. 11am-6pm, 20kr). The Aurland **tourist office** (tel. 57 63 33 13) serves Flåm in the winter (open Mon.-Fri. 8am-7pm, Sat.-Sun. 11am-7pm; Sept.-April Mon.-Fri. 8am-3pm). **Kafé Troll,** in the town center, serves traditional fare outside in the summer.

Ferries run from Flåm and Aurland west through narrow fjords to **Gudvangen** (2 per day, 2½hr., 100kr from Flåm, 90kr from Aurland). From Gudvangen, buses (5-8 per day, 70min., 54kr) run up to **Voss,** birthplace of the canonized American football figure Knute Rockne, east of Bergen on the Oslo rail line. From the train station, turn left when you face the lake and bear right at the fork by the church to find the **tourist office** in Tinghuse (tel. 56 51 00 51; open Mon.-Sat. 9am-7pm, Sun. 2-6pm; Sept.-May Mon.-Fri. 9am-4pm). Turning right from the station and walking along the lakeside road brings you to Voss's large, modern **youth hostel (HI)** (tel. 56 51 22 05) where you can rent canoes and rowboats. (30kr per hr., 85kr per day. Hostel 145kr, nonmembers 175kr. Open mid-Jan. to Oct. Reserve ahead.) The central **Voss Camping** (tel. 56 51 15 97) is right by the lake and tourist office (50kr per tent, 4-person hut 250kr). Local **trains** between Voss and Myrdal stop on demand at **Ørn-aberg,** where a steep 300m path leads you down to the slightly decrepit but incredibly well-located **Mjølfjell Youth Hostel (HI)** (tel. 56 51 81 11). The owner will give

NORWAY

you hiking suggestions and maps. (125kr, nonmembers 150kr. Open June-Sept.; call ahead the rest of the year.)

On the North side of Sognefjord, **Balestrand** is a spectacular mid-way point between Flåm and Bergen or Nordfjord. A ferry leaves Balestrand at midday to cruise up the **Fjærland fjord** to Mundal. Crafty buses meet the boat and transport you to the base of the **Jostedal glacier,** whose blue ice hangs ominously overhead; the ferry returns to Balestrand around 6pm. (Ticket includes stop at interactive glacier museum, 195kr at the tourist office.) The **tourist office** (tel. 57 69 14 57), near the bus station on the quay, can help plan area tours by boat, bike, or foot around Kaiser Wilhelm's garden spot (open June-Aug. Mon.-Sat. 8am-6pm, Sun. 11am-3pm). The Bergen **hydrofoils** serve Balestrand twice a day (4½hr., 355kr, railpasses and ISIC 50% off). **Ferries** to Fjærland connect with buses north over snowy mountains to Stryn in Nordfjord (114kr, ISIC 50% off). The **Balestrand Youth Hostel (HI)** (tel. 57 69 13 03) overlooks the fjord, a 5min. walk up the hill and to the left. (85kr, nonmembers 110kr. Open mid-June to late Aug.) **Sjøtun camping** (tel. 05 69 12 23), 500m down the coastal road, provides tent sites and huts (15kr per person, 30kr per tent, 2-person hut 90kr).

■■■ HARDANGERFJORD

Hardangerfjord, east of Bergen and south of Voss, is the subject of endless sight-seeing tours. Either of these towns can serve as a base of operations, although **Odda** is more central. Odda's **tourist office** (tel. 53 64 12 97) provides assistance for trips to the fjord and distributes the handy *Hardanger Guide '95* (open Mon.-Fri. 10am-8pm, Sat. 10am-5pm, Sun. 11am-6pm; mid-Aug. to mid-June Mon.-Fri. 9am-3pm). A stay at the **Odda Youth Hostel** (tel. 53 64 14 11) will relieve you of 130kr (nonmembers 155kr). Beautiful **Eidfjord,** on the main road RV7, 45km southeast of Voss, *"is a Norwegian fjord,"* according to its brochure. Glad to hear it. Its **tourist office** (tel. 53 66 51 77) will direct you to the marked paths leading to the **Viking Burial Place** at Hereid, dating from 400-800AD. While you're at it, ask them how to find a guest house (singles 130-330kr) or **Saebø Camping** (tel. 53 66 59 27; 70-210kr per cabin, 25kr per tent, 15kr per person). Take an hour-long hike down to **Vøringstossen,** one of Norway's most famous waterfalls, and check out the stunning scenery from RV7, including the **Hardangerjøkulen glacier.**

■■■ NORDFJORD

Twisting over 100km inland to the foot of the **Jostedal glacier,** Nordfjord is less fantastic than its neighbors to the North and South. Wedged between the mountains near the inner end of the fjord, **Stryn** is a summer ski destination. Buses stop at the edge of town; walk past the Esso station to get to the main street, Tonningsgata. Well-versed downhillers should ask at the tourist office about **summer skiing** at Strynefjellet. Take a bus to Briksdalsbreen (departs 10am, 45kr) to probe the crevasses of the Jostedal glacier. The tasteful **HI youth hostel** (tel. 57 87 11 06) is a hefty romp up the hill behind town. (Lockout 10:30am-4pm. Curfew 11pm. 80kr, nonmembers 105kr. Laundry. Open May-Oct.) **Stryn Camping** (tel. 57 87 11 36) is the most central of countless sites (60kr per tent, 10kr per person). The **tourist office** (tel. 57 87 23 32) lies off the main street on the paved square with the *Télé* offices (open June-Aug. 9am-6pm). Stryn is a meeting point for **buses** from Otta on the Oslo-Trondheim rail line via Lom and Jotunheimen (Otta-Stryn 190kr, students 143kr; Lom-Stryn 120kr, students 90kr), from Hellesylt in Geirangerfjord (64kr) and from Fjærland and Balestrand in Sognefjord (118kr, 50% ISIC discount).

bathers can bask on the coast around **Måløy,** at Nordfjord's mouth. Reach hydrofoil from Bergen (424kr, 212kr with ISIC), by daily *Hurtigruten* m Bergen (arrives at 7:30am, 9hr., 460kr) or southbound from Åle-am, 4½hr., 222kr), or by bus from Stryn (109kr). The local **tour-**

ist office (tel. 57 85 08 50), in the town hall, will help you with accommodations (open mid-June to mid-Aug. 10am-6pm).

■■■ GEIRANGERFJORD

Resist the temptation to stay snuggled in bed and take the bus to Geirangerfjord, perhaps the most stunning of the Norwegian fjords, and certainly the most visited. The most southern, inland arm of the fjord system that begins at Ålesund, its 16km of green-blue water reflects stunning cliffs and waterfalls. Watch for the drama of the **Seven Sisters,** the powerful surge of the **Suitor,** and the mist of the **Bride's Veil.** From June through August, several daily ferries (1hr., 30kr) connect the tiny towns of Hellesylt and Geiranger, at opposite ends of the fjord. Otherwise, both towns are accessible only by road. From the south or southeast, go through Stryn; from the north, launch yourself from Åndalsnes or Ålesund. The **Golden Route** is a 85km trail that begins in Geiranger and ends in Åndalsnes; enjoy the spectacular scenery by car, or preferably by bicycle.

Germans come to find their Yellowstone in **Geiranger;** in the summer over 5000 tourists visit each day, and an armada of ocean liners maintains a steady presence off-shore. You can join the flotilla by going on the sight-seeing trip of the fjord (1¾hr., 64kr; call Geiranger Fjordservice 94 66 05 02) or enlarge it by renting a boat near the pier (tel. 70 26 31 23; motorboats 100kr per hr., 400kr per day; open late June and early Aug. 10am-6pm, July 10am-8pm). The Geiranger **tourist office** (tel. 70 26 30 99), just up from the landing, provides camping and hiking information, and finds private rooms (200kr). Ask about the 45min. walk to **Storseter,** which passes under a waterfall (open June-Aug. 9am-7pm). Geiranger has 10 camp-grounds; the closest (and only one with wheelchair access) is **Geiranger Camping** (tel. 70 26 31 20; 15kr per person, 45kr per tent).

At the eastern end of the fjord, tiny, unspoiled **Hellesylt** is a base for mountain hiking in some of the wildest scenery in Norway. Hikers head for the **Eriksdal glacier** and the **Troll's Path.** In the 1800s, cruise ship passengers were led on ponies from Hellesylt to Øye through the extremely narrow **Norangsdalen.** At the turn of the century, a huge avalanche dammed up the valley; farm buildings remain under the murky water. The daily Leknes bus (34kr to Øye) runs through the valley, but the return is the next day. The **tourist office** (tel. 70 26 50 52), right on the ferry landing, rents fishing equipment (15kr per hr.) and provides hiking maps (open mid-June to mid-Aug. 8:30am-5:30pm). The **Hellesylt Youth Hostel (HI)** (tel. 70 26 51 28), up the hill along the road to Stranda, has a ripping view. (Lockout 10am-5pm. 85kr, nonmembers 110kr. Open June-Aug.)

■■■ ÅNDALSNES AND ÅLESUND

The mountains around Åndalsnes are a mecca for mountaineers, rock climbers, and casual hikers. The wagons that split off the Oslo-Trondheim train at Dombås end at Åndalsnes (3 per day, from Oslo 6½hr., 445kr), taking off onto the roller-coaster **Rauma Line** which passes over stunning bridges before making a U-turn in the 1340m Stavems tunnel. The train zips past the ultimate mountaineering challenge, **Trollveggen**—the highest vertical rock wall in Europe—and the most notable peak in the area, **Romsdalshorn.** The Dombås-Åndalsnes buses parallel the train. An equally awesome approach is the dizzying road down **Trollstigen,** traversed by the bus to Geiranger, and featuring no fewer than 11 hairpin turns.

Åndalsnes At the mouth of the Rauma River and the bottom of a wide fjord, Åndalsnes marks the terminus of the Golden Route from Geiranger and the Rauma Line from Dombås. The town centers on the road leading uphill from the train station and boasts the **Norsk Tindemuseum,** housing legendary mountaineer Arne Randers Heen's collection of expedition paraphernalia. Arne climbed Romsdalshorn

NORWAY

a good number of times; the 233rd time he was 80 years old. The museum is on the bank of the river, right by the two small islands. (Open mid-June to mid-Aug. Mon.-Fri. 3-6pm, Sat.-Sun. 2-6pm; other times on request.) The local **tourist office** (tel. 71 22 16 22) is a good source for hiking maps and recreational information (open Mon.-Sat. 9:30am-9:30pm, Sun. 3:30-9:30pm, late Aug.-May Mon.-Fri. 9am-3pm). To get to the **Setnes Youth Hostel (HI)** (tel. 71 22 13 82), walk up Jernberegata and take a left where the road ends onto Storgata. Follow Storgata down to the traffic circle, stay right, pass the gas stations, and cross the river. The hostel is on the left; you can see it from the road. It's a good 30min. walk, but the breakfast makes you forget the miles. (95kr, nonmembers 120kr. Breakfast 55kr. Open mid-May to mid-Sept.) The knowledgable hostess sometimes arranges trips to Geirangerfjord. To hit the mountains, contact **Aak** (tel. 71 22 64 44), 4km east of town on the E69 back toward Dombås; they have beds (55-140kr) with showers and a fireplace and rent canoes (first hr. 100kr, thereafter 30kr per hr.) and cross-country telemark skis (100kr per day). Follow the signs from the hostel to **Åndalsnes Camping** (tel. 71 22 16 29, fax 71 22 63 60), which lets you set up tents for 15kr per person, 40kr per tent; they rent out huts (130-500kr), bikes (30kr per hr., 70kr per day), and canoes (40kr per hr., 150kr per day).

Ålesund The largest city between Bergen and Trondheim enjoys a beautiful cliff-side location and is renowned for its Art Nouveau architecture. For a view of old Åle-sund, the harbor, and the mountains beyond, chug up the 418 steps to **Aksla** (mountain lodge open 10am-10pm in summer). The **Summøre Museum** (10min. by bus 13, 14, 18, or 24, 15kr) displays local fishing boats from days of yore, and a reconstructed Viking ship. (Open Mon.-Fri. 10am-5pm, Sat.-Sun. noon-5pm. 25kr, students 15kr. Admission includes open air museum, boat collection, and medieval museum.) Newly-opened **Hansen Gården,** Kongensgate 14 (tel. 70 13 58 90), provides spotless, cozy rooms (110kr; sheets 40kr; open June 20-Aug. 20). Call ahead for reservations. **Prinsen Strandcamping** (tel. 70 15 52 04), at Gåseid, is 5km outside town (bus 15kr) next to a popular beach. (30kr per tent. Huts or rooms 150-600kr per person. Wheelchair access.) The **tourist office** (tel. 70 12 12 02) is across from the bus station in the city hall (open Mon.-Fri. 9am-6pm, Sat. 9am-3pm, Sun. noon-5pm; Sept.-May Mon.-Fri. 8:30am-4pm). Ålesund is reachable by **road** (3 buses per day from Åndalsnes, 125kr), by **Hurtigruten** (625kr), which docks here daily, or by **hydrofoil** from Bergen (Mon.-Fri. 1 per day).

There's an old Viking site on **Giske,** a short bus ride from Ålesund (34kr). Ornithu-siasts will thrill to the island of **Runde,** sanctuary to more than 500,000 birds. A hydrofoil links Ålesund and Hareid; a *Soreid* bus leaves from there (one way 102kr). From Ålesund, it's 2hrs. by bus and ferry (90kr) to **Molde,** a seaside town known for its **International Jazz Festival** (late July). Ask at Ålesund or Åndalsnes for info.

■■■ TRONDHEIM

Medieval capital of Norway, Trondheim is the natural stopping point between Oslo and destinations above the Arctic Circle. Olav Tryggvason founded Trondheim in 997; his image now presides over an outdoor market from a column in the main town square, **Torvet.** Local boy King Olav Haraldsson became Norway's patron saint after he fought to introduce Christianity. A steady stream of pilgrims prompted the construction of **Nidaros Cathedral,** Scandinavia's largest medieval structure, built over a holy well that sprang up beside St. Olav's grave. Site of all Norwegian coronations, it holds the crown jewels. (Open mid-June to Aug. Mon.-Fri. 9:30am-5:30pm, Sat. 9:30am-2pm, Sun. 1-4pm; reduced hours off-season. 10kr, students ⁻kr.) The view from the top of the 172-step spiral staircase in the tower is worth the ⁻dmission every 30min.). The **Gamle Bybro** (old town bridge) and the 18th-⁻harves are perhaps the prettiest part of town. On the hill across the river ⁻¹ **Kristiansten Fortress.** Exhibits of some of Norway's greatest art ⁻ **Trondhjems Kunst-Forening,** next to the cathedral. Edvard

Munch has a hallway to himself, highlighted by the woodcuts *Lust* and *Jealousy*. (Open 11am-4pm; Sept.-May Tues.-Sun. noon-4pm. 20kr, students 10kr.) Bus 4, direction "Iade," will take you to the intriguing **Ringve Museum of Musical History.** Displays range from a one-stringed Ethiopian violin to the ornate Mozart Room; guides demonstrate the instruments. (Tours in English at 11am, 12:30, 2:30, and 4:30pm in July. 40kr, students 25kr.) Ferry over to **Munkholmen,** an island monastery that became a prison fortress and then flipped again into a quiet beach and picnic spot. (Round-trip 25kr; fortress 15kr, students 10kr.) From late August until May, the city is alive with students; visit the red 'n' round **Studentersenter** across the river from the cathedral to dip your toes in their hectic activity.

Practical Information, Accommodations, and Food The train station faces the center of town, which is circled by the Nid River. From the train station, walk across the bridge, then 6 blocks on Søndregate, turn right on Munkegata, and continue to the main square and the **tourist office,** Munkegata 19 (tel. 73 92 94 05). Its staff books rooms in private homes (180kr), and promotes *Trondheim By Bike*. (Open Mon.-Fri. 8:30am-8pm, Sat. 8:30am-6pm, Sun. 10am-6pm; late Aug.-May Mon.-Fri. 9am-4pm, Sat. 9am-1pm.) The **InterRail Center,** in the train station, has hot plates, showers, and "at-your-own-risk" baggage storage (open early July-late Aug. 7am-10pm). A **DNT office,** Munkegata 64 (tel. 73 52 38 08), above Paul's Indian Restaurant, describes huts and trails to the north and south of Trondheim (open Mon.-Wed. and Fri. 8am-4pm, Thurs. 8am-6pm). All **city buses** leave from the Munkegata-Dronningensgate intersection and require exact change (14kr). **Trains** run to Trondheim from Oslo (7-8hr., 502kr), Stockholm via Storlien (13hr.) and Bodø. **Long-distance buses** leave from the *rutebilstasjonen* on Hans Hagrups gate.

The **InterRail Center,** Elgesetergate 1 (tel. 73 89 95 38), not related to its homonym at the railway station, offers cheap dorms (80kr), free luggage storage, European newspapers, and ping pong. From the station, cross the bridge, and turn right on Olav Tryggvasonsgate, then left on Prinsensgate; it's across the next bridge on the left. Or take bus 41, 42, 48, 49, 52, or 63 to Samfundet (10kr). (Angst-ridden student café open July-late Aug. Dinner 35kr. Disco Tues., Fri. and Sat.) Student-run **Singsaker Sommerhotell,** Rogertsgate 1 (tel. 73 52 00 92), has a grill, pool table, piano, and TV room. (Sleeping-bag accommodations 130kr. Singles 210kr. Doubles 340kr. Open mid-June to mid-Aug.) **Pensjonat Jarlen Youth Hostel (HI),** Kongensgate 40 (tel. 73 51 32 18, fax 73 52 06 35), is smack-dab in the center, its convenience justifying its price (150kr, 175kr non-members). An old school building lookalike, **Trondheim Vandrerhjem (HI),** Weidemannsvei 41 (tel. 73 53 04 90), a 15min. walk from the city center offers dorm rooms (90kr). The closest of multiple campsites is large and crowded **Sandmoen Camping** (tel. 73 88 61 35), 10km south of town. Take bus 44 or 45 from the bus station to Sandbakken. (20kr per tent, 20kr per person.) Camping outside of sites is not permitted in the Trondheim area. Cheap **Rema 1000** stores abound in the town center. Wander along Munkegata, from the **fruit market** at Torvet to the **Ravnkola fish market** by the water, to replenish the vitamins lost to weeks of bread and cheese.

NORTHERN NORWAY

■■■ BODØ AND FAUSKE

Bodø Its provincial charm destroyed in WWII, Bodø (BUD-dha) is the northern terminus of the Norwegian rail line and the starting point for buses and boats farther into the Arctic. **Kjerringøy,** an old coastal trading center 30km north of Bodø, recently opened as a highly reputed outdoor museum; several buses (50kr) and ferries (16kr) make the trip each day. (Guided tours at 11:15am, 1pm, and 3:30pm.

NORWAY

25kr, students 10kr.) The largest maelstrom in the world, **Saltstraumen,** is only 33km from Bodø, but isn't really that exciting; it looks like a patch of mild rapids. Ask at the tourist office for tidal timetables. (Mon.-Fri. 5 buses per day, Sat. 3 buses per day, Sun. 1 bus; 38kr, 19kr with Scanrail.)

Daily **flights** from Oslo cost only 780kr; from anywhere north of Trondheim, 410kr. By **train,** Bodø is 11 hours north of Trondheim (1 day and 1 night train per day). Two **buses** per day run from Bodø north to Narvik (7hr., 305kr). The **tourist office,** Sjøgata 21 (tel. 75 52 60 00), is about 5 blocks toward the center from the train station. They'll give you the all-knowing, all-seeing *Bodø Guide,* and also have maps and hiking info. (Open Mon.-Fri. 9am-5pm and 7-9pm, Sat. 10am-3pm, Sun. 6-9pm; in winter Mon.-Fri. 9am-4pm.) To get to the **Flatvold Youth Hostel (HI)** (tel. 75 02 56 66), turn right on Sjøgata from the bus stop, or left from the ferry landing and train stations; turn left at the traffic circle and walk 10 minutes to the traffic light. It's Nordic clean and modern, with kitchen and laundry facilities. (Reception closed noon-5pm. 95kr, nonmembers 120kr. Open June 20 to mid-Aug.)

Fauske   To make the Trondheim-Narvik run in one day, get off the train one stop before Bodø at Fauske (63km before Bodø), where a bus meets the train and goes directly to Narvik; if you stay on the train to Bodø, the bus will have left. Fauske's **HI youth hostel** (tel. 75 64 67 06) lies 1km south toward Bodø from the station (90kr, nonmembers 120kr; open June to mid-Aug.). **Lundhøgda Camping** (tel. 08 14 39 66) is 3km from town (50kr per tent). Call the Statens Skoger office (tel. 08 14 59 66) for information about hiking in the stunning **Rago National Park,** where trails lead all the way to Jokkmokk and Kvikkjokk in Sweden. **Mo i Rana** is 2½ hours further towards Trondheim. It's home to a hostel (tel. 75 15 09 63; 90kr, nonmembers 115kr; open May to mid-Sept.) and is the base for excursions to the **Svarteisen glacier;** buses (120kr) leave at 10:30am from the local **tourist office** (tel. 75 15 04 21).

■■■ NARVIK

In a land where snow-capped peaks reflect in glimmering fjords, Narvik is a necessary monstrosity, a tangle of tracks and conveyor belts that bring iron ore from trains to ships. If you doubt its importance, wander through the cemeteries just east of the train station, a testament to the cost of the Allies' first victory over the Nazis (May 28, 1940). The **Nordland Red Cross War Museum,** on the main square, tells the story behind the gravestones. (Open early June-late Aug. Mon.-Sat. 10am-10pm, Sun. 11am-5pm; late Aug. to mid-Sept. and early March-early June Mon.-Fri. 11am-5pm. 20kr, students 10kr.) If you doubt Narvik's sheer ugliness, a dock tour may convince you. (Mid-June to mid-Aug. daily 2pm from LKAB guardhouse on Havnegata. 20kr.) In winter, the city basks in the midnight sun—on the rare days when the clouds part—and Narvik becomes a **skiing** center; slopes run from above tree level to sea level. You can ascend the looming peak by foot or take the new **Gondolbanen** (cable car). Undoubtedly the most glorious aspect of Narvik is getting there; Nordic nature in its untamed magnificence is yours on the bus north to Tromsø (251kr, 5hr.) or south to Bodø (305kr, 7hr.), the hydrofoil to Svolvær (255kr; see Lofoten), or the last hour of the train trip through Kiruna in Sweden (3 per day, 154kr).

Practical Information, Accommodations, and Food   Parallel to the ore-loading tracks is Narvik's main street, Kongensgate, on which you'll find the amicable **tourist office,** Kongensgate 66 (tel. 76 94 33 09). From the train station exit, turn right, walk 100m up the hill, then turn left past Gunnars market. The office changes money (bank rates are much better), gives transportation advice, and ...ks private rooms. (Singles 150kr. Doubles 250kr. 20-25kr fee. Open Mon.-Sat. ..., Sun. 11am-7pm; mid-Aug. to mid-June Mon.-Fri. 9am-4pm.) The **bus sta-** ...parking lot just above the tourist office.

...ord-Norge Buss-Ekspressen* buses stop at the **Nordkalotten youth** ...3 (tel. 76 94 25 98); or turn left from the tourist office and

walk 10min. down Kongensgate. (135kr, nonmembers 150kr. 4min. showers 10kr.
Kitchen. Open March-Nov. Reservations recommended.) Back up the hill 100m
toward town, on Kongensgate, the Swedish Church runs an International Seamen's
Center with cheap food, sauna, ping-pong, and showers. **Narvik Camping** (tel. 76
94 58 10) is 2km north of town along the main road. (70kr per tent. 4-person hut
390kr. Open year-round.) The **Rema 1000** discount store is on Snorresgate, 6 blocks
uphill and parallel to Kongensgate (open Mon.-Fri. 10am-8pm, Sat. 10am-6pm).

■■■ LOFOTEN ISLANDS

Yes, there are enchanted islands, and when they're sunny, they are the Lofotens.
Made luscious by the Gulf Stream, their jagged, green-gray mountains shelter fishing
villages, farms, and happy sheep. Sun-spangled puffins pontificate from the cliffs at
Værøy, while stockfish dry on quayside wooden racks. As late as the 1950s, fisherfolk lived in the small *rorbuer*, yellow and red wooden shacks which cluster along
the coast. Today, tourists book the *rorbuer* solid (75-125kr per person in a group of
4 or more). The indispensable brochure *Nordland 1995*—available at any tourist
office from Bodø north—lists them, among other accommodations, while the *Lofoten Info-Guide 1995*, available at tourist offices in the Lofotens (5kr), also furnishes
information on ferries, buses, and sights. The **midnight sun** glows May 27-July 15
over the Lofotens. Any high place or beach is a good vantage point; try **Eggum,**
across Vestvågøy from Stamsund, **Laukvik,** across Austvågøy from Svolvær, or ask
around. Arctic swimming is possible at shallow, white sandy beaches after the sun
has shone for a few days; good places are toward **Utakleiv** on Vestvågøy, where you
can also spot the midnight sun, and the beach by **Ramberg** on Flakstadøy.

   Highway E10 binds the four largest of the Lofotens—Vågen, Vestvågøy, Flakstad,
and Moskenes—which point toward the tiny outlying isles of Værøy and Røst. Narvik and Bodø are the best mainland springboards to the Lofotens; bus service runs
daily from Narvik to Svolvær (7hr., 291kr, railpass and student discount 50%) and
Bodø, through Fauske, to Svolvær (10½hr., 406kr, railpass and student discount
50%). By **boat,** your best and cheapest bet is the car ferries from Bodø to Moskenes
(2-3 per day, 4½hrs., 89kr), stopping 2 or 3 times per week at Røst and Værøy.
Hydrofoils from Bodø serve Værøy (twice daily, 220kr) and Svolvær (once daily,
219kr). From Narvik, hydrofoils skim the channel to Svolvær daily (255kr; return
only Tues.-Sun.). A final approach is the *Hurtigruten,* daily connecting Bodø with
Stamsund (4½hr., 226kr) and Svolvær (6hr., 243kr).

   Try to get to your preferred destination in one ferry swoop from the mainland; the
buses on the four northern islands are infrequent, expensive, and have confounding
schedules. Wave at them to make sure they stop. **Hitching** is easier on the east coast
than on the sparsely populated west coast, but no one's holding their breath. The
best way to experience Lofoten's spectacular scenery is to hike inland away from
Highway E10. Almost every tourist office or hostel owner can give suggestions and
maps.

Røst, Værøy, and Moskenes Røst is the southernmost and smallest of the
Lofotens, reachable only by ferry from Bodø (Tues. and Fri., 5hr., 79kr), and Moskenes (Wed. and Sun.). The **HI youth hostel** (tel. 76 09 61 09) is 500m from the boat
landing and charges a ruthless 75kr for breakfast (100kr, nonmembers 115kr; open
May-Aug.). Though famed for its puffins, uncharacteristically flat Røst can't compare
to craggy **Værøy,** which rises volcano-style between Røst and Moskenes, wallpa-
pered with thousands of seabirds. You can take the car ferry from Bodø (Mon.-
Wed., Fri.-Sat., 4-7hr., 84kr) or from Moskenes (Mon., Wed., Thurs., Sat., Sun. 1¾hr)
to Værøy. Stay at the **Værøy Youth Hostel (HI),** 4km from the ferry stop (tel. 76 09
53 75 or 76 09 53 52; 75kr, nonmembers 100kr; open mid-May to mid-Sept.), and
hike out to the cliffs.

   Ferries to **Moskenes,** the southernmost of the larger Lofotens, dock at the town of
Moskenes. The **tourist office** (tel. 76 09 15 99) by the ferry landing gives advice

rooms and sights (open June 11-Aug. 7 Mon.-Fri. 9:30am-4:30pm, Sat.-Sun. 10am-4pm; early June and mid-Aug. to Sept. closed weekends). About 10km to the south is **Å,** a tiny monosyllabic wooden settlement with a **youth hostel (HI)** (tel. 76 09 11 21, fax 76 09 12 82; 95kr, nonmembers 115kr, reservations essential, open May-Sept.). The hostel also rents *rorbuer,* which are both more rustic and cheaper for groups of 4 or more. If it's full, try **Hennumgården** (tel. 76 09 12 11; 100kr). Half of Å's buildings make up the **Norsk Fiskeværsmuseum,** an open-air museum documenting life in the old fishing days (open June-late Aug. Mon.-Fri. 10am-6pm, Sat.-Sun. 11am-3pm; 25kr). Camp on the cliffs behind the town above a snow-fed lake (free), or take a fishing cruise to the **Moskenesstraumen** (260kr), a maelstrom described in the fiction of both Jules Verne and Edgar Allen Poe. Take a swim here, and it will be your last. A cheap but lovely **fjord cruise** sails daily from Reine (north of Moskenes) to Rostad, Kirkefjord, Engelsnes, Vindstad, and back to Reine (35kr).

Flakstad, Vestvågøy, and Austvågøy Moving north, the next large island is **Flakstad,** centered on the hamlet of **Ramberg.** Flakstad has perhaps the best hiking trails on the islands; get detailed maps at the **tourist office** (tel. 76 09 34 50; open mid-June to Aug. Mon.-Fri. 10am-7pm, Sat.-Sun. 11am-5pm). The island's red-painted church, built of Russian driftwood in 1780, holds concerts during the summer (early July-early Aug.).

The mountain-backed hamlet of **Stamsund** on **Vestvågøy,** the next island north, is home to a **youth hostel (HI)** (tel. 76 08 93 34), where travelers from all over the world come for a night (80kr) and remain for weeks, cooking their freshly caught fish on wood-burning stoves. The benevolent ruler of this island utopia, Roar Justad, keeps bureaucracy to a minimum and will lend you his rowboats and fishing gear for a 100kr deposit. He also rents mopeds (80kr per day plus 0.50kr per km) and mountain bikes (75kr per day) for quests into the Lofoten wilderness. Head to **Borg,** the excavation site of the largest found Viking building and the only proven seat of a Viking chieftain. A fully reconstructed version should be completed in 1995. Two buses run daily to Stamsund from Å (86kr, 50% off with railpass) and Svolvær (72kr, 50% off with railpass) via Vestvågøy's underwhelming main town of **Leknes.**

Svolvær, on the northernmost island of **Austvågøy,** is the bland hub of beautiful Lofoten. The **tourist office** (tel. 76 07 30 00) is right near the ferry dock and will energetically provide info on hiking and sight-seeing possibilities (open Mon.-Fri. 9am-4pm, Sat. 10am-2pm). **Svolvær Sjøhuscamping** offers clean harborside rooms not far from the center, take the 4th right from Torget on Vestfjordgata going north (tel. 76 07 03 36; reception open 9am-2pm and 4-11pm; 100kr). More distant, and far more charming, is the friendly **Marinepollen Sjøhus** (sea houses; tel. 76 07 18 33), north along the E10 for 15 minutes until *fektveien* on the right; the quay-side WWII hospital ship is visible from the road. (Single cabin 100kr. Double 200kr.) Above Svolvær is the two-pronged rock stack called **The Goat;** lunatic rock climbers occasionally attempt the leap from one horn to the other. You can hike up past it to **The Frog,** another weird formation bucking the spine of the mountain. A natural rock bridge at the cliff top overlooks the island's mountains.

■ ■ ■ TROMSØ

Tromsø, city of midnight fun and Norway's gateway to the Arctic Ocean, is about 240km up the coast from Narvik on a small island connected to the mainland by bridge. Locals call the city, with its cafés, discos, and 60 nightclubs, "the Paris of the North"; they are perhaps suffering from cranial frostbite. Nevertheless, Tromsø is a good place to toast the woods and mountains before heading north to Finnmark or snowfields of **Svalbard.** The striking, modern **Arctic Cathedral** has clean white ____ned to blend with ice and snow (open Mon.-Sat. 10am-5pm, Sun. 1-5pm; ___msø Museum,** Lars Thøringsvei 10, features exhibits on the region's ___vell as ethnographic displays on Sami culture. (Open 9am-9pm; ___0am-3:30pm, Sat. noon-3pm, Sun. 11am-4pm. 10kr, students

5kr.) Take bus 21 or 27 to the south end of the island. The 2nd-floor **Polar Museum** chronicles Roald Amundsen's hardy polar exploits, all in Norwegian (open 11am-6pm, mid-Sept. to mid-May 11am-3pm; 20kr). For a sweeping view of the city in the midnight sun (roughly May 21-July 23), take the **cable car** to the top of Tromsdalstind; reach the cable car station aboard bus 28. (Daily 10am-5pm; midnight sun season 9pm-1:30am in good weather. 45kr.)

To sample the nightlife, wander down **Storgata** and its sidestreets. **Vertshuset Skarven,** on Strandskillet, looking onto the harbor, is a spot for all generations. Look for a whitewashed building. (Beer 35kr. Dinner from 50kr. Open Mon.-Thurs. noon-12:30am, Fri.-Sat. noon-1:30am, Sun. 3pm-12:30am.) **Blå Rock Café,** Strandgata 14, is a sleek three-storey eatery in the Hard Rock Café tradition. (0.5L beer 29kr in summer. Large pizza 85kr, small 60kr. Open Mon.-Thurs. 6pm-1:30am, Fri. 2pm-3:30am, Sat. noon-4am, Sun. 6pm-1:30am.) **Middags Kjelleren,** in a basement grotto between Skarven and Blå Rock, has bands most nights. (Cover after 8pm. Open Mon.-Thurs. 3pm-2am, Fri. 3pm-4am, Sat. noon-4am, Sun. 6pm-1:30am.)

Practical Information, Accommodations, and Food Tromsø's location means frequent connections to the rest of the country. The *Nord-Norge Ekspressen* **bus** is 251kr to Narvik and 323kr to Alta. The northbound *Hurtigruten* leaves daily at 6pm; the southbound arrives at 11:45pm. (To Honningsvåg 691kr, Bodø 701kr.) A standby **flight** from Oslo is 800kr. The **tourist office,** Storgata 61/63 (tel. 77 61 00 00), books rooms in private homes for 25kr, and is generally well clued-in. (Open Mon.-Fri. 8:30am-7pm, Sat.-Sun. 10am-5pm; mid-Aug. to May Mon.-Fri. 8:30am-4pm. Singles 150kr. Doubles 200kr.)

The **Elverhøy Youth Hostel (HI)** (tel. 77 68 53 19) is a bland, impersonal student dorm. Take bus 24. (Lockout 11am-5pm. 95kr, nonmembers 120kr, 100kr deposit mandatory for keys. Open June 20-Aug. 19.) Closer but more expensive is **Park Pensjonat,** Skolegate 24 (tel. 77 68 22 08), with spacious, comfortable rooms. (Singles 260kr. Doubles 320kr. Triples 360kr.) **Tromsdalen Camping** (tel. 08 33 80 37) has its share of bare ground but still undercuts the competition. Walk across the river to Tromsdalen, 30 minutes from the town center, or take bus 30 or 36. (2- to 4-person huts 250kr. Tents 100kr.) Next to the open-air market is **Domus,** a large market with a cheap salad bar (open Mon.-Fri. 10am-8pm, Sat. 10am-6pm). Fishermen sell fresh goods near the harbor by a statue memorializing their perils at sea. For a prepared meal of fresh fish, try **Prelaken,** Sjøgaten 12 (full meal 45kr).

■■■ FINNMARK

On most maps, Finnmark appears about as inviting as a walk-in freezer. The sun hides its face here from late November until late January, and only the exquisite colors of the *aurora borealis* (Northern Lights) illuminate the frigid countryside. But in summer the snow-capped peaks, vast stretches of coastal tundra, and inland forest bask under the midnight sun, and, the landscape becomes an arctic wonderland. The wilderness of **Finnmarksvidda** that spreads east from Tromsø is Europe's largest, a highly popular hiking area spotted with tourist huts. Consult the DNT offices in Oslo or Bergen for maps, prices and other information.

Buses run once or twice per day along the E6, the main highway around the top of Norway; spur lines branch south to Sweden and Finland. Both buses and the *Hurtigruten* are *very* expensive. Scanrailers get 50% off on *Nord-Norge Ekspressen* buses from Bodø to Kirkenes, and students may get some reduction on buses run by **FFR.** Some travelers find **hitchhiking** surprisingly successful, though traffic is light and distances are long. Those who thumb it bring a tent and a warm sleeping bag. If you're under 25, **flying** is the cheapest way to get to Finnmark. SAS offers 800kr standby (*Superhaik*) to Alta, and *Widerøe Airlines* will fly between any two cities north of and including Tromsø for 410kr (make reservations); youth standby fares in Sweden (250 Swedish kr from Stockholm to Kiruna or Gällivare in Swedish Lapland) are sometimes an even better option.

NORWAY

Alta and Hammerfest Slate-gray mountains, towering cliffs, and icy green sea make the road from Tromsø north to **Alta,** Finnmark's largest town, the most spectacular bus route in Norway. The **Alta River,** famous for its salmon, runs nearby at the bottom of Europe's longest canyon (tours 110kr). For fishing permits, consult the **tourist office** (tel. 78 43 77 70). The **Alta Museum,** winner of "European Museum of the Year Award 1993," includes Scandinavia's only prehistoric UNESCO World Heritage site: spectacular rock carvings from more than 6000 years ago. Take the city bus to its west end along the E6. (Open summer 8am-11pm, early June and late August 8am-8pm, off-season reduced hours. 30kr, 25kr in winter.) You can stay at the **Frikirkens Elevheim (HI)** (tel. 78 43 44 09; lockout 11am-5pm; 100kr, non-members 125kr; open late June-late Aug.). **Alta River Camping** (tel. 78 43 43 53) is 5km out of town, accessible only by the twice daily bus to Kautokeino. (Reception open 9am-11pm. 50kr per tent, 15kr per person. 4-bed huts 300-350kr. Open mid-June to mid-Aug.) One or two **buses** per day run to Tromsø (7-8hr., 330kr); Hammerfest (3hr., 150kr); Honnigsvåg (5hr., 220kr); Kautokeino (3hr., 140kr); and Karasjok (4hr., 250kr).

At **Hammerfest,** the world's northernmost town, you can become a member of the Royal and Ancient Polar Bear Society (est. 1963)—if you have 95kr to blow. The *Hurtigruten* stops here for 1½ hours. Daily buses head west to Alta and east to Kirkenes. Contemplate the midnight sun from **Salen,** a short, steep hike up the hill from the **tourist office** (tel. 78 41 21 85), up the street from the pier and on the left (open Mon.-Fri. 10am-7pm, Sat.-Sun. 10am-5pm; mid-Aug. to May Mon.-Fri. 10am-3pm). Call Per Bjaaland (tel. 78 41 19 87) to rent one of his two centrally located, furnished **apartments** (300kr plus 25kr per person, max 4 persons, breakfast 50kr).

Nordkapp and Honningsvåg Looming into the Arctic Ocean from the island of Magerøy, the famed **Nordkapp** is much ado about less than you might have hoped. Not even continental Europe's northernmost point (a title held by Knivskjellodden, a peninsula to the west), Nordkapp is an expensive tourist mecca (ticket, including bus, 190kr). Nordkapp's first budget traveler was a 17th-century Italian monk named Francesci Negri, who made the journey by rowboat and foot. Battered by gale and wave and carrying only a letter from his mom for comfort, Negri managed to caulk leaks in his boat with his habit and, once on land, to spark fires on the desolate rock using his own hair. Exhausted, naked, and bald, he arrived in Nordkapp and was ostracized. Perched on and inside the rock is the **Nordkapp Complex,** with a bank, post office, telephones, cafeteria, and a gold-enameled Thai Museum commemorating King Chulalongkorn's visit in 1907. No joke. Around the complex is rough landscape, open ocean bashing beneath the midnight sun (mid-May to July), and a cliff-side champagne bar. Be warned: the complex closes at 2am, and the only rooms are in Honningsvåg (last bus leaves at 1:15am).

To reach Nordkapp, first travel to **Honningsvåg,** 25km south, whose **tourist office** (tel. 78 47 28 94) provides transport info for all of Finnmark (open 8:30am-7pm; Sept.-May Mon.-Fri. 8:30am-4pm). The 33km trip to Nordkapp can be made by bus (4 per day, round-trip 100kr); some thumb it, but get the weather forecast first— Nordkapp is dullsville in the mist. The cold and primitive **Nordkapp Youth Hostel and Camping (HI)** (tel. 78 47 51 13) is 8km up the same road (bus 12kr). There's a kitchen but few utensils, and the toilets are a windy 200m walk away. (100kr, non-members 120kr. 20kr per person, 40kr per tent. Open June-Sept. Reservations recommended.) The **bus** to Honningsvåg from Alta (1-2 per day, 6hr., 220kr with ferry) or Hammerfest (1-2 per day, 4½hr., 160kr) is cheaper than the *Hurtigruten* (from Kirkenes 635kr, Tromsø 655kr, Hammerfest 255kr).

■ Poland (Polska)

US$1 = 23255zł (złoty, or PLZ)	**10000zł =** **US$0.43**
CDN$1= 17323zł	**10000zł =** **CDN$0.57**
UK£1 = 36953zł	**10000zł =** **UK£0.27**
IR£1 = 36604zł	**10000zł =** **IR£0.27**
AUS$1 = 17823zł	**10000zł =** **AUS$0.56**
NZ$1 = 14100zł	**10000zł =** **NZ$0.71**
SAR1 = 6523zł	**10000zł =** **SAR1.53**
Country Code: 48	**International Dialing Prefix: 00**

The first and most gracious of the 1989 Eastern European shakedowns unfolded in Poland with a manner more typical of chess games than revolutions. After over 20 years of anti-government union strikes, economic distress, and political imprisonments, Wojciech Jaruzelski's Central Committee met with Lech Wałęsa and other Solidarity leaders for several weeks of "round-table" discussions. In return for Solidarity's pledge to end strikes, the government agreed to legalize the union, amend the constitution, and hold free elections. Solidarity members swept into all but one of the contested seats, and the editor of its newspaper, Tadeusz Mazowiecki, became Eastern Europe's first noncommunist premier in 40 years. Checkmate.

Now, the largest and most populous of the newly liberated Eastern European nations is gritting its teeth in a determined attempt to rejoin the modern world. In 1990, the Solidarity government opted to take the bitter dose of capitalism in one gulp. To woo western investment, the government eliminated subsidies, froze wages, and devalued currency, throwing the antiquated economy into recession and producing the first unemployment in 45 years. Consumer goods now fill the shelves, and budding capitalists truck in supplies to sell at sidewalk bazaars, though few people have any free cash to spend. Although prices have continued to increase, Poland is still a bargain for Westerners.

Whatever Poland is or becomes, it promises few dull moments. Struggle has been a way of life for Poles, who have enjoyed only 26 years of freedom in this century. Resilient and gracious, they have drawn strength from the Catholic Church and a rich intellectual tradition. Survivor of the devastating Second World War, misman-agement, and environmental carnage, the country offers many riches. The medieval amber shores of the Baltic coast to the north transform into the poppy-strewn plains that dominate Poland's landscape. Along the southern border, the Sudety and Kar-paty Mountains break the lull of the lowlands, culminating in the exhilarating, snow-capped peaks of the Tatry range where *górale* (mountaineer) folklore still thrives.

For more comprehensive coverage of Poland, consult *Let's Go: Eastern Europe*.

GETTING THERE

As of September 1994, citizens of the U.S. and Ireland need no visas for Poland for stays up to 90 days, and citizens of the U.K. for stays up to 6 months. Citizens of Aus-tralia, Canada, New Zealand, and South Africa need visas. Single-entry visas (valid 3 months) cost US$32 (students US$24; Canadians US$50, Canadian students US$38); two-entry visas cost US$60 (students US$45; Canadians US$95, Canadian students US$72), and multiple-entry visas cost US$135 (students US$101; Canadians US$210, Canadian students US$153). Transit visas (valid 48hrs.) cost US$16 (students US$12; Canadians US$25, Canadian students US$19). Regular service takes up to 14 days. In some cases 24hr. rush service is possible, but it requires an additional payment of US$17. For more info, contact an **embassy: U.S.,** 2224 Wyoming Ave., Washington, DC 20008 (tel. (202) 234-2501, fax 328-2152), **Canada,** 443 Daly St., Ottawa 2, Ont., K1N 6H3 (tel. (613) 789-0468, fax 232-3463), **U.K.,** 47 Portland Place, London W1N 3AG, (tel. (0171) 580 43 29, fax 323 40 18), **Ireland,** 05 Ailesbury Rd., Dublin 4 (tel. (01) 22 83 08 55 or 22 83 75 62, fax 269 83 09), **Australia,** 7 Turrana St., Yarralumla ACT 2600 Canberra (tel. (06) 273 12 08 or 273 12 11, fax 273 31 84), **New Zealand,** 17 Upland Rd., Kelburn, Wellington (tel. (04) 71 24 56, fax 71 24 55, **South Africa,** 14 Arnos St., Colbyn, Pretoria 0083 (tel. (012) 43 26 21, fax 346 13 66).

Getting to Poland means an easy if tiresome **train** trip from Berlin, Prague, or Budapest (often overnight). **Polferries ships** from Ystad, Sweden or Copenhagen, Denmark to the port city of **Świnoujście** in northeast Poland; or from Oxelösund, Sweden (near Stockholm) or Helsinki, Finland to **Gdańsk** are excellent options. For further info, contact **Polish Baltic Shipping Co.,** ul. Portowa 41, PL 78-100 Koło-brzeg (tel. (48) 9665 25211, fax (48) 965 26612).

GETTING AROUND

PKP trains run frequently to almost every town; although prices have dramatically increased, they remain an inexpensive mode of travel. The *ekspresowy* trains are listed with an "Ex" in front of the train number. *Pośpieszny* (direct trains) chug along almost as fast. *Osobowy* trains are the slowest and cheapest—about 35% less. Once you figure out which train you want, note the *peron* (platform) number, write down the destination, type of train, date, and time; then hand the information to the clerk. All *ekspresowy* and some *pośpieszny* trains require seat reservations; if you see a boxed R on the schedule, ask the clerk for a *miejscówka* (30,000zł). A *bilet* (ticket) in *pierwsza klasa* (1st class) is 50% more and worth it for overnights—the seats fold back all the way. International train tickets can now be purchased only with złoty. The ISIC entitles cardholders to 25% off on international fares, but only for the Polish portion of the trip. **Eurotrain passes,** available at ALMATUR, offer 40% discounts on train tickets between European cities for those under 26. ALMATUR also sells **Interrail passes** and **Wasteels**. Discount tickets for those under 26 are also sold at all major train stations and ORBIS offices.

Bus travel has become cheaper than the train. **PKS buses** are a particularly good idea for short excursions, which can take hours on an *osobowy* train. Advance tickets may be purchased at the bus station. In the country, PKS markers (like yellow Mercedes-Benz symbols) indicate bus stops, but drivers will often halt elsewhere if you flag them down. Though the domestic airline, **LOT**, is not a real budget option, it does give students under 26 a 25% discount.

Although one may hitch on any road in the country, tourists should be aware that **hitching** is becoming increasingly dangerous. Hand-waving, not a thumb, is the accepted sign. The Polish government has encouraged hitching with the *Autostop Hitchhike Book,* available from PTTK for 40,000zł (valid May-Sept.); it includes an insurance policy, an ID card, a tourist information book, and vouchers that qualify one's drivers for prizes and compensation.

City public transportation (*komunikacja miejska*) is cheap and efficient. Buy tickets from any Ruch kiosk, and punch your ticket (*bilet*) on board. Only Polish students can ride for the lower *ulgowy* fare; if caught by the conductor, you will be fined. In most cities, trams stop running as early as 10pm. **Taxis** will probably rip you off. Search out official vehicles with the city shield on the door. It is generally much cheaper to use one of the Radio Taxi services available in most cities—919 is the country-wide number, but local newspapers publish the telephone numbers of various taxi companies. When you get in the taxi, always check if the meter is turned on. You will be asked to pay for the driver's return trip if you travel outside the city. At night, taxi-drivers use a different meter; it should say "2" on the left side. Consequently, fares increase by 50%. It is not recommended to accept rides from private car owners, even though they might cost less.

POLAND ESSENTIALS

ORBIS is the Polish state travel bureau, with offices in most major hotels and elsewhere in major cities. They sell international (*międzynarodowe*) and domestic (*krajowe*) train tickets and international bus tickets. **ALMATUR,** the Polish student travel organization, sells the ISIC and Eurotrain passes; they can also help find inexpensive university housing during the summer. Both provide maps and brochures, as do **PTTK** and **IT (Tourist Information)** bureaus, on the main street of every town. Since 1989, private tourist agencies have mushroomed all over Poland; their prices are often more competitive than those of ORBIS. (Warning: quite a few of them are nothing more than a hoax.)

The złoty is real money now but still not widely traded in the West. Change back before leaving. For cash, *kantor* offices (private exchange counters) offer marginally better rates than banks or hotels. The most reliable place to exchange traveler's checks and to get Visa or MC cash advances is the **Bank PKO S.A.**, with offices all over Poland. Most ORBIS offices, and branch offices of **Narodowy Bank Polski** in major cities, will exchange traveler's checks. Banking hours are Mon.-Fri. 8am-4pm, though some banks stay open until 6pm. Exchange windows generally operate 9am-6pm, and stay open 24hrs. in some ORBIS hotels as well as in airports, train stations, and border crossings. The black market is extinct. Polish banknotes cause a lot of problems, not just for foreigners, but for locals as well. The smallest banknotes include 50 and 100 zł, which are to be substituted with coins. It is somewhat of a challenge not to confuse the banknotes—the 1000zł bill looks very much like the 100,000zł bill. Currency reform has been officially announced in the papers by the Polish government and the Central Bank, and is supposed to go into effect Jan.1, 1995. Essentially, it means that 4 zeros will be removed from every Polish bill—1 new zł will be worth 10,000 old zł!

Department stores, supermarkets, and boutiques carry many foreign-made goods. Supermarkets and large department stores are usually open from 9am to 8pm, small shops from 11am to 7pm, and grocery stores from 5am or 6am to 6pm or 7pm. Most museums are open Tuesday through Sunday from 10am to 4pm. Legal **holidays** include New Year's Day, Easter Monday, Labor Day (May 1), Constitution Day (May 3), Corpus Christi (variable; a Thursday in May or June), Ascension Day (Aug. 15), All Saints' Day (Nov. 1), National Independence Day (Nov. 11), and Christmas (Dec. 25-26). Museums ordinarily close the day after a holiday as well.

In general, don't do anything your mother wouldn't recommend. You can be seriously **fined** for (among other things) jaywalking, putting your shoes on a train seat, riding a tram or bus without a validated ticket, or playing cards in public.

The transition to capitalism and market economy has brought with it a significant increase in crime rates. Many cities in Poland are plagued by highly organized mafia-like gangs. Tourists are more vulnerable than locals, because they often carry hard currency. Carry only the bare minimum of cash with you. If the need arises, dial 997 for the **police,** 998 for the **fire department,** and 999 for an **ambulance.**

Communication In cities, many Poles know some English. German is more common; try English before Russian. Polish spelling is fully phonetic and easy to figure out. Buy a phrasebook before you arrive. Some key words and phrases include: *Cześć* (tcheshch, "hello"); *Ile kosztuje?* (EE-leh kosh-TOO-yeh, "how much is it?"); *Proszę* (PROH-sheh, "please"); *Dziękuję* (jeng-KOO-yeh, "thank you"); *Do widzenia* (doh veed-ZEN-ya, "goodbye"). *Tak* means "yes," while *nie* (nyeh) is "no." When all else fails, there's always *Nie mówię po polsku* (nyeh MOO-vyeh poh POHL-skoo, "I don't speak Polish"). Women traveling alone may have to deal with a drunken oaf or two; fire away a firm *Odczep się* (OHD-chep sheh, "get lost").

Mail to and from Poland is becoming more and more reliable. Airmail *(lotnicza)* letters usually take 7-10 days to the U.S. For **Poste Restante,** put a "1" after the city name to make sure it goes to the main post office (picking up a letter costs 3000zł). Public pay **phones** now use tokens *(żetony),* which come in 2 denominations (A for inner-city calls, 1,200zł, and C for city-to-city calls, 11,800zł). PPTT phone cards are available for all types of calls, even international ones, and come in several denominations (100 units 117,700zł). Both tokens and phone cards are available at the *poczta* (post office). To reach the AT&T **USADirect operator** dial 01 04 80 01 11 (from outside Warsaw dial a 0 and wait for a tone first); MCI **WorldPhone** 01 04 80 02 22; **SprintExpress** 01 04 80 01 15; **Canada Direct** 01 04 80 01 18; **BT Direct** 044 00 99 48. To make a **collect call,** write the name of the city or country and the number plus "Rozmowa R" on a slip of paper, and hand it to a post office staff member; it'll take some time. Direct international calls to most Western European countries, as well as to the U.S., are available from private phones—just dial 00 plus the country code and the number you are calling.

Accommodations, Camping, and Food At the train station or outside the tourist office, you will likely make the acquaintance of grandmother types offering private rooms. These unofficial accommodations are usually safe, clean, and convenient, but do ask if the room is near the city center. Expect to pay about US$15 per person. **HI youth hostels** *(schroniska młodzieżowe)* are generally crowded, rather primitive and quite uncomfortable, but are absolutely everywhere and cost an average of 60,000zł per night (slightly less for "juniors" under 18 or 26, slightly more for nonmembers). Hot water is chancy. **PTSM** is the national hostel organization. **University dorms** are a smart option during the summer (July-Aug.), when they transform into sparse but cheap tourist housing. Ask at ALMATUR. **PTTK** runs a number of hotels called **Domy Turysty,** where you can stay in multi-bed rooms for 40,000-90,000zł. Many towns have a **Biuro Zakwaterowań,** which arranges stays in private homes. Rooms come in categories I-III. The lower the number, the better the room. Category I rooms are most centrally located and have hot water. Category III rooms almost never have hot water.

Tent sites average 25,000zł per person, 50,000zł with car. Bungalows are often available; a bed costs about 100,000zł. Look for the *Polska Mapa Campingów,* which lists all campgrounds. ALMATUR also runs a number of campgrounds in summer; ask for a list at one of their offices.

Śniadanie (breakfast) is usually consumed 5-8am, and consists of cheese, cold cuts, eggs, and bread. A *drugie śniadanie* (second breakfast), similar to a packed lunch, is not unusual around 9-11am. The main meal of the day is *obiad* (1-5pm). Food is quite cheap in Poland, and more expensive does not always mean better. A *restauracja* or *kawiarnia* (café) has waiters; a *bar* is self-service; a *bar mleczny* (milk bar) is usually super-cheap. While tipping is not mandatory in Poland, it is customary to leave a tip of 10-15% in restaurants and cafés. *Barszcz* is a beet broth served in many different ways, both hot and cold, and usually with potatoes or bread. *Bigos* is *sauerkraut* cooked with meat (beef and sausage), and seasoned. Beware *Flaczki*, it's tripe. *Gołąbki* ("little pigeons") are really cabbage rolls filled with meat and rice. *Kotlet schabowy* is the ubiquitous pork chop. *Pierogi* are dumplings with various fillings (fruit, meat, cheese, potato, cabbage, mushroom) and toppings (butter, sour cream, sweet cream, fruit syrup, bacon bits, browned onions). *Zapiekanka* is a fast-food concoction of mushrooms, melted cheese, and ketchup on French bread, sold at kiosks on the streets. Polish beer is dubious, but try to find *Żywiec* or *Okocim* (if you want it cold, say so). Vodka, the national specialty, comes in many flavors and brands: *Wyborowa*, *Żytnia*, and *Polonez*, to name just a few. Don't leave the country without trying the herb vodka, *Żubrówka*, complete with a blade of grass from the region where the bison (*żubr*) roam.

■■■ WARSAW (WARSZAWA)

Contemnire procellas (to defy the storms) became Warsaw's motto. It survived the partitions and WWI, and fought heroically in WWII. At least two-thirds of its population perished during WWII and by 1945, 85% of the capital's standing structures had fallen. Over 50 years after the German invasion, the faded but colorful façades of the *Stare Miasto* (old town), the cobblestone streets, and the tall, narrow buildings have all been painstakingly restored. Buildings that never existed rose above the rubble, built after plans found in old archives—a resurrection testifying to Warsaw's relentless, defiant spirit.

ORIENTATION AND PRACTICAL INFORMATION

Warsaw, the country's principal air and rail hub, lies in east-central Poland, about 150km from the Belorussian border. The *Śródmieście* (city center) and most major points of interest lie on the west bank of the **Wisła River,** which bisects the city. To the right of the main train station **Warszawa Centralna, ul. Marszałkowska** intersects **Aleje Jerozolimskie,** forming the center of the modern downtown. Beyond, Aleje Jerozolimskie extends toward the river to cross the next major street, **Nowy Świat.** A right on Nowy Świat leads down embassy row to Łazienki and Wilanów palaces; a left leads north to the old town. A good **map** with bus and tram lines is *essential;* purchase one at the *Ruch* (news and tobacco) stand on any street corner, in large hotels or bookstores, in the airport, or in bus and train stations.

Tourist Information and Offices: Centrum Informacji Turystycznej (Tourist Information Center), pl. Zamkowy 1/3 in the Old Town (tel. 635 18 81). Efficient, warm, and English-speaking staff. Maps, guidebooks, listings of hotels, tourist offices, restaurants, and cafés; currency exchange and hotel reservations. Pick up a free issue of the monthly *Welcome to Warsaw* and *Warszawa—What, Where, When*. Open Mon.-Fri. 9am-6pm, Sat. 10am-6pm, Sun. 11am-6pm. **ORBIS,** ul. Bracka 16 (tel. 27 01 72). Entrance on al. Jerozolimskie near Nowy Świat, at the back of the Smyk department store. Train, plane, and bus tickets. Open Mon.-Fri. 8am-7pm, Sat. 8am-3pm. UPS window open Mon.-Fri. 8am-4pm. A mega-office branch at ul. Marszałkowska 142 (tel. 27 67 66, fax 27 11 23), is open Mon.-Sat. 9am-6pm. Both branches change money, do Visa/MC cash advances, and cash traveler's checks for 5% commission. The *Warsaw Voice*, a weekly local newspaper geared to the city's growing international population, includes a section on restaurants and culture, and gives useful tips on finding your way around the city.

Budget Travel: ALMATUR, ul. Kopernika 23 (tel. 26 35 12 or 26 26 39), off Nowy Świat. Good place for travel information and English speakers. Sells ISIC, travel insurance (US$8), international bus tickets, plane tickets at a student discount. Open Mon.-Fri. 9am-6pm, Sat. 10am-2pm. **Room 19,** ul. Krakowskie Przedmie-ście 24 (tel. 26 75 41), is ALMATUR's train ticket department. Go through the main university entrance, and it's the first building on the right. Open Mon.-Fri. 9am-4pm.

Embassies: U.S., al. Ujazdowskie 29/31 (tel. 628 30 41); entrance around the cor-ner at ul. Piękna 12. Open Mon.-Fri. 9am-noon. **Canada,** ul. Matejki 1/5 (tel. 29 80 51). Open Mon.-Fri. 8:30am-1pm and 2-5pm. **U.K.,** al. Róż 1 (tel. 628 10 01). Con-sular office at Wawelska 14 (tel. 25 80 31). Open Mon.-Fri. 9am-noon. **Australia,** ul. Estońska 3/5 (tel. 617 60 81). **New Zealand** citizens should contact the British embassy. **Czech Republic,** ul. Koszykowa 18 (tel. 628 72 21). Open Mon.-Fri. 9am-1pm. **Lithuania,** al. Ujazdowskie 13 (tel. 625 34 10). **Russia,** ul. Belwederska 49, building C (tel. 621 34 53). Open Wed. and Fri. 8am-1pm. **Slovakia,** ul. Litewska 6. (tel. 41 01 12). **Ukraine,** ul. Szuka 7 (tel. 29 64 49).

Currency Exchange: Hotels, banks, and tourist offices, as well as private *kantor* counters (with slightly better rates) throughout the city exchange cash. 24hr. ser-vice at the Railway Station and the International Airport in the departures area. **Bank PKO S.A.** (tel. 637 10 00), in the blue skyscraper at pl. Bankowy 2 cashes all brands of traveler's checks for 0.5-1.5% commission.

American Express, ul. Krakowskie Przedmieście 11 (tel. 635 20 02). Full service. Express cash machine. Open Mon.-Fri. 9am-5pm, Sat. 10am-2pm.

Post Office: Main post office at ul. Świętokrzyska 31/33 (tel. 26 60 01 or 26 04 11). Poste Restante at counter 12. **Postal code:** 00-001. Open 24hrs.

Telephones: at the post office. Long lines during the day. **City Code:** 022 for six-digit numbers, and 02 for seven-digit numbers.

Flights: All flights, domestic and international, use the new and improved **Port Lot-niczy Warszawa-Okęcie** on ul. Żwirki i Wigury, commonly referred to as Termi-nal 1. To the city center, take bus 175 (after 11pm, bus 611). Bus tickets at the *Ruch* stand in the departure hall or at the *kantor* office outside (6000zł). The Air-port City Bus (35,000zł) travels directly from the airport to the center (every 20-30min.). Runs between 5:35am and 11:37pm. Tickets available at the ORBIS desk at the airport, the LOT office in the Marriott Hotel, or from the driver.

Trains: Most trains use **Warszawa Centralna**—in the center of the city. To Berlin (8hr., 654,000zł), Budapest (10hr., 1,382,000zł), Prague (12hr., 822,000zł), Mos-cow (27hr., 1,130,000zł), St. Petersburg (24hr., 1,114,000zł), Minsk (12hr., 630,000zł), Kiev (22hr., 820,000zł), Vilnius (12hr., 570,000zł), Vienna (9hr., 1,400,000zł plus 332,0000zł for couchette), Gdańsk (4hr., 153,000zł), Kraków (2½hr., 135,000zł), Zakopane (8½hr., 171,000zł).

Buses: PKS Warszawa Zachodnia (tel. 23 64 94 or 23 64 95), next to the Warszawa Zachodnia train station at al. Jerozolimskie 144. From the main train station, take bus M or 127 headed west. Open 5am-11pm. International Bus Infor-mation window open Mon.-Fri. 8am-4pm. To Minsk (11hr., 315,000zł), Vilnius (12hr., 326,000zł), Riga (14hr., 643,000zł).

Public Transportation: Bus and tram lines are marked on the standard city map. All day trams and buses (including express lines) cost the same. Fare 6000zł, students 3000zł. Night buses 18,000zł. Large baggage 6000zł per piece. You must buy tick-ets at a *Ruch* stand or street vendor; there are no conductors on buses or trams. Once in the bus or tram, punch both ends of the ticket in the machines on board. If caught without a punched ticket, you'll be nabbed for 250,000zł.

Taxis: Stands marked by blue and white signs. For cheap and reliable 24hr. taxi ser-vice, call 96 22 or 96 24. Taxi meters usually start at 30,000zł. At night, the rates are about 20% higher.

Hitchhiking: Thumbers usually pick up *Książeczka autostopu* (The Hitchhiker's Book), available only at the PTTK office, Rynek Starego Miasta 23 (tel. 31 05 44, open Mon.-Fri. 10am-4pm).

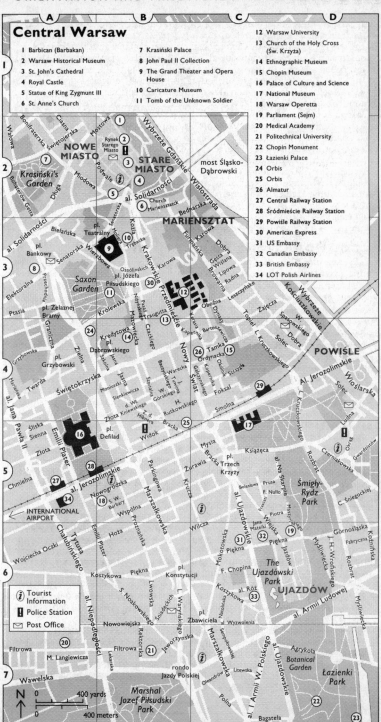

Central Warsaw

1 Barbican (Barbakan)
2 Warsaw Historical Museum
3 St. John's Cathedral
4 Royal Castle
5 Statue of King Zygmunt III
6 St. Anne's Church
7 Krasiński Palace
8 John Paul II Collection
9 The Grand Theater and Opera House
10 Caricature Museum
11 Tomb of the Unknown Soldier
12 Warsaw University
13 Church of the Holy Cross (Św. Krzyża)
14 Ethnographic Museum
15 Chopin Museum
16 Palace of Culture and Science
17 National Museum
18 Warsaw Operetta
19 Parliament (Sejm)
20 Medical Academy
21 Politechnical University
22 Chopin Monument
23 Łazienki Palace
24 Orbis
25 Orbis
26 Almatur
27 Central Railway Station
28 Śródmieście Railway Station
29 Powiśle Railway Station
30 American Express
31 US Embassy
32 Canadian Embassy
33 British Embassy
34 LOT Polish Airlines

(i) Tourist Information
! Police Station
✉ Post Office

POLAND

Luggage Storage: At the bus station open 7am-8pm. 20,600zł per piece per day. At the train station, use the *przechowalnia bagażu* on the level below the main hall. Lockers come in three sizes and operate on tokens 30,000-100,000zł per day.

Bookstores: Klub Międzynarodowej Prasy i Książki, ul. Marszałkowska 116/122, has a good selection of English-language magazines. Open Mon.-Fri. 9am-8pm, Sat. 9am-4pm. **Bookland**, next to the British Institute at al. Jerozolimskie 61 (tel. 625 41 46), sells paperbacks. Open Mon.-Fri 10am-4pm, Sat. 10am-2pm.

Laundromat: ul. Karmelicka 17 (tel. 31 73 17). Take bus 180 north from ul. Marszałkowska, or bus 33 from ul. Jana Pawła II towards Żoliborz and get off at ul. Anielewicza. Open Mon.-Fri. 9am-7pm, Sat. 9am-1pm. Wash and dry 86,000zł per kg. Bring your own detergent.

Crisis Lines: Women's Hotline, tel. 635 47 91, staffed Mon.-Fri. 4-8pm.

Pharmacy: Apteka Grabowski at the central train station. Apteka, ul. Grójecka 76 (tel. 22 28 91). Open 24hrs.

Medical Assistance: For general information about hospitals, pharmacies and the like, call the **Health Info Line** (tel. 26 27 61 or 26 83 00). Mon.-Sat. 7:30am-7:30pm, Sundays 8am-3pm. Doctors available 24hrs. at **Capricorn,** ul. Podwale 11 (tel. 31 89 69 or 31 76 07).

Emergencies: Police Headquarters, tel. 26 24 24.

ACCOMMODATIONS AND CAMPING

The **Syrena** office, ul. Krucza 17 (tel. 628 75 40), pins down rooms in private homes; arrive early. From the train station, turn left (toward downtown) at al. Jerozolimskie, follow it to ul. Krucza and take a right. (Singles 220,000zł. Doubles 340,000zł. Open Mon.-Sat. 8am-7pm, Sun. 8am-5pm.) **Informacja noclegowa** (Mon.-Fri. 10am-5pm tel. 643 95 92; and Mon.-Fri. 5-10pm, Sat.-Sun.11am-5pm tel. 671 58 25) is a phone service which directs people to hotels. They pride themselves on finding rooms that will best meet your tastes, needs, and budget. A third agency that finds private rooms is **Romeo i Julia**, ul. Emilii Plater 15/30 (tel. 29 29 93), directly opposite the central train station. (Open Mon.-Fri. 10am-7pm. Singles 300,000zł. Doubles 430,000zł. For breakfast, add 10,000zł.)

Hotel Bursa Artystów, ul. Miodowa 24a (tel. 635 79 05 or 635 41 74), just before the entrance to the Old Town. Superbly located. Art student dorm becomes a hotel in the summer. Doubles 440,000zł. Triples 660,000zł. Open July-Aug.

Schronisko Młodzieżowe (HI), ul. Smolna 30, top floor (tel. 27 89 52), across from the National Museum. Take bus 158 or 175, or tram 22 from al. Jerozolimskie. Clean and basic. Excellent location. Lockout 10am-5pm. Curfew 11pm. 64,000zł, nonmembers 80-91,000zł. Sheets 15,000zł. English spoken.

Schronisko Młodzieżowe (HI), ul. Międzyparkowa 4/6 (tel. 31 17 66). Close to the river, between two parks. Take tram 2, 18 or 19 northbound from ul. Marszałkowska and get off at ul. Andersa after you see a stadium on your right. 65,000zł, nonmembers 75,000zł. Sheets 18,000zł. Open April 15-Oct.15.

Schronisko Młodzieżowe (HI), ul. Karolkowa 53a (tel. 32 88 29). Tram 22 west from al. Jerozolimskie or train station to Okopowa. Turn left on al. Solidarności, and then right onto ul. Karolkowa. Pretty but out of the way. Lockout 10am-5pm. Curfew 11pm. 70,000zł, nonmembers 75,000zł. Doubles 280,000zł. Triples 120,000zł per person. Sheets 10,000zł. Baggage storage 5000zł. No showers.

Hotel Harenda (PTTK), also known as **Dom Turysty,** ul. Krakowskie Przedmieście 4/6 (tel. 26 26 25). From train station, take bus 175 to Uniwersytet. Walk back to the end of the block and take the first left on Oboźna. Clean, modern showers. Singles 450-600,000zł. Doubles 600-850,000zł. Triples 630,000zł. Quads 660,000zł.

Dom Literata, ul. Krakowskie Przedmieście 2/8 (tel. 635 39 20 or 635 04 04). Prime location, at the entrance to the Old Town, over a posh café full of writers and artists. Singles 300,000zł. Doubles 400,000zł.

Dom Chłopa, pl. Powstańców Warszawy 2 (tel. 27 92 51), between the Pałac Kultury and Nowy Świat. A real hotel, attracting an older clientele. Reception open 24hrs. Singles 400,000zł. Doubles 900,000zł.

POLAND

Your Hostelling International card will allow you stay at over 5,000 hostels in 70 countries for only $5 to $30 per night.

Please sign me on for a full 12 months as a:
❑ youth (under 18) $10
❑ adult $25
❑ family $35,
❑ senior (over 54) $15
❑ Life $250

My payment is enclosed via:
❑ Check
❑ MC/VISA # _____--_____--_____--_____ ___/___

❑ **I do not want to join yet; please send me more information**
Please allow 3 weeks for delivery. For faster delivery options call 1-800-444-6111.

_____

Name _____

Address _____

City _____ | State _____ | Zip _____ | Birth Date (m/y) _____

Phone _____ | Departure Date _____ | Destination _____

IF YOU CAN'T AFFORD TO TRAVEL, JOIN THE CLUB.

432

HOSTELLING INTERNATIONAL

The new seal of approval of the International Youth Hostel Federation.

HOSTELLING INTERNATIONAL®

LET'S GO TRAVEL · EURAIL PASSES
The least expensive way to see Europe

1-800-5-LETS-GO

Eurail Pass	
15 days	$498
21 days	$648
1 month	$798
2 months	$1098
3 months	$1398

Eurail Flexipass	
Any 5 days in two months	$348
Any 10 days in two months	$560
Any 15 days in two months	$740

Eurail Youthpass	
Under 26	2nd class
15 days	$398
1 month	$578
2 months	$768

Eurail Youth Flexipass	
Any 5 days in two months	$255
Any 10 days in two months	$398
Any 15 days in two months	$540

Please see reverse for order card

NO POSTAGE
NECESSARY
IF MAILED
IN THE
UNITED STATES

BUSINESS REPLY MAIL
FIRST-CLASS MAIL PERMIT NO. 13213 WASHINGTON DC

POSTAGE WILL BE PAID BY ADDRESSEE

**HOSTELLING INTERNATIONAL
AMERICAN YOUTH HOSTELS
PO BOX 37613
WASHINGTON DC 20078-4258**

The right Eurail for me is:

Description	Name (Should appear as on passport)	Price
	Total	

Bill my:

☐ Mastercard   ☐ Visa ☐ AmEx ☐ Check or Money Order Enclosed

Card#_____ Exp. Date_____

_____
Name   Birthdate   Date trip begins

_____
Street Address   City   State   ZIP   Phone Number

We also offer Travel Gear Discounted Airfares AYH Cards	Mail Order to **Let's Go Travel** 53A Church Street Cambridge, MA 02138 **1-800-5LETS-GO**	See our full-color catalog in this Guide

Hotel MDM, pl. Konstytucji 1 (tel. 628 25 26). A grand, graying edifice brooding over a noisy, commercial stretch of Marszałkowska south of the centrum. Singles 500-650,000zł. Doubles 900,000-1,100,000zł. Triples 1,300,000zł. Breakfast included. 20% discount for students with valid ID.

Camping Gromada, ul. Żwirki i Wigury 32 (tel. 25 43 91). Take bus 175 "Port Lotniczy" 1 stop past Pomnik Lotnika. 75,000zł per person, 55,000zł per tent. 2-person bungalows 150,000zł, 4-person 300,000zł. Open May-Sept.

FOOD

Many of Warsaw's best restaurants bunch around the **Rynek Starego Miasta,** the market square of the Old Town. Few Poles can afford these places; Warsaw's proletarian cafeterias are infinitely more colorful and cheap. During the day, you can stop by a *sklep spożywczy* (grocery store) and test your food vocabulary.

Bazyliszek, Rynek Starego Miasta 3/9 (tel. 31 18 41). One of Warsaw's finest. Noted for its superb preparation and presentation of game. Goose 210,000zł. Roast duck 270,000zł. Vegetarian entrees include a "vegetable bouquet" 80,000zł. Reserve ahead and dress sharp. Open noon until last guest leaves.

Zapiecek, ul. Piwna 34/36 (tel. 31 56 93), on the corner of ul. Piwna and Zapiecek in the Old Town. Small but opulent. *Barszcz* 20,000zł. Viennese veal 65,000zł. Open 11am-11pm.

El Popo, ul. Senatorska 27 (tel. 27 23 40). Yucca trees, colorful parrots and desert brown hues make it a real Mexican *casa. Nachos con guacamole* (52,400zł). *Fajitas* (190,500zł). Margaritas 97,600zł. Open noon-midnight.

Bar Uniwersytecki, Krakowskie Przedmieście 16/18. Next to the university under the yellow awning. One of the last bastions of cheap Polish food. Rice with apples 6850zł. Home-made soups 7000-11050zł. Pancakes with apples 6600zł. Omelettes 7200zł. Open Mon.-Fri. 7am-8pm, Sat.-Sun. 9am-5pm.

Ekologiczna "Nove Miasto' Restaurant, Rynek Nowego Miasta 13/15 (tel. 31 43 79). New Polish and vegetarian cuisine. Warsaw's first wholefood restaurant. Organically grown vegetarian entrees 69,000-98,0000zł. Bamboo furniture, outdoor seating available. Open 10am-midnight. Wheelchair access.

Parnas, ul. Krakowskie Przedmieście 4/6, in the same building as the Harenda. The best Greek place in town. Classic *argdemono* soup 35,000zł. *Souvlaki* 140,000zł. *Mousaka* 90,000zł. Reservations recommended. Open 1pm-midnight.

Blikle, ul. Nowy Świat 35. Best pastries in the city, by the same Swiss family since the 1870s. Delectables from 3000zł. Open Mon.-Fri. 10am-7pm, Sat. 10am-3pm.

Hotel Bristol Café, ul. Krakowskie Przedmieście 42/44. Polish movie folks flock here to relax and sip *Baronesse*—a strawberry and sherry milk-shake for 95,000zł—a prologue to a stylishly filling *Notre Dame* sandwich with salmon and cream cheese (95,000zł). Smoked chicken salad 90,000zł. Open 9am-9pm.

SIGHTS

Stare Miasto, Nowe Miasto, and Trakt Królewski Warsaw's postwar reconstruction shows its finest face in the **Stare Miasto** (Old Town). Narrow, cobbled streets, colorful, and brick churches give the area a rustic atmosphere. The impressive **Zamek Królewski** (Royal Castle), an early-Baroque structure with Gothic fragments and a Rococo façade was plundered by the Nazis. (Open Tues.-Sun. 10am-6pm. Royal suite: 50,000zł, students 25,000zł. Other interiors: 30,000zł, students 15,000zł. Thurs. free.) As you proceed past the Royal Castle to turn left onto ul. Świętojańska, where the *kasa* to the Castle is located, you will see the **Katedra Św. Jana** (Archcathedral of St. John), the oldest church building in Warsaw, from the turn of the 13th and 14th centuries. Ulica Świętojańska takes you straight to the **Rynek Starego Miasta** (Old Town Market Square), which has emerged from recent renovation in pristine condition. The façades of the Renaissance and Baroque houses charm the visitor with their colors and decorations. Although most of the houses surrounding the Rynek were razed to their foundations during the Warsaw Uprising, a few managed to survive WWII; the house at no. 31 dates back to the 14th century. Most of the buildings on the north side of the square comprise the

POLAND

Muzeum Historyczne miasta Warszawy (the Historical Museum of Warsaw), with the entrance at no. 28 (open Tues. and Thurs. noon-7pm, Wed. and Fri. 10am-3:30pm, Sun. 10:30am-4:30pm; 20,000zł, students 5,000zł, Sun. free). Ul. Krzywe Koło leads from the square to the **Barbakan** (Barbican), a rare example of 16th-century Polish fortifications. Through the Barbican Gate, ul. Freta marks the edge of the **Nowe Miasto** (New Town), which in spite of its name, is actually the second-oldest district in the city. At ul. Freta 16, the great physicist and chemist **Maria Skłodowska-Curie**, winner of two Nobel prizes, was born in 1867; the house is now a museum. (Open Tues.-Sat. 10am-4:30pm, Sun. 10am-2:30pm. 10,000zł, students 4000zł.)

Many of Warsaw's must-sees lie along the 4km **Trakt Królewski**. The city's most attractive thoroughfare, it begins on Plac Zamkowy (Castle Square) in the Stare Miasto and continues all along ul. **Krakowskie Przedmieście**. Fryderyk Chopin gave his first public concert in the **Koniecpolski-Radziwiłł Palace** at no. 46/48; he played on the organ in **Kościół Wizytek** (Church of the Visitation Nuns), one block down the street, and composed in the **Czapski-Krasiński Palace**, which now houses the Academy of Fine Arts and the **Salonik Chopinow**. Chopin's grave is in Père Lachaise Cemetery in Paris, but his heart lies in an urn in the left nave of **Kościół Św. Krzyża** (Holy Cross church). The Chopin **museum** is located in the Ostrogskis Castle at Okólnik 1—to get there walk a few blocks down the street from the Academy, turn left onto ul. Ordynacka and follow it to Okólnik. (Open Mon., Wed., Fri. 10am-5pm, Thurs. noon-6pm, Sat.-Sun. 10am-2pm. 20,000zl, students 10,000zl.)

The Royal Route ends with the striking Neoclassical **Pałac Łazienkowski,** also called **Pałac na Wodzie** (Place on the Water), which harbors galleries of 17th- and 18th-century art. (Open Tues.-Sun. 9:30am-4pm barring rain. 20,000zł, students 12,000zł. Guided tour in Polish 80,000zł, in English 300,000zł.)

Commercial District, the Ghetto, and Wilanów Warsaw's commercial district lies southwest of the Old Town along ul. Marszałkowska. Here, at al. Jerozolimskie 3, is the **Muzeum Narodowe** (National Museum), with stellar though sporadically gruesome collections of 8th- to 12th-century Coptic and medieval art. (Open Tues. and Sun. 10am-5pm, Wed., Fri. and Sat. 10am-4pm, Thurs. noon-6pm. 12,000zł, students 7000zł, Thurs. free.) The best panorama of Warsaw is from the 70-storey, 242m "Stalin Gothic" **Pałac Kultury i Nauki** (Palace of Culture and Science), on ul. Marszałkowska, as this is the only location from which the hulking beast itself is not visible. Below, Plac Zwycięstwa (Victory Square), in front of the Palace, is the site of the dubious **Cricoland**, a miniature amusement park; its various contraptions look none too safe—venture in at your own risk.

Still referred to as "the Ghetto," the modern Muranów neighborhood of Warsaw houses few descendants of what was once a community numbering 400,000. The beautifully reconstructed **Nożyk Synagogue** at ul. Twarda 6 lies just north of the Pałac Kultury. Farther north, at ul. Tłomackiego 3/5, off al. Solidarności (former al. Świerczewskiego), stands **Muzeum Żydowskiego Instytutu Historycznego** (Museum of the Jewish Historical Institute). On ul. Zamenhofa, look for the **Ghetto Uprising Monument**. The **Jewish Cemetery** on ul. Okopowa stretches for miles, a forest-covered treasure of gravestone art (open Mon.-Thurs. 9am-3pm, Fri. 9am-1pm). At **Umschlagplatz,** a huge and moving monument marks the spot where 300,000 Jews were rounded up to be sent to death camps. Farther north, in the Żoliborz section, Father Jerzy Popiełuszko delivered outspoken anti-government sermons at the **św. Stanisława Kostki Church** until his brutal murder by the secret police in 1984. Today his grave is a shrine to both the Church and Solidarity. Take tram 6, 15, 31, or 36 to Plac Wilsona; the church is on ul. Kozietulskiego.

Wilanów can be reached by bus 180 or by express bus B from ul. Marszałkowska. Up to the 17th century, it was a village named Milanowo. After his coronation in 1677, **King Jan III Sobieski,** bought the village and had the existing mansion rebuilt into a Baroque-style palace. Since then, the **Wilanów Palace** has functioned both as a museum and as a residence for the highest ranking guests of the Polish state (open

Wed.-Mon. 9:30am-2:45pm; 28,000zł, students 18,000zł). The pavilion next to the palace houses the **Muzeum Plakatu** (Poster Museum); it boasts an impressive collection of posters from the last hundred years or so—around 50,000 of them (open Tues.-Sun. 10am-4pm; 10,000zł, students 5000zł).

ENTERTAINMENT

Classical concerts fill the Gallery of Sculptures in the **Pomarańczarnia** near the Pałac Łazienkowski on Sundays at 5pm in June and July. Inquire about concerts at **Warszawskie Towarzystwo Muzyczne** (Warsaw Music Society), located at ul. Morskie Oko 2 (tel. 49 68 58). Tickets are available Mon.-Fri. 9am-3pm and before concerts. Also, the **Pomnik Chopina** (Chopin Monument), nearby in the Park Łazienkowski, hosts free Sunday performances by some of Poland's most distinguished classical artists (May-Oct. noon and 4pm). **Teatr Wielki,** Plac Teatralny 1 (tel. 26 30 01), Warsaw's main opera and ballet hall, offers performances almost daily. **Filharmonia Narodowa** (National Philharmonic Orchestra) gives regular concerts in its hall at ul. Jasna 5 (tel. 26 72 81), but is closed during the summer. For information and tickets, visit the **ZASP** *kasy teatralne* (tel. 21 94 54 or 21 93 83), al. Jerozolimskie 25 (open Mon.-Fri. 11am-6pm, Sat. 11am-2pm).

The best place to go for live jazz is the **Akwarium** at ul. Emilii Plater 49 (tel. 20 50 72), open Mon.-Thurs. 11am-11pm, Fri.-Sun. 11am-3am. **Sala Kongresowa** (tel. 20 49 80 or 693 61 40), at the Palace of Culture and Science, hosts "serious" jazz and rock concerts. Herbie Hancock and Bob Dylan performed there recently. The entrance to the Sala Kongresowa is from ul. Emilii Plater.

Much of Warsaw's social life revolves around its *winiarnie* (wine cellars) and *kawiarnie* (cafés). The most popular outdoor cafés are those on the **Rynek Starego Miasta** and along **Nowy Swiat.** In addition to the cafés, discos, jazz clubs, and pubs add flavor to Warsaw night life.

Café Lapidarium, ul. Nowomiejska 6 (tel. 635 68 28 or 31 85 36). Open-air garden, full of the young and famous. Rock concerts Wed.-Sun. 7pm on the Big Stage, 10pm on the Small Stage. Tickets 50,000zł. Foster's on tap 40,000zł. The owners also operate the ship **Barka na Wiśle**, down the hill from the Old Town on ul. Mostowa, where live music vibrates Fri.-Sun. 7pm-2am.

Park, al. Niepodległosci 196 (tel. 25 71 99 or 25 91 65). International disco; one of the more popular student hangouts in Warsaw. Disco Fri.-Sat. 9pm-4am. Cover 60,000zł, students and women 30,000zł. 50% off with ISIC. Beer starts at 15,000zł. Entrees 30,000-60,000zł.

The Irish Pub, ul. Miodowa 3 (tel. 26 25 33). Promotes folk and country music. Concerts start at 7:30pm, free of charge. Not surprisingly, Irish music prevails. Guiness or Kilkenny are the obvious favorites here, at 35,000-70,000zł.

Pub Falcon That's It, ul. Marszałkowska 55/73 (tel. 621 96 75). Free rock'n'roll and funk concerts at 7pm on random evenings. Greek salad 50,000zł, tuna salad 45,000zł.

■■■ SZCZECIN

Settled in the 8th century and chartered in 1278, Szczecin (SHCHEH-cheen) has changed hands repeatedly due to the strategic value of its ports, a cosmopolitan history which found the city in German hands during the Allied bombings of 1944. A few original structures remain, but much of the city's beauty lies in its restorations. A relic of the Prussian settlement, the Baroque **Brama Portowa** (Port Gate) marks the downtown area. Originally called the Brandenburg and later the Berlin Gate, it features a Latin inscription commemorating Frederic Wilhelm I, King of Prussia, and a panoramic view of 18th-century Szczecin. A block away on ul. Wyszyńskiego, the 13th-century **Katedra Św. Jana** (Cathedral of St. James) looms over the town. Destroyed during WWII, it was carefully restored to its original Gothic shape. On ul. Korsarzy, the giant, newly restored **Zamek Książąt Pomerańskich** (Palace of Pomeranian Princes) was the seat of the Pomeranian princes until 1630. It later belonged in turn to the Swedes, the Prussians and the Germans. (Open 10am-6pm. 10,000zł.) Behind the palace, on ul. Panieńska, the abandoned **Baszta Panieńska Siedmiu Płaszczy** (Maiden's Tower or the Tower of Seven Cloaks) stands defiantly.

The old **Ratusz** (Town Hall) now houses one of the city's three branches of the **Muzeum Narodowe** (National Museum); this particular branch illustrates Szczecin's history from the Paleolithic to the present. The rest of the museum, chronicling Pomeranian art from the medieval to the modern, is located in the Baroque **Pomeranian Parliament**, ul. Stromłynska 27/28, north of Castle Hill. (All three branches open Sat.-Sun. 10am-4pm, Tues. and Thurs. 10am-5pm, Wed. and Fri. 9am-3:30pm. 15,000zł, students 10,000zł. Thurs. free.)

Practical Information, Accommodations, and Food Trains arrive at the end of ul. 3-go Maja from Gdansk (5hr., 153,000zł), Poznań (3hr., 109,500zł) and Berlin (2½hr., 360,000zł). **ORBIS**, pl. Zwycięstwa 1 (tel. (091) 431 06), has the same address as the Hotel Policyjny, but is located on the other side of the square (open Mon.-Fri. 9am-5pm and Sat. 9am-1pm). **COIT (Centralny Ośrodek Informacji Turystycznej)**, ul. Wyszyńskiego 26 (tel. (091) 34 04 40), sells maps and brochures (open Mon.-Fri. 9am-5pm).

To get to the **youth hostel**, ul. Monte Cassino 19a (tel. (091) 22 47 41), take tram 3 from the train station or the center to ul. Kołłątaja; then go one stop on bus 67 in the direction of ul. Karola Miarki. (Lockout 10am-5pm. 90,000zł, members 65,000-75,000zł. Sheets 25,000zł.) **Hotel Policyjny**, pl. Zwycięstwa 1 (tel. (091) 51 31 91), offers decent rooms. (Singles 214,000zł. Doubles 235-353,000zł. Triples 288,000zł. Quints 321,000zł.) **Café Vega,** at entrance H of the Palace of Pomeranian Princes, is quick and convenient, with an English menu (entrees 35,000-50,000zł; open 10am-10pm). A sparkling Polish McDonald's clone, **Mic Mac Fast Food**, ul. Niepodległości 13, at the Brama Portowa serves incredibly good food in a spotless neo-Greek interior. (Burgers 25,000zł. Veggie burgers 16,500zl. Open 24hrs.)

■■■ GDAŃSK

The history of Gdańsk (GDA-neesk) is rich in dramatic events. In 1793 it was annexed by Prussia and in 1919 established as a free city by the Treaty of Versailles. In 1939, Gdańsk ceased to be a peaceful city, and a bridge between nations. The German interference in the dispute between Poland and Gdańsk, then called Danzig, was an immediate cause of the World War II, and resulted in many ethnic conflicts. Gdańsk is also known worldwide as the birthplace of *Solidarność,* the first independent workers' union in Eastern Europe, led by Lech Wałęsa, a former electrician at the Gdańsk shipyards.

ORIENTATION AND PRACTICAL INFORMATION

Gdańsk dips its toes in the Baltic Sea, serving as Poland's principal port. From the Gdańsk-Główny train station, the Old Town center lies a few blocks south, across Wały Jagiellońskie, along Motława, tributary of the Wisła River.

- **Tourist Offices: IT,** ul. Heweliusza 27 (tel. 31 43 55, fax 31 66 37). The English-speaking staff sells maps, guides, and tickets to major sights. Open Mon.-Fri. 8am-4pm. **ORBIS**, ul. Heweliusza 22 (tel. 31 44 25), sells ferry, train, and international bus tickets. Open Mon.-Fri. 10am-5pm, Sat. 10am-2pm.
- **Budget Travel: ALMATUR**, 2nd floor of Długi Targ 11 (tel. 31 29 31), in the town center. ISIC, bus, and train tickets. Open Mon.-Fri. 9am-5pm.
- **Currency Exchange:** At hotels, banks, *kantor* desks and certain post offices throughout the city. 24hr. *kantor* at the train station. **Bank Gdański**, ul. Wały Jagiellońskie 14/16 (tel. 37 92 22), cashes traveler's checks for 1% commission.
- **American Express: ORBIS** office of Hotel Hewelius. Replaces lost traveler's checks; cashes them for a 3% commission. Holds mail.

Post Office: ul. Długa 22/25 (tel. 38 91 39). Open Mon.-Fri. 8am-8pm, Sat. 9am-1pm. **Postal Code:** 80-801.

Telephones: Open 24hrs. at ul. Długa 22/25. Ring the bell between 10pm and 6am. **City Code:** 058.

Flights: The **airport** is 22km away at Rebiechowo. Buses 110 and B connect it with the train station.

Trains: PKP information tel. 31 11 12. To Warsaw (4hr., 144,000zł); Kraków (198,000zł); Prague (15hr., 933,000zł), St. Petersburg (36hr., 1,350,000zł).

Buses: PKS information tel. 32 15 32. The bus station is located behind the train station. Enter through the underground passageway. Tickets sold 5:30am-10:20pm. To Toruń (4hr., 106,000zł), and Vilnius (10hr., 300,000zł).

Ferries: Take the commuter rail to the Nowy Port terminal. To Oxelösund, near Stockholm (Mon., Wed. and Sun.; off-season only Thurs.; 440SEK round-trip), Helsinki (Sun. and Thurs., 260FIM one way), Ystad in Sweden (mid-April to mid-Oct. Fri., 360SEK round-trip). To book a place, call the **Polferries Travel Office** in Gdańsk (tel. 43 18 87 or 43 02 12, fax 43 09 75) or the ORBIS travel office.

Taxis: Radio taxi tel. 9197 or 31 59 59 or 41 14 11.

Hitchhiking: Those Warsaw-bound go to ul. Elbląska (near the stadium).

Luggage Storage: At the train station. 7000zl per piece per day. Open 24hrs.

English Bookstore: English Books Unlimited, ul. Podmlynska 10 (tel. 31 33 73). Watch for a black and gold sign and a portrait of Shakespeare. Good selection of books in the English language. Open Mon.-Fri. 10am-6pm, Sat. 10am-5pm.

Pharmacies: At the train station. 24hrs. except 7:30-8am.

Emergencies: Ambulance, tel. 999. **Fire,** tel. 998. **Police,** tel. 997.

ACCOMMODATIONS AND CAMPING

Gdańsk and the resort town of Sopot up the coast claim Poland's most popular beaches and are commensurately swamped in summer. Reserve well in advance. For help in finding a room, try **Biuro Usług Turystycznych,** at ul. Heweliusza 8 (tel. 31 26 34 or 31 17 27), across from the train station. Singles run 165,000zł, doubles 270,000zł. (Open 7:30am-7:30pm.)

Schronisko Młodzieżowe (HI), ul. Wałowa 21 (tel. 31 23 13). Cross the street in front of the train station, head up ul. Heweliusza and turn left at ul. Łagiewniki. Most convenient of the area hostels. Lockout 10am-5pm. Curfew 10pm. 52-60,000zł, over 26: 60-70,000zł. Sheets 11,000zł. Baggage room 10,000zł.

Schronisko Młodzieżowe (HI), ul. Grunwaldzka 244 (tel. 41 16 60). Take tram 6 or 12 to al. Wojska Polskiego. A long walk even after the endless tram ride. Immaculate and efficiently run. Reception open 5-9pm. Lockout 10am-5pm. Curfew 10pm. 60,000zł, over 26 70,000zł. Sheets 10,000zł. Baggage room 10,000zł.

Dom Harcerza, ul. Za Murami 2/10 (tel. 31 36 21), 100m away from the Golden Gate. Hard-to-come-by doubles 214,000zł. Triples 321,000zł. A bed in a 12-person room costs 60,000zł.

Hotel Zaułek, ul. Ogarna 107/108 (tel. 31 41 69). Basic but cheap. Singles 120,000zł. Doubles 220,000zł. Triples 270,000zł. Quads 280,000zł.

Dom Studenta PWSSP, ul. Chlebnicka 13/16 (tel. 31 28 16). A street over from Długi Targ. Dorm of the local art school during the academic year. Doubles, triples, and quads for 100,000zł per bed. Open in summer.

Camping: Gdańsk-Jelitkowo, ul. Jelitkowska 23 (tel. 53 27 31), opposite the Hotel Marina. From Gdańsk-Główny, take tram 2, 4, or 6 to the last stop. One block from the beach. 32,500zł per person, 22,000zł per tent. Bungalows 80,000zł per person (sleep 3-4). 10% discount for students. Open May to mid-Sept.

Private rooms: ORBIS (tel. 31 21 32 or 31 49 44) arranges private rooms in well-kept apartments, all centrally located. (Singles 400,000zł. Doubles 600,000zł.)
  ALMATUR, Długi Targ 11 (tel. 31 29 31), directs travelers to student dorms in July-August. Doubles 270,000zł.

FOOD

From the river walkway, follow the aroma of fresh fish frying. For fresh food of all sorts, try the **Hala Targowa market** on ul. Podmłyńska (open Mon.-Fri. and 1st and last Sat. of the month 9am-6pm). Appease a late-night craving at the **24hr. store,** upstairs at Wały Jagiellońskie, across from the train station.

Bar "Neptun," ul. Długa 33/34 (tel. 31 49 88). Revamped milk bar now serving hearty, homestyle meat dishes alongside vegetarian entrees. 35,000zł per feed. Open Mon.-Fri. 7am-7pm, Sat. 9am-5pm.

Pizzeria Napoli, ul. Długa 62/63 (tel. 31 41 46). Tasty pizza (40-80,000zł) and spaghetti (60-90,000zł). Take-out and delivery available. Open 10am-10pm.

Govinda, ul. Ogarna 107/108, next to Hotel Zaułek. Hare Krishna vegetarian restaurant serving spicy rice (6000zł) with coconut (7000zł) and carrot and beet salads (6000zł). Open noon-8pm.

Złoty Kur, ul. Długa 4 (tel. 31 61 63). Clean tables outside. Chicken 45,000zł. *Gołąbki* a must for 35,000zł. Open 10am-7pm.

Jadłodajnia u Plastyków, ul. Chlebnicka 13/16 (tel. 31 28 16). In the art students' dorm cafeteria. Homestyle lunches for around 30,000zł. Open Mon.-Sat. 11am-5pm, Sun. 11am-4pm.

Palowa, ul. Długa 47 (tel. 31 55 32), in the basement of the town hall. A popular pseudo-medieval café run by the students' union. *Tortes* from 15,000zł per slice. Coffee 7000-35,000zł. Mixed drinks 40-60,000zł. Open 10am-midnight.

SIGHTS AND ENTERTAINMENT

Gdańsk was one of the first Polish cities to undergo an exhaustive postwar facelift. The handsome market square, **Długi Targ,** forms the center of town, where the original 16th-century façade of the **Dwór Artusa** faces out onto the **Fontanna Neptuna** (Neptune Fountain). Next to the fountain, the 14th-century **Ratusz** (Town Hall) houses the **Muzeum Historii Miasta Gdańska** (Gdańsk Historical Museum); don't miss the fantastic *Red Chamber* with a ceiling covered with allegorical paintings by Baroque masters. (Open Tues.-Sun. 10am-5pm. 10,000zł, students 5,000zł.)

One block north of Długi Targ is Gdańsk's grandest house of worship, the 14th-century **Kościół Najświętszej Marii Panny** (St. Mary's church), Poland's largest brick cathedral. Climb the 405 steps up the steeple to rise above the din and clatter of the city. (Open May to mid-Oct. 9am-5:30pm. 10000zł. Binoculars at the top of the tower 2,000zł.) **Ul. Mariacka,** behind the church, is perhaps Gdańsk's most beautiful street. If you follow it through the gate to the Motława River, you will see the enormous **Gothic crane** that unloaded medieval freighters.

On Plac Obrońców Poczty Polskiej, is the **Old Post Office,** which was a rallying point for Polish resistance and since then has become a patriotic symbol. Solidarity flags fly high at the **Gdańsk Shipyard** and at the **monument** to the 1970 uprising, north of the center of town, near ul. Jaracza and only 1 stop from the train station on tram 8. Take a ferry to the island of **Westerplatte,** where you can visit the site of the first shots of WWII. Boats leave from outside the Green Gate at the end of Długi Targ. (May-Sept. 9 per day, 1hr., round-trip 70,000zl, students 50,000zł.)

The Gdańsk area enjoys more sunshine than any other in the country. To get to **Stogi Beach,** the city's best, take tram 8 or 13 "Stogi" from the train station to the end, or bus 112 or 186 also "Stogi" to the last stop, then follow ul. Nowotna and everyone else, although only the brave (or the foolish) actually venture in the water.

The turreted mansion at ul. Wały Jagiellońskie 1 is home to the student club **Żak.** It has a movie theater (35,000zł, students 30,000zł), a pub downstairs (open Sun.-Thurs. 2pm-midnight, Fri.-Sat. 2pm-2am), and a fashionably downtrodden café upstairs (open Sun.-Thurs. 2pm-2am, Fri.-Sat. 5pm-2am). For more jazz, head to the **Cotton Club** on ul. Złotnicka 25/29 or test your detective skills trying to find the **Yellow Jazz Club,** a ship without an address or a phone number on the Motława River, on ul. Rybackie Pobrzeże. It's worth the hunt. Every year during the first 2 weeks of August, Gdańsk erupts in the street fair **Jarmark Dominikański.** The **Jantar Jazz Festival,** which visits the city during July and August, ushers in the September **Polish Film Festival,** held in the **NOT** building next to the Hotel Hevelius. All tickets are available at ORBIS.

POLAND

■ MALBORK AND SOPOT

Malbork Castle, in the unassuming town of the same name, was the main residence of the Teutonic Knights in the 14th century. WWII reduced the fortress—then one of the largest castles in Europe—to just another pile of rubble; reconstruction continues to this day. To get to the castle, follow ul. Dworcowa from the train station towards the center and take the fork marked "Centrum." Go up the steps to cross the highway, then walk up ul. Kościuszki; you'll see the ruddy castle towers atop the hill. (Castle open Tues.-Sun. 8:30am-5pm; Oct.-April 9am-2:30pm. Admission only with guided tour 60,000zł. In English 525,000zł extra.) Malbork is 40min. from Gdańsk by train (49,000zł), which makes it a perfect destination for a day trip. There are 29 **trains** per day from Gdańsk and 7 **buses** per day. The nest of the milk bars on ul. Kościuszki is **Maćko** at no. 7. (Cheese-filled *naleśniki* 15,000zł. Open Mon.-Fri. 8am-5pm, Sat.-Sun. 9am-4pm.) The recently renovated **Café Zamkowa,** located right next to the castle entrance, prepares a regal feast amid the coats-of-arms that hang on the walls. (Entrees 110,000-170,000zł. Open 10am-8pm.)

Located 15min. from Gdańsk by commuter train (10,000zł), **Sopot** features miles of white beaches, the longest pier on the Baltic (512m), a horse-racing course, and a spa park. As a health spa, Sopot is renowned in Poland and abroad—every year, thousands of people come here to treat their rheumatic problems with salt and mud baths. **ORBIS,** ul. Monte Cassino 49 (tel. (058) 51 41 42), sells train, plane, and ferry tickets, as well as tickets to the **Opera Leśna,** an outdoor theater built in 1909, where concerts and festivals are held (open 10am-5pm). At the pier, you can buy tickets for boat trips to the **Hel peninsula** (70min., 150,000zł round-trip, students 120,000zł). The **Pub FM** at ul. Monte Cassino 36, one of the most popular student beer joints, also serves food. *(Pierogi ruskie*—dumplings with potato and cheese filling—30,000zł. Open 12:30pm-2am.)

■■■ TORUŃ AND POZNAŃ

Toruń An astounding number of tourist attractions are packed into Toruń's medieval ramparts. The **Old Town,** commanding the right bank of the Wisła River, was constructed by the Teutonic Knights in the 13th century, and is the birthplace of renowned astronomer Mikołaj Kopernik (Copernicus). Visit his birthplace, **Dom Kopernika,** at ul. Kopernika 15/17 (open Tues.-Sun. 10am-4pm; 10,000zł, students 5000zł). The **Ratusz** (Town Hall), ul. Rynek Staromiejski 1, is in the center of the tourist district and sells tickets to most of the sights in town. It houses the **Muzeum Okręgowe** (Regional Museum. Open Tues.-Sun. 10am-6pm. 15,000zł, students 10,000zł.) For an additional fee of 20,000zł (students 15,000zł), you can climb the medieval 13th-century tower and get a much better look at the layout of the whole city. Among the tall Gothic churches that dot the skyline, the **Cathedral of St. John the Baptist and St. John the Evangelist** is the most impressive. To view the length of the town, stroll along the **Bulwar Filadelfijski,** among fishermen and lingering couples who line the stone steps to the river.

Toruń lies 47km east of Bydgoszcz, halfway between Warsaw and Poznań. There are several **train stations** in the city; the main one, **Toruń Główny,** is located on the opposite side of the Wisła River. The **IT tourist office** in the town hall on the Rynek is extremely helpful (open Mon. and Sat. 9am-4pm, Tues.-Fri. 9am-6pm, Sun. May-Aug. only 9am-1pm). **ORBIS,** ul. Żeglarska 31 in the Old Town (tel. (056) 225 53), sells train and bus tickets, and distributes free information on Toruń and Kopernik (open Mon.-Fri. 9am-5pm). Take bus 22 from the train station to Plac Rapackiego, then bus 10 outside the Old Town gate to the 3rd stop to find the **Dom Turysty (Wycieczkowy),** ul. Legionów 24 (tel. (056) 238 55. Singles 160,000zł. Doubles 240,000zł. Triples 330,000zł. Quads 380,000zł.) For large single beds and doubles with sinks, try **Hotel Polonia,** pl. Teatralny 5 (tel. (056) 230 28), opposite the municipal theater. (Singles 170-280,000zł. Doubles 240-300,000zł.) Vagabonds can pitch tents at **Campground "Tramp,"** ul. Kujawska 14 (tel. (056) 241 87), across

POLAND

from the train station. (15,000zł per tent, 25,000zł per person. 3-person cabins 150,000zł. 4-person bungalows 200,000zł.) A large collection of **fruit and vegetable stands** line up a block east of the Rynek; most restaurants are in the old town. Reacquaint your taste buds with oregano and tomato sauce at **Staromiejska Italian Restaurant**, ul. Szczytna 4. (Entrees 112-270,000zł. Italian *pierogi* (tortellini) 49,000zł. Lasagna 55,000zł. Open 11am-10pm.) A good hangout for English-speaking beer guzzlers, **Pub "Czarna Oberża"** (Black Inn), ul. Rabiańska 9, serves Vietnamese entrees (70-75,000zł) and Chicago style pizza for 38,000zł (open Mon.-Thurs. 1-11pm, Fri.-Sat. 1pm-midnight, Sun. 2-11pm).

Poznań Known as Posen to its Prussian (1793-1918) and German (1939-45) rulers, Poznań first hosted the biannual International Trade Fair in 1921; in fall and spring, business folk from around the world descend upon the city, filling up hotel rooms and bolstering the local economy. Downtown, in the **Stary Rynek,** opulent 15th-century merchant homes surround the multicolored **Ratusz** (Town Hall) which now houses the municipal museum (open Mon.-Tues. and Fri. 10am-4pm, Wed. 10am-6pm, Sun. 10am-3pm; 10,000zł, students 6000zł, Fri. free). On the door of the Ratusz, two metal goats—the symbol of Poznań—fight every day at noon. Behind the town hall, on the northeast corner of the Rynek, starts **Ulica Żydowska** (Jewish Street), the center of the pre-war Jewish district; in 1940 the synagogue was turned into a swimming pool. On the opposite side of the Rynek, the pink frescoed **Kościół Farny Marii Magdaleny** (Parish Church) blesses the end of ul. Świętosławska. In the *Rynek* itself, the **Museum of Historic Musical Instruments,** Stary Rynek 45, stars Chopin's own piano and a collection of instruments from Polynesia and Africa (open Tues. 10am-5pm, Wed. and Fri. 10am-4pm, Sat. 10am-5pm, and Sun. 10am-3pm; 10,000zł, students 6000zł).

The main **train station** is in the southwestern corner of the city, a 20min. walk to the Old Town. To get to the center, take bus 51, 68, or 76 to the end of al. Dworcowa and transfer to any tram headed to the right. The **bus** station is just 200m down the street from the train station. **ORBIS,** ul. Marcinkowskiego 21 (tel. (061) 33 09 41) is open Mon.-Sat. 10am-5pm. **Glob-Tour,** at the train station (tel. (061) 66 06 67 or 69 54 60), arranges private rooms (singles 300,000zł, doubles 400-600,000zł; open 24hrs.). A 10min. walk west of the train station, the **youth hostel (HI),** ul. Berwińskiego 2/3 (tel. (061) 66 36 80) offers spotless rooms (64,000zł, over 26 100,000zł). **Wojewódzki Ośrodek Metodyczny,** the teacher's hostel, ul. Niepodległości 34 (tel. (061) 53 22 51) is more spacious, but less centrally located. Take bus 51 from the train station to the Hotel Polonez and walk back one block (117,000zł, students 72,000zł). For similar prices and better location in the summer, **ALMATUR,** ul. Fredry 7 (tel. (061) 52 74 44), has the scoop on summer hostels. The tastiest and most accessible restaurants are around the **Stary Rynek**. The cheapest places can get very crowded; both locals and tourists are quick to recognize the "best deal in the square." If you are looking for something fast and simple, **Avanti bistro**, Stary Rynek 76, offers tasty spaghetti for a mere 14-21,000zl (open Mon.-Sat. 9am-11pm, Sun. and holidays 11am-10pm). **U Dylla bistro**, Stary Rynek 37, features standard Polish fare. Anything you order will be well done. (Entrees 80,000-12,000zł. Open 4am-11pm.)

■■■ KRAKÓW

Capital of Poland until the 16th century, Kraków is a jewel among European cities. Unlike most of Poland, the city miraculously escaped the obliteration of WWII; instead, the Nazis desecrated Wawel Castle, using Kraków's most precious landmark as their headquarters. Many city buildings bear the scars of severe air pollution from the smokestacks of industrial Nowa Huta, Kraków's "model" suburb to the east. Cobblestone alleys punctuated with Baroque cupolas and church spires now fill with a dynamic young community; shackled for so long, Kraków is renascent.

ORIENTATION AND PRACTICAL INFORMATION

The city fans outward in roughly concentric circles from the large Renaissance **Rynek Główny** (main market square), at the heart of the **Stare Miasto** (old town). The refreshingly green belt of the **Planty** gardens rings the Stare Miasto, and the **Wisła River** skims the southwest corner and **Wawel Hill**. For maps, try **ORBIS** or **COIT**, near the train station.

Tourist Offices: ORBIS, Rynek 41 (tel. 22 40 35), sells ferry, plane, international bus and train tickets. Open Mon.-Fri. 8am-7pm, Sat. 9am-1pm. **PTTK**, ul Wester-platte 15 (tel. 22 20 94), gives tours of the city: 5hr. in English 600,000zł. Open Mon.-Fri. 9am-3pm.

Budget Travel: ALMATUR, Rynek Główny 7/8 (tel. 22 63 52), in the courtyard in back. Eurotrain tickets, bus tickets to Western Europe, and ISIC. Does *not* arrange student accommodations. Open Mon.-Fri. 9am-5pm.

Currency Exchange: At *kantor* booths all over the city, ORBIS offices, and hotels. **Bank PKO S.A.**, Rynek 31 (tel. 22 60 22), cashes traveler's checks and does Visa and MC cash advances. Open Mon.-Fri. 7:30am-7pm, Sat. 7:30pm-1:45pm.

American Express: At **ORBIS**, al. Focha 1, in the Hotel Cracovia (tel. 21 98 80). No wired money or traveler's checks sold. AmEx checks cashed for 1% commission. Mail held for US$1 per piece. Open Mon.-Fri. 8am-8pm, Sat. 8am-3pm.

Post Office: Main office at Westerplatte 20 (tel. 22 48 11 or 22 26 48, fax 22 36 06). Open Mon.-Fri. 7:30am-8:30pm, Sat. 8am-2pm. **Poste Restante** at window 7 Sun. 9-11am. **Postal Code:** 30 001.

Telephones: 24hr. phones at the main post office, and also at the office opposite the train station, ul. Lubicz 4 (tel. 22 14 85 or 22 86 35). **City Code:** 012.

Trains: Kraków Główny (tel. 22 41 82 or 22 22 48) on pl. Kolejowy, an easy 10min. walk northeast from the center of town. To Warsaw (3½hr., 180,000zł), Zakopane (2½hr., 88,500zł), Gdańsk (6-9hr., 180-216,000zł), Tarnów (1½hr., 52,500zł), Wrocław (4hr., 127,500zł).

Buses: The **PKS station** (tel. 936), on ul. Worcella, faces the train station. International bus tickets can be arranged by the travel agent **Sindbad**, located in the main hall of the bus station (tel. 22 12 38), open Mon.-Fri. 8am-6pm.

Luggage Storage: At the train station. 7000zł per piece per day. 24hrs.

Pharmacy: Rynek 13 (tel. 22 41 90). Open Mon.-Fri. 8am-8pm, Sat. 8am-3pm. After hours, check the signs on the door for pharmacies on call.

Emergencies: Police tel. 21 00 20 or 10 71 15.

ACCOMMODATIONS AND CAMPING

Friendly neighborhood room-retrievers **Wawel Tourist** (tel. 22 19 21, fax 22 16 40) reside next to the tourist office at ul. Pawia 8. (Open Mon.-Fri. 8am-9pm, Sat. 8am-3pm. Singles 170-200,000zł. Doubles 250-3200,000zł.) Reservations are vital in summer. **ALMATUR, IT,** or **PTTK** can call ahead for you.

Schronisko Młodzieżowe (HI), ul. Oleandry 4 (tel. 33 82 22). Take tram 15 or 18 from the train station; or walk (15min. from the Stare Miasto). Flexible lockout 10am-5pm. Curfew 11pm. Clean and pleasant if you can get a double (100,000zł). Dorms 80-90,000zł per bed. Members 25% off.

Schronisko Młodzieżowe (HI), ul. Kościuszki 88 (tel. 22 19 51). Take tram 2 from Westerplatte. Run by nuns in a heavenly setting. Reception open Mon.-Fri. 8am-3pm and 5-11pm, Sat. 8am-2pm and 5-11pm, Sun. 8-10am and 5-11pm. Curfew 11pm. Dorms 80,000zł. Members 25% off. Sheets 11,000zł.

Hotel Saski, ul. Sławkowska 3 (tel. 21 42 22, fax 21 48 30). Half a block from the Rynek and the nightlife. Full of international students. Singles 390-510,000zł. Doubles 600-780,000zł. Triples 680-890,000zł.

Hotel Polonia, ul. Basztowa 25 (tel. 22 12 81), next to the Hotel Warszawski. First-rate and cosmopolitan. Singles 375-450,000zł. Doubles 450-695,000zł. Triples 540-810,000zł.

POLAND

PTTK Dom Turysty, ul. Westerplatte 15/16 (tel. 22 95 66), near the central post office. Big, brown, and efficient. Dandy location on park and near Rynek Główny. Reception open noon-10pm. 8-bed dorms 120,000zł per person.

Student Hotel Żaczek, ul. 3-go Maja 5 (tel. 33 54 77). Vast, friendly, and stark. Take tram 15 or bus 119 from the train station. Singles 200,000zł. Doubles 320,000zł. Triples 420,000zł. One bathroom serves four rooms. Open July-Sept.

Camping Krak, ul. Radzikowskiego 99 (tel. 37 21 22 or 37 58 40). Take tram 4, 8, 12, or 44 to Fizyków and walk north. 50,000zł per person. Open May 15-Sept. 15.

FOOD

Obwarzanki (soft pretzels with poppy seeds) are Kraków's street-stand specialty. All the places listed below are within a few blocks of the Rynek Główny.

Różowy Słoń, ul. Straszewskiego 24. Pop art decor and delicious salads. Big bowls of salad around 30,000zł; otherwise 11,000zł per 100g. Open Mon.-Sat. 9am-9pm, Sun 11am-9pm.

Bar Mleczny Uniwersytecki, ul. Piłsudskiego 1 (tel. 22 32 47), across from the Jagiellonian University. A last bastion of proletarian dining—a full meal is under 20,000zł. Egg-salad sandwich 3800zł. Cheese *naleśniki* 11,200zł. Open Mon.-Fri. 6am-8pm, Sat. 7am-4pm, Sun. 7am-3pm.

Akropolis, ul. Grodzka 9 (tel. 21 77 55). Greek grill in the southern part of the Rynek. *Gyros* 45,000zł. Greek salad 30,000zł. Open Sun.-Thurs. 10am-midnight, Fri.-Sat. 10am-2am.

Chiński Pałac Restaurant, in the elegant Hotel Saski, ul. Sławkowska 3 (tel. 21 35 42). Curry chicken 95,000zł. Egg rolls 25,000zł. Take-out. Open 7am-11pm.

Hawełka Restaurant, at Rynek 34 (tel. 22 47 53). Occupies an airy white and green dining hall in the heart of the Old Town. Traditional Polish cuisine. Delicious blueberry *pierogi* 45,000zł. Open 10am-10pm.

Café Malma, at Rynek 25 (tel. 21 98 94). Popular spot, always crowded. American, London, or Kraków-style breakfast 70,000zł. *Tortes* 190-21,000zł. Open 10am-11pm. Lunch and dinner in the cellar noon-8pm.

SIGHTS

At the center of the old town is the **Rynek Główny,** one of the largest and most distinctive market squares in Europe. In its northeastern corner rise the red towers of the **Kościół Mariacki,** a richly decorated cathedral with a 500-year-old carved-wood altarpiece by Wit Stwosz. The invading Nazis dismantled it and stashed it away; Allied forces discovered the buried pieces in Germany at war's end. Reassembled, it is ceremoniously unveiled at noon each day (Mon.-Sat. noon-6pm, Sun. 2-6pm. 5000zł). Diagonally across the square stands the lonely **Ratusz** (Town Hall) **Tower,** spared when the rest of the building was torn down in 1820 (open Wed. and Fri.-Sun. 9am-4pm, Thurs. 11am-6pm; 7000zł). Dividing the square in half, the Italianate **Sukiennice** (Cloth Hall) is as mercantile now as it was in guild times; the ground floor is an enormous souvenir shop. Upstairs, the **Muzeum Narodowe** (National Museum) houses a gallery of 18th- and 19th-century Polish classics (open Wed. and Fri.-Sun. 10am-3:30pm, Thurs. noon-5:30pm; 30,000zł, students 15,000zł, Thurs. free). During the academic year, Polish students cruise the area around the statue of Adam Mickiewicz, Poland's most celebrated Romantic poet.

Kraków's **Jagiellonian University,** over 600 years old, includes astronomer Mikołaj Kopernik and drama scholar Agnieszka Marszałek among its alumni. The university's oldest building is the 15th-century **Collegium Maius,** southwest of the Rynek on ul. Jagiellońska 15, with a bewitching Gothic courtyard and vaulted walkway. (Open Mon.-Fri. 11am-2:30pm, Sat. 11:30am-1:30pm to groups only—join or form one. 20,000zł, students 10,000zł.)

The **Zamek Wawelski** (Wawel Castle) is one of the finest surviving pieces of Renaissance architecture in Poland. Begun in the 10th century, the castle has 71 chambers, a magnificent sequence of 16th-century tapestries commissioned by the royal family, and a series of 8 tapestries from Arras depicting the story of Noah's Ark.

POLAND

The castle is undergoing renovation—not all the chambers are open to the public. At the entrance to the castle, there is a guide office (tel. 22 09 04, fax 37 48 37), where you can purchase an English guidebook. A 3½hr. tour in English costs 375,000zł. (Office open Mon.-Sat. 8am-3pm, Sun. 10am-3pm. Wawel open Mon.-Thurs., and Sat. 9:30am-4:45pm, Sun. 10am-3pm. 30,000zł, students 15,000zł. Wed. free. Treasury free.) To see **Wawel's Oriental Collection,** including the huge embroidered Turkish tent, you have to buy a separate ticket at the general Wawel ticket window. (Exhibit open Mon.-Sat. 9:45am-2:45pm, Sun. 10am-3pm. 20,000zł, students 10,000zł.) Next door is Kraków's **Katedra** (Cathedral), where Poland's kings were crowned and buried. Its former archbishop, Karol Cardinal Wojtyła, is now Pope John Paul II. (Open Mon.-Sat. 9am-5pm, Sun. 12:15-5pm. Ticket window for graves and the **dzwon Zygmunta** (Zygmunt's bell) open Mon.-Fri. 9am-5:15pm, Sat. 9am-4:45pm, Sun. 12:15-5:15pm. 20,000zł, students 10,000zł.)

South of the old town center lies **Kazimierz,** the 400 year-old Jewish quarter. Take tram 6, 8, 10, 18, or 19 from the center or walk down ul. Stradomska from the Castle. The synagogue at the intersection of ul. Podbrzezie and ul. Miodowa, known as **Templ,** was founded by progressive Jews in 1860; it features a polychrome ceiling and 36 splendid stained-glass windows. Poland's oldest synagogue, the **Stara Synagoga** at Szeroka 24, now houses the **Muzeum Judaistyczne,** depicting the history and culture of Kraków's Jews (open Wed.-Thurs. 9am-3:30pm, Fri. 11am-6pm, Sat.-Sun. 9am-3pm; 20,000zł, students 10,000zł). Close to the synagogue, the **Jewish bookstore Jordan,** at ul. Szeroka 2 (tel. 21 71 66), organizes tours of Kazimierz (open Mon.-Fri. 10am-6pm, Sat.-Sun. 10am-4pm). Tours depart from the bookstore and trace the places from *Schindler's List* (2hr., 170,000zł, in English).

ENTERTAINMENT

Student clubs romp from about 8pm to midnight or 1am, and charge a minimal cover. The **Rotunda,** at ul. Oleandry 1 (tel. 33 35 38), has information on student events and concerts; it's the "official" student cultural center. **Pod Jaszczurami,** Rynek Główny 7, features quality jazz (Mon. 6-10pm and Tues. 8pm-1:30am) and a popular disco (Wed.-Thurs. and Sun. 8pm-2am, Fri.-Sat. 8pm-4am). **Stańczyk,** in the cellar under the Town Hall, is a popular café with live jazz Fri.-Sat. at 10pm (open 10am-1am, except for the nights of performances). **Jama Michalika,** ul. Floriańska 45, is Kraków's best-known café. Home of the Green Balloon cabaret, it's festooned with political caricatures and eclectic, plush decor (open 9am-10pm). The cellars of the **Pub Pod Papugami** (Under the Parrots), ul. Św. Jana 18, fill with a cosmopolitan crowd of students (open Mon.-Fri. noon-2am, Sat.-Sun. 4pm-2am). Popular with international free spirits, **Free Pub,** ul. Sławkowska 4, is life on the edge in Kraków.

■ NEAR KRAKÓW

Oświęcim-Brzezinka (Auschwitz-Birkenau) The Nazi concentration camps at Auschwitz (Oświęcim) and Birkenau (Brzezinka) are places of unspeakable horror, debris of an apocalypse that many have begun to forget. An estimated 1.5 million people were murdered; thousands more suffered hideously at the hands of the Nazis. The camps are in **Oświęcim; buses** leave from the central Dworzec PKS across from Kraków Główny (1½hr., 44,000zł). **Trains** also leave from Kraków Główny to the site (1¾hr., 31,000zł). An alternate way of reaching Oświęcim is to take a half-day tour, organized by either Point Tour or ORBIS. Both agencies charge the same prices: 340,000zł, students 250,000zł (5hr.). For details contact **ORBIS** at al. Focha 1 (tel. 22 46 32, fax 22 28 85), or **Point Tour** offices: in the Holiday Inn Hotel at ul. Armii Krajowei 11 (tel. 37 50 44), or in the Hotel Ibis at ul. Przy Rondzie 1 (tel. 21 84 33). Tickets are also sold on the bus; the ORBIS bus leaves at 9:05am from pl. Szczepański 6, and the Point bus leaves at 9:15am from the same place.

Prisoners were originally kept at the smaller **Konzentrationslager Auschwitz I,** within the city limits. By foot, turn right as you exit the train station, go 1 block and turn left; the camp driveway is 1.6km down on your right. Or catch bus 2, 3, 4, or 5;

POLAND

all will drop you near the kiosks outside the driveway. The camp itself is now a museum; barracks and crematoria hold displays detailing Nazi atrocities. An excellent English guidebook is available at the entrance. Begin your visit with the utterly terrifying film shot here by the Soviet Army on January 27, 1945. (Camp open 24hrs. Museum areas open 8am-7pm; May and Sept. 8am-6pm; April and Oct. 8am-5pm; March and Nov.-Dec. 15 8am-4pm; Dec. 15-Feb. 8am-3pm. Free.) You must not leave Oświęcim without visiting the starker and vaster **Konzentrationslager Auschwitz II-Birkenau.** In the countryside, 3km from the original camp and a good half-hour's walk west of the train station, Birkenau was constructed later in the war. There are no pamphlets, brochures, or display cases, only endless rows of barracks and watchtowers and the untouched, collapsing remains of gas chambers and crematoria. In the far right corner of the camp is a pond still gray from the tons of ashes deposited there nearly half a century ago.

Wieliczka Thirteen km southeast of Kraków, visit the 1000-year-old salt mine at Wieliczka, where pious Poles carved an immense 20-chapel complex in salt 100m underground. The most spectacular is **St. Kinga's Chapel.** Today, the Wieliczka salt mine has been declared by UNESCO as one of the 12 most priceless monuments in the world. (Open 8am-6pm; Oct.15-April 15 8am-4pm. Obligatory guided tours; last leaves 1½hr. before closing. 90,000zł, students 50,000zł.) You can get to Wieliczka by signing up for one of the trips organized by **ORBIS** or **Point Tour** (3hr., 340,000zl). The ORBIS bus to Wieliczka leaves daily at 3:10pm from pl. Szczepański 6, and the Point bus leaves daily at 3:20pm from the same place. Or choose the budget option: **trains** travel from Kraków (hourly, 25min., 10,000zł); **private buses** leave from the PKS bus station (every ½hr., 15,000zl). Once in Wieliczka, follow the tracks' former path and then the *do kopalni* (to the mine) signs. A guidebook in English is available at local kiosks.

Tarnów The Romany culture still thrives in Tarnów. At ul. Krakowska 10, the **Ethnographic Museum** traces the history of Polish Gypsies. The English brochure *The Gypsies: history and culture,* gives interesting insights into the subject and is worth the 10,000zł. (Open Tues. and Thurs. 10am-5pm, Wed. and Fri. 9am-3pm, Sat.-Sun. 10am-2pm. 10,000zł, students 7000zł.) In the *Rynek,* the **Town Hall Museum** shows off frescoes, furniture, and porcelain. (Open Tues. and Thurs. 10am-5pm, Wed. and Fri. 9am-3pm, Sat.-Sun. 10am-2pm. 10,000zł, students 7000zł.) **Trains** chug to Kraków (1hr., 35,500zł), Warsaw (4hr., 162,000zł), and Budapest (10hr., 771,000zł). For lodging, try **Dom Wycieczkowy PTTK,** ul. Żydowska 16 (tel. 21 62 29), in the heart of the Old Town. (Triples 240,000zł. Quads 320,000zł. Quints 350,000zł.) Or, **camp** at ul. Piłsudsksiego 30 (tel. 21 51 24). Take bus 30 "Basen"; get off after a left turn from ul. Romanowicza onto ul. Piłsudskiego. (20,000zł per person, 15,000zł per tent. 4- and 6-bed cabins at 45,000zł per bed. Open June-Aug.) **Polonia Restaurant,** in the Hotel Polonia, ul. Wałowa 21 has a vegetarian menu (potato pancakes 42,000zł, soups 10,000-32,000zł).

Częstochowa As Mecca is to Muslims, so is Częstochowa to Catholic Poles. Every year hundreds of thousands of Poles and foreigners make the pilgrimage to the most sacred of Polish icons, the **Black Madonna** in the towering monastery of **Jasna Góra.** (Chapel open 5am-9:30pm. Icon visible 6am-noon, 3-4:40pm, 6:30-7:15pm, and 9-9:15pm.) Countless crutches, medallions, and rosaries strung upon the chapel walls attest to its miraculous power. The monastery also houses the largest **treasury** in Poland, which contains priceless works of art, many of them donations of previous pilgrims: monstrances, chalices, crosses, candelabra, liturgical vestments, jewelry. (Open in summer Mon.-Sat. 9-11:30am and 3:30-5:30pm, Sun. 8am-1pm and 3-5:30pm; in winter Mon.-Sat. 9-10:30am and 3:30-4:30pm, Sun. 9am-12:30pm and 3:30-5pm. Donations encouraged.) Get to Częstochowa by **train** from Kraków (2hr., 81,000zł), Warsaw (3hr., 115,500zł), or Wrocław (3½hr., 103,000zł), but be careful to enquire about where you should get off—some trains stop at the

Częstochowa Główna station (main), others at Częstochowa-Stradom. From Stradom, take bus 15 or a cab (50,000zł) to the center. **WCIT,** al. NMP 65 (tel. 24 13 60, fax 24 34 12), is extremely organized and has detailed information on the town's hotels, but does not direct to private rooms. **ALMATUR,** al. NMP 37 (tel. 24 43 68 or 24 443 78, fax 24 43 78), sells ISIC and directs to summer student hostels (open Mon.-Fri. 9am-5pm, Sat. 10am-2pm). **Dom Pielgrzyma** (The Pilgrims' House), ul. Wyszyńskiego 1/31 (tel. 24 70 11 or 65 66 68, ext. 315), behind the monastery on Jasna Góra, is in a modern, hostel-like building. (Singles 300,000zł. Doubles 300,000zł. Quads 200,000zł.) Simple self-service entrees are prepared for pilgrims and served in a large and modern dining hall with additional seating outside. (Soups 10,000zł. Salads 6000zł. Entrees 35,000zł. Open 7am-8pm.)

■■■ ZAKOPANE

Directly south of Kraków, the placid Polish landscape shoots up 2500m to form the Tatry Mountains. Zakopane is the crowded center of the region. Set in a valley surrounded by jagged peaks and soul-stirring alpine meadows, the town is Poland's premier ski and hiking resort. Short mountain hikes are a specialty of the region, the **Tatrzański Park Narodowy** (National Park). A map is essential—the entrance to the park, at the end of ul. Strążyska, is a starting point for hikes of 2½-6 hours. (8000zł, students 5000zł.) **Giewont** (1090m) is 4½ hours away. The mountain lake of **Morskie Oko** dazzles herds of tourists; take a bus (45min., 10,000zł) from Zakopane to Polana Palenica, then hike 10km (6hr.). For a more dramatic vista, catch a bus to **Kuźnice,** 20min. south of central Zakopane, and hop on the **Kasprowy Wierch** chairlift. (7:30am-8:10pm; Dec.-Feb. 8am-4pm; March-May and Oct. 7:30am-5:40pm; June 7:30am-6:10pm. 115,000zł round-trip.) Go up a cable car to the **Gubałówka** mountain (20,000zł, students 10,000zł) and hike down (easy 25min.), or walk to the **Butorowy Wierch** peak and take a chairlift down to get a beautiful view of Zakopane and the slopes of Gubalowka (15,000zł).

Bus and (slower) **rail** lines link Zakopane to Katowice, Kraków, and Warsaw; a direct train connects to Budapest (Mon., Thurs., and Sat.). The main tourist office in town is **ORBIS,** ul. Krupówki 22 (tel. and fax (0165) 122 38), which gives out tourist info in English, cashes traveler's checks at 5% commission, organizes trips to Morskie Oko (8hr., 65,000zł) and rafting on the Dunajec River (7hr., 260,000zł), and sells plane, ferry, and bus tickets (open Mon.-Fri. 8am-8pm, Sat. 8am-noon). Rent a mountain **bike** at the Bzyk Sport sporting goods store at ul. Krupówki 37. (30,000zł per hour, 200,000zł per day. Open Mon. 10am-4pm, Tues.-Sun. 10am-6pm.)

The **IT tourist office,** ul. Kościuszki 23 (tel. (0165) 122 11), close to the train and bus stations, arranges private accommodations for 150,000zł per person (open 8am-8pm April-May and Nov., otherwise 24hrs.). Since Zakopane is the biggest center of mountain tourism in Poland, it gets very crowded in the summer (July-Sept.) and in the winter, especially around Christmas and during the winter break in February. Prices tend to go up substantially in season. To get to the **youth hostel (HI),** ul. Nowotarska 45 (tel. (0165) 662 03), walk down ul. Kościuszki towards town, then take the second right onto ul. Sienkiewicza and walk 2 blocks. (Lockout 10am-5pm. Curfew 11pm. Doubles 264,000zł, students 208,000zł. Dorms 75,000zł.) The **PTTK Dom Wycieczkowy,** ul. Zaruskiego 5 (tel. (0165) 632 81), is a large traditional chalet in the center of the town. (Singles 220,000zł. Doubles 400,000zł. Triples 600,000zł. 6-8-bed rooms 70,000zł per bed. 12-28-bed rooms 60,000zł per bed.) Pitch a tent at the base of the ski jump at **Camping Pod Krokwią,** ul. Żeromskiego (tel. (0165) 122 56; 25,000zł per person, 25,000zł per tent; open May-Aug.). The local specialty is *oscypek* (goat cheese) made by the Highlanders. Because of its strong and salty flavor, it can only be eaten in small quantities at a time. **Restaurant Śwarna,** ul. Kościuszki 4, is low-budget and tasty. (Breakfast 25,000zł. Trout 39,000zł. *Janosik* pork chop 62,000zl. Open 8am-10pm.)

POLAND

■■■ LUBLIN

Today a town of students, theater, and beautiful parks, Lublin lived through many a grim day during WWII, when the city's large Jewish population was mercilessly murdered in **Majdanek,** the largest concentration camp after Oświęcim (Auschwitz). The site of 360,000 murders, it can be reached by city bus 28 from the main train station or trolley buses 153 from ul. Krakowskie Przedmieście and 156 from ul. Królewska; they all stop at the huge granite monument marking the entrance to the grounds. The former cell-blocks now house moving exhibits chronicling the operations of this death factory, spread over the 5km Black Road near Lublin's southeastern suburbs. The road takes the visitor to the bath-house, the gas chambers, the prisoners' barracks, the assembly area, the crematorium, and ends at the **Mausoleum,** where the ashes of murdered prisoners were deposited. The **State Museum at Majdanek,** founded in 1944 after the liberation of Lublin, is open Tues.-Sun. 8am-6pm in the tourist season (Oct.-April Tues.-Sun. 8am-3pm).

The 19th-century ochre façades of **Krakowskie Przedmieście,** Lublin's main artery, introduce the more ancient buildings of the medieval **Stare Miasto** (old town). The grand **Katedra Św. Jana Chrzciciela i Jana Ewangelisty** (Cathedral of St. John the Baptist and St. John the Evangelist), ul. Królewska, was built 1586-96 by the Jesuits, who also founded a college on the premises; the cathedral's opulent frescoes and gilded altar are well worth the visit. To the left of the square runs ul. Lubartowska, the main artery of the prewar Jewish district in Lublin. Plac Ofiar Getta (Victims of the Ghetto Square) on the left side of the street is the site of **Pomnik Pomordowanych Żydów** (Monument to the Murdered Jews). At no.10 stands **Bożnica,** an early 20th-century synagogue, the only one in Lublin to survive the war. The synagogue also houses **Izba Pamięci Żydów Lublina** (museum commemorating Lublin's Jews). Ul. Krakowskie Przedmieście leads straight through pl. Łokietka to the fortified **Brama Krakowska** (Kraków Gate), which ushers you into the Old Town. Through the arch and straight along ul. Bramowa, leads to the **Rynek Starego Miasta** (Old Town Market Square), lined with early Renaissance houses, the most noteworthy of which are the Klonowice house at no. 2, the Lubomelskich house at no. 8, and the Konopniców house at no. 12. In the middle of the Rynek stands the **Stary Ratusz** (Old Town Hall), seat of the local authorities in the 14th century; redone several times, it ended up an 18th-century Neoclassical style.

Ul. Grodzka, which starts in the northwest corner of the Rynek, across from ul. Bramowa, leads through the 15th-century **Brama Grodzka** (Grodzka Gate) to the massive **Zamek Lubelski** (Lublin Castle). Once the court of a feudal kingdom, the castle served as Gestapo headquarters during WWII, and then as a prison till 1954. The fortified walls now house **Muzeum Lubelskie** (Museum of Lublin), along with archaeological and ethnographic displays (open Wed.-Sat. 9am-4pm, Sun. 9am-5pm; 12,000zł, students 8000zł, Sun. free).

Lublin has an impressive number of **pubs,** many of them run by students. Painters and art students hang out at **Bauhaus Café** at ul. Świętoduska 20, a block north of Krakowskie Przedmieście, where it reaches the Old Town (open Mon.-Thurs. noon-midnight, Fri. noon-2am, Sat. 4pm-2am, Sun. 4pm-midnight). Behind the modern entrance to Lublin's Catholic University (**KUL**) on al. Racławickie is an airy courtyard with perpetually young crowds and a cellar café in the right wing of the building. KUL's English Department graduates run **18 Hester Café** at ul. Okopowa 20 (open Mon.-Fri. noon-midnight, Sat.-Sun. 4pm-4am). In addition to alternative performances, the theater Scena Ruchu, at al. Piłsudskiego 13, runs **Graffiti,** with rock discos Fri.-Sat. 8pm-3am (cover: Fri. 40,000zł, Sat. 50,000zł). Their eponymous pub is open Sun.-Thurs. 4-11pm, Fri.-Sat. 4-8pm. Rock discos also take place at **Hades,** ul. Peowiakow 13, usually on Fri. and Sun. at 8pm (cover 10,000zł).

Practical Information, Accommodations, and Food Lublin lies 175km southeast of Warsaw on the historic trade route to Lviv and Ukraine. The main **train station,** Lublin Główny, pl. Dworcowy 1, south of the Old Town, sends trains to Warsaw (2½hr., 96,000zł), Kraków (4hr., 144,000zł), and Zamość (3hr., 44,000zł). **Buses** leave the PKS bus station (tel. (081) 77 66 49), ul. Tysiąclecia 4, near the Old Town for Warsaw (3hr., 84,000zł), Zamość (2hr., 54,000zł), and Sandomierz (2½hr., 64,000zl). The **IT tourist office,** ul. Krakowskie Przedmieście 78 (tel. (081) 244 12), sells maps (26,000zł) and offers 10% student discount on all prices (open Mon.-Fri. 9am-5pm, Sat. 10am-2pm). **ORBIS,** ul. Narutowicza 31 (tel. (081) 222 56), handles international and domestic train and bus tickets (open Mon.-Fri. 9am-6pm, Sat. 11am-4pm). **Tourist Agency "Horyzont,"** ul. Gazowa 4 (tel. (081) 226 19, fax 267 12), cheerfully directs travelers to hotels and camping sites in Lublin and throughout Poland (open Mon.-Fri. 10am-4pm, Sat. 10am-noon). For **currency exchange,** *Kantors* throughout the city have the best rates. The **post office,** ul. Krakowskie Przedmieście 50, is open Mon.-Fri. 7am-9pm, Sat. 8am-2pm; telephones are available 24hrs.

Lublin lacks a private room-finding agency, but reasonable alternatives are within walking distance of the historic center. **Schronisko Młodzieżowe (HI),** ul. Długosza 6a (tel. (081) 306 28), lies west of the center near the Catholic University. Take bus 13 from the train station to the end of the Saxon Gardens. (Lockout 10am-5pm. Curfew 10pm. Both flexible. Luggage storage. 2- to 12-person rooms. 36-52,000zł. Over 26 40-56,000zł. Nonmembers 44-60,000zł. Sheets 14,000zł.) To get to hostel-esque **ZNP Dom Noclegowy,** ul. Akademicka 4 (tel. (081) 382 85), take bus 13 from the train station just past Ogród Saski. (Singles 155,000zł. Doubles 190,000zł. 6-person rooms 480,000zł.) Ideally located **Hotel Lublinianka,** ul. Krakowskie Przedmieście 56 (tel. (081) 242 61), has lofty ceilings and decent bathrooms. (Singles 236-307,000zł. Doubles 380,000zł. 6-person room 90,000zł per person.)

Canucks get 10% off at **Jazz Pizza,** in a cellar at ul. Krakowskie Przedmieście 55. (English menu: jazzy pizzas 25,000zł, 8000-17,000zł for extra toppings. Open Mon.-Sat. 11:30am-10pm, Sun. 3-10pm.) **Bar Deli Rood,** ul. Krakowskie Przedmieście 21, is a modern and agreeable variation on the fast food theme (open Mon.-Sat. 10am-8pm, Sun. 10am-6pm). **Café and Bar "Zielony Liść"** (Green Leaf), ul. Ewangelicka 6, serves sandwiches and salads under 20,000zł (open 8am-10pm). For Polish specialities (40-60,000zł), try **Restaurant Karczma Słupska,** al. Racławickie 24, past the Catholic University (open Thurs.-Tues. 10am-10pm, Wed. 10am-8pm).

■ ZAMOŚĆ

Zamość, built in the 1580s, is a monumental sight in itself, with its Renaissance layout, the imposing town hall, the peaceful cobblestone **Rynek,** and the surrounding houses with painted façades. Especially worth seeing are the splendidly preserved **Armenian houses** in the northeast corner of the Rynek, at ul. Ormiańska 22, 24, 26, 28, and 30. The house at no. 24 is the headquarters of the **Muzeum Okręgowe** (Regional Museum), which displays artifacts from the region: Lusatian jewelry from 1000B.C., 10th- to 13th-century combs, and other objects of everyday use. (Open Tues.-Sun. 10am-4pm. 10,000zł, students 5000zł.) In the summer, the whole town echoes with life during the annual **Zamojskie Lato Teatralne** (Zamość Theater Summer), when the best experimental groups perform in theaters and on the streets. For more info, contact **WDK,** at ul. Partyzantów 13 (tel. (084) 20 21 or 20 22). In May, jazz musicians from Ukraine and Belarus come to jam with Poles during the **Jazz na Kresach Festival** (Jazz of the Borderlands).

To reach Zamość from Lublin, take the **train** (3hr., 49,000zł) or **bus** (2hr., 54,000zł). **IT,** in the Ratusz, at Rynek 13 (tel. (084) 22 92), arranges guides to Zamość (300,000zł for a minimum of 4hr.) and to the neighboring region of Roztocze (460,000zł per day) and sells maps (open Mon.-Fri. 7:30am-5pm, Sat. 8am-2pm, Sun. 9am-2pm). Accommodations are scarce. The hostel-like **Hotel Marta,** ul. Zamenhoffa 11 (tel. (084) 26 39), used to be the PTTK Dom Wycieczkowy (80,000zł per bed). **Hotel Renesans,** ul. Grecka 6 (tel. (084) 20 01), has a café on the premises. (Singles 250,000zł. Doubles 350,000zł. Café open 7am-11pm. Breakfast 50,000zł. Pool table 30,000zł per hour.)

■■■ WROCŁAW

Under Prussian and German rule between 1741 and 1945, Wrocław's elaborate postwar reconstruction conceals the city's destruction in WWII, when it became *Festung Breslau,* one of the last battling grounds of the Red Army's march to Berlin. The oldest neighborhood of the city, **Ostrów Tumski** (Cathedral Island), lies across the river from the center of town, next to the **Botanical Gardens.** East of the Old Town, the **Panorama Racławicka Museum,** ul. Purkyniego 11, houses a 120m mural lining which recounts the peasant insurrection led by Kościuszko in the late 18th century (open Tues.-Sun. 8am-7pm; 60,000zł, students 30,000zł). Burial place of Ferdinand Lasalle and the family of Thomas Mann's wife, the **Jewish cemetery,** located in a park at ul. Ślężna 37/39, has only recently been opened to the public (open only Sun. at noon May-Oct. 30,000zł). In the theater building at ul. Kuźnicza 29, in the university area, the Art Nouveau **Café "Pod Kalamburem,"** is an artists' haven. Piano concerts are held here every Thursday and Saturday. Pick up a free copy of the *Wrocławski Informator Kuturalny* to find out more about local cultural events. (Open Mon.-Sat. 10am until last guest leaves, Sun. 4pm until last guest leaves.) In the southern area of the city, the **Operetka,** the **Teatr Polski,** and the **Filharmonia** are all on the same stretch of ul. Piłsudskiego. (Ask at ORBIS for tickets.)

Practical Information, Accommodations, and Food The well-stocked, brand new **IT tourist office,** Rynek 14 (tel. (071) 44 31 11), will answer all your questions and supply you with handy maps (open Mon.-Fri. 9am-5pm, Sat. 10am-2pm). **ALMATUR,** ul. Kościuszki 34 (tel. (071) 44 39 51), in the student center Pałacyk, has info on concerts and sells ISICs and international bus tickets (open Mon. and Fri. 9am-4pm, Tues.-Thurs. 9am-5pm, Sat. 10am-2pm). **Trains** arrive from Warsaw (5-7hr., 162,000zł), Kraków (4hr., 127,500zł), Częstochowa (3½hr., 103,000zł), Prague (7hr., 600,000zł), and Budapest (12hr., 1,008,000zł). The main **bus** station is behind the train station, at ul. Sucha 2, and sends coaches to Warsaw (8hr., 242,000zł) and Kraków (7hr., 165,000zł).

The **youth hostel,** ul. Kołłątaja 2 (tel. (071) 338 56), lies directly opposite the train station. (Lockout 10am-5pm. 22,500-63,000zł per person, depending on size of dorm. Doubles 39-66,000zł per bed.) **Biuro Usług Turystycznych** (Tourist Services Center), ul. Piłudskiego 98 (tel. (071) 44 78 85 or 44 41 01), books private accommodations. (Singles 170,000zł. Doubles 300,000zł. Open Mon.-Fri. 8:30am-4pm, Sat. 9am-2pm.) Centrally located between the train station and the Old Town, **Hotel Savoy,** Plac Kościuszki 19 (tel. (071) 440 33 49), has rooms with baths. (Singles 205,000zł. Doubles 300,000zł. Triples 330,000zł.)

Spiffy vegetarian meals at **Bar Vega,** Rynek 27a, cost less than 30,000zł (open Mon.-Fri. 8am-7pm, Sat.-Sun. 9am-5pm). **Bar Miś,** ul. Kuźnicza 48, offers cafeteria-style meals for under 20,000zł. (Rice with blueberries 7900zł. Open Mon.-Fri. 6:30am-6pm, Sat. 8am-5pm.) On the western edge of the *rynek,* **Dwór Wazów,** Rynek 5 (tel. (071) 44 16 33) fits into a classy stone house. (Gypsy pork chop 160,000zł. Ice cream 24-53,000zł. Restaurant open 1pm-midnight; café open 10am-10pm.)

POLAND

District boundaries are shown in light gray. Districts names are the same as the capital cities. Regional areas are named in bold-face: **ALGARVE** Regions have no administrive boundaries

Rio Minho
MINHO
Viana do Castelo ★
Rio Cávado
Serra do Gerês
TRÁS-OS-MONTES
Bragança
★ Braga
●Guimarães
Serra do Marão
Vila Real ★
COSTA VERDE
DOURO LITORAL
DOURO ALTO
Porto ★
Rio Douro
BEIRA ALTA
Salamanca
Aveiro ★
Viseu ★
COSTA DA PRATA
BEIRA LITORAL
Rio Mondego
Serra da Estrela
Guarda ★
SPAIN
Figueira da Foz ★
Coimbra ★
Serra da Gardunha
BEIRA BAIXA
ATLANTIC OCEAN
Leiria ★
Batalha ★
Fátima ★
★ Castelo Branco
Nazaré ★
São Martinho do Porto ●
Alcobaça ●
Tomar ●
Ilhas Berlengas
Caldas da Rainha ●
Cabo Carvoeiro
Óbidos ●
Peniche ●
Rio Tejo
Serra de São Mamede
Cáceres
ESTREMADURA
RIBATEJO
★ Portalegre
Vila Franca
Serra de Aire
Mafra ●
Sintra ●
Cascais ●
☉ Lisboa
Estremoz ★
Elvas ★
Mérida
Estoril ●
Queluz
Setúbal ★
ALTO ALENTEJO
Cabo Espichel
Evora ★
Serra de Ossa
COSTA AZUL
★ Beja
Sines ●
BAIXO ALENTEJO
Rio Guadiana
Rio Mira
Mertola ●
COSTA DOURADA
Serra de Monchique
Portimão ●
Silves ●
ALGARVE
Tavira ●
Cabo São Vicente
Lagos ●
Sagres ●
Faro ★
Olhão ●
Vila Real de Santo Antonio
Golfo de Cádiz

Portugal

US$1	= 159$ (escudos, or PTE)	100$ =	US$0.63
CDN$1	= 118$	100$ =	CDN$0.85
UK£1	= 252$	100$ =	UK£0.40
IR£1	= 249$	100$ =	IR£0.40
AUS$1	= 122$	100$ =	AUS$0.82
NZ$1	= 96$	100$ =	NZ$1.04
SAR1	= 45$	100$ =	SAR2.25
Country Code: 351		International Dialing Prefix: 099 or 098	

PORTUGAL

Centuries ago, Portuguese explorers noticed that the Atlantic Ocean didn't swallow the sun every evening. Their revolutionary navigational and shipbuilding techniques allowed Vasco da Gama to sail around the Cape of Good Hope and Magellan to sail around the world, and their discoveries fed the country's prosperity, transforming art and architecture into the ornate and sometimes eccentric Manueline style. Following the Age of Discovery a period of decline set in, imbuing the culture with a nostalgia still reflected in the folk ballads of *fado*—fate. By 1580, Portugal had exhausted both its resources and its royal line, and after minimal resistance, the Spanish Habsburg Philip II claimed the Portuguese throne. Independence wasn't regained until 1640, when the royal house of Bragança established itself by hooking up with England. An earthquake in 1755 reduced much of Lisbon to rubble, shaking the country's faith and economy so much that when Napoleon invaded in 1807, King Pedro III moved the court of his crumbling empire to Brazil.

A parliamentary republic sprouted in 1910, only to be overthrown by a 1926 military coup. Strongman António Salazar, an economist-turned-dictator, and his successor, Marcelo Caetano, ruled the country for the next 50 years, running down the economy through the exploitation of a domestic peasantry and African laborers under colonial rule. In 1974, a bloodless coup toppled the regime, prompting mass rejoicing—every Portuguese town now has its Rua 25 de Abril to honor the putsch. The new junta granted independence to Portugal's African holdings; the ensuing civil wars in Mozambique and Angola set off a rush of immigration into an already unstable Portugal. In 1986, President Mario Soares and Prime Minister Cavaco Silva supervised Portugal's entry into the European Economic Community, and they initiated a sometimes painful modernization drive for the country. Portugal remains quite poor by European standards; some estimates hold that up to two-fifths of the population now live abroad in search of better jobs and living standards.

Each year, sun-addicts migrate to the sands, cliffs, and sparkling waters of the Algarve; fewer visit the rougher northern coast. Notable architecture abounds in the north: Coimbra and Porto have Romanesque churches, while the area north of the Rio Douro is dotted with Roman and Visigothic ruins. In the center and south are massive fortresses lingering from the Moorish occupation.

For more detailed, energetic, and sunny information on Portugal, grab a copy of *Let's Go: Spain & Portugal*.

GETTING THERE AND GETTING AROUND

International **airports** in Lisbon, Porto, and Faro serve major European and North American cities. Lisbon and Porto are also accessible by daily **trains** from Madrid and Paris.

Eurailpasses are valid on the Portuguese national **train** system, but even passholders must pay extra on express trains. **Caminhos de Ferro Portugueses,** Portugal's national railway, operates throughout the country, but aside from the Braga-Porto-Coimbra-Lisbon line, it's wisest to take the bus. Trains are less comfortable, less frequent, often slower, and reach fewer destinations. **Rodoviária,** the national bus company, has recently been privatized and broken up by region (and switched names to EVA in Algarve). In most places Rodoviária is still known by its old name, and links just about every town. Other private regional companies cover the more obscure routes. Express coach service *(expressos)* between major cities is especially good. **Hitchhiking** in Portugal is not reliable enough to be anyone's main means of transportation.

PORTUGAL ESSENTIALS

The national **tourist board** is the Direcção Geral do Turismo (DGT). Their offices are in virtually every city; look for the "Turismo" sign. They'll give you free maps that usually include brief descriptions of sights, and useful phone numbers. Many *turismos* keep lists of approved accommodations and can point you to a *quarto* (private room).

A strongly Catholic country, Portugal's liveliest festivals are the *festas juninas,* which take place around the feast days of St. John and St. Peter, June 24 and 29. June is bedlam in Lisbon; the feast day of its patron saint Santo Antônio is celebrated June 13 with costume processions and bacchanalian excesses. Two important festivals commemorate the appearances of the Virgin in Fátima (May 12-13 and Oct. 12-13). Holy Week brings processions and crowds to Braga; Easter Sunday marks the beginning of the Portuguese bullfighting season. (The bull is wounded, not killed.) Every town has its patron saint; their feast days are local holidays, accompanied by pilgrimages, village fairs, and often makeshift amusement parks, and closed shops. Everything in Portugal closes on New Year's Day, Carnival Tuesday, Good Friday, Easter Sunday, April 25, Labor Day (May 1), June 10, June 24, Corpus Christi, Assumption, Oct. 5, All Saints Day (Nov. 1), Restoration of Independence (Dec. 1), Immaculate Conception (Dec. 8), Christmas Eve, and Christmas Day.

Portuguese **currency** is divided into escudos and centavos; the $ sign is used in *Let's Go* as a currency symbol. Shops are usually open weekdays from 9am to 1pm and from 3 to 6pm, and on Saturday mornings. Normal banking hours are weekdays from 8:30am to 3pm, but many close for lunch from around 11:45am to 1pm.

Communication Portuguese is a Romance language similar to Spanish, but also accessible to those with a background in French or Italian. In the southern and central provinces, many locals speak English, French, or German.

Mail usually takes 6-8 business days to reach the U.S. or Canada; postage costs 130$. **Posta Restante** pick-up at central post offices costs 55$ per item. A **telegram,** the most reliable means of communication, may be sent from almost any post office; offices with telegram service have signs that read "CTT." A message of 10-15 words costs a flat fee of about 1614$ plus a 84$ per word charge. **Phone booths** marked by signs saying "Credifone" are located at phone offices, on the street, and in some post offices. Direct-dialing from a phone booth is the least expensive way to make an international call. Dial 098 for Europe, 097 for everywhere else. Few pay phones accept coins; the Credifone system uses magnetic cards that are sold at locations posted on the phone booth. Local calls cost 17.50$ by Credifone, 20$ by coin. Phone calls from bars and cafés cost whatever the proprietor decides to charge, typically 30-40$; there's usually a posted sign that indicates the charge. Some helpful numbers throughout Portugal are: **directory assistance,** 118; **local operator,** 142; **international operator,** 099 for inside Europe, 098 for elsewhere. In an **emergency (police, fire, medical):** 115. For MCI's **WorldPhone,** dial 05 017 1234; AT&T's **USADirect** 05 017 1288; **SprintExpress** 05 017 1877; **Canada Direct** 05 017 1226; **BT Direct** 05 05 0044; **Ireland Direct** 05 05 0353; **Australia Direct** 05 017 6110; **SA Direct** 05 017 2700. Women traveling alone will likely receive inordinate amounts of male attention—annoying, but rarely dangerous. See Essentials—Women Travelers, in the front of this book.

Accommodations and Camping The **Associação Portuguesa de Pousadas de Juventude (APPJ),** the Portuguese Hostelling International affiliate, runs the country's HI hostels. To stay in a hostel, an HI card (3000$) is mandatory. In Portugal, these are sold only by APPJ's Lisbon office, Av. Duque D'Avila, 137, 1000 Lisbon (tel. (1) 355 90 81, fax (1) 352 86 21). A bargain bed in a *pousada de juventude* (not to be confused with the sneakily-named opposite, *pousada,* see below) costs 1300-2000$ per night, 1100-1750$ in off-season (breakfast included). Lunch or dinner cost 750$. Rates are slightly higher for guests 26 or older. Hostels are typically some distance away from the town center. Reception hours are from 9am to 12:30pm and 6 to 9pm. Most hostels enforce a lockout 10:30am to 6pm; the early curfews (11pm or midnight) may cramp your style if you club-hop.

Hotels in Portugal are usually more expensive than they're worth. *Pensões,* also called *residencias,* will likely be your mainstay; they're far cheaper than hotels, and offer more privacy than hostels. All are rated by the government on a 3-star scale, and are required to prominently post their category and legal price limits. During high season, many *pensão* owners won't reserve rooms by phone.

The Portuguese love to camp; their 168 official **campgrounds** *(parques de camp-ismo)* come brim-full with amenities and comforts. With such facilities, it's wise to arrive early; urban and coastal parks may require reservations. Recently, police have been cracking down on illegal camping, so don't try it near one of the official campgrounds. Larger tourist office branches stock the *Roteiro Campista,* an indispensable multilingual guide to all official campgrounds; or write to the **Federação Portuguesa de Campismo,** Av. 5 Outubro, 15-3, Lisboa CODEX (tel. (1) 315 27 15, fax (1) 54 93 72). **Orbitur-Intercâmbio de Turismo, S.A.,** a private company, administers 18 of Portugal's poshest, best-run, and most expensive campgrounds. For reservations write to Orbitur at R. Diogo Couto, 1-8, 1100 Lisboa (tel. (1) 815 48 71, fax (1) 814 80 45). **Quartos** are rooms in private residences, sometimes the only choice in small or less touristed towns, particularly in southern Portugal. The tourist office can usually help find them, and restaurant proprietors and bartenders often supply names and directions. A **pousada** (literally, resting place) is a castle, palace, or monastery converted into an expensive and luxurious government-run hotel (Portugal's version of the Spanish *parador nacional).*

Food and Drink Olive oil, garlic, herbs, and sea salt routinely season local specialties. As a whole, the aromatic Portuguese cuisine is heavy on herbs and light on spices. *Sopas* (soups) are hearty and filling. Main dishes run a delectable gamut. Seafood lovers get their fix from grilled *peixe espada grelhado* (grilled swordfish), *lagosta suada* (steamed lobster), *pescada frita* (fried hake, a particularly delicious Atlantic fish), *linguado grelhado* (grilled sole), *polvo* (boiled or grilled octopus), and *mexilhões* (mussels). Pork fiends indulge in *bife de porco à alentejana,* made with clams in a coriander sauce. Those who prefer chicken fork into *frango assado* (roasted on a spit) and *frango no churrasco* (grilled). The entire country feeds on *cozida à portuguesa* (boiled beef, pork, sausage, and vegetables) in winter. Portugal's favorite dessert is *pudim,* a rich caramel custard. Portuguese *vinho* (wine) costs a pittance by North American standards. Sparkling *vinho verde* (literally "green wine"—the name refers to its youth, not its color) comes in red and white versions. Excellent local table wines are Colares, Dão, Borba, Bairrada, Bucelas, and Periquita. Port, pressed (by feet) from the red grapes of the Douro Valley and fermented with a touch of brandy, is a fortified dessert in itself. A unique heating process gives Madeira wines their odd "cooked" flavor.

The Portuguese eat earlier than the Spanish. The midday meal (dinner, "lunch" to Americans) is served between noon and 2pm, supper between 7:30 and 10pm. A good meal costs 1000-2000$ just about anywhere. Oddly, prices don't vary much between ritzy and economy restaurants in Portugal. Half portions *(meia dose)* cost more than half-price but are often more than adequate. The ubiquitous *prato do dia* (special of the day) and *menú* (appetizer, bread, entree, and dessert) satisfy hungry folks. The *ementa turistica* (tourist menu) is usually a way to rip off foreigners. Most restaurants will add a 10% service charge to your bill. It's customary to round off the sum to the next highest unit of currency and leave the change as a tip. Attention vegetarians—every town you visit is likely to have a **mercado municipal** (open-air produce market); for groceries, shop at the **supermercado** (supermarket).

■■■ LISBON (LISBOA)

Although modern problems assail Lisbon—traffic, smog, and urban decay noticeable to most visitors—the city retains some of its imperial grandeur. The city's appeal results from a combination of relaxed urbanity and the significance *Lisboetas* attach to tradition. The city constantly renovates its beautiful and historic monuments, and meticulously maintains the black and white mosaic sidewalks, pastel building facades, and cobbled medieval alleys (some barely an arm's length wide).

N ←

1/8 mile
125 meters

G

R. Bela Vista da Graça
R. dos Sapadores
R. Leite de Vasconcelos
R. Senhora da Glória

GRAÇA

Rua Damasceno
Calçada do Monte
R. da Graça
Rua da Palma
R. de S. Lázaro

R. Instituto Bacteriologico

F

R. de S. Tomé
C. de Santo André
R. do Benformoso
Castelo

ALFAMA

Campo de Santa Clara
Rua dos Remédios
Rua Jardim do Tabaco
C. S. Vicente

3
22
21
16
19

18
16
17
7

Rua da Costa do Castelo
Rua da Madalena
Rua dos Bacalhoeiros
Rua da Alfandega

E

Rua das Portas   de Santo Antão
Avenida da Liberdade

Rua dos Fanqueiros
Rua da Prata
Rua dos Correiros
Rua Augusta
Rua do Ouro

Rua da Conceição
Rua de São Julião

BAIXA

PRAÇA DOM PEDRO IV
PRAÇA FIGUEIRA
PRAÇA DOS RESTAURADORES

PRAÇA DO COMÉRCIO

6
5
8

Rua do Carmo
Rua Nova do Almada

2

D

Jardim Botanico

Rua do Salitre
Rua da Alegria
R. da Con. de Glória
C. da Glória
R. de Dom Pedro V

R. Nova da Trinidade
R. Misericordia
Trav. da Queimada
Rua das Flores
Rua do Alecrim

Rua Garrett
R. A.M. Cardoso
R. Serpa Pinto

Rua do Arsenal
Av. Ribeira das Naus

9
11
10

Rio Tejo

Rua da Escola Politécnica

C

Rua d. Século
Calçada do Combro
R. Cordeiros

PRAÇA LUIS DE CAMÕES
Rua de São Paolo

Rua da Boavista
Rua d. Luis I
Av. Vinte E. Quatro de Julho

4

B

RATO

Rua Nova de S. Mamede
Instituto Nacional
Rua de San Bento
R. N. d. Piedade

BAIRRO ALTO

R. do Poço dos Negros
Rua dos Poiais

Carlos I
Av. Dom

12

A

Av. D. A. de Cabral
Rua Saraiva de Carvalho

R. de Santo Amaro
R. de S. Jorge
R. de Bernado

Calçada da Estrêla
R. Bela Vista
R. da Esperança

Jardim da Estrêla

14
13

To the Museu de Arte Antiga
15

PORTUGAL

Lisbon

1 City Tourist Office	12 Palácio da Assembléia Nacional
2 Main Post Office	13 Basílica da Estrela
3 Estação Santa Apolónia	14 Jardim da Estrêla
4 Estação Cais do Sodré	15 Museo Nacional de Arte Antiga
5 Estação do Rossio	16 Igreja de Madalena
6 Teatro Nacional	17 Sé
7 Casa dos Bicos	18 Castelo de São Jorge
8 Ascensor de Santa Justa	19 Fundação Espíritu Santo Silva
9 Museu de Arqueologico	20 Igreja de São Vicente
10 Museu Nacional de Arte Contemporânea	21 Igreja de Santa Engrácia
11 Igreja de São Roque	22 Museo da Antiharia

ORIENTATION AND PRACTICAL INFORMATION

The **Baixa,** or Lower Town, is Lisbon's downtown and the old business district. Its grid of small streets begins at the **Rossio** (the main square, comprised of the connecting **Praça Dom Pedro IV** and **Praça da Figueira**) and ends at Praça do Comércio, near the **Tagus River** (Rio Tejo). **Praça dos Restauradores,** an active square, is just north of the Rossio. Lisbon's swank shopping district, the **Chiado,** is linked to the Baixa by the **Ascensor de Santa Justa,** an elegant, historic elevator. West of Rua da Misericórdia spreads the **Bairro Alto** (Upper District), a populous working-class area of narrow streets, tropical parks and Baroque churches. To the east, the **Alfama,** Lisbon's famous medieval quarter, stacks tiny whitewashed houses along a labyrinth of narrow alleys and stairways beneath the Castelo de São Jorge. The old and new business districts are connected by **Avenida da Liberdade,** a tree-lined boulevard that begins its uphill climb at Pr. Restauradores. **Belém** (Bethlehem), formerly an autonomous town (about 6km west of Praça do Comércio), is home to several museums and palaces.

Tourist Office: Palácio da Foz, Pr. Restauradores (tel. 346 33 14 or 342 52 31). M: Restauradores. English spoken. Open Mon.-Fri. 9am-8pm, Sat.-Sun. 10am-7pm. Airport branch office open 24hrs.

Budget Travel: Tagus (Youth Branch), Pr. Londres, 9B (tel. 849 53 63). M: Alameda. Books flights on TAP and British Airways. English spoken. **Tagus (Main Office),** R. Camilo Castelo Branco, 20 (tel. 352 55 09). Both offices open Mon.-Fri. 9am-1pm and 2:30-5:30pm.

Embassies: U.S., Av. das Forças Armadas (tel. 726 66 00). **Canada,** Av. Liberdade, 144/56, # 4 (tel. 347 48 92). **U.K.,** R. São Domingos à Lapa, 37 (tel. 396 11 91). Also handles **New Zealand** affairs. **Australians** should turn to the Australian Embassy in Paris. **South Africa,** Av. Luís Bivar, 10 (tel. 353 50 41).

Currency Exchange: Santa Apolónia train station, on the platform. Enormous lines here and at the airport branch. Both open 24hrs. Also at the main post office, most banks, and travel agencies (often for a 1000$ fee and 152$ tax).

American Express: Top Tours, Av. Duque de Loulé, 108 (tel. 315 58 85). M: Rotunda. Exit toward R. Rod. Sampa and walk up Av. da Liberdade toward the Marqués de Pombal Statue, then turn right. This sole Top Tours office handles all AmEx services. Traveler's checks sold and cashed. Mail held. English spoken. Long lines. Open Mon.-Fri. 9am-1pm and 2:30-6:30pm.

Post Office: Correio, Pr. Comércio (tel. 346 32 31). Open for Poste Restante Mon.-Fri. 9am-7pm. Branch office at Pr. Restauradores open for **telegrams,** international express service, stamps and telephones 8am-10pm. **Postal Code:** 1100.

Telephones: Central exchange at Pr. Dom Pedro IV, 68. M: Rossio. For **telegrams,** dial 183. Open 8am-11pm. Credifone cards (not TLP cards, which are valid in Lisboa and Porto only) come in 50 units (750$) or 120 units (1725$). Local calls consume at least 1 unit. One phone takes MC, Visa, and Eurocard. **City Code:** 01.

Flights: Aeroporto de Lisboa (tel. 80 20 60), on the northern outskirts of the city. Local buses 44 or 45 (20min. from downtown). The express bus (Aero-bus or line 91, 400$) is faster. All 3 lines head for the Baixa. Taxis are cheaper for more than 2 people (about 800$ to the Baixa). **TAP Air Portugal** (airport tel. 848 91 81; info 848 91 82). **Iberia** (tel. 358 20 16; reservations 847 50 34).

Trains: (tel. 888 40 25). **Santa Apolónia,** on banks of the Tagus near Alfama, for all international, northern, and eastern lines. **Cais do Sodré** for Estoril and Cascais (40min., 155$). **Barreiro** for the Algarve and southern lines. To reach Barreiro, take a ferry across the Tagus (every 5-10min, 110$, free if coming into Lisbon from the south) from Pr. Comércio. **Rossio** (between Pr. Restauradores and Pr. Dom Pedro IV) for Sintra (45min., 165$) and western lines. Detailed schedules and some assistance at Rossio. Open 8am-11pm. To Evora (3hr., 820$), Porto (5hr., 1690$), Lagos (6½hr., 1540$), Badajoz, Spain (5hr., 2850$), Paris (27hr., 21,135$).

Buses: Rodoviária, Av. Casal Ribeiro, 18 (tel. 54 58 63). M: Picoas. From Pr. Marqués de Pombal take Av. Fontes Pereira de Melo to Pr. Duque de Saldanha and bear right around the roundabout. To Evora (2½hr., 1100$) Coimbra (3hr.,

1200$), Lagos (5hr., 1900$), Porto (5hr., 1600$). Private **Caima** buses, R. Bacal-hoeiros, 16 (tel. 87 50 61) runs express buses to the Algarve and Porto (1700$) and Lagos (2100$).

Public Transportation: Buses, CARRIS (tel. 36 32 02). 140$ within the city. **Metro (M):** 65$ at window, 60$ from vending machines. 500$ for book of 10 at window, 475$ from machines. *Bilhete de assinatura turístico* (tourist pass), good for unlimited travel on CARRIS buses, trolleys, funiculars, and the subway (1-day 400$, 4-day 1440$, 7-day 2030$). The passes are sold in CARRIS booths (open 8am-8pm), located in most network train stations and the busier metro stations. **Trolleys (eléctricos):** Ubiquitous cars (many seem pre-WWI) offer beautiful views of the harbor and older neighborhoods. Line 28 is good for sightseeing (stops in Pr. Comércio, 140$).

Taxis: Rádio Táxis de Lisboa (tel. 815 50 61), **Autocoope** (tel. 793 27 56), and **Teletáxi** (tel. 815 20 16). 24hr. service.

Luggage Storage: At **Estações Rossio** and **Santa Apolónia**. Lockers 350$, 450$, and 750$ for up to 48hrs. At the **bus station**, 130$ per bag per day.

English Bookstore: Livraria Bertrand, R. Garrett, 75 (tel. 346 86 46). Good collection of best-sellers and (mostly fashion) magazines. International maps and travel guides (including *Let's Go*). Open Mon.-Fri. 9am-7pm, Sat. 9am-1pm.

Laundromat: Lavatax, R. Francisco Sanches, 65A (tel. 82 33 92). M: Arroios. Wash, dry, and fold 800$ per 5kg load. Open 9am-1pm and 3-7pm, Sat. 9am-noon.

Medical Assistance: British Hospital, R. Saraíva de Carvalho, 49 (tel. 60 20 20; at night 60 37 85).

Emergency: tel. 115 anywhere in Portugal. **Police,** R. Capelo, 3 (tel. 346 61 41).

ACCOMMODATIONS AND CAMPING

Expect to pay about 2500$ for a single and 4000$ for a double and more in fancier *residencias* or smaller hotels. The vast majority of hotels are in the center of town on **Av. Liberdade** and adjacent sidestreets. Lodgings near the *castelo* or in the Bairro Alto are quieter, nearer to the sights, and more expensive. Be cautious in the Bairro Alto, the Alfama, and the Baixa after dark. If the central accommodations are full, head east to the *pensões* along **Av. Almirante Reis.**

Pousada da Juventude de Lisboa (HI), R. Andrade Corvo, 46 (tel. 353 26 96, fax 352 86 21). M: Picoas. Take a left out of the station and then make 2 successive right turns. HI card required. Recently renovated with spic 'n' span rooms. Handicap access. Max. stay 3 days in high season. No curfew, no lockout. Check-out by noon. Dorms 2000$ per person. Doubles with bath 5000$. Low season 1750$, 4500$. Breakfast included. Reservations (by letter or fax only) recommended.

Pousada da Juventude de Catalazete (HI), Estrada Marginal (tel. 443 06 38), in the coastal town of **Oeiras.** Train from Estação Cais do Sodré to Oeiras (20min., 95$). Exit through the underpass from the side of the train coming from Lisbon, cross the street, and follow Lisboa road signs. At the intersection across from a bus stop (no street signs), turn left and go downhill. At the underpass, go straight and follow HI signs to the INATEL complex. Enter the complex and walk to the end of the path; the hostel is to the left. Beautiful ocean views from the patio and more quiet than the city. Reception open 9:30-10:30am and 6-11pm. Curfew midnight. Dorms 1600$. Doubles 3600-4000$. Oct.-May 1300$, 3000-3500$. Breakfast included. Reservations recommended.

Pensão Beira-Mar, Largo Terreiro do Trigo, 16 (tel. 87 15 28). Clean spacious rooms, some with ocean view. Friendly owner speaks English and picks guests up from the airport or train station. Laundry. Singles 1500$. Doubles 3000$.

Pensão Prata, R. Prata, 71, 3rd fl. (tel. 346 89 08), 2 bl. from Pr. Comércio. A yellow awning hides the sign. Eleven sun-kissed rooms in a peaceful apartment setting. All rooms with double bed 3800$, with shower 4300$, with bath 5000$.

Residencial Florescente, R. Portas de Santo Antão, 99 (tel. 342 66 09), 1 bl. from Pr. Restauradores. Singles and doubles 5000$, with shower 6000$, with bath, TV, and phone 7500$. Large room with full bath and A/C 8500$.

Pensão Campos, R. Jardim do Regedor, 24, 3rd fl. (tel. 346 28 64), on busy pedestrian street between Pr. Restauradores and R. Portas de Santa Antão. Cozy rooms and clean baths. Singles 3000$. Doubles 3500$, with bath 4500$.

Pensão Estrela de Chiado, R. Garrett, 29, 4th fl. (tel. 342 61 10). A tiring climb up 95 stairs, but the rooms are clean, the water hot, and the singles large. Rooms with veranda have views of the castle. Opt for rooms with bath; the common showers aren't appealing. Singles 2000$. Doubles 3500$, with bath 4000$.

Pensão Londres, R. Dom Pedro V, 53 (tel. 346 55 23, fax 346 56 82). Take the funicular by Palácio da Foz in Pr. Restauradores. Facing away from the funicular, walk across to R. Dom Pedro V. Near good inexpensive restaurants. Singles 3000$, with bath 4000$. Doubles 5000$, with bath 7000$. Breakfast included.

Camping: Parque da Câmara Municipal de Lisboa-Monsanto (tel. 70 20 61, fax 70 74 74), on the road to Benfica. Take bus 43 from the Rossio to the Parque Florestal Monsanto. Swimming pool and reasonably priced supermarket. 350$ per person, 300$ or more per tent (depending on size). **Clube de Campismo de Lisboa Costa da Caparica** (tel. 290 01 00), 5km out of Lisbon (take the bus from Pr. Espanha; M: Palhavã). Beaches. Pool. Fun. 700$ per person and per tent.

FOOD

Lisbon has some of the least expensive restaurants of any European capital. A full dinner costs about 1500$. Restaurants in the **Baixa** are more elegant and more expensive, catering largely to tourists. The **Bairro Alto** feeds many locals. Restaurants there, as in the **Alfama,** are correspondingly small, dark, and cheap. Savor seafood specialties such as *bacalhau cozido com grão* (cod with chick-peas and boiled potatoes), a local classic. Other culinary delights include *amêijoas à bulhão pato* (a steamed clam dish), and *creme de mariscos* (seafood chowder with tomatoes).

Bus 40 runs to **Mercado Ribeira,** a market complex on Av. 24 de Julho outside the Cais do Sodré (open Mon.-Sat. until 2pm). There's a larger market in Cascais on Wednesday morning (5min. from the train station). A jumbo supermarket, **Pão de Açucar,** is in the Amoreiras Shopping Center de Lisboa, Av. Duarte Pacheco.

Malmequer Bemmequer, R. de São Miguel, 23-25 (tel. 87 65 35). The name means "He loves me, loves me not." Friendly owner trained on cruise ships serves delicious, reasonably priced seafood dishes. Entrees 800-1300$. Open noon-3:30pm and 7-11pm.

Restaurante Bonjardim, Trav. de Santo Antão, 12 (tel. 342 74 24), off Pr. Restauradores. Delicious roast chickens (995$) and *chouriço asado na brasa* (roast sausage, 290$). Entrees 800-1600$. Open noon-3pm and 6:30-10:30pm.

Lua de Mel, R. Prata, 242-248 (tel. 87 91 51), corner with R. Santa Justa. Ogle the beautiful cakes in the window, and make a bee-line for the fresh, honey-laden pastries (85$). Sandwiches 200-400$. Fruit salads and ice cream sundaes 450$. A/C. Open Tues.-Sat. 7am-midnight.

Celeiro, Rua 1 de Dezembro, 65, right off the Rossio. This "macrobiotic" restaurant located beneath a health food supermarket will satisfy the strictest herbivore. Cafeteria-style (self-serve). Entrees 100-570$. Open Mon.-Fri. 9am-7pm.

Porto de Abrigo, R. Remolares, 16-18 (tel. 346 08 73), near Estação Cais do Sodré. One of the most popular riverside eateries. *Pato com arroz* (duck with rice and olives, 1190$). Entrees 950-1480$. Open Mon.-Sat. noon-3pm and 7-10pm.

Mestre André, Calçadinha de Sto. Estevão, 6 (tel. 87 14 87), off R. Remédios. Eclectic adornment of old movie posters and stills. Brazilian background music. Outdoor seating. Their *morcela frita,* an ugly but savory little blood sausage (400$), and *truta grelhada* (grilled trout, 800$) are favorites among regulars. Entrees 700-1200$. Open Mon.-Sat. noon-3pm and 7-10:30pm.

Cervejaria da Trindade, R. Nova Trindade, 20c-d (tel. 32 35 06). Make a left coming off R. Misericórdia. Regal imagery on shiny *azulejos* in an elegant but noisy atmosphere. The *espetada de tambroil com gambas* (fish and prawn kebab, 1300$) is particularly yummy. Grilled specialties and fish entrees 950-1600$. Open Mon.-Sat. 9am-11:30pm.

PORTUGAL

SIGHTS

Lisbon's 18th-century heart today shows the city's modern and sophisticated side. The center of activity is the **Rossio**; the **Teatro Nacional** marks the former site of the Palace of the Inquisition. After the 1755 earthquake, Marquês do Pombal commissioned the **Baixa,** the grid of streets south of the Rossio, to facilitate communication between the town center and the river. **Rua Augusta,** a pedestrian zone, is lined with shops selling furs, shoes, and perfume, and leads past a triumphal arch to **Praça do Comércio.**

North of the Rossio, **Praça dos Restauradores** commemorates the 1640 "restoration" of Portugal's independence from Spain with an obelisk and a bronze sculpture of the Spirit of Independence. Here begins **Avenida da Liberdade,** the city's most imposing boulevard. Boxed in a fanciful Gothic tower by Eiffel, the **Acensor de Santa Justa** connects the Baixa to the Chiado (140$ each way). On R. da Misericórdia is the **Igreja de São Roque,** noted for its **Capela de São João Baptista** (fourth from the left), a chapel ablaze with precious gems and metals that caused a stir upon its installation in 1747. Three different ships delivered the chapel to Lisbon after it was built in Rome from agate, lapis lazuli, alabaster, and *verde antica*.

A ½hr. walk down Av. Infante Santo and a 10min. jaunt to the left of Calçada da Pampulha is the **Museu Nacional de Arte Antiga,** home to a representative collection of European paintings ranging from Gothic primitives to 18th-century French masterpieces (open Tues.-Sat. 10am-1pm and 2-5pm; 250$, students free). Buses 40 and 60 stop to the right as you leave the museum and head back to the Baixa.

Originally a Visgoth settlement and later home to the Moorish aristocracy, the **Alfama** became the noisy, popular section of town it is today when the Christians recaptured the city. Off **Rua de São Pedro,** the main fish market street, **Igreja de São Miguel** (1812) is arguably Lisbon's finest church with a Rococo gilt altar screen and a ceiling crafted of Brazilian jacaranda wood. (Ask the sacristan to turn on the lights.) Between the Alfama and the Baixa is the quarter known as the **Mouraria** (Moorish quarter), established after Dom Alfonso Henriques and the Crusaders expelled the Moors in 1147. The restored, luxurious **Castelo de São Jorge** looks down at Lisbon from its hill a few blocks up from the cathedral. Built in the 5th century by the Visigoths, this castle was the principal palace of the royal family from the 14th to the 16th centuries. High up on its windswept esplanade shaded by olive trees, the castle gardens are home to odd-looking albino peafowl. (Open 9am-9pm, Oct.-March 9am-7pm. Free.)

Belém lies about 6km west of Praça do Comércio. Take tram 15 or 17 from Pr. do Comércio (20min., 140$) or the train from Estação Cais do Sodré (10min., 100$). From the train station, cross the street to get into town. Rising from the banks of the Tagus behind a sculpted garden, **Mosteiro dos Jerónimos** stands as Portugal's most refined celebration of the Age of Discovery (open Tues.-Sun. 10am-5pm, Oct.-May 10am-1pm and 2:30-5pm; 400$, Oct.-May 250$, students free).

The **Torre de Belém,** built to protect the seaward entrance of the Portuguese capital, rises from the Tagus's north bank. It's a 20min. walk along the railroad tracks from the monastery. The six-cornered turrets, copied from originals in India, and the Venetian balconies and windows typify the crafty eclecticism of Manueline architects. (Open Tues.-Sun. 10am-1pm and 2:30-5pm. 400$, Oct.-May 250$; students and seniors free.)

ENTERTAINMENT

The weekly paper *Sete,* available from kiosks in the Rossio (215$), publishes listings of concerts, movies, plays, exhibits, and bullfights. More comprehensive, though less hip, *Cultura Agenda* is available free from kiosks in the Rossio and the tourist office. **Fado** is a melancholy wailing expression of *saudade,* an enigmatic Portuguese emotion of nostalgic yearning. The sensational tales of lost loves and faded glory performed by *fadistas* are Portugal's equivalent of blues. The Bairro Alto has many *fado* joints off **R. Misericordia,** particularly on sidestreets radiating from the Museu de São Roque. Feel the knife twisting in your heart at **Sr. Vinho,** R. Meio a

PORTUGAL

Lapa, 18 (tel. 347 26 81), in nearby Madregoa. (Min. food and drink charge 2500$. Open 8:30pm-2am.)

Those in search of rowdier fun shouldn't be deceived by the after-dinner lull; nothing starts up until after midnight. Nightlife clusters around **Rua Diário das Notícias** in the Bairro Alto. June is the month of *feiras populares*, outdoor night fairs with plenty of eating, drinking, and dancing to live music. There's a lively one called "Oreal" at **Campo das Cebolas**, near the waterfront in the Alfama (open June Mon.-Fri. 10pm-1am, Sat.-Sun. 10pm-3am).

Boris, Travessa Agua da Flor, 20. A small but trendy place where the drunken singing carries into the street. Open 9pm-2am.

Cena de Copos, R. da Barroca, 105. Postmodern decor, techno-pop music, and the requisite smoky air. Enigmatic cubist painting on the wall makes more sense as the night progresses. Jammed after midnight. A "tourist menu" (750$) is good for 3 drinks. Open 10pm-2am.

Artis, R. do Diário das Notícias, 95 (tel. 342 47 95). Sip beer with a cosmopolitan crowd under the sultry red lights. Eclectic mix of posters and musical instruments adorn the walls. Open 8:30pm-2:30am.

La Folie Discoteca, R. Diario das Noticias, 122-4. Crazy fun with a bar, A/C, and the latest international music. 900$ cover charge includes two beers or one mixed drink. Open Tues.-Sun. 10pm-4am.

Do Outro Lado, R. da Barroca, 129B. Easy-going atmosphere with the latest dance music. A young, trendy crowd. Expensive bar but no cover charge. Ring the bell. Open 10pm-3am.

Memorial, R. Gustavo de Matos Sequeira, 42A (tel. 396 88 91), 1 bl. south of R. Escola Politécnica in the Bairro Alto. A hip gay and lesbian disco-bar. The lights and Europop blast from 10pm, but the fun starts after midnight. The 1000$ cover charge includes two beers or one mixed drink. Open 10:30pm-4am.

■ SINTRA, ESTORIL, AND CASCAIS

After Lord Byron sang its praises in the epic poem *Childe Harold*, **Sintra** became a must for 19th-century English aristocrats on the Grand Tour. While the town's popularity has made it a bit self-conscious, Sintra retains the air of a fairy-tale city and makes a delightful daytrip from Lisbon. Between the train station and the town center stands a storybook village hall; the conical chimneys of the **Paço Real** (Palácio Nacional) loom behind. Once the summer residence of Moorish sultans and harems, the palace and its complex gardens were torn down during the Reconquista and replaced with a vaguely Moorish, mostly Gothic and Manueline building. Inside is the Sala dos Cisnes, a banquet hall where 27 swans in different positions decorate the ceiling. (Open Thurs.-Tues. 10am-12:30pm and 2-4:30pm. Tickets sold 10am-4:30pm. 400$, Oct.-May 200$, Sun. free.) Hike or taxi up the 3km of winding access road to the **Palácio da Pena,** a massive palace built over an old Hieronymite monastery. The palace was built in the 1840s by Prince Ferdinand, the queen's German consort. Nostalgic for his country, the prince commissioned on obscure German architect to design this folly. The utterly fantastic result would do loony Ludwig proud: a Bavarian castle embellished with Arab minarets, Gothic turrets, and a Renaissance dome. (Open Tues.-Sun. 10am-5pm, none admitted after 4:30pm. 400$, Oct.-May 200$; students with ID and seniors free.) Sintra's **tourist office** (tel. 923 11 57, fax 923 51 76) is at Pr. República, in the same building as the regional museum. Sintra, 30km northwest of Lisbon, is accessible by train from the Rossio station (every 16min., 45min., 165$).

The reputation of **Estoril** and **Cascais,** a half-hour west of Lisbon, as playgrounds for the rich and famous, shouldn't deter you from spending a day at the beach. Although they bristle with their share of luxury hotels and restaurants, at least they're relaxed and informal. **Trains** to Estoril leave from the Caís do Sodré station in Lisbon (40min., 300$). **Buses** run between Sintra and Estoril (40min., 300$). Rodoviária **buses** run from Sintra to Cascais, departing from Av. Dr. Miguel Bombarda, across the street from the train station in Sintra (1hr., 300$). The Estoril **tourist office,** Arcadas do Parque (tel. 468 01 13), across from the train station and to the left, offers detailed maps and schedules of events in the area (open Mon.-Sat. 9am-8pm, Sun. 10am-6pm; Oct. 15-June 16 Mon.-Sat. 9am-7pm, Sun. 10am-6pm). Its pastel yellow counterpart in Cascais is on R. Visconde da Luz (tel. 486 82 04), at Av. Combatentes da Grande Guerra (open Mon.-Sat. 9am-8pm, Sun. 10am-6pm; Oct.15-June 16 Mon.-Sat. 9am-7pm, Sun. 10am-6pm). In Estoril, you can find reasonably priced rooms at **Pensão Marylus,** R. Maestro Lacerda, 13 (tel. 468 27 40). From the train station, walk uphill on Av. Marginal, make a left onto Av. Bombeiros Voluntários and walk 3 bl. until R. Maestro Lacerda. (Singles 2500$. Doubles 6000$. Oct.-May 2000$, 4000$. Breakfast included.) For rooms in Cascais, try **Residencial Palma,** Av. Valbam, 15 (tel. 483 77 97, fax 483 79 22; singles and doubles 8000$). For a taste of the Mediterranean, dine at **Joshua's Shoarma Grill,** R. Visconde da Luz, 19 (tel. 484 30 64), half a block uphill from the tourist office (open Mon.-Fri. noon-4pm and 6pm-2am, Sat.-Sun. 1pm-2am).

CENTRAL PORTUGAL

The meadowed **Ribatejo** is a fertile region that fills most of the basin of the Tagus and its main tributary, the Zêzere. Although farmed intensely—yielding vegetables, olives, and citrus fruits—the area is best known in Portugal as a pastureland for Arabian horses and great black bulls. Stretching south and east of the Tagus, the less fortunate **Alentejo** region covers almost one-third of the Portuguese land mass. With a population of slightly over half a million it remains the least populous region. The requisite olive trees and whitewashed hamlets dot the rolling hills.

■■■ TOMAR

For centuries the mysterious Knights Templar schemed and plotted from Tomar, a small town straddling the Rio Nabão. Most of Tomar's monuments reflect its former status as the den of that secretive religious order. The **Convento de Cristo** is a stately fortress established in 1320 as a refuge for the disbanded Knights. Modeled after the Holy Sepulchre in Jerusalem, the **Templo dos Templares** contains an ornate octagonal canopy that protects the high altar. The Knights supposedly attended Mass on horseback, each under one of the arches. (Temple under renovation in 1994.) **Claustro dos Felipes** is considered one of Europe's masterpieces of Renaissance architecture; its graceful spiral staircases, Tuscan columns and Ionic pillars frame a large fountain. Tomar's **Museu Luso-Hebraíco,** in the 15th-century Sinagoga do Arco at R. Dr. Joaquim Jaquinto (a.k.a. R. da Judiaría), 73, is Portugal's only significant reminder of what was once a great European Jewish community. After the expulsion of the Jews, the building served as a prison, a hayloft, and a grocery warehouse until its classification as a national monument in 1921. (Open Thurs.-Tues. 9:30am-12:30pm and 2-6pm. At other times, ring at #104. Free.)

Practical Information, Accommodations, and Food The Rio **Nabão** divides Tomar. The train and bus stations as well as most accommodations and sights lie on the west bank. From Tomar's train or bus station, turn right at the door, left on R. Torres Pinheiro, walk until you reach Av. do Cândido Madureira. Tomar's **tourist office** (tel. (049) 32 34 27), two blocks to the right, offers perhaps the most comprehensive map on the Portuguese mainland (open Mon.-Fri. 9:30am-12:30pm and 2-6pm, Sat.-Sun. 10am-1pm and 3-6pm; Oct.-May Mon.-Fri. 9:30am-12:30pm and 2-6pm, Sat.-Sun. 10am-1pm). The **train station,** on Av. Combatentes da Grande Guerra (tel. (049) 31 28 15), on the southern edge of town, serves Lisbon (2hr., 800$), Coimbra (2hr., 750$), Porto (4½hr., 1235$), and Faro (via Lisbon, 9hr., 1925$). Tomar is the northern terminus of a minor line, so most destinations require a transfer at Entrocamento; you can buy the ticket for both legs here. **Buses** leave from beside the train station for Lisbon (2hr., 1050$), Coimbra (2hr., 1000$), Porto (4hr., 1300$), and Lagos (8hr., 2200$).

The most inexpensive rooms in town are in the **Pensão Tomarense,** R. Torres Pinheiro, 15 (tel. (049) 31 29 48), a block from Nuno Alvares. (Singles 1900$, with shower 2400$. Doubles with bath 3000$.) Another bargain is the **Pensão Nuno Alvares,** Av. Nuno Alvares, 3 (tel. (049) 31 28 73), a block to the right of the bus and train stations. (Singles 1800$. Doubles 3000$, one with bath 4000$.) Dine on a riverside patio with a handsome view of the castle in the **Restaurante A Bela Vista,** Fonte Choupo, 6, across Ponte Velha on your left. (Entrees 800-1700$. Open Wed.-Mon. noon-3pm and 7-9:30pm.) Tomar is the picnic capital of Portugal. The **market** (Mon.-Sat. 8am-2pm, Fri. until 5pm), on the corner of Av. Norton de Matos and R. Santa Iria on the other side of the river, provides all the fixings. A section of the lush Parque Mouchão is set aside just for picnickers.

■■■ SANTARÉM

Capital of the Ribatejo province and its major town, Santarém sits on a rocky mound overlooking the Rio Tejo. This flourishing medieval center boasted 15 convents, making it the capital of Portugal's Gothic style, and is now the primary market for produce in this fertile region. The core of the town is formed by the densely packed streets between **Praça Sá da Bandeira** and the park **Portas do Sol,** below which flows the Río Tejo. **Rua Capelo Ivêns** begins at the *praça.* The austere façade of the **Igreja do Seminário dos Jesuitas** is covered with stone friezes that resemble ropes and Latin mottos from the Bible (usually open 9am-5pm). The 12th-century **Igreja de Marvila** has a 16th-century Manueline portal and a 17th-century *azulejo* interior (closed for restoration in 1994). The early Gothic severity of nearby **Igreja da Graça** contrasts with Marvila's exuberance. In the chapel to the right of the chancel is the tomb of Pedro Alvares Cabral, the explorer who discovered Brazil and one of the few *conquistadores* who stayed alive long enough to be buried in his homeland. Off R. São Martinho stands the medieval **Torre das Cabaças** (Tower of the Gourds), so-called because of the eight earthen bowls installed in the 16th century to amplify the bell's ring. The main exhibit in the **Museu Arqueológico de São João do Alporão,** across the street, is what little of Dom Duarte de Meneses his comrades could salvage from the battlefield: one tooth (open Mon.-Sat. 10am-12:30pm and 2-6pm, Oct.-May Mon.-Sat. 9am-12:30pm and 2-5:30pm; free). Av. 5 de Outubro ends at the **Portas Do Sol,** a lush paradise of gardens and fountains surrounded by old Moorish walls. Climb up the remaining steps of the citadel for an awe-inspiring view of the winding Tagus River and the agricultural fields of the Ribatejo plain.

Practical Information, Accommodations, and Food The **train station,** 2km outside town, with trains to Lisbon (1hr., 500$) and Tomar (1hr., 360$), can be reached by bus (150$) from the **bus station,** which also services Lisbon (1½hr., 700$). Walk through the park, cross busy Av. Marquês Sá da Bandeira, turn right and then left, take R. Pedro Canavarro uphill, and make a right on R. Capelo Ivêns to get to the **tourist office,** R. Capelo Ivêns, 63 (tel. (043) 39 15 12; open Mon.-Fri. 9:30am-12:30pm and 2-6pm, Sat.-Sun. 9:30am-12:30pm and 2-5pm).

Be warned that during the **Ribatejo Fair** (10 days starting the first Friday in June) prices for rooms increase 10-40%. The **Pensão do José,** (a.k.a. **Pensão da Dona Arminda**), Trav. Froes, 14 and 18 (tel. (043) 230 88), under the sign that reads "rooms," has clean, cozy singles for 1500$ and doubles for 3000-3500$. Turn left exiting the bus station, bear right at the end of the block onto R. Mercado, then left onto R. Herculano for **Residencial Beirante,** R. Alexandre Herculano, 5 (tel. (043) 255 47). All rooms come with TV, phone, sparkling bathroom, and an invaluable wall fan. (Singles 3750$. Doubles with double bed 5000$, with two beds 6000$. Triples 7000$. Breakfast included.)

Santarém has a **sweets fair** (last Wed. to Sun. in April) featuring calories from all over Portugal. Put some meat on those spindly bones at the **Festival e Seminário Nacional de Gastronomia** (the last ten days of Oct.), in which each region of Portugal has a day to prepare a typical feast and entertainment. For the rest of the year, you'll have to settle for groceries from the **Minipreço Supermarket,** R. Pedro Canavarro, 31, a street leading from the bus station (open Mon.-Sat. 9am-8pm). Always bustling with locals, **Restaurante Pigalle,** R. Capelo Ivêns, 15, specializes in chicken. (½ bird with fries and salad, 700$. Entrees are 100$ less at the bar than at a table. Open Mon.-Sat. 8am-midnight.) Delicious pastries and croissants make **Pastelaria Venezia, R.** Capelo Ivêns, 99, an excellent stop for a snack or light lunch (open Mon.-Sat. 8am-7pm).

■■■ FIGUEIRA DA FOZ

At the mouth of the Mondego, half-way between Lisboa and Porto, and only an hour or so from Coimbra, Figueira is one of the biggest "party" towns in Portugal, where pleasure-seekers celebrate sunny days and raucous nights. Figueira's festive mode shifts from standard high gear to warp speed during the **Festa de São João** (June 19-24). At 5am, a huge rowdy procession heads for nearby Buarcos, where all involved take a so-called *banho santo* (holy bath) in this town's large beach. The **casino** complex on R. Bernardo Lopes also contains a **nightclub** (cover 300$), a **cinema** (tix 350$), and an **arcade.** To gamble you must be over 18 and show proper ID. There's also a show, usually live music, at night. (Open 3pm-3am.)

Trains connect Figueira da Foz with Coimbra (40min., 300$) and Lisbon (3hr., 1200$). Keeping the river to the left, drag your pack for 25min. along Av. Saraiva de Carvalho, which becomes R. 5 de Outubro at the fountain and then curves into Av. 25 de Abril. On this street, Aparthotel Atlântico marks the location of the **tourist office** (tel. (033) 226 10; open 9am-midnight, Oct.-May Mon.-Fri. 9am-12:30pm and 2-5:30pm). Four blocks inland and parallel to the avenue, **Rua Bernardo Lopes** harbors semi-affordable *pensões* and restaurants. **Pensão Central,** R. Bernardo Lopes, 36 (tel. (033) 223 08), next to Supermarket Ovo, certainly is central to all the action—it's down the street from the casino. (Singles 3000$. Doubles 5000$. Triples 6000$. Breakfast included.) On one of the perpendicular streets, **Pensão Residencial Rio-Mar,** R. Dr. António Dinis, 90 (tel. (033) 230 53), lets comfortable but dark doubles (3000-6000, breakfast included). **Parque Municipal de Campismo** (tel. (033) 327 42 or 231 16) beckons with an Olympic-size pool and tennis courts. From the station, take a taxi (500$), or, with the beach to your left, walk up Av. 25 de Abril and turn right at the roundabout on R. Alexándre Herculano. Turn left at Parque Santa Catarina going up R. Joaquim Sotto-Mayor past Palácio Sotto-Mayor. (Reception open 8am-8pm, Oct.-May 8am-7pm. Silence 11pm-7am. June-Sept. each party must have a minimum of 2 people. 350$ per person, 250$ per tent, 350$ per car. Showers 110$.)

Supermercado Ovo, on the corner of R. A. Dinís and R. B. Lopes, stocks imported foods aimed at tourists (yes, you) and is thus a bit pricey (open Mon.-Fri. 9am-1pm and 3-7pm). Instead, treat yourself to a sit–down meal (350-900$) at Restaurante Rancho, R. Miguel Bombardo, 40-44, two blocks from the tourist office but packed with locals at lunchtime (open Mon.-Sat. 8am-10pm).

■■■ EVORA

One of the only major towns to relieve the empty and sparsely populated Alentejo, Evora rises like a megalith from the rolling plain of olive trees. Portugal's showpiece of medieval architecture, the town also contains a Roman Temple to Diana, Moorish arches, and a 16th-century university. Elegant marble-floored shops flash their wares in the windows, university students chat on the streets, and a steady trickle of tourists visits from Lisbon, about 140km to the west.

ORIENTATION AND PRACTICAL INFORMATION

Evora is easily accessible from Lisbon; several trains per day ply the routes from the capital and Faro. **Praça do Giraldo** is Evora's main square. In the old town on the hill, dozens of winding sidestreets lead in and out of the *praça*, home to most of the monuments and lodgings.

Tourist Office: Pr. Giraldo, 73 (tel. 226 71). Helpful English-, French- and German-speaking staff compensates for the illegible map by calling around until you have a room. Open Mon.-Fri. 9am-7pm, Sat.-Sun. 9am-12:30pm and 2-5:30pm; Oct.-May Mon.-Fri. 9am-12:30pm and 2-6pm, Sat.-Sun. 9am-12:30pm and 2-5:30pm.

Currency Exchange: 24hr. exchange machine outside tourist office.

Post Office: R. Olivença (tel. 233 11), 2 bl. north of Pr. Giraldo. Walk up R. João de Deus, pass under the aqueduct and turn right. Open for mail, Poste Restante, telephones, and telegrams Mon.-Fri. 8:30am-6:30pm. **Postal Code:** 7000.

Telephones: at the post office. **City Code:** 066.

Trains: (tel. 221 25), 1½km from town center. To Lisbon (3hr., 770$) and Faro (6hr., 1380$).

Buses: R. República (tel. 221 21), opposite Igreja de São Francisco. To Lisbon (3hr., 1050$), Faro (5hr., 1380$), and Porto (7hr., 2100$). **Luggage Storage** in the basement (90$ per day).

Laundromat: Lavévora, Largo D'Alvaro Velho, 6 (tel. 238 83), off R. Miguel Bombardo. 350$ per kg. Open Mon.-Fri. 9am-1pm and 3-7pm.

Hospital: R. Velasco (tel. 250 01, 221 32, or 221 33), close to the city wall and intersection with R. D. Augusto Eduardo Nunes.

Emergency: tel. 115. **Police,** R. Francisco Soares Lusitánia (tel. 220 22), near the Temple of Diana.

ACCOMMODATIONS AND CAMPING

Most *pensões* reside around the **Praça do Giraldo.** *Quartos* (rooms in private houses) cost 2500-5000$ and are often reasonably pleasant alternatives to crowded *pensões* in the summer. Ask the tourist office to call around to find you a room.

Pensão Os Manueis, R. Raimundo, 35 (tel. 228 61), around the corner from the tourist office. The main building with rooms and baths is clean and sunny. The annex across the back street is less so, but rooms are still spacious. Singles 3000-3500$, with bath 4000-4500$. Doubles 3500-4000$, with bath 5500-6000$.

Residencial Diana, R. Diogo Cão, 2 (tel. 220 08, fax 74 31 01). Follow R. 5 de Outubro from Pr. Giraldo toward the cathedral; take the third right. Combines *fin-de-siècle* charm with modern amenities. Lofty ceilings and pristine baths. *Salão de chá* (tearoom) nearby. Singles 6500$. Doubles 8000$. Oct.-May: 5750$, 6800$.

Pensão Giraldo, R. Mercadores, 27 (tel. 258 33), 2 blocks from tourist office. Spacious, tidy rooms just off the *praça*. Singles 2400$, with shower 3500$. Doubles 3500$, with shower 4800$. Depending on demand, prices rise in summer.

Camping Orbitur (tel. 251 90), a 2-star park on Estrada das Alcáçovas, which branches off the bottom of R. Raimundo. Only 1 bus to town daily; it's a 40min. walk. Laundry. Small market. Reception open 8am-10pm. 480$ per person, 400$ per tent, 410$ per car. Showers 50$.

FOOD

A **public market** livens up the small square in front of Igreja de São Francisco and the public gardens. Budget restaurants cook in and around the **Praça do Giraldo.** Food is salty in Evora—bring your diuretics. Inhale the thick aroma of roasting fowl as you pass by the monstrous grill inside the cave site of **Café-Restaurante A Gruta,** Av. General Humberto Delgado, 2, outside the city wall on the way to Pr. de Touros. Follow R. República toward the train station and turn right at the end of the park. (½-chicken 500$. Open Sun.-Fri. 11am-3pm and 5-10pm.) **Restaurante A Choupana,** R. Mercadores, 16-20, off Pr. Giraldo, serves elegantly prepared Portuguese nouvelle cuisine. Avoid the astronomical cover charge—up to 800$—by rejecting the bread and small salad. (*Trutas do Minho*, trout, 680$. Entrees mostly 900-1300$. ½-portions 600$. Open 10am-2pm and 7-10pm.)

SIGHTS AND ENTERTAINMENT

Off the east side of the *praça,* Rua 5 de Outubro leads to the colossal 12th-century **sé.** The **Museu de Arte Sacra,** in a gallery above the nave, houses the cathedral's treasury and astonishing 13th-century ivory *Virgem do paraíso.* (Cloister and museum open Tues.-Sun. 9am-noon and 2-5pm. *Sé* free, cloister and museum 200$.) Next door, the **Museu d'Evora** houses Roman artifacts unearthed nearby, and 16th- and 17th-century European paintings (open Tues.-Sun. 10am-12:30pm and 2-5pm, 200$). Across from the museum, Evora's most famous monument, the 2nd-century **Templo de Diana,** stands outlined against the sky. The temple of the goddess of the hunt, the moon, and purity was fittingly used as a slaughterhouse for centuries. The highlight of a visit to Evora is the **Igreja Real de São Francisco.** Its austere bulk hoards the gleefully perverse **Capela de Ossos** (Chapel of Bones). Three tireless Franciscan monks ransacked assorted local cemeteries for the remains of 4000 people to construct it. Enormous femurs and baby tibias neatly panel every inch of wall space, while rows of skulls line the capitals and ceiling vaults. The decayed and shriveled corpses of an adult and an infant dangle on one wall. (Church and chapel open Mon.-Sat. 8:30am-1pm and 2:30-6pm, Sun. 10-11:30am and 2:30-6pm. To chapel 50$; 50$ to take pictures.)

Although most of Evora tucks itself in with the sun, **Xeque-Mate,** R. Valdevinos, 21 (second right off R. 5 de Outubro from the *praça),* and **Discoteca Slide,** R. Serpa Pinto, 135, keep the music blaring until 2am. Only couples and single women need apply. Evora's most popular café-bar hangout is **Portugal,** R. João de Deus, 55. Evora's festival, the **Feira de São João** (last week of June) celebrates the arrival of summer with a full-fledged, Portuguese-style country fair.

ALGARVE

This southern coast has sold its soul to commercial capitalism. After the Moors were driven from Portugal, the Algarve remained a quiet fishing backwater; now increasing tourism and overdevelopment are destroying its trademark villages. Portuguese often come in September, while in July and August foreigners predominate, lured by the region's beaches and sunny, dry weather. Ocean winds cool the mornings, while clear skies bless the evenings.

Hotels and *pensões* usually fill during the peak summer months; try the reasonably priced *quartos* (private rooms). Ask at tourist offices or bars, keep your eyes peeled for signs, or take your chances with the room-pushers who accost incoming travelers at bus and train stations. Local delicacies include *caldeirada* (a chowder of fish and shellfish), *cataplana* (ham, clams, and sausage), and *lulas* (squid, often cooked in its own ink). To gulp it down, try *amenênoda amarga* (almond liqueur) or *medronho* ("firewater" made from miniature strawberries of arbutus trees). Tourist offices sell *The Algarve News* (105$). It runs articles on trendy clubs, local festivals, special events, and topless beaches.

Faro, the Algarve's capital, is at once a transportation hub and a provincial Portuguese city. Low-tech Portuguese trains wheeze into town from Lisbon (6 per day, 7hr., 1550$). Aside from the mobbed resorts (like **Albufeira**), plenty of villages welcome budget travelers (try Salema and Burgau). Other inexpensive spots are **Sagres** (ravishing isolated beaches and sheer cliffs) and the region between **Olhão** and the Spanish border (**Tavira,** for example). Reaching more remote beaches is a snap, as EVA has extensive bus services with convenient schedules and low fares. The train costs less than the bus but only connects major coastal cities, and in some towns the station is a hike from the center.

■■■ LAGOS

For many, many moons, swarms of Europeans have sojourned here to worship the almighty Sun. Most visitors don't care that Lagos was a major Moorish port, the official harbor for the fleet of Prince Henry the Navigator and a center of the African slave trade. The port and old town preserve a measure of local color; along the narrow pedestrian streets, cosmopolitan bars burble to British pop or sway to jazz. To the west, rock tunnels through the sheer cliffs connect secluded sandy coves, while 4km of uninterrupted beach lounges to the east.

ORIENTATION AND PRACTICAL INFORMATION

Running the length of the river, **Avenida dos Descobrimentos** carries traffic in and out of the city. **Rua das Portas de Portugal** marks the gateway leading into **Praça Gil Eanes** and the town's glitzy tourist center. Most restaurants, accommodations, and services hover about the *praça* and **Rua 25 de Abril;** they are usually mobbed.

Tourist Office: Largo Marquês de Pombal (tel. 76 30 31). Take the sidestreet R. Lina Lectão (off Pr. Gil Eanes) which leads to the Largo. Open 9:30am-12:30pm and 2-7pm; July-Sept. open through lunch hours too.

Budget Travel: Club Algarve, R. Marreiros Neto, 25 (tel. 76 23 37), uphill from the tourist office. English spoken. Open Mon.-Fri. 9am-12:30pm and 2:30-6:30pm.

Post Office: R. Portas de Portugal (tel. 76 31 11), between Pr. Gil Eanes and Av. Descobrimentos. Open Mon.-Fri. 9am-6pm; for Poste Restante 9am-noon. **Postal Code:** 8600.

Telephones: Across from the post office. Open 8:30am-6pm. **City code:** 082.

Trains: tel. 76 29 87. On the eastern edge of town, across the river from the bus station. To Lisbon (6½hr., 1700$) and Evora (4½hr., 1380$).

Buses: EVA (tel. 76 29 44), on the eastern edge of town, off. Av. Descobrimentos. To Lisbon (8 per day, 5hr., 1900$) and Faro (2½hr., 850$).

Laundromat: Lavandaria Luso-Britânica, R. Urbaniz Lapinha (tel. 76 02 50), a small street near Pr. João de Deus. Wash and dry 1300$ per 4kg load. Open Mon.-Fri. 9am-1pm and 3-7pm, Sat. 9am-1pm.

Medical Assistance: Hospital, R. Castelo dos Governadores (tel. 76 30 34), next to Igreja Santa María.

Emergencies: Police: General Alberto Silva (tel. 76 29 30), near Pr. da República. **Ambulance:** tel. 76 01 15.

ACCOMMODATIONS, CAMPING, AND FOOD

Rooms in *casa particulares* (private homes) go for 1500-3500$. Be sure to verify that there's hot water and that the location is close to downtown.

Pousada de Juventude de Lagos (HI), R. Lançarote de Freitas, 50 (tel. 76 19 70). From tourist office, walk up R. Garrett, then hang a left onto R. Cândido dos Reis. The street is on your right. Central courtyard with tables encourages social butterflies. All-day reception, curfew 2am. Members only. Dorms 1600$, doubles 4000$. Oct. to mid-June 1300$, 3500$. Kitchen. Summer reservations recommended; make them through Movijoven, Av. Duque D'Avila, 137, Lisboa 1000.

Residencial Rubi Mar, R. Barroca, 70 (tel. 76 31 65), down R. 25 de Abril and then left on Trav. Señora da Graça. Centrally located and comfortable—a good deal if you get here in time to grab one of their eight rooms. Doubles 5000$, with bath 6000$. Quads 7000-8500$. Lower prices Oct.-July 10. Breakfast included.

Camping: Sites are crowded and expensive, resembling high-tech shantytowns. Jam-packed **Parque de Campismo do Imulagos** (tel. 76 00 31) is annoyingly far away but linked to Lagos by a free shuttle bus. Reception open 8am-10pm. 850$ per person, 470$ per tent. Nearer town on the beautiful Praia Dona Ana is **Camping da Trinidade** (tel. 76 38 92). 347$ per person, 367$ per tent. Free showers.

Mullins, R. Cândido dos Reis, 86, is a Lagos hot spot. Servers dance to the tables with huge portions of spicy food, and the crowd quivers with a carnal pulse.

(Chicken *piri-piri* smothered in hot sauce 1125$. Joe free. Open noon-2am.) The owner of **Santa Fe Restaurante,** R. Silva Lopes, 29, a Bostonian blow-in, promises "nothing over 1000$" on the menu of tacos, steaks, and burritos. Open noon-2am.

SIGHTS AND ENTERTAINMENT

Only the altar of **Igreja de Santo António,** off R. São Gonçalo, survived the 1755 earthquake; workers painstakingly rebuilt everything else exactly as before. Extraordinary gilded woodwork embellishes the interior. Adjoining the church, the **Museu Municipal** exhibits costumes and weapons (open Tues.-Sun. 9:30am-12:30pm and 2-5pm; 200$, students and seniors free, Sun. free). On either side of Pr. República, near Igreja de Santa María da Misericórdia, molder the evil remains of the 16th-century **Antigo Mercado de Escravos,** modern Europe's first slave market. Ancient weathered cliffs surround the **beaches.** Follow Av. dos Descobrimentos (the main waterside avenue) west until the sign for **Praia de Pinhão.** Follow this to the shore and continue on the paths until you find a cove to your liking. The rocks afford tremendous views of the inlets.

The streets of Lagos pick up late into the evening; the area between Pr. Gil Eanes and Pr. Luís de Camões bursts with cafés. **Café Gil Eanes,** Pr. Gil Eanes, 20, snares especially large crowds. Stop by **Shots in the Dark,** R. 1 de Maio, 16, parallel to and behind R. Cândido dos Reis, to hang out with the international backpacking crowd.

■■■ ALBUFEIRA

To this, the largest seaside resort in the Algarve, tourists come hell-bent on relaxation. More authentic culture can be found in the winding streets of the **old town,** which come together at **Praça da República,** another touristy area of restaurants and nightclubs. The last holdout of the Moors in southern Portugal, Albufeira tries desperately to preserve graceful Moorish architecture in the old quarters of town. Tiny minarets pierce the small Byzantine dome of **Santana;** an exquisite filigree doorway heralds the **São Sebastiao;** an ancient Gothic one fronts the **Misericórdia;** and a barrel-vaulted interior receives worshippers into the **Matiz.**

Albufeira's spectacular beach, **Praia dos Barcos,** is edged with rocky coves. Nearby beaches include Baleira, Oura, and Inatel. Local artisans sell their wares in the **tropical park** at Largo Engenheiro Duarte-Pacheco. Palm-leaf, wrought iron, and stone pieces are specialties of the region. The hottest clubs in town, **Disco Silvia's** and **Club Disco 7½,** face off on R. São Gonçalo de Lagos, near the east side of the beach. A dandy mingling spot is the **Fastnet Bar** on R. Cândido dos Reis (open 10am-3am). They net tourists with Tequila Sunrises, Blue Hawaiians, and unabandoned *karaoke*. Bands perform almost nightly on the outdoor stage in the *largo*. The tourist office sells **bullfight** tickets (May-Sept. Sat. 5:30pm, tickets 2500-3500$).

Practical Information, Accommodations, and Food The English-speaking **tourist office,** R. 5 de Outubro, 5 (tel. (089) 51 21 44), has maps, brochures, and a list of *quartos* for 3000-5000$ (open 9:30am-7pm). The **train station,** 6km inland, is accessible from the center by bus (every 30min., 140$). Albufeira is on the Lagos-Vila Real de Santo António line, with frequent departures to Faro (45min., 250$) and Lagos (1½hr., 380$). The **bus station** is at the entrance to town, up Av. Liberdade; walk downhill to reach the center. EVA buses head to Faro (1hr., 550$) and Lagos (1½hr., 750$).

Many accommodations are booked solid through travel agents from the last week in June through mid-September. **Pensão Silva,** R. Joaquim M. De Mendoça Gouveia (tel. (089) 51 26 69), off R. 5 de Outubro (if you're facing the ocean, it's a small street on the right), is in an older building with wood floors and chandeliers. (Singles 3500$. Doubles 4500$. Oct.-May 2000$, 3500$.) The modern **Pensão Albufeir-ense,** R. Liberdade, 18 (tel. (089) 51 20 79), 1 bl. from the *largo* through Trav. 5 de Outubro, has a garish interior, comfortable rooms, and a TV lounge. (Singles 3500$. Doubles 5000$. Triples 6500$. Oct.-May: 2000$; 3000$; 4000$.) **Camping**

Albufeira (tel. (089) 58 95 05, fax 58 93 93) is a few km outside town on the road to Ferreiras. More like a crowded shopping mall than a peaceful retreat, the place boasts four swimming pools, three restaurants, three tennis courts, a supermarket, and a hefty price tag. (700$ per person, per car, and per tent.) The new campground effectively prohibits unofficial camping on nearby beaches. Budget restaurants spill across the old fishing harbor east of the main beach. **Cantinho Algarvio,** Trav. Cais Herculano, serves up a nifty *salada de atum* (tuna) and other entrees for 1500-2500$ (open 9am-midnight).

■■■ TAVIRA

Perhaps the loveliest community in the Algarve, Tavira straddles the slow Gilão river. White houses and palm trees fringe the river banks, and festive Baroque churches speckle the hills above. The easy-going fishing port doesn't sweat it over the recent influx of backpackers. In mid-afternoon, fishers sit in small riverfront warehouses repairing nets alongside their beached craft. Local beaches, including **Pedras do Rei,** are nearby. To reach Tavira's excellent beach on **Ilha da Tavira,** an island 2km away, take the "Tavira-Quatro Aguas" bus from Pr. República. The ferry between Quatro Aguas and Ilha da Tavira runs between May and mid-Oct., daily until 8pm (10 per day, 5min., 100$ round-trip; keep ticket stub for the return).

Tavira is easily reached from Faro by **bus** (10 per day, 1hr., 390$) and **train** (every hr., 25min., 255$). The **tourist office** (tel. (089) 225 11) will move in 1995 from Pr. República to R. Galeria, 9, up the street from the bus station (open 9:30am-7pm, winter 9:30am-12:30pm and 2-5:30pm). Tavira has one of the choicest *pensões* in the Algarve, **Pensão Residencial Lagôas Bica,** R. Almirante Cândido dos Reis, 24 (tel. (089) 222 52), on the far side of the river. To reach the *pensão* from Pr. República, cross the bridge and continue straight down R. A. Cabreira; turn right and go down two blocks. (Singles 2200-2500$. Doubles 3500$, with bath 4500$. About 500$ less in winter.) If rooms are full, **Pensão Residencia Almirante** at 51-53 (tel. (089) 221 63), lies right across the street. (Singles 2000$. Doubles 3000$. Triples 4000$. Winter discount.) Seek and ye shall find equally reasonable cafés and restaurants on Pr. República and opposite the garden on R. José Pires Padinha. **Restaurante Bica,** underneath the Pensão Lagôas, serves excellent regional entrees (650-1000$) in a simple atmosphere (open 9:30am-midnight).

NORTHERN PORTUGAL

Although their landscapes and shared Celtic past invite comparison with neighboring Galicia, the **Douro** and **Minho** regions are more populated and faster developing. South of the Rio Minho lies **Braga,** a busy commercial city whose concentration of religious architecture has earned it the title of the Portuguese Rome. Braga's people are considered by some the most pious, by others the most fanatic, and by all the most conservative in Portugal. Buses travel between Braga and Porto (1½hr., 550$).

Farther inland rises a mountainous region composed of three provinces: **Trás-os-Montes, Beira Alta,** and **Beira Baixa.** A recent agricultural boom and the success of the wine trade have transformed the region into a quirky center of upward mobility, but the transportation system remains downright archaic.

■■■ COIMBRA

Portugal's former capital, Coimbra regained importance in the late 16th century as a center of the Inquisition. Centuries later, Salazar (Portugal's longtime Fascist dictator) attended its university. In spite of such unfortunate caveats, Coimbra exudes a self-assured elegance which belies urban woes of grime, filth, and noise. Presiding over the rest of the city, the old town contrasts medieval spires and monumental Fascist building blocks.

ORIENTATION AND PRACTICAL INFORMATION

Coimbra's center, a tangle of narrow streets, splits roughly into 2 areas. The lower town lies between the triangle formed by the river, **Largo da Portagem,** and **Praça 8 de Maio.** The upper town spreads over the adjoining hill, accessible through the **Arco de Almedina.**

Tourist Office: Largo Portagem (tel. 238 86), 2 blocks east of Coimbra-A off Av. Emídio Navarro. Open Mon.-Fri. 9am-7pm, Sat.-Sun. 9am-12:30pm and 2-5:30pm.

Currency Exchange: Hotel Astória, across from the tourist office. 800$ charge per transaction. Open 24hrs. Better rates and no charge for transactions less than 10,000$ at Montepio Geral, C. Estrela. Open Mon.-Fri. 8:30am-3pm.

Post Office: R. Olímpio Nicolau Rui Fernandes (tel. 243 56), just past the Manga rotunda. Central office is the pink powder puff on Av. Fernão de Magalhães. Both open Mon.-Fri. 8:30am-6:30pm, Sat. 9am-12:30pm. **Postal Code:** 3000.

Telephones: In post offices. **City Code:** 039.

Trains: Estação Coimbra-A, Largo das Ameias (tel. 349 98). From the front entrance follow Av. Emidio Navarro along the river all the way to the tourist office. **Estação Coimbra-B** (tel. 341 27). Trains from cities outside the region stop here; regional trains stop at both stations. Frequent shuttles connect the two (5min., 100$). To Porto (3hr., 800$), Lisbon (3hr., 1145$), Paris (22hr., 18,640$).

Buses: Av. Fernão de Magalhães (tel. 270 83). To reach the tourist office, turn right from the station and follow the avenue to Coimbra-A and then Largo da Portagem (15min.). To Lisbon (3hr., 1150$), Porto (6hr., 1000$), Evora (6hr., 1400$), Faro (12hr., 2400$).

Public Transportation: Buses and street cars. Single ticket bought on board 175$; book of 10 costs 515$. Special tourist passes also available. Ticket books and passes sold in kiosks at Largo da Portagem and Pr. República, among other places.

Hospital: Hospital da Universidade de Coimbra (tel. 40 04 00). Near the Cruz de Celas stop on lines 3, 7, 7T, and 29.

Emergency: tel. 115. **Police,** R. Olímpio Nicolau Rui Fernandes (tel. 220 22).

ACCOMMODATIONS AND CAMPING

Notoriously cheap and seedy *pensões* line **Rua da Sota** and the surrounding streets across from Coimbra-A. Anything decent starts at 3500$ for doubles.

Pousada de Juventude (HI), R. António Henriques Seco, 14 (tel. 229 55). From either Coimbra-A or Largo Portagem, take bus 7, 8, 29, or 46, then walk from Pr. República up R. Lourenço A. Azevedo, left of the Santa Cruz park, and take the 2nd right. Enormous sunlit rooms, TV room with VCR, bar, and gray parrot, Jacó. Reception open 9am-noon and 6pm-midnight. Bag drop-off all day. Lockout noon-6pm. Curfew midnight. 1300$. Doubles 3000-3500$. Breakfast included.

Pensão Rivoli, Pr. Comércio, 27 (tel. 255 50), in a mercifully quiet pedestrian plaza off busy R. Ferreira Borges. Neat, well-furnished rooms with white walls. Curfew 1am, but you can borrow a key. Singles 2000$. Doubles 4000$.

Residencial Internacional de Coimbra, Av. Emídio Navarro, 4 (tel. 255 03), in front of Coimbra-A. Fluorescent lighting and lumpy pillows may annoy, but rooms are decent-sized and pleasant. Choice of river view or full-sized bathroom. Singles and doubles 3200$. Doubles with bath 4500$. Winter 2500$, 4000$.

Camping: Municipal Campground (tel. 70 14 97), in a recreation complex ringed by noisy avenues. Take bus 5 "São José" or 1 "Estádio" from Largo Portagem outside the tourist office. The entrance is at the arch off Pr. 25 de Abril. Reception open 9am-10pm, Oct.-March 9am-6pm. 220$ per person, 165-320$ per tent, 280$ per car. 5% IVA not included. Showers free.

PORTUGAL

FOOD

Scout out **Rua Direita,** west off Pr. 8 de Maio, the sidestreets to the west of Pr. Comércio, and Largo da Portagem, and the university district around **Praça da República.** There are university *cantinas* (cafeterias) at several locations, including one in the old college courtyard. Students with ID or student-posers without (easy June-July when the university hosts foreign programs) can receive meals for a mere 250$. **Restaurante Esplendoroso,** R. da Sota, 29, across from Coimbra-A, up R. da Sota, promptly serves excellent Chinese food in a relaxing atmosphere (open noon-3pm and 7-11pm). Frequented by truck drivers and students, **Churrasqueria do Mondego,** R. Sargento Mór, 25, off R. Sota, 1 block west of the Largo da Portagem, allows you to view the slow torture of the *frango no churrasco* (barbecued half-chicken, 330$) over the flaming grill (open noon-3pm and 6-10:30pm). Espresso worshipping has replaced more conventional prayer at **Café Santa Cruz,** Pr. 8 de Maio, in what used to be part of the cathedral (open 7am-2am).

SIGHTS AND ENTERTAINMENT

To reach the old center of town, pass through the **Arco de Almedina,** the remnant of a Muslim town wall. Up a narrow stone stairway looms the hulking 12th-century Romanesque **Sé Velha** (Old Cathedral). R. Borges Carneiro (behind the cathedral) leads to the **Museu Machado de Castro,** famous for its Gothic and Renaissance sculptures, which are illuminated by creepy lighting in the underground passage-ways of the old Roman forum (open Tues.-Sun. 10am-5pm; 500$, seniors and Sun. mornings free).

Rua São Pedro, flanked by the grim façades of new university buildings, leads to the **Porta Férrea** (Iron Gate), a door to the old courtyard of the **universidade.** The staircase at the right leads up to the **Sala dos Capelos,** where portraits of Portugal's kings (6 of whom were born in Coimbra) hang below a beautifully painted 17th-century ceiling (open 9am-noon and 2-6pm). Past the Baroque clock tower are the **capela da universidade** (university chapel) and the 18th-century **biblioteca da universidade** (university library). The library shelters 143,000 books in 3 lofty halls painted with Chinese motifs. (Open 9am-12:30pm and 2-5pm. 250$, students free.)

The **Mosteiro de Santa Cruz** (Monastery of the Holy Cross) on Pr. 8 de Maio, at the far end of R. Ferreira Borges in the lower city, is a 12th-century monastery with all the usual trappings: a splendid barrel-vaulted **sacristía** (sacristy), an ornate **tumulos reais** (where the first two kings of Portugal lie buried), and a 16th-century **claustro** (open 9am-noon and 2-6pm; 150$). In the 14th century, Queen Isabel ordered the construction of the great **Convento de Santa Clara-a-Velha**—smack on top of a swamp. The convent sinks a little deeper each year; today it's more than half underground. (Open 9am-12:30pm and 2-5:30pm.)

To hear the most unrestrained and heartfelt *fado* singers, go after dinner to **Diligência Bar,** R. Nova, 30 (tel. 276 67), off R. Sofia (performances around 10pm-2am). You may find free-form *fado* in the wee hours at **Bar 1910,** above a gymnasium on R. Simões Castro (open until 4am, beers about 200$). The happening discos are **Via Latina,** R. Almeida Garret, 1, near the Santa Cruz garden, and **Scotch,** across the river near Convento Santa-Clara-a-Nova. Both places peak between midnight and 2am. (Occasional cover. Beers about 300$, mixed drinks 500$.)

■■■ PORTO (OPORTO)

As the proverb says, "Coimbra sings, Braga prays, Lisbon shows off, and Porto works." Magnificently situated on a dramatic gorge cut by the Rio Douro, 6km from the Atlantic, Portugal's second city is an attractive harbor town and the industrial and commercial center of the north. For the 1415 invasion of Ceuta, residents slaughtered all their cattle, gave the meat to the Portuguese fleet, and kept only the entrails for themselves. The ever-popular dish *tripas à moda do Porto* commemorates the culinary self-sacrifice. Porto's fame, however, springs from the taste of its

PORTUGAL

vinho. Developed by English merchants in the early 18th century, the port wine industry across the River Douro in Vila Nova de Gaia drives the city's economy.

ORIENTATION AND PRACTICAL INFORMATION

At the heart of Porto, **Avenida dos Aliados** forms a long rectangle bordered on the north by **Praça General Humberto Delgado** and on the south by **Praça da Liberdade.** The **Estação São Bento** lies smack in the middle of town, just off Pr. Liberdade. The **Ribeira,** or Esplanade, district is a few blocks to the south, directly across the bridge from **Vila Nova de Gaia,** the area of wine houses.

Tourist Office: R. Clube dos Fenianos, 25 (tel. 31 27 40), on the west side of city hall. Open Mon.-Fri. 9am-7pm, Sat. 9am-4pm, Sun. 10am-1pm, Oct.-June Mon.-Fri. 9am-12:30pm and 2-5:30pm, Sat. 9am-4pm.

Currency Exchange: An office at the **airport** provides service Mon.-Fri. 9am-8pm, Sat. 9am-4pm. There's a 24hr. **automatic exchange machine** on Pr. Liberdade, right outside Banco Espírito Santo e Commercial de Lisboa.

American Express: Top Tours, R. Alferes Malheiro, 96 (tel. 208 27 85), up R. do Almada from the tourist office. Open Mon.-Fri. 9am-12:30pm and 2:30-6:30pm.

Post Office: Pr. General H. Delgado (tel. 208 02 51), across from the tourist office. Open for stamps Mon.-Fri. 8am-9pm, Sat.-Sun. 9am-6pm. Poste Restante. **Postal Code:** 4000.

Telephones: Pr. Liberdade, 62. Open 8am-11:30pm. Also at the post office. **City Code:** 02.

Flights: Aeroporto Francisco de Sá Carneiro (tel. 948 21 41), accessible by bus 44 and 56 (every 20min.) from Pr. Lisboa.

Trains: Estação de São Bento (tel. 200 27 22), centrally located 1 block off Pr. Liberdade. Receives some local and regional trains. **Estação de Campanhã** (tel. 56 41 41), Porto's main station west of the center. Frequent connections to Estação São Bento (5min., 100$). To Coimbra (2½hr., 800$), Lisbon (4½hr., 1615$), Madrid via Entroncamento (12hr., 7500$), Paris (27hr., 19,000$).

Buses: Garagem Atlântico, R. Alexandre Herculano, 366 (tel. 200 69 54). To Coimbra (1½hr., 950$) and Lisbon (5hr., 1600$).

Public Transportation: *Passe Turístico* discount pass is available for the Porto transportation system (trolleys, buses, etc.). 3-day 1500$. 7-day 2000$.

Laundromat: Penguin, Av. Boavista (tel. 69 50 32), in shopping center Brasília. Follow the same route to the youth hostel, but walk uphill 1 block further to the rotary. 1300$ per 5.5kg load. Open Mon.-Sat. 10am-11pm.

Pharmacy: tel. 118 for info on which pharmacy is "on call."

Medical Assistance: Hospital de Santo António, R. Prof. Vicente José de Carvalho (tel. 200 52 41).

Emergency: tel. 115. **Police,** R. Alexandre Herculano (tel. 200 68 21).

ACCOMMODATIONS AND CAMPING

Most *pensões* lie west of Av. Aliados. Rates for singles are absolutely criminal.

Pousada de Juventude do Porto (HI), R. Rodrigues Lobo, 98 (tel. 606 55 35). Take bus 3, 20, or 52 (10min., 140$) from the stop on the lower west end of Pr. Liberdade and hop off at R. Júlio Dinis (driver knows the hostel stop). Fine kitchen facilities, cramped rooms, game room, and library. If you arrive in town after 10pm, don't bother. 3-day max. stay. Reception open 9-11am and 6pm-midnight. Curfew midnight. 1300$. Doubles with bath 3500$. Breakfast included.

Residencial Paris, R. da Fábrica, 29 (tel. 32 13 96). Across Pr. Liberdade from the train station, make a left onto R. do Dr. Artur de Magalhães Basto, which quickly turns into R. Fábrica. Room sizes vary from adequate to gigantic. Singles 2300$, with bath 3850$. Doubles with shower 3700$, with bath 5100$.

Pensão dos Aliados, R. Elísio de Melo, 27 (tel. 200 48 53, fax 200 27 10), on the left as you walk up Av. Aliados. Living room with TV. Sumptuous rooms with telephones and wall-to-wall carpeting. Singles 4000-5500$. Doubles 4700-6500$. Triples 6000$. Breakfast included. In summer, reserve several days in advance.

PORTUGAL

Camping: Prelada, Parque de Prelada (tel. 81 26 16), 5km from the beach. Take bus 6 from Pr. Liberdade. 430$ per person, 350$ per tent.

FOOD

The most colorful restaurants border the river in the Ribeira district, particularly on **Cais de Ribeira, Rua Reboleira,** and **Rua de Cima do Muro.** You'll find much seedier surroundings near Pr. Batalha on **Rua do Cimo de Vila** and **Rua do Cativo.** Replete with fresh flowers, fruit, and fish, the **Mercado de Bolhão** perfumes the corner of R. Formosa and R. Sá de Bandeira (open Mon.-Fri. 7am-5pm, Sat. 7am-1pm). **Máximo Restaurante-Café,** R. José Falcão, 115, combines a SoHo look, a local clientele, and American food. (Hamburgers 470-710$. Salads 330-790$. Daily specials 700-1200$. Open Mon.-Sat. 8am-10:30pm.) Dirt-cheap meals (most under 1000$) at **Churrasqueira Moura,** R. Almada, 219-223, include *frango no churrasco* (barbecued chicken with fries, 660$; open Mon.-Sat. 11:30am-10pm). Stone walls and nautical decor befit the riverside location of the **Taberna Típica,** R. Reboleira, 12. (*Arroz de polvo* octopus rice, 790$. Satisfying specials 750-1300$. Open Thurs.-Tues. 11am-midnight.)

SIGHTS AND ENTERTAINMENT

The heavy Romanesque husk of Porto's 13th-century **cathedral** glowers on a hill above the Ribeira. To the left of the high altar, the **Capela do Santíssimo Sacramento** shines with solid silver and plated gold. During the Napoleonic invasion, townspeople whitewashed the altar to protect it from vandalism. (Open 9am-noon and 2-5:30pm. To cloister 100$.) West of the cathedral, on Rua da Bolsa at Rua do Comércio do Porto, stands the **Palácio da Bolsa** (Stock Exchange), the epitome of 19th-century elegance. Magnificent parquet floors of inlaid Brazilian wood smell of cedar and jacaranda. Modeled after the Alhambra in Granada, the sparkling Sala Arabe took 18 years to decorate. (Open Mon.-Fri. 9am-6pm, Sat.-Sun. 10am-noon and 2-5pm; Oct.-May Mon.-Fri. 9am-noon and 2-5pm. 400$, students 200$.) Under the floor of the Gothic **Igreja de São Francisco,** famed for its gilded wood interior, thousands of human bones have been cleaned and stored in the *osseria* to await Judgement Day (open Mon.-Sat. 9am-5pm; 250$). South of the Bolsa, the **Ribeira** (Esplanade) is skirted by a marvelous quay filled with shops and restaurants. To see more of the Ribeira, take trolley 1 from the Igreja de São Francisco along the river to the **Foz do Douro,** Porto's beach community.

Just up R. Taipas from the museum and church rises the 82m **Torre dos Clérigos** (Tower of Clerics). Long the city's most prominent landmark, its granite tower glimmers like a splendid processional candle. Mount the 200 steps for a vista of the city and the Rio Douro valley. (Open Mon.-Sat. 10:30am-noon and 3-6pm, Sun. 10:30am-1pm and 8-10pm. Free.) The Portuguese art scene is blessed with a rare modern splash in the **Casa de Serralves (Museu de Arte Moderna),** a recently opened contemporary art museum west of the town center. The building crowns an impressive 44 acres of sculptured gardens, fountains, and even old farmlands which tumble toward the Douro River. Take bus 78 from Pr. D. João I. (Museum open Tues.-Fri. 2-8pm, Sat.-Sun. 10am-8pm. Park closes at sundown.)

Most of Porto's *caves* or *adegas* (wine lodges) lead free tours of the wineries, where both red and white port are aged and blended in huge oak barrels. Now as always, only human feet crush the grapes. Most of the 80-odd Port lodges ferment across the river, in **Vila Nova de Gaia.** Walk across the lower level of the Dom Luís I bridge and take a sharp right. **Sandeman,** Largo Miguel Bombarda (tel. 30 40 81), off Diogo Leite, stocks the best port and features a grape-crushing music video for those who pine for MTV (open 9:30am-1pm and 2-5:30pm, free). The crowds are smaller at **Ferreira,** Av. Diogo Leite, 70 (tel. 370 00 10, ext. 315; open Mon.-Fri. 9:30am-12:30pm and 2-5pm, Sat. 9:30am-noon; free).

Romania

US$1	= 1650lei (ROL)	1000lei =	US$0.61
CDN$1	= 1200lei	1000lei =	CDN$0.83
UK£1	= 2590lei	1000lei =	UK£0.39
IR£1	= 2540lei	1000lei =	IR£0.39
AUS$1	= 1230lei	1000lei =	AUS$0.81
NZ$1	= 900lei	1000lei =	NZ$1.11
SAR1	= 460lei	1000lei =	SAR2.15

Country Code: 40   International Dialing Prefix: EU: 00; USA: 011

Deep in the mysterious Carpathian Mountains, Romanian peasants preserve folk traditions lost to the rest of Europe for centuries. The fortified towns of Transylvania still look like medieval woodcuts, and the green hills of Moldavia remain as serene as the frescoes on their monastery walls. Once the poorest and most totalitarian country in the Soviet bloc, the Romanian regime under Nicolae Ceaușescu ruthlessly destroyed rural villages and herded their inhabitants into factory towns.

In 1989, the country finally erupted in a revolution as bloody and ruthless as the man it pulled down. The revolt started in a minor event in the western city of Timișoara: the arrest of a Hungarian priest by the dreaded *Securitate*, the secret police. Riots ripped across city, then around the country. Clashes with security

ROMANIA

forces in Bucharest on December 21-22 brought hundreds of thousands of protesters into the streets, and Ceauşescu fled the angry crowds. He and his wife were quickly arrested, summarily tried, and executed on Christmas Day. The immense enthusiasm that followed those December days didn't last for long, as power was seized by Ion Iliescu's National Salvation Front, accused by many to be only a continuation of the Communist party. Nonetheless, Iliescu won the 1990 presidential elections with an astonishing 70% of the vote, and his government began to reform the system, albeit slowly, and many say half-heartedly.

With the Romanian economy flushing down the toilet, the initial enthusiasm for democracy is turning into apathy or even disgust towards politics. Iliescu clings to power and his government's steps towards reforming the economy garnered the praise and money of the World Bank and the IMF, but for the victims of reform, the "good old days" of Ceauşescu evoke a certain nostalgia.

The hospitality of the Romanian people will surely be a high point of your visit; though many do not speak English, most will make an effort to understand you. Beware, though, that due to the extreme difficulty of life here, some Romanians might befriend you in the hopes of receiving an invitation to your country (which facilitates their visa process). Westerners are walking gold mines to Romanians: US$55 equals a month's wages here. Awareness rather than paranoia will serve you better; register with your embassy, and watch your wallet at all times.

For more explicit coverage of Romania, brave *Let's Go: Eastern Europe.*

GETTING THERE AND GETTING AROUND

Citizens of the U.S., Canada, the U.K., Ireland, Australia, New Zealand, and South Africa all need **visas** to enter Romania; single-entry (US$31) and multiple-entry (US$68) visas allow a 6-month stay; a transit visa (US$21) is valid for 72hrs. You can obtain a visa at a Romanian embassy or at the border with US$6 surcharge. Direct **trains** arrive in to Bucharest from Budapest, Prague, Warsaw, Sofia, and Moscow. **Buses** connect from Bucharest and Constanta to Varna, İstanbul, and Athens.

Agentie de Voiaj CFR (CHE-FE-RE; in Bucharest, appears as SNCFR) sells domestic and international train tickets. Knowing the number of the train you want is crucial; get a copy of the train timetable *(Mersul Trenurilor;* 650lei, US$0.30; instructions in English, Romanian, French, and German). Tickets can be purchased at CFR offices up to 24hrs. before the train departure; after that the train station will only sell tickets from 2hrs. before the scheduled departure. **Eurail** is not yet valid in Romania, although **Interrail** is accepted.

There are 3 types of trains: *rapid* or *expres* (indicated in green on timetables and at train stations), *accelerat* (red), and *persoane* (black or blue). Try to travel in 1st class *(clasa-întîi,* wagons marked by a yellow stripe on the side) and by *rapid* or *accelerat* trains. The difference in price between 1st and 2nd class is minimal by western standards; comfort and security standards are much higher. If taking an overnight train, again opt for 1st class in a sleeping carriage *(vagon de dormit).* During holiday periods, purchase tickets for *rapid* trains at least five days in advance.

To buy **international tickets,** go to the CFR (SNCFR) office in larger towns and be prepared to wait a while. Budapest-bound trains may exit Romania through either Arad or Oradea; you'll need to specify one when buying a ticket. In southern Romania, it is customary to give your smaller change to the desk officer after purchasing your ticket. It is now possible to pay for international train tickets with lei, but the conditions may test your physical fitness: at the counter you may be given a special receipt saying how much you have to pay; if this happens you must change money at a nearby bank or bureau and then return with the validated receipt. An ISIC entitles you to discounts on tickets throughout Eastern Europe, and if you're lucky, a 50% discount on domestic tickets.

Use the extensive local **bus** system only when trains are not available; though prices are equivalent, buses are usually packed and poorly ventilated. Look for the signs for the bus station *(autogară)* in each town. Old, rickety aircraft make domestic **flights** on TAROM a unique experience, and foreigners are charged four times as

ROMANIA

much as Romanians. However, fares are still lower than in Western Europe, and flying obviously saves time (Bucharest-Satu Mare is 1hr. by plane, 12hrs. by train). **Hitchhiking,** though risky, remains popular throughout the country. Drivers may expect a payment equivalent to 50-100% of the equivalent bus fare for giving you a lift. A wave of the hand, rather than a thumb, is the recognized sign. Women traveling alone should find another means of transportation.

ROMANIA ESSENTIALS

ONT (National Tourist Office), the national tourist bureau, doesn't always give reliable info about the price and availability of cheap rooms. Branches in expensive hotels are often more useful than the main offices. **CTT,** the youth travel agency, is designed for organized groups and will be utterly befuddled by your presence. Some ONT branches have been replaced by private bureaus, which aren't always helpful either. Hotels and restaurants open and close all the time; it's a good idea to double-check all important info.

The most common banknotes in Romania are 500, 1000, and 5000 **lei.** Bills worth 100lei are still in circulation, but are nearly worthless and looked at with suspicion, while new 10,000 lei bills are not widely used. You can pay for almost anything except plane tickets in lei; due to currency fluctuations, however, *Let's Go* lists many prices in U.S. dollars. It's a good idea to keep all receipts for money exchanged and art purchased in Romania. Private exchange bureaus can be found throughout the country now; there's little variation among their rates and commissions. Avoid changing money on the street. Although unofficial trading is still illegal, getting jailed is now less of a risk than getting cheated; train stations require special vigilance. Traveler's checks can be a hassle, and you may be charged higher commissions It is customary to give inexact change, especially if it is under 10-15 lei.

Many banks and more important businesses may be closed on Friday afternoons. Tourist and CFR bureaus are usually open Monday through Friday 8am to 8pm. They may be open on Saturday mornings as well, but almost everything is closed on Sundays. **National holidays** are New Year's Day (stores closed Jan. 1-3), 3-4 days for Orthodox Easter (a week later than Roman Catholic Easter), May Day (May 1), and Christmas (some businesses may be closed Dec. 25-31). Romania is in the same time zone as Bulgaria, one hour ahead of western Europe.

Gypsies are widely mistrusted in Romania. Romany children in the streets of cities, who may seem endearingly sweet, are often all too eager to relieve travelers of their wallets. Many Romanians hold conservative attitudes towards sexuality. Unfortunately, these attitudes may translate into harassment of gay, lesbian, and bisexual travelers.

Public hygiene in Romania will challenge Westerners. Most public restrooms lack soap, towels, and toilet paper. Even "privatized" public bathrooms that charge 10-20 lei may give you only a tiny amount of toilet paper. Feminine hygiene products can sometimes be found in stores now, but will be expensive. Stash basic medicines in your backpack; drug stores (*farmacie*) may not have what you need. If you do buy medicines in Romania, know what you're purchasing: *antinevralgic* for headaches, *piramidon* for colds and the flu, and *saprosan* for diarrhea.

Communication Romanian is a Romance language; travelers familiar with French, Italian, Spanish, or Portuguese can usually decipher public signs. In Transylvania, German and Hungarian are widely spoken. Throughout the country, French is the second language for the older generation, English for the younger. However, spoken Romanian is a trial for the average visitor. The biggest problem is caused by the two additional vowels: *ă* (like the e in hammer) and *â* or *î* (like the sound between d and n in couldn't). The other two characters peculiar to the Romanian alphabet are *ş* (pronounced "sh") and *ţ* (pronounced "ts" or "tz"). Also, *ci* and *ce* are pronounced "chi" and "che," while *chi* and *che* are pronounced "ki" and "ke," as in Italian. In many words ending in *i*, the "i" is very soft (almost unnoticed). A few key phrases in Romanian will smooth your travels considerably. Try the following: *vă*

ROMANIA

rog (VUH-rog; "please"), *multumesc frumos* (mul-tsu-MESK fru-MOZ; "thank you very much"), *bună dimineata/ziua/seara* (BU-na di-mi-NYAH-tsah/ZI-huah/SAH-rah; "good morning/day/evening"), *unde* (UN-de; "where?"), *ce* (CHE, "what?"), *cînd* (KUHND, "when?"), *cît costă* (KUT KOH-stah; "How much does it cost?").

You can now dial abroad directly; the **international prefix** is 00. Orange phones take phone cards; blue phones take coins. Phone cards are available at post and telephone offices in 5000, 10,000, and 20,000 lei denominations. Rates per minute run US$0.50 (870 lei) to neighboring countries, US$0.75 (1230 lei) to most of Europe, and US$1.75 (2970 lei) to the U.S. To reach the AT&T **USADirect** operator, dial 018 00 42 88; **SprintExpress** 018 00 08 77; **Canada Direct** 018 00 50 00; **BT Direct** 018 00 44 44. Many hotels and companies have international direct-dial phones; in Bucharest, these numbers start with 2, 3, or 4 (most people have numbers that start with 6 or 7, which means they may not dial directly abroad, but they can still dial Direct-type services). Local calls cost 20 lei and can be made from any phone; intercity calls can be made from the new phones (orange and blue) or from old phones marked *telefon interurban*. City codes are 3 digits (first digit 0) followed by the 6-digit local number; Bucharest has only 2 digits (01) and local numbers have 7 digits.

It's also possible to make intercity or international phone calls from some post or telephone offices. It's no easy task, but it may be the only option in small cities. At the phone office, write down where you want to call, how long you want to talk, and the telephone number. Operators shout your telephone destination in the most incoherent way possible, so stay nearby. You will pay up front (always ask for the rate per minute).

Accommodations and Camping Hotels in Romania charge foreigners 2-4 times the Romanian price. Hotels are still less expensive than in the West, but don't expect the same quality. As a loose rule, 1-star hotels are nasty, 3-star ones decent. **Private accommodations** are generally the way to go, but hosts rarely speak English, and travelers should note that renting a room "together" means sharing a bed. Through ONT, they run about US$12 per person (breakfast included). Always fix a price before you accept anything. Freelance housing offers should cost under US$6. Your hosts may also expect you to change money with them at a favorable rate. Many towns reserve **university dorms** for foreign students at insanely low prices. Ask at the local university rectorate; the ONT *may* be able to help you. Prices at 2-star hotels start at US$12 for singles and US$24 for doubles (showers cost US$4-5 more). **Campgrounds** are crowded, and their bathrooms redefine the word "foul." Bungalows are relatively cheap but often full in summer (about US$5-10). The tourist map called *Popasuri Turistice* (in French), lists most sites.

Food and Drink Finding food in Romania is no longer such a problem; marketplaces are excellent sources of inexpensive food. It's a good idea to carry a water bottle. There are taps—often actual wells—in train stations and spaced regularly along major roads, although it's always a safer bet to buy bottled water. Wines of the Murfatlar region, near the Black Sea, are world-famous and wonderfully inexpensive (US$3-5 per bottle). A good, cheap local drink is *ţuică* (ts-WI-ca, plum brandy). Three or four shots will be enough to dull your hunger pangs.

With the current exchange rate, even some of the most expensive restaurants are cheap (full meals US$10-12). But double-check your bill and politely ask for an explanation if the amount appears incorrect. Many restaurants list prices per serving of 100 grams, so be sure both you and your waiter understand how much you plan to spend. Except in the more expensive establishments, you are expected to seat yourself wherever there is space available, including at a partially occupied table. Restaurants are generally open from 7am to 10pm but stop serving an hour before closing. Tip by rounding up the bill to the nearest 50 or 100 lei.

■■■ BUCHAREST (BUCUREŞTI)

Polluted, bad-mannered, and anarchic, Bucharest wears the scars of Romania's struggles. First mentioned in a document dated 1459 and signed Vlad Ţepeş (a.k.a. Count Dracula), Bucharest spent centuries as just another stop on the road from the Balkans to Central Europe. Made the capital of a unified Romania in 1859 the city was dubbed "Little Paris" and "Pearl of the Balkans" for its beautiful boulevards, parks, and fine neo-Classical architecture. It takes a vivid imagination to recreate this vision today: Ceauşescu's government demolished historic neighborhoods, replacing them with concrete-box housing projects. Though the streets are now cleaner (some even have trashcans) and new shops and restaurants are shyly cropping up, Bucharest remains a grimy, jaded Gotham that can wipe the smile off the most determined traveler's face.

ORIENTATION AND PRACTICAL INFORMATION

Bucharest is in southeastern Romania, 70km north of the Bulgarian border. Direct trains connect the city with most Eastern European capitals. Armed with a city map (secured at the train station with any luck), head east on **Calea Grivitei** and take a right onto **Calea Victoriei,** which leads to most sights and tourist spots. Walk down another 4 blocks on Strada Biserica Amzei, the continuation of Grivitei, to **Bulevardul Magheru** (which becomes Bd. Bălcescu and then Bd. Brătianu), the main artery in Bucharest. Trolley 79 or the metro to Piaţa Romană will take you to Bd. Magheru.

Tourist Offices: The **ONT** office at the Gara de Nord is apparently just for show. Open Mon.-Fri. 7:30am-8pm, Sat. 7:30am-3pm, Sun. 7:30am-2pm. For reliable help, go to the main office, Bd. Magheru 7 (tel. 614 11 38), next to the *Magazinul Eva* (EVA store), for maps (1000 lei, US$0.60) and info on sights, accommodations, and camping throughout the country. Private rooms US$12 per person (showers and breakfast included); ask a for central location. Open Mon.-Thurs. 8am-4pm, Fri. 8am-2pm. Most major hotels also have ONT desks or newly privatized tourist offices.

Embassies: U.S., Str. Tudor Arghezi 7-9, 1 block behind Hotel Intercontinental. Consulate, Str. Snagov 25 (tel. 10 40 40). Open Mon.-Fri. 8am-5pm. **Canada,** Str. Nicolae Iorga 36 (tel. 50 61 40), near Piaţa Romană. Open Mon.-Fri. 9am-5pm. **U.K.,** Str. Jules Michelet 24 (tel. 12 03 03). Open Mon.-Thurs. 8:30am-5pm, Fri. 8am-1pm. Citizens of **Australia** and **New Zealand** should contact the British embassy. **Bulgaria,** Str. Rabat 5 (tel. 33 21 50). Open Mon.-Fri. 8:30am-12:30pm and 2-5pm. **Hungary,** Str. Jean-Louis Calderon 63 (tel. 614 66 21, 614 66 22, and 614 66 23). Open Mon.-Thurs. 8am-4:30pm, Fri. 8am-3:30pm. **Russia,** Şoseaua Kiseleff 46 (tel. 617 23 22). Open Mon., Wed., and Fri. 9am-1pm.

Currency Exchange: Avoid changing money on the street; there are plenty of currency exchange offices. Banks will usually be slower, and rates aren't that different; many of them are listed in the newspapers. For traveler's checks, try the reception at Hotel Minerva (3% commission).

American Express: Hotel Minerva, Bd. Ana Tpătescu (tel. 312 39 69, fax 312 27 38). Go up to the 2nd fl. and turn left. Replaces lost cards and checks, but won't accept wired money and doesn't cash traveler's checks. Mail held; address it to Minerva International S.A., 2-4 Gh. Manu Str., Bucharest 1, Romania.

Post Office: Str. Matei Millo 10 (tel. 614 40 54), off Calea Victoriei. Open Mon.-Fri. 7:30am-8pm, Sat. 7:30am-2pm. Poste Restante down the street next to the Hotel Carpati. **Postal Code:** 70154.

Telephones: Orange card phones for international calls are located throughout the city center, in the train station, and near the telephone company at Calea Victoriei 37; there you can also order collect or operator-assisted calls. For directory assistance, call 11 51 50. Wait for the English-speaking operator. **City Code:** 01.

Flights: Otopeni Airport (tel. 633 66 02, info 633 31 37), 16km away, handles international traffic. Bus 783 leaves from Piaţa Unirii every 1-2hr.; buy tickets on board. Coming from Otopeni, buses let you off near the Hotel Intercontinental on Bd. Magheru. **Băneasa Airport,** connected with Piaţa Romana by bus 131, han-

ROMANIA

dles domestic flights. Buy international tickets at Str. Brezoianu 10 (tel. 646 33 46; see directions under Trains, below); domestic tickets at the **TAROM** office, Piaţa Victoriei (tel. 659 41 85 or 659 41 25). Both offices open Mon.-Fri. 7:30am-7pm.

Trains: Gara de Nord (tel. 952) is the main station. Domestic tickets can be purchased in advance (though not in English) at the **Agence de Voyage, CFR,** Calea Grivitei 139 (tel. 650 72 47), 2 blocks down from the train station, or Str. Brezoianu 10, 1st floor (tel. 613 26 44), 2 blocks south of Bd. Mihail Kogălniceanu between Calea Victoriei and Cişmigiu Park (use the TAROM entrance). Learn the phrase *Un bilet pentru...* ("One ticket to..."). 1st class to Constanta (4320lei, US$2.70), Braşov (2560lei, US$1.60), Cluj-Napoca (7200lei, US$4.50). **International tickets** must be bought at the CFR office in Piaţa Unirii (tel. 613 40 08). All offices open Mon.-Fri. 7:30am-7pm, Sat. 7:30am-noon.

Buses: Three stations serve Bucharest. **Filaret,** Piaţa Gării Filaret 1 (tel. 641 06 92), and **Rahova,** Şos. Alexandriei 164 (tel. 776 47 95), are both in the southern suburbs; **Băneasa,** Str. I. Ionescu de la Brad 5 (tel. 779 56 45), is to the north. All are madhouses. Scores of buses to İstanbul via Bulgaria leave from the main train station (17hr., US$15; outside and to the right, one company charges US$10). Each representative will *claim* that their bus is air-conditioned. Suspicious dealings with customs officials are common. For buses to Athens, inquire at Hotel Majestic or at the office in room 129 in Hotel Union, Str. I Cîmpineanu (tel. 613 26 40). Generally, trains are a better mode of transportation out of Bucharest.

Public Transportation: Buses, trolleys, and trams all cost 100lei. Tickets available at kiosks near most stops or on the buses. Buses are packed to the gills on busy routes—people literally hang out the doors. Hold on to your valuables. The metro covers all major points in Bucharest for 100lei (open 5am-11pm).

Taxis: tel. 053. Expect 240lei per km. Try to hail "state taxis" with the number 053 on the rear passenger door. Arrange the price (*preti*) before you accept a ride.

Luggage Storage: Gara de Nord.

Pharmacy: At Bd. Magheru 18 (tel. 659 61 15) just across from the ONT office and in the train station. Open 24hrs. Ring the bell at night.

Medical Assistance: Clinica Batiştei, Str. Tudor Arghezi 28, behind the Hotel Intercontinental. **Ambulance,** tel. 961 or 679 43 10.

Emergencies: Police, tel. 955. Also, call your consulate.

ACCOMMODATIONS

The ONT office on Bd. Magheru can arrange private rooms (US$12) or accommodations in hotels starting at US$20. You're better off avoiding offers for private accommodations by individuals at the train station. During the school year (early Sept.-late June), Romanian students will often share their rather drab rooms. Try the dormitories of the **Polytechnic Institute** near the Semănătoarea metro stop.

The hotel situation is not very rosy. Even rat-holes cost more than they should, and it's hard to find nice rooms under US$30 per person. One-star hotels are the cheapest. Most of the rooms in these hotels are similar; the difference lurks in price and location. Check the signboard posted outside the ONT office in the train station for more information. **Hotel Dunărea,** Calea Grivitei 140 (tel 617 32 20), across from the Gara de Nord train station has rooms that are bearable for short layovers, and only 15min. away from downtown. (Singles US$15. Doubles US$24.) Also central, the **Hotel Munteniea,** Str. Academiei 21 (tel. 614 60 10), lies behind Bucharest University. (Singles US$20. Doubles US$40.) On a quiet street near the central post office, **Hotel Carpati,** Str. Matei Millo 16, takes no phone reservations. (Singles US$25. Doubles US$38.) **Hotel Minerva,** Bd. Ana Ipătescu (tel. 311 15 50) offers newly renovated singles (US$46), and doubles (US$60).

FOOD

Try the **open-air markets** on Piaţa Amzei between Calea Victoriei and Bd. Magheru (close to Piaţa Romană); Piaţa Matache, 5min. from the train station towards downtown; and Piaţa Unirii. **Unic,** on Bd. Magheru near the University, has a decent food selection (as well as Kodak film). Try the Greek-owned **food store** in Piaţa 1 Mai

ROMANIA

Bucharest

1 Village Museum	13 Goethe Institute
2 Russian Embassy	14 Canadian Embassy
3 Ministry of Foreign Affairs	15 British Council
4 Geological Museum	16 French Library
5 Romanian Peasant Museum	17 Romanian Development Agency
6 Museum of Natural History	18 Romanian Atheneum
7 Government of Romania	19 State Ownership Fund
8 Dynamo Stadium	20 National Military Museum
9 Emergency Hospital	21 Opera House
10 Bucharest Circus	22 National Art Gallery
11 North Railway Station	23 Great Palace Hall
12 Art Collections Museum	24 Senate

25 Natl. Agcy. for Privatization
26 National Theatre
27 American Library
28 Italian Library
29 Palas
30 Ministry of Justice
31 City Hall
32 National History Museum
33 Caritas
34 Jewish Theatre
35 Progresul Arena
36 Casa Republicii

(four stops on bus 300 outbound from Piața Romanâ). For excellent bread, head for one of the many Turkish bakeries or the **Ana** bakery on Calea Dorobanților.

Restaurant Elegant-Efes, Bd. Magheru 24A (tel. 659 54 30), across from the main ONT office. Opened in summer 1993, it quickly found a following for its *pui* (roasted ½-chicken, US$4) and *crenwurst* (pork sausages, US$1). Wash the meal down with a pint of cold draft beer imported from Turkey. Open until late.

Hanul Lui Manuc, Bd. Iuliu Maniu 30 (tel. 615 33 00), near the southern end of Calea Victoriei. Traditional cuisine in a beautifully restored 17th-century manor. Meals US$6-12. Restaurant open 7am-midnight. *Crama* (cellar) café open Mon.-Fri. 11am-11pm, Sat.-Sun. 10am-midnight. Courtyard *Bar de Zi* (day bar) open Mon.-Fri. 10am-10pm, Sat.-Sun. 10am-11pm.

Restaurant Capșa, Calea Victoriei 36 (tel. 615 61 01), near the University. A Bucharest legend, it used to be popular with writers, artists, and intellectuals. Fair quality. You can enjoy excellent ice cream at the *brasserie* next door.

Spring Time, in Piața Vicotriei. This fast-food place has an outstanding view of the government building. Hamburgers US$1. *Cartofi prăjiți* means french fries. 4 scoops of delicious ice cream only US$2; eat it outside in the Herăstrău Park.

Pizza Julia, on Bd. Nicolae Titulescu, a 10min. walk from Piața Victoriei. One of the best pizza places in town. Slice US$2-4. Popular with students.

SIGHTS

In the heart of downtown is **Piața Universității,** where demonstrators battled Ceaușescu's forces on Dec. 21, 1989, the day before his demise. In the spring of 1990, students protesting the new regime occupied the square and declared it a "communist-free zone." A few hundred meters south runs the famous **Str. Lipscani,** named after the Leipzig merchants who used to do business there. They have been replaced by Gypsies and Turks selling everything you can think of. Bd. Brátianu leads to **Piața Unirii,** home of communist Romania's biggest supermarket, now converted into a weird shopping mall. The nearby marketplace was empty before 1989; locals called it **Circul Foamei** (Circle of Hunger). Ceaușescu drastically rearranged the square, but he spared **Dealul Mitropoliei,** the small hill on the south-western side. On the hill are the **Parliament building** and the main Orthodox Catholic **cathedral.** Downhill west from the square stretches Bd. Unirii to the world's second largest building (after the Pentagon), **Casa Poporului** (People's House). Ceaușescu demolished several historical neighborhoods and spent billions of dollars on a private palace he called the country's "civic center." The new government is not sure what to do with it. In the spring of 1994, Casa Poporului was renovated and hosted a business forum and Israeli-Palestinian peace talks.

Ceaușescu also renovated the shores of **Dîmbovița,** but couldn't make the river any bigger. The most interesting *quai*, Splaiul Independenței, runs along the river west from Piața Unirii; the imposing **Palace of Justice** stands on the southern shore. Twenty minutes away from Piața Unirii is Piața Operei, with the **Opera House.** From the opera, continue west on Bd. Ervilor Sanitari to the **Cotroceni Palace,** residence of the president of Romania. Part of the palace is a museum and can be visited. Turn right, then left on Șos. Cotroceni; across from the palace are the **Botanical Gardens,** and a few hundred yards west is the green campus of the **Polytechnical Institute,** swarming with students during the school year (Oct.-June).

The oldest buildings in Bucharest are northwest of Piața Unirii, in the triangle between the river, Bd. Brátianu, and Bd. Kogálniceanu. Near Piața Unirii are the ruins of the old princely court. Near Calea Victoriei is the **Stavropoleos church,** and a few yards up is the **History Museum of Romania.** Ten min. from Piața Universitații, on the right are the **Cișmigiu Gardens,** the oldest park in Bucharest. Alleys curve elegantly around a small lake; you can rent a **boat** and row through the dark tunnel. In **Piața Revoluției** (also called Piața Palatului) the imposing **Royal Palace,** residence of Romania's kings, then of its communist dictator, is now the **National Art Museum.** The Western European painting collection is small, but includes Italian and Dutch works. The museum was closed for renovations in 1994.

ROMANIA

Bucharest's parks compensate a little for its urban wastescape. Wander through well-groomed central **Cişmigiu Park,** a few blocks west of Calea Victoriei, or the picturesque **Herăstrău Park** to the north. The bars in Herăstrău Park provide ample opportunity to rub elbows with the locals. You can also join the crowds at **Parcul Studentilor** (Student Park) on Lacul Tei; swim or play volleyball, basketball, tennis, or ping pong here. Take bus 282 or trolley 86 to the end and follow the signs.

ENTERTAINMENT

Whatever you do in the evening, pack a map and cab fare; the streets are very poorly lit and buses are unreliable. At the **Casa de Culture Studentilor,** Calea Plevnei 61 (M: Eroilor), behind the Opera, there's a disco where you can groove with Romanian students (open Thurs.-Sun. 7:30pm-midnight). The best disco in town, **Martin,** at the intersection of Calea Dorobanţilor and Bd. Iancu de Hunedoara, has started to invite popular Romanian rock and pop singers for evening jams (open 10pm-5am). **Vox Maris** is a name shared by two fancier nightspots: one at Bd. M. Kogálniceanu 2-4, under the Cercul Militar Naţional (open 10pm-4am) and the other recently opened in Piata Victoriei, across from the Tarom office, drawing soccer stars. For bars, try **007** at Bd. Bălcescu 4, or **Salon Spaniol,** Calea Victoriei 116 (open until 4am).

The magnificent **Atheneum** concert hall in Piaţa Revoluţiei often hosts excellent concerts at incredibly low prices. Tickets for the **Opera House** (tel. 614 69 80) and the **Operetta** near the National Theater (tel. 613 63 48) sell quickly, so buy them well in advance. Many of the theaters are very good, and tickets are extremely cheap; however, most shows are in Romanian. Bucharest has the only **Jewish State Theater** *(Teatru Evreesc)* in Europe, at Str. Iuliu Baraş 15, which performs throughout the summer. The shows are in Yiddish, though the simultaneous headphone translations into Romanian should make everything clear.

■ SNAGOV AND SINAIA

When Bucharest has gotten the better of you, take a daytrip to **Snagov,** a tiny village half an hour north of Bucharest by car or train. Many people hitch. In summer, hordes descend upon **Snagov Park,** 5km west of Snagov village, where people swim in the brownish lake or rent a rowboat and navigate to **Snagov Monastery** (a 30min. row). Here lies the grave of the Vlad Ţepeş (Dracula). Only men may enter the monastery.

Another option is to escape to **Sinaia.** This high mountain resort town lies 1¾ hours from Bucharest toward Braşov by train. Here looms the 19th-century summer castle of King Carol I, the first King of Romania. Be sure also to visit the **Sinaia Monastery,** built in the 17th century and used as a refuge during the Russo-Turkish War.

BLACK SEA COAST

Romania's Black Sea coast used to be jam-packed in summer, but prices are rising too high for many Romanians. Finding a place is easier, but July and August are still crowded. As a foreigner, you'll always be charged more in hotels; there's nothing you can do about it. Trains run from Bucharest to Constanta (8 per day, 1st class 4000lei) where you can catch a bus to the Black Sea resorts.

Constanţa The city, a Greek harbor some 2500 years ago, received its name from the daughter of Emperor Constantine; some residents playfully regard Constantinople as "the fatherland." Escape the innumerable gray apartment blocks that stifle the city by exploring the old town. Take a walk along the waterfront **promenade** past the imposingly elegant *Cazino.* Refreshments are available in the nearby small pub **Vraja Mării** (Charm of the Sea), affectionately nicknamed *Javră Mării*

ROMANIA

(scurvy dog). The **mosque** on Str. Muzeelor is one of the few reminders of Turkish domination and offers a bird's eye view of the town (open 9am-5pm, 100lei). In Piața Ovidiu, behold the **Statue of Ovid,** commemorating the Roman writer who wrote his most famous poems in exile here, then head into the **Archeological Museum** (open 9am-8pm, US$0.60).

No direct **trains** connect south to Varna and İstanbul; you have to make a detour via Bucharest. Direct **buses** are faster; buy tickets at **NURLIN SRL,** in front of the train station (to İstanbul 17hr., US$15). Take trolley 40 or 43 from the train station and get off where Bd. Tomis intersects Bd. Republicu (about 5 stops) for the **ONT tourist office,** Bd. Tomis 66 (tel. (041) 61 48 00). The staff speaks English and can help arrange **private accommodations.** Down Bd. Tomis from the ONT at #20-26, **Hotel Tineretului** (tel. (041) 61 88 55) has average-sized rooms with TVs (singles US$25, doubles US$33). **Hotel Continental,** further up on Bd. Tomis has singles for as little as US$17 (and cashes traveler's checks for a hefty 10% fee). There are plenty of fast-food and pizza places in Constanța; for some ambience, try **Casa cu Lei** (House with Lions), a few yards up from Hotel Intrim (chicken US$1, beef and pork US$2-4). At **Piața Unirii** next to Bd. Republicu, there's a large **food store** and a **fruit and vegetable market.**

South of Constanța The coast south of Constanța is lined with sandy beaches and '70s tourist resorts. Buses run south from Constanța's train station about every half-hour in the direction of **Mangalia** (40km, 500 lei); private buses are cheaper than the state-run service. Bypass humdrum **Eforie Nord** and **Eforie Sud,** and go straight to **Costinești,** a dynamic seaside hotspot catering to a young crowd. You can hike the 3km from the bus stop; hitchers say it's easy enough to get a ride. Try to call ahead for accommodations at **Biroul de Cazare** (tel. (041) 74 29 77), **Hotel Forum** (tel. (041) 74 16 77), or **Hotel Amiral** (tel. (041) 74 16 34) where bunga-lows (US$6 per person) and less desirable rooms (US$3 per person) abound. Across from Hotel Forum, the disco **Vox Maris** is the hippest in town.

Continuing farther south, you'll pass through the resorts **Neptun, Jupiter, Venus,** and **Saturn** before reaching Mangalia. Neptun and its northern affiliate, Olimp, have some of the best beaches, but tend to be more expensive. The **tourist office** in Nep-tun, Dispecerat de Cazare (tel. (041) 73 13 10) can help you find rooms; their prices are 50% lower than those at hotels. One-star hotels run about US$6 per person, and two-star about US$12 (prices rise in July-August).

Probably the village least spoiled by the heavy tourist industry, **2 Mai** is located on the southern end of the Romanian coast. There are no hotels, so bring a tent or arrange private accommodations (set the price before you move into the room). This village seems to be popular among intellectuals, artists, and bohemian students. Most young people camp at the southern end of the village, on the beach, and every night set up campfires and play guitar. From here you can walk to Bulgaria (4km away), and then take a bus to Varna.

Histria A Hellenic colony mentioned by Greek historian Strabo in the 5th century BC, Histria was rediscovered in the early 20th century by Romanian archeologist Vasile Pârvan. The excavations are about 30km north of Constanța, on the shore of Lake Sinoe (a lagoon separated from the sea by a thread of sand). Buses leave from the Tomis Nord station in Constanța, but drop you off 7km from the site. The **museum** and **excavations** follow the city's 14 centuries of recorded history, from the 7th century BC to the 7th century AD. Most explanations are in Romanian, French, and German. Several walls and a few columns still stand, and the museum has carved stones, fragments of statues, and amphorae (some have been claimed by swallows). The ruins are surrounded by stork-infested wilderness. (Museum open until 5pm. 1000lei.).

Danube Delta The scenic Danube Delta occupies the northern half of the coast. **Tulcea** is its main gateway, 5 hours from Bucharest by fast train via Medgidia,

ROMANIA

and 4 hours from Constanta by slow train. The terrain between the three arms of the Danube from Tulcea to the Black Sea is a world of natural and artificial canals cutting their way through kilometers of roads—a paradise for anglers, birdwatchers, and adventurers armed with small boats. The **Eurodelta tourist office** offers boat trips to the Delta and the Ukrainian city of Izmail. Turn right at the Casa de Cultură a Sindicatel, cross Str. Isaccea, and walk up the hill for the ultra-cheap, three-star **Hotel Trei Stele** (tel. 51 67 64) Str. Carpați 16. (No English spoken. Small, dark doubles US$2. Triples US$3.)

TRANSYLVANIA

Though the name evokes a dark, evil land of black magic and vampires, Transylvania (Ardeal) is a pastoral, peaceful land of green hills, descending gently from the Carpathians toward the Hungarian Plains. For centuries, Romans, Hungarians, Germans, Turks, and Russians have fought over the rich Transylvanian plateaus in northwestern Romania. The evidence remains—villages built around fortified churches and citadel ruins stand on nearly every hill. Romania's Hungarians, the country's largest minority group, are concentrated here, especially in the northwest. Many people speak German or Hungarian better than Romanian. Due to location and the influence of Austrian rule, Transylvania is the most westernized part of Romania. Cities are cleaner, services are better, and waiters friendlier than elsewhere. The beautiful medieval centers of Transylvanian towns escaped the bulldozers as communist planners contented themselves with building eyesores on the outskirts. Two different train routes from Budapest merge at Brașov before continuing to Bucharest: trains through Arad stop either in Sibiu or Sighișoara, while those through Oradea stop at Cluj-Napoca and Sighișoara.

■ ■ ■ BRAȘOV

Brașov, rising from the foot of Mt. Timpa, is one of the most beautifully restored cities in Romania and a good base for excursions to the Carpathian mountains. **Piața Sfatului,** in the center of the old town, and the nearby Str. Republicii, provide splendid strolling ground and give a sad glimpse of the beauty Romania lost when the housing projects took over. The fairy-tale **Orthodox Cathedral** in the square was built in 1858 with marble and delicate gold. Uphill from the square along Str. Gh. Baritiu looms the **Black Church,** the most celebrated Gothic building in the country; it received its name after being charred in a fire in 1689. Magnificent organ concerts are offered during the summer several times a week. (Open Mon.-Sat. 10am-6pm. 100lei.) Walk right from the Hotel Aro Palace along Bd. Eroilor for an **ethnographic museum** which houses exhibits of traditional Transylvanian folk costumes and ceramics. (Open Tues.-Sun. 10am-6pm. Students 100lei.) A few doors down at no. 21 is the **Muzeul de Arta** (National Art Museum), featuring the work of Romania's newest talents. (Open Tues.-Sun. 10am-6pm. Students 50lei.)

Practical Information, Accommodations, and Food All Budapest-Bucharest **trains** stop in Brașov. From the train station, ride bus 4 for 10min. On Bd. Eroilor, you'll see the Hotel Aro Palace on your left facing a park; the ONT **tourist office** (tel. (068) 14 16 48) in its lobby has maps and info on hotel accommodations (open 8am-8pm). The **bus station** is near hotel Aro Palace. To walk from the station (2km), head straight on Bd. Victoriei, follow the road to the right around the civic center, then turn right on Bd. 15 Noiembrie, which becomes Bd. Eroilor after Piața Teatrului. The **CFR** office is on Str. Republicii 53 (open Mon.-Fri. 7am-7:30pm). **EXO,** Str. Postbvarului 6 (tel. (068) 14 45 91), near the central square is an agency that offers private rooms at US$17 per person. As you face Hotel Aro Palace, walk 350m left and then make a right onto Str. Republicii. Turn left at the first crossing,

ROMANIA

walk for a block, and turn right onto Str. Postăvarului. (Open Mon.-Fri. 11am-8pm, Sun. 11am-2pm). The cheapest hotel in town is **Hotel Aro Sport,** Str. Sf. Ioan 3 (tel. (068) 14 28 40), behind the Hotel Aro Palace. Spartan but clean rooms share common bathrooms. (Singles US$22. Doubles US$36). Rooms may be available in the student **dormitory** complex off Str. Memorandunului from July to September. Your best bet might be **private rooms.** Just act confused in the train station, or in front of Hotel Capitol or Hotel Aro Sport, where locals roam around in search of lodgers (US$6-10 per person, but you can bargain).

Restaurants cluster near the main square. **Gustări** offers traditional Romanian fare. (Full meals US$2. Open 8:30am-10pm.) For dessert, head across the square and take a right onto Str. Muresenilor to the **Mamamia,** where banana splits, milkshakes, and sundaes are expensive (about US$3), but well worth the treat. Riding up the **Mount Tîmpa** cable car wins you both a transfixing view and a reasonably priced restaurant, the **Panoramic** at the top.

■ POIANA BRAŞOV AND BRAN

Poiana Braşov, one of Romania's most popular mountain resorts, is only 10km away (buses leave from in front of the main building of the university on Bd. Eroilar; 200 lei). Ask for "maşina de Poiana." The green open area among the mountains, perfect for hiking or skiing, is dotted with restaurants and one-star hotels.

Bran, 23km southwest of Braşov, is a picturesque town whose claim to fame is the **Castle of Vlad Ţepeş.** Ostensibly home to the count who inspired Bram Stoker's novel *Dracula,* the castle still poses majestically, though not very mysteriously, on its hill. (Open Tues.-Sun. 9am-4pm.) Actually, Count Dracula had nothing at all to do with this castle; the rumor started because the place needed money for reconstruction. Still, it looks like a vampire *could* have lived there. Locals seek to accentuate the attraction with the **Muzeul Vama Bran,** which contains old photos and relics from the castle, and with an ethnographic **museum** of Transylvania. (Both open Tues.-Sun. 10am-4pm. To castle and museum 150lei, students 50lei.) To get to Bran from Braşov, take the **bus** marked "Bran" from the station on Bd. Eroilor (every hr., 300lei).

■ ■ ■ SIGHIŞOARA (SEGESVÁR, SCHÄSSBURG)

Of all the medieval towns in Transylvania, Sighişoara is perhaps the least spoiled and most enchanting. Surrounded by mountains and crowning a green hill on the railroad line between Cluj and Braşov, its guild towers, old clock tower, steeples, and irregular tile roofs are almost entirely unobstructed by modern buildings. The old walled town is preserved as a museum, and visitors can wander into the surrounding hilly, green farmland. Enter the **Old Town** through the **old clock tower**, a few meters down from Hotel Steaua to Piaţa Hermann Oberth, then uphill. Built in 1556, the tower is 64m high. Watch the clock figures move every hour: they represent Peace and Justice. The ground-level rooms were used as torture chambers. A **museum** inside offers glimpses into the city's past as well as an outstanding panorama of the surrounding area (open Tues.-Sun. 9am-6:30pm). Nearby is the **Museum of Medieval Armory,** whose three rooms display cannonballs, sabers *(iatagan),* and other weapons of Dark Age domination (open Tues.-Sun. 10am-3:30pm). The old Saxon **church,** built between the 14th and 16th centuries, has a 175-step **covered wooden staircase** (closed for renovations in the summer of 1994).

Practical Information, Accommodations, and Food Almost all **trains** on the Bucharest-Budapest and Bucharest-Cluj routes stop on Sighişoara (1½hrs. from Braşov, 4½hrs. from Bucharest, 2½hrs. from Cluj). From the train station, take a right, then a quick left, and follow the main street until it crosses the river. Then take a right onto Str. 1 Decembrie to reach the town's **tourist office** (tel.

ROMANIA

CLUJ-NAPOCA ■ 699

(065) 77 10 72; open Mon.-Fri. 8am-3:15pm, Sat. 10am-1pm) and only hotel. Alternately, you can cross the river on the bridge by the orthodox church, then take a left to reach Str. 1 Decembrie. The **CFR office** is nearby (tel. (065) 77 18 20; open Mon.-Fri., 7am-8pm). Farther down on the main street is the **post office** (open Mon.-Fri. 7:30am-noon and 5-7pm) and the **telephone office** (open 7am-10pm, international calls available).

A few steps from the tourist office, **Hotel Steaua** (tel. (065) 77 19 30, fax 77 19 32) has fairly big rooms and the reception can provide information and maps of the city in English and German. (Singles US$14, with bath US$17. Doubles US$25, with bath US$31. Triples with bath US$35. Breakfast included.) For a **private room,** try the tourist office. You might be offered one by somebody if you act confused in front of the hotel. **Dealul Gàrii** offers **camping** and a 24hr. restaurant on the north side of the rail tracks (tel. (065) 77 10 46). From the station, turn left, then left again across the railway, then head up Str. Dealul Gării.

In the old town, you can have an excellent meal of local delicacies; try the corner house on the 2nd sidestreet after entering through the clock tower. Here, the **Restaurant Cetate,** P-ta Museului 5, is run by a company called Dracula SRL; Vlad Dracul, father of Vlad "Count Dracula" Țepeș lived in this house between 1431-1436. Sit in massive wooden chairs and enjoy a full meal for less than US$5. Try the dungeon-like *berărie* (bar) downstairs, if there's anybody there; a lack of tourists kept the place empty in the summer of 1994. If you take the first sidestreet after the clock tower and walk toward the Lutheran church atop the hill, you'll come to a small square where **Cofetarie Boema** is located. This cozy café offers magnificent cakes with aromatic coffee. (Open 9am-9pm.)

Făgăraș Mountains The Făgăraș lie just to the south of the rail line between Subiu and Brașov. You can hike past snowfields and shepherds' huts and stay cheap in a *cabana* (a primitive mountain lodge with an outhouse and occasionally electricity). The view of the Vallachian plains to the south and the Transylvanian plateau to the north will make up for any fatigue. Bring a map and food—the only available grub may be the Romanian equivalent of Spam—and disinfect water from the streams.

Camping is legal everywhere, but there are not so many spots where you can actually set up a tent and feel safe in it, so keep your eyes open. Fire wood is scarce. The ridge path is marked by a red band bordered by white bands. It starts in the Olt Valley on the railroad from Sibiu to the south, but most hikers dismiss the first portion as uninteresting and enter the ridge at the **Avrig Lake** or the **Puha Saddle** *(Șaua Puha)*. For any of these, take a train to **Avrig** (on the Brașov-Sibiu line), and follow the signs starting at the station. The first 10km or so is rather dull, on a flat and dusty road. The usual route goes from Avrig to the **Poiana Neamțului** *caban* and then climbs for about two hours to Cabana Bărcaciu, from which the ridge is three-four hours away. You should always allow one full day for getting near the ridge.

■ ■ ■ CLUJ-NAPOCA (KÖLOSVAR)

Proud of its Roman past, Cluj even has a statue of Lupina Capitolana with Romulus and Remus sent by "Mother Rome." Kölosvar is officially a bilingual city, and though many ethnic Hungarians are moving back to Hungary, the town's operas and two theaters still perform in both Romanian and Hungarian. The university also adds a foreign flavor to the atmosphere, with many Arab and Greek students. Watch your belongings carefully, but otherwise the city is enjoyable.

To get to the city center from the train station, take either bus 3 or 4 or head straight down the Str. Horea, which changes its name to Str. Gheorghe Doja after crossing the river. At the end of Str. Gheorghe Doja is Piața Unirii, the city's central square (20min. from the train station). A walk around the central square, over which the Gothic steeple of the **Catholic Cathedral** rises majestically, should help you to orient yourself. Cluj has a few interesting museums and churches. A walk up

ROMANIA

Str. Făcliei will bring you to the 15th-century **Biserica Reformată** (Reform Church), which often holds organ concerts. On neighboring Piața Victoriei, the **Catedrala Arhiepiscopală** (Orthodox Cathedral) holds services. (Mon.-Sat. 7:30-9:30am and 6-7pm, Sun. 8:30am-12:30pm and 6-7pm.) Also worth seeing are the **Museum of Transylvanian History,** Str. Constantin Daicoviciu 2 (open Tues. and Thurs.-Sun. 10am-5pm), the **Village Museum** in Park Hoia, and the **Ethnographic Museum of Transylvania,** Str. Memorandumului 21. ISICs earn discounts on admission. On Str. Universității, beginning from the southern end of Piața Unirii, you'll discover the student section of town. The hottest nightspot in town is the **Bianco e Niro** disco and bar, Str. Universității 7-9, with a high-tech sound and light system to keep you moving (300lei with ISIC). The **Nicula Monastery,** 60km towards Heudin, is accessible by bus, while the nearby **Apuseni Mountains** are a wonderful hiking area.

Practical Information, Accommodations and Food Cluj-Napoca can be reached by **train** from Budapest (6hr.), Bucharest (7hr.), and Brașov (4hr.). The tourist office **KmO** is located at Piața Unirii 10 (tel. (064) 19 65 57; open Mon.-Fri. 9am-6pm, Sat. 10am-1pm). Buy a map of the city (200 lei), change money, and ask about **private rooms** or university dorms. Next to KmO is the **CFR** agency (tel. (064) 11 24 75), but to get domestic tickets go to Piața Mihai Vitearul (tel. (064) 11 22 12). A **post office** with international telephones located around back is on Str. Gh. Doja 33 (open 7am-10pm). On the central square screams an insanely crowded **telephone office;** escape to the one 5min. away on Str. G. Barițiu (open 7am-10pm). On Piața Nihai Viteazu 11, you'll find the **TAROM** office (tel. (064) 13 02 34) which sells plane tix to Bucharest for US$44 (open Mon.-Fri. 7am-7pm, Sat. 7am-1pm).

Check the accommodations board at the train station for directions to the hotels in Cluj-Napoca. The **Hotel Vladeasă,** at Str. Gh. Doja 20 (tel. (064) 11 84 91), is the best value for both location and price. (Singles US$16. Doubles US$25, with bath US$28. Triples US$37.) Farther from the town center towards the train station is the old yellow **Hotel Astoria** (tel. (064) 13 01 66), on Str. Horea 3, whose rooms are spacious but bland. (Singles US$17, with bath US$21. Doubles US$25, with bath US$29. Triples US$34. Quads US$38.) **Camping Făget** (tel. (064) 11 62 34) is 8km from the city towards Bucharest. (US$4 for 1 person, US$5 for 2 people, US$6 for 3 people. Open May-Oct. 15.)

A **market** sprawls over Piața Nihai Viteazu (covered section open Tues.-Sat. 8am-4pm). Learn to love the mascot of student hang-out **Pizzeria New Croco,** up Str. Pasteur from Piața Păcii, a cheerful crocodile. Hippies predominate among the clientele inside dolphin-safe **Flipper,** past the Pizzeria New Croco, right on Str. Hașdeu, and then right on Str. Piezișa. Across from Flipper, **Restaurant Spaghetti** serves students beer from barrels. At **Cafetăria Tineretului,** (a.k.a. "Arizona"), university types sip coffee and peer through a cloud of smoke between classes (open Mon.-Fri. 8am-8pm, Sat. 9am-5pm).

Russia (Россия)

US$1 = 2250R (Rubles)	1000R = **US$0.44**
CDN$1 = 1650R	1000R = **CDN$0.61**
UK£1 = 3530R	1000R = **UK£0.28**
IR£1 = 3470R	1000R = **IR£0.29**
AUS$1 = 1680R	1000R = **AUS$0.60**
NZ$1 = 1220R	1000R = **NZ$0.82**
SAR1 = 630R	1000R = **SAR1.58**
Country Code: 7	**International Dialing Prefix: 810**

> In Russia's unstable economy, expect prices to have changed dramatically. As of July 1994, inflation of ruble prices was 10-15% a month, and the exchange rate was going up by 3 rubles to the dollar every day.

Russia is a sprawling agglomeration of east and west, which defies its own logic. With roots in Byzantium, Paris, and Mongolia, it straddles continents and cultures. Boris Yeltsin may sit at a table with the seven leading industrial nations but his country is a chaotic eastern bazaar, with its own ever-changing rules and frustrations. With the collapse of the Soviet Union, held together by the give of totalitarianism, the patchwork of autonomous regions and minority nationalities that make up the country has begun to tear apart. Russia is now redefining itself as a country of nationality as opposed to ideology, and has metamorphosed from the world's largest bastion of socialist power into an enormous, sprawling yard sale. Red banners are visible only in souvenir shops, *babushki* (elderly women) peddle the contents of their *dachas* (summer cottages), and enterprising young capitalists buy and sell western goods on street corners. Russians endure with unique resourcefulness and a heavy dose of black humor, saving, bartering, growing vegetables on their windowsills, and taking refuge around the kitchen table with homemade pickles and a bottle of vodka.

Since the Mongol invasion of the 13th century, Russia has been a nation in a virtually perpetual state of emergency. Early in the 18th century, Peter the Great's crash-westernization cost thousands of lives and precipitated a permanent crisis of cultural identity. Although Nicholas II established a congressional body, the *Duma*, World War I took a tremendous toll on the country, and the Lenin's organizational genius led to the bloodless October 1917 "coup" that cost the Tsars their crown. After the Bolshevik revolution came civil war and the first wave of political executions. Under Stalin, Russia experienced a boom in industrialization and suffered purges that left tens of millions dead. Khrushchev emerged as the new leader of Russia, and a political and cultural "thaw" followed in the early 1960's, before he was ousted by Brezhnev. Andropov and Chernyenko followed him in humorously quick succession, resulting in Gorbachev's tenure as General Secretary from 1985 and the beginning of political and economic reform for the Soviet Union. But what began with *glasnost* (openness) and *perestroika* (rebuilding) gradually turned into a bewildering hodgepodge of semi-anarchy, deepening economic crisis, and cynicism. Despite great popularity in the West (and the 1990 Nobel Peace Prize to show for it), Russian discontent with Gorbachev's reforms and a failed right-wing coup in August 1991 led to his resignation and Yeltsin's election as President of Russia.

Today Russia's future is uncertain. Yeltsin, while trying to construct a new Russian economy, is continually engaged in a power struggle with the Russian Parliament. That Parliament is now dissolved, and Yeltsin is once more on top, but it is anyone's guess what will happen next. Come and see for yourself.

GETTING THERE

Russian visas require an invitation with itinerary and dates of travel and, thus, are inherently difficult to get without a contact in Russia. However, some organizations specialize in supplying invitations and/or visas for individual tourists. **Travellers Guest House,** 50 Bolshaya Pereyaslavskaya 10th fl., Moscow, Russia 129401 (Moscow tel. (095) 971 40 59, fax 280 76 86), arranges visa invitations, will register you once you arrive in Russia, makes reservations, and gets train tickets. With an office in the U.S., **Russia House,** 1800 Connecticut Ave. NW, Washington DC 20009, attn.: Chris Poor (tel. (202) 986-6010, fax 667-4244) provides a visa, reservations, train tickets, etc. In Russia, contact the office at 17 Leningradsky Prospect, Moscow, Russia 125040 (tel. (095) 250 01 43, fax 250 25 03). For Australians, **Red Bear Tours,** 320B Glenferrie Rd., Malvern, Melbourne, Victoria 3144, Australia (tel. (3) 824 71 83 or (008) 33 70 31, fax 822 39 56), provides rail tickets across Russia and assorted tours. Their newsletter has the most recent information on their services. Also try **Russian Youth Hostels,** with offices worldwide: U.S., 409 N Pacific Coast Highway, Building 106, #390, Redondo Beach, CA 90277 (tel. (310) 379-4136, fax 379-8420); U.K., YHA Travel Store, 14 Southhampton St., London, WC2E 7HY (tel. (0171) 836 10 36); Finland, Eurohostel, Linnankatu 9, SF-00160 Helsinki (tel. (90) 66 44 52); Germany, DJH, Templehofer Ufer 32, 10963 Berlin (tel. (030) 264 95 20); and Estonia, Karol Travel Agency, Lembitu 4, EE0001, Tallinn (tel. (2) 45 49 00). Contact **Host Families Association** (HOFA) in Russia (tel. and fax (812) 275 19 92), U.S. (tel. (202) 333-9343), U.K. (tel. (01295) 71 06 48), or in Australia (tel. (03) 725 85 55).

If you have received an invitation, you must apply for the actual visa at a Russian embassy or consulate. Send a photocopy of your invitation, a photocopy of the front pages of your passport, a completed application (contact the embassy or a travel agent for blanks), 3 photographs, a cover letter (with your name, dates of arrival and departure, date of birth, and passport number), and the visa fee (most recently two-week service US$20, one-week US$30, same-day US$100) to the embassy or consulate. Include a return envelope with postage.

Most organizations will register your visa for you on arrival, but if this service is not included, go down to the central OVIR (ОВИР) office (in Moscow, at ul. Cherny-shevskaya 42, called УВИР) to register; many people ignore this step, but it's the law. This is also where you should try to extend your visa, although it can involve bureaucratic hassle. Officially, you can freely travel anywhere that isn't off-limits to foreigners (such as military bases and power plants), but local administration may give you a hard time if the city is not on your visa. It's generally OK to enter Russia through a city not specifically listed on your visa.

Many organizations in the U.S. run special educational tours to Russia. Try contacting **CIEE** (tel. (212) 661-1414) or the **American Council of Teachers of Russian** (ACTR), 1776 Massachusetts Ave. NW, Suite 300, Washington, DC 20036 (tel. (202) 833-7522). **Volunteers For Peace,** 43 Tiffany Rd., Belmont, VT 05730 (tel. (802) 259-2759), has innovative workcamps and language programs across the former Soviet Union which run US$300-700; group airfare to Russia for the programs runs US$950 round-trip. Visa-free cruises are available with many of the major Scandinavian lines, but their prices are prohibitive and not really fit for the budget traveler. **Group tours** are the easy way out, and now that travel has become so much easier in Russia, you risk missing out on the most interesting experiences and glimpses of the country. A little savvy and creativity will get you much farther than any organized itinerary.

Customs enforcement is arbitrary and unpredictable. There's not much you can do except be polite; one day they'll tear your pack apart, the next they'll just nod and dismiss you. If you fly in (especially with a group) your baggage will probably not be inspected. You may encounter more difficulty if you arrive by train or car. Weapons and narcotics are definitely off-limits; if you have any doubts, check with the Russian embassy before you go. Politely answer border officials, but *do not* offer any information that they don't specifically ask for. You can't bring rubles into or out of the country. At the border, you will be given a **Customs Declaration Form** on which to declare all your valuables and foreign currency. *Don't* lose it. Everything listed must be on your person when you leave the country. You *may not* export works of art, icons, old *samovars* (not electric), and antique books—technically, anything published before 1945. Military items such as army belts and flags are nominally contraband, but authorities hardly ever bother with them.

Flying on British Airways to St. Petersburg or Moscow is the most direct way to reach the former Soviet Union. **Rail travel** from Helsinki (7½hr., 265mk, Eurail and Scanrail 148mk) is a fine option; you can reserve in advance by telephone (tel. (90) 010 01 24) and pick up your ticket at a special office in the Helsinki station. The Finnish Moscow-bound train crosses the border before midnight; make sure your visa is valid from the date you leave Helsinki. Daily trains also run to Moscow and St. Petersburg from Eastern European capitals. If you are coming from Warsaw, your train will go through Belarus, now a separate sovereign country, for which you need a transit visa. Get it (US$25) at the Belarussian consulate in Warsaw, *not* at the border, where you will be taken off the train in the middle of the night. Rail travel from the Baltic capitals is an especially cheap and reliable option. **Buses** run from Helsinki via Lahti (8hr. 190-250mk); buy tickets at the station (tel. (90) 97 00 40 00) or on board. The **ferries** that cross from Stockholm and Helsinki to St. Petersburg carry organized tours only.

GETTING AROUND

Foreigners are now allowed free movement in Russia. You are officially required to buy internal plane and train tickets at inflated Intourist prices, but this is only enforced in Moscow and St. Petersburg. Elsewhere, buy your train tickets at the station like everyone else—and run the risk of only being able to get a 3rd-class seat, as trains are often crowded. You cannot buy train tickets originating in a different town, so it is best to use Moscow or St. Petersburg as a base and make a series of round-trip journeys from there.

Russia boasts an extensive **rail** and **bus** network and a vast, not-so-reliable **air** system monopolized by **Aeroflot** (Аэрофлот; LOT and Czech Air fly in Russia too.). **Train** cars are divided into 3 classes: luxury 2-bed "L" (Л) compartments, 4-bed cozy "coupés" (К) and *platskarti* (open-car couchettes; П). *electrichka* (commuter rail, marked on train station signs as пригородные поезда; *prigorodnye poezda*) have their own platforms at each train station; buy tickets from the *kassa* (касса; ticket counter). These trains are often packed; you may have to stand for an hour or more. Buses are slightly more expensive and less crowded than trains; they are a good option for shorter distances. Buy seats on *myakki* (мягкий; "soft") buses and you'll get a seat assignment in a fairly comfy reclining chair. You can usually store your luggage under the bus for about 100R.

Within Russian cities, overcrowded **buses, trams,** and (in major cities) unbelievably efficient **metro** systems ferry citizens for 50-150R per ride. In the metro, buy tokens at the *kassa* and drop them into machines that let you onto escalators. Buy bus tickets at newsstands or from the *babushki* at metro stations. For longer stays, a *yediny bilet* pass is valid on all forms of public transport for a month. On the bus you must validate your ticket in one of the little hole-punchers. Since it's often bone-crushingly crowded, riders often ask their neighbors to pass tickets up to be punched. The same goes for purchasing tickets, which can sometimes be done from the driver. Always buy tickets; fines for getting caught without are punitive (5000R). It is also customary for passengers to tap each other on the shoulder and ask if they are getting off at the next stop (Вы выходите?, "Vee vee-HOAD-it-yeh") so that everyone can push their way to an exit. Metro stations are all in Cyrillic; if you don't read Russian, you can usually recognize stations by memorizing the first and last letters. When two lines intersect, there is often a different station name for each line. You'll want to know the words *vkhod* (вход; entrance), *vykhod* (выход; exit), *vykhod v gorod* (выход в город; exit to the city), and *perekhod* (переход; passage to another line). Metro stations are marked above ground by a fluorescent red *M*. Try to acquire the newest city map possible, for metro stations and street names have been changing wildly in recent years, as tastes in politics have spun. However, in Moscow and St. Petersburg, maps and street signs have all caught up with the times.

Hailing a **taxi** is indistinguishable from hitchhiking. Almost all of those who stop will be private citizens, taking passengers to make a little extra cash. The custom is to step off the curb and hold out the hand; when a car stops, potential riders tell the driver their destination before getting in. He will either refuse the destination and speed off, or nod his head, at which point haggling over the price begins. Meters are non-operational. Those who do not speak Russian will get ripped off, and are lucky to get away for less than 10,000R.

RUSSIA ESSENTIALS

Be flexible. Expect airport delays, tour cancellations, hotel changes, cold showers, and bathrooms *sans* toilet paper. The rules have changed so often no one really knows what they are anymore. Travel in Russia requires ample preparation. Pack carefully; bring your sense of humor and any Western goods you will need. Most toiletries and other items are available in Moscow and St. Petersburg, but for higher prices. Ziplock bags and pocket packs of tissues are indispensable. Roach traps can be a godsend if you are staying in a dormitory.

Changing money in Russia is now easy. Find an *Obmen Valyuty* (Обмен Валюты; "currency exchange") sign. Many places will change Deutschmarks, and some French francs and British pounds along with U.S. dollars, but few will change traveler's checks. You are best off with dollars. Rubles are now convertible, real currency, with a published exchange rate (that is often higher every day). You will have no problem changing unspent rubles back at the end of your trip, but the exchange rate is so unstable, it's best not to change large sums of money at a time.

Russia can be a user-unfriendly society: state shops are crowded, with frustrating inefficiency and long lines. A 3-line process is the rule in stores. In the first line, ogle the products and find out their prices. Then stand in line to tell the cashier their departments and prices; pay and take the receipt. In the 3rd line, present the receipt to the salesperson and pick up your purchase—unless the store has already run out. This will only work in Russian. In Moscow and St. Petersburg there is a whole new crop of small western-style supermarkets selling food, toiletries, and household supplies, often for hard currency or credit cards. For souvenirs, look for enterprising Russians selling pins, dolls, and military gear outside major tourist attractions. The old state-run hard currency souvenir stores have in some cases been converted to private ventures; look for *beriozhka* (берёжка) signs. Because of the recent influx of western goods, token packs of cigarettes and ballpoint pens are no longer accepted as currency, and don't make very good gifts for Russians. When visiting friends, it is better to bring flowers or cookies or candy. Sweatshirts and t-shirts with city of college logos make good larger presents, as do cassettes of western pop music. A bottle of imported wine makes a very special present.

Language Though more and more people speak English in the former Soviet Union, take some time to familiarize yourself with the Cyrillic alphabet. It's not as difficult as it looks and will make getting around and getting by immeasurably easier.

Cyrillic	English	Pronunciation	Cyrillic	English	Pronunciation
А, а	a	d*a*cha	Р, р	r	B*r*ad
Б, б	b	*B*altimore	С, с	s	*S*arala
В, в	v	The *V*illage People	Т, т	t	*T*homas
Г, г	g	*G*alina	У, у	u	kit 'n' cab*oo*dle
Д, д	d	*D*avid	Ф, ф	f	*F*riend
Е, е	ye	*ye*llowtail	Х, х	xh	c*h*utzpah
Ё, ё	yo	*yaw*n	Ц, ц	ts	Let'*s* Go
Ж, ж	zh	*Zh*irinovsky	Ч, ч	ch	*ch*icken tender
З, з	z	*Z*ack	Ш, ш	sh	*Ch*arlotte
И, и	i	W*ee*vil	Щ, щ	shch	Khru*shch*ev
Й, й	y or j	(no sound)	Ъ, ъ	(hard)	(no sound)
К, к	*k*	Corrigan	Ы, ы	y	glottal "i"
Л, л	l	*L*anguid	Ь, ь	(soft)	(no sound)
М, м	m	*M*oscow	Э, э	eh	*A*lexander
Н, н	n	*N*atasha	Ю, ю	yoo	*you*
О, о	o	*L*a*w*	Я, я	yah	*Ya*hoo!
П, п	p	*p*uffin			

On the list of handy phrases-to-know: добрый день (DOH-bree DYEHN; "Good day"), спасибо (spa-SEE-bah; "thank you"), хорошо (hah-rah-SHOH; "OK"), извините (eez-vee-NEET-syeh; "excuse me"), где (gdyeh; "where"), касса (KAH-sah; "cash register" or "ticket office"), and метро (meh-TROH; "metro"). In the Slavic world, plurals of words are usually formed by adding the letter "ы" or "и" to the end, so the plural of *matryoshka* is *matryoshki*. Note that улица (*ulitsa;* abbreviated ул.) means "street"; проспект (*prospect;* пр.) means "avenue"; площадь (*ploshad;* пл.) means "square"; and бульвар (*bulvar;* бул.) is "boulevard." Once you get the hang of recognizing the letters, you can pronounce just about any Russian word—give it a try.

Communication There is neither rhyme nor reason to the former Soviet Union's **mail service.** Delivery can take anywhere from 2 weeks to eternity. It is not recommended that you use the Russian postal service for international mail. **American Express** card and traveler's check holders can receive letters at their travel service bureaus in Moscow and St. Petersburg; this is usually more reliable than Russian mail. **DHL** has offices in Moscow, St. Petersburg, and Nizhny Novgorod; they are expensive but reliable.

Local **telephones** in Moscow take special tokens, sold at metro station *kassas* for 100R; in St. Petersburg they take metro tokens. In most small towns, pay phones are free for local calls. You can make intercity calls from phone booths marked междугородные in each city. Have patience; it will take a while, but you will almost always get through, although calls from small towns are not always possible. Dial 8, wait for the tone, then dial the city code. Direct international calls buzz from telegraph offices and hotel rooms: Dial 8, wait for the tone, then dial 10 and the country code. To make calls from the telephone office, buy tokens and use the *mexhdugorodny aftomat* telephones (междугородный афтомат; "intercity phones"); be sure to press the *otbet* (ответ) button when your party answers, or you will not be heard. If there are no automatic phones, you must pay for your call at the counter and dial it yourself (your money will be returned if you do not get through) or have it dialed for you by the operator. Calls to North America cost 2000-5000R per minute with a 3min. minimum; calls to Europe run 1500-3000R per minute. You cannot call collect. Several hotels in Moscow now have direct-dial booths operated by a special card or credit card. The cost is astronomical (at least US$6 per min. to the U.S.). To reach AT&T **USADirect,** dial 155 50 42 in Moscow. Dial 095 first when calling from another city, you will be paying for the phone call to Moscow. To reach the **Sprint-Express** operator, dial 155 61 33 in Moscow. For **Canada Direct,** dial 810 80 04 97 72 33; **BT Direct** 810 80 04 97 72 66. If traveling independently, leave a copy of your itinerary with the embassy, along with your name, address, date and place of birth, and passport number. Calling into the country can be equally frustrating. The U.S., Canada, and most European countries have direct dial to Moscow and St. Petersburg. For other cities, go through the operator.

Accommodations   Western-style **youth hostels** have begun to arrive in Russia. The **Moscow Travellers' Guest House** and its affiliate, the **Holiday Hostel,** and the **St. Petersburg International Hostel** provide comfortable facilities in the two Russian capitals. Both arrange visas for your stay. Especially during summer, reserve well in advance. Hotels offer several classes of rooms: *Lux,* usually a two-room double with TV, phone, fridge, and bath, is the most expensive. *Pol-lux* is a one-room double of single with TV, phone, and bath. Rooms with bath and no TV, if they exist, are cheaper. The lowest price rooms are *bezudobstv* (безудобств), which means one room with a sink. Many hotels have restaurants on the ground floor, often the best eatery in town; all have at least a buffet or cafeteria—probably the worst food in town. In Russia, hot water gets turned off during part of the summer for pipe repair, so you may have to make do with cold showers.

Another cheap option can be staying in a **university** or institute dorm; many will take in foreign students for US$10 a night. Rooms are liveable, but don't expect sparkling bathrooms or reliable hot water. Make arrangements with an institute from the West.

Food and Drink   Although Moscow and St. Petersburg are now sprinkled with Western restaurants and Georgian cooperatives offering all kids of delicious food options, in the smaller towns and cities, while there is plenty to eat, little of it is actually tasty. Russians look upon food for its principle value—nourishment—and are not concerned much with taste. The standard hotel dinner menu includes *salat* (салат; "salad"), usually cucumbers or beets and potatoes with mayonnaise and sour cream; soup (суп), either meat or cabbage; and *kuritsa* (курица; "chicken") or *myaso* (мясо; "meat"), often called *kutlyeti* (кутлеты; "cutlets") or *bifsteaks* (бифштекс), a distant relative of hamburger. Dessert is *morozhenoye* (мороженое; "ice cream") and coffee (кофе) or *chai* (чай; "tea"). Russian **cafés** (кафе) offer similar-quality food for lower prices; often the tables have no chairs. *Stolovayas* (столовая; "cafeterias") are often unsanitary and should be viewed suspiciously.

RUSSIA

There are essentially three ways to buy food in Russia: on the street, from a store, or at a farmer's market (where prices are high but produce fresh). A **dietas** (Диета) sells goods for people on special diets (such as diabetics), a **produkty** (Продукты) specializes, a **gastronome** (Гастроном) has sorry-looking meat, fish, and dairy, and a **universam** (Универсам) carries packaged goods, fruits and vegetables. The **market** (рынок; *rynok*) in every town has abundant fruits and vegetables, butter, honey, and cheese. Wash everything before you eat it—Russian farmers use pesticides with a liberal hand. Be sure to bring all the containers you need—bags for carrying and pots for honey; these are not provided. If worse comes to worst, the ubiquitous **kiosks** in every town sell sodas, juice, candy bars, and cookies, and all you have to do is point at what you want. Buy booze in a Western grocery store. *Zolotoye koltso, Russkaya,* and *Zubrovka* are the best vodkas around, *Stolichnaya* and *Moskovskaya* are very well known, and the generic brand gets the job done.

Travelers are generally advised not drink the **water** in Russia. While often potable in limited doses, water cleanliness is on the decrease. It is recommended to boil your water for 10min. One final word of advice: take Pepto-Bismol and snack foods such as peanut butter, instant soup, and granola to tide you over on those days when you can't face another sour cream salad. Bon appetit!

■■■ MOSCOW (МОСКВА)

Moscow is huge, apocalyptic, and compelling. Home to one in fifteen Russians (and more every day), the city throbs with energy and noise. On the street, Moscow exhausts and exhilarates. It feels like one huge bazaar, where *mafiosi* selling Japanese televisions out of the back of a truck stand next to grandmothers offering up the potatoes and dill they've been growing at their *dachas* for the past 30 years. In Moscow, anything and everything is possible; after enough time here, the contradictions begin to seem normal. Moscow is the world's third most expensive city and the casino capital of the world; nightclub entrance fees can be upwards of US$50. At the same time, the average pensioner earns the equivalent of US$40 per month and can't afford to buy a banana. Moscow is made by contrasts; the Stalinist edifices make a gray backdrop to churches' and monasteries' splashes of color. And some beauty is not so hard to find; cool and peaceful parks lie along the eight-lane avenues. Here it's easy to forget you're in a city of 10 million.

ORIENTATION AND PRACTICAL INFORMATION

Moscow is laid out in a series of concentric rings, emanating from the Kremlin. The outermost "ring road" forms the city boundary, but most sights of interest to visitors lie within the inner "garden ring." **Red Square** (Красная Площадь; *Krasnaya Ploschad*) and the **Kremlin** (Кремль) mark the center of the city; nearby starts Moscow's popular shopping streets, **Novi Arbat** (Новый Арбат, formerly Prospect Kalinina), running west parallel to the Metro's blue lines, and **ulitsa Tverskaya** (улицаТверская), which goes north along the green line. Ul. Tverskaya was formerly called ul. Gorkovo; the upper half, which leads to the **Garden Ring** (Садовое Кольцо), the original limit of 19th-century Moscow, is now known as ul. Pervaya Tverskaya-Yamskaya. Learn Cyrillic, orient yourself by the **metro,** and you can never get really lost. All buses and trams eventually stop at one of the stations, marked by a red neon **M.** An extensive map of Moscow, including all public transportation routes and a street index, sells at many kiosks for less than a dollar.

Tourist Offices: Intourservice Central Excursion Bureau, ul. Belinskovo 4A (ул. Белинского), (tel. 203 8016 or 203 82 71, fax 200 12 43), around the corner from Intourist Hotel and 2 blocks from Red Square. If you don't speak Russian, you may have to buy your out-of-town excursions here. Open 9am-6pm. The **Moscow Excursion Bureau,** ul. Rozhdestvenka 5 (ул. Рождественка), (tel. 923 89 53), behind Detski Mir. If you speak some Russian, your best bet for out-of-town

RUSSIA

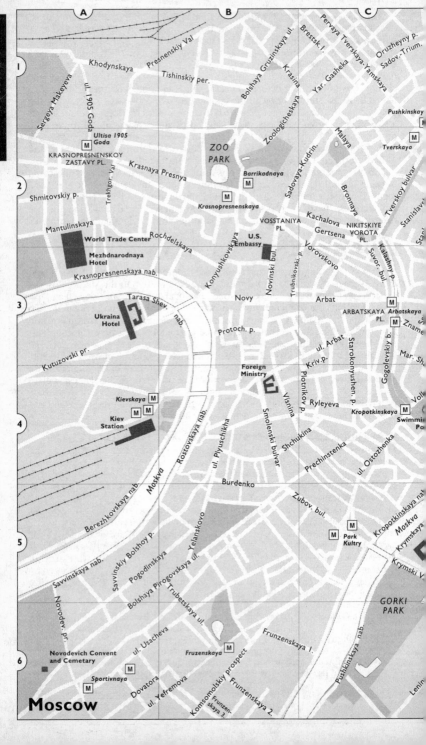

Moscow

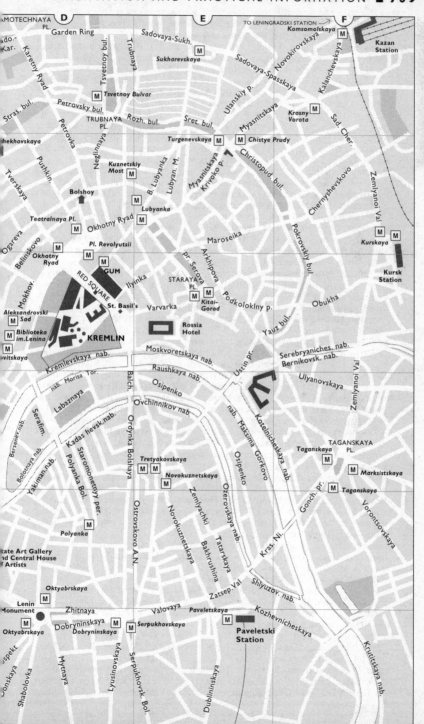

RUSSIA

MOTECHNAYA
PL.
D

Garden Ring

Sadovaya-Sukh.

E

TO LENINGRADSKI STATION

Komsomolskaya

F

M

Kazan
Station

ado.-
Kar.

Karetny Ryad

Tsvetnoy bul.

Trubnaya

Sukharevskaya

M

Sadovaya-Spasskaya

Novokirovskaya

Kalanchevskaya

Stras. bul.

M Tsvetnoy Bulvar

Petrovsky bul.

Rozh. bul.

Ulanskiy p.

Myasnitskaya

Krasny
Vorota

M

Sad Cher.

Petrovka

TRUBNAYA
PL.

Neglinnaya

Sret. bul.

Turgenevskaya

M

M Chistye Prudy

Krasny
Vorota

Chernyshevskovo

Zemlyanoi Val

hekhovskaya

Pushkin.

Kuznetskiy
Most

B. Lubyanka

Lubyan. M.

Myasnitskaya

Krivoko P.

Christopud bul.

Tverskaya

M

Bolshoy

M

M Lubyanka

Maroseika

Pokrovsky bul.

Kurskaya

M

Ogareva

Teatralnaya Pl.

M

Okhotny Ryad

Pl. Revolyutsii

Arkhipova

pr. Serova

Obukha

Kursk
Station

Belinskovo

M

Okhotny
Ryad

M

M GUM

Ilyinka

STARAYA
PL.

Podkolokllny p.

Mokhov.

RED SQUARE

St. Basil's

Varvarka

Kitai-
Gorod

M M

Yauz bul.

Aleksandrovski
Sad

M

KREMLIN

Rossia
Hotel

Serebryaniches. nab.
Bernikovsk. nab.

Biblioteka
im.Lenina

M

Kremlevskaya nab.

Moskvoretskaya nab.

Ustin pr.

Ulyanovskaya

Zemlyanoi Val

vitskaya

M

nab. Morisa Tor.

Raushskaya nab.

Labaznaya

Osipenko

Ovchinnikov nab.

Kadas hevsk.nab.

TAGANSKAYA
PL.

Serafim.

Ordynka Boishaya

Tretyakovskaya

Osipenko

Taganskaya

M

Bolotnaya nab.

Staromonetnny per.

M M

Novokuznetskaya

Kotelnicheskaya nab.

nab. Maksima Gorkovo

Gonch. pr.

M Marksistskaya

Bersenev.nab.

Yakiman.nab.

Polyanka Bol.

M

Zemlyachki

Ozerovskaya nab.

M Taganskaya

Vorontsovskaya

Polyanka

M

Ostrovskovo A.N.

Novokuznetskaya

Bakhrushina

Tatarskaya

Kras. Ni.

ate Art Gallery
nd Central House
f Artists

Oktyabrskaya

M

Shlyuzov. nab.

Zatsep. Val

Kozhevnicheskaya

Lenin
Monument

Zhitnaya

Valovaya

Paveletskaya

Oktyabrskaya

M

Dobryninskaya

M Serpukhovskaya

M

Paveletski
Station

ospekt

Dobryninskaya

Paveletskaya

Kozhevnicheskaya

Jonskaya

Shabolovka

Mytnaya

Lyusinovskaya

Serpukhovsk. Bol.

Dublininskaya

Krutitskaya nab.

RUSSIA

excursions, walking tours, etc. Tours of Moscow plus daytrips to Vladimir and Suzdal, all for rubles. Open 10am-2pm and 3-6pm.

Embassies: U.S., Novinski bul. 19/23 (tel. 252 24 51). M: Баррикадная (Barikadnaya). Open Mon.-Fri. 9am-6pm. **Canada,** Starokonyusheni per. 23 (tel. 241 50 13 or 241 11 11). Open Mon.-Fri. 8:30am-1pm and 2-5pm. **U.K.,** nab. Sofiskaya 14 (tel. 230 63 33, fax 233 35 63). Open Mon.-Fri. 9am-12:30pm and 2:30-6pm. **Ireland,** Grokholsky per. 5 (tel. 288 41 01). **Australia,** Kropotkinski per. 13 (tel. 246 50 12). Open Mon.-Fri. 9am-12:30pm and 1:30-5pm. **New Zealand,** ul. Povarskaya 44 (tel. 290 12 77 or 290 34 85). Open Mon.-Fri. 8:30am-12:30pm and 1:30-5pm; Sept.-May 9am-12:30pm and 1:30-5:30pm. **Czech Republic,** ul. Yuliusa Fuchika 12/14 (tel. 251 05 40). Open Mon.-Fri. 8:30am-5pm. **Hungary,** ul. Mosfilmovskayu 62 (tel. 143 86 11). Open Mon.-Fri. 8:30am-4:30pm. **Poland,** ul. Klimashinka 4 (tel. 255 00 17). Open Mon.-Fri. 9am-5pm.

Currency Exchange: *Moscow Express Directory,* updated biweekly and available free in most luxury hotels, lists places to buy and sell traveler's checks, and exchange money. **Credo Bank,** Leantyersky Per. 10 (tel. 925 80 83), cashes traveler's checks and deals with international money orders.

American Express: ul. Sadovaya-Kudrinskaya 21a (ул. Садовая-Кудринская), (tel. 956 90 00 or 956 90 05). M: Mayakovskaya (Маяковская). Left out of the metro onto ul. Sadovaya-Bolshaya (ул. Садовая-Большая), which becomes ul. Sadovaya-Kudrinskaya. All banking services for cardholders. **ATM** in lobby open 24hrs. Office open Mon.-Fri. 9am-5pm.

Post Offices: Moscow Central Telegraph, ul. Tverskaya 7, a few blocks from the Kremlin. Look for the globe and the digital clock out front. M: Okhotny Ryad. **Poste Restante:** 103009. International mail open Mon.-Fri. 8am-2pm and 3-9pm, Sat. 8am-2pm and 3-7pm, Sun. 9am-2pm and 3-7pm. Poste Restante also at the **Intourist Hotel Post Office,** ul. Tverskaya 3/5. Address mail to До Востребования *(Do Vostrebovania),* K-600, Intourist Hotel, ul. Tverskaya 3/5, Moscow. To mail **packages,** especially books, bring them unwrapped to the Intourist Hotel Post Office or to Moscow Central Telegraph; they will be wrapped and mailed while you wait. Open Mon.-Fri. 9am-1pm and 2-5pm, Sat. 9am-1pm and 2-4pm.

Telephones: At **Moscow Central Telegraph.** Prepay at the counter. Calls to the U.S. cost 2000-6000R per min. Telegrams at windows 7-9 (650R per word). Faxes 10,800R per page. Open 8am-8pm. Branch office at 22 is less crowded. **International telephone cabinets** (международный телефон; *mezhdunarodni telefon)* at M: Boykovskaya (Бойковская) are much less of a wait. Major hotels have direct-dial phone booths at exorbitant prices (1min. to the U.S.: US$6-15). International calls can also be placed from private homes. **Local calls** require either a metal *zheton* (жетон) or a one-ruble coin: these are sold at some (not all) metro stations or kiosks for 150R. **City Code:** 095.

Flights: International flights arrive at **Sheremetyevo-2** (Шереметьево-2) to the north (tel. 578 91 01, 578 71 79, or 578 56 14). Most domestic flights originate at **Vnukovo** (Внуково), (tel. 436 22 81), **Domodedovo** (Домодедово), (tel. 323 86 56), or **Sheremetyevo-1,** (tel. 578 62 20). Buses link all three airports; commuter rail goes to Vnukovo and Domodedovo. Cabs will rip you off like you've never seen—up to 100,000R—but you have no choice.

Trains: 8 mainline stations, most along the metro's Ring Line. Trains to St. Petersburg and some to Estonia depart from **Leningradski vokzal** (Ленинградский Вокзал). M: Komsomolskaya (Комсомольская). Across the street are **Kazanski vokzal** (Казанский Вокзал) and **Yaroslavski vokzal** (Ярославский Вокзал), where the Trans-Siberian leaves (US$250.) Other stations are served by Metro stops: **Paveletski vokzal** (Павелетский Вокзал) and **Kurski vokzal** (Курский Вокзал) serve the south. **Rizhski vokzal** (Рижский Вокзал) serves Rīga, Latvia (16hr.) and Estonia. Trains from Warsaw (22hr.), Vilnius, Lithuania (18hr.), and Prague arrive at **Belorusski vokzal** (Белорусский Вокзал). Trains to Ukraine, the Czech Republic, Slovakia, Bulgaria, and Romania use **Kievski vokzal** (Киевский Вокзал). Train info, tel. 266 90 00. Intourist general info tel. 262 33 42.

Public Transportation: The **Metro (M)** will teach you the importance of learning the Cyrillic alphabet. Вход means "entrance", Выход "exit", Выход в город "exit to the street", and Переход "passage to a different line" and often to a new station: a

RUSSIA

station which serves more than one line will generally have different names. Trains run 6am-1am (fare 150R). Buses and trolleys cost 150R per ride; tickets available in metro station *kassi* (кассы) and sometimes from the driver. *Yedinye bilyeti* (единые билеты; "month-passes") let you ride on any form of transportation (16,500R). Monthly metro passes are more cost-effective (9000R). Purchase either from the *kassi*. Metro maps are included on the back of the Moscow map (free in hotels) or buy one at any kiosk.

Taxis: Tel. 927 00 00, for Kutozovsky, Gruzinsky, Sadovaya, and center tel. 137 00 40, for hard currency only tel. 457 90 05. If you don't speak Russian, it's nearly impossible to get anyone to take you for rubles. Ask around for the going rate before you get in a cab, and agree on a price before you set off. Taxi stands are indicated by a round sign with a green "T." Meters are strictly ornamental.

Laundromat: Unless you want to shell out megabucks for a dry cleaners, there are no laundromats in Moscow. Traveler's Guest House will do your laundry for 6000R per load. Your bathtub might be more convenient.

Medical Assistance: European Medical Center, Gruzinski per. 3, korpus 2 (tel. 253 07 03 or 229 65 36). French joint venture offering walk-in medical care for hard currency (US$76 per visit, students US$61). Open Mon.-Fri. 9am-6pm. The **American Medical Center** provides 24hr. emergency assistance. Located at Shchmitovsky Proezd 3. M: Ulitsa 1905 goda (tel. 256 82 12 or 256 33 66).

Emergencies: Ambulance: tel. 03. **Fire:** tel. 01. **Police:** tel. 02. No coins needed from pay phones. Also try the U.S. Embassy's emergency number (tel. 252 24 51). International SOS tel. is 120 52 51.

ACCOMMODATIONS

Suffice it to say that the concept of budget accommodations for student travelers has yet to arrive in Moscow—nor does it appear to be on the horizon. To get to **Traveller's Guest House,** Bolshaya Pereyaslavskaya 50 (Большая Переяславская), (tel. 971 40 59, fax 280 76 86; M: Prospect Mira), walk north along pr. Mira and go right on Banny Pereulok (Банный Переулок), the 3rd right, then left at the end of the street. If you speak no Russian and know no Muscovites, this will be all you'll ever need; it's also a full-service travel agency with an English-speaking staff. (Dorms US$15. Singles US$30. Doubles US$35. Reservations are a must, especially in the summer.) **Prakash Guesthouse,** ul. Profsoyuznaya 83 (ул. Профсоюзная), (tel. 334 25 98; M: Belyaovo (Беляюго)) is several stops beyond Oktyabrskaya (Октябрьская) on the orange line. From the center, take the exit nearest the first car of the train, and then go all the way to the left, exiting on the left side of the *perehod*. The guesthouse is a block up on the right. A renovated dormitory, it's the only place in Moscow for Indian food. (Singles US$30, payable in dollars or rubles. Doubles US$40. Both with shower and toilet. Breakfast US$5, dinner US$10. Movies—Indian and American—every night. Open 7am-11pm; call ahead if arriving later or earlier.)

FOOD

Eating out in Moscow is a luxury mainly enjoyed by foreigners and the new Russian elite. Meals are outrageously expensive and quality generally leaves a lot to be desired. There are, of course, a few exceptions, but everybody knows them so reservations are a must—simply make a round of calls at noon to secure a table for that evening. Alternately, adopt an early eating schedule; Russians tend to come later and linger until closing, making a meal an extended social outing, although this is becoming somewhat less common as the concept of business meals enters into Russian life. Restaurants with prices listed in dollars usually accept either credit cards or rubles; dollars are no longer legal tender for such transactions. If you're going for ethnic fare, Georgian is usually best—tasty and cheap. If you do go Russian, make sure that you're getting a *chisti stol* (clean table—without a large assortment of appetizers for which you will pay dearly). **Cafés,** substantially cheaper than restaurants, often serve even better food—offering one or two well prepared dishes rather than a selection of mediocre ones; they are also faster and less dark and formal.

RUSSIA

Restaurants

Patio Pizza, ul. Volkhonka 13a (ул. Волхонка) (tel. 201 50 00), opposite Pushkin Museum of Fine Arts. M: Kropotkinskaya. This place rocks, come early. Delicious thin-crust pizzas and a scrumptious array of desserts, without lightening your wallet excessively. Well-stocked all-you-can-eat salad bar US$6. 28cm pizzas US$5-15 (most are US$6). Lasagna US$6. Italian wines from US$7. Chocolate mousse or sinful chocolate nutcake US$4. Open noon-midnight.

Santa Fe, ul. Mantulinskaya 5/1 (ул. Мантулинская) (tel. 256 14 87). M: Ulitsa 1905 goda. A hefty walk—exit onto ulitsa 1905 goda from metro and follow it straight to the Mezhdunarodny, then turn right. It's on your left. A yummy American food oasis even for the budget traveler. Fast service with a smile. Reservations a must. Black bean soup US$4. Cajun burger US$10. Vegetable pasta US$10. Large desserts US$6-10. Open noon-midnight.

American Bar and Grill, Sadovaya Triumfalnaya ul., opposite M: Mayakovskaya (tel. 250 95 25 or 250 79 99). No reservations, but worth the long wait. A good place for large groups and noisy fun. New England clam chowder US$4. BBQ baby back ribs US$12. NY style cheesecake US$6. Open 24hrs. American breakfast served 4am-11am. French toast with maple syrup US$5.

Trenmos Bistro Bar, ul. Ostozhenka 1/9 (ул. Остоженка). Across from M: Kropotkinskaya (tel. 202 57 22). The name (truncated Trenton (NJ)-Moscow) and founders are all-American, as is the menu. Cheeseburger US$7, spaghetti marinara US$5, spinach lasagna US$6, pizza US$7. Restaurant open noon-11pm.

Delhi (Дели), ul. Krasnaya Presnya 23-b (tel. 255 17 66). M: ul. 1905 goda. Left out of the station, heading toward the Stalinist tower. A refreshing number of vegetarian options. Menu in Russian, Urdu, and English. Ask to eat in the ruble room. Both rooms have the same menus with vastly differing prices. Tandoori Chicken US$18 or 7500R. Spicy chick peas US$4 or 5000R. Lamb curry US$11 or 7900R. Open noon-5pm, 7-11pm.

Guria, pr. Komsomolski 7 (tel. 246 03 78). M: Park Kultury. Homey restaurant that serves delicious Georgian fare for some of the lowest prices in the city. A vegetarian meal of *lobio* (beans), *khachapuri*, salad, and Georgian yogurt comes to 10,000R. *Satsivi* (turkey in walnut sauce) 6000R. *Khachapuri* 2000R. Menu in English. Bring your own drinks. Open 11am-11pm.

U Pirosmani (У Пиросмани), pr. Novodevichi 4 (tel. 247 19 26), across from the Novodevichy Convent (giving it one of Moscow's best views). M: Sportivnaya (Спортивная). Specializing in delicately spiced Georgian cuisine, a cooperative above the rest for its flavorful dishes. *Lobio* US$3. *Khachapuri* US$1. *Baklazhany* US$4. Bottle of Georgian wine US$12. Open noon-4:30pm and 6-10:30pm. Dinner reservations a must.

Baku-Liban (Баку Ливан), ul. Tverskaya 24. M: Mayakovskaya. Wait in line for *schwarma* (2500R) and other middle eastern delicacies for deliciously low prices at the stand-up café on the right side. On the left, upstairs, is an elegantly set restaurant of the same name (tel. 299 85 06) which serves *tabbouleh* (US$6), *hommos* (US$7), falafel (US$6), and pricier plates entitled "With love from Lebanon." Open 11am-5pm, 6-11pm. Credit cards accepted at the restaurant.

Aztec, in the Hotel Intourist, ul. Tverskaya 3/5, 20th fl. (tel. 956 84 89). M: Okhotny Ryad. If the super-friendly service and good Latin American food don't entice you, the superb view will. Nachos US$7. Chicken burrito US$15. Cheese enchilada US$13. Sunday brunch 10am-3pm. Restaurant open 24hrs.

Rocky's, Kuznetski Most 7 (tel. 921 25 29). Another oasis for homesick Americans—a bar 'n' grill, complete with Stallone posters and loud American pop music. Some of the waitstaff speak English. Fish and chips US$11. *Chile con carne* US$10. Deluxe burgers US$8. Pint of beer US$5, ½-pint US$3. Open 11am-midnight.

La Cantina, ul. Tverskaya on the right of the Intourist Hotel. M: Okhotny Ryad (tel. 292 53 88). Carefully executed Mexican restaurant with a Russian twist. Nachos and chili US$6. Large chicken enchiladas a whopping US$12. Open 11am-11pm.

Café Margarita (Кафе Маргарита), ul. Malaya Bronnaya 28 at the corner of Maly Kosikhinski (Малый Козихинский), (tel. 299 65 34). Super-trendy café opposite Patriarch's Ponds, where Bulgakov's *The Master and Margarita* begins. Live piano music nightly (cover 3000R). *Lobio* 5000R, *blini* with mushrooms 7000R. Open 2-5pm and 6pm-midnight.

Cafés and Fast Food

Café Russkaya Kykhnya (Кафе Русская Кухня). 2nd floor of GUM department store, at the St. Basil's end. One of the nicest cafés serving Russian food you'll find—clean and bright, with marble floors and fake ivy. Good food at good price. *Borscht* 755R, pizza 1200R, mushroom omelet 2000R. Open 8am-8pm.

Blinchiki (Блинчики). A stand off Tverskaya on Strasnoy Bulvar (Страстной Бульвар) diagonally opposite McDonald's. Scrumptious apricot-filled *blini* ("Russian crêpes") 400R. Open 10am-8pm.

Pizza (Пицца). Next to Blinchiki, also has long lunch lines, and cheap *authentic* pizza, baked on the premises. Slice 1200R. Whole pie 5300R. Open 11am-7pm.

Café Oladi (Оладьи), ul. Pushkinskaya 15, just past the Tchaikovsky Conservatory. The namesake dish are small, sweet pancakes, 400R. Order at the counter and then stand at one of the tall tables to eat. Yum. Open 9am-7pm.

Blini, ul. Myasnitskaya 14/12 (ул. Мясницкая), 2 blocks north of Lubyanka Ploschad. Unassuming Russian café; look for the vertical "Блины" sign outside. Pancakes with chocolate, vanilla, or raspberry sauce 350R. Open Mon.-Sat. 10am-6pm.

McDonald's (Макдоналдс, not that you need the Cyrillic to recognize it), ul. Bolshaya Bronnaya 29, on Pushkin Square. M: Pushkinskaya. You can't miss the golden arches. It's always packed mostly with Russians lining up for a hamburger and *kartofel fri*. Big Mac 3600R, large fries (Большая порция картофеля-фри) 2500R. Cheeseburger 200R. Two other McDs are at ul. Arbat 50/52 (M: Smolenskaya) and Gaznetny per. 17/9, near Central Telegraph (M: Okhotny Ryad). There is relative calm until 2pm, when Russians start feeding.

Kombi's, with locations at 46-48 Prospect Mira near the Traveler's Guest House, Tverskaya ul. 4, M: Teatralnaya, and ul. Tverskaya-Yamskaya 2 off ul. Tverskaya at M: Mayakovskaya. A clean, western-style sandwich shop with subs (3500-5000R), salads (1500-2800R), milkshakes (2100R). English menu. Open 10am-10pm.

Rostik's (Ростик'с), 2nd floor of GUM department store, at the end nearest Kazan Cathedral. Moscow's answer to KFC. 2 pieces of chicken with roll 3200R. 3 pieces 6000R. 16 chicken pieces 26,000R. Fries 1000R, shakes 1400R. The menu is in Russian and English; order and pay at one of the *kassas,* then go get your food. Takeout, too. Open 10am-8pm.

Markets

To replenish your diet after too many potato and sour cream salads, go to a farmer's market—*rynok* (рынок; pronounced "REE-nuk")—where Russians, as well as Georgians, Armenians, Uzbeks, and peasants from all over cart their finest produce to Moscow. Impromptu markets spring up around metro stations; some of the best are at M: Turgenevskaya (Тургеневская), Kuznetski Most (Кузнетский Мост), Aeroport (Аэропорт), and Baumanskaya (Бауманская).

The number of western-style **supermarkets** is expanding monthly as the need to use them decreases. Many of the goods sold here can be found in kiosks and in even smaller combination markets selling Russian and western foods, but little beats the convenience of knowing you can find everything you need all at the same place. **Sadko Arcade,** behind Krasnya Presnya park along the river (M: ulitsa 1905 goda) is a 45min. walk from the Metro, convenient only if you have a car. If you do, this sleek market surprisingly has some of the best prices in town and certainly one of the largest selections. (Open 10am-8pm.) The **Arbat Irish House,** 11 Novi Arbat (M: Arbatskaya), is a supermarket-clothing-electronics store with an Irish Bar to boot. A well-stocked Russian supermarket, **Novoarbatski Gastronom,** flanks the Irish House on the left. (Irish House open Mon.-Sat. 9am-9pm and Sun. 10am-8pm.) **Global USA Supershop,** ul. Usacheva 35 (Усачева) (M: Sportivnaya (Спортивная)) stocks electronics, clothing, and some food, too (open 10am-10pm).

SIGHTS

Red Square (Красная Площадь) There is nothing red about it; *krasnaya* meant "beautiful" long before the Communists took over. Red Square is a 2280ft. long lesson in Russian history and culture: on one side, the **Kremlin**, at once the historical and religious center of Russia and the seat of the Communist Party for 70-odd years; on the other, **GUM** (ГУМ), the *Gosudarstveny Universalny Magazin* (State Department Store), once a market, then the world's largest purveyor of the grim consumer goods of the Soviet economy, now a bona fide shopping mall. **St. Basil's Cathedral** (Собор Василия Блажного; *Sobor Vasiliya Blazhnovo*) with its crazy-quilt onion domes, is the second oldest building in the square. Downstairs is an exhibit on the history of the church and Ivan's campaign against the Tatars, all in Russian. (Cathedral open Wed.-Mon. 10am-5pm. 4000R; tickets on sale until 4:30pm.) The **History Museum** and **Lenin Museum,** both of which are now closed for physical and ideological repair. Indeed, Lenin's historical legacy has finally come into question, and his name and face are coming down all over Moscow. In the glory days, **Lenin's Mausoleum** in front of the Kremlin used to be guarded by fierce goose-stepping guards, and the line to get in was hours long. The guards have now been replaced by one bored cop, and the line has vanished. Entrance to the Mausoleum also gives access to the **Kremlin wall** where Stalin, Brezhnev, Andropov, Gagarin, and American John Reed, among others, are buried. (Open Tues.-Thurs, Sat. 10am-1pm, Sun. 10am-2pm. Both free.) Turn right out of GUM down Nikolskaya Ulitsa (ул. Никольская); this is a nice walking street and leads you to **Lubyanka Ploschad** (пл. Лубянка), site of the headquarters of the KGB and formerly of a huge statue of Fyodor Derzhinsky, the organization's founder. Previously called Ploschad Derzhinskovo, it has now been named Lubyanka—after the name of the KGB prison.

Kremlin (Кремль) Like a spider in her web, the Kremlin sits geographically and historically in the center of Moscow. Here Ivan the Terrible reigned with an iron fist, and Stalin ruled behind the Iron Curtain. Napoleon watched Moscow burn, and the Congress of People's Deputies dissolved in 1991, ending the Soviet Union. Buy tickets at the *kassa* in Aleksandrovsky Sad on the west side of the Kremlin and enter through Borovitskaya gate tower in the southwest corner. Shorts and large bags are not allowed; there is a checkroom. Start at **Cathedral Square,** where the most famous gold domes in Russia rise. All the churches are now museums; buy tickets at the door or an all-for-one ticket at the main *kassa*. The **Annunciation Cathedral** holds the loveliest iconostasis in Russia, with luminous icons by Andrei Rublyev and Theophanes the Greek. Across the way is the square **Archangel Cathedral,** also with vivid icons and frescoes, as well as the final resting place for many Tsars prior to Peter the Great. The centerpiece of Cathedral Square is **Assumption Cathedral,** where Ivan the Terrible's throne stands by the south wall. Behind Assumption Cathedral is **Patriarch's Palace,** site of the Museum of 17th-Century Russian Applied Art and Life and the **Church of the Twelve Apostles,** built by Patriarch Nikon in the 17th century as revenge against Ivan the Terrible's extravagant St. Basil's Cathedral.

Also open to visitors is the **Armory Museum,** just to the left as you enter. All the riches of the Russian Church, and those of the State that are not in the Hermitage can be found in these nine rooms. **The Diamond Fund,** an annex of the Armory, has still more glitter, including a 190-carat diamond given to Catherine the Great by Gregory Onov (a special friend of hers). That's all of the Kremlin you can actually go into, except for the **Kremlin Palace of Congresses,** the square white monster built by Krushchev in 1961 for Communist Party Congresses. It's also a theater, one of the few open in the summer for concerts and ballets. (The Kremlin open Fri.-Wed. 10am-4:30pm. 200R. Each cathedral 5000R, students 2500R. All cathedrals 20,000R, students 10,000R. Armory and Diamond Fund US$10, students US$5, payable in rubles. Patriarch's Palace is 5000R, students 2500R.) **Aleksandrovsky Sad** (Александровский Сад; Alexander Gardens) is more than just the place to buy your Kremlin tickets, this is a pleasant garden and a cool green respite from the carbon monoxide fumes of central Moscow. At the north end is the **Tomb of the Unknown Soldier** where, like those in every city in Russia, an eternal flame burns in memory of the catastrophic losses the country suffered in World War II, the Great Patriotic War.

Pushkin Square, the Arbat, and the Patriarch's Ponds Halfway up ul. Tverskaya from Red Square, **Pushkin Square** (M: Pushkinskaya) is Moscow's favorite rendezvous spot. Amateur politicians gather on the square to argue and hand out petitions and missionary groups try to attract followers. All the major Russian news organizations are located in this region, perhaps one of the reasons the square is the center of free speech. At M: Arbatskaya, the **Arbat,** a pedestrian shopping arcade, was once a showpiece of glasnost, a haven for political radicals, Hare Krishnas, street poets, and *metallisti* (heavy metal rockers). Now, however, it boasts McDonald's, a Baskin Robbins, and the United Colors of Benetton. With these forerunners of capitalism, this formerly infamous street has lost much of its political significance and life. Follow ul. Bolshaya Bronnaya, next to McDonald's, down to the bottom of the hill, turn right and follow ul. Malaya Bronnaya to the **Patriarch's Ponds,** where the action of Mikhail Bulgakov's novel *The Master and Margarita* begins. This region, known as the Margarita, is popular with artsy students and old men playing dominoes by the shaded pond.

Houses of Worship and Parks When you can't take the grime and bedlam any more, escape to one of Moscow's hidden parks or monasteries. Among the most famous is the **Novodevichi Monastir** (Новодевичи Монастырь; convent), near M: Sportivnaya (Спортивная). You can't miss the high brick walls, golden domes, and tourist buses. Buried within the monastery's walls are some well-known 16th-century Russians, but all the truly famous folks are entombed at the cemetery next door. Wandering around the grounds is rewarding on a pleasant day, but a few of the buildings are also open. The **Smolenski cathedral,** in the center of the convent, is stunning inside. Unfortunately, due to staff shortages it is closed in rainy weather, when only the museum, housed in a white building to the left, is open—on sunny days, the museum is closed. Turning right and down the street, the convent's **cemetery** cradles the graves of Gogol, Chekhov, Stanislavsky, Khrushchev, Shostakovich, Mayakovsky, Bulgakov, and other luminaries. The gravestones are often creative representations—visual or symbolic—of the deceased. Buy tickets to the cemetery at the small kiosk across the street from the entrance; if you can read Cyrillic a useful map of the cemetery is sold there (500R). (Open 10am-6pm. 1500R, children 800R.)

Large, airy and lovely, **Moscow Synagogue,** ul. Arkhipova (ул. Архипова), gives a very different feeling than Russia's churches. From M: Kitai-Gorod (Китай-Город), walk up Arkhipova two blocks; it's the yellow building with white columns on the right with the Hebrew over the door. Under the Russian system, Judaism is a race—if you are Jewish, you are not Russian. This is not a Russian place; you could be in any synagogue, anywhere. Services are held daily, morning and evening, during which time women are not allowed downstairs and men must cover their heads. Otherwise, it's open to the public.

To get an understanding of Russian spiritual life, attend an Orthodox service. One 17th-century jewel is the **Church of St. Nicholas** at Komsomolski pr. and ul. Frunze (M: Frunzenskaya). Daily services are at 8:00am and 6pm; women must cover their heads. Another ecclesiastic gem is the 18th-century **Church of Ionna Voina,** on ul. Dimitrova, M: Oktyabrskaya (Октябрьская), named after the patron saint of the tsar's musketeers. (Services 8am and 6pm). The inner south region in general is speckled with numerous, sometimes boarded-up churches; simply walk around the neighborhood to find one you like. The **Yelokhovski Cathedral,** ul. Spartakovskaya 15 (M: Baumanskaya; Бауманская), is Moscow's largest and perhaps most beautiful operational church. Built in 1845, the turquoise exterior is outshone only by the gilded interior. (Services Mon. and Sat. 8am and 6pm, Sun. and holidays 7am and 10am.)

The **Church of St. Nicholas of the Weavers** is one of Moscow's better known churches, mainly because it's very hard to miss. Located at the corner of Komsomolsky prospelet and ul. Timura Frunze across from the very popular Café Guria (M:

Park Kultury), it looks like a church Hansel and Gretel's witch would have designed—white-washed with deliciously artificial green and orange trimming. Enter off ul. Timura Frunze around the back of this functioning church to witness the low-ceilings and colorful interior for yourself (evening service 6pm).

From M: Park Kultury (Парк Культуры), cross the **Krimski Most** bridge to **Gorky Park,** or from M: Oktyabrskaya (Октябрьская) enter through the main flag-flanked gate on Krymski Val. This is Moscow's amusement park, where droves of out-of-towners and young Muscovites promenade and relax, smiling and munching on some sweet delicacy sold at the numerous kiosks in the park. (Open 9am-10pm; Mon.-Thurs. 1000R, Fri.-Sun. 2000R. Most rides 2000R.)

The best time to come to **Izmailovsky Park** (Измайловский Парк), M: Izmailovsky Park, is late Sunday afternoon, when people want to go home and are willing to make a deal. Use you're Russian and you're less likely to get ripped off. Everything is on sale here, from carpets and samovars to military uniforms, pins, and old Soviet money. Some stalls even take orders, delivery in a week. (Bazaar open Sat.-Sun. 10am-4pm. 200R.) Another relatively untourested respite from Moscow's chaos is the tsars' **Kolomenskoye Summer Residence,** on a wooded rise above the Moskva River at M: Kolomenskaya (Коломенская). Peter the Great's 1702 log cabin and Bratsk Prison, where the persecuted Archpriest Avvakum wrote his celebrated auto-biography, have been moved here from Arkhangelsk and Siberia respectively. An exit from the Kropotkinskaya Metro still reads "Бассейн Москва," or **Moscow swimming pool,** but like many unfortunate Soviet creations, this former landmark is no more. It lies empty, waiting to be bulldozed into a public garden.

The **Moscow State University** (МГУ; EM-GEH-OO) a hefty walk from M: Universitet (Университет), lies within a single Stalinist edifice; to fully appreciate its size, you must go inside, which means persuading a student-friend to take you. If you're desperate for foreign company, hang out in the neighborhood: you're bound to run into some of the many foreigners who come to study here. Near Moscow State University, in the **Lenin Hills** (a leafy enclave overlooking the city center) is a one of the city's best viewing areas from which you can see the **Luzhniki Sports Complex,** the **Lenin Stadium** (sites of the infamous 1980 Olympics), and all of Moscow behind it. Considered a highly romantic spot, this could be a Russian make-out point, except for the camera-toting tourists and the not-so-picturesque view. Most of the golden splashes are lost in the sea of gray.

Museums

Well worth a peek is the **Moscow Metro.** All the stations are unique, and those inside the ring line are quite elaborate, with mosaics, sculptures, and crazy chandeliers. And with trains coming every two minutes, you can stay as short or long as you like. Stations Kievskaya (Киевская), Mayakovskaya (Маяковская), and Ploschad Revolutsii (Площадь Революции) are particularly good, as are Novoslobodskaya (Новослободская) and Mendeleevskaya (Менделеевская).

Pushkin Museum of Fine Arts, ul. Volkhonka 12. M: Kropotkinskaya (Кропоткинская). It gained the bulk of its impressive collection after the revolution made sure that every museum would no longer be a museum of private collections. The Egyptian exhibit on the first floor and the French impressionists (mainly Monets) are understandably two major pilgrimage areas, but as the museum frequently rotates its large collection, spending enough time in each section is probably more advisable. The floor plan on each floor is quite detailed, or you can buy an excursion Walkman which lasts 1hr. (4000R) to walk you through the museum. 8000R. Open Tues.-Sun. 10am-7pm, ticket booth to 6pm.

Museum of Private Collections, in the freshly painted aqua building to the left of the main entrance to the Pushkin. A wide collection of 19th- and 20th-century foreign and Russian art. Although the quality of the works varies, it is definitely worth a lengthy visit. 8000R. Open Wed.-Sun. 10am-4pm, ticket office until 3pm.

Tretyakov Art Gallery, Lavrushensky per. 10 (Лаврушенский пер.), M: Tretyakovskaya (Третьяковская). One of Russia's premier art galleries. Undergoing major

RUSSIA

renovation in summer of 1994, the building was due for completion in September, 1994. It holds some of the most important Russian works, both paintings and sculptures, including a magnificent collection of icons. The *Mona Lisa* equivalent here is the 12th-century Vladimir icon *God and Mother,* taken from Constantinople. Open Tues.-Sun. 10am-8pm.

Manege (Манеж), Manezhnaya Ploschad, west of the Kremlin. This one-time riding school for the military (hence the French name) is now the Central Exhibition Hall and often has interesting modern Russian exhibits. Enter from the north end, on the square. 1000R, students 500R. Open Wed.-Mon. 11am-8pm. Ticket window closes one hour early.

New Tretyakar Art Gallery (Государственная Третьяковская Галерея), ul. Krymsky Val 10. M: Oktyabrskaya. Built to house newer works and exhibitions of Russian art, shares a building with the Central House of Artists; the Tretyakov is behind, with an entrance to the right. This is the place to come for comprehensive exhibits on a particular Russian artist. Open Tues.-Sun. 10am-8pm. 7500R, students 3500R. The **Central House of Artists** (Центральный Дом Художника), is the only large museum which does not charge separate prices for foreigners, it houses numerous small and mostly interesting exhibitions—some of which are for sale. Come here for cutting edge Russian art, as well as progressive historical exhibits which come and go quickly. Open Tues.-Sun. 11am-7pm. 500R, students 300R.

Museum of the Revolution (Музей Революции), ul. Tverskaya 21. M: Pushkinskaya (Пушкинская). Covers everything *since* the revolution, although it often has exhibits from previous centuries. Amazingly, this Soviet archive has moved with the times, adding statistics on the ill-effects of socialism as well as eclectic documents such as those on '80s rock bands in the later rooms. The museum shop on the 1st floor is one of the best places to buy Soviet medals, this store also stocks old posters and T-shirts with slogans like "The Party is Over" or "Хард Рок Кафе." Museum open Tues.-Sat. 10am-6pm, Sun. 10am-5pm. 1500R.

Authors' Houses

Russians take immense pride in their formidable literary history, preserving authors' houses in their original state down to the half-empty teacups on the mantelpiece. Each is guarded by a team of *babushki* fiercely loyal to their master's memory.

Leo Tolstoy Estate, ul. Lva Tolstova 21 (ул. Лва Толстого). M: Park Kultury. Where the famous author lived and worked 1882-1901, it's one of the most perfectly preserved house-museums in Moscow. Open Tues.-Sun. 10am-6pm; off-season 10am-3pm; closed last Fri. of the month. 2000R, students 500R.

Dostoevsky Flat Museum, ul. Dostoevskovo 2 (ул. Достоевского) just off Ploschad Kommuny (Площадь Коммуны). M: Novoslobodskaya (Новослободская). Located on the grounds of the hospital where his father was a doctor. Open Thurs., Sat., Sun. 11am-6pm, Wed., Fri. 2-9pm, closed last day of the month. 1000R.

Gorky's Flat Museum, ul. Kachalova 6/2, off ul. Sadovaya-Kudrinskaya. M: Pushkinskaya. A pilgrimage site more for its architectural interest than for its collection of Maxim Gorky's possessions. Open Wed. and Fri. noon-7pm, Thurs., Sat., Sun. 10am-5pm. Closed the last Thurs. of the month. Free.

Stanislavsky Museum (Музей-Дом Станиславского), ul. Stanislavskovo 6. M: Pushkinskaya. More interesting than his upstairs apartment are the collections of costumes in the basement used for such famous productions as Gogol's *Government Inspector* and Shakespeare's *Othello.* Open Thurs., Sat.-Sun. 11am-6pm, Wed., Fri. 2-9pm, closed last Thurs. of the month.

ENTERTAINMENT

Moscow is a large and fast paced city, and it has the entertainment options to show it. The only problem here is that the scene moves so fast it is impossible to keep on top of what's in and what's out. Starting September 1 and running well into June, Moscow boasts very good theater, ballet, and opera, as well as excellent orchestras. If you buy your tickets far enough in advance and/or don't demand front row center, you can go very cheaply. Just purchase them at the *kassa* in the theater, usually open midday to 7pm, when performances start. Tickets to performances at the

Bolshoi and the Tchaikovsky Concert Hall are often snatched up by Intourist and scalpers; if you have no luck at the box office, hang out outside the theater and look foreign. This is especially true at the Old Circus. Try not to look too rich, though: speak some Russian, and you may well get your price, probably US$5-10.

The **Bolshoi Theater** (Большой Театр), M: Teatralnaya Ploschad (Театральная Площадь), literally called "the Big Theater," was unfortunately closed for renovation in 1994. If it is open in '95, it is worth a trip; both the opera and ballet companies are still good, despite multiple defections to the West, and the theater itself is pure pre-Revolutionary elegance. **Tschaikovsky Concert Hall,** Triumphalnaya Square 4/31, M: Mayakovskaya, is well-known and as a result hard to get tickets, except from scalpers. A better bet is the **Tschaikovsky Conservatory,** ul. Gertsena 19 which gives stunning albeit erratic productions for next to nothing. The **Stanislavsky Theater,** ul. Tverskaya 23, M: Tverskaya, named for the famous director, offers mostly avant-garde productions. The **Chekhov Theater,** ul. Kuznetski Most 3 (ул. Кузнетский Мость), M: Kuznetski Most, where Chekhov's *The Seagull* opened successfully after failure in St. Petersburg, has traditionally had more avant garde productions, and annoyed the Soviet government to no end. (*Kassa* open noon-3pm and 4-7pm—on performance days, opens at 11:30am.) The **Old Circus** (Старый Цирк), M: Tsvetnoi Bulvar (Цветной Бульвар), is traditionally better than the new circus near MGU, it usually has animal acts in the first half and a glittery acrobatic performance in the second. (*Kassa* open 11am-2pm, 3-7pm.)

Nightlife

When it comes to nightlife, Moscow isn't Barcelona, Buenos Aires, New York, or Paris. But sometimes it thinks it is. While Moscow may be the casino capital of the world, you won't be able to afford most of the exorbitant cover charges (usually more than US$25). Check the weekend editions of the *Moscow Times* or *Moscow Tribune* for music festival listings (the annual jazz festival thrills Moscow every summer) and club ads. The *Moscow Revue,* free at the Traveler's Guest House and sprinkled around the city, also has good up-to-date listings of what's happening in the city.

Sports Bar, 10 Novy Arbat (tel. 290 42 11). M: Arbatskaya. Next to Melodiye and across from the Irish Bar. The 2 floors fill up fast for big games; otherwise the 2nd floor is the place to be. By 1995, the disco, once one of the city's most popular, should have started up again. Bottle of beer 6300R. Glass of beer 9450R. Hamburger and fries 12,600R. Menu in English. Open 9:30am-midnight.

Arbat Irish Bar, Novy Arbat 13, M: Arbatskaya, is a total scene on weekend nights, and packs out with large groups of Americans, Irish, and Russians. Chicken wings US$3. Bud 6000R. Guiness 8000R. Open 11am-midnight.

Rosie O'Grady's, ul. Znamenko 9/12 (ул. Знаменко), M: Borovitskaya (Боровитская), is a genuine Irish pub in the middle of Moscow, with friendly Irish staff and largely ex-pat clientele. Pint of Guiness 9000R. Salads and sandwiches 8000R. Open noon-1am.

Club 011 gets going around midnight, behind AmEx at ul. Sadvaya-Kudrinskaya 19. Open Thurs.-Sat. 10pm until everyone leaves.

Manhattan Express, on the northwest corner of the Hotel Rossiya. M: Kitai Gorod (Китай Город). This self-proclaimed New York supper club creates weekly extravaganzas—fashion shows, strip shows, and performances by top Russian bands. Cover US$20-25, except Thurs. when foreigners get in free with one guest and proof of passport before 1am. Happy 2hrs. and no cover charge 7-9pm. Open until the wee hrs.—5am.

Hermitage, ul. Karetny Ryad 3 (ул. Каретний Ряд). Between M: Mayakovsky and M: Tsvetnoi Bulvar. A real western-style dance club with occasional live music. Cover 20,000R. Open 10pm-5am.

■ NEAR MOSCOW

An easy trip out of the city and into peaceful, green *dacha* territory is to **Peredel-kino** (Переделкино), where Nobel prize winning writer and poet Boris Pasternak had a *dacha*. The area remained a kind of dissident writers' colony well after Pasternak's death in 1960, and even when it was dangerous to do so, hundreds of visitors came to his grave here every year. It's a 25min. *electrichka* ride from Moscow's Kiev Station; buy a ticket from the *prigorodnye kassi* (пригородные кассы) to the left as you exit M: Kievskaya.

Sergievsky Posad (Сергиевский Посад), more commonly known by its former Soviet name, Zagorsk (Загорск), is possibly Russia's most famous pilgrimage point trekked to by Orthodox believers who wish to pray in the many churches inside the small town's main sight—the **Troitske-Sergieva Lavra** (the "Trinity Monastery of St. Sergius"). Approximately 70km from Moscow, **Sergieva Posad,** the Golden Ring town closest to Moscow, is on the road to Yaroslavl but is often considered one of the capital's outermost sights because of its ease as a daytrip. The stunning monastery, founded in 1340, is again a religious center—the paths between the colorful collection of churches are now dotted with monks in flowing robes. The entire complex, the complete and mystical view of which can be seen in full glory from a distance, contains within its walls a number of different sights.

■■■ ST. PETERSBURG (САНКТ-ПЕТЕРБУРГ)

The brainchild of Peter the Great, St. Petersburg has been heavily shaped and molded by its creator and numerous subsequent adopted parents. It was here that westward-looking tsars tried to drag Russia out of Byzantium, and it was here that Lenin and Trotsky formed the Bolshevik Party that ended the rule of the Romanovs. It is a city of contradictions; it is a gateway to the West on a seaport that is ice-locked five months of the year, it is a graceful European capital of palaces and canals on the edge of the Russian steppe. It is a city of change; Russia's history is written in its name, which has changed to Petrograd and Leningrad and back again in the last 100 years. Three quarters of a century of communist rule have left an indelible mark on St. Petersburg. Yet here and there a bit of the old glitter remains: St. Petersburg boasts some of the world's finest art museums, gorgeous Imperial palaces in the suburbs, and some of the finest ballet in the world.

ORIENTATION AND PRACTICAL INFORMATION

St. Petersburg is in northwestern Russia, just 6 hours' train ride east of Helsinki, Finland, and 9 hours northwest of Moscow. It sits on a former swamp at the mouth of the **Neva River** (Нева), on the **Gulf of Finland** (Финский Залив, *Finsky Zalif*). Several canals run roughly parallel to the river, and the main thoroughfare is **Nevsky Prospect** (Невский Проспект), which runs from the **Admiralty** (Адмиралтейство, *Admiralt-estvo*) on the river to **Uprising Square** (Площадь Восстания, *Ploschad Vosstaniya*) and **Moscow train station** (Московский Вокзал, *Moskovsky Vokzal*) before veering south to Alexander Nevsky Cemetery. Across the river, to the north of the Admiralty is the **Fortress of Peter and Paul**, the historic heart of the city.

> **Tourist Offices:** As of June 1994, your best bet is the **Russian Youth Hostel** on 3rd Sovetskaya ul. M: Ploschad Vosstaniya (Площадь Восстания). They sell maps, offer advice, and will procure train tickets and visas. A new **tourist office,** across from the Grand Hotel Europe on Nevsky Prospect, M: Gostiny Dvor (Гостиный Двор), should be in operation by summer 1995.
>
> **Consulates: U.S.,** ul. Furshtadtskaya 15 (ул. Фурштадтская; tel. 275 17 01). Open Mon.-Fri. 9:15am-1pm and 2pm-5:30pm. **U.K.,** pl. Proletarskoy Diktatury 5 (пл. Пролетарской Диктатуры; tel. 119 60 36). Open Mon.-Fri. 9:30am-5:30pm. **South Africa,** nab. Reki Moyki 11 (наб. Р. Мойки). Open Mon.-Fri. 9:30-noon. **Bulgaria,**

RUSSIA

ul. Ryleeva 27 (ул. Рылеева; tel. 273 73 47). Open Mon.-Fri. 2-4 pm. **Czech and Slovak,** ul. Tverskaya 5 (ул. Тверской; tel. 271 04 59). Open Mon.-Fri. 9:30am-12:30. **Finland,** ul. Chaikovshovo 71 (ул. Чайковского; tel. 273 73 21). Open Mon.-Fri. 9am-5pm. **Hungary,** ul. Marata 15 (ул. Марата; tel. 312 67 53). Open Tues.-Wed., Fri. 10am-noon.

Currency Exchange: Look for the Обмен Валюты (*Obmen Valyuty*) signs. Changing money is easy now, since there's no more on-the-street exchanging. Decent rates at the **Central Exchange Office,** ul. Mikhailovskaya 4 (ул. Михаиловская). M: Gostiny Dvor (Гостиный Двор). Open 10:30am-7:30pm. Expect a long wait.

American Express: ul. Mikhailovskaya 1/7 (ул. Михаиловская; tel. 119 60 09, fax 119 60 11), in the Grand Hotel Europe. Usual services. Mail held for cardholders, no packages. Open Mon.-Fri. 9am-5pm.

Post Office: ul. Pochtamskaya 9 (ул. Почтамская). Open Mon.-Sat. 9am-8pm, Sun. 10am-6pm. **DHL,** Canal Griboyedova 5 (Канала Грибоедова) #325, 2nd fl. (tel. 311 26 49, 311 85 57, 210 75 75; fax 314 64 73). Packages and letters to the U.S. in 3 business days. Holds mail and packages. Open Mon.-Fri. 9am-6pm.

Telephones: Central Telephone and Telegraph, ul. Gertsena 3-5 (ул. Герцена), off Nevsky pr. near Palace Square. Buy a phone card from the *kassa* in the third hall. AT&T **USADirect** in Moscow: tel. 095 155 50 42. You will be charged for calling Moscow. **Local calls** can be made from any phone booth on the street; use metro tokens. For **intercity calls**, use one of the *mezhdugorodni* (междугородный) phone booths at the Central Telephone office; they take special grooved *zhetoni* (жетоны, "tokens") that are sold across from the booths. Open 24hrs., except 12:30-1pm. **City Code:** 812.

Flights: The main **airport** is Pulkovo (Пулково). Take bus 13 from M: Moskovskaya (Московская) or the youth hostels can arrange for you to be taken (or met) by taxi for US$15. A bus also links it with the Aeroflot (Аэрофлот) building at Nevsky and ul. Gertsena (45min.). Buy tickets on the bus.

Trains: St. Petersburg has 4 main stations, all accessible by metro. Trains to Estonia (Tallinnn 28,000R), Lithuania, Latvia, and Poland leave from the **Varshavski Vokzal** (Варшавский вокзал), M: Baltiskaya (Балтийская). To Ukraine (Kiev 61,000R) and Belarus from the **Vitebski Vokzal** (Витебский вокзал), M: Pushkinskaya (Пушкинская). To Moscow (9hr.; 37,000R) and all other points in Russia from the **Moskovski Vokzal** (Московский вокзал), M: pl. Vosstaniya (пл. Восстания). To Helsinki (6hr., 113,700R) from the **Finlyandski Vokzal** (Финляндский вокзал), M: pl. Lenina (пл. Ленина). **Central Ticket Office** (Централны Железнодорожные Кассы, *Centralny Zheleznodorozhny Kassy*), Canal Griboyedova 24 (канал Грибоедева). Open Mon.-Sat. 8am-8pm, Sun. 8am-4pm. Foreign tourists must purchase tickets at the **Intourist** department inside the ticket office (windows 100-104, 2nd floor); they also handle international tickets (windows 90-99. Open 8am-noon and 1-7pm.

Public Transportation: Buses (Автобус) like regular city buses, **tramvayas** (Трамвая) and **trolleybuses** (Троллейбус) run infrequently, irregularly, and often change routes. List of stops are posted on the outside of the bus. The *Traveller's Yellow Pages* map shows all the buslines on its city plan. The **Metro (M)** is rather meager (open 6am-1am; 150R). Bus tickets also cost 150R. Buy them in groups of 10 from the driver. Be sure to punch your ticket; the fine is 5000R if you don't, and they do check. An 8,000R *yedini billet* (Единый Билет), available at metro stations pays for all public transportation for a calendar month.

Laundromat: The **Russian Youth Hostel** has a washing machine but no dryer, and will wash your clothes for US$1. Otherwise, use the sink, and bring your own detergent or buy a western brand.

Emergencies: Fire, 01. **Police,** 02. **Ambulance,** 03. For medical emergencies, **Polyclinic No. 2** (tel. 110 11 02) or **Hospital No. 20** (tel. 108 48 08) are for foreigners. **U.S. consulate 24hr. emergency number,** 274 86 92.

ACCOMMODATIONS

The International Hostel sells *The Traveller's Yellow Pages*, which has current listings of accommodation options. Two hostels in St. Petersburg, together with the Traveller's Guest House in Moscow and establishments in Novgorod and Irkutsk,

RUSSIA

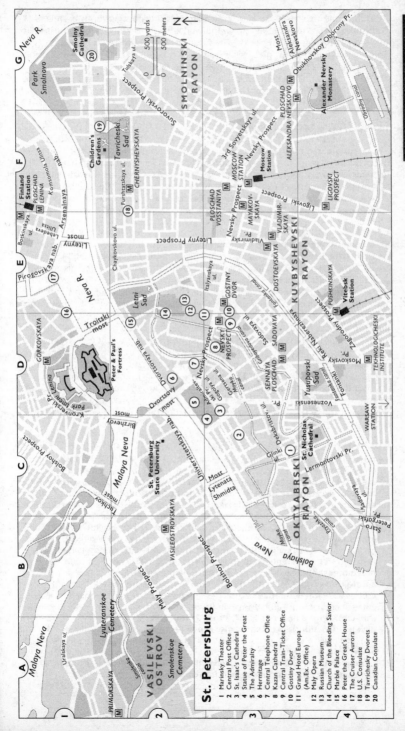

St. Petersburg

1 Marinsky Theater
2 Central Post Office
3 St. Isaac's Cathedral
4 Statue of Peter the Great
5 The Admiralty
6 Hermitage
7 Kazan Cathedral
8 Central Telephone Office
9 Central Train-Ticket Office
10 Gostiny Dvor
11 Grand Hotel Europa (Am.Ex. Office)
12 Maly Opera
13 Russian Museum
14 Church of the Bleeding Savior
15 Marble Palace
16 Peter the Great's House
17 The Cruiser Aurora
18 U.S. Consulate
19 Tavrichesky Dvorets
20 Canadian Consulate

500 yards
500 meters

form the California-based **Russian Youth Hostels** organization. Both hostels in St. Petersburg accept reservations by phone, and are, at this writing, the closest thing to a tourist office in St. Petersburg. The **International Youth Hostel** is in a restored 5-storey building near M: pl. Vosstaniya (пл. Восстания) on 3rd ul. Sovyetskaya 28 (третая ул. Советская). Women and men are on different floors. (Reception open 8am-noon and 2pm-midnight. Check in by 9:30pm. Check-out 11am. Lockout 1am-7am. US$15 includes sheets and breakfast. In Russia to reserve, tel. (812) 277 05 69 or 329 80 18, fax (812) 277 51 02 or 329 80 19. In the U.S. and Canada tel. (310) 379-4316, fax 379-8420.) To get to **Hostel "Holiday,"** ul. Mikhailova #1 (ул. Михайлова). M: Ploschad Lenina (пл. Ленина), exit at Finlandsky Vokzal (Финляндский Вокзал) and turn left on ul. Komsomola (ул. Комсомола), then right on Mikhailova. Just before the river, turn left into a courtyard, then right. Ring the bell. (Open 24 hrs. Check-out at 11am. In Russia, tel. (812) 542 73 64, fax 277 51 02. US$15 includes breakfast and sheets. Dinner US$5.) Travelers who speak Russian may want to consider a **homestay** in an apartment with a Russian family. This can be arranged through the **Traveller's Guest House** in Moscow, either from Moscow or from St. Petersburg (tel. (095) 971 40 59, fax 280 76 86; US$10 per night).

FOOD

Restaurants along **Nevsky** are likely to have better food, but prices will be correspondingly higher. Food at neighborhood places is almost always inedible and no one will speak English; even in restaurants in highly touristed areas, menus are often only in handwritten Cyrillic. Because of the favorable exchange rate, elegant Russian restaurants are often a good deal for foreigners. For more info on restaurants and cafés, check the *St. Petersburg Press*, or ask at the hostel, which keeps a running traveler's notebook. *Tap water is not potable in St. Petersburg.* Get foreign mineral water at hard-currency stores, boil or filter your own, or snag a bottle of western soda. **Markets** (Рынки) stock fresh produce, meat, cheese, honey, and occasionally a prepared dish or two, but they are comparatively more expensive than state-owned stores. The **covered market** at Kuznechni per. 3 (Кузнечный пер.), just around the corner from M: Vladimirskaya (Владимирская), closed 2nd Tues. of the month, and the **Patent Cooperative Trade Center** (Maltsevski Rynok), ul. Nekrasova 52 (ул. Некрасова), at the top of Ligovski pr. (Лиговский пр.), M: Ploshad Vosstaniya (open Tues.-Mon. 8am-7pm, Sun. 8am-4pm), are the biggest and most exciting.

Restaurants

Tbilisi, ul. Sytninskaya 10 (ул. Сытнинская; tel. 232 93 91). M: Gorkovskaya (Горьковская). Wide selection of Georgian appetizers (*satsivi*—chicken in walnut sauce 4500R) and hot dishes (*tolma*—meat wrapped in grape leaves 4500R). Good for vegetarians. Menu in Russian, English, and Finnish. Open 11am-11pm.

Tandoor, ul. Voznesensky (ул. Вознесенский), on the corner of Admiralteysky. The unfamiliar odor of good food wafting onto the street should entice you in. Good food and prices make up for the wait. Tandoori chicken US$5. Open noon-11pm.

Assemblaya (Ассемблая), ul. Bolshaya Konyushenaya 13 (ул. Большая Конюшенная), off Nevsky pr. A beautifully decorated restaurant with pricey yet satisfying courses. Menu in English and Russian. Tongue 5700R. Omelet 1200R. Musical program 5000R, to avoid the charge, leave before 8pm. Open 24 hrs.

Le Café, Nevsky pr. 142, convenient to the Russian Youth Hostel. Oasis for Westerners. Sells foreign fashion magazines and newspapers for reasonable prices. A guitar-accordian duet adds a Russian flavor. *Borscht* US$4.70. Cheeseburger with fries US$7.85. Apple pie US$3.15. Open 11am-11pm.

Koryeiski Domik (Корейский Домик, Korea House), nab. Reki Fontanki 20 (наб. Реки Фонтанки). M: Chernushevskaya (Чернышевская). Korean-style meat cooked before you. Cabbage soup 3000R. Pickled radishes with crab 2500R. Menu in Korean, English, and Russian. Reserve ahead. Choose between sitting on cushions, *Koryeiski*, or at a "European" table. Open 1-10pm.

RUSSIA

Demyanova Ukha (Демьянова Уха), pr. Kronverski 53. M: Gorkovskaya (Горьковская). Fresh-fish dishes in a jovial, hectic atmosphere. Assorted fish 14,350R but tea only 60R. Menu changes daily. Open noon-9pm. Reservations needed even for lunch.

Chebey (Хлебей), on Bolshoy pr. 61 (пр. Большой). M: Petrogradskaya (Петроградская). Serves yummy Chinese and Russian fare for appropriate prices. Lazy Susans and round tables make this good for large groups. Full meal 20,000R. Sweet and sour fish 12,850R. Chicken Gumbo 2510R. Open 11am-7pm.

Chaika (Чайка), Kanal Griboyedeva 14 (Канала Грибоедова), off Nevsky pr. near Dom Knigi. German fare, hard liquor, caviar, and cheesecake for hard currency. Run on a card system, so you pay at the end. Don't lose the card—it costs you 120,000R. Main dishes 2100-3pm.

Café Tet-a-Tet (Кафе Тет-а-Тет spelled Мет-а-Мет on the sign), pr. Bolshoi 65 (пр. Большой). M: Petrogradskaya (Петроградская) on Petrogradskaya side. An elegant, intimate restaurant; live music on grand piano and tables for 2—bring a date. Standard Russian fare with a number of fish dishes, entrees approximately 10,000R. Open 1pm-midnight. Menu in Russian and English. Make reservations.

Balkany (Балканы), Nevsky pr. 27, between the Kazan Cathedral and Gostiny Dvor. Standard Russian fare; just pick a table, sit down, and ask for a menu. Particularly neatly set and clean, complete with plastic ketchup and mustard containers on each table. Main courses 2100-2600R. Open 11am-10pm.

Shanghai, ul. Sadovaya 12 (ул. Садовая). M: Gostiny Dvor. Serves Russian food for rubles and more expensive Chinese menu in dollars. 2nd floor offers Chinese fare—menus in Chinese, Russian, and English. Spicy asparagus US$2. Fried fish in soy sauce US$2.50. Blini with caviar US$2.50. Open noon-11pm.

Literaturnoye Café (Литературное Кафе), Nevsky pr. 18. A famous 19th-century chat spot for writers and artists, gracefully restored to its original elegance. Pushkin had his last meal here. Pricey, but unbeatable for champagne and sweets in the afternoon. *Prix fixe* meal includes caviar, fish, *borscht* and other Russian delicacies, but no alcohol (40,000R). 2500R cover. Reservations recommended. Open noon-5pm and 7-10pm.

Cafés and Fast Food

Baghdad (Багдад), ul. Furshtadtskaya 35. M: Chernyshevskaya (Чернышевская). Delicious Uzbek and Russian cuisine. Hearty bowl of fatty *lagman* (soup with meat) and rice *plov,* 4000R. Very popular with good reason. Open noon-11pm.

Café Morozhenoe (Кафе Мороженое), Nevsky pr. 24, opposite the Kavkazki. St. Petersburg's premier ice cream parlor. Homemade ice cream of various mixed flavors. Large ice cream 4,000R. Turkish coffee 1500R. Open 11am-10pm.

St. Petersburg Café, Canal Griboyedeva (Канала Грибоедова). Tiny but packed, with a healthy mix of Russians and tourists. Order scrumptious apricot tarts and carrot pies at the counter. Full meal 4000R. Open noon-11pm. Take-out available.

Baskin Robbins 31 Flavors, Nevsky pr. 79. M: Ploschad Vosstaniya (Площадь Восстания). As always, pretty in pink, just not quite so well-lit as the usual. Exceptionally artificial colors adorn a rather bizarre assortment of smiling pigs. Menu in Russian and English. Sundae 5100R. Single cone 1700R. Open 10am-10pm. Also Park Lenina, M: Gorkovskaya (Горьковская).

Metekhi (Метехи), ul. Belinskovo 3 (ул. Белинского). Tiny Georgian co-op café with stained glass windows and six tables ladles out a terrific bowl of *kharcho* soup and *lobio* (vegetarian chili) for about 2000R each. *Lavash* (лаваш, very Georgian) 1000R. *Shashlik* (шашлык) 5000R. Open 11am-8pm.

Café Vityaz (Витязь), Stroganoff Palace, across from Nevsky pr. 20. Situated in the crumbling courtyard of a once magnificent palace, this romantic café is open only in summer. Beer 2438R. Tea 335R. Open May 25-Sept. 11am-11pm.

Beer Garden, Nevsky pr. across from Nevsky Palace Hotel. Near the Russian Youth Hostel. Lawn covered with tables and parasols, while a barbecue cooks up tasty meat-treats. Live music on weekends. Menu in English. Beer US$3.50. Barbecued chicken US$5. Open noon-4am. Lunch noon-4pm. Grill 6pm-4am.

SIGHTS

Winter Palace, Russian Museum, and St. Isaac's Cathedral

St. Petersburg's cultural highlight is the magnificent green-and-gold **Winter Palace** in spacious Palace Square, the site of a mass town meeting during the 1991 coup attempt. The building, inhabited by tsars up until the Revolution, stands as a symbol of the enormous power of Russia's pre-revolutionary autocracy. The palace now houses the **Hermitage** (Эрмитаж) museum, one of the world's finest. The Hermitage collection started with Catherine the Great's 24 paintings; it now includes 2½ million items, kept in about 1000 rooms. In Spanish works, it is surpassed only by the Prado in Madrid, while in Dutch paintings (especially Rembrandts) it has no equal. The museum also displays Flemish masters such as Rubens and works by da Vinci, Michelangelo, and Titian. The Impressionist and 20th-century collections are superlative. Among the main halls where the tsars reigned and entertained is the awesome **Malachite Hall,** where Kerensky's Provisional Government met for the last time on November 7, 1917, when Lenin's Bolshevik forces stormed the palace. (Open Tues.-Sun. 10:30am-6pm. Tickets until 5pm. Upper floors start closing an hour early. 16,000R, under 18 9000R. Cameras 6000R, videocameras 14,000R.)

In Mikhailovsky Palace, **The Russian Museum** (Русский Музей; *Russki Muzey*), M: Gostiny Dvor, down ul. Mikhailova (ул. Михайлова) past the Grand Hotel Europe, houses the largest collection of Russian art outside the Tretyakov Gallery in Moscow, chronologically covering icons from the 14th to 17th centuries, and paintings and sculpture of the 18th century. Most of the 20th-century collection is either in storage or out of the country on tours. (Open Wed.-Mon. 10am-6pm. Tickets for sale Mon.-Wed. 10am-5pm 9500R, students 4700R.) **The Summer Gardens and Palace,** behind the museum, are a lovely place to rest and cool off. They can be entered from the north or south end only, and have long paths lined with marble busts of famous Russians. In the northeast corner of the gardens is Peter's **Summer Palace**, a small building that was once part of a larger complex. (Gardens open 8am-10pm in summer, 8am-7pm in winter; free. Palace open Wed.-Mon. 10:30-6pm Closed last Mon. of the month; US$2 adults, with ISIC US$1.)

For an awe-inspiring view of the city's rooftops, climb to the dome of **St. Isaac's Cathedral** (Исаакиевский Собор; *Isaakievski Sobor*), on Isaakievskaya pl., a massive example of 19th-century civic-religious architecture designed by Auguste de Montferrand. The dome of the cathedral is covered with almost 100kg of gold, which in sunlight glints from miles away. The murals and mosaics inside are the works of some of Russia's greatest artists; the chips in the marble columns appear courtesy of German artillery fire during the siege of Leningrad. (Museum open Thurs.-Tues. 10am-6pm; 400R, students 300R. Colonnade open 10am-5pm; 500R, students 200R.) The **Museum of the History of Leningrad**, (Государственный Музей Истории Ленинграда), nab. Krasnaya Flota 44 (наб. Красная Флота), along the embankment, covers the 1941 blockade, at least for now, while the other periods are reinterpreted for shiny, happy democratic digestion. (Open Mon. and Thurs.-Sun. 11am-6pm, Tues. 11am-4pm. US$1, students US$0.50)

Peter and Paul Fortress (Петропавловская Крепость)

Across the river from the Hermitage, the fortress' spreading walls and golden spire beckon. It was begun in May 1703, the birthday of St. Petersburg. Originally built as a defense against the Swedes, it houses the gold-spired cathedral that gives the complex its name, as well as several museums. (Open Thurs.-Mon. 11-5pm, Tues. 11-4pm. Closed last Tuesday of the month. US$2.50, 50% off with ISIC.) The icons are currently under restoration, but in **Peter and Paul Cathedral** you can see the graves of every tsar since Peter the Great. (Thurs.-Mon. 10am-5:40pm, Tues. 10am-4:40pm.) **The State Museum of the History of St. Petersburg,** to the left of Shemyakin's statue, museum houses paintings, clothing, and other kitsch from the late 19th century. (Open Thurs.-Mon. 11am-6pm, Tues. 11am-5pm Closed last Tues. of the month.) **The Trubetskoy Bastion** (Трубецкой Бастион), in the Southwest corner of the fortress, is a reconstruction of the prison where Peter the Great imprisoned and

RUSSIA

tortured his first son, Aleksei. Dostoevsky, Gorky, Trotsky, and Lenin's older brother also spent time there. (Same hours as museum.)

Nevsky Prospect (Невский Проспект) Palace Square (Дворцовая Площадь; *Dvortsovaya Ploschad*), the huge windswept expanse in front of the Winter Palace has been the site of many turning points in Russia's history. Catherine was hailed as Tsarina after she overthrew her husband in a coup. On "Bloody Sunday," 1905, Nicholas II's guards fired into a crowd of peaceful demonstrators, beginning the end for the Romanovs. The landmark Art Deco building **Dom Knigi,** Nevsky pr. 28, was the Russian headquarters of the Singer Sewing Machine company before the revolution. (Open 9am-8pm.)

The colossal edifice across the street from Dom Knigi, modeled after St. Peter's in the Vatican but designed and built by Russian architects and left to decay by the Soviets, is the **Kazan Cathedral** (Казанский Собор; *Kazanski Sobor*), which used to be the **Museum of the History of Religion and Atheism,** but now is called the **Museum of the History of the Russian Orthodox Church**. These days it functions both as a museum and as a church, with morning services in the front part with an eclectic collection of Russian religious artifacts in the back. (Open Mon.-Tues. Thurs.-Fri. 11am-6pm, Sat.-Sun. 12:30pm-6pm. *Kassa* closes at 5pm. 5500R, student 2500R.) Farther down Nevsky pr. at no. 35 stands the **Gostiny Dvor** (Гостиный Двор), St. Petersburg's largest department store. Under renovation in summer 1994, it might return to its former glory as souvenir haven within a year. In any case, bustling with shoppers, this is a major Nevsky pr. landmark and has been since the 18th century. (Open Mon.-Sat. 10am-8pm.)

The **Anna Akhmatova Museum,** (Музей Анны Ахматовы), is housed at Fontanka 34 (Фонтанка), but the entrance is actually at Liteyny pr. 51 (Линтейный пр.), and showcases one of the greatest poets of the Soviet era. (Open Tues.-Sun. 10:30am-6:30pm, *kassa* stops at 5:30pm. 3000R, students 1500R.) The **Dostoevsky Museum** (Достоевский Музей) is in the writer's apartment at Kuznechny per. 5/2 (Кузнечный пер.), around the corner to the right from M: Vladimirskaya (Владимирская). The neighborhood recalls Dostoevsky's Petersburg—tall narrow buildings like the one in which Raskolnikov lived. (Open Tues.-Sun. 10:30am-6:30pm, *kassa* closes 5:30pm; closed last Wed. of month. 3000R, student 1500R.) The halfway point of Nevsky Prospect is marked by the Moscow train station, which faces **Uprising Square** (Площадь Восстанияь; *Ploshad Vosstaniya*). Here were some of the bloodiest confrontations of the February Revolution, and is where the Cossacks turned on the police during a demonstration—hence the name.

At the far end of Nevsky Prospect, opposite M: Ploschad Aleksandrer Nevskovo, is the **Alexander Nevsky Monastery** (Лавра Александра Невского; *Lavra Aleksandra Nevskovo)*, a peaceful spot for a stroll, as well as a major pilgrimage site. The monastery got its name from Prince Alexander of Novgorod, whose body was moved here by Peter the Great in 1724. The graveyard on the left is the small **Lazarus Cemetery,** the oldest in the city, established in 1716. Across the way, or to the right as you walk in, the **Tikhuin Cemetery** is not as old, but larger and its ground holds more famous names. The **Church of Annunciation,** currently under renovation, used to house the **Museum of Urban Sculpture**; now it belongs, once again, to the monastery. (Cathedral open 9am-noon, 5pm-7pm; free. Cemeteries open Fri.-Wed. 11am-5pm; each 1000R, students 500R.)

To truly understand St. Petersburg's obsession with WWII, visit **Piskarovskoye Memorial Cemetery** (Пискаровское Мемораьное Кладбище). During the 900 days the city was under siege by the Germans, close to 1 million people died. This cemetery is their grave. An eternal flame burns while a monument reads, "No one is forgotten; nothing is forgotten." To get there, stop at M: Ploschad Muzhestva (Площадь Мужества) and go left to the street. Walk left to the corner, cross the street in front of you (Непокоренных пр.; *Nepokorennikh pr.*) and catch the 123 bus from the shelter. Ride about 6 stops, 7-10min.

ENTERTAINMENT

St. Petersburg's famed White Nights lend the night sky a pale, bewitching glow from mid-June to early July. During the 3rd week in June, when the sun barely touches the horizon, the city holds a series of outdoor evening concerts as a part of the **White Nights Festival.** Check kiosks and posters for info. **Marinsky Theater** (Мариинский Театр), Teatralnaya pl. 1 (Театральная пл.), M: Sadovaya (Садовая), formerly the Kirov Opera and Ballet, is one of the most famous theaters for ballet in the world. Pavlova, Nureyev, Nijinsky, and Baryshnikov started here and it was here that Tschaikovsky's Nutcracker and Sleeping Beauty premiered. The theater hosts White Nights Festival, for which tickets are easier to get. (From 1000R. *Kassa* open 11am-3pm, 4pm-7pm Wed.-Sun.) Second to the Marinsky for opera and ballet, **Maly Theater** (Малый Театр), pl. Iskusstv 1 (пл. Искусств), has the advantage of being open in July and August when the Marinsky is closed. (*Kassa* open 11am-3pm, 4pm-8pm.) **Shostakovich Philharmonic Hall** (Шостакович), Mikhailovskaya ul. 2 (Михайловская ул.), is a large concert hall with both classical and modern concerts. **Oktyabrskaya Concert Hall** (Концертный зал Октябрьский), Ligovsky pr. 6 (Лиговский пр.), is St. Petersburg's large and modern concert hall for orchestras, ballets, and rock concerts. In June 1994 concerts were held with Run DMC, Falco, A-Ha, Lane Davis, and others. (From 1500R. *Kassa* open 11am-8pm.)

Clubs come and go like the Top-40 groups here; both hostels can recommend the newest places. Soviet rock superstars like Kino and Igry got their starts at **St. Petersburg Rock Club** (Рок Клуб), ul. Rubinshteina 13 (ул. Рубинштайна), M: Dostoevskaya (Достоевская) (cover 3000R). Although **Rock around the Clock,** M: Sennaya Ploschad (Сенная пл.), Sadovaya ul. 27 (Садовая ул.), has a fairly high cover and expensive drinks, the music is good (open 9pm-6am). **Tunnel,** located in an old bomb shelter, is the place to go for techno and dancing. It's located on Lyubansky per. (Любянский пер.) between ul. Blokina (Блокина) and Zverinskaya (Зверинская), M: Gorkhovskaya (Горковская). (Open Thurs.-Sat. midnight-4am.) **Art Café,** ul. Gertsena 58, not far from Marinsky Theater, is a small, informal jazz club in a back room. (Open Fri. and Sat. 7pm-11. Cover 1000R.)

■ PETERHOF AND TSARSKOYE SELO

Ride the suburban *electrichka* trains any spring or summer weekend day and you will witness the Russian love of the countryside. Most Russians own or share a *dacha* outside the city. The 3 major palaces nearby were burned to the ground during the Nazis' retreat, but in one of the great paradoxes of the Soviet regime, Stalin provided the cash to completely rebuild these symbols of the tsars during postwar reconstruction. **Peterhof** (Петергоф), also known as Petrodvoretz (Петродворец), is the most thoroughly restored of the palaces. The entire complex is 300 years old, and many tsars have built on it or expanded existing palaces. The **Grand Palace** (Большой Дворец) was Peter's first residence here. The **Lower Gardens** offer supreme views. Follow the sound of children's shrieks and giggles to the **"joke fountains,"** which, activated by one misstep, suddenly splash their unwitting victims. (2000R, with ISIC 1000R.) **Hydrofoils** leave frequently from Hermitage (10,000R one way). It's also an easy trip by *electrichka* from Baltisky Station, M: Baltiskaya (Балтийская; round-trip 800R). **Trains** leave every 15min. or so. Then catch bus 350, 351, 353 or 356 to the "Fountain" (Фонтаны; *Fontany*).

Twenty-five km south of the city, **Tsarskoye Selo** (Царское Село; "Tsar's Village"), renamed "Pushkin" during the Soviet era—most Russians and train conductors still use that name—harbors Catherine the Great's summer residence, the azure **Yekaterinsky Dvorets** (Catherine's Palace). Take any *electrichka* from Vitebski Vokzal (Витебский Вокзал; M: Pushkinskaya) leaving from Platforms 1, 2, or 3 (one way 300R). Once at the station, take bus 371or 382 almost to the end. An easy bus ride from Tsarskoye Selo, **Pavlovsk** (Павловск) is a modest Classical contrast to both Pushkin or Peterhof. Given to Paul I by his frightening mother, Catherine the Great, on the birth of her grandson the future Tsar Alexander I, Pavlovsk was one of the last imperial palaces to be built. One of the largest landscaped **parks** in the world, speckled with the usual colonnades and temples, is still the biggest draw to Pavlovsk, which has gone through periods of boredom and excitement. (Open 10am-5pm. 1000R, children 50R. Closed first Mon. of month.) From Petersburg, take an *electrichka* from Vitesbski Vokzal (Витебский Вокзал; M: Pushkinskaya) to Pavlovsk, (800R each way). Any of the trains on Platforms 1, 2, and 3 are fine. Take 370 or 383 to the palace. They also go all the way to Pushkin if you wish to combine the visits.

■■■ NOVGOROD (НОВГОРОД)

Novgorod is a particularly proud city, in large part because it fended off the Mongol Tatars that weaker Moscow could not. But a few centuries later, under the rule of Ivan III and then Ivan the Terrible, Moscow brought this once powerful town under its yoke and residents have been grumbling about it ever since. Founded in the 9th century by Prince Rurik, Novgorod ("New Town") grew throughout the Middle Ages. Easily explored in a day (a good daytrip from Moscow or St. Petersburg via the night train), Novgorod is bigger and more thoroughly restored than Pskov; it makes a good introduction to the Russia of the 12th-15th centuries.

Entering the **Kremlin** from the lake side is most impressive, affording a panoramic view of the huge red brick walls, the **Novgorod horseman** (a statue commemorating the city's survival through the ages), and, not quite so appealing, the sandy lakeside spotted in summer with sunbathing Russians. The **St. Sophia Cathedral** (Софийский собор; *Sofiysky Sobor*) is the religious pinnacle of any trip to Novgorod. The oldest stone building in Russia, this 11th century Byzantine cathedral is most imposing from the outside, where the Swedish west doors depict intricately carved scenes from the Bible. The dark interior and heavy iron chandelier make the cathedral oppressively gloomy. (Open 8am-8pm. Services 10am and 6pm. Free.)

Across the footbridge from the Kremlin and to the right, **Yaroslav's Court** is the old market center of Novgorod, and the original site of the palace of the Novgorod princes. There are remains of the 17th century waterfront arcade, several churches from the 13th-16th centuries, and the market gatehouse which is now a **museum** where you can see some of the old frescoes that were in the other buildings (open Wed.-Sun. 10:30am-7:30pm; closed last Thurs. of the month).

The **Yuriev Monastery** and the **Museum of Wooden Architecture** is the last of over 20 that once surrounded Novgorod; it is striking for its location, in the middle of broad and windy marshes, but little else. Take bus 7 from pl. Pobedy (пл. Победы) for about 20min., then walk to the museum. The church has been heavily reconstructed, and most buildings are closed to the public. (Open Wed.-Mon. 10am-4pm.) One km west of the monastery is a **Museum of Wooden Architecture,** a collection of houses and churches from surrounding towns, some dating from the 16th century (open Thurs.-Tues. 10am-6pm).

Look for posters advertising the disco bar and laser-show called **Baccara** (Баккара) on Fridays and Saturdays at 11pm. Visit the **Pushkin Theater** next to the Hotel Intourist, or perhaps catch a performance at the **Concert Hall** in the Kremlin (*kassa* open Mon.-Fri. 2-7pm, Sat. noon-5pm).

Practical Information, Accommodations, and Food Trains arrive from St. Petersburg (4-6hr.) and Moscow (8hr., *Lux* 57,000R, *kupé* 18,000R). More expensive than the bus, trains are a lot more comfortable. For regular tickets more than 24hrs. in advance go to *kassa* 5 or 6 (open 9am-noon and 1-8pm). For *lux* (люкс) or same-day tickets, go to the *sutochnaya* (суточная) *kassa* 3 (open 8am-1pm and 2-7pm). Buses leave from the end of pr. Karla Marxa (пр. Карла Маркса) for Moscow (26,000R), St. Petersburg (9600R), and Pskov (11,000R). South of Yaroslavl's Court on the east side of the river, you'll find a **tourist office** at ul. Nikolskaya (ул. Никольская), (tel. (8160) 353 32). Pass through an archway into a courtyard; there is a plaque reading "Новгородское Бюро." (Open 9am-5pm.) Or, trek to Intourist Hotel, ul. Dmitriyevskaya 16 (ул. Дмитриевская), (tel. (8160) 750 89 or 942 90) which is open 24hrs. Bus 4 and 20 from the station go within 0.5km at the Univermag (Универмаг) stop, or walk along the street next to the earth wall, left from the station for five long blocks until you reach the river; the hotel is directly in front.

Change **currency** at the **Telephone and Telegraph Office,** Ploschad Pobedy (Площадь Победы), at the corner of ul. Gorkhovo (ул. Горхого) and Sovietskaya (Советская; now Oktyabrskaya, ул. Октябрьская). On the left are several phones that dial direct to Moscow. (Open 24hrs. Currency exchange open Mon. Fri. 9am-1pm and 2-8pm, Sat.-Sun. 9am-7pm.)

Prospect Karla Marxa (пр. Карла Маркса), runs from the train station to the earth walls that surround old Novgorod; turn left here for the **Novgorod Hostel,** 27a ul. Komsomolskaya, now ul. Novo-Luchanskaya (ул. Комсомольская, now ул. Ново-Лучанская), (tel. 720 33). The big, red building on the right hand side is the hostel. An oasis for the budget traveler tired of musty, old Intourist hotels, this converted dorm has shabby but clean, bright, and airy rooms with firm beds. (Reception open 24hrs. Singles 36,000R. Doubles with shared bath 31,200R. Doubles with private bath 80,000R.) The corridors are well lit, and the rooms include a proper shower as well as TV and phone at **Hotel Sadko** (Гостиница Садко), Prospect Yuri Gagarin 16 (пр. Юри Гагарина; tel. 753 66). (Reception open 24hrs. Singles 30,000R. Doubles 48,000R. Triples 62,000R.)

The few eateries with any kind of ambience cater primarily to tourists—and raise their prices accordingly. *Shashliki* (шашлыки) and *sloiki* (слойки, a delicious pastry with jam) are available at a stand outside the Kremlin; if it's a sunny day, you're best off taking a picnic and sitting on a bench or by a lake. In a stone tower of the Kremlin, **Restaurant Detinets** (Детинец) serves tasty Russian specialties. (Mushrooms and sour cream 2700R. *Schi*—cabbage soup—1396R. Open 11am-11pm.) Five minutes from the Kremlin and the hostel, **Pri Dvore** (При Дворе), ul. Sovetskaya 3 (ул. Совемская) serves yummy *shashliki* (1500R) outside and has an extensive Russian menu indoors. (Courtyard bar open noon-11pm. Restaurant open noon-4pm and 6-11pm.) **Café Posad** (Кафе Посад), ul. Bolshevikov 14 (ул. Большевиков), now (sometimes) called ul. Rogatitsa (ул. Рогатица) serves up Russian standards for less than the hotel restaurants. (*Borscht* 990R. Beef stroganoff 2700R. Chicken fillet 2800R. Open Mon.-Sat. noon-midnight.)

Slovakia (Slovensko)

US$1 = 31.35SK (Koruny)	10SK =	US$0.32
CDN$1 = 22.94SK	10SK =	CDN$0.44
UK£1 = 49.18SK	10SK =	UK£0.20
IR£1 = 48.26SK	10SK =	IR£0.21
AUS$1 = 23.35SK	10SK =	AUS$0.43
NZ$1 = 17.04SK	10SK =	NZ$0.59
SAR1 = 8.83SK	10SK =	SAR1.13
DM1 = 20.39SK	10SK =	DM0.49
Country Code: 42	International Dialing Prefix: 00	

Survivor of centuries of Tartar invasions, Hungarian domination, and Soviet industrialization, Slovakia has emerged triumphant as a mature country. Natural wonders cover the map: the mountainous and forested north slopes into the gorgeous landscapes of central Slovakia. Hiking and skiing are national pastimes. The countryside is dotted with castle ruins, relics of the defense against the Tartars. In the smaller towns, even suburban factories have not destroyed the old-time atmosphere. Take a deep draught of Slovak wine, put on the hiking boots, and enjoy the freedom.

To hear more about the wonders and sights of Slovakia and its surrounding countries, look for a copy of *Let's Go: Eastern Europe.*

GETTING THERE AND GETTING AROUND

Citizens of Ireland and the U.S. can visit Slovakia visa-free for up to 90 days, and citizens of the U.K. for up to 180 days. Citizens of Australia, Canada, New Zealand and South Africa need visas (US$20 for single-entry; US$47 for multiple-entry; payable money order; cash or personal check accepted if applying in person.) Apply by mail, in person or at the border (additional fee involved).

The main Slovak **railway** starts in Košice and ends in Bratislava; international links to Hungary, Austria, and Poland (but not the Czech Republic) are 35% cheaper for students. EastRail is valid in the Slovak Republic; Eurail is not. **ŽSR** is the national train company; every info desk has a copy of **Cestovný poriadok** (58SK), the master schedule. *Odchody* (departures) and *príchody* (arrivals) are on the left and right sides of schedules and posters, but be sure to check revolving timetables, as the train platform (*náštupište*) often changes. A reservation (*miestenka*, 6-7SK) is required for international voyages (including the Czech Republic), *expresný* trains, and 1st-class seats, but not domestic *rychlík* (fast), *spešný* (semi-fast), or *osobný* (local) trains. Buy a reservation at the boxed-R counter before you buy a ticket. The Czechoslovak **bus** company, **ČSAD**, publishes a master schedule; it's generally easier to let the info desk decipher it. **Bicycling** is popular; **hitchhiking** is legal.

SLOVAKIA ESSENTIALS

Čedok, the Czechoslovak travel bureau, still exists in the Slovak Republic but is being replaced with professional travel companies, often with **Satur.** CKM, the Čedok of Czechoslovak youth, has been renamed **CKM Slovakia** and still operates in most areas. Many small, private travel agencies (*cestovná kancelária*) have emerged, including **Slovakoturist,** but it dedicates more effort to arranging package tours for wealthy Slovaks than to helping foreign visitors and budget travelers.

The old Czechoslovak and the modern Czech coins and bills are not valid in Slovakia; you must use the new coins and Slovak bills. Phones and ticket machines accept only Slovak coins. You cannot buy Western currency or Czech crowns in Slovakia without a Slovak passport; find a Slovak friend to change you extra koruny back into dollars, deutschmarks, or pounds.

The **mail** service is quite modern; Poste Restante mail with a "1" after the city name goes to the main post office. Local **telephone** calls cost 2SK; drop the coin in after you've been connected. The AT&T **USADirect** number is 00 42 00 01 01; MCI **WorldPhone** 00 42 00 01 12; **Canada Direct** 00 42 00 01 51; and **BT Direct** 00 42 00 44 01.

Many Slovaks know German, and English and French are common in Bratislava. The diligent tourist can turn heads with a phrase in Slovak: *Áhoj, Nazdar* (AH-hoy, NAHZ-daar, "hello"); *Do videnia* (DOH vee-dane-yah, "goodbye"); *Ďakujem* (DYAK-oo-yem, "Thank-you"); *Prosím* (PROH-seem, "please"); *Koľko?* (KOHL-koh, "how much?"). *Áno* (AH-noh) means "yes" and *Nie* (NYEH) means "no."

Summers average 71°F; winters 34°F. Everything closes New Year's Day, Easter Sunday and Monday, Cyril and Methodius Day (July 4), October 28, and Christmas (Dec. 25-26). If a holiday falls on Sunday, Monday is a holiday. The week between Christmas and New Year's is nearly void of commerce and public transport.

Visitors are advised not to drink tap water, which is chlorinated and may cause abdominal discomfort. Bottled water is available in grocery stores. There is a reciprocal Health Agreement between Slovakia and the U.K. If you carry a U.K. passport, you are entitled to free medical care while traveling in Slovakia (however, prescribed medication is *not* free of charge). The **emergency phone number** is 158.

Accommodations and Camping In Bratislava, **summertime hostels** open when university students leave; get info at CKM. **Juniorhotels (HI),** though rare, are a step above the usual brand of hostel. In the mountains, **chaty** (chalets) range from plush quarters for 400SK per night to a friendly bunk and outhouse for 100SK. **Hotels** in the boonies provide comparable service to those in cities but are much cheaper. **Campgrounds** abound near the country's national parks but are often open only in summer. A campground map is sometimes available at CKM offices.

Food and Drink Many Slovak dishes resemble those of neighboring Hungary, Austria, and Moravia in the Czech Republic, including the ever-popular *guláš*. Viennese-style *nockerln* (very small fried pieces of dough) or *knedla* (like the Bohemian *knedlík* or Austrian *knödel*) often accompany meat entrees. Native to the mountain regions of Slovakia is *halušky* (potato pasta) with *bryndza*, a soft ewe's milk cheese. Serve yourself to a cafeteria-style meal at a *bufet, samoobsluha,* or *občerstvenie*. It's fast, but you must eat while standing up. A *kaviareň* serves coffee, tea, and often desserts. All grocery stores are closed between Saturday noon and

Monday morning. *Potraviny* (grocery stores) and *ovocie zelenina* (greengrocers) pop up on every other corner. Almost every major city has a vegetarian restaurant.

■■■ BRATISLAVA

Although Slovakia's capital city has fewer than half a million inhabitants, its history is rich and cosmopolitan. In the early 19th century, Bratislava was inhabited by German-speaking Swabians who called the city **Pressburg.** Later, the city acquired a Hungarian character and was called **Pozsony.** In this period, Slovaks referred to it as **Prešporok.** Only in 1918 was it christened **Bratislava.** As much in the 19th century as today, Bratislava was not only a center of intellectual life, but also a city that loved beer. Two entire districts of the city once dedicated themselves to the noble art of brewing beer, but they have since been replaced by highways.

ORIENTATION AND PRACTICAL INFORMATION

Bratislava lies on the banks of the Danube, a proverbial stone's throw from the Austrian and Hungarian borders. Trains and buses connect the city with Budapest and Vienna; hydrofoils also serve Vienna. Traveling by rail to Prague sometimes requires a change at Brno. Avoid getting off at the *Nové Mesto* train station, which is much farther from the center than Bratislava's *Hlavná stanica* (main station).

The Danube runs west-to-east across Bratislava. The Old Town, with its cluster of tourist offices and restaurants, sits just north of the river bank, bordered by the **Staromestská** highway to the west, **námestie SNP** to the north, **Štúrova** to the east, and **Hviezdoslavovo námestie** to the south. From the train station, take tram 1. Buy tickets (5SK) for the tram from the orange automat machines (near major tram stops). Maps of Bratislava range in price 10-50SK. Make sure to buy a new one that has the accurate post-communist street-names. Lenin, Klement Gottwald, and the Red Army are very much out of fashion.

Tourist Offices: BIS (*Bratislavská Informačná Service*), Panská 18 (tel. 33 37 15 or 33 43 25). A rich resource of info, pamphlets, and maps. Open Mon.-Fri. 8am-6pm, Sat. 8am-1pm. **Slovakoturist,** Panská 13 (tel. 33 57 22 or 33 34 66). Colorful pamphlets on Slovakia and, to a lesser extent, Bratislava. Open Mon.-Fri. 9am-5pm. **Satur,** Jesenského 9-11 (tel. 36 76 24 or 36 84 06). The former Čedok office has many useful brochures and maps. Open Mon.-Fri. 9am-6pm, Sat. 9am-noon.

Consulates: U.S., Hviezdoslavovo nám. 4 (tel. 33 33 38), open Mon.-Fri. 8:30am-noon and 2-4pm for regular services. **Czech Republic,** Panenská 33. **Hungary,** Palisády 54 (tel. 33 56 01). **Poland,** Hummelova 4 (tel. 31 52 22 or 31 52 20). **Romania,** Fraňa Kráľa 11 (tel. 49 16 65).

Currency Exchange: VÚB Všeobecná Úverová Banka, Poštová at Obchodná; cashes AmEx checks. Open Mon.-Thurs. 8am-5pm, Fri. 8am-noon. **Ľudová Banka,** nám SNP 15; cashes AmEx checks for 1% fee. Open Mon.-Fri. 8am-5pm.

Post Office: Main office at nám. SNP 35. Poste Restante counter 6. Open Mon.-Fri. 7am-8pm, Sat. 7am-6pm, Sun. 9am-2pm. **Postal Code:** 810 00 Bratislava 1.

Telephones: Kolárska 12. Open 24hrs. **City Code:** 07.

Trains: The main train station (*Bratislava Hlavná stanica*) is located north of the town at the end of Štefánikova (tel. 469 45). International connections to Vienna, Budapest, and Prague. International tickets at counter 13, 14 or 15.

Buses: Main station (*autobusová stanica*) on Mlynské nivy, east of the Old Town at the end of Dunajská (tel. 632 13 or 21 22 22). International connections to Vienna, Budapest, and Prague. Check ticket for bus number (*č. aut.*); several different buses sometimes depart simultaneously.

Hydrofoils: Station next to Slovak National Museum at Fajnorovo náb.

Hitchhiking: Those hitching to Vienna cross the SNP bridge and walk down Viedenská cesta. The same road takes them to Hungary via Győr, though fewer cars head in that direction. Those headed to Prague take bus 104 from the center up Pražská to the Patronka stop.

Pharmacy: *Lekáreň* at Špitálska 3 (tel. 51 01 14). Open 24hrs.

Emergencies: Ambulance: tel. 155. **Fire:** tel. 150. **Police:** tel. 158. The station at Mestská sprava VB, Špitálska 14 (non-emergency tel. 593 41 or 531 71).

ACCOMMODATIONS AND CAMPING

Inexpensive accommodations in Bratislava are not hard to find, whether you want a hostel, a pension, or a private room. Most accommodations agencies are helpful and efficient. **Satur Cestovná Kancelária,** Jesenského 9-11, arranges rooms in the center (300SK per person). **CKM Slovakia,** Hviezdoslavovo 16 (tel. 33 16 07 or 33 41 14; fax 33 56 44), arranges accommodations at hostels for 170SK per person. (English spoken. Open Mon.-Fri. 8:30am-5pm.) **BIS Bratislavská Informačná Služba,** Panská 18, offers several options, including private rooms (singles 500SK, doubles 700SK) located well outside the center and pensions (singles 600SK, doubles 1080SK, triples 1320SK, shower and breakfast included).

Pension Gremium, Gorého 11 (tel. 32 18 18, fax 33 06 53). New and in the heart of the Old Town. Reception on 2nd floor open until 2am. German spoken. Singles 640SK. Doubles 990SK. Shower and breakfast included. Restaurant and café.

American House, Kremnická 7 (tel. 83 88 90). Located on the other side of the Danube; take bus 40, 50, 23, or 47 three stops from the center. English spoken. Rooms 300-600SK, breakfast included.

Bernolák Youth Hostel, Bernolákova 1 (tel. 49 77 21). Trolleybus 210 to Račianské mýto and turn right near the lovely monument. A high-rise student dorm. English spoken. Doubles 234SK, with ISIC 204SK. Call in advance. Open July-Aug.

YMCA na Slovenska, Karpatshá 2 (tel. 49 80 05). Old terraced building two blocks down Šancová from the train station. German spoken. Reception open 8am-11pm. Doubles, triples, quints 150SK per person. Open mid-July to mid-Aug.

Mladá Garda, Račianska 103 (tel. 25 31 36). Cheap rooms in the suburbs. Take tram 3 to the Mladá Garda stop. English spoken. Singles 180SK. Doubles 240SK. Open mid-July to mid-August.

Camping: Motel Zlaté Piesky, ul. Vajnorská (tel. 633 06), in suburban Trnávka. Take tram 2 or 4 to last stop or bus 110 from Trnavské mýto to last stop. Campground and bungalows down by the lakeside, way out of town. Camping 150SK per person. 4-person bungalow 550SK.

FOOD

Most eateries in Bratislava fall into one of two categories—expensive and eager to trap the tourist or very cheap self-serve joints. **AS Potraviny,** at Obchodná 14, is a sizeable grocery store with impressive selections of baked goods, meats, and beer. Fruit-stands are nearby. (Open Mon.-Fri. 6am-7pm, Sat.-Sun. 6:30am-5pm.)

Restaurant Gremium, Gorého 11, 2nd floor (tel. 32 18 18, fax 33 06 53). Expensive, but exquisite. Sumptuous *guláš*. Entrees 50-150SK. Open Mon.-Sat. 11am-8pm.

Občerstvenie Polom, Obchodná 8. Cheap and edible self-serve food. Bottles of *Topvar* beer 12 SK. Open 8am-6pm.

Zelený Dvor, nám SNP 30 (tel. 36 45 86). An outdoor eatery with sausages, *guláš,* and daily specials 40-140SK. ½l of *Zuzana* dark beer 20SK. Open 10am-11pm.

Veľkí Františkání, Františkánske nám 10. Expensive but good. Try the *lečo* or the *Wiener schnitzel.* Entrees 70-170SK, draft *Topvar* 25SK. Open 10am-1am.

SIGHTS AND ENTERTAINMENT

Bratislava's main square is **Hlavné námestie,** at the center of the **Old Town.** Of all the historic buildings that line the main square, the **Old City Hall** *(Stará radnica)* is the most interesting. It is in fact a complex of several buildings, the oldest of which are in Gothic style. The distinctive yellow tower is a hallmark of Bratislava; on warm summer evenings, brass bands play popular tunes on its balcony. The courtyard is in particularly good condition; from here you can enter the **Bratislava Municipal Museum.** With its fascinating collections of Gothic sculpture, aristocratic furniture, bourgeois mugs, old Slovak books, and 19th-century pub signs, this is easily one of the most interesting museums in Bratislava. At a reasonable pace, it can be covered in under an hour. (Open Tues.-Sun. 10am-4:30pm. 10SK, students 3SK). On the other side of the Old Town Hall is the **Primate's Square** *(Primaciálne námestie)*, surrounded by several restored buildings. The most impressive is the Neoclassical **Primate's Palace** *(Primaciálny palác)*, where the victorious Napoleon and the temporarily vanquished Austrian Emperor Franz I signed the Peace of Pressburg (1805). A walk down Panská from Hlavné námestie leads to **St. Martin's Cathedral** *(Dóm svätého Martina)*, the Gothic church, where Hungarian kings were coronated for three centuries. However, the locked doors render the church treasures inaccessible to tourists. North of Hlavné námestie is the **Franciscan Church** with a pretty Gothic tower from the 13th century and a more recent interior. From the church, Zamočnícka leads to **Michalská,** the busiest pedestrian street in Bratislava's Old Town. At the north end of the street is the **Michalská brána** (Michael Tower) a beautiful and tall Baroque structure that once served as a watchtower.

From the banks of the Danube to the historic squares of the Old Town, the imposing four-towered **Castle of Bratislava** remains a visible landmark. Of strategic importance for over a millennium, the castle burned down in 1811, and for many years was nothing more than a romantic ruin. In 1953 it was restored to its 15th-century appearance and housed the leaders of the Slovak Socialist Republic. Today it serves as the meeting place of the Slovak National Assembly. In addition to its political function, the castle is the home of many important collections of the **Municipal Museum** *(Mestské Múzeum)*. This is the place to visit to examine the rich displays on Slovak history, art, and culture. (Open Tues.-Fri. 9am-5pm, Sat.-Sun. 10am-6pm, 40SK, students 12SK.)

For concert and theater schedules, pick up a copy of *Kám* at BIS. Although not in English, the information is easy enough to decipher. The **Slovak Philharmonic** plays regularly on ul. Palackého; buy tickets at the Reduta office behind the concert hall up to 1 hour before performances. **National Theater** tickets are also sold here; the theatre is on Komenského nam. Also look for performances by the internationally-known **Bohdan Warchal Quartet,** based in Bratislava in summer

True to their Central European heritage, Bratislavans prefer the conversation and carousing of a wine pub, beer hall, or café to the thumping of a dance club. What the city has to offer for entertainment certainly reflects this charming preference. **Smíchovský Dvor** is a popular local beer garden on Mariánska at Heydukova (open Mon.-Sat. 10am-10pm). To carouse in one of Europe's largest beer-halls, head for **Stará Sladovňa,** Cintorínska 32, housed in a 19th century malthouse (open 10am-11pm). **Veľkí Františkání,** Františkánske nám 10, is a wine-pub in the heart of the Old Town with a Medieval terrace (open 10am-1am).

■ ■ ■ KOŠICE

Compared to most of Slovakia's towns and cities, Košice has handled a mixture of the old and new very well. While thousands of gray Communist-era apartment blocks surround the city, they do not intrude in Košice's Old Town, which is, in fact, quite well-preserved and almost as a self-contained unit within the city. Its heart is the wide street **Hlavná**. At the widest point is the glorious Gothic **Cathedral of St. Elizabeth** *(Dom sv. Alžbety)*, designed in the 14th century by the French architect Villars d'Honnecourt on request of the Hungarian King Lajos I. To the north of the cathedral is the **Urban Tower** *(Urbanova veža)*, *which* houses the **Metallurgical Museum**, featuring a collection of cast iron bells, pewter doorknockers, and golden candelsticks. (Open Tues.-Sat. 9am-5pm, Sun. 9am-noon. 10SK, students 5SK.) At Mlynská and Hrnčiarska is a **Secessionist Building** *(Secesný dom)* worthy of attention. Far more inspiring, however, is the grand neo-Gothic **Jakab Palace** *(Jakabov palác)* at the corner of Mlynská and Štefánikova, right before the bridge to the park.

Set along most routes from Poland to Bulgaria and Romania and near the halfway point of the 13hr. Kraków-Budapest slog, Košice serves as one of Eastern Europe's **rail** centers. Other connections to Budapest require a change at Miskolc. To the west, trains to Prague (9hr.) and Bratislava (6hr.) are fairly frequent. Eastbound trains to Lviv (8hr.) and Kiev (17hr.) in the Ukraine run at least once a day and often continue all the way to Moscow. In the Slovan Hotel, **Satur,** Hlavná at Rooseveltova (tel. (95) 231 21), provides foreigners with maps and info, albeit grudgingly (open Mon.-Fri. 9am-6pm and Sat. 9am-noon).

Hotel Európa, Štefánikova 4 (tel. (95) 622 38 97), across the park in front of the train station, is an old 19th-century hotel in reasonably good condition. (24hr. reception. Common showers and toilets. Singles 210SK. Doubles 360SK. Triples 480SK.) A large house in the suburbs now serves as **Pension Rozália,** Orvaská 14 (tel. (95) 397 14), with small, but clean rooms at 150SK per person. Beware of the offers of "free" chauffeuring to the city center, as it will actually cost 100SK. **Hotel Coral,** Kasárenské nám. 5 (tel. (95) 260 95 or 268 19, fax 211 56), is clean and modern. (24hr. reception. Singles 340SK. Doubles 450SK.) Good food at reasonable prices awaits at **Reštaurácia Grand,** Kováčska 65. Try *Hovädzie na korení,* a rather mild *guláš,* for 40SK. (Open Mon.-Sat. 10am-10pm, Sun. 3-10pm.) **Tatraburger,** Hlavná 74, offers a Slovak version of guess-what (open Mon.-Fri. 9am-9pm, Sat. 8am-2pm, Sun. 2-8pm; burgers 20SK). Enjoy meatless delights at Košice's only vegetarian restaurant, **Reštaurácia Ajvega,** Orlia 10 (open 10am-11pm).

■■■ THE HIGH TATRAS (VYSOKÉ TATRY)

Slovaks take great pride in the **High Tatras** *(Vysoké Tatry),* a mountainous mecca for hikers, skiers, campers, and nature-lovers. Far taller than the **Little Tatra** *(Malá Fatra)* to the west, the **Low Tatras** *(Nízké Tatry)* to the south, and the **Matras** in Hungary, the High Tatras are a formidable natural barrier between today's Slovakia and Poland. The range, a mere 26km long, is one of the most compact in the world.

The most important transportation center in the Tatras region is **Poprad**, a good starting point for hiking trips; a map of the **Vysoké Tatry** is indispensable (15-50SK). To the north of Poprad lie the ski resorts of **Starý Smokovec** and **Tatranská Lomnica**. Tatranská Lomnica is also a springboard for trips to the Polish Tatras. To the west of Poprad lies the well-endowed hiking and skiing center of **Štrbské Pleso**. To the south of Poprad and on the other side of the Low Tatras lies the **Slovenský Raj National Park,** a paradise of stately pines and untamed wilds. The park also contains several breathtaking caves. The more extensive caves at **Ochtina** are easier to reach from Rožnava, the end of the bus line from Poprad. Also close to Poprad are several lovely medieval **Spiš** towns. **Levoča,** the former capital of the Spiš region and by far the most impressive of the Spiš towns, is difficult to reach from Poprad. **Kežmarok,** on the other hand, is a mere half-hour away and has a gorgeous medieval center.

Poprad With an international airport and excellent train and bus connections to Slovak and international destinations, Poprad is the "gateway to the High Tatras"; it is also a convenient access point to the **Low Tatras** to the south and to the **Slovak Paradise** (Slovenský raj) to the southeast. All main buildings, stores and eateries in Central Poprad are clustered around **námestie sv. Egídia,** a long pedestrian street. The main square, however, boasts a few medieval buildings: the most eye-catching is the fortified **Roman Catholic Church** (Rímsko-katolický Kostol), elevated by Saxons in the Middle Ages. A 15min. walk down Štefánikova and then left on unmarked Kežmarska leads to **Spišská Sobota,** a historic village centered around **Sobotské námestie.** After 45 years of unprecedented neglect under the Communist regime, the whole village is currently the site of extensive restoration.

Poprad Information Agency *(Popradská Informačná Agentúra),* nám. sv. Egídia 2950 (tel. (092) 636 36), can handle almost any inquiry, and offers reasonably priced private rooms (250SK per person). (Open Mon.-Fri. 8:30am-7pm, Sat. 9am-1pm, Sun. 2-6pm.) **Satur,** nám. sv. Egídia 2950 (tel. (092) 234 30, fax 636 19) arranges the cheapest private rooms; expect to pay a mere 150SK per person.

(Open Mon.-Fri. 9am-noon and 1-6pm, Sat. 9am-noon.) **Hotel Európa,** Wolkerova 3 (tel. (092) 327 44 or 237 53), is conveniently next to the train station, with old but clean rooms. (Reception open 24hrs. Shared toilets and baths. Singles 220SK. Doubles 350SK.) **Slovenská Reštaurácia,** 1 mája 9, provides authentic Slovak cuisine in a folkloric atmosphere. (*Halušky* with *bryndza* 30SK. Daily specials 50SK. Live Gypsy music nightly. Open 10am-11pm.) For cheap, stand-up fare under 40SK, go to **Gastrocentrum,** námestie sv. Egídia 21. The sausages are popular. *(Tatran* beer 10SK. Open Mon.-Fri. 8am-6pm, Sat. 7am-noon.) Although the name of **Vináreň Zlatý Kalich,** nám. sv. Egídia 36, suggests a wine pub, it proudly focuses on inexpensive 10SK drafts of *Tatran,* Poprad's very own beer (open Mon.-Fri. 9am-10pm, Sat. 3-10pm).

Kežmarok   At the feet of the High Tatras in the east lies the well-preserved and tidy medieval town of Kežmarok. Although today the town is peripherally connected to Poprad by a slow train, it was once one of the most important economic, cultural, and military centers in the Kingdom of Hungary. During the revolutionary chaos of 1918 a **"Spiš Republic"** was proclaimed in Kežmarok, but the fledgling state became part of Czechoslovakia. Although life is quieter in Kežmarok nowadays, the town remains a popular spot as it is an excellent base for day-trips to the Tatras. Kežmarok is famous for its **Renaissance buildings,** which include a castle that belonged in turn to the Habsburgs, the Thurzos, and the Thökölys. Kežmarok's **námestie Požiarnikov** square is dominated by the **Church of the Holy Cross** (Kostol sv. Križa), a late Gothic Catholic hall church. Open at seemingly random hours, the interior boasts several 15th-century Gothic altars, two organs, and the tomb of the aristocratic Thököly family who resided in Kežmarok Castle in the 16th century. Next to the church is the **watchtower** (Zvonica), the most famous landmark in Kežmarok. From the church down Nová street is the **Kežmarok Castle** (Kežmarský hrad) on Hradné námestie. The gate to the impressive courtyard dates back to the 16th century, when the Thököly famliy owned the castle. Today, the castle hosts the **Kežmarok Museum** in its well-preserved interior. (Open Tues.-Sun. 9am-4pm. 28SK, students 14SK.)

Only 30min. by train from Poprad, Kežmarok is well worth the trip. Accommodations are usually not a problem. **Satur,** Hlavné námestie 63 (tel. and fax (0968) 31 22) provides general tourist info and arranges private rooms for 200SK per person and hotel reservations at 300SK per person. (Open Mon.-Fri. 9am-noon and 1-5pm, Sat. 8am-noon.) A Communist-era hotel with clean rooms, **Hotel Lipa,** Garbiarska 61 (tel (0968) 20 37 or 20 38, fax 20 39), is conveniently located near the main train station. (Reception open 24hrs. Singles 370SK. Doubles 570SK.) Dine on excellent Slovak cuisine at **Club Restaurant,** MUDr. Alexandra, in the Old Town. (*Halušky* 30SK, *gulá*š 50SK, roast beef 90SK. *Tatran* beer 25SK. Open 7am-10pm.)

Starý Smokovec   Founded in the late 18th century, Starý Smokovec is the oldest resort town in the Tatras. Most businesses are trilingual (Slovak, German, English), making it feel truly international. The wonderful hiking through the forested Tatra Mountains are the big attraction of Starý Smokovec. The convenient funicular (every 30min. 6am-7pm; 10SK) to Hrebienok takes you to the heart of hiking country. A 2km ride to **Hrebienok** takes you to an altitude of 1285m above sea level, and an easy 20min. hike from there leds to the foaming **Cold Waterfall** *(Studenovodské vodopada).* The truly ambitious can climb the 2450m **Slavkovský Štit,** whose stony face overlooks Starý Smokovec.

Starý Smokovec is easily reached from Poprad's train station, Poprad-Tatry. The narrow-gauge **Tatra Electric Railway** (TEŽ) trains depart from the upper-level platform (every ½hr. during the day; less frequently after dark; under 20SK). The lack of street names, signs, or a good map makes getting around a real challenge. **Satur** (tel. (0969) 27 10, fax 32 15) is located just above the train station, up a short path. Its wonderful English-speaking staff that provides info and arranges accommodations. (Open Mon.-Fri. 8am-6pm, Sat. 8am-12:30pm.) **Tatranská Informačná Kancelária,** in the Slovenská Sporiteľňa building west of the post office (tel. (0969) 34 40), offers several brochures and maps of the region. (Open 8am-7pm.)

CKM Juniorhotel Vysoké Tatry, in Horný Smokovec 2 stops on TEŽ towards Tatranská Lomnica (tel. (0969) 26 61), offers the cheapest accommodations in the Tatras (140SK per night for ISIC or HI cardholders. Nonmembers 200SK. Call in advance.) Also try the **Hotel Šport,** in Horný Smokovec, two stops on TEŽ towards Tatranská Lomnica. (Reception open 24hrs., or book through Satur. Doubles 940SK, breakfast included.) Relax in the new chalets at **Ternocamp** (tel. (0969) 24 06) down the road or railway to Poprad about 3km from Starý Smokovec. (Singles 570SK. Doubles 1080SK. Breakfast included.) Dozens of stand-up buffets offer delights such as hamburgers (13-23SK) and corn on the cob (4SK). The town's main restaurant is mediocre, but Starý Smokovec has a first-rate grocery store: **Potraviny,** across from the Hotel Grand next door to Satur, or a 3min. walk from the train station (open Mon.-Sat. 6am-8pm, Sat. 10am-6pm).

■■■ PREŠOV

Visited by relatively few tourists, Prešov preserves its authentic flavor well. As Hlavná splits into two main streets, the tower of **St. Nicholas** *(Kostol sv. Mikuláša)* captures the visitor's attention. The proportions and the distinctive turrets of the Gothic church are reminiscent of Saxon churches in Transylvania. On the right (eastern) side of Hlavná is the **Local Museum** *(Vlastivedné múzeum),* featuring displays on the rich history of Prešov (open Tue.-Fri. 10am-5pm, Sat.-Sun. 11am-3pm; 10SK, students 5SK). West of Hlavná, down the alley Švermova, is the **Synagogue** *(Synagóga).* The exterior is undergoing repair, but the ornate and well-maintained late 19th-century interior is open to the public. Part of the synagogue houses the **Museum of Judaica** *(Múzeum Judaík;* open Tues.-Wed. 11am-4pm, Thurs. 3-6pm). From the west side of Hlavná extends a narrow medieval street called Floriánova, at the end of which is **St. Florian's Gate** *(Brána sv. Floriána),* a remnant of an early Renaissance fortification. South of Floriánova along Hlavná is the **Šariš Gallery** *(Šarišská galéria),* housed in a Gothic building. The gallery features a collection of art from the local Šariš region (open Tues.-Fri. 8:30am-4pm; 6SK, students 2SK).

Count on **Tatratour,** Hlavná 129 (tel. (91) 343 00 or 339 62, fax 343 01), for its friendly and patient staff to offer general and accommodations info on Prešov and Šariš county. (German spoken. Open Mon.-Fri. 8am-5pm.) Prešov has several decent and relatively inexpensive hotels which are almost always have space. **Hotel Dukla,** námestie Legionárov 2 (tel. (91) 227 41, fax 321 34), at the corner of Halvná and Grešova just south of the Old Town, boasts a merry English-speaking reception open 24hrs. and newly renovated rooms, with shower and toilet. (Singles 835SK. Doubles 1522SK. Breakfast included.) The older **Hotel Šariš** (tel. (91) 463 51 or 463 52) is at Sabinovská 1, north of Old Town (24hr. reception. Singles 690SK. Doubles 1380SK. Breakfast included.) **Slovenská Reštaurácia,** Hlavná 11, is a very popular restaurant with inexpensive food. Try the *rezeň (schnitzel)* or the *Tokajská mäsová zmes* (assorted pan-fried veal and pork cutlets) for 70SK. (Open 9am-10pm.) Choose from an impressive selection of salads and cold cuts at **Echkhaus Bufet,** Hlavná 21 (open Mon.-Fri. 6am-8pm, Sat. 7am-1pm, Sun. 8am-2pm).

Slovenia (Slovenija)

US$1 = 129SIT	100SIT = US$0.77
CDN$1= 96SIT	100SIT = CAD$1.04
UK£1 = 205SIT	100SIT = UK£0.49
IR£1 = 203SIT	100SIT = IR£49
AUS$1 = 99SIT	100SIT = AUS$1.01
NZ$1 = 78SIT	100SIT = NZ$1.28
SAR1 = 36SIT	100SIT = SAR2.76
Country Code: 386	International Dialing Prefix: 00

Slovenia wants to forget Yugoslavia. Worlds away from the conflict in Bosnia, the most prosperous of the breakaway republics is relishing its independence, rapidly modernizing and turning a hungry eye toward the West. Only half the size of Switzerland, Slovenia is extraordinarily diverse: in the space of a day, you can breakfast in the Alpine peaks, lunch under the Mediterranean sun, and dine in the vineyards of the Plannonian plains. Though the Italian port city of Trieste sits on a chunk of its coastline, Slovenia opens a small window onto the Adriatic. In the northwest, the Julian Alps offer fabulous hiking before gradually descending into gentle hills near the Hungarian plains in the northwest. The river Sava originates in the Alps, circles around Ljubljana, then descends toward the Danube; its valley is marked by hills scattered with castles, manors, monasteries, and churches with tall, slender towers.

For more detailed coverage of Slovenia, pick up a copy of *Let's Go: Eastern Europe.*

GETTING THERE AND GETTING AROUND

Altogether, there are 63 international border crossings in Slovenia. The country is easily accessible by car, train, or plane. Ljubljana has frequent and uncrowded international train connections. Discounts are available for travelers under 26; check at the Ljubljana station (look for the BIJ-Wasteels logo). *"Vlak"* is the word for train; *"prihodi vlakov"* means arrivals; *"odhodi vlakov"* means departures. **Buses** are more expensive and slower, but reach some otherwise inaccessible places. Tickets are sold at the station or on board. There are three international **airports** in Slovenia:

the Ljubljana Airport in Brnik, with a regular bus service for incoming and outgoing flights; the Maribor Airport in the east, with connections to the rest of the world via Belgrade; and the much smaller Portorož Airport on the coast. **Adria Airways** flies direct to Munich, London, Paris, Vienna, and Moscow and offers daily service between Ljubljana and major Yugoslav cities. There is also a regular **hydrofoil** service between Venice and Portorož.

SLOVENIA ESSENTIALS

Citizens of the U.S., Canada, Australia, and New Zealand may visit Slovenia visa-free for up to 90 days. Citizens of Ireland, South Africa and the U.K. need visas. Apply by mail, in person, or at the border. **Tourist offices** are located in most major cities and tourist spots; the staff are generally friendly, speak English, and can help you find accommodations. Most businesses are open Mon.-Fri. 8am-7pm, and Sat. 8am-1pm or 7am-noon. Many restaurants stay open Sundays. **Holidays** in 1995 include: Jan. 1-2, Feb. 8 *(Prešeren* Day), April 16-17 (Easter Sunday and Monday), April 27 (Day of Uprising Against WWII Occupation), May 1-2 (Labor Day), May 22 (Whit Sunday), June 25 (National Day), August 15 (Assumption Day), Oct. 31 (Reformation Day), Nov. 1 (All Saints' Day), Dec. 25 (Christmas), and Dec. 26 (Independence Day).

The national **currency** is the Slovenian **Tolar** (1SIT), divided into 100 **stotins** which you'll probably never need; most shops round up bills to the nearest tolar. Prices in hard currency tend to be stable but are usually set in *deutschmarks* (DM) rather than U.S. dollars, though most establishments accept payments in any hard currency, and exchange offices are plentiful. The exchange rate for marks is slightly better than for U.S. dollars. Banks are usually open Mon.-Fri. 7:30am-6pm, Sat. 7:30am-noon. For purchases of at least 9000SIT you can get a 13% value-added tax refund at the border (ask the store salesperson for a tax-free check).

Communication Post offices in Slovenia are usually open Monday through Friday 8am-6pm, and Saturday 8am-2pm (in larger cities, there is also a night service). When at the post office, stock up on **phone tokens** or purchase a **magnetic phone card** (440SIT). There are two kinds of tokens: "A" for local calls and "B" for long-distance calls. To call abroad from Slovenia, dial 00, followed by the country code and the area code and local number. AT&T **USADirect** and similar services are not yet available. For **operator assistance** in connecting calls, dial 90 in Ljubljana, Kranj, Maribor and Nova Gorica, and 900 in other Slovene cities. Calling the U.S. is expensive (almost US$3 per min.); try calling from a neighboring western country.

If you speak any other Slavic language, you'll be able to decipher many Slovene words. Most young people speak at least some English, but the older generation is more likely to speak German (in the north) or Italian (along the Adriatic). Many cities along the Italian border are officially bilingual. The tourist industry is generally geared toward German speakers, though most tourist office employees speak English. Some useful phrases include: *da* (yes); *ne* (no); *Oprostite!* (excuse me); *Prosim!* (please); *Hvala!* (thank you); *Koliko to stane?* (how much does it cost?); and, *Ali govorite* (do you speak English?).

Accommodations and Camping The coast tends to get crowded as early as June, and is mobbed in July and August. In the mountains, the high season tends to be only July-Aug. Student rooms are commonly available in the mountains during summer vacation (late June-early Sept.) Early June may be the most pleasant time to visit the Alps, however, when the weather is usually fair. **Hotels** are classified into five categories (L (deluxe), A, B, C, D) and tend to be expensive. **Youth hostels** are cheap, but they're generally open only during the summer. The same is true for student dormitories. Usually, the best option is to rent **private rooms;** prices depend on the location, but they are rarely above US$20, and the rooms are usually a delight. In some places you can find rooms advertised on the streets (*sobe* or *zimmer* is "room"); or ask at the local tourist offices for help.

Food and Drink As fast food, self-serve places mushroom in Slovenia, espe-cially in larger, more touristed cities, traditional Slovene cuisine is becoming harder to find. If you can, try the national dish *jota*, a potato, bean, and cabbage soup. Pota-toes are so popular that Slovenes have been dubbed the "potato-eaters." Slovenes also have good pastries; one of their favorite cakes is *potica*, a sheet of pastry, spread with a rich filling and rolled up. The most common and popular of all fillings is the made from walnut kernels (walnut *potica*). Slovenia lies in the center of the so-called European **wine** zone, at nearly the same latitude as Burgundy in France. Better Slovene wines include *merlot*, *cabernet* and *tokay* among reds, and *muscat*, *mal-vazjia*, *pinot blanc* and *sauvignon* among whites. Locals claim that the less familiar *Dolenjski Cviček* has curative properties in addition to a pleasant sourish taste. A specialty of the **Podravje wine region,** which stretches on the Pannonian plains in the northeastern part of the country, is ice wine, produced from frozen grapes.

■■■ LJUBLJANA

Legend has it that Jason the Argonaut, Golden Fleece in tow, fled across the Black Sea, up the Danube to the Sava and Ljubljanica Rivers to escape King Aietes. Trapped by the Barje marshlands, he founded a city on the banks of the Ljubljanica. Ljubljana is now Slovenia's commercial and cultural core. The Old Town charms vis-itors with colorful Renaissance, Baroque and Secessionist façades.

ORIENTATION AND PRACTICAL INFORMATION

Just 40km from the Austrian border, Ljubljana is a major junction between the main north-south and east-west rail lines in the region. It is easily accessible from neigh-boring Italy, Austria, and Hungary.

Tourist Office: TIC-Tourist Information Center, Slovenska 35 (tel. 22 42 22, fax 22 21 15), offers excellent brochures. Open Mon.-Fri. 8am-7pm, Sat.-Sun. 8am-noon and 4-7pm. **Slovenÿaturist,** Slovenska 58 (tel. 31 18 51).

Embassies: U.S., Pražakova 4 (tel. 30 14 27, fax 30 14 01); **U.K.,** Trg Republike 3/IV (tel. 125 71 91, fax. 125 01 74), open Mon.-Fri. 9:30am-noon and 1-4pm; **Aus-tria,** Štrekljeva 5 (tel. 21 34 36, fax 22 17 17); **Hungary,** Dunajska 22 (tel. 11 51 68, fax 11 71 43).

Currency Exchange: At most hotels, travel agencies, and banks. Few charge commission.

American Express: Atlas, Mestni Trg (tel. 22 27 11). Holds mail. Open Mon.-Fri. 9am-5pm, Sat. 9am-noon.

Post Office: Cigaletova 15 (tel. 31 45 73), 3 blocks right of the train station. Open 24hrs. **Postal Code:** 61000.

Telephones: Buy tokens or magnetic phonecards at post offices. **City Code:** 061.

Flights: The airport is in Brnik, 26km away (tel. (064) 22 27 00, fax 22 12 20). Buses leave from the central bus station.

Trains: Trg OF (*Osvobodielne Fronte;* tel. 131 51 67 or 31 67 68). To Venice (6hr.), Trieste (3hr.), Vienna (6hr.), Budapest (10hr.), Salzburg (4½hr.) and Munich (6hr.).

Buses: The station neighbors the train station (tel. 133 61 36). Buses to all major destinations: Bled and Postojna 1hr., Adriatic coast 3hr.

Public Transportation: Buses run until midnight. 60SIT (drop exact change in the box next to the driver), or you can buy tokens for 43SIT at post offices and news-stands. Day, weekly, and monthly passes available at *Ljubljanski potniški promet*, Celovška 160 (tel. 159 41 14).

Hitchhiking: Hitchers to Bled take bus 1 to the last stop. Hitchers to the coast take bus 6 to the last stop or walk out of town along Tržaška cesta.

Emergencies: Police: tel. 92. **Fire:** tel. 93. **Ambulance:** tel. 94.

ACCOMMODATIONS, CAMPING AND FOOD

Private rooms are available through tourist offices. Singles cost about US$10 but are scarce. In July and August, ask about student dorm rooms (US$10 per person) in the **Dom Učencev Tabor** at Vidovdanska cesta 7 (tel. 32 10 67) or the **Dijaški Dom Ivana Cankarja** at Poljanska cesta 26-28 (tel. 133 52 74). The cheapest hotel in town is the **Park Hotel,** Tabor 9 (tel. 133 13 06, fax 32 13 52), near one of the youth hostels (singles US$21, with shower US$27). Camp at **Autocamp Ježica,** Dunajska 270 (tel. and fax 37 13 82); take bus 6 or 8 (US$7 per person; open May-Sept.). For a supermarket, head to **Maximarket,** across from the Parliament building (open Mon.-Fri. 9am-8pm, Sat. 8am-7pm). The Old Town hosts a large **outdoor market** (open Mon.-Sat. until 2pm). The popular cafés lining Mestni Trg and Stari Trg are the haunts of Ljubljana's artsy scene. Enjoy pizzas and pasta in a grotto with stained-glass windows at **Zlata Ladjica,** Jurčičev Trg 1. Gostilna Sestica, Slovenska 40 (tel. 21 95 75) is Ljubljana's oldest restaurant, with a formidable selection of entrees.

SIGHTS AND ENTERTAINMENT

A prominent feature of **Prešernov Trg,** Ljubljana's main square, is **Trimostovje** (Triple Bridge); in the 1930s, the old Špitalski Bridge was revamped by the architect Jože Plečnik, who transformed it into one of Ljubljana's most admired architectural jewels. To the left is the **Zmajski most** (Dragon Bridge), built in 1901 in place of the former wooden "Butcher's Bridge." The bridge was named after Emperor Franz Joseph, but locals call it the Dragon Bridge, because it is decorated with dragons, Ljubljana's mascot.

   Trg Francoske Revolucije (French Revolution Square) and its immediate surroundings were once occupied by Teutonic Knights; the neighborhood is still called **Križanke.** The Knights built a monastery in the square; demolished in the 18th century, the complex was restored under Plečnik's guidance, and now hosts musical, theatrical and dance performances of the **Ljubljana International Summer Festival** (mid-July to end of September). Ljubljana's museums cluster around the Slovene parliament buildings on the train station side of the river. Museums are generally open Tues.-Sat. 10am-6pm, Sun. 10am-1pm. The **Moderna Galerija** (Museum of Modern Art), displays works of 20th-century Slovene artists. Every odd year, it also hosts the **International Biennial of Graphic Art,** the largest exhibition of its kind in the world. To the left stands the **Narodna Galerija** (National Gallery), Cankarjeva 20; it exhibits works by Slovene artists from the Middle Ages to the present. Near the museums stretches **Tivoli park,** with some of the prettiest strolling grounds in Ljubljana, and excellent paths for jogging. The **Slovene Symphony Orchestra** performs regularly at **Cankarjev Dom,** across from the Parliament building. Various events, from violin concerts to grunge music, are held throughout the year; pick up the *Where To?* brochure at tourist offices for listings of the month's cultural events. The most popular disco in town is **Babilon,** at Kongresni Trg 2. For a more underground scene, try **K-4** at Kersinkova 4 or the **Acapulco** and **Eldorado.**

■■■ JULIAN ALPS(JULIJSKE ALPE)

The southern Alps are not as high as their Austrian or Swiss siblings, but they are no less beautiful. The mountains cover the northwest of Slovenia, peaking at 2864m on **Mt. Triglav** in the heart of the **Triglav National Park.** East of Triglav is **Bled,** a world-famous resort. The more peaceful **Bohnij,** southwest of Bled, is the place to get information about climbing Mt. Triglav. A railroad crosses the mountains connecting Jesenice, Bled, Bohinj, and Most na Soči.

Bled In a pleasant valley with a great view of the Alps, Bled has been a world-class resort for more than a century, and is a good base for trips into the mountains and to the nearby ski centers of Straža, Zatrnik and Pokljuka, on the Pokljuka plateau. The **Bled Castle** (*Blejski Grad*) has a wide terrace, from which spreads an incredible view of Bled and its surroundings. (Open 8am-7pm; 200SIT, ages 3-10 100SIT, or free with a deposit of 500SIT towards a meal). Bled's phone numbers are in the process of being converted to six-digit numbers. Check the *1995 Bled Tourist News* for updates. Trains stop in **Lesce,** 5km away from Bled on the Ljubljana-Salzburg-Munich line. Catch one of the frequent buses going from Lesce to Bled, or consider taking a taxi (the 900SIT may be bearable if you pool with someone else). The **tourist office** is by the lake, at Ljubljanska 4 (tel. (064) 772 35 or 772 45, fax 781 81; open Mon.-Sat. 8am-6pm, Sun. noon-6pm). The **youth hostel (HI),** 17 Grajska C. (tel. (064) 782 30), is in a calm location close to the castle. (DM15 per person, with breakfast DM20. Members only. Open most of the year; call ahead.) **Camping Zaka,** C. svobode 13 (tel. (064) 779 32 or 773 25), is on the opposite shore of the lake, 2km from the center. It has a private beach and charges DM12 per person. (Open May-Sept.) The restaurant **Blejski Grad** in the castle, boasts a candle-lit interior with medieval Italian murals. Arrive early to snag a table with a view of the lake. (Menu in Italian. Fish, meat, and pasta specialties. Entrees 800-1400SIT.)

Ribčev Laz Ribčev Laz boasts a beautiful location on the southeastern edge of the **Bohinj Lake.** The Bohinj area is as beautiful as Bled's environs, but more isolated and less touristed, though it can get crowded in July and August. There are no direct bus connections to Ribčev Laz, but the resort is only 5km west of **Bohinjska Bistrica,** and buses run every hour from Bled to the tourist office in Bistrica (260SIT). To get to Ribčev Laz, catch the local bus on the main road in front of the post office (110SIT). All trains on the Bled-Most na Soči line stop in Bohinjska Bistrica (101 SIT to Bled, 377 SIT to Nova Gorica, 470SIT to Ljubljana). Most of the interesting walks and hikes start in Ribčev Laz, so you might as well come here instead of staying in Bohinjska Bistrica. Once in Ribčev, stop by the **tourist office**, located near the main road; the staff is friendly but the office often closes before 6pm. Pick up a walking/hiking map from the Ribčev tourist office. Hiking trips include a visit to the **Savica waterfall**. Bohinj is also a starting point for climbing **Mt. Triglav;** alternate starting points are in the north in the Sava Valley.

Private rooms are generally excellent and inexpensive. Singles run about US$10, breakfast US$4. Ask the tourist office for a room with a Triglav-view. Farther along the lake, there is a **youth hostel** that keeps changing its name (in 1994 it was the Hotel Apollon; inquire at the tourist office). You can feed yourself at any of the hotel restaurants, but also try **Restaurant Triglav,** 15min. away in Stara Fužina, north of Ribčev Laz. Turn right 50m down from the tourist office and cross the bridge. Follow the main road, and admire the picturesque church by the lake on the way. Its a bit expensive (full meals US$10-15) but worth the hike for the excellent food and great views from the terrace; don't forget to ask about national specialties.

Planina pod Golico Planina pod Golico (Planina below Golica) is an idyllic village in the Karavanke mountains, famous for its daffodils. To reach it, first go to **Jesenice** (1hr. north of Ljubljana by train on the Salzburg route or by bus from Bled), which is an industrial city in the east of the Upper Sava Valley and an access point to the Kranjska Gora ski resort. The Karavanke mountains run from west to east, separated from the Julian Alps by the Upper Sava Valley. The border between Austria and Slovenia runs along this thin ridge. Armed soldiers once guarded this border; most controls are now gone, but bring your passport just in case you run into a patrol. Even after the daffodils are gone, the meadows are filled with flowers of all colors of the rainbow. **Kepa** (2143m) lies 3hr. west of Golica on the ridge and **Stol** (2236m) is 4hr. east. Most buses in Jesenice stop in front of the railway station. Don't be misled; the few buses per day to Planina stop across the street. Check the schedules, but unless you're lucky you'll have to walk. If you were lucky enough to catch a bus, get off at the last stop on the main road of Planina, near a small market. Follow the road to reach the **tourist office,** located at 39 Planina pod Golico (tel. (064) 835 47). They arrange private rooms for 1200SIT and stay open late in the evening, but you may need to knock. Possibly the best accommodations option is the **Golica caban** (*koča*). This small hut is slightly above the treeline (1500m) at the end of a steep but relatively easy climb (45-60min. from *Pri Fencu*). Crowded but clean, it offers an impressive view of the Julian Alps. (40 beds. 4-bed room 900SIT, dorm-style attic 700SIT. Modest but nourishing meals. Open May-Sept.)

■■■ SLOVENIAN RIVIERA

Slovenia claims only 40km of the Adriatic coast, but this stretch of green bays, little seaside towns, and beaches with a myriad of recreational facilities, is well worth visiting. The towns of Koper, Izola, and Piran are an attractive bland of Slovene and Italian. The main tourist center is the summer and spa resort of Portorož.

Portorož (Portorose) Built in a Mediterranean style, the town's terraces and houses with red-tiled roofs march down to the sea. Spring may be the best time to see Portorož. Frequent **buses** run here from Ljubljana and Postojna; you can also take a bus to Koper, and from there, a local bus to Portorož. Thomas Mann once said that Venice should be entered only by sea. And indeed, a **ship** makes the Portorož-Venice trip Fri.-Sun. from April to mid-Oct. (departs Portorož 8am, arrives Venice 10:30am; departs Venice 5:30pm, arrives Portorož 8pm). The **bus** station is meters from the sea; across from it is the main **tourist office,** Obala 16 (tel. (066) 763 72, fax 730 54; open Mon.-Sat. 8am-noon and 4-7pm, Sun. 8am-noon). As a rule, hotels are expensive although prices go down drastically in the off-season months. There are a number of **pensions** that offer reasonable rates, but they're frequently packed; check directly or with the tourist office. There are two **campgrounds** in Portorož: **Lucija** (tel. (066) 710 27) and **Strunjan** (tel. (066) 786 38). Rates run DM8-12 per day. For alternatives, try any of the nearby towns: Jzola, Strunjan, Piran, or Koper. There is a **youth hostel** in Koper. Most restaurants are on the waterfront. **FANCY** has a nice terrace and a menu in English. At night, its lights reflect beautifully on the water; beware the mosquitoes as you wait for service. (Pizzas 400-700SIT; small Italian-style smoked ham 700SIT; meat entrees 900-1600SIT.)

Piran Only 3km from Portorož, tiny Piran is just as touristed, but proffers considerably more charm. Built on a peninsula by Venetians, the narrow stone-tiled streets and crowded houses make feel like a little slice of Italy. Buses run frequently from Portorož to Piran; take the ordinary bus (60SIT) or the casino mini-van (70SIT). Once there, follow the wharf to the central square, dominated by a **statue** of the famous violinist and composer Giuseppe Tartini, born in Piran. The narrow streets near the center are worth a look. A short walk uphill is the Baroque-Renaissance **Church of San Giorgio** (built ca. 600 AD, rebuilt in the 14th century), the most prominent church in Piran. Back by the sea, take a walk along the quay to the odd church/lighthouse at the end of the peninsula. There is no real beach here, but you can enjoy a meal in one of the waterfront restaurants. **Pavel** offers entrees for 700-1400SIT. To book a room or for more information on Piran and its environs, visit the **tourist office** in the main square (tel. (066) 74 60 95, fax 74 61 01). Singles run DM13-19, doubles DM19-31. Expect a 50% increase in prices in July-August as well as a 50% surcharge for stays of less than three nights.

Spain (España)

US$1	= 130ptas (pesetas, or ESP)	100ptas =	US$0.77
CDN$1	= 97ptas	100ptas =	CDN$1.04
UK£1	= 206ptas	100ptas =	UK£0.49
IR£1	= 204ptas	100ptas =	IR£0.49
AUS$1	= 99ptas	100ptas =	AUS$1.01
NZ$1	= 79ptas	100ptas =	NZ$1.27
SAR1	= 36ptas	100ptas =	SAR2.75
Country Code: 34		**International Dialing Prefix: 07**	

Phoenicians, Carthaginians, Greeks, Romans, Visigoths, and Muslims were all drawn to Spain's legendary mineral wealth and to its strategic position. The Romans brought their roads, irrigation canals, aqueducts, courtyards, rounded arches, brick masonry, legal code, and language. The Muslims, who invaded in 711, were transmitters and elaborators of classical Greek science and philosophy and of those Eastern artistic traditions crucial to the European Renaissance. Spain inspired the builder in its settlers, and the climate seems peculiarly well-suited for pickling old stone. In Andalusia, the mosque at Córdoba and the Alhambra in Granada are as much fountainheads of architecture as the Parthenon in Athens or Aya Sofya in İstanbul.

After three centuries of Muslim hegemony and another three centuries of Muslim, Jewish, and Christian vernacular syncretism (a prime example of which is Mudejar architecture, which applies Moorish use of tile, brick, and geometric patterns to European structures such as Gothic and Romanesque), Enrique de Trastámara won control of Castile in 1369 and began to build a Christian Spain modeled after high medieval, Latinate European traditions (including rigid religious orthodoxy and intolerance). In 1469, the marriage of Fernando de Aragón and Isabel de Castilla joined Iberia's two mightiest Christian kingdoms. By 1492, the unstoppable duo had captured Granada (the last Moorish stronghold) and had dispatched Columbus, among others, to explore the New World. The daughter of Fernando and Isabel, Juana la Loca (the Mad), married Felipe el Hermoso (the Fair), scion of the powerful Habsburg dynasty. Ms. Crazy and Mr. Handsome spawned Carlos I (known as Charles V of Germany, 1516-1556), who reigned supreme over an immense empire—what is today the Netherlands, and Belgium, as well as part of Germany, Austria, Spain and the colonies in the Americas. In 1713, Felipe IV became king and like his grandfather, Louis XIV, ushered in a regime of palace-building and decadence. Napoleonic occupation and incompetent government inspired Spanish colonies in the Americas to declare their independence and ushered in an era of nationalism and political unrest in Spain itself. The 19th century saw rapid industrialization in some areas (although the majority of the country remained agricultural), and the growth of regional consciousness in nearly all. Sparked by international depression, these tensions erupted in the Spanish Civil War (1936-1939); aided crucially by Hitler and Mussolini, Francisco Franco emerged as the country's dictator and ruled until his death in 1975. Under King Juan Carlos, Franco's hand-picked successor, Spain has become a modern, stable, and democratic constitutional monarchy, and since 1982 has been led by Socialist Prime Minister Felipe González, who narrowly escaped defeat in the 1993 elections to a member of the conservative *Partido Popular.*

Every year, tourists more than double Spain's population of 40 million; much of the crunch comes in July and August. No infrastructure could possibly be expected to bear such a burden. This fact—and Andalusia's searing heat—counsel against summer travel in southern Spain; if you must travel then, choose central or northern itineraries.

For more explicit, hot, and sweaty information about Spain, get your hands on a copy of *Let's Go: Spain & Portugal.*

GETTING THERE AND GETTING AROUND

Airports in Madrid, Barcelona, and Málaga handle most of Spain's international air traffic. Trains chug over the border into France and connect with most major European cities. **Brittany Ferries,** Millbay, Plymouth (tel. (01752) 22 13 21) sail between Plymouth in England and Santander. **P. & O. European Ferries,** Channel House, Channel View Road Dover, Kent CT17 9TJ (tel. (01304) 20 33 88) links Portsmouth England, with Bilbao.

Spanish **trains** are clean, somewhat punctual and reasonably priced, although they don't run to some small towns. The rail network is extremely centralized, radiating from Madrid. **RENFE,** the Spanish national rail system, offers many types of service with a corresponding variety of prices: *AVE* trains are the fastest but currently run only between Madrid and Seville. *Talgos* are elegant low-slung trains that zip passengers in air-conditioned compartments; *electro* are very comfortable and quick, but have more intermediate stops than *talgo. Talgo 200s* are talgo trains on *AVE* rails; currently they offer some services out of Madrid. *Expreso, estrella,* and *rápido* vary greatly in speed. *Cercanías* are commuter trains that radiate from larger cities to suburbs and nearby *pueblos,* making frequent stops and usually lacking air-conditioning. Don't bother with any *tranvía, semidirecto,* or *correo* train—these are ludicrously slow and are now uncommon. Unfortunately, no youth railpass exists (not even the old *Tarjeta Joven*). On blue days (almost every day except for holidays and Friday and Saturday afternoons), round-trip tickets are discounted 10%;

sometimes those with student IDs enjoy further reductions. Buy tickets within 60 days of departure at RENFE travel offices, RENFE train stations and authorized travel agencies. RENFE will refund 85% (75% on "red days"—holidays) of the ticket price for cancellation up to 15 minutes before train departure. **Reservations** are strongly advised on Spanish trains; even if you have a Eurail pass, and the train is half-full, train conductors will either send you off the train to get a reservation (in which case you could well miss the train) or charge you for the reservation plus a fine. The only other train company in Spain is **FEVE,** actually a conglomeration of private companies which has short runs between northern towns not served by RENFE. Those with Eurailpasses need only pay a small reservations fee on trains in Spain.

Bus routes are far more exhaustive than the rail network, are the only public transportation to isolated areas, and almost always cost less. Highway improvements and expansions have cut travel time between major cities by as much as 50% in the past few years, making some bus journeys faster than a slow-train connection. Spain has a multitude of private companies rather than one national bus line, which makes trip planning an ordeal.

Rental cars cost considerably less than in other European countries, but you must be over 21, carry an International Driving Permit, and be prepared to pay for expensive fuel. Renting from abroad is considerably less expensive than doing so once you have arrived in Spain. For rural drives, tourist offices often supply leaflets on local *"Rutas Turísticas."* **Hitching** is reportedly slow and can be dangerous. Spanish hospitality to hitchhikers has dwindled in the wake of increasing crime. The northern areas are regarded as relatively easy to hitch in, as is the Mediterranean coast. Inland hitching is said to be only fair; hitching out of Madrid—in any direction—is nearly impossible. In Andalusia, rides are infrequent and the sun can be intolerable.

SPAIN ESSENTIALS

Most towns have a centrally located **Oficina de Turismo** (tourist office, fondly called *Turismo*) that distributes information on sights and lodgings. They'll give you a free map that usually includes brief descriptions of sights and useful phone numbers. Although most don't book accommodations, many *Turismos* keep a list of approved establishments or can point you to a *casa particular* (private room). **Viajes TIVE,** the national chain of student travel agencies, peddle discount travel tickets, churn out ISICs and HI cards, and dispense transport information.

The northwest regions are rightly called "wet" or "green" Spain, with a humid, temperate climate open to the sea, and a lush, often thickly wooded landscape (both features reappear in those mountain areas of the south and east whose ranges are high enough to catch moisture). The interior has a climate resembling that of Central Europe, with long winters and, in the lowlands, torrid summers. The eastern and southern coasts enjoy a Mediterranean climate, with mild winters. The northeast coast can be humid; the Guadalquivir river basin (including Seville and Córdoba) is the most sweltering part of the country.

Some Spanish men think that foreign women traveling without male or family companions do so *en busca de aventura* (in search of sexual adventure). Women should be extra cautious in big cities, and memorize the **Spanish emergency phone number (091).**

Banks, shops and offices shut down on **legal and religious holidays** in Spain: New Year's Day, Jan. 6, March 29, Easter (April 13-17, 1995), May Day, Corpus Christi (June 15 in 1995), July 25, Aug. 15, Oct. 12, Nov. 1, Dec. 8, and Christmas. Some of these religious celebrations are no longer legal holidays, but business slows down anyway and sometimes stops altogether. The *Semana Santa* (Holy Week), the week before Easter, sees much celebration, especially in Andalusia. Cities and towns strive to outdo one another with ardent displays of adoration. Bullfights feature prominently in most festivals between May and October.

Spanish workers ordinarily start at 9am, go home at 1:30 or 2pm for a long lunch, and go back around 4:30 or 5pm until 8pm. On Saturday, shops are usually open only in the morning, and Sunday is a day of rest for everyone except a few indispensables (not including tourist offices). The smallest denomination of paper **currency** is 1000ptas. Coins come in 1, 2, 5, 10, 25, 100, 200, 500ptas, and the rare 50pta coins. In summer, **banking hours** are Monday through Friday 9am-2pm; in winter, banks are also open Saturday 9am-1pm. The odd bank is open for an afternoon session too. Banks charge a minimum of 500-750ptas for currency exchange. **El Corte Inglés,** a Spanish department store chain, exchanges money from Monday to Saturday 10am-8pm at competitive rates: 1% commission (250ptas min. charge) on traveler's checks; 2% commission (500ptas min. charge) on currency. Beware dastardly rates in after-hours *bureaux de change.*

Communication There are 5 official **languages** in Spain (plus plenty of dialects, such as the Mallorquín of the Balearic Islands). Catalan is the language of choice in Catalonia, Valencian in Valencia. The non-Indo-European Basque (Euskera) language is spoken in north central Spain, and Galician (related to Portuguese) is spoken in the once-Celtic northwest, though both are minority languages even in their own dominions. Spanish (Castilian, or Castellano) is spoken everywhere. In Spanish, "ll" is pronounced like English "y", "j" like "h", soft "c" and "z" like "th", and "h" is not pronounced.

Stamps are sold at post offices, hotels, and tobacconists. An airmail letter takes 7-14 business days to reach the U.S. and Canada; it's faster to the U.K. and Ireland, slower to Australia and New Zealand. Postage for a letter is 90ptas. The Spanish version of Poste Restante is **Lista de Correos.** Most post offices also have fax service. A telegram *(telegrama)* is the most reliable means of communication. Telegraph offices are inside post offices. A message costs 135ptas per word. **Phone** booths are marked by signs that say *Teléfono público* or *Locutorio.* Most bars also have pay phones. Local calls cost 15ptas. A 3min. call to anywhere in Spain is 100ptas. Phonecards in 1000 and 2000ptas denominations are more convenient than feeding coin after coin into a payphone; they're sold at tobacconists. Direct-dialing from a phone booth is the cheapest way to make international calls. It can take up to 30 seconds after you dial to make the connection; dial 07, wait for the high-pitched dial tone, then its country code + city code + phone number. Collect calls *(cobro revertido)* are billed according to pricier person-to-person *(persona a persona)* rates, but may still be cheaper than calls from hotels. *Telefónica* is a central phone office. Other useful numbers include: local operator, 009; national police, 091; and local police emergency 092. For AT&T's **USADirect,** dial 900 99 00 11, MCI's **WorldPhone** 900 99 0014, **SprintExpress** 900 99 00 13, **Canada Direct** 900 99 00 15, and **BT Direct** 900 99 00 44.

Accommodations and Camping **REAJ,** the Spanish Hostelling International (HI) affiliate, runs about 100 youth hostels year-round and over 140 in summer. A bed costs about 700ptas per night. HI cards (1800ptas) are available at Viajes TIVE, other travel agencies and REAJ offices, but are rarely sold at youth hostels.

Accommodations have many an alias in Spain; each name indicates a specific type of establishment. Cheapest and barest are *hospedajes* (called *Casas de Huéspedes* in the south). The categories next higher in quality are *pensiones,* then *hostales,* then *hostal-residencias* (all three similar in amenities), the staples of many budget travelers. These are rated by the government on a 2-star system; even one-star places in this category are usually very comfortable. The highest priced accommodations are *hoteles,* far beyond the reach of budget travelers.

Campgrounds are government-regulated on a 3-class system, rated and priced by the quality of amenities. Tourists offices stock the *Guía de Campings,* a fat guide to all official campgrounds in Spain.

In some areas, tourist authorities promote alternate types of accommodations. Look out for *casas particulares* (private residences), *casas rurales* (rural cottages), *casas rústicas* (farmhouses), *refugios* (rustic huts in the mountains), *colegios mayores* (state university student dorms), and monasteries or convents.

Food and Drink Spaniards start their day with a breakfast of coffee or hot chocolate and *bollos* (rolls) or *churros* (lightly fried fritters). As in the rest of Europe, dinner ("lunch" to Americans) is served between 2 and 3pm, and traditionally consists of several courses. Supper at home is light and devoured around 8pm. Supper out begins after 9pm, usually at 10pm, and is a light meal.

Some restaurants are "open" from 8am until 1 or 2am, but most only serve meals from 1:30 or 2 to 4pm and from 8 until 11pm or midnight. Each city's tourist office rates its restaurants with a row of forks, 5 forks indicating luxury. *Cafeterías* are rated by a row of up to 3 cups. All cafeterias and one- and two-fork establishments are in the budget range. Prices for a full meal range start at about 800ptas in the cheapest bar-restaurants. Restaurants often offer a *plato combinados* (combination platter—includes a main course and side dishes on a single plate, plus bread, and sometimes beverage) or a *menú del día* (two dishes, bread, beverage, and dessert— roughly 800-1100ptas).

Nibbled on or snarfed down at bars, *tapas* are ever so conducive to convivial good spirits. A *tasca,* often also called a *taberna,* is a bar or pub that serves *tapas* at a counter or a few tables in back. *Pinchos* are the equivalent of *tapas* in the North. *Raciones* may be equal to an entree in size. *Bocadillos* are *tapas* served as a sandwich on a hunk of thick bread—often a viable substitute for lunch. Your fork may find its way into: *champiñones al ajillo* (mushrooms in garlic sauce), *jamón serrano* (smoked ham), *atún* or *bonito* (tuna), *calamares fritos* (fried squid), *chorizo* (spicy sausage), *gambas* (shrimp), *ternera* (veal), *lomo* (pork), *judías verdes* (green beans), and *lenguado* (sole).

While the most well known Spanish dishes—*paella* (steamed saffron-flavored rice with chicken stock and an assortment of seafood), *gazpacho* (cold tomato-based soup), and *tortilla española* (potato omelette)—are from Valencia, Andalusia, and Castile, respectively, the most sophisticated and varied cuisines on the peninsula were developed in the Basque country, Navarre, Catalonia, and Galicia.

Food is almost always washed down with alcohol, whether a glass of wine (*vino blanco* is white, *tinto* is red) or of beer *(cerveza)*. Beer is served in bottles or on draught. Aguila, Estrella, and San Miguel are fine national brands; Volldamm (Catalonia), and Alhambra (Andalusia) are fine regional brews. Rioja is a world-renowned grape-growing region, with especially good red wines; there are innumerable fine regional wines. *Sangría* is made of red wine, sugar, brandy, seltzer, and peaches. Another native beverage is sherry *(jerez)*, from the city of the same name.

■■■ MADRID

Although it witnessed the coronation of Fernando and Isabel, Madrid was of no great importance until paper-pushing Habsburg Felipe II plunked down the Spanish court here permanently in 1561; an unlikely choice of capital considering the city's distance from vital ports and rivers. Yet from that moment on, the city became the seat of wealth, culture, and imperial glory, watching over Spain's 16th- and 17th-century Golden Age of literature (Cervantes, Lope de Vega), art (El Greco, Velázquez), and architecture. Today's Madrid owes much of its neoclassical flair, from the Palacio Real to the Museo del Prado, to the 18th-century urban renewal of Bourbon Felipe V. Passionately hostile to Franco's Nationalists, the center was the last city to fall to the dictator save for Valencia. Since then Madrid has kept up a furious pace. In the 1980s, *la movida,* a postmodern, post-Franco cultural movement unleashed a frenzy of sex, drugs and punk on the city. The capital of contemporary Spanish cultural life, surpassing Barcelona as the country's manufacturing and financial center, the city is anything but a museum piece.

ORIENTATION AND PRACTICAL INFORMATION

The *Plano de Madrid* and the *Plano de los Transportes* maps, free at tourist offices, are good maps of the city center, but do not include street indexes; pick up the Falk or Chequepoint map (800ptas) at a newspaper kiosk. The center of Madrid is the

Puerta del Sol, an intersection where 8 streets meet above ground, and metro lines blue 1, red 2, and yellow 3 meet underneath. Four major streets conduct traffic in and out of Sol. Orient yourself with your back to the clock tower on the **police station** (a good landmark). The street leading traffic out of Sol (on your far left) is **Calle del Arenal.** C. del Arenal runs into **Calle de Bailén** at its other end (in front of the Pl. de Oriente and Palacio Real). A right on Bailén leads to **Plaza de España,** with **Parque del Oeste** to the left. The street leading traffic into Sol is **Calle Mayor** (on your near left). Down this street is the **Plaza Mayor. Carrera San Jerónimo** emerges from the other side of Sol. **Plaza Canalejas** is just down the street; **Calle Príncipe** leads out of the right of the plaza to **Plaza Santa Ana** and an area of quality restaurants and bars. **Calle Alcalá** (on your far right) leads from Sol to **Plaza Cibeles** and eventually to **Plaza de la Independencia** and the **Parque del Retiro.**

South of Sol, amid a tangle of streets reached by **Calle de Carretas,** is **Calle de Atocha,** which runs downhill to **Estación de Atocha** (train station). South of C. Atocha lies the neighborhood **Arganzuela.** North of Sol, bounded by the **Gran Vía,** is a major shopping area. **Calle Montera,** the one street with car traffic amidst pedestrian thoroughfares, leads from Sol to Gran Vía and the eponymous metro stop. To the left, Gran Vía runs by **Plaza de Callao** and heads downhill to **Plaza España.** Past Pl. España, the Gran Vía becomes C. Princesa, stretching uphill through the residential **Argüelles** and collegiate **Moncloa** neighborhoods. Even farther north is the **Ciudad Universitaria** (1 to 1½hr. walk). **Calle Fuencarral** leads off the Gran Vía to the north and forms the eastern border of **Malasaña,** a lively middle-class area. Parallel to C. Fuencarral is C. Hortaleza, which heads into the working-class **Chueca,** full of inexpensive restaurants, nightclubs and *hostales* and a site of the city's increasingly open gay scene.

Madrid is safe compared to other major European cities, but the Puerta del Sol, Plaza 2 de Mayo in Malasaña, Plaza de Chueca, and Pl. España (to a lesser extent) are particularly intimidating late at night. Watch out for thieves and pickpockets in the metro and on crowded city streets, and be wary of opportunists whose clever scams are often targeted at tourists. As usual, we advise you to avoid the parks and quiet residential areas after dark.

Tourist Offices: Municipal, Pl. Mayor, 3 (tel. 366 54 77 or 588 16 36, fax 366 54 77). M: Sol. Open Mon.-Fri. 10am-8pm, Sat. 10am-2pm. **Regional/Provincial Office of the Comunidad de Madrid,** C. Princesa, 1, Torre de España (tel. 541 23 25), entrance faces Pl. España. M: Pl. España. A **2nd office** is at C. Duque Medinaceli, 2 (tel. 429 49 51), just off Pl. Cortes. M: Sol. Both open Mon.-Fri. 9am-7pm, Sat. 9:30am-1:30pm. More offices at **Estación Chamartín** (tel. 315 99 76; open Mon.-Fri. 8am-8pm, Sat. 9am-1pm) and the **airport,** in the international arrivals area (tel. 305 86 56; open same hrs. as Chamartín).

Budget Travel: Viajes TIVE: C. Fernando el Católico, 88 (tel. 543 02 08 or 543 74 12, fax 544 00 62). M: Moncloa. Branch at José Ortega y Gasset, 71 (tel. 347 77 00). M: Lista. Discount plane tix, BIJ tix, HI cards, and railpasses sold. Message board for rides, cheap tickets, and apartment sharing notices. Both offices open Mon.-Fri. 9am-2pm, Sat. 9am-noon.

Embassies and Consulates: U.S. (both): C. Serrano, 75 (tel. 577 40 00). M: Rubén Darío. Open Mon.-Fri. 9am-1:30pm and 3-6pm. **Canadian (both):** C. Núñez de Balboa, 35 (tel. 431 43 00). M: Velázquez. Open for walk-in service Mon.-Fri. 9am-12:30pm, for phone service only also 2-5pm. **British Embassy:** C. Fernando el Santo, 16 (tel. 319 02 00). M: Colón. **Consulate,** C. Marqués de la Ensenada, 16 (tel. 308 52 01). Open Mon.-Fri. 8am-2:30pm. **Australian (both):** Po. Castellana, 143 (tel. 579 04 28, fax 570 02 04). M: Cuzco. Open Mon.-Thurs. 8:30am-5pm, Fri. 8:30am-2:15pm. **New Zealand (both):** Pl. Lealtad, 2, 3rd floor (tel. 523 02 26). M: Banco de España. Open Mon.-Fri. 9am-1:30pm and 2:20-5:30pm. **South African Embassy:** Edificio Lista, C. Claudio Coello 91, #6, (tel. 527 31 53).

Currency Exchange: American Express has the best rates. Also at **El Corte Inglés,** C. Preciados, 3 (tel. 532 18 00), M: Sol; C. Goya, 76 (tel. 577 71 71), M:

750

Madrid

1 National Tourist Office
2 Regional Tourist Office
3 City Tourist Office
4 Budget Travel: Viajes TIVE
5 American Embassy
6 Australian Embassy
7 Canadian Embassy
8 New Zealand Embassy
9 U.K. Embassy
10 American Express Office
11 Main Post Office
12 Estación de Chamartín
13 Estación del Norte
14 Estación de Atocha
15 Estación de Nuevos Ministerios
16 Estación de Recoletos
17 Estación de la Plaza de Colón
18 Estación Sur de Autobuses
19 Main Police Station
20 Youth Hostel
21 San Pedro el Viejo
22 Palacio de Santa Cruz

23 Capilla del Obispo, Iglesia
   San Andrés, and San Isidro
24 Convento de las Descalzas Reales
25 Catedral de San Isidro
26 Palacio Real and Catedral
27 de la Almudena
   Academia de San Fernando and
28 Calcografía
   Iglesia de San Francisco
29 Capilla de San Antonio
30 Museo del Prado
31 Centro Reina Sofía
32 Museo Municipal
33 Teatro de la Opera
34 Biblioteca Nacional
35 Palacio de las Cortes
36 Museo Lázaro Galdiano
37 Museo Arqueológico
38 Museo de Artes Decorativas
39 Museo de América
40 Museo Naval
41 Auditorio Nacional

SPAIN

Goya); C. Princesa, 42 (tel. 542 48 00), M: Argüelles. Open Mon.-Sat. 10am-9pm, Sun. noon-8pm. ATMs accept major bank cards, but use only the first four digits.

American Express: Pl. Cortes, 2 (tel. 322 54 24, fax 429 21 78; lost traveler's checks call (900) 99 44 26). M: Sevilla. Holds mail, cashes personal checks in emergency. Express Cash machine. Open Mon.-Fri. 9am-5:30pm, Sat. 9am-noon.

Post Office: Palacio de Comunicaciones, Pl. Cibeles (tel. 396 24 43). M: Banco de España. Information open Mon.-Fri. 8am-10pm. Open for stamps and certified mail Mon.-Fri. 8am-10pm, Sat. 8:30am-2pm, Sun. 9:30am-1pm; for *Lista de Correos* Mon.-Fri. 8am-9:30pm, Sat. 8:30am-2pm; for **telegrams** 24hrs. Telegram assistance available Mon.-Fri. 8am-10pm (at window 27). English and French spoken at information desk. **Postal Code:** 28070.

Telephones: Telefónica, Gran Vía, 30, at C. Valverde. M: Gran Vía. Open Mon.-Sat. 9am-midnight, Sun. 10am-midnight. Almodóvar used to work here. Seriously. The **Palacio de Comunicaciones** (above) is quieter. Open Mon.-Fri. 8am-midnight, Sat.-Sun. and holidays 8am-10pm. **City Code:** 91.

Flights: Aeropuerto Internacional de Barajas, 15km northeast of Madrid. **Bus** to Plaza de Colón (every 15min., 300ptas). **Iberia:** C. Goya, 29 (tel. 587 81 56). Domestic reservations (tel. 411 10 11), international (tel. 329 43 53). 24hrs.

Trains: For general railway information, call 429 02 02. Madrid has 2 *largo recorrido* (long distance) and 2 intermediate stations: **Estación Chamartín,** Agustín de Foxá (tel. 323 21 21). M: Chamartín, line 8 (1 stop from Pl. Castilla stop on blue line 1). Bus 5 runs to and from Sol (45min.); the stop is just beyond the lockers. Chamartín services towns throughout Spain, Portugal, and France. Ticket windows open 6:45am-11:35pm. **Estación Atocha,** Av. Ciudad de Barcelona (tel. 527 31 60). M: Atocha-Renfe (on blue line 1). Newly renovated, serves Castilla-La Mancha, Andalucía, Valencia, Granada, Córdoba, Toledo, Salamanca, etc. Also AVE (Alta Velocidad Española) service to Seville via Córdoba (tel. 534 05 05). Service to Portugal. Ticket windows open 6:30am-11:30pm. Intermediate stop only (trains every 5-10min.): **Estación de Recoletos:** Po. Recoletos, 4 (tel. 232 15 15). M: Colón. **Estación Nuevos Ministerios:** C. Raimundo Fernández Villaverde, on the corner with Po. Castellana. M: Nuevos Ministerios. **RENFE Main Office,** C. Alcalá, 44 (tel. 563 02 02), where Gran Vía hits C. Alcalá. M: Banco de España. Schedules, national and international tickets. Open Mon.-Fri. 9:30am-8pm. Sample *regional-expres* and *largo recorrido* fares to: Ávila (8 per day, 2hr., 710ptas); Segovia (8 per day, 2hr., 650ptas); Toledo (9 per day, 1hr., 535ptas); Salamanca (3 per day, 3½hr.); Lisbon (11hr., 5600ptas); Paris (17-19hr., 12,715ptas).

Buses: Numerous private companies serve Madrid, each with its own station. Buses usually pass through the central **Estación Sur de Autobuses,** C. Canarias, E-16 (tel. 468 45 11) en route. M: Palos de la Frontera, yellow line 3. Amazing computerized ticket information service, on the left near entrance, provides info in English. Private companies include: **Estación Auto Res:** Pl. Conde de Casal, 6 (tel. 551 72 00). M: Conde de Casal. To Salamanca and Cuenca. **Estación Herranz:** C. Fernández de los Ríos (tel. 543 81 67 or 543 36 45), a little booth half a block from the corner of C. Isaac Peral. M: Moncloa. To El Escorial and Valle de los Caídos. In El Escorial call 890 41 00. **Estación La Sepulvedana:** Po. de la Florida, 11 (tel. 547 52 61 or 530 48 00). M: Norte (via extension from M: Opera). To Avila and Segovia.

Luggage Storage: Estaciones de Chamartín and **Atocha** (see trains). Automatic lockers for backpacks 300ptas per day, for large packs and suitcases 500ptas per day. Open 7:30am-11:30pm. **Estación Sur de Autobuses** (see buses). Bags checked (80ptas per bag per day).

Public Transportation: Metro 125ptas; 10-ride ticket *(billete de diez)* 550ptas; tel. 435 22 66 and 552 49 00. Runs 6am-1:30am. The *Plano del Metro* is more concise than the unwieldy *Plano de los Transportes* which should be used to decipher the **bus** system (125ptas, 10-ride *bonobús* pass 600ptas). Buses run 6am-midnight. 11 night buses travel from Sol and Pl. Cibeles to the outskirts every ½hr. midnight-3am, every hr. 3-5am. Night buses (numbered N1-N11) are indicated on a special section on the *Plano*. There are N stops all along the marked routes, not just in Sol and Pl. Cibeles. **Information:** Empresa Municipal de Transportes (EMT) (tel. 401 31 00 or 555 72 96).

ACCOMMODATIONS ■ 751

Hitchhiking: Neither popular nor safe. Hitchers take N-I (north) for Burgos; N-II (northeast) for Zaragoza and Barcelona; N-III (east) for Cuenca and Valencia; N-IV (south) for Andalucía; N-VI (northwest) for Avila, Segovia, Salamanca, and Galicia; E-4 (west) for Extremadura and Portugal; 401 (southeast) for Toledo.

Taxi: Base fare is 200ptas, plus 75ptas per km, plus supplements. Tel. 445 90 08, 447 51 80. Service for the handicapped, tel. 547 82 00, 547 85 00, or 547 86 00.

Car Rental: Don't do it unless you're planning to zoom out of Madrid. **Atesa:** C. Orense, 83 (tel. 571 32 94). M: Tetuán. C. Francisco leads to C. Orense. Open Mon.-Fri. 8:30am-1:30am and 4:30-8pm, Sat. 9am-1pm. Also at the airport (tel. 205 86 60). Open 7am-midnight.

English Bookstores: Librería Turner, C. Genova, 3 (tel. 319 09 26). M: Cólon. Open Mon.-Fri. 10am-8pm, Sat. 10am-2pm. **English Editions,** Pl. San Amaro, 5 (tel. 571 03 21). M: Estrecho. Used novels bought and sold—excellent selection. Open Mon.-Thurs. noon-7pm, Fri. noon-8pm, Sat. 11am-2pm.

Laundromat: Lavandería Donoso Cortés, C. Donoso Cortés, 17 (tel. 446 96 90). M: Quevedo. Self-service: wash 550ptas, dryer 25ptas for five min., detergent 60ptas., iron 50ptas. Open Mon.-Fri. 9am-7pm, Sat. 8:30am-1pm.

Gay and Lesbian Services: The Colectivo de Gais y Lesbianas de Madrid (COGAM), C. Carretas, 12, 3rd fl. (tel. and fax 522 45 17), very close to Puerta del Sol. M: Sol. Provides a wide range of services and activities of interests. Reception hours Mon.-Fri. 5-9pm. COGAM library open 7-9pm. **GAI-INFORM,** a gay information line (tel. 523 00 70) provides information in Spanish about gay associations, leisure-time activities, and health issues Mon.-Fri. 5-9pm.

Crisis Hotlines: Rape, 574 01 10. **AIDS Information,** 445 23 28. **Women's Medical Issues,** 730 49 01. Staffed Mon.-Fri. 3:30-6:30pm. **English-Language Help,** 559 13 93. Staffed 7-11pm.

Medical Assistance: Anglo-American Medical Unit, Conde de Aranda, 1, 1st floor (tel. 435 18 23), to the left. M: Serrano. Not an emergency clinic.

Emergency: tel. 091 or 092. **Ambulance,** tel. 061 or **Red Cross,** tel. 522 22 22. **Fire,** tel. 080. **Police,** C. Luna, 29 (tel. 521 12 36). M: Callao.

ACCOMMODATIONS

Demand for rooms rises dramatically in summer; make reservations. Expect to pay 1700 to 2700ptas per person for a typical *hostal* room, slightly less for a bed in a *pensión*. A/C is not common at all. **Calle Fuencarral** is less expensive and closer to the nightlife of Malasaña and Chueca. The centrally located **Puerta del Sol** and **Palacio Real** zone crawls with tourists. For 225ptas, **Viajes Brújula,** Torre de Madrid, 6th fl. (tel. 559 97 04), at Pl. España (by Alitalia and Kuwait Airlines signs), will book you a room. You must go in person and provide location and price range (youth hostels excluded), they plug them into their magic computer. English spoken. Open Mon.-Fri. 9am-7pm, Sat. 9am-2pm; Oct.-June Mon.-Fri. 9am-2pm and 4-7pm, Sat. 9am-2pm. Branch offices located at: Estación Atocha (tel. 539 11 73), open 8am-midnight; Estación Chamartín (tel. 315 78 94), open 7:15am-11:30pm; and the airport bus terminal in Pl. Colón (tel. 575 96 80), open 8am-10pm.

Albergue Juvenil Santa Cruz de Marcenado (HI), C. Santa Cruz de Marcenado, 28 (tel. 547 45 32). M: Argüelles. Walk down C. Princesa, turn left on C. Serrano Jover, and right on C. Santa Cruz de Marcenado. Modern facilities located near the student district. 3-day max. stay. Reception open 9am-10:30pm. Strict curfew 1:30am. 650ptas, over 26: 800ptas. Members only, or buy HI card (1800 ptas). Tiny breakfast. Lockers. Reserve in writing 15 days in advance, or show up early.

Albergue Juvenil Richard Schirrman (HI), Casa de Campo (tel. 463 56 99). M: El Lago. Turn left (downhill) on leaving the station, left at the paved road which runs parallel to the metro tracks, and look for signs for the hostel. On the outskirts of the city, in an enormous park, close to a lake and municipal swimming pool. DO NOT walk alone through the unlit park at night. Each austere 8-person room has a bath. Lockers. Same members only and reservations policies, maximum stay, and prices as above.

SPAIN

Hostal-Residencia Miño, C. Arenal, 16, 2nd fl. (tel. 531 50 79 or 531 97 89). M: Opera or Sol. Rooms range from large with hardwood floors and balconies to tight quarters with vinyl underfoot. Singles 2200ptas, with shower 2900ptas. Doubles with shower 3900ptas, with bath 4500ptas. Triples 6000ptas.

Hostal Santa Cruz, Pl. Santa Cruz, 6, 2nd fl. (tel. 522 24 41), M: Sol. In the lovely and atmospheric—though extraordinarily touristy—Pl. Santa Cruz, next to the Plaza Mayor. Stately high ceilings and a palatial lounge. Singles sink 1700-2800ptas. Doubles 3600-4400ptas. Triples 4400-5500ptas.

Hostal-Residencia Rober, C. Arenal, 26, 5th fl. (tel. 541 91 75). M: Opera. Possibly the only place in Madrid, except the banks, where smoking is strictly prohibited. Enormous communal bathroom and wall-to-wall industrial carpeting in all rooms. Singles 3000-3800ptas. Doubles 4800ptas. Triples 6000ptas.

Hostal-Residencia Paz, C. Flora, 4, 1st fl. (tel. 547 30 47), on a quiet street parallel to C. Arenal, reached via C. Donados or C. Hileras. M: Sol or Opera. Lovely, spotless rooms with windows overlooking a tree-filled courtyard. Ten recently renovated rooms have quality beds. Singles 2300ptas. Doubles 3400-4000ptas. Triples with shower 4800ptas. Reservations encouraged.

Hostal Aguilar, C. San Jerónimo, 32, 2nd fl. (tel. 429 59 26). M: Sol. More than 50 big, clean rooms, all with telephone, TV, and shower. One of few *bostales* which offer quads. Singles 2700-3000ptas. Doubles 4100-4500ptas. Triples 5500-6500ptas. Quads 7500-8500ptas. Reservations accepted. Visa and MC.

Hostal-Residencia Mondragón, C. San Jerónimo, 32, 4th fl. (tel. 429 68 16). M: Sol. In the same building as the Aguilar and several other *bostales* (Madrid Centro, San Jerónimo, and León). Spain's first motion picture was filmed here in 1898. Large rooms, and a sun-splashed red-tiled terrace. Attractive reception area. Singles 1700ptas. Doubles 2400-2600ptas. Triples 3600ptas. Open March-Dec.

Hostal-Residencia Malagueña, C. Preciados, 35, 4th fl. (tel. 559 52 23), between Pl. Santo Domingo and Pl. Callao. M: Callao. Spacious, airy rooms with high windows and now decorative gas "hearths." No elevator. Singles 2000ptas. Doubles 3000-3600ptas. One triple 3600ptas.

Hostal Palacios-Ribadavia, C. Fuencarral, 25, 2nd fl. (tel. 531 10 58 or 531 48 47). M: Gran Vía. Family-run and renovated in 1994. All rooms have showers. Singles 2300-2800ptas. Doubles 3600-4200ptas. Triples 5300-6000ptas.

Hostal Greco, C. Infantas, 3, 2nd fl. (tel. 522 46 32 or 522 46 31). M: Gran Vía or Chueca. Enormous rooms come with large bathrooms, telephone, personal safe, and emergency light. Singles (only two of these, so you might want to call for a reservation) 3000ptas. Doubles 5000ptas. Triples 6800ptas. Visa, MC.

Hostal Lorenzo, C. Infantas, 26, 3rd fl. (tel. 521 30 57 or 532 79 78). M: Gran Vía or Chueca. Colonial-style rooms, some with plant-filled, glassed-in balconies. Flowers and big beds in all the rooms. Singles 3000- 3500ptas. Doubles 4800ptas. Triples 6500ptas. Visa, MC.

Camping

Tourist offices can provide information about the 13 or so campsites within 50km of Madrid. The same information is in their **Guía Oficial de Campings, España '95,** a big book which they gladly let you look through, but don't give away. **Camping Osuna** (tel. 741 05 10, fax 320 63 65) is located on the Ajalvir-Vicálvaro road (15.5km). Take the metro to Canillejas, then cross the pedestrian overpass, walk through the parking lot, and turn right along the freeway. (475ptas per person, per tent, and per car). **Camping Alpha** (tel. 695 80 69) hides on a shady site 12.4km down the Ctra. de Andalucía in Getafe. From the Legazpi metro station take bus 447, which stops next to the Nissan dealership (every ½hr. until 10pm, 10min.). Ask the driver to let you off at the pedestrian overpass near the Amper building. After crossing the bridge, take an enchanting 1½km walk back toward Madrid along the edge of the busy highway. (525ptas per person and car, 550ptas per tent.) Alpha has a pool. Both campgrounds have phones, hot showers, washers and dryers, safes, currency exchange, medical care, a playground, a bar, and a restaurant.

FOOD

In Madrid, it's not hard to fork it down without forking over too much, unless of course you're intent on elaborate fare and representatives from all the food groups at every meal. Madrid delicacies include *caldereta de cordero* (lamb stewed with tomatoes and peppers), *cocido madrileño* (chickpea stew flavored with chorizo sausage) and *pisto manchego* (a vegetable stew). Keep in mind the following essential buzz words for quicker, cheaper *madrileño* fare: *bocadillo* (200-300ptas), a sandwich on a french bread roll; *sandwich* (150-250ptas), a sandwich on sliced bread, usually grilled; *croissant* (150-250ptas), a croissant sandwich; *ración* (300-500ptas), a plate of meat, cheese, or some other finger food, served with bread; and *empanada* (150-250ptas), a puff pastry with tuna, hake, apple and other fillings.

Chueca is the none-too-closeted gay/glam district, where scenesters crowd the chic gourmet joints and stalk the streets in platform shoes. Highest nose-ring per capita of anywhere in the city. **Calles Echegaray, Ventura de la Vega,** and **Manuel Fernández González** are the budget boulevards. **Argüelles** and **Moncloa** are a bit out of the way, but full of student-priced eateries. In the following listings and Madrid in general, a *restaurante* or *casa* is open from 1 to 4:30pm and 8:30pm to midnight unless otherwise noted. Establishments such as *mesones, cafeterías, bares, cafés, terrazas,* and *tabernas* include a bar and serve drinks, *tapas, raciones,* and *bocadillos* all day until midnight. For **groceries,** try **Mercado de San Miguel,** on Pl. San Miguel, just off the northwest corner of Pl. Mayor, or discount **% Dia,** right behind the Mercado de San Miguel (both open Mon.-Sat. 8am-2pm and 5:30-8pm).

Casa Ciriaco, C. Mayor, 84. M: Sol or Opera. *Castizo* (traditional, pure) Madrid fare without pretensions. Filling bean and ham or chicken plates 1000-1200ptas. *Menú* 2100ptas; entrees about 1500ptas. Open Sept.-July Thurs.-Tues.

Madrid 1600, C. Cava de San Miguel. M: Sol. Another "typical" restaurant, this stone-walled den has decent *cocido madrileño* (see above). *Menú* 1500ptas. Open 1-4pm and 8pm-midnight.

Museo del Jamón, C. San Jerónimo, 6 (tel. 521 03 46), off Puerta del Sol. M: Sol. Five other locations throughout the city. Succulent Iberian ham available in any form your piggish little heart could desire: *bocadillo* (150ptas), *chiquito* (95ptas), *croissant* (150ptas), *ración* (500ptas). *Menú* 850ptas or 1000ptas. Open Mon.-Sat. 9am-12:30am, Sun. 10am-12:30am.

Mesón La Caserola, C. Echegaray, off C. San Jerónimo. M: Sol. Bustling, crowded joint serves a solid *menú* (825ptas) to ravenous locals. Despite its proximity to Puerta del Sol, La Caserola's prices and atmosphere remain *madrileño* as opposed to *turístico*. Cozy atmosphere. Cheap *raciones* and *tapas* during off-hours; many entrees around 600ptas. Closed Mon. noon. A/C.

Restaurante Integral Artemisa, C. Ventura de la Vega, 4, off C. San Jerónimo. M: Sol. A leftist's dream come true: a vegetarian restaurant next to socialist party headquarters. Decent food, though service is slow. Flavorful *potaje* (stew), pizza, purees, and salads. Many salads around 900ptas. Entrees 800-1200ptas; non-vegetarian available as well. A/C. Visa.

La Carreta, Barbieri, 10 (tel. 532 70 42 or 521 60 97), off C. Infantes. M: Gran Vía or Chueca. An Argentine restaurant specializing in Argentine, Uruguayan, and Chilean delights. Try the delicious Martín Fierro dessert, named after the eponymous Argentinian national novel (890ptas). Lunch *menú* 1500ptas. Entrees around 900ptas. Visa, MC, AmEx, DC.

Restaurante La Vascongada, Pl. Vázquez de Mella, 10, on the edge of Chueca toward Gran Vía. Yellow sign visible from C. Infantas near the ugly parking plaza. Typical dishes of Madrid and the Basque country. *Menú* 700ptas. Special offer: half a chicken for 400ptas. Entrees 300-700ptas. A/C.

Nabucco, C. Hortaleza, 108 (tel. 410 06 11), a couple of blocks off Pl. Santa Bárbara. A large pizza-pasta place. Much lower prices than the upscale clientele and atmosphere suggest. Pizzas 500-800ptas, pasta dishes 600-800ptas. Visa, MC, AmEx, DC.

La Granja Restaurante Vegetariano, C. San Andrés, 11 (tel. 532 87 93), off Pl. 2 de Mayo. M: Tribunal, Noviciado, or Bilbao. Attractive dark wood and tile interior.

SPAIN

A vegetarian ecstasy: great food, lot's of it, and cheap. Salads and soups, vegetarian *paella, arroz con algas* (rice with seaweed)—you name it, if it didn't walk or swim, they've got it. *Menú* 850ptas. Closed Sun. Visa.

La Gata Flora, C. 2 de Mayo, 1, and across the street at C. San Vicente Ferrer, 33 (tel. 521 20 20 or 521 27 92). M: Noviciado or Tribunal. Tightly packed tables and a bohemian crowd in a marvelous Italian restaurant. Pizzas and pastas 700-900ptas; big, verdant salads 500-675ptas. Excellent *sangría* 875ptas. Open 2-6pm and 8:30pm-midnight; Fri.-Sat. open until 1am. Visa, MC, DC.

El Bocadillo Americano, C. Cardenal Cisneros, right off C. Luchana, which is off the Glorieta de Bilbao. Spain's first—and so far only—bagel shop. Plain, garlic, onion, and cinnamon-raisin bagels for 100ptas; with cream cheese 200ptas; with lox 425ptas.

SIGHTS

From Plaza Mayor to Puerta de Toledo The arcaded **Plaza Mayor** (M: Sol) is topped with the Habsburgs' elegant black slate roofs and spindly, pagoda-like towers. It was completed in 1620 for Felipe III; his statue is also from the 17th century, although it took the city until 1847 to get it up. The public executions and bullfights that took place here are now but ghosts haunting the plaza's lively cafés. This most picturesque part of Old Madrid is not far from smaller and quieter **Plaza de la Villa.** Legend has it that François—Carlos I's archenemy—was held prisoner in the **Torre de los Lujanes,** a 15th-century building on the eastern side of the plaza. The characteristically Habsburg 17th-century **Ayuntamiento** (or Casa de la Villa) on the plaza was both the mayor's home and the city jail. South of Pl. Mayor on C. Toledo looms **Iglesia de San Isidro,** a 17th-century church designed by the famed Pedro Sánchez and Francisco Bautista. The remains of San Isidro landed here after being tossed from church to church. The church was restored after the interior was burned by rioting workers in 1936. It served as the cathedral of Madrid from the late 19th century until 1993, when a new cathedral was consecrated (see "Palacio Real"). (Open for mass only. M: Latina. Bus 17, 23, 35, and 60.)

Between Sol and Paseo del Prado Picasso's *Guernica* is the centerpiece in the **Museo Nacional Centro de Arte Reina Sofía,** a collection of 20th-century art at C. Santa Isabel, 52, opposite Estación Atocha near the south end of Po. Prado (M: Atocha). When Germans bombed the Basque town of Guernica for the Fascists in Spain's Civil War, Picasso painted this huge work of jumbled and distorted figures to denounce the bloodshed. When asked by Nazi officials if he was responsible for the painting, Picasso answered "No, you are." He gave the canvas to New York's Museum of Modern Art on condition that it return to Spain when democracy was restored. The pink Neoclassical monolith of a museum also contains works by Miró, Julio González, Juan Gris, Picasso and Dalí that illustrate the essential role of Spanish artists in the cubist and surrealist movements. (Open Mon. and Wed.-Sat. 10am-9pm. 400ptas, students with ISIC free.)

In Madrid, only the Prado surpasses the collection of the **Museo de la Real Academia de Bellas Artes de San Fernando,** C. Alcalá, 13. (M: Sol or Sevilla.) Masterpieces in the collection include Velázquez's portraits of Felipe IV and Mariana de Austria and Goya's *La Tirana,* a portrait of the actress María Fernández, dubbed the tyrant after her marriage to an actor who always played despots. *La primavera* (the Spring), the only work in Spain from a handful extant by Habsburg court painter Giuseppe Milán Arcimboldo, depicts a man composed entirely of fruits, flowers and plants. (Open Mon.-Fri. 9am-7pm, Sat.-Mon. 10am-2pm. 200ptas, students free.) Next door the **Calcografía Real** (Royal Print and Drawing Collection) organizes excellent temporary exhibitions of works on paper. (Free with museum admission.)

The **Museo Thyssen Bornemizsa,** on the corner of Po. Prado and C. San Jerónimo (M: Banco de España) is an 18th-century palace transformed to house this fabulous and newly-purchased 775-piece collection of art ranging from the Titian to Hockney. The first-floor array of 20th-century art is stellar, featuring all the major names, the second houses a wide selection of impressionist, realist, and fauvist work.

Finally, the third floor displays Old Masters, fleshing out areas where the Prado is weak: the Titians and Tintorettos are far superior. (Open Tues.-Sun. 10am-7pm. Last entry 6:30pm. 600ptas, students with ISIC and seniors 350ptas.)

The Retiro and Jerónimos **Parque del Retiro,** Madrid's top picnic and suntanning zone, was originally intended to be a *buen retiro* (nice retreat) for Felipe IV. The palace burned down, but the **Museo del Ejército** remains. Alfonso XII and his horse glare at the **Estanque Grande,** a rectangular lake in the middle of the park. (Rowboats 10am-sunset; 400ptas for 2 people, 100ptas for each additional person.)

Museo del Prado Spain's premier museum, and one of Europe's finest, is on Po. Prado at Pl. Cánovas del Castillo. (M: Banco de España or Atocha.) The Neoclassical building has sheltered the royal painting collection since the time of Fernando VII, who cared precious little for art and plenty about making an impression at home and abroad. Over 3000 paintings, many collected by Spanish monarchs between 1400 and 1700, include Spanish and foreign masterpieces, with particular strengths in the Flemish and Venetian Schools. The wonder of the Prado is that *every* work is a masterpiece. Innumerable hours of jostling through herds of schoolchildren cannot do justice to every canvas in the Prado. Decide beforehand what you want to see, and try not to become sidetracked by imitations and wanna-be Rubens. The museum is laid out in a fairly logical fashion and rooms are numbered, but it can be easy to lose sight of the forest for the groves of Goyas once within. Maps are pricey but helpful: the Guide to the Prado costs 1800ptas, and the abridged edition 500ptas. The second floor presents Spanish works from the 16th and 17th centuries, highlighted by the collection of **Diego Velázquez.** The oft-imitated *Las Meninas* (The Maids of Honor)—widely considered Velázquez's ultimate masterpiece—occupies an entire wall. Velázquez is credited with radicalizing the art of portraiture with his unforgiving realism. Portraits of the royal family, especially his renderings of the foppish and fey Felipe IV, are legion. Francisco de Goya is represented by *La Maja vestida* (Clothed Maja) and *La Maja desnuda* (Nude Maja), the hilariously unflattering *La Familia de Carlos IV* and *Los Fusilamientos del tercero de mayo,* which depicts the slaughter of Spaniards by Napoleon's army. Don't miss the large room devoted to Goyas' *Pinturas Negras* (Black Paintings)—works dating from the end of his life, when the artist was in poor health and living in a small country house outside Madrid, since nicknamed the *Quinta del Sordo* (the deaf man's house). Goya painted these chillingly macabre scenes on the walls of his house; years after his death they were placed on canvas and restored.

Among the **El Grecos** (ubiquitous portraits of men with pointed beards and ruffs around their necks), are *La trinidad* (The Trinity) and *La adoración de los pastores* (The Adoration of the Pastors).Works of Spanish painters from the same era fill the first floor, including Murillo, Ribera, and Zurbarán. The Prado also has a formidable stash of Italian works by greats such as Titian, Raphael, Tintoretto, and Botticelli. Because the Spanish Habsburgs long ruled the Netherlands, the Flemish holdings are also top notch, with **Van Dyck,** Roger van der Weyden, Albrecht Dürer, Peter Breughel the Elder, and Rubens. Watch out for Bosch's decadent *Garden of Earthly Delights.* (Open Tues.-Sat. 9am-7pm, Sun. 9am-2pm. 400ptas, students with ISIC and citizens of EU countries under 21 with ID free.)

Your ticket to the Prado also admits you to the nearby **Casón del Buen Retiro,** C. Alfonso XII, 28, facing the Parque del Retiro (M: Retiro or Banco de España). Once part of Felipe IV's Palacio del Buen Retiro, then a porcelain factory, it was destroyed in the war against Napoleon. The rebuilt version has a superb collection of 19th-century Spanish paintings. (Same hrs. as the Prado.)

The Palacio Real and Environs With 20 square km of tapestry and the largest candelabra in Europe, the impossibly luxurious **Palacio Real** was built for first Bourbon King Felipe V to replace the burned-own Alcázar. The shell of it took 40 years and interior decoration of its 2000 rooms dragged on for a century. Spanish

SPAIN

monarchs abandoned it in the war-torn 1930's. To see the palace's collection of porcelain, tapestries, furniture, armor, and art, stroll around or take a guided tour (in Spanish or English, 40min.). (M: Opera. Buses 4, 15, 25, 33, or 39. Palace open, except during royal visits, Mon.-Sat. 9am-6pm, Sun. 9:30am-2pm. 500ptas, students 350ptas, Wed. free for EU citizens. Arrive early to avoid waiting.) The palace faces the **Plaza de Oriente,** a semicircle square contingent on the northwestern side with the serene **Jardines de Sabatini,** the park of choice for romantics. Juan Carlos opened **Campo del Moro** (facing the canal) to the public only 13 years ago; the view of the palace rising majestically on a dark green slope is straight out of a fairy tale. In the heart of downtown, the **Convento de las Descalzas Reales** (Convent of the Royal Barefoot Ones), Pl. Descalzas, between Pl. Callao and Sol. M: Callao or Sol), founded in 1559 sheltered widows of royal families for a few centuries, thus acquiring an exceptional collection of religious artwork—tapestries, paintings, sculptures, and liturgical objects. The Salón de Tapices contains 12 renowned tapestries woven from cartoons by Rubens. Mandatory tour in Spanish. (Open Tues.-Thurs. and Sat. 10:30am-12:30pm and 4-5:30pm, Fri. 10:30am-12:30pm, Sun. 11am-1:30pm. 600ptas, students 200ptas.)

Casa de Campo Catch the cable car *(teleférico,* 250ptas, round-trip 360ptas; noon-9pm) down to the city's largest park, the **Casa de Campo.** Woods, a municipal pool, a zoo, and an amusement park all conspire to leave the city far behind. Don't attempt to explore the park on foot; it's so large it makes Madrid's center look like a clearing in the woods. Avoid straying beyond populated areas such as the zoo and amusement park after sunset. (Amusement park open Mon.-Fri. noon-11pm, Sat. noon-1am, Sun. noon-midnight. M: Lago or Batán. Bus 33 or 65.)

El Pardo Built as a hunting lodge for Carlos I in 1547, El Pardo was subsequently enlarged by generations of Habsburg and Bourbon royalty into the magnificent country palace that stands today—a 15min. bus ride from the city center. Franco resided here from 1940-1975, and the palace is still the official reception site for distinguished foreign visitors. Renowned for its collection of tapestries—several of which were designed by Goya—the palace also holds a little-known Velázquez depicting a deer slain by Felipe IV, and Ribera's *"Techo de los hombres ilustres"* (Ceiling of the Illustrious Men). (Open Mon.-Sat. 9:30am-6pm, Sun. 9:30am-2pm. Compulsory 45min. guided tour in Spanish. 600ptas, student 250ptas; Wed. free for EU citizens. Bus 106 from Paseo de Moret, near M: Moncloa, 115ptas each way.) The palace's **chapel** and the nearby **Casita del Príncipe** created by Villanueva of Prado fame are free.

ENTERTAINMENT

Film, Theatre, and Music The **Parque del Retiro** sometimes shows free movies at 11pm. The state-subsidized *filmoteca* in the renovated Art Deco **Ciné Doré,** C. Santa Isabel, 3 (tel. 369 11 25; M: Antón Martín), is the best for repertory cinema. (Tickets 200-400ptas.) Subtitled films are shown in many private theaters, such as **Alphaville** and **Renoir I** and **2**—check the V.O. (for *versión original)* listings in entertainment guides. The theater district is bounded by Pl. Santa Ana and Pl. Colón (south to north), and Po. Prado-Recoletos and Puerta del Sol (east to west). **Localidades Galicia,** Pl. Carmen, 1 (tel. 431 27 32 or 531 91 31; M: Sol), handles theater tickets, as well as those for soccer games, movies and bullfights. (Open Mon.-Fri. 10am-1pm and 4:30-7pm.) The theater district is bounded by Pl. Santa Ana and Pl. Cólon (south-north) and Po. Prado-Recoletos and Puerta del Sol (east-west). **Teatro Español,** C. Príncipe, 25 (tel. 429 03 18, tickets and info tel. 429 62 97; M: Sevilla), hosts well-known Spanish plays. Tickets around 1300-1700ptas, reduced prices on Wednesdays. The finest classical performances happen at the **Auditorio Nacional,** C. Príncipe de Vergara, 136 (tel. 337 01 00). The grand, granite 19th-century **Teatro de la Opera,** on Pl. Opera, is the city's principal venue for classical ballet and the lyric genre. **Flamenco** in Madrid is tourist-oriented and expensive. If you must, try **Casa Patas,** C. Cañizares, 10 (tel. 369 04 96). The flamenco starts at midnight (Fri.-Sat.); the cover charge varies. (Open 8:30pm-2:30am.)

Sports Spanish sport-fans go ballistic for **fútbol** (soccer)! Every Sunday and some Saturdays between September and June, one of two big local teams plays at home. "Real Madrid" plays at Estadio Santiago Bernebeu, Po. Castellana, 104 (tel. 457 11 12; M: Lima; buses 27, 40, 43). "Atlético Madrid" plays at Estadio Vicente Calderón, C. Virgen del Puerto, 67 (tel. 366 47 07; M: Pirámides or Marqués de Vadillos). Tickets for seats are 2500ptas, for standing-room 1000ptas. If tickets are sold out, shifty scalpers lurk by the stadium during the afternoon or evening a few days before the game. **Corridas** (bullfights) are held during the Festival of San Isidro and every Sunday in summer, less frequently the rest of the year. The season lasts from March to October, signalled by posters in bars and cafés (especially on C. Victoria, off C. San Jerónimo). **Plaza de las Ventas,** C. Alcalá, 237 (tel. 356 22 00), east of central Madrid, is the biggest ring in Spain. (M: Ventas. Bus 21, 53, 110.) Ticket outlets are at C. Victoria, 3, off C. San Jerónimo east of Puerta del Sol (M: Sol), Pl. Carmen, 1 (tel. 531 27 32), and Pl. Toros, C. Alcalá, 237 (M: Ventas). A seat is 2000-2500ptas.

Nightlife *Madrileños* like to say that no one goes to bed until they've killed the night. Some clubs don't even bother opening until 4 or 5am; adjust your body clock accordingly. The weekly *Guía del Ocio* (100ptas at any kiosk) lists complete entertainment minutiae, as do the Friday supplement (*El Mundo's* "Metropoli," *El País's* "Guía," *Diario 16's* "Madrid") and the daily *cartelera* listings in any newspaper. Pl. 2 de Mayo in Malasaña, Pl. Chueca, Pl. España, and the Gran Vía can be intimidating and sleazy. For a city of its size, however, Madrid is fairly safe, and the only places to avoid late at night are the parks.

Coffee at a **classic café** is expensive (200-300ptas)—but an hour or two spent at one of them is a most economical way to soak up a little Madrid (and a lot of secondhand smoke). **Café Comercial,** Glorieta de Bilbao, 7 (M: Bilbao), is a traditional establishment with high ceilings and huge mirrors frequented by artists and Republican aviators alike. Anti-Franco protests started here and the establishment hosts frequent *tertulias* (gatherings of literati and intellectuals). (Beer 250ptas. Open 8am-1am, Fri.-Sat. until 3am.) **Café Gijón,** Po. Recoletos, 21 (M: Colón), has both a breezy terrace and a smoky bar-restaurant. Long a favorite of the literati, this is the sort of place where people bring their books to study and their friends to talk. Coffee 300ptas at the tables. (Open 9am-1:30am.)

As the sun sets and bathes the streets in gold, **terrazas** and **chiringuitos** (outdoor cafés/bars) spill across sidewalks all over Madrid. **Plaza Mayor** is handy for a glass of wine while digesting the tourist office's brochures. **Calle Bailén,** by the Viaducto, has spectacular views of flaming sunsets and couples making out. A number of kiosks and open-air *cafeterías* sprinkled about the **Casa del Campo. Paseos Castellana, Recoletos,** and **Prado** are fashionable and hip areas, hence a bit pricy. **El Viso,** between Po. Castellana and C. María de Molina is a pre-war garden city within the city in which villas, walled gardens, and winding streets exude a charming villagelike aura. Hippies, intellectuals, bohemians, street musicians, and junkies check each other out in the **Plaza 2 de Mayo. Calle San Vincente Ferrer,** with its tattoo parlors, second-hand clothing and leather stores, motorcycle repair shops, and countless pubs is prime Malasaña. **Chueca** is the host to a mainly male gay scene.

For **clubs and discos,** life begins at 1:30am. Many discos have "afternoon" sessions (usually 7-10pm, cover 250-1000ptas) for teens; but the "night" sessions (lasting until dawn) are when to really let your hair down. Don't be surprised if at 5:30am there's still a line of people waiting to get in. Really. Cover *(entrada)* can get as high as 2000ptas, and men may be charged up to 500ptas more than women. The cover charge often includes a drink.

Cervecería Alemana, Pl. Santa Ana, 6, is an ex-Hemingway hangout with a slightly upscale crowd. It's one of a row of three *cervecerías* (brasseries) that all deserve exploration. (Open Sun.-Fri. noon-12:30am, Sat. noon-1:30am.)

Viva Madrid, C. Manuel Fernández González, 7, next to Pl. Santa Ana (M: Antón Martín), is a U.S. expatriate hangout with wonderful tiles and animals carved in wood. (Beer and juice 400ptas, mixed drinks 700-800ptas. Open 8pm-3am.)

Club Andy Warhol's, C. Luchana, 20. 15 minutes of fame, if you can stay up long enough. (Open Mon.-Sat. 5am (yup, am)-10am, Sun. 5am-noon.)

Joy Eslava, C. Arenal, 11 (M: Sol or Opera), is a three-tiered theater turned disco with 3 bars, laser lights, video screen and live entertainment. The young crowd parties to disco music. Cover 1500ptas. Open Mon.-Thurs. from 11:30pm, Fri.-Sat. 7-10:15pm and 11:30pm-5:30am.

Cervecería Ratskeller's, on the corner of C. Luchana and C. Palafox (by the cinema Palafox). Crowds of vacationing American college students give this self-proclaimed House of Beer a Spring Break in Cancún feel. However, if that's what you go for... Open noon-3am

La Tetera de la Abuela, C. Espíritu Santo, 37, brings together writers, actors, and students. Open Sun.-Thurs. 7:30pm-1am, Fri.-Sat. 7:30pm-2am.

Archy, C. Marqués de Riscal, 11 (tel. 308 31 62), off C. Almagro from Pl. Alonso Martínez. Dress to kill or the fashion police at the door might laugh. No cover, but drinks cost 700-900ptas. Open from noon on.

Pacha, C. Barceló, 11 (tel. 446 01 37), near M: Tribunal. Converted from an old theater, and once one of the trendiest clubs in Madrid. As Chueca's gay scene blossomed, Pacha's mainstream clientele scurried away. The place still fills up, however, and the crowd is not overtly gay. Open from 7pm on.

No Se Lo Digas a Nadie, C. Ventura de la Vega, 7, next to Pl. Santa Ana. M: Antón Martín. Look for a black garage door. Don't tell it to anybody, there are enough gyrating bodies downstairs already. Live mellow music starts around 12:15am. Drinks 500-800ptas. Open Tues.-Sat. 8:30am-1pm and 8:30pm-3am, Fri.-Sat. 8:30am-1pm and 8:30pm-4am.

■ EL ESCORIAL

They called El Escorial the eighth wonder of the world, and they were right. It is a fascinating, severe complex that includes a monastery, two palaces, a church, two pantheons, a magnificent library, and innumerable artistic treasures. Located near the charming town of **San Lorenzo** and within easy striking distance of Madrid, El Escorial should be visited early in the day to see it all. *Don't* come on Monday, when the whole complex and most of the town shut down.

The **Monasterio de San Lorenzo del Escorial** was a gift from Felipe II to God, the people, and himself, commemorating his victory over the French at the battle of San Quintín in 1557. The **Palacio Real** includes the *Salón del Trono* (Throne Room) and two **dwellings** in one—Felipe II's spartan 16th-century apartments and the more luxurious 18th-century rooms of Carlos III and Carlos IV. The astonishing **Panteón Real** (known affectionately as *el pudridero,* the rotting chamber) was another brainchild of Felipe II. Although he didn't live to see it finished, he's buried here with Carlos V and most of their royal descendants. On the far side of the complex, the **Salas Capitulares** (chapter rooms) display an outstanding exhibition on the construction of El Escorial, with some wooden models of 16th-century machinery and the buildings themselves. Also in the Salas Capitulares is the **Pinacoteca,** which holds a collection of masterpieces by Bosch, Dürer, El Greco, Titian, Tintoretto, Velázquez, Zurbarán, Van Dyck, and others. (The entire El Escorial complex is open Tues.-Sun. 10am-1:30pm and 3:30-6:30pm; Oct. 16-April 14 10am-1:30pm and 3-6pm. Last admission to palaces, pantheons and museums 1hr. or ½hr. before closing (depending on "zone"), 15min. for the *casitas.* Monastery 800ptas, students 300ptas, Wed. free for EU citizens. *Casitas* 150ptas.)

The easiest way to get to El Escorial from Madrid, and back again, is by **bus. Autocarres Herranz** buses pull right up to the kiosk outside the Moncloa metro station (buy a ticket here), and whisk travelers to El Escorial's **Plaza Virgen de Gracia,** in the center of town, close to the **tourist office,** C. Floridablanca, 10 (open Mon.-Fri. 10am-2pm and 3-4:45pm, Sat. 10am-1:45pm). Get bus tickets back to Madrid at C. Reina Victoria, 3 (tel. (91) 890 41 22) or at the Bar Casino, C. Rey, 3. (1hr., 325ptas, round-trip 600ptas.) **Trains** arrive at Ctra. Estación (tel. (91) 890 04 13), 2km from town, and shuttle buses run frequently to the Pl. Virgen de Gracia. They run to Madrid's Atocha and Charmatín stations (1hr., round-trip 640ptas), Avila (1hr., 640ptas), and Segovia (same info as Avila).

In the shadows of the colossus, lively San Lorenzo willingly hosts those who need another day. The best accommodations can be found at **Hostal Vasco,** Pl. Santiago, 11 (tel. (91) 890 16 19), a charming 19th-century building with a terrace on the plaza and a lounge on each floor. (Singles 1900ptas. Doubles with shower 3800ptas. Triples 4900ptas. Breakfast 375ptas. Lunch and dinner each 1300ptas.) The **Mercado Publico,** C. Rey 9, 2 blocks off C. Floridablanca, sells a large selection of fresh produce, deli meats, cheeses, and other staples for picnics (open Mon.-Wed. and Fri.-Sat. 9am-2pm and 6-9pm, Thurs. 6-9pm). During the **Festivals of San Lorenzo** (Aug. 10-20), parades of giant figures line the streets and fireworks fill the sky.

■ ARANJUEZ

Like several other venerable Habsburg and Bourbon retreats (such as La Granja), Aranjuez no longer hosts monarchs during the summer (it lost out to Mallorca a while back), but the decaying grandeur of its **Palacio Real** nonetheless warrants an excursion. Room after opulent room displays finely worked Vatican mosaics, chandeliers and mirrors from the La Granja crystal factory, Buen Retiro porcelain and Flemish tapestries. The Mozarabic smoking room has its own gaudy copy of the Alhambra. (Open Wed.-Mon. 10am-6:30pm, Oct.-May Wed.-Mon. 10am-5:30pm. Compulsory tour in Spanish. 400ptas, students 275ptas, Wed. free for EU citizens.) River walkways run from the **Jardín de la Isla,** with its banana trees and mythological statuary, to the huge **Jardín del Príncipe,** created for the youthful amusement of Carlos IV, Goya's patron. (Gardens open 8am-8:30pm, Oct.-May 8am-6:30pm. Free.)

The **tourist office** (tel. 891 04 27), is in a kiosk opposite the construction in the Pl. del Puente. The **train station** (tel. 891 02 02) is a pleasant 10min. walk from town along tree-lined Carretera Toledo and serves Toledo (3 per day, ½hr.) and Madrid (45min., round-trip 635ptas). Frequent **buses** run to Madrid (1hr., 365ptas) from C. Infantas, 8 (tel. 891 01 83). **Hostal Infantas,** Av. Infantas, 4 (tel. 891 13 41), rents adequate rooms just minutes away from the traffic circle. All rooms have phones and TVs. (Singles 1550-2300ptas. Doubles 2700-4700ptas. Triples 3510-5900ptas.) The town's strawberries and asparagus have been famed for centuries. *Fresón con nata* (strawberries and cream, 300-400ptas) are staples at kiosks and cafés throughout town. **La Alegría de la Huerta,** on Carretera Andalucía, kitty-corner from the tourist office, has an attractive inner courtyard. (*Menús* 1000-3000ptas.)

CENTRAL SPAIN

In the High Middle Ages, Central Spain was the stage for the power plays of the Spanish nobility. As Christian forces stormed into Muslim Spain, La Mancha became the domain of military orders modeled on such institutions as the Knghts TEmplar. LAter The kingdoms of Castille and Aragon battled for supremacy in the country; the result is a landscape dotted with battlements and castles. The Castilian nobility grew wealthy as it seized more and more land; and well before the famous union with Aragon in 1492, it was clear that Castille had the whip in hand. The concept of a unified Spain—under Castilian command—took root here, and *castellano* (called simply "Spanish" by foreigners) became the dominant language throughout the nation. Green and rolling León (the provinces of León, Zamora, and Salamanca) retorts that

SPAIN

it had 24 kings before Castille even had laws. Between the imperial hauteur of Castille and the provincial pride of León, the region overflows with ego.

■■■ TOLEDO

Cervantes called it that "rocky gravity, glory of Spain and light of her cities." Baroque poet Góngora called it a perpetual avalanche; and Luís Buñuel, André Bretón, and their merry band of Surrealists, lured by Toledo's mystery and intrigue, had head-quarters here. Toledo remains a treasury of Spanish culture, no matter how many armies of tourists and vendors of kitsch pass through. Peaceful coexistence and col-laboration among Christians, Muslims, and Jews have resulted in an unequaled architectural syncretism (both Mudejar and Mozarabic). Roman settlement, capital of the Visigothic kingdom, stronghold of the Emirate of Córdoba and imperial city under Carlos I, Toledo bears a rich history and heritage surpassed by few others in Spain.

ORIENTATION AND PRACTICAL INFORMATION

Getting here is a snap from Madrid; many buses and trains make the 1½hr. journey every day. From a stop to the right of the train station, or from the inside the bus sta-tion, city buses 5 and 6 go directly to **Plaza de Zocodóver,** the center of town (100ptas). No Castilian city is as labyrinthine as Toledo. Streets are well-labeled and the tourist office distributes a fairly detailed map, but it's virtually impossible not to get lost—frequently. Many major sights are near or atop the central hill, which is almost exactly circular.

Tourist Office: (tel. 22 08 43, fax 25 26 48), just outside the Puerta Nueva de Bisa-gra and Po. Merchán, on the north side of town. From the RENFE station, turn right and take the busy right-hand fork; continue past the bus station, skirting the city walls until you reach the gateway. The office is across the road, outside the walls. Open Mon.-Fri. 9am-2pm and 4-6pm, Sat. 9am-3pm and 4-7pm, Sun. 9am-3pm. For a map and rudimentary info, queue up at the gray **information booth,** Pl. Zocodóver. Open Mon.-Sat. 10am-6pm, Sun. and holidays 10am-3pm.

Post Office: C. Plata, 1 (tel. 25 10 66), off Pl. Zocodóver, via C. Comercio and then C. Toledo. Open for all services, including **telegrams,** Mon.-Fri. 8am-9pm, Sat. 9am-2pm; also open Sat. 2-7pm for telegrams only. **Postal Code:** 45001.

Telephones: C. Plata, 20. Open Mon.-Fri. 9:30am-1:30pm and 5-9pm, Sat. 9:30am-2:30pm. **City Code:** 925.

Trains: Po. Rosa (tel. 21 12 72), in a neo-Mudejar building opposite the Puente de Azarquiel. To Madrid's Estación de Atocha (1½hr., 450ptas), passing through Aranjuez (45min., 235ptas). To get anywhere else, transfer in Madrid or Aranjuez.

Buses: (tel. 21 58 50) in the Zona Safón, 5min. from the city gate and tourist office (from Pl. Zocodóver, take C. Armas). To Madrid (1½hr., 540ptas).

Luggage Storage: at the train and bus stations, 300ptas per day. Open 6am-11pm.

Laundromat: Juan Pascual, C. Bolivia, 2 (tel. 22 16 03). Wash and dry 1325ptas per 5kg. Open Mon.-Fri. 9am-1:30pm and 4-8pm.

Medical Assistance: Hospital Virgen de la Salud (tel. 26 92 00), on Avenida de Barber, toward Avila highway. **Red Cross:** tel. 22 29 00.

Emergencies: tel. 091. **Municipal Police,** Ayuntamiento, 1 (tel. 21 34 00).

ACCOMMODATIONS AND CAMPING

Finding a bed during the summer, especially weekends, can be difficult. The tourist office provides a complete and invaluable list of hotels, *hostales,* and *pensiones,* with an address, price, and capacity for each establishment.

Residencia Juvenil "San Servando" (HI), Castillo San Servando (tel. 22 45 54), uphill on the left from the train station (15min.). A 14th-century castle. Pool, TV room, and modern bathrooms. Anyone returning alone at night should take a cab.

Reception open 7:50am-11:50pm. Curfew around 11:50pm. 775ptas, over 26: 950ptas. Hot water 8:30-9:30am and 8-10pm. Reserve ahead.

Pensión Descalzos, C. Descalzos, 30 (tel. 22 28 88), down the steps off Po. San Cristóbal or down the Bajada Descalzos, in the southwest corner of town. Close to the Casa del Greco and Iglesia Santo Tomé. Truly hot showers. Rooms with bath also have music and TV. Singles 1875ptas. Doubles 3000-5000ptas. Triples 6800ptas. Jan.-March 17: 1500ptas; 2500-4000ptas; 5600ptas. Breakfast 150-500ptas. IVA not included. MC, Visa.

Hostal Las Armas, C. Armas, 7 (tel. 22 16 68), just off the low end of Pl. Zocodóver. 200-year-old house, with low ceilings, twisty steps, impossible angles, and flowering patio. 19 small and crepuscular rooms. Curfew 1am. Singles 1900ptas. Doubles 3000ptas. Triples 4200ptas. IVA not included. Open April-Oct.

Segovia, C. Recoletos, 2 (tel. 21 11 24), on a tiny, narrow street off C. Armas. Nine large rooms with religious theme. Cool in summer; portable heating units in winter. No singles. Doubles 1900ptas. Triples 2700ptas. Showers 200ptas.

Camping: Camping El Greco (tel. 22 00 90), 1½km from town on the road to Madrid (C-401), easily reached by bus 7. Wooded and shady 1st-class site between the Tajo and an olive grove. 450ptas per person, tent, or car.

Circo Romano, Av. Carlos III, 19 (tel. 22 04 42). 2nd-class site. Closer but noisier and often in disrepair. 450ptas per person, tent, or car.

FOOD

It would be impossible to swing a dead cat in this city without its whiskers chancing upon a *típico* eatery of one sort or another. Restaurants catering to tourists can be a bit pricey (*menús* hover between 1200 and 1500ptas), but supply well-prepared regional specialties such as *perdiz* (fowl), *cuchifritos* (a melange of sheep, eggs, tomato, and white wine), *venado* (venison), and *carcamusas* (mystery dish). Suck down some *gazpacho* (390ptas) or devour *pollo al ajillo* (garlic chicken, 725ptas) on the outdoor *terraza* at **Restaurante La Cubana,** Po. Rosa, 2, across the river in front of Puente Viejo de Alcántara, down the road from the youth hostel. (Other dishes significantly more expensive. Open 1-4pm and 8-11pm, Fri.-Sat. until midnight.) A brick-walled, cavernous establishment underneath the Fuensalida Palace, the **Cafetería Fuensalida-Manila,** Pl. Conde, 2, in the southwest corner of town, serves 500ptas salads (open 8am-11pm). The **morning market** is held 8:30am-2pm in the Pl. Mayor behind the cathedral every day but Tuesday, when it is set up on Po. Carmen, across from the train station.

SIGHTS AND ENTERTAINMENT

South and uphill from the plaza is the **Alcázar,** Toledo's most formidable landmark. Little remains of the original 13th-century structure; the building was largely reduced to rubble during the Civil War, as besieged Fascist troops held out against acute Republican bombardment. The rooms above ground are now a gung-ho, nationalistic military museum, dedicated to the Spanish foot soldier. (Open Tues.-Sun. 9:30am-1:30pm and 4-6:30pm; winter until 5:30pm. 125ptas.) To the west, the grandiose **cathedral,** with 5 naves, delicate stained glass, and endless ostentation, soars from the city center. As the seat of the Primate of Spain, the cathedral contains an embarrassment of riches. The *Sacristía* (sacristy) hoards El Grecos and 2 Van Dycks. The chains on the outside of the cathedral are from Ronda, where Christian slaves were forced to carry heavy sacks of water up 365 steps into a Moorish castle. (Cathedral open Mon.-Sat. 10:30am-1pm and 3:30-7pm, Sun. 10:30am-1:30pm and 4-7pm. 350ptas.)

Greek painter Domenico Theotocopuli, a.k.a. El Greco, was a *toledano* most of his life, churning out eerie canvases and gloomy portraits of sallow, spindly saints by the hundreds. The **Casa del Greco** at C. Levi, 3, isn't really where he lived but contains a reasonable collection of his paintings (open Mon.-Sat. 10am-2pm and 4-6pm, Sun. 10am-2pm; 200ptas, EU citizens and students with ISIC free). The nearby **Iglesia de San Tomé** sports El Greco's lugubrious *El entierro del conde de Orgaz* (The Burial of Count Orgaz), as well as a Mudejar apse (open Tues.-Sat. 10am-1:45pm and

SPAIN

3:30-6:45pm, Sun. 10am-1:45pm; off-season Tues.-Sat. 10am-1:45pm and 3:30-5:45pm, Sun. 10am-1:45pm; 200ptas).

Two synagogues, both in the **Judería** on the west side, are all that remain of what was once Spain's largest Jewish community. The **Sinagoga del Tránsito** (1366) is a simple building with wonderful Mudejar plasterwork and an *artesonado* (coffered) ceiling. Manuscripts, lids of sarcophagi, inscriptions, and amulets clutter the **Museo Sefardí** inside the synagogue (open Tues.-Sat. 10am-2pm and 4-6pm, Sun. 10am-2pm. 200ptas.) **Sinagoga de Santa María la Blanca** (1180), down the street, was once the city's principal synagogue but was later converted to a church, but somehow looks like a mosque (open 10am-2pm and 3:30-7pm, off-season until 6pm; 200ptas). Less touristed are the remnants of the city's Islamic past, near the Puerta del Sol off C. Real de Arrabal. Both a Muslim and a Christian house of worship at different points in its life, the 10th-century **Mezquita del Cristo de la Luz** is Toledo's oldest building. Its columns support arches inspired by the mosque at Córdoba. The Emirate was also responsible for the **hammams** (baths) on C. Angel.

At night, congregations of young people scarf *tapas* and swill beer to the east and west of Pl. Zocodóver, along **Calle de Santa Fe** and **Calle de la Sillería. Zaida,** Centro Comercial Miradero, downhill on C. Armas, is the place to dance.

■■■ SEGOVIA

Ever since the Romans came and built an aqueduct, Segovia has been milking tourists. Buckets of kitsch advertise the beautiful golden churches and twisting alleyways of the city. Spanning 813m, the **Acueducto Romano** is constructed of great blocks of granite—with no mortar. View it at its maximum height (28.9m) from Plaza del Azoguejo, or catch its profile from the steps on the left side of the plaza. Amazingly, the Romans' feat of engineering, restored by the Catholic Monarchs in the 15th century, was in use until just seven years ago. What 2000 years of turbulent history couldn't do, 20th-century pollution can—the aqueduct is now suffering from structural decay and is currently sheathed in scaffolding. The **Alcázar,** an archetypal late-medieval castle, juts audaciously into space at the far northern end of the old quarter. Isabel was crowned Queen of Castile in the Alcázar in 1474 (hence the streets named in her honor). Inside, instruments of destruction and mounted knights in armor terrorize from every side. In the **Sala de Solio** (throne room), the inscription above the thrones "Tanto monta, monta tanto" can be roughly translated "[She] mounts, as does [he]." This signifies not what your dirty mind suggests, but rather Fernando and Isabel's equal authority as sovereigns. (Alcázar open 10am-7pm; Oct.-March 10am-6pm. 350ptas, seniors 250ptas.) Commissioned by Carlos I in 1525, the **cathedral** towers above Pl. Mayor in the center of town. The late Gothic naves are impressively high, with a striking ceiling pattern of rib vaulting, and the stained-glass windows are ethereal. Skip the snoozy taped tour (50ptas) and luxuriate in the tranquil cloisters. The **museum** holds a fine collection including Ribera's erotic *La caridad romana,* a remarkable Flemish triptych from the 16th century. (All open 9am-7pm; Oct.-March Mon.-Fri. 9:30am-1pm and 3-6pm, Sat. 9:30am-6pm. Cathedral free; admission to museum, cloister, and *Sala Capitular* 200ptas.)

Practical Information, Accommodations, and Food Segovia lies 88km northwest of Madrid (2hr., 600ptas) on the rail line to Medino del Campo and Valladolid. **Buses** trek to Avila (520ptas); Madrid (1¾hr., 715ptas); and Barcelona (5375ptas). To get to the helpful multilingual **tourist office,** Pl. Mayor 10 (tel (921) 43 03 28), take bus 1a, 2a, or 2b from the train station, 1a or 1b from the bus station (100ptas). Ask for their pamphlet listing accommodations options. (Open Mon.-Sat. 9:30am-2pm and 5-7pm.)

During the summer, finding a *hostal* room can be a nightmare; reservations are vital. The regional tourist office helps with reservations and hands out a list of accommodations. Be prepared to pay more than 2000ptas for a decent single. **Hostal Juan Bravo,** C. Juan Bravo, 12, 2nd fl. (tel. (921) 43 55 21), right on the main thoroughfare in the old town, has bright, carpeted rooms that are cool in the summer (doubles 3200-4100ptas, triples 4400-5500ptas). **Camping Acueducto,** Ctra. Nacional, 601 (tel. (921) 42 50 00), 2km from Segovia toward La Granja, is a 2nd-class site in the shadow of the Sierra de Guadarrama (380ptas per person or tent; no hot water; open April-Sept.).

Segovia is famed for sublimely tender roast suckling pig *(cochinillo)* and lamb, but steer clear of pricey Pl. Mayor and Pl. Azoquejo. **Restaurante-Mesón Alejandro,** C. Carbitrería, the first left off C. Cronista Lecea, which is off Pl. Mayor; stirs together a delicious *paella* for 590ptas (good *menú del día* 900ptas; entrees 500-900ptas). **Bar-Mesón Cueva de San Estéban,** C. Valdelaguila, 15, off the top of Pl. San Estéban, which is reached by C. Escuderos, has stone and mortar walls, wooden pygmy footstools for seats, and a reasonable *menú* (800ptas). Cold beer from the font at the rear of the cave is 150ptas.

■ LA GRANJA

The royal palace and grounds of La Granja, 11km southeast from Segovia, were built by the first Bourbon King in Spain, Felipe V; "The Versailles of Spain" was one of four royal summer retreats (with El Pardo, El Escorial, and Aranjuez). Marble everywhere, windows framed by original 250-year-old lace curtains, ceilings painted in false perspective, and lavish crystal chandeliers (made in San Ildefonso's renowned crystal factory) are just the frosting. (Palace open Tues.-Sat. 10am-1pm and 3-5pm, Sun. 10am-2pm. 500ptas; students, professors, and seniors 300ptas; Wed. EU citizens free.) Frequent **buses** leave Segovia for La Granja (10-13 per day, 20min., 95ptas).

■■■ AVILA

Avila's fame is forever ensured by St. Theresa of Avila (1515-1582)—mystic, writer, reformer of monastic life, the nun who founded the Order of the Discalced Carmelites and whose raptures were immortalized in marble by Bernini. Because the city sits on a rocky escarpment high above the Río Adaja valley, Avila keeps cool in the summer while the plain swelters below. Within the classic medieval walls, carved images of bulls and hogs are mute reminders of a Celtiberian culture much older than the ancient fortifications. Avila proudly wears the oldest, most complete fortified medieval belt of any Spanish city. Construction of the **murallas medievales** began in 1090, but most were realized in the next century; the concentrated burst of activity lent the walls their unusual uniformity. Eighty-two massive towers reinforce walls whose thickness averages 3m.

Some believe that the profile of the **cathedral** looming over the watchtowers inspired St. Theresa's metaphor of the soul as a diamond castle. Begun in the 2nd half of the 12th century, the oldest Spanish cathedral in the transitional Romanesque-to-Gothic style recalls the long, turbulent centuries of the Reconquista. Embedded in the city walls, the cathedral participated in Avila's defense system. The small **museum** has a fine collection of gold and silver work, sculptures, and paintings from the 12th to 18th centuries, including a small El Greco. (Cathedral open 8am-1pm and 3-7pm; Oct.-April 8am-1pm and 3-5pm. Free. Museum open 10am-1:30pm and 3-7pm; Oct.-April 10am-1:30pm and 3-6pm. 200ptas.) Most of St. Theresa's mystical experiences took place during the 30 years she spent in the **Monasterio de la Encarnación.** The tiny cell where she lived is through the farthest door in the farthest chapel. Upstairs from the cloister, a museum features a collection of furnishings, letters and other personal effects. (Open 9:30am-1:30pm and 3:30-6pm; winter 9:30am-1pm and 4-7pm. Obligatory tour in Spanish 100ptas.) Locals built the **Convento de Santa Teresa** in the 17th century on the site of her childhood home. Next door, the **Sala de Reliquias** holds relics of the convent's namesake, including her forefinger, the sole of her sandal, and the cord with which she flagellated herself. (Convent open 9:30am-1:30pm and 3:30-9pm. *Sala de Reliquias* open 9:30am-1:30pm and 3:30-7:30pm. Free.)

Practical Information, Accommodations, and Food Avila's **tourist office,** Pl. Catedral, 4 (tel. (918) 21 13 87), is directly opposite the cathedral. From Pl. Santa Teresa, walk through the main gate and turn right up winding C. Cruz Vieja. (Open Mon.-Fri. 9:30am-2pm and 4:30-7pm, Sat. 9:30am-1:30pm and 4:30-8:30pm, Sun. 11:30am-2pm.) The **bus station** is on Av. Madrid at Av. Portugal (tel. (918) 22 01 54), on the northeast side of town. Buses run to Segovia (1hr., 520ptas); Salamanca (1½hr., 875ptas); and Madrid (2hr., 835ptas). To reach the Pl. Santa Teresa, cross the street and walk down C. Duque de Alba. The **train station,** Av. Portugal, 17 (tel. (918) 22 01 88; info tel. 22 65 79), is at the end of Av. José António on the northeast side of town. Trains head to Medina del Campo (1hr., 480ptas; change here for Segovia); Salamanca (2hr., 550ptas); and Madrid (2hr., 575-1050ptas). To reach Pl. Santa Teresa from the train station, follow Avenida José Antonio to Calle de Isaac Peral, bear right, and turn left on C. Duque de Alba. Municipal buses run from nearby the train station to the Pl. Victoria.

Lodgings in Avila are plentiful and reasonably priced. **Residencia Juvenil "Duperier" (HI),** Av. Juventud (tel. (918) 21 35 48), only has 20 beds. From Pl. Sta. Teresa take Av. Alférez Provisional, cross C. Santa Fé onto Av. Juventud, and turn right into the Ciudad Deportiva complex from Av. Juventud. (Curfew 11pm. 800ptas, with breakfast 900ptas. Over 25: 1100ptas, 1250ptas. Open mid-July to Aug.) Stumble into attractive **Hostal Continental,** Pl. Catedral, 4 (tel. 21 15 02), right next to the tourist office and in front of the cathedral. (Singles 2100-2300ptas. Doubles 3500-3900ptas. Triples 4000-500ptas. Lower prices in off-season. Prices don't include IVA. Visa, MC, AmEx.) The **Hostal Santa Ana,** C. Alfonso Montalvo, 2 (tel. (918) 22 00 63), off Pl. Santa Ana, down Av. José Antonio from the train station, is an efficiently run *hostal;* sheets are snow-white, baths are spic and span. (Doubles 3200ptas. Triples 4500ptas. Oct.-July 14: 3000ptas, 4000ptas. Showers 200ptas.)

The city won fame for its *ternera de Avila* (veal) and *mollejas* (sweetbread). The *yemas de Santa Teresa* or *yemas de Avila,* local confections made of egg yolks and honey, and *vino de Cebreros,* the smooth regional wine, are delectable. Every Friday (9am-2pm), a **market** in Pl. Victoria sells fruits, vegetables, meat, and other foodstuffs for cheap (plus tacky clothes and arts and crafts). **Plaza de la Victoria** is a center of budget dining. **Quiros,** C. Caballeros, a few steps from Pl. Victoria, and **Alimentación Barcense,** C. Reyes Católicos, closer to the cathedral, are small bargain grocery stores (both open Mon.-Sat. 9am-1:30pm and 4-7:30pm). For ¡ham!, **Mesón del Jamón,** C. Doctor Fleming, 26, off Av. Portugal, is the place to go (*menú* 1200ptas).

■■■ SALAMANCA

For centuries the "hand of Salamanca," the brass knocker traditionally found on the doors of this city, has welcomed students, scholars, rogues, royals, and saints. Nowhere is the golden glow of sandstone more apparent than in the Baroque **Plaza Mayor,** a trapezoid begun in 1729 during the reign of Felipe V. Between the arches—almost 100 of them—hang medallions with bas-reliefs of famous Spaniards, from El Cid to Franco. One of the city's most celebrated landmarks, the 15th-century **Casa de las Conchas** (House of Shells), is adorned by rows of scallop shells chiseled in sandstone. (Now a public library, but courtyard is open to tourists. Open Mon.-Fri. 9am-9pm, Sat.-Sun. 10am-2pm and 4-7pm. Free.)

Founded in 1218, the **Universidad** is entered from the **Patio de las Escuelas,** off C. Libreros. The university's **entryway** is one of the best examples of Spanish Plat-eresque, a style named for the filigree work of *plateros* (silversmiths). The walls are marked here and there by students' initials in bold red, painted upon graduation in an ink of bull's blood, olive oil, and herbs. Inside the **Escuelas Menores,** also on the Patio de las Escuelas, the *Cielo de Salamanca* (Sky of Salamanca), a 15th-century fresco of the zodiac that covered the ceiling of the ancient library, is preserved in the **University Museum** (open Tues.-Sat. 9:30am-1:30pm and 4-6:30pm, Sun. 9:30am-1:30pm).

Begun in 1513 to accommodate the growing tide of Catholics, the spindly spires of the **catedral nueva** weren't finished until 1733. The Romanesque **catedral vieja** (1140) has an amazing central altarpiece that narrates the story of the Virgin Mary in 53 scenes. Inside the cupola, apocalyptic angels separate the sinners from the saved. (Cathedrals open 10am-2pm and 4-8pm; Oct.-March 10am-1pm and 4-6pm. Old cathedral, cloister, and museum via new cathedral, 200ptas. New cathedral free.)

Ambiente, an inexpensive pamphlet sold at kiosks, lists movies and special events. The **Plaza Mayor** is the social as well as geographic center of town; people overflow from the plaza as far west as **San Vicente.** A lot of the student nightlife also concentrates on the **Gran Vía** and side streets. **Café Novelty,** on the northeast corner of Pl. Mayor, is the oldest café in town and a meeting place for students and professors. Miguel de Unamuno was a regular. Also try **Café El Corrillo,** Pl. Mayor by C. Juan del Rey. **Pub Rojo y Negro,** C. Espoz y Mina sells scrumptious coffee, liquor and ice cream concoctions (250-600ptas) in an old-fashioned setting. There's a dance floor down below. (Open until 12:30am.) Avoid the southwest section of town after dark unless you're accompanied by a friend or bodyguard; Salamanca's drug scene is somewhat notorious.

Practical Information, Accommodations, and Food Most sights and a great deal of cheap food and accommodations lie south of the **Plaza Mayor.** The **Universidad** is south of the Plaza Mayor, near the Plaza de Anaya. Whether you arrive by bus or train, you'll be 20min. from the town center. From the train station, catch the bus that goes to Plaza Mercado (next to Pl. Mayor). From the bus station, either catch bus 4 to Pl. Mercado or walk down Calle de Filiberto Villalobos, cross the busy main road and head down Calle Ramón y Cajal to its dead end; turn left and immediately right up Calle Prior, which runs to Pl. Mayor. The **tourist office,** Pl. Mayor (tel. (923) 21 83 42), is open Mon.-Sat. 9am-2pm and 4:30-7pm, Sun. 10am-2pm. **Trains** chug to Madrid (3½hr., 1250ptas) via Avila (1055ptas), Burgos via Palencia, León (3½hr., 1600ptas), and transfer center Valladolid. **Buses** run to Avila (1-2hr., 765ptas), Segovia (2hr., 1250ptas), Madrid (2½-3hr., 1525-1910ptas), and León (3hr., 1600ptas).

The abundance of students means many rooms. Cheap *pensiones* abound on the side streets off Pl. Mayor, especially on **Calle Meléndez,** just south of the plaza. **Pensión Las Vegas,** C. Meléndez, 13, 1st fl. (tel. (923) 21 87 49) shelters pretty, clean rooms with big windows and balconies. (Singles 1000ptas. Doubles 2000-3000ptas. Triples 3000-4000ptas.) One of the best bargains in town, **Pensión Marina,** C. Doctrinos, 4, 3rd fl. (tel. (923) 21 65 69), between C. Compañía and C. Prado has mammoth bedrooms and two TV lounges with overstuffed furniture. (Single 1600ptas. Doubles 2200ptas.) To camp with all the amenities, head 4km toward Madrid to reach **Regio** (tel. (923) 13 88 88, fax 13 80 44), on the Ctra. Salamanca (425ptas per person or tent, 375ptas for a one-person tent).

Every clique has its favorite café in **Plaza Mayor;** all serve the same moderately good food at a standard, slightly inflated price. A slew of bar-restaurants line streets between the plaza and the university, where a full meal costs no more than 1000ptas. Don't miss *jeta,* a local *tapas* specialty (fried pig lips). The intimate **Restaurante Vegetariano El Trigal,** C. Libreros, 20, near the cathedral and the Patio de las Escuelas, doubles as a yoga center. (Creative *menú* 900 or 1300ptas. *Platos combinados* 675ptas. Open 1-4pm and 8:30-11pm.) **Imbis,** C. Rua Mayor, 29, offers a good selection of *tapas.* (*Platos combinados* about 700ptas. *Menú* 1000-1100ptas. Open 8am-midnight.)

■ CIUDAD RODRIGO

A medieval town characterized by its fabulous masonry and its honey-colored stone, Ciudad Rodrigo rises from the plains near the Portuguese border. The cloister of the cathedral alone merits a trip to the town. Biblical and mythological scenes are illustrated in fascinating stonework. At one corner, monsters devour Muslims; halfway around, two demons smirk as Adam and Eve receive their punishment; at the far end, two birds kiss. The cathedral's museum is filled with strange and thrilling old pieces, including an ancient clavichord, the ornate "ballot box" used to determine the cathedral's hierarchy, and the robes and richly embroidered slippers worn by long-dead bishops and priors. (Cathedral open 10:30am-1:30pm and 4-8pm. Free. Cloister and museum open 10:30am-1:30pm and 4-6pm. 200ptas. Mandatory guided tour in Spanish.) Eight **buses** a day (3 on Sun.) arrive from Salamanca (1hr., 670ptas).

■■■ LEÓN

In Spain the city is called *la ciudad azul* (the blue city), after the dominant hue of the cathedral's stained glass windows. Some think that it should be renamed *la ciudad dingy grey*, but many pleasant parks and quiet plazas dot the otherwise urban landscape. Historically an area of transit, León was founded in 68AD by the Seventh Roman Legion—hence the name which is a demotic corruption of *legío*; the lion emblazoned everywhere postdates the naming of the city.

Proud *Leoneses* claim that their **cathedral** is the most beautiful in the land. A splendid **museum** on the evolution of Romanesque sculpture hides beyond the vast cloister and twisting sculptures. (Museum open 9:30am-1:30pm and 4-6pm. Cloister and museum 300ptas.) The **Basílica de San Isidoro** was dedicated in the 11th century to San Isidoro of Sevilla, whose remains were brought to León while Muslims ruled the south. The corpses of León's royal family rest in the impressive **Panteón Real,** but more lively fun is overhead: remarkably vibrant tempera frescoes cover 2 crypt ceilings. (Open Mon.-Sat. 10am-1:30pm and 4-6:30pm, Sun. 10am-1:30pm. With tour 300ptas.) **Los Botines,** in Pl. Santo Domingo, is one of the few buildings outside of Catalonia designed by *Modernista* Antonio Gaudí. The relatively restrained structure (under renovation until early 1995) displays only hints of the wild stuff to come. **Fiestas** commemorating St. John and St. Peter run together for a week-long celebration (June 20-29) including *la corrida de toros* (bullfight).

Practical Information, Accommodations, and Food León's **tourist office** is at Pl. Regla, 3 (tel. (987) 23 70 82), in front of the cathedral (open Mon.-Fri. 9am-2pm and 4:30-6:30pm, Sat. 10am-1pm). **Trains** leave from **RENFE,** Av. Astorga, 2 (tel. (987) 27 02 02), across the river from Pl. Guzmán el Bueno, at the bend in Av. Palencia for La Coruña (7hr., 3400ptas), Madrid (5hr., 1500-3900ptas), and other locales. The ticket office is at C. Carmen, 4 (tel. (987) 22 05 25; open Mon.-Fri. 9:30am-2pm and 5-8pm, Sat. 10am-1:30pm). **Buses** leave from Estación de Autobuses, Po. Ingeniero Saenz de Miera (tel. (987) 21 10 00; information open Mon.-Sat. 7:30am-9pm; Madrid, 4½hr.; Astorga, 1hr., 385ptas).

For lodging, look on **Avenida de Roma, Avenida de Ordoño II,** and **Avenida de la República Argentina,** which lead into the new town from Pl. Guzmán el Bueno. The **Residencia Juvenil Infanta Doña Sancha (HI),** C. Corredera, 2 (tel. (987) 20 22 01 or 20 38 11), 2 blocks past the Jardín San Francisco, is a clean university dorm during the school year. (800ptas. Over 26, 1100ptas. Often booked solid; call ahead.) The chatty proprietors of **Hostal Oviedo,** Av. Roma, 26 (tel. (987) 22 22 36) offer large rooms with many terraces (singles 1600ptas, doubles 2700ptas, triples 3500ptas; showers 250ptas). Downstairs from the Oviedo, **Hostal Europa** (tel. (987) 22 22 38) is spic and span (singles 1600ptas, doubles 2700ptas; showers 200ptas).

Food in the buff is sold at **Mercado Municipal del Conde,** Pl. Conde, off C. General Mola (open Mon.-Sat. 9am-2pm). Inexpensive eateries cluster by the cathedral and on the small streets off **Av. Generalísimo Franco.** Also seek around **Pl. San Martín.** The **Cafetería-Restaurante Catedral,** by the cathedral at C. Mariano Dominjuez Berrueta, 17, serves a monumental 950pta *menú* (open Mon.-Sat. 1-4pm and 8pm-midnight). **Mesón San Martín,** Pl. San Martín 8, a winding block from Pl. Mayor offers house specialities including *menestra* (a vegetable and ham stew) and *pimientos rellenos* (stuffed peppers) (open Mon. and Thurs. 1-4pm, Tues.-Wed. and Fri.-Sun. 1-4pm and 8-11:30pm). For the early part of the night (around 11pm-2am) the **barrio húmedo** around **Pl. San Martín** sweats with bars, discos and techno-pop.

■■■ BURGOS

Everything in Burgos stands tall, from its starched citizens to the Gothic stone architecture for which it is famous. The *Cabeza de Castilla* (Head of Castile), Burgos rose to prominence as capital of the province, then of the kingdom of Castile, claiming the purest form of Castilian. The town's other claim to fame is Rodrigo Díaz de Vivar, a.k.a. El Cid, Spain's real-life epic hero. Although not born here, his more memorable exploits took place in this suave, graceful city. Today, Burgos belies its conservative reputation with a lively youth culture and the international influence of backpacking pilgrims on their way to Santiago.

ORIENTATION AND PRACTICAL INFORMATION

Burgos lies about 240km north of Madrid on the main route between Madrid and France. The **cathedral** and most other monuments are found in the old city of plazas and curving streets. Across the river hulk the train and bus stations.

- **Tourist Office:** Pl. Alonso Martínez, 7 (tel. 20 31 25). From Pl. José Antonio take Laín Calvo for 3 blocks. A variety of multilingual maps and brochures; even a computer to take you on a video tour of the region. Open Mon.-Fri. 9am-2pm and 4:30-6:30pm, Sat. 10am-1:30pm.
- **Budget Travel: Viajes TIVE** (tel. 20 98 81), in the Casa de Cultura on Pl. San Juan. Unmarked door; hang a left after entering. Student IDs (500ptas) and HI cards (1800ptas). Some English spoken. Open Mon.-Fri. 9am-2pm.
- **Post Office:** Pl. Conde de Castro, 1 (tel. 26 27 50), across the river from Pl. Primo de Rivera, where El Cid points the way. Open for stamps, *Lista de Correos*, and **telegrams** Mon.-Fri. 8am-9pm, Sat. 9am-2pm. **Postal Code:** 09000.
- **Telephones:** Look for booths in plazas. **City Code:** 947.
- **Trains:** at the end of Av. Conde Guadalhorce, across the river from Pl. Castilla (tel. 20 35 60). A 10min. walk southwest of the city center. Information open 7am-11pm. **RENFE,** C. Moneda, 21 (tel. 20 91 31). Open Mon.-Fri. 9am-1pm and 4-7pm, Sat. 9am-1pm. To: León (2hr., 1600ptas); Madrid (3½hr., 1400-2700ptas); Barcelona (8hr., 5200ptas); Santiago (7hr., 4500ptas). Prices vary widely depending on day or time of travel
- **Buses:** C. Miranda, 4 (tel. 20 55 65), off Pl. de la Vega. To: Madrid (3hr., 1720ptas); Barcelona (7hr., 4455ptas); León (2hr., 1655ptas).
- **Medical Assistance: Casa de Socorro,** Conde de Vallellano, 4 (tel. 26 14 10), at C. Ramón y Cajal near the post office.
- **Emergencies:** tel. 091 (police) or 092. **Ambulance,** tel. 23 22 22.

ACCOMMODATIONS AND FOOD

Head either to the streets radiating north from Pl. Alonso Martínez or the neighborhood around Pl. Vega. At **Hostal Hidalgo,** C. Almirante Bonifaz, 14 (tel. 20 34 81), all rooms have high ceilings and wood floors (singles 1800ptas, doubles 3200-3400ptas). For sparkling rooms with a view of the bus station, **Pensión Ansa,** C. Miranda, 9 (tel. 20 47 67) is the place to go. (Singles 2000ptas. Doubles 3400ptas. Triples 4500ptas. Showers included.) **Hostal Niza,** C. General Mola, 12 (tel. 26 19 17) has large rooms, some with balconies. From Pl. Vega, follow C. Madrid and take the 2nd left onto General Mola; the *hostal* is at the end of the block. (Singles 2500ptas. Doubles 3000ptas. Triples 4525ptas. Showers 250ptas.) The "Fuentes

Blancas" bus (from El Cid statue, 65ptas) voyages to **Camping Fuentes Blancas,** 3½km outside Burgos. (Open April-Sept.; 450ptas per person, tent, or car.)

Landlocked Burgos means meat, meat and more meat. There are 2 markets: **Mercado Norte** near Pl. España and the smaller **Mercado de Abastos,** on C. Miranda near the bus station. (Open Mon.-Sat. 7am-3pm. Mercado Norte. also Fri., 5:30-8pm.) For *tapas* paradise, visit C. San Lorenzo at night. At #20, the **Mesón de los Herreros** (between Pl. Mayor and Pl. Alonso Martínez) serves *morritos* (pig nose), *sesos* (lamb brains), and tamer alternatives. (Open Mon.-Sat. 9:30am-3:30pm and 6pm-12:30am, Sun. 11am-3:30pm and 6pm-midnight.) **Restaurante Sotillano,** C. Avellanos, 5 (off Pl. Alonso Martínez) is the hungry bargain-hunter's dream. (*Menú* of local specialties 1000ptas. Open 11:30am-5pm and 8pm-midnight.)

SIGHTS AND ENTERTAINMENT

The slender, lacy spires of the **cathedral** soar above the city. A powerful group of 13th-century gentlemen sheep farmers (the Mesta) paid for this Gothic masterpiece with funds from their extraordinary merino wool. In the **Capilla Mayor,** at the east end, El Cid's bones and those of his wife Jimena rest in marmoreal serenity. Before leaving the cathedral, look for the fly catcher high up near the main door in the central aisle. As it strikes the hours, this strange creature opens its mouth in imitation of the crowds gawking below. (Cathedral open 9:30am-1pm and 4-7pm. Free. Sacristy and museum 350ptas, students 100ptas.) The ruins of a **Medieval Castle** dominate a hilltop rising to the side of the cathedral. From C. San Esteban, follow the paved road up for about 15 minutes, through fields of wildflowers. At the top there are spectacular views of the surrounding countryside and the roof of the cathedral.

After the cathedral, the **estatua del Cid** in Pl. General Primo de Rivera is Burgos's most venerated landmark. Rodrigo Díaz de Vivar (Cid comes from the Arabic for Lord) won his fame in battle against both Moors and Christians. Burgos tradition compels its youth to climb the statue and fondle the testicles of El Cid's horse, thus ensuring their own strength, courage, and fame. Past the **Casa del Cordón,** on C. Santander, where Columbus met with Fernando and Isabel after his second trip to America, and Felipe el Hermoso (the Handsome) died after a trying game of *pelota* (jai-alai), is the **Museo de Pintura Marceliano Santa María.** Rich landscape scenes and portraits by Marceliano Santa María, a 20th-century local artist, hang within. (Open Tues.-Sat. 10am-2pm and 5-8pm, Sun. 10am-2pm. 25ptas, students free.)

The **Cartuja de Miraflores** is a Carthusian monastery that houses the ornate tombs of King Juan II of Castile, Queen Isabel of Portugal, and their son Don Alfonso. Debate rages as to whether Alfonso's early death was caused by scheming noblemen or a bad cold. (Open Mon.-Sat. 10:15am-3pm and 4-6pm, Sun. and holidays 11:20am-12:30pm, 1-3pm, and 4-6pm. Mass Mon.-Sat. 9am, Sun. and holidays 7:30am and 10:15am. Free.) To get here, take the "Fuentes Blancas" bus (4 per day from statue of El Cid, 65ptas) or walk 3km east along the Paseo de La Quinta.

Nightlife in Burgos rivals that of Spain's larger cities. Students congregate in the zone next to the cathedral and **Pl. Huerto del Rey** (known as **Las Llanas**). An even larger student crowd attacks **C. San Juan** and enjoys the spoils at the neon **Picoco** and in **La Faberna Pahl,** with its *sevillanas,* a popular form of flamenco that incites lustful dancing. The elegant and relatively tranquil cafés along Paseo del Espolón draw a slightly more mature crowd. **La Trastienda,** just off the Paseo at the corner of C. Eduardo Martinez de Campo, 4, attracts young members of all sexual orientations. Draft beer 125ptas. Nightlife switches into high gear from June 23 to July 8, when Burgos honors its patron saints Peter and Paul with concerts, parades, fireworks, bullfights, and dances. The day after Corpus Christi, citizens parade through town with the *Pendón de las Navas,* a banner captured from the Moors in 1212.

NORTHERN SPAIN

For ages, religious pilgrims en route to Santiago de Compostela have crossed the French border into northern Spain in search of spiritual knowledge. Whether you seek fulfillment in sun-worship, on a pair of skis, or in front of the fiery nostrils of a bewildered bull, the area remains a haven. The autonomous communities of Aragón, Navarra and Euskadi (the Basque Country) all share a border with France. Cantabria picks up where Euskadi leaves off along the North Atlantic coast, Asturias is west of Cantabria and tiny Galicia occupies the far northwest corner of the country. The Pyrenees loom along most of the border; use Jaca in Aragón as a base for mountain adventure. Out of the mountains in Navarre, Pamplona and its bulls are the most well-known attraction. When you tire of playing Hemingway's game, know that some of the most beautiful beaches in the world stretch along the Atlantic from San Sebastián (Donostia) to Santander (whence ferries leave for Plymouth, England). Both the inland scenery and the politics grow more complex in the restive Basque provinces.

■■■ SANTIAGO DE COMPOSTELA

Embraced by the Ríos Tambre and Ulla, Santiago was founded in 813, when, according to legend, Bishop Teodomiro informed Asturian King Alfonso II of the miraculous discovery of a tomb containing the remains of the Apostle St. James. In his Spanish incarnation, the gruesomely named St. James the Moorslayer (Santiago Matamoros) occasionally appeared on a white charger to lead the Christian forces into battle. Santiago thus became one of Christianity's three holy cities, and—like Rome and Jerusalem—the destination of pilgrimages. The clever Benedictine monks built monasteries to host the pilgrims on the way, giving rise to the first large-scale tourist industry in European history. Pilgrims from all over Spain and Europe still follow the superhighway (Ctra. 120) to Santiago, and are easily identified by their crook-necked staffs and scallop shell necklaces. At any hour of the day or night, the granite streets surrounding Santiago's famous cathedral are filled with musicians, street-walkers, and smiling nuns, all just celebrating the fact that they're there.

ORIENTATION AND PRACTICAL INFORMATION

The **cathedral** marks the center of the old city, which sits higher than the new city. Three streets lead directly to the cathedral from the south side (train station side) of town: **Rúa do Franco** (Calle del Franco), **Rúa do Vilar** (Calle del Vilar) and **Rúa Nova** (Calle Nueva). From the train station, turn right at the top of the stairs and take C. Hórreo to **Praza de Galiza** (do *not* take Avenida de Lugo). From here, it's one more block to **Entrecalles,** from which the 3 cathedral-bound streets spring. From the bus station, take bus 10 to Pr. Galiza (every 10-15min., 35ptas).

> **Tourist Office:** R. Vilar, 43 (tel. 58 40 81), in the old town. English and French spoken. Bus schedules. Open Mon.-Fri. 9am-2pm and 4-7pm, Sat. 10am-1:30pm.
>
> **Budget Travel:** TIVE, Plazuela del Matadero, s/n (tel. 57 24 26). Turn right up R. Fonte Santo Antonio from Pr. Galiza. ISIC 500ptas. HI card 1800ptas. Open Mon.-Fri. 9am-2pm.
>
> **American Express:** Ultratur Viajes, Av. Figueroa, 6 (tel. 58 70 00). Open Mon.-Fri. 9am-2pm and 4:30-7pm, Sat. 9am-2pm.
>
> **Post Office:** Travesa de Fonseca (tel. 58 12 52, fax 56 32 88), on the corner of R. Franco. Open for stamps and *Lista de Correos* Mon.-Fri. 8am-9pm, Sat. 9am-2pm; for **telegrams** Mon.-Fri. 8am-9pm, Sat. 9am-7pm; for faxes Mon.-Fri 8am-9pm, Sat. 9am-9pm. **Postal Code:** 15080.
>
> **Telephones:** C. Bautizados, 13, in the old town off Pr. Toral. Open Mon.-Fri. 10am-11:30pm, Sat. 10am-8pm, Sun. 11am-3pm and 5-9:30pm. **Telephone Code:** 981.

SPAIN

Trains: R. General Franco (tel. 52 02 02). Information open Mon.-Sat. 7am-9pm, Sun. 7am-1pm. To: Madrid (8hr., 4000-6000ptas); Pontevedra (1½hr., 420ptas); La Coruña (1hr., 400-460ptas).

Buses: Estación Central de Autobuses (tel. 58 77 00), C. San Cayetano. Nothing central about it, but 10 bus leaves every 15min. for center (35ptas). Information open 8am-10pm. **ALSA** (tel. 58 64 53). To: Madrid (8-9hr., 5090ptas), San Sebastián (6hr., 3120ptas), and Bilbao (9½hr., 5320ptas). **Castromil** tel. 58 97 00. To: La Coruña (1½hr., 715ptas) and Pontevedra (1½hr., 540ptas). **Empresa Freire** tel. 58 81 11. To: Amsterdam, Paris, Hamburg, and Zürich.

Luggage Storage: At the train station (lockers 400ptas). Open 7:30am-11pm. At the **bus station** (75ptas per bag). Open 8am-10pm.

Laundromat: Lava-Express, C. República El Salvador, 21 (tel. 59 00 95), in the new town at the corner with C. Alfredo Brañas. Self-service wash and dry 550ptas per 4kg. Open Mon.-Fri. 9:30am-2pm and 4-8:30pm, Sat. 10am-2pm.

Medical Assistance: Hospital Xeral, C. Galeras (tel. 54 00 00).

Emergency: Ambulance, tel. 59 36 56. **Policía municipal,** tel. 092.

ACCOMMODATIONS, CAMPING, AND FOOD

Rúa do Vilar and **Calle Raiña** spill over with *hospedajes* and *pensiones,* and every other building in town has a hand-drawn *"habitaciones"* sign. Behind a green door next to the eponymous bar, **Hospedaje Viño,** Pr. Mazarelos, 7 (tel. 58 51 85), shelters spotless singles (1000-1500ptas) and doubles (2000-2500ptas). At Pr. Galiza, take a right onto R. Fonte San Antonio and turn left through a purple-flowered archway. **Hospedaje Ramos,** C. Raiña, 18, 2nd floor (tel. 58 18 59), is simple but comfortable; rooms with private baths are a far better deal (though the public bath is spotless). Every night, *tunas* in the square below will serenade you. (Singles 1300ptas, with bath 1500ptas. Doubles 3000ptas, with bath 3500ptas.) **Camping As Cancelas,** R. 25 de Xullo, 35 (tel. 58 02 66), sits 2km from the cathedral on the northern edge of town. Take bus 6 or 9. Souvenirs, laundry, supermarket and pool make this the Club Med of camping. (495ptas per person, 525 per car or tent.)

Pilgrims need to eat too; Santiago is a budget diner's dream. Most restaurants in the old town south of the cathedral, notably on **Rúa do Villar, Rúa Franco,** and **Calle Raíña. Casa Manolo,** R. Traviesa, 27, near the market and Pl. San Augustín, serves a 650pta *menú* of endless choices. Bread, wine, and *flan* are included. (Open Tues.-Sun. 1-4pm and 8pm-midnight.) **Bar Coruña,** C. Raiña, 17 (tel. 58 39 68) serves just about anything slapped between two slices of bread, from anchovies (185ptas) to tortillas (140ptas; open 9:30am-midnight).

SIGHTS AND ENTERTAINMENT

The entire old town has been designated a national monument; feast your art-historian's eyes on every door and square. The **cathedral's** core is an admirable Romanesque Latin cross with ambulatory and radiating chapels. The cathedral's four façades are masterpieces from different eras; its four entrances open onto four plazas, Pr. Platerías, Quintana, Obradoiro or Azabaxería. The **Pórtico de la Gloria,** facing the Praza da Obradoiro, is often considered the crowning achievement of Spanish Romanesque sculpture. Inside the cathedral, Santiago's revered remains lie beneath the high altar in a silver coffer, while his more savory bejeweled bust sits above. Near Pr. Camino, both the **Museo do Pobo Galego** and the **Museo Municipal** exhibit tidbits of Galician culture in the Gothic **Monasterio de Santo Domingo** (open Mon.-Sat. 10am-1pm and 4-7pm; free).

Crowds of all ages flood the city's cellars for mix-and-match nightlife (women generally no cover, men 400-600ptas). Santiago's **fiestas** occur July 18 to 31. At night, various student singing troupes called **tunas** dress in medieval garb and sing ribald songs and an occasional serenade in the streets of the old city. Dating from the Middle Ages, the *tunas* traditionally performed as a way of feeding themselves while at school; today they offer females lots of flirtatious, if unrequested, attention. Many *tunas,* however, are quite respectable, and in any event this thoroughly Spanish form of entertainment is free.

■ RÍAS BAJAS (RÍAS BAIXAS)

Protected coves lure *gallegos* to the *Rías* (inlets) for weekend visits. Tourism is gradually eclipsing fishing as the main local industry. Quaint stone villages and Celtic ruins speckle the countryside. Public transportation between towns in this area is sparse; either rent a car or plan your itinerary carefully.

North of Santiago North of Santiago, the Rías Altas stretch their watery fingers into the land from the province of Lugo down to Cabo Finisterre. In the misty mountains of Galiza the weather is anything but predictable (even in summer), but views are spectacular year-round. Thanks to a healthy burst of summer tourism from landlocked Spaniards, the Rías Altas have the resources to augment a relatively unspoiled coastline.

La Coruña (A Coruña) makes an ideal base for exploration and also has a stellar nightlife, a historic old town, plenty of waterfront restaurants, and a couple of decent beaches. The **tourist office** is at Dársena de la Marina (tel. (981) 22 18 22), near the waterfront (open Mon.-Fri. 9am-2pm and 4-6pm, Sat. 10:30am-1pm). **Trains** leave from Pr. San Cristóbal, s/n (tel (981) 15 02 02) for Vigo (8 per day, 3hr., 1100ptas) and Santiago (1¼hr., 460ptas). **Buses** serve the Rías Altas and surrounding area from C. Caballeros (tel. (981) 23 96 44), across Av. Alcalde Molina from the train station. Bus 1 (90ptas) runs from the train and bus stations to the tourist office. For accommodations, scour **Calle Riego de Agua** and the area from Pr. Maria Pita down to Pr. San Agustín. Welcoming, cheery rooms await at **Hospedaje María Pita**, C. Riego de Agua, 38, 3rd floor (tel. (981) 22 11 87), 1 bl. behind Av. Marina. (Doubles with sink 2500ptas). There are three other attractive *hostales* in this building.

Excursions to the Rías Altas are many. In La Coruña's northern coast, where buses and trains seldom run and hitching is useless, rain forests give way to soft, empty beaches around the **Rías de Cedeira, Ortigueira** and **Viveiro.** Buses and the occasional FEVE train run inland to Ortigueira from Ferrol, but the sporadic coastal bus from La Coruña is preferable—you can always hop off if you see a place you like.

South of Santiago Chiefly a port city, sprawling **Vigo** is noisy and polluted, but its ferries, buses, and trains shuttle visitors efficiently to the nearby Ría de Vigo and Rio Miño. The **tourist office** is at As Avenidas, s/n (tel. (986) 43 05 77), in the grey circular building right across from the Estación Maritima (open Mon.-Fri. 9am-2pm and 4:30-6:30pm, Sat. 10am-12:30pm). **Trains** leave from Pr. Estación (tel. (986) 43 11 14) to Pontevedra (35min., 195ptas), Santiago de Compostela (2hr., 60ptas), and Porto, Portugal (1500ptas). **Buses** leave from **Estación de Autobuses,** Av. Madrid, (tel. (986) 37 34 11), for Santiago de Compostela (2hr., 835ptas), La Coruña (2½hr., 1500ptas), and Bayona (½hr., 215ptas).

Budgeteers come from far and wide for Vigo's inexpensive rooms, especially those on **Calle Alfonso XIII** (to the right upon exiting the train station). Doubles (1600-2800ptas) in **Hostal-Residencia Madrid,** C. Alfonso XIII, 63 (tel. (986) 22 55 23) are big enough to hold an olympic pool and sunny enough to get a tan. (Singles 1500ptas.) At **Hostal-Residencia Orensano,** C. Lepanto, 9 (tel. (986) 43 51 12), 1 bl. from train station, singles are only 1000-1200ptas (doubles 2000-2500ptas). Innumerable cheap bars and cafés crowd side streets off **Calle Urzáiz.** A popular place for delicious *tapas* is the **Mesón Don Sancho,** 1 C. García Olloqui, 1 bl. up from the Estación Marítima. (Clams in wine and garlic 500ptas. Open 11am-midnight.) Starting in the late afternoon, students pack the streets of the *casco antiguo*, which gets progressively sleazier as the night wears on. Vigo hosts *Expomagia* in mid-June, a celebration of all things occult.

Cangas and Bayona make the best beach excursions from Vigo. A ferry ride across the Ría de Vigo, **Cangas** is hardly an unspoiled paradise, but it does retain a small-town feeling and a white **beach. Ferries** go from Vigo to Cangas (20min., round-trip 330ptas). Inexpensive lodging is scarce. Twenty-one km southwest of Vigo, snug in its own mini-estuary, lies **Bayona** (Baiona), the first European town to receive word of the discovery of the Americas, when La Pinta returned to its port in March, 1493. A stroll along the stone walls of the 16th-century **castillo**-*cum*-hotel—the *parador* that was once the castle of the Condes de Gondomar—provides the most breathtaking sea views in the area (well worth the 100ptas). **Buses** leave Vigo for Bayona (every ½hr., about 1hr., 215ptas).

■■■ BILBAO (BILBO)

Bilbao is capital of the province of Vizkaia and the industrial engine of the entire Basque region. Don't judge the city by the dirt under its nails—with an outstanding art museum, a medieval quarter tucked in the crook of a great river estuary, and orgiastic nightlife, Bilbao rewards the perceptive. The ivy-covered **Museo de Bellas Artes,** ranked among Europe's best, boasts substantial Spanish and Flemish (12th-19th century) holdings, numerous canvases by Basque painters, and a sizeable contemporary abstract art collection. From Pl. Federico Moyúa (with Pl. España behind you), angle right on C. Elcano and follow it to Pl. Museo. (Open Tues.-Sat. 10am-1:30pm and 4-7:30pm, Sun. 10am-2pm. Free.) The **Museo Arqueológico, Etnográfico, e Histórico de Vizcaya,** C. Cruz, 4, housed in a beautiful old stone cloister, displays Basque hand-weaving, blacksmithing, armaments, and life on the sea. The museum is in the old city; walk past Pensión de la Fuente away from C. Correo to Pl. Miguel de Unamuno, whence C. Cruz springs. (Open Tues.-Sat. 10am-1:30pm and 4-7pm, Sun. 10:30am-1:30pm. Free.)

In Bilbao's **casco viejo** (old town) people spill out into the streets to tipple *chiquitos,* small glasses of beer or wine characteristic of the region. Teeny-boppers jam **C. Licenciado Poza.** With 200 bars in 200m, **Calle Ledesma** exerts a similar pull. The most radical bar in town (in all senses) is **Herriko Taberna** (The People's Tavern), C. Ronda, 20. Unmarked save for an outer wall splattered with militant graffiti, its interior is papered with political posters and photos of Basque detainees. If it's closed, don't despair; they're hanging out 6 streets over on **Calle Barrencalle.** Beaches are within easy reach by train, north of the city at **Plencia** (Plentzia) or at **Sopelana** along the way. **Getxo** also lies just a little nearer the surf; its illuminated suspension bridge fords the river, leading to a spate of all-night bars. **Buses** go here from Pl. Ensanche in Bilbao (150ptas), near the market (taxi home 2000-2500ptas).

Practical Information, Accommodations, and Food Bilbao's 6 **train** stations and 16 **bus** stations serve San Sebastián (bus 1¼hr., 960ptas), Burgos (bus 2hr., 1305ptas), Barcelona (train 10¾-11½hr., 4500-5000ptas; bus 7hr., 4450ptas), and Madrid (train 5¾-8¾hr., 3800-4400ptas; bus 5hr., 3035ptas). From any one of the myriad stations, navigate toward the Gran Vía, leading to Pl. España and the **Puente del Arenal** bridge, which spans the river to link the new town with the *casco viejo.* Just across the bridge, skip down the stairs to the right to the **tourist office** (tel. (94) 416 00 22), on Plaza Arriaga, whose booklet about Bilbao (available in English, 200ptas) practically puts us out of business (open Mon.-Fri. 9:30am-1:30pm and 4-8pm, Sat. 9am-2pm, Sun. 10am-2pm). **Plaza Arriaga** and nearby **Calle Arenal** are good starting points for hunting budget pensions. From the plaza, take C. Bidebarrieta and turn left on C. Lotería for **Pensión Ladero,** C. Lotería, 1, 4th fl. (tel. (94) 415 09 32). Every huge room has a chandelier, and most have terraces. (Singles 1500ptas. Doubles 2500ptas.) From the bridge, take C. Bidebarrieta and turn right for **Pensión Mardones,** C. Jardines, 4, 3rd fl. (tel. (94) 415 31 05), with brand spanking new singles (1500ptas), doubles (2600ptas) and triples (4000ptas).

Mercado de la Ribera, on the bank of the river heading left from the tourist office, is the biggest indoor market in Europe. It's worth a trip even if you're not eating. (Open Mon.-Thurs. and Sat. 7:45am-2pm, Fri. 7:45am-2pm and 5-8pm.) The best lunch for its price in Bilbao (900ptas) is served at **Aitxiar,** C. María Muñoz, 8 (open 1:30-3:30pm and 8:30-11pm). Heavenly ham and cheese with hearty bread and a drink go for about 700ptas in the lovable **Charcutería Claudio,** C. Esperanza, 18, past the train station (open 6-11pm).

■■■ SAN SEBASTIÁN (DONOSTIA)

This provincial capital is a blue-blood resort in a come-here-to-die setting. By day, crowds flock to La Concha, the crescent-shaped strip of sand that hugs the Mar Cantábrico. On either side of this giant playground, two steep hills elbow their way into the sea. They call San Sebastián "the seashell with the pearl" because La Concha curves like an oyster round a pearl-like islet in the bay. With the granting of regional autonomy for the Basque Country *(País Vasco)* and the dissipation of support for the ETA, the separatist tensions that once marred this pleasure-loving town have lessened; residents seem eager to ignore the political graffiti lingering on walls, preferring to promote the enjoyment of sun and surf. Enjoy San Sebastián's commodities, but don't expect to cut corners; over a century and a half of exclusivity are still reflected in the prices.

ORIENTATION AND PRACTICAL INFORMATION

The Río Urumea splits San Sebastián in two. The city center and most monuments are on the west side of the river, in a peninsula that juts into the sea. On the north of the peninsula lies the **parte vieja** (old city). To the south, the **Catedral del Buen Pastor** sits on the edge of Calle de San Martín, in the commercial district. The main bridge, **Puente Santa Catalina,** turns into **Avenida de la Libertad** on the west side of the river and runs to the **Playa de la Concha,** which fronts a large bay. To the left, past the tunnel, is **Playa de Ondarreta;** to right is **Monte Urgull.** The east side of the river is home to the **RENFE station.** To get to the *parte vieja*, head straight to Puente María Christina, cross the bridge and then turn right along the river and walk 4 blocks north to Av. Libertad. Turn left and follow it to the **puerto** (port); the *parte vieja* fans out to the right. To get to the **tourist office** from the station, turn right after crossing Puente María Cristina (the southern bridge) and continue past Puente Santa Catalina; Calle Reina Regente will be on the left. The **bus station** is in the south of the city in Plaza de Pío XII. **Avenida de Sancho El Sabio** runs to the right (north), straight toward the ocean and the center of the city.

Tourist Office: Centro de Atracción y Turismo, C. Reina Regente, (tel. 48 11 66), in the vast Teatro Victoria Eugenia. Open Mon.-Sat. 8am-8pm, Sun. 10am-1pm; Oct.-May Mon.-Fri. 9am-1:30pm and 3:30-6:30pm, Sat. 9am-1pm.

Currency Exchange: Agencia de Cambio, C. San Martín, 35 (tel. 43 03 47), at the corner of C. Easo. Mediocre rates but no commission. Open 9am-9pm.

Post Office: C. Urdaneta, s/n (tel. 46 49 14, fax 45 07 94), the street just south of the cathedral. Open for *Lista de Correos* Mon.-Fri. 8am-9pm, Sat. 9am-2pm; for stamps, telegrams, and fax same hrs., plus Sat. until 7pm. **Postal Code:** 20007.

Telephones: C. San Marcial, 29, 1 block from Av. Libertad, toward the cathedral. Open Mon.-Sat. 9:30am-11pm. **City Code:** 943.

Trains: RENFE, Estación del Norte, Av. Francia, s/n (tel. 27 92 56), on the east side of Puente María Cristina. Information (tel. 28 35 99) open 7am-11pm. To: Pamplona (1¾hr., 1200-1700ptas), Burgos (3½-4½hr., 2100ptas), Madrid (6-9hr., 4200-5400ptas), Barcelona (8-9hr., 4300-4800ptas), Santiago de Compostela (11hr., 5300ptas), Valencia (15hr., 5600-6300ptas), Lisbon (15hr., 7500ptas); Paris (9800ptas; change at Hendaye, France).

Buses: Several private companies run from different points in the city. Most leave from Pl. Pío XII (buy tickets on bus or at ticket booths along Av. Sancho El Sabio). **PESA** (tel. 29 95 55, ext. 13). To: Bilbao (1¼hr., 960ptas), Vitoria-Gasteiz (12 per day, 1¾hr., 935ptas). Tickets next door on Av. Sancho el Sabio. **La Roncalesa** (tel. 46 10 64). To: Pamplona (5 per day, 1½hr., 685ptas).

Luggage Storage: From the RENFE station, cross Puente María Cristina, turn right, walk 1 block, then take C. San Martín to the left; after 5 blocks, head left on C. Easo to # 22. 175ptas per day. Open June 21-Sept. 21 8:30am-8:30pm.

Laundromat: Lavomatique, C. Iñigo, 13, off C. San Juan. Wash 450ptas per 4kg load. Dry 50ptas per 7min. Soap 25ptas. Open Mon.-Fri. 10am-1pm and 4-8pm, Sat.-Sun. and holidays 10am-1pm.

Medical Assistance: Casa de Socorro, C. Pedro Egaño, 8 (tel. 46 63 19 or 46 41 20). **Red Cross,** C. Matías, 7 (tel. 21 46 00). **Ambulance,** tel. 22 22 22.
Emergencies: tel. 088. **Police,** tel. 45 00 00, emergency tel. 092.

ACCOMMODATIONS AND CAMPING

Desperate backpackers are forced to scrounge for rooms in July and August—particularly during *Sanfermines* (July 7-14) and *Semana Grande* (the week after Aug. 15). If you get away with 2500ptas a night, consider yourself lucky. Prices are also higher during *Semana Santa* (Holy Week—the week leading up to and including Easter). Budget options congregate both in the **parte vieja** and around the **cathedral.** The tourist office has lists of budget accommodations, and most *pensión* owners know *casas particulares* that take in guests—so don't be afraid to ask for help. The *parte vieja* is a prime location because of its proximity to Playa de la Concha and the port, its nightlife, and a plethora of *pinchos* (bite-size snacks) bars.

Albergue Juvenil la Sirena (HI), Po. Igueldo, 25 (group reservations tel. 31 02 56; guest phone 31 02 56, fax 21 40 90), near Playa de Ondarreta, in the far west end of the city. Bus 24 runs from train and the bus stations to Av. Zumalacárregui (1st stop after the tunnel). Bus 5 drops you off one street further from hostel on C. Matia. From Zumalacárregui, take the street that angles toward the mountain (Av. Brunei) and turn left at its end. Brand-new facilities. 3-day max. stay in summer. Members only (flexible). Midnight curfew; mid-June to Sept. 2am curfew. 1500ptas; winter 1300ptas. Over 26: 1700ptas; 1300ptas. Breakfast included. Lunch or dinner 650ptas. Sheets 350ptas. Luggage storage and washing machines.

Pensión Amaiur, C. 31 de Agosto, 44, 2nd fl. (tel. 42 96 54). From Alameda del Boulevard, go up C. San Jerónimo to the end and turn left. Gorgeous. Showers last only 5min. *Semana Santa* and June 22-Sept. 21: Doubles 4500ptas. Triples 6000ptas. After *Semana Santa*-June 21: 3000ptas; 4200ptas. Sept. 22-before *Semana Santa:* 2500ptas; 3300ptas. 500ptas *Let's Go* discount. Breakfast 200ptas.

Pensión Loinaz, C. San Lorenzo, 17, 2nd fl. (tel. 42 67 14). The people are delightful, the location ideal, the price fair, and the rooms choice. *Semana Santa* and July-Aug. Doubles 4000-4500ptas, triples 6000ptas. *Semana Santa*-June: 3000ptas; 4300ptas. Sept.-*Semana Santa:* 2500ptas; 3500ptas.

Pensión La Perla, C. Loyola, 10, 2nd fl. (tel. 42 81 23), the street directly ahead of the cathedral. All rooms with balconies and showers. English-speaking owner. Singles 3000ptas. Doubles 4500ptas. Oct.-June: 2500ptas; 3000ptas.

Hostal-Residencia Alameda, Alameda del Boulevard, 23, 2nd fl. (tel. 42 16 87 or 42 41 12). Across a tree-lined walk from the old quarter. Thirty-odd rooms, so there is hope. Singles 3500ptas. Everything else 2500-3500ptas per person. Sept.-June: 2600ptas; 2000-2600ptas.

Camping: Camping Igueldo (tel. 21 45 02), 5km west of town. 268 spots fill in the blink of an eye. Bus 16 "Barrio de Igueldo-Camping" leaves from Alameda del Boulevard (roughly every hr. 6:50am-10:30pm, 85ptas). Reception open 8am-midnight. Site (including tent and 1 or 2 people) 1378ptas; 395ptas per additional person. Winter: 905ptas; 335ptas.

FOOD

Pinchos are a religion in San Sebastian. Bars in the lively old city spread an array of enticing tidbits (called *pintxos* in Basque) on toothpicks or bread (8 *pinchos* and a drink, about 1200ptas). Thirty-nine restaurants and bars breathe cheaply on **Calle Fermín Calbetón.** The least expensive hunting ground for a full meal at a *jatetxea* (restaurant in Basque) is the **Gros** neighborhood, on the east side of the river. For history's greatest *pinchos* tour, start at **Bar La Cepa,** C. 31 de Agosto, 7-9, which has to-die-for peppers and a host of other delicacies (*pinchos* 125-250ptas, *bocadillos* 350-700ptas, entrees 900-1250ptas). Then continue across the street at **Gastelv,** C. 31 de Agosto, 22, for exquisite seafood confections (*tapas* 100-200ptas, lunch *menú* 900ptas). Soothing pink walls and elegant decor in **La Barranquesa,** C. Larramendi, 21, 3 bl. behind the cathedral. provide a break from the madness of the *parte vieja.* (*Menú* with *paella* and chicken 850ptas. Open Mon.-Sat. 1:15-3:30pm and 8:15-11:30pm.) Shop *all* your groceries in **Todo Todo 3,** C. Serrano Anguta, between C. Zumalacárregui and C. Matia (open Mon.-Fri. 9am-1pm and 4-8pm, Sat. 9am-1pm).

SIGHTS AND ENTERTAINMENT

The view of the bay—from anywhere—is especially spectacular on weekends after dark, when the base of Isla Santa Clara is lit by banks of floodlights so that it seems to float on a ring of light. The top of **Monte Igueldo,** at the far side of the bay, provides the best view. For the **funicular** to the top, take the hourly bus 16 "Igueldo" from Alameda del Boulevard or walk along the beach and turn left just before the tennis courts. (Funicular every 15min. 10am-9pm; Sept. 25-June 25 11am-8pm. 85ptas.) At the other end of the bay, gravel paths wind through the cool, shady woods of **Monte Urgull.** The overgrown **Castillo de Santa Cruz de la Mota** crowns the summit with cannons and a chapel, and is itself crowned by the statue of the Sagrado Corazón de Jesús which blesses the city (open 8am-8pm; winter 8am-6pm). A more jarring "monument" is the unmarked, white-plaster smear on a rock near the paseo as it rises above the aquarium. A member of ETA (Basque terrorist organization) accidentally blew himself up here trying to plant a bomb. At one end of Paseo Nuevo (the wind-whipped road that rounds the peninsula), the **Museo de San Telmo,** housed in a former Dominican monastery, has an array of Basque artifacts dating to prehistory, a couple of dinosaur skeletons, some El Grecos, and a smattering of contemporary art (open Tues.-Sat. 9:30am-1:30pm and 4-8pm, Sun. 10am-2pm; 350ptas, students 200ptas).

The *parte vieja* pulls out all the stops after dark. The **Bar Uraitz** and **Bar Eibartarra,** C. Mayor, 26, are the two most packed ones on the street, itself virtually impassable after dark. **Calle Fermín Calbetón,** 3 bl. in from Alameda del Boulevard, is also lined with oodles of bars. In the mood to boogie? Check out the modern music and dance mixes of the giant **Iguana,** C. San Jerónimo, in the *parte vieja.*

San Sebastián's five-day **Festival de Jazz** is one of Europe's most ambitious. For information on the 1995 festival, contact the **Oficina del Festival de Jazz** (tel. 48 11 79) at C. Reina Regente, s/n, 20003 San Sebastián (beneath the tourist office). The week of August 15, **Semana Grande** (Big Week) is ablaze with concerts, movies, and an international fireworks festival.

■■■ PAMPLONA

At the city's bullring, a huggable statue of Ernest Hemingway welcomes *aficionados* to Europe's biggest and most primal party: eight days of dancing, drinking, dashing, and satiating the wild beast within. **La Fiesta de San Fermín**—known to locals as **Los Sanfermines** (July 6-14)—is the orgy of bull worship celebrating Pamplona's patron saint San Fermín, who was martyred when bulls dragged him through the streets. The mayor kicks off eight days of craziness by lighting the first rocket, the *chupinazo* from the Ayuntamiento's balcony. Then the fantastical **Riau Riau procession** winds through the streets. The *peñas,* taurine societies more concerned with Bacchus than bullfighting, lead the brouhaha. The **encierro** (running of the bulls) takes place at 8am every morning; hyper-adrenalized men in white shirts and red sashes flee from not-so-innocuous herbivores that charge 825m down the streets to the bull ring *(Plaza de Toros).* It lasts about 2-3min. when the bulls stay packed; isolated bulls are far more dangerous, since they'll run into the crowds. Try not to cower in a doorway; 3 people were recently trapped and killed by bulls this way. Many are injured at the end of the course, where a terribly narrow opening rudely interrupts the bravado. If you decide to participate, watch an *encierro* first. At all costs avoid running with the dangerous, enormous weekend bunch: there's lots of pushing, shoving and pain. To witness the madness, be at the Santo Domingo stairs or inside Pl. Toros itself by 7am. The scene in the **bull ring** is exciting enough for those who would rather not be mauled, but seats (1500ptas or more a head) sell out fast. Two free sections are reserved in the stands for women and children. At day's end, the hoopla moves into the streets with dancing in the alleys, spontaneous parades and a no-holds-barred party on Pl. Castillo. The truly inspired carousing takes place the first few days of the *fiesta*. Nearby towns sponsor *encierros* too—Tudela in the last week of July, Estella in the first week of August, Tafalla the week of August 15, and Sangüesa the week of September 12.

During non-*Sanfermines* time (the other 51 weeks of the year), a different but no less enchanting side of Pamplona emerges. The city is all elegance, with its broad, airy Enlightenment streets and the historic alleyways of the old Jewish quarter. The pentagonal **Ciudadela**, with its duck pond, deer park and strollable gravel paths, sprawls next to the delicious **Jardines de la Taconera.** On weekends, the bars in the **Casco Antiguo** climax with youth activity.

Practical Information, Accommodations, and Food RENFE, off Av. San Jorge, has crappy connections to the outside world. Better to take swift **buses** from the station on C. Conde Oliveto (at the corner of C. Yanguas y Miranda) to Madrid (5 per day, 5½hr., 2905ptas), Barcelona (3-6 per day, 5½hr., 3480ptas, San Sebastián (7 per day, 1½hr., 635ptas), and the Navarrese Pyrenees. Bus 9 (20min., 75ptas) runs from the train station to the head of Po. Sarasate, which leads to central Pl. Castillo. If you have Jedi powers of mind control, the sort of luck that wins sweepstakes, truckloads of cash, or a large gun, you *may* be able to find a room during the first few days of *Sanfermines*. Check papers for **casas particulares** or stay in a nearby town. The **tourist office** is here at C. Duque de Ahumada, 3 (tel. (948) 22 07 41), to help you. They have a functional map and bus info, but provide little information on budget beds. Find the office from Pl. Castillo by turning left off Av. Carlos III onto C. Duque de Ahumada. Information on **currency exchange** and buses to campsites are on the office's bulletin board. (Open Mon.-Sat. 9:30am-2:30pm and 3:30-7:30pm, Sun. 9:30am-2:30pm; Oct.-June Mon.-Fri. 10am-2pm and 4-7pm, Sat. 10am-2pm.) Store **luggage** at the bus station (July 5-14 open 24hrs., 200ptas per day; otherwise, 115-170ptas per day; open 6:15am-9:30pm, Sun. 7am-9:30pm) or the train station (300ptas per day; open 5:30am-1:30am). Be wary; theft multiplies during *Sanfermines,* and the areas by the walls in the *casco antiguo* are a nighttime no-no.

When the bulls stop running, snap up a bed on Calle San Gregorio and its continuation, Calle San Nicolás. **Hostal Bearán,** C. San Nicolás, 25 (tel. (948) 22 34 28), has comfy, pink-trimmed rooms. (Doubles with bath 5000ptas; Oct.-May 2500ptas.) Across the street, Quaker-like rooms await friends inside the **Fonda La Aragonesa** (Singles 3000ptas. Doubles 3500ptas. Oct.-May: 2500ptas; 3000ptas.) Enact your favorite jailbird fantasy in **Hostal Otano,** C. San Nicolás, 5 (tel. (948) 22 50 95), once a prison. It now has gorgeous rooms, tasteful furniture, and oil paintings. (Singles 2000ptas, with bath 2700ptas. Doubles 3500ptas, with bath 5000ptas.) A La Montañesa bus runs from Pl. Toros 4 times per day to **Camping Ezcaba** (tel. (948) 33 03 15; 425ptas per person, tent, car; open June-Oct.). Look on Calle Navarrería (near the cathedral), Calle Estafeta and Calle Mayor for frenzied feeding. At C. San Nicolás, 19-21, **Restaurante Sarasate** serves a nutritious *menú* (1175ptas) amid Indian tapestries (open Mon.-Thurs. 1:15-4pm, Fri.-Sat. 1:15-4pm and 9-11pm).

■ OLITE

Enchanting Olite is absurdly close to the stereotype of the little Spanish town. The Río Cidacos trickles by the slender walls of the **Palacio Real,** which rises proudly out of the flatlands 42km south of Pamplona, in the very center of **Plaza Carlos III el Noble.** In the early 15th century, King Carlos III made this sumptuous palace of pointed turrets, arched windows, soaring stone walls, and flowery courtyards the focus of Navarrese courtly life. Ramparts, spiral staircases, guard towers, lookout perches, moats, alligators, distressed damsels, dragons, armored attackers, poison-dipped arrows, and court jesters—this is the medieval palace of your dreams. (Palace open Mon.-Sat. 10am-2pm and 5-7pm, Sun. 10am-2pm; Oct.-March Mon.-Sat. 10am-2pm and 4-5pm, Sun. 10am-2pm. Free.)

Vitoria-Gasteiz-Zaragoza line **trains** arrive from Pamplona (2-3 per day, 35min., 400ptas). **Conda** (tel. (948) 82 03 42) and **La Tafallesa** (tel. (948) 70 09 79) run **buses** to Pamplona (45min., 380ptas) and Tudela (45min., 390ptas). From the bus stop on Ctra. Zaragoza, turn left (if coming from Pamplona) to reach Pl. Carlos III. The metal staircase in the middle of the plaza leads to the helpful **tourist office** (tel. (948) 71 24 34; open April-Sept. Mon.-Sat. 10am-2pm and 4:30-7:30pm). The luxurious and rarefied air of the court lingers in many of Olite's restaurants and accommodations, and they charge accordingly. An exception is the budget-minded **Fonda Gambarte**, R. Seco, 13, 2nd fl. (tel. (948) 74 01 39), off Pl. Carlos III (doubles 3000ptas; call ahead).

■■■ JACA

Pilgrims to Santiago once recuperated from the trek through the Pyrenees at this first major stop on their route, the ancient capital of the Kingdom of Aragón. Today the pilgrimage has reversed directions; most people now head through Jaca *toward* the Aragonese Pyrenees for spectacular hiking and skiing. The **tourist office** at Av. Regimiento, 2 (tel. (974) 36 00 98), past C. Mayor, has lots of hiking information (open Mon.-Fri. 9am-2pm and 4:30-8pm, Sat. 9am-1:30pm and 5-8pm, Sun. 10am-1:30pm; mid-Sept.-June Mon.-Fri. 9am-1pm and 4:30-7pm, Sat. 10am-1pm and 5-7pm). Shuttle buses run from downtown to train station roughly ½hr. before each train leaves. They stop at Ayuntamiento on C. Mayor or (if closed) at the taxi stop, and at the bus station. The **train station** at northeast end of Av. Juan XXIII serves Zaragoza (3 per day, 3hr., 1065ptas) and Madrid (1 per day, 6½hr., 3200ptas). La **Oscense** (tel. (974) 35 50 60) sends **buses** to Zaragoza (2-3 per day, 2½hr., 1210ptas) and nearby towns.

Jaca's *hostales* and *pensiones* are mainly grouped around C. Mayor and the cathedral. **Albergue Juvenil de Vacaciones (HI),** is at Av. Perimetral, 6 (tel. (974) 36 05 36). Follow Av. Jacetania-Oroel to the left (facing town) halfway around the town's perimeter, and go down the broad stone steps capped by the modern metal sculpture. The hostel is across and to the right. Swarming with youth groups, these barracks scream "summer camp," and are distant from the train station and everything else. (Reception open 8am-4pm and 7pm-midnight. 950ptas per person, over 26: 1100ptas. Nonmembers 100ptas more. Sheets 250ptas.) Several centuries worth of cleanliness and comfort await inside **Hostal Sompart,** C. Echegarery, 11 (tel. (974) 36 34 10), for only 100-200ptas more than surrounding pensiones. (Doubles 4000-4500ptas. Triples 6000ptas. Low-season: 3600-4000ptas; 5500ptas.) **Habitaciones Martínez,** C. Mayor, 53 (tel. (974) 36 33 74), is run by a management that gushes over *Let's Go* travelers. New rooms down the street have elegant bedspreads (1800ptas per person). Older rooms above bar are smaller (1500ptas per person). Camp at **Peña Oroel** (tel. (974) 36 02 15), 3½km down the road to Sabiñánigo, with its wooded grounds and first-rate facilities. (490ptas per person, tent, or car. Open *Semana Santa* and mid-June to mid-Sept.)

■ PARQUE NACIONAL DE ORDESA Y MONTE PERDIDO

The real things to see are the mountains and valleys that surround Jaca. Getting to Parque Nacional de Ordesa y Monte Perdido can mean riding along with the mail for an hour, and then hiking 9km. It would be worth crawling twice that distance to experience the park's primeval majesty, with cascades, rivers, and miles of trails crossing sheer, poplar-covered mountain faces. If you only have a day to spend in Ordesa, the **Soaso Circle** is the most practical hike, especially for virgin mountaineers. A far more rugged climb begins at the Refugio Góriz and climbs **Monte Perdido** (3355m; mountaineering equipment recommended). Count on eight hours there and back from the *refugio* (for details call (974) 48 63 79 or 48 63 75). For any of these hikes, the *Editorial Alpina* topographical map is an absolute must (on sale at the souvenir shop by the parking lot for a hefty 650ptas). Get trail maps (300ptas) and information about the park from the **ICONA office** in Torla on C. Francia (tel. (974) 48 63 48; open in summer 9am-2pm and 4-8pm). The **information booth** at the park entrance is also open in summer.

Buses go only as far as **Torla**, a small stone village 9km short of the park; a mail-delivery bus leaves **Sabiñánigo** Mon.-Sat. at 10am, stopping in Torla at 11:55am before continuing to Aínsa. Sabiñánigo connects easily by bus or train to Jaca and Huesca (2-5 buses per day from Jaca, 15 min., 150ptas; all trains on the Zaragoza-Huesca-Jaca line stop in Sabiñánigo). Renting a car is easier, and Jaca is one of the few places those under 21 can rent one—**Aldecar** on Av. Jacetania, 60 (tel. (974) 36 07 81), left from the bus station and downhill. (3500ptas per day, 25ptas per km.) In the park, **camping** is limited to one night at heights over 2200m above the Soaso Steps, but the 120-bed **Refugio Góriz** (one of many *refugios*), about 4hr. from the parking lot, has winter heating and meager hot showers (950ptas per person). Get a preview of the *refugio* feel while still in Torla in the **Refugio L'Atalaya,** C. Francia, 45 (tel. (974) 48 60 22; 900ptas per person). If you want your own room, go farther up Torla's only crossroad, where **Fonda Ballarín,** C. Capuvita, 11 (tel. (974) 48 61 55) costs 1500ptas for singles, 2700ptas for doubles (mid-Sept. to June 1400ptas; 2500ptas). There's angling in the river at **Camping Río Ara** (tel. (974) 48 62 48), about 1km down the paved path from its sign off Ctra. Ordesa, right before the bridge (380ptas per person, per tent, and per car; open March-Nov.).

CATALONIA (CATALUNYA)

Hemmed in by the Pyrenees to the north and the Rio Ebro delta to the south, Catalonia is a privileged land. This prosperous region has always proudly held itself apart from the remainder of the country, retaining its own culture and tongue. Colonized by Greeks and Carthaginians, Catalonia (or Tarraconensis) was one of Rome's favored provinces. In the second half of the 18th century, Catalonia rapidly developed into one of Europe's premier textile manufacturing centers, and industrial expansion through the 19th century underpinned a flowering of the arts and sciences now known as a Catalan *Renaixença* (Renaissance). Having fought on the losing side in the Civil War, Catalonia lost its autonomy in 1939; Catalan instruction was widely suppressed, and publication in the language was limited. Since autonomy was recovered in 1977, Catalan media and arts have flourished. The language (it's not a dialect) is once again official in Spain and some are currently pushing for the right to speak Catalan in the Senate; the region itself is almost entirely bilingual.

The jagged cliffs of the Costa Brava cut into the Mediterranean Sea from Barcelona north to the French border. Craggy precipices and hairpin turns render parts of the coast unnavigable even by the most modern land transportation; many buses zigzag between the coastal towns and safer inland routes. The juxtaposition of mountains and sea, trees and rocks, make it the paradise of the perambulatory naturalist. Rocky shores have enchanted artists—Chagall set up his canvas here, and Surrealist icon Salvador Dalí hailed from the region.

■■■ BARCELONA

Grand, sprawling, self-confident Barcelona embodies Catalonia's artistic genius and commercial resourcefulness. It boasts a long reputation for being the nation's most cosmopolitan, sophisticated, and progressive city. In Middle Ages, Barcelona was the capital of a fat commercial empire, but the discovery of the Americas turned the Atlantic into the hip trade route and left the Mediterranean neglected. Not until the 19th century did the Industrial Revolution's textile mills restore Barcelona's glory,

Barcelona

1 Regional Tourist Office
2 City Tourist Office
3 City Tourist Office
4 Budget Travel: TIVE
5 American Consulate
6 Canadian Consulate
7 U. K. Consulate
8 American Express Office
9 Main Post Office
10 Estació de França
11 Estació de Sants
12 Estació de la
   Plaça de Catalunya
13 Estació del Passeig de Gràcia
14 Police Station
15 Youth Hostel
16 La Seu
17 Palau de la Generalitat
18 Ajuntament
19 Santa Mafía del Mar
20 Museu Picasso
21 Gran Teatre del Liceu
22 Museu Marítim
23 Temple Expiatori de la
   Sagrada Família
24 Palau de la Música Catalana
25 Palau Nacional
26 Estadi Olímpic
27 Palau Sant Jordi
28 Vila Olímpica

SPAIN

MONTJUÏC

nurturing the bourgeoisie who shared the wealth with a pioneering generation of artists and musicians. The 20th century brought political unrest and the rise of anarchism when, during the Spanish Civil War, the anti-Fascist coalition operated out of Barcelona. In recent decades the city has been receptive to the political activism of feminists, gays, and other groups. Barcelona used the 1992 Olympics to reinvent itself. Substandard hotels fell to the wrecking ball, new parks and sculpture gardens were planted, pedestrian zones expanded, and over 50 monuments restored.

ORIENTATION AND PRACTICAL INFORMATION

On Spain's Mediterranean coast 200km from the French border, Barcelona is Spain's second most important transport connection; most traffic to and from the rest of Europe passes through here. **Plaça de Catalunya** marks the center of the city. From here, **Las Ramblas** and **Via Laietana** run straight to the harbor. From the harbor end of Las Ramblas as you face toward Pl. Catalunya, **Montjuïc**, site of the 1992 Olympic stadium, rises to the left, and the towering **Vila Olímpica** (Olympic Village) is along the shore to the right. The **Barri Gòtic**, centered on the cathedral and Plaça Sant Jaume, lies in between. On the left side of Las Ramblas toward the port is **Barri Xinès**, the city's red-light district. From Pl. Catalunya toward the mountains away from Las Ramblas, the **Eixample** borders the Gran Via de les Corts Catalanes along its lower edge and is bisected by **Passeig de Gràcia.** The upper limit of the grid-planned neighborhood is Avinguda Diagonal, which separates the Eixample from the older neighborhood of **Gràcia,** in the foothills of the mountains encircling Barcelona.

Barcelona is a relatively safe city. Pickpocketing is the most common crime, mainly on and near Las Ramblas and in the train stations. Plaça Reial and Carrer Escudellers should be avoided altogether after dark, and Barri Xinès is not safe for lone walkers at night.

Tourist Offices: La Gran Via de les Corts Catalanes, 658 (tel. 301 74 43). M: Urquinaona (L1, L4) or Pl. Catalunya (L1, L3, L5). 2 blocks from the Pg. Gràcia intersection, in the Eixample. Open Mon.-Fri. 9am-7pm, Sat. 9am-2pm. **Estació Central de Barcelona-Sants,** Pl. Països Catalans, s/n (tel. 491 44 31). M: Sants-Estació (L1, L5). Info on Barcelona only. Open 8am-8pm, Sat.-Sun. 8am-2pm. **Aeroport El Prat de Llobregat,** International Terminal (tel. 478 47 04), 25m to the left of the customs exit. Info on all of Spain. Open Mon.-Sat. 9:30am-8pm, Sun. 9:30am-3pm.

Budget Travel: TUJUCA (TIVE), C. Calàbria, 147 (tel. 483 83 78). M: Rocafort (L1), 2 bl. from the metro. Come early: in summer there's often a wait. Eurotrain tickets, cheap buses, flights, and ISIC. Open 9am-1pm and 4-5:30pm. **Centre d'Informació: Assessorament per a Joves,** C. Ferran, 32 (tel. 402 78 03). More of a local student assistance office than a travel agency. Plenty of free advice and a bulletin board with events for youths. Excellent library of travel guides, including *Let's Go.* Open Mon.-Fri. 10am-2pm and 4-8pm.

Consulates: U.S., Pg. Reina Elisenda, 23 (tel. 280 22 27, fax 205 52 06). M: FFCC, Reina Elisenda. Open Mon.-Fri. 9am-12:30pm and 3-5pm. **Canada,** Via Augusta, 125 (tel. 209 06 34). M: FFCC, Sant Gervase or Muntaner; any line from Pl. Catalunya except Tibidabo. Open Mon.-Fri. 9am-1pm. **U.K.,** Av. Diagonal, 477 (tel. 419 90 44, fax 405 24 11). M: Diagonal (L3, L5). Open Mon.-Fri. 10am-2pm. **Ireland,** Gran Via Carles III, 94 (tel. 330 96 52). **Australia,** Gran Via Carles III, 98 (tel. 330 94 96, fax 411 09 04). M: María Cristina (L3). Open Mon.-Fri. 10am-2pm. **New Zealand,** Travessera de Gràcia, 64 (tel. 209 03 99. **South Africa,** Gran Via de les Corts Catalanes 634-636 (tel. 318 07 97).

American Express: Pg. Gràcia, 101 (tel. 217 00 70, fax 415 37 00). M: Diagonal (L3, L5). The entrance is on C. Rosselló, around the corner. Mail held. Multilingual 24hr. ATM machine outside. Open Mon.-Fri. 9:30am-6pm, Sat. 10am-noon.

Currency Exchange: The best rates are at the **banks** in the Eixample; 1% commission on greenbacks (min. 300ptas). Banking hours are Mon.-Fri. 8:30am-2pm. **El Corte Inglés** (Pl. Catalunya; open Mon.-Sat. 9am-9pm) changes traveler's checks with no commission or minimum. On Sun. you can change money at **Estació de**

Sants (tel. 490 77 70) for a 1% commission on checks and bills (500ptas min.). Open 8am-10pm, except Dec. 25, 26 and Jan. 1, 6. The exchanges on **Las Ramblas** may be temptingly convenient on Sun., but they often charge the maximum commission (9.8%).

Post Office: Pl. Antoni López (tel. 318 38 31), at the end of Via Laietana near the port. M: Jaume I or Barceloneta (L4). Open for stamps Mon.-Fri. 8am-10pm, Sat. 8am-2pm; for *Lista de Correos* (general delivery) Mon.-Fri. 8am-9pm, Sat. 9am-2pm; for **telegrams** Mon.-Sat. 8am-8pm. **Postal Code:** 08002.

Telephones: Central Telephone Exchange, C. Fontanella, 2, just off Pl. Catalunya. M: Catalunya (L1, L3). Open Mon.-Sat. 8:30am-9pm. Another is at Estació Sants. M: Sants-Estació (L3, L5). Open 7:45am-11pm. **City Code:** 93.

Flights: Airport at **El Prat de Llobregat** (tel. 478 50 00), 12km southwest of Barcelona. RENFE Trains (every ½hr., 20min., 260ptas) to **Estació Central-Sants** (M: L1, L5; on the southwestern edge of the city), then **Plaça de Catalunya** (M: L1, L3; in the center). Late-night **bus** service (bus EN) from the airport to the Plaça de Espanya (M 21, 25) 9pm-2:40am, or from Pl. Espanya (on corner of Av. Reina María Cristina and the Gran Via) to the airport 9:40pm-3:15am.

Trains: RENFE information (tel. 490 02 02; open 7:30am-10:30pm). **Estació Sants,** M: Sants-Estació (L3, L4), is the domestic and international hub. To: Madrid (6 per day, 3900ptas); Valencia (14 per day, 4½hr., 3000ptas); Seville (8 per day, 12-14hr., 6900ptas); Milan (1 per day, 18hr., 8825ptas); Paris (5 per day, 9650 ptas). **Estació França,** Av. Marqués de L'Argentera, M: Barceloneta (L3), serves fewer domestic and international destinations. Both stations open 6am-11pm.

Buses: Enatcar, Estació del Nord (tel. 245 25 28). M: Arc de Triomf (L1). Open 6am-1am. To: Madrid (5 per day, 8hr., 2600ptas); Valencia (9 per day, 4hr., 2650ptas). **Julià Via,** C. Viriato (tel. 490 40 00), to the right of Estació-Sants. M: Estació-Sants (L3, L5). Open 9am-8pm. To: Paris (6 per week, 15hr., 9225ptas); Frankfurt (3 per week, 19hr., 11,160ptas). **Sarfa,** Estació del Nord (tel. 265 11 58). Open 8am-8pm. Services many beach towns along the Costa Brava.

Ferries: Transmediterránea, Av. Drassanes, 6 (tel. 317 42 62). M: Drassanes (L3). From the metro, Columbus points the way from his perch to **Estació Marítima** (tel. 317 42 62). Open Mon.-Fri. 9am-1pm and 4-6pm, Sat. 9am-noon. During the summer, voyages most days between Barcelona and Mallorca (8hr.), Menorca (9hr.), and Ibiza (9½hr.). *Butaca* seat 6100ptas, but cabins are cheap too.

Public Transportation: tel. 412 00 00. *Guía del Transport Públic,* available free at tourist offices and at the transport information booth in Pl. Catalunya, maps out all 4 of the city's metro lines and bus routes (day and night). Metro (M) and bus rides cost 120ptas, a 10-ride Metro pass 600ptas, 10-ride Metro and bus pass 625ptas. Hold onto your ticket or pass throughout the trip; riding without a receipt carries a 5000ptas fine. Metro open Mon.-Thurs. 5am-11pm; Fri., Sat., holidays 5am-1am; Sun. 6am-midnight. Routes vary, but day buses usually run 5am-10pm and night buses from 11pm-4am.

Taxis: tel. 358 11 11, 330 08 04, 357 77 55, or 300 38 11. The first 6min. or 1.9km cost 250ptas, then it's 102ptas per km. Airport-Barcelona costs 2000-3500ptas.

Car Rental: Tot Car, C. Josep Terradellas, 93 (tel. 405 34 33). Free delivery and pickup. 2100ptas per day, 21ptas each additional km. Insurance 1100ptas per day. Mon.-Sat. 9am-2pm and 4-8pm.

Hitchhiking: Those hitching to France take the metro to Fabra i Puig, then Av. Meridiana to reach A-7. Those en route to Tarragona and Valencia take bus 7 from Rambla Catalunya at Gran Via. The *autopista* access lies near here. With the proper sign, this approach also puts hitchers on the A-2 to Zaragoza, the beginning of the trek to Madrid. Hitching on *autopistas* (toll roads, marked by an "A") is illegal, but it is permitted on national (N) highways. **Barnastop,** C. Sant Ramon, 24 (tel. 443 06 32), on the corner of Non de Rambla. M: Liceu (L3). Matches drivers with riders. 3ptas per km to driver in Spain, 4ptas per km outside Spain. 1-2ptas per km commission. Open Mon.-Fri. 11am-2pm and 5-8pm, Sat. 5-8pm, or call and leave a message on the machine.

Luggage Storage: Estació Sants. M: Sants-Estació (L1, L3). Lockers 400 and 600ptas. **Estació França.** M: Barceloneta (L1). Lockers 300 and 500ptas. Open 6:30am-11pm. **Estació del Nord,** M: Arc de Triomf (L1). Lockers 300ptas. Open

Mon.-Fri. 7:30am-7pm, Sat. 8am-noon. Many of the hostels will store for about 150ptas per bag per day.

English Bookstores: Librería Francesa, Pg. Gràcia, 91 (tel. 215 14 17). M: Diagonal (L3, L5). Open Mon.-Fri. 9:30am-2:30pm and 4-8:30pm, Sat. 9:30am-2pm.

Laundromats: Lava Super, C. Carme, 63, off Las Ramblas by the Palau Virreina. Wash and dry 1000ptas per 5kg. Open Mon.-Fri. 8am-8pm, Sat. 8am-2pm.

Gay and Lesbian Association: Grup de Lesbianes Feministes de Barcelona, Gran Via de les Corts Catalanes, 549, 4th fl. (tel. 323 33 07). M: Catalunya (L1, L3). Less than 1 bl. from Pg. Gràcia heading away from Pl. Catalunya.

Late-Night Pharmacy: Pharmacies stay open late on a rotating basis. Check signs in pharmacy windows for current listings.

Medical Assistance: Médicos de Urgencia, C. Pelai, 40 (tel. 412 12 12). M: Catalunya (L1, L3), close to the end of the street that meets Las Ramblas and Pl. Catalunya. Hospitals also useful as an emergency drug store.

Emergencies: Ambulance, tel. 061. **Fire,** tel. 080. **Police,** Station at Las Ramblas, 43 (tel. 301 90 60), across from Pl. Real, next to C. Nou de la Rambla. M: Liceu (L3). English spoken. **Municipal Police,** tel. 092. **National Police,** tel. 091.

ACCOMMODATIONS AND CAMPING

Hostal and *pensión* signs catch the eye every 3 doors. Quality varies, but the benefits of the 1992 Olympic frenzy are still evident—newly painted walls, upgraded bathrooms, and new beds, which become a rare commodity during peak season (July-August).

Hostels

Albergue de Juventud Kabul, Pl. Reial, 17 (tel. 318 51 90). M: Liceu (L3). Head toward the port from the metro; turn left after C. Ferran to enter Pl. Reial. Upon entering the plaza, turn right and walk to the end. In the words of their own brochure, "a great party atmosphere." Showers and freshly painted rooms. 5-day max. stay. Open 24hrs. 1000ptas. Sheets 200ptas. Laundry 500ptas per kg. Luggage storage 100ptas per day.

Alberg Juvenil Palau (HI), C. Palau, 6 (tel. 412 50 80). M: Jaume I (L4). 1 bl. from Pl. Sant Jaume: take C. Ciutat to C. Templaris, then take the 2nd left. Friendly, small hostel in the heart of the Barri Gòtic. 6-night max. stay. 2-8 people per room. 1100ptas. Breakfast included. Kitchen open 7-10pm. Sheets 150ptas. Hostel open 7am-midnight and 3-3:15am. Reservations with one night's deposit.

Alberg Mare de Déu de Montserrat (HI), Pg. Mare de Déu del Coll, 41-51 (tel. 210 51 51), beyond Park Güell. Bus 28 from Pl. Catalunya stops across the street from the hostel. Otherwise take the metro to Vallcarca (L3), walk up Av. República Argentina and across C. Viaducte de Vallcarca; from there, signs point the way up the hill. Members only. Renovated villa with its own private woods and a hilltop view of Barcelona. Institutional sleeping areas. 5-night max. stay. Reception open 7:30-9:30am, 5-7:30pm, and 8:30-10pm. Lockout 10am-1:30pm for cleaning. Check-in 5pm. Midnight curfew; doors open at 1 and 2am sharp for stragglers. 1300ptas, over 25 1925ptas, and 500pta deposit for ID card. Breakfast (8-9am) included. Sheets 350ptas. No reservations.

Hotels and Pensions

Barri Gòtic and Las Ramblas

Barcelona's *ciutat vella* (old quarter) has a wealth of accommodations and eateries for the impoverished traveler.

Casa de Huéspedes Mari-Luz, C. Palau, 4 (tel. 317 34 63). M: Jaume I (L4) or Liceu (L3). 1 block from Pl. Sant Jaume. Take C. Ciutat to C. Templaris, then take the 2nd left. After dark it is safer not to approach from Escudellers. Basic rooms, sparkling new showers, keys for 24hr. entry, and a li'l extra TLC. 1200ptas per person (less in winter). Reservations accepted from repeat visitors only.

Hostal Residència Romay, C. Avinyó, 58 (tel. 317 94 14). M: Drassanes (L3). Toward the end of Las Ramblas, turn left onto C. Josep Clavé; C. Avinyó lies on the left after the church. Directly above Pensión Albi. Marble reception, stark white halls, a large comfy chair, some beds. Keys for 24hr. entry. Singles 1500ptas. Doubles 2000ptas, with bath 2500ptas.

Hostal Levante, Baixada de San Miguel, 2 (tel. 317 95 65). M: Liceu (L3). Walk down C. Ferran and turn right on C. Avinyó; Bda. San Miguel is the first left. New sparkly tiled floors and bathrooms. Singles 2000ptas. Doubles 3200ptas, with shower 4000ptas. Reservations and credit cards accepted.

Pensión Bienestar, C. Quintana, 3 (tel. 318 72 83). M: Liceu (L3). 2 blocks from Las Ramblas, off C. Ferran. This quiet *pensión* offers 27 rooms with high ceilings and freshly painted walls. Bathrooms large enough to sleep in. Singles 1500ptas. Doubles 2400ptas. Triples 3600ptas.

Hostal Marítima, Las Ramblas, 4 (tel. 302 31 52). M: Drassanes (L3). At port end of Las Ramblas; follow the signs to *Museo de Cera* next door. Prime location on the main drag has noisy drawbacks. Bathrooms leave much to be desired. Singles 1500ptas. Doubles 2600ptas, with shower 3500ptas. Laundry 800ptas.

Pensión Fernando, C. Volta de Remei, 4 (tel. 301 79 93). M: Liceu (L3). Fourth left off C. Ferran walking from Las Ramblas. Also run by Mari-Luz and Fernando, this *pensión* offers small, affordable rooms stuffed with furniture. Keys for 24hr. entry. 1300ptas per person. Reservations accepted.

Hostal Residència Segura, Junta de Comerç, 11 (tel. 302 51 74), off C. Hospital. M: Liceu (L3). Firm beds and clean bathrooms. Ask for a room with a sink. Singles 1500-2000ptas. Doubles 2500-3000ptas. Triples 3500-4000ptas.

Hostal Residència Marmo, C. Gignás, 25 (tel. 315 42 08). M: Jaume I (L4). From Via Laietana, C. Angel Baixeras narrows into C. Gignás. Spacious rooms with over-sized, polished furniture and vaulted ceilings possess an antique charm. Keys for 24hr. entry. Singles 1500ptas. Doubles 3000ptas.

Pensión Aviñó 42, C. Avinyó, 42 (tel. 318 79 45), next door to Hostal Residència Romay. M: Drassanes (L3). Faux stained-glass windows brought down a peg (and up a few centuries) by pink bathrooms. Singles 1500ptas. Doubles 2000-3000ptas. Prices vary according to length of stay and time of year.

Hostal Layetana, Pl. Ramón Berenguer el Gran, 2 (tel. 319 20 12). M: Jaume I (L4). Less than 1 bl. from the metro, on the far side of the *plaça*. Balconies overlook ancient Roman walls that never imagined they would be so close to immaculate bathrooms with individually wrapped bars of soap. Singles 2000ptas. Doubles 3500ptas-4800ptas. Shower 200ptas. Reservations recommended July-Aug.

Near Plaça de Catalunya

A bit pricier than in the Barri Gòtic, accommodations here are safer and more mod-ern, while still close to the action (and rumble) of Las Ramblas. Ideal for groups of two or more. The metro stop is Pl. Catalunya (L1, L3) unless otherwise specified.

Hotel Toledano/Hostal Residència Capitol, La Rambla, 138 (tel. 301 08 72, fax 412 31 42). Facing Las Ramblas from Pl. Catalunya, it's 50m away on the left. This family owned, split-level hotel-*hostal* has been making tourists happy for 76 years. English-speaking owner. Keys for 24hr. entry. Singles 2500ptas. Doubles 3800-4300ptas. Quads 5600-6300ptas. Prices are for *hostal* only and don't include IVA. Reservations and credit cards accepted.

Pensión Noya, La Rambla, 133 (tel. 301 48 31). Above noisy restaurant Núria, so you can nibble to postpone sleepiness. This 10-room retreat welcomes backpack-ers with open arms. Singles 1600ptas. Doubles 2600ptas. Reservations accepted.

Pensión L'Isard, C. Tallers, 82 (tel. 302 51 83), directly opposite the University. M: Universitat (L1). Quiet, relaxing rooms with new mattresses, tiling, sinks, and bal-cony. Keys for 24hr. entry. Singles 1800ptas. Doubles 3500-4500ptas. Triples 4500ptas. Reservations with deposit.

Hostal Plaza, C. Fontanella, 18 (tel. 301 01 39), down the street from Pensión Aris. Adopted by eager-to-please Americans just starting in the Spanish *pensión* busi-ness. Art and 3-speed fans. Singles 2500ptas. Doubles 3500-4000ptas. Triples 6000ptas. Prices may vary. Laundry 1000ptas per 5kg. Credit cards accepted.

Pensión Estal, C. Santa Anna, 27 (tel. 302 26 18). Rooms offer views of Iglesia Santa Anna. French-speaking owner. Singles 1500-2000ptas. Doubles 3000-4000ptas.

Hostal Residència Lausanne, Av. Portal de L'Angel, 24 (tel. 302 11 39). Amid the shopping promenade, a quiet back terrace provides sanctuary from Barcelona's evening intensity. Singles 2000ptas. Doubles 3000-3990ptas. Triples 4500ptas.

Residència Australia, Ronda Universitat, 11 (tel. 317 41 77). A gregarious English-speaking owner shows that she cares with embroidered sheets and curtains, a spotless bathroom, ceiling fans in rooms, and winter heating. Singles 2350ptas. Doubles 3450-4200ptas. Prices don't include IVA.

Pensión Nevada, Av. Portal de L'Angel, 16 (tel. 302 31 01), just past Hostal Lausanne. Your cozy bedroom away from home on the range. Try to get the room with the Dungeons & Dragons figure. Keys for 24hr. entry. Singles 2000ptas. Doubles 4400ptas.

Residència Victoria, C. Comtal, 9 (tel. 317 45 97). Walking from Pl. Catalunya, take the first left on Av. Portal de L'Angel. Popular with foreign students. Full kitchen, TV, washer/dryer, and open-air dining room. 5-day min. stay. Singles 2000ptas, one month 48,000ptas. Doubles 3000ptas. Reservations required at least 15 days in advance.

Pensión Santa Anna, C. Santa Anna, 23 (tel. 301 22 46). What this place lacks in size and ambience, it makes up with clean bathrooms and firm beds. Singles 2000ptas. Doubles 3000ptas. Triples 3500ptas.

Pensión Aris, C. Fontanella, 14 (tel. 318 10 17), 2 bl. past the Telefónica on the right. Memories of the Olympics hang on white-washed walls with light blue trim. 21st-century windows shut out all sound. Singles 2000ptas. Doubles 3500-4500ptas. Triple 4500ptas.

The Eixample

The most beautiful *hostales* are found here along wide, safe *avingudas.* Most have huge entryways with colorful tiles and steel and wood *Modernista* elevators.

Hostal Residència Palacios, Gran Via de les Corts Catalanes, 629bis (tel. 301 37 92), across from the main tourist office. M: Catalunya (L1, L3) or Urquinaona (L1, L4). Rooms are well-furnished, if a little dark. Singles 2300–3750ptas. Doubles 3500-4500ptas. Breakfast 300ptas. Prices do not include IVA. Reservations and credit cards accepted.

Hostal Residència Windsor, Rambla Catalunya, 84 (tel. 215 11 98), above the Hostal Líder. M: Pg. Gràcia (L4, L3). Aristocratic *hostal* lives up to its name with crimson carpets and palatial quarters. Each room decorated differently—cheers for Anglo-Saxon individualism. Singles 2900-3700ptas. Doubles 4900-6000ptas.

Hostal Residència Oliva, Pg. Gràcia, 32, 4th fl. (tel. 488 01 62), on the intersection with C. Disputació. M: Pg. Gràcia (L4, L3). Sedate lounge with a long, polished wooden table encourages guests to write the great 20th-century novel. Singles 2650ptas. Doubles 4770-5830ptas.

Hostal Residència Montserrat, Pg. Gràcia, 114 (tel. 217 27 00). M: Diagonal (L3, L5, FFCC). Hidden on the right side of Diagonal as you face Tibidabo. Small lounge in the reception area with bloated leather couches. Singles 3000ptas. Doubles 4715ptas. Breakfast 400ptas. Reservations held 24hrs.

Gràcia

In Gràcia, 5-10min. on foot from Diagonal, families and travelers mingle in a calm, neighborhood setting. The accommodations listed here are small and elegant. Neighborhood bars and *pastelerías* remain "undiscovered."

Pensión Norma, C. Gran de Gràcia, 87 (tel. 237 44 78). M: Fontana (L3). Rooms with life-size dressers and tables, but your own house could never be this clean. So newly-renovated as to be austere. Singles 1500ptas. Doubles 3000-4000ptas.

Hostal Bonavista, C. Bonavista, 21 (tel. 237 37 57). M: Diagonal (L3, L5). In a lush neighborhood off the northern end of Pg. Gràcia. Well-kept rooms dotted with pictures of horses and their successors (old-fashioned cars). Keys for 24hr. entry. Singles 1887ptas. Doubles 2642-3680ptas. Showers 300ptas.

Pensión San Medín, C. Gran de Gràcia, 125 (tel. 217 30 68). M: Fontana (L3). Hallways are lined with faux-corkboard wallpaper and long Persian rugs. Each room has new furniture and a phone. Singles 2500-3500ptas. Double 4300-5300ptas. Showers 200ptas.

Camping

While there is no camping in Barcelona, inter-city buses (150ptas) run to these locations in 20 to 45 minutes: **El Toro Bravo** (tel. 637 34 62), just south of El Prat in Vildecans, accessible by bus L93 from Pl. Universitat or L90 from Pl. Goya (550ptas per person, 600ptas per tent); **Filipinas** (tel. 658 28 95; 550ptas per person and 600ptas per tent) and **La Ballena Alegre** (tel. 658 05 04; 500ptas per person and 1100ptas per tent). The latter two are another km down the road.

FOOD

Barcelona is a city of dining out; just about every block has several places to eat. In the **Eixample,** *patisseries* and cafés offer luscious (but expensive) treats under the shady trees. Closer to the port, bars and cafés are more harried. The **Barri Gòtic** is plastered with 850-950ptas *menús*. Catalan specialities include *mariluz a la romana* (white fish in tomato sauce), *butifarra con judias blancas* (sausage with white beans), and *crema catalana* (Catalan pudding). "La Boquería," officially the **Mercat de Sant Josep,** off Rambla Sant Josep, 89, is Barcelona's best market, with fresh fish and produce in an all-steel *Modernista* structure (open Mon.-Sat. 7am-8pm). **Bakeries** are a cheap alternative, as they often sell cold *bocadillos* (sandwiches). Be aware that food options shrink drastically in August, when restaurateurs and bar owners close up shop and take their vacations.

Restaurante Bidasoa, C. Serra, 21 (tel. 318 10 63). M: Drassanes (L3). Take 3rd left off C. Josep Anselm Clavé from Las Ramblas. They'll stir up whatever your heart desires if you're not satisfied by the 43 permutations of eggs, salad, and fish. Meals under 1000ptas. Open Sept.-July Tues.-Sun. 1:30-4pm and 8-11pm.

El Gallo Kirko, C. Avinyó, 19 (tel. 412 48 38). M: Liceu (L3). Walk down C. Ferran, and it's the 4th right. Built around part of a Roman stone wall erected around Barcelona in the 4th century, EGK specializes in *couscous* (with vegetables, 450ptas) and curry (with beef and rice, 450ptas). Open noon-midnight.

Restaurante Self-Naturista, C. Santa Anna, 11-15 (tel. 318 23 88). M: Catalunya (L1, L3). Self-service vegetarian cafeteria with a jazz background. A wide selection of desserts and salads spills over the counter. Variety of bread, mushroom, and artichoke dishes, most under 400ptas. Open Mon.-Sat.11:30am-10pm.

Restaurante El Cid, C. Princesa, 11 (tel. 319 28 25). M: Jaume I (L4). C. Jaume I becomes C. Princesa at the intersection with Via Laietana. Dimly lit tables, mirrored walls, and a polished wooden bar make for a relaxing dinner. *Paella con espárragos* with appetizer 1100ptas. *Menú* 825ptas. Open Mon.-Sat. 8am-10pm.

Restaurante Riera, C. Joaquín Costa, 30 (tel. 442 50 58). M: Liceu (L3) or Universitat (L1). Off C. Carme coming from Liceu, or off Rda. Sant Antoni coming from Universitat. Flocks of gregarious regulars. Meals change daily, but a heaping plate of *paella* is always available. 3-course gorge-fest with dessert 600ptas. Open Sept.-July Sun.-Thurs. 1-4pm and 8:30-11pm, Fri 1-4pm.

Bar Restaurante Los Toreros, C. Xuclá, 3-5 (tel. 318 23 25), on an alley between C. Fortuny and C. Carme, both off Las Ramblas. M: Catalunya (L1, L3). *Platos combinados* from 500ptas, *menú* 700 ptas. Open Mon.-Fri. 8am-1am, Sun. 8am-5pm.

Restaurante Biocenter, C. Pintor Fortuny, 24 (tel. 302 35 67). M: Catalunya (L1, L3). Across the street from the store of the same name, off Las Ramblas. Sounds threateningly futuristic; it's actually a small and friendly vegetarian restaurant. *Menú* with trip to the salad bar, a bowl of soup, a vegetarian dish, and dessert (975ptas). Open Mon.-Sat. 1-5pm and 8:30-11pm.

Restaurant Les Corts Catalanes, Gran Via de les Corts Catalanes, 603 (tel. 301 03 76), just off Rambla Catalunya. M: Catalunya (L1, L3). Vegetarian staples include *tarta de espinacas con guarnición* (savory spinach cake) and crowd-pleasing *zumo de zanahorias* (carrot juice). Salads 700-1000ptas. Most pastas around 1000ptas. Restaurant open 1-4pm and 8-11pm. Bar and store open 9am-midnight.

SIGHTS

During the summer (June 13-Sept. 27) the easiest way to take in the major sights of Barcelona is to hop on the **Bus Turístic,** sponsored by the city's Patronat de Turisme. (Ajuntament tourist offices have a free pamphlet that maps out the bus route.) The tourist offices have a wealth of information and pamphlets. *Barcelona: One and Only* is a *barrio*-by-*barrio* description of the city; *El Barcelonés* is a quick and dirty glance. And don't leave the office without the Ajuntament's large map of the city, which lists all the museums and Gaudís in Barcelona.

Las Ramblas and Barri Gòtic Dubbed "the most beautiful street in the world" by W. Somerset Maugham, tree-lined **Las Ramblas** runs from Pl. Catalunya to the Monument de Colom at the port. Originally composed of 5 segments, this broad pedestrian lane is a veritable urban carnival: street performers swallow knives, beggars hold out their hands and tourists fiddle with their fanny packs. At the port end, the **Monument de Colom,** erected in 1886, towers over the city. (Elevator open 9am-9pm; Oct.-March Tues.-Sat. 10am-2pm and 3:30-7pm, Sun. 10am-7pm; April-May Tues.-Sat. 10am-2pm and 3:30-8pm, Sun. 10am-8pm. 225ptas. Ticket office open until ½hr. before closing.) Barcelona's drive to recover and refurbish its seafront has resulted in not only Vila Olímpica but also **Moll de la Fusta,** between Pg. Colom and the water, a wide pedestrian zone that leads down to the docks, which are ideal for a slow evening *passeig.*

You can ride westward on the small ferry **Las Golondrinas** (tel. 412 59 14) through Barcelona's busy harbor, past a beautiful view of Montjuïc to the isolated peninsula at the breakwater. (Every ½hr. 11am-8:30pm, Nov.-March Sat.-Sun. 11am-6pm, April and Oct. 11am-6pm, June 11am-7pm. Round-trip 355ptas.)

Strictly speaking, the **Barri Gòtic** (Gothic Quarter) is the area surrounding the cathedral, the Ajuntament, and the Generalitat, but the name also extends to the area between Las Ramblas and Via Laietana. Since Roman times, the handsome **Plaça de Sant Jaume** has been the city's main square. The *plaça* is dominated by two of Catalonia's most important buildings: the **Palau de la Generalitat** (seat of Catalonia's autonomous government) and the **Ajuntament** (city hall). The Gothic **Església Catedral de la Santa Creu** is on C. Bisbe next to the Generalitat (look for its high-flying jagged spires) and the smallish **Plaça de la Seu.** (Cathedral open 8am-1:30pm and 4-7:30pm. Cloister open 8:45am-1:15pm and 4-6:45pm. Museum open 11am-1pm. 50ptas. Ask a guard to let you see the *coro* (choral chamber) for 25ptas) On the opposite side of the cathedral, on C. Comtes, is the **Palau Reial** (Royal Palace). Inside, the **Museu Frederic Marès** holds the sculptor's idiosyncratic personal collection and the **Museu d'Historia de la Ciutat** has the ruins of a Roman colony. (Chambers of the royal palace open Tues.-Sat. 9am-8:30pm, Sun. 9am-1:30pm, Mon.3-8:30pm. Museum open Tues.-Sat. 10am-8pm, Sun. 10am-2pm; Oct.-June Tues.-Sat. 10am-2pm and 4-8pm, Sun. 10am-2pm.)

Barri de la Ribera and Parc de la Ciutadella The venerated **Barri de la Ribera** section of the old city grew with Barcelona's development as a major sea power during the Middle Ages. The **Església Santa María del Mar** on Pl. Santa María, is perhaps the zenith of 14th-century Catalan Gothic design. Entrance around back at Pg. Born, 1. (Open 9am-12:30pm and 5-8pm, occasionally closed Sun. for concert preparations.) Off Pg. del Born, C. Montcada runs up to the world-famous **Museu Picasso** at #15-19, housed in what were once 2 adjacent medieval mansions. Thirty rooms trace the master's development during his turn-of-the-century stay in Barcelona. (Open Tues.-Sat. 10am-8pm, Sun. 10am-3pm. 500ptas.)

The peaceful **Parc de la Ciutadella** hosted the 1888 Universal Exposition; it now harbors several museums and a zoo. *Copito de Nieve* (Little Snowflake), the only captive albino gorilla in the world, is the main attraction at the **Parc Zoològic,** south of the Plaça d'Armes. María finds him disgusting. (Open 9:30am-7:30pm, winter 10am-5pm. 900ptas.) On Pl. Armes is Barcelona's **Museu d'Art Modern,** a potpourri of paintings and sculptures mostly by 20th-century Catalan artists (open Wed.-Mon. 10am-9pm).

The Eixample The 1859 demolition of Barcelona's medieval walls symbolically ushered in a *Renaixença* (Renaissance) of Catalan culture. Catalan architect Ildefon Cerdà's design for a new Barcelona, *Pla de Reforma i Eixample* (plan for renovation and broadening), reveals a grid of squares softened by the cropped corners of streets, forming octagonal intersections. Meanwhile, the flourishing bourgeoisie commissioned a new wave of architects to build their houses, reshaping the face of the Eixample with *Modernismo* architecture. The best way to approach this macro-museum of Catalan architecture is with 2 handy guides available free at the tourist office: *Discovering Modernist Art in Catalonia* offers a cogent look at the main buildings. *Gaudí* is a pamphlet describing 9 of the master's magnum opuses.

Many modernist buffs argue that the **Casa Milà** apartment building (popularly known as **La Pedrera**—Stone Quarry), Pg. Gràcia, 92 (entrance on C. Provença), is Gaudí's masterpiece. Note the intricate ironwork around the balconies and the diversity of the front gate's egg-shaped window panes. (Rooftop tours Tues.-Sat. 10am-1pm on the hour. Free.) Gaudí's masterpiece was the **Temple Expiatori de la Sagrada Família,** on C. Marina between C. Mallorca and C. Provença. (M: Sagrada Familia, L5). Its 3 proposed façades symbolize Jesus' nativity, passion, and glory; only the first is finished. Elevators and a maze of symmetrical staircases lead to its towers, bridges, and crannies. The museum has a model of the complete structure. (Open 9am-9pm; May and Sept. 9am-8pm; March-April and Oct. 9am-7pm; Nov.-Feb. 9am-6pm. 700ptas to both church and museum.)

Montjuïc Throughout Barcelona's history, whoever controlled the strategically located **Montjuïc** (mountain of the Jews) ruled the city. Over the centuries, dozens of despotic rulers have modified the **fortress** built on top of the ancient Jewish cemetery at Montjuïc. **Poble Espanyol,** Barcelona's attempt to dissuade you from visiting the rest of Spain, features replicas of famous buildings and sites from every Spanish region: a Plaza Mayor (with a self-service cafeteria), a Calle de la Conquista, a Plazuela de la Iglesia, and so on. Studded with happening bars and clubs, it's also a favorite weekend night-spot. (Open Sun.-Mon. 9am-8pm, Tues.-Thurs. 9am-3am, Fri.-Sat. 9am-4am. Craft shops open 10am-8pm. 650ptas.)

In 1929, Barcelona inaugurated the **Estadi Olímpic de Montjuïc** in its bid for the 1932 Olympic games. Over 50 years later, Catalan architects Federic Correa and Alfons Milá and Italian Vittorio Gregotti renovated the shell (open 10am-6pm) and lowered the playing field to maximize seating for the 1992 Games. The **Palau d'Esports Sant Jordi** is the most technologically sophisticated of the Olympic structures. About 100m down the road from the Olympic stadium is the **Fundació Joan Miró,** including works from all periods of Miró's career. (Open Tues.-Sat. 11am-7pm, Thurs. 11am-9:30pm, Sun. 10:30am-2:30pm. 500ptas, students 250ptas.) To get to Parc de Montjuïc, go first to Pl. Espanya (M: L1, L3), then take bus 61, (every 10 min.), which stops at various points on the mountain. The walk up, along Av. Reina María Cristina, is direct but lengthy.

Park Güell and Tibidabo Take bus 24 from Pg. Gràcia or the metro to Lesseps (L3) to see the **Park Güell,** conceived as a garden city for 60 houses with a splendid view of the city and sea. Gaudí designed its roads, walls, and service buildings. Inside, find an elegant white staircase lined with a multicolored salamander; in the back of the park, elevated paths swerve through hedges and prehistoric plants. The **Casa-Museu Gaudí** is here. (Open 10am-2pm and 4-7pm; Nov.-March 10am-

2pm and 4-6pm. 200ptas. Park open 10am-9pm; April and Sept. 10am-8pm; March and Oct. 10am-7pm; Nov.-Feb. 10am-6pm. Free.)

To step back from all the architecture and art museums, head to the city's highest point at **Tibidabo,** perched atop the encircling mountains. Tibidabo's huge **Temple del Sagrat Cor** has received little artistic attention. The view of Montserrat and the Pyrenees from the bust of Jesus is an eyebrow raiser (round-trip elevator ride 75ptas). 500ptas purchases a view from the Torre de Collserola, 560m above sea level, a communications tower built in 1992 by British architect Norman Foster. To reach the top, either wait 15min. for the *tramvia blau* (blue streetcar; 120ptas, Sat.-Sun. 165ptas) or walk up Av. Tibidabo in the same time. At the top of the street, you have to take a funicular. (Operates 7:15am to ½hr. after the Parc d'Atraccions closes. Round-trip 400ptas.)

ENTERTAINMENT

Every evening around 5pm, a man sets up a box in the middle of C. Porta de l'Angel before the Galerías Preciados and, as a crowd gathers, intersperses opera with commentary. Nightlife in Barcelona starts then and there, winding down about 14 hours later. Having caught word that the city is a perfect combination of exuberance and variety, international youths have poured in over the last few years. The best source of information on movies, concerts, cultural events, bars, and clubs is the weekly *Guía del Ocio* (95ptas), available at newsstands.

Discos, Pubs, and Bars The *passeig* (stroll) is divided into 2 shifts: the post-siesta burst (around 5-7pm), then a second wave after dinner (perhaps 9-11pm). The later *passeig* blends into the beginnings of a drink around 10 or 11pm, but only in a pub, café or bar. After the bars wind down around 2am, the crowds flood the discos for another 4 or 5 hours. Don't refer to a *disco* as a *club*; the latter means "brothel."

The most fashionable, modern, and safe discos are located in the **Eixample.** Head out along **Carrer de Balmes, Avinguda Diagonal,** and any of their cross streets. (M: Diagonal, L3, L5.) **Otto Zutz,** C. Lincoln, 15, is one of the largest and flashiest. (M: FFCC Muntaner. Uptown near Pl. Molina at C. Balmes and Via Augusta. Cover 2000ptas. Drink included. Open until 4:30am.) The bar **La Fira,** C. Provença, 171, M: Diagonal (L3, L5), contains bumper cars, swings, ferris wheel benches, and funhouse mirrors salvaged from amusement parks. No carnival dress: avoid shorts and sandals. (Open Mon.-Thurs. 7pm-3am, Fri.-Sat. 7pm-4am, Sun. 6pm-midnight.) On the block between C. Balmes and Rambla Catalunya, **Nick Havana,** C. Rosselló, 208 (M: Diagonal, L3, L5) gyrates with blaring video screens and flashing lights. (Mixed drinks 900ptas. Cover after midnight 900ptas. Open Mon.-Thurs. 8pm-4am, Fri.-Sat. 8pm-5am, Sun. 7pm-3am.)

Music, Theater, and Film The **Gran Teatre del Liceu,** Rambla de Caputx-ins, 61, founded in 1847, was, until recently, one of the world's leading opera stages: its interior was destroyed by fire in 1994, and the theater is not expected to reopen until the 21st century. At the **Palau de la Música Catalana,** an extraordinary brick *Modernista* building tucked away on C. Francesc de Paula, 2 (tel. 268 10 00), off Via Laietana near Pl. Urquinaona, concerts cover all varieties of symphonic and choral music. Ask about free Tuesday night winter concerts and the October music festival. (Box office open Mon.-Fri. 5-8pm; Sept.-May Mon.-Fri. 11am-1pm and 5-8pm. Tickets 800-1500ptas.)

Films are popular in Barcelona. Besides Spanish and Catalan features, you should be able to find a Hollywood classic or the hottest new flick in English. Check the schedule of the **Filmoteca,** Av. Sarrià, 33 (tel. 430 50 07), run by the Generalitat, for classic, cult, exotic, and otherwise exceptional films. (Always subtitled if not a Castilian- or Catalan-language film. M: Hospital Clínic, L5. 300ptas.)

■■■ GIRONA

A world-class city waiting patiently for the world to notice, Girona rules without vainglorious ceremony over the 235-municipality province of Girona from the banks of the Riu Onyar. The wonderfully schizophrenic Girona contrasts the hushed Medieval masterpiece of stone alleyways on one river bank with a thriving, modern city on the other. Girona was named for the Roman city Gerunda, but owes as many connotations to the renowned *cabalistas de Girona*, who for centuries spread the teachings of Kabbalah (mystical Judaism) in the West. Still a center of culture and home to a large University, it is a magnet for artists, intellectuals, and activists. Most of Girona's sights are in the old city across the coffee-colored Riu Onyar from the train station. **El Call** begins at C. Sant Llorenç, a right turn off C. Força onto a narrow alleyway. The entrance to **Casa de Isaac el Cec** is off C. Sant Llorenç about halfway up the hill. The probable site of the last synagogue in Girona, it now serves as a museum linking the baths, butcher shop and synagogue, all of which surround a serene patio. (Open 10am-6pm; Nov.-May Tues.-Sun. 10am-2pm. Free.) Further uphill on C. Força and around the corner to the right, Girona's cyclopean Gothic **cathedral** rises up a record-breaking 90 Rococo steps from its *plaça*. The northern **Torre de Charlemany** is the only structure which remains from the 11th century; the cavernous interior has one rather than the customary 3 naves, making it the world's widest Gothic vault at 22m. In the trapezoidal cloister, the **Museu del Claustre** hoards some of Girona's most precious possessions, including the intricate and animated **Tapis de la Creació,** which takes up the entire wall of Room IV. Woven in the 11th or 12th century, its illustrations depict the cycle of creation and biblical scenes. (Cathedral and museum open 10am-2pm and 4-7pm; Oct.16-Jan.7 and Feb.-April Tues.-Sun. 10am-2pm and 4-5pm. Museum 300ptas, students 200ptas.)

Practical Information, Accommodations, and Food The **Pont de Pedra** connects the two banks and leads directly into the old quarter by way of C. Ciutadans, C. Carreras Peralta, and C. Força. Girona is the Costa Brava's transport hub: all trains on the Barcelona-Portbou-Cerbère line stop here, scores of buses travel daily to the Costa Brava and nearby cities, and the major national and international car companies have offices here. The RENFE and bus terminals are off **Carrer de Barcelona** on the modern side of town. **Trains** (tel. (972) 20 70 93) chug to Figueras (26-52min., 260ptas), Barcelona (1-2hr.; 600ptas, *talgo* 1600ptas); Valencia (8hr., 3500ptas); Madrid (12hr., *talgo* 9-10hr.; 5100ptas, *talgo* 6500ptas). **Buses** (tel. (972) 21 23 19), depart from around the corner from the train station. **Sarfa** (tel. (972) 20 17 96) travels to Tossa de Mar (505ptas, Sat.-Sun. 480ptas). The **tourist office** Rambla de la Libertat, 1 (tel. (972) 419 54 19), directly on the left as you cross Pont de Pedra from the new town, offers transit schedules, restaurant and accommodations listings with locations marked on maps, and piles of brochures. (Open Mon.-Fri. 8am-8pm, Sat. 8am-2pm and 4-8pm, Sun. 9am-2pm.) There is also a **branch office** at the train station (open July-Aug. Mon.-Fri. 9am-2pm). The office posts indexed street map when closed, with directions to the main office.

Room are hardest to find in June and August. **Alberg-Residència de Girona (HI),** C. Ciutadans, 9 (tel. (972) 21 80 03), lies in the heart of the old quarter, on the street which runs from Pont de Pedra. High-caliber staff, high-fashion sheets. (11pm curfew, but door opens every ½hr. until 1am. 1200ptas, over 25 1625ptas; July-Aug. 1300ptas, 1925ptas.) **Pensió Viladomat,** C. Ciutadans, 5 (tel. (972) 20 31 76), is on the same street and features sparkling clean rooms. Primarily a student residence until late June. (Singles 1800ptas. Doubles 3500ptas. Triples 4000ptas.) Enjoy inexpensive, authentic cuisine in Girona. Chow down at **Café la Torrada,** C. Ciutadans, 18, a block from the youth hostel, which attracts a local student crowd. Catalan menu only. (Entrees 450-1250ptas. Open Mon.-Fri. 9am-4pm and 7pm-1am, Sat.-Sun. 7pm-midnight.) **Larcada,** Rambla de la Libertat, 38, has dozens of tables right on the Rambla. Linger over your meal in true Spanish style near amorous couples flaunting their bliss. Try their crispy, tangy variation on the pizza theme (650-900ptas; open 12:30-4pm and 7-11pm).

Girona takes its evening *passeig* seriously. The Rambla is the place to see and be seen, to chat amicably, to gossip, to politick, to flirt, to desert one's dog, and to dance: there's a live band here every Wednesday in July at 10pm, and *sardanas* most Fridays all summer long. After the *passeig* there's dinner, and after dinner there's bar-hopping, when the throngs move to the newer part of the city. Bars near Pl. Ferran el Catòlic draw big crowds, but during the summer, **Parc de la Devesa,** across the river from the old town and several blocks to the left, has all the *ambiente.* Against a backdrop of towering 140-year-old trees and broad paths, local bars stand in all their splendor. Of Girona's four discotheques, the mightiest is **La Sala de Cel,** C. Pedret, 118, off Pl. Sant Pere in the northern quarter of the city. It's in a building with a small pool and garden. (Open Sept.-July Thurs.-Sun. nights. Cover 2000ptas, includes 2 drinks.) Artsy folk mill around bars and cafés in the old quarter.

■ TOSSA DE MAR AND FIGUERAS

Tossa de Mar is a blissful resort on the lower part of the Costa Brava, about 40km north of Barcelona. Beaches aside, the chief lure is the **Vila Vella** (old town), a collection of 14th- and 15th-century buildings and fortifications on the rocky peninsula above the sea. Bus service is reasonably frequent (every 2hr.) from Barcelona, but is so limited from Girona that travelers may wish to head for Lloret de Mar (10km south) and catch the 15min. bus ride from there to Tossa. The **tourist office** (tel. (972) 34 01 08), in the bus terminal at the corner of Av. Ferran Agulló and Av. Pelegrí, has a godsend map of the city, accommodations, campsites, and services. (Open Mon.-Sat. 9am-9pm, Sun. 10am-1pm; Nov.-May Mon.-Fri. 10am-1pm and 4-7pm, Sat. 10am-1pm.) **Fonda Lluna,** C. Roqueta, 20 (tel. (972) 34 03 65), has small rooms, big beds, grandparent-like attention, and a heartstopping rooftop view of the Vila Vella and the sea. (1500ptas with bath. Open March-Oct.) Eat seafood Poseidon would envy at **Restaurant La Salsa,** Pg. Sa. Sassola s/n (2 person min.).

Tourists once ignored the rather unwelcoming and beachless **Figueras,** 40km north of Girona. But since Salvador Dalí decided to build a museum for his works here, art buffs have swarmed to see the largest single collection of Spain's most notorious Surrealist. Transformed from an old municipal theater, the **Teatre-Museu Dalí,** in Pl. Gala i S. Dalí, parades the artist's capricious projects: erotically nightmarish drawings, extraterrestrial landscapes, and even a personal rock collection. (Open 9am-7:15pm; 900ptas, students and seniors 700ptas. Also open 10pm-1am, 1200ptas (limited admission, so more space). Oct.-June Tues.-Sun. 10:30am-5:15pm; 700ptas, students and seniors 500ptas.) The **tourist office** (tel. (972)50 31 55) on Pl. del Sol offers the standard information about visiting Catalonia. (Open Mon.-Sat. 8:30am-8pm; Oct.-June 20 Mon.-Fri. 8:30am-3pm, Sat. 9am-1pm.) The **HI youth hostel,** C. Anicet de Pagés, 2 (tel. (972) 50 12 13), is a bit of a hike from the train and bus stations. (Lock-in midnight-8am, but opens briefly on the hr. until 4am. Lockout 1-5pm. 1300ptas. Reserve 1 month ahead in July and Aug. through the Barcelona office at (93) 402 11 66 or call the hostel 2-3 days before arrival.)

Teisa buses connect Figueras with Olot (1hr., 400ptas, Sat.-Sun. 510ptas), where there's service to Ripoll, an entrance to the Catalan Pyrenees. RENFE **trains** (tel. (972) 50 46 61) make for Girona (25min.-1hr., 260ptas) and Barcelona (1½-2hr., 850ptas).

■■■ CATALAN PYRENEES

Sheep and cows outnumber people in the Pyrenees, wandering unattended through the rocky outcrops and snow-covered crags that cut through the steep green slopes. Limited bus service and circuitous roads prevent easy access to this section of the Pyrenees (230km long), but the splendor of Parc d'Aigüestortes, filled with clear glacial lakes and waterfalls, renders even the most arduous journey worthwhile. The Department of Commerce and Tourism distributes pamphlets with information on local winter sports or areas of scenic grandeur. Skiers will find the English-language guide *Snow in Catalonia* (free at tourist offices) especially useful. Cyclists should ask for *Valles Superiores del Segre/Ariège,* which covers the Alt Urgell, Cerdanya, and the Val de Ribas. Editorial Alpina publishes a series of indispensable topographical maps bound in red booklets.

Núria and Ripoll   After the Civil War, **Núria** enjoyed about 20 years of fame for its international ski competitions, but because of the popularity of bigger mountains and longer slopes, the town temporarily declined. Núria has carved a new market niche for itself as a resort area with year-round, right-at-your-doorstep hiking and skiing. The Cremallera zips from the Ribas de Freser stop on the Ripoll-Puigcerdá line; the 45min. ride scales 800m through virgin mountain faces to which stubborn sheep, goats, and pine trees cling (6-11 per day depending on season 7:20am-9:30pm, 1750ptas round-trip). Climbers prefer the four-hour hike to **Puigmal** (2913m). In 1988, 11 ambitious mountaineers climbed the peak on 6-ft. stilts, setting a new world record. Ten ski trails offer slopes ranging from *molt facil* (very easy) to *molt difficil* (very difficult or expert) at **Estació de la Vall de Núria.** The "white phone" for ski conditions is in Barcelona at tel. (93) 301 97 77. (Weekend lift tickets 1500ptas, weekdays 1200ptas.) **Information** for the whole valley is available at tel. (972) 72 70 31. From Núria, a modern cable line (670ptas) whisks straight to **Alberg de Joventut Pic de l'Aliga** (tel. (972) 73 00 48), the alternative being an arduous 20min. climb (10min. down). The modern three-story youth hostel loyally maintains Núria's training-camp atmosphere. (1300ptas per person, over 25 1925ptas. Hot showers. Breakfast included. Closed Nov.) **Hotel Vall de Núria** (tel. (972) 73 03 26) is the only other real building in the valley. (Singles from 3500ptas in winter and 7500ptas in summer. Doubles from 5000ptas in winter to 9500ptas in summer.) Free **camping,** with hot showers and toilets, is permitted near the hotel. Bring up a well-stocked picnic basket, as there are no markets in the valley and only a handful of eateries.

Almost everyone comes to **Ripoll** to see the 11th-century portal of the **Monestir de Santa Maria,** with its monstrous gargoyles and local animals in a 12-month calendar. (Open 9am-1pm and 3-9pm. Free.) The well-stocked **tourist office** (tel. (972) 70 23 51) is next to the monastery on Pl. Abat Oliva. (Open Mon.-Fri. 10am-1pm and 5-7pm, Sat. 10am-1pm; Oct.-June Mon.-Fri. 11am-1pm and 4-6pm, Sat. 11am-1pm.) **RENFE trains,** Pl. Nova, 1, serve Puigcerdà (1½hr., 290ptas) and Barcelona (2hr., 600ptas). To reach Ribas de Freser and the Cremallera to Núria, take the Puigcerdà train (125ptas). **Teisa,** one bl. down from RENFE, runs **buses** to Girona via Olot (2¾hr., 855ptas, Sat.-Sun. 975ptas). If gaping at the church portal took longer than you planned, try winter-heated **Hostal Habitacions Paula,** C. Pirineus, 6 (tel. (972) 70 00 11). Pirineus runs off Pl. Abat Oliba; the *hostal* is at the corner of C. Berenguer. Some of the big rooms face the monastery, but the interior singles are more like closets than cloisters. (1300ptas per person plus tax.)

BALEARIC ISLANDS (ILLES BALEARES)

The Balearic Islands are an autonomous province of Spain about 100km off the east coast between Barcelona and Valencia. Although numbers have dwindled somewhat, hundreds of thousands still descend upon the sun-drenched islands each summer, making for a prosperous economy. Those islanders not running a restaurant or *pensión* work in the olive, fig, and almond groves that blanket the countryside. Summers tend to be hot, dry, and crowded—spring and autumn are gorgeous, and the easiest times to find budget accommodations.

SPAIN

Getting There and Getting Around Transmediterránea monopolizes **ferry** movement between the mainland and all the islands except Ibiza and Formentera. Their ships depart from Barcelona (office at Estació Marítima, tel. (93) 443 25 32) and Valencia (office at Av. Manuel Soto Ingeniero, 15, tel. (96) 367 65 12). The one-way fare for a *butaca* (airplane-style seat) is 6100ptas. **Flebasa** (tel. (96) 578 40 11 or 78 42 00), in the city of Denia (on the FEVE rail line between Valencia and Alacant), challenges Transmediterránea in Ibiza. Their boats dock in Port Sant Antoni. The high-speed ferry ticket comes with a bus connection from either of those cities or from Madrid, Albacete, and Benidorm (in summer). (One-way from Madrid 7610ptas, from Alacant or Valencia 5570ptas.)

Flying is the best way to **island-hop.** **Iberia** flies from Palma to Ibiza City, Ibiza (3-4 per day, 20min., 4800ptas) and Mahón, Menorca (2-3 per day, 20min., 4850ptas). Note that the stopover in Palma between Menorca and Ibiza can last up to 4 hours (2-3 per day, 10,650ptas). Planes fill a couple of days in advance in summer, so make reservations. If flying round-trip, ask if the *tarifa-mini* fare is applicable. Seafarers between the islands sail Transmediterránea, whose **ships** connect Palma with Ibiza City (1-2 per week, 4½hr., 4509ptas) and Mahón (1 per week, 6½hr., 4509ptas). Mallorca and Ibiza operate extensive intra-island **bus** systems. Travel costs add up, as bus fares between cities range from 100-700ptas each way. A day's Vespa or **moped rental** costs about 2200ptas while **bicycle rental,** about 800ptas.

Mallorca Mallorca absorbs the bulk of invaders, particularly in July and August. Jagged limestone cliffs line the north coast, while lazy bays scoop into the rest of the coastline. The capital of the province, **Palma** is a showy Balearic upstart; its streets hustle with conspicuously consuming shoppers, and the town boasts a swinging nightlife. Though better **beaches** spread throughout the expanse of the island, decent ones are a mere bus ride from Palma. The beach at **El Arenal** (Platja de Palma, bus 15), 11km to the southeast, is popular—a little over-touristed perhaps. The clear-watered **Palma Nova** and **Illetes** beaches (buses 1 and 3 respectively) are 15 and 9km southwest. Every Friday, *El Día de Mundo* newspaper (100ptas) publishes an entertainment supplement with numerous listings of bars and discos all over Mallorca. Palma nightlife is centered in the **El Terreno** area, with a motherlode of nightclubs centered on Pl. Gomilia and along C. Joan Miró. Drinks appear amid elegant furniture, cooing doves and ducks, piles of fresh fruit and flowers, and hundreds of dripping candles at **ABACO,** C. Sant Joan, 1, in the Barri Gòtic near the waterfront, all to the accompaniment of Handel, Bach, et al. (Fruit nectars 750ptas, cocktails 1300-1400ptas.) The divine **Baccus,** around the corner on C. Lluis Fábregas, 2, attracts lively lesbian and gay hedonists (open until 3am).

In Palma, check the backstreets of the **Barri Gòtic** for a cheap room, or take bus 15 (130ptas) from Pl. Espanya and ask the driver to let you off at Hotel Acapulco for the **Alberg Juvenil Platja de Palma (HI)**, C. Costa Brava, 13 (tel. (971) 26 08 92), in the beach town **El Arenal** (members only, 1000ptas; closed Dec.). **Hostal Ritzi,** C. Apuntadores, 6 (tel. (971) 71 46 10), off Pl. Reina, is a classy *hostal* with ritzy throw pillows and wall-to-wall carpeting. (Singles 1700ptas. Doubles 2800ptas, with shower 3200ptas, with bath 3500ptas. Keys for 24hr. entry.)

Ibiza Once a hippie enclave, Ibiza (Eivissa) is now a summer camp for disco maniacs and tourists with bohemian pretensions. Although the existence of a thriving gay community lends credence to Ibiza's self-image as a "tolerant" center, the island's high-cost-of-touring precludes a true human diversity. Nobody in their right mind hangs out in the city of Ibiza during the day when there are so many beaches about. When the sun sets, however, Ibiza turns into the SoHo of the Mediterranean. Tourists and locals alike jam the outdoor cafés and boutiques clad in outrageously scanty attire: hip-huggers, bangles, and nipple rings. The elbows push into most **bars** along C. Major and the next street parallel, C. Verge. Live jazz wails through the smoky air of **La Cantina** under Teatro Pereyra on C. Comte Roselló every night after 10pm. Gay nightlife hovers around Sa Penya; the bars **Exis** and **Gallery** are especially throbbing. Ibiza's **disco** scene is world-famous and ever-changing. The best information sources are regulars; the second, posters and the *Diario de Ibiza* newspaper (100ptas). Elusive and invaluable is the schedule for the **Discobús,** which runs to and from all the major hotspots (midnight-5am, 200-300ptas). The power of the rising sun draws thousands of solar zombies to the nearby tanning grounds. No beach is within quick walking distance, but **Platja de Talamanca, Platja des Duros,** and **Platja de Figueretes** are close enough to be on the larger city maps. Many more good beaches are accessible by bus, including clean **Salinas,** former hippie hangout **Cala Llonga,** and **Cala Olivera.**

Decent, cheap accommodations in Ibiza are rare, especially in the summer when gobs of Britons et al vie for the few that do exist. "CH," which stands for **casa de huespedes,** marks many doorways, but often the owner must be reached through the phone number tacked on the door. Ibiza's relative safety and up-all-night mentality ensure that owners offer keys for 24hr. entry. **Hostal La Marina,** C. Andenes del Puerto, 4 (tel. (971) 31 01 72), across from Estació Marítima is conveniently located. Salty air floats through the window. (Singles 1500ptas. Doubles 3000ptas, with bath 4500ptas. Credit cards accepted.)

VALENCIA

■■■ VALENCIA

Medieval song describes Valencia as the land of water, light and love. Surrounded by the famed orange groves of the *huerta* (orchard), this lively, modern city is graced by numerous ancient buildings, museums and monuments. Greenthumbs are the majority in Valencia; the lushly exuberant parks and gardens are a local obsession. The regional language is *valenciá,* closely related to Catalan, but residents also speak Castilian Spanish.

ORIENTATION AND PRACTICAL INFORMATION

Avinguda **M. de Sotelo** runs from the train station to **Plaça del Ajuntament,** where the city tourist office is located.

Tourist Offices: Regional, Estació del Nord, C. Xàtiva, 24 (tel. 352 85 73), on the right as you walk off the train. English spoken. Open Mon.-Fri. 10am-6pm. **City,** Pl. Ajuntament, 1 (tel. 351 04 17). Open Mon.-Fri. 8:30am-2:15pm and 4:15-6:15pm, Sat. 9am-12:45pm.

Currency Exchange: El Corte Inglés, C. Pintor Sorolla, 26 (tel. 351 24 44). From Pl. Ajuntament, walk down C. Bareas as it turns into a pedestrian walk; El Corte Inglés sits on the left. Also novels and guidebooks in English, telephones, and a grocery store on the 5th floor. Open Mon.-Sat. 10am-9pm.

American Express: Duna Viajes, C. Cirilo Amorós, 88 (tel. 374 15 62). Next to Pl. América on the edge of Río Turia. Mail held. Open Mon.-Fri. 9:30am-2pm and 5-8pm, Sat. 10am-2pm.

Post Office: Pl. Ajuntament, 24 (tel. 351 67 50). Open for stamps and *Lista de Correos* Mon.-Fri. 8am-9pm, Sat. 9am-2pm. **Postal Code:** 46080.

Telephones: Estació del Nord, C. Xàtiva, 24 (fax 394 27 44). Open 8am-10pm. Faxes sent and received. **City Code:** 96.

Flights: The airport is 15km southwest of the city (tel. 350 95 00). CVT buses (tel. 340 47 15) link the airport with the bus station in Valencia (almost every hr. 6am-8:20pm from airport, 200ptas). **Iberia,** C. Pau (Paz), 14 (tel. 352 05 00). Open Mon.-Fri. 9am-2pm and 4-7pm, Sat. 9am-1:30pm.

Trains: Estació del Nord, C. Xàtiva, 24 (tel. 351 36 12). Information office open 7am-10:30pm (24hr. phone). To Barcelona (4-6hr., 2020-3700ptas), Madrid (5-7½hr., 3000-4500ptas), Seville (9hr., 4900-6000ptas).

Buses: Estació Terminal d'Autobuses, Av. Menéndez Pidal, 13 (tel. 349 72 22), across the river. Take bus 8 (80ptas) at Pl. Ajuntament, 22., or walk 25min. northwest from the center. To Madrid (5hr., 2645ptas), Barcelona (4½hr., 2650ptas).
Public Transportation: EMT Buses (tel. 352 83 99). Most leave from Pl. Ajuntament, 22. Buy tickets aboard or at any newsstand (80ptas, 10-ride ticket 550ptas).
Ferries: Transmediterránea, Av. Manuel Soto Ingeniero, 15 (tel. 367 07 04). To Palma de Mallorca (Mon.-Sat., 9hr., 6900ptas). Or buy tickets (on day of departure only) at the port office, Estació Marítima (tel. 367 39 72). Take bus 4 from Pl. Ajuntament. **Flebasa** (Denia office tel. 578 42 00) ferries to the Balearic Islands leave from Denia (5220ptas includes 3hr. bus to Denia port).
Luggage Storage: At the **bus station,** lockers 200ptas and 400ptas. Or at the **train station,** lockers 300ptas and 600ptas. Both open 24hrs.
Laundromat: Lavandería El Mercat, Pl. Mercat, 12 (tel. 391 20 10), on the left past the market. Self-service wash or dry 425ptas. Open Mon.-Sat. 10am-8pm.
Pharmacy: Check listing in local paper *Levante* (100ptas) or the *farmacias de guardia* schedule posted outside any pharmacy.
Medical Assistance: Hospital Clínico Universitario, Av. Blasco Ibáñez, 17 (tel. 386 26 00), at the corner of C. Dr. Ferrer. Take bus 30 or 40 from Av. M. de Sotelo in front of the train station. English-speaking doctor is often on duty.
Emergencies: tel. 091. **Ambulance,** tel. 352 67 50. **Police,** Jefatura Superior, Gran Via de Ramón y Cajal, 40 (tel. 091).

ACCOMMODATIONS

The business of Valencia is business, so rooms are not hard to find during high the summer. Avoid the areas by the *barrio chino* (red-light district) around Pl. Pilar. The best options cluster around **Plaça Ajuntament** and **Plaça Mercat.**

Alberg Colegio "La Paz" (HI), Av. Port, 69 (tel. 369 01 52). Take bus 19 from Pl. Ajuntament and ask the driver to signal the stop. Forbidding fortress safeguards a peaceful ambience. 2-4 people per room. Reception open 9am-1pm and 5-8pm. Curfew midnight. Members only. 950ptas per person. Over 26: 1300ptas. Breakfast included. Sheets 300ptas. Open July-Sept. 15.
Hostal del Rincón, C. Carda, 11 (tel. 391 60 83). Ample hotel with starched white sheets and squeaky-clean bathrooms. Singles 1000ptas. Doubles 1800ptas.
Hostal-Residencia El Cid, C. Cerrajeros, 13 (tel. 392 23 23), off C. Vicente Mártir between Pl. Ajuntament and Pl. Reina. Pseudo-wooden floors and a little dog named Snoopy radiate a homey feel. Singles 1200ptas. Doubles 2500ptas, with shower 2800ptas, with bath 3500ptas.
Hostal Moratín, C. Moratín, 15 (tel. 352 12 20), 1st street on the left off C. Barcas coming from Pl. Ajuntament. Brilliant-white rooms. Cozy dining room where owner often serves up a great *paella*. Singles 1850ptas. Doubles 3000ptas. Triples 4500ptas. Breakfast 250ptas. Dinner 900ptas.

FOOD

Valencia, of course, gave birth to *paella*. Another regional favorite is *horchata*, a sweet, milky white drink pressed from locally-grown *chufas* (earth almonds). Buckets of fresh fish, meat, fruit and cereals sell at the **Mercat Central** on Pl. Mercat (open Mon.-Thurs. 7am-2pm, Fri. 7am-2pm and 5-8:30pm, Sat. 7am-3pm).

Restaurante La Utielana, Pl. Picadero Dos Aguas, 3 (tel. 352 94 14). Take C. Barcelonina off Pl. Ajuntament, turn left at its end, then a sharp right onto C. Procida. Devilish to find. Choose from a super scoop of scrumptious seafood *paella* (a shocking 325ptas) or *gambas a la plancha* (425ptas). A meal you will not forget. A/C. Open Sept.-July Mon.-Fri. 1:15-4pm and 9-11pm, Sat. 1:15-4pm.
Café Valiente, C. Xàtiva, 8 (tel. 351 21 17). Stainless steel bar winds around the restaurant, accommodating patrons with one ambition—a large helping of *paella* scooped fresh from giant round pans (with chicken 490ptas, with seafood 560ptas). Expect a good 10-15min. wait. *Paella* served religiously 1-4pm. Open Mon.-Sat. 1-4pm and 7-10pm, Sun. 1-5pm.

La Lluna, C. Sant Ramón (tel. 392 21 46). Behind the hanging-bead curtain is a veggie restaurant to moon over. A 4-course *menú* and whole-grain bread served only weekday afternoons (750ptas). Open Mon.-Sat. 1:30-4:30pm and 8pm-midnight.

SIGHTS AND ENTERTAINMENT

Most of the sights line the **Río Túria** or cluster near **Plaça de la Reina.** Taxonomists may lose it when they see the **Jardì Botànic,** C. Beato Gaspar Bono, a university-maintained open-air botanical garden that cultivates 43,000 plants from around the world (open 10am-9pm, Oct.-May 10am-6pm; 50ptas, students free). The banks of the diverted **Túria** are now one of the world's largest urban parks, featuring a gigantic doll of Jonathan Swift's "Gulliver" (open Tues.-Sun. 10am-2pm and 5-9pm, Sept.-June 10am-dusk).

On C. Sant Pius V, the compelling **Museu Provincial de Belles Artes** displays superb 14th- to 16th-century Valencian primitives (influenced by Flemish painters' marked attention to clothing) and works by later Spanish and foreign masters—a Hieronymous Bosch triptych, El Greco's *San Juan Bautista,* Velázquez's self-portrait, Ribera's *Santa Teresa* and a slew of Goyas. (Open Oct.-July Tues.-Sat. 10am-2pm and 4-6pm, Sun. 10am-2pm; Aug. Tues.-Sun. 10am-2pm. Free.)

The Aragonese began the **seu** (cathedral) in Pl. Zaragoza shortly after the *Reconquista.* Seized by a fit of Romantic hyperbole or simply vertigo, French novelist Victor Hugo counted 300 bell towers in the city from the **Micalet** (the cathedral tower) in Pl. Reina—actually there are only about 100. (Tower open 10am-1pm and 4:30-7pm. 100 (not 300) ptas.) The **Museu de la Seu** squeezes a great many treasures into very little space. Check out the overwrought tabernacle made from 1200kg of gold, silver, platinum, emeralds, and sapphires; two Goyas; and the withered left arm of San Vicente, who was martyred in 304 AD. (Open Mon.-Sat. 10am-1pm and 4:30-6pm;, Dec.-Feb. 10am-1pm. 100ptas.)

The newer sections of the city around Pl. Cánovas del Castillo and over the Túria near the university on Av. Blasco Ibáñez are fertile ground for discos. One favorite is **Woody,** C. Menéndez y Pelayo, 137, with a blinking 70s-type dance floor (open Fri.-Sat. 11:30pm-7am, cover 1000ptas). **Distrito 10,** C. General Elío, 10, is another hotspot of mirrors, 3 floors of balconies and a gigantic video screen. (Open Sept.-July Thurs.-Sat. 6-9:30pm and midnight-7am, Sun. 6-9:30pm. Early session 400ptas, late session 1500ptas.) Gay men congregate at **Balkiss,** C. Dr. Monserrat, 23. Lesbians favor **Carnaby Club,** Poeta Liern, 17.

Valencia's most illustrious traditional event is undoubtedly **Las Fallas,** March 12-19. The city's neighborhoods compete to build the most elaborate and satirical papier-mâché effigy; over 300 such *ninots* spring up in the streets. Parades, bullfights, fireworks and street dancing enliven the annual excess, and on the final day—*la nit del foc* (fire night)—all the *ninots* simultaneously burn in one last, clamorous release.

■ JÁTIVA (XÀTIVA) AND GANDÍA

The last foreigner of note to come through **Játiva** was Felipe V, who burned it to the ground. With an imposing mountainous backdrop and land that lends itself equally to *huertas* (orchards) and to vineyards, it's no wonder that Felipe was just one in a long line of conquerors. Although it's quite accessible as a daytrip from Valencia, few tourists visit the city, and its quiet charm remains intact.

The striking ramparts atop the hill in back of town lead to the city's **castell,** made up of two sections, the **castell machor** (larger), on the right as you come in, and the pre-Roman **castell chicotet** (smaller). The former, used from the 13th through 16th centuries, bears the scars of many a siege and earthquake. Its arched stone **prison** has held some famous wrong-doers, including King Fernando el Católico and the Comte d'Urgell, would-be usurper of the Aragonese throne. Referred to in Verdi's *Il Trovatore,* this man spent his final decades here before being buried in the castle's chapel. (Open Tues.-Sun. 10:30am-2pm and 4:30-7pm; in the off-season Tues.-Sun.

10:30am-2pm and 3:30-6pm. Free.) Játiva's **tourist office** is at C. Noguera, 10. (Tel. (96) 227 33 46. Open Tues.-Sun. 9am-2:30pm; Sept. 16-June 14 Tues.-Fri. 9am-2pm and 4-6pm, Sat.-Sun. 10am-2pm.) Frequent **trains** connect to Valencia (1hr., 365ptas, round-trip 730ptas).

Gandía is best known as the hang-out of the Borjas, especially of Francisco de Borja, who renounced his title and wealth to become a Jesuit. Everything you need is a stone's throw from the train station on **Marqués de Campo.** Everything you want is at the **beach,** 4km away. The **tourist office** (tel. (96) 287 77 88) is right across from the train station (open Mon.-Fri. 10am-2pm and 4:30-8pm, Sat. 10am-2pm). **Trains** arrive from Valencia 14 times a day (1¼hr., 625ptas).

Simple flattery does not do justice to **Alberg Mar i Vent (HI),** C. Doctor Fleming, s/n (tel. (96) 289 37 48), the hostel/beachfront resort in Platja de Piles, a town 10km south of Gandía. Take the **La Amistad bus** (tel. (96) 287 44 10), which departs from the right of the train station (check with the tourist office for times; 85ptas). Water laps at the door, there's an outdoor patio and basketball court and they rent bikes and windsurfers. Alcohol is strictly prohibited. (3-day max. stay. Curfew midnight. 770ptas, with 3 meals 1700ptas. Over 26: 915ptas; 2225ptas. Open Feb.-Nov.)

■■■ ALICANTE (ALACANT)

Beyond the polished pedestrian thoroughfares inlaid with meticulously cleaned red tiles lies the old city—paradoxically a modern, urban snarl of lively streets at the foot of the *castillo.* Grittier than their new-quarter counterparts, these streets are full of historic buildings and mouthwatering food. The beaches are nearby, the lodging is plentiful and cheap and the nightlife moves at a steady clip.

ORIENTATION AND PRACTICAL INFORMATION

Esplanada d'Espanya stretches along the waterfront between 2 large jetties. Behind it, the old quarter is a web of streets and *plaças* off the main avenue, **Rambla Méndez Nuñez,** where nearly all services and points of interest cluster.

Tourist Office: Municipal, C. Portugal, 17 (tel. 514 92 95), next to the bus station. Ask for *Alicante at your Fingertips,* a helpful guide to local services. Open Mon.-Fri. 9am-2pm.

Currency Exchange: El Corte Inglés, Maisonnave, 53 (tel. 511 30 01). Zero commission. They also have a great map, novels and guidebooks in English, haircutting, a restaurant and **telephones.** Open Mon.-Sat. 10am-9pm.

Budget Travel: TIVE, Av. Aguilera, 1 (tel. 513 11 58), near the train station off Av. Oscar Esplá. ISIC 500ptas. HI card 1800ptas. Open Mon.-Fri. 9am-1:30pm.

Post Office: Pl. Gabriel Miró (tel. 521 99 84), off C. Sant Ferran. Open Mon.-Fri. 8am-9pm, Sat. 9am-2pm. **Telegrams** (tel. 514 20 01). Open Mon.-Fri. 8am-9pm, Sat. 9am-7pm, Sun. 9am-2pm. **Postal Code:** 03000.

Telephones: Av. Constitució, 10 (tel. 004). Open 9am-10pm. Another office at the **bus station.** Open Mon.-Fri. 9:30am-2pm and 5-9:30pm, Sat.-Sun. 10am-2pm and 5-9pm. **City Code:** 96.

Flights: Aeroport Internacional El Altet (tel. 528 50 11), 10km from town. **Alcoyana** (tel. 513 01 04) sends 13 buses per day between the airport and Av. Constitució (departs town 7am-10pm, departs airport 6:30am-9:20pm; 150ptas).

Trains: RENFE, Estació Término, Av. Salamanca (tel. 592 02 02), west of the city center. Information open daily 7am-10pm. To reach Esplanada d'Espanya from here, walk down wide Av. la Estación to Plaza de los Luceros and hang a right onto Av. Federico Soto, which leads to the waterfront. Most destinations require a transfer. Direct to: Valencia (2hr., 1500-2000ptas); Madrid (4hr., 3400-4400ptas); Barcelona (61hr., 4000ptas). **Ferrocarrils de la Generalitat Valenciana, Estació de la Marina,** Av. Villajoyosa, 2 (tel. 526 27 31), far from town. Take bus C-1 from Pl. Espanya. Local service along the Costa Blanca. Also **night trains** to discos on the beaches near Alacant.

Buses: C. Portugal, 17 (tel. 513 07 00). To reach Esplanada d' Espanya, turn left onto Carrer d' Italia and right on Av. Dr. Gadea; follow Dr. Gadea until the park, then left on the waterfront. For the Costa Blanca, go to **UBESA** (tel. 513 01 43). Enatcar (tel. 512 56 22) runs to Madrid (5½hr., 2895ptas); Granada (6hr., 3090ptas) and Barcelona (8hr., 4290ptas). **Luggage storage** 200ptas per bag. Open 6:45am-9pm.

Ferries: Flebasa (tel. 578 42 00). Service from Denia (includes bus from Alicante) to Ibiza (3 per day, 3½hr., 5220ptas). Open Mon.-Fri. 9am-1pm and 4:30-8pm, Sat. 9am-noon.

Medical Assistance: Hospital Clínico, Maestro Alonzo, 109 (tel. 590 83 00). **Ambulance** (tel. 511 46 76).

Emergency: tel. 091. **Police,** C. Médico Pascual Pérez, 27 (tel. 514 22 22).

ACCOMMODATIONS AND CAMPING

Although there seem to be *pensiones* and *casas de huéspedes* on every corner, stay away from the places along **C. Sant Ferran** (where theft and prostitution are common) and around the **Església de Santa María;** opt instead for the newer section of town. The tourist office keeps accommodations listings.

Residencia Juvenil (HI), Av. Orihuela, 97 (tel. 528 12 11). Take bus G from next to the bus station on the corner of C. Lorenzo and C. Portugal, and get off at the last stop (85ptas). Members only. 3-day max. stay. 770ptas, with breakfast 850ptas, with 3 meals 1700ptas. Over 25: 910ptas; 1240ptas; 2225ptas.

Pensión Las Monjas, C. Monjas, 2 (tel. 521 50 46). Follow C. San Isidro off Rambla Méndez Núñez until it turns into C. Monjas. In the center of the historic district and only a few blocks from the beach. Each room is individually decorated in the owner Pedro's whimsical taste. Singles 1500-2500ptas. Doubles 3000-4000ptas.

Habitaciones México, C. General Primo de Rivera, 10 (tel. 520 93 07), off the end of Av. Alfonso X El Sabio. Laundry service 600ptas per load. Singles 1450ptas. Doubles 2800-3400ptas. Triples 3600-4000ptas.

Camping: Camping Bahía, Playa Albafereta (tel. 526 23 32), 4km away on the road to Valencia. Take bus C-1. 450ptas per person. 500 ptas per tent. Open March 15-Oct. 15.

FOOD

Small family-run establishments in the **old city** (between the cathedral and the steps to the castle) and on side streets around town are the least traveled route. Locals devour tapas in the **Calle Mayor.** The **market** near Av. Alfonso X El Sabio sells fresh fish, meats and produce, plus sandwich meats and bread.

Mesón de Castilla, C. Sant Nicolau, 12 (tel. 520 06 84). The owner juggles 10 plates through the dining room to accommodate the regulars. *Menú especial*—3 courses, fruit, bread, and drink—800ptas. *Paella* option Thurs. and Sun. Open Mon.-Fri. 1-4pm and 7-10pm, Sat.-Sun. 1-4pm.

Restaurante Mixto Vegetariano, Pl. Santa María, 2. Creative vegetarian fare; some meat plates as well. Salad bar and only whole-wheat pizza crust in Spain. *Menú* 975ptas. Open Tues.-Sun. 1-4:30pm and 8pm-midnight.

La Venta del Lobo, C. Sant Ferran, 48 (tel. 514 09 85). A 2-room neighborhood grill ambitious enough to prepare specialties from all over Spain. Try *gazpacho andaluz* for a taste of the south (370ptas) or Valencian *paella. Menú* 900ptas. Multilingual menu. Open Tues.-Sat. 1-5pm and 8:30pm-12:30am, Sun. 1-5pm.

SIGHTS

Complete with drawbridges, clandestine tunnels, fishy passageways, and urine-splashed dungeons, the **Castell de Santa Bárbara** isn't just another castle. Built by the Carthaginians and recently reconstructed, the 200m-high fortress has a dry moat, a dungeon, a spooky ammunition storeroom, and an amazing view of Alicante. A paved road from the old section of Alicante leads to the top; most people take the elevator (200ptas) by the beachfront. (Castle and museum open 10am-

SPAIN

8pm; Oct.-March 9am-7pm. Free.) The **Concatedral de San Nicolás de Bari,** one block north of Méndez Núñez on C. San Isidro, reflects the sober Renaissance style of Agustín Bernadino, while the Baroque communion chapel lavishly compensates for such restraint. Intricate wood carvings embellish the door to the cloister. (Open Mon.-Sat. 8am-2:30pm and 6-8:30pm, Sun. 9am-1:45pm.)

If Alicante's beach doesn't suit you, hop on bus C-1 in Pl. Espanya (75ptas) or board the Alicante-Denia train (85ptas) for the 6km long **Playa de San Juan.** Or, try the **Playa del Saladar** in Urbanova. Buses from the Alicante bus station make the trip to Urbanova (3 per day, 35min., 100ptas).

In summer, nightlife centers on the **Playa de San Juan. Ferrocarriles de la Generalitat Valenciana** runs special **Trensnochador** night trains from Estació de la Marina to several points along the beach (every hr., 11pm-7am, 85-280ptas). A taxi from Alicante (900-1000ptas) to Playa de San Juan and can be shared by up to four people. **Voy Voy** on Av. Niza at the "Discoteca" stop on the night train, swings with outdoor bars, decibels of music, and dancing (open until 6am). Alicante's hottest disco is **Buggatti,** C. Sant Ferran, 27 (tel. 521 06 46), featuring neon-lined bars and candle-lit tables. (Cover including 1 drink 1000ptas. Open nightly until 5:30am.) Gay men convene at **Jardineto** on C. Barón de Finestrat. From June 21 to 29, the town bursts with bacchanalian celebration for the **Festival de Sant Joan,** comprised of romping *fogueres* (symbolic or satiric effigies).

ANDALUSIA

Between the jagged Sierra Morena and the deep blue sea, Andalusia has always inspired fascination with its rich history. Home of several emperors and writers of the caliber of Seneca and Quintilian, it was one of the Roman Empire's richest, most sophisticated provinces. The Moors remained in control of eastern Andalusia longer than elsewhere (711-1492), but the region owes just as much to the Romans' irrigation, cool patios, and red and white stone architecture. The Moors maintained and perfected these techniques; more importantly, they assimilated and elaborated the wisdom and science of Classical Greece and the East, which made the European Renaissance possible. Owing to the long summers, regional cooking is light, depending on such delicacies as *pescaíto frito* (lightly fried fish) and cold soups such as *gazpacho* served *con guarnición* (with garnish), often spooned by the waiter at your table.

■■■ SEVILLE (SEVILLA)

With its brilliant light, whitewashed grace, jasmined balconies, and orange trees laden with fat glowing globes, Seville may convince you that otherworldly cities do exist. Site of a small Roman acropolis founded by Julius Caesar, seat of Moorish culture, focal point of the Spanish Renaissance, and guardian angel of traditional Andalusian culture, Seville has never failed to spark the imagination of newcomers. The 16th-century maxim *"Qui non ha visto Sevilla non ha visto maravilla"*—who has not seen Seville has not seen a marvel—remains true five centuries later.

ORIENTATION

Seville is a major travel hub, connecting Portugal, Cádiz, Córdoba, and Madrid. **Río Guadalquivir** flows roughly north-south through Seville. Most of the city, including the alleyways of the old **Barrio de Santa Cruz,** is on the east bank; some of the most active nightlife and least expensive food is on the west bank in **Barrio de Triana** and **Barrio de los Remedios.** The **cathedral** on **Avenida de la Constitución** marks Seville's center, where the main tourist office, post office, banks, and travel agencies cluster. Seville's shopping district lies north of the cathedral where Constitución fades into **Plaza Nueva.** The neighborhoods surrounding Plaza Nueva, as well as those northeast of the Barrio de Santa Cruz (**Barrio de la Puerta del Carne** and **Barrio de la Puerta de Carmona**) are hunting grounds for *pensión* and restaurant seekers. **The Estación Santa Justa** (train station), is a 40min. walk from the city center. The main bus station at **Prado de San Sebastián** on C. Menéndez Pelayo is much closer (a 10min. walk). Beware, Seville is the Spanish capital of pickpocketing and car theft. Avoid Santa Cruz and Barrio de las Tres Mil Viviendas at night.

PRACTICAL INFORMATION

Tourist Offices: City, Po. Delicias, 9 (tel. 423 44 65), across from Parque de María Luísa by Puente del Generalísimo. Open Mon.-Fri. 9am-1:15pm and 4:30-6:45pm. **Regional,** Av. Constitución, 21B (tel. 422 14 04, fax 422 97 53), 1 block south of the cathedral. Amazing. Open Mon.-Fri. 9am-2pm, Sat. 10am-2pm.

Budget Travel: Viajes TIVE, C. Jesús de Veracruz, 27 (tel. 490 60 22). Downtown near El Corte Inglés. Open Mon.-Fri. 9am-2pm.

Consulates: U.S.: Po. Delicias, 7 (tel. 423 18 83 or 423 18 85). Open Mon.-Fri. 10am-1pm. In emergencies, call U.S. embassy in Madrid at tel. (91) 577 40 00. **Canada:** Av. Constitución, 30, 2nd floor, #4 (tel. 422 47 52, in emergency (91) 431 43 00). **U.K.:** Pl. Nueva, 8B (tel. 422 88 75). In emergencies, call Madrid for referral in Seville. Covers New Zealand affairs. Open Mon.-Fri. 9am-2:30pm.

Currency Exchange: El Corte Inglés: Pl. Duque de la Victoria, 10, near C. Alfonso XII or C. Luis de Morales, 122, near the football stadium. No commission. Grab a **map.** Open Mon.-Sat. 10am-9pm. **Banks** offer better rates, charging 1% commission or 500ptas, whichever is greater. Most open Mon.-Fri. 8:30am-2pm.

American Express: Viajes Alhambra, Teniente Coronel Seguí, 6 (tel. 421 29 23), north of Pl. Nueva. Holds mail (postal code: 41001) and has 24hr. cash machine outside. Open Mon.-Fri. 9:30am-1:30pm and 4:30-8pm. Sat. 9:30am-1pm.

Post Office: Av. Constitución, 32 (tel. 421 95 85), across from the cathedral. Open for stamps and most mail services Mon.-Fri. 8am-9pm, Sat. 9am-7pm. Open for *Lista de Correos* Mon.-Fri. 8am-9pm, Sat. 8am-2pm. Open for **telegrams** (national tel. 422 00 00, international tel. 422 68 60) and **faxes** Mon.-Fri. 8am-9pm, Sat. 9am-8pm. **Postal Code:** 41070.

Telephones: Pl. Gavidia, 7, near Pl. Concordia. Open Mon.-Fri. 10am-2pm and 5:30-10pm, Sat. 10am-2pm. **Telephone Code:** 95.

Flights: Aeropuerto San Pablo, (tel. 451 61 11, ext 1240), 12km from town on Ctra. Madrid. A taxi to the airport from the center of town costs about 1800ptas.

Trains: Estación Santa Justa, Av. Kansas City, s/n (info tel. 454 02 02, reservations 454 03 03). Bus 70 links Estación Santa Justa and the Prado de San Sebastián station. Bus EA goes to the airport and Puerta de Jerez, near regional tourist office. Both buses stop on Av. Kansas City, to the left as you exit the station. There's now special high-speed AVE (*Alta Velocidad Española*) train service between Seville and Madrid that reduces travel time to 2¾hr. **RENFE,** C. Zaragoza, 29 (tel. 421 79 98), near Pl. Nueva. Open Mon.-Fri. 9am-1:15pm and 4-7pm. Sat. 9am-1pm. Trains connect Seville to Córdoba, Cádiz, Málaga, Granada, and Madrid.

Buses: Prado de San Sebastián, C. José María Osborne, 11 (tel. 441 71 11). Bus 70, C1 and C2 link Estación Santa Justa and Prado de San Sebastián. **Transportes Alsina Graells** (tel. 441 88 11). To: Córdoba (2hr., 1100ptas); Granada (8 per day, 3¼-4hr., 2505ptas); **Transportes Comes** (tel. 441 68 58). To: Jerez de la Frontera (2hr., 825ptas); Algeciras (3½hr., 2000ptas). The newer bus station, serving destinations outside of Andalucía and Spain, is at **Plaza de Armas,** Puente Cristo de la Expiración corner with C. Arjona (tel. 490 80 40), on the river bank, facing the ghost-town remnant of Expo92. **Sevibus** (tel. 490 11 60) to Madrid (6hr. non-stop, 2305ptas).

Luggage Storage: At the main bus station (*consigna*) 90-180ptas. Open 6:30am-10pm. At the train station, lockers 300-500ptas per day. Open 24 hrs.

Laundromat: Lavandería Robledo, C. F. Sánchez Bedoya, 18 (tel. 421 81 32), 1 block west of the cathedral, across Av. Constitución. Wash and dry 5kg 950ptas. Open Mon.-Fri. 10am-2pm and 5-8pm, Sat. 10am-2pm.

Hospital: Hospital Universitario Virgen Macareno, Av. Dr. Fedriani, s/n (tel. 437 84 00). English spoken.

Emergency: tel. 091. **Police,** Av. Paseo de las Delicias, (tel. 461 67 76).

ACCOMMODATIONS AND CAMPING

During *Semana Santa* and the *Feria de Abril,* rooms vanish and prices soar. Make reservations if you value your feet. Look in the **Barrio de Santa Cruz,** especially around C. Mateos Gago. Also try the **Plaza de Curtidores** and the **Plaza de Pilatos,** in the Barrios Puerta de la Carne and Puerta de Carmona.

Sevilla Youth Hostel (HI), C. Isaac Peral, 2 (tel. 461 31 54), a few km out of town. Take the 34 bus from Plaza Nueva or the tourist office. 3-day max stay. No curfew or lockout. English spoken. All triples. Members 1007ptas, over 26 1484ptas; non-members 1484ptas, over 26 2650 ptas. Breakfast 160ptas.

Huéspedes Buen Dormir, C. Farnesio, 8 (tel. 421 74 92). From the cathedral follow C. Mateos Gago, bearing left on the main thoroughfare, then turn right on Fabiola; look for the alley opposite #10. Room size varies radically. Tropical birds chirp in the lobby. English spoken. Singles 1500ptas. Doubles 2500-3000ptas, with spotless bath 3500ptas. Triples with bath 4500ptas.

Hostal-Residencia Córdoba, C. Farnesio, 12 (tel. 422 74 98). Family-run with stained-wood doors, modern bathrooms, and spacious rooms. Singles 2500ptas. Doubles 3500-4500ptas. Triples 4800ptas, or request extra beds.

Hostal Bienvenido, C. Archeros, 14 (tel. 441 36 55), near Pl. Curtidores, just off C. Menéndez Pelayo. Welcoming, English-speaking managers are willing to negotiate prices. Small, dark rooms mitigated by a beautiful view from upstairs terrace. Singles 1500ptas. Doubles 3000ptas.

Hostal Galatea, C. San Juan de la Palma, 4 (tel. 456 35 64, fax 456 35 17). From the west end of Pl. Encarnación, take C. Regina; make a right on C. San Juan de la Palma. Young multilingual managers captivate patrons with their warmth and their clean, new *hostal* with TV room and peaceful *terraza*. All rooms with fan. Singles 2900ptas. Doubles 4700ptas, with shower 5800ptas. Triples 6100ptas.

Hostal Lis, C. Escarpín, 10 (tel. 421 30 88). Ostentatious brightly tiled entry and patio—Sevillian tiles on acid. Small *hostal* with large rooms, all with shower. Singles 2000ptas. Doubles 4000ptas. Triples 5600ptas.

Hostal La Gloria, C. San Eloy, 58 (tel. 422 26 73). Striking exterior with ornate wood trim in brick orange. Hot showers. A/C upstairs where most needed. Singles 2500ptas, with bath 3000ptas. Doubles 3500ptas.

Camping Sevilla, Ctra. Madrid-Cádiz, km 534 (tel. 451 43 79), 12km out of town near the airport. From Estación Prado de San Sebastián, take the Empresa Casal bus toward Carmona (approx. every hr. 7am-9:30pm, 225ptas) or bus 70, which stops 800m away at Parque Alcosa. 525ptas per person, 500ptas per car and tent.

Camping Villson, Ctra. Sevilla-Cádiz, km 554, (tel. 472 08 28), about 14km out of the city. Take the Los Amarillos bus that goes to Dos Hermanas via Barriada (every 20-25min. 6:30am-midnight, 130ptas). Adults 400ptas; 425ptas per car and per tent. Hot showers included. Free pool.

FOOD

Seville is renowned for its jams, pastry, and candy, sold in **Plaza del Cabildo** near the cathedral. *Bar-restaurantes* gravitate around Estación de Córdoba on **Calle Arjona** and **Avenida Marqués de Paradas,** and on many streets of **El Arenal** and **Barrio Santa Cruz.** A number of inexpensive, student-oriented restaurants and bars operate during the schoolyear (Sept.-June) on **Avenida Reina Mercedes. Barrio Triana** is Seville's favored venue for the *tapeo* (*tapas*-barhopping), a gloriously active alternative to sit-down dining. *Sangría* and *tinto de verano,* a cold blend of red wine and Casera (sweetened or citrus-flavored tonic water) will quench your thirst. Buy fresh produce from screaming vendors at the **Mercado del Arenal,** near the bullring on C. Pastor y Leandro, between C. Almansa and C. Arenal. Look there for *toro de lidia* (fresh bull meat) (open Mon.-Sat. 9am-2pm).

Restaurante El Baratillo, C. Pavia, 12 (tel. 422 96 51), on a tiny street off C. Dos de Mayo. Friendly owner circulates among the customers and offering tasty samples of her cooking in a room covered with early-eighties posters. Huge *menú,* including wine or beer 500ptas. Excellent *platos combinados* 450-750ptas. Meals served Mon.-Fri. 8am-10pm, Sat. noon-5pm.

Jalea Real, Sor Angela de la Cruz, 37 (tel. 421 61 03), near Pl. Encarnación. From Pl. Encarnación, head 150m east on C. Laraña, and turn left immediately before Iglesia de San Pedro. Young and hip vegetarian restaurant. 2-course lunch *menú* with whole-wheat bread, wine, and dessert 1200ptas. Monumental *platos combinados* 700ptas. Open Mon.-Fri. 1:30-5pm and 8:30-11:30pm, Sat. 1:30-5pm; Oct.-May Tues.-Sat. 1:30-5pm and 8:30-11:30pm, Sun. 1:30-4:30pm.

Bodega Santa Cruz, C. Rodrigo Caro, 1 (tel. 421 32 46). Take C. Mateos Gago, on the north end of the cathedral; the *bodega* is on the first corner on your right. Casual and crowded—locals come at all hours to sample the varied and tasty *tapas* (150ptas), washing them down with beer (110ptas). Open 8am-midnight.

Mesón Serranito, C. Antonia Díaz, 11 (tel. 421 12 43), beside the bullring. Take C. García Vinuesa across from the cathedral and split left on C. Antonia Díaz. Stuffed bull heads line the walls. *Platos combinados* 750-800ptas. Open Mon.-Sat. noon-4:30pm and 8pm-midnight.

Mesón La Barca, C. Santander, 6, across C. Temprado, off Paseo de Cristóbal Colón, up from Torre del Oro. Small restaurant, ample portions. *Platos combinados* from 650ptas. Open Sun.-Fri. 11am-midnight.

Freiduría Santana, C. Pureza, 61 (tel. 433 20 40), parallel to C. Betis, 1 block away from the river. Fresh *pescado* (fish), *calamares*, and *gambas* (shrimp). Free samples ease the wait. Open Sept.-July Tues.-Sun. 7pm-midnight.

Casa Manolo, C. San Jorge, 16 (tel. 433 47 92), north of Puente Isabel II. This local favorite is a madhouse during *fiestas*. *Menú de la casa* 1600ptas, *pescado frito* (fried fish) 850ptas. Meals served Tues.-Sun. 9am-midnight.

SIGHTS

Christians razed an Almohad mosque to clear space for Seville's **cathedral** in 1401, although the famed **La Giralda** minaret survived. The conquerors demonstrated their religious fervor by constructing a church so great that, in their own words, "those who come after us will take us for madmen." The largest Gothic edifice ever built, it took more than a century to complete. Black and gold coffin-bearers guard the **Tumba de Cristóbal Colón** (Columbus's Tomb). The tower and its twins in Marrakech and Rabat are the oldest and largest surviving Almohad minarets. (Tower and cathedral open Mon.-Sat. 11am-5pm, Sun. 2-5pm; Giralda also open Sun. 10am-2pm. Joint admission 550ptas, students 200ptas, senior citizens free.) Outside of the cathedral, on the northeast end, the **Patio de los Naranjos** (orange trees) evokes the bygone days of the Arab caliphate. The winding alleys of the **Judería** (old Jewish quarter) run from the Patio de los Naranjos to the Jardines de Murillo, along the walls of the Alcázar.

The 9th-century walls of the **Alcázar** face the south side of the cathedral. The site was used as early as 712 by the Almohads to control the Guadalquivir, and this palace-fortress is the oldest still used by European royalty. (Open Tues.-Sat. 10:30am-5pm., Sun. 10am-1pm. 600ptas, students free.) The 16th-century **Lonja** was built by Felipe II as a commercial exchange for American trade. In 1784 it was turned into the Archive of the Indies, a collection of over 30,000 documents relating to the conquest of the "New World." Highlights include letters from Columbus to Fernando and Isabel. (Open Mon.-Fri. 10am-1pm. Free.) The **Museo de Arte Contemporáneo** next door (C. Santo Tomaso, 5) has some fab Mirós on the top floor (open Tues.-Fri. 10am-2pm; Oct.-June Tues.-Fri. 10am-7pm, Sat.-Sun. 10am-2pm; free). On C. Temprado, off C. Santander, two blocks west of the Lonja, is the **Hospital de la Caridad,** a compact 17th-century complex of arcaded courtyards. Its founder, Don Miguel de Mañara, is popularly believed to be the model for Don Juan. (Open Mon.-Sat. 10am-1pm and 3:30-6pm. Church 200ptas.)

King Fernando III forced Jews fleeing Toledo to live in the **Barrio de Santa Cruz,** now a neighborhood of winding alleys, flower pots, and excellent art galleries. North of Barrio Santa Cruz off Pl. Pilatos, the **Casa de Pilatos** is the most sumptuous Sevillian palace after the Alcázar (open 9am-7pm; 1000ptas). The **Museo Provincial**

SPAIN

de **Bellas Artes,** Pl. Museo, 9, in a 16th century Andalusian palace and a connected church, has a collection of Spanish masters second only to the Prado (open Tues.-Sun. 9am-3pm; 250ptas, EU citizens under 21 free). Undergoing renovations.

ENTERTAINMENT

The tourist office distributes *El Giraldillo,* a free monthly magazine on entertainment in Seville. Sevillians gather in *bares, terrazas,* and *chiringuitos (*outdoor bars that pulsate to *bacalao* techno-dance music) clustered on the riverside, along Paseo de Cristóbal Colón, between Puente del Generalísimo and Puente de Isabel II. **Bar Capote,** next to Puente de Isabel II, rocks (open Mon.-Thurs. until about 5am, Fri.-Sat. even later). On Po. Delicias, **Alfonso XII, Líbano,** and **Chile** are the bars of choice for ending a *marcha* (an evening of bar-hopping). The gay scene is coming out strong in Seville; popular disco-bars with a mostly international clientele include **Lamentable** and **Cátedra** on Pl. Alfalfa and **Poseidón** on C. Marqués de las Paradas.

The best flamenco in town is on the western edge of Barrio Santa Cruz at **Los Gallos,** Pl. Santa Cruz, 11 (tel. 421 69 81). The cover (3000ptas) includes one drink. (Show times change every couple of weeks; call ahead for listings.) Several booths on C. Sierpes, C. Velázquez and Pl. Toros sell **bullfight** tickets. For information on dates and prices, go to **Plaza de Toros** or call 422 31 52.

Seville's world-famous **Semana Santa** (Holy Week) festival lasts from Palm Sunday to Good Friday. Penitents in hoods guide bejeweled floats, lit by hundred of candles, through the streets. The city explodes in the **Feria de Abril** (April Fair), a week-long festival that began as a popular revolt against foreign influence in the 19th century. The party rages with circuses, folklore displays, and bullfights.

■ NEAR SEVILLE

Cádiz The headquarters of the Spanish treasure fleet, Sir Francis Drake torched the Spanish Armada as it lay at anchor here in 1587. The city is energetically progressive: Cádiz's inhabitants fought fiercely against the Fascists during the 1936-39 Civil War, and today they consistently vote for leftist parties. Socially, the city has a roaring nightlife, open gay life, and the most extravagant carnival in all of Spain. The **tourist office** is on the right-hand corner of the Pl. San Juan de Dios (tel. (956) 24 10 01; open Mon.-Fri. 9am-2pm and 5-8pm, Sat. 10am-2pm). *Hostales* huddle around the harbor and Pl. San Juan de Dios, many on C. Marqués de Cádiz and C. Flamenco. The **Hostal Colón,** C. Marqués de Cádiz, 1 (tel. (956) 28 53 51), is squeaky clean and colorful (doubles 2800-3200ptas). **Hostal Cádiz,** C. Feduchy, 20 (tel. (956) 28 58 01) is friendly and up on things (doubles 2500-3000ptas, triples 3600-4500ptas).

Jerez de la Frontera You can see fermenting sherry in the *bodegas* (wine cellars) of Jerez de la Frontera, one of Andalusia's most commercial cities. **Harvey's of Bristol** (tel. (95) 15 10 30; 200ptas), **González Byass** (tel. (95) 34 00 00; 300ptas), and **B. Domecq** (tel. (95) 33 18 00; free) have multilingual tour guides who distill the complete sherry-making process as you sip free samples. (Call ahead for tour hours.) Avoid visiting the town in August, when many *bodegas* close down for the annual hangover. During the second week in September, the town erupts in the harvest celebration **Fiestas de la Vendimia.** The **tourist office** is at C. Alameda Cristina, 7 (tel. (95) 33 11 50, -62; open Mon.-Fri. 8am-3pm and 5:30-8pm, Sat. 10am-1:30pm; winter Mon.-Fri. 8am-3pm and 5-7pm, Sat. 10am-2pm). **Trains** come from Seville (11 *regionales* per day, 1½hr., 400ptas). Finding a bed in Jerez is as easy as finding wine. Look along **Calle Medina,** near the bus station, and **Calle Arcos,** which intersects C. Medina at Pl. Romero Martínez. The **Albergue Juvenil (HI),** Av. Carrero Blanco, 30 (tel. (95) 34 28 90), is in an ugly urbanization, a 10min. bus ride (bus L-8 leaves near the bus station, every 15min., 80ptas; or bus L-1 from Pl. Arenal) or a 25min. walk from downtown, and definitely worth the hike. (1007ptas, 1166ptas with breakfast. Over 26: 1484ptas; 1643ptas. Nonmembers: 2650ptas; 2809ptas.) *Tapas*-hoppers bounce in, out, and all around **Plaza del Arenal,** or northeast on Av.

Alcalde Alvaro Domeqo around **Plaza del Caballo.** *Jerez,* the local wine of which natives are justifiably proud, is ubiquitous and inexpensive.

Arcos de la Frontera Arcos de la Frontera is a historic monument of a city, a maze of alleyways, medieval ruins, and stone arches in the midst of fields of sunflowers and sherry-grape vines. The **Iglesia de Santa María** offers a dandy view of olive groves and low hills. Built in 1553, the church has a unique interior melange of Gothic, Renaissance, and Baroque styles. A Spanish-speaking guide is available. (Open Mon.-Fri. 10am-1pm and 4-7pm. Mass 8pm, also Sun. noon. 150ptas.) For sleeping, try **Fonda del Comercio,** C. Debajo del Corral, 15 (tel. 70 00 57), with its high, beamed ceilings, and thick white-washed walls. (Singles 1500ptas. Doubles 2600ptas.) The **tourist office** is at C. Cuesta de Belén (tel. (956) 70 22 64), on the continuation of the Corredera (open Mon.-Fri. 9am-2pm and 5-7pm, Sat. 10am-2pm; winter Mon.-Fri. 9am-3pm and 5-7pm, Sat. 10am-2pm). **T.G. Comes** buses travel to Cádiz (1½hr., 615ptas), Jerez (½hr., 255ptas) while **Los Amarillos** (tel. (956) 70 02 57) jaunts to Seville (2½hr., 840ptas), Cádiz (710ptas) and Jerez (255ptas).

■■■ CÓRDOBA

Córdoba has seen Christianity, Islam, and Judaism meet in harmony and strife for centuries. Arab occupation brought the town its greatest prosperity; for a time Córdoba, with its vast library, was one of the largest cities in medieval Europe. The city's whitewashed houses, serene patios and narrow streets typify Spanish Andalusia; Moorish influence lingers as both Muslims and Catholics still congregate in the Mezquita (mosque) every year on the anniversary of its construction.

ORIENTATION AND PRACTICAL INFORMATION

Córdoba sits atop the Andalusian triangle (north of Seville and Granada), about halfway between Madrid and Gibraltar. The city's more modern and commercial northern half extends from the train station on **Avenida de América** down to **Plaza de las Tendillas** in the center of the city; the older, maze-like southern half, known as the **Judería** (old Jewish quarter), extends from Pl. Tendillas down to the banks of the Guadalquivir, winding past the Mezquita and Alcázar.

Tourist Office: Oficina Municipal de Turismo y Congresos, Pl. Judas Levi (tel. and fax 20 05 22), next to the youth hostel. English spoken. Open Mon.-Sat. 9am-2pm and 5:30-7:30pm, Sun. 9am-2pm; Nov.-May Mon.-Sat. 9am-2pm and 4:30-6:30pm.
Post Office: C. Cruz Conde, 15 (tel. 47 82 67), just north of Pl. Tendillas. Open for stamps and *Lista de Correos* Mon.-Fri. 8am-9pm, Sat. 9am-7pm. **Telegrams:** tel. 47 03 45. Open Mon.-Fri. 8am-9pm, Sat. 9am-7pm. **Postal Code:** 14070.
Telephones: Pl. Tendillas, 7. Open Mon.-Fri. 9:30am-1:55pm and 5-9pm, Sat. 9:30am-1:55pm. **City Code:** 957.
Trains: Av. América s/n. (Information: tel. 49 02 02.) To: Seville (*AVE* 45min., 1800-2500ptas; *talgo* 1hr., 1700-2000ptas; *regional* 2½hr., 710ptas); Málaga (*talgo* 2½hr., 1800-2100ptas; *regional* 3hr., 1800ptas); Madrid (*AVE* 1¾hr., 5000-6600ptas; *talgo* 2¼hr., 4600-5200ptas; *expreso* 6¾hr., 3200ptas). **RENFE,** Ronda de los Tejares, 10 (tel. 47 58 54). Open Mon.-Fri. 9am-1:15pm and 5-7:30pm.
Buses: Transportes Ureña and **Empresa Bacoma,** Av. Cervantes, 22 (tel. 47 23 52). To: Valencia (4500ptas); Barcelona (7500ptas). **Alsina-Graells Sur,** Av. Medina Azahara, 29 (tel. 23 64 74). To: Seville (2hr., 1605ptas); Málaga (3½hr. 1395ptas). **Autocares Priego** (tel. 29 01 58 and 29 07 69) runs anywhere on the Sierra Cordobesa; **Empresa Carrera** (tel. 23 14 01) functions in the Campiña Cordobesa; and **Empresa Ramírez** (tel. 41 01 00) runs buses to nearby towns and camping sites.
Luggage Storage: Paquete-Exprés, next to the train station. 300ptas per locker.
Medical Assistance: Urgencias Avenida de América, Av. América, s/n (tel. 47 23 82), ½km east of the train station.

Emergency: Ambulance, tel. 29 55 70. **Fire,** tel. 080. **National Police,** tel. 091. **Municipal Police,** tel. 092.

ACCOMMODATIONS AND CAMPING

Accommodations cluster near the train station, in and around the Judería, and off the Plaza de las Tendillas, and are crowded during *Semana Santa* (around Easter).

Residencia Juvenil Córdoba (HI), Pl. Judas Levi (tel. 29 01 66, fax 29 05 00), next to the municipal tourist office. Impeccably clean, brand-new. Thick plastic divisions instead of walls. English spoken. No curfew. 1007ptas, over 26 1484ptas. Breakfast 159ptas. Non-members pay more. Call ahead in the summer, and confirm a day before arriving.

Hostal-Residencia Séneca, C. Conde y Luque, 7 (tel. 47 32 34), 2 blocks north of the Mezquita. Impeccably maintained by vivacious English-speaking owner with list of places to visit. Doubles 3350ptas, with bath 4350ptas. Triples 4800ptas, with bath 6250ptas. Lower rates in winter.

Huéspedes Martínez Rücker, Martínez Rücker, 14 (tel. 47 25 62), just east of the Mezquita. Airy, arboreal courtyard and charming rooms. Singles 1500ptas. Doubles 3000ptas.

Camping: Municipal, Av. Brillante (tel. 47 20 00; ask for *Camping Municipal*). About 2km north of the train station: turn left on Av. América, left again at Av. Brillante, then walk uphill. Buses 10 and 11, which leave from Av. Cervantes near the station, run to the campsite. 519ptas per person, per tent and per car.

FOOD

The famous Mezquita attracts more high-priced eateries than Mohammed did followers. If you're counting pesetas, find a bargain eatery on **Calle Doctor Fleming**, west of the Judería, or on **Avenida de Menéndez Pidal** in the Barrio Cruz Conde.

Sociedad de Plateros, C. San Francisco, 6 (tel. 47 00 42), between C. San Francisco and the top end of Pl. Potro. Casual atmosphere attracts families by day and British students by night. Wide selection of *tapas*. 300-600ptas, with fresh fish every day. Bar open 8am-4pm and 7pm-1am; meals served 1-4pm and 8pm-midnight. Others scattered throughout Córdoba.

Taberna Salinas, C. Tundidores, 3 (tel. 48 01 35), just south of the Ayuntamiento. A shining example of traditional Cordoban cooking. 600-700ptas. Open Mon.-Sat. 12:30-4:30pm and 8:30pm-midnight.

Mesón de las Cabezas, C. Cabezas, 17 (tel. 47 83 56). Dark, musty, weird and wonderful. Great place to drink wine (half-glass 50ptas)—not much else is served. Cheerful host, quiet patio fountain, and a surreal juxtaposition of decorations: bullfight posters, nude calendars, old metal signs, a stuffed owl, and a boar's head. A nearby rooster crows all day long. Open Tues.-Sun. 11am-3pm and 7-11pm, but hours are as unpredictable as the tastes of the owner and patrons.

SIGHTS AND ENTERTAINMENT

Begun in 784, the **Mezquita** was intended to surpass all other mosques in grandeur. Over the next 2 centuries the spectacular golden-brown building was gradually enlarged to cover an area equivalent to several city blocks. The courtyard features carefully spaced orange trees, palm trees, and fountains. Inside, 850 pink and blue marble, alabaster, and stone columns support hundreds of red- and white-striped 2-tiered arches. In 1523 drastic alterations stuck a full-blown Renaissance cathedral in the middle of the mosque. (Open 10am-7pm; Oct.-March 10am-1:30pm and 3:30-5:30pm. 700ptas, free during mass Mon.-Fri. 8:30-10am, Sun. 10am-1pm.)

Just west of the Mezquita and closer to the river lies the **Alcázar**, a palace for Catholic monarchs that headquartered the Inquisition between 1490 and 1821. Its walls surround a manicured hedge garden with flower beds, terraced goldfish ponds, fountains, and palm trees. (Open Tues.-Sat. 9:30am-1:30pm and 5-8pm, Sun. 9:30am-1; Oct.-April 9:30am-1:30pm and 4-7pm. Gardens illuminated May-Sept. 10pm-1am. 300ptas, free Tues.) Tucked away on C. Judíos, the **Sinagoga** is a solemn reminder of the 1492 expulsion of Spanish Jewry. (Open Tues.-Sat. 10am-2pm and 3:30-5:30pm, Sun. 10am-1:30pm. 50ptas.) The **Museo Taurino y de Arte Cordobés,** at Pl. Maimonides, a bullfighting museum, displays heads of matadors killed by fearless bulls. (Open Tues.-Sat. 9:30am-1:30pm and 5-8pm, Sun. 9:30am-1:30pm; Oct.-April Tues.-Sat. 9:30am-1:30pm and 4-7pm, Sun. 9:30am-1:30pm. 300ptas, free Tues.)

For **flamenco,** join fellow tourists and head for the **Tablao Cardenal,** Cardenal Herrero, 14 (tel. 48 03 46), facing the Mezquita (Tues.-Sat. 10:30pm; 2500ptas, includes a drink). The tourist office keeps a schedule of **bullfights** at Las Califas bullring; tickets range from 800 to 12,000ptas.

During most of the year, Córdoba's youth frequent the pubs and clubs around the **Plaza Tendillas** at night. From the first weekend in June until the heat subsides, the **Brillante** area (uphill from and north of Av. América, or a 500-900ptas cab ride) is the place to be: the Sierra is cool, the beer cold, and the prices not too high.

■ MEDINA AZAHARA

Constructed in the 10th century by Abderramán III, the Medina Azahara is a pleasure palace built into the Sierra Morena, 8km northwest of the city. Before its excavation in 1944, the existence of the site had been mere rumor. (Open Tues.-Sat. 10am-2pm and 6-8:30pm, Sun. 10am-2pm; Oct.-April Tues.-Sat. 10am-2pm and 4-6:30pm, Sun. 10am-2pm. 300ptas, EU citizens free.) Reaching Medina Azahara takes some effort; call ahead to make sure it's open (tel. 23 40 25). The O-1 bus (schedule information tel. 25 57 00) leaves from Av. Cervantes for Cruce Medina Azahara, stopping 3km from the site itself (about every hr. 6:30am-10:30pm, 90ptas).

■■■ GRANADA

As the Christian Reconquista advanced, the Moors enclosed the glorious city of Granada in layer upon layer of fortification. The citadel was bitterly contested until 1492, when Boabdil, its last Arab king, lost the city's keys to Catholic monarchs Fernando and Isabel. Though Granada's mosques were destroyed, the majestic clay-red Alhambra and snow-capped Sierra Nevada still lure travelers here. The 50,000 students of its university help make Granada a lively provincial capital.

ORIENTATION AND PRACTICAL INFORMATION

The center of Granada is **Plaza Nueva,** framed by handsome Renaissance buildings and outfitted with a wide variety of hotels and restaurants. Plaza Nueva sits just north of **Plaza de Isabel la Católica,** which is at the intersection of the two main arteries, **Calle Reyes Católicos** and **Gran Vía de Colón.** From RENFE and all bus stations except Alsina Graells, follow Av. Constitución to Gran Vía de Colón, turn right and walk 15-20min. into town. Municipal **buses** cover nearly all areas of town; bus 11 connects a number of major streets, including Carretera de Madrid, the train and bus stations and the town center. If solo, avoid the small streets at the foot of the Albaycín northeast of Pl. Nueva after dark.

Tourist Office: Pl. Mariana Pineda, 10 (tel. 22 66 88). From Puerta Real turn right onto Angel-Gavinet, and then the 3rd right again. Ask for a map of the Alhambra and the Albaycín since the palace complex itself does not provide one. Open Mon.-Fri. 9am-2pm and 4:30-7pm, Sat. 10am-1pm. **Branch Tourist Office:** C. Mariana Pineda, s/n (tel. 22 59 90). Open Mon.-Fri. 10am-8pm, Sat. 10am-2pm.
Budget Travel: Viajes TIVE, C. Martínez Campo, 21 (tel. 25 02 11) off C. Recogidos. Open Mon.-Fri. 9am-1pm.
Currency Exchange: Look for the **banks** all along Gran Vía, and compare rates.
American Express: Viajes Bonal, Av. Constitución, 19 (tel. 27 63 12), at the north end of Gran Vía de Colón. Open Mon.-Fri. 9:30am-1:30pm and 5-8pm.

Post Office: Puerta Real, s/n (tel. 22 48 35, fax 22 36 41). Open for stamps and *Lista de Correos* Mon.-Fri. 8am-9pm, Sat. 9am-2pm; for telegrams Mon.-Fri. 8am-9pm, Sat. 9am-6pm. Fax service. **Postal Code:** 18080.

Telephones: C. Reyes Católicos, 55, 1 bl. towards Pl. Nueva from Pl. Isabel la Católica. Open Mon.-Sat. 9am-2pm and 5-10pm. **Telephone Code:** 958.

Trains: Av. Andaluces, s/n (tel. 27 12 72). From Pl. Isabel la Católica, follow Gran Vía de Colón to the end, then bear left on Av. Constitución. Turn left on Av. Andaluces. To: Madrid (6-8hr., 3400-5200ptas), Barcelona (14hr., 6500ptas), Algeciras (5hr., 1595ptas), Cádiz (6hr., 2100ptas). The **RENFE office** for information and ticket sales is on C. Reyes Católicos, 63 (tel. 22 71 70).

Buses: The usual mess of companies, including **Alsina Graells,** Camino de Ronda, 97 (tel. 25 13 58), near C. Emperatriz Eugenia in Andalucía, and **Bacoma,** Av. Andaluces, 12 (tel. 28 42 51), near the train station.

Luggage Storage: At the **train station** (200ptas). At the Alsina Graells **bus station** (300ptas).

Laundromat: Lavandería Autoservicio Emperatriz Eugenia, C. Emperatriz Eugenia, 26 (tel. 27 88 20). Exit Alsina Graells bus station to the left and turn at the first right. Wash 300ptas. Dry 200ptas. Open Mon.-Sat. 9am-2pm and 4-8pm.

Medical Assistance: Clínica de San Cecilio, C. Doctor Oloriz, 16 (tel. 28 02 00).

Emergencies: Municipal Police, C. Duquesa, 21 (tel. 092). **Policía Nacional,** Pl. Campos (tel. 091). English and French spoken (theoretically).

ACCOMMODATIONS, CAMPING, AND FOOD

Freshly renovated in 1994, the **Albergue Juvenil Granada (HI),** Ramón y Cajal, 2 (27 26 38, fax 28 52 85) offers doubles with baths and 6 singles with handicapped access. From Alsina Graells station, walk down Camino de Ronda for about 15min., take the right fork to the end, then turn down a gravel road and walk through the tall peach and gray gate. Or take bus 11 from the center. (No curfew. 1007ptas per person, over 26: 1488ptas. Nonmembers 1488ptas, over 26: 2500ptas.) Funkily tiled **Hostal Austria,** Cuesta de Gomérez, 4 (tel. 22 70 75) was remodeled last year and sparkles. All rooms have baths and 8ft windows. (Singles 1500-2000ptas. Doubles 2500-3000ptas.) To be let in by a rope/pulley home invention to the **Hostal Navarro-Ramos,** Cuesta de Gomérez, 21 (tel. 25 05 55), ring the buzzer. (Singles 1200ptas. Doubles 1900ptas, with bath 2900ptas. Triples with bath 3900ptas.) **Hostal Residencia Britz,** Cuesta de Gomérez, 1 (tel. 22 36 52), on the corner of Pl. Nueva, has a cool soft-drink machine in the lobby that says *"Gracias."* Oh, and the rooms are good. (Singles 2120ptas. Doubles 3286ptas, with bath 4505ptas. 6% discount if you flash *Let's Go*.) **Camping** is available at 4 locations near Granada. **Sierra Nevada,** Av. Madrid, 107 (tel. 15 09 54), reached by bus 3 or 5, has lots of shady trees, modern facilities, and free hot showers (460ptas per person, tent, or car).

Restaurante Alcaicería, C. Oficios, 6, is one of the most highly regarded eateries in town. Enter through the vine-covered archway and follow the sounds of the guitar. (*Menú* 1450ptas. Open 1-4pm and 8-11:30pm.) The unassuming façade of **Rincón de Pepe,** Escudo de Carmen, 17, off Pl. Carmen, hides good food and better prices. (*Menú* 525-975ptas. Open noon-4pm and 7:30-11pm.) The **market,** usually located on C. San Augustín, has transferred to Pl. Romanilla beside the cathedral, where it will remain until the architectural dig at the usual spot is done (open Mon.-Sat. 8am-3pm).

SIGHTS

The **Alhambra** is the name of both the hill that dominates Granada and the sprawling palace-fortress atop it. Against the silvery backdrop of the Sierra Nevada, the Christians drove the first Nazarite King Alhamar from the Albayzín to this more strategic hill. Here he built a fortress called the **Alcazaba,** the oldest section of today's Alhambra. The **Alcázar** (Royal Palace) was built for the great Moorish rulers Yusuf I (1333-1354) and Muhammad V (1354-1391). Legend has it that an unexplained force murdered Yusuf I in an isolated basement chamber of the Alcázar; his son Muhammad V was left to complete the palace. After the Christian *Reconquista* drove the Moors from Spain, Fernando and Isabella respectfully restored the Alcázar. Little did they know that two generations later omnipotent Emperor Carlos V would demolish part of it to make way for his **Palacio de Carlos V,** a Renaissance masterpiece by Pedro Machuca, a disciple of Michelangelo. Although it is glaringly incongruous amidst all the Moorish splendor, experts agree that the Palacio is one of the most beautiful Renaissance buildings in Spain. Up the hill past the Alhambra's main entrance is the lush palace greenery of the **Generalife,** the spacious summer retreat of the Sultans that crowns the Alhambra's twin hill, *el cerro del sol* (the sun hill). Enter the Alhambra through Puerta de Granada, off Cuesta de Gomérez. (Alhambra open Mon.-Sat. 9am-7:45pm, Sun. 9am-5:45pm; Oct.-May 9am-5:45pm. 600ptas, Sun. after 3pm free. Generalife only, 150ptas. Box office shuts down about 45min. before closing time.)

Begun 30 years after the Christian reconquest of the city, the **cathedral** (entrance on Gran Vía), intended to outshine the Alhambra, does not even rise out of its shadow. The **Capilla Real** (Royal Chapel) contains the elaborate tomb of Fernando and Isabel, their nutty daughter Juana La Loca, and her handsome husband Felipe el Hermoso, whose corpse Juana dragged around with her for a unpleasantly long time after his demise. (Both open 10:30am-1pm and 4-7pm; Oct.-Feb.10:30am-1pm and 3:30-6pm. 200ptas.)

ENTERTAINMENT

Entertainment listings are near the back of the daily paper, the *Ideal* (90ptas), under the heading *Cine y Espectáculos.* The Friday supplement lists even more bars, concerts, and special events. Avoid the **Cuevas Gitanas de Sacromonte** (gypsy caves). Once home to a thriving Gypsy community, the hill is now just a snare for gullible tourists. Instead, head for the **Albaycín.** Exclusive **Casa de Yanguas,** on C. San Buenaventura off Cuesta del Chapiz, with terraces, balconies, and even a rotating art exhibit surrounding its 15th-century Moorish patio, competes with **Carmen de Aben Humeya,** off Pl. San Nicolás, for the title of Most Romantic Bar in Spain. (Drinks at both start at 600ptas.) If you want to discuss China's economic future, try **Restaurante-Bar Poetas Andaluces II,** C. Pedro A. Alarcán, 43.

■ LA CARTUJA AND FUENTEVAQUEROS

On the outskirts of Granada stands **La Cartuja,** a 16th-century Gothic Carthusian monastery. A marble with rich brown tones and swirling forms (a stone unique to nearby Lanjarón) marks the sacristy of Saint Bruno. To reach the monastery, take **bus** 8 (85ptas) from in front of the cathedral. (Open 10:30am-1pm and 4-7pm; Oct.-Feb. 10:30am-1pm and 3:30-6pm.)

Author of *Bodas de sangre* (Blood Weddings) and *Romancero Gitano* (Gypsy Ballads), poet and playwright Federico García Lorca was born outside of town in tiny **Fuentevaqueros,** near the airport. The ancestral house-*cum*-**museo** has photographs, manuscripts, and even some sketches by the great poet-and dramatist, who was shot by right-wing forces near Granada at the outbreak of the Civil War. The museum is a psychoanalyst's dream—García Lorca spent his formative years there—but few others can get that excited about a place where he lived only nine years. (Open to 15 people every ½hr. Tues.-Sun. 10am-1pm and 6-8pm; Oct.-March Tues.-Sun. 10am-1pm and 4-6pm; April-June Tues.-Sat. 10am-1pm and 5-7pm. 100ptas.) **Buses** (150ptas) run to the house from the train station almost every hour.

■■■ COSTA DEL SOL

The coast has sold its soul to the Devil, and now he's starting to collect. Artifice covers its once-natural charms as chic promenades and hotels seal off small towns from the shoreline. The former Phoenician, Greek, Roman, and Arab ports cater to an international clientele with wads of money and tons of attitude. Although the Costa del Sol officially extends from Tarifa in the southwest to Cabo de Gata east of Almería, the name most often refers to the resorts from Marbella, in the province of Málaga, to Motril, in the province of Granada. Post-industrial Málaga divides the Costa in two. To the northeast, the hills dip straight into the ocean, where the scenery is less spoiled but beaches are usually rocky. To the southeast, the Costa is more built up and water washes almost entirely against concrete.

Nothing can take away the coast's major attraction, however: 8 months of spring and 4 of summer per year. Sun-freaks swarm everywhere in July and August; make reservations or be ready for a search. Prices double in high season. Some sleep on the beaches (solo travelers and women should be cautious), a practice that is winked at on the outskirts of less elegant areas. Alternatively, ask around for *casas particulares*. June is the best time to visit, when summer weather has come to town but most vacationers haven't.

Trains go far as Málaga, Torremolinos, or Fuengirola; private bus lines supply connections along the coast itself. Railpasses are not valid, but prices are reasonable.

MÁLAGA

More style than substance, the city is known gastronomically for wine (not cuisine) and economically for tourism (not industry). Poor Málaga, once celebrated by Hans Christian Andersen, Rubén Darío and native poet Vicente Aleixandre, has lost its looks. Its concrete arms extend down the coast, its beaches are unpleasant and its streets are crowded and dirty. But Málaga is the transportation hub of Andalusia, and its residents some of the most lively, genial people you are likely to meet.

To see the city at its best, stroll the length of the palmy **Paseo del Parque;** it'll take you below the **Alcazaba,** the local Moorish palace. The labyrinthine palace attaches to the **Museo Arqueológico,** where neolithic pottery will capture your attention (open Tues.-Fri. 9:30am-1:30pm and 4-7pm, Sat. 10am-1pm, Sun. 10am-2pm; in summer, also Mon. 9:30am-1:30pm). For a breathtaking view of Málaga and the Mediterranean, climb up to the **Castillo Gibralfaro,** originally constructed by the Phoenicians and later rebuilt by the Arabs. Take bus 35 from the Po. Parque (10 per day, 11am-7:05pm, 100ptas). The **Museo de Bellas Artes,** C. San Augustín, 8, in the old palace of the Counts of Buenavista, hoards a wealth of mosaics, sculptures and paintings, including works by Murillo, Ribera, and native son Picasso (open Tues.-Fri. 10am-1:30pm and 5-8pm, Sat.-Sun. 10am-1:30pm; 250ptas, EU students under 21 free). Po. Parque turns into **Almeda Principal** just east of the **Plaza de la Marina.** The city center, containing most sights and the **cathedral** (called "the little lady with one arm" because no one ever bothered to finish the second tower) is north of Almeda Principal. (Cathedral open Mon.-Fri. 10am-12:45pm and 4-5:30pm.)

Young *malagueños* have two destinations after the sun goes down: either the beaches and nightclubs at **Pedregalejos** (take bus 11), or the bars and discos *"del centro"*—particularly around **Calle Comedia.** The *Guía de Ocio* (160ptas), sold at newsstands, lists the week's events around town.

Practical Information, Accommodations, and Food There's a multilingual **tourist office** at Pasaje de Chinitas, 4 (tel. (95) 221 34 45), off Pl. Constitución (open Mon.-Fri. 9am-2pm, Sat. 9am-1pm). To get to the **train station** (tel. (95) 231 25 00), hop on bus 3 at Po. Parque or bus 4 at Pl. Marina. **RENFE,** C. Strachan, 4 (tel. (95) 260 23 66 or 236 02 02), is less crowded, and more convenient for getting tickets and information (open Mon.-Fri. 9am-1:30pm and 4:30-7:30pm). Trains run to Torremolinos (½hr., 125ptas), Córdoba (3hr., 1700ptas), Madrid (7hr., 4200ptas), and Barcelona (14hr., 6400ptas). The enormous central **bus station,** at Po. Tilos (tel. (95) 235 00 61), lies behind RENFE.

Head toward **Avenida de las Américas, Plaza de la Constitución,** or **Calle Córdoba** for a good night's rest. Many budget establishments cluster north of **Paseo del Parque** and **Alameda Principal.** Be particularly wary of the following neighborhoods after dark: Alameda de Colón, El Perchel (streets northwest of C. Cuarteles), Cruz de Molnillo, streets around the market, and La Esperanza/Santo Domingo (north of El Corte Inglés). Only a 30sec. walk from good ol' McDonald's, **Hostal La**

Palma, C. Martínez, 7 (tel. (95) 222 67 72), off C. Marqués de Larios, is blessed with ceiling fans. (Singles 1500-1800ptas. Doubles 2500-2800ptas. Triples 3300-3600ptas. Quads 4400-4800ptas.) For inexpensive food, try the *pasajes* around the cathedral and **Calle Granada,** or focus on drinking liquids in the bars and cafés on **Paseo Marítimo.** Those in the know dine on the beachfront in **Pedregalejo,** near the eastern edge of town, where a row of crowded and inexpensive restaurants snatches up the day's catch. Wash your fried squid down with either *malagueño* or *moscatel,* Málaga's sweet wines.

TORREMOLINOS

Something about Torremolinos just screams *Love Boat:* hordes of shoppers peering into Duty-Free stickered windows, and tourists downing drinks at kiosk bars, tapping their feet to the likes of Gloria Estefan. Travelers and residents of Málaga intermingle and collectively exude an "I'm-on-vacation" attitude, which evolves from a daytime, beachside lassitude into nocturnal energy. **Buses** and **trains** run frequently to and from Málaga. The **tourist office** is at C. Guetaría, s/n (tel. (95) 238 15 78). **Hostal La Palmera,** Av. Palma de Mallorca, 37 (tel. (95) 237 65 09), above the La Caixa Savings Bank, makes a fine home away from home, 5min. from the beach. (Singles 2000-3000ptas. Doubles 3000-4000ptas. Triples 4000-5000ptas. Cots 600ptas. Breakfast 350ptas.) **Hostal Pizarro,** Pasaje Pizarro (tel. (95) 238 71 67 or 238 71 85), is only a block past C. San Miguel, off Pl. Costa del Sol. (Singles 2500ptas. Doubles 3500ptas. Triples 5000ptas. Quads 6000ptas. Prices 400-600ptas more during Christmas, *Semana Santa,* and July-Aug.) Restaurants dot **Avenida Palma de Mallorca. La Carihuela** is *the* place to be when the sun goes down by virtue of its diverse selection of dishes and see-and-be-seen ambience.

MARBELLA

Glam Marbella, the jewel of the Costa del Sol, caters to the British, Germans, French, Americans, and Swedes (pallid when they arrive, crimson when they leave) who descend upon it each season in a vain attempt to rub elbows with the rich and famous. The city vacuums pesetas quickly, efficiently, painlessly, and in 5 different languages, but it's also possible to steal away from this snooty city with a budgety good time. Marbella has a chic promenade over the beach, leaving its most valuable asset starved for space. If the press of flesh stifles, hop on the Fuengirola bus, stop at **Playa de las Chapas,** 10km east, and walk in either direction to find an open stretch. If you choose to stay in Marbella for the evening, visit **Old Vic,** Av. Ansol, 2, a Spanish neon disco.

Buses leave for Málaga (frequently, 1½hr., 505ptas) from the station on Av. Ricardo Soriano (tel. (95) 277 21 92). To get to the town center, take a left on Av. Soriano until it becomes **Avenida Ramón y Cajal.** The old town is on the left; the waves crash to the right. One of the several multilingual **tourist offices** is at C. Glorieta de la Fontanilla, s/n (tel. (95) 277 14 42; open Mon.-Fri. 9:30am-9pm, Sat. 10am-2pm; winter Mon.-Fri. 9:30am-8pm, Sat. 10am-2pm).

If you don't have reservations, especially from mid-July through August, arrive early and pray. The area in the old part of town behind Av. Ramón y Cajal is loaded with little *hostales* and *fondas,* all of which fill up quickly. Several cheap guest houses line **Calle Ancha, Calle San Francisco, Calle Aduar** and **Calle de los Caballeros,** all of which are uphill on C. Huerta Chica, across C. Ramón y Cajal from the tourist office road. People at bars often know of *casas particulares.* **Hostal del Pilar,** C. Mesoncillo, 4 (tel. (95) 282 99 36), the 2nd left off C. Huerta Chica, has a relaxing bar/lounge with a sociable scene. (Mattresses on the roof in warm months 800ptas. Singles 1500-2300ptas. Doubles 2400-4000ptas. Triples 3500-5000ptas.) **Casa-Huéspedes Aduar,** C. Aduar, 7 (tel. (95) 277 35 78), overflows with roses that compensate for unexceptional rooms. (Singles 2000ptas. Doubles 2000-2900ptas.) **Bar El Gallo,** C. Lobatas, 46, sports a loud TV and louder locals, but lip-smackin' good food. (*San Jacobo*—pork stuffed with ham and swiss—and fries 400ptas. Open 9am-midnight.)

SPAIN

■■■ GIBRALTAR AND ALGECIRAS

A British colony, **Gibraltar** comes complete with bobbies, fish 'n' chips, a changing of the guard, and Marks and Spencer. Gibraltar takes its Britishness very seriously, but unlike their counterparts in London, citizens can switch from the Queen's English to Andalusian Spanish with ease. From the northern tip of the controversial massif known as **Top of the Rock,** there's a remarkable view of Iberia and the Straits of Gibraltar. **Cable cars** carry visitors from the southern end of Main St. to the Top of the Rock, making a stop at Apes' Den, where a colony of monkeys clamber lithely about the sides of rocks, the tops of taxis, and tourists' heads. (Cable car every 10min., Mon.-Sat. 9:30am-6pm. Last tix sold 5:15pm. Round-trip UK£4.65 per person, one-way: UK£3.45 per person. Ticket includes St. Michael's Cave and the Apes' Den. Newly-installed toll booths charge £3 per car and £3 per walker.) **Pubs** linger along Main St. The early evening crowd people-watches from **Angry Friar,** 287 Main St. across from the Governor's Residence, also known as **The Convent,** which occasionally has live music (open 10am-midnight, food served 10am-3pm).

From Spain, dial 07 to access telephone numbers in Gibraltar. The USA Direct code is 88 00. Although *pesetas* are accepted everywhere (except in pay phones), the pound sterling is clearly the preferred method of payment. **Buses** run from **La Línea,** the nearest Spanish town on the border, from the Empresa Comes station in Algeciras behind Hotel Octavio (40min., 195ptas). The main **tourist office** is at 18-20 Bomb House Lane (tel. 748 05; open Mon.-Fri. 10am-6pm, Sat. 10am-2pm). Camping is illegal, and the two affordable places in the area are often full, especially between July and September. In a pinch, crash at one of the *hostales* in La Línea, a 20min. trudge over the border, or in Algeciras. The cheapest beds are at the **Toc H Hostel,** Line Wall Rd. (tel. 734 31), a whitewashed maze of plants, cats, and young people. Show up by 9:30am with your lucky rabbit's foot. (£3 per person. £15 per week.) The other choices are **Miss Serruya Guest House,** 92/1a Irish Town (tel. 732 20; singles £16, doubles £8 per person), and **Queen's Hotel,** 1 Boyd St. (tel. 740 00), through Southport Gate and to the right. (Double £12, with bath £14. Single £16, with bath £18. More than 50% off for Let's Go readers.) Even fast food is expensive. For the cheapest eats, check out the small restaurants and pubs in the alleys of **Main Street.** A bit of advice to Gibraltar's weekend visitors: eat early, as almost all restaurants are closed by 4pm. **Smith's Fish and Chips,** 295 Main St., is run by a cheerful lad who dishes out rotund servings of chicken and fish. (Fish and chips, £2.95 plus some vegetarian dishes. Open Mon.-Fri. 11am-9:30pm, Sat. noon-3pm.) **Uptown Chicago,** 10 Cannon Lane, off Main St., offers splendid English grub and super service. (Burger with fries and salad £2.50. English breakfast £2.95. Take-out cheaper. Open Mon.-Fri. 9am-10pm, Sat. 9am-5pm.)

Most people come to **Algeciras** to leave. On the Spanish side of the Bahía de Algeciras, the port offers cheap rooms and a passage to Morocco. All services necessary for transit to Morocco are clustered around the port. The **tourist office,** C. Juan de la Cierva (tel. 57 26 36), is the gigantic tube-shaped pink and red building (open Mon.-Fri. 9am-2pm, Sat. 10am-1pm). **Trains** run to Málaga (5½hr., 1380ptas), Seville (6hr., 1805ptas), and Granada (2½hr., 1600ptas), and Madrid (7-9hr., 7700ptas). **Ferries** leave hourly 7am-10pm for Ceuta (1½hr., 1834ptas) and Tangier (2½hr., Class A 3440ptas, Class B 2700ptas). Ferry passengers with Eurailpasses get a 20% discount. Lots of convenient lodgings bunch around **Calle José Santacana,** parallel to Av. Marina and one block inland, and **Calle Duque de Almodóvar,** 2 blocks farther from the water. Check **Hostal Vizcaino,** at C. José Santacana, 9 (tel. (956) 65 57 56; singles with bath 1200ptas, doubles with bath 2400ptas). **Hostal Residencia González,** C. José Santacana, 7 (tel. 65 28 43), is another decent bargain close to the port with roomy, tasteful quarters and new wood furnishings. (Singles 1500ptas, with bath 2000ptas. Doubles 3000ptas, with bath 4000ptas.) Relish your final taste of *paella,* or welcome yourself back from Morocco with a *medio pollo asado* (baked ½-chicken) sold in many places along **Av. Virgen del Carmen,** near the port, and **C. Juan de la Cierva.**

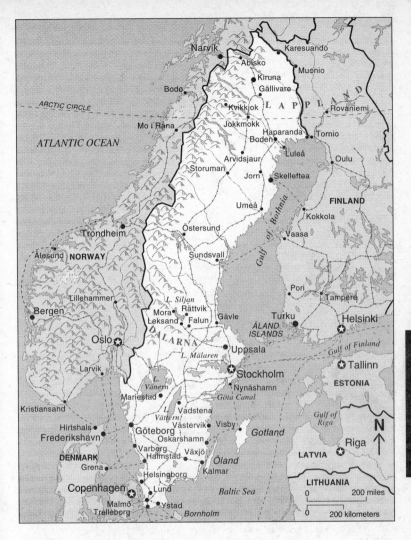

Sweden (Sverige)

US$1 = 7.65kr (kronor)
CDN$1= 5.70kr
UK£1 = 12.17kr
IR£1   = 12.05kr
AUS$1= 5.87kr
NZ$1 = 4.64kr
SAR1 = 2.18kr
Country Code: 46

1kr =   US$0.13
1kr = CDN$0.17
1kr =   UK£0.08
1kr =   IR£0.08
1kr = AUS$0.17
1kr =   NZ$0.22
1kr =   SAR0.47
International Dialing Prefix: 009

Some call Sweden the world's success story, a modern miracle. Fervent social democratic idealism and principled neutrality have made Sweden (Sverige) a land whose affluence is widely shared. Thanks to free health care, education, and other services, Sweden some years ago became the first place on earth where physicians could not tell the social class of children by examining their bodies and growth rates.

Sweden's internationalism is unforgettable: Raoul Wallenberg clambered over the roofs of Nazi trains to hand out Swedish passports that saved thousands of Jews from concentration camps, Dag Hammarskjöld nurtured the U.N., and Prime Minister Olof Palme marched against the Vietnam War and sheltered draft resisters. Today in impoverished East Africa, so much of the incoming aid bears the Swedish colors that many villagers assume Sweden is a global superpower. While extremely informed of and involved in international affairs, Swedes retain a certain provincial mentality: In the national debate preceding the November 1994 referendum over EU membership, two of the most fervently discussed issues were the continued availability of *snus* (dip), of which Swedes are the world's leading consumers, and the potential risk of an increasing inflow of foreigners unacquainted with the obligations inherent in *allemansrätten* (see Sweden Essentials, below), who might trample the country's pristine forests and fields.

The country's 8.3 million citizens—among them tens of thousands of political refugees—inhabit a land the size and shape of California. A whopping 25 hours by train in length, Sweden defies the whirlwind tour, but unless you're an avid mountaineer, you needn't make the pilgrimage north to Lappland's sleepless sun and the alpine huts of the Kungsleden. If logging and coastal scenery inspire you, head to the northeast coastal cities of Luleå and Umeå. Life pulses peacefully in the southern half of the country, where 85% of Swedes reside, many taking their five-week paid vacations in waterside cottages in Dalarna or Småland, or on Viking- and camper-trodden Gotland, an island off the southeast coast. At the center of it all lie the islands of Stockholm, where the ultra-trendy sneer at non-Stockholmer "hicks" (even residents of the nearby suburbs) and emulate Mediterranean café culture in 17th-century vaults.

GETTING THERE AND GETTING AROUND

Sweden is easily accessible by boat or train from Denmark and Germany, by ferry from Poland and Finland, and by train and bus from Norway and Finland. A consistent and reliable series of trains greets travelers in the southern half of the country; in the north, long-distance buses (railpasses not valid), are often a better option. The *buy-in-Scandinavia* **Scanrail pass,** which replaced the Nordturist Railpass, allows 5 days within 15 (1600kr, under 26: 1200kr) or 21 consecutive days (2300kr, under 26: 1700kr) of unlimited rail travel through Sweden, Norway, Denmark, and Finland, as well as many free or discounted ferry rides. This differs from the *buy-outside-of-Scandinavia* **Scanrail pass** which offers 5 out of 15 days (US$159, under 26: US$119), 10 out of 21 days (US$275, under 26: US$206), or 30 consecutive days (US$399, under 26: US$299) of unlimited travel. For holders of the **Reslustkortet** card (150kr, seniors 50kr), fares are reduced 50% on trains marked with a red circle in the timetable (usually trips begun on a Tues., Wed., Thurs., or Sat.), and youths 19-25 can receive another 25% off. **Eurail** is valid, but reservations (20kr) are still required (though rarely enforced) on nearly all long-distance journeys.

For travelers under 25, SAS offers a standby fare of 280-350kr on all their flights between Stockholm and other Swedish cities (call (020) 91 01 50 for details Mon.-Fri. 7am-9pm, Sat. 8am-6pm, Sun. 8am-8pm). **Hitching** in Sweden can be slow near the major cities, but picks up in the north. In this safety-minded country, all must wear seatbelts, and headlights must be on at all times. Sweden is a biker's heaven. Numerous paths cover most of the country, particularly the south; you can complete a trip of Sweden on the hostel-spotted Sverigeleden **bike route.** Contact the Svenska Turistföreningen (STF, see Sweden Essentials) for more information.

SWEDEN ESSENTIALS

Sweden is a nation of many public **holidays** (Jan. 1, Jan. 6, April 14-17, May 1, May 25, June 5, June 24, Nov.4, Dec. 24-26, and Dec. 31 in 1995) and even more festivals. May 1 brings a rousing solidarity parade in Stockholm. **Midsummer** incites Bacchanalian dancing around maypoles. The "Crayfish Premiere" opens August 9, followed by the "Sour Herring Premiere" on August 17, observed particularly in northern Sweden. Sour herring (*surströmming*) is prepared by letting the fish ferment (or rot), after which it is tinned and sold. It is supposed to be a delicacy, but do as the connoisseurs, and wear a clothes peg on your nose while eating it. Plan ahead for holidays, especially Midsummer (June 23-25), as many transportation lines shut down and some hotels close.

Most Swedish **banks** are open weekdays until 3pm (sometimes later in Stockholm). Exchange rates remain constant, but commissions vary. Exchange checks in large denominations, as there is usually a 35kr commission per check. Many **post offices** double as banks and are open weekdays from 9am to 6pm, Saturdays from 10am to 1pm. **Phones** require at least 2kr, although nearly half of all phones in the country only accept phone cards (*Telefonkort;* widely available at newsstands and post offices). Call 079 75 for directory information in Sweden and 079 77 to make a collect call. For AT&T's **USADirect,** dial (020) 79 56 11; MCI's **WorldPhone** (020) 79 59 22; **SprintExpress** (020) 79 90 11; **Canada Direct** (020) 79 90 15; **BT Direct** (020) 79 51 44; **Australia Direct** (020) 79 90 61. For **emergency help** dial 900 00 (free). Almost all Swedes speak some English, and those under 50 are generally fluent. Sweden leads the world in facilities for people with disabilities.

Accommodations, Camping, and Food Sweden's top-notch **youth hostels** (*vandrarhem*), at 90kr for HI members and an additional 35kr for nonmembers, are the only budget option in Sweden; hotels cost at least 300-400kr. If you arrive in the off season and the local hostel is closed (a problem in the north and in smaller towns), staying in private homes is a bearable alternative (100-200kr per night). Book through the local *turistbyrå* (tourist office). Be warned that in some Swedish hostels, sheets are paper disposables so you may want to bring your own (or pay 15kr extra for cotton sheets). The **Svenska Turistföreningen (STF)** runs Sweden's hostels, which fill up quickly in the summer; reserve in advance. Most hostels have kitchen facilities, and receptions are usually open from 8 to 10am and 5 to 9 or 10pm (shorter hours in winter). *Vandrarhem* are often used by Swedish families who can't afford expensive hotels, so beware of screaming children. STF's main office is in downtown Stockholm at Drottninggatan 31, P.O. Box 25, 101 20 Stockholm (tel. (08) 790 31 00, fax (08) 20 13 32); STF also has a branch in Göteborg at Drottningtorget 6, Box 305, 401 24 Göteborg (tel. (031) 15 30 70, fax (031) 15 59 95); and a branch in Malmö at Skeppsbron 1, 211 20 Malmö (tel. (040) 30 22 10, fax (040) 30 22 30). STF will sell you **Hostelling International (HI)** membership (210kr) and distributes a free brochure called *Swedish Youth and Family Hostels*, listing all hostels with phone and fax numbers, and including a map (open Mon.-Fri. 10am-6pm; Aug.-April Mon.-Fri. 10am-5:30pm). The STF also manages mountain huts in the northern wilds.

Many **campgrounds** (80-100kr per site) also offer *stugor* (simple cottages) for around 75-175kr per person. If you don't have an International Camping Card, you'll need a Swedish one (80kr, valid 1 yr.), available with the free booklet *Camping i Sverige,* which is in Swedish. Get these from **Sveriges Campingvärdars Riksförbund (SCR)** (fax (0522) 338 49), Box 255, 451 17 Uddevalla. You may walk or camp for 1 or 2 nights anywhere on *privately* owned land—except for gardens—so long as you respect the privacy of the owners as well as the flora and fauna. Pick up the brochure *The Common Right of Access (Allemansrätten)* at the STF. Don't let the fact that the natives persist in T-shirts and shorts trick you into thinking that the weather is always warm; their thermostats are skewed. Summer days are pleasant (around 20°C in the south, 16°C in the north), but nights can get surprisingly chilly (around 10°C in the south, 5°C in the north).

Food is unbelievably expensive in restaurants and not much cheaper in grocery stores. Rely on supermarkets and outdoor fruit and vegetable markets. Potatoes are the national staple; these and other dishes are invariably smothered with dill. Try tasty milk products like *messmör* (spreadable whey cheese) and *fil,* a fluid yogurt good for dousing your muesli. When you tire of groceries, seek out restaurants that offer a **dagens rätt,** a daily special usually available only at lunch. This may be the only time you can afford a sit-down meal; the price (40-55kr) includes a main dish, salad, bread, and beverage. Alcohol is not a wise option for the budget traveler. A real beer *(starköl)* usually costs at least 15kr in stores and 30-45kr in city pubs and bars. The cheaper, weaker, and lousier low-alcohol alternative is *lättöl* (8-12kr). Note that the drinking age in bars is 18, but you have to be 20 to buy alcohol from the state-run Systembolaget stores, which monopolize the sale of booze (open Mon.-Fri.; expect long lines on Fri.).

■■■ STOCKHOLM

Stockholm is part modern metropolis, part old-world charm, and unfortunately, quite commercial. Although on the surface Stockholm can seem cold and imposing, underneath the frenetic consumerism lies a elegantly majestic city of water, made up of islands and bridges connecting the main districts of Gamla Stan, Norrmalm, Södermalm, Östermalm, Vasastan, Kungsholmen, and Djurgården. At the southern tip of Norrmalm lies the cosmopolitan mecca of trendy shops and even trendier people in platform shoes, a far cry from ABBA's hokey style, and well-aware of it. The rest of the city, however, will be worth your while. Seek out Djurgården's museums, Gamla Stan (the Old Town) and the thousands of islands that make up the archipelago, or just walk along Stockholm's waterfront and take in its beauty.

ORIENTATION AND PRACTICAL INFORMATION

Gamla Stan (Old Town) is the centerpiece of Stockholm's 24,000-island archipelago. To the east lie the museums and hostels of Skeppsholmen island and the cultured greenery of Djurgården; to the south, the artsy island of Södermalm; to the north, the commercial districts of Norrmalm. The main train station, **Centralstation,** stands on the southern tip of Norrmalm. The *tunnelbana* (subway) links it all up, but given the short distances and disproportionate subway fares, a stroll is often preferable.

Tourist Offices: Tourist Information (tel. 789 24 90), in the northeast corner of Kungsträdgården at Hamngatan. From Centralstation, walk up Klarabergsgatan to Sergels Torg (T-bana: T-Centralen), then bear right on Hamngatan. Books hostels (15kr fee) and hotels (40kr fee). Tourist information open Mon.-Fri. 9am-7pm, Sat.-Sun. 9am-5pm; Sept.-May Mon.-Fri. 9am-6pm, Sat.-Sun. 9am-3pm. **Hotellcentralen** (tel. 24 08 80), at the train station. 40kr finding fee for hotels, but just 15kr per person for hostels. No charge if reserved by phone. Also sells a comprehensive color city map (10kr). Open 7am-9pm.

Budget Travel: Kilroy Travels Sweden, Kungsgatan 4 (tel. 23 45 15). Cheap and largely refundable student flight tickets. Branch on university campus at Frescati (tel. 16 05 15). Open Mon.-Fri. 9:30am-5pm. **Transalpino,** Birger Jarlsgatan 13 (tel. 679 98 70). Open Mon.-Fri. 10am-5:30pm. T-bana for both: Östermalmstorg.

Embassies: U.S., Strandvägen 101 (tel. 783 53 00). **Canada,** Tegelbacken 4 (tel. 613 99 00). **U.K.,** Skarpögatan 6-8 (tel. 671 90 00). **Australia,** Sergelstorg 12 (tel. 613 29 00). In emergencies, contact the British Embassy. **South Africa,** Linnégatan 76 (tel. 24 39 50).

Currency Exchange: Forex in Centralstation (open daily 8am-9pm) and in Cityterminalen (open Mon.-Sat. 10am-3pm) take 15kr commission on traveler's check transactions and a 20kr commission to exchange cash. **Valutaspecialisten,** Kungsgatan 30 (tel. 10 30 00), near Hötorget, charges no commission and has good rates. Open Mon.-Fri. 8am-7pm, Sat. 9am-4pm. See also Post Office, below.

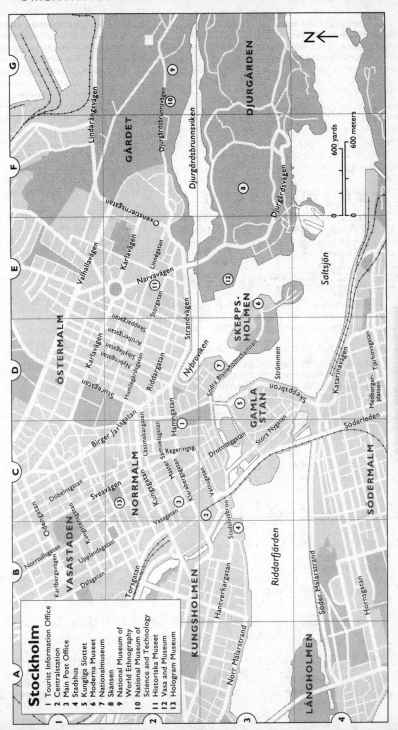

Stockholm

1 Tourist Information Office
2 Centralstation
3 Main Post Office
4 Stadshus
5 Kungliga Slottet
6 Moderna Museet
7 Nationalmuseum
8 Skansen
9 National Museum of World Ethnography
10 National Museum of Science and Technology
11 Historiska Museet
12 Vasa and Museum
13 Hologram Museum

SWEDEN

600 yards
600 meters

N

DJURGÅRDEN
GÄRDET
ÖSTERMALM
NORRMALM
VASASTADEN
KUNGSHOLMEN
GAMLA STAN
SKEPPS-HOLMEN
SÖDERMALM
LÅNGHOLMEN

Saltsjön
Riddarfjärden
Nybroviken
Djurgårdsbrunnsviken
Strömmen

Lindarängsvägen
Oxenstiernsgatan
Djurgårdsbrunnsvägen
Djurgårdsvägen
Valhallavägen
Karlavägen
Narvavägen
Linnégatan
Storgatan
Strandvägen
Karlavägen
Skeppargatan
Artillerigatan
Sibyllegatan
Nybrogatan
Humlegårdsgatan
Riddargatan
Sturegatan
Birger Jarlsgatan
Lästmakargatan
Master Samuelsgatan
Kungsgatan
Regeringsg.
Hamngatan
Klarabergsgatan
Vasagatan
Vattugatan
Drottninggatan
Stora Nygatan
Skeppsbron
Södra Blasieholmshamnen
Söderleden
Katarinavägen
Medborgar-platsen
Tjärhovsgatan
Söder Mälarstrand
Hornsgatan
Norr Mälarstrand
Hantverkargatan
Stadshusbron
Upplandsgatan
Dalagatan
Torsgatan
Sveavägen
Döbelnsgatan
Odengatan
Kungstensgatan
Karlbergsvägen
Norrtullsgatan

American Express: Birger Jarlsgatan 1 (tel. 679 78 80, for 24hr. refund assistance (020) 79 51 55). No fee for cashing traveler's checks; 20kr charge for exchanging cash. T-bana: Östermalmstorg. Open Mon.-Fri. 9am-6pm, Sat. 10am-1pm.

Post Office: Mäster Samuelsgatan 70, near Centralstation. **Postal code:** 101 10 Stockholm 1. Open Mon.-Fri. 8am-6:30pm, Sat. 10am-2pm. Stock up on cheap postcards along Drottninggatan (1kr each).

Telephones: Telecenter, at Centralstation, assists you with international calls. Also sells phone cards for 30, 55, or 95kr. Open 8am-9pm. **City code:** 08.

Flights: Arlanda Airport, 45km north of the city. **Flygbussar** buses (40min., 50kr; public transportation passes not valid) run between the airport and Cityterminalen (see Buses, below), departing either way every 10min., 4:30am-10:30pm.

Trains: Centralstation (T-bana: T-Centralen) is Stockholm's main gateway. Luggage office (40kr per day) near the Vasagatan entrance; **lockers** 25kr per 24hrs. (goods removed after 7 days); **showers** 20kr. Waiting rooms for women *(Damväntsal)* and families *(Familjeväntsal).* Open 5am-midnight. **Train information:** tel. (020) 75 75 75. To Copenhagen (non-stop): 4 per day, 8½hrs., 497kr. To Oslo (non-stop): 3 per day, 6hrs., 529kr. Reservations 20kr.

Buses: The **Cityterminalen,** upstairs from Centralstation, sends buses to the airport (50kr), to the Gotland ferries (50kr), to the Poland ferries (120kr, every other day on even dates), and on routes within Sweden (to Göteborg, 7-8hrs., 240kr; to Malmö, 10-11hrs., 270kr). Reservations required daily on **Swebus** buses, Fri. and Sun. on all other buses (tel. (020) 64 06 40). Open 4:15am-11pm.

Public Transportation: SL: Office in Sergelstorg (tel. 600 10 00), T-bana: T-Centralen, provides information. Open Mon.-Thurs. 8:30am-6:30pm, Fri. 8:30am-5:30pm. Most in-town destinations cost 2 coupons (13kr; 1hr. of unlimited transfer on bus/subway). **Rabatt-kuponger,** (85kr), sold at *Pressbyrån* news agents, are valid for up to 10 trips; the **SL Tourist Card (Turistkort),** valid on buses, subways, commuter trains, and the trams and ferries to Djurgården, costs 56kr (under 18 and seniors 33kr) for 24hrs. of free travel, or 107kr (under 18 and seniors 70kr) for 3 days on all of the above plus free entry to Skansen, Gröna Lund, Kaknästornet, and the Tram Museum. Most subway lines run 5am-2am, after which they are replaced by night buses. The **Stockholmskortet** (Stockholm Card) offers unlimited travel by bus (not airline buses), subway, and local trains, free sight-seeing by boat, and free admission to 70 attractions (175kr per 24hrs.).

Ferries: Silja Line, Kungsgatan 2 (tel. 22 21 40), and **Viking Line,** Centralstation (tel. 714 56 00). Daily to Mariehamn, Turku (Åbo), and Helsinki in Finland. Viking buses to Kapellskär (the embarking point) leave from Cityterminalen (1½hr., 20kr). Silja ferries to Turku and Helsinki free with Eurail and Scanrail, though to Helsinki a cabin must be reserved (100kr per bed with Eurail, 170kr per bed with Scanrail; reserve about 2-3 weeks in advance for cheapest fares). Viking Line ferries are free with Eurail, 33% off with Scanrail. (T-bana: Slussen, then bus 45 (free) to the dock.) Ferries to **Gotland** leave from Nynäshamn, south of Stockholm by bus or SL commuter rail (see Gotland); **Polferries** (tel. (0155) 781 00) ships to Gdańsk, Poland, leave from Oxelösund, further south (1-3 per week; 300kr, students and seniors 230kr).

Bike Rental: Try **Skepp O'Hoj** on Djurgårdsbron (tel. 660 57 57). 110kr per day, 360kr per week. Open daily April-Sept. 9am-9pm.

Hitchhiking: Laborious. Gas stations are the hitcher's best bet; it's illegal to wait on a highway. Those headed south take the T-bana to the gas station Kungens Kurva in Skärholmen. Those going north take bus 52 to Sveaplan and stand on Sveavägen at Nortull, or go farther up the E4 to the junction of Uppsalavägen and Enköpingsvägen.

Bookstore: Akademibokhandeln, Almquist, & Wiksell, Mäster Samuelsgatan 32 (tel. 23 79 90). Truckloads of English books. Open Mon.-Fri. 9:30am-6pm, Sat. 10am-3pm; Sept.-May Mon.-Fri. 10am-4pm, Sat. 10am-3pm.

Laundromat: Rare and expensive. Try **Tvättomaten,** Västmannagatan 61. T-bana: Odenplan. Open Mon.-Fri. 9am-6pm, Sat. 10am-2pm. 65kr per load.

Gay and Lesbian Services: The Swedish Federation for Sexual Equality (RFSL) runs a center at Sveavägen 57 (tel. 736 02 15). T-bana: Rådmansgatan.

SWEDEN

Bookstore open Mon.-Thurs. noon-9pm, Fri. noon-6pm, Sat.-Sun. noon-3pm. Café Diva open 11am-8pm. Restaurant and disco nightly (see Entertainment).

Pharmacy: Apotek C. W. Scheele, Klarabergsgatan 64 (tel. 21 82 80), under the green-and-white "Apotek" signs at the overpass over Vasagatan. T-bana: T-Centralen. Open 24hrs.

Medical Assistance: Call 644 92 00 for a referral to the nearest hospital.

Emergencies: Ambulance, Fire, and **Police,** tel. 900 00 (red button on older pay phones). Police station: Bryggargatan 19, north of Centralstation (tel. 769 51 00).

ACCOMMODATIONS AND CAMPING

Hostels (Vandrarhem)

Summer demands reservations, and most hostels limit stays to five nights. Check-out time is usually 10am, so don't get too wired under the midnight sun and expect to sleep in. HI hostels cost 90kr per night, 125 for nonmembers.

af Chapman (HI) (tel. 679 50 15, fax 611 98 75), a full-rigger 1888 sailing ship majestically moored off Skeppsholmen, to the right as you cross the bridge. Take bus 65 from T-Centralen. 2- to 10-bed cabins. Reception open 7am-noon and 3pm-2am. Lockout 11 am-3pm. Curfew 2am. Breakfast 40kr. Sheets 30kr. In summer reserve 2-3 months in advance or show up 7-8:30am. Open April to mid-Dec.

Skeppsholmens Vandrarhem (HI) (tel. 679 50 17, fax 611 71 55), in the Hantverkshuset, on the shore behind the af Chapman. Less mythic and more institutional, but bigger, plusher rooms. Reception open 7am-2pm and 3pm-2am. Lockout noon-3pm. Curfew 2am. Breakfast 40kr. Lockers 10kr. Sheets 30kr. In summer reserve 2-3 months in advance or show up early. Open Jan. 2-Dec. 23.

Långholmen Vandrarhem (HI), Kronohäktet (tel. 668 05 00, fax 84 10 96), on Långholmen Island. Plush cells in a transmogrified prison, most with TV, phone, and private shower. From T-bana: Hornstull, march north on Långholmsgatan, turn left (before the bridge) onto Högalidsgatan, then right on Bergsundsgatan over the bridge onto Långholmen, then follow the "Kronohäktet" signs. No curfew, no lockout. Reception open 24 hrs. Breakfast 50kr. Dinner 30kr. Sheets 35kr. Some free lockers. Laundry 25kr. Kitchen. Wheelchair access.

Columbus Hotell-Vandrarhem, Tjärhovsgatan 11 (tel. 644 17 17, fax 702 07 64). Three blocks east of T-bana: Medborgarplatsen. Built in 1780, a former brewery, prison, and plague hospital (none within this century), with the cheapest hotel rooms in town (singles 390kr, doubles 490kr). The hostel part has 90 beds, 2-6 per room. Reception open 24 hrs. No curfew. 110kr. Breakfast 45kr. Lockers 5kr. Paper sheets 30kr, cotton sheets 45kr. Credit cards accepted. Open Jan.-late Dec.

Gustaf af Klint, Stadsgårdskajen 153 (tel. 640 40 77, fax 640 64 16). A snug former Navy ship moored 200m east of T-bana: Slussen. Reception open 24hrs. No curfew. TV. 120kr per person in 4-bed cabin, 140kr per person in double, 100kr per person in 14-bed dormitory. Breakfast 40kr. Free backpack-sized lockers. Sheets 35kr. Laundry 25kr. Open mid-Jan. to mid-Dec.

Zinken Hostel (HI), Zinkens Väg 20 (tel. 658 29 00, fax 658 36 64). From T-bana: Zinkensdamm, head south on Ringvägen 3 blocks; turn right on Zinkens Väg, 200m on right. A peaceful, if institutional and out-of-the-way, 340-bed hostel, frequented more by families than by youths; 2-10 bodies per room. Kitchen and TV. No lockout, no curfew. Breakfast 40kr. Luggage room and safe. Lockers in rooms. Sheets 38kr. Laundry 20kr.

Brygghuset, Norrtullsgatan 12N (tel. 31 24 24). Two blocks north of T-bana: Odenplan. Spacious 2- to 8-bed rooms. Limited kitchen. Ping-pong and TV. 53 beds. Reception open 7:30am-noon and 3-10pm. Lockout noon-3pm. Curfew 2am. 110kr. Doubles 150kr per person. Breakfast 30kr. Free lockers. Sheets 30kr. Laundry 30kr. Open June-Aug.

STF Backpackers Inn, Banérgatan 56 (tel. 660 75 15, fax 665 40 39). Two blocks down Valhallavägen from T-bana: Karlaplan. Simple—308 bunk-beds set in Anna's former classrooms—but central, and near the rolling hills of Gärdet (field), which leads into Djurgården. Lockout 11:30am-4pm. Curfew 2am. 75kr, nonmembers

110kr. Breakfast 35kr. Sheets 30kr. Free luggage storage, or bring a lock for your own authentic Junior High School locker. Open July to mid-Aug.

Camping

Bredäng Camping (tel. 97 70 71, fax 708 72 62), 10km southwest of the city center near Lake Mälar. T-bana: Bredäng. Follow the signs down the stairs, past the hulking housing project, and parallel to the train tracks along Stora Sällskapets väg to the campsite (7-10min.). Often crowded. 65kr per person or 125kr per tent, 300kr for a 4-person cabin. Store, laundry, running water, sauna. Open 7am-11pm; Oct.-April 7am-9pm.

Vårberg Camping (tel. 710 63 70 or 710 13 30, fax 710 88 68), 12km southwest of city center, 1km from Lake Mälar. T-bana: Vårberg (25min. from T-Centralen). Follow the signs to Vårbergs Idrottsplats (sports ground). Near Scandinavia's largest mall. Reception open 8am-10pm. 40kr per person or 80kr per tent. Hot water included. Open June 1-Aug. 31.

FOOD

Stockholm's best deals are at lunch, when most restaurants offer a *dagens rätt* for 40-60kr. If that leaves you kronorless, head for the supermarket in the basement of **Åhléns** department store at Klarabergsgatan and Drottninggatan (T-bana: T-Centralen; open Mon.-Fri. 9:30am-9pm, Sat. 9:30am-8pm, Sun. noon-8pm). **Hötorget** and **Östermalmstorg** both host outdoor produce markets and indoor deli malls; the underground **Hötorgshallen** is cheaper (open Mon.-Fri. 9:30am-6pm, Sat. 9:30am-3pm). Copy the locals and picnic in idyllic **Djurgården.**

Herman's Lilla Gröna, Katarina Bangata 17 (tel. 640 30 10), in Söder. T-bana: Medborgarplatsen, 3 blocks south on Götgatan, then left on Katarina Bangata. Generous servings from your choice of Green Cuisine for 53-60kr at lunch. Herman offers *Let's Go* readers 10% off here and at any of the other branches: **Herman's Höjdare,** Fjällgatan 23a (tel. 643 85 11), in Söder; **Herman's Hermitage,** Stora Nygatan 11 (tel. 11 95 00), in Gamla Stan; **Herman's I Sibirien,** Surbrunnsgatan 25 (tel. 612 17 66), T-bana: Odenplan; **Hemma Hos Herman,** Regeringsgatan 91 (tel. 11 58 50), which crosses over Kungsgatan. Open Mon.-Fri. 11am-8pm, Sat. noon-9pm., Sun. noon-7pm.

Café Gråmunken, Västerlånggatan 18 in Gamla Stan. Get your food upstairs, then go down into the crypt-like basement and hang with Stockholm youth. Soup 25kr. Calzones 25-30kr. *Dagens rätt* 30-50kr. Open 10am-11pm.

Restaurang Kristina, Västerlånggatan 68 (tel. 20 05 20), in Gamla Stan. Relatively fancy (but cheap) restaurant with café in front. Pizza 30-55kr. Steak 55kr. Yummy desserts 15-45 kr. Open 11am-11pm.

Café Art, Västerlånggatan 60 (tel. 11 76 61), in Gamla Stan. *Très alternatif* café in a hole in the wall. Watch your step (and your head) as you descend into the crypt. 25-35kr sandwiches and filled baguettes. Open 11am-11pm.

Svea Bar & Matsal, Sveavägen 53 (tel. 31 59 50), T-bana: Rådmansgatan. Treat yourself to a classy restaurant without spending too much. *Dagens rätt* (meat, fish, pasta, or salad) 50kr; dinner slightly more expensive. Open 11am-1am.

SIGHTS

For the ultimate view of Stockholm, walk uphill on Katarinavägen (on the north edge of Södermalm) to the sculpted hand memorializing Spanish Civil War martyrs. Or climb the **Stadshuset** tower. It's a hike (the elevator only goes halfway—you walk the next six floors) but well worth the asthma attack. The **Stadshus** (City Hall), on Stadshusbron near Centralstation, holds 19 million gilded tiles in its Golden Hall; you'll feast here when you win your Nobel Prize. (Tours daily at 10am, 11am, noon, and 2pm; Sept.-May 10am and noon. Tower open May-Sept. 10am-4:30pm; tour and tower 30kr, tower only 15kr.)

The **Gamla Stan** quarter is Stockholm's ancient heart, and it still beats healthily, albeit infused with tourist blood. Stroll along Västerlånggatan, the main drag, and join the young and the glamorous in the local coffee shops. Two-hour **walking**

SWEDEN

tours of the narrow, winding streets start daily at 6:30pm from the obelisk between the palace and the cathedral (summer only, 40kr). At the northwest corner, the 18th-century **Kungliga Slottet** (Royal Palace) hoards within its walls the gold and glitter of menacing weaponry and extravagant living quarters (about 20kr per exhibit). Head over to petite Skeppsholmen Island for such cultured monstrosities as a sculpture of a blue lemon paying homage to a pair of bull's horns, at the **Moderna Museet** (open Tues.-Thurs. 11am-8pm, Fri.-Sun. 11am-5pm; 40kr, under 17 free). For more traditional artistic fare, such as Rembrandt's stunning portrayal of the Batavian conspiracy, try the **Nationalmuseum** at the north end of the Skeppsholmen bridge (open Tues. 11am-9pm, Wed.-Sun. 11am-5pm; 40kr, students and seniors 20kr, Fri. free.)

Sample Swedish internationalism at the **National Museum of World Ethnography** (Etnografiska Museet), Djurgårdsbrunnsvägen 34 (take bus 69 from Norrmalmstorg; open Tues.-Fri. 11am-4pm, Sat.-Sun. noon-5pm; 30kr). The less benign internationalism of Sweden's Viking past is in display at **Historiska Museet** on Narvavägen 13-17, the street that leads to Djurgårdsbron bridge (open Tues.-Wed. and Fri. noon-5pm, Sat.-Sun. 10am-5pm, Thurs. until 8pm; 50kr, students, children and seniors 30kr). Discover more recent Swedish cultural history at the **Nordiska Museet**, at Djurgårdsvägen 6-16, on Djurgården (open Tues.-Sun. 11am-5pm, Thurs. 11am-8pm; 50kr, students 30kr) or at the overplayed Skansen on Djurgården. The oldest open-air museum in the world, **Skansen** consists of 150 buildings from all over Sweden, representing societies from the Middle Ages to the present. Swedish traditional festivals are celebrated here with outdoor concerts and folkdancing (open 9am-10pm, but most buildings close at 5pm; 50kr).

Djurgården, east of Skeppsholmen, is Stockholm's pleasure island, reached by bus 44 or 47 from the center, by foot from Strandvägen, by the Djurgårdslinjen tram from Nybroplan (13kr per day, tourist cards valid but not transportation passes), or by ferry from Nybroplan or Slussen (10kr). Especially wander-worthy is its south coast, where you'll pass house boats, museums, and a former tar factory **(Beckholmen).** Djurgården's and Stockholm's most impressive sight is the **Vasa,** an intact 17th-century warship that sank on her maiden voyage in 1628 and was dredged up in 1961 from the bottom of Stockholm's harbor. The new **Vasamuseet,** built around the ship, uncovers the events leading up to the Vasa's tragedy the process of her salvage. For kicks, go down to the lowest level and look up at the ship (open daily 10am-5pm, Wed. 10am-8pm; 45kr, students 30kr).

ENTERTAINMENT

Let the street musicians of **Gamla Stan** enchant you in the daytime, or wander through **Kungsträdgården,** where young Stockholmers often go just to relax. Sniff out events in the free booklet *Stockholm This Week* (available at any information booth) or ask a newfound Swedish friend to translate the list of events in the Saturday *På Stan* supplement of the *Dagens Nyheter* newspaper. At night, Gamla Stan comes alive with pub-crawlers and discotheques, as do the streets of Birger Jarlsgatan and Sveavägen. **Birger Jarlsgatan,** between Strandvägen and Kungsgatan (T-bana: Östermalmstorg) is lined with bars packed full of mainstream *nollåttor* ("zero-eights," which is how the rest of Sweden spitefully refers to the inhabitants within this telephone area code). Expect a cover charge and a line to get in after 11:30pm. **Sveavägen** also has as few good pubs and clubs near T-bana: Rådmansgatan. Annual happenings include the **Spring Festival** on Djurgården in April; the **Jazz and Blues Festival** on Skeppsholmen island in July; the raucous Stockholm **Water Festival** (the second week of Aug.); and **Christmas markets** in the Old Town and Skansen (starting in early Dec.).

Stiliga Duken, Stora Nygatan 35 (tel. 21 98 25), in Gamla Stan. Where the wild things are. Bar upstairs, restaurant below. Stockholm grunge meets rap in platform shoes. Loud music, crowded beyond belief. Thurs.-Sat. live bands; Wed. reggae night. No cover. Open 5:30pm-1am. Min. age 20.

Hyndans Hörna, Kornhamnstorg 61 (tel. 20 20 15), in Gamla Stan. Stocked bar and a little food in a tiny, crowded pub. More of Stockholm's hippest. No cover. Open noon-3am. Min. age 23.

Kaos, Stora Nygatan 21 (tel. 20 58 86), in Gamla Stan. Kurt Cobain's resting place. Live bands nightly. Frequented by skate brats and grunge rats. Café upstairs, band downstairs. Open nightly 5pm-1am. Min. age 18.

Tre Backar, Tegnérgatan 12-14 (tel. 673 44 00), T-bana: Rådmansgatan. "Three beer crates" (3 floors, 2 underground) filled with mellow young people. Ground floor café/bar lined with bookshelves; mid-level has live bands every night; basement bar. Bands every evening. Cover 40-50kr for the live music. Open Mon.-Wed. 11am-midnight, Thurs.-Fri. 11am-1am, Sat. 6pm-1am. Min. age 18.

The Anchor, Sveavägen 90 (tel. 15 20 00), T-bana: Rådmansgatan. A bar packed with preppier (and drunker) young twenty-somethings. No cover. Open Sun.-Thurs. noon-1am, Fri.-Sat. noon-3am. Min. age 20.

HUSI/Café Diva, Sveavägen 57 (tel. 31 34 80 or 31 55 33), T-bana: Rådmansgatan. Stockholm's premier gay bar (mostly male) with good dance music. Cover Fri.-Sat. 60kr. Open Mon.-Sat. 6pm-3am, Sun. 6pm-midnight. Min. age 18.

Monnet Le Club, Kungsgatan 56 (tel. 20 33 68), T-bana: Hötorget. Frequented by 18-20 year-olds. Bar, casino, and disco. No cover. Open 2pm-3am (disco starts 11pm). Min. age females 18, males 20.

■ THE ARCHIPELAGO AND DROTTNINGHOLM

The peninsulas and islands of Stockholm's surrounding *skärgård* (archipelago) offer relaxing vacation spots. To the west of Stockholm floats **Björkö,** a booming Viking Age trade center, and its recent excavations. (Ferries from Stadshusbron near the Stadshuset leave daily 10am, returning at 4:45pm, Sat.-Sun. at 5:45pm; round-trip 165kr.) Hugging the Baltic coast, the islands of the **outer skärgård** are an ideal escape from urban life. Boats depart from Strömkajen (2-4hrs., one-way 70kr; contact Waxholmsbolaget (tel. 679 59 60) for info). **Vaxholm,** with its mighty fortress and museum, is closer to central Stockholm; contact Waxholmsbolaget or Strömma Kanalbolaget (tel. 23 33 75) about trips out (1hr. 25min., round-trip 70kr) or take bus 676, 671, 672, or 673 from T-bana: Tekniska Högskolan. For excursions that cover the entire Skärgård, contact Waxholmsbolaget, Strömma Kanalbolaget, or Stockholm Sightseeing (tel. 24 04 70). For the best bargain, get the **Båtluffarkortet** card (230kr), which grants unlimited travel for 16 days around the archipelago on Waxholmsbolaget sailings.

The Swedish royal family frolics at the extravagant **Drottningholm** palace amid Baroque gardens and Rococo interiors. Catch the free half-hourly English tour of the palace's **theater** and watch the original stage machinery produce thunderstorm effects. (For more information, call 759 04 06). Ballet or opera are yours for 85-410kr (tel. 660 82 25 for ticket information). **Kina Slott,** Drottningholm's Chinese pavilion, was an 18th-century royal summer cottage. (Palace and Kina Slott open May-Sept. 11am-4:30pm; Oct. Mon.-Fri. 1-3:30pm, Sat.-Sun. noon-3:30pm. Palace 30kr, students and children 10kr. Kina Slott 25kr. Theater open May-Aug. noon-3pm, Sept. 1-4pm; 30kr, children 10kr.) Get to Drottningholm via frequent ferries from Stadshusbron (May-Aug., round-trip 70kr), or on buses 301 through 323 from T-bana: Brommaplan.

GOTLAND

Vacationing Swedes have long cherished Gotland for its narrow cobblestone streets, seductive sands, and wildlife sanctuaries. Once the Baltic's trading center, Gotland lies off the east coast of Sweden, 320km south of Stockholm. According to the legend of Gutasaga, this charming island was discovered by Tjelvar, who rescued it from a curse that caused it to sink every day, only to resurface at night. You can tour the countryside by bike, explore the ruins of medieval churches, and party with the international jet setters who surface at night.

Visby's ancient wall—the oldest medieval monument in Scandinavia—encloses narrow, winding streets, ruined churches, and a wealth of petite squares and rose gardens. At the **Gotlands Fornsal** history museum, you'll discover that in 1361 this wall sheltered the town's privileged merchants, while the peasantry was massacred outside the gates. Exhibits cover the Viking Age, ancient burial rituals, and the town's 15th century sewage system (open 11am-6pm; Sept. to mid-May Tues.-Sun. noon-4pm; admission 30kr, students and seniors 10kr, under 17 free). Learn more from a guided tour of Visby (60kr per person); contact the tourist office for more information (see below). The **Visby Medieval Festival** turns the streets into a museum during the second week of August. Locals don authentic fashions of the Dark Ages, Strandgatan transforms into a medieval market, Danish king Valdemar Atterdag's invasion of Visby and a dramatic jousting tournament are re-enacted, and Visby even pulls this off without turning into EuroDisney®.

Outside the walls, a world of nature awaits. Examine the mystical monoliths on **Fårö,** off the northern tip of Gotland (bus 21, 2hrs.), the blazing beaches of **Tofta,** about 15km south of Visby (bus 31), and the calcified cliffs of **Hoburgen** at the island's southernmost tip. Cycling is a pleasant way to explore Gotland's flat terrain; try **HyrCykel Här,** about 300m to the left of the ferry terminal (45kr per day, 200-225kr per week for 3- to 5-speeds; 75kr per day, 325kr per week for mountain bikes; open daily 5:30am-6pm). Contact the Turistcenter (see below) for more information on bike trips and guided tours of Fårö (200kr per person). Part of northern Gotland is a military area closed to the public.

Practical Information, Accommodations, and Food The simplest way to Gotland is via the **Gotlandslinjen ferries** to Visby from Nynäshamn (5-6hrs.) or Oskarshamn (4-6hrs.). Fares are highest on weekends (162kr; students and seniors 106kr) and cheapest during the week (125kr, students and seniors 79kr). Nynäshamn is linked to Stockholm by **bus** from Cityterminalen (1hr., 50kr) and by *pendeltåg* (commuter train) from Centralstation (1hr., 50kr; *rabattkuponger* valid). For details contact **Gotland City** in Stockholm, Kungsgatan 57A (tel. (08) 23 61 70). Open Mon.-Fri. 9:30am-6pm, Sat. 10am-2pm. Once you're there, find the helpful **tourist office** at Donners Plats, Strandgatan 9 (tel. (0498) 24 70 65), a 10min. walk left from the ferry terminal (open June-Aug. Mon.-Fri. 8am-8pm, Sat.-Sun. 10am-7pm). They change money outside banking hours and offer detailed maps of Gotland and Visby (20-50kr). In the winter, head to **Gotlands Turistförening,** Hamngatan 4 (tel. (0498) 24 70 65; open Sept.-May Mon.-Fri. 9am-5pm). Pick up a **bus** timetable there, at the ferry terminal, or at the Visby bus station, Kung Magnusväg 1 (tel. (0498) 21 41 12; open Mon.-Fri. 8am-noon, 1-5pm).

Private rooms are cheaper outside the wall; reserve one at **Gotlands Turist-center,** Korsgatan 2 (tel. (0498) 27 90 95; open Mon.-Fri. 9am-6pm, Sat.-Sun. 10am-6pm; Oct.-April Mon.-Fri. 9am-6pm; singles 180kr, doubles 320kr). Or stay at the **STF Vandrarhem Visby,** Gamla A7 området (tel. (0498) 26 98 42). From the Visby bus station (Kung Magnusväg 1, outside the eastern wall), head east along the southern edge of the walled sports complex to Artillerigatan. The hostel is on the right. (Reception open 8-10am and 5-9pm. 90kr. Open mid-June to mid-Aug.) For a more rural setting try **Västerhejde Vandrarhem,** 6km south of the center of Visby (tel. (0498) 26 49 95, fax (0498) 29 62 60). Take bus 31 from the bus station, and ask the bus driver to drop you off. **Campgrounds** abound on Gotland. **Kneippbyns Campingplats** (tel. (0498) 26 43 65), 4km south of Visby, the home of Pippi Longstocking's Villa Villekulla, mini-golf, and a water park, dips its toes in the sea and is accessible by bus (80kr per tent, 225kr per person for 2-4 bed cabin and breakfast; open May-Sept. 10am-6pm).

The **Brinken** café, Söder Torg 19, offers a 47kr *dagens rätt* (open Mon.-Fri. 10am-7pm, Sat.-Sun. 11am-6pm). At **Rosa's,** St. Hansgatan 22, daily specials begin at 45kr (open mid-May to Sept. Mon.-Fri. 9am-5pm, Sat. 9am-4pm, Sun.11am-6pm). Admire

SWEDEN

a crumbling church ruin over coffee and crumbling pastry at **St. Hans Konditori,** St. Hansplan 2; it serves large meals from 55kr and metamorphoses into a mellow nightspot, sometimes with live folk music (open May -early Sept. Mon.-Sat. 8:30am-8:30pm, Sun. 9:30am-8:30pm).

SOUTHERN SWEDEN

Islands and skerries line both the east and west coasts of Sweden; the eastern **Småland** coastline, between Västervik and Kalmar, is particularly scenic, while the western **Halland** coast between Gothenburg and Helsingborg is scattered with small resort towns like **Båstad, Falkenberg,** and **Varberg,** whose beaches entice many sun-worshipping Swedes. Inland, clear lakes and limitless woods abound. The island of **Öland,** accessible from Kalmar via Europe's longest bridge, supports a nature reserve; it also has its share of archaeological sites. Famous crystal makers like **Orrefors** and **Kosta** roost in towns by the same name (near Växjö in Småland). **Skåne** (the stub of Sweden across from Copenhagen) and **Blekinge** (around Karlskrona), are Sweden's southernmost provinces; Blekinge is traditionally known as Sweden's garden, and Skåne as its breadbasket. *Pågatågen* (local trains, railpasses valid) run to destinations in most of Skåne (for info, call (040) 720 55).

From **Helsingborg** in northern Skåne, trains bound for Copenhagen cross on ferries to Helsingør in Denmark; reach Helsingborg by SJ train or by *pågatågen* (from Malmö or Lund 50-60kr). **Trelleborg,** in southern Skåne, sees several ferries per day off to Saßnitz (railpasses valid) and Travemünde in Germany; take an SJ train or bus from Malmö (40kr). From **Ystad,** also in southern Skåne, ferries serve Bornholm (see Denmark), and others shuttle to Świnoujście, Poland (2 per day, 290kr, with ISIC 230kr). Reach Ystad by *pågatåg* (from Malmö 70kr).

■■■ MALMÖ

Sweden's third-largest city languishes on the western coast of Skåne; trade and modernization have wiped out most of the city's old cobblestone streets, leaving it rather charmless. The **Form and Design Center,** in an old yellow building at Lilla torg 9, exhibits Sweden's contributions to convenience culture: bike helmets, wheelchairs, and other useful stuff (open Tues., Wed., and Fri. 11am-5pm, Thurs. 11am-6pm, Sat. 10am-4pm, Sun. noon-4pm. Free). From here wander to the **Rooseum,** Gasverksgatan 22, a collection of contemporary art (open Tues.-Sun. 11am-5pm. 20kr, under 15 free). Or meander in the other direction to **Malmöhus,** the city's old fortress, now a group of museums housing everything from historical artifacts to the local aquarium (open Mon.-Sat. noon-4pm, Sun. noon-4:30pm; Sept.-May closed Mon.; 30kr). To find out what's happening in Malmö, consult the tourist office, the **Youth Center,** or the all-knowing *Malmö This Month* guide (free).

Practical Information, Accommodations, and Food The train station and ferry harbor lie just north of the old town. Try **Shopping Linjen** for the cheapest trips to Copenhagen, Denmark (45min., 17kr; call (040) 11 00 99 for more information). Trains arrive from Göteborg (312kr) and Stockholm (487kr). The **tourist office** is in the train station, right by the ferry quay and across the street from the main post office (open Mon.-Fri. 9am-9pm, Sat.-Sun. 9am-8pm; Oct.-May Mon.-Fri. 9am-5pm, Sat. 9am-1pm). For good company and ideas for how to kill time in Malmö, drop by the **Youth Center** on Norra Neptuniusgatan 5 (tel. (040) 34 22 54); they offer free baggage storage, free showers, and free use of their kitchen facilities. You can buy frozen food and nuke it in their microwave. Rent bikes from **Fridhem Cykelaffär,** Tessinsväg 13 (tel. (040) 26 03 35; 35kr per day; open Mon.-Fri. 9am-noon and 1-6pm, Sat. 10am-1pm). Exhange money and cash traveler's checks at

Valutaspecialisten, Hamngatan 1 (tel. (040) 12 15 55; open Mon.-Fri. 8am-8pm, Sat. 9am-5pm). Unlike Forex, they charge no commission.

Sleep in a large, clean room with your own small bathroom at the **HI hostel,** Södergården, Backavägen 18 (tel. (040) 822 20, fax (040) 51 06 59). Take bus 21A to Vandrarhemmet, walk across the main street and follow the youth hostel signs (open mid-Jan. to mid-Dec. 8-10am, 4-8pm; no curfew; 90kr, nonmembers 125kr). **City Room,** Adelgatan 19 (tel. (040) 795 94), will book rooms in private homes (open Mon.-Fri. 10am-5pm; 150kr per night, price per week negotiable). **Sibbarp Camping,** Strandgatan 101 (tel. (040) 15 51 65), is at the end of bus route 11A (tents 120kr).

Browse around **Möllevångstorget** at mealtime; it offers a wide variety of cuisine at the lowest prices, as well as a **vegetable and fruit market** (open Mon.-Fri. 10am-2pm). The least expensive supermarket close to the city center is **AG Favör** on Värnhemtorget (open Mon.-Fri. 9am-7pm, Sat. 9am-3pm).

■■■ LUND

Malmö simply cannot compete with the beauty of its smaller sibling city. Lund, about 30km away. Home to Sweden's second-largest **university,** it throngs with young people in the winter and spring months. Their sophisticated fraternities, called *nationer,* are sleepier during vacations than those of rival Uppsala, but you can try calling the Småland (tel. (046) 12 06 80), Lund (tel. (046) 14 51 20), or Malmö (tel. (046) 12 78 02) *nationer* to see what's up. The campus is north of the town's ancient **cathedral,** an impressive 900 year-old remnant of the time when Lund was the religious epicenter of Scandinavia (open Mon.-Tues. and Fri. 8am-6pm, Wed.-Thurs. 8am-7:30pm, Sat. 9:30am-5pm, Sun. 9:30am-6pm). The cathedral's medieval clock chimes at noon and 3pm on weekdays and Sundays, 1pm and 3pm on public holidays. **Kulturen,** Tegnérplatsen, a collection of old Swedish houses, boasts modern art, archaeological findings, and much more (open 11am-5pm; Oct.-April noon-4pm. 30kr, students 20kr).

Practical Information, Accommodations, and Food

Most intercity **SJ trains** from Malmö stop at Lund; the cities are also connected by *pågatågen* (30kr, railpasses valid). Lund's **tourist office,** Kyrkogatan 11 (tel. (046) 35 50 40), is in the city hall, across the street from the cathedral (open Mon.-Fri. 10am-6pm, Sat.-Sun. 10am-2pm; Sept.-May Mon.-Fri. 10am-5pm; May also Sat. 10am-2pm).

Rest your tired limbs at the unusual **HI Hostel Tåget** (The Train), Bjerredsparken (tel. (046) 14 28 20, fax (046) 32 05 68), with authentic sleeping cars from the 1940's. Turn right as you come from the central station, and follow the signs (reception open 8-10am and 4-8pm; no curfew; 90kr, nonmembers 125kr; kitchen; open Jan. to mid-Dec.). The tourist office books rooms in **private homes** (150kr, 40kr fee). **Camping** is closest at Källbybadet (tel. (046) 35 51 88); take bus 91 "Klostergården" (40kr; open mid-June to Aug.). **Mårtenstorget** has a fresh fruit and vegetable market (open Mon.-Sat. 7am-2:30pm), and **supermarkets** abound (the **ICA** store across from the station is open 9am-9pm). **Chrougen,** the local student hangout, at Sandgatan 2 in the *Akademiska Föreningen* (student union), moonlights as a restaurant and disco. (Restaurant open mid-Aug. to mid-June 7-10pm, music 10pm-2am, cover 60kr.) Enjoy cheap food and Turkish and Oriental music with punks, Marxists, and others into body piercing at **Café Ariman,** Kungsgatan 12e (open Mon.-Sat. 11am-6pm). The **John Bull Pub,** Bantorget 2, serves good pub grub and beer in a congenial atmosphere (open Mon.-Thurs. 11am-1am, Fri.-Sat. 11am-2am, Sun. noon-1am).

■■■ VARBERG

Located in the county of Halland on the coast between Göteborg and Malmö, Varberg draws tourists to its **beaches** that stretch for miles northward and southward. For information on specific beaches, contact the tourist office (see below). Don't bother asking where to find the Swedish Bikini Team; it's only a low-brow U.S. beer commercial fantasy. The **Varberg Fortress,** built originally as a castle in the 14th century and fortified by 1617, looks out onto the sky-blue waters of the Kattegatt. Although you can't go into the castle on your own, you can climb up and around it; there are hourly tours from mid-June to mid-August (10am-5pm; 10kr, children 5kr). The unspectacular **Varberg Museum** boasts the only completely preserved medieval costume in the world (tel. (0340) 185 20; open 10am-7pm; mid-Aug. to mid-June Mon.-Fri. 10am-4pm, Sat.-Sun. noon-4pm; 10kr, children 5kr). Walk along the waterfront or rent a boat (tel. (0340) 798 85) to see the gorgeous coastline. If you're tired of walking, a **bike** is essential; the bus service is wanting. Rent one for 50kr per day at **Team Sportia,** across from the tourist office at Kyrkogatan 18 (open Mon.-Fri. 9:30am-6pm, Sat. 10:30am-2pm).

Practical Information, Accommodations, and Food Varberg is on the Göteborg-Malmö route, 1hr. and 72kr (under 19: 38kr) from Göteborg, 3hr. and 238kr (under 19: 190kr) from Malmö. The **tourist office,** Västra Vallgatan 39 (tel. (0340) 887 70), at Brunnsparken, offers free brochures and maps of the Halland region (30kr). It also books rooms in private homes (single 115kr, double 100kr per person) for a 25kr booking fee (open Mon.-Sat. 9am-7pm, Sun. 3-7pm; April-May and Sept. Mon.-Fri. 9am-5pm, Sat. 10am-1pm; Oct.-Mar. Mon.-Fri. 9am-5pm).

Most of Varberg's hostels and camping grounds lie far from the town center, but the **Crown Jail** of Varberg Fortress will lock you up between June and August (tel. (0340) 887 88; reception open 8-9:30am and 5-8pm, 100kr per bed in 1- to 4-bed rooms; kitchen facilities). Otherwise, commute 7km south to **HI Hostel Vare** (tel. (0340) 410 43) on bus 652 and walk another km, or bike south on Västra Vallgatan and follow the signs (open year-round; 85kr, nonmembers 115kr). Located on a small bay, **Apelvikens Camping** (tel. (0340) 141 78) is a 3km waterfront bike ride away. Or take bus 8 to the end of the line and follow the signs (open late April to mid-Aug.; high season 128kr per day, low season 100kr per day). Neighboring a supermarket, but no less idyllic, **Getteröns Camping** (tel. (0340) 168 85) lies 5km north of Varberg. Take bus 5 to Getteröns (open 8am-9pm in summer, 128kr per day). Eat like royalty in the cafés and restaurants that abound on **Drottninggatan** (the queen's street) and **Kungsgatan** (the king's street).

■■■ GOTHENBURG (GÖTEBORG)

Why are there subway trains in Stockholm, but instead streetcars in Gothenburg? "Because we have nothing to hide," say the *Göteborgare,* who poke fun at Stockholmers for good reason; *nollåttor* (zero-eights) are convinced that the entire country beyond their area code is a backward forest, but they are horribly mistaken. Sweden's second-largest city is as cosmopolitan as the capital, while friendlier and mellower. (In fact, the only thing you can hold against Göteborg is that it spawned the pop group Ace of Base.) For the best view of town (and a perfect place to picnic), climb up to the towering **Masthuggskyrka** (take tram 3 or 4 to Stigbergstorget and follow the signs). Walk back to the city center via Haga Nygata, a cobblestone street with beautifully restored wooden houses. The **Maritime Museum** houses the destroyer *Småland* and submarine *Nordkaparen* (open Mon.-Fri. 9am-4pm, Sat.-Sun. 10am-5pm; 40kr). The mighty **Poseidon statue** stands in front of the **Konstmuseum** (art museum) at the upper end of Kungsportsavenyn (open Mon.-Fri. 11am-4pm, Sat.-Sun. 11am-5pm; Sept.-April closed Mon.; 40kr, under 17 free; wheelchair access). The surrounding *skärgård* (archipelago) is Gothenburg's least expensive pleasure, but parts of it are military zones off-limits to foreigners (check at the tourist office or call (031) 69 20 00). **Vrångö** offers secluded beach serenity (take tram 4 to Saltholmen, then a boat to the island; call (031) 69 64 00 for more information). **Nya Elfsborg** is a fortress where the Göta Älv meets the sea; many a time, this island stronghold saved Gothenburg form the Danish navy. Tours leave Stenpiren early May to early September (7 per day, 60kr).

Bars and clubs line **Kungsportsavenyn** (known simply as Avenyn); the area is packed with young people on weekends, so expect long lines to get in anywhere. Try **Magasinet,** Magasinsgatan 3 (tel. (031) 11 10 53), for a taste of some excellent local bands (open 9pm-2am; free entry every Tues., Wed., Fri., and Sat.). Fantastic jazz swings at **Nefertiti,** Hvitfeldtsplatsen 6 (tel. (031) 11 15 33; open July-May). Consult *Göteborg This Week* for concert and event listings; get tickets at the main tourist office (tel. (031) 13 65 00; booth open Mon.-Fri. 9am-5pm, Sat. 10am-2pm).

Practical Information, Accommodations, and Food The **tourist office,** Kungsportsplatsen 2 (tel. (031) 10 07 40), in the old town, cheerfully advertises the fact that Gothenburg was voted "Sweden's nicest city" in a national survey. Pick up your free copy of the *City Nytt* and *Göteborg This Week* here (open 9am-8pm; early June and late Aug.; Sept.-April Mon.-Fri. 9am-5pm, Sat. 10am-2pm; May Mon.-Fri. 9am-6pm, Sat.-Sun. 10am-2pm.) For budget travel, head for **Kilroy Travels Sweden** at Berzeliigatan 5 (tel. (031) 20 08 60; open Mon.-Fri. 9:30am-5pm). **Exchange currency** at the **Forex** shops (open daily 8am-9pm in Centralstation and Kungsportsavenyn 22; 15kr per traveler's check, 20kr commission on cash), or at **American Express,** at **Ticket,** Östra Hamngatan 35 (open Mon.-Fri. 10am-1:30pm and 2:30-6pm).

Trains arrive at **Centralstation** (to Oslo, 5hr., 381kr; to Stockholm, 3½-5hr., 444kr.), which offers **lockers** (20kr per 24hrs.) and **showers** (20kr; open Sun.-Thurs. 7am-9pm, Fri.-Sat. 7am-10pm), as well as a **waiting room** for women traveling alone. Centralstation lies northeast of elegant Brunnsparken, while Kungsportsavenyn, the city's main boulevard, runs south. **Stena Line ferries** (tel. (031) 775 00 00) sail to Fredrikshavn, Denmark (3hr.; 60kr, 30kr with Scanrail or Eurail) and to Kiel, Germany (14hr.; 600kr, Sat. 700kr). **Sea Cat hydrofoils** (tel. (031) 775 08 00) whisk to Fredrikshavn (1¾hr., 95kr). **Scandinavian Seaways** (tel. (031) 80 55 10) ships sail to Harwich (24hr.; 495kr, mid-June to early Aug. 695kr, Oct. 595kr), and Newcastle, England (22hr.; 495kr, mid-June to early Aug. 695kr, Oct. 595kr), and Amsterdam, Netherlands (20hr.; 420kr, mid-June to early Aug. 520kr).

Public transportation is a must as you move out of the city center. Trams, buses, and even boats in the *skärgård* are accessible with the *magnetkort,* fare cards that come with varying numbers of *kuponger* (valid 1hr.; single ticket (2 *kuponger*) 14kr, 9 *kuponger* 50kr, 22 *kuponger* 100kr). The **24hr. card** (35kr) allows unlimited travel within city limits. All cards are available at the **Tidpunkten** kiosk at Nils Ericsonsplatsen, next to the train station (open Mon.-Thurs. 7am-10pm, Fri. 7am-2:30am, Sat. 9am-2:30am, Sun. 9am-6pm), and in the many **Pressbyrån** kiosks at transit hubs. The **Göteborg Card** gives you free public transportation plus free entry (or discounts) for many attractions and tours (available at tourist offices and hotels; 1 day 120kr, 2 day 200kr, 3 day 250kr).

The **HI hostel** closest to the center of town is the enormous, modern **Ostkupan,** Mejerigatan 2 (tel. (031) 40 10 50). Take bus 64 from Brunnsparken to Gräddgatan (250 beds in dorms; reception open 7:30-11pm; 90kr, nonmembers 125kr; wheelchair access; open June-Aug.). Sleep cheap in the cramped but friendly **Nordengården,** Stockholmsgatan 16 (tel. (031) 19 66 31). Take tram 3 to Stockholmsgatan and walk downhill; it's in the yellow wooden building on your left (reception open 7-10am and 4-9pm; lockout 10am-4pm; 80kr; breakfast 25kr; sleeping bags allowed). Docked among the ships of the Maritime Museum, **Seaside** (tel. (031) 10 10 35), centrally located at Packhuskajen harbor, has newly renovated cabins in a former Norwegian motorship well worth the 100kr—if you don't get seasick (reception open 8am-9pm, check-in after 4pm, no curfew, no phone reservations). The closest **campsite** is **Kärralund Camping,** Olbersgatan (tel. (031) 25 27 61; take tram 5 to Wellangergatan, walk east 200m on Olbersgatan). There are 48 beds in its hostel (reception open 7am-11pm, Sept.-April 8am-noon and 4-8pm; 90kr, nonmembers 125kr; wheelchair access).

Fruits of the sea lend their fragrance to the quasi-ecclesiastical **Feskekörka,** a fish market and restaurant (open Tues.-Thurs. 9am-5pm, Fri. 9am-6pm, Sat. 9am-1:30pm). Munch on a 38-45kr *dagens rätt* at **Plankan,** Vasaplatsen 3 (tel. (031) 11 63 02; open Mon.-Thurs. 10:30am-1am, Fri. 10:30am-2am, Sat. 1pm-2am, Sun. 1pm-1am). Or fuel up with a 30kr vegetarian lunch with the university students at **Norrlands Café,** Västra Hamngatan 20 (open Mon.-Thurs. 9am-11pm, Fri. 9am-2am, Sat. 11am-2am, Sun. noon-9am). The readily available *City Nytt* paper provides a comprehensive list of restaurants.

CENTRAL SWEDEN

■■■ UPPSALA

Once a hotbed of pagan spirituality and the cradle of Swedish civilization, Uppsala is now a Nordic Oxbridge, sheltering the 20,000 students of Sweden's oldest university. Scandinavia's largest cathedral, the magnificent **Domkyrka,** where Swedish monarchs were crowned, looms just over the river (open 8am-8pm; Sept.-May 8am-6pm; free; for tours call 18 72 10). The **Gustavianum,** across from the Domkyrka, lodges the once macabre **Anatomical Theater**—the site of public human dissections—as well as small-scale museums of Nordic, classical, and Egyptian antiquities (open 11am-3pm; Sept.-May Anatomical Theater only noon-3pm; 10kr per museum, 25kr for all 4). The university's millhouse from the 1760s has been converted into **Upplandsmuseet,** a showcase of the province's settlements, as well as its two-billion-year geological history (open noon-5pm; free). For university events, scope the bulletin board at the massive **Carolina Rediviva Library,** Övre Slottsgatan at Drottninggatan (open Mon.-Fri. 8:30am-8pm). A glorious pagan temple stood a millennium ago at **Gamla Uppsala** (Old Uppsala), 4km north of the city center. Little remains save huge burial mounds of monarchs and **Uppsala Kyrka** (Church), one of Sweden's oldest (open Mon.-Sat. 8:30am-8pm, Sun. 12:30-8pm; Sept.-March 8:30am-dusk. Take bus 20 or 24 north from Dragarbrunnsgatan. Return within 90min. to re-use ticket.) After exhausting Uppsala, Baroque aficionados should hop the boat to **Skokloster,** a dazzling many-windowed palace (round-trip 95kr, departs 11:45am and returns 5pm from Islandsbron on Östra Ågatan and Munkgatan. Summer only).

Practical Information, Accommodations, and Food As you exit the Uppsala train station, the center of town is ahead and to the right. The **tourist office,** Fyris Torg 8 (tel. (018) 11 75 00 or (018) 27 48 00), is near the west bank of the River Fyris. From the train station, walk right on Kungsgatan 2-3 blocks, turn left on St. Persgatan, and cross the bridge to pick up a map (31kr) of the city (open Mon.-Fri. 10am-6pm, Sat. 10am-2pm). If you insist on wheels in this walkable town, rent them at **Cykel och Skidstället,** Svartbäcksgatan 20 (tel. (018) 12 67 40), for 65kr per day, 200kr per week (open Mon.-Fri. 9:30am-6pm, Sat. 10am-2pm). **Trains** from Stockholm's Centralstation run about every hour (45min., 50kr).

Sunnersta Herrgård (HI), Sunnerstavägen 24 (tel. (018) 32 42 20), 6km south of town, offers pleasing doubles, a few triples, and swimming in nearby Lake Mälar. Take bus 20 or 50 from Dragarbrunnsgatan to Herrgårdsvägen (12-15min., 15kr), then walk 2 blocks behind the kiosk, turn left and walk 50m (reception open 8-10am and 5-9pm; 90kr, nonmembers 125kr; laundry; sheets 25kr; kitchen; open May-Aug.). By the river and a swimming pool rests **Fyrishov Camping** (tel. (018) 27

49 60), off Svartbäcksgatan 2km from the city center (reception open 7:30am-10pm; tents 85kr, 4-5 bed huts 330kr). Take bus 4 to Fyrishov.

All Uppsala university students belong to refined fraternities called *nations,* which practically give away food and drink (meals average 35kr, beer 25kr) and throw flamboyant fests. If you are a university student and arrive on a summer Thursday, bring your ID (not an ISIC) and your passport to the student union office, Övre Slottsgatan 7 (tel. (018) 10 59 54; open Thurs. 5-7pm), at Åsgränd, for a one-week student card (30kr, 10kr extra for each additional week). Or try the direct approach and show up at a *nation*'s door with a smile and a college ID or ISIC in hand. Your best bets are **Upplands Nation,** St. Larsgatan 11 (tel. (018) 13 24 16), with a disco on Fridays during the school year (open 7pm-1am, beer 20kr), or the laid-back **Södermanland-Nerikes Nation,** St. Olofsgatan 16 (tel. (018) 12 34 91; summer Tues., Fri., and Sun.; school year Tues. and Sun. only; open nightly 6pm-1am, winter 7pm-1am), which serves an all-you-can-munch lunch open to every-body during the academic year (30kr, served Mon.-Fri. 11am-2pm). For cheap nutri-tion, head for the large, cafeteria-like **Landings,** Kungsänggatan 5 (sandwiches from 12kr, free refills of tea and coffee; open Mon.-Fri. 8:30am-8:30pm, Sat. 8:30am-3pm) or the vegetarian café on Drottninggatan 7 (*dagens rätt* 35-45kr; open Mon.-Fri. 11am-3pm, Sat. 11am-2pm). **Camel Club,** Vaksalagatan 10, has a 42kr lunch rang-ing from vegetarian to pasta to traditional Swedish as well as a bar and disco at night (open 10am-2am; disco Wed., Fri., and Sat.; 40kr, free before 10pm).

■■■ DALARNA

An old Ingmar Bergman movie goes by the English title *Wild Strawberries.* The Swedish title, *Smultronstället,* holds two meanings: a place of wild strawberries, or a secret spot where one goes to commune with nature, one's self, and one's signifi-cant other. Dalarna, however hokey, is Sweden's *smultronstället.* Scores of Swedes summer here in tidy red and white farmhouses in the woods. The **Silijansleden,** a 340km cycling and hiking trail, winds its way through forests and over mountains around Lake Siljan. Several trains run from Stockholm via Uppsala to Borlänge, and from there either northeast to Falun or northwest to Leksand, Rättvik, and Mora.

Leksand Over 20,000 people flock to this small town on bluffs above the lake to take part in the ancient **Midsummer** (summer solstice) festivities: the raising of the maypole, a procession of richly decorated longboats that once ferried people to church, exuberant folk music, and the **Siljansrodden,** a two-week series of long-boat-rowing competitions on Lake Siljan. The annual **Musik vid Siljan** festival in Leksand and Rättvik (1st week of July) arranges a mélange of music from all over the earth (call (0248) 102 90 for more info). Also contact the **tourist office,** on Norsga-tan (tel. (0247) 803 00), for details. To get to the office from the train station, walk up Villagatan to Leksandsvägen; turn left, then hang a right on Norsgatan (open Mon.-Sat. 9am-9pm, Sun. noon-9pm; mid-Aug. to mid-June Mon.-Fri. 9am-5pm, Sat. 9am-1pm).

Accommodations are often crowded (packed for Midsummer), but the tourist office can hook you up with a private room for a 25kr fee (doubles from 265kr). Try the **Ungdomsgården** (tel. (0247) 100 90), on Rättviksvägen near Tällbergsvägen, a few minutes from the station. A combination campground, lodge, and country kitchen, the main building is a red farmhouse (reception open 8am-9pm, 60kr per bed, tents 80kr, open mid-June to mid-Aug.). With new facilities and lots of common space, Leksand's **HI hostel** (tel. (0247) 152 50) is 2.5km from the train station. Cross the bridge near the tourist office and head left on Insjövägen (reception open 8-10am and 5-8pm; May and Sept. open 5-7pm.; Oct.-April call before you arrive; 90kr, nonmembers 125k; laundry 30kr; bikes 60kr per day). A 20min. walk on the road toward Tällberg brings you to swimming and **camping** (tel. (0247) 803 13) at Orsandbaden (85kr per tent). Hit **Leksands Kebab & Pizza,** Norsgatan 23, for substantial low-cost pizza (from 30kr; open Mon.-Thurs. 11am-10pm, Fri.-Sat. 11am-midnight, Sun. noon-10pm).

From Leksand's quay there are breezy **boat connections** a few times a week to Rättvik (60kr) and Mora (120kr). For info, call (010) 252 32 92 or (010) 204 77 24.

Rättvik Twenty minutes north by train, the sleepy town of Rättvik blossoms with life during the Musik vid Siljan Festival (see above), and plays no second fiddle to Leksand in celebrating Midsummer. If fiddling is in fact your thing, check out the **Bingsjö Spelmansstämma** (Player's Convention) on the first Wednesday of July (double-check 1995 date with tourist office), when some 30,000 people from all over the world invade a private farm in Bingsjö, 40km from Rättvik, for everything from Swedish folk songs to bluegrass. Nearby attractions include **Rättviks Gammelgård,** a Dalarna farm reincarnated, with local handicrafts and a café. Walk 10 minutes northwest out of the town center towards Sjurberg (open June to mid.-Aug. 11am-6pm; free; guided tours at 1 and 2:30pm, 10kr). Rent a canoe, pedal boat, or windsurfer at **Siljansbadet Sommarland** (tel. (0248) 134 00), behind the train station (20-50kr per hr.).

Rättvik's **tourist office** (tel. (0248) 702 00), across from the train station, sells detailed hiking and biking maps of the Lake Siljan area (15kr) and pins down rooms in private homes starting at 250kr (open Mon.-Fri. 9am-8pm, Sat. noon-4pm, Sun. 11am-6pm; Sept.-May Mon.-Fri. 9am-5pm, Sat. noon-4pm). Built in the old Dalarna blockhouse style, the **HI youth hostel** (tel. (0248) 105 66) sprawls beneath the pines off Centralgatan, 1km behind the tourist office (reception open 8-10am in summer and 5-8pm year-round; 90kr, nonmembers 125kr; laundry 15kr; breakfast 40kr). Massive **Rättviksparkens Camping** (tel. (0248) 116 06, in winter (0248) 102 51) is down the side road that turns off Centralgatan at the youth hostel (reception open 8am-10pm; Sept.-May Sat.-Sun. noon-1pm; 100kr per tent, cabins available). The town center has a small but stocked and relatively cheap ICA **supermarket** (open 9am-7pm). Swedish and American food coexist in harmony at **Mathuset** (open Mon.-Sat. 10am-8pm, Sun. noon-8pm). Gaze at Agneta Svensdotter's *Paradise* or cable TV while eating a late-night pizza at **Rättviks Kebab and Pizzeria**, across from the tourist office (40kr per meal; video games; open Mon.-Thurs. 11am-10pm, Fri.-Sat. 11am-2am, Sun. 11am-10pm).

Mora Head north to more tourist-friendly Mora, which was home to artist Anders Zorn (1860-1920), famous for his paintings of large, naked women. Visit his collection at the **Zornmuseet,** Vasagatan 36 (open Mon-Sat. 9am-5pm, Sun. 11am-5pm; 25kr, students 20kr). **Nusnäs,** 10km east of Mora (take bus 108), is the home of wooden *dalahäst* horses, the Swedish equivalent of American baseball and apple pie. You can tour the factory at **Nils Olsson Hemslöjd** (tel. (0250) 372 50) for free (open Mon.-Fri. 9am-4pm, Sat.-Sun. 10am-4pm; mid-Aug. to May Mon.-Fri. 8am-4pm, Sat. 10am-1pm). **Santa Claus's** humble abode (or one of them; every snowy village claims the title) is in nearby **Gesunda,** accessible by bus 107 from Mora. It's called **Tomteland** (tel. (0250) 290 00; open mid-June to mid-Aug. 10am-6pm, and throughout Dec., of course; 95kr).

Mora's central train station is a hike from civilization; take the train from Morastrand platform, right near the town center. The **tourist office** (tel. (0250) 265 50), on the lakefront by Morastrand, books beds in private homes (160kr) for a 25kr fee (open Mon.-Sat. 9am-8pm, Sun. 11am-8pm; mid-Aug. to mid-June Mon.-Fri. 9am-5pm, Sat. 9am-1pm). Comprised of buildings up to 200 years old and run by missionaries, the hostel at **Åmåsängsgården** (tel. (0250) 133 42) is 4km south from the town center (reception open 10am-noon and 4-8pm; 90kr; open mid-June to mid-Aug.). Mora is a gateway to northern Sweden; the **Inlandsbanan** train route (see Lappland) begins here (1 train per day at 3:50pm).

■■■ ÖSTERSUND

Located at the intersection of the longitudinal Inlandsbanan and the latitudinal railway from Sweden's east coast to Trondheim, Norway, Östersund is a natural stopover (from Trondheim, 5½hr., 278kr; from Stockholm, 6hr., 497kr). Although near the country's geographical heart, this lakeside town is a tad outlandish. No low-key patriots, the inhabitants of Jämtland county boisterously boost their region during **Storsjöyran.** Held the last weekend in July, this "freedom fest" has the locals performing some decidedly un-Swedish dancing in the streets. **Lake Storsjön** is home to a cousin of the Loch Ness monster that King Oscar II and a crew of Norwegian whalers unsuccessfully tried to capture in 1894. Their harpooning equipment is on display at the **Länsmuseet,** 700m north of the city center on Kyrkgatan (open Mon., Wed.-Fri. 9am-4pm, Tues. 9am-9pm, Sat-Sun. noon-4pm; free). Rent a mountain bike at **Cykelogen,** Kyrkgatan 45, for 100kr a day (regular bike 50-75kr) and let gravity draw you over the footbridge to **Fröson Island,** formerly the turf of the (Viking) Aesir gods.

The **tourist office,** Rådhusgatan 44 (tel. (063) 14 40 01), sells mountain hiking maps (65kr) and detailed city maps (55kr), and books private rooms (135-150kr) for a 40kr fee (open Mon.-Sat. 9am-9pm, Sun. 10am-7pm; Sept.-May Mon.-Fri. 8am-5pm). From the train station, walk up the hill on your left and continue down Prästgatan; hang right up Postgränd one block. Ask for the new location of the **HI Youth Hostel,** scheduled to move in 1995. Wild strawberries grow on the thatched roof of **Frösötornets Härbärge hostel** (tel. (063) 11 57 67), which sits at the top of a 176m high ski slope overlooking the city. Take bus 5 from the city center (last one leaves 8:22pm) or endure a hellish climb. (Reception open 9am-9pm. 115kr. Showers 1kr per 2min. Kitchen. Open May-Sept.) Take bus 2 or 6 to **Östersunds Camping** (tel. (063) 14 46 15) at "Fritidsbyn" (tents 95kr). For basic Swedish lunch, try **Wedemark's Konditori,** Prästgatan 27 (sandwiches 15-28kr; open Mon.-Fri. 9am-6pm, Sat. 9am-2pm). Find both Mexican and Creole cuisine in the old-fashioned Swedish interior of **Brunkullans Café/Restaurang,** Postgränd 5. The lunch buffet (55kr) includes rice, bread, salad, and coffee or tea (open Mon.-Sat. 11am-11pm, Sun. 11am-10pm). **Saluhallen,** a gourmet food market on Stortorget, features culinary delights ranging from Chinese chili sauce to Indian cashews to freshly baked bread (open Mon.-Fri. 10am-6pm, Sat. 10am-2pm).

■■■ UMEÅ

Return to the sunnier coast in Umeå (OOM-eh-oh), a pulsating university town at the mouth of the Ume Älv. Defying the general southward migration trend, Umeå has been the fastest growing city in Sweden for the past 15 years, and has one of the youngest populations. **Silja Line** ferries sail to Vaasa (June-Aug. 195kr, Sept.-May Sun.-Wed. 165kr, Thurs.-Sat. 195kr; 50% off with Eurail or Scanrail) and Pietarsaari (1 per day, 175kr, 50% off with Eurail or Scanrail), both in Finland. On weekends many of the younger passengers don't disembark at all; they just go for the cheap booze and slot machines. Check out the world's oldest ski at the **Swedish Ski Museum,** one of seven museums built door-to-door in **Gammlia.** (Indoor museums open 10am-6pm; mid-Aug. to early June 9am-4pm; open-air museum open Midsummer to mid-Aug. noon-5pm. Free.) To brave the **rapids** of Vindelälven in a rubber raft navigated by the staff of **Sotarns Forsränning** (tel. (090) 19 39 90; open July noon-5pm, reservations required May-June and Aug.-Sept.; 130kr), take bus 15 to Vännäs.

Trains run to Umeå from Boden (5hr., 312kr), Luleå (6hr., 346kr), and Stockholm (11½hr., 570kr). To get to the **tourist office,** Renmarkstorget 15 (tel. (090) 16 16 16), stroll down Rådhusesplanaden across from the train station and turn right on Skolgatan. They have a list of contacts for private rooms (150kr) and stacks of useful brochures. (Open Mon.-Fri. 8am-8pm, Sat. 10am-6pm, Sun. noon-6pm; Sept.-May Mon.-Fri. 9am-6pm.) The mellow **HI hostel,** Järnvägsallén 22 (tel. (090) 11 16 50), sits 200m east (left) of the train station. (Reception open 8am-noon and 4-10pm.

SWEDEN

90kr, nonmembers 125kr. Breakfast 45kr. Kitchen. Laundry 5kr. Sauna 10kr per person, 5-person minimum. Open early June-early Aug.) Camp at **Nydala lake** (tel. (090) 16 16 60; 65kr, people-watching included). **Oves Cykelservice,** Storgatan 86 (tel. (090) 12 61 91), rents bikes (30kr per day) to adventurous souls who head up the river around the 30km **Umeleden** bike trail (open Mon.-Fri. 8am-5pm). Along the Umeleden sit old hydropower stations, gardens, restaurants, and **Baggböle Herrgård,** a delightful café in a 19th-century mansion (open Tues.-Sun. noon-8pm).

Dine on a hearty Swedish *dagens rätt* (48kr) at **Carl Gustav,** Magasingatan 17 (open Mon.-Fri. 8am-6pm, Sat. 11am-5pm, Sun. noon-5pm). Collegiate types eat at **Teater Café,** Vasaplan, where lunch specials run from 38 to 49kr; vegetarians are well taken care of (open Mon.-Thurs. 11am-midnight, Fri. 11am-1am, Sat. noon-1am, Sun. 5-11pm). The **Blå Dragon** night club, on Västra Norrlandsgatan by the E4 highway, caters to a young clientele on Wednesday (cover 20kr) and Friday (70kr, before 10pm 35kr; open 8pm-1am). A lively pub atmosphere dominates at **Viskningar och Rop** (despite the fact that it's named after a somber Bergman film). Find it in the Hotel Plaza on Storgatan near Renmarkstorget (no cover; open Mon.-Thurs. 11am-midnight, Fri. 11am-2am, Sat. 3pm-2am, Sun. 3pm-midnight; disco on Wed., Fri., and Sat. nights until 2am).

LAPPLAND

Many "Southerners"—anyone living south of the Arctic Circle—imagine that Lappland consists of herds of reindeer roaming through dense forest, thick snow, unrelenting darkness, and bitter cold for half the year, and perpetual light for the other half. This is all true. Although mining has begun to encroach upon previously virgin land, the lure here is still nature, from swampy birch and pine forests in the vast lowlands to the spectacular fells: old, rounded mountains that rise to meet the Norwegian border. In the lowlands, long clothing and a supple wrist will protect you against the summer's swamp-bred mosquitoes. Many bug repellents were banned for environmental reasons; if you plan on hiking or camping, buy your repellent (75kr) in Lappland to be on the safe side.

Getting There Swedish Lappland is home to 17,000 reindeer-tending **Sami,** to whom the name "Lapps" is derogatory. Jokkmokk, Gällivare, and Kiruna are the three main settlements north of the Arctic Circle, and all make good stopovers on the way to mountains stations such as Kvikkjokk and Abisko, or national parks Muddus, Padjelanta, Sarek, and Stora Sjöfallet. A considerable time-saver going north is flying; enjoy youth standby fares on **SAS** (under 24 only; Stockholm-Kiruna 500kr) or **Transwede** (under 24 only; Stockholm-Gällivare 500kr). There are two **rail routes** to Lappland. The **coastal route** extends from Stockholm through Boden, Gällivare, and Kiruna to Narvik, Norway, along the **Malmbanan** (Stockholm-Kiruna 2 per day in either direction, 18hr., 623kr, reservations necessary). The touristy **Inlandsbanan** (inland railway) stops for reindeer; it also stops for souvenirs and at the Arctic Circle so you can touch the ground and feel special. Traveling the entire length requires overnight stopovers in Östersund. (One per day. Mora-Gällivare 500kr. 50% discount with Eurail and Scanrail. Unlimited travel for 14 days 995kr. Runs early June to mid-Aug.) Connections between the parallel inland and coastal train routes can be made at Uppsala-Mora, Sundsvall-Östersund, and Luleå-Boden-Gällivare. **Buses,** many of which accept no railpasses, are the only way to the smaller towns; pick up a copy of the *Länstrafiken i Norrbotten* company schedule. If you plan to use both buses and trains in the north, consider buying the **Norrlandskortet,** which gives unlimited travel on all SJ trains (2nd class, excluding Inlandsbanan) and Länstrafikens buses in Sweden north of Sundsvall as well as trains to Narvik, Trondheim and Mo i Rana in Norway (890kr, under 19 445kr). The brochure *Summer Routes in Norrland* (available at tourist offices) supplies an exhaustive menu of routes and trails, complete with listings of attractions and events. If you're heading for the mountains, STF's *Turisttrafik i fjällen* brochure is an indispensable transport overview (which unfortunately comes out late in the summer).

Getting Out Transportation out of Lappland can be challenging. Those heading farther north can take the most scenic train ride in Sweden up to Narvik on the Norwegian coast (stop at Abisko Turiststation or lonelier Låktatjåkka for dramatic mountain trails). One bus a day (100kr) links Kiruna to **Karesuando** on the Finnish border, site of Sweden's northernmost **Youth Hostel** (tel. (0981) 202 85, open June-Aug., call ahead). From there you can continue to Skibotn, Norway or Kilpisjärvi and Muonio, Finland, or backtrack south to Finland through **Boden.** Railpasses are valid on all **buses** from Boden to **Haparanda,** on the Finnish border. Be sure to plan ahead: the hostel in **Luleå** (20min. from Boden) is 6km from the city (tel. (0920) 523 25, take bus 6 from Luleå). If you make it to Haparanda, stay at the **HI hostel,** Strandgatan 26 (tel. (0922) 111 71). Remember that Finland is one time zone ahead when consulting schedules.

■■■ LULEÅ

At the mouth of the Lule Älv (river) lies Luleå (LOOL-eh-oh), a small university town with a slow-paced, relaxed atmosphere and plenty of natural beauty. Seven hundred years ago, Luleå was a trading port and fishing region, and when the number of fast days were increased (during which only fish could be eaten), Sweden quickly secured this now-profitable region. The medieval church in **Gammelstad** (Old Luleå), was built in the 1480s. Take bus 8, 9, 10, or 32; 18kr). Return to the 20th century (and your childhood) at the **Teknikens Hus** (Technology Museum), Högskolan, where you can play with lots of techno-toys (open Tues.-Sun. 11am-5pm; late Aug. to mid-June Tues., Thurs., Fri. 9am-4pm, Wed. 9am-8pm, Sat.-Sun. noon-5pm; free). Explore the hundreds of uninhabited islands of the **Luleå Archipelago;** get more info at the **tourist office,** Storgatan 438 (tel. (0920) 29 35 00 or 29 35 05). They rent rooms (150-200kr per person) and bikes in the summer (40kr per day). From the train station, cross Prästgatan, walk diagonally across the park, cross Hermalingsgatan and continue straight up Storgatan; the tourist office is on the right in a yellow building with a red roof (open Mon.-Fri. 10am-7pm, Sat.-Sun. 10am-4pm).

To get to **Örnviks Youth Hostel (HI),** Örnviksvägen 87 (tel. (0920) 523 25), 6km from the city center, take bus 6 and ask the driver to drop you off after the bridge; cross the road, walk back towards the bridge, and follow the path leading into the field on your right. (Reception open 7am-11pm; Sept.-May Mon.-Fri. 7am-11pm, Sat.-Sun. 8am-9pm. 90kr, nonmembers 125kr. Breakfast 45kr. Kitchen.) **EFS Sundet** (tel. (0920) 520 74) is the closest campground; take bus 6 (50kr per tent, 2-bed cabins 120kr). Quell hunger pangs at **Börse Olssons Konditori,** Storgatan 61. (Sandwiches 18-28kr. Open Mon.-Fri. 8am-9pm, Sat. 10am-6pm, Sun. noon-9pm.) Relax the tight grip on your wallet and feast at **Café Pimpinella,** Storgatan 40. (*Dagens rätt* 57kr. Bar at night. Open Mon.-Tues. 11am-11pm, Wed.-Thurs. 11am-midnight, Fri.-Sat. 11am-2am.) Get dessert and coffee at the wonderfully mellow **Café Valvet,** Nygatan 11 (open Mon.-Fri. 9am-6pm, Sat. 10am-4pm; sandwiches: 10-15kr).

■■■ JOKKMOKK AND GÄLLIVARE

A very good reason (and the only reason) to stop in **Jokkmokk** is the outstanding museum of indigenous Sami culture **Ájtte.** (Open Mon.-Fri. 9am-6pm, Wed. until 8pm, Sat.-Sun. 11am-6pm; Sept. to mid-June Mon.-Fri. 9am-4pm, Sat.-Sun. noon-4pm. Oct.-April. closed Mon. 20kr.) See the midnight sun at **Storknabben,** an easy 2km hike from town. Walk east on Storgatan, turn right onto Lappstavägen and follow the signs (café open daily in the summer 7pm-1am). Ask the **tourist office,** Stortorget 4 (tel. (0971) 121 40), about the reconstructed Stone Age village of **Vuollerim,**

45km east of Jokkmokk. The office keeps a list of private rooms (85-150kr per person), stores luggage (15kr), rents bikes (50kr per day, 10kr per hr.), and sells mountain maps (open 9am-7pm; Sept.-May Mon.-Fri. 8:30am-3:30pm). If you didn't intend to head for the mountains, the wilderness photos in **Edvin Nilsson's gallery,** on Klockarvägen, just off Storgatan, may change your mind. (Open July-Aug. 11am-6pm. Free. Try the door in June; if he's home he'll let you take a look.) To get to the **HI Hostel,** walk up Stationsgatan from the train station, and turn left on Storgatan. (Reception open 8-10am and 5-9pm. 90kr, non-members 125kr. Free sauna.) Foot-sore travelers can stay at the **yellow house** across the street from the station (75-85kr). The campsite is 3km outside town at **Jokkmokks Turistcenter** (tel. (0971) 123 70; tents 60kr, 4-bed cabins 540kr). Hike east on Storgatan. **Buses** to Jokkmokk run from Gällivare (5 per day, Sat.-Sun. 1 per day; 1½hr.; 73kr).

Spend some time underground in the mining town of **Gällivare** (YELL-i-varay).The **tourist office** (tel. (0970) 166 60) is at Storgatan 16; from the train station, turn right onto the main road, walk up the hill and cross through the parking lot. (Open 9am-8pm; mid-Aug. to May Mon.-Fri. 9am-4:30pm.) Their weekday tours will bury you in the **copper and iron mines** (mid-June to early-Aug. at 10am to iron mine, 160kr; 1:30pm to copper mine, 140kr). For a real taste of the crags, take a day hike up 820m-high **Dundret mountain** (round-trip 14km, allow 3-6hr.). If hiking doesn't suit you, take the midnight sun trip up Dundret (mid-June to mid-July 11pm; 140kr; includes coffee and waffle). The **HI youth hostel** (tel. (0970) 143 80) is a 5min. walk from the station; cross the bridge over the tracks, then the one over the river. (Reception open 8-10am and 5-10:30pm. 90kr, nonmembers 125kr. Laundry 20kr. Kitchen. Sauna 50kr per hr. Call ahead.) **Gällivare Camping** (tel. (0970) 186 79) is home to friendly people and overfriendly mosquitoes; it's by the river 1½km from the station (75kr per tent; open early June-early Sept.).

■■■ KIRUNA AND KUNGSLEDEN

Kiruna bills itself as the "City of the Future," but it's a rather dystopian vision of mining, missile launching, and satellite operations. The town's major claim to fame is that the first pictures of the Chernobyl disaster were taken by satellites from Kiruna. You can see the world's largest underground iron ore mine here. (Sign up at **Kiruna Guidetour,** across from the tourist office, early June to mid-Sept. 10am, noon, 2pm, and 4pm. 85kr.) The Sami knew about the stuff long before it was "discovered" but didn't tell anyone because they feared (rightly) that they'd be forced to transport the ore with their reindeer and sleighs. The midnight sun lasts from May 28 to July 15, with the all-night **Festival of Light** on the first weekend in July. The **tourist office** is at Lars Janssonsgatan 17 (tel. (0980) 188 80; open Mon.-Fri. 9am-8pm, Sat.-Sun. 9am-6pm; mid-Sept. to March Mon.-Fri. 10am-4pm; April-early June Mon.-Fri. 9am-5pm, Sat. 10am-1pm). The **HI youth hostel** (tel. (0980) 171 95) is at Skyttegatan 16a (reception open 8-9:30am and 4-9:30pm; 90kr, nonmembers 125kr; open mid-June to mid-Aug.). **Camp** at **Radhusbyn Ripan** (tel. (0980) 131 00), 20 minutes from the train station (85kr per tent, 4-person cabins 600-660kr). **Buses** leave across from the city hall on Hjalmar Lundbonsvägen.

A short bus trip from Kiruna or Jokkmokk, the 500km **Kungsleden,** a moderate, well-marked hiking trail, stretches from Abisko in the north (on the Narvik train line) to Hemavan in the south. Many sections, in particular from Abisko to Kvikkjokk, have HI-staffed cabins 8-21km apart (95kr, non-members 125kr). To climb Sweden's highest peak, **Kebnekaise** (2117m), take a bus from Kiruna to Nikkaluokta (52kr) and hike 19km to the Kebnekaise mountain cabin. From there, you can reach the summit in a day. This is rugged country, and there may be snow as late as July. Bring food, maps, full raingear, and warm clothing, and leave a copy of your route with someone in town. Contact **STF (Svenska Turistföreningen)** before heading north (see Sweden Essentials); they run most of the mountain stations and huts, and publish essential brochures and guides for hikers.

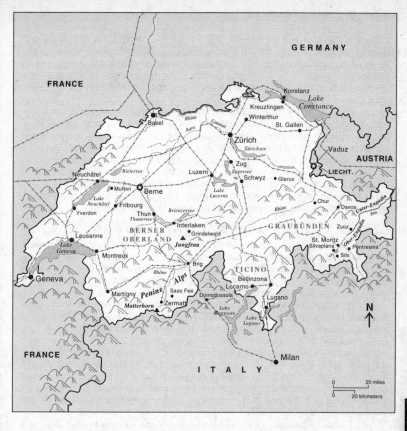

Switzerland (Suisse, Die Schweiz, Svizzera)

US$1 = 1.30SFr (francs)	1SFr = **US$0.77**
CDN$1= 0.97SFr	1SFr = **CDN$1.03**
UK£1 = 2.07SFr	1SFr = **UK£0.48**
IR£1 = 2.05SFr	1SFr = **IR£0.49**
AUS$1= 1.00SFr	1SFr = **AUS$1.00**
NZ$1 = 0.79SFr	1SFr = **NZ$1.27**
SAR1 = 0.37SFr	1SFr = **SAR2.73**
Country Code: 41	**International Dialing Prefix: 00**

Divided by impassable Alpine giants and united by neither language nor religion, it's curious that Switzerland is a nation at all. What is now a confederation of 23 largely autonomous cantons was first conceived in 1291 and jelled into its present form at a slothful pace all the way through the 19th century. Swiss politics have an old-fashioned feel; approximately 3000 local communes retain a great deal of power, and major policy disputes are routinely settled by national referenda. Official neutrality since 1815 has kept the ravages of war away from this postcard-perfect haven. Placidity has also nurtured the growth of Big Money in the staid banking centers of Geneva and Zürich. Spurred by its love of prosperity, Switzerland now seems on the verge of major change. Though the nation remains neutral in relationship to its European neighbors, Swiss citizens have recently become passionate about the country's affairs, albeit to cast their ballots mostly against integration into the European Union.

One aspect of Switzerland will likely always overshadow whatever internal divisions exist: the majestic Alps. Keats, Shelley, and Byron glorify them in their Romantic poetry; others have fallen silent in a landscape that defies words. Snow-capped peaks lord over half the country's area, enticing skiers, bikers, hikers, and paragliders from around the globe to one of the most finely-tuned tourist industries in the world. Victorian scholar John Ruskin called the Swiss Alps "the great cathedrals of the earth"; you're welcome to worship here if you can spare the cash.

For more information on Switzerland, the country defined, more than any other, by its topography, pick up a copy of *Let's Go: Austria & Switzerland*.

GETTING THERE AND GETTING AROUND

Getting around Switzerland is gleefully easy. **Private railways** and yellow **post buses** (railpasses not valid), which serve many of the remote villages, pick up the slack where trains fail to go. **Eurailpasses** clear the way for passage on most lake cruises and portage on state-run trains, but private companies exert a deathgrip on Alpine rail routes, particularly in the Berner Oberland—special passes are needed here.

An array of special passes help beat the ruinous transport costs. The **Swiss Card** entitles you to 50% off all trips on federal and private railroads, postal buses, and steamers. At only 135SFr per month, the card pays for itself in one or two journeys. Less casual and more expensive is the **Swisspass**, available through Rail Europe or any major travel agency in your home country. The Flexipass option buys you 3 days of travel in 15 for US$148; continuous passes cost US$186 for 8 days, US$214 for 15 days, and US$296 for a month (all prices 2nd class); they allow for unlimited travel on all government-operated railways, lake steamers, and most private railways and postal buses, but only a 25-50% discount on the most expensive mountain railways and cable cars.

Postal buses (a barrage of banana-colored, three-brake-system-coaches delivered to you expressly by the Swiss government) take care of transport in rural areas (the only mode of transport near St. Moritz). **Steamers** traverse many of the larger lakes. Fares are no bargain, but a Eurailpass sometimes gets you free passage, and a Swisspass almost always wins a free ride. **Cycling,** though strenuous, is a splendid way to see the country; rental at almost any station is standard at 19SFr per day (return to any station). **Hitching** is difficult. With sufficient stamina, overland **walking and hiking** are the most enjoyable ways to see Switzerland. Thirty thousand miles of hiking trails lace the entire country; yellow signs give directions and traveling times.

SWITZERLAND ESSENTIALS

Switzerland is quadrilingual: French is spoken in the west, Italian in the south, Romansch (a relative of Latin and Etruscan) in the cantons of Engadin and Graubünden, and Swiss German *(Schwyzerdütsch,* a dialect nearly incomprehensible to other German speakers) everywhere else. Most people know at least three languages, including English. **Tourist offices** in every Swiss city *(Verkehrsbüro or Kurverein)* locate rooms, distribute maps, and suggest hiking or biking routes. All official tourist offices are marked by a fat blue **"i"**. The info-service **Anglophone** (tel. 157 50 14) is a 24hr. English-speaking hotline that will answer questions on any aspect of life in Switzerland.

Currency exchange at its easiest (and latest) takes place in train stations; rates are usually the same as banks. **Local phone calls** cost 40 centimes. **Post offices** offer international calling on a phone first, pay later or collect basis. Dial 191 or 114 for English-friendly assistance. For AT&T's **USA Direct,** dial 155 00 11; for **MCI,** dial 155 02 22; for **Sprint,** dial 155 97 77; for **Canada Direct,** dial 046 05 83 30, for **BT**

Direct, dial 155 24 44; and for **SA Direct,** dial 155 35 35. Ring the **police** at 117, an **ambulance** at 144. Most stores are open Mon.-Fri. from 8am to 6:30pm with a break from noon to 2pm, and Saturday mornings. In cities, shops also close Monday mornings. Museums close on Mondays. The country closes down for **national holidays** on Jan. 1, Good Friday (April 14, 1995), Easter Monday (April 17, 1995), Ascension (May 25, 1995), Whit Monday (June 5, 1995), Aug. 1, and Christmas (Dec. 25-26).

Switzerland is justifiably proud of its winter-wonderland reputation. Farsighted planning, and avoiding the hoity-toity resorts, allows for cheap **skiing.** Lift tickets average 30-60SFr per day, rentals 30SFr. Passes usually cover transportation to the lifts as well as uphill carriage. A week of lift tickets, equipment rental, lessons, lodging, and demi-pension (breakfast plus dinner) averages 500-700SFr. Like its terrain, Switzerland's weather varies crazily from area to area. Wear layers. Be prepared.

Accommodations, Camping, Food, and Drink All things Swiss are meticulous, orderly, efficient, and expensive. Few hosteling horror stories apply to Switzerland; the uniformly cheery **HI Jugendherbergen** are bright, clean, and open to all ages (20-40SFr per night; nonmembers 5-7SFr extra; breakfast and sheets included). **Hotels** are generally pretty pricey. In smaller towns, *Zimmerfrei* (private rooms) abound; the tourist office can supply a list and make reservations. As befits a country so blessed by Mother Nature, Switzerland blossoms with over 1200 **camp-grounds.** Some are so beautiful they take on spiritual value; others are glorified backyards (3-10SFr per person and 4-12SFr per tent). This land of order and propriety forbids freelance camping along roads and in public areas. **Swiss Alpine Club (SAC) huts** are modest and extremely practical for those interested in trekking in higher, more remote areas. Bunk rooms sleep 10 to 20 weary hikers, with blankets (but no running water or electricity) provided. SAC huts are open to all, but SAC members get discounted rates. An average one-night stay without food is 30SFr for nonmembers, 20-25SFr for members. Those serious about conquering the summits should contact SAC, Helvetiaplatz 4, 3005 Berne (tel. (31) 351 36 11, fax 352 60 63).

The Swiss are hardly culinary daredevils, but they're very good at what they do. In French Switzerland, try the cheese specialties; *fondue* is always excellent, as is *raclette* (melted cheese with pickled onions and boiled new potatoes). Swiss-German food is heartier. Try *Züricher Geschnetzeltes* (veal strips in a delicious cream sauce) and *Rösti* (hashbrowned potato with onion). Of course, *Lindt* chocolate is a perennial favorite, especially in its home city of Zürich. Supermarkets like Migros and Coop generally carry every imaginable permutation of nuts, filling, and color in the chocolate bars. **Migros** supermarket cafeterias and **Coop** centers are the budgeteer's choice for self-service dining.

GERMAN SWITZERLAND

■■■ ZÜRICH

In many ways, Zürich is the quintessential banker's town; leather briefcases, Bally's shoes a and Armani suits ooze pecuniary stodginess. However, the city retains something of the liberal avant-garde spirit of 1916, the year when artistic and philosophical radicalism shook the calm of Zürich. Living at Universitätstr. 38, James Joyce toiled away on *Ulysses*. Not far away, at Spiegelgasse 14, Russian exile V.I. Lenin read a lot of Marx and dreamed of revolution. At the same time, raucous young artists calling themselves Dadaists—some, legend has it, living next door to Lenin and irritating him immensely—were founding the seminal proto-performance-art collective known as the *Cabaret Voltaire*. Such anarchy laid the basis for the alternative movement of the early 1980s, which stormed through the streets screaming "Züri brennt" (Zürich is burning).

ORIENTATION AND PRACTICAL INFORMATION

Zürich sits on the northern tip of the Zürichsee (Lake Zürich); the River Limmat divides it in half. Swissly efficient trams crisscross the city, operating from 5:30am-midnight (Fri.-Sat. until 2am). Rides cost 1.70-2.80SFr. The 24hr. *Tageskarte* is your best bet (6.40SFr). Buy tickets from machines at tram stops.

Tourist Offices: Main office in the **train station** at Bahnhofplatz 15 (tel. 211 40 00). Exit the station to Bahnhofplatz, and walk to the left. Finds rooms for 5SFr; dispenses maps and the weekly *Zürich News*. Open Mon.-Fri. 8:30am-9:30pm, Sat.-Sun. 8:30am-8:30pm; Nov.-March Mon.-Fri. 8:30am-7:30pm, Sat.-Sun. 8:30am-6:30pm. Also at **airport terminal B** (tel. 816 40 81). Open 10am-7pm.

Consulates: U.S., Zollikerstr. 141 (tel. 422 25 66). Open Mon.-Fri. 9-11:30am, 1:30-4pm. **U.K.,** Dufourstr. 56 (tel. 261 15 20). Open Mon.-Fri. 9am-noon, 2-4pm. **Canadians, Australians,** and citizens of **Ireland** should contact their embassies in Berne. **New Zealand's** consulate is in Geneva.

Currency Exchange: Train station rates comparable to most banks. Open 6:15am-10:45pm (or feed the machine outside the office that magically converts US$20 and US$50 and British pounds into Swiss francs).

American Express: Bahnhofstr. 20, near Paradeplatz (tel. 211 83 70). Usual services. Open Mon.-Fri. 8:30am-5:30pm, Sat. 9am-noon. Traveler's checks **emergency line** toll-free (tel. 046 050 100).

Post Office: Main office at Kasernenstr. 95-97. Open Mon.-Fri. 6:30am-10:30pm, Sat. 6:30am-8pm, Sun. 11am-10:30pm. 1SFr Poste Restante charge after 6:30pm. **Postal Code:** 8021.

Telephones: At the train station. **City Code:** 01.

Flights: Trains from Hauptbahnhof to airport, 10min., railpasses valid.

Trains: tel. 211 50 10. To Berne (42SFr), Geneva (73SFr), Lugano (58SFr), Lucerne (18.60SFr).

Bike Rental: At the baggage counter (*Gepäckexpedition Fly-Gepäck*) in the station. Open 6am-7:40pm. 19SFr per day.

Hitchhiking: Hitchers to Basel, Geneva, Paris, or Bonn take tram 4 to Werdhölzli. For Lucerne, Italy, and Austria, they take tram 5 or 14: Bahnhof Wiedikon and then walk down Schimmelstr. to Silhölzli. Munich-bound thumbers take tram 14: Milchbuck and walk to Schaffhauserstr. Hitchhiking is illegal on the freeway. **Mitfahrzentrale** (tel. 261 68 93) pairs drivers and riders.

Bookstores: Librairie Payot, Bahnhofstr. 9, large selection of English books, including *Let's Go*. Open Mon. 1-6:30pm, Tues.-Fri. 9am-6:30pm, Sat. 9am-4pm.

Laundromat: At the **train station**, 7.50-9SFr per 6kg. Dryer 4.50SFr for 1hr. Soap included. Open 6am-midnight. Located under the tracks. Ask at the shower desk for laundry services.

Pharmacy: Theaterstr. 14 on Bellevueplatz. Open 24hrs.

Emergencies: Ambulance: tel. 144. **Medical Emergency:** tel. 261 61 00. **Police:** tel. 117.

ACCOMMODATIONS AND CAMPING

Expensive as Zürich can be, there are some budget options, mainly hostels. Don't expect the hotel standards that made Switzerland famous. These accommodations are usually somewhat distant from the town center, but easily accessible with Zürich's extensive public transportation system.

Jugendherberge Zürich (HI), Mutschellenstr. 114 (tel. 482 35 44). S-Bahn 1 or 8: Bahnhof Wollishofen. Walk up the hill three blocks to Mutschellenstr. Impeccably clean and busy. Reception open 6-10am and 2-10pm. Checkout 6-9am. 27.50SFr, nonmembers 37SFr. Doubles available on request with 11SFr surcharge (nonmembers 18SFr). Laundry 8SFr. Reserve a few days in advance.

Hotel Biber "The City Backpacker," Schweizerhofgasse 5 (tel. 251 90 15, fax 251 90 24). In the heart of the *Altstadt;* ask the friendly staff for tips on sights and nightlife. 4-6 person dorms 28SFr, 26SFr subsequent nights. Singles 60SFr. Doubles 80SFr. Kitchen facilities, showers included. Sheets 2SFr. Lockers available.

SWITZERLAND

Martahaus, Zähringerstr. 36 (tel. 251 45 50, fax 251 45 40). Simple but comfortable. On the river and very busy. Reception open 7am-11pm. Dorms 30SFr. Singles 60SFr. Doubles 90SFr. Triples 105SFr. Showers and breakfast included.

Pension St. Josef, Hirschengraben 64/68 (tel. 251 27 57, fax 251 28 08). Possibly the most comfortable place to stay in Zürich. Singles 65SFr. Doubles 100SFr. Triples 135SFr. Quads 155SFr. Quints 155SFr. Breakfast buffet included. Reception open Mon.-Sat. 7:30am-10pm, Sun. 7:30am-6pm.

Foyer Hottingen, Hottingerstr. 31 (tel. 261 93 15, fax 261 93 19). Take streetcar 3 "Klusplatz". Guardian nuns admit *women, married couples, and families only*. Curfew midnight. Dorms 22SFr, 25SFr with partitions. Singles 50SFr. Doubles 80SFr. Triples 95SFr. Quads 105SFr. 3min. showers 1SF. Breakfast included.

Hotel Splendid, Rosengasse 5 (tel. 252 58 50). Rooms are small and sparsely furnished. Convenient for Niederdorfstr. bar-hopping, or just for hanging out downstairs. Singles 55SFr. Doubles 90SFr. Breakfast 8SFr. Showers included.

Camping Seebucht, Seestr. 559 (tel. 482 16 12), somewhat far away, but in a scenic lakeside location. Train 7: Wollishofen, and walk the remaining 15min. along the shore to the right; or bus 161 or 165 (from Bürgkliplatz, at the lake-end of Bahnhofstr.): Grenzsteig. 5.50SFr per person, 8-10SFr per tent. Reception open 7:30am-noon and 3-8pm. Open early May to late Sept.

FOOD

The cheapest eats in Zürich are at the *Wurstli* stands (sausage and bread for 3-4SFr) and fresh veggie and fruit stalls peppering the streets.

Mensa der Universität Zürich, Rämistr. 71. Streetcar 6 (from Bahnhofplatz; to return from Tannenstr.): ETH Zentrum, or walk. Stunningly edible. Hot dishes 5.50-6.50SFr with ISIC, salads 6.90SFr. Open Mon.-Sat. 11am-1:30pm and 5-7:30pm. Self-service café open Mon.-Sat. 11am-7:30pm.

Gleich, Seefeldstr. 9, (tel. 251 32 03) behind the opera house. Vegetarian restaurant and bakery delivers fresh salads and creative repasts. Salads 6-11.50SFr. Entrees 9-22SFr. *Menu* 21-34SFr. Open Mon.-Fri. 6am-9pm, Sat. 8am-4pm.

Rheinfelder Bierhalle, Niederdorfstr. 76 (tel. 251 54 64), in the *Altstadt. Rösti* in all variations. A mostly local crowd enjoys the food, but most especially the drink. Entrees 11-30SFr. *Menu* 15-28SFr. Open 9am-12:30am.

Restaurant Raclette-Stube, Zähringerstr. 16 (tel. 251 41 30), near the Central Library. Swiss *fondues* are at their richest, largest, and cheapest at this small restaurant at the outskirts of the *Altstadt. Fondues* 18SFr per person, *raclette* 7SFr per person. Open Sat.-Thurs. 6-11:30pm. Fri. 11am-2pm and 6-11:30pm.

SIGHTS AND ENTERTAINMENT

The stately, colorful, and very expensive shopping promenade **Bahnhofstrasse** runs from the station to the Zürichsee. Halfway down Bahnhofstr. lies **Paradeplatz**, the town center, if indeed Zürich has one. It is said that Zürich's banks keep their gold reserves in safes directly under the ground here. You probably won't spot any golden ingots, so keep walking. To the east loom the rather brutal twin towers of Zürich's **Grossmünster,** a Romanesque cathedral with stark and somber Giacometti stained-glass windows (open Mon.-Fri. 9am-6pm, Sat. 9am-5pm, Sun. after services to 6pm). Across the river, rises the steeple of the dreamier 13th-century **Fraumünster,** a Chagall-decorated wonder (open Mon.-Sat. 9am-noon and 2-6pm; March-April and Oct. 10am-noon and 2-5pm; Nov.-Feb. 10am-noon and 2-4pm). The **Kunsthaus Zürich,** Heimplatz 1, is famed for large Impressionist and Expressionist collections (open Tues.-Thurs. 10am-9pm, Fri.-Sun. 10am-5pm; 4SFr, students 3SFr, Sun. free). James Joyce is buried in the **Fluntern Cemetery.** Next door is the **Zürich Zoo,** Zürichbergstr. 221, with thousands of species making it one of Europe's most famous animal attractions. (Cemetery open 7am-8pm, Mar.-Apr. and Sept.-Oct. 7am-7pm, Nov.-Feb. 8am-5pm. Free. Zoo open 9am-6pm, Nov.-Mar. 9am-5pm. 12SFr, children 6SFr. Take trams 5 or 6: Zoo.) **The Lindt and Sprüngli Chocolate Factory** welcomes visitors to its **chocolate museum** (exhibits in German), and invites guests to watch a film on the history of the company and chocolate production, with

SWITZERLAND

plenty of the confection ready for the taking (open Mon.-Thurs. 9am-noon and 1:30-4pm; call a day ahead). To reach the factory, take the tram (S-1 or S-8) to Kilchberg from the Hauptbahnhof. From there, walk 3min. along the lake or take the bus to the factory. (Tours free.)

Nightlife revolves around Niederdorfstr., Münstergasse, and Limmatquai. These streets are lined with cafés and bars that overflow with people well into the wee hours. Everyone likes **Casa Bar,** Münstergasse 30, a teeny, pricey pub with live jazz (open 7pm-2am; no cover, but drink prices could bankrupt you). The artsy crowd congregates at the **Bar Odeon,** Limmatquai 2, near the Quaibrücke. Thornton Wilder and Lenin got sloshed here. The English-speaking and Scandinavian crowd enjoys Guiness and British beers at **Oliver Twist,** Rindermarkt 6, a Victorian replica bar (open Mon.-Fri. 11:30-midnight and Sat.-Sun. 3pm-1am).

■■■ LUCERNE (LUZERN)

A steady stream of modern visitors flocks to Lucerne to splash in the Vierwaldstätter-see and drink in the history of the city with its medieval streets, bridges, and ramparts. Lucerne's myriad museums keep the masses content on those cloudy days when the Pilatus is inaccessible. Much of Lucerne's tourist culture thrives on the Vierwaldstättersee and the cobblestone streets of the *Altstadt,* spread out on both sides of the Reuss River. The 660-year-old **Kapellbrücke,** a wooden-roofed bridge running from the station to the *Altstadt* and decorated with scenes from Swiss history, has characterized the Lucerne landscape since the Middle Ages. Down the river, grapple with your mortality as you cross the covered **Spreuerbrücke,** adorned with Kaspar Meglinger's eerie *Totentanz* (Dance of Death) paintings. The **Altstadt** is famous for its frescoed houses and *oriel* windows, especially the colorful scenes of the Hirschepl. The ramparts of the medieval city still tower on the hills above the river; climb them and walk from tower to tower for a magnificent view of Lucerne. The city mascot, the great **Lion of Lucerne,** carved out of the base of a cliff on Denkmalstr., gazes over the city with melancholy eyes. The 9m monument honors the Swiss Guard who died defending Marie Antoinette in Revolutionary Paris.

The **Verkehrshaus der Schweiz** (Transport Museum), Lidostr. 5, features a planetarium, a history of transportation over land, sea, and air, and the **Swissorama,** a mind-boggling 360-degree panorama (open 9am-6pm; 15SFr, 13SFr with guest card, students 11SFr). The **Richard Wagner Museum,** Wagnerweg 27, is set in Wagner's secluded former home in the woods overlooking the lake, and displays original letters, scores, and instruments of the composer. Wagner wrote *Siegfried* and *Die Meistersänger* here. (Open Tues.-Sun. 10am-noon and 2-5pm; Oct-April Tues., Thurs. and Sat.-Sun. 10am-noon and 2-5pm. 5SFr, students 4SFr.)

Practical Information, Accommodations, and Food

The **tourist office,** Frankenstr. 1 (tel. (041) 51 71 71), overflows with maps and guides (open Mon.-Fri. 8:30am-6pm, Sat. 9am-5pm; Nov.-March Mon.-Fri. 8:30am-noon and 2-6pm, Sat. 9am-noon). The **post office** is across from the train station at Bahnhofstr., 6000 Luzern 1 (open Mon.-Fri. 7:30am-6:30pm, Sat. 9:30-11am). The station itself (schedule info tel. (041) 21 33 11) houses **currency exchange** (open Mon.-Fri. 7am-8:45pm, Sat.-Sun. 7:30am-7:30pm; Nov.-April Mon.-Sat. 7:30am-7:30pm, Sun. 8am-6pm); **lockers** (2-5SFr); and **bicycle rental** (19SFr).

Hop on bus 18 to Goplismoos for the friendly **Jugendherberge Am Rotsee (HI),** Sedelstr. 12 (tel. (041) 36 88 00). After 7:30pm, take bus 1 to Schlossberg and walk 15min. down Friedentalstr. (Reception open 4pm-12:30am. Lockout 9:30am-4pm. Curfew 11:30pm. 26SFr first night, then 24SFr. Doubles 34-40SFr, then 31-37SFr. Nonmembers 7SFr surcharge. Showers and breakfast included. Reserve early in summer.) The centrally located **Touristen Hotel Luzern,** St. Karliquai 12 (tel. (041) 51 24 74, fax 52 84 14), is by the river. From the station, go underground and exit the complex to the *Altstadt;* walk left along the river, cross the second covered bridge, and turn left onto St. Karliquai. (Singles 60SFr. Doubles 90-110SFr. Triples

126SFr. 6- to 10-bed rooms 33SFr per person. 10% discount with ISIC.) **Privatpension Panorama,** Kapuzinerweg 9 (tel. (041) 36 71 01), overlooks the *Altstadt*. From the station take bus 4 or 5 "Wesemlin" to Kapuzinerweg. (Singles 40SFr. Doubles 60-90Sfr. Breakfast included.) **Camping Lido,** Lidostr. 8 (tel. (041) 31 21 46), is a ½hr. hike from the station, on the Lido beach. Cross the Seebrücke and turn right along the quay, or take bus 2 to Verkehrshaus. Swimming, tennis, and mini-golf are nearby. (Reception open 8am-6pm. 6SFr per person, 3SFr per tent. Dorms 12SFr. Open April-Oct.)

Saturday morning markets along the river purvey fresh fruit, vegetables, and meat for an inexpensive picnic. For sit-down meals, budget *menus* cost 12-15SFr just about everywhere. Find the best vegetarian meals around at the **Restaurant Karibia,** Pilatusplatz. (Spring rolls 9.50SFr, samosas 8.50SFr, and spinach *Strußel* 11.50SFr. Open Tues.-Sat. 9am-midnight, Sun.-Mon. 10am-midnight.) **Krone,** Rössligasse 11, serves good food with cafeteria-style service; be creative with the colored chalk and blackboard walls. (All entrees under 12SFr. Open 9am-11pm.) The city's nightlife revolves around the crowded corridors of the *Altstadt*.

■ MOUNT PILATUS

Soaring 2154m into the sky, the view from Mount Pilatus stretches all the way to Italy on clear days. Join a daily escorted excursion, meeting at 12:30pm at the Luzernerhof on the Nationalquai (tel. (041) 51 20 55); catch a boat to Alpenachstad and ascend by the steepest cogwheel train in the world (75SFr), and return by cable car to Kriens and bus to Lucerne by 4:30pm. (Details at tourist office in Lucerne.) Or, brave bus 1 to Kriens and take the cable car from there, which reduces the price and time of the trip. (Eurail halves the price of the excursions, cable car, and train.) Though banned until the 17th century for fear of angry ghosts, it is now legal to climb Pilatus by foot. The hiking trails require sturdy hiking boots and at least five hours.

■■■ BERNE (BERN)

Switzerland's capital since 1848, Berne is still not the land of fast tracks, power politics or screeching motorcades. Home of Toblerone chocolate and Swiss cheese, Berne has been Europe's leading flower-growing city since 1984. Founded by the Duke of Zähringen in 1191, Berne's mascot and namesake is the bear; spend a few days here and the tourist industry will brand that fact onto your brain. Bears aside, it's an attractive city. Burned to the ground in 1405, Berne was rebuilt in sandstone and mahogany. Today its cobblestone streets twist around brightly painted fountains and long shopping arcades.

NOTE: Berne's telephone system was being changed at the time this book was published. The phone numbers below are subject to change.

PRACTICAL INFORMATION

Tourist Office: Verkehrsbüro (tel. 311 66 11), on the ground floor of the train station. Distributes maps and copies of *This Week in Berne*. Room reservations (3SFr). Open 9am-8:30pm; Oct.-May Mon.-Sat. 9am-6:30pm, Sun. 10am-5pm.

Budget Travel: SSR, Rathausgasse 64 (tel. 312 07 24). Bus 12: Rathaus. BIJ tickets and student discounts. Open Mon.-Wed. and Fri. 10am-6pm, Thurs. 10am-8pm.

Embassies: U.S., Jubiläumsstr. 93 (tel. 357 70 11). Open Mon.-Fri. 8:30am-noon and 2:30-5:30pm. **Canada,** Kirchenfeldstr. 88 (tel. 352 63 81). Open Mon.-Fri. 8am-noon and 12:30-4pm; Oct.-May Mon.-Fri. 8am-noon and 1-4:30pm. Consulate at Belpstr. 11 (tel. 381 22 61). Open Mon., Wed., and Fri. 8am-12:30pm and 1-4pm, Tues. and Thurs. 1-4pm. **U.K.,** Thunstr. 50 (tel. 352 50 21). Open Mon.-Fri. 9am-12:30pm and 2-5pm. **Ireland,** Kirchenfeldstr. 68 (tel. 352 14 42). Open Mon.-Fri. 9:15am-12:30pm and 2-5:30pm. **Australia,** Alpenstr. 29 (tel. 351 01 43). Open Mon.-Thurs. 10am-12:30pm and 1:30-3pm, Fri. 10am-12:30pm. Citizens of **New Zealand** should consult the consulate in Geneva.

Currency Exchange: Downstairs in the train station. Rates comparable to major banks. Open 6:15am-9:45pm.

American Express: in **Kehrli and Oehler,** Bubenbergpl. 11 (tel. 311 94 01). From the train station, walk to the bus area across *Bahnhofplatz*. Mail held. All banking services. Open Mon.-Fri. 8:30am-5:30pm, Sat. 9am-noon.

Post Office: Schanzenpost 1, behind the train station. Open Mon.-Fri. 6am-11pm, Sat. 6am-9pm, Sun. 10am-noon and 4-11pm. *Poste Restante.* Branch at the corner of Aarbergergasse and Genfergasse, across from the train station. Open Mon.-Fri. 7:30am-noon and 1:45-6:30pm, Sat. 7:30-11am. **Postal code:** CH-3000.

Telephones: At the train station. Open Mon.-Sat. 6:30am-10:30pm, Sun. 7am-10:30pm. **City Code:** 031.

Trains: Berne Centrale station (tel. 21 11 11; train info 157 33 33). To: Geneva (2hr., 47SFr), Lucerne (1hr. 20min., 31SFr).

Public Transportation: For all **SVB** buses and trams (tel. 321 88 88), buy a *Touristen-Karte* from the ticket offices downstairs at the station or at Bubenbergpl. 5. 24hr. ticket 7SFr. Swisspass valid. Buses run 5:45am-11:45pm. **Nightbuses** at 12:45am and 2am, 5SFr (no passes valid). SVB offices open Mon.-Wed. and Fri. 6:30am-7:30pm, Thurs. 6:30am-9:30pm, Sat. 6:30am-6:30pm.

Bike Rental: At the station (tel. 680 34 61). 19SFr per day, mountain bike 31SFr per day. 76SFr and 124SFr per week respectively. Open 6:15am-11:45pm.

Hitchhiking: Those headed to Geneva and Lausanne take bus 11 to Neufeld. Those headed to Interlaken and Lucerne take streetcar 5: Ostringgasse. Those trying to reach the *Autobahn* north often take bus 20 to Wyler.

Pharmacy: In train station. Open 6:30am-8pm. To find out which pharmacy is open 24hrs. on a given day, call 311 22 11, or general information at 111.

Emergencies: Police: tel. 117. **Ambulance:** tel. 144. **Doctor's night service:** tel. 311 22 11.

ACCOMMODATIONS AND CAMPING

The outlook is bleak. Unless you stay at the youth hostel, you'll pay at least 40SFr for a single. Guesthouses a few km outside the city offer rooms for less (35-40SFr), and the tourist office helps find accommodations.

Jugendherberge (HI), Weihergasse 4 (tel. 311 63 16). From Bahnhofpl., walk through to Christoffergasse until it ends, continue around the Parliament next to the park. Go through the gate marked "1875" and turn left onto the Bundesstr. Take the *Drahtseilbahn* (funicular) down for 1SFr. Once downhill, turn left onto Weihergasse. Sprawling, brand new, and right on the fringes of the *Altstadt.* Reception open 7-9:30am, 3-6pm, 6:30-10:45pm, and 11:15pm-midnight. Lockout 9:30am-3pm. 15SFr, nonmembers 22SFr. Max. 3-night stay. Laundry 5SFr. Breakfast 6SFr. Lunch or dinner 10SFr. Limited parking.

Hotel National, Hirschengraben 24 (tel. 381 19 88, fax 381 68 78). First left off Bubenbergplatz. Beautiful rooms, central location, and moderately priced restaurant downstairs. Singles 49-65SFr, with shower 85-100SFr. Doubles 84-94SFr, with shower 110-130SFr. Hall showers and breakfast included.

Pension Martahaus, Wyttenbachstr. 22a (tel. 332 41 35). Bus 20: Gewerbeschule, then right onto Wyttenbachstr. Calm, comfortable pension in a suburb. Reception Mon.-Fri. 8am-noon and 3-9pm, Sat.-Sun. 8-11:30am and 4:30-8:30pm. Singles 55SFr. Doubles 90SFr. Triples 120SFr. Quads 140SFr. Breakfast, hall showers included. Laundry 5-6SFr. Limited parking.

Camping: Camping Eichholz, Strandweg 49 (tel. 961 26 02). Streetcar 9: Wabern (last stop). 5.50SFr per person, 4-8SFr per tent. Also sports a few rooms with 2 beds for 14SFr plus 5.50SFr per person. Reserve ahead. Open May-Sept.

FOOD

Shop at markets to beat the pricey restaurants. A daily **fruit market** blossoms at Bärenplatz (open 8am-6pm), Tuesday and Saturday markets are at Bundesplatz and Thursdays at Waisenhausplatz (all open 8am-1pm). The **Migros Restaurant** at Zeughausgasse 31, off Bärenplatz, offers well-prepared meals at reasonable prices.

The **Mensa der Universität,** Gesellschaftstr. 2, northwest of the station and off Sidlerstr. (bus 1: Universität), serves better than average institutional fare, and the students are friendly. *(Menus* 8-12SFr. Kitchen open Mon.-Thurs. 11:30am-1:45pm and 5:45-7:30pm, Fri. 11:30am-1:45pm. Cafeteria open Mon.-Thurs. 7:30am-8:30pm, Fri. 7:30am-5pm. Open mid-Aug. to mid-July.) **Zähringer und Schopbar,** Hallerstr. 19, near the Mensa cooks up great Swiss dishes, such as *rösti* and *späteli,* and helps you wash it down with good old brew. (Open 9am-midnight.) **Schoog-Dee,** Bollwerk 4, behind the train station, is always good for a bite of Thai and other Asian specialties between trains. (Entrees 15-20SFr, *menus* 12-16SFr. Open Mon.-Fri. 11am-2pm and 5-11:30pm, Sat.-Sun. 5pm-11:30pm.)

SIGHTS AND ENTERTAINMENT

Eleven bridges cross the Aare. The **Untertorbrücke** is the oldest, dating back to 1489. Right near the station stands the 18th-century **Church of the Holy Ghost,** decorated in bright pastel colors (open Mon.-Sat. 11am-3pm). Up Spitalgasse stands the old **prison tower,** which served as the city gate from 1256 to 1346. Farther down, near the Rathausgasse, the cobblestoned route takes you past the **Zytglogge** (clock tower), built in the 13th century, now famous for its astronomical clock with moving figures. Join the crowd 4min. before each hour to watch bears dance, jesters beat drums, and to hear the squeaky golden rooster. (Tours of interior May-Oct. at 4:30pm. 3SFr. Tickets at the tourist office.) A walk down Theaterplatz, then Münstergasse to Münsterplatz, leads to the most impressive of Berne's churches, the 15th-century **Münster.** Climb the highest spire in Switzerland for a fantastic view of Berne's mahogany roofs. (Open Mon.-Sat. 10am-noon and 2-5pm, Sun. 11am-noon and 2-5pm; Nov.-Easter Tues.-Fri. 10am-noon and 2-4pm, Sat. 10am-noon and 2-5pm, Sun. 11am-noon and 2-5pm. Tower closes 30min. before church, 3SFr.) Across the bridge is the 500-year-old **Bärengraben** (bear pits), where the city's mascots lumber back and forth. (Open 7am-6pm; Oct.-March 8:30am-4pm.) On Easter, newborn cubs emerge for their first public display. Receive an introduction to Swiss politics at the **Parlamentsgebäude,** in session only four times per year. No time to filibuster here. (Free 45min. tours hourly 9am-noon and 2-4pm. When Parliament is in session, watch from the galleries.)

The **Botanical Gardens** of the University of Berne, Altengrain 21, thrive on the banks of the Aare, with exotic plants from Asia, Africa, and the Americas photosynthesizing cheek by jowl with the native Alpine greens. (Park open March-Sept. Mon.-Fri. 7am-6pm, Sat.-Sun. 8am-5:30pm. Greenhouse open 8-11:30am and 2-5pm. Free.) Take bus 20 to Gewerbeschule and backtrack to the entrance either downhill from the bus stop or the bridge.

Several of Berne's outstanding museums cluster together at **Helvetiaplatz** across the **Kirchenfeldbrücke** (tram 3 or 5). Ask the tourist office or the cashier at the museum for a **day ticket** *(Tageskarte;* 7SFr). The **Kunstmuseum,** Hodlerstr. 8-12, near the Lorrainebrücke, presents the largest Klee collection anywhere (over 2500 works), a brace of Kandinskys, some early Picassos, and a comprehensive collection of regional art, including tons of Ferdinand Hodler. (Open Tues. 10am-9pm, Wed.-Sun. 10am-5pm. 3SFr, more for special exhibits.) **Kunsthalle,** Helvetiaplatz 1, features the contemporary work of a few former starving, young artists. The hall is now full of spots, dots, and occasional plastic chunks of modern art. (Open Tues. 10am-9pm, Wed.-Sun. 10am-5pm. 4SFr, students 2SFr only for special exhibits.) **Albert Einstein's House,** Kramgasse 49, is now filled with photographs and a few of Einstein's letters, but not much else (open Feb.-Nov. Tues.-Fri. 10am-5pm, Sat. 10am-4pm; 2SFr). **Bernisches Historische Museum,** Helvetiaplatz 5, exhibits Flemish tapestries, replicas of rural Swiss rooms, and booty from the Burgundian wars of 1476. In addition to displaying the remains of the fire-gutted **St. Christopher Tor,** this castle-like edifice chronicles the development of everything from cameras to pianos to syringes. (Open Tues.-Sun. 10am-5pm. 5SFr, students 2SFr. Sat. free.)

Bars and late-night cafés line the Bärenplatz. **Reithalle,** in a graffiti-covered warehouse, provides an industrial setting in which to explore Berne's underground

SWITZERLAND

music scene. (Shows Fri. and Sat., and occasionally other nights. Average cover 15SFr.) The **Diagonal Café-Bar** offers a slanted view of Berne in its Spartan bar (open Mon.-Thurs. 7am-1:30pm, Fri.-Sat. 7am-12:30pm, Sun. 9am-11:30pm). A Berne tradition not to be missed is a drink at the **Klötzlikeller Weine Stube,** Gerechtigkeitsgasse 62. Berne's oldest wine cellar lists countless wines for the tasting, and good meals to go with them. (Open Tues.-Sat. 4pm-12:30am.)

■■■ INTERLAKEN

Less than an hour by train from Berne, Interlaken is a starting point for treks into the surrounding mountains and a hub for trains throughout Switzerland. The town lies between the Brienzersee and the Thunersee and offers convenient access to both lakes; it functions better as a way station than as a destination. **Alpin Zentrum,** Interlaken's main "adventure coordinator," offers a myriad of these daredevil activities. On the water, there's **river rafting** (½-day, 61-81SFr) and **canyoning** (½-day 80-155SFr). On land, **climb rocks** (½-day 75SFr); struggle up and grapple with the crags of the Alps. For challenging **guided mountain biking,** fork over 56SFr for a ½-day (bike rental ½-day 25SFr, full day 35SFr). In the air, enjoy the graceful, peaceful beauty of **tandem paragliding** (½-day 100-170SFr, depending on altitude of flight), or experience the free-fall rush of **bungee-jumping** from one of several locations: Mt. Titlis (70m 119SFr; 120m 169SFr), and Schilthorn (100m 129SFr; 180m 259SFr, prerequisite of one previous jump). Alpin Zentrum also offers combined packages of all their activities (300-350SFr). For info and reservations, contact Alpin Zentrum, P.O. Box 3800, Interlaken, Switzerland (tel. (036) 23 43 63, fax 22 73 07).

Höheweg nightlife heats up in tourist season. The party starts at **Buddy's,** Höheweg 33, an Interlaken tradition with the cheapest beer in town. (2.70SFr. Open Sun.-Thurs. 10am-1am, Fri.-Sat. 10am-1:30am; off-season Sun.-Thurs. 10am-12:30am, Fri.-Sat. 10am-1am.) Herds then migrate to Interlaken's oldest disco, **Johnny's Dancing Club,** Höheweg 92, downstairs in the Hotel Carlton. (Sat. cover 5SFr. Drinks from 5.50SFr. Open Dec.-Oct. Tues.-Sun. 9:30pm-2:30am.)

Interlaken's *other* tradition is the summer production of Schiller's *Wilhelm Tell.* Held in a huge amphitheater around the corner from Balmer's, the cast of hundreds includes residents, children, and local horses and cows, which are paraded through the streets before the performance begins. (Shows late June to early July Thurs. 8pm; mid-July to early Sept. Thurs. and Sat. 8pm. Tickets 12-30SFr from the *Tell-büro,* Bahnhofstr. 5 (tel. (036) 22 37 23). English synopsis 1SFr.)

Practical Information, Accommodations, and Food Any train you want probably starts and stops at the **Ostbahnhof** (tel. (036) 22 27 92). The **Westbahnhof** (tel. (036) 22 35 25) stands in the center of town bordering the Thunersee. Each station features a minute **tourist office** that changes currency at good rates. Computers on the platform at either station babble tourist info in English, German, and French. The main **tourist office,** Höheweg 37 (tel. (036) 22 21 21), in the Hotel Metropol near Westbahnhof, finds rooms and provides maps and schedules for free. Ask for their list of rooms in private homes if you'll be staying at least 3 days. (20-30SFr per person. Open Mon.-Fri. 8am-noon and 2-6:30pm, Sat. 8am-noon and 2-5pm, Sun. 5-7pm; Sept.-June Mon.-Fri. 8am-noon and 2-6pm, Sat. 8am-noon.) **Bicycles** can be rented at the train stations (19SFr per day).

Although Interlaken gushes hotels, very few approach affordability. Take bus 5 to Hotel Sonne, or walk 15min. from either station to **Balmer's Herberge,** Haupstr. 23 (tel. (036) 22 19 61, fax 23 32 61). From Westbahnhof go left, veer right onto Bahnhofstr., turn right on Centralstr. and follow the signs. Sign in and return at 5pm, when beds are assigned (no reservations). Balmer's draws a primarily American crowd with its summer-camp atmosphere. "Uncle Erich" provides currency exchange, bike rental, discount excursions, nightly movies, CNN, MTV, book exchange, kitchen facilities (1SFr per 20min.), laundry (8SFr per load), mini department store (open until 10pm), and a super-friendly staff. The staff makes a real effort to get guests out on the trails and slopes, and also encourages adventuring visitors to go **river rafting** (75SFr), **canyoning** (80SFr), **rock-climbing** (75SFr), or **bungee-jumping** (the longest in Europe at 180m; also a 100m jump for the more tame) off a cable car near Lucerne (148SFr); or combine any of these in an Adventure-Package. Some prefer the frigid but fantastic ice-climbing (110SFr) or the beautiful tandem para-gliding off the local mountains (100-170SFr). If beds are filled, you can crash on a mattress. (Reception open 9:20am-noon and 4:30-11pm; winter 6:30am-9am and 4:30-11pm. Dorms 16SFr. Doubles 54SFr. Triples 66SFr. Quads 84SFr. Breakfast included.) **Jugendherberge Bönigen (HI),** Aareweg 21 (tel. (036) 22 43 53), is farther from town; take bus 1 to Lütschinenbrücke. (Reception open 6-9am and 4-9pm. Dorms 23.10SFr. Doubles 60SFr.) **Camping Jungfraublick** (tel. (036) 22 44 14, fax 22 16 19) is 5min. past Balmer's on Gsteigstr. (7.70SFr per person, off-season 5.70SFr; 4-10SFr per tent. Open April-Oct.) Just across the river from Ostbahnhof is the small, waterside **Camping Sackgut** (tel. (036) 24 44 34; 5.90SFr per person, 5-11SFr per tent; open May-Oct.). Five other sites cluster together near the Lombach River in Unterseen. Follow the signs from Seestr. near Westbahnhof.

Interlaken is filled with ridiculously overpriced restaurants. Avoid them and hit the markets and *bäckerei* that abound instead. Stock up for hikes at the **Migros** supermarket across from Westbahnhof (open Mon.-Thurs. 7:30am-7pm, Fri. 7:30-9pm, Sat. 7:30am-4pm). While chocolates are the specialty at **Confiserie Rieder,** Marktgasse 14, the tea room and bakery offer sandwiches and salads for moderate prices (open Tues.-Fri. 8:30am-6:30pm, Sat. 8:30am-6pm, Sun. 1-6pm; 5-17SFr).

■■■ JUNGFRAU REGION

The most famous (and visited) region of the Berner Oberland, the Jungfrau area has attracted tourists for hundreds of years with glorious hiking trails and perennially snow-capped peaks. As the birthplace of skiing (or so they claim), the area offers some of the most challenging slopes in Switzerland. Rail costs are scandalously steep; **Berner Oberland Bahn** does not accept railpasses (except for 50% off trips to Männlichen). The 15-day **Berner Oberland Regional Pass** (175SFr, 140SFr with Swisspass or Half-Fare Card) can save cash with 5 free days and 10 ½-price days.

Appreciate the juxtaposition of the Berner Oberland's calm, peaceful lakes and its stark mountain peaks with a cruise on one of Interlaken's two lakes, the **Thunersee** (to the west) and the **Brienzersee** (to the east). A relaxing excursion, it's also the region's only activity that is free with a Eurailpass. Day passes valid on both lakes can be purchased at Interlaken's station (40SFr; Sept.-June 30SFr; Swisspass and Berner Oberland regional pass valid July-Aug.); otherwise, fares are determined by the number of km traveled on the lake.

SKIING AND HIKING

The Berner Oberland offers visitors some of the best skiing and hiking in the world. Mountain terrain for both alpine and cross-country skiing, as well as for hiking, ranges from the easy to the advanced. Free maps for **hikers** are available from even the most rinky-dink of tourist offices. Climbers should pack sunglasses, water, raingear, and a sweater, and follow standard safety procedures; the Alps are not kind to the unprepared.

There are four types of **ski passes** for the Oberland; the Jungfrau "Top Ski" Region pass is the most extensive and expensive (3-day 136SFr, age 16-21 110SFr, age 6-16 68SFr; valid for ascent only). The **Kleine Scheidegg/Männlichen pass** (1-day 52SFr, age 16-21 42SFr, 2-day 95SFr, age 16-21 76SFr) covers more trails than you'd tire of in a week. The **ski schools** in Grindelwald (tel. (036) 53 20 21) and Wengen (tel. (036) 55 20 22) supply info on classes. A week's worth of group lessons are a bargain, often less than a few hours of a private lesson. Call (036) 53 26 92 for **weather and ski conditions** at Grindelwald/First, tel. (036) 55 44 33 for Kleine Scheidegg/Männlichen, and tel. (036) 55 26 55 for Mürren/Schilthorn (German only).

In Interlaken, **Balmer's Herberge** offers a discount skiing deal. Guests receive transportation to Grindelwald (13SFr), ski rental (downhill 35SFr for 1 day, 60SFr for 2 days, 75SFr for 3 days), ski passes covering a limited area (50SFr for 1 day, 85SFr for 2 days, 130SFR for 3 days), free sleds, and expert trail advice, all at slashed prices. Ask at the desk for departure times and other sundry details.

Grindelwald The town of Grindelwald is a skier and climber's nirvana. The **tourist office** (*Verkehrsbüro*; tel. (036) 53 12 12) provides hiking and skiing maps and can find you rooms in private homes. (Open Mon.-Fri. 8am-7pm, Sat. 9am-7pm; Oct.-June Mon.-Fri. 8am-noon and 2-6pm, Sat. 8am-noon.) Ride a gondola to the **First** mountain for toe-curling scenery. (26SFr, round-trip 40SFr, guests of Balmer's Herberge 20SFr. Regional Pass valid.) Trips to the **Männlichen** mountain snake up from the **Grund** station (26SFr, round-trip 40SFr, 50% off with Eurail); the summit affords a glorious glance at the **Eiger, the Mönch,** and **Jungfrau.**

Budget travelers strike it rich in Grindelwald. The **Mountain Hostel** (tel. (036) 533 900) in Grindenwald is most excellent. The hostel is next door to the Männlichen cable car, a few minutes from the train station. The owners speak English and lead guided hikes through the area. (27-40SFr per person, tack on 20SFr for a dinner voucher to a local restaurant. Breakfast and showers included. Parking available.) Of Grindelwald's four **campgrounds,** the closest is **Gletscherdorf** (tel. (036) 53 14 29), a small site endowed with clean facilities and phenomenal photo opportunities of the mountains. From the station, turn right; take the 1st right after the tourist office, then the 3rd left. (8.50SFr per person, 4-8SFr per tent.) Another option is **Camping Eigernordwand** (tel. (036) 53 42 27), across the river and to the left of the Grund station (9.50SFr per person, 5-7SFr per tent). The budget-minded avoid restaurants and buy provisions at the **Coop** across from the tourist office.

Lauterbrünnen The glacier-cut valleys of the Lauterbrünnen are stark but beautiful, untamed yet serene. Lauterbrünnen town feels small, dwarfed by sheer rock cliffs. The **tourist office** (tel. (036) 55 19 55) is 200m left of the station on the main street (open Mon.-Fri. 8am-noon and 1:30-7:30pm, Sat. 9-11am, Sun. 3-5pm). A delightful farmhouse-turned-hostel, the **Matratzenlager Stocki** (tel. (036) 55 17 54), offers a full kitchen redolent with spices and a mellow atmosphere. Leave the train station from the back, descend the steps, cross the river, turn right, and walk 200m. The sign on the house reads "Massenlager." (10SFr per person. Open Jan.-Oct.) **Camping Schützenbach** (tel. (036) 55 12 68, fax 55 12 75), on the Panorama walkway to the falls, has showers and laundry and kitchen facilities. (6.50SFr per person, 5-14SFr per tent, dorms 14-26SFr.) Follow the signs toward Trümmelbach from the station (15min.). **Camping Jungfrau** (tel. (036) 55 20 10, fax 55 38 18), up the main street from the station toward the large waterfall, provides cheap beds, kitchens, showers, lounges, and a snack bar. (6.80SFr per person, 3-10SFr per tent, dorms 14-18SFr.) Lauterbrünnen's **Coop** roosts between the train station and tourist office.

The fabulous **Trümmelbach Falls,** 10 consecutive glacier-bed chutes, generate mighty winds and a roaring din inside their mountain home. Explore via tunnels, footbridges, and underground funiculars. (Open April-Nov. 8:30am-5:30pm. 8SFr.) Cable cars leave from **Stechelberg** (45min. from the falls) to Gimmelwald (6.80SFr), to Mürren (13.60SFr), to Birg (30.60SFr) and to the top of the **Schilthorn** (45.20SFr), the mountain made famous in the Bond flick *In Her Majesty's Secret Service*. **Mürren,** a car-free skiing and sport resort town, coordinates this area; ask at the **tourist office** (tel. (036) 55 16 16) in the Sports Center (5min. left of the Lauterbrünnen terminus, 10min. right of the Gimmelwald one) for hiking trails and skiing prices. (Open Mon.-Wed. and Fri.-Sat. 9am-noon and 1-6:30pm, Thurs. 9am-noon and 1-8:30pm, Sun. 2-6pm.) The single hostel in the valley rewards those who trek to **Gimmelwald** on the steep Stechelberg trail; the **Mountain Hostel** (tel. (036) 55 17 04) is rustic, inexpensive, friendly, and not the same place as the once in Grindenwald. *Don't arrive without food*—there are cooking facilities, but no restaurants, in this microscopic burg (8.50SFr, showers 1SFr).

Thunersee and Brienzersee The **Thunersee** cruise takes a half hour to reach the **Beatushöhlen,** caves with stalactites, waterfalls, and the ancient cell of the pallid Augustinian monk St. Beatus. (Open April-Oct. 9:30am-5pm. 10SFr, students 9SFr.) Across the lake **Spiez Castle** features authentic period rooms, a mesmerizing tower view, a chapel, and a rose garden. (Open July-Aug. Mon. 2-6pm, Tues.-Sun. 10am-6pm; April-June and Sept.-Oct. Mon. 2-5pm, Tues.-Sun. 10am-5pm. 4SFr, students 1SFr.) Accommodations on the lake are expensive; ask at the tourist offices for *Zimmer Frei* options. **Spiez** and **Thun,** the Thunersee's metropolises, have offices located adjacent to the train stations. (Spiez tel. (033) 54 21 38; open Mon.-Fri. 8am-noon and 1:30-6:30pm, Sat. 9am-noon; June and Sept. Mon.-Fri. 8am-noon and 2-4pm, Sat. 9am-noon; Oct.-May Mon.-Fri. 8am-noon and 2-5pm. Thun tel. (033) 22 23 40; open Mon.-Fri. 9am-noon and 2-5pm, Sat. 9am-noon.) The lone **Jugendherberge (HI)** on the lake is in **Faulensee,** Quellenhofweg 66 (tel. (033) 54 19 88). Most steamers stop at the hostel; check the itinerary at the landing just to be sure. (Reception open March-Oct. 7-9am and 5-9pm. Lockout 9am-5pm. 20.40SFr, nonmembers 27.40SFr. Breakfast included. Reservations encouraged.) **Campgrounds** are countless; try **Panorama Rossen** (tel. (033) 54 43 77) in Aeschi (take the bus to Mustermattli; 20.50SFr including tent; open May-Oct.).

The **Brienzersee** is the more rugged and less developed of the lakes. **Brienz** makes for a serene daytrip from Interlaken (1hr. by boat, 20min. by train). The **Ballenberg Swiss Open-Air Museum,** a 50-hectare park, displays examples of traditional rural dwellings from every region of Switzerland, with Swiss artisans busily at work. The park is about an hour's walk from the train station, but an hourly bus (round-trip 5.60SFr) connects the two. (Open April 15-Oct. 25 10am-5pm. 12SFr, with visitor's card 10.50SFr.) The **tourist office** (tel. (036) 51 32 42) across from the train station gives tips to hikers of all levels. (Open Mon.-Fri. 8am-7pm, Sat. 8am-6pm; Sept.-June Mon.-Fri. 8am-noon and 2-6pm, Sat. 8am-noon.) The train station rents **bicycles.** From the tourist office, cross the tracks, turn left and hug the lake for 15min. to the rustic **Brienz Jugendherberge (HI),** Strandweg 10 (tel. (036) 51 11 52, fax 51 22 60), which rents hiking boots (5SFr) and bikes (10SFr per day, 15SFr per 2 days) to its guests. (Reception open March-Nov. 8-9am, 5-6pm, and 7-9pm. 22.50SFr first night, then 20SFr. Doubles 29.50SFr, then 27SFr) Along the same stretch sprawl two campgrounds: **Camping Seegärtli** (tel. (036) 51 13 51; 7SFr per person, 4-7SFr per tent; open April-Oct.) and **Camping Aaregg** (tel. (036) 51 18 43, fax 51 43 24; 5.50SFr per person, 4-12SFr per tent; open April-Oct.).

■■■ ZERMATT AND THE MATTERHORN

The **Matterhorn** is an ornery giant, its peak often shrouded in thick clouds; the best time to catch a glimpse is at dawn or dusk. To climb this beast, you need a mountain of money and a courageous heart; the hike takes two days and hiring a guide costs over 500SFr. Fortunately, you can hike 388km worth of sign-posted paths around **Zermatt** without grave danger to life or wallet. Find more info at the **Burgführerbüro** (mountaineering office; tel. (028) 67 34 56; open July to mid-Oct. 8:30am-noon and 4:30-7pm), across from the train station. Sturdy boots, warm clothing and raingear are essential. For a spectacular glimpse of the Matterhorn and its splendid valleys, climb to **Hörnli Hütte** (4-5hr.) or the bathtub-sized lake **Schwarzsee** (1½-2hr.) from Zermatt. The less zealous can take a cable car (round-trip 27.50SFr, 20.50SFr with Swisspass). Zermatt has more **summer ski trails** than any other Alpine resort; lifts operate from 7am-2pm depending on the weather. Ski passes cost 60SFr for a day, 204SFr for a week. Flexible passes allow 2 out of 4 days of slopes for 90SFr, 3 out of 6 for 140SFr, and 7 out of 14 for 286SFr (seniors 25% off and children under 16 50% off). Ski rental runs about 40SFr (30SFr if you stay at the youth hostel). For more time on the slopes, rent equipment a day ahead; ski shops are open Monday through Saturday 8am-6:30pm. The **tourist office** (tel. (028) 66 11 81), to the right of the train station, provides specific skiing and hiking maps and other general info (open Mon.-Fri. 8:30am-noon and 1:30-6pm, Sat. 8:30am-noon; July to mid-Sept. also Sat. noon-6:30pm, Sun. 9:30am-noon and 4-6:30pm). For **alpine rescue,** call (028) 67 34 87.

The **Jugendherberge (HI)** (tel. (028) 67 23 20) provides inexpensive, impeccably clean housing, but it's quite a trek. From the train station, walk to the right, down the main street, turn left at the church, cross the river and follow the signs uphill for 15min. (Reception open 6:30-9am and 4-10pm. Lockout 9:30am-4pm. Curfew 11:30pm but silence after 10pm. 36.50SFr, additional nights 34.50SFr. Nonmembers 42SFr, additional nights 40.50SFr. Breakfast, sleep sack, showers, and either lunch or dinner included.) Closer to the station but farther from the mountains is the pleasant **Hotel Bahnhof** (tel. (028) 67 24 06); get off the train and go 100m to the left (dorms 22-26SFr, singles 40SFr, doubles from 70SFr). The lone campground in town is **Camping Matterhorn Zermatt** (tel. (028) 67 39 21), 5min. to the left of the station (7SFr per person; showers and toilets included; open June-Sept.). Cafés are expensive, even for Switzerland. Zermatt's oldest restaurant, the **Café du Pont,** at the end of Bahnhofstr., serves hearty Alpine fare (open 9am-midnight; last orders taken at 10pm; entrees 6-20SFr).

FRENCH SWITZERLAND

■■■ BASEL (BÂLE)

Basel struggles desperately to maintain its medieval quaintness despite its status as Switzerland's second largest city and as headquarters for Roche, Sandoz, and Ciba-Geigy. The resulting balance may disconcert visitors; the guided tour of the city proudly flaunts its chemical factories as well as the Romanesque cathedral. Beyond such disparities, Basel is a city of culture—where Erasmus once lived, Switzerland's first university still stands. The Humanists have been printing books here since the 15th century, and Basel's 30 museums hold some of the best art, antique, historical, and botanical collections in the world.

ORIENTATION AND PRACTICAL INFORMATION

Basel sits in the northwest corner of Switzerland, a stone's throw from Germany and France. The *Gross-Basel* portion of town, where most sights are located, lies on the left bank of the Rhine on two hills separated by the valley of the Birsig; on the right bank lies *Klein-Basel.*

Tourist Office: Schifflände 5 (tel. 261 50 50, fax 261 59 44). Tram 1 (from the SBB station): Schifflände; the office is on the river, near the Mittlere Bridge. Open Mon.-Fri. 8:30am-6pm, Sat. 8:30am-1pm. Grab lists of museums, cultural events, and suggested walking tours for Basel and the surrounding area. Hotel reservations (10SFr) can also be made at the **branch office,** located at the SBB station (tel. 271 36 84). Open June-Sept. Mon.-Fri. 8:30am-7pm, Sat. 8:30am-12:30pm and 1:30-6pm, Sun 10am-2pm; Oct.-March Mon.-Fri. 8:30am-6pm, Sat. 8:30am-12:30pm; April-May Mon.-Fri. 8:30am-7pm, Sat. 8:30am-12:30pm and 1:30-6pm.

Currency Exchange: Rates are nearly uniform throughout town. SBB station bureau open 6am-9pm.

Post Office: Freiestr. 12, at the intersection with Rudengasse. Tram 1, 8, or 15: Marktplatz; go 1 block up Gerbergasse to Rudengasse. Open Mon.-Fri. 7:30am-6:30pm, Sat. 7:30-11am. **Postal Code:** 4000

Telephones: In post office. Mon.-Fri. 7am-8pm, Sat. 8am-6pm. **City Code:** 061.

Trains: The city actually has 3 train stations: the **French (SNCF)** station (tel. 271 50 33) is next door to the **Swiss SBB** station (tel. 272 67 67), but trains originating in Germany, arrive at a separate station (DB), north of the Rhine down Riehenstr. (tel. 695 55 11). The former 2 stations are at the end of Centralbahnstr., near the *Altstadt.* International connections are easily made through the French or German stations. To Zürich (1hr., 29SFr), Geneva (3hr.), Lausanne (2½hr.), Berne (1hr., 33SFr), Innsbruck (5hr.), Salzburg (7hr.), Vienna (10hr.), Paris (4½-5½hr.), and Rome (7hr.)

Buses: Buses leave from the SBB and SNCF to points in France and Germany; there are also buses to Germany departing from the DB.

Public Transportation: Trams and buses move swissly and silently from 5:45am-11:45pm. Most sights are within a single zone (#10). One-zone ticket costs 2.40SFr, day ticket 7.20SFr. Tram tickets dispensed from easy-to-use vendors at all stops. Maps available at tourist office or at train station.

Bike Rental: Next to information in the train station. 21SFr per day. ID deposit required. Open Mon.-Fri. 8am-noon and 1-5pm.

Luggage storage: At all train stations. 5SFr, open 5:30am-12:15am. No lockers.

Emergency: Police: tel. 117. **Medical:** tel. 261 15 15. (All lines English speakers.)

ACCOMMODATIONS AND CAMPING

Don't miss Basel because you didn't *call ahead of time.* There is but one packed hostel and very few hotels even remotely approach budget status. The truly desperate can try **Hecht am Rhein,** Rheingasse 8 (tel. 691 22 20) or **Stadhof,** Gerbergasse 84 (tel. 261 87 11), both of which have showerless rooms in extremely limited numbers (50-75SFr for singles).

Jugendherberge (HI), St. Alban-Kirchrain 10 (tel. 272 05 72). Tram 1: Aeschenplatz, then tram 3 (2 stops). Or, a 10-15min. walk from the SBB station down Aeschengraben, then St. Alban Anlage. Near the river in a calm, verdant stretch. Checkout by 10am. Lockout 10am-3pm. Curfew at midnight. 24.50SFr for the first night, 22SFr each subsequent night. Laundry 8SFr.

Hotel-Pension Steinenschanze, Steinengraben 69 (tel. 272 53 53, fax 272 45 73). From SBB station, left on Centralbahnstr., toward Heuwage-Viadukt and straight ahead. The best deal in Basel: TV, thick mattresses and pillows, bathroom with a shower spouting hot, high-pressure water, and big breakfast. Free luggage storage. No curfew. Singles start at 60SFr, but an ISIC card gets a student rate of 45SFr (3 day max. stay). Doubles with shower 135-170SFr.

Hotel Terminus, Centralbahnstr. 13 (tel. 271 52 50). Next to the SBB train station. Gracious family hotel coddles its guests. Singles 60-70SFr, with shower 100-150SFr. Doubles 80-100SFr, with shower 160SFr to—well, never mind. Breakfast buffet, shower, and satellite TV included.

Camping: Camp Waldhort, Heideweg 16, 4153 Reinach (tel. 711 64 29). Tram 1: Aeschenplatz (one stop), then tram 11: Landhof. Reception open 8am-noon and 2:30-10pm. 6SFr per person, 5SFr per tent. Open March-Oct.

FOOD

Basel is a university town, so relatively cheap eateries are fairly numerous, even in the heart of the city. Check out weekday morning fruit, vegetable, and baked goods stalls on the **Marktplatz.** Numerous cafés also sprinkle the Marktplatz. Grocery shop at **Migros,** Claraplatz or Sternengasse 17, and at the **Coop** centers, Aeschenplatz or Claraplatz (open Mon.-Fri. 7:30am-6:30pm, Sat. 7:30am-5pm).

Hirscheneck, Lindenberg 23 (tel. 692 73 33). Cross the Wettsteinbrücke and take the first left. An unabashedly left-of-center restaurant/bar where dreds and piercings prevail. *Menu* 13SFr. Open Mon. 5pm-midnight, Tues.-Thurs. 8am-midnight, Fri.-Sat. 8am-1am, Sun. 10am-3pm for big breakfast.

Zum Schnabel, Trillengässlein 2 (tel. 261 49 09). Eat alone or play cards with friends in this comfortable restaurant that serves remarkably well-prepared German-style dishes. An 11.50SFr lunch menu could include a deluxe *wurstsalat* with tasty *rösti.* Open Mon.-Sat. 11:30am-11pm.

Gruner Heinrich Pizzeria *(A3-4)*, Glockengasse. Cheap, hearty Italian food *(gnoc-chi* with tomato sauce 11.50SFr). If it's a nice evening, grab a post-dinner ice cream in nearby Marktplatz and walk the cobblestoned streets. Open Tues.-Sat. 9am-midnight, Sun. 5pm-midnight.

Topas Kosher Restaurant, Leimenstrasse 24 (tel. 261 34 43). Chinese-Kosher! Entrees 22-28SFr. An ISIC card will knock 8SFr off the tab. (Be sure to ask the manager.) Open Sun.-Tues. and Thurs. 11:30am-2pm and 6:30-9pm, Fri.-Sat. 11:30am-2pm (Fri. dinner and Sat. lunch only if table reserved in advance).

SIGHTS AND ENTERTAINMENT

Basel's gargantuan **Kunstmuseum** (Museum of Fine Arts), St. Albino-Graben 16, houses the world's oldest public art collection, established in the 16th century, and boasts rooms filled with masterpieces of Holbein, Monet, Matisse, Braque, Chagall, Klee, Rothko, and Picasso (open Tues.-Sun. 10am-5pm; 6SFr, students 4SFr, Sun. free). The **Museum für Gegenwartskunst** (Museum of Contemporary Art), St. Alban-Rheinweg 60 (a painting's throw away from the youth hostel), hosts a discerning collection of art since the 60s, focusing especially on Minimalism and Conceptualism (open Tues.-Sun. 11am-5pm; 8SFr, students 5SFr). The **Sammlung Karikaturen and Cartoons** (Cartoon and Caricature Collection), St. Alban-Vorstadt 9, could make any sourpuss chuckle (open Wed. 4-6pm, Sat. 3-5:30pm, Sun. 10am-4pm; 5SFr, students 2.50SFr).

Within the 11th century walls of the **Münster,** crown jewel of Basel's medieval buildings, are countless sculptures and carvings, as well as Erasmus's bones. Its **tower** boasts the city's best view of *Klein Basel*, the Rhine, and the Black Forest. (Cathedral open Mon.-Fri. 10am-5pm, Sat. 10am-noon and 2-5pm, Sun. 1-5pm; mid-Oct. to Easter Mon.-Sat. 10am-noon and 2-4pm, Sun. 2-4pm. Free.) The gaudily-decorated **Rathaus** (city hall) was erected in the early 1500s to celebrate Basel's entry into the Confederation. The most spectacular of Basel's medieval gates, the **Spalentor,** dating from the 1100s, is just up Spalenvorstadt, and the **Jean Tinguely Fountain** is a refreshingly modern counterpoint to the rambling, medieval *Altstadt*.

Off Marktplatz, Sattlegasse (Saddler's Street) marks the beginning of the **artisan's district,** with street names such as Schneidergasse (Tailor's Street). Find the Elf-tausendjungfern-Gässlein **(Lane of 11,000 Virgins)** and try to count them all. Legend has it that St. Ursula's pilgrimage of girls to the Holy Land during the Children's Crusade passed through here. A colorful Gothic fountain is situated in the **Fischmarkt.**

The annual blow-out for Basel is its carnival, taking place on the Monday *after* Ash Wednesday (March 6, 1995). This centuries-old **Fasnacht** is a colorful three-day affair of fife and drum processions, with revelers hiding behind masks in an attempt to scare away the spirits of winter.

The bar and club scene of this university town will not disappoint. In general clubs do not rev up until the bars close down. **Barfüsserplatz** is a good place to start bar-hopping, though drinks everywhere are quite expensive. Huge parties or "events" thrown in offbeat places (a butcher shop was popular last year) are the in-thing among the trendier party-goers. **Atlantis,** Klosterburg 13 is big, hot, smoky, loud, fun bar that sways to live salsa and reggae during the summer and kicks back to blues and rock in the winter. (Cover charge around 8SFr on weekends. Open Sun.-Thurs. 8am-12:30am, Fri.-Sat. 8am-1:30am.) The **Brauerei Fischerstube,** Rhein-gasse 45, is Basel's smallest brewery, crafting four of the best beers in town. (Open Mon.-Thurs. 9am-midnight; Fri.-Sat. 9am-1am, Sun. 10am-midnight.) The door game's a minor ordeal, but **null-8-fünfzehn** with solid rock music and *relatively* cheap drafts (4.50SFr) can make for a fun, late night. (No cover. Open Mon.-Thurs. 7pm-2am, Fri.-Sat. 8pm-3am, Sun. 8-pm-2am.) On warm summer nights, head over to the elegant **Campari Bar,** near the Tinguely fountain.

S W I T Z E R L A N D

■■■ NEUCHÂTEL

An 18th-century traveler once called Neuchâtel the "City of Butter." He was likely referring to the unique yellow stone that comprises a large part of the city's architecture. Even after the novelty of the color has worn off, the town possesses a remarkably intact medieval beauty. Not surprisingly, the **château** for which the city is named and the neighboring **Eglise Collégiale** dominate the town from their hilltop perches. (Guided tours of the castle in English April-Sept. Mon.-Sat. hourly 10am-4pm, Sun. 2-4pm, free. Church open 8am-6pm). The **Tour des Prisons** is but an arrowshot away on rue de Château, and is worth every centime of the 0.50SFr entry fee. Lock a friend in one of the tiny, wooden cells that were still in use in 1848. The potential for fun is limitless.

Facing the lake, the **tourist office** is in the left corner of the square (tel. (038) 25 42 42; open July-Aug. Mon.-Sat. 9am-12:30pm and 1:30-7pm, Sept.-June Mon.-Fri. 9am-noon and 1:30-5:30pm, Sat. 9am-noon). They provide the *Bulletin Touristique*, which contains a helpful city map, and listings (in French) of sights, museums, bars, and phone numbers. The **Auberge de Jeunesse (HI)**, 35 rue de Suchiez (tel. (038) 31 31 90) boasts friendly and helpful management and a fine view of the lake; too bad you have to hike up 3km to reach it on foot. Take bus 1 "Cormondrèche" from pl. Pury and follow the signs uphill. (Reception open 8-9am, 5-6:30pm, and 7:15-10pm. Curfew 10:30pm, but ask for a key. 24SFr first night, subsequent nights 22SFr. Shower, sheets, and breakfast included. Closed Dec.15-Feb. 15.) Neuchâtel, with its barrage of students, offers good, inexpensive meals. The student hangout **Creperie Bach et Buch** is especially satisfying, located near the university toward pl. Pury, along ave. Premier-Mars (kitchen open Mon.-Thurs. 11:30am-4pm and 5:30-10pm, Fri.-Sat. 11:30am-3pm and 5:30-11:30pm).

■■■ GENEVA (GENÈVE)

If peace has a home on this planet, it is Geneva. The city has exemplified Switzerland's policy of neutrality since it joined the Swiss Confederation in 1815. Center of nascent Protestantism and birthplace of both the Red Cross and the League of Nations, Geneva now hosts the European headquarters of the United Nations, a slew of international organizations (one-third of its 375,000 residents are foreigners) and perpetual negotiations between various and sundry belligerents.

ORIENTATION AND PRACTICAL INFORMATION

Genevois sun themselves on the western shore of **Lac Léman** (Lake Geneva), at the southwestern corner of Switzerland. The Rhône River divides the city. Carry your passport with you at all times; the French border is very close and regional buses frequently cross it.

Tourist Office: In the train station (tel. 738 52 00). Staff books hotel rooms (5SFr fee) and provides free maps, and publications such as *This Week in Geneva*, *What's on in Geneva*, and the monthly *Spectacles et Manifestations*, in French. Open Mon.-Fri. 8am-8pm, Sat.-Sun. 8am-6pm; Sept. 15-June 15 Mon.-Sat. 9am-6pm. **CAR (Centre d'Accueil et de Renseignements),** at the top of rue du Mont Blanc by the Gare Cornavin answers all sorts of questions and stocks the invaluable *Info Jeunes,* listing inexpensive accommodations, restaurants, and other practical info. Open June15-Sept. 15 8am-11pm.

Currency Exchange: In Gare Cornavin. Good rates, no commission on traveler's checks. Open 6am-9:30pm.

American Express: 7, rue du Mont-Blanc, P.O. Box 1032, Geneva 01, CH-1211 (tel. 731 76 00). Mail held. All banking services. Open Mon.-Fri. 8:30am-5:30pm, Sat.-Sun. 9am-noon.

Post Office: Poste Centrale, rue de Mont-Blanc 18, 1 block from the Gare Cornavin in the Hôtel des Postes. Open Mon.-Fri. 7:30am-6pm, Sat. 8-11am. **Postal Code:** 1200 Genève 1.

Telephones: In Gare Cornavin (open 7am-10:30pm), and in post offices (open Mon.-Fri. 8am-6pm). **City Code:** 022.

Flights: Swissair (tel. 799 31 11). Trains leave Gare Cornavin for **Cointrin Airport** (5:28am-11:22pm, every 10min., 5SFr).

Trains: Gare Cornavin (tel. 731 64 50) is the primary station. Zürich (73SFr), Paris (103SFr), Rome (118SFr), Cologne (191SFr), Milan (71SFr), and Barcelona (105SFr). Reservations and info office open Mon.-Fri. 8am-7:15pm, Sat. 8am-6:15pm, Sun. 10am-6:15pm. **Gare Genève Eaux-Vives,** on the eastern edge of the city, serves Annecy and Chamonix.

Public Transportation: (tel. 308 34 34, 8am-noon and 1:30-5pm). The free, if somewhat confusing, map *Le réseau* is available at **Transports Publics Génévois,** next to the tourist office in Gare Cornavin. 2SFr buys an hour of unlimited travel on any bus; 3 stops or less costs 1.20SFr. 24hr., 48hr., and 72hr. passes cost 8.50SFr, 15SFr, and 19SFr respectively. Buses free with Swisspass, but not with Eurail. Buy multi-fare and day tickets at train station, others at automatic vendors at every stop. Buses run roughly 5:30am-midnight.

Ferries: CGN, quai du Mont-Blanc, at the foot of rue du Mont-Blanc (tel. 311 25 21). To Lausanne (3½hr., 44SFr) and Montreux (5hr., 53SFr). Ferries leave at 9:15am and 4:15pm. Eurail and Swisspass valid.

Bike Rental: At the baggage check in Gare Cornavin. From 19SFr per 12hr., 16SFr per 12hr. ID deposit required. Open 7am-7:30pm.

Hitchhiking: Those headed to Germany or northern Switzerland take bus 4/44 to Jardin Botanique. Those headed to France take bus 4/44 to Palettes and switch to line D to St. Julien. Or call **Telstop** (tel. 964 16 64) or check their list of available rides in front of the CAR information office (0.09Sfr per km).

Laundromat: Salon Lavoir St. Gervais, rue Vallin (tel. 731 26 46). Just off the pl. St. Gervais. Wash 4SFr, dry 1SFr per 12min. Open Mon.-Sat. 7:30am-10pm, Sun. 10am-10pm.

Medical Assistance: Hôpital Cantonal, 24, rue Micheli-du-Crest (tel. 372 81 00). Door 3 for outpatient care. Walk-in clinics dot the city; call 320 25 11.

Emergency: Ambulance: tel. 144. **Police:** tel. 117. At 5, rue Pecollat, next to post office.

ACCOMMODATIONS AND CAMPING

Thanks to the large number of hostel and quasi-hostel accommodations, finding a room in Geneva shouldn't be a problem. If the ones below are full, ask the tourist office for the brochure *Youth Accommodation* (**CAR** map lists the same info).

Auberge de Jeunesse (HI), 28-30, rue Rothschild (tel. 732 62 60). Walk 5min. left from the station down rue de Lausanne, then turn right on rue Rothschild. State-of-the-art; huge and well-tended. Flexible 3-night max. stay. Reception open 6:30-10am and 5-11pm. Lockout 10am-5pm. Curfew midnight. 27SFr, nonmembers 27SFr. Showers, breakfast, and sheets included. Laundry 7SFr. Kitchen.

Centre St. Boniface, ave. Mail 14 (tel. 321 88 44). Bus 1 or 9: Cirque, and continue down av. Mail. Large plastic mattresses and a lack of secure lockers, but the location is central, and the price exceptional (14SFr, sheets 7SFr). Singles 39SFr, students 34SFr. Doubles 62SFr, students 54SFr. Kitchen facilities. Reception open Mon.-Fri. 9:30-11:30am and 4:30-7pm, Sat. 9:30am-noon.

Hôme St-Pierre, 4 cours St-Pierre (tel. 310 37 07), in an unforgettable location in front of the cathedral in the *vieille ville.* Bus 5: pl. Neuve (5 stops), or walk 15min., crossing the Rhône at Pont du Mont-Blanc. A residence/hostel for women only (ages 17-30). No lockout. No curfew. Dorms 20SFr. Rarely available singles 35SFr. Doubles 50SFr. Showers and lockers included. Laundry 4SFr. Big breakfast 7.50SFr. Popular and small, so reserve ahead by phone or mail.

Cité Universitaire, 46, av. Miremont (tel. 346 23 55, fax 346 25 10), on the other side of the old town from the station. Take bus 3 "Crte de Champel" from the pl. de 22 Cantons opposite the train station to the last stop. Respectable rooms in a modern high-rise. Reception open Mon.-Fri. 8am-noon and 2-10pm, Sat. 8am-noon and 6-10pm. Curfew 11:30pm. Dorms 15SFr. Singles 38SFr, students 32SFr. Doubles 52SFr, students 46SFr. Showers included.

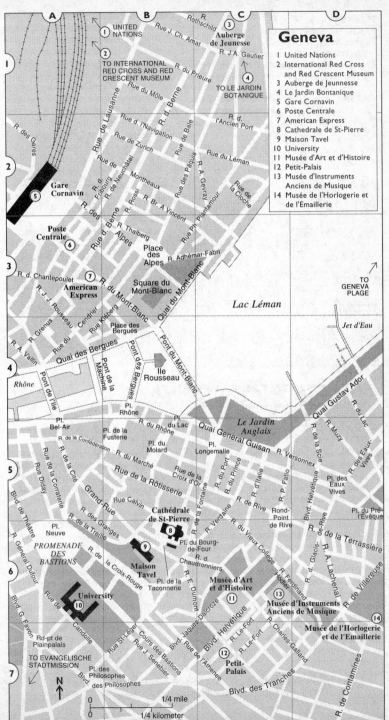

Geneva

1 United Nations
2 International Red Cross and Red Crescent Museum
3 Auberge de Jeunnesse
4 Le Jardin Bontanique
5 Gare Cornavin
6 Poste Centrale
7 American Express
8 Cathedrale de St-Pierre
9 Maison Tavel
10 University
11 Musée d'Art et d'Histoire
12 Petit-Palais
13 Musée d'Instruments Anciens de Musique
14 Musée de l'Horlogerie et de l'Emaillerie

SWITZERLAND

Hôtel St. Gervais, 20 rue des Corps-Saints (tel. 732 45 72). From the train station, cross the street and walk right 3min. down rue Corvain. Simple but luxurious rooms near the station. Reception open 6:30am-midnight. Singles 50-58SFr. Doubles 68-98SFr, shower and breakfast included.

Camping: Pointe-à-la-Bise (tel. 752 12 96). Take bus 9 to Rive stop, then bus E about 7km north to Bise. 6SFr per person, 7SFr per tent. Open April to mid-Oct.

FOOD

You can find everything here from sushi to *paella*, but you may need a banker's salary to cover it. For farm-fresh fruits and cheeses, check out the **market** on rue de Coutance, leading down to the river just above the *ponts de l'Ile* (8am-6pm). The best **cafés** are around **Place du Bourg-de-Four,** below Cathédrale de St. Pierre, and the village of **Carouge** (tram 12: pl. du Marché).

Auberge de Saviese, 20 rue Paquis. Bus 1: Navigation. Santa Barbara students and *Génévois* natives all come here for excellent *fondue au cognac* (17.50SFr). A portion of *raclette* with all the trimmings goes for 4.50SFr. Open Mon.-Fri. 8am-11:30pm, Sat. 11am-11:30pm.

Restaurant Manora, 4, rue de Cornavin, near the station, across from Notre Dame. Huge self-serve restaurant with a selection that's fresh, varied, and of high quality, especially the fruit bar (3.70-6.20SFr) and salad bar (3.90-9.50SFr). *Plats du jour* 7.50 and 9.70SFr. Open Mon.-Sat. 7am-9:30pm, Sun 9am-9pm.

Navy Club, 31, rue Bourg-de-Four (tel. 310 44 98). The *vieille ville* meets the Love Boat. Veal sausage with *rösti* served with salad and bread is a tasty and traditional way to load calories (13SFr). Open Mon.-Fri. 11am-2pm and 6pm-midnight.

Le Zofage, 6, rue des Voisins. Tram 12: Pont d'Arve, then down blvd. Pont d'Arve and left on rue Voisins. University restaurant that serves adequate *plats du jour* for a price that's hard to find elsewhere (8.50SFr until 2pm). Open 7am-midnight.

Le Rozzel, 18 Grand rue (tel. 311 89 29). Créperie with outdoor seating along the nicest street in the *vieille ville.* Large buckwheat or dessert crépes from 3.50-9SFr. Open Mon.-Fri. 8am-7:30pm, Sat. 9am-6pm.

SIGHTS AND ENTERTAINMENT

Climb the north tower of the **Cathédrale de St-Pierre** to view the winding streets and flower-bedecked homes of Geneva's old town. (Cathedral open 9am-7pm; Oct. and March-May 9am-noon and 2-6pm; Nov.-Feb. 9am-noon and 2-5pm. Tower open 11:30am-noon and 2-5:30pm except during services. 2.50SFr, children 1SFr.) **Maison Tavel,** 6, rue du Puits-St-Pierre (tel. 310 29 00), next to the **Hôtel de Ville** (town hall), relates the history of Geneva from the 14th through 19th centuries (open Tues.-Sun. 10am-5pm; free). Calvin & Co. stare at tourists from **le Mur des Réformateurs,** just below the Hôtel de Ville. Opposite the Hôtel de Ville, the **world's longest bench** stretches out to 394ft. The **Petit-Palais,** 2, Terrasse St-Victor, displays a wonderful collection which encompasses the incredibly dynamic period from 1880-1930, ranging from Impressionism, Pointilism, and Cubism to Expressionism, Fauvism, and Primativism (open Mon.-Fri. 10am-noon and 2-6pm, Sat.-Sun. 10am-1pm and 2-5pm; 10SFr, students and seniors 3.50SFr).

Geneva's contemporary monuments stand on the *rive droite,* 10min. from the train station. The guided tour of the **United Nations** at the end of rue Montbrillant is, like Orson Welles' conception of peace, quite dull, despite art treasures donated by all the nations of the world. The constant traffic of international diplomats provides the bulk of the excitement. (Open 9am-noon and 2-6pm; Sept.-Oct. and April-June 10am-noon and 2-4pm; Nov.-March Mon.-Fri. 10am-noon and 2-4pm. 8SFr, seniors and students 6SFr.) More interesting is the nearby **International Red Cross and Red Crescent Museum,** 17, av. de la Paix. A beautifully designed series of films, slide shows and photographs traces the bloody history of the humanitarian organization. (Open Wed.-Mon. 10am-5pm. 8SFr, students 4SFr, under 11 free.)

Geneva's lakefront begs to be strolled. Saunter down **Quai Gustave-Ador** to the world's tallest fountain (140m), the **Jet d'Eau** ("Calvin's Bidet" to irreverent foreigners). **Le Jardin Anglais** is Geneva's most overrated attraction, featuring the **Horloge Fleurie,** a large clock of flowers designed in homage to Geneva's clock industry. Two fine beaches front the lake: **Paquis Plage,** at quai du Mont-Blanc (1SFr), is laid-back and popular with the *Génévois*; upscale **Genève Plage** (5SFr) offers a giant waterslide, volleyball, and basketball tournaments and an Olympic-size pool.

At the tourist office, pick up the free *This Week in Geneva* (English) or *Manifestations et Spectacles*, invaluable guides to nighttime activities. *Fun mag* (in French) lists events and concerts with a decidedly youthful bent. Summer nightlife centers around the cafés and the lakeside quays. Both brimming with cafés, **Place du Bourg-du-Four,** below Cathédrale St-Pierre in the old town and the village of **Carouge** attract young people on sultry evenings. Anglophones gather at **Flanagans,** rue du Cheval-Blanc, where friendly bartenders pull a good beer in a relaxed establishment (music Thurs.-Sat.; open Mon.-Thurs. 10am-1am, Fri.-Sat. 10am-2am, Sun. 5:15pm-midnight). The tiny **Post Café,** rue Chaponnieére, draws a huge crowd (open Mon.-Fri. 6:30am-2am, Sat. 10am-2am, Sun. 5pm-2am; happy hour 5-8pm). **Au Chat Noir,** 13 rue Vautier in Carouge, is popular for its jazz acts, but also features guitar rock and sax-moaning blues (open Sun.-Thurs. 9pm-4am, Fri.-Sat. 9pm-5am).

The party in Geneva is **l'Escalade,** commemorating the dramatic repulse from the city walls of the invading French troops. The revelry lasts a full weekend, around Dec. 11. During the first week in August, three days of international musical and artistic celebration culminate in boat shows and a fabulous fireworks display at the **Fêtes de Genève.** The **La Bâtie Festival,** a folk-music festival traditionally held in September, draws Swiss music lovers down from the hills for two weeks of cabaret, theater, and concerts. Many events are free; students pay half-price for the others (regular prices 10-32SFr).

■■■ LAUSANNE

Wedged between the Alps and Lac Léman (don't dare call it Lake Geneva here!), Lausanne may no longer be the same bohemian and intellectual center it was in the late 18th century, when Voltaire, Lord Byron and others flocked here, but the town's aesthetic sense is still strong. The Ouchy waterfront is a summer retreat for sailors, swimmers, and water-skiers, and the tourist business is a fine-tuned machine making the city's attractions accessible while eschewing all things tacky. For over a century, the town has proudly hosted the headquarters of the International Olympic Committee. At the other end of the city's 5-stop mini-metro, the *vieille ville* (old town) retains an ecclesiastic, medieval air.

Lausanne's Gothic **Cathédrale** was consecrated by Pope Gregory X in 1275. Ogle the famous rose window, then check out the stunning view from the tower. (Open Mon.-Fri. 7am-7pm, Sat. 8am-7pm, Sun. 11:30am-7pm; Oct.-Feb. daily 8am-5:30pm. Free. Tower open Mon.-Sat. 9-11:30am and 1:30-5:30pm, Sun. 2-5:30pm. 2SFr, children 12 and under 1SFr.) The **Collection de l'Art Brut,** 11, av. Bergières, is perhaps Europe's most unusual gallery. Its founder, postwar painter Jean Dubuffet, despised the pretension of the avant-garde art scene, so filled the gallery with the works of "non-artists"—the criminally insane, the institutionalized, and others who considered themselves only dabblers. (Open Tues.-Fri. 10am-noon and 2-6pm, Sat.-Sun. 2-6pm. 6SFr, students 4SFr.) The **Musée Olympique,** 1, quai d'Ouchy, gives a high-tech presentation of the philosophy, history, and greatest moments of the Olympic Games. (Open Tues.-Wed. and Fri.-Sun. 10am-6pm, Thurs. 10am-9:30pm. 12SFr, students 9SFr, children 10-18 6SFr.) Take an evening stroll down the **quai de Belgique** in Ouchy, a lakeside promenade flanked by flowers, immaculate gardens, small fountains, and benches. The best beach area is in the **Bellerive** complex (bus 2: "Bellerive"), a massive park with lots of grassy areas where scantily-clad Europeans bake themselves. (Open Mon.-Thurs. 8am-1am, Fri.-Sat. 8am-2am, Sun. 11am-midnight. 3.50SFr, after 5pm 3SFr.)

SWITZERLAND

Practical Information, Accommodations, and Food The **tourist office,** 2, av. de Rhodanie (tel. (021) 617 14 27), is located across from the lake, in Ouchy. Take the Metro (direction "Ouchy"), or bus 2 to the last stop at Ouchy. The staff is superb, the map free, and the wait short; the staff will also make hotel reservations for 3SFr. (Open Mon.-Sat. 8am-7pm, Sun. 9am-noon and 1-6pm; mid-Oct. to Easter Mon.-Fri. 8am-6pm, Sat. 8:30am-noon and 1-5pm.) Be sure to pick up the staggeringly comprehensive *Useful Information,* the *plan officiel* (map), the guide to public transportation, and a list of the upcoming events. Frequent **trains** service Geneva, Basel, Neuchâtel, Interlaken, Zürich, Madrid and Paris. Lausanne's comfortable **Auberge de Jeunesse (HI),** 1, chemin de Muguet (tel. (021) 617 57 82), across the street from a giant municipal sporting complex, looks out onto the lake and mountains. Take bus 2 "Bourdonette": Théâtre de Vidy, then follow the signs downhill about 200m. (Reception open 7-9am and 5-10pm. Curfew 11:30pm. 24SFr, subsequent nights 20SFr. Get there by 5pm to beat the crunch.) **Jeunotel,** Chemin du Bois-de-vaux (tel. (021) 626 02 022, fax 626 02 26), is a vast complex of dorms and studios with fluffy comforters. Take bus 2 "Bourdonette": Bois-de-Vaux, cross the street and follow the signs. (Dorms 18SFr. Singles 50SFr. Doubles 50SFr. Breakfast 6SFr.) **Camping de Vidy** is at 3, chemin du Camping (tel. (021) 624 20 31; reception open 9am-noon and 5-7pm; 6SFr per person, students 4.50SFr; 6-10SFr per tent). Take av. de Rhodanie west out of the city, loop around the *autoroute* onto rte. de Vidy and turn left onto chemin des Ruines Romaines.

Many restaurants are just spectator sports for the budget traveler. Visit produce **markets** Wednesday and Saturday at pl. de la Riponne (7:30am-12:30) at Ouchy on Sunday from April to mid-October (8am-8pm). Nearby, a local favorite, the **Berguglia Boulangerie,** 10, rue Madeleine, serves up scrumptious and cheap delights ranging from sandwiches to desserts (open Mon. 2:15-6:30pm, Tues.-Fri. 7:30am-12:30pm and 2:15-6:30pm, Sat. 7am-5pm). **Manora Sainf,** 17, pl. de St-François (tel. (021) 320 92 93), is a popular self-service restaurant with fantastic salad, fruit, and dessert bars. *(Menus du jour* 7-15SFr. Open Mon.-Fri. 7am-10:30pm, Sun. 9am-10:30pm.) **Crêperie d'Ouchy,** 7, pl. du Port, is one of the few affordable cafés along the pricey Quai d' Ouchy. (Buckwheat *galettes* 4-15SFr., dessert *crêpes* 4-10SFr, real Normandy *cidre* 2.50SFr. Open 9am-midnight, Sept.-May 11am-9pm.) For some entertainment, wander along the bar-lined **pl. St.-François.** A pungent hole-in-the-wall, **Dolce Vita,** rue de César Roux 30, features frequent live shows of rap, indie, world, and blistering acid jazz (open Wed.-Sun. 11pm-3am, Fri.-Sat. 11pm-4am, off-season closed Thurs.).

■■■ MONTREUX

Popular resort and retirement pad for the wealthy, Montreux also draws footloose young folk to its music festivals, which feature jazz, funk, rap, salsa, blues, and gospel. The most famous, the **Montreux Jazz Festival,** has become a world-famous magnet for exceptional musical talent. Past guests have included Dr. John, Quincy Jones, Santana, Wynton Marsalis, Etta James, Bobby McFerrin, and the B.B. King Blues Band. (Tickets 50-198SFr, festival pass 1400SFr, standing room 30-68SFr.) Write well in advance for info and tickets to **Ciao Travel,** 2707 Congress St. 1F, San Diego, CA 92110 (tel. (619) 297-8112). Full payment is required when you reserve. With luck, the tourist office may have some tickets available when the festival starts, but most are snapped up over a month before the concerts begin.

From late August to early October, the **Classical Montreux-Vevey Music Festival** takes over, featuring a myriad of philharmonics from Moscow to Memphis. Write to **Festival de Musique,** 5, rue du Théâtre, Case Postale 162, CH-1820 Montreux 2 (tickets 30-110SFr). In the U.S., contact **Dailey-Thorp Inc.,** 315 W. 57th St., New York, NY 10019 (tel. (212) 307-1555).

Château de Chillon is a 10min. walk past the hostel. The remarkably well-preserved 13th-century fortress is a delightful site with all the comforts of home: prison cells, torture chamber, weapons room, and terrific views. The *château* inspired narratives by Rousseau, Victor Hugo, and Alexandre Dumas, as well as Lord Byron's *The Prisoner of Chillon*. (Open 9am-6:15pm; April-June and Sept. 9am-5:45pm; Oct. daily 10am-4:45pm; Nov.-Feb. 10am-noon and 1:30-4pm; March 10am-noon and 1:30-4:45pm. 5SFr, students 4SFr.)

Montreux's **tourist office,** pl. du Débarcadère (tel. (021) 963 12 12, fax (021) 963 78 95), sits on the lake. Exit the train station onto av. des Alpes, cross the street, descend the steps to the right and walk about 300m to the left. (Open 9am-noon and 1:30-6pm.) There is also a branch office at the Gare Centrale with maps, guidebooks, and a friendly staff. The newly renovated, wheelchair-accessible **Auberge de Jeunesse Haut Lac (HI),** 8, passage de l'Auberge (tel. (021) 963 49 34), is a 25min. walk along the lake; or, take bus 1 "Villeneuve" to Territet Gare and follow the signs downhill. Due to its view of the lake, fantastic showers, and airy comforters, it's wise to make reservations at least a few days in advance. (Reception open 7-10am and 3-10pm. Curfew 11pm. 24.50SFr first night, then 22SFr, doubles 33.50SFr per person, then 31SFr. Breakfast included. Wheelchair access rooms 41SFr.) Despite its garish storefront façade, **Hôtel Elite-Garni,** 25 av. du Casino (tel. (021) 963 67 33), boasts a solid, old-time look. From the station, cross the street, make a left onto av. des Alpes, continue left to Place de la Paix, bearing left around the bend to av. du Casino. (Reception open all day. Singles 50-55SFr. Doubles 80-120SFr. 10SFr less in winter.) Nearby **Villeneuve** has luxurious lakeside camping at **Les Horizons Bleues** (tel. (021) 960 15 47). Take bus 1 to Villeneuve, then from the bus stop, follow the lake 5min. to the left. (Reception open 7am-noon and 3-8pm. 5.50SFr per person, 4-6SFr per tent. Open April 1-Sept. 30.)

Although a lakeside stroll with an ice-cream cone is affordable, lakeside dining certainly is not. The chic cafés lining the waterfront tend to set prices that match the posh country-club atmosphere. **Caveau des Vignerons,** 30bis, rue Industrielle, however serves *fondue* (16SFr) and *raclette* (5SFr), generally prepared for more than one person. (Open Mon.-Fri. 7am-midnight, Sat. 3:30pm-midnight.) Visit the **Marché de Montreux** every Friday from 7am-7pm at the place de Marché to sample fresh fruits, vegetables, meats, cheeses, breads, and pastries, or to pick up some second-hand clothing and antiques.

ITALIAN SWITZERLAND

The Italian-speaking canton of **Ticino** (Tessin in German) is renowned for its refreshing juxtaposition of Swiss efficiency and Italian *dolce vita.* The ring of Italian accents is not all that sets the region apart from Switzerland—the southern climate turns it into a Mediterranean garden. The emerald lakes, lush mountains, and vineyards that surround defiant stone houses render Ticino's countryside as romantic as Lugano and Locarno, its famed resorts. Although Italian is the official language, many residents also speak German, English, or French.

■■■ LUGANO

Switzerland's third-largest banking center hides from German Switzerland in the dramatic crevassed bay between San Salvatore and Monte Brè. Despite the novelty of Italian motifs in architecture and food, the city is ruthlessly Swiss. The 16th-century **Cathedral of San Lorenzo,** across the street and down the hill from the station, harbors beautifully carved statues and frescoes in its hidden alcoves. The **Museo Cantonale d'Art,** Via Canova 10, features 19th- and 20th-century Swiss and international works (open Tues. 2-5pm, Wed.-Sun. 10am-5pm; permanent collection 5SFr, students 3SFr; special exhibits 8SFr, students 3SFr). For a loftier view of the lake, take a car or ride the funicular to **Monte Brè,** with continuous service year round to the 3059-ft.-high summit. Hike up to the 933m summit for a magnificent view of the city below and the Alps beyond.

Practical Information, Accommodations, and Food Lugano's busy **tourist office,** Riva Giocondo Albertolli 5 (tel. (091) 21 46 64), finds rooms (3SFr fee) and provides general info (open Mon.-Fri. 9am-6:30pm, Sat. 9am-5pm; Oct.-June Mon.-Fri. 9am-6pm). To reach the office from the station, walk left on Piazzale della Stazione, turn right on Via San Gottardo, right on Via Paolo Regazzoni, and a left on Via Cattedrale to reach the Piazza Cioccaro (or take the funicular). From the Piazza, follow via Cattedrale, turn right on Pessina, left on Via del Pesci, then left on Riva Via Vela, which turns into Riva Giocondo Albertolli; the office is to the left. Frequent **trains** head from Lugano to Milan (30SFr), Zürich (58SFr), Berne (65SFr), and Locarno (round-trip 15SFr; change in Bellinzona).

Albergo per la Gioventú (HI), Crocifisso-Savosa (tel. (091) 56 27 28) is a short ride on bus 5 (catch it left of the train station and across the street) to Crocifisso, the 6th stop (backtrack a few steps and turn left on Via Cantovale). The hostel sprawls over a large plot of land featuring flowering gardens, a quiet neighborhood, and a swimming pool. (Reception open 6am-1pm and 3-10pm. Curfew 10pm. Dorms 14SFr, nonmembers 21SFr; singles 22-35SFr, doubles 36-36SFr. Kitchen facilities. Sheets 2SFr. Breakfast 6SFr. Reserve ahead. Open mid-March to Oct.) The **Hotel Pestalozzi,** Piazza Indipendenza 9 (tel. 22 95 95, fax 23 20 95) offers some singles and doubles without showers for reasonable prices (singles 48-67SFr, with shower 78-86SFr; doubles 90-117SFr, with shower 128-144SFr; breakfast included; reserve ahead). **Campers** must catch the Ferrovia Lugano-Ponte-Tresa (across from the train station) to **Agno** (every 20min., 3SFr), where five campgrounds such as **La Palma** (tel. (091) 59 25 61) and **Golfo del Sole** (tel. (091) 59 48 02) settle near the lake. (All cost 5.50-7SFr per person, 3-7SFr per tent, and are open April-Oct.)

Shop or dine at **Migros,** via Pretoria 15, in the town center (market open Mon.-Fri. 8am-6:30pm, Sat. 7:30am-5pm; restaurant open 9am-10pm). For rich Italian dishes, try **Ristorante Gamrinus,** Via Giacomo Luvini (tel. 23 19 55) where spaghetti and risotto are 16-20SFr, salads 10-18SFr, and crêpes 7SFr (open 11:30am-11pm).

■■■ LOCARNO

On the shores of Lago Maggiore, **Locarno** basks in Mediterranean breezes and Italian sun. For much of the interwar era, hopes for peace were symbolized by "the Spirit of Locarno"—a futile attempt in 1925 by England, France, and Italy to appease Germany after World War I. Above the city towers the brilliantly orange church, **Madonna del Sasso** (Madonna of the Rock), the town's landmark and symbol. The 15th-century *Madonna* itself is tucked away in the museum next to the cathedral. (Grounds open 7am-10pm; Nov.-Feb. 7am-9pm. Museum open Sun.-Fri. 10am-noon and 2-5pm. 3SFr, students 1.50SFr.)

To reach Locarno's **tourist office,** Largo Zorzi on Piazza Grande (tel. (093) 31 03 33), walk diagonally to the right from the train station for a block, through a pedestrian walkway, then cross the street on the left (open Mon.-Fri. 8am-7pm, Sat.-Sun. 9am-noon and 1-5pm; Nov.-Feb. Mon.-Fri. 8am-noon and 2-6pm). The friendly **Pensione Città Vecchia,** Via Torreta 13 (tel. (093) 31 45 54), is always full; make reservations weeks in advance (reception open 8am-10pm, singles 20SFr, sheets 4SFr, breakfast 4SFr). The **Albergo la Zingara,** Via delle Motta 8 (tel. and fax (093) 32 35 53), is bright, spacious, and impeccably clean; look for the huge, framed jigsaw puzzles on the walls (34SFr, with breakfast 40SFr; showers included). **Delta Camping** (tel. (093) 31 60 81) a 20min. walk along the lake from the tourist office, offers a sumptuous view of the lake (reception open mid-March to late Oct. 8am-noon and 2-9pm; 9SFr per person, 8-10SFr per tent; bungalows available). Locarno's **open-air market** takes over the Piazza Grande every other Thurs. (8am-1:30pm). The largest number of eateries are to be found near the waterfront, underneath the arcades bordering the Piazza Grande. **Casa de Popolo,** at the top of via della Motto on Piazza della Corporazione, specializes in pizza, fresh pasta, and *gelati,* with a lively clientele. (Entrees 13-15SFr. Open 7am-midnight.)

Turkey (Türkiye)

US$1   = 34483TL (lira, or TRL)   10000TL =   US$0.29
CDN$1 = 25686TL   10000TL = CDN$0.39
UK£1   = 54793TL   10000TL =   UK£0.18
IR£1   = 54275TL   10000TL =   IR£0.18
AUS$1 = 26428TL   10000TL = AUS$0.38
NZ$1   = 20907TL   10000TL =   NZ$0.48
SAR1   = 9672TL   10000TL =   SAR1.03
Country Code: 90   International Dialing Prefix: 00

All prices are quoted in U.S. dollars because rampant inflation in Turkey tends to correspond roughly with the devaluation of the lira.

Turkey has served as both a battleground and a canvas for Eastern and Western cultures and traditions. The iron-forging Hittites controlled Asia Minor in the second millennium BC, developed systems of government and law, and spoke one of the earliest known Indo-European languages. The Aegean coastal cities (Miletus, Ephesus, Pergamon, and Smyrna) enriched Greek culture as much as did Greece proper. Asia Minor became the cradle of the foundling religion of Christianity that ruled Europe for the next 1500 years. In the 11th century the region then shuddered with the advent of Seljuk Turk control.

Perhaps the greatest empire the world has ever known, the Ottomans ruled Turkey (and, at times, a large part of the Eastern Mediterranean) from the early 15th century to the end of World War I. The reign of Süleyman the Magnificent, from 1520 to 1566, marked the apex of the empire, after which point it declined into a stagnant morass of corruption. That modern Turkey exists at all is a tribute to early 20th-century leader Mustafa Kemal (Atatürk) who led the forces that expelled the British, French, Greek, and Russian armies. Equating modernization with westernization, Atatürk abolished the Ottoman Caliphate, romanized the alphabet, outlawed Muslim tribunals, and installed a facsimile of democratic government; for a time he went so far as to command *muezzin* (prayer callers) to sing in modern

■ TURKEY

Turkish, even though, according to Muhammed, the Qur'an is perfect, immutable, and untranslatable.

Atatürk's autocratic reforms, however, could go only so far. Beyond İstanbul and a few other large cities, traditional Islamic customs and attitudes prevailed. In the late 1970s, democracy began to falter as street warfare erupted in İstanbul, prompting military intervention. Elections in 1983 ushered in the centrist party of Turgut Özal, who died in 1993; in that year Tansu Çiller was elected Turkey's first female Prime Minister. In spring of 1994, Çiller turned the problem of Kurdish terrorism over to the military; traditionally heavy-handed, they began razing villages suspected of harboring rebel activity, and thousands of Kurdish villagers are now fleeing to the cities. Turkey was a crucial U.S. ally during the Cold War, but its current position has become more vague. Though the prospect of membership is fairly dim, Turkey will enter into free-trade relations with the European Union in 1996. Turkey is also seeking economic opportunity in the former Soviet republics of Kazakhstan, Tajikistan, and Uzbekistan.

Although some tourist destinations are becoming commercialized, Turkey is still an ideal budget travel destination, at least for men; the traditional, if unofficial, subordinate status of women in Turkey can lead to difficulties and even harassment for women traveling alone.

For more detailed coverage of Turkey, consult *Let's Go: Greece & Turkey.*

GETTING THERE

Bus travel is one of the cheapest methods of arriving in Turkey. Amsterdam, Athens, London and Munich are all centers for private bus lines providing long-distance tours. **Magic Bus** offers cheap, direct service to Europe's major cities. Offices are located at 20 Filellinon St., Syntagma, Athens (tel. (01) 323 74 71); and 32 Tsimiski St., Thessaloniki (tel. (031) 28 32 80). **London Student Travel,** 52 Grosvenor Gardens, London SW1W OAG (tel. (0171) 730 34 02) offers competitive rail, coach, and air fares all over the continent.

Trains to Turkey from Venice, Munich, and Vienna are relatively cheap. They are also inconvenient: Eurail is not valid in Turkey, and the Turkish rail system is rivaled only by the Greek as Europe's most antiquated and least efficient. Be sure to ask for a top bunk and wrap the straps of your luggage around your limbs when you sleep to deter thieves.

Reservations are recommended for many **ferries;** be warned that they run on very irregular schedules. You should check in at least two hours in advance. Make sure you bring along toilet paper and motion sickness medication. There is direct ferry service between Piraeus, Greece and İzmir, but it's cheaper to sail from one of the Greek islands. Three ferries per week also run between Pythagorion and Kuşadası. You can also travel to Turkey by boat from points other than Greece, including Bríndisi, Italy. Be prepared for the Turkish port tax—usually around US$10. If you travel to Greece on a charter flight, you may not be allowed to enter Turkey; check with the travel agent for the specifics.

Turkish Airlines (THY) fares are exorbitant, but a 60% student reduction brings them in line with the budget carriers. THY also has regular service to Turkey from European countries and offers 50% discounts to ISIC holders and those under 22 on some international flights. If you have flown to Greece on certain European charter flights, you are required to stay in Greece for your vacation (in other words, you can't take advantage of cheap fares to Greece in order to visit Turkey). Both **Romanian Airlines (Tarom)** and **Pakistan Air** offer low fares to İstanbul from the U.S. and major European cities.

Many travelers cross Turkey on the way to other Asian countries. Most buses to the east depart directly from Ankara, though some leave from Urfa or Antakya. Transit visas for Syria are easier to obtain than for Iran; Iraq seems a less likely bet. Reaching the former USSR from Turkey is a definite possibility; check locally or with the Russian embassy in Ankara.

TURKEY

GETTING AROUND

Turkey is a budget traveler's dream. Frequent and cheap **buses** run between all sizeable cities. Private bus lines sometimes offer students a 10% discount (flash the ol' ISIC). **Varan Tours** buses, though slightly more expensive, are faster and more comfortable for longer trips (they're air-conditioned). In Anatolia and Eastern Turkey, **Ulusoy** and **METRO Tour** also provide upscale bus transportation. The trade-off for inexpensive **trains** (10% student discount) is the long rides. Also, trains do not run along the western coast. **Shared taxis,** known as *dolmuş,* usually minibuses or vans, fill gaps left by the remarkably comprehensive bus system and also follow fixed routes. They are almost as cheap as buses and leave whenever they fill up *(dolma* means "stuffed"). You can get on and off *dolmuş* whenever you like. **Hitchhiking** in Turkey is quite common, however drivers have been known to ask 50-100% of the equivalent bus fare. The hitching signal is a waving hand.

Those wishing to avoid Turkey's eternal bus and train rides should consider the low domestic fares on **Turkish Airlines;** the student (ages 12-24—bring ID) rate is usually US$42. There is no **ferry** system along the west coast except for a **Turkish Maritime Line** boat from İstanbul to İzmir (3 per week; 1 per week Oct.-June).

TURKEY ESSENTIALS

Turkish government tourist offices and tourist police exist in most major cities and resort areas. Some English, German or French is usually spoken. They help find accommodations and often provide the usual slew of services without charge. In places without an official office, travel agents often serve the same function.

The black market exchange rate in Turkey is only slightly better than the official rate. If you're coming from Greece, spend your *drachmae* before arriving; the few banks that change them do so at an egregious rate. Persistent haggling in shops, over accommodations, and over less regulated transportation fares can save you loads of money. Examine what you buy at bazaars carefully; exporting antiques is a jailable offense, even if you plead ignorance. *If you're caught doing drugs in Turkey, you're screwed.* The horror stories of lengthy prison sentences and dealer-informers are true; embassies are absolutely helpless in all cases. The minimum sentence for possession of even the smallest amount is 16 months. Turkish law also provides for "guilt by association"—those in the company of a person caught are subject to prosecution. As for the foolish notion of smuggling: anyone looking remotely like a backpacker gets searched with a fine-toothed comb arriving back in Europe from Turkey. If you still don't believe us, watch *Midnight Express* for some more detailed depictions of Turkish prisons.

Everything closes on the national **holidays:** January 1, April 23, May 19, August 30 and October 28-29. During Ramadan *(Ramazan* in Turkish; Feb. 1 to March 4 in 1995), pious Muslims will not eat, drink, smoke, or travel between dawn and sunset. Outside İstanbul, Ankara and the coastal resort towns, things really slow down. Hotel rooms are more available during this period, even at resorts. Large celebrations mark Ramadan's conclusion, known as *Bayram;* bus and train tickets or hotel rooms are scarce. During *Kurban Bayram* (the Festival of Sacrifice; May 21-31, 1995), similar chaos ensues. On the first day of the celebration, each family is expected to slaughter a sheep; vegetarians may want to stay indoors.

Museums, archaeological sites, and monuments are generally open from 9am to 5pm; many close on Monday. **Shops** in Turkey are generally open Monday through Saturday from 9am to 1pm and 2 to 7pm. **Government offices** are open Monday through Friday from 8:30am to 12:30pm and 1:30 to 5:30pm. **Banks** are open Monday through Friday from 8:30am to noon and 1:30 to 5pm. In resort town hours are often longer, with the exception of banks, whose only concession is occasional Saturday hours. **Food stores,** bazaars, and **pharmacies** *(eczane)* tend to have longer hours. Despite Turkey's enormity, the entire country lies within the same **time zone**—3 hours ahead of British Standard Time in summer, 2 ahead in winter (Turkey does not observe daylight savings time).

Communication It's rarely a problem finding English-speakers in well-touristed areas. Off the beaten track, sign language and a pocket dictionary usually suffice. German is useful. A few phrases should help smooth the way: *teşekkür* (teh-shehk-KEUR; "thanks"); *...nerede?* (NE-reh-deh; "where is...?"); *Kaç para?* (KACH pah-rah; "How much is it?"); *...istiyorum* (ees-tee-YOH-room; "I want..."); and *anla-madım* (ahn-LA-mah-dim; "I don't understand"). Remember that in Turkey a raise of the chin, sometimes accompanied by a clicking noise made with the tongue, means "no," and putting your palm flat on your chest is a polite way of refusing an offer (the Turks seem to be an inexhaustible fountain of offerings, especially tea).

Turkey has a surprisingly good phone system. Make international calls at post offices, or buy a phone card *(telekart)*. Costs are upwards of US$12 for 3 minutes to North America. Make **collect calls** from a post office and expect 2-hour delays. Callers to the **US** can dial 00 800 122 77 for a **AT&T** operator; for **MCI,** dial 00 800 111 77; for **Sprint,** dial 00 800 144 77. To call **Britain,** dial 00 800 44 11 77; **Ireland,** 00 800 353 11 77; **Australia,** 00 800 61 11 77; **Canada,** 00 800 166 77. To make **collect calls to Europe** dial (9) 9800 144 77. Calling card calls have been known to be terminated after just a few minutes for no apparent reason. **Post offices (PTTs)** are typically open from 8:30am to noon and 1 to 5:30pm; offices in resort towns and central post offices in larger towns keep longer hours. **Poste Restante** should be addressed *Merkez Postanesi.* Mail to or from North America can take anywhere from 10 to 17 days.

Health, Safety, and Climate Toiletries are cheap and readily available in Turkey. Tampons are somewhat uncommon in the east and in small towns, though, and you should always carry toilet paper; expect to encounter quite a number of pit toilets. There are rumors that some of eastern Turkey's feisty mosquitoes carry malaria; to be on the safe side, start a course of anti-malaria pills before you go. Ask your doctor about typhoid, gamma-globulin and tetanus shots. Where the tap water is safe (primarily in the larger cities), it is so chlorinated that for both your taste buds and your health you should buy bottled water. Many tourists' digestive systems find fending off the microscopic fiends in Turkish food quite a task, especially in eastern Turkey. Avoid ground beef and any sort of uncooked meat. Should you succumb to diarrhea, two or three days' rest, dry toast, and oceans of liquid should help you recover. If it persists, see a doctor.

Women traveling in Turkey may have a less pleasant experience than men. In Anatolia and eastern Turkey, most Turkish women are in *purdah* (wear scarves over their hair) and rarely make public appearances; foreign women will be stared at often and approached frequently. When not in heavily touristed areas, women should dress conservatively (always wear a bra and avoid short shorts and tank tops) to avoid verbal and physical harassment. If you feel threatened, visible and audible anger—particularly in public—can be an effective deterrent. Better yet, say you're going to the cops; Turks fear the police, who, in these situations, almost always side with foreigners. Your best bet is to not travel alone in most parts of Turkey.

Turkey is a large country whose climate varies quite a bit. In summer, the Aegean and Mediterranean coasts are hot, with average temperatures around 32°C. Mosquitoes are a problem in some resort towns, so bring repellent. The swimming season from Bodrum south and all along the Mediterranean coast lasts from early May through October. On the Black Sea coast (İstanbul included), the swimming season is shorter (June-early Sept.), and fall brings considerable rainfall; winters are mild and wet. As you move inland, the climate becomes more extreme; the area around Urfa is regularly above 40°C in summer, while the area north of Van is kept relatively cool by its high altitude. In winter, Urfa is quite temperate while most of central and eastern Anatolia is bitter cold and snowy.

Accommodations, Camping, and Food A night's budget accommodation averages US$3-7 per person on the Aegean coast, US$2.50-6 along the Mediterranean and US$1.50-4 in the east. Make sure your hotel has water before paying. If you're traveling in winter, check for heating. Don't expect toilet paper or towels in low-budget hotels. Most Turkish towns have a *hamam,* or bathhouse, where you can get a wonderful steam bath for under US$2. *Hamamlar* schedule different times for men and women. It is not wise to use the *hamam* if traveling alone. **Camping** is popular in Turkey, and cheap campgrounds abound (usually US$1.50 per person), although many official ones still aren't registered with the Ministry of Culture and Tourism. Official government campsites are typically open from April or May through October. Freelance camping is illegal, but not unheard-of.

Restaurants are called *lokanta.* There are always numerous stands selling *şiş kebap* (skewered chunks of lamb) or *döner kebap* (slices cut from a leg of lamb roasting on a spit). In restaurants, it's customary to go to the kitchen yourself and choose after seeing everything. Staple dishes include the tomato *çorbası* (soups) and different varieties of *pilav* (rice). *Meze* refers to appetizer plates, which include *pilaki* (navy beans in a tomato sauce, often with meat), *patlican kızartması* (fried eggplant), and *dolma* (stuffed vegetables served hot or cold and usually filled with meat, rice, onions, and herbs). Salads, widely available, include *çoban salatası* (cucumber and tomato salad) and *karışık salata* (mixed salad). Turkish yogurt and *zeytin* (olives) are terrific. *Lahmacun,* a distant relative of pizza, is flat bread served with your choice of eggs, meat, tomatoes, cheese or spices. Or, try *köfte* (spicy meatballs). If you want to avoid meat, tell the cook or waiter *"et yok"* (without flesh). Travel lore and Turkish public health authorities have it that *ayran,* a popular yogurt and water drink, helps your body combat the summer heat. Beer is called *bira; Efes Pilsen* and *Tuborg* are the most popular brands. The best domestic white wines are *Çankaya, Villa Doluca,* and *Kavaklıdere.* The best red wines are Yakut and Kavaklıdere. The cheapest wines are *Guzel Marmara* (found only in the İstanbul area) and *Buzbağı,* both with fragrant plastic corks. *Rakı,* an anise-flavored spirit, is the powerful national liquor and stronger cousin of *ouzo.*

■■■ İSTANBUL

İstanbul is a feast for the senses. Calls to prayer resonate from grand mosques as the scent of corn wafts from streetside grills. Merchants sell drill bits and silver kettles on twisting streets that lead wanderers to subterranean teahouses. İstanbul's unbridled capitalism assaults you with every step you take, but the glorious remnants of the Byzantine and Ottoman empires preside over today's dynamic, lurching circus.

ORIENTATION AND PRACTICAL INFORMATION

İstanbul is the only city built on two continents: Asia and Europe. Waterways divide the city into three sections. The **Bosphorus Strait** (Boğaziçi) separates Asia Minor from Europe, distinguishing Asian İstanbul from European İstanbul. The Asian side is mostly residential. Almost all historical sites and markets are situated on the southern bank of the **Golden Horn,** an estuary that splits the European half of the city. Budget travelers converge in **Sultanahmet,** the area around the Aya Sofya. The city's main boulevard—leading west from Sultanahmet toward the university, the Grand Bazaar and Aksaray—changes its name from Divan Yolu to Yeniçeriler Cad. to Ordu Cad. Shoppers cram themselves into the district between the **Grand Bazaar,** east of the university just north of Yeniçeriler Cad., and the less touristy **Egyptian Bazaar,** just southeast of Eminönü. The **Kumkapı** district, south of the university and Yeniçeriler Cad., makes navigation a challenge. The tourist office will provide you with a free map; as long as you remain near landmarks you won't get lost.

Don't exchange money with random people on the street—they're most likely passing off counterfeits. Make sure that taxi drivers restart their meters when you get in (night rates midnight-6am). Most areas of İstanbul are relatively safe, but after sunset avoid the **Galata** tower and the back streets of **Beyoğlu,** the area north of İstiklâl Cad. Women are often targets of harassment on the streets of İstanbul, and while not necessarily "unsafe," getting around alone can be unpleasant.

TURKEY

Tourist Information Offices: In **Sultanahmet,** Divan Yolu 3 (tel. 518 18 02), at the northern end of the **Hippodrome,** across from the Sultan Pub. Open 9am-5pm. In **Taksim,** in the Hilton Hotel Arcade (tel. 233 05 92), open Mon.-Sat. 9am-5pm, and near the French Consulate (tel. 245 68 76), same hours. In the **Karaköy Maritime Station** (tel. 249 57 76), open 9am-5pm. In the **Sirkeci Train Station** (tel. 511 58 88), open Mon.-Sat. 8:30am-5:30pm. In the Airport (tel. 663 07 93 or 663 67 38), open 24hrs. Tourist offices supply superb country and city maps.

Budget Travel Offices: Best of the bunch is **Gençtur,** Yerebatan Cad. 15, 2nd floor (tel. 520 52 74 or 520 52 75), right in the center of Sultanahmet. Sells ISICs, youth ID cards, distributes free maps, and provides a Poste Restante service (free; holds mail for 1 yr.). Open Mon.-Fri. 9am-5:30pm, Sat. 9am-1pm.

Consulates: U.S., Meşrutiyet Cad. 104/106, Tepebaşı (tel. 251 36 02). **Canada,** 107 Büyükdere Cad., Gayrettepe (tel. 272 51 74). **U.K.,** N. Meşrutiyet Cad. 34 (tel. 293 75 45 or 252 64 36). **Ireland,** Cumhuriyet Cad. Mobil 6, Pegasus Ezi, Elmadağ (tel. 246 60 25). **Australia,** Tepecik Yolu 58, Etiler (tel. 257 70 50). **New Zealand** nationals should get in touch with the embassy in Ankara. **Bulgaria,** Zincirlikuyu Cad. 44, Levent (tel. 269 04 78 or 269 22 16). **Greece,** 32 Turnacıbaşı, Galatasaray (tel. 245 05 96). Consulates issue visas 10am-noon.

Currency Exchange: Banks' exchange counters open Mon.-Fri. 8:30am-noon and 1:30-5pm. Most don't charge a commission. The exchange booths at the **Yeşilköy Airport** and the **main post office** are open 24hrs. The exchange booth at the **Sirkeci train station** is open 8am-9pm, but accepts only cash. The best rates are given by private exchange companies; they will also change *lira* back into dollars without any questions. **Çetin Döviz Hizmetleri,** İstiklâl Cad. 39 (tel. 252 64 28 or 29) at the Taksim end of İstiklâl Cad. facing the French Cultural Center, does not charge a commission. Open 8am-7:30pm. Remember to keep your receipts; some banks will not change *lira* back into dollars even with a receipt (see Turkey Essentials). Often, the Central Bank has the best rate.

American Express: Türk Express, Cumhuriyet Cad. 91, 2nd floor (tel. 241 02 48), up the hill from Taksim Sq., handles business related to American Express, including lost AmEx checks and credit cards. Open Mon.-Fri. 8:30am-noon and 1-5:30pm.

Post Office (PTT): Main branch at Büyük Postane Sok. 25, 2 blocks southwest of Sirkeci train station. Stamp, telephone and currency exchange, and telegram services 24hrs. Crowded around midday. All PTTs accept packages.

Telephones: International calls can be made at payphones in the Taksim and Central PTTs. Look for the yellow phones marked *Uluslararası* or *Milletlerarası.* To use the AT&T or MCI access number to make a calling card call, deposit a small (US$0.20) or medium (US$0.40) token into a pay phone. **City Code:** 212 and 216.

Flights: Atatürk Airport (tel. 573 04 33) has one terminal for domestic flights and one for international flights, 5km apart and connected by regular bus service. Both terminals are 30min. from downtown. **Türk Hava Yolları** ("THY," or Turkish Airlines; tel. 248 26 31) offers a sizeable reduction to ISIC holders on domestic flights. **Pakistan Air** and **Romanian Air** usually sell the cheapest tickets to and from Europe, though service can be very spotty.

Trains: Europe-bound trains leave from **Sirkeci Station** (tel. 527 00 51) in Eminönü. To Sofia (US$36), Athens (US$46), and Munich (US$130). 10% student discounts for those under 27. **Haydarpaşa Station**, on the Asian side (tel. 348 80 20). Ferries between the station and Karaköy pier #7 run every 30min. (US$0.50, schedule posted on the pier).

Buses: As of November 1994, all buses should leave from the new **Esenler Otobüs Terminalı** (tel. 658 10 10 or 658 00 36). Depending on the progress of the extension of the tram line, you might be able to take it all the way there from Sultanahmet, or you might have to get off at Aksaray (6 stops) and port your stuff about 10min. up Adnan Menderes Bulvarı where you can take the metro right through the center of the terminal. All bus companies should have offices at **Esenler,** and most have offices in Sultanahmet. Only **Varan Tours** (tel. 251 74 74 or 244 84 57) is licensed to operate throughout Western Europe. **Derya Turizm** is also licensed for Greece. Another major bus-line is **Ulusoy** (tel. 251 70 00); **Kamil**

İstanbul City Overview

660 yards
600 meters
0

Bosphorus Strait

TO HAYDARPAŞA RAILWAY STATION

TO YALOVA

Dolmabahçe Cad.

TO BOSPHORUS

Atatürk Kültür Sarayı (Opera House)

Meşe Cad.

İnönü Cad.

Cumhuriyet Cad.

KABATAŞ

TAKSIM

Tarlabaşı Cad.

GALATASARAY

İstiklal Cad.

Mebusan Cad.

TOPHANE

BEYOĞLU

TÜNEL

İstasyon Cad.

Refik Saydam Cad.

Bahriye Cad.

SİŞHANE

Evliya Çelebi Cad.

Kemeraltı Cad.

Yüksek Kaldırım

KARAKÖY

Galata Tower

THY Air Terminal

Gülhane Parkı

Topkapı Palace

Sirkeci Cad.

Galata Br.

New Br.

Tersane Cad.

Atatürk Br.

Ankara Cad.

Sirkeci Station

Hamidiye Cad.

EMİNÖNÜ

SULTANAHMET

Hilaliahmer Cad.

Divan Yolu

Cankurtaran Station

Golden Horn

UNKAPANI

Atatürk Bulvarı

Süleymaniye Camii

İstanbul University

Kapalı Çarşı

Yeniçeriler Cad.

Kumkapı Station

Abdülezel Paşa Cad.

Süleymaniye Cad.

Şenzadebaşı Cad.

Ordu Cad.

LÂLELI

Kennedy Cad.

Demirhisar Cad.

Fethiye Camii

FENER

Draman Cad.

Selimiye Camii

BALAT

Yavuz Selim Cad.

Fatih Camii

Valens Aquaduct

AKSARAY

Mustafa Kemal Cad.

Namık Kemal Cad.

Yenikapı Station

Sea of Marmara

Tekfur Camii

Kariye Camii

Fevzi Paşa Cad.

Keçeciler Cad.

Akkemiz Cad.

Şehzadebaşı Cad.

EDİRNEKAPI

Vatan Cad.

Millet Cad.

Turlı Baruthane Cad.

Oğuzhan Cad.

Hekimoğlu Ali Paşa Cad.

Koca Mustafa Paşa Cad.

TOPKAPI

Rami-Edirnekapı Cad.

Yeni Çevre Yolu

BAYRAMPAŞA

Topkapı-Edirnekapı Cad.

Old Topkapı Bus Station

TO AIRPORT

TO AIRPORT

N

TURKEY

Koç, Pamukkale, and **Çanakkale Seyahat,** are good too. Beware: unlicensed companies offering substantial discounts for Western European destinations and then abandoning their passengers in Eastern Europe. Agencies downtown are clustered on Hüdavendigâr Cad., behind the Sirkeci Railway Station and on İzmir Cad., off Ordu Cad. to the left just before the Aksaray intersection. Frequent buses to Ankara (8hr., US$7-20), Bursa (4hr., US$4-8.50), İzmir (9hr., US$11-22), and Bodrum (13hr., US$15-30).

Ferries: Turkish Maritime Lines, on the waterfront at Karaköy (tel. 244 02 07), just west of the Haydarpaşa ferry terminal—it's the building with blue awnings marked "Denizcilik İşletmeleri." Ferries to İzmir and Trabzon, and points between (US$15-20, meals US$4 extra). For longer trips, reserve well ahead. Local ferries to Kadıköy and Haydarpaşa from Karaköy (US$0.50); the Princes' Islands and the Black Sea (on the Bosporus tour) from Eminönü (round-trip to the islands US$2, Bosporus tour US$6), and Yalova from Kabataş (2½hr.). Faster but more expensive seabuses run to Yalova from Kabataş (1hr., US$6), the Princes' Islands (10 per day, 20min., round-trip US$6) and Bostancı from Karaköy (20min., US$1.50).

Bookstore: Aypa Bookstore, Mimar Mehmet Ağa Cad. 19 (tel. 517 44 92), accepts Visa and MasterCard. Open 7am-8pm.

Laundromat: Hobby Laundry, Caferiye Sok. 6/1, part of Yücelt Hostel building. 1kg wash and dry US$1.50. Open 9am-8pm.

Hospitals: American Hospital, Admiral Bristol Hastanesi, Nişantaşı, Güzelbahçe Sok. (tel. 231 40 50). **German Hospital,** Sıraselviler Cad., Taksim (tel. 243 81 00). The German Hospital is more convenient to Sultanahmet.

Emergencies: Police: tel. 266 66 66. Some speak English. **Tourist Police:** in Sultanahmet, at the beginning of Yerebatan Cad. behind the obelisk in the park across from the information office (24hr. hotline 527 45 03 or 528 53 69). Open 9am-6pm.

ACCOMMODATIONS AND CAMPING

İstanbul's budget accommodations are concentrated in the **Sultanahmet** district. Despite the area's mesmeric setting, İstanbul's Turkish aura is diluted here by droves of backpackers. Prices in Sultanahmet range from US$2.15 for a rooftop to US$20 for a single. Rates go up in July and August. If you're willing to spend a little more, look at third- and fourth-class hotels in the adjacent **Aksaray** district.

Hanedan Hostel, Akbıyık Cad., Adliye Sok. 3 (tel. 516 48 69). Friendly, caring management, 24hr. showers, no curfew, and freshly painted. Pleasant view from terrace. High season prices: dormitory US$4 per person, roof US$2, doubles (some with shower) US$6-8 per person. Breakfast US$1.

Yusuf Guest House, Kutlugün Sok. 3 (tel. 516 68 78), across from the Old Prison, farther towards the Topkapı Palace. Very clean, quiet rooms and knowledgeable, young management in a pink building. Roof (open or covered) US$3. Dorm beds US$5. Doubles US$7 per person. Breakfast US$1. Reservations suggested.

Orient Youth Hostel, Akbıyık Cad. 13 (tel. 517 94 93), near Topkapı Palace. Clean, comfortable, has a cool roof terrace with a small cafeteria. Free belly-dancing every week during the summer, every 2 weeks during winter. Roof US$2, beds in dormitory US$3. Doubles (some with balcony) US$4 per person. Breakfast US$1. Laundry and **Backpacker's Underground Café** across the street.

Hotel Ema, Salkım Söğüt Sok. 18 (tel. 511 71 66). Clean, well-kept rooms, management speaks English and French. Rooms without private baths are also available for US$2 less. Singles US$10. Vast doubles US$15, with private bath. Triples with bath US$20. Breakfast included. *Jeton* phone inside.

Ottoman Guest House, Tevkifhane Sok. 6 (tel. 517 69 09). Take Tevkifhane Sok. across the little park between Aya Sofya and the Blue Mosque. Comfortable, very clean, with a café-bar on the terrace. Doubles with shared bathroom US$15. You can also watch the sound and light show (see Sights, below) from here.

Yücelt Hostel, 6 Caferiye Cad (tel. 513 61 50 or 513 61 51, fax 512 76 28), on the street left of Aya Sofya when you face the gate of the mosque. A great place to meet travelers. Attached cafeteria, with an impressively loud stereo. Dorms

US$4.50 5.50. Doubles US$6.50 per person. Showers included. Reservations recommended in summer. Luggage room and safe on premises. Laundry next door.
Camping: Londra Mocamp (tel. 560 42 00), 1km from the airport, along the noisy and nerve-grating highway to İstanbul. The bus does not stop here; take a taxi. Facilities include cafeteria, bar, pool, and showers. US$2.30 per person, US$1 per tent. 2-person bungalows US$15. Much more pleasant are **Ataköy Mokamp** (tel. 539 60 14 or 539 60 00) and **Yeşilyurt Kamping** (tel. 574 42 30), on Sahil Yolu near the villages. 2 people and a tent US$7.50.

FOOD

If you like eating, you'll love İstanbul. You can count on high quality, kaleidoscopic variety and reasonable prices. The premier eating locales are the **Kumkapı** district, south of the Grand Bazaar, the **Sirkeci** district near the train station and the **Tepebaşı** quarter, near the British consulate. For a quick stand-up lunch, the numerous *kebapçı* or *köfteci* will easily fill you up for less than US$3. For a little more, you can order grilled seafood in the towns of **Sarıyer** or **Rumeli Kavağı**, both a scenic bus (25 from Eminönü) or ferry ride north along the Bosporus. Also try **open-air fruit markets.** Two markets are centrally located: one next to Çiçek Pasajı, in Beyoğlu, and another next to the Mısır Çarşısı (Egyptian Bazaar), near the New Mosque and Eminönü.

Pudding Shop, Divan Yolu 6 (tel. 522 29 70). Known as "the beginning of the hippie trail," from which 1960s wayfarers journeyed east towards Nepal, Oz, and beyond. The hippy allure is gone; now the place seems more like a cafeteria. Full meal US$3.50. Open 7am-11pm.
Hacı Salih, Anadolu Psajı 201, İstiklal Cad. (tel. 243 45 28). Abdullah's parent restaurant, serves great authentic Turkish lunches. Open noon-5pm.
Backpacker's Underground Café, Akbıyık Cad. 14/1, across from Orient Youth Hostel. Home for the alternative crew; owner plays what his patrons (mostly New Zealanders) like to hear. Fish 'n' chips US$1.30. Open 7am-midnight.
Doy-Doy, Şifa Örücüler Sok. 13 (tel. 517 15 88). From the Hippodrome turn left on the second street behind the Blue Mosque. Fast, hot soup with all the bread you want. With *elmalı çay* (apple tea), US$0.50. Breakfast, lunch, and dinner.
Hacı Abdullah, Sakızağcı Cad. 19 (tel. 244 85 61). From İstiklâl Cad. take a right from the Ağacamii (it's surrounded by a big stucco wall). Ask for the special of the day, and don't miss the marinated artichokes in June (US$2). Full meals about US$8. A/C. English menu. Open 11am-11pm.

SIGHTS

Built in 537 by the Emperor Justinian, **Ayasofya** is among the world's most inspiring churches. Constantinople's cathedral for 900 years, it then served as İstanbul's mosque after the Ottoman conquest in 1453. In 1935, Atatürk neutralized it into a museum. The enormous dome was the largest in the world until the construction of St. Peter's in Rome. The grand galleries upstairs display supreme mosaics. (Open Tues.-Sun. 9:30am-5pm; Sept.-June only to 4:30pm. Gallery open Tues.-Sun. 9:30am-noon and 1-4:30pm. US$2, with ISIC US$1.)

Sultan Ahmet I built the **Sultanahmet Camii** (the Blue Mosque) opposite the Ayasofya in a brazen attempt to one-up Justinian. The mosque's silhouette is unforgettable, and stunning, deep blue İznik tiles line the interior. English-speaking Turks often loiter around the entrance during the day, eager to give potentially instructive freelance tours. Agree on the fee beforehand: US$4 for up to 4 people is reasonable. (Mosque open to visitors 9am-5pm, except during prayers. Modest dress required.) To the northwest are the ancient **Hippodrome**, where Byzantine emperors once presided over chariot races and circuses and the 16th-century **İbrahim Paşa Palace**, which beautifully exhibits a collection of Turkish and Islamic art (palace open Tues.-Sun. 10am-5pm; Tues.-Fri. US$2, Sat.-Sun. US$1).

From the mid-15th to the mid-19th centuries, the **Topkapı Sarayı** (Topkapı Palace) was the nerve center of the Ottoman Empire. You can while away a whole afternoon among the exhibits of gold, diamonds, jade, emeralds, ornate miniatures, and fine Oriental porcelain. Take a guided tour of the **Harem** (Wed.-Mon., 3 per day, US$2); it's best to arrive early. The **Circumcision chamber** is exquisitely decorated with blue İznik tiles. According to Turkish tradition, males were circumcised not at birth, but after they had come of age. (Palace open Wed.-Mon. 9:30am-5pm. US$2.) Outside the palace sits **Gülhane Park,** which has a zoo, concession stands and Turkish music playing over loudspeakers. Locals come here to relax, so it's a good place to get away from other tourists.

West along Divan Yolu, the enormous **Grand Bazaar** (Kapalı Çarşı) is probably a better place for visiting than buying. Be prepared to get lost. Hawkers prey on tourists and fake or faulty merchandise is ubiquitous. The summer tourist invasion inflates prices as much as 300-400%. Beware of shoddy imitations of Persian carpets. Few Turks are naïve enough to buy anything here—follow their example.

A full day of the Old City may leave you slightly disoriented. Luckily, the area north of the Golden Horn on the European side is comparatively soothing. The 62m-high **Galata Tower,** built by the Emperor Justinian in 528 AD and rebuilt in 1348 by the Genoese as a low-tech spy satellite for observing the old city, still serves its purpose today. The view mustn't be missed. (Open 9am-6pm. US$1.) Right along the Bosphorus, **Dolmabahçe Palace** was the home of sultans from 1856 until the demise of the Ottoman Empire after World War I. Goose-stepping soldiers guard the royal dock and the memory of Atatürk, who died in the palace at 9:05am (all the clocks were halted at that moment). The chi-chi pseudo-French architecture is testament to the sultans' eclectic pretensions during the decline of their empire, but remains impressive in its vast scale. Be sure to see the collection of imperial treasures, including the famous Spoonmaker's Diamond and an emerald the size of a cabbage. (Open Tues.-Sun. 9:30am-4pm. US$5.) To get to Dolmabahçe from Sultanahmet, take the tram to Eminönü, or walk. From Eminönü, take bus 2 or 25E5. The number of visitors per day is limited, so go early.

After an extended day of sight-seeing, a **cruise** along the **Bosphorus** may revive you. Boats leave from pier #3 in Eminönü at 10:30am and 1:30pm in the winter, and 5 times per day in the summer, and return from the Black Sea in the evening (US$3.50). When the ferry makes its final stop on the Asian side, disembark and treat yourself to fish *kebap*, mussels, or fried *kalamari* for US$2-4 from the street vendors.

ENTERTAINMENT

Interestingly, İstanbul shuts down early—few places are open after midnight. Nocturnal creatures congregate in the restaurants and bars at the foot of Divan Yolu Cad. The **Café Bodrum,** just off Divan Yolu across from the tourist office, draws a large crowd. (Open 7:30pm-midnight. Beer US$1.) Trek up to the **Çiçek Pasajı** (see Food, above) to enjoy an evening of piquant food, potent drink, and traditional Turkish music. *Rakı*, a licorice-flavored spirit nicknamed "Lion's Milk," gushes freely in the many taverns of the "Flower Passage." A few musicians and one or two gypsy dancers often perform in the courtyard. Alternatively, venture to Lâleli or Beyazıt and spend the evening at a Turkish tea house. **Ali Paşa's Bazaar,** a 16th century courtyard near the entrance to the Grand Bazaar on Divan Yolu Cad., is a great place to slurp Turkish tea, meet some locals, and smoke a *nargile* (water pipe).

Whatever you've heard about the straight or gay **nightclubs** off İstiklâl Cad., north of the Horn, definitely avoid going. Most will vacuum you clean out of money with a twist of a swizzle stick. This area is also a popular hangout for thieves. The nightclubs north of Taksim Square along Cumhuriyet Cad. are a bit more respectable, but the choking price of your first drink may make you regret not having stayed at home. If you must swing in İstanbul, try **Hayal Bar,** near the Taksim side of İstiklâl Cad., on Büyükparmakkapı Sok. (drinks US$2-3). **Café Gramafon,** 3 Beyoğlu, charges a US$3 cover and serves US$1.50 beers, closing anywhere from 1am to 3am, depending on the day and the mood of the crowd. If you want to hang out where young Turks do, explore the **Ortaköy** area. (Bus 22E, 22B or 25 from

Eminönü). **Belly-dancing** may sound tantalizing, until you realize how much it costs. Inquire at the tourist office if you're still interested—locations change frequently. On Saturdays and Sundays craftspeople display their works on the sidewalks along the cobblestone streets. Sorry, no booze by the water, but you can get beer on the side streets as well as on the main strip, **Muallim Naci Cad.** (where the bus lets you off), for US$1, along with US$0.25 ice cream cones.

The **İstanbul Festival,** an international festival in its 21st year, unfurls with a flourish in June and July. In the past, performers have ranged from Konya's Whirling Dervishes to Joan Baez. Ask at the tourist office or call 260 45 33 or 260 90 72 for more information. The free **Sound and Light Show** at the Blue Mosque is corny, but offers a gasp-producing view of İstanbul's illuminated minarets and domes. (May-Sept. at 9pm. In English every 4th night. Schedule posted at tourist office.)

■ PRINCES' ISLES AND EDIRNE

Ferries to the **Princes' Isles** leave from Eminönü or Kabataş on the northern side (from Eminönü departures every hr., 7-11am; every 2hr., 2-10pm, US$3). The ferry stops at four of the nine islands of this careless archipelago. Some people prefer the quieter atmospheres of **Burgazada** and **Heybeliada,** but **Büyükada,** the largest and most picturesque of the islands, offers the best swimming (at Yörükalı beach) in the İstanbul area (and this, sadly, is not all that great). In Heybeliada, take a horse-carriage to Deçirmen for a picnic (fix the price beforehand).

Though an easy *dolmuş* from both the Greek and Bulgarian borders, **Edirne** is in many ways the consummate Turkish city, home to some of the finest Ottoman architecture, authentic Turkish baths and, recently, hordes of Romanians and Bulgarians on shopping sprees. Buses depart to İstanbul (3hr., US$4.50) and Bursa (US$10). The **tourist office,** Talatpaşa Cad. 17 (tel. (284) 225 15 18), about 200m west of the Eski Cami, is helpful (open 8:30am-6:30pm; Sept.-May Mon.-Sat. 8:30am-5pm). The **Konak Hotel,** Maarif Cad. 6 (tel. (284) 225 13 48), is a beautiful old wooden house built in the 1870s. (Singles US$2.50. Doubles US$2 per person. Triples US$1.85 per person. Hot baths US$1.) **Hotel Efe,** Maarif Cad. 13 (tel. (284) 213 61 66), has modern plumbing and MTV (Singles US$11. Doubles US$16. Triples US$23. Breakfast included.) Amenities at **Fifi Camping,** E5 İstanbul Çıkışı (tel. 235 79 68), include a swimming pool and a free bus service to town. Take a *dolmuş* (US$0.50) from the bus station, and ask to be let off at the campsite. (Site rental US$2, tent rental US$2, parking US$2. Student discount available.) Need a bath? Try 16th-century **Sokullu Hamamı,** beside Üçşerefeli Cami. You can see the minarets from the tourist office. (Open 6am-midnight for men, 9am-8pm for women; US$2.25, with massage US$4, but bargain.)

On the second or third weekend in June, Edirne hosts the annual **Kırkpınar Wrestling Tournament,** in which young, brawny men grease up and grapple. Check for the exact dates at any tourist office. Tickets can be purchased in Edirne at the **Belediye** (town hall), across from the Eski Cami, or at the Sarayiçi stadium north of the town's center, where the events are held. (Tickets for Fri. preliminaries free, Sat. US$3.25, Sun. finals US$6.45, 3-day pass US$8.) Beds are hard to find during the tournament; phone ahead. The competition has inspired a room in the museum behind Selimiye Cami that displays pictures of famous wrestlers, some of their personal belongings and a history of oil wrestling.

■■■ BURSA

The deep green **Uludağ Mountain,** site of Turkey's leading ski resort, adds welcome color to the city settled at its base whose greatest attractions are the Ottoman monuments scattered throughout the city and the myriad thermal baths in the **Çekirge** (Grasshopper) district. Bursa's tourist route stretches from the Yeşil Cami in the east to Çekirge's thermal baths in the west. Despite their names, the **Yeşil Cami** (Green Mosque) and **Yeşil Türbe** (Green Mausoleum) actually seem blue to many. The

Turkish and Islamic Art Museum, including the **Ethnographic Museum,** is nearby. (Mausoleums and museums open 8:30am-5pm; Oct.-April Tues.-Sun. 8am-noon and 1-5pm. Museum US$0.80, students US$0.40.) Built in the Turkish style common before the conquest of Constantinople, the **Ulu Cami** (Great Mosque) diverges from the popular Ayasofya designs of İstanbul. The rectangular layout and numerous supporting columns characterize the Seljuk architectural style. To go to the **Eski Kaplıca** bathing complex, built by Justinian in the 6th century, take the Çekirge *dolmuş* and get off at the luxurious Kervansaray Hotel (US$0.50). The Eski Kaplıca will be on the right when you face the hotel. After a long day of travel, ask for the "rubbing" and have at least one layer of dead skin exfoliated by the special cloth. They'll show you all the dirt they get off you afterwards. (Open 8am-10pm. US$6 entrance to baths, US$4 rubbing, US$4 massage.)

To reach the **Uludağ Mountain cable car** station, take a *dolmuş* marked "Televiewer" (US$0.30) from the Kafkaf pastry shop on Atatürk Blv., 2 blocks past the statue. The cable car runs to the mid-station (every hr. on the hr., 9am-9pm, round-trip US$1.75), and from the mid-station to a small town perched 2000m up the mountain (every hr. on the ½hr., 20min., US$2.65 there and US$5.00 back). Be prepared for a dose of chill, sudden changes of weather, and pricey.

Practical Information, Accommodations, and Food Bursa is accessible by **express ferry** from Karaköy in İstanbul (Mon.-Fri. 5 per day, US$3.50). On weekends the express ferry launches from Kartal on İstanbul's Asian coast. A **slow ferry** leads to Bursa from Kabataş near the Dolmabahçe Palace in İstanbul (8 per day, US$2). Early ferries, leaving at 8:30 or 9am, beat the crowds. They land in Yalova, where you can hop a *dolmuş* or bus to Bursa (every 30min., US$2). The entire trip takes about 3½ hours. **Buses** to Bursa from İstanbul depart from Esenler Bus Station (hourly, 4hr., US$6-8). **Kamıl Koç** is safe and reliable, as are Ulusoy and Varan, but the latter two are more expensive. Bus routes connect Bursa to Ankara, İzmir and other big cities. To get to the center of town, take a *dolmuş* marked "Heykel" from the bus station (US$0.30) and get off at Ulu Cami (Great Mosque). The **tourist office** (tel. (224) 221 23 59) is near the *heykel* (a huge statue of Atatürk), under the big fountain (open Mon.-Sat. 8:30am-noon and 1:30-5:30pm; Oct.-May Mon.-Fri. 8:30am-noon and 1-5pm). A **branch office** with the same hours has opened in the bus station.

If you must stay in the noisy and distant area around the bus station, try the de-frilled **Otel Ozendim** (tel. (224) 254 94 71) directly across from the depot at 135 Garaj Karşısı. (Singles US$4. Doubles US$3 per person. Triples US$2.50 per person. Quads US$2 per person. Showers included.) **Otel Deniz,** Tahtakale Cad. 19 (tel. (224) 222 92 38) is graced with hot showers on demand. (Singles US$4. Doubles US$6.30.) On the top of Uludağ, **Millıpark Camping** (tel. (224) 214 52 81) charges US$3.50 per person, US$2.50 per tent. (Take a cable car, see above.) *İskender kebap,* an excellent Turkish dish made of lamb with a rich sauce of tomatoes and butter, originated in Bursa, and don't you forget it. Picnickers can stock up in the market on Tahtakale near the budget hotels. Bursa's **Kültürpark** (take a *dolmuş* from the Heykel stop, US$0.30) harbors some decent restaurants and is a fountain of generally elusive alcoholic beverages (as well as concerts, movies and plays).

AEGEAN COAST

With an incomparable collection of classical ruins and a sinuous coastline that conceals dozens of sublime beaches, the once tranquil Aegean Coast is now increasingly fast-paced. Resorts such as Kuşadası and Bodrum are becoming particularly swollen with pensions and souvenir stands as the tourist hordes arrive; come soon.

■■■ ÇANAKKALE TO İZMİR

Çanakkale and Troy (Truva) Blessed with inexpensive accommodations and bus connections to all major cities and nearby sights, **Çanakkale** is an easy base from which to explore Gallipoli and Troy. From the bus station, take a left out the main doors, then your next right onto Demircioğlu Cad. (following the "ferribot" sign), and continue onto the docks. The town clock tower and the **tourist information office,** İskele Meydanı 67 (tel. (286) 217 11 87), will be on your left. Across the street from 14 Fetvane Sok. the **Kervansery Otel,** has hand-pumped showers. (Singles US$3-3.50. Doubles US$4.70-6. Triples US$6-7.75.)

Troy (Truva) is 32km south of Çanakkale. Take a *dolmuş* from the station in Çanakkale (US$1.20, 45min.), and arrange for the *dolmuş* to wait for an hour or two while you explore the ruins. The site slept until Heinrich Schliemann, millionaire-turned-amateur archaeologist, decided to prove that the Homeric myths weren't fiction. His discoveries rocked the archaeological world; the remaining Bronze Age fortifications, given their age, are remarkably well preserved. The tacky wooden horse that assures you that you've reached Troy is not the original. (Open 8am-8pm, off season 8am-5pm. US$1, students US$0.50.)

Pergamon, İzmir, and Çeşme The ruins at **Pergamon** sprawl over 30,000 acres, farther south near the pleasant, modern town of **Bergama.** Though the **Altar of Zeus,** considered the cat's meow of the Hellenistic era, resides in eastern Berlin, the mammoth amphitheater, huge gymnasium and lavishly frescoed House of Attalus make Pergamon more than worthwhile. (Open 8:30am-7pm; Oct.-April 8:30am-5:30pm. Acropolis US$1.50, with ISIC US$0.75.) Bergama's **tourist office,** İzmir Cad. 54 (tel. (541) 318 62; open Mon.-Fri. 8:30am-5:30pm, summer open 8:30am-7pm), is to the right as you exit the bus station. Buses run from Bursa (6½hr, US$12), İzmir (1½hr., US$1.50), and İstanbul (10hr, US$16). The most fetching pension in Bergama is the **Pergamon Pension** (tel. (541) 633 23 95), a 150-year-old Greek-style mansion with high ceilings, a café, and a Turkish bath on the premises. Heading from the bus station, pass the PTT and you'll see a fork; bear to the right—the pension is on the left. (US$5 per person. Breakfast US$1.30.)

İzmir, Turkey's third-largest city and the former Smyrna, is a sprawling metropolis that does not easily reveal its treasures. İzmir's **agora** was built in the 4th century BC by Alexander, destroyed by an earthquake in 178 AD, and rebuilt by Emperor Marcus Aurelius soon thereafter. The rather uninspiring remains are accessible from Anafartalar Cad. Walk south along 941 Sok. from the Otel Saray. (Open 8:30am-5:30pm. US$1, students US$0.50.) Above the city at Mt. Pagos is the most enduring of Alexander's legacies, the **Kadifekale,** literally "velvet fortress" (open 24hrs., free). Bus 33 from Konak Sq. ascends the mount for a flabbergasting panorama of the bay. Frequent buses arrive from İstanbul (9hr., US$14), Bursa (6hr., US$10), Çanakkale (6hr., US$9), Selçuk (1hr., US$2), and Ankara (8½hr., US$11). Find the **tourist office,** Gaziosmanpaşa Blv. 1/1c (tel. (232) 484 21 47), by the landmark Hilton Hotel. (Open Mon.-Fri. 8:30am-7pm, Sat.-Sun. 9am-5pm; Sept.-June Mon.-Sat. 8:30am-5:30pm; smaller branch in bus station open 8am-noon and 12:30-8pm.) The Basmane district is loaded with cheap hotels. The **Otel Saray,** 635 Anafartalar Cad. (tel. (232) 483 69 46), appears to be a transplanted Miami Beach hotel but has nice, airy rooms. (Singles US$3.30. Doubles US$6.70. Triples US$10.) To get there, go straight up Gaziosmanpaşa Blv. from the tourist office and make a left on Anafartalar Caddesi, which is also the street for cheap eats.

One hour west of İzmir chortles the popular seaside resort of **Çeşme.** Buses leave every ½-hour or so from the Üçkuyular bus lot in İzmir. From the bus stop, continue down the main road to the water for the **tourist office,** İskele Meydanı 8 (tel. (232) 712 6653; open Mon.-Fri. 8:30am-7pm, Sat.-Sun. 9am-noon and 1-5pm; Oct.-May Mon.-Fri. 8:30am-noon and 1-5:30pm). It's easy to see why the **Aras Pension** (tel. (232) 712 73 75), by the bus station, has been voted Çeşme's best pension five times—clean, light rooms with toilets, showers, and marble-like floors. (Singles

US$6.70. Doubles US$13.30. Triples US$16.70. Breakfast US$1.70.) An hour's boat ride from Çeşme takes you to Chios in Greece. Contact **Ertürk Ferryboat,** Cumhuriyet Meydanı 11/A (tel. (232) 712 67 68), for schedule information (one way US$25, same day return US$30, open round-trip US$35).

■■■ KUŞADASI AND ENVIRONS

In summer, Kuşadası's proximity to the Greek island of Samos and its place on many Aegean cruise ship itineraries transform the town into a tourist blob. The town of Selçuk, 20km away and only 3km from Ephesus, offers rooms that elate the frugal, but it lacks Kuşadası's nightlife and coastline. The best beaches in the area are sandy **Karovaplajı** (Long Beach) and **Yavansu plajı** (Silver Beach); take any *dolmuş* marked "Davutlar."

Most visitors to Kuşadası arrive by boat, a convenient method given that harbor master, duty-free shop, fish market, passport police, and customs are all in the port area. There is no way around paying the port tax (US$10), and it is generally best to pay it in U.S. dollars to avoid changing-station commissions and weak exchange rates from other currencies. When you do exchange your money, keep heading downhill to find better rates. By bus, Kuşadası is a two-hour ride from İzmir. The bus station is about 2km east of the center and frequent *dolmuş* connect the two. The **tourist office** on İskele Meydanı in the port (tel. (256) 614 11 03) provides pension and campground listings, bus schedules, and maps (open May-June 8am-6pm, June-Aug. 8am-7:30pm, Sept.-May 8am-noon and 1-5:30pm). To get there from the bus station, it's best to take a taxi, but if you want to walk, direct your ox-strong legs out of the station to the right, eventually charge left on Kahramanlar Cad. and follow this street to the water (it changes names to Barbaros Blv.). English-speaking **Ekol Travel,** Liman Çikmazi 3/1 (tel. (256) 614 92 55, fax 614 26 44), in the bazaar at the end of the cruiseliner gangway has cheap flights, ferry tickets, temporary baggage storage, transportation advice, car rentals, and emergency help. (15% discount on ferry tickets for *Let's Go* readers. Open Mon.-Sat. 8:30am-9pm, Dec.-March 8:30am-7:30pm.) The cheaper pensions line Aslanlar Cad. and many small streets higher up. Women should avoid the cheapest places. Try to haggle down high-season prices. **Hotel Rose (Salman's Pension),** Aslanlar Cad., Aydınlık Sok. 7 (tel. (256) 411 11) is bedecked with big, comfy rooms, a lounge, and laundry service (US$2 per kg). (US$4 per person. Roof US$1.50. Dorm US$3. 15% discount for *Let's Go* readers.) **Hülya Pension,** Mah. İleri Sok. 39 (tel. (256) 614 20 75), just down the street, is clean and light. (Singles US$5-6.70. Doubles US$6.70-10. Triples US$9-12. Excellent Turkish dinner US$3.) **Önder** (tel. (256) 614 24 13) and **Yat Camping** (tel. (256) 614 13 33), 2km north of town on Atatürk Bulvarı, have good facilities, including laundry and swimming pools. (Both sites US$1.70 per person. At Önder, US$1 per tent, 2-person bungalows US$12.50. At Yat, US$1.30 per tent, 2-person bungalows US$15. Both include breakfast and are closed Dec.-April.) If you want to meet other backpackers, try pub lane (watch out for the Union Jack), where the nectar never stops flowing.

Ephesus and Selçuk For an archaeological fix, visit **Ephesus** (Efes). The ruins from the Roman and early Christian era are extensive and well-preserved. Tours are expensive (US$24 per day) and cursory, so buy a guidebook (US$5 at entrance) and do it yourself. Bring a water bottle. From the Kuşadası bus station, take a *dolmuş* to Selçuk, and tell the driver you want to get off at Ephesus. From the Selçuk train station, take any *dolmuş* toward Kuşadası. (Site open 8am-7pm. US$2.50, with ISIC US$1.50.) The most important of these remains is the **Vedius Gymnasium** to the left as you proceed down the road to the main entrance. Farther on spread the contours of what must have been an enormous **stadium**. Just before the main entrance stand the ruins of the **Double Church** (Church of Councils) where the notorious Ecumenical Council of Churches met in 431 AD. Once you pass through the main entrance, at the center of the site stretches **Arcadian Street,** a magnificent, colonnaded marble avenue. Up the hill, the imposing ruins of the **Temple of Hadrian** dominate the left side of the road and a little farther on, the ruins of the exquisite **Fountain of Trajan.** Various fragments found on this location have been piled piecemeal to reconstruct the original structure.

Selçuk's main attraction is its proximity to Ephesus; its **Ephesus Museum** highlights over a century of excavations. Its most famous pieces are the statues of Priapus and multi-breasted Artemis. (Open Tues.-Sun. 8:30am-5:30pm. US$2, with ISIC US$1.) On Saturdays during the summer, locals as well as tourists frequent the huge **open-air market,** which features fresh fruits, cheeses, vegetables, tea, spices, and clothing. The **bus station** from which the Kuşadası *dolmuş* (US$1) runs is at the northwest corner of the crossroads. Buses from İzmir also come here (1½hr., US$1.50). You can catch a minibus back to İzmir (every ½hr., US$1) at the bus station or a larger bus back to İzmir on the street in front of the bus station (stand on the opposite side and signal to the driver, buses every ½hr., 1½hr., US$1.50). **Tuncay Pension,** İsabel Mah., Ay Sok. 3 (tel. (232) 892 62 60), offers large and hygienic rooms. From the bus stop, take the third left, then the first right and right again. (US$4 per person in high season, US$3 low season.) Friendly management and decent rooms are on offer at **Australian Pension,** Prof. Miltner Sok. 7 (tel. (232) 892 60 50), behind the museum. (Follow the signs. Rooms US$3.30 per person. Dorm beds US$2.75.)

■■■ PAMUKKALE AND APHRODISIAS

Whether as **Pamukkale** or ancient Hierapolis, this village has been drawing the weary and the curious to its thermal springs for over 23 centuries. The Turkish name—literally "cotton castle"—refers to the snow-white cliffs, shaped over millennia by the accumulation of calcium deposited by mineral springs. Don't leave Pamukkale without a savory dip in the **sacred fountain** at the Pamukkale Motel (75m beyond the archaeological museum). Warm, fizzy waters bubble from the spring's source. (Open 9am-9pm. US$3.30 per hr.) Most of the direct buses that run to Pamukkale leave from Selçuk and Kuşadası before 9am (5-6 per day, US$6, 4½hr.). From Pamukkale, there are direct buses to Bodrum (4-5hr., US$6), Selçuk and Kuşadası (4-5hr., US$5), and İzmir (5hr., US$5). The small **tourist information office** (tel. (258) 272 20 77) is at the end of the row of curio shops and cafés near the main site entrance (open 8:30am-6pm). The manager of **Mustafa Motel** (tel. (258) 272 12 40), on the main road near the center of town, serves PB & J to Yanks, vegemite to Aussies, and cornflakes to Limeys, accompanying each nation's culinary totem with hilarious imitations (clean rooms US$5 per person).

In ancient times, **Aphrodisias** gained fame for its sculpture, and was an important think-tank of Asia Minor. Particularly worth seeing are the surviving Greek **stadium,** with its seating capacity of 30,000, and the elegant **Temple of Aphrodite.** (Museum and ruins open 9am-7pm. Each US$3, with ISIC US$1.50.) The easiest way to see the ruins is as a daytrip from Pamukkale. Pamukkale Turizm **buses** leave at 10am and return to Pamukkale at 5pm (2hr., US$5, round-trip US$9).

■■■ BODRUM

Knotted in serpentine coastline, the Bodrum Peninsula is a heliophile's paradise of beaches centered around a sophisticated resort. Bodrum has a thrilling nightlife, with many opportunities to meet people of all sexes and orientations. Perhaps the only chance in life you'll get to see elderly French women, preppy American students, bisexual Italian models, and Turkish teenyboppers sharing the same dance floor will be at the **Halicarnassus Disco,** Z. Müren Cad. at the end of Cumhuriyet Cad., 1½km from the center of town (it's marked on the tourist map). (Cover US$9. Open until 5am.) Turn left onto Satay Sok. from Neyzen Teufik Cad., to reach the scanty remains of the **Mausoleum of Halicarnassus,** yet another one of the seven wonders of the ancient world. Guarding the harbor, the **Kale,** a solid crusader fortress, now houses Bodrum's **Museum of Underwater Archaeology,** a bizarre assortment of shipwreck flotsam from sites along the surrounding Turkish coastline. (Castle open Tues.-Sun. 8am-5pm. US$1.30, with ISIC US$0.65. Museum open Tues.-Sun. 8am-noon and 1-5pm. US$0.70, with ISIC US$0.35.) The **tourist office** (tel. (252) 316 10 91) at the foot of the castle has accommodations listings and a lousy map (open 8am-8pm., Nov.-March 8am-noon and 1-5pm). If you arrive in the evening in July or August without a reservation, you won't get a room. The going summer rate at the cheaper pensions is about US$6 per person. Often rooms are available in private homes called *ev pansiyons:* look for signs that read "Oda Var" or "Boş Oda Var." Tastefully decorated **Polyanna Pension** (tel. (252) 615 28), lies on Ortanca Sok., just before the Halikarnas Disco end of Cumhuriyet Cad. If coming from the tourist office, turn left off Cumhuriyet Cad. at the White House Restaurant. (US$5 per person. Breakfast US$1.70.) Stock up at the cheap fruit and vegetable stands just down Cevat Şâkir Cad. from the bus station, or at the big **market** that comes periodically on the other side of the station. Along Cumhuriyet Cad., before the harbor, a number of *kebap* salons and stands offer fried mussels (US$0.70) and the usual *pide* and *şiş.*

Bodrum's popularity among Turks stems largely from its location at the head of the enchanting **Bodrum Peninsula.** After a day of swimming and sunning, you can linger over dinner, or partake of Bodrum's rousing nightlife. A few of the beaches on the southern coast of the peninsula are accessible only by tour boats, which leave from the front of the castle (9-11am, returning 5-6pm). Known as *mavi yolculuk* ("blue journey"), these tours are fine alternatives to all the archaic splendor of the ruins and to the Teutonic masses plaguing the beaches around the city. Itineraries for the tours vary widely (check the tour schedule at the dock). Some popular destinations are **Kara Island,** the village of **Akyarlar,** and the beaches at **Baradakçı, Çapa Tatil, Kargı Bay, Bağla,** and **Karaincir.** Boat tours cost around US$9 per person for the day, US$12.50 with lunch. In summer, boats also leave daily from the castle to tranquil **Orak Island** (same prices). These are some of the best swimming spots on the peninsula, pristine and uncrowded; accordingly, there are no cheap accommodations at these places. Daytrips are your best bet. **Gölköy** and **Türkbükü,** once idyllic villages, are now hives for Turkish tourists. A few old windmills dot **Yalıkavak,** at the northwest end of the peninsula, where many even smaller villages are scattered. Each of these towns has a few pensions, usually near the beach. You can camp in Yalıkavak at **Yalı Camping** (tel. (252) 385 41 42), across from Belediye beach at the harbor (US$3.30 per person).

MEDITERRANEAN COAST

Extending from the edges of Greece to the Syrian border, Turkey's Mediterranean coast runs the gamut from chic to garish to remote. Pine forests, secret coves, and sandy beaches garnish the stretch between Fethiye and Antalya. Farther east, broad swatches of sand and concrete are dotted with castles and ruins, making up the stretch of overcrowded shoreline that tourist propaganda has dubbed the "Turquoise Coast." The only factor which puts this area one below the Aegean is the heat: over 40°C in July and August.

■■■ MARMARİS AND THE DATÇA PENINSULA

Marmaris has enough shady palm trees and canopied side streets to compensate for its grimy beach, crowds, and development-choked shoreline, but most people only come to Marmaris on their way to somewhere else. Marmaris is shackled to Rhodes by **ferry** (Mon.-Sat. at 8:30 or 9am, Nov.-April Mon., Thurs., Sat. 9am; US$35, same day round-trip US$65; port tax US$5). Frequent **buses** run to İzmir (5hr., US$6), Bodrum, and Fethiye (both 3hr., US$3.30). The **tourist office**, Kordon Cad. (tel. (252) 412 10 35), right before the marina, can tell you (in English) about **Günnücek National Park** hiking and provide a town map (open 8am-7:30pm, Oct.-April closes at 5pm). From the bus station, cross the bridge over a channel of water and then follow along the coast to reach the tourist office. Both **Interyouth Hostels** offer a 10% discount for HI, ISIC and GO 25. One at Tepe Mah., 42 Sok. No. 45 (tel. (252) 455 32 18) spoils guests with an international phone and MTV (US$4 per person). Perks at the other at Kameraltı Mah., İyiliktaş Mevkii 14 (tel. (252) 412 64 32), include laundry (US$1) and service from bus and ferries. (Roof US$2. Dorm US$3. Triples and quads US$4. Doubles US$5.) Avoid the waterfront eateries; head inland to chow. At the **Marmaris Lokantası**, Fevzipaşa Cad., just inland from the post office, you'll get cheap, hearty food (soup US$0.70, *döner* US$1.70). Hook up with other tourists, along the Kuşadası-style row of pubs behind the tourist office away from the water, or in the **Greenhouse** discotheque.

Stay in Marmaris no longer than necessary; hop a bus to the resplendent **Datça Peninsula** (2hr., US$1.70). Boats depart from Bodrum only in the summer (9am and 5pm, US$7; return at 9am). **Antalyalı Pension** (tel. (252) 712 38 10) is the easiest one to find (on Yalı Cad., the main road). From the bus station, pass the PTT and take the left fork (US$5 per person). Camping is possible on the beach at **Ilıca Camping** (tel. (252) 712 34 00; US$2 per tent and 2 people). Feridun, the campground owner, may take you on a wild boar hunt followed by a wild boar all-you-can-eat feast with salad, wine, and belly dancing (US$12).

The road from Marmaris to Fethiye passes by the ruins of the ancient city of **Caunos,** where archaeologists are turning up new structures as fast as they can dig. The ruins are accessible only by boat from the nearby town of **Dalyan.** Camping by Lake Köyceğiz will undoubtedly acquaint you with the annual convention of the Voracious Mosquitoes Union. Dalyan's **Kristal Pansiyon** (tel. 284 22 63) rescues you with bug-proof windows for a mere US$3.

■■■ XANTHOS AND KALKAN

Xanthos, 22km from the ancient Lycian capital Kalkan, has a large amphitheater and examples of Lycian rock tombs and funeral monuments. Twenty km from Xanthos crumble the ruins of **Patara,** birthplace of St. Nikolas (a.k.a. Santa Claus). But here nothing beats the 18km stretch of deserted, sandy **beach.** At night the beach becomes a turtle sanctuary, so camping is out. It's no great loss, though, because **St. Nikolas Pension** (tel. 843 51 64; US$5 per person) is outstanding, and you may be able to tent-pitch in town. To get to Patara, take any bus going from Fethiye to Kalkan, and get off at the turn-off (US$1.50). From there it's 6km to the beach. From Kalkan, *dolmuş* leave every ½-1hr. and come back at 4 or 5pm (US$1).

Kalkan, between Fethiye and Kaş, is a postcard Turkish fishing village. This is public knowledge and drooling tourists now stomp the narrow streets. Kalkan is famous for its tailors—get those fashionable baggy pants you've swooned over. High prices plague lodgings, though food is reasonable. **Çelik Pansiyon,** Yalı Boyu Hah 9 (tel. (242) 844 21 26), down the hill from the bus stop, to the left, has spacious rooms and a terrace overlooking the harbor (singles US$7, doubles US$10, triples US$17). Many restaurants offer all-you-can-eat buffets. Vegetarians should head straight to the **Jolly Roger** (tel. (242) 844 32 84), down the hill on the extreme right of the fork near the bus stop; look for the "Scottish Spoken Here" sign. (Open 9:30am-1am.)

TURKEY

■■■ ANTALYA AND SIDE

Perched above the sea a scenic but rough 4½hr. bus ride from Kaş, **Antalya** serves as a good base for exploring nearby beaches and Roman ruins. East of Antalya lies the ancient Roman province of **Pamphylia** and its several important, partially excavated sites. The travel agencies that line Cumhuriyet will send you there (daytrips US$15). Antalya's **Archaeological Museum,** on Kenan Evren Blv., showcases many of the artifacts found thus far (open Tues.-Sun. 8:30am-5:30pm, Oct.-May 9am-noon and 1:30-5:30pm; US$1.20).

Connections to major Turkish cities (İstanbul US$54, Ankara US$46) are possible via **Turkish Airlines** (tel. (242) 243 43 84) and by **bus.** To reach the main **tourist office** (tel. (242) 241 17 47) from the bus station, turn left onto Kazım Özalp Cad. and again left on Cumhuriyet Cad. then right at the traffic circle onto Atatürk Cad. Walk down the street and make a right after going through **Hadrian's Gate.** You should now be on Hesapçı Sok., the main street in old town, on which you can find most of the hostels. Go down it and make a right after Abad Otel (about 4 blocks), then continue until you reach the white building set back from the street, across from the Aspen Hotel. Total distance: about 2km. (Open Mon.-Fri. 8:30am-5:30pm.) Sack out cheaply in old Ottoman houses; the best pensions are in the old city (*Kaleiçi*), southeast of the yacht harbor (see directions to tourist office). The **Ani Pansiyon,** Tabakhane Sok. 26 (tel. (242) 247 00 56) is nicer than your own home (doubles US$13.30, breakfast included). The last pension on Hesapçı Sok. before you hit the cliff is **Bermuda Pansiyon** (tel. (242) 247 34 48), where the top room has a balcony and a sea view. (US$3.30 per person. Breakfast US$1.70.)

A theater garnished with marble reliefs, a grand colonnaded avenue, and a supreme stadium conjure a vision of **Perge** in its 2nd-century heyday. To get here from Antalya, take a *dolmuş* to Aksu from the central *dolmuş* station, then walk 2km. No imaginative reconstruction is necessary at **Aspendos,** 49km from Antalya, thanks to the efforts of the Seljuk Turks who used it as a pilgrimage way station. The huge theater is one of the best-preserved in the world; even the marble stage remains almost completely intact. (Site open 8:30am-6:30pm, in winter 8:30am-5:30pm. US$1, students US$0.50.) Take the Manavgat *dolmuş* 5km past the village of Serik; the ruins are another 4km from the turn-off. *Dolmuşes* run infrequently, but taxis are available, and tractors are known to pick up hitchhikers.

Side has all the components of a classic vacation on the Mediterranean coast: Hellenic ruins, a fine museum, a 1km stretch of sandy beach, and acres of tourists. The Hellenistic walls to the city are impressively large (1.7m wide, 10m high). When you enter Side, you'll see the **Nymphaeum** memorial fountain which once had a marble façade depicting punishments administered to those who committed sexual sins or sins against the gods. While most ancient theaters were hewn into the hillsides, the 2nd-century **theater** of Side was built on level ground using arches. It is also the largest in the area (seating 25,000 people) though not as well preserved as that of Aspendos. (Open 8:30am-5:30pm. US$1, students US$0.50.) The ancient Roman baths now house a great **Archaeological Museum** (open Tues.-Sun. 8am-noon and 1:30-7:30pm; US$1, students US$0.50).

Several direct buses go to Side from Antalya. About 200m to the east stretches the best beach in Side, **Büyük Plaj,** where you can unfurl a sleeping bag on the sand or in one of the empty, rickety wooden shacks. From the bus station, walk about 2km with the sea to your right, and turn onto the dirt road leading toward the water. Nearby cafés have showers and toilets open 24hrs. on the beach. Otherwise, **Pettino Pansiyon** (tel. (242) 753 12 72; call for directions) lets clean rooms with bath (US$5) and serves vegemite breakfasts (U$1.50). The nearby **Nymfeum Disco** (tel. (242) 753 10 76) mixes tourists and locals with live music and dollar beers (open 8am-10pm and 11pm-5am.).

■■■ ANTAKYA (HATAY)

Few tourists are to be found in idyllic Antakya (Hatay), and a merciful breeze subdues the summer heat. Little remains from the Biblical days when this was Antioch—a city of half a million, one of the largest in the Mediterranean. Everything that's left—including spectacular mosaics—is in the **Archaeological Museum** (open Tues.-Sun. 8:30am-noon and 1:30-4:30pm; US$1, students US$0.50). Two km from the town center towards Reyhanlı is **San Pierre Kilisesi,** where St. Peter's original congregation coined the word "Christianity" (open Tues.-Sun. 8am-noon and 1:30-5:30pm; free).

From the Atatürk statue in the city center, walk down Atatürk Cad. to the **tourist office** in the park on the opposite side of the circle. (Open Mon.-Fri. 8am-noon and 1:30-5:30pm, occasionally Sat.) For accommodations, walk down İstiklâl Cad. from the bus station toward the town center. **Hotel Saray,** Hürriyet Cad. 3 (tel. (384) 214 9001), across the bridge from Atatürk, presides over squeaky-clean rooms with round-the-clock hot water (singles US$7, doubles US$12, triples US$17) and the recommendable **Restaurant Nuri** (open 5am-1:30am, US$3 for full meal). If you have a Syrian visa (which you should get in İstanbul or Ankara), you can take a bus directly to Aleppo (Halep), 100km away (US$7). You are supposed to exchange US$100 at the border. The jaunt on to Damascus is another 2hr. and US$3.

CENTRAL TURKEY

The rolling miles of stoic Anatolian plateau contain the oldest and newest landmarks of Turkish civilization. Konya, once capital of the Seljuk Empire, bristles with exquisite mosques and tombs, while Ankara, Turkey's capital, testifies to the modernization imposed by the contemporary Turkish state. To the south, Cappadocia's ancient ruins attract the lion's share of tourists.

■■■ KONYA

Konya was the 12th-century capital of the Seljuk sultans and has been Turkey's religious center since the 13th century, when Afghani holy man Celâleddin Rumi, known to his followers as Mevlâna (master), settled here. Founder of the famous order of Whirling Dervishes, Mevlâna believed spiritual perfection and union with the divine was achieved through ecstatic dance. In 1925, Atatürk dissolved the order and now the Dervishes dance but once a year in December (if you can't make it, genuine Dervishes whirl year-round in İstanbul). You can spot the 13th-century **Mevlâna Tekke** by its radiant turquoise tower. Inside this one-time monastery are the *türbe* of Celâleddin and other dervishes, as well as a fascinating museum with prayer rugs, musical instruments, and elaborately decorated garments. (Open Mon. 10am-5:30pm, Tues.-Sun. 9am-5:30pm; US$1.) Konya's other major attractions stud **Alâaddin Tepesi** (Aladdin Hill), several hundred meters up Hükümet Cad. This mound supposedly contains layers of civilization stretching back to the Bronze Age. While in Konya, wander through the enchanting **bazaar,** between the Aziziye Mosque and the **post office** (open 24hrs.) on Alâaddin Cad.

The **tourist office** Mevlâna Cad. 21 (tel. (332) 110 74), is across the street from the Mevlâna Müze (Mevlana Museum). **Çatal Pansiyon,** around the corner from the tourist office (tel. (332) 351 49 81), charges US$7 for doubles and US$10 for triples (US$8-12). **Otel Çeşme,** 35 Akifpaşa Sok. (tel. (332) 351 24 26) offers well-kept rooms adorned with fake brick and stained glass (singles US$7, doubles US$8, triples US$11; all with bath). The local specialty is *firin kebap,* a chunk of oven-roasted lamb. Try it at **Lokanta Şima Restaurant,** near the tourist office on Mevlâna Cad.

Ten **buses** a day roam between Konya and Silifke (3hr., US$4.50), İzmir (8hr., US$7.50), and Ankara 15 times a day (3hr., US$4). Night buses run to and from İstanbul. If you arrive at the bus station in the daytime, take a minibus marked "Mevlâna" to the center; at night try a 3-wheeled cart. After midnight, you'll have to take a taxi. To get back to the bus station take any *dolmuş* marked "Otogar."

■■■ EĞIRDIR

Discovered by tourists about a decade ago, Eğirdir, a fishing town by an azure-blue fresh-water lake in the midst of the Central Tauras mountains, has managed to shield its tranquility from the hordes. Nature-lovers and adventurers, rejoice! 27km to the east lies **Zindan**, a 1½km-long cave which served the Romans as an open-air temple dedicated to Eurymedon. Only 25km south of town, **Kovada National Park** teems with wildlife and draws butterfly collectors in the spring. Avid walkers can follow a popular stretch of the **King's Road** by which Lydian rulers once made their way from Ephesus to Babylon. To reach these places, charter a minibus with some friends or ask at a pension, since no regular bus service is available. The diehard trekker will want to meet Nurtay Yatman, the hardy proprietor of **Donatim Ticaret,** Hükümet Cad. 18 (tel. (246) 311 60 80), a wilderness supply store down the street from the Otel Sinan (open 8am-8pm in summer, 8am-5pm in winter).

Buses arrive from Ankara (7hr., US$7) and Konya (8 per day, 3½hr., US$7). To get to the **tourist office,** 2. Sahil Yolu 13 (tel. (246) 312 20 98) from the bus station, walk left for 200m and follow the signs (open Mon.-Fri. 8:30am-noon and 1:30-6pm). Located in the middle of Yeşilada's south side, **Halley Pension,** Yeşilada Mah. 2. Sok. 6 (tel. (246) 312 36 25) provides congenial family service (singles US$9, doubles US$12, triples US$15). If you have your own tent, camping is free at **Yazla Plaj,** the small public beach one km west of the center of town along 2. Sahil Yolu. Cushier camping can be had a 5min. walk up the road at **Altınkum Plaj,** where you can rent a tent (US$1) and have access to the camp's electricity and showers. Not surprisingly, the people of Eğirdir make a mean fish—carp, bass, and crayfish being the local specialties. Most of the fish restaurants around the town are very similar in price (US$3-4 a meal) and good quality.

■■■ ANKARA

Travelers have often scorned this sprawling, polluted, windy capital, but their criticisms are not entirely valid. Besides its roles as a transport center and museum city, Ankara has many European-style cafés in the **Kızılay** district. Catch the city on a sunny summer day, and you may find it more lively and engaging than its poor reputation would suggest.

ORIENTATION AND PRACTICAL INFORMATION

Get a map at the tourist office; you'll need it to survive in this huge and bewildering city. Most points of interest are in the **Ulus** and **Kızılay** districts. Continue straight on Cumhuriyet Bulvarı to the equestrian statue of Atatürk in the center of Ulus. Remember that the statue faces west; it is a key reference.

Tourist Office: Main office at Gazi Mustafa Kemal Blv. 121 (tel. 488 70 07). From the train station's main platform, descend the stairs into the shoplined tunnel to Tandoğan (marked Tandoğan Kapalı Çarşı). At the end of the tunnel turn left onto Mustafa Kemal Blv.; it will be on the right side of the street after the PTT and the Renault sign. Open Mon.-Fri. 8:30am-6pm, Sat.-Sun. 10am-6pm. Another office at the airport (tel. 398 03 48). Open 24hrs.

Embassies: U.S., Atatürk Blv. 110 (tel. 426 54 70). **Canada,** Nenehatun Cad. 75 (tel. 436 12 75). **U.K.,** Şehit Ersun Cad. 46a (tel. 468 62 30). **Australia,** 83 Nenehatun Cad. (tel. 446 11 80). **New Zealand,** İran Cad. 13 (tel. 467 90 56). **Bulgaria,** Atatürk Blv. 124 (tel. 426 74 55). **Greece,** 9-11 Zia Ül-Rahman Cad. (tel. 436 88 60).

American Express: Services through **Koç Bank,** 58 Atatürk Blv. (tel. 418 18 04). Emergency cash for cardholders and holds mail. Open Mon.-Fri. 9am-4pm.

Post Office: PTT, on Atatürk Bulvarı in Kızılay and in Ulus. Both open 24hrs. In the train station, open 7am-11pm. Poste Restante open Mon.-Sat. 8:30am-5:30pm.

Telephones: At the post office, bus and train station. 24hrs. **City Code:** 312.

Airport: Direct flights to İstanbul, Adana, Diyarbakır, Erzurum, İzmir, and Trabzon. Buses leave from Hipodrom Cad. (next to the train station) and head to the airport, **Esenboğa,** every hour (US$2.50). All domestic flights US$50 or less, students (114-24) get 25% off.

Trains: The **Terminal** bus station is on Hipodrom Cad., down the street from the **Gar** (train station); it's quicker to travel between İstanbul and Ankara by bus, but overnight trains are more comfortable. The *Mavi Tren* leaves Ankara at 11:30pm (9hr., US$6). The *Anadolu Ekspresi* departs at 10pm (9¼hr., US$4-6 plus US$2 if you want a couchette). *Ankara Ekspresi* contains only sleeping compartments and departs at 10:30pm (9hr., couchette US$24). Ankara is also connected by rail to İzmir, Konya, Erzurum, Trabzon, Kayseri and other Turkish cities.

Buses: Frequent departures to Konya (3hr., US$5), İstanbul (6hr., US$8-10), İzmir, Bodrum, Trabzon, Bursa, and Nevşehir, to name a few. Daily to the Iranian border (US$17). Luggage deposit US$0.30.

Medical Assistance: Hacettepe University Hospital, Hasircilar Cad. (tel. 310 35 45). From the statue in Ulus, head south about 2km, turn left onto Talat Paşa Cad., and climb the hill to Hasircilar Cad. Emergency health care. Open 8:30am-5pm.

ACCOMMODATIONS AND FOOD

Most of the less expensive hotels are to the east of **Ulus,** toward the citadel, but this is a busy, noisy part of town, and hotels tend to be rather run-down. First try **Otel Şan,** 8 Şan Sok (tel. 311 09 43), a spotless new hotel in a quieter area of town. (Singles US$5, doubles US$8, triples US$16. Breakfast US$1.50.) The **Hisar Oteli,** Hısarpark Cad. 6 (tel. 311 98 89) is a little noisier, but clean, with a pleasant view. (Singles US$5, doubles US$9). **Otel Yakut,** Hilal Sok. 19 (tel. 312 51 58), is on a small street between the Hacı Bayram mosque and the Roman baths, and has sunny, large rooms. (Singles US$6, with bath US$9; doubles US$10). Ulus, like all of Turkey, is full of cheap *kebapçı.* From Ulus, walk east on Hisarparkı Cad., turn right just before Anafartalar Cad. to find Ankara's big **food market,** with everything from sugared almonds to live chickens.

SIGHTS

The fantastic **Anadolu Medeniyetleri Müzesi** (Museum of Anatolian Civilizations) is near the southern end of the citadel that dominates the old town. Take a taxi (US$1-3) or walk up the hill east from the statue of Atatürk, on Hısarparkı Cad., and right onto İpek Cad. The museum's setting is unique: a restored Ottoman *han* and *bedesten* (covered bazaar), its halls tweeting with scads of canaries, houses a collection of astoundingly old artifacts that trace Anatolian history from the dawn of civilization. (Open Tues.-Sun. 8:30am-5:30pm. US$2, students US$1.) While in the area, stroll through the **bazaar,** the town-within-a-town inside the citadel walls, and the **Alâaddin Mosque.** Don't leave town without visiting **Anıt Kabır,** Atatürk's mausoleum. Its immense scale and the sheer number of Atatürk's personal effects manifest Turkey's reverence for its national hero. The site is in a vast park overlooking the west side of town (a 25min. walk from Kızılay, or take southbound bus 63 on Atatürk Cad.). (Mausoleum open Tues.-Sun. 9am-5pm in summer, 9am-4pm in winter. Free.)

■■■ CAPPADOCIA

300km southeast of Ankara, Cappadocia is the most striking province in Turkey's central plateau. Peculiar volcanic formations, clustered in valleys and along ridges, chisel the sharp-jawed landscape. When Christians arrived here in the 6th century, they carved houses, churches, and entire cities out of the soft volcanic rock.

Göreme Göreme's proximity to rock-hewn churches and the valley of Zelve make it a convenient base. **Guided tours** of Cappadocia's major sites are available from several agencies in town for US$15-30. The most impressive of these are at the **Göreme Open-Air Museum,** 1km out of the village on the Ürgüp road (open 8am-6pm. US$3, students US$1.50). The monks of Cappadocia built the majority of the churches in Göreme between the 4th and 10th centuries, and inhabited the area until the formation of the modern Turkish Republic, when all Anatolian Greeks were relocated in exchange for the Turks living in Greece. Be certain to visit the Church of the Apple (Elmalı) and the Sandal Church in the hill right before the main entrance; both feature superb frescoes. In the last few years, over 60 new pensions have carved a niche for themselves, charging a standard US$4 for a room without a bath. For cave-dwelling with the comfort of a hotel, try **Peri Pension** (tel. (384) 271 21 36); its rooms are in a giant rock cone (US$2.50 per person). The hospitable **Rock Valley Pension** (tel. (384) 271 23 51) offers lots of headroom and high-pressure showers and is a good place to join informal excursions to some of the area's more inaccessible sites (US$2.50 per person). Camp at **Göreme Dilek Camping** (tel. (384) 271 23 96), where phallic rock formations penetrate the campsite (US$2 per person, US$5 includes tent rental). The **Orient,** opposite the Yüksel Motel, satisfies your appetite for US$4-6. The menu includes vegetarian dishes (US$1) and even breakfast pancakes and French toast.

Kaymaklı and Derinkuyu In the villages of **Kaymaklı** and **Derinkuyu,** inauspicious passages lead to two of Cappadocia's most spectacular sites. Two stark but well-preserved underground cities, thought to be over 3000 years old, lurk in an endless warren of tunnels, rooms, stairwells, and hallways. The cities are south of **Nevşehir,** on the road to Niğde; Kaymaklı is 20km away, Derinkuyu 29km. In both cities, the tunnels were built low and tortuous to hamper the progress of invaders. Though marked, the tunnels form a potentially confounding maze. Both cities have unexplored tunnels which are out of bounds, and thus tempting; be careful—there are tales of travelers who never made it back. Even during the hottest days it's dank in the tunnels, so bring a sweater. Buses run to Nevşehir every ½hr. (US$0.50). (Both sites open 8:30am-5:30pm, in winter until 5pm. US$0.70, students US$0.35.)

Ürgüp The leafy town of Ürgüp, 20km east of Nevşehir, makes a pleasant base for exploring. A bus runs every half hour to Nevşehir (US$0.30), where you must transfer from Göreme. There are *dolmuş* and buses to Kayseri for connections to the east (2hr., US$1). The Ürgüp **tourist office** (tel. (326) 341 40 59) is on Kayseri Cad., inside the garden. They'll help you plan daytrips and give tips on cheap hotels. (Open 8:30am-8pm; Oct.-March Mon.-Fri. 8am-5pm.) **Merkez Family Pension,** Hükümet Konağı Arkası 14 (tel. (326) 341 27 46), 200m east of the bus station, is the cheapest. (Singles US$4. Doubles US$4. Triples US$6.) From Cumhuriyet Sq., the center of town, Atatürk turns his back on **Pension Sun,** Hamam Sok. 6 (tel. (326) 341 44 93), beside the Turkish bath (well worth the US$6-8 per person). In the courtyard of an antique inn, the **Sofa Restaurant** serves tasty Turkish fare at fair prices (open 7:30am-11:30pm). Dance at **Harem Disco & Cave Bar,** literally a hole in the wall (no cover). Somewhat risky mopeds are an excellent way to see wineries in the area; try **Hepatu Rent a Motorcycle** (tel. (326) 341 32 33; US$7 per 4hr., insurance US$3) if you have an international driver's license.

Ukraine (Україна)

Country Code: 7   **International Dialing Prefix: 810**

In September 1994, the Ukrainian currency was experiencing hyperinflation. 45,000 Kupony (*Karbonovets*) equaled US$1. Last year they were exchanged at 9000 Kupony per US$. The year before that the rate was 230 per US$. Prices listed reflect costs in July 1994, drastic fluctuations are expected.

Despite Russian influence, Ukraine has held fast to a distinct political and literary tradition for hundreds of years. The fruit of the republic's farms, factories, and mines was shipped to Moscow during the Soviet era, and was a primary reason why Ukraine was considered the "breadbasket" of the Soviet republics, but on December 1, 1991, an overwhelming 90% of Ukraine's citizens voted for complete independence. Ukrainian currency and visas have since appeared, and, ironically, a postwar power play by Stalin (trying to get more votes for the USSR) means that Ukraine already has a seat at the United Nations.

Ukrainian nationalism resurfaced in the 19th century under the banner of the poet Taras Shevchenko, who led a campaign to revitalize the Ukrainian language and safeguard it from Polish and Russian cultural imperialism. In this century, the movement persisted, only strengthened by Soviet acts of mistreatment such as Stalin's forced famine of 1931 (which claimed 7 million lives), the long-standing ban on the teaching of Ukrainian in Soviet schools, and the Chernobyl disaster of 1986.

Although conditions are improving, travel is still quite difficult in Ukraine; many travel restrictions have not yet been lifted. A trip takes significant preparation, careful planning, and a total disregard for comfort. With patience and a positive attitude, however, the traveler to Ukraine will be rewarded with an experience that offers a glimpse not only of beautiful landscapes and the rich cultural heritage of this country, but also of the extraordinary process that struggles to redefine it.

For more detailed coverage of Ukraine, refer to *Let's Go: Eastern Europe.*

GETTING THERE AND GETTING AROUND

Foreign travelers arriving in Ukraine must have not only a **visa** but an **invitation** from a citizen or official organization. Regular visa processing at an embassy (with the correct paper-work) takes up to two weeks and costs US$30. Priority processing (less than 7 days) is US$60, while express (same day service) costs US$100; prices do not include postage or express mail. For more info, contact an **embassy: U.S.,** 3350 M St., NW, Washington, DC 20007 (tel. (202) 333-0606, fax 333-7510), **Canada,** 331 Metcalfe St., Ottawa, Ont. K2P153, (tel. (613) 230-2961, fax 230-2400), **U.K.,** 78 Kensington Park Rd., London W112PL, (tel. (0171) 727 63 12, fax 792 17 08), or **Australia,** 4 Bloom St., Moonee Pons, 3039, Melbourne (tel. (613) 326 01 35, fax 326 01 39). Transit and short-term (72hrs.) visas are also available at the larger border crossings and airports, prices vary but are still exorbitant. Visas may be extended once in the country by contacting the local authorities. Several **private organizations** can arrange visas and invitations (as well as homestays, tickets, etc.) for a slightly increased fee; **Home & Host International** (in the U.S., tel. 1-800-SOVIET-U or (612) 871-0596, fax 871-8853) and **IBV Bed & Breakfast Systems,** (tel. (301) 942-3770, fax 933-0024) 13113 Ideal Drive, Silver Spring, MD 20907 are two such agencies. **Kobasniuk Travel, Inc.,** 157 Second Ave., New York, NY 10003 (tel. (212) 254-8779, fax 454-4005) specializes in travel in Ukraine. It may be more expensive than doing it yourself, but can save time and provide peace of mind.

If you arrive in **Kiev airport** without a visa, you can buy a tourist voucher at window #8 (1-5 days US$5; 6-10 days US$10, etc.) for up to a month, which will serve as an invitation; then go to the window just at the entrance to buy your visa (transit visa US$15, short-term visa US$50). This will allow you to go through customs. You must declare all valuables and foreign currency in order to settle your tab when leaving the country. A copy of your invitation and your letters of introduction should be carried on your person at all times. Upon arrival in Ukraine you must check into a hotel or register with the **Office of Visas and Registration** (VVIR; tel. 225-13-54) in Kiev at bul. Tarasa Shevchenka 34 (бул. Тараса Шевченка), or in police stations of smaller cities, within the first three working days (US$10); visas may also be extended in such offices. Your visa not only lets you into the country but also proves that you are allowed to leave; **don't lose it.** Once you leave Ukraine, your visa becomes invalid. If you bought a double-entry visa you will be given a re-entry slip (въезд) upon your first arrival.

Air Ukraine International (in the U.S., tel. (202) 833-4648) flies from a number of European capitals as well as Chicago, New York, and Washington. Swiss Air, Air France, ČSA, Lufthansa, LOT, Malev, and SAS also fly to Kiev, generally 1-2 times per week. **Trains** run to Ukraine from Warsaw, Prague, Sofia, and Moscow; a weekly train runs from Berlin but tickets must be reserved significantly in advance. Relying on any water transport is risky. The once common **ferries** across the Black Sea have now been reduced to a few routes between Odessa, Yalta and İstanbul.

The good news about **trains** is that they're dirt cheap, go everywhere and are reasonably comfortable. The bad news is that **getting tickets** drives travelers to tears. Officially, foreigners are not allowed to travel without the proper **Intourist covers** on their tickets, which can only be obtained from official Intourist ticket windows. The rules keep changing, and cashiers know this. If you don't like being taken, you can declare "Снимайте!" (Snee-MAHY-tyeh, "Withdraw the ticket request!") and take the bus or come back later; arguing rarely works. Most towns also have a **central ticket bureau** which may also have an Intourist window. The lines here are just as long and the cashiers just as unpredictable, but they are usually closer to the center.

Buses are a little more expensive but less-crowded and the best way to travel across short distances. In large cities, buy tickets at least the night before at the regular ticket-windows with everyone else.

Local **public transportation** is swift and goes everywhere, but is unbelievably crowded. Buy **tickets** for trams, trolleybuses, and local buses at kiosks for next to nothing; punch them on board (large baggage requires an extra ticket). It costs 100Krb for a ticket that says "5Krb"—don't worry, inflation often outruns the printing presses. Tickets must be bought within the city to be valid. Buy **metro** tokens at the *kassa* in any station, and drop them in the slot before going through the turnstile. On **buses,** pay the conductor on board or the driver as you get off. In all cases, the number of people on the bus or tram or car will be well above the designated maximum; don't be afraid to push your way on board. To get off, ask the person in front of you, "Вы сходите сейчас?" (Vih skhah-DEE-tyeh s-chass; "Are you getting off now?") and he or she will move out of the way. Likewise, if asked, you are expected to move aside quickly.

Taxis are generally expensive for foreigners; agree on a price before getting in. State taxi service (recognizable by the checkered signs) is supplemented by what is labeled "private transport." Private transport is unregulated and cannot be recommended by *Let's Go* as a safe means of transportation. In any case, you are expected to pay the driver, making this an uneconomical form of transport for long journeys. State taxis wait for passengers at taxi stands throughout cities, and both taxis and private transport can be hailed by holding the hand at a downward salute.

UKRAINE ESSENTIALS

The breakup of the Soviet Union also brought about the demise of the official state travel agency, **Intourist,** which was responsible for foreigners traveling to Ukraine. **Private tourist offices** are starting to make an appearance, and can be useful places to get maps or hard-to-find train tickets.

The currency of Ukraine is the *karbonovets*, (Крб; Krb) usually referred to as "kupon." Inflation is endemic; expect all prices we list to change considerably. As of July 1994, all domestic train tickets were sold for kupons, but international tickets may still be sold only for US$. **Dollar-stores,** or "*Kashtans*" (Каштан) sell foreign merchandise only for dollars. In prices, "т" simply means "thousand." Exchange of US$ and DM is fairly simple, and can be done at Обмін Валют kiosks. Bring a large stash of US$1 bills; hotels and dollar-stores do not give change in dollars. Exchange of currencies other than US$ or DM is difficult, and **traveler's checks** are rarely accepted. Exchange with individuals is illegal but quite common. Black-market exchangers offer a rate slightly better than the official rate. Fraud is common; an exchanger may ask to see your money, then take it and run.

The loosening of state control and the worsening economic situation in Ukraine has led to an increase in crime. Foreigners can be an appealing target; be discreet with your valuables and never expose large sums of cash, particularly just after changing money. Try not to walk alone after dark, and steer clear of unlit parks and side streets. If you need a ride at night take a state taxi and choose your driver carefully. Women travelers should simply ignore unwanted advances from amorous Ukrainian men and seek out the assistance of the militia (Милиция) if the annoyance persists. If need be, turn to an older woman for help in an uncomfortable situation; her stern rebukes will usually be enough to embarrass the most persistent jerks.

It's a wise idea to register with your embassy once you arrive in Ukraine. Besides making the process of recovering lost passports much quicker, the embassy staff may be able to offer important information on travel or the situation in Ukraine.

Communication Telephones are struggling out of the dark ages; if you want service, you must pay dearly for it. Order an international call at the post office for

UKRAINE

the cheapest rate; when the call is ready, in 5-25min., you'll be pointed to the right booth to take it. In Kiev, **Utel** (Ukraine telephone) has started producing electronic **phonecards;** the phones are still scarce. You can take advantage of Utel's new technology to make **collect calls** from some phones. Dial 27 10 36 and ask for an ITNT operator. AT&T **USADirect** is available from a few phones in a few cities at tel. 81 00 11. **Local calls** are free from any gray pay phone in most cities, ever since the 15-kopeck coin was abandoned. In Lviv, buy tokens at the post office or at kiosks to make them work, although in many cases nothing will make them work. **Mail** is cheap but quite slow; allow min. 2-3 weeks from Kiev to any foreign destination.

Take the time to learn a few key phrases in Ukrainian. English-speakers are rare and most likely to be found among Ukrainian students who generally speak a second language. Pick up a phrase book before setting out and memorize the following phrases: Доброго ранку (Doh-bree-DYEHN; "Good morning"), До Побачення (Doh-poh-BAH-chen-ya; "Good-bye"), Прошу (PRO-shoo; "Please"), Вибач-те (VEE-bach (tye); "Excuse me"), Коли (Koh-LIH; "When?"), Де (Deh; "Where?"), Скільки (SKIL-kee; "How much?"), Дякую (DYA-kou-yoo; "Thank you").

Accommodations, Camping, and Food

Hotels fall into two categories, "hotels" and "tourist bases" called "Турбаза" (TOOR-bah-zah). The latter usually form part of a complex aimed at motoring tourists, but are otherwise nearly indistinguishable from hotels. Though hotel prices in Kiev are astronomical, singles run anywhere from US$2-25 per night throughout the rest of the country. Prices also drop when you ask for rooms without television or telephone. Make sure everything on the bill is really in the room. The phrase "самое дешёвое место" (SAHM-ah-yih dih-SHOHV-ah-yih MYEST-ah) helps—it means "the cheapest place." Your passport may be kept for the duration of your stay. Conditions are usually adequate, although you will nearly always need your own toilet paper (buy it at kiosks or markets) and hot water is a rare gift. Valuables should never be left in the room when you are absent; several people other than you have keys to your room. **Camping** is popular in Ukraine and most cities have a campground on the edge of town. These Soviet complexes can be quite posh, with saunas and restaurants, but are never new. Space in an bungalow with electricity will run US$7-10 per night; tent space costs US$3-8. Free camping is illegal. **Private rooms** are available through a few agencies and directly through bargaining at the train station; prices run US$1-2 per person but conditions vary widely.

With few exceptions, food in **restaurants** is not great and the atmosphere a bit rough. Cheaper and tastier options are available at **cafés,** where you order from the menu posted on the bar and either pick up your food there or have it brought to you. Tipping is optional in principle but expected from foreigners. At the bottom of the scale are little **cafeteria-style** cafés, sometimes only labeled "Кафе," which offer one main dish, soup, a few vegetable side dishes, and tea or milk. They're delightfully cheap; meals rarely run over US$1. **Vegetarians** can usually find enough here to make a decent meal, although you may get tired of cucumbers, tomatoes and carrots. Carnivores and herbivores alike may find themselves frequenting the public **markets,** laid out in enormous warehouses and usually jam-packed (open usually by 10am, they close no earlier than 5pm). **State food stores** are separated into a few categories based on their content. Гастроном mostly sells packaged goods. Молоко sells dairy products. Овочі-Фрукти sells fruits and vegetables, often in large jars, preserved. М'ясо sells meat, Хліб bread, Ковбаси sausage and Риба fish.

■■■ KIEV (КИЇВ)

"Most often of all I soothe my aged imagination with pictures of gold-domed, garden-cloaked and poplar-crowned Kiev," wrote poet Taras Shevchenko from exile. Kiev once ruled the first slavic empire, Kievan Rus, stretching from the Black Sea to the Danube. It has since fallen in political stature and influence, and has only recently begun to wield its own power anew. Life, everyone will admit, can be difficult here for residents and travelers alike. But it is all worth it to see the "mother of all Rus," laced as it is with all that is splendid, glorious, and grandiose.

ORIENTATION AND PRACTICAL INFORMATION

Situated on the lush, steep banks of the Dnieper (Дніпро) River, Kiev is a busy port serving ships headed south to the Black Sea and north to Russia. The city itself is divided into two parts: upper Kiev clings to the hills, while the lower city skirts the riverbanks. **Khreshchatik** (Хрещатик), the city's main boulevard, is lined with theaters, shops, and cafés. Running parallel, **vulitsya Volodimirska** (вулиця Володимирська) harbors a variety of historical sights.

Tourist Office: None as such. On vul. Hospitalna 12 (вул. Госпітальна), just behind the Respublikanski Stadion, the office of **Intourist Kiev** does little more than arrange domestic and international flights as well as train tickets (tel. flights: domestic 224 10 45, international 224 29 50; train tickets 224 25 59). Expect to pay a commission on all tickets—sometimes as high as 2000%. Down the hill at no. 9, **Hotel Rus** (tel. 220 42 55 or 220 52 33), has a map of the city. Service bureau open 8am-8pm.

Embassies: U.S., vul. Kotsyubinskovo 6 (вул. Коцюбинского) (tel. 244 73 49, emergencies after hours 244 73 45, 244 73 44 for 24hr. answering machine). Open Mon.-Fri. 9am-6pm. **Canada,** vul. Yaroslaviv val 31 (вул. Ярославів Вал) (tel. 212 02 12). **U.K.,** vul. Desyatinna 9 (вул. Десятинна) (tel. 288 05 04). **Russia,** Prospekt Kutuzova, 8 (tel. 294 6701). Issues US$50 visas to former Soviet republics Armenia, Azerbaijan, Georgia, etc. Foreign citizens caught traveling in these countries without a visa are fined US$300. Open Mon., Wed., Fri. 9am-noon.

Currency Exchange: Traveler's checks cashed at Hotel Intourist on vul. Gospitalna 12 (вул. Госпітална) behind the Respublikanski Stadion (Республиканськи Стадион) metro stop for 2.5% commission. (Open Mon.-Fri. 8am-noon and 1-7:30pm, Sat.-Sun. 8am-5pm.) Cash (US$, DM) is much easier to change, at any kiosk marked Obmin-Balyut (Обмін-Балют). Most major currencies can be changed at the big hotels for lousy rates.

Post Office: vul. Khreshchatik 24 (Хрещатик), next to Majdan Nezalezhnosti (Майдан Незалежності).

Telephones: Credit card calls can be made from the service bureau of Hotel Rus at Gospitalna 9 (Госпітална). Open 8am-8pm. **Utel phonecards** are available at the post office in denominations of US$10 or US$20, and can be used to make international calls at Utel phones, located in the post office, at large hotels and at the Dim Ukraincki (Дім Український) cultural center across from Hotel Dnipro. Other **international** calls can be made from any post office. **City code:** 044.

Flights: Kiev-Borispol receives incoming flights from most West European cities. A **bus** leaves the parking lot every 30min. and drops you off at the Livoberezha (Лівобережа) metro stop, across the river from most of Kiev (fare 60,000Krb). **Taxis** charge foreigners outrageous prices (up to US$70) because they can.

Trains: Kiev-Passazhirski (Київ-Пассажирський), M: Vokzalna (Вокзальна) or tram 2. **Tickets** can be purchased at the Intourist window on the second floor of the station, window #42, open 24hrs., except 7-8am, 1-2pm and 7-8pm. Direct connections to Vienna, Berlin, Moscow, Warsaw, Bratislava, Chelm, Brest.

Buses: Most long-distance buses leave from the central Avtovokzal (Автовокзал) at pl. Dzerzhinskovo (пл. Дзержинського). Buses to Dnipropetrovsk leave from the Darnica station at pr. Yiruya Gagarina (пр. Юрія Гагаріна). Regional buses to points north leave from Polese at pl. Tarasa Shevchenka, to points south from Juzhnaya at pr. Akademika Glushkova 3 (Академика Глушкова) and from Podol at vul. Nizhnij Val 15a (Нижній Вал). Regional buses to points east leave from Dachnaya at pr. Peremogi 142 (пр. Перемоги).

Public Transportation: Kiev's **metro** (M) system is clean and efficient and abnormally well-buried. Buy a bunch of tokens from the "Каса" at 150Krb a piece or a monthly pass, good for all public transport, from a kiosk for US$0.75. Check the map before you go down the escalator; there are only lists of names at the bottom. Перехід (Perekhid) indicates a walkway to another station, вихід у місто (vikhid u misto) an exit onto the street, and вхід (vkhid) an entrance to the metro. Ticket for **trams, trolleybuses,** and **buses** are available at kiosks for 100Krb and

UKRAINE

must be punched on board. Note that trolleybuses and buses with the same number probably have very different routes.

Taxis: A trip for the foreigner will cost a bundle; try to avoid taxis if you can.

Luggage storage: Located at hotels and the train station. Hotels will often charge less, but only keep luggage if they think you have a room there.

Pharmacy: Apteka 7 vnochi (Аптека 7 вночи) at vul. Artyoma 10 (вул. Артёма), is open 24hrs. Hard-currency pharmacies in the lobbies of both Hotel Intourist and Hotel Rus have many western products.

Medical Assistance: Polyklinik 1, vul. Verkhna 5 (вул. Верхна) (tel. 296 66 68), accepts foreign patients in room 355 for hard currency, but it is not the same service as at home. English spoken.

Emergencies: To be avoided. This is a Ukrainian service made for Ukrainians. **Medical,** tel. 03 (better yet, contact your embassy). **Fire,** tel. 01. **Police,** tel. 02.

ACCOMMODATIONS AND CAMPING

Kiev's tourist industry is aimed at rich foreign businessmen, and as a result, the hotel prices here make budget travelers cringe. During July and August there are some possibilities for staying in vacant dormitories. The **Institute of Foreign Languages,** vul. Chervnoarmiska 73 (вул. Червноармійска) (tel. 269 93 08, fax 227 67 88), rents their dorm beds out at US$3-7 per person July 1-Aug. 25. Call Margarita Dvorzhetskaya Mon.-Fri. 10am-1pm or 2-5pm to arrange a space. **Hotel Mir** (Готел Мип), 40-leji Oktyabrya 70 (40-леійі Октября) (tel. 264 96 46), near Goloceyevskaya pl. (Голосеевская пль) has doubles for US$36 in kupons. At least it has toilets. M: Либіська (Libidska), then tram 4 to the магазин книги Ювілейний (magazin knigi Yuvilejnij) stop, then walk another ½km or so. The restaurant, sauna, and casino at **Motel-Camping "Prolisok,"** pr. Peremogi 179, (tel. 444 12 93) are very popular with foreign tractor trailer drivers. From M: Svyatoshno (Святошно) take trolleybus 7 to the Автостанция Дачна (Avtostantsiya Dachna) stop and walk 2km down the highway. (Dim but comfortable doubles US$65. Bungalows with kitchen and shower US$17.50 per person. Tent space US$7.)

FOOD

Some of the better **cafés** are on **Andriyivsky uzviz** (Андріївський узвіз) and **vul. Karla Marksa** (вул. Карла Маркса). Markets in the summer are well-stocked and active, and many even serve ready-to-eat dishes along with their wide variety of bulk foods. An enormous variety of vegetable products can be bought from **Bessarabski Rynok** (Бессарабський Ринок), vul. Khreshchatik (вул. Хрещатик) and vul. Taras Shevchenko (вул. Тарас Шевченко) (open Tues.-Sun. 7am-7pm, Mon. 7am-5pm). **Livoberezhniy Rynok,** at M: Ливобережна (Livoberezhna), is slightly less expensive, but further from the center. Pay in dollars for not-so-fresh western food at **NIKA,** across from the Bessarabski Rynok on vul. Taras Shevchenko 3 (вул. Тарас Шевченко) (open Mon.-Sat. 10am-8pm, Sun 10am-6pm). Quiet by day, **Spadishchina** (Спадшина), vul. Spask 8 (вул. Спаськ) (M: Контрактова пл., Kontraktova pl.) is swarmed by 26-28 year olds in suits and slinky dresses dancing and drinking many bottles of vodka. The fancy cars and bodyguards speak volumes. (Full meal US$5. Open noon-11pm.) The crowded and underground **Bistro Maksim** (Бистро Максимь), vul. Bogdana Khmelnikovo 21 (вул. Богдана Хмельникого), across from the opera house doles out soup, salad, meat, and potatoes to an international crowd, for under US$3 (open Mon.-Sat. noon-midnight). The best of the hotels restaurants is **Restaurant Khreshchatik,** vul. Khreshchatik 16 (вул. Хрещатик), in the Hotel Khreshchatik. The lunchtime menu is superior to the dinner menu. (Full meal US$5-6. Open 8am-11pm.)

SIGHTS AND ENTERTAINMENT

Downtown Kiev orbits around **vul. Khreshchatik** (вул. Хрещатик), the historical nucleus as well as the contemporary heart of the city. Along Khreshchatik, you can check out the **TsUM** (ЦУМ), the central department store where everything you need is on sale in a terrifically confusing jumble of counters (open Mon.-Sat. 9am-8pm). Farther down, **Maydan Nezalezhnosti** (Independence Square, formerly

October Revolution Square), enclosing large fountains, is filled with people-watchers and with political discussion. Right-wing, left-wing, and tourist literature is sold along the fountain walls, and the occasional street-performer pleases crowds with a show. At the center of **Khreschatiy Park**, the **Arch of Brotherhood**, a huge silver croquet wicket that towers over the park, celebrates the Russian-Ukrainian union. Locals refer to it as "the yoke." Also inside the park is the **Monument to the Brave Soccer Players.** As the story goes, Nazi troops forced the team to play a "death match" against a German SS team. Stirred by local pride, Kiev's Dynamo played their hardest, won the match 3-0, and were promptly executed.

At bul. Tarasa Shevshenka, the **V.I. Lenin monument** continues to stand, even though most of Kiev's major Communist monuments have been long since desecrated. Dedicated to the poet namesake, bul. Taras Shevchenko sweeps past the many-domed ochre **Vladimirska Cathedral,** built to commemorate the 900th anniversary of Christianity in Kiev. At no. 12 the **Taras Shevchenko Museum** is one of the largest and most beautiful literary museums in the former Soviet Union. Exhibits are labeled in Ukrainian and Russian, but an English-speaking guide is under US$1. (Open Tues.-Sun. 10am-5pm. Closed on last Fri. of the month.)

Up the hill from the opera house on vul. Volodimirska (вул. Володимирська), the **Golden Gates** (Золотой Ворота) have stood since 1037, marking the entrance to the city. A museum is now housed inside the gates. (Open Fri.-Tues. 10am-5pm, Wed. 10am-4:30pm.) At vul. Volodimirska 24, the golden onion domes, decorated façades, and 11th-century Byzantine icons of the **St. Sophia Monastery** recall its past as cultural center of Kievan Rus and the site of the first library in Rus (real price US$0.03; foreigners usually US$3).

At the end of vul. Volodimirska, an ancient, winding road leads to the oldest section of Kiev. This is **Andriyivskiy uzviz** (Андріївський узвіз), now an artists' colony, complete with cafés, souvenir shops, and galleries. **St. Andrew's Cathedral** proudly overlooks its street; learn about it and the street just below at the **Andriyivskiy Uzviz Museum** (open Mon.-Fri. 9am-5pm). Downhill, at Andriyivsky uzviz 13, away from St. Andrew's toward lower Kiev and the historic Podol district, is **Bulgakov's House** (open Tues.-Sun.). A stroll down vul. Petra Sahaydachnoho (Петра Сагайдачного) leads toward the scenic **funicular,** which will take you back to upper Kiev for the price of a metro ticket (open 6:30am-11pm, Sundays free).

In the summer, locals café-hop up and down Kreshchatik, and gather to talk at the fountains of Maydan Nezalezhnosti, which are lit up at night. If you desire more spirited company, **Slavuta,** vul. Horkoho 12 (вул. Горкого), is open until midnight and has beer on tap (US$3 per ½l). Take trolleybus 16 or 18 from Maydan Nexalezhnosti to **pl. Lvivska** (пл. Львівська), another café-hopping relay track, for a closer look at the less touristed sections of town.

A seat at the national **opera and ballet theater** costs US$0.25 if you buy a ticket there, vul. Volodymyrska 50. (Ticket office open Tues.-Sat. noon-2pm and 4-7:30pm, Sun. 11am-1:30pm. Shows at noon and 7pm.) The **national theater** across the street (М: Театральна; Teatralna) is just as good a bargain. (Ticket office open Thurs.-Tues. noon-2:45pm and 4-7pm, Wed. noon-2:45pm and 4-6pm. Shows at 7pm.)

■■■ LVIV (ЛЪВÉВ)

Lviv, alternately called L'vov (by the Russians), Lwów (by the Poles), and Lemberg (by the Germans), dates back to 1256, when the city's first fortress arose in a valley at the confluence of Eastern European trade routes. From the start an integral part of East Central Europe rather than the Russian empire, its narrow cobblestone alleys and magnificent Gothic and Baroque cathedrals are startlingly reminiscent of such former Austro-Hungarian jewels as Prague and Kraków. In 1939 Western Ukraine was cut out of Poland and annexed to the rest of the Ukrainian Soviet Socialist Republic, Lviv's predominantly Polish population was deported, scarlet banners were hung, and decades of Sovietization ensued. In the post-Soviet age, Lviv has become the center of Ukrainian national revival. The yellow and blue Ukrainian flag flies over the headquarters of the democratically elected city council, and *Rukh*, the Ukrainian popular front, maintains its headquarters here.

ORIENTATION AND PRACTICAL INFORMATION

The center of the old town is **pl. Rynok** (пл. Ринок), the old market square. Around it a grid of streets forms the old town, and along the western side, **prosp. Svobody** (пр. Свободи) runs from the Opera House to **pl. Mitskievicha** (пл. Міцкевича). Tram 1 runs from the northwest train station to the center of the old town, tram 6 to the north end of prosp. Svobody. Tram 9 goes back the way tram 1 came.

Tourist Offices: Grand Hotel (Гранд-Готель), prosp. Svobody 13 (пр. Свободи), (tel. 76 90 60), is not a tourist office, but the reception desk of this Ukrainian-American venture understands the concept "customer service"; perfect English, free maps for casual passers-by, and questions answered with a smile. **Hotel Georges** (Готель Жорж) **service bureau** plans guided excursions and does possess a lot of information about the city, but only reluctantly lets you have it. (Yes, this used to be Intourist.) Open Mon.-Fri. 9am-5pm.

Currency Exchange: Traveler's checks accepted for 2.5% commission at **Hotel Georges** exchange bureau. Open Mon.-Sat. 9am-5pm, Sun. 9am-3pm. Many western currencies exchanged, including Australian and Canadian dollars, at **Dendi Exchange,** ul. Kopernika 16. Open 8am-8pm. Dollars and DM exchanged at Обмін-Валют kiosks; those that accept Polish złoty are also marked кантор.

Post Office: vul. Slovatskovo 1 (вул. Словацьково), one block from park Ivan Franko, to the right as you face the university. Open Mon.-Fri. 8am-8pm, Sat. 8am-6pm, Sun. and holidays 8am-2pm. Poste Restante. **Postal Code:** 290000.

Telephones: Doroshenka 39 (Дорошенка), around the corner from the post office. Order calls at window #3; at night, window #1. Open 24hrs. **City Code:** 0322.

Trains: Train station on pl. Voksalna (пл. Вокзальна) at the end of vul. Vokzalna (вул. Вокзальна). **Tickets** available at windows #23-25 on the second floor, or at the travel bureau of the Hotel George. Direct trains daily to Sofia, Budapest, Prague, Bratislava; twice daily to Pszemyśl, Poland; on odd days only to Warsaw.

Buses: Station on the outskirts of town at vul. Striycka (вул. Стрийська). Extensive regional service; for long-distances, buy tickets 1 day in advance. To Przemyśl, Poland (4hr.; пермишл), Lublin (Люблін), Warsaw (Варшава), and Krakow (Краків).

Public Transportation: Buy tickets for trams, trolleybuses and buses at kiosks; punch on board.

Pharmacy: Apteka 1 (Аптека), vul. Kopernika 8 (вул. Коперника). Open 24hrs.

ACCOMMODATIONS AND FOOD

Despite recent renovations at **Hotel Georges** (Готель Жорж), pl. Mickiewicza 1 (пл. Міцкевича) (tel. 79 90 11), the elevator doesn't always work and the mirrors in the hallways are a bit cracked. Take tram 1 from the train station to Дорошенка. (Singles US$9-14. Doubles US$17-22.) Wonderfully modern facilities are offered at **Hotel Sputnik** (Готель Спутник), vul. Knyahini Olgi 116 (бул. Княгині Ольги) (tel. 645 82 20). Take trolleybus 5 from the bus station to the 7th stop, then backtrack and take a left onto Knyahini Olgi. (Singles US$15. Doubles US$16-29. Bath and breakfast included.) **Hotel Lviv** (Готель Львів), vul. 700г. Lvova 3 (вул. 700р. Львова), just behind the opera house, is not as pretty as the newer hotels but the beds are comfy and the location central. Take tram 6 from the train station to Оперний Театр, backtrack about 50m and take a left; the hotel is on the right. (Singles US$7-9.50. Doubles US$11-16. Asking for rooms without TV and refrigerator may lower the price.)

Most restaurants and cafés cluster around **pl. Rynok**; the most central **market** stands on Prospect Shevchenko, a block past Hotel George, though it's not as big as **Rynok Noviy** (Ринок Новий), reachable by bus 18. The **Halytski Rynok** (Галицький Ринок), behind the flower stands across from the Church of St. Andrew, has fresh berries, honey, and vegetables (open 7am-6pm). Get a full meal for under US$2 in **Stari Royal** (Старий Рояль), at vul. Stavropitivska Dnestr (вул. Ставропітівська Днестр), next to the pharmacy museum (open noon-11pm). **Restaurant Festival** (Фестивальний), vul. Sichovich Strilsti 12 (tel. 72 20 59), behind the main university building, serves up traditional Ukrainian fare under US$3 and has music and cabaret show 7:30-8:30pm (open noon-11pm). **Pizza Pronto** on vul. Gorodska 61, just down the street from the circus is a busy little restaurant serving hot pizza (open 10am-9pm.) **Pingvin** (Пінгвін), prosp. Svobodi 43 (пр. Свободи) is an extremely popular ice cream parlor, and with good reason—it's one of the best in town (open Mon.-Sat. 9am-2pm and 3-9pm, Sun. 9am-2pm and 3-8pm). Cool off with summertime sherbets at **Korona** (Корона), prosp. Svobodi (пр. свободи), next to the Hotel Ukraina (open 9am-3pm and 4-8pm).

SIGHTS AND ENTERTAINMENT

Lviv's historical center is compact and best seen on foot. The ornate Neoclassical **Opera and Ballet Theater** (Театр Опери та Балету) opens onto a pedestrian mall that runs down the middle of prospect Svobodi, splitting it in two. The **Mickiewicz column,** which honors the Polish poet, is the site of concerts, crowded political discussions and the occasional Hare Krishna singalong. Turn left at the Ukraine movie theater to reach the stone-gray façade of the former 17th-century Bernardine Monastery, now the Greek Catholic **Church of St. Andrew.** The church boasts a cavernous interior covered in frescoes, and a massive gilt altar of rich gold and black granite. Make a sharp left here and take one of the narrow streets leading up to **pl. Rynok,** the historic market square.

On pl. Katedralna rises the Polish **Roman Catholic Cathedral** (open Mon.-Sat. 6am-noon and 6-8pm, Sun. and holidays 6am-3pm and 5:30-8pm.) Next door stands a small Renaissance chapel, whose portal displays a frieze of delicately sculpted stone. At the east end of the square are the massive **Assumption Church** (next to the 60m Korniak belltower) and the Baroque cupola of the **Museum of Religion,** formerly a Dominican monastery and church, whose masterfully carved wooden figures are worth a look (open Fri.-Sun. 11am-6pm). Up above the old city, where the television tower now stands, **High Castle Hill** (Vysoki Zamok; Бысокий Замок), yields stunning panorama of Lviv. Continuing farther east, take tram 2 or walk along vul. Lichakivska to vul. Krupyarska (Крупярська). Walk up the street on the left to the outdoor **Museum of Architecture,** also known as the **Shevchenskivski Hai** (Шевченськивський Гай). Lying on a vast park, the museum harbors a collection of authentic wooden houses brought here from around western Ukraine (open Tues.-Fri. and Sun. 10am-6pm, Sat. 11am-7pm).

When the night comes, Lviv offers comparatively little. Near the arsenal on vul. Vinnichenka is **Pid Veshayu** (Пі́д Вежею; Under the Tower), a popular, rowdy beer hall. Coffee is served upstairs, draft beer in the smoky grotto basement. Part of Lviv's original city wall (c. 1256) is visible downstairs near the bar. (Open 9am-3pm and 4-8pm.) Catch a performance at the **Opera** or the **Symphony,** vul. Chaikovskoho 7. The ticket desks (*teatralni kasi;* театральны касы) are to be found at pr. Svobodi 37. (Open Mon.-Sat. 11am-2pm and 4-7pm.)

■■■ YALTA (ЯЛТА)

The most popular resort in Crimea has much to offer, but after the sun and the Black Sea, everything else is garnish. Strolling along the promenade is a favorite pastime after a hard day of sun-basking. The beaches in Yalta proper are covered with gray, smooth pebbles and can be a bit disheartening at first sight. But the cobalt waters of the Black Sea reach 25°C in summer and are mercifully free of stinging jellyfish, overbearing surfers, and sticky sand. Although there are few spots along **nab. Lenina** where you can bathe for free, one 15,000Krb ticket will give you access to any public beach all day. The **Delfin** beach at the western end of town is a little sandier and a little less crowded than the east-end **Massandtovskiy.**

Chekhov called Yalta home for the last five years of his life. At ul. Kirova 112 (ул. Кирова), the house he built with his own hands and the garden he planted are now a museum. Bus 8 takes you there every 40min. from the Кинотеатр Спартак stop on ul. Pushkinska. A 10min. walk from town on Moskovskaya ul. leads to the **circus**

UKRAINE

(Season: May 28-Oct. 28 Tues.-Sun. Ticket windows open Tues.-Sun. 10am-6pm.) If you aren't feeling childish enough yet, the **Polyana Skazok** (Поляна Сказок) children's park next to the campground takes characters from Russian and Ukrainian fairytales and immortalizes them in larger-than-life figures (open 8am-8pm).

Practical Information, Accommodations, and Food To get to Yalta, take a train to Simferopol from Kiev (19hr., US$4), Odessa (12hr., US$3), Moscow (22hr.), and then take a **trolleybus** (every 10min.). Although all of Greater Yalta was once covered by frequent waterbus service, fuel, and funding shortages have brought the service to a trickle. **Ferries** still run to İstanbul twice weekly. Buy tickets at the port at Roosevelta 5. Traveler's checks are accepted for no commission at the **State Import-Export Bank of the Ukraine,** nab. Lenina 3 (open Mon.-Fri. 8:30am-1pm and 2-5:45pm). At **Xchange Points,** near Hotel Yuzhniya at ul. Roosevelta 8, most major currencies are changed (open 8am-8pm).

In the height of the summer, there are serious crowds here, political unrest or not, in search of serious tans. It's wise to book ahead. If you can't, however, a good first stop is the **service bureau** (Бюро Обслуживанния) at Roosevelta ul. 6, (tel. (0654) 32 78 73), which for a US$3 fee will guide you to rooms in the Hotel Krym and Hotel Yuzhniya, among others. **Hotel Otdykh** (Гостиница Отдых), Drazhinskovo 14 (Дражинского) (tel. (0654) 35 30 79), in the old town above the Massandrovskiy beach offers friendly, helpful service. (Doubles and triples with bath US$4.25 per person.) Find aging elegance at **Hotel Volna** (Гостиница Волна), ul. Sadovaya 4 (ул. Садовая) (tel. (0654) 32 39 40). Take trolleybus 1 to the Кинопрокат (*Kinoprokat*) stop and backtrack 150m. (With bath, US$5 per person.) For a real class-act campground in a charming high-altitude setting, with showers, kitchen facilities, sauna, as well as a café and restaurant, trek to **Motel-Camping Polyana Skazok** (Поляна Сказок), ul. Kirova 167 (ул. Кирова) (tel. (0654) 39 52 19). Take bus 26, 27, or 11 from the upper platform of the bus station to the Поляна Сказок (Polyana Skazok) stop; it's a 20min. walk uphill. (Tents US$1 per person. Bungalows US$3 per person. Motel singles US$14-19. Doubles US$19-24. Campground open June-Oct.) Probably the easiest way to keep your stomach happy in Yalta is to pick and choose from the numerous kiosks and snack stands that litter the street and beaches. For a state store, the **Gastronom** (Гастроном) market on nab. Lenina 4 is surprisingly well-stocked with foreign products. Fresher than usual entrees for under US$1 await at **Café Krym** (Кафе "Крым"), Moskovskaya ul. 1/2 (open 8am-8pm). Wolf excellent meaty food at **Restaurant Gurman** (Ресторан "Гурман"), nab. Lenina, in the alleyway to the left of the Casino Diana building. (Entrees US$1.50-3. Open noon-11pm.)

■■■ ODESSA (ОДЕССА)

Cosmopolitan Odessa is full of markets, quick-changing roadside business, dour but impressive monuments, and strings of sunny, sandy beaches. A lot goes on here; you can feel the activity the minute you step off the train. Everything is available here, from auto parts to exotic Nikes. The sea is always in the background; sailors from the disputed Black Sea Fleet crowd trams and public places.

ORIENTATION AND PRACTICAL INFORMATION

Odessa lies in a long strip along the coastline; the central section is bounded by the train station to the south and the port to the north. All streets are labeled in both Ukrainian and Russian. The main street in Odessa is **vul. Deribasovskaya** (вул. Дерибасовская). The northern end of Deribasovskaya intersects **vul. Sovetskoi Armii** (вул. Советської Армії); in the opposite direction, heading towards the sea, it meets **vul. Pushkinskaya** (вул. Пушкинская). A right onto Pushkinskaya from Deribasovskaya leads to the train station, and a left ushers you onto **Primorski Boulevard** (Приморский бул.), a tree-lined promenade with a panoramic view of the sea.

Tourist Office: For train, plane or bus tickets, the **Intourist Office,** ul. Pushkin-skaya 17 (ул. Пушкинская), in the lobby of the Hotel Krasnaya (Гостиница Красная). Trolleybus 1 or 4 takes you there from the train station. Open 9am-5pm. Just as friendly and a little more likely to speak English, the **service bureau** in the Hotel Chornoye Morye (Готель Чёрное Море), ul. Lenina 59, offers English-language tours of the city (US$10 per hr.).

Currency Exchange: Major European currencies exchanged at **Dendi Exchange,** ul. Pushkinskaya 54 (ул. Пушкинская). Open 8am-8pm. Take trolleybus 1 or 4 from the train station. Traveler's checks accepted at the exchange bureau of the **Hotel Krasnaya** (Гостиница Красная), ul. Pushkinskaya 17, (trolleybus 4 from the train station) for a 2.5% commission. Open Mon.-Fri. 9am-5pm, Sat. 10am-1pm.

Post Office: bul. Sadovaqa 8 (бул. Садовая). Poste Restante at counter #8; postcards and pre-stamped airmail envelopes at #9 (8000Krb). Open 8am-8pm.

Telephones: At the post office. Open 24hrs. For hard currency, the **telephone bureau** on ul. Lenina 19 (ул. Ленина) is a bit cheaper. To western Europe US$1.50 per min. To USA US$2.50 per min. To Australia US$4 per min. Open 8am-8pm. Local calls free from any phone that works. **City code:** 048.

Trains: Zh. D. Vokzal (Ж. Д. Вокзал) on Privokzalnaya pl. (Привокзальная пл.) at the southern end of ul. Pushkinskaya (ул. Пушкинская).

Buses: The main bus station is on ul. Dzerzhinskovo 58 (ул. Дзержинского). To Kiev: 11hr., US$7. **Tinra** (Тинра), 26 ul. Zhukovskovo (ул. Жыковсокого). Services to Varna, Bulgaria (Tues. 7am, 24hr., US$34).

Boats: Schedules are unpredictable. Ask for info at the booking office of the **Black Sea Steamship Line** on Potemkin pl. at the top of the stairs by the same name. To İstanbul US$97, Piraeus US$180. Open Mon.-Thurs. 8am-12:30pm and 1-5pm, Fri. 8am-12:30pm and 1-4pm, Sat.-Sun. 10am-12:30pm and 1-2pm. To the left of the main dock are the ferries that run to the beaches surrounding Odessa.

Public Transportation: The train station is the center of the system; main terminus is at Gretska pl. (Грецька площа). Trams and trolleybuses leave from the south side of the station if they are heading south, the west side if they are heading west, etc. Buy tickets (100Krb) at Абонементы kiosks and punch on board. Buses leave less frequently but cover more territory. Pay the driver on board (3000Krb).

Pharmacy: Apteka (Аптека) 1, ul. Sadovaya 5 (ул. Садовая). Open 8am-8pm; prescriptions filled around the clock. Tampons. No condoms.

Medical services: Polyklinik, Sudostroitelnaya ul. 21 (Судостроительная ул.). Accepts foreign patients for hard currency.

Emergency: Fire, tel. 01, **Police,** tel. 02, **Ambulance,** tel. 03.

ACCOMMODATIONS AND CAMPING

The downtown hotels, crumbling remnants of a glorious marbled past, are often affordable even if prices are quite nebulous—make sure a ghost television or refrigerator isn't added into your bill. Usually you can ask for one place in a triple or quad, and if you don't mind spending the night with strangers, this is the cheapest option. Prices range widely, depending whether you have a sink, toilet, shower, refrigerator, or television. Take tram 3 or 12 from the train station to reach the downtown hotels; they are all located very close to each other. The elegant but aging **Hotel Tsentralnaya** (Гостиница "Центральная"), vul. Sovetskoi Armii 40 (вул. Совeтской Армії) (tel. 26 84 06) offers spacious and bright rooms. (Singles US$21-28. Doubles US$13-26 per person. Triples US$11-15 per person.) The grand, ornate exterior of **Hotel Bolshaya Moskovskaya** (Гостиница Большая Московская), ul. Deribasovskaya 29 (ул. Дерибасовская) (tel. 22 40 16) hides tired, mediocre rooms. (Singles US$19-35. Doubles US$16-27 per person. 4-6 beds US$12-20 per person.) Camp at **Dolphin Camping** (Кемпинг "Дельфин"), dor. Kotovskovo 307 (дор. Котовского) (tel. 55 50 52 or 55 00 66). From the train station, take trolleybus 4 or 10 to the terminus (a small loop in the road) and transfer to tram 7; get off 20min. later at the Лузановка stop and continue along the road for ½km. No kitchen facilities, but the surprisingly elegant and cheap restaurant, the sauna, the bar, and the private beach might make up for it. (Bungalows US$7 per person. Cottages US$5 per person. Tents US$3 per person.) Staying in a **private apartment** is by far the cheapest option, with prices running

US$1-2 per person, but you'll be lucky to get anything near the center of town. Train-station hawkers are recognizable by their signs: usually some variation on "Сдаю комнату." The first thing to ask is "Скiлко?" (SKIHL-koh, "how much?")

FOOD

Odessa is blessed with a few good restaurants, an amazing market, and one or two hip cafés. Curiously, Odessan restaurants are often underground if they're indoors. A number of good options can be found along **vul. Sovetskoi Armii** (вул. Советської Армії) south of **ul. Deribasovskaya** (ул. Дерибасовская). The **Privoz** (Привоз) **market** on Privoznaya ul. (Привозная ул.) will provide any food that Odessa port handles, and more. A shining star in the bitter night of Ukrainian restaurants, **Galaxy Restaurant,** vul. Sovetskoi Armii 23, below the street serves superior, delicately-prepared food with soberly polite service. (English menu. Full meal US$5-7. Open noon-midnight.) The hyper-cool sip foreign liqueurs and discuss where to shop while looking disdainfully across the room at the regular folk enjoying juicy cutlets (US$2) at **Café na Gretseskoe** (Кафе на Грецеское), vul. Gretska 11 (вул. Грецька) (open noon-11pm). For decent food, warm service, and a full meal for US$3-5, descend into **Restaurant Zhanetta** (Ресторан Жанетта), vul. Gretska 23 (вул Грецька) (open 11am-11pm). The cheapest meal in town awaits at simply titled **Café** (Кафе), ul. Karla Marksa 12 (ул. Karla Marksa) (open 8am-8pm). **Pizza Spaghetti,** ul. Lenina 6 (ул. Ленина), serves "traditional" Italian Ukrainian cuisine (Pizza, 2 slices for US$0.75) **Restaurant Fav** (Фав), ul. Tracheskaya 50 (ул. Траческая), serves traditional Ukrainian and Russian to the accompaniment of cabaret performances. (Dinner and show about US$6. Open 6pm-4am.)

SIGHTS AND ENTERTAINMENT

The pedestrian **ul. Deribasovskaya,** as well as being the commercial center of Odessa, is home to musicians, mimes, artists, and a thriving café culture that attracts the young and the fashionable. Turn left on ul. Lenina to find the **Opera and Ballet Theater,** an imposing edifice that towers over the surrounding gardens, and wedding-photo hot-spot. The nearby **Museum of the Black Sea Fleet** (Музей морского флота) at ul. Lastochkina 6 (ул. Ласточкина), was under reconstruction in 1994. At no. 4 on the same street, the **Archeological Museum of Odessa** (Археологичний Музей) houses artifacts found in the Black Sea region, dating back to the Greek and Roman eras. The façade is graced by classical figures; don't forget to look at the garden, too. (Museum open Tues.-Sun. 10am-5pm.) Take a right at the Archeological Museum onto the shady, tree-lined **Primorski Boulevard,** the most popular spot in Odessa to stroll. The statue of the great Russian writer **Alexander Pushkin** has his back unceremoniously turned to city hall, since the local government refused to help fund its construction Down Primorski bul., a statue of the **Duc de Richelieu** gazes toward the **Potemkin stairs** and the more distant **Morskoi Vokzal.** Director Sergei Eisenstein used these stairs in his epic 1925 film *Battleship Potemkin*. If you are too tired to climb back up the stairs, an **escalator** (150Krb) will bring you back. A left at this point will bring you to a **monument** commemorating the actual mutiny of the *Potemkin*. At the end of Primorski the **Palace of Vorontsov,** now a club for schoolchildren, boasts a spectacular view, especially at sunset.

Although it's tough to find a place to stay that's close to the beach, most of Odessa's sandy shore is reachable by public transportation. Tram 5 stops at **Lanzheron beach** (Ланжерон), the closest to central Odessa, at **Vidrada beach** (Видрада), with its pleasant sheltered **forest road** leading into town through the Shevchenko Park, at **Delfin** (Дельфин) **beach,** also on the edge of the park, and at **Arkadia** (Аркадия), the most popular beach in town because of its wide stretches of sand. Arkadia is also reachable by trolleybus 5 and bus 129. To the south, the **Golden Shore** (Золотой Берiг) is a little bit farther away but quite pretty; the sea and surf is most impressive here. Trams 17 and 18 stop here, as well as at **Chayka** (Чайка) and **Kurortniy** (Курортний) beaches.

UKRAINE

LET'S USE CTS

THE YOUTH & STUDENT TRAVEL SPECIALISTS

FROM LONDON

in USD$ one way	✈	🚆
Amsterdam	60	33
Athens	104	172
Berlin	108	76
Dublin	58	41
Edinburgh	63	35
Madrid	90	102
Milan	105	
Munich	108	88
Paris	60	47
Pisa (Florence)	120	91
Prague	113	99
Rome	105	97
Tel Aviv	133	
Venice	105	91

Accommodation • budget hotels, family accommodations and youth hostels in the main tourist destinations. **Rent a car or a van** for 3, 6 or even more days, with chance of a drop-off in a different country. **Ferry boat** • discounted tickets for Greece, Sardinia and Corse. **Eurotrain Explorer Pass** • to use as you like the rail network of Hungary, Poland, Check and Slovakian Republic, Baltic countries, Portugal. **And also** • sightseeings and excursions to the most important European tourist highlights, tours all over Europe, seaside resorts in Greece and all possible budget tourist services.

ONE WAY BUDGET FLIGHT TICKETS FOR THE UNITED STATES AND LONG HAUL AVAILABLE
PUBLISHED PRICES ARE SUBJECT TO CHANGE

YOUTH & STUDENT TRAVEL CENTRE

London ■ 44 Goodge Street W1P 2AD • tel. (071) 5804554/6375601 *Underground station: Goodge Street*

London ■ 220 Kensington High Street, W8 7RA • tel. (071) 9373265 *Underground st.: High Street Kensington*

Rome ■ via Genova, 16 (*off via Nazionale*) tel. (06) 46791 • *Underground station: Repubblica* ■ Corso Vittorio Emanuele II, 297 • tel. (06) 6872672/3/4

Florence ■ via dei Ginori, 25/R • tel. (055) 289721/289570

Milan ■ via S. Antonio, 2 tel. (02) 58304121

Naples ■ via Mezzocannone, 25 • tel. (081) 5527975/5527960

Venice ■ Dorso Duro Ca' Foscari, 3252, tel. (041) 5205660/5205655

Paris ■ 20, rue des Carmes • tel. (01) 43250076 • *Underground station: Maubert Mutualité*

Other 80 CTS offices are to be found in all major italian cities

Index

Also available from St. Martin's Press

"The information here comes from those who ought to know best." — VILLAGE VOICE

THE INSIDER'S GUIDE TO THE COLLEGES
THE STAFF OF THE YALE DAILY NEWS
1995 EDITION

The only college guide written by students, for students that tells what the colleges are really like!
Features include:

- Candid, in-depth profiles of more than 300 schools in all 50 states and Canada. Profiles focus on academic strengths and weaknesses, housing and food, social life, student activities, and the campus and surrounding area.
- Practical insider tips on the application and admissions process
- Up-to-date statistics on current tuition, acceptance rates, average test scores and more.
- Plus: a College Finder, which zeroes in on the right schools in dozens of categories.

Please send me __copies of THE INSIDER'S GUIDE TO THE COLLEGES (0-312-11291-2) at $14.99 each. I have enclosed $3.00 for postage and handling for the first book, and $.75 each additional copy.

Name_____

Address_____

City_____**State**_____**Zip**_____

Send check or money order with this coupon to:
St. Martin's Press • 175 Fifth Avenue • New York, NY 10010
Att: Nancy/Promotion

★ FREE T-SHIRT ★

JUST ANSWER THE QUESTIONS ON THE FOLLOWING PAGES AND MAIL TO:

Attn: Let's Go Survey
St. Martin's Press
175 Fifth Avenue
New York, NY 10010

WE'LL SEND THE FIRST 1,500 RESPONDENTS A LET'S GO T-SHIRT!

(Make sure we can read your address.)

"A crash course that could lead to a summer job — or a terrific party." —BOSTON GLOBE

With THE OFFICIAL HARVARD STUDENT AGENCIES BARTENDING COURSE, you could find yourself mixing drinks professionally and earning great money, or at the least, giving fabulous cocktail parties!

- Over 300 recipes for the most asked-for drinks — including a section on popular nonalcoholic beverages
- Tips on finding top-paying bartending jobs
- How to remember hundreds of recipes
- How to serve drinks and handle customers with aplomb

- -

Please send me ___ copies of THE OFFICIAL HARVARD STUDENT AGENCIES BARTENDING COURSE (0-312-11370-6) at $9.95 each.

I have enclosed $3.00 for postage and handling for the first book, and $.75 each additional copy.

Name_____

Address_____

City _____ State_____ Zip_____

SEND CHECK OR MONEY ORDER WITH THIS COUPON TO:
St. Martin's Press • 175 Fifth Avenue • New York, NY 10010 • Att: Nancy/Promotion

■ LET'S GO 1995 READER ■ QUESTIONNAIRE

1) Name _____

2) Address _____

3) Are you: female   male

4) How old are you?   under 17   17-23   24-30   31-40   41-55   over 55

5) Are you (circle all that apply):   in high school   in college   in grad school
                                                employed   retired   between jobs

6) What is your personal yearly income?
Under $15,000 $15,000 - $25,000 $26,000 - $35,000 $36,000 - $50,000
$51,000 - $75,000 $76,000 - $100,000   over $100,000   not applicable

7) How often do you normally travel with a guidebook?
This is my first trip
Less than once a year
Once a year
Twice a year
Three times a year or more

8) Which *Let's Go* guide(s) did you buy for your trip?

_____

_____

9) Have you used *Let's Go* before?
Yes   No

10) How did you first hear about *Let's Go*? (Choose one)
Friend or fellow traveler
Recommended by store clerk
Display in bookstore
Ad in newspaper/magazine
Review or article in newspaper/magazine
Radio

11) Why did you choose *Let's Go*? (Choose up to three)
Updated every year
Reputation
Easier to find in stores
Better price
"Budget" focus
Writing style
Attitude
Better organization
More comprehensive
Reliability
Better Design/Layout
Candor
Other _____

_____

_____

12) Which of the following guides have you used, if any?
Frommer's $-a-Day
Fodor's Affordable Guides
Rough Guides/Real Guides
Berkeley Guides/On the Loose
Lonely Planet
None of the above

13) Is *Let's Go* the best guidebook?
Yes
No (which is?) _____
Haven't used other guides

14) When did you buy this book?
Jan Feb Mar Apr May Jun
Jul Aug Sep Oct Nov Dec

15) When did you travel with this book? (Circle all that apply)
Jan Feb Mar Apr May Jun
Jul Aug Sep Oct Nov Dec

16) How long was your trip?
1 week   2 weeks
3 weeks   1 month
2 months   over 2 months

17) Where did you spend most of your time on this trip? (Circle one)
cities   small towns   rural areas

18) How many travel companions did you have?   0 1 2 3 4 over 4

19) Roughly how much did you spend per day on the road?
$0-15 $51-70
$16-30 $71-100
$31-50 $101-150
                   over $150

20) What was the purpose of your trip?
(Circle all that apply)

Pleasure   Business

Study   Volunteer

Work/internship

21) What were the main attractions of your trip? (Circle top three)
Sightseeing
New culture
Learning Language
Meeting locals
Camping/Hiking
Sports/Recreation
Nightlife/Entertainment
Meeting other travelers
Hanging Out
Food
Shopping
Adventure/Getting off the beaten path

22) How reliable/useful are the following features of *Let's Go*?
v = very, u = usually, s = sometimes
n = never, ? = didn't use

Accommodations	v u s n ?
Camping	v u s n ?
Food	v u s n ?
Entertainment	v u s n ?
Sights	v u s n ?
Maps	v u s n ?
Practical Info	v u s n ?
Directions	v u s n ?
"Essentials"	v u s n ?
Cultural Intros	v u s n ?

23) On the list above, please circle the top 3 features you used the most.

24) Would you use *Let's Go* again?
Yes
No (why not?) _____
_____

25) Do you generally buy a phrasebook when you visit a foreign destination?
Yes   No

26) Do you generally buy a separate map when you visit a foreign city?
Yes   No

27) Which of the following destinations are you planning to visit as a tourist in the next five years?
(Circle all that apply)

Australia	Hong Kong
New Zealand	Vietnam
Indonesia	Malaysia
Japan	Singapore
China	India

Nepal	U.S. Nat'l Parks
Middle East	Rocky Mtns.
Israel	The South
Egypt	New Orleans
Africa	Florida
Turkey	Mid-Atlantic
Greece	States
Scandinavia	Boston/New
Portugal	England
Spain	The Midwest
Switzerland	Chicago
Austria	The Southwest
Berlin	Texas
Russia	Arizona
Poland	Colorado
Czech/Slovak	Los Angeles
Rep.	San Francisco
Hungary	Seattle
Baltic States	Hawaii
Caribbean	Alaska
Central America	Canada
Costa Rica	British Columbia
South America	Montreal/Que-
Ecuador	bec
Brazil	Maritime Prov-
Venezuela	inces
Colombia	

28) Please circle the destinations you visited on your trip:

U.K.	Ireland	France
Italy	Spain	Portugal
Switzerland	Austria	Belgium
Netherlands	Denmark	Germany
Norway	Sweden	Finland
Ukraine	Russia	Latvia
Lithuania	Estonia	Slovenia
Bulgaria	Iceland	Hungary
Slovak Rep.	Romania	Poland
Czech Rep.	Greece	Turkey

29) What other countries did you visit on your trip? _____
_____

30) How did you get around on your trip?

Car	Train	Plane
Bus	Ferry	Hitching
Bicycle	Motorcycle	

31) Which of these do you own?
(Circle all that apply)

Computer	CD-ROM
Modem	On-line Service

Mail this to:
Attn: Let's Go Survey
St. Martin's Press
175 Fifth Avenue
New York, NY 10010
Thanks For Your Help!

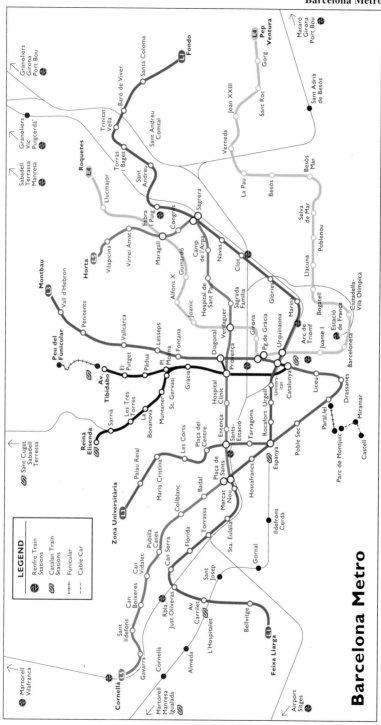

Barcelona Metro

Madrid Metro

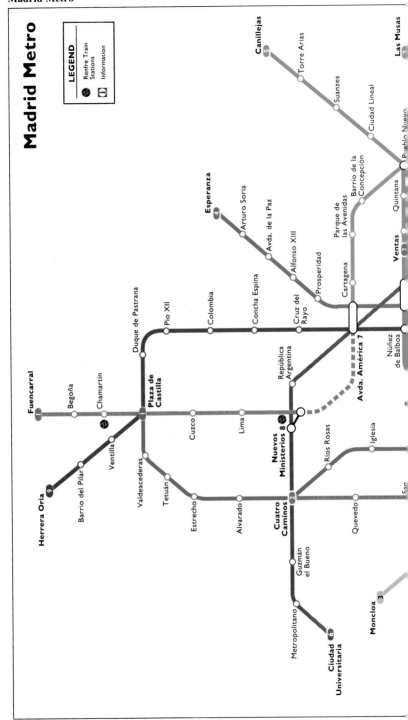

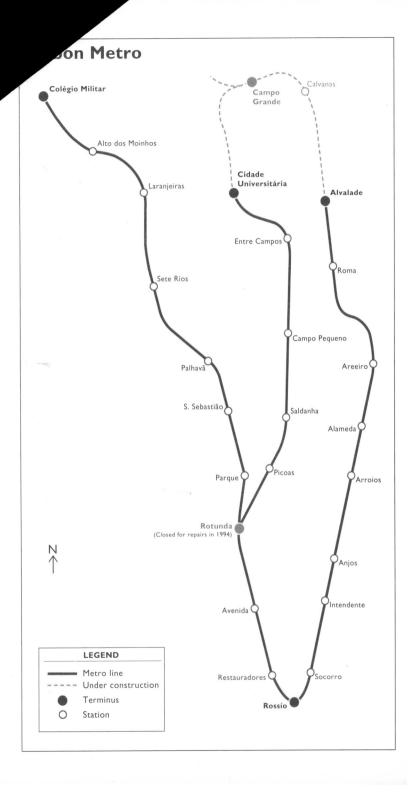

on Metro

Colégio Militar

Campo Grande

Calvanas

Alto dos Moinhos

Laranjeiras

Cidade Universitária

Alvalade

Entre Campos

Roma

Sete Ríos

Campo Pequeno

Areeiro

Palhavã

S. Sebastião

Saldanha

Alameda

Picoas

Parque

Arroios

Rotunda
(Closed for repairs in 1994)

N
↑

Anjos

Intendente

Avenida

Restauradores

Socorro

Rossio

LEGEND
— Metro line
- - - Under construction
● Terminus
○ Station

Paris Metro

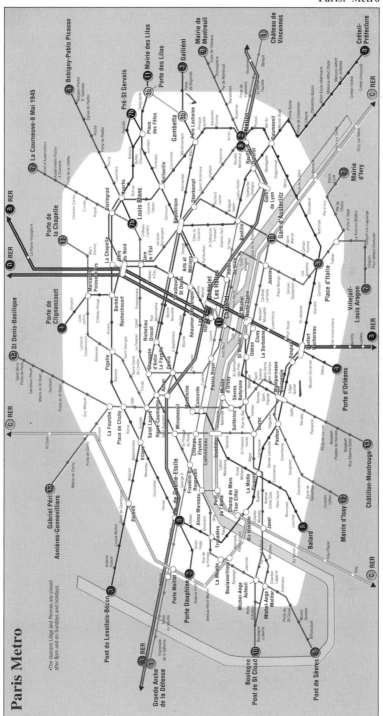

Paris: Metro

• The stations Liège and Rennes are closed after 8pm and on Sundays and holidays.

Paris: Overview and Arrondissements

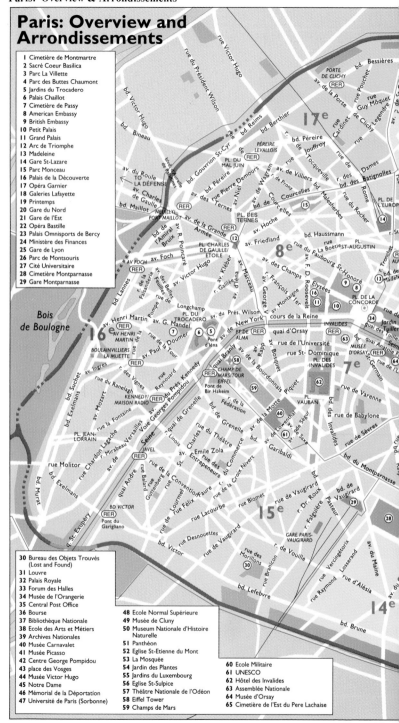

1 Cimetière de Montmartre
2 Sacré Coeur Basilica
3 Parc La Villette
4 Parc des Buttes Chaumont
5 Jardins du Trocadero
6 Palais Chaillot
7 Cimetière de Passy
8 American Embassy
9 British Embassy
10 Petit Palais
11 Grand Palais
12 Arc de Triomphe
13 Madeleine
14 Gare St-Lazare
15 Parc Monceau
16 Palais de la Découverte
17 Opéra Garnier
18 Galeries Lafayette
19 Printemps
20 Gare du Nord
21 Gare de l'Est
22 Opéra Bastille
23 Palais Omnisports de Bercy
24 Ministère des Finances
25 Gare de Lyon
26 Parc de Montsouris
27 Cité Universitaire
28 Cimetière Montparnasse
29 Gare Montparnasse

30 Bureau des Objets Trouvés (Lost and Found)
31 Louvre
32 Palais Royale
33 Forum des Halles
34 Musée de l'Orangerie
35 Central Post Office
36 Bourse
37 Bibliothèque Nationale
38 Ecole des Arts et Métiers
39 Archives Nationales
40 Musée Carnavalet
41 Musée Picasso
42 Centre George Pompidou
43 place des Vosges
44 Musée Victor Hugo
45 Notre Dame
46 Mémorial de la Déportation
47 Université de Paris (Sorbonne)

48 Ecole Normal Supérieure
49 Musée de Cluny
50 Museum Nationale d'Histoire Naturelle
51 Panthéon
52 Eglise St-Etienne du Mont
53 La Mosquée
54 Jardin des Plantes
55 Jardins du Luxembourg
56 Eglise St-Sulpice
57 Théâtre Nationale de l'Odéon
58 Eiffel Tower
59 Champs de Mars

60 Ecole Militaire
61 UNESCO
62 Hôtel des Invalides
63 Assemblée Nationale
64 Musée d'Orsay
65 Cimetière de l'Est ou Pere Lachaise

N

bd. Ney   rue de la Chapelle   bd.   Macdonald

Canal de l'Ourcq

champonnet   **18e**

dener Duhesme

rue Duhesme

ourt

Custine

rue

②   bd. de   bd. de la   Chapelle

L. Rochechouart

av. Trudaine

e

r. l'Evangle

rue Riquet

rue d'Aubervilliers   rue de l'Ourcq

rue Archereau

rue de Flandre

rue de Crimée

③

av. Corentin Carlou

bd. Sérurier

bd. Indochine

av. Jean Lolive

av. Jean   Jaurès

Bassin de la Villette

③

PL. DE STALINGRAD

RER ⑳

②①   Canal St- Martin

r. Armand Carel

av. Secrétan

④

r. David d'Angiers

rue Manin

bd. d'Algérie

19^e

PL. DU COLONEL FABIEN

Châteaudun

rue La Fayette

r. Paradis

③⑦

rue Montmartre

Réaumur

2^e

r. Etienne Marcel

③⑤

③③

RER ④②

e

Louvre

St-Honoré

rue de Rivoli

Pont Neuf

bd. de Magenta

bd. de Strasbourg

r. du Fg. St-Denis

r. d'Hauteville

10^e

av. de la Villette

du Temple

rue du Faubourg

bd. St-Martin

blvd St-Martin

rue de Turbigo

PL. DE LA RÉPUBLIQUE

③⑧

rue St-Martin

rue du Temple

③⑨   ④①

④⓪

bd. Beaumarchais

rue des Archives

3^e

rue Vieille du Temple

④③

rue St-Antoine

④④

bd. du Temple

av. Parmentier

rue St-Maur

rue des Pyrénées

PL. GAMBETTA

bd. Mortier

av. Gambetta

bd. de Belleville

la République

av. de la République

rue Oberkampf

11^e

av. Gambetta

20^e

⑥⑤

bd. R. Lenoir

rue du Chemin Vert

Voltaire

Roquette

rue de la

bd. de Ménilmontant

av. Philippe Auguste

bd. de Charonne

bd. Davout

Ile de la Cité

④⑤

④⑥

Ile St-Louis

bd. Henri IV

②②

rue de la Roquette

rue de Charonne

rue du Faubourg

rue de Montreuil

St-Antoine   NATION   RER

Cours de Vincennes

Michel

St-Quai de la Tournelle

④⑨

des Ecoles

④⑦

LUXEMBOURG

⑤①

⑤②

PL. DE LA CONTRE-SCARPE

④⑧

rue Monge

5^e

quai St-Bernard

G. St-Hilaire

⑤③

⑤⓪

rue Censier   rue Buffon

rue Mouffetard

⑤④

bd. St-Marcel

RER

GARE D'AUSTERLITZ

4^e

rue de Rivoli

rue Ledru Rollin

av. Ledru Lyon

Pont de Sully

RER ②⑤

②④

②③

Pont de Bercy

quai

rue de Bercy

bd. Diderot

PL. DE LA NATION

bd. Picpus

av. Daumesnil

PL. FÉLIX ÉBOUÉ

○

de Bercy

12^e

rue de Picpus

av. du Dr. Arnold Netter

M. Bizot

av. Daumesnil

rue de Charenton

bd. Soult

Parc Zoologique

bd. de Port Royal

bd. Arago

PL. D'ALESIA

bd. A. Blanqui

rue de Tolbiac

13^e

bd. Kellerman

Guy Lussac

C. Bernard

rue

Seine

bd. de l'Hôpital

rue de la Gare

rue de Jeanne d'Arc

av. de Choisy

rue National

av. d'Ivry

rue de Tolbiac

rue Regnault

bd. de Masséna

Chevaleret

Pont de Tolbiac

rue du

de Bercy

Pont National

Pont National

RER   BD. MASSÉNA

rue de Paris

bd. du Gén

bd. Poniatowski

Bois de Vincennes

0   1 mile

0   1 km

9e

Rue Chaussée d'Antin

Rue St-Lazare

R. d'Amsterdam

Richelieu

St Lazare

Chaussée d'Antin

Havre-Caumartin

Boulevard Haussmann

Bd. Haussmann

Rue Auber

Boulevard des Italiens

Rue Pasquier

Rue Tronchet

Rue

Opéra

Auber

Scribe

Bd. des Capucines

RER

Opéra

RER

Rue du Quatre

Sept

Quatre Septembre

Biblio Na

Bd. de la Madeleine

Rue des Capucines

Rue de la Paix

Rue des Petit Champs

Madeleine

Madeleine

La Colonne

PLACE VENDÔME

Avenue de l'Opéra

Pyramides

Rue de Richelieu

Rue Boissy d'Anglas

Rue Royale

Rue St-Honoré

Rue de Castiglione

Rue St-Honoré

Rue des Pyramides

1er

8e

Musée Bouilhet Christofle

Rue de Rivoli

Tuileries

PLACE ANDRE-MALRAUX

Concorde

Jeu de Paume

Palais

PLACE DE LA CONCORDE

PLAC CARRO

JARDIN DES TUILERIES

L'Orangerie

Quai des Tuileries

Pt. de la Concorde

Seine

Pont Solférino

Pont Royal

Pont du Carrousel

Quai Anatole France

Quai Voltaire

Assemblée Nationale

Chambre des Deputés

Musée D'Orsay

RER

Musée d'Orsay

Bd. St-Germain

Rue de Lille

7e

Rue de l'Université

Solférino

Ecole Na Superieu Beau

0		1/8 mile

0		125 meters

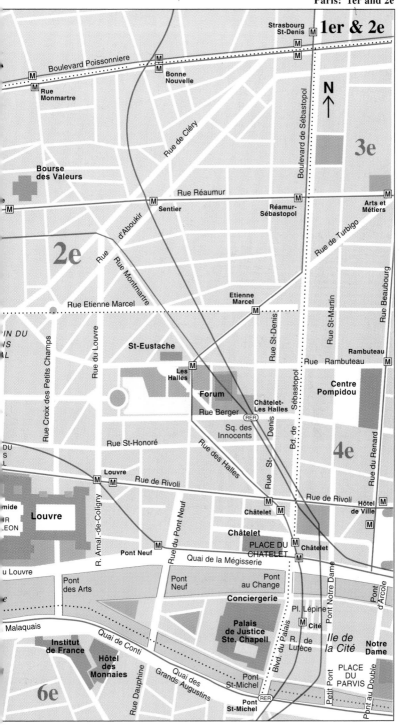

Strasbourg
St-Denis Ⓜ

Boulevard Poissonniere

Ⓜ

Bonne
Nouvelle

Ⓜ
Rue
Monmartre

N
↑

3e

Rue de Cléry

Boulevard de Sébastopol

Bourse
des Valeurs

Rue Réaumur

Ⓜ

Ⓜ Arts et
Métiers

Ⓜ

Ⓜ Sentier

Réamur-
Sébastopol

d'Aboukir

2e

Rue de Turbigo

Rue

Rue Montmartre

Rue Etienne Marcel

Etienne
Marcel
Ⓜ

IN DU
NS
AL

Rue Croix des Petits Champs

Rue du Louvre

St-Eustache

Rue St-Denis

Rue St-Martin

Rue Beaubourg

Les
Halles
Ⓜ

Rambuteau
Ⓜ

Forum

Rue Rambuteau

Centre
Pompidou

DU
S
L

Rue St-Honoré

Rue Berger

Châtelet-
Les Halles
RER

Sq. des
Innocents

Bd. de Sébastopol

Rue St-

4e

Rue du Renard

Rue des Halles

Louvre
Ⓜ Ⓜ Rue de Rivoli

Louvre

Rue de Rivoli

mide
R
EON

R. Amal.-de-Coligny

Ⓜ
Châtelet

Ⓜ Ⓜ

Hôtel
de Ville Ⓜ

Ⓜ

Pont Neuf
Ⓜ

Châtelet

PLACE DU Ⓜ
CHATELET
Ⓜ

Châtelet

u Louvre

Rue du Pont Neuf

Quai de la Mégisserie

Pont Notre Dame

Pont
d'Arcole

Pont
des Arts

Pont
Neuf

Pont
au Change

Malaquais

Conciergerie

Pl. Lépine

Quai de Conti

Palais
de Justice
Ste. Chapell

Ⓜ Cité

Ile de
la Cité

Notre
Dame

Institut
de France

Hôtel
des
Monnaies

Rue Dauphine

Quai des
Grands Augustins

Blvd. du Palais

R. de
Lutèce

Petit Pont

PLACE
DU
PARVIS

Pont au Double

e

6e

Pont
St-Michel

Pont
St-Michel RER

Palais
du Louvre

Pont Neuf

Châtelet

Quai du Louvre

Pont
des
Arts

1er

Pont au
Change

Pont du
Carrousel

Pont
Neuf

Conciergerie

Cité

Quai Malaquais

Quai de Conti

**Ste-
Chapelle**

Pont St-Michel

np Palais

Île de
la Cité

Hô
Die

Rue de la Cité

**Ecole Nationale
Supérieure des
Beaux Arts**

R. Bonaparte

**Institut
de France**

**Hôtel des
Monnaies**

Quai des
Grands
Augustins

Rue de Seine

Rue Mazarine

Rue Dauphine

Pont
St-Michel

RER

Bd.

Rue des Sts-Pères

Rue Jacob

St-Michel

Rue St-Jacques

R. de l'Abbaye

Rue St-André des Arts

Rue Danton

Pl.
St-Michel

**PLACE
ST-GERMAIN-
DES-PRÉS**

**St-Germain
Des Prés**

M

Bd. St-Germain

Bd. St-Germain

**St-Germain
des Prés**

M

Mabillon

Odéon

Boulevard

**Musée
du Cluny**

7e

R. du Four

Rue de l'Odéon

Rue Racine

Sorbonne

R. de Sèvres

R. du Vieux
Colombier

R. du Saint Sulpice

Rue de Tournon

**PLACE DE
L'ODÉON**

St-Michel

**PLACE
DE LA
SORBONNE**

R. du Cherche Midi

**PLACE
ST-SULPICE**

St-Sulpice

Rue Soufflot

R. d'Assas

R. de Rennes

M

St-Sulpice

**Palais du
Luxembourg**

M

Luxembourg

Bd. Raspail

6e

Rue Gay-Lus

Rennes

M

R. de Vaugirard

*JARDIN
DU
LUXEMBOURG*

St Placide

M

**Notre-Dame
des Champs**

Rue d'Assas

Rue du Montparnasse

Rue Vavin

Rue Notre-Dame des Champs

Boulevard St-Michel

**Montparnasse
Bienvenüe**

M

Vavin

M

Boulevard du Montparnasse

Avenue de

la Observatoire

Port Royal

M

R. du Depart

**Edgar
Quinet**

M

Boulevard Raspail

14e

Boulevard Edgar Quinet

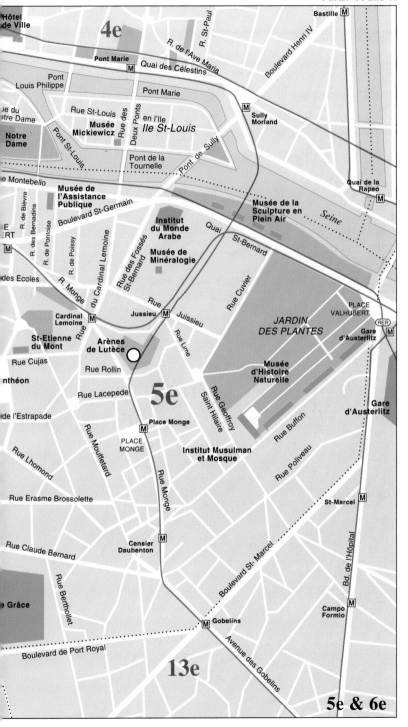

Hôtel de Ville

4e

R. St-Paul

R. de l'Ave Maria

Boulevard Henri IV

Bastille M

Pont Marie M

Quai des Célestins

Pont Louis Philippe

Pont Marie

Rue St-Louis

Rue des Deux Ponts

en l'Ile
Ile St-Louis

Sully Morland M

e du tre Dame

Musée Mickiewicz

Pont St-Louis

Notre Dame

Pont de la Tournelle

Pont de Sully

e Montebello

Musée de l'Assistance Publique

Quai de la Rapeo

Seine

M

E RT M

R. de Blèvre

R. des Bernadins

R. de Pontoise

R. de Poissy

Boulevard St-Germain

Rue des Fossés St-Bernard

Institut du Monde Arabe

Musée de Minéralogie

Musée de la Sculpture en Plein Air

Quai St-Bernard

des Ecoles

R. Monge

Rue du Cardinal Lemoine

Rue Juissieu

Rue Cuvier

PLACE VALHUBERT

Rue Jussieu M

RER

Cardinal Lemoine M

Jussieu M

Rue Linne

JARDIN DES PLANTES

Gare d'Austerlitz

St-Etienne du Mont

Rue

Arènes de Lutèce ◯

Rue Cujas

Rue Rollin

5e

Gare d'Austerlitz

nthéon

Rue Lacepede

Rue Geoffroy Saint Hilaire

Musée d'Histoire Naturelle

de l'Estrapade

Place Monge M

Rue Mouffetard

PLACE MONGE

Institut Musulman et Mosque

Rue Buffon

Rue Lhomond

Rue Poliveau

Rue Erasme Brossolette

Rue Monge

St-Marcel M

Rue Claude Bernard

Censier Daubenton M

Bd. de l'Hôpital

Rue Berthollet

e Grâce

Boulevard St-Marcel

Campo Formio M

Gobelins M

Boulevard de Port Royal

13e

Avenue des Gobelins

5e & 6e

Paris: RER

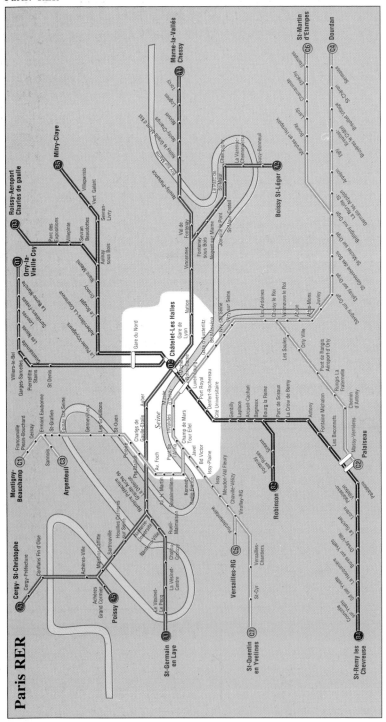

Paris RER

London: Underground

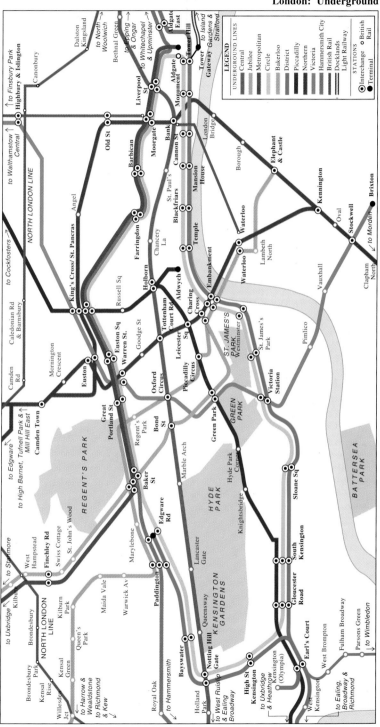

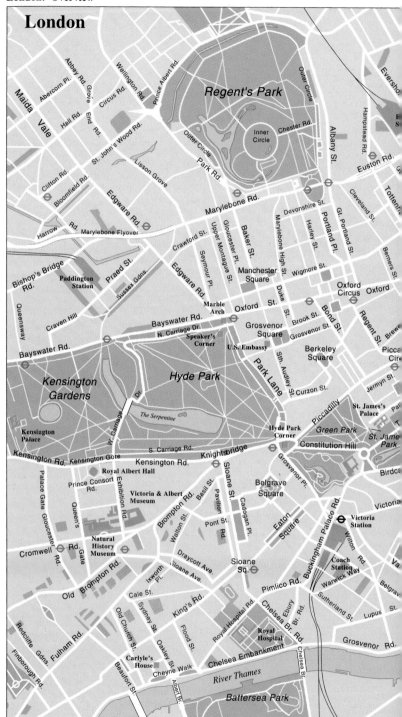

King's Cross Station

Pancras Station

Pentonville Rd.

City Rd.

King's Cross Rd.

Gray's Inn Rd.

Judd St.

Woburn Pl.

Southampton Row

Coram's Fields

Guilford St.

Rosebery Ave.

St. John's St.

Lever St.

Bath St.

Old St.

East Road

Hoxton St.

City Rd.

Kingsland Rd.

Gt. Eastern St.

Shoreditch High St.

Commercial St.

Theobalds Rd.

Clerkenwell Rd.

Farringdon Rd.

Goswell Rd.

Aldersgate

Barbican Centre

Liverpool St. Station

New Oxford St.

Holborn

High

Kingsway

Drury La.

Chancery La.

Fetter La.

Charterhouse St.

Smithfield Market

Holborn Viaduct

Old Bailey

Newgate St.

St. Paul's

London Wall

Moorgate

Bank of England

Bishopsgate

Houndsditch

Leadenhall St.

Fenchurch St.

Law Courts

Aldwych

Fleet St.

Cheapside

Cornhill

Gracechurch St.

St. Eastcheap

Strand

Victoria Embankment

Queen

Victoria St.

Cannon St.

The Tower

National Gallery

Charing Cross Stn.

Whitehall

Blackfriars Br.

Blackfriars Station

Cannon St. Station

Upper Thames St.

Tower Hill

Waterloo Br.

National Theatre

Stamford St.

Southwark St.

Southwark Br.

London Br.

River Thames

Tower Br.

Royal Festival Hall

York Rd.

Waterloo Rd.

The Cut

Blackfriars Rd.

Union St.

Tooley St.

St. Thomas St.

London Bridge Station

Waterloo Station

Houses of Parliament

Millbank

Westminster Br.

Westminster Br. Rd.

Lambeth Palace Rd.

Lambeth Rd.

Borough Rd.

London Rd.

Borough High

Long La.

Tabard St.

Great Dover St.

Harper Rd.

Bridge Rd.

Abbey St.

Tower

Willow Walk

Ferry Rd.

Lambeth Br.

Albert Embankment

Black Prince Rd.

Kennington Rd.

Imperial War Museum

New Kent Rd.

Rodney Pl.

East St.

Flint St.

Old Kent Rd.

Kennington Park Rd.

Manor Pl.

Crampton St.

Walworth Rd.

Portland St.

Thurlow St.

Albany Rd.

Kennington La.

Braganza St.

Vauxhall Br.

Vauxhall Station

Kennington Oval

gate lery

N

0   1/2 mile

0   1/2 kilometer

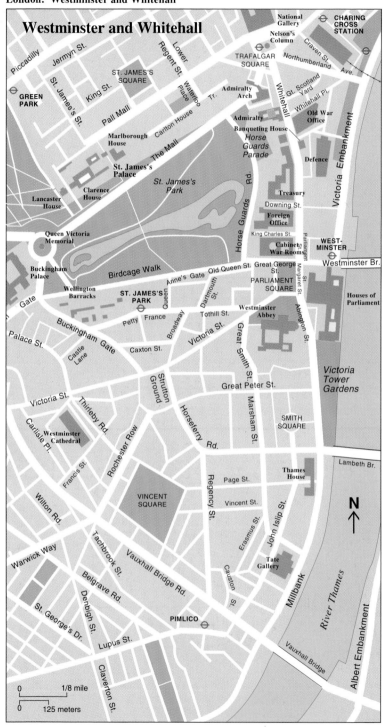

Westminster and Whitehall

GREEN PARK

Piccadilly

Jermyn St.

ST. JAMES'S SQUARE

Regent St.

Lower Regent St.

National Gallery

Nelson's Column

CHARING CROSS STATION

Craven St.

TRAFALGAR SQUARE

Northumberland Ave.

St. James's St.

King St.

Waterloo Place

Pall Mall

Admiralty Arch

Whitehall

Gt. Scotland Yard

Whitehall Pl.

Canton House

Admiralty

Old War Office

Marlborough House

The Mall

Banqueting House

Horse Guards Parade

Defence

St. James's Palace

St. James's Park

Clarence House

Treasury

Lancaster House

Horse Guards Rd.

Downing St.

Foreign Office

Queen Victoria Memorial

King Charles St.

Cabinet War Rooms

WEST-MINSTER

Westminster Br.

Buckingham Palace

Birdcage Walk

Anne's Gate

Old Queen St.

Great George St.

Margaret St.

Parliament St.

PARLIAMENT SQUARE

Houses of Parliament

Gate

Wellington Barracks

ST. JAMES'S PARK

Dartmouth St.

Queen

Westminster Abbey

Abingdon St.

Palace St.

Buckingham Gate

Petty France

Broadway

Tothill St.

Victoria St.

Great Smith St.

Castle Lane

Caxton St.

Victoria Tower Gardens

Victoria St.

Thirleby Rd.

Strutton Ground

Great Peter St.

Marsham St.

Carlisle Pl.

Westminster Cathedral

Horseferry Rd.

SMITH SQUARE

Lambeth Br.

Francis St.

Rochester Row

Page St.

Thames House

Wilton Rd.

VINCENT SQUARE

Regency Rd.

Vincent St.

John Islip St.

N

Warwick Way

Tachbrook St.

Vauxhall Bridge Rd.

Erasmus St.

Tate Gallery

Millbank

River Thames

Belgrave Rd.

Denbigh St.

Causton St.

St. George's Dr.

Lupus St.

PIMLICO

Claverton St.

Vauxhall Bridge

Albert Embankment

Victoria Embankment

0   1/8 mile

0   125 meters

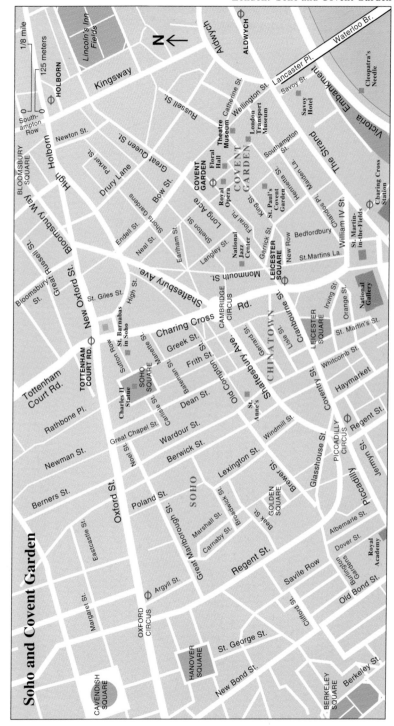

London: Soho and Covent Garden

Soho and Covent Garden

Lincoln's Inn Fields

Kingsway

HOLBORN

Newton St.

BLOOMSBURY SQUARE

Parker St.

Great Queen St.

Drury Lane

Bow St.

Endell St.

Shorts Gardens

Neal St.

Shelton St.

Earlham St.

High Holborn

Bloomsbury Way

Russell St.

Great Russell St.

Bloomsbury St.

St. Giles St.

New Oxford St.

TOTTENHAM COURT RD.

Sutton Row

St. Barnabas in Soho

Manette St.

High St.

Shaftesbury Ave.

Monmouth St.

Langley St.

National Jazz Center

LEICESTER SQUARE

New Row

Bedfordbury

St.Martins La.

St.Martin's St.

St. Martin-in-the-Fields

National Gallery

LEICESTER SQUARE

Irving St.

Orange St.

Cranbourn St.

Charing Cross Rd.

Greek St.

CAMBRIDGE CIRCUS

Gerrard St.

Lisle St.

CHINATOWN

Whitcomb St.

Haymarket

Coventry St.

PICCADILLY CIRCUS

Charing Cross

Tottenham Court Rd.

Rathbone Pl.

Charles II Statue

SOHO SQUARE

Carlisle St.

Bateman St.

Frith St.

Dean St.

St. Anne's

Windmill St.

Old Compton St.

Greek St.

Shaftesbury Ave.

Newman St.

Great Chapel St.

Wardour St.

Berwick St.

Lexington St.

Brewer St.

Glasshouse St.

Regent St.

Berners St.

Noel St.

Poland St.

SOHO

Marshall St.

GOLDEN SQUARE

Beak St.

Jermyn St.

Piccadilly

Eastcastle St.

Oxford St.

Great Marlborough St.

Carnaby St.

Broadwick St.

Albemarle St.

Dover St.

Royal Academy

Burlington Gardens

Old Bond St.

Margaret St.

OXFORD CIRCUS

Argyll St.

Regent St.

Savile Row

Clifford St.

New Bond St.

CAVENDISH SQUARE

HANOVER SQUARE

St. George St.

BERKELEY SQUARE

Berkeley

Russell St.

Catherine St.

Wellington St.

Theatre Museum

London Transport Museum

COVENT GARDEN

Floral Hall

Royal Opera

Long Acre

Floral Pl.

King St.

St. Paul's Covent Garden

Garrick St.

Henrietta St.

Maiden La.

Southampton St.

The Strand

Lancaster Pl.

Savoy St.

Savoy Hotel

Cleopatra's Needle

Victoria Embankment

Charing Cross Station

Chandos Pl.

William IV St.

ALDWYCH

Aldwych

Waterloo Br.

Southampton Row

HOLBORN

N

1/8 mile

125 meters

0

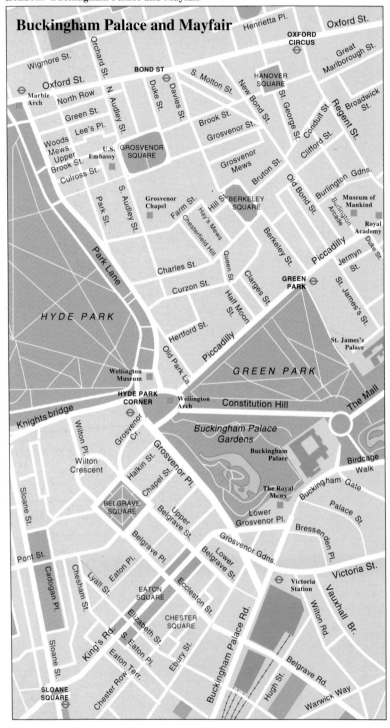

Buckingham Palace and Mayfair